Caribbean Sea
75°W
60°W
15°N
N
Maracaibo
Santa Marta
Barranquilla
Cartagena
CENTRAL AMERICA
Barquisimeto
Coro
Caracas
Barcelona
Cumaná
Maturín
Maracay
Valencia
Mérida
Barinas
Orinoco R.
Ciudad Guayana
Ciudad Bolívar
Cúcuta
San Cristóbal
Bucaramanga
Gulf of Panama
Medellín
Manizales
Pereira
Tunja
Bogotá
Villavicencio
Cali
COLOMBIA
VENEZUELA
GUYANA
Georgetown
Paramaribo
SURINAME
FRENCH GUIANA (France)
ATLANTIC OCEAN
Galápagos Islands (Ecuador)
Neiva
Florencia
Pasto
Esmeraldas
Boa Vista
ECUADOR
Quito
Ibarra
0°
Portoviejo
Ambato
Riobamba
Guayaquil
Cuenca
Machala
Loja
Negro R.
Macapá
Amazon R.
Manaus
Santarém
Belém
São Luis
Iquitos
Piura
Tapajós R.
Xingu R.
Fortaleza
Teresina
Chiclayo
Cajamarca
Trujillo
PERU
Pucallpa
Madeira R.
Rio Branco
Porto Velho
Tocantins R.
Natal
João Pessoa
Chimbote
Huánuco
Cerro de Pasco
BRAZIL
São Francisco R.
Recife
Maceió
Aracaju
Lima
Huancayo
Ayacucho
Cusco
Ica
Trinidad
BOLIVIA
Salvador
Juliaca
La Paz
15°S
Arequipa
Cochabamba
Santa Cruz
Cuiabá
Brasília
Goiânia
Tacna
Oruro
Arica
Sucre
Potosí
PACIFIC OCEAN
Iquique
Paraguay R.
Uberlândia
Campo Grande
Belo Horizonte
Tarija
Pedro Juan Caballero
Vitória
San Salvador de Jujuy
Antofagasta
PARAGUAY
Campinas
Rio de Janeiro
São Paulo
Niterói
Santos
Salta
Asunción
Ciudad del Este
San Miguel de Tucumán
Curitiba
Copiapó
Resistencia
Posadas
Encarnación
Corrientes
Florianópolis
CHILE
Catamarca
Santiago del Estero
La Rioja
La Serena
Paraná R.
Porto Alegre
30°S
Córdoba
Santa Fe
Rivera
Salto
Paysandú
San Juan
Mendoza
Valparaíso
Santiago
San Luis
Rosario
URUGUAY
Rancagua
Buenos Aires
Montevideo
Río de la Plata
Talca
45°W
Concepción
Chillán
ARGENTINA
Bahía Blanca
Mar del Plata
Temuco
Neuquén
Puerto Montt
45°S
Comodoro Rivadavia
Falkland Islands (Islas Malvinas) (U.K.)
Strait of Magellan
Punta Arenas
Ushuaia
South America
Elevation in Feet
15,000
10,000
5,000
2,000
1,000
0
Below sea level
Major Cities
Capital city
Over 5,000,000
1,000,000–5,000,000
500,000–999,999
250,000–499,999
100,000–249,999
Less than 100,000
0 250 500 mi.
0 250 500 km

ENCYCLOPEDIA OF

LATIN AMERICAN HISTORY AND CULTURE

EDITORIAL BOARD

ENCYCLOPEDIA OF

LATIN AMERICAN HISTORY AND CULTURE

SECOND EDITION

Volume 4

J–O

Jay Kinsbruner

EDITOR IN CHIEF

Erick D. Langer

SENIOR EDITOR

CHARLES SCRIBNER'S SONS

A part of Gale, Cengage Learning

Detroit • New York • San Francisco • New Haven, Conn • Waterville, Maine • London

Encyclopedia of Latin American History and Culture

Jay Kinsbruner, Editor in Chief
Erick D. Langer, Senior Editor

For product information and technology assistance, contact us at
Gale Customer Support, 1-800-877-4253.
For permission to use material from this text or product,
submit all requests online at **www.cengage.com/permissions.**
Further permissions questions can be emailed to
permissionrequest@cengage.com

Library of Congress Cataloging-in-Publication Data

Encyclopedia of Latin American history and culture / Jay Kinsbruner, editor in chief; Erick D. Langer, senior editor. -- 2nd ed.
p. cm. --
Includes bibliographical references and index.
ISBN 978-0-684-31270-5 (set) -- ISBN 978-0-684-31441-9 (vol. 1) -- ISBN 978-0-684-31442-6 (vol. 2) -- ISBN 978-0-684-31443-3 (vol. 3) -- ISBN 978-0-684-31444-0 (vol. 4) -- ISBN 978-0-684-31445-7 (vol. 5) -- ISBN 978-0-684-31598-0 (vol. 6)
1. Latin America--Encyclopedias. I. Kinsbruner, Jay.

F1406.E53 2008
980.003--dc22 2008003461

Gale
27500 Drake Rd.
Farmington Hills, MI, 48331-3535

978-0-684-31270-5 (set) 0-684-31270-0 (set)
978-0-684-31441-9 (vol. 1) 0-684-31441-X (vol. 1)
978-0-684-31442-6 (vol. 2) 0-684-31442-8 (vol. 2)
978-0-684-31443-3 (vol. 3) 0-684-31443-6 (vol. 3)
978-0-684-31444-0 (vol. 4) 0-684-31444-4 (vol. 4)
978-0-684-31445-7 (vol. 5) 0-684-31445-2 (vol. 5)
978-0-684-31598-0 (vol. 6) 0-684-31598-X (vol. 6)

This title is also available as an e-book.
ISBN-13: 978-0-684-31590-4 ISBN-10: 0-684-31590-4
Contact your Gale, a part of Cengage Learning, sales representative for ordering information.

Printed in the United States of America
1 2 3 4 5 6 7 12 11 10 09 08

CONTENTS

JAAR, ALFREDO

JAAR, ALFREDO (1956–). Alfredo Jaar (*b.* 1956), Chilean artist. Born in Santiago, Jaar received degrees in filmmaking from the American Institute of Culture (1979) and in architecture from the University of Chile in Santiago (1981). In 1982 he moved to New York, where he received fellowships from the Guggenheim Memorial Foundation (1985), the National Endowment for the Arts (1987), and the Deutscher Akademischer Austauschdienst Berliner Kunstlerprogram (1989). Employing over-life-size and close-up photographs, light boxes, mirrors, and digital signs in his installations, Jaar addresses themes related to environmental decay and the inequality of human groups and nations. The exportation of toxic industrial waste by developed countries to Nigeria was the subject of his *Geography = War* (1991), and the plight of the Vietnamese boat people was depicted in *(Un)Framed* (1987–1991). Jaar has traveled to and meticulously researched each site he selects as a theme. The simplicity of his installations has prompted comparisons with the minimalist artists Robert Morris and Donald Judd.

See also **Art: The Twentieth Century.**

BIBLIOGRAPHY

Ashton Dore and Patricia C. Phillips, *Alfredo Jaar: Gold in the Morning* (1986).

W. Avon Drake et al., *Alfredo Jaar: Geography = War* (1991).

Alfredo Jaar, "Artists' Statements" in *Art Journal* 51 (1992): 18–19.

Additional Bibliography

Baddeley, Oriana. *New Art from Latin America.* London: Academy Editions, 1994.

Jaar, Alfredo. *Alfredo Jaar: Lament of the Images.* Cambridge, MA: Massachusetts Institute of Technology, 1999.

Jaar, Alfredo. *Alfredo Jaar: Studies on Happiness 1979–1981.* Barcelona: ACTAR, 1999.

Jaar, Alfredo. *It Is Difficult: Ten Years.* Barcelona: Actar, 1998.

Jaar, Alfredo. *Let There Be Light: The Rwanda Project 1994–1998.* Barcelona, Spain: ACTAR, 1998.

Jaar, Alfredo; Mark Durden and Craig Richardson. *Face On: Photography as Social Exchange.* London: Black Dog, 2000.

Jacob, Mary Jane; Noreen Tomassi, and Ivo Mesquita. *American Visions: Artistic and Cultural Identity in the Western Hemisphere.* New York, NY: ACA Books in association with Arts International: Allworth Press, 1994.

Johnson, Patricia C. "Sound of Silence Speaks Loudly." *Houston Chronicle,* (March 2006).

MARTA GARSD

JACOBINISM

JACOBINISM. Jacobinism, a term that refers to Brazil's urban radical nationalism, particularly in the early Old Republic (1889–1930). Associated with positivist-influenced militants in the Republican Party, especially those connected with the dictatorial presidential administration (1891–1894) of

General Floriano Peixoto (hence, Florianistas), its adherents were generally middle-class civilians and army officers. Jacobinos defended Peixoto's regime during the Naval Revolt (1893–1894) and engaged in street riots and, more rarely, assassinations (including an attempt on President Prudente de Morais in 1897), targeting monarchists and Portuguese, especially, as threats to the imperiled Republic and as economic parasites.

Rooted in the abolitionist and Republican mobilization and in the economic difficulties of the 1880s and 1890s, and hostile to the political tradition of the monarchy's parliamentary and planter elites, the Jacobin leaders often supported a post-positivist authoritarianism, statist intervention and developmentalism in the economy, and paternalist labor policies. They also feared the restoration of the monarchy and the old agriculture-based oligarchies. Triumphant under Peixoto, Jacobins remained a threat to the emerging power of the state oligarchies and Paulista federal hegemony, at least until the Revolta Contra Vacina of 1904 (the coup and popular revolt associated with the government's forced vaccination against smallpox), and were seemingly influential in the *salvacionista* military coups against state oligarchies of the 1910s. Their thinking remained influential among the military officer corps, the radical-wing elders of the Republican Party, and the political elite of Rio Grande until the Revolution of 1930.

See also **Afrancesado; Brazil, Political Parties: Republican Party (PR).**

BIBLIOGRAPHY

June E. Hahner, *Civilian-Military Relations in Brazil, 1889–1898* (1969).

Afonso Arinos De Melo Franco, *Rodrigues Alves,* vol. 1 (1973).

June E. Hahner, "Jacobinos Versus Galegos," in *Journal of Inter-American Studies and World Affairs* 18, no. 2 (1976): 125–154.

Suely Robles Reis De Queiroz, *Os radicais da república* (1986).

José Murilo De Carvalho, *Os bestializados* (1987).

Jeffrey D. Needell, "The *Revolta Contra Vacina* of 1904," in *Hispanic American Historical Review* 67 (May 1987): 233–269.

Additional Bibliography

Deutsch, Sandra McGee. *Las Derechas: The Extreme Right in Argentina, Brazil, and Chile, 1890-1939.* Stanford, CA: Stanford University Press, 1999.

Reis de Queiroz, Suely Robles. "Reflections on Brazilian Jacobinism of the First Decade of the Republic (1893-1897)." *The Americas.* 48:2 (October 1991): 181-205.

JEFFREY D. NEEDELL

JAGAN, CHEDDI (1918–1997). Cheddi Jagan, a Guyanese political leader, was the grandson of indentured Hindu Indians brought by the British to work the plantations of British Guiana (present-day Guyana). Despite a humble rural background, Jagan, born on March 22, 1918, was sent to secondary school in the capital, Georgetown, where he excelled in his studies and in sports. In 1936 his family pooled all their savings and sent him to Howard University in Washington, D.C. After two years he transferred on a full scholarship to Northwestern University in Chicago, where he earned his degree in dental surgery. In 1943 he married Janet Rosenberg, a committed socialist. That same year he returned to British Guiana to practice dentistry.

In 1946 Jagan entered politics, and in 1947 he was elected to the colonial legislative council. In 1950 he teamed up with another Guyanese of socialist inclinations, the Afro-Guyanese lawyer Forbes Burnham, to found the People's Progressive Party (PPP). The party won the 1953 election and declared that it would "fight" for socialism. By 1955 Jagan and Burnham had split, establishing the basic political and racial divide that survives to this day: a rural, Indian-based PPP and an urban, black People's National Congress (PNC). It is widely accepted that repeated electoral frauds, starting in 1964, kept Jagan and the PPP from power. Burnham's sudden death in 1985 put Desmond Hoyte in the presidency. In 1992, in the first truly democratic elections since 1961, Jagan and the PPP won by a handsome majority. He died of heart failure on March 6, 1997, and was succeeded by his wife, Janet Jagan, who served until 1999.

See also **Guyana; Jagan, Janet.**

BIBLIOGRAPHY

Jagan, Cheddi. *The West on Trial: My Fight for Guyana's Freedom*. London: Joseph, 1966.

Maingot, Anthony P. *The United States and the Caribbean: Challenges of an Asymmetrical Relationship*. Boulder, CO: Westview Press, 1994.

Spinner, Thomas J., Jr. *A Political and Social History of Guyana, 1945–1983*. Boulder, CO: Westview Press, 1984.

ANTHONY P. MAINGOT

JAGAN, JANET (1920–). In December 1997, Janet Jagan (formerly Rosenberg) was elected president of the Republic of Guyana, the only English-speaking country in South America. Born in Chicago on October 20, 1920, to conservative Jewish Republican parents, she became the first American-born woman to be elected president of any country. She left the United States in 1943 with her Guyanese, East Indian, Hindu husband, Cheddi Jagan, to lead the anticolonial, anticapitalist nationalist movement of British Guiana (later Guyana). She relinquished her U.S. citizenship in 1947. In 1953 the People's Progressive Party (PPP) that they had formed three years previously won office in the first elections held under universal suffrage. Cheddi Jagan became the colony's first premier and Janet its first woman cabinet member. Having been elected to the legislature, she also became deputy speaker of Parliament.

Quickly the Jagans became lightening rods in the international cold war. Because they were accused of being communists, Britain (still the colonial power), with U.S. backing, suspended the constitution and ousted the Jagans and the party they led from power. Furthermore, they were both imprisoned. The U.S. government declared Janet *persona non grata*. The Jagans survived unbowed, their firm commitment to democratic socialist transformation intact. This remained the hallmark of their politics. The PPP, relying almost exclusively on the predominantly Hindu East Indian vote, was elected to national office once again in 1957. Cheddi Jagan became chief minister, with Janet holding an important cabinet post as head of the Ministry of Labour, Health, and Housing. In the racially charged politics of the country, Janet Jagan became identified almost exclusively with the country's Hindu population. The party remained in office until 1964 during a period when the country saw significant achievements in education, agriculture, health, welfare, and economic development. While in office, Janet and Cheddi Jagan became poster children in the U.S.-led international campaign against communism. She was labeled as one of the most dangerous communists in the hemisphere. Voted out of office after a constitutional change that favored the opposition, Janet and Cheddi embarked on a campaign for freedom and civil rights until, in 1992, their party was once again elected to office. Cheddi Jagan became the country's executive president. When he died in office in March 1997, Janet Jagan became the country's first woman prime minister. After national elections in December 1997, she served for twenty months as executive president until a heart attack, at the age of eighty-three, forced her resignation in 1999. Even though out of office, she continued to be politically active.

See also **Burnham, Linden Forbes; Guyana; Jagan, Cheddi.**

BIBLIOGRAPHY

Despres, Leo A. *Cultural Pluralism and Nationalist Politics in British Guiana*. Chicago: Rand McNally, 1967.

Hintzen, Percy C. *The Costs of Regime Survival: Racial Mobilization, Elite Domination, and Control of the State in Guyana and Trinidad*. New York; Cambridge, UK: Cambridge University Press, 1989.

Hintzen, Percy C. "Cheddi Jagan (1918–97): Charisma and Guyana's Response to Western Capitalism." In *Caribbean Charisma: Reflections on Leadership, Legitimacy, and Populist Politics*, ed. Anton Allahar. Boulder, CO: Lynn Reinner Publishers, 2001.

Jagan. Cheddi. *The West on Trial*, revised edition. Berlin: Seven Seas, 1980.

Spinner, Thomas J., Jr. *A Political and Social History of Guyana, 1945–1983*. Boulder, CO: Westview, 1984.

PERCY C. HINTZEN

JAGUAR. The jaguar (*Panthera onca*) is the biggest, most powerful New World member of the cat family. A male jaguar can weigh between 200 and 250 pounds. Although jaguars rarely attack human beings, in folklore they are man-eaters. For many ancient and recent cultures in Latin

America, this mighty hunter has symbolized political and military power. The jaguar is also associated with shamans or priests.

For its size and weight, the jaguar has the most powerful bite of any large cat. Its head is flexible, and it has wide-field binocular vision and eye cells that take in all possible light. Its eyes seem mirror-like. Although it prefers moist, lowland, tropical forest, it can survive in many environments. It is a good swimmer, climbs trees, and may sleep in caves or crannies; thus, it fits human symbolic concepts of the levels of the world. Its tawny color makes it a sun symbol in some cultures, and because it hunts at night and seeks dark places, it is also linked to the underworld and the "other" world.

Jaguars are companions and avatars of pre-Columbian gods, whose pictures and statues often include jaguar attributes or show them wearing jaguar skins, although jaguars are rarely gods as such. In the last millennium CE, Olmec art in Mexico and Chavin art in Peru featured jaguar depictions. Later, Classic Maya kings sat on jaguar thrones, wore jaguar-skin garments, and took jaguar names. Jaguar remains have been found in royal Maya burials. On the north coast of Peru, Moche gods had feline fangs, and Moche rulers wore jaguar headdresses. At the time of the Spanish Conquest, the major orders of warriors in Aztec Mexico were named after the jaguar and the eagle. Jaguars were associated with human sacrifice in these cultures. In Toltec sculpture in Mexico, jaguars are shown eating human hearts. South American depictions of a jaguar with a man may be interpreted sometimes as a protector figure, a companion spirit, or alter ego; sometimes as the recipient or agent of human sacrifice; or sometimes as a shaman undergoing initiation.

The words for "jaguar" and "shaman" or "priest" are the same in many indigenous languages. In recent ethnographic literature, accounts of a shaman's transformation into a jaguar to protect his people are widespread. The shaman usually acquires the jaguar's power in ritual by using a psychoactive drug. Jaguar masks, sometimes with mirror eyes, are worn in some regions for special rites. Jaguar teeth or claws are used on shaman's belts or necklaces. Pre-Columbian rulers also had shamanic powers and supernatural aspects and used these to enhance personal power, presumably for the good of their people.

Archaeological objects and recent ethnographic literature suggest that some groups thought of themselves as people or children of the jaguar, with a jaguar ancestor, male or female, in the mythic past. Jaguars are often addressed as father, grandfather, uncle, or mother.

Degradation of the Jaguar's habitat—meaning it has less on which to feed and fewer places to rest and reproduce—has pushed the jaguar toward extinction. Hunting by outdoorsmen and poaching by livestock ranchers have contributed to its decline. Organizations in different countries have classified the jaguar variously as vulnerable, near-threatened, and endangered.

See also **Chavín; LePlongeon, Augustus; Olmecs.**

BIBLIOGRAPHY

Arroyo, Sergio Raúl. *El jaguar prehispánico: Huellas de lo divino.* Mexico City/Monterrey, Mexico: INAH/ Museo de Historia Mexicana, 2005.

Benson, Elizabeth P., ed. *The Cult of the Feline: A Conference in Pre-Columbian Iconography.* Washington, DC: Dumbarton Oaks Research Library and Collections, Trustees for Harvard University, 1972.

Fernández Balboa, Carlos. *Yaguar: Guía para conocer y defender al yaguar americano.* Buenos Aires, Argentina: Editorial Albatros, 1993.

Furst, Peter T. "The Olmec Were-Jaguar Motif in the Light of Ethnographic Reality." In *Dumbarton Oaks Conference on the Olmec*, edited by Elizabeth P. Benson. Washington, DC: Dumbarton Oaks Research Library and Collection, Trustees for Harvard University, 1968.

Rabinowitz, Alan. *Jaguar: Struggle and Triumph in the Jungles of Belize.* New York: Arbor House, 1986.

Saunders, Nicholas J. *People of the Jaguar: The Living Spirit of Ancient America.* London: Souvenir Press, 1989.

ELIZABETH P. BENSON

JAGUARIBE GOMES DE MATOS, HÉLIO

JAGUARIBE GOMES DE MATOS, HÉLIO (1923–). Hélio Jaguaribe Gomes de Matos (*b.* 1923), Brazilian political scientist. During the second half of the twentieth century, Jaguaribe distinguished himself as one of Brazil's foremost social scientists whose research interests and publications consistently presented innovative approaches to issues of political and social development in modern Brazil and Latin America. Best known for his studies on the role of political nationalism and social organization in Brazilian modernization, Jaguaribe's works are widely read among Latin Americanists in the Americas and Europe. Some of his most provocative early writings include the controversial *O nacionalismo na atualidade brasileira* (1958), *The Brazilian Structural Crisis* (1966), and *Economic and Political Development: A Theoretical Approach and a Brazilian Case Study* (1968), as well as collaborations with the journal *Cadernos de nosso tempo.* His later works, including *Crise na república* (1993) and *Brasil: Reforma ou caos* (1989), concentrate on the institutional, social, economic, and political problems involved in the transition from authoritarian to democratic rule, particularly in Brazil.

A native of Rio de Janeiro, Jaguaribe received a law degree from the Pontífica Universidade Católica of Rio de Janeiro (1946) and a doctorate from Mainz University in Germany (1983). After receiving his law degree, Jaguaribe worked as a lawyer, entrepreneur, and industrialist in the states of Rio de Janeiro and Espírito Santo. After entering academics in the mid-1950s, Jaguaribe taught extensively in Brazil, serving as a faculty member of the Instituto Superior de Estudos Brasileiros (1956–1959) and the Universidade de São Paulo, and abroad, as visiting professor at Harvard (1964–1966), Stanford (1966–1967), and the Massachusetts Institute of Technology (1968–1969). In the early 1990s, Jaguaribe served as dean of the Instituto de Estudos Políticos e Sociais do Rio de Janeiro.

Between 1994 and 1999, he worked with UNESCO in determining the principle conditions that influence the emergency and development of the main civilizations in history. This work allowed him to write a book titled *A Critical Study of History*, which was published in 2001.

See also **Brazil: 1808–1889; Brazil: Since 1889; Nationalism.**

BIBLIOGRAPHY

Additional Bibliography

Halper, Stefan A., and John R. Sterling, eds. *Latin America: The Dynamics of Social Change.* New York: St. Martin's Press, 1972.

Jaguaribe, Hélio. *Political Development: A General Theory and a Latin American Case Study.* New York: Harper & Row, 1973.

Jaguaribe, Hélio, et al. *Brasil, sociedade democrática.* Rio de Janeiro: Editora José Olímpio, 1985.

Jaguaribe, Hélio, et al. *Brasil, reforma ou caos.* Rio de Janeiro: Editora Paz e Terra, 1989.

Jaguaribe, Hélio. *Sociedade, Estado e partidos políticos na atualidade brasileira.* Rio de Janeiro: Editora Paz e Terra, 1992.

Jaguaribe, Hélio. *Brasil, homem e mundo–reflexão na virada do século.* Rio de Janeiro: Topbooks, 2000.

Jaguaribe, Hélio. *Um estudo crítico da história.* São Paulo: Editora Paz e Terra, 2001.

Lowenthal, Abraham F., and Gregory F. Treverton, eds. *Latin America in a New World.* Boulder, CO: Westview Press, 1994.

DARYLE WILLIAMS

JAGUNÇO. Jagunço, a bodyguard, hired gun, or assassin. Originating in northeastern Brazil in the early nineteenth century, *jagunços* were an integral part of rural life throughout the country well into the twentieth century. They formed the heavily armed military forces of *coronéis* (local political bosses) during regional power struggles and were also employed as enforcers of property rights against sharecroppers and squatters. Some *jagunços* became Cangaceiros (bandits), while many fought alongside Antônio Conselheiro during the millenarian Canudos conflict in Bahia (1896–1897). As Brazil modernized, they declined, but competition for land in the Amazon Basin has led to their resurgence under the name of *capanga.*

See also **Coronel, Coronelismo.**

BIBLIOGRAPHY

Euclides De Cunha, *Rebellion in the Backlands* (*Os Sertões*), translated by Samuel Putnam (1944).

Jorge Amado, *Jubiabá,* translated by Margaret A. Neves (1984).

Afonso Arinos, *Os jagunços: Novela,* 3d ed. (1985).

Additional Bibliography

Barros, Luitgarde Oliveira Cavalcanti. *A derradeira gesta: Lampião e nazarenos guerreando no sertão.* Rio de Janeiro: Mauad: FAPERJ, 2000.

Grunspan-Jasmin, Elise. *Lampião, senhor do sertão: Vidas e mortes de um cangaceiro.* São Paulo: Editora da Universidade de São Paulo, 2006.

Lins, Daniel Soares. *Lampião: O homem que amava as mulheres: o imaginário do cangaço.* São Paulo: Annablume, 1997.

ROBERT WILCOX

JAINA. Of the many traditions of figurine making among the ancient Maya, the figurines of Jaina Island are the most notable. The reasons are the great number, the duration of facture, and the quality of many individual works.

Jaina Island lies just off the coast of the Mexican state of Campeche, easily accessible by canoe and without relationship to any larger Maya site. A plaza separates two small complexes of architecture from one another on a limestone outcropping that rests above swampy areas below. Although only a small number of graves have been excavated legally, many more have been looted, and the figurines belong to collections of museums worldwide. There may have been tens of thousands of burials on the island; some were secondary burials, suggesting that the island was a choice for funerary veneration.

Román Piña Chán excavated several burials in the 1960s; he found no tombs with masonry chambers, only shallow graves. Because the preservation was poor, he did not determine a relationship between the gender of the figurine and the gender of the interred; interments received multiple figurine offerings, of varying quality, along with items of shell and bone, vessels, and stone tools.

Although artisans fashioned most figurines using molds (multiple examples survive from single molds), they formed the finest ones by hand, shaping solid bodies onto which clothing and other accoutrements could be layered, along with elaborate headdresses, sometimes using mold-made parts. Many depict warriors, captives, artisans, and courtly attendants; almost a quarter represent women, more than in any other medium of Maya art.

Most figurines are from 8 to 12 inches in height, and their gestures have made them appealingly lifelike. A number of paired examples survive, including male-female couples. Many are rattles or whistles, suggesting funerary music and dance. Once fully painted, the figurines retain traces of tenacious Maya blue, white, yellow, and red pigments applied after the firing process.

See also **Art: Pre-Columbian Art of Mesoamerica; Maya, The.**

BIBLIOGRAPHY

Piña Chán, Román. *Jaina, la casa en el agua.* Mexico: Instituto Nacional de Antropología, 1968.

MARY ELLEN MILLER

JALISCO. Jalisco, state in west central Mexico that is sixth largest in the area (30,941 square miles), and fourth largest in population (5,278,987 in 1990). The indigenous population that settled the area beginning about 15,000 years ago was less dense and more linguistically and culturally diverse than that of central Mexico. By the early sixteenth century, the area included well-developed sedentary chiefdoms and numerous nomadic peoples. Nuño Beltran de Guzmán's campaign of conquest (1529–1536) was bloody even by standards of the time. Further conflicts reduced the area's indigenous population by some 90 percent by 1560. Today Indian elements are notably scarce in Jalisco's culture, and with the exception of some 65,000 Indians, mostly *huicholes,* the state is predominantly *criollo* and mestizo. Guadalajara, the chief city, has been the seat of a bishopric since 1548. It was the capital of Nueva Galicia and seat of New Spain's only independent *audiencia* since 1560.

Under Spanish rule in the seventeenth century, the area developed haciendas (great landed estates) as well as an occasionally spurious local nobility. Peninsular Spanish immigrants, who often succeeded as merchants because Guadalajara was such an important entrepôt in New Spain's trade network with the northern provinces, then intermarried with landed families to integrate an oligopoly based on agriculture, commerce, and mining. Discovery of silver at Bolaños initiated a period of growth in 1747 that was boosted by a relaxation of trading restrictions in 1773. This development broadened the economic base, created a more mobile and wage-oriented labor force, and thus laid the groundwork for future industrial development.

The Wars of Independence from Spain, beginning in 1810, devastated the local economy. The insurgents' temporary seizure of Guadalajara in late 1810 foreshadowed a period of several decades when the capital was to be the political and military football first of royalists and insurgents, later of centralists and federalists, then of monarchists and constitutionalists. Real recovery did not begin until the peace imposed by dictator Porfirio Díaz between 1876 and 1910.

By the time the revolution against Díaz broke out in 1910, Jalisco was losing influence relative to Sonora, Nuevo León, and other rival states. As a bastion of conservative Spanish Catholicism, Jalisco in this period is perhaps best remembered as the focal point of the proclerical Cristero Rebellion (1916–1929), a bitter reaction to the anticlerical policies of the revolutionary leaders Alvaro Obregón and Plutarco Elías Calles. Even today, the ruling party (Institutional Revolutionary Party—PRI) is often sharply challenged by opposition parties and prochurch elements with power bases in Jalisco.

Guadalajara was a somewhat distant second to Mexico City in size and influence until the nineteenth century. As early as 1840, the city had begun to develop an industrial base dominated by paper and printing, clothing, and food products. Today, Guadalajara is a major industrial and commercial center, with photographic and electrical goods, textiles, tequila, and steel leading the list of local products. Other important municipalities in the state include Puerto Vallarta (home of the state's second international airport), Lagos de Moreno, Tepatitlán, Ciudad Guzmán, and Ocotlán.

Jalisco is still the country's top maize producer and the second-largest cattle producer, and trade accounts for approximately 20 percent of the state's domestic product. The state is popularly identified with such *criollo* cultural monuments as tequila, *charros* (elaborately costumed cowboys), and mariachi music, and with the international beach resort of Puerto Vallarta. Outsiders encounter the state's culture through the works of such prominent twentieth-century natives as writers Agustín Yáñez and Juan Rulfo and the muralist José Clemente Orozco, as well as through *huichol* yarn paintings, pottery from Tonalá, and hand-blown glass from Tlaquepaque.

See also **Calles, Plutarco Elías; Cristero Rebellion; Díaz, Porfirio; Guadalajara; Guzmán, Nuño Beltrán de; Huichols; Mestizo; Obregón Salido, Álvaro; Orozco, José Clemente; Rulfo, Juan; Yáñez Santos Delgadillo, Agustín.**

BIBLIOGRAPHY

References in English consist mainly of topical monographs and dissertations that can be located through the Library of Congress, *Handbook of Latin American Studies,* and University Microfilms, *Dissertation Abstracts.* The standard source in Spanish is José María Muriá, *Historia de Jalisco,* 4 vols. (1980–1982); a much shorter version, *sans* bibliography, is his *Breve historia de Jalisco* (1988). Relatively recent Spanish-language sources can be found in Jaime Olveda and Marina Mantilla Trolle, *Jalisco en libros* (1985). A more general bibliography is Ramiro Villaseñor y Villaseñor, *Bibliografía general de Jalisco,* 2 vols. (1958, 1983).

Additional Bibliography

Fábregas, Andrés. *El norte de Jalisco: Sociedad, cultura e historia en una región Mexicana.* Zapopán: El Colegio de Jalisco, 2002.

González Navarro, Moisés. *Masones y cristeros en Jalisco.* México, D.F.: El Colegio de México, Centro de estudios históricos, 2000.

Shadow, Robert Dennis. *Tierra, trabajo, y ganado en la región norte de Jalisco: Una historia agraria de Villa Guerrero, Jalisco, 1600–1980.* Zamora, Michoacán: Colegio de Michoacán; Colotlán: Universidad de Guadalajara, Centro Universitario del Norte, 2002.

RICHARD LINDLEY

JAMA-COAQUE. Jama-Coaque, the name originally given to the prehistoric culture occupying northern Manabí Province, Ecuador, during the Regional-Developmental period, (500 BCE–CE 500). More recent research has established that the Jama-Coaque tradition represents four phases of occupation beginning around 550 BCE and continuing until the Spanish conquest in 1531. Although its territory may have fluctuated over time, it minimally extended along the northern Manabí coast from Bahía de Cojimíes in the north to Bahía de Caráquez in the south. To the east, limited archaeological evidence suggests that Jama-Coaque influence extended to the Andean foothills.

Jama-Coaque was originally defined by the Ecuadoran archaeologist Emilio Estrada in the late 1950s, on the basis of limited test excavations at the littoral type sites of Coaque and Jama. The culture is best known for its tradition of elaborate ceramic figurines and modeled vessels depicting a wide range of anthropomorphic and zoomorphic imagery. It shares many characteristics with the Bahía culture to the south, such as ceramic house models and neck rests, suggesting shared Asiatic influences. Also common to both cultures are several vessel forms and decorative techniques, such as negative painting, postfire multicolored painting, and nicked or cutout flattened rims on shallow polypod bowls, but enough differences exist to differentiate the two styles clearly. Jama-Coaque figurines are commonly mold-made, and even the larger, hollow, modeled figurines depicting elite personages or dragonlike animals typically exhibit detailed ornamentation assembled from standardized mold-made pieces. Other typical pottery artifacts include both flat and cylindrical stamps or seals, incised spindle whorls, zoomorphic whistles and flutes, and anthropomorphic masks that may have functioned as pendants. A number of these ceramic objects, as well as specific costumes and ornamentation depicted on figurines, have stylistic parallels in Mesoamerica, suggesting maritime contacts with western Mexico.

Both the costumes depicted on figurines and the evidence of numerous fabric impressions in clay suggest a well-developed textile industry. Featherworking is also depicted on some figurine costumes. Lithic industries included a sophisticated lapidary technology of carved and polished greenstone and jadeite. Obsidian was imported from highland sources near the Quito Basin, and a well-developed prismatic blade industry is present at several sites. Artifacts of cut and polished *Spondylus* shell were crafted into sumptuary ornaments and may have been traded to highlanders for obsidian. The abundance and standardization exhibited by many of these artifact categories suggest a well-developed craft specialization.

Archaeological research in the Jama Valley, at moister higher elevations inland from the coast, have shed new light on the nature of Jama-Coaque settlement dynamics and subsistence production. High population densities and multitiered settlement hierarchies are present throughout the sequence, along with intensified agricultural production based on maize and root crops. The Jama-Coaque polities were stratified chiefdoms that minimally controlled a large river valley. It is also possible that a single paramount from a large ceremonial civic center ruled over all of northern Manabí at various times in the prehistoric past. One such regional center is the site of San Isidro, in the middle Jama Valley some 15 miles inland from the coast. It has over 125 acres of thick habitation refuse and is dominated by a large central platform mound measuring 110 yards in width at the base and some 19 yards in height. Smaller platform mounds have been documented at secondary centers throughout the valley.

By the time of Pizarro's march through Coaque and Pasao in 1531, the Jama-Coaque peoples may have been coming under the progressive domination of the Manteño polity to the south. Although not conclusive, the presence of Manteño burnished black pottery in several Late Integration sites suggests the establishment of enclave communities that perhaps administered tribute payments from the local Jama-Coaque populations.

See also **Archaeology; Atacames; Guangala.**

BIBLIOGRAPHY

Emilio Estrada, *Prehistoria de Manabí* (1957).

Clifford Evans and Betty Meggers, "Mesoamerica and Ecuador," in *Handbook of Middle American Indians,* edited by Robert Wauchope, vol. 4 (1966).

Betty Meggers, *Ecuador* (1966).

Robert A. Feldman and Michael E. Moseley, "The Northern Andes," in *Ancient South Americans,* edited by Jesse D. Jennings (1983).

James A. Zeidler and Deborah M. Pearsall, eds., *Regional Archaeology in Northern Manabí, Ecuador,* vol. 1, *Environment, Cultural Chronology, and Prehistoric Subsistence in the Jama River Valley* (1994).

Additional Bibliography.

Cummins, Thomas B.F. *Arte Prehíspanico del Ecuador: Huellas del pasado: Los sellos de jama-coaque.* Guyaquil: Banco Central de Ecuador, 1996.

James A. Zeidler

JAMAICA. Jamaica, an island in the West Indian archipelago that encircles the Caribbean Sea, has a land area encompassing 4,471 square miles, an area slightly smaller than the state of Connecticut. The climate is mostly tropical, with a temperate interior.

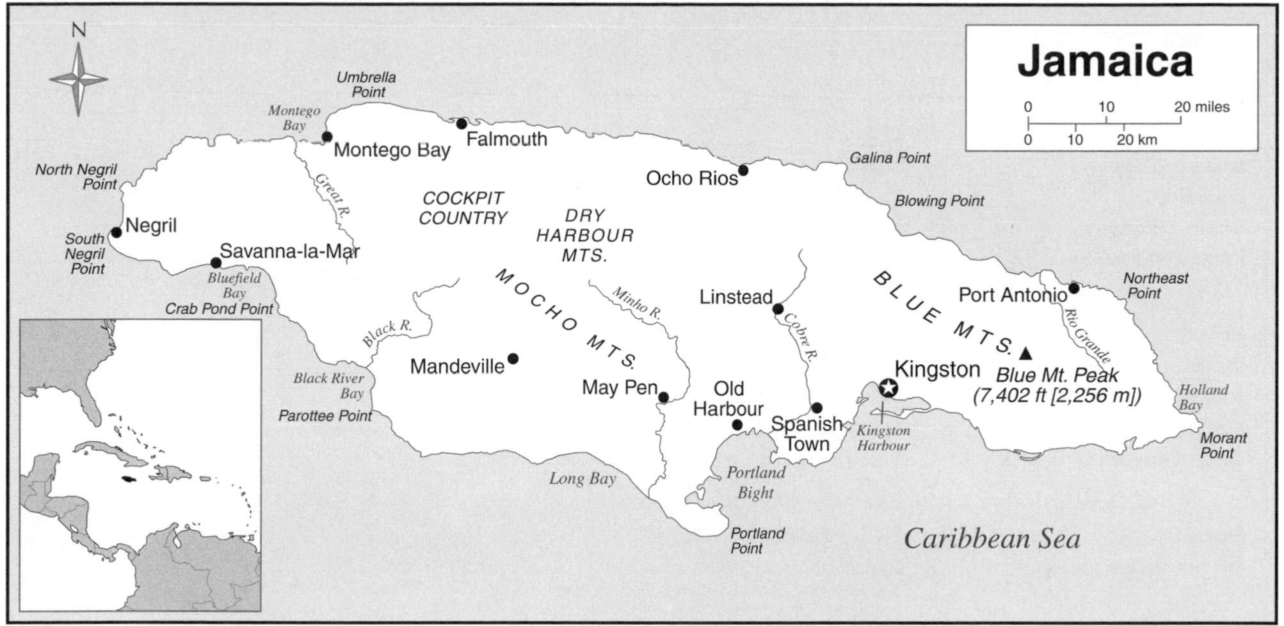

The terrain is predominantly mountainous, reaching a height of 7,400 feet in the Blue Mountain range. The nation's population in 2007 was approximately 2.7 million, 49 percent of which lived in urban areas. The ethnic divisions are as follows: 90 percent African; 7.3 percent multiracial; 1.3 percent East Indian and Afro–East Indian. Ethnic diversity plays a major role in Jamaican history.

Although recorded Jamaican history began with European arrival in the New World, Jamaica has a rich pre-Columbian history. Its earliest inhabitants were the peaceful Arawak Indians who sought refuge from the more aggressive Caribs. Unfortunately, little remains of their culture. Archaeologists have been able to reconstruct some patterns from kitchen middens, burial caves, and other artifacts. Although Jamaica provided the necessary refuge from the Caribs, no such haven could protect the Arawaks from the Europeans.

Christopher Columbus, on his second transatlantic voyage, arrived in Jamaica on May 5, 1494, going ashore at what is now called Discovery Bay. He received a less than hospitable welcome from native inhabitants. On further excursions, he found the natives living on the western part of the island more amiable. As Jamaica was not a source of gold, Spain used it mainly as a supply base. Whereas the first Spanish community, Sevilla la Nueva, was unsuccessful, other settlements and townships, most notably St. Jago de la Vega (Spanish Town), became well established. Settlers introduced the banana and most citrus fruits.

English interest in the island dated from at least 1569, but not until 1643 did the British attach much importance to it. During this time, Spanish-English relations became more tenuous. In 1655, under Cromwell's "Western Design," Admiral William Penn and General Oliver Robert Venables attacked Jamaica after being routed by the Spaniards at Santo Domingo, having relatively little trouble taking the island. The Spaniards, intent on making British occupation temporary, freed their black slaves, who escaped to the mountains and aggravated the British through guerrilla warfare. These guerrillas would later become known as Maroons.

In 1656 some 1,600 colonists came to the island, settling around Port Morant. While the soil was healthy, the surrounding area was swampy, and within three months 1,200 colonists had died. The Spaniards tried at various times to recapture the island but failed. Jamaica was legally ceded to the English by the Treaty of Madrid (1670), but the island received only nominal English attention. It was not until large sugar plantations displaced the small independent settler that the island increased in political importance.

Jamaica	
Population:	2,780,132 (2007 est.)
Area:	4,244 sq mi
Official language:	English
Languages:	English, English patois, Creole
National currency:	Jamaican dollar (JMD)
Principal religions:	Seventh-Day Adventist, 10.8%; Pentecostal, 9.5%; Other Church of God, 8.3%; Baptist, 7.2%; New Testament Church of God, 6.3%; Church of God in Jamaica, 4.8%; Church of God of Prophecy, 4.3%; Anglican, 3.6%; other Protestant Christian, 7.7%; Roman Catholic, 2.6%
Ethnicity:	African, 90%; multiracial, 7.3%; East Indian and Afro-East Indian, 1.3%
Capital:	Kingston (est. pop. 575,000 in 2005)
Other urban centers:	Montego Bay, Portmore, Spanish Town
Annual rainfall:	30 inches on the south coast, up to 200 inches in the mountains and northeast
Principal geographical features:	*Mountains:* Blue Mts., which reach a maximum elevation of 7,402 ft. *Rivers:* Black, Rio Grande, Yallahs *Islands:* Morant Cays, Pedro Cays
Economy:	*GDP per capita:* $4,700 (2006 est.)
Principal products and exports:	*Agricultural:* bananas, coffee, sugar *Manufacturing:* cement, light manufacture, rum *Mining:* bauxite/alumina Tourism is one of the most important components of Jamaica's economy.
Government:	Independence from the United Kingdom, 1962; Constitution, 1962. Constitutional parliamentary democracy. The chief of state is the monarch of the United Kingdom, represented by a governor general appointed on the advice of the prime minister. The prime minister is head of government, the prime minister is technically appointed by the governor general but in practice is the leader of the ruling party or coalition in the legislature. The legislature is a bicameral Parliament, consisting of a 21-seat Senate and a 60-seat House of Representatives. Representatives are elected by popular vote to 5-year terms. Senators are appointed by the governor general on the recommendation of the prime minister, with the majority party receiving 13 seat and the minority 8. There are 13 units of local government (parishes).
Armed forces:	*Army:* 2,500 *Navy:* 190 (Coast Guard) *Air force:* 140 *Reserves:* 950
Transportation:	*Ports:* Kingston, Port Esquivel, Port Kaiser, Port Rhoades, Rocky Point *Roads:* 9,560 mi paved; 3,486 mi unpaved *National airlines:* Air Jamaica, Trans Jamaica Airlines *Airports:* 11 paved runway and 23 unpaved runway airports; international facilities at Kingston and Montego Bay
Media:	4 daily newspapers, including *Daily Star* and *Jamaica Gleaner;* major weeklies include *Thursday Star* and *Sunday Gleaner.* 13 radio and 3 television stations, major broadcasters include Radio Jamaica Limited and Television Jamaica Limited, both privately owned.
Literacy and education:	*Total literacy rate:* 87.9% (2003 est.) Six years of primary education is required. Several colleges and technical schools available, as well as a campus of the University College of the West Indies.

Beginning with the seventeenth century, sugar and slavery were central factors in Jamaica's development. By 1673 sugar had become Jamaica's staple crop, the "gold" sought by the Spaniards. For the most part, absentee ownership was the preferred form of plantation management. Slaves and intensive labor were needed to tend sugarcane. During the eighteenth century, approximately five thousand slaves per year were brought to Jamaica. The slaves brought their customs and religions, which were often an important force in slave rebellions.

The Maroons, the freed Spanish slaves who had escaped to the dense forest interior, also carried out rebellions. They molested the English from the very beginning, swooping down from the hills, raiding farms and towns, and burning fields. Escaped slaves flocked to the Maroons, swelling their numbers and strengthening their position. Conflict with the Maroons lasted until 1796 and cost the British approximately £250,000.

Resolving the Maroon conflict, however, did little to rectify social inequalities for the Jamaican slave. Men and women continued to suffer under the prevailing system. Foreign events promoted the continued use of slavery on Jamaica. First, wars with both the United States and France were costly, and Jamaica's sugar and coffee were important commodities in financing the wars. Second, as ideas from the French Revolution filtered to the Caribbean and especially Haiti, slaves of that nation clamored for freedom. After a failed attempt to take Haiti, but having witnessed its slave rebellions, the British returned to Jamaica determined to prevent similar uprisings.

In 1838, humanitarian efforts in England coupled with resistance to slavery led to emancipation. As in many nations, however, the abolition of slavery brought new social struggles. In Jamaica two distinct societies continued to exist. At times social diversity led to increased tensions, as with the Morant Bay Rebellion of 1865, in which the peasantry revolted against the planter class.

Social tensions exacerbated a declining economy. Jamaica's agricultural industry remained highly susceptible to fluctuating world markets and economic conditions, and continued to decline until the pre–World War II era, when England reinstituted isolationist policies and subsidies for its colonies. This refuge was temporary.

When Jamaica received its independence in 1962, social tensions continued to permeate Jamaican life. The black shoulder continued to bear Jamaica's poverty. Out of these conditions grew the influential Rastafarian religious movement. Founded in the 1930s, the Rastafarians advocated black nationalism and recognized the ties of the people to Africa. Black nationalism was strengthened by the civil rights movement in the United States. In 1963 Jamaicans took to the streets of Kingston, inspired by Martin Luther King, Jr. The Kingston protests were strongly anti-imperialist and pro-socialist; the calls for an end to social injustices, however, fell on deaf ears at the official level.

This intransigence was made all too clear when popular Guyanese lecturer Walter Rodney, an advocate of black power, was denied entrance into Jamaica by Prime Minister Hugh Shearer on October 15, 1968. The following day black Jamaicans once again took to the streets in protest. The demonstration resulted in substantial property damage and the loss of two lives. Shearer labeled Rodney a subversive and a Communist. Although calls for reform sounded from many parts of the country, legislators were slow to respond.

In the 1970s, the failure to respond to social injustice allowed a socialist government under the leadership of Michael Manley and the People's National Party to come to power. Poor economic world trends, however, produced many hardships for Jamaica, and while Manley's government did make gains in social justice, real economic changes were hindered. The socialist experiment failed in 1980, after which Jamaica was ruled by the more conservative Labour Party. Under Prime Minister Edward Seaga, Jamaica reestablished ties with the International Monetary Fund, yet continued to struggle with its debt. Economic and social conditions were exacerbated when, in 1988, Michael Manley once again returned to power. Enacting austerity measures and continuing a free-market approach, the People's National Party was positive about Jamaica's future. Manley was able to convince major world powers to forgive a substantial portion of Jamaica's debt.

Manley stepped down in 1992 and P. J. Patterson of the People's National Party became prime minister until 2006. Fellow party member Portia Simpson-Miller replaced him and became the first female prime minister. However, Bruce Golding of the Jamaican Labour Party defeated Simpson-Miller in the 2007 election. While the economy went through a recession in the mid-1990s, Jamaica has experienced moderate economic growth in the early twenty-first century. Nevertheless, income inequality and high unemployment will continue to be policy concerns.

See also **British-Latin American Relations; Buccaneers and Privateers.**

BIBLIOGRAPHY

Abrahams, Peter. *Jamaica: An Island Mosaic.* London: His Majesty's Stationery Office, 1957.

G. Beckford, George, and Michael Witter. *Small Garden, Bitter Weed: The Political Economy of Struggle and Change in Jamaica.* London: Zed Press, 1982.

Black, Clinton V. *The Story of Jamaica from Prehistory to the Present.* London: Collins, 1965.

Ingram, Kenneth E. *Jamaica.* Oxford, U.K.: Clio, 1984.

Knight, Franklin W. *The Caribbean: Genesis of a Fragmented Nationalism.* Oxford, U.K.: Oxford University Press, 1990.

Knight, Franklin W., and Colin A. Palmer, eds., *The Modern Caribbean* Chapel Hill: University of North Carolina Press, 1989.

Looney, Robert E. *The Jamaican Economy in the 1980s* Boulder, CO: Westview Press, 1986.

Manley, Michael. *Jamaica: Struggle in the Periphery.* London: Third World Media Ltd., 1982.

McCarthy, Lloyd D. *Independence from Bondage: Claude McKay and Michael Manley: Defying the Ideological Clash and Policy Gaps in African Diaspora Relations.* Trenton, NJ: Africa World Press, 2007.

Nettleford, Rex. *Jamaica in Independence.* London: James Currey, 1989.

Payne, Anthony J. *Politics in Jamaica*, rev. edition. New York: St. Martin's Press, 1995.

ALLAN S. R. SUMNALL

JAMES, CYRIL LIONEL ROBERT

(1901–1989). Cyril Lionel Robert James (*b.* 4 January 1901; *d.* 31 May 1989), historian, philosopher, literary critic. C. L. R. James is well known outside his island home of Trinidad and Tobago as one of the twentieth century's leading intellectuals. His illustrious career as a writer spans several disciplines. His contributions to cultural studies, political philosophy, and West Indian creative and historical literature both predict and inform the late twentieth century's preoccupation with postcolonial studies and have earned him a place of high respect as an interpreter of both Marx's and Lenin's philosophies.

Throughout his life James was recognized as a brilliant student and teacher. When he emigrated to England in 1932, he established himself as a keen cricket commentator, writing for the *Manchester Guardian.* Later in his career he combined the history of cricket with autobiography to create a stunning cultural critique of the West Indies in *Beyond a Boundary* (1963). His novel *Minty Alley,* written in 1927, is a foundational text in the Caribbean literary tradition. His historical work, *The Black Jacobins: Toussaint L'Ouverture and the San Domingo Revolution* (1938), remains a universally acclaimed account of the Haitian war for independence in relationship to the French Revolution.

James was a major figure in the Pan-African movement in the 1930s. The continual development of his political ideologies can be traced through his numerous and diverse essays, collected in several volumes. Both his essays and full-length works reflect a keen interest in and healthy skepticism for Marxism, Trotskyism, socialism, and notions of American democracy. In association with Trotsky's organization, with which he later broke, James spent fifteen years in the United States (1938–1953) lecturing and organizing black workers. A casualty of the McCarthy era, he was asked to leave the country because his activities were considered too radical. While awaiting deportation, James wrote *Mariners, Renegades, and Castaways: The Story of Herman Melville and the World We Live In* (1953), a literary critique of Herman Melville's novel *Moby Dick,* but also a political commentary on totalitarianism and American democracy. James periodically revisited the Caribbean and also traveled through Europe and Africa. In 1968, he was allowed to reenter the United States, where he taught at Federal City College for ten years. During the last decades of his life he continued to write and lecture widely, and received awards and accolades from around the world. He died in London, England, his adopted home.

See also **Labor Movements.**

BIBLIOGRAPHY

Paul Buhle, ed., *C. L. R. James: His Life and Work* (1986), and *C. L. R. James: The Artist as Revolutionary* (1988).

Anna Grimshaw, *The C. L. R. James Archive: A Reader's Guide* (1991).

Anna Grimshaw, ed., *The C. L. R. James Reader* (1992).

Paget Henry and Paul Buhle, eds., *C. L. R. James's Caribbean* (1992).

Additional Bibliography

Dhondy, Farrukh. *C.L.R. James: A Life.* New York: Pantheon Books, 2001.

King, Nicole. *C.L.R. James and Creolization: Circles of Influence.* Jackson, MS: University Press of Mississippi, 2001.

Worcester, Kent. *C.L.R. James: A Political Biography.* Albany, NY: State University of New York Press, 1995.

NICOLE R. KING

JANGADA.

Jangada, a raft made of lightweight logs secured with wooden pegs or lianas, used for fishing by various indigenous groups in precolonial Brazil. Pero Vaz da Caminha recorded the first description of a *jangada,* misidentifying it as a pirogue. Tupi names for these vessels were many: *itapaba, igapeba, candandu, piperi,* and *catamarã.* The Portuguese adopted and modified the original raft, eventually labeling it *jangada,* from the Hindustani *janga* with the augmentative *ada,* meaning "larger."

The raft was first made of three logs, had no sail, and was guided by a fisherman who sat with legs extended. It was later expanded to five or six logs with a rudder (also used for a paddle). A stone on a woven rope was, and still is, used to anchor the *jangada.* A mast for a triangular sail was developed by the seventeenth century. There are small (about 10 feet by 2½ feet), medium (about 15 feet by 5 feet), and "classic," or large, *jangadas,* which measure about 26 to 30 feet by 6½ feet and require six to seven logs. The larger rafts may carry a crew of up to four men, each having a special title and function and receiving a certain portion of the catch according to his station, as recorded by noted authority Luís da Câmara Cascudo.

Jangadas are found primarily along Brazil's Northeastern coast from Bahia to Pernambuco to Ceará, and in each state a distinctive vocabulary exists to label the logs, vessel size, auxiliary equipment, and crew. Used today only by the poorest fishermen, the *jangada* has become a symbol of the Northeast, immortalized in prose, poetry, and song.

See also **Precontact History: Amazonia.**

BIBLIOGRAPHY

Luís Da Câmara Cascudo, *Dicionário do folclore brasileiro,* 3d ed. (1972).

Nearco Barroso Guedes Araújo, *Jangadas,* 2d ed. (1990).

GAYLE WAGGONER LOPES

JANITZIO. Janitzio, island in Lake Pátzcuaro (Michoacán, Mexico). Janitzio is home to one of the many distinctive Tarascan communities that settled on and around Lake Pátzcuaro. During the Mexican wars for independence from Spain the insurgents built a fort on the island that was attacked in 1816 by royalist forces. The heroic defense mounted by the insurgents is commemorated by an enormous 132-foot statue of José María Morelos y Pavón (1765–1815). The statue, in its strikingly beautiful setting, along with the picturesque butterfly fishing nets made and used by the island people (today mainly viewed in postcards, in light of the decline of the lake), have made Janitzio the subject of popular songs and a place of tourism.

See also **Morelos y Pavón, José María.**

BIBLIOGRAPHY

Pablo G. Macías, *Pátzcuaro* (Morelia, 1978).

Additional Bibliography

Toledo, Victor M. *Plan Patzcuaro 2000: Presentación, Objectivos, Propuestas.* Morelia, Mexico: SEMARNAP, 1996.

MARGARET CHOWNING

JAPANESE–LATIN AMERICAN RELATIONS. The history of Japanese relations with Latin America dates from the early seventeenth century. By means of the Manila Galleon, Japanese and other Asian merchants developed a thriving trade with New Spain. Throughout most of the Tokugawa shogunate (1639–1857), however, Japan remained isolated from most foreign contact. The impetus for modernization, begun during the Meiji Restoration of the late nineteenth century, led Japan to cultivate commercial and diplomatic relations with the Pacific nations of Latin America. Seeking a precedent for the establishment of co-equal treaties with the major world powers, Japan signed a commercial treaty with Mexico in 1888. These initial trade ventures with Mexico, and later Peru and Chile, were soon overshadowed by Japanese government-sponsored immigration to Latin America. Designed to alleviate increasing economic distress among Japan's agricultural population, these first immigrants (*nikkei*) were recruited mainly from southern Japan and particularly the island of Honshu. Later, these *nikkei* would be joined by immigrants from Okinawa.

While some of the first *nikkei* learned Spanish and converted to Roman Catholicism, most remained determined to promote the Japanese language and culture within their Latin American immigrant communities. Cultural organizations such as Peru's Nihonjin Doshikai (Japanese Brotherhood Association) and Mexico's Confederación de las Asociaciones Japonesas en la República Mexicana, enhanced Japanese cultural awareness and solidarity. Second-generation Japanese (*nisei*) in Latin America were generally educated in Japanese language schools, and the children of prosperous *issei* (first generation) were frequently sent to Japan to complete their education. Ironically, the very success of Latin American *issei* and *nisei* in building prosperous and culturally cohesive communities was at once their greatest strength and most significant vulnerability.

The first Japanese *nikkei* faced the same opposition earlier Chinese immigrants to the Western Hemisphere had encountered. After the Gentlemen's Agreement of 1907, Japanese immigration in the hemisphere was redirected from the United States and Mexico to the South American nations, where the *issei* made their livelihoods in commercial agriculture and later in urban commerce, with Brazil becoming the destination for the vast majority of Japanese. On the eve of World War II, approximately 190,000 of Latin America's 250,000 Japanese resided in Brazil, largely in agricultural cooperatives in São Paulo State.

Japanese militarism in the 1930s and the early financial success of many Latin American *nikkei* exacerbated the existing ill will and suspicion displayed by many Latin Americans toward the highly insular Japanese communities. After Pearl Harbor, nearly 2,000 Latin American Japanese, mostly from Peru, Central America, and Mexico, were deported from their adopted countries and interned in camps in the western United States. The Mexican government adopted a domestic internment policy similar to that of the United States, while Brazil, Bolivia, and Paraguay allowed their *nikkei* populations to remain in relatively isolated agricultural colonies where minimal security measures were taken. Tokyo made only limited attempts to establish espionage networks in Latin America during the war. These efforts were largely confined to the Japanese diplomatic communities in Argentina and Chile before both nations broke relations with the Axis. Japanese nationals in Latin America were generally instructed to maintain a low profile, and the vast majority did so, with the exception of the fanatically nationalistic Shindō Remmei patriotic league in Brazil.

By the early 1950s, Japanese immigration to Latin America resumed with the governments of Paraguay and Bolivia actively seeking these new colonists. As Japan emerged to become an economically powerful nation in the 1960s, many Latin American nations began to perceive themselves as Pacific Rim states and sought active trade relations with Tokyo to counterbalance the dominance of the United States in the hemisphere. By the 1980s, Japanese economic power made that country the second-largest trading partner with Peru and Chile, and the third-largest investor in Mexico. In 2004, Japan signed a free-trade pact with Mexico. Japanese immigration to Latin America effectively ceased by the late 1960s as the Japanese agricultural sector attained unprecedented levels of prosperity.

There have been major changes among the Japanese in Latin America in the 1990s. Thousands of Latin American Japanese, mostly Brazilian *nisei* and *sansei* (third generation), are immigrating to Japan now that foreign-born Japanese can more easily obtain work permits. Over 200,000 Japanese Brazilians live in Japan and are the largest group of Portuguese-speakers in Asia. But given the questionable economic future of many Latin American nations, it now seems clear that the historic pattern of Japanese immigration and settlement is not likely to be renewed. In the future, Japan's influence is likely to grow, but more through trade and culture than through settlement of new groups of pioneering *nikkei*. In Peru the election of *nisei* Alberto Fujimori to the presidency in 1990 elevated public awareness of the Japanese presence in Latin America.

In 1997 Fujimori gained great popularity by rescuing Japanese citizens held hostage at the Japanese embassy by the revolutionary group Movimiento Revolucionario Túpac Amaru (MRTA). Fujimori won the next three presidential elections, but after a scandal in 2000, early in his third term, he went into exile in Japan. There, the Japanese government revealed that he had never given up his Japanese citizenship. Despite Peru's extradition requests, the Japanese state allowed Fujimori to reside in Japan.

See also **Asians in Latin America; Fujimori, Alberto Keinya; Manila Galleon.**

BIBLIOGRAPHY

James L. Tigner, *The Okinawans in Latin America* (1954).

Norman Stewart, *Japanese Colonization in Eastern Paraguay* (1967).

Philip Staniford, *Pioneers in the Tropics: The Political Organization of the Japanese in an Immigrant Community in Brazil* (1973).

Nobuya Tsuchida, "The Japanese in Brazil, 1908–1941" (Ph.D. diss., UCLA, 1978).

Amelia Morimoto, *Fuerza de trabajo immigrante japonesa y desarrollo en el Perú* (1979).

C. Harvey Gardiner, *Pawns in a Triangle of Hate: The Peruvian Japanese and the United States* (1981).

Maria Elena Ota Mishima, *Siete migraciones japonesas en Mexico, 1890–1978* (1982).

Susan Kaufman Purcell and Robert M. Immerman, eds., *Japan and Latin America in the New Global Order* (1992).

Additional Bibliography

Di Tella, Torcuato S., and Akio Hosono, eds. *Japón-América Latina: La construcción de un vínculo.* Buenos Aires: Nuevohacer, Grupo Editor Latinoamericano, 1998.

Murakami, Yusuke. *El espejo del otro: El Japón ante la crisis de los rehenes en el Peru.* Lima: Instituto de Estudios Peruanos, 1999.

DANIEL M. MASTERSON
JOHN F. BRATZEL

JARA, VÍCTOR (1934–1973). Víctor Jara (*b.* 28 September 1934; *d.* 14/15 September 1973), Chilean singer, songwriter, and theater director. One of the leading figures of the New Chilean Song movement of the later 1960s and early 1970s, Jara was born into a peasant family in Lonquén, near Talagante, in central Chile. After his military service (1952–1953), he studied acting at the University of Chile drama school, later acquiring a reputation as a theater director. Given his innate musical skill and his work with folk groups such as Cuncumén, with whom he toured Latin America and Europe, he soon found a place among the musicians gathering at the Peña de los Parra, an informal club founded in 1965 by Ángel and Isabel Parra, which was the focal point of New Chilean Song as it took shape. Several of Jara's songs (many pointed, some controversial) were to become true classics of the period, while his singing gained popularity.

A loyal but undogmatic Communist, Jara was a devoted supporter of President Salvador Allende and became an immediate victim when the military seized power in September 1973. He was arrested, brutally beaten, and shot in one of the most tragic events of a tragic time.

See also **Allende Gossens, Salvador; Theater.**

BIBLIOGRAPHY

Joan Jara, *An Unfinished Song: The Life of Víctor Jara* (1983).

Additional Bibliography

Aguilera, Pilar, Ricardo Fredes, Ariel Dorfman, et al. *Chile: The Other September 11.* New York: Ocean Press, 2003.

Sepúlveda Corradini, Gabriel. *Víctor Jara: Hombre de teatro.* Santiago, Chile: Editorial Sudamericana, 2001.

Sierra I Fabra, Jordi. *Victor Jara: Reventando los Silencios.* Madrid: Joaquin Turina, 2000.

SIMON COLLIER

JARA CORONA, HERIBERTO (1879–1968). Heriberto Jara Corona, born on July 10, 1879, in Nogales, in the state of Veracruz, Mexico, is one of the most symbolic figures of the Mexican Revolution. A distinguished fighter for social causes, he was active in the ranks of Ricardo Flores Magón's Mexican Liberal Party. In 1910 Jara joined the Madero movement, which opposed the reelection of Porfirio Díaz. When Madero won, Jara served as deputy in the twenty-sixth congress, representing the textile region of Orizaba. As a deputy he fought Victoriano Huerta, who had taken over the presidency of Mexico after overthrowing Madero, and in 1913 joined the constitutionalist forces of Venustiano Carranza. In 1914 he served as military governor of Mexico City. At the head of the Ocampo brigade, he oversaw the withdrawal of the U.S. Army from the Port of Veracruz. As a constituent deputy (1916–1917), Jara participated in preparing article 123 of the 1917 constitution, which established the social rights of workers. He collaborated with the government of Lázaro Cárdenas and in 1938 led the Party of the Mexican Revolution. He served as secretary of the navy from 1940 to 1946. After a lifetime devoted to the pursuit of peace, he died on April 17, 1968, in Mexico City.

See also **Cárdenas del Río, Lázaro; Carranza, Venustiano; de la Huerta, Adolfo; Flores Magón, Ricardo; Mexico, Political Parties: Partido Liberal Mexicano; Mexico, Political Parties: Party of the Mexican Revolution (PRM); Mexico, Wars and Revolutions: Mexican Revolution; Río Blanco Strike.**

BIBLIOGRAPHY

González Marín, Silvia. *Heriberto Jara, un luchador obrero en la Revolución Mexicana (1879–1917)*. México, D.F.: Sociedad Cooperativa Publicaciones Mexicanas, 1984.

Zapata Vela, Carlos. *Conversaciones con Heriberto Jara*. México, D.F.: Costa-Amic Editores, 1992.

SILVIA GONZALEZ MARIN

JARAMILLO ALVARADO, PÍO (1884–1968).

Liberal lawyer and sociologist Pío Jaramillo Alvarado (17 May 1884–24 July 1968) is best-known for his critique of the exploitation of indigenous peoples in Ecuador. He was born to a white mestizo family in the southern Ecuadorian province of Loja. Typical of early twentieth century *indigenistas*, he critiqued indigenous realities from a non-indigenous perspective. In 1940 he led the Ecuadorian delegation to the Pátzcuaro Congress in Mexico that founded the Interamerican Indigenist Institute. Three years later he helped found the Ecuadorian Indigenist Institute, for which he subsequently served as director.

Jaramillo Alvarado earned a doctor of jurisprudence degree and engaged in an intensive study of his national reality. He contributed essays to newspapers throughout the country, most significantly under the pseudonym Petronio in the liberal newspaper *El Día*. On occasion, he served as governor and deputy of his native province of Loja. He also taught law at the Central University in Quito and the University of Guayaquil.

Jaramillo Alvarado's best-known work is *El indio ecuatoriano* (The Ecuadorian Indian), originally published in 1922. He significantly rewrote the book for subsequent editions in 1925, 1936, and 1954. This work established him as one of Ecuador's leading intellectuals. *Del agro ecuatoriano* (Of Ecuadorian Land; 1936) extended his discussion of issues facing Ecuador's rural peoples.

See also **Indigenismo.**

BIBLIOGRAPHY

Jaramillo Alvarado, Pío. *El indio ecuatoriano: Contribución al estudio de la sociología indoamericana*, 6th edition. 2 vols. Quito: Corporación Editora Nacional, 1983.

Muñoz Vicuña, Elias, et al. *Vision actual de Pío Jaramillo Alvarado: Documentos del seminario nacional, Loja, 13 al 16 de septiembre, 1988.* Loja, Ecuador: Subsecretaria de Cultura, Dirección Provincial de Educación, Departamento de Cultura de Loja, Fundación Friedrich Naumann, 1989.

MARC BECKER

JARAMILLO LEVI, ENRIQUE (1944–).

Enrique Jaramillo Levi, the Panamanian writer, dramatist, and editor, was born in Colón. He attended La Salle High School and in 1967 received a degree in English from the University of Panama. He earned master's degrees in creative writing (1969) and Latin American literature (1970) from the University of Iowa. In 1973, on a scholarship from the Center for Mexican Writers, he traveled to Mexico, where during the next twelve years he taught at Universidad Autónoma Metropolitana, founded the publishing company Editorial Signos, and published several books, articles, poems, and anthologies. From 1987 to 1990 he was a Fulbright scholar in the United States and also published the anthology *When New Flowers Bloomed: Short Stories by Women Writers from Costa Rica and Panama* (1991). Jaramillo Levi was the first Panamanian to publish a book of stories in the United States and in Spain. Some of his many published works include *Duplicaciones* (*Duplications*, 1973), *Fugas y engranjes, 1978–1980* (*Flights and Gears*, 1982), *Caracol yotros cuentos* (*Snail and Other Stories*, 1998), *Senderos retorcidos* (*Cuentos Selectos: 1968–1998*), *Twisted Footsteps: Selected Stories*, 2001, *Luminoso tiempo gris* (*Luminous Gray Time*, 2002), and *Echar raíces* (*To Take Root*, 2003).

Aside from enriching the innovative literary tradition started by fellow Panamanian writer Rogelio Sinán (b. 1904), Jaramillo Levi's writings have opened new avenues of expression, with emphasis on universality and aesthetic experimentation. He has received many literary prizes. Now living in Panama, he continues to serve as editor of the magazine *Maga*, which he founded in 1984, and as director of Editorial Universitaria.

See also **Literature: Spanish America.**

BIBLIOGRAPHY

Primary Works

Fugas y engranjes. Mexico: Universidad Nacional Autonoma de Mexico, 1982.

When New Flowers Bloomed: Short Stories by Women Writers from Costa Rica and Panama. Pittsburgh, PA: Latin American Literary Review Press, 1991.

Duplications and Other Stories. Pittsburgh, PA: Latin American Literary Review Press, 1994.

Caracol y otros cuentos. Mexico: Alfaguara, 1998.

Senderos retorcidos (Cuentos Selectos: 1968–1998). Mexico: Ediciones Vieira, 2001.

Luminoso tiempo gris. Madrid: Paginas de Espuma, 2002.

Echar raíces. Panama: Universal Books, 2003.

Pequeñas resistencias 2: Antología del cuento centroamericano contemporáneo. Madrid: Páginas de Espuma, 2003.

Secondary Works

Aguilar, Alfredo, ed. *Puertas y ventanas: Acercamiento a la obra literaria de Enrique Jaramillo Levi.* San José, Costa Rica: Editorial Universitaria Centroamericana, 1990.

Birmingham-Pokorny, Elba D. "Las realidades de Enrique Jaramillo-Levi: Una entrevista." *Confluencia* 8–9 (1993): 185–198.

Burgos, Fernando, ed. *Los escritores y la creación en Hispanoamérica.* Madrid: Castalia, 2004.

Foster, David William. *Handbook of Latin American Literature.* 2nd ed. New York: Garland, 1992.

García, Kay. "El agua: Un signo polisémico en la obra literaria de Enrique Jaramillo Levi." *Confluencia* 5, no. 2 (1990): 149–153.

Miró, Rodrigo. *La literatura panameña.* Panama: Editorial Universitaria, 1972.

ELBA D. BIRMINGHAM-POKORNY
KARIN FENN

JÁUREGUI, AGUSTÍN DE (?–1784).

Agustín de Jáuregui (*d.* 27 April 1784), viceroy of Peru (1780–1784). Although the date and place of Jáuregui's birth are uncertain, it is known that he was of noble Navarrese descent and served as equerry to Philip V before a period of military service in Cartagena, Cuba, and Honduras in the 1740s.

Following his return to Spain, he began a new period of service in America in 1773, with his appointment as captain-general of Chile, a post from which he was promoted to Lima in 1780 in succession to the disgraced Manuel de Guirior. His period of office was complicated by widespread internal insurgency (notably the rebellion of Túpac Amaru I), the fear of British attack and the high costs of coastal defense occasioned by this fear, and the administrative reorganization that culminated in the introduction of the intendant system in 1784. Replaced as viceroy by Teodoro de Croix on 3 April 1784, Jáuregui died later that month.

See also **Peru: From the Conquest Through Independence.**

BIBLIOGRAPHY

Sebastián Lorente, ed., *Relaciones de los virreyes que han gobernado el Perú,* vol. 3 (1872).

Rubén Vargas Ugarte, *Historia del Perú: Virreinato (Siglo XVIII) 1700–1790* (1956), esp. pp. 393–433.

Additional Bibliography

O'Phelan, Scarlett. *La gran rebelión en los Andes: De Túpac Amaru a Túpac Catari.* Cuzco, Perú: Centro de Estudios Regionales Andinos "Bartolomé de las Casas," 1995.

Robins, Nicholas A. *Genocide and Millennialism in Upper Peru: The Great Rebellion of 1780-1782.* Westport, CT: Praeger, 2002.

Stavig, Ward. *The World of Tupac Amaru: Conflict, Community, and Identity in Colonial Peru.* Lincoln, NE: University of Nebraska Press, 1999.

JOHN R. FISHER

JAURETCHE, ARTURO M. (1901–1974).

Arturo M. Jauretche (*b.* 13 November 1901; *d.* 25 May 1974), Argentine nationalist intellectual, born in Lincoln, in Buenos Aires Province. Along with Luis Dellepiane and Raúl Scalabrini Ortiz, Jauretche founded the Radical Orientation Force of Argentine Youth (FORJA) in 1935. The FORJA criticized the country's liberal order and especially its quasi-colonial relationship with Great Britain as part of a deep historical revisionism with political goals. Its members embraced a vitriolic anti-imperialism replete with epithets (e.g. *vendepatria*) that would become an integral part of Argentine political discourse over the next several decades. In its scorn for the oligarchy's cosmopolitan, antinational culture, its denunciations of the Roca-Runciman Pact, and criticisms of what it saw as U.S. pretensions to hegemony in Latin America, the FORJa helped contribute to the popular nationalism that would crystallize under Juan Domingo Perón. Jauretche was the most effective disseminator of the FORJA's ideas in books such as *Libros y alpargatas: civilizados o bárbaros* (1983) and *El medio pelo en la sociedad argentina* (1966).

The FORJA remained primarily an intellectual movement; expelled from the Radical Party, it never constituted an independent political force in its own right.

See also **Argentina, Political Parties: Radical Party (UCR); Roca-Runciman Pact.**

BIBLIOGRAPHY

Norberto Galasso, *Jauretche y su época* (1985).

David Rock, *Authoritarian Argentina: The Nationalist Movement, Its History and Its Impact* (1993).

Additional Bibliography

Iturrieta, Aníbel, and Antonio Lago Carballo, eds. *El pensamiento político argentino contemporáneo.* Buenos Aires: Grupo Editor Latinoamericano, 1994.

JAMES P. BRENNAN

JÊ.

See **Gê.**

JECKER BONDS.

Jecker Bonds, promissory notes that provided a pretext for the French Intervention in Mexico (1862–1867). Jecker, Torre, and Company was one of three French banking houses in Mexico City. Late in 1859 the Conservative Miramón regime entered into a bond-conversion arrangement with Jecker. In return for ready cash not even totalling 1 million pesos, Miramón issued bonds whose value came to 15 million pesos. Jecker agreed to pay 3 percent interest on these bonds over a five-year period in return for 15 percent of the face value of each new bond at the moment of conversion of an old bond for a new one. The Duc de Morny, half-brother of Napoleon III, had been Jecker's partner at the time of the issue. His close collaborator, Count Pierre Dubois de Saligny, French minister in Mexico (1860–1863), pressed the Jecker claims. The Juárez government, however, refused to recognize the Jecker debt. But afterwards, the Mexican Empire paid Morny's claim in regular installments until his death in 1865, as provided by the Treaty of Miramar (March 1864).

See also **French Intervention (Mexico).**

BIBLIOGRAPHY

Nancy N. Barker, "The Duke of Morny and the Affair of the Jecker Bonds," in *French Historical Studies* 6 (1970): 555–561, and *The French Experience in Mexico, 1821–1861* (1979).

Additional Bibliography

Steven C. Topik, "When Mexico Had the Blues: A Transatlantic Tale of Bonds, Bankers, and Nationalists, 1862-1910" *American Historical Review* Vol. 105, No. 3 (June 2003): 714-738.

BRIAN HAMNETT

JEFE POLÍTICO.

Jefe Político, a term designating the chief political officer (civil governor) at the provincial or departmental level, especially in nineteenth-century Latin America and Spain. The term was recognized in the Spanish Constitution of 1812 and was incorporated into many subsequent Latin American constitutions. The office of *jefe* (or *gefe*) *político* replaced that of Corregidor and was especially popular with liberal governments that sought to replace Spanish colonial terminology with new terms. Usually appointed by the president, the *jefe político* often exercised great power at the local level. In Argentina, the term is used to designate the chief of police.

See also **Spain, Constitution of 1812.**

BIBLIOGRAPHY

Constitución política de la monarquía española promulgada en Cádiz a 19 de marzo de 1812, título VI (1820).

Mario Rodríguez, *The Cádiz Experiment in Central America, 1808 to 1826* (1978).

Additional Bibliography

García Morales, Soledad. "Francisco M. Ostos Mora, jefe político de la huasteca veracruzana." *La Palabra y el Hombre.* 27:1 (October-December 2000): 123-145.

RALPH LEE WOODWARD JR.

JEREZ, FRANCISCO DE (1497–?). Francisco de Jerez (Xerez, Francisco de; *b.* 1497), Francisco Pizarro's secretary at Cajamarca during the capture of Atahualpa in 1532 and author of one of the earliest and most widely read chronicles of the Conquest. Born in Seville, Jerez came to the New World in 1514 in the fleet of Pedro Arias de Ávila. He accompanied Pizarro on his three trips to Peru in 1524, 1526, and 1531, serving as the conqueror's secretary on all three. He witnessed the encounter with Atahualpa, as well as the Inca's subsequent kidnapping and execution at Cajamarca. While at Cajamarca, Jerez broke his leg, and used his convalescence to write his chronicle. He returned to Spain in 1533, a much wealthier man, and his chronicle was published a year later in Seville. Titled *True Relation of the Conquest of Peru,* and written in part to refute the chronicle of Cristóbal de Mena, it soon became the standard account of the Conquest. Written in dry and unembellished soldier style, it describes in detail Pizarro's march from Tumbes to Cajamarca, the Inca's entourage, his capture, the story of the ransom, and so on. Jerez used his new wealth to establish himself as an important merchant in Seville, but his business failed to prosper. He later petitioned the court to allow him to return to America. Whether he actually returned to the New World is not known, nor is the date of his death.

See also **Atahualpa; Pizarro, Francisco.**

BIBLIOGRAPHY

Raúl Porras Barrenechea, *Cronistas del Perú, 1528–1650* (1962).

James Lockhart, *The Men of Cajamarca* (1972).

Additional Bibliography

Xerez, Francisco de. *Verdadera relación de la conquista del Perú.* Madrid: Historia 16, 1985.

Xerez, Francisco de. *Relazione del conquisto del Perù e della provizia di Cuzco.* Roma: Bulzoni, 1992.

JEFFREY KLAIBER

JEREZ, MÁXIMO (1818–1881). Máximo Jerez (*b.* 8 June 1818; *d.* 11 August 1881), Nicaraguan general and diplomatic figure. Jerez was born in León, the center of Nicaraguan liberalism. Political conditions forced his family to relocate to Costa Rica until 1825, when they returned to Nicaragua. Although his father had hoped he would join the family business as a painter, Jerez instead studied civil and canon law at León's university. He received his degree in 1837 and intended to become a priest; however, his scientific orientation led him to a second degree in philosophy the following year. In 1844 he worked for the noted jurist Francisco Calderón as a member of a diplomatic legation to European parliaments. Despite his youth, Jerez earned a reputation as a hard-working, honest, dedicated, and affable individual. His capabilities prompted President José León Sándoval to name Jerez to his cabinet in 1845. However, Jerez's liberal sympathies were becoming more pronounced, and he declined this position in a government led by a Conservative from Granada; instead, the ministry went to Fruto Chamorro.

Jerez joined the Liberal militia opposed to Sándoval and Chamorro and quickly distinguished himself in action. On 17 August 1845, Jerez was wounded in the battle of Chinandega; he was named colonel and major-general of the army. He recovered and took up the struggle with renewed vigor. In 1847 he was elected representative to the Central American Diet in Nacaome, where he formed an alliance with other Liberals and the prounionists José Sacasa and José Francisco Barrundia and embarked on a lifelong friendship with the Honduran general Trinidad Cabañas. In 1848–1849 Jerez served as secretary of the legation to Great Britain, where he was very much affected by Lord Aberdeen's criticism of Nicaragua's inability to meet its treaty obligations. In 1853, Jerez was a Liberal delegate from León to the Constituent Assembly called by Fruto Chamorro to amend the 1838 Constitution. A crisis ensued when Chamorro overruled the Liberal opposition and exiled Jerez, Francisco Castellón, and José Guerrero on charges of conspiracy.

When William Walker invaded Nicaragua in 1855, Jerez viewed him as the last hope of Central American liberalism and joined Walker's puppet government as cabinet minister for a short while until he grasped the true nature of Walker's designs. Jerez then defected to the opposition and led the Nicaraguan western army into Managua on

24 September 1856. Other Central American and legitimist troops followed. Jerez served as co-president in a provisional coalition with the Conservative Tomás Martínez until November 1857, when Martínez alone was elected to continue. Jerez served in various diplomatic positions until his death in Washington.

See also **Cabañas, José Trinidad; Walker, William.**

BIBLIOGRAPHY

Albert Z. Carr, *The World and William Walker* (1963).

Pedro Joaquín Chamorro, *Máximo Jerez y sus contemporáneos* (1948).

José Dolores Gamez, *Apuntamientos para la biografía de Máximo Jerez* (1910).

Sofonías Salvatierra, *Máximo Jerez Comentario polémico inmortal:* (1950).

William Walker, *The War in Nicaragua* (1860; repr. 1985).

Additional Bibliography

Gudmundson, Lowell, and Héctor Lindo-Fuentes. *Central America, 1821–1871: Liberalism before Liberal Reform.* Tuscaloosa: University of Alabama Press, 1995.

Montúfar, Lorenzo, and Raúl Aguilar Piedra. *Walker en Centroamérica.* Alajuela, Costa Rica: Museo Histórico Cultural Juan Santamaría, 2000.

KAREN RACINE

JESUITS. The Society of Jesus, *Compañía de Jesús* in Spanish, popularly known as the Jesuits, is a Roman Catholic religious order of men founded by the Spaniard Ignatius Loyola in the sixteenth century. In 1534 Ignatius and six companions studying in Paris vowed themselves to poverty, chastity, and work in the Holy Land. In 1540 the Roman Catholic Church approved the establishment of the group as a religious order.

PURPOSE

The purpose of the group was the salvation of their own souls and that of their neighbors. Members include ordained priests, who take the vows of poverty, chastity, and obedience, plus an additional vow of special obedience to the pope, or spiritual coadjutors, priests who take the three vows but not that of obedience to the pope, and lay brothers, who perform tasks for which the priesthood is not needed. Candidates for the priesthood, called scholastics, are also members of the Jesuits.

ORGANIZATION

The Jesuits are highly centralized. A superior general in Rome is the head of the order. Geographic units headed by provincials report to the central office in Rome, and each house or residence, headed by a rector or superior, reports to the provincial. Required written correspondence between a local superior and provincial, and between provincial and the superior general assure a tighly knit bond and a continual flow of information and directives in both directions. Many of these documents dating from the sixteenth century are preserved in the central Jesuit archives in Rome.

The Society of Jesus grew rapidly in the sixteenth and seventeenth centuries. In 1556, at the death of Ignatius Loyola, there were 936 members. In 1626 there were 15,544. In Counter-Reformation Europe, Jesuits founded colleges, wrote theological and philosophical treatises, preached itinerant missions, and were influential at the Council of Trent (1545), thus gaining reputations for superior intellect, theological knowledge, and moral probity.

From the early days of the Jesuits, foreign missions were given high priority. The sixteenth century witnessed the expansion of Europe, and the church saw the opportunity to convert vast numbers of souls to Christianity. Jesuits were sent to the Portuguese colonies of West Africa, Francis Xavier began the evangelization of India (1541), and in 1549 Manuel da Nóbrega began mission work in Brazil. The first Jesuits arrived in French Canada in 1611.

MISSIONS IN LATIN AMERICA

Jesuit mission work in Latin America had a relatively late start. The Spanish king, Philip II (1527–1598), hesitated to send the Jesuits to his domains in the New World. The Dominicans (Hispaniola) and Franciscans (Mexico) had preceded the Jesuits, and the danger of rivalry and jurisdictional disputes made the king uneasy. In addition, the Jesuits, based in Rome, had a certain independence that did not sit well with the king. Nevertheless, because they were well trained and well organized, they were permitted to establish missions in America.

Florida was the first American mission field of the Jesuits. Between 1565 and 1571 the Jesuits worked with the Indians on the shores of eastern and western Florida. Few converts were made, but the Jesuits acquired valuable lessons about the importance of learning the Indian languages and customs, establishing a solid economic base apart from the promises of king and conquistadores, and formulating clear goals for a mission area. These were lessons they carried with them to future mission experiences in America.

The Jesuits left Florida in 1571 and joined a group of Jesuits sent to Mexico in 1572. In Mexico the Jesuits established residences in Mexico City, Oaxaca, and Guadalajara, and later founded colleges in other major towns. Indian and Spanish parishioners were served, and the northern and western frontiers witnessed major Jesuit mission activity. In 1582 Jesuits arrived in Guatemala. In 1568, three decades after Pizarro conquered the Incas, and when there were already 2,500 Spanish settlers in Peru, five Jesuits arrived in Lima. The pattern of establishing a college, residences, and missions for the Indians was followed. In 1585 the Jesuits entered Tucumán, in present-day Argentina, and the following year they traveled north from Lima to Quito. By 1593 a Jesuit house was established in Chile. In the Jesuit expansion north and south, the major focus of their labor was the urban college or university.

COLLEGES AND UNIVERSITIES

The models for the Jesuit colleges founded in Latin America were those of Europe. The college was the spearhead of Jesuit strategy during the Counter-Reformation in Germany, France, and Poland. Indoctrinating young Catholic minds to be wary of the pitfalls of Protestantism was a primary goal. Solid classical learning was another. In Latin America as well, the college was viewed as an instrument for Catholic and secular education. It was also seen as an ideal vehicle for proselytizing. The college always had a church attached to it, and the pulpit served as a powerful means of instruction and persuasion. Itinerant missions that swept through the countryside, exhorting the old faithful and encouraging the new, were initiated in the college. Social works of mercy that encompassed the surrounding neighborhood were also based in the college. So the college was not solely an educational institution; it was supposed to be a storehouse of energy that radiated outward, incorporating numerous ministries and housing Jesuits engaged in a variety of activities.

Large Latin American cities such as Lima, Mexico City, and Córdoba, in Argentina, had colleges with thirty or forty Jesuits. Smaller ones, such as those in Cuenca or Latacunga, in Ecuador, had only four or five. Colleges charged their students no tuition. Financial support came from a complex of farms and estates that each college had to possess as an endowment before being allowed to open. The larger the college, the greater the number of students and Jesuits to be provided for, and the more extensive the estates and farms necessary to provide for them. Large sugar plantations and vineyards on the coast of Peru supported the college in Lima. Sheep farms and associated textile mills were the financial mainstay of the college of Quito, and cattle ranches and farms supplied the Jesuit college in Mexico City with most of its income. Many documents dealing with Jesuit landholdings and agrarian operations are extant, and shed a great deal of light on colonial Latin American rural society and development.

The Jesuits ran eight universities in colonial Latin America. The most famous were Córdoba in Argentina, San Pablo in Lima, and that of Mexico City. A university was a prestigious institution that could confer doctoral degrees. The universities and colleges were a focus of cultural life as well. Philosophical disputations, theater, panegyrics, processions, and degree conferrals added colorful pageantry to colonial life. In 1767 the Jesuits staffed more than thirty-five colleges throughout Latin America.

Brazil had no Jesuit universities, but by 1578 the college in Bahia was conferring master's degrees, and mission work focused on trying to settle surrounding Indians in fixed towns called Aldeias. Financial support was provided by sugar plantations.

EVANGELIZATION

The frontier of the Latin American world beckoned the Jesuit missionary. In 1594 Jesuits began evangelizing Sinaloa, in northwestern Mexico. The mission to the Mainas Indians along the Marañón

River in Peru was begun in 1639 by three Jesuits, and the Moxos Indians were evangelized in 1668. The Indians of Pimería Alta, in northwestern Mexico (Arizona), were evangelized by Eusebio Kino, who also showed that California was not an island (as hitherto had been believed). The Jesuit missions of Baja California operated from 1697 to 1767. During this time fifty-nine Jesuits established a chain of mission farms, villages, and ranches from Cabo San Lucas to the present international border. Jesuits stationed in the Andean regions of Cuzco and La Paz (Bolivia) evangelized the Altiplano.

Jesuits in Brazil traveled up the Amazon and thrust their way into the interior by the end of the sixteenth century. The order founded almost 400 missions in their 200-year history in Brazil. António Vieira became the Indians' most eloquent spokesman, charging Portuguese colonists with killing over two million Indians in their quest for workers and slaves. By the seventeenth century over 258 Jesuits had been sent to Portuguese Brazil. Labor in the mission village was organized for the benefit of the religious order, the crown, or the colonists. In 1757 a royal decree freed Indian villages from missionary control.

THE REDUCTIONS OF PARAGUAY

The most famous of the Jesuit missions in Latin America were the reductions in northern Argentina and Paraguay. The term "reduction" comes from the Spanish noun *reducción,* the closest English meaning of which is "reservation." The first reductions were begun by the Franciscans, but the prototype of the Jesuit reductions was probably the Jesuit mission of Juli, on the shores of Lake Titicaca. The reductions were self-sufficient Guarani Indian settlements. No Spaniards other than missionaries were permitted to enter a reduction. The "corrupting influence" of merchants or settlers was to be kept far from the neophytes. Isolation and indoctrination were the hallmarks of the reductions. A major project of the reductions was Yerba Mate, a tea that when boiled provided a tasty and popular beverage. Indians who sold reduction tea in Buenos Aires received low prices from Buenos Aires middlemen, so the Jesuits took over the sale and eventually the distribution of the tea, which became known as Jesuit tea. As a result, the order was criticized for operating an extensive commercial enterprise.

The reductions protected the Indians from the slave-raiding Bandeirantes, who periodically attacked the missions from São Paulo, Brazil. These villages allowed the missionaries to indoctrinate the Indians on a regular basis. Reduction town planning included elaborately constructed chur-ches, the ruins of which still survive as tourist attractions.

In 1750 Spain and Portugal signed the Treaty of Limits that transferred some of the missions to Brazilian territory. The Jesuits and Indians protested with armed resistance, but to no avail.

When the Jesuits were expelled from the Spanish domains in 1767, government officials immediately repossessed the reductions, expecting to find mines of precious metals and hoards of silver and gold. Nothing was found. Eventually the mission Indians drifted into the mainstream of colonial agrarian society. The charge that the Jesuits had made the Indians thoroughly docile and helplessly dependent was untrue; many Guaraní took up trades in urban centers.

CRITICISM

Animosity and resentment had built up against the Jesuits during the two hundred years that they worked in Latin America. The network of colleges, estates, and slaves working on the estates created a political and economic force unrivaled by colonial economic groups. The Jesuits' economically integrated institutions were able to withstand the wild fluctuations of the colonial economic climate. Those of laypersons could not. Large estates and ostentatious construction fueled rumors of wealth and power. The European Bourbon monarchs, who resented the Jesuits for their own reasons, were confirmed in their wildest suspicions.

A propaganda campaign waged by the prime minister of Portugal, José de Carvalho, Marqués of Pombal, convinced the king that the Jesuits were subverting royal authority and using the missions as economic benefices. In 1759, six hundred Jesuits were expelled from their colleges and missions in Brazil and from the other Portuguese domains. Eventually this was followed by their expulsion from the Spanish domains in 1767, and the order was suppressed in 1773.

EXPULSION

Over 2,000 college, mission, and parish personnel gathered in port cities (the sick and infirm remained) and were exiled to Italy. Jesuit estates, houses, movable property, and real estate were auctioned off by a committee of *temporalidades* (tangible possessions), and the income went to the crown. Schools and colleges were staffed by other religious orders. However, the academic quality of the universities and colleges suffered enormously, Indian missions collapsed, and the cultural and economic life of the region declined. Indian protests and revolts occurred in Mexico and Brazil.

RESTORED SOCIETY

In 1814 the Society of Jesus was restored by the papacy, but Jesuits did not return to Latin America until the middle of the nineteenth century. By then the independence movement and political upheavals had changed the educational and economic structures so the Jesuits never regained the influence that they had enjoyed in education, economics, and politics.

After the Second Vatican Council (1962–1965), the Jesuits in Latin America began to choose what was called the "option for the poor," associating themselves with many of the rural land-reform movements and the creation of Christian base communities (*comunidades de base*). These movements were often locally opposed, and Jesuits were accused of being Communist sympathizers. Liberation theology was another movement that individual Jesuits supported. Jesuit theologians and writers such as Juan Luis Segundo and Gustavo Gutiérrez proposed the Bible as a vehicle for political and individual liberation from oppression. Many Jesuits today in Latin America are in the forefront of economic and theological reforms.

See also **Catholic Church: The Colonial Period; Catholic Church: The Modern Period; Universities: Colonial Spanish America.**

BIBLIOGRAPHY

Peter Masten Dunne, *Pioneer Black Robes on the West Coast* (1940).

Magnus Mörner, *The Economic and Political Activities of the Jesuits in the La Plata Region: The Hapsburg Era* (1953).

Guillermo Furlong Cardiff, *Misiones y sus pueblos de Guaraníes* (1962).

C. R. Boxer, *The Golden Age of Brazil, 1695–1750* (1965).

Magnus Mörner, *The Expulsion of the Jesuits from Latin America* (1965).

Luis Martín, *The Intellectual Conquest of Peru: The Jesuit College of San Pablo, 1568–1767* (1968).

Juan Luis Segundo, *The Liberation of Theology,* translated by John Drury (1976).

Herman Konrad, *A Jesuit Hacienda in Colonial Mexico: Santa Lucía, 1576–1767* (1980).

Nicholas P. Cushner, *Lords of the Land: Sugar, Wine, and Jesuit Estates of Coastal Peru, 1600–1767* (1980); *Farm and Factory: The Jesuits and the Development of Agrarian Capitalism in Colonial Quito, 1600–1767* (1982); *Jesuit Ranches and the Agrarian Development of Colonial Argentina, 1650–1767* (1983).

Dauril Alden, "Sugar Planters by Necessity, Not Choice: The Role of the Jesuits in the Sugar Cane Industry of Colonial Brazil," in *The Church and Society in Latin America,* edited by Jeffrey A. Cole (1984), pp. 139–170.

Additional Bibliography

Castelnau-L'Estoile, Charlotte de. *Les ouvriers d'une vigne stérile: Les jésuites et la conversion des Indiens au Brésil, 1580–1620.* Lisbonne: Fundação Calouste Gulbenkian, Paris: Centre culturel Calouste Gulbenkian; Lisbonne: Commission nationale pour les commémorations des découvertes portugaises, 2000.

Cohen, Thomas M. *The Fire of Tongues: António Vieira and the Missionary Church in Brazil and Portugal.* Stanford: Stanford University Press, 1998.

Flores, Moacyr. *Reduções jesuíticas dos guaranis.* Porto Alegre: EDIPUCRS, 1997.

Millones Figueroa, Luis, and Domingo Ledezma. *El saber de los jesuitas, historias naturales y el Nuevo Mundo.* Madrid: Iberoamericana; Frankfurt am Main: Vervuert, 2005.

Negro Tua, Sandra, and Manuel M. Marzal. *Esclavitud, economía y evangelización: Las haciendas jesuitas en la América virreinal.* Lima: Pontificia Universidad Católica del Perú, Fondo Editorial, 2005.

Santos Hernández, Angel. *Los Jesuitas en América.* Madrid: Editorial MAPFRE, 1992.

NICHOLAS P. CUSHNER

JESUS, CAROLINA MARIA DE (1914–1977). Carolina Maria de Jesus (*b.* 1914; *d.* 1977), Brazilian writer. A fiercely proud black woman, Jesus spent most of her life in obscurity, raising her three children in São Paulo's Canindé Favela, and supporting herself and them by scavenging paper. Her diary, published in 1960 through the help of journalist Audálio Dantas, who discovered her accidentally, made her an overnight sensation. It described the misery of *favela* life and expressed her thirst to escape it and provide a better life for her children. Within a year, it had become Brazil's all-time best-selling book, and it ultimately was translated into thirteen languages and sold in forty countries. But her fame and fortune did not last. She moved out of the *favela* into a house in a middle-class neighborhood, where she was rejected by her new neighbors; she spent much of the money she received unwisely, giving large sums away to needy people she hardly knew; and because she was unwilling to control her outspokenness, she alienated the members of the elite for whom she had been fashionably chic. Even at the height of her fame, most Brazilians never took Jesus seriously. The Left rejected her because she did not speak out against the exploitation of the poor. The literary establishment rejected her writing as childlike; indeed, she enjoyed a much more positive reputation outside of Brazil, where her book was called "one of the most astonishing documents of the lower-class depths ever printed."

All of Jesus's subsequent books lost money, so that within a few years of her exceptional success, she was forced to move out of her house with her children. She became a recluse in a distant semirural district. Times were so hard for her that she had to walk back to the city to scavenge for refuse, and her family again suffered hunger. She died at the age of sixty-three, so poor that her children had to ask for charity to bury her. Her diary, translated into English as *Child of the Dark,* was still in print in many foreign countries, although it had been largely forgotten in Brazil.

See also **Brazil: Literature; Favela.**

BIBLIOGRAPHY

Carolina Maria De Jesus, *Child of the Dark,* translated by David St. Clair (1962).

Robert M. Levine and José Carlos Bom Meihy, *The Life and Death of Carolina Maria de Jesus* (1995).

Additional Bibliography

Feracho, Lesley. "Transgressive Acts: Race, Gender, and Class in the Poetry of Carolina Maria de Jesus and Miriam Alves." *Afro-Hispanic Review* 18:1 (Spring 1999): 38–45.

Ferreira, Débora R.S. "Na obra de Carolina Maria de Jesus, um Brasil esquecido." *Luso-Brazilian Review* 39:1 (Summer 2002): 103–119.

Jesus, Carolina Maria de. *I'm Going to Have a Little House: The Second Diary of Carolina Maria de Jesus.* Lincoln, NE: University of Nebraska Press, 1997.

ROBERT M. LEVINE

JEWS. Varying patterns of immigration, as well as differing degrees of acculturation, adaptation, and assimilation, have characterized the diverse Jewish population in Latin America and the Caribbean. Ashkenazim (Jews of Central and Eastern European ancestry) currently constitute the majority of the approximately half a million Jews in the region, but the first Jews to land in the New World came from Spain and Portugal. Early arrivals have been traced back to the initial voyages of exploration undertaken by Columbus and others sailing on behalf of Spain. These voyages represented Spain's outward expansion and were a direct result of Spanish unification and of the end of the war against the Moors. They were undertaken at the height of the power of the Spanish Catholic Church, during the Inquisition.

The impact of the Inquisition cut a path across the Atlantic, for only those who could document their Catholic ancestry were sanctioned to enter these new lands. Nevertheless, *conversos* and suspect "New Christians" (Jewish converts to Christianity), along with a handful of Jews who managed to elude state edicts, in fact became the earliest Jewish settlers of the Americas. A tolerant environment and distance from the Inquisition's reach were major factors in the initial establishment of Jewish communities in both Spanish- and Portuguese-controlled territories and, shortly thereafter, in the Dutch-ruled possessions of Pernambuco and Bahia on the mainland and Curaçao and Suriname in the Caribbean. The experience of the descendants of Spanish and Portuguese *marranos* (converts to Christianity who secretly maintained their Judaism), who saw themselves as "La Nación," constitutes a unique chapter in the history of Jewish settlements in the Caribbean, which began to flourish in the seventeenth century.

German-Jewish refugees aboard the *St. Louis,* turned away from Havana harbor, 1939. Although some Latin American countries opened their doors to a limited number of European Jewish refugees during World War II, both Cuba and the United States refused to allow those aboard the *St. Louis* to disembark, forcing their return to Nazi Germany. © BETTMANN/CORBIS

It is both ironic and tragic that the best sources for Jewish life in the early colonial period are dossiers that document persecution and autos-da-fé, such as the destruction of Luis de Carvajal and his family in Mexico and the trial of Francisco Maldonado de Silva in Tucumán, then under the aegis of the Viceroyalty of Peru; detailed records of the Inquisition also portray the daily life of New Christians in Brazil. Many of the New Christians were eventually assimilated into the region's mainstream population, and only occasional traces (names and isolated but telling customs) link descendants to their Jewish origins. The modified Jewish traditions still being observed by the inhabitants of Venta Prieta (Mexico), and by some inhabitants of Loja (Ecuador), attest to non-Christian roots.

While a relatively small number of Jews had already settled in Latin America and on several Caribbean islands as the independence movements unfolded (Jews were, for instance, among the supporters of Simón Bolívar), today's Jewish population must be seen in the context of nineteenth-century migration waves linked to World War I and World War II. This holds true for both Ashkenazi and for Sephardic Jews from Northern Africa and the Middle East. Official immigration plans played a role in attracting Europeans, Jews among them, to the nascent republics. Beyond these plans, however, the dominant factor in the migration of Jews to Latin America and the Caribbean, whether in the sixteenth or in the twentieth century, has been the possibility of finding a haven from persecution (oftentimes, since the 1800s, as a second choice to the United States) and access to opportunities that had been foreclosed in European towns and villages.

A notable example of a prompt and coordinated response to persecution—especially pogroms—under czarist Russia was framed by Baron Maurice de Hirsch and, under his guidance, by the Jewish Colonization Association (JCA) by resettling Jews in an agricultural setting in Argentina. The experiment, lauded by Alberto Gerchunoff as an unmitigated success that delivered a new Zion for the Jews, began to falter as the descendants of the colonists opted for urban life. Contrary to patterns elsewhere, a significant segment of the Jewish immigrants to several Latin American nations became an integral part of the urban labor force. Socialist and anarchist tenets among the urban proletariat contributed to anti-Semitic outbursts and pogroms during labor struggles. In 1919, the Semana Trágica (Tragic Week) served as a powerful reminder of Argentina's painful readjustment to the changing economic order and to the reweaving of its social fabric; it was also a reminder that anti-Jewish feeling had taken root on this side of the Atlantic. Today, most of Argentina's approximately quarter million Jews—the largest Jewish community in Latin America—live in Buenos Aires, where over a third of the country's population resides, and are engaged in occupations that range from retail merchandising (one of the earliest Jewish trademarks in the city) and industry to careers in the liberal professions and scientific fields.

In addition to various official plans aimed at attracting European immigrants—plans that varied greatly among the countries that possessed them—conditions that propitiated the establishment of Jewish institutions and allowed for the development of a Jewish way of life were a significant inducement for this minority culture. Following traditional ethnic patterns of immigration, local aid societies were established along trade lines, and by city or area of origin. Religious tolerance and economic incentives, particularly in the form of industrial growth and of an accommodating climate, determined the initial inflow as well as the sustained growth of Jewish communities. In wartime, the availability of visas (or of quasi-legal permits) sufficed to direct passage into one or another country. In this regard, Bolivia and the Dominican Republic (where an agricultural experiment by German-Jewish colonists took place in Sosua), constitute paradigmatic responses to World War II refugees. Other countries soon opened their doors, albeit under quotas, to fleeing Jews.

With few exceptions, the largest Jewish centers in Latin America are in the region's major cities. Buenos Aires, São Paulo, Rio de Janeiro, Montevideo, Santiago, Mexico City, and Caracas are hubs of Jewish life, possessing established communal, religious, and educational networks that reflect the ideological and religious plurality of the community. From strictly Orthodox to secular Zionist to "lay Yiddishist" and, in recent years, to Conservative and Reform trends that replicate those of the United States, Jews have been provided in most Latin American nations with a suitable environment for all aspects of Jewish life.

As elsewhere, Ashkenazic and Sephardic communities have developed independently of each other, with the added splintering that corresponds to points of origin. In some cases, however, they have come together under representative umbrella organizations, such as Asociación Mutual Israelita Argentina (AMIA) and other mutual aid societies. Even before the establishment of the State of Israel in 1948, Zionism had been a mainstay of educational and communal associations. This tends to explain the rapid integration into Israeli life of first- and second-generation Latin American Jews. It is important to note, however, that economic fluctuations, political repression, and anti-Semitic outbursts and sentiments also enter into the equation that motivates immigration to Israel and, particularly since the 1970s, to other countries. Besides Tragic Week, anti-Semitism has included the "Golden Shirts" pro-Nazi elements in Mexico, the July 1994 bombing of the AMIA Building in Buenos Aires, and the ongoing circulation of anti-Semitic publications. It is also important to note that since 1948, relations between Israel and its Arab neighbors have had a direct impact on the Jewish communities (which disagreed on Middle Eastern politics) in Latin America. The 1970s United Nations statement equating Zionism with racism, for instance, generated lost tourist revenue in Mexico and its Jewish community, due to a Jewish-American boycott.

Early life in the major Latin American centers had a distinctly Yiddish flavor: newspapers and magazines—such as *Die Yiddishe Zeitung* and *Die Presse* in Argentina and *Havaner Leben* in Cuba—and theater and radio programs echoed the dominant presence of Ashkenazi Jews. The growth of a vibrant Spanish and Portuguese language journalism in these communities indicate the degree of integration that has occurred in the countries that are home to Latin American Jews. This sentiment is manifested in first-rate literary and cultural

Brazilian president Luis Inácio Lula da Silva blows a shofar, or ram's horn, at a celebration of the Jewish New Year, ten days before Brazil's general elections, 2006. The growing participation of Jews in established and emerging democracies through Latin America testifies to the integration of Jews into Latin American society. EVARISTO SA/AFP/GETTY IMAGES

expressions that continue to earn critical acclaim. In the political arena, integration is also evident—except for periods of heightened anti-Semitism or of official and unofficial proscription—in the number of Jews who have joined their respective governments, as well as in the relatively high proportion of Jewish youth who in the 1970s and early 1980s actively opposed the dictatorial regimes of the Southern Cone, notably in Argentina. Radical political transformations have also produced a different mass reaction, as witnessed by the emigration of most Cuban Jews at the beginning of the revolution and a similar move by the Nicaraguan Jews at the triumph of the Sandinista revolution. These demographic shifts in turn affected several Caribbean locations as well as South Florida.

Today, most Latin American Jews belong to the middle sectors of the socioeconomic spectrum. Beyond their measurable financial security, however, and contrary to widespread popular notions, a significant number of urban Jewish families remain indigent and require communal support for their sustenance. Entry into the Latin American mainstream can also be gauged by the high rate of intermarriage and assimilation, and constitutes a reason for communal concern over the lasting presence of Jewish life in a number of smaller centers. Other indicators are equally significant to an understanding of the current status of Jews in Latin America. These include ongoing Christian-Jewish dialogues that build on the conclusions of the Second Vatican Council (1962–1965), a shift in ethnic politics, the growing participation of Jews in longtime and reestablished democracies, the high profile of Jewish scientists and artists, the open recognition of minority contributions to the mosaic of national cultures, the expansion of moderate religious and cultural practices among younger segments of the population, and the unintended solidarity among persecuted minorities created in response to anti-Jewish terrorism and anti-Semitic acts.

See also **Arab-Latin American Relations; Israeli-Latin American Relations.**

BIBLIOGRAPHY

Boleslao Lewin, *Los judíos bajo la inquisición en Hispanoamérica* (1960).

Anita Novinsky, *Cristãos novos na Bahia* (1972).

Seymour B. Liebman, *The Inquisitors and the Jews in the New World: Summaries of 'Procesos,' 1500–1810, and Bibliographic Guide* (1975).

Comité Judío Americano, Instituto De Relaciones Humanas, *Comunidades judías de Latinoamérica, 1973; 1974; 1975* (1977) [similar reports exist for other years].

Henrique Rattner, *Tradicão e mudanca: a comunidade judaica em São Paulo* (1977).

Martin H. Sable, *Latin American Jewry: A Research Guide* (1978).

Jacobo Schifter Sikora, Lowell Gudmundson, and Mario Solera Castro, *El judío en Costa Rica* (1979).

Robert Weisbrot, *The Jews of Argentina: From the Inquisition to Perón* (1979).

Judith Laikin Elkin, *Jews of the Latin American Republics* (1980).

Seymour B. Liebman, *New World Jewry, 1493–1825: Requiem for the Forgotten* (1982).

Judith Laikin Elkin and Gilbert W. Merkx, eds., *The Jewish Presence in Latin America* (1987).

Leonardo Senkman, comp., *El antisemitismo en Argentina*, 2d ed. (1989).

Haim Avni, *Argentina and the Jews: A History of Jewish Immigration,* translated by Gila Brand (1991).

Gunter Bohm, *Los sefardíes en los dominios holandeses de América del Sur y del Caribe, 1630–1750* (1992).

Judit Bokser De Liwerant, *Imágenes de un encuentro: la prescencia judía en México durante la primera mitad del siglo XX* (1992).

Robert Di Antonio and Nora Glickman, eds., *Tradition and Innovation: Reflections on Latin American Jewish Writing* (1993).

Robert M. Levine, *Tropical Diaspora: The Jewish Experience in Cuba* (1993).

Additional Bibliography

Agosín, Marjorie. *Memory, Oblivion, and Jewish Culture in Latin America.* Austin: University of Texas Press, 2005.

Bodian, Miriam. *Dying in the Law of Moses: Crypto-Jewish Martyrdom in the Iberian World.* Bloomington: Indiana University Press, 2007.

Bokser de Liwerant, Judit, and Alicia G. de Backal, eds. *Encuentro y alteridad: Vida y cultura judía en América Latina.* México, D.F.: Universidad Nacional Autónoma de México; Jerusalem: Universidad Hebrea de Jerusalén; México, D.F.: Asociación Mexicana de Amigos de la Universidad de Tel Aviv: Fondo de Cultura Económica, 1999.

Cohen, Mario E. *América colonial judía.* Buenos Aires: Centro de Investigación y Difusión de Cultura Sefardí, 2000.

Cortina, Guadalupe. *Invenciones multitudinarias escritoras judíomexicanas contemporáneas.* Newark: Juan de la Cuesta, 2000.

Elkin, Judith Laikin. *The Jews of Latin America.* Rev. ed. New York: Holmes & Meier, 1998.

Grinberg, Keila, ed. *Os judeus no Brasil: Inquisição, imigração, e identidade.* Rio de Janeiro: Civlização Brasileira, 2005.

Klich, Ignacio, and Jeff Lesser. *Arab and Jewish Immigrants in Latin America: Images and Realities.* Portland: F. Cass, 1998.

Lesser, Jeff. *Welcoming the Undesirables: Brazil and the Jewish Question.* Berkeley: University of California Press, 1995.

Papiernik, Charles. *Unbroken: From Auschwitz to Buenos Aires.* Albuquerque: University of New Mexico Press, 2004.

Ruggiero, Kristin. *The Jewish Diaspora in Latin America and the Caribbean: Fragments of Memory.* Portland: Sussex Academic Press, 2005.

SAÚL SOSNOWSKI

JÍBARO. Jíbaro, a term describing the rural subsistence population of the inland regions of Puerto Rico. During the 1890s and early twentieth century, the *jíbaro* was characterized as an untrustworthy and uncultured peasant. In the 1960s, under the nationalist program of the Popular Democratic Party and its leader, Luis Muñoz Marín, the *jíbaro* reemerged as a symbol of Puerto Rican identity. While perhaps poor in material wealth, the *jíbaro* was considered to be rich in cultural traits: hospitable, honorable, and hardworking. The virtues of *jíbaro* culture became identified with an idealized political image of Puero Rican nationality. This depiction was adopted by both pro-independence and pro-statehood political groups. Notable among the former was Eugenio María de Hostos, who called them "philosophers of nature" in his 1863 novel *La peregrinación de Bayoán*. Despite the effects of modernization and urbanization, which produced migration from rural to urban areas in the 1940s, the rural image of the *jíbaro* remains a powerful symbol of *puertorique-ñidad*. "Estado Jíbaro" was the term coined by Governor Luis A. Ferré to describe a state in which Puerto Rican culture would exist within a multicultural society. Some Amazonian indigenous groups in Peru and Ecuador have erroneously been called *jíbaros* by outsiders. In the past, some of these groups, such as the Shuar, may have manufactured shrunken heads.

See also **Campesino; Ferré Aguayo, Luis Antonio; Margil de Jesús, Antonio; Muñoz Marín, Luis; Shuar.**

BIBLIOGRAPHY

José C. Rosario, *The Development of the Puerto Rican Jíbaro and His Present Attitude Towards Society* (1935).

Kenneth R. Carr, *A Historical Dictionary of Puerto Rico and the Virgin Islands* (1973).

Raymond Carr, *Puerto Rico: A Colonial Experiment* (1984).

Additional Bibliography

Bolla, Luis. Los Achuar: *Sub etnia del pueblo de los Aínts o jí Baros.* Lima: Centro Amazónico de Antropología y Aplicación Práctica (CAAAP), 2003.

Guerra, Lillian. *Popular Expression and National Identity in Puerto Rico: The Struggle for Self, Community, and Nation.* Gainesville: University Press of Florida, 1998.

Hostos, Eugenio María de. *La peregrinación de Bayoán*. Río Piedras, PR: Editorial Edil, 1970.

María, José de. "Gramática y vocabulario jíbaros." In *Boletín de la Sociedad Ecuatoriana de Estudios Históricos y Americanos.* Vol. 1, nos. 2–3; vol. 2, nos. 4–5. Quito: J. Jijon y Caamaño, 1918.

Torres-Robles, Carmen L. "La mitificación y desmitificación del jibaro como símbolo de la identidad nacional puertorriqueña." *Bilingual Review/Revista Bilingüe* 24, no. 3 (September–December 1999): 241–253.

Heather K. Thiessen

JIJÓN Y CAAMAÑO, JACINTO (1890–1950).

The Ecuadoran archaeologist and historian Jacinto Jijón y Caamaño, born December 11, 1890, was a member of the traditional aristocracy of Quito, heir to several major haciendas, a large textile factory, and the title of Conde de Casa Jijón. He was the first Ecuadoran to undertake field archaeology in his country, a competent self-taught historian, a linguist, a major collector of art, artifacts, books, and manuscripts, a benefactor of the Academia Nacional de Historia (formerly the Sociedad Ecuatoriana de Estudios Históricos Americanos), of which he was a founding member, and politically, a champion and ideologue of the Conservative Party. Dissuaded by his mother from marrying the woman he loved, he eventually wed his cousin María Luisa Flores y Caamaño, a granddaughter of Juan José Flores, the first president of Ecuador (1830–1834, 1839–1845), through whom he inherited the Flores family papers, including those of Juan José's son Antonio Flores Jijón, also a president of Ecuador (1888–1892).

Jijón y Caamaño built one of the largest and most imposing mansion complexes in Quito, the Circasiana, with a separate building for his growing collections, including that of his mentor Federico González Suárez, which Jijón y Caamaño acquired after the archbishop-historian's death in 1917. His former library now houses the Archivo Municipal de Historia. Jijón y Caamaño led the failed Conservative putsch of 1924 and served as *alcalde* (mayor) of Quito, but was happiest in the field and in his study. Although he never graduated from college, he made major contributions to the study of the prehistory and history of Ecuador. Jijón y Caamaño died August 17, 1950, and fortunately his collections have been maintained. His library holdings, including thousands of manuscripts, now constitute the Fondo Jijón y Caamaño in the Banco Central del Ecuador's former Centro de Investigación y Cultura building in Quito, and his collection of archaeological artifacts and colonial art are in the Centro Cultural de la Pontificia Uni-versidad Católica de Quito, as is also the Archivo-Museo Juan José Flores.

See also **Ecuador, Political Parties: Conservative Party; Flores Jijón, Antonio; González Suárez, (Manuel María) Federico.**

BIBLIOGRAPHY

Jijón y Caamaño, Jacinto. *Quito y la independencia de América.* Quito: Universidad Central, 1922.

Jijón y Caamaño, Jacinto. *Solemne pronunciamiento de la capital de Quito y demás pueblos del Sur de Colombia, por el cual se constituye el Ecuador en estado soberano, libre e independiente: Año de 1830.* Quito: Universidad Central, 1922.

Jijón y Caamaño, Jacinto. *Escritos del Doctor Francisco Javier Eugenio Santa Cruz y Espejo.* Vol. 3. Quito: Imprensa Municipal, 1923.

Jijón y Caamaño, Jacinto. *Política conservadora.* 2 vols. Riobamba, Ecuador: La Buena prensa del Chimborazo, 1929–1934.

Jijón y Caamaño, Jacinto. *Sebastián de Benalcázar.* 3 vols. Quito: Imprensa del Clero, 1936–1949.

Jijón y Caamaño, Jacinto. *El Ecuador interandino y occidental antes de la conquista castellana.* 4 vols. Quito: Editorial Ecuatoriana, 1940–1947.

Jijón y Caamaño, Jacinto. *Antropología prehispánica del Ecuador*, 2nd edition. Quito: Museo Jacinto Jijón y Caamaño, 1997.

Larrea, Carlos Manuel. *Las principales publicaciones de Jacinto Jijón y Caamaño sobre la historia ecuatoriana: Reseña cronológica y crítica.* Quito: Editorial Benalcázar, 1977.

Vargas, José María. *Jacinto Jijón y Caamaño: Su vida y su museo de arqueología y arte ecuatoriano.* Quito: Editorial Santo Domingo, 1971.

MICHAEL T. HAMERLY

JIMÉNEZ, ENRIQUE A. (1888–1970). Enrique A. Jiménez (*b.* 1888; *d.* 1970), president of Panama (June 1945–October 1948). Nicknamed "el submarino" for his apparent ability to fire on political opponents and to surface at the most opportune moment, Jiménez was supposed to be an interim president. He was supported by the Partido Renovador and Don Pancho Arias Paredes, who expected to succeed Jiménez but met an untimely death before elections were scheduled. With his support gone, Jiménez faced stiff opposition from Arnulfo Arias Madrid, who unsuccessfully attempted a coup d'état in December 1945, and was imprisoned for most of 1946. Although Jiménez negotiated an agreement with the United States regarding U.S. bases in Panama, anti-Yankee demonstrations led to its rejection by the National Assembly. Jiménez responded to the growing domestic agitation caused by students and labor with the iron fist of the National Police, which was under the leadership of José Antonio Rémon Cantera. Jiménez's political fortunes ended when his chosen successor, Domingo Díaz Arosemena, died of a heart attack (1946) and Remón installed Arias as president.

See also **Arias Madrid, Arnulfo.**

BIBLIOGRAPHY

Leslie Bethell, ed., *The Cambridge History of Latin America*, vol. 7 (1990), pp. 624–626.

Walter La Feber, *The Panama Canal* (1979), 2d ed., pp. 100–101.

Additional Bibliography

Harding, Robert C. *Military Foundations of Panamanian Politics.* New Brunswick, NJ: Transaction Publishers, 2001.

Pizzurno Gelós, Patricia, and Celestino Andrés Araúz. *Estudios sobre el Panamá republicano: 1903-1989.* Panama: Manfer, 1996.

MICHAEL A. POLUSHIN

JIMÉNEZ DE PALACIOS, AURORA (1922–1958). The Mexican politician Aurora Jiménez de Palacios was born on December 9, 1922, in Tecuala, Nayarit, to a family of modest means. She received several government scholarships for the children of workers in Culiacán, Sinaloa, and Mexico City to attend public schools. Jiménez de Palacios graduated in economics from the University of Guadalajara in 1947. She held a number of administrative posts at her alma mater and then moved to Baja California del Norte. In 1954 her state changed its status from a federal territory, and special congressional elections were held. She was elected the first female member of the Mexican congress.

See also **Women.**

BIBLIOGRAPHY

Romero Aceves, Ricardo. *La mujer en la historia de México.* Mexico: Costa Amic, 1982.

RODERIC AI CAMP

JIMÉNEZ DE QUESADA, GONZALO

(1509–1579). Gonzalo Jiménez de Quesada (*b.* 1509; *d.* 16 February 1579), Spanish conquistador. Jiménez was born into a Jewish converso family in Córdoba, which had moved to Granada by 1522. Both he and his father were lawyers who practiced before the Audiencia in Granada. His family's subsequent financial ruin, the result of a lawsuit, made emigration inviting. In 1535, Jiménez joined a New World–bound expedition led by Pedro Fernández de Lugo, the experienced governor of the Canaries and at that time governor of the troubled colony at Santa Marta in what is now Colombia. As lieutenant to Governor Fernández, Jiménez was to oversee judicial and administrative procedures, not to command as conquistador.

The situation in Santa Marta was chaotic and grim: too many Spaniards and hostile Indians, and not enough food or gold. An expedition to the interior was an obvious solution, but Governor Fernández's son abandoned the project and returned to Spain. Suddenly, at the age of twenty-seven, unseasoned and inexperienced, Jiménez was given command as captain-general. Leaving Santa Marta on 5 April 1536, his force of 670 Spaniards made the difficult journey up the Magdalena and Opón rivers before reaching the Eastern Cordillera near Vélez in March 1537. The trek had taken its toll; fewer than 200 had survived.

But then their luck changed. They had reached the Chibchas (Muisca), the largest group of Indians in Colombia. Jiménez and his group seized more than 200,000 pesos in gold and 1,815 large emeralds, distributed the Indians in *encomienda,* founded Santa Fé de Bogotá, and named the rich kingdom New Granada. The sudden appearance of Nicolás Féderman's and Sebastián de Belalcázar's expeditions endangered this success, but Jiménez negotiated astutely. Leaving his brother Hernán in command, Jiménez traveled to Spain with Féderman and Belalcázar. There, however, he faced a hostile and pro-Indian Council of the Indies that ordered his imprisonment. He fled to France, Portugal, and Italy before returning to Spain in 1545. In the interval, the civil war in Peru and chaos in New Granada led the council to reconsider his merits.

Although he was not allowed to govern, Jiménez did return to New Granada in 1551 as *adelantado* (governor), marshal, senior *regidor* (alderman) in the Bogotá cabildo, and chief spokesman for the fast-disappearing conquistadores. He wrote at least four or five works, one running to more than 500 folios, of which only *El epítome* (1547) and *Antijovio* (1567) survive. The latter is an ambitious and complex work whose importance is still being debated.

In 1560 Jiménez exchanged his 2,000-ducat annual salary for *encomiendas* of equal value and joined the *encomendero* class. However, great wealth escaped him. In 1569, at the age of sixty—some say seventy—hounded by debt and lawsuits, still mesmerized by the El Dorado legend, he organized and commanded a disastrous expedition into the llanos. Of 300 Spanish and 1,500 Indians, only 50 Spaniards and 30 Indians returned alive in 1572. Yet, at the request of the Bogotá *audiencia,* he was pacifying hostile Indians in the Central Cordillera near Mariquita in 1574. He died there in 1579, suffering from what was described as leprosy.

See also **Council of the Indies; El Dorado; New Granada, United Provinces.**

BIBLIOGRAPHY

Germán Arciniegas, *The Knight of El Dorado: The Tale of Don Gonzalo Jimenez de Quesada,* trans. Mildred Adams (1942; repr. 1968).

Victor Frankl, *"El Antijovio" de Gonzalo Jiménez de Quesada, y las concepciones de realidad y verdad en la época de la contrarreforma y del manierismo* (1963).

Juan Friede, *El Adelantado Don Gonzalo Jiménez de Quesada,* 2 vols. (1979).

John Hemming, *The Search for El Dorado* (1978).

Gonzalo Jiménez de Quesada *Antijovio* (1952).

Ramos Pérez, *Ximénez de Quesada en su relación con los cronistas y el "Epítome de la conquista del Nuevo Reino de Granada"* (1972).

Additional Bibliography

Avellaneda Navas, José Ignacio. *La expedición de Gonzálo Jiménez de Quesada al mar del sur y la creación del Nuevo Reino de Granada.* Bogotá: Banco de la República, 1995.

MAURICE P. BRUNGARDT

JIMÉNEZ MORENO, WIGBERTO

(1909–1985). Wigberto Jiménez Moreno (December 29, 1909–April 24, 1985), the renowned Mexican historian, geographer, anthropologist, and archaeologist, was born in León, Guanajuato. In 1938 Jiménez

Moreno discovered the old city of Tula and uncovered its role as the Toltec capital. He went on to serve as the director of the National School of Anthropology and History and held numerous positions at the National Museum of Archaeology, History, and Ethnography. His legacy remains alive in the Wigberto Jiménez Moreno Library in his hometown of León, to which he donated more than forty thousand titles on the anthropology, ethnography, and history of Mexico.

See also **Toltecs.**

BIBLIOGRAPHY

Jiménez Moreno, Wigberto, "Mesoamerica before the Toltecs." In *Ancient Oaxaca*, edited by John Paddock. Stanford CA: Stanford University Press, 1966.

Jiménez Moreno, Wigberto. "Síntesis de la historia pretoleca de Mesoamérica." In *Esplendor del México Antiguo*, Vol. 2. México: Centro de Investigaciones Antropológicas de México, 1959.

ALISON FIELDS

JIMÉNEZ OREAMUNO, MANUEL DE JESÚS

JIMÉNEZ OREAMUNO, MANUEL DE JESÚS (1854–1916). Manuel de Jesús Jiménez Oreamuno, the Costa Rican historian and writer about local customs and manners, was a member of one of the most distinguished political families in the country. He was born in Cartago on June 16, 1854, son of Jesús Jiménez Zamora (the three-time president of Costa Rica, and foreign secretarty from 1859 to 1860) and grandson of Francisco Maria Oreamuno, also president of the republic for two short terms (in 1844 and 1856). He was the brother of Ricardo Jiménez Oreamuno, the most influential Costa Rican politician during the first decades of the twentieth century and the only person who has been appointed head of the three powers of the state.

Jiménez Oreamuno was president of the Cartago municipality (1883–1885); congressman in four legislative periods (1886–1888; 1892–1894; 1910–1914; 1914–1916); secretary of foreign affairs (1888–1889; 1903); presidential candidate (1894); and secretary of both treasury and commerce (1902–1904). From 1904 to 1906 he represented Costa Rica as chargé d'affaires and general consul in El Salvador. From 1910 to 1914 he was first designate to the presidency. He died in Alajuela February 25, 1916.

See also **Costa Rica; Jiménez Oreamuno, Ricardo.**

BIBLIOGRAPHY

Jiménez Oreamuno published many historical stories that were collected into two volumes titled *Noticias de antaño* (*News from Yesteryear*).

RODOLFO CERDAS CRUZ

JIMÉNEZ OREAMUNO, RICARDO

JIMÉNEZ OREAMUNO, RICARDO (1859–1945). Ricardo Jiménez Oreamuno (*b.* 6 February 1859; *d.* 4 January 1945), president of Costa Rica (1910–1914; 1924–1928; 1932–1936). Born in Cartago, Costa Rica, Ricardo Jiménez earned his law degree from the University of Santo Tomás in San José in 1884. The following year he was named president of the municipality of San José and sent on a diplomatic mission to Mexico, where he successfully gained Mexican support for Costa Rica's battle against Justo Rufino Barrios, the Guatemalan general who was attempting to create forcibly one Central American republic. Upon completion of his mission, Jiménez left for Washington, D.C., where in January 1886 he published his most notable essay, "Colegio de Cartago," in which he condemned Jesuit control of schools and argued for complete separation of church and state. The essay not only established Jiménez as one of the leading liberal theorists of the Costa Rican Generation of '89, but served as that group's credo.

In the years that followed, Jiménez held several government posts. In November 1886 he was appointed secretary of state in the Office of the Interior, Police, and Public Works. In September 1889 he assumed the post of secretary of state in the Office of Foreign Relations, only to quit after eight days on the job. In November he was named secretary of the interior, foreign relations, and finance, and the following year he was named president of the Supreme Court. In 1892 he resigned his post in objection to the dictatorship of José Joaquín Rodríguez. In 1906 he was elected to the Costa Rican Congress and made a name for himself as the country's chief critic of the United Fruit Company's preferred economic status.

Jiménez was elected and served his first term as president from 1910 to 1914. After a brief retreat from politics he was elected representative of the provinces of San José and Cartago in 1921. He went on to serve as president of Costa Rica twice more (1924–1928 and 1932–1936). Jiménez was a highly accomplished leader best known for his foreign relations successes in protecting the sovereignty and neutrality of Costa Rica amidst Central American political strife. In 1939, at the age of eighty, Jiménez ran for a fourth term of office; however, he withdrew from the race due to a shortage of campaign funds. He remained an active voice in politics during his latter years and was honored as *Benemérito de la Patria* by a unanimous vote of Congress in 1942.

See also **Costa Rica; United Fruit Company.**

BIBLIOGRAPHY

Eugenio Rodríguez Vega, *Los días de don Ricardo Jiménez* (1971).

Joaquín Vargas Coto, *Crónicas de la época y vida de don Ricardo* (1986).

Additional Bibliography

Mahoney, James. *The Legacies of Liberalism: Path Dependence and Political Regimes in Central America.* Baltimore: Johns Hopkins University Press, 2001.

Rodríguez Vega, Eugenio. *Ensayos olvidados sobre don Ricardo Jiménez.* San José, Costa Rica: Universidad Autónoma de Centro América, 1994.

DOUGLAS R. KEBERLEIN

JIMENO Y PLANES, RAFAEL (c. 1760–1825).

Rafael Jimeno y Planes (also Ximeno; *b.* ca. 1760; *d.* 1825), painter. Born into a family of artists, Jimeno was trained at the Academia de San Carlos in Valencia and also spent time in Madrid and in Rome absorbing the neoclassical style. In 1794 he arrived in New Spain to teach painting at the Academia de San Carlos; four years later he became its general director and continued to teach there for the rest of his life. His portraits of fellow academicians Jerónimo Gil and Manuel Tolsá are considered his best work, but just as significant were his paintings in the dome of the cathedral of Mexico City (1809–1810) and in the Capilla del Señor in the Church of Santa Teresa (1813), both lost. Important paintings in the chapel of Tolsá's Palacio de Minería (1812–1813) survive. Jimeno also did drawings for engravings, notably for illustrations of *Don Quixote* in Spain and of the Plaza Mayor of Mexico City after the installation of Tolsá's equestrian statue of Charles IV.

See also **Art: The Nineteenth Century.**

BIBLIOGRAPHY

Xavier Moyssén Echeverría, *El pintor Rafael Ximeno y Planes, su libreta de dibujos* (1985).

Manuel Toussaint, *Colonial Art in Mexico* (1967).

Additional Bibliography

Pierce, Donna, Rogelio Ruiz Gomar, and Clara Bargellini. *Painting a New World: Mexican Art and Life, 1521-1821.* Denver: Frederick and Jan Mayer Center for Pre-Colombian and Spanish Colonial Art, Denver Art Museum, 2004.

CLARA BARGELLINI

JÍVAROS. *See* **Shuar.**

JOÃO I OF PORTUGAL (1357–1433).

João I of Portugal, born on April 11, 1357, was king of Portugal (1385–1433) and founder of the house of Aviz (Avis). The illegitimate son of Pedro I, he ascended to power first as regent in 1383 and then as king despite opposition from the aristocracy and upper clergy. Through the Portuguese defeat of Castilian forces in the Battle of Aljubarrota (1385), the establishment of close alliances with England and Burgundy, and the creation of a new aristocracy with middle-class roots, João centralized power in the hands of the monarchy.

The marriage of João to Philippa of Lancaster, daughter of John of Gaunt, reinforced Portuguese-English relations and produced several children who contributed to the future of independent Portugal. Isabel was wed to Philip the Good, duke of Burgundy, thereby solidifying relations with Flanders. Henrique, or Henry the Navigator, devoted his energies to increasing the economic power of Portugal by attempting to establish a direct trade route to the Far East. Duarte (*b.* 1391) succeeded his father but died in 1438, leaving his brother Pedro as regent. Pedro's regency assured the house of Aviz's position as the ruling dynasty of Portugal until 1580, when Castilian forces seized the throne for Philip II of Spain. The house of Aviz promoted intensive overseas exploration and expansion not only to perpetuate the Aviz name but also to placate their initial supporters, the Portuguese mercantile community. João died on August 4, 1433.

See also **Philip II of Spain.**

BIBLIOGRAPHY

"The Conquest of Ceuta: Being the Chronicle of the King Dom João I." In *Conquests & Discoveries of Henry the Navigator, Being the Chronicles of Azurara*, edited by Virginia de Castro e Almeida, translated by Bernard Miall. London: George Allen & Unwin, 1936.

Livermore, H. V., ed., *Portugal and Brazil.* Oxford, Clarendon Press, 1953.

LESLEY R. LUSTER

JOÃO II OF PORTUGAL (1466–1495).

João II of Portugal, born on March 3, 1466, was the great-grandson of João I and fourth Portuguese king (1481–1495) of the Aviz (Avis) dynasty. Also known as John the Perfect, he succeeded to the throne after the death of his father, Afonso V, in 1481. João is credited with reasserting the power of the Crown over the nobility, reestablishing the Portuguese priority of overseas exploration as a means of economic expansion, and smoothing relations with Ferdinand and Isabella of Castile by successfully negotiating the Treaty of Tordesillas in 1494. The policy of economic growth through exploration led to the establishment of the fortress of São Jorge da Mina (Elmína, in present-day Ghana) in 1482 as a protective measure to encourage Portuguese trade with Guinea, Diogo Cão's discovery of the mouth of the Congo, the successful and lucrative colonization of the Atlantic islands of Madeira and the Azores, and, more important, Bartolomeu Dias's successful rounding of the Cape of Good Hope in 1488. João died on October 25, 1495.

See also **Ferdinand II of Aragon; Isabella I of Castile; João I of Portugal; João III of Portugal; Tordesillas, Treaty of (1494).**

BIBLIOGRAPHY

Burns, E. Bradford. *A History of Brazil*, 3rd edition. New York: Columbia University Press, 1993.

Livermore, H. V., ed., *Portugal and Brazil.* Oxford, Clarendon Press, 1953.

McAlister, Lyle N. *Spain and Portugal in the New World, 1492–1700.* Minneapolis: University of Minnesota Press, 1984.

Winius, George D. "The Enterprise Focused on India: The Work of D. João II." In *Portugal, the Pathfinder: Journeys from the Medieval toward the Modern World, 1300–ca. 1600*, edited by George D. Winius. Madison, WI: Hispanic Seminary of Medieval Studies, 1995.

LESLEY R. LUSTER

JOÃO III OF PORTUGAL (1502–1557).

João III of Portugal, born on June 6, 1502, was king from 1521 to 1557. Also known as John the Pious, he was the great-nephew of João II, son of Manuel I, and the sixth ruler of the Aviz (Avis) dynasty.

Under João the Portuguese development of Brazil began in earnest. He divided the Brazilian coastline into twelve captaincies that he awarded to hereditary proprietors (*donatarios*). He sent Tomé de Sousa to Bahia to establish a government there so as to end the threat of French invasion and Indian revolts. Jesuit priests were sent to pacify, convert, and acculturate the Indians. At home, João established the Inquisition and permitted the entry into Portugal of the Jesuits, whose influence on education became marked during his reign.

Despite the fact that Portugal was at the height of its powers at João's ascension, during his reign the country began its decline. The French and English challenges to the Portuguese monopoly of trade, the falling prices of Asian goods, the tremendous expense of maintaining the fleets and overseas posts, and the burden of crown debt caused by wasteful spending all contributed to the waning of the Portuguese empire that was to culminate under his successors. He died on June 11, 1557.

See also **Brazil: The Colonial Era, 1500-1808; Captaincy System; Jesuits; João II of Portugal; Manuel I of Portugal; Sousa, Tomé de.**

BIBLIOGRAPHY

Burns, E. Bradford. *A History of Brazil*, 3rd edition. New York: Columbia University Press, 1993.

Johnson, H.B. "The Portuguese Settlement of Brasil, 1500–1580." In *The Cambridge History of Latin America*, vol. 1, edited by Leslie Bethell. Cambridge: Cambridge University Press, 1984, pp. 249-286, especially pp. 261–262, 267–268.

Livermore, H. V., ed., *Portugal and Brazil.* Oxford, Clarendon Press, 1953.

Lockhart, James, and Stuart B. Schwartz. *Early Latin America: A History of Colonial Spanish America and Brazil.* Cambridge, U.K., and New York: Cambridge University Press, 1983.

McAlister, Lyle N. *Spain and Portugal in the New World, 1492–1700.* Minneapolis: University of Minnesota Press, 1984.

LESLEY R. LUSTER

JOÃO IV OF PORTUGAL (1604–1656).

João IV of Portugal (*b.* 19 March 1604; *d.* 1656), son of the seventh duke of Bragança, Dom Teodósio, and his wife, Dona Ana de Velasco. Born in the ancestral palace in Vila Viçosa, he married Dona Luísa Francesca de Guzmán of the Spanish house of Medina Sidonia (12 January 1633). Following the success of the December Revolution (1640) against Portugal's Spanish rulers, he was acclaimed king (15 December) and became the founder of the Bragança dynasty, thereby fulfilling 60 years of dreams of his family and his nation. He inherited a government devoid of funds, an effective army, or a competitive navy, but despite these weaknesses his rule survived a serious pro-Spanish conspiracy (1641). He came to rely upon the Jesuits for advice and diplomatic service and the members of his councils, including the Overseas Council, which he created for the management of the empire. Although he was unable to save Portugal's eastern empire, beset by heavy pressure from the Dutch, or to resume the once lucrative silk trade between Macao and Japan, he supported popular Brazilian uprisings against occupying Dutch forces in northeastern Brazil and lived to learn of their definitive surrender (1654). João IV was a conscientious, prudent monarch whose interests were hunting and music and the welfare of his subjects.

See also **Brazil: The Colonial Era, 1500–1808; Jesuits.**

BIBLIOGRAPHY

Joel Serrão, ed., *Dicionário de história de Portugal* (1971), vol. 2, pp. 620–623.

Joaquim Veríssimo Serrão, *História de Portugal*, vol. 5 (1980).

Additional Bibliography

Ames, Glenn Joseph. *Renascent Empire: The House of Braganza and the Quest for Stability in Portuguese Monsoon Asia, c.1640-1683.* Amsterdam: Amsterdam University Press, 2000.

Mello, Evaldo Cabral de. *O negócio do Brasil: Portugal, os Paises Baixos e o Nordeste, 1641–1669.* Rio de Janeiro: Topbooks, 1998.

Pereira, Gerardo. *A restauração de Portugal e do Brasil.* Rio de Janeiro: Biblioteca do Exército Editora, 2004.

Russell-Wood, A. J. R. *The Portuguese Empire, 1415–1808: A World on the Move.* Baltimore: Johns Hopkins University Press, 1998.

DAURIL ALDEN

JOÃO V OF PORTUGAL (1689–1750).

João V, born on October 22, 1689, was king of Portugal from 1706 to 1750. The grandson of João IV, João V, also known as John the Magnanimous, was "neither feared nor owed," thanks to gold and diamond discoveries in Brazil. At the time largely untapped, this great wealth enabled him to build massive royal works, such as the palatial monastery at Mafra (1717–1735) and the Lisbon Aqueduct of Free Waters (1732–1748); to support cultural establishments such as the Royal Academy of History (1720); and to indulge in extended patronage of the Church. It also afforded him freedom from the Cortes, without whose intervention he ruled with increasing absolutism. João experienced recurring bouts of illness (possibly epilepsy) that worsened after 1742, and the queen, Maria Ana of Austria, assumed the regency until his death on July 31, 1750. He was succeeded by his son José I.

See also **João IV of Portugal; José I of Portugal.**

BIBLIOGRAPHY

Almeida, Manuel Lopes de. "Portugal na Época de D. João V: Esboço de interpretação político-Cultural da primeira metade do século XVIII." In *International Colloquium on Luso-Brazilian Studies.* Nashville: Vanderbilt University Press, 1953.

Boxer, Charles R. *The Golden Age of Brazil, 1695–1750: Growing Pains of a Colonial Society.* Berkeley: University of California Press, 1962. 2nd edition, New York: St. Martin's, 1995.

Francis, Alan David. *Portugal, 1715–1808.* London: Tamesis Books, 1985.

Livermore, H. V. *A New History of Portugal,* 2nd edition. Cambridge, U.K., and New York: Cambridge University Press, 1976.

CATHERINE LUGAR

JOÃO VI OF PORTUGAL (1767–1826). João VI of Portugal (*b.* 13 May 1767; *d.* 10 March 1826), regent (1799–1816) and king (1816–1826). João was the second son of Queen Maria I and Pedro III of Portugal who became heir to the crown when his elder brother José died in 1788. In 1785 he married Carlota Joaquina, the daughter of the Spanish king Carlos V. When Queen Maria became mentally ill, João took the government in his hands in 1792 and was officially declared regent in 1799. With the invasion of Portugal by Napoleon Bonaparte's troops in 1807, he embarked with the royal family and his court for Brazil. After a short stay in Bahia, he chose Rio de Janeiro as the seat of his government.

Among his first reforms was the opening of Brazilian ports to international trade, which changed the colony considerably. The capital became crowded with civil servants, aristocrats, and foreigners, a demographic and cultural change for which the police intendant general, Paulo Fernandes Viana, sought to prepare the urban space. The regent and the royal family were housed in a *chácara* (farm) in São Cristóvão that had belonged to a rich merchant. The Portuguese elite took refuge in the beautiful neighborhoods, where they built the noble houses to which they were accustomed in Portugal. The downtown shops and warehouses occupied by Portuguese and foreign merchants began to display European goods and fashions. Court life contributed to the development of a luxury trade, and the lifestyle changed in many aspects: housing, furniture, transportation, fashions.

Dom João soon adjusted to the Brazilian environment and enjoyed the musical events in church and in the palace. Every day he received his subjects in a ceremony called *beija-mão,* and on special occasions he favored them with a promotion in military rank, an honor in the Order of Christ, or a public office in some part of the Brazilian territory. When Bonaparte was defeated in Europe (1815), Dom João and the royal family were supposed to return immediately to Portugal, but the regent preferred to stay in Brazil. On 9 March 1816, after Queen Maria's death, he became King João VI.

The Pernambucan Revolution of 1817 was the result of the struggle between absolutism and liberalism that began after the fall of Napoleon. The conspiracy was put down, but, in Portugal, the king's continued absence was a major grievance. In 1820 the commander in chief of the Portuguese army, the English officer William Carr Beresford (1768–1854), left for Brazil in order to warn the king of the imminence of revolution in Portugal and the urgent need for his return. João VI was not a man of quick decisions. He always listened to his ministers, and since they held differing views about monarchy, the constitution, and the cortes, the king delayed his return.

After many ministerial discussions, the opinion prevailed that the king should return to Portugal, leaving his elder son Pedro in Brazil. João VI and the court finally sailed 26 April 1821, after the city of Rio de Janeiro had been the stage of a violent coup attempt and the persecution of those who defended the immediate adoption of the Spanish Constitution of 1812—unpleasant events for which the king was not directly responsible. Rather, they were the result of Pedro's personal interference and of his fear of a more democratic form of constitutional government. The years before João VI's death in 1826 in Portugal were troubled by the absolutist movement conducted by his younger son Miguel (1802–1866) in 1823 and 1824.

See also **Pernambucan Revolution (1817).**

BIBLIOGRAPHY

Roderick J. Barman, *The Forging of a Nation* (1988).

Pedro Calmon, *O rei do Brasil: Vida de D. João VI,* 2d ed. (1943).

Maria Cândida Proença, *A Independência do Brasil: Relações externas portuguesas, 1808–1825* (1987).

Manuel De Oliveira Lima, *D. João VI no Brasil, 1808–1821,* 2d ed. (1945).

Maria Beatriz Nizza Da Silva, *Cultura e sociedade no Rio de Janeiro, 1808–1821,* 2d ed. (1978).

Angelo Pereira, *D. João VI príncipe e rei* (1953–1956).

Additional Bibliography

Rabello, David. *Os diamentes do Brasil: Na regência de Dom João, 1792–1816: um estudo de dependência externa.* São Paulo: Editora Arte & Ciência, UNIO, 1997.

Schultz, Kirsten. *Tropical Versailles: Empire, Monarchy, and the Portuguese Court in Rio de Janeiro, 1808–1821.* New York: Routledge, 2001.

MARIA BEATRIZ NIZZA DA SILVA

JOÃO PESSOA. João Pessoa, population, 649,410 (2004), capital of the Brazilian state of Paraíba. Known as Parahyba until 1930, when it was renamed in honor of the assassinated governor João Pessoa, the city was founded as Filipéia in 1585. Located six miles from the sea, on several hills overlooking the Paraíba River at its confluence with the Sanhauá, the city included the colonial port of Varadouro, which received ocean vessels until the late nineteenth century. Politically incorporated into adjacent Pernambuco (as part of the province of Paraíba) several times during the colonial period and economically subordinate to the regional entrepôt of Recife, Parahyba exported dyewood, sugar, hides, skins, vegetable waxes, and coffee. Cotton, which gained ascendancy in the nineteenth century, eventually led to Varadouro's decline, since river navigation depended on favorable tides. The Atlantic port of Cabedêlo, eleven miles away and constructed during the cotton boom of the 1920s, enabled Parahyba's exporters to remain competitive.

Famous for its beautiful beaches, the exquisitely restored colonial church of São Francisco, and its museum of regional popular art, and having direct access to the sugar plantation zone, João Pessoa is today an important tourist and convention center.

See also **Cotton.**

BIBLIOGRAPHY

Linda Lewin, *Politics and Parentela in Paraíba: A Case Study of Family-Based Oligarchy in Brazil* (1987).

Additional Bibliography

Aguiar, Wellington. *Cidade de João Pessoa: A memória do tempo.* 2nd ed. João Pessoa: Prefeitura Municipal, 1993.

Menezes, José Luiz da Mota. *Algumas notas A respeito da evoluçáo urbana de Jão Pessoa.* Recife: Pool, 1985.

LINDA LEWIN

JOAQUIM, LEANDRO (c. 1738–c. 1798). Leandro Joaquim (*b.* ca. 1738; *d.* ca. 1798), Brazilian painter and architect. Born in Rio de Janeiro, Joaquim studied with the painter João de Sousa and was a colleague of Manuel da Cunha. He collaborated with the sculptor Valentim da Fonseca E Silva (Mestre Valentim) on the Passeio Público and designed sets for the Teatro de Manuel Luis. Although his oeuvre consists primarily of religious paintings and portraits of governmental dignitaries, his few secular compositions have received particular acclaim. They include *Incendio do Recolhimento do Parto* and *Reconstrução do Recolhimento do Parto* and six oval panels commissioned for a pavilion in the Passeio Público. The latter are aesthetically among his best works but are also iconographically significant because they document social life and urban transformation in late-eighteenth-century Rio. As of 2007, 19 of the oval panels are housed among the Museo Nacional de Bellas Artes and the Museo Histórico Nacional. They include: *Cena maritime, Pesca de Baleia na Baía de Guanabara, Procissão Marítima ao Hospital dos Lázaros, Revista Militar no Largo do Paço, Vista da Igreja da Glória e Vista da Lagoa do Boqueirão,* and *Dos Arcos da Carioca.*

See also **Architecture: Architecture to 1900; Art: The Colonial Era; Rio de Janeiro (City).**

BIBLIOGRAPHY

Arte no Brasil, vol. 1 (1979), esp. pp. 264–267.

Additional Bibliography

Bayón, Damián, and Marx, Murillo. *History of South American Colonial Art and Architecture.* New York: Rizzoli, 1992.

Reber, Vera, and Weber, David J., eds. "Inter-American Notes." *The Americas* 52, no. 3 (Jan., 1996): 393–408.

CAREN A. MEGHREBLIAN

JOASEIRO DO NORTE. *See* **Juazeiro do Norte.**

JOBET BÚRQUEZ, JULIO CÉSAR

(1912–1980). Born in the southern Chilean village of Perquenco in Cautín province on January 2, 1912, Julio César Jobet Búrquez studied at the local secondary school and then moved to Santiago to study history, geography, and civic education at the Instituto Pedagógico of the University of Chile. During his student days in Santiago, he became one of the founders of the Socialist Party, and later a contributor to several journals, including *Travesía, Temuco, Occidente,* and *Revista del Partido Socialista Arauco.*

His interests in social and political thought, set in historical context, are reflected in several important books: *Santiago Arcos Arlegui y la Sociedad de la Igualdad* (1942); *Ensayo crítico del desarrollo económico-social de Chile* (1951) *Luis Emilio Recabarren: Los orígenes del movimiento obrero y del socialismo chileno* (1955); *Los precursores del pensamiento social de Chile,* 2 vols. (1955–1956); *El Partido Socialista de Chile,* 2 vols. (1971); and *Temas históricos chilenos* (1973).

Jobet Búrquez's lifetime interest in the evolution of Chilean educational thought is reflected in his masterful *Doctrina y praxis de los educadores representativos chilenos* (1970), an extraordinary contribution that highlights the educational philosophy of such figures as Manuel de Salas, Andrés Bello, and Valentín Letelier. Although ill since 1973, after the military coup he devoted his last years to the rebuilding of the Socialist Party.

See also **Chile, Political Parties: Socialist Party; Education: Overview.**

BIBLIOGRAPHY

Poblete Guerrero, Victor. "La producción ensayística de Julio César Jobet." *Occidente* 279 (November 1978): 39–42.

Grez Toso, Sergio "Escribir la historia de los sectores populares." In *Anaquel Astral,* edited by Virginia Vidal. Santiago, Chile: Editorial Poetas Antiimperialistas de América, 2006. Also available from http://virginia-vidal.com/anaquel/article_296.shtml.

IVÁN JAKSIĆ

JOBIM, ANTÔNIO CARLOS "TOM"

(1927–1994). Antônio Carlos "Tom" Jobim (*b.* 25 January 1927; *d.* 8 December 1994), Brazilian composer. The most famous Brazilian songwriter, inside and outside of Brazil, Jobim was born in Rio de Janeiro. He studied with Lúcia Branco and Tomas Teran and was profoundly inspired by the works of Brazilian composer Villa-lobos. As a young man, Jobim worked for a time as an architect but soon gave that up to pursue music as a full-time career. He began playing in nightclubs as a pianist around 1950, then got a job with the Continental record label in 1952 transcribing music, followed by a post with Odeon as artistic director, and then worked for various artists as an arranger. During the mid- to late-1950s, he would compose songs (alone and in collaboration with Newton Mendonça, Luiz Bonfá, and poet Vinícius de Moraes) that prefigured and then defined the bossa-nova style. Jobim wrote the music for such enduring songs as "Garota de Ipanema" (The Girl from Ipanema), "Samba de uma nota só" (One Note Samba), "Desafinado" (Off-Key), "Aguas de março" (Waters of March), "Dindi," "Corcovado" (English title: "Quiet Nights of Quiet Stars"), "Insensatez" (English title: "Foolishness"), and other standards often recorded by musicians in many countries. While singer-guitarist João Gilberto provided the bossa-nova style with its beat, Jobim contributed its most important melodic and harmonic elements.

Jobim's compositions are warm and intimate and incorporate difficult harmonies even as the composer strove for a subtle simplicity. He sometimes wrote his own lyrics, but usually collaborated with songwriters such as Vinícius de Moraes, with whom he wrote the ground-breaking bossa standard "Chega de saudade" (No More Blues [1956]), songs for Moraes's play *Orfeu da conceição* (1956), tunes such as "A Felicidade" for the 1959 film *Orfeu Negro* (Black Orpheus), and later classics like "Garota de Ipanema" (1962). Jobim arranged João Gilberto's "Chega de saudade" (1959), considered the first bossa-nova album, and supplied several of its songs.

Jobim achieved international fame as a songwriter in the 1960s and recorded numerous albums over the next three decades as a singer-pianist. Some of Jobim's albums were strictly in the bossa vein, while others, such as *Urubu* (1976), which incorporated Brazilian regional music and evoked impressionistic classical music, ventured into other styles. Jobim (like João Gilberto) had a strong influence on succeeding generations of Brazilian musicians as well as on American jazz musicians in the 1960s and 1970s.

See also **Gilberto, João; Music: Popular Music and Dance.**

BIBLIOGRAPHY

Ruy Castro, *Chega de saudade* (1991).

Augusto De Campos, *Balanço da bossa e outras bossas* (1978).

José Eduardo Homem De Mello, *Música popular brasileira* (1976).

Chris Mc Gowan and Ricardo Pessanha, *The Brazilian Sound: Samba, Bossa Nova, and the Popular Music of Brazil* (1991).

Additional Bibliography

Cabral, Sérgio. *Antônio Carlos Jobim: Uma biografia.* Rio de Janeiro: Lumiar Editora, 1997.

Jobim, Helena. *Antônio Carlos Jobim: Um homem iluminado.* Rio de Janeiro: Editora Nova Fronteira, 1996.

CHRIS MCGOWAN

JOCKEY CLUB. The Jockey Club, an upper-class institution imitating the French model, ostensibly promoted improved thoroughbred racehorses and also served as a center for socialization, communication, and recruitment among Latin American elites and resident foreigners. Exorbitant membership dues guaranteed exclusivity. The two most important Jockey Clubs were established in Mexico City and Buenos Aires. Oligarchs during the era of Porfirio Díaz founded the Mexican club in the capital city in 1881 in the Casa de Azuelos (the famous building covered with titles in the center of town, a famous Sanborn's restaurant in the early twenty-first century) with game rooms, a fencing salon, a restaurant, and a library. The following year the club built its own racetrack. It served as the social center for Mexico City society until the revolution forced its closing in 1914. Argentine president Carlos Pellegrini in 1882 organized the club to promote the breeding of fine horses (with government subsidies). The club offered members access to excellent wine cellars and a collection of European art. An inflammatory speech by Juan Domingo Perón in April 1953 inspired an angry crowd of *descamisados* ("shirtless ones"—Perón's working-class supporters) to sack the building housing the prestigious club, located on La Florida. Argentina's club was later rebuilt; it serves, together with the Palermo racetrack, as one of the finest sporting venues in South America.

See also **Pellegrini, Carlos; Sports.**

BIBLIOGRAPHY

Beezley, William H. *Judas at the Jockey Club and Other Episodes of Porfirian Mexico*, 2nd edition. Lincoln: University of Nebraska Press, 2004.

Edsall, Thomas M. *Elites, Oligarchs, and Aristocrats: The Jockey Club of Buenos Aires and the Argentine Upper Class, 1920–1940.* Ph.D. dissertation, Tulane University, 2000.

Newton, Jorge, and Lily de Newton. *Historia del Jockey Club de Buenos Aíres.* Buenos Aires: Ediciones L. N., 1966.

Richmond, Douglas W. *Carlos Pellegrini and the Crisis of the Argentine Elites, 1880–1916.* New York: Praeger, 1989.

WILLIAM H. BEEZLEY

JODOROWSKY, ALEJANDRO (1929–). Cult filmmaker and author Alejandro Jodorowsky was born on February 7, 1929, in Iquique, Chile, to Russian immigrant parents. He attended university in Santiago but left Chile when he was twenty years old and did not return to his country of origin for forty years. In Paris in the 1950s he studied mime with Marcel Marceau and worked with members of the surrealist movement on film and theater projects and novels. After further work in avant-garde theater in Paris during the 1960s, he made his first feature film, *Fando y Lis* (Fando and Lis) in Mexico in 1967. In 1970 he wrote, directed, and starred in *El topo* (The Mole), which has been categorized as a "mystic western" that employs the surrealist techniques and theory he absorbed in France. With *El topo* he gained one of his biggest supporters, John Lennon of the Beatles, who along with his wife Yoko Ono financed Jodorowsky's third feature film, *La montaña sagrada* (*The Holy Mountain*, 1973). *Santa Sangre* (*Holy Blood*, 1989), a Mexican-Italian co-production directed by Jodorowsky, reestablished him as a cult figure in experimental and surrealist film. He is the author of several novels, including *Donde mejor canta un pájaro* (*Where a Bird Sings Best,* 1994), and collections of essays. Now a naturalized French citizen, he lives in Paris where he works with his *cabaret místico* (mystical cabaret).

See also **Cinema: From the Silent Film to 1990.**

BIBLIOGRAPHY

Alejandro Jodorowsky. Official Web Site. Available from http://www.alejandro-jodorowsky.com.

García Gamboa, Rafael. "Jodorowsky: De lo pánico a la psicomagia." *Archipiélago* 6–7, no. 2 (March–August 1996): 44.

Jodorowsky, Alejandro. *El Topo: The Book of the Film*. Edited by Ross Firestone. Translated by Joanne Pottlitzer. New York: Douglas Book Corp., 1972.

Jodorowsky, Alejandro. *La escalera de Los Ángeles: Reflexiones sobre el arte de pensar*. Barcelona: Ediciones Obelisco, 2006.

STACY LUTSCH

JOHN PAUL II, POPE (1920–2005). Karol Józef Wojtyła was born in Wadowice, Poland, and studied in Rome after World War II. His nationality, theater and philosophy education, and World War II and cold war experiences influenced his religious career. Ordained archbishop of Kraków in 1964 (auxiliary bishop 1958–1964), he rose in prominence by challenging Poland's communist government and by participating in the Second Vatican Council (co-drafting the 1965 *Gaudium et Spes*) and the Synod of Bishops. Created a cardinal by Pope Paul VI (r. 1963–1978) in 1967, he was elected pope after the death of John Paul I, who served for only month, in 1978, becoming the first non-Italian pope since 1522.

John Paul II traveled to every inhabited continent, visiting twenty-four Latin American and Caribbean nations during seventeen trips. He first attended the Third General Conference of Latin American Bishops (CELAM) in Puebla, Mexico, in January 1979, affirming the Church's "option for the poor" but questioning theology based on non-Christian ideology. He served as mediator in several Latin American conflicts, averting war between Argentina and Chile in 1979, and encouraging resolution of the 1982 Falklands/Malvinas crisis. Although he supported the human rights work by bishops' conferences in these nations, he did not specifically admonish their regimes. Nor did he censure the Salvadoran government for its abuses, as Archbishop Oscar Arnulfo Romero had requested before his assassination in 1980. During his 1983 trip to Central America, he prayed at Romero's tomb but broadcast his rebuke of Ernesto Cardenal, priest and minister of culture in Nicaragua's Sandinista government, to the world from the Managua airport runway.

Enforcing orthodoxy and discipline was central to John Paul II's papacy. He openly criticized activists such as Peruvian Gustavo Gutiérrez and Brazilian Leonardo Boff; disciplinary actions continued throughout the 1980s and 1990s. Latin American activism led him to exercise control over the Jesuits (refusing the resignation of, and then deposing, Superior-General Pedro Arrupe) in 1981, and over the Confederation of Latin American Religious in 1991. John Paul II's selections for Latin American bishops, archbishops, and cardinals were conservatives who upheld Roman teachings. He elevated Opus Dei to the status of personal prelature, granting it more influence and autonomy from local church control. As communism weakened and fell in Europe, he continued to criticize Marxism, as during his 1998 visit to Cuba. In Santo Domingo, Dominican Republic (1992) and Mérida, Mexico (1993), he assured indigenous and mixed-race crowds that the Church had come to Latin America for them; yet concurrently the Church targeted pro-indigenous activist Bishop Samuel Ruiz García.

John Paul II also criticized capitalism's "culture of death," including in his last address specific to the region, *Ecclesia in America* (1999). Integrating into this concept opposition to artificial birth control and abortion, he pressed governments and their delegations to international meetings to do the same, thereby antagonizing feminists and progressives. During his papacy, the number of women in religious orders in Latin America and worldwide declined but still outnumbered vowed religious men, and laywomen in nonordained leadership increased; yet in *Ordinatio Sacerdotalis* (1994), John Paul II excluded women from ordination. Nevertheless, John Paul II was esteemed in the region as a spiritual leader, attracting many with his use of communications media, mass events such as World Youth Day, and his beatifications and canonizations of many Latin Americans.

See also **Boff, Leonardo; Cardenal, Ernesto; Catholic Church: The Modern Period; Conference of Latin American Bishops (CELAM); Gutiérrez, Gustavo; Romero, Oscar Arnulfo.**

BIBLIOGRAPHY

Bono, Agostino. "Latin America: Controversy, Strong Stands Marked Pope's Work." *Catholic News Service* 2005. Available from http//www.catholicnews.com/jpii/stories/story09.htm.

Comblin, José. "Changes in the Latin American Church during the Pontificate of John Paul II," part 1. *National Catholic Reporter* 1, no. 14 (2 July 2003). Available from http://www.nationalcatholicreporter.org/globalpers/gp070203.htm.

Comblin, José. "Desperate for Leadership: Changes in the Latin American Church during the Pontificate of John Paul II," part 2. *National Catholic Reporter* 1, no. 15 (9 July 2003). Available from http://www.nationalcatholicreporter.org/globalpers/gp070903.htm.

Dussel, Enrique. "The Catholic Church in Latin America since 1930." *Cambridge History of Latin America*, vol. 6, edited by Leslie Bethell, pp. 547–582. Cambridge, UK, and New York: Cambridge University Press, 1994.

Guzmán Stein, Laura. "The Politics of Implementing Women's Rights in Catholic Countries in Latin America." In *Globalization, Gender, and Religion: The Politics of Women's Rights in Catholic and Muslim Contexts*, edited by Jane H. Bayes and Nayereh Tohidi, pp. 127–155. Basingstoke, Hampshire, U.K., and New York: Palgrave, 2001.

John Paul II. "Ordinatio Sacerdotalis." March 22, 1994. Available from http://www.vatican.va/holy_father/john_paul_ii.

John Paul II. "Ecclesia in America." January 22, 1999. Available from http://www.vatican.va/holy_father/john_paul_ii.

Szulc, Tad. *Pope John Paul II: The Biography*. New York: Scribner, 1995.

Vatican News Service. "Viaggi Apostolici del Santo Padre Sua Santitá Giovanni Paolo II: Statistiche." Updated January 22, 2005. Available from http://www.vatican.va/news_services.

Wynn, Wilton. *Keepers of the Keys: John XXIII, Paul VI, and John Paul II, Three Who Changed the Church*. New York: Random House, 1988.

KRISTINA A. BOYLAN

JONESTOWN. James (Jim) Warren Jones founded the Peoples Temple, originally named Wings of Deliverance, in Indianapolis, Indiana, in 1955, with social justice for poor and working-class peoples of all races as his stated goal. In his previous experience within the Assemblies of God church, he claimed to have been scorned for preaching inclusion of African Americans. In 1960 Jones's church affiliated with the Protestant denomination of Disciples of Christ, and the congregation adopted the name Peoples Temple Christian Church. In 1965 the congregation moved to Redwood Valley, California, to escape the pervasively racist climate in Indiana at the time. Jones also believed that in this location he and his followers could survive a nuclear war.

In 1974 the church came under investigation for tax evasion. Around the same time, ex-members of the church went to the media and government organizations, urging investigations into church practices. In 1974 the Peoples Temple acquired a lease for nearly four thousand acres of land from the Guyanese government to establish an agricultural and religious mission in a remote jungle area in the northwest part of the country. Jones had selected Guyana because it was an English-speaking country with conditions suitable for agriculture. In 1977 Jones and his church made the move, welcomed by the country's black-minority, socialist government. Jones named the closed settlement Jonestown. The Jonestown settlement is notorious for the massacre that occurred on November 18, 1978, in which Jones and 900 of his followers died.

See also **Guyana.**

BIBLIOGRAPHY

Chidester, David. *Salvation and Suicide: An Interpretation of Jim Jones, the Peoples Temple, and Jonestown*. Bloomington: Indiana University Press, 1988.

Hall, John R. *Gone from the Promised Land: Jonestown in American Cultural History*. New Brunswick, NJ: Transaction, 2004.

Reiterman, Tim, and John Jacobs. *Raven: The Untold Story of the Rev. Jim Jones and His People*. New York: E. P. Dutton, 1982.

Religious Movements Homepage Project. University of Virginia. *Peoples Temple (Jonestown)*. Available from http://religiousmovements.lib.virginia.edu/nrms/Jonestwn.html.

KATHRYN PLUMMER

JONGO. Jongo, a Brazilian dance-song indigenous to southern-central Brazil. The jongo is an African slave dance style performed for social and recreational purposes. Many scholars believe the jongo to be of Angolan origin, while others have identified a form of the same title in northern Ghana. Accompanied by a highly syncopated 2/4 drum pattern, the male and female participants of the jongo dance in a circle, moving in a counterclockwise direction. Performing with a rattle in his hand, the singer jumps to the center of the circle and sings a verse. After the singer is answered by the chorus, he stamps his feet and then, near the end of the chorus, rejoins the dancers. The dance resumes when one of the spectators moves to the center of the circle.

Songs of the jongo dance, known as *pontos,* are usually sung in improvised one- and two-line verses, or *voltas,* which parallel the percussion accompaniment. In São Paulo the lead singer and a harmonized second voice are answered by the dancers in an improvised call-and-response pattern. The jongo continues to survive in a few areas within the former southern-central slave regions. Since its founding in 2000, Jongo da Serrinha, a community musical group from São José da Serra in the state of Rio de Janeiro, has gained prominence through its critically acclaimed performances in the urban jongo clubs of Rio.

See also **Music: Popular Music and Dance; Slavery: Brazil.**

BIBLIOGRAPHY

Nicholas Slonimsky, *Music of Latin America* (1972).

Additional Bibliography

Gandra, Edir. *Jongo da Serrinha: Do terreiro aos palcos.* Rio de Janeiro: Giorgio Grafica e Editora, 1995.

Jongo da Serrinha. *Jongo da Serrinha.* Rio de Janeiro: Prefeitura do Rio e Programa de Bolsas da RioArte, 2002.

Teobaldo, Délcio. *Cantos de fé, de trabalho e de orgia: O jongo rural de Angra dos Reis.* Rio de Janiero: E-papers, 2003.

JOHN COHASSEY

JOSÉ I OF PORTUGAL (1714–1777).

José I of Portugal (*b.* 6 June 1714; *d.* 24 February 1777), king of Portugal (1750–1777). Called the "idle king," in contrast to his energetic chief minister, Sebastião José de Carvalho e Melo, Count of Oeiras (known as the Marquês de Pombal), José was eclipsed as Pombal pushed absolutist tendencies to despotic heights following the cataclysmic Lisbon earthquake of 1755. The king never challenged Pombal's attacks on the aristocracy, his suppression of the Jesuits, or his extensive administrative, economic, and fiscal reforms that worked toward a more bourgeois and secular state. José's marriage to the Spanish Bourbon princess Mariana Victoria (1729) produced four daughters. The oldest, the future María I, inherited the throne at his death.

See also **Lisbon Earthquake; Pombal, Marquês de (Sebastião José de Carvalho e Melo).**

BIBLIOGRAPHY

João Lúcio De Azevedo, *O Marquês de Pombal e a sua época* (1922).

Alan David Francis, *Portugal, 1715–1808* (1985).

H. V. Livermore, *A New History of Portugal* (1976), pp. 212–238.

Additional Bibliography

Domingues, Mário. *Marquês de Pombal: O homem e a sua época.* Lisboa: Préfacio, 2002.

Lopes, António. *Enigma Pombal: Nova documentação, tentative de interpreção.* Lisboa: Roma Editora, 2002.

Maxwell, Kenneth. *Pombal: Paradox of the Enlightenment.* Cambridge: Cambridge University Press, 1995.

CATHERINE LUGAR

JOURNALISM.

Latin American journalism is complicated by the tension that exists between the quality of the work and the strategies employed to deal with competitors and enemies of the press. In 2005, the United Nations estimated that almost 10 percent of the region's citizens are illiterate and only 83 percent of primary students finish the schooling cycle. Even though millions do not buy a newspaper, it is a daily habit for many to read the headlines on the front pages of publications in *kioskos* (cabinets that hold newspapers and magazines). Radio and television have reached more *incomunicados* (those beyond communication), but many who are exposed to broadcast media are also tabloid readers. The print medium has had a greater long-term historical impact by influencing opinion makers but is losing that power. The mainstream press, which represents the social and economic interests of its owners, often challenged in the twentieth century by dictators, is under pressure of the powers that be (*poderes fácticos*) such as corporations, populist politicians, and the drug lords in the early twenty-first century.

The first printing press was set up in New Spain (Mexico) in 1535, soon after the Spanish Conquest and a century before the establishment of the first printing press in the British North American colonies. This first press was used primarily to produce religious material to support the Roman Catholic Church. An Italian citizen brought the first printing press to the Viceroyalty of Peru in 1583.

Under close government control, however, the early presses did not print newspapers until the eighteenth century. The first newspaper in Spanish America was *La Gazeta de México y Noticias de Nueva España,* founded in Mexico City in 1722; the first daily paper did not appear until 1805. The early press reported on religious and commercial activities, but as time passed, journalism entered into a vituperative political phase.

The movements for independence from Spain between 1809 and 1825 saw the birth of patriot propaganda organs, such as *El Despertador Americano* (The American Alarm Clock) in Mexico, *Aurora de Chile* (Dawn) in Chile, and *El Peruano* (The Peruvian) in Peru. *El Peruano* suspended publication in 1880 during a war against Chile, but it restarted several years later and was still being published into the twenty-first century. As the nineteenth century progressed, newspapers became a source of information for the masses.

In Chile, for example, *El Ferrocarril* (The Railroad, 1855–1911) was the first newspaper supported mainly by advertising. Likewise, in Mexico the founding by Rafael Reyes Spíndola of *El Imparcial* (1896), which sold for one centavo, removed the press from dependence on political support by widening circulation and thus increasing advertising revenues. Newspapers were also an important medium for fledgling parties, such as *La Vanguardia* for the Argentine Socialist Party.

As an example of the power of the press in early twentieth-century Latin America, U.S. journalist James Creelman's interview with the Mexican dictator Porfirio Díaz (1876–1911), published in *Pearson's Magazine* in 1908, contained Díaz's assertion that he would not run for an eighth term in 1910. Intended only for foreign consumption, the interview was circulated by the underground press in Mexico, which set the political pot bubbling and led to revolution. In the aftermath of the revolution, some conservative Mexico City newspapers, seeking to preserve privilege, undermined the fragile democratic government of Francisco I. Madero (1911–1913).

In Bolivia, the distance between the press and the people was huge. The Big Three tin-mine owners controlled the three leading newspapers until the advent of *La Calle* (The Street, 1936–1946). Politicized by the disastrous Chaco War with Paraguay (1932–1935), *La Calle* supported the Movimiento Nacionalista Revolucionario (Nationalist Revolutionary Movement), which started reforms in Bolivia in 1952.

In Cuba, the corrupt press under Fulgencio Batista (1934–1959) accepted $450,000 a month in bribes to support the dictator. After Fidel Castro gained power in 1959, he instituted state control of the press. *Granma* became the voice of the Cuban Communist Party, and therefore of the state, and Prensa Latina started operations as the Third World's first international news agency.

Other newspapers strove to be independent. In Uruguay, *El Día* championed the progressive programs of President José Batlle y Ordóñez. *La Prensa* of Buenos Aires, founded by Ezequiel Paz in 1869 and the best known Latin American newspaper before its closure by Juan Perón in 1951, refused to accept subscriptions from government employees and vowed not to discuss the private lives of public figures. Bartolomé Mitre founded Argentina's influential *La Nación.*

The liberal *Excélsior* of Mexico, however, was not able to remain exempt from the wrath of the official party Partido Revolucionario Institucional. Founded in 1917, and one of the few successful newspaper cooperatives in the world, *Excélsior* was edited by Julio García Scherer until the government of Luis Echeverría engineered his ouster in 1976. Neither *Excélsior* nor *La Prensa* of Argentina has recovered its international prestige.

In Brazil, during the early Portuguese colonial period, there was no printing press or periodicals, since prohibitions against the press were rigorously enforced. The first Brazilian newspaper was the weekly *A Gazeta do Río de Janeiro,* established in 1808.

The nineteenth century saw the emergence of such distinguished journalists as Joaquim María Machado de Assís (1839–1908), who along with Rui Barbosa (1849–1923) combined journalism with literature. Cuban José Martí did the same for Mexican, American, and Venezuelan newspapers beginning in 1880.

In modern times, giants of the Brazilian press such as *O Estado de São Paulo* and *Jornal do Brasil* opposed the reformist president João Goulart (1961–1964), contributing to his overthrow and ushering in twenty-one years of military rule. But once censorship was lifted in 1978, Brazilian newspapers were instrumental in opposing continued military domination and fostering a return to democracy in 1985.

But nowhere was the dispute between government and press more sharply etched than in Chile during the freely elected presidency of socialist Salvador Allende (1970–1973). While Allende granted freedom of the press, the opposition press undermined his government and made possible the military coup of 11 September 1973. *El Mercurio* (founded 1827) accepted $1,650,000 from the Central Intelligence Agency to wage verbal warfare against Allende. His successor, dictator General Augusto Pinochet, did not permit freedom of expression during his sixteen-year rule.

There were other approaches toward the relationship between government and the press. In Peru a group of military officers who took power in 1968 seized the eight leading newspapers in 1974. They promised to turn these dailies over to various sectors of the people, but this never happened. An elected civilian government returned the papers to their owners in 1980.

Journalism is a prestigious field in Latin America, although underpaid reporters often hold two or more jobs, sometimes unaware of possible conflicts of interest. They are also susceptible to bribes, particularly in remote areas, far from the main capitals.

Government harassment of the press can be fierce. Some 98 newsmen were killed in Argentina during the Dirty War (1976–1983), and some 400 fled the country. Brazilian newsmen also suffered abuses during dictatorship in the 1970s. Journalists also have been on the front lines, sometimes paying with their lives, in the drug wars of Colombia and the Sendero Luminoso (Shining Path) Maoist terrorist activities in Peru.

Direct censorship, such as that wielded by the Sandinistas of Nicaragua against *La Prensa* in the 1980s, is rare because media watchdogs and nongovernmental organizations (NGOs) disseminate alerts immediately. More insidious, however, is *auto-censura* (self-censorship) by which governments or corporations indirectly intimidate journalists, who might not be aware of their adversarial potential against those who rule.

The first journalism school in Latin America was created by the Círculo de Periodistas (Circle of Journalists) in La Plata, Argentina, in 1934, but widespread instruction in the field did not exist until after World War II. In 1994, Colombian writer Gabriel García Márquez created Fundación Nuevo Periodismo Iberoamericano (New Iberoamerican Journalism Foundation), currently the main journalism training organization for practitioners in the region. Based in Cartagena, it promotes quality journalism through workshops and the presentation of annual Nuevo Periodismo (New Journalism) awards. In 2004, there were 1026 departments, schools, and communication programs in 22 countries across Latin America. Most of them offer journalism as a career path; as an example, Brazil had 297 courses recognized with the title "Journalism," while Chile had more than forty public and private universities teaching journalism courses. Investigative journalism *(periodismo de investigación)* started reporting on corruption, violence, and drug trafficking in the 1980s. Investigative journalism often seeks to make state institutions accountable, especially in weak democracies. There are several national and independent investigative journalism networks that maintain vigilance. Some stories have had strong political impact, especially in Argentina, Brazil, Costa Rica, Colombia, México, and Peru.

The Ecuadorian newspaper *Hoy* in 1994 and Peruvian weekly magazine *Caretas* in 1995 offered on-line versions of their publications before the

New York Times and *El País* (Spain) announced their Internet versions.

Blogs (*diarios de referencia*) have been an online feature for leading newspapers since 2005. The authors of the blogs can be either staff or nonstaff journalists. Ricardo Noblat, a Brazilian journalist who independently started a blog, had his work co-opted by the newspaper *O Estado de São Paulo* because it successfully exposed government corruption. In January 2007, Noblat's abandoned the *Estadão* (a colloquial name for the Sao Paulo paper) and moved to *O Globo*, the most important in Rio de Janeiro.

Such literary periodicals as *Etiqueta Negra,* based in Lima (Peru), and *Gatopardo,* based in Bogotá (Colombia), have contributors from Latin America, United States, and Europe and combine writing with innovative design.

See also **Allende Gossens, Salvador; Barbosa de Oliveira, Rui; Batista y Zaldívar, Fulgencio; Batlle y Ordóñez, José; Castro Ruz, Fidel; Chaco War; Díaz, Porfirio; Dirty War; Echeverría Álvarez, Luis; Excélsior (Mexico City); García Márquez, Gabriel; Internet; Journalism in Mexico; Machado de Assis, Joaquim Maria; Madero, Francisco Indalecio; Martí y Pérez, José Julián; Mercurio, El; Mitre, Bartolomé; Nación, La (Buenos Aires); Perón, Juan Domingo; Pinochet Ugarte, Augusto; Prensa, La (de Nicaragua); Radio and Television; Scherer, Julio.**

BIBLIOGRAPHY

Good historical overviews are Gustavo Adolfo Otero, *El periodismo en América* (1946); and Michael Brian Salwen and Bruce Garrison, *Latin American Journalism* (1991). Significant treatments of the Latin American press in the twentieth century are Robert N. Pierce, *Keeping the Flame: Media and Government in Latin America* (1979); and Marvin Alisky, *Latin American Media: Guidance and Censorship* (1981). Elizabeth Fox, ed., *Media and Politics in Latin America: The Struggle for Democracy* (1988), gives more attention to radio and television. For critical national studies, see Juan Gargurevich, *Historia de la prensa peruana 1594–1990,* Lima: La Voz Ediciones, 1991; Jerry Knudson, *Bolivia: Press and Revolution, 1932–1964* (1986); *The Chilean Press During the Allende Years, 1970–73* (1986); Nelson Werneck Sodré, *A História da Imprensa no Brasil* (1966). Twenty-first century journalism analyses include Catherine Conaghan, *Deception in the Public Sphere,* Pittsburgh: University of Pittsburgh Press, 2006; Silvio Waisbord, *Watchdog Journalism in South America: News, Accountability and Democracy,* New York: Columbia University Press, 2000.

JERRY KNUDSON
JACQUELINE FOWKS

JOURNALISM IN MEXICO. The first printing press in the Americas began to operate in Mexico in 1539, but the first newspaper, the *Gaceta de México,* wasn't published until 1722. For half a year it circulated monthly with business and society news. In 1805 the *Diario de México* became the first daily paper in New Spain.

In December 1810, Miguel Hidalgo produced *El Despertador Americano* in Guadalajara and published nine issues. Soon, despite the censorship of the viceregal government, newspapers began to appear, such as *El Ilustrador Nacional* (Sultepec, state of México, 1812), the *Gazeta del Gobierno Americano* (Guanajuato, 1812), and José Joaquín Fernández de Lizardi's *El Pensador Mexicano* (1812).

When the country gained its independence in 1821, literary creation and political factions produced newspapers that were substantial, although they almost always spoke in euphemisms. Some of the first were *El Ensayo Literario* (Puebla, 1838), *El Ateneo Mexicano* (1840), and *El Liceo Mexicano* (1844). Those that enjoyed wide circulation were *La Estrella Polar de los Amigos Deseosos de la Ilustración* (Guadalajara, 1822), *La Concordia Yucateca* (1829), *La Aurora de la Libertad* (1831), and *El Federalista* (1831).

Around the middle of the century, the main newspapers were conservative (such as *La Espada de D. Simplicio,* 1855) or liberal (such as *El Republicano,* 1855, and *El Siglo XIX,* which had four phases between 1841 and 1896). There was ample freedom of criticism. Newspapers supporting workers and socialists appeared later. Some, along with publications such as journalist Filomeno Mata's *El Diario del Hogar,* constituted Porfirio Díaz's more significant opposition. The Flores Magón brothers' *El Hijo del Ahuizote* and later their *Regeneración* (1900–1916) helped to ignite the revolution.

By the end of the war, several newspaper companies had been established. *El Dictamen,* published in Veracruz since 1898, is the oldest daily in the country. *El Universal* (1916) is the dean of the Mexico City press. During the first half of the twentieth century, the press, which was conservative, clashed with governments such as that of Lázaro Cárdenas (1934–1940). It was evident that the hostility was coming to an end when, on June

7, 1951, president Miguel Alemán established Freedom of the Press Day at a reception given for him by José García Valseca, who was to become owner of thirty-seven daily newspapers.

Self-censorship prevailed in most publications. The government was sponsor to almost all of them. In 1976, the board of directors of *Excelsior* (founded in 1917) was dissolved when its members proposed a more autonomous editorial line. Several of them founded *Proceso*, which has been the nation's most important political weekly since 1976. Others founded *Unomásuno* in 1977, from which a group of journalists later split off to form *La Jornada* in 1984.

A more independent press has developed with the liberalization of Mexican politics. There are specialized dailies such as *El Financiero* (1980) and *El Economista* (1988) and newspapers backed by ample business resources, such as *Reforma* (1993) and *Excelsior* (re-founded in 2006). Others, such as *La Crónica* (1996) and *Milenio* (2000), have distinguished themselves among the thirty-five dailies appearing in Mexico City. By the end of the twentieth century, some three hundred dailies were in circulation throughout the country, but the majority were printing only a few thousand copies each.

See also **Excélsior (Mexico City); Journalism.**

BIBLIOGRAPHY

Cano Andaluz, Aurora, ed. *Las publicaciones periódicas y la historia de México.* México, D.F.: Universidad Nacional Autónoma de México, Instituto de Investigaciones Bibliográficas, 1995.

Lawson, Chapell H. *Building the Fourth Estate: Democratization and the Rise of a Free Press in Mexico.* Berkeley: University of California Press, 2002.

Ruiz Castañeda, María del Carmen. *La prensa: Pasado y presente de México.* México: UNAM, 1987.

Trejo Delarbre, Raúl. *Volver a los medios: De la crítica, a la ética.* México, D.F.: Cal y Arena, 1997.

RAUL TREJO DELARBRE

JOVELLANOS, SALVADOR (1833–1881).

Salvador Jovellanos (*b.* 1833; *d.* 1881), Paraguayan president (1871–1874). The decade after the disastrous War of the Triple Alliance was a difficult period for Paraguay, with political factions shifting constantly and foreign armies in control of the streets of Asunción. Under such circumstances, obscure men sometimes achieved high political office. Salvador Jovellanos was one example. He had been chosen by President Francisco Solano López to study in Europe. After López was killed, Jovellanos was chosen as Cirilo Antonio Rivarola's vice president solely, it seems, on the basis of his charming manner. He in turn succeeded to the presidency when opponents forced out Rivarola in 1871. His charm notwithstanding, Jovellanos never gained the trust of any major faction. His administration was marred by four revolts and by two notorious loans negotiated in London in an effort to restore the country's wrecked economy.

See also **War of the Triple Alliance.**

BIBLIOGRAPHY

Charles J. Kolinski, *Historical Dictionary of Paraguay* (1975).

Harris Gaylord Warren, *Paraguay and the Triple Alliance: The Postwar Decade, 1869–1878* (1978), pp. 177–193.

Additional Bibliography

Amaral, Raúl. *Los presidentes del Paraguay: Crónica Política 1844-1954.* Asunción: Biblioteca de Estudios Paraguayos, 1994.

Aramburu, Eduardo. *Demanda de Eduardo Aramburu contra Salvador Jovellanos, Higinio Uriarte y suceciones de Juan B. Gill y Emilio Gill.* Montevideo: Imprenta La Reform, 1876.

Ayala, Eligio. *La Revolución armada: Un tema constitucional.* Asunción: Archivo del Liberalismo, Cuadernos Históricos, no. 11, 1989.

Rivarola, Cirilo A. *Manifiesto.* Buenos Aires, 1983.

THOMAS L. WHIGHAM

JUANA INÉS DE LA CRUZ, SOR (1648–1695).

Sor Juana Inés de la Cruz (*b.* 12 November 1651 or 1648; *d.* 17 April 1695), the major poet of the Spanish colonies. Born in San Miguel de Nepantla, near the capital city of Mexico, Juana Inés de Asuaje y Ramírez was the illegitimate daughter of Isabel Ramírez de Santillana and Pedro Manuel de Asuaje y Vargas Machuca; her illegitimacy

Sor Juana Inés de la Cruz, c. 1651–1695. Often regarded as the last notable poet of the Spanish colonies, Sor Juana Inés de la Cruz offers a richly varied amount of information about the diverse ethnic groups living in Mexico during the latter half of the seventeenth century. In several instances of her work, she uses the voice of minority peoples, such as slaves and Indians, giving modern-day readers a glimpse of people frequently left unrecorded in history. THE GRANGER COLLECTION, NEW YORK

may explain the uncertainty about the year of her birth. Taken to the Spanish viceroy's court as a child prodigy, she became a nun in 1667, first with the Carmelites for a short time and then definitively, in 1669, in the Jeronymite Convent of San Jerónimo, where, with the religious name of Sor Juana Inés de la Cruz, she had her own collection of books and some free time for study and writing. Toward the end of her life she was more strictly ascetic. She died taking care of her sister nuns during a plague.

Almost all of Sor Juana's works were initially published in Spain in three different volumes (1689, 1692, and 1700). Her works include many different genres of poetry, dramatic works in verse, and prose works of a more doctrinal or autobiographical sort.

Personal Lyrics. Her secular lyric poetry is among her best-known work. There are, for example, such highly original works as her verse portrait of her beloved Marquise of Paredes (a viceroy's wife); her sonnet on a painted portrait of herself as a vain attempt to save her body from annihilation; several "carpe diem" sonnets centered on the image of the rose; and various poems on hope and the vanity of human illusions, on feminine fidelity, on absence and the sufferings of love, and on the imagination within which we can imprison the beloved.

Religious Writings and "Villancicos". Among Sor Juana's devotional writings are the interesting prose *Ejercicios de la Encarnación* (Exercises on the Incarnation), in which she presents the Virgin Mary as a model of feminine power and wisdom, almost on the same level as God. Her *villancicos,* or carol sequences, written for festive performance in cathedrals, reveals her religious and social sensibility. This popular genre, with many different voices, permitted the poet to speak for marginal social groups such as black slaves, Indians, and women, and to make fun of masculine clerical types such as the student. These songs present women as intellectual as well as devout, as for example in the figure of Saint Catharine of Alexandria. Her black voices speak a special dialect of Spanish, and her Indians speak Nahuatl, to address God directly and to complain about how they are treated by Spanish representatives of the Church or State.

The "Sueño". Sor Juana's lengthy *Sueño* (Dream) occupies a unique place among her works. In her highly significant autobiographical *Respuesta* (Reply), she refers to the *Sueño* as the only poem that she had written for her own pleasure. It is a compendium of contemporary scholastic and scientific knowledge, ranging from the ancient philosophers and church fathers to Florentine hermetic wisdom and the contemporary ideas of Athanasius Kircher and perhaps even of René Descartes. Literarily, the poem draws on Renaissance poetic commonplaces, recast in Spanish baroque forms. Its narrative structure is based on the arrival and departure of night, framing the dream itself, which is an adventure of the intellectual Soul in search of a complete understanding of the universe, a journey that represents the author's own crisis as a religious woman interested in the physical sciences. She seems to identify with Phaëthon, the illegitimate son of Apollo struck down by his father and thus made famous, and with other mythological figures, mostly feminine, such as Night. The Soul, who is the protagonist of the poem, comes back to earth in the final lines of the poem and is identified with the poet herself, who wakes up and, for the first time, asserts her feminine presence grammatically in the very last word of the poem.

The "Respuesta". In 1690 the bishop of Puebla published Sor Juana's critique of a Portuguese Jesuit's sermon, along with a public letter of his own addressed to her over the pseudonymous signature of a nun. In her critique (*Carta atenagórica* or *Crisis sobre un sermón*), Sor Juana had refuted in a highly sophisticated and learned way the argument of Father Antonio de Vieira, in which he rejected interpretations by the fathers of the church and proposed his own. The letter, although somewhat ambiguous, reveals how much bishop admires her intellectually as he urges her to use her intelligence in the study of divine rather than secular matters. The bishop's critique provided Sor Juana with an excuse for a full-scale apologia in her *Respuesta a sor Filotea de la Cruz.* This eloquent and warmly human document fully explains the nun's intellectual vocation by recalling her childhood eagerness to learn to read and write and her adolescent rejection of marriage and choice of the convent as a place in which to study. She cites many famous women from the Bible and from classical antiquity in her defense of equal feminine access to study and to writing. She implies that women as scientists have empirical advantages when she asserts, "If Aristotle had done some cooking, he would have written even more." Such a feminist apologia is unique in the seventeenth-century Hispanic world. (In a letter, "Carta de Monterrey," a translation of which was published in 1988, which Sor Juana wrote to her confessor long before her *Respuesta,* she defends her rights in even stronger terms.)

Neptuno alegórico (Allegorical Neptune) is, for the modern reader, a difficult work; it is an official *relación* or explanation of the triumphal arch erected in November of 1680 for the reception of the new viceroy, the Marqués of La Laguna, and his wife. The nun presents as an allegorical model for the viceroy the mythological figure of Neptune, in her poetic description of the arch. This is a highly learned text in which she displays her most arcane erudition and ingenuity.

Theater. Sor Juana's theatrical works consist of several *loas* (short dramatic prologues) that are largely mythical and allegorical; three *autos sacramentales,* or allegorical dramatizations of sacramental theology in the tradition of Calderón, written, with their *loas,* for the feast of Corpus Christi; and two full-length "cape and sword" plays in the tradition of Lope de Vega. The *loas* that precede her *autos* are especially interesting for their presentation of Aztec feminine characters, who defend pre-Christian religious practices. Of the *autos, El cetro de José* (Joseph's Scepter) is based on a story from the Bible; *El mártir del Sacramento, San Hermenegildo* (The Martyr of the Sacrament...) is hagiographic; and *El Divino Narciso* (Divine Narcissus), the best of the three, is an ingenious allegorization of the pagan mythological Narcissus as the redeeming Christ. Narcissus (Christ), having rejected the advances of Echo (the Devil), who is the rival of Human Nature, sees the latter reflected in the Fountain of Grace, which unites God to Human Nature at the moment of the Incarnation; then Narcissus, in love with himself as reflected in Human Nature, falls into the fountain and drowns, allegorically crucified. One of the secular plays, *Amor es más laberinto,* was written in collaboration with Juan de Guevara; the other, *Los empeños de una casa,* has strong leading female roles, especially that of Leonor, which is a sort of autobiographical figure. The comic character Castaño, a mulatto servant from the New World, speaks satirically of the machismo of white Spaniards in a metatheatrical scene parodying the "cape and sword" comedy as a literary genre.

From the baroque intellectual world of her convent cell Sor Juana sends messages that intimate her deep concerns as a woman and a *criolla.* She is a key figure for understanding colonial Mexico.

See also **Mexico: The Colonial Period; Theater.**

BIBLIOGRAPHY

Electa Arenal, "Sor Juana Inés de la Cruz: Speaking the Mother Tongue," *University of Dayton Review* 16 (1982): 93–105.

Marie-Cécile Bénassy-Berling, *Humanismo y religión en Sor Juana Inés de la Cruz* (1983).

Jean Franco, *Plotting Women* (1989).

Inundación castálida, edited by Georgina Sabat de Rivers (Madrid, 1982).

Asunción Lavrin, "Unlike Sor Juana? The Model Nun in the Religious Literature of Colonial Mexico," in *Feminist Perspectives on Sor Juana Inés de la Cruz* (1991), pp. 61–85.

Josefina Ludmer, "Tricks of the Weak," in *Feminist Perspectives on Sor Juana Inés de la Cruz* (1991), pp. 86–93.

Obras completas, 4 vols. edited by Alfonso Méndez Plancarte and Alberto G. Salceda (Mexico, 1951–1957).

Obras selectas, edited by Georgina Sabat de Rivers and Elias L. Rivers (Barcelona, 1976).

Octavio Paz, *Sor Juana; or, the Traps of Faith* (1988).

Georgina Sabat-Rivers, *El "Sueño" de Sor Juana Inés de la Cruz: Tradiciones literarias y originalidad* (1976).

Georgina Sabat-Rivers, *"Esta de nuestra América pupila": Hacia Sor Juana Inés de la Cruz: Poetas barrocos de la Colonia* (1991); and "A Feminist Rereading of Sor Juana's 'Dream,'" in *Feminist Perspectives on Sor Juana Inés de la Cruz* (1991), pp. 142–161.

Nina Scott, "'If you are not pleased to favor me, put me out of your mind . . .': Gender and Authority in Sor Juana Inés de la Cruz," (Plus the translation of the "Carta de Monterrey"), *Women's Studies International Forum* 2 no. 5 (1988): 429–438.

"Sor Juana Inés de la Cruz," *Latin American Writers,* edited by Carlos A. Solé and Maria Isabel Abreu, pp. 85–105.

Alan Trueblood, *A Sor Juana Anthology* (Cambridge, Mass., 1988).

Additional Bibliography

Glantz, Margo. *Sor Juana Inés de la Cruz: Saberes y placers.* Toluca, Estado de México: Gobierno del Estado de México, Instituto Mexiquense de Cultura, 1996.

Montané Martí, Julio C. *Intriga en la corte: Eusebio Francisco Kino, Sor Juana Inés de la Cruz, y Carlos de Sigüenza y Góngora.* Hermosillo, México: Universidad de Sonora, 1997.

Kirk Rappaport, Pamela. *Sor Juana Inés de la Cruz: Religion, Art, and Feminism.* New York: Continuum, 1998.

GEORGINA SABAT-RIVERS

JUAN DIEGO

JUAN DIEGO (?–1548?). According to several traditions, Juan Diego was a poor Indian chosen by the Virgin Mary to be her messenger to Brother Juan de Zumárraga (1468–1548), the first bishop of New Spain. The Virgin asked to have a sanctuary built near Mount Tepeyac, north of Mexico City, so that she could provide her love, aid, and protection to the people of the newly conquered land. Whether Juan Diego was actually a real person has been the subject of debate since the late eighteenth century, but the dispute became more intense after Pope John Paul II's visit to Mexico in 1990. At that time the upper hierarchy of the Catholic Church in Mexico officially announced that Diego was on the way to becoming a saint.

Those who wanted sainthood for Juan Diego provided Rome with a "biography" that was a combination of "select" segments from various documents written by indigenous and Spanish individuals. None of them is contemporary to the Virgin's appearances, which, according to this "official version," occurred on December 9 and 12, 1531, ten years after the Spanish conquest of Mexico City, or Tenochtitlan. The lack of contemporary testimonies is one of the strongest criticisms against admitting the veracity of the Virgin's appearance. Zumárraga is the only historical person in the account, but he never mentioned the miracle in his numerous writings.

The reconstructed biography sent to Rome presents Juan Diego as a very poor *macehualli* (the Nahuatl word for "commoner") born in 1474 in Cuauhtitlan, a town located fourteen miles north of Mexico City. His original name in the Nahuatl language was Cuauhtlatoa (He Who Speaks Like an Eagle). Before the arrival of the Spaniards, he had married María Lucía but had decided to live with her in celibacy. Juan Bernardino, Juan Diego's uncle, is the other relevant character. He was favored with one of the Virgin's first miracles, when he was cured of a fatal epidemic disease (a *cocoliztli*). Juan Diego died at age seventy-four, in 1548, and was buried in the first chapel built in Tepeyac, a building he had tended with great care.

See also **Catholic Church: The Colonial Period; John Paul II, Pope; Zumárraga, Juan de.**

BIBLIOGRAPHY

Chávez, Eduardo. *Our Lady of Guadalupe and Saint Juan Diego: The Historical Evidence.* Lanham, MD: Rowman and Littlefield, 2006.

Nobisso, Josephine. *Saint Juan Diego and Our Lady of Guadalupe.* Boston: Pauline Books and Media, 2002.

XAVIER NOGUEZ

JUAN FERNÁNDEZ ISLANDS. Juan Fernández Islands, three volcanic islands belonging to Chile that lie about four hundred miles west of Valparaiso. Although possibly sighted by Magellan, they were discovered in 1574 by the Spanish navigator Juan Fernández. He named them after saints, but those names were soon supplanted by Más a Tierra (Nearer Land) and Más Afuera (Farther Out) for the two principal islands and Santa Clara, or Goat Island, for the small island just off the tip of Más a Tierra. They became important aids to navigation along the Pacific coast of South America and served as bases for Spain's rivals during the seventeenth and eighteenth centuries.

In October 1704 a British privateer marooned Scottish seaman Alexander Selkirk on Más a Tierra, where he remained until rescued by Captain Woodes Rogers in February 1709. Selkirk's story provided the factual basis for Daniel Defoe's *Robinson Crusoe* (1719).

Colonization efforts failed until 1750, when the Spanish established San Juan Bautista at Cumberland Bay, Más a Tierra, to defend the island against rival nations. As a penal colony, it held a number of prominent Chilean creoles during the wars for independence. The Chileans abandoned the island in 1837, following a Peruvian raid. Chileans returned later to San Juan Bautista (today called Robinson Crusoe), used it as a penal colony again, and eventually developed a small fishing and agricultural community. In the twentieth century it became primarily a lobster fishing center.

During World War I, Cumberland Bay was the site of a naval encounter in which British forces sank the German light cruiser *Dresden* in March 1915. Since then the island has attracted some tourist activity. In January 1966 the Chilean government renamed Más a Tierra for Robinson Crusoe and Más Afuera for Alexander Selkirk.

See also **Explorers and Exploration: Spanish America.**

BIBLIOGRAPHY

Benjamín Vicuña Mackenna, *Juan Fernández, historia verdadera de la isla de Robinson Crusoe* (1883).

Ralph Lee Woodward, Jr., *Robinson Crusoe's Island: A History of the Juan Fernández Islands* (1969).

Additional Bibliography

Brescia, Maura. *Selkirk, Robinson, el mito: A tres siglos del solitario en Isla Robinson Crusoe*. Santiago: Editorial Mare Nostrum, 2004.

Cuevas, Jaime G., Marticorena, Alicia, and Cavieres, Lohengrin A. "New Additions to the Introduced Flora of the Juan Fernández Islands: Origin, Distribution, Life History Traits, and Potential of Invasion." http://www.scielo.cl, 2004.

Sánchez-Ostiz, Miguel. *La isla de Juan Fernández: Viaje a la isla de Robinson Crusoe*. Barcelona: Ediciones B., 2005.

Simmons, James C. *Castaway in Paradise: The Incredible Adventures of True-life Robinson Crusoes*. Dobbs Ferry, NY: Sheridan House, 1993.

Yáñez R., Eleuterio, Canales R. Cristian, and Silva G. Claudio. *Evaluación de la langosta explotada en las islas Robinson Crusoe y Santa Clara del archipiélago de Juan Fernández*. Chile: Investigaciones marinas, 2000.

Ralph Lee Woodward Jr.

JUAN SANTOS. *See* **Atahualpa (Juan Santos).**

JUAN Y SANTACILIA, JORGE (1713–1773). Jorge Juan y Santacilia (*b.* 5 January 1713; *d.* 5 July 1773), Spanish scientist. Born in Novelda, near Alicante, Juan was orphaned at three but nevertheless received a first-rate education, first in Malta, then at the prestigious new Spanish naval academy (Guardia Marina) in Cádiz, and finally with the Spanish fleet plying the Mediterranean (1730–1734). In 1734 Philip V chose him and Antonio de Ulloa, another brilliant young naval officer, to join the French scientists Louis Godin and Charles Marie la Condamine on an expedition to the Indies to measure the exact length of a degree on the equator.

Finally reaching Quito in May 1736, the group immediately began their measurements, with Juan assigned to the ostensible leader of the expedition, Louis Godin, with whom he made observations at thirty-two sites. Juan's stay in Ecuador was not without controversy, however. Both he and Ulloa became embroiled with the president of the Audiencia of Quito and also with the French in a protocol dispute over whose names and royal coat of arms were to be placed on the pillars erected on the equator.

Called to Lima early in the War of Jenkins's Ear, the two officers advised the viceroy on military and naval matters before returning to Quito in January 1744 to make their own scientific observations. Late in October they left for Spain, where they began writing a four-volume descriptive work on their travels, *Relación histórica del viage a la América meridional* (Historical Report on the Voyage to America), published in 1748. In 1749 they completed a secret report for crown officials on conditions in the Indies.

Juan never returned to the Indies. After that last assignment, he became a royal troubleshooter in his native country, where he improved ventilation in the mercury mines at Almadén, strengthened the sea walls at Cartagena, built a new arsenal at El Ferrol, and served as ambassador to Morocco, among other duties. Spending his last days in Madrid as head of the Royal Seminary of Nobles, Juan was noted for his deep-seated attachment to Enlightenment ideas, confirmed by the posthumous publication of his book on astronomy in 1774.

See also **Travel Literature; War of Jenkins's Ear (1739–1748).**

BIBLIOGRAPHY

John J. Tepaske and Besse Clement, eds. and trans., *Discourse and Political Reflections on the Kingdoms of Peru*... (1978).

Additional Bibliography

Orozco Acuaviva, Antonio. *Los cirujanos navales de la "Asamblea Amistosa Literaria" de Jorge Juan*. Cádiz, Spain: Fundación Uriach 1838, 2000.

Soler Pascual, Emilio. *Viajes de Jorje Juan y Santacilia: ciencia y política en la España del siglo XVIII*. Barcelona: Ediciones B, 2002.

JOHN JAY TEPASKE

JUÁREZ, BENITO (1806–1872).

Benito Juárez (*b.* 21 March 1806; *d.* 18 July 1872), president of Mexico (1858–1872). Juárez led the liberals and Republicans during the War of the Reform (1858–1861) and the French Intervention (1862–1867). For many Mexicans, and in the official pantheon of national heroes, Juárez is a preeminent symbol of Mexican nationalism and resistance to foreign intervention. His critics, however, continue to charge that Juárez resorted to dictatorial methods to prolong his presidency, undermined the property rights of rural villages, and sacrificed Mexican sovereignty to the United States.

Juárez was born in the village of San Pablo Guelatao, Oaxaca. His parents were Zapotec Indian peasants who died before he reached the age of four. Juárez was raised by relatives and worked in the fields until the age of twelve, when, in hopes of getting an education, he left his village and walked the forty miles to the city of Oaxaca to live with his sister. There, he was taken in by Antonio Salanueva, a bookbinder and Franciscan monk, who immediately took Juárez to be confirmed and encouraged him to attend the seminary for his education. Still lacking a primary education and with no more than the rudiments of Spanish grammar, Juárez began studying Latin. After two years, Juárez convinced his patron to allow him to study the arts since he was still too young to be ordained a priest. Juárez completed his secondary education in 1827. Lacking the financial resources and the inclination to receive holy orders, he rejected an ecclesiastical career in order to study law at the newly established Institute of Sciences and Arts, where he received his degree in 1834.

Even before Juárez received his law degree, his political career had begun with election to the City Council of Oaxaca in 1831. Two years later he was elected to the state legislature. He made a living as a lawyer, and in 1841 he was appointed a civil judge. In 1843, he married Margarita Maza. The following year, he was appointed secretary of government by the state governor, Antonio León, and then to the post of prosecutor with the state supreme court. In 1845, Juárez was elected to the state legislature, but that body was soon dissolved in a conservative rebellion led by General Mariano Paredes. Juárez was then named by liberal forces to the executive committee for the state. Elected to the national congress the following year, Juárez supported President Valentín Gómez Farías in his attempt to use church property to pay for the war with the United States. Organized opposition to these efforts, the Rebellion of the Polkos (1847),

Juárez as icon. Striking teachers in the state of Oaxaca protest under a banner containing the image of Benito Juárez, October 2006. Juárez's portrait became one of the iconic images of the protest, which lasted seven months and resulted in several deaths. AP IMAGES

brought Antonio López de Santa Anna back to the presidency, ended the liberal government, and forced Juárez to return to Oaxaca.

In Oaxaca, liberals regained control of the state and elected Juárez governor in 1847. At the end of his term in 1852, he accepted the post of director of the Institute of Sciences and Arts. When Santa Anna returned to the presidency in 1853, he exiled Juárez and other leading liberals. Juárez eventually ended up in New Orleans, where he met Ponciano Arriaga, Melchor Ocampo, and other opponents of Santa Anna, and where he earned his living making cigars.

With Juárez and his allies providing the political platform for the liberal Revolution of Ayutla in 1854, Juárez traveled to Acapulco to serve as a political aide. When Juan Álvarez forced Santa Anna into exile the following year, liberal exiles were able to return to Mexico. President Álvarez named Juárez his minister of justice and ecclesiastical affairs. Juárez wrote the Ley Juárez (eliminating the right of ecclesiastical and military courts to hear civil cases), which President Álvarez signed in November 1855. Juárez resigned the following month, returning to Oaxaca, where he took office as governor in January 1856 and served for nearly two years. Juárez supported and swore to uphold the Constitution of 1857, but he took no direct role in drafting that document. President Ignacio Comonfort designated Juárez minister of government in November 1857. Elected president of the Supreme Court (and first in line of succession to the presidency), Juárez took the oath of that office on 1 December 1857. Ten days later President Comonfort ordered Congress closed and Juárez arrested. Juárez was freed in January 1858 and escaped from the capital, just before conservative militarists overthrew Comonfort and declared Félix Zuloaga president. The coup notwithstanding, in accordance with the Constitution of 1857, Juárez succeeded Comonfort in the presidency, taking the oath of office on 19 January 1858 in

Guanajuato, thereby leaving Mexico with two presidents and civil war.

During the War of the Reform, or Three Years' War (1858–1860), Juárez fled to Guadalajara, where he was captured and nearly executed by conservative forces. Later he made his way to Colima, then Manzanillo, and by way of Panama, Havana, and New Orleans to Veracruz, where the liberal governor, Manuel Gutiérrez Zamora, allowed Juárez to establish his government. With the support of the radical liberals (known as puros) like Miguel Lerdo De Tejada and Melchor Ocampo, Juárez issued the reform laws separating the church and state, establishing civil marriage and civil registration of births and deaths, secularizing the cemeteries, and expropriating the property of the church. The conservative forces held most of central Mexico but were unable to dislodge the Juárez government from Veracruz. Perennially short of funds to pay and provision the improvised forces that fought the conservatives, the liberal government expropriated and sold church property and negotiated with the United States.

During the war, Juárez authorized arrangements with the United States that have been the source of enduring controversies about his patriotism. The McLane–Ocampo Treaty, which Juárez's secretary of foreign relations Melchor Ocampo negotiated with the U.S. diplomat Robert M. McLane in 1859, permitted United States protection of transit over routes across Mexican territory in exchange for several million dollars. The treaty was rejected by the U.S. Senate. In what is known as the Antón Lizardo incident, President Juárez authorized U.S. ships to attack conservative vessels flying the Mexican flag at anchor in the port of Antón Lizardo, Veracruz, in 1860. Juárez's critics charge that he condoned foreign intervention and sold out to the United States.

Further concessions were not necessary before liberal forces under Jesús González Ortega defeated the conservative army and recaptured Mexico City in December 1860. At the end of Comonfort's term in 1861, there were new elections, which Juárez won. His government's suspension of payments on the foreign debt led to the intervention of Spain, France, and Great Britain. Spanish and British forces soon withdrew, but French forces, supporting the creation of a Mexican empire, advanced toward Mexico City in early 1862, and in 1864 the Austrian archduke Maximilian von Habsburg took the throne as Maximilian I.

The French Intervention (1862–1867) provides conflicting images of Juárez. A heroic Juárez led the Republican forces that tenaciously defended Mexico and its Republican constitution during desperate years of struggle against foreign and imperial armies. But Juárez's critics charge that he illegally extended his presidency when his constitutional term ended in 1865 and that he arbitrarily ordered the arrest and imprisonment of Jesús González Ortega, who ought to have succeeded to the presidency. The defeat of the imperial armies and the execution of Maximilian in 1867 provided a moment of unity for Mexican liberals, but Juárez's attempt to alter the constitution and strengthen the presidency by referendum again prompted critics to charge him with dictatorial methods. Many liberals opposed his reelection, but Juárez retained enough support to win the presidential elections of December 1867.

The liberals divided into three major factions backing Sebastián Lerdo de Tejada, Porfirio Díaz, and Juárez. The president repeatedly resorted to grants of extraordinary power to combat revolts and to maintain order. His critics maintained that Juárez was corrupted by power and increasingly dictatorial. By the time of the 1871 elections, Juárez could no longer count on a majority of votes, and the election passed to Congress, which elected him to another term. Porfirio Díaz resorted to rebellion, but Juárez was able to defeat him, again with an extension of extraordinary powers.

Not long afterward, on the evening of 18 July 1872, Juárez died. Controversial during his lifetime, he became a premier symbol of Mexican nationalism after his death. Ironically, Porfirio Díaz, as president, played a major role in creating the Juárez myth. As a national hero, Juárez has been most commonly invoked by presidents seeking to create an image of continuity with the past during times when stability and economic growth rather than reform have been the major concerns of government.

See also **Anticlericalism; Comonfort, Ignacio; Mexico, Wars and Revolutions: The Reform.**

BIBLIOGRAPHY

Ivie E. Cadenhead, Jr., *Benito Juárez* (1973).

Donathon C. Olliff, *Reform Mexico and the United States: A Search for Alternatives to Annexation, 1854–1861* (1981).

Laurens Ballard Perry, *Juárez and Díaz: Machine Politics in Mexico* (1978).

Ralph Roeder, *Juárez and His Mexico: A Biographical History,* 2 vols. (1947).

Walter V. Scholes, *Mexican Politics During the Juárez Regime, 1855–1872* (1957).

Richard N. Sinkin, *The Mexican Reform, 1855–1876: A Study in Liberal Nation-Building* (1979).

Charles Allen Smart, *Viva Juárez: A Biography* (1963).

Daniel Cosío Villegas, *Historia moderna de México,* vol. 1, *La república restorada, vida política* (1959).

Charles A. Weeks, *The Juárez Myth in Mexico* (1987).

Additional Bibliography

Cunningham, Michele. *Mexico and the Foreign Policy of Napoleon III.* New York: Palgrave, 2001.

Hamnett, Brian R. *Juárez.* London: Longman, 1994.

Villalpando César, José Manuel. *Maximiliano.* México: Clío, 1999.

D. F. STEVENS

JUÁREZ, JOSÉ (1617–1661). José Juárez (*b.* 1617; *d.* 1661), painter. The son of Luis Juárez, José was surely introduced to painting in his father's workshop. He has been considered by some to be the best painter of colonial Mexico. These claims are often accompanied by assertions that he must have received training in Spain. Others consider that the presence of Sebastián López de Arteaga and of original works by Francisco de Zurbarán in New Spain would have been sufficient for someone of his talent to develop as he did. Juárez's works show the influence not only of Zurbarán but also of compositions by Peter Paul Rubens, known in New Spain through prints. Probably his best-known painting is a complex composition depicting martyrdom and glorification, *Saints Justus and Pastor.*

See also **Art: The Colonial Period; Mexico: The Colonial Period.**

BIBLIOGRAPHY

Rogelio Ruíz Gomar, *Historia del arte mexicano,* vol. 2 (1982), pp. 38–40.

CLARA BARGELLINI

JUÁREZ, LUIS (c. 1585–c. 1635). Luis Juárez (*b.* ca. 1585; *d.* ca. 1635), Mexican painter. Juárez was the founder of an important dynasty of colonial Mexican painters. Although the place of his birth is unknown, his mannerist style can clearly be identified as Mexican—influenced, of course, by the Spanish masters who preceded him, particularly the Sevillian Alonso Vázquez, who came to New Spain in 1603 and died there in 1608. The works of Juárez are remarkably uniform in style and feeling, usually showing religious figures in an elegant yet subdued and direct manner. Scattered throughout Mexico are nearly one hundred paintings that can be attributed to Juárez, evidence that he was well and widely known.

BIBLIOGRAPHY

Rogelio Ruíz Gomar, *El pintor Luis Juárez* (1987).

Additional Bibliography

Ciancas, María Ester, and Meyer de Stinglhamber, Bárbara. *La pintura de retrato colonial, siglos XVI-XVIII.* México, D.F.: Instituto Nacional de Antropología e Historia, 1994.

Saucedo, Carmen. "Notas al documento: El pintor Luis Juárez: un trabajo para Santa Teresa la Antigua." *Estudios de Historia y Sociedad* 10, no. 39 (1989): 107–114.

Shorts, Don Allen. *1200 Mexican Artists: An Identification Guide to Painters, Graphic Artists, Sculptors and Photographers (from Colonial Times to the Present).* Ventura, CA: Old California Press, 2002.

CLARA BARGELLINI

JUÁREZ CELMAN, MIGUEL (1844–1909). Miguel Juárez Celman (*b.* 29 September 1844; *d.* 14 April 1909), president of Argentina (1886–1890). Juárez Celman, born in Córdoba, took a strong anticlerical position in promoting secular education. After serving as a legal adviser, legislator, and provincial minister, he became an unconditional supporter of Julio Argentino Roca. He married Roca's sister, and Roca married Juárez Celman's sister. In 1882, Roca decided that his brother-in-law should govern Córdoba. Impressed with Juárez Celman's political machine, Roca then imposed him as president of the republic.

As chief executive, Juárez Celman was self-serving and corrupt. His regime promoted European immigration, foreign investment, public works, and economic growth. Unfortunately, wild speculation, galloping inflation, and a tripling of the public debt occurred. A particularly irresponsible issue of paper currency resulted in the loss of political legitimacy. When Juárez Celman belatedly took measures to head off the financial crisis, his supporters refused to back him in Congress.

Angry investors and those who suffered a decline in their standard of living joined with Catholic activists and the Unión Cívica (Civic Union) in demanding honest government. Three days of rebellion, known as the 1890 Revolution, resulted in Juárez Celman's resignation on 6 August, 1890. Once worth over $30 million, he died in obscure poverty at Capitán Sarmiento Arrecites.

See also **Anticlericalism; Roca, Julio Argentino.**

BIBLIOGRAPHY

Juan Carlos Agulla, *Eclipse of an Aristocracy: An Investigation of the Ruling Elites of Córdoba,* translated by Betty Crouse (1976).

Gustavo Ferrari, "La presidencia Juárez Celman," in *La Argentina del ochenta al centenario,* edited by Gustavo Ferrari and Ezequiel Gallo (1980).

A. G. Ford, *The Gold Standard, 1880–1914* (1962).

Thomas Mc Gann, *Argentina, the United States and the Inter-American System, 1880–1914* (1957).

Additional Bibliography

Pinedo, Enrique. *Los relegados.* Buenos Aires: Corregidor, 2000.

Rock, David. *State Building and Political Movements in Argentina, 1860–1916.* Stanford, CA: Stanford University Press, 2002.

DOUGLAS W. RICHMOND

JUAZEIRO DO NORTE. Juazeiro do Norte (until 1944 Joaseiro or Joazeiro), one of the principal cities of the state of Ceará in Brazil. Located in the Carirí Valley in the uplands of Ceará's interior, the city has an estimated population of 240,638 (2006) and serves as a commercial and manufacturing center, depending primarily on the processing of sugar and cotton.

Drawn by rumors of a miracle, pilgrims flocked from the Brazilian backlands to the town during the 1890s. In 1889 and again in 1891, the host reputedly turned to blood during mass celebrated by local priest Padre Cícero Romão Batista (1844–1934). Although the Catholic Church refused to accept the alleged miracle and threatened Padre Cícero with excommunication if he persisted in insisting on its validity, thousands of peasants regarded the priest as a saint, and Joaseiro's population reached thirty thousand by 1914. Such growth helped to make the city an industrial and commercial center of the Sertão.

Padre Cícero's spiritual power quickly translated into political influence. His actions in state and national politics were closely tied to maneuvers of José Gomes Pinheiro Machado but were also influenced by shifts in Ceará's economy, by the complex interplay of church-state relations, and by the instability of his own relations with the church hierarchy. Maintaining his base in Joaseiro, Padre Cícero held sway over much of the state and was instrumental in toppling the state government of Marcos Franco Rabelo in March 1914.

Despite excommunication in 1916, Padre Cícero retained his spiritual and political influence until his death in 1934. Juazeiro do Norte remains a pilgrimage center as well as an important political bailiwick.

See also **Messianic Movements: Brazil.**

BIBLIOGRAPHY

Amália Xavier De Oliveira, *O Padre Cícero qui eu conheci: Verdadeira história de Juazeiro do Norte* (1969).

Ralph Della Cava, *Miracle at Joaseiro* (1970).

Luitgarde O. C. Barros, *A Terra da Mãe de Deus: Um estudo do movimento religioso de Juazeiro do Norte* (1988).

Additional Bibliography

Camurça, Marcelo Ayres. *Marretas, molambudos e rabelistas: A revolta de 1914 no Juazeiro.* São Paulo: Maltese, 1994.

Freixinho, Nilton, and Antônio Olinto. *O sertão arcaico do Nordeste do Brasi: Uma releitura.* Rio de Janeiro: Imago, 2003.

CARA SHELLY

JUDICIAL SYSTEMS

This entry includes the following articles:
BRAZIL
SPANISH AMERICA

BRAZIL

During the empire, Brazil had a unitary judicial system. Like France, however, administrative or public law disputes were decided by the Council of State, an executive body outside the judiciary. Pursuant to the 1891 Constitution, which was modeled on the U.S. Constitution, Brazil instituted a dual judicial system of federal and state courts. The state courts have general jurisdiction, while the federal courts have limited jurisdiction. The jurisdiction of the federal courts is generally limited to cases in which federal questions are presented, in which the federal government (or its public enterprises or autarchies) has an interest, in which a crime involves federal property or services, or in which an international concern is present. Since 1891, the Brazilian courts have been given jurisdiction over cases involving both public and private law. Brazil also has three specialized court systems within the judiciary: labor, electoral, and military courts.

Brazil has a career judiciary, although there is lateral entry into the higher courts. A Brazilian national between the ages of twenty-three and forty-five, who has practiced law for two years, can begin a judicial career by passing written and oral tests. Those who pass start their careers in entry-level judicial districts (*comarcas de entrância*) and eventually are promoted to the higher courts, either on merit or seniority. Those completing a two-year probationary period are guaranteed tenure until retirement age. Their salaries may not be reduced, nor may they be involuntarily transferred.

THE FEDERAL JUDICIARY

Supreme Federal Tribunal. Brazil's highest court is the Supreme Federal Tribunal (STF), which consists of eleven justices (*ministros*), usually sitting in panels of five. They are appointed by the president, with the approval of an absolute majority of the Senate. The present constitution has redefined the STF's jurisdiction to make it primarily a constitutional court. Direct actions challenging the constitutionality of any federal or state law or normative act can now be brought directly before the STF, whose decision is binding. The right to bring a direct action of unconstitutionality, however, is limited to the president; the procurator general; the executive committees of the Senate, Chamber of Deputies, or state legislatures; state governors; the Federal Council of the Bar Association; any political party represented in Congress; and any syndical confederation or national class (management or labor) entity. The STF has original jurisdiction to decide all requests for issuance of a mandate of injunction, another form of direct constitutional action used to try to make Congress or some other federal agency issue a law or rule necessary to implement a constitutional right.

The STF has ordinary appellate jurisdiction in matters involving habeas corpus, writs of security, habeas data and mandates of injunction decided originally by the Superior Tribunals if they have denied such requests, and in political crimes. The STF also has jurisdiction to hear extraordinary appeals if the appealed decision is contrary to a provision of the Constitution, declares a treaty or federal law unconstitutional, or upholds the constitutionality of a local law or act.

Superior Tribunal of Justice. Directly below the STF in the hierarchy is the Superior Tribunal of Justice (STJ). Created by the 1988 Constitution, the STJ is the court of last resort for much of the appellate caseload formerly decided by the STF. The STJ has thirty-three judges appointed by the president from lists of candidates nominated by courts, the Bar Association, and the Public Ministry. The STJ sits in chambers with five judges each.

The original jurisdiction of the STJ is quite limited, for it functions predominantly as an appellate court. Its ordinary appellate jurisdiction includes cases involving denials of habeas corpus or writs of security by other tribunals below it, and cases in which the parties are a foreign state or an international organization taking legal action against a county or a person resident or domiciled in Brazil. It has jurisdiction to decide on special appeal cases decided by the lower tribunals if the appealed decision is contrary to a treaty or federal law, or denies the effectiveness of a treaty or federal law; upholds a law or act of local government challenged as contrary to federal law; or interprets federal law differently from another tribunal.

Federal Regional Tribunals. Below the STJ are five Federal Regional Tribunals (FRT), located in Rio de Janeiro, Brasília, São Paulo, Pôrto Alegre, and Recife. These courts, each of which has at least seven judges, were created by the 1988 Constitution to replace the former intermediate federal appeals court, the Federal Tribunal of Recourses. The FRTs also have very limited original jurisdiction. Their primary function is to hear appeals from cases decided by federal judges and by state judges exercising federal jurisdiction within their particular region.

Federal Judges. The federal judges are essentially courts of first instance for cases in which the federal government has an interest. Federal judges are career judges, chosen by competitive examinations. If there is no federal judge in a particular judicial district, a state judge may be permitted to decide federal cases. In such event, an appeal may be taken to the FRT.

Labor Courts. The Labor Courts are regular members of the Brazilian federal judiciary. Nevertheless, they differ from the regular judiciary in that their jurisdiction is limited to labor matters and they operate collegially at all levels. Moreover, they are mixed tribunals, composed of both professional judges and lay representatives of labor and management. All Labor Courts have the power to decide any matter connected with labor law. The Labor Court system is exclusively federal; state courts may not decide labor law questions. The Labor Courts have jurisdiction to conciliate and adjudicate individual and collective labor disputes. If collective bargaining negotiations fail to produce an agreement, the parties may appoint arbitrators. If any party refuses to negotiate or to arbitrate, the respective management or labor syndicate may litigate a collective bargaining dispute, and the Labor Courts will establish the rules and conditions for the contractual provisions and the protection of labor.

At the head of the Labor Court system is the Superior Labor Tribunal (SLT), which has twenty-seven judges appointed by the president after approval by the Senate.

Below the SLT are the Regional Labor Tribunals. Every state has at least one Regional Labor Tribunal, as does the federal district. The baseline courts of the Labor Court system are the Boards of Conciliation, which have at least one labor judge and two temporary representatives, one from labor and the other from management.

Electoral Courts. The Electoral Justice system consists of the Superior Electoral Tribunal (SET), the Regional Electoral Tribunals, electoral judges, and the electoral boards. The Electoral Courts are responsible for supervising the integrity of the electoral process. Unlike other Brazilian courts, they are staffed by members of other courts who serve two to four years. Decisions of the SET are not appealable except on constitutional grounds or if they deny writ of habeas corpus or writ of security.

The Regional Electoral Tribunals are misnamed. Each state capital and the federal district has a Regional Electoral Tribunal, whose jurisdiction is statewide rather than regional. The Regional Electoral Tribunals have seven judges, who serve for at least two years, but never more than two consecutive terms.

The baseline courts for the Electoral Justice system are the electoral judges, who sit alone. Usually, the state judge in the electoral district performs the functions of the electoral judge; if there are several judges in the district, the Regional Tribunal selects a judge to serve as electoral judge for a two-year term.

Election returns are supervised by election boards. These boards consist of a law judge and two to four citizens of outstanding reputations nominated by the presiding judge with the approval of the Regional Tribunal.

Federal Military Courts. The Military Courts have jurisdiction to try military personnel (and those equated with such personnel) for military crimes, as defined by law. This court system consists of the Superior Military Tribunal, the Councils of Justice, and professional military judges. The Superior Military Tribunal has fifteen judges with life tenure, appointed by the president with the approval of the Senate.

The judges of first instance are called auditors. They are lawyers and career judges, chosen through competitive examinations. They perform many of the functions of an investigative magistrate or prosecutor. Trials are held before Councils of Justice, made up of one auditor and several military officers.

THE STATE JUDICIARIES

Tribunals of Justice. The highest court in every state is called the Tribunal of Justice. The number of judges, called *desembargadores,* on the Tribunal of Justice varies from state to state. In the more populous states, where the Tribunals of Justice typically have about one hundred judges, they sit in panels (*câmaras*) or groups of panels. In more sparsely populated states, the Tribunals of Justice hear appeals directly from courts of first instance.

Intermediate Appeals Courts. More populous states have an intermediate court of appeals, the *Tribunal de Alçada.* (The busiest court system, São Paulo, has three: two civil and one criminal.) The intermediate court divides jurisdiction with the Tribunal of Justice, hearing appeals relating to leases, labor accidents, fiscal matters, most summary proceedings, and less serious criminal offenses.

State Military Courts. States also have their own systems of military justice. The court of first instance, called the Council of Military Justice, tries military police and firemen for military crimes. In some states appeals from these Councils are heard directly by the state Tribunals of Justice; other states have created their own Tribunals of Military Justice to hear such appeals. These courts usually consist of seven judges, four chosen from colonels in active service in the military police and three civilians.

Courts of First Instance. Each state is divided into judicial districts, and each district has at least one titular law judge (*juiz de direito*). The state courts of the first instance generally sit as a single judge and have jurisdiction over all matters not specifically allocated to the exclusive jurisdiction of other courts by the Constitution or statute.

Jury Tribunals. Intentional crimes against human life are usually tried by a Jury Tribunal, which consists of one professional judge who presides and seven lay jury members chosen by lot from an array of twenty-one persons. The jury decides whether a crime was committed, the nature of the crime, its gravity, and who committed it.

Verdicts of the Jury Tribunal may be appealed, but the appellate tribunal can only modify the decision with respect to the decisions of the presiding judge and only to correct an error or injustice in his application of the penalty. The appellate tribunal may only make the judgment correspond to what the law establishes and what the jury found. If the appellate court determines that the jury's decision was manifestly contrary to the evidence on the record, it will vacate the jury verdict and remand for retrial by the same Jury Tribunal. A second appeal may not be taken after a retrial.

Small Claims Courts. Since authorizing legislation was passed in 1984, many states have created Small Claims Courts, which decide less complex civil cases and minor criminal infractions. Disputes can be resolved inexpensively through conciliation, arbitration, or trial before a law school graduate. Appeals from these Small Claims Courts are decided by groups of judges of the first instance.

Justices of the Peace. At the very bottom of the state judicial system are justices of the peace, who do not enjoy the constitutional guarantees of the regular judiciary. They are nominated by state governors from a list of three prepared by the president of the Tribunal of Justice. They perform marriages and attempt conciliations, but they have no real jurisdictional functions.

CONCLUSIONS

Brazil has a sophisticated and complex judicial system that looks better on paper than it is in practice. Most courts have huge backlogs, and cases generally move slowly through the system. More resources need to be allocated to the judiciary, and more judges need to be appointed, particularly in urban areas. Excessive formalism needs to be pruned from the procedural codes. The judicial system would benefit from streamlining in order to function efficiently. Justice delayed is justice denied, and unfortunately much justice in Brazil is delayed.

See also **Brazil, Constitutions.**

BIBLIOGRAPHY

The jurisdiction and manner of selection of the Brazilian courts is set out in Articles 92 to 126 of the

Constitution of 1988. For detailed commentary on these provisions, see José Cretella Júnior, *Comentários à Constituição Brasileira de 1988* 2d ed., vol. 6 (1993), pp. 2995–3287. Useful diagrams of the various judicial systems appear in Laerte Romualdo De Souza, *III breviário de organização judiciária*, 2d ed. (1990). Helpful overviews are Athos Gusmão Carneiro, "Política judicial no Brasil: Estrutura do poder judiciário brasileiro conforme a Constituição de 1988," *Ajuris* 20 (November 1993): 236–252; Paulo Roberto De Gouvêa Medina, "O poder judiciário na Constituição de 1988," *Revista Forense,* 305 (January–March 1989): 351–371. The law regulating the organization of the judiciary is the Organic Law of the National Judiciary (*Lei orgânica da magistratura nacional*), Complementary Law 35 (14 March 1979). An overview of Brazilian civil procedure appears in Keith S. Rosenn, "Civil Procedure in Brazil," *American Journal of Comparative Law* 34 (1986): 487–525.

Additional Bibliography

Barrios, Feliciano, ed. *El gobierno de un mundo: Virreinatos y audiencias en la América hispánica.* Cuenca: Ediciones de la Universidad de Castilla-La Mancha: Fundación Rafael del Pino, 2004.

Bastos, Aurélio Wander. *Introdução à teoria do Direito.* 2nd. ed. Rio de Janeiro: Lumen Juris, 1999.

Comargo, José Márcio, ed. *Flexibilidade do mercado de trabalho no Brasil.* Rio de Janeiro: Fundação Getulio Vargas Editora, 1996.

Flory, Thomas. *Judge and Jury in Imperial Brazil, 1808–1871: Social Control and Political Stability in the New State.* Austin: University of Texas Press, 1981.

French, John D. *Drowning in Laws: Labor Law and Brazilian Political Culture.* Chapel Hill: University of North Carolina Press, 2004.

Lara, Silvia Hunold, and Joseli Maria Nunes Mendonça, eds. *Direitos e justiças no Brasil: Ensaios de história social.* Campinas: Editora UNICAMP, 2006.

Moraes, Alexandre de. *Jurisdição constitucional e tribunais constitucionais: Garantia suprema da Constituição.* São Paulo: Editora Atlas, 2000.

Pereira, Anthony W. *Political (In)Justice: Authoritarianism and the Rule of Law in Brazil, Chile, and Argentina.* Pittsburgh: University of Pittsburgh Press, 2005.

Sieder, Rachel, Line Schjolden, and Alan Angell. *The Judicialization of Politics in Latin America.* New York; Basingstoke: Palgrave Macmillan, 2005.

Keith S. Rosenn

SPANISH AMERICA

Spanish America's colonial civil-law legacy remains the core of its modern judicial systems. That legacy is most clearly evident in judicial method and approach. The organizational architecture of the modern judicial institutions derives from the nineteenth-century adaptation of the doctrine of the division of powers and the simplified first-, second-, and third-instance hearing process to promote prompt and efficient administration of justice.

After the papacy sanctioned Spain's formal right to rule New World lands in the Treaty of Tordesillas (1494), the Spanish crown introduced and modified Iberian judicial institutions and the civil law inherited from the Roman Empire. At the heart of the Spanish judicial system was the *audiencia.* In Spain an *audiencia* was an ordinary-jurisdiction, local, and regional appellate court. In the Americas the crown expanded *audiencia* duties to include oversight of civil administration and consultation with various colonial fiscal and administrative offices. First introduced in Santo Domingo in 1511, the *audiencia* became the main pillar of Spanish governance in the Americas. At the local level in major Spanish population centers, municipal judges adjudicated most first-instance, ordinary-jurisdiction civil and criminal cases. In towns and villages, Alcaldes Mayores, royal officials with local administrative, fiscal, and judicial responsibilities, adjudicated most of those cases.

During the colonial era the Spanish government created an array of special-jurisdiction courts, ranging from Indian courts and probate courts for intestate peninsulars to tax fraud and mining courts. The regional *audiencia* ministers adjudicated most appellate cases from the special first-instance courts. In addition, the Catholic Church and the military maintained privileged-jurisdiction (fuero) courts for civil and criminal cases in addition to canon-law and military-law cases.

The introduction of the doctrine of the separation of powers and the simplified hearing process accompanied the initiation of a constitutional tradition in Spain in 1812. Following the emergence of new republics, political leaders throughout Spanish America built on those innovations and augmented their political systems with constitutional-jurisdiction courts (supreme courts). Political leaders also sought to restrict ecclesiastical-jurisdiction courts to canon-law cases and military courts to military-law cases; restricting those two jurisdictions emerged as among the most volatile issues, as political leadership sought to transform colonial corporatist polities into republican polities. Most Spanish American republics introduced universal civil- and criminal-law courts and developed universal legal codes within three generations of independence. Today all of the constitutional republics have universal ordinary-jurisdiction courts and constitutional-jurisdiction supreme courts.

The jurisprudential common denominator throughout Spanish America is that all judicial systems are rooted in the colonial civil-law legacy. That legacy includes investigatory or inquisitorial procedures, rather than the accusatory procedures of common-law heritage states, and judicial decision making based on written legal codes and texts, rather than judicial opinions and precedent. Lawmakers in many Spanish American republics have augmented their colonial civil-law legacy with innovative laws to protect individual constitutional rights (Amparo) and to strengthen international laws concerning the scope and significance of sovereignty (the principle of nonintervention). At the same time, national and global support for prosecuting former leaders and regimes for human-rights violations, as well as the creation of international organizations and laws, has affected national judicial systems. For instance, in the face of pressure, courts limited amnesty for ex-officials. Outside their home countries, former dictators faced arrest and criminal charges.

See also **Audiencia; Fueros; Tordesillas, Treaty of (1494).**

BIBLIOGRAPHY

The most comprehensive bibliographic guide in English is American Association of Law Libraries, *Workshop on Latin American Law and Law-Related Reference Sources* (1988), a compilation of workshop papers and annotated jurisdictional bibliographies that survey all fields of law. The principal study in English is Albert S. Golbert and Yenny Nun, *Latin American Laws and Institutions* (1982). For a succinct discussion of the differences between common-law and civil-law heritage systems, see Fernando Orrantia, "Conceptual Differences Between the Civil Law System and the Common Law System," in *Southwestern University Law Review* 19, no. 4 (1990): 1161–1170. The most recent study in English that reflects the depth and scope of that literature on the colonial system is Patricia Seed, *To Love, Honor, and Obey in Colonial Mexico: Conflicts over Marriage Choice, 1574–1821* (1988). The most recent work in Spanish on the colonial legal environment is Victor Tau Anzoátegui, *La ley en América Hispana: Del descubrimiento a la emancipación* (Buenos Aires, 1992). See also Frank Griffith Dawson, "Contributions of Lesser Developed Nations to International Law: The Latin American Experience," in *Case Western Reserve Journal of International Law* 13 (Winter 1981): 37–81; and Marcos Kaplan, comp., *Estado, derecho y sociedad* (Mexico City, 1981).

Additional Bibliography

Barrios, Feliciano, ed. *El gobierno de un mundo: Virreinatos y audiencias en la América hispánica.* Cuenca, Spain: Ediciones de la Universidad de Castilla-La Mancha, Fundación Rafael del Pino, 2004.

Brinks, Daniel M. *The Judicial Response to Police Killings in Latin America.* New York: Cambridge University Press, 2008.

Davis, Madeleine. *The Pinochet Case: Origins, Progress, and Implications.* London: Institute of Latin American Studies, 2003.

Friedman, Lawrence Meir, and Rogelio Pérez Perdomo. *Legal Culture in the Age of Globalization: Latin America and Latin Europe.* Stanford, CA: Stanford University Press, 2003.

Mirow, Matthew C. *Latin American Law: A History of Private Law and Institutions in Spanish America.* Austin: University of Texas Press, 2004.

Sieder, Rachel, Line Schjolden, and Alan Angell. *The Judicialization of Politics in Latin America.* New York and Basingstoke, U.K.: Palgrave Macmillan, 2005.

Twinam, Ann. *Public Lives, Private Secrets: Gender, Honor, Sexuality, and Illegitimacy in Colonial Spanish America.* Stanford, CA: Stanford University Press, 1999.

LINDA ARNOLD

JUDICIARY IN LATIN AMERICA, THE. The historical origin of the Latin American judiciary lies in the constitutions that came into effect in most of the region after 1810 when the individual nations gained their independence. These constitutions draw on the legal concepts prevailing in continental Europe during the period and recognize the existence of three branches of government and the independence of the judicial branch. The political model that was implemented provided for a presidential executive with broad powers, including the power to suspend constitutional rights in emergency situations, along with weak legislative and judicial branches that would be subject to repeated intervention by the executive.

With the exception of the countries belonging to the English-speaking Caribbean, all the nations south of the United States have judiciaries based on the continental European tradition. In its most usual version, this tradition merges principles and practices that clearly differentiate the role of the legislative branch from that of the judicial. The former is responsible for debating and approving generally applicable laws that judges may interpret only in the specific cases they hear. This tradition demonstrates a certain degree of mistrust toward judges' having a creative role in law and does not license judges to weigh decisions differently when factors such as public well-being are at stake, restricting them to a purely exegetical interpretation of the law. This rejection of judicial activism, more characteristic of the North American tradition, was consistent with political systems in which the judiciary lacked full autonomy. The history of these systems is one of ongoing political interference that has weakened or done away with judicial independence. In Argentina in 1946, a Congress dominated by Peronists backed constitutional accusations against all the members of the Supreme Court. The military coup that deposed Juan Domingo Perón in 1957 proceeded to remove all the judges of that court from their positions. More recently, in 1990, Argentine President Carlos Menem added four members to Argentina's Supreme Court to ensure for himself a majority that supported his point of view. There are plentiful examples of similar practices. In Peru there have been three interventions in the judiciary since 1968. A new law approved in Venezuela in 2004 increased the number of Supreme Court judges from twenty to thirty-two, with only a simple majority in the National Assembly required to confirm a nominee, thus permitting government control over the Court. Legislation also facilitated the suspension or removal of Supreme Court judges on unspecified grounds.

The diminished position of the judiciary has been the target of severe criticism. During the 1990s, the beginning of redemocratization in several countries created conditions that fostered a process of judicial branch reform. Governments have implemented this reform with support from professional and human rights agencies that have in turn received technical and financial support from international agencies such as the World Bank, the Inter-American Development Bank, and the U.S. Agency for International Development (USAID). These reforms have been intended to remedy a number of weaknesses, including judiciaries lacking sufficient independence and impartiality, outdated legislation, and procedures that sometimes conflict with constitutional rights. Judiciaries in many countries suffer from a marked shortage of trained, qualified judges, lack of professional management, lack of an effective system for overseeing judicial ethics, and low budgets.

Partial improvements are evident in each one of these areas. Progress has been made in establishing a merit-based method for selecting judges for lower courts and it is complemented by more rigorous training processes based on practical cases. Some countries that have done this well are Chile, Guatemala, the Dominican Republic, and Argentina. With the exception of those in Costa Rica, Argentina, and Brazil, all of Latin America's judicial schools were established in the 1990s. Another point worth noting is that considerable efforts have been made to reform outdated legislation and procedures. The main focus in this regard has been on reforming criminal law procedure, replacing the traditional written inquisitorial system with an oral accusatory system. This reform has taken place in sixteen of the nineteen countries that have continental European juridical traditions and is at various stages of the integration process, ranging from complete effectiveness throughout the national territory (as in Costa Rica and Chile) to partial but ongoing implementation in countries such as Peru. The process has entailed the massive retraining of judges, government attorneys, public defenders, and police. In some countries, such as Chile, it has led to the creation of an Office of the Government Attorney and an Office of the Public Defender. The "Monitoring of Criminal Procedural Reforms" project undertaken by the Centro de Estudios de Justicia de las Americas (Justice Studies Center of the Americas, CEJA) has revealed that the ten countries analyzed have made various levels of progress in the field of criminal procedural reform. In addition to reforming the criminal process, there has been an expansion of the jurisdiction of the courts. In many countries, new courts have been set up to address social conflicts, for example conflicts within families and among young people.

There have also been reforms to the internal management of the judiciary. These include reforms of organization and administration as well as incorporation of information technologies into the work of the courts. Many of these programs have international financing; Venezuela, Guatemala, El Salvador, Peru, and Colombia in particular receive significant funding from external sources such as the World Bank, the Interamerican Development Bank, the United Nations Development Program, and USAID among others. It is also possible to find improvements, although not very significant ones, in human and budgetary resources. Thus, for example, the number of federal judges in Mexico increased by 25 percent between 2000 and 2004 and by 40 percent in Colombia. Funds per capita allocated to the judiciary have been rising in the region, from USD$16 between 2002 and 2003 to $19.30 between 2004 and 2005. These changes are a sign of significant progress.

See also **Argentina, Constitutions; Argentina, Truth Commissions; Bolivia, Constitutions: Overview; Brazil, Constitutions; Chile, Constitutions; Colombia, Constitutions: Overview; Costa Rica, Constitutions; Guatemala, Constitutions; Haiti, Constitutions; Honduras, Constitutions; Inter-American Development Bank (IDB); Menem, Carlos Saúl; Mexico, Constitutions: Constitution of 1917; Nicaragua, Constitutions; Panama, Constitutions; Paraguay, Constitutions; Perón, Juan Domingo; Peru, Constitutions; Peru, Truth Commissions; Truth Commissions; Uruguay, Constitutions; Venezuela, Constitutions; World Bank.**

BIBLIOGRAPHY

Frühling, Hugo. "Judicial Reform and Democratization in Latin America." In *Fault Lines of Democracy in Post-Transition Latin America*, edited by Felipe Agüero and Jeffrey Stark. North-South Center Press, 1998.

Gutiérrez Palma, Mauricio. *Reporte sobre la Justicia en las Américas: 2004–2005.* Santiago: Centro de Estudios de Justicia de las Americas (CEJA), 2005.

Hammergren, A. Linn. *Envisioning Reform: Improving Judicial Performance in Latin America*, University Park: Pennsylvania State University Press. 2007.

Popkin, Margaret. "Efforts to Enhance Judicial Independence in Latin America: A Comparative Perspective." In *Guidance for Promoting Judicial Independence and Impartiality.* Revised ed. Washington, DC: Office of Democracy and Governance, U.S. Agency for International Development, 2002. Online at: http://www.usaid.gov/our_work/democracy_and_governance/publications/pdfs/pnacm007.pdf.

Riego, Cristián. "Segundo Informe comparativo Seguimiento de los procesos de reforma judicial en América Latina." *Revista Sistemas Judiciales* 5 (September 2003): 1–8. Also available from www.cejamericas.org.

Ungar, Mark. *Elusive Reform: Democracy and the Rule of Law in Latin America.* Boulder, CO: Lynne Rienner Publishers, 2002.

HUGO FRÜHLING

JUJUY. Jujuy, province in northwestern Argentina with an area of 20,548 square miles and a population of 611,888 (2001) that stretches from the Andes into their foothills. A great number of the population are descended from the Aymara people of the Bolivian Puna and Altiplano. The landscape is similar in many respects to the southern Bolivian highlands, with extensive salt flats, barren high mountains, and fertile river oases in the piedmont. In 1561 the Spanish explorer Juan Pérez Zurita founded the city of Nieva on the site that would later become Jujuy, but in 1563 the settlement was destroyed by retaliatory raids organized by the original inhabitants of that region, a group of Tahuantinsuyo. In 1563 King Phillip of Spain declared the area a dependency of Tucumán in 1593, intended to protect trade caravans to Alto Peru (Bolivia) from the attacks of Humahuaca and Calchaquí warriors. To pacify and evangelize the indigenous peoples, Franciscan and Jesuit missions were established in the areas with the densest populations. In the Jesuit missions the cultivation of sugarcane and cotton was introduced, while in the settlements dominated by Spaniards, cattle ranching and the cultivation of tobacco, corn, oranges, and rice prevailed. In colonial times these activities lent significance to this northwesternmost corner of the Río De La Plata viceroyalty.

The decline of Jujuy started with the expulsion of the Jesuits in 1767. In 1776 this portion of what had been the viceroyalty of Peru was designated by the Spanish Crown as part of the newly created viceroyalty of Río de la Plata. This was followed by the War of Independence (during which Spanish troops occupied the region on eleven separate occasions) and several decades of internecine wars. It was not until 1853 that Jujuy exited its most turbulent period, but in the meantime the fragile agricultural bases of its economy had been severely damaged.

Irrigation works and the completion of a railroad in 1990 connecting Jujuy with Buenos Aires and another linking it with La Paz (Bolivia) eased that city's isolation while at the same time opening the way for an exodus of natives to Buenos Aires and for an influx of impoverished Bolivians that continues today. Mineral exploitation is an important pillar of the province's economy. Antimony and tin are mined in Rinconada, and Sierra del Aguilar and Nevado del Chañi have the richest deposits of lead, zinc, silver, and iron of Argentina. Iron from the Zapala mine is processed in the iron mill of Palpalá. Sugar refineries and wood-processing plants are elements of the industrial development of the province. There is also significant tourism in the region.

See also **Agriculture; Aymara; Franciscans; Jesuits; Río de la Plata, Viceroyalty of; Tahuantinsuyu; Tucumán.**

BIBLIOGRAPHY

Eugenio Tello, *Descripción de la provincia de Jujuy* (San Salvador, 1989).

Additional Bibliography

Brennan, James P., and Ofelia Pianetto. *Region and Nation: Politics, Economics, and Society in Twentieth-Century Argentina.* New York: St. Martin's Press, 2000.

González, Ricardo. *Imágenes dos mundos: La imágenería cristiana en la puna de Jujuy.* Buenos Aires: Fundación Espigas, 2003.

Santamaría, Daniel J., and Enrique Normando Cruz. *Celosos, amantes, y adúlteras: Las relaciones de género entre los sectores populares del Jujuy colonial.* San Salvador de Jujuy, Argentina: Centro de Estudios Indígenas y Coloniales, Facultad de Humanidades y Ciencias Sociales, Universidad Nacional de Jujuy, 2000.

César N. Caviedes

JULIÃO, CARLOS

JULIÃO, CARLOS (1740–1811). Carlos Julião (*b.* 1740; *d.* 18 November 1811), officer in the Portuguese army and artist. Born in Italy, Julião began a military career in Portugal in 1763 and by 1800 had been promoted to colonel. During his thirty-seven years in military service, he traveled to India, China, and South America. He recorded his travels in a pictorial travel account that was published posthumously in 1960 by the Brazilian National Library. One section of the account consists of forty-three watercolors without text. Entitled *Ditos de figurinhos de brancos, negros dos usos do Rio e Serro do Frio,* the watercolors depict diverse social and cultural aspects of the Portuguese colony of Rio de Janeiro during the late eighteenth century. They show members of the white elite at work and in their domestic life; slaves working in the mines, at festivals, and in the cities; and Indians. These watercolors are iconographically and sociologically significant because they document daily life in colonial Rio de Janeiro through the eyes of a Portuguese official.

See also **Travelers, Latin American.**

BIBLIOGRAPHY

Carlos Julião, *Riscos illuminada de figurinhos de brancos e negros dos usos do Rio de Janeiro e Serro do Frio* (1960).

Additional Bibliography

Russell-Wood, A. J. R. *The Portuguese Empire, 1415–1808: A World on the Move.* Baltimore: Johns Hopkins University Press, 1998.

Caren A. Meghreblian

JULIÃO ARRUDA DE PAULA, FRANCISCO

JULIÃO ARRUDA DE PAULA, FRANCISCO (1915–1999). Francisco Julião Arruda de Paula (*b.* 16 February 1915; *d.* 10 July 1999), honorary president, Peasant Leagues of Brazil. Born to a once-prominent landowning family in Pernambuco State, Julião became a lawyer and politician who defended peasants and advocated land reform. He was twice elected state legislator in 1954 and 1958 and entered Congress in 1962. In 1964 the military imprisoned him, and in 1965 Mexico granted him asylum. Exiled, Julião returned to Brazil once in 1979 and again in 1986, when he ran unsuccessfully for Congress. Rejected by voters, he returned to Mexico.

Julião was a controversial figure in the rural labor movement. He believed that feudalism reigned in Brazil and only a bourgeois revolution could bring progress. He pushed for radical agrarian reform—the quick redistribution of large landholdings without compensating owners in cash—and the complete enfranchisement of the rural poor. Fiercely independent, he devised his own spiritually rich discourse of revolt and resisted the directives of organizations, even his own.

Key supporters of the rural movement, such as the Brazilian Communist Party, distanced themselves from Julião. Within the Peasant Leagues, his independence spawned factionalism, with some members forcefully seizing land and others supporting legal methods of change. All the same, Julião did more to popularize the cause of the rural poor in Brazil and abroad than any other individual.

See also **Brazil, Organizations: Peasant Leagues.**

BIBLIOGRAPHY

Francisco Julião, *Cambão—The Yoke, the Hidden Face of Brazil,* translated by John Butt (1972).

Joseph A. Page, *The Revolution That Never Was: Northern Brazil, 1955–1964* (1972).

Additional Bibliography

Alexander, Robert J. *A History of Organized Labor in Brazil.* Westport, CT: Praeger, 2003.

Castellanos Hidalgo, Diana Guadalupe, and Batista Neto, Jônatas. *Um olhar na vida de exílio de Francisco Julião.* São Paulo, 2002.

Julião, Francisco. *Cambão.* México: Siglo Veintiuno Editores, 1969.

CLIFF WELCH

JUNÍN, BATTLE OF.

Battle of Junín, the decisive engagement of the Peruvian struggle for independence. A patriot army led by General Simón Bolívar defeated the Spanish royalist forces under General José Canterac at the battle of Junín on 6 August 1824. The battle was fought on the 9,000-foot-high Plains of Junín, near the central highland city of Jauja. Bolívar's 9,000-man force was outnumbered by almost 7,000, but in a short, decisive cavalry engagement, the patriots carried the day. Even though casualties were low on both sides, Bolívar gained the critical initiative. Shortly thereafter, after returning in triumph to Lima, Bolívar was recalled to Colombia. However, his lieutenant, General Antonio José de Sucre, went on to defeat the royalist army at the battle of Ayacucho on 9 December 1824, effectively ending three hundred years of Spanish rule in America.

See also **Bolívar, Simon.**

BIBLIOGRAPHY

Timothy E. Anna, *The Fall of Royal Government in Peru* (1979).

Additional Bibliography

Archer, Christon I., ed. *The Wars of Independence in Spanish America.* Wilmington: Scholarly Resources, 2000.

Vargas Ugarte, Rubén, Juan Basilio Cortegana, and Lorenzo Aza. *Historia de las batallas de Junín y Ayacucho.* Lima: Editorial Milla Batres, 1974.

PETER F. KLARÉN

JUNTA

This entry includes the following articles:
BRAZIL
SPANISH AMERICA

BRAZIL

The juntas of Brazil were extralegal governmental boards of prominent men of the local elites that functioned as parallel forms of local government. Displaying an independent spirit, they often challenged the Portuguese governor and ruled at the local level through the municipal *senados da câmara.* Juntas became more common in the early nineteenth century than they had been in the colonial period, although the crown did introduce judicial juntas in the mining regions to inflict capital punishment on the nonwhite population without any appeals. When news of the Portuguese revolution of 1820 reached Brazil, new governments (*juntas administrativas*) were formed in each capital city. José Bonifácio de Andrada E Silva was chosen to be a member of the *junta governativa.* Delegates were sent from Brazil's juntas to the Portuguese Cortes. The delegates were willing to remain within the Portuguese empire provided they were allowed representation in the Cortes. Juntas in the nineteenth century came to represent local interests and elites against the Portuguese ruling class, especially during the independence struggle.

See also **Cortes, Portuguese.**

BIBLIOGRAPHY

Leslie Bethell, ed., *The Cambridge History of Latin America,* vol. 2 (1984).

Emilia Viotti Da Costa, *The Brazilian Empire, Myths and Histories* (1985).

Additional Bibliography

Schultz, Kirsten. *Tropical Versailles: Empire, Monarchy, and the Portuguese Royal Court in Rio De Janeiro, 1808–1821.* New York: Routledge, 2001.

Silva, Maria Beatriz Nizza da. *De Cabral a Pedro I: Aspectos da colonização portuguesa no Brasil.* [Oporto, Portugal?]: Universidade Portucalense Infante D. Henrique, 2001.

PATRICIA MULVEY

SPANISH AMERICA

Junta is the Spanish word for any board or council. During the political crisis of the early 1800s when Napoleon invaded Spain, numerous juntas developed out of the municipal councils of important cities in the New World. When the Central Junta fled from Seville to Cádiz in 1810, the Spanish American juntas took over in the New World. They either declared their support for the exiled Spanish king or declared their right to independence from the Central Junta in Spain.

In the twentieth century, juntas in Spanish America have become associated with groups of military officers who collectively exercise the powers of government. A military junta is usually established following a coup d'état. Juntas are often headed by ranking officers of the army, navy, and air force. The exclusion of all civilians from the executive and the ban on all political parties indicate the military's complete rejection of the previous system and its belief in its ability to define and protect the country's national interest. The Sandinistas' Governing Junta of National Reconstruction (Junta de Gobierno de Reconstrucción Nacional) after 1979 raised many eyebrows in Nicaragua and in the United States because of the diversity of its five members, some of whom were on the left of the political spectrum.

See also **Napoleon I; Nicaragua.**

BIBLIOGRAPHY

Additional Bibliography

Barros, Robert. *Constitutionalism and Dictatorship: Pinochet, the Junta, and the 1980 Constitution.* Cambridge, U.K.: Cambridge University Press, 2002.

Pereira, Anthony W. *Political (In)Justice: Authoritarianism and the Rule of Law in Brazil, Chile, and Argentina.* Pittsburgh: University of Pittsburgh Press, 2005.

Riz, Liliana de. *La política en suspenso, 1966–1976.* Buenos Aires: Paidós, 2000.

HEATHER K. THIESSEN

JUNTA DO COMÉRCIO. Junta do Comércio (Portuguese Board of Trade), established in 1755 to replace the *mesa do bem commun,* whose members had vigorously opposed the crown's formation of monopoly companies. The marquês de Pombal established the Junta do Comércio as a principal part of his strategy to reinvigorate Portugal's economy by creating a central agency that would coordinate the empire's commercial activity. The Junta's statutes, confirmed in 1756, called for a *provedor* (superintendent), secretary, *procurador* (advocate), six deputies (four from Lisbon and two from Porto) together with a judge conservator, and a solicitor of the exchequer. Only well-established businessmen who were Portuguese-born or naturalized could be appointed deputies. The Junta's commission authorized it to supervise "all affairs connected with the commerce and navigation of these kingdoms and dominions." It administrated the Brazil fleets and customhouses, set freight prices, issued passports, oversaw the loading and unloading of cargoes to prevent contraband, and managed the proceedings surrounding bankruptcies. In 1759 it helped establish the Aula de Comércio (Commercial School) to train aspiring merchants. Eventually, it licensed the operation of Lisbon's shops and oversaw apprentice training.

The Junta's charge soon went beyond administrating commerce to directly influencing economic policy. After 1700 it became the basic administrative organ for stimulating Pombal's industrial program by channeling funds and giving special privileges to public and private enterprises. Industries such as cotton and glass manufacturing and the production of luxury goods like silk, china, and jewelry were encouraged toward the goal of making Portugal independent of foreign manufactures. After Pombal's fall, the Junta do Comércio went into eclipse as his successors reversed his centralized administrative structure. In 1788 it became a royal tribunal with the title Real Junta do Comércio, Agricultura, Fabricas, e Navegação, but with considerably less real power, and was finally dissolved in 1834.

BIBLIOGRAPHY

Kenneth Maxwell, *Conflicts and Conspiracies: Brazil and Portugal, 1750–1808* (1973).

Joel Serrão, ed., *Dicionário de história de Portugal,* vol. 2. (1979).

Additional Bibliography

Colmenares, Germán. *Partidos políticos y clases sociales.* Santafé de Bogotá: Universidad del Valle: Banco de la República: Colciencias: TM Editores, 1997.

Llano Isaza, Rodrigo. *Los draconianos: Origen popular del liberalismo colombiano.* Bogotá: Planeta, 2005.

WILLIAM DONOVAN

JUNTAS PORTUGUESAS.

JUNTAS PORTUGUESAS. Juntas Portuguesas, the administrative organs governing Portugal from the revolution of 24 August 1820 until the return of the king from Brazil in 1821. Marking the beginning of Portuguese liberal practice, the leaders of the constitutional movement promised to convoke the General Cortes to draw up a constitution, and they formed a Provisional Junta of the Supreme Government of the Realm, composed of military leaders and representatives of the clergy, the magistracy, and the commercial bourgeoisie of Pôrto. With the adherence of Lisbon to the revolution on 15 September 1820, it became necessary to avoid weakening the revolution by the division of authority. To this end, the governments of Pôrto and Lisbon organized into two distinct bodies, with the Pôrto Junta concerning itself with public administration, and the Provisional Preparatory Junta of the Cortes taking responsibility for all activities necessary for the implementation of the *cortes.* The two juntas gathered the principal leaders of the 1820 movement, including the brigadier Antônio da Silveira Pinto da Fonseca, the judge of the Court of Appeals Manuel Fernandes Tomás, and the Count of Sampaio. Although they attempted to control the workings of the state, the juntas did not cease to proclaim their loyalty to the church and the monarchy, in the person of João VI.

See also **João VI of Portugal.**

BIBLIOGRAPHY

Joel Serrão, "Vintismo," *Dicionário de história de Portugal,* vol. 4 (1971), pp. 321–329.

Joaquim Veríssimo Serrão, *História de Portugal,* vol. 7 (1984), pp. 354–360.

Additional Bibliography

Schultz, Kirsten. *Tropical Versailles: Empire, Monarchy, and the Portuguese Royal Court in Rio De Janeiro, 1808-1821.* New York: Routledge, 2001.

LÚCIA M. BASTOS P. NEVES

JUNTA SUPREMA DE CARACAS. Junta Suprema de Caracas, the highest junta of the Venezuelan government, established by the *cabildo* of Caracas as a result of the *cabildo*'s defiance of the captain-general of Venezuela, Vicente Emparán, and its effective declaration of independence on 19 April 1810. When the *cabildo* of Caracas demanded the resignation of Emparán, the Supreme Governing Junta was created to defend the privileges of Ferdinand VII. This junta assumed control of the government of the province of Caracas and sent delegates to the other provinces to obtain support for the decision not to recognize the regency of Spain.

Once its governing authority was established, the junta sent representatives out of the country to win support for the independence movement, abolished the slave trade, eliminated export duties, and called for elections to establish a constituent congress. The junta dissolved once the Constituent Congress was installed in March 1811.

See also **Ferdinand VII of Spain.**

BIBLIOGRAPHY

Instituto Panamericano De Geografía E Historia, *El 19 de Abril de 1810,* no. 11 (Caracas, 1957).

Andrés Ponte, *La revolución de Caracas y sus próceres* (1960).

P. Michael Mc Kinley, *Pre-Revolutionary Caracas: Politics, Economy, and Society, 1777–1811* (1985).

Additional Bibliography

Ibarra D., Daniel E. *Las articulaciones políticas de una revolución conservadora: El comportamiento político de la élite venezolana en la transición a la república.* Mérida, Venezuela: FUNDARTE, 1999.

INÉS QUINTERO

JURADO, KATY (1924–2002). Best known for her Golden Globe–winning role in the Hollywood western *High Noon* (1952), Mexican actress Katy Jurado (January 16, 1924–July 5, 2002) also starred in many other Hollywood and Mexican films before her death in 2002 at the age of seventy-eight. Born María Cristina Estela Marcela Jurado García in Guadalajara, Jalisco, Mexico, she was nominated for an Academy Award for her work opposite Spencer Tracy in *Broken Lance* (1954), one of only three Hispanic actresses to be nominated. Before coming to Hollywood in 1951, she had already worked with noteworthy Spanish director Luis Buñuel and won three Ariel awards, one of the highest honors in Mexican cinema. Contrary to the career paths of many of her Hollywood colleagues at the time, she did not sign a studio contract, instead preferring to work independently on projects such as Marlon Brando's *One-Eyed Jacks* (1960); *Man from Del Rio* (1956), with Anthony Quinn; and *Stay Away Joe* (1968), with Elvis Presley. She returned to live in Mexico in 1968, where she continued working as an actress on television and earned lifetime achievement awards from the Santa Fe Western Festival (1981) and the Mexican Film Promotion Trust (1992). Upon her death, after six decades in cinema, she had more sixty films to her credit.

See also **Cinema: From the Silent Film to 1990.**

BIBLIOGRAPHY

Cuevas, Concepcion. "Katy Jurado y Diana Bracho, ayer y hoy, dos mujeres en el cine: La mujer en las artes." *Fem* 25, no. 234 (September 2002): 42–43.

STACY LUTSCH

JUSTO, JOSÉ AGUSTÍN PEDRO (1876–1943).

José Agustín Pedro Justo (*b.* 26 February 1876; *d.* 11 January 1943), general and president of Argentina (1932–1938); leader of the Concordancia. Born in Concepción del Uruguay, Entre Ríos Province, Justo gained national prominence as a member of the Argentine army. After graduating from the Military College of San Martín in 1892, he rose rapidly through the ranks. He gained influence over a generation of military officers as the director of his alma mater between 1915 and 1922.

Having achieved the rank of brigadier general, he entered national politics in 1922, when President Marcelo T. de Alvear (1922–1928) appointed him minister of war. Along with other members of the Alvear administration, Justo joined the Anti-Personalist wing of the Radical Civic Union. In opposition to the second administration of President Hipólito Irigoyen (reelected 1928), he joined with the planners of the Revolution of 1930. When the military, led by General José Felíx Uriburu, seized power, he participated in the provisional government as commander-in-chief of the army.

Justo became the leading spokesman for conservative politicians who hoped to impose limits on democracy and to use the government to protect their interests. When support for Uriburu faded in 1931, the provisional government sponsored elections engineered to favor the conservatives, and Justo, with the support of the National Democratic Party and the Anti-Personalist Radicals, was elected president. Serving from 1932 to 1938, he directed the consolidation of the Concordancia, a coalition of conservative political forces that controlled Argentine politics until 1943.

Justo's administration maneuvered Argentina through the Great Depression. The fiscal innovations initiated under Justo, including the Roca–Runciman Pact (1933), the Pinedo Plan, the establishment of a national income tax, and the creation of Argentina's Central Bank, were overshadowed by the growing reliance on electoral fraud, censorship, and repression that maintained the Concordancia in power.

See also **Argentina: The Twentieth Century Concordancia.**

BIBLIOGRAPHY

Robert A. Potash, *The Army and Politics in Argentina, 1928–1945: From Yrigoyen to Perón* (1969).

David Rock, *Argentina, 1516–1987: From Spanish Colonization to Alfonsín,* rev. ed. (1987), pp. 216–231.

Additional Bibliography

Fernández Lalanne, Pedro E. *Justo-Roca-Cárcano: El 30 y otras décadas.* Buenos Aires: Editorial Sinopsis, 1996.

López, Mario Justo, Germán Darío Gómez, and Jorge Eduardo Waddell. *Entre la hegemonía y el pluralismo: Evolución del sistema de partidos politicos.* Buenos Aires: Lumiére, 2001.

Pinedo, Enrique. *Los relegados.* Buenos Aires: Corregidor, 2000.

DANIEL LEWIS

JUSTO, JUAN B. (1865–1928). Juan B. Justo (*b.* 28 June 1865; *d.* 8 January 1928), Argentine Socialist congressman, senator, and party founder. Born in the city of Buenos Aires, Justo graduated from the medical school of the local university in 1888. After travel to Europe, he returned to Argentina in the early 1890s to serve as a surgical specialist at the head of a local clinic and as a professor at the school from which he had recently graduated. In these positions, he introduced modern sanitary and scientific techniques into Argentina's operating rooms.

In the 1890s, Justo's interests began to shift from medicine to politics. His concern with the many environmentally induced illnesses he was called on to treat made him determined to attack the social conditions producing them. In 1893 he began to meet with like-minded professionals and skilled workers to found a socialist newspaper. The result was the appearance in 1894 of *La Vanguardia,* destined to be the most influential socialist publication in Argentina. Soon thereafter, Justo helped found the Socialist Party of Argentina, which in 1896 began to participate in local and national elections on a regular basis.

As the Socialist Party evolved and expanded, Justo emerged as its principal leader and guiding force. A man of great intellectual ability, he molded the party in his own image and directed it along the path—mostly a moderate one—he believed best suited to Argentine conditions. One of the few Argentine Socialists well versed in Marxist theory (he produced the first Spanish translation of *Das Kapital*), he closely followed various European models of socialist theory, organization, and practice, adjusting them whenever necessary to local circumstances and conditions. Among his several publications, *Teoría y práctica de la historia* (1909) best describes and explains Justo's particular brand of socialism.

Under Justo's direction, the Socialist Party of Argentina grew in size, strength, and support. Justo himself was elected three times to the national Chamber of Deputies (1912–1916, 1916–1920, and 1920–1924) and once to the national Senate (1924–1928) from the federal capital. As a legislator, Justo was a forceful advocate for his party's programmatic agenda and an acerbic critic of the governments in power. His speeches were characterized by careful and often compelling reasoning, extensive documentation, frequent references to foreign examples, and sardonic wit. The acknowledged leader of his party, he also served as the head of its congressional delegation.

Justo's brilliance and leadership attracted many like-minded and able young men to the party. He developed a coterie of protegés, notably Nicolás Repetto and Enrique Dickmann, who were closely tied to him not only by philosophy but also by marriage. Throughout the first three decades of the twentieth century, Justo and his allies dominated the editorial board of *La Vanguardia* as well as the main directive positions and candidate lists of the Socialist Party.

Although the party flourished under Justo's direction, there were many who chafed and occasionally rebelled against his tight discipline and the control he exercised from the top. Dissident reaction against the "family elite," a constant and repeated complaint, resulted in several serious schisms within the party in these years. Rarely, however, was open criticism directed against Justo himself, who remained the most widely respected, and by some revered, socialist in Argentina. The impact of Justo's ideas continued to have a substantial influence on the direction of Argentina's Socialist Party well after his death in 1928.

See also **Argentina, Political Parties: Socialist Party; Medicine: The Modern Era.**

BIBLIOGRAPHY

Dardo Cúneo, *Juan B. Justo y las luchas sociales en la Argentina* (1956).

Additional Bibliography

Camarero, Hernán, and Carlos-Miguel Herrera, eds. *El Partido Socialista en Argentina: Sociedad, política e ideas a tráves de un siglo.* Buenos Aires: Prometeo, 2005.

Portantiero, Juan Carlos. *Juan B. Justo: Un fundator de la Argentina moderna.* Buenos Aires: Fondo de Cultura Económica, 1999.

Rocca, Carlos J. *Juan B. Justo y su entorno.* La Plata, Argentina: Editorial Universitaria de La Plata, 1998.

Richard J. Walter

JUZGADO GENERAL DE INDIOS.

Juzgado General de Indios, a court of appeal for Indians. From the earliest days of conquest and settlement, the Spanish crown was concerned about the well-being of the native population. This concern included providing the Indians with access to judicial recourse in civil and criminal matters. In Peru an elaborate but inefficient protective system was developed that involved provincial judges and a staff in Lima, all supported by Indian taxation. In Mexico the crown in 1592 established a special tribunal in Mexico City, the General Indian Court, to hear Indian cases without charge to the individual and supported by a special tax. The Mexican court, which existed until 1820, had jurisdiction in suits of Indians against Indians and Spaniards against Indians, although other courts could hear such cases as well. It also heard numerous complaints by Indians against Spanish officials and clergy. Its existence helped to rein in the excesses of provincial governors, and Indians found it preferable to other judicial alternatives and used it extensively.

See also **Criminal Justice; Judiciary in Latin America, The.**

BIBLIOGRAPHY

Woodrow Borah, *Justice by Insurance: The General Indian Court of Colonial Mexico and the Legal Aides of the Half-Real* (1983).

Additional Bibliography

Kellogg, Susan. *Law and the Transformation of Aztec Culture, 1500–1700.* Norman: University of Oklahoma Press, 1995.

Serulnikov, Sergio. *Subverting Colonial Authority: Challenges to Spanish Rule in Eighteenth-century Southern Andes.* Durham, NC: Duke University Press, 2003.

MARK A. BURKHOLDER

KAGEL, MAURICIO RAÚL (1931–).

Mauricio Raúl Kagel (*b.* 24 December 1931), Argentine composer who became a naturalized German citizen. He was born in Buenos Aires. At the University of Buenos Aires he studied literature and philosophy until 1955. He trained with private instructors, most notably with Juan Carlos Paz. For a few years he worked as a pianist and conductor for opera preparation at the Teatro Colón in Buenos Aires. In 1957 he moved to Germany where he studied with Werner Meyer-Eppler at the Institute for Research in Phonetics and Communications in Bonn. His career developed rapidly as a composer, conductor, writer, and lecturer. He founded the Cologne Ensemble for New Music in 1961.

Since 1965, Kagel has written for what is now called "musical theater," and he has written and directed his own films. His early compositions, written while he was still living in his native country, were very pitch conscious and precisely structured. *The String Sextet* (1953, revised 1957) uses polymetric rhythms and microtonal writing. His more experimental *Musique de tour* for tape with light projections (1953), required a light system projected from a steel tower and sound broadcast from twenty-four loudspeakers. Other influential compositions by Kagel include *Anagrama* for spoken choir, four soloists, and chamber orchestra (1957–1958), based on a palindrome by Dante; *Transición* no. 1 for electronic music (1958–1960); and *Transición* no. 2 for piano and tape recorder (1958–1959). Theatrical components became very important in his works *Sur scène* for instrumental theater (1959–1960); *Pandorasbox* for bandoneon, a type of accordion (1960–1962); *Ludwig van* (1970), a homage to Beethoven that appeared in several versions, including a German television film and a recorded version with Kagel's ensemble playing distorted music of Beethoven; and *Staatstheater* (1970), the prototype of a veritable anti-opera.

Other significant works by Kagel include *Match* for two cellos and percussion (1964); *Tremens,* instrumental theater for two actors and electronically amplified instruments (1963–1965); *Pas de cinq,* variable scenes for five actors (1965); *Music for Renaissance Instruments* (1965–1967); *Halleluja* for voices (1967–1968); *Atem* for one wind instrument, tape recorder, and two loudspeakers (1970); *Con voce* for three silent players (1972); *Zwei Mann Orchester* for two performers (1971–1973); *1898* for children's choir (1972); *Mare nostrum* for contralto, baritone, and chamber ensemble (1973); *Exotica* for non-European instruments (1972); *Die Mutation* for children's voices and piano obbligato (1971); *Siegfriedp* for cello (1971); *Bestiarium* sound fable for three actors, bird calls and other objects, and tape (1974); *Die Umkehrung Amerikas* (1975–1976), a radio play; *Unguis incarnatus est* for piano (1972); *Morceau de concours* for solo trumpet and tape (1971), a competition piece; *Variationen ohne Fuge* for orchestra and two actors, Brahms and Handel (1971–1972); *Tango alemán* for bandoneon (1978); *Vox humana?* cantata for narrator, choir, and orchestra (1979); *Rrrrrr....* a radio fantasy for different instrumental combinations (1982); *Pan* for piccolo flute and string quartet (1985); *Ein Brief* for mezzo-soprano and orchestra (1986); *Zwei Akte* for saxophone and harp (1988–1989); *Les idées fixes,* rondo for orchestra (1989); and *Der Windrose* for salon orchestra (1988).

Films written and directed by Kagel include *Antithèse* (1965); *Match* (1966); *Solo* (1966–1967); *Duo* (1968); *Halleluja* (1967–1968); *Sous tension* (1975); *Blue's Blue* (1981); and *Dressage* (1985). He also wrote the music for the film *MM51* (1977).

See also **Music: Art Music.**

BIBLIOGRAPHY

Rodolfo Arizaga, *Enciclopedia de la música argentina* (1971), pp. 187–188; "Dossier Kagel," in *Musique en jeu,* no. 7 (1972): 98–100, 113, 117–123.

John Vinton, ed., *Dictionary of Contemporary Music* (1974). pp. 386–387.

Gérard Béhague, *Music in Latin America: An Introduction* (1979), pp. 337–338.

Alcides Lanza, "Music Theatre: A Mixed Media Realization of Kagel's 'Ludwig van,'" in *Interface* 8 (1979): 237–248; *New Grove Dictionary of Music and Musicians* (1980).

Additional Bibliography

Heile, Björn. *The Music of Mauricio Kagel.* Burlington, VT: Ashgate, 2006.

Karolyi, Otto. *Modern American Music: from Charles Ives to the Minimalists.* London: Cygnus Arts; Madison, NJ: Fairleigh Dickinson University Press, 1996.

Lochhead, Judith Irene, and Joseph Henry Auner. *Postmodern Music/Postmodern Thought.* New York: Routledge, 2002.

Surrans, Alain. *Mauricio Kagel: Parcours avec l'orchestre.* Paris: L'Arche, 1993.

Tadday, Ulrich. *Mauricio Kagel.* München: Edition Text, 2004.

ALCIDES LANZA

KAHLO, FRIDA (1907–1954). Frida Kahlo (*b.* 6 July 1907; *d.* 13 July 1954), Mexican artist. Kahlo was born in Coyoacán, the daughter of the Hungarian Jewish immigrant photographer Guillermo Kahlo and Matilde Calderón. She studied at the Escuela Nacional Preparatoria, one of thirty-five girls in a student body of two thousand. In 1925, she suffered a fractured spine and pelvis in a traffic accident that left her in constant pain. During her convalescence, she began to paint.

Artist Frida Kahlo in hammock, c. 1950. The talented Mexican painter Frida Kahlo (1907–1954) is best known for her provocative self-portraits. She became well known in her marriage to famed muralist Diego Rivera; her eminence as an artist followed her death. HULTON ARCHIVE/GETTY IMAGES

In 1929 Kahlo married the famed muralist Diego Rivera. Together they became international celebrities, honored by the art world and the political left. Among their friends, they counted Leon Trotsky, Max Ernst, Tina Modotti, Henry Ford, John D. and Nelson Rockefeller, Pablo Neruda, André Breton, and Isamu Noguchi. To complement Diego Rivera's extravagant character, Frida Kahlo created her own flamboyance. Drawing upon the Mexican cultural nationalist movement, she elevated Tehuana dress to haute couture and coiffed her hair in indigenous styles embellished with ribbons, bows, combs, and flowers. Necklaces, earrings, and rings completed her costume along with a prominent cigarette. A vivacious, engaging, and playful presence, Frida Kahlo was a living work of art, self-constructed to fight her constant physical agony and her sorrow at being unable to conceive a child and having to endure her husband's infidelities.

Most of Kahlo's paintings are small, intricately crafted self-portraits combining the real and the fantastic. They capture her spiritual and physical suffering in anatomical, surgical detail cast in traditional Mexican art forms like the *retablo,* using Catholic and pre-Colombian symbolism and imagery. Her subject matter is distinctly female: motherhood, fertility, the womb, childbirth, childhood, children, and family. Her art is precociously feminist in her concern with domestic violence, adultery, and her drive to control her own body. Often interpreted as surrealist, her depiction of flowing blood and wounded bodies in fact derives from Mexican popular culture. In her fantastic depiction of monkeys, prickly pears, and rainforest, she achieves a degree of sensual expression unequalled in Mexican art. André Breton wrote: "There is no art more exclusively feminine, in the sense that, in order to be as seductive as possible, it is only too willing to play alternately at being absolutely pure and absolutely pernicious. The art of Frida Kahlo is a ribbon about a bomb" (Herrera, p. 214).

Kahlo died in July 1954 at the age of forty-seven. By the 1980s, her art had received the international recognition that had eluded her in her lifetime.

See also **Art: The Twentieth Century; Rivera, Diego.**

BIBLIOGRAPHY

MacKinley Helm, *Modern Mexican Painters* (1968).

Hayden Herrera, *A Biography of Frida Kahlo* (1983).

Diego Rivera, with Gladys March, *My Art, My Life: An Autobiography* (1960).

Raquel Tibol, *Frida Kahlo, crónica, testimonios y aproximaciones* (1977).

Bertram D. Wolfe, *The Fabulous Life of Diego Rivera* (1963).

Additional Bibliography

Lindauer, Margaret A. *Devouring Frida: The Art History and Popular Celebrity of Frida Kahlo.* Middletown, CT: Wesleyan University Press, 2003.

Lozano, Luis-Martin, ed. *Frida Kahlo.* México, D.F.: Grupo Financiero Bital, 2001.

MARY KAY VAUGHAN

KAMINALJUYÚ. Kaminaljuyú, a Formative and Classic Period Maya site in (and mostly destroyed by) the suburbs of modern Guatemala City. The source of its importance was the El Chayal obsidian deposits 12 miles northeast. Through exploitation of this resource, it became sufficiently strong to resist Olmec inroads into the southern highlands. Its location provides trade access to the west and north across the Isthmus of Tehuantepec to the Gulf, northward into the Petén and the southern Maya lowlands, and southward to the Pacific Coast and Central America. Though independent of the Olmecs, Kaminaljuyú must have served as a major conduit of cultural influences reaching the Mayas from the Olmec region via Izapa, to which Kaminaljuyú is stylistically linked.

As Teotihuacán rose to power about 150 CE, Kaminaljuyú became a major trading partner or a colony. The distinctive Teotihuacán *talud-tablero* (sloping-table) style of terrace facings on platforms and pyramids appears on several structures in one area of the site tied to this era. Teotihuacán dress on sculptured monuments and funerary furnishings in elaborate tombs further document the Teotihuacán links. (Alfred V. Kidder and E. M. Shook excavated two tombs in Structure E-III-3 and reported finding sacrificial victims, jadeite beads, a mask, headdress, obsidian blades, stingray spines, stuccoed gourds, and quartz crystals.) Some scholars believe that Kaminaljuyú was initially conquered by Teotihuacán warriors, integrated into the Teotihuacán trade networks, and sustained by the rule of the descendants of local marriages. Kaminaljuyú was both a commercial and dynastic link between Tikal and Teotihuacán; and perhaps Curl Nose (ruler of Tikal, late fourth century CE) married into the Tikal ruling lineage from Kaminaljuyú.

Subsequent interpretations of Kaminaljuyú's developmental history suggest even greater links to nearby Maya cities like Tikal, and a broader elite ideology shared by Teotihuacán and Mayan rulers.

See also **Olmecs; Teotihuacán; Tikal.**

BIBLIOGRAPHY

Alfred V. Kidder, J. D. Jennings, and E. M. Shook, *Excavations at Kaminaljuyú, Guatemala* (Carnegie Institution of Washington, publication 561, 1946).

E. M. Shook and A. V. Kidder, *Mound E-III-3, Kaminaljuyú, Guatemala* (Carnegie Institution of Washington, publication 596, 1952).

William T. Sanders and J. W. Michels, *Teotihuacán and Kaminaljuyú: A Study in Prehistoric Cultural Contact* (1977).

Additional Bibliography

Braswell, Geoffrey E. "Dating Early Classic Interaction between Kaminaljuyu and Central Mexico." in *The Maya and Teotihuacan: Reinterpreting Early Classic Interaction* edited by Geoffrey E. Braswell. Austin: University of Texas Press, 2003.

Hatch, Marion Popenoe. *Kaminaljuyú/San Jorge: Evidencia arqueológica de la actividad económica en el Valle de Guatemala, 300 a.C. a 300 d.C.* Guatemala: Universidad del Valle de Guatemala, 1997.

Michels, Joseph W. *The Kaminaljuyu Chiefdom.* University Park: Pennsylvania State University Press, 1979.

Parsons, Lee Allen. *The Origins of Maya Art: Monumental Stone Sculpture of Kaminaljuyu, Guatemala, and the Southern Pacific Coast.* Washington, DC: Dumbarton Oaks Research Library and Collection, 1986.

Valdés, Juan Antonio, and Jonathan Kaplan. "Ground-Penetrating Radar at the Maya Site of Kaminaljuyu, Guatemala." *Journal of Field Archaeology* Vol. 27, No. 3 (Autumn, 2000): 329–342.

WALTER R. T. WITSCHEY

KAQCHIKEL. Kaqchikel, Mayans of south-central Guatemala (1992 pop. 750,000). The Kaqchikel (formerly known as Cakchiquel) came to highland Guatemala between 1200 and 1250 as warriors accompanying the K'iche' (Quiché) and the Tz'utujil (Zutuhil). By 1470 an independent Kaqchikel nation ruled forty towns from the capital, Iximche'. Although by 1520 the population had been decimated by European plagues, continued strife with the K'iche' and Tz'utujil forced the Kaqchikel to enlist Spanish military aid. Pedro de Alvarado (known as Tonatiu) marched into Iximche' as an ally in 1524. But after further joint campaigns against the Pipiles and the Tz'utujil, planned at and launched from Iximche', Alvarado broke with the Kaqchikel, demanding tribute. The Kaqchikel leaders abandoned Iximche' to lead guerrilla resistance that lasted over a decade.

Between 1519 and 1550 the Maya population of Guatemala dropped by 80 percent, and between 1550 and 1800 by another 60 percent.

The centrally located Kaqchikel supplied labor and provender for the Spanish settlements while reestablishing pre-Columbian trade networks through exchange of their minimal excess produce. Many adopted Catholic religious practices, though the sacred 260-day calendar round was maintained. Holy places, particularly the dawn altars, the caves, and the obsidian emblematic stelae brought from Tula, endured as often clandestine centers of worship.

The Indian policies of the Spanish and Guatemalan governments alternated between assimilationism and integrationism. The politically knowledgeable Kaqchikel have consistently used the courts to oppose discrimination and to petition for equal rights. While maintaining their own ethnicity, they have incorporated multiethnic Indian resettlements into Kaqchikel communities. At the time of the downfall of the Liberal regimes of Jorge Ubico and Federico Ponce (1944), they tried to secure their traditional lands. Under Juan José Arévalo, they formed farm labor unions. Successive governments tried to assure access to Indian labor by cultivating dependence through economic and educational subordination.

Through unions, cooperatives, education, and commerce, the Kaqchikel are freeing themselves from debt peonage and manual labor constraints. Although ties to the land are still important, many families are no longer primarily farmers. Robert M. Brown found that most Kaqchikel families have four sources of income in addition to farming. Between the 1964 and the 1981 censuses, both the absolute and the relative population figures for Kaqchikel increased, despite the toll of the 1976 earthquake.

Although the violence of 1979–1985 slowed Kaqchikel population growth, the average educational level, involvement in macropolitical and macroeconomic spheres, and commitment to revitalizing Kaqchikel culture are building steadily. The 1986 Guatemalan constitution recognizes the indigenes' rights to maintain their languages and cultures.

In 1987 the government established official alphabets for Mayan languages. Kaqchikel, as one of the four major indigenous languages, is now served by the national bilingual/bicultural education program. Mayan scholars are again turning to the classic sources of the 1500s, such as the Annals of the Kaqchikels and the Popol Vuh, as inspiration for novels, histories, textbooks, poetry, and for constructing a new worldview, a modern Mayan reality. In 1990 a Kaqchikel poet, Kab'raqän, wrote: "So we too emerge from the heavy shadows, the dark night. Because all of their shadowy voices, the voices of our grandmothers, our grandfathers are crying in our hearts."

See also **Closed Corporate Peasant Community (CCPC); K'iche'; Precontact History: Mesoamerica; Tz'utujil.**

BIBLIOGRAPHY

Francisco Hernández Arana Xajila and Francisco Díaz Gebuta Quej, *Memorial de Tecpán-Atitlán: Anales de los Cakchiqueles*, translated by José Antonio Villacorta C. (1934).

Adrián Recinos, *Crónicas indígenas de Guatemala* (1957).

Sol Tax, *Penny Capitalism* (1963).

Manning Nash, "Guatemalan Highlands," in *Handbook of Middle American Indians,* vol. 7, *Ethnology,* pt. 1 (1969).

Sol Tax and Robert Hinshaw, "The Maya of the Midwestern Highlands," in *Handbook of Middle American Indians,* vol. 7, *Ethnology,* pt. 1 (1969).

Douglas E. Brintnall, *Revolt Against the Dead: The Modernization of a Mayan Community in the Highlands of Guatemala* (1979).

Sheldon Annis, *God and Production in a Guatemalan Town* (1987).

Robert McKenna Brown, *Language Maintenance and Shift Among the Kaqchikel Maya* (1991).

JUDITH M. MAXWELL IXQ'ANIL

KATARISMO.

Katarismo, inspired by eighteenth-century rebel Tupaj Katari, encompasses diverse Bolivian Aymara nationalist groups that blend class consciousness with ethnic demands. It began in the early 1970s, when young intellectuals won control of a *campesino* union outside La Paz. By 1978 they dominated most highland unions and formed a political party, the Movimiento Revolucionario Tupaj Katari (MRTK). The Katarista Campesino Confederation joined the Bolivian Workers Central (COB) in 1979 and formed the Single Union Confederation of Campesino Workers (CSUTCB). During the 1980s the movement split into ten parties, almost all demanding a multinational state. Its ideas still underlie Aymara nationalism in the early twenty-first century.

See also **Aymara; Bolivia: Bolivia Since 1825; Movimiento Indígena Pachacutik; Movimiento Revolucionanrio Tupaj Katari de Liberación (MRTKL).**

BIBLIOGRAPHY

Hylton, Forrest, and Sinclair Thomson. "The Chequered Rainbow." *New Left Review* 35 (September–October 2005): 41–64.

Hurtado, Javier. *El Katarismo.* La Paz: Hisbol, 1986.

Canessa, Andrew. "Contesting Hybridity: Evangelistas and Kataristas in Highland Bolivia." *Journal of Latin American Studies* 32, no. 1 (2000): 115–144.

Rocha Monroy, Ramón. *Líderes Contemporáneos del Movimiento Campesino de Bolivia: Jenaro Flores Santos.* La Paz: CIPCA, 2006.

LINDA FARTHING
BENJAMÍN KOHL

KEARNY, STEPHEN W. (1794–1848).

Stephen W. Kearny (*b.* 30 August 1794; *d.* 31 October 1848), a soldier who gained fame during the Mexican War (1846–1848). Kearny, of Dutch and Irish parentage, was raised in New Jersey and New York City. He served with distinction during the War of 1812 and as an officer commanding various posts on the western frontier. When the Mexican War broke out, he was given the command of the Army of the West. He marched 1,600 troops into Santa Fe, New Mexico, and served as military governor from August to September 1846.

From Santa Fe Kearny led an army of about one hundred to California to assist in the American conquest of the far West. On 6 December 1846, at San Pasqual, near San Diego, in a brief but bloody skirmish, he encountered a Californio force led by Andrés Pico that blocked his advance for several days. Later Kearny assisted in the recapture of Los Angeles. For many months he quarreled with John C. Frémont over who was the chief commander of California. Eventually Kearny was vindicated and Frémont was court-martialed.

In 1847 Kearny was sent to Mexico and served as the civil governor of Vera Cruz and later of Mexico City. He died the following year in St. Louis, of a tropical disease contracted in Vera Cruz.

See also **Mexico, Wars and Revolutions: Mexican-American War.**

BIBLIOGRAPHY

Dwight Clarke, *Stephen Watts Kearny: Soldier of the West* (1961).

Hubert Howe Bancroft, *History of California,* 7 vols. (1884–1890).

Justin Harvey Smith, *The War with Mexico,* 2 vols. (1919).

Allan Nevins, *Frémont* (1922; repr. 1963).

Additional Bibliography

Ricketts, Norma B. *The Mormon Battalion: U.S. Army of the West, 1846–1848.* Logan: Utah State University Press, 1996.

RICHARD GRISWOLD DEL CASTILLO

KEITH, MINOR COOPER (1848–1929). Minor Cooper Keith (*b.* 19 January 1848; *d.* 14 June 1929), Costa Rican railroad builder and founder of United Fruit Company. Born in Brooklyn, New York, Keith received only a grade-school education before beginning to work in the cattle business out west. In 1871 his uncle, Henry Meiggs, obtained and transferred the contract to build the Costa Rican railroad to Minor's elder brother, Henry Meiggs Keith. Henry Keith soon had Minor in Costa Rica working on the railroad, which quickly became Minor C. Keith's project. He completed the Costa Rican Railway on 7 December 1890.

Minor Keith encouraged banana production along the railroad line in order to have a return freight during the period before the railroad reached the Mesa Central. He used the Tropical Trading and Transport Company to control all the banana land in the early decades. Later he organized the Colombian Land Company, Limited, and the Snyder Banana Company as his fruit business expanded. He joined with Andrew W. Preston of Boston Fruit Company to form the United Fruit Company, incorporated in New Jersey on 30 March 1899. Preston became president and Keith first vice president, but Keith ceased any active role in the company by 1912. He had received $4 million in United Fruit shares for his various fruit operations when United Fruit organized.

On 31 October 1883, Keith married Cristina Castro Fernández, the daughter of José María Castro, who served twice as president and once as chief justice of Costa Rica, and Pacífica Fernández de Castro, who designed Costa Rica's flag and coat of arms. Minor and Cristina had no children.

Later in life, Keith pursued other interests. He collected and turned over to the Costa Rican National Museum (founded in 1887) many Costa Rican antiquities. About 1905, he acquired fruit lands in Guatemala for United Fruit and built the International Railroads of Central America by purchasing existing railroads and acquiring concessions for additional lines in Guatemala and El Salvador. He had interests in Brazilian railroads and Cuban sugar mills among his many and varied Latin American business holdings.

See also **Railroads; United Fruit Company.**

BIBLIOGRAPHY

John E. Findling, *Dictionary of American Diplomatic History,* 2d ed. (1989), p. 279.

J. Fred Rippy, "Relations of the United States and Costa Rica During the Guardia Era," *Bulletin of the Pan American Union* 77, no. 2 (1943): 61–68.

Watt Stewart, *Keith and Costa Rica* (1964).

Additional Bibliography

Chomsky, Aviva. *West Indian Workers and the United Fruit Company in Costa Rica, 1870–1940.* Baton Rouge: Louisiana State University Press, 1996.

O'Brien, Thomas F. *The Revolutionary Mission: American Enterprise in Latin America, 1900–1945.* Cambridge: Cambridge University Press, 1996.

Quesada Monge, Rodrigo. *Una lección de estilo empresarial: las inversiones de Keith en Costa Rica, 1885–1929.* Heredia, Costa Rica: Departamento de Filosofía, Universidad Nacional, 2003.

Striffler, Steve, and Mark Moberg. *Banana Wars: Powers, Production, and History in the Americas.* Durham, NC: Duke University Press, 2003.

THOMAS SCHOONOVER

KEMMERER, EDWIN WALTER (1875–1945). Edwin Walter Kemmerer (*b.* 19 June 1875; *d.* 16 December 1945), U.S. financial adviser in Latin America. Born in Scranton, Pennsylvania, Kemmerer attended Wesleyan University (B.A., 1899) and Cornell (Ph.D., 1903). One of the most famous U.S. economists in the opening decades of the twentieth century, Kemmerer was a professor at Cornell (1906–1912) and Princeton (1912–1943). He helped design the Federal Reserve System in 1911, edited the *American Economic Bulletin* and the *American Economic Review,* and became president of the American Economic Association in 1926. He was renowned as an expert on money and banking.

His greatest achievement, however, was his success as an adviser to foreign governments. A product of the Progressive Era, Kemmerer saw himself as a professional technician bringing universal, scientific advances to underdeveloped countries and their poorer citizens. He became known as the "money doctor."

Throughout the world, Kemmerer spread the gospel of the gold standard and central banks. His teams of experts stabilized exchange, modernized financial and fiscal institutions, and thus made countries more attractive to foreign investors, particularly during the lending boom of the 1920s. He played many of the roles later assigned to international financial institutions, principally the International Monetary Fund.

Kemmerer's overseas economic reforms began with the United States–Philippine Commission in 1903–1906. From 1917 to 1934 he conducted similar crusades against inflation in Mexico, Guatemala, Colombia, Germany, Chile, South Africa, Poland, Ecuador, Bolivia, China, Peru, and Turkey. In most cases, Kemmerer and his colleagues were invited independently by foreign governments, although the U.S. State Department heartily approved of his missions.

After the Great Depression, Kemmerer's influence faded, as he continued to espouse monetary stability based on the gold standard. Although his ideas lost sway, his institutions—such as the central bank, the superintendency of banking, and the national comptroller—continued as major instruments of economic policy-making in Latin America. Moreover, the pattern he set for the role of foreign advisers in Latin America's financial development forecast the operations of international institutions, academics, and technocrats in subsequent decades.

See also **Banking.**

BIBLIOGRAPHY

Paul W. Drake, *The Money Doctor in the Andes: The Kemmerer Missions, 1923–1933* (1989).

Edwin W. Kemmerer, "Economic Advisory Work for Governments," in *American Economic Review* 17, no. 1 (March 1927): 1–12.

Robert N. Seidel, "American Reformers Abroad: The Kemmerer Missions in South America, 1923–1931," in *Journal of Economic History* 32, no. 2 (June 1972): 520–545.

Additional Bibliography

Almeida Arroba, Rebeca. *Kemmerer en el Ecuador.* Quito: Facultad Latinoamericana de Ciencias Sociales (FLACSO), Sede Ecuador, 1994.

Rosenberg, Emily S. *Financial Missionaries to the World: The Politics and Culture of Dollar Diplomacy, 1900-1930.* Durham, NC: Duke University Press, 2003.

PAUL W. DRAKE

KENNECOTT COPPER COMPANY.

See **Gran Minería.**

K'ICHE'.

The K'iche' (Quiché) Indians are Guatemala's most numerous Maya ethnolinguistic group, with an estimated total population of between 1.5 and 2 million concentrated in the western departments of Guatemala, the great majority in the highlands and the remainder in the Pacific and northern lowlands. Caught in the middle of a harsh and bloody civil war, since the late 1970s the K'iche' have suffered widespread internal dislocation, involving many deaths and the destruction of numerous communities. Thousands have emigrated to Mexico, the United States, and Canada. Some joined the guerrillas in the 1970s and early 1980s, and many more have been conscripted into the army, whose counterinsurgency campaign of torture and death has claimed thousands of Maya victims.

The Spanish Conquest was characterized by K'iche' and other Maya bravely opposing forces favored by superior technology. Beginning in 1524, the Spanish conquerors enslaved and forcibly resettled (*congregación*) the K'iche'. They destroyed K'iche' cultural-religious symbols and required the people to practice the Catholic religion. The K'iche' were compelled to give labor and tribute to their new lords (*encomenderos*). While late-twentieth-century violence has been horrific for the K'iche', in the 1524–1675 period they lost 80–90 percent of their population, primarily to Old World diseases. The K'iche' population numbered some 925,000 about 1520 and declined to probably fewer than 100,000 in the seventeenth century. Recovery over the next three centuries to more than 1.5 million is ample testimony to the K'iche' ability to survive despite unfavorable odds.

The key to K'iche' resistance to a multitude of destructive forces, including the more subtle Spanish and Guatemalan efforts to integrate the Maya into a colonial or national polity, lies in the strength of K'iche' cultural traditions and the ability to maintain ancestral towns and lands. Both of these factors have deep roots in the pre-Conquest period, when the early K'iche' (ca. thirteenth century) and their predecessors formed villages, then more complex patrilineal clans and chiefdoms, and finally a state structure.

For at least several centuries prior to the Spaniards' arrival, the K'iche' were the dominant highland group, directly ruling both their own regions and those peoples who later broke away to form the independent Tz'utujil and Kaqchikel polities. Other Maya, like the Mam, were subordinate tributaries under indirect K'iche' authority. Lacking a rich resource base near their capital, Gumaarcaj (Utatlán), the K'iche' expanded into lower-lying areas rich in agricultural commodities like cacao and cotton.

Preconquest K'iche' writings include the Popol Vuh, elaborate calendars, and clan histories (*títulos*) by priests and chroniclers. All were lost or destroyed, but Maya versions in the Roman alphabet took their place. Despite Spanish efforts to extirpate the pagan past—notably by destroying temples and killing religious leaders—much survived, often in modified form. Woven textiles for both daily wear and ceremonial occasions are an obvious example.

Such political and cultural achievements bestowed strength, a measure of continuity, and a distinct identity on the K'iche' inhabitants of numerous hamlets and towns. New levels of cultural identity based on these antecedents have emerged, giving the K'iche' both a new pan-Maya identity and a growing sense of belonging to a particular group. Rigoberta Menchú Tum, who was awarded the Nobel Peace Prize in 1992 for her work as an advocate for indigenous rights, is likely the most widely recognized K'iche' Maya in the early 2000s.

Still, the struggle for K'iche' and Maya survival in Guatemala is likely to remain difficult. Institutional violence persists, racism is deeply entrenched, and poverty has increased as population expansion and environmental destruction have put new strains on the carrying capacity of the land.

See also **Kaqchikel; Menchú Tum, Rigoberta; Precontact History: Mesoamerica; Tz'utujil.**

BIBLIOGRAPHY

Fundamental works are Robert M. Carmack, *Quichean Civilization: The Ethnohistoric, Ethnographic, and Archaeological Sources* (1973), and *The Quiché Mayas and Utatlán: The Evolution of a Highland Guatemalan Kingdom* (1981). An intriguing comparison of past and present events is W. George Lovell, "Surviving Conquest: The Maya of Guatemala in Historical Perspective," in *Latin American Research Review*, 23, no. 2 (1988): 25–57.

A number of authors focus on K'iche' towns as a mechanism for analyzing a period stretching from the pre-Hispanic era to the present. Noteworthy are Robert M. Carmack, *Historia social de los Quiché* (1979); Robert M. Hill II and John Monaghan, *Continuities in Highland Maya Social Organization: Ethnohistory in Sacapulas, Guatemala* (1987); and Jean Piel, *Sajcabajá: Muerte y resurrección de un pueblo de Guatemala, 1500–1970* (1989).

Important analyses of postcolonial Guatemalan Maya society are Robert M. Carmack, "Spanish-Indian Relations in Highland Guatemala, 1800–1944," in *Spaniards and Indians in Southeastern Mesoamerica: Essays on the History of Ethnic Relations,* edited by Murdo J. MacLeod and Robert Wasserstrom (1983).

Carol A. Smith, ed., *Guatemalan Indians and the State, 1540–1988* (1990).

Essential for understanding the impact of revolution and institutionalized repression on the K'iche' and other Maya peoples is Robert M. Carmack, ed., *Harvest of Violence: The Maya Indians and the Guatemalan Crisis* (1988).

Additional Bibliography

Grandin, Greg. *The Blood of Guatemala: A History of Race and Nation.* Durham, NC: Duke University Press, 2000.

CHRISTOPHER H. LUTZ

KIKAPOO. The Kikapoo are Algonquian speakers who in 1649 began moving south and west from their homeland in the central Great Lakes region under pressure from the Iroquois. By the late 1700s they reached southern Illinois only to be forced west of the Mississippi in 1819 by encroaching settlement and military losses. There they splintered into groups, some staying on their Missouri reservation while others continued to move south and west, spreading across Oklahoma and Texas. The Missouri group traded for land in Kansas, where they remained to become one of the three federally recognized Kikapoo tribes. In the 1830s unrest in Texas drove the fiercely independent Kikapoos to Mexico, where they were granted land in exchange for protection of Mexican settlements. In 1852 the Mexican Kikapoo established a traditional colony at Nacimiento. Approximately 2,000 of the 3,500 modern Kikapoos live in traditional settings, divided among Oklahoma, Texas, Kansas, and Coahuila, Mexico. Their economy is based on casino operations, seasonal migrant labor, and farming.

See also **Mexico: 1810-1910.**

BIBLIOGRAPHY

Fabila, Alfonso. *La tribu kikapoo de Coahuila.* México, D. F.: Instituto Nacional Indigenista, 2002.

Jablow, Joseph. *Illinois, Kickapoo, and Potawatomi Indians.* New York, Garland, 1974.

SOLVEIG A. TURPIN

KINCAID, JAMAICA (1949–). Elaine Potter Richardson (Jamaica Kincaid) was born in St. John's on the eastern Caribbean island of Antigua on May 29, 1949. She was educated in the British colonial system and raised by her half-Carib mother and her father, a carpenter. Much of Kincaid's work is inspired by her early life: Her novel *Autobiography of My Mother* (1996) imagines the life of a half-Carib woman in Dominica, and her novel *Annie John* (1985) and her short-story collection *At the Bottom of the River* (1983) deal with girlhood in the colonial Caribbean.

In 1965, shortly before Antigua gained its independence from Britain, Kincaid left her home for Westchester, New York, to work as an au pair—a servant, she would later say. Her novel *Lucy* (1990) is based on this experience working abroad to send money home to her family. She attended Franconia College in New Hampshire before pursuing photography at the New School for Social Research in New York City.

She became Jamaica Kincaid in 1973 during a moment of inspired self-invention. Her reasons for choosing this name are vague, except that Jamaica was representative of the Caribbean and its colonial history, and Kincaid flowed well with Jamaica. This renaming was strategic: She achieved the anonymity necessary to write about her experiences at home and abroad without anyone, particularly Antiguans, recognizing her early efforts.

With the encouragement of George Trow, a friend and writer for the *New Yorker*, she submitted her work to the magazine. Her writing caught the attention of the editor, William Shawn, and by 1976 Kincaid had joined the *New Yorker* as a staff writer. She credits Shawn and the *New Yorker* with providing her the opportunity to learn how to write. At the *New Yorker* Kincaid developed a signature style, striking a balance between fiction and nonfiction. Her articles for the "Talk of the Town" column are anthologized in *Talk Stories* (2001).

Her narratives are inspired by the events and people in her life, the facts of which are fictionalized through the filter of her perception. She uses these familiar relationships to discuss the dynamic between the powerful and the powerless, most often as it relates to British colonialism and North American neocolonialism in the Caribbean. More so than her themes, it is her shockingly honest, distinctly feminine West Indian voice that makes her work autobiographical. The urgency and directness of this narrative voice at times seems angry, as in the anticolonial, antitourist essay "A Small Place" (1988), and at other times unsympathetic, as in *My Brother* (1997), her memoir of her youngest brother's death from AIDS.

Kincaid identifies writers from an English literary tradition, including Charlotte Brontë and Virginia Woolf, as primary influences. This complicates critical readings that understand her work's orality in the context of African storytelling, or interpret her postcolonial themes and Caribbean landscapes as derived from a West Indian literary tradition.

Kincaid has two children from her marriage to composer Allen Shawn (William Shawn's son). She teaches at Harvard University, but makes her home in Bennington, Vermont, where she is an avid gardener. In the essay collection *My Garden (Book)* (1999) and the travel narrative *Among Flowers* (2005) Kincaid explores gardening as the ultimate form of conquest.

See also **Antigua; Colonialism; Feminism and Feminist Organizations; Jamaica; Literature: Spanish America; Women.**

BIBLIOGRAPHY

Primary Works

At the Bottom of the River. New York: Farrar, Straus and Giroux, 1983.

Annie John. New York: Farrar, Straus and Giroux, 1985.

Annie, Gwen, Lilly, Pam, and Tulip. New York: Library Fellows of the Whitney Museum of Modern Art, 1986.

A Small Place. New York: Farrar, Straus and Giroux, 1988.

Lucy. New York: Farrar, Straus and Giroux, 1990.

The Autobiography of My Mother. New York: Farrar, Straus and Giroux, 1996.

My Brother. New York: Farrar, Straus and Giroux, 1997.

My Favorite Plant: Writers and Gardeners on the Plants They Love. New York: Farrar, Straus and Giroux, 1998.

My Garden (Book). New York: Farrar, Straus and Giroux, 1999.

Life and Debt. Produced and directed by Stephanie Black. 80 mins. New Yorker Films, 2001. Documentary film.

Talk Stories. New York: Farrar, Straus and Giroux, 2001.

Mr. Potter. New York: Farrar, Straus and Giroux, 2002.

Among Flowers: A Walk in the Himalayas. Washington, DC: National Geographic Society, 2005.

The Best American Travel Writing. Ed. Boston: Houghton Mifflin, 2005.

Secondary Works

Bloom, Harold, ed. *Jamaica Kincaid*. Philadelphia: Chelsea House, 1998.

Bouson, J. Brooks. *Jamaica Kincaid: Writing Memory, Writing Back to the Mother*. Albany: State University of New York Press, 2005.

Ferguson, Moira. *Jamaica Kincaid: Where the Land Meets the Body*. Charlottesville: University Press of Virginia, 1994.

Lang-Peralta, Linda, ed. *Jamaica Kincaid and Caribbean Double Crossings*. Newark: University of Delaware Press, 2006.

LARA B. CAHILL

KINNEY, HENRY L. (1814–1861?). Henry L. Kinney (*b.* 3 June 1814; *d.* July 1861?), U.S. filibuster and borderlands entrepreneur. A Pennsylvanian by birth, Kinney farmed and speculated in land in Illinois in the 1830s. Ruined in the Panic of 1837, he migrated to the Republic of Texas. In 1840, at the mouth of the Nueces River, within territory disputed by Texas and Mexico, he established a trading post/smuggler's nest that became known as Kinney's Rancho. Kinney, who became bilingual, survived border strife by providing information and supplies to Texan and Mexican forces alike, sometimes serving as intermediary between them. His ranch became the nucleus of a boomtown, Corpus Christi, after General Zachary Taylor stationed his army in its vicinity prior to the Mexican–American War. During that conflict, Kinney apparently was division quartermaster on the general staff of the Texas Volunteers and then agent of the U.S. Quartermaster Department, serving as supplier, scout, interpreter, and dispatch carrier.

Kinney served in the Republic of Texas's Ninth and Tenth congresses, as well as the Texas Constitutional Convention of 1845 (where he championed the interests of Spanish-speaking inhabitants). Although elected to the Senate of the first four Texas legislatures, he never took his seat in the second legislature and abandoned his seat in the fourth. After the Mexican–American War, he became involved in the publication of the *Corpus Christi Star* (later the *Nueces Valley*), Texas Ranger affairs, and promotion of Texas's first state fair (1852), held both to boost Corpus Christi and to raise aid for José María Carvajal's Republic of the Sierra Madre.

From 1854 to 1858 Kinney devoted himself to the Central American Land and Mining Company, designed to colonize—really filibuster—Central America's Mosquito Coast, on the basis of an invalid land grant. Kinney ruled Greytown (San Juan del Norte) as "civil and military governor" for part of this period. In 1859, Kinney served as Texas governor Sam Houston's agent to investigate Juan Cortina's raid on Brownsville. Elected a representative in Texas's eighth legislature, Kinney opposed secession and, in March 1861, was forced to give up his seat. Several undocumented accounts assert that he died at Matamoros, Mexico.

See also **Filibustering.**

BIBLIOGRAPHY

William O. Scroggs, *Filibusters and Financiers: The Story of William Walker and His Associates* (1916), esp. pp. 93–132.

Joseph Milton Nance, *After San Jacinto: The Texas–Mexican Frontier, 1836–1841* (1963).

James T. Wall, *Manifest Destiny Denied: America's First Intervention in Nicaragua* (1981), esp. pp. 29–70.

Additional Bibliography

Clayton Anderson, Gary. *The Conquest of Texas: Ethnic Cleansing in the Promised Land, 1820–1875*. Oklahoma: University of Oklahoma Press, 2005.

Gore, W.R. *The Life of Henry Lawrence Kinney*. M.A. thesis; University of Texas, 1948.

Thrall S., Homer. *A Pictorial History of Texas.* St. Louis: Thompson, 1879.

Wilbarger, J.W. *Indian Depredations in Texas.* Austin: State House, 1985.

ROBERT E. MAY

KINO, EUSEBIO FRANCISCO (1645–1711).

KINO, EUSEBIO FRANCISCO (1645–1711). Eusebio Francisco Kino (*b.* 10 August 1645; *d.* 15 March 1711), Jesuit missionary and explorer of northwestern New Spain. A native of Segno, near Trent, in the Italian Tyrol, educated in Austria and Germany, Kino was among the foreign-born Jesuit missionaries permitted by the Spanish crown under quota to serve in the Spanish Indies. He excelled in mathematics, astronomy, and cartography, and could have had a university chair in Europe. Instead, he put these skills to good use during a thirty-year career in New Spain, first as royal cosmographer of Admiral Isidro de Atondo's failed effort to occupy Baja California in the mid-1680s and then as the pioneer missionary of Pimería Alta (present-day northern Sonora and southern Arizona), capstone of the Jesuits' northwest missionary empire.

An irrepressible expansionist, Kino had a restless nature better suited to exploration and first contact with the Pimas and Pápagos (Tohono O'Odam) than for everyday administrative routine at mission Dolores, which he established as his headquarters in 1687. On numerous expeditions, traveling the valleys of the San Pedro, Santa Cruz, Gila, and Colorado rivers, he introduced cattle, created demand for European goods, and mapped the country. His crowning cartographic achievement, which he drew the year before his death, showed California not as an island, a misconception of the seventeenth century, but as a peninsula.

In 1966, Kino's grave was discovered in Magdalena, Sonora, since renamed Magdalena de Kino. The Jesuits in the early twenty-first century promoted his cause for canonization. A mineral, a hospital, a table wine, and much else bear his name, and statues abound.

See also **Jesuits; New Spain, Colonization of the Northern Frontier.**

BIBLIOGRAPHY

Herbert E. Bolton, *Rim of Christendom: A Biography of Eusebio Francisco Kino, Pacific Coast Pioneer* (1936; repr. 1984).

Ernest J. Burrus, e.g., *Kino and the Cartography of Northwestern New Spain* (1965).

Ernest J. Burrus *Kino and Manje, Explorers of Sonora and Arizona, Their Vision of the Future* (1971). See also Charles W. Polzer, *Kino Guide II,* rev. ed. (1987).

Additional Bibliography

Montané Martí, Julio C. *Intriga en la corte: Eusebio Francisco Kino, Sor Juana Inés de la Cruz, y Carlos de Sigüenza y Góngora.* Hermosillo, México: Universidad de Sonora, 1997.

Polzer, Charles W. *Kino, a Legacy: His Life, His Works, His Missions, His Monuments.* Tucson: Jesuit Fathers of Southern Arizona, 1998.

JOHN L. KESSELL

KIRCHNER, NÉSTOR (1950–).

KIRCHNER, NÉSTOR (1950–). Néstor Carlos Kirchner was born on February 25, 1950, in Río Gallegos, in the province of Santa Cruz, and served as president of Argentina from May 2003 to December 2007. His early studies were in his native city, and he then transferred to La Plata (Buenos Aires) to study law. There he joined the Peronist Youth, a leftist movement that supported the Montoneros guerrilla group during the last administration of Juan Perón and the subsequent administration of Perón's wife, María Estela Martínez de Perón. In March 1975 Kirchner married Cristina Fernández, a fellow student and political activist.

Following the military coup of 1976 Kirchner returned to Santa Cruz, abandoned political activity, and devoted himself to his profession. With the return of democracy in 1983 he rejoined the Peronist party and became president of the provincial pension fund (Caja de Previsión Social). In 1987 he was elected mayor of Río Gallegos and held the post until 1991, when he won the election for governor. Thanks to successive reforms of the province's constitution, he was reelected twice, in 1994 and 1998.

As governor he supported the nationwide privatization program implemented by Carlos Menem, particularly the privatization of the state oil company, YPF, which provided Santa Cruz with an abundance of funds for public works and for increasing the provincial government staff. Kirchner's management of the funds received from oil royalties was covert and at his own discretion. His supporters spoke highly of his management, whereas his adversaries accused him of having transformed the province into a fiefdom. He concentrated control of sources of wealth and jobs and overpowered the legislative and judiciary bodies as well as the media, and persecuted rivals and dissidents. He created a nationalist and populist inner sector that he sought to use to launch himself onto the national scene.

When Fernando de la Rúa resigned from the presidency in December 2001, he was succeeded by five interim presidents in the midst of an unprecedented crisis. The fifth, Eduardo Duhalde, supported Kirchner's candidacy in the elections that were finally held in March 2003 and in which he ran against two other Peronist candidates, thanks to a timely amendment to the party's bylaws and the support of the Congress. In the campaign, Kirchner positioned himself as the representative of the progressive, nationalist sector, in opposition to the neoliberal platform on which Menem sought to return to the presidency. He also promised to retain Duhalde's minister of the economy, Roberto Lavagna, who was credited with having begun to reactivate the economy in mid-2002. Although he only won 22 percent of the votes and placed second behind Menem, Kirchner managed to unite all anti-Menem factions and secure the presidency when Menem refused to run in the second round of elections.

Soon after his inauguration, he was able to gain the broad support of public opinion and sectors of his party and of other political forces weakened by the crisis, thanks to measures aimed at accelerating reactivation of the economy and improving the social situation. He renegotiated the $144 billion public debt that was in default, achieving a significant discount. Benefiting from high world prices on commodities, he applied a tax on exports that allowed him to increase social spending without affecting the fiscal surplus. He maintained a high exchange rate that allowed for rapid recovery of industry and a consequent reduction in unemployment, bringing down the proportion of the population in poverty from almost 55 percent to under 30 percent in three years.

With regard to institutional issues, his policies were more ambiguous. He spurred the reopening of trials for human rights violations during the dictatorship, forced the retirement of a large number of military officers, intensified the purge of corruption among some police forces, and propelled the removal of several of the more questionable judges from the Supreme Court. At the same time, he strengthened the executive's discretionary control of the budget, issued an unusual number of emergency decrees through bypassing Congress, persecuted media outlets and independent journalists, and purchased the loyalty of governors, mayors, and legislators of the Peronist party and the forces of opposition, using the augmented Treasury resources. Problems arose on the economic front toward the end of his administration, the result of distortions in relative prices (rates frozen for almost four years, price controls, and cross subsidies) and a growing recklessness in public spending.

See also **Argentina: The Twentieth Century; Duhalde, Eduardo; Menem, Carlos Saúl; Perón, Juan Domingo.**

BIBLIOGRAPHY

Primary Work

With Torcuato S. Di Tella. *Después del derrumbe: Teoría y práctica política en la Argentina que viene; Conversaciones.* Buenos Aires: Galerna, 2003.

Secondary Works

Natanson, José. *El presidente inesperado.* Rosario, Argentina: Homo Sapiens, 2004.

Novaro, Marcos. *Historia de la Argentina contemporánea.* Buenos Aires: Edhasa, 2006.

Marcos Novaro

KISSINGER, HENRY (1923–). Henry Kissinger was a U.S. policy maker who has received considerable criticism for supporting dictatorships in Latin America and Asia while serving as the national security advisor and secretary of state during the 1970s. Born in Germany in 1923, Kissinger and his family moved to New York City to escape Nazi repression. After earning a PhD, he taught international relations at Harvard. Advising New York's Republican governor Nelson Rockefeller in the 1960s, Kissinger became acquainted with Richard Nixon. When Nixon won the U.S. presidency in 1968, he appointed Kissinger as his national security advisor. In 1973, Nixon also appointed Kissinger secretary of state. Despite the resignation of Nixon in 1974, Kissinger continued in this position until 1977 under the administration of Nixon's successor Gerald Ford. Possibly his most significant foreign policy achievement, Kissinger and Nixon reestablished in 1972 relations with communist China. In 1973, Kissinger, along with North Vietnamese diplomat Le Duc Tho, won the Nobel Prize for negotiating an end to the war in Vietnam, even though Tho did not accept the award and hostilities continued until 1975. Since the end of the Vietnam War, critics of Kissinger have noted that he supported the unlawful bombing of Cambodia, Vietnam's neighbor, which allowed the brutal dictatorship Khmer Rogue to gain power and commit genocide.

While Kissinger has been closely tied with the Vietnam War and Asia, his support for dictatorships in Latin America in the 1970s has received notable scrutiny. In 1970, socialist Salvador Allende won the Chilean presidency causing concern in the United States about the spread of communism in South America. Kissinger and the Nixon administration imposed severe economic sanctions to weaken the democratically elected government. When Augusto Pinochet, leader of Chile's armed forces, overthrew Allende's government in 1973, the United States immediately supported the military government. Even though the Pinochet regime openly tortured and killed its political opponents, Kissinger continued aid to Chile and never denounced the brutal, undemocratic tactics. Later, in the 1970s, the Argentine military took over its government. To quell opposition and communism, the armed forces kidnapped, killed, and disappeared leftist students, intellectuals, and workers. Later declassified documents revealed that Kissinger told his Argentine counterpart that the United States would support the regime because of its anti-communist stance. He only urged the dictatorship to "get back to normal procedures" before the U.S. Congress investigated human rights abuses. Moreover, when the U.S. ambassador in Argentina protested the human rights violations, Kissinger threatened to fire him.

Kissinger's actions in Latin America have continued to raise controversy in the early twenty-first century. A court in Spain brought charges against former Chilean dictator Augusto Pinochet, who was in the United Kingdom at the time, for the murder of Spanish citizens. While the United Kingdom allowed Pinochet to return to Chile, Spain's action set a precedent for holding policy makers accountable for human rights violations. Instead of answering a French court's questions in 2001 about the disappearance of French citizens in Pinochet's Chile, Kissinger left the country. Several courts in Spain, Argentina, and Chile would like Kissinger to testify regarding his knowledge of state-sponsored terrorism in Latin America and Asia. A Spanish court in 2002 tried to have Kissinger extradited. Despite these legal issues, Kissinger's consulting firm works with major corporations and Kissinger regularly advised President George W. Bush during the U.S. war in Iraq.

See also **Allende Gossens, Salvador; Kissinger Commission; Pinochet Ugarte, Augusto.**

BIBLIOGRAPHY

Garcés, Joan E., and Christopher Hitchens. *La intervención de Estados Unidos en Chile.* Chile: Editorial 30 Años, 2003.

Hanhimäki, Jussi M. *The Flawed Architect: Henry Kissinger and American Foreign Policy.* New York: Oxford University Press, 2004.

Suri, Jeremi. *Henry Kissinger and the American Century.* Cambridge, MA: Belknap Press of Harvard University Press, 2007.

Byron Crites

KISSINGER COMMISSION.

The Reagan administration convened the U.S. National Bipartisan Commission on Central America in 1984 in hopes of reversing flagging congressional support for its Central American policy, particularly with respect to aid to the Nicaraguan Contras and military assistance for the government of El Salvador. Former Secretary of State Henry Kissinger chaired the conservative, twelve-member commission, whose mandate was to study contemporary conflicts in Central America and make policy recommendations.

The report of the Kissinger Commission was released in January 1984. It contained an overview of Central American development and addressed what the commission believed to be the immediate causes of the military conflicts afflicting the region in the early 1980s. Members of the commission concurred with other observers that peace in Central America was dependent upon improvements in economic and social conditions and that those developments were not likely to occur until the civil wars came to an end.

Regarding the region's economic problems, the report recommended that the United States mount a large aid program for Central America; it envisioned much more external assistance than was actually forthcoming in the 1980s. The sections dealing with security issues, however, created the most public controversy, and only partially succeeded in gaining congressional support. Especially contentious aspects of the report were its insistence that Central American revolutionary movements relied heavily on support from Cuba and the Soviet Union, the commission's refusal to fully acknowledge United States' backing of the Contras, and arguments in favor of increasing U.S. military assistance to El Salvador.

BIBLIOGRAPHY

Report of the National Bipartisan Commission on Central America (1984).

Richard E. Feinberg, "The Kissinger Commission Report: A Critique," in *World Development* 12, no. 8 (1984): 867–876.

William M. Leo Grande, "Through the Looking Glass: The Kissinger Commission Report on Central America," *World Policy Journal* 1, no. 2 (1984): 251–284.

Additional Bibliography

LaFeber, Walter. *Inevitable Revolutions: The United States in Central America*. Second Edition. New York: W.W. Norton, 1993.

LeoGrande, William M. *Our Own Backyard: The United States in Central America, 1977–1992*. Chapel Hill: University of North Carolina Press, 1998.

Rouquié, Alain. *Guerras y paz en América Central*. México, D.F.: Fondo de Cultura Económica, 1994.

MARY A. CLARK

KNOROSOV, YURI (1922–1999). Yuri Valentinovich Knorosov was a Russian-Ukranian linguist, epigrapher, and ethnographer who carried out groundbreaking work in the decipherment of Maya hieroglyphic writing. He was born on November 19, 1922, of Russian parents in Pivdenne near the city of Kharkiv (Kharkov in Russian) in eastern Ukraine. Knorosov's upbringing in Ukraine (his grandmother was Armenian) exposed him to different languages. Perhaps his background explains why Knorosov, who initially studied medicine, eventually turned to cultural anthropology and linguistics at Moscow State University. Later he joined the Institute of Ethnography in Leningrad, which was part of the Soviet Academy of Sciences, and received his Doctorate of Science. Knorosov's publications on languages and ancient scripts began to appear in 1949.

Over the years Knorosov worked with decipherments in Egyptian, Harrapan, and Easter Island scripts, but it is for his contributions to the decipherment of Maya hieroglyphs that he is best known. The story has been widely circulated that Knorosov, who was in the Red Army during World War II, saved a copy of the Maya Dresden Codex from a burning library in Berlin in 1945. However, people close to Knorosov state that he was a military communications engineer behind the lines and that the tale of his library rescue was partially conjured by himself. What did happen was that various books on the Maya were confiscated by the Red Army from a national library in Germany and sent to Moscow, where Knorosov accessed them, including a copy of the Dresden Codex and studies in Maya language and writing.

Knorosov's contributions to Maya hieroglyphic writing are enormous. Until the late 1970s the general interpretation of Maya writing was that it consisted of numbers, calendars, pictographs, and undecipherable signs. Scholars believed that Maya calendar hieroglyphs and astronomy could be studied from their writing, but not their language, culture, or history. Knorosov and others challenged this assumption. As a linguist and anthropologist, Knorosov realized that writing, and particularly ancient scripts, are often syllabic in nature; consonant-vowel combinations (*CV, CV-CV,* or *CVC*) are commonly represented in writing, as in Egyptian hieroglyphs. Equipped with these insights and the Dresden Codex, Knorosov went to work deciphering the ancient Maya script.

Knorosov's breakthrough was derived from his utilization of "Landa's alphabet," which many previous epigraphers had dismissed as being inaccurate. This bilingual text (an important tool for deciphering unknown writing) is part of Bishop Diego de Landa's *Relación de las cosas de Yucatán* (c. 1566), which covers Yucatec Maya culture. Landa, and possibly other priests, attempted to extract the Spanish alphabet from a Maya informant writing Maya signs for Spanish syllables (*ah, be, se*, and so forth). Fortunately, Spanish vowel-consonant combinations are represented in Mayan languages (Spanish "hey" vs. English "gee" for the letter *g*, for instance). Knorosov worked with the entire Landa alphabet and not merely a few signs as others had done.

Another advantage of Knorosov's research was that he examined the Dresden Codex for his decipherments. This codex, containing writing together with paintings on stuccoed paper, was probably created in Yucatán just before the Spanish Conquest. The book exhibits a large corpus of Maya hieroglyphs with patterned substitutions (also necessary for making decipherments). Additional advantages of using the Dresden Codex are that it presents linguistic elements found in Yucatec Mayan, which was familiar to Knorosov, and its texts describe the painted scenes. Thus, he was able to discern Landa's "cu" sign placed over what Knorosov suspected to be a "chu" sign to make *cuch* or "burden." This hieroglyph is associated with images of people carrying burdens. Similarly, "ku" and "tzu" make *kutz* or "turkey," and "ku" alongside its twin render *kuk*, which is "quetzal bird." These signs also appear next to their corresponding avian images. Knorosov also picked out linguistic details in Mayan languages, including the verb ending "ah" in *chukah* ("capture/captured," written as "chu + ka + ah").

Subsequent work in Maya epigraphy has shown that Knorosov was largely correct in his findings regarding the nature of the script. Yet his decipherments were challenged for decades because of East-West antagonisms, Knorosov's peripheral position in Maya studies, and the inaccuracy of some of his proposed readings. However, Knorosov's pivotal work led him to decipher many Maya hieroglyphs, and he opened the door for future research in ancient Maya writing.

Knorosov's contributions made it possible for scholars to examine phonetic elements, attain additional decipherments, and have a greater understanding of the structure of Maya hieroglyphs. The study of syllables and vowel length in Maya writing in the early twenty-first century is based upon Knorosov's advancements. Additionally, a crucial finding stemming from Knorosov's work is that Maya writing contains historical information about ancient Maya elites and events in their lives, including their names and titles, births, wars, coronations, marriages, rituals, and deaths. Students of Maya culture can now read texts about the dedication of buildings and monuments, ownership of objects, and qualities of material culture. Without Yuri Knorosov, it is possible that little would have been currently known about Maya writing beyond calendars, mathematics, and basic life histories of Maya rulers.

See also **Maya, The; Mayan Epigraphy.**

BIBLIOGRAPHY

Coe, Michael D. *Breaking the Maya Code.* London: Thames and Hudson, 1992.

Knorosov, Yuri V. *Selected Chapters from "The Writing of the Maya Indians,"* ed. T. Proskouriakoff; trans. Sophie Coe. Cambridge, MA: Peabody Museum of Archaeology and Ethnology, Harvard University, 1967.

JOEL PALKA
YURIY POLYUKHOVYCH

KNOX–CASTRILLO TREATY (1911).

Knox–Castrillo Treaty (1911), a loan convention signed in Washington, D.C., on 6 June 1911 between U.S. secretary of state Philander C. Knox and Nicaraguan minister Salvador Castrillo. Reflecting the U.S. government's desire to provide financial, and by extension political, stability for Nicaragua, the convention called for the Nicaraguan authorities to negotiate a loan for the purpose of re-funding the nation's internal and external debts. The bonds floated for the loan would be secured by Nicaraguan customs duties, and the customs would be supervised by a collector general approved by the U.S. government. Although ratified almost immediately by Nicaragua, the treaty languished for nearly a year in the U.S. Senate Foreign Relations Committee. In May 1912, when the committee finally voted, the treaty failed to secure the necessary support for a favorable report to the Senate. The Nicaraguan government then decided to negotiate directly with U.S. bankers for a short-term loan, a financial arrangement that did not carry the official sanction and guarantees that treaty status would have provided.

See also **Dollar Diplomacy; United States-Latin American Relations.**

BIBLIOGRAPHY

Papers relating to the Foreign Relations of the United States, 1912 (1919), esp. pp. 1,071–1,104.

Dana G. Munro, *Intervention and Dollar Diplomacy in the Caribbean, 1900–1921* (1964), esp. pp. 186–204.

Additional Bibliography

Gobat, Michel. *Confronting the American Dream: Nicaragua Under U.S. Imperial Rule.* Durham, NC: Duke University Press, 2005.

RICHARD V. SALISBURY

KOELLREUTTER, HANS JOACHIM

(1915–2005). Hans Joachim Koellreutter (*b.* 2 September 1915; *d.* 13 September 2005), German-born teacher and composer, who lived in Brazil from 1937.

Koellreutter's effect on young Brazilian composers has been enormous. In 1939 he formed the group Música Viva Brasil and in 1940 began publishing a magazine of the same name. Through his group and his periodical, Koellreutter set out to introduce new music to Brazilian audiences. He championed the theories and music of Arnold Schoenberg, and encouraged his music students to employ the twelve-tone technique when writing music. He had many famous music students, among them Gilberto Mendes, Roberto Sion, and Diogo Pacheco. Koellreutter's modernist agenda prompted Brazil's principal nationalist composer, Camargo Guarnieri, to write the famous "Carta aberta aos músicos e críticos do Brasil" (Open letter to musicians and critics of Brazil), in which he attacked the idea that serial technique could be a suitable means of expression for nationalist music. Composers such as César Guerra Peixe, Claudio Santoro, and others who studied with Koellreutter went on to develop their own individual styles, but the ideas and teaching of Koellreutter made a major contribution to twentieth-century Brazilian music. He died in São Paulo on September 13, 2005.

See also **Music: Art Music.**

BIBLIOGRAPHY

Gérard Béhague, *Music in Latin America: An Introduction* (1979).

David P. Appleby, *The Music of Brazil* (1983).

Additional Bibliography

Brito, Teca Alencar de. *Koellreutter educador: O humano como objetivo da educaçao musical.* São Paulo: Fundaçao Pieropolis, 2001.

Kater, Carlos. *Música Viva en H.J. Koellreutter: Movimentos em direçao a modernidade.* São Paulo, SP: Musa Editora: Atravez Associação Artístico-Cultural, 2000.

DAVID P. APPLEBY

KONETZKE, RICHARD

(1897–1980). Richard Konetzke was a German historian dedicated to the study of colonial Spanish America. He studied at the University of Berlin. Konetzke's research at the Archivo General de Indias of Seville, Spain produced the three-volume *Colección de documentos para la historia de la formación social de hispanoamérica 1493–1810* (Madrid, 1953–1962). In 1954 he became professor of Spanish, Portuguese, and Latin American history at the University of Cologne.

In 1964 Konetzke cofounded the *Jahrbuch für Geschichte von Staat, Wirtschaft und Gesellschaft Lateinamerikas*, a periodical publication in Latin American studies; this journal publishes articles in various languages such as German, Spanish, English, Portuguese, and French. One of his major works is his survey of colonial Spanish America, first published in German in 1965 and eventually translated into Spanish as *América Latina II: La época colonial* (1972); it has been reprinted several times since its initial release, due in large part to the fact that Konetzke's institutional interpretation has remained fundamental in the study of Latin America. The major criticism of Konetzke's work is his supposed overemphasis on the importance of the state in the formation of colonial Spanish society, principally because he relied completely on official documents, without making distinctions between government and the actual social reality.

BIBLIOGRAPHY

Morner, Magnus. "Richard Konetzke (1897–1980)." *Hispanic American Historical Review* 61, no. 1 (1981): 87–89.

CLAUDIA P. RIVAS JIMÉNEZ

KORN, ALEJANDRO (1860–1936). Alejandro Korn (*b.* 3 May 1860; *d.* 9 October 1936), Argentine philosopher. Together with José Vasconcelos and Antonio Caso in Mexico, Carlos Vaz Ferreira in Uruguay, and Alejandro Deustua in Peru, Korn belonged to a group of Latin American philosophers who were prominent at the end of the nineteenth and beginning of the twentieth centuries and who represented the beginning of a more professional approach to philosophy.

Korn was born in San Vicente, Buenos Aires Province, and educated in medicine at the University of Buenos Aires. He began his career as professor of philosophy at the University of Buenos Aires in 1906, while still engaged in his main profession as a psychiatrist. In the beginning, he was influenced by positivism, but he soon abandoned this position because of its naturalist determinism, which he felt made moral responsibility impossible. His Kantian-based philosophy was later influenced by the work of Europeans such as Wilhelm Dilthey and Henri Bergson.

Korn conceived of philosophy as a knowledge of the subjective, or the human, world, as opposed to science, which was the exact knowledge of the natural world. Philosophy was to him axiology, or the analysis of values and valuations as sources of all human action. Although it is not openly revealed in his philosophical writings, the base of his worldview is an intensely religious, but not dogmatic, feeling. His ethic is voluntarist and considers action as the way out of perplexities of theoretical antinomies. Although he considered Marxism an antiquated philosophy of the nineteenth century, he adhered to "ethical socialism," a form of socialism based on the moral reasoning of social justice.

Korn was the author of a classic work on the interpretation of the history of ideas in Argentina, *Influencias filosóficas en la evolución nacional* (1936). His philosophical writings have been collected in *Obras,* 3 vols. (1938–1940) and *Obras completas* (1949).

See also **Caso y Andrade, Antonio.**

BIBLIOGRAPHY

Solomon Lipp, *Three Argentine Thinkers* (1969).

Juan Carlos Torchia Estrada, *Alejandro Korn: Profesión y vocación* (1986).

Daniel E. Zalazar, *Libertad y creación en los ensayos de Alejandro Korn* (1972).

Additional Bibliography

Rocca, Carlos J. *Alejandro Korn y su entorno.* Argentina: s.n., 2001.

Rocca, Carlos J. *La actividad política de Alejandro Korn.* Argentina: s.n., 2003.

JUAN CARLOS TORCHIA ESTRADA

KÖRNER, EMIL (1846–1920). Emil Körner (*b.* 10 October 1846; *d.* 25 March 1920), German army officer and founder of the modern Chilean army. Emil Körner Henze, as he was called in Chile, was born in Wegwitz, Saxony. He entered the army in 1866. He was a student and later taught at the Artillery and Engineer's School (Charlottenburg) and was decorated after Sedan. He graduated from the Kriegsakademie (staff school) in 1876 and served in Italy, Spain, and Africa. After nearly twenty years of service in the kaiser's army, Captain Körner had established a good record but, as a Saxon and a commoner, had a limited future as an officer of the imperial army. His military career took a sharp turn in 1885 because of the Chilean government's decision to professionalize its army. Impressed with what he had read of Chile's recent victory over Peru (War of the Pacific, 1879–1884), Körner accepted an offer to teach artillery, infantry, cartography, military history, and tactics; to serve as subdirector of the Escuela Militar; and to oversee establishment of a Chilean staff school. In Chile he ultimately rose to the rank of inspector general.

A year after his arrival he helped inaugurate the Academia de Guerra, and the Chilean army began a new life. Under Körner's direction the new staff school provided advanced training and the army adopted the general staff system in order to be prepared for war at any time. By 1889, the popular Körner was advocating wide-reaching reforms in military training. Two years later he helped the forces of the National Congress with the support of the Navy and some Army leaders to win a civil war against President José Manuel Balmaceda. Subsequently Körner was given great latitude in the continual modernization of the army. He attracted several German missions to Chile in the last decade of the century, and by 1910, when he retired, Chile's army was superficially a creole copy of the kaiser's. Körner died in Berlin, but his remains were brought to Santiago in 1924.

See also **War of the Pacific.**

BIBLIOGRAPHY

Frederick M. Nunn, "Emil Körner and the Prussianization of the Chilean Army: Origins, Process, and Consequences, 1885–1920," in *Hispanic American Historical Review* 50 (May 1970): 300–322.

Frederick M. Nunn, *Yesterday's Soldiers: European Military Professionalism in South America, 1890–1940* (1983).

Carlos Sáez Morales, *Recuerdos de un soldado,* vol. 1, *El ejército y la política* (1933).

Additional Bibliography

Núñez P., Jorge. *1891, crónica de la guerra civil.* Santiago de Chile: LOM Ediciones, 2003.

Sater, William F., and Holger H. Herwig. *The Grand Illusion: The Prussianization of the Chilean Army.* Lincoln: University of Nebraska Press, 1999.

FREDERICK M. NUNN

KOSICE, GYULA (1924–). Gyula Kosice (*b.* 26 April 1924), Argentine painter and sculptor, born in Hungary. Kosice came to Argentina at age three. He studied at free academies from 1937 to 1942 and later at the School of Philosophy and Letters of the University of Buenos Aires and at the National School of Fine Arts. He founded the Grupo Madí art movement as well as the Asociación de Arte Concreto-Invención, a nonfigurative group. ("Madí," like Dada, is an arbitrary word.) Kosice designed the Hydrospatial City. He is the creator of hydrokinetic art and neon luminal sculpture. A member of the Argentine Writers' Society (SADE), Kosice wrote eight books, among them *Herbert Read* (1955), *Poème hydranlique* (1960), *Arte Hidrocinético* (1968), *Arte y arquitectura de agua* (1974), and *Arte Madí* (1980, 1982). His works are highly personal and imaginative, effecting a sense of tranquillity.

See also **Art: The Twentieth Century.**

BIBLIOGRAPHY

Vicente Gesualdo, Aldo Biglione, and Rodolfo Santos, *Diccionario de artistas plásticos argentinos* (1988).

Additional Bibliography

Barjalía, Juan–Jacobo. "Kosice, Madí y el vanguardismo." *La Maga,* Buenos Aires: (August 1999).

Bajarlía, Juan–Jacobo, and Gyula Kosice. *Kosice: Un visionario del arte contemporáneo.* Buenos Aires, Argentina: Corregidor, 2001.

Kosice, Gyula. *Arte y filosofía porvenirista: Ensayos.* Buenos Aires: Arte Gaglianone, 1996.

Kosice, Gyula. *Obras, 1944–1990: Museo Nacional de Bellas Artes, Buenos Aires, Argentina, abril/mayo 1991.* Buenos Aires: Museo Nacional de Bellas Artes.

AMALIA CORTINA ARAVENA

KOSMOS LINE. Kosmos Line, a Hamburg shipping line organized in early 1872 primarily to enter the competition for the Pacific coast freight service. Known as the Deutsche Dampfschiffahrts-Gesellschaft Kosmos (German Steamship Service Company Kosmos), it originally served only South America's Pacific coast, but by the early 1880s, it was running ships up to Central America during the six-month coffee season. Later, Kosmos extended its service northward to San Francisco. About 1880, Bremen shippers responded with the formation of the Roland Line to compete with Kosmos for the trade of the Pacific coast. Later Kosmos also developed trade with the Caribbean area, and it received a British mail subsidy to establish the first regular steamer service to Las Malvinas (Falkland Islands). In 1901, the Hamburg-Amerika Linie (HAPAG) obtained a large interest in Kosmos through an agreement by which they shared access to the Pacific coast. Kosmos suspended service to Latin America from 1914 until mid-1921. In 1926, HAPAG absorbed Kosmos, but re-formed a shipping company for Latin American service under this name in 1976.

BIBLIOGRAPHY

Edwin J. Clapp, *The Port of Hamburg* (1911).

Otto Mathies, *Hamburgs Reederei 1814–1914* (1924).

Ludwig Wendemuth and W. Böttcher, *The Port of Hamburg* (1932).

Raymond A. Rydell, *Cape Horn to the Pacific: The Rise and Demise of an Ocean Highway* (1952).

Additional Bibliography

Schoonover, Thomas David. *Germany in Central America: Competitive Imperialism, 1821–1929.* Tuscaloosa: University of Alabama Press, 1998.

THOMAS SCHOONOVER

KOTOSH. Kotosh, an archaeological site in the Huallaga drainage of highland Peru. Known for its monumental architecture, Kotosh was built during the third millennium BCE, centuries before the introduction of ceramics. It is located in a rain shadow along the eastern slopes of the Andes at 6,600 feet above sea level. It is dominated by two mounds, the larger of which reached a height of 45 feet. Excavations showed that the featureless mounds were eroded terraced pyramid-platforms and that their impressive scale was the end product of centuries of intentional filling and renovation, a process sometimes called "ritual entombment." The core of the mounds contains a sequence of similar public structures superimposed one on top of the other.

The most important of these buildings are small stone chambers with a square ground plan and a central subfloor firepit attached to subterranean flues. The structures often feature a distinctive two-level floor in which a recessed zone surrounds the central stone-lined hearth. The exterior and interior walls of these chambers were plastered with light clay, and in some cases the entryway was painted red. These buildings are generally interpreted as chambers designed for rituals involving burnt offerings.

The best known of the Kotosh buildings, the Temple of the Crossed Hands, has two clay friezes flanking the main axis of the building: the eastern one depicts a small set of hands with the left arm overlapping the right, while the western one shows a similar but slightly larger set with the right arm on top of the left. These images constitute one of the oldest known examples of public art in the Americas, and they may symbolize dual opposition, a principle fundamental to later Andean ideology.

Preceramic structures similar to those at Kotosh have been found at other sites, including Shillacoto in Huánuco, Huaricoto in the Callejón de Huaylas, and La Galgada in the Tablachaca drainage. These structures probably housed comparable ceremonies, and the groups responsible for them are thought to have shared a similar belief system, sometimes referred to as the Kotosh Religious Tradition.

Following the Preceramic occupation (known as the Mito phase), Kotosh continued to be occupied during the second millennium BCE by farmers who supplemented their diet with hunted game, especially deer. These groups produced elaborate ceramic assemblages known as the Kotosh Waira-jirca and Kotosh Kotosh styles; the form and decoration of this pottery display link to styles of the tropical forest, highlands, and coast. This pottery and occasional exotic imports from the eastern lowlands constitute evidence of the role that Amazonian cultures played in the development of early Andean civilization. During the first millennium BCE Kotosh developed strong ties to Chavín de Huántar, and the local population participated in the Chavín sphere of interaction.

See also **Chavín de Huántar.**

BIBLIOGRAPHY

A synthesis of Kotosh and the Kotosh religious tradition is presented in Richard L. Burger, *Chavín and the Origins of Andean Civilization* (1992). The University of Tokyo excavations at the site were published in Seiichi Izumi and T. Sono, *Andes 2: Excavations at Kotosh, Peru, 1960* (1963), and S. Izumi and Kazuo Terada, *Andes 4: Excavations at Kotosh, Peru, 1963 and 1966* (1972). Seiichi Izumi discussed the implications of Kotosh investigations in "The Development of the Formative Culture in the Ceja de Montaña" in *Dumbarton Oaks Conference on Chavin,* edited by Elizabeth Benson (1971).

Additional Bibliography

Schjellerup, Inge. *Los valles olvidados: Pasado y presente en la utilización de recursos en la Ceja de Selva, Perú/The Forgotten Valleys: Past and Present in the Utilization of Resources in the Ceja de Selva, Peru.* Copenhagen: National Museum of Denmark, 2003.

Stone-Miller, Rebecca. *Art of the Andes: From Chavín to Inca.* New York: Thames and Hudson, 1996.

Von Hagen, Adriana, and Craig Morris. *The Cities of the Ancient Andes.* New York: Thames and Hudson, 1998.

RICHARD L. BURGER

KRAUSISMO. Alter the revolution of 1868, the Spanish government sent Julián Sanz del Río (1814–1869) to Germany to study the philosophy of education with Georg Wilhelm Friedrich Hegel. For reasons not completely clear, Sanz ended up studying in Dresden with Karl Christian Friedrich Krause (1781–1832), whose eclectic philosophy he brought back to Madrid. By a strange fluke the Puerto Rican Eugenio María de Hostos happened to be in the Spanish capital during those years and became one of Sanz's disciples, imbuing his novel *La peregrinación de Bayoán* with a call to harmony and order, tenets integral to Krause's worldview. Soon thereafter the Cuban patriot José Martí, as a result of his revolutionary activities, found himself exiled to the peninsula, where he also came into contact with the Krausist doctrine of harmonic rationalism which he applied to anti-colonial proposals.

Later, others, such as the Mexican Alfonso Reyes, the Uruguyan José Enrique Rodó, the Peruvian Alejandro O. Deustua, and the Argentine Alejandro Korn absorbed Krausism in varying degrees either during trips to Spain or in Latin America itself. Reyes, for example, spent time at the Residencia de Estudiantes in Madrid and with many graduates of the Institución de Libre Enseñanza, the premier Krausista think tank. For his part, Rodó corresponded with important Spanish Krausist intellectuals such as Leopoldo Alas, Rafael Altamira, and Miguel de Unamuno. There were also women Krausists such as the Peruvian Aurora Cáceres's writing after the 1920s, a result of her interest in Unamuno's philosophy, and before her, the Ecuadorian Marieta de Veintemilla. In Spain, Krausism was a philosophy of educational, social and political reform. It functioned analogously in Latin America, yet in the dissimilar regions of this hemisphere it took on wider and more varied forms and meaning according to the context, representing all the while an idealist challenge to North American utilitarianism.

See also **Arielismo; Deustua, Alejandro O; Hostos y Bonilla, Eugenio María de; Korn, Alejandro; Martí y Pérez, José Julián; Philosophy: Overview; Positivism; Reyes Ochoa, Alfonso; Rodó, José Enrique.**

BIBLIOGRAPHY

Abellán, José Luis. "La dimensión krauso-positivista en Eugenio María de Hostos." *Cuadernos Americanos* 16 (1989): 58–66.

Alvarez Guerrero, Osvaldo. *El radicalismo y la ética social: Irigoyen y el krausismo.* Buenos Aires: Editorial Leviatán, 1986.

Ardao, Arturo. *Espiritualismo y positivismo en el Uruguay*, 2nd edition. Montevideo: Universidad de la República, Departamento de Publicaciones, 1968.

Gómez Martínez, José Luis. "Pensamiento hispanoamericano: El caso del krausismo." In *Actas del II Seminario de Historia de la Filosofía Española*, edited by Antonio Heredia Soriano, pp. 155–172. Salamanca, Spain: Ediciones Universidad de Salamanca, 1982.

Oria, Tomás G. *Martí y el Krausismo.* Boulder, CO: Society of Spanish and Spanish-American Studies, 1987.

Roig, Arturo Andrés. *Los krausistas argentinos.* Puebla, Mexico: Editorial J. M. Cajica, Jr., 1969.

Salazar Bondy, Augusto. "La obra filosófica de Alejandro Deustua." In his *Historia de las ideas en el Perú contemporaneo*, 2nd edition. 2 vols. Lima: Francisco Moncloa, 1967.

Stoetzer, O. Carlos. *Karl Christian Friedrich Krause and His Influence in the Hispanic World.* Köln: Böhlau, 1998.

Ward, Thomas. "El krausismo en las Américas." In his *La teoría literaria: Romanticismo, krausismo y modernismo ante la globalización industrial*, pp. 53–91. University, MS: Romance Monographs, no. 61, 2004.

THOMAS WARD

KRAUZE, ENRIQUE (1947–). Mexican historian and intellectual Enrique Krauze Kleinbort is well known for his popular series of illustrated presidential biographies and for producing historical television programs marketed for the general public. Krauze has authored important historical books on Mexican intellectuals and presidents. His political essays in *Vuelta and Letras Libres* often provoke critical discussion.

Born September 16, 1947, in the Federal District, Krauze, the son of a printer, graduated from the National Autonomous University of Mexico (UNAM) with an engineering degree and earned a PhD from the Colegio de México. He was awarded a Guggenheim Fellowship for 1979–1980. He collaborated closely with Nobel Prize winner Octavio Paz as managing editor and subdirector of *Vuelta* from 1976 to 1996, founded his own intellectual magazine, *Letras Libres*, in 1999, and directs his publishing firm, Editorial Clío. He became a member of the Mexican Academy of History in 1989, and the prestigious National College in 2005.

See also **Paz, Octavio.**

BIBLIOGRAPHY

Krauze, Enrique. *Caudillos culturales en la revolución Mexicana.* Mexico: Siglo Veintiuno Editores, 1976.

Krauze, Enrique. *Mexico, Biography of Power: A History of Modern Mexico, 1810–1996.* Translated by Hank Heifetz. New York: HarperCollins, 1997.

RODERIC AI CAMP

KREUTZBERGER, MARIO (1940–). Mario Kreutzberger was born on December 28, 1940, in Talca, Chile, to German-Jewish parents who had fled Nazi Germany. Initially studying to become a tailor, Kreutzberger spent some time in New York, where he became familiar with television programming in the United States. When he returned to Chile, Kreutzberger started a television show in 1962, *Sábado Gigante,* which initially aired for eight hours every Saturday. With this show he took on his artistic name, Don Francisco. In 1985 *Sábado Gigante* began production in Miami, and in 1987 it became the first regularly and nationally broadcast Spanish-language program in the United States. The variety show runs for three hours during prime time on Saturday nights across forty-two countries, including parts of Latin America and Europe. The show is consistently a top-rated show among Latino audiences in the United States and is a mix of performances, interviews, comedy sketches, and games featuring audience participation and product placement. In 2002 the program celebrated its fortieth anniversary, becoming the longest-running variety show.

See also **Radio and Television.**

BIBLIOGRAPHY

Kreutzberger, Mario. *Don Francisco: Life, Camera, Action!* Morales, Mexico: Grijalbo, 2002.

Winslow, George. "Mario Kreutzberger." *Broadcasting & Cable* 134 (November 8, 2004): 26.

ROCÍO RIVADENEYRA

KRIEGER, EDINO (1928–). Edino Krieger (*b.* 17 March 1928), Brazilian composer. Born in the state of Santa Catarina, Brazil, Krieger was the son of Aldo and Gertrudes Krieger. His father was a well-known violinist, conductor, and composer who undertook the musical instruction of his son when the boy was only seven. During the next seven years, Edino Krieger gave several recitals as a violinist, and at the age of fourteen received a scholarship to study violin at the Conservatório Brasileiro de Música in Rio de Janeiro. In 1944 he wrote an improvisation for solo flute and in 1945 became associated with a group of composers, Música Viva, under the leadership of Hans Joachim Koellreutter, a pupil of Paul Hindemith. Three years later he won first prize in a competition sponsored by the Berkshire Music Center in Massachusetts. He later enrolled in the Juilliard School of Music in New York City, where he studied with Aaron Copland, Peter Mennin, and Darius Milhaud.

Krieger has combined a career as a composer of works of stylistic originality and powerful dramatic qualities with significant achievements as director of the music section of Brazil's National Foundation of the Arts. During his administration, the foundation contributed to a vitalization of musical performance throughout the nation and published scores of historical works by Brazilian composers, providing a heightened sense of the nation's cultural achievements. Important compositions by Krieger include his *Ludus symphonicus,* commissioned by the Instituto de Cultura e Bellas Artes of Venezuela, and his oratorio *Rio de Janeiro,* a dramatic narration of the birth of Brazil from its period of Portuguese colonization. Both these works were performed in Rio de Janeiro in 1988 at a special concert celebrating the composer's sixtieth birthday.

See also **Music: Art Music.**

BIBLIOGRAPHY

David P. Appleby, *The Music of Brazil* (1983).

Additional Bibliography

Coelho, Francisco Carlos, and Mayer, Marion. *Música contemporânea brasileira: Edino Krieger.* São Paulo: Discoteca Oneyda Alvarenga, 2006.

DeBiaggi, Emerson L. *Brazilian Art-Music in the Post-Nationalist Period: Three Compositions for Viola.* Santa Barbara: University of California, 1996.

Gandelman, Saloméa. *36 compositores brasileiros: Obras para piano (1950–1988).* Rio de Janeiro: Ministerio da Cultura, 1997.

Secretaria Municipal de Cultura. *Edino Krieger, catálogo de obras.* Rio de Janeiro: Prefeitura Rioarte, 1996.

DAVID P. APPLEBY

KRIEGER VASENA, ADALBERTO

KRIEGER VASENA, ADALBERTO (1920–2000). Adalberto Krieger Vasena was an Argentine politician and economist who served as minister of the economy during the de facto governments of what has been termed the "Liberating Revolution" between 1957 and 1958, and during the administration of Juan Carlos Onganía from 1967 to 1969.

Krieger Vasena was an economist with liberal roots; during his first term as minister, Argentina joined the International Monetary Fund (IMF). Called on again by the military dictatorship in late 1966 to stabilize the economy, Krieger Vasena (who had the support of the international financial agencies) promoted a plan to control inflation and reactivate the economy with a heavy emphasis on industry. The general lines of the plan were a 40 percent devaluation of the Argentine peso, the introduction of heavy export taxes, and the freezing of wages.

With the *Cordobazo* civil uprising in 1969 (a social protest by students and workers centered in the city of Córdoba), Krieger Vasena had to relinquish his position as minister. In 1973 he was called on to serve as director of the World Bank and two years later became the bank's executive vice president for Latin America, serving until 1978. In addition to his terms as minister, he is remembered for having supported the work of economy minister José Martínez de Hoz during a plan called "The Process" (1976–1982) and Carlos Menem's state reform project (1989–1999).

See also **Argentina: The Twentieth Century; Cordobazo, El; International Monetary Fund (IMF); Martínez de Hoz, José Alfredo; Menem, Carlos Saúl; Onganía, Juan Carlos; World Bank.**

BIBLIOGRAPHY

Brailovsky, Antonio Elio. *Historia de las crisis argentinas.* Buenos Aires: Editorial de Belgrano, 1985.

De Riz, Liliana. *La Política en suspenso, 1966–1976.* Buenos Aires: Paidós, 2000.

Gerchunoff, Pablo, and Lucas Llach. *El ciclo de la ilusión y el desencanto: un siglo de políticas económicas argentinas.* Buenos Aires: Ariel, 1998.

O'Donnell, Guillermo. *El Estado burocrático autoritario.* Buenos Aires: Editorial de Belgrano, 1982.

VICENTE PALERMO

KUBITSCHEK, MÁRCIA

KUBITSCHEK, MÁRCIA (1943–2000). Márcia Kubitschek (*b.* 23 October 1943; *d.* 5 August 2000), Brazilian cultural and political figure. The only natural daughter of President Juscelino Kubitschek (another, Maria Estela, was adopted; he had no sons), she was born in Belo Horizonte, capital of Minas Gerais, while her father was its mayor. With the end of her first marriage, to a Brazilian investment banker, she married the renowned Cuban American ballet dancer, Fernando Bujones, in New York City in 1980. Kubitschek has administered various cultural activities, including the Ballet of Rio de Janeiro, the Ballet of Brazil Foundation, the Brazilian Tourist Authority in New York City, and the Brasília 2000 Olympics Association. A political centrist, she was elected a member of the Brazilian Constituent Assembly of 1987–1988. The assembly reconstituted the country along civilian lines after the military dictatorship of 1964–1985, which had barred her father from campaigning for a second term as president. In the first direct gubernatorial elections held in the Federal District (Brasília), in 1991, she became lieutenant governor of the national capital built just over a generation before by her father. She lost a senatorial bid in 1994 although a record number of five women won seats that year to the Brazilian Senate.

See also **Kubitschek de Oliveira, Juscelino.**

BIBLIOGRAPHY

See *Travel Weekly,* 26 August 1985, for her work at the Brazilian Tourist Authority, and *Veja,* 19 October 1994, for her 1994 senatorial candidacy.

Additional Bibliography

Jardim, Serafim; Luiz Carlos Bernardes, and Orlando Leite. *Juscelino Kubitscheck: onde está a verdade?* Petrópolis: Editora Vozes, 1999.

EDWARD A. RIEDINGER

KUBITSCHEK DE OLIVEIRA, JUSCELINO

KUBITSCHEK DE OLIVEIRA, JUSCELINO (1902–1976). Juscelino Kubitschek de Oliveira (*b.* 12 September 1902; *d.* 22 August 1976), president of Brazil (1956–1961), founder of Brasília (1960). Born in Diamantina, Minas Gerais, an impoverished colonial diamond-mining town, Kubitschek and his older sister were raised on the spare resources of their resolute and independent schoolteacher mother. Their father died when they were very young. A great-uncle had been prominent in early republican (late nineteenth-century) state politics, favoring transfer of the capital from the baroque Ouro Prêto to a new, planned city, Belo Horizonte. Studying grade school with his mother and completing secondary education at a local seminary, Kubitschek entered the medical school of Belo Horizonte in 1922. Supporting himself as a telegraph operator, he became a doctor in 1927.

Income from his first years of medical practice allowed him to pursue specialized study in Europe during most of 1930. He established his own practice in Belo Horizonte the following year. That year he married Sarah Gomes de Lemos, member of a socially and politically prominent family. During an uprising in 1932 by the neighboring state of São Paulo against the federal government, Kubitschek was called to the borderline front as a medical officer. It was at this time that he met and impressed Benedito Valadares, a local politician serving as head of the military police in the region, who became Kubitschek's political mentor.

In 1933 President Getúlio Vargas appointed Valadares interventor, or chief executive, of Minas Gerais. Valadares made Kubitschek his chief of staff. Actively extending the political network of his boss, and building a base for himself in Diamantina, Kubitschek was elected a federal deputy the following year, occupying this position until the Vargas coup of 1937 closed Congress and established the authoritarian Estado Nôvo.

Uneasy about such a regime, he returned to his medical practice and profitably revived it. However, he entered public life again in 1940 when Valadares appointed him mayor of Belo Horizonte. His mayoralty gave singular impetus to the urban infrastructure of the still-developing city, augmenting streets, parks, water, and sewage systems; enhancing real estate; and encouraging commercial and industrial development. The model neighborhood of Pampulha became a signature of his administration with its dramatically modern church, designed by Oscar Niemeyer and bearing murals by Cândido Portinari.

As the strength of the Estado Nôvo withered by 1945 under the victory of democratic forces in World War II, Vargas and his state interventors sought to maintain their political control in the emerging era of political liberty. They organized the Social Democratic Party (PSD) as a powerful opponent to the anti-Vargas forces, which had coalesced in the National Democratic Union (UDN).

Kubitschek became the organizing secretary of the PSD in Minas Gerais, the largest section of the party in the country, extending throughout the state his network of contacts. Removed from the mayoralty of Belo Horizonte with the ouster of Vargas near the end of 1945, Kubitschek was voted in by a substantial margin as a federal deputy that year and began his term in the Constituent Assembly in 1946.

Maneuvering himself within the factions of the PSD of Minas Gerais, Kubitschek ran successfully for the governorship of the state in the election of 1950. He obtained the tacit support of Getúlio Vargas, who won the presidential election the same year through another party he had founded, the trade-union-based Brazilian Labor Party (PTB).

With a campaign slogan of "energy and transportation," Kubitschek began in 1951 an intensive gubernatorial administration dedicated to activating the state's economy through industrialization. He expanded or inaugurated numerous hydroelectric plants; brought the West German steel company, Mannesmann, to the state; enlarged the road network by many hundreds of miles; and built many clinics, schools, and bridges. These projects were financed through federal funds, foreign capital, and mixed public and private enterprises, a pattern he would also apply at the federal level.

Using the success of his administration in Minas Gerais, Kubitschek prepared himself for the presidential succession of 1955. He launched his campaign in the shadow of the August 1954 suicide of Vargas, who had been charged with massive corruption by the military and the UDN. Attempting to acquire the power base of the fallen president, Kubitschek renewed the alliance of the PSD and PTB by selecting as his vice presidential running mate the political heir of Vargas, João Goulart. He thereby also acquired the ire of the anti-Vargas forces. Kubitschek campaigned with an extensive plan for national development, pledging himself to fulfill a series of economic targets that would culminate in the building of a new national capital, Brasília, on the central plateau of the country. He won the October election, however, with

Brazilian president Juscelino Kubitschek (1956–1961) at a press conference inaugurating the new capital of Brasília in 1960. © BETTMANN/CORBIS

only one-third of the votes, the lowest in Brazilian history, since he was relatively unknown in national politics and bore the burden of anti-Vargas sentiment. Only a protective coup the following month allowed Kubitschek and Goulart to take office for their five-year term in January 1956.

Because Kubitschek entered the presidency under such bitter and delicate circumstances, diligent execution of his campaign promise of "fifty years of progress in five" became paramount for solidifying his national support. Campaign targets were achieved as the production of concrete, steel, energy, and other components of industrial expansion dramatically increased. The automobile industry was created, soon making the country almost self-sufficient in such production. The latter years of the Kubitschek government witnessed economic growth at annual rates averaging over 7 percent. In April 1960 he inaugurated the futuristic and controversial new capital, Brasília, with buildings by Niemeyer and an urban design of Lúcio Costa, a bravura feat strikingly affirming national accomplishment.

The cost of such progress, however, was inflation. Kubitschek encouraged extensive foreign investment, and the vast market potential of a growing Brazil attracted it. However, declining income from Brazilian exports created a shortage of capital, pressuring inflation. Kubitschek was cooperative in international relations, suggesting Operation Pan American, a hemisphere-wide approach to Latin American problems, to U.S. president Dwight D. Eisenhower. But in 1959 Kubitschek rejected the International Monetary Fund's (IMF) efforts to make him reduce inflation by cutting his economic expansion program.

As a result, inflation accelerated. This and charges of graft and favoritism, along with the fact that Kubitschek was constitutionally barred from succeeding himself, enabled the candidate of the opposition, Jânio Quadros, to win the 1960 presidential election.

Still popular personally, Kubitschek was elected a senator from Goiás the same year. However, with the establishment in 1964 of a military regime, the political rights of Kubitschek were canceled for ten years, thereby ending his plans to return to the presidency in the election of 1965. He went into intermittent exile in Europe or the United States, supporting an unsuccessful Frente Ampla, a broad front of civilian leaders allied across the political spectrum. After 1967 he remained in Brazil, becoming an investment banking executive. He died in 1976 in an automobile accident on a highway between São Paulo and Rio de Janeiro. His funeral procession in Brasília produced one of the greatest popular outpourings of grief in the history of the city, and the military government was forced to decree three days of official mourning.

Although Kubitschek dominated the Brazilian national scene for a relatively brief period, his memory has proved lasting due to a concentration of exceptional personal, economic, political, and cultural factors. Possessed of great ambition and energy, he was able as an administrator to take advantage of economic opportunities resulting from increased Brazilian exports during World War II and then from the resurgence of international capital in the recovery from that war. He represented a generation of Brazilian elites that legitimized itself through modernization based on industrialization and accommodated itself to trade unionism growing from that development. During his presidency there occurred a rare combination of intensive economic production within a fully functioning democratic government. His administration bore, moreover, a cultural style, expressed in architecture, landscape design, sculpture, and even the rhythms of bossa nova, which projected itself as the embodiment of international modernism, giving Brazilians a sense of confidence and promise.

See also **Brasília; Brazil, Political Parties: Party of Brazilian Social Democracy (PSDB); Estado Novo.**

BIBLIOGRAPHY

Robert J. Alexander, *Juscelino Kubitschek and the Development of Brazil* (1991).

Carlos Heitor Cony, *JK, Memorial do Exílio* (1982).

Francisco De Assis Barbosa, *Juscelino Kubitschek: Uma Revisão na Política Brasileira* (1960).

Abelardo Jurema, *Juscelino & Jango: PSD & PTB* (1979).

Juscelino Kubitschek, *Meu Caminho para Brasília,* 3 vols. (1974–1978), and *Por Que Construí Brasília* (1975).

Francisco Medaglia, *Juscelino Kubitschek, President of Brazil: The Life of a Self-Made Man* (1959).

Osvaldo Orico, *Confissões do Exílio: JK* (1977).

Sílvia Pantoja and Dora Flaksman, "Kubitschek, Juscelino," in *Dicionário Histórico-Biográfico Brasileiro, 1930–1983,* vol. 2 (1984), pp. 1,698–1,717.

Edward Anthony Riedinger, *Como Se Faz um Presidente: A Campanha de J.K.* (1988).

Maria Victória Benevides, *O Governo Kubitschek: Desenvolvimento Econômico e Estabilidade Política, 1956–1961* (1976).

Additional Bibliography

Bojunga, Cláudio. *JK: O artista do impossível.* Rio de Janeiro: Objetiva, 2001.

Cohen, Marleine. *JK: Juscelino Kubitschek: O presidente bossa-nova.* São Paulo: Editora Globo, 2005.

Lafer, Celso. *JK e o programa de metas, 1956–1961: Processo de planejamento e sistema politico no Brasil.* Rio de Janeiro: FGV Editora, 2002.

EDWARD A. RIEDINGER

KUMATE RODRÍGUEZ, JESÚS (1924–).

Mexican health official and medical researcher Jesús Kumate Rodríguez was born November 12, 1924, in Mazatlán, Sinaloa, the son of a small businessman and a school teacher. He graduated from Mexico's Military Medical School in 1946 and in 1963 received a PhD in biochemistry from the National Polytechnic Institute. He also completed advanced studies in the United States. Kumate taught at both the Military Medical School and the National Autonomous University of Mexico (UNAM) for many years, and served as research coordinator of the Children's Hospital, Mexico City, an institution he later directed (1979–1980). A member of the National Academy of Medicine, he received the Carnot Prize for his early research. In 1974 he was invited to become a member of the prestigious National College, and in 1983 the secretary of public health appointed him coordinator of the National Institute of Public Health for the entire country. He became assistant secretary of health in 1985, and in 1988, president Carlos Salinas (1988–1994) selected Kumate as his secretary of health, a position he held until 1994. He is recognized for his work on pediatric medicine, and for policy issues related to children's health generally. Kumate has authored numerous books and articles in his specialty.

See also **Public Health; Salinas de Gortari, Carlos.**

BIBLIOGRAPHY

Kumate, Jesús. *Los niños de México, 1943–2003.* México: El Colegio Nacional, 2004.

RODERIC AI CAMP

KUNA (CUNA). Kuna (Cuna) is the spoken language and common name applied to the Tule peoples of Panama and Colombia. There are four principal groups of the Kuna. The most well-known are those who inhabit the San Blas archipelago off the Caribbean shore of Panama. Other groups include the Kuna Brava, in the center of the Darién jungle; the Bayano Kuna, of the Bayano River region of Panama; and those who live in Colombian villages near the Panamanian border.

The Kuna are descendants of Carib peoples. They are physically short, only slightly taller than pygmies. They have bronze skin and black hair, but also have a high rate of albinism.

The Spanish conquistador Vasco Núñez de Balboa came into contact with the Kuna in the early sixteenth century, but Spanish cruelty under the subsequent rule of Governor Pedrarias Dávila became a highly significant part of Kuna mythology. By the seventeenth century the Kuna, as well as other natives along the eastern coast of Central America, were favoring the English and helping them in their struggles against Spain in this region.

In the nineteenth century the Kuna moved from their mainland villages to the coral islands along Panama's east coast. Of the more than 365 islands of the San Blas archipelago, only about fifty are inhabited, with about a hundred more used for coconut and food production.

Property in Kuna society has traditionally been owned and passed on through the female line. Women are also the ones to choose their mates. The principal wealth in Kuna society is based on coconuts, a business that the women normally own and manage. The Kuna did not intermarry with other peoples and have maintained their own strict standards of morals and conduct. During the building of the Panama Canal, the men were contracted in teams for specific periods of labor, but most returned to their home islands when their contract was up.

After a 1925 skirmish with Panamanian police, the *comarca* (territory) of San Blas became an autonomous region within Panama. Elected Kuna chiefs called *saylas* preside over council meetings. The Kunas own the land, but the Panamanian government has established an office on the island of El Porvenir, where a government official supervises the village chiefs, pays their salaries, and is the connecting link between the San Blas Kuna and the government in Panama City.

In the twentieth century the Kuna became notable for their art forms, whose motifs are very similar to those found on gold and ceramics from the Conte archaeological site in Coclé Province, which date from approximately A.D. 500 to 1100. The Kuna have long worn golden ornaments, but according to legend the atrocities of the Spanish conquistadores caused gold working to become taboo and goldsmiths were prohibited from even landing on the islands. Thereafter, the Kuna purchased gold jewelry from merchants who came to the islands in boats.

The practice of colorful body painting has long been a Kuna trait. In 1680, the buccaneer surgeon Lionel Wafer noted the colors of their body painting as being mostly red, yellow, and blue, depicting "figures of birds, beasts, men and trees or the like." Twenty-first-century Kuna are known for their interpretive needlework, used originally on their *molas,* or blouses. The use of reverse appliqué of Kuna native symbolism, cartoon art, and religious scenes on fine European cottons in solid colors has created an art form sought by major museums and individual collectors. The *molas* developed from the late nineteenth century forward in imitation of traditional body painting, but the styles and techniques of *mola* artisans gradually changed. After World War II the colorful *molas* suddenly burst upon the art scene with unique cartoon images derived from everything from foreign graphic art to domestic political statements, more recently including Christian religious art.

As of the 2000 census, more than 61,000 Kuna lived in Panama. While most continue to live in the San Blas Island region, concentrations of Kuna people can also be found in Panama City, attracted by short-term wage labor opportunities.

See also **Caribs; República de Tule.**

BIBLIOGRAPHY

Clyde E. Keeler, *Cuna Indian Art: The Culture and the Craft of Panama's San Blas Islanders* (1969).

Ann Parker and Avon Neal, *Molas: Folk Art of the Cuna Indians* (1977).

Mary W. Helms, *Ancient Panama: Chiefs in Search of Power* (1979).

James Howe, *The Kuna Gathering: Contemporary Village Politics in Panama* (1986).

Additional Bibliography

Gallup-Diaz, Ignacio. *The Door of the Seas and Key to the Universe: Indian Politics and Imperial Rivalry in the Darién, 1640–1750.* New York: Columbia University Press, 2005.

Howe, James. *A People Who Would Not Kneel: Panama, the United States, and the San Blas Kuna.* Washington, DC: Smithsonian Institution Press, 1998.

Martínez, Atilio, ed. *La migración de los kunas hacia la costa atlántica: Según la historia oral kuna.* Translated by Saila Dummad Iguanabiginia. Panama: Editorial Portobelo, Librería El Campus, 1999.

Tice, Karin E. *Kuna Crafts, Gender, and the Global Economy.* Austin: University of Texas Press, 1995.

Ventocilla, Jorge, Heraclio Herrera, and Valerio Núñez. *Plants and Animals in the Life of the Kuna.* Edited by Hans Roeder. Translated by Elisabeth King. Austin: University of Texas Press, 1995.

SUE DAWN MCGRADY

LABARCA HUBERTSON, AMANDA

(1886–1975). Amanda Labarca Hubertson (*b.* 5 December 1886; *d.* 1975), Chilean educator and feminist. Born in Santiago to Onofre and Sabina Pinto, Labarca studied at the Pedagogic Institute of the University of Chile in Santiago, at Columbia University in New York, and at the Sorbonne in Paris. She married educator and politician Guillermo Labarca Hubertson, a Radical Party activist who was minister of justice and education during the first presidency of Arturo Alessandri. Amanda Labarca taught most of her life and was active in the Radical Party. Her books on women's issues include *A dónde va la mujer?* (Whither Women? 1934) and *Feminismo contemporáneo* (Contemporary Feminism, 1947). Labarca worked in the women's suffrage movement and was president of Mujeres de Chile (Chilean Women). A devoted secondary school teacher, she also served as director of a high school and later taught courses on education at the University of Chile. She wrote important books about education, including *Realidades y problemas de nuestra enseñanza* (Realities and Problems in Chilean Education, 1953), *La esceuela secundaria en los Estados Unidos* (Secondary Schools in the United States, 1919), and *Historia de la enseñanza en Chile* (History of Chilean Education, 1939). Labarca also wrote essays and fiction during her early years, including *La lámpara maravillosa* (1921) and *Impresiones de juventud* (1909). With a handful of Latin American women, Labarca played a prominent role in focusing attention on women's issues and was an active participant in international feminist congresses during the first half of the twentieth century.

See also **Feminism and Feminist Organizations; Philosophy: Feminist.**

BIBLIOGRAPHY

Biblioteca Del Congreso, Chile, *Amanda Labarca: Bibliografía selectiva* (1983).

Roberto Munizaga Aguirre, *Educatores chilenos de ayer y de hoy,* vol. 5 (1983–1992).

Jordi Fuentes et al., *Diccionario histórico de Chile,* 10th ed. (1989).

Additional Bibliography

Boschetto-Sandoval, Sandra M. *The Imaginary in the Writing of Latin American Author Amanda Labarca Hubertson (1886–1975): Supplements to a Feminist Critique.* Lewiston, NY: E. Mellen Press, 2004.

Salas Neumann, Emma S. *Amanda Labarca: Dos dimensiones de la personalidad de una visionaria mujer chilena.* Santiago de Chile: Ediciones Mar del Plata, 1996.

GEORGETTE MAGASSY DORN

LABASTIDA Y DÁVALOS, PELAGIO ANTONIO DE

(1816–1891). Pelagio Antonio de Labastida y Dávalos (*b.* 1816; *d.* 1891), bishop of Puebla, archbishop of Mexico, opponent of the Reform. Born in Zamora, Michoacán, Labastida was ordained in 1839. He became rector of the seminary in Morelia and governor of the diocese in the early 1850s, and was bishop of Puebla from 1855 to 1863. Labastida protested against President

Ignacio Comonfort's 31 March 1856 decree punishing the Puebla clergy for the rebellion of Zacapoaxtla, which he had not supported, and the loss of the city to the Conservatives. Banished from Mexico, he went to Rome and became a strong opponent of liberalism and the Reform movement. Labastida returned with the French Intervention, and on 21 June 1863 General Élie-Frédéric Forey appointed him to the three-man executive power. On 17 November Marshal François Bazaine removed him as an obstacle to French efforts to find a compromise with moderate Liberals. Labastida opposed Maximilian's ecclesiastical policy, which sought to conciliate Liberal opinion by upholding the disamortization (the transfer of corporate properties to private ownership) policies of the period 1856–1863. Exiled in 1867 by Juárez, he attended the First Vatican Council (1869–1870) in Rome. He was allowed to return to Mexico in 1871 and died in Oacalco, Morelos.

See also **Religion in Mexico, Catholoic Church and Beyond.**

BIBLIOGRAPHY

Jan Bazant, *Alienation of Church Wealth in Mexico: Social and Economic Aspects of the Liberal Revolution, 1856–1875*, translated and edited by Michael P. Costeloe (1971).

Michael P. Costeloe, *Church and State in Independent Mexico: A Study of the Patronage Debate, 1821–1857* (1978).

Additional Bibliography

Peloso, Vincent C., and Barbara A. Tenenbaum, eds. *Liberals, Politics, and Power: State Formation in Nineteenth-Century Latin America*. Athens, GA: University of Georgia Press, 1996.

Villalpando César, José Manuel. *Maximiliano*. México: Clío, 1999.

BRIAN HAMNETT

LABOR MOVEMENTS. The history of organized labor in Latin America is rich and varied. From the mid-nineteenth century to the present, workers have sought to further their collective interest by forming unions, by taking direct action, by supporting friendly candidates, and by forming their own political groupings. These efforts have met with uneven success, although at times workers have wrested concessions from their employers and played an important role in shaping national history. Overall, labor's trajectory can be divided into roughly three somewhat overlapping periods. During the first period, spanning roughly 1850 to 1870 until the 1930s, workers' organizations emerged. Workers organized their first significant collective actions and, for the most part, took a marked oppositional and apolitical stance toward the state and toward both the dominant agrarian and the emerging industrial elites. During the second period, covering the 1920s through the decades after World War II, labor became increasingly incorporated into the political and economic equation, and political parties formed that catered to organized labor and workers but often sought to control both, albeit not always successfully. Finally, the 1960s to the present make up a third period, when the traditional labor movement lost much of its power owing to military takeovers and the imposition of neoliberal economic policies.

THE EMERGENCE OF WORKERS' ORGANIZATIONS

Sometime after 1850, urban workers emerged as a group demanding notice in most Latin American societies, although the population remained predominantly rural. This phenomenon coincided with Latin America's entrance into the world economy as an exporter of primary products and importer of manufactured goods, which resulted in a growth of local industry and of urban areas. Rail, port, and mine workers were among the first to organize, although artisans preceded them in many cases. Transport, dock, and mine workers could strike serious blows at local economies by blocking exports and imports. Although such action in the export sector drew immediate hostile attention from the state, workers sometimes managed considerable gains through concerted action.

In the rapidly growing cities there was a large body of artisans who, under pressure from the increasing subordination of labor to the modern large factory, often banded together. With some exceptions, such as the Brazilian textile industries, most enterprises remained small (less than five people), as did the percentage of factory workers within the total numbers of salaried individuals. A modern industrial proletariat really formed only after 1930. Textile factories usually represented the largest enterprises, but flour mills and meatpacking plants in Argentina also employed several hundred people, as did mining companies in Mexico and Chile.

Construction, which was at best part-time or seasonal work, also provided considerable employment.

Obstacles. Many factors, however, hindered organizing. In most countries, a substantial jobless pool existed. In Buenos Aires 10,000 men might appear for the morning shape-up at the docks. São Paulo imported immigrants for the coffee plantations, and the Argentine government recruited in Europe. Competition kept wages close to survival level and jobs at a premium, but skilled workers fared much better. Many immigrants, particularly in the period 1880 to 1910 in the more dynamic Southern Cone economies, for example, thought that they could advance from worker to owner to entrepreneur. Just enough did so to keep the hope alive, but opportunities closed off as industry demanded more capital and technology after 1900. Local bourgeoisies proved intransigent toward workers' demands and organization. These attitudes stemmed from the competitiveness of relatively small industrial establishments and from the fact that owing to lack of mechanization, the wage bill represented a hefty percentage of costs. Ideological and institutional coercion had not yet fully developed, and so repression often proved to be the standard response of owners and the state to workers' movements. Agrarian elites, who were not always directly concerned with urban affairs, agreed that repression was the best answer to agitation.

Foreign ownership of most major export industries (railroads in Argentina, mines in Chile and Mexico, as well as important textile plants in Mexico and Peru, for example) served as a rallying point for workers, particularly native ones. Although workers in foreign enterprises occasionally won a sympathetic hearing from local governments, in most cases the state defended foreign capital as fiercely as local capital. In Brazil, where planters became involved in industrial and commercial activities after the 1890s, a state policy of repression emerged, though its ferocity varied from area to area. Elsewhere, when workers did not directly threaten the export sector, they sometimes could avoid immediate state action. Nevertheless, there were many instances of heavy repression in the period up to 1930, including massacres after strikes in Veracruz at the Orizaba and Río Blanco textile mills (1906 and 1907, respectively) and in the mining areas around Iquique, Chile (1907). Numerous workers and their families lost their lives in these encounters, perhaps more than a thousand in the latter incident.

Other factors pressured workers and their organizations. Governments protected strikebreakers, banned and forcefully dispersed meetings, closed union halls, shut down working-class newspapers, and used agents provocateurs. On the pretext that foreigners lay behind growing labor unrest, Argentina, Brazil, Chile, Cuba, and Uruguay all passed laws allowing for expulsion of foreign-born persons, who formed a significant part of working-class leadership, for disturbing the social peace. Many of the first labor laws, which appeared before 1920, were designed to control rather than protect workers, but some also arose from Catholic social action, which advocated Sunday rest and protection for women and children. Exceptionally, in Uruguay, President José Batlle y Ordóñez (1903–1907, 1911–1915) passed comprehensive social legislation, including social services and protective measures, as part of his larger program that courted popular support to counter the viselike grip of the old agrarian oligarchy.

In countries with the most advanced economies, immigrants, mostly Italians and Spaniards (Portuguese in Brazil), formed the bulk of the urban working class. In Argentina, Uruguay, and southern Brazil, for example, this foreign influence had numerous consequences. Some immigrants brought previous labor-movement experience, though most newcomers possessed little political consciousness. Many immigrants wanted only to make money and return home, and so steered clear of potentially troublesome activities. A refusal by many to become citizens hurt strategies that depended upon working-class votes. Ethnic diversity led to rivalries between foreigners and between foreigners and nationals. Those born abroad became subject to nationalistic campaigns and right-wing jingoism, typified by paramilitary right-wing organizations such as the Argentine Liga Patriótica, which emerged after 1910.

Accomplishments. Workers achieved much before 1930. Living and working conditions helped mobilize people. Workers lived in abysmal circumstances, even compared with salaried or middle-sector employees. Lack of social services and extensive slums were prevalent, and led to alarming public-health problems, but large numbers of workers crowded together helped to build a certain sense of solidarity at home as well as at work. Working-class districts such as La Boca in Buenos Aires and Brás in São Paulo grew into militant centers of activity. Workers in mining camps, mill towns, and plantations developed a similar affinity, often leading to organization. Everywhere, job conditions remained difficult. Owners imposed draconian work rules and applied them arbitrarily. Work hours totaled as much as twelve to sixteen hours a day, six days a week. Few safety measures existed, and occupational diseases represented a serious threat in many industries. Employers fired workers almost at will, particularly if they resisted industrial discipline. Most workers had unstable work histories. The average worker had little or no control over his or her own fate in the labor market, but gravitated both geographically and sectorally to where jobs existed or were rumored to exist. Many workers set up their own small enterprises, failed, then returned to the status of employee. A fortunate few, however, succeeded, giving rise to the proverbial immigrant success story.

ANARCHOSYNDICALISM

Anarchists or utopian socialists controlled the first attempts at organization. Gradually, anarchosyndicalism emerged as the dominant tendency among activists. All shades of anarchists believed in confronting the state and not participating in traditional politics. Later, there emerged a syndicalist current that assigned primacy to unions but concentrated upon immediate economic gains. Strongest in Argentina and Brazil, syndicalists negotiated with governments when necessary. A reformist socialism, akin to that of Europe, also attracted some workers, particularly in the Southern Cone. Because it was dedicated to electoral politics, however, the fact that immigrants could not vote weakened its appeal. Catholic-leaning organizations and independent unions that took no set positions also arose. Most workers, even those who were unionized, probably held no set ideological positions, but acted on the basic desire to improve their living and working conditions however possible. Workers often bargained collectively and sometimes won partial or full victories. Strikes, however, proved to be the most common and effective form of direct action. Mostly these occurred in one or more shops, but sometimes they affected a whole industry and occasionally turned into generalized movements that briefly closed major cities, such as Buenos Aires and Montevideo in the early 1900s and São Paulo in the following decade. Workers also used slowdowns, boycotts, and other tactics to gain their ends.

GROWTH OF THE MOVEMENT

Until 1920, the strongest labor movements had emerged in Argentina, Chile, Brazil, and Mexico. Unions, however, existed in almost every country except for primarily agrarian nations, where only a few artisans organized. In Argentina, Chile, and Brazil significant federations formed, grouping important numbers of unions and workers. The largest of them, the Argentine syndicalist Federación Obrera Regional Argentina (FORA), claimed 20 to 25 percent of Buenos Aires's workforce by 1918. Despite divisions, particularly between anarchists and syndicalists, the Argentine movement remained numerically the strongest. In Chile miners led the way, along with workers in the larger cities. The militant Partido Obrero Socialista (POS) arose in 1912 and elected its leader, Luis Emilio Recabarren (1876–1924), to Congress, though the elites refused to seat him. In Brazil a national confederation, the Confederação Operária Brasileira (COB), emerged in 1908, hewing to an anarchosyndicalist line, and several general strikes shook both Rio de Janeiro and São Paulo in the following years. In Mexico at least 250 strikes took place during the regime of Porfirio Díaz (1876–1911). Also, in some cases, Díaz sided with locals against foreign companies to gain political points. Widespread state repression doomed most of the strikes, but they put social issues squarely on the agenda and undermined Díaz.

Labor and the State. The Mexican Revolution (1910) ushered in a new relationship between labor and the state. Segments of the labor movement, located predominantly in Mexico City, signed a pact in 1915 with the upper-middle-class faction led by Venustiano Carranza (1859–1920) and Álvaro Obregón (1880–1928) under which, in return for support, they could organize freely. But tensions soon arose, and a general strike in Mexico City against unfavorable government policies led to repression that weakened the radical wing of the labor movement and strengthened more collaborationist elements. The Constitution of 1917 incorporated a whole section of labor clauses, but these progressive measures remained largely a dead letter until the 1930s or later owing to a lack of government enforcement. But the document presaged a time when social and labor questions would increasingly become a part of the state's purview throughout Latin America.

After 1917 a close relationship developed between the ruling cliques and labor leaders, such as Luis Morones, who controlled the Confederación Regional Obrera Mexicana (CROM), Mexico's leading labor confederation, which existed with government approval. CROM organized workers and kept more radical elements within the labor movement under check, often aided by state violence. CROM's greatest influence was evident during the 1920s, when its connections allowed it to offer members material benefits. The government often pressured CROM's rivals. This pattern of state-labor collaboration, where power lies with the state, has marked Mexican labor relations ever since. Even today, the relationship between the ruling Institutional Revolutionary Party (PRI) and the largest labor confederation, the Mexican Confederation of Workers (CTM), continues. The government and the CTM sign annual social pacts that limit wage increases. Although these matched or even outran the pace of inflation during the expansionary 1950s and 1960s, from about 1985 to 1995 workers steadily lost ground. By some estimates, real salaries plummeted as much as 60 percent during that period.

WORLD WAR I AND THE 1920S: NEW TRENDS
World War I brought substantial economic dislocations that resulted in mass layoffs and rapid inflation throughout Latin America. This situation was reflected in a burst of labor unrest from 1917 to 1920, which included major general strikes and increased organization, often in trades previously nonunionized. Working-class actions in countries such as Colombia, Cuba, Peru, and Uruguay reached new heights. Labor gained a stronger bargaining position owing to the cutoff of imports and to more demand for skilled labor, which helped some workers attain their goals. Most workers generally achieved limited gains, and many experienced defeats. But the unrest prompted politicians and employers to rethink the question of labor relations.

In the 1920s there were several new trends. A postwar depression halted the upsurge in labor activity. The state and ruling groups strengthened the repressive apparatus and rethought strategies to dampen workers' rebellion and protest. Although comprehensive legal controls emerged only after 1930, their roots lie in this period. Governments sought to coopt labor or at least to neutralize it. Mexico and Uruguay led the way, but the same phenomenon appeared in Argentina and Chile, not coincidentally countries where the labor movement proved to be strongest. Some governments promulgated labor codes that regulated work relations and the ways in which workers could organize. States tried to see that these codes effectively governed relations between labor and capital, but they did not always succeed. Increased social legislation represented an attempt to domesticate labor; with better conditions and wages there would be more contented workers, higher productivity, and thus more profits.

Three other developments shaped the 1920s. First, the failure of confrontational strategies eclipsed anarchism and anarchosyndicalism. Second, workers more often sought to bargain with the state and employers and to resort to direct action only in extreme instances. Third, newly formed Communist parties tried to organize a labor movement with long-term revolutionary objectives, and at the same time pursued electoral ends. The rise of Communist parties that won solid working-class constituencies created new splits within the labor movement, and also frightened both agrarian and industrial elites. Communism was yet another divisive ideology—though Communists at times collaborated with others to oppose foreign capital and the capitalist system—and it provided another reason for official repression of any workers' protest that foreign agitators manipulated a well-intentioned local labor force. But the rise of Communism also opened the way for a more systematic analysis of imperialism, which appealed to workers exploited by foreign capital, and even sometimes to local industrialists.

Rural labor was generally unorganized before the 1930s, but the Mexican Revolution had stirred up considerable peasant agitation and the beginnings of organization. Agrarian tenants' movements also arose. In Argentina, for example, they sometimes connected with urban labor. Strictly rural unions remained scarce, but peons often protested forcefully against working conditions. Nonurban workers, other than those outside agribusiness, seldom joined organizations, let alone led collective action. Still, the massive peasant uprising in El Salvador in 1932 and its brutal repression, in which perhaps 30,000 persons perished; strikes on banana plantations in Central America and Colombia in the late 1920s and early 1930s; and the vast uprisings by estate workers across the Caribbean (1931–1938) show that rural workers were not totally passive.

CULTURAL POLITICS

As workers became more organized, politicians, elites, and the Catholic Church all expressed concern over the culture, values, and morals of laborers. Managers in collaboration with public officials often instituted programs to help inculcate "proper behavior." For instance, the Chilean government and mine owners in the first half of the twentieth century felt that workers were violent and drank to excess, creating public disorder and wrecking business efficiency. Believing that families reduced these problems, the El Teniente copper mine in Chile paid wage bonuses to married men. Furthermore, El Teniente offered classes on family, values, and middle-class consumption for women and men in order to maintain a more stable workforce. Often, workers accepted the ideas taught in these programs, but that did not make them a compliant workforce; instead, Chilean miners through organization and strikes sought greater benefits and better working conditions and pay to achieve the middle-class lifestyle.

The question of morals became especially acute as women entered the workplace. In Medellín, Colombia, women in the first decades of the century began working in the textile industry. City officials and religious leaders became concerned that independent women in the workplace would weaken ethics, increase sexual promiscuity, and eventually destroy the family structure of the whole country. Conservatives generally expected women to be mothers and to take care of their homes. To assuage these concerns, a paternalistic capitalism developed to maintain working women's "morality." Factories did not hire married women, and on the shop floor, nuns in Medellín monitored women's behavior, preventing gossip about sex. During the 1920s and 1930s female employees lived in supervised dormitories. Factory owners considered sex outside of marriage a dismissible offense. Studies of gender and labor in other Latin American countries have similarly shown that workplace issues went far beyond questions of pay and living conditions, reflecting the critical cultural conflicts of the time.

Scholars also have researched how issues of race shaped worker organization, beliefs, and action. During the mid-twentieth century in Peru, white-collar employees (e.g., bank tellers, retail salespersons, office workers) often defined themselves as white in order to elevate the status of their work. This racial self-identification helped these nonindustrial workers differentiate themselves from mestizos. In Brazil, Afro-Brazilian port workers, when forming an alliance with the state, accused employers and managers of racism. This rhetoric helped Afro-Brazilians establish legitimacy because the federal government wanted to craft a strong national identity based on unity, rather than the country's history of slavery. Latin American workers did not follow general rules regarding race, but racial questions influenced the politics of the workplace.

Industrialization. The Great Depression and World War II accelerated industrialization. The working class expanded markedly and, as immigration slowed, the class became more national. Political parties and politicians courted labor support more seriously after 1930, and particularly after 1945, in response to labor's new strength and in hopes of gaining an ally against their enemies. Mechanisms of control over labor also expanded in terms of labor-relations systems and corporatist controls. Global depression after 1930 generated more worker agitation against deteriorating conditions. Some organizations became more collaborationist and others more militant, with mixed results in terms of permanent gains for workers. Repression, however, remained a major response to workers' unrest. Nonetheless, the years 1930 to 1950 ushered in an era during which organized labor slowly emerged as a new force in society.

The Emerging Movement. The democratic movements that grew across Latin America in the immediate postwar years often included a labor component. After years of containing their frustration during economic depressions and wars, workers sought to recover lost ground, with varied results. The war had been fought in the name of democracy, and workers demanded the fruits of the system. Politicians or political movements often coopted these efforts, giving limited economic benefits or more room to organize in return for state support of labor and workers' votes at election time. Peronism is a classic case. In Argentina, General Juan Domingo Perón emerged as leader of a military junta (1943–1946), and labor rallied to his support, attracted by incentives he had granted as secretary of labor and social welfare. Workers formed the backbone of Perón's electoral bids, and their votes carried him to victory in 1946 and 1952. The Peronist-dominated trade union center Confederación General de Trabajo (CGT), however, remained largely under the control of a bureaucracy pledged to Perón. Workers (even rural ones), at least until 1950, received real gains in terms of social and labor legislation and income. Perhaps most important, they gained a sense of dignity and of their collective power. After 1950, when the economy turned down, workers took the brunt of cuts that eroded support for the increasingly dictatorial Perón. Despite this loss, however, the Peronist Party still received the support of a substantial majority of Argentine workers, even after Perón's ouster in 1955; labor did not forget the gains won under him.

In Mexico strikes by white-collar unions and electrical and rail workers in the 1950s and early 1960s led to repression and more state control over the CTM and other labor organizations. There was also significant postwar labor activity in Brazil. From 1945 to 1947 a labor upsurge sparked by Getúlio Dornelles Vargas's Partido Trabalhista Brasileiro (PTB) and the Partido Comunista Brasileiro (PCB) was condemned by upper- and middle-class politicians, who outlawed the PCB and prohibited its elected candidates from office. Nevertheless, Vargas, running as a populist with an appeal to labor, won the Brazilian presidental election in 1950. But labor autonomy remained limited, and docile leaders headed most major unions, although independent elements continued to operate. Vargas's death in 1954 failed to sever labor's links to populist politicians, but the next regimes were markedly less favorable toward workers and unions. Like Perón in Argentina, Vargas, despite his control over the state, could not simply manipulate labor at will. Even with imbalances in power, a degree of negotiation always existed between the two sides.

In Bolivia, the revolution in 1952 depended heavily upon the support of militant miners' unions hewing to leftist doctrines. The Confederación Obrera Boliviana (COB) demanded and received cogovernment of the mines, and the minister of mines came from labor's ranks. Although the ruling party, Movimiento Nacional Revolucionario (MNR), moved steadily rightward, and miners lost their power owing to both economic and political factors, their unions continued to exercise influence at the national level until the tin industry's collapse in the 1980s. In fact, COB became the main vehicle for labor and leftist politics, both in opposition and in government, as during the brief regime of Juan José Torres (1970–1971), when the Asamblea Popular (Popular Assembly) functioned in place of traditional parliamentary bodies.

Institutionalization. The decades after 1950 brought accelerated industrial growth and urbanization. The working class rapidly increased in numbers and became a more important actor at the political level. This situation, in turn, reflected a process of institutionalization designed to contain industrial conflict and mobilize support for elite-led political parties and governments. Organized workers often received or won economic benefits as well as favorable social legislation in return for their support. Real wages for workers in more dynamic industrial sectors probably tended upward, though patterns varied country by country. In Mexico, for example, the ruling PRI tightly controlled organized labor. It accomplished this end through a policy of divide and rule (more than a thousand unions existed by the 1960s), keeping white-collar and peasant unions separate from blue-collar ones; a forceful imposition of corrupt leadership; repression of independent actions; and the granting of real wage gains. Labor also became a battleground between contending political parties and competing ideologies. Occasionally, one party captured the bulk of labor support, as in the cases of Peronism in Argentina and Acción Democrática (AD) in Venezuela. But in Colombia, Catholics and Communists vied for workers' allegiance. In Peru the Peruvian Aprista Party (PAP/APRA) and the Communists did the same. In Chile Socialists, Communists, Radicals, and Christian Democrats all controlled labor blocs in the 1960s.

In Cuba labor was divided between the centrist Auténticos, aided by government intervention from 1944 to 1952, and the Communists, hurt by repression during that same period. After 1952 the Twenty-sixth of July labor movement and Communist-influenced unions, both of which played a role in the struggle against Fulgencio Batista, formed the unified Confederación de Trabajadores de Cuba (CTC). Unions continued to represent workers' interests, but within the bounds of the Revolution, and with often mixed results.

In Chile, organized labor had an important opportunity to see many of its goals realized. Workers solidly backed the Popular Unity ticket, which elected a Socialist, Salvador Allende, to the presidency in 1970. His early policies benefited the working class in material and organizational terms, but when his nationalization measures slowed, militant workers forced his hand by seizing factories. Eventually, they formed worker-run zones (*cordones industriales*), but the reactionary military coup in 1973 found labor almost totally unprepared to defend the regime in any significant manner.

During the 1960s and 1970s there was also marked growth of rural unions in several countries. Agricultural workers' and peasants' unions, for example, became an important segment of the labor movement in Brazil, Bolivia, Chile, Peru, and Central America. Sometimes national federations emerged, as in Chile, Brazil, and Peru. In Mexico an official confederation existed. Despite this phenomenon, however, the vast majority of Latin American rural workers remained unorganized.

LABOR AND THE MILITARY

By the 1960s, before the military takeovers that swept across Latin America, the ranks of organized workers had risen markedly in almost every country, from some 4.5 million in 1945 to 6 to 7 million in 1960 to 1970. The greatest militancy in the labor movement had shifted from transport or dock workers to those in the modernized sectors, such as the metal trades, but not mining and oil. Public-sector unions also grew as government bureaucracy expanded. Labor in most countries had become firmly allied with or tied to specific political parties such as AD in Venezuela, APRA in Peru, Peronism in Argentina, and the PRI in Mexico. These ties created tensions between political platforms and workers' demands. The question became, to what degree should workers bow to the agenda set by non–working- class politicians and abandon labor autonomy? Labor had become a significant actor not only because it influenced or controlled votes, but also because it could threaten to disturb political stability, and that could bring down governments.

The military takeovers from 1964 through the early 1980s brought reactionary forces to power. The military deemed labor organizations subversive and acted to curb their power, usually by force, as in Argentina, Chile, and Brazil. In Brazil, during 1967 not a single major strike took place, but in Argentina, the military governments after 1966 failed to crush the Peronist resistance in the unions, leading to Perón's ill-fated return in 1974. A second round of military dictatorship ending in 1983 fared no better. Everywhere, however, military rule weakened labor by arresting, torturing, and exiling leaders and middle-level organizers.

NEW PATTERNS

The 1970s and 1980s brought other new patterns. First, neoliberal economic policies in conjunction with built-in structural imbalances resulted in a marked shrinkage of the industrial sector. Privatization also reduced the number of blue- and white-collar jobs in the state sector. This situation weakened once strong industrial and public sector unions and labor's traditional bargaining power. The International Monetary Fund mandated austerity programs in a dozen countries, drastically lowering working-class living standards. Despite general strikes against such programs in Argentina, Brazil, Bolivia, Colombia, the Dominican Republic, Ecuador, Peru, and elsewhere, almost nowhere did labor and its allies ultimately succeed in changing economic policies, though occasionally it did postpone or ameliorate them. Second, explosive informal sector growth changed the composition of the working class. Informal sectors proved notoriously difficult to organize because they had no locus of work. Many people opposed collective action, considering themselves to be individual entrepreneurs. Even in cases where unions emerged within the sector, such as that of street vendors in La Paz, they proved fragile and transient. Third, in countries where the military ruled over a long period, years of clandestine or severely limited activity for labor and for progressive political parties served to weaken the traditional links between the two. As a result, labor emerged into the period of redemocratization perhaps less powerful but more independent, opening the possibility that it could forge a more truly autonomous path.

A TURNING POINT

At the start of the 1990s labor appeared to be at a crossroads. Traditionally strong sectors had weakened numerically. In Peru, for example, where a once vibrant labor movement had played a major role in forcing the military out of power in 1980, by 1991 it looked powerless against the strong antilabor policies of the government of Alberto Fujimori. In Argentina a "Peronist" president pursued antilabor measures, and in Mexico the long-term collaboration between the PRI and the CTM seemed to be on the verge of collapse, with labor receiving fewer benefits. But in Brazil, as a result of the massive strikes led by metallurgical workers in the state of São Paulo in the 1970s, a new labor party had formed. Hewing to a social-democratic position, the Partido dos Trabalhadores (PT) soon turned to national politics. Its candidate, the charismatic Luís Inácio Lula da Silva ("Lula"), ran a strong second in the presidential elections of 1990 and 1994, and the PT even captured the city of São Paulo in the first campaign. Lula eventually won the presidency in 2002 and was reelected in 2006. Some on the Left have accused Lula of not enacting significant change, but he still remains widely popular with the poor and working classes.

By the mid-1990s the immediate prospects for Latin American labor seemed far from rosy. Widespread and continuing neoliberal programs undercut unions, and often class solidarity, through massive layoffs and drastic cuts in the public sector. Increased competition in newly formed free-trade areas (such as NAFTA and Mercosur) led companies to downsize and, at least in the latter area, resulted in massive flows of labor from low- to high-wage areas. This trend eroded pay scales in high-wage jobs. After thirteen years, NAFTA in 2007 produced a mixed record for Mexican labor. In northern Mexico, where foreign companies set up factories called *maquiladoras*, new employment opportunities both increased and offered limited opportunities for upward mobility. Established in the early 1970s, these manufacturing facilities have hired mostly women workers, and prohibited union organizing. The prospect of jobs at one of these plants continues to draw migrants, but nongovernmental organizations have found human-rights violations, poor working conditions, and weak labor rights enforcement in this industrial sector. In contrast to the north, southern Mexico continues to be a major source of immigration to the United States because it has seen little development since the mid-1990s. Informal labor (without security) continues to grow rapidly in Mexico with free trade. Nonunionized labor has also increased in Mexico: Wal-Mart is the country's largest employer. Although it affords few labor rights, a Wal-Mart job brings stability and a better salary than the typical informal-market job.

The rest of Latin America, likewise, presents a conflicting picture of neoliberalism. With globalization, generally there has been increased job insecurity and weaker social safety nets. Yet, greater trade has created new jobs and been a source of economic growth. The regional trading pact Mercosur in South America established new nearby markets so that Latin American countries do not have to rely primarily on Europe and North America consumption. Also, with global trade, Latin American countries have found new markets and investors in Asia. By 2007 Latin American countries saw a small but noticeable increase in the middle class, including white- and blue-collar workers. Still, these gains remain precarious. This contradictory data regarding neoliberal policies ultimately does not justify the idealistic predictions of pro-trade economists, nor does it completely validate the critics' negative images of worker despair and exploitation.

Globalization also has increased labor migration. In Argentina and Chile, Bolivian migrants have formed a new underclass with few legal protections. Many Latin American workers have migrated to the United States, both legally and illegally. Undocumented workers receive below-average pay and are subject to substandard working conditions with little recourse. Usually they have been ignored by Mexican politicians, but Vicente Fox (2000–2006), the first opposition candidate to win the presidency in seventy years, became a vocal advocate of Mexican migrants and migrant-labor rights in the United States. U.S. unions, also once antagonistic to foreign labor, have increasingly supported immigration reform, hoping to unionize foreign labor. Although efforts to work out legislation to legalize millions of undocumented Hispanic workers have gained public support in the United States, in 2007 Congress had not gathered sufficient votes to pass such reform. Whether a deal passes or not, Spanish American labor migration has transformed many U.S. cities, with Spanish now a prominent language in much of the country, and a cash-paying population that helps the local economy.

In the 1990s politicians discovered that controlling rampant inflation, which includes holding down wages and benefits, wins more votes than pro-labor platforms. As in the case of the Peronist Party in Argentina and the ruling center-left coalition in Chile, even traditionally labor-friendly parties have distanced themselves from unions. Almost everywhere, labor finds itself on the defensive. Only in Brazil, where the PT remains a significant force, and in Uruguay, where many unions are allied with the Frente Amplio (a progressive electoral coalition that won over 30 percent of the vote in the 1994 elections), do things look more hopeful. By the twenty-first century, neoliberalism's downsides had provoked popular resistance and helped leftist candidates return to office. With the general weakness of organized labor, new, diverse, and less cohesive coalitions protested economic dislocation and demanded new policies. After the Argentine government devalued its currency and defaulted on its public debt in 2001, a mix of unemployed middle-class workers, small-scale entrepreneurs, and unorganized workers engaged in large protests that brought down the government. Néstor Kirchner became Argentina's president in 2003 by promising greater social services for the unemployed and increased equality. Rural labor maintains a critical political role. The Movimiento Sem Tierra (MST) has expropriated and redistributed large agricultural estates throughout Brazil and pressed Lula da Silva for land and housing.

The rise of this new Left has not meant unequivocal support for unionized employees. Venezuela's president Hugo Chávez won on a leftist platform, promising to usher in a new era of socialism, and the poor and nonunion laborers have clearly benefited from Chávez's redistributive policies. But the well-off, conservative oil workers' union generally opposed Chávez and his platform, and when the petroleum unions went on strike in 2003, Chávez eventually put down their protest. Neither has the Left dominated the political scene. The leftist candidate in Mexico lost the 2006 elections by a small margin. Even leftist presidents such as Michelle Bachelet in Chile maintained promarket policies, albeit with a greater emphasis on the humane treatment of labor.

Despite more sympathetic governments, workers must formulate new strategies to meet the challenges of the early twenty-first century and beyond. As prime victims of the restructuring of local and global capital, they must broaden the appeal of their movements to include new groups, such as those in the informal sector, women, Afro-Latin Americans, and even the unemployed. Furthermore, as capital internationalizes, labor organizations must do the same. Indeed, some dialogue between workers inside the free-trade areas has already taken place, with the idea of increasing cooperation between national movements.

See also **Organizations (under individual countries).**

BIBLIOGRAPHY

Bergquist, Charles. *Labor in Latin America: Comparative Essays on Chile, Argentina, Venezuela, and Colombia.* Stanford, CA: Stanford University Press, 1986.

Farnsworth-Alvear, Ann. *Dulcinea in the Factory: Myths, Morals, Men, and Women in Colombia's Industrial Experiment, 1905–1960.* Durham, NC: Duke University Press, 2000.

French, John, ed. *Latin American Labor Studies Bibliography.* Vols. 1–4. Miami: Florida International University, 1989–1993.

Garza Toledo, Enrique de la. *Sindicatos y nuevos movimientos sociales en América Latina.* Buenos Aires: Consejo Latinoamericano de Ciencias Sociales, 2005.

González Casanova, Pablo, ed. *Historia del movimiento obrero en América Latina.* 4 vols. Mexico City: Siglo Veintiuno Editores, 1984–1985.

Hall, Michael, and Hobart Spalding. "The Urban Working Class and Early Latin American Labour Movements, 1880–1930." In *The Cambridge History of Latin America,* vol. 4, edited by Leslie Bethell. Cambridge, U.K.: Cambridge University Press, 1986.

Klubock, Thomas Miller. *Contested Communities: Class, Gender, and Politics in Chile's El Teniente Copper Mine, 1904–1951.* Durham, NC: Duke University Press, 1998.

Murillo, Maria Victoria. *Labor Unions, Partisan Coalitions, and Market Reforms in Latin America.* Cambridge, U.K.: Cambridge University Press, 2001.

Parker, David S. *The Idea of the Middle Class: White-Collar Workers and Peruvian Society, 1900–1950.* University Park: Pennsylvania State University Press, 1998.

Roxborough, Ian. "Labor Since 1930." In *The Cambridge History of Latin America*, Vol. 6, Part 1. Cambridge: Cambridge University Press, 1995.

Spalding, Hobart A. *Organized Labor in Latin America: Historical Case Studies of Workers in Dependent Societies.* New York: New York University Press, 1977.

HOBART A. SPALDING
BYRON CRITES

LABRADOR RUÍZ, ENRIQUE (1902–1991). Enrique Labrador Ruíz (*b.* 11 May 1902; *d.* 1991), Cuban novelist, journalist, and short-story writer. Labrador Ruíz was born in Sagua la Grande in the province of Las Villas. Self-taught, he started out as a journalist for the newspaper *El Sol* in the city of Cienfuegos and eventually became one of its editors. When the paper moved to

Havana, he, too, moved and once there, began to write for other newspapers and magazines. In 1946 he received the National Short Story Prize for "El conejito Ulán." In 1950 he was awarded the National Prize for his novel *La sangre hambrienta,* and in 1951 he received the Juan Gualberto Gómez prize for journalism. His work appeared in publications all over the Americas, including *Orígenes* (Cuba), *The American News* (United States), and *Babel* (Chile).

After the Cuban Revolution of 1959, Labrador Ruíz became editor of the National Publishing House. Although he was initially supportive of the Cuban government, he eventually broke with it and emigrated to Miami, where he died in 1991. His work is considered to be a precursor of the modern Latin American novel.

Among Labrador Ruíz's most important works are the novels *El laberinto de sí mismo* (1933, repr. 1983), *Cresival* (1936), *Carne de quimera: Novelines neblinosos* (1947, repr. 1983), and *La sangre hambrienta* (1950), and the short stories *El gallo en el espejo* (1953) and *Cuentos* (1970).

See also **Cuba, Revolutions: Cuban Revolution; Literature: Latin America.**

BIBLIOGRAPHY

Rita Molinero, *La narrativa de Enrique Labrador Ruíz* (1977) and *Homenaje a Enrique Labrador Ruíz* (1981).

Additional Bibliography

Garrandés, Alberto. *Aire de Luz: Cuentos cubanos del siglo XX.* La Habana: Editorial Letras Cubanas, 1999.

ROBERTO VALERO

LA BREA Y PARIÑAS. La Brea y Pariñas, since colonial times a tar-producing estate in the province of Talara in northern Peru, which was later developed into the Negritos oil field, a source of dispute between several Peruvian governments and foreign oil companies until its expropriation by the military government in 1968. Through dubious legal means, Genaro Helguero bought the Hacienda La Brea y Pariñas and then obtained tax exemptions and property rights over surface and subsoil. In 1888 he sold the property to Herbert Tweddle, who organized the London and Pacific Petroleum Company under British law. In 1913, Standard Oil of New Jersey bought control of the British firm and under Canadian law merged it into the International Petroleum Company. This company exported Peruvian oil at huge profits made possible by advantageous tax deals with the Peruvian government (paying only 6 percent tax on its profits since 1916). The other local and foreign companies that controlled two other important oil fields in northern Peru, Lobitos and Zorritos, paid a higher tax rate. The legal dispute over Negritos was one of the main reasons for President Fernando Belaúnde's ouster by a military coup in 1968. According to studies, Peru's economy would have been better off without the presence of the International Petroleum Company.

See also **Petroleum Industry.**

BIBLIOGRAPHY

Adalberto Pinelo, *The Multinational Corporation as a Force in Latin American Politics: A Case Study of the International Petroleum Company in Peru* (1973).

Rosemary Thorp and Geoffrey Bertram, *Peru, 1890–1977: Growth and Policy in an Open Economy* (1978).

Additional Bibliography

Jochamowitz, Luis. *Crónicas del petróleo en el Perú.* Lima: Grupo REPSOL YPF, 2001.

ALFONSO W. QUIROZ

LACALLE HERRERA, LUIS ALBERTO (1941–). Luis Alberto Lacalle Herrera (*b.* 13 July 1941) was elected president of Uruguay in 1989 and took office on March 1, 1990. He was the first Blanco (National Party) president of Uruguay elected in the twentieth century. The grandson of the great Blanco leader Luis Alberto de Herrera, Lacalle graduated from law school and gravitated toward a political career. He was elected a deputy to Congress in 1971 but lost his position in 1973 when Congress was closed in the coup that brought the military to power for the next twelve years.

In 1981 Lacalle founded a political group within the Blancos known as the National Herrerist Council, and by 1982 he was on the Blanco board of directors. In the national elections permitted by the military in November 1984, Lacalle was elected to the Senate. In 1987 he served as vice president to the Senate. In July 1988, Lacalle declared himself a presidential candidate. With the 1988 death of the last political caudillo, Blanco Senator Wilson Ferreira Aldunate, Lacalle emerged as the leader of the party. On November 26, 1989, aided by infighting in the ruling Colorado Party and a stagnant economy, Lacalle was elected president, with his party receiving 39 percent of the vote.

Lacalle, an articulate, center-right politician, attempted to steer Uruguay away from its welfare-state orientation. His major goals were to privatize, or at least to bring mixed ownership to, such state-owned operations as the airline and telephone company. He also attempted to reform the social-security system, which was a heavy drain on government resources. On March 26, 1991, he signed an agreement with the presidents of Brazil, Argentina, and Paraguay for the creation by 1995 of a common market (Mercosur) among these nations. In 1999 he won the primary elections but was defeated in the general elections. He ran again for president in 2004 but was defeated in a two-to-one margin by the other candidate for his party, Jorge Larrañaga. Lacalle has written on political and economic matters, and he authored a book about his grandfather, *Herrera, Un nacionalismo oriental* (1978).

See also **Herrera, Luis Alberto de; Mercosur; Uruguay, Political Parties: Blanco Party.**

BIBLIOGRAPHY

Martin Weinstein, "Consolidating Democracy in Uruguay: The Sea Change of the 1989 Elections" (Bildner Center for Western Hemisphere Studies of the Graduate Center of the City University of New York, Working Paper Series, 1990).

Charles G. Gillespie, *Negotiating Democracy: Politicians and Generals in Uruguay* (1991).

Additional Bibliography

Martínez, Durán. *Vivir es combatir.* Montevideo: Ediciones de la Plaza, 2004.

García Pintos, Pablo. *Faltan 60 meses: Peripecias del gobierno blanco (1990–95).* Montevideo: Ediciones Cruz del Sur, 2006.

Garrido, Atilio. *Lacalle, con alma y vida.* Montevideo: Gussi Libros, 2001.

MARTIN WEINSTEIN

LACANDONES. The Lacandon Maya, or *los lacandones* as they are known in Mexico and Guatemala, were found in dispersed settlements throughout the tropical forests of lowland Chiapas and Petén in the mid-nineteenth century. However, by the mid-twentieth century Lacandon populations dwindled and became concentrated in the villages of Najá, Mensabak (Metzabók), and Lacanjá in Chiapas due to pressure from loggers and ranchers and waves of migrations by foreign settlers. The Lacandon are recognized by their white gowns, long hair, and particular dialect of the Yucatec Mayan language. There are two main groups which are separated by slight cultural and linguistic differences: the northern and southern Lacandon. They are slash-and-burn horticulturalists who raise maize, beans, squash, root crops, bananas, and a large variety of plants in their fields and gardens. Additionally, the Lacandon subsist by hunting, fishing, and gathering resources from the surrounding forests. Today the Lacandon also make a living through tourism, wage earnings, and by selling lumber and farming rights to their lands. The Lacandon were well known for their non-Christian religious practices which until about 1980 included offering incense, food, and drink to their native deities through "god pots," or incense burners, and burning anthropomorphic rubber figurines. At this time roads brought extensive social and economic changes to the Lacandon, who are slowly losing many of their aboriginal customs and domestic practices.

Historical and archaeological evidence points to the cultural origins of the Lacandon Maya. The northern part of the geographical area where they are found was populated by Yucatec Mayan speakers and the southern portion by Cholan speakers during the Spanish colonial period. The tropical forests of the Maya lowlands were a remote refuge for Maya escaping the Spanish conquest in Yucatan and the Maya highlands, and the new migrants interacted and intermarried with the native Maya groups. This blend of peoples and cultures led to the creation of the Lacandon in the late colonial period; they retained Yucatec Mayan and certain behaviors from Cholan and migrant groups. The earliest known descriptions of the Lacandon and their lifeways are found in Spanish documents dating to the 1780s, but some of the Lacandon material culture has affinities with remains from the Late Post-Classic to early historic periods (ca. 1400–1700) in Yucatan, Petén, and lowland Chiapas. At the end of the colonial period the Lacandon had large populations located in villages and scattered extended families which were organized around political leaders or head men. When populations decreased to only a few hundred people at the turn of the twentieth century, the Lacandon sociopolitical and economic structure was reduced to local bands.

Archaeologists have found Lacandon incense burners in ancient Maya ruins throughout Petén in Guatemala and Chiapas in Mexico, left there over the course of the twentieth century, which speaks to the importance of these sites for the Lacandon. In traditional Lacandon beliefs the ruins are the homes of gods, who must be given offerings to cure people or to bring rain for crops. The geographical extension of these finds also points to the fact that Lacandon populations were much larger and more dispersed in the past. Lacandon settlements were found near sacred lakes and cliff paintings in Chiapas, and Lacandon deities are depicted in the precontact rock art found on lakeside cliffs, an indication of their ancient roots. Excavations in nineteenth-century Lacandon settlements demonstrate that despite a remote existence, the Lacandon maintained trade with foreigners for metal tools such as knives, axes, machetes, and scissors, and for other exotic goods including painted pottery, glass bottles, and metal pots. The evidence also shows that they shunned items such as guns, canned goods, and Christian artifacts.

Historically, the Lacandon are known for interesting behaviors no longer witnessed ethnographically. Some nineteenth-century Lacandon were associated with cannibalism, homicide, and blood letting rites in which religious practitioners offered their blood to the gods. Other Lacandon used poisoned arrows during conflicts and blowguns for hunting birds and small animals. Disease, conflict, and assimilation affected Lacandon populations and resulted in elaborate visitation rituals at Lacandon settlements in which outsiders shouted their intentions to hidden settlements and left their arrows and machetes in the bush. Lacandon women were often victims of violence and neglect. Historically women were captured in their settlements by men seeking wives or traded to outsiders for goods. Lacandon men were frequently polygamous, gaining allies through marriage and economic power through extra labor, but women often controlled the domestic units and influenced their husbands in undertaking trade expeditions to obtain personal and household goods.

See also **Indigenous Peoples; Maya, The.**

BIBLIOGRAPHY

Anguiano, Raúl. *Journal of an Expedition to the Lacandon Jungle, 1949.* Mexico City: Quálitas Compañia de Seguros, 1999.

Boremanse, Didier. *Hach Winik: The Lacandon Maya of Chiapas, Southern Mexico.* Albany, NY: Institute for Mesoamerican Studies, 1998.

Marion Singer, Marie-Odile. *Los hombres de la selva: Un estudio de tecnología cultural en medio selvático.* Mexico City: Instituto Nacional de Antropología e Historia, 1991.

McGee, R. Jon. *Watching Lacandon Maya Lives.* Boston: Allyn and Bacon, 2002.

Nations, James D. *The Maya Tropical Forest: People, Parks, and Ancient Cities.* Austin: University of Texas Press, 2006.

Palka, Joel. *Unconquered Lacandon Maya: Ethnohistory and Archaeology of Indigenous Culture Change.* Gainesville: University Press of Florida, 2005.

Perera, Victor, and Robert D. Bruce. *The Last Lords of Palenque: The Lacandon Maya of the Mexican Rainforest.* Berkeley: University of California Press. 1985.

Soustelle, Jacques. *The Four Suns: Recollections and Reflections of an Ethnologist in Mexico.* Translated by E. Ross. New York: Grossman Publishers, 1970.

Vos, Jan de. *La paz de Dios y del Rey: La conquista de la selva Lacandona, 1525–1821.* Mexico City: Fondo de Cultura Económica, 1988.

JOEL W. PALKA

LACANDON FOREST. Lacandon Forest (*Selva Lacandona*), the largest surviving tropical wilderness area in modern Mexico and a major segment of the once vast rain forest belt of Middle America. Located in the Usumacinta River basin in the states of Chiapas and Tabasco, it harbors a considerable, if largely unstudied, diversity of flora and fauna. This humid, lowland region was once a part of the heavily populated heartland of Classic Maya civilization that flourished between 300 and 900 CE. The forest is named for the later Lacandon peoples, who fled to the region from the direction of the Yucatán Peninsula in the centuries following the abandonment of the ancient cities.

This great forest, which covered at least 520,000 square miles in 1875, was, in spite of much manual lumbering of hardwoods, largely intact and isolated until 1950. Yet by 1990 it had suffered extreme alteration and at least a 70 percent reduction, to approximately 156,000 square miles, as a result of mechanized lumbering, road construction, excessive settlements, extensive cattle ranching, massive uncontrolled burning, and large-scale energy projects for oil exploration and planned hydroelectric dams. During the last decade of the twentieth century, efforts were undertaken to regulate the forest area and to formalize the Montes Azules Biosphere Reserve to preserve a significant remaining upland portion.

The Selva Lacandona has received increased attention from the international community due to the January 1994 rebellion of the EZLN (*Ejército Zapatista de Liberación Nacional / Zapatista Army of National Liberation*), a revolutionary group made up of both indigenous and non-indigenous members that is based out of the forest. The subsequent militarization and continued conflict in the region demonstrate the tenuous relationships and divergent priorities of the Mexican government, the indigenous population of the Lacandon, and national and international environmental conservation groups.

See also **Forests; Mexico, Zapatista Army of National Liberation.**

BIBLIOGRAPHY

Frans Blom and Gertrude Duby, *La Selva Lacandona* (1955).

Gertrude Duby Blom, *Bearing Witness* (1984).

S. Jeffrey K. Wilkerson, "The Usumacinta River: Troubles on a Wild Frontier," in *National Geographic Magazine* 168 (October 1985): 514–543.

S. Jeffrey K. Wilkerson, "The Last Forest: Exploring Mexico's Lacandon Wilderness," in *America's Hidden Wilderness: Lands of Seclusion*, edited by Donald J. Crump (1988), pp. 36–61.

S. Jeffrey K. Wilkerson, "Damming the Usumacinta: The Archaeological Impact," in *Sixth Palenque Round Table* 8 (1991): 118–134.

Additional Bibliography

Jan de Vos, *Una tierra para sembrar sueños: Historia reciente de la Selva Lacandona.* Mexico City: Fondo De Cultura Economica, 2002.

Karen O'Brien, *Sacrificing the Forest: Environmental and Social Struggles in Chiapas.* Boulder, CO: Western Press, 1998.

S. JEFFREY K. WILKERSON

LA CENTINELA. La Centinela, the capital of the Chincha kingdom. The archaeological site of La Centinela lies near the modern town of Chincha Baja and near the mouth of the Chincha valley. It consists of a group of impressive adobe compounds that were built during the period of the Chincha kingdom but continued to function during the following period of Inca domination. In the midst of these local architectural compounds the Inca built a compound of their own. While the earlier Chincha construction was of the coursed adobe known as *tapia,* the Inca compound was constructed of adobe bricks. It also contained a rectangular plaza and had the trapezoidal niches and doorways typical of Inca architecture. But alongside the buildings that appear to have served as an Inca palace stood a pyramidal platform more reminiscent of earlier Chincha architecture even though it was constructed of adobe bricks and constituted a formal part of the compound of the dominant Inca. Several of the compounds built of *tapia* had been modified with adobe bricks, in one case extensively, indicating Inca alteration of existing structures. Scholars suspect that these local compounds were related to Chincha social units and were the settings for important ceremonies and rituals, probably including initiation, marriage, and other rites of passage. Archaeological evidence of extensive manufacturing or other purely economic activities has not been found.

Differences in Inca architectural modification to the Chincha compounds may have been related to differences in the ways the Inca supported and controlled various groups. Though they exerted control indirectly, the Inca were obviously not content to leave the mechanisms by which they carried it out entirely in local hands. Elements of Inca identity were made evident at many points in the social and political ceremonies that held together the upper levels of local society. However, pottery design, which employed both Inca and Chincha elements, survived into the Spanish colonial period.

La Centinela was probably part of a broader network of population centers and other kinds of sites in the Chincha valley. These were linked by a system of roads, one of which was part of the Inca road system during the times of the Inca Empire. The nearby sites of Tambo de Mora and La Cumbe were perhaps visualized as part of the same large complex during pre-Columbian times. La Cumbe served mainly as a cemetery.

See also **Archaeology; Indigenous Peoples.**

BIBLIOGRAPHY

Max Uhle, "Explorations at Chincha," in *University of California Publications in American Archaeology and Ethnology* 21, no. 2 (1924): 55–94.

Additional Bibliography

Sandweiss, Daniel H. *The Archaeology of Chincha Fishermen: Specialization and Status in Inka Peru.* Pittsburgh: Carnegie Museum of Natural History, 1992.

Wing, Elizabeth S., and Jane C. Wheeler. *Economic Prehistory of the Central Andes.* Oxford: B.A.R., 1988.

CRAIG MORRIS

LACERDA, CARLOS FREDERICO WERNECK DE

LACERDA, CARLOS FREDERICO WERNECK DE (1914–1977). Carlos Frederico Werneck de Lacerda (*b.* 30 April 1914; *d.* 21 May 1977), famous for combative oratory and journalism that contributed to the fall of Brazilian presidents. According to historian José Honório Rodrigues, "No single person exerted as much influence on the Brazilian historical process" from 1945 to 1968.

Lacerda, born in the city of Rio de Janeiro, was a rebellious, intense youth who preferred to educate himself by reading instead of taking formal courses. In 1935 he dropped out of the Faculdade Nacional de Direito (Rio Law School) without obtaining a degree. His ardent oratorical and journalistic work for communism ended in 1940 with his "expulsion" from the Communist Party, which he had in fact never joined. Continuing to condemn the dictatorship of Getúlio Vargas, he contributed to the achievement of democracy in 1945. His articles, such as those after 1949 in his own *Tribuna da Imprensa,* gained him admirers as an anticommunist and a courageous crusader against corruption. After his revelation of scandals in the final Vargas administration (1951–1954), supporters of the president killed a military officer while trying to assassinate Lacerda. Following Vargas's suicide (24 August 1954), mobs shouted "death to Lacerda." The latter, however, became the congressman who received the greatest number of votes.

Calling for a reform of the political system, Lacerda demanded in 1955 that President-elect Juscelino Kubitschek be prevented from taking office. Kubitschek, inaugurated with the help of a military coup, in turn would not allow Lacerda, Brazil's most sensational orator, to broadcast, and tried unsuccessfully to have him removed from Congress. As congressional opposition leader, Lacerda secured passage of legislation to reform education and was active in advancing the campaign that brought Jânio Quadros to the presidency early in 1961.

When Quadros, attacked by Lacerda for harboring dictatorial plans, unexpectedly resigned in August 1961, the presidency went to Vice President João Goulart, despite Lacerda's wishes. Lacerda, who had been elected governor of Guanabara state, gave his state a brilliantly constructive administration while denouncing Goulart and the president's Communist allies in labor unions. During the military coup that overthrew Goulart in 1964, Lacerda dramatically prepared the governor's palace against a possible assault by Goulart's forces.

As a presidential candidate, Lacerda denounced the new military regime and its unpopular anti-inflation measures. After an institutional act ended direct presidential elections, he found allies in Kubitschek and Goulart for organizing an antidictatorial front. The increasingly repressive military regime jailed him for a week in 1968 and deprived him of his political rights for ten years. Lacerda then concentrated on business affairs, writing, and book publishing, activities to which he had turned in 1965 following a political setback. He died of a heart attack.

See also **Journalism; Lacerda, Maurício Pavia de.**

BIBLIOGRAPHY

José Honório Rodrigues, Introduction to *Carlos Lacerda, Discursos parlamentares* (1982).

Additional Bibliography

Dulles, John W. F. *Carlos Lacerda, Brazilian Crusader,* Volume 1: *The Years 1914–1960* (1991); Volume 2: *The Years 1960–1977* (1996). University of Texas Press (Austin).

McCann, Brian. "Carlos Lacerda: The Rise and Fall of a Middle-Class Populist in 1950s Brazil." *The Hispanic American Historical Review* 83 (November 2003): 661–696.

Mendonça, Marina Gusmão de. *O demolidor de presidentes: A trajetória política de Carlos Lacerda, 1930–1968.* São Paulo: Códex, 2002.

JOHN W. F. DULLES

LACERDA, MAURÍCIO PAIVA DE

LACERDA, MAURÍCIO PAIVA DE (1888–1959). Maurício Paiva de Lacerda (*b.* 1 June 1888; *d.* 23 November 1959), popular politician and journalist who contributed to the collapse of Brazil's Old Republic in 1930 through his passionate oratory. Always attacking those in power, Lacerda stirred the masses in the streets and encouraged workers to strike. He named his son Carlos Frederico, after Marx and Engels.

Maurício de Lacerda was born in Vassouras, Rio de Janeiro State. He was the oldest son of Sebastião de Lacerda, a prominent politician of the state who became a cabinet minister and supreme court justice. Before the willful Maurício obtained his degree at the Rio Law School, he was a student leader, director of a newspaper in Vassouras, and participant in an ineffective antigovernment conspiracy. As a congressman (1912–1920) from his home state of Rio de Janeiro, Lacerda introduced labor legislation. The antigovernment revolts of 1922 and 1924 were insufficiently labor-oriented to attract him, but he was nevertheless arrested on both occasions. Following his imprisonment (1924–1926) he allied himself with the "Cavalier of Hope," Luís Carlos Prestes, leader of the revolutionary Long March (1925–1927), but in 1929–1930 he angered Prestes by supporting the Liberal Alliance and its uprising, which brought Getúlio Vargas to the presidency.

Lacerda denounced the economic policies and what he saw as the fascist viewpoints of the new Vargas regime, and in 1935 he joined the Aliança Nacional Libertadora, whose honorary president, Prestes, was by then a Communist in hiding. Following the unsuccessful uprising of Prestes and his followers that year, Lacerda was jailed, again without cause, for a year. During most of the Vargas dictatorship (1937–1945), he did legal work for the Rio de Janeiro municipality. He ran unsuccessfully for Congress when the dictatorship fell.

See also **Lacerda, Carlos Frederico Werneck de; Vargas, Getúlio Dornelles.**

BIBLIOGRAPHY

Michael L. Conniff, *Urban Politics in Brazil: The Rise of Populism, 1925–1945* (1981).

John W. F. Dulles, *Anarchists and Communists in Brazil, 1900–1935* (1973).

John W. F. Dulles, *Carlos Lacerda, Brazilian Crusader,* vol. 1 (1991).

Additional Bibliography

McCann, Brian. "Carlos Lacerda: The Rise and Fall of a Middle-Class Populist in 1950s Brazil." *The Hispanic American Historical Review* 83 (November 2003): 661–696.

Mendonça, Marina Gusmão de. *O demolidor de presidentes: A trajetória política de Carlos Lacerda, 1930–1968.* São Paulo: Códex, 2002.

JOHN W. F. DULLES

LACERDA, OSVALDO

LACERDA, OSVALDO (1927–). Osvaldo Lacerda (*b.* 23 March 1927), Brazilian composer and teacher. Lacerda's formal music training started at age nine, when he began piano study in the city of São Paulo, where he was born. From 1945 to 1947 he studied harmony, and in 1952 he became a composition student of Camargo Guarnieri. In 1963 he became the first Brazilian to win a Simon Guggenheim grant for study in the United States. He studied with Vittorio Giannini in New York City, and with Aaron Copland at Tanglewood. In 1965 he participated in the Inter-American Seminar of Composers at Indiana University and in the Third Inter-American Composers Seminar, held in Washington, D.C. In an era in which most Brazilian composers reject obvious national elements in their works, Osvaldo Lacerda remains an important spokesman for neonationalism with compositions such as nine *Brasiliana* suites for piano based on Brazilian themes and dances. He also excels in writing songs and choral works, such as

Poema da necessidade, for four-part chorus, based on a poem by Carlos Drummond de Andrade.

See also **Music: Art Music.**

BIBLIOGRAPHY

Marcos Antônio Marcondes, ed., *Enciclopédia da música brasileira: Erudita, folclórica e popular* (1977).

Gérard Béhague, *Music in Latin America: An Introduction* (1979).

David P. Appleby, *The Music of Brazil* (1983).

Additional Bibliography

Appleby, David. "Trends in Recent Brazilian Piano Music." *Latin American Music Review* (Spring 1981): 91–102.

Mariz, Vasco. *Figuras da Música Brasileira Contemporanea.* Brasília: Universidade de Brasília, 1970.

DAVID P. APPLEBY

LA CIUDADELA.

LA CIUDADELA. La Ciudadela, a fortress in the center of Mexico City. It was the scene of many military rebellions. Antonio González Velázquez built it in 1793 as the Royal Cigar and Cigarette Works. It obtained its military features from Miguel Costansó and Ignacio Castera when in 1808 they finished transforming it into a gunpowder storage facility for the Spanish army. The rebel leader José María Morelos was imprisoned in La Ciudadela in 1815. In the period of Santa Anna (late-1820s–mid-1850s) it served as the bastion for the generals in revolt, and its importance continued during The reform (1857–1860) and the French intervention. In 1871, Sóstenes Rocha seized it in order to crush a rebellion against Benito Juárez. In 1913, Manuel Mondragón and Félix Díaz rebelled against Francisco Madero and for ten days (Decena Trágica) bombarded the center city and principal neighborhoods from La Ciudadela. The treaty that the rebels signed there with their adversary, General Victoriano Huerta, was backed by U.S. Ambassador Henry Lane Wilson and resulted in the assassination of Madero and the dictatorship of Huerta from 1913 to 1914.

After the Revolution, La Ciudadela was declared a historic monument and became a center of fine culture. In its surroundings began the student movement of 1968. Between 1987 and 1991 it was refurbished under the direction of Abraham Zabludovsky and today houses the Mexican Library.

See also **Mexico City.**

BIBLIOGRAPHY

La Ciudadela: Biblioteca México (1991).

Antonio Saborit et al., *La Ciudadela de fuego: A ochenta años de la decena trájica* (1993).

Additional Bibliography

García Cantú, Gastón. *La intervención francesa en México.* México: Clío, 1998.

J. E. PACHECO

LA DEMOCRACIA.

LA DEMOCRACIA. La Democracia, a town in the Pacific coastal department of Escuintla, Guatemala, notable for its central park, which is adorned with sculptures from the site of Monte Alto and contains an archaeological museum.

The site of Monte Alto, on the Pacific coast of Guatemala, has about fifty earthern mounds and is notable for its colossal stone heads, full-figure boulder sculptures, and full-round potbelly sculptures, which most likely date between 500 and 200 BCE. The boulder heads, which are bald, have closed eyes and closed mouths, indicating that they represent deceased individuals. These heads appear to depict severed trophy heads of elites. Full-figure boulders have expansive bodies, their limbs are wrapped around them, and their faces are similar to the boulder heads. The full-round potbelly sculptures are smaller and squatter than the boulder sculptures, but otherwise have similar stylistic features.

Excavations at Monte Alto revealed that sculptures had specific placements. One sculpture was located on the central north-south axis of the site. Colossal stone heads and human-effigy boulder sculptures were found in irregular rows on the east and west sides of the mound group; these may not have been their original placements.

Stylistic affinities of these sculptures with those of the Olmecs, combined with their comparative crudity, suggest that they might predate the Olmec (1200–500 BCE). They were considered evidence that the beginning of Mesoamerican civilization was in the Pacific lowlands of Guatemala. Secure dating of potbellied figures in El Salvador shows that they postdate the Olmec, thus suggesting that they are a regional development outside of the Olmec heartland.

See also **Archaeology; Mesoamerica.**

BIBLIOGRAPHY

Jeffrey Parsons, "Excavation at Monte Alto, Escuintla, Guatemala," in *National Geographic Society Research Reports* (1976), pp. 325–332, and "Post-Olmec Stone Sculpture: The Olmec-Izapan Transition on the Southern Pacific Coast and Highlands," in *The Olmec and Their Neighbors: Essays in Memory of Matthew W. Stirling,* edited by Elizabeth P. Benson (1979), pp. 257–288; Arthur Demarest, *The Archaeology of Santa Leticia and the Rise of Maya Civilization,* Middle American Research Institute (Tulane University) Publication 52 (1986).

Additional Bibliography

Chévez Van Dorne, Rubén. *Cultura Monte Alto: Explicación de las piezas: Description of the pieces.* Guatemala: Division de Educacion y Cultura, 1987.

Evans, Susan Toby. *Ancient Mexico and Central America: Archaeology and Culture History.* London: Thames & Hudson, 2004.

Orellana, Sandra L. *Ethnohistory of the Pacific Coast.* Lancaster, CA: Labyrinthos, 1995.

EUGENIA J. ROBINSON

LADINO. Ladino, a Spanish word derived from the Latin *latinus,* meaning a person who spoke the Latin language, in contrast to speakers of Arabic. In medieval Spain, the word was used to describe Moors who had learned the Spanish language with such care and precision that they were scarcely distinguishable from Spaniards. From there, the word's meaning (documented as early as 1596, and also described as such in Covarrubias's 1611 *Tesoro de la lengua castellana*) was broadened to designate a crafty person, one who is cunning or astute, especially in learning foreign languages. In Spain, it was applied to the Moors and Spanish Jews (the Sephardic Jews of the Spanish diaspora are still known as ladinos), or any "foreigner" who learned the Spanish language, and implied a certain adaptation to Spanish customs. In the New World, usage expanded to incorporate New World Indians, African slaves, and the offspring of Spanish and Amerindians (mestizos), who were proficient Spanish-speakers and reasonably well-adapted to Spanish customs. Generally, the term described a person of non-Hispanic ethnic or racial background who successfully learned the Spanish language and customs of the Spaniards. In Guatemala, although originally applied to mestizos, it now connotes any person who is culturally not Mayan. This purely cultural significance means that it describes both individuals of European descent and those of purely indigenous descent whose cultural identity and language align them with European rather than Amerindian culture.

See also **Spanish Language.**

BIBLIOGRAPHY

Sebastián De Covarrubias, *Tesoro de la lengua castellana o española* (1611).

Joan Corominas and José A. Pascual, *Diccionario crítico etimológico castellano e hispánico* (1980).

Thomas M. Stephens, *Dictionary of Latin American Racial and Ethnic Terminology* (1989).

Additional Bibliography

Hale, Charles R. *Más que un Indio= More than an Indian: Racial Ambivalence and Neoliberal Multiculturalism in Guatemala.* Santa Fe: School of American Research Press, 2006.

Harris, Tracy K. *Death of a Language: The History of Judeo-Spanish.* Newark: University of Delaware Press; London: Associated University Presses, 1994.

Nelson, Diane M. *A Finger in the Wound: Body Politics in Quincentennial Guatemala.* Berkeley: University of California Press, 1999.

Reeves, René. *Ladinos with Ladinos, Indians with Indians: Land, Labor, and Regional Ethnic Conflict in the Making of Guatemala.* Stanford, CA: Stanford University Press, 2006.

Taracena Arriola, Arturo. *Invención criolla, sueño ladino, pesadilla indígena: Los Altos de Guatemala: De región a estado, 1740-1871.* Rev. ed. Antigua: Centro de Investigaciones Regionales de Mesoamérica,1999.

J. DAVID DRESSING

LADRÓN DE GUEVARA, DIEGO (1641–1718). Diego Ladrón de Guevara (*b.* 1641; *d.* 9 November 1718), bishop and viceroy of Peru (1710–1716). Born in Cifuentes, Ladrón studied in Alcalá and Sigüenza before entering the church, serving as a canon in both Sigüenza and Málaga. He was sent to America in 1689 as bishop of Panamá and was subsequently promoted to Huamanga (Peru) in 1699, and Quito in 1703.

Following the death in office in 1710 of the viceroy of Peru, marqués de Castelldosríus, Ladrón, as the audiencia's third choice as interim successor, took office when the other two nominees died. Although recalled to Spain in 1713, he remained in office until 1716 and stayed in Lima for two further years to defend himself (unsuccessfully) against charges of corruption, permitting contraband, and incompetence in defending shipping in the Pacific against English intruders. He left Peru for Acapulco in March 1718 and died in Mexico City later that year.

See also **Peru: From the Conquest Through Independence.**

BIBLIOGRAPHY

Rubén Vargas Ugarte, *Historia del Perú: Virreinato (Siglo XVIII) 1700–1790* (1956), esp. pp. 67–96.

Geoffrey J. Walker, *Spanish Politics and Imperial Trade, 1700–1789* (1979), esp. pp. 61–62, 80–83.

Additional Bibliography

Andrien, Kenneth J. *Andean Worlds: Indigenous History, Culture, and Consciousness under Spanish Rule, 1532–1825.* Albuquerque: University of New Mexico Press, 2001.

JOHN R. FISHER

LA ESCALERA, CONSPIRACY OF.

In December 1843 Esteban Santa Cruz de Oviedo, a planter with major holdings in the western province of Matanzas, Cuba, claimed to have uncovered a conspiracy to promote revolt by the slaves of Cuba's sugar plantation heartland. The authorities tortured suspects, then executed the "confessed" ringleaders. Captain-General Leopoldo O'Donnell, Cuba's new chief executive, doubting that all the guilty had been found, widened the circle of investigation. Persecution and torture spread throughout much of western Cuba in the first months of 1844. Officials eventually concluded that a vast revolutionary conspiracy involving slaves, free people of color, Cuban-born whites, and foreigners existed. They implicated Domingo Del Monte and José de la Luz y Caballero, two of Cuba's preeminent dissident intellectuals; they convicted in absentia David Turnbull, an abolitionist and former British consul in Havana, of being the "prime mover" behind the conspiracy; and they executed the prominent free mulatto poet Plácido for being the leader of a revolutionary faction of people of color. By the end of 1844, thousands of people of color, free and slave, had been banished, imprisoned, tortured, or executed; many others had simply disappeared. The alleged conspiracy acquired the name La Escalera—the Ladder—from the principal instrument to which suspects were bound before interrogation accompanied by the lash. The year 1844 has gone down in Cuban history as el Año del Cuero, the Year of the Lash.

Generations of Cuban scholars have debated the reality of the conspiracy. Although it was clearly exaggerated by unscrupulous officials who wanted to silence dissidence, by venal whites who wanted to despoil rising members of Cuba's free colored class, and by panic-stricken slaveholders who feared a replay of the Haitian Revolution, La Escalera probably existed as a conjunction of several different conspiracies. Each drew energy from British abolitionism; each had distinct cores involving whites, slaves, and free people of color; each overlapped, if only in some cases, at the margin; and each expanded or contracted at different points between 1841 and 1844.

La Escalera decimated the leadership of Cuba's free colored class and encouraged many Cuban whites to look more favorably upon Cuba's annexation by the United States. It was the last major act of collective resistance by Cuba's people of color before their participation in the Ten Years' War.

See also **Cuba: The Colonial Era (1492-1898); Slavery: Spanish America.**

BIBLIOGRAPHY

David R. Murray, *Odious Commerce* (1980), chaps. 8 and 9.

Enildo A. García, *Cuba: Plácido, poeta mulato de la emancipación, 1809–1844* (1986).

Robert L. Paquette, *Sugar Is Made with Blood* (1988).

Additional Bibliography

Childs, Matt D. *The 1812 Aponte Rebellion in Cuba and the Struggle against Atlantic Slavery.* Chapel Hill: University of North Carolina Press, 2006.

Cooper, Frederick, Thomas Holt, and Rebecca Scott. *Beyond Slavery: Explorations of Race, Labor, and*

Citizenship in Post-emancipation Societies. Chapel Hill: University of North Carolina Press, 2000.

Helg, Aline. *Our Rightful Share: The Afro-Cuban Struggle for Equality, 1886–1912.* Chapel Hill: University of North Carolina Press, 1995.

Schmidt-Nowara, Christopher. *Empire and Antislavery: Spain, Cuba, and Puerto Rico, 1833–1874.* Pittsburgh, PA: University of Pittsburgh Press, 1999.

ROBERT L. PAQUETTE

LA GALGADA. La Galgada, Peruvian site of ruins dating from the Late Preceramic period (3000–2000 BCE). Andean South America is one of the regions where civilization arose independently before 3000 BCE. The ruins of La Galgada (Rockslide) have provided some of the richest evidence in Peru of early cultural development. Located 72 miles from the coast on the banks of the Tablachaca, a tributary of the Santa River, the largest river on Peru's Pacific coast, the town was a center on routes connecting the coastal desert, the highlands, and the Amazon Basin. Isolation and aridity account for the well-preserved buildings, irrigation canals and field patterns, and burial tombs containing offerings of gourd vessels, baskets, cotton and bast cloth, stonework, shell and turquoise jewelry, and even feathers. The similarity of the material from La Galgada to that from such contemporary sites as Kotosh, Huaricoto, and Huaca Prieta reveals a widespread shared culture before the introduction of pottery about 2000 BCE.

The earliest excavated structures, about 2800 BCE, are small circular or rectangular temples with plastered stone walls painted white and flat roofs. The rituals seem to have included putting food offerings in the small central fire pit. The temple chambers were converted into tombs by building a stone roof supported by a massive stone column. The tomb was buried under earth fill, leaving a shaft to the surface, and a new temple was built on top. Four levels of such temple–tombs are known, spanning the period 2600–2000 BCE.

Cotton, the principal crop, was used to make cloth by pre-loom techniques, much of it evidently for trade. Several dye colors are among the oldest specimens known. With the introduction of the heddle loom along with pottery about 2000 BCE, there were style changes in cloth, jewelry, and architecture, heralding the Chavín style, which dominated northern Peru for the next two millennia.

See also **Archaeology.**

BIBLIOGRAPHY

Terence Grieder and Alberto Bueno Mendoza, "Ceremonial Architecture at La Galgada," in *Early Ceremonial Architecture in the Andes,* edited by Christopher B. Donnan (1985), pp. 93–109.

Terence Grieder, "Preceramic and Initial Period Textiles from La Galgada, Peru," in *The Junius B. Bird Conference on Andean Textiles,* edited by Ann Pollard Rowe (1986), pp. 19–29.

Terence Grieder, Alberto Bueno Mendoza, C. Earle Smith, Jr., and Robert M. Malina, *La Galgada, Peru* (1988).

Additional Bibliography

Burger, Richard L. *Chavín and the Origins of Andean Civilization.* London: Thames and Hudson, 1995.

Moseley, Michael. *The Incas and Their Ancestors: The Archaeology of Peru.* London: Thames & Hudson, 2001.

Rodríguez López, Luis Francisco. *Costa Norte: Diez mil años de prehistoria.* Lima: Ministerio de la Presidencia: Consejo Nacional de Ciencia y Tecnología, 1994.

Schobinger, Juan. *The Ancient Americans: A Reference Guide to the Art, Culture, and History of Pre-Columbian North and South America.* Armonk, NY: Sharpe Reference, 2001.

TERENCE GRIEDER

LAGOA SANTA. Lagoa Santa is an archaeological and paleontological province in Brazil. Formally the term refers to the city of Lagoa Santa, approximately 30 kilometers from Belo Horizonte, the state capital of Minas Gerais, but it is most often used in the scientific literature to refer to the karst where the city of Lagoa Santa is located. The province was first explored by Peter Lund, a Danish naturalist, who investigated the local caves and shelters from 1833 to 1843. Lund described an impressive number of new genera and species of extinct large mammals (megafauna) based on the fossils he collected in Lagoa Santa. The most important site he excavated in the region was Sumidouro Cave, where he found human skeletal remains that were apparently associated with the extinct megafauna. As a consequence, Lund proposed that the Americas were occupied much earlier than what was believed in the nineteenth century. Since then Lagoa Santa has become an icon in the international literature on the occupation of the New World by humans. Although during the twentieth century the region was explored by several successive Brazilian and international missions, the coexistence hypothesis raised by Lund was confirmed only in 2002–2003 by AMS (accelerator mass spectrometry) radiocarbon dating on fossil bones. The region is also one of the few areas in the Americas where a large number of human skeletal remains dated to the Pleistocene-Holocene transition have been found. Among these skeletons, "Luzia," found at Lapa Vermelha IV, is by far the most prominent. She is thought to be one of the earliest, if not the earliest, human skeletons ever found in the New World, estimated to be between 11,000 and 11,500 years old.

See also **Archaeology.**

BIBLIOGRAPHY

Laming-Emperaire, Annette, Andre Prous, Águeda Vilhena de Moraes, and Maria da Conceição Beltrão. *Grottes et abris de la region de Lagoa Santa, Minas Gerais, Brésil.* Cahiers d'Archeology dAmérique du Sud 1. Paris: École Pratique des Hautes Études, Sciences Économiques et Sociales, 1975.

Neves, Walter A., and Mark Hubbe. "Cranial Morphology of Early Americans from Lagoa Santa, Brazil: Implications for the Settlement of the New World." *Proceedings of the National Academy of Science USA* 102 (2005): 18309–18314.

Piló, Luís Beethoven, Augusto S. Auler, Walter A. Neves, Xianfeng Wang, Hai Cheng, and R. Lawrence Edwards. "Geochronology, Sediment Provenance, and Fossil Emplacement at Sumidouro Cave, a Classic Late Pleistocene/Early Holocene Paleoanthropological Site in Eastern Brazil." *Geoarchaeology* 20, no. 8 (2005): 751–764.

WALTER A. NEVES

LAGOS, RICARDO (1938–). Ricardo Lagos (*b.* 2 May 1938), a leader of Chile's moderately socialist Partido por la Democracia (PPD) and minister of education (1990–) in the government of President Patricio Aylwin Azcócar. Lagos studied law at the University of Chile and earned his doctorate in economics from Duke University in 1966. As a former member of the Radical Party, Lagos staunchly supported the Popular Unity government of Salvador Allende, who nominated him ambassador to the Soviet Union. However, Allende was overthrown by a military coup and ousted by dictator Augusto Pinochet in 1973, before Lagos could assume his post. Lagos then went into exile in the United States. In 1978, he accepted a position working for the United Nations.

In the early 1980s, Lagos returned to Chile. He was soon nominated president of the anti-Pinochet Democratic Alliance of political parties. In a television appearance early in 1987, he issued a direct challenge to General Pinochet that helped to launch the eventually successful plebiscite campaign. That same year, he was briefly jailed for his political activites. Afterward, he founded the Partido por la Democracia. Although he far outpolled all senatorial candidates in the 1989 general election except the Christian Democrat who was his running mate, Lagos was denied the second seat from Santiago because their combined totals fell just short of the requisite two-thirds of the votes cast.

In 1999, Lagos was nominated for the presidency by Chile's Socialist Party, and in 2000 he took office as Chile's first socialist president since the ousted Allende. During his years in office, he refused to shelter Pinochet from prosecution. Chile's economy flourished, and many of his democratic reforms were sucessfully adopted. In 2006, Lagos was suceeded by another Socialist president, Michelle Bachelet, the first woman president in Chile's history.

See also **Chile: The Twentieth Century; Chile, Political Parties: Popular Unity; Chile, Political Parties: Socialist Party.**

BIBLIOGRAPHY

Partido por la Democracia (*Chile*) (1989), and *Qué es el PPD: Documentos oficiales* (1989); A. Cavallo et al., *La historia oculta del regimen militar* (Santiago, 1989).

P. Constable and A. Valenzuela, *A Nation of Enemies* (1991).

Additional Bibliography

Claude, Marcel. *El retorno de Fausto: Ricardo Lagos y la concentración del poder económico.* Santiago: Ediciones Política y Utopía, 2006.

Funk, Robert L. *El gobierno de Ricardo Lagos: La nueva vía chilena hacía el socialismo.* Santiago: Ediciones Universidad Diego Portales, 2006.

Mares, David R., and Francisco Rojas Aravena. *The United States and Chile: Coming in from the Cold.* New York: Routledge, 2001.

MICHAEL FLEET

LAGUERRE, ENRIQUE ARTURO

(1906–2005). Enrique Arturo Laguerre, Puerto Rico's foremost novelist, was born on May 3, 1906, in Moca, a rural community in the western part of the island. Educated at the University of Puerto Rico, in 1924. Laguerre embarked upon a lifelong teaching career spanning from elementary to postgraduate education.

Laguerre's twelve novels form a saga of Puerto Rico's land, people, and history in the late nineteenth and twentieth centuries. Two of them, *El laberinto* (1959; *The Labyrinth,* 1960) and *Los amos benévolos* (1976; *Benevolent Masters,* 1976); are available in English. *La llamarada* (The Blaze), a classic since its publication in 1935, deals with the exploitation of the sugarcane worker. *Solar Montoya* (Montoya Plantation, 1941) takes place in the coffee fields, and *Los dedos de la mano* (The Fingers of the Hand, 1951) in tobacco country. Other novels deal with the Puerto Rican in San Juan, New York, and abroad; university life, feminism, and the religious practices of Santería. Puerto Rican identity and values are central themes in *Cauce sin río* (Riverbed without a River, 1962), *El fuego y su aire* (Fire and Its Air, 1970), and *Infiernos privados* (Private Infernos, 1986). Associated with the 1930s generation, Laguerre creates a historical consciousness by enriching the past with legends, folklore, and myths, especially in *La resaca* (The Undertow, 1949) and *Los gemelos* (The Twins, 1992). Laguerre's novels treat the plight of oppressed women, children, and workers; the effects of affluence and power on the individual; and conflicts of conscience. In his writing he has embraced both traditional and innovative forms. In 1999 he was nominated for the Nobel Prize in Literature. He died on June 16, 2005, one month short of his one-hundredth birthday, and was buried in his native town of Moca.

See also **Literature: Spanish America.**

BIBLIOGRAPHY

Luis O. Zayas Micheli, *Lo universal en Enrique A. Laguerre: Estudio conjunto de su obra* (1974).

Estelle Irizarry, *Enrique A. Laguerre* (1982), *"La llamarada," clásico puertorriqueño: Realidad y ficción* (1985) and *La novelística de Enrique A. Laguerre: Trayectoria histórica y literaria* (1987).

Additional Bibliography

Irizarry, Estelle. *Estudios sobre Enrique A. Laguerre.* San Juan, P.R.: Editorial Instituto de Cultura Puertorriqueña, 2005.

ESTELLE IRIZARRY

LAGUNA, SANTA CATARINA.

Santa Catarina Laguna, a seaport in southern Brazil, founded in 1684 by Domingos de Brito Peixoto. In an effort to drive out the encroaching Spanish Jesuits, the Portuguese crown encouraged settlement at Laguna. Between 1682 and 1706 the Spanish Jesuits founded the missions of the Seven Peoples, the Sete Povos, which flourished in what is now Rio Grande do Sul. The presence of the Sete Povos threatened Portuguese territorial ambitions in the region. Moving with geopolitical and economic motivations, Portugal staked its claim to the region. Settled by Paulistas and Azorean couples sent by the crown, Laguna quickly became part of Portuguese Brazil. By 1694 settlers had transformed the region from a farming-fishing community to one dependent on grazing. Laguna later developed into an out-migration area as Lagunistas themselves migrated south to the plains of Rio Grande do Sul. In the eighteenth century a newly opened road for the livestock trade linked Laguna to São Paulo and the mines of Minas Gerais.

See also **Brazil, Geography.**

BIBLIOGRAPHY

Leslie Bethell, ed., *The Cambridge History of Latin America,* vol. 2 (1984), p. 472.

Rollie E. Poppino, *Brazil: The Land and People,* 2d ed. (1973), p. 83

Additional Bibliography

Brancher, Ana, Silvia Maria Fávero Arend, and Rodrigo Lavina. *História de Santa Catarina, séculos XVI a XIX.* Florianópolis: Editora da UFSC, 2004.

ORLANDO R. ARAGONA

LALEAU, LÉON (1892–1979). Léon Laleau (*b.* 3 August 1892; *d.* 1979), Haitian writer, journalist, and diplomat. Léopold Sédar Senghor cited Laleau as "one of the best representatives among Haitian poets using the vein of blackness." Laleau made many contacts with European and Latin American writers during his diplomatic assignments in Rome, Paris, London, Lima, and Santiago de Chile. Influenced by French symbolism at first, he later became acutely conscious of the catastrophic effects of the U.S. occupation of Haiti (1915–1934). He began to move toward the writers of *La revue indigène* and to use Haitian themes in the volume of verse, *Musique nègre* (1931), and in his novel about the occupation, *Le choc* (1932). Laleau also managed *Haïti journal, Le nouvelliste,* and *Le matin* at different periods. He wrote for the *Mercure de France, Le divan, Le Figaro littéraire,* and *Paris soir,* among other French journals. A collective volume of Laleau's *Oeuvre poétique* ("À voix basse," 1919; "La flèche au coeur," 1926; "Le rayon des jupes," 1928; "Abréviations," 1929; "Musique nègre," 1931; "De bronze et d'ivoire," 1978) won the literary prize of Éditions Henri Deschamps for 1978.

Other works include *Amitiés impossibles* (theater, with Georges Léger, 1916); *Une cause sans effet* (theater, 1916); *L'étau* (theater, 1917); *La pluie et le beau temps* (theater, 1919); *La danse des vagues* (novel, 1919); *Le tremplin* (theater, 1921); *Maurice Rostand intime* (biography, 1926); and *Apothéoses* (essays, 1952).

See also **Haiti; Literature: Latin America.**

BIBLIOGRAPHY

F. Raphaël Berrou and Pradel Pompilus, *Histoire de la littérature haïtienne illustrée par les textes,* vol. 2 (1975), pp. 480–514, 666–691, 737–750.

Conjonction, nos. 87–88 (1963), special issue dedicated to Laleau.

Naomi M. Garret, *The Renaissance of Haitian Poetry* (1963), pp. 48–50; 139–144.

Additional Bibliography

Charles, Christophe. *Littérature haïtienne.* Port-au-Prince: Editions Choucoune, 2001.

CARROL F. COATES

LA LIBERTADORA REVOLUTION. La Libertadora Revolution (1901–1903), the last in a series of civil conflicts that plagued Venezuela during the nineteenth century. When Cipriano Castro took power in 1899, he began a process of military and political transformation that tended to centralize power and eliminate the political factionalism that was typical of the nineteenth century. The urgent need for financial resources and the chaotic budgetary situation of the country pitted Castro against the most notable bankers, creating a climate of tension which led to the revolution.

The uprising was financed and organized by Manuel Antonio Matos, an important Caracas banker, backed by the New York and Bermúdez Company, whose interests in the asphalt business were being affected by Castro's rule, as well as by important caudillos in the country. The revolution broke out in 1901 and rapidly spread throughout the entire country. The last battle took place in 1903. The government's triumph consolidated the politics of centralism and ended the politics of *caudillismo,* which had characterized late nineteenth-century politics in Venezuela.

See also **Castro, Cipriano; Caudillismo, Caudillo.**

BIBLIOGRAPHY

Eleazar López Contreras, *Páginas para la historia militar de Venezuela* (1945).

Orray Thurber, *Orígenes del capital norteamericano en Venezuela* (1983); and Inés Quintero, *El ocaso de una estirpe: La centralización restauradora y el fin de los caudillos históricos* (1989).

Additional Bibliography

Diaz, Arlene J. *Female Citizens, Patriarchs, and the Law in Venezuela, 1786-1904.* Lincoln: University of Nebraska Press, 2004.

Krispin, Karl. *La Revolución Libertadora.* Caracas: Banco de Venezuela, 1990.

INÉS QUINTERO

LAMADRID, GREGORIO ARÁOZ DE (1795–1857). Gregorio Aráoz de Lamadrid (*b.* 28 November 1795; *d.* 5 January 1857), Argentine military and political leader in the Río de la

Plata during the independence and early national periods. Born in Tucumán, Lamadrid entered the local militia in 1811. His revolutionary duties included fighting under Manuel Belgrano, José Rondeau, and José de San Martín in 1812–1820. Lamadrid sided with the Unitarists of Buenos Aires against the Federalists of the interior and, accordingly, fought against Juan Facundo Quiroga of La Rioja after assuming the governorship of Tucumán in 1825. He later fought against the dictatorship of Juan Manuel de Rosas. In addition to his personal service in the struggles for Argentine independence and nation building, Lamadrid wrote two basic sources concerning these events: his autobiography and a work on José María Paz that he completed shortly before his death in Buenos Aires.

See also **Rosas, Juan Manuel de; Wars of Independence: South America.**

BIBLIOGRAPHY

Lily Sosa De Newton, *Lamadrid* (1971).

Ernesto Quesada, *Lamadrid y la Coalición del Norte* (1965).

Jacinto R. Yaben, *Biografías argentinas y sudamericanas,* vol. 1 (1938–1940), pp. 278–285.

Additional Bibliography

Herrero, Fabián, and Klaus Gallo. *Revolución, política e ideas en el Río de la Plata durante la década de 1810.* Buenos Aires: Ediciones Cooperativas, 2004.

Lynch, John. *Argentine Caudillo: Juan Manuel de Rosas.* Wilmington, DE: SR Books, 2001.

Szuchman, Mark D., and Jonathan C. Brown, eds. *Revolution and Restoration: The Rearrangement of Power in Argentina, 1776–1860.* Lincoln: University of Nebraska Press, 1994.

FIDEL IGLESIAS

LAMAR, MIRABEAU BUONAPARTE

(1798–1859). Mirabeau Buonaparte Lamar (*b.* 16 August 1798; *d.* 19 December 1859), president of the republic of Texas (1838–1841). Born near Louisville, Georgia, Lamar founded (1828) and published the Columbus *Enquirer,* and served as secretary to Georgia governor George M. Troup and as state senator before moving to the Mexican province of Texas in 1835. Lamar was soon caught up in Texas's revolt against Mexico. His distinguished military service led to a succession of elected and appointed offices, including secretary of war, commander in chief of the army, vice president, and president of the Republic of Texas.

Lamar's presidency was characterized by many innovative, and often radical, programs. Texas became the first nation in the world to ensure that a person's home and livelihood could not be taken away because of debts. Lamar also established a system of public education endowed entirely from the public domain. But improvident adventures, such as the Santa Fe Expedition, which tried to wrest that trade center from Mexico in 1841, and the republic's continued financial troubles overshadowed the positive aspects of Lamar's administration. Following his retirement from the presidency, Lamar spent much of his time writing poetry and history. He also served in the Mexican-American War (1846–1848) and as minister to Nicaragua and Costa Rica (1858–1859). He died in Richmond, Texas, two months after returning from Central America.

See also **Texas; Texas Revolution.**

BIBLIOGRAPHY

Asa K. Christian, *Mirabeau Buonaparte Lamar* (1922).

Philip Graham, *The Life and Poems of Mirabeau B. Lamar* (1938).

Charles A. Gulick, ed., *The Papers of Mirabeau Buonaparte Lamar,* 6 vols. (1968).

Stanley Siegel, *The Poet President of Texas: The Life of Mirabeau B. Lamar, President of the Republic of Texas* (1977).

Additional Bibliography

Winders, Richard Bruce. *Crisis in the Southwest: The United States, Mexico, and the Struggle over Texas.* Wilmington, DE: SR Books, 2002.

MICHAEL R. GREEN

LAMARQUE, LIBERTAD

(1908–2000). Known as "The Bride of America," this Argentine actress and singer had one of the longest careers of any artist in Latin America. Born in Rosario on November 24, 1908, Lamarque began acting before the age of ten, with her father's support, in the theaters of her native city. She moved to Buenos

Aires in 1924 to start her professional career in the theater. Two years later she made her foray into tango, and themes such as "Madreselva," "Besos brujos," and "Gaucho del Sol" paved her way to success and into film. The timber of her voice was unique and lent her singing great expressivity in songs the public valued. In 1933, she was in the cast of *Tango*, the first talking picture in the history of Argentine film. During the 1930s and 1940s she was one of the most in-demand stars in Argentina, a country whose popular culture scene was then dominated by the tango and a flourishing film industry. In the following years she played in more than twenty films.

During the filming of *La Cabalgata del Circo*, Lamarque got into a heated argument with one of the other actresses in the cast, Eva (Evita) Duarte, who already had connections with future president Juan Domingo Perón. In the face of political pressures, she emigrated to Mexico, where, in 1947, she appeared in *Gran Casino*, a film by the Spanish director Luis Buñuel. She began to make trips back to Buenos Aires after 1955, when Perón was no longer in power. Her more than 400 musical recordings are a total unattained by any other Argentine singer. Although she revisited her native country several times to take leading roles in films and to record albums, she would always return to her beloved Mexico. There she spent her most active years and subsequently the final years of her life. She died on December 12, 2000.

See also **Argentina: The Twentieth Century; Buñuel, Luis; Perón, Juan Domingo; Perón, María Eva Duarte de; Rosario.**

BIBLIOGRAPHY

Lamarque, Libertad. *Libertad Lamarque*. Buenos Aires: J. Vergara Editor, 1986.

ELENA MOREIRA

LAMARQUE PONS, JAURÉS (1917–1982). Jaurés Lamarque Pons (*b.* 6 May 1917; *d.* 11 June 1982), Uruguayan composer and pianist. Lamarque Pons was born in Salto, where he began his music studies with María Victoria Varela (piano). Later he moved to Montevideo and took advanced piano lessons with Wilhelm Kolischer. He took courses in harmony, counterpoint, and instrumentation with Tomás Mujica and Guido Santórsola. In 1949 he enrolled in the composition classes of the Spanish composer Enrique Casal-Chapí. His *Aires de milonga* premiered in 1943. Lamarque's earlier music was universalist in character and included piano pieces, chamber music, and vocal works. He later composed in the nationalist style, using popular urban melodies, such as old tangos and *milongas* and the rhythms of the Afro-Uruguayan *tamboril.* From that period came his opera *Marta Gruni* (1965), with a libretto from the Uruguayan playwright Florencio Sánchez. After its 26 February 1967 premiere at the Teatro Solís under his baton, it became one of the most frequently performed Uruguayan operas. Other important works of Lamarque Pons include the ballet *Suite según Figari* (1952), *Suite Rioplatense* (1954), and the ballet-pantomime *El encargado* (1956). He also composed music for stage and films. Lamarque Pons died in Montevideo.

See also **Music: Art Music; Theater.**

BIBLIOGRAPHY

Composers of the Americas, vol. 16 (1970), pp. 102–107.

Susana Salgado, *Breve historia de la música culta en el Uruguay,* 2d ed. (1980).

Additional Bibliography

González Puig, Beatriz. *Jaurès Lamarque Pons.* Montevideo: Arca, 1995.

SUSANA SALGADO

LAMBADA. Lambada, musical style and dance from northern Brazil. *Lambada* became nationally popular at the end of the 1980s and flourished briefly as an international dance craze. Lambada originated in the mid-1970s in the state of Pará, where musicians such as Joachim de Lima Vieira were fusing Afro-Brazilian *carimbó* with merengue and elements of other Caribbean styles. The sensual *lambada* dance, in which the partners' thighs press close together, was a hybrid of the *maxixe, forró,* and merengue. *Lambada* gained popularity in Bahia and from there was exported to Europe and Spanish-speaking regions of Latin America. In 1989, the song "Lambada" (based on Gonzalo and Ulises Hermosa's "Llorando se fue") by the band Kaoma, was the number-one hit in fifteen countries.

See also **Music: Popular Music and Dance.**

BIBLIOGRAPHY

Chris McGowan and Ricardo Pessanha, *The Brazilian Sound: Samba, Bossa Nova, and the Popular Music of Brazil* (1991).

Additional Bibliography

Browning, Barbara. "The Daughters of Gandhi: Africanness, Indianness, and Brazilianness in the Bahian Carnival." *Women & Performance* 7.14–15 (1995): 151–169.

CHRIS MCGOWAN

LAMBAYEQUE. Lambayeque, the name of a modern Peruvian town, district, province, and department. The department, which was created by law 10 December 1874, is bounded by the department of Piura on the north, the department of La Libertad on the south, the department of Cajamarca on the east, and the Pacific Ocean on the west. Its territory encompasses the desert coast; fertile, irrigated river valleys; and the western slopes of the Andes Mountains.

The town of Lambayeque became increasingly important during the colonial period. Encompassing a large community of Indians, at the time of the Spanish Conquest, Lambayeque became a very valuable *encomienda* entrusted by Francisco Pizarro in 1536 to Juan de Barbarán, his loyal supporter and confidant. By the earliest years of the seventeenth century, the town had become an important stopover on the overland route to Lima. Twice thereafter, the town became a refuge for the provincial elite: first, on 14 February 1619, following an earthquake that damaged Trujillo, and second, after the flood of 1720, which destroyed the provincial capital of Saña. As a consequence of the flood, Saña's citizens made Lambayeque the de facto administrative center of the area, a function it performed into the nineteenth century.

During the early nineteenth century, Lambayeque was the third department, after Ica and Tarma, to choose independence. In the late twentieth century, the department was known for its sugar production. It also became known nationally for a pastry called "King Kong," still a sought-after item found in markets across Peru. The town of Lambayeque has been eclipsed by the departmental capital and bustling commercial emporium of Chiclayo. In 1987 archaeologist Walter Alva discovered an extraordinarily rich archaeological site outside of Chiclayo. Known as Sipán, the Moche burial site somehow escaped the rampant looting that damaged and destroyed many other archaeological sites throughout Peru's northern coastal region. Artifacts found there include metalwork in gold and silver, as well as various masks and jewelry pieces made of precious stone.

See also **Moche; Sipán; Sugar Industry; Tarma.**

BIBLIOGRAPHY

Ricardo A. Miranda, *Monografía general del Departmento de Lambayeque* (1927).

David P. Werlich, *Peru: A Short History* (1978).

Hans Heinrich Brüning, *Estudios monográficos del Departmento de Lambayeque* (1989).

Additional Bibliography

Fernández Alvarado, Julio César. *Sinto, señorío, e identidad en la costa norte lambayecana.* Chiclayo, Peru: Consultores y Promotores Turísticos del Norte (COPROTUR), 2004.

Ibáñez, Eugenio W. *Lambayeque: Mitología y realidad.* Peru, 1997.

Pillsbury, Joanne, ed. *Moche Art and Archaeology in Ancient Peru.* Washington, DC: National Gallery of Art; New Haven, CT: Distributed by Yale University Press, 2001.

Ramírez, Susan E. *Provincial Patriarchs: Land Tenure and the Economics of Power in Colonial Peru.* Albuquerque: University of New Mexico Press, 1986.

SUSAN E. RAMÍREZ

LAMBITYECO. Lambityeco was one of the principal Zapotec settlements in the Valley of Oaxaca occupied during the Monte Albán IV period (750–1000). During this period Monte Albán, which had served as the regional capital for over 1,200 years, was gradually abandoned. As its political and economic power waned, other centers in the valley such as Lambityeco, Macuilxochitl, and Jalieza increased in power and influence. This decentralization was accompanied by a low degree of formal political integration and a secularization of authority, trends that characterized the postclassic throughout Mesoamerica.

Located in the eastern arm of the Valley of Oaxaca, a little over a mile west of the modern town of Tlacolula, Lambityeco is the Period IV sector of a larger site known as Yegüih, which has more than 200 mounds over an area of about 188 acres. Lambityeco, in the northwest sector of the site, consists of about seventy mounds.

Excavations in two of the larger mounds (Mounds 190 and 195) revealed that they were elite residences. In their earliest versions, they were simple houses with a single patio. Mound 190 was reconstructed at least five times, and Mound 195 was rebuilt at least once before being converted into a pyramid. Both structures had family tombs. The tomb in Mound 195 had lifelike stucco representations of a man and a woman above the door and two stucco friezes each depicting a man and a woman in possible marriage scenes. The tomb in Mound 190 contained a large number of ceramic vessels characteristic of Period IV, carved bones, bone tools, and unfired clay vessels.

The unfired clay vessels and millions of pottery sherds on the surface suggest local ceramic production at Lambityeco, and a clay source has been identified at the site. A standardized bowl form apparently was produced on a massive, commercial scale. Another important local industry was salt production. It also seems likely that the site served an important function as a central marketplace.

See also **Archaeology.**

BIBLIOGRAPHY

John Paddock, "Lambityeco," in *The Cloud People: The Divergent Evolution of the Zapotec and Mixtec Civilizations,* edited by Kent V. Flannery and Joyce Marcus (1983), pp. 197–204.

Richard E. Blanton, Stephen A. Kowalewski, Gary Feinman, and Jill Appel, *Ancient Mesoamerica: A Comparison of Change in Three Regions,* 2d ed. (1993).

Additional Bibliography

Flannery, Kent V., and Joyce Marcus. *Early Formative Pottery of the Valley of Oaxaca.* Ann Arbor: Museum of Anthropology, University of Michigan, 1994.

Kowalewski, Stephen A. *Prehispanic Settlement Patterns in Tlacolula, Etla, and Ocotlan, the Valley of Oaxaca, Mexico.* Ann Arbor: Regents of the University of Michigan, Museum of Anthropology, 1989.

Marcus, Joyce, and Kent V. Flannery. *Zapotec Civilization: How Urban Society Evolved in Mexico's Oaxaca Valley.* New York: Thames and Hudson, 1996.

William R. Fowler

LAME, MANUEL QUINTÍN (1883–1967). Manuel Quintín Lame (*b.* 31 October 1883; *d.* 7 October 1967), Colombian indigenous leader and author. The son of Páez sharecroppers, Lame organized the Indians of the departments of Cauca and Tolima. His efforts, which met with severe repression by Colombia authorities, revolved around the following demands: (1) defense of the *resguardo,* a communal landholding corporation of indigenous people; (2) consolidation of the *cabildo* (*resguardo* council) as a center of political authority; (3) reclaiming of lands usurped from the *resguardo;* (4) refusal by sharecroppers to pay rent; and (5) reaffirmation of indigenous cultural values.

Although Lame's program was obstructed in Cauca, where his 1910–1921 campaign provoked military occupation, police violence, and the eventual imprisonment of Lame and his associates, his efforts in Tolima were more successful. The pressure exerted by the growth of the coffee economy upon indigenous landholdings in Tolima resulted in the division of *resguardos.* Lame's campaign, which lasted from 1922 to 1939, restored the *resguardo* status of Ortega and Chaparral, thus reversing over a century of land loss under capitalist expansion.

Lame is best known for a 118-page manuscript, "Los pensamientos del indio que se educó dentro de las selvas colombianas" (The Thoughts of the Indian Who Was Educated in the Colombian Forests). Although it was completed in 1939, *Los pensamientos* was published only posthumously in 1971 as *En defensa de mi raza* (In Defense of My Race). This autobiographical treatise outlines Lame's political philosophy, offers an idiosyncratic vision of indigenous history, and denounces specific crimes against Colombian Indians. *Los pensamientos* is a philosophical attack on capitalism, called "civilization" by its author, and is strongly messianic in character.

See also **Resguardo.**

BIBLIOGRAPHY

Diego Castrillón Arboleda, *El indio Quintín Lame* (1973).

Gonzalo Castillo-Cárdenas, *Liberation Theology from Below: The Life and Thought of Manuel Quintín Lame* (1987).

Joanne Rappaport, *The Politics of Memory: Native Historical Interpretation in the Colombian Andes* (1990)

Additional Bibliography

Espinosa Arango, Mónica Lucía. "Of Visions and Sorrows: Manuel Quintín Lame's Indian Thought and the Violences of Colombia." Ph.D. diss., University of Massachusetts Amherst, 2004.

Romero Loaiza, Fernando. *Manuel Quintín Lame Chantre: El indígena ilustrado, el pensador indigenista.* Pereira: F. Romero Loaiza, 2005.

JOANNE RAPPAPORT

LAMPIÃO (1897–1938).

LAMPIÃO (1897–1938). Lampião (Virgulino Ferreira da Silva: *b.* 7 July 1897; *d.* 28 July 1938), Brazilian bandit. Brazil's best-known bandit of all time, Lampião was a world-class bandit as well. Son of a modest rancher and hauler in the backlands of Pernambuco, he went astray when he and his brothers began to feud with neighbors. As violence increased on both sides, the Ferreiras, of lower social status than their adversaries, were branded, not unjustly, as outlaws. After 1922, Lampião became the preeminent figure in the *cangaço,* the name given to the organized brigandage that flourished in the region from the 1870s to the 1930s. He seemingly verged on legality in 1926, when Father Cícero Romão Batista of Juàzeiro had him commissioned a captain in forces hastily raised to oppose Luís Carlos Prestes's wandering revolutionaries. But the patent proved to be worthless, and he reverted to outlawry. For sixteen years, roaming over seven states; living from extortion, robbery, and abductions; and enjoying protection from sometimes reluctant ranchers, political bosses, and even for a time a state governor, he and his band so vanquished police and army forces sent against them that they virtually dominated portions of the backlands. Conscious of his image and ever catering to the press, he became one of the nation's most newsworthy figures, and the story of his exploits reached abroad. Partly the result of strengthened efforts, but largely by luck, the police killed him, his companion, Maria Bonita, and several others of his band in a surprise attack in Sergipe in 1938. Thus the *cangaço* ended. Lampião, whose preserved head long lay in a museum in Salvador, survives in folkore and history.

See also **Banditry; Cangaceiro.**

BIBLIOGRAPHY

Billy Jaynes Chandler, *The Bandit King: Lampião of Brazil* (1978).

Optato Gueiros, *"Lampião": Memórias de um oficial excommandante de forças volantes* (1952).

Ranulpho Prata, *Lampeão* (1934).

Additional Bibliography

Barros, Luitgarde Oliveira Cavalcanti. *A derradeira gesta: Lampião e nazarenos guerreando no sertão.* Rio de Janeiro: Mauad: FAPERJ, 2000.

BILLY JAYNES CHANDLER

LAM Y CASTILLA, WIFREDO (1902–1982).

LAM Y CASTILLA, WIFREDO (1902–1982). Wifredo Lam y Castilla (*b.* 9 December 1902; *d.* 11 September 1982), Cuban painter. Born in Sagua la Grande of a Chinese father and mulatto mother, Lam received a scholarship from the town council in 1921 to study in Havana. From 1923 to 1937 he studied in Madrid, and from 1937 to 1939 he worked in Paris with Pablo Picasso and rediscovered his African ancestry. The events of World War II forced Lam to Marseilles in 1939 and out of France in 1941 with a group of three hundred intellectuals who chose exile from the Vichy government. Seven months after leaving France, he returned to Cuba. In 1942–1943, he painted *The Jungle,* his best-known work. He lived in Paris, New York, and Havana from 1946 to 1964, finally settling in the Italian town of Albissola Marina. In 1966, he returned to Cuba and painted *The Third World* for display in the Presidential Palace. His works run the gamut from postimpressionist to surrealist to postcubist styles, yet he never lost his devotion to the African influence. His paintings are unique in depicting African Cuban vodun spirits in a style based on Picasso and West Indian devices. Internationally acclaimed, he stands as Cuba's foremost modern painter.

See also **Art: The Twentieth Century.**

BIBLIOGRAPHY

Max-Pol Fouchet, *Wilfredo Lam* (1976).

Antonio Núñez Jiménez, *Wilfredo Lam* (1982).

Antonio Núñez Jiménez *Exposición antológica "Homenaje a Wilfredo Lam" 1902–1982,* issued by the Museo Nacional de Arte Contemporaneo, Madrid (1982).

Additional Bibliography

Noceda, José Manuel. *Wifredo Lam: La cosecha de un brujo.* La Habana: Letras Cubanas, 2002.

Sims, Lowery Stokes. *Wilfredo Lam: And the International Avant-garde, 1923–1982.* Austin: University of Texas Press, 2002.

Wilson, Andrew R., ed. *The Chinese in the Caribbean.* Princeton, NJ: M. Wiener Publishers, 2004.

JACQUELYN BRIGGS KENT

LANDA, DIEGO DE (1524–1579). Diego De Landa (*b.* 1524; *d.* 1579), Castilian Franciscan missionary. Born in Cifuentes, Landa entered the monastery of San Juan de los Reyes in Toledo when he was sixteen. In 1549 he journeyed to Yucatán, where he learned the Maya language and ministered to the Maya people. Landa, one of the earliest Franciscans in Yucatán, helped convert the Maya to Christianity, only to discover that they refused to abandon their traditional religion. Suspecting them of carrying out human sacrifice using Catholic ritual, he organized an inquisition (1562) that eventually led to the imprisonment and torture of 4,400 Indians. After extracting confessions, and after more than 170 people had died under torture or by committing suicide, Landa held an auto-da-fé (day of judgment, punishment, and penance) on 12 July 1562 and pardoned the survivors. He was later charged with misconduct in the affair but defended himself successfully and in 1564 returned to Spain, where he wrote his book about Maya history and culture (*Relación de las cosas de Yucatán*). He returned to Yucatán in 1573 as bishop and died there seven years later without further controversy.

See also **Franciscans; Maya, The; Yucatán.**

BIBLIOGRAPHY

Inga Clendinnen, *Ambivalent Conquests: Maya and Spaniard in Yucatán, 1517–1570* (1987).

Juan Francisco Molina Solís, *Historia de Yucatán durante la dominación española,* vol. 1 (1904).

Additional Bibliography

Chuchiak, John F. "'In Servitio Dei': Fray Diego de Landa, The Franciscan Order, and the Return of the Extirpation of Idolatry in the Colonial Diocese of Yucatán, 1573–1579." *The Americas* 61:4 (April 2005): 611–646.

Timmer, David E. "Providence and Perdition: Fray Diego de Landa Justifies his Inquisition against the Yucatecan Maya." *Church History* 66:3 (September 1997): 477–488.

ROBERT W. PATCH

LANDALUZE, VÍCTOR PATRICIO DE (1828–1889). Víctor Patricio de Landaluze (*b.* 1828; *d.* 8 June 1889), Cuban painter and cartoonist who is considered the precursor of graphic political satire in Cuba. Born in Bilbao, Spain, Landaluze emigrated in the 1850s to Havana, where he founded the newspaper *Don Junípero* (1862). Between 1868 and 1878, he was the political cartoonist for *La Charanga, El Moro Muza* (under the pseudonym of Bayaceto), *Don Circunstancias,* and *Juan Palomo,* weekly journals through which he satirized the Cuban struggle for independence. He was both professor at and director of the Academy of San Alejandro in Havana.

In oil and watercolor paintings, he depicted popular Cuban stereotypes such as the *guajiro* (a rustic type), the landowner, the slave, and the *ñanigo* (a member of a secret black society), and illustrated the books *Tipos y costumbres* (Types and Customs) and *Cuba pintoresca* (Picturesque Cuba), both published in 1881.

His ironic attitude toward the Cuban independence movement earned him the antipathy of art critics. Ironically, his painting of the backward *campesino* Liborio became a Cuban national symbol. With the exception of an oil painting of a fugitive slave cornered by dogs and soldiers (*El cimarrón* [The Runaway Slave]), Landaluze's work is often considered biased in his presentation of blacks as lazy and lascivious. Much of his production, however, recorded with exactitude the costumes and rituals of the different nations of Cuban blacks. He died in Guanabacoa.

See also **Campesino; Journalism.**

BIBLIOGRAPHY

Dawn Ades, *Art in Latin America: The Modern Era, 1820–1980* (1989), p. 85.

Adelaida De Juan, *Pintura cubana: Temas y variaciones* (1980), pp. 25–26, 33–36, 46.

Additional Bibliography

Landaluze, Víctor Patricio de. *Víctor Patricio Landaluze.* La Habana: Editorial Letras Cubanas, 1991.

MARTA GARSD

LANDÁZURI RICKETTS, JUAN

LANDÁZURI RICKETTS, JUAN (1913–1997). Juan Landázuri Ricketts (*b.* 19 December 1913; *d.* 16 January 1997), archbishop of Lima and primate of Peru (1955–1988), cardinal (1962–1997). Landázuri led the Peruvian Catholic church through a period of transformation in that institution's understanding of its mission in society. A Franciscan, and considered a Church moderate, Landázuri championed the Church's commitment to the reform of social and economic structures. Enjoying great prestige among fellow bishops, he copresided over the Second Conference of Latin American Bishops (CELAM) at Medellín, Colombia, in 1968 and served as the vice president of the Latin American Bishops' Council at the time of its third general conference in Puebla, Mexico (1979). Under his leadership, the Peruvian church distanced itself from the state and traditional elites, democratized church decision-making procedures, and turned its attention to organizing the poor. Though famous for his mediation skills, Landázuri's defense of the Liberation Theology of Gustavo Gutiérrez, a Peruvian priest, culminated in the 1980s in clashes with the Vatican and division among an increasingly conservative Peruvian hierarchy.

See also **Catholic Church: The Modern Period; Conference of Latin American Bishops; Liberation Theology.**

BIBLIOGRAPHY

Catalino Romero, *Iglesia en el Perú: Compromiso y renovación (1958–1984)* (1987).

Penny Lernoux, *People of God* (1989), esp. pp. 98–102, 114–115.

Additional Bibliography

Figari, Luis Fernando. *Horizontes de reconciliación.* Lima: Vida et Espiritualidad, 2004.

MATTHEW J. O' MEAGHER

LANDÍVAR, RAFAEL

LANDÍVAR, RAFAEL (1731–1793). Rafael Landívar (*b.* 27 October 1731; *d.* 1793), Guatemalan Jesuit priest and writer, born in Santiago de los Caballeros de Guatemala, today known as Old Guatemala City. He graduated from San Borja School and earned his Ph.D. in philosophy from the Pontifical University of San Carlos at the age of sixteen. Later he traveled to Mexico (1749) and in 1750 joined the Jesuit order. Five years later he was ordained a priest. In 1761 he returned to Guatemala, where he assumed the position of rector at the College of San Francisco de Borja.

When Charles III expelled the Jesuits from the American continent six years later, Landívar and his colleagues roamed the ports of Europe for a year, an odyssey which finally ended when the Jesuits were allowed to settle in Italy. Though Charles III prohibited the members of the Jesuit order from performing priestly duties and writing books, this did not prevent Landívar from writing in Bologna. His works include *Oración fúnebre a la muerte del arzobispo de Guatemala, Francisco Figueredo y Victoria,* two odes in Latin and one in Castilian, and the collection of poems entitled *Salva cara parens.* His most outstanding work, however, is *Rusticatio mexicana,* a mournful song of his native land in which he describes its natural attributes, its customs, and its disasters such as volcanic eruptions and earthquakes. The first edition was published in Modena in 1781 and the second in Bologna in 1782. It is the first ode to the Guatemalan homeland by a political exile and is considered the best verse about Latin America ever written in Latin.

See also **Charles III of Spain; Jesuits.**

BIBLIOGRAPHY

Catalina Barrios y Barrios, *Rafael Landívar: Vida y obra* (1982).

Antonio Batres Jáuregui, *Landívar e Irisarri: Literatos guatemaltecos,* 2d ed. (1957).

José Mata Gavidia, ed., *Landívar, el poeta de Guatemala* (1979).

Additional Bibliography

Higgins, Antony. *Constructing the Criollo Archive: Subjects of Knowledge in the Bibliotheca Mexicana and the*

Rusticatio Mexicana. West Lafayette, IN: Purdue University Press, 2000.

Recinos, Ivonne N. "La 'Rusticatio Mexicana' y su relación con las reformas borbónicas." *Revista Iberoamericana* 94 (July–August 2002): 147–174.

FERNANDO GONZÁLEZ DAVISON

LAND LAW OF 1850 (BRAZIL). The Lei de Terra made purchase the only means of acquiring public lands by abolishing the right to acquire legal title through simple occupancy. Containing 108 articles, the law was subject to long debate. Passed on 18 September 1850, it was not published and put into effect until 30 June 1854. The law created a service called the General Bureau of Public Lands (*Repartição Geral das Terras Públicas*) to control access and promote colonization.

The Land Law represented a reformulation of land policy in Brazil. During the colonial period land was acquired through effective occupation, purchase, inheritance, or donation. Donations (*sesmarias*) were crown grants of public lands awarded to petitioners in recognition of their service to the crown, or for the purpose of settlement. At independence, donations of *sesmarias* were abolished and effective occupation, purchase, and inheritance of land became the prevailing forms of acquisition until 1850.

The Land Law vested the ownership of all free land in the state. It confirmed the pre-1850 claims of existing occupants and provided for the official registration and surveying of those claims, upon presentation of proof concerning effective occupation and cultivation. The Land Law limited the size of claims to the dimensions of the largest *sesmaria* in each district. It required a vast bureaucracy at the local level, since it delegated to police officers and judges the responsibility for informing the government of the existence and location of public lands. It also empowered parish priests to register lands after local civil servants located and measured the claim. Funds from land sales and the registration of private claims were to be dedicated to measuring public lands and defraying the costs of settling European colonists.

According to some interpretations, the intent of the Land Law was to stimulate the occupation and colonization of public lands, while others link the abolition of the transatlantic slave trade and the passage of the Land Law to a reevaluation of public policy regarding land and labor. In conjunction with a general refocusing of the national economy, from the sugar production of the Northeast to the coffee farming of the Center South, the public regulation of land and labor restricted access to land in favor of the increasing demands of the external capitalist market. The clause that linked the official recognition of claims to a deed of purchase permitted the establishment of a complex bureaucracy to control access to public lands, thus favoring commercial use of land. As a result, the Land Law of 1850 transformed land into a marketable product and legitimized the alienation of unclaimed lands by monied and propertied interests, thereby reinforcing the tendency toward land concentration begun by the *sesmarias*.

Lack of human resources to implement the registration and measurement of lands, a weak bureaucracy at the local level, and resistance by local landowners contributed to the minor impact the law had on the agrarian structure of the country.

See also **Fazenda, Fazendeiro.**

BIBLIOGRAPHY

Emília Viotti Da Costa, *The Brazilian Empire: Myths and Histories* (1985).

Additional Bibliography

Aguiar, Maria do Amparo Albuquerque. *Terras de Goiás: Estrutura fundiária, 1850-1920.* Goiânia: Editora UFG, 2003.

Holston, James. *Insurgent Citizenship: Disjunctions of Democracy and Modernity in Brazil.* Princeton, NJ: Princeton University Press, 2008.

Silva, Ligia Maria Osório. *Terras devolutas e latifúndio: Efeitos da lei de 1850.* Campinas: Editora da Unicamp, 1996.

NANCY PRISCILLA SMITH NARO

LAND TENURE, BRAZIL. There are two principal types of land tenure in Brazil. The first dates back to the legal ownership of land by deed, officially granted by Sesmarias (crown grants) in the sixteenth century. The other form of land tenure, which paralleled that of legal claim, was related to title through occupation or squatting and through cultivation of the land. After Brazilian independence in 1822, the granting of *sesmarias* was discontinued. Until the Land Law of 1850, claim to land was recognized by its effective occupation and cultivation.

Land usage varied throughout Brazil. A *chácara,* or country establishment on the outskirts of a town or city, was typically a small or medium-sized farm where the proprietor owned both the land and its produce, often foodstuffs. Other small holdings for subsistence cultivation and some livestock breeding usually contained a small cabin or two and might also have included primitive processing facilities for manioc, beans, and corn. These units existed on unclaimed plots of land and also within fazendas (large rural properties). They were referred to variously as *roças, sítios,* and *situações.* Their occupants were squatters or leaseholders (*posseiros*), renters (*arrendatários*), tenants (*foreiros*), or sharecroppers (*parceiros*), many of whom paid an annual rent in cash and labor services to the landowner and owned small numbers of slaves. During the nineteenth century, small farms within the confines of large ones or within plantations could be freely exchanged or sold by their occupants without the prior knowledge of or consultation with the landowner. This arrangement began to change when landowners, faced with increasing production costs and diminishing prices for slave labor in the 1880s, began to control land use and labor through contracts and other formal agreements.

See also **Fazenda, Fazendeiro; Sesmaria.**

BIBLIOGRAPHY

Nancy Priscilla Smith Naro, "Customary Rightholders and Legal Claimants to Land in Rio de Janeiro, Brazil, 1850–1890," in *The Americas* (April 1992).

Additional Bibliography

Garfield, Seth. *Indigenous Struggle at the Heart of Brazil: State Policy, Frontier Expansion, and the Xavante Indians, 1937–1988.* Durham, NC: Duke University Press, 2001.

Miller, Shawn William. "Stilt-Root Subsistence: Colonial Mangroves and Brazil's Landless Poor." *The Hispanic American Historical Review.* 83:2 (May 2003): 223–253.

NANCY PRISCILLA SMITH NARO

LAND TENURE, SPANISH AMERICA.

See **Hacienda.**

LANUSSE, ALEJANDRO AGUSTÍN

(1918–1996). As a member of the Argentine military and a politician, Lanusse became the last de facto president of the Argentine Revolution (1966–1973). Born August 28, 1918, he entered the army's Military Academy in 1938. He was a determined anti-Peronist and in 1951 took part in the failed coup against Perón (ruled 1946–1955) led by General Benjamin Menéndez. He was sentenced to life in prison but was released following the overthrow of Perón in 1955. Ambassador to the Holy See in 1956, in 1960 he was appointed assistant director of the Higher School of War. A member of the "Legalist" (blue) faction of the army, in June 1966 he played an active role in the military coup that removed President Arturo Illia from office.

In 1968 Lanusse was appointed commander in chief of the army. After the civil uprising known as the *Cordobazo* in 1969 and the kidnapping of General Pedro Aramburu in 1970, Lanusse forced the resignation of de facto president Juan Onganía through the Junta of Commanders. With the regime cornered by the political and social crisis, and with guerrilla violence increasing, after the brief presidency of General Roberto Levingston, Lanusse assumed the presidency in March 1971, with the aim of pushing forward a transition to democracy. He promoted the Great National Accord reestablishing political party activity, and called for elections for 1973. He lifted the ban on Peronism and ordered the corpse of Eva Duarte to be returned to Perón. However, owing to his political aspirations, as well as to the tensions he had to deal with from within the military regime, he considerably manipulated the political process by imposing ad hoc rules that kept Perón from running as a candidate.

Following Hector Cámpora's triumph in the presidential elections, Lanusse virtually withdrew from active politics, although he was to be very critical of the subsequent military dictatorship (1976–1983). In 1985 he testified in the trial of the military juntas for the torture and disappearance of his former press secretary and his cousin. Lanusse died in Buenos Aires on August 26, 1996.

See also **Aramburu, Pedro Eugenio; Argentina: The Twentieth Century; Cámpora, Héctor José; Cordobazo, El; Illia, Arturo Umberto; Levingston, Roberto Marcelo; Onganía, Juan Carlos; Perón, Juan Domingo; Perón, María Eva Duarte de.**

BIBLIOGRAPHY

Halperín Donghi, Tulio. *La larga agonía de la Argentina Perónista.* Buenos Aires: Ariel, 1994.

Lanusse, Alejandro Agustín. *Mi testimonio.* Buenos Aires: Lasserre, 1977.

ÓDonnell, Guillermo. *El Estado burocrático autoritario.* Buenos Aires: Editorial UB, 1982.

Rouquié, Alain. *Poder militar y sociedad política en la Argentina.* Buenos Aires: EMECE, 1981.

VICENTE PALERMO

LANZA, ALCIDES (1929–). Alcides Lanza is an Argentine-Canadian composer. Born in Rosario, Argentina, on June 2, 1929, Lanza studied composition with Julián Batista and Alberto Ginastera. He continued his studies at the Instituto Di Tella in Buenos Aires (1963–1964). From 1959 to 1965 he was a member of the artistic staff of the Teatro Colón in Buenos Aires, where he became one of the founding members of Agrupación Música Viva. Awarded a Guggenheim Fellowship in 1965, he studied with Ussachevsky and Mimaroglu at the Columbia-Princeton Electronic Music Centre in New York. Since 1971, he has been professor of composition and electronic music at McGill University in Montreal, becoming a naturalized Canadian in 1976.

Showing the influence of his earlier architectural studies, his scores are based on ideograms, graphisms, and drawings, all intended to give a direct representation of his musical ideas. A substantial amount of Lanza's production includes electroacoustics either on tape, live processing, or both. Notable are several pieces written for his life and artistic partner the actress-singer Meg Sheppard, with whom he has performed extensively in Canada and elsewhere promoting his music and that of many Latin American and Canadian avant-garde composers. Lanza's scores and recordings are published by Editions Shelan Publications in Montreal.

See also **Ginastera, Alberto Evaristo; Music: Art Music.**

BIBLIOGRAPHY

John Vinton, ed., *Dictionary of Contemporary Music* (1971).

Gérard Béhague, *Music in Latin America: An Introduction* (1979).

Andrée Laurier, "Le compositeur À l'ère de l'électronique et des nouvelles facilités de la composition," in *Le compositeur canadien* (March 1984): 15–19.

Additional Bibliography

Jones, Pamela. *Alcides Lanza: Portrait of a Composer.* Montreal: McGill-Queen's University Press, 2008.

SERGIO BARROSO

LA OROYA. La Oroya, town and mineral smelting center in the central highlands of Peru (1990 population 33,594). At 12,200 feet, La Oroya stands at the crossroads of the central railway and highway systems connecting the mining center of Cerro de Pasco and the commercial city of Huancayo with the country's capital, Lima. The railway reached La Oroya in 1893 and a year later the Cerro De Pasco Corporation, formed with U.S. investment capital (Guggenheim interests), began to establish a smelting complex to treat minerals from Cerro de Pasco, Morococha, and other nearby mining areas. This gave the Cerro de Pasco Corporation the technological advantage to displace foreign and domestic competition. The smelter was upgraded by 1922. Pollution from the smelter modified the agrarian landscape and made possible the purchase of rich pasture lands formerly owned by the native Cattlemen's Society of Junín. With the nationalization of mining interests between 1968 and 1975, La Oroya smelter was managed by a state company.

BIBLIOGRAPHY

Florencia Mallon, *The Defense of Community in Peru's Central Highlands: Peasant Struggle and Capitalist Transition, 1860–1940* (1983).

Elizabeth Dore, *The Peruvian Mining Industry: Growth, Stagnation, and Crisis* (1988).

Additional Bibliography

Pajuelo, Ramón. *Medioambiente y salud en La Oroya: Sistematización de un programa de intervención.* Lima: CooperAcción, Acción Solidaria para el Desarrollo, 2005.

ALFONSO W. QUIROZ

LAPA VERMELHA. The archaeological site Lapa Vermelha, a complex of rock-shelters and caves, is located at Pedro Leopoldo, approximately 30 kilometers from Belo Horizonte, the state capital of Minas Gerais, Brazil. Lapa Vermelha IV is one of the shelters and caves to be systematically excavated. Excavations at Lapa Vermelha IV, which stopped at approximately 13 meters below the surface, were carried out from 1971 to 1976 by a French-Brazilian mission led by Annette Laming-Emperaire. In general, the site was very poor in terms of evidence of human occupation, with occasional hearths and dispersed stony debris of quartz distributed along the geologic layers. Dates from present until circa 23 BCE were obtained by regular carbon-14 applied to charcoal. Stone tools unequivocally produced by humans were found until circa 10 BCE. However, a very fine stone tool and some stone flakes were found associated to a level dated to circa 13 BCE. Natural vertical transportation from higher levels could not peremptorily be ruled out as a possible explanation for such an early date. The most important finding at Lapa Vermelha IV was the human skeleton later known as "Luzia," one of the oldest, if not the oldest, human skeleton ever found in the Americas. Like other early human skeletons from South and Central America, Luzia exhibits a cranial morphology very different from late and modern Amerindians, showing a remarkable similarity with present Australians and Melanesians.

See also **Archaeology.**

BIBLIOGRAPHY

Laming-Emperaire, Annette. "Missions archéologiques franque-brésiliennes de Lagoa Santa, Minas Gerais, Brésil: Lê grand abris de Lapa Vermelha (P.L.)." *Revista de Pré-História* 1, no. 1 (1979): 53–89.

Neves, Walter Alves, Joseph Powell, and Erik Ozolins. "Extra-Continental Morphological Affinities of Lapa Vermelha IV, Hominid 1: A Multivariate Analysis with Progressive Numbers of Variables." *Homo* 50, no. 3 (1999): 263–282.

Prous, André. "L'archéologie au Brésil: 300 Siècles d'occupation humaine." *L'Anthropologie* 90, no. 2 (1986): 257–306.

WALTER A. NEVES

LA PAZ. La Paz, city and region of Bolivia, located in the western part of the nation; the city is situated some 50 miles southeast of Lake Titicaca. Covering an area of 51,732 square miles, the department of La Paz contains four distinct ecological zones: altiplano (12,000 feet or higher), high valley (12,000–8,000 feet), *yungas* or steep valleys (8,000–4,000 feet), and the Amazon Basin (4,000–1,000 feet). Each is characterized by distinct agricultural production. Potatoes and barley are grown on the altiplano, corn in the valleys, and tropical fruits at lower elevations. The city of La Paz is located in a high valley zone and in 2006 had a population of 835,000. The urban agglomeration amounted to 1.7 million people out of a departmental total of 2,672,800 inhabitants.

When Alonso de Mendoza founded the city of La Paz on 20 October 1548, he chose a site amid densely populated Aymara villages. The tribute lists of the first *encomiendas* (1560) showed why La Paz attracted Spanish settlers. Items delivered to the *encomenderos* included wool in the form of manufactured garments, llamas, sheep, pigs, corn, salt, fish, eggs, potatoes, coca, and cotton. *Encomiendas* also regularly supplied labor for the Spanish farms near the city and for the alluvial goldfields in the province of Larecaja.

After the demise of the *encomienda*, Aymaras continued to be important components of the Spanish economic system. The large number of surviving villagers on the altiplano paid tribute in coin derived from their labor at the Potosí mine and the marketing of their agricultural surplus in urban centers. Other villagers migrated to the Spanish-owned haciendas either on the altiplano or in the valley zones, where they became resident Colonos fulfilling obligations of labor and personal service to the owners. By the 1830s, out of a total Indian population of 500,000 in the department of La Paz, 70 percent resided in Indian villages and 30 percent on haciendas.

For the Spaniards, the city of La Paz served not only as a repository of goods from the immediate area but also as a trade center on the route from Potosí to Lima and an administrative center for Spanish authorities. Because of those functions, the city grew from a population of almost 6,000 in 1586 to 30,000 by independence in 1825.

During the colonial period only two uprisings occurred: an artisan tax revolt of 1661 led by Antonio Gallardo and an Indian uprising of 1781 led by Julián Apaza Túpac Catari. After the Indian siege had been lifted by Spanish troops in 1781, and rebel leaders had been executed, the memory of the rebellion reminded Indians and creoles alike of the deep divisions in colonial society.

During the early independence period, 1825–1880, regional caudillos, many of whom received their military training in the republican armies, dipped their hands generously into the treasury of La Paz, which was the largest in Bolivia because of Indian tribute payments. Thus, although Sucre was the official capital, La Paz became the de facto center of government. Once in power, however, caudillos altered colonial social relations very little.

In 1880 silver barons from southern Bolivia seized political control and stressed export-led development. They not only opened trade, built railroads, and established banks but also removed government protection for Indian communities and sponsored hacienda expansion. In the department of La Paz between 1880 and 1916, approximately 30 percent of Indian communal householders sold their land to elite residents of the city of La Paz. Meanwhile, La Paz became the official "second" capital of Bolivia, confirmed in the Federalist War of 1899. After the railroad reached the city in 1905, La Paz became the terminus of the import trade and the business headquarters for banks and exporters involved in the rubber and tin trade. By 1942 the city of La Paz had about 287,000 inhabitants and included a large, politically active middle class.

During the 1940s, the National Revolutionary Movement (MNR) galvanized the latent political strength of the urban middle class when the party branded the government a tool of the tin mine owners. The 1952 revolution took place in the streets of La Paz and ushered in a reform government. But while MNR leaders expropriated the largest tin mines, implemented an agrarian reform that returned land to the tillers, and opened the electorate to all adults, other demographic and political forces proved stronger than the reform program. Despite having legal access to land, Indians increasingly moved into the city because population growth exceeded available land resources. Simultaneously, the government enlarged the bureaucracy and expanded state-run enterprises, and private, small-scale capitalists developed a manufacturing sector, particularly in textiles and food processing. Under these conditions, the city population increased to 992,000 by 1985. Thus, alongside modern office buildings and cosmopolitan hotels, Indians have their own markets and form the majority of inhabitants in certain sectors of the city.

Cholos (mestizos) comprise the largest portion of the city's population. They are defined by their cultural characteristics. *Cholos* speak both Spanish and Aymara, dress in a Western style, and participate in the national economy and political system. Their jobs and incomes vary greatly. They are waiters, truck drivers, merchants, mechanics, store owners, factory employees, white-collar workers, construction workers, and artisans of all sorts. *Cholos* comprise the rank and file of urban political parties and staff the government's bureaucracy and army. They are proud of their Indian heritage but do not consider themselves Indian. They value education highly, but they are not unified politically.

La Paz, one of Bolivia's most densely populated urban areas, with a large Aymara population, is a multi-ethnic city in which Indian and Western cultures collide daily. The outcome of these cultural collisions is not so much the blending of cultures as it is the creation of distinctions and the establishment of boundaries among social groups.

The city is home to several universities, including the University Mayor de San Andrés and the Universidad Católica Boliviana. As the nation's administrative capital, La Paz is the center of the legislative and executive branches of government. President Juan Evo Morales Ayma in 2005 became Bolivia's first head of state of Indian ethnicity.

See also **Bolivia, Political Parties: Nationalist Revolutionary Movement (MNR); Encomienda; Mestizo.**

BIBLIOGRAPHY

Alberto Crespo R., *El corregimiento de La Paz 1548–1560* (1972).

Wolfgang Schoop, *Ciudades bolivianas* (1981), 47–89.

Herbert S. Klein, *Bolivia: The Evolution of a Multi-Ethnic Society* (1982).

Additional Bibliography

Baptista Gumucio, Mariano. *La Paz vista por viajeros extranjeros y autores nacionales, siglos XVI al XX.* La Paz: Gobierno Municipal, 1997.

Dávila, Amanda, and Jitka Silva J. *Historia oral de los barrios paceños.* La Paz: Ediciones Casa de la Cultura, Gobierno Municipal, 1998.

Gamarra Zorrilla, José. *La Paz: Estudio e interpretación de su historia.* La Paz: Editorial Salamandra, 1995.

García Linera, Alvaro. *Reproletarización: Nueva clase obrera y desarrollo del capital industrial en Bolivia (1952–1998): El caso de La Paz y El Alto.* La Paz: Muela del Diablo, 1999.

López Beltrán, Clara. *Alianzas familiares: Élite, género y negocios en La Paz, S. XVII.* Lima: Instituto de Estudios Peruanos, 1998.

Medinaceli, Ximena. *Balance bibliográfico de la ciudad de La Paz: La ciudad en sus textos.* La Paz: Universidad Mayor de San Andrés, 1999.

Villagómez, Carlos. *La Paz ha muerto: Arte, arquitectura, ciudad: Textos.* La Paz: Plural Editores: Colegio Departamental de Arquitectos de la Paz, 2004.

ERWIN P. GRIESHABER

LAPLANTE, EDUARDO (1818–?). Eduardo Laplante (*b.* 1818; *d.* ?), Cuban lithographer and painter. Born in France, Laplante was among the first to portray Cuban rural life as it existed in reality. He devoted particular care to details in his art making his work useful for historians and students of mid-nineteenth-century Cuban planter society. Laplante is most famous for his collection of twenty-eight lithographs, *Los ingenios de Cuba* (1857), which provides detailed views of both external appearances and internal social conditions in Cuba's major sugar plants. With these lithographs Laplante achieved a realistic portrait of Cuban race and class relations as well as the operation of the rural sugar economy.

See also **Art: The Nineteenth Century.**

BIBLIOGRAPHY

Adelaida De Juan, *Pintura Cubana: Temas y variaciones* (1978) and *Two Centuries of Cuban Art, 1759–1959* (1980).

Additional Bibliography

Cantero, J.G. *Los ingenios de Cuba.* Coral Gables: La Moderna Poesía, 1994.

Consejo Nacional de las Artes Plásticas. *Subasta Habana 2005.* La Habana Vieja: Comité Organizador Subasta Habana, 2005.

KAREN RACINE

LA PLATA. La Plata, an island approximately 5.5 square miles in size, lying just south of the equator, 14 miles off the central coast of Ecuador. Archaeological evidence indicates that the island was an important offertory and religious center during the pre-Columbian era. Findings of Valdivia, Machalilla, Chorrera, Bahía, Jama-Coaque, Manteño, and Inca pottery at various sites around the island indicate that it was utilized from the Early Formative Period (around 2450 BCE) through the Inca conquest.

Large quantities of broken clay figurines, engraved stones, and processed *Spondylus* (thorny oyster) shell have been found at archaeological sites on La Plata. The figurines exhibit a wide range of styles and are generally of crude manufacture. The nature of the deposits suggests that they were ritually smashed and left as offerings. The engraved stones are found in similar offertory contexts. *Spondylus* shell was highly valued by Andean cultures throughout the pre-Columbian era. The amount of *Spondylus* shell found on La Plata suggests that it may have been an important source of this material, which in turn may have contributed to the ritual significance of the island.

In 1892 George A. Dorsey was the first to undertake archaeological investigations on La Plata. His discovery of an Inca burial on the island marks the northernmost limits of Inca expansion along the Pacific coast. The grave was found to contain a wealth of materials including gold, silver, and copper figurines, a gold bowl, *tupus* (metal pins), and Inca polychrome pottery. The type of figurines found in this burial is known from only a limited number of sites around the empire, most of which were of extreme ritual importance to the Inca. It has been suggested that the burial on La Plata may have been associated with the state rite of *capac hucha,* which involved the ceremonial sacrifice of children and served to define the sacred and political boundaries of the Inca Empire.

See also **Archaeology.**

BIBLIOGRAPHY

George A. Dorsey, *Archaeological Investigations on the Island of La Plata, Ecuador* (1901), Field Columbian Museum, Anthropological Series, Publication 56, vol. 2 (1901), and Jorge Marcos and Presley Norton, "Interpretación sobre la arqueología de la Isla de La Plata," in *Miscelánea antropológica ecuatoriana* 1 (1981): 136–154.

Additional Bibliography

University of Bristol. *Isla de la Plata Expedition.* Bristol: University of Bristol, 1991.

TAMARA L. BRAY

LAPRIDA, FRANCISCO NARCISO DE (1786–1829). Francisco Narciso de Laprida (*b.* 28 October 1786; *d.* 28 September 1829), Argentine patriot. Born in San Juan and educated in Buenos Aires and Santiago de Chile, Laprida returned to his native city in 1811 to practice law and participate in local politics. He was president of the Congress of Tucumán when, on 9 July 1816, it adopted the Argentine declaration of independence.

Laprida served briefly as acting governor of San Juan in 1818. As a liberal professional and eager to promote progressive innovations, he collaborated from 1822 to 1824 with the radical reformist government of Salvador María del Carril in his home province and then with the abortive national government of Bernardino Rivadavia and his Unitarist party. He was vice president of the Constituent Congress that issued the centralist 1826 Constitution. In the civil strife that followed adoption of the Constitution, he was a committed Unitarist. Laprida was killed by victorious Federalists in the immediate aftermath of the battle of Pilar, in Mendoza province.

See also **Rivadavia, Bernardino.**

BIBLIOGRAPHY

Emilio Maurín Navarro, "Dr. Francisco Narciso de Laprida," in his *Precursores cuyanos de la independencia de América y patriotas sanjuaninos de la hora inicial* (1968).

José F. Sivori, *Francisco Narciso de Laprida* (1971).

Additional Bibliography

Halperin Donghi, Tulio. *Revolución y guerra: Formación de una elite dirigente en la Argentina criolla.* Buenos Aires: Siglo XXI Editores Argentina, 2002.

Herrero, Fabián, and Klaus Gallo. *Revolución, política e ideas en el Río de la Plata durante la década de 1810.* Buenos Aires: Ediciones Cooperativas, 2004.

Szuchman, Mark D., and Jonathan C. Brown, eds. *Revolution and Restoration: The Rearrangement of Power in Argentina, 1776–1860.* Lincoln: University of Nebraska Press, 1994.

DAVID BUSHNELL

LA QUEMADA. La Quemada, one of the principal settlements of Mesoamerica's northern periphery, located in central Zacatecas, Mexico, on the grasslands bordering the eastern slope of the Sierra Madre Occidental. The main occupation of La Quemada apparently dates to the Epiclassic period (600–900 CE), although earlier and later dates have been recovered. The site was established atop the dominant peak in the valley, a readily defensible location. By construction of numerous terraces, many of which are interconnected by stairways and causeways, the peak was transformed into an imposing architectural space. It contains perhaps fifty patio complexes, one central ball court that is among the longest in Mesoamerica, at least two smaller ones, thirteen or more pyramids, a large colonnaded hall, and a massive wall that encloses the central parts of the site that are not protected by natural cliffs. In the valley below are numerous present-day villages, many of which are linked by a system of ancient roads that centered on La Quemada. Archaeologists assume that La Quemada was the elite administrative and religious center of this group of settlements.

In virtually all parts of the site excavated to date, extensive human skeletal deposits have been found, including piles of disarticulated, cut, and burned bone, suspended skulls and long bones, and subfloor burials. Some of the bones are probably those of revered ancestors, and others belonged to enemies. All apparently were displayed to symbolize a social order rooted in violence.

Archaeologists have varying opinions about the causes of growth and decline of La Quemada, as well as whether it should be included in the Chalchihuites culture. Some perceive colonization by more sophisticated societies to the south as an important force, whereas others see the developments as indigenous. The new chronological evidence that places La Quemada's occupation within the Epiclassic Period does not support the previously popular notion that La Quemada was built to serve as an outpost for Toltec (900–1150 CE) trade in turquoise with the American Southwest. By the time the Toltecs were in their ascendancy, La Quemada was apparently abandoned or much reduced in size. The late dates obtained from the nucleus of the site may represent its occasional, postoccupational use as a camp or shrine.

See also **Precontact History: Mesoamerica.**

BIBLIOGRAPHY

J. Charles Kelley, "Settlement Patterns in North-Central Mexico," in *Prehistoric Settlement Patterns in the New World,* edited by Gordon R. Willey (1956), pp. 128–139.

Phil C. Weigand, "The Prehistory of the State of Zacatecas: An Interpretation," in *Anthropology* 2, no. 1 (1978): 67–87, and no. 2 (1978): 103–117.

Marie-Areti Hers, *Los toltecas en tierras chichimecas* (1989).

Peter Jiménez Betts, "Perspectivas sobre la arqueología de Zacatecas," in *Arqueología* 5 (1989): 7–50.

Charles D. Trombold, "A Reconsideration of the Chronology for the La Quemada Portion of the Northern Mesoamerican Frontier," in *American Antiquity* 55, no. 2 (1990): 308–323.

Ben A. Nelson, J. Andrew Darling, and David A. Kice, "Mortuary Practices and the Social Order at La Quemada, Zacatecas, Mexico," in *Latin American Antiquity* 3, no. 4 (1992): 298–315.

Additional Bibliography

Foster, Michael S., and Shirley Gorenstein, eds. *Greater Mesoamerica: The Archaeology of West and Northwest Mexico.* Salt Lake City: University of Utah Press, 2000.

Nelson, Ben A. "A Place of Continued Importance: The Abandonment of Epiclassic La Quemada," in *The Archaeology of Settlement Abandonment in Middle America.* Takeshi, Inomata, and Ronald W. Webb, eds. Salt Lake City: University of Utah Press, 2003.

Strazicich, Nicola M. "Manufactura e intercambio de cerámica en la región de Alta Vista y La Quemada, Zacatecas (400-900 d.C.)," *Estudios cerámicos en el occidente y norte de México* edited by Williams, Eduardo, and Phil C. Weigand. Zamora: El Colegio de Michoacán; Morelia: Instituto Michoacano de Cultura, 2000.

Wells, E. Christian. "Pottery Production and Microcosmic Organization: The Residential Structure of la Quemada, Zacatecas." *Latin American Antiquity* Vol. 11, No. 1 (Mar. 2000): 21–42.

Ben A. Nelson

LARA, AGUSTÍN (1900–1970). Agustín Lara (*b.* 30 October 1900; *d.* 6 November 1970), renowned Mexican composer of popular songs. Lara was born in Tlacotalpan, Veracruz. He began composing in the mid-1920s, when the regional music of Mexico had not yet become popular, and joined Radio XEW with his own program, "Hora Azul" (Blue Hour), on which he showcased his own compositions, often playing them on the piano. He wrote almost 600 songs, mostly in the International Latin style, including "Farolito," "Enamorada," "Mujer," "Cada noche un amor," and "Solamente una vez" ("You Belong to My Heart"), which achieved global fame. His choice to use an international rather than native Mexican styles brought extensive criticism from many Mexican musicians, scholars, and critics, who regarded his work as not truly Mexican. The song "Granada" became so popular in Europe and the Americas that he received honorary Spanish citizenship.

See also **Music: Popular Music and Dance; Radio and Television.**

BIBLIOGRAPHY

New Grove Dictionary of Music (1980).

Claes Af Geijerstam, *Popular Music in Mexico* (1976).

Additional Bibliography

Buraya, Luis Carlos. *Agustín Lara.* Las Rozas: Dastin, 2003.

Torres, José Alejandro. *Agustín Lara.* México, D.F.: Grupo Ed. Tomo, 2004.

Guy Bensusan

LAREDO BRU, FEDERICO (1875–1946). Federico Laredo Bru (*b.* 23 April 1875; *d.* 8 July 1946), president of Cuba 1936–1940. A veteran of the war of independence, Bru served as governor of Las Villas Province and as secretary of the interior under President José Miguel Gómez. In 1923 he led an uprising of disgruntled veterans against President Alfredo Zayas. Bru was elected vice president of Cuba in January 1936, and when President Miguel Mariano Gómez was impeached by a Senate subservient to army chief Fulgencio Batista, he was installed as the new figurehead president. He nevertheless discharged the duties of his office with great aplomb and dignity, counterbalancing military interference as much as possible. A law completely restructuring the sugar industry, one of the most important pieces of legislation of the period, was passed during his term in office. It was also under Laredo Bru that the 1940 constitution was framed by a freely elected constituent assembly.

See also **Cuba, War of Independence.**

BIBLIOGRAPHY

Herminio Portell-Vilá, *Nueva historia de la República de Cuba* (1986), pp. 474–510.

Additional Bibliography

Whitney, Robert. *State and Revolution in Cuba: Mass Mobilization and Political Change, 1920-1940.* Chapel Hill: University of North Carolina Press, 2001.

JOSÉ M. HERNÁNDEZ

LARKIN, THOMAS (1802–1858). Thomas Larkin (*b.* 16 September 1802; *d.* 27 October 1858), California merchant and U.S. consul in Monterey, California. A Bostonian, Thomas Larkin came to California in 1832 to work for his half-brother, Captain Juan Bautista Rogers Cooper, in Monterey. Larkin soon began his own successful career trading in flour and hides, provisioning vessels, and collecting debts for eastern U.S. merchants. His wide network of merchant contacts in Mazatlán, Mexico, Honolulu, Hawaii, and the United States made natural his appointment as U.S. consul in 1843. His diligence and his wide circle of acquaintances among the leading citizens of Mexican California led to his appointment as confidential agent by President James K. Polk in 1846. Larkin was successful in warding off European influence in California, in persuading leading *Californios* to favor acquisition by the United States, and in mediating between them and Americans intent on acquiring California by force. He later became a major land speculator in the San Francisco area.

See also **California; Californios.**

BIBLIOGRAPHY

Harlan Hague and David J. Langum, *Thomas O. Larkin, a Life of Patriotism and Profit in Old California* (1990).

George P. Hammond, ed., *The Larkin Papers: Personal, Business, and Official Correspondence of Thomas Oliver Larkin, Merchant and United States Consul in California,* 10 vols. (1951–1968).

John A. Hawgood, ed., *First and Last Consul: Thomas Oliver Larkin and the Americanization of California,* 2d ed. (1970).

E. JEFFREY STANN

LARRAZÁBAL UGUETO, WOLFGANG (1911–2003). Wolfgang Larrazábal Ugueto was a Venezuelan naval officer and politician. Born on March 5, 1911, in Carúpano, Larrazábal studied at the Escuela Naval (1928–1932). He became commander of the naval base at Puerto Cabello and held successively higher posts, finally rising to commander of the navy in 1957. As the senior navy officer, he joined forces with other military and civilian leaders to overthrow Marcos Pérez Jiménez in January 1958. When the dictator fled, Larrazábal headed the interim governing junta (January 23–November 13, 1958) as provisional president. Prior to elections in December, he resigned from the military to run as a presidential candidate of the Democratic Republican Union and the Communist Party. His enormous personal popularity in Caracas and other cities enabled him to capture 34 percent of the popular vote. He lost to Rómulo Betancourt of Democratic Action, however, who received 50 percent. Larrazábal is noted for his support of democracy at a time when many military leaders preferred to rule. He backed the electoral process and encouraged the military to support the transition to civilian rule during his transition government. Larrazábal ran for president again in 1963 as the Popular Democratic Force candidate but won only 9.4 percent of the vote. He remained a political figure in the 1980s but broke with the Force to form a splinter group. In 1993 he retired from politics; ten years later, on February 27, 2003, he died of a respiratory malfunction.

See also **Venezuela, Political Parties: Communist Party.**

BIBLIOGRAPHY

José Umana Bernal, *Testimonio de la revolución en Venezuela* (1958).

John D. Martz, *Acción Democratica: Evolution of a Modern Political Party* (1966).

Agustin Blanco Muñoz, *El 23 de enero: Habla la conspiración* (1981).

Judith Ewell, *Venezuela. A Century of Change* (1984).

Additional Bibliography

Baloyra, Enrique A., and John D. Martz. *Political Attitudes in Venezuela: Societal Cleavages and Political Opinion.* Austin: University of Texas Press, 1979.

Penniman, Howard R., ed. *Venezuela at the Polls: The National Elections of 1978.* Washington, DC: American Enterprise Institute for Public Policy Research, 1980.

KATHY WALDRON

LARREA, JUAN

LARREA, JUAN (1782–1847). Juan Larrea (*b.* 1782; *d.* 1847), Spanish-born merchant and member of the first Argentine patriot junta. Larrea arrived in Buenos Aires prior to 1806. He fought British invaders as a captain in the battalion of Volunteers of Catalonia. An early champion of independence, he was initially associated with the Spanish-dominated Partido Republicano, which controlled the *cabildo,* or town council. In 1810 Larrea joined Mariano Moreno and other creoles participating in the *cabildo abierto* on 22 May, and became a member of the first patriot junta. During the ensuing controversy between federalists and centralists, Larrea continued to support Moreno and was exiled to San Juan after Moreno's resignation and the revolt of May 1811. In January 1813 Larrea represented Buenos Aires at the constitutional assembly. Named minister of the treasury under Supreme Director Gervasio Antonio de Posadas, Larrea and Carlos María de Alvear were charged to acquire a naval squadron. Larrea accomplished this with the aid of the North American merchants Guillermo Pío White and William Brown. The unraveling of the "united" provinces in 1815 forced Larrea, once again, into exile and obscurity. Reestablished as a merchant, he was appointed Argentine consul general in France several years later. Larrea eventually returned to Buenos Aires, where he died.

See also **Catalonian Volunteers; Creole; Moreno, Mariano.**

BIBLIOGRAPHY

Carlos Alberto Floria and César A. García Belsunce, *Historia de los Argentinos,* vol. 1 (1971), pp. 244 and 322–337.

Diego Abad De Santillán, *Historia Argentino,* vol. 1 (1965), pp. 516–528.

Ione S. Wright and Lisa M. Nekhom, *Historical Dictionary of Argentina* (1978), pp. 476–477.

Additional Bibliography

Halperin Donghi, Tulio. *Revolución y guerra: Formación de una elite dirigente en la Argentina criolla.* Buenos Aires: Siglo XXI Editores Argentina, 2002.

Herrero, Fabián, and Klaus Gallo. *Revolución, política e ideas en el Río de la Plata durante la década de 1810.* Buenos Aires: Ediciones Cooperativas, 2004.

Szuchman, Mark D., and Jonathan C. Brown., eds. *Revolution and Restoration: The Rearrangement of Power in Argentina, 1776–1860.* Lincoln: University of Nebraska Press, 1994.

CHRISTEL K. CONVERSE

LARRETA, ENRIQUE RODRÍGUEZ

LARRETA, ENRIQUE RODRÍGUEZ (1873–1961). Enrique Rodríguez Larreta (*b.* 4 March 1873; *d.* 7 July 1961), Argentine dramatist. Enrique Rodríguez Larreta was born in Buenos Aires of Uruguayan parents and belonged to the cattle-baron oligarchy; he earned a doctorate in law from the University of Buenos Aires. Larreta exemplifies the phenomenon of the gentleman literatus made possible by the enormous economic prosperity and international ties that characterized Argentine life in the federal capital of Buenos Aires and the province of Buenos Aires between 1880 and 1930. True to his class, Larreta specialized in a literature (basically narrative and lyrical dramas) that focused on questions of national identity from the perspective of the ruling creoles. This meant an emphasis on a chthonic definition of Hispanic roots, with or without the dimension of their forceful domination of indigenous elements. Larreta's most famous work, *La gloria de don Ramiro; una vida en tiempos de Felipe II* (1908), in the context of a decadent prose with important French parallels, explores contradictions of the Hispanic substratum of Latin American society and is most notable for its rereading of the Spanish racialistic obsession with the "purity of the blood." Larreta correlates Don Ramiro's nonpurity with his failure in the New World, a plot configuration that has strident ideological implications for early-twentieth-century political beliefs in an Argentina that opposed immigration (especially its Jewish components) and non-Hispanic liberalism, while at the same time calling for a reaffirmation of an authentic Hispanic heritage. Larreta, thanks in great part to the strains of literary decadence to which he was exposed, may not have been as facile in these matters as Leopoldo Lugones (1874–1938) or the harsh-minded nationalists, but there is no question that his writing strikes a counterpoint to the dominant cultural liberalism of the modernists. One cannot help but be struck by the juxtaposition in Larreta of significant manifestations of an aesthetist posture and the mythmaking force of an austere Spanish traditionalism, a feature of his writing also evident in *Zogoibi* (1926), set in the legendary Argentine pampas.

See also **Jesus; Race and Ethnicity.**

BIBLIOGRAPHY

Amado Alonso, *Ensayo sobre la novela histórica: El modernismo en* La gloria de don Ramiro (1942).

Juan Carlos Ghiano, *Análisis de* La gloria de don Ramiro (1968).

Gabriella Ibieta, *Tradition and Renewal in "La gloria de don Ramiro"* (1986).

Additional Bibliography

Fernández-Levin, Rosa. *El autor y el personaje femenino en dos novelas del siglo XX.* Madrid: Editorial Pliegos, 1997.

Torres-Pou, Joan. "La 'novela de los orígenes' como subtexto en *La gloria de don Ramiro* y *Zogoibi: El dolor de la tierra* de Enrique Larreta." *Confluencia.* 16:2(Spring 2001): 92–98.

DAVID WILLIAM FOSTER

LARS, CLAUDIA. *See* **Brannon de Samayoa Chinchilla, Carmen.**

LA SALLE, RENÉ-ROBERT CAVELIER, SIEUR DE (1643–1687).

René-Robert Cavelier, Sieur de La Salle (*b.* 22 November 1643; *d.* 19 March 1687), French explorer. A native of Rouen, France, La Salle was educated by the Jesuits but left the order and went to Canada in 1666 to enter the fur trade. In 1679 he built and launched the first sailing vessel to ply the Great Lakes. By canoe, he descended the Mississippi River to its mouth in 1682, claiming for France all the lands of its drainage.

La Salle envisioned a warm-water port on the Gulf of Mexico to serve his commercial aims and French designs of empire. Returning to France, he won royal support for a voyage to the Mississippi through the Gulf to establish a colony on the lower river. He sailed from La Rochelle on 24 July 1684. Because of geographical uncertainty, he missed the mouth of the Mississippi and landed his 280 colonists at Texas's Matagorda Bay on 20 February 1685. Realizing his error, he sought his post on the Illinois River by land, but was slain by a disenchanted follower near the Trinity River in eastern Texas.

La Salle was responsible for opening the Mississippi Valley for development. His Gulf of Mexico expedition sparked a renewal of Spanish exploration in the Gulf that led to Spanish occupation of eastern Texas and Pensacola Bay. Because of La Salle, the United States asserted a claim to Texas as part of the Louisiana Purchase, giving rise to a boundary dispute with Spain that lasted until 1819.

See also **Explorers and Exploration: Spanish America; Mexico, Gulf of; Texas.**

BIBLIOGRAPHY

Patricia K. Galloway, ed., *La Salle and His Legacy: Frenchmen and Indians in the Lower Mississippi Valley* (1982).

Francis Parkman, *La Salle and the Discovery of the Great West* (repr. 1963).

Robert S. Weddle, ed., *La Salle, the Mississippi, and the Gulf: Three Primary Documents* (1987).

Robert S. Weddle, *The French Thorn: Rival Explorers in the Spanish Sea, 1682–1762* (1991), esp. pp. 3–84.

Additional Bibliography

Johnson, Donald S. *La Salle: A Perilous Odyssey from Canada to the Gulf of Mexico.* New York: Cooper Square Press, 2002.

ROBERT S. WEDDLE

LAS CASAS, BARTOLOMÉ DE (1474–1566).

Bartolomé de Las Casas (*b.* ca. August 1474; *d.* ca. 17 July 1566), remains one of the most controversial figures in Latin America's conquest period. His exposé of Spanish mistreatment of Amerindians produced public outrage that was directed at both the conquistadores who were committing the atrocities and at the writer who had made them public. Las Casas's vast output of political, historical, and theological writing forms one of the basic sources for contemporary understanding of the conquest period and of some of the most important individuals involved in the initial colonization of the Spanish Indies.

The early years of Las Casas's life seemed destined to propel him toward the newly discovered Indies and

Mutilation of Native Americans by Spanish Conquistadores, by Theodore de Bry, in *Historia de las Indias* (1566), by Bartolomé de Las Casas. Las Casas was an outspoken critic of the brutal treatment of indigenous populations by their Spanish conquerors. SNARK/ART RESOURCE, NY

its inhabitants. He was the son of a Seville merchant, Pedro de Las Casas. In 1493 the young Bartolomé saw Christopher Columbus's triumphant return to Spain and the small group of Taino Indians Columbus brought with him. Las Casas remained at home in school while his father and other members of his family accompanied Columbus as colonists on the second voyage to the Indies. Five years later Pedro ?>de Las Casas returned to Spain for a short period, bringing with him a Taino boy named Juanico. While his father was at home, Bartolomé declared his desire to become a priest and went to Salamanca to learn canon law. He also began to learn about the Indies from Juanico, with whom Las Casas struck up a lifelong friendship. In 1502 Las Casas quit school and sailed to the West Indies. His first years in Hispaniola were spent helping his father and aiding in the provisioning of Spanish military expeditions. At the same time, young Las Casas began learning several native languages and befriending local Indians; he had already begun deploring the violence he witnessed. He returned to Europe, first to Spain and then to Rome where, in 1507, he was ordained a priest.

In 1510 Las Casas returned to Hispaniola. These years were to be crucial both for Las Casas and for the nature of Spanish-Indian relations. His return coincided with the arrival of the Dominicans. In 1511 the Dominican priest Antonio de Montesino represented his order in a highly public condemnation of the *encomienda* system that outraged the island's entire Spanish community. The message was not lost on Las Casas, who then held Indians as an *encomendero* (land grantee). Las Casas was ordained priest in 1512 or 1513, and in 1513 he joined Diego de Velázquez and Pánfilo de Narváez in the conquest of Cuba. Las Casas preached to and converted the natives in preparation for the Spanish conquistadores, and those efforts largely succeeded. In reward for his services, Las Casas received land together with a grant of Indians and by all appearances had established himself as a typical *encomendero.*

The decimation of Cuba's native population by Spanish *encomenderos* through overwork, starvation, and murder made Las Casas realize that the real solution for Indian mistreatment lay not with challenging the conduct of individual *encomenderos* but by calling into question the entire system and its relationship to Christian mortality. In 1514 he astonished his parishioners by condemning the *encomienda* in its entirety, freeing his Indians, and then vigorously interceding with local authorities on the natives' behalf. Failing to convert even a single *encomendero* to his position, he went to Europe in 1515 to plead his case with the king of Spain. Las Casas spent the next six years arguing that the period for military conquest of the Indians had passed. The time had arrived, he claimed, for peaceful conversion of natives and the promotion of agricultural colonization. He did not stand alone in condemning Spanish cruelties against Indians. Other voices had begun to sound in the Americas, and a small but influential group of royal ministers and Spanish churchmen supported the goal of protecting Indians. After heated debate, Emperor Charles V (Charles I of Spain) sided with Las Casas in 1519, ruling that the Indies could be governed without the force of arms. The ruling, however, had little practical effect in the distant Western Hemisphere.

During the next quarter century, Las Casas repeatedly suffered defeats in his efforts to defend the Americas' native populations. In 1520 he left Spain to establish a settlement in Venezuela, hoping to peacefully convert local Indians and create an economically self-sufficient community. But opposition from *encomenderos* and colonial officials helped to incite an Indian rebellion that wrecked the project. Despondent over its failure, he entered the Dominican order as a monk in 1523. The years that followed were ones of intellectual growth and personal frustration for Las Casas. He outlined his program for peaceful conversion, in opposition to military conquest, in *Del único modo de atraer a todos los pueblos a la verdadera religión* (1537; *The Only Way*). While in the monastery, he began his monumental *Apologética historia* (*In Defense of the Indians*) and the *History of the Indies* and continued a lifelong passion of collecting documents. One of Las Casas's critics charged that he once arrived in Tlaxcala, Mexico, "with twenty-seven or thirty-seven [Indian] carriers—and the greatest part of what they were carrying was accusations against the Spaniards, and other rubbish."

Although colonial Spaniards scorned any attempt to ameliorate the Indians' plight, moral encouragement arrived from Europe in the form of Pope Paul III's bull *Sublimis Deus* (1537), which proclaimed that American Indians were rational beings with souls, whose lives and property should be protected. During the same year Charles V supported an effort by Las Casas and the Dominicans to establish missions in Guatemala based on the precepts laid out in *Del único modo*. The high point of the crown's efforts came in 1542 with the so-called New Laws, which forbade Indian slavery and sought to end the *encomienda* system within a generation by outlawing their transference through family inheritance. Las Casas, who was in Spain at the time, directly influenced the direction of the New Laws in part by reading the first version of *The Devastation of the Indies* (a much longer text than the one he published in 1552) to a horrified royal court.

In 1544 he sailed to the Indies for a brief and tempestuous tenure as the bishop of Chiapas. Although he had been offered the Cuzco bishopric, the richest in the Americas, Las Casas instead accepted one of the poorest. When he tried to implement the New Laws in his see, local clergy who had ties to *encomenderos* defied him. After Las Casas denied final absolution to any Spaniard who refused to free his Indians or pay restitution, he received threats against his life. Proclamation of the New Laws brought outright revolt in parts of Spanish America and fierce antagonism everywhere. Even the Viceroyalty of New Spain and its high court openly refused to enforce them. In 1545 colonial opposition persuaded Charles V to revoke key inheritance statutes in the New Laws. Las Casas went to an ecclesiastical assembly in Mexico City and persuaded his fellow bishops to support a strongly worded resolution defending Indian rights. At the same time he publicly humiliated the viceroy, Antonio de Mendoza, for attempting to silence him. But he left his most defiant act for last.

Just after arriving, Las Casas issued a confessor manual for the priests in his diocese that essentially reinstituted the inheritance statutes of the New Laws. His *Confesionario* produced public outrage by reiterating that all Spaniards seeking last rites must free their Indians and make restitution, even if the Indians were part of a deeded estate. Las Casas justified his decision by arguing that all wealth acquired through *encomiendas* was ill-gotten, declaring, "There is no Spaniard in the Indies who has shown good faith in connection with the wars of Conquest." This last statement put at issue the very basis of Spain's presence in the Americas. Las Casas contended that the Spanish had acquired all their wealth by unjustly exploiting Indians; if all of their activities since Columbus's landing were unjust, so too, logically, was the crown's American presence. Not surprisingly, the Council of the Indies recalled Las Casas to Spain in 1547 and ordered all copies of *Confesionario* confiscated.

Colonial and Spanish opposition to Las Casas coalesced around Juan Ginés de Sepúlveda, one of Spain's leading humanists. Sepúlveda used Aristotle's doctrine of just war to defend Spanish conduct in the Americas. The vigor of Las Casas's counterattack led the Council of the Indies to call for a court of jurists and theologians to ascertain "how conquests may be conducted justly and with security of conscience." Charles V then ordered the two men to debate their positions before the court.

Much popular misconception has surrounded the 1550 "great debate" between Las Casas and Sepúlveda in the Spanish city of Valladolid. The two men never debated face to face but stated their cases individually before the court. Sepúlveda's three-hour defense of just wars against Indians rested on four points. First, the Indians had committed grave sins by their idolatry and sins against nature. Second, their "natural rudeness and inferiority" corresponded with Aristotle's view that some men were born natural slaves. Third, military conquest was the most efficacious method of converting Indians to Christianity. Finally, conquering Indians made it possible to protect the weak amongst them. In rebuttal, Las Casas took five days to read his *Apologética historia sumaria*. In the end, the majority of judges sided with Las Casas but, perhaps fearing controversy, refused to render a public decision. Legislation by the crown continued to move slowly toward the abolition of Indian slavery and some of the egregious features of the *encomienda* system.

Las Casas left Chiapas in 1547 and, in August 1550, resigned the Chiapas bishopric. He assumed residency in the Dominican San Gregorio monastery, where in 1552 he produced his most important work, *The Devastation of the Indies: A Brief Account. A Brief Account* was immediately translated into several languages and ignited a firestorm of controversy that continues today. Next came his two largest works. The first, *Apologética historia sumaria*, argued for the rationality of American Indians by comparing them favorably to the Greeks and Romans. After research in Hernando Columbus's library, he rewrote his three-volume *History of the Indies*, which remains a standard source on Columbus and Spain's first decades in the Americas.

Las Casas continued to champion Indian rights in the final phase of his life. His last great success occurred in 1555, when Peruvian conquistadores offered 8 million ducats to Philip II in exchange for perpetual *encomiendas*. Las Casas adroitly had the decision postponed while he gained the power of attorney, enabling him to act officially on the Indians' behalf. With their backing, he made a counteroffer that surpassed the conquistadores' bribe and led to its summary withdrawal. Despite that triumph, Las Casas's final years were characterized by urgent pleas about the Indians' circumstances and the belief that God might destroy Spain for its sins against them. On the day he died, Las Casas voiced regret for not having done more. He was buried in the convent chapel of Our Lady of Atocha in Madrid.

Today Las Casas is largely remembered for *A Brief Account* and his role in the controversy surrounding the Black Legend of Spanish conquest. Whether or not Las Casas exaggerated Spanish atrocities, as his critics claim, does not alter the fact that *A Brief Account* remains one of the most important documents ever written on human rights. The issues Las Casas raised in 1552 remain pertinent today. Modern scholarship has supported Las Casas's staggering toll of native deaths but assigns the principal responsibility to Afro-European diseases rather than Spanish cruelty. Recent work has also refuted the claim that Las Casas promoted the African slave trade as a substitute for Indian slavery, pointing out that his *History of the Indies* explicitly condemns African slavery. Although Las Casas never claimed to be an impartial historian, his historical texts continue to provide information on the conquest period. Ultimately, however, it is Las Casas as a crusader and symbol of the struggle for human rights that keeps him in our historical memory. Perhaps no one else in history has been more insistent or clear in articulating Western culture's moral responsibility to the oppressed.

See also **Black Legend; Charles I of Spain; Columbus, Christopher; Dominicans; Encomienda; Mendoza, Antonio de; Narváez, Pánfilo de; New Laws of 1542; Philip II of Spain; Sepúlveda, Juan Ginés de; Slave Trade; Velásquez, Diego de.**

BIBLIOGRAPHY

Lewis Hanke, *Aristotle and the American Indians* (1959); Henry R. Wagner, *The Life and Writings of Bartolomé de las Casas* (1967); Charles Gibson, ed., *The Black Legend: Anti-Spanish Attitudes in the Old World and the New* (1971); Gustavo Gutiérrez, *Las Casas: In Search of the Poor of Jesus Christ* (1994).

Additional Bibliography

Iglesias Ortega, Luis M. *Bartolomé de las Casas: Cuarenta y cuatro años infinitos.* Sevilla, Spain: Fundación José Manuel Lara, 2007.

Vickery, Paul S. *Bartolomé de las Casas: Great Prophet of the Americas.* Mahwah, NJ: Paulist Press, 2006.

WILLIAM DONOVAN

LA SERENA. La Serena, city of 154,521 inhabitants (2002), on the mouth of the Elqui River and on the Pan-American Highway some 265 miles north of Santiago, Chile, and capital of the Coquimbo region (2002 population 627,622). The city was founded in 1544 by Juan Bohón, one of Pedro de Valdivia's lieutenants, to secure the land route toward southern Peru. It became a center of the mining activities conducted in the southern part of the Norte Chico and of the fruit and brandy industry of the Elqui Valley. The well-protected port of Coquimbo, 10 miles to the south, has served as its outlet to the sea. Overwhelmed by the political hegemony of Santiago and the commercial prowess of Valparaíso, La Serena has become a placid provincial city without major ambitions, beautified by the public works with which past president Gabriel González Videla commemorated his city of birth.

See also **Chile, Geography.**

BIBLIOGRAPHY

Guido Veliz Cantuarias, "Conurbación La Serena–Coquimbo," in *Revista Geográfica* (Mexico) 111 (1990): 219–258.

Additional Bibliography

Cavieres Figueroa, Eduardo. *La Serena en el s. XVIII: Las dimensiones del poder local en una sociedad regional.* Valparaíso: Ediciones Universitarias de Valparaíso, Universidad Católica de Valparaíso, 1993.

Villarejo, Avencio. *La Serena, de Cenicienta a princesa: Monografía de la IV Región de Coquimbo desde la prehistoria hasta nuestro días.* Santiago: Ediciones Agustinianas, 1995.

CÉSAR N. CAVIEDES

LA SERNA, JOSÉ DE (1770–1832). José de La Serna (*b.* 1770; *d.* 6 July 1832), last viceroy of Peru and commander of the Spanish forces at the Battle of Ayacucho (1824). A native of Jerez de la Frontera, Spain, he was a professional soldier who fought in the defense of Ceuta in 1790, and later against England and France. He was sent to Peru in 1816 as one of the generals under Viceroy Joaquín de la Pezuela. He criticized the latter's decision to hold on to Lima at all costs, and in 1821, following Pezuela's overthrow, he was acclaimed viceroy by his fellow commanders. He negotiated briefly with General José de San Martín, especially over the idea of placing Peru under a crowned head. The negotiations came to naught, and in July 1821, he abandoned Lima and took his army to the highlands, where he established his seat of command in Huancayo and later in Cuzco. On 9 December 1824, on a plain near Ayacucho, he led the last royal army in South America against General Antonio José de Sucre, Simón Bolívar's chief lieutenant. La Serna was defeated, and with that loss Spain's empire in the New World, save its Caribbean possessions, disappeared. La Serna was taken prisoner and returned to Spain, where he received the title Count of the Andes. He subsequently held the post of captain-general of Granada (1831). He died in Seville.

See also **Ayacucho, Battle of; Huancayo.**

BIBLIOGRAPHY

Timothy E. Anna, *The Fall of the Royal Government in Peru* (1979).

Rubén Vargas Ugarte, *Historia general del Perú,* vol. 6, *Emancipación (1816–1825)* (1966).

Additional Bibliography

Fisher, John Robert. *Bourbon Peru, 1750-1824.* Liverpool: Liverpool University Press, 2003.

Montoya Rivas, Gustavo. *La independencia del Perú y el fantasma de la revolución.* Lima: Instituto Francés de Estudios Andinos: Instituto de Estudios Peruanos, 2002.

JEFFREY KLAIBER

LAS HERAS, JUAN GREGORIO DE (1780–1866). Juan Gregorio de Las Heras (*b.* 11 June 1780; *d.* 6 February 1866), Argentine general and hero of the wars of independence. Born in Buenos Aires and seemingly destined for a commerical career, he enrolled in the militia and fought against the British during the "English invasions" of 1806–1807. In 1813 he went to Chile with a force of Argentine auxiliaries and distinguished himself in the early campaigns of Chile's wars of independence. Following the collapse of patriot Chile (October 1814), he joined José de San Martín's Army of the Andes, in which he commanded a division. He fought in many other actions, including the battles of Chacabuco (12 February 1817) and Maipú (5 April 1818), and later served as San Martín's chief of staff on the expedition to liberate Peru (1820–1821).

When San Martín withdrew from Peru, Las Heras returned to his native land. He became governor of Buenos Aires Province in 1824 and chief executive of Argentina in 1825. During his brief period in office, war was declared on Brazil. With Bernardino Rivadavia's assumption of the Argentine presidency (1826), Las Heras returned to Chile and resumed his military career. He was cashiered in 1830 for refusing to recognize the new Chilean Conservative regime. He was reinstated in 1842, after which he immediately retired. He spent the rest of his life in Chile. His remains were repatriated to Buenos Aires in 1906.

See also **Wars of Independence, South America.**

BIBLIOGRAPHY

Additional Bibliography

Halperin Donghi, Tulio. *Revolución y guerra: Formación de una elite dirigente en la Argentina criolla.* Buenos Aires: Siglo XXI Editores Argentina, 2002.

Herrero, Fabián, and Klaus Gallo. *Revolución, política e ideas en el Río de la Plata durante la década de 1810.* Buenos Aires: Ediciones Cooperativas, 2004.

Szuchman, Mark D., and Jonathan C. Brown., eds. *Revolution and Restoration: The Rearrangement of Power in Argentina, 1776–1860.* Lincoln: University of Nebraska Press, 1994.

SIMON COLLIER

LASO, FRANCISCO (1823–1869).

Francisco Laso (*b.* 8 May 1823; *d.* 14 May 1869), Peruvian artist and writer. A painter influenced by the French romantic tradition who focused on Peruvian subjects, Laso was born in Tacna and studied at the Academy of Painting and Drawing in Lima, where he was assistant to Ignacio Merino, director of the academy. He went to Paris in 1842 to study with the painter Hippolyte Delaroche. On visits to Rome and Venice he was influenced by Titian and Veronese. In 1847 he returned to Peru and traveled throughout the countryside, sketching Indians. During a second trip to Europe he studied with the genre painter Marc Gabriel Charles Gleyre in Paris. In Gleyre's atelier, Laso finished his famous *El indio Alfarero* (The Indian Potter, also known as Dweller in the Cordillera, 1855), a painting of a young Indian holding a Mochica ceramic piece, which is considered a forerunner of Peruvian indigenist art in the twentieth century. Upon his return to Peru in 1856, he was commissioned to paint *The Four Evangelists* for the Cathedral of Lima and the *Saint Rose of Lima* (1866) in the municipal palace. Laso worked as a Red Cross volunteer during the yellow fever epidemic of 1868 in Peru and fell victim to it. He died at the height of his career.

See also **Art: The Nineteenth Century.**

BIBLIOGRAPHY

Dawn Ades, *Art in Latin America: The Modern Era, 1820–1980* (1989), p. 39.

Oriana Baddeley and Valerie Fraser, *Drawing the Line: Art and Cultural Identity in Contemporary Latin America* (1989), p. 17.

Juan E. Ríos, *La pintura contemporánea en el Perú* (1946).

Additional Bibliography

Majluf, Natalia. "The Creation of the Image of the Indian in 19th-century Peru: The Paintings of Francisco Laso (1823-1869)." Ph.D. diss., University of Texas at Austin, 1995.

MARTA GARSD

LASTARRIA, JOSÉ VICTORINO (1817–1888).

José Victorino Lastarria (*b.* 22 March 1817; *d.* 14 June 1888), intellectual and politician, the most active and brilliant mid-nineteenth-century Chilean Liberal. Lastarria had more than a touch of vanity. "Tengo talento y lo luzco" (I have talent, and it shows), he once told the Chilean congress. He *did* have talent. As a politician, his finest moments were in 1849–1850, when he was congressional leader of the resurgent Liberal opposition to the Conservative regime, a role for which he was arrested in November 1850 and briefly exiled to Peru. In 1851 he was expelled from congress. Later he held the office of minister of finance (1862) and minister of the interior (1876–1877). He was elected six times to the Chamber of Deputies (1849, 1855, 1858, 1864, 1867, 1870) and was a senator from 1876 to 1882. His many public services included diplomatic missions to Peru (1863), Argentina (1864), and Brazil (1879), and membership on the supreme court (1882–1887).

Lastarria's talent for active politics and diplomacy was limited. His true interests were intellectual and literary. He contributed to numerous newspapers and journals, serving as editor of *El Siglo* (1844–1845) and helping to found *La Revista de Santiago* (1848). An indefatigable "cultural entrepreneur," he was instrumental in founding the Sociedad Literaria (Literary Society) of 1842, an event regarded as the first real stirring of cultural life in postcolonial Chile. In a notable opening address to this society, Lastarria pleaded for an authentic national literature within the canons of modern romanticism. His own fiction, for example, *Don Guillermo* (1860), does not read well today, but his promotion of literature was tireless, and the several circles and academies he sponsored are vividly described in his *Recuerdos literarios* (1878), a remarkable intellectual autobiography. At his death, he left unfinished a prologue he had promised Rubén Darío (1867–1916) for his path-breaking *Azul* (1888).

Lastarria urged a "philosophical" approach to historical writing and engaged in a famous polemic on the subject with Andrés Bello (1781–1865), whose ideas proved more enduring. Of greater positive influence was Lastarria's political-constitutional thought. Consistently liberal and democratic, it is best represented in his books *Elementos de derecho constitucional* (Elements of Constitutional Law, 1846), *Bosquejo histórico de la Constitución chilena* (Historical Outline of the Chilean Constitution, 1847), *Historia constitucional de medio siglo* (Constitutional History of Half a Century, 1853), and *Lecciones de política positiva* (Lessons in Positive Philosophy, 1874), the last of which reflects positivist influence, Lastarria having assimilated the thought of Auguste Comte (though not uncritically) in the 1860s.

See also **Bello, Andrés; Chile, Political Parties: Liberal Party.**

BIBLIOGRAPHY

Bernardo Subercaseaux, *Cultura y sociedad liberal en el siglo XIX: Lastarria, ideología y literatura* (1981).

José Victorino Lastarria, *Obras completas,* 14 vols. (1906–1934).

Allen Woll, *A Functional Past: The Uses of History in Nineteenth-Century Chile* (1982), chaps. 1–2.

Additional Bibliography

Meléndez, Mariselle. "Miedo, raza y nación: Bello, Lastarria y la revisión del pasado colonial." *Revista Chilena de Literatura* 52 (April 1998): 17–30.

Subercaseaux, Bernardo. *Historia de las ideas y de la cultura en Chile.* Santiago: Editorial Universitaria, 1997.

Troncoso Araos, Ximena. "El retrato sospechoso: Bello, Lastarria y nuestra ambigua relación con los mapuche." *Atenea* 488 (2003): 153–176.

SIMON COLLIER

LASUÉN, FERMÍN FRANCISCO DE

(1736–1803). Fermín Francisco De Lasuén (*b.* 7 June 1736; *d.* 26 June 1803), Franciscan missionary in California. Born in Victoria, Spain, Lasuén arrived in New Spain in 1759, posted first in Baja California and later in Alta California. While stationed at San Francisco de Borja mission in Baja California between 1768 and 1773, he directed the construction of a large adobe church and other buildings, the ruins of which still exist behind a later Dominican-constructed stone facade.

Between 1773 and 1803 Lasuén was stationed at the San Gabriel, San Diego, and San Carlos missions in Alta California. In 1785 he became the superior of the Alta California missions, directing the development of the missions until his death at San Carlos. During his tenure as superior, nine missions were established, including four in the summer of 1797 alone. As part of the maturation of the mission system, mission herds expanded and the Franciscans planted larger crops. The danger of food shortages passed, and the missionaries recruited larger numbers of Indians. To accommodate growing populations of converts, the Franciscans directed ambitious building projects, including the construction of larger churches. The stone structure that Lasuén began constructing at San Carlos in 1793 became the church that stands today.

See also **California; Missions: Spanish America.**

BIBLIOGRAPHY

Zephyrin Engelhardt, O.F.M., *Missions and Missionaries of California,* 4 vols. (1929–1930).

Maynard J. Geiger, O.F.M., *Franciscan Missionaries in Hispanic California, 1769–1848: A Biographical Dictionary* (1969).

Additional Bibliography

Sandos, James A. *Converting California: Indians and Franciscans in the Missions.* New Haven, CT: Yale University Press, 2004.

ROBERT H. JACKSON

LAS VEGAS. Las Vegas, the culture characteristic of the people of southwestern Ecuador in the preceramic period between 10,000 and 6,600 years ago (based on 22-radiocarbon dates). The Las Vegas culture may be a local variant of the preceramic culture distributed in the coastal zones of northern Peru, Colombia, and Panama in the same period. In Ecuador, it is the only preceramic-stage culture reconstructed in detail. Las Vegas lithic technology lacked stone projectile points and bifacial flaking techniques, both of which were characteristic of the preceramic tool kits found in the highlands of Ecuador.

The way of life of the Las Vegas people has been reconstructed from abundant remains excavated at Site 80, a large camp or village on the seasonal Las Vegas River, and from limited excavations and surface reconnaissance of thirty-one sites on the semiarid and recently deforested Santa Elena Peninsula. Lithic, shell, and bone artifacts; 192 human skeletons; faunal remains; charcoal; pollen; phytoliths; minerals; and settlement data have been analyzed. The human skeletons recovered from the site show that the people, who lived there 6,600 to 8,250 years ago, were biologically like other early Native Americans, and that they were relatively healthy and did not suffer from the deleterious effects of intensive agriculture (such as anemia and tooth decay). The sample included 122 adults and 70 subadults who were buried in various ways, reflecting a complex set of burial customs probably associated with ancestor worship. This is evidence that there was an intensification in the social activities of the local group in the period after 8,000 years ago.

The Las Vegas people were unspecialized gatherers, hunters, and fishermen living in a tropical, littoral zone with high biotic potential. The people exploited comprehensively an environment which included a seasonally dry tropical forest, more heavily wooded river bottoms, limited mangrove swamps, estuaries, beaches, and a very productive marine ecosystem. The animal bones recovered from the midden at Site 80 suggest that the ancient environment was similar to the present one (semiarid), although it had not yet suffered the desertification caused by deforestation: the ancient environment was not very moist, because tropical forest animals were not identified from bones in the Las Vegas sites.

Counting the animal bones recovered from Site 80 suggests that the people consumed calories from animal sources in the following proportions: terrestrial fauna (like deer) accounted for about 54 percent of the calories, while fish contributed about 35 percent and shellfish about 11 percent. It is likely that plant food contributed most to the people's diet, but ancient plant remains are only rarely preserved in these sites. Evidence of squash, bottle gourd, and primitive maize found in Site 80 indicates that the people added plant cultivation to their subsistence system before 8,000 years ago. At that time they occupied Site 80 on a semipermanent basis, moving irregularly to subsidiary camps. A trench suitable for supporting the wall poles of a shelter is evidence that the earliest Las Vegans built circular huts about 6 feet in diameter.

Preceramic people like those of Las Vegas probably inhabited both the lowlands of the Guayas River basin and the littoral zones of the coast of Ecuador, where they exploited a wide variety of tropical resources from permanent villages, but regrettably preceramic sites have been identified only on the Santa Elena Peninsula, and there is a gap of over 1,000 years at the end of the preceramic period. Still, the proto-agricultural way of life of the Las Vegas preceramic people on the coast and in the Guayas basin may have been the foundation for the development of the ceramic-stage Valdivia culture around 5,000 years ago.

See also **Archaeology; Puná Island.**

BIBLIOGRAPHY

Three interpretive works by Karen E. Stothert describe the Las Vegas data: "Review of the Early Preceramic Complexes of the Santa Elena Peninsula, Ecuador," in *American Antiquity* 48, no. 1 (1983): 122–127; "The Preceramic Las Vegas Culture of Coastal Ecuador," in *American Antiquity* 50, no. 3 (1985): 613–637; and *La prehistoria temprana de la peninsula de Santa Elena: Cultura Las Vegas* (1988).

KAREN E. STOTHERT

LATIFUNDIA. Latifundia, a system of land tenure dominated by large rural estates (latifundios). Concentration of landownership began during the Conquest, with sizable royal grants establishing a system of land concentration that persists in much of Latin America. Figures from Milton Esman indicate that in 1978, 60 percent of rural Mexican households were landless or near landless; the figure was 66 percent in Colombia and 70 percent in Brazil. Latifundia has been especially persistent in cattle-ranching regions.

Chile is among the extreme cases of a latifundia-dominated society. From colonial times onward, a rural elite controlled the best lands in the central valley around Santiago. In 1924 fewer than 3 percent of farms in the fertile central valley controlled 80 percent of the arable lands. The rural poor (*huasos; inquilinos,* or sharecroppers; migrant workers; and squatters) remained subservient to a powerful patron. The Christian Democratic government of Eduardo Frei (1964–1970) passed but did not enforce land-reform legislation. The socialist regime of Salvador Allende (1970–1973) attempted unsuccessfully to reform the latifundia system.

Mexico's landowners established the first association in the Western Hemisphere to promote rural interests. In 1529 town councilmen in Mexico City organized the Mesta, patterned on a powerful organization of sheep ranchers in Spain. While not as powerful as its Spanish predecessor, the Mexican Mesta appointed many important rural officials and shaped rural legislation. As a public official recorded in 1594, ranching and agriculture were "in the hands of the rich and of those possessing Indians under the encomienda system." While latifundia was not universal in Mexico, on the northern grazing lands the large haciendas ably described by François Chevalier dominated into the twentieth century. Even the great upheaval of the Mexican Revolution only replaced one set of latifundistas with another.

Similar circumstances prevailed in Uruguay and Argentina. Spanish colonial policy promoted land concentration and the marginalization of the gauchos and others of the rural lower classes. Rich, landed Uruguayan families—the Viana, de la Quadra, and others—dominated the countryside and, after Independence, the country. Argentina, with vast lands and a small population, also experienced latifundia, especially on the Pampas. Colonial and national policies granted control of the vast plains to the few.

Great estates (*hatos*) also developed on the Venezuelan and Colombian Llanos during the early eighteenth century. In mid-eighteenth-century Venezuela, about thirty families owned forty ranches covering 219 square leagues on which about 300,000 cattle grazed.

Independence speeded land concentration in much of Latin America. Land granted to war veterans quickly passed to the hands of caudillos and wily speculators. Venezuelan caudillo José Gregorio Monagas distributed land to followers in 1848, but more than half the total went to ten concessions. Owing to the income and prestige of landownership, latifundistas have retained strong political clout. Through rural societies and associations, they continue to promote their interests at the regional and national levels.

See also **Estancia; Fazenda, Fazendeiro; Fundo; Hacienda.**

BIBLIOGRAPHY

François Chevalier, *Land and Society in Colonial Mexico,* translated by Alvin Eustis, edited by Lesley Byrd Simpson (1963).

Charles H. Harris III, *A Mexican Family Empire: The Latifundio of the Sánchez Navarros, 1765–1867* (1975).

Brian Lovemen, *Struggle in the Countryside: Politics and Rural Labor in Chile, 1919–1973* (1976).

Milton J. Esman, *Landlessness and Near-Landlessness in Developing Countries* (1978).

Richard W. Slatta, *Cowboys of the Americas* (1990).

Additional Bibliography

Azcuy Ameghino, Eduardo. *El latifundio y la gran propiedad colonial rioplatense.* Buenos Aires, Argentina: F.G. Cambeiro, 1995.

Rodríguez Mirabal, Adelina C. *Latifundio ganadero y conflictos sociales en los llanos de Apure, 1700–1800.* Caracas: Fondo Editorial Tropykos, Facultad de Ciencias Económicas y Sociales, 1995.

Richard W. Slatta

LATIN AMERICA.

LATIN AMERICA. Latin America, term commonly used to describe South America, Central America, Mexico, and the islands of the Caribbean. As such, it incorporates numerous Spanish-speaking countries, Portuguese-speaking Brazil, French-speaking Haiti and the French West Indies, and usually implies countries such as Suriname and Guyana, where Romance languages are not spoken. The term *Latin America* originated in France during the reign of Napoleon III in the 1860s, when the country was second only to England in terms of industrial and financial strength. The French political economist Michel Chevalier, in an effort to solidify the intellectual underpinnings of French overseas ambitions, first proposed a "Pan-Latin" foreign policy in the hopes of promoting solidarity between nations whose languages were of Latin origin and that shared the common cultural tradition of Roman Catholicism. Led by France, the Latin peoples could reassert their influence throughout the world in the face of threats from both the Slavic peoples of eastern Europe (led by Russia) and the Anglo-Saxon peoples of northern Europe (led by England). In the Western Hemisphere, Pan-Latinists distinguished between the Anglo north and the Latin south, which they gradually began to refer to as *América latina.* From the French *l'Amérique latine,* the term came into general use in other languages.

BIBLIOGRAPHY

John L. Phelan, "Panlatinismo, la intervención francesa en México y el origen de la idea de latinoamerica," in *Latino América aunuario/estudios latinoamericanos* 2 (1969): 119–141.

Additional Bibliography

Galeano, Eduardo H. *Las venas abiertas de America Latina.* España: Catalogos, 2001.

González Casanova, Pablo. *El Estado en America Latina Teoría y Practica* México: Siglo XXI de México, 2000.

Mignolo, Walter. *La idea de America Latina.* México: Gedisa, 2007.

Rousso-Lenoir, Fabienne. *America Latina.* New York: Assouline, 2002.

J. David Dressing

LATIN AMERICAN FREE TRADE ASSOCIATION (LAFTA).

LATIN AMERICAN FREE TRADE ASSOCIATION (LAFTA). Latin American Free Trade Association (LAFTA), an organization comprised of eleven nations dedicated to furthering economic integration in Latin America. Established by a treaty signed in Montevideo, Uruguay, on February 18, 1960, the Latin American Free Trade Association (LAFTA) served as a forum for the creation of greater economic ties among Latin American nations. The Montevideo agreement was initially signed by representatives of Argentina, Brazil, Chile, Colombia, Ecuador, Mexico, Peru, and Uruguay. Bolivia, Paraguay, and Venezuela became members shortly thereafter.

The treaty signed at Montevideo proposed the gradual easing of trade barriers between the member nations, culminating with completely free trade by 1973. A permanent body was created to facilitate periodic tariff reductions and regular negotiations between the members. LAFTA met with some early success, as these nations had traded very little in the years preceding the agreement. However, progress toward integration moved slowly throughout the 1960s as the disparities of the member nations became more apparent.

Frustrated by the slow process of integration, the LAFTA nations signed the Caracas Protocol in 1969, thereby extending the deadline for free trade to 1980. The divisiveness and imbalance that had threatened LAFTA throughout the 1960s only increased during the 1970s. Many members, whose level of industrialization at this time might be described as intermediate, felt ill-equipped to compete with the large industrialized nations—Argentina, Brazil, and Mexico. The perceived inequity inherent in LAFTA led to the 1969 ratification of the Andean Pact by Bolivia, Chile, Colombia, Ecuador, Peru, and, later, Venezuela, which pursued their own agendas for integration independent of LAFTA, an action which further inhibited LAFTA's original goal of free trade throughout the hemisphere. In 1980, the year in which free trade in Latin America was to have occurred, the members of LAFTA formed the Latin-American Integration Association (LAIA), initiating a renewed effort toward integration.

In the early 1990s, the United States began establishing free-trade agreements with individual countries. The most prominent among them was the North American Free Trade Agreement (NAFTA), which created a free-trade zone between Mexico, Canada, and the United States. This new trade again sparked interest in a larger free-trade area of the Americas. Consequently, in 1993 the Organization of American States proposed the Free Trade Area of the Americas (FTAA) to be implemented in 2005. However, as of 2007, political opposition in the United States and Latin America has prevented its adoption. Nevertheless, more Latin American countries have established free-trade agreements with the United States, and in 2004 the United States and Central America signed a free-trade pact. In 2007 the United States was still in the process of negotiating economic agreements with Peru and Colombia.

See also **Andean Pact; Free Trade Area of the Americas (FTAA); North American Free Trade Agreement.**

BIBLIOGRAPHY

Edward S. Milenky, *The Politics of Regional Organization in Latin America: The Latin American Free Trade Association* (1973).

Additional Bibliography

Magariños, Gustavo. *Integración económica latinoamericana: Proceso ALALC/ALADI 1950–2000.* Montevideo, Uruguay: ALADI, 2006.

JOHN DUDLEY

LATIN AMERICAN STUDIES ASSOCIATION.

The Latin American Studies Association, commonly known as LASA, is the world's largest organization of scholars interested in Latin American studies. Founded in 1966, it is comprised of more than 5,000 members from around the world, but especially from the western hemisphere. LASA holds international conferences for the exchange of scholarly discourse, and publishes the highly regarded multidisciplinary scholarly journal *Latin American Research Review*. LASA also takes public stands on issues important to contemporary Latin America.

BIBLIOGRAPHY

Latin American Studies Association. Available from http://lasa.international.pitt.edu/.

JAY KINSBRUNER

LATORRE, LORENZO (1840–1916).

Lorenzo Latorre (*b.* 28 July 1840; *d.* 18 January 1916), military leader and president of Uruguay (1876–1880). Latorre was the country's strongman after the uprising of 1875. His dictatorship from March 1876 until his resignation in March 1880 initiated the militarist period. The son of an immigrant warehouse-keeper, he began his military career as a soldier in Venancio Flores's Colorado revolution and, later, as a professional soldier fought in the War of the Triple Alliance (1865–1870) against Paraguay. The Blanco caudillo Timoteo Aparicio's civil war between 1870 and 1872 created a power vacuum. The government that ruled until 1875 was one of cultured professionals, but lacked support from the military and the dominant economic groups—factors that provided the conditions for the establishment of militarism.

Latorre's program responded to the interests of the rural upper classes and to those of the financial and commercial classes who supported the gold standard and resisted the introduction of paper currency. His administration saw the escalation of fencing on the ranges that had begun in 1872, the reform of the Rural Codes, which tended to guarantee landownership and order in rural areas, and the extension of the authority of the army and the police. It sought balance in fiscal matters and guaranteed the continuation of the gold standard. Latorre was granted constitutional legitimacy in 1878.

Upon his resignation in 1880, Latorre was replaced by Francisco A. Vidal, president of the Senate. In 1882 another military leader, General Máximo Santos, assumed control of the government. Latorre, who settled in Buenos Aires after his resignation, was taken by surprise by a decree of permanent exile issued by the new dictator. Another military leader, Máximo Tajes, succeeded Santos and began the slow transition to civilian government.

See also **Military Dictatorships: 1821–1945; War of the Triple Alliance.**

BIBLIOGRAPHY

Enrique Méndez Vives, *El Uruguay de la modernización* (1977).

Alberto Zum Felde, *Proceso histórico del Uruguay,* 5th ed. (1967).

Additional Bibliography

Allende, Alfredo. *Lorenzo Latorre, el estadista: La construcción del estado uruguayo (1876–1880).* Montevideo: Editorial El Galeón, 2003.

Nahum, Benjamín. *Latorre y los ingleses: La reanudación de las relaciones diplomáticas entre Uruguay y Gran Bretaña, 1878–1879.* Montevideo: Ediciones de la Banda Oriental, 1996.

FERNANDO FILGUEIRA

LAUGERUD GARCÍA, EUGENIO KJELL (1930–). Eugenio Kjell Laugerud García, born on January 25, 1930, was a brigadier general who became president of Guatemala in 1974, succeeding Carlos Arana Osorio. He served until 1978. It is widely believed that the 1974 elections were fraudulent and that Efrain Ríos Montt was the actual winner.

Laugerud initially tried to implement a program of slight social and political reform. During his first years in office, membership in labor unions nearly tripled. Laugerud also inaugurated colonization programs for landless peasants in the Petén and along the Mexican border.

Laugerud's reform programs were cut short when a massive earthquake on February 4, 1976, caused enormous destruction and catalyzed social unrest. The last years of Laugerud's presidency were overshadowed by growing political violence. In May 1978, the army massacred one hundred civilians thought to be subversives in the village of Panzós, Alta Verapaz. One month later, Fernando Romeo Lucas García succeeded Laugerud as president of the republic. In 1983 Laugerud was forced to retire from the army.

See also **Guatemala.**

BIBLIOGRAPHY

Jim Handy, *Gift of the Devil: A History of Guatemala* (1984).

Richard F. Nyrop, ed., *Guatemala: A Country Study,* 2d ed. (1984).

Additional Bibliography

Booth, John A. "Socioeconomic and Political Roots of National Revolts in Central America." *Latin American Research Review* 26, no. 1 (1991): 33–73.

VIRGINIA GARRARD-BURNETT

LAUTARO (c. 1535–1557). Lautaro (*b.* 1535?; *d.* 29 April 1557), Araucanian warrior and leader. Captured at an early stage of the warfare between the Araucanians and the Spaniards under Pedro de Valdivia (1500–1553), Lautaro spent some time as a groom in the conquistador's entourage, where he learned much about Spanish military capacity. Escaping back to Araucanian territory, he emerged as a great military leader of his own people. Toward the end of 1553 his forces successfully attacked and destroyed the Spanish fort at Tucapel: a desperate counterattack by Valdivia himself led to the conquistador's death (December 1553). From this resounding victory, Lautaro went on to defeat the Spaniards at Marigueñu (February 1554) and to force the evacuation of Concepción. Re-founded by the Spaniards, the settlement was attacked and destroyed a second time by Lautaro in December 1555. The following year the brilliant Araucanian launched an offensive to the north of the river Maule. But the Araucanians were never as effective away from their own territory as they were on home ground. Repulsed by Pedro de Villagra (1508?–1577) near the river Mataquito in November 1556, Lautaro fell back on a safe position near the mouth of the Itata. On 29 April 1557 a second attack to the north of the Maule was countered by Francisco de Villagra (1511–1563) at the battle of Peteroa (sometimes called the second battle of

Mataquito), in which Lautaro received a fatal wound either from an arrow or a sword.

Lautaro's deeds were frequently evoked as an inspiring precedent by creole patriots at the time of independence. His name (like those of other Araucanian heroes of the period) has often been used as a given name for Chilean boys even in the twentieth century.

See also **Araucanians.**

BIBLIOGRAPHY

Fernando Alegría, *Lautaro, joven libertador de Arauco* (1981).

Additional Bibliography

Dillehay, Tom D. *Monuments, Empires, and Resistance in the Andes: The Araucanian Polity and Ritual Narratives.* Cambridge; New York: Cambridge University Press, 2007.

Ferrando Keun, Ricardo. *Y así nació la frontera—: Conquista, guerra, ocupación, pacificación, 1550-1900.* Santiago: Editorial Antártica, 2000.

SIMON COLLIER

LAUTARO, LOGIA DE. Logia de Lautaro, a lodge founded in Buenos Aires in 1812 by José de San Martín, Carlos María de Alvear, and José Matías Zapiola, following the models of the lodges of Spain and England. Its most important goal was to spread the idea of independence, and many of the sympathizers of independence belonged to it. A highly disciplined political pressure group, the Lautaro Lodge helped revitalize the Sociedad Patriótica of Buenos Aires. In October 1812, the Lautarianos played a key role in the overthrow of the first triumvirate (then the executive body of Argentina), of which Juan Martín de Pueyrredón was a member. However, dissension soon appeared, and the lodge had to be reorganized in 1815. The lodge was instrumental in the mobilization of resources for San Martín when he was preparing the expedition to liberate Chile. After San Martín left, and without his influence, dissension arose once again, and the lodge became more and more involved in the intricate web of the Argentine politics of the period. By 1820 it had lost practically all of its influence.

BIBLIOGRAPHY

Antonio R. Zúñiga, *La Logia "Lautaro" y la independencia de América* (1922).

Ricardo Rojas, *San Martín: Knight of the Andes,* translated by Herschel Brickell and Carlos Videla (1945).

Ricardo Piccirilli, *San Martín y la Logia Lautaro: Conferencia pronunciada el 13 de agosto de 1958* (1958).

Jaime Eyzaguirre, *La Logia Lautariana y otros estudios sobre la independencia* (1972).

Additional Bibliography

Maguire, Patricio José, and Patricio José Maguire. *La masonería y la emancipación del Río de la Plata.* Buenos Aires, Argentina: Editorial Santiago Apóstol, 2000.

JUAN MANUEL PÉ REZ

LAVALLE, JUAN GALO (1797–1841). Juan Galo Lavalle (*b.* 17 October 1797; *d.* 9 October 1841), Argentine general. Born in Buenos Aires, Lavalle entered the military soon after the outbreak of revolution against Spain. He earned a reputation for valor tinged with rashness, distinguishing himself both in José de San Martín's crossing of the Andes and in later service with Argentine expeditionary forces in Peru and Ecuador. He returned to Buenos Aires in 1824 and won further distinction in the war of 1825–1828 against Brazil.

Like most of the professional military, Lavalle was a supporter of the Unitarist faction against the Federalists. He thus opposed the Federalist governor of Buenos Aires, Manuel Dorrego, whom he accused of inflicting a disorderly and arbitrary rule upon the province and of ending the Brazilian war on unfavorable terms. On 1 December 1828, Lavalle seized power in Buenos Aires by a coup. Twelve days later he had the former governor shot, thereby setting off a backlash of anger that in the end doomed Lavalle's government. Faced with counterrevolutionary uprisings throughout Buenos Aires Province, he held power less than a year.

For roughly ten years Lavalle lived as an exile in Uruguay, until in 1839 he launched a major invasion of Argentine territory, aiming to overthrow the Federalist dictatorship established by Juan Manuel de Rosas. He penetrated deeply into Buenos Aires Province, but Rosas was able to assemble superior forces. In the meantime, Lavalle's alliance with the French forces intervening in the Río de la Plata made him vulnerable to charges of betraying national interests. He withdrew to the Argentine interior, where he suffered eventual defeat at the hands of Rosas's allies in 1841. Fleeing toward Bolivia, he was assassinated in Jujuy. Lavalle would remain a dashing hero to some; but the execution of Dorrego dogged his historical image just as it did his entire subsequent career.

See also **Andes; Rosas, Juan Manuel de.**

BIBLIOGRAPHY

Pedro Lacasa, *Vida militar y política del general argentino don Juan Lavalle* (1973).

John Lynch, *Argentine Dictator: Juan Manuel de Rosas 1829–1852* (1981).

Lily Sosa De Newton, *Lavalle* (1967).

Additional Bibliography

Pasquali, Patricia. *Juan Lavalle: Un guerrero en tiempos de revolución y dictadura.* Buenos Aires: Planeta, 1996.

Zenequelli, Lilia. *Tiempos de guerra, tiempos de paz: Juan Galo Lavalle, José María Vilela.* Buenos Aires: Editorial Dunken, 1999.

David Bushnell

LAVALLEJA, JUAN ANTONIO (1784–1853).

Juan Antonio Lavalleja (*b.* 20 June 1784; *d.* 22 October 1853), Uruguayan military leader and a hero in the struggle for Uruguayan independence. Born in Santa Lucía to a family of cattle ranchers, he began his military career in 1811 in José Artigas's revolutionary movement for independence from the Spanish dominion. From 1816 to 1818 he fought against the invaders from the Luso-Brazilian Empire, and in 1818 he was taken prisoner and confined for three years in Río de Janeiro. Once freed, he returned to his homeland, now called the Cisplatine Province, and joined the revolutionary movement for independence. Discovered, he was forced into exile in Buenos Aires, where he prepared the "liberation crusade." The final epic of national independence, Artigas's offensive was brought to a close in 1828 with a preliminary peace agreement and finally ended in 1830 with the establishment of a constitutional government.

Lavalleja's adherence to federalist ideals caused him on more than one occasion to favor forms of political unity with Argentina, but he finally renounced these to pursue an independent nation. The liberation crusade was the zenith of his career as well as the beginning of his rivalry with the other national caudillo, President Fructuoso Rivera, against whom Lavalleja rose up in arms in 1832 and 1834. Defeated, he went into exile in Brazil. He returned in 1836 to fight against Rivera again, this time along with the constitutionalist forces of then President Manuel Oribe. He defeated Rivera at the battle of Carpintería, where for the first time the colors symbolizing the traditional parties of Uruguay, red (*colorado*) for Rivera and white (*blanco*) for Oribe, were used. The war ended in 1851, and in 1853, Lavalleja joined the governing triumvirate—a short-lived one, since he died that same year.

See also **Cisplatine War; Rivera, Fructuoso.**

BIBLIOGRAPHY

Anibal Barrios Pintos, *Lavalleja: La patria independiente* (1976).

Alfredo Castellanos, *La Cisplatina, la independencia y la república caudillesca* (1974).

Additional Bibliography

Goldman, Noemí, and Richardo D. Salvatore, eds. *Caudillismos rioplatenses: Nuevas miradas a un viejo problema.* Buenos Aires: Eudeba, Universdad de Buenos Aires, 2005.

Magdalena Gutiérrez

LAVALLE URBINA, MARÍA (1908–1996).

María Lavalle Urbina was a lawyer, public official, and early Mexican feminist. Born on May 24, 1908, in Campeche, she grew up in an important political family. After working as an elementary school teacher, she became the first woman to graduate in law from the state university in 1945 and immediately entered public life. A member of the Institutional Revolutionary Party (PRI), in 1947 she became the first female magistrate of the superior court of justice of the Mexican Federal District. From 1954 to 1964 she worked in the secretariat of the interior. In 1964 she became the first female president of the Mexican senate to be elected from her home state. She served on United Nations and national commissions and presided over the Alianza de Mujeres de México (Alliance of Mexican Women) in the 1960s and the Academia Mexicana de Educación (Mexican Academy of Education). From 1976 to 1980 she served as undersecretary of public education, and from 1982 to 1984 directed the nation's textbook commission. The author of many articles on delinquency, human rights, and women, she received awards such as Woman of the Year (1963), the United Nations Prize in the Field of Human Rights (1973), the Justo Sierra Medal from the state of Campeche (1981), the Belisario Dominguez Medal from the Mexican Senate (1985), and the René Cassin Prize from the Mexican *Tribuna Israelita*. She died on April 23, 1996.

RODERIC AI CAMP
CLAUDIA CARBALLAL BENAGLIO

LA VENTA. La Venta, an important center of the archaeological Olmec culture located on a swamp island 30 miles west of Villahermosa, Tabasco, Mexico. Excavations conducted at La Venta in the 1940s and 1950s have played a pivotal role in shaping current interpretations of Olmec culture. Dating to as early as 1150 BCE, La Venta appears to have reached its apogee between 800 and 400 BCE. Originally interpreted as an empty ceremonial center, the site is now known to have supported a considerable population of fishermen and agriculturalists who made their homes on the banks of the many creeks and rivers that surrounded the site center. The ceremonial precinct of La Venta was dominated by a court enclosed by a fence constructed of basalt columns and a 33-foot-high great pyramid resembling a fluted cone. Scattered throughout La Venta were a large number of stone monuments, including four colossal heads. The majority of these monuments are currently displayed at La Venta park in Villahermosa. During the 1950s the site of La Venta was in danger of destruction due to both the construction of a nearby petroleum refinery and the encroachment of the modern town of La Venta. The site is now protected as an archaeological park.

See also **Olmecs.**

BIBLIOGRAPHY

Philip Drucker, Robert F. Heizer, and Robert J. Squier, *Excavations at La Venta, Tabasco* (1959).

Michael D. Coe, *America's First Civilization* (1968).

Rebecca González Lauck, "Proyecto arqueológico La Venta," in *Arqueología* 4 (1988): 121–165.

William F. Rust and Robert J. Sharer, "Olmec Settlement Data from La Venta, Tabasco, Mexico," in *Science* 242 (1988): 102–104.

Additional Bibliography

Diehl, Richard A. *The Olmecs: America's First Civilization.* New York: Thames & Hudson, 2005.

González Lauck, Rebecca. "La Venta: An Olmec Capital" in *Olmec Art of Ancient Mexico.* Benson, Elizabeth P., Beatriz de la Fuente, and Marcia Castro-Leal, eds. Washington, DC: National Gallery of Art, 1996.

F. KENT REILLY III

LAVISTA, MARIO (1943–). Mario Lavista, born on April 3, 1943, is a Mexican composer, editor, and administrator. Lavista was among the talented group of young musicians who in the 1960s matriculated at the Carlos Chávez composition workshop in the National Conservatory of Mexico. Others were Eduardo Mata and Hector Quintinar, the latter also one of Lavista's teachers. Study with leaders of Europe's avant garde—Karlheinz Stockhausen, György Ligeti, and Iannis Xenakis—and his own pioneering creative impulses led Lavista to discoveries of new sonorities coaxed from traditional instruments; however, he has not eschewed electronic sound synthesis, which he studied in Japan. Lavista has taught theory and composition at the National Conservatory, edited the music journal *Pauta,* and headed the music section of the National Council for Culture and the Arts. In 1991 he won the Premio Nacional de Artes y Ciencias and the Medalla Mozart.

See also **Mata, Eduardo; Music: Art Music; Quintanar, Héctor.**

BIBLIOGRAPHY

José Antonio Alcaraz et al., "Período contemporáneo," in *La música de México,* edited by Julio Estrada, vol. 1, pt. 5 (1984).

Additional Bibliography

Moreno Rivas, Yolando. *La composición en México en el siglo XX*. Mexico: Consejo Nacional para la Cultura y las Artes, 1994.

ROBERT L. PARKER

LAVRADIO, MARQUÊS DO

LAVRADIO, MARQUÊS DO (1729–1790). Marquês do Lavradio (Dom Luís de Almeida Portugal Soares Alarção Eça Melo Pereira Aguilar Fiel de Lugo Mascarenhas Silva Mendonça e Lencastre; *b.* 27 June 1729; *d.* 2 May 1790), governor of Bahia and viceroy of Rio de Janeiro. Born in Lisbon, the son of an army officer who served as captain-general of Angola and briefly as the last viceroy of Brazil at Bahia de Todos os Santos, Lavradio became the forty-fifth governor and captain-general of Bahia (1768–1769) before being promoted to Rio de Janeiro, where he became the third viceroy to reside there (1769–1779). As had his predecessors, Lavradio found his authority far more circumscribed than his exalted title would suggest. His regime coincided with the climax of a century-long dispute between Spain and Portugal over the temperate lands between present-day São Paulo and the Río de la Plata. In spite of his best efforts, he was unable to prevent vastly superior Spanish forces from gaining control over the southern portions of that disputed territory. Acutely aware of the fact that Brazil's first gold boom was already over, Lavradio tried to stimulate new sources of royal income by encouraging the production of tobacco, cereals, fibers, whale products, and dyestuffs and to curtail illicit foreign trade with Brazilian ports. Toward the end of his viceregency he drafted an illuminating, markedly modest account of his administration, one of the few such terminal reports ever prepared by senior administrators of colonial Brazil. Subsequently, he became a member of the Council of War and president of the senior judicial tribunal of the kingdom, the Desembargo do Paço, but left no trace of his role in either body.

See also **Bahia; Brazil: The Colonial Era, 1500–1808.**

BIBLIOGRAPHY

Dauril Alden, *Royal Government in Colonial Brazil* (1968).

John Armitage, *The History of Brazil... 1808 to... 1831*, 2 vols. (London, 1836), 2: 161–242.

Additional Bibliography

Maxwell, Kenneth. *Conflicts & Conspiracies: Brazil and Portugal, 1750-1808*. New York: Routledge, 2004.

Oliveira, Cecilia Helena de Salles, Maria Lígia Coelho Prado, and Maria Helena Capelato. *A independência e a construção do império, 1750-1824*. São Paulo-SP: Atual Editora, 1995.

DAURIL ALDEN

LAVRADOR DE CANA

LAVRADOR DE CANA. Lavrador de Cana, in Brazil a farmer who planted and harvested sugarcane, which was then sent to a mill for processing into sugar. In colonial Bahia, cane farmers were associated with the dominant sugar export economy, slavery, and the political interests of the sugar sector. Most *lavradores* were white and were socially an adjunct of the mill-owner elite, although many were themselves people of humble background and resources. However, the racial composition of the *lavradores* changed at the beginning of the nineteenth century. The records of one mill show that 44 percent of the *lavradores* were nonwhite.

Land determined one's social position and the relationship of cane farmers to the mill. Those who owned land outright, who were the most privileged, generally divided the pressed cane on a fifty–fifty basis with the mill owners. Among the less fortunate were those who owned land that was under obligation, and sharecroppers and tenants, who leased or rented Engenho lands with restrictions both on land use and on the disposal of the cane produced. *Lavradores de cana* owned varying numbers of slaves and in some cases also had capital sufficient to purchase or negotiate access to the oxen, lumber, and firewood necessary for sugar production.

See also **Plantations; Slavery: Brazil; Sugar Industry.**

BIBLIOGRAPHY

Stuart B. Schwartz, *Sugar Plantations in the Formation of Brazilian Society: Bahia, 1550–1835* (1985).

Additional Bibliography

Araújo, Tatiana Brito de. *Os engenhos centrais e a produção açucareira no Recôncavo Baiano, 1875–1909*. Salvador, Brazil: FIEB, 2002.

Barickman, B. J. *A Bahian Counterpoint: Sugar, Tobacco, Cassava, and Slavery in the Recôncavo, 1780–1860*. Stanford, CA: Stanford University Press, 1998.

García Fernández, Ramón V. "Os lavradores de cana de São Sebastião." *Revista do Instituto de Estudos Brasileiros.* 40 (1996): 173–190.

NANCY PRISCILLA SMITH NARO

LAW OF THE SEA. The Latin American and Caribbean states were very active in the Third United Nations Conference on the Law of the Sea (UNCLOS III), 1973–1982. In fact, three Latin American states (Chile, Ecuador, and Peru) precipitated a controversy in the 1950s when they claimed a 200-mile zone to protect tuna, a claim that had to be resolved at the conference. Their claim was on the basis of the Declaration of Santiago on the Maritime Zone (1952), which the United States particularly opposed on the ground that it violated the traditional area of the high seas considered to be open to all—most states accepted that this was the area beyond the three-mile territorial sea. (Other states in the region soon followed suit with similar claims.) The enforcement of these states' claimed right to regulate tuna fishing resulted in the Tuna War when Ecuador and Peru seized and fined United States private fishing boats in the 1950s and 1960s.

In preparation for the conference, the Caribbean states met in the Dominican Republic in 1972 and approved the Declaration of Santo Domingo, which set the territorial sea and fishing limits for these states. The first session of UNCLOS III was held in New York in 1973, the second in Caracas, Venezuela, in 1974 (the other sessions were held mainly in New York and Geneva). This long conference differed from the earlier ones—UNCLOS I (1958) and UNCLOS II (1960)—in that it had some 150 participants versus some 80 for them. While the earlier ones had been on an East (Soviet bloc)–West (led by the United States) political axis, this conference was on a North (developed and industrialized)–South (developing) economic and political axis. The latter group of states, a majority, used the conference to challenge the North and to bring about the New International Economic Order (NIEO). This would help transform the traditional system so that it would better serve the interests and needs of the South, especially economically. The Group of 77 (G-77), formed in the 1960s and including Latin America, developed a unified bloc in the United Nations in general and in UNCTAD (UN Conference on Trade and Development) in particular to advance the movement toward the NIEO. The UN General Assembly passed a declaration on the establishment of an NIEO in 1974 and later the same year approved the Charter of Economic Rights and Duties of States.

During UNCLOS III the South used bloc caucusing and bargaining to deal with the North. The G-77 was one bloc along with both an African group and a Latin American group (it had twenty-eight members), all trying to have a common position on major issues. Several Latin American and Caribbean states were especially influential at UNCLOS III: the Bahamas, Brazil, Chile, Jamaica, Mexico, Peru, Trinidad and Tobago, and Venezuela. Two compromises between the North and the South that favored the latter were a territorial sea of 12 miles and an Exclusive Economic Zone of 188 miles (200 miles total). In the final vote on the 1982 Law of the Sea Convention, only four states voted against it (including the United States and Venezuela); seventeen abstained (among the North); the South, including Latin America and the Caribbean, voted for it. The required sixty ratifications were obtained in late 1993; they included twelve Commonwealth Caribbean and seven Latin American states. The Convention went into effect in November 1994. The United States signed in August 1994; Senate approval was still needed.

See also **Fishing Industry.**

BIBLIOGRAPHY

Robert L. Friedheim and William J. Durch, "The International Seabed Resources Agency Negotiations and the New International Economic Order," in *International Organization* 31, no. 2 (Spring 1977): 349–352, 378–382.

Edward Miles, "The Structure and Effects of the Decision Process on the Seabed Committee and the Third United Nations Conference on the Law of the Sea," in *International Organization* 31, no. 2 (Spring 1977): 161–166, 177–179, 185–192.

Douglas M. Johnston, ed., *Regionalization of the Law of the Sea: Proceedings* (1978).

Bernard H. Oxman, David D. Caron, and Charles L. O. Buderi, eds., *Law of the Sea: U.S. Policy Dilemma* (1983), chaps. 2 and 4.

Francisco Orrego Vicuña, *Exclusive Economic Zone: A Latin American Perspective* (1984).

Additional Bibliography

Galdorisi, George, and Kevin R. Vienna. *Beyond the Law of the Sea: New Directions for U.S. Oceans Policy.* Westport, CT: Praeger, 1997.

Klein, Natalie. *Dispute Settlement in the UN Convention on the Law of the Sea.* Cambridge: Cambridge University Press, 2005.

LARMAN C. WILSON

LEAGUE OF NATIONS. Hoping to counterbalance the growing political and economic power of the United States and the economic dominance of Britain in Latin America, nine Latin American countries (Bolivia, Brazil, Cuba, Guatemala, Haiti, Honduras, Nicaragua, Panama, and Peru) became charter members of the League of Nations in 1919, followed by several others that joined during the 1920s.

After World War I, Latin America continued to fear the possibility of direct foreign intervention in hemispheric affairs, not having forgotten European attempts, both direct and indirect, to do so during the 1800s and the U.S. buildup in the Caribbean in Theodore Roosevelt's day. The "big stick," the Roosevelt Corollary to the Monroe Doctrine, and dollar diplomacy had left their mark. In spite of Woodrow Wilson's declaration on 27 October 1913 that the United States would never again seek territory through conquest, and of some goodwill he gained by accepting Latin American leadership in the mediation of the Mexican Revolution, Latin American political leaders sought clarification of the Monroe Doctrine in the international arena. Just as Baron Rio Branco had closely aligned Brazil with unpopular U.S. policies in order to use the prestige of the U.S.-Brazilian alliance to escape British domination while establishing a favorable western boundary, Latin American leaders aligned themselves with the League of Nations.

Unfortunately, the League usually ignored Latin America and proved to be the wrong forum for negotiation, since the U.S. Senate failed to ratify the League's Covenant and the United States thus did not become a member. During the 1920s and 1930s, U.S. manufactured goods flooded Latin American markets while U.S. investments, particularly in Brazil, dominated Latin American economic development.

The League did get involved, however, in two incidents of open fighting in Latin America. In July 1932, the League began to investigate sporadic fighting between Bolivia and Paraguay over an area called the Gran Chaco. Paraguay formally declared war on 10 May 1933. More than 100,000 lives were lost while the League's fact-finding commission, headed by Álvarez del Vayo of Spain, investigated and made its way back to Geneva in December of that year. The League proposed a peace treaty, which both sides rejected, and then an arms embargo. The Chaco War dragged on mainly because, despite U.S. imposition of a separate arms embargo, existing arms contracts to Bolivia for the defense of the oilfield owned by Standard Oil of New Jersey were not affected. The war ended 14 June 1935 when Paraguay ran out of matériel.

The League was even less effective in settling open fighting between Peru and Colombia over Leticia, a small town with a strategic location on the upper Amazon. Both sides ignored League mediation efforts, but the conflict came to an end when Peru's president, Luis Sánchez Cerro, was assassinated in 1933. League commissioners administered the area around Leticia for a year and then returned it to Colombia.

By 1938, Chile, Brazil, Paraguay, Nicaragua, Guatemala, Costa Rica, and Honduras had dropped out of the League, which they viewed as powerless, and turned to direct negotiations with the United States.

See also **Chaco War; Monroe Doctrine; Roosevelt Corollary; Wilson, Woodrow.**

BIBLIOGRAPHY

E. Bradford Burns, *The Unwritten Alliance: Rio-Branco and Brazilian-American Relations* (1966).

Joseph S. Tulchin, *The Aftermath of War: World War I and U.S. Policy Toward Latin America* (1971).

Elmer Bendiner, *A Time for Angels: The Tragi-comic History of the League of Nations* (1975).

Robert F. Smith, ed., *The United States and the Latin American Sphere of Influence* (1981).

F. S. Northedge, *The League of Nations: Its Life and Times, 1920–1946* (1986).

Additional Bibliography

Irurozqui, Marta. *"A bala, piedra y palo": La construcción de la ciudadanía política en Bolivia, 1826-1952.* Seville: Diputación de Sevilla, 2000.

Lorini, Irma. *El nacionalismo en Bolivia de la pre y posguerra del Chaco (1910-1945).* La Paz: Plural Editores, 2006.

Segura, Jorge Rhenán. *La Sociedad de las Naciones y la política centroamericana: 1919-1939.* San José, Costa Rica: Euroamericana de Ediciones, 1993.

LESLEY R. LUSTER

LEAGUE OF UNITED LATIN AMERICAN CITIZENS.

LEAGUE OF UNITED LATIN AMERICAN CITIZENS. Struggling for civil rights, citizenship, and economic advancement, Mexican Americans formed the League of United Latin American Citizens (LULAC) in Corpus Christi, Texas, in 1929. The war between the United States and Mexico (1846–1848) had left a legacy of prejudice and animosity among Anglos, Mexicans, and Mexican Americans. By the 1920s several Mexican American civic organizations began addressing this situation and decided to join forces. By uniting, they hoped to strengthen their political clout in combating the daily discrimination experienced by Mexican Americans in employment, residence, schools, and elections. After debating whether the new organization should include noncitizens, the delegates, in a move to gain public credibility, made a controversial decision to establish a citizens-only membership. Benjamin Garza, head of the Sons of America in Corpus Christi, was the first president general.

By 1932 local LULAC chapters had formed in Arizona, Colorado, New Mexico, and California. In 1934 women organized a national office. LULAC launched successful legal challenges to Mexican Americans' second-class citizenship in the United States. In 1945, 1946, and 1948, they disputed Mexican American children's segregation in California and the public school system in Texas. The organization provided financial backing for the farm workers' struggle in the 1960s. In the twenty-first century LULAC remains influential, representing not only Mexican Americans in the Southwest but Hispanics throughout the United States and Puerto Rico.

BIBLIOGRAPHY

Kaplowitz, Craig A. *LULAC, Mexican Americans, and National Policy.* College Station: Texas A&M University Press, 2005.

Márquez, Benjamin. *LULAC: The Evolution of a Mexican American Political Organization.* Austin: University of Texas Press, 1993.

San Miguel, Guadalupe, Jr. *"Let All of Them Take Heed": Mexican Americans and the Campaign for Educational Equality in Texas, 1910–1981.* Austin: University of Texas Press, 1987.

MEREDITH GLUECK

LEAL, FERNANDO

LEAL, FERNANDO (1896–1964). Fernando Leal (*b.* 1896; *d.* 1964), Mexican painter. Born in Mexico City, Leal studied briefly at the San Carlos Academy of Fine Arts and at the Open Air Painting School in Coyoacán under Alfredo Ramos Martínez. He was a teacher of drawing and printmaking at the Open Air School for seven years. In 1921, together with Jean Charlot, he devoted himself to woodcuts, reviving the once popular medium with images of contemporary life. Leal was among the first Mexican painters to use subjects from the Mexican Revolution in his canvases, including *Zapatista Camp* (1922). Later that year, he was invited by Education Minister José Vasconcelos to paint on the walls of the National Preparatory School. The result was the large encaustic mural *The Feast of Our Lord of Chalma,* which depicted the Indian dances dedicated to the Black Christ of the village of Chalma. In 1927 Leal decorated, in fresco, the entrance to the laboratories of the Department of Public Health. In 1931, again using encaustic, he painted the vestibule of Bolívar Hall, incorporating various events from the Wars of Independence in South America.

Unlike many of his contemporaries, who were leftists and anticlerical, Leal was a devout Catholic, and in the late 1940s he was involved in mural decorations for the Church of Our Lady of Guadalupe in Mexico City. He also served as art critic for the newspaper *El Nacional Revolucionario* in 1934–1935. Although he ceased mural painting in the last decade of his life, he continued to produce many easel paintings of landscapes, figures, and still lifes, as well as woodcuts, until his death.

See also **Art: The Twentieth Century.**

BIBLIOGRAPHY

Jean Charlot, *The Mexican Mural Renaissance* (1962).

Antonio Rodríguez, *A History of Mexican Mural Painting* (1969).

Additional Bibliography

Folgarait, Leonard. *Mural Painting and Social Revolution in Mexico, 1920-1940: Art of the New Order*. Cambridge: Cambridge University Press, 1998.

Pellicer, Carlos, and Rafael Carrillo Azpéitia. *La Pintura mural de la Revolución Mexicana*. México: Fondo Editorial de la Plástica Mexicana, 1998.

ALEJANDRO ANDREUS

LEANTE, CÉSAR

LEANTE, CÉSAR (1928–). César Leante (*b.* 1 July 1928), Cuban novelist and essayist. Leante was born in Matanzas and spent part of his childhood in Mexico. From 1944 to 1950 he was a member of the Socialist Youth Movement and later the Popular Socialist Party. In 1954 he began writing radio scripts and continued until 1959, the year he joined the staff of the newspaper *Revolución*. In 1961 he became an editor for the news agency Prensa Latina. He also taught theater at the National School for Instructors in the Arts until 1963, when he was named cultural attaché at the Cuban embassy in Paris. Leante went on to represent his country officially in international activities and to occupy prestigious posts at the Ministry of Foreign Relations and at the Cuban Union of Writers and Artists (UNEAC), which recognized his novel *Padres e hijos* with an honorable mention in 1965. He translated into Spanish the works of Simone de Beauvoir and Antoine de Saint-Exupéry.

Leante served as literary adviser to the National Council on Culture and enjoyed favorable treatment from the Cuban regime until opting not to return to Cuba while on an official trip to Europe. Since then he has published in Spain, his adopted home, and elsewhere in the Americas. One of his best-known works is the 1973 novel *Muelle de caballería*. Among his other works are *Tres historias* (1977), *Calembour* (1988), and *Fidel Castro* (1991). His novels have been translated into several languages.

See also **Literature: Spanish America.**

BIBLIOGRAPHY

Madrid, Lelia M. "*Calembour:* Las traiciones de la univocidad: Entrevista con César Leante." *Inti* 32–33 (Fall–Spring 1990–1991): 181–188.

Madrid, Lelia M. "Entrevista con César Leante: Lugar y fecha: Editorial Pliegos, Madrid, 13/1/90." *Hispania USA* 74:4 (Dec. 1991), 950–953.

Prado Oropreza, Renato. "Historia y literatura en Cabrera Infante, César Leante, y Cintio Vitier." *Texto Crítico* 9 (Jan. 1983): 65–91.

ROBERTO VALERO

LE BRETÓN, TOMÁS ALBERTO

LE BRETÓN, TOMÁS ALBERTO (1868–1959). Tomás Alberto Le Bretón (*b.* 1868; *d.* 1959), Argentine politician and statesman. Born in Buenos Aires, Le Bretón trained as a lawyer at the university there and received his degree in 1891. He became a specialist in patent law and used this expertise to represent Argentina at the 1904 Berlin Industrial Property Congress as well as at a subsequent congress in Stockholm. Although Le Bretón is now remembered mostly for his dominant role in Radical Party politics after his election to the Chamber of Deputies in March 1914, he was also instrumental in promoting land colonization in the Chaco region as part of a process of government support for the nascent cotton industry there. He probably became interested in the matter as a member of the Administrative Commission of Land and Colonies in 1920, but he did not become officially active in this regard until 1923, following a term in the United States (1919–1922) as Argentine ambassador. As minister of agriculture from 1922 to 1925 he thoroughly reorganized the ministry, paying particular attention to the prospects of cotton cultivation. Le Bretón contracted with U.S. agronomist Dr. Ernest Tutt to provide the most modern agricultural and marketing information. These resources, along with the opening of government lands to settlers and provision by the government of free cotton seed to farmers, together served to promote the rapid development of this industrial fiber.

Le Bretón's links to the Antipersonalist Radical Civic Union led to his reentry into politics. In later years the conservative governments of General José

Augustín P. Justo and Roberto M. Ortiz appointed him to several important diplomatic posts. In 1936 Le Bretón was called upon to represent Argentina in commercial negotiations with Great Britain. He also served as Argentine ambassador to Great Britain from 1938 to 1941.

See also **Argentina: The Twentieth Century; Cotton.**

BIBLIOGRAPHY

Additional Bibliography

Persello, Ana Virginia. *El partido radical: Gobierno y oposición, 1916–1943.* Buenos Aires: Siglo veintiuno editores Argentina, 2004.

DONNA J. GUY

LECHÍN OQUENDO, JUAN (1914–2001).

Juan Lechín Oquendo (*b.* 19 May 1914; *d.* 27 August 2001), Bolivian labor leader. Born in the small mining town of Corocoro to an Arab father and a mestizo mother, Lechín studied at the American Institute in La Paz. He was a founding member of Bolivia's Federation of Miners (Federación Sindical de Trabajadores Mineros de Bolivia—FSTMB) and for over forty years (1944–1986) served as its permanent secretary. In 1952, Lechín joined the revolution of the Nationalist Revolutionary Movement (MNR) that nationalized the mining industry, declared universal suffrage, and carried out an extensive land reform program, playing a key role in the formation of the new regime. As minister of labor, Lechín was instrumental in the establishment of the Bolivian Workers Central (COB), an umbrella organization in which he presided as secretary general until the mid-1980s. He was also instrumental in securing worker cogovernment and comanagement in Comibol (the Mining Corporation of Bolivia).

In 1960, Lechín was elected vice president of Bolivia on the MNR ticket headed by Víctor Paz Estenssoro. This relationship, however, was short-lived as Lechín resigned from the MNR to form his own Revolutionary Party of the Nationalist Left (Partido Revolucionario de Izquierda Nacionalista—PRIN) and then conspired with the military to topple Paz Estenssoro in 1964.

Lechín's support for the military coup did not prevent his joining the MNR leadership in exile while the new military government cracked down on labor. Ironically, between 1982 and 1985 Lechín was largely responsible for the erosion of labor's power. In an attempt to replay the 1950s, he demanded and obtained worker comanagement in Comibol; significantly, he rejected worker cogovernment. At the same time, however, Lechín launched numerous general strikes that crippled the government's attempts to stabilize the economy.

A year after the launching by the MNR of Bolivia's New Economic Policy in 1985, Lechín suffered a humiliating defeat when the miners he had served since 1944 refused to reelect him permanent secretary of the FSTMB. Earlier he had lost his position as secretary general of the COB. From 1986 until his death in 2001, Lechín was a marginal player in labor and in Bolivian politics.

See also **Bolivia, Organizations: Bolivian Workers Central (COB); Bolivia, Political Parties: Nationalist Revolutionary Movement (MNR).**

BIBLIOGRAPHY

Lupe Cajías, *Historia de una leyenda: Vida y palabra de Juan Lechín Oquendo* (1988).

James M. Malloy and Eduardo Gamarra, *Revolution and Reaction: Bolivia, 1964–1985* (1988).

Additional Bibliography

Calla, Ricardo. *La derrota de Lechín.* La Paz: Ediciones del Tigre de Papel, 1986.

EDUARDO A. GAMARRA

LECLERC, CHARLES VICTOR EMMANUEL (1772–1802).

Charles Victor Emmanuel Leclerc (*b.* 17 March 1772; *d.* 2 November 1802), commander of the French military expedition to Saint-Domingue in 1802. In December 1802 a French funeral ship docked at Marseilles. On board were the body of Leclerc and his grieving widow, Pauline. Napoleon officially declared his court in mourning and announced a state funeral for his brother-in-law.

Leclerc, a native of Pontoise, first served under Napoleon at the siege of Toulon (1793) and attained the rank of general in 1797 for his service in Italy. Leclerc married Pauline Bonaparte in 1797 and played an important role in Napoleon's coup against the Directory in 1799.

In 1801, Napoleon selected Leclerc to lead a French expedition against Toussaint Louverture and the black rebels of Saint-Domingue. Leclerc encountered unexpected resistance from the rebels, attempted to restore slavery in the former colony, and arrested Toussaint L'Ouverture. He then contracted yellow fever and died at Cap Français. At the time of his death, Jean-Jacques Dessalines had organized the island's blacks for victory and independence from France.

See also **Dessalines, Jean Jacques; Louverture, Toussaint.**

BIBLIOGRAPHY

Cyril L. R. James, *The Black Jacobins* (1938).

Georges Lefebvre, *Napoleon,* 2 vols., translated by Henry F. Stockhold (1969).

James Leyburn, *The Haitian People* (1941).

Thomas Ott, *The Haitian Revolution, 1789–1804* (1973).

Additional Bibliography

Dubois, Laurent. *Avengers of the New World: The Story of the Haitian Revolution.* Cambridge, MA: Belknap Press of Harvard University Press, 2004.

Fick, Carolyn. *The Making of Haiti: The Saint Domingue Revolution from Below.* Knoxville: University of Tennessee Press, 1990.

Geggus, David Patrick, ed. *The Impact of the Haitian Revolution in the Atlantic World.* Columbia: University of South Carolina, 2001.

Mézière, Henri. *Le général Leclerc (1772–1802) et l'expédition de Saint-Domingue.* Paris: Tallandier, 1990.

THOMAS O. OTT

LECONTE, MICHEL CINCINNATUS

LECONTE, MICHEL CINCINNATUS (?–1912). Michel Cincinnatus Leconte (*d.* 8 August 1912), president of Haiti (1911–1912). Leconte was one of six Haitian presidents who ruled for very brief periods between 1911 and 1915, an era of chronic political instability that encouraged the U.S. military to intervene in Haitian affairs in 1915. Leconte staged a successful coup against President Antoine Simone. Lasting only from 14 August 1911 to 8 August 1912, Leconte's presidency was subject to the pressures produced by U.S. and German banking and commercial interests that were competing for control over Haitian economic life. With the support of the German merchants in Haiti, Leconte sought to appease native elite elements unhappy about the corruption that had occurred in Simone's dealings with U.S. bankers and railroad businessmen. U.S. diplomatic pressure, as epitomized by the visit of U.S. Secretary of State Philander Knox, encouraged him to impose order upon the country. Leconte reorganized the army and began developing a system of public education before he was killed in a mysterious explosion at the presidential palace in Port-au-Prince.

See also **Haiti.**

BIBLIOGRAPHY

Rayford W. Logan, *Haiti and the Dominican Republic* (1968).

David Nicholls, *From Dessalines to Duvalier* (1979).

Additional Bibliography

Berloquin-Chassany, Andrés Avelino. *Haïti, une démocratie compromise, 1890-1911.* Paris: Harmattan, 2004.

PAMELA MURRAY

LECUONA Y CASADO, ERNESTO

LECUONA Y CASADO, ERNESTO (1895–1963). Ernesto Lecuona y Casado (*b.* 6 August 1895; *d.* 29 November, 1963), Cuban pianist and composer. Lecuona, born in Guanabacoa, began to play the piano when he was barely four years old—he had to climb on a box to reach the keyboard. As the great Ignacy Jan Paderewski once noted, he gave the impression that "he had nothing to learn. Nature had made him a prodigious pianist." Thus pianists sometimes have difficulty playing many of his works because they were composed by an extraordinary master of the keyboard. He had the same natural gift for composing. Many times his works went straight to the publisher without Lecuona's having played them even once.

In this somewhat undisciplined fashion Lecuona's creative genius produced three groups of works. The first encompasses the bulk of his early *boleros, guarachas,* and *criollas*—Cuban music with

European roots. The second is made up of Afro-Cuban compositions, which he began to write around 1920, the best known of which is probably the elegant and sensuous dance "La Comparsa." The third, less numerous group is his Spanish-style works, among which the seven pieces that form his suite *Andalucía* stand out. It is said that the celebrated French musician Maurice Ravel believed that the semiclassic "Malagueña," one of these Spanish-style works, was more melodic and beautiful than his own "Bolero." Lecuona also wrote a number of works for the theater, from frivolous revues to tragic zarzuelas (Spanish operettas). Many of his best-known songs come from his stage work, among them "Siboney," one of his most popular pieces outside Cuba.

Plácido Domingo, the world-acclaimed tenor, won the 1985 Grammy Award for Latin American songs for his performance of "Always in My Heart," the theme song that Lecuona wrote for the film of the same title, released in the early 1940s. Lecuona died in Santa Cruz de Tenerife, Spain.

See also **Bolero; Theater.**

BIBLIOGRAPHY

Gloria Castiel Jacobson, "The Life and Music of Ernesto Lecuona" (Ph.D. diss., University of Florida, 1982).

José I. Lasaga, *Cuban Lives: Pages from Cuban History* (1988), vol. 2, pp. 411–424.

Additional Bibliography

León, Carmela de. *Ernesto Lecuona: El maestro.* Ciudad de La Habana: Editora Musical de Cub, 1995.

José M. Hernández

LEDUC, PAUL (1942–). Paul Leduc is a Mexican film director. Leduc was born on March 11, 1942, in Mexico City, where he attended the National Autonomous University of Mexico (UNAM) and studied architecture and theater before receiving a scholarship to study film direction at the Institute of Graduate Film Studies in Paris. Upon his return to Mexico in 1967, he organized numerous film clubs and began his career as an assistant director and producer of various important documentaries. Under the government of Luis Echevarria (1970–1976), Leduc took advantage of the increased support for alternative film production and was able to gain financial support for his first feature film. This debut was his acclaimed *Reed: México insurgente* (1970), which depicts and demystifies the Mexican Revolution. A series of noted and controversial films followed. *Frida, naturaleza viva* (1985) played an important part in establishing Leduc's reputation. One of the most creative and original directors of current Latin American cinema, Leduc is equally adept at narrative film and documentary. He has consistently preferred to work as an independent film director. Leduc's other films are *Historias prohibidas de Pulgarcito* (1981), *La cabeza de la hidra* (1983), *Como vas* (1989), *Barroco* (1990), *Latino Bar* (1991), *Dollar Mambo* (1993), and *El Cobrador: In God We Trust* (2006).

See also **Cinema: Since 1990.**

BIBLIOGRAPHY

Luis Reyes De La Maza, *El cine sonoro en México* (1973).

E. Bradford Burns, *Latin American Cinema: Film and History* (1975).

Carl J. Mora, *Mexican Cinema: Reflections of a Society: 1896–1980* (1982).

John King, *Magical Reels: A History of Cinema in Latin America* (1990).

Additional Bibliography

Lynd, Juliet. "Art and Politics in Paul Leduc's Frida: Naturaleza viva." *Romance Languages Annual* 10, no. 2 (1998): 696–702.

Paranaguá, Paulo Antonio, ed. *Mexican Cinema.* Translated by Ana M. López. London: British Film Institute, 1995.

David Maciel

LEEWARD ISLANDS. The Lesser Antilles of the eastern Caribbean are divided into the Leeward and the Windward Islands. The Leeward Islands were so named because ships sailing south from the Atlantic did so on the leeward (sheltered, or facing the direction toward which the wind blows) side of the islands. The islands are administered by the United States (the U.S. Virgin Islands), the Netherlands (Saba, St. Eustatius, and the southern part of St. Martin), France (Guadeloupe, the northern part of St. Martin, St. Barthélemy, and a few

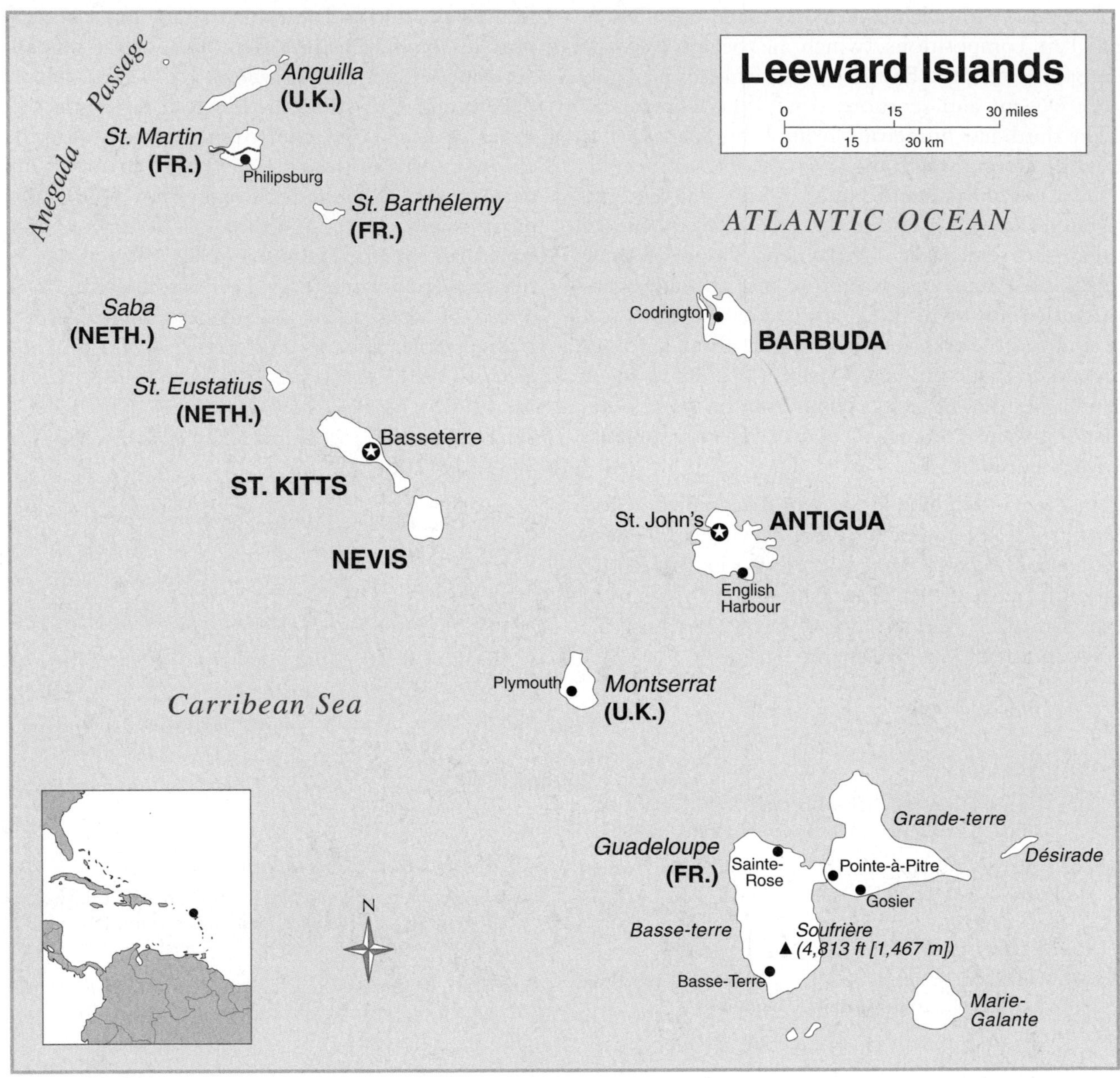

others), and the United Kingdom (the British Virgin Islands). Several of the islands that were formerly British colonies were part of a West Indies Federation, dissolved in 1962: Anguilla, Antigua, Barbuda, the British Virgin Islands, Montserrat, Nevis, Redonda, St. Kitts, and Sombrero.

Columbus visited the Leewards but, not finding any precious metals, considered them *islas inutiles* (useless islands). The English, French, and Dutch were less disdainful and indeed fought over them. Even Sweden had a colony (present-day French St. Barthélemy, also known as St. Barts). They were important strategically and as sugar and tobacco colonies. British Admiral Lord Nelson stationed his fleet in Antigua. At the Battle of the Saintes (off Guadeloupe) in 1782, the English fleet defeated the French fleet, stopping any further French conquests in the Caribbean region.

Dominica, independent since 1978, has at various points in its history been considered part of the Leeward Islands and the Windward Islands. Twice declared a neutral Carib sanctuary, it was nevertheless colonized by the French because of its strategic location between the French islands of Guadeloupe and Martinique (part of the Windward Islands). After winning the Battle of the Saintes, England gained the island and dominated the Caribbean.

Every one of the Leewards has made a more or less smooth transition from colonialism to either outright independence or Dependent Territorial status, that is, keeping a link to the United Kingdom but with full internal self-governance. The area has not been without its conflicts, however. In 1967 Anguilla seceded, preferring to be linked with London than with Saint Kitts and Nevis. In Antigua in 1990, the eldest son of the prime minister, Vere Bird Jr., was involved in a scandal involving the sale of Israeli guns to the Colombian Medellín drug cartel. Hurricanes and volcanic eruptions have also played a destructive role. Half the island of Montserrat has remained uninhabitable since 1995, when the Soufrière Hills volcano became active after a long dormancy. There are volcanoes also called Soufrière in Guadeloupe, St. Lucia, and St. Vincent.

The transition away from sugar economies has been difficult for the islands. By the end of the twentieth century the British Virgin Islands was relying on tourism and offshore financial services, and Antigua on Internet gambling. All the islands are members of the Organization of Eastern Caribbean States and of the Caribbean Community (CARICOM). It is expected that the CARICOM Single Market and Economy (CSME) plan will bring some benefits to these well-governed but economically fragile states.

See also **Windward Islands.**

BIBLIOGRAPHY

Fergus, Howard A. *A History of Education in the British Leeward Islands, 1838–1945.* Mona, Jamaica: University of West Indies Press, 2003.

ANTHONY P. MAINGOT

LEGUÍA, AUGUSTO BERNARDINO

(1863–1932). Augusto Bernardino Leguía (*b.* 19 February 1863; *d.* 7 February 1932), Peruvian politician, businessman, and landowner, and twice president of Peru (1908–1912, 1919–1930) at a time of distressing economic modernization and social upheaval. Initially an important representative of the Civilista political elite, and an example of the rise of the more business-oriented sector of the Peruvian agro-export elite, Leguía broke with the Civilista Party over issues of executive initiative and state interventionism. In his second presidential term, Leguía used both popular and elite support to enhance the role of the state aided by foreign loans which became excessive after 1925.

Leguía was born in Lambayeque and studied accounting in a British school in Valparaíso. After the War of the Pacific he was tied through marriage to agro-exporting landed interests. He also developed financial ties with foreign and local banks and insurance companies. He established the British Sugar Company in 1896 and the South America Insurance Company in 1900. He rose meteorically in politics, first serving as finance minister under Presidents Manuel Candamo and José Pardo. As a presidential candidate with the official Civilista Party blessing, Leguía was elected president in 1908. His first term of office was traumatic. In an attempted coup in 1909, Leguía almost lost his life but also demonstrated considerable courage. His attempts at modernizing the state lost him favor among the Civilistas. From 1908 to 1910 Leguía also had to face international crises with neighboring Ecuador, Colombia, and Chile. In his second term Leguía was able to settle most of these old boundary disputes.

After 1913 Leguía lived abroad, mainly in London. In 1918 he returned to Peru with strong popular support. Leguía won the presidential elections of 1919, but fearing congressional opposition by his political enemies, he rallied military support for a coup to reinforce his presidential powers. Subsequently, his efforts to establish a New Fatherland (*Patria Nueva*) resulted in rigged reelections in 1924 and 1929. He exiled or imprisoned many of his political adversaries. His public works in Lima and the provinces (road construction, urbanization), state modernization, and encouragement of local capitalist interests seriously floundered during the financial crisis that led to the depression of the 1930s. He was ousted by a military coup led by Colonel Luis Sánchez Cerro and died in prison in Callao.

See also **Peru, Political Parties: Civilista Party; Sánchez Cerro, Luis Manuel; War of the Pacific.**

BIBLIOGRAPHY

Manuel Capuñay, *Leguía, vida y obra del constructor del gran Perú* (1952).

Alfonso Quiroz, *Domestic and Foreign Finance in Modern Peru, 1850–1950: Financing Visions of Development* (1993).

Additional Bibliography

Sánchez, Luis Alberto. *Leguía: El dictador.* Peru: Editorial Pachacútec, 1993.

ALFONSO W. QUIROZ

LEGUIZAMÓN, MARTINIANO (1858–1935).

A writer from Rosario del Tala in the province of Entre Ríos, Argentina, Martiniano Leguizamón was born in 1858 and spent his early years on his father's ranch of Gualeguay. He started writing poetry and comedy at a young age, during his schooling at the Colegio de Concepción del Uruguay. In 1880 he traveled to Buenos Aires to study law and entered journalism to make a living, contributing to *La Pampa, La Patria Argentina, La Razón, La Prensa, La Nación, El Día* (La Plata), and the weekly, *Caras y Caretas.* Passing the bar in 1885, he held administrative positions and worked as a teacher from 1885 to 1889. His first literary title was *Recuerdos de la tierra* (1896; Earth Memories), a fictional reconstruction of his childhood on the ranch, following the model established by Rioja native Joaquín V. González in *Mis montañas* (1893; My Mountains).

Leguizamón's comedy on country customs, *Calandria* (1897), had a great impact, as it was read and celebrated as a response to the gaucho police story—depicting the gaucho as a criminal or as a disenfranchised victim who had to take justice into his own hands—deriving from the novel, *Juan Moreira* (a serial by Eduardo Gutiérrez published in his family's newspaper, *La Patria Argentina*, between 1879 and 1880). Leguizamón's *Calandria* was adopted by José Podestá of the Podestá-Scotti company for performances in the circus ring as the second part of the circus shows that his company offered on tour from village to village. Fray Mocho (the pseudonym of José Álvarez), who was editor of *Caras y Caretas* in his early years and later a renowned native writer, also from Entre Ríos, wrote in the *Tribuna*, a pro-government daily (May 23, 1896), that this was a depiction of "the real gaucho of his homeland ... mischievous, cheerful, not killing or stealing, but wandering from ranch to ranch, expressing his sorrows on the guitar and enamoring young girls in the little dances."

Alma nativa (1906) was a series of sketches and tales that highlighted the joy of rural work ("Junto al fogón"), glossing over the fatigue it caused, loyalty to the landowner ("La maroma cortada"), and the landowner's paternalism ("La minga," "El precio de un pial") and portrayed typical characters ("El curandero," "Mama Juana"). He also wrote the novel *Montaraz* (1900), the essays, *Páginas argentinas* (1911), and a series of historical studies (including *Rasgos de la vida de Urquiza* [1920; Characteristics of the Life of Urquiza] and *El gaucho* [1932]), as well as the first biography of eastern poet Bartolomé Hidalgo, one of the initiators of Río de la Plata gaucho poetry (*De cepa criolla,* [1908; Of Creole Stock]).

See also **González, Joaquín Víctor; Literature: Spanish America.**

BIBLIOGRAPHY

Ara, Guillermo. "Martiniano Leguizamón y el regionalismo literario." In *Leguizamón, Martiniano: De cepa criolla.* Buenos Aires: Hachette, 1961.

González, Joaquín V. "Introducción." In *Recuerdos de la tierra.* Buenos Aires: Hachette, 1957.

Payró, Roberto. "Prólogo: La portada y el scenario." In *Leguizamón, M. Montaraz. Costumbres argentinas.* Buenos Aires: Hachette, 1962.

Romano, Eduardo. "Prólogo." In *El cuento argentine: Antología 1900–1930 y el fascículo.* Buenos Aires: Centro Editor de América Latina, 1980.

EDUARDO ROMANO

LEIGHTON GUZMÁN, BERNARDO (1909–1995).

Bernardo Leighton Guzmán, a Chilean politician, was born on August 16, 1909. He served as minister of the interior during the first half of Christian Democrat Eduardo Frei's presidency in the mid-1960s. Along with Frei, Radomiro Tomic, and Rafael Agustín Gumucio, he was among the many young, middle-class Chilean Catholics attracted to the liberal currents of Catholic social thought that emerged during the 1920s and 1930s. After several years of burrowing from within the country's traditional Conservative Party, this group left the party in 1938 to establish the Falange Nacional, which in 1957 became the Christian Democratic Party (PDC).

Known affectionately as Hermano Bernardo (Brother Bernard), Leighton was one of the most congenial and widely respected of the Christian Democrats. He served in the cabinets of Liberal (Arturo Alessandri) and Radical (Gabriel González Videla) governments, and throughout his career maintained cordial relationships with virtually all political forces, particularly those of the Left. Although one of the most trusted confidants of the strongly anticommunist Frei, he was among the minority of Christian Democrats who condemned the 1973 military coup and publicly criticized those who encouraged and supported it. He and his wife were shot and left for dead by unknown assailants in Rome in 1978. Shortly thereafter the Chilean government permitted Leighton and his wife to return to Chile. He eventually recovered but remained partially paralyzed until his death on January 26, 1995.

See also **Chile, Political Parties: Christian Democratic Party (PDC).**

BIBLIOGRAPHY

Michael Fleet, *The Rise and Fall of Chilean Christian Democracy* (1985).

Additional Bibliography

Boye, Otto. *Hermano Bernardo: 50 años de vida política vistos por Bernardo Leighton.* Santiago: Editorial Aconcagua, 1986.

Mayorga Marcos, Patricia. *El cóndor negro: El atentado a Bernardo Leighton.* Santiago: El Mercurio, Aguilar, 2003.

MICHAEL FLEET

LELOIR, LUIS F.

LELOIR, LUIS F. (1906–1987). Luis F. Leloir (*b.* 6 September 1906; *d.* 2 December 1987), Argentine scientist and winner of the Nobel Prize in chemistry in 1970. Born in Paris to a wealthy Argentine landowning family, Leloir was brought to Argentina when he was two years old. He received an M.D. from the University of Buenos Aires in 1932, after which he briefly practiced medicine. In 1934 he joined the research team at the Institute of Physiology under the leadership of Dr. Bernardo A. Houssay, the pioneering Argentine scientist and 1947 Nobel Prize winner in physiology and medicine. From 1936 to 1937, Leloir pursued his interest in the young field of biochemistry at Cambridge University, England, with Sir Frederick Gowland Hopkins, another Nobel Prize winner (1929). He returned to Buenos Aires and rejoined the Institute of Physiology (1937–1943), where he studied the oxidation of ethanol and fatty acids, and later worked on the mechanism of renal hypertension.

In 1944, disagreements with the Juan Perón government led Leloir (and many other scientists) to pursue research abroad. Initially, he worked on the formation of citric acid as a research associate at Washington University in Saint Louis, and later joined the Enzyme Research Laboratory at the College of Physicians and Surgeons in New York City. In 1947, he returned to Argentina and became the first director of the Biochemical Research Institute in Buenos Aires, a research group formed and led by Leloir and financed by businessman Jaime Campomar. On Campomar's death in 1957, the U.S. National Institutes of Health provided a grant that allowed the institute to continue its research.

Leloir was awarded the 1970 Nobel Prize for the work he and his staff did at the institute in the late 1940s and early 1950s that led to the discovery of sugar nucleotides and their role in the biosynthesis of carbohydrates. His more than seventy scientific articles have been published in international scientific journals. Leloir's dedication and many scientific successes, despite an often astonishing lack of financial support for even basic equipment and laboratory space, attest to his genius and contradict the image of Latin American disinterest in science.

See also **Medicine: The Modern Era; Science.**

BIBLIOGRAPHY

Luis Leloir, *Opera selecta* (1973) and "Far Away and Long Ago," in *The Excitement and Fascination of Science,* edited by Joshua Lederberg, vol. 3, pt. 1 (1990), pp. 367–381.

Additional Bibliography

Nachón, Carlos A. *Luis Federico Leloir, 1906-1987: Premio Nobel de Química 1970: (ensayo de una biografía).* Buenos Aires: Fundación Banco de Boston, 1994.

J. DAVID DRESSING

LEMÁCHEZ, QUIRINO. *See* **Henríquez, Camilo.**

LEMUS, JOSÉ MARÍA (1911–1993). José María Lemus was president of El Salvador from 1956 to 1960. Born on July 22, 1911, in La Unión of humble origins, Lemus attended the National Military Academy. He served as El Salvador's undersecretary of defense (1948–1949), and as President Oscar Osorio's (1950–1956) minister of the interior (1950–1955); in the latter post he antagonized his colleagues by fighting corruption. Lemus was Osorio's choice to succeed him, and in 1956 he won a disputed election.

A man of democratic impulses, he brought a number of distinguished civilians into government. He repealed Osorio's antisedition law and permitted political exiles to return to El Salvador, thereby antagonizing the military. He also offended the press by requiring newspapers to print replies to news stories and editorials.

The use of production controls to combat the 1958 drop in coffee prices infuriated the growers, while rising prices and unemployment alienated the workers. A disputed congressional election in 1960 exacerbated tensions. Lemus responded by announcing reforms in health, education, and minimum wages. With the support of the Roman Catholic Church, he organized a mass rally in support of the government. This was followed by student demonstrations praising the Cuban revolution. The subsequent roundup of students and other dissidents led to Lemus's arrest and exile on October 26, 1960. He lived in exile in New York with his wife and eight children until death, from Hodgkin's disease, on March 31, 1993.

See also **El Salvador; Osorio, Oscar.**

BIBLIOGRAPHY

Franklin D. Parker, *The Central American Republics* (1964).

Stephen Webre, *José Napoleón Duarte and the Christian Democratic Party in Salvadoran Politics, 1960–1972* (1979).

James Dunkerly, *The Long War: Dictatorship and Revolution in El Salvador* (1982).

ROLAND H. EBEL

LENCA. The Lenca are a group of people who inhabited central, south, and western Honduras and southeast El Salvador at the time of the Spanish conquest. Origins of the Lenca are still unclear. Ancestors may have been Late Preclassic populations of central Honduras. The Salvadoran Lencas built the Classic-Period Quelepa on the Pacific coastal trade route. The term *Lenca* encompasses the Potón, Guaquí, Care, Chato, Dule, Paraca, and Yara Indians. The Lencan language family includes extinct Honduran Lenca and Salvadoran Lenca, of which there are few surviving speakers.

The Lenca gathered foods and cultivated maize, beans, curcubits (squash and pumpkins), chiles, tobacco, cacao, and plantains. Their stratified political organization was headed by caciques (high chieftains) and lesser chiefs, followed by priests, soldiers, and commoners. Chiefdoms made up at least four provinces: Care, Cerquín, Potón, and Taulabe.

War was important to the Lenca way of life; their main weapon was the poison-tipped lance. They also built mounds and hilltop fortresses called *penoles.* The Lenca made peace agreements and formed alliances against the Spanish, who enslaved them for work in mines and the Repartimiento system of labor partitioned by the Spanish for their own use.

Disagreement among scholars on whether to include the Lenca in the Mesoamerican cultural category is due to their mix of northern and southern cultural traits. Mesoamerican traits include agricultural and religious practices, the use of wooden swords with obsidian and cotton armor for war, and a calendar of eighteen months of twenty days each. Poisonous weapons and the panpipe, however, are characteristic of South American cultures.

Although most speak Spanish, the Lenca are still Honduras's largest indigenous group (approximately 100,000), residing primarily in the western Honduran mountains and a small portion of El Salvador. Life for the Lenca people is marked by extreme poverty and inadequate access to both medical services and education. Since the late twentieth century, however, cooperatives that produce, market, and sell exquisite pottery using traditional methods and designs have improved living conditions for many Lenca families.

See also **Indigenous Peoples; Mesoamerica; Repartimiento.**

BIBLIOGRAPHY

Doris Stone, *The Archaeology of Central and Southern Honduras* (1957).

Anne Chapman, "Los Lencas de Honduras en el siglo XVI," *Estudios Antropológicos e Históricos,* no. 2 (1978).

John M. Weeks, Nancy Black, and J. Stuart Speaker, "From Prehistory to History in Western Honduras: The Care Lenca in the Colonial Province of Tencoa," in *Interaction on the Southeast Mesoamerican Frontier,* edited by Eugenia J. Robinson (1987), vol. 1, pp. 65–94.

Additional Bibliography

Chapman, Anne MacKaye. *Los hijos del copal y la candela.* Mexico: Universidad Nacional Autónoma de México, 1985–1986.

LAURA L. WOODWARD

LENCINAS, CARLOS WÁSHINGTON

(1889–1929). Carlos Wáshington Lencinas (*b.* 13 November 1889; *d.* 10 November 1929), Argentine caudillo. Born in Rivadavia in the province of Mendoza, Argentina, Lencinas studied law at the University of Córdoba. Upon returning to Mendoza, he followed in the political footsteps of his father, José Néstor Lencinas, who in 1918 became the first governor from the Radical Civic Union (UCR) to rule the province. When his father died in office in 1920, Lencinas, who that year had been elected a representative to Congress, took the reins of the party and eventually formed a new one, the Lencinista UCR. In 1922 he was elected governor of Mendoza and ruled in a populist fashion. He was popularly called "el gauchito Lencinas." In 1924 his government was "intervened," an Argentine constitutional device that under specific conditions allows Congress or the central government to assume administrative control of a province; thus ended Lencinas's short-lived governorship. Two years later Lencinas was elected national senator by Mendoza's legislature, but his credentials were rejected by Congress. On 10 November 1929, Lencinas was assassinated while addressing a crowd in Mendoza. As his assailant was also shot and killed, the motivation for the crime was never clearly determined. A popular and charismatic leader, Lencinas established pioneer social reforms such as the minimum-wage salary, the eight-hour workday, and an employee pension system. These provincial measures were the harbinger of national social reforms instituted a generation later by Juan Domingo Perón.

See also **Argentina, Political Parties: Radical Party (UCR).**

BIBLIOGRAPHY

Pablo Lacoste, "Carlos Wáshington Lencinas: Su vigencia póstuma," in *Todo es historia* 23, no. 270 (1989): 82–97.

Dardo Olguín, ". . . Y en el medio de mi pecho Carlos Wáshington Lencinas . . .!" in *Todo es historia,* no. 24 (1969): 8–35.

Celso Rodríguez, *Lencinas y Cantoni, el populismo cuyano en tiempos de Yrigoyen* (1979).

Additional Bibliography

Brennan, James P., and Ofelia Pianetto. *Region and Nation: Politics, Economics, and Society in Twentieth-century Argentina.* New York: St. Martin's Press, 2000.

Persello, Ana Virginia. *El partido radical: Gobierno y oposición, 1916-1943.* Buenos Aires: Siglo veintiuno editores Argentina, 2004.

CELSO RODRÍGUEZ

LEÑERO, VICENTE

(1933–). Vicente Leñero is a Mexican writer and journalist. Leñero was born on June 9, 1933, in Guadalajara, Jalisco. He earned a degree in engineering, which he practiced very briefly. During the early 1960s Leñero was a full-time journalist, and subsequently he continued working in that profession. He has published short stories, novels, dramas, and cultural reports, and he has made decisive contributions to some of the most important journalistic and cultural enterprises in recent Mexican history. Since 1976 he has served on the board of the magazine *Proceso.*

Inspired by the exemplary works of Juan Rulfo and Juan José Arreola, Leñero published his first book, *La polvareda y otros cuentos,* in 1959. Published two years later was his first novel, *La voz adolorida,* a revised version of which later appeared under the definitive title *A fuerza de palabras.* This work began a novelistic career unique in Mexican literature. Perhaps because of his engineering background, Leñero is very conscious of the structure of his novels and in each of them displays a will to master a radically different and complex structure. This formal preoccupation has produced at least one masterpiece, *Los albañiles* (1964), winner of the Biblioteca Breve Prize for a novel in 1963, at that time the most prestigious recognition that existed in the Spanish language.

Although some critics consider the spontaneity of Leñero's works excessive and even distracting, his approach has led him to explore the most diverse novelistic subgenres while reflecting with clarity and honesty on some of the most critical moral problems of our time. His screenplays for *El callejón de los Milagros* (1995) and *El Crimen del Padre Amaro* (2002), one of Mexico's highest-grossing films, have earned him great acclaim in that genre.

See also **Arreola, Juan José; Cinema: Since 1990; Journalism; Literature: Spanish America; Rulfo, Juan.**

BIBLIOGRAPHY

Danny J. Anderson, *Vicente Leñero: The Novelist as Critic* (1989).

Additional Bibliography

Rea, Joan. "El conflicto de conciencias en los dramas de Vicente Leñero." *Latin American Theater Review* (Spring 1998): 97–105.

JORGE AGUILAR MORA

LENG, ALFONSO (1894–1974). Alfonso Leng (*b.* 11 February 1894; *d.* 11 November 1974), Chilean composer. Born in Santiago, Leng was largely a self-taught composer, he attended the conservatory in Santiago for less than a year (1905). Leng was a member of the *Grupo de los diez* (Group of the Ten), which had been formed by fellow composers Próspero Bisquertt, García-Guerrero, Acario Cotapos, and Carlos Lavín, whose works introduced the concept of modernism into the Chilean cultural aesthetic. By about 1906 Leng had acquired his definitive style, as shown in such compositions as *Preludio no. 2* (1906) and his five *Doloras* for piano (1901–1914). In 1921 he composed *La muerte de Alsino,* a symphonic poem. Leng's style was strongly connected with German late romanticism. He wrote a considerable number of works for voice and piano as well as choral works. He was awarded the National Art Prize in Music in 1957. A noted dentist, he wrote several major papers on odontology. He died in Santiago.

See also **Music: Art Music; Music: Popular Music and Dance.**

BIBLIOGRAPHY

Revista Musical Chilena (Leng issue), 98 (1966); *Composers of the Americas,* vol. 15 (1969), pp. 156–160.

John Vinton, ed., *Dictionary of Contemporary Music* (1974); *New Grove Dictionary of Music and Musicians,* vol. 10 (1980).

Additional Bibliography

Ficher, Miguel, Martha Furman Schleifer, and John M. Furman. *Latin American Classical Composers: A Biographical Dictionary.* Lanham: Scarecrow Press, 1996.

SUSANA SALGADO

LEO XIII, POPE (1810–1903). Pope Leo XIII (*b.* 2 March 1810; *d.* 20 July 1903), considered the first modern pope (1878–1903). Although he retained many of the attitudes of his predecessor, Pius IX, toward the modern world, especially his reservations regarding liberalism and the application of scientific method to religion, Pope Leo opened the doors for Catholics notably in the realm of social thought. After a short diplomatic career he served as bishop of Perugia, Italy, for thirty-two years. Elected pope in 1878, he attempted to give a more positive response to many of the great intellectual and social questions of the day: industrialism, capitalism, democracy, and nationalism. He is most famous for his encyclical *Rerum Novarum* (1891), the first major papal statement on the rights of workers and social justice. In that and other writings, Leo XIII criticized socialism and economic liberalism, but he also called for a just and democratic social order. His ideas inspired the creation of the Christian Democratic parties of Europe and Latin America. At his invitation, the bishops of the Catholic Church in Latin America held a plenary council in Rome in 1899.

See also **Catholic Church: The Modern Period.**

BIBLIOGRAPHY

Edward T. Gargan, ed., *Leo XIII and the Modern World* (1961).

Lillian Parker Wallace, *Leo XIII and the Rise of Socialism* (1966).

Additional Bibliography

Viaene, Vincent. *Diplomatie vaticane, opinion catholique et politique internationale au temps de Leo XIII, 1878-1903.* Leuven, Belgium: Leuven University Press, 2005.

JEFFREY KLAIBER S.J.

LEÓN.

León, the second city of Nicaragua and the traditional center of liberal political groups. León was first established on the western shores of Lake Managua in 1524. It was moved a few miles to the west to its present site in 1610 as the result of an eruption of nearby Momotombo volcano. During the colonial period, it shared leadership of the country with the rival city of Granada but was the provincial capital within the captaincy general of Guatemala. León's cathedral is the largest in Central America. The present structure, designed by the prominent colonial architect Diego de Porres, was completed in 1780. Built of cut stone, it withstood repeated earthquakes. On occasion it has served as a fortress. Rubén Dário (1867–1916), Nicaragua's most beloved poet, spent much of his early life in León. He is buried within the cathedral under a statue of a lion, and his home has been converted into a museum. The city has grown in recent years, but not as rapidly as Managua. León is estimated to have a population of 174,051 (2005).

See also **Darío, Rubén.**

BIBLIOGRAPHY

Alfonso Arguello, *Historia de León Viejo* (1969).

Additional Bibliography

Arellano, Jorge Eduardo. *León de Nicaragua: Tradiciones y valores de la Atenas centroamericana.* Managua: Fondo Cultural CIRA, 2002—.

Tünnermann Bernheim, Carlos, and Denis Torres P. *León Viejo y otros escritos.* Managua: Universidad Politécnica de Nicaragua, 1997.

Werner, Patrick S. *Epoca temprana de León Viejo: Una historia de la primera capital de Nicaragua.* Managua: Asdi: Instituto Nicaragüense de Cultura, 2000.

DAVID L. JICKLING

LEÓN, ALONSO DE (1637–c. 1691).

Alonso de León (*b.* 1637; *d.* ca. 25 March 1691), first governor of Coahuila (1687–1691) and leader of early colonization efforts in Texas. The son and namesake of an important chronicler of Nuevo León, León was born in León, Spain. He grew up on Mexico's northern frontier, earned a reputation as an explorer and soldier, and rose to the rank of general in 1687. That same year, León became the first governor of the newly created province of Coahuila, which was intended to serve as a bulwark against the threatening French presence in the Gulf of Mexico. At first, he concentrated on internal affairs, distributing land grants and mining licenses, reorganizing the presidio system, and attempting to pacify the indigenous population. But imperial matters soon took precedence. In 1689 and 1690, León led expeditions to Texas. The first came across the remains of a French fort built by Sieur de La Salle, already destroyed by Indians. On the second, León's party founded the first Texas mission, San Francisco de los Tejas. However, such missionary activity—underfinanced, poorly supplied, and insufficiently defended—could not be sustained in the face of a hostile Indian response and was abandoned within a few years. Spain would not establish a permanent base in Texas until 1716. León died in Santiago de Monclova, which he had founded in 1689.

BIBLIOGRAPHY

Vito Alessio Robles, *Coahuila y Texas en la época colonial* (1938).

David J. Weber, *The Spanish Frontier in North America* (1992).

R. DOUGLAS COPE

LEÓN DE LA BARRA, FRANCISCO

(1863–1939). Francisco León de la Barra (*b.* 16 June 1863; *d.* 22 September 1939), president of Mexico (26 May 1911–6 November 1911). The son of a Chilean immigrant who fought for the Liberals in the War of the Reform, León de la Barra was a native of Querétaro. He graduated in 1886 from the School of Jurisprudence that was later absorbed into the National University. An outstanding international lawyer and career diplomat, León de la Barra was Mexico's ambassador to the United States when the Revolution of 1910 began. After being elevated constitutionally to the presidency by the Treaty of Ciudad Juárez, he presided over the most democratic elections held until that time.

Nicknamed the "White President" because of his apolitical behavior, León de la Barra walked with some success the slippery tightrope between demands for peace and order and the quest for social change. Although some interpretations have made his presidency the scapegoat for Francisco Madero's inadequacies, more recent studies have been more favorable, pointing out that he allowed a free press and initiated labor and agrarian reforms. León de la Barra served Victoriano Huerta briefly as secretary of foreign relations (1913), was ambassador to France in 1913–1914, and then retired to Europe, where he played a role in the post–World War I settlement. He died in Biarritz, France.

See also **Madero, Francisco Indalecio.**

BIBLIOGRAPHY

Stanley R. Ross, *Francisco I. Madero: Apostle of Mexican Democracy* (1955).

Presidencia De La República, *Los presidentes de México: Discursos políticos, 1910–1988* (1988), vol. 1, esp. pp. 17–21.

Additional Bibliography

Avila Espinosa, Felipe Arturo. *Entre el porfiriato y la revolución: El gobierno interino de Francisco León de la Barra.* México, D.F.: Universidad Nacional Autónoma de México, 2005.

Henderson, Peter. *In the Absence of Don Porfirio: Francisco León de la Barra and the Mexican Revolution.* Wilmington, DE: Scholarly Resources, 2000.

PETER V. N. HENDERSON

LEONI, RAÚL (1906–1972). Raúl Leoni (*b.* 26 April 1906; *d.* 5 July 1972), Venezuelan president (1964–1968). Raúl Leoni was one of the founding fathers of Venezuela's most important twentieth-century political party, Acción Democrática (AD). He began his political career when, as president of the Venezuelan Students Federation, he organized a Students' Week in February 1928 to protest the repressive regime of Juan Vicente Gómez. Although the protest sparked a more general outcry against the regime, including an aborted rebellion led by young army officers, it also forced Leoni and his colleagues into exile for eight years. While in Barranquilla, Colombia, Leoni and other exiles plotted their return and drew up the *Plan de Barranquilla,* a nationalist reform document that foreshadowed the program of the AD. The plan stressed the need for political democracy and social justice in Venezuela and sought to curb the virtually unbridled power of the country's foreign-owned petroleum companies. Leoni returned to Venezuela after the death of Gómez, and in 1936 he was elected to the Venezuelan Chamber of Deputies as a member of the Partido Democrático Nacional (PDN), precursor of AD. However, Leoni was deported by President Eleazar López Contreras in 1937 and was unable to take his seat.

After earning a law degree at the Universidad Nacional de Colombia in Bogotá, Leoni returned to Venezuela, where he became one of the main organizers of AD, which was legally recognized in September 1941. Leoni and Rómulo Betancourt led the party into power for the first time by cooperating with dissident army officers who, in 1945, overthrew dictator General Isaías Medina. As minister of labor during the heady years that followed, Leoni oversaw the unionization of Venezuelan workers and supervised the first collective bargaining agreement between the oil companies and their workers in 1946. When AD fell victim to its own mistakes and a military coup against President Rómulo Gallegos in November 1948, Leoni left the country again, this time to work for the International Labor Organization of the United Nations and with fellow AD exiles who formed part of a larger community of exiled Caribbean democratic-left leaders.

With the fall of the dictatorial General Marcos Pérez Jiménez in January 1958, Leoni returned to Venezuela to help his party regain power. After becoming president of AD the following year, he succeeded his old ally Rómulo Betancourt as president of Venezuela between 1964 and 1968. Relying initially on support from the AD-affiliated labor groups, Leoni largely continued the nationalist, reformist policies inaugurated by Betancourt. These included promotion of industrialization, agrarian reform, and expansion of public education. Leoni also proved to be an innovator by seeking conciliation with the radical Left which had launched a guerrilla war several years earlier, and by legalizing the Communist Party in 1968. Finally, by proposing a law to levy an excess profits tax on the oil companies, he goaded the latter into accepting a compromise arrangement that increased the industry's benefit to the national government. This step paved the way for future efforts to increase the government's share of Venezuelan oil wealth.

See also **Pérez Jiménez, Marcos; Venezuela, Political Parties: Democratic Action (AD).**

BIBLIOGRAPHY

Robert J. Alexander, ed., *Biographical Dictionary of Latin American and Caribbean Political Leaders* (1988).

John Martz, *Acción Democrática: The Evolution of a Modern Political Party in Venezuela* (1966): Charles D. Ameringer, *The Democratic Left in Exile: The Antidictatorial Struggle in the Caribbean, 1945–1959* (1974).

Additional Bibliography

Arráiz Lucca, Rafael. *Raúl Leoni: (1905–1972).* Caracas: Editora El Nacional: Banco del Caribe, 2005.

Rivas, Ramón. *Acción Democrática en la historia contemporanea de Venezuela, 1929–1991.* Mérida: Universidad Popular "Alberto Carnevali," 1991.

PAMELA MURRAY

LEÓN-PORTILLA, MIGUEL (1926–).

Miguel León-Portilla is a leading Mexican scholar of ancient Mexican literature, philosophy, and culture. Born on February 22, 1926, in Mexico City, Léon-Portilla received B.A. degrees at the Instituto de Ciencias in Guadalajara (1944) and Loyola University in Los Angeles (1948). In 1951 he graduated with an M.A. from Loyola and received a Ph.D. from the National University of Mexico in 1956. León-Portilla has held several positions since then, including professor in the Faculty of Philosophy and Letters at the National University of Mexico; director of the Inter-American Indigenist Institute (1960–1963); director of the Institute of Historical Research of the National University of Mexico (1963–1975); and delegate of Mexico to UNESCO. His honors include Mexico's 1981 National Prize in the Social Sciences, History, and Philosophy. León-Portilla's revised Ph.D. dissertation, *La filosofía Nahuatl estudiada en sus fuentes,* first published in 1959, set the stage for his lifelong scholarly endeavors. His more than 40 monographs, over 200 professional articles, instrumental involvement in the publication of numerous primary sources, and his editorships of *Estudios de cultura Nahuatl* and *Tlalocan* demonstrate his pivotal role in developing and furthering Aztec studies.

Among León-Portilla's major contributions has been his willingness to grapple with questions of Aztec worldview and philosophy, based on documentary sources that are incomplete and subject to interpretation. His translations of primary Aztec documentation have made a large and complicated corpus accessible to intensive study; his interpretations and analyses have stimulated scholarly research and debate; and his numerous syntheses of Aztec literature and culture have extended an understanding of ancient Mexico to a worldwide audience. Having translated and interpreted several compilations of Nahuatl works, he is regarded as one of the primary scholars of Nahuatl literature and thought. His work in this field has contributed to the push for establishing bilingual education in rural Mexico in part to support the indigenous language.

See also **Aztecs; Literature: Spanish America; Nahuatl.**

BIBLIOGRAPHY

Among León-Portilla's many influential works are *Visión de los vencidos* (1950); *Aztec Thought and Culture* (1963); *Trece poetas del mundo azteca* (1967); *Pre-Columbian Literatures of Mexico* (1969); *Pueblos originarios y globalización* (1997); and *Visión de los vencidos: Relaciones indígenas de la conquista* (2003). For background, see the preface by Jorge Klor De Alva, "Nahua Studies, the Allure of the 'Aztecs,' and Miguel León-Portilla," in León-Portilla's *The Aztec Image of Self and Society* (1992), vii–xxiii.

Additional Bibliography

Moraña, Mabel, ed. *Ideologies of Hispanism.* Nashville, TN: Vanderbilt University Press, 2005.

FRANCES F. BERDAN

LEOPOLDINA, EMPRESS (1797–1826).

Empress Leopoldina (Maria Leopoldina de Hapsburg; *b.* 22 January 1797; *d.* 11 December 1826), empress consort of Brazil (1822–1826). Daughter of Emperor Francis I of Austria, Archduchess Leopoldina married Pedro, prince of Brazil and heir to the Portuguese throne, in ceremonies in Vienna and Rio de Janeiro in 1817. The marriage became a factor in the acceptance of Brazil's independence from Portugal—declared by Pedro with Leopoldina's strong support in 1822—by Austria and the "Holy Alliance" of conservative European monarchies. Pedro and Leopoldina were proclaimed emperor and empress of Brazil on 12 October 1822.

Intelligent and well educated, especially in the natural sciences, Leopoldina came under the intellectual influence of her husband's chief minister, José Bonifácio de Andrada E Silva, though she retained her innate political conservatism. Pedro's banishment of José Bonifácio in 1823 distressed her, and subsequent revelations of her husband's infidelities added to her unhappiness. While the emperor's political enemies publicly sympathized with his long-suffering wife, Leopoldina remained devoted to the unfaithful Pedro. She bore him four daughters, including the future Queen Maria II of Portugal, and two sons, one who died in infancy and one who became Emperor Pedro II of Brazil. Barely a year after the birth of her second son, Leopoldina died of complications following a miscarriage.

See also **Brazil: 1808–1889.**

BIBLIOGRAPHY

Amilcar Salgado Dos Santos, *Imperatriz D. Leopoldina* (1927).

Carlos H. Oberacker, Jr., *A imperatriz Leopoldina: Sua vida e sua época* (1973).

Additional Bibliography

Barman, Roderick J. *Citizen Emperor: Pedro II and the Making of Brazil, 1825–1891.* Stanford, CA: Stanford University Press, 1999.

Buonfiglio, Monica. *Imperatriz Leopoldina: O anjo da independência do Brasil.* São Paulo: Oficina dos Anjos, 2002.

NEILL MACAULAY

LEPE, DIEGO DE (?–c. 1513). Diego De Lepe (*d.* before 1513), Andalusian explorer, possible discoverer of the Orinoco River in present-day Venezuela. A native of Palos, in southwest Spain, Lepe was one of several leaders of a series of minor expeditions from Spain's southern Atlantic ports that led to important advances in geographic knowledge of New World coasts. Leading a small fleet of two boats, Lepe left Seville in mid-November 1499, pursuing the course set two weeks earlier by Vicente Yáñez Pinzón, who commanded four ships. Lepe followed the route of Pinzón, passing the Cape Verde Islands, then sailed to Cape San Agustín (Pinzón reached it on 26 January 1500) on the Brazilian coast. Pinzón seems to have been the first European to discover the Amazon estuary and enter the great river; he sailed upstream for a time and made contact with peoples along its banks. Diego de Lepe and his men followed within days.

At this point the account becomes confused. Some say Lepe sailed southward along Brazil's coast as far as the Río de la Plata; others argue he went northwestwardly, encountering several important rivers, including the Orinoco, of which he took possession in the name of the Spanish monarchs, calling it the Marañón. In skirmishes he lost eleven men but captured thirty-six Native Americans, whom he later presented as slaves to Bishop Juan de Fonseca in Seville. Given that Lepe's fleet and that of Pinzón came together in the Gulf of Paria, the second version of Lepe's voyage seems most likely.

From the north coast of South America, Lepe's boats headed to the Isla de San Juan (Puerto Rico) in May 1500, while the Pinzón group sailed to Hispaniola's north coast in June of the same year. From Puerto Rico, Lepe sailed directly to Spain, reaching Seville several weeks earlier than Pinzón. He had an audience with the monarchs in Granada on 15 November 1500, and later secured an agreement for a new voyage on 14 September 1501. It is unclear if this expedition ever took place. Lepe died in Portugal sometime before 1513.

Both Pinzón and Diego de Lepe came upon Brazil several months prior to the official Portuguese discovery of Pedro Alvares Cabral on 22 April 1500. Their logs, maps, and reports were used by cartographer Juan de la Cosa for his famous world map of 1500.

See also **Explorers and Exploration: Spanish America.**

BIBLIOGRAPHY

Juan Manzano Manzano, *Los Pinzones y el descubrimiento de América* (1988).

Francisco Morales Padrón, *Andalucía y América* (1988).

Additional Bibliography

Espínola, Rodolfo. *Vicente Pinzón e a descoberta do Brasil.* Fortaleza: COELCE; Rio de Janeiro, 2001.

NOBLE DAVID COOK

LÉPERO. Lépero, a pejorative term used primarily in the nineteenth century to refer to Mexico City's underclass. During the long period of economic stagnation and political instability after Independence in 1821, Mexico City's elite grew obsessed with the suspected volatility, moral turpitude, and criminal activities of the vast majority of the urban population, who led lives of poverty and uncertainty. The term *lépero* or *populacho* indiscriminately lumped together underemployed artisans and manual laborers with beggars and criminals. Successive governments implemented various legal measures, such as a special vagrancy court, to fight the perceived infestation of idlers and thieves, but such legislation did little to eliminate the city's problems, which were primarily a result of the country's chronic political and economic crises and not the criminal proclivities of its residents.

The term *lépero* is of obscure origin and was also used as a pejorative in parts of Central America and Ecuador. In Cuba, however, it was equivalent to Ladino.

See also **Acordada, Revolt of; Parián.**

BIBLIOGRAPHY

Torcuato S. Di Tella, "The Dangerous Classes in Early Nineteenth Century Mexico," in *Journal of Latin American Studies* 5, no. 1 (1973): 79–105.

Frederick J. Shaw, Jr., "Poverty and Politics in Mexico City, 1824–1854," (Ph.D. diss., University of Florida, 1975).

Silvia M. Arrom, "Popular Politics in Mexico City: The Parián Riot, 1828," in *Hispanic American Historical Review* 68 (May 1988): 245–268.

Eric Van Young, "Islands in the Storm: Quiet Cities and Violent Countrysides in the Mexican Independence Era," in *Past & Present* 118 (1988): 130–155.

Additional Bibliography

Arrom, Silvia Marina, and Servando Ortoll. *Riots in the Cities: Popular Politics and the Urban Poor in Latin America, 1765-1910.* Wilmington, DE: Scholarly Resources, 1996.

Illades, Carlos. *Hacia la república del trabajo: La organización artesanal en la Ciudad de México, 1853-1876.* México, D.F.: Colegio de México, Centro de Estudios Históricos: Universidad Autónoma Metropolitana-Iztapalapa, 1996.

Lida, Clara E., and Sonia Pérez Toledo. *Trabajo, ocio y coacción: Trabajadores urbanos en México y Guatemala en el siglo XIX.* México, D.F.: Universidad Autónoma Metropolitana, Unidad Iztapalapa, Casa Abierta al Tiempo, División de Ciencias Sociales y Humanidades, Departamento de Filosofía: Porrúa, 2001.

Piccato, Pablo. *City of Suspects: Crime in Mexico City, 1900–1931.* Durham, NC: Duke University Press, 2001.

Warren, Richard A. *Vagrants and Citizens: Politics and the Masses in Mexico City from Colony to Republic.* Wilmington, DE: Scholarly Resources, 2001.

RICHARD WARREN

LE PLONGEON, AUGUSTUS (1826–1908). Amateur archaeologist and photographer Augustus Le Plongeon (May 4, 1826–December 13, 1908) and his wife Alice spent close to twelve years investigating Yucatán sites such as Chichén Itzá and Uxmal. Arriving in 1873, they lived continuously at Yucatán until 1885, recording monuments and searching for cultural connections between the Maya and ancient Egypt.

Although Le Plongeon invited criticism with his monogenetic theories of the Maya as the cradle of civilization, he was a pioneer in systematic photographic documentation. More than 500 photographs provide information about the appearance of structures and objects subsequently damaged, moved, or destroyed. Taking hundreds of three-dimensional photographs, he documented entire structures such as the Governor's Palace at Uxmal. He also photographed miscellaneous sculptures including a rare *in situ* photograph of a phallic sculpture from the Nunnery Quadrangle. At Chichén Itzá he excavated and made cross-section drawings of the Platform of Venus and excavated a Chacmool figure from the Platform of the Eagles and Jaguars.

Although Le Plongeon's theories were deemed outlandish by contemporaries Alfred Maudslay and Teobert Maler and were nearly forgotten as a result, his methodical approach and dedication to understanding Maya culture provide scholars with valuable visual and contextual information. His work also provides insight into the nineteenth-century fascination with Maya culture.

See also **Chacmools; Chichén Itzá; Jaguar; Uxmal; Yucatán.**

BIBLIOGRAPHY

Brunhouse, Robert L. *In Search of the Maya: The First Archaeologists*. Albuquerque: University of New Mexico Press, 1973.

Desmond, Lawrence Gustave. "Augustus Le Plongeon: A Fall from Archaeological Grace." In *Assembling the Past: Studies in the Professionalization of Archaeology*, edited by Alice B. Kehoe and Mary Beth Emmerichs. Albuquerque: University of New Mexico Press, 1999.

Desmond, Lawrence Gustave, and Phyllis Mauch Messenger. *A Dream of Maya: Augustus and Alice Le Plongeon in Nineteenth-Century Yucatan*. Albuquerque: University of New Mexico Press, 1988.

Le Plongeon, Alice. "Ruined Uxmal." *New York World*, June 27, 1881.

Le Plongeon, Augustus. *Maya/Atlantis: Queen Moo and the Egyptian Sphinx*. Blauvelt, New York: R. Steiner Publications, 1976.

LAURA M. AMRHEIN

LERDO DE TEJADA, MIGUEL (1812–1861). Miguel Lerdo de Tejada (*b.* 1812; *d.* 22 March 1861), Mexican politician, author of the Ley Lerdo, and brother of Sebastián Lerdo de Tejada. A native of the city of Veracruz, Lerdo was elected to the Mexico City *ayuntamiento* (city council) in 1849 and became its president in 1852. Lerdo was a close associate of many of the *agiotistas* (moneylenders) of Mexico City and Veracruz and a consistent advocate of infrastructure development. Lerdo was deputy minister and later minister of development during the last presidency of Antonio López de Santa Anna (1853–1855). As finance minister for Ignacio Comonfort, Lerdo issued the Law Disamortizing Urban and Rural Property, commonly called the Ley Lerdo, on 25 June 1856. Lerdo served Benito Juárez as finance minister (1858–1859, 1859–1860) and as minister of development (1859, 1860). On 12 July 1859, after Lerdo had threatened to resign, the liberal government issued a decree nationalizing all property of the regular and secular clergy, suppressing religious orders, and separating the church and the state. Lerdo hoped to use church property as collateral for a loan from the United States to adequately fund the liberal government and its war against the conservatives. He traveled to New Orleans, New York, and Washington, D.C., in 1859, but was unsuccessful in acquiring funds. Lerdo resigned in June 1860, when Juárez rejected his proposal to suspend payment on the foreign debt, but the real difference between the two men was Lerdo's position in favor of either negotiating peace with the conservatives or inviting U.S. intervention, neither of which Juárez would accept. After the liberal victory, Lerdo became a candidate for the presidency of the republic. During the campaign he died of typhus in Mexico City.

See also **Anticlericalism; Ley Lerdo.**

BIBLIOGRAPHY

Carmen Blázquez, *Miguel Lerdo de Tejada: Un liberal veracruzano en la política nacional* (1978).

Richard N. Sinkin, *The Mexican Reform, 1855–1876: A Study in Liberal Nation-Building* (1979).

Barbara A. Tenenbaum, *The Politics of Penury: Debt and Taxes in Mexico, 1821–1856* (1986), pp. 133, 156–163.

Additional Bibliography

Fowler, Will. *Mexico in the Age of Proposals, 1821–1853.* Westport, CT: Greenwood Press, 1998.

Villegas Revueltas, Silvestre. *El liberalismo moderado en México, 1852–1864.* México, D.F.: Universidad Nacional Autónoma de México, 1997.

D. F. STEVENS

LERDO DE TEJADA, SEBASTIÁN (1823–1889). Sebastián Lerdo de Tejada (*b.* 1823; *d.* 1889), president of Mexico (1872–1876). The younger brother of Mexican politician Miguel Lerdo de Tejada, Sebastián Lerdo was born in Jalapa, Veracruz. After renouncing an ecclesiastical career, he moved to Mexico City in 1841. Lerdo took a teaching post at the Colegio de San Ildefonso in 1849 and became rector in 1852. President Ignacio Comonfort appointed him minister of foreign relations in 1857, but Lerdo remained in Mexico City as the rector of San Ildefonso and took no part in the War of the Reform. In 1861, he was elected to the national legislature, where he served as president of the Congress on three occasions. During the French Intervention, Lerdo accompanied President Benito Juárez as a representative of the Congress. Juárez appointed Lerdo to head the ministries of government and foreign relations.

Along with Juárez and José María Iglesias, Lerdo was among the most prominent politicians in the Republican government. He wrote decrees (8 November 1865) explaining the extension of Juárez's presidential term until the end of the war and eliminating the possibility of succession for Jesús González Ortega. According to some sources, Lerdo convinced Juárez not to pardon Maximilian. Lerdo wrote the *convocatoria* of 1867, which sought to increase presidential power through an unconstitutional plebiscite.

Despite increasing opposition to him, Lerdo was elected vice president. He inherited the presidency on the death of Juárez in July 1872 and later that year was elected to a constitutional term. His presidency was marked by the completion of the Mexico City–Veracruz railroad (1873), the elimination of several regional caciques, and anticlerical reforms. As minister of foreign relations, Lerdo had consistently resisted U.S. encroachments on Mexican territory. As president, he delayed railroad construction in the north, saying "Between strength and weakness, the desert," but finally granted a concession to a U.S. firm. After announcing his intention to seek reelection in 1876, Lerdo faced two opposition movements, one led by José María Iglesias, the other by Porfirio Díaz. Although Lerdo was reelected, he was not able to defeat his armed opponents. He resigned the presidency on 20 November 1876 and fled into exile on 25 January 1877. He died in New York City.

See also **French Intervention (Mexico); Juárez, Benito.**

BIBLIOGRAPHY

Laurens Ballard Perry, *Juárez and Díaz: Machine Politics in Mexico* (1978).

Daniel Cosío Villegas, *Historia moderna de México, Vol. 1: La república restorada, La vida política* (1959).

Frank A. Knapp, *Sebastián Lerdo de Tejada, 1823–1889: A Study of Influence and Obscurity* (1951; repr. 1968).

Richard N. Sinkin, *The Mexican Reform, 1855–1876: A Study in Liberal Nation-Building* (1979); *Diccionario Porrúa de historia, biografía y geografía de México,* 5th ed. (1986), vol. 2, pp. 1654–1655.

Additional Bibliography

Aguilar Rivera, José Antonio. *El manto liberal: Los poderes de emergencia en México, 1821–1876.* México: Instituto de Investigaciones Jurídicas, Universidad Nacional Autónoma de México, 2001.

Luna Argudín, María. *El congreso y la política mexicana (1857–1911).* México, D.F.: Fondo de Cultura Económica, 2006.

D. F. STEVENS

LERMA RIVER. Lerma River, a waterway in west-central Mexico. Beginning in the Toluca basin, in the state of Mexico, the river drops sharply into the basin of Guanajuato, winds through the fertile agricultural basin known as the Bajío, and empties into Lake Chapala in Jalisco, 350 miles away. From Chapala, the river continues as the Río Grande de Santiago, which flows through the agricultural lands of Jalisco before plunging over the western edge of the central plateau toward the Pacific. Collectively, the Lerma-Chapala-Santiago system forms the largest river basin located wholly within the borders of the Republic of Mexico.

Since the Lerma is one of the largest perennial waterways serving the densely populated southern portion of the central plateau, it is used extensively for drinking water, irrigation, and hydroelectric power. Water diversion from the Lerma began during the colonial period, to irrigate the important wheat- and cornfields of the Bajío, the breadbasket of Mexico. Much of the river is also diverted by aqueduct to meet the growing water needs of Mexico City.

Throughout the twentieth century, human and natural stresses on the Lerma have deteriorated its water quality and flow. Such problems are exemplified by the receding shores of Lake Chapala.

BIBLIOGRAPHY

David Barkin and Timothy King, *Regional Economic Development: The River Basin Approach in Mexico* (1970), pp. 68–69, 113–115.

Jorge L. Tamayo, *Geografía moderna de México,* 9th ed. (1980), pp. 239–275.

Michael E. Murphy, *Irrigation in the Bajío Region of Colonial Mexico* (1986), esp. pp. 1–8.

Additional Bibliography

Fabián Ruiz, José. *Lerma y Balsas, crónica de dos ríos.* Morelia, México: Foro Cultural Morelos, 1998.

Faugére-Kalfon, Brigitte. *Entre Zacapu y Río Lerma: Culturas en una zona fronteriza.* México: Centre Français d'Études Mexicaines et Centraméricaines, 1996.

MARIE D. PRICE

LÉRY, JEAN DE (1534–1611). Jean de Léry (*b.* 1534; *d.* 1611), Huguenot pastor who traveled to Brazil in 1556 as part of a colony established by French adventurer Durand de Villegagnon near present-day Rio de Janeiro. In 1578 Léry published *Histoire d'un voyage fait en la terre du Brésil,* in which he recalled his voyage to the New World, his flight from the French colony, and the two months he spent living among the Tupinambá Indians. Léry's remarkably comprehensive and largely sympathetic discussion of Indian life included descriptions of physical appearance, housing, cuisine, ceremonial rituals (including cannibalism), warfare, marriage customs, and child rearing.

See also **Indigenous Peoples; Travel Literature.**

BIBLIOGRAPHY

Olivier Reverdin, *Quatorze Calvinistes chez les Topinambous: Histoire d'une mission genevoise au Brésil* (*1556–1558*) (1957).

Janet Whately, "Une révérence réciproque: Huguenot Writing on the New World," in *University of Toronto Quarterly* 57, no. 2 (Winter 1987–1988): 270–289.

Additional Bibliography

Greenblatt, Stephen. *New World Encounters.* Berkeley: University of California Press, 1993.

Silva, Wilton Carlos Lima da. *As terras inventadas: Discurso e natureza em Jean de Léry, André João Antonil e Richard Francis Burton.* São Paulo: Editora UNESP, 2003.

KATHLEEN JOAN HIGGINS

LESCOT, ÉLIE (1883–1974). Élie Lescot (*b.* 1883; *d.* 1974), Haitian dictator (1941–1946). Lescot, a native of Saint-Louis-du-Nord, was educated in Cap Haitien and received his doctorate from Laval University in Québec. Subsequently he was secretary of public education, justice, and the interior; envoy to the Dominican Republic; and a diplomat in the United States. His regime was known for its tyranny and corruption as well as for its close cooperation with U.S. government and business interests. Lescot established his dictatorship, in part, by taking advantage of circumstances produced by U.S. national and hemispheric security concerns after the outbreak of World War II. In the name of protecting Haiti from the Axis powers, he not only confiscated the property of Germans and Italians within the country, but also suspended the Haitian constitution. The regime also benefited from an influx of U.S. military and economic aid during the war period. U.S.-sponsored development projects went to enrich Lescot's family and friends. These included a project to grow sisal financed by the U.S.-controlled Société Haïtienne-Américaine du Développement Agricole (SHADA), to which Lescot made huge land concessions and which, in turn, led to the displacement of thousands of peasants.

Lescot's policies favored members of the country's mulatto elite and, generally, denied the aspirations and interests of blacks. Lescot excluded blacks from important positions in his government. He also attacked black folk culture by supporting the Roman Catholic Church's campaign against the vodun religion. Although this attack proved short-lived, it helped provoke widespread nationalist opposition to the regime. Lescot altered the constitution in order to extend his term of office and postponed elections, ostensibly because of World War II. By the end of 1945, students, workers, and intellectuals openly demanded an end to the dictatorship. Following the Revolution of 1946, Lescot was forced to resign on 11 January 1946. He was exiled to Canada.

See also **World War II.**

BIBLIOGRAPHY

David Nicholls, "Haiti Since 1930," in *The Cambridge History of Latin America,* vol. 7, edited by Leslie Bethell (1990), pp. 545–577.

Michel Rolph-Trouillot, *Haiti: State Against Nation* (1990).

Additional Bibliography

Smith, Michael J. *Shades of Red in a Black Republic: Radicalism, Black Consciousness, and Social Conflict in Postoccupation Haiti, 1934–1957.* Ph.D. diss., University of Florida, 2002.

PAMELA MURRAY

LESSEPS, FERDINAND MARIE, VICOMTE DE (1805–1894).

Ferdinand Marie, Vicomte de Lesseps (*b.* 19 November 1805; *d.* 7 December 1894), French statesman who organized construction of the Suez Canal in the 1860s and attempted to build a canal in Panama in the 1880s.

Born into a distinguished diplomatic family with connections in the Middle East, de Lesseps entered the foreign service in the 1820s and received a number of postings, including a seven-year tour in Egypt. While there he became acquainted with a group of development-minded engineers from France committed to material progress, Saint-Simonians, who tried to build a canal linking the Red Sea and the Mediterranean.

After his removal from the foreign service following the 1848 revolution, de Lesseps temporarily retired from public life. However, two of the connections he had made were to lead to eventual triumph: his cousin married the Emperor Napoleon III, providing access to the court, and a prince he had known became Viceroy of Egypt. De Lesseps soon parlayed these advantages into a project to build a canal at Suez modeled on the Saint Simonians' plans. For fifteen years he mesmerized Europe with his tremendous vigor and promotional talents, and he received world acclaim upon opening the canal in 1869.

Within a few years de Lesseps determined to repeat his triumph in Central America, and he devoted his energies to organizing a new company for the project. He sponsored a series of meetings to make geographical and engineering plans, but he steered that planning toward a decision he had already made: to build a sea-level canal in Panama. In 1879, ready to raise capital, he formed the Compagnie Universelle du Canal Interoceanique de Panama and acquired a concession from the Colombian government. The following year he managed to raise a vast sum of money through public subscription, a tribute to his reputation as *le Grand Français.* Work began in February 1881.

For eight years the French company labored heroically in Panama but accomplished only a fraction of the necessary excavation. It went bankrupt in 1889, a victim of many ills. First, de Lesseps's insistence on a sea-level canal was mistaken, given the technology and resources available. Second, from the beginning he had spread around graft and spent with such extravagance that his capital soon ran out. Third, yellow fever, malaria, smallpox, tuberculosis, and other diseases devastated the French and West Indian work forces. By now old and infirm, de Lesseps was shielded from the tremendous scandal that accompanied the crash of the Compagnie Universelle.

The French debacle eventually led to the U.S. canal project of the 1900s. The year de Lesseps died, stockholders and receivers created a new company to manage the assets and preserve the Colombian concession. The French excavations, maps, buildings, and equipment helped convince the U.S. government to build there rather than in Nicaragua.

See also **Panama Canal.**

BIBLIOGRAPHY

Gerstle Mack, *The Land Divided* (1944).

David McCullough, *The Path Between the Seas* (1977).

Maron J. Simon, *The Panama Affair* (1971).

James M. Skinner, *France and Panama* (1989).

Additional Bibliography

Banville, Marc de. *Canal Francés: La aventura de los franceses en Panamá.* Panamá: Canal Valley, 2005.

MICHAEL L. CONNIFF

LETELIER DEL SOLAR, ORLANDO

(1932–1976). Orlando Letelier del Solar served as Chilean ambassador to the United States and cabinet minister under President Salvador Allende. Born April 13, 1932, in Temuco to an upper-class family, Letelier graduated from the University of Chile with degrees in law and economics. After several years in the government's Department of

Copper, he worked for Felipe Herrera at the Inter-American Development Bank in Washington, D.C., from 1960 to 1971. A long-time Allende supporter, he was appointed Allende's ambassador to the United States, a post in which he faced a hostile Nixon administration committed to subverting the Chilean government. During Allende's hectic final four months in office, Letelier served in his cabinet as minister of foreign relations, interior, and defense, successively.

He was arrested in the September 11, 1973, coup and, with other ranking officials and supporters of the fallen government, was sent to a prison camp on Dawson Island in the frigid Strait of Magellan. Exiled a year after the coup, Letelier went to Venezuela before accepting a position as associate fellow at the Institute for Policy Studies in Washington, D.C., where he was prominent among Chileans attempting to rally opposition to the Augusto Pinochet regime. Agents of the Dirección Nacional de Inteligencia (DINA) blew up his automobile on September 21, 1976, killing him and his assistant Ronni Moffitt. U.S. courts tried and sentenced five DINA agents: U.S. citizen Michael Townley and four Cuban exiles.

When the Pinochet dictatorship issued an amnesty decree in April 1978 exonerating the military and police of crimes committed since the coup, it pointedly excluded the Letelier assassination in order to reduce friction with the U.S. administration of President Jimmy Carter. Nonetheless, Pinochet refused requests for the extradition of former DINA commander Manuel Contreras Sepúlveda and sub-commander Pedro Espinoza Bravo, both indicted in the United States. Following the dictatorship's end, a Chilean court in November 1993 sentenced Contreras and Espinoza to seven and six years, respectively. The Supreme Court upheld the sentence in May 1995. While some denounced the sentences as too lenient, others saw them as weakening the military's heretofore absolute impunity for the human rights violations committed during the dictatorship.

See also **Allende Gossens, Salvador; Carter, Jimmy; Chile: The Twentieth Century; Pinochet Ugarte, Augusto.**

BIBLIOGRAPHY

Branch, Taylor, and Eugene M. Proper. *Labyrinth.* New York: Viking Press, 1982.

Dinges, John, and Saul Landau. *Assassination on Embassy Row.* New York: Pantheon, 1980.

Matus Acuña, Alejandra, and Francisco Javier Artaza. *Crimen con castigo.* Santiago: Ediciones B, Grupo Zeta: La Nación, 1996.

THOMAS C. WRIGHT

LETELIER MADARIAGA, VALENTÍN

LETELIER MADARIAGA, VALENTÍN (1852–1919). Valentín Letelier Madariaga (*b.* 16 December 1852; *d.* 20 June 1919). Chilean thinker and political figure, often considered the chief Chilean disciple of positivism. Born in Linares City, he qualified as a lawyer in 1875 and later held a number of official jobs, including the secretaryship of Chile's legation in Germany (1880–1885). He was a deputy in the Congress of 1888–1891 and, as a leader of the Radical Party, was one of the signers of the act deposing President José Manuel Balmaceda in January 1891 (for which he was later imprisoned and exiled by Balmaceda). In 1906 Letelier became rector of the University of Chile, where he instituted important reforms. At the third Radical Party convention in 1906, Letelier successfully advocated "socialist" (i.e., social reform) principles that were the direct opposite of the "individualism" espoused by his chief adversary, the brilliant speaker Enrique Mac iver Rodríguez. Letelier's pen was rarely idle; his numerous works, which incline to the ponderous, cover history, law, sociology, and philosophy.

See also **Positivism.**

BIBLIOGRAPHY

Luis Galdámes, *Valentín Letelier y su obra* (1937).

Solomon Lipp, *Three Chilean Thinkers* (1975).

Additional Bibliography

Fuentealba Hernández, Leonardo. *La filosofía de la historia en Valentín Letelier.* Santiago de Chile: Taller Gráfico de la Editorial Universitaria, 1990.

SIMON COLLIER

LETELIER VALDÉS, MIGUEL FRANCISCO

LETELIER VALDÉS, MIGUEL FRANCISCO (1939–). Miguel Francisco Letelier Valdés is a Chilean organist and composer. Born on September 29, 1939, in Santiago, Letelier Valdés is the son of composer Alfonso Letelier Llona. He received his early musical education at the National Conservatory of the University of Chile. Later studies included work in France with Max Deutsch, André Jolivet, and Jean-Jacques Grünenwald. In Argentina, where he temporarily took up residence, he studied with Alberto Ginastera. He later moved back to Chile to join the faculty at the Universidad de Chile. Letelier Valdés, who has given recitals throughout South America and Germany, has composed for orchestra, piano, chamber groups, and voice. The originality of his work makes it difficult to identify him with a particular style or tendency, but his later music shows an affinity with the work of György Ligeti and Luciano Berio.

See also **Music: Art Music.**

BIBLIOGRAPHY

John Vinton, ed., *Dictionary of Contemporary Music* (1971).

Samuel Claro Valdés and Jorge Urrutia, *Historia de la música en Chile* (1973).

SERGIO BARROSO

LETICIA DISPUTE. The Leticia Dispute was a conflict in the 1930s between Colombia and Peru over control of the Amazon River town of Leticia and surrounding territory (about 4,000 square miles). Under the Salomón-Lozano Treaty (1922), meant to settle a long-standing boundary dispute, the border between the two countries was set at the Putumayo River, except for the Leticia Quadrilateral or Trapezium, which stretches south from the Putumayo to the northern bank of the Amazon. The treaty was unpopular among Peruvians, who had founded Leticia in 1867, had recently controlled rubber extraction in the region, and still had economic interests there.

On September 1, 1932 an armed force of about two hundred Peruvian civilians and soldiers seized Leticia and expelled the Colombian residents. On October 21, Peruvians captured Tarapacá, a Colombian town on the Putumayo. President Luis Sánchez Cerro of Peru did not authorize the action at Leticia but was pressured by public opinion to use the incident to secure revision of the 1922 treaty. Colombia's president, Enrique Olaya Herrera, was determined to regain Leticia and dispatched an expedition of a thousand men and five ships, which reached the disputed area by sailing to Pará, Brazil, and thence up the Amazon. The Colombians also hastily assembled an air force of U.S.- and European-made planes piloted mainly by German employees of the Colombian airline SCADTA. Early in 1933 the Colombians recaptured Tarapacá and took the Peruvian fort at Güepí, also on the Putumayo. Further hostilities were averted by the assassination of Sánchez Cerro in April and the accession of Oscar Benavides, who was more amenable to the return of Leticia to Colombia. This finally was accomplished on June 19, 1934 through the efforts of the League of Nations and the mediation of Afrânio de Melo Franco, foreign minister of Brazil. The 1934 agreement ended the conflict, but Leticia remained isolated from the rest of Colombia and the government presence weak, though it developed close ties with the neighboring border towns of Tabatinga, Brazil, and Santa Rosa, Peru. As a result, by 2000 the region had become a center for trafficking in narcotics and other illegal goods. In 2005 the municipality of Leticia had a population of nearly 32,500.

See also **Amazon River; Benavides, Oscar Raimundo; Drugs and Drug Trade; Melo Franco, Afrânio de; Olaya Herrera, Enrique; Sánchez Cerro, Luis Manuel.**

BIBLIOGRAPHY

Basadre, Jorge. *Historia de la República del Perú.* 6th ed. Vol. 14. Lima: Editorial Universitaria, 1968.

Donadio, Alberto. *La Guerra con el Perú.* Bogotá: Planeta, 1995.

Restrepo, Juan Camilo, and Luis Ignacio Betancur. *Economía y conflicto Colombo-peruano.* Bogotá: Villegas Editores, 2001.

Wood, Bryce. *The United States and Latin American Wars, 1932–1942.* New York: Columbia University Press, 1966.

HELEN DELPAR

LETRADOS. Letrados, university graduates (literally "men of letters") and synonymous with lawyers and judges. *Letrados* comprised a special group, equal to knights and noblemen (*fidalgos*), who occupied most of the judicial and many of the administrative positions of government. Lusophone members of this group usually were educated at the University of Coimbra in Portugal and were schooled in canon law or civil law before entering royal service. *Letrados* were closely associated with the crown and often were appointed to one of the king's councils, to knighthoods and to military orders. As members of the bureaucracy, *letrados* established and ran the administration of the Portuguese Empire, including colonial Brazil.

In the Hispanic world *letrados* were educated at the Universities of Salamanca and Alcalá before taking positions in the colonial government. Very early on, New World universities such as the Universidad de San Marcos in Lima were established, allowing for the creation of a secondary class of *letrados,* the Creole elite.

In all cases the *letrados* read books and frequently indulged in literature. Early Ibero-American literature was written by *letrados* who dominated the literary scene throughout the colonial era. Some early and diverse *letrados* who wrote foundational chronicles that helped to establish an Ibero-American literary tradition were Pero Vaz de Caminha (1450–1500), Hernán Cortés (1485–1547), and José de Acosta (1539–1600). *Letrados* participated in the wars for independence oftentimes as ideological nation-builders and continued to have importance throughout the nineteenth and twentieth centuries.

BIBLIOGRAPHY

Stuart B. Schwartz, *Sovereignty and Society of Colonial Brazil* (1973).

Additional Bibliography

Calaça, Carlos Eduardo. *Anti-semitismo na Universidade de Coimbra: Cristãos-novos letrados do Rio de Janeiro, 1600–1730.* São Paulo: Humanitas, 2005.

Díaz Caballero, Jesús. "El incaísmo como primera ficción orientadora en la formación de la nación criolla en las Provincias Unidas del Río de la Plata." *A Contracorriente* 3, no. 1 (Fall 2005): 67–113.

González, José Eduardo. "Los nuevos letrados: Posboom y posnacionalismo." *Revista Iberoamericana* 194–195 (2001): 175–190.

Prado Arnoni, Antonio. Boêmios, letrados e insubmissos: Nota sobre cultura e anarquismo. *Revista Iberoamericana* 208–209 (2004): 721–733.

Rama, Angel. *La ciudad letrada.* Montevideo, Uruguay: Arca, 1998.

Ross Wilkinson
Thomas Ward

LEVENE, RICARDO (1885–1959).

Ricardo Levene (February 7, 1885–March 13, 1959) was one of the principal figures involved in the study of Argentine history in the first half of the twentieth century.

Levene attended secondary school in the city of Buenos Aires and in 1906 earned a doctorate of jurisprudence and law at the University of Buenos Aires. He had a long career as a professor and authority in the Philosophy and Letters faculties at the University of Buenos Aires and in the faculty of Humanities at the National University of La Plata. Among other positions, he was twice president of the latter university, from 1930 to 1931 and from 1932 to 1935.

Levene played a central role in the process of institutionalizing and professionalizing historical studies in Argentina. For much of the first half of the twentieth century, he was president of the Board of American History and Numismatics (Junta de Historia y Numismática), an organization that became the National Academy of History (Academia Nacional de la Historia) in 1938.

Levene is also known for his extensive work as a historian. Worth mentioning among his vast range of works are his role as director general of the *Historia de la Nación Argentina* (History of the Argentine Nation), a collective work whose first volume was published in 1939, and his historical *Ensayo histórico sobre la revolución de mayo y Mariano Moreno* (2 vols., 1920–1921; Essay on the May Revolution and Mariano Moreno, 1927).

See also **Moreno, Mariano.**

BIBLIOGRAPHY

Carbia, Rómulo. *Historia crítica de la Historiografía argentina.* Buenos Aires: Imprenta y Casa Editoria Coni, 1940.

Scenna, Miguel Angel. *Los que escribieron nuestra historia,* Buenos Aires: Ediciones La Bastilla, 1976

Pablo Buchbinder

LEVINGSTON, ROBERTO MARCELO (1920–).

Roberto Marcelo Levingston (*b.* 10 January 1920), president of Argentina (18 June 1970–March 1971). With the fall of Juan Carlos Onganía, Alejandro

Lanusse stayed in the background while the military junta recalled Levingston from the post of military attaché in Washington, D.C., to assume the presidency. The first item on his agenda after taking office was to salvage Onganía's stabilization plan. When that attempt failed, Levingston brought in Aldo Ferrer as economic minister. By October 1970 he and Ferrer had expanded credit, initiated a 6 percent pay hike, and promoted exports through a "buy Argentine" campaign.

Levingston's reform program notwithstanding, unrest burgeoned among labor, guerrillas, and political parties, with the latter forming a broad coalition, including Peronists, called the "Hour of the People." When Córdoba's governor, José Luis Camilo, dubbed some political agitators "vipers," he sparked the *viborazo,* a guerrilla insurrection. Alarmed, the military deposed Levingston and installed Lanusse as president, marking the end of the "Argentine Revolution."

See also **Argentina: The Twentieth Century.**

BIBLIOGRAPHY

Andrew Graham-Yooll, *De Perón a Videla* (1989).

Additional Bibliography

Amézola, Gonzalo de. *Levingston y Lanusse, o, El arte de lo imposible.* La Plata: Editorial de la U.N.L.P, 2000.

Perina, Rubén. *Onganía, Levingston, Lanusse: Los militares en la política argentina.* Buenos Aires: Editorial de Belgrano, 1983.

ROGER GRAVIL

LEVINSON, LUISA MERCEDES (1914–1988).

Luisa Mercedes Levinson (*b.* 5 January 1914; *d.* 4 March 1988), Argentine writer. Born in Buenos Aires, Levinson was part of the *La Nación* dynasty, the oligarchic Buenos Aires daily whose literary supplement continues to be a powerful voice in Argentine letters. Perhaps best known as the mother of writer Luisa Valenzuela, Levinson exemplifies one literary alternative in Argentina during the turbulent 1950s and 1960s: the projection of an internationalist commitment to contemporary themes such as the individual against the "massification" and cultural commodification of society, the problematics for a woman of sustaining an intrinsic dignity and integrity in the wasteland of modern life, and the psychological depth of solitary lives. *La pálida rosa de Soho* (1959) deals in a highly poetic fashion with the experiences of a London prostitute, while the stories of *La hermana de Eloísa* (1955) were written in collaboration with Jorge Luis Borges, with whom she was long associated. *El último zelofonte* (1984) is especially notable for its psychopathic eroticism and the possibilities it presents as a political allegory of contemporary Argentina.

See also **Literature: Latin America; Philosophy: Feminism.**

BIBLIOGRAPHY

Bernardo A. Chiesi, *La manifestación del animus en "A la sombra del búho"* (1981).

Celia Correas De Zapata, "Elementos fantásticos y mágicos-Realistas en la obra de Luisa Mercedes Levinson," in her *Ensayos hispanoamericanos* (1978), pp. 245–277.

Perla Giorno, *Soledad y búsqueda: Dos novelas latinoamericanas* (1976).

Delfín Leocadio Garasa, "Prólogo," in Luisa Mercedes Levinson, *Obra completa,* vol. 1 (1986), pp. 7–14.

Solomón Lipp, "Los mundos de Luisa Mercedes Levinson," in *Revista Iberoamericana* 45, nos. 108–109 (1979): 583–593.

Additional Bibliography

Arlt, Mirta. *Luisa Mercedes Levinson: Estudios sobre su obra.* Buenos Aires: Corregidor, 1995.

Sabino, Osvaldo R. *Luisa Mercedes Levinson: Revolución, redención y la madre del nuevo Mesías: Alusión mítica y alegoría política en La isla de los organilleros.* Buenos Aires: Corregidor, 1993.

Suárez, María del Carmen. *Potencia del símbolo en la obra de Luisa Mercedes Levinson.* Buenos Aires: Ediciones Ultimo Reino, 1993.

DAVID WILLIAM FOSTER

LEVY, ALEXANDRE (1864–1892).

Alexandre Levy (*b.* 10 November 1864; *d.* 17 January 1892), Brazilian composer, pianist, conductor, and critic. A composer of French and Swiss descent, he enjoyed the musical advantages of being a member of one of São Paulo's most renowned musical families. His father was a clarinetist and owner of Casa Levy, a music store as well as a recital hall in which concerts of local and visiting artists took place.

Alexandre Levy performed in public for the first time at the age of eight in a concert in which he and his brother played the piano, and his father the clarinet. Since his father owned a publishing business, several of the compositions he wrote as a teenager were published.

The last two decades of the nineteenth century in Brazil were marked by rising republican sentiment which culminated in the end of the empire and the establishment of the republic in 1889. The importance of Levy's work as a composer consisted of the fact that a respected Brazilian musician with excellent European training began to employ systematically the use of Brazilian folk and popular music in his compositions at a time when Brazilian musicians were attempting to break the bonds of European artistic domination. Levy also introduced Brazilian audiences to a significant number of European works unknown to them in his programming of works for the Haydn Club, of which he was program director and frequent conductor. Two of Levy's best-known works are *Variations on a Brazilian Theme* (Vem cá, Bitú [1887]), and *Suite brésilienne* (1890). On 17 January at a dinner on the country estate of his family, he complained of feeling unwell and died before the family was able to summon a physician. He was only thirty-one years old.

See also **Music: Popular Music and Dance.**

BIBLIOGRAPHY

David P. Appleby, *The Music of Brazil* (1983).

Gérard Béhague, *Popular Musical Currents in the Art of Music of the Early Nationalistic Period in Brazil* (Ph.D. diss., Tulane Univ., 1966).

Additional Bibliography

Lago, Manoel Aranha Correa do. "Brazilian Sources in Milhaud's Le Boeuf sur le Toit: A Discussion and a Musical Analysis." *Latin American Music Review* 23:1 (Spring–Summer 2002): 1–59.

DAVID P. APPLEBY

LEWIS, ROBERTO (1874–1949). Roberto Lewis (*b.* 1874; *d.* 1949), Panamanian painter. In the 1890s, Lewis studied under Albert Dubois and Leon Bonnat in Paris, where he was later named Panamanian consul (1904–1912). Upon returning to Panama, he became director of the Academia Nacional de Pintura from its founding until the late 1930s.

Lewis is well known for the official neoclassical paintings with which he decorated the interiors of public buildings such as the Teatro Nacional, the Palacio de Gobierno, and the Presidencia. He also painted many portraits, including all of the national presidents from 1904 to 1948. Unlike the academic portraits, Lewis's landscapes, including the famous *Tamarindos de Taboga* (1936), are characterized by the luminous colors and lively brushwork which reflect the influence of post-impressionism on his style.

See also **Art: The Twentieth Century.**

BIBLIOGRAPHY

Rodrigo Miró, "Lewis, Amador, Ivaldi," in *Revista Lotería,* no. 219 (May 1974): 72–80.

P. Prados, *Exposición Maestros-Maestros* (1987).

Additional Bibliography

Rajer, Anton. *París en Panamá: Roberto Lewis y la historia de sus obras restauradas en el Teatro Nacional de Panamá.* Menasha: Banta Book Publishing Corporation; Madison: University of Wisconsin Press, 2005.

MONICA E. KUPFER

LEY, SALVADOR (1907–1985). Salvador Ley (*b.* 2 January 1907; *d.* 21 March 1985), Guatemalan composer and pianist. Ley was born of German parents who had settled in Guatemala City. At the age of fifteen Ley won a scholarship to study music in Berlin. He remained in Germany from 1922 until 1934, when he returned to Guatemala to teach and serve as the director of the National Conservatory of Music. In 1937, Ley moved to New York City, where he made his North American debut in January 1938. His subsequent tour of the United States included a performance at the White House. Ley returned to Guatemala and resumed the directorship of the National Conservatory from 1944 to 1953. In the latter year he returned to the United States and taught at the Westchester Conservatory of Music in White Plains, New York. Ley has composed orchestral works, including *Copla triste* and *Danza exótica,* the opera *Lera,* and works for piano and voice.

See also **Music: Art Music.**

BIBLIOGRAPHY

Otto Mayer-Serra, *Música y músicos en Latinoamérica,* vol. 2 (1947), pp. 556–557.

J. Victor Soto De Ávila, *Quién es quién en Centroamérica y Panamá* (1954), p. 111; Enrique Anleu Díaz, *Esbozo histórico-social de la música en Guatemala* (1978), p. 97.

STEVEN S. GILLICK

LEY DE LEMAS. *See* **Uruguay, Electoral System.**

LEY IGLESIAS. Ley Iglesias, a Mexican law regulating the cost of church sacraments, named for José María Iglesias, its principal author. The law was promulgated 11 April 1857, while its author was minister of justice under President Ignacio Comonfort. The law stipulated that the poor were not to be charged for baptisms, marriage banns, weddings, or burials. All who earned no more by their honest toil than would provide for their daily subsistence were to be considered poor. All others could be charged reasonable fees. The Comonfort administration had earlier taken from the church the responsibility for registering births, marriages, adoptions, and deaths. Registration of these events and the administration of cemeteries were turned over to civil officials, but these changes were not technically part of the Ley Iglesias. These Reform Laws were later adopted as part of the Constitution of 1857.

See also **Anticlericalism.**

BIBLIOGRAPHY

Walter V. Scholes, *Mexican Politics During the Juárez Regime, 1855–1872* (1957).

Thomas Gene Powell, *El liberalismo y el campesinado en el centro de México, 1850–1877* (1974).

Thomas Gene Powell, "Priests and Peasants in Central Mexico: Social Conflict During 'La Reforma,'" in *Hispanic American Historical Review* 57, no. 2 (1977): 296–313.

Additional Bibliography

Carbajal, Juan Alberto. *La consolidación de México como nación: Benito Juárez, la constitución de 1857 y las leyes de reforma.* México: Editorial Porrúa, 2006.

Matute, Alvaro, Evelia Trejo, and Brian Francis Connaughton Hanley, eds. *Estado, Iglesia y sociedad en México, siglo XIX.* México, D.F.: Facultad de Filosofía y Letras, UNAM: Grupo Editorial, Miguel Angel Porrúa, 1995.

D. F. STEVENS

LEY JUÁREZ. Ley Juárez, a Mexican law abolishing military and ecclesiastical fueros (privileges) named for Benito Juárez, its principal author. The law, dated 11 November 1855, was promulgated by President Juan Álvarez, while Juárez was his minister of justice. The law contained seventy-seven main articles that had the effect of abolishing all special tribunals except the military and ecclesiastical courts. Although the Ley Juárez did not abolish these courts, it did end the military and ecclesiastical *fueros* in civil cases. Priests and military officers could no longer change the venue of trials for civil offenses to the ecclesiastical or military courts. Sinkin argues that the law accepted the basic corporate structure of society and did not abolish the entire *fuero* system since the church courts retained the right to hear criminal cases. As the first of the Reform Laws, the Ley Juárez was approved as part of the Constitution of 1857.

See also **Anticlericalism; Juárez, Benito.**

BIBLIOGRAPHY

Richard N. Sinkin, *The Mexican Reform, 1855–1876: A Study in Liberal Nation-Building* (1979), pp. 98–99, 123–124.

Additional Bibliography

Arnold, Linda. *Política y justicia: La Suprema Corte mexicana (1824–1855).* México, D.F.: Universidad Nacional Autónoma de México, Instituto de Investigaciones Jurídicas, 1996.

Ramos Medina, Manuel, ed. *Memoria del I Coloquio Historia de la Iglesia en el Siglo XIX.* México, D.F.: Centro de Estudios de Historia de México Condumex, 1998.

D. F. STEVENS

LEY LERDO.

LEY LERDO. Ley Lerdo, a Mexican law disamortizing property held by the Catholic Church and civil institutions, was named for Miguel Lerdo De Tejada, its principal author. The law was promulgated 25 June 1856, while Lerdo served as finance minister for President Ignacio Comonfort. It declared that civil and ecclesiastical corporations, such as the Catholic Church and local and state governments, would be prohibited from owning real property not directly used in everyday operations. The church could retain its sanctuaries, monasteries, convents, and seminaries, and local and state governments their offices, jails, and schools, but both had to sell all other urban and rural real estate. Tenants were given preference during the first three months the law would be in effect, and the annual rent was considered as 6 percent of the value of the property for sale. The government would collect a 5 percent tax on these sales. The law prohibited civil and ecclesiastical corporations from acquiring property in the future, but it did not confiscate their wealth. The *Ley Lerdo* also targeted the *ejido*, the communally held land of indigenous and peasant villagers, demanding its sale. Intended to raise revenue and promote the development of markets, the actual effects on property ownership are disputed, but it seems to have raised little revenue for the government. The Ley Lerdo was adopted as part of the Constitution of 1857. It was later superseded by decrees confiscating church property.

The Ley Lerdo was one of several laws ending church privileges adopted in Mexico during the revolutionary era known as "La Reforma" (the Reform) from 1854 to 1876. In response to the liberal and modernizing reforms approved in the 1857 constitution, religious, military, and peasant leaders rose up in protest and civil war ensued. The Catholic Church excommunicated authorities who had signed the constitution. Ultimately, the liberals succeeded, though not without lasting consequences. While Catholicism remained strong into the twenty-first century, the Ley Lerdo and La Reforma marked the beginning of a formal feud and separation between church and state that has slowly been resolved, particularly with Mexico's 1992 constitutional reforms.

See also **Anticlericalism; Lerdo de Tejada, Miguel.**

BIBLIOGRAPHY

Jan Bazant, *Alienation of Church Wealth in Mexico: Social and Economic Aspects of the Liberal Revolution, 1856–1875* (1971).

Thomas Gene Powell, *El liberalismo y el campesinado en el centro de México, 1850–1876* (1974).

Robert J. Knowlton, *Church Property and the Mexican Reform, 1856–1910* (1976).

Charles R. Berry, *The Reform in Oaxaca, 1856–76: A Microhistory of the Liberal Revolution* (1981).

Additional Bibliography

Chasteen, John Charles, and James A. Wood. *Problems in Modern Latin American History: Sources and Interpretations, Completely Revised and Updated.* Wilmington, DE: SR Books, 2004.

Hamnett, Brian. *Juárez.* New York: Longman, 1994.

Jackson, Robert H., ed. *Liberals, the Church, and Indian Peasants: Corporate Lands and the Challenge of Reform in Nineteenth-Century Spanish America.* Albuquerque: University of New Mexico Press, 1997.

Juárez, José Roberto. *Reclaiming Church Wealth: The Recovery of Church Property after Expropriation in the Archdiocese of Guadalajara, 1860–1911.* Albuquerque: University of New Mexico Press, 2004.

Kourí, Emilio. *A Pueblo Divided: Business, Property, and Community in Papantla, Mexico.* Stanford, CA: Stanford University Press, 2004.

Matute, Alvaro, Evelia Trejo, and Brian Francis Connaughton, eds. *Estado, Iglesia y sociedad en México, siglo XIX.* México, D.F.: Facultad de Filosofía y Letras, UNAM, Grupo Editorial, Miguel Angel Porrúa, 1995.

Thomson, Guy P. C. *Patriotism, Politics, and Popular Liberalism in Nineteenth-Century Mexico: Juan Francisco Lucas and the Puebla Sierra.* With David G. LaFrance. Wilmington, DE: Scholarly Resources, 1999.

D. F. STEVENS

LEYVA SOLANO, GABRIEL (1871–1910).

LEYVA SOLANO, GABRIEL (1871–1910). Gabriel Leyva Solano (*b.* 1871; *d.* 13 June 1910), precursor of the Revolution in Sinaloa. From northern Sinaloa, educated at the state *colegio* (preparatory school) in Culiacán, Leyva became a schoolteacher on a large rural estate. There, and in neighboring villages, he observed the misery and the atrocities of local political authorities which the country folk suffered. This, combined with reading of Porfirian abuses in the nation, led him to cultivate opposition sentiment among peasants. In time, as a lawyer's assistant, Leyva began representing the dispossessed in legal proceedings. An avid follower of Francisco Madero, after the latter's tour of the state in 1909, Leyva espoused the Maderista cause among peasants and workers in northern Sinaloa. Harassed by authorities, he gathered a revolutionary band around him in May 1910. But within a month he was betrayed, captured, and executed without trial, an early martyr of the Revolution.

See also **Madero, Francisco Indalecio.**

BIBLIOGRAPHY

Amado González Dávila, *Diccionario geográfico, histórico y estadístico del Estado de Sinaloa* (1959).

Ernesto Higuera, *Gabriel Leyva Solano: Ensayo biográfico* (1954).

Hector R. Olea, *Breve historia de la Revolución en Sinaloa* (1964).

STUART F. VOSS

LEZAMA LIMA, JOSÉ (1910–1976).

José Lezama Lima (*b.* 19 December 1910; *d.* 9 August 1976), Cuban poet and novelist. Possibly the greatest Cuban novelist and one of the greatest Cuban poets of all time, Lezama Lima was born in Havana. He graduated from the law school of the University of Havana in 1929 and worked as a lawyer until 1941, when he received a post at the cultural office of the Ministry of Education. Aside from his own arduous literary creations, he promoted literature in Cuba by founding and directing four literary publications that were pivotal to the development of Cuban literature: *Verbum,* while he was a law student; *Espuela de Plata,* with Guy Pérez Cisneros and Mariano Rodríguez (1939–1941); *Nadie Parecía,* with Ángel Gaztelu (1942–1944); and *Orígenes,* with José Rodríguez Feo (1944–1956). This last publication became the center of Cuban literary and artistic life. It published only previously unpublished material and provided a forum for the work of Cuban writers of merit, both known and unknown, including Alejo Carpentier, Virgilio Piñera, Lydia Cabrera, Eliseo Diego, and Eugenio Florit. It also published the graphic work of great Cuban artists, among them Wilfredo Lam and Amelia Peláez, as well as a section of reviews. Aside from attracting the best talent in Cuba, *Orígenes* also published the work of varied figures of international renown, such as Albert Camus, Gabriela Mistral, Juan Ramón Jiménez, Octavio Paz, Paul Valéry, giving Cuban cultural activity an unprecedented entry into the international scene.

Lezama Lima's official standing after the Cuban Revolution of 1959 was initially good. He was almost enthusiastic about the new regime, and he occupied several key posts in the Cuban cultural establishment: he was one of the vice presidents of the National Union of Cuban Writers and Artists (UNEAC), director of the Department of Literature and Publications of the National Council of Culture, and researcher and consultant at the Institute of Literature and Linguistics at the National Academy of Sciences. Although he never publicly dissented from the government, in his later years he was harassed and marginated because he failed to be actively supportive of official aims and policy.

Lezama Lima's best-known work, the novel *Paradiso,* was published in Cuba in 1966 to immediate acclaim there and abroad. Yet its distribution in Cuba was extremely limited, and shortly after its publication it mysteriously disappeared from bookstores and became very difficult to obtain. He became an internationally known and revered author, receiving many invitations to cultural events abroad, but the Cuban government repeatedly denied him permission to travel. He lived in Cuba until his death.

Lezama Lima is one of the most complex, baroque authors in the history of the Spanish language. An unabashed proponent of "art for art's sake" in a milieu that favored art as an instrument for social change, he spurned references to reality and sought to create a hermetic and self-referent world through language. His best-known works include *Oppiano Licario* (1977), the sequel to *Paradiso;* the essay *Las eras imaginarias* (1971); and a volume of his poetic work, *Poesía completa,* published in 1975. His novels and poetry have been translated into many languages.

See also **Cuba: Cuba since 1959; Literature: Spanish America.**

BIBLIOGRAPHY

Emilio Bejel, *José Lezama Lima: Poet of the Image* (1990).

Gustavo Pellón, *José Lezama Lima's Joyful Vision: A Study of "Paradiso" and Other Prose Works* (1989).

Raymond Souza, *The Poetic Fiction of José Lezama Lima* (1983).

Additional Bibliography

Arcos, Jorge Luis. *Los poetas de "Orígenes."* Mexico City: Fondo de Cultura Económica, 2002.

Cella, Susana. *El saber poético: La poesía de José Lezama Lima.* Buenos Aires: Nueva Generación: Facultad de Filosofía y Letras, Universidad de Buenos Aires, 2003.

Salgado, César Augusto. *From Modernism to Neobaroque: Joyce and Lezama Lima.* Lewisburg: Bucknell University Press; London: Associated University Presses, 2001.

Varela Jácome, Benito. *Asedios a la literatura cubana: Textos y contextos.* Santiago de Compostela: Universidad de Santiago de Compostela, Servicio de Publicaciones e Intercambio Científico, 2002.

Vilahomat, José R. *Ficción de racionalidad: La memoria como operador mítico en las estéticas polares de Jorge Luis Borges y José Lezama Lima.* Newark, DE: Juan de la Cuesta, 2004.

ROBERTO VALERO

LIAUTAUD, GEORGES (1899–1991). Georges Liautaud (*b.* 1899; *d.* 1991), Haitian artist and sculptor. Liautaud, who has been described as Haiti's most consistently original artist, did not begin his career until middle age. He received an above-average education but also expressed an early interest in mechanics. He spent several years in the Dominican Republic working as a repairman for the railroads before returning to Haiti as a blacksmith and manufacturer of hardware. In 1953 DeWitt Peters, the director of the Centre d'Art in Port-au-Prince, discovered Liautaud's metal crosses and began to commission more such works of pure art. After this Liautaud shifted to one dimensional figures, especially representations of a half-woman, half-fish spirit known as Maîtresse La Sirène. In the early 2000s his unique pieces can be found in galleries in Paris, New York, and Rotterdam.

See also **Art: The Twentieth Century.**

BIBLIOGRAPHY

Eleanor Ingalls Christensen, *The Art of Haiti* (1975).

Selden Rodman, *The Miracle of Haitian Art* (1974).

Ute Stebich, *Haitian Art* (1978).

Additional Bibliography

Cerejido, Elizabeth. *Lespri endepandan: Discovering Haitian Sculpture.* Miami: Patricia & Phillip Frost Art Museum, 2004.

Rodman, Selden. "Cutting Fantastic Figures: Figments of the Master's Imagination." *Américas* 40:1 (January–February, 1988): 26–30.

KAREN RACINE

LIBERALISM. Liberalism was at first a European and later a worldwide intellectual and political movement whose aim was to promote greater freedom and liberty for the individual. It had its roots in the struggle for power between church and state during the Middle Ages. Liberals tended to see both institutions as inimical to the interests of the individual and therefore wanted to limit their power. The political agenda of nineteenth-century liberalism was to liquidate the remaining power of the medieval church, already broken in northern Europe as a result of the Protestant Reformation, and to promote individual economic and political power, under the doctrine of laissez-faire, against the political power of the state. Liberals hoped that the economic growth from such reforms would expand the size of the middle class, increase the number of citizens admitted to political power, and thereby bolster the ranks of liberalism.

Latin American liberalism was part of this wider movement. Since the Iberian world had been untouched by the Protestant Reformation, its liberals faced a far more powerful church antagonist than the liberals of northern Europe, a reality that explains the primacy of anticlericalism in the liberal movement in Spain, Portugal, and Latin America. Moreover, Europe's experience with economic development, civil war, and revolution was such that the state's power to impose corporate and economic restraints on the individual was much weaker there by the nineteenth century than in the Iberian/Latin American world.

The battle against the power of the church was pan-European and began in the Enlightenment, whose secular and optimistic vision of the future greatly molded liberal thinking. In Iberia, the opening round was the expulsion of the Jesuits from the Portuguese and Spanish empires in 1759 and 1767, respectively. Their properties were confiscated, for a brief time administered by the state, and eventually auctioned off. The second round took place during the Napoleonic Wars, when the state's economic problems produced similar results. In 1798 the Spanish Bourbons ordered the forced sale of all church property in Spain that sustained chantries and pious foundations. In 1804 the measure was extended to Spanish America. Already in the air, therefore, were some of the components that would mark future liberal thinking.

The seeds of other liberal issues of the Iberian world—greater economic and political freedom—also go back to the Bourbon Reforms of the eighteenth century. While the goal of many was greater absolutism, the particulars of the agenda could just as easily be pushed forward in the name of individual freedom. Free trade, for example, advanced on various fronts by fits and starts, so that by the end of the century mercantilism was in decline. On the political front, the introduction of the Intendancy System and local militias gave the central government a real presence at the provincial level, but it also created the regional organizational structures that enabled regions to resist central authority and set the stage for the federalist-centralist struggles of the nineteenth century.

Much of liberal ideology was crystallized in the Spanish Constitution of 1812. The constitutional crisis brought on by the 1808 French invasion of Spain prompted an immediate "modernization" of the political system. The constitution severely limited monarchical government, ended the Inquisition, restricted the military and ecclesiastical fueros, created provincial deputations and militias as a counterweight to centralized authority, and provided for universal manhood suffrage. The constitution also went into effect in Mexico and Central America, where elections were soon held. The constitution was annulled in 1814 by Ferdinand VII, but was forced on him again in 1820. Mexican and Central American leaders broke definitively with Spain in 1820 in order to avoid a return of its version of liberalism. The 1812 Constitution socialized a generation of Mexican and Central American liberals and accounts for some of the virulence of the federalist-centralist struggles there.

Liberals identified with federalism and the separation of powers because they provided a check on the absolute power of the centralized state and tended to enhance the autonomy and freedom of the individual. The problem of what the proper balance between central and provincial authority should be occupied liberals from early on. They were not always consistent in their answer. They frequently acted illiberally and imposed their own views on others. Liberals were often selective in what principles they chose to support; their decisions usually depended on the political, economic, and social context of their own region and what was in their personal interest and/or what was politically possible. Pragmatic considerations such as survival, self-defense, access to power, and domination often won out over ideological consistency in the liberal agenda, especially in the area of the federalist-centralist debate. This debate was especially intense in Mexico, Central America, Colombia, Brazil, and Argentina.

Regarding the economic order, liberals wanted to liquidate much of the colonial legacy of state control, state taxation, and church, corporate, and state interference in economic matters. In general, liberals supported the movement toward free trade and a lowering of the tariff. They believed that these changes would produce more trade and commerce, which in turn would prompt the economic growth that would transform the whole economy. An end to state subsidies and monopoly rents like tobacco and *aguardiente* were logical parts of the liberal program. But where falling government revenues endangered the ability of the central government to pay its soldiers and bureaucrats, or where the reaction from sugar, tobacco, and cotton growers or artisan producers was too great, liberals usually moderated their principles.

A basic premise of liberalism was the right of the individual to be treated equally before the law. Thus it was logical that Indian tribute and communal lands, special categories like ecclesiastical and military *fueros,* entailed estates, and slavery and other forced labor institutions would come under attack. Freedom of the press and many civil liberties taken for granted elsewhere were not always espoused by, let alone supported by, Latin American liberals. Liberals in multiracial and unequal societies frequently compromised and even betrayed their principles. Such was the case in Mexico, Guatemala, Ecuador, Peru, and Bolivia, where liberals excluded Indians from their push to increase individual liberties, and in

Brazil, Venezuela, and Cuba, where liberals closed their eyes to the plight of the enslaved.

Since the church had been such a close partner of the state in the colonial period, it had held onto functions and powers that the churches of post-Reformation Europe and North America had long since relinquished. The church's role as the recorder of vital statistics, such as births, marriages, and deaths, was a frequent battleground between the Latin American church and its liberal opponents. Religious toleration and church control of education were other areas of conflict. State control of church appointments and tithes, the colonial *patronato*, was claimed by the liberals, and used to mold and "modernize" the church hierarchy. What to do with the religious orders was a thorny problem. For many liberals, they were a vestige of the Middle Ages. Their suppression had several advantages from the liberal point of view. A sell-off of their wealth would raise money for the state, put property back into circulation that had been in "dead" hands, and eliminate some of the financial support for, and hence the attractiveness of joining, the clerical estate. The church-state conflict was especially bitter in Mexico, Guatemala, and Colombia.

The liberal advance in Latin America was anything but uniform. Country-by-country differences are a testimony to Latin America's fabled diversity. The bewildering possibilities for just one country are captured in Gabriel García Márquez's portrayal of the liberal struggle in Colombia in his novel *One Hundred Years of Solitude*. But each region is a case study that frequently disproves the general rule. In Central America, liberals from the outlying provinces had won a seemingly definitive victory in their struggle with conservative centralists in Guatemala City in the late 1820s, and thought they would have the power to force Guatemala to share its income and resources with the rest of Central America. Beginning in 1830, the liberal federation president, Francisco Morazán of Honduras, pursued a centralist policy and carried out the most radical liberal program in Latin America up to that time, with the abolition of tribute, the ecclesiastical *fuero*, regular orders, and compulsory tithes. These measures, as well as a head-tax, making divorce legal, and allowing civil marriage, led to an inevitable reaction.

In Guatemala it coalesced around the proclerical Caudillo Rafael Carrera, who led the conservatives to victory over Morazán in 1840. Guatemalan conservatives, fearing a resurgence of liberal power throughout the isthmus, flip-flopped and adopted a federalist stance. Liberal aid in Nicaragua to the interventionist effort of the American filibuster William Walker confirmed conservative fears and discredited liberals throughout Central America. Walker's intervention plus Carrera's reign until 1865 delayed a return to liberal rule in Central America. When Liberals did recover power in Guatemala under Justo Rufino Barrios in 1871, their disestablishment of the church was even more total than that in Mexico later. With the social control provided by the church gone, liberals ruled Guatemala's Indians in a repressive and exploitative fashion.

In Mexico the colonial church, establishment, and legacy, especially in Mexico City, were much stronger. Liberals were not immediately victorious as in Central America, and had to proceed in a more piecemeal fashion. They had to ensure that the institutional framework protected their liberal base in the provinces, especially against special interest groups in Mexico City like the army. The liberal agenda in the 1820s and 1830s was pushed forward on the federal structure outlined in the 1824 constitution by regional politicians like Valentín Gómez Farías of Zacatecas, José María Luis Mora of Guanajuato, and Lorenzo de Zavala of Yucatán. The individual states had considerable powers, including their own state legislatures, state militias, and state-elected governors.

Liberals finally achieved national power when Antonio López de Santa Anna overthrew the centralist government of Anastasio Bustamante in 1832 and installed Gómez Farías as acting president in 1833. Liberal laws closed down the clerically run national university, secularized Franciscan missions, disentailed church property, and ended compulsory tithes. But other liberal measures, such as ending tariff protection, abolishing the tobacco monopoly, decreasing the size of the army, and ending the military *fuero*, threatened too many vested interests. Santa Anna sided with the centralists in 1834 and defeated a coalition of state militias headed by Zacatecas. But Texas escaped and became an independent republic in 1836 with Zavala as its vice president. The debacle continued and soured many liberals on federalism.

A divided house was obviously a conquered one, and the loss of much of northern Mexico in the Mexican-American War (1846–1848) confirmed the suspicion that federalism put liberals at a competitive disadvantage both nationally and internationally. When liberals drew up the Constitution of 1857, they made sure it was much more centralist than the Constitution of 1824. It also enshrined the Ley Juárez and Ley Lerdo that abolished the ecclesiastical and military *fueros* and provided for the sale of corporately owned church and Indian real estate. The church's belligerent reaction and support for the conservatives in the War of the Reform (1858–1861) and French intervention (1862–1867) made the liberals determined to establish the church completely. While the disestablishment was reconfirmed in the Constitution of 1917, the church continued to endure in Mexico.

In Argentina liberals faced a weaker colonial establishment, traded directly with Europe, and resided in the capital of Buenos Aires rather than in the provinces (as in Mexico). Under the leadership of Bernardino Rivadavia and other Porteño leaders, they imposed a Unitario or centralist order, first on the province of Buenos Aires in 1820 and then on the rest of the country with their rigorously centralist constitution of 1826. The liberals' program of modernization was truly impressive. They took the *fuero* from the army and church, reduced the size of the former, and took over assets and property, and many of the educational and welfare functions, of the latter. In their economic program liberals pushed infrastructure development, greater foreign trade, increased immigration, and new investment. But religious freedom, tax modernization, and the war with Brazil over Uruguay were too radical for the interior provinces, and the liberal experiment ended in 1827 in civil war, Rivadavia's departure, and Juan Manuel de Rosas's rise to power. With the defeat of Rosas in 1852, the Unitario liberals regained power in Buenos Aires, and within ten years they had forced themselves on the rest of Argentina. While the Constitution of 1853 was federalist and the capital was eventually federalized, the constitutional right of the president to intervene in the provinces, and the income and growth of Buenos Aires, ensured a centralization in favor of *porteño* liberals that would have gladdened the hearts of the Unitarios.

In Brazil the chief force for liberalism was the monarch Dom Pedro I, more liberal than his subjects. Favoring a constitutional monarchy, religious toleration, civil liberties, and an end to slavery, he pushed the Constitution of 1824 on his reluctant subjects. But it was not long before the parliamentary system he created evolved to the point where the majority resisted his liberalism and centralization. As a result he abdicated in 1831 in favor of his five-year-old son, Dom Pedro II. By 1842 a system had developed by which the emperor would dissolve parliament, and the elections would be fixed to favor the opposition party; conservative or liberal made no difference. This sham continued until the monarchy was overthrown in 1889.

In Colombia, Venezuela, and Ecuador, independence colleagues Francisco de Paula Santander, José Antonio Páez, Juan José Flores, and Vicente Rocafuerte provided strong leadership and carried out some liberal reforms without them being recognized as such, and a formal liberal-conservative division was postponed until the 1840s. When Colombia's liberal reform came in earnest in the 1850s and 1860s, it surpassed Mexico's in its laissez-faire and individual and states' rights. With the backing of the relentless Tomás Cipriano Mosquera, it imitated the Mexican example in suppressing religious orders and seizing all church property.

In Chile, too, federalism produced disorder and chaos in the 1820s. While the problems with ultrafederalism were not admitted by liberals until the second half of the nineteenth century, ultrafederalism was out of step with the need for a state to be strong enough to face the world, maintain order, and get infrastructure projects like transportation and port systems developed so commerce and trade could evolve effectively. This was Chile's response under the guidance of Diego Portales and the Constitution of 1833, and the nation's unparalleled success by the end of the nineteenth century was an important lesson for the rest of Latin America. In Colombia, where a shortage of national revenues led to a shedding of national government functions and a turn to extreme federalism from 1863 to 1885, the results were such that the liberal Rafael Núñez Moledo drew the same conclusions Portales had, and orchestrated a rapprochement with the conservatives and the church; together they produced the highly centralized Constitution of 1886.

Toward the end of the century, reaction had set in among other liberals as well. In Mexico under Porfirio Díaz, in Venezuela under Antonio Guzmán Blanco, and in Central America under other liberal dictators, the "order and progress" doctrines of the Positivists brought more authoritarian and centralized rule. Although liberal in economic and religious matters, these dictators and their supporters sacrificed other liberal principles, such as an independent judiciary, a free press, and political democracy, for the economic progress order was supposed to bring. On the other hand, in Chile liberals chipped away at presidential power and moved toward parliamentarism, while Brazil moved toward decentralization. And in Argentina, liberal reform brought the middle class to power for the first time in 1916, when the radicals won as a result of the 1912 Sáenz Peña election law.

As the twentieth century opened, the worldwide economic development brought by the industrial revolution had created powerful new forces like corporate businesses that threatened the individual. As a consequence, the political agenda of liberalism changed and increasingly had a social program that looked once again, as it had in its struggle against the church, to the state to protect the individual from the awesome economic power of private capitalism. This change in liberalism was evident in the rule of José Batlle y Ordóñez in Uruguay, Hipólito Irigoyen in Argentina, Arturo Alessandri Palma in Chile, and Alfonso López Pumarejo in Colombia.

In many places the demands of the middle classes and the masses were not met by liberalism, and the old order was swept away, as was the case in the Mexican Revolution of 1910. At the same time, economic difficulties and the worldwide Great Depression of the 1930s saw the rise of mass-based authoritarian political movements. Fascism and communism spread throughout Latin America while the APRa (Alianza Popular Revolucionaria Americana) appeared in Peru, the PRI (Partido Revolucionario Institutional) in Mexico, and the Peronist Party in Argentina. Many saw these groups as national and international threats; where liberals held power, they invoked the countervailing power of the state for protection. For some this worldwide struggle culminated in World War II. With the victory of the Allies, the global threat of fascism was virtually eliminated, but the postwar settlement left the world divided between East and West. As the twentieth century came to a close, the perceived threat from international communism was much reduced by the collapse and breakup of the Soviet Union, and many mass-based formerly authoritarian political movements like APRA, PRI, and Peronism tried to gain respectability by transforming themselves into something akin to liberal parties.

Liberals were now more openly divided over the role of the state. Those who focused on economic concerns like the threat of inflation, budgetary deficits, trade problems, and the inability of the state to solve a wide array of social ills were known as "Neoliberals." They called for a reduced role for the state, a sell-off of state-run enterprises, and a return to the laissez-faire principles of nineteenth-century liberalism. Others looked at the same economic problems, the rise of the third world, nuclear proliferation, and environmental pollution as the main causes of an unstable world order and as the chief threats to individual liberties, and they argued for a continued strong role for the state. Whatever the case, all liberalism—whether old or new, right or left—was about restraining power for the benefit of the individual.

See also **Bolivia, Constitutions: Overview; Bourbon Reforms; Brazil, Constitutions; Chile, Constitutions; Cuba, Constitutions; Ecuador, Constitutions; Guatemala, Constitutions; Peru, Constitutions; Spain, Constitution of 1812.**

BIBLIOGRAPHY

For a clearly written and cogently argued survey of liberalism in general, see Harry K. Girvetz, *From Wealth to Welfare: The Evolution of Liberalism,* rev. ed. (1966). On Latin America, the best survey by far is David Bushnell and Neill Macaulay, *The Emergence of Latin America in the Nineteenth Century,* 2d ed. (1994). For church-state relations, see John L. Mecham, *Church and State in Latin America: A History of Politico-Ecclesiastical Relations,* rev. ed. (1966), which, though overly legalistic, is still serviceable. Individual country surveys in which the role of liberalism is particularly well explained include David Bushnell, *The Making of Modern Colombia: A Nation in Spite of Itself* (1993); Ralph L. Woodward, Jr., *Central America: A Nation Divided,* 2d ed. (1985), and Hugh Thomas, *Cuba: The Pursuit of Freedom* (1971). For the role of the Constitution of 1812, see Nettie Lee Benson, *The Provincial Deputation in Mexico: Harbinger of Provincial Autonomy, Independence, and Federalism* (1992) and Nettie Lee Benson, ed., *Mexico and the Spanish Cortes, 1810–1822* (1966). An excellent in-depth political history of liberalism and federalism in early independent

Chile is Simon Collier, *Ideas and Politics of Chilean Independence, 1808–1833* (1967). The study of liberalism as intellectual history in a single country has no equal to Charles A. Hale, *Mexican Liberalism in the Age of Mora, 1821–1853* (1968) and *The Transformation of Liberalism in Late Nineteenth-Century Mexico* (1989). The crucial Mexican Reform period is superbly handled by Richard N. Sinkin, *The Mexican Reform, 1855–1876: A Study in Liberal Nation-Building* (1979). The impact of the expropriation of church wealth is analyzed in Jan Bazant, *Alienation of Church Wealth in Mexico: Social and Economic Aspects of the Liberal Revolution, 1856–1875* (1971). Although liberalism in the twentieth century has not been adequately studied, the economic issues are outlined in Joseph L. Love and Nils Jacobsen, eds., *Guiding the Invisible Hand: Economic Liberalism and the State in Latin American History* (1988).

Additional Bibliography

Aguilar Rivera, José Antonio. *The Divine Charter: Constitutionalism and Liberalism in Nineteenth-Century Mexico.* Lanham, MD: Rowman & Littlefield Publishers, 2005.

González Prada, Manuel. "Nuestros Liberales." in *Horas de lucha* with *Páginas libres.* Cáracas: Biblioteca Ayacucho, 1976: 269-276.

Gootenberg, Paul. *Imagining Development: Economic Ideas in Peru's "Fictitious Prosperity" of Guano, 1840–1880.* Berkeley: University of California Press, 1993.

Paim, Antônio. *História do liberalismo brasileiro.* São Paulo, Brasil: Editora Mandarim, 1998.

Rodríguez O., Jaime E. *El manto liberal: Los poderes de emergencia en México, 1821–1876.* Jurídicas, Universidad Nacional Autónoma de México, 2001.

Tosto, Milton. *The Meaning of Liberalism in Brazil.* Lanham, MD: Lexington Books, 2005.

MAURICE P. BRUNGARDT

LIBERAL PARTY (CENTRAL AMERICA). Central American liberalism arose during the movement toward independence—achieved in 1821—in the heart of the Captaincy General of the Realm of Guatemala. Those who opposed the continuance of the system of privileges authorized by the crown and defended by the conservatives, who were considered crooked and reactionary, founded a group to advance the ideas of the French Enlightenment. They referred to the conservatives as "fevers" or "cowards." They were self-declared defenders of the ideology of the French Revolution and placed hope in the Spanish liberalism of the period.

In the beginning, both liberals and conservatives were criollos. The former desired federalism as a system of government for the United Provinces of Central America, while the latter sought centralism. The tension between these two factions would cause hate and bloodshed lasting into the twentieth century. After Central American independence, the liberals held power for several decades. In the 1830s Francisco Morazán headed a government that confronted the disinterest of the provinces, which failed to provide enough funds for its very existence. The conservatives capitalized on this situation, and the United Provinces were divided into the several states currently found on the isthmus. The conservatives dominated the political scene through the first half of the nineteenth century, the only exception being Costa Rica, where a patriarchal democracy predominated until 1948.

In Guatemala, the 1871 triumph of the so-called Liberal Revolution had a determining influence on the diffusion of liberalism in the other countries, especially in Honduras and El Salvador. Two decades earlier, the president of El Salvador, Gerardo Barrios, promoted both liberal principles and coffee production. In so doing, he followed the lead of Costa Rica's coffee industry under that country's liberal President Braulio Carrillo. In Guatemala, Justo Rufino Barrios increased coffee production and put an end to the conflicts between liberals and conservatives by imposing liberal absolutism. This was more forceful in Guatemala, El Salvador, and Honduras than in Nicaragua. A good number of new, land-owning mestizos were incorporated into the ranks of the liberals.

Liberal ideology spread by intellectuals such as Guatemala's Lorenzo Montúfar adopted the principles of French positivism and became rooted in the liberal, anticlerical, Latin American world of the time. Those who called themselves liberals defended freedom of expression, secular education, abolition of the death penalty, and limited terms of office for those in power. But they were far from actually realizing these ideals. In essence—excepting Costa Rica once again—the expanding coffee industry revitalized the feudal system. Democratic principles such as freedom of work and movement were impossible with the state finding it necessary to use its power to forcibly recruit laborers. Also, in an attempt to avoid the disorder caused by conflicts with the conservatives, freedom of thought and expression were also restricted. And although the liberals considered themselves anticlerical due to the relationship that existed between the church and the conservatives, liberal governments permitted the functioning of the church, and their members attended Mass, even, as in Guatemala, at churches whose possessions had been confiscated. All the Central American countries except Costa Rica distanced themselves from predominant liberal ideologies in the decades surrounding 1900.

The contradiction between what was preached and what was practiced was evident. The Liberal Party produced such memorable dictators as Justo Rufino Barrios, Manuel Estrada Cabrera, and Jorge Ubico in Guatemala, Terencio Sierra in Honduras, and José Santos Zelaya and Anastasio Somoza in Nicaragua. In their time, just as the conservatives did, the liberals resorted to foreign intervention for partisan rather than national reasons, inhibiting the march of progress. A mark in favor of liberal governments is that they established infrastructural bases that would aid free trade and production in archaic societies: the railroad, the telegraph, and electricity. This brought about the rise of a small, urban middle class. Nevertheless, social development was scarce. The economic growth that did occur was at the expense of peasants, who only grew poorer.

At the beginning of the twentieth century, the Central American isthmus became a colony for ever-increasing foreign interests: bananas for North America, coffee for Germany, and sugar for Great Britain. These interests surpassed the power of the state and brought about liberal dictatorships. Rather than being driving forces behind democracy, these foreign interests maintained the liberal status quo. The conservatives of course took every advantage to criticize the liberals, whose governments began to fall. In turn-of-the-century El Salvador, differences with conservatives dissolved when the oligarchy agreed to a power-sharing arrangement. Guatemala saw the fall of the dictator Jorge Ubico in 1944 and Nicaragua that of the Somoza dynasty in 1979. The survival of liberalism in Honduras is due to its articulating relatively democratic principles, as was the case in Costa Rica with its Revolution of 1948. Despite the fact that liberalism was no longer an important ideological tendency in the mid-1990s, the Liberal International had various Central American political parties as members.

See also **Liberalism.**

BIBLIOGRAPHY

Mario Rodríguez, *The Cádiz Experiment in Central America, 1808 to 1826* (1978).

R. L. Woodward, Jr., "The Rise and Decline of Liberalism in Central America: Historical Perspectives on the Contemporary Crises," in *Journal of Inter-American Studies and World Affairs,* 26 (1984): 291–312, and *Central America: A Nation Divided* (1985).

Additional Bibliography

Argueta, Mario. *La primera generación liberal: Fallas y aciertos (1829-1842).* Tegucigalpa: Banco Central de Honduras, 1999.

Gudmundson, Lowell, and Héctor Lindo-Fuentes. *Central America, 1821-1871: Liberalism before Liberal Reform.* Tuscaloosa: University of Alabama Press, 1995.

Mahoney, James. *The Legacies of Liberalism: Path Dependence and Political Regimes in Central America.* Baltimore: Johns Hopkins University Press, 2001.

FERNANDO GONZÁLEZ DAVISON

LIBERATION THEOLOGY. Liberation Theology represents a major change in the way Christianity approaches the social problems of Latin America. The changes began in the 1960s with the Second Vatican Council and the growth of Christian Base Communities. The first major publication was the Spanish edition of Gustavo Gutiérrez's *A Theology of Liberation* (1971). Gutiérrez is still a key figure.

Liberation theology has eight basic themes: (1) praxis (our action in the world) is the starting point of theology; (2) history is the locus of theology (God acts in historical time); (3) the world should be viewed as a whole, favoring the Hebraic holistic view over Greek dualism; (4) sin is social and systemic, not just individual; (5) God is on the side of the oppressed; (6) the present world order must be transformed; (7) the purpose of theology is primarily to act and to change the world, not just to understand it; (8) the kingdom of God (the reign of God) has begun in this life, and the purpose of humanity is to increase the kingdom by human actions in the world.

In the colonial period and until about 1960, the church generally promoted the fatalistic view that the poor would receive their reward in the afterlife, implying that they should not strive for social change in this life. Liberation theology uses biblical themes like the Exodus to teach the poor that God is on the side of the oppressed and favors their liberation. Thus the post-Vatican II Church (Second Vatican Council) has a "preferential option for the poor." The focus is to work for justice and social change in solidarity with the poor.

Liberation theology is closely connected to Christian base communities (*comunidades eclesiales de base*), small communities that began about 1960 to empower the poor to work for social change. There are thousands of base communities all over Latin America. The movement is strongest in Brazil, Nicaragua, and El Salvador, and weakest in Bolivia and Colombia.

There is much controversy over liberation theology and the base communities. They are a challenge to the current power structures in both civil society and the Catholic Church. Because they have empowered the poor in many countries, the Vatican fears a laity that sees power as coming from the grass roots and not just from the hierarchy. Liberation theology has redefined the church. Thus, Leonardo Boff's *Ecclesiogenesis: The Base Communities Reinvent the Church* (1986) defines the church as the people, and deemphasizes the institutional church. Governments are threatened by the poor masses who are organizing as a result of this movement and who have rising expectations of more control over their lives. These organized groups work for social change, sometimes in a revolutionary mode, as happened in Nicaragua in the 1980s.

Liberation theology is often linked with Marxism, but most liberation theologians do not accept all of Marxism, and certainly not its atheistic materialism. Rather they use Marxism as a source for their questions, not their answers. Liberation theologians use Marxist economic analysis to ask probing questions about the economic injustice endured by the poor in Latin America.

Leading Liberation theologian Leonardo Boff, Brazil, 1986. Beginning in the 1960s, the theology of liberation transformed the Catholic Church in Latin America and had a profound impact on society. Liberation theology aims to empower the poor and encourages faith-directed social action.

Liberation theology defines theology as reflection on praxis (experience); that is, theology is the work of the corporate community of Christians reflecting on the happenings in their lives in light of the Scriptures. Thus the poor who are members of base communities reflect on their economic and political oppression and see that God liberated his people in the Exodus and elsewhere. Their faith in the Scriptures gives them hope, and the organization of their Christian communities gives them the means. The power of religion is no longer a magic formula reserved for priests; it is also held by the people, according to liberation theology. Power is to be used for good, so politics is a proper field for Christian action.

Liberation theology has been criticized for being too naive about Marxist economics and Dependency Theory. In its early years biblical scholars criticized its weakness in exegesis (interpretation). Over the decades, the Catholic Church hierarchy, including the Vatican, largely has not supported the theology of liberation; it has appointed more conservative clergy in an attempt to restrain the movement. Its greatest competition from within Christianity comes from the Pentecostal and Evangelical groups, which concentrate on individual conversion and avoid community politics and social issues. These groups do not require literacy and commitment to social action, as the base communities usually do. In some areas of Brazil, for instance, the base communities are in direct competition with Pentecostals for the population in poor barrios or *favelas* (slums). Despite philosophical differences, however, these groups have on occasion collaborated.

Major Latin American liberation theologians include Gustavo Gutiérrez, a priest who lives in a poor section of Lima; Leonardo Boff, a former Franciscan seminary professor from Brazil who resigned his priesthood in 1992, after many battles with the Vatican; Juan Luis Segundo, an Uruguayan Jesuit; Jon Sobrino, a Spanish Jesuit who has lived in El Salvador for many years; Hugo Assmann, a Brazilian priest who founded the Departamento Ecuménico de Investigaciones (DEI) in Costa Rica, a Christian institute that publishes books on liberation theology; José Míguez Bonino, an Argentine Methodist pastor; Segundo Galilea, a Chilean priest who was director of the Latin American Pastoral Institute for many years and writes on Christian spirituality; and Pablo Richard, a Chilean priest who has worked at DEI in Costa Rica for many years. All but Gutiérrez and Galilea have spent most of their careers as university professors. A major publisher of liberation theology books is Orbis Books, in Maryknoll, New York.

In the history of ideas, liberation theology may be the first intellectual movement from Latin America that has been adopted as part of a global culture. European and U.S. cultures have sought, translated, and integrated a Latin American idea system into their own.

Liberation theology remains relevant in the twenty-first century despite a changed global context—the breakup of the Soviet Union and democratization throughout Latin America. Priests and laypeople demanding a "preferential option for the poor" generally face less violence than did their predecessors. Those who espouse liberation theology are paying attention to new issues, such as the environment, race, gender, and feminism. Protestantism continues to pose challenges to Catholicism, though some progressive Protestants have adapted liberation theology tenets and joined with Catholics in their struggles.

See also **Gutiérrez, Gustavo; Religion in Mexico, Catholic Church and Beyond.**

BIBLIOGRAPHY

Gustavo Gutiérrez, *A Theology of Liberation: History, Politics, and Salvation,* translated and edited by Sister Caridad Inda and John Eagleson (1973).

José Míguez Bonino, *Doing Theology in a Revolutionary Situation* (1975).

Jon Sobrino, *The True Church and the Poor,* translated by Matthew J. O'Connell (1984).

Phillip Berryman, *Liberation Theology: The Essential Facts About the Revolutionary Movement in Latin America and Beyond* (1987).

Leonardo Boff and Clodovis Boff, *Introducing Liberation Theology,* translated by Paul Burns (1987).

Juan Luis Segundo, *The Liberation of Theology* (1988).

Arthur F. Mc Govern, *Liberation Theology and Its Critics* (1989).

Alfred Hennelly, ed., *Liberation Theology: A Documentary History* (1990).

Warren Edward Hewitt, *Base Christian Communities and Social Change in Brazil* (1991).

Ronald G. Musto, *Liberation Theologies: A Research Guide* (1991).

Additional Bibliography

Barber, Michael D. *Ethical Hermeneutics: Rationality in Enrique Dussel's Philosophy of Liberation.* New York: Fordham University Press, 1998.

Boff, Leonardo. *Ecology and Liberation: A New Paradigm.* Translated by John Cumming. Maryknoll, NY: Orbis Books, 1995.

Dussel, Enrique D., and Eduardo Mendieta, eds. *Beyond Philosophy: Ethics, History, Marxism, and Liberation Theology.* Lanham, MD: Rowman and Littlefield, 2003.

Hopkins, Dwight N. *Introducing Black Theology of Liberation.* Maryknoll, NY: Orbis Books, 1999.

Schüssler Fiorenza, Elisabeth, ed. *The Power of Naming: A Concilium Reader in Feminist Liberation Theology.*

Maryknoll, NY: Orbis Books; and London: SCM Press, 1996.

Tombs, David. *Latin American Liberation Theology*. Boston: Brill Academic Publishers, 2002.

THOMAS NIEHAUS

LIBRARIES IN LATIN AMERICA. While its antecedents reach back to antiquity, the modern library emerged in the seventeenth century. Its features include a designed space, a catalog of the collection, and the concept of a repository of learning. But what most distinguishes the modern library from its predecessors is the elevation of service to its principal raison d'etre. The monastic custodians from Umberto Eco's *The Name of the Rose* who poisoned pages to deter their consultation are replaced by librarians whose mission is to minimize the interval between a request for information and its delivery.

As institutions, libraries reflect the values of the cultures they inhabit and the groups that sponsor them. Their histories reveal intellectual movements, trends in scholarship, and, most importantly, the importance of information to a society. Libraries in Latin America generally follow the same trajectory as their counterparts in Anglo-America and Western Europe. However, due to circumstances peculiar to the region and to countries within it, Latin American libraries have developed their own approaches to providing collections and services to their readers.

THE DEVELOPMENT OF NATIONAL LIBRARIES

Private and institutional libraries played an important role in the intellectual life of the colonial period. Wills and other inventories of property record the contents of early private libraries and demonstrate that literate citizens of the Iberian colonies had access to the full range of European science and humanistic thought. The Catholic Church, which monopolized theology and dominated education, constituted the colony's largest literate institution. Libraries built by secular clergy and religious orders served the colonial church and later became the foundational collections for repositories established by Latin American republics in the nineteenth century. One early ecclesiastical library that survived the vicissitudes of revolutionary struggle and republican anticlericalism is the Biblioteca Palafoxiana in Puebla, Mexico, which opened in 1646.

Independence brought the foundation of libraries, throughout Latin America, dedicated to the proposition that an educated citizenry would reject tyranny. Belief in the virtue of libraries inspired many revolutionary leaders to endow them with their prestige and with their personal collections. And prominent Latin American politicians, such as Domingo Faustino Sarmiento in Argentina and Mexico's José Vasconcelos, closely associated themselves with libraries, declaring them inseparable from progress. However, enthusiastic foundation did not insure continued prosperity. Many nineteenth-century libraries languished in an environment of war and regime change. An extreme case is the Peruvian National Library which was twice destroyed and rebuilt: when its collection was sacked in 1879 as a result of the nation's defeat by Chile in the War of the Pacific, and after its destruction by fire in 1943.

The current information landscape features a national library in nearly every Latin American country and a myriad of government, public, school, special, and university libraries. These institutions, some 4,000 in one reliable count, provide their users with a highly variable set of resources. Some rules of thumb apply. Most book and periodical collections show little treatment of subjects beyond national frontiers. National libraries are located in capital cities, though Sucre, not La Paz, is home to Bolivia's Biblioteca Nacional. Public libraries are not well developed, although Colombia provides a notable exception. However, recent developments—investments made from domestic and international sources, the onset of functioning library networks, and, most importantly, the advent of digital technologies—offer the prospect of fundamental change.

National libraries, sometimes closely linked to national archives, preserve important parts of their countries' cultural patrimony. Their collections vary in size, from the 150,000 items reported by Ecuador to Brazil's 5,000,000. National libraries hold the largest and richest historical collections of books and periodicals published in their countries, many acquired through deposit laws that require publishers to supply copies of their works to the national library before they can be sold to the public. These repositories also guard some truly distinguished special collections of books and manuscripts. Among the most illustrious are the Chilean Biblioteca Americana José Toribio Medina, of early American imprints; Colombia's Fondo Cuervo, 5,726 volumes specializing in linguistics; Guatemala's Sección del Fondo Antiguo, an aggregation of former monastic and conventual libraries; and Mexico's Sala Mapoteca, whose cartographic materials include some the earliest representations of American geography.

Since the nineteenth century, national libraries have enhanced access to their collections by publishing important edited series. Brazil's monumental *Anais da Biblioteca Nacional* (1876–) and Argentina's *Anales de la biblioteca* (1900–1915) are pioneers of a genre emulated by *Revista del Archivo Nacional* (1972–) from Peru, among others. National libraries have also provided bibliographic leadership in their countries. They compile and publish most of the region's national bibliographies and introduced professional education for librarians in Peru and Argentina.

PUBLIC LIBRARIES

Although Carnegie libraries were built in the English-speaking Caribbean as early as the 1910s, Latin America's public libraries are largely a development of the post–World War II era. Much of the impetus came from the United States and international organizations that promoted libraries as instruments for democratic change in Latin America. In words reminiscent of the early nineteenth century, UNESCO, the Organization of American States and Pope Paul VI's Vatican extolled libraries' democratizing, liberating, and educating virtues. The high point in this wave of library promotion came in 1968 with the foundation of the Escuela Interamericana de Bibliotecología (Interamerican Library School), with a grant from the Rockefeller Foundation.

Though international support flagged in the 1970s, two countries developed their own programs, each of which linked a system of public libraries with the national library. Cuba made public libraries a component of its highly effective literacy campaign. In the 1960s it developed a program that assembled book collections and provided professional staff training at the Biblioteca Nacional José Martí. In Venezuela, oil revenues and the work of a charismatic and well-connected national librarian resulted in the Red de Bibliotecas Públicas (1974–1994) (Public Library Network), which acquired, processed, and delivered collections of representative works to public libraries throughout the country.

A convergence of events in the past decade has produced renewed attention to libraries in Latin America. Projects long on the drawing board have come to fruition in new buildings for the national libraries of Peru and Bolivia. In both cases, their former homes were refitted to provide public and school library services. Colombia, which boasts what has long been one of Latin America's premier public libraries in Bogotá's Biblioteca Luís Angel Arango, has seen a resurgence of interest in public libraries. The Bill and Melinda Gates Foundation jumpstarted the enterprise by funding Red Capital de Bibliotecas Públicas (Capital Network of Public Libraries) in Bogotá. Not surprising given the donors' orientation, the libraries emphasize digital rather than paper information. Less predictable is the new libraries' architecture, designed to establish them as community centers in a country with a very difficult political climate. Recently, Medellín's mayor has taken a page from the Gates' notebook, constructing several attention-grabbing library buildings in some of the city's poorest areas.

DIGITAL LIBRARIES

Twenty-first century libraries have been fundamentally changed by the Internet. And while there is insufficient space to describe more than the broadest contours of the transformation, digital technologies will have the last words of this entry. The greatest noncommercial potential of digital libraries lies in its ubiquitous presentation of information. Several studies of digital libraries published in the 1990s suggest that Latin America and other regions of the developing world have the opportunity to bypass paper collections as they construct their research infrastructure. Where copyright barriers are low, Latin America has made considerable strides to develop this potential. The pioneering work of SciELO, the Scientific Electronic Library Online, the Red de Bibliotecas Virtuales de Ciencias Sociales de America Latina y el Caribe (Latin American and Caribbean Network of Social Science Virtual Libraries), and Hemeroteca Cientifica en Linea (Online Library of Scientific Periodicals) makes thousands of articles freely available to anyone with an Internet connection. Brick-and-mortar libraries in the region have used digital technologies to scan books, newspapers, and other sources of information in their collections, originally printed on paper. And government entities maintain portals that have become the sole sources of many official publications. Brazil is particularly active in distributing government publications in digital form; its Portal Oficial do Governo do Brasil is a model for the genre. Latin Americanists in search of single port of entry to the digital world should first consult the Latin American Network Information Center developed and maintained at the University of Texas.

See also **Education: Overview; Literacy; Universities: The Modern Era.**

BIBLIOGRAPHY

Asociación de Bibliotecas Nacionales de Iberoamérica. *Historia de las bibliotecas nacionales de Iberoamérica: Pasado y presente.* 2nd ed. Mexico City: Universidad Nacional Autónoma de México, 1995.

Krzys, Richard, and Gaston Litton. "Latin American Librarianship." In *Encyclopedia of Library and Information Science.* Vol. 14, edited by Allen Kent and Harold Lancour. New York: Marcel Dekker, 1975.

Leonard, Irving A. *Books of the Brave.* Berkeley: University of California Press, 1992.

Libraries Online

Archivo y Biblioteca Nacionales de Bolivia, Bolivia: http://www.archivoybibliotecanacionales.org.bo/.

Biblioteca Nacional del Perú: http://www.bnp.gob.pe/portalbnp/.

Biblioteca Palafoxiana, Puebla, Mexico: http://www.bpm.gob.mx/.

Hemeroteca Cientifica en Linea (Online Library of Scientific Periodicals), Universidad Autónoma del Estado de México, Mexico City: http://redalyc.uaemex.mx/.

Latin American Network Information Center, University of Texas at Austin: http://lanic.utexas.edu.

Portal Oficial do Governo do Brasil: http://www.brasil.gov.br/.

Red de Bibliotecas Virtuales de Ciencias Sociales de America Latina y el Caribe (Latin American and Caribbean Network of Social Science Virtual Libraries), Buenos Aires: http://sala.clacso.org.ar/biblioteca.

Red Capital de Bibliotecas Públicas (Capital Network of Public Libraries, BiblioRed), Bogotá: http://www.biblored.org.co/).

Scientific Electronic Library Online (SciELO), São Paulo: http://www.scielo.org.

DAVID BLOCK

LIBRARY OF CONGRESS, HISPANIC DIVISION.

The Hispanic Division of the Library of Congress oversees a collection of thirteen million items in all formats related to the Luso-Hispanic world. The interest of the Library of Congress in Iberia and the hemisphere began in 1815 when it acquired the private collection of Thomas Jefferson (1743–1826). Interest in the Americas grew in wake of the Mexican-American War (1846–1848) and the Spanish-American War (1898). In 1926 Archer Milton Huntington (1870–1955), a philanthropist, poet, and founder and president of the Hispanic Society of America, established a series of trust funds for the purchase of materials related to Spanish, Portuguese, and Latin American arts, crafts, literature and history. In 1929 Huntington provided for an ongoing consultant in Hispanic culture. The Spanish Augustinian friar and literary critic David Rubio served as consultant from 1931 to 1942. In 1936 Huntington made a donation to "equip and maintain a Hispanic reading room" and established the Hispanic Foundation, which in 1979 was renamed the Hispanic Division. The reading room opened its doors to the public on Columbus Day in 1939 and began playing a preeminent role in the emergence and development of Luso-Hispanic and Caribbean studies.

Lewis U. Hanke served as director of the Hispanic Foundation from 1939 to 1951. He brought with him from Harvard University a resource he had founded in 1935, the *Handbook of Latin American Studies* (published until 1950 by Harvard University Press and subsequently by the University of Texas Press). The *Handbook*, a collaborative undertaking of a network of scholars, was sponsored by the American Council of Learned Societies and the Social Science Research Council. Hanke made the *Handbook* the reference and bibliographic center of the Hispanic reading room.

In 1942 the Chilean literary critic Francisco Aguilera became the first full-time specialist in Hispanic culture, and in the 1950s he also served as editor of the *Handbook*. In 1943 Aguilera started recording Spanish and Latin American poets for the Library with the encouragement of Librarian of Congress Archibald MacLeish, himself a poet. The resultant Archive of Hispanic Literature currently contains recordings by 680 poets, prose writers, playwrights and essayists from Iberia, the Caribbean, and Latin America, as well as U.S. Latino and Hispanic writers, including eight Nobel laureates.

Another innovative scholar followed Hanke in 1952. Howard F. Cline was director of the Hispanic Foundation until his untimely death in 1971. He began including the growing number of social science publications in the *Handbook*. In 1966 he founded with a group of scholars the Latin American Studies Association, which in the early twenty-first century has about 6,000 members. Cline also reorganized the Conference on Latin American History and made it an affiliate of the American Historical Association. Cline was one of the founders of the Spanish and Portuguese Historical Studies. In 1955 Cline and Aguilera were among the founding members of the Seminar for the Acquisitions of Library Materials, an organization of librarians and area specialists. Cline also was instrumental in opening a Library of Congress field office in Rio de Janeiro. During the Cline years the Hispanic Foundation published numerous works in cooperation with scholarly associations and university presses. Cline's crowning achievement is the sixteen-volume *Handbook of Middle American Indians*, a collaborative undertaking of ethnohistorians, archaeologists, and anthropologists.

Mary Ellis Kahler, a historian of Brazil and Portugal as well as a librarian, served as chief from 1973 until 1978, when she left to become the director of the Library's field office in Rio de Janeiro. Under her leadership the division published major guides to Hispanic manuscript collections, such as the Harkness and Kraus collections.

William E. Carter, the director of Latin American Studies at the University of Florida and an anthropologist, served as chief from 1979 until his death in 1983. He changed the name of the division to "Hispanic Division," in keeping with the intention of the original founder. The division published a comprehensive *National Directory of Latin Americanists.* Carter took an interest in streamlining the Library's acquisitions activities. The literary critic Sara Castro Klaren was chief from 1984 until 1986, when she accepted a professorship at the Johns Hopkins University in Baltimore. During her tenure the division mounted a major exhibition on Miguel de Cervantes (1547–1616).

Cole Blasier, a political scientist and expert on international relations, and former director of the Center for Latin American Studies at the University of Pittsburgh, led the division from 1988 until 1993. He had been one of founders of the Latin American Studies Association, and is an expert on Latin American–Soviet relations. Blasier appointed John R. Hébert, assistant chief of the Hispanic Division, to coordinate the Library of Congress Quincentenary Program, which featured the major exhibit "An Ongoing Voyage, 1491–1992" and several publications. Keenly interested in the future, he supported automating the preparation of the *Handbook of Latin American Studies*, which in 1990 became the first automated annotated bibliography of the Library of Congress. He named Ieda Siquiera Wiarda the division's first Luso-Hispanic specialist and Barbara Tenenbaum the first Mexican specialist.

The historian Georgette M. Dorn became chief in 1994. She had been head of the Hispanic Reading Room and specialist in Hispanic Culture. Dorn and Dolores Moyano Martin, the editor of the *Handbook of Latin American Studies*, raised funds from the Andrew W. Mellon Foundation and the Fundación MAPFRE of Madrid, Spain, to carry out the retrospective conversion of the *Handbook*'s first fifty volumes, which was accomplished in 1995. Dorn also secured grants for bringing academic interns from Iberia, Latin America, and the United States to the Library. A major publication in 1995 was *Hispanic Americans in Congress, 1822–1995.* In 1996 the division developed Spanish and Portuguese interfaces to the Hispanic Reading Room and the *Handbook* Web sites. The division organizes public events, and the Hispanic Reading Room offers reference services in person and through electronic communications.

See also **Cline, Howard F.; Handbook of Latin American Studies (HAPI); Libraries in Latin America.**

BIBLIOGRAPHY

Library of Congress. *National Directory of Latin Americanists.* 3rd edition. Washington, DC: Author, 1982.

Library of Congress. *Library of Congress Hispanic and Portuguese Collections: An Illustrated Guide.* Washington, DC: Author, 1996.

Library of Congress. *Library of Congress Information Bulletin* 63 (December 2004): 239–242.

Library of Congress, Hispanic Division. Hispanic Reading Room Web site. Available from http://www.loc.gov/rr/hispanic.

Wauchope, Robert, ed. *Handbook of Middle American Indians*, 16 vols. Austin: University of Texas Press, 1964–1976.

GEORGETTE MAGASSY DORN

LIDA, RAIMUNDO (1908–1979). Raimundo Lida (*b.* 15 November 1908; *d.* 20 June 1979), Argentine literary scholar. Born in Lemberg, Austria (Lvov, Poland), Lida arrived with his family in Argentina at the age of two and was educated at the University of Buenos Aires, as a student of Amado Alonso and Pedro Henríquez Ureña. His literary scholarship represented the best of the philological tradition, while displaying a strong interest in aesthetics, philosophy of language, and newer critical methodologies. Lida became secretary of the Institute of Philology at the University of Buenos Aires under the directorship of Alonso. In 1948 Alfonso Reyes appointed him director of the Center of Linguistic and Literary Studies of the Colegio de México, where he also became the founding managing editor of the *Nueva Revista de Filología Hispánica (NRFH).* Lida's distinguished career as professor at Harvard University began in 1953; in 1968 he became Smith Professor of Romance Languages. His *Letras hispánicas: Estudios, esquemas* (1958) is a collection of essays on philosophy, Latin American literature (Rubén Darío, Gabriela Mistral, and Jorge Luis Borges, among others), and the prose works of Francisco de Quevedo, to which he dedicated much of his scholarly career. Nine of his later articles on Quevedo were collected posthumously as *Prosas de Quevedo* (1981). *NRFH* published a special issue titled *Homenaje a Raimundo Lida* (vol. 24, no. 1) in 1975. Known for his scholarly precision in addressing historical contexts and stylistic questions, and for the economy and subtle wit of his own critical style, Lida placed great emphasis on his role as mentor to several generations of Hispanists who shaped U.S. scholarship on the literature of medieval and early modern Spain and present-day Latin America.

See also **Alonso, Amado.**

BIBLIOGRAPHY

Ana María Barrenechea, "Bibliografía de Raimundo Lida," in *Nueva Revista de Filología Hispánica* 24, no 1 (1975): v–x; "En Memoria de Raimundo Lida," in *Revista Iberoamericana* 46, no. 112–113 (July–December 1980): 517–521.

Jorge Guillén, "Raimundo Lida," in *Insula: Revista Bibliográfica de Ciencias y Letras* 36, no. 421 (December 1981): 1, 3.

Iris M. Zavala, "Las letras hispánicas de Raimundo Lida (1908–1979)," in *Insula: Revista Bibliográfica de Ciencias y Letras* 36, no. 421 (December 1981): 4–5.

Additional Bibliography

Lida de Malkiel, María Rosa, and Victoria Ocampo. *Homenaje a Maria Rosa Lida de Malkiel y Raimundo Lida.* Buenos Aires, 1982.

EMILIE BERGMANN

LIENDO Y GOICOECHEA, JOSÉ ANTONIO (1735–1814). José Antonio Liendo y Goicoechea (*b.* 3 May 1735; *d.* 2 July 1814), Central American educator and scientist, founding member of the Economic Society of Guatemala. Born to a creole family in present-day Cartago, Costa Rica, Goicoechea was instrumental in introducing the Enlightenment to late colonial Central America. He entered the Franciscan order in his native Costa Rica, and it was during his studies to enter the order that he was first exposed to scientific training. In 1767 he earned a bachelor's degree from the University of San Carlos. He moved to Guatemala sometime during the late 1760s, and in 1769 he published a paper on experimental physics. In the 1780s Goicoechea visited Spain, where he was exposed to the "new learning" so popular at the time. He examined the libraries, botanical gardens, and natural history exhibits of Spain, an experience that provided him with the basis for his later work in Guatemala. He returned to Guatemala in 1788.

Along with other "enlightened" figures, on 20 November 1794 Goicoechea signed a petition to the crown calling for the establishment of an economic society modeled on those existing in Europe. He and his associates hoped that the society could help to enliven Guatemala's moribund economy, so backward in comparison with what Goicoechea had seen in Spain. But economic revival threatened many entrenched interests, and the crown ordered the suppression of the society in 1800, ostensibly because Goicoechea and another member, Antonio Muró, argued that Indians should be allowed to wear European-style clothing.

Goicoechea taught a generation of Guatemalans destined to lead the former Spanish colony as an independent nation. In addition to his article on

Indian clothing, he wrote articles on indigo cultivation, the Indians of Comayagua, and poverty in the capital city. He died in Santiago de Guatemala.

See also **Guatemala, Economic Society of.**

BIBLIOGRAPHY

John Tate Lanning, *The Eighteenth-Century Enlightenment in the University of San Carlos de Guatemala* (1956).

Elisa Luque-Alcalde, *La Sociedad Económica de Amigos del País de Guatemala* (1962).

Robert Jones Shafer, *The Economic Societies in the Spanish World, 1763–1821* (1958).

Ralph Lee Woodward, Jr., *Class, Privilege, and Economic Development: The Consulado de Comercio of Guatemala, 1793–1871* (1966).

Additional Bibliography

Raventós de Marín, Nury. "Dr. Fray José Antonio Liendo y Goicoechea, hombre de la ilustración." *Revista de la Universidad de Costa Rica* 31 (September 1971): 71–90.

MICHAEL POWELSON

LIHN, ENRIQUE (1929–1988). Enrique Lihn (*b.* 3 September 1929; *d.* 10 July 1988), Chilean poet. Lihn was the prominent Chilean poet of his generation and one of the most original voices of contemporary Latin American poetry. *La pieza oscura* (1963) (*The Dark Room and Other Poems* [1978]) marks the initial maturity of his poetry of biographical experience and the manifestation of the strange and ominous. *Poesía de paso* (1966) develops a poetry of circumstance, which emanates from visits to art museums and famous cities and travel to foreign countries. It parodies art criticism and the language of travelogues. *Escrito en Cuba* (1969) and *La musiquilla de las pobres esferas* (1969) present an ironic vision of life and poetry, which marks a new stage of Lihn's work.

During the military dictatorship Lihn produced a series of books, which included *Por fuerza mayor* (1974), *París, situación irregular* (1977), *A partir de Manhattan* (1979), *Estación de los desamparados* (1982), *El paseo Ahumada* (1983), *Pena de extrañamiento* (1986), *Al bello aparecer de este lucero* (1983), *La aparición de la Virgen* (1988), and *Album de toda especie de poemes* (1989), published posthumously. These books played with all kinds of allusions to social, cultural, and political circumstances. Lihn also wrote three novels of parody, a collection of short stories, *Agua de arroz* (1964), plays, and numerous essays, and he did a number of original drawings. *Diario de muerte* (1989) is a collection of poems written when the author was suffering from cancer.

See also **Literature: Spanish America.**

BIBLIOGRAPHY

Rodrigo Cánovas, *Lihn, Zurita, Ictus, Radrigán* (1986).

Cedomil Goic, *Historia y crítica de la literatura hispanoamericana* (1990), vol. 3, pp. 241–243.

Pedro Lastra, *Conversaciones con Enrique Lihn* (1980).

Dave Oliphant, "On translating the poetry of Enrique Lihn," *Dactylus* 6 (1986): 61–63.

Additional Bibliography

Aguilera Garramuño, Marco Tulio, and Fernando Burgos. *Los escritores y la creación en Hispanoamérica*. Madrid: Editorial Castalia, 2004.

Polanco Salinas, Jorge. *La zona muda: Una aproximación filosófica a la poesía de Enrique Lihn*. Valparaíso: Universidad de Valparaíso; Providencia: RIL Editores, 2004.

CEDOMIL GOIC

LIMA. Lima, capital city of Peru, a large metropolitan area with a population of 7.75 million (2005); also a province and department of the same name. Like other Latin American megalopolises, Lima's size continues to increase as people move from the interior provinces seeking better economic opportunities. Lima is by far the most important industrial, commercial, banking, and political center of the country. It is situated in the central coastal region and connected with the rest of the country by a network of highways, including the longitudinal coastal Pan-American Highway and the Central Highway, which reaches the central highlands. On the Pacific Ocean coast, the port of Callao was once separated from Lima by a few miles but now is part of a continuous urban sprawl. This area, known as the Metropolitan Area of Lima and Callao (AMLC), has a population of 8.2 million (2007), more than one-fourth of Peru's total population. In 1995 the area produced 44 percent of Peru's gross domestic product, illustrating its economic, financial, and industrial primacy.

Lima extends from and beyond the Rímac River valley, a narrow fringe of dwindling agricultural land similar to other valleys (Huara, Chancay, Chillón, Mala, Cañete) in the department that sporadically interrupt the vast coastal desert. These valleys were among the most productive sugar and cotton areas up to the 1920s, when the decline of export prices and growing real estate developments helped drastically reduce the arable land. Although situated in a tropical region, Lima has a humid and mildly cold climate during the months of April to November because of cloud cover from the effects of the cold Humboldt current off the coast. During the summer months of December to March, the weather is sunny and hot.

Before the arrival of the Spaniards, the valley of Lima was under the influence of the important religious center of Pachacámac. This god was accepted by Inca rulers and worshipped as the one responsible for the periodic earthquakes. For defensive reasons Francisco Pizarro abandoned his initial plan to make the central highland town of Jauja the political center of the conquered Incan territory. He decided instead to establish the future administrative center of the Viceroyalty of Peru in the valley of Lima. Thus Ciudad de los Reyes (City of the Kings), as Lima was known in early colonial times, was founded on 18 January 1535.

Under Spanish colonial rule, Lima consisted of well-protected squared blocks of dwellings at the center of which was the Plaza de Armas, the square bordered by the government and municipal palaces and Lima's cathedral, as well as the most notable families' houses. This core, characterized by one- and two-story houses of distinct colonial architecture, Moorish balconies, and ornate baroque and rococo churches, is today known as the downtown area of Old Lima. In one of the city's old sections, Pachacamilla, the syncretic and popular religious cult of the Señor de los Milagros (Lord of Miracles), invoked for protection against earthquakes (the most destructive of which occurred in 1630, 1687, 1746, 1941, and 1970), began initially among the urban slaves of the owner of the Pachacamac estate just south of Lima.

Lima's old boundaries were modified by the mid-nineteenth century, when Henry Meiggs was contracted to demolish the remnants of the old colonial wall surrounding Lima. At the time, Lima, Callao, and the port of Pisco south of Lima were the main beneficiaries of the income produced by the booming export of guano, a fertilizer deposited on islands off the central coast by seabirds. Beyond the post-Independence political struggle that made Lima the target of conspiracies and coups by military chieftains, a rising civilian economic and social elite built new houses and summer ranches in Lima, Miraflores, and Chorrillos. However, by the end of the War of the Pacific and the Chilean occupation of the city (1881–1883), Lima's urban development was in decline.

Starting in the first two decades of the twentieth century, and especially in the 1920s, Lima's real estate boom began in earnest. New avenues and streets raised the price of land in and around Lima. New neighborhoods funded by profitable financial institutions extended considerably the urban area. A process of gradual industrialization, a growing urban market, and a rise in commercial and other services since the 1890s provided jobs and entrepreneurial opportunities. By the 1950s, however, the first slums appeared on Lima's outskirts, the result of a housing shortage as the massive immigration from the interior provinces steadily increased. By the 1970s, Lima was surrounded by an impressive and populous ring of slums, which by the 1990s contained almost a third of the city's population. In these vast and precarious concentrations, called *pueblos jóvenes*, or "young towns," inhabitants seek better urban services. Some have been successful. Through organization, residents of older settlements such as Villa El Salvador and Comas obtained not only basic city services, but also legal standing. The city's growth rate began to slow in the 1970s.

As a political and cultural center, Lima is the head of the government and the judicial system and is home to several universities, among them the oldest in the Americas, San Marcos University. It is a city that has inspired the witty anecdotes of Ricardo Palma, the tragicomic short stories of writer Julio Ramón Riveiro, and the skeptical novels by Mario Vargas Llosa. The main financial center of Peru, Lima possesses disproportionate financial and economic resources as a result of the unequal distribution of wealth and income in Peru. Since Peru's return to democracy, which was consolidated in 2001, Lima's voting population has been decisive. The city continues to grapple with growth and administration of water, electricity, and sewage, and the municipalities of Lima and Callao still struggle with systematic problems in urban transportation. Despite the extended poverty and obvious corruption in the Peruvian capital, people in Lima can enjoy a wide variety and richness of food and folklore representing a blend of ethnic origins.

See also **Pachacamac.**

BIBLIOGRAPHY

José Barbagelata and Juan Bromley, *Evolución urbana de Lima* (1945).

David Collier, *Squatters and Oligarchs: Authoritarian Rule and Policy Change in Peru* (1976).

Alberto Flores Galindo, *Aristocracía y plebe: Lima, 1760–1830* (1984).

María Rostoworowski, *Pachacámac y el Señor de los Milagros* (1992).

Alfonso Quiroz, *Domestic and Foreign Finance in Modern Peru, 1850–1950: Financing Visions of Development* (1993).

Additional Bibliography

Charney, Paul. *Indian Society in the Valley of Lima, Peru, 1532–1824.* Lanham, MD: University Press of America, 2001.

Dietz, Henry A. *Urban Poverty, Political Participation, and the State: Lima, 1970–1990.* Pittsburgh, PA: University of Pittsburgh Press, 1998.

Higgins, James. *Lima: A Cultural History.* New York: Oxford University Press, 2005.

Jaime, Joseph A. *La ciudad, la crisis y las salidas: Democracia y desarrollo en espacios urbanos meso.* Lima: Alternativa Centro de Investigación Social y Educación Popular, 2005.

Jouve Martín, José Ramón. *Esclavos de la ciudad letrada: Esclavitud, escritura y colonialismo en Lima (1650–1700).* Lima: Instituto de Estudios Peruanos, 2005.

Ludeña Urquizo, Wiley. *Piqueras, Belaúnde, la Agrupación Espacio: Tres buenos tigres: Vanguardia y urbanismo en el Perú del siglo XX.* Lima: Urbes, 2004.

Mills, Kenneth. *Idolatry and Its Enemies: Colonial Andean Religion and Extirpation, 1640–1750.* Princeton, NJ: Princeton University Press, 1997.

Pérez-Mallaína Bueno, Pablo Emilio. *Retrato de una ciudad en crisis: La sociedad limeña ante el movimiento sísmico de 1746.* Seville, Spain: Escuela de Estudios Hispano-Americanos, 2001.

Sifuentes de la Cruz, Luis Enrique. *Las murallas de Lima en el proceso histórico del Perú: Ensayo acerca de la historia y evolución urbana de la ciudad de Lima entre los siglos XVII y XIX.* Lima: Consejo Nacional de Ciencia y Tecnología, 2004.

Van Deusen, Nancy E. *Between the Sacred and the Worldly: The Institutional and Cultural Practice of Recogimiento in Colonial Lima.* Stanford, CA: Stanford University Press, 2001.

Alfonso W. Quiroz

LIMA, ALCEU AMOROSO (1893–1983). Alceu Amoroso Lima (*b.* 11 December 1893; *d.* 14 August 1983), Brazilian writer, publicist, and Catholic leader, whose career started in 1919 as a literary critic for the recently founded Rio de Janeiro newspaper *O Jornal.* Cautious that his activities as a writer could detract from the respectability of his position as an industrialist, he chose the pen name Tristão de Athayde, which was destined to make him famous. As an intellectual and a writer, he embraced many different roles simultaneously. These included social activist on Catholic issues, political doctrinaire, essayist at large, professor of literature and, of course, literary critic, which was his main persona throughout his life, with only sporadic interruptions.

His life was marked and divided by the year 1928, when, hitherto religiously indifferent, he converted not only to Catholicism but to militant Catholic causes. For a long time he was an intellectual of the rightist, conservative, ideology, but, after the military political coup of 1964 in Brazil, he identified himself progressively with left-of-center positions. As a matter of fact, he eventually belonged to the so-called Catholic Left, not going so far, however, as to accept Liberation Theology.

Lima's influence was enormous, although it abated somewhat after his death. In any case, he personified the traditional Catholic thinker par excellence. Although he wrote hundreds of books and essays, the five volumes of his *Estudos* (1927–1933) may be taken as a largely representative introduction to the whole of his work.

See also **Liberation Theology.**

BIBLIOGRAPHY

Carlos Dante De Moraes, *Tristão de Athayde e outros ensaios* (1937).

M. A. M. Ancilla O'Neill, *Tristão de Athayde and the Catholic Social Movement in Brazil* (1939).

Vera Regina Teixeira, "Alceu Amoroso Lima," in *Latin American Writers,* edited by Carlos A. Solé and Maria Isabel Abreu, vol. 2 (1989), pp. 781–790.

Antônio Carlos Villaça, *O pensamento católico no Brasil* (1975) and *O desafio da liberdade* (*A vida de Alceu Amoroso Lima*) (1983).

Additional Bibliography

Andrade, Djalma Rodrigues de. *O paradoxo cristão: História e transcendência em Alceu Amoroso Lima.* São Paulo: Edições Loyola, 1994.

Reis, Vera Lucia dos. *O perfeito escriba: Política e letras em Alceu Amoroso Lima.* São Paulo: Annablume, 1998.

WILSON MARTINS

LIMA, JORGE DE (1895–1953). Jorge de Lima (*b.* 23 April 1895; *d.* 16 Nov. 1953), Brazilian poet, physician, politician. Lima was born in the northeastern state of Alagoas, where he completed secondary school. While drawn to the priesthood, he chose medicine as a career and went to Salvador to study. Having specialized in public health, he returned in 1915 to practice in Alagoas. In 1926, he became involved in public affairs, winning election to the state chamber of deputies as a candidate of the Republican Party. In 1930 he moved to Rio, where he was active in political causes while continuing his medical career. In 1946, he served on the governing council of the Federal District, and in 1949 he began to teach at the University of Brazil and the Catholic University.

Like many well-known intellectuals of the period, he participated in the Catholic movement of renovation. While the first poetry he published followed Parnassian models, Lima achieved recognition only in the second phase of modernism as a member of a spiritually oriented group in Rio. His poetry, inspired by his Christian faith, gave way to surreal verse of self-searching abstraction. In literary circles, Lima's most admired single work is *Invenção de Orfeu* (Invention of Orpheus, 1952), a dense ten-canto lyrical epic.

In terms of cultural nationalism, Lima's cult of northeastern regionalism, especially of the black cultural presence, is noteworthy. He was born into a family that had been active in the abolition movement, and a concern for the black experience marks his writing from the 1920s on. One of his most noteworthy works is *Poemas Negros* (1947), which invokes African deities. In addition to eighteen books of verse, Lima wrote five works of long fiction, but they are not of the same distinction as his verse. He also produced children's literature, biography, and art criticism.

See also **Modernism, Brazil.**

BIBLIOGRAPHY

Richard A. Preto-Rodas, "The Black Presence and Two Brazilian Modernists: Jorge de Lima and José Lins do Rego," in *Tradition and Renewal: Essays on Twentieth-Century Latin American Literature and Culture,* edited by Merlin Forster (1975).

Marie F. Sovereign, "The Double Itinerary of Jorge de Lima's Poetry," in *Luso-Brazilian Review* 11, no. 1 (1974): 105–113.

Luciana Stegagna Picchio, "Jorge de Lima: Universal Poet," in *Portuguese Studies* 1 (1985): 151–167.

Additional Bibliography

Espinheira Filho, Ruy. *O Nordeste e o negro na poesia de Jorge de Lima.* Salvador: Fundação das Artes, Empresa Gráfica da Bahia, 1990.

Farias, José Niraldo de. *O surrealismo na poesia de Jorge de Lima.* Porto Alegre: EDIPUCRS, 2003.

CHARLES A. PERRONE

LIMA, TREATY OF (1929). Treaty of (1929) Lima, a diplomatic agreement between Chile and Peru, signed on 16 April 1929, that finally resolved the Tacna-Arica Dispute. Under the Treaty of Ancón, signed in 1883, Chile retained temporary possession of the two provinces Arica and Tacna. It refused, however, to carry out the remaining terms of the treaty, which called for a plebiscite to determine the ownership of this territory. After years of haggling, Peru and Chile signed the Treaty of Lima. According to this arrangement, Chile retained Arica but Tacna was awarded to Peru along with 6 million pesos. While it settled the long-simmering boundary dispute between Chile and Peru, the Treaty of Lima unfortunately did not deal with Bolivia's loss of its seacoast, an issue (dating from the War of the Pacific) which continues to complicate the relationship between Santiago and La Paz to this day.

See also **Ancón, Treaty of (1883); Tacna-Arica Dispute; War of the Pacific.**

BIBLIOGRAPHY

Fredrick B. Pike, *Chile and the United States, 1880–1962* (1963), pp. 229–230.

William F. Sater, *Chile and the United States: Empires in Conflict* (1990), pp. 100–101.

WILLIAM F. SATER

LIMA BARRETO, AFONSO HENRIQUES DE (1881–1922).

LIMA BARRETO, AFONSO HENRIQUES DE (1881–1922). Afonso Henriques de Lima Barreto (*b.* 13 May 1881; *d.* 1 November 1922), Brazilian author. A fin-de-siècle realist writer, memorialist, and journalist from Rio de Janeiro, he produced novels, stories, and essays containing scathing critiques of the Brazilian plutocracy, the bureaucratic state, racism, and social injustice. The grandson of African slaves on both sides, he was for decades compared—almost always unfavorably—with Joachim Maria Machado De Assis. Although both wrote urban fiction set in Rio, Machado's style was generally considered more sophisticated in form, whereas Lima Barreto's fiction was seen as a poorly articulated paraphase of his own life.

His fictional works, including his four major novels—*Recordações do escrivão Isaías Caminha* (1909; Memoirs of the Clerk Isaías Caminha), *O triste fim de Policarpo Quaresma* (1915; *The Patriot,* 1978), *Vida e morte de M. J. Gonzaga de Sá* (1919; *The Life and Death of M. J. Gonzaga de Sá,* 1979), *Clara dos Anjos* (1923; *Clara dos Anjos,* 1979)—were based on an aesthetic in which literature is seen as "liberating from all forms of prejudice." Initially devalued as romans à clef or autobiographical recollections, these works have more recently received favorable critical reappraisals for their antiliterary attitude and direct prose style.

A fierce opponent of the highly rhetorical, French-inspired "literature of the salons" promoted by his contemporary Henrique Coelho Neto, Lima Barreto was also a self-proclaimed anarchist who espoused virulent anti-Americanism. His best-known novel, *O triste fim de Policarpo Quaresma,* is a utopian novel and an overt attack on the Republican government of Floriano Peixoto. The hero, a fanatic nationalist obsessed with Brazil's redemption, dies a madman. In his diaries, Lima Barreto, who died at age forty-one, describes his own life as a tragic one, marked by alcoholism, discrimination, and economic hardship.

See also **Coelho Neto, Henrique; Literature: Brazil.**

BIBLIOGRAPHY

Francisco De Assis Barbosa, *A vida de Lima Barreto* (1975).

Francisco De Assis Barbosa, "A. H. de Lima Barreto," in *Latin American Writers,* edited by Carlos. A. Solé and Maria Isabel Abreu, vol. 2 (1989), pp. 565–573.

Robert Herron, "*Isaías Caminha* as a Psychological Novel," in *Luso-Brazilian Review* 8 (December 1971): 26–38.

Maria Luisa Nunes, ed. and comp. *Lima Barreto: Bibliography and Translations* (1979).

Additional Bibliography

Dacanal, José Hildebrando. *Romances brasileiros: Contexto histórico, enredo, personagens principais, estructura narrativa, comentário crítico e exercícios.* Porto Alegre: Novo Século, 2001.

Nolasco-Freire, Zélia. *Lima Barreto, imagem e linguagem.* São Paulo: Annablume, 2005.

Oakley, R. J. *The Case of Lima Barreto and Realism in the Brazilian 'Belle Epoque'.* Lewiston: E. Mellen Press, 1998.

MIRIAM AYRES

LIMA CONFERENCE (1847–1848).

LIMA CONFERENCE (1847–1848). Lima Conference (1847–1848), a meeting of representatives of the republics of Bolivia, Chile, Ecuador, New Granada, and Peru at Lima. Initiated by Peruvian President Ramón Castilla, it was an attempt to revive the Bolivarian ideal of Latin American solidarity, and an early antecedent of the Pan-American Union, which sought to confront the dangers of European intervention through a defensive confederation. (In 1846 conservative Ecuadorian politician and former dictator Juan José Flores had conspired in Spain and France to establish a European monarchy in Ecuador.) The conference also considered the consequences and dangers for Latin America of the outcome of the Mexican-American War and the French and British intervention in Argentina. The Lima Conference was followed by a similar meeting in Santiago in 1856.

See also **Pan-Americanism.**

BIBLIOGRAPHY

Jorge Basadre, *Historia de la República del Perú,* vol. 2 (1963).

Additional Bibliography

Bushnell, David, and Neill Macaulay. *The Emergence of Latin America in the Nineteenth Century.* New York: Oxford University Press, 1994.

St. John, Ronald Bruce. *The Foreign Policy of Peru.* Boulder, CO: L. Rienner Publishers, 1992.

ALFONSO W. QUIROZ

LIMA E SILVA, LUÍS ALVES DE

(1803–1880). Luís Alves De Lima e Silva (duque de Caxias; *b.* 25 August 1803; *d.* 7 June 1880), patron of the Brazilian army and Brazil's most famous soldier. Caxias began his military career at age five as a cadet. His father, Francisco de Lima e Silva, was prominent in national politics and served as a member of the Regency from 1831 to 1835. Caxias saw action in the struggle for independence. During the Regency period (1830–1841), in which three political parties were grappling for power following the abdication of Dom Pedro I, he served the goals of the moderate Chimango Party by dissolving the unruly army created by the former ruler. Then, with a corps of four hundred loyal officers (the Sacred Battalion) heading up units of the newly created National Guard, Caxias suppressed various regional uprisings. In 1840 he was appointed president of Maranhão Province, which was in rebellion. The seizure of the town of Caxias was crucial in bringing that area under control, and he was given the title of baron (later viscount, count, marquis, and duke) of Caxias. Subsequently, he was able to suppress revolts in the provinces of São Paulo, Minas Gerais, and Rio Grande do Sul.

Caxias is remembered as the providential figure in establishing and maintaining political stability for the empire and as a very active member of the Conservative Party, serving as minister of war, deputy, senator, and, on two occasions, as prime minister. He characterized himself as being "more of a soldier than a politician." Others described him as "the most civilian soldier." Although he demonstrated his military abilities in the campaign to topple the Argentine dictator Juan Manuel de Rosas in 1852, it was as commander of Allied forces during the Paraguayan War (1865–1870) that Caxias met his greatest test both militarily and politically. Certain Liberal Party leaders in power at that moment subjected Caxias to a constant barrage of criticism in Parliament and the press, to which Caxias responded with a threat to resign. Dom Pedro II removed the Liberal regime and, although the episode was complicated by other factors, Liberal leaders blamed the whole affair on "militarism."

Caxias, his health broken, and bitter over the way civilian leaders had allowed partisan considerations to affect their obligation to support him and the army in the war, returned home to further evidences of ingratitude. No hero's welcome was arranged, he continued to be criticized in Parliament, and the size of the army was cut drastically against his wishes. Although he subsequently served in various governmental positions, Caxias died disillusioned with the treatment accorded him and the army by civilian political leaders of the empire.

In the view of Brazilian military leaders, Caxias stands as the example of how the army, under the leadership of patriotic officers, could serve as the principal institution for maintaining the national unity needed for governing an essentially undisciplined society whose civilian leaders purportedly have lacked an adequate sense of patriotism. Thus, the term *Caxiasism* becomes synonymous with the term *civics.*

See also **Rosas, Juan Manuel de; War of the Triple Alliance.**

BIBLIOGRAPHY

E. Bradford Burns, *A History of Brazil,* 2d ed. (1980), pp. 177–178, 282.

Affonso De Carvalho, *Caxias,* 2d ed. (1940).

Olyntho Pillar, *Os patronos das forças armadas* (1966), pp. 15–56.

Paulo Matos Peixoto, *Caxias: Nume tutelar da nacionalidade,* 2 vols. (1973).

Additional Bibliography

Izecksohn, Vitor. *O cerne da discórdia: A Guerra do Paraguai e o Núcleo Profissional do Exército Brasileiro.* Rio de Janeiro: Biblioteca do Exército Editora, 1997.

ROBERT A. HAYES

LIMANTOUR, JOSÉ YVES (1854–1935). José Yves Limantour (*b.* 26 June 1854; *d.* 26 August 1935), Mexican secretary of the treasury (1892–1911), a leader of the *científicos.* In 1892 Limantour became secretary of the treasury in the government of Porfirio Díaz after serving for a year as *oficial mayor* of the ministry under Matías Romero. Faced with a severe economic crisis, he initially was forced to secure a series of foreign loans at disadvantageous terms, to maintain Mexico's solvency, but eventually he reformed government finances to the extent that he produced a surplus in 1895 and for years thereafter. In 1899 he renegotiated the nation's foreign loans at significantly better rates.

His most pressing dilemma, however, was the decline in the value of silver during the 1890s. He determined that the best solution was to convert Mexican currency to the gold standard, and he did so in 1904.

Limantour presided over the period of Mexico's most dynamic economic development until after 1940. His policy was based on the encouragement of foreign investment. After 1900, however, Limantour, like Díaz, became increasingly concerned about the vast economic presence of U.S. investors in the country. In 1902, worried by the likelihood that the two largest U.S.-owned railroad companies, the Mexican Central and the Mexican National, would swallow up other lines, Limantour initiated the government purchase of two railroad companies, the Interoceanic and the National. When this jeopardized the delicate financial situation of the Mexican Central, Limantour engineered its takeover by the government in 1906. Two years later, he merged all these lines together to form the Ferrocarriles Nacionales de Mexico. In 1908 Limantour sponsored a new banking law that reined in the unfettered growth of banks and attempted to curb abuses and corruption that marked the banking system.

Despite his reforms, the Mexican economy experienced a severe downturn in 1907 due to the decline in mineral prices on the world market. Foreign investment temporarily dried up and the country plunged into a depression, which, when coupled with a series of disconcerting political developments, badly destabilized the Díaz regime.

Between 1900 and 1910 Limantour led the *científicos,* one of two major factions within the Díaz dictatorship. Technocrats who sought to modernize the nation through positivist principles, they believed fervently in rational decision making. The opposing faction was a group of Porfirian generals, the most notable of whom was Bernardo Reyes Ogazón, the political boss of Nuevo León. Their politics centered around personal relations with those who depended on their goodwill.

The rivalry between Limantour and Reyes took in more importance in 1904, when the aged dictator agreed to run for president for another term with a vice president for the first time. Two years earlier the finance minister had won a cabinet struggle that resulted in Reyes's ouster as minister of war and he triumphed again when Díaz chose *científico* stalwart Ramón Corral Verdugo as his vice president. During this period, the *científicos* obtained the governorships of several key states. The division in *Porfirista* elite ranks badly weakened the government when it confronted the challenge of rebellion in 1910.

On 25 May 1911 Limantour resigned his post as finance minister and went into exile in France, where he lived for the next twenty-four years.

See also **Díaz, Porfirio; Reyes Ogazón, Bernardo.**

BIBLIOGRAPHY

Daniel Cosio Villegas, ed., *Historia moderna de México,* 9 vols. (1955–1970).

Charles Hale, *The Transformation of Liberalism in Late Nineteenth Century Mexico* (1989).

José Y. Limantour, *Apuntes sobre mi vida pública* (1965).

Antonio Manero, *La revolución bancaria en México* (1957).

Walter F. McCaleb, *Present and Past Banking in Mexico* (1920).

Additional Bibliography

Maria y Campos, Alfonso de. *José Yves Limantour: El caudillo mexicano de las finanzas, 1854–1935.* Mexico City: Grupo Condumex, 1998.

MARK WASSERMAN

LINARES, JOSÉ MARÍA (1808–1861). José María Linares (*b.* 10 July 1808; *d.* 6 October 1861), president of Bolivia (1857–1861). Linares was born in Tilcala into an important Spanish family from colonial Potosí. Heir to one of the largest fortunes in Bolivia, he became the first civilian president in Bolivia's history. After the death of General José Ballivián in exile, Linares became the undisputed champion of the enemies of Manuel Isidoro Belzú (president, 1848–1855), who had mobilized Bolivia's lower classes to remain in power. A widely read and charismatic man, Linares, with his supporters, known as the "Rojo," conspired ceaselessly to overthrow the government. When they finally did so, he quickly established a dictatorship because he felt that this was the only way to reform Bolivian society. In particular, Linares attempted to rid the government of the corruption inherent in previous military regimes. Although a devout Catholic and proclerical, on other issues Linares was a precursor to later liberal administrations, fostering the mining industry and free trade and trying to inculcate European culture into Bolivian society. He tried to do this through dictatorial means, however, and ultimately failed. He was overthrown by members of his own administration in 1861.

See also **Ballivián, José.**

BIBLIOGRAPHY

Alcides Arguedas, *Historia de Bolivia: La dictadura y la anarquía* (1926).

Manuel Frontaura Argandoña, *El dictador Linares* (1970).

Herbert S. Klein, *Bolivia: The Evolution of a Multi-Ethnic Society* (1982), pp. 130–134.

Additional Bibliography

Vazquez Machicado, Humberto. *La diplomacia boliviana en la corte de Isabel II de España: La mision de José María Linares.* La Paz: Libreria Editorial "Juventud," 1991.

ERICK D. LANGER

LINARES, PEDRO (1906–1992). Pedro Linares (*b.* 29 June 1906; *d.* 26 January 1992), a Mexican papier-mâché artist (*cartonero*) who developed an expressive, one-of-a-kind style from folk art forms and traditional, ephemeral fiesta accoutrements. He is best known for two genres—the *alebrije* (fantastic animal) and the *calavera* (animated skeleton)—based on Holy Week Judas and Day of the Dead *calavera* miniatures.

Trained as a child by his father, Linares passed the family métier on to his three sons—Enrique, Felipe, and Miguel—who extended the imaginative possibilities of the medium. Grandsons Leonardo, Ricardo, and David have also taken up the work.

Alebrijes, a term coined by Linares, combine the body parts of serpents, scorpions, lions, reptiles, and butterflies and accentuate a playful outlook on reality. Intricate surface patterning in an array of bright colors and detailed tactile textures (spikes, bumps, curves) add dimension. Linares's *calaveras* touch on a pre-Hispanic rooted belief that death is an extension of life. Thus, *calaveras* engage in a wide variety of activities, such as guitar-playing, picture-taking, and skateboarding. Many of Linares's *calavera* scenes are inspired by the prints of José Guadalupe Posada, most notably La Catrina, El Panteón, Don Quixote, and revolutionary figures.

See also **Dia de muertos, Calaveras.**

BIBLIOGRAPHY

Rodolfo Becerril Straffon and Adalberto Ríos Szalay, *Los artesanos nos dijeron...* (1981).

Carlos Espejel, *Las artesanías tradicionalis en México* (1972); Judith Bronowsky, *Artesanos Mexicanos* (1978).

Victor Inzúa Canalis, *Artesanía en papel y cartón* (1982) and *El imaginativo mundo de los Linares* (1987).

Susan N. Masuoka, *En Calavera: The Papier-Mâché Art of the Linares Family* (1994).

SUSAN N. MASUOKA

LINARES ALCÁNTARA, FRANCISCO (1825–1878). Francisco Linares Alcántara (*b.* 13 April 1825; *d.* 30 November 1878), president of Venezuela (1877–1878). Linares Alcántara began his political and military career before the Federal War (1859–1863). He participated in that as a proponent of liberalism and remained a prominent figure in the Liberal Party. In 1873 President Antonio Guzmán Blanco named him first appointee of the republic, and as such he took on the duties of the first magistracy on various occasions.

With Guzmán's support Linares Alcántara was elected president in 1877. He brought together a cabinet composed mostly of civilians, promoted the politics of reconciliation by declaring a general amnesty, and supported freedom of the press and an administrative decentralization of funds destined for construction of public works. During his administration, a reaction against Guzmán, which Linares Alcántara tacitly encouraged, gained strength, and there were calls for a return to the Constitution of 1864. After Linares Alcántara's sudden death, his followers continued to participate in the reaction against Guzmán. The reinstatement of the Constitution of 1864 and the nullification of General Guzmán Blanco's statutes resulted in the Revindicadora (Revindicating Revolution) of December 1878, by which power was returned to Guzmán.

See also **Guzmán Blanco, Antonio Leocadio; Venezuela, Constitutions.**

BIBLIOGRAPHY

Francisco González Guinán, *Historia contemporánea de Venezuela,* vols. 10 and 11 (1954).

INÉS QUINTERO

LINATI, CLAUDIO (1790–1832).

LINATI, CLAUDIO (1790–1832). Claudio Linati (*b.* 1790; *d.* 1832), Italian printer. Linati was born in Parma, Italy. At seventeen he belonged to the Engraving Society in Parma. In 1809 he went to Paris, where he attended the atelier of Jacques-Louis David. In Belgium, Linati met the Mexican diplomat Manuel E. Gorostiza, who awarded him a loan and a contract from the Mexican government to bring the first lithographic press to Mexico. In 1825, Linati arrived in Veracruz with Gaspar Franchini, whom he knew through his political activities in Parma with the Carbonaris. In Mexico he founded *El Iris,* and in 1826 he joined Florencio Galli and the Cuban writer José María Heredia. Later joined by Onazio de Attellis, marques de Santangelo, an Italian, they used their printing skills in polemics. A liberal and revolutionary opposed to all forms of tyranny, Linati was exiled. The press, however, remained at the Academy of San Carlos, where a course in lithography was offered for one year; however, use of the press to illustrate publications was tightly restricted.

Back in Europe, Linati completed and published in Brussels a series of lithographs entitled *Les costumes civils, militaires, et religieux du Méxique* (1826?), which portrayed various Mexican costumes and customs. It is an important book in that it provides a glimpse of the way in which Europeans imagined the social life of a country that so attracted them. Linati died in Tampico, Tamaulipas, Mexico.

See also **Art: The Colonial Era.**

BIBLIOGRAPHY

Edmundo O'Gorman, *Documentos para la historia de la litografía en México* (1955).

Manuel Toussaint, *La litografía en México en el siglo XIX* (1934).

Additional Bibliography

Mathes, W. Michael. *Mexico on Stone: Lithography in Mexico, 1826-1900.* San Francisco: Book Club of California, 1984.

Solà, Angels. "Escocés, yorkinos y carbonarios: La obra de O. de Attellis, marqués de Santangelo, Claudio Linati y Florencio Galli en México en 1826." *Boletín Americanista* 26:34 (1984): 209-244.

ESTHER ACEVEDO

LINDLEY LÓPEZ, NICOLÁS (1908–1995).

LINDLEY LÓPEZ, NICOLÁS (1908–1995). Nicolás Lindley López, born on November 16, 1908, was one of the important Peruvian army leaders of the institutional military coup of July 18, 1962. The coup was officially justified by the allegation that the contested elections of that year had been fraudulent. None of the three main contenders in the elections, Víctor Raúl Haya De La Torre, Fernando Belaúnde, and Manuel Odría, had been able to obtain the number of votes necessary to become president. The formation of a coalition between the Aprista Party and Odría's party and the congressional designation of Haya as president prompted the anti-Aprista forces in the military to stage the coup.

Together with generals Ricardo Pérez Godoy (army) and Pedro Vargas Prada (air force) and Vice Admiral Juan Francisco Torres Matos, Lindley López formed the executive of an interim government that held new elections in 1963, which were won by Belaúnde. After the forced retirement of Pérez Godoy, Lindley López became the de facto president. The military government restored constitutional guarantees, attempted a localized agrarian reform, and confronted strikes and armed insurrections led by Hugo Blanco and Javier Heraud. The new technocratic attitude among the military was the basis for the far more consequential coup of 1968. Lindley López later served as the ambassador to Spain and resided there until his death on February 3, 1995.

See also **Peru, Political Parties: Overview.**

BIBLIOGRAPHY

Arnold Payne, *The Peruvian Coup d'état of 1962: The Overthrow of Manuel Prado* (1968).

Daniel Masterson, *Militarism and Politics in Latin America: Peru from Sánchez Cerro to "Sendero Luminoso"* (1991).

Additional Bibliography

Kuczynski, Pedro-Pablo. *Peruvian Democracy under Economic Stress: An Account of the Belaúnde Administration, 1963–1968.* Princeton, NJ: Princeton University Press, 1977.

Philip, George D. E. *The Rise and Fall of the Peruvian Military Radicals, 1968–1976.* London: Athlone Press, 1978.

ALFONSO W. QUIROZ

LINDO ZELAYA, JUAN (1790–1857).

Juan Lindo Zelaya (*b.* 1790; *d.* 24 April 1857), president of Honduras (1847–1852) and El Salvador (1841–1842). Lindo was born in Comayagua, Honduras, the son of Joaquín Fernández Lindo and Barbara Zelaya. He studied in Mexico as a youth and later was appointed interim colonial governor of Honduras by Governor José Gregorio Tinoco de Contreras (ruled 1819–1821). The Constituent Assembly of Honduras, then reappointed him to the post, at which he served from 21 November 1821 to 11 February 1824. While president of El Salvador, he established in 1841 the Colegio de la Asunción, which was later elevated in status, becoming the University of El Salvador in 1847. He also raised the Honduran Academía Literaria in status and renamed it the University of Honduras (1847). Its curriculum, under his direction, included law, philosophy, and Latin.

On 12 February 1847, Lindo became president of Honduras with the support of Honduran Conservatives and the approval of neighboring Guatemala. Technically, his term expired on 16 July 1848, when the 4 February 1848 constitution took effect, and his second term began on the same date and lasted until 1 January 1852. Domestic unrest due to disputes with Great Britain over loan agreements marred his term of office, as did Liberal revolts in Tegucigalpa on 4 February 1849 and 12 February 1850, which forced him to flee. Liberal forces under General Santos Guardiola, his successor, were eventually suppressed with the aid of Guatemala and El Salvador. Lindo's refusal to run for reelection and his belief in the 1848 constitution led him to allow a Liberal to take office unopposed.

See also **Guardiola, Santos; Honduras.**

BIBLIOGRAPHY

Rómulo E. Durón y Gamero, *Biografía de don Juan Nepomuceno Fernández Lindo* (1932).

Luis Mariñas Otero, *Honduras,* 2d ed. (1983).

Additional Bibliography

Mejía, Medardo. *Don Juan Lindo: El frente nacional y el anticolonialismo.* Tegucigalpa: Editorial Universitaria, 1993.

JEFFREY D. SAMUELS

LINE OF DEMARCATION (1493).

Line of Demarcation (1493), papal donation of temporal authority in the Indies to the Spanish crown. Following the successful completion of Christopher Columbus's first voyage to the New World, Pope Alexander VI (a Spaniard) extended to the crown of Castile by a series of bulls (May–September 1493) dominion over all those lands and peoples to the west of a meridian that were not already under the control of another Christian prince. The line ran roughly 100 leagues west of the Azore or Cape Verde Islands. Other western European seafaring nations, especially England and

France, questioned the claims: Francis I purportedly asked to be shown the clause in Adam's will excluding the French from a share in the newly discovered lands; the English outright rejected papal authority in the matter; and the Portuguese demanded bilateral discussions with the Spanish to redraw the boundary, which resulted in the Treaty of Tordesillas.

See also **Tordesillas, Treaty of (1494).**

BIBLIOGRAPHY

C. H. Haring, *The Spanish Empire in America* (1963).

Lyle N. McAlister, *Spain and Portugal in the New World: 1492–1700* (1984).

Additional Bibliography

Bernand, Carmen. *Descubrimiento, conquista y colonización de América a quinientos años.* México: Consejo Nacional para la Cultura y las Artes, 1994.

Elliott, John Huxtable. *Empires of the Atlantic World: Britain and Spain in America, 1492-1830.* New Haven, CT: Yale University Press, 2006.

Fernández-Armesto, Felipe. *The Americas: A Hemispheric History.* New York: Modern Library, 2003.

Kamen, Henry. *Empire: How Spain Became a World Power, 1492-1763.* New York: HarperCollins, 2003.

NOBLE DAVID COOK

LINHA DURA.

Linha Dura (hard line), the term used to characterize the authoritarian views of a faction of young officers (called *duristas,* or hard-liners) in the Brazilian military following the 1964 coup d'état. Aimed first at armed revolutionaries and left-wing political activists, the hard-line was expanded to include union leaders, social workers, journalists, students, and teachers, under the alleged effort to fight communism. The ascendancy of the hard-liners (1968–1974) was heralded on 13 December 1968 by the declaration of Institutional Act 5, which abrogated civil liberties, suspended habeas corpus, adjourned Congress indefinitely, and gave the government discretionary power to purge the bureaucracy, military, universities, and trade unions. The incapacitation by a stroke in 1969 of President Artur da Costa E Silva, who had argued for a quick return to constitutional government, further facilitated the in-house coup known as "the revolution within the revolution." General Emílio Garrastazú de Médici was named president (1969–1974) by the military high command and presided over the most violent and repressive period of the regime. While the economy boomed, arrests, torture, and illegal detention aroused vociferous opposition domestically and internationally. The 1974 inauguration of Ernesto Geisel, who with his colleague General Golbery Couto y Silva represented moderate factions within the military government, marked the beginning of a politics of *abertura,* or "opening." The strategy of gradual liberalization was repeatedly challenged by hard-liners, but prevailed through a precarious alliance with civil groups, including women's movement organizations, labor organizers, the Brazilian Bar Association, and leaders of the Brazilian Catholic Church. Geisel's dismissal of hard-liner Army Minister Sylvio Frota in 1977 and the amnesties extended to political exiles and prisoners in 1978 and 1979 signaled the ascension of *abertura* politics and the decline of the hard-line.

See also **Institutional Acts.**

BIBLIOGRAPHY

Peter Flynn, *Brazil: A Political Analysis* (1978).

Maria Helena Moreira Alves, *State and Opposition in Military Brazil* (1986).

Alfred Stepan, ed., *Democratizing Brazil* (1989).

Additional Bibliography

Alonso, Angela Maria. *Idéias em movimento: A geração 1870 na crise do Brasil-Império.* São Paulo: ANPOCS: Paz e Terra, 2002.

Castro, Celso. *Os militares e a república: Um estudo sobre cultura e ação política.* São Paulo: Rio de Janeiro: J. Zahar Editor, 1995.

Couto, Ronaldo Costa. *História indiscreta da ditadura e da abertura: Brasil: 1964–1985.* Rio de Janeiro: Editora Record, 1998.

FRANCESCA MILLER

LINIERS Y BREMOND, SANTIAGO DE

(1753–1810). Santiago de Liniers y Bremond (*b.* 25 July 1753; *d.* 26 August 1810), viceroy of Río de la Plata (1807–1809). Born in Niort,

France, Liniers was the son of a French naval officer from the Poitou region. At age twelve, he joined the Order of Malta as page to the grand master. He entered the service of the Spanish king in 1774 as an army officer in the Moroccan campaigns. Liniers first arrived in the Río de la Plata with the Cevallos expedition (1776) and returned in 1788. Married to María Martina de Sarratea, daughter of Martín de Sarratea, a prominent Spanish-born merchant, Liniers served as the head of the naval squadron charged with the protection of Montevideo, and then as interim governor of Misiones.

Present at the time of the second British invasion (1806–1807), Liniers was instrumental in reorganizing the militia that defeated the British invaders. Awaiting the arrival of a new viceroy to replace the discredited Sobremonte, who had fled during the invasions, Liniers was named interim viceroy and given the title of count of Buenos Aires. He was instrumental in putting down the Álzaga rebellion of January 1809 and ruled until replaced by the newly arrived Viceroy Cisneros in August 1809. He then retired to Alta Gracia, Córdoba.

Upon hearing of the dramatic action of the *cabildo abierto* (open town council meeting) of Buenos Aires, Liniers helped organize the royalist opposition to the Buenos Aires revolutionary troops. He was captured and executed as a traitor to the revolutionary cause.

See also **Río de la Plata.**

BIBLIOGRAPHY

Paul Groussac, *Santiago de Liniers* (1943).

Enrique Udaondo, *Diccionario biográfico colonial argentino* (1945), pp. 502–505.

Additional Bibliography

Aguirre, Gisela. *Santiago de Liniers.* Buenos Aires: Editorial Planeta Argentina, 2000.

Lozier Almazán, Bernardo P. *Liniers y su tiempo.* Buenos Aires: Emecé Editores, 1990.

SUSAN M. SOCOLOW

LINS, OSMAN DA COSTA (1924–1978).

Osman da Costa Lins (*b.* 5 July 1924; *d.* 8 July 1978), Brazilian writer. A prolific author whose body of work includes short stories, drama, essays, and teleplays, Lins is best known for several novels exemplifying an important existentialist trend in Brazilian literature between the 1950s and the early 1980s. Lins's themes concerned the moral and ethical issues that must be confronted in everyday life, while the formal aspect of his fiction steadily evolved from simplicity to complex experimentation in language. His efforts to create innovative narrative techniques stand out in one of his best novels, *Avalovara* (1973; Eng. trans. 1980).

See also **Literature: Brazil.**

BIBLIOGRAPHY

Anatol Rosenfeld, "The Creative Narrative Processes of Osman Lins," in *Studies in Short Fiction* 8, no. 1 (1971): 230–244.

Additional Bibliography

Ferreira, Ermelinda. *Vitral ao sol: Ensaios sobre a obra de Osman Lins.* Recife: Editora Universitária da UFPE, 2004.

Igel, Regina. *Osman Lins: Uma biografia literária.* São Paulo: T.A. Queiroz Editor em convênio com o Instituto Nacional do Livro [e] Fundação Nacional Pró-Memória/MINC, 1988.

Simas, Rosa. *Circularity and Visions of the New World in William Faulkner, Gabriel Garcia Marquez, and Osman Lins.* Lewiston, NY: E. Mellen Press, 1993.

PEDRO MALIGO

LINS DO REGO, JOSÉ (1901–1957).

José Lins Do Rego (*b.* 3 June 1901; *d.* 12 September 1957), Brazilian writer. Author of numerous volumes of speeches, personal and travel memoirs, and children's literature, Lins do Rego is known principally as a novelist, most notably for the six volumes of the Sugarcane Cycle. Critics have traditionally included him in a group referred to as the Northeastern Generation of 1930, a half dozen novelists whose fiction came to dominate the Brazilian literary scene during the 1930s and 1940s. Indeed, he and another member of the group, Jorge Amado, took turns writing many of the best-sellers at the time, and both had a sufficiently high profile to merit the attentions, generally unfavorable, of the government of Getúlio Vargas. He was also affiliated with the Region-Tradition movement founded in 1926 by Brazilian sociologist Gilberto Freyre, at least in the sense that his novels seemed to be the most faithful to the tenets of the regionalist movement.

Lins do Rego was born into the rural aristocracy and thus had a unique insider's perspective on the society he depicted in his works. He was born on his grandfather's plantation in Paraíba, was raised by his maiden aunts after his mother's death when he was only eight months old, and attended both a boarding school and law school in Recife. Each of these episodes is the theme of one of the novels of the cycle. A common criticism of his work as a novelist, in fact, is that he was more of a memorialist than a creator, but this perceived shortcoming is an advantage from the perspective of social history, for his novels provide perhaps the most complete, and certainly the most readable, portrait of the rural Brazilian society of the period. Lins do Rego is regarded as one of the masters of the "sociological novel," a rather vague category referring to his portrayal of characters who are at once affecting and convincing.

Freyre's notion of regionalism, detailed in his *Manifesto regionalista de 1926*, grew out of his opposition to the modernists of Rio de Janeiro and São Paulo, whom he considered too citified, too cosmopolitan, and too European to qualify as spokesmen for a still essentially rural Brazil. Today the manifesto sounds almost quirky, with its praise for regional cuisine and such things as palm thatch roofing, but it was at the time as much at the center of intellectual debate as the political question of left versus right, a matter rendered nearly moot by the Vargas coup of 1930 and utterly so by the declaration of the Estado Novo in 1937.

The modernists became urbane vanguardists, and the regionalists of the Generation of 1930 defined themselves as chroniclers of that "other," more real Brazil with its mansions and shanties, a Brazil in which the heritage of a colonial past lay just beneath the surface. Regionalism versus modernism was at the center of intellectual ferment of the period, although in hindsight it is clear that both groups were attempting, by quite different avenues, to accomplish the same end—to create a literature that could be clearly identified as truly Brazilian. The unstated agenda, and the factor that made Lins do Rego such an important writer of the time, was that the regionalists were consciously writing social documents, a posture that whether intentional or not, made the creation of art a secondary part of the exercise. There is no doubt that the public preferred such artlessness, but it is a factor that inhibits such documents from translating well into subsequent decades. From a historical perspective, however, this unadorned memorialism has its positive value, because the appeal of these works at the time of their publication was based in large degree on the fact that the Brazilian reading public *recognized* the characters and scenes and stories, which meant that their fidelity to the realities of Brazilian society was the key to their success.

It is not clear why the Vargas government regarded such writing as a threat to its well-being, but perhaps the very accuracy of the social portrayals made the government edgy. There is also some suspicion that Lins do Rego's works were targeted simply as a matter of guilt by association, because he was associated in the minds of many with other members of the generation who were in fact also members of the illegal Communist Party and whose works often made these sympathies more than evident. But the clearest sentiment evident in his works themselves is probably nostalgia, hardly a subversive quality.

The Sugarcane Cycle is largely a chronological account of the life of Carlos de Melo, who, like Lins do Rego, is the scion of a wealthy planter family. The first novel, *Menino de Engenho* (1932), deals with the early years of the timid and lonely young man, and the second, *Doidinho* (1933), continues with his trials at boarding school. *Bangüê* (1934) chronicles the years spent in Recife in law school, and *O Moleque Ricardo* (1935) tells the similar story of the black childhood companion of Carlos, who moves to the city and becomes involved in a union movement. *Usina* (1936) recounts the death of Ricardo and the transformation of the Santa Rosa plantation from the old labor-intensive plantation system into a modern, mechanized (and dehumanized) factory.

The final novel, not originally included in the cycle by its author, is also universally regarded as his best—*Fogo Morto* (1943). This volume, a tripartite narrative centering on three very different people, contains not only the best-drawn characters but also the fullest insights into a society on the verge of decadent collapse. The first central character is a saddle maker who lives on the plantation of Seu Lula, the second character, a member of the hereditary aristocracy who is the central character of the second part of the novel. The final segment features the third character, a local eccentric and his manic and misdirected exploits. Although each character is from a different social stratum and each has his own foibles and strengths, the narrative is in essence the story of a social system in which the fabric seems to be unraveling, where all assumptions about outcomes are thwarted. Lins do Rego also wrote fiction about other uniquely Brazilian and mostly rural issues, such as messianic movements and banditry, but his best works remain those most closely drawn from his own experiences. It is certainly this latter body of work that assures his place as one of the most important Brazilian writers of the century.

See also **Literature: Brazil; Modernism, Brazil; Regionalism.**

BIBLIOGRAPHY

José Aderaldo Castelo, *José Lins do Rego: Modernismo e regionalismo* (1961).

Bobby J. Chamberlain, "José Lins do Rego," in *Latin American Writers,* vol. 2, edited by Carlos Solé and Maria Isabel Abreu (1989), pp. 909–913.

Eduardo F. Coutinho and Ângela Bezerra de Castro, *José Lins do Rego* (1990).

Fred P. Ellison, *Brazil's New Novel: Four Northeastern Masters* (1954), pp. 45–79.

Claude L. Hulet, *Brazilian Literature,* vol. 3 (1975), pp. 271–272.

Wilson Martins, *The Modernist Idea* (1975), pp. 285–288.

Fogo Morto Borzoi Anthology of Latin American Literature, vol. 1 translated by Susan Hertelendy (1977), pp. 446–458.

Álvaro Lins, Otto Maria Carpeaux, and Franklin Thompson, *José Lins do Rego* (1952).

João Pacheco, *O mundo que José Lins do Rego Fingiu* (1958).

Plantation Boy, translated by Emmi Baum (1966).

Pureza: A Brazilian Novel, translated by Lucie Marion (1948).

Additional Bibliography

Antunes, Fatima M. R. Ferreira. *"Com brasileiro, não há quem possa!": Futebol e identidade nacional em José Lins do Rego, Mário Filho e Nelson Rodrigues.* São Paulo: Editora UNESP, 2004.

Russotto, Márgara. *Arcaísmo y modernidad en José Lins do Rego: Doidinho y la formación del narrador.* Caracas: Fondo Editorial Tropikos, 1990.

Trigo, Luciano. *Engenho e memória: O nordeste do açúcar na ficção de José Lins do Rego.* Rio de Janeiro: Academia Brasileira de Letras: Topbooks, 2002.

JON S. VINCENT

LINSEED. The flax plant has been cultivated in Europe, North Africa, and the Middle East—especially Egypt, the Caucasus, and the Black Sea—since antiquity. In Latin America it has been cultivated in Mexico, Chile, and Brazil. In Argentina, however, it became an especially important crop that provided the necessary infrastructure for several industries. Agronomist Martín José de Altolaguirre first introduced it to Argentina as an experiment in 1784. He grew the plant at his farm near the convent of La Recoleta in Buenos Aires and then extracted oil from the seed (linseed). In Argentina the plant was more greatly appreciated for that seed than for its use in the production of linen. After 1850 European immigrants began to cultivate the plant in Buenos Aires, Santa Fe, Córdoba, and Entre Ríos provinces. From 1899 until the 1940s, the acreage devoted to its cultivation steadily increased.

At the beginning of the twentieth century, the Bemberg Company began growing linseed in Baradero and Rojas in the province of Buenos Aires. A key ingredient in the production of paints and printer's ink, linseed was exported as raw material for European manufacturers until the 1950s. By 1913 Argentina was exporting more than a million tons of linseed each year and was devoting more acreage to this crop than any other country. The value of Argentine linseed exports was exceeded only by that of wheat, corn, and oats.

During World War I, Argentine exporters began to ship crushed, rather than whole, seed in order to reduce cargo space. The Depression and the development of modernized seed processing stimulated import substitution so that companies previously involved in exporting seed began to invest in domestic processing plants to extract oil and other by-products. World War II accelerated the growth of domestic seed oil production, and exports of Argentine linseed oil grew dramatically until the industry began a gradual decline after the 1960s. Overall world demand has not changed dramatically since the 1960s. Still, Argentina remains the largest exporter of linseed oil.

BIBLIOGRAPHY

Carlos De Alberti Girola, *El cultivo del trigo para la producción de la semilla en la Argentina* (1915).

Raúl Ramella, *El lino oleaginoso* (1944).

Emilio A. Gruget, *Aprovechamiento industrial de los rastrojos del lino oleaginoso* (1949).

Carlos Remussi, *El lino textil* (1951).

Additional Bibliography

Barsky, Osvaldo, and Jorge Gelman. *Historia del agro argentino: Desde la conquista hasta fines del siglo XX.* Buenos Aires: Grijalbo Mondadori, 2001.

DONNA J. GUY

LIRCAY, BATTLE OF.

LIRCAY, BATTLE OF. Battle of Lircay (17 April 1830), a seminal military encounter which brought the Conservative Party to power in Chile. Tired of political unrest, a combination of Conservative and regional interests selected General Joaquín Prieto Vial to lead a coup. Pro-government forces under General Ramón Freire Serrano advanced from Santiago, only to be defeated at the Lircay River. The Conservative triumph, while perhaps issuing in what became known as the "weight of the night" ended the political anarchy that had plagued Chile since the fall of Bernardo O'Higgins in 1823. After Lircay, Chile would enjoy stability, albeit at some substantial damage to political rights, that would bring economic recovery and national progress.

See also **Chile, Political Parties: Conservative Party.**

BIBLIOGRAPHY

Luis Galdames, *A History of Chile* (1941), p. 236.

Simon Collier, *Ideas and Politics of Chilean Independence, 1808–1833* (1967), pp. 327–328, 348.

Additional Bibliography

Collier, Simon. *Chile: The Making of a Republic, 1830-1865.* New York: Cambridge University Press, 2003.

Eyzaguirre, Jaime. *Historía de Chile.* 2 v. in 1. Santiago, Zig-Zag, 1973.

WILLIAM F. SATER

LISBOA, ANTÔNIO FRANCISCO.

See **Aleijadinho.**

LISBOA, JOAQUIM MARQUES (1807–1897).

Joaquim Marques Lisboa (Almirante Tamandaré; *b.* 13 December 1807; *d.* 20 March 1897), patron of the Brazilian navy. Tamandaré graduated from the Naval Academy in 1826. He was appointed to noble status (baron, viscount, count, and marquis Tamandaré) by Dom Pedro II for suppressing various rebellions, including the Confederation of the Equator (1824), the Balaiada Rebellion (1838–1841), and the Praieira Revolt (1848–1849). As commander of Brazilian naval forces in the Rio de La Plata in 1864, Tamandaré was involved in bringing pressure on the Uruguayan regime of Atanásio Cruz Aguirre by leading the attacks against Salto and Paissandú. He supported the mission of Counselor José Antônio Saraiva, who was seeking satisfaction of Brazilian claims against the Uruguayan government. Tamandaré's testy, impulsive nature created problems for himself and the Brazilian government. He incurred the displeasure of the diplomatic corps when he tried to impose a blockade on Montevideo during a time of peace. He quarreled bitterly with other leaders of the high command of the forces of the Triple Alliance, and, despite numerous minor victories, he was strongly criticized for hesitating to attack the Paraguayan stronghold of Humaitá. He was finally relieved of his command in December 1866 and returned to Brazil, where, because of his long service, he was maintained on the active list until shortly after the creation of the Republic (1889). Tamandaré carried out an endless campaign to exonerate his name, a goal that was finally achieved via the Supreme Military Tribunal a few days before his death. His birthday is celebrated as Sailors' Day.

See also **War of the Triple Alliance.**

BIBLIOGRAPHY

Pedro Calmon, *História do Brasil,* vol. 7 (1963), pp. 1788, 1791–1792, 1824, 1871, 1890.

Pelham Horton Box, *The Origins of the Paraguayan War* (1967), pp. 124, 130, 220–224, 233, 237–239.

Charles J. Kolinski, *Independence or Death! The Story of the Paraguayan War* (1965), pp. 13, 58, 106, 128, 139.

Olyntho Pillar, *Os patronos das forças armadas,* vol. 1 (1961), pp. 148–153.

Additional Bibliography

Lima, José Francisco de. *Marquês de Tamandaré, patrono da Marinha: (seu perfil histórico).* Rio de Janeiro: F. Alves, 1983.

Vianna Filho, Arlindo. *As razões e as paixões do patrono de Marinha do Brasil.* Rio de Janeiro: Imprensa Naval, 1991.

ROBERT A. HAYES

LISBON EARTHQUAKE. The Lisbon earthquake, a devastating disaster, occurred on the morning of November 1, 1755, the Feast of All Saints. It struck with extraordinary intensity in a series of violent shocks that left Lisbon's central commercial district and major public buildings, churches, and palaces in ruins. But the major cause of damage derived from the ensuing fire, which in the following six days razed most of the city's other neighborhoods. Although casualty figures vary enormously, at least 15,000—and perhaps as many as 30,000—people died from the quake and fire. Hundreds of thousands were left homeless, and extensive damage remained conspicuous into the nineteenth century.

The earthquake had an enormous effect on Portugal's economy and politics. It ruined many Lisbon merchants, and the enormous cost of rebuilding the city and its infrastructure consumed much of the country's and empire's revenues for years to come. The earthquake precipitated the political rise to power of Sebastião de Carvalho, the future marquês de Pombal, who used the emergency to assume vital dictatorial power, which he held until 1777. The rebuilt city owed much to Pombal's energy and vision. From the ashes of medieval Lisbon arose a symmetrical city whose wide streets, open squares, and central grid reflected Enlightenment ideas of harmonious architecture and rational city planning.

See also **Earthquakes; Pombal, Marquês de (Sebastião José de Carvalho e Melo).**

BIBLIOGRAPHY

Kendrick, Thomas Downing. *The Lisbon Earthquake.* London: Methuen, 1956.

Sousa, Maria Leonor Machado de. *The Lisbon Earthquake of 1755: British Accounts.* Translated by Judith Nozes. Lisbon: British Historical Society of Portugal, 1990.

WILLIAM DONOVAN

LISCANO VELUTINI, JUAN (1915–2001). Juan Liscano Velutini, born in Caracas on July 7, 1915, was a Venezuelan poet, folkorist, literary critic, essayist, and editor. Following early studies in Europe, Liscano returned to Venezuela, where he was a central figure in national literary and intellectual life and founder and director of several journals, most notably the literary supplement of *El Nacional* (1943–1950) and *Zona Franca* (1964–1984), and of the publishing houses Monte Avila (1979–1983) and Mandorla. He participated in resistance activities during the dictatorship of Marcos Pérez Jiménez and spent the years 1953–1958 exiled in Europe. An independent thinker of greater erudition, he wrote extensively, often polemically, on literature and art and on cultural, social, philosophical, and political issues. He is one of the most important literary critics of Venezuela. Although he won the Premio Nacional de Poesía in 1952, his best work is found in the more than a dozen books of poetry published after that date. In his early poetry, which culminates in the neoepic *Nuevo Mundo Orinoco* (1959), the themes of American nature, history, and experience predominate. His later work explores individual perception, metaphysics, and universal myth. More modern essays reflect his interest in the erotic, psychology, esoterica, and historical cultural patterns. Toward the end of his career he began to reflect on the state of Venezuela in such works as *Pensar a Venezuela: Testimonios de cultura y política* (1995). He died in Caracas on February 16, 2001.

See also **Literature: Spanish America.**

BIBLIOGRAPHY

Tiempo desandado (1964) and *Fuegos sagrados* (1990) contain good selections of Liscano's rich and varied essayistic production. His *Panorama de la literatura venezolana actual* (1973) and *Lecturas de poetas y poesía* (1985) are basic contributions, as are his several books on Rómulo Gallegos. *Nombrar contra el tiempo* (1968) is a useful anthology of his early poetry. *Nuevo Mundo Orinoco* (1959; 2nd ed. 1976; 3rd ed. 1992), *Rayo que al alcanzarme* (1978), *Fundaciones* (1981), *Myesis* (1982),

Vencimientos (1986), and *Domicilios* (1986) contain his mature poetry. Arlette Machado, *El apocalipsis según Juan Liscano* (1987) is a largely autobiographical document in interview form. Oscar Rodríguez Ortiz has edited a volume containing the major criticism on Liscano's work, *Juan Liscano ante la crítica* (1990).

Additional Bibliography

Pineda, Rafael. "La poesia de Juan Liscano." *Revista Nacional de Cultura (Caracas)* (1962): 59–67.

MICHAEL J. DOUDOROFF

LISPECTOR, CLARICE (1925–1977). Clarice Lispector (*b.* 10 December 1925; *d.* 9 December 1977), Brazilian writer. After nine novels, six collections of stories, four children's books, translations, interviews, and a wealth of *crônicas* (newspaper columns), Lispector's literary reputation rests on three features, all of which, from the early years of her career, were a positive influence on Latin American narrative: a lyrical and metaphoric style conveying her philosophical subject matter; a structure based chiefly on interior monologue and stream of consciousness; and themes concerning anxiety, isolation, and the need for self-realization. A writer of greatly refined poetic prose, but one with a strong social conscience, Lispector is one of Latin America's most original and powerful authors of the post–World War II era.

The youngest of three daughters of Ukrainian immigrants, she read avidly, doing little else in her spare time, whether as a student or journalist. In general, her life seems to have paralleled the content, themes, and style of her works. Existential and mystical in nature, they reveal her innermost self acting upon more than reacting to exterior reality. Never very methodical, she finally learned at least to jot down her ideas and feelings as they came to her and before they were lost forever. Later she could piece them together as she understood them, and, except for *A maçã no escuro,* all her works were composed in this rather unstructured manner.

Never a popular author in the sense that great numbers of people read her works, she was from the beginning of her career in 1942 an important author, one whose achievements had already attracted a discerning international audience as well as a national one. Lispector was less interested in events than in the repercussions these events produced in the minds of her characters—an approach to fiction writing that put her largely at odds with what was then current in the Brazilian novel and short story. Not surprisingly, then, very little happens in a typical Lispector tale: plot, if defined in terms of the traditional realistic novel, is virtually nonexistent. The conflict of the work is based, almost invariably, in the mind of the character most centrally involved, the character whose hermetic and at times even claustrophobic point of view dominates both the telling and the structuring of the story. More than anything else, Lispector's narratives, her novels and her shorter pieces, are philosophical and poetic exercises that probe the complex and shifting inner realities of modern men and women. Her work has been praised for its brilliant use of language, its structural inventiveness, and its depiction of the alienated and frustrated modern human condition.

As a Brazilian writer, Lispector is best remembered for having opened new roads for Brazilian narrative, for having helped to lead it away from the productive but ultimately limiting kind of regionalism that had dominated the literary scene in Brazil for several decades. Lispector's first novel, *Perto do coração selvagem* (1942), broke radically with this deeply rooted tradition and established a new set of criteria that would help internationalize Brazilian literature and end its cultural and linguistic isolation.

The storm center of *Perto do coração selvagem,* and a character who, in her inner verisimilitude and complexity, can be taken as the prototype for later protagonists of Lispector, is a young woman, the first of a series of striking female characters the author would create. Ranging from timid Ermelinda (*A maçã no escuro*), to the middle-class housewife Ana ("Amor"), to the hopelessly crippled refugee Macabéa (*A hora da Estrela*), to the existential voice of *Um sopro de vida,* Lispector's characters, whether female or male, all relate in one way or another to the issues of feminism, fulfillment, courage, freedom, and love.

Although many critics find her stories superior to her novels, because of the striking dramatic intensity that characterizes them, there can be no doubt that Lispector was a major precursor of the "new novel" in Latin America.

See also **Literature: Brazil.**

BIBLIOGRAPHY

Olga De Sá, *A escritura de Clarice Lispector* (1978).

Earl Fitz, *Clarice Lispector* (1985).

Benedito Nunes, *O mundo de Clarice Lispector* (1966), and *Leitura de Clarice Lispector* (1973).

Additional Bibliography

Feracho, Lesley. *Linking the Americas: Race, Hybrid Discourses, and the Reformulation of Feminine Identity.* Albany: State University of New York Press, 2005.

Kahn, Daniela Mercedes. *A via crucis do outro: Identidade e alteridade em Clarice Lispector.* São Paulo: Associação Editorial Humanitas: FAPESP, 2005.

Pontieri, Regina Lúcia. *Clarice Lispector: Uma poética do olhar.* Cotia: Ateliê Editorial, 1999.

Rosenbaum, Yudith. *Metamorfoses do mal: Uma leitura de Clarice Lispector.* São Paulo: Edusp: FAPESP, 1999.

Zorzanelli, Rafaela Teixeira. *"Esboços não acabados e vacilantes": Despersonalização e experiência subjetiva na obra de Clarice Lispector.* São Paulo: Annablume, 2006.

RICHARD A. MAZZARA

LITERACY. Literacy, in its most basic definition, the ability to read and write simple messages. An issue of concern affecting the general populace, it has been widely addressed in Latin America, primarily in the last half of the twentieth century. Before 1950, the formal education systems of the region were largely designed to serve the interests of the ruling elite. After 1960, informal, community-based, or "popular education," programs were mounted on a large scale. According to Miguel Roca, as late as 1950, 40 percent of the population of Latin America fifteen years of age or older was illiterate, and the mean level of education for this group was less than one year. By 1985, however, illiteracy had dropped to approximately 17 percent in the same age group. While the overall percentage of illiterates declined, however, the absolute numbers of illiterates remained relatively stable. This marked improvement in the literacy rate can be explained in large part by the expansion of the formal education system and by the provision of informal, or popular, education programs for adults who either never entered or dropped out of the formal system.

The expansion of educational opportunities was dramatic after 1950 for reasons that were economic, political, and social. Moreover, the commitment of such international groups as UNESCO, UNICEF, the Organization of American States, and the Economic Commission for Latin America and the Caribbean to educational development in the region was significant. Finally, several regional meetings of Latin American ministers of planning and education held during this period served to establish a region-wide educational agenda. These efforts notwithstanding, marginal populations disproportionately represented by women, indigenous groups, and rural populations continued to lack access to schools, attended infrequently, repeated grades, and/or dropped out at a high rate during the first years of primary schooling.

By the 1960s, national-level literacy campaigns were a visible manifestation of the effort to reach marginalized groups. The two campaigns that stand out—those in Cuba in 1960 and in Nicaragua in 1980—were both associated with revolutionary governments. They were both acclaimed internationally as having achieved unparalleled success. Cuba, for example, was credited with practically eliminating illiteracy within a single year. Similarly, in Nicaragua, literacy brigades in the department with the highest rate of illiteracy (Río San Juan) reduced illiteracy from 96 percent in 1979 to 3.7 percent in 1987. Not all literacy campaigns have been associated with revolutionary governments, however. Once illiteracy was seen as an obstacle to economic development, numerous campaigns were begun in the 1960s and 1970s, including those in Argentina, Bolivia, Brazil, Colombia, Chile, Ecuador, El Salvador, Honduras, Jamaica, Mexico, Peru, the Dominican Republic, and Venezuela.

Literacy education in Latin America received additional impetus at the Regional Conference of Ministers of Education (1979). From this conference came the Major Project of Education, an ambitious twenty-year plan organized and administered by UNESCO to overcome the region's educational problems. This region-wide project pledged by 1999 to ensure universal access to

Bolivian woman in adult literacy class, Chapare, 2006. National campaigns significantly reduced illiteracy in Latin America during the twentieth century. Nearly 90 percent of adults in most countries can read and write. © JORGE UZON/CORBIS

schooling, eliminate illiteracy, expand educational opportunities for adults, and improve the quality of education at all levels. Unfortunately, the economic recession of the 1980s adversely affected progress toward these goals, and illiteracy remained a serious problem into the 1990s, especially among the traditionally underserved groups. On the eve of the United Nations National Literacy Year (1990), there were still an estimated 44 million illiterates in Latin America (virtually unchanged from 1970, at 44.4 million, and 1980, at 44.3 million).

Most of the literacy campaigns mentioned appear to have concentrated on imparting an ability to read and write a simple message. This definition, while helping boost claims of success, does not consider the uses to which literacy is put. Those who argue for *functional literacy* define it as a person's capacity to make decisions concerning his or her economic, civic, political, and day-to-day life. In fact, enabling people to enjoy meaningful and active participation in all areas of national life constitutes the greatest challenge to literacy campaigns in Latin America—the challenge of ensuring that people will retain and use their newly acquired literacy skills.

Literacy recidivism—the relapse to illiteracy—is widespread and serious in Latin America and threatens to undermine the success of both literacy campaigns and government efforts to universalize primary education. This phenomenon leaves its victims worse off than ever, more destitute and less motivated. Bernard Dumont proffers several recommendations for postliteracy programs that serve to maintain and expand literacy skills, including production of appropriate educational materials (easy-to-read, practical general education books; rural newspapers and supplements in urban newspapers containing current and practical information and written specifically for the newly literate; entertaining comic books and picture stories; and radio, film, and TV programs), creation of "literary environments" (through, for example, road signs and newspapers), and access to positions of higher responsibility. It is clear that to be successful, future programs must focus on the postliteracy needs of the newly literate.

See also **Education: Overview; Education: Nonformal Education.**

BIBLIOGRAPHY

Paulo Freire, *Pedagogy of the Oppressed,* translated by Myra Bergman Ramos (1972).

Valerie Miller, *Between Struggle and Hope: The Nicaraguan Literacy Crusade* (1985).

Irene Campos Carr, "The Politics of Literacy in Latin America," in *Convergence* 23, no. 2 (1989): 58–68.

José Rivero, "Learning for Autonomy," in *International Review of Education* 35, no. 4 (1989): 445–461.

W. Ross Winterowd, *The Culture and Politics of Literacy* (1989).

Juan B. Arrien, *Nicaragua: Mobilizing the Local Community for Literacy and Post-Literacy* (ERIC Document: ED321043, 1990).

Bernard Dumont, *Post-Literacy: A Pre-Requisite for Literacy* (ERIC Document: ED321058, 1990).

Miguel Soler Roca, *Literacy in Latin America: Progress, Problems, and Perspectives* (ERIC Document: ED321054, 1990).

Additional Bibliography

Belle, T.J.L., and Carlos Alberto Torres. "The Changing Nature of Non-formal Education in Latin America." *Comparative Education* 36:1 (2000): 21-36.

Kueper, Wolfgang, and Teresa Valiente Catter. *Educación de los adultos en Africa y Latinoamérica: Experiencias interculturales en un encuentro multicultural.* Quito: Abya-Yala, 1999.

EVERETT EGGINTON

LITERATURE

This entry includes the following articles:

BRAZIL
SPANISH AMERICA

BRAZIL

Although there is some debate among scholars as to what period and what specific works mark the beginning of Brazilian literature—one written by a Brazilian population aspiring to or conscious of an identity that is separate from that of its colonial master—the earliest written account of Brazil dates back to 1500 and is part of the vein of chronicles of the New World. Written by Pero Vaz de Caminha (1450–1500), the *Carta do a El-Rei Dom Manuel sobre o achamento do Brasil* (Letter of the Discovery of Brazil) is an account of the territory and people found by Admiral Pedro Álvares Cabral's expedition to the northeast of Brazil. Its lyrical descriptions reflect an idealization of Brazilian indigenous peoples that continued to have currency, albeit inflected with different meanings, through the rise of Brazilian modernism and well into the twentieth century.

COLONIAL LITERATURE

Colonial literature can be divided into chronicles, travel narratives, and pedagogical Christian, or "salvationist" literature written for indigenous people's evangelization. The most significant author of the sixteenth century is Father José de Anchieta (1534–1597), a Jesuit imbued with the spirit of the Council of Trent (1545) who arrived in Brazil in 1553 and whose didactic theater pieces—medieval *autos*, reminiscent of Gil Vicente—attempt to reconcile local cultural vocabularies with a Catholic evangelizing message. His *Autos de São Lourenço*, for example, incorporates Tupi names and imagery, including them as both townspeople in need of defense and salvation and as the cohort of demons—Guaixará, Saravaia, and Aimbirê, all of them Dionysiac in their lust for earthly pleasures—against whom São Lourenço battles. The poetic works of the period, influenced by medieval verse structures, also propagate the Catholic religion.

In 1601 Bento Teixeira (1561–1600) published *Prosopopéia*, notable for being the first book of poetry written by a man born in Brazil—though some scholars have claimed he was in fact born in Portugal—rather than for its quality. Regardless of Teixeira's birthplace, this work is the first epic poem in Brazilian literature and inaugurates its Baroque period. It was not until Gregório de Matos's (1633–1696) forceful *nativismo*, however, that Brazilian poetry came into its own. Matos produced a poetry steeped in the European Baroque tradition that at the same time incorporated the flora, fauna, landscape, and sociopolitical context of Brazil. Noted for his strong poetic personality and caustic critical voice, Matos earned the nickname "Boca do inferno"—Hell's Mouth. He also produced religious sonnets and lyrical love poems. Another remarkable figure of the Baroque period was Antônio Vieira (1608–1697), whose sermons exemplify the ideal of *conceptismo*, a style known for its rhetorical mastery and concise expression of complex ideas. Critical of the flourish and luxuriating linguistic complexity that characterized Baroque *culteranismo*, Vieira endeavored to produce sermons of clarity and rhetorical force. Among his noted works are the "Sermon of the Sexegesima," the "Sermon for the good success of Portuguese forces against those of Holland," and the "Sermon of Saint Anthony to the Fish."

In the eighteenth century, with the boom in gold and diamond mining, Minas Gerais rose to become the new economic center of Brazil. Young people from the region went to Portugal to be educated and returned drenched in the ideals of the European Enlightenment. They absorbed aesthetic innovations encouraged by the rise of the bourgeoisie—the adoption of classical paradigms as a counterblow against the Baroque, seen as a reflection of the excesses of the aristocracy. Absorbing this influence, but consciously seeking a national mode of writing in the later eighteenth century, the Mineira school of writers founded Arcadia Ultramarina in 1768–1769; the name of this poetic academy alluded to Brazil's distance from Portugal (hence *ultramarina*, "beyond the sea") and consolidated the Mineira school. The most notable of the Mineira school and indeed the most important lyric poet of his time was Tomás Antônio Gonzaga, who took the pastoral name "Dirceu"; his love poems were collected in *Marília de Dirceu*. Along with the other members of the Mineira school, Gonzaga took part in the 1789 rebellion against Portuguese rule, known as the *Inconfidência Mineira*. The plot was discovered and the rebellion stifled, its leaders exiled or executed. Among the other participants were the poets Claudio Manuel da Costa (1729–1789), Alvarenga Peixoto (1744–1793), and Silva Alvarenga (1749–1814). Claudio Manuel da Costa's epic poem *Villa Rica* tells the story of the emergence of Ouro Preto, the city at the heart of Brazil's eighteenth-century golden age, and confers heroic status on the *bandeirantes*—Brazilian pioneers.

This period of transition to romanticism is also marked by epic poems that engage the ideal of the "noble savage" within the context of Brazilian history. In *Caramuru* (1781), José de Santa Rita Durão (1722–1784) recounts the history of the discovery of Bahia. In the epic poem *O Uraguay* (1769), Basílio da Gama (1741–1795) describes the massacre of the indigenous peoples of the Sete Povos das Missões; the poem is also notable for its formal innovations, as it is written in blank verse and without strophic divisions (traditionally *oitavas reais*, or decasyllabic eight-line stanzas with an abababcc rhyme scheme). These poems present idealized images of Brazilian indigenous peoples and the landscape that surrounds them, and find an echo in later romantic mythologizing of Brazilian heroes.

ROMANTICISM

In Brazilian poetry, 1836 marks the beginning of the romantic period. In that year Gonçalves de Magalhães published his poetry collection *Suspiros Poéticos e Saudades* and launched *Nitéroi*, a journal of Brazilian letters in Paris. In *Nitéroi*, Magalhães published his "Discurso Sobre a História da Literatura do Brasil," a romantic manifesto that exhorts his countrymen to produce a literature reflective of the nation's independence, gained in 1822. This Brazilian specificity finds expression in the rejection of the influence of classicism and Latinizing expression, and in nationalist portrayals of nature where Brazilian flora and fauna were represented in their own terms, rather than as local versions of European *loci amoeni*. In many ways, these trends, and the emergence of indianismo, are heirs to the innovations of the Mineira school.

If Domingos José Gonçalves de Magalhães is the ideological leader of early romanticism in Brazil, Antônio Gonçalves Dias (1823–1864) is undoubtedly its best lyrical poet. His "Canção do Exílio" (Song of exile) in which he evokes, with poignant simplicity, the Brazilian landscape and the intense longing (*saudade*) for his homeland (he was in Comigra, Portugal, from 1838 to 1845) reverberates through later poetic representations of Brazil. Casimiro de Abreu (1839–1860), for example, wrote his own "Canção do Exílio," echoing the longing for the "birdsong of the Sabiá," a birdsong that functions as a metonym for the ideal Brazil of Gonçalves Dias. Gonçalves Dias exploration of the local also manifests itself in his Indianist poetry; "I-Juca-Pirama" is the quintessential idealized, indigenous Brazilian hero. Manuel Araújo Porto-Alegre (1806–1879), also a member of this first generation of romantics, through his contributions to the journal *Nitéroi* and his

Brasilianas (poems) aided in the consolidation of the romantic movement in Brazilian letters.

The second generation of romantic poets is one of pessimism and *mal-de-siècle.* Luís José Junqueira Freire (1832–1855), Manuel Antônio Alvares de Azevedo (1831–1852), and Luís Nicolau Fagundes Varela (1841–1875) are the most notable poets of this period. Their solipsistic poetry, exploring the subjectivity of a cosmopolitan poetic self, was for the most part indifferent to the project of Brazilian specificity. These poets are not concerned with Brazilian nativism, landscape, *saudade*, or mythologizing of an indigenous past; rather, they represent a current of Brazilian poets whose preoccupations were in keeping with romantic expressions—of the unreachable, the contradictory, the fragile division between reality and dream—across Europe and the American continent.

The third generation of romantic poets turned its gaze toward its historical, political, and social context. The most representative poet of this socially conscious generation is Antônio de Castro Alves (1847–1871). Although he also wrote beautiful love lyrics, he is best known for his social critiques in verse, especially "Navio Negreiro," which marks the high point of abolitionist poetry. The Brazilian historian Capistrano de Abreu named this generation the *condoreiros* (from the word "condor"), suggesting their high-flying aspirations. Joaquim de Sousa Andrade (1833–1902), known as Soussândrade, though not very successful in his own era, was rediscovered by the *concretismo* poets (concrete poetry movement) in the 1960s. They popularized his *Guesa Errante* (1888), and literary critics have come to regard him as one of the best poets of the romantic period.

Gonçalves de Magalhães played a role in launching romantic theater with *Antonio José ou O poeta e a Inquisição* (1838); but it was Luís Carlos Martins Pena (1815–1848) who consolidated Brazilian drama by introducing and perfecting the *costumbrista* play, a sort of comedy of manners depicting provincial customs. Romantic prose developed the vein of *indianismo*—a nationalist idealization of indigenous Brazilians that seeks to establish Brazilian identity as distinct from, and often antagonistic to, Portuguese and European identities. José Martiniano de Alencar (1829–1877) is the most important representative of romantic *indianismo.* His novels *O Guarani* (1857) and *Iracema* (1865) exhibit the nationalist impetus to create and fortify Brazilian literature; Alencar's regional descriptions and love stories between indigenous heroes and sympathetic Europeans contributed to a new set of foundational myths that mark the separation of Brazilian culture from European literary traditions. In his literary autobiography *Como e porque sou romancista* (How and Why I Am a Novelist, 1893), Alencar notes his readings of James Fenimore Cooper, Walter Scott, and especially René Chateaubriand, but insists that his novels' overriding aesthetic is drawn from a knowledge of the nature he encounters in Brazil. Most critics agree that his works—not only his Indianist writings, but also his urban, psychological, and historical novels—laid the foundation for the Brazilian novel.

Other novelists of note during this period are Joaquim Manuel Macedo (1820–1882), who published *A Moreninha* in 1844, and Manuel Antônio de Almeida (1831–1861). Almeida's *Memórias de um Sargento de Milícias* (1854–1855), which explores the underbelly of Brazilian society with seedy characters and antiheroes, is often seen as the first *costumbrista* novel in Brazil. He is widely recognized as the precursor of realism and naturalism in Brazilian literature. The first naturalist work, *O Mulato* (1881) by Aluísio Azevedo (1857–1913), was published in 1881; although the influence of the Portuguese realist José Maria de Eça de Queirós and the French naturalist Émile Zola is evident, Azevedo's novels spring from a local impetus: He is an abolitionist and broaches questions of race and slavery specific to a critique of Brazilian society.

REALISM

Several writers of the romantic period began to experiment with narrative styles such that they dovetailed with realist conventions. Joaquim Maria Machado de Assis (1839–1908) is the most significant bridge between romanticism and realism in Brazil. Machado wrote romantic poetry and short stories, but his most remarkable works were the novels *Memórias póstumas de Brás Cubas* (*The Posthumous Memoirs of Brás Cubas*, 1880), widely seen as the inauguration of realism in Brazil; *Quincas Borba* (1892); and *Dom Casmurro* (1900). A contemporaneous work by Euclides da Cunha (1866–1909), *Os Sertões: Campanha de Canudos* (Rebellion in the Backlands, 1902), concerning the decimation of an apocalyptic religious enclave in northeastern Brazil, combines elements of realist narrative, journalistic reporting, sociological study, and personal testimony. Like many naturalist works, it exhibits the influence of positivism and geographic determinism. Da Cunha's work marks the end of realism and naturalism and the beginnings of modernist literature in Brazil. Afonso Henriques de Lima Barreto (1881–1922), whose works do not fit neatly into any particular movement, had a significant impact on Brazilian intellectuals' debates on national identity and culture. Barreto's work, in particular the novel *Triste fim do Policarpo Quaresma* (The Sad End of Policarpo Quaresm, 1915) offers a scathing critique of Brazilian racism in portraying the lives of Rio de Janeiro's underprivileged classes. His direct style and simple prose anticipated the modernist rebellion.

Because of its rejection of certain romantic parameters and its search for objective approaches to poetic subjects, Parnassianism can be understood in broad terms as the poetic counterpart of realism. This movement encompasses the works of Olavo Bilac (1865–1918), Alberto de Oliveira (1857–1937), Raimundo Corréia (1859–1911), and Vicente Carvalho (1866–1924). Like European Parnassianism, it seeks to cultivate form and turn away from the free verse and blank verse of the romantics. It uses the search for the perfection of form not as an end in itself but as a device to create an objective distance. This is a period of meditative and philosophical poetry and of a return to classicism.

SYMBOLISM

The publication of two books in 1893—*Missal* and *Bróqueis*—by João da Cruz e Sousa (1863–1898) marks the beginning of symbolism in Brazilian literature. Aside from being the most important exponent of symbolism in Brazil, Cruz e Sousa also expresses an internal fragmentation related to race and culture. The son of freed slaves, Cruz e Sousa experienced numerous obstacles in his professional endeavors because he was black. In his poetry, he explored the ways in which his embrace of Parnassianism and then symbolism distanced him from his race and culture; but he adhered to the maxim of art for art's sake and to the cult of beauty as two absolutes in his work. Another symbolist poet of note is Alphonsus de Guimaraens (1870-1921), notable for his mystical poetry. Augusto dos Anjos (1884–1914) is the most important poet between the end of symbolism and the rise of modernism. His original lyrical mode reached into scientific language and other surprising imagery to present meditations on existence and love and sympathy for the suffering of others. His collection *Eu* ("I"), published in 1912, is still widely read.

MODERNISM

Marking the moment when *modernismo* took root in the national culture, in 1922 the city of São Paulo celebrated Semana de Arte Moderna ("Modern Art Week"). The keynote speech of the writer and diplomat José Pereira da Graça Aranha (1868–1931), an important figure in the modernist movement, introduced a series of lectures, readings, and art exhibits. *Modernismo* shares with other avant-garde movements the impulse to redefine poetic language and revise traditional conventions and ideals of beauty, to explore a radically free verse, and to rethink the relationship of the artist to society. It also has a strong impetus to continue the search for a national and culturally independent literature. Oswald de Andrade's (1890–1954) famous 1928 "Manifesto Antropófago" (Anthropophagous Manifesto) declared metaphoric cannibalism as the new aesthetic ideal, and the Tupi people as the symbol of both Brazilian otherness and the absorption of European influence. "Tupi or not Tupi, that is the question," he wrote, suggesting that the use, ingestion, and digestion of all foreign cultures that had an impact on Brazil, paired with creativity and irreverence, may lead to a newfound identity that supersedes imitation and that might open the floodgates of originality. Other proposals for a new literature are Mário de Andrade's (1893–1945) *Paulicéia Desvairada* (Hallucinated City, 1922), a long poem organized as a carnivalesque stroll through the twists and turns of the city of São Paulo. His *Macunaíma* (1928) was another fundamental modernist text. The urban turn of literary nationalism also signals the interest of the *modernistas* in negotiating a national identity that would encompass both the Brazilian metropolis and the large expanses of rural land in the interior of the nation.

A less radically experimental manifestation of modernism emerged in Rio de Janeiro, with Cecilia Meireles (1901–1964) as one of its foremost exponents. Despite her more lyrical and symbolist tendencies, she was associated with a literary journal that also espoused *brasilidade* (Brazilianness) and universality as joint precepts. Before 1922 several poets had produced works that engaged in a modernist aesthetic. The poems in *A Cinza das Horas* (1917), by Manuel Bandeira (1886–1968), displayed a marked symbolist influence; but his subsequent collections, such as *Carnival* (1919), experimented with dislocated rhythms, ridiculed sentimentalism, and played with language in ways that foreshadowed modernist experiments. Other poets who emerged during the first phase of *modernismo* reshaped the movement in the 1930s—Carlos Drummond de Andrade (1901–1987), Murilo Mendes (1901–1975), Jorge de Lima (1895–1953), and Vinicius de Moraes (1913–1980). Whether explicitly politicized or not, the poetry of this period looks toward the world and distances itself from the metapoetic experimentalism of the first wave of *modernismo*. In the 1950s João Cabral de Melo Neto (1920–1999) became one of the most influential poetic innovators; his *Morte e Vida Severina* (Death and Life of Severino, 1954–1955) is a poetic rendering of the life and death of a simple man in the economically depressed region of northeastern Brazil.

The prose of the 1930s and 1940s tended to be socially conscious and regionalist. Among the representative authors of the period are Jorge Amado (1912–2001), Raquel de Queiroz (1910–2003), Graciliano Ramos (1892–1953), and José Lins do Rego (1901–1957). Among urban novelists, Cyro dos Anjos (1906–1994) stands out with *O amanuense Belmiro* (Diary of a Civil Servant, 1937) and *Abdias* (1945). The generation that followed focused on psychologically complex explorations of individuals, whether set in the backlands or in middle-class urban households. A study by the sociologist Gilberto Freyre (1900–1987), *Casa Grande e Senzala* (*The Masters and the Slaves*, 1933), which discussed Brazil's colonial heritage and history of slavery, had an impact well beyond the confines of the social sciences. João Guimarães Rosa (1908–1967) published *Grande Sertão: Veredas* (The Devil to Pay in the Backlands, 1956), widely considered one of the best novels of the twentieth century in Brazil. At this time also Clarice Lispector (1920–1977) published her lucid short stories. In the theater, Ariano Suassuna (b. 1927) was the most influential playwright.

In the 1950s and 1960s *concretismo*, an approach to a poem as a visual and musical object, was followed by a neoconcretist movement. In between, Haroldo de Campos (1929–2003) and Decio Pignatari (b. 1927) experimented not only in response to modernist literature, but also to other art forms including film. The repressive dictatorship that began in 1964 created a shift in certain poets, with many of them beginning to write social and political critiques. Carlos Drummond de Andrade in the meantime passed from a politically engaged period (notably with *A Rosa do Povo* (The Rose of the People, 1945) to an intimist meditative poetry in *Claro Enigma* (Clear Enigma, 1951).

In the late 1960s through the 1980s, the atmosphere for writers was heavy with politics. It was a period of introspection but not of solipsism, when novels and short stories were quests for the elements that define Brazilian society. Such explorations often entailed deconstructing popular images of the nation and its foundations—hence the popularity of the historical novel genre. Of note in this period are José Cândido de Carvalho (1914–1989), Nélida Piñon (b. 1937), João Ubaldo Ribeiro (b. 1941), and Moacyr Scliar (b. 1937). Silvano Santiago (b. 1936), and Marcio Souza (b. 1946) both explore the genre of the New Historical Novel. A special place deserves to be saved for the shining chronicles of this period. Already announced as a new creative genre since Rubem Braga (1913–1990) published *Um Pé de Milho* (A Foot of Maize, 1948), the chronicle became a creative and fruitful field with Nelson Rodrigues (1912–1980), and Luis Fernando Verissimo (b. 1936). The urban short story was a fruitful genre, with Dalton Trevisan's (b. 1925) *O Vampiro de Curitiba* (The Vampire of Curitiba, 1965) striking an irreverent note; dark, violent, and abject characters populate Rubem Fonseca's (b. 1925) short story collections.

POETRY AND POPULAR MUSIC

After the 1960s Brazilian poetry grew in popularity through a collaboration with musicians. Songwriters' influence crossed over into the realm of letters, as with Chico Buarque (b. 1944), Torquato Neto (1944–1972), Caetano Veloso (b. 1942), and Gilberto Gil (b. 1942). *Tropicalismo* emerged in the late 1960s and picked up on the innovations of the numerous avant-gardes in Brazil, including the concretist movement and its offshoots, and the politically informed poetry of *violão de rua* ("guitar of the streets"). In the 1980s political poetry reacted to years of dictatorial repression, notable examples being João Cabral de Melo Neto's *A Escola das Facas* (The School of Knives, 1980) and Alex Polari's (b. 1951) *Inventário de cicatrizes* (Inventory of Scars, 1987). Other significant poets of the late 1970s and 1980s are Paulo Leminski (1944–1989), Ana Cristina César (1952–1983), Adélia Prado (b. 1935), and Sebastião Uchoa Leite (1935–2003). Glauco Mattoso (b. 1951) was active in the "marginal poets" group of the 1970s but his poetry has only recently begun to be included in poetry anthologies.

From 1990 to 2006, poetry sees a new turn, with the context of globalization and the emergence of the Internet as another means for poems to circulate. Several significant literary journals emerge strictly in the virtual world and literary blogs begin to have an influence in determining the fate of poems and poets. The 1990s can be characterized by a popularization of poetry through mass media, and a productive erosion of the division of high and popular culture. Alberto Martins (b. 1958), Claudia Roquette-Pinto (b. 1963), Paulo Lins (b. 1958), Moacir Amâncio (b. 1949), Arnaldo Antunes (b. 1960), Carlito Azevedo (b. 1961), and Contador Borges (b. 1954) are among the poets who provide a glimpse of the many trends of the 1990s. Other poets of note are Jussara Salazar (b. 1959) and Paulo Henriques Britto (b. 1951). The turn of the millennium has also witnessed some remarkable young poets, such as Micheliny Verunschk (b. 1972) and Ademir Assunção (b. 1961). In prose, novelists and short story writers who explore the chaos and contradictions of Brazilian modernity are João Gilberto Noll (b. 1946), Bernardo Carvalho (b. 1960), Fernando Bonassi (b. 1962), and Chico Buarque (b. 1944). Other notable novelists are Alberto Mussa (b. 1961) and Milton Hatoum (b. 1952).

See also **Alencar, José Martiniano de; Amado, Jorge; Anchieta, José de; Andrade, Carlos Drummond de; Andrade, Mário de; Andrade, Oswald de; Bilac, Olavo; Campos, Haroldo de; Castro Alves, Antônio de; Concretism; Cruz e Sousa, João da; Cunha, Euclides da; Durão, José de Santa Rita; Freyre, Gilberto (de Mello); Gonzaga, Tomás Antônio; Graça Aranha, José Pereira da; Indianismo; Lima, Jorge de; Lima Barreto, Afonso Henriques de; Lins do Rego, José; Lispector, Clarice; Machado de Assis, Joaquim Maria; Matos, Gregório de; Meireles, Cecília; Melo Neto, João Cabral de; Modernism, Brazil; Pena, Luís Carlos Martins; Piñon, Nélida; Pôrto Alegre, Manuel Araújo; Queiroz, Rachel de; Ramos, Graciliano; Ribeiro, João Ubaldo; Rosa, João Guimarães; Science Fiction in Latin America; Scliar, Moacyr; Suassuna, Ariano Vilar; Tupi; Vieira, Antônio.**

BIBLIOGRAPHY

Aguilar, Gonzalo. *Poesía concreta brasileña: Las vanguardias en la encrucijada modernista.* Rosario, Argentina: Beatriz Viterbo, 2003.

Baden, Nancy T. *The Muffled Cries: The Writer and Literature in Authoritarian Brazil, 1964–1985.* Lanham, MD: University Press of America, 1999.

Bandeira, Manuel. *Apresentação da poesia brasileira.* Rio de Janeiro: Ouro, 1967.

Barbosa, Frederico, and Claudio Daniel, eds. *Na virada do século: Poesia de invenção no Brasil.* São Paulo: Landy, 2002.

Barbosa, Frederico, ed. *Cinco séculos de poesia: Antologia da poesia clássica brasileira.* São Paulo: Landy, 2000.

Buarque de Hollanda, Helóisa, ed. *Esses Poetas: Uma antologia dos anos 90.* Rio de Janeiro: Aeroplano Editora, 1998.

Candido, Antonio. *Formação da literatura brasileira: Momentos decisivos.* São Paulo: Livraria Martins, 1964.

Costigan, Lúcia Helena. "Historiografia, discurso e contra-discurso na colônia: Gregório de Matos e Juan del Valle y Caviedes." *Hispania* 75, no. 3 (1992): 508–515.

Coutinho, Afranio. *An Introduction to Literature in Brazil.* Translated by Gregory Rabassa. New York: Columbia University Press, 1969.

Cyntrão, Sylvia Helena, ed. *A forma da festa: Tropicalismo: A Explosão e seus estilhaços.* São Paulo: Imprensa Oficial do Estado, 2000.

Fitz, Earl E. *Brazilian Narrative Traditions in a Comparative Context.* New York: MLA, 2005.

Gonzaga, Sergius. *Manual de literatura brasileira.* Porto Alegre: Mercado Alberto, 1995.

Hamilton, D. Lee. "A vida e as obras de José de Anchieta." *Hispania* 26, no. 4 (1943): 407–424.

Lemos de Oliveira, Celso. "Brazilian Literature and Art: From Colonial to Modern." *Hispania* 75, no. 4 (1992): 988–999.

Martins, Wilson. "O teatro no Brasil." *Hispania* 46 (1963): 239–251.

Menton, Seymour. *La Nueva Novela Histórica de la América Latina: 1979–1992.* Mexico: Fondo de Cultura Económica, 1993.

Paulino Bueno, Eva. "Brazilian Naturalism and the Politics of Origin." *MLN* 107, no. 2 (1992): 363–395.

Perez, Renard. *Escritores Brasileiros Contemporâneos,* 2nd edition. Rio de Janeiro: Civilização Brasileira, 1970.

Schwarz, Roberto. "A Brazilian Breakthrough." *New Left Review* 36 (2005): 91–107.

Voigt, Lisa. "'Por Andarmos Todos Casy Mesturados': The Politics of Intermingiling in Caminha's *Carta* and Colonial American Anthologies." *Early American Literature* 40 (2005): 407–439.

Verberckmoes, Johann. "Amerindian Laughter and Visions of a Carnivalesque New World." *Zeitsprünge* (Frankfurt) 7 (2003): 264–284.

Wasserman, Renata. "The Red and the White: The 'Indian' Novels of José de Alencar." *PMLA* 98, no. 5 (1983): 815–827.

Claret M. Vargas

SPANISH AMERICA

Spanish American literature shares many European literary and cultural patterns and at the same time gives voice to a distinct and different American reality. For the most part, period styles in Spanish American literature correspond to those in Europe (for example, Renaissance, baroque, neoclassicism, romanticism, realism). Vigorous national literatures are in evidence in a number of Spanish American countries (the most notable examples being Mexico, Cuba, Colombia, Peru, Chile, and Argentina), and many first-rank individual writers have achieved international distinction.

THE LITERATURE OF SPANISH AMERICA: PRE-COLUMBIAN TO 1995

Well-defined national literatures, it could be argued, make ineffective the use of the more general Spanish American construct that is here being applied. There is a large degree of commonality among the national literatures, stemming in large part from the relative constancy of the Spanish language and the numerous similarities in literary movements and period styles. In spite of some legitimate concerns about its usefulness, the Spanish American construct offers a valid framework for literary study and commentary in this diverse area of the world.

Terminology and Periodization. An even more complex question is the particular approach to be used in considering the development of a multifaceted literary expression in Spanish America. One could focus, for example, on the various literary genres (Spanish American poetry, for example, or the Spanish American novel), on various aesthetic or thematic patterns that transcend national boundaries (the literary conceptualization of Spanish America, the regionalist "novel of the land," social and political themes in literature), or on a series of major figures who exemplify the peculiar mix of European and local elements in Spanish America. The most productive design for a general discussion, however, is a combination of several of those approaches, in which political period, epoch style, and genre development find expression in a complex literary interweaving that has been in process for nearly five centuries. The principal periods can be divided into pre-Hispanic literature; the colonial period (extending from 1520 to 1820 and including accounts of exploration, conquest, and consolidation during the sixteenth century; baroque literature during the seventeenth century; and neoclassicism during the eighteenth and early nineteenth centuries); independence and the development of national literatures from 1820 until 1915 (including romanticism, realism-naturalism, and modernism); and the development of modern literature after 1915.

Pre-Hispanic Literature. Any consideration of Spanish American literature should take as a point of departure the cultural richness of the well-developed pre-Columbian civilizations in the Western Hemisphere, a richness that is expressed in languages other than Spanish. The principal indigenous cultures encountered in the European conquest were those of the Nahuatl-speaking Aztecs in central Mexico, the Mayas of southern Mexico and Guatemala, and the Quechua speakers of the Andean Incan Empire. Other cultures were those of the Otomí, the Zapotecs, the Mixtecs, and the Tarascans in Mexico; the Cunas in Central America; Arawaks and Caribs in the Caribbean; and the Chibchas, Aymaras, Guarani, and Araucanians in South America. At the time of the Conquest all those cultures enjoyed a more or less developed literary expression, most often in orally transmitted form, although in some areas written transcription was in use.

In the Nahuatl-speaking area of Mexico a very elaborate historical and artistic expression was recorded and transmitted in both oral form and by means of pictographic codices inscribed on such materials as *amate* paper or leather. A few of these documents survived the Conquest, but most of our present-day information comes from the efforts of

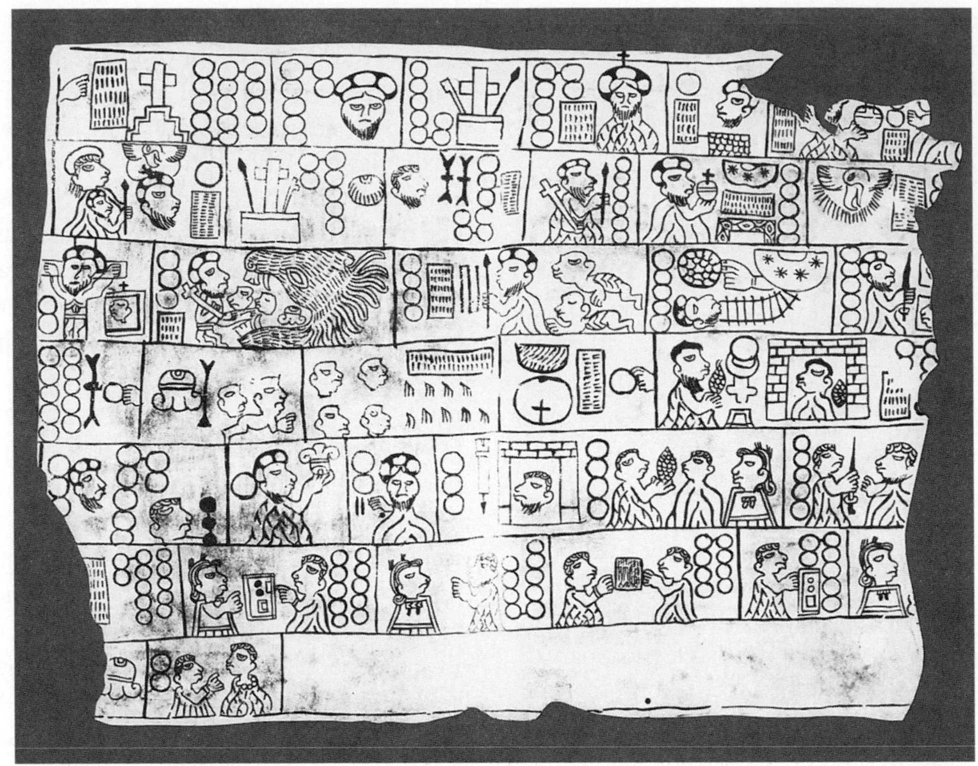

Mexican pictographs. A catechism from sixteenth-century colonial Mexico.

certain Spanish clerics, in particular Fray Bernardino de Sahagún, whose informants transcribed Nahuatl materials using the Latin alphabet. Poetry (religious, warmaking, epic, lyric, dramatic) is the most significant literary genre, showing a notable richness of imagery and awareness of form. Several individual poets can be identified, foremost among them Netzahualcóyotl (king of Tetzcoco, 1402–1472).

The Maya culture in Yucatán and Central America showed a much greater variation in linguistic patterns than the Nahuatl but had a similar combination of oral and written traditions. An ideographic/phonetic system was developed in the lowlands, and various kinds of historical and literary materials were recorded on paper codices and engraved on stone. As in central Mexico, however, the most important collections of literary materials are those transcribed after the Conquest using the Latin alphabet. The most famous of these texts, for example, is the Popol Vuh or *Libro del Consejo*, a narrative and mythological text transcribed from Guatemalan K'iche'-Maya and translated into Spanish in the eighteenth century by Fray Francisco Ximénez. The various mytho-historical texts known as the Chilam Balam books were transcribed from Yucatecan Maya; the best known, the *Chilam Balam de Chumayel*, was found and published in the mid-nineteenth century. In those same years the K'iche' tragedy *Rabinal Achí* was also transcribed from an ancient theatrical tradition.

The Quechua-speaking cultural area in the Andes (the Inca Empire) also had a well-developed literary tradition, but in contrast to the high cultures to the north it lacked a formalized writing system. The cords, knots, and colors of the mnemonic *quipu* apparently aided in the transmission of statistical, historical, mythical, and even literary information, but the system was essentially different from the pictographs or the ideographs used in the other centers. Once again, the principal sources of cultural and literary information in this area are the post-Conquest chronicles, in particular Cristóbal de Molina's *Relación de las fábulas y ritos de los Inkas* (1575), Juan Santacruz Pachacuti's *Relación de antigüedades de este Reyno del Perú* (1598), and El Inca Garcilaso De La Vega's *Comentarios reales* (1609). As in the Nahuatl area, poetry was the

Netzahualcóyotl, fifteenth-century king of Texcoco, shown here receiving tributes from native chiefs, was also a poet in the Nahuatl language. THE ART ARCHIVE/NATIONAL ARCHIVES MEXICO/MIREILLE VAUTIER. REPRODUCED BY PERMISSION OF THE PICTURE DESK INC.

preferred literary genre, and anonymous creators used a number of traditional forms to express their ideas (e.g., the sacred or heroic *jailli*, the sentimental *arawi*, the musical *wayñu*, or the funereal *wanka*). The Quechua-language *Ollantay*, an anonymous dramatic text discovered in the early years of the nineteenth century, is generally considered to be of pre-Hispanic origin.

Exploration, Conquest, and Consolidation (1520–1620). An essentially Hispanic culture was established and refined in the New World, a culture built around the linguistic, social, and religious values imposed by a European power structure that attempted to repress all vestiges of indigenous cultures. That very process of colonization and *mestizaje* (racial mixing), which brought together in differing proportions the European settlers, the aboriginal populations, and imported African slaves, is the hallmark of what has come to be seen as a distinctive Spanish American society. Literature was an essential component of that developing Hispanic society. The New World attracted the attention and, on occasion, the presence of distinguished Spanish writers, among them Gutierre de Cetina, Tirso de Molina, and Mateo Alemán. Such figures, together with the clerics and other educated persons who were a part of the early colonization efforts, were very much influenced by the humanistic Renaissance style then current in Europe, a circumstance that ensured that most of the early literature in Spanish America followed that same Renaissance model.

The most important literary genres from this early period are the *crónica* (an expository prose text of exploration and conquest, including letters, accounts, histories, etc.) and epic poetry. The earliest of the chroniclers are Christopher Columbus (1451–1506), whose diary and letters (perhaps the best known of which is a letter dated 1493 to Luis de Santangel, a secretary to Ferdinand and Isabella) describe and justify his discoveries in the New World, and Hernán Cortés (1485–1547), who recounted his exploits in the conquest of Mexico to King Charles I in his *Cartas de relación* (1519–1536). More compelling as a chronicle of conquest is the account of one of Cortés's foot soldiers, Bernal Díaz del Castillo (ca. 1495–1584), whose *Historia verdadera de la conquista de la Nueva España* (finished in 1568 but not published until 1632) presents the most vivid and readable account of the conquest of Mexico. The most famous chronicler of the period is probably Fray Bartolomé de Las Casas (1474–1566), whose polemical treatise *Brevísima relación de la destrucción de las Indias* (1552) was translated rapidly into a number of other languages and contributed to the so-called Black Legend of the Spanish conquest. Most of Las Casas's other voluminous writings were not published until well after his death.

The first major chronicler born in the New World was El Inca Garcilaso De La Vega (1539–1616), the mestizo son of an Inca princess and a Spanish captain. Following his early years in Cuzco, the Inca Garcilaso completed his education and spent the remainder of his life in Spain. His most important works, *La Florida del Inca* (1605) and the *Comentarios reales* (1609, 1617), reflect a unique dual culture. On the one hand, El Inca is clearly a Hispanic writer, and, on the other, his command of Quechua and his access to primary sources through personal family experience give unusual authority to his historical commentary.

The most important epic poet was Alonso de Ercilla y Zúñiga (1533–1594), who as a young Spanish officer took part in the wars of conquest against the Araucanians in Chile. His personal experiences were the basis for *La araucana* (published in three parts in 1569, 1578, and 1589), a long narrative poem that in many ways can be seen as a rhymed chronicle of the Spanish conquest of Chile. At the same time Ercilla's poem is probably the best example of the Renaissance epic (on the model of Ariosto and others) in Spanish literature. *Arauco domado* (1596), by Pedro de Oña (1570–ca. 1643), follows in the epic tradition set by Ercilla. Bernardo de Balbuena (ca. 1562–1627) wrote *Grandeza mexicana* (1604), a descriptive epic in terza rima on Mexico City, as well as the heroic epic *El Bernardo, o Victoria de Roncesvalles* (1624). *La Cristíada* (1611) was a religious epic on the Passion of Christ written by Diego de Hojeda (ca. 1571–1615).

Baroque (1620–1750). By the mid-seventeenth century a solid Hispanic social structure had been consolidated in the Spanish American colonies, with the viceregal capitals of Mexico City and Lima as the two political and cultural centers. The relative turbulence of the Conquest had long since passed, and colonial life was carried forward with a sense of stability and coherence, most especially in the upper levels of society. Affluence and conspicuous luxury were much in evidence, and the often exaggerated forms of the European baroque were used as models in colonial art, architecture, music, and literature.

The first major literary figure in this period was Juan Ruiz de Alarcón y Mendoza (1580–1639), a poet and playwright whom Alfonso Reyes has called the "first universal Mexican." Alarcón spent most of his life in Spain, where he wrote and saw produced a number of first-rank dramas, among them *La verdad sospechosa* and *Las paredes oyen* (both published with other plays in 1628 and 1634). The central figure of the baroque period, however, was Sor Juana Inés de la Cruz (ca. 1648–1695), an extraordinary Mexican writer and intellectual whose works place her in the first rank of Spanish American authors from all periods. Her literary work is varied and extensive, including a number of dramas of different types, several significant prose texts, and a large body of poetry. Her best-known plays are *Los empeños de una casa* (1683) and *El Divino Narciso* (1690); her prose works include *Carta athenagórica* (1690), a learned commentary on a sermon by Antonio Vieira, and *Respuesta a Sor Filotea de la Cruz* (1691), an unusual autobiographical justification of her intellectual life. The best of her poetry is to be found, perhaps, in a series of masterly love sonnets and in *Primero sueño* (1692).

The acerbic verses of the satirical Peruvian poet Juan del Valle y Caviedes (ca. 1652–ca. 1697) circulated widely in manuscript outside his local area (for example, Sor Juana wrote from her convent in Mexico requesting copies of his texts), but his *Diente del Parnaso* was not published definitively until 1873. Carlos de Sigüenza y Góngora (1645–1700), a leading Mexican intellectual and scientist, produced a number of literary works, among them a gongorine poem titled *Primeravera indiana* (1668) and *Los infortunios de Alonso Ramírez* (1690), a first-person narrative chronicle. Another leading figure is the Peruvian intellectual Pedro de Peralta Barnuevo y Rocha (1663–1743), whose accomplishments as a scientist, historian, and creative writer place him in the transition between the seventeenth-century baroque and the Enlightenment of the eighteenth century. His best-known work is a long epic poem on Pizarro titled *Lima fundada* (1732).

Enlightenment and Neoclassicism (1750–1820). The eighteenth century in the Spanish colonies was a period of further cultural and political development in which the liberal ideas of the French Enlightenment provided a kind of ideological framework. By the middle of the century, the extremes of the baroque style in art and literature had largely been replaced by the more playful lightness of the rococo, which in turn soon gave way to more controlled neoclassical patterns. In politics the impact of the American and French revolutions was widely felt; by the end of the century the now rather frail colonial institutions seemed ripe for change, which swept through the colonies in the early decades of the nineteenth century.

The most notable representative of Enlightenment ideas in Spanish America was Andrés Bello (1781–1865), who had a distinguished career as a public figure, educator, scholar, and writer in both

Venezuela and Chile. Among his best-known works are the neoclassical *silvas* "Alocución a la poesía" (1823) and "La agricultura de la zona tórrida" (1826). The Ecuadorian José Joaquín de Olmedo expressed in heroic style several of the battles in the struggle for independence. The most striking is *La victoria de Junín, canto a Bolívar* (1825), a long silva that celebrates Bolívar's 1824 victory with grandiose images. José María Heredia y Heredia (1803–1839) is a transitional figure between the waning of neoclassicism and a developing romanticism. Born in Cuba, he spent most of his life in exile; the resulting tension is visible in many of his poetic works. His two best-known texts are neoclassical odes. "En el Teocalli de Cholula" (1820) uses the Mexican pyramid for a reflection on tyranny and the passage of time; "Niágara" (1824) describes the famous cataract in precise terms but at the same time is an impassioned comment on exile.

Two major prose writers of this period should be mentioned. Under the pseudonym "Concolorcorvo," Alonso Carrió de la Vandera (ca. 1715–1783) wrote *El lazarillo de ciegos caminantes* (1773), a first-person picaresque description of a journey from Buenos Aires and Montevideo to Lima. José Joaquín Fernández de Lizardi (1776–1827), known also by his pseudonym "El Pensador Mexicano," was strongly influenced by Enlightenment ideas and by a desire for social reform. His most famous work is *El Periquillo Sarniento* (1816), a four-volume picaresque novel sharply critical of social conditions in prerevolutionary Mexico and often considered to be the first Spanish American novel. The best dramatist of this period was Manuel Eduardo de Gorostiza (1789–1851), whose work was identified both with Mexico and Spain. He wrote a number of plays and adaptations, the best known of which is *Contigo pan y cebolla* (1833).

Romanticism (1820–1880). The coming of independence in Spanish America initiated an extended period of national definition. In the post-conflict decades many of the developing national entities were either anarchic or dominated by dictatorial strongmen, and it was not until well into the latter part of the nineteenth century that the now independent Spanish American nations were able even to glimpse the stability and democracy envisioned by the liberators.

Literary expression during these decades was centrally influenced by romanticism, which placed itself in opposition to the rational streams of neoclassicism and proposed to give a dominant place to strong human emotions. In keeping with a culture in the process of consolidation, the Spanish American romantics differed in many ways from the Europeans. They described a distinct landscape, for example, with regional languages and customs and with indigenous people and the gaucho as romantic heroes. They expressed as well the ongoing Spanish American conflict between rural and urban values or, as Domingo Faustino Sarmiento (1811–1886) expressed it, between civilization and barbarism.

After extended residence in Paris the Argentine Esteban Echeverría (1805–1851) became one of the principal standard-bearers for romanticism in Spanish America. He found himself in conflict with the despotic Juan Manuel de Rosas, and his literary associations and publications are colored by that tension. His best-known poem is "La cautiva" (1837), a work that applies European aesthetic ideas to an Argentine reality. He is most remembered, however, for his vivid short story "El matadero," a brutal denunciation of Rosas probably written in 1839 but not published until 1871.

Several romantic poets should be mentioned here. The most memorable works of the Cuban mulatto poet "Plácido" (Gabriel de la Concepción Valdés, 1809–1844) are the ballad "Jicoténcal" and the ode "Plegaria a Dios." Gertrudis Gómez de Avellaneda (1814–1873) was born in Cuba but spent much of her life in Spain, and in many ways was the prototypical anguished romantic. She wrote poetry (including such emotional texts as "Al partir" and "Al destino"), theatrical works, legends, and novels. Perhaps her most remembered work is the antislavery novel *Sab* (1841). Gaucho poetry in the River Plate region developed as a significant late romantic expression. Among the foremost poets are two Argentines: Estanislao del Campo (1834–1880), whose comic poem *Fausto* (1866) makes a unique contribution to this subgenre, and José Hernández (1834–1886), whose two-volume mock epic *Martín Fierro* (*El gaucho Martín Fierro*, 1872; *La vuelta de Martín Fierro*, 1879) has become Argentina's national work. In Hernández's poem the gaucho is no longer comic or folkloric, but in the person of Fierro rather a tragic figure who must deal with the contradictory demands of modern society. The Uruguayan poet Juan Zorrilla de San Martín (1855–1931) wrote an extensive lyrical epic titled *Tabaré* (1888), whose indigenous theme and musical language represent a point of transition between romanticism and modernism.

The prose writing of the period was varied and included both narrative and expository forms. Sarmiento, a central Argentine figure of romanticism, wrote the classic prose work *Civilización i barbarie: La vida de Juan Facundo Quiroga* (1845), generally known simply as *Facundo*, which is neither novel nor history; rather, it is a dialectical attempt to capture the essence of an area under development. The novel as such was carried forward by such writers as the Argentine José Mármol (1817–1871), whose *Amalia* (1851) was the best political novel of the period; by the Colombian Jorge Isaacs (1837–1895), whose *María* (1867) was the prototypical sentimental romantic novel; and by the Chilean Alberto Blest Gana (1830–1920), whose *Martín Rivas* (1862) used realistic detail to depict the society of its time. The Peruvian Ricardo Palma (1833–1919) occupies a unique place among late romantic prose writers. His *Tradiciones peruanas*, published in several series beginning in 1872, are short narrative pieces that allow Palma to make effective use of an encyclopedic knowledge of the colonial period and an unusual verbal inventiveness. The major essayist of the period was Juan Montalvo (1832–1889) of Ecuador, whose masterwork *Siete tratados* (1882) placed him among the best prose writers in the Spanish language. Also important is *Moral social* (1888), by the Puerto Rican Eugenio María de Hostos y Bonilla (1839–1903).

Realism-Naturalism (1880–1915). By 1880 the majority of the Spanish American nations had enjoyed some fifty years of political independence, and from that point through the turn of the century they began to enjoy a modicum of stability and economic prosperity. Reflecting a concern for renovation, the literary expression of these decades can best be seen in two distinct and parallel dimensions: first, the development of prose fiction and other associated genres influenced by realism and naturalism and, second, the studied cultivation of poetic discourse in what came to be designated as modernism.

The beginnings of realism in Spanish America can be traced to Blest Gana and other writers of the preceding period. During the decades around the turn of the century, however, there are several very significant novelists and short-story writers who bring this focus to fuller development. First among them might be the Peruvian Clorinda Matto de Turner (1852–1909), whose *Aves sin nido* (1889) is considered to be the first true *indigenista* novel in Spanish America. Tomás Carrasquilla (1858–1940) of Colombia developed an engaging regionalist view of his own native area, in which popular language and situations are used effectively. His best works are *Frutos de mi tierra* (1896) and *En la diestra de Dios Padre* (1903). Roberto J. Payró (1867–1928) presented a picaresque view of Argentine life in *El casamiento de Laucha* (1906) and *Pago Chico* (1908).

Naturalism, especially the work of Émile Zola, was a determining influence for several Spanish American writers. Carlos Reyles (1868–1938) of Uruguay, for example, wrote naturalistic novels, among them *Beba* (1894) and *La raza de Caín* (1900). Another Uruguayan, Javier de Viana (1868–1926), used the gaucho setting for a number of collections of naturalistic short stories, such as *Campo* (1896), *Leña seca* (1911), and *Yuyos* (1912). The Chilean coal mines, factories, and farms provided settings for the short stories of Baldomero Lillo (1867–1923), who was clearly influenced by Zola. *Sub terra* (1904), a very successful collection protesting mine conditions, contains such well-known texts as "El chiflón del diablo" and "La compuerta número 12." *Sob sole* (1907), a second collection dealing with the problems of peasants and other workers, is not of the same quality.

It is appropriate to consider under realism the works of the Uruguayan playwright Florencio Sánchez (1875–1910), who is the first major figure of the modern Spanish American theater. His principal works—*M'hijo el dotor* (1903), *La gringa* (1904), and *Barranca abajo* (1905)—represent in realistic terms the tension between rural and urban values.

Modernism (1880–1915). The period of relative political stability after 1880 favored the parallel development of what is now known as modernism, which extended over some three or four decades, well into the new century, and gave rise to major literary centers (Mexico City and Buenos Aires, among others) and to significant literary journals (such as *Revista Azul* and *Revista Moderna*). Modernist writers, central among them such figures as José Martí, Rubén Darío, and Leopoldo Lugones, were motivated by the desire to revitalize what they saw as antiquated literary discourse in Spanish, and, using the French Parnassian and symbolist poets as models, they strove for musicality and perfection of form in their works. Figurative language was rich and sensorial, with preference given to chromatic imagery and elegant symbolism (i.e., the color blue or the graceful figure of the swan). Themes were exotic or introspective, and a profound disenchantment with mediocre surroundings led many modernists to take refuge in invented "ivory tower" worlds.

The multifaceted literary work of the Cuban patriot José Martí (1853–1895) is at the center of a first group of modernist writers. Martí's political activities forced him to spend much of his life in exile, and his sizable literary production is closely related to his life-long profession as a journalist. His prose writings (essays, *crónicas*, short stories, and *Amistad funesta*, a novel published in 1885) represent an important contribution to the renovation of prose style during the modernist years. His books of poetry are, however, his most significant literary contribution: *Ismaelillo* (1882), short poems written to his absent son, and *Versos sencillos* (1891), a collection of musical eight-syllable poems containing some of Martí's best-known lines. Two other collections, *Versos libres* (written around 1882 but not published until 1913) and *Flores del destierro* (written between 1882 and 1891 but not published until 1933), appeared after Martí's death. Other early modernists were the Mexican Manuel Gutiérrez Nájera (1859–1895), the Cuban Julián del Casal (1863–1893), and the Colombian José Asunción Silva (1865–1896). Nájera, a recognized journalist, founded the well-known modernist journal *Revista Azul.* His musical and strikingly chromatic verses appeared largely in literary journals and were collected after his death as *Poesías* (1896). Casal's sensorial poetry, particularly that published in *Nieve* (1892) and *Bustos y rimas* (1893), expressed in a most poignant way modernism's pessimistic dimension. Silva's poems also appeared first in literary journals, and only after he committed suicide were they finally collected and published as *Poesías* (1908). Silva's "Nocturno" is his best-known single work; its sensuality and novel use of a four-syllable rhythmic foot earned the poet a considerable international reputation.

Rubén Darío (pseudonym of Nicaraguan writer Félix Rubén García Sarmiento, 1867–1916) is the central figure of a second grouping, and indeed can be seen as the quintessential modernist presence. He left his native Central America as a young man and with varied diplomatic and journalistic assignments spent many years in South America and Europe. His extensive literary production, which includes short stories, essays, and travel commentaries, as well as a number of volumes of poetry, reflects a varied international life. Darío's *Azul...* (1888; 2d ed., 1890) combines prose and poetry and is often cited as a key early modernist work. More innovative than his poems are Darío's lyrical short stories (e.g., "El pájaro azul"), especially in the 1888 edition. The *Prosas profanas y otros poemas* (1896; 2d ed., 1901) is the high point in Darío's luxuriant and aristocratic modernist art. The third work is *Cantos de vida y esperanza. Los cisnes y otros poemas* (1905), perhaps Darío's best single poetry collection and one that represents at the same time a period of maturity in modernist development. Darío's later collections, *El canto errante* (1907) and *Poema del otoño y otros poemas* (1910), continue this same introspection but do not reach the level attained in *Cantos de vida y esperanza.*

Other poets who with Rubén Darío contributed to the second modernist group include the Bolivian Ricardo Jaimes Freyre (1868–1933), the Mexican Amado Nervo (1870–1919), the Colombian Guillermo Valencia (1873–1943), the Peruvian José Santos Chocano (1875–1934), and the Uruguayan Julio Herrera y Reissig (1875–1910). In his unusual work *Castalia bárbara* (1899), Jaimes Freyre made novel use of Nordic myths and imagery and also experimented with metrical form. Nervo's voluminous work revolves around religious and existential concerns, in particular the anguish resulting from the loss of a loved person. In form, his poetry moved from the modernist patterns of *Perlas negras* and *Místicas*, both published in 1898, toward the spare presentations of *Serenidad* (1914) and *Elevación* (1917). Valencia's *Ritos* (1899) shows modernist elegance and precision in its attention to metrical form and chromatic imagery. Chocano's principal work, and the one most closely aligned with modernism, is the torrential *Alma América; poemas indo-españoles* (1906). One of the most fascinating and difficult figures of the entire movement, Herrera y Reissig represented in many ways the epitome of a bohemian and extravagant modernist lifestyle, and his published poetic work, collected the year of his death in a volume entitled *Los peregrinos de piedra* (1909), has at its center a most demanding metaphorical structuring.

The central figure in a third modernist group is the Argentine Leopoldo Lugones (1874–1938), whose some thirty-five published volumes include poetry, prose fiction, political commentary, historical treatises, and literary and cultural studies. His very sizable contributions to prose fiction came with such titles as *La guerra gaucha* (1905) and *Las fuerzas extrañas* (1906); similar contributions to history, culture, and literary studies are in *Historia de Sarmiento* (1911) and *El payador* (1916). His major poetic works are *Las montañas del oro* (1897), a collection of rather audacious texts using an innovative prose-like form; *Los crepúsculos del jardín* (1905), a volume of carefully worked texts in modernist style; *Lunario sentimental* (1909), a curious mix of poetry, fiction, and dramatic pieces using the lunar theme; and *Las horas doradas* (1922), simple contemplations on the beauties of the natural world.

Other poets to be considered in this third group are the Mexicans Enrique González Martínez (1871–1952) and José Juan Tablada (1871–1945), and the Peruvian José María Eguren (1874–1942). The early works of González Martínez are very much within the modernist poetic, but his sonnet "Tuércele el cuello al cisne" (in *Los senderos ocultos*, 1911) appeared to call for a violent end to Darío's modernism. Tablada published a collection of modernist verses under the title of *El florilegio* (1899), and then, in books like *Li-Pó y otros poemas* (*poemas ideográficos*) (1920), turned to experimentations with miniature Oriental forms and visual poetry. Eguren's delicately chromatic verses, generally in short lines and also with figures in miniature, were collected in *Simbólicas* (1911) and *La canción de las figuras* (1916).

Three other modernist prose writers deserve mention. The most important novel by Venezuelan Manuel Díaz Rodríguez (1871–1927) is *Sangre patricia* (1902), a poetic work that uses a shifting point of view to examine the internal dimensions of its central character. The best modernist narrative work, however, is *La gloria de don Ramiro* (1908), a historical novel written by the Argentine Enrique Larreta (1873–1961) in which sixteenth-century Ávila, Spain, is brought to life in a veritable symphony of places, persons, and sensorial impressions. The principal essayist of modernism is the Uruguayan academic José Enrique Rodó (1872–1917), whose most famous work is *Ariel* (1900), a philosophical essay in six chapters that uses Shakespeare's character to speak in support of morality and beauty and to inveigh against materialism, especially that of the United States. *Motivos de Proteo* (1909) is a fragmented gathering of parables, exhortations, confessions, and allegories that together illustrate Rodó's working out of a kind of spiritual autobiography.

Connecting the final stages of modernism and the beginning experimentation of the vanguardists is a transitional grouping, to which the Mexican Ramón López Velarde (1888–1921) clearly belongs. His first two poetry collections, *La sangre devota* (1916) and *Zozobra* (1919), are largely in the modernist tradition; his later work, published posthumously as *El son del corazón* (1932), anticipates a number of the stylistic complexities of the vanguardists. Another major figure is Chilean Gabriela Mistral (pseudonym of Lucila Godoy Alcayaga, 1889–1957), who in 1945 was the first Spanish American to be awarded the Nobel Prize for literature. Her principal collections—*Desolación* (1922), *Tala* (1938), and *Lagar* (1954)—reveal a poetic discourse that evolved away from the decorative aspects of modernism toward an impassioned and anguished simplicity. Also a part of this group are the Uruguayan Juana de Ibarbourou (1895–1979), whose sensual verses appeared in *Las lenguas de diamante* (1919) and *Raíz salvaje* (1922); the Uruguayan Delmira Agustini (1886–1914), whose best-known work is *Los cálices vacíos* (1913); and the Argentine Alfonsina Storni (1892–1938), whose acid feminist verses are best represented in *Ocre* (1925).

Several essayists belong to this transitional group. The Mexican Alfonso Reyes (1889–1959), a talented poet as well as a novelist and an essayist, produced in *Visión de Anáhuac* (1917) a major contribution to the consolidation of a Spanish American cultural unity. A fellow Mexican, José Vasconcelos (1882–1959), commented on the cultural role of the mestizo and the indigenous people in *La raza cósmica* (1925), and the Peruvian José Carlos Mariátegui (1894–1930) dealt with similar concerns in his *Siete ensayos de interpretación sobre de la realidad peruana* (1928). The writings of Pedro Henríquez Ureña (1884–1946) of the Dominican Republic displayed wide interest in language, culture, and literature; one of his best works is *Seis ensayos en busca de nuestra expresión* (1928).

Vanguardism (1915–1945). Three major political events during the second decade of the twentieth century introduced a period of rejection of established values: the Mexican Revolution (1910–1917), World War I (1914–1918), and the Russian Revolution (1917). As was the case in the preceding period, Spanish American literary expression in the two or three decades following 1920 once again developed essentially in two distinct but parallel dimensions: the intense and multiform experimentations in poetic discourse now generally designated as vanguardism and the equally significant exploration of Latin American problems and values in regional *criollista* prose fiction.

Vanguardism was strongly influenced by such experimental European movements as Cubism, Futurism, and Surrealism, but in its Latin American setting vanguardism was primarily a rejection of the modernist aesthetic. Truth and beauty were no longer to be found in musicality, order, and careful delineation; the destruction of such "antiquated" concepts was necessary in order to fashion altered poetic worlds envisioned by the "new" poet or those to be found in the disordered flow of the subconscious. Free verse took the place of metered form; nonregular structures, hermetic imagery, and visual typographic experimentations became hallmarks of vanguardist poetic discourse.

The most important vanguardist figure is without doubt the Chilean Vicente Huidobro (1893–1948), who spent significant periods of his life in France and Spain and whose work includes both the elaboration of a theory he called "creationism" and a very substantial poetic praxis. At the center of Huidobro's theory are the concepts that the "new" poet has divine powers in his small realm (Huidobro averred in one of his most famous lines that the poet is a minor god) and that imitative conventionalities should not interfere with those powers. Huidobro's poetry was published in both Spanish and French, with such titles as *El espejo de agua* (1916), *Horizon carré* (1917), and *Poemas árticos* (1918). His masterwork is *Altazor, o el viaje en paracaídas* (1931), whose descending imagery is at once the culmination and the destruction of the poet's theoretical ideas.

A second major figure, though one not so centrally identified with the theoretical issues of vanguardism, is the Peruvian César Vallejo (1892–1938). Vallejo also spent significant portions of his life in Europe, principally in France and Spain, and in his essays and prose fiction took a committed political stance. His best works, however, are still his three volumes of poetry. In *Los heraldos negros* (1918), *Trilce* (1922), and *Poemas humanos* (1939), Vallejo experiments with structure and figurative language but at the same time communicates a profound and tragic vision of human existence. Other important figures in a first vanguardist group are the Argentines Oliverio Girondo (1891–1967) and Jorge Luis Borges (1899–1986), and the Cuban Mariano Brull (1891–1956). Girondo and Borges made major contributions to the development of Ultraism in Argentina, the first with his collections *Veinte poemas para ser leídos en el tranvía* (1922) and *Calcomanías* (1925), and the second with *Fervor de Buenos Aires* (1923), *Luna de enfrente* (1925), and *Cuaderno de San Martín* (1929). Brull's playful sonorities are best represented in *Poemas en menguante* (1928).

A second vanguardist group followed the central figure of the Chilean Pablo Neruda (pseudonym of Neftalí Ricardo Reyes Basoalto, 1904–1973), whose voluminous poetic production extended over almost five decades and earned him the Nobel Prize for literature in 1971. In contrast to Huidobro, Neruda paid little attention to theoretical concerns, preferring to express in poetry the ever-changing vision of the world around him. His first major work, *Veinte poemas de amor y una canción desesperada* (1924), over the years became Neruda's most popular book. His most vanguardist verses are *Tentativa del hombre infinito* (1926) and *Residencia en la tierra* (1933, 1935), the second reflecting Neruda's often anguished consular service in Southeast Asia. Beginning with *España en el corazón* (1937), an incandescent protest volume on the Spanish Civil War, a political and openly Marxist commitment became increasingly evident in Neruda's poetry: *Tercera residencia* (1947); *Canto general* (1950), which includes the well-known "Alturas de Macchu Picchu" (the Incan fortress city); *Canción de gesta* (1960), a

Reader with a newspaper bearing Nobel Prize–winning Colombian author Gabriel García Márquez's image, Mexico City, Mexico, 2007. In addition to following elements of European literary styles, Latin American literature also shows a distinctive influence from the indigenous peoples who related stories by oral tradition thousands of years before the arrival of the Spanish. RONALDO SCHEMIDT/AFP/GETTY IMAGES

celebration of the Cuban Revolution; and *Incitación al Nixonicidio* (1973), a scathing denunciation of the United States. Neruda also developed a spare, columnar poetic form to represent the small details of his surrounding world. These novel texts appeared first in *Odas elementales* (1954) and were continued in several additional collections during the 1950s.

Other important figures in the second vanguardist group are the Puerto Rican Luis Palés Matos (1898–1959), the Cuban Nicolás Guillén (1902), and the Mexicans José Gorostiza (1901–1973) and Xavier Villaurrutia (1903–1950). Palés Matos and Guillén are the most important representatives of the vanguardist experimentation in Afro-Antillian forms and rhythms, Palés with *Tuntún de pasa y grifería* (1937) and Guillén with *Motivos de son* (1930), *Sóngoro consongo* (1931), and *West Indies, Ltd.* (1934). Gorostiza and Villaurrutia combined complexities of language and death imagery with carefully worked poetic form; Gorostiza's *Muerte sin fin* (1939) is one of the great twentieth-century poems in the Spanish language, and Villaurrutia's major collection is *Nostalgia de la muerte* (1938).

The Regional Novel and Short Story (1915–1945). Prose fiction during these decades showed a pattern of development parallel to but distinct from that of the experimental poetic forms of vanguardism. The jungles, the plains, the cities, and the conflicts of modernization became the settings for a number of compelling works, as first-rank writers established an international readership and set the stage for the Boom period in the latter half of the century.

The Mexican Revolution of 1910 provided the motivation for one of the most significant examples of a regionally specific prose fiction. The central figure is Mariano Azuela (1873–1952), a novelist and medical doctor who himself fought in the Revolution. His most famous novel, and the prototypical novel of the Revolution, is *Los de abajo* (1915), in which Azuela depicts with graphic detail and a cyclic structure the disorderly development of the conflict. Other significant novels by Azuela are *La Malhora* (1923) and *La luciérnaga* (1932). The most famous work of Martín Luis Guzmán (1887–1976) is *El águila y la serpiente* (1928), not really a novel but rather a representation of important personalities and events during the revolutionary years. Once again, the author was himself a participant, and his personal view of such figures as Carranza and Villa make his account an especially compelling one. José Rubén Romero (1890–1952) wrote several novels on the Revolution, among them *Mi caballo, mi perro y mi rifle* (1936), but he is probably best known for his salacious depiction of Mexican life contained in the picaresque *La vida inútil de Pito Pérez* (1938).

Both the Venezuelan Rómulo Gallegos (1884–1969) and the Colombian José Eustasio Rivera (1888–1928) situate their novels in northern South America. Gallegos's masterwork, *Doña Bárbara* (1929), is set on the Venezuelan *llano*, and depicts through a strong female central character the struggle between the same antagonistic forces of civilization and barbarity that Sarmiento had earlier studied. Rivera chose the rubber-growing region of the Colombian jungle as the setting for *La vorágine* (1924). His protagonist is ultimately swallowed up by the "green hell" of the jungle, and Rivera's vivid first-person descriptions remain the most significant dimension of the novel.

Social protest is a central concern of the indigenist novel, particularly that set in the Andean region. In his *Raza de bronce* (1919) the Bolivian Alcides Arguedas (1879–1946) represented the unresolved conflict between indigenous people and landowners, though more in a spirit of submission than protest. The protest is intensified in the works of the Ecuadorian Jorge Icaza (1906–1978), whose *Huasipungo* (1934) is probably the most representative indigenist novel. The indigenous community mounts a disorganized and unsuccessful rebellion against the despotic landholders who want to remove them from their small parcels of land (*huasipungos*). The most famous work of the Peruvian Ciro Alegría (1909–1967) is *El mundo es ancho y ajeno* (1941), a novel that once again deals with the dispossession of indigenous community lands by a rapacious landowner.

Many of the short stories of the Uruguayan Horacio Quiroga (1878–1937), most especially those from *Cuentos de amor, de locura y de muerte* (1917), reveal a sharp awareness of both the remote Argentine-Uruguayan setting of Misiones and the unusual narrative techniques of Edgar Allan Poe. The Argentine Ricardo Güiraldes (1886–1927) wrote poetry and short stories but is best known for his splendid gaucho novel *Don Segundo Sombra* (1926). The "master" Don Segundo is seen through the eyes of his young admirer Fabio, and becomes the shadowy embodiment of the entire gaucho tradition.

The Chileans Eduardo Barrios (1884–1963) and Pedro Prado (1886–1952) should be considered here, through their best novels are not necessarily regional in setting. Barrios is best known for *El hermano asno* (1922), a psychological study of the closed world of a monastery; Prado's masterwork is *Alsino* (1920), a fanciful poetic novel about a young boy who grows wings.

Poetry, Drama, and the Essay, 1945–1995. The last half of the twentieth century was a period of considerable tension, brought on by the Cold War, the Cuban Revolution, widespread guerrilla movements, and the growing drug trade. Against that backdrop, however, literary expression has shown extraordinary development in all genres. In poetry the major figure is the Mexican Octavio Paz (1914–1998), whose imposing work won him the Nobel Prize in 1990. *Libertad bajo palabra* (1949, expanded in 1960) is a compilation of his earlier poetry; *Blanco* (1967), *Pasado en claro* (1975), and *Árbol adentro* (1987) represent his later work. Paz was also a brilliant cultural and literary essayist; *El laberinto de la soledad* (1950), a commentary on modern Mexican culture, and *Los hijos del limo* (1974), on the interconnections between romanticism and the avant-garde, are only two of many influential works. Other important poets who are roughly contemporaneous with Paz are the Cuban José Lezama Lima (1910–1976), the Nicaraguan Pablo Antonio Cuadra (1912–2002), and the Chileans Nicanor Parra (*b.* 1914) and Gonzalo Rojas (*b.* 1917). Lezama's anguished and self-reflective poetry found its fullest expression in *La fijeza* (1949) and *Dador* (1960); both his essays and his novel *Paradiso* (1966) reveal similar complexities. Cuadra's poetry develops a central view of his native country; *Cantos de Cifar* (1971), set in the central lake region of Nicaragua, and *Siete árboles contra el atardecer* (1980), a totemic vision of a multiple Nicaraguan reality, are examples of that view. Parra is best known for *Poemas y antipoemas* (1954), which set in motion a denunciatory poetic style. Rojas is passionate, irreverent, and at the same time brilliantly sensorial in his poetic language. *Materia de testamento* (1988) is an excellent collection of his recent work.

A number of writers born in the 1920s or later have made significant contributions to the development of contemporary poetry, but there is space here only for the most schematic of representations. Important poets born in the 1920s, for example, would include Álvaro Mutis (Colombia, 1923), Ernesto Cardenal (Nicaragua, 1925), Rosario Castellanos (Mexico, 1925–1974), Jaime Sabines (Mexico, 1925), Roberto Juárroz (Argentina, 1925), Carlos Germán Belli (Peru, 1927), and Enrique Lihn (Chile, 1929–1988). Significant poets born in the 1930s include Juan Gelman (Argentina, 1930), Roque Dalton (El Salvador, 1935–1975), Alejandra Pizarnik (Argentina, 1936–1972), Óscar Hahn (Chile, 1938), and José Emilio Pacheco (Mexico, 1939). Among those poets born in the 1940s or later who should be mentioned are José Kozer (Cuba, 1940), Antonio Cisneros (Peru, 1942), Rosario Ferré (Puerto Rico, 1942), Arturo Carrera (Argentina, 1948), Néstor Perlongher (Argentina, 1948), David Huerta (Mexico, 1949), and Coral Bracho (Mexico, 1951).

The drama has enjoyed spectacular development over the past several decades, a transformation that critics have referred to as the "new" Spanish American theater. Significant initial contributions to that development were made by the Mexicans Xavier Villaurrutia (1903–1950) and Rodolfo Usigli (1905–1979). Villaurrutia's best full-length play is a reworking of the Hamlet theme titled *Invitación a la muerte* (1943; staged in 1947); Usigli is best known for his use of Mexican culture and history, particularly in *El gesticulator* (1943; staged in 1947) and *Corona de sombra* (1943; staged in 1947). René Marqués (Puerto Rico, 1919–1979), Carlos Gorostiza (Argentina, 1920), and Carlos Solórzano (Guatemala, 1922) made substantial contributions in the 1950s. Marqués's best plays are the ever-popular *La carreta* (1952), which depicts the disintegration of Puerto Rican rural life, and *Los soles truncos* (1959), in which the pressures of the modern world produce the suicide of three aging sisters. In *El juicio* (1954) and *El pan de la locura* (1958), Gorostiza uses realistic staging for pointed social commentary. *Las manos de Dios* (1956), Solórzano's best play, also carries a strong social message but one that is expressed in the more symbolic terms of traditional religious drama.

In the 1960s, a group of brilliant younger dramatists began to make their presence known and have continued to express themselves up to the present. Emilio Carballido (Mexico, 1925) is a major figure, whose extensive work includes such successes as *Yo también hablo de la rosa* (1970), a commentary on multiple reality, *Tiempo de ladrones* (1983), a long melodramatic presentation based on the bandit-hero Chucho el Roto, and *Rosa de dos aromas* (1986), a double-sided spoof on traditional machismo. The plays of Egon Wolff (Chile, 1926), especially *Los invasores* (1964) and *Flores de papel* (1970), depict the invasion and destruction of middle-class values. Loss of freedom and movement is the dominant theme in the plays of Griselda Gambaro (Argentina, 1928), as seen sharply in *Los siameses* (1967) and *El campo* (1967, staged in 1968). Fellow Argentine Osvaldo Dragún (1929) is best known for his *Historias para ser contadas* (1982), a series of whimsical but often sharply critical one-act plays. *El cepillo de dientes* (1967), depicting bizarre everyday rituals by El and Ella, is an obvious incursion into theater of the absurd by Jorge Díaz (Chile, 1930). Equally absurdist but considerably more violent is *La noche de los asesinos* (1965, staged in 1966) by José Triana (Cuba, 1933): the three characters act out over and over the murder of their parents. The plays of Eduardo Pavlovsky (Argentina, 1933) deal with the violence of recent Argentine history: *El señor Galíndez* (1973), for example, is set in a well-equipped torture chamber that becomes increasingly visible as the play progresses. Vicente Leñero (Mexico, 1933) makes adroit use of everyday Mexican language in his *Jesucristo Gómez* (1986; staged in 1987), a present-day reworking of the Gospel of Luke in which Christ becomes an ordinary bricklayer, and in his *Nadie sabe nada*

(1988), a searing denunciation of Mexican journalism and public life.

Prose Fiction, 1945–1995. The novel and the short story have also enjoyed extraordinary development over the past several decades, and critics have used the stock-market term "boom" in discussing what has been seen as the new narrative in recent Spanish American literature. This development really began before 1945, with the publication of *La última niebla* (1934) and *La amortajada* (1938) by the Chilean María Luisa Bombal (1910–1980). These two novels represent a sensitive probing of the feminine psyche but at the same time make effective use of a poetic style and experimentation in point of view. In the 1940s the movement toward a new narrative can be seen clearly in the works of Jorge Luis Borges (Argentina, 1899–1986), whose brilliant short fiction was collected first in *Ficciones* (1944) and then in *El aleph* (1956). The labyrinthine circularities of Borges's best tales, among them "La biblioteca de Babel," "El jardín de senderos que se bifurcan," "La muerte y la brújula," and "Las ruinas circulares," call into question the very processes of writing and reading. *El informe de Brodie* (1970) contains some of Borges's best later work. Miguel Ángel Asturias (Guatemala, 1899–1974) is best known for *El señor presidente* (1946) and *Hombres de maíz* (1949), two novels that combine sophisticated narrative technique, social message, and indigenous myths. Asturias was awarded the Nobel Prize for literature in 1967. Eduardo Mallea (Argentina, 1903–1982) was a prolific and expansive novelist; his best works are *La bahía de silencio* (1940) and his masterpiece, *Todo verdor perecerá* (1941), both intense psychological studies presented in a complex narrative style. The unusual historical and musical background of Alejo Carpentier (Cuba, 1904–1980) found brilliant expression in his novels and short stories, especially in *El reino de este mundo* (1949), a novel based on the Haitian revolution, and the shorter historical pieces of *Guerra del tiempo* (1958). Agustín Yáñez (Mexico, 1904–1980) is best remembered for *Al filo del agua* (1947), a novel that uses sophisticated narrative techniques to present the tensions of a small Jalisco village at the beginning of the Mexican Revolution. Juan Carlos Onetti (Uruguay, 1909) is a prolific novelist and short-story writer, whose masterworks are *La vida breve* (1950), a complex interplay between fiction and reality, and *El astillero* (1961), in which the pointless rebuilding of a ruined shipyard becomes an allegorical reference to Uruguayan reality.

Author Julio Cortázar, Paris, France, 1969. Latin American authors such as Cortázar began to receive wide notoriety and acclaim from the literature community in the 1960s and 1970s. PIERRE BOULAT/TIME LIFE PICTURES/GETTY IMAGES

In the 1950s other younger writers began to contribute to the developing new narrative. José María Arguedas (Peru, 1911–1969) published *Los ríos profundos* (1958), an unusual novel that uses both Spanish and Quechua in the communication of a multicultural Andean reality. Augusto Roa Bastos (Paraguay, 1917–2005) received international attention for *Hijo de hombre* (1960) and *Yo, el supremo* (1974), the second a contribution to the so-called dictator novel. Juan Rulfo (Mexico, 1918–1986) produced two masterworks. The first is *El llano en llamas* (1953), a collection of short stories set in rural

Gabriel García Márquez's birthplace, Aracataca, Colombia. Local officials have pledged to rebuild the decaying museum dedicated to García Márquez in the town that inspired the fictional Macondo in his *One Hundred Years of Solitude*. AP IMAGES

Jalisco, and the second is the extraordinarily complex *Pedro Páramo* (1955), a novel in whose pages the living hell of the created town of Comala and its inhabitants can be experienced. Juan José Arreola (Mexico, 1918–2001) is best known for his brilliant and highly intellectual short fiction, collected first in *Confabulario* (1952) and then in *Confabulario total* (1962). In *Balún Canán* (1957) and *Oficio de tinieblas* (1962), Rosario Castellanos (Mexico, 1925–1974) uses the indigenous setting of her native state of Chiapas in making a memorable contribution.

The 1960s and 1970s saw the publication of an unusually large number of first-rank narrative works, and the consequent coining and wide use of the Boom terminology to characterize the production of those decades. The oldest of the principal figures is Julio Cortázar (Argentina, 1914–1984), whose novel *Rayuela* (1963) was one of the opening salvos in this war of innovation. The most celebrated feature of the novel is an open-ended "Table of Instructions," which invites readers to follow an idiosyncratic and rather whimsical pattern established by the author or to invent their own approaches to the reading of the novel. The first novel by Carlos Fuentes (Mexico, 1928) was *La región más transparente* (1958), a mythical-realistic incursion into the roiling world of Mexico City; in *La muerte de Artemio Cruz* (1962) Fuentes uses an unusual triadic structure to delve into a contradictory personality that is representative of post-Revolutionary Mexico. *La ciudad y los perros* (1963), a complex narration set in a real Lima military academy, was the prize-winning first novel by Mario Vargas Llosa (Peru, 1936); even more involved was his second novel, *La casa verde* (1966). Guillermo Cabrera Infante (Cuba, 1929–2005) published the highly inventive and very Cuban *Tres tristes tigres* in 1967. The best-known work of Gabriel García Márquez (Colombia, 1928), who received the Nobel Prize in 1982, is *Cien años de soledad* (1967), the paradigmatic Boom novel. Set in the banana-growing region of

Colombia, the work develops the history, often in magical terms, of the fictional town of Macondo and its leading family. García Márquez's successful later novels include *Crónica de una muerte anunciada* (1981) and *El amor en los tiempos de cólera* (1985). The principal contributions of Manuel Puig (Argentina, 1932–1990) came with *La traición de Rita Hayworth* (1968) and *Boquitas pintadas* (1969), novels that demonstrated connections to the cinema and other popular art forms. José Donoso (Chile, 1924) contributed to the wave of new fiction with *El obsceno pájaro de la noche* (1970), a dark representation of Chilean society, and then with *Casa de campo* (1978), an allegory of the 1973 military coup.

There are a number of post-Boom prose fiction writers who deserve attention, among them are Severo Sarduy (Cuba, 1936–1992), Luisa Valenzuela (Argentina, 1938), José Emilio Pacheco (Mexico, 1939), Alfredo Bryce-Echenique (Peru, 1939), Gustavo Sainz (Mexico, 1940), Antonio Skármeta (Chile, 1940), Eduardo Galeano (Uruguay, 1940), Cristina Peri Rossi (Uruguay, 1941), Isabel Allende (Chile, 1942), Rosario Ferré (Puerto Rico, 1942), and Reinaldo Arenas (Cuba, 1943–1990).

MERLIN H. FORSTER

THE LITERATURE OF SPANISH AMERICA SINCE 1995

Since the mid-1990s, there has been a noticeable break with past generational models, as new writers shaped by more recent history have arisen, and new genres and forms have gained prominence.

Prose Fiction. The most pronounced characteristic of Spanish American fiction since the mid-1990s is its distance from the writing models associated with Magical Realism, the literary genre that predominated in the Spanish-language editorial market during the 1980s. At least two important milestones indicate this transition. The first is the appearance in 1996 of the controversial anthology of short stories *McOndo*, coedited by Alberto Fuguet (Chile, b. 1964), who became known in the early 1990s for his novel *Mala Onda* (Bad Vibes, 1991). The second milestone is the upsurge of another Chilean, Roberto Bolaño (1953–2003), on the literary scene in the mid-1990s. As suggested by the title, *McOndo* (an ironic allusion to García Márquezś mythical town of Macondo) proposes a writing style inserted into an urban, globalized, transnational setting—the anthology indistinctly incorporates both Spanish and Hispano-American writers—profoundly affected by the mass media. In the same spirit has emerged the self-proclaimed "Crack Generation" of Mexican writers, who announced themselves with a collective manifesto in 1996. In this generation of prolific writers, the most prominent include Jorge Volpi (Mexico, b. 1968), author of the novels *En busca de Klingsor* (1999; *In Search of Klingsor*, 2002) and *El fin de la locura* (The End of Insanity, 2003) and Ignacio Padilla (Mexico, b. 1968), author of *Amphitryon* (2000; *Shadow without a Name*, 2003). These writers are represented in the anthologies *Líneas aéreas* (Airlines, 1999) and *Se habla español* (2000), the latter edited by Fuguet and Edmundo Paz Soldán (Bolivia, b. 1967) and distributed in the United States.

Perhaps the most influential Hispano-American writer at the turn of the twenty-first century is Robert Bolaño, author of the groundbreaking novel *Los detectives salvajes* (1998; *The Savage Detectives*, 2007) and the monumental posthumous novel *2666* (2004). Bolaño's importance however is not limited to his own work, but rather to the elaboration of a personal canon that has provided an alternative to that established by the Boom. Bolaño identifies literary figures who have renovated Spanish American literature of the late twentieth century, such as Sergio Pitol (Mexico, b. 1933), author of the celebrated novel *El arte de la fuga* (The Art of the Fugue, 1966), Fernando Vallejo (Colombia, b. 1944), who was internationally recognized for his novel *La virgen de los sicarios* (Our Lady of the Assassins, 1994) and the critic and novelist Ricardo Piglia (Argentina, b. 1940), who, following his acclaimed work *Respiración artificial* (1980; *Artificial Respiration*, 1994), published two novels during the 1990s, *La ciudad ausente* (1992; *The Absent City*, 2000) and *Plata quemada* (1997; *Money to Burn*, 2003). The noteworthy writers born approximately during the 1950s include Diamela Eltit (Chile, b. 1949), author of an important work dating back to the 1980s and Pedro Lemebel (Chile, b. 1951), author of urban chronicles who is also a performance artist. Daniel Sada (b. 1953), who has been praised for his radical handling of the language, the acclaimed novelist and poet Carmen Boullosa (b. 1954), and the novelist, chronicler and short story writer Juan Villoro (b. 1956) are a few of the most important Mexican writers within this same period. Some significant literary aspects of writers within this period are the "dirty realism" of Pedro Juan Gutiérrez (Cuba, b. 1950), in which eroticism coexists with humor and violence, the minimalist and laconic work of Rodrigo Rey Rosa (Guatemala, b. 1958), and the irreverent irony of Ana María Shua (Argentina, b. 1951). One of the most recognized members within this group is the prolific and eccentric Argentinean writer César Aira (b. 1949), who to date has published approximately fifty novellas in addition to numerous literary essays and a heterodox *Diccionario de autores latinoamericanos* (Dictionary of Latin American Authors, 2001). The literary figures born around the 1960s who merit emphasis include the Mexican authors Mario Bellatin (b. 1960), Cristina Rivera Garza (b. 1964) and David Toscana (b. 1961), and the Argentineans Alan Pauls (b. 1959) and Rodrigo Fresán (b. 1963).

The characteristics of the narrative production of the past few years include the current relevance of the detective genre (and, in some ways, the new historical novel), in addition to the increasing prevalence of the theme of social and political violence, reflecting the extreme violence that still plagues the region. Mayra Santos Febres (Puerto Rico, b. 1966), Leonardo Padura Fuentes (Cuba, b. 1955), the prolific Hispano-Mexican writer Paco Ignacio Taibo II (b. 1949), Élmer Mendoza (Mexico, b. 1949), and Santiago Gamboa (Colombia, b. 1965) are among this genre's leading figures. Authors such as the Argentineans Guillermo Martínez (b. 1962) and Pablo de Santis (b. 1963) are also associated with a revival of the analytical detective novel, although in a more Borgesian than hard-boiled way. Political and social violence in areas devastated by internal warfare, drug trafficking, and corruption over the past twenty years can be found in the work of Horacio Castellanos Moya (El Salvador, b. 1957), of the Colombians Fernando Vallejo, Laura Restrepo (b. 1950), and Carlos Franco (b. 1962), and of the Peruvians Alonso Cueto (b. 1954), and Santiago Roncagliolo (b. 1975).

Poetry. The publication of the anthology (or "sample," as it is called) *Medusario* in 1996, which introduced the concept of neobaroque poetry, referred to as *neobarrosa* in the Río de Plata, marks a phenomenon of rupture within 1990s poetry similar to that in narrative prose. Joining established poets such as Marosa di Giorgio (Uruguay, 1934–2004), Gerardo Deniz (Spain, b. 1934), and Rodolfo Hinostroza (Peru, b. 1941), several younger and less publicized poets, all born around the 1950s, appeared on the sccene, including Eduardo Milán (Uruguay, b. 1952), Coral Bracho (Mexico, b. 1951), Eduardo Espina (Uruguay, b. 1954), Tamara Kamenszain (Argentina, b. 1947), and the Peruvian settled in Argentina Reynaldo Jimenez (b. 1959). The neobaroque poets have reacted against the Anglo-Saxon conversational poetic tradition imposed by the continental poets of the Generation of 1950 (continued in the so-called social poetry of the 1970s and 1980s). Other important names of poets born since 1940 include the Peruvians José Watanabe (1946–2007), Carmen Ollé (b. 1947), Enrique Verástegui (b. 1950), and Mario Montalbetti (b. 1953); the Salvadoran Jacinta Escudos (b. 1953); the Chileans Gonzalo Millán (1947-2006), Raúl Zurita (b. 1950), and Marjorie Agosín (b. 1955); the Colombian Juan Gustavo Cobo Borda (b. 1948); the Mexican David Huerta (b. 1949); the Argentine María Negroni (b. 1951); and the Guatemalan Humberto Ak'abal (b. 1952). There are also a number of older poets who have acquired iconic status among the young: Peruvians Jorge Eduardo Eielson (1924–2006) and Blanca Varela (b. 1926), and the Chilean Jorge Teillier (1935–1996).

JUAN CARLOS GALDO

See also **Agustini, Delmira; Alegría, Ciro; Allende, Isabel; Arenas, Reinaldo; Arguedas, Alcides; Arguedas, José María; Arreola, Juan José; Asturias, Miguel Ángel; Azuela, Mariano; Balbuena, Bernardo de; Barrios, Eduardo; Bello, Andrés; Blest Gana, Alberto; Bolaño, Roberto; Bombal, María Luisa; Borges, Jorge Luis; Boullosa, Carmen; Brull, Mariano; Bryce Echenique, Alfredo; Carballido, Emilio; Cardenal, Ernesto; Carrasquilla, Tomás; Casal, Julián del; Castellanos, Rosario; Chilam Balam; Chocano, José Santos; Cortázar, Julio; Cuadra, Pablo Antonio; Dalton García, Roque; Darío, Rubén; Díaz del Castillo, Bernal; Díaz, Jorge; Donoso, José; Dragún, Osvaldo; Echeverría, Esteban; Eguren, José María; Ercilla y Zúñiga, Alonso de; Ferré, Rosario; Fuentes, Carlos; Galeano, Eduardo Hughes; Gallegos, Rómulo; Gambaro, Griselda; García Márquez, Gabriel; Garcilaso de la Vega, El Inca; Gauchesca Literature; Gómez de Avellaneda y Arteaga, Gertrudis; González Martínez, Enrique; Gorostiza Acalá, José; Guillén, Nicolás; Güiraldes, Ricardo; Gutiérrez Nájera, Manuel; Guzmán, Martín Luis; Henríquez Ureña, Pedro; Hernández, José; Herrera y Reissig, Julio; Hostos y Bonilla, Eugenio María de; Huidobro Fernández,**

Vicente; Ibarbourou, Juana de; Icaza Coronel, Jorge; Isaacs, Jorge; Larreta, Enrique Rodríguez; Las Casas, Bartolomé de; Leñero, Vicente; Lezama Lima, José; Lihn, Enrique; Lugones, Leopoldo; Mallea, Eduardo; Mariátegui, José Carlos; Mármol, José Pedro Crisólogo; Marqués, René; Martín Fierro; Matto de Turner, Clorinda; Mistral, Gabriela; Montalvo, Juan; Mutis, Alvaro; Neruda, Pablo; Nervo, Amado; Olmedo, José Joaquín de; Oña, Pedro de; Pacheco, José Emilio; Palés Matos, Luis; Parra, Nicanor; Paz, Octavio; Peri Rossi, Cristina; Pitol, Sergio; Pizarnik, Alejandra; Popol Vuh; Prado, Pedro; Quiroga, Horacio; Rabinal Achi; Reyes Ochoa, Alfonso; Rivera, José Eustasio; Roa Bastos, Augusto; Rodó, José Enrique; Romero, José Rubén; Rulfo, Juan; Sahagún, Bernardino de; Sánchez, Florencio; Sarduy, Severo; Science Fiction in Latin America; Sigüenza y Góngora, Carlos de; Silva, José Asunción; Skármeta, Antonio; Solórzano, Carlos; Storni, Alfonsina; Tablada, José Juan; Theater; Triana, José; Usigli, Rodolfo; Valdés, Gabriel de la Concepción; Valencia, Guillermo León; Valenzuela, Luisa; Valle y Caviedes, Juan del; Vallejo, César; Vargas Llosa, Mario; Vasconcelos Calderón, José; Villaurrutia, Xavier; Wolff, Egon.

BIBLIOGRAPHY

Albuquerque, Severino João. *Violent Acts: A Study of Contemporary Latin American Theatre.* Detroit, MI: Wayne State University Press, 1991.

Alegría, Fernando. *Nueva historia de la novela hispanoamericana.* Hanover, NH: Ediciones del Norte, 1986.

Anderson Imbert, Enrique. *Spanish-American Literature: A History.* 2nd ed. Revised and updated by Elaine Malley. Translated by John V. Falconieri. Detroit, MI: Wayne State University Press, 1969.

Balderston, Daniel, and Mike Gonzalez, eds. *Encyclopedia of Latin American and Caribbean Literature 1900–2003.* London and New York: Routledge, 2004.

Becerra, Eduardo, ed. *Líneas aéreas.* Madrid: Lengua de Trapo, 1999.

Brotherston, Gordon. *Latin American Poetry: Origins and Presence.* Cambridge, U.K. and New York: Cambridge University Press, 1975.

Brushwood, John S. *The Spanish American Novel: A Twentieth-Century Survey.* Austin: University of Texas Press, 1975.

Brushwood, John S. *Genteel Barbarism: Experiments in Analysis of Nineteenth-Century Spanish-American Novels.* Lincoln: University of Nebraska Press, 1981.

Covington, Paula H., ed. *Latin America and the Caribbean: A Critical Guide to Research Sources.* Westport, CT: Greenwood Press, 1992.

Echavarren, Roberto, José Kozer, and Jacobo Sefamí, eds. *Medusario: Muestra de poesía latinoamericana.* Mexico City: Fondo de Cultura Económica, 1996.

Forn, Juan, ed. *Buenos Aires: Una antología de la narrativa argentina.* Barcelona: Anagrama, 1992.

Forster, Merlin H. *Historia de la poesía hispanoamericana.* Clear Creek, IN: American Hispanist, 1981.

Foster, David William. *Handbook of Latin American Literature.* 2nd ed. New York: Garland, 1992.

Foster, David William. *Sexual Textualities: Essays on Queer/ing Latin American Writing.* Austin: University of Texas Press, 1997.

Franco, Jean. *An Introduction to Spanish-American Literature.* 3rd ed. Cambridge, U.K. and New York: Cambridge University Press, 1994.

Fuguet, Alberto, and Sergio Gómez, eds. *McOndo.* Barcelona: Mondadori, 1996.

Goić, Cedomil. *Historia y crítica de la literatura hispanoamericana.* 3 vols. Barcelona: Editorial Crítica, 1988–1991.

Kristal, Efraín, ed. *The Cambridge Companion to the Latin American Novel.* Cambridge, U.K. and New York: Cambridge University Press, 2005.

Leal, Luis. *Breve historia de la literatura hispanoamericana.* New York: Knopf, 1971.

Lockhart, Darrell B., ed. *Jewish Writers of Latin America: A Dictionary.* New York: Garland, 1997.

Lyday, Leon F., and George W. Woodyard, eds. *Dramatists in Revolt: The New Latin American Theater.* Austin: University of Texas Press, 1976.

Medina, José Ramón, and Nelson Osorio T., eds. *Diccionario enciclopédico de las letras de América Latina.* 3 vols. Caracas: Biblioteca Ayacucho; Monte Avila Editores Latinoamericana; Consejo Nacional de la Cultura, Venezuela (CONAC; vol. 3 only), 1995–1998.

Oviedo, José Miguel. *Historia de la literatura hispanoamericana.* 4 vols. Madrid: Alianza Editorial, 1995–2001.

Paz Soldán, Edmundo, and Debra A. Castillo, eds. *Latin American Literature and Mass Media.* New York: Garland, 2001.

Peden, Margaret Sayers. *The Latin American Short Story: A Critical History.* Boston: Twayne, 1983.

Rela, Walter, ed. *A Bibliographical Guide to Spanish American Literature: Twentieth-Century Sources.* New York: Greenwood Press, 1988.

Rivera-Rodas, Óscar. *La poesía hispanoamericana del siglo XIX: Del romanticismo al modernismo.* Madrid: Alhambra, 1988.

Sefamí, Jacobo, ed. *Contemporary Spanish American Poets: A Bibliography of Primary and Secondary Sources.* Westport, CT: Greenwood Press, 1992.

Solé, Carlos A., and Maria Isabel Abreu, eds. *Latin American Writers.* 3 vols. New York: Scribner, 1989.

Stabb, Martin S. *In Quest of Identity: Patterns in the Spanish American Essay of Ideas, 1890–1960.* Chapel Hill: University of North Carolina Press, 1967.

Taylor, Diana. *Theatre of Crisis: Drama and Politics in Latin America.* Lexington: University Press of Kentucky, 1991.

Williams, Raymond Leslie. *The Twentieth-Century Spanish American Novel.* Austin: University of Texas Press, 2003.

Zapata, Miguel Ángel, ed. *Nueva poesía latinoamericana.* Mexico City: Universidad Nacional Autónoma de México (UNAM); Xalapa, Mexico: Universidad Veracruzana, 1999.

BIBLIOGRAPHY ASSEMBLED BY
MERLIN H. FORSTER
JUAN CARLOS GALDO

LIVESTOCK

Origins. People in southeastern Europe domesticated wild cattle (*B. primigenius*) at least 8,500 years ago. Herders in southern Asia domesticated *Bos indicus* (zebu or Brahman cattle) about the same time. Since then, humankind has taken advantage of the wide range of useful products that cattle provide: meat, leather, milk, power, and tallow.

The zebu comes from India. These animals tolerate heat and resist disease and insect attacks better than most breeds. Their distinctive hump of cartilage and fat above the neck and withers give the large zebu a somewhat menacing look. Colors range from various shades of gray to red. Unlike most breeds, zebus can tolerate hot, humid climates. Ranchers from Texas to Venezuela and Brazil have raised the breed. A relative newcomer to western-hemisphere ranching is the Charolais, a native to France. Beef producers initially thought very little of this large, muscular, all-white breed. However, the Charolais's fast growth and heavier weight at a younger age soon attracted adherents.

Specialized markets have opened new opportunities to livestock raisers. The venerable Corriente breed, for example, is much in demand for team roping competitions. The Corriente developed in colonial Mexico from cattle imported from Spain. Like its cousin, the Longhorn, the hardy Corriente is a tough survivor.

An indigenous woman with llama near Lake Titicaca, Bolivia. Llamas were domesticated more than five thousand years ago and continue to be important to the livelihood of the Andean peoples. PHOTOGRAPH BY ANNE KALOSH. REPRODUCED BY PERMISSION

Animal husbandry—raising and domesticating animals for food, transportation, power, clothing fiber, or building materials—is an ancient activity. South Americans of the pre-Columbian era domesticated many animals, including the alpaca and the llama. After the arrival of the Spanish, cattle, sheep, mules, and goats joined the ranks of indigenous livestock.

Llamas, alpacas, vicuñas, and guanacos—members of the family Camelidae—were native to the Andean highlands. Guanacos, never domesticated, were hunted for their meat. Llamas, alpacas, and vicuñas may have been domesticated by about 2000 BCE. They stand about 4 feet high at the shoulders, may reach more than 4 feet in length, and weigh up to 300 pounds. Indians wove their wool into yarn and used their flesh as food. Llamas also were used as pack animals.

The Colonial Era. Thanks to Spanish explorers and rich grasslands, herds of wild cattle proliferated quickly in the Río de la Plata during the early colonial period. Indians learned to herd horses and cattle, and developed a livestock trade across the Andes to Chile. Gauchos (most often Indian or mestizo) hunted the wild cattle for their hides.

By the mid-eighteenth century, ranchers established Estancias and began domesticating wild cattle and claiming control of land and water. They raised the tough, rangy creole cattle for their hides and increasingly for the salted meat trade to Brazil and Cuba. Oxen, the most important draft animals, pulled high-wheeled carts across the pampas and up to Alta Peru.

During the latter decades of the nineteenth century, ranchers began improving their creole stock with imported breeds, in order to compete in the growing refrigerated beef export market. Thanks to their control of the pampas, Argentina's wealthy livestock producers remained politically powerful into the twentieth century.

Longhorns. Longhorn cattle are descended from the creole cattle brought to Mexico and South America during the sixteenth century. During the eighteenth century, Spanish priests brought the breed to missions that they established in Texas, New Mexico, and California. Longhorns likewise provided the basis for the beef industries of Brazil and Argentina. Their hardiness made the Longhorn well-suited to less hospitable ranges, such as the semi-desert regions of northern Mexico and the south Texas brush country.

Growing up wild on open range or in the dense thickets of the Texas brush country, Longhorns did not take kindly to being herded. Longhorns come in an amazing variety of colors and patterns. With horn spreads sometimes exceeding ten feet, they posed dangers to horses and riders. Fiercely protective, they used their horns against wolves and other enemies.

Despite their virtues, Longhorns had deficiencies that ultimately doomed them as the mainstay of the beef cattle industry. They take longer to mature: ten years versus six years for so-called "American breeds," such as Herefords, Angus, Devon, and Shorthorn. Longhorns are a lean breed, and the beef-eater's pallet came to demand fatty, marbled beef. Finally, the unwieldy horns created havoc in close quarters, such as the confines of feedlots. During the late nineteenth century, other breeds pushed aside the venerable Longhorn.

In 1927 the U.S. Forest Service acted on a congressional mandate to establish a national herd of

Argentinian rancher with cattle, 1999. Rancher Edmundo Moore inspects the cattle on his ranch in Lobos, Argentina. Despite challenges, Argentina remains a major world producer of cattle and sheep. AP IMAGES

Longhorns. Rangers could locate only three bulls, twenty cows, and four calves. They removed those animals to the Wichita Mountains Wildlife Refuge at Cache, Oklahoma. During the following decades, government and private efforts established the "Seven Families" of different gene pools to rebuild the breed. Today breeders raise tens of thousands of Longhorns.

Brazil. Like livestock producers everywhere, those in the Brazilian Northeast faced many problems. Rustlers, runaway slaves, and bandits posed threats to cowboys and herds. Droughts still strike the region periodically. Despite the problems, by the early eighteenth century Bahia held an estimated 500,000 cattle and Pernambuco 800,000. This marked the high point of *vaqueiro* life.

During the eighteenth century, the economy, population, and political power in Brazil shifted south toward Rio de Janeiro. This demographic shift left the Northeast politically and economically marginalized and contributed to a decline in the northern livestock industry toward the end of the eighteenth century. Minas Gerais, also a mining center, became Brazil's new livestock center. Still further to the south gaúchos herded cattle in Rio Grande do Sul. Jesuit missionaries moved some livestock into southern Brazil in the 1620s. Ranchers and priests brought many more animals during the following decade. The Brazilian southern plains, called Campo Gerais during the colonial era, had an abundance of well-watered pasture land.

In 1793 the captaincy of Rio Grande exported 13,000 arrobas of dried meat. About a decade later the figure had jumped to 600,000 arrobas as *charqueadas*(beef-drying plants) multiplied. (An arroba is 11.5 kg or about 25 pounds.) Slaves in Cuba provided a ready market throughout the nineteenth century.

Not until the mid-nineteenth century did ranchers in southern Brazil begin to furnish cattle with salt. Some ranchers added wire fencing after the 1880s, but borderlands cattle production, work techniques, and social relations changed very little. Ranchers in Rio Grande and nothern Uruguay continued to raise cattle for the traditional hides and jerky markets for decades after ranchers elsewhere diversified into the more lucrative chilled beef trade.

Mules and Sheep. The Spanish and Brazilians also bred mules, the sterile offspring of a donkey and a mare. In mountainous regions, such as Salta, mules served as mounts. In many areas, including mining centers, like Potosí, they were used as work and pack animals. Muleteers (*arrieros*) drove long trains of more than eighty mules from Potosí and Chile to cities in the Río de la Plata. During the colonial period, the pampas around Córdoba became an important mule-breeding center.

Sheep have long been raised, especially for their wool and meat. Beginning in the 1820s, British ranchers began importing sheep and grazing them in cooler areas of the Argentine pampas. Despite resistance from traditional cattle ranchers, the sheep population grew gradually. Initially, ranchers raised merino sheep and exported wool to French and British textile mills. Both men and women earned relatively high wages during the busy shearing season. During the 1860s, thicker fleeced Rambouillet sheep replaced the merinos. With the development of the technology to ship refrigerated meat, ranchers imported Lincoln and Romney Marsh sheep, breeds that provided good mutton and wool. By 1895, Argentina's sheep population numbered nearly 75 million head. Today Argentina remains among the world's top ten sheep and cattle producers.

In 2001, a foot-and-mouth disease outbreak lead to the banning of Argentine beef abroad. However, the Argentine government aggressively tackled the problem. Exports have become so valuable that they have caused rapid price hikes for domestic consumers, leading the government to impose export restrictions in 2006.

See also **Agriculture; Saladero; Vaquería.**

BIBLIOGRAPHY

J. Frank Dobie, *The Longhorns* (1941).

John E. Rouse, *World Cattle* (1970).

Richard W. Slatta, *Gauchos and the Vanishing Frontier* (1983) and *The Cowboy Encyclopedia* (1994).

David Rock, *Argentina, 1516–1987* (1987).

Additional Bibliography

Barsky, Osvaldo. *Historia del capitalismo agrario pampeano.* Buenos Aires: Siglo Veintiuno Editores Argentina, 2003.

Bell, Stephen. *Campanha Gaúcha: A Brazilian Ranching System, 1850–1920.* Stanford, CA: Stanford University Press, 1998.

RICHARD W. SLATTA

LIVINGSTON CODES.

LIVINGSTON CODES. Livingston Codes, a set of civil penal reform codes written by U.S. lawyer and statesman Edward Livingston in the 1820s and later adopted by Guatemala. Written for Louisiana, that state rejected his *System of Penal Law* in 1826. When Livingston became Andrew Jackson's secretary of state in 1831, he offered the codes to Guatemala's liberal governor, José Francisco Barrundia, who viewed it as a needed replacement for his country's Hispanic criminal code. With the help of Barrundia's active advocacy in the legislature, the codes were adopted by Guatemala in December 1835 during the administration of Governor Mariano Gálvez. They went into effect on 1 January 1836.

The Livingston Codes provided trial by jury, habeas corpus, and jails with separate cells; they also vested the appointment of all judges in the governors of the various states within Guatemala. Despite their progressive nature, they proved to be impractical for Guatemala and quickly resulted in the alienation of a number of sectors of Guatemalan society, in particular attorneys and rural peasants who were conscripted into forced labor gangs to construct new jails. Trial by jury proved impractical, especially in rural areas, and the change in the appointment system of judges alienated powerful landed interests. The association of the Livingston Codes with centralization efforts of the Liberals in Guatemala City also aroused opposition to them. Rafael Carrera demanded the abolition of the Livingston Codes during his 1837 rebellion, and after he gained power the codes were repealed in 1839.

See also **Carrera, José Rafael.**

BIBLIOGRAPHY

Mario Rodríguez, "The Livingston Codes in the Guatemalan Crisis of 1837–1838," in *Applied Enlightenment: Nineteenth Century Liberalism,* Middle American Research Institute, Tulane University, Publication 23, no. 1 (1972), pp. 1–32, is the best source for this topic. On the origins of the codes, see Grant Lyons, "Louisana and the Livingston Criminal Codes," in *Louisiana History* 15 (1974): 243–272, and Ira Flory, Jr., "Edward Livingston's Place in Louisana Law," in *Louisiana Historical Quarterly* 19 (1936): 328–389. For the resistance to the codes, see Ralph Lee Woodward, Jr., *Rafael Carrera and the Emergence of the Republic of Guatemala, 1821–1871* (1993), pp. 53–83.

Additional Bibliography

Woodward, Ralph Lee. *Rafael Carrera and the Emergence of the Republic of Guatemala, 1821–1871.* Athens: University of Georgia Press, 1993.

HEATHER K. THIESSEN

LLAMA.

LLAMA. The llama, alpaca, guanaco, and vicuña are four species of camelid native to the high-altitude zones of the central and southern Andes in Peru. Raised by Andean peoples on the grasslands of the high plateau, the domesticated camelids, llamas and alpacas, are valued primarily for their wool, hides, and meat. Although not as large as the Old World camel, llamas are prized as pack animals for transporting food products to and from lower altitudes. The wild vicuña, the smallest of the species, is used mainly for its soft fine wool. The undomesticated and increasingly rare guanaco is hunted for meat and especially for pelts. Ranchers consider guanacos a threat to pastureland needed for livestock.

Llamas and alpacas have been central to the livelihood of Andean peoples since their domestication between 4000 and 3000 BCE. In the Inca state (c. 1430–1532) Andean communities developed large herds of llamas and alpacas in order to maintain a steady supply of wool, meat, and animals for ritual sacrifice. As a hedge against famine the Inca state promoted the storage of dried llama meat (*charqui*). Mountain pastoralists under Spanish colonial rule produced alpaca wool for export. For most of the nineteenth and early twentieth centuries the economy of southern Great Peru revolved around the export of high-grade alpaca wool to Britain. The collapse of the wool export boom in the 1920s, coupled with the expansion of cattle raising, has led to a sharp reduction in camelid herds. Nevertheless, the Peruvian government has begun to assist mountain communities in building up alpaca herds.

See also **Wool Industry.**

BIBLIOGRAPHY

Orlove, Benjamin S. *Alpacas, Sheep, and Men: The Wool Export Economy and Regional Society of Southern Peru.* New York: Academic Press, 1977.

Franklin, William L. "Biology, Ecology, and Relationship to Man of the South American Camelids." In *Mammalian Biology of South America,* edited by M. A. Mares and H. H. Genoways, 457–489. Linesville, PA: Pymatuning Laboratory of Ecology/University of Pittsburgh, 1982.

Masuda, Shozo, Izumi Shimada, and Craig Morris, eds. *Andean Ecology and Civilization.* Tokyo: University of Tokyo Press, 1985.

STEVEN J. HIRSCH

LLANOS (COLOMBIA). The eastern tropical plains of Colombia cover approximately 98,000 square miles, or one–fifth of the national territory. Stretching eastward from the Eastern Cordillera to the Venezuelan border, the llanos are bounded on the north by the Arauca River and on the south by the Guaviare River. Included within the sparsely populated region are the departments of Arauca, Casanare, Meta, and Vichada, which had a combined population of about 880,000 in 1993. Villavicencio, the capital of Meta and the largest city in the llanos, had a population of 253,000 in 1993.

Cut off from the heart of Colombia by the Eastern Cordillera, the llanos have played a marginal role in the country's history. Although Europeans seeking El Dorado began to explore the region in the 1530s, few Spaniards settled there. In 1778 the llanos were home to only 1,535 whites, who were devoted mainly to cattle raising. In the mid–seventeenth century missionaries moved into the area to proselytize the original inhabitants, who were gathered into mission towns, which numbered thirty-one by 1760.

The llanos became a battleground during the Wars of Independence as well as a place of refuge for patriots during the Spanish reconquest (1816–1819). The region suffered population loss and economic disruption because of the conflict and experienced little growth during the nineteenth century. One significant nineteenth-century change was the decline of the northern llanos and the shift of population south to Meta. Villavicencio, founded in 1850, had a population of nearly 5,000 by 1918.

After 1930 the national government regularized regional administration and created an infrastructure to encourage settlement and development. Cattle raising remained a major economic activity, supplemented by petroleum production and the cultivation of rice and other commercial crops. The llanos were a center of Liberal guerrilla activity during La Violencia, especially during the period 1949–1953, and the scene of agrarian conflict during the 1970s and 1980s.

By 1994 Casanare had become Colombia's leading oil–producing department because of the exploitation of large reserves (about two billion barrels) found there by British Petroleum in association with Ecopetrol, the state petroleum agency, and other foreign firms. Production in the Casanare fields of Cusiana and Cupiagua peaked in 1999, producing 434,000 barrels daily.

See also **Wars of Independence, South America.**

BIBLIOGRAPHY

Jane Rausch, *A Tropical Plains Frontier: The Llanos of Colombia, 1531–1831* (1984).

Jane Rausch, *The Llanos Frontier of Colombia, 1830–1930* (1993).

Jane Rausch, *Columbia: Territorial Rule and the Llanos Frontier* (1999).

HELEN DELPAR

LLANOS (VENEZUELA). The low-lying plains of the Orinoco basin, occupying almost one-third of Venezuela's national territory, run from the Andes to the Atlantic. Approximately 600 miles long and 200 miles wide, they are bounded on the north by coastal mountains and on the south by the Guiana Highlands. Treeless, they are covered largely by a mixture of savanna and scrub woodland. The climate of the llanos is divided into a rainy season from roughly April to November and a dry season from November to April. The rainy season causes extensive flooding during which the lowlands along the streams are inundated and livestock are driven to safer ground to the north. The dry season is characterized by severe drought. As the waters recede and the grasses are scorched by the sun, livestock must retreat toward the Orinoco River to seek food and water.

The human population of the llanos is sparse, owing to drought and flooding, extreme heat, abundance of insects, and disease. Most of the population is clustered in river towns, the largest and more important of which is Ciudad Bolívar, which lies 200 miles up the Orinoco. Traditionally cattle raising has been the principal economic activity despite weather extremes, transportation problems, poor-quality forage, and disease. The local cowboys, or *llaneros*, are legendary for their independence and for their fighting skills, which they demonstrated in the independence wars and the civil wars of the nineteenth century. Their regionalism helped to thwart Simón Bolívar's dream of a Gran Columbia of which Venezuela was a part.

In the later twentieth century there has been significant agricultural development in the northern llanos, facilitated by land settlement, irrigation projects, and the construction of a major dam on the Guárico River. Large oil and gas deposits lie beneath the eastern portion of the llanos, including the Orinoco Heavy Oil Belt in Venezuela (*Faja Petrolífera del Orinoco*). In 2006, President Hugo Chávez claimed that Venezuela had the largest oil reserves in the world, taking into consideration the extra–heavy deposits in the Orinoco Oil Belt. Previously thought to be too costly to produce, Orinoco oil is now more attractive as world oil costs rise.

See also **Petroleum Industry.**

BIBLIOGRAPHY

American University, *Foreign Area Studies Division, Area Handbook for Venezuela* (1964).

Raymond E. Crist and Edward P. Leahy, *Venezuela: Search for a Middle Ground* (1969).

John V. Lombardi, *Venezuela: The Search for Order, the Dream of Progress* (1982).

Preston E. James and C. W. Minkel, *Latin America,* 5th ed. (1986).

Additional Bibliography

Baudilio Mendoza Sánchez, *El moderno desarrollo agrícola en Venezuela* (2000).

WINFIELD J. BURGGRAAFF

LLANQUIHUE. Llanquihue, province of southern Chile. With a population of 321,493 (2007), it is the core of the Lake Region. The province was created in 1861, and until 1925, its area included what is today the Aisén region of Chile. In 1970 it became part of what is known as Chile's Lake Region, which also includes Chiloé, Osorno, Palena, and Valdivia provinces. The green landscape dotted with lakes and mountain peaks—most of them snow-capped volcanoes—attracted Chilean and European colonists during the second half of the nineteenth century. Dairy and grain-growing farms, interspersed with large cattle ranches, prospered. Labor for many of these enterprises was supplied by migrant workers from Chiloé. Today, nearly 40 percent of the population is of European ancestry, and the rest are natives from Llanquihue and Chiloé. The largest city is Puerto Montt (2000 population 138,138), which connects with the island of Chiloé via ferry, with the province of Aisén in northern Patagonia via an all-weather road, and with Bariloche (Argentina) via the Pérez Rosales Pass and Puerto Blest.

See also **Chile, Geography.**

BIBLIOGRAPHY

Jean-Pierre Blancpain, *Les allemands au Chili (1816–1945)* (Cologne, 1974).

Instituto Geográfico Militar, "La región de Los Lagos," in *Geografía de Chile,* vol. 32 (1986).

Additional Bibliography

Schmid Anwandter, Peter. *Pioneros del Llanquihue, 1852–2002: Edición conmemorativa de los 150 años de la inmigracíon alemana a Llanquihue.* 2nd ed. Santiago de Chile: Liga Chileno Alemana, 2002.

Zamudio Vargas, Orlando. *Chile: Historia de la división político-administrativa, 1810–2000.* Santiago, Chile: Instituto Nacional de Estadísticas, 2001.

CÉSAR N. CAVIEDES

LLERAS, LORENZO MARÍA (1811–1868). Lorenzo María Lleras (*b.* 7 September 1811; *d.* 3 June 1868), Colombian politician. As an educator, publicist, and politician, Lleras voiced a moderate liberalism that characterized an important current in early national Colombian politics. Born in Bogotá, Lleras received his education in his native city. His activity as a lawyer facilitated his political activity with General Francisco de Paula Santander and Florentino González in the 1830s, especially as editor of *La Bandera Nacional.* Lleras was rector of the Colegio Mayor de Nuestra Señora de Rosario (1842–1846) before establishing the Colegio Mayor de Espíritu Santo, where he trained numerous influential Liberals. His *El Neo-Granadino* promulgated Draconiano Liberalism in the 1850s, an ideology he championed in the congress and in the cabinet of President José María Obando.

Lleras's association with members of the Democratic Society of Artisans led to his brief incarceration after the 1854 coup of José María Melo. He backed anti-Conservative forces in the 1859–1862 civil war and was a delegate to the Rionegro Convention (1863). Lleras and Clotilde Triana, his second wife, parented fifteen children, establishing a lineage that included Liberal presidents Carlos Lleras Restrepo (1966–1970) and Alberto Lleras Camargo (1958–1962).

See also **Columbia, Organizations: Democratic Society of Artisans.**

BIBLIOGRAPHY

Robert H. Davis, "Acosta, Caro, and Lleras: Three Essayists and Their Views on New Granada's National Problems," (Ph.D. diss., Vanderbilt University, 1969).

Andres Soriano Lleras, *Lorenzo María Lleras* (1958).

Additional Bibliography

Sowell, David. "'La teoria i la realidad': The Democratic Society of Artisans of Bogota, 1847–1854." *The Hispanic American Historical Review* 67:4 (November 1987): 611–630.

Sowell, David. *The Early Colombian Labor Movement: Artisans and Politics in Bogotá, 1832–1919.* Philadelphia: Temple University Press, 1992.

DAVID SOWELL

LLERAS CAMARGO, ALBERTO (1906–1990). Alberto Lleras Camargo (*b.* 3 July 1906; *d.* 4 January 1990), president of Colombia (1945–1946 and 1958–1962). Born into a middle-class Bogotá family, Lleras Camargo briefly attended university but was quickly drawn into Liberal journalism and politics. Elected to Congress in 1930, he became the youngest interior minister in Colombian history during the first term of Alfonso López Pumarejo (1934–1938). In López's troubled second term (1942–1945), Lleras was ambassador to the United States; he completed López's term upon the latter's resignation in July 1945, a period of severe political and labor unrest. He served as secretary general of the Organization of American States (1948–1954) and rector of the University of the Andes in Bogotá (1954). In 1956–1957 he negotiated with exiled Conservative leader Laureano Gómez the agreements that formed the basis for the bipartisan National Front; in May 1958 he was elected president under that agreement. Lleras's regime faced serious problems of pacification and rehabilitation after more than a decade of violence; the western department of Caldas, plagued by murderous *bandoleros*, proved especially intractable. Reform projects inspired by the Alliance for Progress, such as a 1961 Agrarian Reform Law, produced indifferent results. After leaving office, Lleras edited the magazine *Visión;* in 1978 he retired from public life, though not before expressing dissatisfaction with the Liberal leadership of the late 1970s.

See also **Colombia, Political Parties: Liberal Party; Organization of American States (OAS).**

BIBLIOGRAPHY

Ignacio Arizmendi Posada, *Presidentes de Colombia, 1810–1990* (1990), pp. 245–248.

Robert H. Dix, *Colombia: The Political Dimensions of Change* (1967).

John Martz, *Colombia: A Contemporary Political Survey* (1962).

Additional Bibliography

Téllez, Edgar, and Alvaro Sánchez. *Ruidos de sables.* Bogota: Planeta, 2003.

Villar Borda, Leopoldo. *Alberto Lleras: El último republicano.* Bogota: Planeta, 1997.

RICHARD J. STOLLER

LLERAS RESTREPO, CARLOS (1908–1994). Carlos Lleras Restrepo (*b.* 14 April 1908; *d.* 27 September 1994), president of Colombia (1966–1970). The son of a prominent but poor Bogotá scientist, Lleras Restrepo was already a rising Liberal politician when he received his law degree in 1930. He served as comptroller and finance minister during the regimes of Alfonso López Pumarejo and

Eduardo Santos (1934–1942). A leader of the Liberals' "civil resistance" during the Conservative regime of Mariano Ospina Pérez (1946–1950), he was forced into exile in 1952, during the presidency of Laureano Gómez. A leading backer of the bipartisan National Front, he reached the presidency in 1966 promising an analogous "national transformation" on the social and economic fronts. A technocrat by temperament, Lleras Restrepo organized "decentralized institutes" in fields as diverse as sports and scientific research. In 1968 he forced through a constitutional reform increasing the executive's budgetary and planning powers. In the late 1970s, through his influential magazine *Nueva Frontera,* Lleras Restrepo was a vocal opponent of the Liberal regime of Julio César Turbay. Lleras Restrepo's writings include the multivolume autobiography, *Historia de mi propia vida* (1983–).

See also **Colombia, Political Parties: National Front.**

BIBLIOGRAPHY

Ignacio Arizmendi Posada, *Presidentes de Colombia, 1810–1990* (1990), pp. 275–280.

Additional Bibliography

Morales Benítez, Otto. *Carlos Lleras Restrepo: Perfil de un estadista.* Bogotá: Ediciones Academia Colombiana de Jurisprudencia, 2000.

RICHARD J. STOLLER

LLORENS TORRES, LUIS (1876–1944). Luis Llorens Torres (*b.* 14 May 1876; *d.* 16 June 1944), Puerto Rican poet. Born into a comfortable family in Juana Díaz, in southern Puerto Rico, Llorens began writing verse at the age of twelve. He studied law in Barcelona and Granada, Spain, where he also wrote articles on Puerto Rican and Caribbean history for several periodicals. Llorens practiced law in Puerto Rico, while at the same time engaging actively in journalistic writing. In 1913 he founded and directed the journal *Revista de las Antillas,* which established new directions for the poetry of Puerto Rico, and two years later established the satirical weekly *Juan Bobo* (with Nemesio R. Canales). He published articles under the pseudonym Luis de Puerto Rico and in 1914 wrote a historical drama, *El grito de Lares* (The cry of Lares, 1927). Llorens defined his philosophy of art as "everything is beauty" and "everything is poetry." Llorens wrote poems of intense patriotic sentiment about Spanish American history and the Caribbean; about Puerto Rico's towns, women, customs, heroes, history, folklore, natives, and landscape, and verse both admiring and protesting the United States. He was also a member of Puerto Rico's House of Representatives from 1908 to 1910, and was a supporter of self-determination for Puerto Rico. When Llorens became gravely ill in New York in 1944, President Franklin D. Roosevelt arranged to have him flown to Puerto Rico, so that he could die in his homeland.

His major works are *América* (1898), *Al pie de la Alhambra* (At the foot of the Alhambra, 1899), *Sonetos sinfónicos* (Symphonic sonnets, 1914), "*La canción de las Antillas*" *y otros poemas* ("Song of the Antilles" and other poems, 1929), *Voces de la campana mayor* (Voices of the great bell, 1935), and *Alturas de América* (Heights of America, 1940).

See also **Puerto Rico; Roosevelt, Franklin Delano.**

BIBLIOGRAPHY

Daisy Caraballo-Abreu, *La prosa de Luis Llorens Torres: Estudio y antología* (1986).

Carmen Marrero, *Luis Llorens Torres: Vida y obra (1876–1944)* (1953).

Theresa Ortiz De Hadjopoulos, *Luis Llorens Torres: A Study of His Poetry* (1977).

Nilda S. Ortiz García, *Vida y obra de Luis Llorens Torres* (1977).

Additional Bibliography

Axelrod, Steven Gould, Camille Roman, and Thomas J. Travisano, editors. *The New Anthology of American Poetry. Volume Two, Modernisms 1900–1950.* New Brunswick, NJ: Rutgers University Press, 2005.

Cabrera de Ibarra, Palmira. *Luis Lloréns Torres: Ante el paisajes.* San Juan: Editorial Yaurel, 1990.

ESTELLE IRIZARRY

LLORENTE Y LAFUENTE, ANSELMO (1800–1871). Anselmo Llorente y Lafuente (*b.* 1800; *d.* 1871), bishop of Costa Rica (1851–1871). In 1850 Pope Piux IX created the diocese of Costa

Rica, separating it from the diocese of León, Nicaragua. On 7 November 1851 Llorente, a native of Cartago, was consecrated its first bishop. Aside from failing to convince the legislature to provide funds for a seminary, Llorente had a harmonious relationship with the government until 1858, when the legislature, supported by President Juan Rafael Mora, passed a hospital tax. Since clergymen were not exempt from the tax, Llorente publicly opposed it, ordering his priests not to pay it. Consequently, he was expelled from the country. He went to Nicaragua but was able to return in August 1859, when Mora was overthrown, largely due to outrage at the bishop's banishment. From then until his death, Llorente maintained a cordial relationship with civil authorities.

See also **Anticlericalism; Mora Porrás, Juan Rafael.**

BIBLIOGRAPHY

Victor Sanabria Martínez, *Anselmo Llorente y Lafuente, primer obispo de Costa Rica: Apuntamientos históricos* (1933).

Philip J. Williams, *The Catholic Church and Politics in Nicaragua and Costa Rica* (1989), pp. 99–100.

EDWARD T. BRETT

LOAS. *See* Lwa.

LOBO, HÉLIO (1883–1960).

A Brazilian diplomat and writer, Hélio Lobo was born on October 17, 1883, in the city of Juiz de Fora, Minas Gerais. He was the son of Fernando Lobo, a government minister and Brazilian senator, and Maria Barroso. After graduating in 1903 from the Faculdade de Direito do Rio de Janeiro (Rio de Janeiro School of Law), he became a diplomat at the invitation of the Baron of Rio Branco. He served as an assistant in the Brazilian-Bolivian and Brazilian-Peruvian arbitration courts from 1907 to 1909. He was named a first secretary in the Brazilian diplomatic corps in 1914 and was elected to the Academia Brasileira de Letras (Brazilian Academy of Language and Literature) in 1918, succeeding João Carneiro de Sousa Bandeira. In 1919 Lobo served on the Secretary of Brazil's delegation to the Versailles Conference. He was a consul-general in London and New York between 1920 and 1926. He taught a course in the College of Sciences, Economics, and Politics of the University of Columbia and inaugurated the Portuguese Chair of the University of Princeton in New Jersey.

Lobo's writings include several books that deal mainly with historical aspects of Brazilian diplomacy in the late nineteenth century and early decades of the twentieth century. In books and at international conferences of American nations, he defended the development of closer diplomatic and business relations between Brazil and the United States. In that sense he shared Joaquim Nabuco's view of the Monroe Doctrine, which Lobo defined as "the keystone of pan-Americanism" (Lobo 1912, p. 34). He distinguished between two interpretations of that doctrine: one of "mutual application among equal sovereign nations" and one of unilateral application "at the discretion of the United States" (Lobo 1939, p. 5). In his view, pan-Americanism, as originated in the Monroe Doctrine, "is above all an aspiration, an understanding among the countries of the American continent for the common good" (1939, p. 2). As he saw it from his pacifist perspective, Brazil was destined to be "a balancing point between Latins and Anglo-Saxons on this side of the Atlantic" (Lobo 1926, p. 163), an agent for harmony in the Americas. Hélio Lobo died in Rio de Janeiro on January 1, 1960, in his seventy-seventh year.

See also **Brazil: Since 1889; Monroe Doctrine; Pan-Americanism; United States-Latin American Relations.**

BIBLIOGRAPHY

Primary Works

De Monroe a Rio Branco. Rio de Janeiro: Imprensa Nacional, 1912.

Brasilianos e yankees. Rio de Janeiro: Livraria Pimenta e Mello, 1926.

O pan-americanismo e o Brasil. São Paulo: Companhia Editora Nacional, 1939.

Secondary Works

Corrêa Filho, Virgílio. "Helio Lobo." *Revista do Instituto Histórico e Geográfico Brasileiro* 248 (July–September 1960): 81–91

DANIEL MESQUITA PEREIRA

L'OLONNAIS, FRANCIS (1630–1670).

Francis L'Olonnais (*b.* 1630; *d.* 1670), notorious French buccaneer who preyed upon Spanish shipping in the Caribbean and terrorized settlements along the Spanish Main and the coast of Central America. He was born Jean David Nau but known as L'Olonnais after his birthplace, Sables d'Olonne in Brittany. L'Olonnais came to the West Indies as an indentured servant but on gaining his freedom, he quickly earned respect as a successful and unusually murderous buccaneer. With the support of the governor of Tortuga, L'Olonnais used that island as his base of operations, equipping his expeditions there and drawing his crew from its unsavory population. His greatest achievement was the capture and plunder of treasure from the relatively well-defended towns of Maracaibo and San Antonio de Gibraltar in the Gulf of Venezuela. L'Olonnais died at Islas Barú, Darién, Panama at the hands of a group of Indians allied to the Spanish. The natives tore his body apart and threw it, limb by limb, into a fire.

See also **Buccaneers and Freebooters.**

BIBLIOGRAPHY

Alexander O. Exquemelin, *The Buccaneers of America* (1993).

Jenifer Marx, *Pirates and Privateers of the Caribbean* (1992).

Additional Bibliography

Apestegui Cardenal, Cruz. *Piratas en el caribe: Corasarios, filibusteros y bucaneros: 1493–1700.* Barcelona: Lunwerg, 2000.

J. DAVID DRESSING

LOMBARDO TOLEDANO, VICENTE (1894–1968). Vicente Lombardo Toledano (*b.* 16 July 1894; *d.* 16 November 1968), Mexican labor leader, intellectual, and opposition party leader. Along with Manuel Gómez Morín and Alberto Vázquez del Mercado, Lombardo was a member of the important intellectual generation known as the "Seven Wisemen," which founded the Society of Conferences and Concerts. His intellectual orientation began with Christian Democracy and early in his adult life moved toward socialism. He was a labor activist best remembered as an organizer and secretary general of the Mexican Federation of Labor (CTM), Mexico's most powerful union. He lost control over this union to a group that included Fidel Velásquez, who dominated it from the mid-1940s to the 1990s. In 1948, disenchanted with the government, Lombardo Toledano founded his own opposition Partido Popular, which predated the Popular Socialist Party (1960), later an ally in Cuauhtémoc Cárdenas's 1988 electoral front.

Born in Teziutlán, Puebla, he was a childhood friend of Manuel Ávila Camacho. His grandparents were Italian immigrant peasants, and his father, who married into an old Spanish family, served as mayor of his hometown. Two of his sisters married leading intellectual contemporaries, Alfonso Caso and Pedro Henríquez Ureña. Lombardo Toledano completed his preparatory studies at the National Preparatory School and went on to obtain a law degree and an M.A. from the National University in 1919 and 1920, respectively. A professor for many years, he founded and directed the night-school program at the National Preparatory School (1923) and the Workers University of Mexico (1936–1968). A student leader in college, he worked for the Federal District, and at the age of twenty-nine, became interim governor of his home state, Puebla. He served in the Chamber of Deputies from 1924 to 1928 and again from 1964 to 1966, and held major union posts as secretary general of the National Federation of Teachers and secretary general of the Federation of Workers of the Federal District. When he lost his influence as the government co-opted labor unions after 1940, he founded and presided over the Federation of Latin American Workers from 1938 to 1963. He also organized and served as secretary general of the Socialist League (1944). He contributed many essays to popular magazines and newspapers.

See also **Mexico, Organizations: Federation of Mexican Labor (CTM).**

BIBLIOGRAPHY

Enrique Krauze, *Caudillos culturales en la revolución mexicana* (1976).

Robert P. Millon, *Vicente Lombardo Toledano, Mexican Marxist* (1966): Vicente Lombardo Toledano, *A un joven socialista mexicano* (1967).

Additional Bibliography

Bolívar Meza, Rosendo. *Vicente Lombardo Toledano: Vida, pensamiento y obra.* Mexico City: Instituto Politécnico Nacional, 2005.

Fernando Alvarez, Luis. *Vicente Lombardo Toledano y los sindicatos de México y Estados Unidos.* Mexico City: Universidad Nacional Autónoma de Mexico: Editorial Praxis, 1995.

Gutiérrez Lombardo, Raúl. *Vicente Lombardo Toledano: Apuntes para una biografía.* Mexico City: Centro de Estudios Filosóficos, Políticos y Sociales Vicente Lombardo Toledano, 2003.

RODERIC AI CAMP

LONARDI, EDUARDO (1896–1956).

A member of the Argentine military, Eduardo Lonardi served as de facto president of the nation from September 23 to November 13, 1955, after having led the Revolución Libertadora (Liberating Revolution), the military coup that overthrew President Juan Domingo Perón on September 16.

Lonardi studied at the Military School and at the Higher School of War. In 1951 he took part in an unsuccessful military coup against Perón, and then went into retirement. In that same year Perón was reelected president, but in the middle of his second term he lost the backing of the Catholic Church, with whom he was having increasingly serious conflicts, as well as the backing of important military and business sectors, in the midst of growing economic difficulties. Relations between the government and the opposition, already tense, became even more strained. In September 1955 General Lonardi led a new coup d'état; its success was not assured until it was joined by the navy under the command of Isaac Rojas and by army divisions led by Pedro Aramburu.

Lonardi assumed the de facto presidency on September 23, established an advisory board composed of non-Peronist politicians, and dissolved the congress. Representing the nationalist Catholic sector of the armed forces under the slogan "neither victorious nor vanquished," he attempted to implement a policy of reconciliation toward the Peronists. He did not take over control of the unions and did not ban the Peronist Party (though the party was stripped of its leader). The liberal military sector and the political forces that had supported the uprising were not happy with his conciliatory approach, and in November Lonardi was deposed by General Aramburu, who gave a hard-line, anti-Peronist orientation to the Liberating Revolution. Lonardi died of cancer in 1956.

See also **Aramburu, Pedro Eugenio; Argentina: The Twentieth Century; Argentina, Political Parties: Justicialist Party; Perón, Juan Domingo; Rojas, Isaac.**

BIBLIOGRAPHY

Caimari, Lila. *Perón y la Iglesia católica: Religión, estado y sociedad en Argentina (1943–1955).* Buenos Aires: Ariel, 1995.

Novaro, Marcos. *Historia de la Argentina contemporánea: De Perón a Kirchner.* Buenos Aires: Edhasa, 2006.

Potash, Robert A. *El ejército y la política en la Argentina: 1945–1962, de Perón a Frondizi.* Buenos Aires: Sudamericana, 1984.

Torre, Juan Carlos. *La vieja guardia sindical y Perón.* Buenos Aires: Sudamericana, 1990.

VICENTE PALERMO

LONDON, TREATY OF (1604).

Treaty of (1604) London, agreement between Spain and England ending a protracted conflict highlighted by the famous defeat of the Spanish Armada in 1588. Issues raised in negotiations during the summer of 1604 included English demands for trade with Spanish colonies, but the demands were denied and there is no mention of them in the final treaty signed 19 August 1604. The treaty was restricted to arrangements in Europe and included an end to English aid to the Dutch and protection of Spanish ships in the English Channel. Outside Europe ("beyond the line"), war between the colonial powers and England's policy of "effective occupation" continued unabated. The treaty, however, ended a war that was disastrous for Spain and marked the end of the age of Queen Elizabeth and Sir Francis Drake and the beginning of Anglo-Spanish cooperation (aided by the accession [1603] in England of James I).

See also **Drake, Francis; Spanish Empire.**

BIBLIOGRAPHY

Charles Howard Carter, *The Secret Diplomacy of the Habsburgs, 1598–1625* (1964).

SUZANNE HILES BURKHOLDER

LONGINOS MARTÍNEZ, JOSÉ

(c. 1755–1803). José Longinos Martínez (*b.* ca. 1755; *d.* 1803), naturalist in New Spain (1787–1803). A native of Calahorra, Spain, Longinos studied botany at the Royal Botanical Garden in Madrid before traveling to Mexico in 1787. Longinos preferred the study of animals and spent his time in Mexico studying birds, butterflies, fish, and mammals. He traveled through Lower and Upper California in 1791 and 1792, and kept a detailed journal on Indian life and customs, geography, and fauna and flora. Following his assignment in California, Longinos went to Guatemala, where he opened a small museum and gave lessons in botany. He died of tuberculosis on a trip to Campeche in Yucatán.

BIBLIOGRAPHY

Lesley Byrd Simpson, ed. and trans, *Journal of José Longinos Martínez: Notes and Observations of the Naturalist of the Botanical Expedition in Old and New California and the South Coast, 1791–1792* (1961).

Iris H. W. Engstrand, *Spanish Scientists in the New World: The Eighteenth-Century Expeditions* (1981).

Additional Bibliography

Bernabéu Albert, Salvador, editor. *Diario de las expediciones a las Californias de José Longinos.* Aranjuez: Doce Calles, 1994.

Maldonado Polo, J. Luis. *De California a El Petén: El naturalista riojano José Longinos Martínez en Nueva España.* Logroño: Gobierno de La Rioja, Instituto de Estudios Riojanos, 1997.

IRIS H. W. ENGSTRAND

LÓPEZ, AMBROSIO

(1809–1881). Ambrosio López (*b.* 1809; *d.* 19 June 1881), Colombian artisan and political activist. Ambrosio López illustrates the potential social mobility afforded by nineteenth-century patron-client relations. Born in Bogotá to the tailor Jerónimo López and the *chichera* (brewer) Rosa Pinzón, López used political associations with, first, General Francisco de Paula Santander, and then Tomás Cipriano de Mosquera to secure various appointments. López helped found the Democratic Society of Artisans in 1847, only later (1851) to quit the organization because he thought that Liberal anti-Catholicism had corrupted it. Ambrosio supported Mosquera in opposing the 1854 revolt of José María Melo, for which he was rewarded with the post of director of waters for Bogotá during the 1860s. He participated in several Catholic mutual aid organizations, favored a more traditional political economy, and opposed Liberalism on most points. In the 1870s, Ambrosio ran the distillery Los Tres Puentes, owned by the Samper brothers. His association with the Sampers later enabled his son, Pedro, to become an important banker; his grandson, Alfonso López Pumarejo, served as president of the country in the 1930s.

See also **Colombia, Organizations: Democratic Society of Artisans.**

BIBLIOGRAPHY

Ambrosio López, *El desengaño o confidencias de Ambrosio López, primer director de la Sociedad de Artesanos de Bogotá, denominada hoi "Sociedad Democrática" escrito para conocimiento de sus consocios* (1851).

Alfonso López, *Mi novela: Apuntes autobiográficos de Alfonso López,* edited by Hugo LaTorre Cabal (1961).

Additional Bibliography

Guerra, Sergio. *Los artesanos en la revolución latinoamericana: Colombia, 1849–1854.* Havana: Editorial Pueblo y Educación, 1990.

Sowell, David. "'La teoria i la realidad': The Democratic Society of Artisans of Bogota, 1847–1854." *The Hispanic American Historical Review* 67:4 (November 1987): 611–630.

Sowell, David. *The Early Colombian Labor Movement: Artisans and Politics in Bogotá, 1832–1919.* Philadelphia: Temple University Press, 1992.

DAVID SOWELL

LÓPEZ, CÁNDIDO

(1840–1902). An Argentine artist of considerable subtlety, Cándido López is principally known for series of fifty-eight panoramic paintings that depict scenes of battle and camp life during the 1864–1870 war with Paraguay. He was born on August 29, 1840, in Buenos Aires, where he studied drawing with the Italians Ignazio Manzoni (1797–1888) and Baldessarre Verazzi (1819–1896), and photography with the Argentine-born Carlos Descalzo (1813–1879). His earliest works show the influence of these three mentors and depict standard themes in a fairly derivative way, revealing little of his future promise. By the early 1860s López was working as a portrait painter in several of the smaller towns of the Bonaerense countryside. In that capacity, he attracted the attention of government officials, who in 1862 commissioned him to paint a formal portrait of President Bartolomé Mitre. The great turning point for López came in mid-1865, however, when he joined the San Nicolás Battalion of the National Guard as a second lieutenant and official campaign artist. In that capacity, he sketched scores of scenes of violence and devastation as the Argentine army advanced. He was an eyewitness at the August 1865 battle of Yataí and, then, after the Allied armies had crossed into Paraguay, at the engagements of Estero Bellaco and Tuyutí, both in May 1866. López had always intended to use his pencil sketches as models for later paintings. His efforts were interrupted, however, on September 22, 1866, when his unit was decimated by Paraguayan fire at the disastrous battle of Curupayty. López received a terrible wound in his right arm, and after evacuation to Corrientes, underwent an emergency operation in which doctors amputated the arm. His recovery, spent mostly in Buenos Aires, proved difficult and painful, and he only slowly adapted to the use of his left hand. In 1872 he married Emilia Magallanes, a widow with a child whose family provided the wounded veteran with work as a farmer and ranch manager at several estancias near Buenos Aires. The couple had twelve children of their own and evidently led a happy life together. The awful memories of the war never left López, however, and starting in the early 1880s he quietly began to paint again, now focusing almost exclusively on the war scenes he had witnessed as a young man. These paintings provide detailed images of military action, as in *Batalla de Yatay. Agosto 17 de 1865,* troop movements, as in *Embarque de las tropes argentines en el Paso de los Libres, Agosto 23 de 1865,* and life in the army camps, as in *Campamento argentino en los montes de la costa del río Paraná, frente a Itapirú, Abril 12 de 1866.* Friends soon learned of these dramatically rendered and colorful paintings and begged López to exhibit them in Buenos Aires, which he was finally able to do in March 1885. The exhibition featured twenty-nine works in oil and was an instant success. His work made a great name for him among veterans, who attested to the veracity of his many details, and to the power of the violent scenes that had been burned into their memories as well as his. General Mitre, who was still very active in his late sixties, remarked of López that his "paintings are veritable historical documents thanks to their graphic fidelity; they are destined to conserve the glorious memory of the events they record." On September 22, 1887, the twenty-first anniversary of the battle of Curupayty, the Argentine Congress authorized the purchase of the twenty-nine paintings and thus assured López's fame and financial stability in the twilight years of his life. He established a gallery within the precincts of the army's Cuerpo de Inválidos in Buenos Aires where he continued to paint similar war scenes, for a total of fifty-eight, most of which are currently divided between the collections of the Museo Histórico Nacional and the Museo Nacional de Bellas Artes. He died in the Argentine capital on the last day of 1902. Interest in his work has revived among art historians throughout South America and Europe, and in 2005 the Argentine filmmaker José Luis García produced a documentary film about his life that has been shown in Rio de Janeiro, Asunción, Bologna, Berlin, and Paris as well as in Buenos Aires.

See also **Art: The Nineteenth Century; Curupayty, Battle of; Mitre, Bartolomé; War of the Triple Alliance.**

BIBLIOGRAPHY

Fèvre, Fermín. *Cándido López.* Buenos Aires: Editorial El Ateneo, 2000.

Pacheco, Marcelo E. *Cándido López.* Buenos Aires: Ediciones Banco Velox, n.d.

Roa Bastos, Augusto. *Cándido López.* Parma, Italy: Franco Maria Ricci, 1976.

THOMAS L. WHIGHAM

LÓPEZ, CARLOS ANTONIO (1792–1862). Carlos Antonio López (*b.* 4 November 1792; *d.* 10 September 1862), president of Paraguay (1844–1862). López was the second of the three major nineteenth-century, post-Independence rulers of Paraguay, after José Gaspar Rodríguez de Francia. Elite contemporaries and traditional historians have viewed him as a benevolent despot who discouraged opposition but was less ruthless, more self-interested, and more receptive to foreigners and the elite than was Francia. Revisionist historians see

López's administration as having modernized Paraguay and developed commerce and foreign ties.

Born and educated in Asunción, López graduated from the Real Colegio y Seminario de San Carlos. He won a competition in 1814 for the chair of arts and another in 1817 for the chair of theology. A lucrative law practice served to introduce him to influential clients and friends. When Francia gained control of the elite, López retired to his family home in Recoleta. In 1826 he married Juana Pabla Carillo, who had an *estancia* in Olivares, southeast of Asunción. They had five children.

In February 1841, when Colonel Mariano Roque Alonso, an uneducated soldier, won the power struggle that ensued at the death of Francia, López became his secretary. On March 12 a national congress appointed Alonso and López to a three-year joint consulate and elected López president in 1844, 1854, and 1857.

During his first term, López continued many of Francia's foreign and domestic policies. Paraguay, continuing its isolation from the countries along the Río de la Plata, regulated foreign commerce and migration. In his second and third terms, López sought to modernize Paraguay. The bureaucracy grew and taxes increased, but the budget was balanced. The government strengthened its army, developed a river navy, and improved internal transportation and communication. In 1852 the López government established steamship service between Asunción, Paraná, Rosario, Buenos Aires, and Montevideo. In 1853, López signed commercial treaties with Great Britain, France, and the United States that brought Paraguay international recognition. Although government regulation of major exports—yerba maté, lumber, and hides—continued, commercial treaties signed with Brazil in 1850 and with Argentina in 1856 defined borders, permitted free navigation of the Paraguay and Paraná rivers, and increased trade. In 1861, López inaugurated a railroad from Asunción to Santísima Trinidad, which was extended almost to Areguá before his death.

Pursuing his program of modernization further, López expanded rural primary schools, reopened the seminary that Francia had closed, and encouraged European immigration. He also contracted with European and North American technicians, engineers, educators, and advisers who, among other things, carried out a national geological survey; established medical services; developed industries such as a gun factory, iron foundry, and shipyard; and encouraged education and artistic endeavors. Although López limited free expression, he supported publication of Paraguay's first newspapers: *El Paraguayo Independiente* (1845–1852) and *El Semanario de Aviso y Conocimientos Útiles* (1853–1868). Under López agricultural production expanded and the government helped improve the quality of Paraguay's export cotton and tobacco. López ended the African slave trade, recognized Indian villagers as Paraguayan citizens, and used the army to end indigenous border raids.

Although López's vision for Paraguay was more self-serving than Francia's, his administration ensured that the Guaraní peasantry remained the basis of Paraguayan society. López bequeathed a unified, prosperous nation without foreign debt to his eldest son, Francisco Solano López.

See also **Alonso, Mariano Roque; Slave Trade.**

BIBLIOGRAPHY

Julio César Chaves, *El Presidente López,* 2d ed. (1968).

Fundación Cultural Republicana, *Mensajes de Carlos Antonio López* (1987), is a useful collection of López's speeches.

John Hoyt Williams, *The Rise and Fall of the Paraguayan Republic, 1800–1870* (1979).

Thomas J. Page, *La Plata, the Argentine Confederation, and Paraguay* (1859).

Juan F. Pérez Acosta, *Carlos Antonio López, obrero máximo, labor administrativa y constructiva* (1948).

Peter A. Schmitt, *Paraguay y Europa 1811–1870* (1990), translated from the German by Frank M. Samson.

Charles A. Washburn, in *The History of Paraguay, with Notes of Personal Observations and Reminiscences of Diplomacy Under Difficulty,* 2 vols. (1871).

Additional Bibliography

Heyn Schupp, Carlos Antonio. *Iglesia y Estado en el Paraguay durante el gobierno de Carlos Antonio López, 1841–1862.* Asunción: Universidad Católica Nuestra Señora de la Asunción, 1987.

Rivarola Paoli, Juan Bautista. *El régimen jurídico de la tierr: Época del Dr. Francia y de los López.* Asunción: J.B. Rivarola Paoli, 2004.

Viola, Alfredo. *Cárceles y otras penas: Época de Carlos Antonio López.* Asunción: Fondo Nacional de Cultura y las Artes: Servilibro, 2004.

Vera Blinn Reber

LÓPEZ, ENRIQUE SOLANO (1859–1917).

Enrique Solano López (*b.* 2 October 1859; *d.* 19 November 1917), Paraguayan journalist, teacher, and politician who left a large library and archives. Son of Francisco Solano López and Elisa Lynch, he worked ceaselessly to revive his late father's reputation, which had been shattered due to his haste in bringing Paraguay into the bloody and disastrous War of the Triple Alliance in 1864. López traveled throughout Europe, and directed the conservative Colorado Party newspaper *La Patria*. He served as the national superintendent of primary schools (1897–1899) and was a Colorado Party senator (1912–1917) and mayor of Asunción in 1912. He ended his illustrious political and writing career as a professor at the National University.

See also **Paraguay, Political Parties: Colorado Party; War of the Triple Alliance.**

BIBLIOGRAPHY

Osvaldo Kallsen, *Asunción y sus calles* (1974).

Charles Kolinsky, *Historical Dictionary of Paraguay* (1973).

MIGUEL A. GATTI

LÓPEZ, ESTANISLAO (1786–1838).

Estanislao López (*b.* 22 November 1786; *d.* 15 June 1838), governor of the province of Santa Fe (1818–1838). Born in the city of Santa Fe, Argentina, López studied in the local convent school. At the age of fifteen he joined the Blandengues who patrolled the northern frontier, where he learned the hit-and-run tactics that his *montonero* soldiers would later use. He participated in the reconquest of Buenos Aires (1806) and in the struggles for independence in the littoral. San Martín early won him over to his ideas. On 23 July 1818, López separated the province of Santa Fe from Buenos Aires by proclaiming himself its interim governor; the following year, he was elected governor, and remained so until his death. In 1819 he gave the province its first constitutional statute. He joined José Gervasio Artigas and Francisco Ramírez in their war against Buenos Aires. He and Ramírez defeated Buenos Aires at Cepeda (1 February 1820) and compelled its *cabildo* to dissolve the national congress and to sign the Treaty of Pilar (23 February). Peace was reestablished between Buenos Aires and Santa Fe with the Treaty of Benegas (24 November). With the death of Ramírez in 1821, López became the dominant leader in the littoral. On 22 January 1822 he signed the Quadrilateral Treaty, and on the eve of the Brazilian invasion of Uruguay he approved an alliance with Montevideo (13 March 1823).

In 1828, López presided over the national convention in Santa Fe that approved the peace treaty with Brazil and appointed him commander of the national army to fight the unitarian José María Paz. At his initiative, the Federalist Pact was negotiated and signed in Santa Fe (4 January 1831). As governor, he encouraged trade and economic development, pushed the provincial borders farther into the Chaco, improved the administration of justice, and established elementary schools, including one in an Abipón village, and a secondary school. His influence diminished as that of Juan Manuel de Rosas increased.

See also **Rosas, Juan Manuel de; Santa Fe, Argentina.**

BIBLIOGRAPHY

Leslie Bethell, ed., *Spanish America After Independence, 1820–1870* (1987).

Joseph T. Criscenti, ed., *Sarmiento and His Argentina* (1993).

H. S. Ferns, *Britain and Argentina in the Nineteenth Century* (1960).

Tulio Halperín-Donghi, *Politics, Economics, and Society in Argentina in the Revolutionary Period,* translated by Richard Southern (1975).

John Lynch, *Argentine Dictator: Juan Manuel de Rosas, 1829–1852* (1981).

Ysabel F. Rennie, *The Argentine Republic* (1945).

José Luis Romero, *A History of Argentine Political Thought,* translated by Thomas F. McGann (1963).

Additional Bibliography

Hoffmann, Andrea. *El discurso político de Estanislao López.* Santa Fe: Asociación Amigos del Archivo General de la Provincia, 1998.

JOSEPH T. CRISCENTI

LÓPEZ, FRANCISCO SOLANO (1826–1870).

Francisco Solano López (*b.* 24 July 1826; *d.* 1 March 1870), president of Paraguay (1862–1870) and the third of its three major nineteenth-century post-Independence administrators. Paraguayans traditionally have viewed López as a national hero, whereas revisionists have judged him to be an ambitious nationalist who overestimated the economic significance and military strength of Paraguay and involved it in the disastrous War of the Triple Alliance.

Born in Asunción as the eldest son of Carlos Antonio López, raised on the family *estancia* in Olivares, and privately educated by tutors, López became his father's principal adviser, confidant, and heir apparent. When Carlos Antonio López declared war on Juan Manuel de Rosas of Argentina in 1845, he made eighteen-year-old Francisco Solano a brigadier general. From 1853 to 1854, the younger López negotiated contracts for technicians and arms in Europe, where he met Elisa Alicia Lynch, who became his mistress and bore him five sons. As commander of the army and vice president, he dominated the triumvirate that ruled at his father's death. On 16 October 1862 a congress elected him president of Paraguay for a ten-year term.

General López continued the political system and economic policies of his father. He sought to make Asunción similar to European capitals—socially vibrant and culturally stimulating, with regular theater performances and fashionable events. He encouraged trade and provided government loans for commercial enterprises, railroad expansion, and telegraph construction. His administration increased the number of doctors, engineers, teachers, and skilled workers and also centralized education and the economy. Although López accumulated his own land and wealth, he was well accepted by both the peasantry and the elite.

When López sought to increase Paraguay's international role in the Río de la Plata area, he clashed with Argentina and Brazil. After leading the armed forces in the War of the Triple Alliance (1864–1870) for more than five years, he was killed at the battle of Cerro Corá.

See also **Cerro Corá, Battle of; Paraguay: The Nineteenth Century.**

BIBLIOGRAPHY

R. B. Cunninghame Graham, *Portrait of a Dictator* (1933).

Juan Emiliano O'Leary, *El Mariscal Solano López,* 3d ed. (1970).

John Hoyt Williams, *The Rise and Fall of the Paraguayan Republic, 1800–1870* (1979).

Additional Bibliography

García, Cristina. *Francisco Solano López.* Madrid: Historia 16: Quorum: Sociedad Estatal para la Ejecución Programas del Quinto Centenario, 1987.

Mattos, Joaquim Francisco de. *A guerra do Paraguai: História de Francisco Solano Lopez, o exterminador da nação paraguaia.* Brasília: Centro Gráfico do Senado Federal, 1990.

Rodríguez Alcalá, Guido, compiler. *Residentas, destinadas y traidoras.* Asunción: RP Ediciones-Criterio, 1991.

VERA BLINN REBER

LÓPEZ, JOSÉ HILARIO (1798–1869).

José Hilario López (*b.* 18 February 1798; *d.* 27 November 1869), president of Colombia (1849–1853). Born in Popayán, López joined the patriots in 1814 and was imprisoned by the royalists from 1816 to 1819. Freed, he fought in Venezuela and in southern Colombia, becoming a colonel in 1826. He rejected Simon Bolívar's dictatorship, and at the Ocaña Convention in 1828 he remained antidictator. Later that year, López and Colonel José María Obando defeated Bolívar's surrogate, Colonel Tomás Cipriano de Mosquera, and won control of Cauca. In 1830 López was promoted to general, and with Obando he raised an army that ousted General Rafael Urdaneta in May 1831. López served in key gubernatorial posts from 1833 to 1837 and was the Colombian chargé d'affaires to the Vatican (1839–1840).

López did not join Obando in the War of the Supremes (1839–1842). Having married into the Neiva elite, he devoted himself to managing his estates until he was elected president. As chief executive, he carried out a liberal agenda. Education was made more secular, the clergy put on salary, the Jesuits expelled, tithe collection secularized, the ecclesiastical *fuero* abolished, clerical posts made elective, and Archbishop Manuel José Mosquera exiled. Also, slavery was abolished and legislation aimed at improving the status of women was enacted. López fought against the Melo Revolt (1854). He joined the Liberal Revolution (1860–1862) late, but contributed to its victory. He participated in the Rionegro Convention (1863).

See also **Obando, José María.**

BIBLIOGRAPHY

Abel Cruz Santos, *General José Hilario López, 1869–noviembre 27–1969* (1969) and *José Hilario López, o el soldado civil* (1970).

Juan Pablo Llinas, *José Hilario López* (1983). See also López's *Memorias del general José Hilario López* (1857), which covers 1814 to 1839.

Additional Bibliography

Gutiérrez Jaramillo, Camilo. *José Hilario López: Un hombre de su siglo.* Bogotá: C. Gutiérrez Jaramillo, 1997.

J. León Helguera

LÓPEZ, NARCISO (1797–1851). Narciso López (*b.* 19 October 1797; *d.* 1 September 1851), Cuban revolutionist. A native of Caracas, Venezuela, López joined the Spanish army in his mid-teens, participated in campaigns against Simón Bolívar's independence movement, and achieved the rank of colonel. When Spanish forces withdrew to Cuba in 1823, López accompanied the army to the island. There he married the sister of a creole planter, and acquired landholdings and mines. In 1827 López went to Spain, where, during the Carlist wars, he served as aide-de-camp to General Gerónimo Valdés in support of the queen-regent, María Cristina, and her daughter, Isabella, against the claims to the succession of Don Carlos, brother of the late Ferdinand VII. While in Spain, López rose to the rank of brigadier general. López returned to Cuba when Valdés became captain-general of the colony in 1841. During Valdés's tenure, López served as president of the Executive and Permanent Military Commission and governor of Trinidad Province—posts which he lost when General Leopoldo O'Donnell replaced Valdés in 1843. This loss of patronage, as well as financial setbacks, may have contributed to López's conversion to anticolonialism in the mid-1840s.

López's overt revolutionary activities commenced in 1848 with a plot named after his mines—Conspiracy of the Cuban Rose Mine. Set to erupt in late June, the uprising was postponed until mid-July in deference to the wishes of the Havana Club, which favored annexation of Cuba to the United States. Alerted by the U.S. government to the pending revolt, Spanish authorities took preemptive action. Having escaped arrest in the resultant crackdown, López reached the United States, where he organized a private military—or "filibustering"—expedition to liberate Cuba. In 1849 the Zachary Taylor administration thwarted this effort, which, like all filibustering expeditions, violated U.S. neutrality statutes, by blockading López's troops assembled at Round Island, off the Gulf coast, and by seizing his ships and supplies in New York City.

Undaunted, López and associated exiles announced a junta based in New York City but with a Washington, D.C., address. On 19 May 1850, López and some 520 followers captured Cárdenas, on Cuba's northern coast. His forces outnumbered by Spanish reinforcements, López fled to Key West, Florida. He was indicted in June 1850 for violating American neutrality laws but never stood trial (charges were dismissed after three juries failed to convict a coconspirator).

Federal authorities upset his next invasion scheme when, in April 1851, they seized the vessel *Cleopatra* in New York and arrested several filibuster leaders. However, that August, López eluded federal authorities and invaded Cuba with some 453 men. His force debarked the coasting packet *Pampero* near Bahía Honda, west of Havana. López mismanaged the ensuing military campaign, which was doomed to failure because Spanish authorities repressed developing resistance prior to the landing. Many of López's followers died in battle. The rest, except for a couple of officers who had returned to the United States for reinforcements, were captured. Spanish authorities released a few, but executed fifty invaders on 16 August and later sent some 160 captives to imprisonment in Spain. López was garroted in Havana on 1 September, in a public display. News of the 16 August executions sparked riots in New Orleans, Mobile, and Key West that did thousands of dollars' worth of damage to Spanish property. Disputes arising from the López invasions complicated for years diplomatic relations between the United States, Spain, and Great Britain and France—the latter two seeking to dominate the Gulf-Caribbean region economically—and left a legacy of fear of American intentions among Spanish officials ruling Cuba.

Some authorities, noting the disproportionate number of Americans in López's filibuster armies, his flag modeled upon the banner of the Republic of Texas, and his contacts with both Americans and Cubans favoring the annexation of Cuba to the United States as a new slave state, portray López as a conservative who intended to integrate Cuba into the United States. A few scholars, however, view López as a liberal nationalist—an early martyr to the cause of Cuban independence.

See also **Cuba: The Colonial Era (1492–1898); Filibustering.**

BIBLIOGRAPHY

Charles Henry Brown, *Agents of Manifest Destiny: The Lives and Times of the Filibusters* (1980), esp. pp. 21–108.

Robert G. Caldwell, *The López Expeditions to Cuba, 1848–1851* (1915).

Philip S. Foner, *A History of Cuba and Its Relations with the United States,* vol. 2 (1963), esp. pp. 41–65.

Herminio Portell Vilá, *Narciso López y su época,* 3 vols. (1930–1958).

Basil Rauch, *American Interest in Cuba, 1848–1855* (1948).

Additional Bibliography

Chaffin, Tom. *Fatal Glory: Narciso López and the First Clandestine U.S. War Against Cuba.* Charlottesville: University Press of Virginia, 1996.

May, Robert E. *Manifest Destiny's Underworld: Filibustering in Antebellum America.* Chapel Hill, NC: University of North Carolina Press, 2002.

Zeuske, Michael. "!Con López a Cuba!: Los voluntarios alemanes en la expedición de Narciso López, 1851–1852." *Montalbán* 29 (1996): 111--139.

ROBERT E. MAY

LÓPEZ, VICENTE FIDEL

LÓPEZ, VICENTE FIDEL (1815–1903). Vicente Fidel López (*b.* 24 April 1815; *d.* 30 August 1903), Argentine historian and political figure. Born in Buenos Aires and the son of Vicente López y Planes, who wrote Argentina's national anthem, López as a young intellectual became involved during the 1830s in Esteban Echeverría's Asociación de Mayo. Fearing possible persecution by the Juan Manuel de Rosas dictatorship, López fled to Chile, where he worked as an educator and liberal publicist. Returning to Buenos Aires after the fall of Rosas in 1852, he served briefly in the provincial government, then emigrated to Uruguay until national unity was finally effected.

Once permanently reestablished in Buenos Aires, López served as university rector, finance minister, and in other capacities, as well as practicing journalism. However, he is best known for his work as a historian. That career began in Chile with the publication of historical novels and essays, and it culminated when he both published historical documents and authored a series of major works of Argentine history, notably his ten-volume *Historia de la República Argentina* (1883–1893). His writing was highly partisan and made use of a lively imagination rather than depending on rigorous documentation, a trait that drew him into a bitter polemic over historical method with Bartolomé Mitre. He was, however, a skilled writer and enjoyed a wide following in his time.

See also **Echeverría, Esteban; Rosas, Juan Manuel de.**

BIBLIOGRAPHY

Rómulo D. Carbía, *Historia crítica de la historiografía Argentina* (1939), pp. 121–148.

Ricardo Piccirilli, *Los López: Una dinastía intelectual* (1972).

Additional Bibliography

Lettieri, Alberto Rodolfo. *Vicente Fidel López: La construcción histórico-política de un liberalismo conservador.* Buenos Aires: Editorial Biblos: Fundación Simón Rodríguez, 1995.

Madero, Roberto. *El origen de la historia: Sobre el debate entre Vicente Fidel López y Bartolomé Mitre.* Mexico City; Buenos Aires: Fondo de Cultura Económica, 2001.

Madero, Roberto. *La historiografía entre la república y la nación: El caso de Vicente Fidel López.* Buenos Aires: Catálogos, 2005.

DAVID BUSHNELL

LÓPEZ, WILEBALDO

LÓPEZ, WILEBALDO (1944–). Wilebaldo López (*b.* 3 July 1944), Mexican playwright. Born in Queréndaro, he studied acting, received a Writers' Guild Fellowship, and was the first dramatist of his generation to achieve recognition. Two of his early plays were widely staged in Mexico: *Los arrieros con sus burros por la hermosa capital* (1967) and *Cosas de muchachos* (1968). His others include *Yo soy Juárez* (1972) and *Malinche Show* (1977), adaptations of Mexican history in modern terms. His recent works have not enjoyed the same popularity with audiences and critics as the earlier ones.

See also **Theater.**

BIBLIOGRAPHY

Malkah Rabell, *Decenio de teatro 1975–1985* (1986).

Guillermo Schmidhuber De La Mora, "*Los viejos* y la dramaturgia mexicana," *Cahiers du C.R.I.A.R.*, no. 7 (1987): 127–133.

Ronald D. Burgess, *The New Dramatists of Mexico* (1991).

GUILLERMO SCHMIDHUBER

LÓPEZ ARELLANO, OSWALDO (1921–).

Oswaldo López Arellano was the dominant military officer in Honduras from 1957 until 1975. Born on June 30, 1921, in Danlí, López Arellano joined the armed services in 1939 and was schooled in military aviation in the United States. As commander of the armed forces beginning in 1956, he was installed as provisional president after the coup of October 3, 1963. This coup, carried out ten days before scheduled elections, reflected the Conservatives' and the military's displeasure with the prospect for a victory by the Liberal candidate, Modesto Rodas Alvarado. López continued as provisional president until a new constitution confirmed him as president in 1965. During his presidency the poor performance of the military in the war with El Salvador (1969) brought discredit on the armed services. López maintained a mild military dictatorship during his term, which continued until 1971. The National Party became his personal political vehicle.

In 1971 Ramón Ernesto Cruz was elected president, but López, as chief of the armed forces, remained in control. In 1972, López again seized power and acted as president until he was toppled by his fellow officers in 1975. At that time, he was charged with corruption in accepting a bribe from United Brands (formerly United Fruit) to obtain lower banana export taxes. López subsequently became the president of the now bankrupt national airline, Servicio Aereo de Honduras, S.A. (SAHSA). He is a retired businessman.

See also **Honduras, National Party (PNH).**

BIBLIOGRAPHY

Raúl Alberto Domínguez, ed., *Ascenso al poder y descenso del General Oswaldo López Arellano* (1975).

James A. Morris, *Honduras: Caudillo Politics and Military Rulers* (1984).

Additional Bibliography

Domínguez, Raúl Alberto. *Ascenso al poder y descenso del General Oswaldo López Arellano.* Tegucigalpa: Imprenta Calderón, 1975.

DAVID L. JICKLING

LÓPEZ BUCHARDO, CARLOS (1881–1948).

Carlos López Buchardo (*b.* 12 October 1881; *d.* 21 April 1948), Argentine composer and teacher. Born in Buenos Aires, López Buchardo began his musical studies with Héctor Belucci and studied piano with Alfonso Thibaud. He studied harmony with Luis Forino and Constantino Gaito. Later he moved to Paris to attend the composition classes of Albert Roussel. Returning to Buenos Aires, López Buchardo founded the eponymous Conservatorio López Buchardo (1924) and directed it until his death.

López Buchardo began to compose as a young man, starting with pieces for the stage, some musicals, and an early opera, *Il sogno di Alma,* which premiered in Buenos Aires on 4 August 1914. He was an excellent melodist with an extraordinary gift for vocal works, and his numerous song cycles, which are based on Argentine folk tunes and themes, were popular worldwide. Among his symphonic works is the *Escenas argentinas* (1920), in which he utilized two popular dances, the *milonga* and *gato;* it premiered under Felix Weingartner with the Vienna Philharmonic Orchestra in Buenos Aires in 1922. The following year López Buchardo received the Municipal Prize in Music. He was founder and director of the school of fine arts at the University of La Plata, where he was professor of harmony. He was also president of the Wagnerian Association, twice member of the board of Teatro Colón, and director of music and art for the stage for the Ministry of Public Instruction. He died in Buenos Aires.

See also **Music: Art Music; Music: Popular Music and Dance.**

BIBLIOGRAPHY

Composers of the Americas, vol. 12 (1966).

Abraham Jurafsky, *Carlos López Buchardo* (1966); *New Grove Dictionary of Music and Musicians,* vol. 11 (1980).

Additional Bibliography

Weiss, Allison L. "A Guide to the Songs of Carlos López Buchardo (1881–1948) Argentina." M.A. Thesis. University of Portland, 2005.

SUSANA SALGADO

LÓPEZ CAPILLAS, FRANCISCO

LÓPEZ CAPILLAS, FRANCISCO (c. 1615–c. 1673). Francisco López Capillas (*b.* ca. 1615; *d.* ca. 18 January 1673), Mexican composer and organist. López Capillas may have been born in Andalusia and was probably a pupil of Juan de Riscos, the *maestro de capilla* of Jaén. Ordained a priest, he was named organist and bassoonist for the Puebla cathedral in December 1641. In 1645 he became first organist and singer. In May 1648 he went to Mexico City, where he was hired by the cathedral organist Fabián Ximeno, who had heard López Capillas on a visit to the Puebla cathedral and been impressed with his talent. He presented a volume of his choir compositions to the Mexico cathedral in April 1654, and on 21 May he was appointed *maestro de capilla* and organist of the cathedral. He was supervisor of the musical services and presented the cathedral with several excellently illuminated choirbooks. López's compositions are considered among the best written in New Spain; his eight Masses, eight Magnificats, and numerous other religious works are composed with extraordinary artfulness. His use of the polyphony, canon, and difficult mensural practices were remarkably competent. The arrival in Madrid of some of his choirbooks generated a court decree (1672) to bestow him a full prebend, but he died in Mexico City before the order became effective.

See also **Music: Art Music.**

BIBLIOGRAPHY

Robert Stevenson, "Francisco López Capillas," in *Heterofonía* 6 (1973), and *Renaissance and Baroque Musical Sources in the Americas* (1970); *New Grove Dictionary of Music and Musicians,* vol. 11 (1980).

SUSANA SALGADO

LÓPEZ CHÁVEZ, JULIO

LÓPEZ CHÁVEZ, JULIO (?–1869). A Mexican peasant, socialist thinker, and military leader, Julio López Chávez (sometimes referred to as Chávez López) was born in or near Texcoco, in the Valley of Mexico. After becoming a disciple of Plotino Rhodakanaty's school of utopian socialism in nearby Chalco, he devoted himself to a radical vision of communal village autonomy that was anarchist in its hostility toward both the church and the centralizing and modernizing project of the liberal state. He led the Chalco Rebellion beginning in 1868, until he was captured by the Mexican army and executed on September 1, 1869.

López Chávez was working on an hacienda near Texcoco when he became a member of Rhodakanaty's school, La Escuela del Rayo y del Socialismo (The Lightning and Socialism School), founded in Chalco in 1865. López Chávez soon attracted the attention of Rhodakanaty and his follower Francisco Zalacosta, who also taught at the Chalco school. Whereas Rhodakanaty eschewed violent tactics and held, in the tradition of Proudhon and Fourier, that revolutionary change would come through education and persuasion, López Chávez believed that violence was necessary to resist the oppression of government. The example of López Chávez's peasant-led militia influenced the next generation of socialist leaders and paved the way for the agrarian uprisings of the coming decades.

BIBLIOGRAPHY

Hart, John M. *Anarchism & the Mexican Working Class, 1860–1931.* Austin: University of Texas Press, 1978.

Valadés, José C. *El socialismo libertario mexicano (siglo XIX).* Mexico: Universidad Autónoma de Sinaloa, 1984.

JAMES ELLIOT MCBRIDE

LÓPEZ CONTRERAS, ELEÁZAR

(1883–1973). Eleázar López Contreras (*b.* 5 May 1883; *d.* 2 January 1973), president of Venezuela (1936–1941). Having completed high school in 1898, López Contreras joined the army of Cipriano Castro in 1899. In 1908, he left the army with the rank of colonel, but in 1913 he returned as commander of the barracks of Ciudad Bolívar, and in 1914 assumed command of an infantry regiment at Caracas. In 1919 he became minister of war and marine, and undertook the acquisition of war matériel from Europe and the United States. As a loyal supporter of Juan Vicente Gómez, he used military force against students, workers, dissident army officers, and other opposition groups. For his reward, he rose through the ranks during the 1920s, taking over as commander in chief in 1930. From 1931 until December 1935, he again served as minister of war and marine.

Following Gómez's death López became president of the republic. He quickly ended popular demonstrations by students and workers. In so doing, he became the first Venezuelan president to speak to the nation by radio. In February 1936, he introduced a broad reform program aimed at appealing to everyone. On the one hand, he checked the power of the army. On the other, he followed Arturo Uslar Pietri's call to "sow the petroleum" by using oil revenues to finance educational and institutional reforms. The government established a new teacher training institution, the Instituto Pedagógico (1936), and gave further assistance to child care by creating the Consejo Venezolano del Niño (1939), the Instituto Preorientación para Menores (1939), and the Casa de Maternidad Concepción Palacios (1938). New cabinet departments included the Ministry of Agriculture and Livestock and the Ministry of Labor and Communications.

López's administration guided Venezuela toward a more democratic government. He tolerated opposition movements, although he exiled Communists and radicals. Like Gómez, he followed an anticommunist policy and limited the activities of labor organizations. The government also imposed more control over the economy by creating the Industrial Bank and the National Exchange Office, as well as the Central Bank of Venezuela.

In 1938, the López government enacted petroleum legislation aimed at giving the nation more control over the industry and a larger share in the revenue, but for various reasons, including corruption, little was done to enforce the laws. In 1941, López stepped down from power, the presidential term having been reduced from seven to five years, and turned the government over to his chosen successor, Isaías Medina Angarita. Following the overthrow of the latter, López Contreras went into exile and effectively dropped out of politics.

See also **Goméz, Juan Vicente; Medina Angarita, Isaías.**

BIBLIOGRAPHY

Henry J. Allen, *Venezuela: A Democracy* (1941).

Winfield J. Burggraaff, *The Venezuelan Armed Forces in Politics, 1935–1959* (1972).

Judith Ewell, *Venezuela: A Century of Change* (1984).

Eleázar López Contreras, *Proceso político social, 1928–1936* (1965).

Emilio Pacheco, *De Castro a López Contreras* (1984).

Alfred Tarre Murzi, *López Contreras: De la tiranía a la libertad,* 2d ed. (1982); *López Contreras, el último general* (1983).

Additional Bibliography

Battaglini, Oscar. *Legitimación del poder y lucha política en Venezuela, 1936–1941.* Caracas: Universidad Central de Venezuela, 1993.

Capriles Ayala, Carlos. *Vida y muerte de la democracia: López Contreras y Medina Angaria vs. Rómulo Betancourt y Pérez Jiménez.* Caracas: Consorcio de Ediciones Capriles, 1999.

Dávila, Luis Ricardo. *El estado y las instituciones en Venezuela (1936–1945).* Caracas: Academia Nacional de la Historia, 1988.

Moleiro, Rodolfo. *De la dictadura a la democracia: Eleazar López Contreras, lindero y puente entre dos épocas.* Caracas: Editorial Pomaire Venezuela, 1993.

WINTHROP R. WRIGHT

LÓPEZ DE ARTEAGA, SEBASTIÁN

(1610–1652). Sebastián López de Arteaga (*b.* 15 March 1610; *d.* 1652), painter. Born in Seville, López de Arteaga was examined as a painter in 1630. In 1638 he was in Cádiz; around 1640 he embarked for New Spain, where in 1642 he erected and decorated an arch with mythological subjects to celebrate the arrival of Viceroy García Sarmiento De Sotomayor y Luna. López de Arteaga is credited with introducing into New Spain the tenebrist style of Francisco de Zurbarán, who some scholars claim had been his teacher. He sought, and with some success won, the patronage of the Inquisition. Although documents attest to López de Arteaga's considerable activity, only eight paintings can be ascribed to him with certainty, and even some of those are problematic. One of the most famous is the *Incredulity of Saint Thomas* (1643). More difficult is the *Marriage of the Virgin,* quite dissimilar and the subject of much discussion over what constitutes this master's style.

See also **Art: The Colonial Era; New Spain, Viceroyalty of.**

BIBLIOGRAPHY

Xavier Moyssen, "Sebastián de Arteaga, 1610–1652," in *Anales del Instituto de investigaciones estéticas* 59 (1988): 17–34.

Manuel Toussaint, *Colonial Art in Mexico* (1967).

CLARA BARGELLINI

LÓPEZ DE CERRATO, ALONSO

(c. 1490–1555). Alonso López de Cerrato (also Cerrato, Alonso López; *b.* ca. 1490; *d.* 5 May 1555), president of the Audiencia of Santo Domingo (1543–1547); president of the Audiencia de los Confines, later Guatemala (1548–1555). Of obscure origins but educated and enjoying royal favor, Cerrato was appointed to serve in Santo Domingo and then Guatemala to enforce the New Laws of 1542 and other pro-indigenous legislation. Stern and uncompromising, he freed Indian slaves in both jurisdictions, lowered tributes, and corrected abuses in Central America. Supported by Bartolomé de Las Casas (1474–1566) and other reformers and indifferent to local public opinion, he earned the enmity of Spanish settlers, who accused him of nepotism. He died while serving his *residencia.*

See also **Las Casas, Bartolomé de; Residencia.**

BIBLIOGRAPHY

Lovell, W. George, Christopher H. Lutz, and William R. Swezey. "The Indian Population of Southern Guatemala: An Analysis of López de Cerrato's Tasaciones de Tributos." *The Americas* 40:4 (April 1984): 459–476.

Rodríguez Becerra, Salvador. *Encomienda y conquista: Los inicios de la colonización en Guatemala.* Seville: Universidad de Sevilla, 1977.

Sherman, William L. "Indian Slavery and the Cerrato Reforms." *Hispanic American Historical Review* 51:1 (February 1971): 25–50.

MURDO J. MACLEOD

LÓPEZ DE COGOLLUDO, DIEGO

(c. 1612–c. 1665). Diego López de Cogolludo (*b.* ca. 1612; *d.* ca. 1665), Franciscan historian and missionary. Born in Alcalá de Henares, Spain, Friar López de Cogolludo arrived as a missionary in Yucatán in 1634, and after years of work among the Maya he rose to be the chief (provincial) of the Franciscan province. In the 1650s he wrote *Historia de Yucathan,* a major source not only for the history of Yucatán but also for the study of Maya culture. The book was published posthumously in Madrid in 1688; later editions appeared in 1842 (Campeche), and 1846 and 1867–1868 (Mérida). Reprints and new editions also appeared in the twentieth century.

See also **Franciscans.**

BIBLIOGRAPHY

Gabriel Ferrer De Mendiolea, "Historia de la historiografía," *Enciclopedia yucatanense,* vol. 5 (1944), pp. 815–846.

J. Ignacio Rubio Mañé, "Preface," in Diego López De Cogolludo, *Historia de Yucathan,* 3 vols. (1954–1957).

ROBERT W. PATCH

LÓPEZ DE LEGAZPI Y GURRUCHÁTEGUI, MIGUEL

(1510–1572). Miguel López de Legazpi y Gurruchátegui (*b.* 1510; *d.* 1572), *escribano mayor* (senior clerk of the Mexico City *cabildo* (municipal council) from January 1542 to 3 June 1557. López perhaps epitomizes the career of a sixteenth-century bureaucrat who, arriving late in a conquest area, had to work to achieve upward mobility. An *hidalgo* (nobleman) from Zumárraga, Guipúzcoa, in the Basque country, López departed for New Spain in 1528. On 19 January 1530 he became the *escribano de cabildo* of Mexico City, serving in that capacity until the end of 1541. For a period after 1535 he was secretary in the government of Viceroy Antonio de Mendoza. After serving as *escribano mayor* of the *cabildo,* he transferred his rights to his son, Melchor de Legazpi.

López's offices, while not providing the opportunity to acquire an *encomienda* (grant of tribute from an indigenous polity) in New Spain, did permit the development of contracts, status (his wife, Isabel Garcés, was the sister of Julián Garcés, first bishop of Tlaxcala), and other assets that he parlayed into a license to settle the Philippine Islands. On 21 November 1564 his armada of 5 ships, 150 sailors, 200 salaried employees, some 25 settlers, and 4 Augustinian friars left Mexico. The navigator for the expedition was the Augustinian friar Andrés de Urdaneta. López was governor of the Philippines when he died in Manila.

See also **Cabildo, Cabildo Abierto; Encomienda; Hidalgo.**

BIBLIOGRAPHY

Ignacio Bejarano, *Actas de cabildo de la Ciudad de Mexico,* vols. 2, 4, and 6 (1889).

José Rogelio Álvarez, ed., *Enciclopedia de México,* vol. 8 (1975), p. 4785.

Peter Boyd-Bowman, *Índice geobiográfico de cuarenta mil pobladores españoles de América en el siglo XVI,* vol. 2 (1968).

Additional Bibliography

Kelsey, Harry. "Finding the Way Home: Spanish Exploration of the Round-Trip Route Across the Pacific Ocean." *Western Historical Quarterly.* (Spring 1986): 145–164.

Lopez, Rafael. *The Christianization of the Philippines.* Manila: University of San Agustín, 1965.

ROBERT HIMMERICH Y VALENCIA

LÓPEZ DEL ROSARIO, ANDRÉS.

See **Andresote.**

LÓPEZ DE QUIROGA, ANTONIO

(c. 1620–1699). Antonio López de Quiroga (*b.* ca. 1620; *d.* late January 1699), silver mine owner in Potosí. López de Quiroga was born near Triacastela in the province of Lugo, in northwestern Spain. He was the leading silver producer of Potosí (and possibly of all Spanish America) in the seventeenth century, owning mines and refineries at Potosí itself as well as at other sites widely scattered over its district. Between 1661 and 1699, these operations provided about 14 million ounces of silver, a seventh or an eighth of the Potosí district's total output in that period.

About 1648 López came to Potosí, where he used his prior commercial experience to set himself up as an importing merchant. He quickly married Doña Felipa Bóveda y Savavia, daughter of a prosperous local family from Galicia, close to his own birthplace in Spain. He benefited from an investigation of coinage adulteration at the Potosí mint, which led to the removal of most of the existing *mercaderes de plata* (silver traders and coinage supervisors) thereby paving the way for his eventual entrance to that profession in the 1650s. From this position, he moved into silver production about 1660, and in that decade rapidly expanded his holdings of mines and refineries in Potosí. In the 1670s and 1680s he extended his activities to Porco, Ocurí, San Antonio del Nuevo Mundo, and other sites in the district, often reviving old mines through the excavation of deep drainage galleries. To expedite this process, about 1670 he introduced the technique of blasting with gunpowder, probably for the first time in Spanish-American silver mining.

López placed many relatives in governmental positions in the Potosí district during the 1670s and 1680s, thus safeguarding his own interests. He became a large landowner and used his estates to supply goods useful in mining. Though he was unsuccessful in acquiring a title of nobility, he ended his days an already quasi-mythical figure in Potosí.

See also **Mining: Colonial Spanish America.**

BIBLIOGRAPHY

Bartolomé Arzáns De Orsúa y Vela, *Historia de la Villa Imperial de Potosí,* edited by Lewis Hanke and Gunnar Mendoza I. 3 vols. (1965), vol. 2.

Peter Bakewell, *Silver and Entrepreneurship in Seventeenth-Century Potosí: The Life and Times of Antonio López de Quiroga* (1988).

PETER BAKEWELL

LÓPEZ DE ROMAÑA, EDUARDO

(1847–1912). Eduardo López de Romaña (*b.* 1847; *d.* 1912), president of Peru from 1899 to 1903. When President Nicolas de Piérola created the post of minister of development, he chose López de Romaña to fill it. López de Romaña successfully undertook an ambitious public works program and pledged to continue Piérola's progressive plans if the president in turn agreed to support him as the next president. On the basis of that agreement and with an alliance formed between Democrats and Civilistas, López de Romaña became president in 1899. In 1901 he began to reorganize the nation's schools to give more emphasis to technical skills in higher education. But his political naïveté made him susceptible to Civilista manipulation, and other progressive programs had less success. By the 1903 election the coalition of parties had split, some members joining the new Liberal Party and others returning to the Civilista Party. Even Piérola had abandoned him in favor of an old friend, Manuel Candamo, the Civilista candidate who won the election. The elite political machinations of the post-Piérola years thus kept power in the hands of the national oligarchy.

See also **Peru, Political Parties: Civilista Party.**

BIBLIOGRAPHY

Alfonso W. Quiroz, *Domestic and Foreign Finance in Modern Peru, 1850–1950: Financing Visions of Development* (1993).

Steve Stein, *Populism in Peru: The Emergence of the Masses and the Politics of Social Control* (1980).

Additional Bibliography

Leiva Viacava, Lourdes. *Nicolás de Piérola.* Lima: Editorial Brasa, 1995.

McEvoy, Carmen. *La utopía republicana: Ideales y realidades en la formación de la cultura política peruana, 1871–1919.* Lima: Pontifica Universidad Católica del Perú, Fondo Editorial, 1997.

VINCENT PELOSO

LÓPEZ JORDÁN, RICARDO

(1822–1889). Ricardo López Jordán (*b.* 30 August 1822; *d.* 22 June 1889), military leader and staunch defender of provincial autonomy. Born in Paysandú, Uruguay, López Jordán was a nephew of Francisco Ramírez and Justo José de Urquiza. He attended the Colegio de San Ignacio in Buenos Aires, and began his military career at the age of nineteen as a soldier in the escort of Urquiza. He served in the forces of Urquiza and the Uruguayans Manuel Oribe, Eugenio Garzón, Lucas Moreno, and César Díaz. Twice military commandant of Concepción del Uruguay, he became extremely popular when he stopped an invasion of his jurisdiction by General Juan Madariaga. He later taught military science at the Colegio del Uruguay, where among his students was Julio A. Roca (who later defeated him in battle and became president of Argentina). He represented Paraná in the national congress (1858) and accompanied Urquiza to Asunción to settle an international dispute (1859). López Jordán served as minister of government in the provincial government of Urquiza (1860) and as president of the provincial legislature (1863–1864), but was unsuccessful in his candidacy for governor because of Urquiza's opposition (1864).

During the War of the Triple Alliance, López Jordán's troops were the only ones not to disband at Basualdo, and he escorted Urquiza home. The day after Urquiza was assassinated, an act for which he assumed responsibility, he was elected governor (12 April 1870). When President Sarmiento refused to recognize the election and ordered the intervention of the province, the legislature authorized López Jordán to defend provincial autonomy. Sarmiento then besieged the province. Warships patrolled the Uruguay and Paraná rivers, and federal troops, eventually armed with imported Remington rifles, advanced into the province from Gualeguaychú and Corrientes.

López Jordán was supported by the people, many young intellectuals, and the partisans of Adolfo Alsina. His secretary at the time was José Hernández, author of the epic poem *Martín Fierro.* Defeated at Naembé (26 January 1871), he fled to Brazil. Following an unsuccessful invasion in 1873, he returned to Brazil. His secretary now was Francisco F.

Fernández. In 1876, in his last attempt at revolution, which received weak support, López Jordán was captured in Corrientes, but he was able to escape to Montevideo. In 1888, President Juárez Celman granted him a pardon. He returned to Buenos Aires, where he was assassinated. Some view him as the last defender of provincial autonomy.

See also **Roca, Julio Argentino.**

BIBLIOGRAPHY

Joseph T. Criscenti, ed., *Sarmiento and His Argentina* (1993), p. 83.

María Amalia Duarte, *Urquiza y López Jordán* (1974) and *Tiempos de rebelión, 1870–1873* (1988).

Ysabel F. Rennie, *The Argentine Republic* (1945), pp. 117–118.

Additional Bibliography

Duarte, María Amalia. *Prisión, exilio y muerte de Ricardo López Jordán*. Buenos Aires: Academia Nacional de la Historia, 1998.

Salduna, Bernardo I. *La rebelión jordanista*. Buenos Aires: Editorial Dunken, 2005.

JOSEPH T. CRISCENTI

LÓPEZ MATEOS, ADOLFO (1910–1969).

Adolfo López Mateos (*b.* 26 May 1910; *d.* 22 September 1969), president of Mexico (1958–1964). The accession of López Mateos to the presidency in 1958 represented the control of a postrevolutionary generation of politicians who, for the most part, were born in the first two decades of the twentieth century. López Mateos also represented politicians who had opposed the Mexican establishment in the 1929 presidential campaign, in which he and a prominent group of students joined forces with José Vasconcelos in a bitter and unsuccessful campaign. During the transitional period of his presidency, from 1958 to 1959, López Mateos faced a most difficult labor strike, that of the railroad workers' union, led by Valentín Campa. This strike revealed the union leadership's failure to represent the rank and file and demonstrated the willingness of the new, untried president, who had achieved the office largely on the basis of his skill as labor secretary in avoiding such confrontations, to apply force when necessary. As a result of his use of army intervention, government-dominated union leadership strengthened its hold over this and other unions. In 1960 López Mateos briefly risked his early political successes by refusing to join the United States and most of the rest of Latin America in breaking relations with Castro's Cuba. In fact, he only succeeded in reinforcing Mexico's independent course in foreign affairs—a strategy followed by most of his successors.

On the economic front, López Mateos inherited a devalued peso, but in spite of pressures to devalue once again, he pursued a moderate economic philosophy, promoting the stabilization of the peso and the gradual, steady expansion of the economy. He appointed as treasury secretary Antonio Ortiz Mena, who became the financial architect of an unprecedented twelve years of growth and continued at the helm of the treasury in the next administration. The López Mateos administration's repressive control of the urban working classes extended to the countryside, as exemplified by the notorious execution of peasant leader Rubén Jaramillo while in the hands of government troops. The forced sacrifices of the Mexican working class were what made possible the economic growth of the 1958–1964 period. This expansion in turn produced a growing middle class and the beginnings of an important industrial infrastructure. There is probably no president in recent times who inherited a better economic and political situation than López Mateos's successor, Gustavo Díaz Ordaz.

López Mateos was born in Atizapán de Zaragoza, México. His father, a dentist, died when he was quite young, leaving his mother to support five children. He attended the Colegio Francés in Mexico City on a scholarship, and completed his secondary and preparatory studies in Toluca, México. A student activist at a young age, he joined the Anti-reelections movement in 1929, working as a librarian to support himself. He attended law school at the National University (1929–1934). Disenchanted with Vasconcelos's failure to win the presidency, he attached himself to the president of the ruling National Revolutionary party (1931–1933). In 1934, he began working for the government printing office, becoming a labor representative of the National Workers Development Bank in 1938 and later serving in the secretariat of public education. President Miguel Alemán Valdés, whom López Mateos represented on numerous assignments abroad, selected him as one of the PRI's candidates for senator from his home state in 1946. In 1951, while still a senator, he became secretary general of the party, organizing the campaign committee for Adolfo Ruiz Cortines's presidential bid (1951–1952). Ruiz Cortines rewarded him for his efforts by appointing him secretary of labor, a position he served in successfully until his own candidacy for the presidency in 1957. He became the only person in the history of the party to win the presidential office from the labor post. After he left the presidency in 1964, president Díaz Ordaz asked him to organize the 1968 Olympic Games in Mexico City. Severe illness prevented him from fulfilling this assignment, and he died after a stroke.

See also **Díaz Ordaz, Gustavo; Mexico, Political Parties: Institutional Revolutionary Party (PRI); Ortiz Mena, Antonio.**

BIBLIOGRAPHY

Frank Brandenburg, *The Making of Modern Mexico* (1964).

Tomás Contreras Estrada, *México y Adolfo López Mateos* (1959).

L. Vincent Padgett, *The Mexican Political System* (1966).

Olga Pellicer De Brody and José Luis Reyna, *Historia de la Revolución Mexicana, 1952–1960,* vol. 22 (1978).

Olga Pellicer De Brody and Esteban L. Mancilla, *Historia de la Revolución Mexicana, 1952–1960,* vol. 23 (1978).

Robert E. Scott, *Mexican Government in Transition,* rev. ed. (1964).

Additional Bibliography

Krauze, Enrique. *El sexenio de López Mateos.* México: Clio, 1999.

Novo, Salvador. *La vida en México en el periodo presidencial de Adolfo López Mateos.* México, D.F.: Consejo Nacional para la Cultura y las Artes, 1997–98.

RODERIC AI CAMP

LÓPEZ MICHELSEN, ALFONSO (1913–2007).

Alfonso López Michelsen was president of Colombia from 1974 to 1978. Born on June 30, 1913, the son of Alfonso López Pumarejo (president 1934–1938 and 1942–1945), López Michelsen was educated in Bogotá, the United States, and Europe, and received his law degree in 1936. In 1958 he organized the leftist Liberal Revolutionary Movement (MRL) in opposition to the bipartisan National Front. A decade later López rejoined the official Liberal fold, becoming governor of Cesar Department in 1967, and later foreign minister. In 1974 he won the first post-Front presidential election; his program included a series of fiscal reforms and an opening to the nonviolent left. Growing popular discontent fueled by rising inflation turned violent in the general strike of September 1977. The resurgence of guerrilla activity led López, once a critic of emergency powers, to impose a state of siege in June 1975. Running again in 1982, López was defeated by the Conservative Belisario Betancur Cuartas. López's writings include *Cuestiones colombianas* (1955); the novel *Los elegidos* (1953); *Colombia en la hora cero* (1963), which he coauthored with Indalecio Liévano Aguirre; and his reflections on Colombia, *Visiones del siglo XX colombiano a través de sus protagonistas ya muertos* (2003). He died of a heart attack in Bogotá on July 11, 2007.

See also **Colombia, Political Parties: Liberal Party.**

BIBLIOGRAPHY

Hernando Gómez Buendía, *Alfonso López Michelsen* (1978).

Ignacio Arizmendi Posada, *Presidentes de Colombia, 1810–1990* (1990).

Additional Bibliography

Tirado, Thomas C. *Alfonso López Pumarejo, el conciliador.* Bogotá: Planeta, 1986.

RICHARD J. STOLLER

LÓPEZ OBRADOR, MANUEL ANDRÉS (1953–).

Leading Mexican politician and presidential candidate Manuel Andrés López Obrador, born November 13, 1953, grew up in Tepetitán, Tabasco. He completed his elementary education locally, and continued his studies in the state capital, eventually graduating from the National Autonomous University of Mexico (UNAM) with a degree in political science. After graduating, he served as coordinator of the National Indigenous Institute (INI) in his home state until 1982. The following year he joined Enrique González Pedrero, a prominent political figure, and coordinated his successful campaign for governor of Tabasco, becoming state president of the Institutional Revolutionary Party (PRI). He joined the Democratic Current and abandoned the PRI in 1987, becoming a candidate in 1988 of the National Democratic Front for governor of Tabasco.

Six years later he again ran for governor as the Party of the Democratic Revolution (PRD) candidate, in a election characterized by widespread fraud. Continuing his opposition to the PRI, López Obrador emerged as a force within the PRD, taking over the party's leadership from 1996 to 1999. Using his political success, he ran victoriously for head of the Federal District, which he governed from 2001 to 2005, when he resigned to become his party's presidential candidate. His candidacy sparked controversy, but he held a strong lead throughout most of the campaign, promising a new emphasis on poverty and social justice. He lost to Felipe Calderón by less than .5 percent of the vote and contested the election, resulting in Mexico's Federal Electoral Tribunal (TRIFE) ruling on the outcome. López Obrador refused to accept the decision against him, and established his own parallel presidency, which he has used to criticize the incumbent administration.

See also **Mexico, Political Parties: Democratic Revolutionary Party (PRD); Mexico, Political Parties: Institutional Revolutionary Party (PRI).**

BIBLIOGRAPHY

Grayson, George W. *Mesías mexicano: Biografía crítica de Andrés Manuel López Obrador.* México, D. F.: Grijalbo, 2006.

Grayson, George W. *Mexican Messiah: Andrés Manuel López Obrador.* University Park: Pennsylvania State University Press, 2007.

RODERIC AI CAMP

LÓPEZ PORTILLO, JOSÉ (1920–2004). José López Portillo was president of Mexico from 1976 to 1982. López Portillo took office at a time when Mexico first began undergoing a series of political and economic crises, beginning a long cycle of problems extending to the 1990s. When his predecessor, Luis Echeverría, left office, he also left a legacy of devaluation, an unstable peso and inflation (for the first time in recent history), the distrust of the private sector, and a populist political heritage. Those disenchanted with the Echeverría administration were hopeful when López Portillo was inaugurated. The new president, with some intellectual credentials, and without a long career in the federal government, seemed to offer something new to expectant Mexicans. To mend fences with the alienated business leadership, the president made it clear that he would need its assistance to reverse the economic deficits created by his predecessor and that the government wanted to reestablish a cooperative relationship with the business community. With the participation of many of Mexico's leading capitalists, he succeeded in creating the Alliance for Production. Initially, this association enjoyed considerable success, and until the last year of his administration, the economy appeared to be growing steadily. But by 1982, after another devaluation, and the near bankruptcy of Mexico's leading industrial enterprise, Grupo Industrial AIFA, confidence in the government declined precipitously and capital flight rose to new highs. Mexico's foreign debt reached an estimated $83 billion. In desperation, the president took the extraordinary measure in his 1 September 1982 State of the Union address of nationalizing the domestically owned banking industry, blaming the bankers and, indirectly, the private sector for Mexico's economic woes. The president's decision to nationalize the banks not only failed to restore public confidence in the economy but also raised doubts about his ability to govern. His political decisions brought Mexico to the point of its lowest political legitimacy in modern times, leaving his successor, Miguel de la Madrid, with nearly insurmountable political and economic problems.

Politically, López Portillo, under the direction of Jesús Reyes Heroles, briefly flirted with serious party and electoral reforms, but failed in his attempts. The president, perhaps fearful of internal instability as well as problems caused by the presence of Central American refugees in Mexico, increased the size and budget of the Mexican military, beginning a pattern of increasing modernization. On the intellectual front, he further alienated support when, in the last year of his administration, he censored his most vociferous critic, the leftist weekly *Proceso,* publicly announcing in April that he would require all government agencies to withdraw advertising from the magazine. His actions produced a pall over the media, underlining their dependency on government goodwill. The level of popular dissatisfaction with his political and economic legacy was reflected in the vote tallies for Miguel de la Madrid in the 1982 elections, in which he obtained 71 percent, leaving López Portillo with the lowest figure up to that date for a government party candidate.

López Portillo was the son of engineer José López Portillo y Weber, a military officer, and Margarita Weber y Narvárez, and the grandson of a prominent political figure in the administration of Victoriano Huerta (1913–1914). He was born on June 16, 1920, in Mexico City, where he completed all of his schooling. He and his predecessor, Luis Echeverría, were high school classmates. After graduating from the National University in 1946, he became a professor of general theory of the state there and founded the course in political science and government policy in Mexico. He obtained a doctorate in law from the University of Santiago, in Chile. During these years he also practiced law.

López Portillo did not hold his first public office until 1960, when he became director general of the federal board of material and moral improvement of the secretariat of national properties. In 1965, he served as director of legal advisers to the secretariat of the presidency, and three years later, became the assistant secretary of the presidency. In 1970, in the administration of Luis Echeverría, he became assistant secretary of national properties. During a mid-term cabinet shuffle, the president appointed him secretary of the treasury May 29, 1973, and he served in this capacity until his September 22, 1975, nomination as the official party presidential candidate. With at least half a dozen potential candidates, López Portillo was considered a dark horse. After leaving the presidency he lived both abroad and in Mexico. He died in Mexico City on February 17, 2004, of a pneumonia-related heart problem.

See also **Mexico, Political Parties: Institutional Revolutionary Party (PRI).**

BIBLIOGRAPHY

Susan K. Purcell, ed., *Mexico-United States Relations* (1981).

Miguel Basáñez, *La lucha por la hegemonía en México* (1982).

Judith A. Hellman, *Mexico in Crisis,* 2d ed. (1983).

Roberto G. Newell and Luis F. Rubio, *Mexico's Dilemma: The Political Origins of Economic Crisis* (1984).

Peter Ward, *Welfare Politics in Mexico: Papering Over the Cracks* (1986).

Daniel Levy and Gabriel Szekeley, *Mexico: Paradoxes of Stability and Change,* 2d ed. (1987).

Judith A. Teichman, *Policymaking in Mexico: From Boom to Crisis* (1988).

José López Portillo, *Mis tiempos: Biografía y testimonio político,* 2 vols. (1988).

Additional Bibliography

Castañeda, Jorge G. *La herencia: Arqueología de la sucesión presidencial en México.* Mexico: Aguilar, Altea, Taurus, Alfaguara, 1999.

Robledo, Elisa. *El presidente y sus amadas.* Mexico: Océano, 2002.

RODERIC AI CAMP

LÓPEZ PUMAREJO, ALFONSO (1886–1959). Alfonso López Pumarejo (*b.* 31 January 1886; *d.* ca. 20 November 1959), president of Colombia (1934–1938, 1942–1945). One of the most influential presidents in the history of Colombia, López's impact can be measured by the fact that almost all legislation that "modernized" Colombia was passed during his first term in office.

Born in Honda (Tolima), López studied at the College of San Luis Gonzaga and then at the Liceo Mercantil (Mercantile Lyceum) in Bogotá, specializing in business. Afterward, he took courses at Bright College in England and worked in New York before returning to Colombia. He never completed a degree, but his life experience prepared him well to work in economics and politics. In 1904, he returned to Bogotá and for twelve years in business experience alongside his father. He began his career in politics in 1915 with Colombia's Partido Liberal. At the same time, he began writing political commentary for the *Diario Nacional* and *La Republica.*

The 1929 world depression exposed the weakness of the Conservative Party—in power since 1886—which had no program to cope with economic collapse and social unrest. López became president in 1934 and, accompanied by an energetic group of young Liberal reformers, began pushing a "New Deal" type of economic, social, labor, and educational legislation to which the patriarchal society was unaccustomed. The most controversial of López's reforms, the Land Law 200 of 1936, has been misnamed the Agrarian Reform Law. In essence, what this law tried to accomplish was the legalization of titles to land and the affirmation of the "social function" of property, particularly landed property. These activities earned his administration the nickname "revolución en marcha," or government on the move. However, his many proposals faced staunch opposition from conservatives.

The domestic and international situation was quite different during his second term (1942–1946). World War II adversely affected the industrial sector in Colombia and weakened its economy. Conservative opposition to López mounted, and in July 1944 he was actually held prisoner by a rebel army colonel named Diógenes Gil. Although he was released, López was forced to resign in 1945 because of the opposition of both the Conservatives and a sizable fraction of his own party, which together effectively blocked most of his initiatives.

See also **Colombia, Political Parties: Liberal Party.**

BIBLIOGRAPHY

Eduardo Zuleta Angel, *El Presidente López* (1966).

Gerardo Molina, *Las ideas liberales en Colombia, 1915–1934* (1978).

Thomas C. Tirado, *Alfonso López Pumarejo, el Conciliador* (1986).

Alvaro Tirado Mejía, "López Pumarejo: La Revolución en marcha," in *La nueva historia de Colombia, I: Historia política, 1886–1906,* edited by Dario Jaramillo Agudelo (1976), pp. 305–348.

Robert J. Alexander, ed., *Biographical Dictionary of Latin American and Caribbean Political Leaders* (1988), pp. 265–266.

Additional Bibliography

Acosta, Pedro. *López Pumarejo en marcha hacia su revolución.* Bogotá: Universidad de Bogotá Jorge Tadeo Lozano, 2004.

Aguilera Peña, Mario. *Alfonso López Pumarejo y la Universidad Nacional de Colombia.* Bogotá: Universidad Nacional de Colombia, 2000.

Tirado Mejía, Alvaro. *Aspectos políticos del primer gobierno de Alfonso López Pumarejo, 1934–1938.* 2nd ed. Bogotá: Planeta Colombiana Editorial, 1995.

José Escorcia

LÓPEZ REGA, JOSÉ (1916–1989).

José López Rega, born October 17, 1916, entered the Argentine Federal Police as a corporal in mid-1940 and was later involved in Argentine politics; he served as private secretary to Juan Perón during his exile. He practiced a combination of spiritualism and esotericism and became spiritual adviser to Perón's second wife, Isabel (María Estela Martínez de Perón), after meeting her in 1965. A short time later he moved to Madrid, where he worked as bodyguard and later private secretary to Perón. Nicknamed *El Brujo* (The Wizard), he exercised a strong yet inconsistent influence on Perón. When the electoral ban on the Peronist Justicialist Party was lifted in 1973, he returned to Argentina. Following the election of Héctor Cámpora, López Rega served as minister of social welfare. In that position he organized the Argentine Anti-Communist Alliance (Triple A), a far-right paramilitary group responsible for the assassination of numerous left-wing militants between 1973 and 1975.

In what became known as the Ezeiza Massacre, officers under the command of López Rega fired into the vast crowds assembled to welcome Perón back to Argentina in June 1973. Shooting at close range from the presidential box, they killed a number of young militants of the Peronist left. When Cámpora resigned from the presidency in July, Raúl Lastiri, López Rega's son-in-law, assumed the interim presidency. With the left out of the government, López Rega's influence increased. Following the September elections, Perón again assumed the presidency, with his wife, who remained under the strong influence of López Rega, as vice president. Isabel assumed the presidency following Perón's death in July 1974 and López Rega acquired enormous control over the cabinet.

The government granted broad repressive powers to the army and the Triple A increased its activities. By mid 1975, López Rega managed to get Celestino Rodrigo appointed as minister of economy. This dark character applied a brutal program of economic adjustment, the *Rodrigazo.* The powerful Peronist unions reacted strongly, forcing the resignations of López Rega and Rodrigo in July 1975, and then reached an agreement with businesses for wage increases that ultimately brought on massive inflation. Isabel appointed López Rega as special ambassador to Spain. After the military coup of March 1976, he remained a fugitive for ten years. In 1986 he was arrested and extradited to Argentina, where he died on June 9, 1989.

See also **Argentina: The Twentieth Century; Argentina, Political Parties: Justicialist Party; Cámpora, Héctor José; Perón, Juan Domingo; Perón, María Estela Martínez de.**

BIBLIOGRAPHY

De Riz, Liliana. *La política en suspenso: 1966–1976.* Buenos Aires: Paidós, 2000.

James, Daniel. *Resistencia e integración: El peronismo y la clase trabajadora argentina, 1946–1976.* Buenos Aires: Sudamericana, 1990.

Torre, Juan Carlos. *Los sindicatos en el gobierno.* Buenos Aires: CEAL, 1983.

VICENTE PALERMO

LÓPEZ TARSO, IGNACIO (1925–).

Film, television, spoken word, and stage actor Ignacio López Tarso was born on January 15, 1925, in Mexico City. During World War II, he crossed the U.S. border and worked as a *bracero* (day laborer) in California. After suffering an injury that left him immobile for a year, he returned to Mexico and in 1949 began studying at Mexico City's School of Fine Arts. While an acting student, he was part of the Teatro Estudiantil Autónomo (Autonomous Student Theater) and performed in plays throughout the city. He made his professional theater debut in *Nacida ayer* (Born Yesterday) in 1951, and his film debut the following year in *Hambre nuestra de cada día* (1952). A highly respected actor, he has appeared in more than 100 theatrical works, 50 films, and 25 telenovelas. The San Francisco International Film Festival awarded him two Golden Gate acting awards, for his roles in *Macario* (1960) and *El hombre de papel* (The Paper Man, 1963). In 2007 he was awarded a special Golden Ariel by the Mexican Academy of Cinematic Arts and Sciences. He has also been involved in Mexican politics.

See also **Cinema: From the Silent Film to 1990; Theater.**

BIBLIOGRAPHY

Valdés Medellín, Gonzalo. "Ignacio López Tarso: El de la sabia Figura: Miguel de Cervantes Saavedra." *Siempre!* April 30, 2006.

STACY LUTSCH

LÓPEZ TRUJILLO, ALFONSO (1935–).

Alfonso López Trujillo, Colombian churchman, as president of the Council of Latin American Bishops (CELAM) led a conservative movement against Liberation Theology and other progressive tendencies in the Latin American Catholic Church. Born on November 8, 1935, in Villahermosa, department of Tolima, he entered the seminary in Bogotá and was ordained a priest in 1960. He received a doctorate in philosophy at the University of Saint Thomas Aquinas, Colombia. In 1971 he was appointed auxiliary bishop of Bogotá. He became archbishop of Medellín in 1978 and was raised to the rank of cardinal in 1983. From 1987 to 1990 he was president of the Colombian episcopal conference. He was elected secretary-general of CELAM in 1972 and served as its president from 1979 to 1983. As secretary of CELAM he was in charge of the third meeting of the Latin American bishops, held in Puebla, Mexico, in 1979. In 1990 he was named president of the Pontifical Commission on the Family, in Rome. In 2001 he became a Bishop of Cardinals and has since fought resolutely against government authorization of gay marriage as well as emphasizing abstinence as the only ordained form of birth control.

See also **Catholic Church: The Modern Period.**

BIBLIOGRAPHY

Alfonso López Trujillo, *Liberación marxista y liberación cristiana* (1974).

Penny Lernoux, *People of God: The Struggle for World Catholicism* (1989).

Additional Bibliography

Gómez Orozco, Horacio. *El Cardenal Alfonso López Trujillo.* Santa Fe de Bogotá: Plaza and Janes Editores, 1997.

Salazar Palacio, Hernando. *La Guerra secreta del cardenal López Trujillo.* Santa Fe de Bogotá: Temas de Hoy, 1996.

JEFFREY KLAIBER

LÓPEZ VALLECILLOS, ITALO (1932–1986).

Italo López Vallecillos (*b.* 15 November 1932; *d.* 9 February 1986), Salvadoran journalist, historian, playwright, poet. As leader of the Generación Comprometida (Committed Generation) that emerged about 1950, López called for revision of Salvadoran literary values. His early poetry, most notably *Imágenes sobre el otoño* (1962), expressed the Committed Generation's sensitivity to the need for social change and relevance in literature. López raised Salvadoran historiography to a higher level of professionalism with his *Biografía de un hombre triste* (1954); *El periodismo en El Salvador* (1964), articles on the independence of El Salvador; *Gerardo Barrios y su tiempo* (1967); and many articles on twentieth-century El Salvador. As director of the press of the Universidad Centroamericana and as a frequent contributor to *ECA—Estudios Centro Americanos,* he was an important intellectual leader of the country in the difficult period after 1972. The versatile López also wrote plays, notably *Las manos vencidas* (1964), *Burudi Sur* (1969), and *Celda noventa y seis* (1975).

See also **Literature: Spanish America.**

BIBLIOGRAPHY

Luis Gallegos Valdés, *Panorama de la literatura salvadoreña del período precolombino a 1980,* 3d ed. (1989), esp. pp. 140, 150–153, 168, 415–445.

Additional Bibliography

Cea, José Roberto. *La generación comprometida: Unos documentos y testimonios para su historia social, ética y estética.* San Salvador, El Salvador: Canoa Editores, 2003.

RALPH LEE WOODWARD JR.

LÓPEZ VELARDE, RAMÓN (1888–1921).

Ramón López Velarde (*b.* 15 June 1888; *d.* 19 June 1921), Mexican poet. López Velarde was born in Jerez, Zacatecas, and died in Mexico City. He was educated in the Seminarios Consiliares of Zacatecas and Aguascalientes and the Instituto Cientifico y Literario de Aguascalientes and received a degree from the Law School in San Luis Potosí. A lawyer, literary historian, and militant in the National Catholic Party, he occupied posts in revolutionary governments. As a poet, he abandoned Latin American modernism and in some respects moved toward the avant garde. *La sangre devota* (1916) expresses the conflict of provincial people, forced from their towns by the Revolution of 1910–1917, and the drama of a young Catholic who confronts his sexuality and a world that has rejected traditional beliefs. The great poetry of López Velarde springs from his relationships with two women with whom he never became intimate: Fuensanta (Josefa de los Rios), who represents childhood and the idyllic, and Margarita Quijano, symbol of the city and a woman of high culture who introduced him to French poetry. *Zozobra* (1919) carries rhyme and free verse beyond the point at which Leopoldo Lugones had left them and speaks of death and passion in a way that is both diaphanous and mysterious. His celebrated poem "La sauve patria," written in 1921 during the period of nationalist renewal associated with José Vasconcelos, was included posthumously in *El son del corazón* (1932). His prose poems and chronicles are collected in *El minutero* (1923), *El don de febrero* (1952), and *Prosa política* (1953). The best critical edition of his *Obras* is that of José Luis Martínez (2d ed., 1990). Several of his poems appear in *Mexican Poetry* (1985), translated by Samuel Beckett. López Velarde died in Mexico City.

See also **Literature: Spanish America.**

BIBLIOGRAPHY

Octavio Paz, "El camino de la pasión," in *Cuadrivio* (1965).

Allan W. Phillips, "Ramón López Velarde," in *Latin American Writers,* edited by Carlos A. Solé and Maria Isabel Abreu, vol. 2 (1989).

Guillermo Sheridan, *Un corazón adicto* (1989).

Additional Bibliography

Arreola, Juan José. *Ramón López Velarde: El poeta, el revolucionario.* México, D.F.: Alfaguara, 1997.

Paredes, Alberto. *El arte de la queja: La prosa literaria de Ramón López Velarde.* México, D.F.: Editorial Aldus, 1995.

J. E. PACHECO

LÓPEZ Y FUENTES, GREGORIO (1892–1966).

Gregorio López y Fuentes (*b.* 1892; *d.* 1966), Mexican novelist and journalist. As a young man, López fought in the Mexican

Revolution. In the post-Revolution period, he began a distinguished career as a journalist at *El Universal,* becoming general editor of the newspaper in 1948 and serving in that capacity until the 1960s. Considered one of the major exponents of the "novel of the Revolution," López addressed in his works the principal social issues of his time. His novels include *Acomodaticio; Arrieros; Campamento; Cuentos campesinos de México; El Indio; Entresuelo, Huasteca; Los peregrinos inmoviles; ¡Mi general!; En Milpa, potrero y monte;* and *Tierra.* He also wrote a series of short stories for children entitled *Cartas de niños* and *El campo y la ciudad.* His fiction is distinguished by the anonymous nature of the characters; representation of types takes precedence over the individual.

See also **Journalism; Mexico, Wars and Revolutions: Mexican Revolution.**

BIBLIOGRAPHY

Additional Bibliography

Negrín, Edith. "'Huasteca' de Gregorio López y Fuentes: El inmenso rumor fragmentado." *Literatura Mexicana* 10:1–2 (1999): 161–185.

Pouwels, Joel Bollinger. "Novels about the Twentieth-Century Mexican Presidential Succession during Four Crisis Periods." *Canadian Journal of Latin American and Caribbean Studies* 27:54 (2002): 215–250.

DAVID MACIEL

LORENZANA Y BUITRÓN, FRANCISCO ANTONIO DE (1722–1804).

Francisco Antonio de Lorenzana y Buitrón (*b.* 22 September 1722; *d.* 17 April 1804), Spanish intellectual, archbishop of Mexico (1766–1772), and cardinal-archbishop of Toledo, Spain (1772–1804). Born in León, Spain, Lorenzana studied under the Jesuits in that city. He served as bishop of Plasencia (1765–1766), then as archbishop of Mexico, where he founded the Home for Abandoned Children in 1767. Among his accomplishments was the Fourth Mexican Provincial Council, held in 1771. Known as a promoter of culture and charity, Lorenzana was elected a cardinal in 1789 and was named envoy extraordinary to the Holy See by Charles IV of Spain in 1797. He organized the conclave at Venice that in 1800 elected the successor to Pope Pius VI. He then accompanied the new pope, Pius VII, to Rome, where he resigned his archbishopric. Lorenzana died in Rome.

Lorenzana's writings include *Concilios provinciales primero, y segundo* (1769); *Cartas pastorales y edictos* (1770); *Concilium mexicanum provinciale III* (1770); *Historia de Nueva España escrita por su esclarecido conquistador Hernán Cortés* (1770); *Missa gothica seu mozarabica* (1770); and *SS. PP. Toletanorum,* 3 vols. (1782–1783).

See also **Charles IV of Spain; Jesuits.**

BIBLIOGRAPHY

Luis Sierra Nava-Lasa, *El cardenal Lorenzana y la ilustración* (1975).

Francisco Sosa, *El episcopado mexicano,* edited by Alberto María Carreño (1962).

Additional Bibliography

Sánchez Sánchez, Isidro. *El Cardenal Lanzana y la Universidad de Castilla-La Mancha.* Cuenca, Spain: Universidad de Castilla-La Mancha, 1999.

Zahino Peñafort, Luisa. *El Cardenal Lanzana y el IV Concilio Provincial Mexicano.* México: Miguel Angel Porrúa, 1999.

W. MICHAEL MATHES

LORENZO TROYA, VICTORIANO (1864–1903).

Victoriano Lorenzo Troya (*b.* 1864; *d.* 15 May 1903), native leader in the Panamanian province of Coclé during the War of the Thousand Days (1900–1903). In 1891, Lorenzo was accused of murder and the following year was sentenced to nine years in prison. He remained in jail until 1898. When the war broke out, he joined the liberal side and fought with Belisario Porras in Panama (then a department of Colombia) hoping that a liberal victory would end the abuses against the Indians. Lorenzo and his Indian followers made a formidable fighting force, practically unbeatable in the mountains. Their exploits became widely known during the war. After the failure of the liberals to take Panama City with their defeat at the Calidonia bridge (24 July 1900), Lorenza went back to Coclé, where he organized a guerrilla group and rejoined Porras. In 1902 he was betrayed by the liberal general Benjamín Herrera, who handed him over to the government. Despite the fact that he should have been protected under the terms of the peace of 21 November 1902, which ended the civil war between liberals and conservatives, the government executed him by a firing squad.

He execution was considered by many a great miscarriage of justice and there are many theories as to why he was executed. First, General Herrera, a Colombian liberal always looked with disdain to the Panamanian liberal leaders and wanted to impose his own authority on them. The fact that Lorenzo was only loyal to Porras—who at the time of his execution was in El Salvador—may have contributed to his arrest by Herrera. Second, the conservative government feared him a great deal and he was seen by them as an obstacle to a permanent peace. During the war, the conservatives had sent an expeditionary force to Coclé to capture him, but failed. Many Panamanian historians speculate that during the peace negotiations between liberals and conservatives, a secret agreement was reached by which the liberals would hand Lorenzo to the conservatives. In 1966, the Panamanian National Assembly, as a tribute to this popular leader, invalidated the proceedings in Lorenzo's trial, indicating that it was a violation of the peace treaty.

See also **War of the Thousand Days.**

BIBLIOGRAPHY

Jorge Conte Porras, *Panameños ilustres* (1978) and *Diccionario biográfico ilustrado de Panamá*, 2d ed. (1986).

Ernesto De Jesús Castillero Reyes, *Historia de Panamá*, 7th ed. (1962).

Additional Bibliography

Galindo H., Julio Roberto. *Benjamin Herrera, Jorge Eliécer Gaitán: Grandes caudillos liberals, gestores de la Universidad.* Santa Fé de Bogotá: Corporación Universidad Libre, 1998.

Pedraja Tomán, René de la. *Wars of the Latin America, 1899–1941.* Jefferson, NC: McFarland & Co., 2006.

JUAN MANUEL PÉREZ

LORETO. Loreto, the largest department of Peru (135,000 square miles) and one of the least populated (2005 population 919,505), encompassing most of the Peruvian Amazonian rain forest. Loreto has only one major highway, which links its western boundary with Tarapoto and Yurimaguas. The department's capital, Iquitos, is the easternmost port in Peru, a major tourist attraction, and the region's most active commercial center, with 40 percent of Loreto's population. Located between two affluents of the Amazon, Iquitos has no highway connection with other Peruvian provinces but has an international airport. With a population estimated at 367,000 in 2000, it is often considered to be the world's largest city that cannot be reached by road. Iquitos has traditionally traded mostly with Peru's neighbor, Brazil, especially since its impressive growth due to the rubber boom of the early years of the twentieth century. Loreto's production includes timber, rubber, agricultural products (yuca, rice, corn), and oil from the area of Trompeteros, which is linked to the coast through a system of oil pipes. Approximately 60 percent of Peru's oil is extracted here. The region also draws tourism.

BIBLIOGRAPHY

Richard Collier, *The River That God Forgot: The Story of the Amazon Rubber Boom* (1968).

Edmundo Morales, *Cocaine: White Gold Rush in Peru* (1989).

Additional Bibliography

Santos-Granero, Fernando, and Federica Barclay. *Tamed Frontiers: Economy, Society, and Civil Rights in Upper Amazonia.* Boulder, CO: Westview Press, 2000.

Vílchez Vela, Percy. *El linaje de los orígenes: La historia desconocida de los Iquito.* Iquitos, Peru: Editora Regional, 2001.

ALFONSO W. QUIROZ

LOSADA, DIEGO DE (1511–1569). Diego de Losada (*b.* 1511; *d.* 1569), Spanish conquistador and founder of Caracas, Venezuela. Losada traveled to America as part of the conquistador armies. He passed through Puerto Rico and later, in 1533, joined Antonio Sendeño's expedition on the Meta River. When Sendeño was assassinated, Losada moved on to the city of Coro. From there he was sent eastward with Juan de Villegas in 1543 to search for provisions and men.

Losada later traveled to Santo Domingo and returned to Venezuela in 1546 in the company of Juan Pérez De Tolosa, governor and captain-general of the province. He took part in the founding of Nueva Segovia de Barquisimeto, received various Indian *encomiendas,* and performed diverse duties within the colonial administration.

In 1565 Losada was assigned the mission of subduing the Caraca Indians, a task at which others had failed. After heavy fighting, he occupied the valley of El Guaire, where he founded the city of Santiago de León de Caracas on 25 July 1567. Losada attempted to win the post of governor and captain-general of the province of Venezuela. To this end he traveled to Santo Domingo to send his petition to the king, but his attempt was unsuccessful.

See also **Caracas; Conquistadores.**

BIBLIOGRAPHY

Felipe Felipe Ferrero, *Don Diego de Losada, o el fundador de Caracas* (1968).

José María Cruxent, *La ruta de Losada* (1971).

Hermano Nectario María, *Diego de Losada, fundador de Caracas* (Caracas, 1967).

Additional Bibliography

Angulo Perdomo, A. Oswaldo. *El de Villegas: "Un gran poblador."* Valencia: s.n., 2005.

Inés Quintero

LOS ALTOS. Los Altos, a region in western Guatemala, bounded on the north and west by Mexico and on the south by the Pacific Ocean. The Sierra Madre crosses the region from northwest to southeast, producing a great deal of geographic and climatic diversity. The surface elevations of its area of 9,200 square miles range from near sea level to more than 12,000 feet in the northern uplands of the Cuchumatanes; its fertile mountain valleys, at altitudes of about 8,000 feet, have been home since pre-Columbian days to a dense population of Maya descent. Its population, estimated to be about 3.5 million in 1990, is about 40 percent of the national total.

When the Spaniards arrived in 1524, Los Altos was dominated by four distinct and warring ethnic states: the Mam, the K'iche', the Kaqchikels, and the Tz'utujils. After a bloody and protracted war, Pedro de Alvarado finally imposed Spanish rule in 1528. Following his death, the region functioned as the *alcaldía mayor* of Zapotitlán, a subdivision of the Audiencia of Guatemala. Crown officials and missionaries were charged with consolidating Spanish political-military and spiritual control over the area and, more important, with collecting the royal tribute from the conquered communities.

Devoid of mineral and agricultural wealth, Los Altos attracted relatively few Spanish colonists. Thus, left relatively unmolested, its Mayan communities were able to recover successfully from the demographic disaster that accompanied the Conquest. Most continued to engage in subsistence agriculture and textile weaving on their communal lands.

The Bourbon Reforms of the eighteenth century substantially altered this traditional pattern. The indigo boom of the latter half of the century integrated the region into the expanding Central American economic network. Attracted by the growing commercial opportunities in cloth and food staples, new Spanish as well as mestizo colonists established themselves in the area, often at the expense of indigenous land and labor. As a result, urban centers such as Quetzaltenango and Totonicapán became dynamic centers of economic and, later, political activity.

By the early nineteenth century, these new colonists had consolidated their hold on the region. Quetzaltenango, the most prosperous village, became the focus of a vigorous regionalist movement whose chief goal was to secure for Los Altos greater political and economic autonomy vis-à-vis the financial and administrative control of the capital. Led by the Quetzalteco patricians, the efforts of Los Altos finally crystallized in 1838, when the region became the sixth state of the Central American Federation. The Federation collapsed, however, and the area was forcibly reintegrated into Guatemala by the Conservative dictator Rafael Carrera in 1840. Following Carrera's temporary ouster in 1848, the region again seceded, but the movement was easily suppressed by an army under the orders of the Liberal government in Guatemala City. In 1871 Los Altos General Justo Rufino Barrios led the revolution that restored the Liberals to power in Guatemala for the next seventy years. Barrios became Guatemalan dictator in 1873 and proceeded to develop the economic infrastructure of Los Altos as well as to encourage the cultivation of coffee, the new cash crop destined to become the mainstay of the nation's economy. The piedmont area of Los Altos remains an important coffee-producing region.

Juan José Arévalo's revolution of 1944 tried to relieve the plight of the indigenous people, but despite numerous decrees, the Liberal land tenure system remained intact. Under Jacobo Arbenz Guzmán (1951–1954), thousands of acres were distributed among peasants, vagrancy laws were abolished, and a national syndicate of peasants was organized.

In 1954, however, those gains were lost to a military coup which restored to power the Liberal land-owning elite, who were this time allied with the military. While paying lip service to reform, the new regimes continued to dispossess peasants and encourage the growth of large agro-export enterprises. Organized resistance has been met with brutal repression by the army.

See also **Bourbon Reforms; Guatemala; Indigenous Peoples; Maya, The; Quetzaltenango.**

BIBLIOGRAPHY

Hazel Ingersoll, "The War of the Mountain" (Ph.D. diss., George Washington University, 1972).

Carol Smith, *The Domestic Marketing System in Western Guatemala* (1972).

Jorge H. González, "Una historia de Los Altos, el sexto estado de la federación centroamericana" (M.A. thesis, Tulane University, 1989).

George Lovell, *Conquest and Survival in Colonial Guatemala: A Historical Geography of the Cuchumatán Highlands, 1500–1821* (1992).

Additional Bibliography

Benítez Porto, Oscar Rodolfo. *Guatemala y el estado de los altos: Estudio histórico-político.* Guatemala: s.n., 1998.

Lutz, Christopher. *Territorio y sociedad en Guatemala: Tres ensayos históricos.* Guatemala: Centro de Estudios Urbanos y Regionales, Universidad de San Carlos de Guatemala, 1991.

Taracena Arriola, Arturo. *Invención criolla, sueño ladino, pesadillo indígena: Los Altos De Guatemala: De región a Estado, 1740–1850.* Antigua, Guatemala: Centro de Investigaciones Regionales de Mesoamérica, San José, Costa Rica: Porvenir, 1997.

JORGE H. GONZÁLEZ

LOTT, HENRIQUE BATISTA DUFFLES TEIXEIRA (1894–1984). Henrique Batista Duffles Teixeira Lott (*b.* 16 November 1894; *d.* 19 May 1984), Brazilian minister of war (1954–1960), politician, and presidential candidate (1959). A native of Sítio, in Minas Gerais, Lott attended the military school of Realengo in Rio de Janeiro. Upon graduation he enlisted in the army in 1911 and was commissioned five years later.

A dedicated professional, Lott remained loyal to the government during the military upheavals of the 1920s and on through the Revolution of 1930, the São Paulo constitutional revolt of 1932, the Communist uprising of 1935, and the 1938 Fascist putsch.

Lott studied abroad at the Superior War College in Paris and at the U.S. Army Command and General Staff College in Fort Leavenworth, Kansas. These courses further enhanced his well-deserved reputation as an instructor at the general staff school and other Brazilian military academies, where he became known for strong opinions and stern discipline. Posted to Italy with the Brazilian Expeditionary Force (FEB) during World War II, he was denied command, thus widening the split with the so-called Sorbonne Group of military reformers. Promoted to general at the age of fifty, he commanded the Second Military Region in São Paulo.

The suicide of President Getúlio Vargas in 1954 brought Lott into politics with his appointment by acting president João Café Filho, who named him minister of war because of his reputation for being apolitical. Café Filho's resignation in November 1955, ostensibly for health reasons, brought in Carlos Luz, president of the chamber of deputies, as chief executive. Allied with the Sorbonne Group, he soon resigned when Lott pronounced in favor of Nereu Ramos, the senate's president.

This institutional crisis coincided with the disputed presidential election of Brazilian Labor Party candidate Juscelino Kubitschek. Lott favored Kubitschek's inauguration as the legitimate candidate, thus easing unrest and ensuring his own reappointment as war minister. He held this post until February 1960, although he retired, with the rank of marshal, in 1959 to run for president on the Labor Party ticket. Defeated by reformist Jânio Quadros, Lott nevertheless remained a powerful figure, opposing both the military interventions against Vice President João Goulart in 1961 and his ousting as acting president in April 1964. Lott's 1965 attempt to present himself as a candidate for the governorship of the state of Guanabara was vetoed by the revolutionary military regime.

See also **Kubitschek de Oliveira, Juscelino; Vargas, Getúlio Dornelles.**

BIBLIOGRAPHY

E. Bradford Burns, *A History of Brazil* (1980).

John W. F. Dulles, *Unrest in Brazil: Political-Military Crises, 1955–1964* (1970).

Robert Ames Hayes, *The Armed Nation: The Brazilian Corporate Mystique* (1989).

Irving L. Horowitz, *Revolution in Brazil* (1964).

Alfred C. Stepan, *The Military in Politics: Changing Patterns in Brazil* (1971).

Additional Bibliography

William, Wagner. *O soldado absoluto: Uma biografia do marechal Henrique Lott.* Rio de Janeiro: Editora Record, 2005.

LEWIS A. TAMBS

LOUISIANA. Louisiana, a Spanish colonial province that included the Louisiana Purchase territory and, at certain periods, lands in the area from the junction of the Ohio and Mississippi rivers to Pensacola, Florida.

Spain's interest in the northern coast of the Gulf of Mexico was dictated by desires to protect the mines of northern Mexico and shipping transiting the northern Gulf of Mexico on the way to Havana. This interest dictated its initial (1699–1723) efforts to dislodge the French colony of Louisiana and its acceptance in 1763 of Louis XVI's gift of the part of Louisiana that lay west of the Mississippi River and the line defined by Bayou Manchac, the Amite River, and lakes Maurepas and Pontchartrain.

This interest dictated that Spain take advantage of Great Britain's involvement in the U.S. Revolutionary War to seize in 1779–1781 the areas north and east of that border that had been given to Great Britain in 1763. Once in control of the Mississippi Valley below the Ohio River, Spain attempted to prevent American settlement west of the Appalachian Mountains by denying those settlements use of the Mississippi for trade (1784–1788) and then, when that policy failed, to extend its influence over those settlements by conspiring with James Wilkinson and others, leaders in Kentucky and Tennessee, to foment rebellion in the West. This expansive policy began to collapse with Kentucky's statehood in 1792 and the opening of New Orleans to friendly and allied shipping in 1793, and came to an end with the implementation of Pinckney's Treaty (1795) in 1798. Weakened by defeats at the hands of the French (1793–1795) and the British, Spain could do no more than make the best trade possible with France: Louisiana for the Kingdom of Etruria, for Charles IV's brother-in-law, Prince Louis of Parma. When Napoleon I decided to sell Louisiana (as defined in 1763) to the United States, Spain protested in vain. The United States took possession on 20 December 1803.

Spain's trade and "Indian" policies in Louisiana differed sharply from those elsewhere in its empire. Although the long-term goal remained the integration of Louisiana into the system of imperial *comercio libre* (free trade), officials on the spot had to tolerate British smuggling that accounted for as much as 85 percent of the colony's ship traffic from 1763 to 1777, and then a French and French West Indian commerce that accounted for about 60 percent of the colony's shipping from 1777 to 1793. After 1793, U.S. ships carried 45 percent to 60 percent of the colony's trade (depending on year). Spanish shipping never amounted to more than 35 percent of the colony's total, and generally was under 25 percent. By their very nature, Louisiana's exports of indigo, tobacco, skins and furs, and lumber and imports of flour, alcoholic beverages, and manufactures did not fit well with the imperial economic system, even as modified during the 1760s and 1770s. Well before 1803, Louisiana had become part of the U.S. economy.

Spain's policies involved forging alliances with, and arming, the Creek, Choctaw, and Chickasaw rather than attempting to subjugate them in a mission system. The goal was to use these peoples and their lands as a barrier to check advancing American settlement. The Nogales Treaty of 1793 culminated this policy, which was abandoned with the implementation of Pinckney's Treaty. Another unusual feature of Spain's Indian policy was that it relied on the Scots firm of Panton, Leslie, and Company to supply the trade goods and presents needed for the alliance system, since Spanish firms did not produce products of the right types and qualities.

Demographically, Louisiana grew from a total of 13,000 persons to 50,000 persons, largely because of immigration. More than half of the population were African slaves. Acadians, Canary Islanders, and Germans were notable minorities.

See also **Fontainebleau, Treaty of (1807); Louisiana Revolt of 1768.**

BIBLIOGRAPHY

Arthur P. Whitaker, *The Spanish-American Frontier, 1783–1795* (1927), and *The Mississippi Question, 1795–1803* (1934).

Lawrence C. Ford, *The Triangular Struggle for Spanish Pensacola, 1689–1739* (1939).

John F. Bannon, *The Spanish Borderlands Frontier, 1513–1821* (1974).

Juan José Andreu Ocariz, *Luisiana Española* (1975).

Antonio Acosta Rodríguez, *La población de Luisiana Española (1763–1803)* (1979).

William S. Coker and Thomas Watson, *Indian Traders of the Southeastern Spanish Borderlands: Panton, Leslie, & Company and John Forbes & Company, 1783–1847* (1989).

Paul E. Hoffman, *Luisiana* (1992), in Spanish.

Additional Bibliography

Axtell, James. *The Indians' New South: Cultural Change in the Colonial Southeast.* Baton Rouge: Louisiana State University Press, 1997.

Din, Gilbert C. *Spaniards, Planters, and Slaves: The Spanish Regulation of Slavery in Louisiana, 1763–1803.* College Station: Texas A&M University Press, 1999.

Teja, Jesús F. de la, and Ross Frank, eds. *Choice, Persuasion, and Coercion: Social Control on Spain's North American Frontiers.* Albuquerque: University of New Mexico Press, 2005.

PAUL E. HOFFMAN

LOUISIANA REVOLT OF 1768.

Louisiana Revolt of 1768, rebellion against Spanish rule by French colonists of Louisiana. The revolt was the result of a conspiracy by the leading merchants and planters of New Orleans against the colony's first Spanish governor, Antonio de Ulloa. Without any bloodshed, they succeeded in driving him out of the colony with the help of colonists who had been both tricked and bullied into supporting the rebel cause.

Confusion had surrounded Ulloa's arrival in 1766, well after the 1762 Treaty of Fontainebleau, which transferred Louisiana from French to Spanish rule. Ulloa kept his distance, both socially and politically, from the local elite, which had been accustomed to a prominent role in all decision making. More than this reticence, what most upset the leading colonists, however, were Ulloa's trade reforms eliminating contraband and regulating the fur trade. Yet even with the support of the former French governor, Charles Philippe Aubry, Ulloa lacked the military force to impose his will. On 28–29 October 1768, the Spanish regime was overthrown and Ulloa and other officials fled to Spain.

Many colonists withdrew their initial support for the rebels after Ulloa's removal. A chaotic period followed until General Alejandro O'Reilly arrived in August 1769 with 2,000 troops to put down the revolt. The five ringleaders (Nicolas Chauvin de La Frenière, Pierre Marquis, Pierre Caresse, Jean Baptiste Noyan, and Joseph Milhet) were executed. A sixth, Joseph Villeré, died before the execution, and six others received lesser sentences. O'Reilly calmed fears with a general pardon, reestablished order, and became the second Spanish governor.

See also **Louisiana; Ulloa, Antonio de.**

BIBLIOGRAPHY

Charles Gayarré, *History of Louisiana,* vol. 2, *The French Domination* (1885), pp. 158–361.

Vicente Rodríguez Casado, *Primeros años de dominación española en la Luisiana* (1942), pp. 99–350.

John Preston Moore, *Revolt in Louisiana: The Spanish Occupation, 1766–1770* (1976).

Additional Bibliography

Calloway, Colin G. *The Scratch of a Pen: 1763 and the Transformation of America.* Oxford: Oxford University Press, 2006.

Din, Gilbert C., and Abraham Phineas Nasatir. *The Imperial Osages: Spanish-Indian Diplomacy in the Mississippi Valley.* Norman: University of Oklahoma, 1983.

Menerey, Wilbur E. *The Rebellion of 1768 in Louisiana and the Manifesto of the Inhabitants.* Harahan, LA: Jefferson Parish Historical Commission, 1997.

PHILIPPE L. SEILER

LOUVERTURE, TOUSSAINT (1746?–1803). Born a slave in the French colony of Saint-Domingue (modern Haiti), Toussaint Louverture (May 20, 1746?–April 7, 1803) died before he was sixty, a figure of international renown. He rose to power as a general and statesman during the Haitian Revolution of 1791–1804, which ended slavery in the Caribbean's wealthiest colony and created the Americas' second independent state. Toussaint's contribution to both these achievements, however, remains controversial, as does his role in the slave uprising from which they emerged.

PRE-REVOLUTIONARY YEARS

According to a nineteenth-century memoir by his son, Isaac, Toussaint's father was an African of royal lineage. Toussaint learned the Aja-Fon language of his forbears as well as the local Creole, and he eventually acquired a basic command of French. He became a Christian and learned to read and, in middle age, to sign his name. Toussaint's experience of slavery was relatively benign; he worked first as a stable lad and then as a coachman. Living with his enslaved wife and children on the Bréda plantation until the slave insurrection of 1791, Toussaint was long assumed to be a member of the slave "elite" at the outbreak of the Haitian Revolution. Many of his contemporaries thought so, and this was the image he cultivated until his death. However, documents published in 1977 show that he had been free since before 1776 and that he had owned and rented both land and slaves, albeit in very small quantities. He was thus a propertied black freedman from the lower ranks of colonial society's free colored middle sector, like several other leaders of slave rebellions or conspiracies in the late eighteenth and early nineteenth centuries. Toussaint's familiarity with African, Creole, and European cultures helps explain his political acuity and versatility as a leader.

TOUSSAINT AS A MILITARY OFFICER

There have long existed two contradictory versions of Toussaint's role in the 1791 uprising, which was the largest slave revolt in American history. Some believe he secretly helped organize the uprising as an intermediary in a white counterrevolutionary plot against colonial democrats. Others argue that he was not involved at all, but instead belatedly joined the slave rebels' ranks and only in the course of 1792 emerged as one of their top military commanders. Like most insurgents, Toussaint joined the invading Spanish forces that in 1793 sought to seize Saint-Domingue from the French, and he immediately began to distinguish himself as a charismatic and cunning leader. Historians disagree to what extent Toussaint was a pragmatic opportunist or an idealistic visionary. In negotiations with the whites, he occasionally supported a compromise peace that would have forced most rebels back into slavery. Unlike other slave leaders, however, he did not sell black prisoners and noncombatants to the Spanish, and clearly he was not fighting for his own freedom. There is no proof that he championed a complete end to slavery before beleaguered French radicals in Saint Domingue took up the idea in August 1793. Yet it was about this time that he adopted the name L'Ouverture, with its cryptic connotation of a new beginning, and he soon became identified with the cause of liberty for all, even while fighting for the proslavery Spanish. In the spring of 1794, he transferred his allegiance to the French Republic around the time it officially declared slavery abolished.

During the following four years of constant warfare against Spanish and British invaders, Toussaint's ragged soldiers continually lacked for food, clothing, and ammunition. They suffered terrible casualties, but in the process, Toussaint forged a formidable army that eventually prevailed. The French made him lieutenant governor of the colony in April 1796 and commander-in-chief of its army the following year. At the same time, he deftly outmaneuvered the French officials sent to control him. In the bitter War of the South (1799–1800), the black leader drove out his erstwhile ally, André Rigaud, a free man of color and his last remaining rival. Ignoring French instructions, he then annexed the neighboring colony of Santo Domingo, which though ceded to France in 1795, was still administered by Spain. He thereafter ruled unchallenged the whole island of Hispaniola.

Toussaint Louverture meets with defeated British generals, 1798. © BETTMANN/CORBIS

TOUSSAINT AS A RULER

Most white colonists fled during the 1790s, and many of Saint Domingue's plantations passed into the hands of Toussaint's black officers, who sequestered abandoned property. Seeking to revive the plantation economy, Toussaint continued the French republican policy of compelling former slaves to continue working on the plantations in return for a share of the produce, and he used the army to impose labor laws that included the use of corporal punishment. The policy was unpopular, as the masses preferred to become independent peasant smallholders. They also resented Toussaint's purchasing Africans from slave ships to supplement the workforce that had been decimated in the revolution. With no export economy, however, there would be no revenue to maintain the black army. And without the army, the social gains of the revolution would be at the mercy of France's unstable politics. Toussaint also encouraged the return of white planters. Some say this was because he believed in a multi-racial future for Saint-Domingue in which he saw a role for European expertise; others regard it as disguised hostage taking, as many planters were not given their estates back.

While acting the role of loyal servant of France, Toussaint conducted his own foreign policy, signing in 1799 a nonaggression treaty with Britain and the United States, which were then at war with France. In July 1801 he angered the new head of state, Napoleon Bonaparte, when he promulgated his own constitution, which made him dictator for life. While maintaining the system of remunerated serfdom for former slaves, the document blended the egalitarianism of the French Revolution with some culturally conservative features reflecting Toussaint's piety. In politics, it anticipated Bonaparte's own military authoritarianism. Above all, it allowed France no effective role in the colony. Toussaint stopped short of declaring independence, perhaps because the provocation might have caused Britain and the United States to cut off the commerce on which his army depended. Or perhaps he was more interested in the substance of statehood than in its symbolism.

Bonaparte wanted to restore France's authority and then reintroduce racial discrimination and slavery. He sent a large military expedition that reached Saint Domingue in February 1802. Caught unawares and uncertain of Napoleon's intentions, Toussaint resisted but failed to rally his followers under the banner of independence. Defeated in a three-month campaign, he surrendered and was deported to France. He died in prison in April 1803 but left behind others who finally expelled the French and founded the state of Haiti.

ASSESSMENTS

In his lifetime, biographies of Toussaint were published in France, England, Sweden, and the United States. He was popular with France's enemies because he stood up to Bonaparte, and he was celebrated by abolitionists and radicals as a symbol of black accomplishment and antislavery. Generally vilified as sanguinary and duplicitous by French writers, he was an inspiration to enslaved and free blacks around the Caribbean. Some slave owners in the U.S. South praised him for his respectful attitude toward whites and for imposing forced labor on the former slaves. Modern biographers have variously depicted him as a revolutionary idealist, a black nationalist, or the first of many postcolonial dictators.

See also **Haiti; Slave Revolts: Spanish America; Slavery: Spanish America.**

BIBLIOGRAPHY

Bell, Madison Smartt. *Toussaint Louverture: A Biography.* New York: Pantheon, 2007.

Geggus, David. "Toussaint L'Ouverture and the Haitian Revolution." In *Profiles of Revolutionaries on Both Sides of the Atlantic: 1750–1850*, edited by R. William Weisberger. New York: Columbia University Press, 2007.

James, C.L.R. *The Black Jacobins: Toussaint L'Ouverture and the San Domingo Revolution.* London: Allison and Busby, 1890.

Laurent, Gérard M. *Toussaint Louverture à travers sa correspondance.* Madrid: G. Laurent, 1953.

Pluchon, Pierre. *Toussaint Louverture: Un révolutionnaire noir d'Ancien Régime.* Paris: Fayard, 1989.

DAVID GEGGUS

LOYNAZ, DULCE MARÍA (1902–1997). The poet and writer Dulce María Loynaz was born in Havana to a family of the Cuban elite. Her father and great uncle were heroes of the War of Independence (1895–1898). Her mother, an arts enthusiast, descended from one of the country's most prominent families. Her privileged upbringing included private tutors, foreign travel, and exposure to a wide range of artistic and cultural experiences. She began writing poetry very early, seeing her first poem published in 1919 in the newspaper *La Nación.* Her poems were featured in prestigious national journals such as *Orígenes*, *Revista Bimestre Cubana*, and *Social.* In 1927 Loynaz earned a law degree from the University of Havana.

In the 1930s Loynaz's home became the gathering place for important writers and artists including the Cuban novelist Alejo Carpentier, and the Spanish poets Federico García Lorca (1898–1936) and Juan Ramón Jiménez (1881–1958). Loynaz's first compilation of poetry—*Versos, 1920–1938*—appeared in 1938. Also dating to this period is her only novel, *Jardín*, which was not published until 1951. In this original work, Loynaz anticipated the magical realism that characterized Latin American narrative of the "boom period" (1960s to 1970s). The themes of her poems (love, solitude, and nature) express the same deep intimate lyrical sentiment typical of Latin American women's poetry of the first half of the twentieth century. Throughout the 1950s, Loynaz wrote chronicles for the international press, published one travel book, *Un verano en Tenerife* (One summer in Tenerife), and two new books of poetry, *Poemas sin nombre* (Unnamed poems) and *Últimos días de una casa* (Last days of a house). She also composed *Ensayos literarios* (Literary essays), a book of literary criticism in which she discussed her views on art and literature. Her autobiography, *Fe de vida* (Life's faith), appeared in 1993.

At the time of her death in 1997, Loynaz was president of the Cuban Academy of Language. She had received Cuba's National Literary Award in 1987 and the prestigious Miguel de Cervantes Prize, the highest honor for literature written in Spanish, in 1992.

See also **Cuba, War of Independence.**

BIBLIOGRAPHY

Montero, Susana A. "Loynaz, Dulce María." In *Diccionario enciclopédico de las letras de América Latina*, edited by José Ramón Medina. Caracas: Biblioteca Ayacucho; Monte Avila Editores Latinoamericana, 1995.

West-Durán, Alan. "Loynaz, Dulce María (1903–1998)." In *Encyclopedia of Cuba: People, History, Culture*, edited by Luis Martínez-Fernández. Westport, CT: Greenwood Press, 2003.

LUIS A. GONZÁLEZ

LOZADA, MANUEL (1828–1873). Manuel Lozada (*b.* 1828; *d.* 19 July 1873), Mexican cacique and rebel leader. Considered by some to be a precursor of later agrarian reformers, Lozada was a mestizo bandit whose extreme violence and invincibility earned him the attribute "El Tigre de Alica." Although still a controversial figure, he led one of the most serious uprisings of the nineteenth century.

Cacique of the Cora and Huichol Indians of western Jalisco, Lozada worked as a peon on the Hacienda de Mojarras. After a dispute with the administrator, he fled to the sierra. In his absence, the administrator was said to have maltreated Lozada's mother, misconduct for which Lozada returned to kill him. A self-designated general, he assumed leadership of the ongoing Indian resistance to European penetration of the Nayarit zone.

Armed conflict broke out in 1847 and reached a climax after the disamortization law of 1856. In his defense of community lands against privatization and hacienda penetration, he received the private support of the San Blas-based Barron and Forbes Company, which was heavily involved in contraband. His tacit support of the Conservative cause during La Reforma (the Civil War of the Reform, 1858–1861), together with his control of western Jalisco, threatened the Liberal position in Jalisco and Sinaloa. In March 1864, however, Lozada rallied to the empire, received a cash subsidy, and was decorated with the Legion of Honor. He abandoned the imperial cause in December 1866 and was thereafter virtually protected from his enemies by Juárez.

Lozada's circular of 12 April 1869 had a distinctly agrarian character and provided for direct action by villages for the recovery of land. His power was broken at Mojonera, near Guadalajara, by General Ramón Corona, after an ill-considered invasion of central Jalisco. Betrayed, he was executed on 19 July 1873.

See also **Cacique, Caciquismo; Hacienda.**

BIBLIOGRAPHY

José María Muriá Et Al., *Historia de Jalisco,* vol. 3 (1981), pp. 348–357.

Jean Meyer, "El ocaso de Manuel Lozada," in *Historia Mexicana* 18, no. 4 (1969): 535–568.

Silvano Barba Gonzalez, *La lucha por la tierra: Manuel Lozada* (1956).

Additional Bibliography

Aldana Rendón, Mario A., and Manuel Salinas Solís, eds. *Manuel Lozada: Luz y sombra.* Tepic, Mexico: Universidad Autónoma de Nayarit, 1999.

BRIAN HAMNETT

LOZANO, PEDRO (1697–1752).

Pedro Lozano (*b.* 16 September 1697; *d.* 1752), Jesuit historian. Lozano was born in Madrid, and a year after entering the Society of Jesus (at fourteen years of age), he was sent to the Province of Paraguay. It was fairly common at the time to send young Jesuits to America for their novitiate training. In theory, they adapted more readily to the customs of the place and learned the local languages more easily. Lozano was assigned for most of his life to the College of Córdoba, where he taught philosophy and theology. He traveled extensively throughout the province, visiting missions and consulting Jesuit records in Santa Fe, Esteco, and Buenos Aires.

In 1730 Lozano began writing the first of the histories for which he became known, *Descripción corográfica del Gran Chaco Gualamba* (1733). He also wrote *Historia de la Compañía de Jesús en la Provincia del Paraguay* (2 vols., 1754–1755), and five volumes of the *Historia civil del Río de la Plata,* as well as two volumes titled *Historia de las revoluciones de la Provincia del Paraguay (1721–1735).* His most famous history, now a classic, is *Historia de la conquista de la Provincia del Paraguay, Río de la Plata y Tucumán* (1905). In 1750 he was given the task of preparing a report on why the Treaty of Limits (1750) would be harmful to the Indians. Lozano died in Humahuaca.

See also **Córdoba; Jesuits.**

BIBLIOGRAPHY

Meliá, Bartomeu, and Liane Maria Nagel. *Guaraníes y jesuitas en tiempo de las misiones: Una bibliografía didáctica.* Asunción: Centro de Estudios Paraguayos, 1995.

Reiter, Frederick J. *They Built Utopia: The Jesuit Missions in Paraguay, 1610–1768.* Potomac, MD: Scripta Humanistica, 1995.

NICHOLAS P. CUSHNER

LOZANO DÍAZ, JULIO (1885–1957).

Julio Lozano Díaz, president of Honduras (November 1954–October 1956). Vice president under Juan Manuel Gálvez, Lozano Díaz seized the presidency at a time of political ferment and trade-union agitation in Honduras. In 1954 a strike against the United Fruit and Standard Fruit and Steamship companies coincided with a three-way contest for the presidency between the Liberal Party candidate

Ramón Villeda Morales, Abraham Williams of the Movimiento Nacional Reformista, and Tiburcio Carías Andino of the Partido Nacional. Although Villeda Morales had garnered nearly 50 percent of the vote, the Carías-controlled Congress refused to sanction a Liberal presidency and Lozano Díaz settled the issue by declaring himself interim president in November 1954. He successfully warded off an attempted coup on 1 August 1956 and orchestrated the victory of his party, the Partido Union Nacional, in the 7 October congressional election. The three opposition parties declared the election fraudulent, and on 21 October members of the Honduran military, led by General Roque J. Rodríguez, brought down the Lozano Díaz dictatorship and established a military junta. He died in Miami on August 20, 1957.

See also **Honduras.**

BIBLIOGRAPHY

Ralph Lee Woodward, Jr., *Central America: A Nation Divided* (1976), pp. 255 and 301.

James A. Morris, *Honduras: Caudillo Politics and Military Rulers* (1984), esp. pp. 11–12.

Leslie Bethell, ed., *The Cambridge History of Latin America,* vol. 7 (1990), pp. 298–299.

Additional Bibliography

Ans, André-Marcel 'd. *Honduras: De un liberalismio al otro.* Tegucigalpa: Centro de Documentación de Honduras, 1999.

Barahona, Marvin. *Honduras en el siglo XX: Una síntesis histórica.* Tegucigalpa: Editorial Guaymuras, 2005.

Martínez B., Juan Ramón. *El asalto al Cuartel San Francisco: El día que la juventud hizo temblar a la dictadura.* Tegucigalpa, Honduras: Ediciones 18 Conejo, 2003.

MICHAEL A. POLUSHIN

LOZZA, RAÚL (1911–). Raúl Lozza, an Argentine painter, craftsman, and illustrator, was born on October 27, 1911, in Alberti, Buenos Aires Province, and was self-taught. He was a founding member of the Asociación de Arte Concreto-Invención, a nonfigurative group, as well as the creator of *perceptismo,* a theory of color and open structure in painting that he called "cualimetría de la forma plana." Lozza's two- and three-dimensional works reveal an almost scientific concern for the intelligent use of technology, and the tonal values in his paintings are intensified or reduced with mathematical precision. Lozza has had numerous exhibitions, including a retrospective in 1985 at the Fundación San Telmo in Buenos Aires. He is the recipient of several awards, including the Palanza Prize (1991) and the Konex Award (1992). In 1997 the Museo de Arte Moderno of Buenos Aires organized an important retrospective exhibition in his honor.

See also **Art: The Twentieth Century.**

BIBLIOGRAPHY

Raúl Lozza. Cuarenta años en el arte concreto (sesenta con la pintura), Catalog of the Fundación San Telmo Exhibition, 22 July–18 August 1985.

Vicente Gesualdo, Aldo Biglione, and Rodolfo Santos, *Diccionario de artistas plásticos en la Argentina* (1988); *Raúl Lozza. Pintura y arte concreto, 1945–1955.* Catalog of the Fundación Banco Patricios Exhibition, 8 September–1 October 1993.

Additional Bibliography

Tomasini, María Cecilia. *Una revision a la relación arte-ciencia en la obra de Raúl Lozza.* Buenos Aires: Centro Cultural Borges, 2002.

AMALIA CORTINA ARAVENA

LUCAS GARCÍA, FERNANDO ROMEO (1924–2006). Fernando Romeo Lucas García, born on July 4, 1924, was a brigadier general who became president of Guatemala in July 1978, succeeding Kjell Laugerud. It is widely believed that the 1978 election was fraudulent, and that Enrique Peralta Azurdia was the real winner.

Lucas García presided over an administration that was generally perceived to be riddled with corruption, cronyism, and violence. During Lucas's tenure the Guerrilla Army of the Poor (EGP) gained significant support and territory from the mainly indigenous inhabitants of the western highlands. Political violence from the Far Right increased, particularly in urban areas, where students, union members, and professionals were regularly "disappeared" by death squads. During this period, the U.S. government under Jimmy Carter refused military aid to Guatemala because of human rights violations.

By 1980 Guatemala's once-vital economy had begun to weaken, due to world recession and a decline in tourism. Dissatisfaction with Lucas García within the military became acute, and on March 23, 1982, he was overthrown in a coup. Lucas was succeeded by a three-man junta consisting of General Efrain Ríos Montt, General Horacio Maldonado Schad, and Colonel Francisco Gordillo. In 1999 the Audiencia Nacional of Spain began criminal proceedings against Lucas García for accusations of torture and genocide against the Maya population. In 2000 Guatemala's Association for Justice and Reconciliation also sought prosecution. Both attempts failed, as Lucas García was living in Venezuela, which denied an extradition request, and was in any event incapacitated by Alzheimer's disease and other ailments. He died in Venezuela on May 27, 2006.

See also **Guatemala; Human Rights; Laugerud García, Eugenio Kjell; Ríos Montt, José Efraín.**

BIBLIOGRAPHY

Jim Handy, *Gift of the Devil: A History of Guatemala* (1984).

Richard F. Nyrop, ed., *Guatemala: A Country Study,* 2d ed. (1984).

Jean-Marie Simon, *Guatemala: Eternal Spring, Eternal Tyranny* (1987).

Additional Bibliography

"Gen. Romeo Lucas García, 85, Former Guatemalan President, Dies." *New York Times,* May 29, 2006.

VIRGINIA GARRARD-BURNETT

LUDWIG, DANIEL KEITH (1897–1992). Daniel Keith Ludwig (*b.* 24 June 1897; *d.* 27 August 1992), American billionaire. In 1967, Ludwig purchased property on both sides of the Jari River in western Pará and Amapá for $3 million and named it Jari. He bought this Brazilian property, the size of Connecticut, so he could grow and manufacture pulpwood. President Humberto Castello Branco granted Ludwig such concessions as ten-year tax exemptions and a guarantee that he could run his operation as he pleased without interference from the Brazilian government. Jari included housing for workers at Monte Dourado, the town Ludwig had built; 2,500 miles of dirt roads; and 50 miles of railroad tracks.

Although Ludwig planned to plant most of the area in *Gmelina arborea* seedlings, a fast-growing East India tree, the huge machines used to level the forest packed down the nutritionless soil, and most of the *Gmelinas* died. He finally covered one-third of Jari in the hardier Caribbean pine, which survived but takes sixteen years to mature. Ludwig did profit from rice he had planted around the Jari River; kaolin, used in the manufacture of porcelain; and bauxite deposits. These earnings, however, did not offset his losses because the remaining *Gmelina* seedlings failed to mature on schedule.

Despite this setback, in 1976 Ludwig spent $269 million on a pulpwood processing factory with a wood-burning power plant that was built in Japan and floated 15,500 miles across the ocean up the Amazon River to Jari. Ludwig had neither enough pulpwood to operate the factory at full capacity nor enough wood to keep his power plant fueled. He realized he would never recover his $1 billion investment. He sold Jari in 1982 for $300 million to a consortium of twenty-three companies backed by the Brazilian government. Jari continues to operate and has made profits from kaolin.

See also **Castello Branco, Humberto de Alencar.**

BIBLIOGRAPHY

Susanna Hecht and Alexander Cockburn, *The Fate of the Forest: Developers, Destroyers, and Defenders of the Amazon* (1990).

Gwen Kinkead, "Trouble in D. K. Ludwig's Jungle," in *Fortune,* 20 April 1981.

Jerry Shields, *The Invisible Billionaire, Daniel Ludwig* (1986).

Roger D. Stone, *Dreams of Amazonia* (1985).

Additional Bibliography

Little, Paul E. *Amazonia: Territorial Struggles on Perennial Frontiers.* Baltimore, MD: Johns Hopkins University Press, 2001.

Posey, Clayton E., and Harold K. Steen. *An Interview with Clayton E. Posey.* Durham, NC: Forest History Society, 1995.

CAROLYN JOSTOCK

LUGONES, LEOPOLDO (1874–1938).

Leopoldo Lugones (*b.* 13 June 1874; *d.* 18 February 1938), Argentine poet and social historian.

Lugones occupies a central position in the history of Hispanic-American modernism for his perfection of form and rich, original imagery in works such as *Los crepúsculos del jardín* (Garden Twilights, 1905). Lugones used his prodigious intellect and formidable learning to make his ideas known in literature, education, politics, government, and public affairs. He began his career as a journalist at the age of sixteen, writing articles for a newspaper in his native Córdoba. He came to Buenos Aires in 1896 and there published his first book of poems, *Las montañas de oro* (The Golden Mountains, 1897). In 1897, he cofounded *La Montaña* as a forum for his socialist—and at times anarchist—ideas. In 1899, he became director of the General Archives of the postal services and in 1904 general inspector of the secondary schools.

Lugones strongly opposed the ultraliberal revolutionary activities of 1904 and in 1907 launched a virulent attack on President Figueroa Alcorta from the columns of *El Diario*. When the Argentine Congress passed an electoral reform bill in 1912, Lugones protested strenuously. His views, which were frequently self-contradictory, suffered radical changes throughout his life. After World War I, he extolled the Versailles Treaty and was critical of German military leadership. Yet he also attacked democracy and was convinced that the use of force was necessary to secure social order and progress. Lugones supported the Argentine university reform laws enacted in 1918, but he opposed universal suffrage and populist solutions to national problems. With the reelection of Hipólito Irigoyen as president in 1928, Lugones's militarism became more extreme, and he participated actively in the September 1930 revolution that overthrew that regime. In his later years he began using a religious approach in his writing. He took his own life on 18 February 1938.

Best known as a poet and prose writer, Lugones is also the author of numerous books revealing his ardent nationalism, his profound insights into Argentine history, and his identification with the people and traditions of Argentina's provincial regions. Such works as *El imperio jesuítico* (1904), *Historia de Sarmiento* (1911), and *El estado equitativo* (1932) have had a strong impact on the way Argentines view themselves and have contributed to Lugones's stature as one of the foremost intellectual figures of his time.

See also **Literature: Spanish America.**

BIBLIOGRAPHY

Alfredo Canedo, *Aspectos del pensamiento político de Leopoldo Lugones* (1974).

Juan Carlos Ghiano, *Poesía Argentina del siglo XX* (1957), pp. 29–40.

Julio Irazusta, *Genio y figura de Leopoldo Lugones* (1968).

Daniel C. Scroggins, "Leopoldo Lugones' Defense of the Monroe Doctrine in the *Revue Sudaméricaine*," in *Rivista Interamericana de Bibliografía* 28, no. 2 (1978): 169–175.

Carlos A. Solé and Maria Isabel Abreu, *Latin American Writers*, vol. 2 (1989), pp. 493–502.

Additional Bibliography

Bischoff, Efraín U. *Leopoldo Lugones: Un cordobés rebelde.* Córdoba, Argentina: Editorial Brujas, 2005.

Luna, Félix. *Leopoldo Lugones.* Buenos Aires: Planeta, 2001.

MYRON I. LICHTBLAU

LUISI, LUISA (1888–1940).

Luisa Luisi (*b.* 1888; *d.* 1940), Uruguayan poet, critic, and educator; her work is grouped with the generation of Uruguayan "realist poets" between 1885 and 1935. Luisi's books of poetry include *Sentir* (1916), *Inquietud* (1921), *Poemas de la inmovilidad y canciones al sol* (1926), and *Polvo de dias* (1935). Her early poetry was conceptual and based on philosophical ideas, but an illness that left her without the use of her legs brought forth in her later poetry an anguish over her immobile state. Her tone became melancholic and reflected a spiritual restlessness and dismay that she was unable to realize her full potential. Luisi's critical prose include *A través de libros y autores* (1925).

Luisi was educated in Montevideo in both private schools and at the Normal Institute for Girls, qualifying to teach in the first, second, and third grades. She later became a school principal, taught reading and declamation in the Normal Institute for Girls, and remained active in Uruguayan education her entire life, despite retiring from teaching in 1929. Luisi, along with her two remarkable sisters, Clotilde and Paulina, broke down many barriers in Uruguayan society for female intellectual activity and for the advancement of women in other areas. Clotilde Luisi distinguished herself as the first woman lawyer in Uruguay and as professor of moral philosophy and religion at the Normal Institute for Girls. Paulina Luisi, one of the few and among the earliest Uruguayan women to become a doctor, held teaching posts and headed the gynecological clinic at the Faculty of Medicine.

See also **Literature: Spanish America; Uruguay: The Twentieth Century.**

BIBLIOGRAPHY

William Belmont Parker, *Uruguayans of Today* (1921), pp. 307–308.

Sarah Bollo, *Literatura uruguaya, 1807–1975* (1976).

Mercedes Pinto, "Las poéticas," in Carlos Reyles, ed., *Historia sintética de la literatura uruguaya,* vol. 2 (1931).

Additional Bibliography

Cabrera de Betarte, Silvia.

Larre Borges, Ana Inés and Cielo Pereira. *Mujeres uruguayas: El lado femenino de nuestra historia.* Montevideo: Fundación Banco de Boston, Extra Alfaguara, 1997-2001.

Paulina Luisi: Una socialista para conocer, querer y emular. Montevideo: Partido Socialista, 2001.

J. DAVID DRESSING

LUISI, PAULINA (1875–1950).

Paulina Luisi (*b.* 22 September 1875; *d.* 17 July 1950), physician, educator, feminist, diplomat, social reformer. Luisi was the first Uruguayan woman to receive a medical degree. Her lifelong work on behalf of children (president of the Uruguayan delegation to the First American Congress of the Child, Buenos Aires, 1916) and women's health (Uruguayan delegate to the International Congress on Social Hygiene and Education, Paris, 1923; member of the League of Nations consultative committee on the Treaty to End Traffic in Women and Children, 1922, 1923, 1924, 1925) was paralleled by her commitment to woman suffrage and female education. She founded the Uruguayan branch of the National Women's Council in 1916 and represented Uruguay at the International Congresses of Women in Geneva and Cristiana, Norway, in 1920 and Rome in 1925. She was the first woman in the Western Hemisphere to represent her government as an officially appointed delegate to an intergovernmental conference (Fifth International Conference of American States, Santiago, 1923). Luisi also served as head of the Uruguayan delegation to the League of Nations. With her colleague, Argentine feminist and socialist Alicia Moreau De Justo, Luisi believed that female education and equal political rights were crucial to improving working conditions and health care for women and children.

See also **Feminism and Feminist Organizations; League of Nations.**

BIBLIOGRAPHY

Inter-American Commission Of Women, *Libro de Oro* (1980), and Marifran Carlson, *¡Feminismo! The Woman's Movement in Argentina from Its Beginnings to Eva Perón* (1988).

Additional Bibliography

Cabrera de Betarte, Silvia. *Paulina Luisi: Una socialista para conocer, querer y emular.* Montevideo: Partido Socialista, 2001.

Henault, Mirta. *Alicia Moreau de Justo: "Dad paso a la honradez, al trabajo, a la justicia."* Argentina: CUATA Ediciones, 2002.

FRANCESCA MILLER

LUÍS PEREIRA DE SOUSA, WASHINGTON (1870–1957).

Washington Luís Pereira de Sousa (*b.* 26 October 1870; *d.* 4 August 1957), president of Brazil (1926–1930). Although known as the consummate defender of the political and economic interests of the state of São Paulo, Luís was born and schooled in the state of Rio de Janeiro. After moving to São Paulo in 1888, Luís steadily rose within São Paulo's political circles, serving as state deputy (1904–1906, 1912–1913), state secretary of justice (1906–1914), mayor of the city of São Paulo (1914–1919), governor of the state of

São Paulo (1920–1924), and senator (1924–1926). In 1926 Luís was elected president of Brazil. He remained president until October 1930, when he was forced from office and into exile during the one-month civil war later known as the Revolution of 1930.

Luís was one of the most prominent members of the Partido Republicano Paulista (PRP), and his political career was representative of the oligarchic-led politics of Brazil's First Republic (1889–1930). He was a fiscal conservative who promoted state autonomy (particularly for the state of São Paulo) and economic policies favorable to coffee cultivation, nascent industrialization, and infrastructural improvements (especially in rail and roads). An advocate of stricter policing and opponent of organized labor, Luís coined the republican elite's dictum that the social question was a police question. However, his close association with the oligarchic interests of the First Republic also proved to be his downfall, as Luís failed to convince the reformist interests from Minas Gerais and Rio Grande do Sul supporting Getúlio Vargas's 1930 presidential candidacy that Luís's hand-picked successor, *paulista* Júlio Prestes, could best manage Brazil's extremely precarious position amidst the onset of the Great Depression. During the Revolution of 1930, Luís and President-elect Prestes were stripped of their political powers and Vargas became chief of the provisional government. Exiled, Luís lived in Europe and the United States. Upon returning to Brazil in 1947, Luís remained far from politics, concentrating his energies on his personal life and his interest in *paulista* history and culture.

See also **Brazil: Revolutions: Revolution of 1930; São Paulo (State).**

BIBLIOGRAPHY

Joseph L. Love, *São Paulo in the Brazilian Federation, 1889–1937* (1980).

"Luís, Washington," in *Dicionário histórico-biográfico brasileiro, 1930–1983,* vol. 3 (1984), pp. 1,952–1,955.

Thomas E. Skidmore, *Politics in Brazil, 1930–1964: An Experiment in Democracy* (1967), pp. 1–8.

Additional Bibliography

Debes, Célio. *Washington Luís.* São Paulo: Imprensa Oficial do Estado, Instituto Histórico e Geográfico de São Paulo, 1994.

Pereira, Robson Mendonça. *Washington Luís e a modernização de Batatais.* São Paulo: FAPESP, Annablume, 2005.

DARYLE WILLIAMS

LUJÁN. Luján, city of 66,448 inhabitants (2001) located 35 miles west of Greater Buenos Aires. Its origin dates to a shrine to the Virgin Mary, erected in 1630, which has become the major Argentine center of religious pilgrimage. In the central nave, the gothic-style basilica commemorates the adherence to Catholicism of the Argentine provinces and in the two lateral aisles, the loyalty of Uruguayans and Paraguayans. The city is also known for its *cabildo* (local council house), built in 1750, and the colonial museum of Buenos Aires. Greater Buenos Aires's western gateway to the Pampa, Luján is an important hub of the General San Martín railway and the starting point of the highway leading to the region of Cuyo and Chile.

See also **Argentina, Geography.**

BIBLIOGRAPHY

José R. Torre, *La casa cabildo de la villa de Luján* (Buenos Aires, 1942).

Felisa C. Echeverría, *Romancero de la villa de Luján* (Luján, 1975).

Additional Bibliography

Bertrand, Jean-René, and Cristina T Carballo. *Estudio sobre los territorios urbanos.* Luján: Universidad Nacional de Luján, Departamento de Ciencias Sociales, División Geografía, 2004.

Guglielmino, Osvaldo. *La Virgen de Luján y nuestra nacionalidad.* Buenos Aires: Instituto Nacional de Investigaciones Históricas Juan Manuel de Rosas, 1997.

Presas, Juan Antonio. *Anales de Nuestra Señora de Luján: Trabajo histórico-documental, 1630-2002.* 4th ed. Buenos Aires: Editorial Dunken, 2002.

CÉSAR N. CAVIEDES

LUJÁN, VIRGIN OF. The Virgin of Luján is the most popular figure of devotion and most venerated shrine in Argentina. Around 1630 a Portuguese ranch owner had two images of the

Virgin Mary brought from Brazil for his chapel. When one of the images, borne by oxen, "refused" to move beyond a certain point, a site thirty-six miles west of Buenos Aires, local inhabitants took it as a sign that the Virgin wished to stay there. A popular devotion grew around the image, and the *villa* of Luján itself grew up around the chapel housing the virgin. It soon became the center of Argentine Catholic religiosity. Generals Manuel Belgrano and José de San Martín paid their respects to the Virgin of Luján. Because of the shrine's popularity, Pope Leo XIII honored the statue with a papal coronation in 1887. A major basilica to house the image, under the care of the Vincentian fathers, was begun in 1887 and opened in 1910. Declared the patroness of Argentina, the Virgin of Luján attracts many pilgrims each year, especially in the months of November and December. Miniature body parts and votive offerings fill the shrine in testament to the healing miracles devotees believe the Virgin has granted. A cloak of white and blue, the colors of Argentina's flag, often covers the image for protection.

See also **Leo XIII, Pope.**

BIBLIOGRAPHY

Jorge María Salvaire, *Historia de Nuestra Señora de Luján* (1885).

Rubén Vargas Ugarte, *Historia del culto de María en Iberoamérica,* 3d ed., vol. 1 (1956).

Additional Bibliography

Guglielmino, Osvaldo. *La Virgen de Luján y nuestra nacionalidad.* Buenos Aires: Instituto Nacional de Investigaciones Históricas Juan Manuel de Rosas, 1997.

Presas, Juan Antonio. *Anales de Nuestra Señora de Luján: Trabajo histórico-documental, 1630–2002,* 4th edition. Buenos Aires: Editorial Dunken, 2002.

JEFFREY KLAIBER

LULA. *See* **Silva, Luis Inácio Lula da.**

LUMBER INDUSTRY. Much of Latin America is denuded of commercial timber, but select areas have supplied specialized markets. Europeans were early attracted to the variety of subtropical trees, both dyewoods and construction wood, formerly available only from the Orient. Craftsmen and builders prized Caribbean mahogany; textile manufacturers coveted brazilwood, Nicaragua wood, and logwood. The best wood commanded high prices in European markets, but the quality was inconsistent and the risks of obtaining it were considerable. Valuable trees such as mahogany were widely scattered. Finding and removing them was a major undertaking. Costs were proportional to overland haulage; the greater the distance, the higher the cost. The competition for accessible trees that consequently arose often provoked international controversy. The dyewood trade suffered from inroads by such other natural dyes as Mexican and Guatemalan cochineal and was destroyed by synthetic dyes after 1856.

Brazilwood, which yielded a brilliant red dye, was the premier wood. It grew along the coast from the state of Pernambuco (Recife) to that of Rio de Janeiro, and provided the economic base for the first Portuguese settlements in the early sixteenth century. Overcoming a French challenge, the Portuguese crown monopolized the brazilwood trade for 300 years. The trade peaked before 1600 and was followed by a sharp drop attributed to the decimation of the coastal forests and Indian laborers. Exports in the seventeenth century averaged only 100 tons annually, even less in the eighteenth century, and ceased altogether in 1875.

Nicaragua wood, a brazilwood substitute that furnished a less intense and less durable red coloring, grew on the Pacific coast of Central America, particularly near Lake Nicaragua. The trade enjoyed a brief boom in the 1830s, when ships rounded Cape Horn to trade along the Pacific.

Logwood yielded a bluish-red dye that was the basic fixing dye for almost every other color used in the textile industry. The major source was the Yucatán, where the Spanish monopoly was threatened in the seventeenth century by English interlopers from Belize. Failing to expel them, Spain finally conceded woodcutting privileges in 1786. By then most of the logwood had been shipped overseas. Moreover, technical changes adopted by the dyemakers, plus the availability of better natural dyes, reduced the demand for logwood. Consequently, loggers shifted to the mahogany resources of the region.

Agents of Brazil's Institute of the Environment and Renewable Natural Resources check to verify the legality of a lumber shipment, 1990. Illegal logging remains a serious problem in the Amazonian rainforest, greatly exceeding legal lumber production according to some estimates. H. JOHN MAIER JR./TIME LIFE PICTURES/GETTY IMAGES

The market for mahogany expanded in the nineteenth century to include building construction, shipbuilding, and railway carriages. Although mahogany grew elsewhere in the Caribbean, the Bay of Honduras was by far the major supplier for the boom that lasted into the 1850s, when exports from the region averaged 25,000 tons annually. As accessible mahogany within the Belize borders became exhausted, aggressive cutters expanded into Mexico, Guatemala, and Honduras, thereby precipitating controversies that questioned the status of both Belize and the resurrected Mosquito Kingdom. As the market declined, the tensions that had accompanied the expansive phase subsided.

Lumber in the twenty-first century remains a limited export. Brazil continues to be the primary exporter, sending mainly mahogany and virola to the United States. Bolivia and Peru also export mahogany and Ecuador primarily trades in balsa wood.

See also **Brazilwood; Forests.**

BIBLIOGRAPHY

Arthur M. Wilson, "The Logwood Trade in the Seventeenth and Eighteenth Centuries," in *Essays in the History of Modern Europe,* edited by Donald Cope McKay (1936, repr. 1968), 1–15.

Alexander N. Marchant, *From Barter to Slavery: The Economic Relations of Portuguese and Indians in the Settlement of Brazil, 1500–1580* (1942, repr. 1966).

William J. Griffith, *Empires in the Wilderness: Foreign Colonization and Development in Guatemala, 1834–1844* (1965).

Susan Fairlie, "Dyestuffs in the Eighteenth Century," in *Economic History Review* 2d ser., 17 (April 1965): 488–510.

Robert A. Naylor, "The Mahogany Trade as a Factor in the British Return to the Mosquito Shore in the Second Quarter of the 19th Century," in *Jamaica Historical Review* 7 (1967): 40–67; *Influencia británica en el comercio centroamericano 1821–1851* (1988); and *Penny Ante Imperialism: The Mosquito Shore and the Bay of Honduras, 1600–1914* (1989).

Additional Bibliography

Miller, Shawn William. *Fruitless Trees: Portuguese Conservation and Brazil's Colonial Timber.* Stanford, CA: Stanford University Press, 2000.

Scholz, Imme. *Overexploitation or Sustainable Management: Action Patterns of the Tropical Timber Industry: The Case of Pará (Brazil), 1960–1997.* London and Portland, OR: Frank Cass, 2001.

Seminario sobre Industria y Comercialización de Productos Forestales en Latinoamérica. *La Industria y la comercialización de productos forestales en Latinoamérica.* Heredia, Costa Rica: Instituto de Investigación y Servicios Forestales (INISEFOR), 2003.

ROBERT A. NAYLOR

LUNA PIZARRO, FRANCISCO JAVIER DE (1780–1855). Francisco Javier De Luna Pizarro (*b.* 1780; *d.* 9 February 1855), Peruvian Roman Catholic priest. Born in Arequipa, in his youth he admired liberal ideas and found politics as practiced in the United States to be worthy of emulation. After the protectorate of José de San Martín ended in 1822, Luna Pizarro organized the liberal leadership in the national congress that formulated the constitutions of Peru from 1823 through 1834. This leadership favored free trade, administrative decentralization, a carefully restricted electorate, establishment of Roman Catholicism as the religion protected by the state, and the prohibition of all other views. Churchmen and the military retained the special privileges awarded them in the colonial era. Luna Pizarro later abandoned his support of the government's right to protect the church and appoint its priests. Regaining the favor of Rome, he then became a conservative archbishop of Lima (1845–1855).

See also **Peru: Constitutions.**

BIBLIOGRAPHY

Jeffrey L. Klaiber, *Religion and Revolution in Peru, 1824–1976* (1977).

The Catholic Church in Peru, 1821–1985: A Social History (1992), esp. pp. 38–58.

Additional Bibliography

Villanueva, Carmen. *Francisco Javier de Luna Pizarro.* Lima: Editorial Brasa, 1995.

VINCENT PELOSO

LUNA Y ARELLANO, TRISTÁN DE (c. 1500–1573). Tristán De Luna y Arellano (*b.* ca. 1500/10; *d.* 16 September 1573), soldier and governor of La Florida (1559–1561). Born in Aragón, Luna came to New Spain with Hernán Cortés around 1530, returned to Spain, and came back to New Spain in 1535. In 1558 Luna, a veteran of the Coronado expedition to the American Southwest as well as of military exploits in Oaxaca, received a charter to establish a colony on the Gulf coast. Planned and outfitted in Mexico, the expedition of eleven vessels, five hundred soldiers, and a thousand colonists and servants (including Mexican natives) sailed from San Juan de Ulúa on the Gulf coast of Mexico on 11 June 1559 for the port of Ochuse (Pensacola Bay).

A hurricane sank most of the ships with their supplies before they could be offloaded. The colony quickly fell into disarray, a process hastened by Luna's illness, which at times incapacitated him. Colonists and scouting parties sent into the interior to seek food and shelter from native peoples were largely unsuccessful. In March 1561, Luna was relieved of the governorship and ordered to Spain; the colony was withdrawn.

See also **Cortés, Hernán.**

BIBLIOGRAPHY

Charles Hudson, Marvin T. Smith, Chester B. De Pratter, and Emilia Kelley, "The Tristán de Luna Expedition, 1559–1561," in *First Encounters: Spanish Explorations in the Caribbean and the United States, 1492–1570,* edited by Jerald T. Milanich and Susan Milbrath (1989).

Herbert I. Priestley, ed. and trans., *The Luna Papers: Documents Relating to the Expedition of Don Tristán de Luna y Arellano for the Conquest of La Florida in 1559–1561,* 2 vols. (1928; repr. 1971).

Robert S. Weddle, *Spanish Sea: The Gulf of Mexico in North American Discovery, 1500–1685* (1985), esp. pp. 251–284.

Additional Bibliography

Flint, Richard, and Shirley Cushing Flint. *The Coronado Expedition to Tierra Nueva: The 1540-1542 Route across the Southwest.* Niwot, CO: University Press of Colorado, 1997.

JERALD T. MILANICH

LUNDU. Lundu, a Brazilian dance and song form. Of African, most probably Angolan, origin, *lundu* was popular in the eighteenth century. Like Batuque and samba, the dance form consisted of a couple performing within a *roda* (spectators' circle) by tapping their feet, accentuatedly swaying their hips, and engaging in the characteristic *umbigada* (smacking of stomachs). Often compared with the Spanish fandango and the Portuguese *fofa* in its dance form, *lundu* was popularized as a song form with humorous lyrics by the Brazilian poet Domingos Caldas Barbosa at the Portuguese court in the eighteenth century. In its song form, *lundu* is played in 2/4 time, with the first beat syncopated. According to Mário de Andrade, it was the first black musical form to be widely accepted into Brazilian "high" society, and left its formal imprint on Brazilian music through its "systematization of syncopation" and the "reduced seventh."

See also **Maxixe; MPB: Música Popular Brasileira.**

BIBLIOGRAPHY

Oneyda Alvarenga, *Música popular brasileira* (1982).

Mário De Andrade, *Dicionário musical brasileiro,* coordinated by Oneyda Alvarenga and Flávia Camargo Toni (1982–1989).

Charles A. Perrone, *Masters of Contemporary Brazilian Song* (1989).

Additional Bibliography

Barros, José Carlos. *Pequena introdução crítica á história da música popular brasileira.* Salvador: Módulo, 2001.

D'Amorim, Elvira, and Dinalva Araújo. *Do lundu ao samba: Pelos caminhos do coco.* João Pessoa: Idéia, 2003.

Livingston-Isenhour, Tamara Elena, and Thomas George Caracas Garcia. *Choro: A Social History of Brazilian Popular Music.* Bloomington: Indiana University Press, 2005.

Robert Myers

LUNFARDO. The Italian dialect word *lunfardo*, meaning a criminal, began as *lombardo*, then became *lumbardo*, and finally *lunfardo.* It was applied to all criminal slang, which—along with brothel slang and the flood of immigrants in the late nineteenth century—gave a major boost to Argentine argot, to the extent that the boundary between Lunfardism and Argentinism is sometimes vague. This lexicon lost or assimilated terms over time while some words changed meanings: *ortiva* was first synonymous with informer but came to mean embittered.

The manifest expressive force of Lunfardo spread throughout society and was expressed in artistic and journalistic forms (for example, *costumbrista* poems and articles in the magazine *Caras y Caretas* and in the newspapers *Última Hora* and *Crítica,* until the 1930s). It also strengthened the repertoire of folk singers, including the lyrics for tango music and the *género chico criollo*, or short, light plays. It was also found in some naturalist novels. With *Versos rantifusos* (1916) by Yacaré (Francisco Fernández) and *La crencha engrasada* (1926) by Carlos de la Púa (Carlos Muñoz del Solar), Lunfardo reached poetic heights. Roberto Arlt incorporated it into his novels (beginning with *El juguete rabioso*, 1926) and his *Aguafuertes porteñas,* in the daily, *El Mundo*, between 1928 and 1933. In the 1960s Ernesto Sábato, Julio Cortázar, and many writers, poets, and dramatists took it up. But it was especially radio and television comedy programs that renewed this legacy and disseminated it down to the end of the twentieth century, although in the last decades of the century young people and the music they sing—from "national" rock to *cumbia villera*—have been the main proponents of Lunfardo. There are many dictionaries of Lunfardo's vocabulary. The initial compilations of Leopoldo Lugones, Luis MariaDrago, Antonio Dellepiane, Luis Villamayor, and others were later systematized by José Gobello in *Lunfardía* (1953), Oscar Conde in *Diccionario etimológico del lunfardo* (1998), and others.

See also **Cortázar, Julio; Sábato, Ernesto; Spanish Language.**

BIBLIOGRAPHY

Conde, Oscar. *Diccionario etimológico del lunfardo.* Buenos Aires: Perfil Libros, 1998.

Gobello, José. *Lunfardía: Introducción al estudio del lenguaje porteño.* Buenos Aires: Argos, 1953.

Eduardo Romano

LUPERÓN, GREGORIO (1839–1897). Gregorio Luperón (*b.* 8 September 1839; *d.* 21 May 1897), president of the Dominican Republic

(6 October 1879–1 September 1880). A black, born in Puerto Plata in the north, Luperón won great distinction as a general during the War of Restoration (1863–1865) and the defeat of Spain. He became a leading soldier-statesman and patriot dedicated to ending turmoil and uniting the country. For many years, he was a strong supporter of Ulises Espaillat, who urged Luperón to become president in 1876. He regularly resisted assuming the office but finally agreed to serve as a provisional president in 1879. As president he reorganized the army and local administration, paid government workers their back pay of three years, and adjusted all foreign claims. In the early 1880s, he served as a diplomat in Paris, representing the democratically elected government of his successor, Father Fernando Arturo de Meriño.

See also **Dominican Republic; Espaillat, Ulises Francisco.**

BIBLIOGRAPHY

Frank Moya Pons, *Manual de historia dominicana* (1977), pp. 367–368, 371–374, 384–402, 407–416.

Emilio Rodríguez Demorizi, *Luperón y Hostos* (1939), pp. 14–15, 20–21, 26, 31–32.

Hugo Tolentino Dipp, *Gregorio Luperón (Biografía Política)* (1977), chap. 2.

Sumner Welles, *Naboth's Vineyard: The Dominican Republic, 1844–1924,* vol. 1 (1966), chap. 6.

Additional Bibliography

Castro Ventura, Santiago. *Andanzas patrióticas de Luperón.* Santo Domingo, República Dominicana: S. Castro Ventura, 2002.

Hernández Flores, Ismael. *Luperón–Peña Gómez, paralelismos.* Santo Domingo, República Dominicana: Editora de Colores, 2004.

LARMAN C. WILSON

LUQUE, HERNANDO DE (?–1534).

Hernando de Luque (*d.* 1534), an early-sixteenth-century Spanish cleric who accompanied Pedro Arias de Ávila (Pedrarias) in 1514 on an expedition to colonize Panama. When Pedrarias took command at Darién, de Luque's friendship with the governor allowed him to establish a number of influential contacts. In Panama, de Luque joined in a business partnership with the conquistadores, Francisco Pizarro and Diego de Almagro. In the early 1520s, the three men embarked on a plan to explore the regions south of Panama and to undertake the conquest of Peru. De Luque was instrumental in raising the necessary funds for the 1524 and 1526 expeditions into the Andean region. Acting as an agent for wealthy investors, including the judge Gaspar de Espinosa, who condemned Balboa, de Luque raised two hundred pounds of gold bars. He was nicknamed "Fernando de Loco," the mad priest, for undertaking the venture. Later scholars have suggested it was de Luque who planned and organized the expeditions as well as arranged for the necessary financial backing. He did not accompany Pizarro and Almagro on the expeditions, remaining instead in Panama to manage their business affairs. De Luque died before the conquest was completed.

See also **Almagro, Diego de; Pizarro, Francisco.**

BIBLIOGRAPHY

Leslie Bethell, ed., *Colonial Spanish America* (1987).

Mark A. Burkholder and Lyman L. Johnson, *Colonial Latin America* (1990).

C. Hedrick Basil, and Ann K. Hedrick, *A Historical Dictionary of Panama* (1970).

Frederick A. Kirkpatrick, *The Spanish Conquistadors* (1934).

James Lockhart and Stuart B. Schwartz, *Early Latin America: A History of Colonial Spanish America and Brazil* (1983).

Additional Bibliography

Castro Vega, Oscar. *Pedrarias Dávila, la ira de Dios.* Costa Rica: s.n., 1996.

Mena García, María del Carmen. *Temas de historia panameña.* Panamá: Editorial Universitaria, 1996.

HEATHER K. THIESSEN

LUSINCHI, JAIME (1924–).

Jaime Lusinchi, born on May 27, 1924, was president of Venezuela from 1984 to 1989. While studying medicine at the Central University of Venezuela and the University of the East, Lusinchi became active in Venezuela's Democratic Action (Acción Democrática—AD). From 1952 to 1958 he was exiled by the military dictatorship. After his return, the young pediatrician became a member of the national executive committee of AD. He also served in the Chamber of Deputies and the Senate. From 1980 to 1983 he was the party's secretary-general. In the 1983 presidential election he defeated Rafael Caldera, the candidate of the Social Christian COPEI (Comité de Organización Política Electoral Independiente) Party. As president, Lusinchi presided over a period of low oil prices and rising discontent; scandals also plagued his administration. Nevertheless, he left office with high public approval ratings. He lives in Miami, Florida.

See also **Venezuela, Political Parties: Democratic Action (AD).**

BIBLIOGRAPHY

Olmedo Lugo, *Políticos de Venezuela* (1969).

Jaime Lusinchi, *Frente al futuro* (1983).

Judith Ewell, "Venezuela Since 1930," in *The Cambridge History of Latin America,* edited by Leslie Bethel, vol. 8 (1991), pp. 785–789.

Additional Bibliography

Leizaola, Zuriñe. *El discurso politico venezolano en el siglo XX.* Caracas: Fundación Carlos Eduardo Frias, 1996.

Rodríguez-Valdés, Angel. *Los oscuros sostenes del poder.* Caracas: Linea, 1991.

WINFIELD J. BURGGRAAFF

LUSO-BRAZILIAN. Luso-Brazilian, term that is used to describe a person or to refer to the mixture of Brazilian and Portuguese culture. *Luso* refers to Portugal and more specifically to Lusitania, the name of Portugal during the Roman Empire. Luso-Brazilian culture evolved from the mixture of Portuguese, African, and coastal Amerindian influences. Portuguese colonists imposed some Western-oriented cultural traditions on the indigenous society, such as the Roman Catholic Church, but the farther away they were from coastal towns, the more likely were colonists and their descendants to adopt Tupi Indian language and customs. Importation of African slaves, which began in the sixteenth century, introduced a new cultural element. Brazil retained many features of Portuguese life, but was distinct from Portugal because of the preponderance of people of color. The society that evolved in Brazil was marked by racial and ethnic diversity, but also by a social hierarchy based on plantations, slavery, and polygamous patriarchal paternalism. Another reflection of the mix of cultures is in language. During colonial times, many words from the Tupi languages came into use alongside Portuguese. Africans, from diverse linguistic groups, added to the vocabulary. Portuguese spoken in Brazil, therefore, includes African as well as Tupi terms.

See also **Race and Ethnicity.**

BIBLIOGRAPHY

Gilberto Freyre, *The Masters and the Slaves* (1946).

Joaquim Mattoso Câmara, Jr., *The Portuguese Language* (1972).

Bailey W. Diffie and George D. Winius, *Foundations of the Portuguese Empire, 1415–1850* (1978).

Stuart B. Schwartz, *Sugar Plantations in the Formation of Brazilian Society: Bahia, 1550–1835* (1985).

Additional Bibliography

Fausto, Boris. *A Concise History of Brazil.* New York: Cambridge University Press, 1999.

Quinlan, Susan Canty, and Fernando Arenas, eds. *Lusosex: Gender and Sexuality in the Portuguese-Speaking World.* Minneapolis: University of Minnesota Press, 2002.

Ribeiro, Darcy. *The Brazilian People: The Formation and Meaning of Brazil.* Trans. Gregory Rabassa. Gainesville: University Press of Florida, 2000.

Sweet, James. *Recreating Africa: Culture, Kinship, and Religion in the African-Portuguese World, 1441-1770.* Chapel Hill: University of North Carolina Press, 2003.

ROSS WILKINSON

LUTZ, BERTHA MARIA JULIA (1894–1976). Bertha Maria Julia Lutz (*b.* 2 August 1894; *d.* 16 September, 1976), the principal leader of the Brazilian woman's suffrage movement. Bertha Lutz was born in São Paulo to a Swiss-Brazilian father, Adolfo Lutz, a pioneer in the practice of tropical medicine in Brazil, and an English mother, Amy Fowler, a former volunteer nurse who cared for lepers in Hawaii. Lutz was educated first in Brazil and then in Europe, receiving her licencié ès sciences from the Sorbonne in 1918. Later, in 1933, she earned a degree from the Faculty of Law in Rio de Janeiro.

Following seven years of study in Europe, Lutz returned to Brazil and helped to initiate a formal woman suffrage movement. Unlike many of her contemporaries, she felt that this was the time to organize, rather than just inform and educate, women. In 1920 she founded her own women's rights organization. Two years later, immediately after Lutz's return from the United States, where she had served as Brazil's official delegate to the first Pan American Conference of Women, this small local group was transformed into the Brazilian Federation for Feminine Progress (Federação Brasileira pelo Progresso Feminino—FBPF), affiliated with the International Woman's Suffrage Alliance. Lutz served as its president from 1922 to 1942. The main suffrage organization in Brazil, the FBPF led the campaign for the vote, because no other suffrage association attained a similar size, geographic range, or network of personal contacts. In 1932, it achieved its major goal when a new civil code enfranchised women under the same conditions as men (illiterates of both sexes were still denied the vote).

More than other leaders of the FBPF, Lutz linked women's economic emancipation with their political and social emancipation. She repeatedly warned women that the franchise was not an end in itself, and she understood that without access to education and jobs, political rights would remain mere abstractions. In print and in public, she spoke out against the exploitation of the working class, and particularly of its lower-class women. But even though the professional women leading the FBPF tackled problems of concern to the working class, such as salaries, shorter working hours, working conditions, and maternity leaves, interclass linkages were not very strong.

Following the promulgation of the 1932 civil code that enfranchised women, Bertha Lutz served on the committee that drafted a new constitution for Brazil. The Constitution of 1934 confirmed the women's 1932 victory by specifically guaranteeing women the vote and equal political rights with men. Lutz ran twice for Congress; elected as an alternate deputy, she entered the Chamber of Deputies late in 1936 to fill the vacancy created by the death of the incumbent. During her year in Congress, she helped create the Commission on the Code for Women, which she headed. Through the commission, she pushed vigorously for enactment of a statute on women, a comprehensive law concerning women's legal status and social rights. But the establishment of the dictatorial Estado Nôvo in 1937 ended electoral politics and women's participation in them until 1945.

Although Lutz, like the FBPF, never regained a preeminent position as a voice for Brazilian women, she continued to work for women's rights in Brazil while also pursuing her own scientific work in botany and herpetology. In 1973 she published a major work on Brazilian species of hyla. She also participated in international women's rights activities, attending numerous women's conferences abroad, including the International Women's Year conference held in Mexico City in 1975, a year before her death at the age of eighty-two.

See also **Brazil, Constitutions; Feminism and Feminist Organizations; Women.**

BIBLIOGRAPHY

June E. Hahner, *Emancipating the Female Sex: The Struggle for Women's Rights in Brazil, 1850–1940* (1990).

Additional Bibliography

Besse, Susan K. *Restructuring Patriarchy: The Modernization of Gender Inequality, 1914–1940.* Chapel Hill: University of North Carolina Press, 1996.

Castellanos, Gabriela, and Simone Accorsi, eds. *Género y sexualidad en Colombia y en Brasil.* Cali: Editorial La Manzana de la Discordia, 2002.

Souza, Lia Gomes Pinto de. "Para ler Bertha Lutz." *Cadernos Pagu* 24 (Jan.–June 2005): 315–325.

JUNE E. HAHNER

LUTZENBERGER, JOSÉ (1928–2002). José Antônio Lutzenberger, born December 17, 1928, was a Brazilian ecologist. Lutzenberger served as Brazil's first secretary of the environment (1990–1992), a cabinet-level post created by President Fernando Collor de Mello in part to address growing international criticism of Brazil's Amazon policy as articulated during predecessor José Sarney's presidency. Lutzenberger, an agronomist with a special interest in the Amazon region and a native of Rio Grande do Sul, had long been a critic of government development policies. He accepted the cabinet post only after Collor de Mello guaranteed that his administration would halt expansion of the controversial BR-364 highway across the southern Amazon, respect the rights of the indigenous peoples of the Amazon, and end all economic incentives to environmentally destructive development projects. Lutzenberger also supported debt-for-nature swaps, unlike the Sarney administration.

Lutzenberger was known for making bombastic gloom-and-doom pronouncements and was often criticized for his adherence to the scientifically unproven "Gaia" theory, which held that the Earth is a closed physiological system capable of altering the planet's climate at will. In late 1991, the Brazilian Chamber of Deputies, along with conservative politicians and the military, complained that Lutzenberger was "internationalizing" the Amazon to the point of compromising Brazilian national sovereignty and hence called for his resignation. Color de Mello replaced him in March 1992.

Lutzenberger enjoyed an international reputation, initially based on his active opposition to the use of pesticides. In 1971 he was a founder of the Association for the Protection of the Natural Environment of Rio Grande do Sul (Associação Gaúcha de Proteção Ambiente Natural—AGAPAN), the first ecological entity organized in Brazil. He was the 1988 recipient of the Swedish government's Right Livelihood Award, the environmental equivalent of the Nobel Prize. Upon his death on May 14, 2002, he was buried in keeping with his wishes close to a tree farm in the Pantano Grande in Rio Grande do Sul state.

See also **Environmental Movements.**

BIBLIOGRAPHY

"Um verde do outro lado," in *Veja* 23 (7 March 1990): 35; "New President Appoints Ecologist to Head Environmental Secretariat," in *International Environment Reporter: Current Report* 13 (11 April 1990): 152–153.

Nira Broner Worcman, "Brazil's Thriving Environmental Movement," in *Technology Review* 93 (October 1990): 42–51.

Additional Bibliography

Kumar, Satish. *Visionaries: The 20th Century's 100 Most Important Inspirational Leaders.* White River Junction, VT: Chelsea Green, 2007.

Place, Susan E., ed. *Tropical Rainforests: Latin American Nature and Society in Transition*, revised and updated edition. Wilmington, DE: Scholarly Resources, 2001.

LAURA JARNAGIN

LUZ Y CABALLERO, JOSÉ DE LA

(1800–1862). José de la Luz y Caballero (*b.* 11 July 1800; *d.* 22 June 1862), Cuban philosopher and educator. Luz y Cabellero was one of the three most influential Cuban thinkers of the nineteenth century, the other two being Father Félix Varela y Morales and José Antonio Saco. A native of Havana, he initially studied for the priesthood but ended up a lawyer, although he never practiced law. Instead, he traveled extensively in Europe and the United States, becoming acquainted with most of the important writers of his time. He was influenced by the work of Francis Bacon, Étienne Bonnot de Condillac, and René Descartes, and came to embrace John Locke's nominalism, the denial that abstract entities or universal principles have real existence.

In Cuba, Luz y Caballero was a respected and popular teacher at the San Carlos Seminary (Cuba's most prominent institution of higher learning at the time) and later at the Colegio El Salvador, which he founded. His ideas and his teaching methods involved him in ardent polemics that provoked the hostility of the Spanish authorities, especially when he was accused of participating in the Conspiracy of la Escalera (1844), an attempted slave revolt. Luz y Caballero opposed violence, however, and held that Cuba was not prepared for self-government. His approach to the problem of slavery was cautious; he believed it should end gradually, by means of the suppression of the slave trade. Despite his timidity, however, he represented a progressive tendency in Cuban society; through his lectures and writings he helped to develop strong nationalistic feelings in a whole generation of Cubans. Luz y Caballero died in Havana.

See also **Slave Trade.**

BIBLIOGRAPHY

Manuel Sanguily y Garrite, *José de la Luz y Caballero* (1926). See also Medardo Vitier, *Las ideas en Cuba* (1969), vol. 2.

Additional Bibliography

Monal, Isabel, and Olivia Miranda Francisco. *Pensamiento cubano, siglo XIX*. La Habana: Editorial de Ciencias Sociales, 2002.

JOSÉ M. HERNÁNDEZ

LWA. *Lwa* (*loas*) are spiritual beings of the Haitian religion vodou (voodoo), regarded as "different aspects of one cosmic Principle" (Desmangles, p. 98). *Lwa* are thought to be present in nature (trees, rivers, mountains, etc.). They are connected to human activities (healing, fighting, farming) and aspects of nature (thunder, rain, storm). *Lwa* are believed to have the power to influence human destiny. They can materialize in a human body by "possessing" or "mounting" people (*monte chwal*). "Serving the *lwa*" is the centripetal religious practice of vodou. The relationship between *lwa* and human beings is based on the concept of reciprocity. Human beings must honor them in order to avoid punishment and misfortune. Apart from Haiti and the Haitian diaspora, *lwa* are also worshiped in parts of the United States (e.g., Louisiana). In West Africa (in particular, Benin) they are called "vodun" (*vodu*).

ETYMOLOGY AND CATEGORIZATION

The term *lwa* is translated as "spirits," "deities," or "gods," but no term corresponds to the whole notion. They are also called in Kreyol *mistè* (mysterie), *espri* (spirit), *anj* (angel) or, rarely, *dye* (god). According to most scholars the term *lwa* derives from a Fon language, though some (e.g., Desmangles) affiliate *lwa* with the French word *loi* (law); neither derivation, however, can be verified.

Lwa show similarities with orishas (*orixás*), the principle divine beings of the Cuban religion Regla de Ocha (Santería) and the Brazilian religion Candomblé, who are also worshiped in the Orisha religion in Trinidad and Tobago. The analogy developed partly because of a common West African origin and partly because of a similar "translation" process during slavery. While Vodou is based mainly on Ewe and Fon elements with some Yoruba influences, Regla de Ocha and Candomblé are based mainly on Yoruba traditions with various other influences. The translatability of Yoruba religious concepts into Ewe and Fon and vice versa facilitated the process of fusion and syncretism (Kubik, p. 30).

Most *lwa* have derived from African deities, but some others from nature spirits or even from human beings (after death), in particular, Maroons, former enslaved people who successfully fled into freedom. *Lwa* are represented as Catholic saints with whom they have in common the function as intermediary between God (*Bondye*) and human beings. The adaptation of Catholic iconography was a form a resistance against oppression, an active possession of the images by African spirits and ancestors. Joan Dayan argues that the forced conversion "might well have goaded the amorphous Dahomean nature spirits into the powerful, anthropomorphized embodiments we now call lwa" (p. 244). Despite the iconography, *lwa* and saints are separate beings of two different systems.

There exists an infinite number of *lwa*. They are categorized in families (*nanchons*), each with its own characteristics (rites, music, songs, dances, offerings, and other attributes). Of the seventeen *nanchons*, Rada, Kongo, and Petro are the most significant. Sometimes the *nanchons* are sorted into just two branches, Rada and Petro. Some scholars interpret the *nanchons* with reference to ethnic origins. Rada derives from Arada, the name of a kingdom in Dahomey, West Africa, during the colonial time. These *lwa* are also called *lwa-Ginen* or the good spirits. Nago, which comprise Yoruba spirits, are sometimes seen as part of Rada. *Lwa* of the Kongo family are identified with the West African Bakongo region. Petro are Creole *lwa*, seen sometimes as derived from Dom Pedro, a mythical leader of a Maroon rebellion in the late eighteenth century (Desmangles). While Rada are characterized as good and harmonious, Petro are seen as aggressive, envious, and bitter. They played a crucial role in the slave uprisings of 1791 and the establishment of Haiti in 1804.

Despite this classification it is not possible to bifurcate them dualistically. Every *lwa* has multiple aspects; even both genders are united in every *lwa*. Many Rada *lwa* have Kongo or Petro counterparts that express different aspects of their identity. According to Alfred Métraux it is not important to which *nanchon* a *lwa* belongs because the *nanchon* signifies the various characteristics that are shared by all *lwa* (p. 77).

PANTHEON OF *LWA*

Each *lwa* has a specific field of responsibility and a variety of traits (speech pattern, body movements, character, preferences in food and clothes), some ambivalent.

Legba opens the gates and guards the crossroads. He is dressed in red and is honored with Rada rites. He is represented as Saint Peter (as guardian of the heaven), as Saint Lazarus (as an old man leaning on a crutch) or as Saint Anthony. In Cuba and Brazil, Legba parallels Eshú (Exu).

Dambala, Legba's opponent, also belongs to the Rada family though he appears in other rites too. His color is white and he is identified by snakelike movements. Dambala is regarded as good and wise. His Catholic image is Saint Patrick. In Rada he characterizes the healing power of the wise old men, while in Petro he demonstrates his violent and aggressive side. His female aspect is called Ayida, who is sometimes called Dambala's consort.

Ogou (Ogun in Cuba, Ogum in Brazil) derives from a Yoruba deity, in the Nago *nanchon*. He is a blacksmith and warrior. His color is red. Saint James or Saint Joseph is his Catholic image.

Erzulie is the only major female *lwa*, part of the Rada *nanchon*. Her colors are blue and pink. She does not parallel a Yoruba deity though she is associated with love, beauty, and grace similar to Oshún in Cuba and Brazil. Erzili Freda is a mother figure similar to Yemaja, whereas the dagger-wielding Erzili Dantò, who belongs to the Petro family, carries similarity to Oya/Yansa.

Baron Samdi is the superior of the **Gédés**, the *lwa* of the dead in Haiti, who according to legend represent a West African ethnic group that was conquered by the royal family of Abomey and sold to slave traders. Baron Samdi is also called Baron Cimetière (Baron of Cemetery) or Baron La Croix (Baron of the Cross). He has no Catholic parallel. Often portrayed wearing black clothes and a top hat, he is honored in both Rada and Petro rites. In material form he behaves obscenely and provocatively.

The twins **Marassa** (parallels Ibeji in Brazil and Cuba) are identified with the Catholic saints Cosmas and Damian. They appear in all rites. Often portrayed as children, they are very powerful because of their dual existence.

Other important *lwa* are **Azaka, Agwe,** and **Simbi.**

See also **African-Latin American Religions: Brazil; Candomblé; Haiti; Orixás; Santería; Vodun, Voodoo, Vaudun.**

BIBLIOGRAPHY

Barnes, Sandra T., ed. *Africa's Ogun: Old World and New.* 2nd exp. ed. Bloomington and Indianapolis: Indiana University Press, 1997.

Bellegarde-Smith, Patrick, ed. *Fragments of Bone: Neo-African Religions in a New World.* Urbana and Chicago: University of Illinois Press, 2005.

Blier, Suzanne P. *African Vodun: Art, Psychology, and Power.* Chicago and London: University of Chicago Press, 1995.

Cosentino, Donald J., ed. *Sacred Arts of Haitian Vodou.* Los Angeles: UCLA Fowler Museum of Cultural History, 1995.

Dayan, Joan. *Haiti, History, and the Gods.* Berkeley: University of California Press, 1995.

Deren, Maya. *Divine Horsemen: The Living Gods of Haiti.* London and New York: Thames and Hudson, 1953; New Paltz, NY: McPherson, 1983.

Desmangles, Leslie. *The Faces of the Gods: Vodou and Roman Catholicism in Haiti.* Chapel Hill: University of North Carolina Press, 1992.

Hurbon, Laënnec. *Voodoo: Search for the Spirit.* Translated by Lory Frankel. New York and London: Harry N. Abrams, 1995.

Hurbon, Laënnec. *Religions et lien social: L'église et l'état moderne en Haïti.* Paris: Cerf, 2004.

Kubik, Gerhard. "West African and African-American Concepts of Vodu and Òrìṣà." In *Ay BōBō: African-Caribbean Religions.* Part 2: *Voodoo*, edited by Manfred Kremser, 17–34. Vienna: WUV-Universitätsverlag, 1996.

Métraux, Alfred. *Le vaudou haïtien* [1958]. Paris: Gallimard, 1998.

BETTINA E. SCHMIDT

LYNCH, BENITO (1880–1951). Benito Lynch (*b.* 25 July 1880; *d.* 23 December 1951), Argentine journalist and writer. Lynch came from an old, distinguished family of *estancieros* (ranchers) and spent his childhood on an *estancia* in Buenos Aires Province. In 1890 he settled in La Plata, where he later worked for the conservative newspaper *El Día*. From 1904 to 1941 he devoted himself to writing fiction. His novels *Los caranchos de la Florida* (1916; *The Vultures of La Florida*) and *El inglés de los güesos* (1924; *The English Boneman*), both later adapted for stage and film, made him one of the most prominent Hispanic novelists. However, to preserve his privacy, Lynch shunned the trappings of success, refusing royalties and academic honors. A member of the generation presided over by Leopoldo Lugones and Ricardo Rojas, Lynch maintained his reclusiveness, his keen loyalty to his social class, his conservatism, and his divorce from contemporary political and literary life even when confronted with the innovative Martín Fierro group. His narratives almost exclusively concern life on the *estancias* of Buenos Aires Province around the beginning of the twentieth century, contrasting city life with the sedentary, stable life of the peasantry. An admirer of Zola, his naturalism contrasts with a sentimental vision of love and friendship, despite his basic distrust of the human race. Lynch's novels are considered models of linguistic frugality and well-adjusted plots.

See also **Literature: Spanish America.**

BIBLIOGRAPHY

Gerald L. Head, "Characterization in the Works of Benito Lynch" (Ph.D. diss., University of California, Los Angeles, 1964).

"La muerte del paisano de Benito Lynch," in *Romance Notes* 12 (1970): 68–73, and "El extranjero en las abras de Benito Lynch," in *Hispania* 54 (1971): 91–97.

Elba Torres De Peralta, "Actitud frente a la vida de los personajes en *El inglés de los güesos* de Benito Lynch," in *Explicación de textos literarios* 5 (1976): 13–22.

David William Foster, "Benito Lynch," in *Latin American Writers,* edited by Carlos A. Solé and Maria Isabel Abreu, vol. 2 (1989), pp. 559–563.

Additional Bibliography

French, Jennifer. *Nature, Neo-Colonialism, and the Spanish American Regional Writers.* Hanover, NH: Dartmouth College Press, 2005.

ANGELA B. DELLEPIANE

LYNCH, ELISA ALICIA (1835–1886). Elisa Alicia Lynch (*b.* June 1835; *d.* 27 July 1886), Irish mistress of Paraguayan dictator Francisco Solano López.

Born into impoverished circumstances, Lynch left Ireland at age fifteen when she married Xavier Quatrefages, a French military surgeon. Theirs was evidently a loveless marriage, and within a few years Lynch was on her own in Paris. In 1853, after having lived with several lovers, she met Solano López, son of the Paraguayan president Carlos Antonio López, who was then on an official tour of Europe.

Unable to marry López because of her then undocumented marital status, Lynch nonetheless accompanied him back to Paraguay. She was less than well received by the Paraguayan elites, who regarded her in a scandalous light. López installed her in a sumptuous residence in Asunción, however, and there she attempted to re-create in Paraguay a salon that included musicians, literary figures, and interesting foreign visitors. She introduced the piano in Paraguay, and popularized Parisian fashions. She had five children with López. Upon his accession to the presidency in 1862, Lynch became de facto first lady.

The outbreak of the War of the Triple Alliance in 1864 found Lynch at the front, together with her consort. Detractors later claimed that she was responsible for many of López's excesses, particularly the mass executions at San Fernando in 1868. Two years later, after a long and sanguinary retreat, López was killed in the northeastern region of Cerro Corá. Lynch witnessed his death, as she did that of their firstborn son, an army colonel.

At the end of the war, the Brazilian authorities deported Lynch, but after a few years she returned to Asunción to try to lay claim to lands that had been transferred to her name during the fighting. These legal efforts failed and she returned to Paris, where she died penniless in 1886. In the 1960s, the Stroessner government repatriated her remains.

See also **López, Francisco Solano; War of the Triple Alliance.**

BIBLIOGRAPHY

Fernando Baptista, *Madame Lynch: Mujer de mundo y de guerra* (1987).

William E. Barrett, *Woman on Horseback: The Biography of Francisco López and Eliza Lynch* (1938).

Gilbert Phelps, *Tragedy of Paraguay* (1975) *passim;* Elisa A. Lynch, *Exposición y protesta* (1987).

Additional Bibliography

Cawthorne, Nigel. *The Empress of South America.* London: Heinemann, 2003.

Rees, Siân. *The Shadows of Elisa Lynch: How a Nineteenth-Century Irish Courtesan Became the Most Powerful Woman in Paraguay.* London: Review, 2003.

MARTA FERNÁNDEZ WHIGHAM

LYNCH, MARTA (1925–1985). Marta Lynch (*b.* 8 March 1925; *d.* 8 October 1985), Argentine writer. Born in Buenos Aires, Lynch was the daughter of an important political figure and the wife of a powerful corporate director. She is notable for making use of the circumstances of her socioeconomic privilege to portray a complex network of cultural oppressions in Argentina, with special reference to the victimization of middle-class women whose lives project a facade of passive comfort. *La señora Ordóñez* (1967) may be the first Argentine treatment of a woman's explicit sexual discontent, while *Al vencedor* (1965) centers on class conflict and its humiliations in Argentina during the so-called Argentine Revolution that followed the Peronist period. But Lynch's best writing focuses on the devastating social and personal price paid by Argentines for the Dirty War of the late 1970s, especially in the short stories of *Los dedos de la mano* (1976), *La penúltima versión de la Colorada Villanueva* (1978), and *Informe bajo llave* (1983). With her death, Lynch joined a line of notable Argentine women authors who have committed suicide.

See also **Argentina: The Twentieth Century; Literature: Spanish America; Women.**

BIBLIOGRAPHY

Diane S. Birkemoe, "The Virile Voice of Marta Lynch," in *Revista de Estudios Hispánicos* 16, no. 2 (1982): 191–211.

David William Foster, "Raping Argentina: Marta Lynch's *Informe bajo llave,*" in *Centennial Review* 3, no. 3 (1991): 663–680.

Naomi Lindstrom, *Women's Voice in Latin American Literature* (1989), pp. 73–95.

Eliana Moya Raggio, "Conversación con Marta Lynch," in *Letras Femeninas* 14, no. 1–2 (1988): 104–111.

Martha Paley De Francescato, "Marta Lynch," in *Hispamérica* 4, no. 10 (1975): 33–44.

Birgitta Vance, "Marta Lynch," in *Spanish American Women Writers: A Bio-Bibliographical Source Book* (1990), pp. 292–302.

Additional Bibliography

Mucci, Cristina. *La señora Lynch: Biografía de una escritora controvertida.* Buenos Aires: Grupo Editorial Norma, 2000.

DAVID WILLIAM FOSTER

MACAS, LUIS (1950–). A Quichua (Saraguro) intellectual and political leader, Luis Macas is perhaps the most important contemporary indigenous political figure in Ecuador. Born in the southern province of Loja, Macas has been a social movement leader, parliamentarian, minister of agriculture, university president, and candidate for president. As founder and president (1990–1996, 2005–) of the Confederacion de Nacionalidades Indígenas del Ecuador (Confederation of Indigenous Nationalities of Ecuador, CONAIE), Macas has been at the forefront of powerful mobilizations, beginning with the historic 1990 *levantamiento* (uprising). He has also founded and led indigenous academic institutions including the Instituto Científico de Culturas Indígenas (Scientific Institute of Indigenous Cultures, ICCI) and the Amawtay Wasi Intercultural University of Indigenous Nationalities and Peoples.

In 2005 Macas was once again elected to the presidency of CONAIE to help the organization rebuild after a bitter and short-lived experience of co-government with the administration of Lucio Gutiérrez (2002–2005). In 2006 he was chosen to be the presidential candidate of the Pachacutik party.

See also **Confederación de Nacionalidades Indígenas del Ecuador (CONAIE); Gutiérrez Borbúa, Lucio; Indigenous Organizations; Movimiento de Unidida Plurinacional Pachacutik (MUPP); Movimiento Indígena Pachacutik.**

BIBLIOGRAPHY

Confederacion de Nacionalidades Indígenas del Ecuador. Available from http://www.conaie.org.

Instituto Científico de Culturas Indígenas (Institute for Science and Indigenous Cultures). Available from http://icci.nativeweb.org/english.html.

Macas, Luis. *El levantamiento indígena visto por sus protagonistas.* Quito: ICCI, Amauta Runacunapac Yachay, 1991.

Macas, Luis, Linda Belote, and Jim Belote. "Indigenous Destiny in Indigenous Hands." In *Millennial Ecuador: Critical Essays on Cultural Transformations and Social Dynamics*, ed. Norman E. Whitten Jr. Iowa City: University of Iowa Press, 2003.

Selverston-Scher, Melina. *Ethnopolitics in Ecuador: Indigenous Rights and the Strengthening of Democracy.* Coral Gables, FL: North-South Center Press at the University of Miami, 2001.

José Antonio Lucero

MACCIÓ, RÓMULO (1931–). Rómulo Macció (*b.* 24 March 1931), Argentine artist. Born in Buenos Aires, Macció was trained as a graphic designer and worked as an illustrator in advertising agencies. He took up painting in 1956, joining the New Figuration group in 1961. His early work consisted of paintings of anthropomorphic fragments, halfway between abstraction and figuration. After 1964 he began to paint distorted figures in expressionistic and surrealistic styles. He consciously sought to generate visual and thematic contradictions, such as the overlapping of planar and volumetric structures and the coexistence of two different subjects in the same painting. In 1967 he won the International Di Tella Prize.

A rational and orderly composition characterized his paintings of the mid-1970s, although surreal traits remained present in melancholic portraits of lonely figures, often self-portraits (*Self-Portrait with Easel,* 1976; *At Seven O'Clock in Highbury Place,* 1976). In the late 1970s, he painted human figures as stylized silhouettes with spiritual and mystical connotations (*Amalfi,* 1980; *Adriatic,* 1979). Macció's tendency to expressionism became more evident in the 1980s (*Castel Sant' Angelo,* 1980). His most recent paintings are views from his atelier and subjects with some classical mythological overtones. He participated in the Venice Biennale in 1988 and exhibited in Paris, Milan, and Rome in 1991. In 1996, he had an exhibition at Mexico City's Museo Cuevas. He also exhibited twice in Buenos Aires in the late 1990s: at the Fundación PROA in 1997, and the Centro Cultural Recoleta in 1999. In March 2007, he had a major exhibition at Mexico City's Museo Nacional de Bellas Artes.

See also **Art: The Twentieth Century.**

BIBLIOGRAPHY

Gilbert Chase, *Contemporary Art in Latin America* (1970), pp. 152–153.

Rómulo Macció, *Rómulo Macció: Selected Paintings, 1963–1980,* translated by Kenneth Parkin (1980).

Félix Angel, "The Latin American Presence," in *The Latin American Spirit: Art and Artists in the United States, 1920–1970,* by Luis R. Cancel et al. (1988), p. 259.

Miguel Briante et al., *Nueva Figuración: 1961–1991* (1991); p. 59.

Additional Bibliography

Grieder, Terence. "Argentina's New Figurative Art." *Art Journal*: 24 (Autumn 1964): 2-6.

Solar, Xu, et al. *Cuatro aspectos de la pintura argentina contemporánea.* Buenos Aires, Argentina: Fondo Nacional de las Artes, 1997.

MARTA GARSD

MACEDO, JOAQUIM MANUEL DE

(1820–1882). Joaquim Manuel de Macedo (*b.* 24 June 1820; *d.* 11 April 1882), Brazilian novelist. Joaquim Manuel de Macedo was not the first Brazilian to publish novels, but he was the great popularizer of the genre in the nation's literature. His two earliest novels, *A moreninha* (1844) and *O moco loiro* (1845), achieved enormous popularity; indeed, *A moreninha* is still widely read and enjoyed in Brazil, particularly by adolescent readers. Macedo's sentimental tales of adventure and romance never challenged established social norms; after a good many implausible plot devices, his aristocratic young heros and heroines always manage to find precisely the mates society and family would have chosen for them. The primary value of his texts is their detailed documentation of upper-class mores in Imperial Rio de Janeiro. (Macedo was tutor to the children of Princess Isabel.) Macedo continued to publish fiction after *O moco loiro,* but his skills as a novelist did not develop and his reputation as a writer was increasingly overshadowed by that of José de Alencar. The most interesting of Macedo's later works, none of which attracted the audience his earliest novels had enjoyed, is *As vítimas-algozes* (1869), a collection of three anti-slavery novellas.

See also **Literature: Brazil.**

BIBLIOGRAPHY

Antônio Cândido, "O honrado e facundo Joaquim Manuel de Macedo," in *Formação da Literatura Brasileira,* 5th ed. (1975), vol. 2, pp. 136–145.

José Antônio Pereira Ribeiro, *O universo romântico de Joaquim Manoel de Macedo* (1987).

Additional Bibliography

Mattos, Selma Rinaldi de. *O Brasil em lições: A história como disciplina escolar em Joaquim Manuel de Macedo.* Rio de Janeiro: Access Editora, 2000.

Serra, Tania Rebelo Costa. *Joaquim Manuel de Macedo, ou, Os Dois Macedos: A luneta mágica do II Reinado.* Brasília: Editora UnB, 2004.

DAVID T. HABERLY

MACEHUALLI.

Macehualli (pl. *macehualtin*), a Nahua social category taken into Spanish as *macehual* (pl. *macehuales*), that usually refers to an indigenous commoner. It also had the occasional meaning of "vassal," reflecting the political dimension of a commoner's life, and, when pluralized, "the people." Forming the majority of the population of central Mexico in pre-Hispanic and colonial times, *macehualtin* farmed, fished, and produced utilitarian goods. As members of *calpulli* and *altepetl* (neighborhoods, towns, and regional states), they had usufruct rights to land. With those rights came the responsibilities of tribute and labor drafts owed to local authorities. Over time, the concepts of *macehualli* and *indio* merged, reflecting changes in colonial society.

See also **Caste and Class Structure in Colonial Spanish America; Nahuas.**

BIBLIOGRAPHY

Jacques Soustelle, *Daily Life of the Aztecs on the Eve of the Spanish Conquest* (1961).

Frances F. Berdan, *The Aztecs of Central Mexico* (1982).

James Lockhart, *The Nahuas After the Conquest* (1992), pp. 95–96, 114–115.

Additional Bibliography

Horn, Rebecca. *Postconquest Coyoacan: Nahua-Spanish Relations in Central Mexico, 1519-1650.* Stanford, Calif.: Stanford University Press, 1997.

Pastrana Flores, Gabriel Miguel. *Historias de la Conquista: Aspectos de la historiografía de tradición náhuatl.* México, D.F.: Universidad Nacional Autónoma de México, 2004.

Stephanie Wood

MACEIÓ. Maceió (formerly Macayo), capital of the state of Alagoas, Brazil, with a population of about 922,463 (2005 est.). Founded in 1815 when a small settlement received official recognition, Maceió became the state capital in 1839. On the Atlantic Coast approximately 120 miles south of Recife, the city's port deals mainly in sugar, cotton, and rum. The primarily industrial economy of Maceió encompasses sugar refineries, textile mills, distilleries, chemical factories, and steel, iron, and zinc foundries. The city is famous for a lighthouse built on an eminence in a residential area about a half mile from the ocean, and local beaches are considered among the best in Brazil.

See also **Brazil, Geography.**

BIBLIOGRAPHY

Additional Bibliography

Albuquerque, Maria de Fátima M de. *O corpo do desejo: Mulheres & imagem corporal no espaço urbano de Maceió.* Maceió: EDUFAL, 2002.

Vieira, Maria do Carmo. *Daqui só saio pó: Conflitos urbanos e mobilização popular: a Salgema e o Pontal da Barra.* Maceió: EDUFAL, 1997.

Cara Shelly

MAC ENTYRE, EDUARDO (1929–). Eduardo Mac Entyre (*b.* 20 February 1929), Argentine artist. A self-taught painter, Mac Entyre was born in Buenos Aires, where he still lives.

In 1959 Mac Entyre, with Ignacio Pirovano and Miguel Angel Vidal, founded a movement called Generative Art, which they defined as "engendering a series of optical sequences which are produced by the evolving of a given form." Mac Entyre uses geometrically precise sequences of exquisitely colored lines that give the canvas a magical effect of depth and appear to generate their own movement as they glide or whirl through space. In liberating his paintings from a static state, he achieved an important goal of twentieth-century avant-garde artists.

A pillar of geometric art in Argentina, Mac Entyre still adheres to the same principles while creating a tremendous variety of forms of his poetic geometry. In 1986 the Organization of American States and the Museum of Modern Art of Latin America honored Mac Entyre for his contribution to the development of the modern art of the Americas. In 1992, he won the first prize at the first annual Bienal de pintura espíritu de Grécia, and in 1996 he won first prize in the Argentinian Maria Calderón de la Barca competition. In 2001, the Vatican Academy of Sciences awarded him the Cristo de Luz prize. His son Christian Mac Entyre is also a well-known artist.

See also **Art: The Twentieth Century.**

BIBLIOGRAPHY

Samuel Paz, "Los diez Últimos años de pintura y escultura argentina, 1950–1960," in *150 años de arte argentino* (Buenos Aires, 1961).

Rafael F. Squirru, *Eduardo Mac Entyre* (1981); *Selections from the Permanent Collection of the Museum of Modern Art of Latin America* (Washington, D.C., 1985); *Mac Entyre* (Buenos Aires, 1993).

Additional Bibliography

Heine, Ernesto. *Antonio Berni, Virginia Jones, Eduardo Mac Entyre, Francisco Matto, Manuel Pailos, y Nelson Ramos.* Montevideo, Uruguay: s.n., 1986.

Mac Entyre, Eduardo. *Eduardo Mac Entyre: Arte negro africano: Colección Campomar.* Buenos Aires, Argentina: Galería Arroyo, 2001.

IDA ELY RUBIN

MACEO, ANTONIO (1845–1896). Antonio Maceo (*b.* 14 June 1845; *d.* 7 December 1896), second in command of Cuba's independence army. Maceo was one of the greatest guerrilla fighters of the nineteenth century and certainly the most daring soldier ever born on Cuban soil. Cubans familiarly refer to him as the Titan of Bronze, as he was dubbed by an admiring speaker at a patriotic rally in New York City in 1895.

Maceo was the son of a Venezuelan mulatto émigré and a free Cuban black, Mariana Grajales, the mother of thirteen children, all of whom swore at her behest to free their country from Spanish domination or die in the attempt. When Cuba's Ten Years' War began in 1868, Maceo enlisted in the rebel army as a private; five years later he achieved the rank of general. From the outset he showed a superior ability to outsmart and outmaneuver the Spanish commanders and occasionally inflicted heavy losses on them. He also displayed extraordinary leadership and determination. Throughout his military career, which spanned the Ten Years' War and the 1895–1898 war, it is estimated that he fought in more than 900 actions. Since he never sought the safety of the rear guard, he sustained twenty-six wounds. Perhaps his greatest military feat was to lead an invasion of western Cuba in 1895–1896, a brilliant operation during which he covered more than a thousand miles in 92 days while engaging the Spanish army in 27 battles or skirmishes and capturing more than 2,000 rifles and 80,000 rounds of ammunition. When Maceo was killed, in a scuffle of little consequence, he had risen to the rank of second in command of the Cuban liberating army.

Maceo's place in Cuban history is as a symbol of tenacity and unwavering patriotism. On 11 February 1878 most of the generals of the Cuban liberating army realized that it would be impossible to defeat the Spanish forces and thus accepted the Pact of Zanjón to end the Ten Years' War. At this juncture Maceo refused to capitulate. He held a historic meeting, known as the Protest of Baraguá, with Spanish marshal Arsenio Martínez Campos, at which he demanded independence for Cuba and the total abolition of slavery. When Martínez Campos rejected these conditions, Maceo resumed fighting. Since the situation of the liberators was truly hopeless, Maceo eventually had to desist and ultimately leave Cuba. But his gesture remained a source of inspiration for future combatants and earned him the acclaim of Cubans and foreigners alike. The American and Foreign Anti-Slavery Society was among the groups praising him warmly for his stand on slavery.

Maceo identified closely with the predicament of the men and women of his race. Although he himself suffered the attacks of racists within the Cuban liberating army, who accused him of attempting to create a black republic in Cuba, his defense of the rights of blacks was based on the theoretical notion of the rights of men rather than any ethnic affinity. "The revolution has no color" was his indignant rejoinder to his accusers. He trusted that "Now, tomorrow, and always there shall exist in Cuba men who will do justice to the people of my race." For this reason, he wrote, "I enjoin my own people not to ask for anything on the basis of the color of their skin."

This confidence in the ability of Cubans was probably the key to Maceo's attitude toward the United States. He favored the recognition of Cuban belligerency by the powerful republic to the north, but he did not think that American intervention was needed to defeat Spain. He believed that Cubans should depend on their own efforts, adding that it was better to rise or fall without help than to contract debts of gratitude with a neighbor as powerful as the United States. He wrote to the *New York World:* "I should not want our neighbor to shed their blood for our cause. We can do that for ourselves if, under the common law, we can get the necessary elements to overthrow the corrupted power of Spain in Cuba." And on another occasion he said: "Do you really want to cut the war down? Bring Cuba 25,000 to 35,000 rifles and a million bullets.... We Cubans do not need any other help."

See also **Cuba, War of Independence.**

BIBLIOGRAPHY

José Luciano Franco, *Maceo, apuntes para una historia de su vida,* 3 vols. (1975).

José Miró Argenter, *Crónicas de la guerra, las campañas de invasión y de occidente, 1895–1896,* 3 vols. (1945).

Philip S. Foner, *Antonio Maceo: The "Bronze Titan" of Cuba's Struggle for Independence* (1977).

Additional Bibliography

Escalona Chádez, Israel. *José Martí y Antonio Maceo: La pelea por la libertad.* Santiago de Cuba, Cuba: Editorial Oriente, 2004.

Tone, John Lawrence. *War and Genocide in Cuba, 1895–1898.* Chapel Hill: University of North Carolina Press, 2006.

Vargas, Armando. *Idearium Maceísta: Junto con hazañas del general Antonio Maceo y sus mambises en Costa Rica, 1891–1895.* San José, Costa Rica: Editorial Juricentro, 2001.

José M. Hernández

MACGREGOR, GREGOR (1786–1845).

Gregor MacGregor (*b.* 1786; *d.* 4 December 1845), British soldier of fortune and speculator in colonization. MacGregor was often regarded as either a visionary idealist or an unscrupulous promoter. A young man of twenty-five with some experience in the British army, this flamboyant Scottish army captain arrived in Venezuela in 1811 to support the cause of independence. MacGregor fought with distinction under Francisco de Miranda and Simón Bolívar and was decorated. During his years with the insurgents he cruised the Caribbean from Florida to Venezuela. At some point he saw his fortune interwoven with the lush tropical environment he had adopted.

Sailing for New Granada in 1819, MacGregor occupied the island of San Andrés off the Nicaragua coast and later landed on the desolate Mosquito Coast, where an assortment of European adventurers had long maintained close ties with the Indians. The imaginative MacGregor concocted a visionary scheme to establish an overseas Acadia on the Mosquito Coast as a haven for surplus population in his native Scotland and as a staging point for introducing the Presbyterian faith to the natives. On 29 April 1820 he received from the compliant Mosquito king, George Frederick, title to the Black River (Río Tinto) district of Honduras, abandoned by the British in 1787.

Styling himself "His Excellency General Sir Gregor MacGregor, Prince of Poyais," he returned home in 1821 to launch his grandiose project on an unsuspecting public, looking to Scotland for settlers and to London for funds. Although preoccupied with financing, MacGregor sent four ships with more than 300 settlers to Black River, where Governor Hector Hall had elaborate instructions on how to proceed. Totally unprepared for frontier survival, two-thirds of the settlers died of malaria, yellow fever, or dysentery. Belize Superintendent Edward Codd authorized Marshall Bennett and George Weston to evacuate the survivors in 1823. About forty-five eventually reached England, where their revelations blackened the name of MacGregor.

Still seeking support, MacGregor returned to England, paid a fine, and then was arrested in France in 1825 but acquitted. Attempts by Poyais bondholders to revive the project in 1837, under various names, failed. MacGregor gave up, leaving England in 1839 for Venezuela, where he was reinstated in his former military rank and granted a pension.

See also **Mosquito Coast; Poyais.**

BIBLIOGRAPHY

Victor Allen, "The Prince of Poyais," in *History Today* 2 (1952): 53–58.

William J. Griffith, *Empires in the Wilderness: Foreign Colonization and Development in Guatemala, 1834–1844* (1965).

Alfred Hasbrouck, "Gregor MacGregor and the Colonization of Poyais Between 1820 and 1824," in *Hispanic American Historical Review* 7 (1927): 438–459.

Robert A. Naylor, *Penny Ante Imperialism: The Mosquito Shore and the Bay of Honduras, 1600–1914* (1989).

Additional Bibliography

Bennett, Charles E. *General MacGregor, Hero or Rogue?* Jacksonville, FL: Mid Nite Books, 2001.

Sinclair, David. *Sir Gregor MacGregor and the Land that Never Was: The Extraordinary Story of the Most Audacious Fraud in History.* London: Review, 2003.

Robert A. Naylor

MACHADO, GUSTAVO (1898–1983).

Gustavo Machado (*b.* 1898, *d.* 1983), leader of Venezuelan Communist Party. Born into a wealthy Caracas family, Machado, while still in high school, became a revolutionary in opposition to the dictatorship of Juan Vicente Gómez (1908–1935). Over the course of his political career, he spent many years in exile and in prison for his revolutionary and Communist activities. During the Democratic Action *trienio* (1945–1948), the Communist Party now legalized, he was a vocal member of the Constituent Assembly and later of the Chamber of Deputies. In 1947 Machado ran for president on the Communist ticket, finishing third and last. After the military dictatorship (1948–1958) Machado returned from exile and was again elected to the Chamber of Deputies (1958), where he served as head of the Communist delegation. He was subsequently imprisoned (1963–1968), however, for allegedly fomenting guerrilla insurgency. After his release he resumed command of the Communist Party, but he renounced armed violence and instead stressed the peaceful road to socialism. From 1973 to 1978, he served in Congress, eventually retiring altogether from public life. In 1981, he was awarded an honorary doctorate from the Universidad de Los Andes in Merida, Venezuela. He died in Caracas in 1983.

See also **Venezuela, Political Parties: Movement to Socialism (MAS).**

BIBLIOGRAPHY

Robert J. Alexander, *The Communist Party of Venezuela* (1969).

Juan Bautista Fuenmayor, *Historia de la Venezuela política contemporánea, 1899–1960,* 10 vols. (1978–).

Robert J. Alexander, ed., *Biographical Dictionary of Latin American and Caribbean Political Leaders* (1988).

Additional Bibliography

Azpúrua E., Miguel. *El último general: Vida y obra revolucionaria del Dr. Gustavo Machado.* Venezuela: s.n., 1999.

Moran Beltran, Lino, Lorena Velazquez and Vileana Melean. "Gustavo Machado and the origins of Marxism in Venezuela." *Revista de Filosofía* 49 (Jan 2005): 28-46.

Nazóa, Anibal, and José Agustín Catalá. *Gustavo Machado, caballero de la revolución.* Caracas, Venezuela: Ediciones Centauro, 1985.

Rangel, Domingo Alberto. *Gustavo Machado: Un caudillo prestado al comunismo.* Caracas, Venezuela: Centauro Ediciones, 2001.

WINFIELD J. BURGGRAAFF

MACHADO DE ASSIS, JOAQUIM MARIA (1839–1908).

Joaquim Maria Machado de Assis (*b.* 21 June 1839; *d.* 29 September 1908), the greatest figure in Brazilian letters. Machado was a novelist, short-story writer, poet, essayist, playwright, and literary critic; fiction, however, gave him eminence in Brazilian literature. A contemporary of the romantics, who to some extent influenced him in his formative years, Machado developed a highly personal style.

Machado was born in a slum of Rio de Janeiro, the son of a black house painter and a Portuguese woman from the Azores Islands. At an early age, he became an orphan and began to earn his own living. He did not receive much formal education. He worked as a typesetter, proofreader, editor, and staff writer. In 1869 he married Carolina, the sister of his friend the Portuguese poet Faustino Xavier de Novais. At thirty-five he joined government service.

When still very young, Machado entered the field of letters, writing poetry, plays, opera librettos, short stories, newspaper articles, and translations. Active in artistic and intellectual circles, he was, however, a man of restrained habits who spent thirty-five years as a civil servant. Some of his biographers believe that the bureaucratic routine permitted Machado to devote himself completely to letters. Others view his hardships as having benefited his literature. Machado's anxieties regarding his race and social origin, the epilepsy that tortured him, and his stuttering all had powerful influences on his art. Literature was his relief.

Machado's first volume of poems, *Crisálidas* (Chrysalis), was published in 1864. Other publications followed: *Falenas* (Moth, 1870), *Contos fluminenses* (Tales of Rio de Janeiro, 1870), his first novel, *Ressurreição* (Resurrection, 1871), *Histórias da meia-noite* (Midnight Tales, 1873), *A mão e a luva* (The Hand and the Glove, 1874), *Americanas* (American Poems, 1875), *Helena* (1876), and *Iaiá Garcia* (1878).

In spite of this substantial accomplishment, Machado had not yet defined his identity, still searching for his own creative principles. At thirty-nine, sick and exhausted, he was granted a leave of absence, which he spent in the resort city of Nova Friburgo, near Rio. This period marks a turning point in his work. After his return to Rio he began one of the masterpieces that characterize the second part of his writing career, *Memórias póstumas de Brás Cubas* (1881; *Epitaph of a Small Winner,* 1952).

This rise to greatness has been explained in different ways. Most modern critics, however, interpret his achievement as the consequence of a long desire for perfection and as the result of the struggle between romantic ideals and Machado's creative intuition with which they conflicted. There was not a sudden change between the two phases; the first phase prepared the second. It was a maturation process. After 1875 the technique of his short stories improved. As a result, the collections published after 1880 include several true masterpieces, such as "Missa do galo" (Midnight Mass), "Noite de almirante" (An Admiral's Evening), "A causa secreta" (The Secret Cause), "Uns braços" (A Pair of Arms), "O alienista" (The Alienist), "O enfermeiro" (The Male Nurse), "A cartomante" (The Fortune Teller), and "O espelho" (The Mirror).

Machado's first novel of the second phase, *Memórias póstumas de Brás Cubas,* is a fictional autobiography written by the dead hero. Starting with his death and funeral, the novel represents a complete break with the literary conventions of the time and Brazilian literature, which allowed an exploration of themes not utilized before. With psychological acuity, the author observes people in trivial, cynical, and egocentric conditions. He also portrays Brazilian society at the end of the empire.

The next novel is *Quincas Borba* (1891; *Quincas Borba: Philosopher or Dog?,* 1954). Rubião, a teacher from Minas Gerais, inherits from Quincas Borba a huge amount of money and a crazy philosophy. As he leaves for Rio, Rubião meets a pair of crooks, Christiano Palha and his beautiful wife, Sofia, with whom he falls in love. The couple, who become Rubião's close friends, slowly steal everything from him. Many other people belonging to a marginal and mobile society are involved. Rubião ends up poor and insane. The conclusion proclaims universal indifference in the face of human suffering and the abandonment of man by supernatural forces.

Machado reached the highest expression of his art in *Dom Casmurro* (1890; *Dom Casmurro,* 1971). This masterpiece is artistically superior to his other works; novelistic elements such as narrative structure, composition of characters, and psychological analysis are employed with incomparable genius. Bento Santiago wanted to join the two ends of life and restore youth in old age. For this purpose he had a replica of his childhood home constructed. Because the plan did not work, he decided to write about his past. Bento and Capitu are in love, but he must become a priest to comply with his mother's vow. Capitu's plotting convinces Bento's mother to allow him to leave the seminary. Bento receives his law degree, and finally the couple are united in a blissful marriage. They have only one child. Escobar, Bento's best friend, has married Capitu's best friend, and the two couples live in perfect friendship. As Escobar dies, Bento becomes convinced that his friend and Capitu have committed adultery. Bento tells his own story, which seems smooth on the surface. Implicitly, however, this is a tragic tale of evil, hatred, betrayal, and jealousy. This content, along with the outstanding artistic qualities of the book, makes *Dom Casmurro* Machado's most powerful work.

In *Esaú e Jacó* (1904; *Esau and Jacob,* 1965), Machado adds a new dimension to his treatment of symbolic and mythical elements. The novel contains more political allegories than do any of his other works. Two identical twins, Pedro and Paulo, differ from each other in every respect but their love for the same girl, Flora. The political atmosphere of the newly proclaimed Brazilian Republic is incorporated into the narrative.

Also in 1904, Machado was overwhelmed by the death of his wife. He wrote a very touching poem, "À Carolina," which appeared as an introduction to a new collection of short stories, *Relíquias da casa velha* (Relics of an Old House, 1906). *Memorial de Aires* (1908; *Counselor Ayres' Memoirs,* 1972), his last novel, is a love story and reminiscence of his life with Carolina. Very ill and frail, Machado died the same year.

Machado de Assis was a powerful writer who is intellectually and emotionally impressive. His writing is predominantly psychological, but the best of his fiction combines the social, philosophical, and historical dimensions with the psychological to make a whole. His extraordinary ability to evoke the past is one of the secrets of his success. His stylistic traits include a simple, exact, and clear syntax and short, discontinuous sentences without rhetorical effects. Metaphor and simile are evident in his writing, but conciseness marks his style and is responsible for its greatness. The underlining philosophy is a pessimistic one that envisions humankind as solitary, depraved, and lost. Compatible with his tragic view of life, his themes embrace death, insanity, cruelty, ingratitude, disillusion, and hate. Machado found refuge for his nihilism in beauty. His heaven is the aesthetic ideal.

Additional collections of short stories included *Papéis avulsos* (1882), *Histórias sem data* (1884), *Várias histórias* (1896), *Páginas recolhidas* (1899), and *Outras relíquias* (1910). Many of these stories have been published in English. A three-volume collection of his complete works is *Obra completa* (1959).

See also **Literature: Brazil.**

BIBLIOGRAPHY

Helen Caldwell, *The Brazilian Othello of Machado de Assis: A Study of "Dom Casmurro"* (1960).

Helen Caldwell, *Machado de Assis* (1970).

Afrânio Coutinho, *Machado de Assis na literatura brasileira* (1960).

Afrânio Coutinho, "Machado de Assis," in *Latin American Writers,* edited by Carlos A. Solé and Maria Isabel Abreu, vol. 1 (1989), pp. 253–268.

John Gledson, *The Deceptive Realism of Machado de Assis: A Dissenting Interpretation of "Dom Casmurro"* (1984).

Claude Hulet, "Machado de Assis," in *Brazilian Literature,* edited by Claude Hulet, vol. 2 (1974), pp. 95–118.

Maria Luísa Nunes, *The Craft of an Absolute Winner: Characterization and Narratology in the Novels of Machado de Assis* (1983).

Marta Peixoto, "Aires as Narrator and Aires as Character in *Esaú e Jacó,*" in *Luso-Brazilian Review* (Summer 1980): 79–92.

Additional Bibliography

Chalhoub, Sidney. *Machado de Assis, historiador.* São Paulo, Brazil: Companhia das Letras, 2003.

Fuentes, Carlos. *Machado de la Mancha.* México: Fondo de Cultura Económica, 2001.

Graham, Richard, ed. *Machado de Assis: Reflections on a Brazilian Master Writer.* Austin: University of Texas Press, 1999.

MARIA ISABEL ABREU

MACHADO Y MORALES, GERARDO

(1871–1939). Gerardo Machado y Morales (*b.* 28 September 1871; *d.* 29 March 1939), president and dictator of Cuba (1925–1933). A man of humble origins, Machado joined the rebels during Cuba's second war of independence (1895–1898), rising to the rank of brigadier general. After peace returned, he became a prominent politician and businessman. In association with American capitalists, he invested in public utilities. He had become wealthy by the early 1920s, when he managed to win control of the Liberal Party and, with a platform of national "regeneration," was elected president in 1924 in a relatively fair election.

Although Machado is usually condemned by historians for eventually turning into a dictator, in his first presidential term not only did he appear to be genuinely concerned with "regenerating" the nation, but he also embarked on an impressive public works program that included the completion of a much-needed central highway and the construction of a national capitol building. In addition, he made a serious attempt to regulate sugar production and became the first president to promote Cuban sovereignty vis-à-vis the United States. His most important step in this direction was a tariff reform bill he sponsored in 1927 that provided protection to emerging Cuban industries.

Betraying his electoral promises, however, Machado did contract several loans with U.S. banks to finance his public works program. He also showed a disposition to resort to force in order to solve problems, so that striking workers, restless students, and other dissidents at times suffered from his actions. On the whole, however, in 1928–1929 he was still popular and had a grip on the political situation.

Ironically, this control proved to be Machado's undoing, for through bribes and threats he brought all the opposition parties under his influence and subordinated the Congress and the judiciary to his will. He was consequently able to push forward a change in the constitution that allowed reelecting himself virtually unopposed for a new six-year term.

At the time of his second inauguration, 20 May 1929, he was still being hailed as the savior of the fatherland. But after that the number of people forced into active opposition increased considerably, and when shortly afterward the shock waves of the worldwide depression reached Cuba, the anti-Machado movement assumed the characteristics of a revolutionary upheaval.

In 1930 there were several antigovernment demonstrations, the most serious of which culminated in the closing of all the schools in the country. The following year, the leaders surviving from the wars of independence staged a full-scale military uprising in the countryside. Machado succeeded in crushing these revolts because he could count on the army, which he had transformed into the overseer of the civil government. But not even the full resources of the army could prevent the revolutionary struggle from degenerating into a vicious fight (as it did from 1932 onward) between the government's brutally repressive forces and clandestine opposition groups such as the so-called ABC movement and the Student Directorate, which were bent upon overthrowing the regime through sabotage and terrorism.

When Franklin D. Roosevelt became president of the United States in 1933, political stability was seen as essential for the successful development of New Deal Cuban policy. Thus, Sumner Welles was sent as ambassador to Havana for the purpose of finding a peaceful solution to the Cuban imbroglio. At first he tried to mediate between the Machado government and its opposition, but as the negotiations went on, he began to push Machado toward making concessions to his enemies. Playing for time, Machado accepted some of the conditions, but he soon drew the line and refused to yield to further pressure, paradoxically assuming the same nationalistic stand as radical opposition groups such as the Student Directorate, which had earlier rejected Welles's good offices. Thus the attempted mediation ended in a deadlock that was resolved only when a general strike paralyzed the nation. Machado then offered favorably disposed Communist labor leaders legal recognition and official support if they would use their influence to end the strike. This maneuver failed, however, and on 12 August 1933 Cuba's armed forces, fearing U.S. armed intervention, moved against the president.

Thus the defiant Machado, who even at the last minute sought to arouse the populace to defend Cuba against a U.S. landing, was finally forced to take a plane to Nassau in the Bahamas. He eventually settled in the United States, where he died, six years later, in Miami Beach. Cuban governments since have refused to authorize the transfer of his remains to his native soil.

See also **Cuba, Revolutions: Revolution of 1933.**

BIBLIOGRAPHY

Luis E. Aguilar, *Cuba 1933: Prologue to Revolution* (1972).

Additional Bibliography

Argote-Freyre, Frank. *Fulgencio Batista: From Revolutionary to Strongman*. New Brunswick, NJ: Rutgers University Press, 2006.

Fuente, Alejandro de la. *A Nation for All: Race, Inequality, and Politics in Twentieth-Century Cuba*. Chapel Hill: University of North Carolina Press, 2001.

Ibarra Guitart, Jorge Renato. *La mediación del 33: Ocaso del machadato*. La Habana, Cuba: Editora Política, 1999.

Valdéz-Sánchez, Servando. *Fulgencio Batista: El poder de las armas (1933-1940)*. La Habana, Cuba: Editora Historia, 1998.

Whitney, Robert. *State and Revolution in Cuba: Mass Mobilization and Political Change, 1920-1940*. Chapel Hill: University of North Carolina Press, 2001.

José M. Hernández

MACHITO (1909–1984). Machito was one of the outstanding bandleaders during the golden age of Cuban music. He was born Francisco Pérez on February 16 (various sources give his birth year as 1908, 1909, or 1912), to Cuban parents (he later chose to use the name Grillo instead). He is said to have been born in either Tampa, Florida, or Havana. He certainly grew up in Havana in a neighborhood in which Afro-Cuban religious and musical traditions were well entrenched. His musical family encouraged him to sing, but he preferred to sing harmony rather than lead. His skills with the maraca led Ignacio Piñeiro to hire him as singer in his Septeto Nacional in 1929, and over the next few years he performed with other major Cuban groups. Machito met Mario Bauzá in 1931; in 1936 the latter married one of Machito's sisters.

Machito's career took off when, encouraged by Bauzá, he moved to New York City in October 1937. His musical evolution from that point was heavily influenced by the New York environment, although it remained unmistakably Cuban. He became a lead vocalist in a number of Latin bands and recorded with Xavier Cugat and Noro Morales. Influenced by the black pride exemplified by the lingering influence of the Harlem Renaissance and Pan-Africanist movement, he formed the Afro-Cubans with Bauzá in 1940. Bauzá credited Machito with having introduced the clave to the United States. Machito became known for his clever vocal improvisations and began to write songs as well. The group soon developed a following not only in the Bronx and Harlem among working-class Latin audiences but also among white audiences in midtown Manhattan. The band added the conga, which had been used by Arsenio Rodríguez and others in Cuba but which had not been used by New York Latin bands. The Afro-Cubans began to record for Decca Records in 1941. Machito's sister Graciela joined the band in 1943. The group's artful blending of jazz instrumentation and Cuban rhythms made them an extremely influential band in an era in which Cuban music was at its peak of popularity in the United States. "The marriage of Cuban music with jazz was not a conventional union," Machito argued. "It was a marriage of love" (quoted in Austerlitz, p. 43).

Machito developed a productive association with the jazz concert and record producer Norman Granz. He recorded with many of the major figures in modern jazz, including not only Latin music fans like Dizzy Gillespie and Stan Kenton but also with musicians less devoted to and knowledgeable about the music such as Charlie Parker. A January 1947 concert in New York's Town Hall, which featured a double bill of Kenton and Machito, is believed to be the first such pairing in a concert setting. In March of that year Kenton paid tribute to Machito by recording a composition named after him. Machito prospered during the mambo craze of the late 1940s and early 1950s and played in different parts of the United States from Florida to California. Strangely enough, although his music was popular in Cuba, the band never played there. By the 1960s Cuban music was no longer popular in the United States. In the 1970s Machito had a steady job as a social worker in Latin neighborhoods in New York. In the mid-1970s he split with his longtime musical partner Bauzá and formed an octet. His career began to revive and he took full advantage of European interest in his music. He died in London of a cerebral hemorrhage on April 15, 1984, while on tour.

See also **Bauzá, Mário; Cugat, Xavier; Music: Popular Music and Dance.**

BIBLIOGRAPHY

Austerlitz, Paul. "Machito and Mario Bauzá: Latin Jazz in the U.S. Mainstream." In *Jazz Consciousness: Music, Race, and Humanity.* Middletown, CT: Wesleyan University Press, 2005.

Orovio, Helio. *Cuban Music from A to Z.* Durham, NC: Duke University Press, 2004.

Roberts, John Storm. *The Latin Tinge: The Impact of Latin American Music on the United States,* 2nd edition. New York: Oxford University Press, 1999.

ANDREW J. KIRKENDALL

MACHU PICCHU. Machu Picchu, the most famous Inca settlement. A royal estate of the emperor Inca Pachacuti, Machu Picchu lies about fifty-four miles northwest of the city of Cuzco at approximately 9,000 feet above sea level, in the cloud forest of the rugged *montaña* region on the eastern watershed of the Peruvian Andes. Machu Picchu is believed to have been abandoned at the time of the Spanish Conquest and was never found by the conquistadores. It lay in obscurity until Hiram Bingham's 1911 expedition in search of the last Inca capital, Vilcabamba. His explorations were publicized by the National Geographic Society, and Machu Picchu became famous as the "Lost City of the Incas."

In fact Machu Picchu was neither lost nor a city. Bingham found local farmers living there when he arrived, and the site was known to the local people. Agustín Lizárraga, a landowner from Cuzco, seems to have been the first outsider to visit the site perhaps more than once between 1894 and 1902. Bingham was the first, however, to clear the site extensively and to recognize it as a major Inca monument. The function of Machu Picchu has long been debated. Bingham believed it to be the last capital of Vilcabamba, the Inca rump state established after the Conquest. Recent research, however, indicates that the site was not a city but an estate of the emperor Pachacuti. Machu Picchu's importance, aside from its beauty and aesthetic qualities, lies in the fact that the Spanish never discovered it. It is therefore one of only a very few examples of an imperial Inca installation that was not altered or affected by the European invasion. It recently has become an obligatory stop for North American and European tourists, although most Peruvians can not afford the airfare to Cuzco and the subsequent train fare to Aguas Calientes, the town from which the bus takes sightseers to the summit.

See also **Archaeology; Bingham, Hiram; Incas, The; Pachacuti; Quechua; Vilcabamba.**

BIBLIOGRAPHY

Sources on Machu Picchu include Hiram Bingham, *Machu Picchu, a Citadel of the Incas* (1930) and *Lost City of the Incas* (1948); Paul Fejos, *Archaeological Explorations in the Cordillera Vilcabamba, Southeastern Peru* (1944); John Hemming, *Machu Picchu* (1981); and Johan Reinhard, *Machu Picchu the Sacred Center* (1991).

Additional Bibliography

Burger, Richard L., and Lucy C. Salazar, eds. *Machu Picchu: Unveiling the Mystery of the Incas.* New Haven, CT: Yale University Press, 2004.

Cuba Gutiérrez, Cosme D. *Machupicchu en la historia de los Inkas.* Perú: s.n., 2005.

Sánchez Macedo, Marino Orlando. *De las sacerdotisas, brujas y adivinas de Machu Picchu.* Lima: M. O. Sánchez Macedo, 1989.

Wright, Kenneth R., Alfredo Valencia Zegarra, et al. *Machu Picchu: A Civil Engineering Marvel.* Reston, VA: American Society of Civil Engineers, 2000.

GORDON F. MCEWAN

MAC-IVER RODRÍGUEZ, ENRIQUE

(1845–1922). Enrique Mac-Iver Rodríguez (*b.* 15 July 1845; *d.* 21 August 1922), a prominent Chilean lawyer, political figure, intellectual, and journalist. As a deputy to Congress, Mac-Iver supported the rebellion against President José Manuel Balmaceda Fernández in 1890–1891. He also served as a senator (1900–1922) and as a government minister, and was a grand master of the Masonic Order. An astute social critic, he lamented the decline in Chile's political morality, the nation's international reputation, and the quality of its leaders. In a 1906 convention of the Radical Party, Mac-Iver unsuccessfully argued against Valentín Letelier Madariaga that the state should not become involved in developing the economy and backing social reforms. At the same time, he questioned the capacity of the lower classes to participate in political life.

See also **Chile, Political Parties: Radical Party.**

BIBLIOGRAPHY

Fredrick B. Pike, *Chile and the United States, 1880–1962* (1963).

Karen L. Remmer, *Party Competition in Argentina and Chile* (1984).

Additional Bibliography

Bañados Espinosa, Julio. *Balmaceda: Su gobierno y la Revolución de 1891.* Santiago, Chile: Eds. Centro de Estudios Bicentenario, 2005.

Núñez P., Jorge. *1891, crónica de la guerra civil.* Santiago de Chile: LOM Ediciones, 2003.

WILLIAM F. SATER

MACULELÊ.

Maculelê, an African Brazilian warrior dance, possibly of southern Angolan, Congolese, Mozambican, and Portuguese origin, traditionally found in Salvador, Bahia, on the feast of Our Lady of the Immaculate Conception. The dance is performed by ten or twenty men dressed in white cotton shirts, holding wooden sticks in each hand. The dancers, in animated synchronicity, perform a mock battle, rhythmically cross-striking their wooden bastinadoes. Similar stick dances date to at least the nineteenth century in Brazil. Exhibitions of *maculelê* may be seen in Salvador and Rio de Janeiro during Carnival. They are often danced by the same men who perform Capoeira.

See also **Music: Popular Music and Dance.**

BIBLIOGRAPHY

Luis Da Camara Casudo, *Dicionário do folclore brasileiro,* 5th ed. (1984).

Mary C. Karasch, *Slave Life in Rio de Janeiro* (1987).

Additional Bibliography

Biancardi, Emília. *Raízes musicais da Bahia. The musical roots of Bahia.* Salvador, Bahia: Secretaria da Cultura e Turismo, 2000.

BERNADETTE DICKERSON

MADEIRA ISLANDS. Madeira Islands, Atlantic island group 400 miles west of Morocco. Madeira was unoccupied before its discovery by the Portuguese in 1420. João Gonçalves Zarco and Tristão Vaz, lieutenants of Henry the Navigator, were the first to land on Madeira. Shortly after, colonies were established with financial support from the revenues of the military order of Christ. The capital was called Funchal, the Portuguese word for "fennel," which grew abundantly on the island. The island was ruled by Donatários until 1497, when the captaincies were abolished and the Portuguese crown took direct control of Madeira.

The Portuguese first established sugar plantations on Madeira, an experiment that introduced the islands to the African slave trade. During the late fifteenth century, Madeira was at the height of its prosperity as the world's largest producer of sugar. This condition changed, however, when the Madeira model for sugar production was introduced to Brazil. By 1620 the sugar industry on the island was in decline as the competition from Brazil proved overpowering. There was a brief respite while the island was under Spanish domination (1580–1640) during the Eighty Years' War, but when the Dutch were forced out of Brazil in 1654, Madeira's sugar industry gradually declined, in spite of strong protectionist legislation meant to save it.

Twice during the nineteenth century the island was occupied by the British, who developed a taste for the local wine. It was believed that the wine was improved by a visit to the tropics, so it was shipped first to Brazil before it was returned to Europe and sold in England.

See also **Explorers and Exploration: Spanish America; Henry the Navigator; Sugar Industry.**

BIBLIOGRAPHY

Elizabeth Nicholas, *Madeira and the Canaries* (1953).

C. R. Boxer, *Four Centuries of Portuguese Expansion, 1415–1825* (1969).

Alfred W. Crosby, *Ecological Imperialism: The Biological Expansion of Europe, 900–1900* (1986).

Additional Bibliography

Brown, Samler A., González Cruz, Isabel, Pascua Febles, Isabel, and Bravo Utrera Sonia del Carmen. *Madeira, Islas Canarias y Azores.* Las Palmas de Gran Canaria: Ediciones del Cabildo de Gran Canaria, 2000.

Hammick, Anne. *Atlantic Islands: Azores, Madeira, Canary and Cape Verde Islands.* St. Ives, Cambs.: Imray Laurie Norie and Wilson, 1994.

Hoe, Susanna. *Madeira: Women, History, Books and Places.* Oxford: Holo, 2004.

Silva, Donald J. *An Annotated Bibliography and Internet Guide for the Madeira Islands.* Lewiston, NY: Edwin Mellen Press, 2005.

Touring Club, Anaya. *Madeira (Guiarama).* Madrid: Madrid ed., 2006.

Vieira, Alberto. *O público e o privado na história da Madeira.* Funchal: Centro de Estudos de História do Atlântico, 1996.

SHEILA L. HOOKER

MADEIRA-MAMORÉ RAILROAD. Madeira–Mamoré Railroad, a transportation company linking Bolivia and Brazil. Ever since the first Europeans descended the treacherous falls and rapids between the Mamoré and Madeira rivers in the eighteenth century, developers dreamed of opening a more direct connection between them. Upriver were great quantities of rubber, quinine, sarsaparilla, hardwoods, and other forest products.

A railroad was first proposed by U.S. entrepreneur George E. Church. Between 1869 and 1872 he obtained Bolivian and Brazilian concessions to build a 220-mile line around a dozen major falls. He raised money in London and began work, but within a year the project collapsed. In 1878 he launched another attempt, this time financed in Philadelphia. It, too, failed; and in 1881 the Brazilian government shut it down with only 11 miles of track laid.

The U.S. magnate Percival Farquhar completed construction of the line early in the twentieth century. Having been successful in his ventures in southern Brazil, he won contracts to modernize the port of Belém. At the same time he acquired the Amazon Navigation Company, which earned great profits by transporting rubber from the headwaters.

The railroad was inaugurated in 1912, just as the rubber boom was being undermined by cheap rubber exports from Asia. Farquhar lost the railroad, as well as his holdings in the port of Pará and the steamships. The railroad ceased operation in 1972.

See also **Farquhar, Percival; Railroads.**

BIBLIOGRAPHY

Frank W. Kravigny, *The Jungle Route* (1940).

Charles A. Gauld, *The Last Titan: Percival Farquhar* (1964).

Additional Bibliography

Carvalho, Vania Carneiro de, and Solange Ferraz de Lima. *Trilhos e sonhos: Dreams and Tracks: Ferrovia madeira-mamore railroad.* Rio de Janeiro: Museu Paulista/ USP, 2000.

Pinto, Emanuel Pontes. *Rondonia: Evolução histórica.* Rio de Janeiro: Expressão e cultura, 1993.

MICHAEL L. CONNIFF

MADEIRA RIVER. Madeira River, an Amazonian tributary that competes with the Amazon for the volume of water that flows through it. Four major rivers merge to form the Madeira before it begins its 2,000-mile journey to join the Amazon 90 miles east of Manaus: the Madre de Dios, the Beni, the Mamoré, and the Guaporé, which forms the border between Rondônia and Bolivia. Jesuits and slave raiders began pushing up the river in 1639. Along their way, the Jesuits converted and captured Indians until after 1719, when the Portuguese settlers eliminated the Torá Indians, who lived near the Madeira's mouth. The Mura, who were brilliant at guerrilla warfare, reclaimed the Torá's territory and prevented settlement along the upper Madeira for most of the eighteenth century.

During the rubber boom of the late nineteenth century, the Madeira and its tributaries were used to transport rubber to waiting markets. Steamships began operating on the river in 1873 and could navigate for 800 miles before encountering the Alto Madeira Falls. After that point, rapids and turbulent waters extend for 260 miles and make passage impossible. When the rubber boom ended, Brazilians fished the Madeira mainly for local consumption.

No other major product was extracted from the river until the gold rush of the 1980s. Indians found gold in the river's bottom where the Madeira passes through Rondônia. An estimated half million prospectors battle with malarial mosquitos and other prospectors as they work in rapids and waters up to 60 feet deep to bring up gold from the deep. The mercury used to extract gold from the sand has polluted the Madeira and has poisoned the fish.

See also **Amazon Region; Amazon River; Gold Rushes, Brazil.**

BIBLIOGRAPHY

R. Kay Gresswell and Anthony Huxley, eds., *Standard Encyclopedia of the World's Rivers and Lakes* (1965).

Alex Shoumatoff, *The Rivers Amazon* (1986).

David Cleary, *Anatomy of the Amazon Gold Rush* (1990).

Susanna Hecht and Alexander Cockburn, *The Fate of the Forest: Developers, Destroyers, and Defenders of the Amazon* (1990).

Additional Bibliography

Craig, Neville B. *Recollections of an Ill-Fated Expedition to the Headwaters of the Madeira River in Brazil.* Whitefish, MT: Kessinger Publishing, LLC, 2007.

Francis, Pauly. *O garimpeiro: Fievre de l'or sur le Rio Madeira.* Paris: R. Laffont, 1991.

Michigan Historical Reprint Series. *The Amazon and Madeira Rivers: Sketches and Descriptions from the Notebook of an Explorer.* Ann Arbor, MI: Scholarly Publishing Office, 2005.

CAROLYN JOSTOCK

MADERO, FRANCISCO INDALECIO (1873–1913). Francisco Indalecio Madero (*b.* 30 October 1873; *d.* 22 February 1913), revolutionary leader and president of Mexico (1911–1913). Madero is best known for his key role in the overthrow of the dictator Porfirio Díaz in 1911 and his forced

Francisco Indalecio Madero (1873–1913) during the Mexican Revolution, 1911. Black and white photograph by a Mexican photographer (20th century). PRIVATE COLLECTION/ THE BRIDGEMAN ART LIBRARY

resignation and assassination in February 1913 by antirevolutionary elements headed by Victoriano Huerta.

Madero was born on the Hacienda de El Rosario, Parras de la Fuente, Coahuila, to one of the wealthiest industrial and landowning families in Mexico, headed by his grandfather, Evaristo Madero, and his father, Francisco Madero Hernández. He studied in Parras, Coahuila, and at the Jesuit Colegio de San Juan, Saltillo, Coahuila, before taking business courses at Mount Saint Mary's College near Baltimore, Maryland (1886–1888). In France he attended the Liceo de Versailles and the Higher Business School in Paris (1887–1892). Subsequently he took classes in agriculture at the University of California at Berkeley (1893). Upon his return to Mexico, Madero founded a business school in San Pedro de las Colonias, Coahuila, where he also administered a family business and practiced homeopathic medicine, spiritism, and vegetarianism.

While working in rural Mexico, Madero came into direct contact with many of its problems, which he attributed to the lack of a liberal, democratic political system. When Porfirio Díaz claimed in the Creelman interview that he would be willing to step down and allow free and open elections, Madero published *La sucesión presidencial en 1910* (The Presidential Succession of 1910 [1908]), which called for freedom of suffrage, nonreelection of high public officials, and rotations in office. The book's appeal (the initial run of 3,000 copies sold out in three months) and its author's dogged determination and persuasive powers led to the formation in May 1909 of the Anti-Reelectionist Center of Mexico.

Within a few months, Madero's anti-reelectionist movement, and then party, had attracted a large enough following to pose a serious threat to the dictatorship. Madero traveled constantly throughout the country, dedicating himself to propagandizing, recruiting, and helping establish political clubs for the cause. The party's national convention, held in Mexico City in April 1910, attracted nearly 200 delegates from all the states and territories but four.

In early June 1910 authorities arrested Madero in Monterrey, Nuevo León, and then transferred him to the city of San Luis Potosí. He was incarcerated in order to remove him from the political scene until after the 26 June 1910 election, which Díaz and his vice presidential running mate, Ramón Corral Verdugo (1854–1912), using fraudulent means, won handily. During that summer in San Luis Potosí, Madero made the decision to escape and challenge the Díaz regime with arms. In early October he fled north to San Antonio, Texas, where he and others drew up the Plan of San Luis Potosí, which called for revolution on 20 November 1910.

The arrests of Madero agents resulted in the confiscation of documents outlining the revolutionary plans for all of central Mexico, thus forcing the conspirators' hands. As a result, Aquiles Serdán (1877–1910) prematurely and futilely raised his revolt on 18 November in the state of Puebla, thus ending any chance of catching the government by surprise. The rebellion sputtered and nearly died, and Madero fled back to Texas for safety.

Only in the state of Chihuahua did any significant rebel activity continue, principally under the leadership of Pascual Orozco. His successes, along with others in the northwest part of the country, convinced Madero to return to Mexico in mid-February 1911. Within weeks the insurgency spread to many areas of the nation and involved thousands of fighters, including followers of Emiliano Zapata (1879–1919) in Morelos. On 10 May 1911, the important border city of Ciudad Juárez, Chihuahua, fell. On 21 May Díaz signed the Treaty of Ciudad Juárez, thereby relinquishing power to an interim government headed by his ambassador to Washington, Francisco León De La Barra. Madero's revolutionaries took control of the country.

Following elections, Madero assumed the constitutional presidency on 6 November 1911, but much of the popular support he had enjoyed the previous May had already disappeared. Once in office Madero proved incapable of stemming the disintegration of his movement.

Madero's difficulties arose from several complex and interrelated factors. First, Madero's social and political outlook had little in common with that of the majority of his followers. He came from a moderately conservative upper-class family that believed in elite rule and a paternalistic relationship with the lower classes. Madero felt comfortable with the upper classes and barely related to the peasants and workers in his movement, most of whom had rural, traditional backgrounds.

Madero's social values in turn shaped his political ideas. He believed that the establishment of a liberal, constitutional, democratic political system would ensure the free election of good men who then would deal with such problem areas as labor, land, education, and taxes. He therefore rejected many of his lower-class and rural supporters' calls for rapid and far-reaching socioeconomic reforms and advocated the more conservative positions of middle- and upper-class elements, many of whom were former supporters of the Díaz regime.

Second, the heterogeneous and disorganized nature of Madero's movement contributed greatly to its demise. The revolution between November 1910 and May 1911 mobilized several thousands of mainly radical, rural, and lower-class fighters throughout the country. The vast majority took advantage of Madero's call to arms to seek redress of local and sometimes personal grievances; they were unaware of or indifferent to Madero's pronouncements. This large, dispersed, and varied movement wanted immediate satisfaction of its demands. Incapable of satisfying his more radical supporters, Madero lost control in the rural areas where they were mainly based.

Third, Madero made a series of political decisions in the weeks following Díaz's surrender that quickly alienated his more radical adherents (and some moderates) and gave his conservative opponents a chance to regroup. Although professing a policy of nonintervention in state and local affairs (he left the Porfirian-era state legislatures intact), Madero intervened in the selection of many other state and local officials. For example, he named governors who generally were middle-aged, educated, and urban-oriented rather than the revolutionary leaders who fought to put him into power.

Madero also alienated many of his followers when he created a new political party, the Constitutionalist Progressive Party (PCP) to replace the Anti-Reelectionist Party. They felt that Madero was discarding an important symbol of the revolution and betraying a loyal supporter, Francisco Vázquez Gómez (1860–1934), whom Madero replaced as his vice presidential running mate. At the same time, Madero compounded the ill feeling toward him by agreeing to the ouster from his cabinet of Emilio Vázquez Gómez (1858–1926), Francisco's brother and one of the staunchest defenders of the left wing of the movement.

Maderista officers and troops also chafed over Madero's decision to demobilize them and maintain the Porfirian army as the only official force in Mexico. When they resisted and clashed with federal units (most notably in Puebla City in mid-July 1911), Madero resorted to the hated draft to build up the regular army and converted newly demobilized insurgents into *rurales* (rural police during Díaz's regime) to fight their former colleagues.

Finally, Madero proved slow to implement the reform program he had promised. The federal government could and did undertake some measures, such as the creation of a labor department and the construction of schools. However, the lack of resources, Madero's belated assumption of the presidency, his selective reluctance to interfere in nonfederal governmental affairs, and the fact that most reforms directly involved state and local levels of administration meant that Madero mostly had only an indirect say in what reforms were implemented.

Beginning in the summer of 1911, the disillusionment of much of his left wing and the continued adamant opposition of the conservatives, supported in part by backsliding moderate Maderistas who feared the increasingly violent masses, led to a series of rebellions, two of which most seriously threatened the regime.

After Díaz's fall, the Zapatistas waited for Madero's government to fulfill its promises, especially those regarding the restitution and protection of communal lands. They became especially angered when federal authorities demanded their demobilization. Zapata tried to reason with Madero, but President León de la Barra, who considered the Zapatistas rural bandits, sent General Victoriano Huerta to subdue them. Thus provoked into rebellion in August 1911, the Zapatistas were soon operating over a wide area of south-central Mexico. In November 1911, they issued the Plan of Ayala, their formal declaration of rebellion, which called for agrarian reform and the overthrow of Madero. Although never able to topple the national government during the Madero period, the Zapatistas made life miserable for provincial authorities and elites, sapped the government's resources, and undermined its military and political credibility.

The second major rebellion occurred in Chihuahua, where Pascual Orozco, financed by the conservative Terrazas-Creel clan, rebelled in early March 1912. His defeat of the federal army at Rellano, Chihuahua, on 23 March forced Madero to turn to Huerta to save the regime. Huerta defeated Orozco's forces at Rellano on 23 May 1911. The Orozquistas fled to the mountains from where they, too, carried on guerrilla warfare, thus also sapping the limited resources of the regime and forcing Madero to focus on a military solution to his problems.

In early 1913, with his movement in tatters, his credibility gone, and his government bankrupt and besieged, Madero faced a rebellion (whose events are referred to as the *decena trágica*, or tragic ten days [9–19 February 1913]) within the federal army, which was led by Félix Díaz, Manuel Mondragón, and Bernardo Reyes. The seriousness of the revolt forced Madero once again to turn to Huerta to save his government. During the ensuing battle, Huerta, with the aid of U.S. Ambassador Henry Lane Wilson (1857–1932), plotted with the rebels against Madero. On 19 February, Huerta forced Madero to resign and assumed the interim presidency. On 22 February, government agents executed Madero and his vice president, José María Pino Suárez (1869–1913), probably upon Huerta's orders.

Madero became a martyr, and his name entered the pantheon of revolutionary heroes as the father of the Mexican Revolution of 1910. He has been portrayed as a well-meaning, progressive democrat who was betrayed by the dark forces of dictatorship and foreign intervention. A more recent assessment, however, depicts him as the person who catalyzed the heterogeneous and dispersed revolutionary movement that managed to overthrow the Díaz regime, yet who did not have the ability or vision to institutionalize that movement and carry out the fundamental socioeconomic reforms necessary to meet the demands of the vast majority of his followers who put him into power. In fact, he oftentimes used autocratic methods to keep those very followers in check to the benefit of Mexico's more conservative and economically privileged groups.

See also **Decena Trágica; Mexico, Wars and Revolutions: Mexican Revolution.**

BIBLIOGRAPHY

Héctor Águilar Camín, *La frontera nómada: Sonora y la revolución mexicana* (1977).

William H. Beezley, *Insurgent Governor: Abraham González and the Mexican Revolution in Chihuahua* (1973).

William H. Beezley, "Madero: The 'Unknown' President and His Political Failure to Organize Rural Mexico," in *Essays on the Mexican Revolution: Revisionist Views of the Leaders,* edited by George Wolfskill and Douglas W. Richmond (1979), pp. 1–24.

Charles C. Cumberland, *Mexican Revolution: Genesis Under Madero* (1952).

François-Xavier Guerra, *Le Méxique de l'ancien régime à la révolution,* 2 vols. (1985).

John M. Hart, *Revolutionary Mexico: The Coming and Process of the Mexican Revolution* (1987), esp. pp. 237–262.

Alan Knight, *The Mexican Revolution,* 2 vols. (1986).

David G. La France, *The Mexican Revolution in Puebla, 1908–1913: The Maderista Movement and the Failure of Liberal Reform* (1989).

David G. La France, "Many Causes, Movements, Failures, 1910–1913," in *Provinces of the Revolution: Essays on Regional Mexican History, 1910–1929,* edited by Thomas Benjamin and Mark Wasserman (1990), pp. 17–40.

Stanley R. Ross, *Francisco I. Madero: Apostle of Mexican Democracy* (1955).

Ramón Eduardo Ruíz, *The Great Rebellion: Mexico, 1905–1924* (1980), esp. pp. 139–152.

Alfonso Taracena, *Francisco I. Madero: Biografía* (1969).

Additional Bibliography

Katz, Friedrich. *De Díaz a Madero.* México, D.F.: Ediciones Era, 2004.

Méndez Reyes, Jesús. *La política económica durante el gobierno de Francisco I. Madero.* México: Instituto Nacional de Estudios Históricos de la Revolución Mexicana, 1996.

McLynn, Frank. *Villa and Zapata: A History of the Mexican Revolution.* New York: Carroll & Graf Publishers, 2001.

DAVID LAFRANCE

MADRAZO, CARLOS A. (1915–1969).

Carlos Alberto Madrazo Becerra (July 7, 1915–June 4, 1969) was a prominent Mexican political leader and a president of the Institutional Revolutionary Party (PRI). He was born in Villahermosa, Tabasco, where he pursued his early education before attending the National Preparatory School (ENP) and law school at the National Autonomous University of Mexico (UNAM) in Mexico City, graduating in 1937. Associated with progressive groups, he was a spellbinding orator and leader in the Bloc of Revolutionary Youth of the Red Shirts (1933–1935) under Tabasco's radical governor Tomás Garrido Canabal. He served as private secretary to Luis I. Rodríguez, his political mentor, during the latter's tenure as governor of Guanajuato (1937–1938) and from 1938 to 1939 was president of the Party of the Mexican Revolution (PRM), forerunner to the PRI. He served in the national Chamber of Deputies from 1943 to 1946; his friendship with Gustavo Díaz Ordaz, later president of Mexico (1964–1970), dated from this time. He served as governor of his home state from 1959 to 1964, and as president of the PRI from 1964 to 1965.

A controversial figure, Madrazo's significance for modern Mexican political life stems mainly from his failure as president of the PRI to make the party more democratic and independent of the presidency. Defeated by an alliance of state governors and cabinet ministers, Madrazo remains a symbol for the still-unrealized renovation of the party. Ironically, his son Roberto Madrazo, who became the party's president and then presidential candidate in 2006, was instrumental in opposing significant internal party reforms in the 1990s and 2000s.

See also **Garrido Canabal, Tomás; Madrazo, Roberto; Mexico, Political Parties: Institutional Revolutionary Party (PRI).**

BIBLIOGRAPHY

Cruz Pereyra, Diogenes de la. *Carlos A. Madrazo: Una historia política en el contexto del estado mexicano.* Villahermosa: Editorial Chontal, 1996.

Hernández Rodríguez, Rogelio. *La formación del politico mexicano: El caso de Carlos A. Madrazo.* México, D.F.: Colegio de México, 1991.

RODERIC AI CAMP

MADRAZO, ROBERTO (1952–).

Mexican politician Roberto Madrazo Pintado is the son of Carlos A. Madrazo, reformist president of the Institutional Revolutionary Party (PRI) in 1964–

1965. Roberto was born in the Federal District on July 30, 1952. He joined the PRI while he was still a law student at the National Autonomous University of Mexico (1971–1974), and served as secretary general of the PRI's National Revolutionary Youth Movement from 1977 to 1978. He pursued a series of posts within the PRI, including general delegate to the national executive committee, and as the committee's secretary of promotion (1984–1987) and of organization (1988–1989). Among his political mentors was Carlos Hank González, an influential political figure.

Madrazo represented Tabasco in the Chamber of Deputies from 1976 to 1979 and 1991 to 1994, and in the Senate from 1988 to 1991. He served as governor of Tabasco from 1995 to 2001, after a bitter campaign involving widespread fraud, defeating among other opponents Manuel Andrés López Obrador. He failed to win his party's nomination as its presidential candidate in 1999, but became president of the PRI in 2002 after defeating his reformist opponents, a position he resigned in 2005 to run for the presidency of Mexico on the PRI ticket. He ran a distant third against Felipe Calderón from the National Action Party (PAN) and López Obrador from the Party of the Democratic Revolution (PRD) in the 2006 elections, destroying his party's chance for a return to the presidency.

See also **López Obrador, Manuel Andrés; Madrazo, Carlos A; Mexico, Political Parties: Institutional Revolutionary Party (PRI).**

BIBLIOGRAPHY

Grayson, George W. *Mesías mexicano: Biografía crítica de Andrés Manuel López Obrador*. México, D.F.: Grijalbo, 2006.

Trelles, Alejandro. *Anatomía del PRI: Claves para entender a Roberto Madrazo*. Mexico: Plaza y Janés, 2006.

RODERIC AI CAMP

MADRID, TREATY OF (1670). Treaty of (1670) Madrid, agreement between England and Spain that recognized England's possessions in the New World. It was one of a series of treaties between Spain and other European powers recognizing "effective occupation" in return for promises not to trade with Spanish colonies. By 1680 European colonial powers were collaborating in an attempt to restrain the activities of buccaneers. The Treaty of Madrid superceded the Treaty of Tordesillas (1494) which had proved unworkable and had been repeatedly violated. The new basis for determining colonial boundaries was effective possessions (at the time of the Treaty of Madrid) rather than prior discovery or an imaginary line.

See also **Tordesillas, Treaty of (1494).**

BIBLIOGRAPHY

Parry, John Horace. *The Spanish Seaborne Empire*. Berkeley: University of California, 1990.

SUZANNE HILES BURKHOLDER

MADRID, TREATY OF (1750). Treaty of (1750) Madrid, agreement between Spain and Portugal that affected Brazil and the Río de la Plata. In the Treaty of Madrid, Portugal ceded to Spain Colônia, an important center of contraband trade, lands adjoining the Río de la Plata, and its free navigation of the river in exchange for two areas along the border of Brazil and an agreement to move seven Jesuit missions (along with thirty thousand Guaraní Indians) located in one of the territories. Signed on 3 January 1750, the treaty's terms faced vehement opposition in both countries. Among its detractors were the powerful Portuguese minister Pombal (Sebastião José de Carvalho e Melo), the future Charles III (1716–1788) of Spain, and the Jesuits, who protested but obeyed. The Portuguese did the most to subvert the treaty, but the Jesuits in Spain (and government supporters of the order) suffered the most from its political repercussions when the attempt to evacuate the missions was met with bloody resistance in 1754 and 1756. The Treaty of Madrid was annulled by the Treaty of El Pardo (12 February 1761) which restored the Jesuits to their missions but renewed territorial disputes.

See also **Jesuits.**

BIBLIOGRAPHY

Guillermo Kratz, *El tratado hispano-portugués de límites de 1750 y sus consecuencias* (1954).

Additional Bibliography

Cortesaão, Jaime. *Alexandre de Gusmão e o Tratado de Madrid* (1750). Rio de Janeiro: Ministério das

Relações Exteriores/Instituto Rio Branco, 1950. Tomo I, parte II.

Pondé, Francisco de Paula e Azevedo. "A defesa das fronteiras terrestres, 1750-1780 (de acordo com o Tratado de Madri)." *Revista do Instituto Histórico e Geográfico Brasileiro,* 155:382 (Jan-Mar 1994), 197-226.

SUZANNE HILES BURKHOLDER

MADRID HURTADO, MIGUEL DE LA

MADRID HURTADO, MIGUEL DE LA (1934–). Miguel de la Madrid Hurtado served as president of Mexico from 1982 to 1988, taking office at the Mexican presidency's lowest level of legitimacy in modern times. Confronted with a major economic crisis created by rapidly increasing inflation, a downturn in growth, high rates of unemployment, extraordinary capital flight, and massive external debt, the president pursued an orthodox strategy of economic austerity. Having achieved only moderate economic success, de la Madrid is likely to be remembered more for laying the groundwork for his successor's liberalization and privatization programs. However, de la Madrid's administration did bring inflation under relative control, renegotiate the debt, and begin the process of selling off state-owned enterprises.

Politically, de la Madrid restored the shattered relationship between the private and public sectors, a step necessary for the success of his economic strategy. Whereas he initially attempted moderate electoral reforms, he reversed this strategy midway through his presidency. The government's mishandling of earthquake rescue efforts in 1985 provoked the development of numerous popular opposition movements. Electoral fraud in Chihuahua in 1986 caused further problems and brought, for the first time in four decades, formal denunciations from the church hierarchy and encouraged a more activist church posture in politics. In 1986, de la Madrid introduced a new electoral code mandating an increase in the number of proportional seats in the Chamber of Deputies from one hundred to two hundred (raising the total number of seats from four hundred to five hundred), setting the stage for the extraordinary representation of the opposition in the 1988 chamber.

Internally, de la Madrid reinforced the growing tendency of the two preceding administrations toward the dominance of political technocrats: younger, bureaucratically experienced, highly educated (often abroad), urban decision makers with few ties to the president's Institutional Revolutionary Party (PRI) or the electoral scene. The control of these leaders continued to exacerbate internal disputes between the more traditional leadership and reform-minded younger technocrats. Finally, de la Madrid's designation of Carlos Salinas as his party's 1988 presidential candidate and the unbending treatment of party dissidents Cuauhtémoc Cárdenas and Porfirio Muñoz Ledo, who formed their own party, led to the most disputed presidential election in the party's history, in which it captured only a bare majority of the votes cast under conditions of widespread evidence of fraud.

Miguel de la Madrid was born December 12, 1934, in Colima, Colima, the son of Miguel de la Madrid Castro, a lawyer and government employee murdered by wealthy landowners after he defended peasant rights. His mother, Alicia Hurtado, took Miguel and his sister to Mexico City, where he attended the Colegio Cristóbal Colón and the National Autonomous University of Mexico (UNAM) law school, from which he graduated with honors on August 8, 1957. An outstanding student, de la Madrid had the second-highest grade point average of his 732 law school classmates. In 1965, on a fellowship from the Bank of Mexico, de la Madrid obtained a masters degree in public administration from Harvard University; he would become the first Mexican president with a graduate degree as well as the first with a degree from abroad. He also taught constitutional law at UNAM from 1958 to 1967. As a student, he worked in the National Foreign Trade Bank under Ricardo J. Zevada, his professor, to support himself at school. After graduation, he obtained his first government post at the Bank of Mexico as an adviser to Mario Ramón Beteta. Beteta became the president's early mentor, and when Beteta moved to the treasury department, he took de la Madrid along as his subdirector general of credit (1965–1970).

In 1970 de la Madrid became assistant director of finances for the government oil company, Pemex, but moved back to his mentor's agency as director general of credit (1972–1975). When Beteta became treasury secretary in 1975, he appointed de la Madrid assistant secretary of credit, a post he continued to hold in the next administration. On May 17, 1979, president José López Portillo (1976–1982) appointed him secretary of programming and planning. Although considered a dark horse candidate for the presidential nomination, he became the party's candidate on September 25, 1981. His ties to José López Portillo, who chose him as his successor, extended back to law school, where he studied under López Portillo. After de la Madrid left the presidency in 1988, his successor, Carlos Salinas, appointed him director of the government-funded publishing firm Fondo de Cultura Económica. De la Madrid often participates in intellectual and policy conferences, where he is viewed as a valued contributor to debates on contemporary public issues.

See also **Cárdenas Solorzano, Cuauhtémoc; Mexico, Political Parties: Institutional Revolutionary Party (PRI); Muñoz Ledo Lazo de la Vega, Porfirio; Salinas de Gortari, Carlos.**

BIBLIOGRAPHY

Bailey, John J. *Governing Mexico: The Statecraft of Crisis Management*. New York: St. Martin's Press, 1988.

Dornbierer, Manou. *El hombre gris: El sexenio de Miguel de la Madrid, 1982–1988*. México, D.F.: Grijalbo, 1999.

Gentleman, Judith, ed. *Mexican Politics in Transition*. Boulder, CO: Westview Press, 1987.

Loret de Mola, Rafael. *Radiografía de un presidente*. México, D.F.: Grijalbo, 1988.

Madrid Hurtado, Miguel de la. *Cambio de rumbo: Testimonio de una presidencia, 1982–1988*. México, D.F.: Fondo de Cultura Económica, 2004.

RODERIC AI CAMP

MADUREIRA, ANTÔNIO DE SENA

(1841–1889). Antônio de Sena Madureira (*b.* 1841; *d.* 1889), Brazilian military leader. Sena Madureira graduated from the military academy with a degree in science and mathematics. He was training in Europe when the War of the Triple Alliance (1864–1870) broke out, and served in the war with distinction. An abolitionist and a republican, Madureira's historical significance stems from his launching, in 1884, of the famous "military question," concerning the civil rights of the military. This occurred when his command gave a hero's welcome to the celebrated abolitionist Francisco de Nascimento. The minister of war labeled the episode a breach of discipline and censured Madureira. A related incident followed when a liberal colonel cited some irregularities in a command headed by a captain with conservative leanings. The captain felt aggrieved and turned to a conservative deputy, who verbally attacked the colonel in the Chamber of Deputies. The colonel responded in the press and was censured by the minister of war. Madureira joined in the debate by writing provocative articles in a republican newspaper. The minister of war sought to administer discipline but found that Madureira was under the direct command of General Deodoro da Fonseca, the most prestigious military officer in the army. Fonseca refused to censure his subordinate, since the matter involved Madureira's criticism of civilian authority, and not a breach of military hierarchy. The affair centered on the rights of the military to express their political views publicly. The Supreme Military Tribunal ruled in favor of the officers, and Madureira's punishments were revoked. The split between military and monarchist leaders remained, however, and the monarchy was overthrown by a military coup in 1889.

See also **Military Question of the 1880s.**

BIBLIOGRAPHY

Robert A. Hayes, *The Armed Nation: The Brazilian Corporate Mystique* (1989).

João Pandiá Calógeras, *A History of Brazil,* edited and translated by Percy Alvin Martin (1939).

Nelson Werneck Sodré, *História Militar do Brasil* (1965), esp. pp. 143–153; *Dicionário de História do Brasil* (1976).

Additional Bibliography

Alves, Claudia Maria Costa. *Cultura e política no século XIX: O exército como campo de constitutenção de sujeitos políticos no Império.* Bragança Paulista, Brazil: CDAPH, 2002.

ROBERT A. HAYES

MÃE MENININHA. *See* **Menininha do Gantois, Mãe.**

MAGALHÃES, BENJAMIN CONSTANT BOTELHO DE. *See* **Constant Botelho de Magalhães, Benjamin.**

MAGALHÃES, DOMINGOS JOSÉ GONÇALVES DE (1811–1882).

Domingos José Gonçalves de Magalhães (*b.* 1811; *d.* 1882), considered the "father" of Brazilian romanticism. Magalhães was a doctor, a poet, and an influential diplomat of the empire who enjoyed the favor of Emperor Dom Pedro II. While living in Paris he fell under the influence of the European romantics. In 1836, along with the romantic painter and poet Manuel de Araújo Porto Alegre (1806–1879) and Alberto Torres Homem, he cofounded a literary review, *Niterói: Revista Brasiliense.* While his early poetical works reflected the conservatism of the neoclassical literary canon, they also contained slight echoes of nascent liberalism.

His first collection of poems, *Suspiros poéticos e saudades* (1836), offered a pantheistic view of life: Nature is omnipresent in, and consequently the major influence on, the poetic art. That same year, influenced by the romantic concept of nationalism, he published the first "history" of Brazilian literature, "Discurso sobre a história da literatura do Brasil." Romantic nationalism is also evident in his most notable drama, *António José; ou, O poeta e a inquisição* (1839), about the eighteenth-century Luso-Brazilian writer condemned by the Inquisition. Although he continued to write throughout his lifetime, his last major work (and the one for which he remains best known today) is the epic poem *A confederação dos Tamojos* (1856), in which he legitimizes the total destruction of an Indian tribe in the pursuit of independence and the establishment of the empire.

See also **Literature: Brazil.**

BIBLIOGRAPHY

David Miller Driver, *The Indian in Brazilian Literature* (1942).

Raymond Sayers, *The Negro in Brazilian Literature* (1956).

Additional Bibliography

Campato Júnior, João Alberto. *Retórica e literatura: O Alencar polemista nas Cartas sobre a Confederaçao dos Tamoios.* São Paulo, Brasil: Scortecci Editora, 2003.

Huppes, Ivete. *Gonçalves de Magalhães e o teatro do primiero romantismo.* Lajeado, Brasil: Fundaçao Alto Taquari de Ensino Superior, 1993.

Teixeira, António Braz. *O pensamento filosófico de Gonçalves de Magalhães.* Lisboa, Portugal: Instituto de Filosofia Luso-Brasileira, 1994.

IRWIN STERN

MAGALLANES.

Magallanes, the name given to the territories around the Strait of Magellan and the southernmost province of Chile (1992 population 143,058), has the second smallest population of any of Chile's regions. Punta Arenas (1990 population 120,030) is the capital city. Most of the territory consists of fjords, channels, glaciated mountains, and impenetrable rain forests or peat moss. This makes it an ideal location for viewing local wildlife, including condors, penguins, and guanacos. The cold steppes of Chilean Patagonia, east of the Andes, hold some potential for raising sheep, the major centers of which are in Puerto Natales and Porvenir. Oil discovered in 1940 near Cerro Sobrero (Tierra del Fuego) met the nation's needs until the mid-1960s. In 1978 Chile and Argentina almost went to war over the possession of the Picton, Lennox, and Nueva islands, which are part of the Magallanes region. (The dispute is known as the "Beagle conflict.") Due to fallout from this dispute, the Chileans supported the United Kingdom against Argentina in the Falklands War of 1982. In 1984 the dispute ended when Argentina and Chile signed the Peace and Friendship Treaty, which granted the islands themselves to Chile and the maritime rights to Argentina. Since the early 1990s there has been a resurge in petroleum exploitation in the eastern segment of the Strait of Magellan. Wool and mouton exports also contribute to the region's economy.

See also **Chile, Geography; Punta Arenas.**

BIBLIOGRAPHY

Alberto M. De Agostini, *Magallanes y canales fueguinos* (Punta Arenas, 1960); and *Instituto Geográfico Millitar,* "La región de Magallanes y la Antártica chilena," in *Geografía de Chile,* vol. 34 (Santiago, 1987).

Additional Bibliography

Brebbia, C. A. *Patagonia, A Forgotten Land: From Magellan to Perón.* Boston; Southampton, U.K.: WIT Press, 2007.

Collier, Simon, and William F. Sater. *A History of Chile, 1808–1994.* New York; Cambridge: Cambridge University Press, 1996.

Gallez, Paul. *Cristóbal de Haro: Banqueros y pimenteros en busca del Estrecho Magallánico.* Bahía Blanco, Argentina: Instituto Patagónico, 1991.

Martinic Beros, Mateo. *Archipélago patagónico: La última frontera.* Puntas Arenas, Chile: Ediciones de la Universidad de Magallanes, 2004.

Martinic Beros, Mateo, and Julio Fernández Mallo. *Faros del estrecho de Magallanes: Un patrimonio histórico y arquitectónico.* 2nd ed. Punta Arenas, Chile: La Prensa Austral, 2002.

Massone, Mauricio. *Los cazadores despúes del hielo.* Concepción, Chile: Museo de Historia Natural; Santiago: Centro de Investigaciones Diego Barros Arana, 2004.

CÉSAR N. CAVIEDES

MAGAÑA, SERGIO (1924–1990).

Sergio Magaña (*b.* 24 September 1924; *d.* 23 August 1990), Mexican dramatist and novelist. Magaña contributed to the formation of a new generation of playwrights with his first play, *La noche transfigurada* (1947), and mainly with his popular play *Los signos del zodíaco* (1951), which depicts the lower class in Mexico City through the simultaneous staging of various scenes. With the collaboration of Emilio Carballido, he founded a literary group called Atenea, which later became the School of Philosophy and Letters theater group, and exerted a great deal of influence on the avant-garde scene. Both *Los argonautas* (1953) and *Moctezuma II* (1954) concern the Spanish Conquest, while *Santísima* (1980), a stylized musical about a prostitute's life, uses characters from Federico Gamboa's novel *Santa.* He has also written novels, such as *El molino del aire* (1953).

See also **Theater.**

BIBLIOGRAPHY

Willis Knapp Jones, *Behind Spanish American Footlights* (1966).

Carlos Solórzano, *Testimonios teatrales de México* (1973).

Additional Bibliography

Vásquez Rentería, Víctor Hugo. *Inventa la memoria: Narrativa y poesía del sur de México.* México, D.F.: Alfaguara, 2004.

GUILLERMO SCHMIDHUBER

MAGDALENA RIVER.

Magdalena River, a waterway in Colombia, important for centuries as the principal artery linking the interior of the country with the Caribbean Sea. Navigable for most of its length of 956 miles, the Magdalena flows northward between the Central and Eastern Cordilleras and empties into the Caribbean near Barranquilla. Its major tributary is the Cauca River.

The mouth of the river was first sighted by Rodrigo de Bastidas and Juan de la Cosa in 1501. With the establishment of Santa Marta nearby in 1526, Spaniards became interested in exploring the river in order to move south and possibly reach Peru. In 1536 the ships of the expedition led by Gonzalo Jiménez De Quesada reached a point on the river near modern Barranca-Bermeja before Jiménez abandoned the river to strike inland to the east. From the founding of Bogotá in 1539 until well into the twentieth century, the Magdalena offered the only practical means of transporting cargo and passengers between the interior and the Caribbean coast. Indian canoes and keelboats were initially used to navigate the river; steam-powered vessels began to flourish in the mid-1840s. By the late twentieth century, the construction of roads and railways and the development of aviation had lessened the economic importance of the river, but it remained a vital part of Colombia's transportation system.

The Magdalena River Basin is the most important region of Colombia in terms of development and economy. About 80 percent of the nation's population lives in this basin, and historically, its waters have produced more than 60 percent of fish consumed in the country. However, from a production high of nearly 80,000 tons per year in the 1970s, in 2006 the basin's fisheries produced only one-tenth of that amount. This fall in production was due to overfishing by landless, displaced peasants trying to survive as fishermen.

In early 2007 oil drilling and extraction activities in the upstream areas of the basin were altering wildlife habitats by consuming large quantities of water and releasing pollutants. In addition, there have been frequent spills and leakages from oil pipelines.

See also **Colombia, Pacific Coast; Fishing Industry.**

BIBLIOGRAPHY

Robert Louis Gilmore and John P. Harrison, "Juan Bernardo Elbers and the Introduction of Steam Navigation on the Magdalena River," in *Hispanic American Historical Review* 28 (1948): 335–359.

Additional Bibliography

Galvis, Germán, and José Iván Mojica. "The Magdalena River Freshwater Fishes and Fisheries." *Aquatic Ecosystem Health and Management* 10, no. 2 (April 2007): 127–139.

Peñuela Ramos, Aristides. *Los caminos al Río Magdalena: La frontera del Carare y el Opón, 1760–1860.* Santa fé de Bogotá: Insituto Colombiano de Cultura Hispánica, 2000.

Posada-Carbo, Eduardo. *The Colombian Caribbean: A Regional History, 1870–1950.* New York: Oxford University Press, 1996.

Rodríguez Cuenca, José Vicente, and Arturo Cifuentes Toro. *Los Panches: Valientes guerreros del valle alto del río Magdalena.* Bogotá: Secretaría de Cultura, 2003.

HELEN DELPAR

MAGDALENA VALLEY. The Magdalena is the principal river of Colombia, and a diverse and long archaeological sequence has been recognized in its valley. The early evidence of human occupation begins with hunters and gatherers. Projectile points and choppers were found in the region of Carare in the middle Magdalena Valley (8500–8000 BCE). More archaeological information is found for ceramic times in the lower Magdalena Valley and includes the sites of Bucarelia and El Bongal (4000–3000 BCE). Both belong to the Puerto Hormiga tradition. Other pottery complexes such as Monsú, Guájaro, and Malambo (2600–1000 BCE) are also present and yield evidence of populations that subsisted on riverine resources as well as on collection of food plants. Sites such as Malambo have been considered by some authors to be part of the Barrancoid pottery tradition. This tradition has been reported to occur from the Magdalena Valley to the lower Orinoco and Amazon rivers, and appears to be related to the peopling of the Lesser Antilles. In relation to the development of agriculture and settled life in the valley, nothing is known. In more recent times (300 BCE–700 CE), complex adaptations to the flooded region of the Mompos Depression occurred. The Mompos Depression has more than 250,000 acres of modified landscape in the form of raised fields that work as agricultural drainage systems for the area during the rainy season. Settlements were dispersed along the artificial channels. High-ranking individuals were buried in earth mounds with pottery and goldwork. Goldwork manufacture illustrating faunal iconography was present.

Another archaeological expression of the Magdalena Valley is what has been called the burial urn horizon. This horizon is characterized by the urns depicting a regional diversity of style that were always used for secondary burials (bones reburied in a pottery container made specifically for them). Examples include the anthropomorphic urns of Tamalameque, Puerto Serviez, Puerto Nare, Honda, Girardot, and El Espinal. The burial urn horizon seems to be a late development (900–1600). Some authors link this horizon to a migration of Carib speakers to the area. The horizon also is considered to be related to ethnic groups that the Spanish encountered, such as the Pantágoras, Pijao, Panche, and Carare. Information related to these settlements is scarce (Mayaca site). However, settlements seem to have included a common long house similar to the Maloca known in the Amazon River region. No hard evidence has been found concerning the subsistence base, but it very likely centered on maize, manioc, and fishing. The archaeological information for the upper Magdalena Valley is more complete and centered on the town of San Agustín, which gave its name to the culture.

See also **Anthropology; Orinoco River.**

BIBLIOGRAPHY

On the middle Magdalena Valley, see Carlos Eduardo López, *Investigaciones arqueológicas en el Magdalena Medio* (1991). For the lower Magdalena Valley, see Gerardo Reichel-dolmatoff, *Arqueología de Colombia* (1986).

Additional Bibliography

Castro Blanco, Elías. *Geografía humana: Desarrollo social y político en la provincia de Mariquita y el valle del Magdalena en el nuevo reino de Granada: La tenencia de la tierra (encomiendas, mitas y resguardos) 1556–1856.* Bogotá, D.C., Colombia: Centro de Investigaciones, 2003.

Llanos Vargas, Héctor. *Presencia de la cultura de San Agustín en la depresión cálida del valle del río Magdalena: Garzon–Huila.* Santafé de Bogotá, D.C.: Fundación de Investigaciones Nacionales, 1993.

Rodríguez Cuenca, José Vicente and Cifuentes Toro, Arturo. *Los panches: valientes guerreros del valle alto del río Magdalena.* Bogotá: Secretaría de Cultura, 2003.

Salgado López, Héctor. *Antiguos pobladores en el valle del Magdalena Tolimense, Espinal-Colombia.* Ibagué, Colombia: Universidad del Tolima, 2006.

AUGUSTO OYUELA- CAYCEDO

MAGDALENO, MAURICIO (1906–1986). Mauricio Magdaleno (*b.* 13 May 1906; *d.* 30 June 1986), Mexican writer. Born in Villa del Refugio, Magdaleno wrote drama, novels, and movie scripts, most of which address the achievements, failures, and contradictions of the Mexican Revolution. In the 1930s Magdaleno founded the theater group Teatro de Ahora in partnership with Juan Bustillo Oro; he also published his most important novel, *El resplandor* (Sunburst, 1937). In the 1940s Magdaleno wrote many successful screenplays for the growing Mexican film industry. Named to the Mexican Academy of Language in 1957, Magdaleno later held a variety of bureaucratic and political offices, including a period as senator for the state of Zacatecas (1958–1964).

See also **Literature: Spanish America; Theater.**

BIBLIOGRAPHY

John S. Brushwood, *Mexico in Its Novel: A Nation's Search for Identity* (1966), pp. 19–21, 217–218, 226.

Guillermo Schmidhuber, "Díptico sobre el teatro mexicano de los treinta: Bustillo y Magdaleno, Usigli y Villaurrutía," in *Revista Iberoamericana* 55, no. 148–149 (1989): 1221–1237.

Joseph Sommers, *After the Storm: Landmarks of the Modern Mexican Novel* (1968), pp. 23–36.

Additional Bibliography

Salazar, Severino. *Zacatecas: Cielo cruel, tierra colorada: Poesía, narrativa, ensayo y teatro, 1868-1992.* México, D.F.: Consejo Nacional para la Cultura y las Artes, 1994.

DANNY J. ANDERSON

MAGELLAN, FERDINAND (1480–1521). The Portuguese explorer Ferdinand Magellan (in Portuguese, Fernáo de Magalháes; known in Spanish as Fernando de Magallanes) was the first man to lead a fleet that circumnavigated the globe. He was born around 1480 in northern Portugal near Oporto. He came from a noble family of the lesser nobility and was orphaned at a young age. He served as a page at the court of the Portuguese queen. It may be there that in 1497 he met Christopher Columbus, who influenced his idea to sail westward to find a passage to Asia.

In 1505 Magellan entered the service to the Portuguese crown under Francisco de Almeida, first viceroy of Portuguese India. As a soldier he served with distinction in Portuguese East Africa (present-day Mozambique) and participated in the conquest of India and Morocco. He fought battles with the Muslims in India and successful attacks on Goa and Malacca in 1511. He was seriously wounded in battles in service to the Portuguese king. After fighting in Morocco, he returned to Lisbon where he was denied a military promotion and pension by King Manuel. Anger at the Portuguese king led him to renounce his Portuguese citizenship and go to Spain, where he married a Spanish noblewoman, to seek aid from King Charles I. He persuaded the king to sponsor a voyage to Asia to verify Spanish claims to the Spice Islands granted under the Treaty of Tordesillas (1494).

Magellan sailed from Spain on September 20, 1519, for the Spice Islands with five ships and 265 men in search of a westward route to Asia, to complete Columbus' dreams. There were problems with the crew from the start, as only one-third were Portuguese and the rest Spanish. Magellan was highly secretive, and the captains and crew objected to being kept in the dark about the extent of the journey. The fleet sailed from Seville to Tenerife in the Canary Islands, then to the Cape Verde Islands, arriving at the coast of Brazil. The fleet had to avoid contact with the Portuguese because Magellan was considered a traitor. They stopped at Rio de Janeiro, hiding in the islands of Guanabara Bay and avoiding any contacts with the Portuguese. The fleet sailed southward looking for an outlet to the Pacific, reaching the Rio de la Plata region in present-day Argentina. They sailed onward to Tierra del Fuego and Patagonia, where the sailors saw the coastal fires of indigenous tribes. It was during this time that Magellan faced a serious mutiny from the Spanish captains and sailors, which he quickly crushed by hanging the ringleaders. The colder waters and temperature of the South Atlantic caused serious problems for the crew. When Magellan reached the tip of South America, one ship deserted the fleet and returned to Spain.

On October 21, 1519, he reached the tip of South America. It took him more than four weeks to go through what was later named the Strait of Magellan to the Pacific Ocean, which he named for its peaceful surface. On November 28, Magellan started sailing on the "unknown sea," but he misjudged the distance across the Pacific to Asia. The journey was exceedingly difficult; because they could not find land, they did not have any fresh food for more than three months. The crew suffered from hunger and scurvy, with nineteen dying en route. The fleet reached Guam on March 6, 1521. After reprovisioning, Magellan sailed again and discovered the Philippine Islands. He persuaded the ruler of the island of Cebú to accept Christianity, but he became involved in a local war. On April 27, 1521, Magellan was killed in a fight with the natives of Mactan Island. He died with his brother-in-law Duarte Barbosa in a skirmish in which his right foot was wounded by a poisoned arrow. He could not retreat from the battle but died with his men. His body was never recovered.

Various accounts dispute the reason for his death. Some paint Magellan as a villain demanding too much food and livestock from the natives whose patience with the Europeans became exhausted. Other accounts describe Magellan and his men as taking sides in a civil war among rival chieftains in the Philippine Islands.

Juan Sebastián de Elcano (c. 1476–1526) assumed command and piloted one ship, the *Victoria*, to the Moluccas. The ship, loaded with spices, sailed for Spain with forty-seven Europeans and thirteen natives of the islands, reaching Seville on September 8, 1522. Only eighteen Europeans were still alive. Although Magellan himself did not complete the first circumnavigation, his skill and ruthless determination made that achievement possible.

Magellan never did reach the Spice Islands but part of his surviving crew did. Historian Charles R. Boxer calls this voyage the most outstanding voyage of its time because Magellan was the first European navigator to sail into unknown waters in the South Atlantic and the Pacific Ocean and circumnavigate the globe, which was a significant nautical feat for the time.

See also **Charles I of Spain; Columbus, Christopher; Elcano, Juan Sebastián de; Explorers and Exploration: Spanish America; Manuel I of Portugal; Tordesillas, Treaty of (1494).**

BIBLIOGRAPHY

Bergreen, Laurence. *Over the Edge of the World: Magellan's Terrifying Circumnavigation of the Globe.* New York: Morrow, 2003.

Boxer, Charles R. *The Portuguese Seaborne Empire 1415–1825.* New York: Knopf, 1969.

Thomas, Hugh. *Rivers of Gold: The Rise of the Spanish Empire, from Columbus to Magellan.* New York: Random House, 2003.

Zweig, Stefan. *Conqueror of the Seas: The Story of Magellan*, trans. Eden and Cedar Paul. New York: Viking Press, 1938.

Patricia A. Mulvey

MAGELLAN, STRAIT OF. Strait of Magellan, a narrow body of water, about 330 miles long and 2.5 to 15 miles wide, separating mainland South America from Tierra Del Fuego and the numerous other islands to the south. Named after its discoverer, Ferdinand Magellan, a Portuguese navigator in the service of King Charles I of Spain, the strait, except for the eastern mouth, which is Argentine, lies entirely within Chile. It provides a protected inland waterway between the Atlantic and Pacific oceans, but is difficult to navigate because of its winding course and the fog and wind that prevail.

Embarked on a voyage of global circumnavigation, Magellan wanted to establish that the Spice Islands (the Moluccas) lay in the Spanish sphere of influence under the 1494 Treaty of Tordesillas. His voyage took him to Brazil, the Rio de la Plata, Patagonia, and, on 21 October 1520, to the strait which bears his name. The passage through the strait was difficult, taking him thirty-eight days. Magellan was killed in the Philippines a few months later, but one of his captains, Juan Sebastian de Elcano, completed the voyage.

In the nineteenth century the Chilean city of Punta Arenas on the strait was an important coaling station, but its value diminished markedly with the opening of the Panama Canal in 1914. In recent years the region has grown in importance as Chile's principal oil and gas production area, as well as the staging base for Antarctic tourism and logistical support. Punta Arenas, along with Ushuaia in Argentina, are the southernmost cities in the world, and were the first to feel the impact of the depletion of the ozone layer over Antarctica.

See also **Beagle Channel Dispute.**

BIBLIOGRAPHY

Antonio Pigafetta, *Magellan's Voyage Around the World* (1906).

Hubert C. Herring, *A History of Latin America* (1963).

Additional Bibliography

De Córdoba, Antonio. *A Voyage of Discovery to the Strait of Magellan*. Stroud, U.K.: Nonsuch, 2006.

Kent, Rockwell. *Voyaging Southward from the Strait of Magellan*. Hanover, NH: University Press of New England, 1999, 1924 75th Anniversary Ed.

Martini Beros, Mateo, Dahl, Victor, and Rees, Earl L. *Voyagers to the Strait of Magellan*. Worthington, OH: Renaissance Publications, 1990.

Martinic Beros, Mateo, and Oportot, Mónica. *Estrecho de Magallanes: Puerta de Chile*. Santiago, Chile: LOM Ediciones, 2002.

Oyarzun Iñarra, Javier. *Expediciones españolas al estrecho de Magallanes y Tierra de Fuego*. Madrid: Ediciones de Cultura Hispánica, 1999.

Sarmiento de Gamboa, Pedro and Batista, Juan. *Viajes al Estrecho de Magallanes*. Las Rozas, Madrid: Dastin, 2000.

Valenzuela Solis de Ovando, Carlos. *El portugués que descubrió Chile*. Santiago de Chile: Edit. Anduijar, 2001.

JACK CHILD

MAGLOIRE, PAUL EUGÈNE (1907–2001). Paul Eugène Magloire, president of Haiti (1950–1956) was born in Cap Haitien into a family of the country's black elite. Magloire received an education at the Lycée Philippe Guerrier, at the military academy, and at the National University, where he earned a law degree. As commander of the Palace Guard, he and two mulatto officers organized the coup that toppled the dictatorship of Élie Lescot in January 1946. After serving as minister of the interior under President Dumarsais Estimé, Magloire again conspired against his superior: when Estimé sought to prolong his rule in violation of Haiti's constitution, Magloire joined in the coup to overthrow him.

Supported by the Roman Catholic Church, the Haitian military, and the U.S. government, Magloire's presidency, from December 1950 to December 1956, represented a return to power of Haiti's mulatto elite in cooperation with blacks like Magloire himself. Instead of continuing the social reforms started by his predecessor, Magloire focused on economic modernization with the help of private, foreign (mainly U.S.) investments, U.S.-government aid programs, and U.S.-backed international agencies like UNESCO. While lavishing money on showy development projects such as the Point Four–sponsored irrigation project in the Artibonite Valley, the regime did little for the bulk of the country's population. It not only suppressed civil liberties and independent unions, but also aggravated conditions for the peasantry by allowing the country's best land to be taken over by foreign-owned agro-export industries. By increasing Haiti's dependence on agro-exports, Magloire contributed to the ecological and human disaster that explains the poverty of most Haitians today as well as the heavy migratory overflow that has characterized the country since his time. At the end of his term, he fled abroad due to intense political pressure. When François "Papa Doc" Duvalier became president in 1957, Magloire became the country's favorite scapegoat, and he was even stripped of his Haitian nationality. In 1986, when the Duvaliers lost power, Magloire returned from exile. In 1988 he was made an adviser to the Haitian army. He died in 2001 at the age of ninety-three.

See also **Duvalier, François; Haiti.**

BIBLIOGRAPHY

David Nicholls, *From Dessalines to Duvalier: Race, Colour, and National Independence in Haiti* (1979).

Michel-Rolph Trouillot, *Haiti: State Against Nation* (1990).

Additional Bibliography

Abbott, Elizabeth. *Haiti: The Duvaliers and Their Legacy*. Rev. and updated ed. New York: Simon and Schuster, 1991.

Bernardin, Raymond. *General Paul Eugène Magloire: Une biographie politique*. Coconut Creek, FL: Educa Vision, 2004.

Trouillot, Michel-Rolph. *Haiti, State against Nation: The Origins and Legacy of Duvalierism*. New York: Monthly Review Press, 1990.

PAMELA MURRAY

MAGOON, CHARLES EDWARD (1861–1920). Charles Edward Magoon (*b.* 5 December 1861; *d.* 14 January 1920), joined the U.S. War Department in 1899, served as governor-general of the Panama Canal Zone in 1905–1906, and was named by President Theodore Roosevelt as provisional governor of Cuba during the U.S. occupation of 1906–1909. His role in Cuba is very controversial. Cuban historians blame Magoon for wasting the monies amassed by the first Cuban president, Tomás Estrada Palma, through granting sinecures and promoting questionable public works, thus establishing the pattern of venality that plagued successive Cuban governments. In actuality, he was not corrupt but inclined to reward a generation of former revolutionary Liberals with posts, which prevented effective enforcement of the civil service law. He was also accused of letting public works contracts to favored U.S. firms. His secretary of justice, General Enoch Crowder, presided over the writing of Cuba's electoral law.

See also **United States-Latin American Relations.**

BIBLIOGRAPHY

David Lockmiller, *Magoon in Cuba: A History of the Second Intervention, 1906–1909* (1969).

Allan R. Millett, *The Politics of Intervention: The Military Occupation of Cuba, 1906–1909* (1968).

Additional Bibliography

Mellander, Gustavo A., and Nelly Maldonado Mellander. *Charles Edward Magoon, the Panama Years.* Rio Pedras, Puerto Rico: Editorial Plaza Mayor, 1999.

LESTER D. LANGLEY

MAHOGANY. *See* **Lumber Industry.**

MAHUAD, JAMIL (1949–). Jamil Mahuad, an Ecuadorian political leader, was born in Loja on July 29, 1949, to a Lebanese father and German mother. He received his doctorate in jurisprudence and law from the Catholic University of Ecuador in 1979 and a master's in public administration from Harvard University in 1989. After fifteen years in Guayaquil, Mahuad moved to Quito in 1981, where he joined the conservative Popular Democracy (DP) party. He served as minister of labor under Osvaldo Hurtado in 1983–1984. He was elected mayor of Quito in 1992 and, after receiving much support for installing a trolley car system, was reelected in 1996.

In 1998 Mahuad was elected president of the republic. During his brief presidency he reached a definitive peace agreement with Peru (following a war in 1995) and conceded the use of an Ecuadorian military base to the United States as part of the controversial "Plan Colombia." Amid economic crisis, he initiated a number of unpopular austerity measures: privatization, dollarization, a freezing of private bank accounts, an increase in the value added tax (IVA), and the elimination of gasoline subsidies. After seventeen months in office he was removed by a military coup (January 2000) and replaced by his vice president, Gustavo Noboa. Mahuad took "temporary absence" in Peru and later Chile. In July 2000 the supreme court of Ecuador indicted him on violations of constitutional rights and corruption on several counts. However, he had already taken up residency in the United States, where he became a fellow at the Kennedy School of Government at Harvard University, giving lectures on political ethics.

See also **Noboa, Gustavo.**

BIBLIOGRAPHY

Gerlach, Allen. *Indians, Oil, and Politics: A Recent History of Ecuador*. Wilmington, DE: Scholarly Resources, 2003.

"Jamil Mahuad Witt." Fundació Cidob: Centro de Investigación de Relaciones Internacionales y Desarrollo. http://www.cidob.org/es/documentacion/biogra fias_lideres_politicos/america_del_sur/ecuador/jamil_mahuad_witt.

SUZANNE CASOLARO

MAINE, U.S.S., SINKING OF THE. The United States battleship *Maine* was sent to Havana in January 1898, at the height of Cuba's second war of independence, for the purpose of protecting American lives and property should the turmoil prevailing in that country make it necessary. At 9:40 P.M. on February 15 the ship blew up in Havana harbor, where it was anchored. Out of a complement of 355 officers and men, a total of 260 were killed. It is likely that the explosion was caused by the detonation of the *Maine*'s own gunpowder, but official inquiries conducted at the time were inconclusive. Inflamed by the yellow press and certain U.S. government officials, public opinion in the United States quickly placed the responsibility for the tragedy on the Spaniards. Two weeks later, Congress appropriated $50 million for war preparations, and on April 11 President William McKinley sent to Congress a war resolution. For this reason, the destruction of the *Maine* traditionally has been regarded as the chief causal explanation of the Spanish-American War. More recently, however, historians have emphasized the need to reconceptualize the origins of the war in the context of U.S. policy toward Cuba in the nineteenth century. For even if the explosion of the *Maine* had faded into the background of the Cuban War of Independence, the fact remains that the United States and Spain were on a collision course because of Cuba and neither showed any willingness to turn aside.

See also **Cuba, War of Independence.**

BIBLIOGRAPHY

Louis A. Pérez, Jr., "The Meaning of the *Maine:* Causation and the Historiography of the Spanish-American War," in *Pacific Historical Review* 58, no. 3 (Aug. 1989): 293–322.

Guillermo G. Calleia Leal, "La voladura del *Maine*," in *Revista de Historia Militar* 34, no. 59 (Spain, 1990): 163–196. The latter is especially interesting in that it reflects the Spanish perspective on the episode.

Additional Bibliography

Carrasco García, Antonio. *En guerra con Estados Unidos: Cuba 1898.* Madrid: Almena Ediciones, 1998.

Pérez, Louis A. *The War of 1898: The United States and Cuba in History and Historiography.* Chapel Hill: University of North Carolina Press, 1998.

José M. Hernández

MAIPO RIVER. Maipo River, a 150-mile-long waterway located at the southern edge of the basin of Santiago, 12 miles from the city's center. It springs from the foothills of the Volcán Maipo and is fed by winter rains and spring snowmelt. The soils on both sides of the Maipo River are rich in mineral nutrients from the volcanic and fluvial deposits carried from the Andes. Here the best vineyards of the country thrive, and the choicest wines of Chile bear the Maipo Valley provenance labels.

See also **Santiago, Chile.**

BIBLIOGRAPHY

Additional Bibliography

Cai, Ximing, Claudia Ringler, and Mark W. Rosegrant. *Modeling Water Resources Management at the Basin Level: Methodology and Application to the Maipo River Basin.* Washington DC: International Food Policy Research Institute, 2006.

César N. Caviedes

MAIPÚ, BATTLE OF. Battle of Maipú, a conflict that took place near Santiago, Chile, on 5 April 1818. A revolutionary army composed of Argentines and Chileans and commanded by General José de San Martín defeated a royalist army composed primarily of American loyalists and commanded by General Mariano Osorio. This decisive victory eliminated Spanish influence in Chile. The battle raged for six hours and the entire royalist army was destroyed. Two thousand royalists were killed and 2,432 captured. Only a handful, including General Osorio, escaped. The insurgents sustained about 1,000 casualties. The victory at Maipú was an important milestone in San Martín's grand strategy to cross the Andes, defeat the royalists in Chile, and then attack Peru by amphibious assault. Revolutionary forces had previously tried to attack Peru via the land route through Bolivia but were repeatedly defeated.

See also **San Martín, José Francisco de.**

BIBLIOGRAPHY

Martin Súarez, *Atlas histórico-militar argentino* (1974).

Christián García-Godoy, ed., *The San Martín Papers* (1988).

Additional Bibliography

Archer, Christon I., ed. *The Wars of Independence in Spanish America.* Wilmington, DE: Scholarly Resources, 2000.

Jocelyn-Holt Letelier, Alfredo. *La independencia de Chile: Tradición, modernización y mito.* Madrid: Editorial MAPFRE, 1992.

Pasquali, Patricia. *San Martín: la fuerza de la misión y la soledad de la gloria: biografía.* Buenos Aires: Planeta, 1999.

ROBERT SCHEINA

MAÍZ, FIDEL (1828–1920). Fidel Maíz (*b.* 1828; *d.* 1920), Paraguayan cleric and figure in the War of the Triple Alliance. Born in the tiny hamlet of Arroyos y Esteros, Maíz was little more than an obscure country priest until the late 1850s, when he gained the attention of the all-powerful López family. One story has it that Maíz was the only Paraguayan priest willing to baptize the offspring of Francisco Solano López (the future president) and his Irish mistress Eliza Lynch. In any case, Maíz went on to officiate at the September 1862 funeral of President Carlos Antonio López, and to participate in the subsequent congressional meetings called to choose a new government. Some ill-chosen words at the latter assembly put Maíz in prison for several years, but in 1866, he was reprieved by Solano López and named army chaplain.

Two years later, Maíz played an infamous role in one of the ugliest episodes of the war: he acted as government prosecutor at a series of conspiracy trials, often referred to as the *tribunales de sangre.* Convened at San Fernando, the trials were characterized by their expediency and, more particularly, by the use of torture to obtain confessions. In this fashion, Maíz elicited confessions from scores of men said to be plotting against López. Many were condemned and bayoneted to death on the same day. In fact, however, historians today question whether any conspiracy ever existed.

After the war, Maíz was imprisoned for a time by the Brazilians and then censured by the Roman Catholic church. He traveled to Rome to appeal his case to the pope, was absolved, and returned to Arroyos y Esteros, where he spent the remainder of his life composing polemical tracts, memoirs, and textbooks for the little church school he ran.

See also **Paraguay: The Nineteenth Century.**

BIBLIOGRAPHY

Fidel Maíz, *Etapas de mi vida* (1919).

Carlos Zubizarreta, *Cien vidas paraguayas,* 2d ed. (1985), pp. 172–176.

Additional Bibliography

Godoi, Juan Silvano. *Documentos históricos: El fusilamiento del obispo Palacios y los tribunales de sangre de San Fernando.* Asunción, Paraguay: Lector, 1996.

Rees, Siân. *The Shadows of Elisa Lynch: How a Nineteenth-Century Irish Courtesan Became the Most Powerful Woman in Paraguay.* London: Review, 2003.

THOMAS L. WHIGHAM

MAIZE. Maize (*Zea mays mays*), a coarse annual plant of the grass family (*Gramineae*). The staple crop of most Latin American countries, it is the most important native crop in the Western Hemisphere and is second only to wheat in commercial value. Maize is also the most photosynthetically efficient of the domesticated grains.

On 5 November 1492 two sailors returned from a reconnaissance mission into the interior of Cuba and reported to Columbus a grain called "maiz ... a grain which was well tasted, bak'd, dry'd and made into flour." At that time maize was grown from southern Canada to southern Chile, from sea level to 10,000 feet. In the English-speaking world maize became known as Indian corn, "corn" being a common European term for cereal grain. In Latin America it continued to be called *maíz.*

There are six major types of maize, all developed by Native Americans in response to various environmental and cultural factors: (1) flint corn, with its hard kernels, is resistant to fungus and stores well in cooler and damper climates; (2) flour corn, with its soft, easily ground kernels, is best suited to warmer and drier climates; (3) dent corn, the most common "field corn," combines the hard features of flint with a flour "dent" over its soft center; (4) sweet corn, which accounts for only 3 percent of overall production because it cannot be dried and stored as easily as the preceding types; (5) popcorn, characterized by small and extremely hard kernels that must be parched or exploded before they can be further processed or eaten; and (6) pod corn, which is raised as a curiosity and represents a "primitive" race in that each kernel is surrounded by its own chaff (husk). Maize is unusual among the domesticated grains because it cannot effectively seed itself. Its seeds (kernels) are

Harvested maize in Ocopata, Peru, late 20th century. Native to the region, corn is a staple food throughout Latin America. © ENZO AND PAOLO RAGAZZINI/CORBIS

enclosed in a modified leaf (husk) and are so tightly attached to the spike (cob) that they cannot be easily dispersed.

ORIGIN

Considerable controversy has surrounded the origin of domesticated maize. Unlike other major cereals, wild races of maize have not been discovered. Two competing theories have been proposed to explain the origin of domesticated maize. Paul Mangelsdorf, Richard MacNeish, and others have argued that maize was domesticated from a wild form that subsequently became extinct. They base their arguments on excavated material from the Valley of Tehuacán, Puebla, Mexico, which they dated as early as 5000 B.C.E. (now redated to 3600 B.C.E.), and on maize pollen from Valley of Mexico lake sediments originally dated as early as 80,000 B.C.E. (now redated to as recent as the beginning of the common era). George Beadle, Hugh Iltis, and others have argued that maize was domesticated from one of the subspecies of teosinte (*Zea mays mexicana, Zea mays parviglumis*), a closely related wild grass. Current research on plant genetics utilizing molecular analysis supports the teosinte theory, and points to the Balsas River drainage of southwestern Mexico as the most probable region for first domestication.

Once domesticated, the cultivation of maize spread rapidly, first as a supplement to the diet of hunting and gathering populations. It may have reached the highlands of Peru as early as 4000 B.C.E., and southern South America soon after. As new races of maize were developed in South

America they hybridized with the more ancient races from Mexico, which led to the rapid evolution of hundreds of varieties of domesticated maize.

Maize also spread north. By 2000 B.C.E. it was present at Bat Cave in west-central New Mexico. Within 600 years these first primitive ears found north of Mexico were followed by more productive varieties. Similar varieties, *chapalote* and *naltel,* are still grown in Mexico.

Unraveling the origin of maize has important consequences for the future of Latin American farmers. Current research on the recently discovered perennial teosinte species *Zea diploperennis* holds the promise of providing genetic material that can be used to increase the disease resistance of *Zea mays.* The incorporation of genetic material from ancient races of Mexican maize into modern hybrids can increase resistance to environmental stresses.

HISTORY

From its humble beginnings as a dietary supplement, maize was rapidly transformed into the essential crop that supported the growth of the first civilizations of the Americas. It was prepared with lime water or wood ash to release chemically bonded nutrients. When maize was combined with beans, squash, chiles, and small amounts of animal protein, it provided a diet far superior to any known in sixteenth-century Europe.

Throughout temperate Latin America maize was the staff of life. In the tropical lowlands of Mexico and Central America it became the dominant crop, and in Amazonia it became an important supplement to manioc-based diets. Maize was grown to its environmental limits in the Andes, but in the higher altitudes it was often replaced as a staple by potatoes and quinoa. It is not surprising that maize was incorporated into the religious life of all pre-Columbian civilizations.

When maize was first introduced to Europe, prominent herbalists referred to it as Turkish corn or wheat. Maize then had a brief vogue in the Mediterranean countries, but it was not prepared properly, nor nutritionally balanced with other crops. As a result, the dietary-deficiency disease pellagra became common in areas where maize was farmed, and it was abandoned as a food crop.

Since maize was associated with the conquered people of the Western Hemisphere, it remained unpopular among Europeans, and was thought by some to be, in the words of English herbalist John Gerard, "a more convenient food for swine than for man" (Charles B. Heiser, Jr., *Seeds to Civilization,* new ed., 1990, p. 92). This colonial attitude did not develop in sub-Saharan Africa, however, where maize was soon incorporated into indigenous subsistence systems and cuisines. Maize also became a staple crop in areas of India and China.

In Latin America maize remains the basis of most traditional meals and is prepared in over 300 ways; even the pollen and fungus (smut) is eaten; in Mexico, the latter, known as *huitlacoche,* is considered a delicacy. Maize also is fermented to produce the traditional maize beer (*chicha*) of the Andes.

TODAY

Almost 350 million acres of maize were planted worldwide in 1985–1986. In North America it is primarily grown for animal feed and industrial products, while in Latin America it is primarily grown for food. Latin America accounts for approximately 42 million acres of the world's maize production. Four countries, China, Brazil, India, and Mexico, account for more than 50 percent of the total area planted to maize in the Third World.

Today, most processed foods contain starch, oil, or sugar from maize. Biodegradable products from diapers to "paper" bags are being produced from processed corn starch, and ethanol, an alcohol distilled from corn starch, is being mixed with gasoline for fuel. A quality-protein maize nearly twice as nutritious as normal maize is currently under development.

Corn has been at the center of debates concerning globalization and free trade. In 1994 Mexico signed a free-trade pact with Canada and the United States, which created the North American Free Trade Association (NAFTA). This agreement removed many trade barriers immediately and called for the end of all trade barriers on agricultural products like corn and beans by 2007. This latter deadline, however, generated criticism from many Mexicans, because the U.S. promotion of corn-based ethanol caused a dramatic rise in maize prices. This increase in turn pushed up the price of tortillas, a staple in the Mexican diet, causing them to be too expensive for many consumers.

See also **Agriculture; Globalization.**

BIBLIOGRAPHY

Paul Weatherwax, *Indian Corn in Old America* (1954).

Alexander Grobman, *Races of Maize in Peru* (1961).

Paul C. Mangelsdorf, Richard S. MacNeish, and W. C. Galinat, "Domestication of Corn," in *Science* 143 (1964): 538–545.

Howard Walden, *Native Inheritance: The Story of Corn in America* (1966).

George W. Beadle, "The Ancestry of Corn," in *Scientific American* 242 (1980): 112–119.

Hugh H. Iltis, "From Teosinte to Corn: The Catastrophic Sexual Transmutation," in *Science* 222 (1983): 886–894.

Stephen J. Gould, "The Short Way to Corn," in *Natural History* 93 (1984): 12–20.

Paul C. Mangelsdorf, *Corn: Its Origin, Evolution, and Improvement* (1984).

Ranulfo Cavero Carrasco, *Maíz, chicha y religiosidad andina* (1986).

Bruce F. Benz, "Racial Systematics and the Evolution of Mexican Maize," in *Studies in the Neolithic and Urban Revolutions,* edited by Linda Manzanilla (1987).

International Maize and Wheat Improvement Center, *The 1986 CIMMYT World Maize Facts and Trends: The Economics of Commercial Maize Seed Production in Developing Countries* (1987).

Museo Nacional De Culturas Populares, *El maíz, fundamento de la cultura popular mexicana,* 3d ed. (1987).

National Research Council, *Quality-Protein Maize* (1988).

Proceedings of the Global Maize Germplasm Workshop, *Recent Advances in the Conservation and Utilization of Genetic Resources* (1988).

Flavio Rojas Lima, *La cultura del maíz en Guatemala* (1988); *Maydica* 35 (1990), special issue devoted to *Zea diploperennis;* Charles B. Heiser, Jr., *Seeds to Civilization: The Story of Food,* new ed. (1990).

Simposium Nacional Del Maíz, *El maíz en la década de los 90* (1990).

Robert E. Rhoades, "The Golden Grain," in *National Geographic* 183 (1993): 92–117.

Additional Bibliography

García, Martha; Sandra Luz; and Mauricio García Sandoval. *El maíz: Sustento del pasado y presente en la cultura popular nacional.* Toluca, Mexico: Universidad Autónoma del Estado de México, 1999.

McAfee, Kathleen. "Corn Culture and Dangerous DNA: Real and Imagined Consquences of Maize Transgene Flow in Oaxaca." *Journal of Latin American Geography* 2:1 (2003), 18–42.

Torres Torres, Felipe. *La industria de la masa y la tortilla: Desarrollo y tecnología.* Mexico City: Universidad Nacional Autónoma de México, 1996.

DONALD E. MCVICKER

MAJANO, ADOLFO ARNOLDO (1938–). Adolfo Arnoldo Majano (*b.* 1938), Salvadoran army officer and member of the provisional junta (1979–1980). Majano was briefly the most visible representative of reformist forces within El Salvador's officer corps. A participant in the coup d'état that overthrew the regime of Carlos Humberto Romero on 15 October 1979, Majano later served as one of two military members on the junta that replaced him. Considered honest and progressive, Majano supported the junta's reforms and urged greater respect for human rights and an opening to the Left. But he was not an effective leader, and rightist forces within the military eventually outmaneuvered him. Ousted from the junta in December 1980, Majano went into exile the following year. In 2001, he sued the Salvadoran government, claiming that the loss of his military salary and retirement fund was a violation of his constitutional rights.

See also **El Salvador; Romero, Carlos Humberto.**

BIBLIOGRAPHY

Tommie Sue Montgomery, *Revolution in El Salvador: Origins and Evolution* (1982).

Shirley Christian, "El Salvador's Divided Military," in *Atlantic Monthly* (June 1983): 50–60.

Additional Bibliography

Bosch, Brian J. *The Salvadoran Officer Corps and the Final Offensive of 1981.* Jefferson, NC: McFarland & Co., 1999.

Grenier, Yvon. *The Emergence of Insurgency in El Salvador: Ideology and Political Will.* Basingstoke, U.K.: Macmillan, 1999.

Menjívar Ochoa, Rafael. *Tiempos de locura. El Salvador, 1979–1981.* San Salvador: FLASCO, 2006.

STEPHEN WEBRE

MALARIA. *See* Diseases.

MALASPINA, ALEJANDRO (1754–1810).

Alejandro Malaspina (*b.* 5 November 1754; *d.* 9 April 1810), Spanish naval officer and explorer. Alejandro Malaspina, a Spanish subject born in Mulazzo, in the Duchy of Parma, Italy, entered Spain's navy in 1774 as a midshipman and rose quickly through the ranks. After serving in Gibraltar, he circumnavigated the earth from 1786 to 1788 as commander of *La Astrea.* As a captain, Malaspina was given command of a five-year around-the-world scientific exploratory mission departing from Cádiz on 30 July 1789. The expedition sailed around the tip of South America and surveyed various Spanish ports. From Acapulco, Malaspina explored northward to the sixtieth parallel, visiting Alaska, Nootka Sound (Vancouver Island), and Monterey, California. His men gathered scientific data and charted the coastline before returning to Mexico. The ships sailed for the Philippines and Australia before recrossing the Pacific to South America and Spain. Prior to publishing his materials, Malaspina fell victim to court intrigue in 1795; he was imprisoned and stripped of his rank. After about eight years in jail, Malaspina was exiled to Parma, where he died.

Not until 1885 did a one-volume account of his expedition appear in print. In the early twenty-first century, however, Malaspina's work has added valuable scientific and visual data to existing knowledge about the natural history of New World areas during the late eighteenth century.

See also **Explorers and Exploration: Spanish America.**

BIBLIOGRAPHY

Donald C. Cutter, *Malaspina in California* (1960).

Iris H. W. Engstrand, *Spanish Scientists in the New World: The Eighteenth-Century Expeditions* (1981).

Pedro Novo y Colson, ed., *Viaje político-científico alrededor del mundo por las corbetas Descubierta y Atrevida* (1885, 1984).

Carmen Sotos Serrano, *Los Pintores de la Expedición de Alejandro Malaspina* (1982).

Additional Bibliography

Manfredi, Dario. *Alejandro Malaspina: La América imposible.* Madrid: Compañía Literaria, 1994.

Pimentel, Juan. *La física de la monarquía: Ciencia y política en el pensamiento colonial de Alejandro Malaspina (1754–1810).* Aranjuez (Madrid): Doce Calles, 1998.

IRIS H. W. ENGSTRAND

MALDONADO.

Maldonado is a department in the southeastern corner of Uruguay (2005 population 144,107), on the Atlantic Ocean. The major town is Maldonado (2004 population 54,603), 80 miles from Montevideo and famous for its several monuments dating to colonial times. The town has been overshadowed by the dramatic development of the neighboring sea resort Punta Del Este (population 7,200 in 2007), which the *New York Times* called "the Hamptons of South America" in 2007. Elites from across South America, and especially Buenos Aires, spend the winter months on the beaches of Playa Mansa and Playa Brava. In this coastal area of Maldonado, the major economic activity is tourism. Sheep graze in the rugged hills of the interior, and on the flatter terrain, vegetables, sugar beets, and wheat are grown. A cement factory as well as granite and marble quarries add extractive industries to the economic profile of Maldonado.

See also **Livestock; Punta del Este.**

BIBLIOGRAPHY

Elzear Giuffra, *La república del Uruguay* (Montevideo, 1935).

Additional Bibliography

Delgado Clavijo, Daniel. *Canarios en la región de Maldonado: Primera mitad del siglo XIX.* Montevideo: Torre del Vigía Ediciones, 2005.

Martínez Rovira, Eduardo. *A pie y a caballo: Apuntes del campo de Maldonado (R.O. del Uruguay).* 2nd ed. Montevideo: A.M.D.G. Ediciones, 2002.

Nicoletti, Marisol C. *Así es Maldonado.* Punta del Este, Uruguay: Mar y Sol Ediciones, 2000.

CÉSAR N. CAVIEDES

MALDONADO, FRANCISCO SEVERO

(1775–1832). Francisco Severo Maldonado (*b.* 1775; *d.* 1832), Mexican politician and reformer. Born in Tepic, Nayarit, Maldonado studied in Guadalajara and became a priest and a scholar. Joining Hidalgo's movement when the insurgent army arrived in Guadalajara in 1810, he published the revolutionary *El despertador americano* and began drafting a constitution. After the battle of Calderón, Maldonado was put on trial. He renounced his earlier views and began to write for a royalist periodical, *El telégrafo de Guadalaxara* (1811). He supported both the Constitution of 1812 and the Plan of Iguala, and served in the early congresses. His social and political ideas, expressed in various editions of a work he called *Nuevo pacto social* and *Contrato de asociación* (1823), may have influenced Mariano Otero. Maldonado's plans are, in the words of Charles Hale, "an odd blend of liberal individualism, utopian socialism, and traditional corporate theory." His views on land reform and corporate society have been seen by some as presaging the Constitution of 1917.

See also **Mexico, Wars and Revolutions: War of Independence.**

BIBLIOGRAPHY

Charles A. Hale, *Mexican Liberalism in the Age of Mora, 1821–1853* (1968), pp. 74–75; *Diccionario Porrúa de historia, biografía y geografía de México,* 5th ed. (1986).

Additional Bibliography

Benítez González, Florencio. *El Plan de Iguala: En la historiografía de su época.* México: Comuna Municipal, 2001.

Magallón Anaya, Mario. "El pensamiento filosófico y político de Francisco Severo Maldonado." *Cuadernos Americanos* 85, Nueva época (Jan–Feb 2001): 193–207.

D. F. Stevens

MALDONADO, RODRIGO DE ARIAS

(1637–1716). Rodrigo de Arias Maldonado (*b.* 25 December 1637; *d.* 23 September 1716), the moving force behind the organization in Guatemala of the religious order of Bethlehemites to serve the poor. Born into the Spanish nobility, Maldonado went with his parents as a child to Costa Rica, where his father served as governor. He took over the governorship when his father died in 1662. As governor of Costa Rica he subdued the Talamanca Indians, and he was expected to go on to higher posts. He moved to Santiago de Guatemala, opened a great house, and lived ostentatiously. He then came under the influence of Hermano Pedro de Bethancourt, who had established a hospital and was extending services to the poor. The king appointed Maldonado marquis de Talamanca, but he refused the honor and turned to a life of service. When Hermano Pedro died, leadership of the group known as the Bethlehemites passed to Maldonado, called Rodrigo de la Cruz within the church. Maldonado went to Rome in 1674 and again in 1685 to gain authorization to establish the order of the Bethlehemites. He then traveled to Mexico and Peru, founding hospitals and churches in the name of the new order. Upon his death he was buried in one of the churches that he had established in Mexico City.

See also **Bethlehemites.**

BIBLIOGRAPHY

Joseph García de la Concepción, *Historia Belemitica,* 2d ed. (1956).

Additional Bibliography

Lobo, Manuel. *El hermano Pedro, un santo par ahoy: Relación de la vida y virtudes del beato hermano Pedro de San José de Betancourt.* Guatemala: Librerías Artemis Edinter, 2002.

David L. Jickling

MALESPÍN, FRANCISCO

(1790–1846). Francisco Malespín (*b.* 1790; *d.* 25 November 1846), president of El Salvador (1844–1845). Following Rafael Carrera's defeat of Francisco Morazán, Carrera imposed Malespín as commander of El Salvador's army in March 1840. Regarded as Carrera's puppet, Malespín effectively resisted Morazán's attempt to return to El Salvador in 1842. Collaborating with Bishop Jorge Viteri y Ungo, Malespín broke with Salvadoran President Juan José Guzmán in December 1843 and took over the presidency on 1 February 1844. He stopped ex-President Manuel José Arce's attempt to return to El Salvador to regain office, but his involvement in the liberal-conservative intrigues of the period led him into war with Nicaragua in October 1844. He captured León on 24 January 1845, but Gerardo

Barrios and Trinidad Cabañas meanwhile pressured Acting President Joaquín Guzmán to depose Malespín on 2 February 1845. When Malespín ordered a priest executed later that year, Bishop Viteri y Ungo excommunicated him. Malespín's efforts to regain power led to war between Honduras and El Salvador in mid-1845. Malespín launched a new invasion of El Salvador in November 1846, but was murdered in a personal dispute at San Fernando, Chalatenango.

See also **El Salvador.**

BIBLIOGRAPHY

Philip Flemion, *Historical Dictionary of El Salvador* (1972), pp. 83–84.

Carlos C. Haeussler Yela, *Diccionario general de Guatemala,* vol. 2 (1983), pp. 950–951.

Ralph Lee Woodward, Jr., *Rafael Carrera and the Emergence of the Republic of Guatemala, 1821–1871* (1992). Translated into Spanish as *Rafael Carrera y la creación de la República de Guatemala, 1821-1871.* La Antigua, Guatemala: Centro de Investigaciones Regionales de Mesoamérica, 2002.

Additional Bibliography

Sullivan-González, Douglass. *Piety, Power, and Politics: Religion and Nation Formation in Guatemala, 1821-1871.* Pittsburgh, PA: University of Pittsburgh Press, 1998.

RALPH LEE WOODWARD JR.

MALFATTI, ANITA CATARINA (1889–1964). Anita Catarina Malfatti (*b.* 2 December 1889; *d.* 6 November 1964), Paulista artist who helped ignite the Brazilian modernist movement. Her oils, drawings, engravings, pastels, and watercolors were exhibited for fifty years in museums in Brazil, France, the United States, Argentina, and Chile.

Malfatti's Italian-born father died before she was thirteen. Her mother, a North American of German descent, was her first art teacher. Born with an atrophied right arm and hand, Malfatti received extensive training to use her left hand. After attending the Escola Americana, Malfatti graduated from Mackenzie College, and later taught at both institutions. Her uncle, Jorge Krug, sent her to Berlin (where she studied with Fritz Burger, Lovis Corinth, and Bischoff-Culm from 1910 to 1914). From 1914 to 1916 she took classes in New York at the Art Students League and at the Independent School of Art with Homer Boss. In 1915 her illustrations appeared in *Vogue* and *Vanity Fair* and she also painted some of the oils (*O japones, O homen amarelo, a boba, a mulher de cabelos verdes*) that led to the "Anita Malfatti Affair."

After returning to São Paulo in 1916, Malfatti painted two other controversial oils, *Tropical* and *O saci,* which were shown at her "Exposicão de pintura moderna" in São Paulo from December 1917 through January 1918. At first the exhibit was a success. But then an influential newspaper critic's hostile remarks led to demands for refunds and a flood of articles pro and con. Following this "Anita Malfatti Affair," a small group of young writers, other artists, and musicians began planning an event, the Modern Art Week, held in São Paulo in 1922, to vindicate her "martyrdom" and to modernize the Brazilian arts. The event did not change public opinion, however. With other members of the "Grupo dos Cinco" (Mario de Andrade, Tarsila do Amaral, Oswaldo de Andrade and Menotti del Picchia) and other Brazilians, including Lucilia Guimarães Villa-Lobos, Heitor Villa-lobos, Victor Brecheret, and Emiliano Di Calvalcanti, Malfatti traveled to Europe, where she stayed until 1928.

Malfatti had many exhibitions in Brazil, including major shows at the Salão Paulista de Arte Moderna (1932), the Salão de Arte de Feira Nacional de Indústrias (1941), the Salão Bahiano de Belas Artes (1949), and the Bienales do Museu de Arte Moderna (1951, and retrospective 1963). She was president and director of the Sindicatos dos Artistas Plásticos from 1941 to 1946.

See also **Art: The Twentieth Century; Modernism, Brazil.**

BIBLIOGRAPHY

Mary [Luciana] Lombardi, "Women in the Modern Art Movement in Brazil: Salon Leaders, Artists, and Musicians, 1917–1930" (Ph.D. diss., University of California at Los Angeles, 1977).

Marta Rossetti Batista, *Brasil.* Vol. 1, *Tempo Modernista—1917/29: Documentacão* (1972), and *Anita Malfatti (1889–1964)* (1977).

Additional Bibliography

Camargos, Marcia. *Semana de 22: Entre vaias e aplausos.* São Paulo, Brazil: Boitempo, 2002.

Jardim, Eduardo. *Mário de Andrade: A morte do poeta.* Rio de Janeiro: Civilização Brasileira, 2005.

Prada, Cecília. "As mulheres de '22." *Problemas Brasileiros* 33: 314 (Mar–Apr 1996): 41–44.

MARY LUCIANA LOMBARDI

MALINALCO. In Malinalco, a small town in southwestern México state, an important Mexica-Tenochca (Aztec) ceremonial-administrative site was built on the south side of Texcaltepec (Hill of the Idols). The site comprises a set of buildings dating from the early sixteenth century. The most exceptional is known as the Monolithic Temple, or Cuauhcalli, a truncated pyramid worked directly from volcanic tuff, a unique example in ancient Mexico of stone carving of enormous dimensions.

The upper façade of the temple's chapel is guarded by an open-mouthed sculpture of Cipactli (Earth Monster), a primeval mythical being associated with the creation of the universe and also with the earthly forces of fertility, particularly those emanating from caves. Despite highly reprehensible acts of vandalism in recent times, the interior of the chapel has been preserved in good condition. Within a space of about 19 feet (5.80 meters) in diameter, four stone carvings are arranged on the floor and on a semicircular bench around the walls. In the center, carved from the living rock of the floor, is an eagle, which faces the entrance. On the east and west sides are two more magnificent eagle sculptures. A carved jaguar rests in the center of the bench, situated on an approximate north-south axis.

This monolithic temple is believed to represent the meeting place of the forces of the upper world, in particular the sun (represented by the eagle), and the lower world: the earth (represented by the jaguar) and nature. In the magical-ritual world of the Aztecs, the two opposing forces needed to merge or complement each other so the universe would continue in balance, for the good of gods and human beings.

This temple is one of many constructions in a group scattered over a wide terrace formed artificially by excavating part of the mountainside and adding large quantities of fill. The other structures principally used masonry in their construction. One of the more interesting is Building III, with two chambers, one rectangular and the other semicircular. The floors of both contain square depressions where fire-related rituals were apparently practiced, so the roofs must have had smoke holes. The vestibule has wide benches attached to the east and west walls. The remains of a mural depicting warriors in procession were discovered in the chamber.

The town of Malinalco is home to the National Autonomous University of Mexico's Dr. Luis Mario Schneider Museum, located at the bottom of the road ascending to the archeological site. Inaugurated on May 18, 2001, the Museum provides a public space where the historical, cultural, artistic, and environmental heritage of Malinalco and its environs can be exhibited and stored.

See also **Aztecs.**

BIBLIOGRAPHY

García Payón, José. *Los monumentos arqueológicos de Malinalco.* México: Biblioteca Enciclopédica del Estado de México, 1974 [1947].

Noguez, Xavier. "El templo monolítico de Malinalco, Estado de México." *Arqueología Mexicana* 13, No. 78 (2006): 68–73.

Townsend, Richard F. "Malinalco and the Lords of Tenochtitlan." In *The Art and Iconography of Late Post-Classic Central Mexico*, edited by Elizabeth P. Benson and Elizabeth Hill Boone. Washington, DC: Dumbarton Oaks, Trustees for Harvard University, 1982.

XAVIER NOGUEZ

MALINCHE (between 1498 and 1505–1527?) Malinche is the first significant native female character to appear in the historical record after the Spanish arrived in Mexico in 1519. Several indigenous and Spanish chronicles mention her, but their information often does not coincide. Her biography has woven legend with reality. She is known by a variety of names: Malintzin, Malinche, or Doña Marina. Her original name was Malinalli (Twisted Grass), one of the twenty signs of the days on the Nahua calendar. Telepal appears as her second name.

Malinche was born sometime between 1498 and 1505 on the cost of the Gulf of Mexico, in the vicinity of Coatzacoalcos, Veracruz. She was the daughter of the chief of Painalan or Teticpac, a Nahuatl-speaking region. For reasons that are not clear she left her community as a slave and was sold to merchants from the region of Xicalanco, an important commercial enclave on Laguna de Términos, Campeche, where the Maya culture met the culture of central Mexico. It was there that she became familiar with the Maya language and culture.

When Hernán Cortés was exploring the coast of the present state of Tabasco in the spring of 1519, one of the local chiefs gave him several female slaves. One was Malinalli. From that moment on, the life of Doña Marina—the name the Spanish gave her—was bound to the captain of the Spanish expedition and she became not only a translator, at first with the aid of Jerónimo de Aguilar, who knew the Maya language, but also a loyal confidante and adviser on many important matters. Her presence in the company of Cortés was so well known that he came to be called "Señor Malinche," "Marina's captain," or "Marina's *huehue*" (old man).

Malinche was first given to Alonso Hernández Portocarrero, but she maintained an intimate relationship with Cortés, with whom she had an unspecified number of children. The most famous was Martín Cortés, who was born in 1522 or 1523 and received the title of knight of Santiago. In 1524 Malinche accompanied Cortés on his unsuccessful expedition to Las Hibueras (Honduras) and during the journey was given in marriage to Juan Jaramillo, with whom she had a daughter named Maria. Little is known of Malinche's last years, but she died in Mexico City in 1527, possibly from one of the terrible smallpox epidemics that struck the native population.

Illustration of La Malinche or Doña Marina, center, with Tlaxcalan chief and the Spanish Hernán Cortés, 16th century. The woman known as La Malinche (1504–1527) played an important role in the Spanish conquest of Mexico in her capacity as an interpreter. She symbolizes a controversial founding myth of modern Mexico. THE GRANGER COLLECTION, NEW YORK. REPRODUCED BY PERMISSION

The life and actions of this notable woman have made her in modern times the symbolic origin of a social and psychological state characterized by "submission to the foreign and disdain for one's own." This is the source of the term *malinchismo,* which has an openly negative connotation, implying surrender of one's national identity in favor of a foreign identity. But La Malinche also represents the beginning of *mestizaje*, or racial mixing, the biological and cultural union of the Mesoamerican peoples with the Spanish. There is presently a trend among Mexican and Chicano (Mexican-American) writers to attempt to salvage her image, not only with regard to gender, but also to give her a more objective place in history, due to the undeniable personal talents she always displayed.

See also **Cortés, Hernán; Cortés, Martín; Maya, the.**

BIBLIOGRAPHY

Díaz del Castillo, Bernal. *The Discovery and Conquest of Mexico: 1517–1521.* Edited by Genaro García; translated with an introduction and notes by A. P. Maudslay; new introduction by Hugh Thomas. Cambridge, MA: Da Capo Press, 2003.

Martínez, José Luís. *Hernán Cortés.* México, D. F.: Universidad Nacional Autónoma de México y Fondo de Cultura Económica, 2003.

Núñez Becerra, Fernanda. *La Malinche: De la historia al mito.* México, D.F.: Instituto Nacional de Antropología e Historia, 2002.

Karttunen, Frances. "Rethinking Malinche." In *Indian Women of Early Mexico*, edited by Susan Schroeder, Stephanie Wood, and Robert Haskett. Norman: University of Oklahoma Press, 1997.

XAVIER NOGUEZ

MALLARINO-BIDLACK TREATY.

See **Bidlack Treaty (Treaty of New Granada, 1846).**

MALLEA, EDUARDO (1903–1982). As a storyteller, essayist, and cultural critic, Argentine writer Eduardo Mallea (August 14, 1903–November 12, 1982) found in literature a space in which he could reflect on the effects of the Great Depression of the 1930s. As a consequence, he became one of the nation's most popular intellectuals to the mid-twentieth century.

After participating briefly in the vanguard movements of the 1920s, Mallea published his first book of short stories, *Cuentos para una inglesa desesperada* (1926; Stories for an English desperate). After that, his story and essay writing focused on examining Argentina's great national problems through the psychological and existential construction of subjectivities in crisis.

In the 1930s, faced with the great political, social, and cultural dilemmas resulting from the coup d'état of September 1930, Mallea wrote *Conocimiento y expresión de la Argentina* (1935: Knowledge and Expression of Argentina) and his best essay, *Historia de una pasión argentina* (1937: History of an Argentine Passion). In them he dealt with the questions concerning the destiny of a country that had lost its way. Far from expressing the pessimism that marked his contemporaries, however, Mallea believed that the values thought to be lost were only submerged in what he called "the invisible Argentina" (which he contrasted to the purity of the visible Argentina), formed by false, "adventitious men" who had not responded to the truth of the national identity and to the authentic nature of the Argentines.

The break between a visible and an invisible Argentina, the proposal of existential solutions to the spiritual crisis of modernity, the search for an order that would reestablish the lost networks of solidarity are the underpinning themes of Mallea's thought and are developed in his later essays and novels: *La bahía del silencio* (1940; The Bay of Silence), *Todo verdor perecerá* (1941; All Verdor Will Perish), *El sayal y la púrpura* (1941; The Sayal and the Purple), *Las Águilas* (1943; The Eagles), *Rodeada está de sueño* (1944; Surrounded by a Dream), *El Retorno* (1946; The Return), *Los enemigos del alma* (1950; The Enemies of the Soul), *La torre* (1950; The Tower), *Chaves* (1953), and *La sala de espera* (1953; The Waiting Room), among others. Similar subjects, figures, and motifs reappear in these writings and underline the role of an intellectual committed to an ethical program. In Mallea's work, reflection on the national entity of Argentina is paramount, and so is the construction of the writer's image as a figure who legitimizes reflection on nationalist ideology. This, then, guarantees the production of intellectual work.

See also **Literature: Spanish America.**

BIBLIOGRAPHY

Canal Feijoó, Bernardo. "Historia de una pasión argentina." *Sur*, no. 38 (November 1937): 74–82.

Dabini, Atilio. "Intelectualismo y existencialismo: Mallea." In *Historia de la literatura argentina*, vol. 4, ed Susana Zanetti. Vol. 4. Buenos Aires: Centro Editor de América Latina, 1982.

Gramuglio, María Teresa. "Posiciones, transformaciones y debates en la literatura." In *Crisis económica, avance del estado e incertidumbre política (1930–1943)*, Vol. 7: *Nueva Historia Argentina*, ed. Alejandro Cattaruzza. Buenos Aires: Sudamericana, 2001.

Mónaco, Ricardo. "La ficción como una pasión ensayística: Eduardo Mallea." In *El oficio se afirma*, Vol. 9: *Historia crítica de la literatura argentina*, ed. Sylvia Saítta. Buenos Aires: Emecé, 2004.

Rest, Jaime. *El cuarto en el recoveco.* Buenos Aires: Centro Editor de América Latina, 1982.

Rodríguez Monegal, Emir. "Eduardo Mallea visible e invisible." In *Narradores de esta América.* Buenos Aires: Alfa Argentina, 1977.

Rozitchner, León. "Comunicación y servidumbre: Mallea." *Contorno*, nos. 5–6 (September 1955): 27–35.

Sarlo, Beatriz. "La imaginación histórica." *Una modernidad periférica: Buenos Aires, 1920 y 1930.* Buenos Aires: Nueva Visión, 1988.

Sylvia Saítta

MALOCA. Maloca, a Portuguese word of Araucan origin, *malocan* was transformed by the Spanish into *maloca*. It was used originally to mean hostile or aggressive actions. The conquest of the pampas added a new meaning to the word, which also came to designate "Indian village." Today, the term refers to "Indian home," "shelter," or "hiding place," giving rise to the Brazilian Portuguese verb *malocar* (to hide or fool). The indigenous *maloca* is a large building of strong beams with large diameters, which support smaller, flexible pieces of wood, over which is woven a roof of straw made from palm or banana leaves or grass. Brazilian and Amazonian Amerindian cultures produced many forms of *malocas* to shelter extended families.

See also **Architecture: Architecture to 1900; Pampa.**

BIBLIOGRAPHY

Additional Bibliography

Marussi, Ferruccio. *Arquitectura vernacular amazónica: La maloca, vivienda colectiva de los Boras.* Lima: Editorial Universitaria, Universidad Ricardo Palma, 2004.

HAMILTON BOTELHO MALHANO

MALONES. Malones (also called *malocas*), a term from the Mapuche *malocan,* meaning "hostilities toward or among enemies involving raiding of goods and property." In Chile, the term *malocas* was used by Spanish colonists in the sixteenth century to describe Mapuche hostilities, but when the Mapuches expanded into the Argentine pampas at the turn of the nineteenth century, the Argentines called the raids *malones.*

In the course of four centuries of resistance, first to Inca and then to Spanish conquest, the Mapuche *malon* functioned as a formidable defense. In classical historiography, the "Indian" *malones* usually have been viewed as obstacles to progress or modernization but have not always been analyzed in cultural context. More recent analytical literature, which has begun to document the quantity and extent of Mapuche *malones* against Creole property, indicates dramatic changes within Mapuche society as a result of the integration of European goods and resources obtained through *malones* within Mapuche systems of exchange and redistribution.

As an institution, intra-Mapuche *malones* functioned to regularize the distribution of material resources, status, and wife-exchange. Allegations of malevolence and witchcraft affecting the health of individuals in a community or band prompted *malones* against other bands and also motivated Mapuche *malones* against creole frontier settlements in Chile and Argentina.

Over the centuries, the organization of the *malones* changed. By the eighteenth century, *malones* were organized, interband military operations, in some cases mirroring Spanish military forms. By the nineteenth century, the intertribal *malones* against Argentine *estancias* were clearly motivated by market objectives as well as by anger at treaty violations. In the course of these developments, however, Mapuche participation in the *malones* continued to be at the discretion of each individual kin leader, rather than dictated through a hierarchy. Even so, by the late nineteenth century, confederations involving over 200 individual bands organized major *malones* against ranching interests in Argentina. It was not until boundary issues between Chile and Argentina were resolved that those national governments were able to effectively combat the Mapuche *malon.*

See also **Araucanians; Calfucurá; Namuncurá, Manuel; Pehuenches; Ranqueles.**

BIBLIOGRAPHY

Madaline W. Nichols, "The Spanish Horse of the Pampas," in *American Anthropologist* 41 (January 1939):119–129.

Alfred Tapson, "Indian Warfare on the Pampa During the Colonial Period," in *Hispanic American Historical Review* 42 (February 1962):1–28.

Judith Ewell and William Beezeley, eds., *The Human Tradition in Latin America: The Nineteenth Century* (1989), pp. 175–186.

Leonardo Leon Solis, *Maloqueros y conchavadores en Araucanía y las Pampas, 1700–1800* (1990).

Additional Bibliography

Rojas Lagarde, Jorge Luis. *Malones y comercio de ganado con Chile: Siglo XIX.* Buenos Aires: El Elefante Blanco, 2004.

KRISTINE L. JONES

MALUF, PAULO SALIM (1931–). Paulo Salim Maluf (*b.* 3 September 1931), a Brazilian politician, was born in São Paulo, the son of Salim Farah Maluf and Maria Estefano Maluf. He married Silvia Luftalla, with whom he had four children. Although trained as an engineer, Maluf has been a longtime political figure both locally and nationally. Owner of Eucatex and other enterprises, Maluf started his political career in 1967, when President Costa e Silva appointed him president of the Caixa Econômica Federal (Federal Savings Bank) of São Paulo, a post he held for two years. In 1969, he was appointed *prefeito* (mayor) of his hometown and served until 1971, when he was appointed secretary of transportation for the state of São Paulo. In 1979, Maluf was indirectly elected under the ARENA Party banner as state governor. In spite of corruption charges, the politician was elected federal deputy in 1982, having received more than 600,000 votes.

Maluf ran for the presidency in 1984, but in spite of military backing was defeated in the electoral college by Tancredo de Almeida Neves. Later, he suffered additional defeats in his campaigns for governor of São Paulo state in 1986 and mayor of São Paulo in 1988, and in his candidacy for the presidency in 1989. The former governor attempted to regain the São Paulo governorship in 1990, but without success. Maluf was accused of a money-laundering scandal involving some family members on the Channel Islands. In 2001 he was formally convicted of corruption and allowed no further appeal. He was forced to pay R$500,000 to the Brazilian government. In September 2005 he and his son, Flávio Maluf, were briefly arrested and detained for three weeks on charges of intimidating witnesses in an ongoing investigation in which they were suspects. In March 2007 the Manhattan district attorney's office in the United States indicted him for his involvement in a money-laundering public works scheme, in which he allegedly stole $11.6 million. His reputation is so poor in Brazil that his name is commonly used as a verb—*malufar*—meaning "to steal public money."

See also **São Paulo (City).**

BIBLIOGRAPHY

Additional Bibliography

Amaral, Walter D. *Aqui, as provas contra Maluf.* São Paulo: Global Editora, 1984.

Maluf, Paulo Salim, with Heródoto Barbeiro. *Paulo Salim Maluf: Partido Democrático Social: Entrevista.* Vila Mariana, Brazil: Editora Harbra, 1989.

Martins, Rui. *O dinhero sujo da corrupção: Por que a Suíça entregou Maluf.* São Paulo, Brazil: Geracão Editorial, 2005.

Puls, Mauricio. *O malufismo.* São Paulo: Publifola, 2000.

Iêda Siqueira Wiarda

MALVINAS, LAS. *See* **Falkland Islands (Malvinas).**

MAM. Mam, one of twenty-nine extant Mayan languages spoken in Guatemala, Mexico, Belize, and Honduras. With approximately 600,000 speakers it is among the four largest languages and is spoken in fifty-six townships in the departments of Huehuetenango, Quetzaltenango, and San Marcos in Guatemala, as well as in the hills surrounding the border towns in Mexico such as Mazapa, Amatenango, Motozintla, and Tuzantán. Mam belongs to the Mamean branch of the Eastern Division of Mayan languages, along with Tektiteko (Teco/Tectiteco), Awakateko (Aguacateco), and Ixil. It is bordered by Q'anjob'alan (Kanjobalan) languages to the north and K'ichean (Quichean) languages to the east. It is the most internally divergent Mayan language, with three major dialect zones each consisting of a number of separate dialects. Mam diverged from other Mamean languages between 1,500 and 2,600 years ago. It is spoken today in a territory similar to that occupied in 1524, though somewhat reduced, through K'iche' (Quiché) incursion, from its maximum area. Although Mamean languages are historically most closely related to the K'ichean, Mam shows a number of innovative similarities to Q'anjob'alan (Western Division) languages that are due to long-term contact in the Huehuetenango region. Mam is suffering extensive loss in the western area, some loss in the south, and very little loss in the north.

See also **Maya, The.**

BIBLIOGRAPHY

See Nora C. England, *A Grammar of Mam, a Mayan language* (1983), for a reference grammar, and "El Mam: Semejanzas y diferencias regionales" in *Lecturas sobre la lingüística maya,* edited by Nora C. England and Stephen R. Elliott (1990), for dialect differences.

Additional Bibliography

B'aayil, Zoila Blanca Luz García Jiménez, and Ajb'ee. *Tx'ixpub'ente tiib' qyool= Variación dialectal en mam.* Guatemala: Cholsamaj, 2000.

Comunidad Lingüística Mam. *Toponimias Mayas mam.* Guatemala: Academia de Lenguas Mayas de Guatemala, 2002.

Gutiérrez Alfonzo, Carlos and Rosalva Aída Hernández Castillo. *Los mames: Exodo y renacimiento.* Mexico City: Instituto Nacional Indigenista, 2000.

Nora C. England

MAMACOCHA. The Incas revered the Pacific Ocean as the goddess Mamacocha, which translates from the Quechua as "Lady Sea" or "Mother Sea." Streams and springs, considered to be daughters of the sea, were venerated and given offerings of shells.

See also **Incas, The.**

BIBLIOGRAPHY

John H. Rowe, "Inca Culture at the Time of the Spanish Conquest," in *Handbook of South American Indians,* vol. 2 (1946), pp. 183–330. See also Burr Cartwright Brundage, *The Empire of the Inca* (1963).

Additional Bibliography

Cobo, Bernabé, *Historia del nuevo mundo* (1653). Sevilla: Impresa de E. Rasco, 1890–1895.

Silverblatt, Irene. *Moon, Sun, and Witches: Gender Ideologies and Class in Inca and Colonial Peru.* Princeton, NJ: Princeton University Press, 1987.

GORDON F. MCEWAN

MAMAQUILLA. Mamaquilla is a lunar deity in the Inca pantheon who served as the basis for the lunar calendar, which guided agricultural cycles. Because Mamaquilla was also the wife of the Inti, or Sun, she constituted one-half of a dual system that was gender based. The Inti and the Mamaquilla complemented each other as did the gold and silver that represented each of them respectively. Just as the Inca king descended from the Inti, the Coya queen was descended from the Mamaquilla. In the dualist structure of governance in the Andes, the moon was the goddess of all women, establishing a theological structure whereby, as Irene Silverblatt argues, the Coya held unquestioned governmental sway over all women.

See also **Incas, The; Inti.**

BIBLIOGRAPHY

Garcilaso de la Vega, El Inca. *Royal Commentaries of the Incas (and General History of Peru).* Translated by Harold V. Livermore and edited by Karen Spaulding. Indianapolis, IN: Hacket, 2006. See p. 17.

Silverblatt, Irene. *Moon, Sun, and Witches: Gender Ideologies and Class in Inca and Colonial Peru.* Princeton, NJ: Princeton University, 1987.

THOMAS WARD

MAMBISES. The term *mambises* refers to the Cuban guerrillas who fought against the Spanish during the Ten Years' War (1868–1878) and the War of Independence (1895–1898). The mambises are named after black Spanish officer Juan Ethninius Mamby, who joined the fight for Dominican independence in 1846 in Santo Domingo. The Spanish began to refer to the guerrillas as "the man of Mamby," or "mambies" as a derogatory term. When the Ten Years' War began many of the soldiers that fought in Santo Domingo were reassigned to Cuba where they applied the related term "mambises" to Cuban fighters; the Cuban fighters adopted the name with pride.

The mambises comprised of a mixture of indigenous, Afro Cuban, Asian Cuban, and Spanish descendants. They called on agricultural workers and freed slaves to join them. They were mainly poor men, who wore typical white and straw hats. They were poorly armed and outnumbered by the Spanish. Because the mambises had no access to conventional weaponry they had to use guerrilla-style tactics and were known for their use of the machete.

During the War of Independence they were led by General Máximo Gómez and General Antonio Maceo Grajales. Generals Maceo and Gómez led the forces west, to the greatest concentration of wealth and government. They traveled over a thousand miles in ninety-two days, fighting twenty-seven battles against numerically superior Spanish forces. Maceo was known as the "Bronze Titan" for being an outstanding leader. Despite Maceo's death in December 1896, the mambises continued the fight until U.S. intervention in 1898.

Another important figure was General Valeriano Weyler y Nicolau, who led the Spanish forces against the mambises. He became known for the "re-concentration" camps used to separate common people from fighters. Anyone caught outside the camp would be considered the enemy and be killed.

See also **Gómez y Báez, Máximo; Maceo, Antonio; Ten Years' War; Weyler y Nicolau, Valeriano.**

BIBLIOGRAPHY

Barnet, Miguel. *Biography of a Runaway Slave.* Translated by W. Nick Hill. Willimantic: Curbstone Press, 1994.

Foner, Philip S. *A History of Cuba and its Relations with the United States (Volume II, 1845–1895)*. New York: International Publishers, 1963.

Moreno Fraginals, Manuel. *Cuba-España, España-Cuba Historia Común*. Barcelona: Grijalbo Mondadori, 1995.

Pando, Magdalen M. *Cuba's Freedom Fighter: Antonio Maceo: 1845–1896*. Gainesville: Felicity Press, 1980.

ALINNE B. OLIVEIRA

MAMBO. Mambo was the predominant Latin popular music and dance style in the Americas throughout the 1950s. Although the term, coined about 1946, refers specifically to a syncopated rhythm, mambo was a cultural phenomenon, its influence evident in literature, film, modern dance, and classical music as well as popular music and dance. Most historians agree that the Cuban *charango* (an ensemble of piano, strings, flute, percussion, and vocals) Arcaño y sus Maravillas was the first to experiment with established rhythmic and formal structures toward a *danzón*-mambo style. The group's 1940 recording *Rarezas* features these developments.

By 1943 Cuban *conjunto* leader Arsenio Rodríguez had recorded *son* music, which featured similar structural and rhythmic innovations. Cuban musicians and arrangers René Hernández, Bebo Valdés, and Dámaso Pérez Prado quickly followed, implementing syncopated figures in specific sections of their arrangements for various Cuban big bands. Of these early figures, Prado, known as the "King of Mambo," became by far the most internationally well-known mambo stylist and bandleader. In 1949 he moved to Mexico City, where he recorded with RCA, releasing records such as *Mambo No. 5* that established him and his style as the personification and quintessence of the mambo among international audiences. Prado's appearances and the use of his music in Mexican films contributed to the dissemination and popularization of his music. As mambo music and dance garnered popularity throughout the Americas, local and regional styles also formed, the most significant of which was in New York City. Important purveyors included Machito and His Afro-Cubans, Tito Puente, and Tito Rodríguez.

See also **Machito; Music: Popular Music and Dance; Pérez Prado, Dámaso; Puente, Tito; Rodriguez, Tito; Son.**

BIBLIOGRAPHY

Garcia, David. *Arsenio Rodriguez and the Transnational Flows of Latin Popular Music*. Philadelphia: Temple University Press, 2006.

Giro, Radames, ed. *El Mambo*. La Habana: Editorial Letras Cubanas, 1993.

DAVID F. GARCIA

MAMELUCO. Mameluco, a person of mixed blood, that is, of Portuguese and indigenous parents. While the term is not used in modern Brazil, *mameluco* appears frequently in the historical documents of the sixteenth and seventeenth centuries. *Mameluco* men participated in many Entradas into the interior, for their facility with Amerindian language, customs, and terrain made them valuable middlemen between the coastal townsfolk and the inhabitants of the wilderness. *Mameluca* women assimilated easily into Portuguese society by marrying Portuguese men. *Mamelucos* profoundly influenced frontier societies such as São Vicente and Maranhão, which were characterized by extensive interactions with the interior and the late introduction of significant numbers of African slaves.

See also **African Brazilians, Color Terminology.**

BIBLIOGRAPHY

John Hemming, *Red Gold: The Conquest of the Brazilian Indians* (1978).

Alida C. Metcalf, *Family and Frontier in Colonial Brazil* (1992).

Additional Bibliography

Carvalho, João Renôr Ferreira de. *Resistência indígena no Piauí colonial: 1718–1774*. Imperatriz: Ética, 2005.

Langfur, Hal. *The Forbidden Lands: Colonial Identity, Frontier Violence, and the Persistence of Brazil's Eastern Indians, 1750–1830*. Stanford, CA: Stanford University Press, 2006.

Metcalf, Alida C. *Go-betweens and the Colonization of Brazil, 1500–1600*. Austin: University of Texas Press, 2005.

ALIDA C. METCALF

MAÑACH Y ROBATO, JORGE (1898–1961). Jorge Mañach y Robato (*b.* 14 February 1898; *d.* 25 June 1961), Cuban writer, born in Sagua la Grande. Mañach was learned in Cuban history and culture and participated in Cuban political life as senator of the Cuban republic (1940–1944) and as minister of state (1944). After studying in Cuba and going to Spain in 1907, where he attended Escuelas Pías in Getafé from 1908 to 1913, he was educated at Harvard, from which he graduated in 1920. In France he studied law at the Sorbonne and experienced the rich cultural and artistic life of Paris during the 1920s. Back in Cuba, Mañach took up a career in journalism (1922) on the famous journal *Diario de la Marina*. His first book, *Glosario* (1924), is a collection of the chronicles of his European and Cuban travels. This work comprises three genres: travel chronicles, *cuadros costumbristas* (works of local color), and essays of literary and art criticism. His essay *Indagación del choteo* (1928), which brought him recognition, deals with the humorous peculiarities and irreverent spirit of the Cuban personality. In *Martí: El apóstol* (1933), a biography in novel form, praise for the Cuban patriot José Martí is based on historical facts rather than on the subjective view of Martí given by the first republican generation. Exalting Martí as a hero, Mañach sought to restore political health to Cuba, which was then under the dictatorship of Gerardo Machado (1925–1933). Mañach rejected autocratic systems and considered the individual's inalienable right to freedom to be the foundation necessary for a social and political regime. And though his writings in the magazine *Bohemia* supported Fidel Castro, Mañach ultimately rejected the tenets of both Castro and Fulgencio Batista. Other important works by Mañach are *Examen del quijotismo* (1950), a phenomenological study of *Don Quijote*, and *Teoría de la frontera* (1970), which synthesizes the values of North American and Latin American culture, and suggests the potential for a good relationship between the two.

See also **Cuba: Cuba Since 1959.**

BIBLIOGRAPHY

Nicolás Emilio Álvarez, *La obra literaria de Jorge Mañach* (1979).

Jorge Luis Martí, *El periodismo literario de Jorge Mañach* (1977).

Rosalyn K. O'Cherony, "The Critical Essays of Jorge Mañach" (Ph.D. diss., Northwestern University, 1970).

Additional Bibliography

Argote-Freyre, Frank. *Fulgencio Batista*. New Brunswick, NJ: Rutgers University Press, 2006.

Díaz Infante, Duanel. *Mañach o la República*. La Habana: Letras Cubanas, 2003.

Fuente, Alejandro de la. *A Nation for All: Race, Inequality, and Politics in Twentieth-Century Cuba*. Chapel Hill: University of North Carolina Press, 2001.

JUAN CARLOS GALEANO

MANAGUA. Managua, the capital of Nicaragua. Located on the southern shores of Lake Managua, the city's site had been an ancient Indian settlement of the Chorotega called Manahuec. Before 1855, however, it was an obscure village. At that time it was chosen as a compromise capital to avoid conflict between the competing centers of León and Granada. The city grew rapidly after the completion of the railroad to coffee-producing areas in 1898 and to the Pacific port of Corinto in 1903. Although it was a late starter among Central American capitals, Managua is now the commercial and political center of Nicaragua. U.S. Marines came to Managua in 1912 to back a Conservative Party revolt. They returned in 1927 to enforce a political settlement between the Conservatives and Liberals. Remaining until 1932, they also supervised elections and trained the National Guard.

A severe earthquake destroyed a large part of the city in 1931, and a major fire caused widespread destruction in 1936. Another earthquake in December 1972 leveled the center of the city. Over 10,000 people were killed, and 300,000 were left homeless. A pattern of decentralization was decided upon in rebuilding, because the fault lines clearly concentrated in the city center. The principal commercial ventures moved to the southern part of the city.

In 1978–1979 the city led the general strikes held to oppose the government of Anastasio Somoza Debayle. Heavy fighting with the Sandinista opposition took place in the city's slum areas in 1979. After more than a decade of peace, Managua continues to grow, contributing to housing shortages and high real estate prices. The population reached 937,489 in 2005, with more than 1.2 million people in the metropolitan area, representing one-fourth of the total population of Nicaragua. It is nearly ten times the size of León, the second-largest city of the country. Managua is governed as a national district under the control of the central government, rather than as a typical municipality. It shares with León the main campuses of the National Autonomous University (UNAN). The Central American University (UCA), a Jesuit institution, was founded in Managua in 1962. The Central American Institute of Business Administration (INCAE) has its original campus to the south of the city.

See also **Catholic Church: The Modern Period; Coffee Industry; Nicaragua.**

BIBLIOGRAPHY

Gratus Halftermeyer, *Historia de Managua* (1971).

Additional Bibliography

Koonings, Kees, and Dirk Kruijt, eds. *Fractured Cities: Urban Violence, State Failure, and Social Exclusion* New York: Zed, 2006.

Lungo, Mario, and Mario Polèse. *Economía y desarrollo urbano en Centroamérica*. San José: FLACSO, Sede Costa Rica, 1998.

Traña Galeano, Marcia, and Adolfo Díaz Lacayo. *Apuntes sobre la historia de Managua*. Managua: Aldilá, 2000.

DAVID L. JICKLING

MANAUS. Manaus, capital of the Brazilian state of Amazonas. Founded in 1669, Manaus is located on the Rio Negro, about 1,000 miles upriver from the mouth of the Amazon, and is the main port in the Amazonian interior.

Manaus was a small settlement in 1867, when the Brazilian government opened the Amazon River to international trade. The forests surrounding Manaus were rich in rubber trees, and from the 1870s on, Brazilian and foreign merchants flocked to the inland capital to profit from the booming rubber trade.

The city entered its heyday in the 1890s, when Manaus became the major center for Amazonian exports; by 1910 the urban population had grown to nearly 100,000 inhabitants. A classic boomtown, Manaus boasted the first electric street lighting in Brazil, piped water and gas, a system of floating docks, an ornate customshouse, and an elaborate opera house, crafted almost entirely from imported materials.

As an entrepôt that relied almost entirely on the rubber trade, Manaus was hit hard by the collapse of the wild rubber market in 1911. Population declined, trade plummeted, and the abandoned, decaying opera house stood as a monument to the excesses of the boom years. However, as the sole significant urban center in the western Amazon, Manaus survived the boom-bust cycle. In an effort to revive the Amazonian economy, in 1967 the Brazilian government declared Manaus a free port, thus generating a sharp increase in commercial activity and industrial development. Along with factories processing local products, Manaus is now home to several large, foreign-owned manufacturing plants producing consumer durables for the Brazilian market. As of 2006, Manaus had an estimated population of 1,688,524.

See also **Amazon Region; Amazon River; Rubber Industry.**

BIBLIOGRAPHY

E. Bradford Burns, "Manaus, 1910: Portrait of a Boom Town," in *Journal of Inter-American Studies* 7, no. 3 (1965): 400–421.

Richard Collier, *The River that God Forgot* (1968).

Barbara Weinstein, *The Amazon Rubber Boom, 1850–1920* (1983).

Additional Bibliography

Aguiar, José Vicente de Souza. *Manaus: Praça, café, colégio e cinema nos anos 50 e 60.* Manaus: Editora Valer: Edições Governo do Estado, 2002.

Markusen, Ann R., Yong-Sook Lee, and Sean DiGiovanna. *Second Tier Cities: Rapid Growth Beyond the Metropolis.* Minneapolis: University of Minnesota Press, 1999.

Oliveira, José Aldemir de, José Duarte Alecrim, and Thierry Ray Jehlen Gasnier. *Cidade de Manaus: Visões interdisciplinares.* Manaus: EDUA, 2003.

BARBARA WEINSTEIN

MANCO CAPAC. Manco Capac, founder of the Inca dynasty (the dates of his reign are unknown). In Inca myth Manco Capac emerged, together with his three brothers and four sisters, from three caves at Pacariqtambo, the Inca place of origin in the Peruvian highlands, a few miles southwest of the valley of Cuzco. Manco married his sister Mama Ocllo, founding the Inca bloodline, and led his siblings into the valley of Cuzco, establishing the city of Cuzco and the Inca dynasty around 1200.

According to the legend, at the end of his life, Manco Capac turned into a stone that became one of the most sacred *huacas* of the Incas.

See also **Incas, The.**

BIBLIOGRAPHY

Sources on Manco Capac and the founding of the Inca dynasty include John H. Rowe, "Inca Culture at the Time of the Spanish Conquest," in *Handbook of South American Indians,* vol. 2 (1946), pp. 183–330; Burr Cartwright Brundage, *The Empire of the Inca* (1963); Gary Urton, *The History of a Myth: Pacariqtambo and the Origin of the Incas* (1990).

Additional Bibliography

Espinoso Apolo, Manuel. *Hablan los Incas: Crónicas de Collapiña, Supno, Inca Garcilasco, Felipe Guaman Poma, Titu Cusi y Juan Santacruz Pachacuti.* Quito, Ecuador: Taller de Estudios Andinos, 2001.

Minelli, Laura Laurencich, ed. *The Inca World: The Development of Pre-Columbian Peru, A.D. 1000–1534.* Norman: University of Oklahoma Press, 1999.

Vilcapoma I., José Carlos. *El retorno de los incas: De Manco Cápac a Pachacútec.* Peru: Universidad Nacional Agraria la Molina, Instituto de Investigaciónes y Desarrollo Andino, 2002.

GORDON F. MCEWAN

MANCO INCA (c. 1516–1545). Manco Inca (*b.* ca. 1516; *d.* 1545), Inca emperor during the early colonial period (reigned 1533–1545). Manco Inca was one of the sons of the emperor Huayna Capac. After the deaths of his brothers Atahualpa, Huascar, and the first Spanish puppet Inca, another brother named Topa Huallpa, Manco Inca was chosen by the Spanish conquistadores to rule as Inca emperor under their control. Crowned in 1533, he was treated badly by the Spanish, who abused him and his family and publicly insulted them. As a result, in 1536 he rebelled and fled with a large group of followers into the *montaña* region of eastern Peru, where he formed the rump state Vilcabamba. Leading a vigorous resistance to the Conquest, he was killed by the Spanish.

See also **Incas, The.**

BIBLIOGRAPHY

John Hemming, *The Conquest of the Incas* (1970).

Burr Cartwright Brundage, *The Lords of Cuzco: A History and Description of the Inca People in Their Final Days* (1967).

Additional Bibliography

Vega, Juan José. *Manco Inca.* Lima, Peru: Editorial Brasa, 1995.

Vilcapoma I., José Carlos. *El retorno de los incas: De Manco Cápac a Pachacútec.* Peru: Universidad Nacional Agraria la Molina, Instituto de Investigaciónes y Desarrollo Andino, 2002.

GORDON F. MCEWAN

MANDAMIENTO. In the political and economic chaos of Guatemala immediately after independence, there was little need for the forced wage labor (*repartimientos*) that had characterized the late colonial period. The onset of large-scale coffee production after 1860, however, prompted the state and expectant planters to revive and expand coerced labor, now universally labeled *mandamientos* (from *mandar,* "to order"). The labor law of 1877, for example, gave Guatemala's Indian population the choice of accepting contracts for seasonal work on the coffee plantations or of finding themselves subjected to repeated forced drafts for the same purposes. Under the *mandamiento* system a planter in need of labor might request workers from one of the regional governors, paying the necessary wages and travel expenses in advance; the governor designated a community to supply the workers and required local Indian officials to mobilize and deliver them. Coercion kept wages low, but because *mandamiento* Indians were a reluctant and resentful work force, planters turned to them only in emergencies or to staff properties notorious for egregious abuse or particularly unhealthful conditions. The more important function of *mandamientos* was to force Indians into debt peonage. Officially abolished in the 1890s, *mandamientos* in fact persisted until the overthrow of President Manuel Estrada Cabrera in 1920.

See also **Coffee Industry; Debt Peonage; Repartimientos.**

BIBLIOGRAPHY

Chester Lloyd Jones, *Guatemala: Past and Present* (1940), chap. 12.

David Mc Creery, "'An Odious Feudalism': *Mandamiento* Labor and Commercial Agriculture in Guatemala, 1858–1920," in *Latin American Perspectives* 13, no. 1 (Winter 1986): 99–117.

Additional Bibliography

Cambranes, J.C. *Coffee and Peasants: The Origins of the Plantation Economy in Guatemala, 1853–1897.* Stockholm, Sweden: Institute of Latin American Studies, 1985.

McCreery, David. *Rural Guatemala: 1760–1940.* Stanford, CA: Stanford University Press, 1994.

Reeves, René. *Ladinos with Ladinos, Indians with Indians: Land, Labor, and Regional Ethnic Conflict in the Making of Guatemala.* Stanford, CA: Stanford University Press, 2006.

Taracena Arriola, Arturo. *Etnicidad, estado y nación en Guatemala.* Antigua: Centro de Investigaciones Regionales de Mesoamérica, 2002-2004.

DAVID MCCREERY

MANDU LADINO (?–1719). Mandu Ladino (*d.* 1719), leader of one of the largest Indian rebellions in the Brazilian colonial period. Mandu Ladino was a "civilized" (ladino means "latinized" or "civilized") Indian, who had been educated by the Jesuits. The revolt began in 1712 because of Tapuia resentment of forced labor in support of a Portuguese garrison. The Tapuia also wanted to avenge Indian killings committed by the Portuguese commander, Antônio da Cunha Souto-Maior, and his men, whose brutality including decapitating Indians for sport.

Mandu's 400 men sacked military garrisons, burned ranches, and killed Portuguese soldiers and settlers in Ceará, Piauí and Maranhão, but they spared missionaries. When Portuguese troops attacked a group of Tupi Indians, they too joined the rebellion and killed 88 people. Rebels destroyed at least 100 ranches, causing substantial losses.

Several Portuguese military expeditions against Mandu failed. The governor of Maranhão led one expedition in 1716 and surrounded Mandu's village, but a premature shot alerted the Indians and allowed them to escape. A rival group of the Tapuia, the Tobajara, defeated Mandu Ladino in a series of engagements, reducing his force to about 50 men. They killed him as he attempted to escape across a river.

See also **Slavery: Indian Slavery and Forced Labor; Tapuia.**

BIBLIOGRAPHY

John Hemming, *Red Gold* (1979).

Additional Bibliography

Cunha, Manuela Carneiro da, and Francisco M Salzano. *História dos índios no Brasil.* São Paulo: Fundação de Amparo á Pesquisa do Estado de São Paulo, 1998.

Prezia, Benedito, and Eduardo Hoornaert. *Brasil indígena: 500 anos de resistência.* São Paulo: FTD, 2000.

ROSS WILKINSON

MANILA GALLEON. From 1571 to 1814, the richly laden Manila galleons sailed across the Pacific Ocean between Mexico and Manila in the Philippines. This trade route linked America with Asia, and more particularly, the Viceroyalty of New Spain with its farthest province, the Philippine Islands. The galleon trade was noted for the length and duration of its voyages—over 6,000 miles and six to nine months' sail from Manila to Acapulco. It was also notable for the enormous size of many of the galleons (up to 2,000 tons, comparable only to the largest of the Portuguese East Indiamen) and the mystique of the Asian luxuries it made available.

In 1571, after gaining control of the Malay trading center of Manila for Spain, Miguel López De Legazpi sent two ships back to Mexico laden with Chinese silks and porcelains, to be exchanged for needed provisions. In this way the Manila galleon trade was established. Spain was uniquely well prepared to conduct this commerce because of the convenient geographical location of Manila and America's large supply of silver. Chinese merchants, eager for silver, carried to Manila fine silks, damasks and other fabrics, gemstones, finely worked gold jewelry, and porcelain. Other products shipped aboard the galleons were brought from India (cottons and other fabrics); Japan (lacquerware and screens); the islands of the Indonesian archipelago (aromatic substances, pepper, cloves, nutmegs, mace); Indochina (gemstones and hard woods); and the Philippine Islands themselves (cinnamon, coconut products, beeswax, and fabrics).

Merchants in Spain found that inexpensive, high-quality merchandise from Asia competed too successfully with Spanish exports to America, and argued for severe restrictions on the volume of the trade—over the loud complaints of Mexican and Philippines advocates. This purposeful limitation after 1593 led to the proliferation of contraband trading.

Precise estimates of the extent of illegal trade are elusive for obvious reasons, but scattered information gleaned from official records, secondhand commentary, testimony from English captors of galleons, and accounts of infrequent inspections suggest that as much as ten times the permitted amount of cargo was being shipped. Contraband trading was fairly common throughout the Spanish Empire, but that on the Pacific galleons was notorious.

The westbound galleons rode the trade winds, and typically reached Manila without incident in three months. Eastbound galleons faced the harder challenge. Oversized, with decks piled high and provisions frequently foregone in order to carry additional merchandise, the unwieldy galleons sailed from Cavite, in Manila Bay. It took a month for the galleons to clear the Philippine archipelago and sail out into the open water of the Pacific. This leg of the journey needed to be completed before the onset of the typhoon season, which required that the galleons depart Manila by the end of June. This feat was rarely achieved, however, and many ended their journeys wrecked in fierce typhoons—as many as forty-four are known to have been lost—or by making the return (*arribada*) to Manila.

Even a successful voyage from Manila to Acapulco could be trying, lasting from six to nine months. This made the problems of provisions and health daunting. It was not unusual for more than 100 persons to die en route.

When first news arrived of the approach of the galleons to Acapulco—usually in January or February—plans were made for a festive trade fair. The ships were met by officials who came from Mexico City for the occasion. The sick were disembarked, ships' manifest and cargo cursorily examined, and merchandise unloaded to be sold at the fair. Residents of the Spanish colonies, both Spaniards and Amerindians, festooned themselves and their homes with Oriental goods.

The Manila galleon trade made significant contributions to colonial Spanish culture. It helped to fashion the very society of the Philippines, which relied upon its income, its merchandise, and the services of Chinese, Malay, and other participants. In Mexico, the infusion of Chinese goods and art forms into Hispanic and Native American material culture remains visible today.

The economy of the whole empire was affected by the trade. From the Spanish (and official Mexican) point of view, the Philippine colony and its commerce were liabilities, even though much sought-after Chinese products were acquired. Manila and the galleons cost enormous sums to maintain and succeeded in directing vast quantities of American silver away from the imperial treasury. Many individual merchants risked and lost their lives, but sizable fortunes were accrued. Upon arrival at Acapulco in 1634, the traveler Fray Sebastián Manrique noted, "this profit made all hardships and dangers appear as nothing."

See also **New Spain, Viceroyalty of; Silk Industry and Trade.**

BIBLIOGRAPHY

William Lytle Schurz, *The Manila Galleon* (1939).

Pierre Chaunu, *Les Philippines et le Pacifique des Ibériques* (1960).

Giovanni Francesco Gemelli Careri, *A Voyage to the Philippines, 1696–1697* (1963).

Nicholas Cushner, *Spain in the Philippines* (1971).

Robert R. Reed, *Colonial Manila: The Context of Hispanic Urbanism and Process of Morphogenesis* (1978).

O. H. K. Spate, *The Spanish Lake* (1979).

Carmen Yuste López, *El comercio de la Nueva España con Filipinas, 1590–1785* (1984).

Louisa Schell Hoberman, *Mexico's Merchant Elite, 1590–1660* (1991), esp. pp. 183–222.

Additional Bibliography

Díaz-Trechuelo Spínola, María Lourdes. *Filipinas: la gran desconocida, 1565–1898.* Pamplona: Ediciones Universidad de Navarra, 2001.

Lang, M.F. *Las flotas de la Nueva España (1630–1710): despacho, azogue, comercio.* Sevilla: Muñoz Moya, 1998.

WILLIAM MCCARTHY

MANIOC. Manioc, a tropical root crop, also known as mandioca, cassava, aipim, or yuca. The manioc plant (*Manihot esculenta*) grows from 5 to 12 feet in height, with edible leaves of five to seven lobes. What most people use for food, however, are the roots, which are 2 to 6 inches in diameter and 1 to 2 feet in length. Each plant may yield up to 17 pounds of roots. When fresh, the roots are a source of carbohydrates, whereas the leaf has protein and vitamin A. Fresh roots may also contain calcium, vitamin C, thiamine, riboflavin, and niacin.

Of the two principal varieties of manioc, the sweet ones can be harvested in six to nine months, peeled, and eaten as a vegetable. The bitter varieties, however, require twelve to eighteen months to mature and have high levels of prussic acid, which must be removed by grating and soaking in water to avoid poisoning.

The indigenous populations of Latin America mastered the technology to render bitter manioc harmless and useful. Amerindian women wash, peel, and grate the roots to convert them into a snowy white mass, which they put into a cylindrical basket press, the *tipiti*. One end of the *tipiti* is tied to a tree, the other to the ground in order to squeeze out excess liquid. The pulpy mass is removed, put through a sieve, and then toasted on a flat ceramic griddle or metal basin. The starchy pulp may also be boiled in a mush, baked into a bread, and even eaten as a pudding (tapioca). Manioc meal (farinha) can be preserved and stored in a tropical climate.

Manioc was domesticated in the Americas; possible areas of origin include Central America, the Amazon region, and the northeast of Brazil. Although the oldest archaeological evidence comes from the Amazon region, actual remains of manioc date from 1785 BCE in and near the Casma Valley of Peru. In Mexico manioc leaves and manioc starch found in human coprolites are 2,100 to 2,800 years old. Manioc was also a staple of the Mayas in Mesoamerica. Evidence of ancient manioc cultivation also exists for the Caribbean, where the Arawaks and Caribs utilized manioc griddles and named the plant *kasabi* (Arawak) and *yuca* (Carib).

The first European description of what the Spanish came to call *yuca* is that of Peter Martyr (1494), who reported on "venomous roots" used in preparing breads. The Portuguese soon thereafter discovered manioc on the coast of Brazil. Two early descriptions are by Hans Staden (1557) and Jean de Léry (1578). Coastal settlers and their slaves rapidly adopted manioc as a principal food staple in South America. The Iberian conquerors also doled out manioc bread to their troops in the frontier wars, and it has been a military ration since the sixteenth century.

By the end of the colonial period, manioc was widely cultivated by small farmers, the enslaved, and the impoverished of tropical Latin America, either for their own families or for sale to sugar planters, towns, and cities. Its cultivation, transport, and commerce contributed significantly to the internal economy of the tropics, but manioc did not become a cash crop for export, possibly because the Portuguese introduced it to the rest of the world in the sixteenth century. It was, however, widely used in the slave trade between Brazil and Africa from at least the 1590s to 1850. In the twentieth century, most manioc production occurs outside of Latin America—Asia and Africa accounted for three-fourths of global production in contrast to Latin America's one-fourth in the 1980s. However, Brazil still remains the largest single producer and accounts for 86 percent of Latin America's production. The export market for manioc remains limited because of the number of close abundant substitutes.

See also **Martyr, Peter; Slave Trade.**

BIBLIOGRAPHY

Hans Staden, *Duas viagens ao Brasil,* translated by Guiomar de Carvalho Franco ([1557], 1974).

Jean De Léry, *History of a Voyage to the Land of Brazil, Otherwise Called America,* translated by Janet Whatley ([1578], 1990).

Leon Pynaert, *Le manioc,* 2d ed. (1951).

William O. Jones, *Manioc in Africa* (1959).

Milton De Albuquerque, *A mandioca na Amazônia* (1969).

Donald W. Lathrap, *The Upper Amazon* (1970).

Anna Curtenius Roosevelt, *Parmana: Prehistoric Maize and Manioc Subsistence Along the Amazon and Orinoco* (1980).

Pinto De Aquiar, *Mandioca—Pão do Brasil* (1982).

James H. Cock, *Cassava: New Potential for a Neglected Crop* (1985).

Robert Langdon, "Manioc, a Long Concealed Key to the Enigma of Easter Island," *Geographical Journal* 154, no. 3 (1988): 324–336.

Timothy Johns, *With Bitter Herbs They Shall Eat It: Chemical Ecology and the Origins of Human Diet and Medicine* (1990).

Maguelonne Toussaint-Samat, *History of Food*, translated by Anthea Bell (1992).

Additional Bibliography

Barickman, B. J. *A Bahian Counterpoint: Sugar, Tobacco, Cassava, and Slavery in the Recôncavo, 1780–1860.* Stanford, CA: Stanford University Press, 1998.

MARY KARASCH

MANLEY, MICHAEL NORMAN (1924–1997). Michael Norman Manley was born in 1924, the youngest son of Jamaican "national hero" Norman Manley and Jamaican sculptor Edna Manley. He was educated at the best schools in Jamaica and then at the London School of Economics. Faced with a serious challenge from the Marxist Left, Norman Manley asked his son to return to reorganize the National Workers Union, the fundamental base of the social democratic People's National Party (PNP). This he did with great success, introducing Jamaicans to his extraordinary charisma and organizational skills. In 1969 Manley replaced his father as head of the PNP, and in 1972 he led the party to a resounding victory over the Jamaican Labour Party (JLP). In 1974 Manley shifted his rhetoric and his policies to the Left. A new platform of "democratic socialism" included new levies on the vital U.S.-owned bauxite industry as well as a decided reorientation of foreign policy from Washington, D.C. to Communist Cuba. Another PNP landslide electoral victory in 1976 encouraged Manley to accelerate this leftist orientation, with unfortunate results. By 1977 serious petrol and food shortages led to widespread political violence. Manley claimed that there was a U.S.-led "destabilization" plan behind the riots and discontent, a claim he never documented. What he faced was the continued flight of capital (both domestic and foreign), the virtual collapse of the tourist industry, and hoarding and speculation that made life expensive and difficult; all of these eroded his own and the PNP's popularity. In 1980 they were soundly defeated by the pro-business JLP. Manley made a comeback in 1989 with a decidedly more moderate program. Faced with a serious recurring illness, Manley resigned in 1992, and died in 1997.

See also **Jamaica; Manley, Norman Washington.**

BIBLIOGRAPHY

Huber-Stephens, Evelyne, and John D. Stephens. *Democratic Socialism in Jamaica: The Political Movement and Social Transformation in Dependent Capitalism.* Princeton, NJ: Princeton University Press, 1986.

Payne, Anthony J. *Politics in Jamaica.* London: Hurst, 1988.

ANTHONY P. MAINGOT

MANLEY, NORMAN WASHINGTON (1893–1969). Norman Washington Manley was chief minister of Jamaica from 1955 to 1962, and a leading figure in the Jamaican independence movement. Manley was born on July 4, 1893, in Roxborough, Jamaica. He was an excellent athlete and talented scholar who won a prestigious Rhodes scholarship to attend Oxford University in 1914. While there he enlisted in the British army and fought in World War I. Upon his return to Jamaica, he witnessed the 1938 union strikes and riots, in which Jamaican workers lobbied for better conditions and pay. Their struggle inspired him to become involved in politics. That same year, he founded the left-wing People's National Party (PNP) and became the party's president. The PNP quickly became a dominant force in Jamaican politics.

In 1944 the efforts of Manley and his party resulted in the adoption of a new constitution that gave full suffrage to all Jamaican adults for the first time. In 1955 his party won the national elections and he became chief minister (later, prime minister) of Jamaica, a post that he held through 1962. That same year, Jamaica became a member of the Federation of the West Indies, an institution the British Crown had created to oversee governance of its Caribbean territories. Although he was in favor of remaining attached to the British Commonwealth through the Federation of the West Indies, in 1961 Manley agreed to hold a popular referendum to decide whether to remain with the federation. The people chose to separate, and this led Jamaica down the road to independence. On August 6, 1962, Jamaica was declared an independent nation. Although his term as prime minister ended in 1962, Manley continued to serve as leader of the PNP until his death on September 2, 1969. His son Michael Manley became prime minister of Jamaica in 1972.

See also **Jamaica; Manley, Michael Norman.**

BIBLIOGRAPHY

Manley, Norman Washington. *Norman Washington Manley and the New Jamaica: Selected Speeches and Writings, 1938–1968*. New York: Africana Publishing Company, 1971.

Thomas, Deborah A. *Modern Blackness: Nationalism, Globalization, and the Politics of Culture in Jamaica.* Durham, NC: Duke University Press, 2004.

Walters, Ewart L. *Resistance and Vision: The Making of Jamaica's National Heroes.* Ottawa: Boyd McRubie Communications, 1997.

EMILY BERQUIST

MANN, THOMAS CLIFTON (1912–1999). Thomas Clifton Mann, a career diplomat, was born 11 November 1912 near the border town of Laredo, Texas, and became bilingual at an early age. After working in the family law firm, he joined the State Department in 1942, specializing in Latin American affairs. He became a foreign service officer in 1947 and served as ambassador to El Salvador and as one of President Lyndon B. Johnson's principal advisers on Latin American policy. Mann advocated private, rather than public, investment and feared that Communists manipulated local nationalist movements in the Western Hemisphere. Therefore, he supported the Central Intelligence Agency's planned overthrow of Guatemala's Jacobo Arbenz Guzmán in 1954. Mann served as Assistant Secretary of State for Economic Affairs in the Eisenhower administration (1957–1960) when it shaped many of the policies subsequently found in the Alliance for Progress. After a stint as Ambassador to Mexico, Mann became Under Secretary of State for Economic Affairs in 1965. His advocacy of unilateral action by the United States in the Dominican Republic crisis of 1965 caused widespread criticism and contributed to his resignation in 1966. That same year President Johnson presented him with the President's Award for Distinguished Federal Civilian Service, and the Pan-American Society of New York awarded him its Gold Insignia. From 1967 to 1972 he was president of the Automobile Manufacturer's Association. In 1997 his alma mater, Baylor University in Waco, Texas, honored him as a Distinguished Alumnus. He died in Austin in 1999.

See also **Dominican Revolt (1965).**

BIBLIOGRAPHY

Abraham F. Lowenthal, *The Dominican Intervention* (1972).

Stephen G. Rabe, *Eisenhower and Latin America: The Foreign Policy of Anticommunism* (1988).

Federico Gil, "The Kennedy-Johnson Years," in *United States Policy in Latin America: A Quarter Century of Crisis and Challenge, 1961–1986,* edited by John D. Martz (1988).

Additional Bibliography

Grandin, Greg. *Empire's Workshop: Latin America, the United States, and the Rise of the New Imperialism.* New York: Metropolitan Books, 2006.

Raymont, Henry. *Troubled Neighbors: The Story of U.S.-Latin American Relations, from FDR to the Present.* Cambridge, MA: The Century Foundation, 2005.

Sweig, Julia E. *Friendly Fire: Losing Friends and Making Enemies in the Anti-American Century.* New York: Public Affairs, 2006.

THOMAS M. LEONARD

MANNING, THOMAS COURTLAND (1825–1887). Thomas Courtland Manning (*b.* 14 September 1825; *d.* 11 October 1887), Louisiana lawyer, public official, and U.S. minister to Mexico. Manning was educated at the University of North Carolina before reading law. On 18 January 1848, he married Mary Blair. Before moving to Louisiana in 1855, he taught school and practiced law in North Carolina. During the Civil War he was a brigadier general in the Confederate army. He served as an associate justice of Louisiana's Supreme Court in 1864–1865 and 1882–1886, and as chief justice from 1877 to 1880.

He was envoy extraordinary and minister plenipotentiary to Mexico from 30 August 1886 until

21 September 1887. In December 1886, he filed a claim against Mexico for the killing of Captain Emmet Crawford, a U.S. citizen, by Mexican rural volunteers. During his short service he intervened on behalf of various U.S. entrepreneurs, especially in mining, railroads, and real estate.

See also **United States-Latin American Relations.**

BIBLIOGRAPHY

James Morton Callahan, *American Foreign Policy in Mexican Relations* (1932); *Dictionary of American Biography,* vol. 6 (1961), p. 253.

National Cyclopedia of American Biography, vol. 4 (1892), p. 344; *Biographical and Historical Memoirs of Louisiana,* vol. 1 (1892), pp. 93, 97, 112.

Luis G. Zorrilla, *Historia de las relaciones entre México y los Estados Unidos de América, 1800–1958,* 2 vols. (1965–1966).

Additional Bibliography

Duarte Espinosa, María de Jesús. *Frontera y diplomacia: Las relaciones México-Estados Unidos durante el porfiriato.* México: Secretaría de Relaciones Exteriores, 2001.

Johnson, Richard L. *Manning: The Life & Times of Thomas Courtland Manning (1825-1887).* Baltimore, MD: Gateway Press, 2005.

THOMAS SCHOONOVER

MANRIQUE DE ZÚÑIGA, ALVARO

MANRIQUE DE ZÚÑIGA, ALVARO (?–c. 1593). Alvaro Manrique de Zúñiga (marqués de Villamanrique; *d.* ca. 1593), seventh viceroy of New Spain. Villamanrique is thought by some to have been the low point of viceregal government in Mexico in the sixteenth century. Governing from 1585 to 1590, Villamanrique is credited with having begun the process whereby the northern frontier was pacified. He sought to increase royal control over the distribution and sale of mercury, wine, and meat. In keeping with royal legislation of 1574, Villamanrique helped strengthen royal control over the Catholic Church. Because of these and other policies many residents of New Spain opposed the viceroy. In 1588 a jurisdictional dispute with the neighboring Audiencia of New Galicia was portrayed in Madrid as approaching a civil war, a prospect that prompted the crown to remove Villamanrique and to subject him to a judicial review. In 1589 he was arrested by the bishop of Puebla, don Diego Romano, and returned to Spain, suffering the sequester of his personal possessions.

See also **Mexico: The Colonial Period.**

BIBLIOGRAPHY

Richard Greenleaf, "The Little War of Guadalajara, 1587–1590," in *New Mexico Historical Review* 43 (1968): 119–135.

Additional Bibliography

Cañeque, Alejandro. *The King's Living Image: The Culture and Politics of Viceregal Power in Colonial Mexico.* New York: Routledge, 2004.

Rivera Cambas, Manuel. *Alvaro Manrique de Zúñiga.* Mexico City: Editorial Citlaltépetl, 1970, 1872.

JOHN F. SCHWALLER

MANSILLA, LUCIO VICTORIO

MANSILLA, LUCIO VICTORIO (1831–1913). The son of General Lucio N. Mansilla and Juan Manuel de Rosas's sister, Agustina, Lucio Victorio Mansilla (December 23, 1831–October 3, 1913) was one of the most important Argentine writers of the nineteenth century. He began writing after being discharged from the army for insubordination. As a member of the military, Mansilla served in the Paraguayan War, or War of the Triple Alliance (1866–1870), and he also played a role in extending Argentina's borders into indigenous territory during the presidency of Domingo F. Sarmiento (1868–1874). Both experiences mark the writing of his principal work, *Una excursion a los indios ranqueles,* published in serial form in the Buenos Aires daily, *La Tribuna* (*A Visit to the Ranquel Indians,* 1870). *Una excursión* approaches the world of the Ranquel tribes with an eye devoid of prejudice. The book discusses the Sarmiento dichotomy of civilization versus barbarism, the political and cultural opposition between the country under Rosas's regime and Sarmiento's political project, coined in his *Facundo,* and in its form and structure, it displays an originality and a modernity rarely surpassed in the century. After having been dismissed from the army, Mansilla took on different political positions and supported diverse political regimes. Nevertheless, his first and principal continuous occupation was writing.

In the 1880s Mansilla published his famous *Causeries de los jueves* in the periodical *Sud-América.* The first issues of *Causeries* were published in five volumes (1889–1890), but some causeries remained unpublished the twentieth century. During the 1890s and until his death in 1913, he settled in Paris, and traveled from there to Buenos Aires and around the rest of Europe.

Other important works by Mansilla include *Estudios morales o el diario de mi vida* (1888; Moral Studies of My Life's Journal), *Retratos y recuerdos* (1894; Portraits and Memories), *Rozas: Ensayo histórico-psicológico* (1898; Rozas: Historical-Psychological Essay), *Mis memorias. Infancia-adolescencia* (1994; My Memories. Infancy and Adolescence, 1904), *En vísperas* (1903; On the Eves), and *Un país sin ciudadanos* (1907; A Country without Citizens).

Mansilla's eccentric image is the result of his extravagant attitude as a public man and an intense, provocative writing. At times his writings blend various genres: autobiography, memory, reporting, biography, and plays.

See also **Sarmiento, Domingo Faustino; War of the Triple Alliance.**

BIBLIOGRAPHY

Molloy, Sylvia. "Imagen de Mansilla." In *Ferrari, Gustavo y Ezequiel Gallo, la Argentina del Ochenta al Centenario.* Buenos Aires: Sudamericana, 1980.

Viñas, David. "Mansilla, Arquetipo Del *Gentleman-Militar* (1870)." *Indios, Ejército y Frontera.* Buenos Aires: Santiago Arcos, 2003.

CRISTINA IGLESIA

MANSO DE MALDONADO, ANTONIO

MANSO DE MALDONADO, ANTONIO (c. 1670–c. 1755). Antonio Manso de Maldonado (*b.* ca. 1670; *d.* 5 November 1755?), military figure and president of the Audiencia of Santa Fe de Bogotá (1724–1731). Drawn from the officer corps of the Barcelona garrison, Manso went to America as *audiencia* president and governor and captain-general of the New Kingdom of Granada in order to conduct the *residencia* (end-of-tenure review) of the first viceroy of New Granada, Jorge de Villalonga (1719–1724), under whose leadership viceregal rule had failed to meet royal expectations, and to oversee the reestablishment of political order in the colony. Manso arrived in New Granada in February 1724 and immediately began to gather testimony on Villalonga. Although faced with voluminous contradictory reports, he largely absolved the former viceroy of wrongdoing. The difficulties of rule, the opposition to his authority, and his scandalous private life left the president bitter and anxious to return to a military post in Spain. Manso's administration is generally considered to have been ineffective or even inept. Returning to Spain in 1731, he served as governor of Cueta and then as inspector of Spanish and foreign infantry.

See also **New Granada, Viceroyalty of.**

BIBLIOGRAPHY

An important and straightforward examination of Manso's role in the experiment with viceregal rule in New Granada is María Teresa Garrido Conde, *La primera creación del virreinato de Nueva Granada (1717–1723)* (1985). See also the discussion in Sergio Elías Ortiz, *Nuevo Reino de Granada: El virreynato, 1719–1753,* in *Historia extensa de Colombia,* vol. 4 (1970), pp. 61–95; and Manso's own report of his administration in Germán Colmenares, ed., *Relaciones e informes de los gobernantes de la Nueva Granada,* vol. 1 (1989).

Additional Bibliography

Kalmanovitz, Salomón. *Economía y nación: Una breve historia de Colombia.* Bogotá: Grupo Editorial Norma, 2003.

Restrepo Tirado, Ernesto. *Gobernantes del nuevo reinado de Granada durante el siglo XVIII.* Buenos Aires, Argentina: Imprenta de la Universidad, 1934.

Silva, Renán. *La ilustración en el virreinato de Nueva Granada: Estudios de historia cultural.* Medellín, Colombia: La Carreta Editores, 2005.

LANCE R. GRAHN

MANSO DE VELASCO, JOSÉ ANTONIO

MANSO DE VELASCO, JOSÉ ANTONIO (1688–1767). José Antonio Manso de Velasco (*b.* 1688; *d.* 5 January 1767), count of Superunda and viceroy of Peru, 1745–1761. Born in Logroño, Spain, Manso followed a military career from an early age, rising to lieutenant general. From 1737 to 1745 he governed Chile with vigor and ability, founding a number of settlements.

On 24 December 1744, King Philip V named Manso viceroy of Peru, the first of the military officers who governed the viceroyalty in place of the traditional noblemen and diplomats. After the earthquake and tidal wave that devastated Lima and Callao in 1746, Manso rebuilt the city and port.

He put down an Indian rebellion in Huarochirí but had less success with that of Juan Santos. For his services, King Ferdinand VI named him count of Superunda in 1748. Manso established the royal tobacco monopoly (*estanco de tabaco*) in 1752 and reformed the mints in Lima and Potosí. His sixteen-year tenure, until 12 October 1761, was the longest of any Peruvian viceroy.

Returning to Spain, he was in Havana when the British captured the port in 1762. As the senior official present, although in transit, Manso was blamed for the debacle. Sentenced to exile in Granada, he died there in 1767, a sad end to a distinguished career.

See also **Peru: From the Conquest through Independence; Spain.**

BIBLIOGRAPHY

Diego Ochagavía Fernández, "El I Conde de Superunda," in *Berceo* 58–63 (1961–1962).

José A. Manso De Velasco, *Relación y documentos de gobierno del virrey del Perú, José A. Manso de Velasco, Conde de Superunda (1745–1761),* edited by Alfredo Moreno Cebrián (1983).

Additional Bibliography

Fisher, John Robert. *Bourbon Peru, 1750–1824.* Liverpool, U.K.: Liverpool University Press, 2003.

Moreno Cebrián, Alfredo, and Núria Sala i Vila. *El "premio" de ser virrey: Los intereses públicos y privados del gobierno virreinal en el Perú de Felipe V.* Madrid: Consejo Superior de Investigaciones Científicas, Instituto de Historia, 2004.

KENDALL W. BROWN

MANTEÑO. Manteño is the name given to the prehistoric culture occupying much of the Ecuadorian coast during the Integration Period (500–1531). Manteño's territorial boundaries extended from the Bahía de Caráquez in the north to the Gulf of Guayaquil in the south, where it is sometimes referred to as the Huancavilca culture. It is widely considered the preeminent society of coastal Ecuador prior to the Spanish Conquest because of its monopoly on balsa raft navigation and a far-flung network of maritime trade, which included a wide variety of sumptuary goods such as artifacts of gold, silver, and copper; elaborate textiles of cotton and wool; richly decorated ceramic vessels and figurines; turquoise, greenstone, and lapis lazuli; and the highly prized *chaquira* (small beads of red and white marine shell).

With the Puná Islanders, the Manteños formed a League of Merchants, although it is unclear to what extent this exchange was strictly commercial or an extraction of religious tribute from dominated coastal peoples. The Manteños themselves were probably subject to Inca influence in a peripheral zone of that expanding empire. Although no permanent Inca presence has been documented in coastal Ecuador, La Plata Island, off the coast of southern Manabí, has yielded clear evidence of a royal Inca burial ritual commonly employed as a territorial marker throughout Tawantinsuyu.

The largest regional centers of Manteño culture were divided in quadripartite fashion, with one of the four local communities playing a paramount sociopolitical role. The two most important of these centers, or *señoríos,* were Salangome in southern Manabí (at present-day Agua Blanca), and Jocay in central Manabí (at present-day Manta). Others existed in inland riverine settings, such as Picuazá (near present-day Portoviejo), but have received less archaeological attention. Many of these sites are true urban centers having well-ordered platform mounds and numerous public buildings with stone wall foundations organized around principles of dual division, tripartition, and quadripartition. Jocay is reported to have had an important religious shrine where regular pilgrimages were made on ritual occasions. There is also a substantial Manteño settlement of the hill country of central and southern Manabí in areas such as Cerro de Hojas, Cerro Jaboncillo, and Cerro de Paco. Sites here are usually smaller than those on the coast and represent habitation sites often associated with agricultural terracing on hillsides.

One of the chief hallmarks of Manteño culture is the use of stone carving for the manufacture of large ceremonial objects. These include heavy U-shaped seats placed over three-dimensional feline or anthropomorphic imagery, and large rectangular stelae with heraldic female figures carved in bas-relief. The seats are widely considered to be associated with high-status, civic/ceremonial functions involving formal seating rituals and may symbolize authoritative powers of the chiefly elite.

A second hallmark of Manteño culture is its distinctive pottery, characterized by burnished black designs on grayware bowls, pedestaled *compoteras* with zoomorphic modeled figures, grayware ollas with fine-line incision, and anthropomorphic figurine-vessels with flaring rim on the head and a pedestal base. Solid mold-made figurines as well as larger, hollow, modeled figurines are common. The latter often depict elite personages with elaborate tattooed designs, especially on the shoulders and neck.

A complex social division of labor is indicated by occupational specialization in economic pursuits as well as in craft manufacture; certain settlements were dedicated exclusively to a narrow range of subsistence and craft pursuits. For example, numerous *albarradas*, or human-made earthen catchment basins, found throughout coastal Guayas province reflect the complexity of Manteño agricultural pursuits and demonstrate a sophisticated management of hydrological resources. Uncovered at Los Frailes in the *señorío* of Salangome was an extensive shell artifact workshop that was dedicated to the manufacture of plaques, sequins, beads, and other ornaments from the pearl oysters, *Pteria sterna* and *Pinctada mazatlantica*, as well as beads and pendants of the thorny oyster *Spondylus*. Because of their very strong symbolic connotations, these were highly sought-after luxury items throughout the Andean Area.

The existence of a complex social hierarchy in these *señoríos* is also suggested by the diversity of human burial patterns found throughout Manteño territory. These include primary interments in simple pits, primary burials in platform mounds, secondary urn burials, and deep shaft-and-chamber tombs in hilltop ceremonial centers such as Loma de los Cangrejitos in the southern Manteño area.

See also **Archaeology; Atacames; Jama-Coaque.**

BIBLIOGRAPHY

Feldman Robert A., and Michael E. Moseley. "The Northern Andes." In *Ancient South Americans*, ed. Jesse D. Jennings. San Francisco: Freeman, 1983.

Marcos, Jorge G. *Los pueblos navegantes del Ecuador prehispánico.* Quito, Ecuador: Ediciones Abya-Yala, 2005.

Marcos, Jorge G., and Martín Bazurco Osorio. "Albarradas y camellones en la región costera del antiguo Ecuador." In *Agricultura ancestral, camellones y albarradas: Contexto social, usos y retos del pasado y del presente*, ed. Francisco Valdez, pp. 93–108. Quito, Ecuador: Ediciones Abya-Yala, 2006.

McEwan, Colin. *"And the Sun Sits in His Seat": Creating Social Order in Andean Culture.* PhD dissertation, Department of Anthropology, University of Illinois, Urbana-Champaign, 2003.

Meggers, Betty J. *Ecuador.* New York: Praeger, 1966.

Mester, Ann M. "Un taller Manteño de madre de perla del sitio Los Frailes, Manabí, Ecuador." In *Miscelánea antropológica ecuatoriana* 5 (1985): 101–111.

Norton, Presley, "El señorío de Salangone y la Liga de Mercaderes." In *Miscelánea antropológica ecuatoriana* 6 (1986): 131–144.

JAMES A. ZEIDLER

MANTILLA, MANUEL FLORENCIO (1853–1909). Manuel Florencio Mantilla (July 2, 1853—October 17, 1909) was one of the most notable figures in the intellectual and political life of the Argentine province of Corrientes during the second half of the nineteenth century. He played an active role in government and parliament and is also known for his work as a historian and publicist. Mantilla pursued studies in jurisprudence at the University of Buenos Aires and later, in Corrientes, held the positions of government attorney and minister of government. In 1879 Mantilla was elected to the National Chamber of Deputies, a position to which he won reelection in 1894. In 1898 he was elected a national senator; he was reelected in 1904.

Mantilla's work in the field of history has particular significance. His principle writings include *Estudios biográficos sobre patriotas correntinos* (1884; Biography Studies of Correntinos Patriots), *Bibliografía Periodística de la Provincia de Corrientes* (1887; Bibliography of Corrientes State), and *Narraciones Históricas* (1888; Historical Narratives).

His most important work, however, is undoubtedly the *Crónica Histórica de la Provincia de Corrientes* (1928–1929; Historical Chronicle of Corrientes State). This work, published posthumously and apparently written during the last year of his life, is a synthesis of the history of the province, practically from the foundation of the city of Corrientes to the second half of the nineteenth century.

See also **Corrientes.**

BIBLIOGRAPHY

Carbia, Rómulo. *Historia crítica de la Historiografía argentina.* Buenos Aires: Imprenta y Casa Editoria Coni, 1940.

Scenna, Miguel Angel. *Los que escribieron nuestra historia,* Buenos Aires: Ediciones La Bastilla, 1976

PABLO BUCHBINDER

MANUEL I (1469–1521). Manuel I (*b.* 31 May 1469; *d.* 13 December 1521), king of Portugal (1495–1521). Born in Alcochete, Manuel was the youngest child of Prince Fernando, second duke of Viseu and first duke of Beja, master of the Orders of Christ and Santiago, and Dona Beatriz, daughter of Prince João. Both parents of Manuel were grandchildren of King João I (reigned 1385–1433), and Prince Fernando was the younger brother of King Afonso V (reigned 1438–1481). One of Manuel's sisters, Leonor, was married to King João II (reigned 1481–1495). Another sister, Isabel, was married to Dom Fernando, third duke of Bragança, who was executed for treason in 1483. An older brother of Manuel was Dom Diogo, fourth duke of Viseu and third of Beja, master of the Order of Christ, who was stabbed to death in 1484 by King João II for conspiring against the monarch. Manuel, who was only fifteen years old at the time of Diogo's death, had earlier been adopted by King João II, his cousin and brother-in-law, and was allowed to succeed his deceased brother as duke of Viseu and Beja and master of the Order of Christ. In July 1491, João II's only legitimate child, Crown Prince Afonso, who had married Princess Isabel, daughter of the Catholic monarchs Ferdinand of Aragon and Isabella I of Castile, was fatally injured in a horseback-riding accident. Although João II had an illegitimate son, Dom Jorge, who by 1492 had become master of the Orders of Santiago and Avis, the monarch was pressured to name Manuel as heir to the throne and did so in his last will and testament.

When João II died in 1495, Manuel was acclaimed king of Portugal on 25 October. In 1496, King Manuel recalled the Braganças to Portugal from exile in Castile and restored that family's properties and titles, which earlier had been confiscated by the crown. In 1498, Manuel named his nephew, Dom Jaime, fourth duke of Bragança, heir presumptive to the Portuguese throne. The previous year, in hopes of unifying the Iberian Peninsula under Portuguese rule, Manuel married Isabel, the widow of Prince Afonso. Isabel, who had become crown princess of Aragon and Castile because of the death of her brother Juan, died in childbirth in 1498. Manuel and Isabel's son, Miguel, heir to the thrones of Portugal, Castile, and Aragon, died in 1500. King Manuel then married Isabel's younger sister, Maria. Among their many children were future King João III (reigned 1521–1557); Princess Isabel (who married Emperor Charles V in 1526); Cardinal-King Henrique (reigned 1578–1580), who was also Grand Inquisitor of Portugal; Prince Luis (father of the illegitimate Dom Antônio, prior of Crato, pretender to the Portuguese throne in 1580); and Prince Duarte (father of Dona Catarina, sixth duchess of Bragança and grandmother of King João IV, the first of Portugal's Bragança monarchs). In 1518, following Queen Maria's death the previous year, King Manuel married Leonor, oldest sister of Charles V and Catherine of Austria (future wife of Manuel's son, King João III).

The most controversial action of Manuel's reign was the forced conversion to Christianity of all Jews living in Portugal. At the prodding of Princess Isabel and her parents, Manuel issued an edict in December 1496, giving all Jews in Portugal from January to October of 1497 to convert to Christianity or to leave Portugal. Contrary to what is frequently written, relatively few Jews were expelled or allowed to depart from Portugal since Manuel did all in his power to prevent them from leaving the country. With few exceptions, Jews in Portugal either voluntarily accepted Christianity or were forcibly baptized. Among the crown's incentives to conversion was the taking of all children under fourteen years of age from Jewish parents who would not convert and giving them to Christians throughout Portugal to raise. By the end of 1497, the process of forced conversion was completed. In 1498, Manuel issued an edict allowing twenty years' grace regarding the sincerity of the conversions. An additional sixteen years was later granted. The result of this forced conversion was a new group in Portuguese society called "New Christians," who later were hounded by the Inquisition and subjected to "purity of blood" statutes until 1773, when King José I (reigned 1750–1777), at the urging of the marques de Pombal, abolished these distinctions.

During his reign, Manuel I presided over numerous financial, legislative, and administrative reforms, including an updated codification of Portuguese law. The monarch replaced the Ordenaçoes Afonsinos of his uncle with the Ordenaçoes Manuelinas, which began to be printed in 1512. A new corrected edition was published in 1521, the year of Manuel's death. Manuel's reign is probably most famous for the great overseas discoveries he sponsored. On 8 July 1497, he sent Vasco da Gama and four ships to find a sea route to India. This aim was achieved with da Gama's arrival in Calicut on 20 May 1498. By the end of August of 1499, two of da Gama's ships had arrived back in Portugal. On 9 March 1500, a follow-up expedition of thirteen ships, headed by Pedro Álvares Cabral, left Lisbon. On 22 April, Monte Pascoal in Brazil was sighted, and on 2 May, Cabral continued to India, but not before sending his supply ship back to Portugal with news of his discovery. In 1501, Manuel sent three ships under the command of Gonçalo Coelho to explore the eastern coast of Brazil. Upon Coelho's return the following year, Manuel leased out Brazil for three years to a consortium headed by Fernão de Loronha. However, Manuel was more interested in North Africa, East Africa, and Asia than in America, and concentrated his energies on those regions.

See also **Gama, Vasco da; Portuguese in Latin America.**

BIBLIOGRAPHY

Damião De Góis, *Crónica do Felicissimo Rei D. Manuel,* first published in 1566–1567. The best modern edition was published in four volumes, 1949–1955.

Elaine Sanceau, *The Reign of the Fortunate King, 1495–1521* (1969).

Additional Bibliography

Bedini, Silvio A. *The Pope's Elephant.* Nashville, TN: J. S. Sanders & Co., 1998.

Costa, João Paulo Oliveira. *D. Manuel I, 1469–1521: Um príncipe do renascimento.* Rio de Mouro: Círculo de Leitores, 2005.

FRANCIS A. DUTRA

MANUMISSION. Manumission, the voluntary freeing of slaves. Throughout Latin America and the Caribbean, the freeing of captives (who, from the mid-sixteenth century onward, were largely Africans or of African descent) implied that enslavement constituted a legal status that was not necessarily permanent. This transformation from slavery to freedom, requiring the relinquishing of control over "property" or "human capital," was of considerable significance to all individuals directly involved in the change, as well as to governing officials and family relations of both masters and slaves. The actual act of freeing an individual slave was, therefore, regularly recorded, most commonly in a notarized letter of liberty (in Spanish a *carta de libertad;* in Portuguese a *carta de alforria*).

The historical significance of manumission rests on an evaluation of such factors as its frequency or availability within a given slave society, the motivations of masters in releasing individual slaves from their control, and the impact that manumission had on freed slaves, their descendants, and the larger slave societies in which both groups lived. Studies of such factors indicate that the significance and impact of freeing a slave or of becoming a freed slave depended on where one lived in Latin America. When one lived in a particular slave society was also quite crucial, as the quality of liberty for an ex-slave and the impact of the newly freed slave on the larger society varied according to the climate for manumission at a particular historical moment. An understanding of slave manumission in Latin America is, therefore, tied to the differing contexts in which it occurred.

Slaves were freed primarily through the individual action of a slaveholder. (The exceptions were the cases of colonial, revolutionary, or national governments who emancipated slave soldiers fighting on their behalf.) Whether these masters freed their captives as an act of charity or in exchange for market value, or in order to relieve themselves of a financial burden, their view of the deed was fundamentally limited to one involving themselves and their human property. The impact upon the slaveholder's community was not as significant a concern as the personal gain to be derived from the act. Even when it benefited the freed slave, manumission was, at bottom, not a social act but a selfish one.

It was the job of government officials, not slaveholders, to concern themselves with the long- and short-term consequences of manumission: independent wage workers who could decide when and for whom to work; sick or elderly freed captives too weak to care for themselves and dying on the streets; healthy and reproductive slaves who competed, or threatened to compete, with free whites for economic standing, social status, and in some cases the numerical majority within the free population as a whole. Throughout Latin America, colonial and later national governments bemoaned what the emancipating slaveholders had wrought—a nonslave population of color struggling for security amid difficult material conditions and unwelcoming free whites.

In both the colonial and national periods, there were laws that formally discriminated against freed slaves and their freeborn descendants. In addition, the Catholic church barred ex-slaves from the priesthood, and some churches segregated nonwhites from whites in their services, brotherhoods, and burial grounds. Whites also petitioned their governments to bar free blacks and mulattoes from training in crafts and entrance into artisan guilds. Despite the clear and persistent evidence that manumission did not protect a freed individual from legal and illegal acts of discrimination, slaves throughout Latin America continued to seek grants of manumission from their owners, preferring a restricted state of freedom to none at all.

The distribution of grants of manumission among slaves in Latin America was neither random nor entirely consistent. Certain subgroups of the slave population, such as male and female children and adult women, were overrepresented among the manumitted, but several studies have shown that the proportions of these subgroups within manumitted populations differed according to regions and, within a region, could change over time. In addition, grants of manumission contained a wide variety of terms, which ranged from dismissal without further obligation to payment and/or further years of service by the slave. Grants sometimes required that a slave wait until the owner's death before his or her release, and sometimes stipulated that a period of service be rendered to the owner's heirs. The specific terms of manumission have been linked to such mutable factors as the economic conditions within a given slave society, the relationship of the slave to the manumittor, and the emergence in some places of large numbers of female slaveholders.

To date, every empirical study of manumission in Latin America and the Caribbean has indicated that less than 2 percent of slaves were freed annually. Nonetheless, manumissions contributed to the freed and free people of color ultimately representing a significant percentage of the total populations of many slave regimes—in some areas of Brazil as much as 40 percent. A mechanism that allowed individual masters considerable flexibility in manipulating the labor and lives of their human property, manumission could have the unintended and unwelcome impact of threatening the numerical majority of whites in the free population. Thus, the practice was cautiously tolerated, but not wholeheartedly embraced, as a method of social control within Latin American slave societies.

See also **Slavery: Indian Slavery and Forced Labor; Slavery: Abolition; Slave Trade.**

BIBLIOGRAPHY

David W. Cohen and Jack P. Greene, eds., *Neither Slave Nor Free: The Freedman of African Descent in the Slave Societies of the New World* (1972).

Katia M. Queirós Mattoso, "A próposito de cartas de alforria na Bahia, 1779–1850," in *Anais de História* 4 (1972): 23.

Stuart B. Schwartz, "The Manumission of Slaves in Colonial Brazil: Bahia, 1684–1745," in *The Hispanic American Historical Review* 54 (November 1974): 603–635.

Frederick P. Bowser, "The Free Persons of Color in Lima and Mexico City: Manumission and Opportunity, 1580–1650," in *Race and Slavery in the Western Hemisphere: Quantitative Studies,* edited by Stanley L. Engermen and Eugene D. Genovese (1975).

James Patrick Kiernan, "The Manumission of Slaves in Paraty, Brazil, 1789–1822" (Ph.D. diss., New York University, 1976).

Lyman L. Johnson, "Manumission in Colonial Buenos Aires, 1776–1810, in *The Hispanic American Historical Review* 59 (May 1979): 258–279.

Jerome S. Handler and John T. Pohlman, "Slave Manumissions and Freemen in Seventeenth-Century Barbados," in *William and Mary Quarterly* 3, 41 (July 1984).

Rosemary Brana-Shute, "The Manumission of Slaves in Suriname, 1760–1828" (Ph.D. diss., University of Florida, 1985).

Kathleen J. Higgins, "Manumissions in Colonial Sabará," chap. 4 in "The Slave Society in Eighteenth-Century Sabará, A Community Study in Colonial Brazil" (Ph.D. diss., Yale University, 1987).

Mary C. Karasch, "The Letter of Liberty," in her *Slave Life in Rio de Janeiro, 1808–1850* (1987); "Special Issue: Perspectives on Manumission," in *Slavery and Abolition* 10, no. 3 (December 1989).

Additional Bibliography

Aguirre, Carlos. *Agentes de su propia libertad: Los esclavos de Lima y la desintegración de la esclavitud: 1821-1854.*

Lima: Pontificia Universidad Católica del Perú, Fondo Editorial, 1993.

Gaspar, David Barry and Darlene Clark Hine, eds. *Beyond Bondage: Free Women of Color in the Americas.* Urbana: University of Illinois Press, 2004.

Giolitto, Loredana. "Esclavitud y libertad en Cartagena de Indias: reflexiones en torno a un caso de manumisión a finales del periodo colonial." *Fronteras de la Historia.* 8 (2003): 67–96.

Nishida, Mieko. "Manumission and Ethnicity in Urban Slavery: Salvador, Brazil, 1808–1888." *Hispanic American Historical Review.* 73:3 (August 1993): 361–391.

KATHLEEN JOAN HIGGINS

MANZANO, JUAN FRANCISCO (1797–1853). Juan Francisco Manzano (*b.* 1797; *d.* 19 July 1853), Cuban poet, narrator, and playwright. The only slave in Spanish American history to become an accomplished writer, Manzano is one of the founders of Cuba's national literature. Born to Toribio Manzano and María Pilar Infazón and slave to Doña Beatriz de Justiz, Marquesa de Justiz de Santa Ana, Manzano published his first collections of poems, *Poesías líricas,* in 1821, and *Flores pasageras* [*sic*] in 1830.

In 1835, at the request of the literary critic and opponent of slavery Domingo Del Monte, Manzano wrote his autobiography. In it, Manzano tells of his good and bad moments under slavery: he was treated as a privileged slave by his first mistress and was punished as a common one by the marquesa de Prado Ameno. Manzano concludes with his escape from his last mistress in 1817. Manzano learned to read and write on his own and his autobiography contains numerous grammatical errors. To make it more presentable, it was corrected but also altered by Anselmo Suárez y Romero, who made the slave's antislavery stance even stronger than Manzano intended. This version was translated into English by Richard Madden as "Life of the Negro Poet," and published in London in 1840. The original was lost until 1937.

After writing his autobiography and reading his autobiographical poem "Thirty Years" in the Del Monte literary circle in 1836, Del Monte and other Cuban intellectuals purchased Manzano's freedom for 800 pesos. Manzano continued to write poetry, publishing much of it in periodicals of the period, and he wrote a continuation of his autobiography, which was lost by Ramón de Palma. In addition, Manzano published his only play, *Zafira,* in 1842. In 1844 Manzano and Del Monte were falsely accused by the mulatto poet Gabriel de la Concepción Valdés (Plácido) of participating in the antislavery Ladder Conspiracy. Manzano was imprisoned for one year. Once released, and fearful that his writing might implicate him in other liberal activities, he never wrote again.

See also **Slavery: Abolition.**

BIBLIOGRAPHY

José Luciano Franco, "Juan Francisco Manzano, el poeta esclavo y su tiempo," in his *Autobiografía, cartas y versos de Juan Francisco Manzano* (1937).

Roberto Friol, *Suite para Juan Francisco Manzano* (1977).

William Luis, "Autobiografía del esclavo Juan Francisco Manzano: Versión de Suárez y Romero," in *La historia en la literatura iberoamericana* (1989), pp. 259–268; *Literary Bondage: Slavery in Cuban Narrative* (1990), pp. 82–100.

Anselmo Suárez y Romero, *Autobiografía de Juan Francisco Manzano y otros escritos,* edited by William Luis (forthcoming).

Additional Bibliography

Branche, Jerome. "'Mulato entre negros' (y blancos): Writing, Race, the Antislavery Question, and Juan Francisco Manzano's 'Autobiografía'." *Bulletin of Latin American Research* 20:1 (January 2002): 63–87.

Burton, Gera. *Ambivalence and the Postcolonial Subject: The Strategic Alliance of Juan Francisco Manzano and Richard Robert Madden.* New York: Peter Lang, 2004.

Miller, Marilyn Grace. "Rebeldía narrativa, resistencia poética y expresión 'libre' en Juan Francisco Manzano." *Revista Iberoamericana* 71:211 (April–June 2005): 417–436.

WILLIAM LUIS

MAPOCHO RIVER. Mapocho River, stream arising in the Andes of Santiago and draining the northern portion of the Santiago basin in Chile. After a short but precipitous course (62 miles), it joins the Maipo River at El Monte. Santiago was chosen by Pedro de Valdivia as the capital of his governancy because the river offered the water needed by the settlement. Cerro Santa Lucía on the southern bank served as a defense post against Indian attacks, and both riverbanks were densely populated by natives engaged in successful agricultural production in the fertile soils along the Mapocho. In the early 1990s the waters had become badly contaminated by city sewage and industrial waste.

See also **Santiago, Chile.**

BIBLIOGRAPHY

Benjamín Vicuña-Mackenna, *Historia de Santiago* (Santiago, 1938).

Jean Borde, *Les Andes de Santiago et leur avant-pays* (Bordeaux, 1966).

Additional Bibliography

Agard–Lavallé, Francine, and Lavallé, Bernard. *Del Garona al Mapocho: Emigrantes, comerciantes y viajeros de Burdeos a Chile (1830–1870)*. Santiago de Chile, 2005.

Palacios, Jorge. *Del Mapocho al Sena*. Santiago: LOM Ediciones, 2001.

Rojas Valdebenito, Wellington. "Otra Mirada al Río Mapocho." *El Heraldo Austral,* Puerto Varas, Chile, (Agosto 2002): 3–4, http://www.bncatalogo.cl

César N. Caviedes

MAPUCHE. The contemporary Mapuche number 1.2 million people, one of the largest indigenous populations in South America. The word *Mapuche* means "people of the land," from *mapu* (land) and *che* (people). The ancestral lands of Mapuche communities are concentrated in the provinces of Arauco, Bío-Bío, Malleco, Cautín, Valdivia, Osorno, and Chiloé in Chile and the provinces of Neuquén, Rio Negro, and Santa Cruz in Argentina. The Mapuche language, Mapudungun ("language of the earth"), is spoken by the older generations and Mapuche traditional authorities. The young either speak Spanish, the official language of Argentina and Chile, or are bilingual.

The Mapuche were once accomplished guerrilla warriors who resisted the Incas and Spaniards. After independence from Spain in the nineteenth century, Chilean and Argentine armies defeated the Mapuche, seized their territories, and massacred their people. The Mapuche were placed on reservations. Many Mapuche lands were sold to non-Mapuche Chilean farmers. The landless Mapuche had to work as wage laborers for farmers and forestry companies or migrate to the cities to become impoverished secondary citizens. Eighty percent of Mapuche inhabit urban areas. Nevertheless, territory, land, and landscape remain central to their cosmology and identity.

The Mapuche in Chile suffered further assimilation under the military dictatorship of General Augusto Pinochet (1973–1990), but the return to democracy saw the passage of indigenous laws recognizing Mapuche culture and language, and the creation of the National Corporation of Indigenous People (CONADI). The democratic governments of Eduardo Frei (1994–2000), Ricardo Lagos (2000–2006), and Michelle Bachelet (2006–), however, built highways and hydroelectric dams on Mapuche lands and supported the rapid exploitation of forests that threaten Mapuche communities and livelihoods.

Mapuche organizations have protested and are struggling to gain recognition as a Mapuche nation. They filed a petition to the Chilean government for the recovery of their territories, cultural and land rights, self-determination, autonomy, greater political participation within the state, and the release of Mapuche political prisoners. These demands have not been met by the government, but are supported by large sectors of the Chilean civilian population, nongovernmental organizations (NGOs), and the United Nations Commission on Human Rights. Many Mapuche are using their common experiences of colonization and domination to strengthen Mapuche identity and create awareness of the Mapuche as a nation that spans Chile and Argentina. This is one of the purposes of *Azkintuwe*, the first Mapuche Internet newspaper, created in 2003.

See also **Calfucurá; Malones; Ranqueles.**

BIBLIOGRAPHY

Bacigalupo, Ana Mariella. *Shamans of the Foye Tree: Gender, Power, and Healing among Chilean Mapuche.* Austin: University of Texas Press, 2007.

Bengoa, José. *Historia de un conflicto: El estado y los Mapuches en el siglo XX.* Santiago, Chile: Editorial Planeta/Ariel, 1999.

Instituto de Estudios Indígenas, Universidad de la Frontera. *Los derechos de los pueblos indígenas en Chile.* Santiago, Chile: LOM Ediciones, 2003.

Richards, Patricia. *Pobladoras, Indígenas, and the State: Conflicts over Women's Rights in Chile.* New Brunswick, NJ: Rutgers University Press, 2004.

Ana Mariella Bacigalupo

MAQUILADORAS. *Maquiladoras* is the term used for foreign assembly plants, particularly in Mexico, but also in Central America and the Dominican Republic. These plants play an important role in the process of globalization and are usually located in countries with relatively low labor costs. Typically, components and other manufacturing inputs produced by capital-intensive processes in industrialized countries are assembled in labor-intensive processes in developing countries, then reexported to markets throughout the world. These assembly plants are often located in free trade zones (FTZs), export-processing zones (EPZs), or bonded facilities in industrial parks.

ORIGINS AND TERMS

Assembly plants in Mexico that rely on imported components operate under the Maquiladora Decree, which governs both the Maquiladora Program and the Programa de Importación Temporal para la Exportación program (PITEX; Temporary Import Program for Exportation). Under the Maquiladora Decree, machinery, components, and supplies are imported duty free as long as the assembled articles are exported. Until November 2006, maquiladoras were exempt from certain taxes that were applicable to companies that manufactured goods strictly for the domestic market in Mexico. Prior to the entry into force of the North American Free Trade Agreement (NAFTA) in 1994, no duty was applied to the value of U.S.-made components contained in articles imported from assembly plants in Mexico. However, under NAFTA all goods from Mexico are imported free of duty, provided the articles meet NAFTA's rules of origin requirements.

The Maquiladora Program was established in Mexico in 1965 to encourage investment in manufacturing operations along its northern border. A key objective was to create jobs for agricultural workers displaced by termination of the Bracero Program in the United States at the end of 1964. The government of Mexico was concerned that the lack of job opportunities for the newly unemployed bracero workers, many of whom had families that had resettled in Mexico's northern border cities, would lead to political instability in the region.

EXPANSION

Confined to Mexico's northern border until 1972, the maquiladora industry grew slowly until the Mexican economic crisis of the early 1980s, when the devaluation of the Mexican peso made the cost of Mexican labor inexpensive in dollar terms and competitive with labor costs in other parts of the developing world. Initially, all assembled goods had to be exported, but by 1994 maquiladoras were permitted to sell up to 50 percent of their production in the Mexican market, and in 2001 all maquiladora products could be sold throughout Mexico. By 1993 the maquiladora industry included more than 2,000 plants and nearly one-half million employees; by the end of 2000, the industry employed 1.3 million workers in 3,700 plants, and 60 percent of these facilities were in the border area. Maquiladora plants produce electronic articles, motors and generators, engines and other auto parts, appliances, apparel, and furniture.

The PITEX Program was established in 1985 to give assembly plants producing motor vehicles, auto parts, and computers for both the Mexican and U.S. markets tax incentives comparable to those for the maquiladora plants. Unlike the Maquiladora Program prior to 1994, there were no restrictions on where PITEX operations could be located or the portion of a company's production that could be sold in the domestic market. Differences between the programs became so subtle that the November 2006 Maquildora Decree merged PITEX with the Maquiladora Program. In 2004 companies operating under the Maquiladora Decree accounted for 82 percent of Mexico's total exports to the United States, with maquiladoras accounting for two-thirds of that total and PITEX companies the remaining one-third.

CONTROVERSY

The maquiladora industry has attracted controversy. Critics claim that maquiladoras export large numbers of jobs from the United States, that they cause severe pollution problems in Mexican and U.S. border cities, that they exploit the largely female workforce, and that they are not integrated with the Mexican economy. Furthermore, critics say that maquiladoras have caused infrastructure shortages in border cities, that they close operations and leave the country at the first sign of labor difficulties, and that they have not produced significant transfers of technology. Proponents of the Maquiladora Program point to the stability of most firms in the industry, the job creation in the stagnant Mexican economy, improved environmental management systems, the growing capital-intensive nature of maquiladoras, increased training and transfers of technology (including managerial skills), high levels of worker satisfaction, and the generation of foreign exchange as benefits of the industry. Opponents of NAFTA, including U.S. labor unions and their supporters, focused on the maquiladora industry in their attacks on the treaty and on globalization.

NAFTA AND A U.S. RECESSION

Implementation of NAFTA began January 1, 1994, and gradually many of the special privileges enjoyed by maquiladoras were extended through programs such as PITEX to all firms manufacturing in Mexico. The transition from the special protections provided by the Mexican maquiladora regulations to the more open NAFTA regime was not handled smoothly by the Mexican government. This created uncertainty and the perception of risk during the time that the U.S. economy was in a recession, from 2001 to 2002. During that period, U.S. producers lost U.S. market share to imports from Asia or shifted production from North America to suppliers in China and elsewhere in Asia. The U.S. recession and global restructuring had a significant effect on the maquiladora industry. Employment in the maquiladora industry fell by 250,000 workers during the U.S. recession, with plants assembling computer equipment, telecommunications equipment, and apparel taking the hardest hits. Only by early 2007 had employment in the maquiladora industry recovered to near the employment figures of the year 2000.

EVOLUTION

Since 1965 the maquiladora industry has evolved away from primarily low-technology, labor-intensive assembly operations to more sophisticated, capital-intensive undertakings requiring a more skilled workforce and employing more technical personnel and engineers. By 2007, electrical equipment for industrial customers, aircraft and automotive parts, and large-screen televisions dominated the product mix, with apparel, consumer electronics (except televisions), and furniture on the decline. Assembly in Mexico continues to be an important component of the strategies for many North American industries to remain competitive with imports from Asia, particularly for products with high transportation costs, whose customers demand just-in-time deliveries, that are subject to frequent style changes or short production runs, and for which protection of intellectual property is important.

See also **Economic Development; North American Free Trade Agreement.**

BIBLIOGRAPHY

Cañas, Jesús, and Roberto Coronado. "Maquiladora Industry: Past, Present, and Future." *Business Frontier* no. 2 (2002). Available from http://www.dallasfed.org/research/busfront/bus0202.pdf

Christman, John H. "Mexico's Maquiladora Industry Outlook, 2007–2012." Presentation at LVIII Maquiladora Industry Outlook Meeting, Tijuana, Baja California, January 26, 2007. Boston and Mexico City: Global Insight, 2007.

Clement, Norris C., Stephen R. Jenner, Paul Ganster, and Andrea Setran. *Exploring the Mexican In-Bond/Maquiladora Option in Baja California.* San Diego, CA: Institute for Regional Studies of the Californias, San Diego State University, 1986.

Dussel Peters, Enrique. *Economic Opportunities and Challenges Posed by China for Mexico and Central America.* Bonn: German Development Institute, 2005.

Grunwald, Joseph, and Kenneth Flamm, eds. *The Global Factory: Foreign Assembly in International Trade.* Washington, DC: Brookings Institution,1985.

Sklair, Leslie. *Assembling for Development: The Maquiladora Industry in Mexico and the United States*, expanded edition. San Diego: Center for U.S.-Mexican Studies, University of California, 1993.

Vargas, Lucinda. "The Maquiladora Industry in Historical Perspective, Part I and II." *Business Frontier* nos. 3 and 4 (1998). Available from http://www.dallasfed.org/research/busfront/bus9803.html (Part 1) and http://www.dallasfed.org/research/busfront/bus9804.html (Part 2).

Watkins, Ralph. "Mexico versus China: Factors Affecting Export and Investment Competition." *Industry Trade and Technology Review* (July 2002): 11–26.

PAUL GANSTER
RALPH WATKINS

MAR, JOSÉ DE LA (1778–1830). José de la Mar (*b.* 1778; *d.* 1830), one of the first military presidents of Peru (1827–1829). Born in Cuenca, Ecuador, he was trained as a royalist officer in Spain.

He was appointed governor of the Callao fortress in 1816. After initially fighting against the naval attacks led by Lord Thomas Cochrane, La Mar capitulated to General José de San Martín's independence forces in 1821. In 1822, La Mar received the title of grand marshal and, when San Martín left Peru, he was put in charge of the government until his dismissal because of his lack of success against the loyalist resistance. However, Simón Bolívar later recruited La Mar to fight in the definitive battles of Junín and Ayacucho against the remaining Spanish forces. In 1827, La Mar was elected president but, while in a campaign against Colombian forces, a coup in 1829 forced him out of office and into exile. He died in San José, Costa Rica.

See also **Battle of Ayachucho; Battle of Junín.**

BIBLIOGRAPHY

Jorge Basadre, *Historia de la República del Perú,* vol. 1 (1963).

Celia Wu, *Generals and Diplomats: Great Britain and Peru 1820–40* (1992).

Additional Bibliography

Montoya Rivas, Gustavo. *La independencia del Perú y el fantasma de la revolución.* Lima, Peru: Instituto Francés de Estudios Andinos: Instituto de Estudios Peruano, 2002.

Morote, Herbert. *El militarismo en el Perú: Un mal comienzo, 1821–1827.* Lima, Peru: Jaime Campodónico Editor, 2003.

Walker, Charles. *Smoldering Ashes: Cuzco and the Creation of Republican Peru, 1780–1840.* Durham, NC: Duke University Press, 1999.

ALFONSO W. QUIROZ

MARACAIBO. Maracaibo, second largest city in Venezuela, is a major seaport situated on the western bank of the channel between Lake Maracaibo, the largest, oldest lake in South America, and the Gulf of Venezuela. Maracaibo is the capital of the state of Zulia. Its population grew from less than 50,000 in 1915 to over an estimated 1.4 million in 2007. Settled first by Ambrosio Alfinger, it was officially founded in 1571 under the leadership of Alonso Pacheco Maldonando. The city has long served as a major port for western Venezuela and eastern Colombia, especially for the export of mountain-grown coffee. In 1667 the Dutch attacked Maracaibo, and in 1669 Henry Morgan captured it. During the twentieth century the city has flourished due to the discovery of oil in the region. Indeed, the largest oil fields in the country are found in the Lake Maracaibo basin, and they figure significantly in Venezuela's status as the world's fifth largest oil exporter. Throughout its history, Maracaibo has served as the center of numerous separatist movements. Its population includes descendants of German immigrants, who comprise a significant part of the city's merchants.

See also **Morgan, Henry; Venezuela: The Colonial Era.**

BIBLIOGRAPHY

John V. Lombardi, *People and Places in Colonial Venezuela* (1976) and *Venezuela: The Search for Order, the Dream of Progress* (1982).

Judith Ewell, *Venezuela: A Century of Change* (1984).

Additional Bibliography

Amodio, Emanuele, Teresa Ontiveros, and Iris Rosas. *Historias de identidad urbana: Composición de identidades en los territorios populares urbanos.* Caracas, Venezuela: Fondo Editorial Tropykos, 1995.

Castro Aniyar, Daniel. *El entendimient: Historia y significación de la música indígena del Lago de Maracaibo.* La Habana, Cuba: Fondo Editorial Casa de las Américas, 1997.

Parra Contreras, Reybar. *Los intelectuales de Maracaibo y la centralización gubernamental en Venezuela (1890–1926).* Maracaibo, Venezuela: Universidad Católica Cecilio Acosta, 2004.

Salazar-Carrillo, Jorge, and Bernadette West. *Oil and Development in Venezuela during the Twentieth Century.* Westport, CT: Praeger, 2004.

WINTHROP R. WRIGHT

MARACATU. Maracatu, an Afro-Brazilian dance procession performed during Carnival in Recife, Pernambuco. The *maracatu* originated in the seventeenth and eighteenth centuries, when plantation owners allowed slaves to elect kings and queens and parade during holidays—singing, dancing, and drumming—while dressed in the costumes of European royal courts. These groups, which were then known as Congadas and were linked to black religious brotherhoods, mixed Catholicism with African religious practices. After the abolition of slavery (1888) this tradition was incorporated into the Carnival celebrations of Recife and given the name *maracatu.* These groups now parade during carnival dressed in elaborate Louis XV costumes of various stock characters: king, queen, princes, princesses, ambassadors, Roman soldiers, *baianas* (Bahian women), and slaves. A central figure is the *dama do paço* (court lady), who carries a small doll representing an ancestor of the group.

Accompanying the royal court is a large percussion orchestra of double-headed drums, metal shakers, and large iron bells. The rhythms are elaborate, interlocking, and highly syncopated, with large *bombos* (bass drums) taking the lead role. *Toadas* (songs) are sung by a lead singer and chorus in a call-and-response form that typically combines Portuguese and Yoruba words. In the 1940s, the *maracatu rural,* a new type of group combining Afro-Brazilian and mestizo traditional patterns developed in the sugarcane area around Recife.

See also **Music: Popular Music and Dance.**

BIBLIOGRAPHY

César Guerra-Peixe, *Maracatus do Recife,* 2d ed. (1980).

Katarina Real, *O folclore no carnaval do Recife,* 2d ed. (1990), esp. pp. 55–82.

Additional Bibliography

Galinsky, Philip. *"Maracatu Atomico": Tradition, Modernity, and Postmodernity in the Mangue Movement and the "New Music Scene" of Recife, Pernambuco, Brazil.* London: Routledge, 2002.

Real, Katarina. *Eudes, o rei do Maracatu.* Recife: Fundacão Joaquim Nabuco, 2001.

Larry N. Crook

MARADONA, DIEGO ARMANDO

(1960–). Diego Armando Maradona, born October 30, 1960, is an Argentine soccer player who is considered one of the best players in the history of the sport. Throughout his career, Maradona had significant athletic achievements with the Argentine national team, with which he won the 1986 FIFA World Cup, as well as with the various clubs for which he played: Argentinos Juniors, Boca Juniors (Argentina), FC Barcelona and Sevilla FC (Spain) and SSC Nápoli (Italy). Although he is an offensive midfielder rather than a born goal scorer, Maradona has produced some of the most famous goals in the history of soccer, including as the two he scored against England in the quarter-finals of the 1986 World Cup. The first, known as the Hand of God, was actually scored with his left hand. In the second, which FIFA (Fédération Internationale de Football Association) chose as the Goal of the Century, he took the ball from midfield and dribbled past six British players and the goalkeeper to score the goal.

His athletic achievements have often contrasted with his addiction to drugs and with the various lawsuits he has been involved in. After his retirement in 1997, he entered rehabilitation in Cuba and in Argentina for his cocaine use. In 2005 he underwent surgery for weight problems and debuted as a host on the *La Noche del Diez* television program. In Argentina and several other parts of the world fans have set up the Maradonian Church, a parody of religion relating to the cult of Maradona as supreme god.

See also **Sports.**

BIBLIOGRAPHY

Borg, Ed. "Diego Maradona: The Most Thrilling—and Disappointing—Star of Our Time." *Soccer Jr.* 5, no. 6 (November–December 1996), 28–30.

Maradona, Diego, with Daniel Arcucci and Ernesto Cherquis. *Maradona: The Autobiography of Soccer's Greatest and Most Controversial Star,* tr. Marcela Mora y Araujo. New York: Skyhorse, 2007.

Telander, Rick. "Prima Dona." *Sports Illustrated* 72, no. 20 (May 14, 1990): 96–106.

Elena Moreira

MARAJOARA.

Known since the nineteenth century for its elaborate polychrome funerary pottery and numerous monumental earthen mounds, the Marajoara culture at the mouth of the Amazon in Brazil was attributed by early professional archaeologists to an invasion from the Andes, because the tropical forest was considered to be too poor to support large human populations and complex cultures. However, the habitat of the Marajoara is not *terra firme* (upland) tropical forest lowland but floodplain, so the influence of the habitat need not have been as limiting as assumed earlier. The culture has now been dated with twenty-four radiocarbon dates, and these reveal that the culture is earlier than related Andean cultures, and the physical anthropology of the people affiliates them with Amazonian populations, rather than Andeans. Thus, Marajoara now must be presumed a local development of the tropical lowlands. The Marajoara mounds had been characterized by earlier archaeologists as purely ceremonial, but recent geophysical surveys and excavations show them to be large platforms for entire villages of earth, pole, and thatch longhouses with adjacent cemeteries and garbage dumps. The fishbones, seeds, and tools of exotic rocks in the mounds indicate a mixed economy of fishing, gathering, trade, and horticulture, and several carbonized maize specimens were recovered in the excavations.

Recent research has shed light on Marajoara chiefdoms, social stratification, and culture, suggesting that a complex religious system developed over differences in resource access; a study along the Camuntins River linked the location of mounds to areas with control over aquaculture systems.

See also **Amazon Basin, Archaeology; Amazon Region.**

BIBLIOGRAPHY

Helen Constance Palmatary, *The Pottery of Marajó Island, Brazil* (1950).

Betty J. Meggers and Clifford Evans, *Archaeological Investigations at the Mouth of the Amazon* (1957).

Anna Curtenius Roosevelt, *Moundbuilders of the Amazon: Geophysical Archaeology on Marajó Island, Brazil* (1991).

Additional Bibliography

Meggers, Betty J. *Amazonia: Man and Culture in a Counterfeit Paradise.* Rev. ed. Washington, DC: Smithsonian Institution Press, 1996.

Prous, André. *Arqueologia brasileira.* Brasília, DF: Editora Universidade de Brasília, 1991.

Schaan, Denise Pahl. "The Camutins Chiefdom: Rise and Development of Social Complexity on Marajó Island, Brazilian Amazon." Ph.D. diss. University of Pittsburgh, 2004.

ANNA CURTENIUS ROOSEVELT

MARAJÓ ISLAND. Marajó Island, an island located at the mouth of the Amazon River on the Atlantic coast of Brazil. Approximately 45,000 square miles in area, Marajó is the world's largest river island. The climate of the island is tropical savanna, and rain falls seasonally from January to July (80–100 inches per year). During the rainy season most (70 percent) of the island floods. Evidence of human habitation on Marajó dates back to the early Holocene period (3,000 to 8,000 B.P.). The island was home to the Pre-Colombian Marajoara culture, which, according to evidence, developed elsewhere and then moved to the island. At the time of European arrival, the population of Marajó may have stood at 36,000.

The people on Marajó Island resisted European encroachment for over 150 years, until Padre Vieira persuaded the Nheengaiba and other tribes to accept Portuguese rule in 1659. After the Portuguese took control, the island was entrusted to the Jesuits, who began raising cattle with Indian cowboys to manage the herds. Around 1900, Indian water buffalo were introduced into the Marajó ecology. According to local tradition water buffalo that were originally intended for British Guiana arrived via a shipwreck. Today, cattle and water buffalo are raised commercially for meat and transportation needs.

See also **Amazon Basin, Archaeology; Amazon Region; Marajoara.**

BIBLIOGRAPHY

Betty J. Meggers, *Amazonia: Man and Culture in a Counterfeit Paradise* (1971).

John Hemming, *Red Gold: The Conquest of the Brazilian Indians, 1500–1760* (1978).

Anna C. Roosevelt, *Moundbuilders of the Amazon: Geophysical Archeology on Marajó Island, Brazil* (1991).

Additional Bibliography

De Assis, Célia, Bauer, Renate, and Tomaz, Kika. *Ilha de Marajó: Paisajem, cultura e natureza.* São Paulo, SP.: Banco Sudameris Brasil, 1996.

Meggers, Betty Jane. *The Archeological Sequence on Marajo Island, Brazil: With Special Reference to the Marajoara Culture.* New York: Columbia University, 2002.

MICHAEL J. BROYLES

MARANHÃO. Maranhão (Modern) is a state in northeastern Brazil bounded by the Atlantic Ocean to the north, Piauí to the east/southeast, Pará to the west, and the Tocantins

River to the south/southeast. Maranhão is relatively flat: more than 90 percent of its total area (about 131,000 square miles) is less than 990 feet above sea level. The climate is hot (average year-round temperature of 75F) and rainy (approximately 81 inches per year) owing to its location near the equator. Northeastern Maranhão is pre-Amazon rain forest, while the babassu (*Orbignya martiana*) palm forest dominates the southwest, along with significant concentrations of buriti and carnauba palms. South America's largest coral reef lies off the coast. Mangrove swamps, which help sustain rich coastal marine life, are rapidly disappearing.

Maranhão's population of 6,184,538 (est. 2006), 43 percent of which is urban, has an average density of nine inhabitants per mile. The largest cities are the capital of São Luís (998,395), Imperatriz (232,560), Caxias (144,387), and Codó (115,098). São Luis was declared a world heritage site in 1997. Historically, most Maranhenses have inhabited the low coastal and river basins in the Northeast, where agriculture predominates. Armed land conflicts between wealthy property owners and poor squatters have intensified in recent years.

Agricultural production remains the base of the state's economy, with significant exports of rice, corn, beans, soybeans, and manioc. Because of drought and pest infestations, the state's harvest fell almost 60 percent in 1990. Babassu and carnauba, along with hardwoods, are exported, as are substantial quantities of fish and seafood. Since 1984 exports of pig iron, iron ore, manganese, aluminum, and alumina have grown steadily. An annual trade of more than 36 million tons established the Maranhão port system as the second in total tonnage nationwide for 1990.

The state has only 1,797 miles of paved roads, including the two federal highways that link the capital to neighboring Belém in Pará (480 miles) and Teresina in Piauí (295 miles), the latter also connected by railway. In 1984, the Companhia Vale do Rio Doce (CVRD) inaugurated a railway for mineral exports linking Carajás in Pará with São Luís (534 miles). CVRD also built a deepwater port in the capital. The Norte-Sul Railway joining Goiânia in Goiás and Açailândia in Maranhão (900 miles) is partially completed. The Alcântara Satellite Base, begun in 1985, is now in operation.

Since 1984, with the opening of the CVRD railway and port, the Alumar (Alcoa/Billiton-Shell) aluminum factory, and the satellite base, the state has regained national importance. Maranhão is also the birthplace of former president José Sarney, whose term (1985–1990) encompassed this period of expansion and development.

See also **Agriculture; Sarney, José; Tocantins; Tocantins River.**

BIBLIOGRAPHY

Paulo Lyra for Alcoa Alumínio S/A, *Maranhão* (1981).

Additional Bibliography

Caldeira, José de Ribamar Chaves. *A criança e a mulher tupinambá: Maranhão—século XVII.* São Paulo: Scortecci Editora, 2000.

Coehlo, Elisabeth Maria Beserra. *Territórios em confronto: A dinâmica da disputa pela terra entre índios e brancos no Maranhão.* São Paulo: Editora Hucitec, 2002.

Santos, Maria do Rosário Carvalho. *O caminho das matriarchas Jeje-Nagô: Uma contribução para história da religião afro no Maranhão.* São Paulo: Imprensa Oficial, 2005.

Gayle Waggoner Lopes

MARANHÃO, ESTADO DO. Estado do Maranhão, one of several administrative centers in colonial Brazil. Because prevailing winds made northern Brazil more accessible by sea from Lisbon than from Salvador, the state of Maranhão was formed as a separate government in 1621. It initially included the captaincies of Ceará (later made dependent upon Pernambuco), Maranhão, and Grão Pará, which included the Amazon Valley. During the seventeenth century the capital moved between the towns of São Luís do Maranhão and Belém do Pará, but when cacao, harvested from the Amazonian rainforest, became the leading export in the eighteenth century, Belém, the leading port, also became the permanent capital. Until their removal in 1759–1760, the Jesuits were the dominant missionaries, but they were joined by Carmelites, Franciscans, and Mercedarians. The expulsion of the Jesuits coincided with the legal end of Indian slavery in Maranhão and the introduction of substantial numbers of African slaves. The arrival of the blacks led to the development of plantation-produced staple exports, mainly cotton and rice. As part of the administrative reorganization of Brazil during the 1760s and 1770s, the state was abolished as a separate entity in 1774.

See also **Amazon Region; Cotton; Rice Industry.**

BIBLIOGRAPHY

Cézar Augusto Marques, *Diccionário histórico-geográphico do Maranhão* (Maranhão, 1870).

Rodolfo Garcia, *Ensaio sôbre a história política e administrativa do Brasil (1500–1810)* (Rio de Janeiro, 1956), chap. 11.

Additional Bibliography

Almeida, Rita Heloísa de. *O diretório dos índios: Um projeto de "civilização" no Brasil do século XVIII.* Brasília: Editora UnB, 1997.

Costa, Wagner Cabral da. *História do Maranhão: Novos estudos.* São Luís: EDUFMA, 2004.

Santos Neto, Manoel dos. *O negro no Maranhão.* São Luís: Clara Editora: Edições Guarnicê, 2004.

DAURIL ALDEN

MARAÑÓN RIVER. Marañón River, an important waterway that joins the Ucayali River to form the Amazon River in the rainforest or Montaña region of Peru. Originating in the Peruvian central Andes, the Marañón flows northward until its confluence with the Santiago River and then eastward in the low Montaña region, where it is joined by the Huallaga River and later the Ucayali. It is a navigable river used commercially since the introduction of steamships in 1866, its banks supporting both industry and agriculture, including the mining of gold and limestone and the production of coffee, cacao, wheat, and fruits. In 1542, Francisco de Orellana, the Spanish explorer, was able to navigate through it and across the Amazonian jungle to reach Spain.

See also **Amazon River; Mining: Colonial Brazil.**

BIBLIOGRAPHY

Javier Pulgar-Vidal, *Análisis geográfico sobre las ocho regiones naturales del Perú* (1967).

Additional Bibliography

Ferreira, Ramón. *Comunidades vegetales de la cuenca superios de los ríos: Marañón, Huallaga y Ucayali.* Iguitos, Perú: IIAP, 1996.

Rodríguez, Manuel, and Durán, Angeles. *El descubrimiento del Marañón.* Madrid: Alianza Editorial, 1990.

ALFONSO W. QUIROZ

MARA SALVATRUCHA, LA. La Mara Salvatrucha (also known as MS or MS-13), whose name roughly translates as "the gang of the clever Salvadorans," is a youth gang with more than 100,000 members organized in cliques or factions. It is active mainly in thirty-one U.S. states, Mexico, and Central America, and also has a presence in Spain and Canada. Academic, journalistic, and government studies of La Mara Salvatrucha are divided between those that focus on its origins and those that analyze the consequences of its activities.

La Mara Salvatrucha was created in around 1983 by the sons of Central American (mainly Salvadoran) political refugees in Los Angeles as a strategy for surviving in streets populated by traditional Mexican-American gangs and in an environment with scarce means of social integration. In 1989, when La Mara Salvatrucha had only 500 members, the Los Angeles police and some officials of the U.S. Immigration and Naturalization Service considered them criminals, and deported many of them who had records for felonies ranging from murder to possession of stolen property. Some of the deportees quickly returned to the United States and extended the group's organization to other states; others stayed in their parents' country of origin, where they were culturally alienated. Those deportees recruited new members, too. Salvadoran sociologists calculate that for every member of La Mara Salvatrucha deported, twenty to twenty-five new members were recruited in their destination country.

Since the 1980s the public image of La Mara Salvatrucha has changed from an organization of excluded youth to a transnational criminal organization. The Salvadoran government claims that gangs are responsible for around 80 percent of the violent deaths in their nation, and that gangs have been the main national-security concern of Central American countries since the end of the civil war in 1992. In 2003 the government of El Salvador announced the toughening of legal punishments against gang members. In the United States enforcement agencies such as the FBI initiated raids against gangs in 2005.

See also **Central America; El Salvador; Guatemala; Honduras; Mexico: Since 1910; Migration and Migrations; United States-Mexico Border.**

BIBLIOGRAPHY

Cordova, Carlos B. *The Salvadorian Americans.* Westport, CT: Greenwood Press, 2005.

Lara Klahr, Marco. *Hoy te toca la muerte: El imperio de las maras visto desde adentro.* México: Planeta, 2006.

FROYLÁN ENCISO

MARBLEHEAD PACT (1906).

On 20 July 1906 official representatives of Guatemala, El Salvador, and Honduras met aboard the U.S.S. *Marblehead,* anchored off the Guatemalan port of San José. Honorary representatives of Costa Rica and Nicaragua were also present. The United States and Mexico, sponsors of the conference, had brought the isthmian nations together in an effort to resolve the conflict that had erupted between El Salvador and Honduras, on the one hand, and Guatemala on the other. The Marblehead Pact, signed by the three belligerents, called for the ending of hostilities, the release of political prisoners, expanded efforts to control the activities of political émigrés, and a commitment to negotiate, within two months, a general treaty of "peace, amity, and navigation." The conferees designated San José, Costa Rica, as the site for the forthcoming isthmian conference and agreed that in the interim any difficulties involving the signatory powers would be submitted to the arbitration of the presidents of Mexico and the United States.

See also **San José Conference of 1906; Washington Treaties of 1907 and 1923.**

BIBLIOGRAPHY

Papers Relating to the Foreign Relations of the United States, 1906 (1909), esp. pp. 835–852.

Dana G. Munro, *Intervention and Dollar Diplomacy in the Caribbean, 1900–1921* (1964), esp. pp. 144–146.

Additional Bibliography

Buchenau, Jÿrgen. "Counter-Intervention Against Uncle Sam: Mexico's Support for Nicaraguan Nationalism." *The Americas,* Vol. 50, No. 2 (October 1993): 207-232.

Stansifer, Charles L. "Application of the Tobar Doctrine to Central America." *The Americas,* Vol. 23, No. 3 (January 1967): 251-272.

RICHARD V. SALISBURY

MARCELIN BROTHERS.

Marcelin Brothers (Philippe Thoby-Marcelin [*b.* 11 December 1904; *d.* 13 August 1975]; Pierre Marcelin [*b.* 20 August 1908]), Haitian writers.

Philippe Thoby-Marcelin added to his own name that of an uncle who adopted him. He published early verse in *La nouvelle ronde* and in *La revue indigène.* Studying in Paris, Philippe met Valéry Larbaud, who published some of his poems in *La revue européenne* (1928). He worked along the lines of the Indigenist movement to cast off French influence and write in a Haitian vein. From the forties onward, Thoby-Marcelin continued to make contact with a number of major writers—Nicolás Guillén, Alejo Carpentier, Aimé Césaire, André Breton, Malcolm Lowry (who dedicated the French translation of *Under the Volcano* to him), Langston Hughes, and others. He was cofounder of the Haitian Popular Socialist Party in 1946. He later served as an employee of the Haitian Department of Public Works and the Pan American Union.

Pierre Marcelin received his early schooling at Saint-Louis de Gonzague in Port-au-Prince. He lived in Cuba with his diplomat father for several years and published fiction in collaboration with his brother. Their *Canapé-Vert* (1942) was awarded first prize for the Latin American novel in 1943. The fiction of both Marcelins has been accused of offering a superficially touristic view of Haiti, but it has achieved greater readership than that of many Haitian writers.

See also **Literature: Spanish America.**

BIBLIOGRAPHY

Philippe Thoby-Marcelin: *La négresse adolescente* (poetry, 1932); *Dialogue avec la femme endormie* (poetry, 1941); *Lago-Lago* (poetry, 1943); *À fonds perdu* (poetry, 1953); *Panorama de l'art haïtien* (1956); and *Art in Latin America Today: Haiti* (1959).

Philippe Thoby-Marcelin and Pierre Marcelin: *La bête de Musseau* (novel, 1946), translated as *The Beast of the Haitian Hills* (1951); *Le crayon de Dieu* (novel, 1946), translated as *The Pencil of God* (1951); *Contes et légendes d'Haïti* (1967), translated as *The Singing Turtle and Other Tales* (1971); and *Tous les hommes sont fous* (novel, 1980), translated as *All Men Are Mad* (1970).

See also Edmund Wilson, "The Marcelins—Novelists of Haiti," *The Nation* (14 October 1950): 341–344; Naomi M. Garret, *The Renaissance of Haitian Poetry* (1963), pp. 93–106; "In Memoriam, Philippe Thoby-Marcelin (1904–1975)," *Présence Haïtienne* 2 (September 1975): 11–15; F. Raphael Berrou and Pradel Pompilus, *Histoire de la littérature haïtienne illustrée par les textes,* vol. 3 (1977), pp. 143–150.

Additional Bibliography

Aub-Buscher, Gertrud, and Beverly Ormerod Noakes. *The Francophone Caribbean Today: Literature, Language, Culture.* Barbados: University of the West Indies Press, 2003.

Balutansky, Kathleen M., and Marie-Agnés Sourieau. *Caribbean Creolization: Reflections on the Cultural Dynamics of Language, Literature, and Identity.* Gainesville: University Press of Florida, 1998.

San Miguel, Pedro Luís. *The Imagined Island: History, Identity, & Utopia in Hispaniola.* Chapel Hill: University of North Carolina Press, 2005.

Carrol F. Coates

MARCHA. *Marcha*, a political, intellectual, and cultural weekly review, founded in Montevideo in 1939 by Carlos Quijano. By November 1974, when it was finally closed by Uruguay's military dictatorship, *Marcha* had published 1,676 issues, with a circulation reaching 30,000, and had established an international reputation for its vigorously independent and principled views. Reflecting the growing strength of anti-imperialist sentiment and disaffection with the traditional political parties in Uruguay during the 1960s, its editorials became increasingly confrontational, which assured its closure after the coup in 1973.

Throughout its history *Marcha* was central to the cultural and intellectual life of Uruguay, but in spite of the prestigious names who wrote for it, *Marcha* always remained closely identified with its founder. Quijano had been a member of the Independent Nationalist faction of the Blanco Party in the 1930s, in opposition to the Herrarists who had backed Gabriel Terra's coup in 1933. After 1938, Quijano took little part in party politics, abstaining until 1946 and abandoning his Blanco affiliation in 1958. His social-democratic convictions eventually led him to support the left-wing Frente Amplio coalition, formed to contest the 1971 elections. Quijano died in exile in 1984, as Uruguay negotiated its return to democracy.

See also **Uruguay: The Twentieth Century.**

BIBLIOGRAPHY

Hugo R. Alfaro, *Navegar es necesario: Quijano y el semanario "Marcha"* (1984).

Gerardo Caetano and José Pedro Rilla, *El joven Quijano, 1900–1933* (1986).

Additional Bibliography

Peirano Basso, Luisa. *Marcha de Montevideo* (2001).

Herrera, Nicolás. *El pueblo desarmado: Uruguay 1970–1973: El testimonio de Marcha* (2004).

Henry Finch

MARCHA DE LOS CUATRO SUYOS. The Marcha de los Cuatro Suyos (Rally of the Four Suyos) was a series of rallies that took place on July 26–28, 2000, in Peru. Convoked to protest the second reelection of President Alberto Fujimori (1990–2000), they gathered tens of thousands of people. The reference to "four suyos"—administrative units of the ancient Inca Empire—was meant to convey the entire nation's rejection of this reelection. The last day of the rallies saw significant violence that resulted in loss of property and life when six guards of the Banco de la Nación (Bank of the Nation) in downtown Lima were trapped in a fire and died. The Fujimori regime blamed the organizers for the fire, but the organizers accused the security forces of setting it.

See also **Fujimori, Alberto Keinya.**

Julio Carrion

MARCH OF THE EMPTY POTS. The first march by this name took place in December 1971 in Santiago de Chile. The demonstration, headed mainly by middle- and upper-class women, was a protest against the economic and social policy of Salvador Allende's socialist administration (1970–1973). Restrictions on merchants, wage increases for workers, and strict price controls had created an acute shortage in the food market and high inflation. The demonstration, led by the Poder Femenino (Feminine Power) women's group, occurred during Fidel Castro's visit to Chile. Left-wing militants who supported the government attacked the women and the government declared a state of siege. The march was part of the political climate that preceded the 1973 military coup led by Augusto Pinochet.

Chilean women used this type of street protest (banging on empty pots to express the people's discontent with the government) again in 1983, this time to demonstrate against the Pinochet dictatorship. It was also used in other parts of Latin America. In Venezuela in 1990, urban sectors called for the resignation of President Carlos Andrés Pérez by banging on pots. In late 2001, numerous *cacerolazos* (pot-bangings) occurred in Argentina, led by the middle classes protesting against the policies of the Fernando de la Rúa administration. These protests intensified once the president, futilely, declared a state of siege, with the protestors joining the street demonstrations organized by the poorer, unemployed classes, and also getting involved in looting and disturbances partially organized by municipal and provincial authorities in opposition to the federal government. De la Rúa relinquished his position on December 20, 2001. Similar demonstrations took place in Uruguay in 2002, against President Jorge Batlle, and even in Spain in 2004, in repudiation of José María Aznar, for his ill-advised political reaction to the Madrid terrorist attack on March 11.

See also **Allende Gossens, Salvador; Chile: The Twentieth Century; Chile, Political Parties: Popular Unity; Pinochet Ugarte, Augusto.**

BIBLIOGRAPHY

Lewkowicz, Ignacio. *Sucesos argentinos: Notas ad hoc.* Buenos Aires: Lewkowicz & Asociados, 2002.

Power, Margaret. *Right-Wing Women in Chile.* University Park: Pennsylvania State University Press, 2002.

Sigmund, Paul E. *The Overthrow of Allende and the Politics of Chile, 1964–1976.* Pittsburgh: University of Pittsburgh Press, 1977.

Svampa, Maristella. *Entre la ruta y el barrio: La experiencia de las organizaciones piqueteras.* Buenos Aires: Biblos, 2003.

VICENTE PALERMO

MAR DEL PLATA. Mar del Plata is a coastal city of Argentina in the province of Buenos Aires, 250 miles from the capital. This bustling city (2001 population 560,274), founded in 1874, has developed into the favorite seaside resort of the inhabitants of the capital. Especially during the first presidential terms of Juan Perón, (1946–1955), with the construction of hotels run by labor unions, Mar del Plata developed into an accessible destination for working- and middle-class tourists. The nearby spa of Huincó, where the mineral water has a moderate calcium carbonate content, attracts many patients with lung problems. Mar del Plata is also an important fish-processing center, with packing plants, paper mills, grain mills, and apparel manufactories. Two universities, the University of the Province of Buenos Aires and the Catholic University Stella Maris, as well as an institute of marine biology, enhance the cultural life of the city. The city has hosted many conventions, including the Fourth Summit of the Americas in 2005, which generated protests. The navy station at Mar del Plata ensures the presence of the Argentine armed forces in the Atlantic.

Following a resurge of tourism in the early 1990s, Mar del Plata experienced a downturn during the country's economic crisis but has since rebounded, despite continuing unemployment.

See also **Buenos Aires; Perón, Juan Domingo.**

BIBLIOGRAPHY

Roberto Cava, *Síntesis histórica de Mar del Plata* (Mar del Plata, 1968).

Additional Bibliography

Bartolucci, Mónica I., and Adriana Alvarez. *Mar del Plata: Imágenes urbanas, vida cotidiana y sociédad, 1874–1990.* Mar del Plata, Argentina: Universidad Nacional de Mar del Plata, 2002.

Cignoli, Alberto. *La Cuestión urbana en el posfordismo: La dinámica reciente del desarrollo urbano de Mar del Plata.* Rosario, Argentina: Homo Sapiens Ediciones, 1997.

Mantobani, José M., and Lorena C. Thesz, eds. *Entre el trigo y la espuma: Mar del Plata y el problema de la creación de los pueblos balnearios del Sudeste de la provincia de Buenos Aires a fines del siglo XIX.* Mar del Plata, Argentina: Universidad Nacional de Mar del Plata, 2002.

Orden, María Liliana da. *Inmigración española, familia y movilidad social en la Argentina moderna: Una mirada desde Mar del Plata, 1890–1930.* Buenos Aires: Editorial Biblos, 2005.

Pastoriza, Elisa, ed. *Las puertas al mar: Consumo, ocio y política en Mar del Plata, Montevideo y Viña del Mar.* Buenos Aires: Universidad Nacional de Mar del Plata, 2002.

César N. Caviedes

MARECHAL, LEOPOLDO (1900–1970). Leopoldo Marechal (*b.* 11 June 1900; *d.* 26 June 1970), Argentine novelist, poet, playwright, and essayist. Born in Buenos Aires, Leopoldo Marechal re-creates in his works his life experiences: his childhood in Buenos Aires, the countryside of Maipú, years spent as a teacher, and trips to Europe are revealed through the written word. His first book, *Los aguiluchos* (1922), is a poetic vision of enjoyment found in the beauty of nature. *Días como flechas* (1926), a second book of poetry, alludes to the biblical story of creation and shows greater structure and harmony in the platonic world constructed by the poet. Marechal collaborated on *Martín Fierro* (1924), a seminal literary review that reflected experimental and stylistic changes in literature as they occurred in Europe, and he also contributed to *Proa,* an avant-garde literary journal.

In his longest, most complex, and highly influential novel, *Adán Buenosayres* (1948), Marechal explores themes that remained constant throughout his works. As an effort to reinterpret biblical themes symbolically through a protagonist simultaneously representing Adam and a contemporary resident of Buenos Aires, the novel oscillates between the symbolic and the realistic, examining the transformations of Argentine society brought about by massive immigration and industrialization. In spite of a favorable review by Julio Cortázar, then a critic and aspiring writer aligned with Victoria Ocampo's *Sur,* the novel was coolly received and left unattended for more than twenty years. This has been attributed, in part, to Marechal's identification with the Peronist Party. More recent writers consider the novel as one of their primary influences and as a precursor to the technical and thematic literary experimentation of the 1960s.

El banquete de Severo Arcángelo (1965), considered to be Marechal's most important experimental novel, reflects the interplay of illusion and reality also found in plays such as *Antígona Vélez* (1951) and *Las tres caras de Venus* (1966), as well as in his essays, including *Cuaderno de navegación* (1966). Marechal is best known for his use of religious and mystical motifs, for the poetic qualities interwoven throughout his narrative and essays, and the epic narrative style of his poetry. He died in Buenos Aires.

BIBLIOGRAPHY

Alfredo Andrés, *Palabras con Leopoldo Marechal, Reportaje y antología: Alfredo Andrés* (1968).

Daniel Barros, *Leopoldo Marechal, poeta argentino* (1971).

Graciela Coulson, *Marechal: La pasión metafísica* (1974); *Poesía: 1924–1950 por Leopoldo Marechal* (1984).

Valentín Cricco et al., *Marechal, el otro: Escritura testada de Adán Buenosayres* (1985).

Leopoldo Marechal et al., *Interpretaciones y claves de Adán Buenosayres* (1966).

Elbia Rosbaco de Marechal, *Mi vida con Leopoldo Marechal* (1973).

Rafael F. Squirru, *Leopoldo Marechal* (1961).

Additional Bibliography

Cheadle, Norman. *The Ironic Apocalypse in the Novels of Leopoldo Marechal.* Woodbridge, Suffolk, U.K.: Tamesis, 2000.

Martínez Pérsico, Marisa E. *La república de Leopoldo Marechal.* Buenos Aires: Ediciones de la UNLA, 2005.

Maturo, Graciela. *Marechal, el camino de la belleza.* Buenos Aires: Biblos, 1999.

Danusia L. Meson

MARGARITA. Margarita, an island about 12 miles off the eastern coast of Venezuela, which, with Tortuga, Cubagua, and Coche, comprises part of the state of Nueva Esparta. It was discovered in 1498 by Christopher Columbus. The Spanish set up pearl fisheries at Cubagua in 1515. In 1524,

Emperor Charles V gave Margarita to Marceto Villalobos. In 1561, Lope de Aguirre plundered Asunción before going on to raid the mainland. Besides pearls, the island's population depended upon fishing and saltmaking for their livelihoods.

Margarita played a crucial role in the return of Simón Bolívar from exile in Haiti. In 1816, he landed on Margarita and in early 1817 defeated royalist troops before he moved his headquarters to the Orinoco region. In return for its loyalty, Bolívar made Margarita part of a new state and promised to create a free trade zone there. This finally occurred in the final quarter of the twentieth century, and as a result the island has become a major tourist attraction.

See also **Columbus, Christopher; Cubagua; Tortuga Island.**

BIBLIOGRAPHY

John V. Lombardi, *People and Places in Colonial Venezuela* (1976) and *Venezuela: The Search for Order, the Dream of Progress* (1982).

Judith Ewell, *Venezuela: A Century of Change* (1984).

Additional Bibliography

Goerdeler, Carl D., Bannier, Anneliet, and Harmans, Gerard. *Venezuela, Isla Margarita.* Houten: Van Reemst, 2000.

López Bohorquez, Alí Enrique. *Margarita y Cubagua en el paraíso de Colón.* Mérida, Venezuela: Gobernación del Estado Nueva Esparta, 1997.

Navarro, Nicanor. *Margarita bajo ruedas.* Mérida, Venezuela: Universidad de los Andes Ediciones del Rectorado, 1995.

O'Bryan, Linda, Zaglitsch, Hans, and Stoks, Frans T. *Venezuela, Isla Margarita.* Haarlem: Gottmer, 1998.

Subero, Efraín. *Los orígenes históricos de Margarita.* Pampatar, Nueva Esparta, Venezuela: Fondo Editorial Fondene, 1996.

WINTHROP R. WRIGHT

MARGIL DE JESÚS, ANTONIO (1657–1726). Antonio Margil de Jesús (*b.* 18 August 1657; *d.* 6 August 1726), missionary and founder of missionary colleges in Guatemala and New Spain. A native of Valencia, Spain, Antonio Margil was ordained a Franciscan priest in 1682 and the following year volunteered for service in New Spain. Shortly after his arrival in the New World, he was sent to Central America, where he served in Yucatán, Guatemala, Costa Rica, and Nicaragua from 1684 to 1697. In 1701, during a second tour in Guatemala, he founded the Colegio de Cristo Crucificado, a missionary college.

Following his appointment as guardian of the new missionary college of Nuestra Señora de Guadalupe de Zacatecas in 1706, Margil spent the remainder of his life working in northern New Spain. From his base at the college, he conducted missionary activity among both Spanish and Indian populations of Nayarit, Nueva Galicia, Zacatecas, Nuevo León, and Coahuila. He participated in the permanent occupation of Texas, founding three missions in the eastern part of the province in 1716–1717 and another in San Antonio in 1720.

See also **Catholic Church: The Colonial Period.**

BIBLIOGRAPHY

Peter P. Forrestal, "The Venerable Padre Fray Antonio Margil de Jesús," in *Preliminary Studies of the Texas Catholic Historical Society* 2, no. 2 (1932).

Eduardo E. Ríos, *Fr. Margil de Jesús, apóstol de América* (1955).

Additional Bibliography

Arricivita, Juan Domingo, and Vivian C. Fisher. *Apostolic Chronicle of Juan Domingo Arricivita: The Franciscan Mission Frontier in the Eighteenth Century in Arizona, Texas, and the Californias.* Berkeley, CA: Academy of American Franciscan History, 1996.

JESÚS F. DE LA TEJA

MARGINAL, MARGINALIDADE. Marginalidade Marginal. A *marginal* is an individual peripheral to or excluded from mainstream Brazilian society. In the colonial period this term referred to the landless, colored poor occupying a stratum between masters and slaves. As neither slaves nor salaried workers in an export-based, slave economy, they were denied steady employment. The Portuguese state tried to repress them and subject them to the most menial and dangerous forms of occasional employment, including manning frontier forts and capturing Indians, runaway slaves, and criminals.

In the late nineteenth century, *marginalidade* became associated with vagabondage. It was linked to modernization, urbanization, social dislocation, racial discrimination, and the breakdown of traditional social controls such as personal honor and rural patronage. The criminalization of socially deviant forms of behavior such as drunkenness, unemployment, and banditry, and of the Afro-Brazilian form of self-defense known as Capoeira, provided a source of free labor that eased the transition from slavery. Persons guilty of these forms of social deviance were arrested and forced to labor on public works projects, for private landowners, or as army recruits as part of their social redemption. Marginality offered a structural challenge to political stability and public order, two values that the Brazilian Empire and First Republic held dear. Today "marginality" is still used to describe the criminal behavior of those on the fringes: the poor, the homeless, the racially mixed, and the unemployed.

See also **Coronel, Coronelismo.**

BIBLIOGRAPHY

Patricia Ann Aufderheide, *Order and Violence: Social Deviance and Social Control in Brazil, 1780–1840* (1976).

Laura De Mello E Sousa, *Desclassificados do ouro. A pobreza mineira no século XVIII* (1982).

Boris Fausto, *Crime e cotidiano: A criminalidade em São Paulo* (1984).

Martha Knisely Huggins, *From Slavery to Vagrancy in Brazil* (1985).

Additional Bibliography

Dalcastagnè, Regina. "Violência, marginalidade e espaço na narrativa brasileira contemporânea." *Diálogos Latinoamericanos* 11 (2005): 72–82.

Severino, Francisca Eleodora Santos. *Memória da morte, memória da exclusão: Prostituição, inclusão marginal e cidadania*. Santos, SP: Editora Universitária Leopoldianum: Universidade Católica de Santos, 2004.

JUDY BIEBER FREITAS

MARIA I (1734–1816). Maria I (*b.* 17 December 1734; *d.* 20 March 1816), queen of Portugal (1777–1816). Born in Lisbon, Maria I was the oldest of four children (all girls) born to the future King José I of Portugal (reigned 1750–1777) and his Spanish queen, Mariana Vitória. As heir presumptive to the throne, Maria was given the title of princess of Beira at her birth. When her father became king, she inherited the title of princess of Brazil. On 6 June 1760, Princess Maria married her father's younger brother, Prince Pedro, and they established their residence at Queluz palace. For the most part, Maria was removed from affairs of state during her father's reign. The marquês de Pombal had hopes that Maria would abdicate her right to the throne and Prince José, oldest son of Maria and Prince Pedro, would succeed his grandfather as king. However, this plan fell through. In February 1777, just days before José I died and Maria succeeded him as ruler of Portugal, Prince José, then fifteen years of age, married his mother's younger sister, thirty-year-old Princess Maria Francisca Benedita. Prince José died of smallpox a little more than a decade later in 1788, leaving his younger brother Prince João to inherit the throne as João VI.

Maria I's reign is frequently described as the *viradeira* (turnabout) because of the reversal of many of the policies promulgated by the marquês de Pombal, her father's chief minister. However, the extent of the changes has sometimes been exaggerated. Maria's husband, who was given the honor and title of King Pedro III, died in 1786. It is not known exactly when Maria began showing signs of mental illness, due possibly to the loss of her father, husband, and son within a short period. However, by late January or early February of 1792, it was clear that she was unable to rule. By a decree of 10 February of that year, her surviving son, Prince João, took over the government of Portugal but was not officially given the title of regent until 1799. In November of 1807, the insane queen accompanied the Portuguese court when it fled to Brazil during the French invasion of Portugal. She died in Rio de Janeiro.

See also **José I of Portugal.**

BIBLIOGRAPHY

Caetano Beirão's *D. Maria I, 1777–1792,* first published in 1934, has gone through a number of editions.

Additional Bibliography

Alves, José Augusto dos Santos. *A opinião pública em Portugal (1780–1820)*. Lisboa: Universidade Autónoma de Lisboa, 2000.

Brandão, Fernando de Castro. *De D. João V a Dona Maria I: 1707–1799: Uma cronologia*. Odivelas: Heuris, 1993.

FRANCIS A. DUTRA

MARIA II (1819–1853). Maria II (*b.* 4 April 1819; *d.* 15 November 1853), queen of Portugal (1834–1853). Maria da Glória was born in the Palace of São Cristóvão in Rio de Janeiro, the oldest child of Crown Prince Pedro and his wife, Archduchess Leopoldina, daughter of the emperor of Austria, Francis I. When Maria was three years old, her father became Pedro I, emperor of Brazil. When Pedro's father, King João VI, died in Portugal on 10 March 1826, Pedro I of Brazil was acclaimed Pedro IV of Portugal. Shortly after receiving this news, Pedro, while still in Brazil, drew up a constitutional charter for Portugal and promised to abdicate the Portuguese throne in favor of Maria da Glória, who was then seven years old, on the conditions that Maria marry her father's younger brother, Prince Miguel, an exile in Vienna, and that Miguel accept the new constitution. In the meantime, Pedro's younger sister, Isabel Maria, would continue to serve as regent of Portugal. Miguel pledged to marry his niece and observe the new constitution. On 29 October 1826, the betrothal took place in Vienna by proxy.

On 5 July 1828, Maria departed from Rio de Janeiro for Vienna in the charge of Brazilian-born Felisberto Caldeira Brant Pontes, first marquis of Barbacena, to complete her education under the watchful eye of her maternal grandfather. However, after arriving at Gibraltar on 2 September 1828, Maria discovered that her husband-to-be Prince Miguel, had returned to Portugal from exile and had been acclaimed king of Portugal by an absolutist-controlled traditional Portuguese *côrtes* of the three estates. Sailing on to England and later to France, Maria met resistance to her claim to the throne by governments of George IV of England and Charles X of France, who were wary of the constitutional liberalism inherent in Pedro's charter of 1826. Therefore, Maria da Glória, along with the marquis of Barbacena and her father's wife-to-be, Amélia, returned to Brazil, arriving in Rio de Janeiro on 16 October 1829.

On 7 April 1831, Pedro I abdicated the Brazilian throne in favor of Maria's brother, his five-year-old son Pedro, and, along with the Empress Amélia, sailed for Europe in the English corvette *Volage* while Maria traveled on the French brig *La Seine*. On 18 September 1834, after years of bitter civil war, fifteen-year-old Maria da Glória was acclaimed Maria II, queen of Portugal, by the newly elected Portuguese *côrtes*. On 28 January 1835, she married Prince Auguste Beauharnais, duke of Leuchtenberg (brother of her father's second wife, Empress Amélia), who died two months later. On 9 April 1836, Queen Maria II married Prince Ferdinand of Saxe-Coburg-Gotha, who in 1837 assumed the title of King Ferdinand II of Portugal. Two of their sons were also kings of Portugal: Pedro V (reigned 1853–1861) and Luis I (reigned 1861–1889). After a troubled reign, Maria II died in Lisbon while giving birth to her eleventh child.

See also **Pedro I of Brazil.**

BIBLIOGRAPHY

Neill Macaulay, *Dom Pedro: The Struggle for Liberty in Brazil and Portugal, 1798–1834* (1986).

Afonso Eduard Martins Zuquete, ed., *Nobreza de Portugal e do Brasil*, vol. 2 (1960), pp. 51–78.

Julio De Sousa E Costa, *D. Maria II* (1947).

Ester De Lemos, *D. Maria II (A Rainha e a Mulher)* (1954).

Additional Bibliography

Bonifácio, Maria de Fátima. *D. Maria II*. Lisbon: Círculo de Leitores: Centro de Estudos dos Povos e Culturas de Expressão Portuguesa, 2005.

FRANCIS A. DUTRA

MARIACHI. Mariachi, an ensemble usually consisting of three violins, a six-string guitar, a bass (*guitarrón*), and two trumpets; also a member of such a group. Although the exact origins of mariachis are disputed and are variously traced to the Coca Indians, the French Intervention serenaders, or to colonial string bands, they have come to be regarded as typically Mexican. Local bands flourished in the west-central state of Jalisco in the late 1800s. They began to travel during the 1910 revolution and later became popular over Radio XEW. Sometime between 1860 and 1930 Gaspar Vargas began the Mariachi Vargas (de Tecalitlán), which was continued and expanded by his son Sylvestre. Early band members played by ear, but later musicians read music, especially after Rubén Fuentes became the arranger.

In the 1940s village mariachis and popular mariachis diverged in style, although both remained wandering troubadours who played for tips. In the 1950s bands began to experiment with new instruments (marimba, harp, clarinet, accordion, and organ), diversify their repertory, and arrange their music for concert halls. The best-known tunes are "La Negra" and "Guadalajara."

See also **Music: Popular Music and Dance.**

BIBLIOGRAPHY

See *New Grove Dictionary of Music* (1980).

Claes Af Geijerstam, *Popular Music in Mexico* (1976).

Additional Bibliography

Nevin, Jeff. *Virtuoso Mariachi.* Lanham, MD: University Press of America, 2002.

Ochoa, Alvaro. *Mitote, fandango, y mariacheros.* Zamora, Michoacán: El Colegio de Michoacán, 1994.

Sheehy, Daniel Edward. *Mariachi Music in America: Experiencing Music, Expressing Culture.* New York: Oxford University Press, 2006.

GUY BENSUSAN

MARIÁTEGUI, JOSÉ CARLOS (1894–1930).

José Carlos Mariátegui (*b.* 14 June 1894; *d.* 16 April 1930), Peruvian essayist and political thinker. Born in Moquegua to a poor family, he was able to obtain only a primary education. In 1909, Mariátegui began as copy boy at the Lima daily *La Prensa;* four years later he was promoted to reporter. He worked as a columnist at several newspapers until his departure for Europe in 1919. There, he broadened his education and married an Italian girl. Won over by Marxism, Mariátegui returned to Peru in 1923, where he became an outstanding leftist personality while earning his livelihood as a freelance writer. His house became a meeting place for avant-garde intellectuals and artists, university students, and labor leaders before and after both his legs were amputated because of an illness dating from his childhood. In 1925 he and his brother established a publishing house that printed two of his books. Mariátegui's prestige rests primarily on his *Siete ensayos de interpretación de la realidad peruana* (1928), translated into several languages; his editorship of the journal *Amauta* (1926–1930), the organization of the Peruvian General Federation of Workers (1929), and the founding of the Socialist Party of Peru (1928).

Traditionally, more emphasis has been placed on Mariátegui's contributions to politics than on his literary writings of his early youth (1914–1919) and mature publications (1920–1930). However, his articles on cultural events, short stories, poems, and plays, all written before 1920, have been reappraised because certain constant elements of this period remained in his later works: profound religiosity, romantic antipositivism, antagonism toward academia, exaltation of heroism, and heterodoxy. During the last seven years of his life Mariátegui molded European ideological and aesthetic currents in order to conform them to his own preferences and originality.

Just as Mariátegui's perception of Marxism exerted influence on his religious ideas, so his religiosity in turn modified his political outlook; he added a mystical dimension to his interpretation of socialism. Religion acquired a new meaning: it became a belief in the supreme good, translated into revolutionary action. At the same time his eclectic-Marxist approach to literature led him beyond a strict analysis of a work. Mariátegui felt the need for a global perspective that would blend previously utilized points of view with the Marxist position on art. He was a Marxist when he viewed art as an economic superstructure, conditioned by class struggle and subject to the changes in the market of intellectual work. He was an eclectic when, compelled by his basic precepts, he adopted heterodox ideas to check dogmatism, arbitrary authority, and the presumed infallibility of the high priests of intelligence, art, and politics. Mariátegui's open-ended ideology and his eclectic methodology of analysis presaged for him the ushering in of a new art, consonant with the socialist society he envisioned.

See also **Amauta.**

BIBLIOGRAPHY

José Carlos Mariátegui, *Seven Interpretive Essays on Peruvian Reality,* translated by Marjory Urguidi (1971).

Eugenio Chang-Rodríguez, *Poética e ideología en José Carlos Mariátegui* (1983).

Eugenio Chang-Rodríguez, "José Carlos Mariátegui," in *Latin American Writers* (1989), vol. 2, pp. 791–796.

Antonio Melis, ed., *José Carlos Mariátegui: Correspondencia* (1984).

Harry E. Vanden, *National Marxism in Latin America: José Carlos Mariátegui's Thought and Politics* (1986).

Additional Bibliography

Beigel, Fernanda. *El itinerario y la brújula: El vanguardismo estético-político de José Carlos Mariátegui.* Buenos Aires: Biblos, 2003.

Escajadillo, Tomás G. *Mariátegui y la literatura peruana.* Lima, Peru: Amaru Editores, 2004.

Stein, William W. *Dance in the Cemetery: Jose Carlos Mariategui and the Lima Scandal of 1917.* Lanham, MD: University Press of America, 1997.

EUGENIO CHANG-RODRÍGUEZ

MARICHAL, JUAN (1937–). A native of Laguna Verde, the right-handed pitcher Juan Marichal, the "Dominican Dandy," was known for his high leg kick, pinpoint control, and such intimidating tactics as head-high, brush-back pitches and aggressive base running. Pitching primarily for the San Francisco Giants, he finished his sixteen-season career (1960–1975) with 243 victories, 142 losses, 244 complete games, 2,303 strikeouts, and a 2.89 earned run average over 3,507 innings. His image was marred when he attacked Dodger catcher John Roseboro in the head with a bat. Still, he was named to nine All-Star teams and elected to the Hall of Fame (1983). He later served as the Dominican Republic's minister of sports and also was a radio announcer.

See also **Sports.**

BIBLIOGRAPHY

Bjarkman, Peter C. *Baseball with a Latin Beat: A History of the Latin American Game.* Jefferson, NC: McFarland, 1994.

Cruz, Héctor J. *Juan Marichal: La historia de su vida.* Santo Domingo, República Dominicana: Alfa & Omega, 1983.

JOSEPH L. ARBENA

MARIEL BOATLIFT. The Mariel boatlift was a massive exodus from April to September 1980 of over 125,000 Cubans to the United States and other countries. Beginning in Havana as a dispute between Cuba and other Latin American countries, especially Peru, over the granting of political asylum, a crisis developed when thousands of Cubans seeking asylum took refuge on the grounds of the Peruvian embassy in Havana. U.S. president Jimmy Carter denounced the Cuban government's refusal to allow asylum seekers to leave the country and pointed to the crowd on the grounds of the Peruvian embassy as an illustration of the unpopularity and bankruptcy of the Cuban regime.

Cuban president Fidel Castro responded by allowing all who wished to leave Cuba to do so via the port of Mariel on the northern coast of the island. To this end Castro allowed small boats from Florida to enter the Cuban port to carry asylum seekers back to the United States. This move clearly caught the Carter administration off guard and at first it declared that all Cubans illegally entering U.S. waters would either be returned to Cuba or jailed in the United States. The Cuban government seized on this policy and charged the Carter administration with hypocrisy. Caught by what many believed was a brilliant move by Castro, President Carter was forced to change policy and announce that the U.S. would accept all Cuban refugees.

The Carter administration's reversal, however, only exacerbated the problem since it encouraged even greater numbers of Cubans to make the difficult crossing to Florida. In addition, Cuba further embarrassed the U.S. by allegedly releasing thousands of prison inmates and mentally handicapped Cubans from jails and hospitals and allowing them, too, to immigrate to the United States. This created an atmosphere of panic in those areas of the United States that received Mariel refugees. Coupled with outbreaks of violence in refugee camps in the United States, U.S. response to the Mariel boatlift was a major foreign policy blunder for the Carter administration and a clear victory for Castro and the Cuban government. Since so many of the refugees were young, Castro was able to convey to the youth at home the pitfalls of leaving Cuba, which included not only a dangerous sea crossing, but also hostility and imprisonment once they entered the United States. Because of the size of the Mariel exodus, it was the Carter administration, not the Cuban government, that was finally forced to halt the influx of Cuban refugees to the United States.

See also **Asylum.**

BIBLIOGRAPHY

Kenneth N. Skoug, *The U.S.-Cuba Migration Agreement: Resolving Mariel* (1988).

U.S. House of Representatives, Committee on the Judiciary, Subcommittee on Immigration, Refugees, and International Law, *Mariel Cuban Detainees* (1988).

Additional Bibliography

Fernández, Gastón. *The Mariel Exodus Twenty Years Later: A Study on the Politics of Stigma and a Research Bibliography.* Miami: Ediciones Universal, 2002.

MICHAEL POWELSON

MARIGHELLA, CARLOS (c. 1904–1969). Carlos Marighella (*b.* ca. 1904; *d.* 4 November 1969), Brazilian architect of Latin American urban guerrilla warfare. Marighella was born in Salvador, the son of an Italian immigrant and, on his mother's side, the descendant of African slaves. He studied engineering at the Salvador Polytechnic but dropped out. He joined the Brazilian Communist Party (PCB) in 1927 and was imprisoned after the party's attempted armed revolt of 1935. Released in 1937, Marighella moved to São Paulo.

Disenchanted with the party's conservatism, he urged violent revolution and a guerrilla struggle. He was elected a deputy from the state of São Paulo to the new Congress in 1946, but was forced underground following the ban on the PCB in 1947. His 1960 acceptance of an invitation to Havana extended to the PCB leadership, which they refused, initiated a break with the party that was complete by 1964. Having rejected the revolutionary theory made popular by Ernesto (Che) Guevera as too spontaneous, and therefore doomed to failure, Marighella founded the Action for National Liberation (ALN) in 1968. His "Mini-Manual of the Urban Guerrilla," written in 1969 as a training manual for the ALN and other guerrilla groups, is a mechanistic theory of urban guerrilla warfare and the most famous document to emerge from the urban struggle in Brazil. Marighella was killed in a police ambush in São Paulo.

See also **Brazil, Political Parties: Brazilian Communist Party (PCB).**

BIBLIOGRAPHY

Robert Moss, "Marighella: Letter from South America," in *Encounter* 39, no. 1 (1972): 40–43.

Additional Bibliography

José, Emiliano. *Carlos Marighella: O inimigo número um da ditadura militar.* São Paulo: Sol Chuva, 1997.

Nova, Cristiane, and Jorge Nóvoa, eds. *Carlos Marighella: O homem por trás do mito.* São Paulo, Editora UNESP, 1999.

Rollemberg, Denise. *O apoio de Cuba à luta armada no Brasil: O treinamento guerrilheiro.* Rio de Janeiro: Mauad, 2001.

Rollemberg, Denise. "A ALN e Cuba: Apoio e conflito." *Cadernos Arquivo Edgard Leuenroth.* Campinas: Unicamp, vol. 8, ńs 14/15, 1̊ e 2̊ semestres de 2001. Dossiê "Tempo de ditadura," edited by Marcelo Ridenti.

Rollemberg, Denise. "Clemente." In *Perfis cruzados: Trajetórias e militância política no Brasil*, edited by Beatriz Kushnir. São Paulo, Imago, 2002.

Rollemberg, Denise. "Esquerdas revolucionárias e luta armada." In *O Brasil Republicano: O tempo da ditadura; Regime militar e movimentos sociais em fins do século XX*, edited by Jorge Ferreira and Lucília de Almeida Neves Delgado. Vol. 4. Rio de Janeiro: Civilização Brasileira, 2003.

Rollemberg, Denise. "Carlos Marighella e Carlos Lamarca: Memórias de dois revolucionários." In *Esquerdas no Brasil República*, edited by Daniel Aarão, Reis Filho and Jorge Ferreira. Rio de Janeiro: Civilização Brasileira, 2007.

Sacchetta, Vladimir, Márcia Camargos, and Gilberto Maringoni,eds. *A imagem e o gesto: Fotobiografia de Carlos Marighella.* São Paulo: Fundação Perseu Abramo, 1999.

MICHAEL L. JAMES

MARIJUANA. *See* **Drugs and Drug Trade.**

MARIMBA. Marimba, a percussion instrument consisting of parallel, graduated, tuned wooden bars that are struck with a mallet. Known as the national instrument of Guatemala, the marimba is also found in southern Mexico, Central America, Cuba, Colombia, Ecuador, Brazil, and Peru. In the controversy over the marimba's origin, the Central Americans are nationalistic, but the earliest documentation dates only to the 1680s. Scholarly opinion favors the theory of African descent because of the similarity with the African xylophone, the linguistic parallel between the Peruvian and the Bantu word for the instrument, and the lack of early archaeological evidence in America.

Marimbas evolved in America, using local woods and gourds for buzzing and resonation. A nineteenth-century variation substituted wooden boxes for gourds, and another variation used a shoulder strap instead of supporting legs. In the 1890s the early diatonic tuning was modified into the fully chromatic scale played on the *marimba doble* by the Hurtado brothers (The Royal Marimba Band).The *grande* has eighty bars and is played by four musicians, while the *cuache* has fifty bars and is played by three. Village marimbas still use the older diatonic scale, while acculturated Indians prefer the chromatic scale and the popular and international repertory. Beginning in the late 1970s a revival of folk groups in Chile and Peru, which spread to Ecuador, Bolivia, Colombia, Venezuela, Mexico, the United States, and Europe, featured players such as Zeferino Nandayapa, who adapted Bach, Mozart, and Handel for use in concert halls as well as for television and commercial recordings.

See also **Music: Popular Music and Dance; Musical Instruments.**

BIBLIOGRAPHY

See listings in *New Grove Dictionary of Music* (1980); F. Maccalum, *The Book of the Marimba* (1968).

Additional Bibliography

Beck, John. *Encyclopedia of Percussion.* New York: Routledge, 2007.

Navarrete Pellicer, Sergio. *Maya achi marimba music in Gautemala.* Philadelphia: Temple University Press, 2005.

Vela, David. *La marimba: Estudio sobre el instrumento nacional.* Guatemala: Dirección General de Cultura y Artes, 2006.

GUY BENSUSAN

MARINELLO, JUAN (1898–1977). Juan Marinello (*b.* 2 November 1898; *d.* 27 March 1977), Cuban poet and essayist. Marinello was born in Jicotea in Las Villas Province and received degrees in public and civil law from the University of Havana, where he was an outstanding student, receiving a scholarship for a year at Madrid's Central University (1921–1922). He was politically active from his student days, organizing and taking part in student protests and groups. He was among the founders of the Hispano-Cuban Culture Institution (1926) and the publication *Revista de avance* (1927). He was imprisoned repeatedly for his political activities, especially during the regimes of Cuban presidents Gerardo Machado and Fulgencio Batista. A lifelong dedicated Communist and political activist, he embraced the Cuban Revolution of 1959 and in turn was wholeheartedly supported and promoted by the Castro regime until his death. Marinello became president of the University of Havana in 1962 and Cuban ambassador to UNESCO in 1963; he was elected by the Central Committee of the Cuban Communist Party to help draft the constitution of the Cuban socialist state. He also received such international honors as the Lenin Medal (1970) and was a part of the executive council of UNESCO in 1974. Although Marinello cultivated poetry in his youth, he is mostly known for his essays and literary criticism. He compiled several anthologies on Cuban literary giant José Martí, whose prose deeply influenced him. His best-known works are the essays *Españolidad literaria de José Martí* (1942), *Creación y revolución* (1973), and *Escritos sociales* (1980).

See also **Cuba: Cuba Since 1959; Cuba, Political Parties: Communist Party.**

BIBLIOGRAPHY

María Luisa Antuña, *Bibliografía de Juan Marinello* (1975); "Cuba, les étapes d'une liberation: hommage a Juan Marinello et Noël Saloman," Actes du Colloque International des 22, 23 et 24 Novembre 1978 (Toulouse, 1979).

Additional Bibliography

Gutiérrez Coto, Amauri Francisco. *Polémica literaria entre Gastón Baquero y Juan Marinello (1944).* Sevilla: Espuela de Plata, 2005.

López Lemus, Virgilio. *Juan Marinello, la palabra trascendente.* La Habana, Cuba: Editora Política, 1998.

ROBERTO VALERO

MARINHO, ROBERTO (1905–2003). Roberto Marinho was the owner of the Globo Group. With a net worth of $1 billion, he was the third richest man in Brazil. This fortune was derived primarily from the TV Globo Network, other media, computer and telecommunications firms, as well as real estate and insurance companies (100 companies total in the group). He founded *O Globo,* one of the four main newspapers in Brazil, and Radio Globo, one of the most popular radio stations in Rio de Janeiro. In 1962, Marinho established TV Globo in joint venture with Time-Life. In 1968, after considerable controversy, that arrangement was found to violate the Brazilian Constitution, and Time-Life was bought out by Marinho, giving him 100 percent ownership of TV Globo. By 1968, TV Globo had the first true network with simulcast programs in Brazil and began a dominance of audience ratings that has continued until today, although competition has grown. TV Globo was favored with military government advertising and infrastructure, such as satellite and microwave links.

The Brazilian managers Marinho hired took advantage of the growing Brazilian advertising market and built up a television production system that has been compared with the old Hollywood studios. TV Globo often produces twelve or more hours of programming a day for itself, including *telenovelas* (prime-time serials), music, news, comedy, public affairs, and talk shows. The Globo Group has expanded into records (Som Livre), magazines (*Globo Rural,* comic books), video and film distribution (Globo Video), and direct satellite broadcasting (GloboSat). In 1989 Marinho used his media power to influence the presidential elections, effectively ruining the campaign of the left-wing candidate, Luis Ignácio Lula da Silva.

Marinho also moved into telecommunications and information technologies through joint ventures with NEC of Japan in areas including cellular telephony and a bid for the second generation of Brazilian telecommunications satellites. His charitable foundation, Fundação Roberto Marinho, produced television programs for education and funds historical preservation. Marinho died on 6 August 2003. Despite their former rivalry, President da Silva (elected in 2002) declared three days of mourning in his honor. Marinho's media empire was distributed among his three sons: Roberto Irineu inherited the television division; José Roberto was given the radio interests; and João Roberto inherited the newspaper.

See also **Radio and Television.**

BIBLIOGRAPHY

Joseph Straubhaar, "Brazilian Television: The Decline of American Influence," in *Communication Research* 11 (April 1984): 221–240.

Additional Bibliography

Amorim, Paulo Henrique, and Maria Helena Passos. *Plim-plim: A pelea de Brizola contra a fraude eleitoral.* São Paulo, Brazil: Conrad Livros, 2005.

Bial, Pedro. *Roberto Marinho.* Rio de Janeiro: Jorge Zahar Editor, 2005.

Machado, Roméro C. *Afundação Roberto Marinho.* 2 vols. Porto Alegre, Brazil: Tchê, 1988–1992.

JOSEPH STRAUBHAAR

MARIÑO, SANTIAGO (1788–1854).

Santiago Mariño (*b.* 25 July 1788; *d.* 4 September 1854), Venezuelan Independence leader. From 1811 to 1821 the aristocratic General Mariño led patriot forces against Spanish rule, especially in his native eastern Venezuela, where he was the most powerful caudillo. Although he several times sought to assert his independence from Simón Bolívar, Mariño served under him for many years and was Bolívar's chief of staff at the battle of Carabobo (1821), which assured Venezuela's independence from Spain. Later he was elected vice president of the ill-fated Gran Colombia confederation. After he lost the 1834 election for president of Venezuela, he rebelled unsuccessfully against the government of José María Vargas (1835–1836). Defeated for the presidency again in 1850, Mariño closed his career as a caudillo by participating in the Revolution of May (1853) that sought to overthrow José Gregorio Monagas.

See also **Gren Colombia; Venezuela since 1830.**

BIBLIOGRAPHY

Julio Cárdenas Ramírez and Carlos Saenz De La Calzada, eds., *Diccionario biográfico de Venezuela* (1953).

Guillermo Morón, *A History of Venezuela* (1964).

Caracciolo Parra Pérez, *Mariño y la independencia de Venezuela,* 5 vols. (Madrid, 1954–1957).

Jesús Manuel Subero, *En defensa del General Santiago Mariño* (1975).

Additional Bibliography

Méndez, Noris, and Pedro Pablo Olivares. "Santiago Mariño y la revolución de las reformas." *Revista Iberoamericana* 82:327 (July-September 1999): 348–360.

Zahler, Reuben. "Honor, Corruption, and Legitimacy: Liberal Projects in the Early Venezuelan Republic, 1821–50." Ph.D. diss., University of Chicago, 2005.

WINFIELD J. BURGGRAAFF
INÉS QUINTERO

MARISOL (1930–). The Venezuelan pop art sculptor Marisol was born Marisol Escobar on May 22, 1930, in Paris, France, to Venezuelan parents. Marisol has lived in Europe, Venezuela, and the United States. She studied in France and in the United States with Hans Hofmann (1950–1954). In the 1950s she changed her interest from painting to sculpture following her introduction to pre-Colombian art. Her sculptures typically are wooden life-size figures in bright colors, with superimposed elements such as portraits of public figures, family members, friends, and herself. She also incorporates diverse objects made from plaster, metal, plastic, fabrics, and all types of recycled materials. She uses these discarded objects with historical background to represent scenes of everyday life, sometimes with a caustic perception or empathic vision. She was awarded the Gabriela Mistral Inter-American Prize for Culture in 1997 by the Organization of American States. Among her works are "The Party" (1965–1966) and "Poor Family I" (1987).

See also **Art: The Twentieth Century.**

BIBLIOGRAPHY

Marisol. Exhibition catalog. Grounds for Sculpture, 1977.

Marisol. Exhibition catalog. Art Museum of the Americas and Brenau University Galleries, 1999.

Marisol en la colección. Exhibition catalog. Museo de Arte Contemporáneo de Caracas Sofía Imber and Maccsi Trasnocho Cultural, 2002.

CLAUDIA P. RIVAS JIMÉNEZ

MARKHAM, CLEMENTS ROBERT (1830–1916). Clements Robert Markham (*b.* 20 July 1830; *d.* 30 January 1916), British writer, translator, geographer, and historian. Born in Stillingfleet, Yorkshire, Markham was the son of the Reverend David F. and Catherine Markham. He studied at Westminster School and then, in 1844, he entered the navy.

Markham traveled and studied widely in Latin America and Asia. He spent a year in Peru (1852–1853), where he examined Inca ruins, learned the Quechua and Spanish languages, and translated some materials into English. He served as secretary (1858–1886) and later president (1889–1909) of the Hakluyt Society and translated and edited twenty-two books for that organization. He was also elected secretary (1863–1888) and president (1893–1905) of the Royal Geographical Society. In 1892, Markham wrote his *History of Peru.* Meanwhile, he sought to use some of what he learned in Peru to assist British development in India. In addition, he studied the irrigation systems of southeastern Spain. Critics claimed that while he had a remarkable career and eventually was knighted by the British government, his interests were too diverse and his work sometimes weakened by spreading himself too thin over too wide an academic area.

See also **British-Latin American Relations.**

BIBLIOGRAPHY

Harry Bernstein and Bailey W. Diffie, *Sir Clements R. Markham as a Translator* (1937).

Bailey W. Diffie, "A Markham Contribution to the Leyenda Negra," in *Hispanic American Historical Review* 16 (1936): 96–103.

Albert H. Markham, *The Life of Sir Clements R. Markham* (1917).

JACK RAY THOMAS

MARLEY, BOB (1945–1981). Bob Marley (born Robert Nesta Marley) is often credited with popularizing Jamaican reggae music around the world. Born on February 6, 1945, in the country town of Saint Ann to a white father and a black mother, Marley moved with his mother, after his father's death, to Jamaica's capital city of Kingston. By the age of fifteen he recorded *Judge Not,* his first record in the ska style (a precursor to reggae), under the name Robert Marley. In 1963 he formed a trio called the Wailers with friends Peter Tosh (born Peter McIntosh) and Bunny Wailer (born Neville Livingston), each of whom would later become famous in his own right. That same year they recorded their first big hit, "Simmer Down." Their career mirrored the changes in Jamaican music throughout the 1960s, moving through musical styles known as rude boy and rock steady to reggae (written in common time with an accent on the offbeat and in general harmonically simple). Throughout their career, the Wailers collaborated with famous reggae producers such as Leslie Kong and Lee "Scratch" Perry. In 1971 they recorded their most successful album, *Trenchtown Rock.* But by 1974 tensions among the three led to a breakup of the original group.

Marley continued without Tosh and Wailer as the head of a new group renamed Bob Marley and the Wailers. He built upon the Wailers' old sound, adding female vocals supplied by his wife, Rita, and electric guitars that appealed to the rock and roll audience.

He became known in this period for the political messages in his music, especially in his 1979 album *Survival* and his subsequent release *Uprising* (1980). Through his fame he also spread knowledge of the Rastafarian faith, which he followed. After refusing treatment for cancer because of his religious beliefs, Marley died on May 11, 1981. He was awarded the Jamaican Order of Merit while on his deathbed. Following his death, a compilation of his hits, *Legend* (1984), became the best-selling reggae album of all time. In 1994 he was inducted into the Rock and Roll Hall of Fame, and in 2001 he was honored with a Grammy Lifetime Achievement Award.

See also **Music: Popular Music and Dance; Rastafarians.**

BIBLIOGRAPHY

Farley, Christopher John. *Before the Legend: The Rise of Bob Marley.* New York: Amistad, 2006.

Frith, Simon, Will Straw, and John Street, eds. *The Cambridge Companion to Pop and Rock.* New York: Cambridge University Press, 2001.

White, Timothy. *Catch a Fire: The Life of Bob Marley,* revised and enlarged edition. New York: Henry Holt, 2006.

EMILY BERQUIST

MÁRMOL, JOSÉ PEDRO CRISÓLOGO

(1817–1871). José Pedro Crisólogo Mármol (*b.* 2 December 1817; *d.* 9 August 1871), Argentine poet, novelist, and journalist. Born in Buenos Aires, Mármol became one of the main literary figures of his time in the fight against the tyranny of General Juan Manuel de Rosas. His works include *El poeta: Drama en cinco actos en verso* (1842), *A Rosas el 25 de mayo* (1843), *Amalia* (in two parts, 1844, 1850), and *Cantos del peregrino* (1846–1847). Most of his works were published in Uruguay. His complete works, including *Armonías* and *El cruzado, drama en cinco actos,* were published posthumously. His novel *Amalia* is considered one of the classics of Spanish American literature. It portrays life in Buenos Aires during the dictatorial regime of Juan Manuel de Rosas from the viewpoint of the opposition (the Unitarios).

Mármol suffered financial hardship during his childhood (the years he lived in Montevideo, his mother's city of origin) and after his mother's death in Brazil. His father distanced himself from his son, who returned to Buenos Aires and began his studies at the University of Buenos Aires.

In 1839, Mármol was jailed by the Rosas regime. In 1840 he was back in Montevideo, where he joined Esteban Echeverría's group of patriots in their fight against the Rosas government in Buenos Aires. His literary mentor was Juan Cruz Varela, who also became his friend and supporter. Works from this period deal with the political battles against the tyranny of Rosas as well as with disagreements among the three political groups fighting Rosas: the Unitarios, the older political theoreticians among the Federales, and Echeverría's group, the Young Argentine Generation. In Rio de Janeiro, Mármol met Juan Bautista Alberdi, who was returning from a trip to Europe. Alberdi convinced Mármol to go to Chile, where he could be more effective in the fight against Rosas, but Marmol's ship was not able to reach Chile. This experience is the source of his *Cantos del peregrino* (Songs of the Pilgrim).

After his abortive trip to Chile, Mármol returned to Brazil, where he remained until 1846. His exile, as well as that of his peers, ended in 1852, when Rosas was defeated by General Justo José de Urquiza's army in the battle of Caseros. During the years that followed, he wrote many articles on political issues, but he never completed the unfinished cantos of the

Cantos del peregrino. Appointed director of the Public Library of Buenos Aires in 1858 (a post he held until his death), Mármol was much admired as the heir to the political ideas of Esteban Echeverría. He is an important writer of the generation of the Romantics, whose life and work centered on beliefs in liberty and democracy for Argentina and South America.

See also **Echeverría, Esteban.**

BIBLIOGRAPHY

Stuart Cuthbertson, *The Poetry of José Mármol* (1935).

Delfín Leocadio Garasa, "José Mármol," in *Latin American Writers,* edited by Carlos A. Solé and Maria Isabel Abreu, vol. 1 (1989).

Additional Bibliography

Civantos, Christina. "Exile Inside (and) Out: Woman, Nation, and the Exiled Intellectual in José Mármols's 'Amalia'." *Latin American Literary Review* 30:59 (January–June 2002): 55–78.

Furlan, Luis Ricardo. *José Mármol: Un destino militante.* Buenos Aires: Círculo de Legisladores de la Nación Argentina, 1999.

MAGDALENA GARCÍA PINTO

MAROONS (CIMARRONES). Maroons (Cimarrónes), African fugitive slaves. *Marronage*—the flight of enslaved men and women from the harsh discipline, overwork, and malnutrition associated primarily with plantations—was a common occurrence in the Americas and Caribbean from the sixteenth through the nineteenth centuries. Originally believed to be of Spanish origin (*cimarrón;* French *marron*), the term "maroon" is now thought to derive from a Hispaniola Taino root meaning "fugitive," which converged with the Spanish *cimá* (mountaintop). The term was originally applied to livestock in the Hispaniola hills and to fugitive Amerindian slaves.

Grand marronage (desertion leading to the establishment of permanent, autonomous settlements on the fringes of plantations or in remote forest, swamp, or mountain areas) must be distinguished from *petit marronage* (individual absenteeism or permanent flight from country to town or sea, from one colonial society to another, where the fugitive could pass for free). This discussion concentrates on *grand marronage,* since neither absentees nor urban and maritime fugitives separated themselves permanently from the slaveowner's society.

Known variously as *quilombos* (Jaga *ki-lombo,* "war camp"), *mocambos* (Mbundu *mu-kambo,* "hideout"), and *palenques* (palisades or stockades), Maroon settlements developed from the southern United States to South America. Maroon communities were more numerous and longer-lived in territories where enslaved Africans vastly outnumbered Europeans.

Maroons developed a variety of military, social, and political relations with Amerindians as allies, domestic slaves, spouses, and advisers of chiefs. In northern Ecuador, for instance, the republic of Esmeraldas emerged in the sixteenth century from the wreckage of a slave ship whose slave passengers escaped and settled among Amerindians. Their Zambo, or Afro-Amerindian offspring, dominated the new state. In sixteenth-century Venezuela, fugitive slave miners lived peacefully with the Jirajara on the San Pedro River in the first of numerous Maroon settlements uniting Africans and Amerindians. African Maroons and their Afro-Carib offspring came to dominate the Carib on the island of St. Vincent. In other instances, such as the Amerindian Miskito of Nicaragua and Honduras and Florida's Seminoles, Amerindians enslaved African fugitives. In the Seminole case, Maroons retained a separate identity and acted as political advisers. In other cases, however, Amerindians assisted Europeans in capturing or killing Maroons and destroying their communities.

Founded by west, central, and east Africans, Maroon societies blended many African, Amerindian, and European cultural traditions in ways based on the contemporary colonial situation, one aspect of which was the disproportion between women and men resulting from the slave trade, as well as from the low fertility of women in monocultural plantation environments. As long as Maroons remained at war with Europeans, the hardships of warfare and bush life tended to suppress fertility. Maroon men tried to solve the shortage of women by kidnapping women for wives, a major reason for raids on plantations and Amerindian settlements. Peaceful Maroon relations with Amerindians provided alternative access to wives, and one of the benefits of peace between Maroon communities and colonial states

Jamaican Maroons at the 264th Annual Accompong Maroon Festival, 2002. The festival, held to commemorate the birthday of Maroon leader Captain Cudjoe and his victory over the British in 1738, features traditional Maroon food, dancing, and other festivities. AP IMAGES

was a rise in the Maroon birthrate and a corresponding increase in the female Maroon population.

Their initial scarcity enhanced the value of Maroon women. As farmers and processors of food, women were responsible for the Maroon food supply. Women presided over Maroon villages; they assumed responsibility for children and the elderly while young men engaged in hunting, surveillance, war, and later in migrant wage labor that took them from the villages.

Females exercised authority through their role as spirit mediums. In the 1730s, an eastern Jamaican Maroon woman, Nanny, founded Nanny Town, later Moore Town, in the Blue Mountains, as a women's and children's refuge from English attacks. Maroons consider Nanny the greatest female Maroon sorcerer, crediting her with repulsing the English by supernatural means and averting Maroon starvation with pumpkin seeds obtained from the spirit world. In Suriname, 80 percent of the mediums of the three main Djuka Maroon spirit cults were women.

Like spirit mediums, twentieth-century female composers also enunciated women's grievances. Indeed, a career as a renowned singer preceded Ma Fiida's rise to leadership in the male-dominated Gaan Gadu cult. With lyrics expressing love and happiness tempered by sadness, rejection, jealousy, and despair, songs provided outlets for female grievances and aggression and brought fame and status to female composer-singers.

In spite of occasional male-female conflicts, Maroons maintained sufficient unity for the task of self-defense. They established stockaded, booby-trapped settlements of various sizes, strategically located in inaccessible swamps and forests or on hills or mountains. Networks of slave and Amerindian allies provided intelligence to Maroons and acted as middlemen in the exchange of Maroon produce and goods for arms and tools. Slaveowners and state officials feared Maroon raids, desertion of laborers, and the undermining of slave discipline.

Europeans counterattacked by passing fugitive slave acts, offering bounties for captured fugitives, and by dispatching armed units, including specially commissioned slave, free black, and Amerindian soldiers. Captured Maroons incurred severe punishment, including imprisonment and execution, hamstringing, wearing of spiked metal collars, and deportation. Marronage could not be eradicated, however. Some settlements were destroyed, but others emerged and many have survived until the present time. Many Maroon groups forced colonial authorities to negotiate peace treaties that recognized Maroon semiautonomy and ceded land to Maroons in return for their cooperation in suppressing slave rebellions and hunting slave fugitives.

The extent of Maroon cooperation with European authorities varied, and peace treaties were broken repeatedly by both sides. Suriname's Maroons continued to welcome new fugitive slaves, for instance, and the Brazilian government and the seventeenth-century Maroon state of Palmares frequently broke peace treaties until the final conquest of Palmares in 1697.

Mature Maroon communities developed complex economies. They grew a wide variety of fruits and vegetables, including rice, and often harvested surpluses. They also produced forest products like timber, salt, and palm wine, as well as building materials and utensils, hammocks, ropes, and beeswax candles. What they did not make they acquired by trade, developing widespread commercial networks with slaves, free people of color, and European settlers.

From the late nineteenth century, colonial economic development began to encroach on many Maroon communities, drawing them into the economic life of colonies and republics and, in some cases, depriving them of their lands. Colombia's San Basilio remained isolated until the early twentieth century, when men began to work in the expanding sugar industry and on the Panama Canal. Cuba's eastern Maroons played an important role in the island's first and second wars of independence in 1868 and 1899, only to lose their farms to North American land speculators and sugar companies and to be ousted from the labor market by Spanish and West Indian immigrants. They rebelled unsuccessfully in 1912. Post–World War II bauxite mining and dam construction proletarianized and displaced Suriname Maroons, alienating them from the urban ruling class. Between 1986 and 1991, Maroons formed the insurrectionary Jungle Commando, which gained control of most of southern and eastern Suriname. Their fate remained uncertain after their leader, Ronnie Brunswijk, negotiated a secret peace with the Suriname government in 1991.

See also **Slave Revolts: Spanish America.**

BIBLIOGRAPHY

José Luciano Franco, *Los palenques de los negros cimarrones* (1973).

Angelina Pollak-Eltz, "Slave Revolts in Venezuela," in *Comparative Perspectives on Slavery in New World Plantation Societies,* edited by Vera Rubin and Arthur Tuden (1977), pp. 439–445.

Richard Price, ed., *Maroon Societies: Rebel Slave Communities in the Americas* (1979).

Kenneth M. Bilby and Filomena Chioma Steady, "Black Women and Survival: A Maroon Case," in *The Black Woman Cross-Culturally,* edited by Filomena Chioma Steady (1981), pp. 451–467.

Richard Price, *First Time: The Historical Vision of an Afro-American People* (1983).

Sally Price, *Co-wives and Calabashes* (1984).

Gad Heuman, ed., *Out of the House of Bondage: Runaways, Resistance, and Marronage in Africa and the New World* (1986).

Juan José Arrom and Manuel A. Garcia Arévalo, *Cimarron* (1986).

Mavis Campbell, *The Maroons of Jamaica, 1655–1796* (1988).

H. U. E. Thoden Van Velzen and W. Van Wetering, *The Great Father and the Danger: Religious Cults, Material Forces, and Collective Fantasies in the World of the Surinamese Maroons* (1988).

Additional Bibliography

Bryant, Sherwin K. "Enslaved Rebels, Fugitives, and Litigants: The Resistance Continuum in Colonial Quito." *Colonial Latin American Review.* 13:1 (June 2004): 7-46.

Gomes, Flávio dos Santos. *A hidra e os pântanos: Mocambos, quilombos e comunidades de fugitivos no Brasil (séculos XVII-XIX).* São Paulo: UNESP, 2005.

Thompson, Alvin O. *Flight to Freedom: African Runaways and Maroons in the Americas.* Kingston: University of West Indies Press, 2006.

MONICA SCHULER

MARQUÉS, RENÉ (1919–1979). René Marqués (*b.* 4 October 1919; *d.* 22 March 1979), Puerto Rican author. René Marqués showed an early interest in theater and cinema as a child in his native Arecibo. While studying drama at Columbia University, he wrote *Palm Sunday* (1956) in English; the book deals with a tragic episode in Puerto Rico's history. After returning to his homeland, Marqués began a seventeen-year association with the Department of Education's community education program in 1950 as a writer and head of the publishing section. In 1958 the Puerto Rico Athenaeum awarded him first prize in four genres: short story, novel, essay, and drama. Marqués taught courses and theater workshops at the University of Puerto Rico, in Río Piedras.

Marqués's first staged work was *El sol y los MacDonald* (The Sun and the MacDonald Family, 1950), a tragedy set in the southern United States. His most celebrated work is *La carreta* (The Oxcart, 1952), about the trials of a family displaced from rural Puerto Rico to the island's capital and then to New York. Another masterwork of intense national and poetic symbolism is *Los soles truncos* (The Truncated Suns), staged in the First Puerto Rican Theater Festival in 1958. Historical events are featured in *La muerte no entrará en palacio* (Death Shall not Enter the Palace, 1958) and *Mariana o el alba* (Mariana or the Dawn, 1965); biblical events in *Sacrificio en el Monte Moriah* (Sacrifice on Mount Moriah, 1969) and *David y Jonatán. Tito y Berenice* (1970); and futuristic events in *El apartamento* (The Apartment, 1965).

Marqués's writings, which include essays and criticism, theater, movie scripts, short stories, poetry, and a novel, show deep concern with the destiny of Puerto Rico and its dependence on the United States. The problem of national identity and cultural conflict is likewise central to his innovative books of short stories, *Otro día nuestro* (Another Day, 1955), *En una ciudad llamada San Juan* (In a City called San Juan, 1960 and 1970), and *Inmersos en el silencio* (Immersed in Silence, 1976).

See also **Puerto Rico.**

BIBLIOGRAPHY

Bonnie Hildebrand Reynolds, *Space, Time, and Crisis: The Theatre of René Marqués* (1988).

Eleanor J. Martin, *René Marqués* (1979).

Charles Pilditch, *René Marqués: A Study of His Fiction* (1977).

Additional Bibliography

Vargas, Margarita. "Dreaming the Nation: René Marqués' 'Los soles truncos'. " *Latin American Theatre Review* 37:2 (Spring 2004): 41–55.

Wasserman, Kimberly. "The New Puerto Rican-American Literature in Spanish, volume 1: Beyond Politics and Displeasure in the Fiction of René Marqués." Ph.D. diss., 2004.

ESTELLE IRIZARRY

MARQUESADO DEL VALLE DE OAXACA. Marquesado del Valle de Oaxaca, the vast estate encompassing 23,000 indigenous vassals granted by the crown to Hernán Cortés in 1529. By the end of the sixteenth century, the marquesses enjoyed the rights to tribute, justice, and administration in seven major jurisdictions: Charo, Coyoacán, Cuatro Villas de Oaxaca, Cuernavaca, Jalapa, Toluca, and Tuxtla. The marquessate's administrative structure was very similar to the royal government's, and until 1771 its indigenous citizens had recourse to either bureaucracy. The *estado,* as the marquessate was also known, was frequently embroiled in litigation concerning the exact scope of the grant, and it was sequestered by the crown on several occasions. In 1629 the marquessate passed to the fourth marquess's niece, wife of the duke of Terranova, and by the end of the century, by a similar process, into the hands of the Neapolitan Pignatellis, the dukes of Monteleone. Thereafter, the marquesses, and the dukes of Terranova and Monteleone, resided in Spain and Italy, leaving the direction of the state to its chief administrator in Mexico.

The marquessate weathered the wars of independence and early national period with difficulty, and in 1825 the duke of Monteleone and Terranova asked his friend, Lucas Alamán, to oversee the liquidation of the estate, which was completed by the end of 1849.

See also **Aztecs; Cortés, Hernán.**

BIBLIOGRAPHY

An excellent source for the administrative history of the marquessate is Woodrow Borah, *Justice by Insurance: The General Indian Court of Colonial Mexico and the Legal Aides of the Half-Real* (1983). There have been studies of several of the estado's jurisdictions and enterprises, including Ward Barrett, *The Sugar Hacienda of the Marqueses del Valle* (1970); G. Micheal Riley, *Fernando Cortés and the Marquesado in Morelos, 1522–1547* (1973); Cheryl English Martin, *Rural Society in Colonial Morelos* (1985); and Robert Haskett, *Indigenous Rulers: An Ethnohistory of Town Government in Colonial Cuernavaca* (1991). The basic study of the estate remains Bernardo García Martínez, *El marquesado del Valle: Tres siglos de régimen señorial en Nueva España* (1969).

ROBERT HASKETT

MÁRQUEZ, JOSÉ IGNACIO DE (1793–1880).

José Ignacio de Márquez (*b.* 7 September 1793; *d.* 21 March 1880), president of New Granada (1837–1840). Born in Boyacá, Márquez received a law degree from the Colegio de San Bartolomé in Bogotá at age twenty. In 1821 he served in the Congress of Cúcuta and was elected presiding officer. In 1830–1831, Márquez served as finance secretary, and his 1831 *Memoria de hacienda* stands as the classic statement of protectionist thought in nineteenth-century Colombia. From March to October 1832, Márquez served as acting president pending the return to New Granada of Francisco de Paula Santander, whereupon he assumed the vice presidency. In 1837 he was elected president by the Congress after a bitterly divisive three-way contest against José María Obando and Vicente Azuero. Although Márquez was a sound administrator with some mildly progressive ideas, his presidency was poisoned by the rivalry between his ministerial grouping and the defeated *progresistas* gathered around Santander. Márquez's purge of *progresista* officials further exacerbated political tensions. In 1839 a rebellion erupted in the southwestern Pasto region, initially directed against a Márquez decree on the suppression of small convents, but which soon came under the leadership of Obando. Throughout 1840 other regional rebellions, known collectively as the War of the Supremes and led by quasi-retired military men and disgruntled local elites, snowballed into a major crisis for the Márquez regime, especially after Santander's death in May 1840 removed a major brake on *progresista* intrigues. On 7 October 1840, after receiving news of a government defeat at Polonia (near Socorro in the northeast), Márquez temporarily stepped down from the presidency—ostensibly for health reasons—but resurfaced in Popayán two weeks later, rallying government forces. Márquez never returned to office, but by early 1842 the rebellions were defeated. He later served as representative for Tunja (1842–1845), interior secretary (1845–1846), and senator for Bogotá (1847–1850).

See also **War of the Supremes.**

BIBLIOGRAPHY

Carlos Cuervo Márquez, *Vida del doctor José Ignacio de Márquez,* 2 vols. (1917).

Additional Bibliography

Carrizosa Argáez, Enrique. *Linajes y bibliografías de los gobernantes de nuestra nación, 1830-1990.* Bogotá, Colombia: Instituto Colombiano de Cultura Hispánica, 1990.

RICHARD STOLLER

MÁRQUEZ, LEONARDO (1820–1913).

Leonardo Márquez (*b.* 1820; *d.* 1913), Mexican general. His military career began in the 1830s in the Texas campaign. During the War of the Reform (1858–1860), he fought on the side of the Conservatives and later to support the monarchy of Maximilian during the period of the French Intervention (1862–1867). He is best known for three episodes: his order to execute captured Liberal officers and some doctors and medical students after the battle of Tacubaya (11 April 1859), an act that earned him the nickname of "Tiger of Tacubaya"; his 1861 orders to execute Melchor Ocampo, leading Liberal statesman, and General Leandro Valle; and his role in the mid-1867 siege of Querétaro, where he left Maximilian to find reinforcements and never returned, thus leaving the emperor to his fate. After the fall of the empire, Márquez went into exile in Cuba. He returned to Mexico in the 1890s, but upon the ouster of Porfirio Díaz, he went back to Havana, where he died three years later.

See also **Mexico, Wars and Revolutions: The Reform.**

BIBLIOGRAPHY

Jesús De León Toral, *Historia militar: la intervención francesa en México* (1962).

Leonardo Márquez, *Manifiestos (el imperio y los imperiales)* (1904).

Additional Bibliography

Hamnett, Brian R. *Juárez.* New York: Longman, 1994.

Rodríguez O, Jaime E. *The Divine Charter: Constitutionalism and Liberalism in Nineteenth-century Mexico.* Lanham, MD: Rowman & Littlefield Publishers, 2005.

CHARLES R. BERRY

MARRIAGE AND DIVORCE. Before the Europeans' arrival in Latin America, in the main cultures of the Andes and Mexico the great majority of commoners were monogamous, but the nobles practiced polygamy. To them, it was a useful privilege that allowed them to form close political alliances and reinforce military victories. The polygamous kings married women not only of the same social class but also women of inferior social classes.

INDIGENOUS SOCIETIES

In the Andes the main social unit was the *ayllu*, a group of relatives that had mythic ancestors in common. During the Inca Empire (Tawantinsuyo) the state controlled the marriages celebrated in each *ayllu*. By doing this, a new tributary union was formed. Before marriage, the young single people of the Andes had a certain degree of sexual liberty, particularly in communal celebrations. Royalty was organized around *panacas*, which were formed by the descendants of an Inca (except the successor, who would found another *panaca*). The blood links in a *panaca* were very deep, because the main wives of the Incas used to be the Incas' own sisters. During the colonial period, some Indians tried to continue practicing polygamy through bigamy or relationships with concubines.

After the Conquest, very few Indians married white women because the Spanish refused to give a woman to a man of a lower rank. Nevertheless, some Mexican nobles were probably the most important exception of this rule. During the sixteenth century, marriages between Indian women and white men were more common, especially if the woman was an heiress of a *cacicazgo*. But the society designed by Spanish colonizers had clear barriers in order to preserve separate "republics" of Spaniards and Indians. Very soon, the mestizos challenged that ideal separation.

COLONIAL PERIOD THROUGH THE NINETEENTH CENTURY

Throughout the colonial period in Latin America, the nurturance and preservation of Catholic marriages and the family were a primary concern of the state and the Church. In the case of women, their "predestination" to marriage and the domestic sphere was sanctioned by the Church.

Race and Class. The Iberian sense of *pureza de sangre* (blood purity), which determined how honorable a person was, changed in Latin America quite early on. It began to be related not only to the absence of Jews, Muslims, or illegitimate ancestors but also to racial mixture. In this sense, the selection of a spouse was very important in defining not only one's own social status but also that of one's family and descendants. Nevertheless, racial mixture (through legal marriage, concubinage, or simply sporadic sexual relations) progressively increased and made social divisions complicated. Some scholars have pointed out that in the eighteenth century, many cities with Spanish colonies saw a loosening of such behaviors. Indeed, the *castas* increased considerably, and race became only one of many factors to consider in marriage. In the end, a person was able to turn "white" through a legal procedure. In spite of those changes, Spaniards and Indians continued to be relatively highly endogamous groups at the end of the colonial period.

As a response to the decline of social order with regard to marriage, in 1774 the crown decreed the Ley Pragmática (Pragmatic Law), which was extended to the American colonies two years later. This royal decree allowed parents to prohibit marriage of their offspring under twenty-five years of age according to the parents' criteria of "notorious inequality." The term *calidad* (quality) employed in this period comprehended a wide array of considerations in judging the value of a bride or a fiancé, such as family, economic status, and certainly race. However, this law probably only contributed to the decrease in nuptiality in cities such as Mexico City and Lima. People who adhered to the social values imposed by the Spanish order may have had difficulty finding adequate candidates for marriage.

Economics. An additional reason that could explain the low marriage rates among Spaniards, Creoles, and even some mestizos of certain cities in colonial Latin

Double wedding between two Inca women and two Spaniards in 1558, c. 1750 (panel) by Spanish School (18th century). NUESTRA SENORA DE COPACABANA, LIMA, PERU/ THE BRIDGEMAN ART LIBRARY

America was the practice of assigning inheritance to the firstborn son, in order to preserve the family power. It made it difficult for the other sons to reach an income level high enough to offer adequate status to a "respectable" bride. Marriage rites too were complicated and expensive during the colonial period and most of the nineteenth century. But the most important economic consideration was the marriage itself, because marrying a woman could mean assuming responsibility for the bride's extensive family.

Consensual Unions and Consanguinity. Many persons avoided or delayed marriage, forming consensual unions instead. Although a woman's honor was said to be lost if she entered a premarital sexual relationship, the frequency of such relationships was high. In many cases women had premarital involvements because of the promise of marriage, which was legally binding. After deflowering a woman, a man who wished (or was forced) to marry her would request ecclesiastic authorities to grant him dispensation from the impediment of previous sexual relationships. The argument often used to support his petition was that the woman would otherwise be dishonored.

The morality argument was also helpful in circumventing the consanguinity limits for spouses. Canon law did not allow marriages within four degrees of kinship or between ritual kin. However, endogamous marriages within elite Latin American families represented a common strategy for consolidating property and for political mobilization. These marriages between cousins, or between uncles and nieces, were not unequal marriages. Although the Catholic Church objected to them on moral grounds, in most cases ecclesiastical authorities were less concerned about consanguineous marriages than they were about irregular sexual relationships and illegitimate births. This order of concern is obvious from the dispensation records. For example, in nineteenth-century Chile, three-fourths of couples seeking the dispensation of consanguineous impediments cited sexual involvement as a justification, and half of these had conceived at least one child

Illegitimacy. Studies of several nineteenth-century cities have found that, on average, 20 to 60 percent of births were illegitimate (in general terms, Latin American illegitimacy was more a phenomenon of cities rather than of rural zones). At the lowest extreme, regions such as the Valle Central in Costa Rica registered only 10 to 20 percent illegitimacy in the first half of the nineteenth century. Cities such as Havana, San Juan de Puerto Rico, and Lima were on the opposite spectrum because illegitimacy was the most common birth status for black women's children: during the second half of the nineteenth century, 70 to 80 percent of them were illegitimate. This situation was not solely because other groups refused to accept black women as wives. For example in Cuba, a poor black woman would often prefer a consensual union with a higher-class male than marriage with a man of her own class, because the former could support her and her children financially. Nevertheless, in certain cities during nineteenth century endogamy among Spaniards and Indians continued at a high rate. For example, in the second half of the nineteenth century, the Havana elite became more rigorous in guarding against "black stains" in their families.

TWENTIETH CENTURY TO THE PRESENT

While changes occurred at different stages among specific countries, more socially conscious governments in the twentieth century spurred an expansion in legal marriages through increased social rewards for married citizens such as social security, family allowances, and health care. Other changes, often associated with the expansion of education, were a higher age for marrying (or coupling) and a decline in fertility and illegitimacy.

Types of Relationships. In general terms, visiting relationships—in which a woman usually has her own house, though occasionally lives with her parents, at the same time that her male companion provides some financial support for her and, typically, their children—continues to be a common type of sexual relationship in Latin America. Research on Colombia, Peru, Panama, Jamaica, and Trinidad indicates that visiting and consensual unions have some stability, as well as financial and social cooperation, built into them. In Jamaica the visiting relationship is practiced by all classes, often as a prelude to marriage. Many women express a preference for the visiting relationship over common-law marriage because common-law unions demand too much, and men fail to take responsibility for their children.

Another common sexual relationship in Latin America is the consensual union, which is like a marriage except that it is not formalized. Consensual union or concubinage has been very common among lower social classes in many Latin American cities. Nevertheless, the proportion of people who legally marry at some point is growing. Illegitimacy is also declining, though undoubtedly the data understates its incidence. In many countries, the increase in legal civil marriages is associated with advantages related to taxes, subsidies, and inheritance. Moreover, women with higher education are marrying later and having fewer children, whereas men are generally marrying somewhat earlier.

Family values in the lower classes (but also in the middle and upper classes), include different priorities of relationships for men and for women. Scholars assert that lower-class children in Venezuela and Chile are bound more to their mothers than to their fathers, and the child stays with the mother if the marriage dissolves. Men may desert their families, but instances of maternal desertion are rare and subject to severe criticism. Children of single mothers are frequently reared by their maternal grandmothers while their mothers work outside the home as domestics.

Divorce. During the colonial period, divorce was not allowed by the Catholic crowns of Spain and Portugal. Unhappy marriages might be dissolved either through annulment—available only if a marriage had not been consummated or the family was powerful enough to "convince" the Catholic Church of that condition—or through a separation of board and bed. There were numerous suits in Brazil and in Spanish America of the latter type, predominantly instituted by women because of desertion, physical violence, or lack of support. The return of the dowry was a major issue in many cases, because the dowry was supposed to provide security for the woman. Civil codes allowing divorce and remarriage were enacted in most countries of Latin America in the twentieth century, some as recently as the last two decades of the twentieth century. However, divorce has not been easy or common, and women and men have often been treated differently by the law. For example, although adultery was considered grounds for divorce according to the 1917 Family Relationship Law, a wife's adultery always constituted grounds, but a husband's only in certain cases. This difference in treatment did not change until the Civil Reform Code in 1983.

See also **Family; Sexuality.**

BIBLIOGRAPHY

Arrom, Silvia. *The Women of Mexico City, 1790–1857.* Stanford, CA: Stanford University Press, 1985.

Bernard, Carmen, and Serge Gruzinski. "Los hijos del Apocalipsis: La familia en Mesoamérica y en los Andes." In *Historia de la familia*, Vol. 2: *El impacto de la modernidad*,, ed. André Burguière et al., pp. 163–216. Madrid: Alianza Editorial, 1988.

Carrasco, Pedro. "Matrimonios hispano-indios en el primer siglo de la colonia." In *Cincuenta años de historia en México*, vol. 1, pp. 103–118. Mexico: El Colegio de México, 1991.

Ellefson, Bernardo. *Matrimonio y sexo en el Incario.* La Paz: Editorial Los Amigos del Libro, 1989.

Gonzalbo Aizpuru, Pilar. *Familia y orden colonial.* Mexico: El Colegio de México, 1998.

Gutiérrez, Ramón A. *When Jesus Came, the Corn Mothers Went Away: Marriage, Sexuality, and Power in New Mexico, 1500–1846.* Stanford, CA: Stanford University Press, 1991.

Johnson, Lyman L., and Sonya Lipsett-Rivera, eds. *The Faces of Honor: Sex, Shame, and Violence in Colonial Latin America.* Albuquerque: University of New Mexico Press, 1998.

Kuznesof, Elizabeth. "Household and Family Studies." In *Latinas of the Americas: A Source Book*, ed. K. Lynn Stoner, pp. 305–388. New York: Garland, 1989.

Lavrin, Asunción. "In Search of the Colonial Woman in Mexico: The Seventeenth and Eighteenth Centuries." In *Latin American Women: Historical Perspectives*, ed. Asunción Lavrin, pp. 4–23. Westport, CT: Greenwood Press, 1978.

Lavrin, Asunción, ed. *Sexuality and Marriage in Colonial Latin America.* Lincoln: University of Nebraska Press, 1989.

Mannarelli, María Emma. *Pecados públicos: La ilegitimidad en Lima, siglo XVII.* Lima: Flora Tristán, 1993.

Martínez-Alier, Verena. *Marriage, Class, and Colour in Nineteenth-Century Cuba: A Study of Racial Attitudes and Sexual Values in a Slave Society.* London and New York: Cambridge University Press, 1974.

McCaa, Robert. *Marriage and Fertility in Chile: Demographic Turning Points in the Petorca Valley, 1840–1976.* Boulder, CO: Westview Press, 1983.

O'Phelan, Scarlett, and Margarita Zegarra. *Mujeres, familia y sociedad en la historia de América Latina, siglos XVIII–XXI.* Lima: Instituto Riva-Agüero, CENDOC-Mujer, 2006.

Rodríguez Saénz, Eugenia. *Hijas, novias y esposas: Familia, matrimonio y violencia doméstica en el Valle Central de Costa Rica (1750–1850).* San José, PR: EUNA, 2000.

Stolcke, Verena. *Racismo y sexualidad en la Cuba colonial.* Madrid, Alianza Editorial, 1992.

Alicia del Águila
Elizabeth Kuznesof

MARROQUÍN, FRANCISCO (c. 1499–1563).

Francisco Marroquín (*b.* ca. 1499; *d.* 9 April 1563), first bishop of Guatemala (1537–1563). Probably a native of Santander, Spain, Marroquín was a diocesan priest and a protégé of Francisco García de Loaysa, bishop of Osma and president of the Council of the Indies. In 1528, when Juan de Zumárraga was named bishop of Mexico, Marroquín accompanied him to the New World. At the invitation of Pedro de Alvarado, he settled in Guatemala in 1530 and served as a parish priest there. In 1532, Marroquín was appointed bishop of the new diocese of Guatemala, and following papal approval, he was consecrated at Mexico City in 1537. Marroquín spent the rest of his life in Guatemala. During his long episcopacy, he showed great interest in the conversion of the Indians, in the settlement and development of the colony, and in education, especially for the Spanish population. He served briefly as co-governor of Guatemala (1541–1542) and thereafter collaborated closely with the presidents of the Audiencia of Los Confines, which was established in 1542. From his earliest days in Central America, Marroquín had a long and stormy relationship with Bartolomé de Las Casas, with whom he disagreed regarding the best method of dealing with the native population.

See also **Catholic Church: The Modern Period; Guatemala, Audiencia of.**

BIBLIOGRAPHY

Lázaro Lamadrid, "Bishop Marroquín: Zumárraga's Gift to Central America," in *The Americas* 5, no. 3 (1949): 331–341.

Carmelo Sáenz De Santa María, *El licenciado don Francisco Marroquín, primer obispo de Guatemala (1499–1563): Su vida, sus escritos* (1964).

Additional Bibliography

Bendaña, R. *La Iglesia en Guatemala: Síntesis histórica del catolicismo guatemalteco: Parte I, 1524–1951.* Guatemala: Librerías Artemis Edinter, 2001.

STEPHEN WEBRE

MARROQUÍN, JOSÉ MANUEL (1827–1908). José Manuel Marroquín (*b.* 6 August 1827; *d.* 19 September 1908), acting president (7 August 1898–3 November 1898), president of Colombia (31 July 1900–7 August 1904). Marroquín, a member of the upper class, is better remembered for his literary achievements than for his political performance. As a writer, he was concerned with form as well as substance, and published works on Spanish poetics and rhetoric. His poetry has been hailed as charming and assured. He was a charter member of the Mosaico group of *costumbristas* ("sketch of manners" writers) and probably was the best of them, employing gentle satire to prod and instruct his readers. He was also a novelist; his best-loved work in that genre, *El Moro* (1897), is a sentimental tale about a horse. As president and nominal head of a disintegrating faction of the Conservatives, Marroquín had the ill fortune to preside ineffectually over a Colombia being torn apart by the War of the Thousand Days (1899–1903) and dismembered by the U.S.-sponsored secession of Panama (1903).

See also **Colombia, Political Parties: Conservative Party.**

BIBLIOGRAPHY

Charles W. Bergquist, *Coffee and Conflict in Colombia, 1886–1910* (1978), pp. 51–80, 196–219.

Frank M. Duffey, *The Early Cuadro de Costumbres in Colombia* (1956), pp. 59–67.

José Manuel Marroquín Osorio, *Don José Manuel Marroquín íntimo* (1915).

Additional Bibliography

Morales Benítez, Otto. *Sanclemente, Marroquín: El liberalismo y Panamá.* Santafé de Bogotá, Colombia: Stamato Editores, 1998.

J. LEÓN HELGUERA

MARSHALS OF AYACUCHO. Several future Peruvian presidents served under General Antonio José de Sucre at the battle of Ayacucho, which ended Spanish rule in South America in 1824. They included Agustín Gamarra of Cuzco (b. 1785), Miguel San Román of Puno (b. 1802), Manuel Ignacio Vivanco (b. 1806), Felipe Santiago Salaverry (b. 1805), and Juan Crisostomo Torrico (b. 1808), all of Lima. The military and political skills of these generals, together with the public renown they received by serving at Ayacucho, helped them to reach the pinnacle of political power, however briefly, during the turbulent post-Independence period known as the "age of the caudillos."

See also **Ayacucho, Battle of; Caudillismo, Caudillo.**

BIBLIOGRAPHY

Timothy E. Anna, *The Fall of Royal Government in Peru* (1979).

Additional Bibliography

Puente Candamo, José A. de la. *La Independencia del Perú.* Madrid: Editorial MAPFRE, 1992.

Walker, Charles. *Smoldering Ashes: Cuzco and the Creation of Republican Peru, 1780–1840.* Durham, NC: Duke University Press, 1999.

PETER F. KLARÉN

MARTÍ, AGUSTÍN FARABUNDO (1893–1932). Agustín Farabundo Martí (*b.* 1893; *d.* 1 February 1932), Salvadoran Communist leader and labor organizer. Martí's father, a moderate landholder in Teotepeque, reputedly adopted his surname in honor of the Cuban patriot José Martí. Young Farabundo grew up surrounded by poor campesinos, with whom he identified later in life. His biographers describe him as a precocious, sensitive child who could not understand the differences between men. When his father decided against dividing the family land among his sons, Martí enrolled in the Faculty of Jurisprudence and Social Sciences at the National University. From the beginning, however, he felt frustrated by the lack of open discussion in his college and began independently reading anarchist and communist texts in the library. He became involved in the nascent labor movement and participated in the first strikes held in El Salvador (1920). At this same time, he provoked a duel with his professor, Victoriano López Ayala, over the nature of cognition. For this, Martí and his friend José Luís Barrientos were exiled to Guatemala in 1920.

There are only fragmentary records of Martí's movements for the period from 1920 to 1925, but it is generally believed that he spent this time living among the Quiché Maya and making contacts among the rural salaried workers of Guatemala. He traveled frequently, working as a baker and bricklayer and doing other odd jobs in Guatemala and Honduras; he also served with the Red Battalions in Mexico, becoming a sergeant. Martí apparently took a pessimistic view of the latter country's still-young revolution, for he once remarked, "Disgracefully, the workers of Mexico have been captured by the bourgeoisie." In 1925, Martí and a few other dissident intellectuals founded the Central American Socialist Party in Guatemala City, which pledged to work for the unity of the isthmus. They had some brief success in persuading the legislatures of Guatemala, El Salvador, and Honduras to sponsor a tripartite republic but lacked support in Costa Rica and Nicaragua, and the party disintegrated.

Martí then found his way back to El Salvador, where he tried to raise the class consciousness of the rural workers. In 1928, President Alfonso Quiñones Molina exiled Martí to Nicaragua. This move allowed Martí to link up with Augusto César Sandino and serve as personal secretary to the Nicaraguan patriot. Martí failed to convert Sandino to Marxism-Leninism and returned to El Salvador in 1929, but Martí retained the highest personal regard for Sandino. Shortly before his execution in 1932, Martí declared that there was no greater patriot in all of Central America than General Sandino. For his own part, Martí was a hardened internationalist and a devout admirer of Leon Trotsky; throughout the 1920s he wore a lapel pin that featured an image of Trotsky within a red star.

Martí spent the closing years of the 1920s in and out of Salvadoran jails, with intermittent periods of exile. He spent some time in California, where he met several sympathetic members of the International Labor Defense and secured a position as Salvadoran representative of the Socorro Rojo (Red Aid), a socialist labor organization. He made his way back to El Salvador in time for the December 1930 election campaign. That year, Martí and a few close associates, including Miguel Mármol, founded the Communist Party of El Salvador. Contrary to the established Moscow-directed approach, the Salvadoran Communists refused to participate in elections and instead concentrated their efforts on organizing the dispossessed rural peasantry. The Communists initially lost ground to the reformist experiment of President Arturo Araujo, but gained strength after a coup in December 1931 brought the military to power. A mass uprising was planned for 22 January 1932, but the government uncovered the plot and executed Martí, along with two student accomplices, on 1 February. The period of repression that followed is known as the Matanza, or massacre. In 1980 several guerrilla groups joined forces and christened their umbrella organization the Farabundo Martí Liberation Front (FMLN) in honor of their model.

See also **El Salvador.**

BIBLIOGRAPHY

Thomas P. Anderson, *Matanza: El Salvador's Communist Revolt of 1932* (1971).

Jorge Arias Gómez, *Farabundo Martí: Esbozo biográfico* (1972).

James Dunkerley, *The Long War: Dictatorship and Revolution in El Salvador* (1982).

FMLN (Frente Farabundo Martí para la Liberación Nacional), *Farabundo Martí* (1982).

Additional Bibliography

Castellanos, Juan Mario. *El Salvador, 1930-1960: Antecendentes históricos de la guerra civil.* San Salvador, El Salvador: Dirección de Publicaciones e Impresos, 2002.

KAREN RACINE

MARTÍNEZ, ANTONIO J. (1793–1867).

Antonio J. Martínez (*b.* 1793; *d.* 1867), Roman Catholic priest, publisher, and political leader of New Mexico under Spanish, Mexican, and U.S. rule. Born in Abiquiu, New Mexico, Martínez was widowed after only one year of marriage. He subsequently studied for the priesthood in Durango, Mexico. As a pastor in Taos, Padre Martínez founded schools and published books and a newspaper called *El Crepúsculo de la Libertad* (The Twilight of

Liberty). His was the first printing press west of the Mississippi River. Martínez's labors were characterized by a deep conviction about the importance of education for his people. He is best known for the often bitter controversies between himself and the first archbishop of Santa Fe, Jean-Baptiste Lamy, which exemplified the cultural conflicts between New Mexico (Hispano) Catholics and the European, especially French, priests sent to work in New Mexico after the territory passed to the United States in 1848. The clash revolved around the efforts of the Europeans, who viewed their ministry as being both religious and social, to Americanize the New Mexico Hispanics. They urged the New Mexicans to abandon their "old-fashioned" Catholicism for a more "modern" Jansenist Catholicism appropriate for Catholics in a Protestant nation. The Europeans, who were trained for the ministry in the austere seminaries of France, knew little about the deep cultural roots of New Mexican Catholicism. Padre Antonio J. Martínez has come to be viewed as a hero of New Mexico history and a forerunner of the Hispanic or Latino civil rights movement of the 1960s.

See also **Catholic Chruch: The Colonial Period; New Mexico.**

BIBLIOGRAPHY

Luciano Hendren, *Fronteras: A History of the Latin American Church in the USA Since 1513* (1983), esp. pp. 195–207.

Carey Mc Williams, *North from Mexico* (1968), esp. pp. 118–119.

Additional Bibliography

De Aragon, Ray J. *Padre Martínez and Bishop Lamy.* Santa Fe, NM: Sunstone Press, 2006.

ALLAN FIGUEROA DECK S.J.

MARTINEZ, DENNIS (1955–). Dennis Martinez was the Latin American pitcher with the most victories in major league baseball when he retired in 1998 after a long career. Born on May 14, 1955, in Granada, Nicaragua, he played for the national team and had studied civil engineering before being signed by the Baltimore Orioles in December 1973. The pencil-thin right-hander made his first major-league appearance late in the 1976 season. Martinez was an important part of a number of great Orioles teams. He led the league in games (39), complete games (18), and innings pitched (292) for the 1979 team, which played in the World Series that year. He tied three other pitchers in the American League for the most wins (14) in the strike-shortened season of 1981. Drinking problems, however, limited his appearances on the 1983 World Series championship team.

Martinez was traded to the Montreal Expos in June 1986. He made a comeback there and led the National League in earned run average (ERA) and shutouts in 1991; he became the fourteenth pitcher in history to pitch a perfect game on July 28 of that year. He moved on to the Cleveland Indians in 1994. At the age of forty in 1995, he pitched a shutout and won his first postseason game against Randy Johnson in Seattle. He also pitched in the World Series that year. He played with Seattle in 1997 and ended his career with the Atlanta Braves in the following year. He pitched in 692 games in 23 seasons and had a career record of 245 wins and 193 losses, a 3.70 ERA, 30 shutouts, and 122 complete games. Having stayed aloof from the internecine struggles in his home country, he was spoken of as a possible presidential candidate in the 1990s; he has had to settle for the nickname El Presidente. In 1998 the national stadium in Managua was renamed in his honor. The Dennis Martinez Foundation has built and maintains children's shelters, schools, and little league baseball stadiums, and engages in other charitable works. The Orioles have employed him as a spring training instructor.

See also **Sports.**

BIBLIOGRAPHY

Arbena, Joseph L. *Latin American Sport: An Annotated Bibliography, 1988–1998.* Westport, CT: Greenwood Press, 1999.

The Baseball Encyclopedia. New York: Macmillan, 1993.

Eisenberg, John. *From 33rd Street to Camden Yards: An Oral History of the Baltimore Orioles.* Lincolnwood, IL: Contemporary Books, 2001.

Pluto, Terry. *Our Tribe: A Baseball Memoir.* New York: Simon and Schuster, 1999

ANDREW J. KIRKENDALL

MARTÍNEZ, ESTEBAN JOSÉ (1742–1798). Esteban José Martínez (*b.* 9 December 1742; *d.* 28 October 1798), Spanish naval officer, explorer of the Pacific Northwest. Born in Seville, Martínez studied at the Real Colegio de San Telmo. He was second pilot in the Department of San Blas in 1773 and sailed as provisional ensign with Juan Pérez to southern Alaska the following year. From 1775 to 1785 he commanded supply ships that sailed to Loreto, San Diego, Monterey, and San Francisco. Martínez was promoted to first pilot in 1781; commanded the *Princesa* and the *Favorita,* and met the expedition of Jean François de La Pérouse at Monterey in 1786; and became an ensign in 1787. With González López de Haro he searched the Northwest Coast for foreign encroachment as far as Unalaska and Kodiak islands. Martínez was commandant of Nootka in 1789 and, after fortifying it, returned to San Blas in December of that year. Subsequently, the British captain James Colnett was arrested for encroachment upon assumed Spanish territory, an event that led to conflict and to the convention of 1790. Martínez was posted to La Coruña in 1792 and returned to San Blas, as a lieutenant, in 1795. He died in Loreto. Among the proposals he had made to the crown were the occupation of the Sandwich Islands (modern Hawaii) and the establishment of a sea otter trade in the Californias.

See also **Explorers and Exploration: Spanish America.**

BIBLIOGRAPHY

Roberto Barreiro-Meiro, *Esteban José Martínez (1742–1798), Colección de diarios y relaciones para la historia de los viajes y descubrimientos,* vol. 6 (1964).

Warren L. Cook, *Flood Tide of Empire: Spain in the Pacific Northwest, 1543–1819* (1973).

Additional Bibliography

San Pío, María Pilar de. *Expediciones españolas del siglo XVIII: El paso del noroeste.* Madrid: Editorial MAPFRE, 1992.

W. MICHAEL MATHES

MARTÍNEZ, JUAN JOSÉ (c. 1782–c. 1863). Juan José Martínez (*b.* c. 3 January 1782; *d.* c. 25 July 1863), a hero of Mexican independence whose existence has been widely questioned. When Miguel Hidalgo besieged Guanajuato in September 1810, the Spaniards fortified themselves in the Alhóndiga de Granaditas granary. According to the legend, Martínez, a miner nicknamed Pípila (Turkey), joined the insurgents in their attack on the Alhóndiga. In the heart of battle he reached the great door of the granary by crawling under the protection of slab and set fire to the building, thus allowing the insurgents to enter. Lucas Alamán, the greatest historian of the epoch, doubted that Martínez had existed, but his critic, José María de Liceaga, insisted on the veracity of the tale. In recent years, the Guanajuato historian Fulgencio Vargas has published articles claiming to possess documents that prove the existence of the hero.

See also **Hidalgo y Costilla, Miguel; Mexico: 1810-1910; Mexico, Wars and Revolutions: War of Independence.**

BIBLIOGRAPHY

Lucas Alamán, *Historia de Méjico desde los primeros movimientos que prepararon su independencia en el año 1808 hasta la época presente,* vol. 1 (1849), p. 430.

José María De Liceaga, *Adiciones y rectificaciones a la historia de México que escribió D. Lucas Alamán* (1868), pp. 113–114.

José María Miquel I Vergés, *Diccionario de insurgentes,* 2d ed. (1980), p. 364.

Additional Bibliography

Rionda Arreguín, Isauro. *El Pípila, héroe popular de la insurgencia.* Guanajuato, Mexico: Archivo General del Estado, 1995.

Van Young, Eric. *The Other Rebellion: Popular Violence, Ideology, and the Mexican Struggle for Independence, 1810–1821.* Stanford, CA: Stanford University, 2001.

JAIME E. RODRÍGUEZ O.

MARTINEZ, PEDRO (1971–). Born in Manoguayabo, Dominican Republic, on October 25, 1971, the fifth of six children of a single mother, Martinez is one of the outstanding Latin American pitchers in Major League Baseball. Despite his unimpressive height and physique, Martinez in his prime had a fastball that could reach up to 97 miles per hour. He had a changeup the equal of which teammate Johnny Damon said he had never seen, as well as a great curve ball. Combined with his pinpoint control and an aggressive approach toward batters who crowd the plate, he has been an extremely intimidating pitcher. Martinez's best years have been compared favorably to those of the best in the game—Sandy Koufax, for example. He has the highest all-time winning percentage of any starting pitcher with more than 200 decisions.

Martinez followed his brother Ramón, also a pitcher, into the major leagues. He was signed by the Los Angeles Dodgers in 1988 and first pitched in the major leagues in September 1992 but was traded after the 1993 season to the Montreal Expos. By 1997 Martinez was one of the game's best, playing on one of the weakest teams, winning seventeen games that year with a league-leading 1.90 earned run average (ERA), a strikeout total of 305, and his first Cy Young Award. Despite these impressive achievements, it was during his seven seasons with the Boston Red Sox, beginning in 1998, that he became a star, compiling a 101-28 record with the team. He led the American League in ERA four times and won the Cy Young Award an additional two times. No pitcher before him had ever been a unanimous choice for the award two years running (1999 and 2000).

Over the next five years, he had the majors' highest number of victories. His most impressive individual statistics came in the 1999 season with the Boston Red Sox; in that year he had a 23-4 record and was named the most valuable player in the All-Star Game. He out-pitched Roger Clemens twice in the American League Championship Series in 1999 and 2003. In the 2003 postseason, he struggled when left in too long and could not hold a lead in the eighth inning of a game in which the Red Sox were ahead.

Martinez has not been as durable a pitcher as one might like, which explains, in part, why, in an age of specialization, he has only won twenty or more games in a season twice and why he rarely averages more than 200 innings per season. A rotator cuff injury cost him much of the 2001 season. The peak of his Red Sox career came in the 2004 season, when his team swept the St. Louis Cardinals in the World Series. In his first and only World Series appearance, Martinez stifled the Cardinal offense in a 4-1 victory in the third game. Following the World Series championship, Martinez joined the New York Mets after they gave him a contract worth $54 million over four years. As of the beginning of the 2007 season he had a lifetime 206-92 record, 2,998 strikeouts, and a 2.81 ERA. Injuries kept him from pitching for most of the 2007 season; in his first game back on the 3rd of September, he recorded his 3,000th strikeout.

See also **Sports.**

BIBLIOGRAPHY

Damon, Johnny, with Peter Golenbock. *Idiot: Beating "The Curse" and Enjoying the Game of Life.* New York: Crown Publishers, 2005.

Kisseloff, Jeff. *Who Is Baseball's Greatest Pitcher?* Chicago: Cricket Books, 2003.

Kolb, Elliott. *Who's Better, Who's Best in Baseball?* New York: McGraw Hill, 2005.

Mnookin, Seth. *Feeding the Monster: How Money, Smarts, and Nerve Took a Team to the Top.* New York: Simon & Schuster, 2006.

ANDREW J. KIRKENDALL

MARTÍNEZ, TOMÁS (1820–1873). Tomás Martínez (*b.* 21 December 1820; *d.* 12 March 1873), president of Nicaragua (1859–1867). In his early life Martínez was involved in commerce and agriculture, only later turning to the military. He became president in 1859, after the ouster of U.S. filibuster William Walker during the National War (in which Martínez emerged as a central figure). His administration developed a program that included the reorganization of agriculture, increased coffee cultivation, state support for secular schools, industrial growth, limitations on government monopolies, separation of church and state, abolition of the death penalty, establishment of trial by jury, and a plan for direct elections.

Ironically, although his administration ushered in thirty years of Conservative Party rule, his plan for direct elections ultimately caused the Conservative Party to split into four factions, creating a tumultuous situation that led to the installation of Liberal José Santos Zelaya as president in 1893.

See also **Nicaragua.**

BIBLIOGRAPHY

Sara Luisa Barquero, *Gobernantes de Nicaragua, 1825–1947* (1945), esp. pp. 117–124.

Francisco Ortega Arancibia, *Cuarenta años (1838–1878) de historia de Nicaragua* (1975).

Benjamin I. Teplitz, "The Political and Economic Foundations of Modernization in Nicaragua: The Administration of José Santos Zelaya, 1893–1909" (Ph.D. diss., Howard University, 1973), esp. p. 7.

Additional Bibliography

Cruz, Arturo J. *Nicaragua's Conservative Republic, 1858–93.* New York: Palgrave, 2002.

Velázquez P., José L. *La formación del Estado en Nicaragua, 1860–1930.* Managua, Nicaragua: Fondo Editorial, Banco Central de Nicaragua, 1992.

SHANNON BELLAMY

MARTÍNEZ, TOMÁS ELOY (1934–).

Tomás Eloy Martínez is a well-known Argentinean writer and an outspoken critic of the military dictatorship of Juan Domingo Perón. Born in the Argentinean town of Tucumán in 1934, Martínez completed his undergraduate education at the University of Tucumán, where he studied Spanish and Latin American literature. In 1957 he began his career writing as a film critic for the newspaper *La Nación* in Buenos Aires. He published his first book, *Sagrado* (Sacred), in 1969, then worked as a reporter in Paris for a year. In 1970 he received his M.A. in literature from the Université de Paris.

During the years of military dictatorship in Argentina (1975–1983), Martínez was forced into exile in Caracas, Venezuela. The three books he wrote during that time—*Los testigos de afuera* (Witnesses Outside, 1978; *Lugar común, la muerte* (Common Place, Death, 1979); and *Retrato del artista enmascarado* (Portrait of the Artist, Masked, 1982) were published in Argentina when the military dictatorship ended. His best-known work is *La novela de Perón* (The Peron Novel, 1985), an historical novel that deals with Perón's return to Argentina in 1973 after eighteen years in exile. The book caused a scandal: Because Martínez had conducted many interviews with Perón, the public wondered whether some of the novel's details were true rather than fictionalized. His book *Santa Evita* (1995), about Perón's beloved wife, is the most translated book in Argentinean history, appearing in more than thirty languages.

In 1995 Martínez became director of Latin American Studies at Rutgers University in New Jersey, a position which he still held in 2007. His 2002 novel *El vuelo de la reina* (The Flight of the Queen) won the prestigious Spanish Alfaguara Award for best novel. He has received seven honorary doctorates and a grant from the Guggenheim Foundation, and has been a fellow at numerous institutions, including the Wilson Center.

See also **Perón, Juan Domingo.**

BIBLIOGRAPHY

Domínguez Cáceres, Roberto. *Santa Evita: Los entremanos del lector y sus obras.* Mexico: Miguel Angel Porrúa, 2003.

Zelarayán, Carolina. *Deseo, desencanto y memoria: La narrativa de Tomás Eloy Martínez.* Tucumán, Argentina: Universidad Nacional de Tucumán, 2003.

Zuffi, María Griselda. *Demasiado real: Los excesos de la historia en la escritura de Tomás Eloy Martínez (1973–1995).* Buenos Aires: Corregidor, 2007.

EMILY BERQUIST

MARTÍNEZ DE HOZ, JOSÉ ALFREDO (1925–).

José Alfredo Martínez de Hoz (born August 13, 1925) served as Argentina's minister of economy from 1976 to 1981, during the Argentine military dictatorship of Jorge Rafael Videla. He promoted the extensive transformation of the economy under a so-called liberal economic program, with highly negative consequences.

Martínez de Hoz was an attorney by profession and served as minister of economy for the province of Salta during the military dictatorship of 1955, and, in 1962, as secretary of agriculture during the interim administration of José María Guido (1962–1963). He served on the board of directors of several multinational companies and business associations and was president of Acindar Industria Argentina de Aceros (ACIN).

When the armed forces installed a new dictatorship in 1976, the military junta appointed Martínez de Hoz minister of the economy. His objective was to stabilize the economy, which was in deep crisis, and to end the model of state intervention and a semi-closed economy that had been in effect since the 1940s. The initial adjustment measures were ineffective, bringing real wages down by 40 percent. Martínez de Hoz promoted a rapid liberalization of financial markets as well as an unequal opening of the economy, but did not oppose the continual rise in public subsidies for certain large companies, military spending, and state company spending. This imbalance led to increasing public and private foreign debt.

The persistence of inflation spurred Martínez de Hoz to experiment with a system of scheduled devaluation known as *la tablita* that accumulated a phenomenal exchange delay and greatly encouraged financial speculation. Many small and medium-sized national companies went bankrupt, whereas a small group of large companies grew strong on the benefits of state subsidies. In 1981 Martínez de Hoz resigned his position, along with President Videla, leaving the economy on the edge of a massive crisis that struck almost immediately afterwards. Private foreign debt was taken over by the state and Argentina's democratically elected government inherited a practically shattered state.

Martínez de Hoz was tried for his participation in state terrorism during the dictatorship and for defrauding the state, but was pardoned in 1990 by President Carlos Saúl Menem.

See also **Argentina: The Twentieth Century; Dirty War; Neoliberalism; Videla, Jorge Rafael.**

BIBLIOGRAPHY

Cavarozzi, Marcelo. *Autoritarismo y democracia, 1955–1996: La transición del estado al mercado en la Argentina.* Buenos Aires: Ariel, 1997.

Gerchunoff, Pablo, and Lucas Llach. *El ciclo de la ilusión y el desencanto: Un siglo de políticas económicas argentinas.* Buenos Aires: Ariel, 1998.

Novaro, Marcos, and Vicente Palermo. *La dictadura militar.* Buenos Aires: Paidós, 2003.

VICENTE PALERMO

MARTÍNEZ ESTRADA, EZEQUIEL

(1895–1964). Ezequiel Martínez Estrada (*b.* 14 September 1895; *d.* 5 November 1964), Argentine writer. Born of Spanish parents in San José de la Esquina, province of Santa Fe, Martínez Estrada was one of the most important Argentine writers of the twentieth century. Some consider him as influential as Domingo Faustino Sarmiento had been for the nineteenth century. His reputation is even more remarkable considering that he had little formal schooling and no university education.

With Martínez Estrada an intellectual movement began in Argentina, the major preoccupation of which was the reassessment of the country's character following the political decadence that began after the military coup of 1930. His book *Radiografía de la pampa* (1933; The X-Ray of the Pampa) is a condemnation of the elite for trying to impose European modes on the Argentine reality, rejecting what Martínez Estrada considered native traits. In this book he dissected Argentine society and searched for its true nature, as it struggled between urban and rural models. When he raised these questions, he brought everything into the open; he criticized those who emphasized only fragments of Argentine life. Basically, his works represented a search for the essence of Argentina's soul, and, therefore, he called on the Argentines not merely to evaluate their past but also to change the way in which they assessed it.

His literary work is characterized by a great sense of pessimism about the country's future as a result of the political decadence that had come about since 1930. His pessimism grew with the military revolts of the 1940s and with Juan Domingo Perón's anti-intellectual attitude. Martínez Estrada went into self-imposed exile from Buenos Aires to Bahía Blanca and from there to Mexico and Cuba. He wrote two other important books, *The Head of Goliath* (1940) and *Sarmiento* (1946), which also deal with social and political thoughts about Argentine society.

See also **Literature: Spanish America.**

BIBLIOGRAPHY

Peter G. Earle, *Prophet of the Wilderness: The Works of Ezequiel Martínez Estrada* (1971).

Pedro G. Orgambide, *Genio y figura de Ezequiel Martínez Estrada* (1985).

Juan José Sebreli, *Martínez Estrada: Una rebelión inútil* (1986).

Additional Bibliography

Alfieri, Teresa. *La Argentina de Ezequiel Martínez Estrada.* Buenos Aires: Leviatán, 2004.

Rosman, Silvia Nora. *Being in Common: Nation, Subject, and Community in Latin American Literature and Culture.* Lewisburg, PA: Bucknell University Press, 2003.

JUAN MANUEL PÉREZ

MARTÍN FIERRO.

MARTÍN FIERRO. *Martín Fierro,* the classic poem of Argentine Gauchesca literature, published in two parts (1872 and 1879). The poem contains a strong ethical, social, and political message, which its author, José Hernández, also delivered in his journalism and political life. Hernández sought to depict the destitute existence of a specific social class, re-creating its world view and particular language. He embodied that class in a fictional gaucho, Martín Fierro, who narrates his life before and after he was compulsorily sent to the frontier to fight the Indians—robbed of his family, home, and all his belongings. He escapes from virtual slavery at the fort, lives as a *gaucho matrero* (cunning outlaw), together with his friend Sargeant Cruz, and finds refuge among the Indians. Upon returning to his "pago" (the region in which he used to live), Martín Fierro finds two of his sons and the one of Cruz. After hearing the father's wise advice the four agree, for reasons not explained in the poem, to lead separate lives.

A vivid depiction of life in the fort and of Indian *malones* (surprise attacks), of Fierro's humiliating experiences as an unsalaried soldier, as well as of the abuses of his orphaned children, the poem is a denunciation of the profound injustices inflicted on the gauchos. An epic and lyrical piece of 7,210 verses, the poem not only achieved Hernández's sociopolitical purposes, but also won popular acclaim. Martín Fierro has ever since been the archetypical gaucho, symbolizing the "barbaric" inhabitants of the Pampas who were decimated in the name of "civilization."

See also **Gauchesca Literature; Hernández, José; Literature: Spanish America.**

BIBLIOGRAPHY

Nettie L. Benson, "*Martín Fierro* at the University of Texas," in *Library Chronicle of the University of Texas* 8, no. 4 (1968): 13–27.

Ted Lyon, "*Martín Fierro:* Narrative Fluctuation (as Key to Interpretation)," in *Chasqui* 1, no. 3 (1972): 26–35.

Nettie L. Benson, "*Martín Fierro,* Best Seller," in *Américas* 25, no. 2 (1973): 8–12.

Frank G. Carrino et al., trans., *The Gaucho Martín Fierro* (1974).

Fermín Chavez, "*Martín Fierro:* Sus contenidos ideológicos y políticos," in *Cuadernos Hispanoamericanos* 357 (March 1980): 525–540.

Michael J. Casey, "El cantor y el mudo: Speech and Silence in *Martín Fierro,*" in *Chasqui* 11, no. 1 (1981): 53–57.

Nancy Vogeley, "The Figure of the Black *Payador* in *Martín Fierro,*" in *CLA Journal* 26, no. 1 (1982): 34–48.

Rodolfo A. Borello, "La originalidad del *Martín Fierro,*" in *Cuadernos Hispanoamericanos* 437 (November 1986): 65–84, and "El *Martín Fierro* y la poesía gauchesca," in *Boletín de la Academia Argentina de Letras* 54, nos. 211–212 (1989): 97–129.

Additional Bibliography

Alposta, Luis. *La culpa en Martín Fierro.* Buenos Aires: Corregidor, 1998.

Astrada, Carlos. *El mito gaucho.* Buenos Aires: Fondo Nacional de las Artes, 2006.

Borello, Rodolfo A. *La poesía gauchesca, una perspectiva diferente.* Mendoza: EDIUNC, 2000.

Hanaway, Nancy. *Embodying Argentina: Body, Space and Nation in Nineteenth-Century Narrative.* Jefferson: McFarland & Co. Publishers, 2003.

Hernández, José. *Martín Fierro.* Nanterre: Allca XX, Université Paris X, 2001.

Martínez Estrada, Ezequiel. *Muerte y transfiguración de Martín Fierro: Ensayo de interpretación de la vida argentina.* Rosario: Beatriz Viterbo Editora, 2005.

Pérez, Alberto Julián. *Los dilemas políticos de la cultura letrada: Argentina, siglo XIX.* Buenos Aires: Corregidor, 2002.

Quiroga Lavié, Humberto. *Memorias de Fierro.* Buenos Aires: Librería Histórica, 2003.

ANGELA B. DELLEPIANE

MARTINIQUE AND GUADELOUPE.

MARTINIQUE AND GUADELOUPE. Martinique and Guadeloupe, Départements d'Outre-Mer (DOMs) of France since 1946. Each elects three representatives to the French National Assembly and two to the Senate. The northernmost of French territories in the eastern Caribbean, the DOM of Guadeloupe consists of the large islands of Basse-Terre and Grande Terre and five dependencies: Marie-Galante, Désirade, Îles des Saintes, Saint Barthélémy, and half

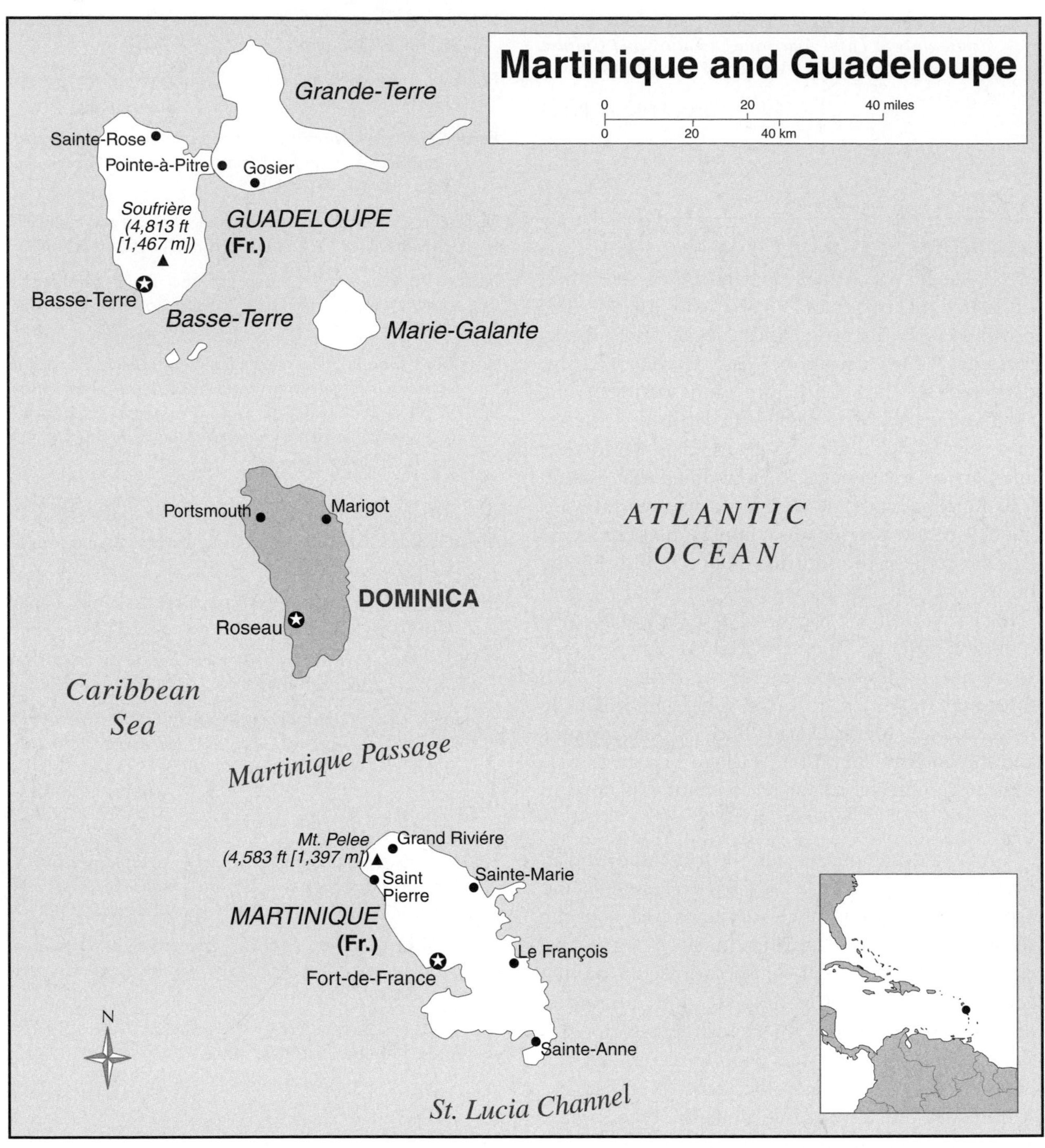

of Saint Martin. Most of the population of 440,189 (2003) is concentrated on the two large islands, primarily in Point-à-Pitre, the commercial center and major port, and secondarily in the political capital of Basse-Terre. Martinique has about a third of its 425,966 population in Fort-de-France, its capital and economic center, which has one of the best harbors in the Caribbean.

There are active volcanoes: Soufrière on Guadeloupe and Pelée on Martinique. The latter created a modern Pompeii in 1902 when it devastated Saint Pierre, then the largest city on Martinique, killing over 30,000 inhabitants in moments.

The first French settlers appeared on Martinique and Guadeloupe in 1635. Carib opposition and weak merchant support slowed the establishment of

Martinique and Guadeloupe

Population:	Martinique: 425,966; Guadeloupe: 440,189 (2003 est.)
Area:	Martinique: 429 sq. mi; Guadeloupe: 687 sq. mi
Official language:	French
Language:	Creole patois
National currency:	Euro
Principal religion:	Predominantly Roman Catholic
Ethnicity:	Mixture of black, white, and Carib Amerindian
Capital:	Martinique; Fort-de-France; Guadeloupe; Point-à-Pitre
Annual rainfall:	Martinique: Averages 75 in; Guadeloupe: Varies from 39 in on La Désirade (outlying island) to 200–400 in on the mountains of Basse-Terre

profitable plantations. In 1664 the French finance minister Jean-Baptiste Colbert, instituted policies that greatly stimulated sugar production with African slave labor and brought the colonies under firm crown control. The *exclusif* ended local attempts at economic diversification and competition with French industry. Local councils were only advisory, and officials were French. Governors answered to the governor-general in Martinique.

By the eighteenth century, French planters in Martinique, Guadeloupe, and Saint Domingue (later Haiti) were producing more sugar than the English, and selling it cheaper, even expanding their trade in British North America, which was legally a closed British market.

The end of plantation slavery began with a massive slave rebellion in Saint Domingue (Haiti) in 1793. In 1794, the French Revolutionary government declared the end of slavery in all French colonies (the British occupation of Martinique made the declaration void there). In 1802 Napoleon decreed a reimposition of slavery in the remaining French possessions. The French agreed to end the African slave trade to their colonies in 1815. Abolition came with a new Revolutionary government in 1848. After emancipation the planters were compensated for their lost slaves, and France offered support in locating indentured labor, primarily from India. From 1850 to 1914, about 25,000 Indians arrived in Martinique and 37,000 in Guadeloupe. Many died or migrated after their contracts were over.

The major political initiatives have come from the working class: a riot on Martinique (1870) and strikes on both Martinique and Guadeloupe in the 1890s and at the beginning of the twentieth century. Sugar and its derivatives continue to dominate the economy, as well as labor and social relations.

The contemporary social structure of Martinique reflects the legacies of a plantation society. The social and landed elite is made up of whites, the Békés, many of whom claim descent from the original colonizers. They maintain marriage with inheritance strictly within their group. The Békés reflect the values of the plantocracy.

"Metropolitans" (whites who immigrated to Martinique, mostly from France) form part of the middle class. The larger part of the middle class is composed largely of *mulâtres,* most of whom are of mixed racial ancestry as a result of sexual liaisons between whites and blacks during slavery (particularly through the concubinage commonly practiced by white males); of marriages among "free coloreds" during slavery; and, more recently, of marriages between "metropolitans" and descendants of Asian indentured laborers and blacks. This middle class, which began its ascent after 1848, now dominates commerce, the professions, and political and bureaucratic offices.

The majority of the population and the lowest economic group is the *noirs* (blacks), although some members of this group are of mixed ancestry. The *noirs* tend to be more rural and to work in agriculture, many as wage laborers on plantations. Some ply trades, often in addition to agriculture; others reside on plantations for lack of their own land and employment alternatives; some are fishermen. The upper level of this class overlaps with the *mulâtres* as shopkeepers, bureaucrats, lawyers, and teachers in rural areas.

The Guadeloupan social structure closely resembles that of Martinique, except that the white elite is not as large, powerful, or racially exclusive. The comparative weakness of the white group is due in good part to the decimation it suffered at the hands of Victor Hugues, the French Jacobin who instituted the Terror in Guadeloupe, executing over 800 whites. Many of the remaining whites fled the island.

Both Martinique and Guadeloupe are intimately tied to the distant French metropole from which they derive their standard of living (very high, compared with their Caribbean neighbors); their defense, education, and health and welfare funding; their official language; and their Roman Catholicism. Independence is not a likely popular choice, largely because of the fear of economic decline without massive French subsidies. However, a growing awareness of cultural similarities to their Caribbean neighbors continues to fuel the search for greater local autonomy within the French nation.

See also **Slave Revolts: Spanish America; Slavery: Spanish America.**

BIBLIOGRAPHY

Lafcadio Hearn, *Two Years in the French West Indies* (1890).

Nellis Maynard Crouse, *The French Struggle for the West Indies, 1665–1713* (1966).

Walter Adolphe Roberts, *The French in the West Indies* (1971).

Léo Elisabeth, "The French Antilles," in *Neither Slave nor Free: The Freedman of African Descent in the Slave Societies of the New World,* edited by David W. Cohen and Jack P. Greene (1972).

Bridget Brereton, "Society and Culture in the Caribbean: The British and French West Indies, 1870–1980," in *The Modern Caribbean,* edited by Franklin W. Knight and Colin A. Palmer (1989).

Dale Tomich, *Slavery in the Circuit of Sugar: Martinique and the World Economy, 1830–1848* (1990).

Additional Bibliography

Adélaïde-Merlande, Jaques, René Bélénus, and Frédéric Régent. *La rébellion de la Guadeloupe, 1801–1802.* Gourbeyre: Archives départementales de la Guadeloupe, 2002.

Berrian, Brenda F. *Awakening Spaces: French Caribbean Popular Songs, Music, and Culture.* Chicago: University of Chicago Press, 2000.

Browne, Katherine E., and Rod Salter. *Creole Economics: Caribbean Cunning under the French Flag.* Austin: University of Texas Press, 2004.

Dubois, Laurent. *A Colony of Citizens: Revolution & Slave Emancipation in the French Caribbean, 1787–1804.* Chapel Hill: University of North Carolina Press, 2004.

Forster, Elborg, and Robert Forster, eds. *Sugar and Slavery, Family and Race: The Letters and Diary of Pierre Dessalles, Planter in Martinique, 1808–1856.* Baltimore, MD: Johns Hopkins University Press, 1996.

Kadish, Doris Y., ed. *Slavery in the Caribbean Francophone World: Distant Voices, Forgotten Acts, Forged Identities.* Athens: University of Georgia Press, 2000.

Pérotin-Dumon, Anne. *La ville aux Iles, la ville dans l'île: Basse-Terre et Pointe-à-Pitre, Guadeloupe, 1650–1820.* Paris: Karthala, 2000.

Price, Richard. *The Convict and the Colonel: A Story of Colonialism and Resistance in the Caribbean.* Durham, NC: Duke University Press, 2006.

Zebrowski, Ernest. *The Last Days of St. Pierre: The Volcanic Disaster that Claimed Thirty Thousand Lives.* New Brunswick, NJ: Rutgers University Press, 2002.

ROSEMARY BRANA-SHUTE

MARTÍ Y PÉREZ, JOSÉ JULIÁN

(1853–1895). José Julián Martí y Pérez (*b.* 28 January 1853; *d.* 19 May 1895) is the father of Cuba's independence. Even if he had done nothing for his native land, Martí would have gone down in history as a great literary figure. But besides being a poet, journalist, and orator of genius, Martí was a revolutionary and a politician, the architect and organizer of Cuba's 1895–1898 war against Spanish colonialism. For this reason he is best known as the apostle of Cuba's independence. Cubans today revere his memory and regard his teachings as the living gospel of the fatherland.

EARLY CAREER

Born in Havana of poor Spanish immigrants, Martí was able to go to high school owing to the support of Rafael María Mendive, an enlightened schoolmaster whose influence outweighed all others on his early youth. Martí was still in school when the first Cuban war of independence, the Ten Years' War, broke out in 1868. Like many of his classmates, he embraced the cause of freedom. In January 1869, aged sixteen, he founded his first newspaper, which he appropriately named *La Patria Libre* (Free Fatherland). Shortly afterward he was arrested and sentenced to six years of hard labor in a rock quarry, merely because he wrote a letter denouncing a pro-Spanish fellow student as an "apostate." After serving only a few months, however, Martí's sentence was commuted to banishment to Spain, where he arrived early in 1871. That same year he published his celebrated essay *El presidio político en Cuba,* a passionate indictment of conditions in Cuba's prisons.

After this, his first exile (during which he completed his schooling at the universities of Madrid and Saragossa), Martí revisited Cuba only twice before 1895: in 1877 for less than two months, and again from 31 August 1878 to 25 September 1879. Altogether Martí spent twenty-three years away from the land of his birth, during which period he worked as a journalist in Mexico, the United States, and Venezuela, and as a professor in Guatemala. Nevertheless, for the most part he made his home in New York, which was the center of his activities from 1881 until just before his death in 1895.

LITERARY WORK

It was during this period that Martí gained recognition throughout the hemisphere, partly as a chronicler of life in the United States. He was a keen observer of the grandeur and miseries of the nation during the Gilded Age, and he reported what he saw in his columns for the *Opinión Nacional* of Caracas, *La Nación* of Buenos Aires, and more than twenty other Spanish American newspapers. In 1884 Martí was famous enough to be appointed vice-consul of Uruguay in New York. By this time he had become one of the forerunners of literary modernism in Spanish with the publication of *Ismaelillo* (1882), a collection of poems for his only son. In 1889 Martí delighted Spanish-speaking youngsters with his *Edad de Oro,* a magazine for children written entirely by him, and in 1891 he published his *Versos sencillos,* which in many ways marks the culmination of his poetic career. Martí's literary output at this point of his life was enormous and included several translations from English, a not very successful novel, and a romantic play. Nowhere is his genius revealed, though, as in the highly personal style of his articles and essays, his mesmerizing speeches, his political documents, and even his private correspondence. His prose is among the best in the Spanish language.

Statue of José Martí in Havana's Revolution Square, Cuba, December 2, 2006. Remembered not only for his accomplishments in literature, Martí is also considered one of the architects of Cuba's independence movement. Though he was killed during the early years of Cuba's rebellion in 1895, Martí's writings continue to instill patriotism in Cubans today. JOE RAEDLE/GETTY IMAGES

CUBAN INDEPENDENCE

Martí spent many of his years in exile plotting the independence of Cuba, a Herculean task. Not only did he have to hold in check those who favored the autonomy of the island under Spain or who endorsed its annexation to the United States, but he also had to cope with the threat of American expansionism and the authoritarian proclivities of the veteran generals of the Ten Years' War. Martí maintained that in order to avoid these pitfalls, Cuba's struggle for independence would have to be brief (so as to minimize the chances for U.S. intervention) and conducted with "republican method and spirit" (in order to prevent the island from falling prey to a military dictatorship after independence). Somewhere around 1887 he concluded that he would have to assume political leadership if these ends were to be attained. For this purpose, in 1892 Martí formed the Cuban Revolutionary Party, an essentially U.S.-centered organization through which he subsequently channeled his efforts to overthrow Spanish domination in Cuba. For more than three years, he worked untiringly until, by early 1895, he was ready to launch a new and more formidable rebellion on the island. The veteran generals would still be in command of the expeditions to sail from Fernandina, Florida, but they were now under the authority of the party and its leader.

At the last minute, however, U.S. authorities seized the boats and the war materials that Martí had clandestinely procured, and he could only join the fighting that had already started in Cuba on the sufferance of the military leaders. His leadership role declined as a result of the Fernandina fiasco. Once in Cuba, the generals challenged the principle of civil supremacy so dear to him, and he began to think of returning to the United States in order to cope with the threat of military authoritarianism that he had long feared. Thus, he was in a somber mood when he was killed in a skirmish of little consequence. The struggle continued, but his political doctrine had very little influence on subsequent developments. After the war ended, there were very few who thought that his statue should be erected in Havana's Central Park.

INTELLECTUAL AND POLITICAL LEGACY

Gradually, however, Martí became better known in Cuba. In 1905 the state sponsored a presentation of the first national statue of Martí. When the island was swept by a shock wave of nationalism in the late 1920s and early 1930s, he emerged as the political, moral, and spiritual mentor of a new generation of Cubans. It was at this time that the cult-like Cuban attitude toward Martí and his preachings took on its present form and substance.

Martí was so prolific that it is nearly impossible to offer an adequate insight into his thought. Often what may be considered as representative ideas are offset by completely different or even contradictory ones. For this reason he appears to be ambivalent on many subjects, while in other cases it seems that he simply refused to record an opinion. We look in vain, for example, for a passage stating his political program, the political system he preferred, or his constitutional doctrine.

It is not surprising, therefore, that leftist scholars and politicians should have found a Marxist slant in his writings. But Martí rejected the notion of the class struggle as well as the high level of violence employed by some of the labor leaders of his time. Furthermore, he condemned the idea of entrusting to the state the satisfaction of man's material needs. Therefore, while Martí may have sympathized with Marx's concern for the worker, he certainly was no Marxist.

Martí was not anti-American, nor did he ever intend to make an enemy of the United States, despite his well-known anti-imperialist stance. If anything, his view of the country, which he chose as his haven in exile, was critical, in the strictest sense of the word. He was aware of the sordid facets of life within its boundaries—and denounced them. But Martí also proclaimed his admiration for the dynamism and industry of Americans as well as his esteem for American thinkers and writers and "the wonderful men who framed the constitution of the United States of America." As Martí himself once said, he loved the land of Lincoln as much as he feared the land of Francis Cutting (a nineteenth-century adventurer who once tried to annex northern Mexico to the United States).

Although Martí was a pugnacious nationalist, when he worried about Cutting-like predators he was thinking not only about Cuba, but about Spanish America as well. He envisioned Spanish America as forming, from the Rio Grande to Patagonia, one single, colossal nation, which he called "our America," and which in his view would have a great future, "not as a conquering Rome but as a hospitable nation." Like Simón Bolívar, therefore, he thought in hemispheric terms, and that is no doubt the reason why Rubén Darío, the great Nicaraguan poet, said that he belonged not to Cuba alone, but to "an entire race, an entire continent."

Throughout the twentieth and twenty-first centuries, politicians across the political spectrum used the writings and images of Martí to promote their agendas. Fidel Castro, who led Cuban Revolution in the late 1950s, emphasized in his speeches Martí's desire for social and racial equality and labeled Martí a revolutionary. Cuban exiles, who vocally oppose Castro's Communist regime, have cited Martí's writings in their protests. The United States government funds Radio Martí, which critiques the Communist government in its broadcasts to Cuba.

See also **Cuba: The Colonial Era (1492-1898); Cuba, Political Movements, Nineteenth Century; Literature: Spanish America.**

BIBLIOGRAPHY

Peter Turton, *José Martí: Architect of Cuba's Freedom* (1986)

Christopher Abel and Nissa Torrents, eds., *José Martí: Revolutionary Democrat* (1986).

Additional Bibliography

Guerra, Lillian. *The Myth of José Martí: Conflicting Nationalisms in Early Twentieth-century Cuba.* Chapel Hill: University of North Carolina Press, 2005.

Lolo, Eduardo. *Después del rayo y del fuego: Acerca de José Martí.* Madrid, Spain: Editorial Betania, 2002.

Zanetti, Susana. *Legados de José Martí en la crítica latinoamericana.* La Plata, Argentina: Facultad de Humanidades y Ciencias de la Educación, Universidad Nacional de La Plata, 1999.

José M. Hernández

MARTORELL, ANTONIO (1939–).

Antonio Martorell (*b.* 18 April 1939) is a Puerto Rican artist. Martorell received his early training with Julio Martín Caro in Madrid (1961–1962). He studied printmaking with Lorenzo Homar from 1962 to 1965 at the Institute of Puerto Rican Culture's graphics workshop in New York City. In 1968 he founded the Taller Alacrán (Scorpion's Workshop). Martorell has also worked as a set designer, book illustrator, caricaturist, textile and graphic designer, art critic, and writer. Since 1985, he has worked collaboratively with Rosa Luisa Márquez as performer and set designer for graphic-theatrical performance pieces. He has taught at the National School of Fine Arts in Mexico City, the Institute of Puerto Rican Culture, and the Universidad Interamericana in San Germán, Puerto Rico. His posters, paintings, and installations have been exhibited internationally, and he has won numerous awards. Martorell has two studios, one in New York City and one in Ponce, Puerto Rico. He is also an artist in residence at the Universidad de Puerto Rico in Cayey. His daughter, Alejandra Martorell, is a famous modern dancer.

See also **Art: The Twentieth Century.**

BIBLIOGRAPHY

Instituto De Cultura Puertorriqueña, *Antonio Martorell, Obra gráfica 1963–1986. Exposición homenaje* (1986).

Martorell, Antonio. *La piel de la memoria* (1992).

Museo Del Barrio (New York City), *Antonio Martorell and Friends: La Casa de Todos Nosotros/A House for Us All* (1992).

Additional Bibliography

Carrero, Angel. *Apuntes éticos: Para la ciudadanía boricua.* San Juan, Puerto Rico: Ediciones Anawin, 1999.

Martorell, Antonio, and María E. Somoza. *Jaulabra en la labra: Antonio Martorell y sus amigos.* San Juan, Puerto Rico: Museo de Arte Contemporáneo de Puerto Rico, 2004.

Rivera, Nelson. *Los carteles de Martorell.* New York: Hostos Culture & Arts Program, 1987.

Rivera, Nelson. *Visual Artists and the Puerto Rican Performing Arts, 1950–1990: The Works of Jack and Irene Delano, Antonio Martorell, Jaime Suárez, and Oscar Mestey-Villamil.* New York: P. Lang, 1997.

Miriam Basilio

MARTYR, PETER (1459–1526).

Peter Martyr (also Pietro Martire d'Anghiera; *b.* 1457 or 1459; *d.* 1526), early historian of the discovery and exploration of the New World. Born in Arona, Italy, Martyr moved to Rome in 1477 and became a noted academic. In 1487 he went to Spain, where he became a cleric and adviser to the Spanish monarchs Isabella I and Ferdinand V, and became a friend of Christopher Columbus. In 1520 he became court historian and secretary to the Council of the Indies. His close relationship to the Spanish court and with the early conquistadores during the time of the Conquest of America provided him with much data, from which he wrote *De orbe novo* (The New World). The first history of the Spanish Conquest, this work was published in eight parts, beginning in 1511. Although it contains many errors as a result of Martyr's heavy use of the reports of the conquistadores, who often embellished their accounts or relied on memory rather than documentary sources, it remains one of the most important of the early chronicles and reflects the Renaissance spirit of the explorations.

See also **Conquistadores.**

BIBLIOGRAPHY

De orbe novo, translated by Richard Eden (1612).

De orbe novo: The Eight Decades of Peter Martyr d'Anghera, translated by Francis Augustus MacNutt (1912).

SUE DAWN MCGRADY

MARYKNOLL ORDER. In 1911 the Catholic Foreign Mission Society of America, popularly known as Maryknoll, was founded in Ossining, New York. In 1920 the Maryknoll Sisters officially became a separate congregation. Prior to U.S. entrance into World War II, Maryknoll mission activities were limited to the Far East. Since the war forced Maryknoll to cut back on that commitment, it decided to expand to Latin America, where it established missions in Bolivia in 1942 and opened its Instituto de Idiomas in Cochabamba, the largest of the order's language schools. It offers instruction in Spanish, Quechua, and Aymara, and trains missionaries for Maryknoll and thirty other Catholic religious orders, as well as for several Protestant groups. So successful has its program been that between 1965 and 1982 alone it taught about 3,500 missioners.

In 1942 Maryknoll also opened missions in Peru and Chile, and by the end of 1943, it had opened additional missions in Mexico, Guatemala, and Ecuador. Later Maryknoll expanded into El Salvador (1961), Venezuela (1966), Nicaragua (1971), Brazil (1976), and Honduras (1981). Its Ecuadoran operations, however, were terminated in 1948. Since a primary goal was to increase indigenous priestly vocations, Maryknoll opened a minor seminary in Puno, Peru, in 1944. Although more than 800 boys studied there, only 12 became priests. The seminary was closed in 1969.

When Maryknoll first entered Latin America, its superior general, James E. Walsh, noted that its missioners were "not going as exponents of any so-called North American civilization." Nevertheless, until the late 1960s the order's work was undeniably colored in part by a sense of U.S. superiority and an anticommunist mentality. Parishes were based on the U.S. Catholic model and when possible included a parochial school. The extensive North American presence in the area was seen as a positive force, and missioners often relied on local North American businessmen for moral and monetary support. Numerous development projects were started under the auspices of the Alliance for Progress, but many eventually failed because of local injustice and an overreliance on outside financial help.

As a result of the Second Vatican Council's emphasis on social awareness, Maryknoll began to rethink its role. In its 1966 general chapter, a new mission rationale was produced, placing more stress on the needs of the poor. Encouraged by the Second General Conference of Latin American bishops at Medellín, Colombia, in 1968, the society increased its efforts in training Catholic lay leaders. *Cursillos* (three-day retreats for lay people, followed by weekly meetings) were held. Catechetical training centers were opened, and Christian Base Communities were organized. At its 1973 general chapter, Maryknoll emphasized its responsibility to make U.S. citizens aware of Third World poverty and injustice, and of the role the First World plays in their perpetuation. Already in 1970 it had created Orbis Books, in an attempt to offer the best of Third World theology to North American readers. After two decades, Orbis has become well known for its English translations of liberation theology, publishing works by such notables as Gustavo Gutiérrez, Leonardo Boff, Jon Sobrino, and Juan Luis Segundo. Its School of Theology at Maryknoll, New York, soon created programs in Hispanic ministry and in justice and peace studies, opening its doors to lay people as well as clergy and to non-Catholics and Catholics alike. In 1975 it began an innovative lay missionary program, which has become a model for other religious orders. It has since offered programs for short-term volunteers. Over the years Maryknoll has produced eight Latin American bishops. Five of its members were murdered while carrying out their duties: Father Bill Woods was killed in Guatemala in 1976, and Sisters Maura Clarke, Ita Ford, Dorothy Kazel, and associate Jean Donovan were murdered by El Salvador's armed forces in 1980. In 2006, with over 650 religious and lay missionaries stationed in ten Latin American countries, along the U.S.-Mexican border, and around the globe, Maryknoll members continue to maintain their reputation for a strong and active commitment to the poor.

See also **Catholic Church: The Modern Period; Missionaries of Charity; Missions: Brazil; Missions: Jesuit Missions (Reducciones); Missions: Spanish America.**

BIBLIOGRAPHY

There is no study that offers a general overview of Maryknoll in Latin America. For the early years see Albert J. Nevins, *The Meaning of Maryknoll* (1954), pp. 201–251. For Maryknoll sisters, see Penny Lernoux, *Hearts on Fire: The Story of the Maryknoll Sisters* (1993). Although not specifically treating Maryknoll, Gerald M. Costello, *Mission to Latin America: The Successes and Failures of a Twentieth Century Crusade* (1979), contains some important information. The periodicals *Mission Forum* and *Maryknoll*, a bilingual (Spanish/English) publication since 1980, are especially valuable.

Additional Bibliography

Behrens, Susan Fitzpatrick. *Confronting Colonialism: Maryknoll Catholic Missionaries in Peru and Guatemala, 1943–1968.* Helen Kellogg Institute for International Studies, Working Paper no. 338, May 2007. Available from University of Notre Dame, Kellogg Institute, http://www.nd.edu/~kellogg.

Daniels, Jim. *Lives of Service: Stories from Maryknoll.* Maryknoll, NY: Orbis Books, 2001.

Ford, Ita. *Here I Am, Lord: The Letters and Writings of Ita Ford*, edited by Jeanne Evans. Maryknoll, NY: Orbis Books, 2005.

Kita, Bernice. *What Prize Awaits Us: Letters from Guatemala*, 2nd edition. Maryknoll, NY: Maryknoll Sisters of St. Dominic, 1998.

EDWARD T. BRETT

MAS CANOSA, JORGE (1939–1997).

Jorge Mas Canosa was a Cuban exile in Miami, Florida, who became one of the most prominent opponents of Cuba's Communist regime under Fidel Castro. His organization, the Cuban American National Federation (CANF), founded in 1981 with support from the administration of President Ronald Reagan, became the most influential lobbying group on Cuban affairs. Sponsored by the U.S. government, CANF produced Radio Martí and TV Martí to provide alternative information and anti-Castro messages to the island. The Cuban government accused CANF of also financing terrorism to bring down Castro.

Mas and his organization were instrumental in crafting and passing the 1992 Cuba Democracy Act, which relaxed travel restrictions for academics but generally strengthened the U.S. trade embargo against Cuba. When Cuba shot down two unarmed, private planes operated by a Miami-based Cuban refugee support organization in 1996, Mas used the incident to push for passage of the Helms-Burton Act, which established penalties for foreign companies that did business with Castro's government. Moreover, the act required the U.S. Congress to meet stringent requirements to lift trade sanctions. The death of Mas, on November 23, 1997, weakened the Cuban exile community's opposition to the Castro government. In 2001 CANF split over tactics. Even though Cuban-Americans have become more ideologically diverse in the early twenty-first century, the laws that Mas helped pass still define U.S. policy toward Cuba's communist government.

See also **Cuba: Cuba Since 1959.**

BIBLIOGRAPHY

Torres, María de los Angeles. *In the Land of Mirrors: Cuban Exile Politics in the United States.* Ann Arbor: University of Michigan Press, 1999.

Vargas Llosa, Alvaro. *El exilio indomable: Historia de la disidencia cubana en el destierro.* Madrid: Espasa, 1998.

BYRON CRITES

MASCATES. *See* **War of the Mascates.**

MASFERRER, ALBERTO (1868–1932).

Alberto Masferrer (*b.* 24 July 1868; *d.* 4 September 1932), Salvadoran journalist and political figure, most famous for his *mínimum vital*, a nine-point program designed to provide a minimum standard of living to his countrymen. As a youth Masferrer displayed exceptional sensitivity to the social problems he encountered throughout Central America. He objected to the outmoded, restrictive system of education and the appalling conditions in which many Salvadorans, particularly those in rural areas, lived. His basic ideas, present in their most rudimentary form in his first work, *Niñerías* (1892), were refined over the next four decades.

In 1895, President Rafael Gutiérrez appointed Masferrer consul to Costa Rica. Here he also began to dabble in journalism and forge links with the nascent labor movement, two interests that were to continue throughout his life. He was reassigned to Chile in 1901 and Belgium in 1911 but left the diplomatic corps in 1914 to pursue a career in journalism. Masferrer returned to El Salvador in 1916 and quickly espoused the cause of the working classes. In 1918 he organized the First Workers' Congress, which featured the future president Arturo Araujo, a landlord, as its keynote speaker. Throughout the 1920s, Masferrer continued to campaign for an improved standard of living and to achieve official respect for the working classes. He served as the editor of several short-lived journals before founding *La Patria* in 1928. In his opening editorial, Masferrer pledged that his newspaper would describe the life of Salvadorans as it actually was and committed himself to working for "the health, welfare, prosperity, culture, liberty, peace and contentment of all." He wrote a series of articles known collectively as "El mínimum vital" (1928–1929) which called for adequate food, housing, clothing, education, work, recreation, and justice for all Salvadorans. In the 1930 campaign for the presidency Masferrer endorsed Arturo Araujo, who borrowed Masferrer's concept of *vitalismo* as his platform. Araujo easily won office after General Maximiliano Hernández Martínez withdrew from the race, but his term lasted less than a year. Masferrer quickly realized that the Araujo administration was corrupt and powerless to effect real reforms, and left for self-exile in Guatemala. Upon hearing of the 1932 Matanza, wherein thousands of Salvadorans were killed by government troops, Masferrer became despondent and sank into deep depression. He died of a cerebral hemorrhage later that year.

Masferrer is an important figure in the intellectual history of Central America. His thought is part of a broad anti-positivist movement that flourished in Latin America in the early decades of the twentieth century. Though his writings shied away from addressing directly the need for political reform, Masferrer's ideas included a clear social and economic agenda which implied that such changes were needed for a more smoothly functioning society. In his mind any truly national culture had an obligation to provide for its people their minimum spiritual and material well-being. His ideas reveal a strong affinity with the Roman Catholic church after *Rerum Novarum,* the 1891 papal encyclical that rejected both capitalism and socialism as paths for human development. His notion of an organic, harmonious nation that was hierarchical in organization and functioned along the lines of Christian charity and the dignity of all work is clearly typical of the intellectual flirtation with fascism that characterized so many thinkers of his generation. Masferrer was a reformer who did not seek to tear down the whole social order; he merely wanted to rid it of its worst abuses. Thus his ideas led directly into the Salvadoran Christian Democratic movement that flourished in the 1960s and similarly sought to improve general conditions through cooperation and conciliation rather than revolution. Masferrer remains a popular figure in El Salvador today.

See also **El Salvador.**

BIBLIOGRAPHY

Matilde Elena López, *Masferrer: Alto pensador de Centroamérica* (1954).

Matilde Elena López, *Pensamiento social de Masferrer* (1984).

Alberto Masferrer, *Obras Escogidas* (1971).

Manuel Masferrer C., *Biografía del escritor Alberto Masferrer* (1957).

Rafael Antonio Tercero, *Masferrer: Un ala contra el huracán* (1958).

María Luisa Zelaya de Guirola, *Masferrer: Un grito en la noche de Centroamérica* (1975).

Additional Bibliography

Casaús Arzú, Marta Elena. "La influencia de Alberto Masferrer en la creación de redes teosóficas y vitalistas en América Central, 1920–1930." *Cuadernos Americanos* 99 (May–June 2003): 197–238.

Racine, Karen. "Alberto Masferrer and the Vital Minimum: The Life and Thought of a Salvadoran Journalist, 1868–1932." *The Americas* 54:2 (October 1997): 209–237.

KAREN RACINE

MASONIC ORDERS. Freemasonry claims traditions that go back to ancient times, but its modern form and meaning reside in such principles as religious tolerance, social equality, philanthropy, and the belief in a powerful Grand Architect of the universe. In the Iberian colonies in the eighteenth century, records of the Inquisition show that several individuals charged with practicing Freemasonry were tried and punished, but Masonic lodges with a primarily Creole composition and purpose did not make a formal appearance until the early nineteenth century.

Masonic societies are secret, primarily in terms of rites of initiation, ceremonies, and forms of identification and salutation. Since the nineteenth century, those in Latin America have been the most public of secret societies. They have been involved in many of the central issues affecting the region; their leaders have been publicly known as Freemasons; and they have made their views known through numerous publications. Probably the major significance of Latin American Freemasonry is the role the lodges played during Independence and their position with respect to church-state relations.

The origins of masonic orders having a specific Latin American orientation remain unclear, but Francisco de Miranda is widely believed to have played a role in their creation during his stay in Europe in the 1790s and the early years of the nineteenth century. The most significant lodge for the process of independence, the Lautaro lodge, first established in Cádiz, was carried to Buenos Aires in 1812 and then to Mendoza and Santiago. Such prominent creoles as Simón Bolívar, Andrés Bello, Vicente Rocafuerte, José de San Martín, Mariano Moreno, and Bernardo O'Higgins were initiated into this network of lodges. Although some may have been genuine believers in some Masonic rites, Independence leaders utilized the lodges primarily as vehicles for the struggle against Spain. Fifty-three such lodges were created between 1809 and 1828 in the Andean countries alone. In Brazil, Masons were a decisive force in the achievement of independence in 1822. Dom Pedro himself was initiated in the Comércio e Artes lodge and became grand master of the Brazilian Grand Orient. Throughout the region, the composition of the lodges reveals a membership of merchants, lawyers, army officers, some artisans, and even members of the clergy.

Independence resulted in the decline of Freemasonry, but only temporarily. The major issue that allowed Freemasonry to flourish was the increasingly acrimonious struggle between church and state. Although Freemasonry welcomed Catholics, the lodges opposed the papacy at a time when the Latin American church sought to strengthen its ties with the Vatican. The very participation of Catholics in Masonic lodges—and the participation of Freemasons in Catholic associations—became a matter of contention. In Brazil, a serious crisis developed in the early 1870s, when the government imprisoned the bishops who upheld papal bulls anathematizing Freemasonry. At issue was the authority of the government to exercise patronage over the church. Freemasonry became the focus of attention in a struggle that eventually led to the separation of church and state in 1890.

Probably under the influence of the increasingly anti-Catholic stands of Freemasons influenced by the so-called Scottish rite, Latin American Freemasonry developed into a liberal, anticlerical force that fought for modernization and secularization, and paid preferential attention to education. In Argentina, such prominent Freemasons as Domingo Faustino Sarmiento and Bartolomé Mitre worked first for the unification of the country and then concentrated on secularization of society and the advancement of lay education. In Mexico, Porfirio Díaz, himself a high-ranking Freemason, utilized the lodges as a vehicle to obtain the backing of business groups and the middle class for the advancement of his modernizing schemes. Mexican Freemasonry had been sharply divided in the 1820s, when the two main branches of Freemasonry, the Yorquinos and the Escoceses, engaged in a bitter struggle over federalism and the expulsion of the Spaniards. By the late nineteenth century, consensus over Díaz's policy of industrialization and foreign investment had muted somewhat the tensions between the rites, but they exploded again during the revolution, when Freemasons became divided over the refusal of President Woodrow Wilson of the United States to recognize Victoriano Huerta.

During the twentieth century, such prominent leaders as Arturo Alessandri Palma, Lázaro Cárdenas, and Hipólito Yrigoyen were Freemasons. The institutionalization of political parties, however, during the century overshadowed the political influence of Freemasonry. Separation of church and state in most Latin American countries deprived Freemasons of a major issue, although echoes of the struggle continued to be heard in Argentina in the 1950s. The lodges continued to serve as vehicles for the transmission of Masonic traditions, but played a diminished social and political role.

See also **Anticlericalism; Miranda, Francisco de.**

BIBLIOGRAPHY

Sister Mary Crescentia Thornton, *The Church and Freemasonry in Brazil, 1872–1875: A Study in Regalism* (1948).

Américo Carnicelli, *La masonería en la independencia de América,* 2 vols. (1970).

José Ferrer Benimeli, *Masonería e Inquisición en Latinoamérica durante el siglo XVII* (1973).

Thomas B. Davis, *Aspects of Freemasonry in Modern Mexico: An Example of Social Cleavage* (1976).

Robert Macoy, *A Dictionary of Freemasonry* (1989).

Additional Bibliography

Armas Asin, Fernando. *Liberales, protestantes y masons: Modernidad y tolerancia religiosa: Perú siglo XIX.* Lima: Fondo Editorial de la Pontificia Universidad Católica del Perú: Cusco: Centro de Estudios Regionales Andinos "Bartolomé de Las Casas," 1998.

Balam Ramos, Yuri Hulkin. *La masonería en Yucatán: El caso de la Gran Logia Unida "La Oriental Peninsular".* Mérida: Universidad Autónoma de Yucatán, 1996.

Bastian, Jean-Pierre, ed. *Protestantes, liberales, y francmasones: Sociedades de ideas y modernidad en América Latina, siglo XIX.* México: Comisión de Estudios de Historia de la Iglesia en América Latina: Fondo de Cultura Económica, 1990.

Boccia Romañach, Alfredo. *La masonería y la independencia americana: Mitos e historia de las sociedades secretas.* Asunción: Servilibro, 2003.

Callaey, Eduardo Roberto. *El otro imperio cristiano: De la Orden del Temple a la francmasonería.* Madrid: Ediciones Nowtilus, 2005.

Carvajal Muñoz, Jorge. *Masonería y temas de la sociedad actual: Intervenciones públicas del Gran Maestro de la Gran Logia de Chile.* Santiago: Ediciones Club de la República, 2002.

Corbière Emilio J. *La masonería.* Buenos Aires: Sudamericana, 1998–2001.

Gran Logia Femenina de Chile. *Mujeres con mandil: Una historia femenina de la masonería en Chile, 1959–2003.* Santiago de Chile: Gran Logia Femenina de Chile, 2003.

González Navarro, Moisés. *Masones y cristeros en Jalisco.* México, D.F.: El Colegio de México, Centro de Estudios Históricos, 2000.

Torres-Cuevas, Eduardo. *Historia de la masonería cubana: Seis ensayos.* La Habana: Imágen Contemporánea, 2004.

IVÁN JAKSÍ

MASSERA, EMILIO EDUARDO

MASSERA, EMILIO EDUARDO (1925–). Emilio Eduardo Massera was a member of the Argentine military. As commander in chief of the navy, he was part of the military junta of 1976 to 1978 and directed the Naval School of Mechanics, the dictatorship's main center for kidnapping, torturing, and "disappearing" people (1976–1983).

Massera entered Argentina's Naval Military School at age seventeen. After graduating in 1946 he continued his studies in the School of the Americas (now called the Western Hemisphere Institute for Security Cooperation), a training facility in Panama created by the U.S. Army to train members of the Latin American military in counterinsurgency methods. On returning to Argentina, President Juan Domingo Perón (1973–1974) promoted him to commander-in-chief of the navy. After Perón's death in July 1974, Perón's wife, María Estela Martínez, assumed the presidency and granted broad repressive powers to the armed forces to eliminate the active guerrilla groups. With violence escalating between armed groups of the Left and the Right (the latter financed by the government), the government under powerful pressure from the unions, and the nation in economic crisis, the armed forces intervened. On March 24, 1976, the military junta composed of General Jorge Rafael Videla, Brigadier Orlando Ramón Agosti, and Admiral Massera took control of the government and formulated long-term plans to ensure its survival.

During its time in power, the military government consolidated its plan of systematic repression as state terrorism. With presidential ambitions, Massera soon opposed the economic policy of de facto president Videla. Between 1976 and 1978 Argentina's largest secret detention center, under Massera's authority, was responsible for the disappearance of thousands of people. In September 1978 Massera retired from the military. He was among the members of the military most inclined to war with Chile over the Beagle Channel conflict at the end of 1978.

In 1985 Massera was sentenced to life in prison for the human-rights crimes he committed during "the Process." He was pardoned by President Carlos Menem (1989–1999) in 1990, but was returned to prison in 1998 for kidnapping children and ordering tortures, executions, and illegal confinements during the military dictatorship.

See also **Argentina: The Twentieth Century; Beagle Channel Dispute; Dirty War; Menem, Carlos Saúl; Perón, Juan Domingo; Perón, María Estela Martínez de; Videla, Jorge Rafael.**

BIBLIOGRAPHY

Munck, Gerardo. *Authoritarianism and Democratization: Soldiers and Workers in Argentina, 1976–1983.* University Park: Pennsylvania State University Press, 1998.

National Commission on the Disappearance of Persons (CONADEP). *Nunca más.* Buenos Aires: Eudeba, 1984.

Novaro, Marcos, and Vicente Palermo. *La dictadura militar.* Buenos Aires: Paidós, 2003.

VICENTE PALERMO

MASSERA, JOSÉ PEDRO (1866–1942).

José Pedro Massera (*b.* 1866; *d.* 1942), Uruguayan philosopher, professor, and politician. From 1887 to 1927 Massera taught philosophy at the University of the Republic in Montevideo. His only published work during his lifetime was *Reflexiones sobre Rodó* (1920), but various of his essays were published posthumously, on subjects such as the works of Carlos Vaz Ferreira and Ribot, moral values, and moral philosophy. In 1937 he gave up teaching to pursue a political career in the national Senate.

See also **Uruguay: The Twentieth Century.**

BIBLIOGRAPHY

Additional Bibliography

Real de Azúa, Carlos. *Historia y política en el Uruguay.* Montevideo: Cal y Canto, 1997.

Terán, Oscar, and Gerardo Caetano. *Ideas en el siglo: Intelectuales y cultura en el siglo XX latinoamericano.* Argentina: Fundación OSDE; Buenos Aires: Siglo Veintiuno Editores Argentina, 2004.

WILLIAM H. KATRA

MASTRETTA, ÁNGELES (1949–).

The Mexican writer and journalist Ángeles Mastretta is well known for creating evocative female characters and literary works that reflect the social and political realities of Mexico. Born in Puebla on October 9, 1949, Mastretta studied journalism and communication at the Universidad Nacional in Mexico City. She began her writing career working as a journalist for the magazine *Siete* and later did some television interviewing. In 1974 she won a scholarship to the Centro Mexicano de Escritores (Mexican Writers' Center), where she came into contact with such writers as Juan Rulfo and Salvador Elizondo. This decisive life experience gave her the discipline and commitment to become a professional writer. Her first novel, *Arráncame la vida* (1985; translated into English as *Mexican Bolero* [1989] and *Tear This Heart Out* [1997]), was an immediate literary success and earned her the Mazatlán Prize for Literature for Best Book of the Year. In 1996 Mastretta won the Rómulo Gallegos Prize for her novel *Mal de amores* (1996; *Lovesick*, 1997). She has also written *La pájara pinta* (1975), *Mujeres de ojos grandes* (1990; *Women with Big Eyes*, 2003), *Puerto libre* (1993), *El mundo iluminado* (1998), and *Ninguna eternidad como la mía* (1999).

BIBLIOGRAPHY

De Beer, Gabriela. "Angeles Mastretta." In her *Contemporary Mexican Women Writers: Five Voices.* Austin: University of Texas Press, 1996.

Foster, David William. *Handbook of Latin American Literature.* 2nd ed. New York and London: Garland, 1992.

JUAN CARLOS GRIJALVA

MASTROGIOVANNI, ANTONIO (1936–).

Antonio Mastrogiovanni (*b.* 26 July 1936), Uruguayan composer. Born in Montevideo, Mastrogiovanni began musical studies with Nieves Varacchi and

Héctor Tosar. He studied composition under Carlos Estrada at the National Conservatory of Music (1963–1968), and was technical director of the music-publishing project at the conservatory. His *Monotemáticas* for violin and piano was well received at its premiere during the Second Latin American Festival of Montevideo (1966). He was awarded several prizes by the SODRE, the Association of Music Students, and the National Conservatory, and was honored by the Uruguayan Ministry of Culture (1960, 1961, 1963). *Sinfonía de Cámara* for orchestra (1965) and the piano concerto (1967) belong to that period. With *Contrarritmos* (1967), for two string orchestras and percussion, Mastrogiovanni shifted toward new composition techniques, in recognition of which he received a scholarship at the Latin American Center of Advanced Music Studies of the Di Tella Institute in Buenos Aires, where from 1969 to 1970 he studied under Gerardo Gandini (analysis), Francisco Kröpfl (composition), and von Reichenbach (electronic music). He received grants from the Organization of American States that enabled him to travel to Rome and Mexico to explore new composition techniques. His *Reflejos* and *Secuencial I* both won the Dutch Gaudeamus Foundation Prize (1970; 1971) and were premiered by the Utrech Symphony Orchestra. Other works of his include *Secuencial II* for tape (1970) and *Maderas* for ensemble (1974).

Since 1971, Mastrogiovanni's works have premiered throughout South America and Europe and have earned the composer awards both at home and abroad. He has taught at several prestigious institutions, including the Conservatorio Nacional de Música in Montevideo (1972–1973), the Conservatorio Nacional Juan José Landaeta in Caracas (1979–1988), and Montevideo's Escuela Universitaria de Música (1986–1993), where he also has served as director since 1988. In addition to composing commissioned works and conducting vocal and instrumental ensembles in Venezuela and Uruguay, he founded and organized an annual competition for advanced music students in Montevideo.

See also **Music: Art Music; Musical Instruments.**

BIBLIOGRAPHY

John Vinton, ed., *Dictionary of Contemporary Music* (1974); *New Grove Dictionary of Music and Musicians* (1980).

Susana Salgado, *Breve historia de la música culta en el Uruguay,* 2d ed. (1980).

Additional Bibliography

Amarilla Capi, Mirta. *La música en el Uruguay.* Montevideo: M. Amarilla Capi, 1983–2000.

Salgado, Susana. *The Teatro Solís: 150 Years of Opera, Concert and Ballet in Montevideo.* Middletown, CT: Wesleyan University Press, 2003.

SUSANA SALGADO

MATA, EDUARDO (1942–1995). Eduardo Mata (*b.* 5 September 1942; *d.* 4 January 1995), Mexican-born composer and conductor. His studies at the National Conservatory of Mexico focused on percussion and composition (with Carlos Chávez and Julian Orbón). He studied conducting with Max Rudolf and Eric Leinsdorf at the Berkshire Music Center in 1964. Mata has concentrated less on composition since his meteoric rise as a conductor, beginning in 1965 with orchestras at Guadalajara and the Free University of Mexico, and followed with Phoenix (1971–1977) and Dallas (1977–1991). He was appointed Fine Arts Opera director in Mexico City (1983) and was a guest conductor of the London Symphony Orchestra.

See also **Music: Art Music.**

BIBLIOGRAPHY

José Antonio Alcaraz et al., *Período contemporáneo,* in *La música de México,* edited by Julio Estrada, vol. 1, pt. 5 (1984).

Additional Bibliography

Flores Aguilar, Verónica. *Eduardo Mata: A varias voces.* México: Conaculta, 2005.

Wagar, Jeannine. *Conductors in Conversation: Fifteen Contemporary Conductors Discuss their Lives and Profession.* Boston: G.K. Hall, 1991.

ROBERT L. PARKER

MATACAPÁN. Matacapán, Middle Classic period (A.D. 400–700) urban center on Mexico's Gulf Coast in the Tuxtlas Mountains of southern Veracruz. The Tuxtlas lay within a region of remnant rain forests, numerous volcanoes, and a long rainy season that today supplies water to extensive areas cleared for agriculture and cattle production. Recent research at the site has uncovered the Formative and Olmec origins of settlement in the region, which now appear to stretch back into the second millennium B.C. Throughout the succeeding millennia the area was periodically devastated by volcanic eruptions that blasted nearby hillsides with enormous basaltic "bombs" and covered the surrounding countryside with a thick mantle of rich ash. Human occupation and population growth in the area, fueled by its agricultural potential, comprised a set of episodes punctuated by volcanic disasters. The longest period of growth culminated in the relatively dispersed urban sprawl at Matacapán with a resident population of perhaps 20,000 people distributed across an area perhaps as large as 5 square miles.

At its height Matacapán was the center of a diversified regional economy that specialized in industrial-level ceramic production, as evidenced by innumerable and well-preserved pottery kilns that have been uncovered throughout the ancient city. Matacapán also maintained far-flung economic and political links to the giant urban metropolis of Teotihuacán in the central Mexican highlands as well as to the more numerous Maya population centers of the eastern lowlands. More than one hundred enormous earthen mounds comprising the monumental core of the Middle Classic city were mapped by archaeologists during the 1980s. Most of these monuments, however, have been leveled and destroyed by wealthy export tobacco farmers who control the region.

See also **Archaeology; Mesoamerica.**

BIBLIOGRAPHY

Robert S. Santley, Ponciano Ortíz Ceballos, and Christopher A. Pool, "Recent Archaeological Research at Matacapán, Veracruz: A Summary of the 1982 to 1986 Field Seasons," in *Mexicon* 9 (1987): 41–48.

Thomas W. Killion, "Residential Ethnoarchaeology and Ancient Site Structure: Contemporary Farming and Prehistoric Settlement Agriculture at Matacapán, Veracruz, Mexico," and Robert S. Santley, "A Consideration of the Olmec Phenomenon in the Tuxtlas: Early Formative Settlement Pattern, Land Use, and Refuse Disposal at Matacapán, Veracruz, Mexico," in *Gardens of Prehistory: The Archaeology of Settlement Agriculture in Greater Mesoamerica,* edited by Thomas W. Killion (1992), pp. 119–149, 150–183.

Additional Bibliography

Santley, Robert S. *The Prehistory of the Tuxtlas.* Albuquerque: University of New Mexico Press, 2007.

Schwartz, Glenn M. and Steven E Falconer. *Archaeological Views from the Countryside: Village Communities in Early Complex Societies.* Washington, DC: Smithsonian Institution Press, 1994.

Stark, Barbara L. and Philip J. Arnold. *Olmec to Aztec: Settlement Patterns in the Ancient Gulf Lowlands.* Tucson: University of Arizona Press, 1997.

THOMAS W. KILLION

MATAMOROS Y GURIDI, MARIANO

(1770–1814). Mariano Matamoros y Guridi (*b.* 14 August 1770; *d.* 3 February 1814), Mexican Independence leader and corevolutionary of Father Miguel Hidalgo. Born in Mexico City, Matamoros studied theology at the Colegio de Santa Cruz de Tlateloco. In 1811, he was interim curate of Jantetelco. He offered his services to the insurgent chief José María Morelos, who named him a colonel and commissioned him to raise military forces. Matamoros accompanied Morelos to Taxco and was at Cuautla during the siege by the royalist army of Félix Calleja. Ordered to obtain provisions, on 21 April 1812, Matamoros and 100 dragoons broke through the royalist lines. When Morelos fled Cuautla, he dispatched Matamoros to reorganize the insurgent forces at Izúcar. A gifted military commander, Matamoros was a close adviser of Morelos during the Oaxaca campaign and was promoted to field marshal and later to lieutenant general. He was with Morelos at the abortive attack on Valladolid, Morelia, in 1814. Later, at Puruarán, Matamoros was captured by the royalists and executed.

See also **Cuautla, Siege of.**

BIBLIOGRAPHY

Lucas Alamán, *Historia de México desde los primeros movimientos que prepararon su independencia en el año de 1808 hasta la época presente,* 5 vols. (1849–1852; repr. 1942).

José María Luis Mora, *México y sus revoluciones,* 3 vols. (1961).

Wilbert H. Timmons, *Morelos: Priest Soldier Statesman of Mexico* (1963).

Additional Bibliography

Agraz García de Alba, Gabriel. *Mariano Matamoros Guridi héroe nacional.* México: Edición del Autor, 2002.

Archer, Christon. *The Birth of Modern Mexico, 1780–1824.* Wilmington, DE: Scholarly Resources, 2003.

CHRISTON ARCHER

MATANZA. Matanza, the name given in El Salvador to the massacre perpetrated by the government after the abortive Communist-led revolt of January 1932. the revolt grew out of the anger of coffee workers and peasants over depressed living conditions and the agitation of Communist Party leaders, especially Secretary-General Augustín Farabundo Martí. The revolt followed a coup d'état on 2 December 1931 that had overthrown the elected government of President Arturo Araújo and replaced it with a military dictatorship headed by General Maximiliano Hernández Martínez.

The Communists' revolt began in a confused manner on the night of 22 January, after Martí and other key leaders had been arrested four days earlier. It took place largely to the west of the capital in the departments of Ahuachapán, Santa Anna, and Sonsonate and just east of San Salvador, around Lake Ilopango. The rebels, armed mostly with machetes, failed to take any major garrisons and killed only a small number of civilians, along with some soldiers and police. By 25 January, military forces had largely regained control of the areas in revolt.

Although unsuccessful in seizing power, the rebellion created a great fear among the upper classes, and General Hernández Martínez decided on a policy of frightful repression in the department where the revolt took place. He instituted the Matanza (slaughter or massacre). Utilizing the regular army, police units such as the Policía Nacional and the Guardia Nacional, and the volunteer Guardia Cívica, drawn from among the upper classes, the government rounded up not only those known as Communists or as rebels, but also large numbers of peasants, often of Pipil Indian origin, and proceeded to execute them by firing squad. The bodies were then buried in mass graves.

Estimates of the number of persons killed in the Matanza vary widely, running from 3,000 to 30,000. A reasonable guess is about 10,000 killed. Since Indians were especially targeted, the Pipil culture of western El Salvador was largely destroyed. Martí and his lieutenants, Alfonso Luna and Mario Zapata, were given the formality of a trial before being executed in the capital. One leader, Miguel Mármol, survived his firing squad and fled into exile. The effect of the massacre was to create a climate of fear among the masses that inhibited agitation for social change for some forty years.

See also **Coffee Industry; El Salvador.**

BIBLIOGRAPHY

Joaquín Méndez H., *Los sucesos comunistas en El Salvador* (1932).

Jorge Schlesinger, *Revolución comunista* (1946).

Thomas P. Anderson, *Matanza: El Salvador's Communist Revolt of 1932* (1971).

Roque Dalton, *Miguel Mármol,* English ed. (1987).

Additional Bibliography

Anderson, Thomas P. *Matanza: The 1932 "Slaughter" that Traumatized a Nation, Shaping US-Salvadoran Policy to This Day.* Willimantic, CT: Curbstone Press, 1992.

Tilley, Virginia. *Seeing Indians: A Study of Race, Nation, and Power in El Salvador.* Albuquerque: University of New Mexico Press, 2005.

THOMAS P. ANDERSON

MATÉ. *See* **Yerba Maté.**

MATIENZO, BENJAMÍN (1891–1919). Benjamín Matienzo (*b.* 9 April 1891; *d.* May 1919), pioneer Argentine aviator. Born in San Miguel de Tucumán, son of a Bolivian-born jurist of the same name, Matienzo followed a military career. He became an aviation enthusiast at an early age and attended the Escuela de Aviación Militar in Palomar. In May 1919 he and two companions set out to fly over the Andes to Chile. Bad weather caused his companions to return to Mendoza; Matienzo, however, pushed ahead. His plane was forced down near Las Cuevas. While attempting to walk into the town, he froze to death. A monument commemorates his determination and sacrifice.

See also **Aviation.**

RONALD C. NEWTON

MATIENZO, JOSÉ NICOLÁS (1860–1936).

José Nicolás Matienzo (*b.* 4 October 1860; *d.* 3 January 1936), Argentine jurist and statesman. Matienzo, a native of San Miguel de Tucumán, specialized in constitutional law. He was a professor at the universities of Buenos Aires and La Plata, wrote extensively on constitutional matters (see his *Cuestiones de derecho público argentino,* 1924, and *Lecciones de derecho constitucional,* 1926), and served as a member of the Supreme Court of the province of Buenos Aires (1910–1913) and as attorney general (*procurador general*) (1917–1922). He also drafted a project for a criminal code, in collaboration with Norberto Piñero and Rodolfo Rivarola. A liberal of reformist inclinations, he was the first president of the National Department of Labor (1907–1909). In 1910 Matienzo published *El gobierno representativo federal en la República Argentina,* a detailed study of the workings of the country's political system, which he described as oligarchical. He shared with other members of his generation, particularly his friend Rivarola, editor of the *Revista Argentina de Ciencias Políticas,* a passionate interest in the reform of the country's political system. In 1922 he was appointed minister of the interior by President Marcelo Alvear, and in 1931 he was a candidate for the vice presidency on the ticket headed by Augustín Pedro Justo. He was elected to the National Senate in 1932, where he remained until his death in 1936.

See also **Argentina, The Twentieth Century.**

BIBLIOGRAPHY

Natalio Botana, *El orden conservador: La política argentina entre 1880 y 1916* (1979).

Ezequiel Gallo, "Argentina: Society and Politics, 1880–1916," in *The Cambridge History of Latin America,* edited by Leslie Bethell, vol. 5 (1986).

Francisco Luis Menegazzi, *Biobibliografía de José Nicolás Matienzo* (1940).

Additional Bibliography

Rock, David. *State Building and Political Movements in Argentina, 1860–1916.* Stanford, CA: Stanford University Press, 2002.

EDUARDO A. ZIMMERMANN

MATO GROSSO.

Mato Grosso is a state in central-west Brazil, bordered on the southwest by Bolivia, on the south by the Paraguay River, on the east by the Araguaia River, and on the north by various Amazon tributaries. The Chapada dos Parecis mountain range lies on the western border of the state. Mato Grosso also contains the Pantanal National Park in the southwest, and Xingu National Park in the Northeast.

The first Europeans to establish permanent settlements within Mato Grosso's interior were missionaries during the early seventeenth century, but until mid-century such settlements were frequently decimated by Bandeirantes, the frontiersmen and entrepreneurs of São Paulo in search of indigenous slaves. In the first quarter of the eighteenth century the discovery of gold in Mato Grosso launched the first significant ranching settlements, and established the boom town of Cuiabá.

Transportation and distance have historically impeded the economic development of Mato Grosso. In 1914 the railroad reached southern Mato Grosso, making Campo Grande the economic hub of the region; prior to this time most transportation depended upon Mato Grosso's waterways. Partially to protect the water route from Rio de Janeiro to this western frontier, by way of Asunción and Buenos Aires, Brazil entered the War of the Triple Alliance in 1864. After World War II railroads were also instrumental in bringing coffee production to Mato Grosso.

In 1977 Mato Grosso was divided into two states, Mato Grosso and Mato Grosso do Sul. As of 2000, the population of Mato Grosso was about 2.5 million, and the total area was 352,400 square miles. The capital of Mato Grosso is Cuiabá (population 500,000). Roughly half of the state remains forested, rural, agriculture-based and dependent upon coffee, cotton, timber, and rubber harvesting.

See also **Brazil, Geography; Rio de Janeiro (City).**

BIBLIOGRAPHY

D. G. Fabre, *Beyond the River of the Dead,* translated by Eric L. Randall (1963).

Rollie E. Poppino, *Brazil: The Land and People* (1968).

Additional Bibliography

Diacon, Todd A. *Stringing Together a Nation: Candido Mariano da Silva Rondon and the Construction of a Modern Brazil, 1906–1930.* Durham, NC: Duke University Press, 2004.

Meade, Theresa A. *A Brief History of Brazil.* New York: Facts on File, 2003.

Vincent, Jon S. *Culture and Customs of Brazil.* Westport, CT: Greenwood Press, 2003.

CAROLYN E. VIEIRA

MATO GROSSO DO SUL. Mato Grosso do Sul is a state created from the southern portion of Mato Grosso State in 1977. It lies in central-west Brazil and is bounded by Bolivia and Paraguay on the west, Paraguay on the south, and the Paraná River on the east. In 2000 the population of Mato Grosso do Sul was 2,074,877; its area was 140,219 square miles. The capital is Campo Grande. The economy is dependent upon agriculture, cattle raising, and mineral exploration.

See also **Brazil, Geography; Mato Grosso.**

BIBLIOGRAPHY

Meade, Theresa A. *A Brief History of Brazil.* New York: Facts on File, 2003.

Swarts, Frederick A., ed. *The Pantanal: Understanding and Preserving the World's Largest Wetland.* 2nd ed. St. Paul, MN: Paragon House, 2000.

Vincent, John S. *Culture and Customs of Brazil.* Westport, CT: Greenwood Press, 2003.

CAROLYN E. VIEIRA

MATOS, GREGÓRIO DE (1636–1696). Gregório de Matos (*b.* 20 December 1636; *d.* 1696), Brazilian poet and satirist. Born in Salvador, Bahia, the son of a rich Portuguese immigrant and a lady of the local aristocracy, Matos was educated in Jesuit schools and then sent to law school in Coimbra, Portugal, in 1652. He graduated in 1661 and, after a period in Brazil, took up practice in Portugal as a guardian of orphans and as a criminal judge. He remained in the metropolis until his return to his native city in 1681. After taking minor religious orders, he was appointed by the archbishop to positions in the bishop's office and the treasury department.

His calling notwithstanding, Matos led a notorious bohemian life and earned a reputation locally as a poet and social observer. His verse was of three fundamental types: devotional, amorous, and satirical. He was especially sensitive to moral decay, corruption, exploitation, and injustice. Many of his poems are quasijournalistic in nature, commenting on local events and personages. His biting verse earned him the nickname "Boca do Inferno" (Mouth of Hell) and the disfavor of powerful citizens. His unrelenting critical writing led to his exile in Angola (1686–1695). He died in Recife, Brazil, one year after his return from banishment.

Matos is generally considered the most important poet of the baroque period in Brazil. His work is an excellent example of the literary practice of his time, a style of conceit and formal play involving liberal borrowing and imitation. He did not publish a book in his lifetime; his poems circulated in manuscript form or were recited. It was not until the late nineteenth century that his work became widely known. The Brazilian Academy of Letters published his works in six volumes (1923–1933); a later commercial edition (1969) has seven volumes. The attribution of many texts, however, remains in dispute.

See also **Literature: Brazil.**

BIBLIOGRAPHY

Nora K. Aiex, "Racial Attitudes in the Satire of Gregório de Matos," in *Studies in Afro-Hispanic Literature,* vol. 1 (1977), pp. 89–97.

Earl E. Fitz, "Gregório de Matos and Juan del Valle y Caviedes: Two Baroque Poets in Colonial Portuguese and Spanish America," in *Inti* 5–6 (1977): 134–150.

Additional Bibliography

Hansen, João Adolfo. *A sátira e o engenho: Gregório de Matos e a Bahia do século XVII.* Cotia: Ateliê Editorial; Campinas: Unicamp, 2004.

Peres, Fernando da Rocha, Waly Salomão, and Maria Vitória de Seixas Caldas. *Gregório de Mattos: O poeta devorador.* Rio de Janeiro: Manati Produções Editoriais, 2004.

CHARLES A. PERRONE

MATTA ECHAURREN, ROBERTO SEBASTIÁN ANTONIO (1912–2002).

Roberto Sebastián Antonio Matta Echaurren was a Chilean painter and printmaker. Known simply as "Matta," he was born in Santiago, Chile, and received his early education from French Jesuits. He went on to earn an architectural degree in 1933 from the Catholic University in Santiago, Chile. He took drawing classes in Santiago at the Academia de Bellas Artes. Matta left Chile in 1935 for Paris, where he worked for the architect Le Corbusier until 1937, by which time he had become a member of the surrealist group. He lived and worked in New York from 1939 to 1948. Shunned by the artistic community upon his return to Paris, he went to Rome. In the late 1950s he slowly regained acceptance in Paris, where, having become a French citizen, he spent part of each year. Matta resisted being labeled a Latin American artist; rather, he saw himself in a universal context, as one who integrated into his art elements of the many cultures with which he came into contact. Throughout the 1960s his work had mainly political and spiritual themes and involved such subjects as the Vietnam War and the civil rights struggle in the United States. In 1968 he was a keynote speaker at the Havana Cultural Congress in Cuba, where he discussed the relationship between art and revolution. He had a retrospective at London's Hayward Gallery in 1977. Eight years later the Pompidou Center in Paris launched another exhibition based on his life's work. In his old age, he maintained residences in Paris, London, Milan, and Tarquinia, Italy. He died there on 23 November 2002.

See also **Art: The Twentieth Century; Santiago, Chile.**

BIBLIOGRAPHY

Valerie Fletcher, *Crosscurrents of Modernism: Four Latin American Pioneers* (1992), pp. 228–287.

Additional Bibliography

Escallón, Ana María, and Patricia Cepeda. *Roberto Matta: El arquitecto del Surrealismo.* Washington, DC: Art Museum of the Americas, 2003.

Fer, Briony; Betti-Sue Hertz; Justo Pastor Mellado; and Anthony Vidler. *Transmission: The Art of Matta and Gordon Matta-Clark.* San Diego, CA: San Diego Museum of Art, 2006.

Garcia Yello, Maria. *Matta.* Córdoba, Spain: Fundación Provincial de Artes Plásticas "Rafael Botí," 2004.

Oyarzún R., Pablo. *Tentativas sobre Matta.* Santiago, Chile: Delirio Poético Ediciones, 2002.

KATHERINE CLARK HUDGENS

MATTO DE TURNER, CLORINDA

(1852–1909). Clorinda Matto de Turner (Grimanesa Martina Matto Usandivaras; *b.* 11 November 1852; *d.* 25 October 1909), Peruvian novelist and journalist. She was born and raised in the ancient city of Cuzco. The family lived in the city as well as in the Hacienda Paullu Chico. Her mother died when she was ten years old, and she was sent to a Catholic school to be educated. At age eighteen she left school to look after her younger brothers. She learned English to prepare herself for study in the United States, but failed to travel to that country. She married Joseph Turner, an Englishman, in 1871. The couple first settled in the small town of Tinta, in the province of Canchis, which later served as the model for the imaginary Killac, the city of her most widely read work, *Aves sin nido* (Birds without Nest). While living in Tinta she developed two of her major intellectual preoccupations: defending the rights of women and protesting the cruel exploitation of the Indians.

In 1876 Matto returned to Cuzco, where she directed the literary magazine *El Recreo del Cuzco* (Cuzco's Entertainment). As an active journalist during these years, she became a well-known celebrity in Peru. She traveled to Lima in 1877 and was warmly received by the intellectual elite. She attended the *salón literario* organized by Juana Manuela Gorriti and was hailed as an important literary voice of Peruvian letters.

When Matto's husband died in 1881, leaving her in dire economic straits, she returned to Tinta to manage her hacienda personally. During this time Chile and Peru were engaged in the War of the Pacific, which left the defeated Peru devastated. Matto aided her compatriots by raising funds for military equipment and donating her farmhouse for medical assistance to the troops. In 1883 she lost her hacienda and she went to Arequipa, where she again worked as a journalist. In 1884 she published *Tradiciones cusqueñas: leyendas, biografías y hojas sueltas* (Cuzco's Traditions: Legends, Biographies, and Other Writings), a volume of articles published in newspapers and literary magazines between 1870 and 1882, with a preface by Peruvian writer Ricardo Palma. In 1886 she published a second volume, *Tradiciones cusqueñas: crónicas, hojas sueltas,* with a preface by José Antonio Laval. These short stories (*tradiciones*) follow the model of the genre created by Palma.

In 1887, Matto returned to Lima and organized a *salón literario* that became an important meeting place for Peruvian intellectuals. She joined the Ateneo de Lima and Círculo Literario literary groups. Connected to these groups was the literary publication *El Peru Ilustrado,* of which Matto was appointed director in 1889. She insisted that the magazine reflect Peruvian concerns above all others. Together with writer Manuel González Prada, she became known as a defender of the Indians. In 1889 she also published her best-known novel, *Aves sin nido.* It was the first indigenous novel that portrayed the life and social condition of the Indian population of Peru and the first favorable literary representation of the Indian cause, including a partial history of the abuse of the Indian by whites, mestizos, and the clergy in Spanish America. In 1892, Matto published her only play, *Hima sumac.* In 1893 she published *Leyendas y recortes.* Her other novels, *Indole* (1891) and *Herencia* (Inheritance, 1895), continue the Indian theme. *Boreales, miniaturas y porcelanas,* published in Buenos Aires in 1902, documents the difficult years of political turmoil in Peru and how they affected Matto. In 1895 she left Lima for Buenos Aires, where she wrote for *La Nación* and *La Prensa.* She founded the magazine *El Búcaro Americano* in 1897 and traveled to Europe in 1908. Her memoirs are collected in *Viaje de recreo* (Vacation Trips, 1910). She died in Buenos Aires of pneumonia, and her remains were returned to Peru in 1924.

BIBLIOGRAPHY

Antonio Cornejo-Polar, *La novela peruana* (1980; 2d ed. 1989).

Efraín Kristal, "Clorinda Matto de Turner" in *Latin American Writers,* edited by Carlos A. Solé and Maria Isabel Abreu, vol. 1 (1989).

Alberto Tauro, *Clorinda Matto de Turner y la novela indigenista* (1976).

Additional Bibliography

Meyer, Doris. *Reinterpreting the Spanish American Essay: Women Writers of the 19th and 20th Centuries.* Austin: University of Texas Press, 1995.

Peluffo, Ana. *Lágrimas andinas: Sentimentalismo, género y virtud republicana en Clorinda Matto de Turner.* Pittsburgh, PA: Instituto Internacional de Literatura Iberoamericana, Universidad de Pittsburgh, 2005.

MAGDALENA GARCÍA PINTO

MAUÁ, VISCONDE DE (1813–1889). Visconde de Mauá (Irineu Evangelista de Souza; *b.* 28 December 1813; *d.* 21 October 1889), Brazilian merchant, banker, industrialist, railroad magnate, rancher, and national politician who rose from obscure beginnings to become a major protagonist in imperial Brazil's banking, transportation, and industrial infrastructure. Born in Rio Grande do Sul, Mauá initiated his business-entrepreneurial career in Rio de Janeiro at age eleven as a cashier in a cloth store and was later employed in a British firm, where he learned British business methods and successively held the positions of partner and sole manager by the 1830s, when the firm's founder returned to England.

Mauá invested in a variety of modernizing endeavors, most of which initially were aimed at improving Brazil's transportation and industrial infrastructure. From the establishment of an iron foundry that supplied pipes for a new water system in Rio de Janeiro, Mauá acquired concessions for a tramway line, the first gas-lamp system built in the country, and the first steamship company to operate on the Amazon River. An investor in the Second Bank of Brazil, he founded the Bank of Mauá in 1854, the same year he constructed Brazil's first railroad line from the port of Mauá on Guanabara Bay in Rio de Janeiro to the interior highlands, where coffee production for the foreign market was the mainstay of the Brazilian economy. That year he also received the title of baron.

Mauá represented his native province of Rio Grande do Sul in the Chamber of Deputies from 1856 to 1873, and he received the title of viscount in 1874 after laying the first submarine cable between Brazil and Europe.

Mauá's widespread banking network extended to London, and his business ventures expanded to Argentina and Uruguay, where he held control over Uruguayan railroads, shipyards, gasworks, livestock farms, and meat-processing plants. His economic liberalism was not popular among conservative economic sectors in Brazil and Uruguay, and his creditors were not sympathetic to the losses he suffered in the Río de la Plata region during the War of the Triple Alliance (1864–1870). His finances declined in the 1870s, and in 1878 he was forced into bankruptcy. His "Exposition to the Creditors of Mauá and Company and to the Public," written in that year, attributed the reversal of his fortunes to his placing the well-being of the country before personal concerns, rather than to mismanagement or misdeeds. Mauá spent the remainder of his life managing a modest investment business.

See also **Brazil: 1808–1889.**

BIBLIOGRAPHY

Roderick J. Barman, "Business and Government in Imperial Brazil: The Experience of Viscount Mauá," *Journal of Latin American Studies* 13, no. 2 (1981): 239–264.

Lidia Besouchet, *Mauá e seu tempo* (1978).

Anyda Marchant, *Viscount Mauá and the Empire of Brazil: A Biography of Irineu Evangelista de Sousa, 1813–1889* (1965).

Additional Bibliography

Caldeira, Jorge. *Mauá: Empresário do Império.* São Paulo, Brazil: Companhia das Letras, 1995.

Rato de Sambuccetti, Susana. *Urquiza y Mauá: El MERCOSUR del siglo XIX.* Buenos Aires: Ediciones Macchi, 1999.

NANCY PRISCILLA SMITH NARO

MAULE. The Maule region, with approximately 900,000 inhabitants (National Census, 2002), is the seventh of Chile's thirteen administrative divisions. It borders the Libertador General Bernardo O'Higgins region to the north and the Bío-Bío region to the south. The region is divided into four provinces: Curicó, Cauquenes, Talca, and Linares. Its capital city is Talca and it has a temperate Mediterranean climate. Agricultural production and forestry are its main economic activities. The region is rich in traditions. Its leading tourist attractions are the traditional area of Vichuquén, the church of San Francisco de Curicó, the Constitución resort area, many national reserves, and the hot springs complex of Quinamávida. It was in the city of Talca that Bernardo O'Higgins signed Chile's declaration of independence in 1818, after battling the Spanish army.

The Spaniards settled in the area in the midst of the seventeenth century. Its capital, Talca, was founded in 1692 by Tomás Marín de Poveda.

See also **Chile: The Nineteenth Century; Chile: The Twentieth Century; O'Higgins, Bernardo.**

BIBLIOGRAPHY

Bethell, Leslie, ed: *Historia de América Latina*, Barcelona, Crítica, 1992–1998. Available in English as *The Cambridge History of Latin America*, 11 vols. New York: Cambridge University Press, 1984–2002.

VICENTE PALERMO

MAURITS, JOHAN (1604–1679). Johan Maurits (John Maurice, Count of Nassau-Siegen; *b.* 17 June 1604; *d.* 20 December 1679), governor-general of Dutch Brazil (1637–1644). Born in Dillenburg in what is now Germany, Maurits was the eldest son of Johann VII, count of Nassau-Siegen (1561–1623), and his second wife, Margaretha, princess of Holstein-Sonderburg. Johan's paternal grandfather was Johann VI (1536–1606), younger brother of William the Silent of Orange. Maurits served with distinction in a number of campaigns in the Thirty Years' War with the army of the Dutch States-General. In August 1636, Maurits formally accepted an offer from the Dutch West India Company to be governor-general of Netherlands Brazil. Soon after his arrival in Recife on 23 January 1637, he successfully ousted the Portuguese military forces from the region north of the Rio São Francisco and forced them to retreat across the river to the captaincy of Sergipe del Rey. The entire captaincy of Pernambuco fell into Dutch hands.

Maurits then returned to Recife to restore order and encourage the Portuguese inhabitants to settle down and continue sugar production. As incentive, he allowed both Catholics and Jews to worship publicly and promised them good treatment. At the same time, he improved fortifications, formed alliances with the neighboring Indians, and tried to encourage more northern European immigration. Later that year, he sent an expedition under Colonel Hans Coen to capture São Jorge da Mina (Elmina) on Africa's Gold Coast. Another expedition, under Admiral Jan Corneliszoon Lichthart, sailed along the coast of Brazil to intercept Portuguese shipping and raided the captaincy of Ilheus, south of Bahia. In November 1637, Colonel Sigismund von Schoppe attacked the captaincy of Sergipe del Rey. By the end of Maurits's first year in Brazil, the northern captaincy of Ceará was also in Dutch hands.

On 17–18 May 1638, Maurits attempted to capture the Brazilian capital of Bahia, but failed even though he had a force of 3,600 Europeans and 1,000 Indians. In 1640, he successfully defended Dutch Brazil from the count of Torre's large Spanish-Portuguese armada. In reprisal for the damage done by Portuguese troops to plantations in Dutch Brazil, Maurits sent another expedition under Lichthart to attack Portuguese sugar mills in the region around Bahia, and twenty-seven of them were destroyed. Other raids were made along the Brazilian coast, but not all were successful. After the Portuguese overthrow of Spanish rule (December 1640) and while a treaty between Portugal and the Netherlands was being negotiated, Maurits sent 3,000 men, including 240 Indians, to capture Luanda and Benguela in Angola, the islands of São Tomé and Ano Bom, and the fortress of Axim on the coast of Guinea, a task successfully completed during the second half of 1641 and early 1642. In November 1641, São Luis do Maranhão was captured, giving the Dutch control over more than a thousand miles of Brazilian coastline. At this point, the Dutch West India Company reached its greatest territorial extension in the Atlantic world.

During his seven-year stay in Brazil, Maurits rebuilt Recife and founded a new town (Mauritsstad) on the neighboring island of Antônio Vaz. He also built two country houses (Vrijburg and Boa Vista) on the island. On his properties he collected a wide variety of Brazilian flora and fauna. Maurits brought with him to America a large entourage of scholars, artists, and craftsmen. The most important were Georg Marcgraf (1610–1644), the German naturalist and astronomer; Willem Piso (1611–1678), the governor-general's personal physician, who published on tropical medicine and diseases; the landscape painter Frans Post (1612–1680); and Albert Eckhout (ca. 1610–1665), whose paintings depicted Brazilians and the country's animals and plants. Also of interest are the paintings by the amateur Zacharias Wagener, a German soldier in the service of the Dutch West India Company.

After more than seven years of rule, Maurits, greatly beloved by the populace of Dutch Brazil, was recalled by the directors of the Dutch West India Company. He left for Europe in May of 1644. He became stadholder of Cleves (1647–1679) and was made a prince of the Holy Roman Empire in 1652. He served in various Dutch military posts, distinguishing himself in battle as late as 1674.

See also **Dutch in Colonial Brazil.**

BIBLIOGRAPHY

José Antônio Gonsalves de Mello, *Tempo dos flamengos: Influencia da ocupaçao Holandesa na vida e na cultura do norte do Brasil* (1947).

Pieter J. Bouman, *Johan Maurits van Nassau, de Braziliaan* (1947).

Charles R. Boxer, *The Dutch in Brazil, 1624–1654* (1957).

E. Van Den Boogaart, ed., *Johan Maurits van Nassau-Siegen, 1604–1679: A Humanist Prince in Europe and Brazil* (1979).

Hermann Wätjen, *Das Hollandische Kolonialreich in Brasilien* (1921).

Peter J. P. Whitehead and Marinus Boeseman, *A Portrait of Dutch 17th Century Brazil: Animals, Plants, and People by the Artists of Johan Maurits of Nassau* (1989).

Additional Bibliography

Herkenhoff, Paulo, and Evaldo Cabral de Mello. *O Brasil e os holandeses, 1630–1654.* Rio de Janeiro: Sextante Artes, 1999.

Mello, Evaldo Cabral de. *O negócio do Brasil: Portugal, os Países Baixos e o Nordeste, 1641–1669.* Rio de Janeiro: Topbooks, 1998.

Francis A. Dutra

MAURO, HUMBERTO (1897–1983). A pioneer of Brazilian cinema, Humberto Mauro made films pursuing Brazilian themes over a fifty-year period. Until the mid-1930s, his work focused on his native state of Minas Gerais. In his first film, *Valadião, o Cratera* (1925), a five-minute silent short, Mauro showed a group of thieves and indigents robbing and marauding in the Minas Gerais mountains. His masterpiece, *Ganga Bruta* (Rude gang) (1933), is a work of formal experimentation that combined expressionism and editing techniques developed in the Soviet cinema. It tells the story of an aristocratic man who kills his bride during their honeymoon in order to rebuild his life. The generation of Cinema Novo in the 1960s saw Mauro as a paradigm of avant-gardism and creativity. Mauro was one of the first filmmakers to show the everyday life of a Brazilian *favela* (slum) in *Favela dos meus Amores* (Favela of my loves), in 1931.

See also **Cinema: From the Silent Film to 1990; Cinema Novo.**

BIBLIOGRAPHY

Johnson, Randal, and Robert Stam, eds. *Brazilian Cinema*, expanded edition. New York: Columbia University Press, 1995.

Schvarzman, Sheila. *Humberto Mauro e as imagens do Brasil.* São Paulo, Brazil: UNESP, 2004.

PAULA HALPERIN

MAXIMILIAN (1832–1867). Maximilian (*b.* 6 July 1832; *d.* 19 June 1867), emperor of Mexico (1864–1867). Born in the Schönbrunn Palace in Vienna, Maximilian was the younger brother of Emperor Francis Joseph. He served as Austrian governor of Lombardy and Venetia from February 1857 until April 1859, when his liberal policies caused a breach with the Vienna authorities. In July 1857, he married Charlotte (known in Mexico as Carlota), daughter of Leopold I of the Belgians, who had earlier declined the Greek throne and the offer of a Mexican crown on the grounds that financial support had been lacking. Carlota, however, fervently believed in the Mexican imperial idea.

Rather than a politician, Maximilian was a romantic who wanted to do something for humanity. Before Napoleon III's suggestion of the Mexican crown, he had traveled the Mediterranean, and by the end of 1859, had also visited Madeira and Brazil. Francis Joseph, reluctant to be drawn into the Mexican scheme, left the matter of the crown to Maximilian, who verbally accepted the offer on 3 October 1863. Following Maximilian's acceptance, Napoleon, in the secret convention of Miramar, agreed to maintain an army of 20,000 men in Mexico until 1867 and the Foreign Legion until 1873, while in exchange, Mexico would cover the entire cost as well as pay back its past debts. In September-October 1863, he was apparently studying Lucas Alamán's *Historia de México*, a pro-monarchy tract. On 10 April 1864, Maximilian formally accepted the crown offered to him by a delegation of Mexican monarchists. Four days later he and Carlota set sail, by way of Rome, where they received the blessing of Pope Pius IX, reaching Mexico City on 12 June, after a *Te Deum* celebrated at the shrine of Our Lady of Guadalupe by Archbishop Labastida. Maximilian had no intention of restoring the position of the church to that held before the Reform Laws, an attitude that led to intense conflict with the bishops and the papal nuncio. He ignored the pope's request to suspend Liberal measures, which he himself had ratified, and issued imperial decrees confirming purchases of ecclesiastical properties (28 December 1864) and continuing sales—though providing for division of rural properties (26 February 1865).

Maximilian also was determined to free himself of the French and disliked Marshal François Bazaine, the French commander in chief in Mexico, who had abandoned the attempt to create a Mexican army late in 1864. The French army encountered fierce guerrilla resistance across Mexico. At the same time, Maximilian made the serious mistake of sending Miguel Miramón and Leonardo Márquez, the best Conservative generals, on missions in Europe.

Maximilian's Council of State and cabinet consisted in the main of moderates, since there existed little basis of support for the empire among Conservatives and the clergy. The emperor's competition for the middle ground was undermined further by Napoleon III's determination from late 1866 to evacuate all French forces. After Miramón's return to France in November, Maximilian for the first time became dependent on the Conservatives for his survival. He had in the meantime withdrawn to Orizaba for one month to ponder the question of abdication and indulge his passion for catching butterflies. Meanwhile, Carlota went to France to appeal to Napoleon III to save the empire by committing more funds. She reached Paris in August 1866, but to no avail.

Maximilian's decision to remain on the throne was made public on 30 November 1866. A junta of notables voted on 14 January 1867 in Mexico City to uphold the empire by one vote, in spite of Bazaine's reservations concerning the empire's military position. Maximilian refused to abandon Mexico City with the last French troops and departed for the interior to take personal command of his army. He was captured by forces loyal to President Benito Juárez and was summarily tried and executed at Querétaro on 19 June 1867. The case against him rested on Juárez's decree of 25 January 1862 for the execution of all collaborators, and the death sentence, which Juárez refused to commute, was determined by the imperial decree of 3 October 1865, which had established the death penalty for all members of rebel bands or bandit groups. Juárez refused all appeals for clemency and delayed sending the corpse to Europe.

Maximilian had attempted to alleviate agrarian problems in his imperial decrees of 26 June 1865, which vested communal ownership in village inhabitants in reversal of Liberal policy, and in those of 1 November 1865, which granted laborers the right to leave employment at will. He did not consider himself to be the dupe of Napoleon III or the pawn of the French army. His decision to remain in Mexico after February 1867 reflected his determination to uphold his honor as a Hapsburg. He had sought to identify with Mexico and believed that the country could attain peace under his rule. Anxious to rally moderate opinion to the throne, he alienated Mexican Conservatives and the Catholic hierarchy. Moreover, Maximilian was hampered by his own lack of political skill.

See also **Napoleon III.**

BIBLIOGRAPHY

Egon Caesar Corti, *Maximilian and Charlotte of Mexico,* 2 vols., translated by Catherine A. Phillips (1928).

Émile de Kératry, *L'elévation et la chute de l'émpereur Maximilian* (1867).

Additional Bibliography

Duncan, Robert. "For the Good of the Country: State and Nation Building during Maximilian's Mexican Empire, 1864–67." Ph.D. diss., 2001.

Hamnett, Brian R. *Juárez.* New York: Longman, 1994.

Rodríguez O, Jaime E. *The Divine Charter: Constitutionalism and Liberalism in Nineteenth-century Mexico.* Lanham, MD: Rowman & Littlefield, 2005.

BRIAN HAMNETT

MAXIMÓN.

Maximón, a Maya cult existing in the western highlands of Guatemala, practiced principally in Santiago Atitlán, San Jorge La Laguna, Nahualá, and Zunil. The cult of San Simón of San Andrés Itzapa is closely related to that of Maximón and has more Ladino followers. The Maximón is a wooden image that is kept in a chapel or at home and dressed as a wealthy Indian or in a suit or military uniform. In exchange for prayers and offerings of money, cigars, liquor, tortillas, candles, and incense, Maximón performs miracles. While Maximón is considered a guardian of moral behavior, he is also associated with vices and sexual disorder.

Maximón is important as a representation of the mixing of Maya and Catholic religions characterized by both the destruction of the native religion and the lack of acceptance of Catholicism. Though unknown, his origins are related to beliefs about San Miguel (Saint Michael), Pedro de Alvarado, San Andrés, San Pedro, Judas Iscariote, and the Maya god Mam. He appeared at the end of the eighteenth century or the beginning of the nineteenth century. The Catholic Church has been unsuccessful in efforts to Crush the cult, and in Santiago Atitlán, Maximón parades with the Catholic saints during Holy Week.

See also **Maya, The; Syncretism.**

BIBLIOGRAPHY

E. Michael Mendelson, "Maximón: An Iconographical Introduction," in *Man* 59, no. 87 (1959): 57–60.

Mario Ricardo Pellecer Badillo, *Un Encuentro con San Simón en San Andrés Itzapa* (1973).

Diego F. Molina, *Las confesiones de Maximón* (1983).

Additional Bibliography

Pieper, Jim. *Guatemala's Folk Saints: Maximón/San Simon, Rey Pascual, Judas, Lucifer, and Others.* Los Angeles: Pieper and Associates, 2002.

LAURA L. WOODWARD

MAXIXE. Maxixe, Brazilian song and dance form. Performed in syncopated 2/4 time, the maxixe was created from a fusion of elements of the European polka, the habanera, the Lundu, and the Brazilian tango. The maxixe was popular from its first appearance in Rio de Janeiro around 1870 until approximately 1920. It has been variously described as the "first ... truly national genre" by Charles Perrone, and "the first urban dance created in Brazil" by Oneyda Alvarenga. Its historical importance derives from its being the immediate and often indistinguishable precursor of the *samba carioca* (Rio de Janeiro samba). The best-known maxixe composers are Ernesto Nazareth and Marcelo Tupinamba, although both referred to their compositions as tangos.

See also **MPB: Música Popular Brasileira.**

BIBLIOGRAPHY

Oneyda Alvarenga, *Música popular brasileira* (1982).

Gérard Béhague, "Popular Music," in *Handbook of Latin American Popular Culture,* edited by Charles Tatum and Harold Hinds (1986).

Mário De Andrade, *Dicionário musical brasileiro,* coordinated by Oneyda Alvarenga and Flávia Camargo Toni (1982–1989).

Charles A. Perrone, *Masters of Contemporary Brazilian Song* (1989).

Additional Bibliography

Chasteen, John Charles. *National Rhythms, African Roots: The Deep History of Latin American Popular Dance.* Albuquerque: University of New Mexico, 2004.

Livingston-Isenhour, Tamara Elena, and Thomas George Caracas García. *Choro: A Social History of Popular Brazilian Music.* Bloomington: Indiana University Press, 2005.

Neves, Maria Helena Franca. *De La Traviata ao maxixe: Variações estéticas da práctica do Teatro São João.* Salvador, Bahia: Secretaria da Cultura e Turismo, Fundação Cultural do Estado: Empresa Gráfica da Bahia, 2000.

ROBERT MYERS

MAYA, THE. The Maya are one of the largest indigenous groups of the Americas, with a modern population estimated at more than six million. The largest concentration of modern Maya peoples is in Guatemala, where they make up over 40 percent of the population. In Mexico, Yucatecan Mayan speakers are the second largest indigenous group in the country. The Mayan language family, which includes twenty-four to thirty related but mutually unintelligible languages, is the most populous and diversified language family in Mesoamerica. With the exception of Huastec in the Mexican states of Veracruz and Tamaulipas, Mayan speakers are found today in northern Yucatán, Belize, Chiapas, and highland Guatemala. Linguists have estimated that the Mayan languages began diverging around 4,100 years ago. Before about 2200 BCE, ancestral Mayan speakers presumably spoke a single parent language, known as proto-Mayan, with their homeland possibly in the northwestern highlands of Guatemala.

The territory of the ancient Maya included the entire Yucatán Peninsula, Belize, most of Guatemala, western Honduras, and western El Salvador. This area is extremely varied topographically and physiographically, and differences in elevation, temperature, rainfall, soils, availability of water, natural plants and animals, and the distribution of natural resources such as salt and obsidian have resulted in great environmental diversity. The northern lowlands of Yucatán are low and flat, hot, relatively dry (rainfall averages less than seventy-eight inches annually), and characterized by poor soils and low forest and bush vegetation. The central lowlands, or the Petén region of Guatemala, are moister, with annual rainfall averaging more than seventy-eight inches, and are distinguished by many lakes, seasonal swamps, deep soils in some places, and good availability of natural resources such as chert, limestone, and hardwoods. The tropical forest in the central lowlands is lush, and animal life is rich and diverse. South of the Petén, the southern lowlands provide a transitional zone to the highlands. This region is characterized by abundant rainfall (78 to 117 inches annually), rich soils, and thick tropical rain forest. The Motagua Valley, which links the southern lowlands with the northern highlands, was an important source of precious greenstone.

The northern highlands are composed of the rugged mountains of the Sierra Madre of Central America, spanning Chiapas and Guatemala. This region is the natural habitat of the quetzal, whose feathers were coveted by Maya lords for resplendent headdresses. The southern highlands are made up of the great chain of volcanoes paralleling the Pacific coastal plain, some of which are still active. The most important mineral resource of the southern highlands is obsidian, or volcanic glass, used for making cutting and scraping implements. Both highland regions feature fertile valleys and basins with rainfall averaging 78 to 117 inches annually. Vegetation in the cool northern highlands consists of rich highland rain forest on higher slopes, and semitropical pine and oak forest on lower slopes. The original vegetation of the southern highlands, which are lower and warmer, probably consisted of mixed evergreen and deciduous forest; the region is so densely inhabited—and this has been true for thousands of years—that the natural environment has been completely altered by human activity. Finally, the Pacific coastal plain and piedmont are hot and wet, with annual rainfall averaging more than 117 inches. Soils here are rich, the tropical vegetation luxurious, and animal life abundant and varied. One of the most important products of the piedmont was cacao—from which chocolate is produced—one of the most important commercial crops of ancient Mesoamerica.

Statue of a Mayan noble woman. Inhabiting portions of Central America and southern Mexico, Mayan civilization reached its zenith from 250 to 900 CE. The ancient Mayans developed a written language, built elaborate temples and palaces, and engaged in robust trade with their neighbors. © CHARLES & JOSETTE LENARS/CORBIS

The earliest secure evidence of human presence in the Maya area has been found in the northern highlands of Guatemala, where fluted projectile points similar to those known as the Clovis type, used by early hunters and gatherers in Northern and Middle America and dated to about 10,600 to 11,300 years ago, have been found at the sites of San Rafael and Los Tapiales. A Clovis-type point is also known from Ladyville, Belize. Belize also has a number of Archaic-period sites tentatively dated to about 7500–2000 BCE, but these sites may be much younger. A recent revision dates the Belize Archaic no earlier than about 2500 BCE. On the Pacific coastal plain of Chiapas, Late Archaic-period sites have been found dating to around 3000–2000 BCE. One of these, Tlacuachero, has produced evidence that shrimp processing was an important activity. During the Archaic period, semisedentary hunters and gatherers living in isolated villages depended primarily on natural plant and animal resources for their livelihood. Coastal dwellers probably traded salt, dried fish and shrimp, and shellfish for highland products such as obsidian and domesticated plant foods such as maize.

Proto-Mayan vocabulary reconstructed by means of comparisons of modern Mayan languages provides a glimpse of the habitat, plants, and animals of the ancestral Mayas of the Archaic period. In addition to a number of terms for highland plants and animals, names for some lowland species also occur. The inference is that proto-Mayan speakers inhabited a highland zone bordering on the lowlands. Names for lowland plants and animals include crocodile, coyol palm, and ceiba tree. Other names for trees refer to the willow, oak, cypress, and pine. Referents for cultivated plants include avocado, chile, yellow squash, maize, sweet potato, bean, cotton, and tobacco. Domestic animals include the dog and turkey. Other animals are jaguar, cougar, deer, fox, squirrel, mouse, gopher, weasel, coyote, agouti, skunk, armadillo, crow, buzzard, hummingbird, owl, bat, hawk, toad, turtle, and fish. Names for insects include bee (which also means honey), fly, gnat, ant, spider, louse, tick, butterfly, and scorpion. Other important items of proto-Mayan vocabulary include words for food preparation (*metate* [grinding stone], to grind, to roast), containers (gourd, trough), construction and tools (bench, cord, mat, house, bed, axe), ritual (drum, rattle, to jump-dance-sing, paper, writing). There is no proto-Mayan word for ceramics, which did not appear in the Maya area until about 1800 BCE. Nor are there terms for *comal* (ceramic griddle) or tortilla, which were absent in the Maya area until probably the Postclassic period.

Early Preclassic villages on the coast of Chiapas, Guatemala, and western El Salvador, dated to 1800–1500 BCE, are characterized by elaborate and well-made ceramics. The presence of highland obsidian and foreign ceramics indicates long-distance trade. Differences in architecture and grave goods and a two-level settlement hierarchy provide evidence for emerging social ranking and political integration. These coastal villagers were probably speakers of Mixe-Zoquean, not Mayan. They had a mixed subsistence economy based on the cultivation of maize, beans, and squash; root crops such as sweet potato and manioc; and the harvesting of coastal and riverine resources.

Toward the end of the Early Preclassic, by about 1200 BCE, the Olmec civilization had emerged on the Gulf Coast of Mexico. By the Middle Preclassic (1000–400 BCE), all of Mesoamerica was connected by networks of elite interaction, and through such ties the Olmecs had a strong impact on other societies, including the Maya. These networks were extremely complex, involving multidirectional economic, social, political, and religious interaction, which had a mutual transformational effect on all participating societies. Nevertheless, it is obvious that the Gulf Coast Olmecs, who were predominantly Mixe-Zoquean speakers, played a principal role in these developments. Many of the important forms and themes of Olmec monumental art, such as carved stelae and altars and portraits of named rulers linked with powerful cosmological forces, foreshadow those that appear later among the Maya. Early steps in the development of calendrics, astronomy, and hieroglyphic writing, which would later become intellectual hallmarks of Classic Maya civilization, were taken by the Olmecs and the Olmec-affiliated Zapotecs of Oaxaca during the Middle Preclassic.

A population increase occurred throughout the Maya area during the Middle Preclassic, and by about 800 BCE the highlands and the lowlands were probably dotted with hundreds of agricultural villages, although very few are known archaeologically. While most were simply large villages, some, such as Kaminaljuyú in the southern highlands and Nakbe in the central lowlands, were extremely complex, with large temple platforms with elaborate architectural decoration. These sites were the centers of hierarchical chiefdoms with tributary economies.

The trends toward greater social complexity and expanding populations were intensified in the Late Preclassic (400 BCE–CE 100) and the Protoclassic (CE 100–250). A number of large chiefly centers developed from their Middle Preclassic antecedents whose rulers vied with one another for economic and political advantage. Ritualized warfare became an important manifestation of elite competition. Widespread homogeneity in ceramics attests to a high level of achievement in craft specialization and strong economic ties throughout the lowlands and the highlands. Networks of communication between the elites of major centers, such as El Mirador and Tikal in the central lowlands, Kaminaljuyú and Chalchuapa in the southern highlands, and Abaj Takalik on the Pacific piedmont, served as the crucible for the development of early Maya civilization.

The Classic period (CE 250–900) witnessed the emergence of state-level polities in the lowlands. While state formation was truncated in the southern highlands by the cataclysmic eruption of Ilopango volcano in El Salvador about CE 250, the lowland centers continued the trends begun earlier. Population increased to as high as ten million during the Late Classic (CE 600–900). Stratified, class-based society with a complex division of labor was fully developed by the beginning of the Classic period. About a dozen major centers became the capitals of regional kingdoms whose territories were in constant flux, depending on the successes or failures of their military and political ventures. Each center was ruled by a shamanistic king who traced

Mayan pyramid at Tikal, Guatemala. The great city of Tikal declined and was eventually abandoned around 900 CE. This mid-twentieth-century illustration shows a temple at Tikal covered by vegetation and what it might look like after restoration. THE LIBRARY OF CONGRESS

his royal descent to a founding ancestor. Carved stone monuments recorded the kings' genealogies and commemorated their important deeds and achievements. Maya lords and their wives were obliged to perform blood sacrifice on special occasions to validate their status and perpetuate their royal lineage. Royal courts of the lowlands financed elite arts and crafts, sponsored religious ceremonies, and organized armed expeditions against competing kingdoms.

Classic Lowland Maya civilization collapsed in the ninth century CE. During the Postclassic period (CE 900–1524), the metropolises of the Petén were reclaimed by the jungle. The central and southern lowlands were virtually depopulated, and political organization reverted to the village level. The northern lowlands experienced great growth during this period. Chichén Itzá was established in the Early Postclassic (CE 900–1200) under the aegis of the Toltecs as the center of a large tributary state dominating the northern lowlands. This period was marked by the rise of the Putun, or Chontal, Maya. Their homeland was in the Tabasco lowlands of the Gulf Coast region, and their cultural traditions were Mexicanized. They were warriors and merchants, whose movements were motivated by a desire to seize resources and trade routes. Initially concerned with controlling the old riverine and overland routes in the central and southern lowlands, they eventually came to control the coastal routes around the Yucatán Peninsula, and ultimately commerce between Gulf Coast Mexico and Central America. Ports in this network included colonies of resident Putun merchants. Putun expansion culminated in the tenth or eleventh century when they, in alliance with Toltec warriors from Tollan, established a new capital at Chichén Itzá.

According to the chronicles, Chichén hegemony was broken in CE 1221. Mayapán rose to power as the new dominant center in Yucatán. There is a great overlap between Chichén Itzá and Mayapán in art style, iconography, architecture, and settlement pattern. The rulers of Mayapán were of the Cocom lineage, descendants of Hunac Ceel, the destroyer of Chichén Itzá. The Cocoms ruled over a fairly unified Yucatán for about 250 years. Shortly before CE 1450, Ah Xupan, a noble lord of the Xiu lineage, led a successful revolt against the Cocoms. Mayapán was sacked and looted. On the eve of the Spanish Conquest, northern Yucatán was divided into sixteen autonomous petty states.

In highland Guatemala, the Toltec-influenced Putun ancestors of the ruling lineages of the Quiches (K'iche'), the Cakchiquels, and the Tz'utujils established themselves in the region in the Late Postclassic (CE 1200–1524). They built fortified mountaintop centers at the sites of Utatlan, Iximché, and Atitlán. Other highland Maya groups included the Mams, who built their capital of Zaculeu in the west, and the Pokomams who built Mixco Viejo and Chinautla Viejo. The Late Postclassic was a period of intense military competition and political fragmentation in the southern highlands.

This pattern was broken by the appearance of European invaders in the early sixteenth century. Sailing from their New World foothold in Cuba, the Spaniards launched their expedition of conquest under Hernán Cortés in 1519, and their first contact with Mesoamerican societies was with the Mayas of Yucatán. With the conquest of the Mexica Aztecs complete in 1523, Cortés dispatched a force from Mexico under the command of Pedro de Alvarado to Guatemala and El Salvador in 1523–1524. The conquest of Yucatán was led by Francisco de Montejo and his son Francisco the Younger from 1527 to 1546.

The conquest of the Maya has been described as a never-ending process of conflict, resistance, accommodation, and integration. Many Maya groups resisted conquest for a long time, and some Maya groups were never conquered by the Spaniards. The Itzás, for example, retained their independence on the island stronghold of Tayasal until 1697, and the Mopans, the last independent Maya group, were driven to extinction by British loggers in Belize in the late eighteenth century.

The invisible ally of the Spaniards, epidemic disease, had a tremendous impact on Maya (and all native New World) populations. Virulent epidemics preceded the arrival of Spanish troops in 1515 or 1516 in Yucatán and 1519–1521 in highland Guatemala. These scourges probably killed at least one-third of the population. By the end of the sixteenth century, the Maya population in most areas was reduced by as much as 90 percent from their pre-Conquest levels.

During the next two centuries the Maya endured forced resettlement from villages scattered throughout the countryside into centralized villages and towns. Once relocated, they were exploited for labor by the crown, clergy, and colonists and forced to pay tribute to *encomenderos* and the crown.

In the nineteenth century the Maya peoples found themselves caught up in the expansion of the plantation economies of southern Mexico and Central America. Whether it was cotton in Guatemala, coffee in Chiapas, or sugar in Yucatán, high levels of international demand for export crops made large-scale commercial agriculture highly

Rigoberta Menchú, Guatemala City, Guatemala, November 9, 2003. Much of today's Mayan population is concentrated in Central America and southern Mexico, often suffering from government oppression. Winner of the 1992 Nobel Peace Prize, Menchú became internationally known as a proponent of the rights of women and indigenous peoples.

profitable, and plantation owners turned to Maya communities for their labor needs. Contractors would entice Maya men to work with high loans that could only be repaid with plantation wages, and the infamous company store, or *tienda de raya,* trapped many in debt peonage. In addition, plantation demands for land and other resources put pressure on Maya holdings, particularly after liberal regimes came to power in the mid- to late nineteenth century and allowed the usurpation of village lands. This dispossession not only forced more Maya to become plantation laborers, but it also seriously disrupted traditional subsistence patterns.

The increasingly desperate economic situation, coupled with repressive local governments, pushed many Mayas into open revolt in the nineteenth century. Perhaps the best-known revolt was the Caste War of Yucatán, which began in 1847. By 1848 the Maya had managed to gain control of most of the peninsula, and they laid waste to the sugar plantations that had been the source of many of their problems. A significant number of Maya rebels retreated into the deep forests of Quintana Roo, where they established autonomous villages with their own military and religious organization.

Despite the temporary success of the Caste War, the plantation became the backbone of the southern Mexican and Central American economies. The agrarian reform carried out after the Mexican Revolution broke up many large estates, but it bypassed large areas of Chiapas, where debt peonage still exists, and Maya peoples continue to provide the bulk of the labor for the large coffee and cotton plantations of Guatemala. The unequal distribution of land and state repression weigh heavily on the Mayas. Tens of thousands of highland villagers were murdered in the 1970s and 1980s by Guatemalan military and paramilitary forces. On New Year's Day 1994 an armed revolt began in Chiapas, which remains unresolved.

The Mayas have traditionally lived in rural communities, with each community distinguished by a unique style of dress, distinct social conventions, and, in places such as Aguacatán and Sacapulas, their own language. Although most Maya remain rural agriculturists, there is a growing number of Maya teachers, university professors, writers, merchants, engineers, doctors, and other professionals. Rigoberta Menchú, a Maya woman of the northern highlands of Guatemala, won the Nobel Peace Prize in 1992.

See also **Alvarado y Mesía, Pedro de; Annals of the Cakchiquels; Calendars, Pre-Columbian; Caste War of Yucatán; Chichén Itzá; El Mirador; Forests; Indigenous Peoples; Kaqchikel; K'iche'; Mayan Alphabet and Orthography; Mayan Epigraphy; Mayan Ethnohistory; Mesoamerica; Olmecs; Tikal; Tz'utujil.**

BIBLIOGRAPHY

Murdo J. MacLeod, *Spanish Central America* (1973).

Terrence Kaufman, "Archaeological and Linguistic Correlations in Mayaland and Associated Areas of Meso-America," in *World Archaeology* 8 (1976): 101–118.

Robert Wasserstrom, *Class and Society in Central Chiapas* (1983).

Sandra Orellana, *The Tzutujil Mayas* (1984).

Robert M. Hill and John Monaghan, *Continuities in Highland Maya Social Organization* (1987).

Grant D. Jones, *Maya Resistance to Spanish Rule* (1989).

Nancy M. Farriss, *Maya Society Under Colonial Rule* (1992).

Robert M. Hill, *Colonial Cakchiquels* (1992).

W. George Lovell, *Conquest and Survival in Colonial Guatemala* (1992).

Michael D. Coe, *The Maya,* 5th ed. (1993).

Thomas C. Kelly, "Preceramic Projectile-Point Typology in Belize," in *Ancient Mesoamerica* 4 (1993): 205–227.

Robert J. Sharer, *The Ancient Maya,* 5th ed. (1994).

Additional Bibliography

León-Portilla, Miguel. *Tiempo y realidad en el pensamiento maya: Ensayo de acercamiento*, 2nd edition. Mexico: Universidad Nacional Autónoma de México, 1986. English translation: *Time and Reality in the Thought of the Maya.* Translated by Charles L. Boilès, Fernando Horcasitas, and the author. Norman: University of Oklahoma Press, 1988.

Restall, Matthew. *The Maya World: Yucatec Culture and Society, 1550–1850.* Stanford, CA: Stanford University Press, 1997.

William R. Fowler
John D. Monaghan

MAYAN ALPHABET AND ORTHOGRAPHY. Through Government Accord 1046–87, published in the *Diario Oficial* on 30 November 1987, the Guatemalan government made official the Unified Alphabets for the Mayan Languages of Guatemala. This accord invalidated

Mayan hieroglyphics, Palenque, Mexico, c. 750 CE. The writing system of the ancient Mayans combined the use of over 800 symbols, each representing a different syllable in the Mayan language. DONNE BRYANT/ART RESOURCE, NY

the 1950 decree regarding Mayan alphabets; it also superseded various other alphabets authorized by the Instituto Indigenista Nacional in 1962, 1966, and 1975. The Unified Alphabets were made official to reduce the ambiguities and confusion of multiple written forms.

The Mayan languages of Mesoamerica had an early written tradition. The Classic lowland Maya used a complex writing system based on iconographic and morphophonemic glyphs that survive in stone and ceramics. There is no evidence of a writing system in the Postclassic Guatemalan highlands; bark paper codices from Yucatán are the only record of Maya writing in the Postclassic period.

The Spanish missionaries who came to Guatemala following the Conquest in 1524 propagated Christian doctrine and recorded some Mayan ethnohistoric and cultural accounts, as well as native language vocabularies, in an accommodated Latin alphabet. The Popol Vuh and the *Memorial de Tecpán Atitlán* are two examples of transcribed narratives using Latin characters.

In the eighteenth, nineteenth, and early twentieth centuries, little was written in or about the Mayan languages. Noteworthy works of this period include Brasseur De Bourbourg's *Dictionnaire, grammaire et chrestomathie de la langue maya* (1862) and Otto Stoll's *Zur Ethnographie der Republik Guatemala* (1884). These early works used an orthography congruent with their authors' own linguistic orientations.

It was not until 1949, at the First Congress of Linguists, that systematic alphabets were first proposed for the four majority Mayan languages of Guatemala. These were made official and published in 1950 as *Alfabeto para los cuatro idiomas indígenas mayoritarios de Guatemala: Quiché, cakchiquel, mam y kekchí*. The 1950 official alphabets, like all those approved by the Instituto Indigenista Nacional during the next several decades, were developed largely by foreign linguists and missionaries. These alphabets imposed conventions of Spanish in order to standardize Mayan orthography and facilitate the transfer of

Mayan language alphabets: summary of distinguishing graphemes

Phoneme	Early[a] missionaries	Late[a] missionaries	Official 1950	Official 1975	ALMK[b]	PLFM[c]	Official 1987
/6/	b	b	b´	b	ƀ	b´	b´
/k/	c/qu	c/qu	c/q	c/qu	k	k	k
/k´/	4	q	c´/q´	c/q´u	γ	k´	k´
/q/	k	k	k	k	λ	q	q
/q´/	ϵ	g	k´	k´	⌖	q´	q´
/c/	4h	qh	ch´	ch´	*	ch´	ch´
/t´/	tt	t	t´	t´	đ	t´	t´
/¢´/	4,	tz	tz	tz´	x	tz´	tz´
/s/	x	x	x	x/ẍ	sh	x/xh	x/xh
/w/	v,uh[#]	v,uh	w´	w; u/c_v	w	w	w
/?/	—	—	´	´	´	7	´

[a]Alphabet used by missionaries of the colonial period (1524–1821) for Ki'che' Kaqchikel, and Tz'utujil (Terrence Kaufman, *Proyecto de alfabetos*, p. 42).
[b]Alphabet created by Adrian Inéz Chávez and adopted by the Academia de la Lengue Maya Ki-chè(ALMK).
[c]Alphabet proposed by Terrence Kaufman and modified and adopted by Proyecto Linguistico Francisco Marroquín (PLFM).

Table 1

literacy skills from Spanish to the vernacular languages.

Despite the existence of official alphabets since 1950, institutions and individuals working in the Mayan languages tended to develop and disseminate Mayan-language materials in different alphabets. Most adhered to Spanish orthography; only the alphabet of Adrián Chávez to write K'iche' (1967) and that of the Proyecto Lingüístico Francisco Marroquín (1976) made concerted efforts to avoid the overt imposition of Spanish orthographic conventions on the Mayan-language writing systems.

The 1987 Mayan-language alphabet was proposed at the first seminar of the Academy of Mayan Languages of Guatemala. At this seminar, Mayan-language speakers and linguists moved to adopt a common core alphabet to write the Mayan languages of Guatemala. The criteria were that the alphabets be systematic, phonemic, and accessible, and that they promote Mayan literacy, reduce dialect differences, and affirm the cultural identity of the Maya.

At the seminar, nine graphemes—those at the center of the alphabet controversy—were approved to represent phonemes common to the Mayan languages: *b*ʕ, *k*, *k*ʕ, *q*, *q*ʕ, *ch*ʕ, *t*ʕ, *tz*ʕ, ʕ. At later regional meetings the remaining graphemes were selected and accommodated to the specific languages.

The phonemic alphabets approved by Government Accord 1046–87 recognize twenty-seven letters shared by the twenty-one Mayan languages of Guatemala, and an additional twenty-six letters used to represent sounds distinctive to specific languages or language groups. Glottalized stops are marked with an apostrophe; no distinctive symbols are used to distinguish whether they are implosive or explosive. Long vowels are represented as digraphs (*vv*) and relaxed vowels are marked with diaeresis (*v̈*).

As an important element of culture and symbol of ethnic pride, the Mayan movement and communities have struggled for the languages' official recognition. In addition to recognizing the alphabet, in 1991 the Mayan Language Academy of Guatemala (ALMG) became a federal institution. With the adoption of the Peace Accords, the government made further commitments to indigenous languages. In 1997 a Committee for the Officialization of Mayan Languages was created, and projects aimed at standardization at the written and spoken levels continue. Elementary school materials are available in both Spanish and Mayan languages. Yet in a 1998 referendum on constitutional reforms, Guatemalans voted not to make the more than twenty Mayan languages official. Spanish remains Guatemala's official language. However, in May 2003 the congress issued a decree called the Law of National Languages, which guaranteed rights and provisions for Mayan, Xinca, and Garifuna languages. Disagreements about vowel use in the orthography persist.

See also **Mayan Epigraphy.**

BIBLIOGRAPHY

A comprehensive study of the Mayan glyphs, including an important discussion of the verb morphology and syntax of the Mayan writing system, is in Linda Schele and David Freidel, *Forest of Kings* (1990). Lyle Campbell discusses the orthographic conventions employed by the early missionaries in "Quichean Linguistics and Philology" in *Word Anthropology: Approaches to Language*, edited by William C. McCormack and Stephen A. Wurm (1978). For a discussion of the 1949 First Congress of Linguists and the 1950 official Mayan alphabets, see Julia Becker Richards, "The First Congress of Mayan Language of Guatemala," in *The Earliest Stage of Language Planning: The "First Congress" Phenomenon,* edited by Joshua Fishman (1992). The general topic of Mayan language alphabets is reviewed by Terrence Kaufman in *Proyecto de alfabetos y ortografía para escribir las lenguas mayances* (1976); and Margarita López Raquec, *Acerca de los alfabetos para escribir los idiomas mayas de Guatemala* (1989).

Additional Bibliography

Brody, Michal. *The Fixed Word, the Moving Tongue: Variation in Written Yucatec Maya and the Meandering Evolution toward Unified Norms.* Ph.D. dissertation, University of Texas at Austin, 2004.

Coe, Michael D., and Mark Van Stone. *Reading the Maya Glyphs*, 2nd edition. London: Thames and Hudson, 2005.

Garzon, Susan, et al. *The Life of Our Language: Kaqchikel Maya Maintenance, Shift, and Revitalization.* Austin: University of Texas Press, 1998.

Guatemala. *Ley de idiomas nacionales: Decreto 19-2003.* Guatemala: Academia de las Lenguas Mayas de Guatemala, 2003.

Guatemala. *Oficialización de los idiomas indígenas de Guatemala: Propuesta de modalidad (resumen).* Guatemala: Proyecto Q'anil B, 1999.

Marcos Méndez, Esperanza. *Kanwi'kon ka pejki'k y ka tz'ijb'i'k tama e jun ira.* Guatemala: Academia de las Lenguas Mayas de Guatemala, 1995.

Montgomery, John. *Dictionary of Maya Hieroglyphs.* New York: Hippocrene Books, 2002.

Montgomery, John. *How to Read Maya Hieroglyphs.* New York: Hippocrene Books, 2002.

Julia Becker Richards

MAYAN EPIGRAPHY. Mayan hieroglyphic texts were probably created for two thousand years, from before 300 BCE until the fall of the Itzás in 1697. Texts were mostly painted, and many writers were skilled artists. Most writers and readers were probably calendar priests who were members of royal families, but beautifully executed royal inscriptions were carved on stone monuments for semipublic display; most surviving texts are from this genre.

The language or languages written in these texts were ancestors of some of the roughly thirty Mayan languages spoken today. The Ch'olan and Tzeltalan languages may descend from the language of the earliest texts. There is consensus among epigraphers that, in the Classic period (c. 250–900 CE), Southern Lowland inscriptions were written in a form of Ch'olan, though they differ on whether it was an ancestor of all the Ch'olan languages or only of modern Ch'ortí and now-extinct colonial Ch'oltí. Many Lowland Northern texts exhibit Yucatecan features; some epigraphers argue that most or all texts at some of these sites were Yucatecan, others that they were written in Ch'olan as a prestige language.

PRINCIPLES

The basic principles of Mayan writing are well understood. Most signs are logograms, representing whole words; epigraphers transcribe them in capital letters, thus WHITE or **SAK** for the logogram spelling *sak*, "white." All other signs (syllabograms) represent syllables; they are transcribed in lowercase bold letters.

Because every syllable in ancient Lowland Mayan languages began with a consonant followed by a vowel, so does every syllabogram—indeed, almost all represent a simple consonant-vowel sequence (a few represent a consonant-vowel-consonant sequence). However, many Mayan syllables (including the last in most words) end in a consonant. Accordingly, in phonetic spellings there is a mismatch between the structure of the script and that of the language it represents. Faced with the final *l* of a word pronounced *tajal*, for example, scribes had two choices: they could fail to spell the consonant at all, or they could spell it as though it were a syllable beginning with *l*. Almost always, they chose to spell the consonant—in this case, using the sign **la**.

Words could be spelled by logograms alone or by syllabograms alone. Often, syllabograms were used as phonetic complements to logograms,

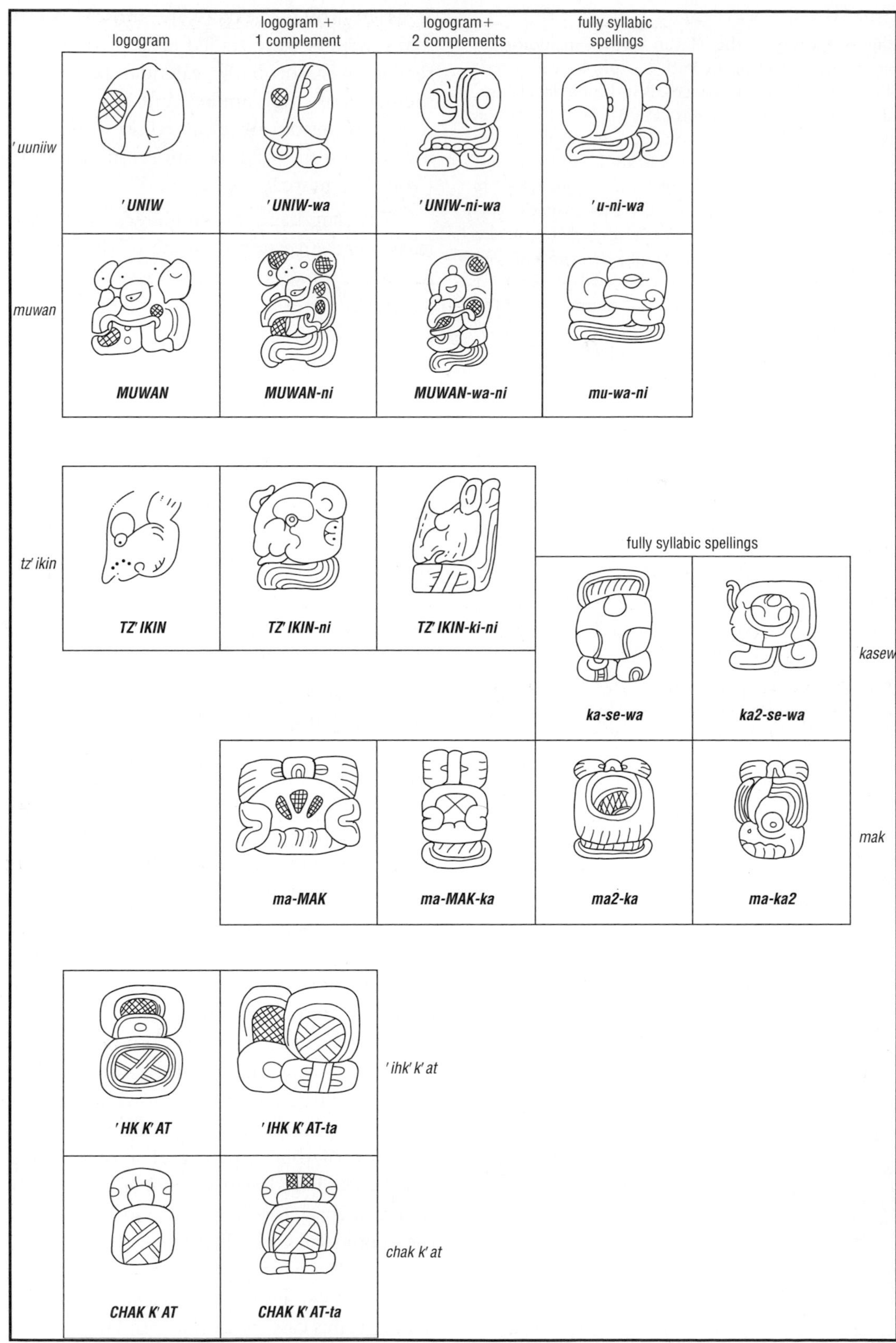
logogram
logogram + 1 complement
logogram+ 2 complements
fully syllabic spellings
'uuniiw
'UNIW
'UNIW-wa
'UNIW-ni-wa
'u-ni-wa
muwan
MUWAN
MUWAN-ni
MUWAN-wa-ni
mu-wa-ni
tz' ikin
TZ' IKIN
TZ' IKIN-ni
TZ' IKIN-ki-ni
fully syllabic spellings
kasew
ka-se-wa
ka2-se-wa
mak
ma-MAK
ma-MAK-ka
ma2-ka
ma-ka2
'ihk' k' at
'HK K' AT
'IHK K' AT-ta
chak k' at
CHAK K' AT
CHAK K' AT-ta

Figure 1

indicating the pronunciation of the beginning or ending of a word. Grammatical affixes were spelled by syllabograms; when attached to logograms, these spellings may have originated as instances of phonetic complementation.

Several syllable types existed in early Lowland Mayan languages. Using *C* to stand for any consonant, and *V* to stand for any vowel, these syllables were *CV, CVV, CVC, CVVC, CVhC, CVjC,* or *CV'C*. However, individual syllabograms do not distinguish vowel length or the presence versus absence of preconsonantal *h, j,* or *'*. Outside of compound words, there is no definite example of preconsonantal *h, j,* or *'* being written explicitly by a *CV* sign; epigraphers disagree on whether such distinctions were made in word-final syllables by spelling conventions, using unpronounced vowels in *CV* signs that spell word-final consonants.

Hieroglyphic writing was not a static system. Over time, Mayan scribes increased their use of phonetic spellings, seemingly in large part by extending the use of particular signs from contexts in which they were already established to other, phonetically or grammatically similar contexts.

DECIPHERMENT

Signs for numerals were recognizable from their tally-like structure, with bars for fives and dots for ones. They were usually juxtaposed with names of the months, or (1 through 13 only) with signs for the twenty named days of the 260-day divinatory calendar. This, together with ethnographic and ethnohistoric parallels, made it possible to reconstruct the calendar system. Calendrical data—especially differences among dates associated with specific glyphic expressions—permitted the recognition of a broad range of content, including a variety of calendrical expressions (e.g., names of days and months, and words for several time periods), astronomical phenomena (e.g., eclipses), and historical data (e.g., names of rulers and dates in their lives, whose span, at a particular site, do not exceed a human lifetime).

The most useful early aid to decipherment was the close correspondence between the content of text and imagery in divinatory manuals from Postclassic Yucatán. The Dresden and Madrid screenfolds in particular include hundreds of images accompanied by short hieroglyphic captions or comments. These image-caption pairs are grouped into "almanacs" treating particular topics; in the captions, at least one feature—the action, the location, the subject, or the object—remains relatively constant throughout the almanac, while at least one of them varies. This correspondence made it possible to identify glyphic expressions associated with particular supernaturals, plants, animals, birds, locations, and activities. Often, the correspondence had independent support, for example when a logogram closely resembled the corresponding element or the glyphic word occurred in the scene corresponding to itself. The imagery helped epigraphers understand the overt meaning of these passages, however obscure their point remained.

Large colonial dictionaries of Yucatec—the native language of the Mayas of Yucatán—were searched for words corresponding to these entities. A large number of signs could be assigned *CV* pronunciations because these signs occur in spellings of two or more words of appropriate meaning in which the corresponding *CV* sequence occurs; in many cases, the same sign spells a consonant at the end of a word. The close match of Yucatec vocabulary to that of these manuals was crucial to advancing Mayan decipherment; historically, this process was helped by a kind of bilingual text, Diego de Landa's representation of the Spanish alphabet in hieroglyphs, but this was not essential and was not even properly understood until the decipherment was well established.

Ethnographically attested Mayan month names made it possible to identify signs for several words

'och-i	*'uht-i*	*ch'am-ay-i*	*cham-i*	*hul-i*
ENTER-chi	'u-ti	GRAB-yi	DIE-mi	VISIT-li, hu-li
he/she/it entered	it happened	it got grabbed	he/she died	he/she visited

Table 1

and syllables in Classic spellings of these names. This provided the first direct evidence that the Classic month names were Ch'olan; a Ch'olan identity for the Southern Lowland inscriptions was already suggested (by 1920) on geolinguistic grounds.

Systematic grammatical analysis was, uncharacteristically, the last major phase of Mayan decipherment. The spelling system interfered with the recognition of some grammatical elements in the most complex part of Mayan grammar, the structure of verbs. To cite one example, intransitive verbs ordinarily ended with a suffix *-i*, as in Table 1.

This suffix was hard to recover because the same sign does not represent it in each occurrence: it must be spelled by a sign for the preceding consonant *+i*, so by at least with twenty different signs. As a result, this common verb type was one of the last to be understood or even recognized.

See also **Mayan Alphabet and Orthography; Knorosov, Yuri.**

BIBLIOGRAPHY

Bricker, Victoria R. "Mayan." In Roger D. Woodard, editor, *The Cambridge Encyclopedia of the World's Ancient Languages*. Cambridge: Cambridge University Press, 2004.

Coe, Michael D. *Breaking the Maya Code*. Revised edition. New York: Thames and Hudson, 1999.

Harris, John F., and Stephen K. Stearns. *Understanding Maya Inscriptions: A Hieroglyph Handbook*. Philadelphia: University of Pennsylvania Press, 1997.

Kettunen, Harri, and Christophe Helmke. *Introduction to Maya Hieroglyphs*. 2005. Available online at http://www.mesoweb.com/resources/handbook/WH2005.pdf.

JOHN JUSTESON

MAYAN ETHNOHISTORY. Mayan history in the sense of a chronologically placeable text begins with a carved stone monument of 199 CE known as the Hauberg Stela. Its provenience is unknown. It is possible that it was anticipated by similar monuments of the Olmec culture, such as Stela 10 from Kaminaljuyú, Guatemala (147 BCE) or even earlier Zapotec and Olmec inscriptions. None of these texts has been read, and in any case they are not Mayan. The Maya are generally confined to the territories of the states of Yucatán, Quintana Roo, Campeche, and Chiapas in Mexico, the republics of Belize and Guatemala, and the westernmost sections of Honduras and El Salvador.

By the end of the third century scholars begin to be able to piece together the fragmentary dynastic histories of particular Mayan cities, and after the sixth century these become relatively complete and continuous. The relevant texts are almost entirely inscribed on stone monuments and the surfaces of buildings, though they are supplemented by other "primary sources": hieroglyphic texts on murals or stone and ceramic objects. The latter are historical sources, but unlike the monumental inscriptions, they are not in themselves history. Though the dynastic histories came to an end in the tenth century, when they ceased to be carved in stone, the tradition of hieroglyphic writing continued on less permanent objects of wood and paper, virtually all of which have been destroyed. The sole surviving pre-Conquest paper manuscript is the Dresden Codex, the dating of which is still debated. Three other codices survive from the sixteenth century (Madrid, Paris, and Grolier), and may be copies of pre-Conquest originals. Though they reveal a great deal about Mayan culture, the codices were not intended as history but rather as mythical, ritual, astrological, and astronomical almanacs.

The decipherment and reading of the pre-Spanish history of the Maya is proceeding rapidly and demonstrates that the Maya may have been the only truly historical people of the Americas from the third to the sixteenth century, although much work remains in deciphering the Andean quipu (or khipu). The conversion of these thirteen centuries from prehistory into history is the most remarkable recent development in the study of the Maya. This historical tradition was confined to only two of the score or so of the Mayan languages of the time: Yucatec and Chol.

To some extent, the historical gap between the tenth century and the sixteenth can be filled, not by the codices but by histories written by the Maya after the Spanish arrived. Although the Mayan alphabet was adequate for writing two of the Mayan languages, and could even have been used to write Spanish (it was used to write Nahuatl), many of the Mayan peoples, particularly the Chontal and Yucatec of Mexico and the Quiche (K'iche') and Cakchiquel (Kaqchikel) of

Guatemala, rapidly adopted the Latin-based alphabets designed by the Franciscan missionaries. Much of what they wrote was their own history.

Some of the sources for this history may have been hieroglyphic manuscripts since lost, but it is likely that the more important source was oral tradition. Nonetheless, the rigor of the Mayan calendar was such that people may very well accept as historical some rather fragmentarily reported events as early as the ninth century (the occupation of Chichén Itzá by the Itzá Maya in 869–880 and their rule of the city until 1009).

Historiographically the Mayan histories present a number of distinctive problems. In their present form, none of them are sixteenth-century manuscripts. The dates given below are *termini ante quem*, indicating the probable dates of the extant copies. All of them were composed over a period of time, sometimes centuries, and by different authors. (The Popol Vuh may be an exception.)

The six fullest and most important of these sixteenth-century Mayan histories are the *Books of Chilam Balam of Tizimin* (1837), *Chumayel* (1837), and *Mani* (1837) in Yucatec; the *Chronicles of Acalan-Tixchel* (1604) in Chontal; the *Popol Vuh* (1704) in Quiche; and the *Annals of the Cakquiquels* (1604) in Cakchiquel. Like the histories of the Classic period (third to tenth century), these works are primarily dynastic. They trace the ruling lineages of their respective areas with varying degrees of historicity and time depth: the Itzá (ninth–eighteenth century) in eastern Yucatán, the Xiu (thirteenth–seventeenth century) in western Yucatán, the Paxbolon (fourteenth–seventeenth century) in western Campeche, the Cavek (thirteenth–sixteenth century) in west-central Guatemala, and the Zotzil (fifteenth–seventeenth century) in east-central Guatemala. In the main they are highly local in reference, though they overlap geographically in some degree, and they refer to places as far afield as southern Veracruz, Cozumel, southeast Chiapas, and the Guatemalan Peten. All of them describe the coming of the Spaniards.

An additional, if problematic, native source is the *Rabinal Achí* (1855), a Quiche drama that appears to refer to fifteenth-century events, preserved in oral and eventually written form, and discovered in the nineteenth century.

The manuscripts have not always been copied in their original order (particularly the *Books of Chilam Balam*), and copyists' errors are frequent. The problems can often be overcome because of the Mayan passion for chronology and accuracy, but it is not always easy. The Mayan cyclical view of time also gets in the way: sometimes the material is both history and prophecy at the same time, on the theory that what happens on a given date will recur on the same date in the next cycle. Dynastic lists are often distorted because of lineage rivalries, and generations may have been added or deleted even in ancient times for political reasons. Mayan history must be attentively and critically read and interpreted.

The historical preoccupations of the Maya that emerge from these sources are unique. Not only are the pre-Conquest histories dynastic, they are also ritualized history. The present owes the past the duty of emulation. Thus the Mayan historian describes the past in terms of its ritual achievements, generalizing it in mythological terms as a basis for the prediction of the future. For the Maya, furthermore, such prophecy was a positive guide to action. Having predicted their future on the basis of the past, they made every effort to make the prediction come true. A famous example is the cycle of 260 *tuns* (approximately 256 years), the end of which was supposed to occur on a day named 8 Ahau. In Classic times this date was supposed to end dynasties, and it often did. It was a great political advantage to potential usurpers to argue that they had the sun on their side. In colonial times, it was on 8 Ahau 1697 that the Itzá Maya of the Peten surrendered and converted to Christianity, having sent to Mérida for missionaries for the purpose. In social terms, Mayan history is strongly hierarchical; in philosophical terms it is profoundly fatalistic. Always it is religious.

Even after the Spanish Conquest, the Maya wrote their own history in a continuous tradition of colonial literacy that lasted in some areas (notably in Yucatec and Quiche) until the nineteenth century. Apart from adding to the early chronicles, they provided the written records, all in Mayan, that are the stuff of history: land documents; wills, *cofradía* ordinances; letters; medical, astrological, and astronomical handbooks; government reports; ritual poetry and drama. These are paralleled by an increasing volume of Catholic materials: catechisms, sermons, missals, church calendars, even occasional translations of secular European narratives.

From many of the Mayan historical sources one may almost gain the impression that the Spanish conquest did not take place. The event itself is described, to be sure, but thereafter the Spanish largely disappear, being fundamentally irrelevant to Mayan history. Mayan resistance to the Europeans was prolonged and stubborn, both overtly and covertly.

Something similar is true for the vast majority of the Spanish chronicles. The Indians existed only as the passive objects of conquest and conversion. In fact, it took the combined efforts of four Franciscans and three Dominicans over a period of three centuries to come close to describing the Maya as well as Bernardino de Sahagún and Alfonso Molina had depicted the Aztecs in central Mexico. The Franciscans are Diego de Landa, Antonio de Ciudad Real, Diego López De Cogolludo, and Domingo de Vico, all of the sixteenth century. The Dominicans are Bartolomé de Las Casas (sixteenth century), Antonio de Remesal (seventeenth century), and Francisco Ximénez (eighteenth century). In varying ways and to varying degrees these authors were interested in the Maya and endeavored to understand them.

The most important Spanish works relevant to Mayan ethnohistory are Landa's *Relacíon de las cosas de Yucatán,* Ciudad Real's *Diccionario de Motul,* Cogolludo's *Historia de Yucatán,* Vico's *Theologia Indorum,* Las Casas's *Apologética historia,* Remesal's *Historia general de las Indias occidentales* and Ximénez's *Historia de la provincia de San Vicente de Chiapa y Guatemala de la orden de Predicadores.* To these may be added the seventeeth-century secular work of Francisco Antonio Fuentes y Guzmán, *Recordación florida.* Landa, Cogolludo, and Ciudad Real deal with Yucatán; Vico, Las Casas, Remesal, and Fuentes y Guzmán treat Guatemala; Ximénez covers Guatemala and Chiapas. Together they come close to blanketing the territory of the Maya, and they are backed up by an enormous archive of secondary sources and historical materials of all kinds, the most significant of which are the sixteenth-century Relaciones Geográficas.

The autistic historical traditions of the Maya and the Spanish meet and begin to merge in these early chronicles. Like the Mayan histories, the Spanish ones show a deepening comprehension of the other tradition over time, though only Ciudad Real (Yucatec) and Vico (Quiche) may be said to have had a firm comprehension of a Mayan language. The only Mayan author with a comparably sophisticated command of Spanish was Gaspar Antonio Xiu, credited with the compilation of many of the *Relaciones geográficas* in Yucatán.

By the end of the nineteenth century, the colonial historical tradition had ended in both Yucatec and Quiche. The Latin-based alphabets were replaced by new ones, and although native language historical materials were produced in them, they are relatively minor. Explicit history was not written.

There has been an enormous growth of interest in Mayan ethnohistory, though this is primarily among "foreign" scholars not resident in Mayan territory. There are, however, some notable exceptions: Alfredo Barrera Vásquez and Alfonso Villa Rojas in Yucatán, and Adrián Recinos and José Antonio Villacorta y Rodas in Guatemala. Nonetheless, the gulf in historical awareness between the Maya and the non-Maya remains almost as formidable as when Landa sat down to write his *Relación* after burning the most valuable sources.

The most significant development in Yucatán, Chiapas, and Guatemala in the modern period may turn out to be the renascent historical consciousness among the Mayan people themselves. This is particularly evident among the Tzotzil, Yucatecans, Quiche, and Cakchiquel, but is also shared by many of their Mayan neighbors. The modern Maya are increasingly interested in their history and more and more knowledgeable about it. They may even take a hand in shaping their future by writing their past again in their own language.

See also **Annals of the Cakchiquels; Chilam Balam; Mayan Alphabet and Orthography; Mayan Epigraphy; Popol Vuh.**

BIBLIOGRAPHY

Charles Étienne Brasseur De Bourbourg, *Dictionnaire, grammaire et chrestomathie de la langue maya* (1862), which includes *Rabinal Achí;* Francisco Ximénez, *Historia de la provincia de San Vicente de Chiapa y Guatemala de la Orden de Predicadores,* 3 vols. (1929–1931).

Antonio De Remesal, *Historia general de las India Occidentales,* 2d ed., 2 vols. (1932).

José Antonio Villacorta C., *Memorial de Tecpán-Atitlán* (1932).

Francisco Antonio De Fuentes y Guzmán, *Recordación florida,* vols. 6–8 (1932–1933).

Alfred M. Tozzer, *Landa's Relación de las Cosas de Yucatán,* Papers of the Peabody Museum of Anthropology, Archaeology and Ethnology, Harvard University, 18 (1941).

Ralph L. Roys, *The Indian Background of Colonial Yucatán* (1943).

Alfonso Villa Rojas, *The Maya of East Central Quintana Roo* (1945).

Adrián Recinos, *Memorial de Sololá: Anales de los Cakchiqueles* (1950).

Diego López De Cogolludo, *Historia de Yucatán,* 5th ed., 2 vols. (1957).

Nelson Reed, *The Caste War of Yucatán* (1964).

France Vinto Scholes and Ralph L. Roys, *The Maya Chontal Indians of Acalan Tixchel* (1968).

Munro S. Edmonson, *The Book of Counsel: The Popol Vuh of the Guatemalan Quiche* (1971).

Howard F. Cline, "The Relaciones Geográficas of the Spanish Indies, 1577–1648," in *Handbook of Middle American Indians,* vol. 12 (1972), pp. 183–242.

Robert M. Carmack, *Quichean Civilization* (1973).

Eugene R. Craine and Reginald Reindorp, trans. and eds., *The Codex Pérez and the Book of Chilam Balam of Mani* (1979).

Alfredo Barrera Vásquez, ed., *Diccionario maya cordemex* (1980), which includes Ciudad Real's *Diccionario;* Victoria R. Bricker, *The Indian Christ, the Indian King* (1981).

Frauke Riese, *Indianische Landrechte in Yukatan um die Mitte des 16. Jahrhunderts* (1981).

Munro S. Edmonson, *The Ancient Future of the Itza: The Book of Chilam Balam of Tizimin* (1982).

René Acuña, "El Popol Vuh, Vico y la Theologia indorum," in *Nuevas perspectivas sobre el Popol Vuh,* edited by Robert M. Carmack and Francisco Morales Santos, (1973).

Robert M. Carmack and Francisco Morales Santos, eds., *Nuevas perspectivas sobre el Popol Vuh* (1973).

Munro S. Edmonson, *Heaven Born Merida and Its Destiny: The Book of Chilam Balam of Chumayel* (1986).

Grant D. Jones, *Maya Resistance to Spanish Rule: Time and History on a Colonial Frontier* (1989).

Additional Bibliography

Castañeda, Quetzil. "We Are *Not* Indigenous: An Introduction to the Mayan Identity of Yucatan" in *Journal of Latin American Anthropology* vol. 9, no. 1 (June 2004): 36–63.

Hanks, William F. and Don S. Rice, eds., *Word and Image in Maya Culture: Explorations in Language, Writing, and Representation.* Salt Lake City: University of Utah Press, 1989.

MUNRO S. EDMONSON

MAYAPAN. Mayapan (meaning "Standard [Banner] of the Maya") is a Late Postclassic Maya site located twenty-four miles southeast of Mérida, Yucatán. According to Bishop Diego de Landa, the city was established by a Chichén Itzá lord named Kukulcan, who decreed that the native lords of Yucatán should live there. After Kukulcan's departure, Mayapan was ruled by the Cocom, an Itzá lineage who established themselves between 1263 and 1283. Mayapan subsequently was the capital of Yucatan's northern plains until its Cocom rulers were deposed by the rival Tutul Xiu lineage during the Katun 8 Ahau between 1441 and 1461.

Mayapan traditionally was referred to as Ichpa ("within the enclosure"), and archaeology has confirmed that Mayapan was a walled city, containing a population of 11,000 to 12,000. Some 3,500 buildings occupy about 1.6 square miles, including about 100 larger masonry temples or ceremonial structures.

Dominating Mayapan is the centrally located Castillo or Temple of Kukulcan (structure Q-162), a radially symmetrical pyramid temple that is a small, poorly constructed imitation of the Castillo at Chichén Itzá. Nearby is a circular building derived from, but smaller than, Chichén Itzá's Caracol structure. "Colonnaded halls," rectangular-plan buildings with frontal and medial colonnades and benches along the rear walls, front several plazas grouped around the central temples.

Located near Mayapan's center are elite residential buildings with open front rooms and one or more private rear chambers that may contain small "family shrine" altars. These "palaces" have crude block walls, beam-and-mortar roofs, and a thick plaster facing, often modeled into architectural sculpture. Some 2,000 smaller houses, with perishable upper walls and thatch roofs, surrounded the upper-class dwellings.

Mayapan possesses thirteen carved stelae, one of which, Stela 1, features a 10 Ahau glyph probably corresponding to 11.11.0.0.0 (A.D. 1441). Its distinctive polychrome hollow ceramic figurine *incensarios* (Chen Mul Modeled Type) portray both Maya and central Mexican deities.

See also **Caracol; Chichén Itzá; Landa, Diego de; Quetzal.**

BIBLIOGRAPHY

Diego De Landa, *Landa's Relación de las cosas de Yucatán*, translated by Alfred M. Tozzer (1941).

H. E. D. Pollock, Ralph L. Roys, Tatiana Proskouriakoff, and A. Ledyard Smith, *Mayapan, Yucatán, Mexico* (1962).

Robert E. Smith, *The Pottery of Mayapan: Including Studies of Ceramic Materials from Uxmal, Kabah, and Chichén Itzá* (1970).

Additional Bibliography

Masson, Marilyn A., Timothy S. Hare, and Carlos Peraza Lope. "Postclassic Maya Society Regenerated at Mayapán." In *After Collapse: The Regeneration of Complex Societies.* edited by Glenn M. Schwartz and John J. Nichols. Tucson: University of Arizona Press, 2006.

Pugh, Timothy W. "The Exemplary Center of the Late Postclassic Kowoj Maya." *Latin American Antiquity* 14, No. 4 (Dec. 2003): 408–430.

Sharer, Robert J., and Loa P Traxler. *The Ancient Maya.* 6th ed. Stanford, CA: Stanford University Press, 2006.

JEFF KARL KOWALSKI

MAYORAZGO. Mayorazgo, a privilege allowing an individual to entail his estate so that his property, real or personal, could be passed on intact to a successor who, following the rule of primogeniture, preferably would be the oldest male son or the nearest relative. The legal basis for such establishments was Castilian law, in particular the 1505 Leyes de Toro. These laws allowed any subject above the rank of peasant to entail his property and thus acquire the privileges of *hidalguía* (nobility), including the title of *don* (gentleman), which forbade his entering any profession attached to commerce or industry on pain of loss of status.

In America rich individuals who could afford to petition the crown or its representatives for the royal decree permitting the establishment, entailed houses, stores, mills, mines, large rural estates, slaves, furniture, and silver and jewelry. The *mayorazgo* became a sought-after privilege of many leading families as a means of preserving the control of property within a kin group and maintaining the lineage and its collective memory. Thus, it became an important institution that perpetuated the elite class.

See also **Castile.**

BIBLIOGRAPHY

William B. Taylor, *Landlord and Peasant in Colonial Oaxaca* (1972).

José F. De La Peña, *Oligarquía y propiedad en Nueva España (1550–1624)* (1983).

Additional Bibliography

Gutiérrez R., Jairo. *El mayorazgo de Bogotá y el marquesado de San Jorge: Riqueza, linaje, poder y honor en Santa Fé: 1538–1824.* Santafé de Bogotá: Instituto Colombiano de Cultura Hispánica, 1998.

Vargas-Lobsinger, María. *Formación y decadencia de una fortuna: Los mayorazgos de San Miguel de Aguayo y de San Pedro del Alamo, 1583–1823.* México: Universidad Nacional Autónoma de México, 1992.

SUSAN E. RAMÍREZ

MAYORGA, SILVIO (1936–1967). Silvio Mayorga (*b.* 1936; *d.* 27 August 1967), Nicaraguan leader and cofounder of the Sandinista National Liberation Front. Mayorga was born in Matagalpa at approximately the same time as Carlos Fonseca. They grew up together and in 1954 entered law school at the National Autonomous University in León. Mayorga immediately became a student leader and joined the Nicaraguan Socialist Party in 1955. Like Fonseca, he soon rejected the passive character of the Socialists and encouraged more aggressive student radicalism. He became active in the Nicaraguan Patriotic Youth organization in the late 1950s and joined Fonseca's New Nicaragua Movement in 1960. In July 1961 Mayorga founded the Sandinista National Liberation Front with Fonseca and Tomás Borge.

Mayorga was one of the principal commanders of guerrillas based in the village of Walaquistan. There he cooperated closely with Borge in planning the first Sandinista attack at Río Coco in 1963. He was gravely injured in an attack at San Carlos in the same year and spent several months recuperating. He reappeared in 1964 as a student organizer in León and Managua. For the next three years, Mayorga encouraged students and the urban poor to support the Sandinistas. In 1967, he led an expedition to explore Quinagua as an alternative guerrilla base in the mountains of Las Segovias. Mayorga's forces had little military experience, and some of his soldiers were teenagers. This proved disastrous when they attacked Pancasán in August 1967. Mayorga and fifty combatants were killed by the National Guard. His death and the Pancasán fiasco forced the Sandinista leadership to suspend frontal attacks on the Guard and seriously reevaluate its political and military strategy over the next two years. Mayorga was the first original Sandinista to fall in combat.

See also **Nicaragua, Sandinista National Liberation Front (FSLN).**

BIBLIOGRAPHY

Frente Estudiantil Revolucionario, *Historia del FSLN* (1975).

Donald Hodges, *The Intellectual Foundations of the Nicaraguan Revolution* (1986).

U.S. Department Of State, Bureau Of Public Affairs, *Nicaraguan Biographies: A Resource Book* (1988).

Additional Bibliography

Díaz Araujo, Enrique. *El sandinismo nicaragüense.* Mendoza, Argentina: Ediciones la Rosa Blanca, 2004.

Flakoll, D.J., and Claribel Alegría. *Nicaragua, la revolución sandinista: Una crónica política, 1855-1979.* Managua, Nicaragua: Anama Ediciones Centroamericanas, 2004.

MARK EVERINGHAM

MAY PACTS (1902). The Pactos de Mayo were a series of four diplomatic treaties between Chile and Argentina negotiated in 1902. Since the mid-nineteenth century, Buenos Aires and Santiago had disputed the location of their common border. The arguments became so hostile that both nations began modernizing their armies as well as engaging in a costly naval arms race in preparation for war. Great Britain convinced the two countries to negotiate a settlement, which resulted in the Pactos de Mayo.

The treaties achieved several goals: they established a mechanism for the peaceful settlement of the outstanding boundary issues and ended the naval competition by setting a rough parity between the two nations' fleets. More significantly, each country recognized the other's hegemony on its own coasts: Argentina promised not to intervene in the Pacific basin, and Chile respected Argentina's domination of the Atlantic. Thus, the treaties not only provided a mechanism for resolving their long-festering border dispute, they also recognized the rights of the signatories in their respective spheres of influence, thereby avoiding future possible irritants to international peace.

See also **Argentina: The Nineteenth Century; Chile: The Nineteenth Century.**

BIBLIOGRAPHY

Luis Galdames, *A History of Chile* (1941), pp. 406–407.

Robert N. Burr, *By Reason or Force: Chile and the Balancing of Power in South America, 1830–1905* (1965), pp. 252–256.

WILLIAM F. SATER

MAZA, MANUEL VICENTE DE (1779–1839). Manuel Vicente de Maza (*b.* 1779; *d.* 27 June 1839), Argentine patriot and public official. Maza studied in his native Buenos Aires and in Chile, where he became a lawyer. After being imprisoned at Lima in 1810 as a patriot sympathizer, he returned in 1815 to Buenos Aires, where he held a number of government positions. A friend of Juan Manuel de Rosas, he was a Federalist, and in 1829 he was deported by the Unitarist regime of Juan Lavalle, returning the same year. However, he was a moderate who, as acting governor of Buenos Aires in 1834–1835, dismissed some of Rosas's strongest military supporters. He resigned the governorship in the aftermath of the assassination of Juan Facundo Quiroga, but continued to serve in the legislature and as special judge of those accused of the murder. In 1839, after his son was involved in a plot against Rosas, Maza was assassinated in Buenos Aires.

BIBLIOGRAPHY

John Lynch, *Argentine Dictator: Juan Manuel de Rosas 1829–1852* (1981), pp. 159–162, 171–173, 204.

Jacinto R. Yaben, *Biografías argentinas y sudamericanas,* vol. 3 (1939), pp. 721–723.

Additional Bibliography

Ŝbato, Hilda, and Alberto Rodolfo Lettieri. *La vida política en la Argentina del siglo XIX: Armas, votos y voces.* Buenos Aires: Fondo de Cultura Económica, 2003.

DAVID BUSHNELL

MAZATLÁN. Mazatlán, Mexican port in the state of Sinaloa with a population of 403,888 (2005). A simple landing after 1806, after independence it quickly became the country's leading port on the west coast. At the entrance to the Gulf of California, centrally located on the Pacific Coast, Mazatlán steadily expanded its commercial hinterland into the interior, becoming the commercial entrepôt for western Mexico. Foreign merchants quickly came to dominate the port's commerce. Their mercantile rivalry with Culiacán (with its satellite port of Altata) resulted in a forty-year struggle between the two cities for control of the state government and location of the state capital. Mazatlán's relative commercial position declined in the late nineteenth century, as railroads took away its competitive advantage in the interior and San Francisco, California, gradually absorbed the direct trade in Asian commerce. In 1873 the Porfirio Díaz–backed political clique led by Francisco Cañedo secured the permanent location of the capital in Culiacán but strove to promote the interests of both cities. The port's merchant-capitalists (by then a blend of native and foreign) began diversifying into other economic sectors (especially industry) and captured more and more of the wholesale trade generated by the growing economic activity within the state.

A railroad link with Guadalajara (1912) provided better access to the western interior of the country, but through the twentieth century, the rise of Mazatlán as a major tourist center has been a driving force in the city's continuing growth.

See also **Díaz, Porfirio.**

BIBLIOGRAPHY

John R. Southworth, *El Estado de Sinaloa—sus industrias, comerciales, mineras y manufacturas* (1898).

Stuart F. Voss, "Towns and Enterprise in Northwestern Mexico: A History of Urban Elites in Sonora and Sinaloa, 1830–1910" (Ph.D. diss., Harvard University, 1972), and *On the Periphery of Nineteenth-Century Mexico: Sonora and Sinaloa, 1810–1877* (1982).

Additional Bibliography

Carrillo Rojas, Arturo, and Guillermo Ibarra Escobar, eds. *Historia de Mazatlán.* Ayuntamiento de Mazatlán/UAS. Culiacán Rosales: Universidad Autónoma de Sinaloa, Facultad de Historia; Mazatlán: H. Ayuntamiento de Mazatlán, 1998.

Román Alarcón, Rigoberto Arturo. *Comerciantes extranjeros de Mazatlan, 1880–1910.* Culiacán: Colegio de Bachilleres del Estado de Sinaloa, 1998.

STUART F. VOSS

MAZOMBOS. Mazombos, descendants of settlers from Portugal. These white Brazilians of the colonial period were similar to the *criollos* of New Spain, but they were more likely to have nonwhite ancestors. Their high social position was linked to elite family membership, proprietorship of vast estates (*fazendas* or *engenhos*) with hundreds of slaves, political posts on the Senado da Câmara, appointment as high-ranking officers in the white militias, or service on the boards of elite white brotherhoods (*irmandades*) of the Catholic Church. In spite of their wealth, the Portuguese crown and the Reinóis limited their role in colonial society, which eventually led to demands for independence from the mother country.

See also **Senado da Câmara.**

BIBLIOGRAPHY

Vianna Moog, *Bandeirantes and Pioneers* (1964).

Additional Bibliography

Mello, Evaldo Cabral de. *A fronda dos mazombos: Nobres contra mascates, Pernambuco, 1666–1715.* São Paulo: Editora 34, 2003.

SHEILA L. HOOKER

MAZORCA. Juan Manuel de Rosas established a repressive dictatorship over the province of Buenos Aires, from 1829 until his overthrow by Justo José de Urquiza in 1852. In addition to censoring the press and exiling political enemies, Rosas established the *Mazorca,* the terrorist arm of his political support group, the Sociedad Popular Restauradora. The term (meaning an ear of corn) symbolized strength through unity. Members tortured and terrorized suspected unitarians, especially during the extremely violent month of October 1840. The terrorists made a slit throat and public display of decapitated heads their trademarks. The Mazorca's terror was so widespread that it became a frequent theme in literature, appearing as a central theme in novels by José Mármol and Juana Manuela Gorriti.

See also **Argentina, Movements: Federalists; Buenos Aires; Gorriti, Juana Manuela; Mármol, José Pedro Crisólogo; Rosas, Juan Manuel de.**

BIBLIOGRAPHY

John Lynch, *Argentine Dictator: Juan Manuel de Rosas, 1829–1852* (1981).

Additional Bibliography

Adelman, Jeremy. *Republic of Capital: Buenos Aires and the Legal Transformation of the Atlantic World.* Stanford, CA: Stanford University Press, 1999.

Gálvez, Manuel. *Vida de Juan Manuel de Rosas.* Buenos Aires: Claridad, 1997.

Gorriti, Juana Manuela. "The Mazorquero's Daughter." In *Dreams and Realities: Selected Fiction of Juana Manuela Gorriti.* Translated by Sergio Waisman. Edited by Francine Masiello. New York: Oxford University Press, 2003.

Mármol, José. *Amalia.* Translated by Helen R. Lane. Edited by Doris Sommer. Oxford and New York: Oxford University Press, 2001.

Ramos Mejía, José María. *Rosas y su tiempo.* Buenos Aires: Emecé, 2001.

RICHARD W. SLATTA

MBAYÁ INDIANS.

The Mbayá (variant: Mbyá) are one of the ethnic groups that make up the vast Tupí-Guaraní group, with whom they share many aspects of religion, language, culture, and social organization. They are seminomads inhabiting regions of Paraguay, Bolivia, Brazil, and Argentina. The central focus of their nomadic wandering is their search for the legendary "land without evil," where they can recover the state of perfection of the first earth and share the immortality of the gods. Their language has survived the pressure of the dominant cultures. They practice a polytheist religion, little of which has been put into writing, that sees acts of nature as part of daily life. There is no priestly caste because everyone is capable of approaching the divine. Nevertheless, there are certain mediators (*paí, caraí*) who are privileged due to their greater sensitivity. They have and continue to produce a large number of ritual texts, the knowledge of which is forbidden to white people. These manifestations form a marginal, underground current in the literary canon. The word is considered sacred; they believe its existence predates mankind, and is an element of cohesion in their social structure. Although Jesuit missions encouraged the Guaraní to mix racially, they otherwise brought about an absolute rejection of Catholicism, and the "other" religion became relegated to secrecy. Because the Mbayá never accepted contact with Roman Catholics, it was not until the publication of León Cadogan's *Ayvu-rapytá* (1959) that Mbayá culture was brought to light. In *El Canto resplandeciente* (1991), Carlos Martínez Gamba collected some Mbayá texts from Missiones, Argentina, from oral accounts by Lorenzo and Benito Ramos and Antonio Martínez.

See also **Indigenous Peoples.**

BIBLIOGRAPHY

Cadogan, León. *Ayvu-rapytá: Textos miticos de los Mbyá-Guarani.* São Paulo: Universidade de São Paulo, 1959.

Gamba, Carlos Martínez. *El Canto resplandeciente: Plegarias de los Mbyá-Guaraní de Misiones.* Buenos Aires: Ediciones del Sol, 1991.

MERCEDES GARCÍA SARAVÍ

MCLANE–OCAMPO TREATY (1859).

McLane–Ocampo Treaty (1859), an agreement between the United States and Mexico regarding transit rights. Negotiations were conducted during the War of the Reform (1858–1860) by Robert M. McLane (1815–1898), United States ambassador to the Liberal government of Benito Juárez in Veracruz, and Melchor Ocampo, Minister of Foreign Affairs. The treaty gave U.S. citizens transit rights across the Isthmus of Tehuantepec and also across northern Mexico from the Gulf of California to the vicinity of the lower Rio Grande, and allowed the U.S. government to send in military personnel to protect the route and U.S. citizens in transit. U.S. citizens would not be charged for transit at a rate different from that charged to Mexicans. In exchange for these transit rights, the United States was to pay Mexico $4 million, half upon ratification and the other half to be applied to the claims of citizens of the United States against the government of Mexico. The treaty was rejected by the U.S. Senate in 1860 and a subject of much controversy in Mexico, where some feared the loss of significant territory to the United States. Had it been ratified, it would have given the United States a large measure of control over areas of Mexico that were considered to be crucial to the passage of persons and goods to and from California.

See also **Ocampo, Melchor; United States-Latin American Relations.**

BIBLIOGRAPHY

Edward J. Berbusse, "The Origins of the McLane-Ocampo Treaty of 1859," in *The Americas* 14 (1958): 223–243.

Agustín Cue Cánovas, *El tratado McLane-Ocampo: Juárez, los Estados Unidos y Europa*, 2d ed. (1959).

Salvador Ysunza Uzeta, *Juárez y el tratado McLane-Ocampo* (1964).

CHARLES R. BERRY

MEAT INDUSTRY. The meat industry processes and transforms various animals for marketing. During the eighteenth century, meat preparation was intended for local markets. The development of the meat industry came about with the preparation of dried beef jerky for export. In the next two centuries, Argentina and Uruguay and other countries with adequate pasturage made meat their principal export. The salting of meat continued until the late nineteenth century, when Brazil, the Antilles and other consumer markets were lost due to the fall of meat consumption among the slaves after the abolition of slavery in those countries.

As jerky production began to decline in the late nineteenth century, merchants began preparing meat extract, and German chemist Justus Von Liebig installed factories in Uruguay and Argentina. Changes in cattle raising and the new technology of refrigeration in the late nineteenth century, which permitted long-distance transportation and created a growing demand in countries such as Great Britain, drove the development of the industry, and frozen and refrigerated beef became vital to the economies of Argentina and Uruguay, and, to a lesser extent of Brazil's.

The meat industry went through several stages in its development. The first stage, from 1870 to 1930, was an era of growth, during which the industry expanded through the use of refrigeration technologies. Initially, tallow chandleries and salteries were reconditioned to provide refrigerated meat, but soon British and U.S. capital made its initial investments, and subsequently these nations exercised an oligopolistic control of prices and trade and together monopolized the ship holds needed for transportation. The best-known establishments were Anglo, Swift, and Armour.

The second stage, from 1930 to 1958, was a period of stagnation. The industry languished as a result of the Great Depression, which led to a reordering of foreign trade. The Imperial Economic Conference of Ottawa (1932–1938) imposed new conditions on the meat trade. It is true that there were periods in which production revived, in particular during World War II with the preparation of products for military consumption and through agreements reached between meat companies and governments, with the aim of holding up the level of exports. In addition, there were some bilateral contracts such as the Roca-Runciman Treaty (1933), signed between Argentina and Great Britain, aiming at maintaining meat exports by awarding companies of British capital with taxing benefits. The treaty, and others like it, was periodically renewed without substantial changes. Nevertheless, during this second stage exports declined for the Río de la Plata meat industry.

The third stage, beginning in 1958 and ending in 1975, was a period of changes in the structure of the industry and of a slight growth of production. These changes included a diversification of industrialized products such as processed meats and prepared meals, the emergence of supermarkets, and new consumption trends. Other changes were the aging and obsolescence of plants, which required new investments of capital; a trend away from concentration in the industry, and, therefore, the declining importance of the traditional oligopoly; and a re-concentration in national markets and specific products. Organizations such as the World Bank and the Inter-American Development Bank became involved in the industry, providing not only credit but also information and recommendations that stimulated sector activities.

The fourth stage, which began in 1975 and continues into the early twenty-first century, has been a period of industrial heterogeneity and specialization in production and marketing, with differences developing between plants producing for export and those producing for domestic consumption in terms of installations and operating conditions. Some integrated, modern establishments have diversified their production and now combine exporting with production for the domestic market.

See also **Inter-American Development Bank (IDB); Livestock; Roca-Runciman Pact (1933); World Bank.**

BIBLIOGRAPHY

Bergquist, Charles. *Los trabajadores en la historia latinoamericana. Estudios comparativos de Chile, Argentina, Venezuela y Colombia*. Colombia: Siglo XXI, 1988.

Buxedas, Martin. *La industria figorífica en el Río de La Plata 1959-1977*. Buenos Aires: Clacso, 1983.

Lobato, Mirta Zaida. *La vida en las fábricas: Trabajo, protesta y política en una comunidad obrera, Berisso (1904-1970)*. Buenos Aires: Prometeo libros, 2001.

Smith, Peter H. *Carne y política en la Argentina*. Buenos Aires: Paidós, 1985.

MIRTA ZAIDA LOBATO

MEDEIROS DA FONSECA, ROMY MARTINS

MEDEIROS DA FONSECA, ROMY MARTINS (1921–). Romy Martins Medeiros da Fonseca (*b.* 30 June 1921), Brazilian women's rights activist. Daughter of José Gomes Leite da Fonseca and Climéria da Fonseca Martins, Medeiros da Fonseca was born in Rio de Janeiro. She married the jurist and law professor Arnoldo Medeiros da Fonseca, with whom she had two children. A graduate of the law school at the Federal University of Rio de Janeiro, Romy Medeiros served as counselor to the State Council on the Rights of Women and has been a leader of the Brazilian Lawyers' Organization (OAB). In addition, she has served as president of the National Council of Brazilian Women (CNMB), an organization founded by Jeronyma Mesquita, a pioneer for women's suffrage.

Medeiros was a coauthor of the Married Woman's Statute, a law that defined social and family rights and supplanted civil code stipulations, which considered married women as "relatively incompetent." In 1972, she organized the First Congress of Women, in which national and international participants debated women's roles in political development. She has served as Brazil's delegate to the Inter-American Commission for Women at the Organization of American States and has been a formal and informal presidential adviser on women's issues since 1947. As a stalwart defender of women's rights, Romy Medeiros has long promoted women's integration into the country's military services and was instrumental in the passage of Brazil's divorce statute. She also published articles and books on women's issues, including *Justiça social e aborto* (1982) and *A Condiçao femenina* (1988.)

See also **Brazil, Liberal Movements; Feminism and Feminist Organizations.**

BIBLIOGRAPHY

Additional Bibliography

Duquette, Michel. *Collective Action and Radicalism in Brazil: Women, Urban Housing, and Rural Movements.* Toronto, Canada: University of Toronto Press, 2005.

Hahner, Judith Edith. *Emancipating the Female Sex: The Struggle for Women's Rights in Brazil, 1850–1940.* Durham, NC: Duke University Press, 1990.

Muraro, Rose Marie. *Memórias das mulheres do exílio: Obra colectiva.* Rio de Janeiro, Brazil: Paz e Terra, 1980.

IÈDA SIQUEIRA WIARDA

MEDELLÍN

MEDELLÍN. Medellín is the second largest city in Colombia and capital of the department of Antioquia. In 2005 the city's population was 2,223,660. Medellín is located in the fertile valley of Aburrá in the Central Cordillera at an altitude of 5,000 feet. The valley already had some 3,000 inhabitants when the city was formally established in 1675. By 1787 nearly 17,000 people lived in the territory under the city's jurisdiction.

After independence, Medellín became the seat of government for the state (later department) of Antioquia. The continued importance of gold mining in Antioquia coupled with the subsequent rise of coffee production allowed Medellín to emerge as Colombia's industrial center in the early twentieth century. Even earlier, local foundries were producing machinery for the processing of coffee and other agricultural products. After 1900 Medellín and its environs were home to several modern textile mills, among the most notable of which were the Compañía Antioqueña de Tejidos (1902) and the Compañía Colombiana de Tejidos (1907). Known as Coltejer, the latter became the largest textile enterprise in Colombia, employing 8,500 people in four plants in and around Medellín by 1967. The cut-flower industry around Medellín has grown in recent years.

In the late twentieth century, Medellín gained notoriety as the headquarters of a violent narcotics cartel. Conflict among drug traffickers and between them and the authorities cost thousands of lives as the number of violent deaths in Medellín rose from 730 in 1980 to 5,300 in 1990, with 4,000 still in 2000. Colombian and international efforts led to the dissolution of the Medellín cartel. Although drug traffickers remain active, *paisas* (residents) have witnessed a reduction in criminal and political violence through governmental measures. In 1995 the city unveiled an elevated metro system.

See also **Coffee Industry; Drugs and Drug Trade.**

BIBLIOGRAPHY

Ann Twinam, "Enterprise and Elites in Eighteenth-Century Medellín," in *Hispanic American Historical Review* 59 (1979): 444–475.

Jorge Restrepo Uribe and Luz Posada De Grieff, *Medellín: Su origen, progreso y desarrollo* (1981).

Alma Guillermoprieto, "Letter from Medellín," in *The New Yorker,* 22 April 1991, pp. 96–109.

Additional Bibliography

Botero Herrera, Fernando. *Estado, nación y provincia de Antioquia: Guerras civiles e invención de la región 1829–1863.* Medellín, Colombia: Hombre Nuevo Editores, 2003.

Farnsworth-Alvear, Ann. *Dulcinea in the Factory: Myths, Morals, Men, and Women in Colombia's Industrial Experiment, 1905–1960.* Durham, NC: Duke University Press, 2000.

Jaramillo Mejía, William; Luis Enrique Rodríguez Baquero; Andrés Roncancio Parra; and Jorge Tomás Uribe Angel. *Nobles, blancos y mestizos en la villa de Nuestra Señora de la Candelaria de Medellín: Probanzas de nobleza, familia y mestizaje del cabildo, 1674–1812.* Santafé de Bogotá, Colombia: Instituto Colombiano de Cultura Hispánica, 1998.

Londoño-Vega, Patricia. *Religion, Culture, and Society in Colombia: Medellín and Antioquia, 1850–1930.* New York: Oxford University Press, 2002.

Riaño Alcalá, Pilar. *Dwellers of Memory: Youth and Violence in Medellín, Colombia.* New Brunswick, NJ: Transaction Publishers, 2006.

Roldán, Mary. *Blood and Fire: La Violencia in Antioquia, Colombia, 1946–1953.* Durham, NC: Duke University Press, 2003.

Ruiz Gómez, Darío. *Medellín: Diario de ciudad.* Medellín, Colombia: Editorial Universidad Pontificia Bolivariana, 2005.

HELEN DELPAR

MEDELLÍN CARTEL. *See* **Drugs and Drug Trade.**

MEDIA ANATA.

Media Anata, an assessment of a half-year's salary imposed on officials taking posts in the Spanish Indies. In a royal order in council (*cédula*) of 21 July 1625, establishing the impost, Philip IV set the assessment initially at one month's salary (*mesada*) but in 1632 raised it to a half-year's stipend, where it remained for the rest of the colonial epoch. As the colonial epoch wore on, revenues from this source began dropping, largely because of the increasing number of exemptions from the assessment, including those for military officers and employees of the tobacco and powder factories. In the 1790s *medias anatas* produced revenues in Mexico of approximately 40,000–50,000 pesos annually, in Peru 8,000–15,000 pesos.

See also **Colonialism; New Spain, Colonization of the Northern Frontier.**

BIBLIOGRAPHY

Recopilación de leyes de los Reynos de las Indias, 4 vols. (1681; repr. 1973), libro VIII, título XIX.

DAILY LIFE

Vegetables for sale, Chichicastenango, Guatemala. Twice a week, vendors come from miles around to sell their wares at this market town in the highlands of Guatemala. © John D. Norman/Corbis

High school students walk through a city park, Santiago, Chile. Schoolchildren in Latin America are highly visible due to their school uniforms. The cost of obtaining a uniform can be a barrier to access to education for families from lower socioeconomic classes. RICHARD NOWITZ/NATIONAL GEOGRAPHIC IMAGE COLLECTION

RIGHT: At school, Boye, Mexico, 2006. Children listen as their teacher gives a lesson at newly built school in a small Mexican town. Money sent back by local residents working north of the border paid for the school and other improvements in town. AP IMAGES

BELOW: An informal game of fútbol (soccer) in a Rio de Janeiro shantytown. Soccer, a popular sport throughout Latin America, provides a diversion for many and a means of escape from crushing poverty for a lucky few. © JOAO LUIZ BULCAO/CORBIS/CORBIS

Unloading the daily catch, Rio Negro, Brazil. Work, rather than school, comprises the typical day for many of the children of Latin America's poorer classes. © Ronald C. Modra/Sports Imagery/Getty Images

TOP: **Bringing charcoal by donkey, Jeremie, Haiti, 2003.** In a country where electricity, kerosene, and gas are in short supply, wood charcoal serves as Haiti's primary source of fuel for cooking and other tasks. The practice of burning trees to create charcoal has devastated what very little remains of Haiti's forests. THONY BELIZAIRE/AFP/GETTY IMAGES

MIDDLE: **Interior of a bar and grocery store on the island of Grenada.** Small general stores such as this are a familiar sight in even the smallest communities and out-of-the-way places throughout the Caribbean. © BOB SACHA/CORBIS

BOTTOM: **A shepherd with his flock of alpaca in the highlands of the Andes mountains, Ucha Ucha, Bolivia.** AP IMAGES

ABOVE: Senior citizens' club having lunch in La Trinité, Martinique. © Owen Franken/Corbis

LEFT: Playing dominoes, Havana, Cuba. Dominoes, traditionally played by older men, is the national game of Cuba. © Alejandro Ernesto/epa/Corbis

RIGHT: A barber's stall in an outdoor market, Chiapas, Mexico. Many different vendors throughout Latin America set up stalls in outdoor markets, selling goods and services. GINA MARTIN/NATIONAL GEOGRAPHIC IMAGE COLLECTION

BELOW: Vina del Mar beach, Chile, 2006. Tourists and local people pack Latin American beaches during the high season from December to the Easter holiday. © KEREN SU/CORBIS

ABOVE: Repairing a car, Havana, Cuba, 1999. Old American cars are ubiquitous in Cuba, where a great deal of ingenuity and creative repair is required to keep these vehicles on the road. American manufacturers stopped shipping cars to Cuba when a trade embargo was imposed after the 1959 revolution. AP IMAGES

LEFT: Train station at rush hour, São Paulo, Brazil, 2006. Thousands of commuters vie for space in South America's biggest city, the third largest metropolis in the world. © PAULO WHITAKER/REUTERS/CORBIS

BELOW: A man reads a newspaper on a city bus in Cuernavaca, Mexico. Traveling by bus is one of the most common and efficient methods of transportation in Mexico, both for long trips and everyday commuting. GINA MARTIN/NATIONAL GEOGRAPHIC IMAGE COLLECTION

Joaquín Maniau, *Compendio de la historia de la Real Hacienda de Nueva España* (1914).

Additional Bibliography

Jáuregui, Luis. *The American Finances of the Spanish Empire: Royal Income and Expenditures in Colonial Mexico, Peru, and Bolivia, 1680–1809.* Albuquerque: University of New Mexico Press, 1998.

Klein, Herbert S. *La real hacienda de Nueva España: Su administración en la época de los intendentes, 1786–1821.* México: Universidad Nacional Autónoma de México, Facultad de Economía, 1999.

JOHN JAY TEPASKE

MÉDICI, EMÍLIO GARRASTAZÚ

(1905–1985). Emílio Garrastazú Médici (*b.* 4 December 1905; *d.* 9 October 1985), military leader and president of Brazil (1969–1974). Médici was born in Bagé, Brazil, a village in southern cattle country close to the Uruguayan border. He entered a military school in Pôrto Alegre when he was twelve and enlisted in the cavalry nine years later. In 1934 he joined the Command and General Staff School in Rio de Janeiro. He was serving as an intelligence officer in Rio Grande do Sul in 1953 when Artur da Costa e Silva, commander of the Third Military Region, named him chief of staff. Eight years later Médici was promoted to brigadier general and appointed commander of the National Military Academy in Agulhas Negras.

Médici was the military attaché at the Brazilian Embassy in Washington, D.C., at the time of the military coup against President João Goulart in 1964. He left the army in 1966 to become civilian head of the National Intelligence Service, returning three years later to take command of the Third Army.

When President Costa e Silva suffered a stroke in August 1969, a three-man junta composed of the military service chiefs assumed control of the government. They bypassed the successor designated in the Constitution of 1967, Vice President Pedro Aleixo, who was perceived as being too much of a politician. After consulting 100 generals, the 10 generals of the Army High Command settled on Médici as the next president. He was then nominated by the government party, the National Renovating Alliance (ARENA), elected by the Brazilian National Congress, and sworn in 30 October 1969.

Médici promised a move toward democracy but instead practiced political repression. He permitted federal elections to Congress in November 1970, but allowed only one opposition party, the Brazilian Democratic Movement (MDB), to compete against ARENA. Before the election, the military carried out a mass crackdown of dissidents and arrested about 5,000 people. According to the Brazilian Amnesty Committee, 170 political opponents were killed during Médici's presidency.

The military considered suppression of dissent necessary for maintaining the stability needed to achieve economic growth. Médici's administration also helped to sustain the "economic miracle" that began in 1968. It attracted foreign loans for large-scale economic development projects and spent heavily on roads, railways, and utility projects—the infrastructure for heavy industry. Government-owned enterprises dominated steel, mining, and petrochemical industries. In 1974, 74 percent of the combined assets of the country's 100 largest firms belonged to state enterprises; state banks accounted for 56 percent of total deposits and 65 percent of loans to the private sector. This created further inequality of wealth among people and regions. Médici attempted to correct this imbalance in 1970 with construction of the Transamazon Highway, which was intended to encourage immigration and development in northeastern Brazil, the nation's poorest region. High government spending, along with the infusion of foreign capital, boosted economic growth rates to between 7 percent and 11 percent during Médici's years in office, but 80 percent of the population remained mired in poverty. Médici died in Rio de Janeiro.

See also **Brazil, Economic Miracle (1968–1974).**

BIBLIOGRAPHY

Werner Baer, *The Brazilian Economy: Growth and Development* (1989).

Thomas E. Skidmore, *The Politics of Military Rule in Brazil, 1964–85* (1988).

Additional Bibliography

Mattos, Marco Aurélio Vannucchi Leme de, and Walter Cruz Swensson. *Contra os inimigos da ordem: a repressão política do regime militar brasileiro (1964–1985).* Rio de Janeiro: DP & A Editora, 2003.

Rezende, Maria José de. *A ditadura militar no Brasil: repressão e pretensão de legitimidade, 1964–1984.* Londrina, Brazil: Editora UEL, 2001.

Souto, Cíntia Vieira. *A diplomacia do interesse nacional: a política externa do Governo Médici.* Porto Alegre, Brazil: Editora da UFRGS, 2003.

ROSS WILKINSON

MEDICINAL PLANTS. Upon their arrival in what is today Latin America, European conquerors found an impressive array of healing plants used by the natives. Accompanying the conquerors were missionaries and occasionally a physician, and it is from their chronicles that we know about medicinal plants of pre-Conquest America. Among them, the accounts of Father Bernardino de Sahagún and especially those of the physician Francisco Hernández in Mexico describe a large number of medicinal plants used by the peoples of Mesoamerica in the sixteenth century. These accounts, however, cover only a fraction of the plants actually used, their applications, and mode of use, since medicine men were understandably reluctant to reveal the secrets of their healing plants to the invaders.

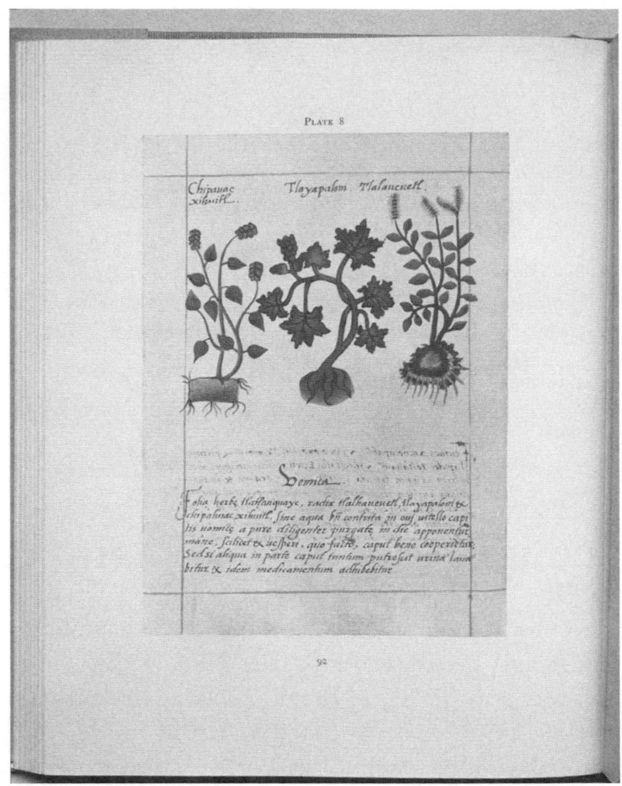

Herbal remedies. A page from the Badianus Manuscript (1552), a compendium of medicinal plants used by the Aztecs at the time of the Conquest. MARK THIESSEN/NATIONAL GEOGRAPHIC IMAGE COLLECTION

Medicine men and women were involved not only in healing individual patients but also in maintaining the integrity of their community. Their highly sophisticated knowledge of healing plants came from years of apprenticeship in well-established traditions and a lifetime of practice that included familiarity with healing plants, their habitats, their effects and interactions; their remedies almost always used plants in combination. During some healing rituals, medicine men consumed hallucinogenic plants. Considered magical and the quintessential medicine, hallucinogenic plants were used as guides to find the causes of challenging illnesses and to foresee events. Christian missionaries labeled these practices diabolic, and medicine men and women were ruthlessly persecuted.

With the social disintegration of the conquered peoples in the fifteenth and sixteenth centuries and the severe disruption of healing traditions, untold knowledge of medicinal plants was lost. However, because of their highly effective cures, native herbalists were eagerly sought after during colonial and postcolonial times. After the Conquest, missionaries continued using and recording the properties of medicinal plants; the religious orders that followed profited from their trade. Nonetheless, most plants considered magical or sacred by the natives were banished as instruments of the devil. Native classifications of plants such as "male" or "female" were replaced by concepts such as "hot" or "cold," which were then prevalent in European medicine. Healing plants of European, African, and Asian origin were added to the colonial pharmacopoeia; some were readily adopted by native herbalists.

Plants gained or lost favor according to economic and social circumstances. A few examples illustrate this point. In 1569, the writings of the Spanish physician Nicolás Monardes popularized many American medicinal plants in Europe; of these plants, balsam of Peru, the resin from the tree *Myroxylon balsamum,* became a worldwide treatment for wounds, infections, and skin ailments and was used as incense by the Roman Catholic Church (for both ritual and fumigatory purposes). The Pacific coast of El Salvador was the most important producer. Since the advent of antibiotics in the 1930s, the economic importance of this plant diminished considerably.

A different fate befell the forest vines of special species of *Chondrodendron,* used as traditional ingredients of curare, the powerful arrow poison from the Amazon that produces muscle paralysis. One of the active chemicals of curare, tubocuraine, is medically used to reduce convulsions caused by tetanus or electric-shock therapy and as a temporary muscle relaxant in some surgeries and in neuropathological spasms. Similarly, in Mesoamerica, the tubers of wild yams (certain species of *Dioscorea*), used since pre-Columbian times by women to control menstruation and for their soaplike suds, never received wide notice by colonial Europeans. Yet today, thanks to a discovery by a Japanese chemist in 1938, they are very important sources of steroidal sapogenins, from which pharmaceutical companies in Mexico synthesize corticosterol-based anti-inflammatories, androgens, estrogens, progesterones, and oral contraceptives. On the other hand, the barks of several species of Cinchona trees from the northern Andes, for which there is no evidence of use before the seventeenth century, became extremely important antimalarial drugs from then onward, thereby making European colonial expansion to the world's tropics more feasible. They are today the source of quinine and its derivatives and are also used to treat hemorrhoids, varicose veins, and cardiac arrhythmias.

Mention must be made of two "medicine" plants held in the highest esteem during pre-Columbian times: the first, coca (several species of *Erythroxylon*), cultivated from Bolivia and Brazil to Nicaragua, was almost universally considered a sacred plant. Restricted to men and, among the Incas, to athletes, message runners, and the nobility, the partaking of the leaves for chewing was a highly ritualized social occasion. Its effect was mostly to suppress tiredness and hunger. Some missionaries disapproved of coca, and in the early 1600s the Inquisition bitterly condemned its use. By that time, however, several religious orders were profiting handsomely from coca production and trade, and their members frequently chewed the leaves. After silver was discovered in Peru in the mid-1500s, enormous quantities of coca were brought in to keep the Indian forced laborers in the mines from feeling tired or hungry. Coca became an important commercial crop in colonial Peru and Ecuador. Cocaine, one of the many alkaloids present in coca, was first isolated in 1858; today, several compounds derived from cocaine are important anesthetics. Cocaine is also used as a recreational drug because of its euphoric and stimulant properties. Unfortunately, cocaine consumption is erroneously confused with traditional coca chewing, a very different activity both socially and physiologically. Recreational cocaine is today an illegal drug; its trade, fueled by a seemingly insatiable demand in the United States and in Europe, has brought grave social and political disruptions to Colombia, Peru, Bolivia, and other Latin American countries.

The second plant, tobacco (*Nicotiana tabacum*), was considered a powerful protector of medicine men and warriors, who drank infusions of the leaves, applied them to their bodies, or inhaled smoke from burned leaves. Tobacco was a common component of the hallucinogenic mixtures prepared by medicine men for diagnosis and divination. It also had more mundane uses: to relieve headaches, to cure skin infections, to heal wounds, to kill and repel insects. With the social disruption following the Spanish Conquest, tobacco use was no longer restricted, and the conquered men and women took to inhaling its smoke to soothe their distress. Christian priests at first disapproved of this practice, then took it up themselves; African slaves readily followed.

Tobacco was introduced to Europe in the sixteenth century as a sedative, especially for painful illnesses, but soon its narcotic properties and the novelty of "drinking smoke" or snuffing the powdered leaves turned it into a recreational substance favored by European intellectuals and the colonial elites. Indians, however, continued using tobacco mostly as a medicine; their gardens invariably included a few tobacco plants. Because of the demand, tobacco production was rapidly commercialized, and its preparation and use were standardized. By the seventeenth century, some areas of the colonies, especially in Cuba, Trinidad, and Venezuela, had been selected for production. In those areas, "industrial" cultivation was associated with large-scale hacienda systems and African slave labor;

elsewhere, tobacco growing was commonly in the hands of small landholders, poor peasants, and runaway slaves. Eventually, small tobacco growers became important in the popular uprisings that led to independence from Spain. Today, the medicinal properties of tobacco are virtually unknown, and its use is mostly as a legal recreational narcotic.

Advances in chemistry during the late eighteenth century and through the nineteenth century led to the extraction and purification of physiologically active compounds from medicinal plants, allowing medical doctors better control of the effects of their prescriptions and permitting the establishment of a pharmaceutical industry. European countries, interested in learning about plant resources that might yield economic benefits, sponsored systematic searches of the American flora through scientific expeditions. In the late eighteenth century, the explorations of Alexander von Humboldt and José Celestino Mutis enriched knowledge about medicinal plants in the upper Amazon basin and northern Andes, as did Richard Spruce's reports in the nineteenth century. In the twentieth century, scientific explorations intensified, involving universities and government agencies in various countries and resulting in improved botanical and pharmacological information.

In the 1930s, with the advent of antibiotics—called "miracle drugs"—the prestige of skillfully marketed synthetic drugs started to eclipse the importance of medicinal plants, and for several decades the latter were considered less reliable agents of healing; since the 1970s, however, pathogens resistant to antibiotics have evolved, and evidence has accumulated of toxic secondary effects and improper use of pharmaceutical products that cause severe health problems. For these reasons, and also because of the prohibitive cost of synthetic drugs to large segments of the Latin American population, some governments have started programs studying their medicinal herbal lore, especially in countries where large Indian populations have kept the herbal tradition alive. Mexico, for example, has produced several government publications on its medicinal flora, and Bolivia has developed successful programs integrating the biomedical traditions of Western medicine with ethnomedical systems such as those of the highly reputed Kallawaya herbal healers.

Pharmaceutical companies continue to send scientific expeditions to Latin America in search of pharmacologically useful plants. A major debate today concerns whether these European and U.S. companies can have exclusive patent rights—and access to potentially high profits—for synthetic drugs developed from plants found on Latin American soils.

See also **Drugs and Drug Trade; Medicine: Colonial Spanish America; Medicine: The Modern Era.**

BIBLIOGRAPHY

An outstanding source of historical material about Latin American medicinal plants is Victor Manuel Patiño, *Plantas cultivadas y animales domésticos en América equinoccial*. Vol. 3, *Fibras, medicinas, misceláneas* (1967). Excellent information about the best-known medicinal plants, including pharmacological and historical aspects of some Latin American natives, is given in Julia Morton, *Major Medicinal Plants: Botany, Culture, and Uses* (1977). Regional reference material can be found for Mexico in Maximino Martínez, *Las plantas medicinales de México* (1990); and Xavier Lozoya L., *Flora medicinal de México* (1982). For the Amazon forest, see Richard Schultes, *The Healing Forest: Medicinal and Toxic Plants of the Northwest Amazonia* (1990); for Colombia, consult Hernando García Barriga, *Flora medicinal de Colombia* (1974); for the mid-Andean region, especially Bolivia, see Joseph Bastien, *Healers of the Andes: Kallawaya Herbalists and Their Medicinal Plants* (1987). On specific plants, *Cultural Survival Report* 23, "Coca and Cocaine—Effects on People and Policy in Latin America" (1985).

Additional Bibliography

Campos-Costero, Isaac. "Marijuana, Madness, and Modernity in Global Mexico, 1545–1920." Ph.D. diss., Harvard University, 2006.

Ortiz Echániz, Silvia. *La medicina tradicional en el norte de México*. México, D.F.: Instituto Nacional de Antropología e Historia, 1999.

Montañez Anaya, Alfred. *Utilización de plantas medicinales en el chamanismo como cultura amazónica*. Florencia, Caquetá [Colombia]: Fondo Mixto para la Promoción de la Cultura y las Artes, 1997.

Mors, Walter B., Carlos Toledo Rizzini, Nuno Alvares Pereira, and Robert A. DeFilipps. *Medicinal Plants of Brazil*. Medicinal Plants of the World, 6. Algonac, MI: Reference Publications, 2000.

Stasi, Luiz Claudio di, and Clélia Akiko Hiruma-Lima. *Plantas medicinais na Amazônia e na Mata Atlântica*. São Paulo, SP: Editora UNESP, 2002.

CARMENZA OLAYA FONSTAD

MEDICINE

This entry includes the following articles:
COLONIAL SPANISH AMERICA
THE MODERN ERA

COLONIAL SPANISH AMERICA

Spanish-American medicine in the colonial period began with entirely new crises in public health. Few professional medical services existed in Europe at the time, and the scientific knowledge to cure diseases such as smallpox did not exist. Though at times colonial authorities attempted to meet the shortage of trained practitioners by imposing rigorous standards, reality demanded a more practical approach. Indeed, the New World context shaped medicine as exchanges between diverse cultures about disease and treatments took place.

During the first generation of colonization, tens of thousands of Native Americans succumbed to European diseases—smallpox, typhoid, measles, and pneumonia. (Spanish commentators were struck more by the magnitude of the epidemics than by specific symptoms.) Although during the sixteenth century, Native Americans suffered the greatest mortality, periodic epidemics plagued all levels of society throughout the colonial period. Donald Cooper identified at least five major epidemics (most likely smallpox or typhoid) in eighteenth-century Mexico City alone, which cumulatively cost at least 50,000 lives.

The first European physician arrived in the New World with Columbus on his second voyage (1493), a colonizing expedition. Few followed, however; by 1545 there was, for example, only one licensed physician in Mexico City. Self-proclaimed practitioners, or *curanderos,* indigenous, African, and European, took up the slack. Though colonial administrators came from a legal tradition concerned with assuring quality control over the practice of medicine, they faced the stark reality with pragmatism.

The Royal Protomedicato. Since the reign of Ferdinand and Isabella, the Spanish monarchy had assumed responsibility for public health. Its concept of public health, centered on safeguarding the public from unlicensed and unqualified practitioners. Regulation of the medical profession fell to the Royal Protomedicato, a board of physicians appointed by the crown. The Protomedicato licensed all medical practitioners, punished quacks, and provided medical advice to the crown. Hence the corporate society that was late-medieval Spain entrusted the regulation of the practice of medicine to the elite of the medical profession itself. At best this elite endeavored to impose high standards, standards that were generally unrealistic for conditions in the New World. At worst, they sought only to preserve the prerequisites for the minority of practitioners who possessed licenses.

The practice of western medicine in Spanish America, such as it was, remained restricted to the larger towns and to the European population. Municipal governments competed for practitioners who could serve in public institutions, care for the officials themselves, and assume nominal responsibility for public-health standards and the health needs of the poor. Desperate to secure the services of any practitioner, authorities readily overlooked the prohibitions against "foreigners" practicing medicine, and often winked at the dubious credentials applicants presented. The vast majority of the population was served by unlicensed practitioners, some probably as effective as those with proper credentials; others no doubt dangerous quacks. Necessity required that any practitioner be tolerated as long as he maintained a relatively low profile and did not openly resort to magic that would offend the clergy.

Colonial authorities were convinced that the shortage of qualified practitioners was the single most important threat to public health. The solution, they believed, lay in re-creating in America the medical institutions of Spain. Public hospitals, supported by endowments from local authorities or religious orders, were established in major cities. Many were designated for the treatment of the poor; some, such as the Royal Indian Hospital in Mexico City, founded in 1553, were created exclusively for Native Americans. (As in Europe, hospitals were usually a last resort for those who had no one to care for them.)

Universities in Mexico City and Lima had faculties of medicine with curricula identical to those in Spain. Protomedicatos were established in Mexico City and Lima during the seventeenth century. Unlike the protocol in Spain, members of the university faculties served on the Protomedicato, thereby eliminating the traditional Spanish distinction between the educating and licensing functions that had been designed as a check on both. There were simply too few qualified physicians to go around.

Academic Medicine. In both Spain and Spanish America the medical profession was divided into countless categories of practice, each with it own restrictions, privileges, and prerequisites. Physicians (*médicos*), the elite of the profession, possessed a university degree. They had a monopoly on positions in the university, the Protomedicato, and many government posts, all of which carried with them a guaranteed salary as well as the opportunity for private practice. Ironically, the "internal medicine" on which they had a legal monopoly was probably the least effective branch of medicine in practice. Academic medicine, which distinguished the physician from other practitioners and which was the basis of his exalted status, remained deeply rooted in the Aristotelian tradition until the late eighteenth century. "Internal medicine" was an intellectual endeavor, not an empirical one. This medieval tradition looked at the body as a holistic organism; disease resulted from an imbalance of bodily humors. As a result, education consisted of learning the general principles of nature recorded by Hippocrates in the fourth century BCE Galen in the second century CE, and Avicenna (Ibn Šiña) in the eleventh century. Although the formal curriculum remained unchanged throughout the colonial period, academic medicine incorporated contemporary ideas from Europe into its traditional structure. John Tate Lanning's studies have demonstrated that graduates in the late eighteenth century were familiar with such contemporary authors as Hermann Boerhaave and Johannes de Gorter.

In both Spain and Spanish America, medicine had little status within the university. Its faculty was poorly paid, its chairs frequently went unfilled, and few students were attracted to the profession. During the seventeenth century, for example, the University of Mexico granted an average of only three bachelor's degrees in medicine per year. In Guatemala, less a part of the colonial mainstream, only one bachelor's degree was awarded every four years. Medical faculties were hard pressed even to supply enough physicians to educate and administer the profession; law and the church offered far more lucrative opportunities. Indeed, only the universities in Mexico City and Lima were authorized to fill three chairs of medicine, the minimum required by Spanish statutes.

Nonacademic Medicine. Nonacademic medicine represented another culture, a culture of experience and practice, not theory. These practitioners—surgeons, bonesetters, bleeders, midwives—learned their craft as informal apprentices, often on a trial-and-error basis. If licensed, they had also passed an examination before the Protomedicato. They provided the untidy everyday procedures of practical medicine like minor surgery. Yet the empirical nature of their training and everyday practice led some to acquire a considerable reputation for the effectiveness of their prescriptions or the swiftness of their surgery. Others, no doubt, had little knowledge of what they were doing. As a rule, the lower the status of the medical practice, the weaker the efforts to enforce the legal prerequisites for practice. Midwives, the only practice open to women, were seldom subjected to any examination; as in Spain, the profession tended to pass from one generation to the next. While "nonacademic" and professional medicine have been viewed separately and in opposition, recent scholarship often considers them interactively.

In addition to demonstrating competence, applicants for a license—as well as young men seeking to enter a university—had to prove their *limpieza de sangre* (purity of blood). *Limpieza de sangre,* that is, proof of legitimacy and the absence of any conviction by the Inquisition for three generations, had become common in sixteenth-century Spain as an artifice to exclude non-Christians from universities and the professions.

For the first 200 years of colonization these restrictions, like those prohibiting the practice of foreigners, were generally ignored. Toward the end of the seventeenth century, growing competition for affluent clients in the major cities led to a number of lawsuits designed to force compliance with *limpieza de sangre* standards on both the university and the Protomedicato. In addition, "legitimate" practitioners used their influence to prohibit all blacks and mulattoes from entering a university—the first time *limpieza de sangre* was used for purely racial objectives. The controversy over qualifications was apparently also related to the dual culture of medical practice. Physicians, who controlled the enforcement apparatus, both envied the success and scorned the methods of certain mulatto surgeons. Their efforts to restrict the practice of medicine to whites, preferably physicians, were largely unsuccessful.

Reforms in Medical Education. The Enlightenment precipitated significant reforms in medical education in both Spain and Spanish America. On both continents the pattern was similar: the initiative came from individual reformers, well-read and optimistic, who sought the backing of the crown to implement their ideas. In Spain the crown supported new royal colleges because they curbed the traditional autonomy of universities and the Protomedicato. In America, where the medical elite was smaller, reformers were less inclined to meet opposition from entrenched local medical authorities but faced the more serious obstacle of insufficient funds and lack of interest of colonial authorities.

At issue was the purely theoretical nature of academic medicine and the purely practical nature of apprenticeships. Reformers argued the need for hands-on experience in anatomy and clinical studies on the one hand and the need for academic training for surgeons on the other. Chairs of anatomy were established in universities, and public anatomical demonstrations were held in hospitals. Independent colleges of surgery opened in Mexico City (1770) and Lima (1811). Gradually the distinction between pure theory (physicians) and pure practice (surgeons) broke down.

Progressive men of medicine in America were in frequent contact with their colleagues in Spain; indeed, reform in America occurred simultaneously with reform in Spain. Although such prominent physicians as Narciso Esparragosa y Gallardo (a Guatemalan who developed elastic forceps) and José Hipólito Unánue (a Peruvian who established clinical lectures) were in the minority, the best of Spanish-American medicine was in no way behind that of Europe. Inoculation against smallpox was introduced in 1780, and vaccination became fairly widespread after 1800.

Spain addressed many social problems by transferring peninsular institutions to the New World. Spanish America came to possess the hospitals, medical faculties, regulatory agencies, and highly structured profession of Spain. But challenges of public health in colonial Spanish America were too vast for the limited resources of premodern Western medicine. And policies designed to restrict access to a profession that needed more, not fewer, practitioners had limited success. Yet the New World opened up entirely new possibilities for the future of medicine.

See also **Diseases; Medicinal Plants; New Spain, Colonization of the Northern Frontier.**

BIBLIOGRAPHY

Donald B. Cooper, *Epidemic Disease in Mexico City, 1761–1813* (1965).

John Tate Lanning, *Pedro de la Torre: Doctor to Conquerors* (1974).

Michael E. Burke, *The Royal College of San Carlos: Surgery and Spanish Medical Reform in the Late Eighteenth Century* (1977).

David A. Howard, *The Royal Indian Hospital of Mexico City* (1980).

John Tate Lanning, *The Royal Protomedicato: The Regulation of the Medical Professions in the Spanish Empire,* edited by John J. TePaske (1985).

Additional Bibliography

Astrain Gallart, Mikel. *Barberos, cirujanos y gente de mar: La sanidad naval y la profesión quirúrgica en la España ilustrada.* Madrid: Ministerio de Defensa, 1996.

Cook, Noble David, and W. David Lovell, eds. *Secret Judgements of God: Old World Disease in Colonial Spanish America.* Norman: University of Oklahoma Press, 1992.

Fajardo Ortiz, Guillermo. *Los caminos de la medicina colonial en Iberoamérica y las Filipinas.* México: Universidad Nacional Autónoma de México, Coordinación de Humanidades, Facultad de Medicina, 1996.

Foster, George M. *Hippocrates' Latin American Legacy: Humoral Medicine in the New World.* Langhorne, PA: Gordon and Breach, 1994.

García Cáceres, Uriel. *Juan del Valle y Caviedes, cronista de la medicina: Historia de la medicina en el Perú en la segunda mitad del siglo XVII.* Lima: Banco Central de Reserva del Perú: Universidad Peruana Cayetano Heredia, 1999.

Hernández Sáenz, Luz María. *Learning to Heal: The Medical Profession in Colonial Mexico, 1767–1831.* New York: Peter Lang, 1997.

Morales Cosme, Alba Dolores. *El Hospital General de San Andrés: La modernización de la medicina novohispana*

(1770–1833). México, D.F.: Universidad Autónoma Metropolitana, 2002.

Schifter Aceves, Liliana, Patricia Aceves Pastrana, and Alba Dolores Morales Cosme. *Medicina, minería e inquisición en la Nueva España: Esteban Morel, 1744–1795*. México: Universidad Autónoma Metropolitana, Unidad Xochimilco, 2002.

Solano Alonso, Jairo. *Salud, cultura y sociedad: Cartagena de Índias, siglos XVI y XVII*. Barranquilla, Colombia: Universidad del Atlántico, 1998.

Zenequelli, Lilia. *Historia de los médicos y boticarios en el Buenos Aires antiguo, 1536–1871*. Buenos Aires: Editorial Dunken, 2002.

MICHAEL E. BURKE

THE MODERN ERA

After the nineteenth-century independence movements in Latin America, liberal governments moved to secularize medical education. In setting up government-supported medical schools they eschewed the influence of religious orders and Iberian models and turned instead to the French model, whose influence continued into the twentieth century. The standard of instruction in most medical schools was poor: Many of the best creole physicians had been killed in the wars of independence. Moreover, political turbulence from the 1830s to the 1860s caused schools to function irregularly and prevented the formation of a scientific community large enough to generate original medical ideas.

THE EARLY MODERN ERA

There were, however, some original medical contributions during the nineteenth century. In the first half of the century the most interesting works were published by physicians who, according to the theory of the relation between climate and disease, correlated local diseases with meteorological conditions. Examples include *Du climat et des maladies du Brésil; ou, statistique médicale de cet empire* (On the climate and diseases of Brazil; or, medical statistics of this empire, 1844) by Joseph F. X. Sigaud, a French physician practicing in Brazil, and *Observaciones sobre el clima de Lima* (Observations on the climate of Lima, 1806), by the Peruvian José Hipólito Unanue (1755–1833). Other important contributions were made by the German-Portuguese physician Otto Wucherer (1820–1873), who initiated parasitological investigations in Brazil, and Carlos J. Finlay (1833–1915), a Cuban who hypothesized in 1881 that yellow fever was transmitted by the Aëdes mosquito. Finlay's theory was ignored until 1899, when the U.S. army tested his mosquito hypothesis and proved him correct.

From the 1880s, the medical profession expanded its prestige in several areas. It gained considerable control over medical practice in urban areas, creating a discrepancy between western medical processes in the cities and the rich traditions of folk medicine in the rural areas of Latin America. Medical schools achieved stability in teaching, more students graduated and went on to practice medicine, and doctors successfully organized themselves into professional associations and began to publish a variety of medical journals. Drawing on the French and English sanitation movements, doctors were at the forefront of campaigns to improve environmental conditions. Their position was further consolidated when nineteenth-century epidemics (e.g., cholera and yellow fever) that threatened the region's ability to make economic progress spurred governments to expand public-health services and to delegate power to the physicians who served on newly established sanitation boards. The development of bacteriology and advances in knowledge concerning insect vectors highlighted doctors' scientific authority, earned them greater respect, and led governments to support the establishment of research centers.

Although the medical establishment gained prestige, public-health programs still relied on local healers. In late-nineteenth-century Costa Rica, the state recruited practitioners of popular medicine to introduce modern treatments because it did not have the resources to reach rural areas. Moreover, people living in small communities often did not trust the national government, and instead relied on medical advice from traditional physicians. Thus, science and medicine often had to take into account local and cultural dynamics.

In the early decades of the twentieth century, the rising tide of nationalism and the belief that science could solve the problems of underdevelopment led to one of the most successful periods in the history of Latin America medicine, especially in the overlapping area of public health and medicine. During this period the Brazilian Oswaldo Cruz

(1872–1917) led the first Brazilian public-health campaign (1903–1909), which rid Rio de Janeiro of yellow fever and bubonic plague, though Cruz's attempts to make the smallpox vaccination mandatory were stalled by political opposition. Cruz also promoted experimental research in Brazil by turning the Cruz Institute (established in 1899), into a highly regarded microbiological and protozoological research center; previously it had mostly imported ideas and techniques from Europe. The institute's best known researcher was Carlos Chagas (1879–1934), who in 1908 discovered that American sleeping sickness (*Trypanosomiasis americana*) is caused by a trypanosome harbored in a Reduviid bug infesting the walls of rural huts.

Another example of important medical research during this period was the study of biological adaptation to high altitudes. Nineteenth-century high-altitude studies had "proved" that the natives of the highlands were mentally impaired. In an attempt to parry the charges of inferiority, in 1927 the Peruvian physician Carlos Monge Medrano (1884–1970) led an expedition to Cerro de Pasco, where he demonstrated the process of physical adaptation to the oxygen deficiency characteristic of high-altitude environments, and discovered the high-altitude disorder—known today as Monge's disease—caused by the loss of tolerance to high altitudes. The discovery led to the establishment of the Instituto de Biología y Patología Andina (1931), which also studied a variety of occupational disorders such as pneumoconiosis. The long collaboration between the Rockefeller Foundation and Latin American countries began in the 1920s with the foundation's hookworm and yellow fever eradication campaigns in Brazil, Peru, Ecuador, and Mexico.

POSTWAR DEVELOPMENTS

After World War II, the influence of the United States eclipsed that of France, and Latin Americans flocked to North American universities to study science and medicine. Moreover, U.S. philanthropies deepened their linkages to Latin America by selectively funding research centers at the region's universities and by supporting the establishment of national councils for higher scientific research in order to create a network of complementary investigative work. U.S.-funded projects grew, in part as a response to the cold war: Officials in Washington, D.C., felt that by improving public health and living conditions in Latin America, the United States could eliminate the social conditions that give rise to communist movements. In the 1950s, international organizations, with funding from the United States, began a malaria eradication campaign in Mexico. Making this a nationalistic cause, Mexico's public-health administrators surpassed the initial project goals. Successful public-health projects such as this helped national governments by allowing them to establish a presence in rural communities, where the government had limited oversight.

Cuba in particular developed well-known medical schools and facilities in the aftermath of their revolution. They also established universal health care, which focused especially on early intervention. Despite its relative poverty, Cuba now has the same life expectancy as the United States (77) and a much lower infant mortality rate. With funding from the Soviet Union, Cuba built the largest medical school in Latin America, which in 2007 had 10,000 students, mostly from other countries in Spanish America. Cuba's medical program became intertwined with politics when the nation started sending its doctors to other countries in Spanish America and Africa in the 1970s. These missions contrasted with the U.S.-led health initiatives during the cold war.

Latin America also saw major growth in terms of experimental medicine, with Argentina leading the way. The most prominent Argentine researcher of this century was Bernardo A. Houssay (1887–1971), whose work on the physiology of the pituitary gland led to the recognition of the role of the anterior pituitary in carbohydrate metabolism; for this work he won the Nobel Prize in medicine in 1947. His colleague Luis F. Leloir (1906–1987) expanded Houssay's findings, showing how complex carbohydrates are broken down into simpler sugars; his research earned him the Nobel Prize in chemistry in 1970. Mexican researchers have combined applied research into tropical disorders and experimental research. Especially prominent in experimental research was Arturo Stearns Rosenblueth (1900–1970), a neurophysiologist who, together with the American physiologist Walter B. Cannon (1871–1945), deciphered the workings of the sympathetic regulatory action. With the mathematician Norbert Weiner (1894–1964), Rosenblueth helped establish cybernetics as a serious area of inquiry. Other areas of original research are genetic studies with the drosophila in Brazil, and psychoanalysis in Argentina. In 1967 the Argentine cardiologist René G. Favaloro (1923–2000) performed the first nonemergency coronary bypass surgery and helped perfect the technique, making it one of the most important procedures in modern medicine.

Despite Latin America's advances in medical research, the political problems and severe economic crises of the 1980s led to a "brain drain," eroded health-care institutions, and allowed the reappearance of preventable diseases. Also, the emergence of AIDS created new debates on medicine. In the late twentieth and early twenty-first century, scientists developed relatively successful treatments against AIDS. Brazil committed itself to providing free access to AIDS medication, but the high costs of treatment made it unaffordable for the poor. Brazil, as well other nations, proposed that drug companies sell the drugs for cheaper prices in developing countries, but the large international pharmaceutical corporations balked, fearing that less costly drugs would make their way back into the U.S. and European markets, eroding profits. Despite threats of trade sanctions, in 2007 the Brazilian government ignored the patent rights of Merck, a large U.S. drug producer, and began buying the medication from a supplier in India for less than half the cost in the United States. Recently, treatments of diseases also have highlighted the social dynamics of medicine. For example, because AIDS is transmitted primarily through sexual intercourse, its emergence raised cultural debates about sex and sexuality throughout the region. In another example, during cholera outbreaks in the early 1990s many commentators felt that the initial medical response placed too much blame on the victim.

Finally, medicine has shaped contemporary policy discussions on the environment and indigenous rights. Many groups and individuals argue that important but environmentally sensitive areas such as the Brazilian rain forest should be protected because these areas have tremendous biological diversity that might provide clues about disease and new medicine. In 1975 the U.S. company Squibb, a large drug producer, took the venom from an Amazon snake to create a popular blood-pressure medicine, captoril; however, Brazil received little benefit from capotoril. More recently, in the Amazon state of Campinas, indigenous groups have been using the slime from a poisonous tree frog to treat a variety of ailments, and in 2006 international drug companies began to investigate using the slime as an anesthetic. However, Brazil has taken an aggressive stance against foreign companies, fearing biopiracy. International and national organizations also have shown a renewed interest in indigenous health care, which advocates a more holistic view of diseases and health care than western medicine provides. Consequently, there is a debate about whether or not the U.S. model of pure research and highly technological and costly medicine is the best one for the region.

See also **Chagas, Carlos Ribeiro Justiniano; Cruz, Oswaldo Gonçalves; Houssay, Bernardo A; Leloir, Luis F; Rosenblueth, Arturo Stearns.**

BIBLIOGRAPHY

Alvarez, Adriana, Irene Molinari, and Daniel Reynoso. *Historias de enfermedades, salud y medicina en la Argentina de los siglos XIX–XX.* Mar del Plata, Argentina: Universidade Nacional de Mar de Plata, 2004.

Bowers, John Z., and Elizabeth F. Purcell. *Aspects of the History of Medicine in Latin America.* New York: Josiah Macy Jr. Foundation, 1979.

Cooper, Donald. "The New 'Black Death': Cholera in Brazil, 1855–56." *Social Science History* 10 (1986): 467–488.

Cueto, Marcos. "Excellence in the Periphery: Scientific Activities and Biomedical Sciences in Peru." Ph.D. diss., Columbia University, 1988.

Cueto, Marcos. "The Rockefeller Foundation's Medical Policy and Scientific Research in Latin America: The Case of Physiology." *Social Studies of Science* 20 (1990): 229–254.

Cueto, Marcos. *Cold War, Deadly Fevers: Malaria Eradication in Mexico, 1955–1975.* Washington, DC: Woodrow Wilson Center Press, 2007.

Danielson, Ross. *Cuban Medicine.* New Brunswick, NJ: Transaction, 1979.

Lowy, Ilana. "Yellow Fever in Rio de Janeiro and the Pasteur Institute Mission (1901–1905): The Transfer of Science to the Periphery." *Medical History* 34 (1990): 144–163.

Ortiz Echániz, Silvia. *La medicina tradicional en el norte de México.* México, D.F.: Instituto Nacional de Antropología e Historia, 1999.

Schendel, Gordon. *Medicine in Mexico: From Aztec Herbs to Betatrons.* Austin: University of Texas Press, 1968.

Silva, Mozart Linhares da. *História, medicina e sociedade no Brasil.* Santa Cruz do Sul, Brazil: Edunisc, 2003.

Stepan, Nancy. *Beginnings of Brazilian Science.* New York: Science History Publications, 1981.

JULYAN G. PEARD
BYRON CRITES

MEDINA, HUGO (1897–1998).

Hugo Medina (*b.* 29 January 1897; *d.* 22 May 1998), Uruguayan general and politician, was a key figure in the transition to civilian rule in Uruguay that took place in the mid-1980s. Commander of the Third Military Region in 1984, he was considered a staunch professional soldier who favored following the timetable established by the military for their withdrawal from executive power. Medina was a member of the military's Political Affairs Commission (COMASPO) from 1980 to 1981. On 7 June 1984, with the retirement of General Hugo Arano, he assumed command of the army. His working relationship with Julio Maria Sanguinetti of the Colorado Party would prove crucial to the talks that resulted in the Naval Club Pact that led to the November 1984 elections. Medina retired from the army in January 1987, after having staunchly defended the armed forces against any trials for human rights violations. Late in 1987, President Sanguinetti appointed Medina minister of defense, a position from which he continued to pressure public opinion against overturning the amnesty law for the military that had been passed in 1986. The referendum on the amnesty law took place in April 1989. The law was upheld, giving Medina excellent credibility with his former military comrades. He continued to serve as minister of defense until the end of the Sanguinetti government in 1990. In a 1991 interview, he admitted he gave orders for torture during the military regime, becoming the first Uruguayan military figure to do so. He died on 22 May 1998, in Montevideo.

See also **Uruguay: The Twentieth Century.**

BIBLIOGRAPHY

Brito, Alexandra Barahona de. *Human Rights and Democratization in Latin America: Uruguay and Chile.* Oxford: Oxford University Press, 1997.

Kaufman, Edy. *Uruguay in Transition: From Civilian to Military Rule.* New Brunswick, NJ: Transaction Books, 1979.

Weinstein, Martin. *Uruguay, Democracy at the Crossroads.* Boulder, CO: Westview Press, 1988.

Weschler, Lawrence. *A Miracle, a Universe: Settling Accounts with Torturers.* New York: Pantheon Books, 1990.

MARTIN WEINSTEIN

MEDINA, JOSÉ TORIBIO (1852–1930).

José Toribio Medina (*b.* 21 October 1852; *d.* 11 December 1930), Chilean historian and bibliographer, and the most remarkable Latin American scholar of his time. Although he was offered a seat in Congress and (in 1871) the secretaryship of the National (*Montt-Varista*) party, Medina preferred the life of scholarship. It was interrupted only by two short-term diplomatic jobs, in Peru (1875–1876) and Spain (1884–1886), and by public service during the War of the Pacific as military adviser and judge. Medina's support for President José Manuel Balmaceda in the 1891 civil war made it advisable for him to live abroad until 1895. In fact he always enjoyed travel, making five extended journeys to Europe (always with Spain as his most cherished destination) and twice visiting the United States. In 1928, aged nearly seventy-six, he presided at the opening of the Twenty-third International Congress of Americanists in New York. He was honored by a wide variety of learned societies in America and Europe.

Medina was the author or editor of 408 books, essays, and articles. Some 185 of these publications were printed (1888–1919) on his own private presses. His copious writings embrace history, bibliography, biography, literary criticism, geography, cartography, palaeography, numismatics, and many other subjects. Of particular note are the series of books he wrote on the Inquisition in colonial Spanish America (he discovered the Inquisition papers in the Simancas archive in Spain), and the extraordinary sequence of bibliographical studies covering the output of colonial printing presses in more than thirty Spanish-American cities. His devotion to Ercilla y Zúñiga yielded the classic modern study of that poet. Both Harvard University and the John

Carter Brown Library offered Medina large sums for his magnificent collection of books and manuscripts. He donated it to the Chilean National Library, where it is kept in the beautifully appointed Sala Medina on the upper floor over the main entrance.

See also **Inquisition: Spanish America.**

BIBLIOGRAPHY

Guillermo Feliú Cruz, *José Toribio Medina* (1952).

Sergio Villalobos R., *Medina, su vida y sus obras* (1952).

Additional Bibliography

Rovira, José Carlos. *José Toribio Medina y su fundación literaria y bibliografica del mundo colonial americano.* Santiago, Chile: Ediciones de la Dirección de Bibliotecas, Archivos y Museos, Centro de Investigaciones Diego Barros Arana, 2002.

SIMON COLLIER

MEDINA ANGARITA, ISAÍAS (1897–1953). Isaías Medina Angarita (*b.* 6 July 1897; *d.* 15 September 1953), president of Venezuela (1941–1945). In 1941, Medina became the handpicked successor of President Eleázar López Contreras, whom he had served briefly as minister of war in 1936. Medina, who entered the Military School in 1912, represented the new professional army officers who emerged during the Juan Vicente Gómez era (1908–1935). During his military career he taught at the Military School, served as secretary to the Ministry of War and Marine, and headed military delegations to Ecuador (1930) and the United States (1940).

As president, Medina introduced a number of political reforms. Constitutional revisions instituted direct elections of national deputies and suffrage for women in municipal elections. Medina also introduced the first income tax law. In 1943, a petroleum law gave the government higher revenues through new taxes and royalties, and the petroleum companies gained more security. An agrarian reform law of 1945 addressed some of the nation's basic rural labor problems. Medina had success in negotiating border settlements with Colombia and Great Britain. In 1943 he headed his own party, the Venezuelan Democratic Party (Partido Democrático Venezolano), which advocated moderate reforms. In October 1945, a military-civilian coalition overthrew Medina.

See also **Venezuela: Venezuela since 1830.**

BIBLIOGRAPHY

Nora Bustamente, *Isaías Medina Angarita* (1985).

Tulio Chiossone, *El decenio democrático inconcluso* (1989).

Judith Ewell, *Venezuela: A Century of Change* (1984).

José Eduardo Guzmán Pérez, *Medina Angarita: Democracia y negación* (1985).

Isaías Medina Angarita, *Gobierno y época del presidente Isaías Medina Angarita,* 17 vols. (1987).

Additional Bibliography

Battaglini, Oscar. *El medinismo: Modernización, crisis política y golpe de estado.* Caracas, Venezuala: Monte Avila Editores Latinoamericana: Dirección de Cultura, Universidad Central de Venezuala, 1997.

Ramírez López, Eduardo, and Constantino Quero Morales. *Isaías Medina Angarita: Presidente de la Transformación.* Caracas, Venezuela: Universidad Católica Bello, 2005.

WINTHROP R. WRIGHT

MEIGGS, HENRY (1821–1877). Henry Meiggs (*b.* 7 July 1821; *d.* 29 September 1877), American entrepreneur who oversaw the construction of railroads in Chile and Peru. Business reverses led the New York–born Meiggs to move to California, where he initially enjoyed great commercial success during the gold rush. Then bad economic times and a willingness to forge documents forced Meiggs, almost a million dollars in debt, to flee his creditors in the United States. In 1854 he arrived in Chile, where he breathed new life into a faltering railroad industry. Beginning in 1861, the informally trained engineer supervised the building of a railroad linking the capital to the south. As promised, he completed the Santiago–Quillota spur in 1863. He later helped construct a rail line between the capital and Chile's principal port, Valparaíso, in less than four years. Meiggs enjoyed enormous success because he paid his workers well and did not maltreat his employees. Apparently well liked, the high-living Meiggs, who built himself a palatial mansion, expanded his activities by trading in guano and opening a bank in La Paz, Bolivia.

Meiggs left Chile in the late 1860s for Peru, where he constructed a railroad between Lima and La Oroya, high in the Andes. This task proved to be particularly difficult to complete, since the rail line ran from the coast to the Altiplano, over 14,000 feet above sea level. Although the railroad clearly benefited the Peruvian economy, it hurt Chile's; some twenty-five thousand Chileans in search of work migrated north, never to return to their homeland. Their departure damaged Chilean *hacendados* (landowners) by depriving them of needed agricultural labor. Meiggs's overall contribution proved substantial, however, helping both the Chileans and the Peruvians develop economically by facilitating the export of their raw materials to the United States and Europe.

See also **Railroads.**

BIBLIOGRAPHY

Watt Stewart, *Henry Meiggs: Yankee Pizarro* (1946).

Thomas C. Wright, *Landowners and Reform in Chile* (1981), p. 145.

Additional Bibliography

Kemp Heiland, Klaus. *El desarrollo de los ferrocarriles en el Perú.* Lima, Peru: Universidad Nacional de Ingeniería, Proyecto Historia, 2002.

Thomson, Ian, and Dietrich Angerstein. *Historia del ferrocarril en Chile.* Santiago, Chile: Dirección Bibliotecas, Archivos y Museos, Centro de Investigaciones Diego Barros Arana, 2000.

WILLIAM F. SATER

MEIRELES, CECÍLIA (1901–1964). Cecília Meireles (*b.* 7 November 1901; *d.* 9 November 1964), Brazilian poet and educator. Born in Rio de Janeiro, Meireles lost her parents at an early age and was raised by her Portuguese Azorian grandmother. She studied in public schools and became a schoolteacher, later completing a graduate degree. In 1919 she published her first book, *Espectros,* sonnets in a Parnassian mold. In 1922, year of the Modern Art Week in São Paulo, she married a Portuguese artist who committed suicide in 1935. From 1930 on, she was a regular contributor to the Rio cultural press, and in 1934 she founded the first library of children's literature in Brazil. An authority on national folklore, she was professor of Luso-Brazilian literature at the University of the Federal District from 1936 to 1938. Following a second marriage, she visited the United States, teaching in one of the earliest programs for Brazilian literature (the University of Texas).

Meireles matured during the modernist period, but her work always maintained a very personal character, influenced above all by symbolism and Portuguese traditions. While thematic and linguistic nationalism became dominant in Brazil, she remained close to the Portuguese lyrical heritage. She published twenty books in her lifetime, the most noted of which, *Romanceiro da inconfidência* (1953), is a cycle of ballads about colonial conspirators for independence. She is one of the outstanding names in Brazilian literary history and is generally considered the nation's most important woman poet. Posthumously, she received the highest prize of the Brazilian Academy of Letters.

See also **Literature: Brazil.**

BIBLIOGRAPHY

John A. Nist, *The Modernist Movement in Brazil* (1967).

Marta Peixoto, "The Absent Body: Female Signature and Poetic Convention in Cecília Meireles," in *Bulletin of Hispanic Studies* 65, no. 1 (1988): 87–100.

Raymond Sayers, "The Poetic Universe of Cecília Meireles," in *From Linguistics to Literature: Romance Studies Offered to Francis M. Rogers,* edited by Bernard Bichakjian (1981).

Additional Bibliography

Gouveia, Maria Margarida Maia. *Cecília Meireles, uma poética do "eterno instante."* Lisbon: Impr. Nacional-Casa da Moeda, 2002.

Oliveira, Ana Maria Domingues de, Jane Christina Pereira, and Luciana Ferreira Leal. *Estudo crítico da bibliografia sobre Cecília Meireles.* São Paulo, Brazil: Humanitas, FFLCH/USP, 2001.

CHARLES A. PERRONE

MEIRELES DE LIMA, VÍTOR (1832–1903). Vítor Meireles de Lima (*b.* 18 August 1832; *d.* 22 February 1903), Brazilian painter. Along with Pedro Américo, Meireles is one of

Brazil's most important historical painters of the Second Empire. Born in the southern province of Santa Catarina, Meireles commenced his formal artistic formation in 1847 at the Imperial Academy of Fine Arts in Rio de Janeiro. In 1852 he won a travel stipend, the academy's top student honor. During his eight years in Europe, he produced his first important historical painting, and one of his greatest works, *A primeira missa no Brasil.*

Upon his return to Brazil, Meireles devoted his life to painting whether working as the academy's professor of history painting, fulfilling governmental commissions, or readying canvases for presentation in the academy's exhibitions. Between 1866 and 1879, he received three important governmental commissions to produce paintings with military themes. Sought to bolster the Second Empire's image after Brazil's participation in the victorious but draining War of the Triple Alliance (1864–1870), these military paintings represent his most celebrated works. They include *Combate naval do Riachuelo* and *Passagem de humaitá* (1872), which re-create events from the war, and *Primeira Batalha dos Guararapes* (1879), which documents a 1648 battle in which black, Indian, and Brazilian troops fought against Dutch colonial domination. Beyond these historical compositions, Meireles produced numerous portraits, an Indianist painting, *Moema,* and various landscapes and panoramas.

See also **Art: The Nineteenth Century.**

BIBLIOGRAPHY

Quirino Campofiorito, *História da pintura brasileira no século XIX* (1983).

Angelo de Proença Rosa, *Vítor Meireles de Lima (1832–1903)* (1982).

Argeu Guimarães, *Auréola de Vítor Meireles* (1977).

Caren A. Meghreblian, "Art, Politics, and Historical Perception in Imperial Brazil, 1854–1884" (Ph.D. diss., UCLA, 1990).

Additional Bibliography

Xexéo, Monica F. B. *Vitor Meireles: Um artista do império.* Rio de Janeiro: MNBA; Curitiba: Museu Oscar Niemeyer, 2003.

CAREN A. MEGHREBLIAN

MEJÍA, TOMÁS (1820–1867).

Tomás Mejía (*b.* 1820; *d.* 19 June 1867), Mexican general. Born in Pinal de Amoles, Querétaro, Mejía became an important military officer while retaining his ethnic ties to the Indian villagers of the Sierra Gorda. An Indian cacique, he led troops from his native region in support of the conservative cause during the Revolution of Ayutla, the War of the Reform, and in support of Maximilian's empire.

Mejía began his career in 1841 as a second lieutenant in the militia, engaging migratory Indians in the North in his first campaigns. He fought against the invading U.S. troops in Monterrey, Angostura, and Buena Vista in 1847 and was promoted to squadron commander in 1849. He reached the rank of lieutenant colonel during the Revolution of Ayutla and division general during the Three Years War. Defeated by Jesús González Ortega in 1860, Mejía later became one of Emperor Maximilian's most trusted generals, and one of the most feared by his republican counterparts. As Maximilian's empire collapsed, Mejía chose to join the emperor in Querétaro, where he was captured, tried, condemned to death, and executed by firing squad alongside Maximilian and Miguel Miramón.

See also **French Intervention (Mexico); Mexico, Wars and Revolutions: Mexican-American War.**

BIBLIOGRAPHY

Diccionario Porrúa de historia, biografía y geografía de México, 5th ed. (1986).

Alfred Jackson Hanna and Kathryn Abbey Hanna, *Napoleon III and Mexico: American Triumph over Monarchy* (1971).

Additional Bibliography

Duncan, Robert. "For the Good of the Country: State and Nation Building during Maximilian's Mexican Empire, 1864–67." Ph.D. diss., 2001.

Hamnett, Brian R. *Juárez.* New York: Longman, 1994.

Reed Torres, Luis. *El general Tomás Mejía frente a la Doctrina Monroe: La guerra de reforma, la intervención y el Imperio a través del archivo inédito del caudillo conservador queretano.* México: Editorial Porrúa, 1989.

Rodríguez O, Jaime E. *The Divine Charter: Constitutionalism and Liberalism in Nineteenth-century Mexico.* Lanham, MD: Rowman & Littlefield Publishers, 2005.

D. F. STEVENS

MEJÍA DEL VALLE Y LLEQUERICA, JOSÉ JOAQUÍN (1775–1813).

José Joaquín Mejía del Valle y Llequerica (also Lequerica; *b.* 24 May 1775; *d.* 27 October 1813), spokesperson for the rights of colonial Americans under Spanish imperialism. Mejía, a native of Quito, served as a substitute delegate of the Viceroyalty of New Granada to the Cortes of Cádiz (1810–1814). He ably led the American delegation in their struggle for equal representation in both the congress and the subsequent new constitution. The problem was population: That of Spain at this time was about 10.5 million, whereas that of Spain's overseas holdings totaled about 15–16.9 million. However, only whites enjoyed full citizenship in Spain and its colonies, and the New World had far fewer whites (2.5–3.2 million) than did Spain (10.5 million). Naturally, Spain was utterly unwilling to surrender political control of its empire to overseas whites.

During the Cádiz debates, Mejía advanced a proposal that the New World's free blacks and Indians, if not its slaves, be counted for purposes of proportional representation. The Cortes agreed to include creoles, Indians, and mestizos, but not Africans and mulattoes. Most historians agree that Mejía was the best orator in Cádiz. He died during a yellow fever epidemic in Cádiz.

See also **Caste and Class Structure in Colonial Spanish America.**

BIBLIOGRAPHY

On events in Spain and at the Cortes of Cádiz, see Timothy E. Anna, *Spain and the Loss of America* (1983).

Additional Bibliography

Comenge, Rafael. *Antología de las cortes de Cádiz.* Pamplona, Spain: Analecta Editorial, 2004.

Estrada Michel, Rafael. *Monarquía y nación entre Cádiz y Nueva España: El problema de la articulación política de las Españas ante la revolución liberal y la emancipación Americana.* México: Editorial Porrúa, 2006.

Morán Orti, Manuel and Miguel Artola. *Las Cortes de Cádiz.* Pamplona: Analecta Editorial, 2004.

RONN F. PINEO

MEJÍA GODOY, CARLOS (1943–).

Carlos Mejía Godoy is the most important singer-songwriter associated with the Sandinista revolution. Born June 27, 1943, to a musical family in Somoto in northern Nicaragua, he contemplated a career in either law or journalism. He dropped out of college after spending time in West Germany on a scholarship to pursue the life of an artist. In the late 1960s he sought to introduce lyrics into the instrumental musical styles of his *patria chica* on radio shows that melded storytelling and folklore. In the 1970s he lived a semi-clandestine life as a member of the Guerra Popular Prolongada (Prolonged People's War) faction of the Sandinistas, and performed his songs as an accordionist and singer in churches in poor neighborhoods. In the latter half of the decade he lived in Europe, spending much of the time in post-Franco Spain. His song "El Cristo de Palacagüina" brought him fame and notoriety for its portrayal of Jesus Christ as a guerrilla. In 1978 he composed an album of songs, *Guitarra Armada* (Armed guitar), with his brother, Luis Enrique Mejia Godoy. Their songs were intended to teach people practical ways to participate in the ongoing revolution. During the rebellion his songs were broadcast on the clandestine radio station Radio Sandino. In the months prior to the triumph of the Sandinistas he and his brother played before international audiences sympathetic to the struggle of the Sandinista National Liberation Front (FSLN). One of his most famous works is "La Misa Campesina Nicaragüense," set to writings by peasants in the Solentiname collective of the poet and priest Ernesto Cardenal. First performed in 1976 and recorded in 1981, it outraged many for its typically Sandinista melding of Christian and revolutionary language and imagery. He was employed briefly by the ministry of culture in the Sandinista government, but left to concentrate on performing and composing.

Mejía Godoy has hosted a television show and has run a café in Managua where he and other like-minded musicians play. Following the death of the presidential candidate Henry Lewites in 2006, Mejía Godoy became the vice presidential candidate (he was not elected) for the Movimiento Renovador Sandinista, which is made up of Sandinistas who are disillusioned with the leadership of Daniel Ortega.

See also **Cardenal, Ernesto; Nicaragua, Sandinista National Liberation Front (FSLN); Patria Chica.**

BIBLIOGRAPHY

Cabezas, Omar. *Fire from the Mountain: The Making of a Sandinista.* New York: Crown, 1985.

Judson, Fred. "Sandinista Revolutionary Morale." *Latin American Perspectives* 14, no. 1 (1987): 19–42.

Mejía Godoy, Luis Enrique. *Relincho en la sangre: Relatos de un trovador errante.* Managua: Anamá, 2002.

Pring-Mill, Robert. "The Roles of Revolutionary Song: A Nicaraguan Assessment." *Popular Music* 6, no. 2 (1987): 179–189.

Scruggs, Thomas M. "Carlos Mejía Godoy." *The New Grove Dictionary of Music and Musicians*, 2nd edition. Edited by Stanley Sadie. New York: Grove, 2001.

Scruggs, Thomas M. "'Let's Enjoy as Nicaraguans': The Use of Music in the Construction of a Nicaraguan National Consciousness." *Ethnomusicology* 43, no. 2 (1999): 297–321.

ANDREW J. KIRKENDALL

MEJÍA VICTORES, OSCAR HUMBERTO

MEJÍA VICTORES, OSCAR HUMBERTO (1930–). Oscar Humberto Mejía Victores was chief of state of Guatemala (1983–1986). Brigadier General Mejía Victores served as minister of defense under Efraín Ríos Montt (1982–1983). After taking part in the 9 August 1983 coup d'état that ousted Ríos Montt from power, Mejía became chief of state, but declined to name himself president of the republic.

Guatemala's economy declined precipitously under Mejía's administration. However, Mejía oversaw the "transition to democracy" under which the military permitted the creation and promulgation of a new national constitution and the election of a civilian to the presidency. In 1986, Mejía stepped down to allow Marco Vinicio Cerezo Arévalo, a civilian and member of the Christian Democratic Party, to become president of the republic. In July 2006 the Spanish government issued warrants against Mejía and Ríos Montt. They were charged with genocide, torture, terrorism, and illegal detention. Human rights groups claim the two are responsible for some of the worst atrocities of Guatemala's civil war, in which by some estimates 200,000 people died. In a 2007 interview with the Associated Press, Mejía claimed that those events were in the past and therefore did not merit further discussion.

See also **Guatemala.**

BIBLIOGRAPHY

Bettina Corke, ed., *Who Is Who in Government and Politics in Latin America* (1984).

Jean-Marie Simon, *Guatemala: Eternal Spring, Eternal Tyranny* (1987).

Additional Bibliography

García, Prudencio. *El genocidio de Guatemala: A la luz de la sociología militar.* Madrid, Spain: Sepha Edición y Diseño, 2005.

Perera, Victor. *Unfinished Conquest: The Guatemalan Tragedy.* Berkeley: University of California Press, 1993.

Short, Nicola. *The International Politics of Post-conflict Reconstruction in Guatemala.* New York: Palgrave Macmillan, 2007.

Torres-Rivas, Edelberto. *Guatemala: Causas y orígenes del enfrentamiento armado interno.* Guatemala: F&G Editores, 2006.

VIRGINIA GARRARD BURNETT

MELÉ, JUAN N.

MELÉ, JUAN N. (1923–). Juan N. Melé (*b.* 15 October 1923) is an Argentine painter and sculptor. Born in Buenos Aires, he studied at the Prilidiano Pueyrredón School of Fine Arts. In 1948–1949 he received a grant from the French government and studied at the Louvre under Georges Vantongerloo, Cesar Domela, Robert Delauney, and Constantin Brancusi, among others. Melé has had a distinguished career in abstract painting and sculpture. In Argentina he joined the Asociación Arte Concreto-Invención, a group of nonfigurative artists. His work is a fine example of highly personal abstract art combining purely plastic form and a sensitive treatment of color. From 1974 to 1986 Melé lived and worked in New York. He has had numerous individual shows throughout the world, including one in 1987 at the Museo de Arte Moderno in Buenos Aires and another in 2001 at the Galerie Slotine in Paris. In 2002 he was named a member of the National Academy of Fine Arts of Argentina. As of 2007, he split his time between Buenos Aires and Paris.

See also **Art: The Twentieth Century; Buenos Aires.**

BIBLIOGRAPHY

Vicente Gesualdo, Aldo Biglione, and Rodolfo Santos, *Diccionario de artistas plásticos en la Argentina* (1988).

Additional Bibliography

Argentina en el arte. Buenos Aires: Ediciones Institucionales, 2002.

Perazzo, Nelly. *El arte concreto en la Argentina en la década del 40*. Buenos Aires: Ediciones de Arte Gaglianone, 1983.

Ramírez, Mari Carmen. *Cantos paralelos: La parodia plástica en el arte argentino contemporáneo*. Austin: Blanton Museum of Art, College of Fine Arts, University of Texas, 1999.

Siracusano, Gabriela. *Melé*. Buenos Aires: Fundación Mundo Nuevo, 2005.

Amalia Cortina Aravena

MELÉNDEZ CHAVERRI, CARLOS

MELÉNDEZ CHAVERRI, CARLOS (1926–). Carlos Meléndez Chaverri (*b.* 3 June 1926, *d.* 12 June 2000), Costa Rican historian, diplomat, and university professor.

Carlos Meléndez Chaverri is recognized as the most productive and insightful twentieth-century Costa Rican historian. He has focused his research and writing on the colonial period in Costa Rica. His works on the colonial period culminated in the valuable monograph *Conquistadores y pobladores* (1982). He has published general histories of Costa Rica for different educational levels, biographies, a study of blacks in Costa Rica, monographs on other Central American topics, and a scholarly work on the national hero, Juan Santamaría.

Heredia-born Meléndez is a scholar-teacher in the full sense of the term, having taught at two high schools before joining the faculty of the University of Costa Rica (1958). There he served as the director of the School of History and Geography and was responsible for the formation of a more professional generation of Costa Rican historians. In addition to these academic functions, he held other public positions such as head of the anthropology and history section of the National Museum (1953–1966), president of the Academy of History and Geography, and Costa Rican ambassador to Spain.

Among his many honors are national literary awards, election to geographic and historical societies throughout Central America, and an honorary doctorate from Tulane University (1979). From 1985 to 1986, he served as the ambassador of Costa Rica in Spain. In 1993, he received another honorary doctorate from the University of Nicaragua. That same year, Costa Rica awarded him the Premio Nacionál de Cultura Magón. He died on June 12, 2000. The following morning at 8:45, the University of Costa Rica held a minute of silence in his honor.

See also **Costa Rica.**

BIBLIOGRAPHY

One of the few examples of Meléndez's writings in English, "Land Tenure in Colonial Costa Rica," is contained in Marc Edelman and Joanne Kenen, eds., *The Costa Rica Reader* (1989), pp. 13–28. See also Carlos Meléndez Chaverri, *Conquistadores y pobladores* (1982); Kenneth J. Grieb, ed., *Research Guide to Central America and the Caribbean* (1985).

Additional Bibliography

Meléndez Chaverri, Carlos. *Don Manuel José Arce: Una vida al servicio de la libertad*. San Salvador, El Salvador: Editorial Delgado, 2000.

Meléndez Chaverri, Carlos. *Santa Rosa: Un combate por la libertad*. Alajuela, Costa Rica: Museo Histórico Cultural Juan Santamaría, 2001.

Chaverri Carlos Meléndez

MELÉNDEZ FAMILY

MELÉNDEZ FAMILY. Meléndez family, a Salvadoran family that held the presidency for three consecutive terms (1913–1927) during the period known as the Meléndez-Quiñónez dynasty era. The Meléndez presidents' fourteen-year occupancy of the nation's highest office is the most obvious example of the restrictive, elitist nature of Salvadoran politics. The Meléndez clan was part of the original Salvadoran landowning oligarchy dating from the early nineteenth century. Originally producers of indigo, they were among the first to grow coffee on a large scale.

President Carlos Meléndez (*b.* 1 February 1861; *d.* 8 October 1918) took office in 1913 following the assassination of Manuel Araujo. He had made many trips to the United States and wished to promote industrialization and the diversification of El Salvador's agrarian economy into henequen and cotton. However, his tenure in office is most notable for two policies: his decision to keep El Salvador neutral in World War I, despite heavy pressure from the United States, and his claim to the Gulf of Fonseca as a condominium territory. The latter resulted in the issuing of the so-called Meléndez Doctrine, which challenged Nicaragua's right to grant the United States a naval base in the Gulf of Fonseca as stipulated by the Bryan-Chamorro Treaty of 1913. Meléndez took his case to the Central American Court of Justice in 1914 and won a judgment in his favor.

Carlos Meléndez passed the presidency to his younger brother Jorge (*b.* 15 April 1871; *d.* 22 November 1953) when his health failed in 1918. Jorge ruled for four turbulent years punctuated by military uprisings, urban labor protests, and demonstrations in San Salvador. Of these, the most serious were a February 1922 revolt of students at the Military Polytechnic School and a popular demonstration in December of that same year which was put down by the army and police. Jorge Meléndez continued his brother's program of modernization by opening the first airport, announcing a campaign to eradicate illiteracy, and creating a monetary commission. However, Jorge Meléndez is remembered also for his increased usage of the Liga Roja (Red League), a shadowy paramilitary group designed to thwart labor organization.

The Meléndez's brother-in-law Alfonso Quiñones Molina was president from 1923 to 1927 and continued the same form of elite-dominated politics as his predecessors. The Meléndez-Quiñónez dynasty governed El Salvador during a crucial period in its modern history. In the 1980s, their descendant, Jorge Antonio Meléndez, fought with the People's Revolutionary Army (ERP) as part of the FMLN-FDR coalition against the government.

See also **El Salvador.**

BIBLIOGRAPHY

Manuel Beltrand, ed., *Orientaciones económicas del Señor Presidente Meléndez* (1917).

Salvador Rodríguez González, *El Golfo de Fonseca y el Tratado, Bryan-Chamorro; La doctrina Meléndez* (1917).

Carlos Meléndez, *Relations Between the United States of America and El Salvador* (1918).

María Leistenschneider and Freddy Leistenschneider, *Gobernantes de El Salvador* (1980).

Tommie Sue Montgomery, *Revolution in El Salvador* (1982).

Additional Bibliography

Castellanos, Juan Mario. *El Salvador, 1930–1960: Antecedentes históricos de la guerra civil.* San Salvador: Dirección de Publicaciones e Impresos, 2002.

Holden, Robert H. *Armies Without Nations: Public Violence and State Formation in Central America, 1921–1960.* Oxford: Oxford University Press, 2004.

Martínez Peñate, Oscar. *El Salvador, Diccionario: Personajes, hechos históricos, geografía e instituciones.* San Salvador: Editorial Nuevo Enfoque, 2004.

KAREN RACINE

MELGAREJO, MARIANO (1820–1871). Mariano Melgarejo (*b.* 15 April 1820; *d.* 23 November 1871), president of Bolivia (1864–1871). Born in Tarata, Cochabamba, General Melgarejo was the archetypical bad caudillo during whose disastrous administration Bolivia gave up large territories to its neighbors, the first systematic assault on the Indian communities occurred, and the public financial system was ransacked. Melgarejo, a mestizo who had risen through the ranks of the army, achieved power after overthrowing General José María Achá and later killing former president Manuel Isidoro Belzú. Extremely corrupt and with the government always in deficit, Melgarejo and his cronies took advantage of the prosperity of the peripheral regions of Bolivia by selling them to its more powerful neighbors. Thus, in the Chilean treaty of 1866, Melgarejo agreed to all Chilean territorial claims in the nitrate-rich Mejillones region of the Atacama Desert. In 1868, Melgarejo signed a treaty in which he ceded 40,000 square miles to Brazil in the Amazon region.

In a desperate attempt to gain more revenue, Melgarejo also further debased Bolivian silver coinage. The dilution of the silver content in coins, though practiced by virtually every Bolivian administration, was so massive under Melgarejo that it led to difficulties in trade, especially in regions of adjacent countries that heavily used Bolivian coinage for circulation. Melgarejo's sales of Indian community lands in 1866 and 1868 also were tainted by corruption. The terms were exceedingly onerous for the Indians; if they did not purchase their own land within ninety days, it was put on the auction block for the highest bidder. Purchasers bought many lands with government bonds and others were given to friends and relatives, thus depriving the government of needed cash revenue. Most affected by these laws were community lands in the La Paz altiplano and the Cochabamba region.

Although his regime continuously had to combat movements against the government, Melgarejo was ousted in 1870 only when the creole opposition allied itself with the altiplano Indians. A massive Indian revolt forced Melgarejo to flee to Peru, where he died the following year. As a result of the revolt, Indian rebels retook many of their community lands.

See also **Caudillismo, Caudillo.**

BIBLIOGRAPHY

Alberto Gutiérrez, *El melgarejismo antes y después de Melgarejo* (1916).

Herbert S. Klein, *Bolivia: The Evolution of a Multi-Ethnic Society* (1982), pp. 135–141.

Additional Bibliography

Baixeras, José Luis. *Melgarejo: Osadía, poder y muerte.* La Paz, Bolivia: Ediciones Capricornio, 2002.

Peralta Ruiz, Victor, and Marta Irurozqui. *Por la concordia, la fusión y el unitarismo: Estado y caudillismo en Bolivia, 1825-1880.* Madrid: Consejo Superior de Investigaciones Científicas, 2000.

ERICK D. LANGER

MELGARES, FACUNDO (1775–c. 1835). Facundo Melgares (*b.* 1775; *d.* c. 1835), Spanish governor of New Mexico. Born in Villa Carabaca, Murcia, Spain, Melgares, nephew of a judge of the Audiencia of New Spain, entered military service in 1803 as a second lieutenant at the presidio of San Fernando de Carrizal, 75 miles south of El Paso del Norte, New Mexico. When a number of Spanish detachments marched from New Mexico and Texas to intercept American explorers in 1806, Melgares brought reinforcements from Carrizal and led his troops into Pawnee territory. After a party headed by Zebulon Pike, sent by the new governor of the Louisiana Territory to find the sources of the Red and Arkansas rivers, had become lost, a Spanish detachment rescued and arrested the men in 1807. Melgares and his soldiers accompanied Pike from Taos to Santa Fe and then down the Rio Grande to Chihuahua for further interrogation.

During Miguel Hidalgo's revolt of 1810, Melgares led royalist troops from Carrizal against the insurgents at Saltillo, Coahuila. Later he commanded an unsuccessful attack against Ignacio Allende, then participated in Allende's capture near Monclova, Coahuila, on 21 March 1811. By 1817, Melgares was commander of the Santa Fe presidio. In July 1818 he brought troops from Chihuahua to defend New Mexico against Comanche-American attacks, taking over as acting governor. He received permanent appointment to the post one month afterward, and spent the rest of the period of Spanish rule defending the territory against periodic reports of American moves and leading numerous retaliatory campaigns against the Navajos. In August 1819, Melgares successfully concluded a formal peace between Navajos and Spanish.

After Mexico became independent, Melgares refused to allow the colonists in New Mexico to swear allegiance to the new republic until he received a direct order from the commandant general. As a result, he was relieved as governor in April 1822, after citizens of the province brought charges against him on 5 July 1822.

See also **Mexico: The Colonial Period; Mexico: 1810–1910.**

BIBLIOGRAPHY

Zebulon Montgomery Pike, *The Journals of Zebulon Montgomery Pike*, 2 vols., edited by Donald Jackson (1966).

David J. Weber, *The Spanish Frontier in North America* (1992).

Arthur Gómez, "Royalist in Transition: Facundo Melgares, the Last Spanish Governor of New Mexico," in *New Mexico Historical Review* 68, no. 4 (1993): 371–387.

Additional Bibliography

Brooks, James S. *Captives and Cousins: Slavery, Kinship, and Community in the Southwest Borderlands.* Chapel Hill: University of North Carolina, 2002.

Burke, James T. *This Miserable Kingdom:The Story of the Spanish Presence in New Mexico and the Southwest from the Beginning until the 18th Century*. Albuquerque, NM: Our Lady of Fatima, 1994.

Forbes, Jack D. *Apache, Navajo, and Spaniard*. Norman: University of Oklahoma Press, 1994.

ROSS H. FRANK

MELLA, JULIO ANTONIO (1905–1929).

MELLA, JULIO ANTONIO (1905–1929). Julio Antonio Mella (*b.* 1905; *d.* 10 January 1929), cofounder and first secretary-general of the Cuban Communist Party. Mella received his early political training in the 1920s as a leader of the movement for university reform. He helped organize the first National Student Congress in 1923, the same year he took part in the famous "Protest of the Thirteen," in which thirteen of Havana's young intellectuals walked out of the Academy of Science when President Alfredo Zayas's minister of justice entered the hall.

Mella was also the editor of *Juventud,* a student literary journal, and it was his efforts as a student reformer that brought him in contact with Cuban Marxists, especially Carlos Baliño, a supporter of the Bolshevik Revolution. Along with Baliño, Mella cofounded the Cuban Communist Party in 1925 and was elected the party's first secretary-general. After the founding of the party, Mella gave weekly classes in politics for Havana labor unions, and he also led efforts to organize students in opposition to the Cuban dictator Gerardo Machado. Mella was arrested that same year when he led a student strike that shut down the University of Havana. In prison Mella organized a hunger strike that gained international attention.

In 1927 Mella was deported to Mexico, where he continued his work against the Machado regime and where he also served briefly in 1928 as the secretary-general of the Mexican Communist Party. On 10 January 1929, Mella was assassinated in Mexico City. Fidel Castro's government later claimed that Mella was killed by agents of the Machado government. But it is also possible that internal squabbles may have led to Mella's death, since two weeks before his assassination Mella was expelled from the Mexican Communist Party.

See also **Cuba, Political Parties: Communist Party.**

BIBLIOGRAPHY

Samuel Farber, *Revolution and Reaction in Cuba, 1933–1960* (1976).

Louis A. Pérez, Jr., *Cuba: Between Reform and Revolution* (1988).

Ramón Eduardo Ruiz, *Cuba: The Making of a Revolution* (1970).

Additional Bibliography

Cabrera, Olga. *Mella: Una historia en la política mexicocubana*. Guadalajara, Spain: Universidad de Guadalajara, 2002.

Cupull, Adys, and Frolián González. *Julio Antonio Mella y Tina Modotti contra el fascismo*. Havana, Cuba: Casa Editora Abril, 2005.

MICHAEL POWELSON

MELLA, RAMÓN MATÍAS (1816–1864).

MELLA, RAMÓN MATÍAS (1816–1864). Ramón Matías Mella (*b.* 25 February 1816; *d.* 4 July 1864), Dominican revolutionary, active in the nationalist movement that led to the establishment of the Dominican Republic in 1844. In 1822 the island of Hispañola fell under the control of Haitian bureaucrats and soldiers. In 1838 Mella and other Dominican nationalists organized a secret society, La Trinitaria (The Trinitarian), for the purpose of overthrowing the corrupt Haitian dictator, Jean-Pierre Boyer. Mella and the Trinitarians aligned themselves, for tactical reasons, with La Réforme, a Haitian reform movement led by Charles Hérard.

Once Boyer was defeated in 1843, however, Hérard turned on his Dominican allies and had Mella and other Trinitarians arrested and incarcerated at Port-au-Prince. A revolt against Hérard that broke out in 1843 in Port-au-Prince was quelled only with the help of Mella and his Dominican troops. As a reward Mella and his Dominican regiment were released by Hérard. Soon after their arrival in Santo Domingo, the eastern part of the island of Hispañola, Mella and his followers began the process of retaking it and proclaiming independence. On 27 February 1844, Mella and his forces secured the city of Santo Domingo and declared independence from Haiti. Mella was named a member of the new ruling junta that was given the task of organizing the new government. But even after the defeat of the Haitians, Mella's life was not safe, since bitter fighting broke out among the new rulers of the republic. By the summer of 1844, the powerful rancher Pedro Santana took over the ruling junta and had Mella imprisoned. In 1848 Mella accepted a general amnesty and was released from prison.

See also **Dominican Republic.**

BIBLIOGRAPHY

Louise L. Cripps, *The Spanish Caribbean: From Columbus to Castro* (1979).

John Edwin Fagg, *Cuba, Haiti, and the Dominican Republic* (1965).

Additional Bibliography

Cassá, Roberto. *Matías Ramón Mella: el patriotismo hecho acción.* Santo Domingo, Dominican Republic: Tobogan, 1999.

Cruz Sánchez, Filiberto. *Mella: biografía política.* Santo Domingo, Dominican Republic: Editora El Nuevo Diario, 1996.

MICHAEL POWELSON

MELLO, ZÉLIA MARIA CARDOSO DE (1953–). Zélia Maria Cardoso de Mello (*b.* 20 September 1953) served as the Brazilian minister of economy (1990–1991). The daughter of Emiliano Cardoso de Mello and Auzélia Cardoso de Mello, Mello was born in São Paulo. An economist by training, she was an analyst at the Banco Auxiliar de São Paulo in 1977 and an analyst at the Dumont Assessoria e Planejamento in 1978. She taught at the school of economics and business administration at the University of São Paulo until 1991, when she married television personality and comedian Chico Anysio.

Mello held her first political post in 1983, during the administration of André Franco Montoro, governor of the state of São Paulo. She also served as adviser to the executive board of the Companhia de Desenvolvimento Habitacional do Estado de São Paulo. In 1985, during the administration of President José Sarney, Mello was invited by Minister of the Treasury Dilson Funaro to work with André Calabi on negotiations regarding the debts owed to the federal government by the states and municipalities. At that time she became acquainted with Fernando Collor De Mello (no relation), the governor of Alagoas and later president of Brazil (1990).

In 1987, at the time of Minister of Treasury Dilson Funaro's resignation, she left the Sarney administration and founded the firm ZLC-Consultores Associados, which advised public and private enterprises in business negotiations. One of the firm's first major clients was Governor Fernando Collor de Mello. Upon his decision to run for the presidency, Mello joined his campaign. In 1990, she was appointed minister of economy, treasury, and planning, the first woman to hold such a position. She was in charge of implementing economic strategies outlined in the Brasil Novo (New Brazil) plan. Mello's affair with a fellow married cabinet member led to her resignation, and she left the government on 9 May 1991 to resume her teaching and consulting career. She then returned to the University of São Paulo and continued consulting in Brazil. In 1995, she moved to New York to become a visiting scholar at Columbia University's Institute of Latin America and Iberian Studies. In 1998, she and her husband Anysio, divorced. They have two children. As of 2003, she was Brazil adviser to ORIX Trade Capital in New York.

See also **Economic Commission for Latin America and the Caribbean (ECLAC); Economic Development.**

BIBLIOGRAPHY

Barrosso, Pessoa. *Zélia: Tesão? Paixão? Ou traiçao?* São Paulo: P. Barrosso, 1992.

Sabino, Fernando Tavares. *Zélia, uma paixão.* Rio de Janeiro: Editora Record, 1991.

ÎÊDA SIQUEIRO WIARDA

MELO, CUSTÓDIO JOSÉ DE (1846–1902). Custódio José de Melo (*b.* 9 June 1846; *d.* 15 March 1902), Brazilian veteran of the Paraguayan War and principal figure in a naval revolt during the civil war of 1893. Melo, whose father was a career army officer, distinguished himself in numerous battles during the Paraguayan War. In the Brazilian military he held various positions of command, mostly on ships. Bahian delegate to the Constitutent Assembly of 1890–1891, Melo opposed the dissolution of Congress by President Manoel Deodoro da Fonseca on 3 November 1891 and launched a rebellion of the fleet that produced Fonseca's resignation. Vice

President Floriano Peixoto took control and named Melo minister of the navy.

A debate over interpretation of the constitution concerning whether Peixoto should have called new elections plus his clash with the Federalists of Rio Grande do Sul brought on the civil war of 1893 and a second revolt of the fleet under Melo. Peixoto resisted and Melo found himself facing a test of arms. Shore batteries at the military forts challenged the naval ships, some of which escaped, one with Melo aboard, and sailed to Santa Catarina, where they made contact with the Federalist rebels. Agreement between Melo and the rebels proved impossible, and Melo sailed toward Buenos Aires. By March 1894 Vice President Peixoto had acquired warships from Europe and the United States, and his superior naval strength, coupled with the support of five large U.S. naval vessels in the harbor, made the position of the rebel ships in Guanabara Bay untenable. Melo took refuge aboard a Portuguese ship and sailed into exile. He was eventually pardoned and returned to Rio to write his memoirs.

See also **War of the Triple Alliance.**

BIBLIOGRAPHY

Custódio José de Melo, *Apontamentos para a história da revolução de 23 de novembro de 1891,* 2 vols. (1895), and *O governo provisório e a revolução de 1891* (1938).

José Maria Bello, *A Modern History of Brazil,* translated by James L. Taylor (1966).

Olinto Lima Freire de Pilar, *Os Patronos das Forças Armadas* (1966).

June E. Hahner, *Civilian-Military Relations in Brazil, 1889–1898* (1969), pp. 49–72.

Additional Bibliography

Corrêa, Carlos Humberto. *Militares e civis num governo sem rumo: O governo provisório revolucionário de Desterro, 1893–1894.* Florianópolis, Brazil: Editora da UFSC, co-edição Editora Lunardelli, 1990.

ROBERT A. HAYES

MELO, JOSÉ MARÍA (1800–1860).

José María Melo (*b.* 9 October 1800; *d.* 1 June 1860), Colombian military leader. A consummate professional military officer, Melo revolted in 1854 in defense of a permanent military institution. Born in Ibagué in west-central Colombia, Melo entered the patriot army in 1819 and participated in the battle of Ayacucho. He served in the Venezuelan military from 1830 to 1835, when he was expelled for his role in the Revolution of the Reforms. Melo served for three years at a Bremen military academy, after which he joined the War of the Supremes (1840–1842) against the Colombian government. President Tomás Cipriano de Mosquera restored his military rank in 1849. José María López appointed Melo commanding general of the department of Cundinamarca in 1849. The efforts of the Gólgotas to eliminate the permanent military led Melo to found the promilitary *El Orden* in 1852. Melo's ill-fated 17 April 1854 revolt failed to attract the support of leading Draconian Liberals. In exile, Melo continued his military career in Central America and Mexico, only to be killed in service to Benito Juárez.

BIBLIOGRAPHY

Alirio Gómez Picón, *El golpe militar del 17 de abril de 1854: La dictadura de José María Melo, el enigma de Obando, los secretos de la historia* (1972).

Dario Ortiz Vidales, *José María Melo: La razón de un rebelde* (1980).

Additional Bibliography

Homenaje al general José María Melo, soldado de Bolívar sacrificado en Chiapas. Tuxtla Gutiérrez, Mexico: Ayuntamiento, 1989.

Vargas Martínez, Gustavo. *José María Melo: Los artesanos y el socialismo.* Bogota, Colombia: Planeta, 1998.

DAVID SOWELL

MELO, LEOPOLDO (1869–1951).

Leopoldo Melo (*b.* 15 November 1869; *d.* 6 February 1951), Argentine politician, lawyer, and university professor. Melo was born in Diamante, in the province of Entre Ríos, and graduated from law school in 1891. An expert in maritime and business law, he taught these subjects for over thirty years at the University of Buenos Aires. He served as a national deputy to Congress from Entre Ríos from 1914 to 1916, and as a senator from 1917 to 1930. In the 1928 elections he was the presidential candidate of the conservative wing of the Radical Civic Union (UCR), but he was defeated by Hipólito Yrigoyen, the candidate of the Personalist faction. Melo served as minister of the interior (the political arm of the executive power in Argentina) under the conservative president Agustín P. Justo from 1932 to 1936. He presided over the Argentine delegations to the Inter-American conferences in Panama (1939) and Havana (1940), and wrote extensively on juridical matters. Melo died in Pinamar, in the province of Buenos Aires.

See also **Argentina, Political Parties: Radical Party (UCR).**

BIBLIOGRAPHY

Lacoste, Pablo. *La Unión Cívica Radical en Mendoza y en la Argentina, 1890-1946: Aportes para el estudio de la inestabilidad política en la Argentina.* Mendoza: Ediciones Culturales de Mendoza, 1994.

Persello, Ana Virginia. *El partido radical: Gobierno y oposición, 1916-1943.* Buenos Aires: Siglo veintiuno editores Argentina, 2004.

CELSO RODRÍGUEZ

MELO E CASTRO, MARTINHO DE

(1716–1795). Martinho de Melo e Castro (*b.* 11 November 1716; *d.* 24 March 1795), Portuguese diplomat (1751–1770), overseas minister (1770–1795). Born in Lisbon, Melo e Castro was a younger son of Francisco de Melo e Castro, Governor of Mazagão in North Africa (1705–1713), and Dona Maria Joaquina Xavier da Silva. His older brother, Manuel Bernardo de Melo e Castro, became the first and only viscount of Lourinha in 1777, after having served as governor and captain-general of Grão Pará and Maranhão (1759–1763). In his youth Melo e Castro followed an ecclesiastical career and studied at Évora and Coimbra. At what time he changed careers is not clear. From 1753 to 1755 he served as envoy to the Netherlands. The following year he was transferred to London, where he held the post of envoy extraordinary and minister plenipotentiary from 1756 to 1762. In that latter year he traveled to France, where he represented Portugal as minister plenipotentiary at the peace talks at Fontainebleau (1762) and Paris (1763) that ended the Seven Years' War (1756–1763). Following the signing of the treaties, Melo e Castro briefly visited Portugal before returning to England, where he continued to serve as envoy extraordinary and minister plenipotentiary until 1770.

On 4 January 1770, he was named secretary of state for naval and overseas affairs, a post he held until his death in 1795. His correspondence during that twenty-five-year tenure is of great importance for understanding Brazil during some of the most critical years of its history. Jacome Ratton, the French-born but naturalized Portuguese merchant, industrialist, memoirist, and contemporary of Melo e Castro, described him as honest, though very stubborn and pro-English. He was well aware of the importance of Portuguese America. In 1779 he wrote: "Portugal without Brazil is an insignificant power." A strong opponent of mercantilism, Melo e Castro was in favor of monopoly companies, against "workshops and manufactories" in Brazil, and greatly concerned about the defense of Portuguese America and the extensive illegal trade carried on there. However, he was outvoted regarding the fate of Brazil's commercial companies, and the Company of Grão Pará and Maranhão lost its monopoly status in 1778, as did the Company of Pernambuco and Paraíba two years later. Melo e Castro was minister during the difficult period of adjustment in Minas Gerais in the aftermath of the gold boom. The Minas conspiracy of 1788–1789 was uncovered while he was in power.

See also **Trading Companies, Portuguese.**

BIBLIOGRAPHY

Kenneth R. Maxwell, *Conflicts and Conspiracies: Brazil and Portugal, 1750–1808* (1973).

Jacome Ratton, *Recordaçoens... sobre occurrencias do seu tempo em Portugal...* (London, 1813).

José Vicente-Serrão, "Melo e Castro, Martinho de," in *Diccionário ilustrado da história de Portugal,* vol. 1 (1985), p. 459.

FRANCIS DUTRA

MELO FRANCO, AFONSO ARINOS DE

(1905–1990). Afonso Arinos de Melo Franco (*b.* 27 November 1905; *d.* 27 August 1990), Brazilian constitutional lawyer, politician, writer, and diplomat. The son of diplomat Afrânio de Melo Franco, Afonso Arinos was born into a distinguished family of the state of Minas Gerais. A lawyer, he initially devoted himself to legal and historical writing, leaving politics to his father and brother, Virgílio Martins de Melo Franco. At the death of his father in 1943, Afonso Arinos joined the Friends of America to continue his father's opposition to the Estado Novo. He advocated economic and political liberalism and, in 1945, helped found the União Democrática Nacional (UDN), the opposition party to Getúlio Vargas and later Juscelino Kubitschek. He served as a federal deputy (1947–1959), a senator (1959–1961), and as minister of foreign relations under Jânio Quadros (1961) and, briefly, João Goulart (1962). Melo Franco was an architect of Brazil's increasingly independent foreign policy vis-à-vis the United States. Under Quadros, he declined to support U.S. pressure on Cuba, advocated seating the People's Republic of China in the United Nations, and sought to restore diplomatic ties with the Soviet Union. However, as Goulart allied with the left, Melo Franco supported the president's overthrow. Only after the military indicated its intention of staying in power did Melo Franco oppose the regime, leading the congressional debate against the Constitution of 1967. When it passed, stripping the Congress of its powers, Melo Franco declined to run again for office, returning to academia (his works on history and law total nearly forty) until asked by President José Sarney in 1985 to organize the drafting of a new, democratic constitution. He later served again as a senator.

See also **Brazil, Political Parties: National Democratic Union of Brazil (UDN).**

BIBLIOGRAPHY

Israel Beloch and Alzira Alves De Abreu, eds., *Dicionário Histórico-Biográfico Brasileiro, 1930–1983* (1984).

Peter Flynn, *Brazil: A Political Analysis* (1978).

Thomas E. Skidmore, *Politics in Brazil, 1930–1964: An Experiment in Democracy* (1967).

Thomas E. Skidmore, *The Politics of Military Rule in Brazil, 1964–1985* (1988).

Additional Bibliography

Arinos Filho, Afonso. *Diplomacia independente: Um legado de Afonso Arinos.* São Paulo, Brazil: Paz e Terra, 2001.

Lattman-Weltman, Fernando. *A política domesticada: Afonso Arinos e o colapso da democracia em 1964.* Rio de Janeiro: FGV Editora, 2005.

ELIZABETH A. COBBS

MELO FRANCO, AFRÂNIO DE (1870–1943).

Afrânio de Melo Franco (*b.* 25 February 1870; *d.* 1 January 1943), Brazilian politician and diplomat. Afrânio de Melo Franco was born into a prominent family of the state of Minas Gerais. Trained as a lawyer, he joined with other students in 1889 to support Brazil's transition to a republican government dominated by powerful states ("Rule of the Governors"). During the First Republic he served as secretary of the legation to Uruguay, a federal deputy (1906–1929), and eventually as Brazil's representative to the League of Nations (1924–1926). As a leading *mineiro,* Melo Franco benefited from the political power of Minas Gerais and São Paulo, known as the "café com leite" (coffee with milk) alliance. In 1929 Melo Franco threw his support to Getúlio Vargas in the national contest for power leading to the Estado Novo. Vargas made Melo Franco his first minister of foreign relations (1930–33), giving him a relatively free hand in the running of Itamaraty. Melo Franco reorganized the ministry, emphasizing foreign trade and, in light of growing world tensions, Pan-Americanism. Along with Oswaldo Aranha, Melo Franco viewed cooperation with the United States as the surest road to national security and the key to Brazil's growing power within Latin America. Melo Franco represented Brazil at the Inter-American Conference of 1938, where he helped induce Argentina to join in the Declaration of Lima. He broke with Vargas in 1933 over a question of political patronage and, just before his death, joined the Friends of America, a group seeking democratization and an end to the Estado Novo.

See also **Estado Novo.**

BIBLIOGRAPHY

Alfonso Arinos de Melo Franco, *Um estadista da república: Afrânio de Melo Franco e seu tempo,* 3 vols. (1955).

Israel Beloch and Alzira Alves de Abreu, eds., *Dicionário Histórico-Biográfico Brasileiro, 1930–1983* (1984).

Peter Flynn, *Brazil: A Political Analysis* (1978).

Stanley E. Hilton, *Brazil and the Great Powers, 1930–1939* (1975).

Additional Bibliography

Soares, Alvaro Teixeira. *Afrânio de Melo Franco, diplomata e internacionalista.* Rio de Janeiro: Ministério das Relações Exteriores, Seção de Publicaçoes, 1970.

ELIZABETH A. COBBS

MELO NETO, JOÃO CABRAL DE

(1920–1999). João Cabral de Melo Neto (*b.* 9 January 1920, *d.* October 1999), Brazilian poet. Born in Recife, Pernambuco, Melo Neto spent his childhood on a sugarcane plantation and attended Catholic schools. In 1942 he published his first collection of poems and moved to Rio de Janeiro to study for the foreign service. During his long diplomatic career, he resided in England, France, Switzerland, and Senegal, as well as in Spain and Spanish America. From the late 1940s his literary reputation grew steadily, and near the end of the twentieth century he was widely regarded as the most important Brazilian poet of the century's second half.

A unique figure in the cultural sphere, Melo Neto has commanded respect both for pure aesthetic principles and for the social perspectives of his work. He has influenced such diverse genres as concretism, regional verse, literature of commitment, and the poetry of song (Música Popular Brasileira). His is not a conventional lyricism of self-expression but rather a controlled objective discourse, often connected to the actual settings and human realities of the northeastern region. In 1968, he was elected to the Brazilian Academy of Letters. He received the prestigious Camões Prize in 1990 for lifetime literary achievement in Portuguese and two years later the Twelfth Neustadt International Prize for Literature (sponsored by *World Literature Today*). When he lost his sight in 1994, he stopped writing poetry. In 1995, his *Selected Poetry, 1930–1990* was published in English. He died in October 1999 in Rio de Janeiro.

See also **Literature: Brazil.**

BIBLIOGRAPHY

Selected Poetry, 1937–1990 (various translators), edited by Djelal Kadir (1994). See also Antônio Carlos Secchin, *João Cabral: A poesia do menos* (1985).

Marta Peixoto, "João Cabral de Melo Neto," in *Dictionary of Brazilian Literature,* edited by Irwin Stern (1988).

Additional Bibliography

Baptista, Abel Barros. *O livro agreste: Ensaio de curso de literatura brasileira.* Campinas: Editora Unicamp, 2005.

Castello, José. *João Cabral do Melo Neto: O homem sem alma; Diário de tudo.* Rio de Janeiro: Bertrand Brasil, 2006.

Suttana, Renato. *João Cabral de Melo Neto: O poeta e a voz da modernidade.* São Paulo: Scortecci Editora, 2005.

CHARLES A. PERRONE

MELVILLE, THOMAS AND MARGARITA.

Thomas and Margarita (Marjorie) Melville are U.S. Catholic missionaries in Guatemala who became revolutionaries. Margarita Bradford (*b.* 19 August 1929) was born in Irapuato, Mexico, and studied at Loretto Academy in El Paso, Texas. She became Maryknoll Sister Marion Peter and was assigned in 1954 to teach at an upper-class school in Guatemala City. Influenced by the *cursillo de capacitación social* (short course of social empowerment) movement, she began to spend time teaching the urban poor and organizing vacation projects for affluent students in poverty-stricken rural areas. Thomas Melville (*b.* 5 December 1930), from Newton, Massachusetts, joined the Maryknoll order and, after ordination in 1957, was sent to work with Indians in the Guatemalan highlands. He helped them form cooperatives. Later he organized an Indian resettlement program in the Petén.

Both missioners became involved with radical university students, some of whom had contact with guerrillas. Frustrated by what they felt was a lack of commitment to the poor by church leaders, they decided to join the guerrilla movement, in order to give it a "Christian presence." Their plan was discovered, and they were expelled from Guatemala in 1967. Soon both left Maryknoll, and they were married in 1968. They then joined a group of Vietnam war protestors burning draft cards in Catonsville, Maryland. They both served time in federal prison for these activities. They later earned doctoral degrees in anthropology and wrote *Guatemala: The Politics of Land Ownership* (1971). In 2005, Thomas published *Through a Glass Darkly: The U.S. Holocaust in Central America.*

See also **Guatemala; Maryknoll Order.**

BIBLIOGRAPHY

The Melvilles defend their actions in Guatemala in *Whose Heaven, Whose Earth?* (1971), an autobiography.

Additional Bibliography

Berhens, Susan Fitzpatrick. *Confronting Colonialism: Maryknoll Catholic Missionaries in Peru and Guatemala, 1943–1968.* Notre Dame, IN: The Helen Kellogg Institute for International Studies, 2007.

Pullapilly, Cyriac K. *Christianity and Native Cultures: Perspectives from Different Regions of the World.* Notre Dame, IN: Cross Cultural Publications, 2004.

EDWARD T. BRETT

MENCHÚ TUM, RIGOBERTA (1959–). Rigoberta Menchú Tum (*b.* 9 January 1959) is the recipient of the 1992 Nobel Peace Prize. Menchú is a Maya-Quiché Indian woman from Guatemala and the first indigenous Latin American so honored. She is a member of the Coordinating Commission of the Committee of Peasant Unity (CUC) and a founding member of the United Representation of the Guatemalan Opposition (RUOG). She was born in Chimel, near San Miguel de Uspantán, to Vicente Menchú and Juana Tum, Maya peasants and Catholic lay leaders. Self-educated, from the age of eight she accompanied her parents to harvest export crops on south coast plantations, and later worked for two years as a domestic in Guatemala City. She participated with her parents in local pastoral activities.

In the 1970s, expropriation of Indian land in El Quiché threatened Maya subsistence and prompted her family's political activism and involvement with the CUC. In the late 1970s, Menchú organized local self-defense groups, armed with rocks and machetes, in response to the government's escalated counterinsurgency war in the highlands. In January 1980, her father was burned to death in the occupation of the Spanish embassy in Guatemala City by campesinos with the support of trade unionists and students. Menchú continued organizing efforts in local Maya communities until forced to flee in 1981; since then she has lived in Mexico City.

A powerful speaker, Menchú has continued to work for peace and the rights of indigenous people in Guatemala in international forums. She has participated in the U.N. Working Group on Indigenous Populations, the U.N. Subcommission on Prevention of Discrimination and Protection for Minorities, and the U.N. Conference on the Decade of Women. She is a credentialed observer of the U.N. Human Rights Commission and the General Assembly. She serves on the board of the International Indian Treaty Council and was a member of honor at the Second Continental Gathering of the "500 Years of Resistance" Conference. Among other awards, she has received the 1988 Nonino Prize special award, the 1990 Monseñor Proaño Human Rights Prize, the 1990 UNESCO Education for Peace Prize, and the 1991 French Committee for the Defense of Freedoms and Human Rights Prize.

Since the end of the Guatemalan civil war in 1996, Menchú has continued her involvement with politics. In 1999 she pressured the Spanish government to prosecute former Guatemalan government and military figures for the atrocities they committed or ordered. (Such charges cannot be brought in Guatemalan courts.) In December 2006, Spain called for the extradition of two of the main military leaders who had been involved. The Spanish government also declared that genocide committed abroad could be brought to trial in Spain, even if no Spanish citizens had been involved. Menchú is also involved with Mexican government efforts to bring low-cost generic medicines to the public. She ran in the September 2007 Guatemalan presidential election but was eliminated in the first round.

Menchú was also at the center of a heated controversy when anthropologist David Stoll researched her story and claims for his 1999 book, *Rigoberta Menchú and the Story of All Poor Guatemalans.* He maintained that in fact she altered many details of her life story in order to make it more compelling. Based on these falsifications, some called for her prize to be revoked, but the Nobel Committee has refused to do so.

See also **Human Rights.**

BIBLIOGRAPHY

Elisabeth Burgos-Debray, ed., *I, Rigoberta Menchú: An Indian Woman in Guatemala,* translated by Ann Wright (1983).

Additional Bibliography

Arias, Arturo, ed. *The Rigoberta Menchú Controversy.* Minneapolis: University of Minnesota Press, 2001.

Morales, Mario Roberto, and Elisabeth Burgos-Debray. *Stoll-Menchú: La invención de la memoria*. Guatemala: Consucultura, 2001.

Sánchez, David de Frutos. *Rigoberta Menchú*. Madrid: Edimat Libros, 2005.

Stoll, David. *Rigoberta Menchú and the Story of All Poor Guatemalans*. Boulder, CO: Westview Press, 1999.

MARILYN M. MOORS

MENDES, GILBERTO

MENDES, GILBERTO (1922–). Gilberto Mendes (*b.* 13 October 1922), Brazilian composer, teacher, critic. Gilberto Mendes has been associated with experimental movements in Brazilian music, most notably the Música Nova group. The *Manifesto música nova,* published in 1963, expressed a commitment to explore every aspect of contemporary musical language, including concertism, impressionism, polytonalism, atonality, serialism, phonomechanical sound, and all aspects of electronic media. Composers associated with the Música Nova group included Willy Correia de Oliveira, Rogério Duprat, Damiano Cozzella, and Júlio Medaglia.

Mendes studied composition with Henri Pousseur, Pierre Boulez, and Karlheinz Stockhausen. One of his best-known compositions, "Beba Coca-Cola" (Drink Coca-Cola), is a satire on a Coca-Cola commercial. In 1970 his composition "Blirium a-9" was chosen by the International Council of Composers of UNESCO for broadcast in Europe. In 1974 his composition "Santos Football Music" won an award from the Associação Paulista de Críticos de Artes as the best experimental work. In 1973 "Pausa e Menopausa" (Pause and Menopause), a composition based on a poem of Ronaldo Azeredo, explored the idea of indeterminacy, in which music could be written as poetry without text, music without sound, and visual impressions without sound. In 1978–1979 Mendes accepted an appointment at the University of Wisconsin–Milwaukee. In 1983 he was a visiting professor at the University of Texas at Austin. During this period numerous performances of his works were given in the United States. He has received many honors, including the Premio Carlos Gomes, the Premio Santos Vivo and the 2003 Premio Sergio Mota, all in Brazil.

See also **Music: Popular Music and Dance.**

BIBLIOGRAPHY

Gérard Béhague, *Music in Latin America* (1979).

David P. Appleby, *The Music of Brazil* (1983).

Additional Bibliography

Bezerra, Márcio. *A Unique Brazilian Composer: A Study of the Music of Gilberto Mendes through Selected Piano Pieces.* Brussels: A. van Kerckhoven, 2003.

Gandelman, Saloméa. *36 compositores brasileiros: Obras para piano (1950–1988).* Rio de Janeiro: Ministro da Cultura, Funarte, 1997.

Santos, Antonio Eduardo. *O antropofagismo na obra pianística de Gilberto Mendes.* São Paulo: Annablume: FAPSEP, 1997.

DAVID P. APPLEBY

MENDES FILHO, FRANCISCO ("CHICO") ALVES

MENDES FILHO, FRANCISCO ("CHICO") ALVES (1944–1988). The Brazilian environmental activist and labor leader Chico Mendes was born in inland Acre on December 15, 1944. The son of rubber tappers, he went to work at age eleven with his father harvesting rubber. Rubber tappers cut trees to gather latex, the raw material for rubber. Tapping is a sustainable method that does not harm the trees, much less the forest.

In the early 1970s the Amazon rain forest was invaded by cattle ranchers who cleared trees to make room for their herds. The Rural Workers' Union of Brasiléia formed in 1975 and Mendes was chosen as its secretary-general. Leading a group of fellow rubber tappers who depended on the forest for their livelihood, Mendes decided to fight against deforestation. His approach, known as "the impasse," consisted of hugging the trees, using one's body to prevent them from being cut down. This peaceful form of protest earned him the nickname "Gandhi of the Rain Forest."

In 1977 he became a councilor in his native town of Xapuri. His increasingly high profile led to death threats, and his term in office was very nearly suspended. Because of infighting among the Council members, Mendes was able to take over as Council president. Between June and September 1979 he turned the Council into a major forum for debates among union, grassroots, and religious leaders. The reaction of the foes within the Council was strong.

Accused of subversion, he was subjected to harsh interrogation by authorities: Brazil was under a dictatorship so Chico was arrested and tortured without a warrant. Under heavy political pressure, he resigned as Council president in October 1979. He founded the Workers Party in Acre in 1980 and ran unsuccessfully for state representative (1982) and mayor of Xapuri (1985).

Following a period of heightened conflict in which both trade unionists and ranchers were killed, Mendes was interrogated again. Under the National Security Act he was ultimately charged with inciting landowners to violence. The trial was held in 1981 in the Manaus Military Tribunal. With no money for a lawyer, Mendes was defended with support from various organizations and released on probation. Another trial, three years later, cleared him because of lack of evidence.

In 1981 he became the director of the Xapuri Workers' Union. His struggle began to draw national attention, with support from civil rights workers. Four years later he chaired the first national conference of rubber tappers, held in Brasilia, resulting in the creation of the National Rubber Tappers' Council He also helped create the Forest Peoples Alliance for the benefit of the natives and rubber tappers and to defend the Amazon rain forest.

American environmentalists and members of the United Nations Environment Programme visited Xapuri in 1987, and Mendes showed them the devastation wrought by projects financed by international banks. Later he went to the United States to participate in the Inter-American Development Bank's annual conference and to explain rain forest issues to the U.S. Congress. He managed to get the financing revoked, but ranchers and politicians accused him of hindering progress in the region. Internationally his actions won him various awards, including the UN's Global 500 Prize. In 1988 Mendes continued his fight amid an increasing number of death threats. He died in an ambush on December 22. Two of the suspects were arrested, while one remains at large.

On the same day of Mendes' death, the Chico Mendes Committee was created. It is an articulation of non-governmental, unions' and students' organizations that fights for the punishment of the murderers and to keep Mendes' struggle and his memory alive. As Mendes once said, "At first I thought I was fighting to save rubber trees, then I thought I was fighting to save the Amazon rain forest. Now I realize I am fighting for humanity."

See also **Brazil: Since 1889; Forests.**

BIBLIOGRAPHY

Comitê Chico Mendes. "O homem da floresta." Available from http://www.chicomendes.org/chicomendes01.php.

Souza, Marcio. *O empate contra Chico Mendes.* São Paulo: Marco Zero, 1988.

Additional Bibliography

Martins, Edilson. *Chico Mendes: Um povo da floresta.* Rio de Janeiro: Garamond, 1998.

Souza, Márcio. *Chico Mendes.* São Paulo, Brazil: Callis Editora, 2005.

Ventura, Zuenir. *Chico Mendes, crime e castigo: Quinze anos depois, o autor volta ao Acre para concluir a mais premiada reportagem sobre o heroói dos Povos da Floresta.* São Paulo, Brazil: Companhia das Letras, 2003.

CARMEN LUCIA DE AZEVEDO

MENDES MACIEL, ANTÔNIO VICENTE.

See **Conselheiro, Antônio.**

MÉNDEZ BALLESTER, MANUEL (1909–2002). Manuel Méndez Ballester (*b.* 4 August 1909, *d.* 24 January 2002), Puerto Rican dramatist. Born in Aguadilla, Puerto Rico, Méndez Ballester began his career in theater as an actor with the Teatro Rodante (Traveling Theater). His first publications were *Isla cerrera* (Wild island, 1937), a historical novel about the resistance of the Puerto Rican Indians to the Spanish Conquest, and *El clamor de los surcos* (1940), a rural drama. In 1939 he studied under a Rockefeller grant in New York, where he penned his famous *Tiempo muerto* (Dead time, 1940), a tragedy about the sugarcane worker during the idle season. His 1958 drama about Puerto Ricans in New York, *Encrucijada* (The crossroads), was staged at the First Puerto Rican Theater Festival. *El milagro* (1957), an avant-garde metaphysical play, debuted the next year in English in New York as *The Miracle.* Two of his well-known satirical works are *Bienvenido, don Goyito* (Welcome, Mr. Goyito, 1966) and *Arriba las mujeres* (Long live women, 1968).

In addition to writing, producing, and directing theatrical productions, Méndez Ballester served as assistant secretary of labor from 1954 to 1962 and subsequently, until 1968, as a member of the House of Representatives, where he initiated environmental reforms. In 1970, he wrote a drama entitled "Invasión y jugando al divorcio." In 1975, he completed a comedy, "Los Cocorocos." A versatile dramatist, Méndez Ballester has cultivated classical tragedy, historical theater, the theater of the absurd, social satire, farce, and zarzuela (operetta). The conflict of material and spiritual values is an abiding theme in his writing, which in addition to novels and drama includes stories, essays, and a humorous column in *El Nuevo Día*. In 1992 the Institute of Puerto Rican Culture published a two-volume collection of his plays. In 1998, the Inter-American University of Puerto Rico established a "Sala Manuel Mendez Ballester," in his honor. He died in San Juan on January 24, 2002.

See also **Theater.**

BIBLIOGRAPHY

Robert A. Riccio, "Studies in Puerto Rican Drama I: *Encrucijada*," *Atenea* (Mayagüez, Puerto Rico) 1, no. 4 (1964): 15–20.

Francisco Arriví, "La generación del treinta: El teatro," *Literatura puertorriqueña: 21 Conferencias* (1969), pp. 387–396.

Additional Bibliography

Cazurro García de Quintana, Carmen. *Medio siglo de periodismo humorístico-satírico: El humor como fórmula artística de significación en el periodismo de Manuel Méndez Ballester.* San Germán, PR: Universidad Interamericana de Puerto Rico, 1993.

Méndez Ballester, Manuel. *En broma y en serio.* San Juan: Biblioteca de autores puerrtoriqueños, 1992.

Vissepó-Altman Torres, Dora. *La obra literaria de Manuel Méndez Ballester.* Madrid, Spain: Verbum, 2003.

ESTELLE IRIZARRY

MÉNDEZ FLEITAS, EPIFANIO (1917–1985).

Epifanio Méndez Fleitas (*b.* 1917; *d.* 22 November 1985), Paraguayan political leader. An early associate of President Federico Chaves (1949–1959), Méndez Fleitas first rose to a position of prominence when the latter came to power in 1949. As chief of police, Méndez Fleitas worked to defend Chaves's interests. He was named director of the Agrarian Reform Institute and later president of the Central Bank. At the same time, he rose rapidly within the "leftist" faction of the ruling Colorado Party, in part because of Chaves's patronage but also because of his own exceptional energy and forceful oratorical style.

Wishing to rise still further, Méndez Fleitas organized a plot with the help of General Alfredo Stroessner, head of the artillery section of the army. In early May 1954, the coup was carried out, but shortly thereafter, Stroessner exiled his fellow conspirator to Buenos Aires and went on to impose a dictatorship that lasted until 1989.

In the Argentine capital, Méndez Fleitas published polemical writings and composed folk music. He also established the Movimiento Popular Colorado (MOPOCO), an emigré group composed of Colorados who had turned against Stroessner. MOPOCO continued to be a major center of opposition to the dictator, though its founder encountered a loss of prestige when it was alleged in the 1970s that he had accepted money from the Central Intelligence Agency. Méndez Fleitas died in Buenos Aires.

See also **Paraguay, Political Parties: Colorado Party.**

BIBLIOGRAPHY

Charles J. Kolinski, *Historical Dictionary of Paraguay* (1973).

Paul H. Lewis, *Paraguay under Stroessner* (1980), *passim.*

Additional Bibliography

Méndez-Faith, Teresa. *Antología del recuerdo: Méndez Fleitas en la memoria de su pueblo.* Asunción, Paraguay: Editorial El Lector, 1995.

Seiferheld, Alfredo M., and José Luis de Tone, editors. *El Asilo a Perón y la caída de Epifanio Méndez: Una visión documental norteamericana.* Asunción, Paraguay: Editorial Histórica, 1988.

THOMAS L. WHIGHAM

MÉNDEZ MONTENEGRO, JULIO CÉSAR (1915–1996).

Julio César Méndez Montenegro, (*b.* 23 November 1915, *d.* 30 April 1996), president of Guatemala (1966–1970). Born in Guatemala City, Méndez Montenegro interrupted his legal studies at the University of San Carlos to participate in the 1944 October Revolution. He was the first president of the Frente Popular Libertador (FPL), which supported Juan José Arévalo for president in 1945. After receiving his *licenciatura* in 1945, he taught at the National University until 1965, rising to dean of the law school.

After the mysterious death of his brother, two-time Partido Revolucionario (PR) presidential candidate Mario Méndez Montenegro (1912–1965), he agreed to substitute for him in the 1966 elections. He defeated the military-backed PID (Institutional Democratic Party) candidate by 45,000 votes but, because he did not receive an absolute majority, had to bargain with the military and its legislative supporters to secure the confirmation of the Congress. As a result, Méndez gave the military both a free hand in conducting the war against the guerrillas in the eastern departments of the country and virtual control of the countryside.

The Méndez Montenegro administration is remembered primarily for the "scorched earth" rural pacification campaigns led by Colonel Carlos Arana Osorio (his successor in office [1970]), the kidnapping of Archbishop Mario Casariego (1968), and for the emergence of the Mano Blanca (White Hand) and other right-wing terrorist organizations. However, his government pushed through some reform measures, most notably the nationalization of the railroad owned by the United Fruit Company. Schools, public hospitals, port facilities, and a major hydroelectric plant were constructed. Some *campesino* organizing and limited land distribution were attempted, but the regime was frustrated in its agrarian reform efforts. Attempts to overhaul the tax code were defeated by street demonstrations.

After leaving office, Méndez Montenegro held a law professorship at the University of San Carlos. He died April 30, 1996.

See also **Guatemala; United Fruit Company.**

BIBLIOGRAPHY

Thomas Melville and Marjorie Melville, *Guatemala—Another Vietnam?* (1971).

William E. Thoms, "Civilian President Julio César Méndez Montenegro and His Guatemala" (M.A. thesis, Tulane University, 1977).

Michael Mc Clintock, *The American Connection,* vol. 2, *State Terror and Popular Resistance in Guatemala* (1985).

James Dunkerley, *Power in the Isthmus: A Political History of Modern Guatemala* (1988).

Additional Bibliography

Brockett, Charles D. *Political Movements and Violence in Central America.* Cambridge: Cambridge University Press, 2005.

Jonas, Susanne. *The Battle for Guatemala: Rebels, Death Squads, and U.S. Power.* Boulder, CO: Westview Press, 1991.

Soto Rosales, Carlos Rafael. *El sueño encadenado: El proceso político guatemalteco, 1944–1999.* Guatemala: Tipografía Nacional, 2002.

ROLAND H. EBEL

MÉNDEZ MONTENEGRO, MARIO

(1912–1965). Mario Méndez Montenegro (*b.* 30 November 1912; *d.* 31 October 1965), mayor of Guatemala City (1944–1948) and founder of the Partido Revolucionario (PR). Born in Santa Rosa, he interrupted his law studies, which he completed in exile, to participate in the October Revolution (1944). He served as undersecretary of the junta and as secretary general of the presidency under Juan José Arévalo (1945–1951). In 1947 he broke with the radicals in the Revolutionary Action Party (PAR) and reconstituted the center-left Popular Liberation Front (Frente Popular Libertador—FPL), which he had helped found in 1944.

In 1957 Méndez Montenegro organized the PR from among the moderate supporters of Arévalo. When the PR was denied legal registration for the elections of 1957, Méndez Montenegro supported the street demonstrations led by General Miguel Ydígoras Fuentes (president, 1958–1963) that annulled them. He became the legal PR candidate for the January 1958 electoral rerun and received 28 percent of the vote. Opposed both ideologically and politically to the Ydígoras Fuentes regime, he backed the 1963 military coup that overthrew Fuentes. He died from a gunshot wound in October 1965, shortly before being nominated as the PR presidential candidate for the elections of 1966. Whether Méndez Montenegro was assassinated or committed suicide remains unclear.

See also **Guatemala, Political Parties: Revolutionary Action Party.**

BIBLIOGRAPHY

Francisco Villagrán Kramer, *Biografía política de Guatemala: Los pactos políticos de 1944 a 1970* (1993).

ROLAND H. EBEL

MÉNDEZ PEREIRA, OCTAVIO (1887–1954). Octavio Méndez Pereira (*b.* 1887; *d.* 1954), prominent Panamanian educator. He was born in Aguadulce and graduated from the University of Chile in 1913. He taught at and was president of the National Institute, served as minister of education, and became the first president of the University of Panama when it was founded in 1935. Méndez Pereira founded numerous schools and learned journals. He published essays on literature, education, and a variety of historical subjects. He wrote biographies of Vasco Núñez de Balboa and Justo Arosemena, and he founded the Panamanian Academy of Language and the Panamanian Academy of History.

See also **Panama.**

BIBLIOGRAPHY

Jorge Conte Porras, *Panameños ilustres* (1978).

Additional Bibliography

Arosemena Jáen, Roberto. *Prisma de una república: Biografía de Octavio Méndez Pereira.* Panama [?]: Ecssa, 1983.

JUAN MANUEL PÉREZ

MENDIBURU, MANUEL DE (1805–1885). Born in Lima on January 21, 1805, Manuel de Mendiburu is considered Peru's foremost historian of the early republic and the forerunner to Jorge Basadre. He was in fact a man of many careers—diplomat, government minister, and military officer. Mendiburu was involved in the highest levels of government for most of his adult life. No doubt the apex of his political accomplishments came when, at the height of his political influence as the prefect of Tacna, he vigorously opposed the Peru-Bolivia Confederation of Andrés Santa Cruz (1829–1836). He briefly was minister of finance and war in the early years of Ramón Castilla's presidency and later was president of the council of state. He served the government of José Rufino Echenique as minister of finance and then as ambassador to London while the government was negotiating a settlement of the external debt. For the first five months of the War of the Pacific (1879–1883), he served as minister of war. Between these assignments he compiled the invaluable *Diccionario histórico-biográfico del Perú* (8 vols., 1874), a descriptive catalog of colonial Peruvian public figures with heavy emphasis on the sixteenth century. He wrote many other studies, numbers of them unpublished, focusing primarily on diplomatic events of his own era.

See also **Basadre, Jorge; War of the Pacific.**

BIBLIOGRAPHY

Anna, Timothy E. *The Fall of the Royal Government in Peru.* Lincoln: University of Nebraska Press, 1979.

Basadre, Jorge. *Historia de la República del Perú, 1822–1933,* 7th edition, rev. and enl. Lima: Editorial Universitaria, 1983.

Denegri Luna, Félix. *Manuel de Mendiburu, prefecto en Tacna, 1839–1842.* Tacna, Peru: Ediciones de la Casa de la Cultura de Tacna, 1965.

Gootenberg, Paul. *Imagining Development: Economic Ideas in Peru's "Fictitious Prosperity" of Guano, 1840–1880.* Berkeley: University of California Press, 1993.

Riva Agüero, José de la. *La historia en el Perú: Tesis para el doctorado en letras,* 2nd edition. Madrid: Imprenta y Editorial Maestre, 1952.

VINCENT PELOSO

MENDIETA, SALVADOR (1882–1958). Salvador Mendieta (*b.* 24 March 1882; *d.* 28 May 1958), Nicaraguan literary figure and Central American unionist leader. Born in Diriamba to a well-liked, hard-working merchant family, Mendieta grew up to become an ardent Central American unionist. Alejo Mendieta was committed to securing a good education for his sons and, when health problems threatened to intervene, sent young Salvador to Guatemala to finish primary school. He completed his baccalaureate in 1896 with a thesis entitled "The Constituents and the Federal Constituent Assembly of 1824." His doctoral thesis in law, titled "Organization of Executive Power in Central America" (Honduras, 1900) further underscores Mendieta's early commitment to the idea of union.

Mendieta's early activities were not confined to the classroom. In 1895 he organized the Minerva Society, a literary-scientific salon with marked unionist sentiments. In 1899 he cofounded another discussion group, El Derecho, which sponsored a journal of the same name. That same year Mendieta ambitiously declared the existence of the Central American Unionist Party, in response to political upheavals throughout the isthmus. He quickly aroused the animosity of Guatemalan dictator Manuel Estrada Cabrera, his lifelong nemesis, who then expelled Mendieta to Honduras in 1900. Nevertheless, the determined young man refused to be dissuaded and set about extending the Unionist Party to other Central American countries.

Mendieta established a newspaper, *Diario Centroamericano,* in Managua, which led President José Santos Zelaya to imprison Mendieta in 1903. During the first decade of the twentieth century, Mendieta traveled throughout the isthmus and began to write some of his most important works: *Páginas de Unión* (1902), *La nacionalidad y el Partido Unionista Centroamericano* (1905), *Partido Unionista Centroamericano* (1911), and *Cómo estamos y qué debemos hacer* (1911). Mendieta's most famous and enduring work was *La enfermedad de Centro América* (1906–1930), in which he focused on the obstacles to Central American development. Mendieta pointed to the lack of education, poor health and hygiene, unequal distribution of wealth and power, and the generally low level of public consciousness as the roots of the isthmus's infirmities.

Mendieta's ideas of union and social justice did not endear him to the oligarchical political elites of Central America, and he found it difficult to get his masterwork published. He traveled to Europe in search of support and finally reached an agreement with Maucci in Barcelona. Back in Nicaragua, Mendieta served as rector of the Universidad Nacional, but he resigned in protest of his inability to effect needed reforms. Seriously ill with a liver ailment, Mendieta nonetheless continued to head the Unionist Party, for which efforts he was sentenced to jail in 1955 by Anastasio Somoza. Fleeing on horseback, the aging Mendieta escaped Somoza's secret police and lived in San Salvador until his death.

See also **Central America.**

BIBLIOGRAPHY

Thomas Karnes, *The Failure of Union: Central America, 1824–1975* (1976).

Juan Manuel Mendoza, *Salvador Mendieta* (1930).

Warren H. Mory, *Salvador Mendieta: Escritor y apóstol de la unión centroamericana* (1971).

KAREN RACINE

MENDIETA Y MONTEFUR, CARLOS

(1873–1960). Carlos Mendieta y Montefur (*b.* 4 November 1873; *d.* 29 September 1960), president of Cuba (1934–1935). A colonel in the war of independence and afterward a congressman for more than twenty years, Mendieta was also a vice presidential candidate in 1916. Three years later he became editor of *Heraldo de Cuba,* where he achieved considerable fame as a combative political journalist. He was generally regarded as an honest man, and for a long time he was held by many to be the "hope of the Republic," until army chief Fulgencio Batista appointed him Cuba's provisional president on 18 January 1934.

Mendieta proved to be an inept and weak president whose main administrative skill was the ability to organize ephemeral compromises among party leaders. For this reason he was quickly dubbed Batista's puppet. During his brief term in office the revolutionary impetus that had begun the previous year came to an end when a general strike against the government was harshly repressed by the military. Mendieta's administration, however, was not altogether counterrevolutionary, for it confirmed much of the social legislation passed by the preceding revolutionary regime. It was also under Mendieta that women were enfranchised, and the Platt Amendment (1901), perceived by many Cubans as an infringement on their sovereignty, was finally abrogated by a treaty signed with the United States on 29 May 1934. Mendieta resigned on 10 December 1935.

See also **Cuba: The Republic.**

BIBLIOGRAPHY

Herminio Portell-Vilá, *Nueva historia de la República de Cuba* (1986): 429–455.

Additional Bibliography

Aguilar, Luis. *1933: Prologue to the Revolution*. Ithaca, NY: Cornell University Press, 1972.

Pérez, Louis A., Jr. *Cuba under the Platt Amendment, 1902-1934*. Pittsburgh, PA: University of Pittsburgh Press, 1986.

JOSÉ M. HERNÁNDEZ

MENDINUETA Y MÚZQUIZ, PEDRO DE (1736–1825). Pedro de Mendinueta y Múzquiz (*b.* 7 June 1736; *d.* 17 February 1825), viceroy of New Granada (1797–1803). Born near Pamplona, Navarre, Spain, Mendinueta pursued a military career. He served as sub-inspector general of the army of New Spain (1785–1789), held a successful command during the French War (1793–1795), and had secured promotion to lieutenant general by the time of his assignment to New Granada. A leader of good ability and sound judgment, Mendinueta ruled during difficult times, facing a plethora of conspiracies inspired by the French Revolution and the threat of invasion during the First British War (1796–1802). Rather than assume personal command on the coast, which was the normal wartime practice for viceroys, he remained in Santa Fe to address questions of domestic security. Mendinueta is well remembered for his strong dedication to public health and the establishment of a school of medicine in Santa Fe. He was replaced by Antonio Amar y Borbón and returned to Spain, where he assumed a position on the Supreme Council of War and later became councillor of state. He died in Madrid.

See also **New Granada, Viceroyalty of.**

BIBLIOGRAPHY

Allan J. Kuethe, *Military Reform and Society in New Granada, 1773–1808* (1977).

José María Restrepo Sáenz, *Biografías de los mandatarios y ministros de la Real Audiencia, 1671–1819* (1952), esp. pp. 219–225; *Historia extensa de Colombia,* vol. 4, *Nuevo reino de Granada: El virreynato* (1970), esp. pt. 2, pp. 393–420.

Additional Bibliography

Mendinueta, Pedro, with notes by John S. Leiby. *Memoria sobre el Nuevo Reino de Granada, 1803. A Report Concerning the Viceroyalty of New Granada*. Lewiston, NY: Edwin Mellen Press, 2003.

Ortiz, Sergio Elías. *Nuevo Reino de Granada: El Virreynato, tomo 2, 1753-1810*. Bogota, Colombia: Academia Colombiana de Historia and Ediciones Lerner, 1970.

ALLAN J. KUETHE

MENDOZA. Mendoza is a city in western Argentina and capital of Mendoza Province. Mendoza was founded on 2 March 1561 by Captain Pedro del Castillo, by order of the governor of Chile, García Hurtado de Mendoza. Its twenty-one square miles are set on a semiarid plain, about 2,475 feet above sea level at the foot of the Andes. It is surrounded mostly by vineyards and wineries, the principal industry of the province. In colonial times it was an isolated trade center between Buenos Aires, 800 miles to the east, and Chile, across the Andes. In 1861 Mendoza was practically destroyed by an earthquake; it was rebuilt close to the old settlement. In the 1880s the city underwent vast technological change: In 1884 the railway line reached Mendoza, opening a flourishing trade with Córdoba, Buenos Aires, and other provinces of the littoral, but weakening the trade with Chile. In 1885 a streetcar system was established, as well as the first telephone lines. In 1882 Adolfo Calle founded the newspaper *Los Andes,* which continues to serve the city and region. Because of Mendoza's dependence on irrigation, water is of critical importance. The oasis provided by the Mendoza River contributed to the city's continuous growth. From 9,900 inhabitants in 1869, the population of Mendoza reached 58,800 in 1914, 109,000 in 1960, and 126,400 in 1985. While the 1990s and 2001 census found decreases in population to 105,818, a phenomenal demographic expansion took place in Mendoza's outlying areas, which today constitute Greater Mendoza (Godoy Cruz, Las Heras, Guaymallén, Maipú, and other adjacent towns). In 2001 this area reached 871,998 inhabitants, 56 percent of the total population of the province, 1,563,838. The arrival of immigrants, especially from Italy and Spain, made an extraordinary commercial, industrial, and cultural contribution to the development of the city. Immigration reached its peak during the pre–World War I years. According to the 1914 census, 31 percent of the population of the capital were Europeans. Today, the city and surrounding areas continue to attract immigrants, particularly from Chile and Bolivia. In 1939 the National University of Cuyo was established (Cuyo is the name given to the region formed by the contiguous provinces of Mendoza, San Luis, and San Juan). Besides this public institution, there are three private universities in the city. The cleanliness of Mendoza is one of its most outstanding characteristics. The irrigation ditches, or *acequias,* open in every street, transform the semidesertic landscape into a charming oasis. The city's wide avenues, plazas, and the attractive General San Martín Park, contribute to the pleasant environment of what constitutes the major urban center in western Argentina.

In the twenty-first century Mendoza province has more than 1,000 wineries, and the recent growth of the industry has increased tourism to the city, which serves as a base for tours to local vineyards. The *Vendimia* (wine harvest) festival celebrated in the city each March is a growing attraction.

See also **Argentina, Geography; Tourism; Wine Industry.**

BIBLIOGRAPHY

Jorge M. Scalvini, *Historia de Mendoza* (1965).

Miguel Marzo and Osvaldo Inchauspe, *Geografía de Mendoza,* 2 vols. (1967).

Rosa T. Guaycochea De Onofri, *Arquitectura de Mendoza* (1978).

Pedro Santos Martínez, *Historia de Mendoza* (1979).

James R. Scobie, *Secondary Cities of Argentina: The Social History of Corrientes, Salta, and Mendoza, 1850–1910* (1988).

Additional Bibliography

Bragoni, Beatriz. *Los hijos de la revolución: Familia, negocios y poder en Mendoza en el siglo XIX.* Buenos Aires: Taurus, 1999.

Brennan, James P., and Ofelia Pianetto. *Region and Nation: Politics, Economics, and Society in Twentieth-Century Argentina.* New York: St. Martin's Press, 2000.

García Vázquez, Cristina B. *Los migrantes, otros entre nosotros: Etnografía de la población boliviana en la provincia de Mendoza, Argentina.* Mendoza, Argentina: Editorial de la Universidad Nacional de Cuyo, 2005.

Gudiño, María Elina. *Estrategias de integración y transformaciones metropolitanas: Santiago de Chile y Mendoza, Argentina.* Mendoza, Argentina: Editorial de la Universidad Nacional de Cuyo, 2005.

Martínez, Pedro Santos. *Historia económica de Mendoza durante el Virreinato, 1776–1810.* 2nd edition. Buenos Aires: Ciudad Argentina, 2002.

Ponte, Jorge Ricardo. *La fragilidad de la memoria: Representaciones, prensa y poder de una ciudad latinoamericana en tiempos del modernismo: Mendoza, 1885–1910.* Mendoza, Argentina: Ediciones Fundación Centro Regional de Investigaciones Científicas y Tecnológicas, 1999.

Richard Jorba, Rodolfo A. *La región vitivinícola argentina: Transformaciones del territorio, la economía y la sociedad, 1870–1914.* Buenos Aires: Universidad Nacional de Quilmes Editorial, 2006.

Celso Rodríguez

MENDOZA, ANTONIO DE (1490–1552). Antonio de Mendoza (*b.* 1490/94; *d.* 21 July 1552), count of Tendilla, Spain's ambassador to Hungary, and viceroy of Peru (1551–1552). Mendoza, probably born in Granada, was also the first viceroy of Mexico (1535–1549). Chosen to represent the king and the Council of the Indies as well as to provide a check on the personal power of Hernándo Cortés, he brought to the office the prestige of the high nobility. Mendoza reached New Spain fourteen years after the military conquest of central Mexico had been completed. Typically, Spanish institutions arrived on the scene as the viability of new colonies became obvious and greater crown control seemed necessary. Yet, once in the colony, Mendoza's direct tie to the crown was relatively loose, considering that fleets containing official letters and orders sailed once a year. Mendoza, like other viceroys, occasionally avoided complying with royal pronouncements, such as his delay in enforcing the New Laws of the Indies that sought to limit *encomiendas* (grants of Indian labor and tribute). (The first viceroy of Peru lost his life in a rebellion following the implementation of the New Laws in that colony.)

Judicial matters and many ecclesiastical ones fell outside Mendoza's domain, but he administered nearly all other social, political, territorial, and economic concerns of the colony. Enhancing revenues through legislation covering taxation, trade, and transportation was probably one of his more pressing goals. Mendoza also supervised matters relating to the indigenous people of the new colony, ironically seeking to protect their rights and to see that they were subjugated and Hispanicized.

See also **New Spain, Viceroyalty of.**

BIBLIOGRAPHY

Arthur Scott Aiton, *Antonio de Mendoza: First Viceroy of New Spain* (1927; repr. 1967).

Michael C. Meyer and William L. Sherman, *The Course of Mexican History,* 3d ed. (1987), pp. 144–150.

Additional Bibliography

Ruiz Medrano, Ethelia. *Gobierno y sociedad en Nueva España: segunda audiencia y Antonio de Mendoza.* Zamora, Mexico: El Colegio de Michoacán; Gobierno del Estado de Michoacán, 1991.

STEPHANIE WOOD

MENDOZA, CARLOS ANTONIO (1856–1916).

MENDOZA, CARLOS ANTONIO (1856–1916). Carlos Antonio Mendoza (*b.* 1856; *d.* 1916), Panamanian lawyer and politician and author of Panama's declaration of independence. He headed the radical wing of the Liberal Party. A mulatto, he was very popular with the lower classes. Mendoza served as deputy to the National Assembly and was a member of the Panama City Council. He was also president of the national directorate of the Liberal Party. In 1910 he occupied the presidency for seven months after the death of President José Domingo Obaldía and prior to Pablo Arosemena, who completed Obaldía's term.

See also **Panama.**

BIBLIOGRAPHY

Baltasar Isaza Calderón, *Carlos A. Mendoza y su generación: Historia de Panamá: 1821–1916* (1982).

Additional Bibliography

Araúz, Celestino Andrés. *Mendoza, Secretario de Hacienda y Presidente: Obra de gobierno, 1908–1910,* 3 volumes. Bogota, Colombia: Stamato Editores, 1999.

JUAN MANUEL PÉREZ

MENDOZA, JAIME (1874–1939). Born July 25, 1874, in Sucre, Jaime Mendoza was, together with Alcides Arguedas and Armando Chirveches, one of the most important Bolivian realist writers. After obtaining a medical degree in Sucre, Mendoza's career took him to the mining centers of Uncía and Llallagua. Living and working in the depressed centers deeply influenced his novel *En las tierras de Potosí* (1911). The War of the Acre found Mendoza in the Bolivian tropics: the conditions of extreme poverty there are reflected in his novel *Páginas bárbaras* (1914). Mendoza later traveled to Europe and lived in France and Spain. While in Europe, he contacted Arguedas, the Nicaraguan Rubén Darío, and other important Latin American writers. Arguedas, who wrote the prologue to *En las tierras de Potosí,* called Mendoza "the Bolivian Gorki" for the social realism that characterized his novels. Also an essayist, Mendoza wrote *Tesis andinista* (1933) and *El macizo andino* (1935), both comparative studies of Bolivia to the Pacific Ocean and the Argentine Río de la Plata basin. In response to the Spanish essayist Carlos Badía Malagrida, who believed that Bolivia was incapable of developing a stable political society, Mendoza used this geography to counteract Badía's negative opinions, and to assert Bolivia's right to exist as an independent nation. He died January 26, 1939, in Sucre.

See also **Arguedas, Alcides; Literature: Spanish America.**

BIBLIOGRAPHY

Arnade, Charles W. "The Historiography of Colonial and Modern Bolivia." *The Hispanic American Historical Review* 42, no. 3 (1962): 333–384.

Zulawski, Ann. "Hygiene and 'The Indian Problem': Ethnicity and Medicine in Bolivia, 1910–1920." *Latin American Research Review* 35, no. 2 (2000): 107–129.

Examines the proposals of Jaime Mendoza and Nestor Morales for improving the health of the native population in the context of the larger national debate about ethnicity and citizenship.

JAVIER SANJINÉS C.

MENDOZA, PEDRO DE (1487–1537).

Pedro de Mendoza (*b.* 1487; *d.* 23 June 1537), first *adelantado* (frontier military commander) of Río de la Plata (1536–1537). Born in Guadix, Spain, Mendoza probably served in the Italian campaigns of Charles V. As part of an attempt by the Spanish crown to control Portuguese expansion in the New World, he was charged with populating the Río de la Plata area in 1534. Although he fell seriously ill before departing Sanlúcar da Barrameda, he had recovered sufficiently by August 1535 to embark on the expedition, which was composed of eleven ships and more than 2,000 men (and a few women) drawn primarily from the Basque region, Andalusia, and the Low Countries.

In February 1536, Mendoza founded a fortified city on the banks of the Río de la Plata, a city that he christened Santa María del Buen Aire. Within a year he and his men were forced to abandon their settlement because of the hostility of the Querandí Indians and the resultant lack of food. Suffering from hunger, recurring sickness, and Indian attack, Mendoza decided to return to Spain in early 1537; he died at sea. Those who had remained in Buenos Aires were compelled to abandon it in 1541 and to withdraw 1,000 miles upstream to the city of Asunción.

See also **Buenos Aires; Río de la Plata.**

BIBLIOGRAPHY

Enrique Udaondo, *Diccionario biográfico colonial argentino* (1945), pp. 582–587.

Additional Bibliography

Aguirre, Gisela. *Pedro de Mendoza*. Buenos Aires: Planeta, 1999.

SUSAN M. SOCOLOW

MENDOZA CAAMAÑO Y SOTOMAYOR, JOSÉ ANTONIO DE (c. 1668–1746).

José Antonio de Mendoza Caamaño y Sotomayor (Marqués de Villagarcía; *b.* ca. March 1668; *d.* 14 December 1746), viceroy of Peru (1736–1745). A grandee of the illustrious Mendoza family who had served Philip V as Spanish ambassador to Venice and as viceroy of Cataluña, Villagarcía took office in Lima on 4 January 1736. Described as a person of limited intelligence and little administrative ability with a certain pious perversity because of his great pleasure in presiding over the *autos de fe* of the Lima inquisition, Villagarcía's overweaning task as viceroy was that of bolstering the Pacific fleet and shoring up coastal defenses against the onslaughts of British naval forces. In 1742 he subdued a serious Indian uprising led by Juan Santos (Apu Inca) in Jauja and Tarma. So great were his military expenditures that Villagarcía ran up a debt of almost 3 million pesos, most of which was unpaid salaries for soldiers, sailors, and militiamen.

In Lima the contentious Villagarcía was constantly at odds with the town council (*cabildo*), merchant guild (*consulado*), royal treasury officials, and the Jesuits, and in the interior, with provincial administrators (*corregidores*). Besides his successful defense of Peru during the War of Jenkins's Ear, his other principal achievement was eliminating the practice at the University of San Marcos of awarding university degrees for gifts of money rather than for academic merit. Accused of mismanagement he was summarily relieved of office on 12 July 1745. He died off Cape Horn on a vessel taking him back to Spain.

See also **Peru: From the Conquest Through Independence; War of Jenkins's Ear (1739–1748).**

BIBLIOGRAPHY

Manuel De Mendiburu, *Diccionario histórico-biográphico del Perú*, vol. 7 (1937). See also Villagarcía's report on his tenure in office in *Memorias de los virreyes que han gobernado el Perú* (1859).

Additional Bibliography

Fisher, John Robert. *Bourbon Peru*. Liverpool, England: Liverpool University Press, 2003.

Marks, Patricia H. *Deconstructing Legitimacy: Viceroys, Merchants, and the Military in Late Colonial Peru.*

Philadelphia: Pennsylvania State University Press, 2007.

Pearce, Adrian John. *Early Bourbon Government in the Viceroyalty of Peru, 1700–1759.* Liverpool, England: University of Liverpool, 1998.

JOHN JAY TEPASKE

MENDOZA Y LUNA, JUAN MANUEL DE

MENDOZA Y LUNA, JUAN MANUEL DE Juan Manuel de Mendoza y Luna (marquis of Montesclaros), viceroy of Peru (1608–1615). Facing a sharp decline in state revenues, Montesclaros sought to rejuvenate the silver and mercury mining industries and increase remittances to Spain. His main efforts were directed at increasing Indian tribute and labor. The first viceroy to attempt radical changes in the Toledo resettlement system, Montesclaros proposed that Indian migrants be forced to pay taxes and participate in the state labor system. More important, Montesclaros tried to end the colonial practice of issuing licenses to those who employed yanaconas, Indians who effectively escaped state demands. Montesclaros also denounced the crown's policy of selling *juros,* annuities that depended on colonial revenues both as security for the purchasers' investments and as the source of interest payments. Although the sale of *juros* was halted in 1615, Montesclaros left office that same year still awaiting crown approval of his policies on Indian labor, which had been bitterly contested by Peru's agricultural and mining elites. His successor, the prince of Esquilache, would reverse most of the Montesclaros program.

See also **Peru: From the Conquest Through Independence.**

BIBLIOGRAPHY

Kenneth J. Andrien, *Crisis and Decline: The Viceroyalty of Peru in the Seventeenth Century* (1985), esp. pp. 135–136.

Ann M. Wightman, *Indigenous Migration and Social Change: The Forasteros of Cuzco, 1570–1720* (1990), esp. pp. 24–27.

Additional Bibliography

Drinot, Paulo and Leo Garofalo. *Más allá de la dominación y resisténcia: Estudios de la historia peruana, siglos XVI–XX.* Lima: IEP, 2005.

Escobar Gamboa, Mauro. *El tabaco en el Perú colonial, 1752–1796.* Lima, Peru: Universidad Nacional Mayor de San Marcos, 2004.

Guibovich Pérez, Pedro. *Censura, libros e inquisición en el Perú colonial, 1570–1754.* Sevilla, Spain: CSIC, 2003.

ANN M. WIGHTMAN

MENEM, CARLOS SAÚL

MENEM, CARLOS SAÚL (1930–). Carlos Saúl Menem (*b.* 2 July 1930), president of Argentina (1989–1999). Menem is the son of Syrian immigrants who settled in the northern province of La Rioja. Active in politics from university days, he was elected to the legislature of his native province on the Peronist ticket in 1955, and subsequently elected and re-elected its governor (1973, 1983, 1987). His career was interrupted by the military regime that deposed President Isabel Perón in March 1976, during which time he spent five years in prison. In 1989, defying all predictions, he defeated Antonio Cafiero for the presidential nomination of the Peronist Party, and won a relatively easy victory in the national elections.

Menem's presidency was a revolutionary one, for Argentina and for Peronism. He reversed a fifty-year-old trend toward statism-populism, opening up the economy by drastically reducing taxes and tariffs, and wiping out huge budgetary deficits by privatizing large state-owned industries. A "convertibility plan" established a stable exchange rate for the Argentine peso in relation to the dollar and permitted the peso's free exchange for foreign currencies. Formerly politically sensitive areas like oil and hydrocarbons have been opened to foreign investments.

At the same time, Menem reversed historic trends in Argentine foreign policy, openly aligning the country with the United States and offering cooperation with United Nations efforts at peacekeeping. Though frequently criticized for his rather haphazard style of administration, as well as for the corrupt practices of family members and immediate aides, such has been Menem's popularity that he was been able to convince the opposition Radical Party to support changes in the Argentine Constitution that allowed him to run for another term—for four, rather than six years—in 1995. He

Former Argentine president Carlos Menem greeted by followers at a political rally on the outskirts of Buenos Aires in July 2002. © REUTERS/CORBIS

won reelection, but could not run for a third term in 1999.

While Menem successfully completed his second term, his currency policy helped produce a severe economic crisis in the early twenty-first century. When the dollar value continued to rise, the Argentine peso also became stronger, making exports too expensive in international markets. Finally, in early 2002 Argentina had to devalue its currency leading to a year of economic depression and political insecurity. Although Menem received considerable criticism for the economic downturn, he tried to run for the presidency in 2003 and made it to a run off with Néstor Kirchner, but withdrew knowing he would loose the election. In 2007, he ran for governor of La Rioja but lost. Also, in 2007, Menem was charged with corruption and embezzlement. Still, Menem has stated that he hopes to return to Argentine politics.

See also **Alfonsín, Raúl Ricardo; Argentina, Political Parties: Justicialist Party; Argentina, Political Parties: Radical Party (UCR); Neoliberalism.**

BIBLIOGRAPHY

Alfonsín, Raúl. *Memoria política transición a la democracia y derechos humanos.* Buenos Aires: Fondo de Cultura Económica de Argentina, 2004.

Levitsky, Steven, and Maria Victoria Murillo, eds. *Argentine Democracy: The Politics of Institutional Weakness.* University Park: Pennsylvania State University Press, 2005.

MARK FALCOFF

MENÉNDEZ DE AVILÉS, PEDRO

(1519–1574). Pedro Menéndez de Avilés (*b.* 1519; *d.* 17 September 1574), Spanish naval officer. Menéndez, a native of Avilés, Asturias, was appointed captain-general of the Indies fleet by Philip II in 1560. In a 1565 patent, he was named *adelantado,* governor, and captain-general of Florida; he agreed to settle and pacify the area at his own expense. In return, Menéndez received tax exemptions, a large land grant, and, in addition to those listed above, the title of marqués. At that time, Florida extended from Newfoundland to the Florida Keys; it was enlarged in 1573 to include the Gulf coast. When Philip II learned of the French establishment at Fort Caroline, he furnished royal support for the Menéndez expedition.

Menéndez sailed to Florida and defeated the French, killing many of them. He founded Saint Augustine on 8 September 1565, and established garrisons at San Mateo (the renamed Fort Caroline) and elsewhere in the Florida peninsula. In 1566, Menéndez established the city of Santa Elena on Parris Island, in present-day South Carolina; he left garrisons there and in Guale (present-day Georgia). Menéndez planned a line of fort-missions from Santa Elena to present-day Mexico, and sent Captain Juan Pardo on an expedition that reached as far as the Appalachian Mountains. First Jesuit and then Franciscan missionaries went to Florida to evangelize the Native Americans.

Despite this and the coming of more than 200 settlers, Menéndez's Florida enterprise failed, largely due to difficulties between the Native Americans and the Spaniards. After the death of Menéndez in Santander, Spain, and the abandonment of Santa Elena, only Saint Augustine remained—the oldest permanent European settlement in the present United States.

See also **Explorers and Exploration: Spanish America.**

BIBLIOGRAPHY

Bartolomé Barrientos, *Pedro Menéndez de Avilés, Founder of Florida,* translated by Anthony Kerrigan (1965).

Woodbury Lowery, *The Spanish Settlements Within the Present Limits of the United States,* 2 vols. (1901–1905).

Eugene Lyon, *The Enterprise of Florida* (1976).

Eugenio Ruidíaz y Caravía, *La Florida: Su conquista y colonización por Pedro Menéndez de Avilés,* 2 vols. (1893).

Félix Zubillaga, *La Florida: La misión jesuítica (1566–1572)* (1941).

Additional Bibliography

Lyon, Eugene. *Pedro Menéndez de Avilés.* New York: Garland Publishing, 1995.

Mercado, Juan Carlos, editor. *Menéndez de Avilés y la Florida: Crónicas de sus expediciones.* Lewiston, NY: Edwin Mellen Press, 2006.

EUGENE LYON

MENININHA DO GANTOIS, MÃE

(1894–1986). Mãe Menininha do Gantois (Maria Escolástica da Conceição Nazareth; *b.* 10 February 1894; *d.* 13 August 1986), the fourth priestess of Ilê Iya Omin Axé Iya Massé, known popularly as the Terreiro do Gantois. Born in Salvador, Bahia, Menininha was the great-niece of Maria Julia da Conceição Nazareth, who founded the Terreiro de Gantois in 1849 after a divergence with Engenho Velho, one of the oldest Candomblé communities in Bahia. The women of the Conceição Nazareth family, who have led Gantois since its foundation, trace their lineage to the city of Abeokuta in Nigeria and preserve many of their cultural traditions through Candomblé. Menininha was initiated as a devotee of the Orixá Oxum at eight months, and named senior priestess of Gantois at the uncharacteristically young age of twenty-eight; hence, her nickname, which means "little girl." For sixty-four years she was spiritual counselor and inspiration to many well-known politicians, artists, and scholars, including Jorge Amado, Carybé, Caetano Veloso, Maria Bethania, and Antonio Carlos Magalhães. Mãe Menininha's openness helped to dispel widespread prejudice against the Afro-Brazilian Candomblé tradition. By the time of her death, she was the most beloved and widely venerated Candomblé priestess in Brazil. Her home in Bahia is now a memorial and museum.

See also **African-Latin American Religions: Brazil.**

BIBLIOGRAPHY

Braga, Julio Santana. *Na gamela do feitiço: Repressão e resistência nos candomblés da Bahia.* Salvador, Brazil: EDUFBA, 1995.

Portugal, Afra Marluce Guedes. *O poder do Candomblé: Com aspectos da religiosidade do Gantois.* Rio de Janeiro: Editora Tecnoprint, 1986.

Voeks, Robert A. *Sacred Leaves of Candomblé: African Magic, Medicine, and Religion in Brazil.* Austin: University of Texas Press, 1997.

KIM D. BUTLER

MENNONITES.

Mennonites, a pacifist, Anabaptist sect that originated in the Low Countries in the early 1540s. Throughout their history, the Mennonites have often been victims of religious persecution because of their beliefs, including their insistence upon separation of church and state, refusal to bear arms, renunciation of participation in secular affairs, refusal to take oaths, and their insistence that their children be educated in religious schools taught in Plattdeutsch, the German spoken by members of the sect.

The Mennonites' desire to remain apart from society at large resulted in frequent mass migrations (*Auswanderungen*) to new lands. A large-scale *Auswanderung* of Mennonites to Latin

America took place after World War I and a smaller one after World War II, when the Mennonites' refusal to bear arms and their Germanic ways seemed to call their loyalty into question. In 1922, over two thousand Mennonites migrated from Manitoba, Canada, to Chihuahua, Mexico, where they were joined by Mennonites from Russia fleeing the Bolshevik Revolution. By 1930, the Chihuahua colony had a population of more than six thousand and had acquired land in Durango. In the mid-1950s, a faction of the Mexican Mennonites, fearful of the government's plans to integrate the sect into the social security system, migrated to British Honduras (Belize), where they established a new colony at Santa Elena, near the Guatemalan border.

Substantial numbers of Mennonites also migrated to other parts of Latin America, most often seeking regions with sizable German populations and land policies that were amenable to the establishment of large agricultural holdings that could be privately owned by the sect. Large numbers of Mennonites emigrated to Paraná, Brazil, and to Paraguay, where, in 1926 and 1927, Canadian and Sommerfelder (South Russian) Mennonites founded the Menno colony in the Chaco Region, south of Puerto Casado. In the 1930s, German-Russians and Polish Mennonites escaped Nazi persecution and Stalinist purges by immigrating to the Chaco, where they established a colony near Menno, called Colonia Ferheim. During the 1940s, a third wave of German-Russian and Russian Mennonites escaped political turmoil in Europe by moving to the Chaco, where they founded yet another large Mennonite settlement, known as Colonia Neuland. The Paraguayan Chaco is now home to one of the largest Mennonite populations in the world.

See also **German-Latin American Relations; Protestantism.**

BIBLIOGRAPHY

Joseph Winfield Fretz, *Mennonite Colonization in Mexico* (1952).

Karl Ilg, *Pioniere in Brasilien: Durch Bergwelt, Urwald und Steppe erwanderte Volkskunde der deutschsprachigen Siedler in Brasilien und Peru* (1972).

Annemarie Elizabeth Krause, *Mennonite Settlement in the Paraguayan Chaco* (Ph.D. diss., University of Chicago, 1952).

Moisés Gonzáles Navarro, *La colonización en México, 1877–1910* (1960); *The Mennonite Encyclopedia*, 4 vols. (1955–1959).

Harry Leonard Sawatzky, *They Sought a Country: Mennonite Colonization in Mexico* (1971).

Additional Bibliography

Bennion, Janet. *Desert Patriarchy: Mormon and Mennonite Communities in the Chihuahua Valley.* Tucson: University of Arizona Press, 2004.

Epp, Marlene. *Women Without Men: Mennonite Refugees of the Second World War.* Toronto: University of Toronto Press, 2000.

Hinkley, Katherine, and Thomas H. Guderjan. *A Mennonite Landscape: The Blue Creek Community.* San Antonio: St. Mary's University, 1997.

Romero Lévera, Mario Aníbal. *Las tres grandes colonias mennonitas del Chaco y su influencia sobre el desarrollo económico del Paraguay.* Paraguay: s.n., 2003.

Stoesz, Edgar, and Muriel Thiessen Stackley. *Garden in the Wilderness: Mennonite Communities in the Paraguayan Chaco, 1927–1997.* Winnipeg: CMBC Publications, 1999.

Thiesen, John D., Theron F. Schlabach, and John J. Friesen. *Mennonite and Nazi? Attitudes among Mennonite Colonists in Latin America, 1933–1945.* Kitchener: Pandora Press, 1999.

VIRGINIA GARRARD-BURNETT

MENNONITES IN LATIN AMERICA. Mennonites in Latin America established themselves according to their points of origin and the countries they entered. The first group came from the United States and Canada and settled in Argentina. The second group, consisting of Russian and German immigrants, organized churches in Paraguay, Mexico, and Brazil. Latin Americans who had early contact with North Americans made up the last group. The Evangelical Mennonite churches of El Salvador and the K'ekchi' Mennonite church in Guatemala exemplify this homegrown form of Mennonite worship. The K'ekchi' church operates an educational center known as Bezaleel, home to more than a hundred secondary- and vocational-school students. Mennonite church tenets call for plain living and dress, separation of church and state, condemnation of slavery, pacifism, refusal to take judicial oaths or hold public office, and the Anabaptist concept of adult baptism.

Since the late twentieth century in Latin America Mennonite church growth has been steady. In addition to the above-mentioned countries, Mennonites established communities in Belize, Bolivia, Chile, Colombia, Costa Rica, Cuba, Dominican Republic, Ecuador, Haiti, Honduras, Jamaica, Nicaragua, Panama, Peru, Uruguay, and Venezuela. As of 1995, Mexico and Paraguay were home to the largest numbers of Mennonites in Latin America—44,000 in Mexico and 29,200 in Paraguay. The Mennonite Central Committee founded in 1920 and the Mennonite Mission Network established in 2002 have been important to the denomination's development in Latin America. For the most part, although not exclusively the former broke ground in South America while the latter opened missionary fields in Central America and the Caribbean. In addition, in 1890 a Hispanic Mennonite Church began operations in the United States.

In Argentina the first Mennonites arrived in 1917 and established the Iglesia Menonita Evangélica Argentina. In 1946 later generations of Mennonites entered the Argentine Chaco to begin work among indigenous people. This work in northern Argentina inevitably brought Mennonite missionaries into southern Bolivia. In 1971 Bible study workers entered, and in 1975 the first Mennonite baptism in Bolivia took place. In Brazil the initial group of Mennonites consisted of German-speakers from the Soviet Union. Arriving in 1930, they settled in southern Brazil where they lived as subsistence agriculturalists. In the 1950s North American Mennonites began missionary endeavors among Portuguese-speaking Brazilians. This brought about the formation of the Associação Evangélica Menonita, which in turn led to a foreign missionary service with Brazilians going to Africa and the Balkans. In Mexico, Mennonite missionary efforts began in earnest in 1958 when workers started planting congregations in Mexico City. In the 1990s these urban congregations joined to carry out a ten-year project to fashion a network throughout Mexico. Of special interest were the relationships formed between the Mennonite Church USA and Mexican congregations on the United States–Mexico border.

Paraguay is the home to the most prosperous Mennonite community in Latin America. German-speakers from Europe and North America, faced with anti-German sentiment during World War I, settled there in the 1920s. During the 1930s and 1940s others followed, fleeing Stalinist purges in the Ukraine and the Soviet Union. Many settled in Filadelphia, the capital of Fernheim colony, which along with the older Menno and newer Neuland colonies are the Mennonite population centers in the Chaco. In the long term this led to the establishment of the German General Conference and Convención Evangélica Menonita Paraguaya.

In the early twenty-first century, Mennonites in Paraguay are wealthy landowners, the country's largest suppliers of dairy products, the leading producers of cotton and peanuts, and exporters of beef. Their children, no longer trained to work in agriculture, are educated in the best Paraguayan schools and join the professional ranks as doctors, engineers, and scientists. In Filadelphia the ready availability of beer and tobacco challenge Mennonite ways, and an alcoholism treatment center has been established. Video games and the Internet also intrude on Mennonite traditionalism, and many remain unbaptized. Some have married outside the faith.

In Paraguay conflict over land has come to the forefront. The wealth of the Mennonite communities has created tensions with the Lengua and Nivaclé Indians of the Chaco. Although 80 percent of these indigenous people are Mennonites, converted over the decades, the European and North American Mennonites control almost four million acres of land. This inequality has relegated the indigenous people, who work as day laborers for landowners, to second-class status and has caused uneasy relationships between the two groups. The landowning Mennonites, who do not worship together with the indigenous people, are ambiguous about building ties with them, whereas the Indians are concerned about maintaining traditions. Mennonite prosperity in the Paraguayan Chaco has affected native peoples who do not share the benefits the wealth created.

See also **Germans in Latin America; Immigration, Paraguay; Protestantism; Protestantismo en México.**

BIBLIOGRAPHY

Falcón, Rafael. *The Hispanic Mennonite Church in North America, 1932–1982.* Scottsdale, PA: Herald Press, 1986.

Goodman, Joshua. "Cultivating Faith on the Chaco." *Americas* 55 (May–June 2003): 39–45.

Peterson, Anna L. *Seeds of the Kingdom: Utopian Communities in the Americas.* Oxford and New York: Oxford University Press, 2005.

ALVIN M. GOFFIN

Additional Bibliography

Fonte, Luisa. *La nación cubana y Estados Unidos: Un estudio del discurso periodístico (1906-1921).* Mexico City: El Colegio de México: Universidad Autónoma Metropolitana-Iztapalapa, 2002.

Ibarra, Jorge. *Cuba, 1898-1921: Partidos políticos y clases sociales* Havana, Cuba: Editorial de Ciencias Sociales, 1992.

ALLAN S. R. SUMNALL

MENOCAL, MARIO GARCÍA (1866–1941). Mario García Menocal (*b.* 17 December 1866; *d.* 1941), president of Cuba (1913–1921). Born in Jaguey Granada, Cuba, Menocal attended Cornell University in New York, receiving an engineering degree in 1888. Upon completion of his studies, Menocal went to work with his uncle, Ancieto G. Menocal, a noted canal engineer. Both men worked in Nicaragua, then a proposed transisthmian canal route.

Menocal participated in the Cuban War of Independence, he was appointed assistant secretary of war in the revolutionary government (1895), and fought with General Calixto García in the Oriente campaign. In 1897, after a strategic success at Tunas he was promoted to general. Menocal cooperated with the U.S. intervention and was named Havana's chief of police. He ran for president on the Conservative Party ticket in 1908 but was defeated by the Conservative turned Liberal José Miguel Gómez. Renominated in 1912, Menocal won, serving two terms. His presidency was fraught with corruption (including 372 indictments against public officials) and disrespect for the law. Indictments of government officials were rarely taken seriously and convictions were often negated through presidential pardons or congressional declarations of amnesty. Menocal's third attempt for the presidency in 1924 met with failure.

See also **Cuba: The Republic (1898–1959).**

BIBLIOGRAPHY

William Fletcher Johnson, *The History of Cuba* (1920).

Louis A. Pérez, *Cuba: Betweeen Reform and Revolution* (1988).

MERA, JUAN LEÓN (1832–1894). An Ecuadorian writer and politician, Juan León Mera was born on June 28, 1832, in Ambato. He was a member of the Conservative Party, held the position of senator, and was twice governor and also minister of the State Auditing Office. He founded the Ecuadorian Academy and promoted an awareness of national literature. This concern for national culture is reflected in his essay *Ojeada histórico-crítica sobre la poesía ecuatoriana* (1868) and in a letter he wrote to Marcelino Menéndez y Pelayo in 1883. Mera wrote the words of Ecuador's national anthem, the verses of *Melodías indígenas* (1858), and the Inca legend in verse *La virgen del Sol* (1861). His most popular work, *Cumandá; o,Un drama entre salvajes* (1879), falls into the melodramatic Indianist literary genre—a New World extension of Romanticism—because it tells of the thwarted love of the Indian siblings Carlos and Cumandá, who were unaware that they were brother and sister. It is the culmination of the Indianist genre in America, which addressed indigenous issues from folk or idealist perspectives and, unlike the twentieth-century Indigenist novel, ignored the social and ethnic consequences of inequalities between races and social classes.

Mera is considered Ecuador's best poet and novelist between independence (1830) and the twentieth century, and both his political and literary activity have a marked Catholic character. He promoted his country's Concordat with the Holy See when he held important positions in the government of Gabriel García Moreno and, in *Cumandá*, stressed the spiritually, culturally, and materially positive work done among indigenous peoples by

Spanish priests in the New World. As a literary critic and historian, he fostered in Ecuador popular knowledge of literature, poetry in particular, and, from his political position in the administrations of García Moreno, encouraged younger generations to value and devote themselves to literature. He died on December 13, 1894.

See also **García Moreno, Gabriel; Literature: Spanish America.**

BIBLIOGRAPHY

Gálvez, Marina, editor. *Coloquio Internacional "Juan León Mera,"* 2 vols. Ambato, Ecuador: Casa de Montalvo, 1998.

Garcés, Víctor Manuel. *Vida ejemplar y obra fecunda de Juan León Mera.* Ambato, Ecuador: Ed. Pío XII, 1963.

Guevara, Darío C. *Juan León Mera; o, El hombre de cimas.* Quito: Ministerio de Educación Pública, 1944.

Pazos, Julio, ed. *Juan León Mera: Una visión actual.* Quito: Corporación Editora Nacional, 1995.

ANGEL ESTEBAN

MERCEDARIANS. Mercedarians (Order of Our Lady of Mercy for the Ransom of Captives), a Roman Catholic religious order founded in Barcelona by Saint Peter Nolasco in 1218. As indicated in the official title of the order, one of its principal missions was the ransom of captives, specifically Christians taken by Muslims. The order enjoyed rapid growth and sustained support in Spain and Portugal, although it was also successful in France, England, and Germany. The order was instrumental in the Spanish Conquest and settlement of the Americas.

Although the Franciscans, Dominicans, and Augustinians constituted the first important missionary orders in Latin America, in many instances their activities were predated by the Mercedarians. The first Mercedarian in the New World was reputedly Friar Jorge de Sevilla, who sailed on Columbus's second voyage in 1493. The first Mercedarian house in the Americas was not founded, however, until 1514 in Santo Domingo.

Several Mercedarians accompanied the early expeditions. For example, Friar Bartolomé de Olmedo was Hernán Cortés's personal chaplain. Friar Francisco de Bobadilla was active early in Panama and Nicaragua. While Friar Vicente de Valverde, a Dominican, accompanied Francisco Pizarro to Cajamarca in Peru, the first organized missionary effort was that of the Mercedarians. Under the leadership of Friar Miguel de Orones, five Mercedarians arrived in 1532, prior to the taking of Atahualpa in Cajamarca, and established a house at San Miguel Piura. In 1535 the order founded its first monasteries in Lima and Cuzco.

While the Mercedarians enjoyed early successes in Peru, the order did not become established in Mexico immediately following the Conquest, in spite of Olmedo's participation. They did, however, establish a monastery in León, Nicaragua, in 1527, which was the first step in building what would later become an important Central American base.

The first Mercedarian expedition to Guatemala was organized in 1538 under the leadership of Friar Juan de Zambrana, who, at the invitation of the local bishop, Francisco de Marroquín, arrived with three others to found their house. Although the Franciscans and Dominicans had sent earlier expeditions to the region, it was the Mercedarians who would enjoy the greatest success, especially in the remote parts of the kingdom, which had largely been ignored by earlier missionary efforts.

At the end of the sixteenth century, the Mercedarians finally had established themselves in Mexico, the heart of New Spain, with their foundation in 1594. It was not until 1616 that Mexico became a province independent of Guatemala.

While the order quickly spread out over the American continents, their efforts were still generally controlled from Spain. It was not until 1564–1566 that independent provinces were established in the Americas, when Guatemala, Lima, Cuzco, and Chile were formally recognized as separate provinces, apart from the order in Spain. Other Latin American provinces included Tucumán, Santo Domingo, Mexico, Quito, Colombia, and the vice province of Marañón. Oversight of the provinces was handled by a vicar who served under the master general of the order.

Normally the vicar for the Spanish Indies was the provincial of Castile, in keeping with the development of the provinces. From 1587 until 1790, there were two vicars general, one for New Spain, the other for the viceroyalty of Peru. The vice province of Marañón was controlled by the Portuguese province. There were only three Brazilian convents, and in 1787 one of these was suppressed.

Unlike other missionary orders, the Mercedarians initially had cool relationships with the crown. On several occasions the Spanish authorities even threatened to expel the order from the New World. During the colonial period, they were often referred to as "mercenaries" (*mercedarios* versus *mercenarios* in Spanish), an allusion to their acquisition of lands and other rewards for service. A late-seventeenth-century reform ended this tradition, and in 1690 the order was proclaimed a mendicant order by the pope.

By the beginning of the seventeenth century, there were about 250 Mercedarians in Latin America. That number would grow to about 1,200 by 1750. The greatest concentration of the order occurred in Central America, where the order had twenty-nine convents, followed by Peru, with twenty-six, and Mexico, with twenty-two. By 1900, there were fewer than ten convents in all of Latin America.

In spite of the modest size of the order, it made some significant contributions, especially in the colonial period. Friar Diego de Porres was one of the leading Mercedarians in the province of Cuzco. About 1551 Porres arrived in Peru in the company of the newly appointed viceroy, don Antonio de Mendoza, and for the next thirty years he engaged himself in missionary work. Near the end of his life he claimed to have baptized 80,000 Indians, married some 30,000, and built no less than 200 churches.

Not all Mercedarians were seen as saintly. Felipe Guamán Poma De Ayala describes the misadventures of Friar Morúa, a Mercedarian assigned to the village of Yanaca. According to the Indian chronicler, Morúa forced the natives to weave clothing which he would in turn sell. The natives could seek no assistance from the local magistrate since Morúa served as a judge for him. Moreover Morúa imposed on the Indians his own choice of chief, a man who continued in idolatrous ways, without reprimand from the priest.

The Mercedarians played an important role in the educational life of Latin America. In many cities they established schools for the training of the local elite. The Mercedarian schools had as their principal goal the training of novices for the order. Several Mercedarians came to occupy important positions in the universities of Latin America.

See also **Catholic Church: The Colonial Period.**

BIBLIOGRAPHY

Mariano Cuevas, *Historia de la iglesia en México,* 5 vols. (1928).

Rubén Vargas Ugarte, *Historia de la iglesia en el Perú,* 3 vols. (1953–1954).

Pedro Nolasco Pérez, *Historia de las misiones mercedarias en América* (1966).

Alfonso Morales Ramírez, *La Orden de la Merced en la evangelización de América (siglos XVI–XVII)* (1986).

Additional Bibliography

Aparicio Quispe, Severo. *La Orden de la Merced en el Perú: Estudios históricos.* Cuzco: Provincia Mercedaria del Perú, 2001.

Black, Nancy Johnson. *The Frontier Mission and Social Transformation in Western Honduras: The Order of Our Lady of Mercy, 1525–1773.* New York: E. J. Brill, 1995.

Proaño, Luis Octavio. *Nuestra Señora de la Merced en la colonia y en la República del Ecuador.* Quito: L. O. Proaño, 1993.

Rangel, Magdalena E. de and José Miguel Romero de Solís. *Los mercedarios en Colima: Haciendas y trapiches.* Colima: Archivo Histórico del Municipio de Colima, Ayuntamiento de Colima: Gobierno del Estado de Colima, Secretaría de Cultura: Universidad de Colima, 1999.

Taylor, Bruce. *Structures of Reform: The Mercedarian Order in the Spanish Golden Age.* Boston: Brill, 2000.

Zaporta Pallarés, José. *Religiosos mercedarios en Panamá (1519–1992): Con testimonios históricos de Tirso de Molina.* Madrid: Revista "Estudios," 1996.

JOHN F. SCHWALLER

MERCEDES. Mercedes, city of 42,359 (2005) inhabitants in Uruguay located at the junction of the Río Negro and the Uruguay River and capital of the department of Soriano. Mercedes was founded in 1781, along with other settlements, to discourage Brazilian incursions into the country. Ruling over a vast agrarian hinterland dedicated to grain growing and the raising of livestock, Mercedes competes with Fray Bentos on the Uruguay River as the major agricultural center of western Uruguay, also known as Littoral.

See also **Uruguay, Geography.**

BIBLIOGRAPHY

Elzear Giuffra, *La república del Uruguay* (Montevideo, 1935).

Additional Bibliography

Piccone, Aurelio, Ernesto Daragnès Rodero, Juan Antonio Varese, and Manuel Santos Pírez. *Memorias del río Negro.* Montevideo: Torre del Vigía-Ediciones, 2003.

CÉSAR N. CAVIEDES

MERCOSUR. In March 1991 Argentina, Brazil, Paraguay, and Uruguay signed the Treaty of Asunción, creating Mercosur (in Spanish, Mercado Común del Sur; in Portuguese, Mercado Comum do Sul, known in Brazil as Mercosul), the Southern Common Market. It was founded to promote regional integration by establishing a common external tariff, coordinated macroeconomic policies, a common business policy toward outside parties, and free circulation of goods, services, and factors of production. The structure of Mercosur (Council, Group, and Business Commission) was defined in December 1994 through the Ouro Preto Protocol. A Permanent Arbitration Panel, based in Asunción, Paraguay, was created in February 2002, and implementation of the Mercosur Parliament began in Montevideo, Uruguay, in December 2006. Signatories to the Treaty of Asunción are full members, and Venezuela began the process of joining in 2006. Chile, Bolivia, Peru, Colombia, and Ecuador are all associate members.

As the largest economic bloc in Latin America, Mercosur had a population of more than 250 million people in 2006, with a gross domestic product in excess of US$1 trillion, nearly 76 percent of South America's GDP. Trade among member countries grew from US$5.1 billion in 1991 to $21.1 billion in 2005, with a positive trade balance of $54.1 billion that year with countries outside the zone.

With respect to other regional blocs, the U.S.-led initiative to form the FTAA (Free Trade Area of the Americas) has been all but paralyzed since 2004, owing to the joint decisions undertaken by members and difficulties in securing trade benefits. Similar causes and effects have virtually incapacitated the agreement with the European Union, the foundations for which were laid in 1992. However, significant progress has been made with respect to trade with Chile and the Andean Community (Peru, Ecuador, Bolivia, and Colombia) as well as concerning agreements with the World Trade Organization to remove restrictions blocking trade with developing countries, resulting in signed agreements with India and South Africa. The main intrazonal challenges include consolidation of a common customs policy, institutional optimization, and reducing the concerns felt by smaller countries that derive few benefits from trade. The Mercosur Structural Convergence Fund was created in December 2004 to address this last issue.

See also **Economic Development; Free Trade Area of the Americas (FTAA).**

BIBLIOGRAPHY

Barbosa, Rubens Antônio, ed. *Mercosul 15 anos.* São Paulo: Imprensa Oficial do Estado de São Paulo, 2007.

Instituto para la Integración de América Latina y Caribe. *Informe Mercosul 11.* Series Informes Subregionales de Integración. Buenos Aires: BID/INTAL, November 2006.

Manzetti, Luigi. "The Political Economy of Mercosur." *Journal of Interamerican Studies and World Affairs* 35, no. 4 (1993–1994): 101–141.

LUIGI MANZETTI
MARIA LETÍCIA CORRÊA

MERCURIO, EL. *El Mercurio* was Chile's most widely read morning newspaper for most of the twentieth century and remains so into the present day, with editions in Santiago and Valparaiso. Owned for generations by the wealthy, Anglo-Chilean Edwards family, it has played a prominent, and decidedly conservative, role in Chilean politics for most of the twentieth century. It vigorously opposed both the reformist Christian Democratic government of Eduardo Frei Montalva (1964–1970) and the Popular Unity government of Marxist Salvador Allende (1970–1973). In an effort to blunt its criticism, Allende withdrew governmental subsidies and support (advertising contracts, etc.), but the paper continued to be published thanks to generous financial support from the U.S. government. It hailed the 1973 coup, and during the ensuing sixteen years of military rule, it enthusiastically supported Pinochet's neoliberal economic policies, downplayed the extent of poverty and human rights abuse, and generally sought to discredit the government's civil and religious critics. Its conservative position continues in the twenty-first century.

See also **Allende Gossens, Salvador; Frei Montalva, Eduardo; Journalism; Pinochet Ugarte, Augusto.**

BIBLIOGRAPHY

Guillermo Sunkel, *El Mercurio: Diez años de educación política-ideológica* (1983).

Fernando Reyes Matta et al., comps., *Investigación sobre la prensa Chile* (1986).

P. Sigmund, *The United States and Democracy in Chile* (1993)

Additional Bibliography

Durán, Claudio. *El Mercurio: Ideología y propaganda, 1954-1994: Ensayos de interpretación bi-lógica y psicohistórica.* v. 1. Santiago: Ediciones Chile y América-CESOC, 1995.

MICHAEL FLEET

MERCURIO PERUANO. *Mercurio Peruano,* Peruvian periodical of the early 1790s. The *Mercurio Peruano* was a biweekly paper published in Lima, beginning in 1791, by a small group of officials, university faculty members, and other citizens who sought to improve Peru. Articles in the *Mercurio* provided Peruvians with information about the viceroyalty and suggestions for improving their daily lives. For example, they analyzed the viceroyalty's commerce, supported more efficient mining techniques, and recommended ways to improve the health of the citizenry. Supported and encouraged by Viceroy Francisco Gil De Taboada y Lemos, the *Mercurio* demonstrated that Lima had a number of self-proclaimed adherents of enlightened ideas, including José Baquíjano y Carrillo, Ambrosio Cerdán y Pontero, José Rossi y Rubí, and Hipólito Unanue. Its demise in 1795, however, reflected how small that number was. At no time did the number of subscribers total four hundred.

See also **Gazetas; Journalism.**

BIBLIOGRAPHY

Mercurio peruano de historia, literatura y noticias públicas que da a luz la Sociedad Académica de Amantes de Lima, 12 vols. (1791–1795; repr. 1964–1966).

Mark A. Burkholder, *Politics of a Colonial Career: José Baquíjano and the Audiencia of Lima* (1980), pp. 86–91.

Additional Bibliography

Clément, Jean-Pierre, *El Mercurio peruano, 1790–1795* (1997–1998).

MARK A. BURKHOLDER

MERELLO, TITA (1904–2002). Tita Merello was an Argentine actress and singer who appeared in more than twenty films during a career that spanned seven decades. Born Laura Ana Merello to a working-class Uruguayan mother and Argentine father in a tenement house in Buenos Aires' poor neighborhood of San Telmo, she began her career as a dancer before moving to the theater stage and to motion pictures. Her filmography includes Luis José Moglia Barth's *¡Tango!* (1933), Argentina's first "Movietone" picture, and Eduardo Morera's *Así es el tango* (1937). Merello appeared on television in the early 1960s and returned to theater before her final motion-picture appearances in *Los miedos* (1980) and *Las barras bravas* (1985). Known for her liveliness, Merello received the Pablo Podestá Prize from the Association of Argentine Actors in 1991 before receding from the public eye in the early 1990s due to health problems.

See also **Cinema: From the Silent Film to 1990.**

BIBLIOGRAPHY

Cabrera, Gustavo. *Tita Merello (1904–2002): El mito, la mujer y el cine.* Buenos Aires: Marcelo Héctor Oliveri Editor, 2006.

Romano, Néstor. *Se dice de mí: La vida de Tita Merello.* Buenos Aires: Sudamericana, 2001.

PATRICK BARR-MELEJ

MERENGUE. Merengue is a fast-paced musical genre with many styles and influences, identified by its distinctive beat and accompanying hip-swaying dance. It was created in the Dominican Republic in the late 1800s from a creolized tradition of African, indigenous Taino, and Spanish peoples. In the Dominican Republic, merengue maintained a regional diversity, with variations in style, use of instruments, and lyrical content, until 1931 when the dictator Rafael Trujillo took power and adopted merengue from the region of Cibao as the national music.

Merengue *cibaeño* was taken to New York by emigrating Dominicans in the 1960s. In the United States, merengue has been influenced by a variety of other musical genres, such as rock-and–roll, as well as other Latin American music. Contemporary merengue is typically lively and animated, playing constant variations of a theme in major mode. Its fast dance tempo is an innovation of artists in the 1960s, when rock-and-roll influenced a number of Latin American musical genres.

See also **Music: Popular Music and Dance; Trujillo Molina, Rafael Leónidas.**

BIBLIOGRAPHY

Austerlitz, Paul. *Merengue: Dominican Music and Dominican Identity.* Philadelphia: Temple University Press, 1997.

HANNAH GILL

MÉRIDA. Mérida, capital and principal city of the state of Yucatán in Mexico, located in the northwestern part of the Yucatán peninsula, about 22 miles south of the port of Progreso (and the Gulf of Mexico). Mérida was founded on 6 January 1542 by the conquistador Francisco de Montejo on the site of the semideserted Maya town of T'ho. Formerly known as Ichcaazihó (which means Five Mountains in Maya), T'ho was within the Maya city-state of Peches, which allied itself with the conquering Spaniards against rival Maya city-states. It is believed that the conquistadores chose the name Mérida because T'ho's indigenous ruins reminded them of the Roman remains in the city of Badajoz in their native Estremadura.

Since the Spanish lacked the military capability to pacify the entire peninsula, their colonizing strategy hinged on the establishment of garrison towns such as Mérida during the colonial period. Mounted troops were dispatched to trouble spots to maintain peace and subdue Indian uprisings. Mérida's physical layout echoed the classic style of the Spanish Renaissance. Crown authorities had insisted on the traditional grid pattern of wide, straight streets intersecting at right angles to form rectangular blocks and open squares. If the city's architecture replicated the Moorish style in vogue at the time in Spain, its simplicity also reflected the dearth of material wealth found in the province. Throughout the colonial era, Mérida remained the seat of the captaincy-general, a self-governing administrative unit independent of the Viceroyalty of New Spain.

At the beginning of the nineteenth century, Mérida was a small town of 10,000 inhabitants. It grew appreciably during the first twenty years after Independence as the regional economy prospered. An unfortunate result of economic progress, however, was the escalation of tensions between expansionistic sugar planters and Maya peasants on the state's southeastern frontier. Ultimately, the apocalyptic Caste War of Yucatán erupted in 1847, reducing Yucatán's population by more than a third. Ironically, Mérida (and the northwestern portion of the peninsula) benefited economically and demographically from the hostilities, as residents of the southeast fled to escape the attacks of the rebel Mayas.

Political factionalism in Mérida and neighboring Campeche during the first fifty years following Independence also contributed indirectly to the state capital's growth: when campechanos seceded from Yucatán in 1862, Mérida remained the only viable commercial center in the state. By 1883, the city numbered roughly 40,000, the only state capital to record a sizable increase during the Mexican nation's turbulent first half-century.

By the beginning of Porfirio Díaz's dictatorship (1876–1911), Mérida was positioned to assume a dominating role in the rapidly expanding Henequen (hard fiber) industry. The northwest quadrant of the peninsula was converted into large henequen estates, as *hacendados* lived in Mérida and managed their haciendas through overseers. During the henequen boom, a peninsular railway network, built, financed, and managed by indigenous entrepreneurs, was routed through Mérida to transport the monocrop. The combination of henequen monoculture, the railroad, the Caste War, and the secession of Campeche (and later in 1902, the partition of the southeastern territory of Quintana Roo) all contributed to Mérida's steady ascent to the leading city in the region. By 1910, the capital's population had grown to more than 60,000; Valladolid, the second-largest city in the state, had fewer than 12,000 residents.

The late-nineteenth-century henequen boom radically changed the city. During Olegario Molina's gubernatorial administration (1902–1909) the most sweeping changes occurred. The Molinista regime taxed the lucrative monocrop and, with the support of the private sector, transformed housing, transportation, communications, public health and sanitation, education, the arts, and the urban landscape. Mérida soon earned the sobriquets "The White City" and "The Paris of Mexico." It was clean, well lit, paved with asphalt, and increasingly modernized.

Since World War I, henequen monoculture has gradually dissipated, but the state capital has remained the political, economic, and cultural hub of the peninsula. Migration and immigration throughout the twentieth century have swelled the population dramatically. More recently, the city has benefited from tourism (as visitors flock to Maya archaeological sites) and as a service sector for the new Caribbean resorts of Cancún and Cozumel. In the early 2000s, with a population in excess of a half million, Mérida functions as the unchallenged primary city in the peninsula.

See also **Maya, The; Yucatán.**

BIBLIOGRAPHY

Enrique Dulanto, "Apuntes históricos y anecdóticos sobre Mérida," in *Artes de Mexico* 20, nos. 169–170 (1973): 7–61.

Rodolfo Ruz Ménendez, *Mérida, bosquejo biográfico* (1983).

Asael T. Hansen and Juan R. Bastarrachea M., *Mérida: Su transformación de capital colonial a naciente metrópoli en 1935* (1984).

Allen Wells and Gilbert M. Joseph, "Modernizing Visions, Chilango Blueprints, and Provincial Growing Pains: Mérida at the Turn of the Century," in *Mexican Studies/Estudios mexicanos* 8 (1992): 167–215.

Additional Bibliography

Peraza Guzmán, Marco Tulio, and Pablo A. Chico Ponce de León. *Arquitectura y urbanismo virreinal.* Mérida: Unidad de Posgrado e Investigación, Facultad de Arquitectura, Universidad Autónoma de Yucatán; Mexico City: Consejo Nacional de Ciencia y Tecnología, 2000.

Reyes Domínguez, Guadalupe. *Carnaval en Mérida: Fiesta, espectáculo y ritual.* México, D.F.: Instituto Nacional de Antropología e Historia; Mérida: Universidad Autónoma de Yucatán, 2003.

Rodríguez, Edgar. *Ciudad blanca.* Merida: Maldonado editores del mayab, 1999.

Rugeley, Terry. *Yucatán's Maya Peasantry and the Origins of the Caste War* Austin: University of Texas Press, 1996.

Allen Wells

MÉRIDA, CARLOS (1891–1984). Carlos Mérida (*b.* 2 December 1891; *d.* 22 December 1984), artist. Although born in Guatemala, Mérida is most often associated with the modern art movement in Mexico. In 1910 he traveled to Paris to study with Kees van Dongen (1877–1968) and Hermen Anglada-Camarasa (1873–1959), becoming closely associated with Pablo Picasso and Amadeo Modigliani. In 1914, Mérida returned to Guatemala to begin experimenting with folkloric themes in his painting. He exhibited his work in the National Academy of Fine Arts in Mexico in 1920, and his uniquely Latin American themes made him one of the pioneers of the Mexican artistic revolution.

The mural renaissance in Mexico in the 1920s greatly influenced his work. He was commissioned in 1921 to do two murals in the Ministry of Education in Mexico City. After a New York exhibition, Mérida again traveled to Europe, where he exhibited his work in Paris (1927). He returned to Mexico in 1929 to continue his work with plastic painting, gradually developing the abstract and plastic-surrealist style for which he is best known. Among his better-known works are mosaic murals in the Benito Juárez housing development in Mexico City (1952) and in the Municipal Building in Guatemala City (1956).

See also **Art: The Twentieth Century.**

BIBLIOGRAPHY

Jean Charlot, *The Mexican Mural Renaissance, 1920–1925* (1979).

Carlos Mérida, *Modern Mexican Artists* (1968), pp. 105–113.

Carlos Mérida, *Carlos Mérida* (1990).

Additional Bibliography

Cardoza y Aragón, Luis, and Renato González Mello. *La nube y el reloj: Pintura mexicana contemporánea.* Mexico: Universidad Nacional Autónoma de México, Instituto de Investigaciones Estéticas: Landucci, 2003.

Lara Elizondo, Lupina. *Referencias de Picasso en México: Ocho pintores (1900-1950): Angel Zárraga, Diego Rivera, Carlos Mérida, Manuel Rodríguez Lozano, Alfonso Michel, Rufino Tamayo, Francisco Gutiérrez, Federico Cantú.* Mexico City: Qualitas Compañía de Seguros, 2005.

SARA FLEMING

MERINO CASTRO, JOSÉ TORIBIO

MERINO CASTRO, JOSÉ TORIBIO (1915–1996). José Toribio Merino Castro (*b.* 14 December 1915, *d.* 30 August 1996), Chilean naval officer. Born in La Serena, Merino entered the Chilean Naval Academy in 1931 and graduated as a midshipman in 1936. He specialized in gunnery and fire control. During the last year of World War II he served as an anti-aircraft battery officer on board the U.S. cruiser *Raleigh.* During his career he commanded the corvette *Papudo,* the transport *Angamos,* and the destroyers *Almirante Williams* and *Almirante Riveros.* Between 1956 and 1957 Merino served in the Chilean naval mission to Great Britain.

In 1963 Merino became chief of staff of the fleet. For the next four years he served as the assistant chief of the General Staff and the director of the Bureau of Weapons. In 1970 he became commander in chief and the naval judge of the fleet, the senior naval command afloat, and in 1973 he was named commander in chief and naval judge of the First Naval Zone.

Merino and other naval officers initiated a plot to overthrow the government of Salvador Allende, informing General Augusto Pinochet, commander of the Chilean army that the navy would act on 11 September 1973. This forced Pinochet to advance a plot of his own from 14 to 11 September. With the overthrow of the Allende government, Admiral Merino served as a member of the junta and the commander of the navy until his retirement on 8 March 1990. He died on August 30, 1996, after an extended illness.

See also **Chile: The Twentieth Century; Pinochet Ugarte, Augusto.**

BIBLIOGRAPHY

Augusto Pinochet, *The Crucial Day* (1982); "Cambio de mando institucional" in *Revista de Marina* (Valparaíso) 2 (1990): 217–220; *El Mercurio* (Valparaíso), 9 March 1990, pp. 1, 12.

Additional Bibliography

Arce, Luz. *The Inferno: A Story of Terror and Survival in Chile.* Madison: University of Wisconsin Press, 2004.

Dinges, John. *The Condor Years: How Pinochet and His Allies Brought Terrorism to Three Continents.* New York: New Press, 2004.

Meneghello Matte, Raimundo. *Merino: El segundo hombre.* Santiago, Chile: Universidad Finis Terrae, 2004.

ROBERT SCHEINA

MESA, CARLOS

MESA, CARLOS (1953–). An accomplished journalist, Carlos Mesa briefly served as Bolivia's president during a time of turmoil. Born in La Paz, he studied in both Bolivia and Spain, graduating with a degree in literature from the Universidad Mayor de San Andrés in La Paz. Working in many media, he became an award-winning journalist, television personality, and historian noted for numerous documentaries and books. He also achieved financial success with the creation of a national television network. In 2002 Gonzalo Sánchez de Lozada asked Mesa, who had no political experience or affiliation, to be his running mate in the presidential elections. His political inexperience may have been advantageous because of growing discontent with the political class. After a very close contest, Sánchez de Lozada and Mesa took office in August 2002.

A variety of protests plagued the government from the beginning, and controversial natural gas proposals provoked fierce demonstrations and violent clashes with security forces. In response to the rising death toll, Mesa withdrew his support from Sánchez de Lozada, who resigned on October 17, 2003, leaving Mesa as president. Although he had distanced himself from his predecessor, Mesa still faced the same difficulties and, as an independent, lacked partisan support in Congress. He took several steps to alleviate tensions, including holding a referendum on the contentious gas issue. Although he was somewhat successful with that referendum in July 2004, opponents were not satisfied and again took to the streets. Pressure mounted in early 2005, leading Mesa to threaten his resignation and propose early elections. Warning that the country was on the verge of civil war, he again submitted his resignation on June 6, 2005. This time Congress accepted it and offered the job first to the speaker of the senate, who declined, and then to supreme court head Eduardo Rodríguez.

See also **Bolivia, Political Parties: Overview.**

BIBLIOGRAPHY

Salman, Ton. "The Jammed Democracy: Bolivia's Troubled Political Learning Process." *Bulletin of Latin American Research* 25, no. 2 (2006): 163–182.

ROBERT R. BARR

MESA DA CONSCIÊNCIA E ORDENS.

Mesa da Consciência e Ordens (Board of the King's Conscience and of the Military Orders), a Portuguese court created in 1532 to supervise the administration of religious affairs. Regarding the colonies, its importance as an instrument of royal power was tantamount to that of the Conselho Ultramarino (Overseas Council). The military orders' concerns were incorporated into the Mesa da Consciência after 1551, when the king became Grand Master of the Orders of Christ, Aviz, and Santiago. In addition, the board took care of an amazing range of responsibilities, which included the appointment of ecclesiastics to the overseas dominions; the management of the inheritances of all those subjects who had died outside the realm; the surveillance of royal chapels, almshouses, hospices, and hosteleries; and, until 1790, the inspection of Coimbra University. According to the 1603 Statutes, the board was composed of a president, five deputies, and four notaries; it was permitted to summon the King's Confessor, the Chancellor of the Orders, and experts in law and theology for advice. Over the years, the board amassed considerable influence, which was called into question only in the beginnning of the nineteenth century. It was abolished in 1828 (Brazil) and 1833 in Portugal.

See also **Portuguese Empire; Portuguese in Latin America.**

BIBLIOGRAPHY

António Sérgio et al., eds. "Mesa," in *Grande enciclopédia portuguesa e brasileira,* vol. 17 (1934–1935), pp. 17–18.

Ruy D'abreu Torres, "Mesa da Consciência e Ordens," *Dicionário de história de Portugal,* edited by Joel Serrão, vol. 3 (1968), pp. 42–43.

Francisco Luiz Teixeira Vinhosa, *História administrativa do Brasil,* pt. 2, vol. 8, *Brasil sede da monarquia* (1984), p. 141.

Arquivo Nacional, *Fiscais e meirinhos: A administraçao no Brasil colonial* (1985), pp. 39, 120.

Additional Bibliography

Dutra, Francis A. *Military Orders in the Early Modern Portuguese World: The Orders of Christ, Santiago, and Avis.* Burlington, VT: Ashgate, 2006.

Neves, Guilherme Pereira das. *E receberá mercê: A Mesa da Consciência e Ordens e o clero secular no Brasil, 1808–1828.* Rio de Janeiro: Arquivo Nacional: Ministério da Justiça, 1997.

GUILHERME PEREIRA DAS NEVES

MESADA ECLESIÁSTICA.

Mesada Eclesiástica, an assessment amounting to one month's stipend that was imposed on all clergy taking posts in the Spanish Indies beginning in 1626. This assessment fell on all ecclesiastics from the august dean and canons of New World cathedrals to priests or regular clergy serving in the most isolated mission posts. All revenues from *mesadas* were allocated to pay the salaries of the Council of the Indies. In 1777 Charles III established an additional assessment of a half-year's stipend (Media Anata Eclesiástica) on all clergy having an annual income of more than three hundred pesos—bishops excluded. After 1777 ecclesiastics in this category had to pay both assessments. By 1800 annual income from the two levies combined was approximately 46,000 pesos in Mexico and 30,000 pesos in Peru.

See also **Charles III of Spain.**

BIBLIOGRAPHY

Recopilación de leyes de los Reynos de las Indias, 4 vols. (1681; repr. 1973), libro I, título XVII.

Gabriel Martínez Reyes, *Finanzas de las 44 Diócesis de Indias, 1515–1816* (1980).

Additional Bibliography

García Pérez, Rafael D. *El Consejo de Indias durante los reinados de Carlos III y Carlos IV.* Pamplona: Ediciones Universidad de Navarra, 1998.

Taylor, William B. *Magistrates of the Sacred: Priests and Parishioners in Eighteenth-century Mexico.* Stanford, CA : Stanford University Press, 1996.

JOHN JAY TEPASKE

MESCALA, ISLAND OF.

Island of Mescala. Located in Lake Chapala, to the south of Guadalajara in western central Mexico, the small island was seized and fortified late in 1812 primarily by Indian insurgents from the lakeside villages. Repeated military attacks against the entrenched rebel forces proved unsuccessful. These failures not only embarrassed the Spanish commander José de la Cruz but also drew off royalist forces from more vital antiguerilla action in western Mexico. Eventually weakened by a combination of naval blockade, plague, and offers of amnesty and land, the rebels surrendered in late 1816 after a four-year siege. Subsequently the island served for some years as a high-security penitentiary.

See also **Guadalajara.**

BIBLIOGRAPHY

Vicente Riva Palacio, *México a través de los siglos,* vol. 3 (1940).

Brian R. Hamnett, *Roots of Insurgency: Mexican Regions, 1750–1824* (1986), esp. pp. 190–192.

William B. Taylor, "Banditry and Insurrection: Rural Unrest in Central Jalisco, 1790–1816," in *Riot, Rebellion, and Revolution: Rural Social Conflict in Mexico,* edited by Friedrich Katz (1988).

Additional Bibliography

Santoscoy, Alberto. "Defensa Heroica de la Isla de Mezcala en el Lago de Chapala, por los valientes Indios Insurgentes de la Región." http://www.epmassoc.com.

Schroeder, Susan. *Native Resistance and the Pax Colonial in New Spain.* Lincoln: University of Nebraska Press, http://www.questia.com, 1998.

ERIC VAN YOUNG

MESILLA, LA.

See **Gadsden Purchase.**

MESOAMERICA.

Mesoamerica, a cultural and geographical term used to define a vast area embraced by central and southern Mexico, Guatemala, Belize, El Salvador, the westernmost parts of Honduras and Nicaragua, and the Nicoya Peninsula of Costa Rica. At the time of the Spanish Conquest, there existed within this area populous, well-adjusted societies capable not merely of meeting basic human needs but also of achieving remarkable results in terms of art and architecture, astronomy, mathematics and the measurement of time, plant domestication, environmental management, written or pictographic communication, and the building of towns and cities. Mesoamerica thus denotes a key area where an advanced culture may be said to have prevailed, distinct from viable but less sophisticated cultures as in such peripheral parts as the Spanish borderlands, the Caribbean littoral, and the Greater and Lesser Antilles.

Elaboration of the term is commonly attributed to the anthropologist Paul Kirchhoff (1900–1972), but the great German scholar Eduard Seler (1849–1992) used the term *Mittel Amerika* to apply to the same conjunction of territory and civilization. The Mesoamerican peoples alive and flourishing at the moment of contact, the Mexicas (Aztecs) foremost of all, are the ones whose accomplishments the historical record has best preserved. These peoples must, however, be seen as but specific expressions of a great cultural tradition that stretches back into the pre-Columbian past and forward, in the cases of Mexico and Guatemala, to our day.

The political and organizational skills characteristic of the Mesoamerican mindset are nowhere better evidenced than in the example of the Aztecs. When Bernal Díaz del Castillo, the conqueror and a chronicler in the making, entered the Aztec capital of Tenochtitlán in 1519, he marveled at the beauty and refinement of the city that met his eyes, later to be even more impressed (as were his fellow countrymen) with the extent and output of the Aztec tribute state, a far-flung dominion whose southern reaches included commercial enclaves in Guatemala and beyond.

Perhaps the single most illuminating measure of the vitality of Mesoamerican culture is the number of people the social system, its structures of privilege and authoritarianism notwithstanding, may have been able to support. Estimates by William T. Sanders place the contact population of the Aztec Empire at between 5 and 6 million, with Mesoamerica as a whole inhabited by between 12 and 15 million. More detailed investigations by Woodrow Borah and Sherburne F. Cook suggest a population for central Mexico alone of 25 million. Even the lower estimates indicate a situation in which the land was worked purposely and fruitfully, to good effect. The Spanish Conquest, most notably the destructive aftermath of warfare, disease, enslavement, forced labor, and culture shock, shattered the Mesoamerican order forever.

See also **Aztecs; Belize; El Salvador; Guatemala; Honduras; Nicaragua; Tenochtitlán.**

BIBLIOGRAPHY

Paul Kirchhoff's classic "Mesoamérica: Sus límites geográficos, composición Étnica y caracteres culturales," in *Acta Americana* 1 (1943): 92–107, has been superseded in English by William T. Sanders and Barbara J. Price, *Mesoamerica: The Evolution of a Civilisation* (1968), which emphasizes ecological adaptation. Sanders's discussion of how many people the social system could support is found in "The Population of the Central Mexican Symbiotic Region, the Basin of Mexico, and the Teotihuacán Valley in the Sixteenth Century," in William M. Denevan, ed., *The Native Population of the Americas in 1492* (1976): 85–150. A counterview is afforded by Woodrow Borah and Sherburne F. Cook, "Conquest and Population: A Demographic Approach to Mexican History," in *Proceedings of the American Philosophical Society* 113 (1969): 177–183. The eyewitness account by Bernal Díaz Del Castillo, *The Discovery and Conquest of Mexico,* translated by A. P. Maudslay (1956), retains its intoxicating headiness centuries later. And few render the complexity of Mesoamerican culture at contact, or document more powerfully the manner of its change and destruction, than Charles Gibson, *The Aztecs Under Spanish Rule: A History of the Indians of the Valley of Mexico, 1519–1810* (1964). Other contributions which afford a Native American, as opposed to a Spanish Colonial, perspective on land and life in Mesoamerica are Miguel León Portilla, *The Broken Spears: The Aztec Account of the Conquest of Mexico* (1962, expanded and updated edition 1992); James Lockhart, *The Nahuas after the Conquest: A Social and Cultural History of the Indians of Central Mexico, Sixteenth Through Eighteenth Centuries* (1992); and Matthew Restall, Lisa Sousa, and Kevin Terraciano, *Mesoamerican Voices: Native-Language Writings from Colonial Mexico, Oaxaca, Yucatan, and Guatemala* (2005). Also see Linda Manzanilla and Leonard López-Lujan, *Historia antigua de México* (1994-1995) and Yólotl González-Torres and Juan Carlos Ruiz Guadalajara *Diccionario de mitología y religión de Mesoamérica* (1995) for broad introductions.

W. GEORGE LOWELL

MESSÍA DE LA CERDA, PEDRO DE

(1700–1783). Pedro de Messía de la Cerda (Messía de la Zerda, Marqués de la Villa de Armijo; *b.* February 1700; *d.* 1783), military figure and viceroy of the New Kingdom of Granada (1761–1772). Born in Córdoba, he pursued a naval career upon completion of his schooling and took part in the Spanish "reconquest" of Sicily and in Mediterranean battles with the English. In 1721 he made his first cruise to the Americas. He was promoted to captain in 1745. He became a knight commander of the Order of Malta. Messía de la Cerda served in the southern Caribbean (1750s). He thus came to his viceregal post with firsthand knowledge of the defense and commercial difficulties that he would face. Important, too, with regard to Messía's qualifications and mandate as viceroy, he was concurrently the commandant general of the Caribbean squadron in charge of the fight against contraband traffic.

In the 1760s the viceroy authorized José Celestino Mutis to introduce the academic study of mathematics and the sciences at the *colegio mayor* of Nuestra Señora del Rosario in Santa Fe de Bogotá, established the tobacco monopoly, and oversaw the expulsion of the Jesuits. By 1767, Messía complained of failing health and sought to return to Spain, which he did in 1772, when Manuel de Guirior (1772–1776) relieved him. He died in Madrid.

See also **New Granada Viceroyalty of.**

BIBLIOGRAPHY

Antonio Moreno y Escandón, in Germán Colmenares, ed., *Relaciones e informes de los gobernantes de la Nueva Granada,* vol. 1 (1989).

Sergio Elías Ortiz, *Nuevo Reino de Granada: El virreynato, 1753–1810* in *Historia extensa de Colombia,* vol. 4 (1970).

Additional Bibliography

Andrien, Kenneth J. "Economic Crisis, Taxes and the Quito Insurrection of 1765." *Past and Present* 129 (November 1990): 104–131.

Domínguez Ortega, Montserrat. "Análisis metodológico de dos juicios de residencia en Nueva Granada: D. José Solís y Folch de Cardona y D. Pedro Messía de la Cerda, 1753-1773." *Revista Complutense de Historia de América* 25 (1999): 139–165.

McFarlane, Anthony. "The 'Rebellion of the Barrios': Urban Insurrection in Bourbon Quito." *The Hispanic American Historical Review* 69: 2 (May 1989): 283–330.

LANCE R. GRAHN

MESSIANIC MOVEMENTS

This entry includes the following articles:
BRAZIL
SPANISH AMERICA

BRAZIL

Messianism, the expectation of sudden intervention by a divine or superhuman being in human history, has been connected with Brazil since its colonization. The diverse religious movements following apocalyptic prophecies have been so persistent that recent scholars have interpreted the salvific theme to be integral to the Luso-Brazilian cultural identity. Although some groups may have roots in indigenous religions, the most noted messianic movements appeared in the nineteenth century as the outgrowths of popular Catholic emphasis on the approaching cataclysmic end of time, the exclusive redemptive kingdom of the Last Days, and the Second Coming of Jesus.

In the sixteenth century, several religious movements exhibited aspects often associated with messianic groups. Coastal Tupi-Guarani tribes undertook dramatic migrations under shamanic guidance, seeking a utopian "land without evil." Similarly, Portuguese immigrants, native Brazilians, and biracial colonists in Bahia joined in the *Santidade* ("Holiness") movement; directed by leaders called Pope and Mother of God, the community expected an imminent cosmic disaster and reversals in the power structure. Later rural movements, such as the twentieth-century devotees of the Beato of Caldeirão (Pedro Batista da Silva) and of Padre Cícero, also followed prophetic leaders who articulated contemporary discontent and promised remedies for social and spiritual needs.

Messianic movements interweaving Christian revelations and Portuguese folklore began in the early 1800s in the Northeast, in marginal communities faced with political upheavals. Three movements, the first led by Silvestre José dos Santos at Rodeador, Pernambuco, in 1817, the second by João Antônio dos Santos and João Ferreira at Pedra Bonita in the 1830s, and the third by Antônio "Conselheiro" Maciel in Canudos in the 1890s, drew upon the legends of Portuguese Sebastianismo. Each community awaited the return of King Sebastião (1557–1578) to overthrow local religious and secular order and establish an earthly paradise with his triumphant angelic army. Armed militia extinguished each of these groups, yet their messianic influence continues in the Northeast, where Antônio Conselheiro himself is now considered a savior.

Messianic movements have also occurred in southern Brazil. In Rio Grande do Sul, a small community formed in the 1870s to follow Jacobina Maurer as the new Christ, and in 1910 a "holy war" was launched in Santa Catarina, aiming military and religious force against the new laws of the republic. Although the latter Contestado Rebellion ended in battle in 1914, its themes persist in regional beliefs.

See also **Catholic Church: The Colonial Period; Catholic Church: The Modern Period.**

BIBLIOGRAPHY

Euclides Da Cunha, *Rebellion in the Backlands,* translated by Samuel Putnam (1944).

Abelardo F. Montenegro, *Antônio Conselheiro* (1954).

René Ribeiro, "O episódio da Serra do Rodeador 1817–20: Um movimento milenar e sebastianista," in *Revista de Antropologia* 8 (1960): 133–144.

Donald Warren, Jr. "Portuguese Roots of Brazilian Spiritism," in *Luso-Brazilian Review* 5 (1968): 3–34.

Ralph Della Cava, *Miracle at Joaseiro* (1970).

Jovelino P. Ramos, "Interpretando o fenômeno Canudos," in *Luso-Brazilian Review* 11 (1974): 65–83.

Maria Isaura Pereia De Queiroz, *O Messianismo, no Brasil e no mundo,* 2d ed. (1976).

Hélène Clastres, *Terra sem mal,* translated by Renato Janine Ribeiro (1978).

José Carlos De Ataliba Nogueira, *Antônio Conselheiro e Canudos: Revisão Histórico,* 2d ed. (1978).

Carole A. Myscofski, *When Men Walk Dry: Portuguese Messianism in Brazil* (1988).

Todd A. Diacron, *Millenarian Vision, Capitalist Reality: Brazil's Contestado Revolution, 1912–1916* (1991).

Robert M. Levine, *Vale of Tears: Revisiting the Canudos Massacre in Northwestern Brazil, 1893–1897* (1992).

Additional Bibliography

Arruda, João. *Canudos: Messianismo e conflicto social.* Fortaleza, Brazil: Editora UFC, 2006.

Lopreato, Christina da Silva Roquette. *Milagres da fé: Messianismo e repressão política no Brasil dos anos 70.* Campinas, Brazil: Editora da Unicamp, 1999.

Pessar, Patricia R. *From Fanatics to Folk: Brazilian Millenarianism and Popular Culture.* Durham, NC: Duke University Press, 2004.

Thomé, Nilson. *Os iluminados: Personagens e manifestações místicas e messianicas no Contestado.* Florianópolis, Brazil: Insular, 1999.

CAROLE A. MYSCOFSKI

SPANISH AMERICA

In Christian belief, the millennium will come when Christ, as He promised, returns and establishes His kingdom of peace and plenty on earth for 1,000 years. Based on the biblical books of Daniel and Revelation, the period is to be ushered in by the Apocalypse, a time of travail and devastation, and end with the Last Judgment, when Satan and his followers shall be forever vanquished. In popular thought, the term is associated with the inauguration of an ideal period, perhaps the return of an imagined golden age of harmony, happiness, and prosperity among all peoples. Many cultures harbor this general belief in messianic movements or millenarianism, with or without the return of their own particular hero.

Such millennial beliefs tend to permeate the ways in which many people understand and practice their daily lives; occasionally, but in no predictable patterns, they can mobilize groups, even masses, for social actions called messianic or millenarian movements. The origins, nature, and outcomes of these disturbances (the state labels them "rebellions," although many millenarians claim to have no quarrel with the government) provoke debate. Most seem to have occurred during periods of social crisis or moral breakdown, but religious belief also can spark movements on its own. Each appears to be based on local concerns and to attract people from all social configurations and classes. Most culminate in a bloodbath, the faithful suppressed by the regime at great cost in men, matériel, and reputation. Nevertheless, Latin Americans continue to yearn for a sanctified and idealized world, and rally around their self-styled prophets for relief. Their leaders, often viewed as messiahs, have received much attention, both in their own times and among more recent scholars. Their charisma derives from their followers, who decide how close the leader is to God and when he or she deserves the title of *santo.* Often the followers are divided, and in the debate that follows, millenarian assemblies may splinter or collapse. People join millenarian groups for reasons other than religious belief; they can include merchants hoping to sell their wares and politicians looking for adherents. Bandits, too, seem to have an affinity for millenarian activities, perhaps because regimes are so quick to label them both "outlaws"—that is, outcasts from society.

Strains of millenarian thought were evident in Latin America prior to the European conquest, have been a vital force in numerous social movements, and continue today. The Aztecs awaited the return of Quetzalcoatl, and the Incas anticipated the restoration of Viracocha, their Creator God.

Even the conquistadores came to the New World driven by a millenarian impulse embedded in their heritage, and the promised return of great Christian kings such as San Sebastián and Charlemagne are still awaited with great anticipation by many Latin Americans.

In the aftermath of the Conquest, messianic movements began to appear that are preserved in scholarly works, movies, novels, songs, poetry, comic books, oral traditions, and lore. Just before his execution at the hands of the Spaniards, the God/ruler of the Incas, Atahualpa, assured that his father, the sun, would resurrect and return him to his earthly kingdom. According to Spanish accounts, thousands of Indians living in Huamanga, Peru, in the 1560s participated in the Taki Onqoy (dancing sickness), believing that an alliance of gods throughout the Inca empire would defeat the Spanish God and banish the colonizers. The movement manifested itself through "demonic possession," whereby Indians began singing and dancing uncontrollably, renounced their belief in Christianity and obedience to Spanish authority, and reembraced their ancestral gods. Colonial religious authorities in the area launched a thorough anti-idolatry campaign to suppress the movement. Another confrontation occurred among Tzeltal-speaking natives in Chiapas, Mexico, who in 1712 received through their prophets admonitions and guidance from the Virgin Mary that ignited and sustained an armed struggle to oust the colonial presence and to usher in the return of an idealized pre-Hispanic glory. In southern Colombia, the Páez enthusiastically followed the preachings of their new spiritual leader, Undachi.

During much of the second half of the nineteenth century, the Maya in Yucatán worshiped a speaking cross that they believed would defend their homeland against the encroachments of outsiders. And northern Arawaks, who lived in Venezuela, Brazil, and Colombia, followed Venancio Kamiko in messianic-style protest. In the 1890s, at Tomochic in Mexico's Sierra Madre Occidental, followers of a teenage girl named Teresa Urrea, whom they declared a *santa,* valiantly defied the bayonets of Porfirio Díaz's dictatorship for the right to practice their religion. More recently, messianism has fueled Jamaica's Rastafarian fervor.

Today the millenarian impulse in Latin America remains strong, with strains in all sorts of religious ideology and practices from liberation theology to evangelicalism to *costumbrismo* (traditional native belief). It is embedded in a variety of current social movements, such as that of the Zapatistas, which erupted in Chiapas, in southern Mexico, on 1 January 1994, and is bound to appear even more forcefully in many more to come.

See also **Catholic Church: The Colonial Period; Catholic Church: The Modern Period.**

BIBLIOGRAPHY

Euclides Da Cunha, *Rebellion in the Backlands,* translated by Samuel Putnam (1944).

Nelson Reed, *The Caste War of Yucatán* (1964).

Heriberto Frias, *Tomochic* (1968).

Victoria Reifler Bricker, *The Indian Christ, the Indian King: The Historical Substrate of Maya Myth and Ritual* (1981).

Mario Vargas Llosa, *Guerra al fin del mundo,* 7th ed. (1984).

Todd A. Diacron, *Millenarian Vision, Capitalist Reality: Brazil's Contestado Revolution, 1912–1916* (1991).

Kevin Marlin Gozner, *Soldiers of the Virgin: The Moral Economy of a Colonial Maya Rebellion* (1992).

Robert M. Levine, *Vale of Tears: Revisiting the Canudos Massacre in Northwestern Brazil, 1893–1897* (1992).

Paul J. Vanderwood, "'None but the Justice of God': Tomochich, 1891–1892," in *Patterns of Contention in Mexican History,* edited by Jaime E. Rodríguez O. (1992).

Steven J. Stern, *Peru's Indian Peoples and the Challenge of Spanish Conquest: Huamanga to 1640,* 2d ed. (1993).

Paul J. Vanderwood, "Using the Present to Study the Past: Religious Movements in Mexico and Uganda a Century Apart," in *Mexican Studies/Estudios Mexicanos* 10 (Winter 1994): 99–134.

Additional Bibliography

Fernández, Eduardo, and Michael F. Brown. *Guerra de sombras: La lucha por la utopía en la Amazonía peruana.* Lima, Perú: CAAAP; Buenos Aires: CAEA-CONICET, 2001.

Pessar, Patricia R. *From Fanatics to Folk: Brazilian Millenarianism and Popular Culture.* Durham: Duke University Press, 2004.

Porro, Antonio. *O messianismo Maya no período colonial.* São Paulo, Brazil: FFLCH-USP, 1991.

Robins, Nicholas A. *El mesianismo y la rebelión indígena: La rebelión de Oruro en 1781.* La Paz: Hisbol, 1997.

Vanderwood, Paul J. *The Power of God Against the Guns of Government: Religious Upheaval in Mexico at the Turn of the Nineteenth Century.* Stanford: Stanford University Press, 1998.

PAUL J. VANDERWOOD

MESTA. Mesta, Spanish sheep owners guild. Chartered by Alfonso X in 1273, the Mesta was granted important pastoral privileges and protection by the Castilian crown in exchange for financial contributions. It represented the interests of migratory sheepowners, whose flocks moved seasonally between northern and southern parts of Spain in search of pasture. In 1500 the organization came under the control of a royal council, thus giving the crown monopoly control over the wool, and in 1501 the Mesta received the right to use in perpetuity land it had once leased for a low rent. It was a source of increasing income for Ferdinand II (1452–1516) and Isabella I (1451–1504), who extended the traditional tax on herds to a tax on each sheep in the pasture. Frequently the source of hostile pasture disputes, the Mesta's privileges came under attack in the eighteenth century and were abolished during the reign of Charles III in 1780, when his minister Campomanes became president of the guild. The organization itself was finally destroyed by the liberals in 1836.

In Latin America, a similar institution took root and expanded in New Spain and enabled Spanish authorities some control over pastoral activities. Unlike Spain, the New World adaptation of the institution was designed to benefit all stockmen, not just members of a sheep-raising guild. Liberal opposition brought an end to it in 1812. Although the Spanish crown provided that the Mesta be established elsewhere in Spanish America, in other parts local *cabildos* managed grazing and pastoral affairs.

See also **Ferdinand II of Aragon; Livestock.**

BIBLIOGRAPHY

Julius Klein, *The Mesta: A Study in Spanish Economic History* (1920).

William H. Dusenberry, *The Mexican Mesta* (1963).

Nina Mikun, *La Mesta au XVIII siècle: Étude d'histoire sociale et économique de l'Espagne au XVIII siècle* (1983).

Jean Paul Le Flem, "El Valle de Alcudia en el siglo XVIII," in *Congreso de Historia Rural: Siglo XV al XIX* (1984).

Additional Bibliography

Pérez Marín, Tomás. *Don Vicente Paíno y Hurtado: Defensor de Extremadura en la lucha contra la Mesta.* Mérida, Badajoz: Editora Regional de Extremadura, 2000.

SUZANNE HILES BURKHOLDER

MESTIZO. Mestizo, a term used in the colonial era to refer to a person of evenly mixed Indian and Hispanic ancestry. The first generation of mestizos were the sons and daughters of Spanish soldiers and settlers who had sexual relationships with Indian women but rarely married them. The most famous mestizo of the sixteenth century was the accomplished writer Garcilaso De La Vega, the son of a lesser Spanish noble and an Inca royal princess. So many mestizos were illegitimate that the terms "mestizo" and "illegitimate" were at times used interchangeably throughout the colonial era.

The Spanish crown found it necessary to determine whether the numerous offspring of Spanish men and Indian women were to be treated as Indians and made to pay tribute, or exempted as were Spaniards. While Spanish authorities opted not to class them as tribute payers, they nevertheless gradually developed a series of discriminatory measures that barred them from access to the priesthood, the university, and political posts on local councils, and excluded them from membership in the most exclusive artisan guilds, those of gold- and silversmiths. Unlike many of the other terms for racial groups in colonial Latin America, mestizo was an official designation for purposes of tribute collection or exemption, which came to be used on both christening and marriage records as well.

During the colonial era, mestizo came to designate any person with both Spanish and Indian ancestry. Such persons were often identified as much by social and economic criteria as by physical ones. Although rarely wealthy, mestizos tended to belong to skilled occupations, lived in Spanish-style housing, and adopted Hispanic dress, which distinguished them from natives.

De Espanol e India Nace Mestizo (From a Spaniard and an Indian Woman Is Born a Mestizo), unknown artist, 18th century.

With independence, particularly in Mexico, the category became a term of pride, indicating that the nation was the product of both native and European civilization. In the contemporary era the term has lost its connection to biology and biography and has come to reflect a variety of different activities. In sociological and anthropological studies a mestizo is a person who mediates between indigenous and regional or national markets or bureaucracies. Mestizo and similar terms such as Ladino and Cholo commonly denote people who sell the textile and agricultural products of native communities to local markets. In art history, architecture, and literature, the term mestizo has become widely used to refer to any art form or writing style that incorporates indigenous as well as Hispanic elements. In this usage it refers not to the creator's biography, as it would have in the colonial era, but to the artistic or literary object created. What the word has retained is the sense of being neither Spanish, nor Indian, but somewhere in between.

See also **Race and Ethnicity.**

BIBLIOGRAPHY

Nicolás León, *Las castas del México colonial* (1924).

Lyle McAlister, "Social Structure and Social Change in New Spain," in *Hispanic American Historical Review* 43, no. 3 (1963): 349–370.

Magnus Mörner, *Race Mixture in the History of Latin America* (1967).

John K. Chance, *Race and Class in Colonial Oaxaca* (1978).

Patricia Seed, "Social Dimensions of Race: Mexico City, 1753," in *Hispanic American Historical Review* 62, no. 4 (1982): 569–606.

Patricia Seed and Philip Rust, "Estate and Class in Colonial Oaxaca Revisited," in *Comparative Studies in Society and History* 25 (1983): 703–709, 721–724.

Rodney Anderson, "Race and Social Stratification: A Comparison of Working-Class Spaniards, Indians, and Castas in Guadalajara, Mexico, in 1821," in *Hispanic American Historical Review* 68, no. 2 (1988): 209–243.

Douglas Cope, *Limits of Racial Domination* (1993).

Additional Bibliography

Appelbaum, Nancy P., Anne S Macpherson and Karin Alejandra Rosemblatt, eds. *Race and Nation in Modern Latin America.* Chapel Hill: University of North Carolina Press, 2003.

Basave Benítez, Agustín F. *México mestizo: Análisis del nacionalismo mexicano en torno a la mestizofilia de Andrés Molina Enríquez.* México: Fondo de Cultura Económica, 1992.

De la Cadena, Marisol. *Indigenous Mestizos: The Politics of Race and Culture in Cuzco, Peru, 1919–1991.* Durham, NC: Duke University Press, 2000.

Gould, Jeffrey L. *To Die in This Way: Nicaraguan Indians and the Myth of Mestizaje, 1880–1965.* Durham, NC: Duke University Press, 1998.

Hedrick, Tace. *Mestizo Modernism: Race, Nation, and Identity in Latin American Culture, 1900–1940.* New Brunswick, NJ: Rutgers University Press, 2003.

Miller, Marilyn Grace. *Rise and Fall of the Cosmic Race: The Cult of Mestizaje in Latin America.* Austin: University of Texas Press, 2004.

PATRICIA SEED

METHUEN, TREATY OF (1703).

Treaty of Methuen (1703), an agreement between Portugal (represented by the marquês de Alegrete) and Britain (represented by John Methuen) that formalized existing trade patterns between the two countries and laid the groundwork for Portugal's economic dependence on Britain for the remainder of the eighteenth century. On 27 December 1703, Portugal agreed to purchase English wheat, textiles, and manufactured goods in exchange for preferential duties on such Portuguese products as olive oil and wine.

Neither Portugal nor Britain anticipated Brazilian gold and diamond strikes in Minas Gerais, Goiás, and Mato Grosso during the early eighteenth century, nor the impact these newly found riches would have on Portuguese-British trade. Portugal's imports began to escalate as the new sources of wealth were used to purchase increasing amounts of raw materials from Britain's North American colonies and luxury imports from Britain. British industrialization boomed as Portugal neglected its manufacturing. During the early eighteenth century, the trade imbalance was paid for with Brazilian treasure. After 1755, as the Brazilian mines began to play out, Portugal became increasingly dependent on Britain's imports and goodwill to maintain Portuguese independence.

As Portuguese colonists, Brazilians found that decisions regarding their future were often dominated by British priorities, which increased the frustration of the already antagonized Brazilian upper class, who wanted free trade, open ports, and an end to Portuguese restrictions on the development of Brazilian industries.

See also **Commercial Policy: Colonial Brazil; Trade, Colonial Brazil.**

BIBLIOGRAPHY

Alan David Francis, *The Methuens and Portugal, 1691–1708* (1966).

E. Bradford Burns, *A History of Brazil* (1980), pp. 79–80.

Leslie Bethell, ed., *The Cambridge History of Latin America,* vol. 1 (1984), pp. 461–487.

LESLEY R. LUSTER

MEXICAN LIBERAL AGRARIAN POLICIES, NINETEENTH CENTURY.

Nineteenth-century liberal agrarian policy focused on the abolition of corporate landholding. The disentailment of church lands and the division of indigenous communal lands were both seen as essential to the formation of an independent state, the basis of which would be the individual property-owning citizen. Liberals touted the end of corporate landholding as a necessary requirement for the country's economic, political, and financial progress: It would put more land into market circulation; theoretically ensure equality through the elimination of corporate privileges; generate new national allegiances by breaking the material basis for communal loyalties; and create a larger rural property tax base (communal lands were not subject to direct property taxes) and a source of credit for the fledgling state.

After Mexico gained independence, the Catholic Church and indigenous communities held extensive amounts of arable land in the central and southern parts of the country as corporate or entailed properties. Although the Cortes of Cádiz in 1813 had called for an end to corporate landholding, the Mexican constitution of 1824 had no such provisions. Individual states passed their own decrees, but these had limited, if any, success in the decades immediately following independence. At the national level the advent of liberal agrarian policy can be dated from the June 1856 implementation of the Lerdo Law (named after treasury minister Miguel Lerdo de Tejada, 1812–1861), which explicitly called for the sale of church lands not used for religious purposes and the division of indigenous communal lands into individual, private plots.

Part of a broader assault on the church at mid-century, the law decreed that the church's urban and rural real estate be sold and the church prohibited from acquiring land again in the future. Church lands would be offered first to existing tenants at a reduced rate to encourage their purchase, but, many tenants, out of loyalty to the church, refused to buy. In such instances, the land was sold at public auction, often ending up in the hands of hacendados and speculators. Similarly, the law took aim at lands held in usufruct by largely indigenous communities based upon colonial land grants. Systems of tenure within communities were quite diverse, with forms of private ownership mixing with forms of communal tenure. As well as lands under cultivation by villagers, there were lands rented to bring in cash, and *ejidos*, which were pasture and woodland areas initially not subject to the Lerdo Law. Liberal policies sought to divide such lands into individual, private plots in order to turn communal landworkers into small landholders, and stipulations were put in place that, in theory, would permit Indian villagers to purchase the land they worked at a nominal fee.

Although expropriations of the church lands began immediately upon the passage of the Lerdo Law, the surveying and division of indigenous lands proceeded haphazardly. In many parts of the country lands continued to be held communally until well in to the Porfiriato (1876–1910). When land divisions did proceed apace, at times they were promoted as much by sectors within villages that were eager to capitalize on changing markets and policies as by federal officials or large landowners.

These liberal land policies were complemented by the surveying and sale of so called *terrenos baldíos*, or vacant lands, particular in the far north of the country during the Porfiriato. Such lands theoretically belonged to the federal government but were often used by villagers for grazing and hunting. These activities were increasingly curtailed as survey companies delineated the bounds of the baldíos, receiving a third of the land in payment with the remaining two-thirds offered up for sale. As was the case with communal land divisions, the newly surveyed lands often ended up in the hands of hacendandos, speculators, and foreign investors. By the end of Porfirio Díaz's reign in 1911 it is estimated that much of the land in Mexico had been divided, surveyed, and put into circulation. Though the ideal may have been to create a large class of small-landowners, in reality land became increasingly concentrated in fewer hands in much of the country. To this the liberals had little response, given their primary allegiance to private property, although critics such as Wistano Luis Orozco and Andrés Molina Enríquez soon arose. Their voices proved prophetic: Nineteenth-century liberal agrarian policy is often directly linked to the coming of the Mexican Revolution in 1910.

See also **Agrarian Reform; Lerdo de Tejada, Miguel; Religion in Mexico, Catholic Church and Beyond.**

BIBLIOGRAPHY

Bazant, Jan. *Los bienes de la Iglesia en Mexico, 1856–1875. Aspectos economicos y sociales de la Revolucion liberal.* Mexico, D.F.: El Colegio de México, 1971.

Hale, Charles. *Liberalism in the Age of Mora.* New Haven, CT: Yale University Press, 1968.

Hernández Chávez, Alicia. *Anenecuilco: Memoria y vida de un pueblo.* Mexico City: El Colegio de Mexico, 1991.

Holden, Robert. *Mexico and the Survey of Public Lands: The Management of Modernization, 1876–1911.* DeKalb: Northern Illinois University Press, 1994.

Kourí, Emilio. *A Pueblo Divided: Business, Property, and Community in Papantla, Mexico.* Palo Alto, CA: Stanford University Press, 2004.

Molina Enríquez, Andrés. *Los grandes problemas nacionales.* [1909]. Mexico City: Ediciones Era, 1978.

Nugent, Daniel. *Spent Cartridges of Revolution: An Anthropological History of Namiquipa, Chihuahua.* Chicago: University of Chicago Press, 1993.

RAYMOND B. CRAIB

MEXICO

This entry includes the following articles:

THE COLONIAL PERIOD

Indo-Mexico on the eve of European contact consisted of complex societies, established territorial entities, and an empire. The intrusion of strangers upset the political balance established by the Mexica of the central valley: Foreign contact came at a critical moment, as the region grappled with evolutionary pressures. Expansion of trade created regional interdependence on resources, bringing merchants in contact with new ideas, different gods, and an array of chiefdoms. An expanding circle of cooperation made force less effective and encouraged consolidation, and an initial amalgamation in the valley of Mexico created the triple alliance of three cities in the valley of Mexico: Tenochtitlan, Texcoco, and a weaker Tacuba. This alliance (c. 1430) created an imperial core of shared interests, and that made possible a bicoastal empire stretching from the Atlantic to the Pacific. Deification of the paramount chief in order to provide political stability had not been solidified by 1519. A legal code developed by Nezahualcóyotl, the philosopher-chief of Texcoco, represented an emerging universal legal philosophy. Spain arrived in the hemisphere at a moment of transition in Indo-Mexico and openness to change.

The expedition of Hernán Cortés (1519) and the subsequent fall of Tenochtitlan (1521) marked the end of indigenous sovereignty. Castile's imperialism, following the Iberian experience, did not seek to extinguish the existing organization and laws of its Indian subjects. Spain recognized two republics (in the sense of distinctly organized peoples): the Republica de los Españoles, which governed Europeans in Mexico, and the Republica de los Indios, which applied to indigenous people. Theoretically, two parallel societies existed, joined in the person of the monarch; the difficulty lay in finding an acceptable way for the two to interact within an overarching sociopolitical structure. Conflict over booty threatened to fragment a weakly consolidated indigenous empire and dash the Crown's plan to modify without destroying. The struggle to reach an acceptable balance among the interests of the indigenous population, the Spanish settlers, and the monarchy lasted for decades. The fight began almost immediately over the issue of slavery.

Classic Maya style pottery bowl with earth deity seated under band of glyphs, from Pre-Columbian period. Spanish church and state competed in dominating the Maya peoples of Mexico's Yucatán in the sixteenth century. CORBIS

Slavery was the first major issue that divided the monarchy and those that toppled the Mexica. Thousands of men, women, and children became slaves as a consequence of war, presenting a moral issue for the Crown. Slavery conflicted with the papal trusteeship of the New World to introduce

Illustration depicting the meeting of Aztec leader Moctezuma and Spanish explorer Hernán Cortés in November 1519, in present-day Mexico. To defeat the vast Aztec empire of Mexico, the Spanish forged alliances with discontented indigenous groups under Aztec domain. THE BETTMANN ARCHIVE/CORBIS

Christianity. The Spanish Crown considered itself to be a benevolent power introducing a unifying social template across the region, and indigenous slavery complicated that process. Nevertheless, it could be eliminated only as the monarchy established its directive authority.

The initial organization of New Spain relied upon the municipality as the basic foundation. A hierarchy of urban settlements in a descending chain placed cities at the apex with authority over towns that in turn directed villas that controlled subordinate *pueblos* (villages) and so on down to *lugares* ("small places"). Theoretically, instructions could be filtered down to the lowest levels, and responsibility for enforcement was shared. Cities, which functioned as the overarching territorial units, had recognized municipal councils, and their authority applied until the border of one municipality touched another.

A parallel indigenous structure involved a modification of the Indian political traditions rather than its replacement. It reassured indigenous leaders that they had a place and a political role in New Spain. Subdivision of regions into *cabeceras* under an elected Indian official, the *juez-gobernador*, mirrored the role of the preconquest hereditary *tlatoani.* Consequently, theoretically, elected officials tended to stay in office, or circulated from one position to another over a lifetime. Indians modified the structure even further, referring to their governor as the *gobernadoryotl.* Each *cabecera* had a municipal council drawn from the ranks of recognized leaders, *prinicipales*, and *caciques.* Indian officials interacted with the viceroy, *audiencia* (high court), and lower levels of the Spanish system. In Mexico City two indigenous municipal council governed the two former Indian cities of the vice regal capital.

Cortés assumed the initial governorship of New Spain, employing his prestige as the conqueror to influence both Indians and the Europeans. Cortés's diplomatic skills and reassurance of the indigenous population played a large part in the transition from one empire to another and accounted for his popularity among the Indians. A suspicious Crown worried that he might declare himself a New World monarch. Consequently, Madrid appointed an *audiencia* to curb Cortés under the ruthless Nuño Beltrán de Guzmán.

Conflict among the Spaniards over Cortés's awarding of land, encomiendas, and other favors to his supporters threatened stability. Encomiendas assigned tribute-paying Indians to a Spaniard who had the theoretical obligation to maintain armed men to be mobilized in case of an Indian rebellion. Tribute could be paid in labor, making it possible for those who acquired land to bring it to cultivation. (Land had no direct connection with the grant of an encomienda.) Cortés reserved an encomienda of 21,000 for himself, but most had only a few thousand. Cortés became a sugar planter and miner—he realized that land and labor, not booty, represented wealth. The Indians were familiar with the concept of tribute, and they adjusted to new demands, as well as to the notion that negotiated cooperation constituted the heart of the monarchy's ruling system.

The failure of the first *audiencia* led the Crown to dispatch professional lawyers in 1530 to establish a more respectable institution. The second *audiencia* proved to be a success. Cortés returned to Spain to defend himself before royal officials. A relieved monarch elevated him to the nobility as the Marques del Valle, and confirmed land grants and other actions of the conqueror. He was allowed to return to Mexico, but prohibited from entering Mexico City by a wary Crown still concerned about his ambitions. The Crown selected a high nobleman, Antonio de Mendoza, to be the first viceroy of the Kingdom of New Spain (1535), which was joined with the other kingdoms of Spain only through the monarch. Colonial Mexico became a political entity theoretically equal in status to all other kingdoms, not a colony in the modern sense. As a kingdom it could expect Emperor Carlos V (Carlos I of Spain) to pay attention to its well-being.

ROLE OF RELIGION

While security and organizational issues distracted Madrid, the religious struggle for the minds and souls of the king's new subjects proceeded with notable success. Religion set the parameters of acceptable behavior for both Europeans and the Indians. Cortés requested missionaries to begin the process of conversion to Christianity, and a small group of Franciscan friars arrived in 1524, followed by twelve Dominicans two years later. Mass conversions with almost nonexistent instruction in the faith constituted more a political act than a spiritual one. Spain could not tolerate non-Catholic subjects, and the Indians understood that they had to adopt the religion of the dominant power. Some immediate benefits accompanied conversion to Christianity: The new religion did not require human sacrifice, protected adherents from enslavement, acknowledged the humanity of the indigenous population, confirmed that they were entitled to be treated as members of the faith, and established their equality before God. Nevertheless, Spain understood that the abrupt acceptance of Catholicism required a spiritual apprenticeship, and so the Inquisition (introduced in 1571) excluded Indians, leaving guidance—and discipline—in the hands of bishops. The Indians' second-class religious status played a major role in creating social inferiority. Subsequently, in the next century, the cult of our Lady of Guadalupe (1648) provided an indigenous manifestation of an important Catholic figure.

THE SOCIAL STRUCTURE

Catastrophe played a role in shaping society. Pandemics swept away an unknown number of Indians in populated regions, and penetrated into mountain ranges and dense jungles. Smallpox, measles, plague, yellow fever, and other diseases that arrived with the Europeans attacked the indigenous population, which had no immunity. In the last days of the besieged city of Tenochtitlan, smallpox thinned the ranks of its defenders. Indigenous leaders, who were more likely to have contact with Europeans, were particularly vulnerable. Disease spared those with immunity to European and African diseases: Spaniards and their mixed-parentage offspring, the mestizos, and blacks had a biological advantage. As the population declined, land was abandoned and the encomienda became less effective as a source of Indian workers. This accelerated the movement to various forms of wage-contract labor and distribution of workers through a *repartimiento* system to Spanish agriculturists. Lands abandoned and confiscated from the pre-European state increased settlers' holdings as haciendas emerged.

A series of epidemics in the 1540s again swept through the Indian population. The source of these diseases is not known, but may have been a result of drought that drove rodents into close contact with human beings in rural villages. Combined with cultural shocks, epidemics created psychological turmoil in indigenous societies, and this made them conducive to both reactionary retreats and abrupt abandonment of pre-European ties to groups, customs, and traditions. Indians who abandoned traditional dress, learned Spanish, changed their diet, and adopted an approved ceremonial life became cultural mestizos detached from Indian society.

The hierarchy of races was more a theoretical than an actual fixing of status. Spaniards born in the mother country were at the top of the racial hierarchy, followed by creoles (Europeans born in the New World), mestizos, mulattoes, Indians, and blacks. A small number of Spanish women went to Mexico. In the middle of the first century, women made up only 16.5 percent of immigrants; their numbers peaked in 1600 at 28 percent. A gender ratio of one female to four males meant that population replacement and growth depended on native-born Mexican women.

Consequently, racial factors were only one element fixing an individual's place in society. Attachment to European culture, religion, occupation, wealth, and marriage alliances combined to determine status. The New World constituted a biological and social frontier where one could invent a past, become a self-declared *hidalgo* (petty noble), or otherwise elevate one's social position, and all of these choices could be legitimized by success and wealth. The fact that most Spaniards arrived in Mexico as servants or were poor relatives of rich merchants could be forgotten. Cultural identification transformed Indians into mestizos, and later, in several generations, perhaps into Creoles. Racial fluidity created a distinct Mexican race in the cities and towns, whereas in the countryside the population remained largely indigenous.

THE CONQUEST OF PERMANENCE

In 1541 the Mixton War shook the foundations of New Spain. Up until then, the relatively smooth acceptance of Spanish authority in central Mexico indicated a pragmatic adaptation to a political and religious system able to maintain peace, encourage trade, negotiate differences, and impose responsibilities. In the north, nomadic groups of less civilized Indians maintained a state of warfare, raiding and burning settlements well into the nineteenth century. If similar massive resistance had occurred in central Mexico, the survival of New Spain would have been in danger, but instead the Indians rallied to defend Spanish sovereignty.

The Mixton War was the consequence of the violent activities of European predators. Under Nuño Beltrán de Guzmán, life in the weakly held western fringe of royal authority was intolerable, as marauders swept across the settlements, looting and killing. When the Indians in the vicinity of Guadalajara revolted, Viceroy Mendoza fruitlessly called on the *encomenderos* for help. The desperate viceroy then turned to Indian leaders, and a force of 3,000 indigenous soldiers along with 300 Spaniards suppressed the rebellion. It became obvious that the king's new Indian subjects provided a more solid sociopolitical foundation than did the Spanish conquerors, whose claims to privileges and status as a new colonial nobility eroded after 1541.

In 1542 the Crown prematurely issued the New Laws of the Indies, which directly attacked many of the privileges that *encomenderos* assumed had become settled custom. Moreover, the law prohibited the granting of new *encomiendas*. Outraged Spaniards verged on rebellion. Viceroy Mendoza quickly suspended the New Laws pending an appeal. The threat of a civil war forced the Crown to permit new grants of *encomiendas*, though there were some new restrictions. Royal officials, the *corregidores*, began the task of converting tribute-paying *encomienda* Indians into regular taxpayers. The institution underwent progressive modifications that rendered it harmless, ending the attempt to create a feudal elite. Nevertheless, the struggle between the monarchy and the aspirational European elite continued to be a matter of concern.

Another crisis occurred in 1563 with the arrival in Mexico of Martín Cortés, the conqueror's son and legitimate heir. The young marques, an immature aristocrat, enjoyed great respect among the indigenous population, and seemed to offer a new option to disgruntled *encomenderos*. Conspirators envisioned manipulating Martín Cortés, declaring him a king and legitimizing their coup with an assembly of notables, but an indecisive Cortés delayed, enabling the *audiencia* to lure him into their chambers and arrest him. With the arrival of a new viceroy, Cortés returned to Spain to explain his role in the affair. The two major conspirators were convicted of treason and beheaded; this served as a warning to *encomenderos*.

THE ECONOMY

Land, and the agricultural production and livestock it supported, constituted the basic form of wealth. In 1528 Carlos V instructed Hernán Cortés to distribute land to his men based on their status. Because all claimed *hidalgo* status, most received grants of 44 hectares at least, with many receiving two or more grants. Cattle, sheep, pigs, and domestic fowl, which were first introduced on the islands, soon arrived in Mexico. Cattle feasted on the abundance of native grasses until European grasses inevitably replaced them. Cattlemen established *estancias* but grazed their herds across croplands, causing damage and giving rise to complaints, so vice-regal authorities directed them northward away from agricultural regions.

Spaniards understood that the domestic market for foodstuffs constituted their primary market: Europeans in Mexico demanded wheat, mutton, and familiar vegetables. In contrast, Europe had little need for American agricultural products, and moreover, transportation costs made low-value exports too expensive. Most crops could be grown in Europe from seed, and it took many years to develop European demand for tropical items such as cacao and tobacco. Early focus on urban markets created an internal economy that was soon affirmed by the development of mining, particularly of silver. Silver, a high-value export, could absorb transatlantic transportation costs. Silver facilitated imports of wines, olive oils, fine cloth, fashionable shoes, and more mundane items such as plows and farm implements.

Trade with Spain relied upon an annual convoy. European pirates (who were tacitly supported by European powers that believed they had been excluded unfairly from the riches of the New World) and North African coastal pirates forced Spain to convoy ships. The arrival of trade goods in large volume distorted prices: Usually they were sold at the trade fair in Jalapa to merchant distributors who were able to take advantage of overabundance to drive hard bargains, then sold at progressively higher prices before the next convoy. This had important economic consequences. Demand for reasonably priced goods and consistent supply led to contraband activity by foreign vessels. Avoidance of customs levies provided a price advantage and cut out middlemen who bought items in other countries then transshipped them on the convoy.

The merchant community had its own guild, the Consulado de Comercio, which was established in Mexico City (1592) and composed of the principal merchants (*almancenros*, or wholesalers). It served as a commercial court, and represented their interests to the viceroy and lobbied officials in Spain. The Casa de Contratacion, Spain's trade board (1503), set imperial trade policy and acted on appeals. The Consulado of Seville and the Casa shared many of the same responsibilities.

Merchant activity functioned on a number of levels, but combined, it constituted the commercial engine of New Spain. Large-scale distributors, the *aviadores*, arranged for sale of imported goods to regional merchants. Regional merchants linked to merchants in Mexico City represented only the skeletal trade structure. Peddlers at the bottom of the scale carried items into rural villages, then sold or extended on credit to small stores in minor towns. In addition, Indian porters, mule drivers who transported goods across the region, engaged in trading on their own account as well as carried the goods of others. *Leperos* (urban vagrants, petty criminals) recycled stolen property and sold it to small stall owners in what aptly became known as the thief's market.

Money remained in short supply, making credit important. Although the Crown established a mint in Mexico City in 1535, export demand for silver drained species out of New Spain. Financing the production of domestic food crops to supply the needs of urban centers, as well as the production of agricultural items with European demand such as cochineal (red dye), depended on credit extended under the *repartimento de comercio*. The *repartimento* distributed goods on credit against harvests. It included items such as animals, seeds, and consumer items. Credit terms could be exploitive; nevertheless, production and consumption depended on the survival of the primary producer and consumer. The church served as a basic source of credit in the absence of modern banking. Reasonable interest rates facilitated purchase of land and urban property. Debt could be rolled over from one generation to a purchaser facilitating land transfers. The church preferred a steady income to support hospitals, orphanages, convents, and other facilities and services.

MINING

New Spain had minor sources of gold, but vast silver deposits. Cortés worked silver mines in Taxco as early as 1525. The first mining boom resulted from the discovery of a huge deposit in Zacatecas in 1546. Four years later, prospectors uncovered a rich vein in Guanajuato; this was followed by a series of strikes in San Luis Potosí, Real de Monte, Pachuca, Parral, and elsewhere. The great mines of Guanajuato produced an estimated 20 to 25 percent of New Spain's silver; the Valenciana mine may have been the most profitable mining enterprise in Mexico. In the early period, miners worked silver out of croppings close to the surface. As the easy available ores ran out, mining became more expensive. Deep shafts required complex drainage, shoring, and pumps (introduced in 1609). Consequently, large enterprises displaced individual miners, except in marginal silver operations. Deep shaft mines in the eighteenth century could absorb a capital investment of a million pesos and years of work.

Usually located in high table land far from food resources, the mining industry had an insatiable demand for supplies of all types. Mining fueled the internal economy. By the eighteenth century the industry depended increasingly on deep shafts that went below the water table, requiring lumber to shore up tunnels and vast amounts of hand tools. Wool clothes; hides for ores; waterproofing material; mules, horses, and oxen for motive power and transportation; fodder for animals; and innumerable other items made mining efficient and life more bearable.

The demand for supplies and the tranport of ores by high-wheeled wagons to smelters required a road network that reached far beyond the mines. Wages for mine labor tended to be attractive, and mine workers constituted a privileged segment of the labor market. Successful investors and silver merchants (*mercaderes de plata*) became a plutocratic elite. Silver pesos financed trade with China by way of Manila through the annual galleon to the west coast port of Acapulco. Crown taxes on mining required one-fifth payment, a rate that could be reduced by various artful dodges or Crown concessions. New Spain absorbed most of the wealth generated by silver. Peripheral parts of the viceroyalty and financial dependencies such as Cuba and others represented a Mexican subimperial structure.

WOMEN AND FAMILY

The importance of Indian women in the family and comparable Spanish notions molded the role and place of women in Mexican society. Both cultures placed the male at the head of the family and subordinated the female. A protective web isolated wives and children from all but the extended family. Lineage, whether real or imagined, conveyed status and had to be preserved; consequently, marriages had to be carefully considered to avoid loss of social standing. Moreover, a dowry negotiated too generously might strain the resources of the family. Dowries could be paid in any thing of recognized value, but they remained the property of the wives, and although they could be managed by the husbands, they could not be squandered. Incidents of wives suing husbands over dowries or failure to acknowledge dowry payments testify to its importance. In the case of catastrophe, the dowry supported the widow.

Marriage was an economic institution, but that did not necessarily preclude love and affection. A man typically had several spouses serially during his lifetime because of maternal deaths during childbirth. Marrying a deceased wife's sister would preserve wealth within the family; another common arrangement involved marriages between second cousins. The further down one stood in the social structure, the less important marriage became, until finally common-law arrangements were acceptable. Within the family, the male possessed legal authority over family members. Both male and female children remained legal minors until age twenty-five and shared the same rights to own property, to enter contracts, to serve as witnesses, and to enjoy other responsibilities. With marriage, responsibility shifted to the male head of household. A widow regained her legal rights, and depending on her personality, could become a powerful matriarch, conduct business, and protect family interests. The extended family and, at times, distant relatives, supplied the employees of family businesses. Actual and theoretical legal rights had little importance at the lower social levels.

Convents, another option for young women and the family, provided a protected, respected place for women and required a smaller dowry than what might be required by a marriage. In some cases, families anxious to avoid the marriage expenses forced young women into convents, but for others, convents were a socially acceptable way to avoid marriage. Convent life—with servants, black slaves, personal items, books, musical instruments, and comfortable quarters—could be pleasant for the nuns, though they could opt for a more rigorous regime if desired. Nuns ran schools for girls, wrote verse, and explored the life of the mind.

EDUCATION

Education in New Spain began with the Indians. The Franciscan lay brother Pedro de Gante taught European knowledge, including Spanish and Latin. In 1536 the Franciscans established a secondary school, Santa Cruz de Tlalteloco, for the indigenous elite. Among other objectives, Franciscan missionaries sought to establish and train an Indian priesthood. The Dominicans did not share such hopes, and as preconquest religious practices persisted, the clergy in general abandoned the notion of an educated Indian priesthood. In the early period, women directed by Catalina Bustamante taught Indian women, but as attitudes changed, that ended, too.

Laws specified that municipalities maintain at least one primary school, but many avoided the expense. Individual priests taught rudimentary literacy skills to selected students regardless of race. Mestizos, whether biological or cultural, could not be excluded from education or the priesthood as their numbers grew, so there were schools for young mestizo girls and boys up to the secondary level, often endowed by benefactors. Tutors might be engaged by the wealthy.

The University of Mexico began to function in 1553 with a course of theology and Latin. It was theoretically closed to mixed-race individuals, but such restrictions could be bypassed. Women could not attend. By 1775 it had conferred 29,882 bachelor degrees and 1,162 masters degrees.

EIGHTEENTH-CENTURY COLONIAL MATURITY

By the late seventeenth century New Spain had developed a dynamic economy and a unique society. It appeared to be self-sufficient—that is, able to manufacture what it needed or buy reasonably priced contraband goods from a competitive array of smugglers of different European nationalities. Meanwhile, Spain declined into an economic depression marked by food riots and the abandonment of rural districts. Transatlantic trade atrophied. The number of Spanish merchant ships arriving at the port of Veracruz declined drastically. In Madrid an unaffordable, bloated bureaucracy struggled to keep the government afloat. To add to the country's woes, a succession crisis occupied court politicians. Finally, Carlos II died in 1700 without an heir, setting off the War of the Spanish Succession (1700–1713).

Only after Felipe V, the grandson of Louis the XIV of France, assumed the Spanish throne was attention paid to revitalizing the empire. There were muted indications of reform even in the darkest days of the previous century, but with the new Bourbon dynasty, recovery began to be evident. The introduction of regional administrators in Spain that reported directly to the king was a model that eventually was introduced in the Latin American empire. In 1743 José Campillo, Felipe V's minister of war and finance, circulated the Nuevo Sistema de Goberieno para la America (New System of Economic Governance in America), a report that suggested cutting taxes to eliminate contraband trade, rationalizing maritime transportation, and distributing land to Indians to make them more productive and to provide a new source of tax revenues. The Enlightenment focus on economics underpinned such plans. But planners and bureaucrats failed to consider that New Spain's merchants, miners, and agriculturalists had adapted to global commerce, tax avoidance, and a host of minor, prohibited, but collectively profitable activities that negatively impacted royal revenues and Spanish trade. Conflict between a prosperous New Spain and a suddenly demanding mother country anxious to repair its fortunes seemed inevitable.

Imperial defense became an issue with the Seven Years' War (1756–1763). The fall of Manila and Havana to the British shocked Madrid and Mexico City. Concern that the 10,000 British troops in North America could capture Veracruz and then Mexico City could not be brushed aside. Even after the return of Havana under the terms of the peace treaty, future conflict had to be anticipated. New Spain had only 3,000 regular army soldiers, mostly on the northern frontier, and poorly trained militias suitable for warding off pirates perhaps, but not much else. Creating a colonial army could not be delayed. In 1764 the Regiment of the Infantry of America, along with a cadre of officers to train the newly reorganized militias, disembarked in Veracruz. To encourage recruitment, the military *fuero* (privileges) covered those in militia units as well as the regular units.

With the reign of Carlos III (1759–1788), another reality became evident. The former Hapsburg monarchs negotiated to establish accepted arrangements and compromises. The new Bourbon monarchy relied on administration by civil and often military bureaucrats rather than politics. Imperial administration reflected the authoritarianism inherent in the Enlightenment's scientific approach. The implication of the new approach arrived in New Spain in the form of the inspection tour of José de Gálvez (1765–1771). An impatient man intent on confirming his preconceived notions and rebalancing the imperial arrangement in favor of the mother country, Gálvez attacked the traditional vice-regal structure, including the *audiencia*. He hoped to eliminate symbols of independent internal sovereignty and replace them with a commandant-general and powerful regional officials, the intendants. On the local level, he anticipated substituting *alcaldes* (mayors) with *subdelegados*, allegedly to end corrupt practices and increase revenues. What Gálvez saw as long overdue reforms, Mexicans considered arbitrary acts that injured their interests. The sudden expulsion of the Jesuits in 1767 from all Spanish domains seemed almost beyond comprehension to many in New Spain. The Society of Jesus had operated the most prestigious secondary schools, educating the sons of the elite.

In 1786 the division of New Spain into twelve intendancies began the implementation of Gálvez's reorganization plan. Earlier, in 1776, a regent had been appointed to assume some of the duties of the viceroy, including presiding over the *audiencia*. As anticipated, tax revenues increased. Nevertheless, resistance to externally imposed reforms delayed the more ambitious plan to eliminate the viceroy, and limited funds weakened the resolve of Madrid's planners. As New Spain entered its last decade, its institutions remained caught between the weakened traditional structure and partially imposed reforms. Nevertheless, the changes in trade policies benefited New Spain's cotton exports and stimulated the economy of the more entrepreneurial regions of Spain. In general, the Bourbon reforms engendered truculence but not rebellion, and in their weakened state could be adjusted to by merchants and others.

The establishment of the United States, followed by the French Revolution (1789) and the Haitian Revolution (1792), began the unraveling. Napoleon threw the European power balance into disarray, and the French blackmail of Spain drained it of money. After exhausting its resources, including church property in Spain, Madrid turned to its empire. The 1804 Law of Consolidation ordered the confiscation of church assets in America. New Spain's viceroy obeyed, in spite of the risk of an economic collapse. Gathering church funds required calling in loans and forcing owners to sell what they could to raise money. Resentment over the economic damage and fear of a French seizure of Mexico led to pressure for political autonomy.

In 1810 Father Miguel Hidalgo began a revolt, initiating a period of insurgency that lasted until 1821. The Spanish Cortes in Cadiz, in the face of the crisis caused by the Napoleonic invasion, embraced transatlantic constitutionalism, elaborating the Spanish Constitution of 1812. It might have worked, but the restoration of the monarchy in 1814 suspended the 1812 charter, then a revolt in 1820 reestablished it. Sporadic instability undermined Spain's credibility. Those who had previously favored autonomy now backed a complete break. Agustín Iturbide's Plan of Iguala (1821) proclaimed independence.

See also **Audiencia; Bourbon Reforms; Cortés, Hernán; Cortés, Martín; Creole; Diseases; Dominicans; Encomienda; Franciscans; Gálvez, José de; Guzmán, Nuño Beltrán de; Indigenous Peoples; Jesuits; Mestizo; Mining: Colonial Spanish America; New Laws of 1542; Race and Ethnicity; Religion in Mexico, Catholic Church and Beyond; Repartimiento; Slavery: Spanish America; Tenochtitlán.**

BIBLIOGRAPHY

Chocano Mena, Magdalena. *La Forteleza Doctra: Elite Letrada y Dominación Social en Mexico Colonial, Siglos XVI–XVII.* Barcelona: Ediciones Bellaterra, 2000.

Estrada, Dororthy Trank de. *Pueblos de Indios y Educación en el Mexico Colonial, 1750–1821.* Mexico DF: Colegio de Mexico, 1999.

Hassig, Ross. *Time, History, and Belief in Aztec and Colonial Mexico.* Austin: University of Texas Press, 2001.

Lockhart, James. *The Nahua after the Conquest: A Social and Cultural History of the Indians of Central Mexico.* Stanford, CA: Stanford University Press, 1992.

MacLachlan, Colin M., and Jaime E. Rodriguez O. *The Forging of the Cosmic Race: A Reinterpretation of Colonial Mexico.* Revised 2nd edition. Berkeley: University of California Press, 1990.

Miño Grijalva, Manuel. *El Mundo Novohispano: Población, Cuidades Economía, Siglos XVII–XVIII.* Mexico DF: Fondo de Cultura Económica, 2001.

Seed, Patricia. *To Love, Honor, and Obey in Colonial Mexico: Conflict over Marriage Choice, 1574–1821.* Stanford, CA: Stanford University Press, 1992.

COLIN M. MACLACHLAN

1810–1910

By 1800 many Mexicans had grown restless with colonial rule and formed groups dedicated to discussing material progress and eventual self-government. They grew so emboldened that upon hearing the news in 1808 of the forced abdication of the monarchs in Spain in favor of Joseph Bonaparte, they were ready to seize power from the pro-Creole viceroy José de Iturrigaray, perhaps with his support. Word of their plans leaked out, however, and the Spaniards staged a preemptive coup and replaced the viceroy with one they could control.

INDEPENDENCE WARS

Independence wars soon followed, triggered by another betrayal of creole conspirators. On 16 September 1810, a parish priest in the town of Dolores, Miguel Hidalgo y Costilla, proclaimed the famed *Grito de Dolores,* usually recorded as "Viva la independencia y mueran los gachupines" ("Long live independence and death to the Spaniards") despite the fact that it was never written down. According to Juan Aldama, present at discussions prior to the *grito,* Hidalgo meant to rally a fighting force under the banner of the Virgin of Guadalupe pledging loyalty to Ferdinand VII and vowing to protect New Spain from the French usurpers of the Spanish crown, sentiments akin to those of the Tupac Amaru II rebellion in Peru ("Death to Bad Government"), for example. Secondarily, Hidalgo was seeking to avoid arrest for treason and certain execution. When his coconspirator, Colonel Ignacio Allende, was unable to mobilize local units of the colonial army on such short notice, Hidalgo was forced to rely on a large and unorganized army of rebellious agricultural workers seeking to redress centuries-old grievances that had grown worse in the eighteenth century. This fighting force would become an important factor in the development of the Mexican state as it struggled to defend its sovereignty against a string of foreign invaders.

After Hidalgo's followers had pillaged San Miguel and Celaya, they approached the silver-rich town of Guanajuato. Its intendant, Juan Antonio de Riaño, refused to surrender the city, and Spanish-born residents took up positions at the Alhóndiga de Granaditas, the public granary. The city soon fell, and for the next day and a half Guanajuato was terrorized by looters and those eager for revenge. During the following month, Zacatecas, San Luis Potosí, and Valladolid (now Morelia) surrendered in terror before the insurgent forces. Hidalgo's forces had just reached Toluca on 29 October when they faced 2,500 royalist troops under the command of Colonel Torcuato Trujillo at the Battle of Monte de las Cruces. Although they won the battle, the insurgents suffered severe losses and retreated on 3 November. By this time most Mexicans, including Indians living in indigenous communities, had refused to support Hidalgo. Subsequently Spanish forces under General Félix Calleja defeated the insurgents at Puente de Calderón on the Lerma River, some thirty-five miles east of Guadalajara. Following this defeat, the mass of troops deserted, and on 21 March 1811, royalists captured Hidalgo and Allende at Nuestra Señora de Guadalupe de Baján and marched them in chains to Chihuahua, where both were executed and their heads hung on public display until 1821.

Creoles still maintained their hopes for eventual self-government despite their revulsion at Hidalgo's tactics. Their optimism was bolstered by the Spanish struggle for independence from the oppressive rule of Napoleonic France. Liberals in the peninsula called a cortes in Cádiz in 1810; from June through August 1810, Mexicans from Yucatán to Santa Fe held popular elections for the first time to select their delegates. The Cortes of Cádiz, which remained in session from 24 September 1810 until 20 September 1813, divided New Spain into seven provincial deputations and established the constitutional Cabildo. Both Viceroy Francisco Javier Venegas and his successor, Félix Calleja, reacted to these changes with repression and the imprisonment of creole leaders. The insurgency continued under the leadership of Ignacio Rayón, who tried to make peace with Calleja, and then José María Morelos y Pavón. Morelos, a parish priest from southern Mexico, carefully maneuvered his small, well-disciplined army toward an encirclement of Mexico City. In the spring of 1813, in order to cope with the reaction to the Constitution of 1812, he called an eight-man Constitutional Congress in Chilpancingo (in present-day Guerrero). General Calleja and his troops broke through the encirclement of Mexico City and captured areas to the south and west, forcing the delegates to flee to Apatzingán, where they approved their constitution on 22 October 1814. Meanwhile, Ferdinand VII was restored to the Spanish throne and promptly nullified the Constitution of 1812 on 4 May 1814. Between 1811 and 1815, 15,000 Spanish troops had arrived in New Spain to restore peace to the colony. In the autumn of 1815, Colonel Agustín de Iturbide captured Morelos, who was executed in December.

Historians previously believed that nothing much occurred in the independence struggle from 1815 to 1820, but further research has produced a complex picture of guerrilla struggle "led" by Vicente Guerrero and Guadalupe Victoria, among others, and Spanish defense in a hostile environment with troops frequently changing sides. This was a difficult period for Mexicans, who were forced to live under a repressive state of siege with some creoles continuing to appear loyal to the crown while supplying aid to the insurgents. A liberal revolution in Spain in 1820 reignited hope, however, with the constitution restored and the Cortes convened once more with delegates from New Spain in attendance. Provincial deputations and constitutional *cabildos* appeared while Mexicans at the Cortes proposed autonomy for New World colonies.

The Spanish Cortes was unable to accept even autonomy, so creoles seized their opportunity, profiting from regional rage against Mexico City and devised a compromise for independence. They convinced General Agustín de Iturbide to put forward what would become known as the Plan De Iguala, promising a constitutional monarchy, Roman Catholicism as the state religion, and the equality of creoles and Spaniards. Iturbide then persuaded Guerrero, on 24 February 1821, to create a united force, the Army of the Three Guarantees, under Iturbide's command. By 24 August 1821, Viceroy Juan O'Donojú signed the Treaty of Córdoba, recognizing Mexican sovereignty.

EARLY INDEPENDENCE

Iturbide and O'Donojú immediately selected a regency to act as an executive with Iturbide as presiding officer to govern with an independent Congress, but an empty treasury, mountains of debts, the devastation of the silver mines, and an internal economy ruined by eleven years of war created serious obstacles for the new nation. Iturbide intimidated Congress and then declared himself emperor on 18 May 1822, only to abdicate less than a year later when the provinces rose against him. After over a year of parliamentary and regional struggle, a Constituent Congress issued the Constitution of 1824, proclaiming Mexico a federal republic with an elected president and Congress. That year and the next, Mexico, like other newly independent Latin American states, received substantial loans from British banking houses. Buoyed by the additional capital, President Guadalupe Victoria (1824–1829) became the only president to serve a full term in office until 1848.

For most of the rest of the century, Mexico could not collect enough revenue to pay for its governments. The years from 1824 to 1834 saw the construction of a federalist regime complete with state militias. During that time the nation established diplomatic relations with the major powers of Europe and the United States. Membership in Masonic lodges formed the basis for rudimentary political parties that gained in strength and ferocity following the passage of a law expelling Spaniards on 20 December 1827. When Manuel Gómez Pedraza was elected president in 1828, the followers of his opponent, Vicente Guerrero, staged the Revolt of the Acordada that included the sacking of a Spanish-owned shopping arcade, the Parían, and brought Guerrero to power.

During this time, Mexico followed up on a Spanish plan to bring foreigners to colonize its largely unsettled northern frontier. In 1822 it permitted Moses Austin and his son Stephen to bring up to 300 Catholic families to Texas, provided they agreed to live under Mexican law. Conditions were so enticing that immigrants, many of them Americans with their slaves, soon outnumbered Mexican settlers. In 1829 Guerrero outlawed slavery, and in April of the following year Congress prohibited further immigration from contiguous nations.

As the money from foreign loans ran out and Mexico defaulted on its repayments, its treasuries began short-term borrowing at high rates of interest from merchants known as Agiotistas, using customs revenues as guarantees of payment. Inevitably that system only depleted treasuries further. Concern over the presence of Spaniards reignited when Spain attempted to reconquer its former colony by force, landing troops at Tampico in July 1829, but a combination of heat, disease, and water shortages helped the Mexican army under the command of Manuel Mier y Terán and Antonio López de Santa Anna to defeat the invaders. Following further expulsions of Spaniards, other concerns became paramount. Mexican liberals split into federalists, who favored the creation of a more secular society and the ending of clerical mortmain, and centralists, who wanted to strengthen national authority over the states and protect the church's traditional privileges. In December 1829, the centralists under General Anastasio Bustamante rebelled against Guerrero and took power. They established a repressive regime with a censored press and borrowed heavily to preserve army support. During their rule, former president Guerrero was assassinated, the last Mexican president to suffer such a fate until 1913.

In 1832 a coalition of groups overthrew Bustamante and elected Santa Anna president. As would become his custom over the next fifteen years, the new president quickly retired to his hacienda, Manga de Clavo, in Veracruz, while Vice President Valentín Gómez Farías and his radical and liberal supporters attempted to create what they thought would be a more progressive Mexico by substantially reducing the power of the Catholic Church. They proposed that the church no longer hold a monopoly over education, be forced to sell nonessential property and pay a sales tax to the government, and relinquish its other special privileges. Unfortunately, Gómez Farías and his supporters alienated many potential supporters by persecuting former officials both in the capital and in the states. Perhaps influenced by clerical pronouncements that a virulent cholera epidemic had been caused by such impious activity, a countrywide outcry ensued, drawing Santa Anna into the fray. Although the movement started out simply as a way to stop the reforms, ultimately it led to a renunciation of federalism altogether and the enactment of the centralist Constitution of 1836.

The period from 1836 to 1846 was the heyday of Mexico's first epoch of centralism; but continued excessive borrowing, church–state controversies, and foreign invasions undermined Mexican hopes for stability. The emerging centralist regime prompted serious revolts in Zacatecas and Texas. The army, partly comprised of unsuspecting "recruits" gathered along the way, successfully defeated the federalists in Zacatecas and then marched 1,500 miles to San Antonio de Béxar (present-day San Antonio), where the men led by Santa Anna captured the Franciscan mission known as the Alamo in March 1836. Later, Santa Anna ordered the execution of all prisoners taken at the battle of Goliad, strengthening ill will toward Mexico in the United States. In April 1836, after losing the battle of San Jacinto, Santa Anna "agreed" to the independence of Texas from the Mexican nation, an agreement that Congress in Mexico City was quick to disavow. Since no territory had ever abandoned Mexican sovereignty before, Mexicans assumed that one day they would regain Texas, while Americans were in no hurry to admit a vast new slave state to the Union and quickly recognized the independence of the Republic of Texas in March 1837.

In 1837, Anastasio Bustamante returned to the presidency and created policies designed to favor moneylenders at the expense of the treasury. In a sense this was a calculated maneuver in which *agiotistas* were reimbursed so they would lend again, leading to that point when the Treasury was finally empty and the lenders had nothing but worthless promissory notes. In 1838 Mexico was invaded yet again, this time by the French ostensibly seeking revenge for the damage of a countryman's pastry shop during a revolt. Santa Anna led one of the armies that successfully drove the French out of Veracruz during this Pastry War; in so doing, he lost a leg and somewhat rehabilitated his reputation.

The 1840s saw a considerable unrest throughout the nation; the economy declined, unemployment grew, and crime and social upheaval increased. Consequently, national leaders insisted upon creating a strong government that might restore order and economic prosperity. As a result, a hierarchical and corporate political structure embodied in the 1843 Constitution (the Bases Orgánicas) replaced the centralist constitution of 1836 (the Siete Leyes), but it, too, failed to achieve either goal.

THE MEXICAN–AMERICAN WAR

In early 1845 the U.S. Congress voted to annex the independent Republic of Texas, and President James K. Polk sent John Slidell to Mexico City to negotiate for the Rio Grande (Río Bravo in Mexico) as its southern boundary as well as for the sale of present-day California and part of New Mexico. Word leaked out, and the Mexicans refused to meet with Slidell. President Polk ordered U.S. troops south of the Nueces River, which the Mexicans considered part of their country. Since he could not buy the land he wanted, Polk was prepared to fight for it and had written the declaration of hostilities before news had even arrived of the 9 May 1846 clash near the Rio Grande between Mexican forces and troops led by General Zachary Taylor. On 13 May 1846 the U.S. Congress declared war on Mexico. It was an unequal contest; the United States had a much larger population and resource base on which to draw, its troops had modern cannon and other weaponry, plenty of ammunition, superb leadership from West Point graduates like Winfield Scott and Robert E. Lee, whose scouting expertise proved invaluable, as well as battle-tested veterans like Taylor. The troops received training before setting out; even the volunteers carried their own guns and were skilled shots. Although the Mexicans had more soldiers, they had been recruited as usual, had no training, and minimal equipment and supplies. Taylor (Army of the Center) marched through the central north, capturing Monterrey and Saltillo, while Stephen Kearny (Army of the West) went through New Mexico and then divided his troops in thirds. One group, headed by Colonel Sterling Price, remained in Santa Fe; a second, under Alexander Doniphan, took Chihuahua, and Kearny marched up California. In March 1847, Winfield Scott (Army of Occupation) landed in Veracruz and laid siege to the city. Having taken the port after heavy shelling, he pushed his way to Mexico City. Although six heroic Mexican cadets threw themselves off Chapultepec Castle rather than surrender (Los Niños Heroes), American troops occupied the capital in September. Throughout the war, Mexico was hampered by divided leadership; for example, when Gómez Farías, vice president once again, decreed that the church provide 15 million pesos for the war effort, clerical leaders paid soldiers to overthrow the government (the Revolt of Los Polkos). American troops finally left the capital in May 1848 after the ratification of the Treaty of Guadalupe Hidalgo, which gave the United States 55 percent of Mexican territory (including present-day California, Arizona, New Mexico, Texas, and parts of Utah, Nevada, and Colorado) in exchange for an indemnity of $15 million, used to repay foreign and moneylender loans.

FROM THE END OF THE MEXICAN–AMERICAN WAR TO THE END OF THE FRENCH EMPIRE

By the time U.S. troops had left Mexico City, the nation's population had grown from 4.5 million in 1800 to 7.5 million, one-third of whom were Indians living in small, often isolated, rural villages. Mestizos inhabited small rural towns, spoke Spanish, and participated in a more market-oriented economy. Few rural mestizos or Indians held loyalties outside their immediate area (the Patria Chica). Provincial cities grew rapidly: Puebla had a population of 71,000 creoles, mestizos, and some Indians, with Guadalajara a close second; nearly all boasted theaters, bullrings, bookstores, a wide array of foreign and domestic merchandise, and daily or weekly newspapers. By 1852, 170,000 people lived in Mexico City, where the rich, professionals, shopkeepers, artisans, and the lame, infirm, and indigent known collectively as Léperos mingled as they emerged from the opera, the university, the Art Academy of San Carlos, the botanical garden, the libraries, the museums, or sumptuous private residences, or simply went about their business.

Although the society was patriarchal, women retained control over their dowries and held property in their own right. Like their sisters everywhere, they went to primary school in great numbers but rarely received a fraction of the secondary education afforded males. Widows often ran their own lives, families, and businesses without the intervention of male relatives.

The presence of U.S. troops in the Mexican capital provoked great soul-searching among Mexican intellectuals. A new generation of liberals followed their predecessors in blaming the church for its refusal to instill individual responsibility and its stranglehold over Mexican society, while their opponents, now calling themselves conservatives, believed that Mexico had gone astray because it tried to follow foreign models while neglecting national institutions. At first it appeared that Mexico had found the road to stability, for its first postwar president, José Joaquín de Herrera, served his full term. But when the indemnity funds ran out, the same pattern of revolt began once more when Santa Anna returned to the presidency in 1853. The new administration sold off a strip of territory known as La Mesilla for $10 million to the United States (the Gadsden Purchase) that it needed for a transcontinental railway.

Santa Anna, mired in the past, planned to use the funds to destroy his political enemies. First he ordered his opponents into exile; many of them found their way to New Orleans and met to discuss strategy. Putting their faith in venerable Juan Álvarez, leader of the newly formed state of Guerrero on the Pacific coast, the young liberals and the old federalist launched the Revolution of Ayutla. Santa Anna resigned in August 1855 as the period known as the reform began. During the presidencies of Álvarez and his protégé Ignacio Comonfort, Mexico enacted the Ley Juárez, which severely restricted the special legal privileges of the church and the army, and the Ley Lerdo, which compelled the sale of property held by corporations such as the church and Indian communities. In 1857, the government decreed state control over birth and death registries and cemeteries; and the Ley Iglesias reduced the high fees often charged for the performance of sacraments. The new federalist Constitution of 1857 codified Mexico's acceptance of free enterprise capitalism and its tenets of individualism, private property, and equality under the law, and created civil education. The church announced that it would excommunicate any Mexican swearing obedience to the new constitution. Its position created a genuine moral dilemma for many Mexicans, including President Comonfort—if government workers did not publicly support the law, they lost their jobs; if they did, they faced eternal damnation. General Félix Zuloaga led a coup against the government with Comonfort's support, only to turn against his mentor and dissolve Congress. Comonfort resigned and was succeeded by Benito Juárez, who had just been elected president of the Supreme Court, and had fled north to avoid arrest.

For the next three years the liberals, headquartered in Veracruz, and the conservatives, in Mexico City, fought each other for control over the national future. Zuloaga nullified the Reform laws while Juárez stiffened them. Although troops under the conservative general Miguel Miramón won most of the battles, he was unable to take Veracruz. Finally, on 22 December 1860, the liberal general Jesús González Ortega and his army defeated conservative troops under Miramón at San Miguel Calpulalpan in Mexico State and entered Mexico City on 1 January 1861. Following his election to the presidency in March, Juárez declared a two-year moratorium on payments on the foreign debt. The following October, the creditor powers—England, Spain, and France—agreed to a joint occupation of Mexican ports to collect their claims. Their troops arrived in December, but subsequent discussions revealed that the French intended to conquer Mexico and establish an empire there. The Spanish and British troops left; a month later, 4,500 more French troops arrived.

There were many reasons for the failed but highly significant French attempt to establish an empire in Mexico. Although it formed part of Emperor Napoleon III's global plan to extend French power, the intrigues of Mexican conservatives at his court, coupled with Empress Eugenie's Spanish origins, played their part as well. Buoyed by overly optimistic visions of welcome in a pro-clerical Mexico, the French troops found surprisingly strong resistance in conservative Puebla as they marched toward Mexico City. On 5 May 1862, peasant armies under General Ignacio Zaragoza and Brigadier General Porfirio Díaz defeated the invaders at Puebla, an event immortalized in Cinco De Mayo, an important national holiday.

Ultimately, however, the French were not to be denied, and by the end of May of the following year, they entered Mexico City as Juárez retreated north to San Luis Potosí. On 16 June 1863 the French general selected a temporary government of thirty-five notables with an executive committee of generals Juan Almonte and Mariano Salas, and Bishop of Puebla and Archbishop-elect of Mexico City Pelagio Antonio de Labastida. In October a group of Mexican conservatives went to visit Maximilian, younger brother of Emperor Franz Joseph of Austria, and persuaded him to accept the throne, granting his condition that the Mexican people vote its approval. The putative emperor met with Napoleon III and signed the Convention of Miramar, whereby Maximilian would gain command over French troops in exchange for a pledge to pay the costs of the French conquest of Mexico, the salaries of the French army, and all claims outstanding, thus tripling Mexico's foreign debt. Maximilian and his wife Charlotte (Carlota) arrived in liberal Veracruz in May 1864 to a chilly reception, but emotions warmed considerably as they made their way to the capital.

Maximilian brought European concepts to Mexico that would have a far-reaching effect long after he had departed the scene. He toured the countryside, ordered the construction of a broad avenue from Chapultepec Castle to the Palacio Nacional (which after his fall would be renamed the Paseo de la Reforma), and approved the establishment of the first bank. He commissioned statues honoring Columbus and Mexican independence, insisting on Mexican materials and Mexican artists. He declared a free press and amnestied all political prisoners. Most significantly, he alienated his conservative supporters by refusing to return church lands and declare Roman Catholicism the national religion. In seeking a middle ground that had long since been discredited, Maximilian courted disaster. Juárista forces, aided by a combination of foreign events—the close of the American Civil War, permitting the export of weapons to the liberals, and growing hostilities between France and Prussia that forced the return of French troops to Europe—began winning victories in the spring of 1866. Maximilian surrendered after the battle of Querétaro in May 1867, was court-martialed, and was executed by firing squad on 19 June.

THE RESTORED REPUBLIC AND PORFIRIATO, 1876–1910

The end of the empire was the beginning of modern Mexico. Soldiers who fought to defend their land against the foreign invaders began to identify with the Mexican nation as well as with their *patria chica.* At the same time, the imperial experience left deep scars on the Mexican psyche that have taken over a century to heal. Even before his election to a third term in 1867, Juárez was determined to punish those nations that had invaded and recognized the empire. His government refused to make any payments on the foreign debt and concentrated, for a short while at least, on its internal obligations. Juárez established a rural police force, the *rurales,* to secure the roads and focused on improving the national economy without recourse to foreigners. Railroads were desperately needed; the line uniting Mexico City with Veracruz was inaugurated on 1 January 1873. Localities built new schools to accommodate free and compulsory primary education—not that every villager's child actually attended. In 1871, Juárez ran for his fourth term against General Porfirio Díaz and Minister of Foreign Relations Sebastían Lerdo De Tejada. Since none of the candidates had a clear majority, the pro-Juárista Congress decided on their venerable leader. Díaz soon "pronounced" himself in revolt with the Plan of La Noria, which advocated term limitations. The rebellion was still limping along when Juárez died on 8 July 1872. The new chief justice of the Supreme Court, Sebastían Lerdo de Tejada, became interim president and was elected to that position in October. Joining forces with the Juáristas to oppose Díaz, Lerdo concentrated his efforts on expanding railroad lines, inaugurating telegraph services, and building schools.

In March 1876 Díaz issued the Plan of Tuxtepec, accusing the president of negotiating overly generous railroad contracts and violating state and municipal sovereignty. He also called for effective suffrage (genuine elections) and no reelection. Díaz entered Mexico City triumphantly on 21 November 1876. Although his comrade in arms Manuel González would serve as president from 1880 to 1884, the period from 1876 until 1911 is known as the Porfiriato in tribute to the man who dominated Mexican political life in the late nineteenth century. It is also the period whose meaning is most disputed among both historians and the Mexican population. Some see the epoch as one of unprecedented development and modernization with significant flaws, while others view it as a shameful time when Mexico was for sale to the highest foreign bidder and its people virtually enslaved by the needs of international commerce.

As Mexico entered the Porfiriato, its leaders embraced a new civic religion—positivism. As articulated in 1867 by Gabino Barreda, founder of the National Preparatory School, "Liberty, Order, and Progress," or the sensible application of scientific knowledge and method, would lead Mexico to its great future. During the first Díaz presidency, the nation tried to articulate its self-image and official history as it tentatively opened itself to the world. The United States recognized the Díaz regime in 1877, and Mexico reestablished relations with France in 1880. During this time the Mexican establishment articulated a national past that stressed identification with the mestizo rather than the creole, and with pre-Columbian culture in general and the Aztecs in particular. In a subtle gesture of protest at the stealthy reestablishment of relations with France, the Mexican Congress forbade foreign scholars from exporting archaeological artifacts uncovered at national sites; soon after, Mexico became the first nation in Latin America to fund its own excavations.

By the close of González's term, his government was accused of unbridled corruption and most of the customs revenue was mortgaged to pay foreign debts. Relations were reestablished with Great Britain in 1884 and a national bank of issue organized under foreign auspices, but the public refused to permit the government to settle the debt outstanding since 1825. The years from 1884 to 1911 mark the true Porfiriato, when Mexico developed at breakneck speed while minimizing concern for the liberty and economic security of the vast majority of its people. The national government tightened its grip as Mexico entered its second and much more centralist period, facilitated by the construction of railroads and telegraph lines. Inseparable from the successes and failures of this progress were the minister of the interior (*gobernación*) and Díaz's father-in-law, Manuel Romero Rubio (1884–1895), and the minister of finance, José Yves Limantour (1893–1911). Romero Rubio strengthened the national government by seizing control over state elections so that he and Díaz could put their friends and allies in office. Limantour paid off the foreign debt in 1888, only to borrow much more heavily, and abolished the state Alcabala (sales tax) that had been the economic mainstay of most cities outside the capital.

The order and progress that Barreda had championed were self-reinforcing. Technology aided order, and order produced foreign recognition, lending, and esteem. Foreign-owned companies laid 15,000 miles of railroad track, enabling many Mexican products to be shipped to faraway destinations; lands previously isolated could now be profitably brought into production. Consequently, the Porfirians tried to apply the Reform laws to dispossess Mexican Indians from their communally owned lands. Proud villagers in states like Chiapas, Yucatán, and Veracruz often became sharecroppers and agricultural wage laborers, attached to haciendas producing for export. With the increasing development of railroad traffic, regions could specialize in marketable commodities: Yucatán produced sisal fiber; Morelos, sugar; and Sonora and Chihuahua, cattle for shipment north. Tax revenues increased, and Mexico was able to buy most of its railroads by 1908. Some historians have argued that by 1910, Americans owned as much as 20 percent of the land surface of the country. In 1884 the Díaz administration had passed laws permitting proprietors to acquire ownership of property including its subsoil.

By 1908 Mexican mines, largely foreign owned, yielded 40 million pesos in gold and 85 million in silver, and large amounts in copper and zinc annually. Oil exploration accelerated after the turn of the century, with the British-owned El Águila Company producing over 100,000 barrels of crude in eight years. The first steel plant, located in Monterrey, was turning out 60,000 tons by 1911. Factories sprang up in provincial cities to produce beer, glassware, textiles, cement, cigarettes, soap, bricks, furniture, and other commodities, but Monterrey became the most industrialized. Mexico City benefited from the installation of a new drainage system. The government also commissioned improvements in port facilities and lowered tariffs. Imports and exports grew from 50 million pesos in 1876 to 488 million pesos in 1910, with exports taking the lead.

These changes had created a sizable new middle class, both urban and rural, particularly in the north, where trade with the United States had produced a certain level of prosperity. Economic benefits, as usual, were not evenly distributed. Many countries in the Western Hemisphere had undergone similar changes, but unlike Argentina or the United States, for example, Mexico had not modernized on the backs of immigrants. Many Mexicans bore the brunt of the upheaval without the salve of dreams for a better future for their children. In fact, for many, life had grown demonstrably worse.

The Porfirians maintained tight control over every facet of political life. They censored the press and used the army and the *rurales* to maintain the peace when required. As historians have recently shown, the Porfiriato was not as vicious as previously claimed in forcing Indians off their ancestral lands, but by 1910 over 50 percent of all villagers were sharecroppers or wage laborers working on 8,245 large haciendas owned by families like the Terrazas-Creel clan in Chihuahua, whose acreage ran into the millions. Some of these peons, illiterate and poorly paid (often in credits on the hacienda store rather than cash), struggled to survive amid poverty and hopelessness as they lived on stagnant wages and watched at least one child in four die before his or her first birthday. Nevertheless, the population almost doubled—from 8,743,000 (1874) to 15,160,000 (1910)—and residents of the capital numbered 471,066. By the 1890s, women had begun careers as teachers, an important first step to the other professions, to feminism, and to politics. The first feminist organization, the Admiradoras de Juárez, was founded in 1904. The middle class expanded considerably while the upper class lived ever more lavishly and danced the cancan, rode bicycles, and played baseball.

Ultimately the contradictions implicit in the Porfiriato—greater material development facilitated by foreign investment leading to substantial dislocation and an ideology based on a self-protective nationalism funded by increasing foreign capital—would, among many other factors, lead to the Mexican Revolution. Contact with other places through intense migration inside Mexico from the country to the city, and from the poorer south and center to the thriving north, as well as treks to the United States raised expectations and levels of sophistication. So did substantial interracial relationships (*mestizaje*), spreading education, and growing literacy. For example, according to the 1910 census, only 15 percent of Mexicans spoke only an indigenous language. While worldwide industrialization had spawned resentment toward those who had benefited from modernization at the masses' expense, its beneficiaries—the Mexican middle classes—yearned for democracy and political freedom.

Much as the ideas of the Enlightenment influenced the independence movement, new concepts created a ferment in Mexico after 1900. The anarchist Flores Magón brothers and their magazine *Regeneración* found an audience among the workers at the American-owned Cananea Consolidated Copper Company, who resented their relegation to more menial jobs for less pay while the better positions went to employees from the United States. On 1 June 1906 they went on strike, and in the melee over twenty Mexicans and two U.S. managers were killed, followed by a general uproar as the workers fired on American residents. Arizona Rangers crossed the border to restore order; the strike was broken and the leaders hanged. By the end of the year workers in textile mills in Puebla, Orizaba, and Tlaxcala had also struck, followed by a massive confrontation at the Río Blanco textile mill in Veracruz on 7 January 1907, where it appears over 100 died.

Nevertheless, the Porfirians believed all was well. In 1908 Díaz told reporter James Creelman that he planned not to run in 1910, when he would be eighty years old. The announcement sparked the publication of two major books: *The Great National Problems* by Andrés Molina Enríquez and *The Presidential Succession in 1910* by Francisco Madero. These works outlined the two major crises facing Mexico; the former called for the agrarian reform desperately desired by the agricultural work force, and the latter championed political liberty yearned for by the middle class. In 1907 a depression hit the United States, seriously affecting the economy of the border states like Chihuahua, Coahuila, and Sonora. In 1909, villagers in Morelos under the leadership of Emiliano Zapata began taking back their ancestral lands by force from sugar haciendas. In 1910 in a fraudulent election Díaz was reelected (Francisco Madero won just 186 votes). On 16 September there was a lavish celebration of the centennial of the Grito de Dolores. Less than two months later, the country was in revolution.

See also **Agiotista; Alcabalas; Aldama y González, Juan de; Allende, Ignacio; Almonte, Juan Nepomuceno; Álvarez, Juan; Austin, Moses; Barreda, Gabino; Bonaparte, Joseph; Bustamante, Anastasio; Cabildo, Cabildo Abierto; Calleja del Rey, Félix María; Chapultepec, Battle of; Cinco de Mayo; Ferdinand VII of Spain; Gómez Farías, Valentín; González, Manuel; González Ortega, Jesús; Guerrero, Vicente; Hidalgo y Costilla, Miguel; Iturrigaray, José de; Kearny, Stephen W; Ley Iglesias; Ley Juárez; Ley Lerdo; Limantour, José Yves; Maximilian; Mexico, Wars and Revolutions: Mexican-American War; Mier y Terán, Manuel; Morelos y Pavón, José María; O'Donojú, Juan; Pastry War; Plan of Iguala; Plan of La Noria; Plan of Tuxtepec; Polk, James Knox; Positivism; Romero Rubio, Manuel; San Jacinto, Battle of; Santa Anna, Antonio López de; Taylor, Zachary; Three Guarantees, Army of the; Venegas de Saavedra, Francisco Javier; Victoria, Guadalupe; Zaragoza, Ignacio; Zuloaga, Félix María.**

BIBLIOGRAPHY

Some works that span the century include John Tutino, *From Insurrection to Revolution in Mexico: Social Bases of Agrarian Violence, 1750–1940* (1986), and Mary Kay Vaughan, "Primary Education and Literacy in Nineteenth-Century Mexico: Research Trends, 1968–1988," in *Latin American Research Review* 25, no. 1 (1990): 31–66.

For the independence period, see Hugh M. Hamill, Jr., *The Hidalgo Revolt* (1966); Virginia Guedea, *En busca de un gobierno alterno: Los Guadalupes de México* (1992); and Nettie Lee Benson, *La diputación provincial y el federalismo mexicano* (1955). A good summary can be found in Colin M. Mac Lachlan and Jaime E. Rodríguez O., *The Forging of the Cosmic Race* (1990), chap. 10.

For insights into the early republican period, see the essays in Jaime E. Rodríguez O., ed., *The Independence of Mexico and the Creation of the New Nation* (1989); Barbara A. Tenenbaum, *The Politics of Penury: Debts and Taxes in Mexico, 1821–1856* (1986); Silvia M. Arrom, *The Women of Mexico City, 1790–1857* (1985); Donald F. Stevens, *Origins of Instability in Early Republican Mexico* (1991); Cecilia Noriega Elío, *El Constituyente de 1842* (1986); Guy P. C. Thomson, "Traditional and Modern Manufacturing in Mexico, 1821–1850," in *América Latina en la época de Simón Bolívar,* edited by Reinhard Liehr (1989); David J. Weber, *The Mexican Frontier 1821–1846: The American Southwest Under Mexico* (1982); Charles A. Hale, *Mexican Liberalism in the Age of Mora, 1821–1853* (1968); and Ciro F. S. Cardoso, ed., *Formación y desarrollo de la burguesía en México: Siglo XIX* (1978).

On the historiography of the Reform and the French intervention, the reader can start with Ralph Roeder, *Juárez and His Mexico,* 2 vols. (1947); Jan Bazant, *Alienation of Church Wealth in Mexico: Social and Economic Aspects of the Liberal Revolution* (1971); Richard N. Sinkin, *The Mexican Reform, 1855–1876: A Study in Liberal Nation-Building* (1979); Robert J. Knowlton, *Church Property and the Mexican Reform, 1856–1910* (1976); Jack A. Dabbs, *The French Army in Mexico, 1861–1867* (1962); David A. Brading, "Liberal Patriotism and the Mexican *Reforma*" in *Journal of Latin American Studies* 20, no. 1 (May 1988): 27–48.

Studies of the restored republic and the Porfiriato include William H. Beezley, *Judas at the Jockey Club* (1987); Charles A. Hale, *The Transformation of Liberalism in Late Nineteenth Century Mexico* (1989); Paul Vanderwood, *Disorder and Progress: Bandits, Police, and Mexican Development* (1981); Robert H. Holden, "Priorities of the State in the Survey of the Public Land in Mexico, 1876–1911," in *Hispanic American Historical Review* 70, no. 4 (November 1990): 579–608; and François-Xavier Guerra, *Le Mexique de l'ancien régime à la Révolution,* 2 vols. (1985).

Additional Bibliography

Altamirano, Ignacio M. *Historia y política de México.* PRI, 1985.

Beezley, William H., and David E. Lorey, eds. *Viva Mexico! Viva la independencia!: Celebrations of September 16.* Wilmington, DE: SR Books, 2001.

Garfias M., Luis. *Guerrilleros of Mexico: Famous Historical Figures and Their Exploits, from the Independence to the Mexican Revolution.* Trans. David Castledine. Panorama Editorial, 1980.

Hunter, Amy N. *History of Mexico.* Philadelphia: Mason Crest Publishers, 2003.

Ratt, Dirk W., ed. *Mexico, from Independence to Revolution, 1810-1910* Lincoln: University of Nebraska Press, 1982.

Rodríguez O., Jaime E. *The Mexican and Mexican American Experience in the 19th Century.* Tempe, AZ: Bilingual Press/Editorial Bilingüe, 1989.

Servín, Elisa, Leticia Reina, and John Tutino, eds. *Cycles of Conflict, Centuries of Change: Crisis, Reform, and Revolution in Mexico.* Durham, NC: Duke University Press, 2007.

Wasserman, Mark. *Everyday Life and Politics in Nineteenth Century Mexico: Men, Women, and War.* Albuquerque: University of New Mexico Press, 2000.

Barbara A. Tenenbaum

SINCE 1910

During the twentieth century, Mexicans experienced the world's first social revolution (1910–1946); an era of economic expansion so dramatic that it became known as the "Mexican Miracle" (1946–1982) and a time of financial, political, and natural disasters that concluded with a series of institutional and political changes that climaxed in 2000 with the election of the first president not from the revolutionary party since 1910. The overwhelming experience of the century was the revolution; its violence; and its institutionalization in government, education, the economy, and daily activities. The revolution began in 1910 as a protest against the political and economic regime of President Porfirio Díaz, who had ruled, with only a four-year gap, since 1876. Quickly it became a popular mobilization that, in many ways, reshaped government, economic activities, and even everyday life.

THE REVOLUTION

In 1910 the disinherited were everywhere. Despite the impressive national growth achieved in transport and exports (via mining and commercial agriculture) during the Porfirian years (1876–1911), the benefits had gone to a small group of national elites and foreigners. For the 80 percent of the 1910 population of 15 million that depended on agriculture, for the 96 percent of rural households that were landless, and for the 50 percent of the rural population tied to the great haciendas, life had become increasingly difficult. Subsistence farmers experienced continuing misery derived from their increasing descent into landlessness, a development spurred by Díaz's program of land consolidation that resulted in massive holdings that in turn led to dramatic decline in income, in corn and bean production, and ultimately in per capita consumption of these staple foods. Workers in the boom sectors of mining, transportation, utilities, and manufacturing, roughly 8 to 15 percent of the adult labor force, experienced economic contraction in the years immediately before the onset of revolution that contributed to their heightened sense of insecurity and economic jeopardy. Because the regime had been unable to attract sufficient national capital, the Díaz government permitted foreign investors to play leading roles in transport (especially railroads), mining, petroleum, industry, manufacturing, and increasingly in agriculture. This created a growing anti-foreign sentiment and provided a source of political discontent. Together these factors resulted in bitter labor conflicts, especially in the mining centers of the north. In perhaps the starkest measure of general conditions, life expectancy was only thirty years for the average Mexican. Porfirio's old, technocratic capital city associates ignored these conditions. They had developed an exclusive society and burgeoning economy based on foreign investment and on their understanding of Auguste Comte and Social Darwinian principles. The Comtian principles, incorporated into the motto of "Order and Progess," promoted economic development and political continuity and justified programs that excluded, criminalized, or ignored provincial, rural, worker, and indigenous groups across the nation, creating a disenfranchised and disadvantaged national community.

Initially, the eighty-year-old Díaz announced he would not stand for reelection in 1910, allowing other candidates to emerge. Anti-Porfirian opposition coalesced around Francisco Madero, from the northern state of Coahuila, and quickly gained supporters from across the nation. Madero's followers, who would become revolutionaries, were generally young, ambitious individuals from outside the capital city. They joined Madero in his opposition to the continuation of the Porfirian regime. Madero, himself a wealthy landowner from the north, had an agenda for political reform including no reelection of the president and effective suffrage, that is, honest voting, by the nation's voters. His supporters included disaffected provincials from nearly all classes who believed that Díaz's government offered them little opportunity for political or economic participation. Díaz's modernization project had excluded provincial elites while benefiting his inner circle. Díaz, after reversing his decision not to run again for president, ended Madero's presidential campaign by having him arrested.

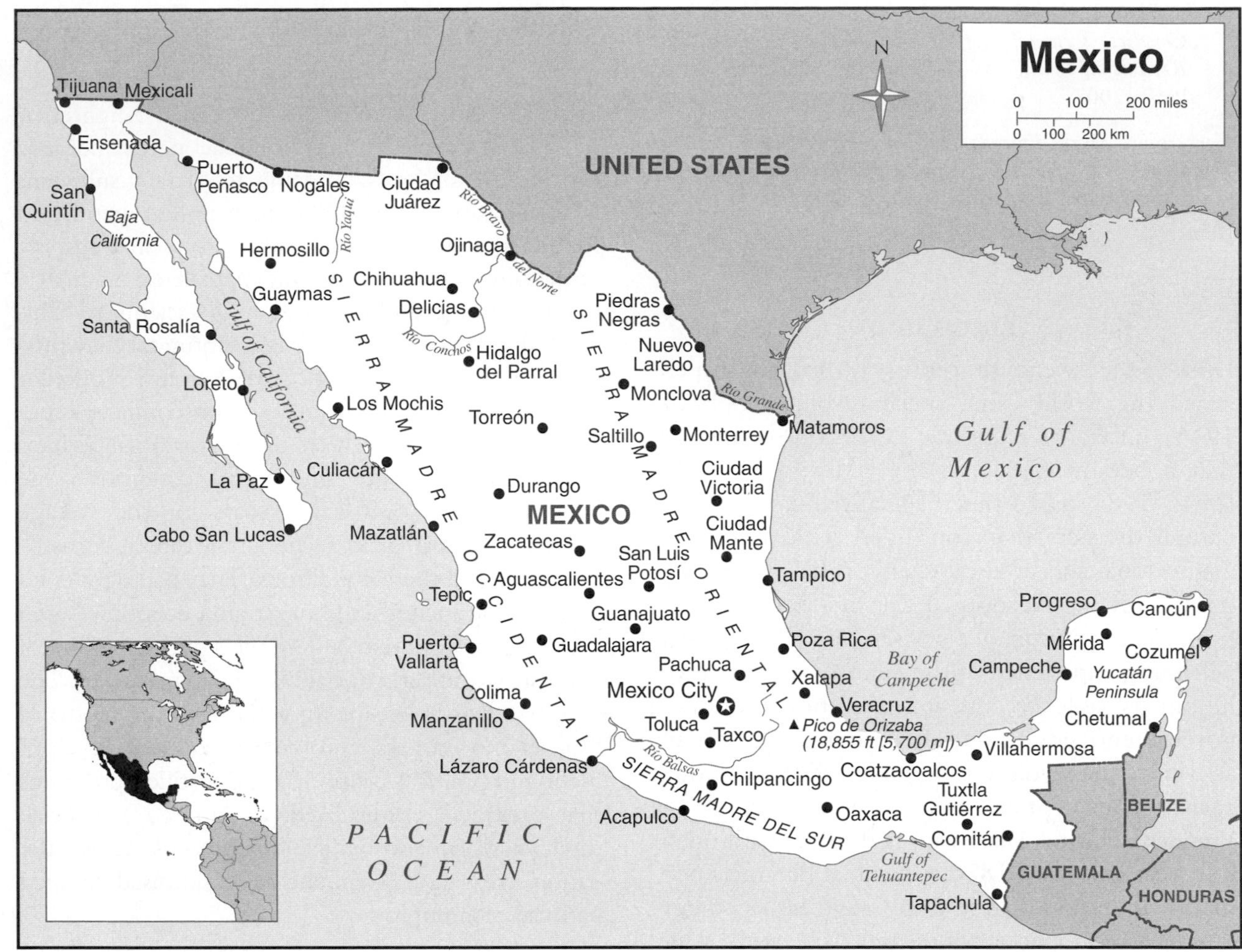

Madero Becomes President. Following Díaz's successful sixth reelection in July 1910, Madero escaped house arrest, fled into exile in the United States, and issued a call for revolution in his Plan of San Luis Potosí that designated November 20, 1910 as the date for the insurrection to begin. On that day, what became the revolution barely sputtered into life, with action being taken only by tiny rebel groups led by Pascual Orozco and Pancho Villa in the state of Chihuahua; quickly, other small bands of rebels began dotting the countryside. These individuals were determined to reclaim the nation for all Mexicans. The widespread emergence of rebellions, even though each involved only small numbers of rebels, shattered both the complacency and the confidence of the president. In April 1911 the Madero forces in Chihuahua defeated federal troops and the following month entered Ciudad Juárez, across the Rio Grande from El Paso, Texas, giving them a port of entry to the United States through which to import guns and ammunition and mobilize recruits. Facing the growing insurrectionary forces that had sprung up across the country and the rebel victory at Ciudad Juárez, Díaz resigned the presidency and left for exile in Paris.

Madero, elected president in 1911 on a platform of moderate political reform, quickly disappointed those within his coalition who wanted an agenda of radical social change. Revolutionary forces with a variety of social and economic goals launched a series of local rebellions that rejected Madero's cautious political reforms and demanded major social programs, in particular, land and labor reforms. The president also earned the bitter opposition of leaders of rural-based rebellions, including Emiliano Zapata of Morelos, whose call for land for those who worked it was

Mexico

Population:	108,700,891 (2007 est.)
Area:	761,606 sq mi
Official languages:	Spanish
Languages:	Spanish, Nahuatl, Maya, Zapotec, Otomi, and Mixtec
National currency:	Mexican peso (MXN)
Principal religions:	Roman Catholic, 76.5%; Protestant, 6.3%
Ethnicity:	mestizo (Amerindian-Spanish), 60%; Amerindian or predominantly Amerindian, 30%; white, 9%; other, 1%
Capital:	Mexico City (est. pop. 18,660,000 in 2005)
Other urban centers:	Ciudad Juárez, Guadalajara, León, Monterrey, Puebla, San Luis Potosí, Tijuana, Toluca, Torreón
Annual rainfall:	ranges from 10 inches in Baja California to 200 inches on the southern Gulf coast; most areas away from the coast are relatively dry, especially in the north
Principal geographical features:	*Mountains:* Cordillera Neovolcanica, includes major peaks of Orizaba (18,701 ft), Popocatépetl (17,887) and Ixtacihuatl (17,342 ft); Sierra Madre de Chiapas, Sierra Madre del Sur, Sierra Madre Occidental, Sierra Madre Oriental, *Rivers:* Balsas, Río Bravo del Norte (Rio Grande) *Lakes:* Chapala *Islands:* Ángel de la Guarda, Cozumel, Marías, Mujeres, Tiburón *Other:* Mesa Central between the Sierra Madre Occidental and Sierra Madre Oriental forms much of the northern part of the country; deserts in the north; rainforest in the south
Economy:	*GDP per capita:* $10,700 (2006 est.)
Principal products and exports:	*Agricultural:* coffee, cotton, fresh fruit, sugar, tobacco, tomatoes *Manufacturing:* assembly, chemicals, clothing, consumer durables, food and beverages, motor vehicles, steel, petroleum, textiles *Mining:* cadmium, celestite, cement, copper, fluorspar, gold, gypsum, manganese ore, molybdenum, oil, salt, silver, sulfur, zinc
Government:	Independence from Spain, 1810. Constitution, 1917. Federal republic. The president is elected by popular vote for a 6-year term, and is both chief of state and head of government. The legislature is a bicameral National Congress, with a 128-seat Senate and 500-seat Federal Chamber of Deputies. Most members of both chambers are chosen through direct, popular election. Some seats are assigned based on popular votes achieved by each party. Senators serve 6-year terms, deputies serve 3-year terms. Cabinet appointed by the president, attorney general requires approval of the Senate. 31 states and 1 federal district.
Armed forces:	*Army:* 144,000 *Navy:* 37,000 *Air force:* 11,770 *Paramilitary:* 11,000 Federal Representative Police; 14,000 rural defense militia *Reserves:* 300,000
Transportation:	*Rail:* 10,976 mi *Ports:* Altamira, Manzanillo, Morro Redondo, Salina Cruz, Tampico, Topolobampo, Veracruz *Roads:* 72,545 mi paved; 73,892 mi unpaved *Airports:* 231 paved runway and 1,603 unpaved runway airports, 1 heliport; 9 major international airports
Media:	Many major newspapers, including *La Prensa, El Norte, El Occidental, El Sol de Tijuana, El Sol de Tampico, El Universal,* and *Esto.* 850 AM and 545 FM radio stations. Over 200 television stations including several government-owned stations. Privately-owned Televisa and TV Azteca are the most prominent television broadcaster.
Literacy and education:	*Total literacy rate:* 91% (2004 est.) Ten years of education are compulsory and free, almost all children attend school. There are more than 1,550 institutions of higher learning, including Autonomous University of Guadalajara, Autonomous University of Nuevo León, Guadalajara University, Iberoamericana University, National Autonomous University and the National Polytechnic Institute.

put forward in the November 1911 Plan of Ayala, and the northern leader Pascual Orozco, who had fought for even more ambitious social reforms. Revolts by these two were followed by other rebellions against Madero's authority. Madero placed General Victoriano Huerta in charge of defeating the rebel forces. Despite Huerta's connections with anti-democratic, conservative interests, many tied to the Díaz camp, he ultimately forged an alliance with elements of the rebel forces he had been attempting to quell, declaring his intention to restore order and stability and to safeguard the nation's integrity. Huerta had the support of the U.S. ambassador, Henry Lane Wilson, who had bitterly opposed Madero's rule, actively threatening intervention and eventually participating in actions that led to a coup against the president. Huerta overthrew the Madero regime in February 1913 and connived at Madero's assassination on February 22.

Pancho Villa (center) leading Mexican rebels on horseback, 1916. Villa's incursion into the United States in 1916 compounded the violence of an already bloody and drawn-out civil war. © HULTON-DEUTSCH COLLECTION/CORBIS

A Three-Year Civil War. Mexico exploded with revolution as Mexicans were determined to avenge Madero (immortalized as a martyr) and to achieve a more equitable society by excluding foreign profiteers and redistributing the nation's resources. His death created a political vacuum that unleashed a new torrent of political conflict. The revolutionaries, calling themselves the Constitutionalists and led by Venuestiano Carranza, united against Huerta. For the next three years a violent civil war raged, engulfing the country in a wave of death and destruction that finally subsided in late 1916. The Constitutionalists first drove Huerta into exile in July 1914. His ability to battle the revolutionaries had been weakened by his diplomatic conflicts with U.S. president Woodrow Wilson, which had resulted in the U.S. blockade of Tampico and the invasion of that port and Veracruz in April 1914. Once the Constitutionalists forced Huerta into exile, they destroyed the federal army and turned on each other. Pancho Villa, one of the prominent rebel generals, called a convention in Aguascalientes, held in October–November 1914, that divided the Constitutionalists. The ensuing conflict dramatically illustrated the gulf that separated rival revolutionary forces, in particular the breach between the revolution's agrarian-based elements and the revolutionaries who were chiefly interested in urban, including worker, issues.

Alvaro Obregón proved to be a brilliant Constitutionalist commander who successfully defeated the armies of the convention, pushing Zapata into his home state of Morelos and Villa into Chihuahua. In a desperate act to prevent total defeat by inciting a foreign intervention that would unite all the revolutionaries, Villa attacked the town of Columbus, in the U.S. state of New Mexico. In response, the United States sent a punitive expedition into Chihuahua, led by General John J. Pershing, who with 11,000 troops unsuccessfully pursued Villa's forces for nine months. Although opposed to the U.S. intervention, other rebels refused to join with Villa. The incessant violence of the period resulted in a staggering loss of life. The bloody toll rose to at least 1.5 million deaths, roughly 10 percent of the 1910 population. The arrival of the Spanish flu epidemic in 1919 compounded the death total, and nearly a million people fled into exile, for the most part to the United States. Few Mexican families were left untouched by the fighting, and the economic cost of the conflict was devastating.

The Constitution of 1917. Obregón's victories pacified the country to the point that Carranza could hold elections, which he won in March 1917. He had convened a convention to modify the constitution in Querétaro in December 1916. Only Constitutionalists could stand as delegates; nevertheless, major revolutionary goals were expressed in the deliberations. Divisions among the delegates revealed the deep fissure between civilian and military interests, with the civilians espousing a more moderate, liberally oriented vision while the military advocated a more nationalist, statist, interventionist, even radical agenda. The Constitution of 1917 went far beyond the president's reformist inclinations and incorporated far-reaching nationalist and social reform goals—all of which required enabling legislation and enforcement, which Carranza did not seek to enact. The document enhanced the power of the central government to confront land, commercial agriculture, and mining (including foreign) and land corporations and the Roman Catholic Church. Provisions called for land reform to restore village, including indigenous, properties; to provide land to those who worked it; and to return ownership of the subsoil, and thus minerals, oil, and water rights, to the federal government. The document contained the most advanced statement on behalf of workers at the time, giving them the rights to organize and strike, arbitration, safe working conditions, fair wages, and reasonable hours; it also protected women and children workers. The constitution attempted to ensure the general well-being of the people through anti-monopoly provisions that alluded to fair costs for food, rent, and transport and other provisions that outlined education and public health programs. The delegates nationalized all church property, removed the political rights of clerics, and restricted their social activities. Overall, the new constitution set forth a nationalist agenda.

REVOLUTIONARY CONSOLIDATION, 1920–1946

The new political order did not return the nation to peace. For the next two decades, violence continued at high levels as revolutionary military leaders dominated the government and were challenged by others. Assassinations remained commonplace, especially to eliminate presidential challengers. The list of assassinations included Zapata in 1919, Carranza in 1920, Villa in 1923, and Obregón in 1928. These were but the most prominent individuals killed.

The nation suffered from severe war-related disruptions and economic contraction as well as rapid population and urban growth, the latter due to the intensity of the war in the countryside and the continuing deprivation faced by rural people. Obregón was elected president in 1920 and remained in office until November 1924. He was the first of the Sonoran dynasty, whose members enacted the social programs called for in the constitution. He strove for economic recovery and made some progress toward agrarian reform while undertaking only a lukewarm application of the anticlerical laws. Although Obregón and his successor, Plutarco Elías Calles, showed more commitment to the agrarian agenda than had Carranza, it would not be until the 1930s, with the advent of Lázaro Cárdenas's presidency, that the agrarian sector would become the focus of serious reform. Less than a tenth of the rural population directly benefited from the reform prior to the Cárdenas regime. In part, the reluctance to pursue agrarian reform more energetically stemmed from concerns about the potential loss of production, especially in view of the global economic recession following World War I that had hurt Mexico's exports.

Restoring Central Authority. The focus of revolutionary political normalization included the restoration of central political authority, the curbing of the ambitious local political chiefs and regional bosses, and the taming of the resentful leadership of the Roman Catholic Church, a

Execution of Miguel Agustín Pro Juárez before a firing squad, Mexico City, 1927. Longstanding conflict between the Catholic Church and the Mexican state reached a high point during the armed Catholic uprising from 1926 to 1929 known as the Cristero Rebellion. © UNDERWOOD & UNDERWOOD/CORBIS

segment of which still hoped to forestall the secular transition under way in the society—although another segment believed the church should participate in the social programs. In addition, the new leaders sought to direct the development of labor and peasant organizing efforts. While the Confederación Regional Obrera Mexicana (CROM; Regional Confederation of Mexican Labor) under Luis Morones benefited from government patronage and Obregón's support, that support was designed to establish control over the organization rather than to promote its independent development. Other unions suffered government oppression, including groups linked to the Communist and anarchosyndicalist movements as well as those identified with the church. Under Obregón, labor militancy declined and the government initiated a pattern of co-optation and incorporation vis-à-vis labor that would serve as a key to regime stability for decades.

Obregón's government initiated efforts to promote both urban and rural education. The secretary of the newly created ministry of education, José Vasconcelos, developed an extensive campaign to achieve national literacy. One leading accomplishment of the Obregón period was the successful management of the always difficult relationship with the United States, effectively staving off further direct interventions and securing U.S. diplomatic recognition for the new government in 1923. The president also tried to move toward civilian control over the revolutionary army by retiring a number of powerful generals.

The Calles Presidency. In what would become a permanent feature of the political system,

Obregón designated his successor, and in 1924 another of the revolutionary generals took the presidency, albeit with benefit of a "legitimizing" election. Plutarco Elías Calles ruled from 1924 to 1928 and subsequently, following the assassination of Obregón by a radical Catholic (Obregón having been reelected president for another term), had great influence during the brief presidencies of Emilio Portes Gil (1928–1930), Pascual Ortiz Rubio (1930–1932), and Abelardo Rodríguez Luján (1932–1934). Calles gave every sign of intending to perpetuate this pattern but was stymied by ill health, the strong-minded Rodríguez, and finally by independent Lázaro Cárdenas, the next military officer selected for the presidential post, who became president in 1934.

Besides having launched a series of impressive social and economic development initiatives, Calles stepped up the pace of agrarian reform, distributing three times as much land as Obregón. Even more critical for the nation's stability was his effort to impose civilian dominance over the military, reducing military spending while working to professionalize the officer class and to divorce it from political involvements. Calles's energies were also devoted to enforcing the anticlerical features of the constitution, and the government took concrete and decisive steps to dismantle the church's infrastructure in terms of personnel and property. Most critical was Calles's successful suppression of the Cristero Rebellion (1926–1929, a pro-Catholic religion uprising,) in a struggle that eventually cost at least 90,000 lives and led to a negotiated settlement of the conflicting temporal claims between the government and the church.

Authoritarianism. At the same time, Calles's self-designation as the Jefe Máximo was emblematic of the regime's marked inattention to even the veneer of political democratization; during Calles's tenure, the government grew progressively authoritarian, with power increasingly centralized in the presidency. By no means, however, was his rule entirely self-serving. Instead, Calles had a clear vision of the developmental direction the nation should take. To achieve national prosperity, he believed that the middle class would have to be substantially expanded, along with the class of small farmers. Together, these groups constituted what Calles believed to be the most promising social and economic basis for capitalist development. Among his most important economic initiatives was the creation of a central financial institution, the Banco de México, and an array of public works projects, including roads and water supplies.

Establishing the Ruling Party. One of Calles's most important political initiatives was the 1929 organization of the new official party, the Partido Nacional Revolucionario (PNR), which would undergo several name changes and reorganizations to become the present-day the Partido Revolucionario Institucional (PRI; Institutional Revolutionary Party). Calles's initiative derived from his interest in civilianizing the regime and creating a stable basis for mediating conflict. From the outset, the official party created by Calles was never viewed as an electoral mechanism designed to contest elections, but as a vehicle for interest aggregation and conflict mediation. The creation of the party afforded competing interests within the revolutionary circle the opportunity to negotiate the critical problem of presidential succession without resort to violence. Initially, the PNR consisted of a broad coalition of military leaders, pro-government labor and agrarian leaders, and regional political bosses. Government employees were required to join the party, and most existing political parties were forced to merge with the PNR. For Calles, the PNR proved to be an important vehicle for the pursuit of his own ambition, enabling him to continue to exercise influence even after his tenure in office had ended.

The Cárdenas Presidency. Elected in 1934 as Calles's handpicked candidate, Lázaro Cárdenas was regarded as someone who would give voice to the long-deferred social agenda of the revolution without challenging the established order. As a party loyalist and former head of the PNR, as a general of the revolution, as a personal friend of Calles and minister in the Calles government, and as a political leader with an impressive record of social reform as governor (1928–1932) of Michoacán, Cárdenas was viewed as the best choice to oversee a shift in political emphasis designed to restore confidence among those disappointed by the revolution's failure to accomplish social reform. The party also provided him with a six-year plan with renewed emphasis on social reforms, already initiated to some extend by Rodríguez.

Although Mexico had begun an economic recovery in the mid-1920s, the global depression that hit in the late 1920s stalled the economy once again, with GNP falling to below pre-revolutionary levels. Cárdenas inherited an economy in 1934 that had changed little in its overall sectoral and labor composition from pre-revolutionary days. Little had been achieved in land reform except the replacement of some traditional landholders, although some land had been distributed to the new *ejidos* (communal holdings, individually worked). What had begun to develop was a new entrepreneurial group linked to the state.

Mexico was not immune to the cultural and communication transformations that were the vanguard of industrial modernization; the impact of such change was notable in the urban arena. Some efforts had been launched to extend education and especially to expand instruction in Spanish among indigenous, non–Spanish-speaking groups. Further, efforts had been made to begin to broaden public health services. Unfortunately, the impact of the Great Depression undercut much of the reform initiative that had been put into place.

Internationally, the critical and highly strained postwar relationship with the United States had been largely repaired as a result of the Bucareli Conferences of 1923, which resolved a number of issues related to U.S. claims against Mexico and Mexico's efforts to protect its sovereignty under the terms of the 1917 constitution. Obregón's conciliatory position toward U.S. oil companies had further patched up the relationship.

Popular Reform. Cárdenas soon showed himself willing to chart an independent course and to establish his own authority, diminishing Calles's role in the process and eventually sending the former president into exile in 1936 after a bitter dispute over the handling of labor mobilization. During his six-year rule, Cárdenas steered politics in a new direction, one that was popular-nationalist and that took a collectivist approach to agrarianism. He created a rationale for a strong role for the state as political overseer of the popular sectors in the name of their self-defense; as the promoter of collectivist ideals, especially within popular education; and as the director of the economy.

In addition to his highly vaunted agrarian reforms that succeeded in distributing twice as much land as had his revolutionary predecessors, along with the nationalization of the railroads and the petroleum industry, Cárdenas was responsible for the creation of a corporatist political structure for the inclusion of popular sectors under regime control. He revamped the official party, renaming it in 1938 the Partido de la Revolución Mexicano (PRM; Mexican Revolutionary Party), and reinforced the corporatist design within the party for sectoral incorporation. Within this framework, labor organization evolved further, and it was with Cárdenas's support that Vicente Lombardo Toledano founded in 1933 the Confederación General de Obreros y Campesinos de México (CGOCM; General Confederation of Workers and Peasants of Mexico) and organized a new labor group, the Confederación de Trabajadores de México (CTM; Confederation of Mexican Workers). In a similar vein, the Confederación Nacional Campesina (CNC; National Peasant Confederation) was created, pulling together a broad variety of autonomous peasant organizations into an officially sponsored peasant confederation, another pillar of solid support for the regime.

On other fronts, Cárdenas pursued bold reforms that addressed the unmet expectations for the defense of national sovereignty. The nationalization of the railroads served as precedent for the nationalization all foreign-owned petroleum companies in March 1938, following years of labor disputes in the sector, largely involving U.S. companies. His seizure of these companies catapulted Cárdenas's popularity to new heights while souring relations with the United States and other nations. Cárdenas's initiatives in agriculture, in the labor sector, and with respect to foreign investment had a decisively chilling effect upon domestic and foreign private investment that persisted throughout his regime, provoking the emergence of a substantial economic difficulties. Nevertheless, despite difficulties in traditional sectors such as mining, oil, and agriculture, manufacturing production increased.

Cárdenas devoted considerable energy to the task of further subordinating the armed forces to civilian political authority. He succeeded in continuing the trend toward the centralization of political authority and the diminution of regional power. Cárdenas ultimately became one of the most influential architects of modern political evolution, incorporating popular groups and giving voice to nationalist sentiment.

The Results of Reform. Nevertheless, by 1938 Cárdenas recognized that the redistributive program alone could not bring national prosperity, so he launched a campaign of industrial development and the promotion of entrepreneurial interests within the private sector. By the end of the Cárdenas era, agriculture accounted for 10 percent of GNP, although fully 80 percent of the population remained in the countryside (albeit with larger numbers now living in rural towns and villages). The national population had risen to roughly 20 million. The percentage of illiterates in the population had declined, although the absolute number had increased. Rising numbers of indigenous people had adopted Spanish as a second language, thereby improving their educational prospects. Despite the land reform, some improvements in electrification and transportation, and the Cardenista focus on education, especially in rural areas, most people continued to suffer the poverty of traditional rural life and were excluded from the nation's modernization. For the urban population, substantial modernization was achieved as income became concentrated in manufacturing and industry.

This was also an era of cultural flowering, known as the golden age of the national film, radio, and recording industries. Many stars emerged, especially singers of both *boleros* and *rancheros.* The revolution affected all of the arts and literature, especially those related to the new mass media.

The Camacho Presidency. Manuel Ávila Camacho's victory in 1940 over the opposition candidate Juan Andreu Almazán. Cárdenas's selection of Ávila Camacho, his minister of war with a reputation as a moderate, a traditionalist, and a Catholic, reflected growing concerns about the state of the economy and the belief that more pragmatic, less politicized policies would have to be adopted in the economic realm. Ávila Camacho's administration (1940–1946) marked the continuation of Cárdenas's move toward industrialization and economic growth as necessary prerequisites for further social reform. The development of the national finance bank, Nacional Financiera (NAFIN), contributed to these efforts, and by the end of the Ávila Camacho administration, national income had tripled. Dramatic policy shifts, including the adoption of a less accommodating approach to labor and its entitlements, opened the door to direct foreign investment.

Internationally, in 1942 Mexico became one of two Latin American states to declare war against Germany, following shipping losses at German hands. Mexico's cooperation with the Allied war effort drew a favorable U.S. response and led the way to military cooperation with the United States. The Mexican Squadron 201 fought in the Pacific and won accolades for its valor. Also, the United States and Mexico agreed on the pathbreaking bracero program, which sent Mexicans as guest workers to the United States. Domestically, production grew in industry and manufacturing, helping to boost national income. Growth was notable in iron, textiles, beer, food processing, chemicals, and cement. Mexican entrepreneurs sought to become self-sufficient, in particular in manufactures utilized domestically.

THE ECONOMIC MIRACLE, 1946–1970

The administration of Miguel Alemán (1946–1952) represented a change in generations, with younger men coming into government who were not veterans of the revolution. This young, civilian president sharply curtailed military spending and strongly emphasized the nation's economic development, shaping a protectionist strategy to stimulate the growth of local business and pursuing an aggressive program of public works. Alemán was also responsible for the further reorganization of the official party and its internal consolidation into three sectors: labor, agrarian, and the so-called popular sector, while the military sector was eliminated.

Adolfo Ruíz Cortines (1952–1958) and Adolfo López Mateos (1958–1964) maintained the broad outlines of the policy direction established in the Alemán presidency. Ruíz Cortines's election in 1952 reflected the government's continuing commitment to economic growth but also stemmed from emerging concerns about the regime's tarnished image, damaged in the Alemán years by growing corruption. Although he had served as Alemán's secretary of the interior and had been deeply involved in the political structure as the governor of Veracruz, Ruíz Cortines's anticorruption drive recaptured some credibility for the regime. In an important political reform, the government granted women the right to vote in 1953. On the economic front, the administration consolidated programs launched in the Alemán period as it presided over dynamic economic growth. New problems were gaining recognition, including the high population growth rate, high urbanization rate, low labor absorption rate in the burgeoning cities, and a worrisome pattern of rising social inequality. The nation's poorest 50 percent of families saw their income share drop from 19 percent to 16 percent during the Alemán period, whereas the top 20 percent saw their income rise to a 61 percent share. Economic growth had failed to helped many in society but had spawned the development of a middle class that benefited from the development program. By 1960 the middle class had doubled in absolute numbers since the revolution.

The López Mateos Presidency. Adolfo López Mateos's administration (1958–1964) accomplished a telling political breakthrough by crushing the challenge of a rail workers' strike and jailing its leader, Demetrio Vallejo, in 1959, demonstrating that even those leaders thought to be sympathetic to labor (López Mateos had been Ruíz Cortines's secretary of labor) were fully prepared to use force to support an industrial policy tied to cheap labor. For labor, López Mateos sought to improve wages by promoting a profit-sharing plan that had its roots in the constitution.

At the same time, in a striking departure from his immediate predecessors, López Mateos launched a series of new state entrepreneurial initiatives along with proposals for social welfare reform and rural education. Furthermore, the government pursued a vigorous land reform campaign that was outpaced only by the Cárdenas administration in terms of the amount of land distributed. This distribution did not favor the *ejido* collectives but individual claimants. Also, despite the acreage involved, the percentage of the rapidly growing population that could benefit from such programs diminished over time, leaving many to wonder about the feasibility of such efforts in the future. Indeed, the impressive national economic growth was outpaced by the exploding population growth rate of 3.1 percent, doubling the population between 1938 and 1958 to a total of 32 million. Not only had the population doubled, but thousands had raced to the cities from the countryside. In 1940 only 8 percent of the population resided in large cities of more than half a million residents, but by 1960 the figure had risen to nearly 20 percent. The cities could not absorb the labor influx, a situation that resulted in the development of the burgeoning informal sector.

Ordaz's Hard-Line Presidency. The relative political calm evaporated during the administration of Gustavo Díaz Ordaz (1964–1970). Because he had been López Mateos's secretary of the interior and was a conservative from the state of Puebla, a stronghold of Catholicism, expectations concerning the new president varied as the administration took office. Politically, it became apparent that the government was prepared to press a hard political line and to reject growing calls for a political opening that had become more insistent during the López Mateos administration. Díaz Ordaz not only reversed the liberalizing intent of López Mateos's congressional representation reform but fired the reform-minded head of the PRI, Carlos Madrazo, who died in 1969 in what came to be viewed as a suspicious accident. Further, the conservative opposition party, the Partido Acción Nacional (PAN; National Action Party), saw several clear electoral victories annulled by the government, actions provoking considerable discontent.

The most serious political crisis faced by the administration involved student protests over the regime's apparent political hard line, political prisoners, and a host of other political issues, including the government's use of force against the opposition and the enormous expenditures involved in hosting the Olympics in 1968. In the final act of the escalating political crisis, on October 2, 1968, the government's security forces shot and killed hundreds of students and bystanders in the Plaza de las Tres Culturas (Plaza of the Three Cultures) at Tlatelolco in Mexico City. The "Generation of 1968" was born of that moment, and the government's claims to revolutionary legitimacy would thereafter ring increasingly hollow, despite impressive rates of aggregate economic growth and substantial social expenditure.

The Echeverría Presidency. The administration of Luis Echeverría (1970–1976) witnessed not only a continuation of the political turmoil that began in 1968 but also the onset of a chronic economic crisis. Politically, Echeverría sought to reestablish lost credibility as the Mexican miracle faded by energetically pursuing a "shared development" initiative that emphasized economic nationalism and a populist revival to include expanded state commitments to social development, rural development, indigenous programs, and state intervention in the economy.

His efforts to revive presidential populism along the lines of Lázaro Cárdenas saw his government adopt programs sponsoring national arts, including traditional handicrafts, and programs aimed at indigenous communities. Most important was the administration's support for regional congresses leading to the El Primer Congreso Nacional de Puelbos Indigenas de Mexico (First National Congress of Indigenous Peoples in 1975). The government also initiated the most rapid expansion of state entrepreneurial efforts in the nation's history. As a result, the Echeverría administration came to be perceived by the business community as having violated implicit understandings between the government and the private sector concerning their respective roles and responsibilities. Echeverría's escalating interventionist posture not only antagonized the private sector but also engendered grave economic difficulties for the public sector. By the end of his term, his administration faced a severe crisis in the external sector and rising deficits in the public sector. Consequently, Mexico staggered into a stabilization agreement with the International Monetary Fund (IMF) in 1976 that was designed to restore the state's financial health and its ability to shoulder its international responsibilities by curtailing public expenditures. Further, the protectionist policies had left Mexico's industry in an uncompetitive position, contributing to the nation's enormous balance-of-payments difficulties.

The limitations imposed on the regime as a result of the financial impasse struck at the heart of Echeverría's initiative and spurred the government to adopt new political tactics to boost the president's credentials as a spokesman for third world views and as a potential United Nations secretary-general. In the foreign policy arena, Mexico's independent stance vis-à-vis the United States on such issues as Cuba, the 1973 coup against Salvador Allende in Chile, and the U.S. role in the hemisphere generally was now bolstered by its new restrictions on foreign investment. Most notable on the domestic front was the unprecedented escalation of the expansion of the parastate along with the government's support for a series of peasant land occupations in the north, designed to undercut the president's northern antagonists who opposed his ambitious governmental initiatives.

The bitter medicine of economic stabilization and austerity imposed by the IMF would never be fully implemented because the international financial community became aware of major new petroleum reserves by 1978. The international community now came to view Mexico as eminently bankable, sitting as it was on a virtual sea of black gold. With energy price restructuring well under way in the international market, the national growth rate rose to 4 percent per annum.

Meanwhile a series of guerrilla groups appeared in Guerrero and other poverty-stricken states. The regime undertook a campaign of eliminating these insurgents, who were inspired by the Cuban Revolution and the 1968 student movement. Only in the early twenty-first century is the systematic repression of these insurgencies coming to light.

López Portillo's Administration. Domestically, the political health of the regime was tested by the failure of the standard opposition parties to contest the 1976 presidential election, forcing the PRI's candidate, Echeverría's finance minister, Jose López Portillo (1976–1982), to run virtually alone. While no opposition party had ever won a significant election since 1910, opposition candidacies provided a "democratic" veneer to the political process and facilitated the conduct of elections as primarily exercises in regime legitimation. Further concern stemmed from a growing tendency toward abstention even in "contested" elections.

In response to the dual challenges of overcoming the nation's financial impasse and restoring waning political legitimacy, the López Portillo administration launched bold initiatives on the political and economic fronts. Politically, having succeeded in destroying budding guerrilla

Earthquake reconstruction efforts, Tlalteloco area, Mexico City, Mexico, late 1980s. Amid an economic crisis, a powerful earthquake struck Mexico City in 1985, destroying homes, infrastructure, and leaving thousands dead. Yet the rebuilding efforts, led by ordinary citizens and community groups, catalyzed greater democracy. © SERGIO DORANTES/CORBIS

movements, the regime undertook a major reform in 1977 that permitted the registration of new parties and offered new opportunities for representation, but importantly, it placed time limits upon the window of opportunity, forcing skeptics within the opposition to register soon or lose the opportunity. The reform succeeded in channeling political interest into the electoral arena and did much to suggest that a real political opening lay ahead.

Economically, the plans were even more ambitious. The López Portillo agenda included the rapid development of petroleum resources, paving the way to overcoming underdevelopment. The skyrocketing population, booming urban centers, and jobless millions were to benefit from the new oil wealth. The latter was urgent, because by the late 1970s the nation suffered from severe unemployment problems, with nearly 50 percent of the economically active population unemployed or underemployed.

By 1981 Mexico ranked fourth in world oil production. Unfortunately, the quality of the oil resources proved lower than initial reports had stated, and by 1982, public-sector finances once again had reached the point of collapse. Several factors combined to bring the nation from boom to bust, forcing it to declare a financial crisis in the external sector in mid-1982 that led to a U.S.-initiated financial rescue later that year. The corruption of the government investment enterprise certainly played a substantial role, but even more important was the combined impact of the collapse of the international market price for oil and a dramatic jump in interest rates. In a final act of desperation that caused widespread negative political fallout, the López Portillo administration nationalized the banking system, hoping to counter the impact of a massive capital flight out of the country.

CRISIS AND RECOVERY, 1982–2006

The 1980s opened a period of dramatic decline for the economy and a plummeting of regime legitimacy from the point of view of both elites and masses. The combination of economic factors, but the devaluation in particular, forced Mexicans of every social group to adjust their day-to-day way of living. The continuing inflation made the thought of saving foolish, as the peso's value declined daily. Buying consumer goods as quickly as possible followed, but these products became the target of criminals or individuals thrown out of work, who turned to robbery to survive.

Kidnapping and carjacking became common urban practices, and rural people flooded across the northern border. Mexicans lost confidence in the government's ability to provide personal security. The regime undertook a full-scale reassessment of the development model, no doubt greatly influenced by the daily experience of citizens, the austerity package imposed by the IMF in 1982 and 1983, and the perspectives of the international financial community, which was gravely concerned about both the practical and symbolic effects of a potential governmental collapse.

Population growth continued to race ahead, reaching 80 million in 1985; wages fell dramatically, by as much as 50 percent during the 1980s, as did national investment; and domestic and foreign debt continued to skyrocket. The public sector underwent a dramatic period of austerity launched in 1983–1984 under the direction of President Miguel de la Madrid (1982–1988) and his economic czar, Carlos Salinas De Gortari, who would become president in 1988. The devastating 1985 earthquake that hit Mexico City further damaged the government's efforts to restore the nation's economic health, as did revelations concerning the extent of corruption in the previous administration. As both civilian and military leaders talked about the natural disaster, community groups undertook rescue, salvage, and rebuilding projects, established community kitchens, and organized bootstrap community projects to survive the earthquake. This activity restored the confidence of common citizens in themselves and resulted in political demands that by 2000 would displace the PRI as the ruling party.

By the end of the 1980s, PRI leaders chose to implement a "modernization" program designed to liberalize the economy, dismantle the structure of protectionism, redirect efforts toward export promotion, implement deep cuts in the scope and commitments of the public sector, and fundamentally redefine government obligations to the people. While continuing to embrace the role of leader of the economy, the administration declared its intention to deregulate and to remove itself from the production sphere, divesting itself of hundreds of public enterprises.

Economic Neoliberalism and Politics. The so-called neoliberal policy shift prompted bitter divisions within the ruling political elite, leading to the rupture that spawned the candidacy in 1988 of Cuauhtémoc Cárdenas, former governor of Michoacán and son of the national leader of the 1930s. Claiming that the revolution had been betrayed by the neoliberal agenda of the new ruling technocrats, who had little feel for popular aspirations, the Cardenista opposition mounted an unprecedented challenge to the regime through the Partido Revolucionario Democratico (PRD). It claimed victory in the 1988 presidential contest following the massive fraud that shut down the computerized vote count, but Salinas was declared the winner.

The conservative opposition, the PAN, had found a new basis for accommodation with the PRI, especially given the government's new economic initiatives. As a means of rebuilding legitimacy, the regime sought to normalize relations with the Roman Catholic Church. Under Salinas's leadership, the official party recaptured sufficient political ground after 1988 to restore some measure of economic growth, to reestablish a selective political opening (to the right), and to weather the political repercussions from the government's aggressive violations of electoral procedures. Salinas undertook difficult measures to change the land reforms, allowing the mortgaging or sale of *ejido* lands in a step that many regarded as the end of the revolution. Moreover, he introduced a program intended to utilize local community initiatives for social reforms that bypassed the national bureaucracy to avoid its inevitable skimming off of funds. Called Solidaridad in imitation of the internationally popular Hungarian Solidarity program, its striking successes outnumbered its failures. Most important to Salinas's efforts to regain the

Mexican farmers protest NAFTA, 2003. The farmers, fearing increased competition from the United States, called for the renegotiation of the North American Free Trade Agreement to protect Mexican agriculture. © REUTERS/CORBIS

economic initiative came when Mexico joined the General Agreement on Tariffs and Trade (GATT) and when Salinas was able to enter into a free trade arrangement with the United States and Canada. The North American Free Trade Agreement (NAFTA) that went into force in January 1994 reflected the increasing weight of trade and international investment in the economy and would have done much to refurbish the regime's image had it not been for two pivotal events in 1994 that stunned the nation: the Chiapas uprising of January 1994 by the Ejército Zapatista de Liberación Nacional (Zapatista Army of National Liberation) and the March 1994 assassination of the official party's presidential candidate, Luis Donaldo Colosio. These events were soon followed by murder charges against the president's brother and increasing evidence of the president's personal corruption involving the deposit of millions of pesos in Swiss banks. After leaving office, Salinas sought protective exile in Ireland.

The 1994 presidential election nevertheless demonstrated once again the official party's recuperative powers. The PRI's replacement candidate, Ernesto Zedillo Ponce de Léon, was elected with official results showing just over 50 percent of the vote for the PRI together with a massive defeat for the Cardenistas and their standard-bearer, Cuauhtemoc Cárdenas, along with some growth in support for the PAN. Some observers argued that the public had voted to retain the PRI because of fears arising out of recent instability. Others maintained that the electoral playing field still remained so uneven that the government's opponents ultimately were prevented from building more support.

In 1997 Cárdenas won election as mayor of Mexico City, where he achieved a reputation for outstanding and efficient government. The charges of corruption in the presidential election reached such a pitch that a new Instituto Federal Electoral (IFE; Federal Election Institute) was established

A fight erupts between lawmakers of opposing parties on the floor of the Mexican National Congress before the inauguration of Felipe Calderón, December 2006. In Mexico's 2006 presidential elections, Felipe Calderón from the governing PAN defeated leftist PRD contender Andrés Manuel López Obrador by less than 1 percent of the vote. This extremely close outcome caused fights and protests to break out between PAN and PRD supporters in the streets and within the legislature. © ERICH SCHLEGEL/DALLAS MORNING NEWS/CORBIS

and began developing practices to ensure fair elections in 2000. The Zedillo administration had to live with the heritage of the Salinas's regime's corrupt policies and gangster politics, the disputed presidential election, the ongoing indigenous challenge presented by the Zapatista Army of National Liberation, and continuing debate on the North American Free Trade Agreement.

The PRI Loses Power. As the nation approached the turn of the century, Zedillo's government faced a host of far-reaching opportunities and challenges. With Latin America's second largest economy, Mexico anticipated reaching a population of 100 million by the turn of the century, and with unprecedented urban growth, Mexico City anticipated a population from 23 to 25 million by the end of the 1990s. In the last years before the millennium, the presidential election of 2000 overwhelmed all other issues. The PRI and the PRD both offered candidates, with the PAN candidate, Vicente Fox capturing national attention. The voting in July 2000 took place within a sea of anticipation, hope, and apprehension, and when the IFE announced the results, Vicente Fox was declared the winner. For the first time since 1910 a presidential candidate of a nonrevolutionary party had been elected. Zedillo acted with the dignity that marked his six-year term as turned the office over to the PAN president.

During the six years of Vicente Fox's administration, features of the national government previously dormant now became apparent. For all of his good intentions, Fox and the nation learned that Congress had a good deal of power when controlled by the opposition party, at this point the PRI. This ignored branch of government blocked or slowed down presidential projects. Fox also had public relations difficulties as a consequence of his new wife Marta's involvement in politics (many charged she had designs on the presidential office in the next term), of financial actions of some of his cabinet members, and of diplomatic difficulties surrounding his relationships with both the United States and Cuba. Migration represented a controversial and difficult problem as thousands of citizens continued to leave their homeland and attempt to join the many millions already residing legally and illegally in the United States. The push of these immigrants came from the fact that an estimated 40 percent of the population suffered from malnutrition, so that the pressure upon the border remained significant.

The elections of 2006 brought intense campaigning, with the PRD candidate Andrés López Obrador, mayor of Mexico City, heir to reputation of Cuauthemoc Cárdenas, and an engaging populist, the early leader. When he refused to participate with the other candidates in a national television debate, his popularity plummeted. Following statements that suggested that Hugh Chávez in Venezuela might serve him as a role model, many middle-class (including left-leaning academics) voters turned against him. In the election the PAN candidate, Felipe Calderón, narrowly won. López Obrador refused to concede and tried to establish a parallel government; his supporters in congress tried to block the inauguration. Nevertheless, as of 2007 Calderón rules a nation with a vibrant democracy and substantial challenges for the future.

See also **Alemán Valdés, Miguel; Ávila Camacho, Manuel; Banco de México; Calles, Plutarco Elías; Cárdenas del Río, Lázaro; Cárdenas Solorzano, Cuauhtémoc; Colosio Murrieta, Luis Donaldo; Commissions Regarding 1968 Massacres in Tlaltelolco; Cristero Rebellion; Díaz, Porfirio; Díaz Ordaz, Gustavo; Echeverría Álvarez, Luis; Ejidos; Huerta, Victoriano; International Monetary Fund (IMF); López Mateos, Adolfo; López Portillo, José; Madero, Francisco Indalecio; Madrazo, Carlos A; Madrid Hurtado, Miguel de la; Mexico, Constitutions: Constitution of 1917; Mexico, Wars and Revolutions: Mexican Revolution; Morones, Luis; North American Free Trade Agreement; Obregón Salido, Álvaro; Orozco, Pascual, Jr; Ortiz Rubio, Pascual; Plan of Ayala; Plan of San Luis Potosí; Portes Gil, Emilio; Rodríguez Luján, Abelardo; Ruiz Cortines, Adolfo; Salinas de Gortari, Carlos; United States-Latin American Relations; United States-Mexico Border; Villa, Francisco "Pancho"; Wilson, Henry Lane; Wilson, Woodrow; Zapata, Emiliano; Zedillo Ponce de León, Ernesto.**

BIBLIOGRAPHY

Aguilar Camín, Héctor, and Lorenzo Meyer. *In the Shadow of the Mexican Revolution: Contemporary Mexican History, 1910–1989.* Translated by Luis Alberto Fierro. Austin: University of Texas Press, 1993.

Büchenau, Jurgen. *Plutarco Elias Calles and the Mexican Revolution.* Boulder, CO: Rowland & Littlefield, 2006.

Camp, Roderic Ai. *Intellectuals and the State in Twentieth-Century Mexico.* Austin: University of Texas Press, 1985.

Camp, Roderic Ai. *Entrepreneurs and Politics in Twentieth-Century Mexico.* New York: Oxford University Press, 1989.

Camp, Roderic Ai. *Intellectuals and the State in Twentieth-Century Mexico.* Austin: University of Texas Press, 1985.

Foweraker, Joe, and Ann L. Craig, eds. *Popular Movements and Political Change in Mexico.* Boulder, CO: L. Rienner, 1990.

Gentleman, Judith, ed. *Mexican Politics in Transition.* Boulder, CO: Westview Press, 1987.

Hansen, Roger D. *The Politics of Mexican Development.* Baltimore: John Hopkins Press, 1971.

Hellman, Judith Adler. *Mexico in Crisis.* 2d ed. New York: Holmes and Meier, 1983.

Knight, Alan. *The Mexican Revolution.* 2 vols. New York; Cambridge University Press, 1986.

Levy, Daniel, and Gabriel Szekely. *Mexico: Paradoxes of Stability and Change.* 2d ed. Boulder, CO: Westview Press, 1987.

Meyer, Michael C., and William H. Beezley, eds. *The Oxford History of Mexico.* New York: Oxford University Press, 2000.

Michaels, Albert. "Mexican Politics and Nationalism from Calles to Cardenas." Ph.D. diss., University of Pennsylvania, 1966.

Mitchell, Stephanie E., and Patience Schell, eds. *The Women's Revolution in Mexico.* Boulder, CO: Rowland & Littlefield, 2006.

Muñoz, María O. "The First National Congress of Indigenous Peoples." Master's thesis, Nebraska, 2004.

Newell G., Roberto, and Rubio F. Luis. *Mexico's Dilemma: The Political Origins of Economic Crisis.* Boulder, CO: Westview Press, 1984.

Porter, Susie S. *Working Women in Mexico City.* Tucson: University of Arizona Press, 2003.

Reyna, José Luis, and Richard S. Weinert, eds. *Authoritarianism in Mexico.* Philadelphia: Institute for the Study of Human Issues, 1977.

Riding, Alan. *Distant Neighbors: A Portrait of the Mexicans.* New York: Knopf, 1985.

Rubenstein, Ann. *Bad Language, Naked Ladies and Other Threats to the Nation: A Political History of Comic Books in Mexico.* Durham, NC: Duke University Press, 1998.

Sanderson, Steven E. *The Transformation of Mexican Agriculture: International Structure and the Politics of Rural Change.* Princeton, NJ: Princeton University Press, 1985.

Schell, Patience. *Church and State Education in Revolutionary Mexico City.* Tucson; University of Arizona Press, 2003.

Smith, Peter H. *Labyrinths of Power: Political Recruitment in Twentieth-Century Mexico.* Princeton, NJ: Princeton University Press, 1979.

Story, Dale. *Industry, the State, and Public Policy in Mexico.* Austin: University of Texas Press, 1986.

Zolov, Eric. *Refried Elvis: The Rise of the Mexican Counterculture.* Berkeley: University of California Press, 1999.

WILLIAM H. BEEZLEY

MEXICO, CENTRALISM. When Mexico first became an independent nation, it faced the problem of creating a system of government within a liberal constitutional framework. Following the failure of the monarchy led by Agustín de Iturbide (1822-1823), the viable options were those of either a federal or unitary republic. Federalism prevailed in 1824. From that time on, the proponents of centralism believed that the federal system was not appropriate for Mexico because regional interests would divide the nation. The first experiment in Mexican federalism reached a crisis point in 1834. The centralists came to power and were able to establish two systems of centralized national organization between 1835 and 1846: the República de las Siete Leyes (Republic of the Seven Laws, 1835-1841) and the República de las Bases Orgánicas (Republic of Organic Foundations, 1843-1846). The centralist system sought to make political order compatible with political freedoms for Mexicans: it attempted to rein in military caudillos (charismatic, authoritarian leaders) and prevent undue influence by the army; it sought a better balance of powers; it abolished the sovereignty of the Mexican states and limited that of municipalities, while awarding departments (which took the place of the states) the necessary autonomy to ensure their welfare; it placed restrictions on political participation, as was common in most of the world; and finally, it centralized the national treasury.

Centralism did not last long in the nineteenth century, given the highly conflictive domestic and international contexts. In retrospect, it was an isolated phenomenon in the history of Mexican political organization. However, several concepts of this centralism were incorporated into Mexico's constitutional system: an express declaration of the rights of all Mexicans, the strengthening of the national government vis-à-vis that of the states, the suppression of the vice presidency, and the need to establish a body to oversee the constitutional order and protect the rights of citizens from abuses by entities of the state.

See also **Federalism.**

BIBLIOGRAPHY

Costeloe, Michael P. *The Central Republic in Mexico, 1835–1846: Hombres de bien in the Age of Santa Anna.* Cambridge, U.K., and New York: Cambridge University Press, 1993.

Sordo Cedeño, Reynaldo. *El Congreso en la Primera República Centralista.* Mexico: El Colegio de México-ITAM, 1993.

REYNALDO SORDO CEDEÑO

MEXICO, FEDERAL DISTRICT. Mexico, Federal District, is the seat of Mexico's national government, covering an area of approximately 592 square miles. It is dominated by Mexico City, which was built over the ruins of the Aztec capital of Tenochtitlán. Today the city and its suburbs, referred to as the Zona Metropolitana, have sprawled northward beyond the district, into the adjacent state of Mexico. Much of the city is built on the drained lake beds of the central valley, and as the underlying silts have dried, buildings have settled tens of feet over the centuries. This unstable subsoil also has increased Mexico City's susceptibility to severe damage from earthquakes, the most recent one devastating the city in 1985.

The Constitution of 1824 authorized Congress to identify a seat of government and establish a Federal District. It selected Mexico City and defined the district as a circle with a radius of 5.5 miles centered on the Plaza Mayor, which formed an area of about 95 square miles. This Federal District disappeared in 1836 as the territory was incorporated into the Department of Mexico. The 1857 Constitution, however, reestablished the Federal District as a state, and its borders with the neighboring states of Mexico and Morelos were finalized in 1898. The Federal District lost its status as a state and became a special political entity under the direct rule of the president in 1928. It was subdivided into sixteen *delegaciones* in 1970. The district is governed by the *jefe del departamento,* who is appointed by the president. The city government is concerned with environmental issues and in 1989 began a program called Hoy no Circula, banning 20 percent of registered vehicles from driving on each weekday.

In 1990 the Federal District proper had a stable population of about 9 million, but the surrounding metropolitan area continued its explosive growth. Its population increased from 3.1 million in 1950 to 18.7 million in 2003. The Mexico City area accounts for 37–38 percent of the nation's gross domestic product and about half of the manufacturing industries, but it has suffered badly from overcrowding, pollution, and pressure on basic services. The Programa de Reordenación Urbana y Protección Ecológica del Distrito Federal is intended to control pollution, development, and further industrialization; increase green areas; and improve overall services. In 2003 construction ended on the city's Torre Mayor on the central Paseo de la Reforma, which as of 2007 was the tallest building in all of Latin America. In 2006 the National Autonomous University of Mexico (UNAM) in Mexico City was ranked seventy-fourth in the world by the *Times Higher Education Supplement*, which makes it the Spanish-speaking world's highest-rated institution of higher learning.

See also **Mexico, Constitutions: Constitutions Prior to 1917.**

BIBLIOGRAPHY

Todo México: Compendio enciclopédico, 1985 (1985), pp. 121–125; *Atlas de la Ciudad de México* (1987).

Jonathan Kandell, *La Capital: The Biography of Mexico City* (1988).

Peter Ward, *Mexico City: The Production and Reproduction of an Urban Environment* (1990).

Additional Bibliography

Arrom, Silvia Marina. *Containing the Poor: The Mexico City Poor House, 1774–1871.* Durham, NC: Duke University Press, 2000.

Curcio-Nagy, Linda A. *The Great Festivals of Colonial Mexico City: Performing Power and Identity.* Albuquerque: University of New Mexico Press, 2004.

Lear, John. *Workers, Neighbors, and Citizens: The Revolution in Mexico City.* Lincoln: University of Nebraska Press, 2001.

Warren, Richard A. *Vagrants and Citizens: Politics and the Masses in Mexico City from Colony to Republic.* Wilmington, DE: Scholarly Resources, 2001.

JOHN J. WINBERRY

MEXICO, GULF OF. The Gulf of Mexico is a body of water that is bordered by the United States on the north and Mexico on the west and south; its eastern boundary is a line drawn from the western tip of the Florida Keys to the northeastern corner of the Yucatán Peninsula. The European discoverer of the Gulf was Sebastián de Ocampo, who sailed around the western end of Cuba in 1508. The earliest maps referred to the Gulf as Seno Mejicano or Golfo de la Nueva España, but it was named Golfo Mexicano on the 1569 Mercator map. The Gulf covers about 590,000 square miles and is bordered by continental shelves that vary between 30 and 90 miles in width. The Campeche Bank on the northern and western coasts of the Yucatán, however, is 150 miles wide at its greatest extent. The Sigsbee Depression, located toward the western side of the basin, forms the deepest point in the Gulf—13,124 feet.

The geologic history of the Gulf of Mexico is related to the breakup of Pangaea, the ancient continent that held all the world's landmasses, between 200 million and 300 million years ago. The Gulf began to form 130 million to 150 million years ago with the separation of North and South America, but its final shape was realized only within the last 30 million years.

The Gulf is dominated by a northward flow of water formed by the part of the South Equatorial (Caribbean) Current that rushes through the Yucatán Channel. This flow divides and curves east and west along the Gulf's north shore. The eastward-flowing waters pass through the Florida Straits to form the Gulf Stream. The waters of the Gulf are quite warm, varying between 73 and 84 F, and this creates the warm, wet maritime tropical air mass that affects the climate of the adjacent mainlands. The warm waters of the Gulf also contribute to the formation or strengthening of hurricanes that cross the Gulf to strike either the United States or the Mexican mainland. The 1995 hurricane season was one of the most active ever recorded. There were twenty-one named storms, and five crossed the northeastern Gulf of Mexico.

One of Mexico's most important resources is petroleum, and production areas on the Gulf continental shelves include the Marine Golden Lane off Tampico and the Akal and Bacab fields on the Campeche Bank, discovered in the mid 1970s. In 2006 oil companies discovered a massive reserve of oil in U.S.-owned Gulf waters that could conceivably boost oil reserves by fifty percent. Veracruz was Mexico's leading port during the colonial period and the nineteenth century, and Gulf ports still account for 75–80 percent of Mexico's maritime foreign commerce.

See also **Florida, Spanish West; Petroleum Industry; Yucatán.**

BIBLIOGRAPHY

Jorge Tamayo, *Geografía general de México,* 2d ed., vol. 2 (1962), pp. 626–644.

Robert S. Weddle, *The Spanish Sea: The Gulf of Mexico in North American Discovery, 1500–1685* (1985).

Additional Bibliography

Barbosa, Fabio. "Petróleo en los hoyos de dona: Una Mirada a lo desconocido. (El petróleo en los hoyos de dona y otras dreas desconocidas del Golfo de México." Translated by David Shields. *Siempre* 50, no. 2649 (March 2004): 48–50.

Gore, Robert H. *The Gulf of Mexico.* Sarasota, FL: Pineapple Press, 1992.

Grafenstein, Johana von, Laura Muñoz Mata, and Antoinette Nelken-Terner. *Un mar de encuentros y confrontaciones: El Golfo-Caribe en la historia nacional.* México, D.F.: Secretaría de Relaciones Exteriores, 2006.

Rezak, Richard, Tom J. Bright, and David W. McGrail. *Reefs and Banks of the Northwestern Gulf of Mexico: Their Geological, Biological, and Physical Dynamics.* New York: John Wiley and Sons, 1985.

Skerritt Gardner, David. *Colonos franceses y modernización en el Golfo de México.* Veracruz, México: Universidad Veracruzana, 1995.

Trujillo Bolio, Mario A. *El Golfo de México en la centuria decimonónica: Entornos geográficos, formación portuaria y configuración marítima.* México D.F.; CIESAS, 2005.

JOHN J. WINBERRY

MEXICO CITY. From the earliest settlement to the present day, the site of Mexico City has been an impressive one. The Anáhuac Valley in which it is located is more than 7,000 feet above sea level, and is surrounded by volcanic mountains, two of which rise a further 12,000–16,000 feet above the valley floor. The origins of Mexico City date to the former Aztec capital of Tenochtitlán, located, according to legend, where the Aztec tribe saw an eagle perched on a cactus devouring a snake—now the *escudo* (emblem) on the nation's flag. While many other civilizations had flourished before the Aztecs, Tenochtitlán was the city that Cortés and his followers conquered and razed, and it provided the foundations for their city. In the early twenty-first century, little is left of the Aztec ruins except for some foundations and lower levels of temples that have been excavated and exposed to public view, most notably at the Templo Mayor located behind the central plaza, and at the Plaza of the Three Cultures (Aztec, colonial Spanish, and modern).

THE COLONIAL AND INDEPENDENT PERIODS

During the sixteenth and seventeenth centuries, Mexico City flourished as the political and economic center of New Spain, ruled through a series of viceroys until independence in 1821. Thereafter, the city was the seat of power for a series of rulers whose legitimacy was sometimes dubious and spurious—such as the self-proclaimed emperor Agustín de Iturbide (1822–1823) and Archduke Maximilian, imposed by a French expeditionary force in 1864. They were succeeded by a series of elected presidents, the most notable of whom was Benito Juárez, whose death in 1872 was followed by the rise of the dictator Porfirio Díaz (1876–1880,

Map of Tenochtitlán (Mexico City), designed by Hernán Cortés, 1524. © CORBIS

1884–1911), who was ultimately overthrown during the Revolution.

The central city ground plan reflects the grid pattern prescribed by the Spanish monarchy and later embodied in the Laws of the Indies established by Philip II in 1573. The central plaza, or (STET) Zócalo, was the seat of the principal council buildings, the treasury, and the cathedral, while the rich lived in mansions and palaces on the main streets running east and north. Once established, the colonial city expanded slowly, growing from 2.5 to 4 square miles between 1700 and the mid-nineteenth century. Not until the relative stability and economic growth experienced during the Porfiriato (the reign of Porfirio Díaz) did physical expansion begin in earnest, largely to the south and west of the *primer cuadro* (the central historic core of the city).

TWENTIETH-CENTURY GROWTH AND DEVELOPMENT

The years after the Mexican Revolution (1910–1917) saw a sharp rise in population. Between 1921 and 1930 the city grew from around 615,000 to more than 1 million. And as the pace of economic growth and industrialization quickened, so did the rate of city expansion, from 4 percent per annum during the 1930s to more than 6 percent annually between 1940 and 1950. Until the 1970s, when the growth rate began to decline appreciably, annual growth rates were steady, averaging around 5.5 percent—approximately doubling the city population every twelve to thirteen years. Thus Mexico City grew from 1.64 million in 1940 to 5.4 million in 1960 and 9.2 million in 1970. In 1990 the total metropolitan population was 17.3 million, and in 2005 it was 19.2 million, with growth rates more or less steady, and with just over one-half of the population living outside the Federal District in the surrounding municipalities of the state of México, such as Ecatepec (1.69 million) and Netzahualcóyotl (1.14 million).

Particularly during the earlier phases of this rapid growth, in-migration was the key factor, accounting for approximately 70 percent of the decennial increase. However, this quickly led to a population age structure dominated by young adults with most of the family-building part of their lives ahead of them, so that natural increase took over as the principal component of growth. Since the mid-1970s Mexico's active population control policy has begun to take effect, and the annual rate of city growth has declined significantly, although it still exhibits a high degree of urban primacy, with just over 18 percent of the total national population living in the metropolitan area (down from 20 percent a decade earlier). Since 2000, net migration is slightly negative, as people move out of the central core and the inner suburbs to new provincial locations or to peri-urban townships in nearby municipalities that have become relative hot spots of economic and servicing activity tied to the core.

Mexico City is one of the largest metropolitan regions of the Americas and has experienced enormous problems associated with rapid growth and change of spatial and functional orientation as its structure shifted from being one of city and central plaza to city and suburbs to that of a mega-city. Physically the city grew from 47 square miles to

A view of Mexico City at night. A statue celebrating Mexican independence stands at the center of a traffic circle on Mexico City's Paseo de la Reforma, considered one of the finest boulevards in the city. © RANDY FARIS/CORBIS

nearly 300 square miles between 1940 and 1970, and in the early 1990s covered approximately 500 square miles. Spatially, population growth has led to a wave of settlement moving outward, first across the Federal District area itself, and then into the surrounding state of Mexico. For several decades the population of the city center has been declining, and from the 1960s onward the peripheral municipalities in the east and north began to experience dramatic growth.

Indeed, much of the built-up area of Mexico City, such as Netzahualcóyotl, began as illegal settlement, which was the only way low-income groups could own homes, because their needs were not met by the government and their incomes were too low for them to be considered creditworthy by formal housing institutions. Between 40 and 50 percent of the built-up area developed without authorization and initially without basic services. Through community mutual aid, household self-help, and personal home-building, combined with incremental government assistance to provide services and legal titles, these initial shantytown settlements were consolidated and upgraded into brick-built working-class neighborhoods (*colonias proletarias*). By 2007 the urban frontier for newly established settlement was in the distant periphery of places such as Chalco, some 25 to 30 miles east of the center.

Mexico City's social ecology shows a broad pattern of rich residential sectors in the west and southwest, and rings of old and newly established "irregular" (i.e. illegally developed) working-class settlements in the north and east. Nevertheless, opportunities for illegal land occupation by poorer groups in the south and in parts of the west, together with the attraction of living in old village centers absorbed into the city as it grew outward, means that spatial segregation is neither absolute nor rigid. Indeed, segregation seems to be declining at least in macro terms, although there has been a notable hardening of segregation lines between neighborhoods at the micro level, as gated neighborhoods separate the rich from the poor irregular settlements that abut them. Rising violence and insecurity became major concerns in the 1990s both as a result of intensifying social inequality and as the country democratized and sought to improve the efficacy of its policing and criminal justice systems, both of which required complete overhaul. In the short term this led to intensification of insecurity and conflict as corrupt police officials were sidelined and were replaced by new cadres of criminal justice personnel.

ECONOMY AND THE LABOR MARKET

Economically the importance of the city relative to the nation is disproportionately large. As a result of state-led investment programs during the 1940s and 1950s that favored Mexico City, the rate of return on the production of industrial goods produced in the city was systematically higher than elsewhere. Almost two-fifths of the national gross domestic product (GDP) is generated by the city, and while it accounts for slightly less than one-third of industrial production, approximately half of all manufacturing activities are located here. Much of this production is oriented to national and local markets, and other areas of the country are more geared to meeting Mexico's increasingly important export-led strategy of industrial and manufacturing production. After the relative stagnation and economic instability of the 1980s, economic recovery in the early 1990s has emerged from two principal sources: the restructuring of the city's economic base and efficiency, with growth rates of more than 3 percent per annum from 1993 to 1997; and growth in the service sector, which is now the second most important sector in terms of GDP as well as job creation. High-level services (professional services, finance, real estate, etc.) grew dramatically (by more than 60 percent) during the decade.

Unfortunately, due to industrial restructuring the growth of new and well-paid jobs in manufacturing has declined significantly, and the slack is increasingly taken up by informal sector activities (such as street trading, unregulated services, and domestic labor). Always a bellwether to macroeconomic conditions, the informal sector increased from around 34 percent of the economically active population in 1981, when there were labor shortages in many formal industries and activities, to almost 40 percent in 1987, as workers shifted from one sector to another due to the recession and as participation rates of household members increased in order to generate an income that might adequately support the family. Wages in the early 2000s continued to be generally low, and statutory wage levels declined to half that of their 1982 level. But rising household participation rates, and the fact that most firms pay considerably more than the statutory minimum, have cushioned the social costs of austerity and recession to a certain extent. In the 1990s the average wage stood at around seven dollars per day and remained around that level a decade later. Not surprisingly, perhaps, Mexico City has become an important exporter of labor to the United States, and this flow generally comprises a rather more educated and skilled labor force than that of the traditional rural regions of west-central and southern Mexico. Mexico City is an important receptor of remittances, and Chilangos (natives of the Federal District) are increasingly found within the emerging transnational community.

GOVERNMENT AND PLANNING

Despite an apparently serious commitment to decentralization during the early 1980s, little was done to reduce Mexico City's economic and social dominance, although at the political level some measure of deconcentration and devolution was attempted. Nor do people appear to want to leave the congestion and pollution of a city that many years ago lost its status as *La región más transparente* (*Where the Air Is Clear*, the title of a novel by Carlos Fuentes). Not even the earthquakes of September 1985, which caused great destruction and loss of life, especially in the downtown tenement areas, led to a decentralization of population to the provinces—although it offered a clear opportunity to do so. Quite the contrary: Most of the reconstruction of dwellings was undertaken in situ. However over the past decade, a greater commitment to decentralization and the democratic opening that has led to greater autonomy for regional and city governments have led to some centrifugal loosening of population, politics, and economic activity, making life outside of the primary metropolitan center both viable and often quite attractive.

Pollution, contamination, and traffic gridlock have accelerated the desire of some to leave the city. Local authorities have responded positively in their attempts to reduce levels of air pollution, closing down noxious industries and servicing and paving many peripheral irregular settlements, thereby reducing the dust blown across the city from desiccated eastern lake-bed areas. But the fact that 85 percent of pollution emanates from vehicles, particularly from private cars, often goes unrecognized by the city's critics. Measures including tighter controls on exhaust emissions, a well publicized one-day-per-week ban on cars without new emission regulators, and wider utilization of unleaded gasoline have been introduced since the late 1980s and have had a significant effect in controlling pollution. Ironically, however, the more effective and accurate daily monitoring systems of the 2000s actually makes it appear that conditions are getting worse, which is not the case. Pollution tends to be most intense during the winter months, when temperature inversions prevent the dispersal of pollutants. While there have been significant improvements in public transportation, with an excellent subway system, most middle-income residents continue to use their private car without heavy financial penalty; indeed, the 2002-07 major project in the Federal District has been the construction of a second tier (*segundo piso*) to the western perimeter motorway (*perférico*), which almost exclusively benefits private transportation.

Governance of the city is divided between two political entities: the Federal District, which is split into sixteen boroughs or *delegaciones,* and the twenty-one of the fifty-eight municipalities in the state of Mexico, as well as a single municipality of the state of Hidalgo, all of which form part of the contiguous urban area. Inevitably this division of governance generates its own problems, such as lack of overall planning control, poorly integrated provision of services, a lack of connection of transportation networks in the two entities, and sharp fiscal imbalances and budgetary appropriations. In terms of political weight, the mayor (or Jefe de Gobierno as he is called) of the Federal District is the dominant actor. Until the 1996 constitutional reform allowed for direct elections from 1997 onward the mayor (then called the *Regente*) was always a senior cabinet position appointed by the President and loyal to him. That changed in 1997 when elections led to the Party of the Democratic Revolution (PRD) taking control of the Federal District, as well as a number of the internal boroughs and surrounding municipalities. Since that time the other two major parties, the National Action Party (PAN) and the Institutional Revolutionary Party (PRI), have also shared the spoils, although the PRI lost much of its influence in the 2006 elections. However, the state of Mexico, the richest state in the country, forms a large part of the city and remained in the hands of the PRI.

This means that Mexico City's metropolitan area is a patchwork of different party-led executive governments, in which the two dominant figures since 2000 have been from different parties than the national president, and who must work with their respective local congresses. No executive tier of metropolitan government exists, making effective integration of planning extremely difficult. Until either the political-administrative structure of Mexico City is reorganized, or until some level of metropolitan authority is established, it seems unlikely that city politicians will have the mandate or the authority to bring citywide vision to the key development tasks: job creation, housing, planning land use for future growth, the development of infrastructure and public transportation systems, the reduction of pollution and maintenance of ecological stability, and effective policing and safeguards for personal security and property. Without such changes the city will survive but is unlikely to thrive.

See also **Aztecs; Díaz, Porfirio; Iturbide, Agustín de; Juárez, Benito; Maximilian; Mexico, Federal District; Mexico, Political Parties: Democratic Revolutionary Party (PRD); Mexico, Political Parties: Institutional Revolutionary Party (PRI); Mexico, Political Parties: National Action Party (PAN); Netzahualcóyotl; Templo Mayor; Tenochtitlán.**

BIBLIOGRAPHY

Aguilar, Adrían G., and Peter M. Ward. "Globalization, Regional Development, and Mega-City Expansion in Latin America: Analyzing Mexico City's Peri-Urban Hinterland." *Cities* 20, no. 1 (February 2003): 3–21.

Davis, Diane E. *Urban Leviathan: Mexico City in the Twentieth Century.* Philadelphia: Temple University Press, 1994.

Garza, Gustavo, ed. *La Ciudad de México en el fin del segundo milenio*. México: El Colegio de México y el Gobierno del Distrito Federal, 2000. This huge and impressive text is a revised and updated version of *El atlas de la Ciudad de México,* 1987. See especially Gustavo Garza, "Servicialización de la economía metropolitana 1960–1998," pp. 178–181; María Eugenia Negrete Salas, "Dinámica demográfica," ch. 4.3, pp. 247–252; Brígida García and Olandina de Oliveira, "El mercado de trabajo, 1930–1998," ch. 4.6, pp. 279–283; Arturo Alvarado, "La seguridad pública," ch. 5.11, pp. 410–419; Carlos Martínez Assad, "Gobierno en transción," ch. 8.4, pp. 667–671; and Gustavo Garza, "La megalópolis de la Cd. de México, según escenario tendencial 2020," ch. 10.3, pp. 753–762.

Gilbert, Alan, ed. *The Mega-City in Latin America*. New York: United Nations University Press, 1996.

Kandell, Jonathan. *La Capital: The Biography of Mexico City*. New York: Random House, 1988. An interesting journalistic account, but will not satisfy most scholars.

Ward, Peter M. *Mexico City*, revised 2nd edition. New York: Wiley, 1998. See also the revised and extended edition: *Mexico megaciudad: Desarrollo y política, 1970–2002*, 2nd edition. México: Colegio Mexiquense y Miguel Angel Porrúa, 2004.

Ward, Peter M. "Mexico City in an Era of Globalization and Demographic Downturn." In *World Cities beyond the West: Globalization, Development, and Inequality*, ed. Josef Gugler. New York: Cambridge University Press, 2004.

PETER M. WARD
C.B. SMITH JR.

MEXICO CITY CONFERENCE (1945).

See **Pan-American Conferences: Mexico City Conference (1945).**

MEXICO, CONSTITUTIONS

This entry includes the following articles:
CONSTITUTIONS PRIOR TO 1917
CONSTITUTION OF 1917

CONSTITUTIONS PRIOR TO 1917

Throughout the nineteenth century, Mexico, like many other western nations, developed its constitutional system in a climate of political instability, economic crisis, and conflicts with foreign powers. The principal inspirations of the Mexican constitutional movement were the Constitution of the United States, the several constitutions of the French Revolution, and the Spanish Constitution of 1812. There were four constitutions in Mexico before 1917: the Federal Constitution of 1824, amended in 1847; the centralist constitutions of the Seven Laws (1836) and Organizational Foundations (1843); and the Federal Constitution of 1857. The Constitution of 1824 established a federal system similar to the United States's, but with many limitations on the powers of the president. The Seven Laws of 1836 formed a fourth power, known as the Supreme Conservative, to regulate the acts of the other branches of government. This constitution divided the republic into departments with restricted responsibilities and subject to central control. The Foundations of 1843 proposed a centralism that gave more liberties to the departments than did the Seven Laws. The Constitution of 1857 was written following the triumph of the Ayutla Revolution (1854–1857), and in it the liberals became a symbol of struggle against the Conservative Party, the French invasion, and the empire of Maximilian (1857–1867). The Constitution of 1857 enshrined the liberal principles of the previous constitutions and definitively established federalism in the nation. It also included reformist measures aimed at secularizing the state and society. Although it did not establish freedom of worship, this constitution abolished ecclesiastical immunity, declared freedom of teaching, and forced the sale of property belonging to civil and religious organizations. Until 1917 the Constitution of 1857 was the symbol of the freedoms that were lost under the dictatorship of Porfirio Díaz (1877–1911).

See also **Federalism.**

BIBLIOGRAPHY

Cosío Villegas, Daniel. *La Constitución de 1857 y sus críticos*. México: Editorial Fondo de Cultura Económica-Clío-El Colegio Nacional, 2007.

Galeana, Patricia, ed. *México y sus constituciones*. México: Editorial Fondo de Cultura Económica, 2003.

REYNALDO SORDO CEDEÑO

CONSTITUTION OF 1917

The constitutionalist movement, headed by Venustiano Carranza, arose through the Guadalupe Plan of March 26, 1913, following the assassination of President Francisco I. Madero. The alleged purpose of the movement was to restore the Constitution of 1857, but deep discontent among peasant farmers and workers over the dispossession of their lands and harsh working conditions in factories, clashes between different political groups, and years of armed struggle made it necessary to consolidate a number of reforms (additions to the Guadalupe Plan, dated December 12, 1914). This led to the convening of a constituent congress.

On November 21, 1916, the Constitutional Congress began its preparatory meetings. Carranza presented a moderate reform plan for the Constitution of 1857. However, the so-called radical faction, whose views eventually prevailed, was interested in implementing the proposals of the Mexican Liberal Party (July 1, 1906) and the Ayala Plan (November 28, 1911) and proved successful in asserting itself.

The Political Constitution of the United Mexican States was signed on January 31, 1917, and proclaimed fives day later (February 5) in Querétaro. The document took effect on May 1, 1917, and has been amended more than 300 times. It consists of nine sections called titles, and its great improvement over the preceding constitution was the establishment of individual rights—to a free, secular education, to health care and decent housing, to agrarian distribution, and to labor regulation (Articles 3, 4, 27, and 123)—as well as municipal freedom that transformed the political administration of the nation's territory.

Its amendments are diverse, some even going so far as to counteract some of the Constitution's original principles. This is the case of changes to Articles 3, 27, and 130, enacted in 1992 within the framework of reestablishing relations between the Vatican and the Mexican Government during the administration of Carlos Salinas de Gortari (1988-1994). The amendment to Article 3 removed the ban on religious bodies, their ministers, joint stock companies and companies linked to religious groups offering primary and secondary education, teachers' education, and education for laborers and peasants. Article 27 was amended to cut back on agrarian cooperatives and make it possible for religious associations and charity institutions to acquire property. The amendment to Article 130 acknowledged some civic rights for clergy and allowed churches and religious groups to establish legal entities.

Furthermore, an amendment to Article 28 during the administration of Ernesto Zedillo Ponce de León (1994–2000) authorized private investment in communications. During Zedillo's administration, the requirements and powers of the Judiciary (Articles 94 through 107) were also modified and legislation was enacted on electoral matters (Articles 41, 54, and 60).

In the early twenty-first century, reforms of unquestionable social significance have been the prohibition of the death penalty (Articles 14 and 22), the recognition of the free determination and autonomy of indigenous peoples and communities (Article 2), and the increase in the number of grades in mandatory basic education (Articles 3 and 31). These three reforms were enacted during the administration of Vicente Fox Quezada (2000–2006).

See also **Carranza, Venustiano; Religion in Mexico, Catholic Church and Beyond.**

BIBLIOGRAPHY

Branco, H. N., and L. S. Rowe. "The Mexican Constitution of 1917 Compared with the Constitution of 1857." *Annals of the American Academy of Political and Social Science*, 71, Supplement (May 1917), pp. i-v1-116.

Bullington, John P. "Problems of International Law in the Mexican Constitution of 1917." *American Journal of International Law*, Vol. 21, No. 4 (October 1927), pp. 685–705.

Márquez Rábago, Sergio R. *Constitución Politica de los Estados Unidos Mexicanos. Sus reformas y adiciones.* México: Editorial Porrúa, 2003.

Palavicini, Félix F. *Historia de la Constitución de 1917.* México: Consejo Editorial del Gobierno del Estado de Tabasco, 1980, t. I-II.

Tena Ramírez, Felipe. *Leyes fundamentales de México 1808–1997.* 20ª ed. México: Editorial Porrúa, 1997.

Irina Córdoba Ramírez

MEXICO, CONSTITUTIONS: CONSTITUTION OF 1824. *See* Mexico, Constitutions: Constitutions Prior to 1917.

MEXICO, CONSTITUTIONS: CONSTITUTION OF 1857. *See* Mexico, Constitutions: Constitutions Prior to 1917.

MEXICO, CONSTITUTIONS: CONSTITUTION OF APATZINGÁN (1814). *See* Mexico, Constitutions: Constitutions Prior to 1917.

MEXICO, EXPULSION OF THE SPANIARDS. Between 1827 and 1835 Mexico's republican governments attempted to expel all males born in Spain. At least five national laws of expulsion were implemented, in varying degrees, and often counterpart laws were enforced in the states. To remain in Mexico, a Spaniard had to gain exceptions to both national and state laws. The nativist hatred of *gachupines* (Spaniards) originated in the colonial experience and in the Hidalgo and Morelos revolts. Ferdinand VII had threatened reconquest. The Spaniards retained control of the fortress of San Juan de Ulúa in Veracruz harbor, thereby threatening trade. With the restoration of absolutism in Spain, San Juan de Ulúa bombarded the city of Veracruz intermittently from September 1823 until the fortress's capitulation in November 1825, fueling anti-Spanish sentiment. Mexico was forced anew to declare war on Spain. Perhaps half the Spaniards still living in Mexico had been royalist soldiers in 1821. The pro-Spanish and monarchist Arenas Conspiracy of January 1827 was found to include a number of Spaniards, thus providing the *cause célèbre* the nativists needed to press for the expulsion of all Spanish males. The Spaniards General Gregorio Arana and five friars were among the fourteen men executed for treason. York-rite Masonic clubs led the persecution in 1827–1829, whereas Scottish-rite Masonic lodges defended the Spaniards' civil rights. First, the *empleos* (employees) law of 10 May 1827 removed Spaniards from government posts. Then the expulsion law of 20 December 1827 included single men, mainly *capitulados* (Spanish-born expeditionary troops who capitulated to Agustín de Iturbide's army) and clergy. Together, these two laws accounted for the departure of roughly 27 percent of Mexico's more than 6,600 Spaniards. Dissatisfaction with these piecemeal remedies led to demands for "total" expulsion, which resulted in the law of 20 March 1829, targeting married men and merchants. Only incapacitating illness could gain exception. In practice congress and medical juntas granted exceptions, but 29 percent of the remaining Spaniards were expelled. Many wives worked to place spouses' names on congress's lists of exceptions. In the summer of 1929, the vanguard of a Spanish army of reconquest, led by General Isidro Barradas, landed near Tampico. The invasion became a fiasco as Mexican forces, aided by an epidemic of malaria, forced Barradas's surrender. A larger invasion force failed to embark from Cuba in 1830, when Ferdinand VII grew timid in light of the social revolt in Paris.

In 1830, President Anastasio Bustamante began to allow *expulsos* to land, whereupon many claimed illness. The sight of prominent returnees led to demands for "reexpulsion." Tampico rebels commenced expulsions anew in 1832. In early 1833, President Manuel Gómez Pedraza attempted to identify Spaniards possessing legitimate exceptions. A 16 January 1833 law reviving the 1829 law was aimed at unmarried illegal returnees. Fathers of families were allowed to return. Few Spaniards were expelled. Vice President/Interim President Valentín Gómez Farías perpetuated Pedraza's exceptions. *Expulsos* were still permitted to land and claim medical exceptions. A 7 June 1833 law declared Spaniards "nonnaturalized foreigners" and permitted the expulsion of antifederalists. The *ley del caso* of 23 June 1833 ordered the expulsion of all remaining Spanish clergy.

Expulsion enforcement stagnated in 1834 for lack of funds. Between May 1834 and December 1836, when Spain recognized Mexican independence, the plight of Spanish residents eased considerably. In 1834, President Antonio López de Santa Anna revoked all remaining expulsion laws, and in 1835, President José Antonio Barragán attempted reconciliation. Ferdinand VII's death and Spain's abandonment of reconquest plans helped, as did the reversion of citizenship questions from the states to the national government. By 1836, *expulsos* returned at will, and Spanish survivors regained the right to their old government posts.

See also **Mexico, Wars and Revolutions: War of Independence; Spanish Empire.**

BIBLIOGRAPHY

Harold Dana Sims: *La expulsión de los españoles de México (1821–1828)* (1974), *Descolonización en México: El conflicto entre mexicanos y españoles (1821–1831)* (1982), *La reconquísta de México: La historia de los atentados españoles, 1821–1830* (1984), and *The Expulsion of Mexico's Spaniards, 1821–1836* (1990).

Additional Bibliography

Levinson, Irving W. *Wars Within War: Mexican Guerillas, Domestic Elites and the United States of America, 1846–1848.* Fort Worth: Texas Christian University Press, 2005.

Orozco, Victor. *Hidalgo o Iturbide? Un viejo dilema y su significado en la construcción del nacionalismo mexicano (1821–1867.)* Mexico: UACJ, Doble Helice, 2005.

Ruiz de Gordejuela Urquijo, Jesús. *La expulsión de los españoles de Mexico y su destino incierto, 1821–1836.* Madrid, Spain: CSIC, 2006.

HAROLD DANA SIMS

MEXICO, ORGANIZATIONS

This entry includes the following articles:

FEDERATION OF MEXICAN LABOR (CTM)

This major Mexican union organization was founded on February 25, 1936, during Lázaro Cárdenas's presidency (1934–1940). The CTM is Mexico's most influential, government-coopted labor federation. Originally it consisted of the National Chamber of Labor, the General Federation of Workers and Peasants of Mexico, the Mexican Unified Labor Federation, and important industrial unions such as those in mining, electrical, and petroleum industries. Initially headed by Vicente Lombardo Toledano, an important intellectual and socialist, the union's leadership was taken over by one of the original founders, Fidel Velázquez Sánchez in 1940, who remained in charge through 1995, providing the longest leadership of any union organization in Mexico, and perhaps in Latin America. In 1946 the CTM, and its peasant counterpart, the National Peasant Federation (CNC), became essential pillars of the incumbent Institutional Revolutionary Party (PRI), which established a semi-corporatist structure divided among organized labor, peasants, and a "popular," or professional, middle-class sector.

The CTM, rather than successfully defending the bread-and-butter issues important to workers, has largely functioned as a channel through which the majority of the organized working class has been controlled and manipulated either by its own leadership, or in collusion with government officials. Although at times the CTM under Velázquez attempted to resist government-sanctioned economic policies inimical to real wage earnings, it has generally acceded to economic strategies that have contributed to the decline in working-class standards of living. The CTM, through its formal linkages with the governing party, also has attempted to guarantee representation among the political leadership in the Chamber of Deputies, among governors, and among party officials. Although it provides the largest single base of party members, it is underrepresented among influential decision makers, further affecting adversely its influence on prolabor social and economic policies. Its declining influence and prestige are reflected in its lower union membership, a situation that was exacerbated during the Carlos Salinas administration (1988–1994), when many state-run industries, and thus employers, were privatized, along with other market reforms. Although initially opposed to the North American Free Trade Agreement (NAFTA), Velázquez later endorsed it. His death in 1997 signified the end of an era. Furthermore, because of its close ties with the PRI, the CTM's viability was called into question with the watershed presidential election of PAN opposition party candidate Vicente Fox in 2000. The Fox administration, as well as that of Enrique Calderón, elected in 2006, continued to work with CTM leadership. Yet overall, its influence in Mexican politics remains diminished.

See also **Mexico, Political Parties: Institutional Revolutionary Party (PRI).**

BIBLIOGRAPHY

Kevin J. Middlebrook, *The Paradox of Revolution, Labor, the State, and Authoritarianism in Mexico* (1995).

Dan La Botz, *Mask of Democracy: Labor Suppression in Mexico Today* (1992) and *Unions, Workers, and the State in Mexico* (1989).

Additional Bibliography

Aguilar García, Javier. *Historia de la CTM, 1936–1990: El movimiento obrero y el estado mexicano.* Mexico: Facultad de Ciencias Políticas y Sociales, Instituto de Investigaciones Sociales, Facultad de Economía, Universidad Nacional Autónoma de México, 1990.

Aguilar García, Javier, and Reyna Vargas Guzmán. *La CTM en el periodo de la globalización: Del sexenio de Carlos Salinas al gobierno de Vicente Fox.* Toluca, Mexico: Universidad Autónoma del Estado de México, 2006.

Brown, Jonathan C., ed. *Workers' Control in Latin America, 1930–1979.* Chapel Hill: University of North Carolina Press, 1997.

Burgess, Katrina. *Parties and Unions in the New Global Economy.* Pittsburgh, PA: University of Pittsburgh Press, 2004.

Hernández Vicencio, Tania. *Los gremios de taxistas en Tijuana: Alternancia política y corporativismo cetemista.* Tijuana, Mexico: El Colegio de la Frontera Norte, Departamento de Estudios Sociales, 1995.

Reyes Sahagún, Carlos. *El movimiento obrero cetemista en Aguascalientes, 1937–1962.* Aguascalientes, Mexico: Instituto Cultural de Aguascalientes, 1993.

Sánchez, Sergio G. Guadalupe. *Del nuevo sindicalismo maquilador en la ciudad de Chihuahua: Un ensayo sobre el poder entre la nueva clase obrera.* Tlalpan, Mexico: CIESAS, 2000.

Sánchez González, Agustín. *Los primeros cien años de Fidel Velázquez.* Mexico: Nueva Imagen, 1997.

Snodgrass, Michael. *Deference and Defiance in Monterrey: Workers, Paternalism, and Revolution in Mexico, 1890–1950.* Cambridge, U.K., and New York: Cambridge University Press, 2003.

Roderic Ai Camp

MEXICAN REGIONAL LABOR CONFEDERATION (CROM)

The Confederación Regional de Obreros Mexicanos (CROM) was a powerful but short-lived labor organization that played an important role in the Mexican Revolution from 1918 to the late 1920s. Founded by Luis N. Morones, a former anarchist and electrical worker, the organization joined General Álvaro Obregón Salido in the political agitation that led to the overthrow of President Venustiano Carranza in 1920. During the presidency of Obregón, CROM expanded its membership, established a major political presence in Mexico City, and developed a close relationship with the American Federation of Labor in the United States, led by Samuel Gompers.

CROM reached the high point of its influence in the presidency of Plutarco Elías Calles. Morones was both leader of the union and minister of industry, labor, and commerce in the Calles cabinet. Although CROM's claim of 2 million members was inflated, the approximately 100,000 active members became a significant force in both unionization and politics. The Calles government, pressured by Morones, supported CROM against employers in the settlement of strikes and also favored CROM over other unions. At the end of Calles's term, CROM, which the intellectual and future labor leader Vicente Lombardo Toledano had joined, was the dominant union in the country. Still, the union faced competition from the independent Confederación General de Trabajadores (CGT), and despite the national leadership's power, militant CROM locals did act autonomously.

The assassination of Obregón in 1928, however, marked the beginning of a sudden decline for CROM and Morones, though the syndicate leader had opposed Obregón's bid for reelection. In the political uncertainty that followed, rival unions asserted themselves while the corrupt practices of Morones and his cronies discredited CROM. President Calles withdrew state support for the CROM and Morones. By the early 1930s, CROM was only a minor factor in Mexican labor and politics, replaced by the Confederation of Mexican Workers (CTM).

See also **Calles, Plutarco Elías; Mexico: Since 1910.**

BIBLIOGRAPHY

Marjorie Ruth Clark, *Organized Labor in Mexico* (1934, 1973).

Barry Carr, *El movimiento obrero y la política en México, 1910–1929,* 2 vols. (1976).

John M. Hart, *Anarchism and the Mexican Working Class, 1860–1931* (1987).

Gregg Andrews, *Shoulder to Shoulder? The American Federation of Labor, the United States, and the Mexican Revolution, 1910–1924* (1991).

Additional Bibliography

Basurto, Jorge. *El proletariado industrial en México, 1850–1930.* Mexico: Universidad Nacional Autónoma de México, Instituto de Investigaciones Sociales, 1975.

Guadarrama, Rocío. *Los sindicatos y la política en México: La CROM (1918–1928).* Mexico: Ediciones Era, 1981.

Guajardo Elizondo, Horacio. *Movimiento obrero mexicano.* Mexico: Ediciones Gernika, 2001.

Lear, John. *Workers, Neighbors, and Citizens: The Revolution in Mexico City.* Lincoln: University of Nebraska Press, 2001.

Leff Zimerman, Gloria. *Los pactos obreros y la institucion presidencial en México, 1915–1938.* Azcapotzalco, Mexico: Universidad Autonoma Metropolitana-Azcapotzalco, Seccion Editorial; and Mexico: Gernika, 1991.

Robles Gómez, Jorge Alfredo, and Luís Angel Gómez. *De la autonomía al corporativismo: Memoria cronológica del movimiento obrero en México, 1900–1980.* Mexico: El Atajo Ediciones, 1995.

Torres Parés, Javier. *La revolución sin frontera: El Partido Liberal Mexicano y las relaciones entre el movimiento obrero de México y el de Estados Unidos, 1900–1923.* Mexico: Universidad Nacional Autónoma de México, Facultad de Filosofía y Letras: Ediciones y Distribuciones Hispánicas, 1990.

John A. Britton

NACIONAL FINANCIERA (NAFIN)

Nacional Financiera (NAFIN) is a national development bank in Mexico. Beginning in 1925 with the establishment of the Bank of Mexico, the nation's central bank, the Mexican government organized more than a dozen public credit institutions to aid in the reconstruction of the financial system and to support the development of specific sectors of the economy. NAFIN was formed in 1934 to carry out a variety of functions, chief among them to promote the development of a stock exchange and a market for public bonds. In 1940 NAFIN was reorganized and given responsibility for industrial promotion.

Public-sector support through NAFIN for industrial development was an important element in Mexico's revolutionary program to construct a modern, capitalistic economy while reducing the nation's reliance on foreigners. During the 1940s large public-sector infrastructure projects accounted for most of NAFIN's loans and investments. Although the development bank nominally was autonomous, its board and officers worked closely with the Treasury Ministry and the Bank of Mexico. Nacional Financiera's resources, which were derived largely from foreign borrowing and the sale of its own certificates, were channeled into irrigation, transportation, and communication. The bank was also instrumental in the "Mexicanization" of electrical power generation.

During the late 1940s NAFIN, while not abandoning its commitment to the nation's infrastructure, became deeply involved in the financing of heavy industry, particularly manufacturing. The development bank not only extended credits, but also often adopted the role of entrepreneur by taking majority or minority positions in large-scale industrial enterprises in the steel, cement, paper, and transportation equipment industries. Bank management's rationale for its aggressive involvement in such projects was that they could not or would not be undertaken by private investors because of the financing requirements and technical complexities. By the early 1960s NAFIN was the majority stockholder in thirteen business firms and was creditor, investor, or guarantor for 533 others.

Sensitive to criticism from the private sector, NAFIN has worked closely with private investor groups to organize and finance businesses. It has also established a unit to assist small and medium-size business and has opened branches in provincial capitals. In 1985, with Mexico experiencing its worst economic crisis in modern history, NAFIN was charged with a new task, export promotion, and its budget was doubled in order to facilitate the government's industrial reconversion and export policies.

Despite NAFIN's status as the preeminent industrial development bank in Mexico, and perhaps in all of Latin America, it has not escaped criticism. Nacional Financiera's access to resources, financial power, and influence came to overshadow that of the private banking system. Some segments of the Mexican private sector are wary of NAFIN's aggressive incursions into certain industrial activities, arguing that the bank has preempted opportunities for private investors, and that as a result the Mexican government has overstepped its bounds. It has also been accused, through its activities, of favoring a small group of Mexican investors and large projects to the detriment of small business. On balance, however, NAFIN's contribution to the building of modern economy in Mexico has been positive and innovative, particularly through its financing of the economic and social infrastructure.

In the 1990s, the Mexican government liberalized the financial sector and allowed foreign banks to invest in Mexico, but NAFIN continued to be an important lender. Since this time, NAFIN has focused more aggressively on small and medium size enterprises (SMEs). By 2006, NAFIN had made loans to approximately 125,348 SMEs; this type of company received nearly 80 percent of NAFIN's credit. In the twenty-first century NAFIN has also expanded outside its borders by providing loans to Hispanic-owned companies in the United States.

See also **Banking: Overview; Economic Development.**

BIBLIOGRAPHY

Charles W. Anderson, "Bankers as Revolutionaries," in *The Political Economy of Mexico,* edited by William P. Glade, Jr., and Charles W. Anderson (1963).

Calvin Blair, "Nacional Financiera: Entrepreneurship in a Mixed Economy," in *Public Policy and Private Enterprise in Mexico,* edited by Raymond Vernon (1964).

Douglas Bennett and Kenneth Sharpe, "The State as Banker and Entrepreneur: The Last Resort Character of the Mexican State's Economic Intervention, 1917–1970," in *Brazil and Mexico: Patterns in Late Development,* edited by Sylvia Ann Hewlett and Richard S. Weinert (1982).

Jeff Brannon, "The Nationalization of Mexico's Private Banking System," in *Mexico, a Country in Crisis,* edited by Jerry R. Ladman (1986).

James M. Cypher, *State and Capital in Mexico* (1990).

Additional Bibliography

Garrido, Celso. *Desarrollo económico y procesos de financiamiento en México: Transformaciones contemporáneas y dilemas actuales.* Mexico City: Universidad Autónoma Metropolitana; Azcapotzalco: Siglo Veintiuno Editores, 2005.

Stallings, Barbara, and Rogério Studart. *Finance for Development: Latin America in Comparative Perspective.* Washington, DC: Brookings Institution Press; Santiago: UN Economic Commission for Latin America and the Caribbean (ECLAC), 2006.

JEFFREY T. BRANNON

NATIONAL PEASANT FEDERATION (CNC)

Founded under president Lázaro Cárdenas (1934–1940) to support peasant interests, the CNC, Mexico's largest peasant union, in reality functioned as an important institution in the corporatist structure of the Institutional Revolutionary Party (Partido Revolucionario Institucional—PRI) and its antecedents. The CNC forms the primary basis of one of the party's three sectors (agrarian, labor, popular), but it has exerted the least influence within the party and governmental leadership, in terms of both policy and personnel. Its leadership has been co-opted by the government, and its members have the least representation in legislative and national party committees. In the early 1990s, however, the CNC did protest some of the PRI's free trade policies. Under President Carlos Salinas de Gortari, Mexico entered into a free trade agreement with Canada and the United States (establishing NAFTA, the North American Free Trade Association), which subjected peasants to stiff foreign agricultural competition. Also, in 2000 Mexico made a partial transition to democracy, when for the first time an opposition candidate won the presidency. This electoral win weakened the CNC's overall strength, as the PRI lost its substantial control over the federal government.

See also **Cárdenas del Río, Lázaro; Mexico, Political Parties: Institutional Revolutionary Party (PRI).**

BIBLIOGRAPHY

Moisés González Navarro, *La Confederación Nacional Campesina* (1977).

Steven Sanderson, *Agrarian Populism and the Mexican State* (1981).

Additional Bibliography

Díaz Soto y Gama, Antonio, with Pedro Castro. *Historia del agrarismo en México.* Mexico City: Era, 2002.

Rojas Herrera, Juan José. *Auge y decadencia del corporativismo agrario en México, 1934–1997.* Chapingo, México: Universidad Autónoma Chapingo, 1998.

RODERIC AI CAMP

MEXICO, POLITICAL PARTIES

This entry includes the following articles:

NATIONAL ACTION PARTY (PAN)
NATIONAL REVOLUTIONARY PARTY (PNR)
PARTIDO COMUNISTA MEXICANO
PARTIDO LIBERAL MEXICANO
PARTY OF THE MEXICAN REVOLUTION (PRM)

DEMOCRATIC REVOLUTIONARY PARTY (PRD)

The Democratic Revolutionary Party (Partido Revolucionario Democrático, PRD) is one of the three main political parties in Mexico. The PRD was established in 1989 after the surprising success of the 1988 electoral challenge by Cuauhtémoc Cárdenas, who ran second as a presidential candidate representing a coalition of small left-wing parties. Cárdenas, a former government official, and Porfirio Muñoz Ledo, a former president of the Institutional Revolutionary Party (PRI), were the key leaders in founding the party, an amalgam of leftist parties and dissident members from the reformist wing of the PRI, who split during the 1987–1988 presidential succession battles within the government leadership. The PRD has become the major left-of-center party, and one of the three competitive parties nationally, providing a populist, pro-statist platform. In addition to its opposition to many of the government's economic liberalization reforms, it has been the most vociferous advocate of political competition pluralization prior to the critical 2000 presidential campaign. It recruits its leadership in larger numbers from the working class than the other two major parties do.

The PRD achieved its greatest electoral victory among candidates taking office in the 1997–2000 congress, but Cárdenas, its standard bearer in the 1994 presidential race, came in third in the presidential election. In 2000 Cárdenas campaigned as the party's presidential candidate a third time, coming in a distant third in an election that brought Vicente Fox and the National Action Party (PAN) to power nationally. The party has suffered from numerous divisions; nevertheless it has strengthened the left substantially through greater national unity and deeper grassroots organizing. It has the smallest partisan support and is the least well-represented at the state level, measured by the number of governorships it has won. In the 2006 presidential race, it put forth Andrés Manuel López Obrador, the front-runner for most of the race, who lost by less than half a percent of the vote. López Obrador did not increase the party's long-term partisan supporters, but dramatically strengthened their presence in the 2006–2009 congress.

See also **Cárdenas Solorzano, Cuauhtémoc; López Obrador, Manuel Andrés; Muñoz Ledo Lazo de la Vega, Porfirio.**

BIBLIOGRAPHY

Bruhn, Kathleen. *Taking on Goliath: The Emergence of a New Left Party and the Struggle for Democracy in Mexico.* University Park: Pennsylvania State University Press, 1997.

Gómez López, Alicia. *Juegos políticos: Las estrategias del PAN y del PRD en la transición mexicana.* Guadalajara: Universidad de Guadalajara, 2003.

Reveles Vázquez, Francisco, ed. *Partido Revolucionario Institucional: Crisis y refundación.* México, D. F.: Gernika, 2003.

Roderic Ai Camp

INSTITUTIONAL REVOLUTIONARY PARTY (PRI)

The Institutional Revolutionary Party, or PRI (Partido Revolucionario Institucional), one of the three major political parties in Mexico, was established in 1946 by president Manuel Ávila Camacho (1940–1946) as the successor to the National Revolutionary Party, or PNR (1929–1938) and to the Party of the Mexican Revolution, or PRM (1938–1946). It was originally founded by president Plutarco Elías Calles (1924–1928) and his closest collaborators as a means of continuing Calles's personal dominance over Mexican politics and as a vehicle for creating national control over local and regional political affiliates. Under president Lázaro Cárdenas (1934–1940), the PNR was reformed with the introduction of a corporatist structure, through which individuals became members by virtue of their affiliation with other occupational organizations, such as labor unions which in a modified form continues to characterize the party. In 1946, with the decline of labor and the rise of middle-class sectors, elements of the party pressured president Manuel Ávila Camacho to reform its internal structure and to rename the party.

In practice, as opposed to the intent of the internal party statutes, the party is governed by a national executive committee and a broader national political committee, whose head is commonly known as the president of PRI. The party president served at the disposal of the president of Mexico until 2000, when after seventy-one years in power the party lost the presidency to the National Action Party (PAN) candidate. The party is divided into three semi-corporate sectors—agrarian, popular, and labor—each of which normally is represented on the executive committee by a prominent sector leader who simultaneously holds a position in Congress. Thus the party structure links the legislative branch, interest groups, and party leadership. The popular sector is by far the most influential in internal party affairs, and in producing future political leaders, who come from major sectoral organizations represented in the National Front of Organizations and Citizens (FNOC). The most influential organizations in that sector have been the national teachers union (National Union of Education Workers; SNTE) and the union of federal workers (Federation of Government Workers Unions; FSTSE). The national executive committee ultimately is in charge of designating candidates for political office, especially at the national and state levels. These choices create considerable tension between national and local leadership. On the state level, various factions, led by competing political figures, have vied for control of the nominating function.

Observers and critics of the PRI have acknowledged its contributions to the continuity of the Mexican political process, most notably as an electoral machine and as the primary channel for grassroots support of government leadership and national policies. On one hand, it remains the most well-organized of the Mexican parties, with the largest core partisan membership. On the other hand, its long identification with the government and its many failed policies, as well as its history of electoral abuses, has led to cynicism on the part of the electorate and widespread rejection of the party's appeals nationally. Its presidential candidate ran a distant third to PAN and the Party of the Democratic Revolution (PRD) in 2006. Nevertheless, it remains the strongest of the three parties at the state and local level, accounting for 42 percent of voter support in the 2000s, and won a plurality of the seats in congress in 2003.

Internal changes were introduced in the 1990s, nearly all of which concerned the reduction of the national leadership's control over the nomination process. Of the three major parties in Mexico, it has the most democratic and broad nomination process—a genuine, open primary—for its presidential candidate. Despite this important structural change, the traditionalist wing of the party retained control through 2006. Their poor showing in that presidential race is likely to strengthen a younger, reformist leadership within the party in the immediate future, and introduce other, notable changes in the party's orientation and structure.

See also **Ávila Camacho, Manuel; Calles, Plutarco Elías; Cárdenas del Río, Lázaro.**

BIBLIOGRAPHY

Crespo, José Antonio. *PRI: De la hegemonia a la oposición, un estudio comparado de 1994–2001.* México, D. F.: Centro de Estudios de Política Comparada, 2001.

Garrido, Luis Javier. *El partido de la revolución institucionalizada.* México, D.F.: Siglo Veintiuno Editores, 1986.

Poiré, Alejandro. "Bounded Ambitions: Party Nominations, Discipline, and Defection: Mexico's PRI in Comparative Perspective." Ph.D. diss. Harvard University, 2002.

Reveles Vázquez, Francisco, ed. *Partido Revolucionario Institucional, crisis y refundación.* México, D. F.: Gernika, 2003.

Story, Dale. *The Mexican Ruling Party: Stability and Authority.* New York: Praeger, 1986.

Roderic Ai Camp

NATIONAL ACTION PARTY (PAN)

The National Action Party, or PAN (Partido de Acción Nacional), is one of the three major political parties in Mexico. Until 2000, PAN was Mexico's most influential opposition party, founded in 1939 by disgruntled former supporters of the government to oppose the policies of president Lázaro Cárdenas (1934–1940) and to provide a viable alternative to the National Revolutionary Party (PNR). The principal founders of the party were Manuel Gómez Morín, a leading intellectual figure in the 1920s, and Efraín González Luna, a prominent lawyer and Catholic lay leader from Guadalajara. As the party's leader until 1949, Gómez Morín attracted a distinguished group of former government officials and intellectuals, many of them activist Catholics, thus stamping the party with a pro-Catholic orientation. With the support of its rank and file, made up largely of middle-class professionals, businessmen, and Catholic student activists, the party succeeded in sending a small contingent of candidates to the Chamber of Deputies by the 1940s. During the 1950s, after Gómez Morín left the party leadership, his successors converted the PAN into a Christian democratic organization.

Although the party continued to expand its influence in the 1960s, it was characterized by numerous rifts within the party leadership over its ideological direction. Those differences often focused on whether the party should become a secular party opposed to state capitalism and the various political abuses of the Institutional Revolutionary Party (PRI) or whether it should function as a Christian democratic party. In the 1970s a faction controlling the party, believing that the party served only to legitimize the PRI, decided to boycott the 1976 presidential elections by refusing to nominate its own candidate. PAN's support declined precipitously. Reversing that strategy in 1982, it regained its previous strength and reassumed its role as the major opposition party, winning approximately 15 percent of the votes cast. In the 1988 presidential elections, under its charismatic presidential candidate Manuel Clouthier, it did extremely well in major cities, but for the first time in its electoral history, it took a back seat to another opposition party, Cuauhtémoc Cárdenas's electoral alliance.

In the 1990s PAN candidates began winning gubernatorial races, strengthening a new kind of political leadership, generally businessmen turned politicians. Using its electoral victories at the local level, these politicians vied for leadership of the party and competed for the party's presidential nominations. The most notable of these noncareer politicians was Vicente Fox (2000–2006), who captured the PAN nomination for president in 2000. Fox created a citizen organization, the Amigos de Fox, which dramatically increased support for the PAN, overcoming its small partisan base and enabling the party to win a dramatic presidential election in 2000. Fox, however, was unable to use a coattails effect to significantly increase support for PAN legislative candidates. PAN obtains most of its support for national candidates among younger, urban, well-educated, and middle-class voters, especially in the north and west central areas. Leadership of the party shifted back to more traditional PAN politicians in 2006, and drawing from independent voters and defections from the PRI, its presidential candidate, Felipe Calderón, narrowly won the presidency with 36 percent of the vote, and PAN obtained 42 percent of the congressional seats.

See also **Cárdenas del Río, Lázaro; Cárdenas Solorzano, Cuauhtémoc; Clouthier del Rincón, Manuel J; Fox Quesada, Vicente; Gómez Morín, Manuel.**

BIBLIOGRAPHY

Gómez López, Alicia. *Juegos politicos: Las Estrategias del PAN y del PRD en la transición mexicana.* Guadalajara: Universidad de Guadalajara, 2003.

Mizrahi, Yemile. *From Martyrdom to Power: The Partido Acción Nacional in Mexico.* Notre Dame, IN: University of Notre Dame Press, 2003.

Shirk, David A. *Mexico's New Politics: The PAN and Democratic Change.* Boulder, CO: L. Rienner, 2005.

RODERIC AI CAMP

NATIONAL REVOLUTIONARY PARTY (PNR)

Ex-president Plutarco Elías Calles (1924–1928) and other leading government officials founded the historic PNR in 1929 to provide an institutionalized means for maintaining the post-revolutionary leadership, specifically that of Calles and his collaborators, in control following the assassination of recently reelected President Álvaro Obregón. The party brought together numerous regional and local political organizations headed by important figures loyal to the national leadership, and it was financed through membership fees paid by government bureaucrats and members of government-affiliated unions. The party played a formative role in developing allegiances among influential political groups, most notably organized labor, organized peasants, and members of professional organizations, especially teachers and government employees. Members of these organizations formally were required to become party members, thus providing it with a broad national membership and a secure financial base.

The PNR became one of the most important vehicles through which Mexico was able to achieve political continuity unlike that of any other Latin American country, and, equally important, to subordinate the military to civilian control. Initially, it proved to be important in the career backgrounds of future Mexican presidents, and Lázaro Cárdenas (1934–1940) was the last president to serve as the party's president. Under his presidential leadership, the PNR was transformed in 1938 to the Party of the Mexican Revolution Party (PRI), having won every presidential contest from 1929 through 2000. Although the PNR established a national development plan in 1934, with strong ideological convictions, the party evolved largely into a pragmatic electoral vehicle capable of electing its members, with or without fraud, to local, state, and national offices. In the 2000 presidential race Vicente Fox of the Partido Acción Nacional (PAN) defeated the PRI's candidate. In 2006 the PRI fell to third place in the presidential election.

See also **Calles, Plutarco Elías; Cárdenas del Río, Lázaro; 'Mexico, Political Parties: Institutional Revolutionary Party (PRI).**

BIBLIOGRAPHY

Robert C. Scott, *Mexican Government in Transition* (1964).

Frank Branderburg, *The Making of Modern Mexico* (1964).

L. Vincent Padgett, *The Mexican Political System* (1966).

Luis Javier Garrido, *El Partido de la revolución institucionalizada* (1982).

Dale Story, *The Mexican Ruling Party* (1986).

Additional Bibliography

Alanís Enciso, Fernando Saúl. *El gobierno del general Lázaro Cárdenas, 1934–1940: Una visión revisionista.* San Luis Potosí, Mexico: El Colegio de San Luis, 2000.

Fallaw, Ben. *Cárdenas Compromised: The Failure of Reform in Postrevolutionary Yucatán.* Durham, NC: Duke University Press, 2001.

Vaughan, Mary K. *Cultural Politics in Revolution: Teachers, Peasants, and Schools in Mexico, 1930–1940.* Tucson: University of Arizona Press, 1997.

RODERIC AI CAMP

PARTIDO COMUNISTA MEXICANO

Partido Comunista Mexicano (Mexican Communist Party) is a small political party founded on September 25, 1919, with the collaboration of leaders from the U.S. Communist Party. It maintained a long history of opposition to the Institutional Revolutionary Party until 1981. Its leadership in the 1920s pursued the Soviet Union's Third International's political philosophy, and attempted to influence the Mexican labor movement away from organic anarchosyndicalism, important among workers prior to the 1910 Revolution. Valentín Campa (1904–1999), a major figure in the party, founded Confederación Sindical Unitaria de México (the Only Mexican Labor Federation) in an attempt to draw workers into a party-affiliated union. Many of the leaders, including Campa, were imprisoned or assassinated in the 1920s, and the party was forced to go underground from 1929 to 1934. When Lázaro Cárdenas became president in 1934 the party collaborated with the Federation of Mexican Labor (CTM), the leading labor organization in Mexico and a pillar of the Partido Revolucionario Institucional. Eventually, the Communist Party leaders were expelled, and the party's influence declined. Its leaders continued to affiliate with various strikes and political movements, the most influential of which were the 1959 railroad strike and the national liberation movement in 1961. Campa ran as the party's presidential candidate in 1976, before it lost its registration. Numerous party members in the 1960s and 1970s joined and founded small leftist parties such as the Socialist Workers Party, Mexico's United Socialist Party, and the Democratic Revolutionary Party (PRD) in 1989. Some members of Congress in the 2006 to 2012 administration were early members of these parties.

See also **Campa Salazar, Valentín; Labor Movements.**

BIBLIOGRAPHY

Campa Salazar, Valentín. *Mi testimonio: experiencias de un comunista mexicano.* Mexico: Ediciones de Cultura Popular, 1978.

Carr, Barry. *Communism in Twentieth-Century Mexico.* Lincoln: University of Nebraska Press, 1992.

De Neymet, Marcela. *Cronologia del Partido Communista Mexicano.* Mexico: Ediciones de la Cultural Popular, 1981.

RODERIC AI CAMP

PARTIDO LIBERAL MEXICANO

Symbolizing the growing discontent before the Mexican Revolution in 1910, the Partido Liberal Mexicano (PLM) was formed in 1906 in opposition to the dictatorship of Porfirio Díaz, who had controlled Mexican politics since 1876. The party's origins began in 1901 when Camilio Arriaga, a member of a wealthy family, organized an initial meeting of Díaz opponents in San Luis Potosí. The more radical working class intellectuals, Ricardo and Enrique Flores

Magón, who with their newspaper *Regeneración* critiqued Díaz, attended this meeting and later became the PLM's principal leaders. Faced with government repression, Arriaga and the Flores Magón brothers fled to Texas in 1904. There in 1906 they officially established the PLM and issued the party's manifesto, calling for the overthrow of the Díaz government, demanding presidential term limits and labor rights.

The PLM gained notoriety because it helped the working class in major strikes in Cananea (1906) and Rio Blanco (1907). However, the party broke up during the revolution. Both the Mexican and the U.S. government cracked down on the PLM. Arrested in 1918, Ricardo Flores Magón died in a U.S. prison in 1923. Also, other party leaders like Arriaga, differed from the Flores Magon brothers' increasingly radical orientation. Still, the PLM's ideology influenced the Mexican Revolution. Díaz Soto y Gama, one of the party's founding members, went on to join the Zapatistas, whose struggle for peasants' rights and land distribution became a major accomplishment of the revolution. The PLM's support for labor was established in article 123 of the 1917 constitution.

See also **Díaz, Porfirio; Flores Magón, Ricardo; Río Blanco Strike; San Luis Potosí; Zapata, Emiliano.**

BIBLIOGRAPHY

Gómez-Quiñones, Juan. *Sembradores, Ricardo Flores Magón Y El Partido Liberal Mexicano: A Eulogy and Critique.* Los Angeles, Aztlán Publications, 1973.

Knight, Alan. *The Mexican Revolution.* Cambridge, U.K.: Cambridge University Press, 1986.

BYRON CRITES

PARTY OF THE MEXICAN REVOLUTION (PRM)

A national political party (1938–1946), the Party of the Mexican Revolution (Partido de la Revolución Mexicana—PRM) is the second antecedent of the Institutional Revolutionary Party (PRI), Mexico's official party. President Lázaro Cárdenas (1934–1940), partly in response to the strengthening control of his loyalists over the party, and in order to enhance their strength, dismantled its original predecessor, the National Revolutionary Party (PNR) in the early months of 1938. The party took on basically a corporate structure, dividing itself into four sectors—popular, labor, agrarian, and military. The most controversial change engineered by Cárdenas was recognition of the military as a separate sector. His successor, General Manuel Ávila Camacho (1940–1946), eliminated the military sector, leaving the party with its basic tripartite structure. The popular sector, although smallest in affiliates, became the arena for the most successful political careers through the party ranks. The PRI went on to govern Mexico until 2000, when Vicente Fox of the Partido Accion Nacional (PAN) won in the presidential election. In 2006 the PRI fell to third place in the presidential race.

See also **Ávila Camacho, Manuel; Cárdenas del Río, Lázaro; Fox Quesada, Vicente; Mexico, Political Parties: Institutional Revolutionary Party (PRI).**

BIBLIOGRAPHY

Robert E. Scott, *Mexican Government in Transition,* rev. ed. (1964).

Luis Javier Garrido, *El partido de la revolución institucionalizada* (1982), 5th ed. (1989).

Dale Story, *The Mexican Ruling Party* (1986).

Additional Bibliography

Alanís Enciso, Fernando Saúl. *El gobierno del general Lazaro Cardenas, 1934-1940: Una visión revisionista.* San Luis Potosí, Mexico: El Colegio de San Luis, 2000.

Navarro, Aaron William. "Political Intelligence: Opposition, Parties, and the Military in Mexico, 1938-1954." Ph.D. diss., Harvard University, 2004.

RODERIC AI CAMP

MEXICO STATE. Mexico State, state in central Mexico that surrounds the nation's capital, the Federal District, on three sides, with a population of 14,077,495 in 2005. At independence, Mexico State included most of the former Intendancy of Mexico. Gradually, new political entities were formed from this expanse: the Federal District and Querétaro, Guerrero, Hidalgo, and Morelos states. The modern boundaries were set in 1869. The state capital, Toluca, is located to the west. Many of the state's inhabitants have strong links to neighboring Mexico City.

In the colonial period, the regions that came to comprise Mexico State typified central Mexico. A dense pre-Hispanic population of Nahuas, Otomís, and Mazahuas (many of whom were subject to the Aztecs) quickly came under Spanish control. By the mid-sixteenth century, Spanish estates shared fertile valleys with Nahua and Otomí villages. Indigenous population and cultural influence remained strong well into the nineteenth century. The large Mexico City market long shaped production by haciendas (wheat, livestock) and pueblos (crafts, charcoal, produce). Silver mines at Zacualpan, Sultepec, and Temascaltepec drew labor and resources in the colonial period, as did gold at El Oro in the nineteenth century.

The city of Toluca exerted little influence beyond its immediate environs in the colonial period. The city's modest size (1,000 families in 1746) can be explained by the fact that it had neither mines nor the patrimonial functions associated with cities that served as diocesan seats. Named the state capital in 1830, Toluca experienced steady growth from then on. The construction of the city's *portales* (1832–1836) anticipated Toluca's transformation into a bustling commercial and administrative center by the late nineteenth century. In recent decades, Toluca has become a major industrial city, home to numerous national and foreign-owned factories, and to a population of 487,630 (1990).

Mexico State today shows the modern face of its colonial past. With highways, buses, and even a metro line, *mexiquenses* are more linked than ever to Mexico City. From outlying areas, white-collar workers and landless laborers commute daily to jobs in the capital. Like Toluca, one-time indigenous villages such as Naucalpan and Cuautitlan have become important industrial cities in their own right. Elsewhere, Mexico City sprawls beyond its borders into Chalco, Texcoco, and other municipalities, spawning huge *ciudades perdidas.* These "lost cities" are inhabited largely by the working poor, many of whom migrated from elsewhere in Mexico. Throughout the state more traditional villages have managed to survive; in some, indigenous languages are still spoken.

See also **Guerrero; Hidalgo; Mexico: 1810-1910; Mexico: Since 1910; Mexico, Federal District; Mexico City; Morelos; Querétaro (State).**

BIBLIOGRAPHY

James Lockhart, "Capital and Province, Spaniard and Indian: The Example of Late Sixteenth-Century Toluca," in *Provinces of Early Mexico: Variants of Spanish American Regional Evolution,* edited by Ida Altman and James Lockhart (1976) pp. 99–123.

John Tutino, *From Insurrection to Revolution in Mexico: Social Bases of Agrarian Violence, 1750–1940* (1986).

Fernando Rosenzweig, "La formación y el desarrollo del estado de México," in *Breve historia del estado de México* (1987) pp. 191–252.

Deborah E. Kanter, "Hijos del Pueblo: Family, Community, and Gender in Rural Mexico, the Toluca Region, 1730–1830" (Ph.D. diss., University of Virginia, 1993).

Additional Bibliography

Chowning, Margaret. *Rebellious Nuns: The Troubled History of a Mexican Convent, 1752-1863.* Oxford; New York: Oxford University Press, 2006.

Gonzales, Michael J. *The Mexican Revolution, 1910-1940.* Albuquerque: University of New Mexico Press, 2002.

Knight, Alan. *Racismo, revolución e indigenismo, México, 1910–1940.* Puebla, Mexico: Instituto de Ciencias Sociales y Humanidades–BUAP, 2004.

Van Young, Eric. *The Other Rebellion: Popular Violence, Ideology, and the Mexican Struggle for Independence, 1810-1821.* Stanford, CA: Stanford University Press, 2001.

DEBORAH KANTER

MEXICO, TRUTH COMMISSIONS. Although Mexico never officially established a formal truth commission, President Vicente Fox Quesada (2000–2006) in 2002 appointed a special prosecutor to investigate state-sponsored atrocities in the 1960s and 1970s. The government under the Institutional Revolutionary Party (PRI), which held power from 1929 to 2000, had not attempted to prosecute the perpetrators of government-organized killings and kidnappings because its own party members and officials approved and managed extralegal violence. When Fox, the candidate of the National Action Party (PAN), became president in 2000, both Mexican and international organizations pressured him to form a truth commission to report on the PRI's past crimes. Instead, Fox made Ignacio Carrillo Prieto special prosecutor, drawing substantial complaints from human rights groups because Carrillo Prieto had worked under the attorney general and therefore was not completely impartial. Still, Carrillo Prieto brought charges of genocide against former president Luis Echeverría Álvarez (1970–1976) for approving the massacre of students during the 1968 protests at Tlatelolco, in Mexico City.

Trying Echeverría proved difficult because court decisions were reversed several times. Ultimately, a federal court in 2007 suspended the trial. Dissatisfied nongovernmental organizations criticized Carrillo Prieto's work because he indicted only a few individuals besides Echeverría. In 2006 the Mexican government closed the special prosecutor's office and the new president, Felipe Calderón Hinojosa, did not make past state crimes a priority issue for his administration.

See also **Echeverría Álvarez, Luis; Fox Quesada, Vicente; Mexico, Political Parties: Institutional Revolutionary Party (PRI).**

BIBLIOGRAPHY

Human Rights Watch. *Lost in Transition: Bold Ambitions, Limited Results for Human Rights under Fox.* New York: Human Rights Watch, 2006.

Scherer García, Julio, and Carlos Monsiváis. *Los patriotas: de Tlatelolco a la guerra sucia.* México, D.F.: Aguilar, 2004.

BYRON CRITES

MEXICO, WARS AND REVOLUTIONS

This entry includes the following articles:

COUP D'ÉTAT OF 1808
MEXICAN-AMERICAN WAR
MEXICAN REVOLUTION
REVOLT OF 1832
THE REFORM
WAR OF INDEPENDENCE

COUP D'ÉTAT OF 1808

When in July 1808, news reached Mexico City that the Spanish kings had abdicated in favor of Napoleon, the Ayuntamiento of Mexico proposed establishing a junta to govern until an assembly of cities was convened. The creole sectors of Mexico City backed this proposal but, fearful that such action could affect its interests and those of peninsular Spaniards, the Audiencia of Mexico proposed instead recognizing one of the juntas formed in Spain. Viceroy José de Iturrigaray, who backed the ayuntamiento, held several meetings to discuss its proposal, in which the positions of the two groups became radicalized. To prevent the creation of a governing junta, the audiencia encouraged a coup d'état. On the night of 15 September 1808, Gabriel de Yermo, at the head of 300 peninsular Spaniards, arrested the viceroy. They also detained several members of the ayuntamiento, as well as other autonomists. The audiencia and the new viceroy, Pedro Garibay, justified the coup by claiming it was based on popular demand, but they convinced no one. Thereafter, the colonial regime lost legitimacy, and the conflict between *criollos* and *peninsulares* became more acute until it erupted into armed struggle.

See also **Azcárate y Lezama, Juan Francisco de; Talamantes, Melchor de.**

BIBLIOGRAPHY

Enrique Lafuente Ferrari, *El virrey Iturrigaray y los orígenes de la independencia de México* (1940).

José Manuel De Salaverría, "Relación Ó historia de los primeros movimientos de la insurrección de Nueva España . . . ," in *Documentos históricos mexicanos,* edited by Genaro García, vol. 2 (1985).

Virginia Guedea, "El golpe de estado de 1808," in *Universidad de México* 488 (Sept. 1991): 21–24.

Additional Bibliography

Archer, Christon I. *The Birth of Modern Mexico, 1780–1824.* Wilmington, DE: Scholarly Resources, 2003.

Hamnett, Brian R. *Roots of Insurgency: Mexican Regions, 1750–1824.* Cambridge: Cambridge University Press, 2002.

Rodríguez O., Jaime E. *The Independence of Mexico and the Creation of a New Nation.* Los Angeles: UCLA Latin American Cener Publications, 1989.

Van Young, Eric. *The Other Rebellion: Popular Violence, Ideology, and the Mexican Struggle for Independence, 1810–1821.* Stanford, CA: Stanford University Press, 2001.

VIRGINIA GUEDEA

MEXICAN-AMERICAN WAR

When James Knox Polk opened his presidential campaign in 1844, he promised to enlarge the United States by annexing the Oregon territory and the Republic of Texas, disregarding the fact that Mexicans believed Texas still to be part of their nation. Polk's promise was merely the latest salvo in a long campaign of U.S. territorial aggrandizement that some have characterized as "manifest destiny." Following his election and the settlement of the Oregon issue, the United States Congress voted to annex Texas in 1845.

Upon hearing the news, Mexicans charged that their sovereignty had been violated. Months of negotiations and threats between the two nations failed to resolve the issue. Major General Mariano Paredes appealed to Mexicans' frustration with this lingering issue and seized power from General José Joaquín de Herrera, contending that he failed adequately to defend Mexican honor. With Paredes in power, Mexico intensified its preparations to assert its sovereignty over Texas, mobilizing troops near the mouth of the Rio Grande, avoiding the disputed territory between it and the Nueces River, the traditional border of Texas. Meanwhile, President Polk appointed John C. Slidell as negotiator with orders to buy California. Slidell's offers infuriated Mexican officials, who rebuffed him. Simultaneously, U.S. warships were sighted in Mexican waters near Veracruz. On 23 June 1845, Brevet Brigadier General Zachary Taylor, commanding approximately 1,500 regulars, left Fort Jesup, Louisiana, for Texas. Mexican intelligence reports revealed that by the end of July 1845, Taylor and his army had camped at Corpus Christi, near the mouth of the Nueces. On 8 March 1846, after Slidell's failure to purchase Mexican land, Polk ordered Taylor to move his troops southward to Point Isabel, into disputed territory. Another detachment had been moved to Fort Texas, opposite Matamoros. By April, the 2,200-man U.S. army was well established in southern Texas; the Mexicans made no attempt to dislodge them. On 4 April 1846, General José María Tornel y Mendivil, minister of war, appointed Major General Mariano Arista to command the Army of the North. Proceeding from Monterrey to Matamoros, Arista mobilized an army of 5,200 troops. In the first week of May, the two nations stood on the brink of war.

Events began to move swiftly in south Texas. On 24 April a clash had taken place at Carricitos, where Mexican troops had routed a U.S. detachment. And between 3 and 9 May, Fort Texas had suffered casualties from the intermittent bombardments by Mexican artillery. Although several U.S. troops, including Major Jacob Brown, for whom Brownsville was later named, had been killed in the encounter, it was the skirmish at Carricitos that furnished the circumstances that Polk used to ask Congress for a declaration of war, claiming that U.S. blood had been shed on U.S. soil. Congressman Abraham Lincoln challenged his colleagues to show him where in U.S. territory that had occurred. By 11 May, two days after Taylor's communiqué had arrived in Washington, the House of Representatives approved a bill authorizing war against Mexico. The next day the Senate voted in favor of war, and on 13 May, Polk signed the measure.

Meanwhile, on the flat plains of Texas, as Taylor attempted to reinforce Fort Texas, he was blocked at Palo Alto by the Mexican army. Just after noon on 8 May, the Battle of Palo Alto, the first major engagement of the Mexican-American War, began. Taylor pitted his 2,200 troops against 3,200 Mexican soldiers under Arista. The Mexican battle line was a mile and a quarter long; the U.S. army was deployed in smaller units. U.S. horse-drawn "flying" artillery dominated the battle, and the Mexican army sustained heavy casualties. The next day, at the Battle of Resaca de la Palma, the Mexicans were routed and sent reeling back to Matamoros. Within days, Matamoros fell to the advancing U.S. army (18 May), and Arista retreated to Linares, where he was relieved of command.

General Pedro Ampudia was given command and decided to make a stand at Monterrey, a city surrounded by natural barriers. While Ampudia was preparing the defenses, Paredes was overthrown in Mexico City by the liberals, headed by Valentín Gómez Farías, and Antonio López de Santa Anna returned from exile. Ampudia, perhaps influenced by the fall of his patron, frequently changed his plans to defend Monterrey, thus confusing and demoralizing his army. Taylor assaulted Monterrey in September with unceasing artillery barrages. Initially the battle went poorly for the U.S. troops, but they successfully outflanked the Mexican defenses. The Mexican defensive perimeter began to shrink. Numerous civilians were trapped inside the city and were killed. In order to win the city, Taylor had agreed to permit the Mexican army to march out with a limited amount of war matériel. Monterrey surrendered on 25 September.

By late 1846, U.S. troops had captured all of northern Mexico as far south as Monterrey with few exceptions and held the initiative. However,

Mexico showed no signs of suing for peace. U.S. forces believed it impractical to cross the desert south of Monterrey, so they decided to halt the offensive in the north and to attack Veracruz and drive on to Mexico City. To accomplish this, Taylor was ordered to send the best half of his army (the regulars) to join Winfield Scott, who had been selected to attack Veracruz.

General Antonio López de Santa Anna, now commanding the Mexican army, intercepted a dispatch that outlined this plan. In response, he boldly led his ill-prepared troops northward from San Luis Potosí in an attempt to catch Taylor by surprise. The two armies met at Buena Vista in February 1847, and again the U.S. artillery was too much for the Mexican army, and Santa Anna was defeated. He now rushed south in order to put down a rebellion in Mexico City and to meet Scott's army, which was advancing from Veracruz.

Mexico had not fared any better with the campaigns in the northwest and the south. In the north, Brigadier General Stephen Watts Kearny and the Army of the West had seized New Mexico, and next prepared to march through Arizona to capture California, which was already in turmoil. Northern California resisted the efforts of John C. Frémont, while in southern California, Andrés Pico and his lancers almost annihilated Kearny at San Pascual, near San Diego. Meanwhile, Colonel Alexander William Doniphan's sweep from New Mexico through Chihuahua, Nuevo León, and Tamaulipas and back through Mier, Camargo, and Reynosa had seriously impaired Mexico's ability to mount any form of counterattack. Having taken the port of Veracruz following a bloody bombardment on 29 March 1847, Scott's inland victories at Cerro Gordo, Contreras, Churubusco, and Molino del Rey demonstrated how ill prepared Mexico was for war, particularly its lack of modern weaponry and ammunition. After a short but stiff resistance by the Niños Héroes at Chapúltepec, U.S. forces entered Mexico City. Finally, on 14 September 1847, Scott entered the capital and took possession. Mexican resistance continued for a short time at Puebla, Huamantla, Atlixco, and other places through which American supplies and reinforcements passed. Throughout the winter of 1847–1848 peace talks continued that resulted in the Treaty of Guadalupe Hidalgo. With the acceptance of the treaty, the war came to an end and the United States emerged victorious, having wrested away half of Mexico's land. Mexico's losses included the present states of Arizona, California, Colorado, Nevada, New Mexico, and Utah in addition to Texas. The United States paid Mexico $15 million and assumed the responsibility for $3.5 million in claims by U.S. citizens against the Mexican government. Mexicans living in the ceded territories were to be treated as citizens of the United States. The treaty was ratified on 10 March 1848 by the United States and 19 May 1848 by Mexico.

See also **Ampudia y Grimarest, Pedro de; Arista, Mariano; Frémont, John Charles; Gómez Farías, Valentín; Guadalupe Hidalgo, Treaty of (1848); Herrera, José Joaquín Antonio Florencio; Kearny, Stephen W.; Monterrey; Niños Héroes; Paredes y Arrillaga, Mariano; Polk, James Knox; Santa Anna, Antonio López de; Taylor, Zachary; Tornel y MendÚvil, José María.**

BIBLIOGRAPHY

In addition to such classical books as *Apuntes para la guerra entre México y los Estados Unidos* (*Notes on the War between Mexico and the United States*) by Manuel Payno, Guillermo Prieto, and other witnesses to the events, significant contributions have been made in more recent years to the study of this war, focusing on the advance of the U.S. troops and the defense put up by the Mexicans. On the subject of the resistance offered by Mexico City, the most original and interesting may be *Sueñan las piedras: alzamiento ocurrido en la ciudad de México, 14, 15 y 16 de septiembre* (*The Stones Are Dreaming: The Uprising in Mexico City, September 14, 15, and 16*) by Luis Fernando Granados (Mexico: Era, National Institute of Anthropology and History, 2003). On the subject of tensions between the Mexican leaders, the defense battles, and how the U.S. army reached Mexico City's main square, there is *Crónica del 47* (*Chronicle of '47*) by José Emilio and Andrés Reséndiz (Mexico: Clío, 1997). For a more general overview, focusing on the military movements and other aspects, there are the books written by Josefina Zoraida Vázquez: *México al tiempo de su guerra con Estados Unidos (1846–1848)* (*Mexico in the Time of War with the United States: 1846–1848*, México: Fondo de Cultura Económica, Secretaría de Relaciones Exteriores, El Colegio de México, 1997) and *La intervención norteamericana* (*The North American Intervention*, México: Secretaría de Relaciones Exteriores, 1997). The more recent studies also include a highly interesting compilation of letters sent from all the states in the Mexican Republic, dealing with their defense against the invading army. The best is *Testimonios de una Guerra:*

México 1846–1848 (*Testimonies of a War. Mexico: 1846–1848*) by Mercedes de Vega and María Cecilia Zuleta (Mexico: Secretaría de Relaciones Exteriores, 2001).

JOSEPH P. SÁNCHEZ
VÍCTOR VILLAVICENCIO (BIBLIOGRAPHY)

MEXICAN REVOLUTION

This bloody upheaval (1910–1920), which left more than 1 million dead, brought profound political and economic change to Mexico. It caused the fall of the dictatorship of Porfirio Díaz (1877–1911), produced the radical Constitution of 1917, and furnished Mexico with a regime that has lasted more than seventy years.

The Revolution went through several stages. The first, the maderista era (1910–1913), encompassed the outbreak of rebellion, the victory of Francisco I. Madero over Díaz in May 1911, the interim presidency of Francisco León De La Barra, and the presidency of Madero until his murder in February 1913. The second comprised the reactionary dictatorship of General Victoriano Huerta, who ousted Madero, from 1913 to 1914. The third, the war of the winners, included the civil war between Venustiano Carranza (called the First Chief), Francisco "Pancho" Villa, and Emiliano Zapata, the latter two of whom were loosely allied. The fourth incorporated the victory of Carranza and his presidency (1916–1920). The final stage covered Carranza's failure and overthrow.

The Revolution had its origins in the changes brought about by the rapid economic growth that took place during the dictatorship of Porfirio Díaz. During this period, economic development, fueled by foreign investment in export industries, permanently altered the Mexican class structure and created widespread unrest. The construction of a nationwide railroad network after 1880 enabled Mexico to compete on the world market for minerals and agricultural products. A burgeoning mining industry helped engender a growing working class that sought improved wages and working conditions. Flourishing commercial agriculture raised land values, which set off periods of land expropriations of small landholders and villages by owners of haciendas. These expropriations alienated peasants, who were forced to immigrate to the cities, mining camps, and across the border to the United States in search of employment.

The expanding economy and government produced a new middle class that, in the face of unfair privilege, sought equal access to politics and economic advancement. All of this dissatisfaction simmered beneath the surface for the most part until the first decade of the twentieth century, when two crises converged to spark the Revolution.

The first crisis was political. Porfirío Díaz would be eighty in 1910, when a new presidential election was to take place. His profession in 1908 that it was time to retire gave rise to a "loyal opposition" led by Madero, the scion of a rich Coahuilan family. Campaigning around Mexico despite threats and imprisonments, Madero won a large following.

The second crisis was economic. A worldwide depression that lasted from 1907 to 1909 adversely affected the export sector, causing a precipitous rise in unemployment that in great part ruined the new middle class. Desperate workers would join the Revolution in 1910, as would members of the middle class who saw no way other than violence to obtain a fair system.

The Revolution erupted in the fall of 1910, when rebels in the northern state of Chihuahua, under the leadership of Pascual Orozco, Jr., staged a series of guerrilla attacks in the name of the Anti-reelectionist movement, headed by Madero. Other regions, most notably Morelos and Sonora, also spawned armed movements. The federal army, incompetently led, undermanned, and badly trained, was overextended and unable to put down the rebellion. When Orozco, ignoring the orders of the timid Madero, captured the important border city of Ciudad Juárez in May 1911, dictator Díaz abdicated and went into exile. The victorious *Maderistas* installed a holdover from the Díaz dictatorship, Francisco León De La Barra, as head of an interim government. Madero was subsequently elected president of Mexico in October 1911. He took office on 6 November.

Madero found himself in an impossible situation, between the still-entrenched *ancien régime,* whose army was intact, and radicals who demanded land and labor reform. The new president, whose father, uncles, and brothers were great landowners and industrialists, was disposed to proceed slowly toward reform. The peasant revolutionary Emiliano Zapata refused to lay down his arms. To convince him, Madero sent the Porfirian army, which was unsuccessful.

Zapatistas marching to Xochimilco, 1914. Beginning as a political crisis, the Mexican Revolution (1910–1920) developed into a broader struggle about peasants' rights, land reform, and social justice. © BETTMANN/CORBIS

In December the reactionaries led by General Bernardo Reyes Ogazón rose against the regime. Emiliano Vázquez Gómez added to the turmoil by proclaiming his revolt along the northern border in February. Pascual Orozco, Jr., disgruntled by Madero's passing him over in favor of Abraham González for the governorship of Chihuahua and backed by funds from the great landholder-political boss Luis Terrazas, rebelled the next month. Attempted coups and labor strikes added to the chaos. Madero's Mexico was being pulled apart by opposition from the states. His refusal to quicken the pace of economic reform badly eroded his support in the countryside. In February 1913, after ten tragic days of artillery fire and slaughter in Mexico City (La Decena Trágica), Victoriano Huerta betrayed Madero and overthrew him on 18 February. Madero and his vice president, José María Pino Suárez, were murdered four days later. Through a series of political machinations, Huerta took over as president on 19 February.

The "usurper," as he became known to Mexicans, confronted three dangerous adversaries: Emiliano Zapata and his strong peasant-based movement in Morelos; Francisco "Pancho" Villa and his peasant–worker–middle-class coalition from Chihuahua and Durango; and Venustiano Carranza and his reformist followers from Coahuila and Sonora. The three joined against Huerta in an uneasy, mutually suspicious alliance, the Constitutional coalition, that would disintegrate with victory.

Primarily as a result of the military talents of Villa and Carranza's most important general, Álvaro Obregón Salido, and the diplomatic and armed intervention of the United States, the Constitutionalist coalition defeated Huerta. In a series of bloody battles in the center of the country (Torreón and Zacatecas), Villa defeated and demoralized the Huertista army.

President Woodrow Wilson undermined the dictator by refusing to recognize his government and by shutting off access to arms and munitions supplies. In April, ostensibly because a Mexican officer in Tampico refused to apologize for a minor incident involving U.S. sailors, Wilson dispatched occupation forces to both Tampico and Veracruz, Mexico's two major ports. U.S. forces deprived Huerta of easy access to supplies and of the use of customs revenues. The dictator resigned on 15 July 1914; the U.S. occupation ended in late November.

The most destructive part of the revolution lay ahead. At a convention the winners held in Aguascalientes in October 1914, it quickly became evident that the allies had widely disparate goals, and moreover that Villa and Carranza had become personal enemies. The rough, former bandit and man of the people could not have been more different from the haughty, aloof *hacendado.*

Carranza withdrew support from the convention, thus assuring the split between him and the Zapatistas and Villistas, who then joined forces against him. A costly, brutal civil war ensued. It is estimated that between October 1914 and October 1915 200,000 soldiers died, a total surpassed only by the suicidal battles of World War I in Europe during the same era.

Carrancista general Obregón defeated Villa in a series of battles at Celaya, León, and Aguascalientes between April and July 1915. In March 1916 a group of Villista raiders crossed the border into Columbus, New Mexico, provoking the second military intervention by the United States in the Mexican Revolution. U.S. troops, led by General John J. "Black Jack" Pershing, futilely chased Villa for nearly a year until February 1917. At several points clashes with Carrancista troops came close to sparking full-scale war.

Carranza convoked a congress of revolutionaries at Querétaro in November 1916. The Convention of Aguascalientes (1914) produced a new constitution that offered a program of far-reaching reform over the bitter objections of the more conservative Carranza. By contrast, the Constitution of 1917 was notable for three aspects: its virulent anticlericalism, its radical land reform, and its wide-ranging intervention in labor-management relations. Carranza, however, ignored most of the new reforms, and actually reversed the process of land reform.

Carranza won the presidential election of March 1917 and assumed office on 1 May. He still faced diminished but stiff opposition from Villa in Chihuahua and from Zapata in Morelos. Zapata was killed in an ambush in 1919, but Villa outlived the First Chief. The primary goals of the victorious Constitutionalists were to restore order and rebuild the economy. As Carranza's popularity plummeted, he sought allies among the old prerevolutionary elite to whom he returned lands expropriated by Villa and others.

Carranza fell when he tried to impose his successor, Ignacio Bonilla, a civilian, as president. The army would not stand still for this imposition and overthrew the First Chief in the April 1920 revolt of Agua Prieta. A month later Carranza was killed trying to escape. Obregón won election to the presidency.

The violence of the Revolution was unrelenting (and lasted long after 1920). All of its major leaders were murdered: Madero and Pino Suárez at the hands of Huerta; Orozco and Huerta in aborted efforts to organize revolts from the United States; Zapata in an ambush; Villa by assassins in 1923; and Obregón by a religious fanatic in 1928. Some whole families were wiped out. Although it is impossible to calculate with certainty, between 1.5 and 2 million Mexicans (perhaps one of eight) perished in the decade of the Revolution. The economy lay in ruins. The nation would not regain the level of development reached in 1910 for another twenty years.

Recent trends in the study of the Mexican Revolution continue to broaden the historical perspective. Marjorie Becker examines the cultural history of the Cárdenas era in order to highlight the process of state building. Along with Katherine Bliss, Becker also pays special attention to gender relations in the Revolution. A recent general study that is useful for teaching the Revolution to undergraduate students is Michael Gonzales's *The Mexican Revolution* (2002). In 2006 Adolfo Gilly published an updated version of his classic Marxist history of the Mexican Revolution.

See also **Mexico, Constitutions: Constitution of 1917.**

BIBLIOGRAPHY

The magisterial two-volume study by Alan Knight, *The Mexican Revolution* (1986), is the best single work on the Revolution. Friedrich Katz, *The Secret War in Mexico: Europe, the United States, and the Mexican Revolution* (1981), is the standard examination of the role of other nations in the upheaval. See also Frank Tannenbaum, *Peace by Revolution* (1933); Charles C. Cumberland, *Mexican Revolution: Genesis Under Madero* (1952), and

Mexican Revolution: The Constitutionalist Years (1972); Robert Quirk, *The Mexican Revolution, 1914–1915* (1960); John Womack, *Emiliano Zapata and the Mexican Revolution* (1970); Michael C. Meyer, *Huerta: A Political Portrait* (1972); Adolfo Gilly, *The Mexican Revolution,* translated by Patrick Camiller (1983); and John M. Hart, *Revolutionary Mexico: The Coming and Process of the Mexican Revolution* (1987).

Additional Bibliography

Becker, Marjorie. *Setting the Virgin on Fire: Lázaro Cárdenas and the Redemption of the Mexican Revolution.* Berkeley: University of California Press, 1995.

Bliss, Katherine Elaine. *Compromised Positions: Prostitution, Public Health, and Gender Politics in Revolutionary Mexico City.* Philadelphia: Pennsylvania State University Press, 2002.

Gilly, Adolfo. *The Mexican Revolution: A People's History.* New York: New Press, 2006.

Gonzalez, Michael J. *The Mexican Revolution, 1910–1940.* Albuquerque: University of New Mexico Press, 2002.

Tutino, John. *From Insurrection to Revolution in Mexico: The Social Bases of Agrarian Violence, 1750–1940.* Princeton, NJ: Princeton University Press, 1987.

Vaughan, Mary Kay, and Stephen E. Lewis, eds. *The Eagle and the Virgin: National and Cultural Revolution in Mexico, 1920–1940.* Durham, NC: Duke University Press, 2006.

MARK WASSERMAN

REVOLT OF 1832

This rebellion led to the downfall of the government of Mexico. Late in 1831, following a pattern established during the independence period (1810–1821), a group of congressmen and prominent Mexico City individuals formed a secret committee to oppose the oppressive regime of Anastasio Bustamante. They convinced the Veracruz garrison to initiate a revolt in January 1832 and obtained the participation of General Antonio López de Santa Anna. The committee subsequently convinced leaders in other states to rebel. Although the revolt drove Bustamante from power in December 1832 and resulted in the election of a liberal government, it also contributed to the fall of the federal system in 1834–1835.

Cast as a hero by the committee, Santa Anna won the presidency for the first time in several attempts, thus initiating his career as a broker among contending political groups. The national army, which supported Bustamante, destroyed or so severely weakened the militias of the major states that they were unable to defend federalism effectively in 1834–1835.

The fratricidal conflict of 1832, which not only divided the nation but also obstructed national efforts to control the emigrants to Texas, so depressed General Manuel Mier y Terán, the most prominent candidate for the 1833 presidential elections and the leading figure in the north, that he committed suicide. His death ended the possibility of a peaceful solution to either the national conflict or the Anglo-American problems in the north, particularly in Texas.

See also **Bustamante, Anastasio; Santa Anna, Antonio López de.**

BIBLIOGRAPHY

Jaime E. Rodríguez O., ed., *Patterns of Contention in Mexican History* (1992), pp. 145–205.

Additional Bibliography

Gonzalez, Michael J. *The Mexican Revolution, 1910–1940.* Albuquerque: University of New Mexico Press, 2002.

Tutino, John. *From Insurrection to Revolution in Mexico: The Social Bases of Agrarian Violence, 1750–1940.* Princeton, NJ: Princeton University Press, 1987.

Vaughan, Mary Kay, and Stephen E. Lewis., eds. *The Eagle and the Virgin: National and Cultural Revolution in Mexico, 1920–1940.* Durham, NC: Duke University Press, 2006.

JAIME E. RODRÍGUEZ O.

THE REFORM

This era (1855–1876), initiated by the Plan of Ayutla in March 1854, capped a long struggle between liberals and conservatives over the character of independent Mexico. Individual rights were the cornerstone of a liberal program that also sought to subordinate the military to civilian authority and to remove the church from secular affairs. A parliamentary system and municipal autonomy within a federal government were favored to prevent a despotic central government and to guarantee individual liberties, while allowing local or state caudillos to retain their dominance. The reformers clashed with the military, Indian communities, and the Catholic Church, which defended corporate structures and privileges.

After coming to power in 1855, the liberals fought for their program through a decade of civil war and foreign intervention (1857–1867). Major reform measures established equality before the law (Ley Juárez, 1855); prohibited civil and ecclesiastical corporate ownership or administration of real estate (Ley Lerdo, 1856), and nationalized virtually all other church wealth; regulated parish fees (Ley Iglesias); suppressed religious orders; separated church and state; established marriage as a civil contract; placed cemeteries and vital statistics under civil control; proclaimed freedom of religion, speech, and the press; and secularized schools and charities. The 1857 Constitution enshrined the reformers' aspirations.

Many Mexicans suffered terribly during the years of turmoil. The contradictory demands of church and state were impossible to obey. For example, the liberal government required officeholders to take an oath of loyalty to the 1857 Constitution, while church authorities forbade the faithful to take the oath. To disobey the government meant the loss of employment; to disobey the church meant denial of the sacraments. Furthermore, during the civil war (1858–1860) the conservative government in Mexico City annulled the liberal laws and Constitution; the liberal government, headquartered in Veracruz, promised to punish those who obeyed the conservatives and issued more extreme measures against its enemies, especially the church.

Prevailing over the French-imposed rule of the Austrian Archduke Maximilian in 1867, the liberals at last had the opportunity to implement their program. They achieved only partial success: the principle, but not the reality, of legal equality for all was established; the decade of conflict undermined the effort to establish a parliamentary system and paved the way for executive dominance; the political and economic power of the church was largely eliminated, but charities and schools suffered; restrictions on the church belied the principle of separation of church and state; the hope that reducing village lands to individual ownership would create a large number of small landowners, which in turn would encourage rural democracy and economic prosperity, largely went awry—privatization facilitated acquisition of village lands by outsiders and by some enterprising villagers; and constitutional guarantees for the individual did little to protect the lower class. Still, the Reform years fostered the growth of nationalism and a sense of nationhood while laying the bases for Porfirian economic development and authoritarian political rule.

See also **Anticlericalism; Catholic Church: The Colonial Period; Mexico, Constitutions: Constitutions Prior to 1917.**

BIBLIOGRAPHY

Charles A. Hale, *Mexican Liberalism in the Age of Mora, 1821–1853* (1968).

Jan Bazant, *Alienation of Church Wealth in Mexico: Social and Economic Aspects of the Liberal Revolution, 1856–1875,* edited and translated by Michael P. Costeloe (1971).

Robert J. Knowlton, *Church Property and the Mexican Reform, 1856–1910* (1976).

Laurens Ballard Perry, *Juárez and Díaz: Machine Politics in Mexico* (1978).

Richard N. Sinkin, *The Mexican Reform, 1855–1876: A Study in Liberal Nation-Building* (1979).

Charles R. Berry, *The Reform in Oaxaca, 1856–76: A Microhistory of the Liberal Revolution* (1981).

Leslie Bethell, ed., *The Cambridge History of Latin America,* vol. 3, *From Independence to ca. 1870* (1985) and vol. 4, *ca. 1870–1930* (1986).

Additional Bibliography

Arrom, Silvia. *Containing the Poor: The Mexico City Poor House, 1774–1871.* Durham, NC: Duke University Press, 2000.

Benítez Treviño, V. Humberto. *Benito Juárez y la trascendencia de las Leyes de Reforma.* Toluca, Mexico: Universidad Autónoma del Estado de México, 2006.

Carbajal, Juan Alberto. *La consolidación de México como nación: Benito Juárez, la constitución de 1857, y las leyes de reforma.* México: Editorial Porrua, 2006.

Monsiváis, Carlos. *Las herencias ocultas de la reforma liberal del siglo XIX.* México, DF: Debate, 2006.

ROBERT J. KNOWLTON

WAR OF INDEPENDENCE

This struggle followed the September 1808 overthrow of Viceroy José de Iturrigaray and culminated in Mexico's final liberation from Spain thirteen years later. In the wake of disruptive plots and conspiracies, the denunciation of the Querétaro conspiracy forced Father Miguel Hidalgo to launch his rebellion on September 16, 1810. For the first weeks, the rebels appeared invincible as enormous numbers of Indians and mestizos joined to pillage royalist properties. Following the fall of the Alhóndiga in Guanajuato (September 28, 1810) and atrocities directed against the elites elsewhere, most Mexican Creoles understandably supported the royalist side. Although

Hidalgo protested Spanish governance, the motives of peasants and indigenous communities are less clear. Some studies have examined how the Bourbon reforms of the eighteenth century threatened local community identity and culture, whereas others have examined how population pressures created tension and frustration with the colonial system. Moreover, the causes of revolt varied greatly based on individual and communal grievances.

The uprising caught the army of New Spain by surprise, and some units in the rebellious regions joined Hidalgo. At San Luis Potosí, Félix Calleja formed the royalist Army of the Center. This force dispersed the rebels at the battles of Aculco (November 7, 1810), Guanajuato (November 25, 1810), and Puente de Calderón (January 17, 1811). However, even prior to the capture and execution of Hidalgo and his leadership, the rebellion had expanded and become a multicentered guerrilla war. Despite the implementation of effective counterinsurgency programs and the militarization of Mexican society, the royalists found themselves bogged down in a war they could not win.

In 1812, Calleja's army marched out of the Bajío provinces north of Mexico City to confront the insurgents of José María Morelos. Although Morelos was defeated at the siege of Cuautla, he reorganized his forces, expanded the rebellion from Acapulco to Veracruz, and occupied the province of Oaxaca. In 1815, after a failed assault on Valladolid, Morelia, Morelos was captured, tried, and executed. His movement was more successful than that of Hidalgo in actually declaring independence, forming a congress, and writing the 1814 Constitution of Apatzingán.

Although many historians have argued that by 1815 the revolt had declined into common banditry, entrenched guerrilla war continued. In Veracruz province, the mountainous regions southwest of the capital, and in other isolated districts, the royalists occupied urban centers but lost control of the countryside except during sweeps by powerful divisions. Calleja's counterinsurgency program to mobilize the population in order to free the army for campaigns against insurgent centers, drained Mexico of funds and manpower. Gradually, the war exhausted both sides and fragmented the centralized viceroyalty. The restoration of the Spanish Constitution in 1820 was interpreted by Mexicans as a prohibition of local taxation for military support. As the militias disbanded, Agustín de Iturbide issued the Plan of Iguala and attracted both royalists and insurgents into the Army of the Three Guarantees. After eleven years of war, the royalists collapsed, and Iturbide's army entered Mexico City on September 27, 1821.

See also **Hidalgo y Costilla, Miguel; Mestizo; New Spain, Viceroyalty of.**

BIBLIOGRAPHY

Lucas Alamán, *Historia de México desde los primeros movimientos que prepararon su independencia en el año de 1808 hasta la época presente,* 5 vols. (1849–1852; repr. 1942).

Timothy E. Anna, *The Fall of the Royal Government in Mexico City* (1978).

Brian R. Hamnett, *Roots of Insurgency: Mexican Regions, 1750–1824* (1986).

John Lynch, *The Spanish American Revolutions, 1808–1826,* 2d ed. (1986).

Jaime E. Rodríguez O., ed., *The Independence of Mexico and the Creation of the New Nation* (1989).

Additional Bibliography

Archer, Christon I. *The Birth of Modern Mexico, 1780–1824.* Wilmington, DE: Scholarly Resources, 2003.

Guarisco, Claudia. *Los indios del valle de México y la construcción de una nueva sociabilidad política, 1770–1835.* Zincantepec, Mexico: Colegio Mexiquense, 2003.

Herrero Bervera, Carlos. *Revuelta, rebelión y revolución en 1810: Historia social y estudios de caso.* Mexico: Centro de Estudios Históricos Internacionales, 2001.

Van Young, Eric. *The Other Rebellion: Popular Violence, Ideology, and the Mexican Struggle for Independence, 1810–1821.* Stanford, CA: Stanford University Press, 2001.

CHRISTON I. ARCHER

MEXICO, ZAPATISTA ARMY OF NATIONAL LIBERATION. The Zapatista Army of National Liberation (Ejército Zapatista de Liberación Nacional, EZLN) emerged as a significant political force in Mexico after seizing San Cristóbal de las Casas and several surrounding communities in Chiapas on January 1, 1994, demanding social justice and economic benefits for the poor. The guerrilla forces are largely peasants of indigenous origins in the highland region of Chiapas, a poor, rural state bordering Guatemala in southern Mexico. The initial attack and the response of the Mexican army resulted in at least 100 deaths, primarily civilians and guerrillas. The guerrillas' action drew international media attention, embarrassing the administration of President Carlos Salinas. The government responded by firing the government cabinet secretary in charge of national security and appointing a peace commissioner, Manuel Camacho Solís, to negotiate with the EZLN. Successful negotiations began in late February 1994, mediated by Bishop Samuel Ruiz, a long-time defender of peasants in his Chiapan diocese. But conflict was renewed in early 1995 after the government identified and tried to capture the Zapatista leader, Rafael Sebastián Guillén Vicente, known as Subcomandante Marcos.

In 1996 the government and the Zapatistas signed the San Andrés accords, but the provisions were never implemented. The central issue of these agreements was the granting of greater autonomy to indigenous communities in Mexico. When Vicente Fox became president in 2000, he promised to solve the stalemate between the government and the movement, with little success. The Zapatistas are no longer treated as a guerrilla movement, but rather as a political force. They tried to influence the 2006 presidential race, but their impact was negligible.

The immediate political consequences of the uprising included heightened tensions between hard-liners and political progressives within the administrations of Salinas and Ernesto Zedillo (1994–2000). The political debate in Mexico also began to focus on the serious deficiencies of the neoliberal economic policies pursued by the ruling Institutional Revolutionary Party (PRI). The uprising created potential conflicts between civilian and military leaderships and enhanced the role and prestige of the Catholic Church as a significant political mediator. The guerrilla actions inspired similar demands elsewhere in Mexico.

The Zapatistas had significant long-term consequences as well. They served as a major catalyst for reforms within the Mexican armed forces: in response to the Zapatistas' use of the Internet and the media to generate public support nationally and internationally, the army introduced important structural changes affecting professionalism and strategy. The success of the Zapatistas further spurred the growth of a wide range of nongovernmental organizations committed to nonviolent means of influencing government policy, thus contributing to democratization. The Zapatistas' policy goals also placed the concept of local autonomy on the forefront of the national political agenda, complementing a newfound emphasis on indigenous rights in the region. Finally, the demands of the rural underclass sharpened the focus on alleviating poverty, shifting the stress to redistribution of economic resources.

See also **Camacho Solís, Manuel; Chiapas; Guerrilla Movements; Salinas de Gortari, Carlos; Subcomandante Marcos.**

BIBLIOGRAPHY

Benjamin, Thomas. *A Rich Land, a Poor People: Politics and Society in Modern Chiapas*, rev. ed. Albuquerque: University of New Mexico Press, 1996.

Collier, George. *Basta!: Land and the Zapatista Rebellion in Chiapas*, 3rd ed. Oakland, CA: Food First Books, 2005.

García de León, Antonio. *Fonteras interiors: Chiapas, una modernidad particular.* Mexico: Océano, 2002.

Harvey, Neil. *The Chiapas Rebellion: The Struggle for Land and Democracy.* Durham, NC: Duke University Press, 1998.

Ramírez Paredes, Juan R. *Nunca más sin rostros: Evolución histórica del proyecto del EZLN.* Mexico: Eón, 2002.

RODERIC AI CAMP

MEYER COSÍO, LORENZO (1942–). The Mexican historian Lorenzo Meyer Cosío was born in Mexico City in 1942. He completed his undergraduate and doctorate degrees at the Colegio de México in 1967, and a master's degree in political science at the University of Chicago in 1970. He has been a full-time researcher at the Colegio de México since 1970, and the founding director of their U.S.–Mexican relations program since 1977. He also has served as academic dean, and has held visiting posts at the Woodrow Wilson Center for International Scholars (1984–1985), Ortega y Gasset University (1991–1992 and 2001–2002), and Stanford University (1998–1999). He received the national prize in journalism in 1989 for his criticisms of Mexican politics. His scholarly work, which has a strongly nationalist perspective, focuses on U.S.–Mexican relations and the Mexican Revolution, and, more recently Mexican democracy. Meyer is best known as a pointed, weekly commentator in Mexico's leading newspapers, and as a leading advocate of the democratic transformation since 1988.

See also **Journalism.**

BIBLIOGRAPHY

Meyer Cosío, Lorenzo, and Héctor Aguilar Camín. *In the Shadow of the Mexican Revolution: Contemporary Mexican History, 1910–1989.* Austin: University of Texas Press, 1993.

Meyer Cosío, Lorenzo, and Josefina Zoraida. *The United States and Mexico.* Chicago: University of Chicago Press, 1985.

RODERIC AI CAMP

MICHELINA, SANTOS (1797–1848).

Santos Michelina (*b.* 1 November 1797; *d.* 12 March 1848), Venezuelan politician who became Venezuela's first secretary of finance in 1830. After briefly participating in the War of Independence, Michelina was imprisoned, then freed and expelled from the country. He settled in Philadelphia, where he studied economics, law, and business. In 1821 he returned to Venezuela and took up various public posts connected with financial affairs. In 1830 he became secretary of finance and foreign affairs and established the foundation for the financial organization of the republic. He took charge of managing the Venezuelan foreign debt and served as negotiator for the country in the working out of diverse international treaties. Later he filled other important public posts. He was elected representative to Congress and was wounded in the assault on Congress of 24 January 1848. He died in Caracas seven weeks later.

BIBLIOGRAPHY

Tomás Michelena, *Reseña biográfica de Santos Michelena. Parte histórica, administrativa y política de Venezuela, desde 1824 a 1848,* 2d ed. (1951).

César A. Tinoco Richter, *Santos Michelena (1797–1848)* (1952).

Pedro José Vargas, *Santos Michelena: Biografía y esbozo de su tiempo* (1972).

Additional Bibliography

Botello, Oldman. *Santos Michelena y su familia.* Caracas, Venezuela: Congreso de la República, Ediciones de la Cámara de Diputados, 1997.

Carrillo Batalla, Tomas Enrique. *El pensamiento económico de Santos Michelena.* Caraca, Venezuela: Academia Nacional de Ciencias Economicas, 1992.

INÉS QUINTERO

MICHELINI, ZELMAR (1924–1976).

Zelmar Michelini (*b.* 24 March 1924; *d.* 20 May 1976), Uruguayan senator and founder of the Movement for a People's Government, a splinter faction of the Colorado Party, known as List 99, which later became the Party for a People's Government (PGP). Michelini abandoned his law school studies and position as general secretary of the Federation of University Students (FEUU) to become an organizer in the Bank Employees Union (AEBU). An active member of the Colorado Party, he was elected to the Chamber of Deputies in 1953 as a close associate of Luis Batlle Berres. Michelini was reelected as a deputy in 1958 and 1962. Growing disagreements with the leadership led Michelini and others to form List 99 within the Colorado Party. With the party's return to the presidency in 1966, Michelini was given the post of minister of industry and commerce. On the death of President Oscar Daniel Gestido and the ascension of Jorge Pacheco Areco to the presidency amid ongoing social tension and political conflict, Michelini, now a senator, took his group out of the Colorado Party in December 1970. In February 1971, Michelini's group, later known as the PGP, joined the Christian Democratic and the Socialist and Communist parties to form the Frente Amplio (Broad Front), a coalition modeled after Unidad Popular in Chile.

Michelini was reelected a senator in 1972 but this time as a member of the Frente Amplio. From this position he protested eloquently against the increased authoritarianism of President Juan María Bordaberry and the growing role of the armed forces. The 27 June 1973 coup found Michelini in Buenos Aires, where he went into permanent exile. He spent the next three years fighting the dictatorship and denouncing its violations of human rights. He testified on these matters before the Bertrand Russell War Crimes Tribunal in Rome in March 1974. His tireless efforts on behalf of political prisoners and his work with other exiles led to his abduction by Uruguayan and Argentine security forces on 18 May 1976. His body was found two days later along with that of a fellow Uruguayan, Héctor Gutiérrez Ruíz. In the 1990s Michelini's PGP, as an independent party, was the dominant force in a social-democratic political movement known as the Nuevo Espejo (New Model). Michelini's son Rafael was a PGP deputy to the Chamber of Deputies.

See also **Uruguay, Political Parties: Broad Front; Uruguay, Political Parties: Colorado Party.**

BIBLIOGRAPHY

César di Candia, ed., *Ni muerte, ni derrota: Testimonios sobre Zelmar Michelini* (1987).

Mario Juanaren, ed., *El pueblo vencerá: Discursos, entrevistas y artículos de Zelmar Michelini* (1985).

Additional Bibliography

Trobo, Claudio. *Asesinato de estado: Quién mató a Michelini y Gutiérrez Ruiz?* Montevideo, Uruguay: Ediciones del Caballo Perdido, 2003.

MARTIN WEINSTEIN

MICHOACÁN. Michoacán, central-western Mexican state. Located between Mexico and Jalisco, it has a population of 3,966,073 (2005) and its capital is Morelia.

Originally populated by Nahuatl groups, the region was conquered in the twelfth century by the peoples who later came to be known as Tarascans. The Tarascan civilization, with centers in the Lake Pátzcuaro region and in the so-called Meseta Tarasca (the western highlands), produced builders and artists of some note, though it is most renowned for having repeatedly resisted conquest by the empire-building Mexicas.

The Tarascans resisted the Spanish conquest as well, especially after Nuño de Guzmán's assassination of their chief, Tangáxoan. Much of the responsibility for pacifying the region lay with ecclesiastical personnel, most notably the saintly humanitarian Vasco de Quiroga (1470–1565; bishop of Michoacán from 1538). "Tata Vasco," as he was kown among the Tarascans, epitomized both the church's defense of pre-Columbian peoples and its desire to mold them into Hispanized Christians. The artisanal skills that Quiroga taught the many communities in the Pátzcuaro region are, in many cases, still practiced.

After the Spanish Conquest, Michoacán's economy developed slowly but steadily, especially after 1650. Its most dynamic sectors were mining, in Tlalpujahua and Inguarán, and sugar production, in the Balsas river basin. By 1810 the fertile valleys in the northern part of the state were producing wheat for sale in out-of-region markets, and the *tierra caliente* (tropical lowlands) had also diversified into rice, indigo, and cotton production. The city of Valladolid (today Morelia) was an important commerical, financial, and administrative center; it was the seat of the bishopric of Michoacán.

Many of the leaders of the Mexican movement for independence came from Michoacán, including Miguel Hidalgo y Costilla (1753–1811), José María Morelos y Pavón (1765–1815), and Ignacio López Rayón (1773–1832). The state was the principal battleground of the wars and it suffered considerable losses from which it took decades to recover. These losses and the patchy and unequal nature of the postwar recovery contributed to the fact that during the next significant challenge to the political status quo—the mid-century Reform—Michoacán again provided key leadership, most notably Melchor Ocampo.

Although the state underwent rapid economic modernization after 1890, a long process of marginalization from the mainstream of national economic life was already underway. In an economic sense, Michoacán had always done many things fairly well, and its diversity of resources, combined with an abundance of labor, had given the state economy a certain buoyancy. But the belated creation of a rail network in the late nineteenth century permitted other regions to compete nationally and even locally with the state's products.

In the twentieth century, Michoacán provided another of Mexico's great leaders, Lázaro Cárdenas (1895–1970), and became a testing ground for Cárdenas's social reformism in the 1930s. Yet, agrarian reform could not prevent the further erosion of the state's ability to support its population. Today Michoacán ranks among the top states in only one area: the number of its inhabitants who migrate to the United States. One result is that Michoacán was the only state to reject the PRI (Institutional Revolutionary Party) candidate in the 1988 presidential elections (to support its native son Cuauhtemoc Cárdenas), and thus remains, as it has always been, in the vanguard of dissident political thought.

See also **Mining: Colonial Spanish America; Nahuatl; Tarascans.**

BIBLIOGRAPHY

Gonzalo Aguirre Beltrán, *Problemas de la población indígena de la cuenca del Tepalcatepec* (1952).

Paul Friedrich, *Agrarian Revolt in a Mexican Village* (1970).

Luis González y González, *San José de Gracia: Mexican Village in Transition* (1974).

Elinore M. Barrett, *La cuenca de Tepalcatepec,* 2 vols. (1975).

Claude Morin, *Michoacán en la Nueva España del siglo XVIII: Crecimiento y desigualdad en una economía colonial* (1979).

Enrique Florescano, ed., *Historia general de Michoacán,* 4 vols. (1989).

Additional Bibliography

Boyer, Christopher R. *Becoming Campesinos: Politics, Identity, and Agrarian Struggle in Postrevolutionary Michoacán, 1920–1935.* Stanford, CA: Stanford University Press, 2003.

Krippner-Martínez, James. *Rereading the Conquest: Power, Politics, and the History of Early Colonial Michoacán, Mexico, 1521–1565.* University Park, PA: Penn State University Press, 2001.

Warren, Fintan B., OFM. *Vasco de Quiroga and his Pueblo-Hospitals of Santa Fe.* Washington, DC: Academy of American Franciscan History, 1963.

Margaret Chowning

MIDDLE EASTERNERS. Middle Eastern and North African immigrants from various ethnic, religious, and linguistic backgrounds came to Latin America as part of the predominantly Ibero–Italian influx that spanned the period from the latter decades of the nineteenth century to the 1950s. Most were Arabic speakers from Ottoman or post–World War I Lebanon, Syria, and Palestine (Mashriq). They were preceded by the less numerous waves of mainly Spanish–speaking Jews from Morocco and Algeria (Maghrib). Some 200 years after the flowering of a Maghribi Jewish presence in Brazil, economic and demographic factors combined with a bout of xenophobia stemming from the Moroccan–Spanish conflagration (1859–1860) to add new impetus to individual departures to Latin America, which had resumed earlier that century. Impelled by such a combination of events, more Jews from Morocco—and eventually from Algeria too—set their sights on reaching Gibraltar, the Spanish mainland (Algeciras, Cádiz, and Málaga), and the Canary Islands (Las Palmas and Santa Cruz de Tenerife), en route to a fresh start across the Atlantic. Favorable economic conditions at their final destination and the fact that some Moroccan Jews hailed from Portugal were among the reasons reportedly pulling the departees in the direction of Brazil. Later, Argentina and Venezuela and, to a considerable lesser extent, other Latin American states became their primary destinations. An indication of the scale of such migration is provided by the Argentine census of 1914, which recorded the presence of nearly a thousand Maghribis: 802 Moroccans and 125 Algerians.

Unlike the North Africans, the Mashriqis' first choice apparently was not Latin America, but rather the United States, presumably because of the greater attention the latter received in nineteenth–century Arabic–language geography books and press. Nevertheless, the economic and other factors that pushed increasing numbers of Lebanese, Syrians, and Palestinians to leave their homes during and after the 1870s, together with stringent health tests in the United States and the eventual introduction of quotas, prompted travel agents to redirect many Mashriqis to the countries south of the Rio Grande. The absence of direct links between the migrants' places of birth and the main Latin American ports required transshipment in France, Italy, Spain, or other European countries. Moreover, Ottoman restrictions prompted numerous travelers to disguise their voyage's ultimate destination as a trip to Egypt. Hence, many of those classed in Latin American immigration registers as Egyptians were in fact Lebanese, Syrians, and Palestinians, just as countless Algerians were Moroccan.

Latin America's principal countries of immigration, Argentina and Brazil, were also the favorites among the Lebanese, Syrians, and Palestinians. Argentine records show some 180,000 entries from the Mashriq during the period 1890–1950. Whereas the Syrians are believed to have been the single largest Middle Eastern group in Argentina, the Palestinians occupied that position in Chile and Honduras. As the main waiting–room republics for Arabic speakers and others intent on crossing into the United States, Cuba and Mexico also witnessed the arrival of thousands of Mashriqis. Not surprisingly, the U.S. government repeatedly prodded the Cuban and Mexican authorities into cooperating to stem the flow of this human contraband. That is not to say that all the Arabic speakers who arrived in these countries sought to leave or aimed to contravene U.S. sanitary and other regulations. Most Arabic speakers were Christian, in particular Greek (Melkite) and Maronite Catholics, or Orthodox. Undeniably, followers of other Christian denominations, Druze, as well as Muslims (Alawi, Shia, and Sunni) and Jews were also among them. In fact, the emigration of Arabic–speaking Jews from Aleppo, Damascus, and Beirut occurred at the same time as that of their Ladino counterparts from continental (European and Near Eastern) Turkey and the eastern Mediterranean isles. Ottoman and Young Turk policies no doubt provoked an Armenian exodus as well. That some Latin American states received nearly as many Turkish and Arabic speakers is highlighted by the fact that from 1901 to 1924 Cuba admitted nearly 14,000 Turkish and Mashriqi aliens, with 5,807 listed as Turks and 8,128 as Arabs, Syrians, or Palestinians.

Most Spanish and Arabic speakers arrived before the 1930s, when the combination of economic crisis and nationalism in Latin America translated into greater selectivity of immigrants. Since the end of World War II, however, the region's Palestinians as well as its Maghribi and Mashriqi Jews represented a powerful magnet for a new wave of their confreres. Hundreds of Palestinian refugees of the first Arab–Israeli war (1948–1949) moved to Brazil, Venezuela, and other countries, and a few thousand Moroccan and Egyptian Jews flocked to Brazil, Chile, and Uruguay. The resettlement of these Jews was one of the side effects of the waning of the French presence in the Maghrib, the Israeli–Egyptian war of 1956, and the fears aroused by the ascendancy of Nasserite Pan–Arabism throughout the Arab world. Known as *turcos*—a label used with inadvertent irony with respect to Turks, Arabs, and Armenians—the Arabic speakers were likewise referred to as *moros* in Cuba, presumably owing to Spain's influence on the island. The immigrants tended to perceive the *turco* sobriquet as pejorative, especially after the Ottoman Empire's demise resulting in Lebanese and Syrian arrivals with French travel documents or Palestinians with papers issued by their country's British mandatory authorities. Many Lebanese, the Maronites in particular, were keen to stress a French identity even before World War I, much in the same way as numbers of Moroccan Jews described themselves as Andalusian Catholics.

Like other new arrivals, the Middle Easterners, or at the very least a significant portion of them, initially saw themselves as sojourners, striving to amass wealth before returning to their birthplace to enjoy the fruits of hard work. Indeed, a number of Maghribis and Mashriqis fulfilled the expectation of moving back to their home countries, so it is hardly surprising to find some of the most successful of them serving as honorary consuls for several Latin American states before the close of the nineteenth century. Moroccans and Algerians first and then Arabic speakers took advantage of Latin America's undeveloped retail trade and devoted themselves almost exclusively to commerce, at the outset as peddlers, then as shopkeepers, and later as wholesalers. Catering to the needs of the least well–off, they helped to expand the market; to achieve this end, they provided credit by operating a rudimentary system of payment by installments.

Most Middle Easterners settled permanently in Latin America. They proved wrong those among the local liberals who, like others, had argued against their immigration, whether on grounds that their occupations differed markedly from official expectations of recruiting agricultural labor or that their ethnoreligious backgrounds stood in the way of assimilation. Nevertheless, the concern over occupations persuaded some of Argentina's better established Syro–Lebanese to promote the channeling of newly arrived kinsmen to farm work early in the twentieth century and to attempt their own screening in Beirut of immigration candidates in the late 1920s. Likewise, concern about their adherence to beliefs other than Catholic was among the contributing factors for Muslim self-effacement throughout the region. Latin Americans of Arab parentage—especially, but not only, the Christians among them—rose to political prominence in countries that once sought to limit the influx of their kinsmen. From the 1930s on, the region saw some become parliamentarians; others were entrusted with ministerial portfolios, pursued military careers, or were coopted into the diplomatic corps; a few ruled—or sought to do so—as elected or de facto heads of state. To name but a few, such are the cases of the three following presidents: Argentina's Carlos Saúl Menem (of Syrian Muslim parentage), Bolivia's Juan Pereda Asbún (whose mother was a Palestinian Christian), and Colombia's Julio César Turbay Ayala (whose father was a Lebanese Maronite).

See also **Arab-Latin American Relations; Jews.**

BIBLIOGRAPHY

Liliana Ana Bertoni, "De Turquía a Buenos Aires: Una colectividad nueva a fines del siglo XIX," pp. 67–93.

Jorge O. Bestene, "Formas de asociacionismo entre los sirio–Libaneses en Buenos Aires (1900–1950)," in *Asociacionismo, trabajo e identidad étnica: Los italianos en América Latina en una perspectiva comparada,* edited by Fernando J. Devoto and Eduardo J. Miguez (Buenos Aires, 1992), pp. 115–133.

Narciso Binyan, "Arabs and Armenians in Latin America," in *Patterns of Prejudice* (November–December 1979): 5–11.

Louise Fawcett De Posada, *Libaneses, Sirios y Palestinos en Colombia* (Barranquilla, 1991).

Nancie L. González, *Dollar, Dove, and Eagle: One Hundred Years of Palestinian Immigration to Honduras* (1992).

Roberto Grün, *Negócios y familias: Armônios em São Paulo* (São Paulo, 1992).

Liz Hamul De Halabe, *Los judíos de Alepo en México* (Mexico, 1989).

Gladys Jozami, "La identidad nacional de los llamados turcos en la Argentina," in *Temas de Asia y Africa* (December 1993): 189–204.

Ignacio Klich, "Criollos and Arabic Speakers in Argentina: An Uneasy *Pas de Deux,* 1888–1914," pp. 243–284.

Ignacio Klich, "La posibilidad del asentamiento de Palestinos en la Argentina (1948–1952): Una perspectiva comparada," pp. 115–141, in *Estudios Migratorios Latinoamericanos* (April 1994).

Luz María Martínez Montiol, *La gota de oro* (Veracruz, 1988).

David Nicholls, "Lebanese of the Antilles: Haiti, Dominican Republic, Jamaica, and Trinidad," pp. 339–360, in *The Lebanese in the World: A Century of Emigration,* edited by Albert Hourani and Nadim Shehadl (London, 1992).

Brenda Gayle Plummer, "Race, Nationality, and Trade in the Caribbean: The Syrians in Haiti, 1903–1934," in *International History Review* (October 1981): 517–539.

Alberto Tasso, *Aventura, trabajo y poder: Sirios y Libaneses en Santiago del Estero 1880–1980* (Buenos Aires, 1989).

IGNACIO KLICH

MIER NORIEGA Y GUERRA, JOSÉ SERVANDO TERESA DE (1765–1827).

MIER NORIEGA Y GUERRA, JOSÉ SERVANDO TERESA DE (1765–1827). José Servando Teresa de Mier Noriega y Guerra (*b.* 18 October 1765; *d.* 3 December 1827), Mexican political theorist and independence leader. Born in Monterrey, Nuevo León, Mier entered the Dominican order, obtained a doctorate in theology, and became notorious on 12 December 1794 when he delivered a sermon questioning aspects of the account of the Virgin of Guadalupe and arguing that the Apostle Thomas had introduced Christianity to America before the arrival of the Europeans, thus questioning the Spanish mandate to govern the New World. Exiled to Spain by the archbishop, he traveled through Europe. After the 1808 coup in New Spain, he became the paid defender of the ousted viceroy José de Iturrigaray in Spain. As a result, he published the first history of the struggle for independence, *Historia de la Revolución de Nueva España* (1813).

An avid polemicist, Mier wrote extensively in support of independence, alleging that the New World had possessed an unwritten constitution since the sixteenth century. In 1817 he joined the ill-fated Mina expedition to free New Spain and was captured and jailed until 1820 when he managed to escape. He traveled to the United States, where he sought support for his country's independence.

Returning to Mexico in 1822, Mier was elected to Congress and numbered among those congressmen opposed to Emperor Iturbide. Subsequently he distinguished himself in Congress as the champion of a strong federal system. He died in 1827, a patriot and an honored legislator.

By exalting Indian society, Mier created the myth of an ancient Mexican empire, thus establishing the foundations of Mexican nationalism. He was also a brilliant political thinker who integrated the Indian past with Hispanic constitutionalism to form a unique Mexican political ideology.

See also **Mexico, Wars and Revolutions: War of Independence.**

BIBLIOGRAPHY

Nettie Lee Benson, "Servando Teresa de Mier, Federalist," in *Hispanic American Historical Review* 28 (November 1948): 514–525.

John V. Lombardi, *The Political Ideology of Fray Servando Teresa de Mier* (1968).

Edmundo O'Gorman, ed., *El hetorodoxo guadalupano,* 3 vols. (1981).

Jaime E. Rodríguez O., ed., *La formación de un republicano* (1988).

Additional Bibliography

Arenas, Reinaldo. *Hallucinations: Being an Account of the Life and Adventures of Fray Servando Teresa de Mier.* New York: Harper & Row, 1971.

Mier Noriega y Guerra, José Servando Teresa de. *The Memoirs of Fray Servando Teresa de Mier.* New York: Oxford University Press, 1988.

Van Young, Eric. *The Other Rebellion: Popular Violence, Ideology, and the Mexican Struggle for Independence, 1810–1821.* Stanford: Stanford University Press, 2001.

JAIME E. RODRÍGUEZ O.

MIER Y TERÁN, MANUEL (1789–1832).

MIER Y TERÁN, MANUEL (1789–1832). Manuel Mier y Terán (*b.* 18 February 1789; *d.* 3 July 1832), Mexican military figure and independence leader. Born in Mexico City, Mier studied at the School of Mines. In 1812 he joined the insurgents, distinguishing himself in combat. After the death of José María Morelos in 1815, he tried, but failed, to assume unified command of the insurgent movement. Later, he served as minister of war and marine. He was subsequently appointed inspector general of the army.

In 1827 Mier assumed command of the commission to define the boundary between Mexico and the United States, a task that highlighted the dangers that Anglo-American immigration posed to Texas. Although he successfully participated in the 1832 revolt against the regime of Anastasio Bustamante and was widely considered the leading candidate for the presidency, he became deeply depressed by the situation in Texas and took his life in a vain effort to galvanize his countrymen to action.

See also **Mexico, Wars and Revolutions: Revolt of 1832.**

BIBLIOGRAPHY

Lucas Alamán, *Historia de Méjico desde los primeros movimientos que prepararon su Independencia en el año de 1808, hasta la época presente,* 5 vols. (1985).

Ohland Morton, *Terán and Texas: A Chapter in Texas-Mexican Relations* (1948).

Additional Bibliography

Jackson, Jack, editor. *Texas by Terán: The Diary Kept by General Manuel de Mier y Terán on His 1828 Inspection of Texas.* Austin: University of Texas Press, 2000.

JAIME E. RODRÍGUEZ O.

MIGNONE, FRANCISCO (1897–1986).

Francisco Mignone (*b.* 3 September 1897; *d.* 19 February 1986), Brazilian pianist, composer, conductor, and leading figure in the nationalist movement in music. Son of an Italian immigrant musician, he studied piano and flute with his father. At an early age he played both instruments in local dance orchestras and demonstrated an amazing facility for improvisation and the ability to absorb the various styles of popular music. His first compositions date from the year 1917 and display a romantic improvisational style as well as an interest in national subjects. In 1920 Mignone received a scholarship for European study from the São Paulo Committee of Artistic Grants and left Brazil in August to study composition at the Giuseppe Verdi Conservatory in Milan, Italy. Most of his teachers had received their musical training in France (Vincenzo Ferroni, his composition teacher, had been a pupil of Massenet). Following the completion of his formal studies in 1922, Mignone stayed for several years in Europe, occasionally conducting, presenting programs of his own works, and studying opera repertoire. His first opera, *L'innocente,* received its premiere in Brazil in 1928, shortly after Mignone's return to his native country. A review of the performance by Mário de Andrade, leader of the nationalist movement, praised the musical qualities of the work while at the same time challenging Mignone to reconsider his position and abilities as a national composer. Mignone accepted the challenge and embarked on a serious period of writing works on national subjects and works based on urban musical ideas.

The period from 1929 to 1959, his most productive period of composition, revealed an intense interest in folk and popular traditions. Mignone's facile pen, improvisational facility, and keyboard skills have produced a large number of works of uneven quality. His compositional style is perhaps best described by Luiz Heitor Correa de Azevedo, who wrote: "His [Mignone's] is a singular spirit, practical and shrewd, capable of perceiving and adapting itself to the more subtle variations of popular taste. The enormous musical facility he possesses gives to all his works a quality of improvisation which takes its path through many diverse positions" (*Música e músicos,* p. 301).

In works such as his *Festa das igrejas* (1940), Mignone demonstrates a brilliance and originality of conception which have charmed audiences in Brazil, Europe, and the United States. His twelve *Valsas de esquina* (Street-corner Waltzes) give the listener sophisticated moments of sounds of bygone days in Rio de Janeiro when popular musicians roamed the streets in night-long revelries. His four *Fantasias brasileiras* represent some of his best writing. Although Mignone had a lifelong attraction to opera, he is at his best in short piano works. A great admirer of Heitor Villa-Lobos, he wrote *Sexta missa,* a mass honoring the eightieth anniversary of the birth of Villa-Lobos in 1967. Mignone is remembered by his colleagues and friends for his gracious spirit of generosity.

See also **Music: Art Music.**

BIBLIOGRAPHY

David P. Appleby, *The Music of Brazil* (1983).

Luíz Heitor Correa De Azevedo, *Música e músicos do Brasil* (1950).

Marion Verhaalen, "The Solo Piano Music of Francisco Mignone and Camargo Guarnieri" (Ed.D. diss., Columbia Univ., 1971).

Additional Bibliography

Capparelli, Cristina. *Três estudos analíticos: Villa-Lobos, Mignone e Camargo Guarnieri.* Porto Alegre, Brazil: Programa de Pós-Graduação em Música, UFRGS, 2000.

Mariz, Vasco. *Francisco Mignone: O homem e a obra.* Rio de Janeiro: Ministério da Cultura, Funarte: EDUERJ, 1997.

DAVID P. APPLEBY

MIGRATION AND MIGRATIONS.

All humans, at least all those living outside our East African cradle, descend from immigrants, from those Homo sapiens who began leaving humanity's ancestral homeland some 50,000 years ago and eventually spread throughout the planet. But this condition is particularly true of the inhabitants of the New World. *Orbe novo,* a term coined soon after Columbus's first voyage, reflected the specific perspective of late-fifteenth-century Europeans but it conveys too an ampler reality. The New World is also "new" in the context of humanity. It was the last major region of the planet to be populated, and it was populated by immigrants from all other continents.

The first to arrive did so, according to moderate estimates drawn from physical evidence, some 14,000 years ago across the land bridge that became later the Bering Strait. Other anthropologists using DNA studies posit at least four separate migrations taking place between thirty and nine thousand years ago. Whatever the dates of arrival, geneticists maintain that the actual number of immigrants from northwestern Asia was relatively small—no more than a few hundred individuals—and that the Amerindian population grew basically by natural increase, reaching anywhere from forty to one hundred million by 1500.

This essay will cover population movements after that date in three sections. The first examines immigration to Latin America during the colonial period from Africa and particularly from Europe since there is an entry on slavery in this encyclopedia. The second covers European and Asian immigration after independence, especially during the peak period between the middle of the nineteenth century and the World Depression of 1930. The third examines emigration from Latin America, and international movements within the region, mainly after the 1950s.

COLONIAL IMMIGRATIONS, 1492–1820

The largest human inflow to the Western Hemisphere during the colonial period originated in Western Africa between the Senegal and Congo rivers and in Angola and Mozambique. Before 1820 Africans outnumbered Europeans more than three to one among arrivals to the Americas (8.4 versus 2.4 million), even though the resident white population outnumbered that of blacks then twelve to eleven million because of their higher rates of survival and reproduction. It was only after the middle of the nineteenth century that the European inflow surpassed the one out of Africa. The African slave trade was by no means restricted to the Americas. Slave trades across the Sahara and Indian Ocean had began much earlier (the ninth century), lasted longer (into the twentieth century), and carried a similar number of people (twelve million who ended up in North Africa, the Middle East, and the Indian Ocean basin). Nonetheless, the transatlantic passage is clearly one of the largest long-distance slave traffics in human history. Between 1492 and the 1860s some 11.3 million Africans were forcibly taken to the New World according to the latest estimates. The trade peaked in the eighteenth century. But one-third of the total arrived after the official abolition of the slave trade by the British parliament in 1807, heading mainly to Cuba and Brazil, the last two countries to abolish slavery in the Americas, in 1886 and 1888 respectively.

The African slave population concentrated along the tropical or semitropical coastal lowlands of the Western Hemisphere, where tropical cash crops could be planted and easily taken to ports for export. Close to 40 percent of the total were sent to Brazil, originally to the coastal Northeast and later also to Minas Gerais (during the gold boom of the first half of the eighteenth century) and to São Paulo (during the coffee boom of the second half of the nineteenth century). The proportion that headed to Spanish America varied dramatically with time. Before the middle of the seventeenth century, when only one-twentieth of the total inflow of slaves to the Americas had arrived and when British and French colonies had barely entered the trade, Spanish America accounted for six-tenths of the imports. But that proportion dropped to less than one-tenth during the eighteenth century and increased to one-fourth during the nineteenth century, almost all of it to Cuba. In total, Spanish America, other than Cuba, did not represent a major destination. Indeed more slaves went to tiny Saint-Domingue (later Haiti) or even tinier Jamaica than to the entire Spanish American mainland. Overall, only about 8 percent of the total went there, concentrating on the Caribbean coast, particularly of Venezuela and Colombia, and the Pacific coast of Colombia, Ecuador, and Peru; another 9 percent headed for the Spanish Caribbean, mainly Cuba, and mainly during the nineteenth century.

Neither did slaves represent a high proportion of the total population in the Spanish mainland colonies. The highest case, Venezuela in 1800, reached only 6 percent, and 26 percent on the coast. By comparison, that same year about half of the population in Brazil and one-third in Cuba were enslaved. The proportion in Cuba reached a peak of 43 percent in 1841, a figure similar to that of the U.S. South (40 percent) before abolition. These proportions have only been matched in world history by Italy during the first century of the Roman Empire, and they were surpassed by islands in the West Indies such as Jamaica and Haiti, where 90 percent of the population was enslaved by the end of the eighteenth century. So although slavery may be one of the most common and widespread labor systems in human history, slave societies like those that developed in the plantation complexes of the Americas are actually quite rare. And it is reasonable to assume that the negative legacies of such systems are equally unusual in their force and persistence.

Europe. Although scattered individuals from all over the world could be found in the Americas during colonial times, the other important migratory stream came from Europe. Explorers and settlers came from

Emigration to Latin America during the colonial and national periods

[in thousands]

Colonial period[a]		National period		%
European		European[b]		
From Spain	900	Italy	6,710	39.9
From Portugal	700	Spain	5,380	32.0
Total Europe	**1,600**	Portugal	1,850	11.0
		Germany	470	2.8
African		Eastern European		
To Brazil	4,030	Jews	420	2.5
To Spanish		Levant	410	2.4
America	1,662	France	360	2.1
Total Africa	**5,692**	Others	1,220	7.3
		Total Europe	**16,820**	**100**
		Asian[c]		
		China	360	42.1
		Japan	320	37.4
		Korea (post-1950)	175	20.5
		Total Asia	**855**	**100**

[a]colonial period=up to 1820 for Europe and 1860s for Africa
[b]Some 81 percent of all postcolonial European immigration (13.6 million) arrived before 1930; 1 percent (.25 million) between 1930 and 1945; and the remaining 18 percent (3 million) after World War II.
[c]73 percent of the Japanese and 90 percent of Chinese arrived before World War II; almost all Koreans arrived after the 1950s.

Table 1

important colonial powers such as France and the Netherlands, minor ones such as Denmark and Sweden, and even noncolonial polities such as Italian city-states. But the bulk arrived through three specific streams. Some 450,000 Spaniards came to the Indies during the first century-and-a-half of explorations and conquest and a similar number arrived during the rest of the colonial period (see Table 1). The total figure approximates the one million Europeans (three-quarters of them British and the rest mainly from German states) that reached the British domains in the mainland and the Caribbean before 1800. Data for colonial Portuguese migration to Brazil are less reliable. The highest estimates reach a million and the most common ones half that number, agreeing that the bulk arrived in the eighteenth century after the discovery of gold and diamonds in Minas Gerais in 1695.

The impact of this inflow on the Americas is difficult to exaggerate. At the most primary or ecological level, human migration brought along other organisms of all sizes, from bacteria to cattle, that radically transformed the local flora and fauna. Wheat, barley, lettuce, cabbage, onions, garlic, carrots, lentils, spinach, eggplant, grapes, apples, pears, peaches, oranges, sugar cane, bananas, pigs, rabbits, horses, donkeys, sheep, goats, dogs, cats, chickens, bees, and numerous other plants and animals were introduced to the Western Hemisphere by Spaniards. Rats, smallpox, other pathogens, and most of the unwanted grasses or "weeds" in the Americas tagged along. This transformation of the hemisphere's biota had momentous demographic, economic, and social consequences. Smallpox and other Old World viruses for which the indigenous population had little immunity caused the greatest demographic catastrophe in human history, killing as many as nine-tenths of the New World's aboriginal inhabitants. Plow animals and cereal made possible extensive agriculture and large landed estates. Sugar cane had a similar effect on the tropical lowlands of the hemisphere. Cattle and horses allowed the formation of the ranching economies and cultural types of the American plains, from the gauchos of the River Plate region and the *llaneros* of Venezuela to the *charros* of northern Mexico and cowboys of the U.S. West.

The sociocultural influence of the Iberian newcomers was obviously most pronounced in the regions where they and their descendants came to represent a larger proportion of the total population: temperate South America and smaller areas such as the uplands of Antioquia and Caldas in Colombia, parts of northern Mexico, the central highlands of Costa Rica and Puerto Rico, and Cuba before the middle of the eighteenth century. These became basically areas of European settlement during the colonial period similar to those in northeastern Anglo- and Franco-America. But the Iberian cultural influence was dramatic even in regions where *peninsulares* and their American-born descendants were a minority.

This influence is palpable and obvious in language, literature, law, religion, urban planning, public and domestic architecture, eating habits, music, and high and folk art. In colonial Brazil more than two hundred languages disappeared in the confrontation with Portuguese. In Spanish America, the fact that during the first century of colonization the inflow came basically from Andalusia, Estremadura, and New Castile, rather than Spain in general, reinforced the Castilian roots of the region—just as the English, rather than British, nature of immigration to North America during the first century of colonization buttressed the Anglo foundations of the United States and Canada. Even some Latin American cultural artifacts that came to be seen as quintessentially indigenous—such as the bowler hats, traditional *polleras* (skirts), and *charangos* (small guitars) of the Andean region—are actually Castilian imports from the sixteenth century.

This history of immigration distinguishes Latin America from the rest of the developing or postcolonial world. Nowhere in the Afro-Asiatic world did European culture penetrate so deeply.

In some regions the Iberian colonizers and their descendants came to represent the majority, making these areas more akin to a southern European version of Australia than to any postcolonial country in Africa or Asia. Where this did not happen, populations nonetheless became much more Hispanized or Lusitanized than people in colonies in Africa or Asia became Gallicized or Anglicized. Even in the least Europeanized countries of the region—say, Guatemala or Bolivia—Spanish and Christianity are almost universal, in dramatic contrast to the situation in India, Indonesia, Indochina, Iraq, Iran, or the Ivory Coast, to use just one letter in the postcolonial alphabet. Moreover, European colonialism in Latin America began and ended much earlier and lasted much longer. This often made the Iberian cultural imprint invisible precisely because it was so deep and buried in time that it appeared to most observers as local, natural, indigenous.

Iberian colonial immigration—and the vast majority of arrivals were immigrants rather than conquistadors or even colonizers—thus gave Latin America whatever cultural meaning it has as a concept or category. The Iberian cultural imprint is the only commonality that warrants including countries like the Dominican Republic (where 90 percent of the population traces its roots, at least partially, to Africa), Guatemala (where a similar proportion descends fully or partially from the pre-Columbian population), and Argentina (where more than half of the population is of non-Spanish European stock) in the same category. We often tend to stress the diversity of Latin America. Some would even point out the arbitrariness of the concept. But in comparison to any other continent, the concept is anything but arbitrary, and what is remarkable about Latin America is the degree of cultural unity and shared codes over such a vast geographical expanse. After all, a Dominican, a Guatemalan, and an Argentinean can laugh at the same joke, while a Greek, a German, and a Pole would have to use a lingua franca and probably miss the pun in translation.

Iberian immigration not only gave Latin Americans a shared culture but also, and somewhat ironically, a separate sense of identity from the motherlands that was forged in part through exclusion. Arrivals from Spain consistently excluded the colonial-born Creoles from the top echelons of the imperial government. They accounted for all but four of the 170 viceroys in the history of colonial Spanish America; and even the four Creoles had been the sons of Spanish officials. Of 602 governors and captain generals all but fourteen had been born in the Old World. The situation was similar within the church's hierarchy, with the Spanish-born accounting for more than four-fifths of all the bishops and archbishops that ever served in the colonies. During the seventeenth and first half of the eighteenth centuries Creoles at least had been able to acquire mid-level government positions, often by purchasing them from a chronically bankrupt crown. The last five or six decades of colonial rule, however, witnessed a reassertion of imperial control. These so-called Bourbon Reforms, and Pombalian in the case of Portuguese America, were rooted ideologically in enlightened despotism and mercantilism. But it was an upsurge of Iberian immigration that made them possible.

The surge arrived through two different channels. One was recruitment by imperial institutions: the civil administration, army, and church. This one provided the personnel for the reinvigorated imperialism that some historians claim amounted to a reconquest of the colonies. It supplied the legion of intendants, or new regional officers, who centralized royal control by fusing other provincial posts and reporting directly to the viceroy and directly to king on matters of finance. It also supplied many of the officers and soldiers for an imperial army that for the first time became an important presence in the colonies. The other flow was channeled through private mechanisms of kinship and commercial networks that resembled those of postcolonial migration to Latin America or the Americas in general. Most of these folks arrived penniless or at least in modest pecuniary conditions. But most of them also arrived with connections to well-to-do relatives (the stereotypical case being an uncle) or *paisanos*, people from the same town or *comarca* (a micro-region or socio-geographic space that is not necessarily an administrative unit, where people have face-to-face interaction; the closest English translation being "shire"). These connections, plus hard work and determination, allowed many of the newcomers to rise within the colonial social ladder and, as a group, to control international and wholesale trade and much of the mining economy.

The immigrants' political and economic dominance inevitably provoked resentment from the local population and other factors intensified such feelings. The fact that the European-born made up only one percent of the white population, which in turn accounted for about one-fifth of all the inhabitants of Ibero-America circa 1800, could not help but underscore the disproportion of their power and influence. People of color—who were excluded from political office, schools, and certain trades by law—would presumably resent white privilege in general. Their most direct exploiters, landlords and plantation owners, tended to be Creole, and during the wars of independence they often took the loyalist side. But support for the king could, and did, coexist with popular Hispanophobia, as the mob's cries during Hidalgo's revolt in Mexico indicated: "Viva Fernando VII and death to the *gachupines*!" [a term of scorn for Spaniards].

The immigrants' success grated on Creoles more directly. Unlike the population of color, they were not officially excluded from public positions or any economic activity. But legal equality raised aspirations that it did not meet and made factual inequality seem more blatant. Creole exclusion from high- and mid-level public office was so thorough as to make it evident that it could not be the result of anything else but systematic discrimination. The source of the Iberian newcomers' commercial success was less apparent. Some of it had to do with their work ethic and resolve. Creoles themselves portrayed the newcomers as hard-working and thrifty, neither of which was necessarily meant as a compliment. But Spaniards' control of transatlantic trade through their *consulado*, or merchant guild, made it clear that their success also rested on monopoly. They were indeed the most visible beneficiaries of the resurgent imperial mercantilism that grieved everyone else by curtailing contraband, limiting consumer choices, and raising prices.

A shift in the regional origins of the immigrants, from the southern half of the peninsula (Andalusia, Estremadura, Castile, and southern and central Portugal) to the northern half (Galicia, Mino, Catalonia, and the Basque country), aggravated the situation. These were people whose native language was not Spanish, that is, Castilian. Their ethnic identities were different from those of the ancestors of most Creoles. Basques, the most numerous and the most commercially successful of these northerners, seemed particularly foreign. They spoke a language that was completely incomprehensible to the residents of the colonies. This, their ethno-cultural distinction in general, and their overrepresentation in the guilds that monopolized transatlantic trade made them seem particularly clannish. The ethno-cultural differences of these northern Iberian immigrants and their economic success amplified the arrogance that colonizers habitually display vis-à-vis the colonized. They often depicted Creoles as indolent and unreliable and—not unrelated—as of dubious racial purity. The fact that most of the arrivals were single young men—plus their economic upward mobility—intensified their competition with Creoles for available white women. It is no coincidence that laws prohibiting Spaniards from marrying Creole women were among the first pieces of legislation passed by the new Latin American republics.

The origins of political independence thus can be found, in large part, in Iberian immigration. Patriotic manifestos made grand pronouncements against the crown and for liberty. But Creoles' sense of an identity separate from that of the imperial motherland, a sine qua non of any anticolonial struggle, was fueled less by gripes against a faraway monarch than by resentment against immigrant neighbors and their monopoly of political office and international trade, their privilege in other occupations, their competition in the marriage market, and their imperious attitudes. As with other political creeds, Creole protonationalism was not simply inspired by the ideals of the French Enlightenment, the example of the United States, or other ideological influences. It also had less abstract, more quotidian and existential roots.

POSTCOLONIAL IMMIGRATION

The three or four decades following emancipation witnessed an early population outflow from, and a modest inflow to, the newly independent nations of Latin America. Early on, many Spaniards and other loyalists left for Cuba and Puerto Rico or returned to Spain. The Mexican government expelled seven thousand of them between 1827 and 1833. As to the arrivals, among the first were mercenaries and volunteers who had fought on the patriot side during the wars of independence. Six thousand Irish and British soldiers fought with Simón Bolívar's armies, and many of those who survived stayed in South America. So did some of the four thousand Irish and German mercenaries recruited by the Brazilian government in 1827–1828 to fight against Argentina, an episode that included the Great Mercenary Revolt of June 1828 in Rio de Janeiro.

Merchant-adventurers, mostly British, seeking opportunities in markets recently opened to free international trade, plus a motley crew of clerks, technicians, artisans, sailors, and artisans formed a second type of early comers and settled mostly in port cities. A British traveler claimed two thousand compatriots lived in Valparaiso in 1828. The cities of the Río de la Plata developed the largest concentration. By the early 1840s some 60 percent of Montevideo's 31,000 inhabitants were foreign born. Across the river, one-third of the 91,000 denizens of Buenos Aires in 1855 had been born overseas, with Italy, France, Spain, and Britain showing the highest numbers.

Farmers, usually recruited by government agencies and/or private contractors for rural colonization schemes, made up the third and largest group of immigrants before the mid-1800s. Many were German-speaking people. Between 1824 and 1850 ten thousand of them founded rural colonies in the southern Brazilian states of Rio Grande do Sul and Santa Catarina. The first of more than sixty German agricultural colonies in Argentina appeared in 1826. About five thousand Germans had settled in southern Chile by the 1850s. Canary Islanders were another common group among these early recruited colonists. They made up the majority of the 13,000 foreigners who entered Venezuela between 1810 and 1860, as they had done during the colonial period in that region of the empire. In the 1830s they appear as contracted laborers in Cuba, Uruguay, and Argentina. The latter two countries also received tens of thousands of French and Spanish Basque and Irish shepherds during this early period. They pioneered the formation of what would become the largest sheep herds in the world by the end of the century, playing an instrumental role in the agro-pastoral development of the pampas.

An estimate given by various historians of 200,000 Europeans entering Argentina, Uruguay, and Brazil between 1816 and 1850 seems high but accurately conveys the disproportionately southern concentration of the inflow already by this early period. At mid-century a few square blocks in Montevideo housed more immigrants than all of Colombia, where the entire European and North American population numbered 850. The only exception to this Southern Cone predominance had already surfaced in Cuba, which received some 50,000 Europeans, mainly Spaniards, between 1820 and 1850.

The transatlantic crossings that had begun modestly after the Napoleonic and Latin American independence wars gathered steam after the mid-century, became massive after the 1880s, and lasted—with a pause during World War I—until the Great Depression. During the entire period, more than 51 million Europeans and about 2 million Asians headed for the New World. Nothing remotely resembling this movement had ever happened before anywhere in the planet. By the outbreak of World War I, more people had come to the New World during the preceding decade than had done so, from both Europe and Africa, during the entire colonial period. Indeed, by then more Europeans had disembarked in the port of Buenos Aires alone during the previous *three years* (1.1 million) than had arrived in all of Spanish America during more than *three centuries* of colonial rule.

Overall, 13.6 million Europeans came to Latin America from the end of the independence wars to 1930 (see Table 2). This represented almost one quarter (24%) of the 56 million Europeans who left their continent during the period and 27 percent of all those who went to the New World. The regional sources, however, differed from the flow elsewhere. Emigration to Australia, New Zealand, Canada, and South Africa—which together received 10 million Europeans, or 18 percent of the total exodus—originated overwhelmingly in northwestern Europe, particularly the British Isles. In the United States—which received 32.6 million European immigrants, or 58 percent of the total—the flow originated also from northwestern Europe almost exclusively (97 percent) before 1880. After that the proportion dropped to 42 percent as southern and eastern Europe joined the stream. In Latin America the inflow was heavily southern European. Italy alone accounted for almost four-tenths of all newcomers, Spain for three-tenths,

European immigration to Latin American countries, c. 1840–1930

Country	Number (in thousands)	% of total
Argentina	6,501	47.9
Brazil	4,361	32.1
Cuba	1,394	10.3
Uruguay	713	5.3
Mexico	270	2.0
Chile	90	0.7
Venezuela	70	0.5
Puerto Rico	62	0.5
Peru	35	0.3
Paraguay	21	0.2
Others	50	0.4
Total	**13,567**	
		% going to Latin America
All European emigration	56,238	24.1
All European emigration to New World	51,244	26.6

Table 2

and Portugal for one one-tenth. The two peninsulas of southwestern Europe thus supplied close to 80 percent of the arrivals. Regional origins within these southern European countries were, however, heavily northern.

In the case of Italy, the northern preponderance reflected time of arrival. Unlike European migration in general, which acquired massive dimensions in the United States earlier than it did in Latin America, Italian migration to South America reached massive numbers earlier in Latin America. During the nineteenth century the stream toward that region was twice as large as that to North America. By 1900 the Italian community in Buenos Aires was larger than the ten largest in North America combined; and São Paulo, Montevideo, and Rosario had more Italians than any U.S. city other than New York. The fact that the upper strip of the peninsula dominated the transatlantic exodus for much of the nineteenth century gave these early Italian enclaves in Latin America a strong northern imprint. Liguria (the coastal region surrounding Genoa) supplied the single largest contingent in Argentinean cities; the Piedmont played that role in the pampas and the Veneto in Brazil. During the twentieth century the Mezzogiorno increased its participation. But northerners retained an overall majority for the entire period in Latin America, in stark contrast to the United States, where southerners accounted for four-fifths of all Italian immigrants.

The northern prevalence had even earlier origins in the case of Spain. As noted before, the Cantabric seaboard had replaced Andalusia and the South as the main source of migration to the Indies already by the eighteenth century. The trend continued during the nineteenth century in spite of significant migration from the Canary Islands to Cuba and Venezuela. Basques became the Iberian equivalent of the Piedmontese in the River Plate region: pioneer settlers of the grasslands. Their early arrival and concentration on pastoral activities earned them enough wealth and prestige to popularize the idea that the *estanciero* oligarchy was mostly ethnically Basque. Asturians were particularly numerous in Mexico and Cuba. Catalans spread throughout much of Spanish America. These so-called Jews of Spain seem to have shared the same dichotomous stereotype as frugal entrepreneurs or radical anarchists. At least the second half of the cliché may not have been an arbitrary invention. Catalans and Jews were the most overrepresented ethnic groups in the anarchist movement both in Europe and the Americas. Galicians became the largest group in all receiving countries. Their numbers and visibility made *gallego* a generic term for "Spaniards" in Latin America, and "gallego jokes" became in Spanish America the equivalent of Polish jokes in the United States or Portuguese jokes in Brazil.

The northern shift among the latter group was also well established already in the late colonial period. By the early 1800s the small region of Minho in the northwestern corner of Portugal provided half of all immigrants in Brazil. Around 1850 more than a third of the Portuguese residents of Rio de Janeiro had been born in the city of Porto, in the Douro region just south of Minho. From this northwestern corner emigration spread to other northern regions, and by the early twentieth century Trás-os-Montes in the northeast and the Beiras just to the south had become major sources. Brazil attracted the bulk (about four-fifths) of Portugal's exodus. But this predominance of the northern mainland characterized only the movement to Brazil rather than Portuguese migration in general. As in the case of Italy we find a sharp contrast between crossings to South America and those to the United States, where 70 percent of Portuguese immigrants originated in the Azores and much of the remainder in Madeira and the Cape Verde Islands.

The remaining one-fifth of European immigrants in Latin America who did not come from the Italian and Iberian peninsulas numbered close to 3 million people, and ethnic Germans represented the largest single group. The majority came from Germany itself. But large numbers came from elsewhere and are difficult to identify in international migration records that categorize people by state or empire of provenance rather than by ethno-linguistic criteria. If one assumes conservatively that half of the Swiss arrivals, one-fifth of those originating in Austro-Hungary, and one-tenth of those from Russia were ethnic Germans (Volga Germans in the latter case), and adds the number to those officially counted as Germans, 300,000 German-speaking people entered Argentina up to the 1930s and a similar number went to Brazil. Southern Chile and Uruguay received more than 30,000 each. And smaller Germanophone communities can be found throughout Latin America, from Plautdietsch-speaking Mennonites in the Paraguayan

Chaco and in Chihuahua and Durango in Mexico to the Austrian Tyrolese towns of Oxapampa and Pozuzo in the Selva Alta of Peru and the Puerto Plata region in the Dominican Republic. A German geographer estimated the number of his co-ethnics in Latin America at 2 million in 1930. Estimates of German descendants in the region today range from 8 to 14 million.

Other immigrants came from a variety of places in Europe. France joined early and accounted for as much as one-tenth of the stream in the nineteenth century but diminished its participation after 1900. Overall, it sent about 340,000 of its citizens to Latin America, or less than 3 percent of the European total. Close to three-quarters of these went to Argentina. Eastern Europeans were more numerous but difficult to identify because of the multiethnic nature of the polities in the region, their changing boundaries, and even their shifting existence. Argentina, for example, recorded the entry of 180,000 Poles and 48,000 Yugoslavs after World War I but none before. Both groups were simply included then among the 177,000 "Russians" and 111,000 Austro-Hungarians listed in Argentinean entry records. It is difficult to say what proportion of this half-million immigrants consisted of Slavic people of various and shifting nationalities. But if half were, the figure would approximate the 240,000 "Slavs" an American geographer claimed resided in the three southernmost Brazilian states in 1930.

Jews made such a large proportion of eastern European immigrants that *ruso*, and less often *polaco*, became generic terms for the Ashkenazim in South America. Unlike Italian immigration, which acquired massive dimensions in South America before it did in the United States, Jewish migration there took off even later than to the north. The first significant movement appears in 1889 with the arrival of a thousand settlers at Moisés Ville, an agricultural colony in the Argentinean province of Santa Fe funded by the Munich-born philanthropist Baron Maurice de Hirsch. Fifteen more of these colonies were founded in the pampas in the following decades, and by 1920 they housed about 30,000 "Jewish gauchos"—to use the title of a famous novel by Alberto Gerchunoff. By then, however, Jewish immigration had become massive, spontaneous rather than recruited by the colonization association, and urban. Between 1880 and 1930, 200,000 Jews arrived in Argentina, some nine-tenths of them from eastern Europe. Another 45,000, mainly refugees, made it between 1930 and 1943. A municipal census of 1936 counted over 120,000 Jews residing in Buenos Aires. Although Jews migrated during the period to all Latin American countries, only two other countries received significant, although smaller, numbers: Brazil, 65,000; and Uruguay, 22,000.

Overall, Europeans came from every corner of their native continent, and even from elsewhere. Afrikaner refugees left South Africa after the Boer War to settle in Patagonia and, in smaller numbers, Mexico. Some 50,000 people, many of them European-born, left the United States and Canada for Cuba during the first two decades of the twentieth century, including rural settlers who founded eighty agricultural colonies. Between 8,000 and 10,000 Southerners emigrated to Latin America, mainly to Mexico, after the Confederate defeat in the American Civil War. And Middle Eastern emigration, restricted mainly to European Turkey and the Levant, formed part of the late phase of the transatlantic wave rather than of Asian migration.

Many of the 340,000 Middle Easterners who came to Latin America (175,000 of them to Argentina, 95,000 to Brazil, and 70,000 elsewhere) entered as *turcos* because they traveled with Ottoman passports. But few were actually Turks or even Muslims. The vast majority were members of religious minorities in the Ottoman Empire and its successor states. Sephardim (the descendants of Spanish and Portuguese Jews) from Constantinople, Salonica, and North Africa, and Mizrahim (Arab Jews) from Aleppo and other towns in the Levant migrated to the River Plate region, where they were heavily outnumbered by Ashkenazim, and also to countries such as Mexico and Cuba, where they made up a larger proportion of local Jewry. Armenians, a group that was already dispersed throughout the Middle East before moving across the Atlantic, came from a variety of countries. Those in Argentina, which today has the ninth-largest Armenian population in the world (130,000), came mostly from Cilicia (the southeastern coast of Turkey) after the massacres of Adana in 1909. The two next-largest Armenian communities in Latin America are in Brazil (40,000) and Uruguay (19,000). Palestinians from Bethlehem and a handful of other Christian towns went mostly to Chile, which has the largest concentration of Palestinians in the world outside of the Middle East; Honduras, where they make up 2 percent of the national population; and El Salvador. Christian Maronites from Mount Lebanon moved in large numbers to the classic countries of immigration in South America. But they found their way to every single country in the Western Hemisphere. Even within the traditional host countries they moved to regions, such as the Andean Northwest of Argentina and the Northeast of Brazil, where few European newcomers settled.

Besides those who came from the Middle East, about 580,000 Asians came to Latin America before World War II. Six-tenths of these were Chinese and the rest mostly Japanese. The first Asians to arrive as an organized group in the New World did so in 1810, when a hundred Chinese tea workers were brought to São Paulo to help introduce tea cultivation in that state. But this failed to generate a steady flow (only 5,000 Chinese went to Brazil in the next two centuries), and the first massive Asian movement in the Americas headed for Cuba. Between 1847 and 1875 as many as 175,000 Chinese coolies arrived on the island to work on sugar plantations, and Cuba had the largest Chinese community in the world outside of Asia well into the twentieth century. Coastal Peru became the second-largest recipient of Chinese coolies during the period (as many as 100,000). And northern Mexico (with some 30,000) was the only other important destination for the Chinese in Latin America, most arriving as free laborers rather than coolies and decades later than in Cuba and Peru. Japanese migration to Latin America is also a later phenomenon. The first Japanese group landed in São Paulo in 1908. By the outbreak of World War II some 188,000 had arrived, and another 66,000 came after the war, making Brazil the country with the largest population of Japanese origin in the world outside of Japan. Peru, which received about 30,000, was the second most important destination, with Mexico and Argentina following with 15,000 and 5,000 respectively.

Why Did They Come? Why did more than 14 million people migrate to Latin America between the middle of the nineteenth century and the 1920s? The most common single answer to this question emphasizes the efforts of governments and economic elites to attract and recruit immigrants. This does explain most of Asian immigration, which consisted mainly of Chinese coolies and Japanese contracted laborers. It also explains migration to the coffee regions of São Paulo and many other smaller flows, particularly to countries of little immigration, that were organized by political authorities and/or planters. But it does not explain the immigration of the vast majority of the 13.6 million Europeans who arrived during that period.

Ruling classes across Latin America did attempt to promote European immigration to "whiten" and "civilize" their countries during the nineteenth and early twentieth centuries. But elite desiderata had little to do with the actual inflow of people. Politicians, planters, and bureaucrats in the ten countries that run along or close to the Pacific from Bolivia to Guatemala concocted all sorts of plans—from giving free passages to granting free land—to recruit Europeans as an antidote to "native indolence." Yet all of these countries combined received fewer European immigrants in a century than a single Argentinean province did in a month. And most of the newcomers to the latter country arrived when its political class had long ceased to view them as civilizing agents and had turned rather xenophobic. The "whitening" and "civilizing" rhetoric of Latin American leaders therefore had more to do with the history of elite racism than with the history of the actual migration of millions of people.

The actual migration of millions clearly obeyed mightier laws than those produced in national legislatures. The depiction of the stream to Latin America as officially recruited, in contrast to the "spontaneous" movements to the United States, is simply erroneous. Ninety-eight percent of the Europeans who migrated to Argentina, the principal destination in Latin America, paid for their passages with their own money or with remittances sent by family and friends. This was also the case for the majority of European migrants to Latin America in general. These crossings resulted from, and formed part of, vast transformations that during the nineteenth century remained mostly Atlantic-based and later became global. These forces were the same that unleashed the movement of 51 million Europeans to the New World in general. The massive movement of people across the Atlantic was part and parcel of other forms of massification that constructed the modern world.

The most primary of these was the massification of human reproduction. The basic outline of Homo sapiens' demographic history is quite simple: ups and downs, stagnation, and protracted growth for

160,000 years with explosive increase in the last two centuries. It took humanity five thousand generations to reach the first billion (in 1804) and just four generations to reach the second billion (in 1927). This first stage of what eventually would be a global demographic revolution took place in Europe. Fueled by declining mortality rates related to basic improvements in public sanitation and midwifery, that continent's population tripled from 140 million in 1750 to 430 million in 1900, as its share of the world's inhabitants rose from 17 to 25 percent. This "vital revolution" directly fed the massive transatlantic exodus. It also facilitated that exodus indirectly by creating a mass market for New World temperate foodstuff that had not existed in the colonial period. Migration and trade became intimately tied. Europe exported people mostly to the regions from which it imported grain and, later, meat. Indeed, over 90 percent of the 56 million Europeans who left their native continent during this period headed for those wheat- and beef-exporting regions (temperate South and North America and Australia/New Zealand).

The massification of production associated with the Industrial Revolution fueled transatlantic emigration in a variety of ways. During its early stages it displaced more workers than it could employ. It promoted internal mobility and urbanization, which often served as a stepping-stone to overseas movement. Urbanization, in turn, further increased the demand for American staples from people who did not grow their own food. Besides this demand for food, industrialization made possible the general international division of labor on which the commercial integration of the Atlantic world rested. It created direct demands for a variety of American raw materials: hides for machine belts and tallow for soap and lubricants from the huge feral cattle herds of the River Plate early in the century; wool from the same region after the industrialization of woolen production in the mid-1800s; natural rubber from the Amazon after Charles Goodyear developed vulcanization around the same time; timber from Canada; flax for textiles, oil paints, and printer's ink from the pampas and the prairies. The increasing variety of articles churned out by industry generated a different sort of demands and desires particularly among the young, the principal font of transatlantic migrants. Contemporary popular theater in Europe abounds with characters who blame the exodus on this consumer culture, on the younger generation's acquisitiveness and their cravings for factory-made shoes and garments instead of homespun espadrilles and blouses, for watches, guns, phonographs, bicycles, and other gadgets of the industrial age.

Emigration "fever" (a metaphor that surfaced in the nineteenth century across Europe) spread mostly through primary transnational social networks but could not have diffused so far and so densely without the technological and organizational transformations that made mass communication possible. The appearance of the telegraph (1844), the photograph (1840s), cheap, machine-made, wood-pulp paper (1850s), the mail system and the postage stamp (1850s), typewriters (1860s), the Universal Postal Union (which unified international postal regulations, 1875), the telephone (1876), photoengraving (1880s), the linotype (1886), and the radio (1895) spawned a veritable revolution in mass communication that made the mass movement of people possible then and not before.

The mail system and the telegraph facilitated the circulation of another essential connective element in mass migration: money. Immigrant remittances flowed eastward and paid for the passages of new streams of people moving westward. European financiers sent much of the surplus capital generated by the industrial revolution to the countries where the remittances were coming from. These investments and loans stimulated economic growth in the receiving countries, which in turn stimulated more emigration to them and more remittances from them. It is no coincidence that the four most important receivers of European immigrants in the nineteenth century (the United States, Argentina, Canada, and Brazil) also became the four most important recipients of British investment and the four fastest-growing economies in the Western Hemisphere.

Mass transoceanic migration required, however, inexpensive means to move not only information, photographs, and dreams but also people, and it was the trade of the Industrial Revolution, rather than trade in general, that provided the impetus for technological innovation. International trade before the nineteenth century was limited to precious minerals, luxury goods, and the slave labor to produce them. Galleons, sails, and sextants could easily accommodate this trade. But as heavy and bulky items with limited value per weight or mass (such as coal, iron, machinery, timber, cotton, wool, or wheat) became the main commodities of trade, advancements in the means of transporting them became a necessity, and the technological innovations that the Industrial Revolution unleashed made them possible. From the mid-1800s on, steamships, screw propellers, iron (and later steel) hulls, and diesel marine engines kept cutting down fuel consumption and pushing up speed. Refrigerated ships made possible the export of South American beef and mutton to Europe. Trains extended the pool of prospective emigrants from a few port areas into the European hinterland. Trains took them across the American continents. Trains allowed the riverless Argentinean pampas to become the second major exporter of cereals in the world, and most of that grain was shipped across the Atlantic along the same routes, and often in the same ships, that brought the millions who farmed the grain. The nineteenth-century innovations in marine and land transportation were thus a sine qua non of both massive transatlantic trade and massive transatlantic migration, movements that were intimately connected.

The connections of liberalism and migration were equally multifaceted. The impressive expansion of transatlantic commerce between the 1860s and World War I, which reached an intensity then unmatched before or after, would not have been possible without a significant level of political commitment to free trade. Neither would mass migration have been possible without a similar level of political commitment to freedom of movement. On the western shores of the Atlantic, liberalism provided the ideological fuel for the independence movements that ended the restrictions on entries that colonial gatekeepers had kept. On the other side, liberalism lifted mercantilist restrictions on exits in one European country after another. By strengthening property rights, lifting restrictions, and promoting competition, liberalism stimulated the privatization of commons and the commercialization of agriculture in the Old World. This in turn encouraged transatlantic ties in various ways. It created a demand for New World fertilizers such as Chilean nitrates. It encouraged migration as a means of earning cash to purchase private land plots in the places of origin. It created, in general, greater opportunities and greater insecurity in the European countryside, elements that normally lead, and led in this case, to increased population movement across the land and across the ocean.

Poverty itself, however, was not, contrary to popular assumption, a common cause of emigration. Transatlantic crossings began and acquired greater intensity precisely in the richest countries of Europe, in the most advanced regions within these and other countries, and in the most economically dynamic counties and municipalities within these regions. As we saw, even in the poorer countries of southern Europe that provided the bulk of the emigrants to Latin America, the majority came from the more developed northern regions. Crossing an ocean is an expensive enterprise that requires various forms of capital (money, knowledge, social connections). The poor tended to stay or migrate short distances. Those who went to the Americas were on average better-off and more educated than those who stayed behind. For example, the literacy rates of Italians, Spaniards, and Portuguese in Argentina, Brazil, and Cuba were higher than those of their compatriots back home.

The mass, long-distance movement of people to Latin America cannot be explained, then, either by the policies of Latin American receiving countries or by the poverty of the European sending countries. Instead, mass migration should be seen as an integral part of a broader process of modernization that included the emergence of mass demographic reproduction, mass production, mass communications and transportation, mass trade and financial flows, mass residential patterns (urban societies), and eventually mass politics and consumption. This represented an integrated process that formed the first mass societies in human history and brought about a new level of global integration to parts of the Atlantic world. None of its components would have been possible without the others.

The principal reason European emigrants went to specific destinations was higher wages. Real wages in Argentina and Uruguay were between 1.5 and 3 times higher than in Italy, and higher still than in Spain and Portugal, during the mass migration period. In the other principal destinations in Latin America, southern Brazil and Cuba, they were between 1.5 and 2 times higher than in the southern European sources of immigration. But wages themselves are not some natural, ahistorical arrangement. They were the result of the modernization process that also produced mass migration, of the transition from domestic to capitalist modes of productions. And so were wage differentials. At the most elemental level, high wages in the destination regions of the Americas resulted, as Adam Smith argued, from the positive ratio of natural resources to labor. But this was also the case before 1800, and few Europeans migrated there then. The demand for labor and the resulting high wages in receiving regions came not simply from abundant natural resources and sparse populations but from the development of dynamic economies connected to a transformed Atlantic market.

The case of Argentina illustrates why this became possible in the nineteenth century and not before. The most elemental and potential source of the country's wealth was always there: the pampas, one of the two most fertile and extensive plains in the world. But in 1800 a still small and overwhelmingly rural European population could provide neither a market for the articles the pampas could produce nor the laborers that those thinly populated grasslands needed to produce them (by 1914, 70% of the farmers in the pampas were foreign born). Even if they could have, mercantilist restrictions on the flow of people and goods on both sides of the Atlantic would have prevented it. Even if political restrictions had not existed, technological ones would have prevented it. Oxcarts and sailing vessels could not have taken millions of people and millions of tons of cereals, beef, and mutton from the hinterland to the port and then across the Atlantic. And the capital to build the required infrastructure did not exist on either side of the ocean. As the nineteenth century matured, the dramatic growth of the European population, its increasing urbanization, the emergence of consumer societies, industrialization, steamers, railroads, the lifting of mercantilist restrictions on trade and migration, and sufficient accumulation to usher in the age of international financial capitalism overcame these obstacles, transforming the region from a backwater of the Spanish Empire into the sixth-richest country in the world.

The Consequences of European Immigration. As the last sentence suggests, European immigration and the accompanying transition from mercantile capitalism and colonial status to industrial capitalism and republican semi-dependency shifted the social, economic, and political centers of the Western Hemisphere. Before 1800 the colonial success stories had been based on a combination of indigenous labor and precious metals, or African slavery and tropical cash crops. The silver of Zacatecas and Potosi had turned Mexico and Peru into the shining stars in the firmament of the Spanish Empire. Sugar and slavery had turned Saint-Domingue and Barbados into some of the richest colonies in the world, worth many times more to the French and British than Quebec or the future United States. In terms of the scale, efficiency, and market orientation of production, the most modern economies in the Americas around 1800 could be found in the mining complex of the Mexican Bajío and in the plantations of the West Indies. A century later economic modernity had moved to the factories and commercial farms in regions of European settlement. Free immigration and its accompanying processes had turned the poorest colonies in the Western Hemisphere into its richest countries.

A similar reversal occurred within countries. Argentina's economic center shifted during the nineteenth century from the Northwest or Andean region that had formed part of the silver mining complex of Upper Peru to the Atlantic-facing and immigrant-receiving littoral on the east. In Brazil, the plantation societies of Bahia and the Northeast were replaced as the country's economic center by the previously marginal São Paulo and the South. In the United States, the shift went in the other geographical direction—from the South to the Northeast—but in the same social track from a region of slavery and plantations to one of farms, factories, and immigrants.

The shift in the distribution of urban centers in the Americas illustrates this overall reversal. Before 1800 urban development had concentrated in the Iberian domains which contained forty-five of the fifty largest towns in the New World. The largest, Mexico City, had a larger population than the five largest cities in the United States combined. Whatever their nominal political status, forty-six of the fifty largest cities, including the ten largest, were within the silver/indigenous-labor or plantation/African-slaves complexes that formed the colonial cores. By 1910 the United States and Canada had seventy-seven of the largest one hundred cities in the Americas. The largest, New York, now had more than ten times the population of Mexico City, which had dropped to twelfth place. Whether in South or North America, this reversal was fueled by European immigration. Buenos Aires had risen from fourteenth place in Latin America in 1790 to first a century later. By 1910 the largest eleven cities in the Americas, and eighty-one of the top one hundred, were cities of immigrants. And the five most urban countries (Uruguay, Cuba, Argentina, the United States, and Canada) were the ones with the highest proportion of European immigrants in their populations. Insofar as modernity, whatever its definition, is unfailingly situated in urban spaces, one can argue that the sites of the modern in the Western Hemisphere shifted during the nineteenth century from the colonial cores in Indo/mestizo- and Afro-America to Euro-America, the temperate ends of the hemisphere that had also been its socioeconomic margins, and to Cuba.

Modernity not only shifted spatially but also in its internal content. Economically it shifted—in the new regions of European immigration of the Americas—to a system that was capitalist not only in terms of exchange and commercialization (as it had been in the old colonial core) but also in terms of social relations of production, based on free labor rather than slavery and semi-bondage arrangements. Economic growth acquired here a stronger connection to social welfare.

The regions of European immigration developed the largest and most powerful labor movement in Latin America and one of the most powerful in the world. They had the highest levels of civic participation in mutual aid societies and other voluntary associations; the earliest and most inclusive forms of political participation; the highest nutritional levels; the highest life expectancy and lowest mortality; the highest levels of popular participation in banking and savings; the highest literacy rates; and the highest per capita levels of printed material, theater performances, sport clubs and activities, and other cultural products.

These represented the first mass societies in Latin America. Economic and sociocultural resources were not only more abundant there but also more equally distributed not only than in the rest of Latin America but also—as both Adam Smith and Karl Marx had predicted from opposite ideological perspectives—than in most of Europe. By the 1920s real wages in Argentina and Uruguay were higher than in every European country except England and Switzerland, with which they were tied. Water consumption and home-ownership rates were higher than in any country in the Old World. The children of immigrants grew on average two inches taller than their European-born parents no matter their ethnic origins. The high levels of popular consumption in turn fomented the early development of domestic markets in regions that also had the highest levels of per capita exports in the New World.

The reversal of the socioeconomic regional rank within the Western Hemisphere produced by immigration during the nineteenth century had a lasting effect. Despite the uneven economic performance of the River Plate countries since the 1960s, the rank in social development indicators within Latin America has shown much continuity over the past century. Those countries or regions that immigration had turned into the most urban and socially developed by 1900 (eastern Argentina, Uruguay, southern Brazil, Cuba, and to a lesser degree Chile) are still so today. In terms of literacy, life expectancy, infant mortality, nutrition, and other indicators of social welfare, they continue to rank closer to Europe (now at the level of eastern European countries such as Poland) than to the poorer Latin American countries.

The impact of immigration was particularly multifaceted in the stretch of temperate South America that runs from Patagonia to São Paulo. The demographic impact here was among the highest in the world. For example, immigrants accounted for 30 percent of the population in Argentina on the eve of World I, compared with 20 percent in Australia and 15 percent in the United States. The newcomers and their descendants came to account for over 80 percent of the population in temperate South America. They were thus necessarily spread over the entire social spectrum, although underrepresented at the very top at the beginning. But, as in the United States, later internal and international nonwhite migrations pushed the earlier European arrivals and their descendants out of the lowest socioeconomic and occupational rungs. Mestizos from Andean Argentina and neighboring countries and Afro-Brazilians from the Northeast not only arrived later, in itself a disadvantage; they also arrived with fewer urban skills and at a time, after the 1920s, when the economy was less dynamic and open. Moreover, they increasingly had to compete not with other migrants but with their urban-born children, who excluded migrants of color through mechanisms that ranged from the hiring of co-ethnics to covert or overt racial discrimination.

Given their demographic weight, immigrants also had a tremendous impact in shaping the popular culture of this region. They diversified a carnivorous diet, turning items such as pasta and wine into national staples. They introduced sports and leisure activities such as bocce, Basque handball, polo, zarzuelas, and soccer. It is no coincidence that this region of South America has won nine of the eighteen soccer World Cups ever played, with Europe winning the other nine. They introduced musical instruments and styles and shaped the tango. They did not have the political power to change the national languages formally. But they had the numbers to change it phonetically, the reason why River Plate Spanish sounds like Italian to most foreigners.

Immigrants eventually assimilated to the national cultures that they had shaped. There is some debate about whether these societies are most appropriately represented by the metaphor of a melting pot or a salad bowl. But it is clear that the historical trend moved from the latter to the former, from a more multilingual and multicultural condition to a more monolingual and monocultural situation. By global standards, what is striking is the absorption capacities of these countries. For example, Yiddish existed as minority language in eastern Europe for centuries but disappeared in Latin America and the United States in two or three generations. Ethnic Chinese in Southeast Asia have preserved a separate identity, language, and institutions for centuries, but European immigrants in the New World have lost them in a few generations.

The process of absorption was also relatively free of violence. While massacres of immigrants have been common in Europe, Africa, and Asia, they have been rare and small in the New World. This was particularly true for European immigrants. The most brutal anti-immigrant episodes in the Americas were the massacre of more than 15,000 Haitians in the Dominican Republic in 1937 and of Chinese in Sonora during the Mexican Revolution.

The impact of immigration has been less multifaceted but economically significant in countries that received relatively few immigrants. A small number of German farmers accounted for more than one-third of coffee production in Guatemala in the early twentieth century. Palestinian Christians make up less than 3 percent of the population in Honduras but owned more than half of the businesses in San Pedro Sula already in the 1920s and a disproportionately high number of industrial and commercial establishments in the country in the first decade of the twenty-first century. The same is true in Ecuador with the Lebanese. People who trace their ancestry to a handful of Maronite villages have been elected to so many local and national offices (including the vice presidency and two presidencies) that political rivals have complained about the "Bedouization of Ecuador." European immigrants in Mexico make up less than 1 percent of the population but have played a dominant role in the country's economy and industrialization.

This is true in all other countries of Latin America and the Caribbean where immigration was not a mass phenomenon. The arrivals and their descendants here came to occupy a privileged class position with a sense of cultural superiority. This situation resembled the experiences of so-called middlemen minorities such as the Chinese in Southeast Asia, the Indians in East Africa, and the Lebanese in West Africa, more than those of countries of immigrations in the Americas. Yet even in these Latin American countries of limited immigration, the separation between the immigrant-descendants and indigenous population was never as sharp and tense as in Asia and Africa, in large part because the existence of native upper- and middle-classes of European (Hispano-Creole) descent made the newcomers less visible.

Post-1930 Immigration. International migration to Latin America and elsewhere declined sharply after the Great Depression of 1930. The following decade witnessed only a few large streams. The continuing immigration of 101,000 Japanese to Brazil was among the largest. So was the arrival of 111,000 Jewish refugees in Latin America between 1933 and 1943, the largest group going to Argentina (45,000), followed by Brazil (25,000), Chile (12,000), Uruguay (7,000), and Cuba (6,000). About 20,000 Republican exiles found refuge in Latin America after the Spanish Civil War, the single largest group heading for Mexico, where they were welcomed by the leftist government of Lázaro Cárdenas.

Emigration to Latin America revived after World War II. The sources were similar to the previous inflow, with Italy, Spain, and Portugal accounting for about three-quarters of the European arrivals, and so were the destinations. Argentina kept its leading position with some 1.5 million arrivals between 1945 and 1960. Brazil followed with three-quarters

Undocumented Bolivian immigrants in Argentina, 2006. An estimated two billion undocumented immigrants from Bolivia and Paraguay live in Argentina. A March 2006 fire in a clandestine factory, which killed six Bolivian immigrants, four of them children, revealed the horrifying working conditions many of these immigrants face. AP IMAGES

of a million. But now Venezuela surpassed Uruguay and Cuba as the next important destination, receiving also about 750,000 Europeans. The most important Asian current during the period was the arrival of 60,000 Japanese in Brazil. However, this inflow, like those from Europe, declined sharply in the early 1960s and basically ended after that with the Japanese and European "economic miracles." Since then the only significant inflow into Latin America has come from Korea, with some 100,000 going to Brazil, 35,000 to Argentina, 15,000 to Paraguay and Mexico each, and smaller groups to countries from Guatemala to Chile.

Since the 1960s most flows into Latin American countries have originated from their neighbors. These intra-regional movements had existed before. The best-known case is the migration early in the twentieth century of West Indians to Panama, the Atlantic coast of Costa Rica, and Cuba and of Haitians to the Dominican Republic and Cuba. But their importance has increased dramatically since the 1960s. The two largest streams have been from neighboring countries such as Paraguay and Bolivia into Argentina and from Colombia to Venezuela. Most of these crossings are undocumented, so official figures are unreliable. But the number of illegal immigrants in both countries has been estimated at around 2 million. As with these two cases, the other significant movements flow into relatively richer neighbors: from Nicaragua to Costa Rica, from Guatemala to Mexico and Belize, from Bolivia and Peru to Chile, and from Haiti to the Dominican Republic, while Dominicans move to Puerto Rico and Venezuela. The exception to this rule has been the exile of middle-class émigrés such as Argentineans and Chileans to Venezuela and Mexico and Cubans to Puerto Rico.

EMIGRATION FROM LATIN AMERICA

Latin America was for almost all of its history an importer rather than exporter of people. The first emigrants were probably the peninsular Spaniards and loyalists who left during and after the wars of independence. Other than European and Asian immigrants returning home, the next two outflows consisted of Mexicans crossing the border north and Cuban exiles and cigar workers settling in Key West, Tampa, and New York from the mid-nineteenth century on. The movement across the Rio Grande increased dramatically during the Mexican Revolution, spreading throughout the Southwest of the United States and establishing an important enclave in Chicago and nearby industrial towns. Since the mid-1990s Mexican immigrants have expanded beyond those original areas of settlement to much of the rest of the country as their numbers have swollen to 11.5 million, or 31 percent of all immigrants in the United States and a tenth of the population of Mexico. The stream out of Cuba remained small until the triumph of the 1959 revolution and its radicalization in the following years, which provoked an exodus of more than a million exiles in the next decades, representing also more than a tenth of the country's population. Most of it headed to Miami and to a lesser degree northern New Jersey. In 2006 there were 936,000 Cuban-born residents in the United States. Smaller streams headed for Spain, Venezuela, and Puerto Rico.

The latter island provided the third important flow out of Latin America before the 1960s. The first significant departures involved 5,000 contracted laborers who left in 1901 to work in the sugar plantations of Hawaii. But the stream to New York had already surpassed this one by the years after World War I, reaching a peak in the two or three decades after the next world war. Altogether, the net emigration from Puerto Rico to the United States reached 1.2 million during the twentieth century. Out-migration decreased dramatically during the 1970s but revived during the next two decades among young and middle-class professionals rather than peasants and workers as in its heyday. By 2000 the number of Puerto Ricans residing in the mainland (3.4 million) almost matched those living in the island (3.6 million). They had now dispersed beyond their original destination. While in the 1940s almost nine-tenths of Puerto Ricans in the United States resided in New York City, and two-thirds still did so in the 1960s, by the end of the century less than a quarter lived in the Big Apple.

The Dominican Republic joined its Caribbean neighbors as an important exporter of people in the 1970s. Many actually went to Puerto Rico as undocumented immigrants. The first recorded *yola*, wooden boats, arrived in 1972, and since then the U.S. Coast Guard has intercepted close to 30,000 Dominicans trying to reach the island. The ratio of undocumented to legal Dominican immigrants is six times higher than in the United States. An estimated 100,000 to 150,000 resided mainly illegally in Puerto Rico in 2007, and San Juan had the largest concentration of Dominican expatriates outside of New York City. There, the 293,000 Dominican residents make up the largest foreign-born group in the city. The census bureau estimated that 766,000 Dominicans resided in the United States in 2006, a figure that represents close to one-tenth of the population of the Dominican Republic. Since the 1990s about 60,000 Dominicans have headed for Spain, more than 80 percent of them women who work mainly as domestic servants.

During the second half of the 1970s a combination of economic decline and political repression turned Argentina into a net exporter of people for the first time in its history. About 20,000 Jews made *aliyah* to Israel then, and another 40,000 more would join them later. A larger number headed to Spain. At the beginning most were children or grandchildren of Spanish immigrants who could claim Spanish citizenship and often moved with the help of relatives there. But they were joined later by those who could claim Italian or other European Union citizenship through ancestry and preferred moving to Spain rather than to their "ancestral" lands. Others were illegal migrants. Whatever their ethnic background, this was a highly skilled migration. About four-tenths were professionals, some of whom popularized psychoanalysis in their new country. Some 262,000 Argentineans are estimated to reside in Spain as of 2007, 166,000 in the United States (where their socio-occupational profile resembles that of their compatriots in Spain), and about 25,000 in Italy.

Brazil, another traditional country of immigration, joined the outflow somewhat later than Argentina but has surpassed it in absolute numbers. In 2002 the consulate service estimated the number of Brazilians residing outside of their country at 1.96 million. Four-tenths of these lived in the United States, mainly in New York, Boston, and Miami. Many had settled in old Portuguese neighborhoods, perhaps simply because of the language or perhaps

Children play in Gonzaga, Brazil, 2005. Gonzaga is a center for migration, chiefly undocumented, from Brazil to the United States and Europe. Brazilians have become one of the fastest growing groups of illegal immigration to the United States since 2000. AP IMAGES

through family connections with Portuguese immigrants in Brazil. One-quarter lived in bordering countries, mainly in Ciudad del Este, a cosmopolitan tax-free city in Paraguay home to large numbers of other immigrants from Taiwan, Iran, and the Middle East. One-fifth lived in Europe, mainly in Portugal, home to about 90,000 Brazilians. And 274,000 resided in Japan, almost all *dekasegui*, descendants of Japanese immigrants who began going in 1990 when the Japanese government extended the right to "return" to the Nikkei, or second- and third-generation immigrants. Most of them have limited Japanese language skills and work mainly in factories.

Emigration in Central America acquired some importance during the civil wars of the 1980s and basically affects the region's five northernmost countries. Panama and Costa Rica have very low emigration rates and receive more people than they send out. El Salvador has the highest emigration rate in the region (with 1 million out of a population of 7 million living in the United States), followed by Guatemala, Honduras, and Nicaragua. The latter country sends more (and poorer) emigrants to Costa Rica than to the United States; there are an estimated 400,000 Nicaraguans in the former and 237,000 in the latter. But all the others share the unidirectionality of their Mexican neighbors in moving overwhelmingly to the United States. Even Guatemala, which sends a tenth of its emigrants across the border to Mexico, still sends the vast majority (85%) to the United States.

Within the Andean region, Colombia was the first country to experience a significant exodus beginning in the 1960s to Venezuela (where the number of mainly undocumented Colombian residents has been estimated as high as 2 million) and soon after to the United States (where close to 600,000 reside). A more recent flow since the 1990s has swollen the Colombian community in Spain to 269,000. Ecuadorian emigration, which began later than Colombia's but has surpassed it in intensity, headed originally mostly to the United States, where 385,000 reside, later to Spain, where an estimated 414,000 Ecuadorians represent the largest Latin American community, and also to Italy, where more than 50,000 reside. Peru has a similar number of its emigrants in Italy, about 126,000 in Spain, and 382,000 in the United States. Bolivia, the last to join the exodus, has 136,000 of its natives living in Spain and 73,000 in the United States. Chile's net emigration rate is negative as it has become a country of immigration rather than emigration.

The intensity of emigration thus varies greatly within the Americas. The highest net emigration rates (between 6 and 12 per thousand in 2007) can actually be found in the West Indies and Guyana. The highest in Ibero-America belongs to Mexico (4.08 per thousand), which also has the highest in the world for a country with a similar-size population (other countries with higher rates such as Botswana, Liberia, Albania, and Jordan have significantly smaller populations). El Salvador, the Dominican Republic, Guatemala, and Ecuador all have rates higher than 2 per thousand, which places them among the top twenty-five countries of emigration in the world. Cuba, Honduras, Nicaragua, Bolivia, and Peru rank above the global average and the rest of the countries in the region below that line.

In terms of destinations, the United States continues to rank at the top. Its census bureau estimates the number of Ibero-Americans residing there in 2006 at 18.7 million, or half of all immigrants in the country. Spain's Latin American population trebled from 2000 to 1.8 million in 2007. The rest of Europe has close to a million Latin American residents, with Italy holding a quarter of them, followed by the United Kingdom and Germany with more than 100,000 each, and Portugal, France, and Switzerland with somewhat lower numbers. Canada's Latin American population increased from 70,000 in 1981 (when a good number of them were still Chilean exiles) to 217,000 in 2001, when El Salvadorans and Mexicans led a more diverse group. Chileans were also the first to arrive in significant numbers in Australia in the 1970s. In 2007 they still make up a third of the 75,000 Latin Americans there. Argentineans and Uruguayans account for another third; and the recently arrived El Salvadorans for an eighth. Some 430,000 Latin American–born adults resided in Japan in 2005, 82 percent of them Brazilians and 14 percent Peruvians.

Chileans of Spanish descent inquire about Spanish citizenship at the Spanish consulate in Santiago, January 2003. Economic downturns in Latin America, along with a new Spanish law allowing individuals with Spanish parents or grandparents to apply for citizenship, have led to an influx of Latin American nationals moving to Spain in the early twenty-first century. AP IMAGES

Similar to the European movements of the past, international migration in the early twenty-first century is more related to relative affluence than to poverty. Just as in the nineteenth century, post–World War II emigration began and acquired greater intensity in the better-off countries and regions. Mexico is actually classified as an upper-middle-income country, ranked as number 71 among the world's 208 countries and territories, and within that country emigration began and acquired massive dimensions in the richer states of the north. The other pioneers of emigration in Latin America—Cuba, Puerto Rico, and later the Southern Cone—are even more developed than Mexico. As in the past also, emigrants continue to be self-selected and of higher socioeconomic and educational background than those who stay behind.

However, several factors, now and then, affect the level of socioeconomic selectivity of the flow. One is time. Emigration tends to spread to poorer places and regions. In Latin America it spread in the late twentieth century to the south of Mexico, Central America, and the Andean region, just as it had spread in the nineteenth century from northern Europe to the less developed southern and eastern regions of the continent. Even within the same region, the flow becomes less selective with time. As social networks linking the place of origin and destination become denser, the assistance they provide lowers the cost of emigrating, making it possible for folks with fewer resources to do so.

The condition of the emigrants is also clearly affected by the level of socioeconomic development in the countries they come from. In the early twenty-first century those from the Southern Cone are on average more educated than those from Mexico or Central America, just as English or Germans were once more skilled than the Irish or Italians. As Table 3 shows, Argentineans, Uruguayans, and Chileans in the United States are four to nine times more likely to have a college degree or higher than Mexicans, Guatemalans, and El Salvadorans. However, distance (as a proxy for cost) increases the selectivity factor to a degree than can trump the level of socioeconomic development of the country of origin. So, for example, the educational attainment of Bolivians in the United States is six times higher than that of Mexicans, even though Mexico is a significantly richer and more developed country.

This combination of factors affects the skill levels of Latin American emigrants and thus their economic success in the host country. The 2000 U.S. census shows that Latin Americans are significantly less educated and more likely to live in poverty, and that their median family income is at least $14,000 lower than that of natives and all major immigrant groups (see Table 3). The same is true in Canada.

These overall figures, however, conceal important differences. Historically, highly selected and educated immigrants such as Chilean émigrés and Cuban exiles before the Mariel boatlift of 1980 had education and income levels higher than most groups, native or not, in North America. Today, immigrants from the most developed countries of South America may have lower levels of education than immigrant groups such as Indians, Nigerians, and Filipinos, but they are equal to or higher than those of the native-born population. Argentineans and Uruguayans have a higher median family income than natives, and Chileans come close. Other immigrants from South America, Panamanians, Cubans, and Costa Ricans have educational and income levels that are not far from the country's averages.

The low ranking of Latin Americans as a whole therefore is due to the low educational and income levels of Mexicans, Central Americans (specifically Guatemalans, El Salvadorans, and Hondurans), and Dominicans, who together make up seven-tenths of all Latin Americans in the United States. The cause of this phenomenon is not simply the poverty of the home countries. After all, even the poorest of the Central American countries, not to mention Mexico, have much higher per capita incomes and literacy than India and Nigeria, whose immigrants have among the highest income and education levels in the United States. The geographical proximity and longer history of going to the United States have simply lowered the cost of migrating for Mexicans, Central Americans, and Dominicans who are less socioeconomically select and more representative of the populations of their countries in general than are immigrants from Asia and Africa.

The economic success of the latter also demonstrates that racism cannot be a significant explanation for Latinos' relatively low socioeconomic standing in the United States. Indeed, contrary to common assumptions, racial discrimination against immigrants

Latin Americans and other selected foreign-born population in the United States, 2000

Place of birth	Population (in thousands)	Percentage high school graduate or higher (age 25+)	Rank	Percentage bachelor's degree or higher (age 25+)	Rank	Percentage of families living under the poverty level	Rank	Median family income	Rank
Top group									
India	1,023	88.2	2	69.1	1	5.4	2	$74,630	1
Philippines	1,369	86.9	4	45.4	3	4.6	1	$65,765	2
Nigeria	135	93.9	1	58.6	2	9.8	7	$52,586	4
Argentina	125	79.5	11	34.5	6	9.0	5	$55,276	3
Native-born	**250,314**	**83.3**	**5**	**24.5**	**10**	**8.3**	**3**	**$50,976**	**7**
Bolivia	53	82.9	6	25.9	9	8.6	4	$47,358	10
Chile	81	81.0	9	29.4	8	9.6	6	$47,821	8
Venezuela	107	87.6	3	43.2	4	13.3	13	$45,424	11
China	1,192	70.8	15	42.7	5	11.5	11	$52,579	5
Middle group									
Peru	278	81.0	8	23.2	12	10.2	8	$44,073	14
Paraguay	12	72.3	12	23.8	11	10.5	9	$44,916	12
Panama	105	82.7	7	22.9	13	12.4	12	$44,302	13
Brazil	212	80.2	10	32.0	7	14.0	14	$41,148	15
Uruguay	25	71.7	14	22.1	14	14.0	15	$52,362	6
Vietnam	988	60.9	18	19.1	16	14.2	17	$47,380	9
Cuba	873	58.7	20	18.5	17	11.4	10	$40,823	16
Colombia	510	72.1	13	21.6	15	14.6	18	$39,583	18
Costa Rica	72	68.9	16	18.1	18	14.1	16	$40,675	17
Lowest group									
Ecuador	299	61.5	17	13.0	20	15.1	19	$39,439	19
Nicaragua	220	59.6	19	13.6	19	15.3	20	$37,879	20
Latin America	**16,087**	**43.9**	**23**	**9.6**	**21**	**20.7**	**23**	**$33,421**	**21**
El Salvador	817	34.8	25	4.9	25	19.2	21	$32,934	22
Guatemala	481	37.3	24	6.0	24	20.1	22	$31,532	23
Honduras	283	44.4	22	8.1	23	22.2	24	$30,308	25
Dominican Republic	688	47.8	21	9.4	22	28.3	26	$27,977	26
Mexico	9,177	29.8	26	4.3	26	24.4	25	$30,689	24

Note: Ranked from 1, most successful (the average of higher education, higher income and lower poverty rates) to 26, least successful. The top group is above or close to the native-born population; the second not far from the national averages; and the third significantly below

Table 3

in general is less harsh now than it was in the past against European groups that today are considered white but were then seen as inferior races. The first immigration restrictions in the United States excluded the Chinese (in 1882) and southern and eastern Europeans (in 1924) openly and specifically for their supposed racial and cultural inferiority. Today one would be hard put to find such explicitly racist arguments even among the most bigoted public figures. The required circumlocutions, codes, and euphemisms necessarily complicate and dilute xenophobic discourse, which may be on an upswing in the early twenty-first century but not at a historically high peak.

Anti-immigrant rhetoric indeed has shown much continuity in the United States over the last two centuries. The volume and stridency of the rhetoric has tended to increase: (1) with the volume of the actual inflow; (2) during periods of economic contractions or uncertainty; and (3) when some politicians and members of the media calculate that the gains (in votes, readers, or viewers) from exploiting xenophobia will be higher than the cost of any possible backlash. Business leaders, who benefit from an increase in the labor supply, have consistently been pro-immigration; labor leaders have been less so, except in the cases where the membership is made up of recent arrivals. Education and income have continued to be positively related to tolerance of foreigners. The complaints against the newcomers have shown as much consistency: they are not as good as previous immigrant groups, do not want to assimilate, take jobs away from the natives and lower wages, and increase crime or terrorism.

The substance behind the complaints ranges from valid (or at least factual) to exaggerated to completely bogus. Immigrants do not switch identities and loyalties when they land in the receiving country. But, for better or worse (inasmuch as assimilation also implies some loss, of language for example), Latin Americans in the United States have followed a pattern similar to that of European immigrants in Latin America (or the United States) before. Every new generation in the host country becomes less distinguishable from the rest of the population in habits, norms, and behaviors (from what one does, eats, and speaks to where one lives and whom one socializes with or marries). Immigration does lower wages. But normally only in the sectors where the newcomers are numerous and rarely by more than 10 percent. Immigration has in many places and times (e.g., the northeastern cities of the United States in the nineteenth century or western Europe today) increased street crime. But in the present-day United States, Latin Americans and other immigrants have much lower crime rates than the native born. In some cases, for example Mexicans, the rate actually increases significantly among the American-born generation, but even then it simply matches that of the rest of the native-born population. And the attempt to link immigration and terrorism conceptually has been less successful in the United States than in western Europe because public opinion associates the two phenomena with different groups: immigration with Mexicans and terrorism with Middle Easterners.

In the early twenty-first century there are two unprecedented grievances against immigrants. One is that they abuse social services, a gripe that did not exist before the development of these programs in the 1930s. The proportion of Latin Americans receiving public assistance (6.4%) and the average amount that they receive ($3,676 annually) is higher than among the native population (3.2% and $2,859). But immigrants utilize fewer medical services (mainly because of their much lower average age) and contribute disproportionately to the Social Security fund (because most undocumented immigrants pay taxes into the fund but will not collect). At any rate, the more restricted, and declining, scope of the welfare state in the United States has made gripes about immigrants abusing it less common and strident than in western Europe.

The other new complaint relates to illegality. Such grumbles were almost nonexistent in the previous migration wave to the United States because there were no significant laws restricting the free flow of people into the country other than those prohibiting the entry of bigamists, anarchists, prostitutes, and contracted laborers. The actual act performed by immigrants today—moving from one country to another—is the same as it was a century before. It simply has been criminalized by the only entity that has the capacity to so: the state. But although not all laws enjoy equal legitimacy in the public eye, and others lose it almost completely (for example slavery or racial segregation), the ingrained respect for the rule of law, John Adams's constantly quoted maxim about the United States being "a government of laws, not men," and the automatic equation of illegality and immorality has infused the discourse on illegality with the legitimacy that those on the racial and cultural inferiority of newcomers once had.

North American attitudes toward Latin American or other immigrants continue to exhibit the peculiar ambiguities of the past. On the one hand, looking down upon the latest arrivals has always served as an assertion of belonging for those who came before and their descendants. On the other, immigration has consistently supplied the crucial element in the construction of the nation's identity and myths. Many countries have had and have larger proportions of immigrants in their population than the United States, which in 2007 ranks sixty-fifth in the world in this measure. But few have defined themselves as "a country of immigrants." In the Americas, only Argentineans and Uruguayans come close in this self-description, as expressed in their popular saying that Mexicans descended from the Aztecs, Peruvians from the Incas, and they themselves from boats. But in the United States this self-definition also contains a paean to the most individualist form of capitalism. The immigrant, in this lore, is the quintessential seeker: restless, ambitious, and asking for opportunity rather than security, so that the American Dream is the immigrant dream.

That dream fuels others back home. About three-quarters of Latin American immigrants in the United States, Europe, and Japan send remittances to their home countries. In 2006 they sent close to $60 billion. Development experts debate how much of this is used for consumption rather than investment in infrastructure and production. But whatever the uses, remittances into Latin America now surpass foreign direct investment and represent an inflow of money twenty times larger than foreign aid. Unlike foreign investment, none of that money is repatriated as profits. Unlike foreign aid, which has always been prone to intermediary corruption and has become increasingly militarized, remittances reach their beneficiaries directly, and whatever its uses, the purchase of armaments is not one of those.

See also **Agriculture; Cities and Urbanization; Coffee Industry; Creole; Diseases; Indigenous Languages; Indigenous Peoples; Industrialization; Jews; Minas Gerais; Mining: Colonial Spanish America; Pampa; Race and Ethnicity; Railroads; Slavery: Brazil; Slavery: Spanish America; Sugar Industry; Trade, Colonial Brazil; Wars of Independence, South America.**

BIBLIOGRAPHY

Brading, D. A. *The First America: The Spanish Monarchy, Creole Patriots, and the Liberal State, 1492–1866.* Cambridge, U.K.: Cambridge University Press, 1993.

Euraque, Dario A. *Reinterpreting the Banana Republic: Region and State in Honduras, 1870–1972.* Chapel Hill: University of North Carolina Press, 1996.

Herzog, Tamar. *Defining Nations: Immigrants and Citizens in Early Modern Spain and Spanish America.*New Haven, CT: Yale University Press, 2003.

Klich, Ignacio. *Arab and Jewish Immigrants in Latin America: Images and Realities.* New York: Routledge, 1998.

Lesser, Jeffrey. *Negotiating National Identity: Immigrants, Minorities, and the Struggle for Ethnicity in Brazil.* Durham, NC: Duke University Press, 1999.

Moya, Jose C. *Cousins and Strangers: Spanish Immigrants in Buenos Aires, 1850–1930.* Los Angeles: University of California Press, 1998.

Narotzky, Susana, and Gavin Smith. *Immediate Struggles: People, Power, and Place in Rural Spain.* Los Angeles: University of California Press, 2006.

Novo, Carmen Martinez. *Who Defines Indigenous?: Identities, Development, Intellectuals, and the State in Northern Mexico.* Rutgers, NJ: Rutgers University Press, 2005.

Robinson, David J., ed. *Migration in Colonial Spanish America.* Cambridge, U.K.: Cambridge University Press, 1990.

Skidmore, Thomas E. *Black into White: Race and Nationality in Brazilian Thought.* Durham, NC: Duke University Press, 1993.

Stein, Stanley, and Barbara H. Stein. *The Colonial Heritage of Latin America: Essays on Economic Dependence in Perspective.* Oxford, U.K.: Oxford University Press, 1970.

JOSE C. MOYA

MILITARY.

See **Armed Forces.**

MILITARY DICTATORSHIPS

This entry includes the following articles:

1821–1945

Authoritarian rule under military dictatorships assumed two primary characteristics in Latin American before 1945: domination by nonprofessional military *caudillos* (strong leaders, from the Latin *capitellum*) and institutional rule by professional armed forces officers seeking consensus within the military establishment. The roots of authoritarianism exemplified by the ancient Spanish expression "Del rey abajo ninguno" (after the king no one is superior to me) were fixed in the mentality of Hispanic colonial leaders from Hernán Cortés and Francisco Pizarro to the regional and local *caciques* (chiefs). Spain's fear of local military autonomy prevented the establishment of well-trained colonial militias that could effectively defend the colonies or provide a basis for a professional military immediately after independence. The nearly complete lack of effectiveness of Peru's colonial militia in putting down the widespread rebellion of Tupac Amaru II (José Gabriel Condorconqui) in the early 1780s is a prime example of the weakness of these colonial militias.

After independence, caudillos often ruled without the constraints of well-integrated political or military systems. The careers of Antonio López de Santa Anna in Mexico and Juan Manuel de Rosas in Argentina stand out in this regard. These charismatic leaders ruled mainly by default because no legitimate civilian or military rivals could construct a power base. Of course, opposition to these caudillos and others was often weakened by state-sponsored terror of the kind that would become the hallmark of most institutional military dictatorships in the modern era.

By Samuel Huntington's classic definition of military professionalism, which identifies four components of military forces—expertise, responsibility, corporateness, and ideology—most nineteenth-century military establishments were woefully amateurish. An important exception was the Paraguayan army headed by Francisco Salano López, which was as well-trained and disciplined as any in Latin America. Yet in the tradition of many power-hungry caudillos, Solano López sacrificed his army and his nation in a quixotic attempt for dominance in South America during the War of the Triple Alliance (1864–1870).

A very few of these caudillos, such as Ramón Castilla in Peru and Porfirio Díaz in Mexico, were nation-builders. Although the national structures these leaders created were badly flawed, their careers manifested a concern for modernization rarely seen among the parochial nineteenth-century military dictators. Still, in the late nineteenth and early twentieth centuries, Peru, Chile, Brazil, and to a lesser extent Mexico, influenced by social Darwinism and the rise of mass armies in Europe, contracted military and naval missions from Germany, France, Britain, and the United States to help build professional military institutions and rid their armed forces of *caudillismo*. But except for the operational experience of Brazil and Argentina in the War of the Triple Alliance and Chile's successful campaign against Peru and Bolivia in the War of the Pacific (1879–1882), the larger armies and navies of South America remained largely in their barracks. Argentina, for example, would not put its army in the field for nearly a century before confronting the British in the Malvinas (Falkland Islands) War of 1982. Thus officers in these nations, with little to call upon by way of a battlefield tradition, began reshaping the traditional meaning of national defense to include important components of formerly civilian-dominated sectors of their national economies. The experience of the Brazilian army during World War II stands out against this tendency to sublimate professional missions. The Brazilian Expeditionary Force (BEF) was recruited from all sectors of the country, and fought well in Italy with the Allies in 1944 and 1945. It was hoped that this battlefield experience would establish prominence for Brazil in the postwar world. In fact, many veterans of the BEF played leading roles in military government that seized power in Brazil in 1964. Their confidence was bolstered by their wartime experience. But the Brazilian generals lacked any real sense of limits regarding the military's role in national affairs. The military dominated Brazil through a series of faceless institutional presidents for more than two decades after 1964.

Juan Perón, Augusto Pinochet, and Hugo Chávez reflect sociopolitical conditions that are grounded in the era before 1945. The armed forces of Latin America of that era never securely established the concept of a military career that would have enabled younger officers to look to their profession and not to political forces to gain what a career soldier seeks—professional satisfaction, regular advancement through merit, a salary adequate to raise a family, and operational experience to demonstrate hard-earned expertise. Prolonged political and economic instability caused mainly by caudillismo deprived the military of the opportunity of creating apolitical and professionally stable military establishments. This legacy would become woefully apparent following World War II.

See also **Armed Forces; Castilla, Ramón; Caudillismo, Caudillo; Díaz, Porfirio; Military Dictatorships: Since 1945; Perón, Juan Domingo; Rosas, Juan Manuel de; State of Siege; Túpac Amaru (José Gabriel Condorcanqui); War of the Pacific; War of the Triple Alliance.**

BIBLIOGRAPHY

Castro, Celso, Vitor Izecksohn, and Hendrick Kraay. *Nova historia militar Brasileira.* Rio de Janeiro: FGY: Bom Texto, 2004.

Díaz Díaz, Fernando. *Caudillos y caciques: Antonio López de Santa Anna y Juan Álvarez.* Mexico City: El Colegio de México, 1972.

Hamill, Hugh M., ed. *Caudillos: Dictators in Spanish America.* Norman: University of Oklahoma Press, 1992.

Huntington, Samuel P. *Political Order in Changing Societies.* New Haven, CT: Yale University Press, 1968.

Lynch, John. *Caudillos in Spanish America, 1800–1850.* Oxford: Clarendon Press and New York: Oxford University Press, 1992.

Masterson, Daniel. *Fuerza armada y Sociedad en el Perú moderno: Un estudio sobre relaciones civiles militares, 1930–2000.* Lima: Instituto de Estudios Políticos y Estratégicos, 2001.

McCann, Frank D. *Soldiers of the Pátria: A History of the Brazilian Army, 1889–1937.* Stanford, CA: Stanford University Press, 2004.

Nunn, Frederick M. *Yesterday's Soldiers: European Military Professionalism in South America, 1890–1940.* Lincoln: University of Nebraska Press, 1983.

Potash, Robert A. *The Army and Politics in Argentina*, Vol. 1: *1928–1945: Yrigoyen to Perón*. Stanford, CA: Stanford University Press, 1969.

Scheina, Robert L. *Latin America's Wars: The Age of the Caudillo, 1791–1899.* Washington, DC: Brassey's, 2003.

DANIEL M. MASTERSON

SINCE 1945

Military rule had been endemic to Latin America, particularly in the 1970s and 1980s, but has nearly vanished since the 1990s. While its origins may be traced back to Spanish colonialism, its prevalence during most of the second half of the twentieth century was attributable largely to the weakness of civilian political institutions and the failure of elected governments to secure popular legitimacy.

Postwar socioeconomic development in much of South America expanded the political participation and influence of the growing middle and working classes. By the 1960s the previously excluded rural and urban poor were demanding a greater political voice. Rather than strengthening democratic institutions, however, increased political mobilization, coupled with wide socioeconomic inequalities, often intensified political polarization. Frequently, students and intellectuals radicalized the debate. In some cases, rising class tensions and civil unrest eroded democratic institutions and renewed military intervention.

Prior to the 1960s, military rule often took the form of personalistic dictatorships. Using the armed forces as a vehicle for upward social mobility, *caudillos* (commanders, authoritarian strongmen) seized power based on personal or regional loyalties and concentrated authority overwhelmingly in their own hands. Most caudillos lacked ideological or programmatic agendas, their objectives often being limited to personal aggrandizement and enrichment.

Personalistic dictators have persisted until relatively recently in Latin America's less developed nations. Notable examples include Panama's Manuel Noriega in the 1980s, the Somoza clan in Nicaragua (1937–1979), and Cuba's Fulgencio Batista (1933–1944, 1952–1958). In the last two cases, extensive corruption and repression delegitimized the political system, opening the way for radical revolutions.

As the armed forces became more strongly institutionalized, however, the number of personalistic dictatorships declined. Caudillos were incapable of dealing with the demands of a modernizing military and a more complex civil society. Paraguay's Alfredo Stroessner (1954–1989) was, perhaps, the region's last personalistic dictator.

During the Cold War, as a consequence of enhanced military education, overseas training, and the development of advanced academies for military officers, Latin American armies became more professionalized. Unexpectedly, however, increased professionalism often enhanced the military's proclivity for political intervention.

Institutional military dictatorships were created by more bureaucratized and cohesive armed forces. Whereas a single leader, such as Chile's Augusto Pinochet (1973–1990), occasionally dominated, authority was normally vested in a collective leadership. Typically, one officer served as president, and he was limited to a single term in office.

Institutional military regimes were often more repressive and brutal than personalistic dictatorships. Their governing style, however, was more sophisticated, commonly drawing on the talents of trained civilian technocrats. They were also more likely to espouse a coherent political ideology and program. Political objectives included the repression of mass political movements, political stability, and economic growth. During the 1960s and 1970s a new type of institutional military government was established in some of Latin America's most advanced nations: Argentina (1966–1973, 1976–1983), Brazil (1964–1985), Chile (1973–1990), and Uruguay (1973–1985). Unlike previous dictatorships, these bureaucratic-authoritarian regimes envisioned a fundamental reordering of society.

Two factors underlay the rise of such regimes. First was the perceived leftist threat to the economic and political order. A Marxist president, Salvador Allende, had been elected in Chile in 1970, and a leftist electoral coalition attracted considerable support in Uruguay. In all four countries, the military and their industrialist allies felt besieged by labor unrest or guerrilla activity. Second, the armed forces wished to extricate their countries from the severe inflation and economic stagnation in which they had become mired.

From the perspective of the military and their technocratic allies, stability and growth necessitated a fundamental restructuring of political and economic institutions. Consequently, authoritarian rule had to be more intensive and enduring than under previous military dictatorships. Lacking sufficient expertise, the military delegated economic decisionmaking to conservative técnicos drawn from the private or state sector. Their policies were designed to eliminate budget and trade deficits, control wages, reduce inflation, stimulate foreign investment, and reduce the size of the state sector (including social welfare programs).

Because these structural adjustments initially reduced popular living standards sharply, and because the military feared a resurgence of working-class and student mobilization, bureaucratic-authoritarian economic policies required substantial political repression. Political party activity was banned, at least temporarily; strikes were prohibited; unions were crushed; and thousands were imprisoned and tortured. In Argentina and Chile many people were killed or "disappeared."

Peru's institutional military dictatorship followed a very different approach toward controlling radical political activity (primarily among the rural poor) and developing the nation's economy. Unlike bureaucratic-authoritarian regimes, General Juan Velasco Alvarado's left-nationalist government (1968–1975) considered Peru's oligarchy, not the Marxist left, to be the primary source of the country's problems. Consequently, it implemented a sweeping land reform, increased the economic role of the state, and tried, with little success, to mobilize the masses behind its programs. Far less radical and ambitious Peruvian-style military dictatorships emerged in Ecuador and Panama. All of these military governments were far less repressive than bureaucratic-authoritarian regimes had been.

Starting in the late 1970s, military dictatorships throughout Latin America gradually stepped down in the face of declining legitimacy and, other than Chile, poor economic performance. Military rulers were more successful at crushing the radical left, often at great cost to human rights.

The end of the cold war eliminated military governments' professed role as protectors of their nations against communist subversion and the wave of democratization that has swept much of the Third World has deligitimized military rule. In particular, the United States has abandoned its erstwhile permissive attitude toward military coups in the hemisphere. In many Latin American nations, however, the military continues to influence the political system and reserves for itself the right to remove "unacceptable" civilian presidents.

See also **Allende Gossens, Salvador; Argentina, Organizations: United Officers Group (GOU); Batista y Zaldívar, Fulgencio; Brazil, Revolutions: Revolution of 1964; Caudillismo, Caudillo; Military Dictatorships: 1821-1945; Noriega Moreno, Manuel Antonio; Pinochet Ugarte, Augusto; Somoza Debayle, Anastasio; Somoza Debayle, Luis; Somoza García, Anastasio; Stroessner, Alfredo; Velasco Alvarado, Juan.**

BIBLIOGRAPHY

Biglaiser, Glen. *Guardians of the Nation?: Economists, Generals, and Economic Reform in Latin America.* Notre Dame, IN: University of Notre Dame Press, 2002.

Collier, David, ed. *The New Authoritarianism in Latin America.* Princeton, NJ: Princeton University Press, 1979.

Garretón Merino, Manuel Antonio et al. *Por la fuerza sin la razón: análisis y textos de los bandos de la dictadura militar.* Santiago: LOM Ediciones, 1998.

Pion-Berlin, David, ed. *Civil-Military Relations in Latin America: New Analytical Perspectives.* Chapel Hill: University of North Carolina Press, 2001.

Silva, Patricio, ed. *The Soldier and the State in South America: Essays in Civil-Military Relations.* New York: Palgrave Macmillan, 2001.

Howard Handelman

MILITARY ORDERS

This entry includes the following articles:
PORTUGAL
SPAIN

PORTUGAL

By 1500 three national clerico-military orders existed in Portugal: The Order of Christ, with its headquarters at Tomar; the Order of Santiago, based at Palmela; and the Order of São Bento de Avis, at Avis. Except for the Order of Christ, founded in 1319, they had their origins in the twelfth century and played major roles in the reconquest of Portugal from the Muslims. Each of the orders had members living a monastic life as well as warrior-monks living in the world and fighting the infidel. All members made vows of poverty, chastity, and obedience. From the beginning, knights of Santiago could marry. However, it was not until 1496 that Pope Alexander VI allowed knights of the orders of Christ and Avis to do the same. By the dawn of the sixteenth century, the vows had been so diluted that the spiritual obligations of the knights were little more than those required of devout Christians.

By that time, the military orders had long since lost their original reason for existence. In the years since the reconquest, the orders had taken on new dimensions. In the sixteenth century, the immense wealth of the orders was used by the Portuguese monarchs to reward royal service. The granting of knighthoods in the orders had become an important tool of royal patronage. At the same time, these knighthoods were highly desired and were symbols of high social rank. Possession of commanderies in the order was even more prestigious as well as lucrative. Members showed great pride in wearing the habits of their respective orders with their distinctive crosses, and they included these insignia in their portraits. Acknowledgment of membership in one of the Portuguese military orders was frequently made in official documents and correspondence of the time. By 1551, when the papacy made King João III and his successors perpetual masters, governors, and administrators of the three Portuguese military orders, the number of new knights in each order had increased significantly, and the Order of Christ was the largest and most prestigious of the three.

Knights, along with their parents and grandparents, were expected to be noble, with no history of manual labor or artisan activity. They also had to be of "pure blood," that is to say, free from any Jewish or Muslim heritage. Background investigations of candidates were undertaken to ensure that these standards were met. By 1572, with the issuance of purity of blood statutes for the three military orders, membership also became desirable as a proof of this purity. During the next hundred years, the great majority of candidates with "New Christian" (converted Jewish) ancestry were denied entrance into the orders, although dispensations were provided for a select few. However, these exceptions ceased shortly after Prince Pedro seized the throne from his brother, King Afonso VI, in 1667. Dispensations became easier to obtain for defects of nobility, especially as the seventeenth and eighteenth centuries progressed. Key provisos were that the service being rewarded by the crown be significant and personal and that the non-noble heritage not be grossly base. Since a knighthood in a military order automatically ennobled, membership was greatly desired by those commoners having pretensions to nobility.

The reformed statutes of all three orders, which went into effect in the late 1620s, also required that prospective members be of legitimate birth, have no pagan ancestry, be no younger than eighteen nor older than fifty years of age, and be in good health. Dispensations from these last requirements were usually easy to obtain. As master of all three orders, the king could grant dispensations to whomever he wished. Usually, he followed the advice of the Mesa Da Consciência E Ordens, which was the watchdog over the standards of the orders. This is the reason that a significant number of men who were awarded memberships, especially those lacking nobility or purity of blood, never received the necessary authorization to become knights. The award of membership in the order did not guarantee the actual receipt of knighthood.

As the years of Portuguese exploration and discovery brought into being a vast maritime empire, the crown was accustomed to use the military orders to reward services performed in North Africa, the Estado da India, West Africa, and on armadas, as well as on the Iberian Peninsula. As the Portuguese crown established a solid presence in America, Brazilian services also had to be acknowledged. Some of the earliest known Brazilian services rewarded with knighthoods in the military orders were those involving the capture of Rio de Janeiro from the French and its early settlement. The third governor-general of Brazil, Mem de Sá; his nephew, Estácio de Sá; and Cristóvão de Barros, son of Portuguese America's first *provedor-mor da fazenda* (chief treasury official), were awarded knighthoods in the Order of Christ in 1566. Salvador de Sá, another nephew of the governor-general, was awarded a knighthood in the Order of Santiago in 1574, after completing a three-year term as governor of Rio de Janeiro (1568–1571). His grandson, sixteen-year-old Salvador Correia de Sá E Benavides, was awarded a similar knighthood in

1618 while residing in Brazil. Both later transferred to the Order of Christ.

The French threat to Maranhão and Pará, the Dutch capture of the Brazilian capital of Bahia in 1624, and the Dutch wars in the rest of northeastern Brazil (1630–1654) provided opportunities for a growing number of Brazilian-born and longtime residents of Brazil to become knights in the orders of Christ, Santiago, and Avis. During the reign of King João IV (1640–1656), when some knights of the Order of Christ—most of them sugar planters—claimed that they were exempt from paying tithes on sugar because of the special relationship the Order of Christ had with Portuguese America, Brazilian residents, especially those with extensive properties, were allowed to become knights only of Santiago and Avis. After the controversy ended in 1658, a small percentage of these knights were allowed to transfer to the Order of Christ.

In the aftermath of the Dutch wars, the percentage of Brazilians who became knights in one of the three military order seems to have decreased. Those fighting hostile Indians or the runaway slaves resisting capture at Palmares and those opening up new territories were occasionally awarded such knighthoods. Memberships in the military orders were also used as dowries. A number of wealthy Brazilian merchants and sugar plantation owners without significant services of their own married women for these dowries. A handful of Brazilian Indians, as well as mulattoes, became knights in the military orders. But, because of the stigma of slavery, no blacks, even the few who were awarded knighthoods, actually became members. Most of the governors-general and viceroys were already knights and commanders in one of the three orders before they arrived in America. An increasing number of judges on the high court, governors of captaincies, and other important officials were also knights or were promised knighthoods for agreeing to serve in Brazil. As time went on, it was not unusual for the crown to hold out similar promises of knighthoods to lesser officials, surgeons, and officers in militias and garrisons as an encouragement to accept Brazilian service. Most of these men were not born in Brazil, although many developed close ties with the country.

The Order of Christ also played another role in Brazil, which it did not share with the orders of Santiago and Avis. The head of the Order of Christ had ecclesiastical jurisdiction over Portuguese America. While Prince Henry (the Navigator) was master, Pope Calixtus III, by the bull "Inter Caetera," of 13 March 1456, gave the Order of Christ spiritual jurisdiction over all regions conquered or to be conquered by the Portuguese. Beginning with Manuel I, who was master of the order before he became king in 1495 and continued to be so after his coronation, all kings of Portugal were also masters, governors, and administrators of the Order of Christ. With the discovery of Brazil by Pedro Álvares Cabral in 1500, Portuguese America thus came under the ecclesiastical jurisdiction of the Order of Christ.

See also **Catholic Church: The Colonial Period.**

BIBLIOGRAPHY

The best overall treatment of the Portuguese military orders is found in Fortunato De Almeida, *História da igreja em Portugal,* 4 vols. (1967–1971). For aspects of the social history of the military orders, see Francis A. Dutra, "Membership in the Order of Christ in the Seventeenth Century: Its Rights, Privileges, and Obligations," in *The Americas* 27, no. 1 (1970): 3–25. See also his "Blacks and the Search for Rewards and Status in Seventeenth-Century Brazil," in *Proceedings of the Pacific Coast Council on Latin American Studies* 6 (1977–1979): 25–35. The effects of the Dutch wars on the demands for rewards are discussed in Cleonir Xavier De Albuquerque, *A remuneração de serviços da guerra Holandesa* (1968). See also Francis A. Dutra, "Evolution of the Portuguese Order of Santiago, 1492–1600," in *Mediterranean Studies* 4 (1994): 63–72.

Additional Bibliography

Dutra, Francis A. *Military Orders in the Early Modern Portuguese World: The Orders of Christ, Santiago, and Avis.* Aldershit, Hampshire: Ashgate, 2006.

Francis A. Dutra

SPAIN

As part of the effort to reconquer Spain from the Moors during the twelfth century, the chivalric orders of Santiago, Calatrava, and Alcántara were founded in Castile, and the orders of Montesa and Saint John were founded in Aragon. Their focus was Christian military service, and their success brought material rewards. By the close of the Middle Ages, the three Castilian orders controlled extensive lands in Estremadura and Andalusia and had jurisdiction over perhaps a million vassals. In the late fifteenth century Ferdinand of Aragon became the grand master of the Castilian orders, bringing the crown substantial financial resources and securing a new source of patronage. A Council of Orders was created in 1499 to administer them, and in 1523 Pope Adrian VI authorized the crown to hold the masterships of the orders in perpetuity.

Together the Castilian orders had 183 encomiendas or seigneurial estates assigned to *comendadores.* The estates produced income that, in the early seventeenth century, varied from less than 1,000 ducats to more than 10,000 ducats. Most estates, however, produced between 1,000 and 3,000 ducats. In addition to the *comendadores,* the orders had *caballeros* or knights who held no *encomienda* but were permitted to wear *hábitos,* the robes and distinctive insignia of their order, and to enjoy their order's legal privileges.

Although their military purpose disappeared after the Reconquest, the orders remained important because membership, awarded only after an increasingly detailed genealogical investigation, confirmed one's lineage was "untainted" by Jewish or Moorish ancestry in a society obsessed with blood purity and inherited nobility. By the seventeenth century, if not earlier, noble families without a member or ancestor who belonged to an order were suspect. The demand for a *hábito* was so intense that the crown augmented its revenue by selling the knighthoods to theoretically qualified buyers, a practice that peaked during the reign of Philip IV. One consequence was an increase in the number of *caballeros.* Another was that knighthoods were granted to infants and children.

Except for one brief instance in Santo Domingo, the military orders held no land in the Spanish colonies. Nonetheless, peninsular knights arrived in the New World from the time of Columbus, and the first generation of American-born Spaniards began seeking *hábitos* when they came of age. From the late 1520s to 1615, only thirty-one Creoles were successful. The number then increased rapidly, with sixty-two men becoming knights from 1641 to 1650. The high point of Creole success was from 1691 to 1700, when seventy-five entered the three Castilian orders. By 1810, 511 Creoles had entered Santiago; 168, Calatrava; and 78, Alcántara. The *audiencia* of Lima was particularly well represented with a total of well over 300, more than twice the number of knights from Mexico. Every *audiencia* had at least a few locally born men who succeeded in gaining the coveted *hábito* and the prestige it conferred.

See also **Catholic Church: The Colonial Period.**

BIBLIOGRAPHY

Guillermo Lohmann Villena, *Los americanos en las órdenes nobiliarias (1529–1900)*, 2 vols. (1947).

John Huxtable Elliott, *Imperial Spain 1469–1716* (1964).

L. P. Wright, "The Military Orders in Sixteenth and Seventeenth Spanish Society: The Institutional Embodiment of a Historical Tradition," in *Past and Present* 43 (May 1969): 34–70.

Henry Kamen, *Spain 1469–1714: A Society of Conflict,* 2d ed. (1991).

Additional Bibliography

Martínez Díez, Gonzalo. *La cruz y la espada: Vida cotidiana de las órdenes militares españolas.* Barcelona: Plaza & Janés, 2002.

SUZANNE HILES BURKHOLDER

MILITARY QUESTION OF THE 1880S.

The Military Question of the 1880s was a dispute concerning the right of Brazilian army officers to criticize government leaders in the press without the consent of the civilian war minister. Disgruntled with low pay and parsimonious defense funding, some officers violently intimidated their critics and dueled with politicians in polemic editorials. A few officers, rallied by Colonel Antônio de Sena Madureira's acerbic pen, committed a series of insubordinate acts to defy the war minister's censorship and defend the military's honor. The government attempted to punish these malcontents despite the Supreme Military Council's ruling that officers, like civilians, had a right to freedom of expression. Alienated by this and other imperial policies, officers toppled the monarchy in 1889, which was deeply unpopular with wealthy elites, Liberal politicians, and the general public. The military government under Field Marshal Manoel Deodoro da Fonseca issued many arbitrary decrees, held off a navy coup, and dissolved an uncooperative Congress. Generally unpopular, the army held onto power until 1894.

See also **Brazil: 1808-1889; Fonseca, Manoel Deodoro da; Madureira, Antônio de Sena.**

BIBLIOGRAPHY

On the institutional causes of military unrest see William S. Dudley, "Professionalization and Politicization as Motivational Factors in the Brazilian Army Coup of 15 November, 1889," *Journal of Latin American Studies* 8:1 (May 1976): 101–125. For the events which precipitated the military question consult Raimundo Magalhães, *Deodoro: A espada contra o império* (1957).

Additional Bibliography

Alonso, Angela Maria. *Idéias em movimento: A geração 1870 na crise do Brasil-Império.* São Paulo: ANPOCS: Paz e Terra, 2002.

Castro, Celso. *Os militares e a república: Um estudo sobre cultura e ação política.* Rio de Janeiro: J. Zahar Editor, 1995.

PETER M. BEATTIE

MILITIAS

This entry includes the following articles:

COLONIAL BRAZIL

A militia system was planned for Colonial Brazil by the first governor-general, Tomé de Souza in 1548, which called for two types of troops. The first was a permanent militia (*tropas auxiliares*) formed by unpaid conscription among the local men capable of taking the field. Officers in each captaincy would be commissioned by the governors. The second formation (*ordenanças*) would be conscripted from the remaining men unfit for the field. It would supplement the small regular garrisons of the colonial forts and carry out police duties in both urban and rural areas. As conceived, both of these forces would supplement the small core of regular regiments sent at intervals from Portugal (*tropa paga*).

Until a colonial population capable of supporting this planned system could emerge, real militia power in the sixteenth century lay in the hands of the *bandeiras.* These were armed bands of local settlers (*moradores*) including the racially mixed mamelucos living among them, who used local Indian allies to hunt Indians of the interior for use as slaves. These Bandeirantes were freelance fighters, and were supplemented in each captaincy by the Capitão Do Mato or "bush captain" and his company of Indian allies. These latter served the militia as scouts, and were essential to the discovery and destruction of the quilombos of runaway slaves. One advantage of unpaid militia service was the possibility of gaining slaves without having to purchase them.

The militia underwent considerable change during the Dutch Wars of 1624–1654. Mathias de Albuquerque, appointed governor and commander in chief of the four northern provinces in 1629, found himself handicapped by a lack of arms and training among the militia, apathy, and desertion among the *moradores.* To combat the Dutch, he created a series of fortified posts at the edge of the forest surrounding each Dutch enclave, and *capitanias de emboscadas* or "strong fighting patrols" capable of ambushing the Dutch. At least half the militia was involved in guerrilla warfare, and this premium on bush-craft allowed the expansion of the militia to include Indians, free mulattoes (*pardos*), and free blacks. Companies of Indians and free blacks were later brigaded into regiments (*terços*) under their native leaders, Dom Felipe Camarão, a Potiguar Indian, and Henrique Dias, a free-born black, and served bravely throughout the war. Use of *pardo* and free black regiments (now called *Henriques*) continued in the 18th and 19th centuries. Both provided excellent service during the French incursions at Rio de Janeiro in 1710 and 1711.

Poor performance by the Portuguese regular army at home and in the colonies during the Seven Years' War (1756–1763), led to major financial and military reforms in the 1760s. Under Count William of Schaumburg-Lippe, the Portuguese home army was reformed. His student, Dom Luis Lavradio, similarly altered the Brazilian militia system. The training of the colonial *auxiliares* was raised to equal that of the regular regiments, while the training of all was upgraded under a uniform system. The semi-independent status of the captaincies was reduced in financial and military areas to one requiring centralized reporting and mutual military assistance. Each captaincy was to maintain at least four militia regiments, two white, one *pardo,* and one free black, with additional militia companies recruited for police work in the urban areas. Militia regiments of horse cavalry existed in several captaincies. Finances were also reformed, allowing the militia to serve longer periods, gain minimal training, and campaign longer when needed. This reformed system prevailed until after independence, when the colonial militia system of Brazil merged into the National Guard.

See also **Armed Forces.**

BIBLIOGRAPHY

Charles R. Boxer, *The Dutch in Brazil, 1624–1654* (1957) and *The Golden Age of Brazil, 1695–1750* (1974).

Richard M. Morse, *The Bandeirantes: The Historical Role of the Brazilian Pathfinders* (1965).

Dauril Alden, *Royal Government in Colonial Brazil, 1769–1779* (1968).

John Hemming, *The Conquest of the Brazilian Indians* (1978).

Additional Bibliography

Bracco, Diego. *Charrúas, guenoas y guaraníes: Interacción y destrucción: indígenas en el Río de la Plata.* Montevideo: Linardi y Risso, 2004.

Figueiredo, Luciano. *Rebeliões no Brasil Colônia.* Stanford: Stanford University Press, 2001.

Kraay, Hendrik. *Race, State, and Armed Forces in Independence-Era Brazil: Bahia, 1790s-1840s.* Rio de Janeiro: Jorge Zahar Editor, 2005.

DANIEL J. SEGEL

COLONIAL SPANISH AMERICA

Following the sixteenth-century conquest of Mexico and Peru, most Spanish settlers turned away from military activities. In New Spain, Peru, and other provinces, the crown enacted military regulations that required Spanish *encomenderos* to keep arms and horses available to defend the new society against Indian uprisings, frontier raids, or foreign intrusions. Although the Mixtón War (1540–1541) on the northern frontier of Mexico required the mobilization of settlers to crush a desperate native attempt to turn back the Conquest and Viceroy Francisco de Toledo y Figueroa ordered Peruvian *encomenderos* to campaign in person and at their own expense against Inca holdouts at Vilcabamba (1572), by the end of the century there was little need for organized militia forces. Occasionally, inexperienced militiamen from the coasts and interior districts served at Cartagena, Veracruz, Havana, Callao, and other coastal fortifications, but often they lacked the resolve to withstand determined raiders.

Infrequently taxation, rising food prices, or political quarrels provoked urban riots and looting that led to demands for organized militia forces. In 1624 Viceroy Marqués de Gelves of New Spain failed to deploy the militia to suppress urban violence in the capital when the creoles who formed these units took sides against him. Similarly, in Peru the dangers of Dutch raids during the 1620s did not appear as threatening as the prospect of mobilizing the 1,800 artisans and laborers of Lima who had been organized into a militia force. In 1692 a violent insurrection of Mexico City's lower classes that destroyed property compelled the authorities to assemble a force of merchants and guildsmen in what became the Urban Regiment of Commerce as well as several cavalry squadrons that were sponsored by the pork butchers, bakers, and tanners. The merchants subsidized ten companies and sent their young assistants to participate in occasional exercises, guard duty, and parades. The regime sanctioned the creation of similar urban units elsewhere, but during peacetime such militias tended to decline in effectiveness.

By the eighteenth century, the external military threat to Spanish America posed by Britain took precedence over internal concerns. The stunning loss of Havana in 1762 during the Seven Years' War caused the government of King Charles III to dispatch Field Marshal Alejandro O'Reilly to Cuba, where he studied the problems of defending the enormous expanses of Spain's American empire. He concluded that Spanish American militiamen would have to play a major role in defense. Each province was to raise a small regular force of infantry and dragoons, sometimes supported by rotating battalions or regiments from the European army. These troops would serve as a training cadre and core for a larger army of provincial militiamen. In Mexico chaotic preparations during the recent war rushed untrained men from the interior to defend Veracruz, where they deserted or soon perished from yellow fever. In 1764 the crown sent Lieutenant General Juan de Villalba to Mexico with a Spanish infantry regiment and a contingent of officers who organized the regular forces and the regional provincial militia units.

As might be expected, some Spanish observers pointed out the inherent dangers of a program designed to arm and train American creoles and the hardy *pardos* and *morenos* who defended coastal regions and strategic ports. Throughout the latter decades of the eighteenth century, defense planners tinkered with the balance of militiamen to regular soldiers. Many professional officers opposed dependence upon potentially untrustworthy provincial militia regiments and battalions, recommending instead small regular armies of American and European soldiers that could be reinforced by untrained colonial reserves in wartime crises. In Peru militiamen exhibited doubtful loyalty in suppressing tax revolts during 1780, and in the case of the massive Túpac Amaru rebellion beginning the same year, the authorities often bypassed militia units in favor of using regular troops and loyal Indians commanded by Spanish officers. The militias of New Granada played a more significant role in containing the Comunero Revolt (1781), but the European officers resisted promotions of the creoles to senior commands. However, because of the high costs of regular units and the fact that with the outbreak of the French Revolution the Spanish army could not spare regiments during wartime, the colonial armies had to be composed of creoles, mestizos, mulattoes, and even Indians, who in theory were exempt from militia recruitment.

Wealthy creoles often paid large sums to purchase senior militia commissions, which offset the costs of arming and uniforming their units. The imperial government offered minor privileges and granted the *fuero militar* (the right of military personnel to be tried in military courts, *see* fueros) to part-time officers and sometimes to soldiers. Although the government had no intention of granting militiamen exemptions from the regular legal system, a few used the *fuero militar* and access to martial courts as a means to protect themselves from prosecution. This practice led to acrimonious disputes involving the mining, merchant, and other legal jurisdictions that resisted any diminution of their powers. While the Crown opposed any militarization of society or the fostering of praetorian attitudes, the need to attract manpower in an era of invasion threats made military privileges one means to satisfy Creole hunger for social recognition and honors.

For many Creoles, lengthy wartime mobilizations and active duty away from their homes and normal occupations offset any privileges or social status that came with showy uniforms. Officers sought to avoid monthly training exercises and claimed ill health or the pressures of business to escape garrison duty or service in cantonments. Terror of yellow fever at the coasts for unacclimatized men of the highlands provoked desertions by militiamen and resistance to recruitment by those who faced lotteries in their home jurisdictions to fill local companies, battalions, and regiments. In New Spain after 1800, ten territorial militia brigades of regiments, battalions, companies, and coastal forces totaled almost 25,000 men at peacetime strength. Adding untrained militia reserves, the regime possessed a theoretical force of some 40,000 men. During a British invasion threat in 1806–1807, Viceroy José de Iturrigaray mobilized an operational army of about 12,000 militia and regular troops to interdict the invasion route inland from Veracruz. In the same years, Buenos Aires militiamen played important roles in repelling two British attacks on the Viceroyalty of La Plata.

With the outbreak of the revolutions for independence in 1810, some provincial militia units turned their guns against the Spanish government. In Mexico, where most militia units remained loyal to Spain until the revolt of Agustín de Iturbide in 1821, much of the Eighth Provincial Brigade based in the Bajío provinces, including captains Ignacio Allende and Mariano Abasolo of the Queen's Provincial Dragoon Regiment based in Guanajuato, joined the rebellion of Father Miguel Hidalgo. In regions torn by chronic revolutionary warfare, new royalist urban and rural militias emerged to garrison their territories and to pursue guerrilla forces, theoretically freeing regular forces to track down major rebel army concentrations. With independence, many former militia officers and soldiers who had served both sides managed to survive the transition to serve the new nations.

See also **Forts and Fortifications, Spanish America.**

BIBLIOGRAPHY

Most studies on the Spanish American militias focus upon the eighteenth century and neglect the earlier period. One exception is Santiago Gerardo Suárez, *La milicias: Instituciones militares hispanoamericanas* (1984). For studies concerning Bourbon militia reforms, see Bibiano Torres Ramírez, *Alejandro O'Reilly en las Indias* (1969); Juan Marchena Fernández, *Oficiales y soldados en el Ejército de América* (1983); Julio Albi, *La defensa de las Indias, 1764–1799* (1987). For studies on New Spain, see María Del Carmen Velázquez, *El estado de guerra en Nueva España, 1760–1808* (1950); Lyle N. McAlister, *The "Fuero Militar" in New Spain, 1764–1800* (1957); and Christon I. Archer, *The Army in Bourbon Mexico, 1760–1810* (1977). For South America, see Leon G. Campbell, *The Military and Society in Colonial Peru, 1750–1810*

(1978), and Allan J. Kuethe, *Military Reform and Society in New Granada, 1773–1808* (1978). For the independence period, see Jaime E. Rodríguez O., ed., *The Independence of Mexico and the Creation of the New Nation* (1989), and Julio Albi, *Banderas olvidadas: El ejército realista en América* (1990).

Additional Bibliography

Blanes Martín, Tamara. *Fortificaciones del Caribe.* La Habana, Cuba: Letras cubanas, 2001.

Marchena Fernández, Juan. *Ejército y milicias en el mundo colonial americano.* Madrid: Editorial MAPFRE, 1992.

Serrano Alvarez, José Manuel. *Fortificaciones y tropas: El gasto militar en tierra firme, 1700–1788.* Sevilla: Diputación de Sevilla, 2004.

Vinson, Ben. *Bearing Arms for His Majesty: The Free-Colored Militia in Colonial Mexico.* Stanford, CA: Stanford University Press, 2001.

CHRISTON I. ARCHER

MILLAS JIMÉNEZ, JORGE (1917–1982).

Jorge Millas Jiménez (*b.* 17 January 1917; *d.* 8 November 1982), Chilean philosopher. Jorge Millas was born and educated in Santiago, where he studied philosophy and law in the 1930s. He also studied psychology at the University of Iowa and held teaching appointments at Columbia University and the University of Puerto Rico. Millas's first major work was *Idea de la individualidad* (1943), a book in which he affirmed the essential individuality of human nature and followed Enrique Molina Garmendia's tradition of separating philosophy from politics. He became one of the founders of Chilean philosophical professionalism in the 1950s, a period in which the study of the discipline became highly specialized and responsive to European, especially German, philosophical currents. In response to social and political change in the 1960s, Millas defended spiritual and humanistic values against the pressures of mass society. His most important works during this period are *El desafío espiritual de la sociedad de masas* (1964) and *Idea de la filosofía* (1970). A philosopher who argued that both philosophy and the university should be free from external pressures, Millas produced an influential set of essays collected under the title *Idea y defensa de la universidad* (1981). During the period of military rule in the 1970s and early 1980s, his articulate defense of the rights of the university gave him great public prominence. He became a leader of the academic organization Andrés Bello and an outspoken opposition voice until his death.

BIBLIOGRAPHY

Enrique Molina Garmendia, *La filosofía en Chile en la primera mitad del siglo XX* (1953).

Iván Jakšić, *Academic Rebels in Chile: The Role of Philosophy in Higher Education and Politics* (1989).

Additional Bibliography

Kourím, Zdenek. "Memoria de tres filósofos latinoamericanos." *Cuadernos Hispanoamericanos* 589/590 (July/August 1999): 69–88.

Sanabria, José Rubén. "En torno a la filosofía latinoamericana." *Revista de Filosofía* 25:75 (September/December 1992): 360–417.

IVÁN JAKSÍC

MILLA Y VIDAURRE, JOSÉ (1822–1882).

José Milla y Vidaurre (*b.* 4 August 1822; *d.* 30 September 1882), Guatemalan writer. Born in Guatemala City, the son of Honduran Colonel Justo Milla and Mercedes Vidaurre, a daughter of one of the city's leading families, "Pepe" Milla was the leading literary figure of nineteenth-century Guatemala and the principal intellectual supporter of the conservative regime of Rafael Carrera (1839–1865). After Francisco Morazán exiled his father in 1829, Milla grew up in the care of his uncle, Santiago Milla. He was educated under the guidance of Father José María Castilla, who had been a leader in the Central America independence movement. His literary talent, much influenced by European Romanticism, was recognized early, and he abandoned legal training to devote his time to editing and writing essays, novels, poetry, and history. He also abandoned a youthful attachment to liberalism and, as editor of the government's gazette (*Gaceta oficial,* later *Gaceta de Guatemala*) and of several independent newspapers, he eloquently defended the Guatemalan conservatives and Rafael Carrera's regime. He also served on the Council of State, in the legislature, and on several diplomatic missions throughout the period of conservative control.

Milla wrote under the anagrammatic pseudonym Salomé Jil. His novels, history, poetry, and descriptions of customs reflected his Romantic ideals but also drew heavily on Guatemalan themes, and in this sense he was a forerunner of Miguel Ángel Asturias. He was Guatemala's most popular novelist well into the twentieth century, his best-known works being *Los nazarenos* (1867), *El visitador* (1869), *La hija del adelantado* (1866), *Historia de un Pepe* (1882), *Memorias de un abogado* (1876), *Cuadros de costumbres* (1865), and *Viaje al otro mundo pasando por otras partes* (1875).

After the Liberal Reforma of 1871, Milla left public service, traveled widely in the United States and Europe, and retired to his hacienda at Quezada, near Jutiapa, in eastern Guatemala, where he wrote the first two volumes of his projected *Historia de la América Central* (1879), commissioned by the Guatemalan government. These volumes, covering the period 1502–1686, reflected his romantic attachment to Hispanic tradition as well as his sensitivity to the indigenous peoples of Guatemala.

See also **Literature: Spanish.**

BIBLIOGRAPHY

Francisco Albizúrez Palma, *Vida y obra de José Milla: Biografía mínima* (1982).

Francisco Albizúrez Palma and Catalina Barrios y Barrios, *Historia de la literatura guatemalteca,* vol. 2 (1981), pp. 269–288.

José Roberto Carrera Molina, *Consideraciones sobre temas, personajes y humorismo de los cuadros costumbristas de José Milla* (1972).

Carlos C. Haeussler Yela, *Diccionario general de Guatemala,* vol. 2 (1983), pp. 1019–1020.

Walter A. Payne, *A Central American Historian: José Milla (1822–1882)* (1957).

Additional Bibliography

Payne, Walter A. *José Milla: un historiador centroamericano, 1822–1882.* Guatemala: Editorial José de Pineda Ibarra, 1982.

Skinner, Lee Joan. "Colonial (Dis)order: Inheritance and Succession in José Milla's Historical Novels." *Latin American Literary Review* 27:54 (July–December 1999): 80–95.

RALPH LEE WOODWARD JR.

MILLENARIAN MOVEMENTS.

See **Messianic Movements: Brazil; Messianic Movements: Spanish America.**

MILONGA.

MILONGA. Milonga, an Argentine term with several distinct meanings, perhaps most commonly applied to the dance that was probably the immediate forerunner of the Argentine tango. The *milonga* of the 1860s and 1870s became, especially after its revival in the 1930s at the hands of talented composers such as Sebastián Piana, part of the standard repertoire of tango bands. The word also means the place where the dance was performed. Hence its development in the 1920s into a virtual synonym for "nightclub" or "cabaret." The young women frequenting such locales also became known, somewhat confusingly, as *milongas* or *milonguitas.* The term seems to have been used originally to describe the *payadas,* the competitive performances of *payadores* (folksingers accompanying themselves on guitar) common in nineteenth-century Argentina and Uruguay. In colloquial Río de la Plata Spanish, *milonga* can also mean "difficulty" (as in the expression "life is a *milonga*") or "vain words." There are two distinct types of *milonga*: *milonga lisa,* or "simple" *milonga,* which calls for the dancer to step on every beat of the music; and *milonga con traspíe,* a version that focuses on countersteps, in which the dancer constantly changes weight from one foot to the other.

See also **Music: Popular Music and Dance; Tango.**

BIBLIOGRAPHY

Roberto Selles et al., *La historia del tango,* vol. 12 (1978).

Additional Bibliography

Nudler, Julio. *Tango judío: Del ghetto a la milonga.* Buenos Aires: Editorial Sudamericana, 1998.

Rosboch, María Eugenia. *La rebelión de los abrazos: Tango, milonga y danza; Imaginarios del tango en sus espacios de producción simbólica; La milonga y el espectáculo.* La Plata, Argentina: Universidad Nacional de la Plata, 2006.

Thompson, Robert Farris. *Tango: The Art History of Love.* New York: Pantheon, 2005.

SIMON COLLIER

MINA.

MINA. Mina, one of the most common terms used to define the ethnicity of Africans in Brazil. "Minas" came from a broad region in West Africa, usually between Cape Mount and Cape Lopez, which the Portuguese called the Costa da Mina. The name derived from the castle São Jorge da Mina (or Elmina), founded in 1482 by the Portuguese on the Gold Coast (modern Ghana). In the colonial period Bahian merchants traded directly with the Mina coast, exchanging tobacco for gold and slaves. Minas were highly valued for their mining skills in the gold-producing captaincies of Minas Gerais and Goiás. In the nineteenth century, however, Minas were often Arabic-speaking Muslims, that is, Hausas or Yorubas from what is now Nigeria. In the cities of Salvador and Rio de Janeiro, Mina slaves were especially successful at buying their freedom and return passage to West Africa.

See also **Africa, Portuguese; Slavery: Brazil; Slave Trade.**

BIBLIOGRAPHY

Philip D. Curtin, *The Atlantic Slave Trade* (1969).

Pierre Verger, *Bahia and the West African Trade, 1549–1851* (1970).

Mary C. Karasch, *Slave Life in Rio de Janeiro, 1808–1850* (1987).

Additional Bibliography

Klein, Herbert S. *The Atlantic Slave Trade.* Cambridge: Cambridge University Press, 1999.

Landers, Jane and Barry Robinson. *Slaves, Subjects, and Subversives: Blacks in Colonial Latin America.* Albuquerque: University of New Mexico Press, 2006.

Silva, Maria Beatriz Nizza da. *Brasil: Colonização e escravidão.* Rio de Janeiro: Nova Fronteira, 2000.

MARY KARASCH

MINAS GERAIS.

MINAS GERAIS. Minas Gerais, a mountainous, landlocked state in southeastern Brazil, encompassing some 225,000 square miles, roughly the size of France. It is the second most populous state, and traditionally one of the three most powerful states in Brazil. To the south, it borders on the other two traditional powers in national politics, the states of São Paulo and Rio de Janeiro.

The Tupi people, probably in sparse numbers, inhabited this densely forested region for several thousand years before the arrival of the first Europeans in the seventeenth century. In the 1690s the discovery of gold in the mountain streams of the interior set off the first great gold rush in the Western world. Thousands of colonists and their African slaves poured into the region during the next fifty years, traveling overland from the port of Rio de Janeiro, or moving down out of northeastern Brazil along the São Francisco River.

The area soon became known as the "General Mines" (Minas Gerais in Portuguese), and in 1720 became a new captaincy of Brazil. The mining camps of Sabará, Mariana, and Vila Rica (present-day Ouro Prêto) were named imperial *vilas* (towns), and became the major population centers in the mining zone. Diamonds were discovered in 1729 to the north of the gold-mining zone, and Tejuco (present-day Diamantina) became the major center for the diamond fields.

The enormous wealth generated by gold and diamond production made the Portuguese monarchy one of the richest in Europe in the eighteenth century, and provided the European economy with 80 percent of its gold supply. Wealthy miners financed the construction of churches, homes, and public buildings in Minas Gerais in a distinctive baroque style. Colonial Brazil's most famous artist and architect, Antônio Francisco Lisboa (1730–1814), better known as Aleijadinho (the little cripple), produced some of Brazil's greatest artistic treasures in the late eighteenth century.

With the exhaustion of placer gold deposits in the 1770s, Minas Gerais entered a period of economic stagnation. But in the mid-nineteenth century coffee production boomed in the southern part of the province, while cattle ranching and dairy farming emerged as major economic activities in the central, northern, and western regions. Gold mining experienced a small revival in the 1820s and 1830s, and even today plays a part in the state's economy.

Despite falling behind the states of São Paulo and Rio de Janeiro in economic growth in the nineteenth century, Minas Gerais maintained a very powerful role in national politics. From the 1890s to the 1930s it dominated presidential politics along with São Paulo.

Since the 1940s the state has become a major manufacturing center, with most of its heavy industry located around the state capital, Belo Horizonte.

Production and processing of raw materials such as iron ore, bauxite, and manganese remain vital to the state economy. Minas Gerais is also famous for its beef and dairy products.

The state continues to play a central role in national politics. *Mineiros* are known for their conservatism and commitment to traditional social values.

See also **Brazil, Geography; Gold Rushes, Brazil; Mining: Colonial Brazil; Tupi.**

BIBLIOGRAPHY

Richard F. Burton, *Explorations in the Highlands of Brazil* (1869).

Charles R. Boxer, *The Golden Age of Brazil, 1695–1750* (1969).

John D. Wirth, *Minas Gerais in the Brazilian Federation, 1889–1937* (1977).

E. Bradford Burns, *A History of Brazil* (1980).

Additional Bibliography

Kiddy, Elizabeth W. *Blacks of the Rosary: Memory and History in Minas Gerais, Brazil.* University Park, PA: Pennsylvania State University Press, 2005.

Langfur, Hal. *The Forbidden Lands: Colonial Identity, Frontier Violence, and the Persistence of Brazil's Eastern Indians, 1750–1830.* Stanford, CA: Stanford University Press, 2006.

Maxwell, Kenneth. *Conflicts and Conspiracies: Brazil and Portugal, 1750–1808.* New York: Routledge, 2004.

Paiva, Eduardo França. *Escravidão e universo cultural na colonia: Minas Gerais, 1716–1789.* Belo Horizonte, Brazil: Editora UFMG, 2001.

MARSHALL C. EAKIN

MINA Y LARREA, JAVIER (1789–1817). Javier Mina y Larrea (*b.* 1 July 1789; *d.* 11 November 1817), Mexican insurgent leader. Born in Otano, Spain, he fought against the French in Spain until he was captured and sent to France. After Napoleon's defeat in 1814, he returned to Spain, then under the absolutist rule of Ferdinand VII (1784–1833), to lead a conspiracy to restore the Constitution of 1812. When the movement failed, he fled to London, where he met Lord Holland, an Englishman sympathetic to the Mexican insurgency, and Fray Servando Teresa de Mier (1765–1827). Together the three planned an expedition to New Spain to fight there against absolutism. In May 1816 he departed for the United States, where he obtained credit, money, and men. He landed in Soto la Marina in April 1817. Leaving some of his forces there, he continued inland to join the insurgents. Although he threatened the regime and was successful in several actions, his enterprise was doomed because the organized insurgency had disappeared with the death of José María Morelos y Pavón (1765–1815). Mina then joined José Antonio Torres (1770–1818) at the fortress of El Sombrero. After El Sombrero fell, he attacked the convoys that laid siege to the fortress of Los Remedios. He was captured at the ranch of El Venadito on 27 October 1817 and shot at Los Remedios.

BIBLIOGRAPHY

Martín Luis Guzmán, *Javier Mina, héroe de España y México,* 3d ed. (1972).

José María Miquel I Vergés, *Mina, el español frente a España* (1945).

William Davis Robinson, *Memoirs of the Mexican Revolution* (1820).

Additional Bibliography

Ortuño Martínez, Manuel. *Xavier Mina: Fronteras de libertad.* Mexico City: Porrúa, 2003.

Torre Saavedra, Ana Laura de la. *La expedición de Xavier Mina a Nueva España: Una utopía liberal imperial.* Mexico City: Instituto Mora, 1999.

VIRGINIA GUEDEA

MINDLIN, JOSÉ EPHIM (1914–). A reporter, attorney, and business owner, Mindlin was born in São Paulo on September 8, 1914, to Russian Jewish immigrant parents. He founded his company, Metal Leve, in 1950. It manufactured engine pistons and grew to be the largest of its kind in Brazil. In the 1990s, after facing a serious crisis caused by the Brazil's financial crisis, Mindlin sold his shares.

He subsequently has devoted most of his time to running the Biblioteca Brasiliana Guita e José Mindlin. A famous book lover, he has amassed more than thirty thousand titles since he was thirteen years old, of which approximately ten thousand are rare and two thousand are among the rarest. His collection on the history of Brazil is the largest ever assembled, even more comprehensive than that of the National Library in Rio de Janeiro.

Despite constant offers from foreign universities, Mindlin announced on May 17, 2006, that he had decided to donate his books to the University of São Paulo, which in December of that year started construction of a library to house them, expected to be completed by the end of 2009. For ninety-nine years after the death of its donor, the library will remain under the Mindlin Foundation's control, with full ownership turned over to the university thereafter.

Mindlin wrote very little, but his passion for books earned him membership in the Brazilian Academy of Letters in June 2006.

See also **Libraries in Latin America.**

BIBLIOGRAPHY

Mindlin, José. *Uma Vida entre livros* São Paulo: EDUSP, 1997.

Mindlin, José. *Destaques da biblioteca indisciplinada.* São Paulo: EDUSP, 2006.

CARMEN LUCIA DE AZEVEDO

MINEIROS. *See* Minas Gerais.

MINING

This entry includes the following articles:
COLONIAL BRAZIL
COLONIAL SPANISH AMERICA
MODERN

COLONIAL BRAZIL

Little is known about the mining of precious metals and gemstones in Brazil prior to the arrival of Europeans. Indian legends of silver and gold whetted the appetites of Portuguese pathfinders (known as Bandeirantes) who found some alluvial gold in the interior of the captaincies of Bahia and São Paulo in the sixteenth and seventeenth centuries. But only after the discovery of gold, and then diamonds, in the rugged interior of southeastern Brazil at the close of the seventeenth century did mining become an important economic activity in Brazil.

The discovery of gold in the 1690s sparked the Western world's first great gold rush. Thousands of Portuguese streamed into the densely forested mountains of the Rio das Velhas basin some 250 miles north of the small port of Rio de Janeiro. Immigrants made a month-long journey up the São Francisco River from settlements in the northeast, or an equally long trek overland from São Paulo or Rio de Janeiro.

By the 1720s the mining zone was known as Minas Gerais (General Mines). Prospectors also moved northward and westward into what today are the states of Goiás and Mato Grosso, sparking smaller gold rushes. Another small-scale gold rush took place in the interior of the captaincy of Bahia. About 150 miles north of the gold-mining zone prospectors found rich diamond deposits in the Sêrro Frio region that the Portuguese crown eventually closed off and controlled through a royal monopoly.

During the first few decades of the eighteenth century the mining zone was a chaotic and violent region. The incoming immigrants drove out or killed off local Indian tribes, and fought bitterly among themselves for control of regional governments. The immigrants also brought with them large numbers of African slaves. By 1750 Minas Gerais was the most populous captaincy in the colony, and it had a black majority.

The Portuguese crown established the captaincy of Minas Gerais in 1720, consisting of several royal towns and four administrative districts, as an attempt to impose order on the mining region.

Most of the gold and diamonds mined during this period was located in rivers and streams, or in land deposits close to the surface. Mining techniques were rudimentary, even by eighteenth-century standards: the Portuguese did not employ deep-shaft mining like that found in Spanish Peru and Mexico. Most miners turned to panning in streams and rivers. The largest operations stripped hillsides using hydraulic techniques and slave labor.

By the 1750s most of the more easily recovered alluvial and surface deposits had been exhausted, and the mountains of the mining zone had been deforested and defaced. Gold production declined throughout

Slaves washing diamonds, Brazil, c. 1770s. Mining for both gold and diamonds in colonial Brazil relied on the labor of African slaves. © KRAUSE, JOHANSEN/ARCHIVO ICONOGRAFICO, SA/CORBIS

the last half of the eighteenth century; indeed, the gold-mining economy had stagnated by the end of the century. However, even as gold production declined, Brazil remained the world's principal producer of diamonds until the 1870s.

The highly dispersed nature of gold mining in eighteenth-century Brazil, and the enormous difficulties the crown faced in attempting to tax mining production, condemned to failure efforts to suppress contraband. (In theory the crown was to receive one-fifth of all production.) The inability of the monarchy to control and measure production also makes it virtually impossible for modern researchers to determine how much gold Brazil actually produced in the eighteenth century.

The most widely accepted "guesstimates" place eighteenth-century production around 25 to 30 million ounces (roughly the same amount produced in California during the gold rush in the mid-nineteenth century). Minas Gerais alone produced three-quarters of the total, with production peaking in the 1750s.

The gold rush transformed Brazil, Portugal's empire, and the European economy. The gold rush stimulated the first effective European colonization of the Brazilian interior, and intensified the decline of the old sugar plantation economy in the Northeast. Rio de Janeiro, once a sleepy backwater port, became a thriving commercial entrepôt, and after 1763 the capital of Brazil. Since the eighteenth century, the center of economic, social, and political power has been firmly entrenched in the Southeast.

Gold and diamonds made Brazil the economic heart of the Portuguese world empire, but they also helped intensify Portugal's economic dependence on England. Brazilian gold paid for the importation of English manufactures and stimulated British rather than Portuguese industry. The enormous wealth of Brazil made the Portuguese monarchy one of the richest in eighteenth-century Europe; these Brazilian riches diminished the need of the monarchy for support from the nobility or other social groups, reinforcing Portuguese absolutism.

Finally, Brazil supplied 80 percent of the gold in circulation in eighteenth-century Europe, stimulating the economic expansion of the European economy in the aftermath of the seventeenth-century depression.

See also **Gold Rushes, Brazil; Slavery: Indian Slavery and Forced Labor.**

BIBLIOGRAPHY

Richard M. Morse, ed., *The Bandeirantes* (1965).

Caio Prado, Jr., *The Colonial Background of Modern Brazil*, translated by Suzette Macedo (1967).

Charles R. Boxer, *The Golden Age of Brazil, 1695–1750* (1969).

James Lang, "Brazil: The Golden Age, 1690–1750," in *Portuguese Brazil: The King's Plantation* (1979).

A. J. R. Russell-Wood, "The Gold Cycle, ca. 1690–1750," in *Colonial Brazil*, edited by Leslie Bethell (1987).

Additional Bibliography

Higgins, Kathleen J. *"Licentious Liberty" in a Brazilian Gold-mining Region: Slavery, Gender, and Social Control in Eighteenth-century Sabará, Minas Gerais.* University Park: Pennsylvania State University Press, 1999.

Santos, Márcio. *Estradas reais: Introdução ao estudo dos caminhos do ouro e do diamante no Brasil.* Belo Horizonte: Editora Estrada Real, 2001.

MARSHALL C. EAKIN

COLONIAL SPANISH AMERICA

Despite Spanish America's fame as the land of El Dorado, colonial mining produced comparatively little gold but huge quantities of silver. Official imports of American bullion between 1500 and 1650 probably drove up European gold stocks by 5 percent and silver stocks by 50 percent—and the age of greatest Spanish American silver production did not even begin until about 1700. Output of the Spanish colonial mines lowered the value of silver relative to gold, in Europe, from 10.5 to 1 around 1500 to 15.5 to 1 by 1800. (The Brazilian gold boom beginning in the 1690s stopped silver's further decline.)

"Gold constitutes treasure," wrote Columbus to Ferdinand and Isabella, "and anyone who has it can do whatever he likes in the world." If bullion gave Spanish adventurers the freedom they yearned for, American gold and silver also magically transformed the Spanish monarchy into a world power, seemingly freed from material constraints, to champion Catholicism against Protestant heresy, defend Habsburg imperial ambitions, and send an Invincible Armada against the English.

Colonial mining concentrated almost exclusively on precious metals. Although aware of deposits of copper and iron, Spaniards could generally import base metals more cheaply from Europe than they could produce them in America. Aside from gold and silver, mercury was the only metal mined in large quantities during the colonial period. The main, and indeed sole significant, center for mercury was Huancavelica, in Peru, discovered in 1563. The Spanish worked alluvial gold deposits in the Caribbean, Mexico, and the Andes (especially in New Granada).

Spanish settlers located all the main silver-bearing zones of Latin America in the sixteenth century. Some deposits of silver ore had been known to the native cultures. Knowledge of these led the settlers, often with success, to seek other neighboring deposits. A prime example of this progression is the Spaniards' exploitation, from 1538, of the ores of Porco in present southwestern Bolivia, which the Incas had mined and refined, and from Porco their discovery in 1545 of the far larger deposits of Potosí, twenty miles to the northeast. The main silver regions found by 1600, and still active in the early twenty-first century, were located in the central Andes (in present-day southern Peru and western Bolivia) and in a 600-mile band of Mexican territory running northwest from Pachuca to Santa Bárbara. This band included the major Mexican centers: the two just mentioned as well as Guanajuato, Zacatecas, and Sombrerete. Other lesser silver centers arose in western and southern-central Mexico before 1600, after which a few major strikes were made in the north. The geographical bounds of colonial Spanish mining essentially were drawn in the sixteenth century. Very little silver ore was ever discovered or worked in Portuguese America.

Most of the ores were found at considerable height: in the 6,000 to 8,000 feet range in Mexico and from 10,000 to 16,000 feet in the central Andes. The ore-bearing veins had been formed during Tertiary orogenesis, when the great sierras of Mexico and the Andes underwent their most recent uplifting. During those movements, hot water carrying metallic salts rose from the earth's interior to fill cracks near the surface. Silver sulfides were among those salts, along with compounds of such elements as tin, copper, lead, bismuth, and antimony. In many cases these silver sulfides (called *negrillos* by the Spanish) were later enriched by the action of descending water, often being converted by oxygenation into silver chlorides (known as *pacos* or *colorados*). Thus enriched, the ores near the surface often yielded high gains to the first miners to attack them. Colonial miners found little native silver (at Huantajaya in northern Chile nearly pure wire silver was extracted) but great quantities of enriched ores. These initial profits provided the capital needed for investment in shaft mining and complex refining machinery once the shallow ores had been taken.

TECHNIQUES

Silver production in its first three decades in both Mexico and the Andes drew on native skills. The Tarascans of western Mexico appear to have placed their copper-smelting knowledge at the disposal of Spaniards wanting silver. In comparison with the central Andean peoples, however, Mexican natives were backward in metal production. Early Spanish miners in what is now Bolivia drew heavily on both the Andeans' abilities in subterranean mining and their refining techniques. Particularly important was the *wayra*, a small,

Llamas and diagrams concerning mineral extraction, engraving by French School (18th century) from *Relation du voyage de la mer du sud aux cotes du Chily et du Perou* by A. F. Frezier, 1716 (b/w photo). PRIVATE COLLECTION/ THE BRIDGEMAN ART LIBRARY

wind-blown smelter. Up to the 1570s Spanish silver "miners" in the central Andes tended to leave extraction and processing of ore to native experts, simply taking a rent in exchange for access to the ore deposits. Some mining and refining technology was, of course, imported from Spain. Especially important as carriers of technology from Spain were the Basques, in whose home economy iron production had long played a prominent part. Another important, perhaps crucial, source of knowledge was the miners of Central Europe, who were present in the New World from the 1520s, though their movements are hard to track. And Central European notions may have been carried across the Atlantic by Spaniards. Finally, the possibility of technical contributions from Africa, though not yet explored, cannot be discounted. Many of the early African slaves in Spanish America came from the extreme west of Africa, where producing and working iron were ancient skills. Their techniques were crucial in the Brazilian goldfields.

The important technical role of Native Americans in silver production came to an end in the 1560s and 1570s. The main reason was the development of ore processing by amalgamation with mercury. The principles of amalgamation had been known in Europe since Roman times, but the industrial development of the process took place in Mexico in the 1550s. Bartolomé de Medina, a Spanish Dominican, is generally credited with devising the process in the mid-1550s, particularly mixing *magistral*) (copper sulfate) with ground silver ore and mercury. In its genesis (still far from clear), Central European experience seems to have played a large part.

Refining by amalgamation consisted essentially of grinding the ore to a coarse dust and sprinkling a small amount of mercury over it. In time (typically, several weeks) the mercury would amalgamate with the silver atoms in the ore, forming a pasty substance. From this, pure silver could be obtained by applying enough heat to volatilize the mercury. Other ingredients were added to increase the speed and effectiveness of the process: water, to bind the dust into a loose mud; common salt, iron filings, and copper sulfate to increase the yield of silver. In Mexico after 1600, the various substances were spread out on a paved yard and there blended. Hence Spanish American amalgamation is often called the *patio* process. But on account of low ambient temperatures, *patios* were not used in the Andes. There, amalgamation was done in tanks, which were sometimes built over vaults in which fires could be set.

To supply mercury for amalgamation in the Americas, the crown established a monopoly over the only two significant quicksilver mines within the empire, at Huancavelica (Peru) and at Almadén (Spain). Huancavelica generally supplied the needs of Andean refiners, with its surplus rounding out shipments to Mexico from Almadén. Prior to 1700 this arrangement favored Andean refiners because Huancavelica provided more abundant stocks than did decadent Almadén. Lack of mercury probably limited silver output in Mexico during the 1600s. In 1698 new discoveries at Almadén led to a steady expansion in mercury production, while depletion of its richest ores by 1760 made Huancavelica less reliable for the Andes. During the latter half of the 1700s, Almadén made large shipments to South America, besides supplying massive amounts of mercury to Mexico. During the mid-1600s and late 1700s, the crown occasionally purchased mercury from Idrija

(Slovenia) when imperial production failed to satisfy the silver refiners' demand.

The silver boom of the 1700s would have been impossible without the surge in mercury output. Mexican silver refiners received further incentive to step up production when the crown cut mercury prices by 50 percent between 1767 and 1778. Attempts to pass on such savings to Andean refiners never permanently materialized, in part because of production difficulties at Huancavelica and also because the government tried to profit from the sale of the mercury. Attempts to find significant mercury deposits in Mexico failed during colonial times. Ironically, however, important discoveries were made soon after independence near Santa Clara, California. Mercury from the New Almadén and New Idria mines made an important contribution to the recovery of silver mining in the new Spanish American nations.

Once amalgamation became established in Mexico during the 1550s and in the Andes during the following decade, silver production passed largely to the Spanish. One great advantage of the process was the ability to handle large volumes of low-grade ore. Its development was indeed spurred by the depletion of the rich surface ores that had previously been smelted. But pulverizing ore on a large scale demanded the building of many trituration mills, powered by animals or waterwheels. Herds of mules and horses had to be bred; dams had to be built. Mines grew deeper and longer as the economies of scale inherent in the new process became apparent. The lower workings began to flood, requiring the installation of pumps and winches. All this meant the deployment of capital that native miners did not possess and the building of machines that had European, but no American, antecedents. Indians were thus largely reduced to the role of manual laborers once amalgamation took hold; they did to some degree (occasionally quite large) continue to use native smelting techniques on the margin of the Spanish-dominated industry. Indeed, at Potosí during the late colonial period, indigenous mining and smelting operations may have produced as much as half the silver coming from the Rich Hill.

LABOR

Almost all manual workers in silver mining and refining were Native Americans. In the early decades, Indians in encomienda were often sent by their masters to work mines and smelters; some of them, as suggested earlier, really operated with a substantial degree of independence. Indian slave labor too was common enough in mining, particularly in Mexico, before enslavement of natives was reigned in by the authorities in the 1550s.

Subsequently, however, the dominant work arrangements in mining were drafts and wage labor. For draft labor, precedents had existed in both the Aztec and Inca empires (*coatequitl* and *mit'a*, respectively), which undoubtedly made it simpler for the Spanish to extract forced labor from native communities. The most notorious draft was the *mita* of Potosí, formally created in the 1570s by Viceroy Francisco de Toledo. At least in its early years, it brought annually more than 13,000 Indian men to work in Potosí. Toledo also established a *mita* for Huancavelica, to supply cheap labor for the mercury mines there. In Mexico the draft was called *repartimiento*. In both cases, the employer paid the draftee a small wage. It was, however, insufficient to maintain the worker, let alone the family who often accompanied him in the Andean case.

Indian wage labor in silver mining appeared almost at the same time as drafts were organized. Once amalgamation was operating, demand for labor grew fast. The drafts of the 1570s were set up mainly to meet this demand but quickly proved inadequate. Mine and mill owners needing workers then began hiring individual Indians, some of them from the drafts themselves (which were thereby depleted). The wage paid to the hired men was up to five times higher than what the draftees received. Using wage workers gave employers another benefit besides a more stable labor supply: the skills that the permanently hired man was more likely than the draftee to acquire.

By 1600 most mining and refining workers were salaried. In Mexico the total labor force producing silver was by then about 9,000 men. Of these, some 68 percent were waged, 18 percent drafted, and 14 percent African slaves. Draftees worked only in the southern mines, in or near the center of Mexico, where the native population had long been sedentary. The northern nomads were not amenable to *repartimiento*. How many men were employed in central Andean mining by 1600 is not known. But in Potosí, which alone produced well over half the Andean silver at the time, 11,000 to 12,000 men were usually at work, barely 40 percent of them draftees in the *mita*. The rest were salaried Indians. In the smaller mining centers that by then had developed around Potosí, *mita* labor was all but unknown. Hence by 1600 the proportion of waged workers in central Andean silver production was close to that found in Mexico. Over the following two centuries, wage labor remained dominant. Drafts all but disappeared in Mexican mining but continued to provide a minority of workers in the Andes until 1812.

It is striking how few workers Spanish American silver production employed. Allowing for lesser mines in South America not mentioned here, the total workforce cannot have exceeded 25,000 in 1600. This was a small part even of the drastically shrunken native population that had survived the sixteenth-century epidemics. It also challenges allegations that the unhealthy and often dangerous labor in the mines annihilated millions of indigenous workers.

Mine owners in the seventeenth century often petitioned the crown to subsidize supplies of African slaves to remedy the deficiencies of the drafts. The crown never obliged. Mexican miners and refiners found it worthwhile to invest in small numbers of black slaves, as the figures given earlier show. But at Andean altitudes and temperatures, Africans quickly succumbed to disease when put to heavy underground labor. Africans, slave and free, were certainly present there, however, as craftsmen engaged in tasks connected with mining, such as carpentry and smithing.

PRODUCTION

Between 1560 and 1685 Spanish American mines produced 25,000 to 30,000 tons of silver and between 1686 and 1810 more than double that amount. In the first period, the central Andean mines dominated production, with Potosí leading the field, even though it reached its peak in the 1590s. After that, depletion of the better ores and rising costs of extraction and labor brought a steady decline of Potosí, which lasted until the 1730s. The contraction of Potosí itself was somewhat offset by discoveries of ore in the surrounding area—above all, at Oruro, 160 miles to the northwest, which burst onto the scene in 1606–1607. It too subsided after 1620, though it remained an important Andean producer throughout colonial times. The Andean seventeenth-century decline was severe enough to produce a falling trend in total Spanish American production from about 1630 to 1700.

In Mexico before 1685 the major producing region was Zacatecas, which embraced the important subdistrict of Sombrerete. Zacatecas was pursued closely after 1630 by Santa Bárbara and Parral and rather more distantly from about 1600 by San Luis Potosí. Other high-yielding Mexican mining centers to about 1700 were Pachuca, Taxco, Guanajuato, and Sultepec. Mexican silver output rose steeply between 1560 and 1630. The rate of growth then slackened or even leveled off, but there was definitely no broad decline of the Andean sort. Doubtless, growing costs of extraction and labor hindered Mexican mining after 1600. A major difficulty after 1630 was the preference that the crown—which controlled the distribution of quicksilver—gave to the Andean mines in the supply of this essential reagent. The Andes were favored because, although production there was dropping, they were still the largest silver-producing zone in the empire. The ensuing shortage of mercury in Mexico restricted silver production there. A return to smelting seems to have solved this difficulty after 1660, perhaps allied with the use of underground blasting. (Both the resurgence of smelting and the use of blasting need further research. Blasting was definitely being used in the Andes around Potosí by the early 1670s. Its earliest known use so far in Mexico is in the early eighteenth century.)

By 1700 Mexico was clearly ahead of the Andes in output. Pachuca, Zacatecas, and Parral flourished in the early 1700s, and San Luis Potosí began to rise rapidly after 1750. After 1730, however, all were dominated by Guanajuato. Though the enormous amounts of silver emerging from Mexican mines after 1770 catch the attention, the highest growth in output may well have taken place before 1750. Rising costs, aggravated by a declining relative value of the silver produced, seem likely to have reduced the growth rate in the late eighteenth century.

Potosí experienced a revival in the 1740s that lasted for sixty years, though in about 1800 maximum output barely reached half the levels achieved in the 1590s. This recovery was propelled by low labor costs as well as by a tax cut in 1736 from the fifth, or *quinto real*, that the crown had levied on Andean silver production from the beginning, to the tenth (*diezmo*), long paid by miners as royalty almost everywhere else in Spanish America. In the Andes a more striking development, however, was the upsurge of production from mines in Peru proper, particularly at Cerro de Pasco, from the late 1770s. This was partly a response to the increased demand for silver in Peru after the Audiencia of Charcas—in which Potosí and Oruro were located—had been assigned in 1776 to the new Viceroyalty of the Río de la Plata. Silver from Charcas now flowed out legally through Buenos Aires, and the merchants of Lima found themselves short of cash with which to trade. The result was larger investment than before in silver production in Peru itself.

Both Mexico and the central Andes benefited in the eighteenth century from a steady growth of quicksilver production at Almadén after new deposits were found there in 1698. This increase more than sufficed to offset faltering mercury production at Huancavelica. Both silver-producing regions, but especially Mexico, also responded after about 1770 to Bourbon governmental policies designed to stimulate mining, which included tax cuts, lower mercury prices, the creation of mining guilds and colleges, dispatch of teams of European experts to update production methods, and awards of titles of nobility to successful miners.

The supply of capital to mining also became more sophisticated in the eighteenth century, with Mexico again the site of the greatest advances. The main source of investment funds in both major producing areas had long been the great merchants who ran the transatlantic and transpacific trades. In late colonial Mexico these merchant houses took on functions quite close to those of banks. Their heavy investments allowed the scale of mining enterprises in Mexico to grow impressively, possibly accompanied by a rise in efficiency. In the Andes, for reasons still to be clarified, mining remained a smaller-scale and more primitive business, although the first steam engine to be used in Spanish American mining was installed in Cerro de Pasco, in Peru. This did not happen, however, until 1816.

The significance of silver mining for colonial Spanish America, for Spain itself, and for the rest of the world, is hard to exaggerate. Silver production sent ripples throughout the imperial economy; mining's fortunes affected almost every sector of colonial life. Mining monetized the Spanish American economy, drew Indians into colonial economic activities, created American demand for American products and European and Asian manufactures, and filled (if only briefly) the coffers of the Spanish crown. It also bears much responsibility for the damage that traditional Indian village life suffered under Spain, for inflation in the economy of Europe, and for lasting pollution, particularly in the form of mercury, of the mining zones' environment. Whereas silver stimulated economic life, mining also absorbed much of the capital available in the colonies and so hindered development of other economic sectors. The monarchy's emphasis on bullion production reinforced Spanish America's colonial status.

SILVER MINING AFTER INDEPENDENCE

All the major regions that yielded silver in colonial times continued to produce it after Independence, though almost everywhere the wars damaged the mining industry. Destruction of machines and mines was not the most serious problem. Worse was the hiatus that the wars caused in maintenance and investment. Machinery decayed and workings often flooded or collapsed for lack of attention. After the wars, though capital was available from local and foreign (particularly British) sources, so much needed to be put right that restoration was slow. Nevertheless, silver production did not slump so severely in the post-Independence decades as has sometimes been thought. In Peru, average annual production from 1800 to 1804 was 531,000 marks (265,000 lbs.). The corresponding figure for 1820 to 1824 was 161,000 marks (80,000 lbs.); for 1830 to 1834, 295,000 marks (147,500 lbs.); and for 1840 to 1844, 500,000 marks (250,000 lbs.), close to the pre-conflict level. Much the same happened in Mexico, which, having produced 62 percent of the world's new silver between 1801 and 1810, continued to yield between 50 and 60 percent of the total to 1860. The quinquennium of highest-ever colonial production in Mexico was 1805–1809, with an annual average of some 20 million pesos (about 600 tons). Only half this amount was produced in 1822, the nineteenth-century nadir of output, but it was equaled again, after a slow recovery, in the period 1848 to 1850. In Chile, where gold had been the precious metal of colonial times, no restoration of silver was needed. But an important strike at Chañarcillo, near Copiapó, in 1832 created an instant silver boom that was sustained by further discoveries, culminating in that of Caracoles in 1870. This site was in

Bolivia but was worked largely by Chileans crossing their northern border. It became Chilean in the War of the Pacific (1879–1883). Northern Chile, however, turned predominantly to copper production about 1900.

Recovery by mid-century was followed by expansion, accelerating toward 1900. New ore deposits were found and new refining methods applied. In Peru, for example, the working of fresh deposits at Casapalca and Morococha undermined the long-standing ore predominance of Cerro de Pasco. Lixiviation, a leaching process introduced to Peru in 1890, partly replaced the traditional smelting and amalgamation of silver ores. The method also was tried in Mexico, where cyanidation, introduced in the 1890s, proved a more useful refining method. Everywhere in the late nineteenth century, mechanization of mining and refining increased, often as a result of rising foreign investment, especially from the United States.

In the long term, since Independence, Mexico has been the largest Spanish American source of silver; it is still among the foremost producers in the world. In the years 1983 to 1987, for example, it ranked first, with an annual average of some 2,463 tons. Production has run at similar levels for much of the twentieth century. By the start of the twentieth century, in the central Andes, silver was yielding pride of place to other base metals often found in association with it—copper in Peru, tin in Bolivia—that proved more profitable, given shifts in world demand. Nevertheless, Peru, after wide variations in its output of silver in this century, in the mid-1980s ranked second in the world, with an annual average of some 1,969 tons. Much Peruvian silver is a by-product of copper refining.

See also **Inti; Mamaquilla; Repartimiento; Slavery: Indian Slavery and Forced Labor; Toledo y Figueroa, Francisco de.**

BIBLIOGRAPHY

Bakewell, Peter. *Silver Mining and Society in Colonial Mexico: Zacatecas, 1546–1700.* Cambridge, U.K.: Cambridge University Press, 1971.

Bakewell, Peter. *Miners of the Red Mountain: Indian Labor in Potosí, 1545–1650.* Albuquerque: University of New Mexico Press, 1984.

Bakewell, Peter. "Mining in Colonial Spanish America." In *The Cambridge History of Latin America*, edited by Leslie Bethell. Vol. 2: *Colonial Latin America.* Cambridge: Cambridge University Press, 1984.

Bargalló, Modesto. *La minería y la metalurgía en la América española durante la época colonial.* Mexico: Fondo de Cultura Económica, 1955.

Brading, David A. *Miners and Merchants in Bourbon Mexico, 1763–1810.* Cambridge, U.K.: Cambridge University Press, 1971.

Brown, Kendall W. "Workers' Health and Colonial Mercury Mining at Huancavelica, Peru." *The Americas* 57, no. 4 (April 2001): 467–496.

Cole, Jeffrey A. *The Potosí Mita, 1573–1700: Compulsory Indian Labor in the Andes.* Stanford, CA: Stanford University Press, 1985.

Deustua, José R. *The Bewitchment of Silver: The Social Economy of Mining in Nineteenth-Century Peru.* Athens, OH: Ohio University Press, 2000.

Fisher, John R. *Minas y mineros en el Perú colonial, 1776–1824.* Lima: Instituto de Estudios Peruanos, 1977.

Garner, Richard L. "Long-Term Silver Trends in Spanish America: A Comparative Analysis of Peru and Mexico." *American Historical Review* 93, no. 4 (1988): 898–935.

Haring, Clarence H. "American Gold and Silver Production in the First Half of the Sixteenth Century." *Quarterly Journal of Economics* 29 (1915): 433–479.

Humboldt, Alejandro von. *Ensayo politico sobre el reino de la Nueva España.* Critical edition by Vito Alessio Robles. 5 vols. Mexico: Robredo, 1941.

Lohmann Villena, Guillermo. *Las minas de Huancavelica en los siglos XVI y XVII.* Seville, Spain: Escuela de Estudios Hispano-Americanos, 1949.

Mitre, Antonio. *Los patriarcas de la plata: Estructura socio-económica de la minería boliviana en el siglo XIX.* Lima: Instituto de Estudios Peruanos, 1981.

West, Robert C. *Colonial Placer Mining in Colombia.* Baton Rouge: Louisiana State University Press, 1952.

Whitaker, Arthur P. *The Huancavelica Mercury Mine: A Contribution to the History of the Bourbon Renaissance in the Spanish Empire.* Cambridge, MA: Harvard University Press, 1941.

Zulawski, Ann. *They Eat from Their Labor: Work and Social Change in Colonial Bolivia.* Pittsburgh: University of Pittsburgh Press, 1995.

KENDALL W. BROWN
PETER BAKEWELL

MODERN

Mining is a mixed economy in present-day Latin America although historically it was a state-chartered monopoly. Mining was at one time a mainstay of the colonial economy in Mexico, Peru, and Brazil, but its relative importance in their national economies was eclipsed soon after their independence. Alexander von Humboldt reported that agriculture was the chief source of wealth and revenue for Mexico on the eve of that country's independence. However, the wars for independence in Mexico and the Andean countries devastated their mining industries. Slackening overseas demand, especially in Europe, also contributed to the collapse of mining. Not until the second half of the nineteenth century did mining reemerge in Latin America as a viable, profitable economic activity.

Between 1850 and 1930, the apogee of private capitalism and liberal democracy in Latin America, mining was a private enterprise. In this system the state granted a private operator a concession to explore and an economic right (permit) to exploit. The mine operator financed exploration, production, beneficiation (turning minerals into metals), transportation, and marketing. In addition to concession and permit fees, the operator paid royalties ranging from 0 to 20 percent, based on the colonial levy of a royal fifth. In addition to colonial mines of gold and silver, the diversified industrial economies of the United States and Europe stimulated the development of new metallic and nonmetallic minerals. Guano, or bird droppings, became an important export item for Peru for nearly half a century, from 1840 to 1890, as fertilizer and as raw material for munitions. Chile first experienced a boom in nitrates (*salitre*) in the 1880s as an alternative to guano, then developed copper mining by the early part of the twentieth century. By 1970 copper was generating more than 80 percent of Chile's export revenues, and it continues to remain the single most important export, generating about 45 percent of the country's total export revenue in the early 1990s. Copper continues to be critical to the Chilean economy in the early twenty-first century. As of 2004, Chile produced 35 percent of world production.

Overall, Latin America emerged as a world-class producer of such base metals as iron, bauxite, copper, tin, and manganese, but it also produces energy minerals. Coal mining is an important economic activity

Mining for borax in the Atacama Desert, Chile. JOEL SARTORE/NATIONAL GEOGRAPHIC IMAGE COLLECTION

in Colombia and Venezuela and is marginally significant in Argentina, Brazil, and Chile. The extraction of hydrocarbon resources such as petroleum and natural gas is important for several countries, primarily Venezuela, Ecuador, Trinidad and Tobago, Brazil, Peru, Colombia, Mexico, and Argentina. The first three were members of OPEC (Organization of Petroleum Exporting Countries), but only Venezuela remained in the cartel by 1994.

During the 1930s, the failing free-enterprise system led to a series of economic reforms throughout Latin America. One facet of this reform movement involved either buying out or expropriating both foreign- and domestic-owned mining and energy companies. These nationalized firms then became state corporations. The trend of nationalization and expropriation, with or without compensation, continued to the 1970s. In Brazil, iron-ore mining was the monopoly of the state or, more precisely, the Companhia Vale Do Rio Doce (after 1944), and under the 1988 Brazilian Constitution, foreigners were prohibited from mining. In Chile, copper mining was a state monopoly during the Salvador Allende years (1970–1973), but it since has been opened to private participation. In Mexico, major changes took place in the late 1980s, especially under the Carlos Salinas De Gortari government, when mining was privatized and Mexican and foreign investors bought up formerly state-held mineral properties. One Mexican investor alone holds more than three-fourths of the country's copper concessions.

Such major nonpetroleum state-owned mining companies as Comibol (Bolivia), MineroPeru and Hierro Peru, CVRD (Brazil), Cananeia (Mexico), Guayana and Minerven (Venezuela), Codelco and Enami (Chile), Yacimientos Carboníferos Fiscales (Argentina), and others are currently going through structural changes, either being sold off to private investors or reorganizing to meet shifting markets. Every country in Latin America has opened up mining concessions to both domestic and international investors, although the degree of participation allowed to private investors is still regulated by the state. The mining boom that hit first in Chile during the 1980s, then in other Latin American countries in the 1990s, was brought on by economic liberalization and deregulation measures that were based on the belief that private mining is more efficient and productive than public-sector operation. Hence, state corporations were seen as wasteful and too expensive to taxpayers. Many such companies are still exempted from tax obligations, but lack the capital resources to invest in new projects.

Mining possesses great growth potential. In Brazil, mining represented less than 2 percent of the country's gross domestic product (GDP) in 1990. Argentina has enormous mineral riches in its Andes but has not developed them. (Mining represents less than 0.4 percent of its GDP.) In Mexico, Colombia, Venezuela, Peru, and Chile, mining is an important activity, but none of these countries relies exclusively on minerals for its revenues. To develop the continent's immense mineral resources, however, Latin America is joining the global trend toward privatization, liberalization, and deregulation of the economy.

Latin America boasts the world's largest copper mine (Chuquicamata, in Chile) and the largest iron-ore mine (Carajás, in Brazil), but it also offers a variety of mining activities. Chile will have more than 60 percent of world-class operations (over 50,000 tons of copper ingot) by the end of this century, while the Carajás iron-ore reserve alone constitutes 18 billion metric tons (19.8 billion tons), or a supply for 530 years at current levels of Brazil's export and domestic consumption of 35 million tons. Gold mining has also become an important activity in several countries. Mexico, Brazil, Venezuela, Chile, Argentina, Ecuador, Costa Rica, and Honduras offer immense potential for gold exploitation. Mining activities stimulated the building of infrastructure such as roads, ports, and power-generation stations, as well as the creation of a coterie of component and supply companies for local industry, thus contributing to the growth of total national economies.

Styles of managing mineral resources and developing them vary from country to country. In Chile, mining is an economic activity shared between the private sector and such state corporations as Codelco in copper and Enami in noncopper minerals. A simplified rule now makes private participation and investment in mining easy and lucrative. In Brazil, for 1990–1991 alone, more than 5,900 mining concessions remained idle, because of a dearth of investment capital and the constitutional prohibition of international participation. In Venezuela and Mexico, private domestic and international capital is welcome. With diminishing ore quality and stringent environmental rules in the United States, major U.S. corporations are moving out to overseas sources, including Latin America.

In the early twenty-first century, Latin America's mining sector has benefited from the overall increase in commodity prices on world markets. China's rapid industrialization and the growth of the world economy have caused a dramatic increase in demand for minerals. Giving U.S. companies competition, Chinese enterprises are now looking to develop and invest in mineral resources in Latin America.

See also **Copper Industry; Gems and Gemstones; Iron and Steel Industry; Tin Industry.**

BIBLIOGRAPHY

Theodore H. Moran, *Multinational Corporations and the Politics of Dependence* (1974).

Malcolm Gillis et al., *Taxation and Mining: Nonfuel Minerals in Bolivia and Other Countries* (1975).

June C. Nash, *We Eat the Mines and the Mines Eat Us* (1979).

José Maria Gonçalves De Almeida, ed., *Carajás: Desafio político, ecologia e desenvolvimento* (1986).

Adrian W. De Wind, Jr., *Peasants Become Miners: The Evolution of Industrial Mining Systems in Peru, 1902–1974* (1987).

Marshall C. Eakin, *British Enterprise in Brazil* (1989).

Ricardo A. Godoy, *Mining and Agriculture in Highland Bolivia: Ecology, History, and Commerce Among the Jukumanis* (1990).

Additional Bibliography

Delgado Wise, Raúl, and Rubén Del Pozo Mendoza. "Mexicanization, Privatization, and Large Mining Capital in Mexico." *Latin American Perspectives* 32, no. 4 (July 2005): 65–86.

García Flores, Pedro Pablo. *La minería en Bolivia*. Bolivia: Observador, 2005.

Sánchez Albavera, Fernando, Georgina Ortiz, and Nicole Moussa. *Mining in Latin America in the Late 1990's*. Santiago, Chile: Naciones Unidas, ECLAC, 2001.

EUL-SOO PANG

MINISTER OF THE INDIES. Minister of the Indies, chief administrator of Spain's New World colonies, 1714–1790. Soon after his victory in the War of the Spanish Succession, Philip V reorganized the administration of Spain and the Indies. In 1714 he named a minister of the Indies, also known as the secretary of state for the Indies, and granted him extensive executive and legislative authority previously reserved for the Council of the Indies. This reform centralized administrative authority over New World affairs in the hands of one person and, once effective, left the council with primarily judicial responsibilities.

The first office of minister of the Indies lasted only five months. It was reestablished in January 1721 and was held by some of the most important government officials of the day: José de Patiño (1726–1736), José del Campillo (1741–1743), and the Marqués de La Ensenada (1743–1754), all of whom also held other ministerial portfolios. The longest ministerial tenure began in 1754 with the appointment of Julián de Arriaga y Rivera, a career naval officer who had previously served as governor of Venezuela and president of the House of Trade. Like several of his predecessors, he served simultaneously as minister of the navy (*marina*). Upon Arriaga's death José de Gálvez, the former visitor-general to New Spain and councillor of the Indies, became minister. During Gálvez's tenure (1776–1787), the ministry was at the apogee of its power and served as the impetus for numerous reform efforts in the New World. The great power Gálvez wielded led to the division of the ministry into two parts upon his death. One, headed by Antonio Valdés, handled the affairs of war, finance, commerce, and navigation for the Indies. The other, headed by Antonio Porlier, a former audiencia minister in Peru, handled grace and justice (*gracia y justicia*). This arrangement persisted until 1790, when the administrative responsibilities for the Indies were united with analogous responsibilities for Spain in five ministerial portfolios. After this reorganization, coupled with the demise of the House of Trade in the same year, the Council of the Indies was the only institution in Spain solely responsible for American affairs.

See also **Council of the Indies.**

BIBLIOGRAPHY

Gildas Bernard, *Le secrétariat d'état et le conseil espagnol des Indes (1700–1808)* (1972).

Additional Bibliography

Mariluz Urquijo, José María. *El agente de la administración pública en Indias.* Buenos Aires: Instituto Internacional de Historia del Derecho Indiano, 1998.

MARK A. BURKHOLDER

MIÑOSO, MINNIE (1925?–). Major League left fielder and occasional third baseman Minnie Miñoso (Saturnino Orestes Armas Miñoso Arrieta) was born, by his account, in El Perico, Cuba, some 108 miles from Havana, on November 29, 1925, though many official records mark the event three years earlier. An Afro-Cuban of humble socioeconomic origins, he signed with the Cleveland Indians in 1948 after playing professionally in Cuba and the U.S. Negro leagues; between 1964 and 1976 he also played and managed in Mexico.

Although he played for four Major League teams, he is most often associated with the Chicago White Sox, for whom he starred (1951–1957, 1960–1961, 1964, 1976, 1980) and who retired his number 9; he was later a White Sox coach and roving goodwill ambassador. During his seventeen Major League seasons he participated in 1,835 games, hit 186 home runs, and had a .298 batting average. He was Sporting News Rookie of the Year (1951), a seven-time All-Star, a three-time Gold Glove winner, and led the American League at least one year in each of these categories: hits, doubles, triples, hit by pitch, sacrifice flies, or stolen bases.

In 1976 he became the second-oldest player to get a base hit in the majors and, thanks to appearances with the independent Northern League team the St. Paul Saints in 1993 and 2003, he appeared in professional baseball games during seven decades. In achieving all this, he recalled that he had faced and experienced the same discrimination and bias as others of his race, culture, and class. An outspoken critic of Fidel Castro and communism, he never returned to Cuba after 1961. The first true Latin American star in the majors, the man known as the Cuban Comet or Mr. White Sox became an inspiring hero for an emerging generation of (especially black) Latino players and a beloved fan favorite in Chicago.

See also **Sports.**

BIBLIOGRAPHY

Lindberg, Richard C. *The White Sox Encyclopedia.* Philadelphia: Temple University Press, 1997.

Miñoso, Minnie. "Introduction." In *White Sox: The Illustrated Story,* by Richard Whittingham. Coal Valley, IL: Quality Sports Publications, 1997. Numerous references to Miñoso also in text.

Miñoso, Minnie, with Fernando Fernández and Robert Kleinfelder. *Extra Innings: My Life in Baseball.* Chicago: Regnery Gateway, 1983.

Miñoso, Minnie, with Herb Fagen. *Just Call Me Minnie: My Six Decades in Baseball.* Champaign, IL: Sagamore Publishing, 1994.

JOSEPH L. ARBENA

MINTS. *See* **Currency.**

MINUJIN, MARTA (1940–). Marta Minujin (*b.* 30 January 1940), Argentine sculptor and painter. Born in Buenos Aires, Minujin studied at the School of Visual Arts from 1953 to 1959. She received a Guggenheim Fellowship in 1966. In New York she oversaw a series of art "happenings," including "Interpenning" and "Kindapenning," which were held in 1972 and 1973, respectively, in the gardens of the Museum of Modern Art. One of her most famous works from the 1980s is "Partenón de libros" (1983), displayed in Buenos Aires. It is a replica of the Parthenon built from books that were outlawed during the Argentinean military dictatorship. Her bronze and plaster sculptures find their inspiration in Greek art. Liberated from traditional rules and stripped of context, they constitute a new spatial conception that proposes the possibility of linking sculpture with architecture through a different idea of movement through the use of constructive kinetics. She has exhibited in New York City as well as throughout Latin America. In 1999 the Museum of Fine Arts in Buenos Aires presented an exhibition of her work titled "Vivir en arte."

See also **Art: The Twentieth Century.**

BIBLIOGRAPHY

Marta Minujin: Recent Sculptures, catalog of Yvonne Séguy Gallery, New York (1984).

Vicente Gesualdo, Aldo Biglione, and Rodolfo Santos, *Diccionario de artistas plásticos en la Argentina* (1988).

Additional Bibliography

Fusco, Coco. *Corpus Delecti: Performance Art of the Americas.* London: Routledge, 2000.

Glusberg, Jorge. *Marta Minujín.* Buenos Aires: Museo Nacional de Bellas Artes, 2000.

AMALIA CORTINA ARAVENA

MIR, PEDRO (1913–2000). Pedro Mir (*b.* 3 June 1913; *d.* 11 July 2000), Dominican poet, novelist, short-story writer, essayist, and teacher. The popular and critically acclaimed dean of contemporary Dominican poets, Mir was born in San Pedro de Macoris, the son of a Puerto Rican mother and a Cuban father. He earned a law degree from the University of Santo Domingo in 1941. Mir's radical opposition to the Rafael Leónidas Trujillo dictatorship led, in 1947, to long years of exile. Effectively assuming a collective voice and condition, the intimate, politically charged poetry of *Hay un país en el mundo* (1949; There Is in the World a Country), *Contracanto a Walt Whitman: Canto a nosotros mismos* (1952; Countersong to Walt Whitman: Song to Ourselves), *Seís momentos de esperanza* (1953; Six Moments of Hope), *Amén de mariposas* (1969; Amen to Butterflies), and *Viaje a la muchedumbre* (1971; Journey to the Multitude) offer lyrically powerful testimony to the patriotic constancy of that exile and the years of crisis and struggle immediately after. Mir's vigorous denunciation of the cruel realities of the Trujillato and a U.S. imperial presence throughout the hemisphere includes contrapuntal emphasis on the epic historical journey of the common people in a Latin America where the conceit and miscarried promise of the Whitmanesque "I" "is no longer / ... / the word fulfilled / the touchstone word to start the world anew. / ... / [where] now the word is / us" (*Viaje a la muchedumbre,* p. 62). Mir returned to the Dominican Republic for two years in 1963, and he reestablished himself there definitively in 1968. In 1974 the secretary of education of the Dominican Republic recognized his essay, "Las raíces dominicanas de la Doctrina Monroe" (The Dominican Roots of the Monroe Doctrine), with an Annual History Award. In 1978, his only novel, *Cuando amaban las tierras comuneras* (When They Loved the Communal Land), was published to acclaim in Mexico. In 1984 the Dominican Congress named him national Poet Laureate. In 1991 he was awarded an honorary doctorate from Hunter College in New York City. Two years later he received the Dominican National Literature Award in recognition of his lifetime of contributions. Mir also held a faculty and research appointment at the Universidad Autónoma de Santo Domingo. He died on 11 July 2000.

A poet of great complexity, technical skill, and intellectual authority, his work combines an elegiac mood with a prophetic vision of hope. An exacting stylist and multifacetic chronicler of his country's social and cultural history, his writings include two other books of verse; a poetic historicist novel, *Cuando amaban las tierras comuneras* (1978); and the elegant narratives of *La gran hazaña de Limber y después otoño* (1977); and *¡Buen viaje, Pancho Valentín!* (1981). His works of historical interpretation, aesthetic philosophy, and art criticism include the two-volume *La noción de período en la historia dominicana* (1981–1983), *Tres leyendas de colores: Ensayo de interpretación de las tres primeras revoluciones del nuevo mundo* (1969), *Las raíces dominicanas de la doctrina Monroe* (1974), *Apertura a la estética* (1974), *Fundamentos de teoría y crítica de arte* (1979), and *La estética del soldadito* (1991).

See also **Literature: Spanish America; Trujillo Molina, Rafael Leónidas.**

BIBLIOGRAPHY

Víctor Fernández-Fragoso, "De la noche a la muchedumbre: Los cantos épicos de Pedro Mir" (Ph.D. diss., Univ. of Connecticut, 1978).

Manuel Matos Moquete, "Poética política en la poesía de Pedro Mir," *Revista Iberoamericana* 53, no. 142 (1988): 199–211.

Silvio Torres-Saillant, "Caribbean Poetics: Aesthetics of Marginality in West Indian Literature" (Ph.D. diss., New York Univ., 1991).

Pedro Mir, *Countersong to Walt Whitman and Other Poems,* translated by Jonathan Cohen and Donald D. Walsh (1993).

Additional Bibliography

Beiro Alvarez, Luis. *Pedro Mir en familia.* [Dominican Republic]: Fundación Espacios Culturales, 2001.

Mir, Pedro. *Homenaje a Pedro Mir y José P.H. Hernández.* Río Piedras, Puerto Rico: Universidad de Puerto Rico, 1994-1995.

Torres-Saillant, Silvio. *Caribbean Poetics: Toward an Aesthetic of West Indian Literature.* Cambridge: Cambridge University Press, 1997.

ROBERTO MÁRQUEZ

MIRAMÓN, MIGUEL (1832–1867). Miguel Miramón (*b.* 1832; *d.* 19 June 1867), Mexican Conservative general and president, executed with Maximilian. Born in Mexico City, Miramón defended Chapultepec as a cadet in 1847. As lieutenant colonel, he fought with Santa Anna in 1854–1855 against the revolution of Ayutla. Miramón played a major part in Puebla's resistance to the Comonfort administration in 1856, for which he was imprisoned in April 1857. After escaping, he became the principal Conservative general in the Civil War of the Reform (1858–1861). Victorious at Salamanca (10 March 1858), Barrancas de Atenquique (2 July 1858), Ahualulco (29 September 1858), and Estancia de las Vacas (12 November 1859), he failed twice to take the Liberal seat of government, Veracruz, in the spring of 1859 and again in February–March 1860.

He was president within the Conservative zone from 15 April 1860 until his defeat at Calpulalpán on 22 December. Following the Liberal victory, he went into exile in Europe, but declined to participate in the French Intervention. After returning to Mexico in July 1863, his relations with Marshal François Bazaine deteriorated, since the French commanders found the presence of a former Conservative leader an embarrassment. This initial trust in Maximilian evaporated after he was consigned to Berlin in November 1864 to study artillery tactics. Miramón's absence (along with that of Leonardo Márquez) delayed the formation of a Mexican imperialist army.

Against his wife's pleading, he returned to Mexico late in 1866, believing he could save the empire after the evacuation of French forces. A swift thrust at Zacatecas late in January 1867 nearly led to the capture of Juárez and his ministers, but Mariano Escobedo trapped Maximilian, Miramón, and Tomás Mejía in Querétaro, where in June 1867 they were captured, summarily tried, and executed. The plea of Miramón's wife and children for clemency was unheeded by an implacable Juárez.

Still a controversial figure, Miramón combined military skill with political miscalculation. Although a Conservative, he was neither specifically monarchist nor imperialist and he remains a legendary figure for Conservatives.

BIBLIOGRAPHY

José Fuentes Mares, *Miramón: El hombre* (1985).

Luis Islas García, *Miramón: Caballero del infortunio,* 2d ed. (1957).

Additional Bibliography

Galeana de Valadés, Patricia. "Los conservadores en el poder: Miramón." *Estudios de Historia Moderna y Contemporánea de México* 14 (1991): 67–87.

Villalpando, José Manuel. *Miguel Miramón.* Mexico City: Planeta DeAgostini, 2003.

BRIAN HAMNETT

MIRANDA, CARMEN (1909–1955). Carmen Miranda (*b.* 9 February 1909; *d.* 5 August 1955), Portuguese-born Brazilian singer and entertainer. Flamboyantly dressed and gifted with a comic personality, Miranda is best remembered as the international "Ambassadress of the Samba." Born Maria Do Carmo Miranda da Cuhna, near Lisbon, Miranda arrived with her family in Rio de Janeiro in 1910. She attended Catholic schools, where she sang and appeared in plays. After singing sambas and tangos at local engagements, Miranda met Josue de Barros, a composer and guitarist who helped prepare her for professional appearances and radio broadcasts.

Signing with RCA Victor in 1930, Miranda emerged as a recording and stage star across South America. During the decade she recorded 281 songs, many of which were also performed by the famous sambista Pixinguinha. In 1939 producer Lee Shubert signed Miranda to star in the hit Broadway show *Streets of Paris.* Billed as the "Brazilian Bombshell," she appeared in numerous American films, including *Down Argentine Way* (1940) and *That Night in Rio* (1941). As her film career waned, she found success in nightclubs in New York, Las Vegas, and London. In 1955, after taping a number for the *Jimmy Durante Show*, she died in Hollywood, California.

See also **Music: Popular Music and Dance.**

BIBLIOGRAPHY

Martha Gil-Montero, *The Brazilian Bombshell: The Biography of Carmen Miranda* (1989).

Additional Bibliography

Castro, Ruy. *Carmen: Uma biografia.* São Paulo, Brazil: Companhia das Letras, 2005.

Coelho, José Ligiéro. "Carmen Miranda: An Afro-Brazilian Paradox." Ph.D. diss., New York University, 1998.

Mendonça, Ana Rita. *Carmen Miranda foi a Washington.* Rio de Janeiro: Editora Record, 1999.

O'Neil, Brian. "Carmen Miranda: The High Price of Fame and Bananas." In *Latina Legacies: Identity, Biography, and Community*, Vicki Ruíz and Virginia Sánchez Korrol, editors. New York: Oxford University Press, 2005.

Sá, Simone Pereira de. *Baiana internacional: As mediações culturais de Carmen Miranda.* Rio de Janeiro: MIS Editorial, 2002.

JOHN COHASSEY

MIRANDA, FRANCISCO DE (1750–1816). Francisco de Miranda (*b.* 28 March 1750; *d.* 14 July 1816), leader of the First Venezuelan Republic (1811–1812). Miranda was born and raised in Caracas. His father was a successful merchant from the Canary Islands who shared with many of his countrymen a scorn for the local planter aristocracy. In order to enhance his status and power, Miranda opted for a career as an officer in the Spanish army. Unable to secure a commission in the local Caracas Battalion—the officer slots were reserved for peninsulars—in 1771 he migrated to Spain and purchased a commission in the army. He served in North Africa and in the Caribbean during the American Revolutionary War. Although he rose to the rank of colonel by his early thirties, there is nothing in the record to indicate Miranda was blessed with a great military mind. In 1783 he fled to the United States to avoid charges of misuse of funds brought against him by the Spanish military. For the rest of his life Miranda promoted the political independence of Spanish America.

For the next two decades following his departure, Miranda traveled widely in the United States and Europe, during which time he became increasingly convinced that Spanish America should follow the example of British North America and become independent. For two years Miranda traveled in the United States, examining the newly independent country and meeting many influential figures. In 1785 he returned to Europe, touring the Continent and Great Britain and observing firsthand the wide variety of rulers and the consequences of their political philosophies. In Russia, for example, Miranda spent nearly two years attempting to convince the Empress Catherine the Great to invest 20,000 rubles in his liberation plans. Although he was unsuccessful, Catherine did grant him 1,000 rubles and ordered Russian embassies to assist him. His writings from the period are a rich source for comparative history. By the time of his return to London in 1789, Miranda had become an active plotter against the crown in Spain. Until 1805, with time out to fight in the French Revolution and obtain the rank of general in the French army, he tried unsuccessfully to obtain backing to revolutionize Spanish America.

Unable to obtain sufficient support in London, Miranda returned in 1805 to the United States, where he found another government unwilling to support his cause. He did, however, succeed in raising a volunteer force of approximately two hundred men, with which he sailed from New York for Venezuela in February 1806. En route he chartered two schooners in Santo Domingo, and the British navy in the Caribbean lent some support to the enterprise. Well aware of Miranda's intent, Spanish military leaders in the captaincy general were fully prepared when he arrived off the Venezuelan coast. With a force comprising three ships and one hundred fifty men, Miranda first attempted to land in April 1806 just west of Puerto Cabello. It was a total fiasco, with Miranda losing two ships and sixty men. Miranda then fled to Barbados, where he was assisted by the British admiral Thomas Cochrane. In August 1806 Miranda returned with a force of ten ships and approximately five hundred men, landing just north of the

Painting of Francisco de Miranda signing the Act of Independence, Venezuela, July 5, 1811. A former officer in the Spanish army, Miranda traveled throughout the United States, becoming convinced that Spanish colonies in the Americas must seek independence. Despite several failed attempts, Miranda eventually succeeded at ousting the Spanish from Venezuela, in 1811, if only for a few years. THE GRANGER COLLECTION, NEW YORK

city of Coro. This time the population fled inland and allowed Miranda and his force to enter the town. He spent a few days trying to convince local leaders to join in rebellion against the Spanish crown, but found no support among the people of Coro. When he and his invasion force were attacked by the local militia, he fled to Trinidad, and from there he returned to England in late 1807.

Miranda's failure in 1806 to spark a general revolt against the Spanish crown is an important event when analyzing the wars for independence that would break out in Venezuela within a few years. The very people who would be the primary actors in the call for Venezuelan independence—namely the local planter and merchant elite—contributed heavily to his defeat. Miranda was seen as being linked to the ideals of the French Revolution, and in 1806 this was not the road down which the reform wing of the Caracas elite wanted to travel.

Nevertheless, Miranda had cast his lot with those wanting separation from Spain, and when revolution did break out in Venezuela in 1810, he returned to lend his support and leadership. Independence was declared on 5 July 1811, and Miranda was selected to suppress the loyalist counterrevolutionaries in Valencia. He was successful in this mission, but he was unable to convince the patriot leaders of the Venezuelan Congress to form a strong centralized government with himself as the leader. In 1812, after a number of royalist victories under General Juan Domingo Monteverde and a disastrous earthquake in Caracas had brought the patriot cause to naught, Miranda was given dictatorial powers. The royalist forces under Domingo Monteverde were too strong for Miranda and his followers. Miranda capitulated to Monteverde on 25 July 1812, ending the First Republic. This capitulation is a source of considerable historical controversy in Venezuela. Many patriot leaders, including Simón Bolívar, suspected Miranda's action bordered on treason. Bolívar, in fact, prevented Miranda's departure, which caused Monteverde to charge that the patriots had violated the terms of the capitulation. The royalists arrested Miranda and sent him to prison in Cádiz, Spain, where he died four years later.

As an international revolutionary activist, Francisco de Miranda is perhaps best remembered for doing more than anyone else to lay the groundwork outside South America for the continent's separation from Spain. He was not a great military leader, however, and the heroes of the Venezuelan independence movement would be those who made their mark on the battlefield. This was, perhaps, as much a condition of his age—he was in his sixties—as of his misunderstanding of the revolutionary cause due to his long absence from Venezuela. But Miranda was no mere footnote in the independence struggle. By the beginning of the nineteenth century, revolutionary struggle was an international undertaking. Miranda realized this reality and promoted his revolution internationally.

See also **Venezuela: The Colonial Era.**

BIBLIOGRAPHY

Joseph O. Baylen and Dorothy Woodward, "Francisco de Miranda and Russian Diplomacy, 1787–88," in *The Historian* 13 (1950): 52–68.

James Biggs, *The History of Don Francisco de Miranda's Attempt to Effect a Revolution in South America* (1910).

Francisco de Miranda, *The New Democracy in America: Travels of Francisco de Miranda in the United States, 1783–84* (1963).

Láutico García, *Francisco de Miranda y el antiguo régimen español* (1961).

Caracciolo Parra Pérez, *Historia de la Primera República de Venezuela,* 2 vols. (1959).

Demetrio Ramos, "La ideología de la revolución española de la guerra de Independencia en la emancipación de Venezuela y en la organización de su Primera República," in *Revista de Estudios Políticos* (Madrid) 125 (1962): 211–272.

William S. Robertson, *The Life of Miranda,* 2 vols. (1929).

Joseph F. Thorning, *Miranda: World Citizen* (1952).

Additional Bibliography

Fernández Nadal, Estela. *Revolución y utopía: Francisco de Miranda y la independencia hispanoamericana.* Mendoza: EDIUNC, 2001.

Maher, John. *Francisco de Miranda: Exile and Enlightenment.* London: Institute for the Study of the Americas, 2006.

Racine, Karen. *Francisco de Miranda, a Transatlantic Life in the Age of Revolution.* Wilmington, DE: Scholarly Resources, 2003.

Zeuske, Michael. *Francisco de Miranda y la modernidad en América.* Aranjue, Spain: Doce Calles and Madrid: Fundación Mapfre Tavera, 2004.

GARY MILLER

MIRÓ, CÉSAR (1907–1999). César Miró (*b.* 1907, *d.* 8 November 1999), Peruvian novelist, poet, composer, and essayist. A professor of art history at San Marcos University for many years and a graduate in journalism, Miró began his literary career with a revolutionary book of poetry, *Cantos del arado y de las hélices* (1929). While he was influenced by the romance of Federico García Lorca's work—especially by its short, eight-syllable verse, vivid imagery, and narrative style—his poetry maintained a Peruvian perspective. In *Nuevas voces para el viento* (1948), the romance evolved to include new themes and language. Miró entered the political arena with such novels as *Teoría para la mitad de una vida* (1935), *El tiempo de la tarántula* (1973), and *La masacre de los coroneles: Sinfonía barroca en tres tiempos* (1982), which deal with themes of political oppression and rebellion. At age twenty, Miró, imprisoned because of political protest, declared a hunger strike, which demonstrated his commitment to fighting political dictatorship. The tarantula symbol in his work represents world threats against humankind: atomic explosions, the war in Vietnam, cataclysm in Peru. Miró stands out for his journalism and critical essays. *Mariátegui: El tiempo y los hombres* (1989) is a collection of essays that reconstruct the political world during and after which José Carlos Mariátegui, the first Latin American essayist to use a Marxist framework of analysis, lived (1894–1930), from Pablo Neruda to the Sendero Luminoso. Miró also wrote travel literature describing the city of Lima. *La ciudad del río hablador* (1944) captures from a modern perspective the mystique and nostalgia of Lima during colonial times. He was 92 years old when he died on November 8, 1999.

See also **Literature: Spanish America.**

BIBLIOGRAPHY

Gloria Videla De Rivero, "La convergencia de indigenismo y vanguardia poética en dos poemas de César Alfredo Miró Quesada," in *Revista chilena de literatura* 34 (November 1989): 43–53.

Additional Bibliography

Miró, César. *Mariátegui, el tiempo y los hombres.* Lima: Empresa Editora Amauta, 1989.

Rivara de Tuesta, María Luisa. *La intelectualidad peruana del siglo XX ante la condición humana.* Lima: s.n., 2004.

DICK GERDES

MIRÓ CARDONA, JOSÉ (1907–1974). José Miró Cardona (*b.* 28 July 1907; *d.* 10 August 1974), Cuban political leader, lawyer, and professor. Miró Cardona graduated from the University of Havana Law School in 1938. He held numerous positions throughout his life, including chief of the archives of the Liberation Army, librarian of the National Institute of Criminology in Havana, professor of penal law and dean of the law school at the University of Havana, secretary of the Democratic Revolutionary Front, and professor of penal law at the University of Río Piedras in Puerto Rico.

In 1959 he became the first prime minister in the revolutionary government and was Cuba's ambassador to Spain in 1960. He subsequently broke with the Castro regime and became president (1961–1963) of the Cuban Revolutionary Council in Miami, which helped prepare the Bay of Pigs Invasion in 1961.

See also **Cuba, Revolutions: Cuban Revolution.**

BIBLIOGRAPHY

Benjamin, Jules R. *The United States and the Origins of the Cuban Revolution: An Empire of Liberty in an Age of National Liberation.* Princeton, NJ: Princeton University Press, 1990.

Smith, Wayne S. *The Closest of Enemies: A Personal and Diplomatic Account of U.S.-Cuban Relations Since 1957.* New York and London: W.W. Norton, 1987.

MARÍA DEL CARMEN ALMODÓVAR

MIRÓ QUESADA FAMILY.

MIRÓ QUESADA FAMILY. The Miró Quesada Family is a wealthy and notable Peruvian family, owner of the daily newspaper *El Comercio* since 1876, and very influential in twentieth-century politics in Peru. Through intermarriage with other wealthy families of Peru, the Miró Quesadas' interests have been an important part of the coastal elite groups that dominated Peruvian economic activities during and after major export boom cycles. Under the leadership of merchant and journalist José Antonio Miró Quesada (1845–1930), the family consolidated its wealth and reputation by the 1890s through its strong involvement with the Civilista Party. José Antonio's eldest son, Antonio Miró Quesada de la Guerra (1875–1935), was elected congressman between 1901 and 1912 and took charge of *El Comercio.* During the second regime of Augusto B. Leguía (1919–1930), Antonio lived in Europe as a political oppositionist. Upon his return to Peru, he and his wife were assassinated by an Aprista follower in 1935.

Aurelio (1877–1950) and Luis Miró Quesada de la Guerra (1880–1976), brothers of Antonio, shared thereafter the management of the newspaper. In 1974 the military government of Juan Velasco Alvarado, as part of its Plan Inca, expropriated the family's newspaper business and assigned it formally to peasant organizations. In 1980, however, *El Comercio* was returned to the Miró Quesada family, represented by Aurelio Miró Quesada Sosa (b. 1907) and Alejandro Miró Quesada Garland (b. 1915). In 2004, Quesada Garland was working as the editor of Lima's daily *El Comercio* newspaper when a high-profile businessman named Fernando Zevallos sued him, the newspaper, and a reporter over several stories which linked Zevallos to drug traffickers.

See also **Journalism.**

BIBLIOGRAPHY

Carlos Astiz, *Pressure Groups and Power Elites in Peruvian Politics* (1969).

Dennis Gilbert, "The Oligarchy and the Old Regime in Peru" (Ph.D. diss., Cornell University, 1977), translated as *La oligarquía peruana: Historia de tres familias* (1982).

Alfonso Quiroz, "Financial Leadership and the Formation of Peruvian Elite Groups, 1884–1930," in *Journal of Latin American Studies* 20 (1988): 49–81.

ALFONSO W. QUIROZ

MISERICÓRDIA, SANTA CASA DA.

Santa Casa da Misericórdia, the most prestigious white religious brotherhood established in the Portuguese world. Originally founded in Lisbon in 1498, it was an elite charitable organization that established hospitals and helped prisoners, widows, sailors, slaves, orphans, and the indigent. From its inception, the kings of Portugal, starting with Manuel I, granted exclusive royal privileges and endowments to the Santa Casa, giving the brothers the right to collect alms and bury the dead. The brotherhood was dedicated to Our Lady, Mother of God, Virgin Mary of Mercy. Branches were founded in Nagasaki, Macao, Goa, Luanda, Salvador, Rio de Janeiro, and elsewhere. Their main social services involved providing dowries, charity, prison relief, hospital treatment, and burial services.

The original Portuguese *misericórdia* had a membership of 100 brothers, half of whom were gentry and the other half of plebian origin. Membership was divided into two classes: brothers of higher standing and lower standing. Because of royal patronage and prestige, the *santas casas* attracted a majority of their members from the upper class. In Brazil applications for membership were scrutinized for purity of blood. A person could be denied membership or expelled from the brotherhood if he or his spouse had Jewish, Moorish, or African ancestors. All branches of the Santa Casa were governed by the same *compromissos* (charters) with common privileges, administrative structures, and similar banners. They also preserved the same traditions of mutual assistance and celebrated the same festivals on All Saints' Day, the Visitation, and Holy Thursday. Restrictions on the admission of clergymen were another feature common to all branches.

The first and most important *misericórdia* in Brazil was established in Salvador da Bahia in the middle of the sixteenth century. Later, other branches were founded in Santos, Espírito Santo, Vitória, Olinda, Ilhéus, Rio de Janeiro, São Paulo, Pôrto Seguro, Sergipe, Paraíba, Itamaracá, Belém, Igarassú, and São Luís de Maranhão. The discovery of gold and diamonds in the 1690s brought the *misericórdia* to the mining cities of Minas Gerais.

The building of the first hospitals in the port cities of Brazil was the most important social function of the Santa Casa. With their resident physicians, nurses, and chaplains, the hospitals were open to all classes and races serving the needs of sailors and slaves. The provision of dowries to orphans and poor white women helped to increase the number of marriages in colonial Brazil. The creation of a foundling wheel and retirement houses provided assistance to orphans, unwanted children, and single women. Prison aid was another vital service performed by the Santa Casa, since the colony of Brazil was often a dumping ground for criminals. The brothers had the right to feed prisoners, provide legal counsel, and to accompany condemned prisoners to the gallows. The tradition of clemency for prisoners who fell from the scaffold was defended in Bahia, Lisbon, Luanda, Goa, and Macao. The Santa Casa was the only brotherhood in Brazil to provide funeral services for persons who were not members. It also paid for masses for the dead and built churches for the local population, thus providing a source of income for the church.

For their impressive network of social services, the Santa Casa depended on private charity, membership dues, interest from loans, rent on property, and legacies of money, land, and slaves. So extensive were its social services that some of the *santas casas* in Brazil fell into bankruptcy in the late colonial period and had to curtail some of their works of charity. All branches of the *misericórdia* within the Portuguese world provided badly needed local social welfare and philanthropy not supported by the state authorities, because the royal government neglected public welfare programs, relying instead on private charity. Through its hospitals, the *misericórdias* offered some measure of public-health assistance in a colony where tropical disease often reached epidemic proportions. The social philanthropy of the *santas casas da misericórdias* can still be seen in modern Brazil, where its hospitals survive.

See also **Catholic Church: The Colonial Period.**

BIBLIOGRAPHY

Charles R. Boxer, *The Golden Age of Brazil, 1695–1750* (1962).

A. J. R. Russell-Wood, *Fidalgos and Philanthropists: The Santa Casa da Misericórdia of Bahia, 1550–1755* (1968).

Additional Bibliography

Diniz, Jaime C. *Mestres de Capela da Misericórdia da Bahia, 1647-1810.* Salvador: Centro Editorial e Didático da UFBA, 1993.

Silva Gracias, Fatima da. *Beyond the Self: Santa Casa da Misericórdia de Goa.* Panjim: Surya Publications, 2000.

Venâncio, Renato Pinto. *Famílias abandonadas: Assistência à criança de camadas populares no Rio de Janeiro e em Salvador: Séculos XVIII e XIX.* Campinas: Papirus Editora, 1999.

Vianna, Arthur Octavio Nobre. *A Santa Casa da Misericórdia Paraense: Notícia histórica 1650-1902.* 2nd ed. Belém: Secretaria de Estado da Cultura, 1992.

PATRICIA MULVEY

MISIONES. Misiones is an Argentine province located in the northeast, bordering on the west with Paraguay and on the north, south, and east with Brazil. It has 970,000 inhabitants, 250,000 of them in its capital city of Posadas. The Spanish conqueror Álvar Núñez Cabeza de Vaca arrived in the territory in 1541. Later, in the seventeenth century, the Jesuits settled in the area, which was inhabited at that time by indigenous people (mostly Guaraní). Misiones was a national territory until 1953, when it was made a province.

The climate of Misiones is subtropical without a dry season, and its topography consists of plateaus. Although deteriorating due to deforestation, jungle covers 35 percent of the province's area. The main economic activities are forestry, sawmills, production of wood panels and cellulose paste, and paper industries. Tea, maté, and tobacco crops are important to the province. Tourism is significant. Iguazú Falls (with its 227 individual falls) in Iguazú National Park and the Jesuit mission of San Ignacio are the area's main attractions.

See also **Argentina: The Nineteenth Century; Argentina: The Twentieth Century; Cabeza de Vaca, Alvar Núñez; Jesuits; Yerba Mate Industry.**

VICENTE PALERMO

MISKITOS. Miskitos (also Mosquitos or Miskitus), a mixed indigenous–black rural population of about 150,000 persons, make up the majority population of eastern Nicaragua and Honduras (the Miskito Coast). Although they have been isolated, the history and lifestyle of the Miskito, particularly those in Nicaragua, have been inextricably meshed with European and Caribbean (Jamaican) settlers, traders, and missionaries who have frequented the region since the late seventeenth century.

During the colonial era eastern Honduras and Nicaragua remained unsettled by Hispanic populations. Instead, the predominant colonial power was Great Britain, replaced by the United States in the late-nineteenth and twentieth centuries. Reflecting colonial British sentiments, the Miskitos have long disliked Hispanic peoples while welcoming English-speakers. Protestant missionaries, most notably Moravians, have predominated. Although Miskito remains the mother tongue, Miskito men generally learn English as a second language, and many speak Spanish as well. Miskito women tend to speak only Miskito.

The Miskitos originated in the late seventeenth century, when a small indigenous population living near Cape Gracias a Dios, at the mouth of the Río Coco, which now forms the border between Nicaragua and Honduras, mixed with freed or escaped African slaves seeking refuge on the coast. The men of this racially mixed population, excellent hunters and fishermen, procured food for European pirates who raided ships in the Caribbean and utilized the isolated Miskito shore for rest and rendezvous. In return, the Miskitos received material goods, including guns and ammunition. With this weaponry the Miskitos expanded territorially north into Honduras, south along the Nicaraguan coast, and west toward the interior, subjugating other indigenous populations and becoming the dominant native group.

Miskito men continued to seek employment with Europeans, leaving home communities for extended periods to work as wage laborers in rubber tapping, lumbering, and mining enterprises or on banana plantations. Miskito women remained in their villages and continued traditional slash-and-burn agriculture, growing rice and beans as cash crops and as basic staples in addition to traditional root crops (especially manioc), plantains, and bananas as well as pejibaye palm. When wage labor was unavailable, the men hunted and fished. This dual economy, combining wage labor with traditional subsistence activities, allowed the Miskitos to survive and flourish even when periodic economic depressions afflicted the extractive European wage economy. Similarly, although traditional village life has been heavily influenced by missionary endeavors, many aspects of traditional kinship and domestic life continue.

During the 1980s the Nicaraguan Sandinista Revolution greatly affected life on the Miskito Coast; many Nicaraguan Miskitos were forced to flee to refugee settlements or to Honduras. When hostilities ceased, villages slowly were reestablished. The long-term effect of this disruption of Miskito life remains unclear. Greater Hispanization of coastal life in general is likely to occur, although the 2003 passage of Nicaraguan Law 455, a state-designed plan for demarcating indigenous territories, has the potential to support Miskito autonomy and to allow more traditional lifeways to continue.

See also **Indigenous Peoples; Nicaragua.**

BIBLIOGRAPHY

Excellent historical background and description of twentieth-century Miskito life prior to the revolution is in Mary W. Helms, *Asang: Adaptations to Culture Contact in a Miskito Community* (1971), and in Bernard Nietschmann, *Between Land and Water* (1973). Eduard Conzemius, "Ethnographical Survey of the Miskito and

Sumu Indians of Honduras and Nicaragua," *Smithsonian Institution Bureau of American Ethnology Bulletin* 106 (1932), describes many traditional cultural practices. An autobiographical account of boyhood on the Miskito Coast is Charles Napier Bell, *Tangweera: Life and Adventures Among Gentle Savages* (1899; repr. 1989). Another description of early-nineteenth-century coast life is Orlando W. Roberts, *Narrative of Voyages and Excursions on the East Coast and in the Interior of Central America* (1827; repr. 1965). Historical background is in Troy S. Floyd, *The Anglo-Spanish Struggle for Mosquitia* (1967).

Additional Bibliography

Dunbar-Ortiz, Roxanne. *La cuestión miskita en la revolución nicaragüense.* Mexico: Editorial Línea, 1986.

Jenkins-Molieri, Jorge. *El desafío indígena en Nicaragua: El caso de los miskitos.* Mexico: Editorial Katún, 1986.

MARY W. HELMS

MISSIONARIES OF CHARITY.

MISSIONARIES OF CHARITY. Missionaries of Charity, an international organization to help the extremely poor. The Missionaries of Charity was founded in Calcutta on 7 October 1950 by Agnes Gonxha Bojaxhiu, an Albanian and former Sister of Loreto, who became universally known as Mother Teresa.

In 1946 Sister Teresa, a geography teacher, was inspired to begin "a mission of compassion and love to the poorest of the poor...." In the 1950s and 1960s, many young women joined the congregation, which spread to Darjeeling, in Bengal; Goa; and Trivandrum, in Kerala, among other places throughout India. On 1 February 1965, when the Holy See accepted the congregation as one of pontifical right, there were over three hundred sisters. Their first overseas mission was to Cocorote, Venezuela, on 26 July 1965. The sisters opened houses for the destitute, day-care centers, and soup kitchens in Haiti, Peru, Panama, Paraguay, Uruguay, and Brazil in the 1970s, and in Argentina, Bolivia, Chile, Colombia, and Ecuador, as well as in the Caribbean in Trinidad, Grenada, Jamaica, and Guyana, in the 1980s.

In 1979 Mother Teresa of Calcutta was awarded the Nobel Peace Prize in recognition of her promotion of peace "in the most fundamental manner, by her confirmation of the inviolability of human dignity." Lay workers who shared the vision of Mother Teresa were organized into the Co-Workers of Mother Teresa in 1954, and the Missionaries of Charity Brothers was founded in 1963. Lay workers and religious serve the poorest of the poor and visit the lonely, the rejected, the aged, and the shut-ins. In the early 1990s, the Missionary Sisters of Charity numbered over four thousand in 450 houses in more than ninety countries. During the same period, houses were opened in Russia and China.

See also **Catholic Church: The Modern Period.**

BIBLIOGRAPHY

Desmond Doig, *Mother Teresa: Her People and Her Work* (1976).

Eileen Egan, *Such a Vision of the Street: Mother Teresa, the Spirit and the Work* (1985).

Additional Bibliography

Teresa, Mother, and Lucinda Vardey. *A Simple Path.* New York: Ballantine Books, 1995.

SISTER M. NOEL MENEZESR.S.M.

MISSIONS

This entry includes the following articles:

BRAZIL

When Pope Alexander VI divided the world between Spain and Portugal in the Treaty of Tordesillas of 1494, he gave each the right to "discover and acquire" unknown lands. But this papal donation also imposed an exclusive obligation to win the people of those unknown lands to Christianity. Thus, when the King of Portugal, João III, decided to plant the first permanent colonies on the coast of South America, he declared, "the main reason which has led me to colonize Brazil is to convert the people therein to our holy Catholic faith."

When the first governor-general of Brazil, Tomé de Sousa, reached Salvador da Bahia in 1549, he was accompanied by six fathers of the Company of Jesus, a new missionary order founded a few years earlier as a militant and intellectual defender of the papacy. Although the Jesuits rapidly dominated missionary effort in Portugal's vast colony, other religious orders were also active in Brazil—the Franciscans, Carmelites, and Benedictines, who along with the Jesuits were subject to the Padroado Real (royal patronage) in Lisbon. Two other orders—the Capuchins and the Oratorians—depended for support on the Propaganda Fide in Rome, founded in 1622 to centralize missionary work.

The Jesuits first instructed and baptized Indians around Salvador, Bahia. Lacking missionaries, they adopted a dangerous policy of persuading Indians to congregate in specially built villages (Aldeias) rather than taking the gospel to them in their own homes. This system was disastrous for the Indians. Many disliked the regimented life in villages, whose huts and layout differed from their custom, and farming plots near sedentary villages were soon exhausted. More seriously, the *aldeias* were close to colonial towns: mission Indians were soon required by law to labor for many months each year for the settlers or colonial government. Although nominally free Christian subjects of the king of Portugal, they were treated as virtual slaves.

The new mission residents were also fatally vulnerable to a range of imported diseases against which Brazilian natives had no genetically inherited immunity. Smallpox, measles, plague, tuberculosis, influenza, and other epidemics took an appalling toll of otherwise strong and fit Indians. Jesuit fathers gave harrowing accounts of entire villages with every person dead or dying. The few survivors were too weak to bury their dead, or to plant for their own sustenance, so that famine followed pestilence. During the twenty years after 1563, some 60,000 mission Indians and 40,000 slaves died in the area around Bahia; countless thousands more perished in the interior and in villages along the coast.

In 1616 the Portuguese, having advanced up the entire coast of Brazil, established the settlement of Belém do Pará near the mouth of the Amazon. Throughout the next 150 years the few colonists of Pará wrought terrible destruction on the tribes living along thousands of miles of Amazonian rivers. Every year, troops of slavers paddled up the rivers to bring back Indian slaves, either luring them by deception or capturing them at gunpoint. Once downriver in Pará and Maranhão, the wretched captives died by the thousands, from imported diseases, overwork, and despair.

Franciscan missionaries were present at the beginning of this expansion into Amazonia, although their leader, Friar Cristovão de Lisboa, withdrew in disgust at the settlers' abuses. The Jesuits started operations on the Amazon in 1654, led by Father Antônio Vieira, one of the finest preachers of his age and a powerful figure at the Portuguese court. During the ensuing decades, Jesuit missionaries made expeditions up many tropical rivers and lured back entire tribes—who were then decimated by the effects of disease and forced labor. The Jesuits and other orders established thriving *aldeias* under their own control, particularly on Marajó Island at the mouth of the Amazon, where they had large herds of cattle. The prosperity of these missions and the fathers' defense of Indians aroused the fury of settlers, who briefly expelled the missionaries from Maranhão in 1661 and again in 1684.

Throughout almost three centuries of colonial rule, the Portuguese crown vacillated between missionary-inspired legislation protecting the Indians and laws permitting slavery to meet the settlers' incessant demands for Indian labor.

The management of mission villages was codified in the Regulations of Missions of 1686, which fixed daily routines and work quotas. In 1693, the government divided the vast Amazon basin among four missionary orders. The Franciscans and Brothers of Mercy (Mercedarians) were awarded the north bank, while the Jesuits were given the south bank of the Amazon. The Negro, Solimões, Japurá and other rivers were granted to the Carmelites. A less severe and intellectual order than the Jesuits, the Carmelites established some twenty prosperous *aldeias* on their rivers. Amazonian tribes responded better to the relaxed Carmelite attitude than to Jesuit discipline. Missionaries caused much havoc by "descending" tribal Indians to restock their *aldeias*, and they were required by law to accompany slaving expeditions to legitimize the victims' servile status. By the mid-eighteenth century 50,000 Indians were settled in *aldeias* under the Jesuits, Carmelites, or Franciscans.

Second only to the Amazon as an arena of missionary activity was the Northeast. In the sixteenth century the Jesuits based in Salvador established missions along the Bahian coast. To the north, the Franciscans set up a base at Olinda in Pernambuco, and labored especially between Paraíba and Alagoas. Also based in Olinda were the Carmelites. In the seventeenth century, the Jesuits and Franciscans, accompanied by the Capuchins and Oratorians, left the coast for the hinterland of the Northeast along the Rio São Francisco. The Italian Capuchins used a system of "ambulatory missions"; the Jesuits, in contrast, built their mission villages far from the towns and plantations to avoid settler abuse of Indian labor.

In the mining states of Minas Gerais, Mato Grosso, and Goiás, mission activity was largely in the hands of parish priests, who preached to the Indians and baptized their children as part of their clerical duties. Since they attended to the religious needs of the mining towns, they had little free time to devote to the *aldeias.*

In the south the Jesuits and Franciscans were also active in Rio de Janeiro and São Vicente. In 1554 the Jesuits moved inland to build a college at São Paulo, from which they attempted to defend the Indians against labor abuse. Their efforts were so threatening that local settlers forced them out between 1640 and 1653.

At this same time, Spanish Jesuits established themselves among the Guarani-speaking tribes of what is now Paraguay. The Guarani were by nature a highly spiritual people. They also lived in large, well-ordered communities and farmed extensively. They therefore accepted what the Jesuits had to offer: intensive religious teaching and observance, regimented existence from cradle to grave, and instruction in large-scale agriculture. Cattle imported from Europe thrived on the grasslands of the Guarani homeland. Spanish Jesuits thus created a theocracy based on forty populous "reductions" (*reduções*) of Guarani Indians. Each reduction had a large baroque church and missionaries' quarters. The Indians lived simply in tidy rows of rectangular huts without chimneys and with minimal furniture.

In the early decades of the seventeenth century, bands (Bandeiras) of Luso-Brazilians from São Paulo marauded deep into the interior in search of natives to enslave. In 1629, these ruthless *bandeirantes* attacked Paraguayan missions and led their Christian Indians to captivity in Brazil. Under pressure from *bandeirante* attack, the Spanish Jesuits had to abandon missions in what are now the Brazilian states of Paraná and southern Mato Grosso. The conflict was reversed in 1641, when at the battle of Mboreré the Portuguese were defeated by mission Indians, who had been armed and trained by Jesuits with military experience. The Paraguayan reductions were left to flourish in peace for over a century.

In 1750 the Treaty of Madrid divided South America between the colonial empires of Spain and Portugal, roughly establishing the frontiers of modern Brazil. In the south, the boundary was fixed along the Uruguay River, which isolated seven large Spanish Jesuit reductions within Portuguese Brazil. The Christian Guarani of those reductions refused to accept this change of sovereignty or to move to new locations west of the Uruguay. The tragic outcome was a campaign by a Spanish-Portuguese military force that slaughtered 1,400 Guarani converts at the battle of Caibaté (1756).

Meanwhile, the colonists' envy and hatred of the Jesuits on the Amazon was bearing fruit. The virtual dictator of Portugal, the future marquis of Pombal, developed a passionate loathing of the black-robed fathers, which culminated in the expulsion of Jesuits from all Portuguese dominions in 1759, followed by their banishment from Spanish South America in 1767. Many mission villages were put under lay "directors," and their Indians suffered terribly from these rapacious new masters. During the centuries of missionary rule, thousands of natives underwent Christian instruction and conversion. But tribal populations declined so catastrophically, their tribal societies were so damaged, and their *aldeias* were so shattered after the departure of the missionaries, that there is little lasting legacy of all that religious effort.

See also **Missions: Jesuit Missions (Reducciones); Slavery: Indian Slavery and Forced Labor.**

BIBLIOGRAPHY

John Hemming, *Red Gold: The Conquest of the Brazilian Indians, 1500–1760* (1978).

Eduardo Hoornaert, "The Catholic Church in Colonial Brazil," in *The Cambridge History of Latin America,* edited by Leslie Bethell (1984).

Additional Bibliography

Azevedo, Francisca L. Nogueira de, and John M. Monteiro. *Confronto de culturas: Conquista, resistência, transformação.* Rio de Janeiro: Expressão e Cultura; São Paulo: Edusp, 1997.

Castelnau-L'Estoile, Charlotte de. *Les ouvriers d'une vigne stérile: Les jésuites et la conversion des Indiens au Brésil, 1580–1620.* Lisbonne: Fundação Calouste Gulbenkian; Paris: Centre culturel Calouste Gulbenkian; Lisbonne:

Commission nationale pour les commémorations des découvertes portugaises, 2000.

Cohen, Thomas M. *The Fire of Tongues: António Vieira and the Missionary Church in Brazil and Portugal.* Stanford, CA: Stanford University Press, 1998.

Flores, Moacyr. *Reduções jesuíticas dos guaranis.* Porto Alegre: EDIPUCRS, 1997.

Golin, Tau. *A expedição: imaginário artístico na conquista militar dos Sete Povos jesuíticos e guaranis.* Porto Alegre: Editora Sulina, 1997.

Pompa, Cristina. *Religião como tradução: missionários, Tupi e Tapuia no Brasil colonial.* Bauru: EDUSC; São Paulo: ANPOCS, 2003.

Santos, Júlio Ricardo Quevedo dos. *Rio Grande do Sul: Aspectos das missões.* Porto Alegre: Martins Livreiro, 1991.

Tavares, Eduardo, and Renato Dalto. *Missões.* São Leopoldo: UNISINOS, Universidade do Vale do Rio dos Sinos, 1999.

JOHN HEMMING

JESUIT MISSIONS (REDUCCIONES)

The Jesuits founded about fifty missions in the upper Río de la Plata between 1610 and 1764. Their purpose was to "reduce [the Indians] to civilized life," meaning to transform to European political, economic, and social patterns and Christian belief and ritual, the Native Americans of the region. In Jesuit Paraguay, an area larger than the modern nation, missionaries worked in the Gran Chaco among Abipones, Tobas, Mocobís, Mbayás, Guanás, Lules, Isistines, Toquistines, Vilelas, Omoampas, and Pasaines, but the famed "Jesuit Republic" refers to the near-legendary thirty (actually thirty-two) Guarani missions located in present-day Paraguay, Argentina, and Brazil. These missions housed a maximum of 140,000 Guaranis in 1732 but generally sheltered about 100,000. The lasting fame of the mission province, called by whites an earthly paradise, rests on its symbolic value. Such Jesuit authors as Pierre Charlevoix praised the mission complex, while opponents of the Jesuits, such as Voltaire, condemned it. Such twentieth-century socialists as R. B. Cunninghame Graham, who saw in the missions a "vanished arcadia," also found in them a historical model for their own political causes.

Although Jesuits arrived in Paraguay in 1588, the first missions were established in 1610. In the area of the later "mission state" between the Alto Paraná and Uruguay rivers, in Guairá along the Paranapanemá River—now Paraná, Brazil—and in Itaty, well north of Asunción, Jesuits went among the Guaranis to teach them Christianity and European ways, but the Guaranis who joined these missions were not aboriginal, having encountered European culture three-quarters of a century before the Jesuits arrived. Indians accepted mission life for the material benefits that they received from the Jesuits, especially iron artifacts and domesticated animals, for the promise of physical security, and for the protection of Guarani women from exploitative sexual relations with Spaniards. The Guaranis rejected Roman Catholic beliefs for a generation or two, although they participated in Catholic rituals at once.

Paulista slave raiders from Brazil and mounted Guaycuruans from the Chaco pushed the northern missions in Guairá and Itaty to the rich agricultural and pasture lands south of the Paraná. On the most dramatic journey, Father Antonio Ruíz de Montoya in 1631 led thousands of Guaranis from Guairá 400 miles south to the center of the mission country. There Jesuits and Guaranis organized militias that halted the Portuguese advance in the 1640s and thereafter protected the missions from external threats until 1767.

Fathers Marcello Lorençana, Roque González De Santa Cruz, and other Jesuits in southern Paraguay and northeastern Argentina undertook the spectacular program of mission expansion that aroused worldwide admiration and envy of the Jesuit order. Paternalistically organized by Jesuits, Paraguayan missions followed physical and social models established by Franciscans in sixteenth-century Mexico. Founders located the church, cemetery, workshops, Guarani quarters, and priests' houses close to the town square. Then they built a sound economy. Mission prosperity resulted from efficient management, continuity of economic rhythms, and the rich lands of the missions. Guaranis cultivated traditional crops, including manioc, sweet potatoes, and maize, and also grew such European imports as wheat and oranges. Vast herds of cattle, horses, and sheep contributed to the prosperity of the missions. The sale of high-quality Yerba Maté, carefully cultivated on Jesuit plantations, earned the profits to pay for the import of such needed European goods as iron tools and weapons; Jesuit *yerba maté* competed with that of Creole merchants, who marketed an inferior product.

Drawing of a Jesuit mission in the Gran Chaco, Paraguay, by Austrian missionary Father Florian Paucke, 18th century. The efficient cultivation of indigenous and European crops, such as the orchards portrayed here, contributed to the prosperity of these missions. © BOJAN BRECELJ/CORBIS

Often labeled "primitive communism," the mission economy and governance were actually based on individual plots for Guarani families, inalienable under Spanish law, and common lands, called *tupambae,* for crops and cattle. These holdings resembled early modern European practices rather than collective farms of the twentieth century. Jesuits only slightly altered the aboriginal sexual division of labor but were responsible for introducing marked status distinctions among men, especially for Guarani officials who assisted priests, including militia commanders and holders of posts on *cabildos.* Traditional chiefs, called caciques by Spaniards, continued to articulate Guarani opinions and often clashed with priests and their Indian appointees. Jesuits controlled surpluses in mission storehouses, and Guarani voices periodically asked for greater involvement in how to use them, because profits from Guarani missions provided capital grants for new missions. In the 1700s, sedentary Chaco peoples of the Argentine northwest, such as the Lules (1711) and Villelas (1735), accepted Jesuit offers to establish missions for them. After 1743, nomadic Chaco Guaycuruans also began settling in missions staffed by Jesuits. Subventions for these foundations came from the abundance of Guarani missions.

Exempt from manual labor in Jesuit missions were the caciques, Indian *corregidores* (magistrates), members of the *cabildo* (the mission's town council), skilled artisans, and captains in the militia companies. Tribute to the Crown was one peso annually paid by all nonexempt men from age eighteen to fifty, a low rate of taxation that partly reflected Jesuit influence at court and royal thanks for Guarani military services to the empire.

Missions were generally staffed by two priests; they reported to a superior who administered the Guarani missions from his headquarters at Candelaria, a large mission town on the Río Paraná. The superior answered to the provincial in Córdoba, who obeyed the Jesuit general in Rome. Although periodic reports of Jesuit arrogance circulated in Spain and America, officials of the Jesuit mission province of Paraguay were loyal to the crown. Like other interest groups in early Spanish America, however, the Society of Jesus often delayed implementing injurious royal decrees and sought to reverse them through political influence in Madrid, Lima, and Asunción. The monarchy wanted missionaries to be Spanish subjects, but manpower needs and Jesuit lobbying forced the crown periodically to relax the rules. The society recruited missionaries in Italy, Germany, and occasionally Britain. Most Jesuits in Paraguay were able men, fluent in several languages and often masters of such specialties as agriculture, artisan trades, commerce, music, and war.

The missions always had enemies. The Jesuits were politically active. They cooperated with and co-opted royal officials, and conflicts arose. The unsuccessful anti-Jesuit efforts of, and unfortunate ends to, the careers of Bishop Bernardino de Cárdenas in the 1640s and Governor José de Antequera y Castro in the 1720s show how influential the agents of the missions were.

From the beginning, the Jesuit monopoly on Guarani labor clashed with the interests of settlers. Paraguayan employers' attitudes toward Guarani workers were formed by the early Franciscan foundations, which integrated the Native American work force into the fabric of the civil province. The Society of Jesus, in contrast, jealously protected its Guarani neophytes against exploitation by private employers, and Jesuits allowed mission Guaranis few opportunities to choose their own ways of work and leisure.

Colonists of Paraguay and Corrientes thus envied the Jesuits' control of native labor and feared the missions' military potential, occasionally used against rebellious settlers. Other adversaries included members of more nationalistic religious orders in Spain, who resented the ultramontane Society of Jesus for its loyalty to the pope. Modernizing bureaucrats of Bourbon Spain after 1700 resented the society's corporate privileges. Royal officials in the 1760s tired of Jesuit privileges, made notorious by Guarani military resistance to the Treaty of Madrid of 1750, which would have transferred seven missions on the Uruguay River to Portuguese control. Some administrators also envied the society's wealth. In early 1767, Charles III ordered the Jesuits expelled from his dominions, and officials in the Río de la Plata executed the order in 1767 and 1768.

After the expulsion, imperial bureaucrats and land-hungry colonists conspired to acquire mission lands, and the Guarani missions slowly declined. Indians with marketable skills took advantage of more relaxed controls to leave the missions and join Hispanic communities of the upper Río de la Plata. They never returned to the wild, as some accounts allege. Although a few missions in the Chaco disappeared after the Jesuits' departure, others were founded. Questions about how great was the contribution of the Jesuit missions to the empire and how much they benefited the Indians are still topics of debate, now invigorated by recent interest in Native American views of the institutions that controlled them.

See also **Catholic Church: The Colonial Period; Missionaries of Charity.**

BIBLIOGRAPHY

Martin Dobrizhoffer, *An Account of the Abipones: An Equestrian People of Paraguay,* 3 vols., translated by Sara Coleridge (1822; repr. in 1 vol. 1970).

Robert B. Cunninghame Graham, *A Vanished Arcadia* (1901).

Magnus Mörner, *The Political and Economic Activities of the Jesuits in the La Plata Region: The Hapsburg Era* (1953).

Guillermo Furlong [Cárdiff], *Misiones y sus pueblos Guaranies* (1962).

Magnus Mörner, ed., *The Expulsion of the Jesuits from Latin America* (1965).

Philip Caraman, *The Lost Paradise: The Jesuit Republic in South America* (1976).

Branislava Susnik, *Los aborígenes del Paraguay,* 7 vols. (1978–1987).

Additional Bibliography

Bailey, Gauvin A. *Art on the Jesuit Missions in Asia and Latin America, 1542–1773.* Buffalo, NY: University of Toronto Press, 1999.

Gálvez, Lucía. *Guaraníes y jesuitas de la tierra sin mal al paraíso.* Buenos Aires: Editorial Sudamericana, 1995.

Flores, Moacyr. *Reduções jesuíticas dos guaranis.* Porto Alegre: EDIPUCRS, 1997.

Hernández Palomo, José Jesús, and Rodrigo Moreno Jeria. *La Misión y los jesuitas en la América española, 1566–1767: Cambios y permanencies.* Madrid: Consejo Superior de Investigaciones Científicas, Departamento de Publicaciones, 2005.

Negro Tua, Sandra and Manuel M. Marzal. *Un reino en la frontera: Las misiones jesuitas en la América colonial.* Lima: Pontificia Universidad Católica del Perú: Ediciones Abya-Yala, 1999.

Olsen, Margaret M. *Slavery and Salvation in Colonial Cartagena de Indias.* Gainesville: University Press of Florida, 2004.

Querejazu, Pedro and Plácido Molina Barbery. *Las misiones jesuíticas de Chiquitos.* La Paz: Fundación BHN, Línea Editorial: La Papelera, 1995.

James Schofield Saeger

SPANISH AMERICA

From the start of the colonial enterprise, missionaries were partners with the Spanish crown in the invasion, conquest, and subsequent settlement of the so-called New World. The first friars came with the conquerors. Mendicant orders established themselves on the island of Hispaniola in the Caribbean as early as 1500. Fray Bartolomé de Olmedo, a Mercedarian, accompanied Hernán Cortés to Mexico. A Dominican traveled with Francisco Pizarro to Peru. From these centers, orders eventually established themselves throughout what became the Spanish domain: to the north, including present-day California, New Mexico, and Arizona; along the southeastern seaboard of North America; and south to the river Bío-Bío. Thus, Spanish American missions proved to be early and ubiquitous institutions found wherever the number of native peoples warranted a "spiritual conquest," to use a phrase coined by Robert Ricard. Their dispersal stretched and guaranteed the frontiers of Spanish power and came to define the extension of the Spanish American Empire.

Different orders developed their own character or reputation, depending on where they were located, which could and did change over time, condition (permanently established or on a frontier), or specialization (such as education or medical care). The Franciscans, for example, steadfastly respected their vow of poverty, beginning as itinerant missionaries and only later building their residences among the Indians. They were the only order that refused to acquire more land than was needed for churches and houses and that depended on the contributions of the faithful for their subsistence. They focused on the northeastern mission field on the frontier of New Spain, especially in Coahuila, Nuevo León, Nuevo Santander, New Mexico, and Texas. The Jesuits, in contrast, became famous for their fine schools; their efficiently run, self-supporting, and even rich haciendas; and, most important, for their missions to the Guarani and Guaycuru of Bolivia, Paraguay, and northwestern Argentina and to the peoples on the northwestern frontier of Mexico, especially in Sinaloa, Sonora, Chihuahua, the Californias, and Arizona. Meanwhile, the Augustinians became known for grandiose and costly monasteries, especially in Mexico.

From the start, conversion remained the missionaries' first and foremost goal. Evangelization, the saving of souls, and the battle against what the Spanish believed to be the devil gave missionaries the courage to explore the land, to make contact with indigenous groups, to live among them, and even to suffer martyrdom at their hands. But Christianization proved a slow and frustrating process. Two formidable obstacles were the language barrier and the relatively small numbers of religious compared to the millions to be converted to the Spanish God.

Despite the study of native languages in order to render them better able to translate and explain such basic concepts as the Trinity, and despite efforts to document and thus understand native cultures, the missionaries' efforts at conversion were never completely effective. Even years later, local native religious beliefs and practices survived. In both the Mexican and Peruvian heartlands, the natives customarily incorporated the gods of the newcomers into the local pantheon. Jesus Christ, then, could be added to their belief system and sacred hierarchy without undue reluctance. Early eyewitnesses reported seeing Christian images alongside native idols. Indigenous peoples often equated their traditional gods with Christian saints and images and continued burning incense and making blood sacrifices to them.

Battling such practices and beliefs and spreading the Christian faith were part of the missionaries' work of "civilizing" or Hispanicizing the natives. In the process, native cultures were altered to varying degrees. In some places entire communities were reshaped, which affected their viability as production units. Under the aegis of the missionaries, monogamy became the standard for lords and commoners alike. Abortion and infanticide were outlawed. There is growing evidence that women lost status because of European-introduced ideas supporting patriarchy and paternalism. And in some native societies, gender roles were reversed by ethnocentric friars. Life in the missions also sometimes meant accepting political hierarchies that were altered or replaced to suit Spanish civil and even military needs. Living with the friars might also imply learning a different language and novel concepts of time, accepting a different calendar, using new agricultural techniques, and eating new foods.

To convert and Hispanicize, the missionaries tried several tactics. Early Franciscans and Dominicans relied on word and example, or "peaceful persuasion," and considered force unnecessary to their efforts. But in the face of incontrovertible evidence of continuing idolatrous practices and other forms of native resistance, the missionaries soon changed their approach. Physical force and punishment quickly became established practice. Lashing, flogging, and other forms of torture extracted admissions of idolatry, sacrifice, and other evidence of the devil's evil influence. Harsh treatment and other abuse were met with dissimulation, feigned ignorance, evasion, slow or reluctant compliance, and silence, typical weapons of the weak. Friars all over Spanish America interpreted this behavior as docility. Regarding the Indians en masse as ignorant and confused children, the missionaries treated them as such, assuming the roles of guides, teachers, and protectors.

Finally, missionaries served in peripheral areas as explorers, diplomatic agents, peace emissaries to hostile tribes, and chroniclers of expeditions. From fortified mission enclosures, sometimes supported by colonial troops, they were also expected to hold the line against nomadic, nonmission Indians as well as other European powers.

An assessment of the success or failure of the missionaries depends on one's point of view. Everywhere their efforts were conditioned by their small numbers and by language barriers, as pointed out above, but also by the poor moral example set by the friars, secular priests, and Spanish and creole settlers. Competition among the orders and the state policy of secularization (that is, reassigning established missions to the authority of members of the secular clergy to give the state better control) limited the geographical theater of their efforts and also reduced the time they had to accomplish their ends. It is an unholy irony that successful missions were among the first to be secularized because once the Indians were Hispanicized, their missionary work was done; the conscientious friars were sent to the frontier to begin anew as if punished by the very God they worshipped. Yet as James Axtell points out, from the Native American point of view the missions may be judged at least a qualified success; although they entailed massive cultural change, they also fostered ethnic identity and survival by teaching native languages and giving the Indians another ethnic group with which they could make comparisons.

See also **Catholic Church: The Colonial Period; Missions: Jesuit Missions (Reducciones).**

BIBLIOGRAPHY

Herbert E. Bolton, "The Mission as a Frontier Institution in the Spanish-American Colonies," in *American Historical Review* 23 (1917):42–61.

Robert Ricard, *The Spiritual Conquest of Mexico: An Essay on the Apostolate and the Evangelizing Methods of the Mendicant Orders in New Spain, 1523–1572,* translated by L. B. Simpson (1966).

James Axtell, "Some Thoughts on the Ethnohistory of Missions," in *Ethnohistory* 29, no. 1 (1982): 35–41.

Inga Clendinnen, "Disciplining the Indians: Franciscan Ideology and Missionary Violence in Sixteenth-Century Yucatán," in *Past and Present* 94 (1982): 27–48.

Fred Spier, *Religious Regimes in Peru* (1992).

Additional Bibliography

Acuña, René, and Roberto Heredia Correa. *Fray Julián Garcés: Su alegato en pro de los naturales de Nueva España.* México: Universidad Nacional Autónoma de México, Instituto de Investigaciones Filológicas, Centro de Estudios Clásicos, 1995.

Bruno, Cayetano. *Iglesia y Estado en indias.* Buenos Aires: Centro de Estudios Salesiano de Buenos Aires (CESBA), 2004.

Langer, Erick D., and Robert H. Jackson. *The New Latin American Mission History.* Lincoln: University of Nebraska Press, 1995.

Mörner, Magnus. *La Corona Española y los foráneos en los pueblos de indios de América.* Madrid: Agencia Española de Cooperación Internacional, Ediciones de Cultura Hispánica, 1999.

Ramos, Gabriela and Solange Alberro. *La venida del reino: religión, evangelización y cultura en América, siglos XVI–XX.* Cuzco, Peru: Centro de Estudios Regionales Andinos "Bartolomé de Las Casas," 1994.

SUSAN E. RAMÍREZ

Gabriela Mistral receiving the Nobel Prize in Literature, 1945. © BETTMANN/CORBIS

MISTRAL, GABRIELA (1889–1957). Gabriela Mistral (*b.* 7 April 1889; *d.* 10 January 1957), Chilean poet. The first female Latin American writer of international stature, Mistral won the Nobel Prize for Literature in 1945. Born Lucila Godoy Alcayaga, in Vicuña, in the province of Coquimbo, Mistral began her career as a teacher and administrator; she directed various secondary schools in different regions of the country from Antofagasta to Punta Arenas. In 1922 Mistral left Chile, not to come back again except for short visits. Invited by President Álvaro Obregón Salido of Mexico to contribute to the educational reforms of Minister José Vasconcelos, she resided in Mexico until 1924. Her official and unofficial trips to South America and the Caribbean brought her public acclamation and the recognition of her peers. She served numerous diplomatic functions as consul in Rome, Marseille, Guatemala, Nice, Aix-en-Provence, Madrid, Lisbon, Paris, Veracruz, Niterói, Petrópolis, Los Angeles, Naples, Miami, and Roslyn Harbor. She was a Chilean delegate to the First Assembly of the United Nations Subcommittee on the Juridical Status of Women in San Francisco, and she took part in the creation of UNICEF. In 1953 Mistral represented Chile in the United Nations General Assembly, and in 1955, at the request of Secretary-General Dag Hammarskjöld, she addressed the U.N. on human rights. During the cold war, her essay "La palabra maldita" (The Damned Word [peace]), denouncing the tensions between East and West, circulated widely. Mistral kept in contact with the Spanish American world through her journalistic pursuits, publishing articles in the main journals of Caracas, Buenos Aires, Santiago, and other major cities. Her poetic works were widely featured in the literary magazines of Chile, Spain, and Latin America before she published her first book.

The poetry of Gabriela Mistral is composed of five major works: *Desolación* (1922), *Ternura* (1924), *Tala* (1938), *Lagar* (1954), and the posthumously published *Poema de Chile* (1967). *Desolación* is divided into four sections: "Vida" (Life), "La Escuela" (The School), "Dolor" (Pain), and "Naturaleza" (Nature). The best-known section is "Dolor," which has served, somewhat inadequately, as a foundation on which to build a biography of the poet. The section is a sequence of twenty-seven poems loosely narrating a story of love and tragedy that describes a couple's first meeting, followed by the glowing experience of romantic love, the fears and insecurities of the enamored woman, the lover's betrayal and his unexpected suicide, the unbearable pain that followed, the healing period, and ultimately, serenity. The intense poetic tone and expression of unbridled passion are unique in Spanish poetry. The language is natural, showing only traces of modernist style; its allegiance is to the spoken language rather than to literary or poetic forms. The personal, intimate mood the poems evoke is also a reaction against the distancing quality of elegant literary expression. In the last section, Mistral aligns herself with the new poetry of the avant garde, with its imagistic and creationist style. One of the section's poems is a close imitation of Vicente Huidobro's poetry of those years.

Mistral's second book, *Ternura,* contains a section of the first edition of *Desolación* and, in its 1945 edition, a section from *Tala.* It is a collection of poems for children: cradle songs, rhymes, *albricias* (rewards), and *jugarretas* (playful tricks). The compositions are full of charm and verbal creativity. The third book, *Tala,* is the definitive example of Mistralian poetry, with selected emphasis on simple matters, nocturnal elegies, and American hymns. The language is particularly close to colloquialism. Many cultural directions are represented, from biblical and classical to modern European and American Indian. Especially notable is a section called "América," which includes the hymns "Sol del trópico" (Tropical Sun) and "Cordillera" (The Andes Mountains). *Lagar* develops the themes of the previous book and builds upon forms introduced in *Tala,* among them the famous *recados* (messages) of which Mistral said, "These letters carry with them my very tone, the most recurrent, the rural lilt in which I have lived and in which I will die." The posthumous *Lagar II* (1991) is a collection of Mistral's theretofore unpublished poems, most of them unfinished or lacking the final approval of the poet. *Poema de Chile,* also published posthumously, was not reviewed by Mistral for final publication, but it is believed that the poem itself was conceived as an open form, constantly to be changed by subtraction or addition. The poem tells the story of a journey, from north to south along the Chilean territory, of an old woman's spirit accompanied by the phantoms of a child and a small deer. The tone is one of nostalgia. Familiarity with and praise of nature and ordinary things is a major theme. The flowers, herbs, fruits, birds, mountains, and rivers described refer to different regions of Chile. Mistral's extensive journalistic articles, letters, and essays have been collected in many volumes. Her poetic work makes her one of the most universal as well as one of the most singular and distinctive voices in Chilean and Spanish American literature.

See also **Literature: Spanish America.**

BIBLIOGRAPHY

Margot Arce de Vázquez, *Gabriela Mistral: The Poet and Her Work,* translated by Helene Masslo Anderson (1964).

Margaret Bates, "The Definitive Edition of Gabriela Mistral's Poetry," in *Revista Interamericana de Bibliografía* 16, no. 4 (1966): 411–415.

Marie-Lise Gazarian-Gautier, *Gabriela Mistral, the Teacher from the Valley of Elqui* (1975).

Cedomil Goic, "Gabriela Mistral," in *Latin American Writers,* edited by Carlos A. Solé and Maria Isabel Abreu, vol. 2 (1989), pp. 677–691.

Sister Mary Charles Ann Preston, *A Study of Significant Variants in the Poetry of Gabriela Mistral* (1964).

Martin C. Taylor, *Gabriela Mistral's Religious Sensibility* (1968).

Additional Bibliography

Agosín, Marjorie. *Gabriela Mistral: The Audacious Traveler.* Athens: Ohio University Press, 2003.

Arrigoitia, Luis de. *Pensamiento y forma en la prosa de Gabriela Mistral.* Río Piedras: Editorial de la Universidad de Puerto Rico, 1989.

Fernández, Jesse. *El poema en prosa en Hispanoamérica: Del modernismo a la vanguardia: Estudio crítico y antología.* Madrid: Hiperión, 1994.

Figueroa, Lorena, Keiko Silva, and Patricia Vargas. *Tierra, indio, mujer: Pensamiento social de Gabriela Mistral.* Santiago, Chile: LOM Ediciones: Universidad Arcis, 2000.

Lillo, Gastón, and Juan Guillermo Renart. *Re-leer hoy a Gabriela Mistral: Mujer, historia y sociedad en América Latina (simposio de Ottawa)L.* Ottawa, Canada: University of Ottawa, 1997.

Münnich Busch, Susana. *Gabriela Mistral: Soberbiamente transgresora.* Santiago, Chile: LOM Ediciones, 2005.

CEDOMIL GOIC

MITA. Mita, a colonial Andean system of rotating forced Indian labor assigned by the state to designated beneficiaries. The Spanish conquerors derived the *mita* from the Quechuan *mit'a,* whereby Andean society made temporary assignments of workers for community projects.

Viceroy Francisco de Toledo (1569–1581) established the colonial mita, issuing laws regarding the size of the draft levies, the wages to be paid the workers, and the frequency with which an individual worker served. Without approval of the crown (which remained ambivalent about the morality of coerced labor but willing to profit from it), Toledo instituted a formal mita for the silver mines and mills at Potosí between 1572 and 1575. Each year it mobilized over 11,000 Indians from the highland provinces between Potosí and Cuzco. Toledo established another important mita at the Huancavelica mercury mines. Particularly before the catastrophic decline in the indigenous population, viceregal officials occasionally assigned mitas to other mines and to Spanish towns, making cheap but unspecialized labor available to other sectors of the colonial economy. Such a mita provided textile sweatshops in Quito with much of their labor.

The mitas coerced reluctant Indians into participating in the colonial economy and subsidized economic production through low wages. *Mitayos* (mita workers) sometimes stayed on to earn the higher wages paid free labor. By the 1700s, the number of *mitayos* who worked at Potosí or Huancavelica was only a tiny fraction of the assigned quota. Some villages successfully resisted fulfillment of the mita obligation. Other villages paid colonial administrators to hire substitutes from the pool of voluntary laborers. Thus, free labor was available, but the Spaniards preserved the mita because it subsidized mining through low wages. Poor ore quality at Potosí made production unprofitable without the mita subsidy during the eighteenth century.

The mita elicited opposition on humanitarian grounds, but many complaints about it also came from priests, governors, *kurakas* (Indian leaders), and landowners who wanted to retain the Indians for other forms of economic exploitation. The cortes of Spain finally abolished the mita in 1812, but it survived at least into the nineteenth century. Clorinda Matto de Turner's 1889 novel *Aves sin nido* shows how forced labor in the form of *pongos* is extracted from Quechua speakers. The *pongo* system has survived in fact until the present day.

Other regions of Latin America had similar systems of forced labor such as the *tequitl* in the Nahuatl-speaking territories of Central Mexico.

See also **Huasipungo; Mining: Colonial Spanish America; Slavery: Indian Slavery and Forced Labor.**

BIBLIOGRAPHY

Aquiles R. Pérez, *Las mitas en la real audiencia de Quito* (1947).

Guillermo Lohmann Villena, *Las minas de Huancavelica en los siglos XVI y XVII* (1949), esp. pp. 91–100.

David L. Wiedner, "Forced Labor in Colonial Peru," in *The Americas* 16, no. 4 (1960): 357–383.

Enrique Tandeter, "Forced and Free Labour in Late Colonial Potosí," in *Past and Present* 93 (1981): 98–136.

Peter J. Bakewell, *Miners of the Red Mountain: Indian Labor in Potosí, 1545–1650* (1984), esp. pp. 54–105.

Jeffrey A. Cole, *The Potosí Mita, 1573–1700: Compulsory Indian Labor in the Andes* (1985).

Additional Bibliography

Matto de Turner, Clorinda, *Torn from the Nest.* Ed. Antonio Cornejo Polar. Trans. John Herman Richard Polt. New York: Oxford University Press, 1998.

Premo, Bianca. "From the Pockets of Women: The Gendering of the Mita, Migration, and Tribute in Colonial Chucuito, Peru." *The Americas* 56:4 (April 2000): 63-93.

Tandeter, Enrique. *Coercion and Market: Silver Mining in Colonial Potosí, 1692–1826.* Albuquerque: University of New Mexico Press, 1993.

KENDALL W. BROWN

MITA, GUATEMALA. Guatemala Mita, a region that roughly corresponds to the eastern highlands of Guatemala, south of the Motagua River. The territory is now occupied by the departments of Santa Rosa, Jalapa, and Jutiapa and borders El Salvador. Mita was unique in Guatemala in that it became *ladino*, or Hispanicized, in the late eighteenth and early nineteenth centuries. Under such conditions of social change, the region erupted in political violence on several occasions. Indeed, it became the home of peasant leader Rafael Carrera, whose revolutionary activities led to the downfall of liberal rule in 1838 in Guatemala and the eventual destruction of the United Provinces of Central America. Thereafter, as Carrera controlled the political life of the nation for the next three decades, a disproportionate number of Guatemala's military and political leaders came from the region.

See also **Guatemala.**

BIBLIOGRAPHY

Pedro Tobar Cruz, *Los Montañeses* (1959).

Additional Bibliography

Grandin, Greg. *The Blood of Guatemala: A History of Race and Nation.* Durham, NC: Duke University Press, 2000.

Shea, Maureen E. *Culture and Customs of Guatemala.* Westport, CT: Greenwood Press, 2001.

MICHAEL F. FRY

MITLA. Mitla was a preeminent Postclassic Zapotec religious center (CE 1000–1521). Mitla is located in Oaxaca's Tlacolula Valley, approximately 24 miles east of Oaxaca City, Mexico. The name Mitla is a corruption of *Mictlán,* the Nahuatl term for the afterworld. The Zapotec name is Lyobba, or "Place of Rest." Before the Conquest, Mitla had reputedly been the residence and court of the Huijatao, or "great seer," an oracular priest whom later Spanish chroniclers compared to a Christian pope in authority.

Five mound groups, the North Group (Church Group), the Group of the Columns, the Arroyo Group, the Adobe Group, and the South Group, have been the focus of considerable archaeological study. The ruins are famous for their distinctive architectural forms. They are composed of impressive one-story palaces built around two or more quadrangular patios. Access to these inner courtyards was highly restricted, in keeping with the privileged status of the buildings' occupants. Elaborate ornamental wall friezes were produced either by carving the limestone surface directly or by constructing fretted mosaics with smaller stones. Traces of the red background color remain. The southern court of the Group of the Columns contains two cruciform tombs, which may correspond to historical accounts of underground passageways where the funerary remains of ranking Zapotec lords were enshrined.

Mitla's prominence derived from its unique sociopolitical status. During the Postclassic period Zapotec authority had become distributed among a number of petty kings who reckoned their control over tributary lands on the basis of descent from common deified ancestors. As the head of the funerary cult, a high priest of Mitla not only was endowed with sacred authority as the principal mediator with the divine but also wielded considerable secular power, apparently serving as chief councillor who arbitrated between the various Oaxacan political factions as well.

Though the earliest structural remains correspond to Zapotec rule, Mitla experienced significant growth between CE 750 and 1521, a period marking the end of Zapotec reign and the ascendance of the Mixtec, who based their power in Mitla, and whose style can also be seen in the archaeological evidence. In the seventeenth century, the Spanish constructed the San Pablo Catholic Church, which stands on the footprint of a former courtyard, is adjacent to the Church Group, and was built using Mitla temple stone. The present-day town of San Pablo Vila de Mitla grew up around the ruins.

See also **Oaxaca (State); Zapotecs.**

BIBLIOGRAPHY

William Henry Holmes, *Archaeological Studies Among the Ancient Cities of Mexico* (1895–1897).

Nelly M. García Robles, Alfredo José Moreira Quiros, Rogelio González Medina, and Victor Jiménez Muñoz, *Mitla.* (1989).

Additional Bibliography

Feinman, Gary M., and Linda M. Nicholas. *Hilltop Terrace Sites of Oaxaca, Mexico: Intensive Surface Survey at Guirún, El Palmillo and the Mitla Fortress.* Chicago: Field Museum of Natural History, 2004.

González Licón, Ernesto. *Zapotecas y mixtecas: Tres mil años de civilización precolombina.* Barcelona, Spain: Lunwerg, 1992.

Pohl, John M. D. "The Lintel Paintings of Mitla and the Function of the Mitla Palaces." In *Mesoamerican Architecture as a Cultural Symbol,* edited by Jeff K. Kowalski. New York: Oxford University Press, 1999.

Robles García, Nelly M. *Las canteras de Mitla, Oaxaca: Tecnología para la arquitectura monumental.* Nashville, TN: Vanderbilt University, 1994.

JOHN M. D. POHL

MITMAES. Mitmaes (also *mitimaes, mitima, mithma, mitmac*), from the Quechua word *mitmaq,* meaning "outsider" or "stranger." *Mitmaes* were people, sometimes whole ethnic groups, who were relocated by the Incas as a matter of policy. It was common imperial practice to move whole populations around the empire in order to break up old political units that might provide the basis for organized revolt. *Mitmaq* communities brought in from loyal provinces were expected to set an example, spread Inca customs, and to serve as an Inca garrison. Conversely, the most recalcitrant elements of the newly incorporated areas were transplanted to loyal and secure areas of the empire, where they could be monitored and would be in the minority.

After the Spanish invasions these microethnic groups used the resulting instability to rebel against the Incan state, often allying themselves with Pizarro's forces. Later, *mitmaq* peoples were seen as intruders by their latter-day ethnic communities. Perhaps the most famous *mitmaq* family was that of Guaman Poma de Ayala, who initiated lawsuits to recover his usurped lands in the post-Conquest period.

See also **Forasteros; Guaman Poma de Ayala, Felipe.**

BIBLIOGRAPHY

For a discussion of *mitmaes,* see John H. Rowe, "Inca Culture at the Time of the Spanish Conquest," in *Handbook of South American Indians,* vol. 2 (1946), pp. 183–330; and John Victor Murra, *The Economic Organization of the Inca State* (1980).

GORDON F. MCEWAN

MITRE, BARTOLOMÉ (1821–1906).

Bartolomé Mitre (*b.* 26 June 1821; *d.* 19 January 1906), president of Argentina (1862–1868) and one of the modern nation's founders. Along with Domingo Faustino Sarmiento, Mitre best represents the liberal reformism that infused Argentina after the overthrow of Juan Manuel de Rosas in 1852. Mitre acted simultaneously as statesman, soldier, journalist, and historian in order to set in motion and later consolidate the program laid out in the Constitution of 1853–1860.

Exile and Rise to Power. From early on, Mitre was a member of the opposition to Rosas, and in 1837 he and his family were exiled to Montevideo, Uruguay. For the next fifteen years he worked intensively as a soldier and publicist in Montevideo; La Paz, Bolivia; and Santiago, Chile. He served as an artillery officer in the defense of Montevideo against the troops of Manuel Oribe, and it was then that he began his historiographical labors, work he would continue until the end of his days. He spent a brief time in La Paz in order to organize a military academy, and he brought his years of exile to a close as a journalist in Chile.

When the uprising against Rosas began, Mitre participated in the campaign of Justo José de Urquiza, governor of Entre Ríos, which ended 3 February 1852 at the battle of Caseros. From that moment on, Mitre played a decisive role nationally. He disagreed with Urquiza in June 1852 by opposing the ratification of the accord of San Nicolás and by participating in the revolution of 11 September, which separated the province of Buenos Aires from the confederation of governors who supported Urquiza. Against the most extreme localist positions of the *porteño* (Buenos Aires) leaders, Mitre defended a conception of national liberalism that, after the defeat at Cepeda on 23 October 1859, brought about on 11 November the signing of the Pact of San José de Flores. As a result, Mitre was elected governor of the province of Buenos Aires in 1860, and the National Convention for Constitutional Reform accepted his anticentralist ideas, which resembled the North American constitutional model. Despite this success, during the rule of Urquiza's successor, Santiago Derqui, there arose new complications in San Juan which led to a definitive confrontation, ending in Mitre's victory at the battle of Pavón on 17 September 1861.

Presidency. In 1861 Mitre's leadership was recognized throughout much of the country. With Urquiza defeated, Mitre's intellectual vision for Argentina joined with his control over military resources and a constitutional organization that was finally recognized by all the provinces. Derqui resigned after Pavón left Mitre to carry out a complete reorganization of the executive, legislative, and judicial powers. On 12 October 1862 Mitre assumed the presidency, unanimously elected by the electoral college. That began a regular succession of constitutional presidents every six years in Argentina, interrupted only by the coup d'état of 6 September 1930.

Three major concerns dominated Mitre's presidency. The first was programmatic. By 10 June 1865 (when power was handed to Vice President Marcos Paz because of the war with Paraguay—the War of the Triple Alliance), Mitre's administration had established the basis for the organization of the three components of state power, to which was added a rigorous fiscal policy, with funds from customs at the port of Buenos Aires becoming part of the national treasury. Likewise, Congress passed a commerce code, and civil, penal, and judicial codes were recommended. The grant for the railway from Rosario to Córdoba was authorized and special attention was paid to the development of educational policy. National secondary schools were founded in Buenos Aires, Concepción del Uruguay (previously established by Urquiza), Catamarca, Salta, Tucumán, San Juan, and Mendoza. An exiled French republican, Amédée Jacques, was the first rector of the Buenos Aires school.

The second concern facing Mitre was institutional. With Urquiza withdrawn to the province of Entre Ríos, the national government could not declare the city of Buenos Aires capital of the republic because of the division in that province brought about by the followers of Adolfo Alsina. Thanks to a compromise, the national government resided in Buenos Aires even though the city could not be federalized. Similarly, the rest of the provinces, with the exception of Entre Ríos and Santiago del Estero, were shaken by violent insurrections and by the reappearance of the *montoneras.* All these rebellions were drastically suppressed through federal intervention by the national government.

The third concern before Mitre was the War of the Triple Alliance. In April 1865, because of the invasion of the province of Corrientes by the troops of Marshal Francisco Solano López during a forced march to Brazil, the Argentine government declared war on Paraguay and a state of siege in all the territory. With the signing of the Treaty of the Triple Alliance with Uruguay and the Brazilian Empire, President Mitre was designated commander in chief of the Allied forces. The war ended with the death of Solano López in 1870. It reduced the population of Paraguay (from 1.1 million to 220,000).

From Opposition to Political Accord. At the end of his term as president, Mitre resolved not to intervene in the designation of his successor. The election of 1868, although divided, turned the office over to Domingo F. Sarmiento, another important member of the group to which Mitre belonged. The following year Mitre was appointed national senator, and in 1870 he founded the newspaper *La Nación.* During Sarmiento's presidency, relations between the provinces and the national government changed. A new coalition of governors, allied with Adolfo Alsina, defeated Mitre in the presidential election of 1874. Mitre and his party did not accept the victory of Nicolás Avellaneda and revolted. They were defeated that same year by the national army in the battles of La Verde and Santa Rosa.

Mitre was tried and removed from his senatorial office and stripped of his military rank. With this defeat the political center shifted to the interior, although it did so by strengthening the authority of the national government. Halfway through the presidency of Avellaneda, Mitre communicated a policy of conciliation to Alsina, through which his military rank was restored. This underscored the style of compromising with his adversaries that he had exercised earlier with Urquiza.

In the election of 1880, Julio A. Roca ran against Carlos Tejedor, governor of Buenos Aires and one of the most extreme proponents of *porteño* localism. Mitre had been elected national representative in 1878. In the conflict that arose between Tejedor and Avellaneda when the former rebelled against the national government, Mitre defended Buenos Aires and later negotiated a peace agreement. With the city of Buenos Aires federalized, a strong coalition over which Mitre had no control was consolidated under the leadership of Roca.

The government that came to power in 1880 was shaken by the economic crisis of 1889–1890. Mitre actively participated in opposing Roca's successor, Miguel Juárez Celman, and in forming a new group, the Civic Union, but he traveled to Europe to avoid the civil and military uprising of July 1890. In 1891 the Civic Union announced the presidential ticket of Mitre–Bernardo de Irigoyen, which was supported by Leandro Alem. For his part, Mitre urged an understanding with Roca, which resulted in a Mitre–José Evaristo Uriburu ticket. This caused a split in the Civic Union. Given the lack of consensus, Mitre renounced his candidacy and along with Roca supported the Luis Sáenz Peña–Uriburu ticket in the presidential election of 1892.

Again elected national senator in 1894, Mitre maintained his stance as a nationalist until he retired from public life in 1901, never diminishing his demands for a free vote or his criticisms of electoral corruption. When he died in Buenos Aires in 1906, Carlos Pellegrini affirmed that "Mitre's thoughts and actions are so intimately tied to our national life that his biography will be the history of the politics of the Argentine people during the second half of the nineteenth century."

As Historian. Mitre's work as a historian, publicist, critic, author, and literary translator was far-reaching. He was the founder of the historiography of Argentina's revolution and the nation's subsequent independence. Two great biographies crown this achievement: *Historia de Belgrano y de la independencia argentina* (1858–1859) and *Historia de San Martín y de la emancipación sudamericana* (1887). Mitre worked with methods based on documentary criticism and introduced his findings into a historical synthesis that emphasized the roles of individual actors as well as the profound effects of social, economic, and institutional factors. His polemic with Vicente Fidel López, summarized in *Comprobaciones históricas* (1882), reveals this orientation and the republican philosophy that inspired it.

See also **Argentina, Constitutions.**

BIBLIOGRAPHY

Archivo del general Mitre, 28 vols. (1911–1914).

Natalio R. Botana, *La libertad política y su historia* (1991). Mitre's library of unedited documents and archives are found in what was his home, today the Mitre Museum.

Ramón J. Cárcano, *Guerra del Paraguay,* 2 vols. (1939–1941). The most recent biography is José S. Campobassi, *Mitre y su época* (1980).

Guillermo Furlong, "Bartolomé Mitre: El hombre, el soldado, el historiador, el político," in *Investigaciones y ensayos,* no. 11 (July–December, 1971): 325–523.

Ricardo Levene, "Presidencia de Mitre" in *Historia argentina contemporánea: 1862–1930,* vol. 1 (1963).

Obras completas de Bartolomé Mitre (1938–1972).

James R. Scobie, *The Struggle for Nationhood: Argentina, 1852–1862* (1964).

Additional Bibliography

Gallardo, Jorge Emilio. *Indígenas y afroargentinos en el sentir de Mitre.* Buenos Aires: Idea Viva, 2002.

Marco, Miguel Angel de. *Bartolomé Mitre: Biografía.* Buenos Aires: Planeta, 1998.

Pasquali, Patricia. *La instauración liberal: Urquiza, Mitre y un estadista olvidado, Nicasio Oroño.* Buenos Aires: Planeta, 2003.

NATALIO R. BOTANA

MIXCO VIEJO. Mixco Viejo was the Pocomam Maya capital in late prehistoric times, and later the Kaqchikel regional center from which the modern municipality of San Martín Jilotepeque was formed. The area came under the domination of Iximché in the late fifteenth century. Although the site might more appropriately be called Jilotepeque Viejo, the name Mixco Viejo is likely to persist.

The site is located approximately 38 miles by car north of Guatemala City in a spectacular setting overlooking the Motagua Valley in the present-day department of Chimaltenango. Its proximity to an important commercial route, the Motagua River, further attests to the city's significance. Like many other Late Postclassic period sites, it is on an easily defended plateau surrounded by deep ravines. Inhabited and flourishing at the time of the Spanish conquest, Jilotepeque Viejo fell in the 1520s only after a lengthy siege laid by Pedro de Alvarado, who then burned the city to the ground.

There are over ninety major structures at Mixco Viejo, residential and civic, built primarily from cut schist slabs. Within the four principal plaza groups are temples, altars, ball courts, and palace platforms. Archaeologists have worked at the site since the 1950s, and today much of the site is restored.

See also **Alvarado y Mesía, Pedro de; Guatemala City; Kaqchikel; Maya, The.**

BIBLIOGRAPHY

John W. Fox, *Quiché Conquest* (1978), esp. pp. 203–210.

Henri Lehmann, *Guide to the Ruins of Mixco Viejo,* translated by Andrew McIntyre and Edwin Kuh (n.d.).

Additional Bibliography

Nance, C. Roger; Stephen L. Whittington; and Barbara E. Jones-Borg; with contributions by George Guillemin and Sergio Rodas Manrique. *Archaeology and Ethnohistory of Iximché.* Gainesville: University Press of Florida, 2003.

Paz Cárcamo, Guillermo. *Chwa Nima Ab'äj: Mixco Viejo.* Guatemala City: Editorial Cholsamaj, 2004.

JANINE GASCO

MIXTECS. Mixtecs, an indigenous people of western Mexico. Mixtec-speaking people presently occupy the northern and western portions of the state of Oaxaca and adjacent areas of Guerrero and Puebla. The traditional homeland is further subdivided into three climatic zones called the Mixteca Alta, the Mixteca Baja, and the Mixteca Costa. There are nearly a quarter of a million Mixtec people living today, most of whom subsist by farming. Nevertheless, depleted agricultural resources, particularly in the Mixteca Alta, have necessitated community out-migration to other parts of the country, including Mexico City, as well as to the United States.

Although the archaeology of the region is still in its infancy, Mixtec cultural evolution is defined by four phases following the emergence of early villages from the hunting and gathering bands of the Archaic Period. These are named Cruz (1500–200 BCE), Ramos (200 BCE–CE 300), Las Flores (CE 300–1000), and Natividad (CE 1000–1520). The Las Flores and Natividad phases correlate with the broader definition of the Mesoamerican Classic and Postclassic periods.

Pioneering work by Alfonso Caso and later archaeologists indicates that between 200 BCE and CE 900, the developing city-states of the Mixteca Alta were dominated by Monte Albán, the Zapotec capital located in the Valley of Oaxaca. Prominent Mixtec communities surrounding the strategic Nochixtlan Valley were located at Yucuita, Yucunudahui, Cerro Jasmin, Jaltepec, and the Yucu Yoco-Mogote del Cacique complexes located between the modern communities of Jaltepec and Tilantongo.

Between 1000 and 1100, the region witnessed a dramatic shift in social organization. The large centralized Classic communities were abandoned and numerous small royal estates succeeded them during the Postclassic period. The precise reasons for such drastic settlement fissioning remain unexplained but were undoubtedly linked to the broader developments that were taking place throughout Mesoamerica at the same time.

Eight native historical manuscripts, called the Mixtec codices, record the foundation of powerful Postclassic kingdoms and their principal dynasties. According to these pictorial accounts, at least, Classic period centers were plagued by internal disputes among multiple ruling families. The succeeding period witnessed the rise of a factionalized secondary nobility, epitomized by the culture hero "8 Deer Jaguar Claw," whose biography is found in Codices Zouche-Nuttall, Bodley, and Colombino-Becker. At the time of the Spanish arrival in the region, Tilantongo had emerged as the highest-ranked of the Mixtec royal houses.

The Mixtecs were never subject to the devastation of the Conquest in the same way as were their bitter enemies, the Aztecs of the Triple Alliance. Between 1525 and 1530 many encomiendas had been awarded to conquistadores. Dominican friars constructed several churches, the most famous being the fortified monastery at Yanhuitlán. By 1545, conflicts between native *caciques* (nobles), Spanish *encomenderos* (high-ranking landholders), and the Dominican friars, however, threatened to destroy delicate social contracts. The church acted as mediator between opposing interests. Eventually, the power of the Spanish *encomenderos* was eroded, and Mixtec *caciques* continued to control much of the land until Mexican independence from Spain.

See also **Aztecs; Codices; Indigenous Peoples; Precontact History: Mesoamerica.**

BIBLIOGRAPHY

Alfonso Caso, *Interpretation of Codex Bodley 2858* (1960).

Ronald Spores, *The Mixtec Kings and Their People* (1967).

Robert Ravicz and Kimball A. Romney, "The Mixtec," in *Handbook of Middle American Indians,* vol. 7, edited by Evon Z. Vogt (1969), pp. 367–399.

Mary Elizabeth Smith, *Picture Writing of Ancient Southern Mexico: Mixtec Place Signs and Maps* (1973).

Ronald Spores, *The Mixtecs in Ancient and Colonial Times* (1984).

Additional Bibliography

Boone, Elizabeth Hill. *Stories in Red and Black: Pictorial Histories of the Aztecs and Mixtecs.* Austin: University of Texas Press, 2001.

Byland, Bruce E., and John M. D. Pohl. *In the Realm of Eight Deer: The Archaeology of the Mixtec Codices.* Norman: University of Oklahoma Press, 1994.

Evans, Susan Toby. *Ancient Mexico and Central America: Archaeology and Culture History.* London: Thames & Hudson, 2004.

Fox, Jonathan, and Gaspar Rivera-Salgado. *Indigenous Mexican Migrants in the United States.* La Jolla, CA: Center for U.S.-Mexican Studies, UCSD/Center for Comparative Immigration Studies, UCSD, 2004.

Monaghan, John. *The Covenants with Earth and Rain: Exchange, Sacrifice, and Revelation in Mixtec Sociality.* Norman: University of Oklahoma Press, 1995.

Rossell, Cecilia, and María de los Angeles Ojeda Díaz. *Las mujeres y sus diosas en los códices prehispánicos de Oaxaca.* México: CIESAS: Porrúa, 2003.

Terraciano, Kevin. *The Mixtecs of Colonial Oaxaca: Ñudzahui History, Sixteenth through Eighteenth Centuries.* Stanford, CA: Stanford University Press, 2001.

Velasco Ortiz, M. Laura. *Mixtec Transnational Identity.* Tucson: University of Arizona Press, 2005.

JOHN M. D. POHL

MIXTÓN WAR. Mixtón War (1541–1542), a rebellion of the Chichimecs of Nueva Galicia, Mexico, that nearly rid the region of Spaniards. Reacting to the brutal legacy of Nuño de Guzmán, more recent abuse by *encomenderos,* and the attempted imposition of alien ways, these semi- and nonsedentary peoples were aroused by their religious leaders, who promised divinely sanctioned victory and a variety of spiritual and material rewards. Early Spanish attempts to defeat the rebels in their hilltop strongholds, including one known as Mixtón, failed; Pedro de Alvarado was killed in one attack after his horse fell on him. By late 1541, Guadalajara was in danger, and the Spanish prevailed only after Viceroy Antonio de Mendoza stormed into the area with a force of around 180 mounted Spaniards and thousands of indigenous central Mexican allies. These were commanded by their own nobility, who were given the right to ride horses, carry Iberian weapons, and enslave captured enemies—a right also enjoyed by Spaniards. Some of the allies helped establish fortified settlements on the route north. Ultimately, the pacification of Nueva Galicia paved the way for the discovery of the silver mines of Zacatecas in 1546, and thus the development of New Spain's economic underpinning.

See also **Chichimecs; Guadalajara.**

BIBLIOGRAPHY

This critical episode in the establishment of colonial New Spain has not received much scholarly attention in recent times. A standard account can be found in Arthur Scott Aiton, *Antonio de Mendoza: First Viceroy of New Spain* (1927). The war receives briefer treatment in Philip Wayne Powell, *Soldiers, Indians, and Silver: The Northward Advance of New Spain, 1550–1600* (1952). Peggy K. Liss, *Mexico Under Spain, 1521–1556: Society and the Origins of Nationality* (1975). A narrative by an indigenous leader, Francisco De Sandoval Acazitli, *cacique* of Tlalmanalco, can be found in Joaquín García Icazbalceta, ed., *Colección de documentos para la historia de México,* vol. 2 (repr. 1971), pp. 307–333.

Additional Bibliography

Weigand, Phil C., and Celia García de Weigand. *Los orígenes de los caxcanes y su relación con la guerra de los nayaritas: Una hipótesis.* Zapopan, Jalisco: El Colegio de Jalisco, 1995.

ROBERT HASKETT

MIZQUE. Mizque, region of the eastern Andes. The present-day province of Mizque is located in central Bolivia. At the eve of the Conquest this once extensive region was populated by the Cotas, Chuyes, Chiriguanos, Guarayos, Moxos, Atacames, and Chiquitos other groups whom archaeologists are still seeking to identify.

Spain conquered Peru in the 1530s, established its viceroyalty, and in 1559 created the Audiencia of Charcas (today Bolivia, Paraguay, Argentina, and part of Brazil). The colonial jurisdiction of Mizque was located in this sub-puna region of the eastern Andes, with Santa Cruz to the east, La Plata (today Sucre) toward the southeast, and Potosí to the south. Before the arrival of the Spaniards, the Incas had incorporated this large, fertile, ecologically multizoned province into their expanding empire. By the late fifteenth century, the Inca leadership had rearranged local ethnic groupings and moved the Cotas and the Chuyes from the northwestern Cochabamba area into the eastern reaches of Mizque (specifically Pocona and Totora) to defend the empire against the aggressive, tropical lowland Chiriguano people. These invaders—a hostile, seminomadic, allegedly cannibalistic nation of the Guaraní language group —had also entered the area in the fifteenth century. Although they were often repelled by the Inca defense and later by Spanish settlers, considerable time passed before full pacification, and they continued to raid and massacre into the early seventeenth century. Other Indian groups inhabiting the lowland area were the Guarayos, Moxos, Atacames, and Chiquitos.

Before the arrival of the Spaniards, the Incas had also reorganized native agricultural practices and assigned groups of highland workers to the fertile eastern valleys. Thus, the state had established agriculture as a collective enterprise to serve the empire and its military operations, imposing its own stamp on existing concepts of reciprocity and exchange. Similarly, after the Conquest, Spanish imperial policy called for relocations of Andean people into Repartimientos (specified groupings) in order better to control draft labor and agricultural production for tribute purposes. Long before the Conquest, Andeans had produced coca in Mizque's tropical zones. After the Conquest, they continued coca cultivation, now to fuel mine workers—silver was discovered in Potosí in 1545—rather than the Inca elite. *Repartimiento* Indians also became prolific wine producers.

By the mid-sixteenth century, disease introduced by the Europeans swept through the region and reduced the native population by perhaps 87 percent, which in turn affected *repartimiento* production. Concurrently, private entrepreneurs recognized this fertile zone's potential. As early as 1558, Spaniards established agricultural estates, enticing *repartimiento* Indians to join as Yanaconas (dependent agricultural laborers). With its ecological advantages, Mizque soon produced all manner of European grains, fruits, vegetables, sugar, livestock, and wine, as well as native foods and coca.

By 1630, Mizque served as an important trade and transport link, connecting distant Santa Cruz to the La Plata–Potosí network. By 1787, however, Intendant Francisco de Viedma lamented that Mizque, once a productive region, had suffered a major economic decline, blaming the local population for the relapse. In 1882 another author expressed similar criticisms, contrasting the region's former productivity to its present decay and abandon. We can only speculate as to the causes of this dramatic economic reversal.

See also **Andes; Bolivia: The Colonial Period; Incas, The; Repartimiento; Yanaconas.**

BIBLIOGRAPHY

Francisco De Viedma, *Descripción geográfica y estadística de la provincia de Santa Cruz de la Sierra* (1836), pp. 80–106.

Eufronio Viscarra, *Apuntes para la historia de Cochabamba; Casos históricos y tradiciones de la ciudad de Mizque* (1882), pp. 50–54.

Josep M. Barnadas, *Charcas: Orígenes históricos de una sociedad colonial* (1973), pp. 23–24, 351, 427.

Brooke Larson, *Colonialism and Agrarian Transformation in Bolivia: Cochabamba, 1550–1900* (1988), pp. 25, 28, 30, 31. "La dinámica de la historia regional: Mizque y 'la' puente de 1630," in *Historia y Cultura* (Lima, 1994).

Additional Bibliography

Brockington, Lolita Gutiérrez. *Blacks, Indians, and Spaniards in the Eastern Andes: Reclaiming the Forgotten in Colonial Mizque, 1550–1782.* Lincoln: University of Nebraska Press, 2006.

Querejazu Lewis, Roy. *El arte rupreste de la cuenca del río Mizque.* Cochabamba, Bolivia: Sociedad de Investigación del Arte Rupestre de Bolivia, 2001.

Rojas Vaca, Hectór Luis. *Población y territorio: Una perspectiva histórica, Mizque y Ayopaya.* Cochabamba, Bolivia: Centro de Comunicación y Desarrollo Andino, 2001.

LOLITA GUTIÉRREZ BROCKINGTON

MOBILE, BATTLE OF. Battle of Mobile (26 February–14 March 1780), part of the conflict between the British and the Spanish over West Florida. Bernardo de Gálvez led his Spanish troops from New Orleans to Mobile, where soldiers from Cuba joined them. Temporarily stopped at the entrance to Mobile Bay by sand bars, the Spaniards established their first encampment on Dog River. They soon moved to Spanish River and built an artillery battery west of Fort Charlotte. A heavy bombardment of the fort began on 12 March. Two days later, Capt. Elias Durnford surrendered. Reinforcements en route to Mobile received word of the surrender and returned to Pensacola. The fall of Mobile set the stage for the battle of Pensacola. Spanish victories over the British on the Gulf coast benefited the American colonies during the War for Independence against Great Britain.

See also **Florida, Spanish West.**

BIBLIOGRAPHY

Bernardo De Gálvez, "Conquista de la Movila y puestos del Río Misisipi," Havana, 28 November 1780, Archivo General de Simancas, Guerra Moderna, legajo 6912, Simancas, Spain.

John Walton Caughey, *Bernardo de Gálvez in Louisiana, 1776–1783* (1934; repr. 1972), pp. 171–186.

William S. Coker and Hazel P. Coker, *The Siege of Mobile, 1780*, in *Maps* (1982).

Joseph Barton Starr, *Tories, Dons, and Rebels: The American Revolution in British West Florida* (1976), pp. 161–174.

Additional Bibliography

Chavez, Thomas E. *Spain and the Independence of the United States: An Intrinsic Gift.* Albuquerque: University of New Mexico Press, 2002.

LaFarelle, Lorenzo G. *Bernardo de Gálvez: Hero of the American Revolution.* Austin: Eakin Press, 1992.

Medina Rojas, Francisco de Borja. *José de Ezpeleta, gobernador de La Mobila, 1780-1781.* Sevilla: Escuela de Estudios Hispano-Americanos de Sevilla, C.S.I.C.: Excma. Diputación Foral de Navarra, 1980.

William S. Coker

MOCAMBO. *See* **Quilombo.**

MOCHE. Moche (Mochica) culture, named by archaeologists for the valley in which its principal site is located, emerged by about 200–100 BCE. Originally centered in the Moche-Chicama valley system, the Moche people expanded over time to control about 330 miles of the north coast of Peru, including the valleys from Lambayeque in the north to Nepeña in the south. Inland they controlled the valleys up to the point where the floodplain was no longer cultivable.

The Moche appear to have been an aggressive, warlike people who spread by conquest over the north coast. The nature of their political organization has been the subject of much controversy. Some have argued that the Moche created one of the first state-level governments in the Andes. Because of the absence of true cities and urban centers, others believe that the Moche were more likely a highly organized, predatory chiefdom without the administrative hierarchy of control characteristic of a centralized government. The Moche appear to have developed true urban centers or cities very late in their history and were probably on the threshold of becoming a true state when their society collapsed between CE 600 and 750.

Moche engineers designed and built fortifications, and public works projects such as roads and canals, in addition to domestic and ritual architecture. The agricultural economy of the Moche led them to construct elaborate irrigation systems, with canals bringing water from the upper valleys to increase the amount of arable land. The construction and maintenance of these systems required a sophisticated knowledge of hydrological engineering and a high level of organization and coordination within Moche society.

Much of what is known of the Moche comes directly from their art. They developed a lifelike style that was so accurate that plants and animals are often easily identified. Realistic portraits of individuals show what the people looked like and provide a great amount of detail about costume. Almost every imaginable aspect of culture was depicted in Moche art, ranging from the familiar and commonplace, including tools, weapons, clothing, houses, plants, and animals, to representations of supernatural beings and scenes from mythology.

Moche society was organized into a hierarchy. Nobles and other important men are shown richly costumed, presiding over ceremonies and rituals. The rulers probably also functioned as the high priests in a theocratic government. Recent archaeological discoveries at Sipán, in the Lambayeque valley, indicate that the highest-ranking members of Moche society controlled vast quantities of gold, silver, and other precious commodities.

Ordinary people were frequently shown engaged in mundane activities such as eating and drinking, bathing, sleeping, fishing, and hunting. Specialized roles in society such as healers and shamans, and even witches, are also shown. Lifelike figurines modeled in clay show Moche people engaged in nearly all common human activities. Portraits of the sick are accurate enough that some diseases can be identified by modern doctors.

The Moche visual style that conveys this information appeared in a wide variety of media. Best known are Moche ceramics, but Moche artists also wove textiles, painted murals, and worked in stone, wood, shell, and metal. Saline soil and increased moisture on the north coast has destroyed all but a few Moche textiles, but the other art forms have survived in abundance.

At the beginning of the Middle Horizon (540–900), the Moche polity appears to have suffered a series of severe crises that led to its collapse. A climatic fluctuation is often cited as a possible cause of these crises. Internal social stress resulting from reduced economic productivity is sometimes mentioned as a factor as well. Another frequently cited cause is the expansion of the Huari Empire from the south. It seems likely that all of these factors played some role in the disappearance of the Moche culture.

In recent years archaeological teams under the guidance of Santiago Uceda of the University of Trujillo, Steve Bourget of the University of Texas at Austin, and John Verano of Tulane University, have discovered evidence suggesting that the Moche practiced ritual warfare, human sacrifice, and excarnation. The 2005 discovery by this same team of a 1,500-year-old tattooed female mummy in the El Brujo ceremonial site promises to reveal a great deal more about Moche culture in the near future. The woman was buried with the some of the most elaborate war clubs and spears found to date.

See also **Archaeology; Sicán.**

BIBLIOGRAPHY

The principal sources on the Moche include Christopher B. Donnan, *Moche Art of Peru,* rev. ed. (1978), and "Iconography of the Moche: Unraveling the Mystery of the Warrior-Priest," in *National Geographic* 174, no. 4 (1988): 550–555; Elizabeth Benson, *The Mochica, a Culture of Peru* (1972); Rafael Larco Hoyle, *Los Mochicas,* 2 vols. (1938–1939); Gordon R. Willey, *Prehistoric Settlement Patterns in the Virú Valley, Peru* (1953); Walter Alva, "Discovering the New World's Richest Unlooted Tomb," in *National Geographic* 174, no. 4 (1988): 510–550. See also Luis G. Lumberas, *The Peoples and Cultures of Ancient Peru* (1972); and Walter Alva and Christopher B. Donnan, *Royal Tombs of Sipán* (1993)

Additional Bibliography

Sutter, Richard C. "The Nature of Moche Human Sacrifice: A Bio-Archeological Perspective." *Current Anthropology* 46:4 (2005), 521–549.

Wilford, John Noble. "A Peruvian Woman Warrior of A.D. 450." *New York Times*, May 17, 2006.

GORDON F. MCEWAN

MOCOVÍ.

MOCOVÍ. The Spanish name *Mocoví* derives from *Emocovit* (the term pertains to the Guaycuru languages and names this partiality) and is the name for an ethnic group that is part of the great Guaycurú branch. The Mocoví originally lived west of the regions occupied by the Abipones in the present-day provinces of Santa Fe and Chaco in Argentina. They were mainly hunters and gatherers. The tribes were led by a chief and a council of elders. After the horse became central to their culture, they used it in attacks on some Spanish populations, generally joining with other indigenous groups. In the eighteenth century, when they were expelled from their lands by the Spanish they moved south to the rural zone around Santa Fe. Jesuits eventually founded a Mocoví mission colony nearby, that of San Francisco Javier, in 1743.

With the loss of their land the Mocoví lost their culture's ancient organization. In the early twenty-first century their settlements can be found north of Santa Fe, in central and southern Chaco, and in towns in Corrientes, Entre Ríos, and Santiago del Estero. Santa Fe has more than 85,000 people of Mocoví origin scattered throughout 125 settlements. Many live within the general population, but some form communities with Mocoví identities on the periphery of cities or in rural areas. They work as rural laborers, woodcutters, harvesters, and employees in sawmills or for municipalities. Those who have a small plot of land grow modest crops of cotton, vegetables, and corn. Some fashion handcrafts that they sell for a little money or exchange for used clothing. They lack labor and social protection, and conservation of their language is suffering under pressure from the Spanish. The Mocovi suffered under the Spaniards and continue to suffer in the early twenty-first century.

See also **Indigenous Peoples.**

BIBLIOGRAPHY

Gualdieri, Beatriz. *Apuntes sociolingüísticos sobre el pueblo mocoví de Santa Fe (Argentina).* Available from www.essarp.org.ar/bilinglatam/papers/gualdieri.pdf.

Martínez Sarasola, C. *Nuestros paisanos, los indios. Vida, historia y destino de las comunidades indígenas de la Argentina.* Buenos Aires: Emecé Editores, 1992.

MERCEDES GARCÍA SARAVÍ

MOCTEZUMA. *See* **Motecuhzoma I.**

MODERADOS. *See* **Brazil, Political Parties: Moderados.**

MODERADOS (MEXICO).

MODERADOS (MEXICO). Moderados (Mexico), literally "moderates," a term applied to moderate liberals in nineteenth-century Mexico to distinguish them from the other liberal faction, the *puros*. The terms apparently date from divisions that arose during Valentín Gómez Farías's attempt to use church property to pay for the war against the United States in 1846–1847. *Moderados* opposed the measure in the legislature, then supported a revolt (known as the Rebellion of the Polkos) that forced withdrawal of the decree and the replacement of Gómez Farías with Antonio López de Santa Anna as president. The *moderados* later negotiated the Treaty of Guadalupe Hidalgo, ending the war and ceding California, Arizona, New Mexico, and Texas to the United States in return for $15 million. The *puros* opposed the treaty, favoring continued resistance. The resulting split continued through the era of the reform and the French Intervention, with the *moderados* moving cautiously toward the disamortization of church property and the *puros* pushing for more rapid and radical changes. The *moderados* generally opposed explicit religious toleration during the Constitutional Convention of 1856–1857. Some *moderados,* such as Pedro Escudero y Echánove and José Fernando Ramírez, were able to support the emperor Maximilian, who was something of a liberal himself.

See also **Guadalupe Hidalgo, Treaty of (1848).**

BIBLIOGRAPHY

Walter V. Scholes, *Mexican Politics During the Juárez Regime, 1855–1872* (1957).

Jesús Reyes Heroles, *El liberalismo mexicano,* 3 vols. (1957–1961).

Michael P. Costeloe, "The Mexican Church in the Rebellion of the Polkos," in *Hispanic American Historical Review* 46 (May 1966):170–178.

Charles A. Hale, *Mexican Liberalism in the Age of Mora, 1821–1853* (1968).

Richard N. Sinkin, *The Mexican Reform, 1855–1876: A Study in Liberal Nation-Building* (1979).

Donald F. Stevens, *Origins of Instability in Early Republican Mexico* (1991).

Additional Bibliography

Aguilar Rivera, José Antonio. *The Divine Charter: Constitutionalism and Liberalism in Nineteenth-Century Mexico.* Lanham: Rowman & Littlefield Publishers, 2005.

Rodríguez O., Jaime E. *El manto liberal: Los poderes de emergencia en México, 1821–1876.* Jurídicas, Universidad Nacional Autónoma de México, 2001.

D. F. STEVENS

MODERATIVE POWER. Moderative Power, one of the four constitutional powers of the Brazilian monarchy (along with the executive, legislative, and judiciary). This was the neutral power advocated by the French philosopher Benjamin Constant de Rebecques that kept the balance among the other powers and acted as arbiter. It gave the emperor power to select senators, dissolve the Chamber of Deputies, call extraordinary sessions of the General Assembly, sanction legislative bills, temporarily approve or suspend acts of provincial assemblies, appoint and dismiss ministers, suspend magistrates, commute sentences, and grant amnesty. This power could be exercised only after consultation with the Council of State.

The prerogatives of the moderate power became a point of contention between Liberals and Conservatives after the 1860 senatorial election, when Pedro II did not choose the candidate with the most votes. Thereafter, its use became increasingly associated with the exercise of personal power and in differentiating a constitutional monarchy from an absolute one. Liberals and Conservatives accepted its existence in principal, but Liberals wanted its acts endorsed by the cabinet, whereas Conservatives maintained that such a requirement was unconstitutional. Although its prerogatives were never changed, Pedro II used it sparingly and in consultation with the Council of State.

See also **Brazil, The Regency.**

BIBLIOGRAPHY

Visconde De Uruguay, *Ensaio sobre o Direito Administrativo* (1960), pp. 253–307.

Paul Bastid, *Benjamin Constant et sa doctrine* (1966).

Additional Bibliography

Needell, Jeffrey D. *The Party of Order: The Conservatives, the State, and Slavery in the Brazilian Monarchy, 1831-1871.* Stanford, CA: Stanford University Press, 2006.

LYDIA M. GARNER

MODERN ART WEEK.

Modern Art Week (Semana de Arte Moderna), a cultural festival held at São Paulo's Teatro Municipal on 13, 15, and 17 February 1922. The young women and men who produced and participated in this three-day series of concerts, readings, lectures, dances, and exhibitions of art were self-consciously declaring their cultural independence from traditional forms and styles, and announcing the arrival of Brazilian modernism. Exhibiting paintings, architecture, and sculpture in the foyer of the theater were Anita Malfatti, Emiliano Di Cavalcanti, John Graz, Martins Ribeiro, Zina Aita, Vicente do Rego Monteiro, Vitor Brecheret, and Antonio Moya. On stage lectures and poetry readings were given by Menotti del Picchia, Guilherme de Almeida, Ronald de Carvalho, Mario de Andrade, Oswaldo de Andrade, Sérgio Milliet, and Renato Almeida. Chamber music concerts featured Guiomar Novaes, Ernani Braga, Heitor Villa-Lobos, Lucília Guimarães Villa-Lobos, Alfredo Gomes, and Paulina d'Ambrósio. Yvonne Daumerie danced. Providing moral and financial support were a few elders: Graça Aranha, who also gave opening remarks, and generous Paulista salon leaders Paulo and Dona Marinette Prado and Dona Olivia Guedes Penteado, among others. D. Marinette Prado had suggested patterning the Brazilian Modern Art Week after a similar one held in Deauville, France.

The public's extremely hostile reactions to the week's events included jeers, catcalls, curses, and other disruptive behavior. Angry people poked canvases with their canes. Men tried to keep discussions of these shocking events from the ears of women and children. This intense response, reminiscent of the "Anita Malfatti Affair" (2 December 1917–January 1918), which inspired Modern Art Week's events, provided the young generation of artists with further evidence of Brazil's cultural backwardness and its need for modernist revolution.

Throughout the rest of the decade of the 1920s, many of Modern Art Week's leaders and participants, including the "Grupo dos Cinco" (Anita Malfatti, Mario de Andrade, Tarsila do Amaral, Oswaldo de Andrade, and Menotti del Picchia) and other Brazilians (Lucília Guimarães Villa-Lobos, Heitor Villa-Lobos, Victor Brecheret, and Emiliano di Cavalcanti) spent much of their time traveling between Brazil and Europe, especially Paris.

See also **Art: The Twentieth Century.**

BIBLIOGRAPHY

Marta Rossetti Batista, *Brasil,* vol. 1, *Tempo Modernista—1917/29: Documentação* (1972).

Mary Lombardi, "Women in the Modern Art Movement in Brazil: Salon Leaders, Artists, and Musicians, 1917–1930" (Ph.D. diss., University of California at Los Angeles, 1977).

Additional Bibliography

Bonaventura, Maria Eugenia de Gama Alves. *22 por 22: A Semana de Arte Moderna vista pelos seus contemporaneos.* São Paulo: Edusp, 2000.

Camargos, Marcia. *Semana de 22: Entre vaias e aplausos.* São Paulo: Boitempo, 2002.

Jackson, K. David. *Literature of the São Paulo Week of Modern Art.* Austin: University of Texas Press, 1987.

Mary Luciana Lombardi

MODERNISM: SPANISH AMERICA.

See **Literature: Spanish America.**

MODERNISM, BRAZIL.

Brazilian modernism began in São Paulo in 1922 and lasted through several phases until 1945. In its beginnings it was principally an aesthetic and cultural revolution. Its objective was to break down a colonial mentality in art and letters that largely ignored national realities in order to imitate foreign currents in these areas. It did not intend to limit itself to São Paulo, or to art and letters, but to embrace the whole nation and to integrate activities in every sphere. It was successful in bringing about a vast transformation in Brazilian life through studies in the arts and sciences, particularly the social sciences. In theory and practice the great leader of modernism from its inception to its close was Mário de Andrade, whose death in 1945 coincided with the end of the movement.

The movement not only modernized Brazilian thought and action but revealed a more integrated Brazil to the world. The nation became liberated, independent at the same time that it continued to adapt foreign materials, and able to contribute to world culture. Regional culture, traditions, folklore, and language, including the contributions of the principal races of Brazil, took on new national meaning for Brazilian intellectuals who revitalized them in their works, whether creative, scholarly, or critical. They no longer felt cultural or intellectual life away from the metropolis was impossible, and many preferred to remain in their native states rather than move to the capital.

From the beginning there was constant emphasis not only on the independence of Brazilian letters but also on the aesthetic value and autonomy of a work of literature. Most of the numerous polemics of modernism dealt with questions of form and technique rather than content, with the result that later Brazilian authors, perhaps more intent than their predecessors, have generally been marked by greater professionalism. Another important question was that of developing linguistic studies and a Brazilian Portuguese suitable for literary purposes. The time of amateurism or dilettantism of authors for whom literature was a youthful or leisure occupation had passed. Modernism was a breath of fresh air to academicism. Despite the problem of making a living, still a great one for writers in Brazil, more of them devoted their talents and energies exclusively to their work than had been the case in the past, when other occupations or peripheral literary activity had taken most of their time.

A certain reaction against positivism, the materialistic philosophy that prevailed in Brazil in the late nineteenth century, in favor of more spiritual values placed emphasis on the reform of poetry during the first phase of modernism. After 1930, however, the reform spread to prose fiction. Modernism was to serve as the necessary catalyst for the production of something new from the several "isms" with which Brazilian novelists had already experimented. The result was a more nationalistic regionalism, sometimes propagandistic as in the early Jorge Amado, sometimes documentary as in José Lins Do Rego's Sugarcane Cycle or Amado's later works of the Cacao Cycle. The psychological novel continued to develop as with Érico Veríssimo or, especially, Graciliano Ramos. As for the short story, modernism abandoned the well-made type à la Maupassant for evocative, impressionistic, slice-of-life pieces such as those Ramos composed. Again, it took some time for formal and linguistic problems to be resolved satisfactorily. The Brazilian *crônica,* a subjective reaction to some current event or situation, much like the American newspaper column or informal English essay, was one highly satisfactory solution, despite its somewhat circumstantial, transitory nature. While modernism tended to avoid the historical and the concrete for the spontaneous and spiritual, it sought to develop works of lasting, universal value.

Modernism was by no means a completely unified movement, but for the first few years all reactions and counterreactions were centered in São Paulo. Then two related but different modernisms developed in other parts of the country. The first, beginning in 1926 in Recife, was regionalism, and the second, the "Testa" or spiritualist group, began in 1927 in Rio de Janeiro. Both were traditionalistic and conservative, especially the latter, which was Catholic in inspiration and hostile to the writers of São Paulo. The chief goal of the one was to base modernism more soundly on cultural traditions, principally those of the Northeast; that of the other was to structure its aesthetics along more classical lines. Neither goal corresponded very well with those of modernism, which gave rise to numerous polemics. While regionalism remained largely unknown outside of Recife, the second group, having originated in the capital, gained national fame immediately. Both had elder statesmen, Gilberto Freyre and Tasso da Silveira, respectively, each of whom longed to be the new Mário de Andrade and to establish the dominance of his group.

By the time modernism reached the Northeast, it had abandoned its purely aesthetic approach and already had acquired some political direction, leftist or rightist. Between 1925 and 1927 modernism appeared to be leftist, and the writers of Recife saw a real need to reaffirm the cultural values of the Northeast. Nevertheless, the modernists were still fundamentally concerned with literature and the fine arts, while the future regionalists emphasized culture in a broader and more popular sense—for example, cookery, crafts, and the like—for some time to come. The birth of a modern northeastern literature therefore owes at least as much to São Paulo in its initial stages as to Recife. Regionalism and modernism were complementary, after all, differing only in degrees of traditionalism and cosmopolitanism. Yet regionalism was elaborated by Freyre chiefly as antimodernist, in large part to prove its independence. Regionalism was in fact to enjoy its most brilliant period in the 1930s and 1940s with the flowering of the Northeast novel, which by and large followed a program already proposed in 1922 by the modernists, who had accomplished a literary revolution. Among its Brazilian proponents, the northeasterners were the most significant members to participate in the revolution through letters. The nationalization of literature during the ferment of the 1920s resulted in the political polarization of northeasterners as well as *paulistas,* who adhered to nationalistic political parties of either extreme. Modernism depended heavily on regionalism to achieve its program of nationalization.

See also **Amado, Jorge; Andrade, Mário de; Freyre, Gilberto (de Mello); Literature: Brazil; Modern Art Week; Paulistas, Paulistanos; Positivism.**

BIBLIOGRAPHY

Aguilar, Gonzalo Moisés. *Poesia concreta brasileira: As vanguardas na encruzilhada modernista.* São Paulo: Edusp, 2005.

Johnson, Randal. "Rereading Brazilian Modernism." Texas Papers on Latin America No. 89-04. Austin: Institute of Latin American Studies, University of Texas at Austin, 1989. Available from http://lanic.utexas.edu/project/etext/llilas/tpla/8904.pdf.

Johnson, Randal. "Brazilian Modernism: An Idea out of Place?" In *Modernism and Its Margins: Reinscribing Cultural Modernity from Spain and Latin America,* edited by Anthony L. Geist and José B. Monleón, 186–214. New York: Garland, 1999.

Martins, Wilson. *The Modernist Idea: A Critical Survey of Brazilian Writing in the Twentieth Century* . Translated by Jack E. Tomlins. New York: New York University Press, 1970.

Nist, John. *The Modernist Movement in Brazil.* Austin: University of Texas Press, 1967.

Schwartz, Jorge, ed. *Caixa modernista.* São Paulo: Edusp, Imprensa Oficial, Governo do Estado de São Paulo; and Belo Horizonte: Editora UFMG, 2003.

Sullivan, Edward J., ed. *Brazil: Body & Soul.* New York: Guggenheim Museum, 2001.

RICHARD A. MAZZARA

MODINHA.

MODINHA. Modinha, a sentimental song genre of Brazilian and Portuguese origin cultivated in the eighteenth and nineteenth centuries. The *modinha* derives its name from the word *moda,* meaning "song" or "melody." The first known Brazilian *modinhas* date from the late eighteenth century. During the 1700s the Brazilian *modinha* became immensely popular among bourgeois circles in the salons of Rio de Janeiro and Lisbon. Although *modinhas* were originally written for piano or harpsichord accompaniment, the guitar became the main instrument of serenaders. By the Second Empire the *modinha* acquired the character of an Italian opera, and over time incorporated a love song style reminiscent of French romantic ballads.

In the nineteenth century there appeared two distinct forms of the *modinha:* the operatic aria type, reflecting Italian cantabile influences, and a sentimental ballad style rooted in European romantic song. Brazilian *modinhas* of this period are characterized by embellishments in the vocal line, romantic lyrics, and frequent use of melodic sequence. As many scholars point out, the *modinha* is the only Brazilian popular music form that did not emerge solely from folk music influences. In the twentieth century the spirit of the *modinha* has survived in the music of such Brazilian popular composers as Heitor Villa-Lobos.

See also **Music: Popular Music and Dance.**

BIBLIOGRAPHY

Gérard Béhague, *Music of Latin America* (1979).

David P. Appleby, *The Music of Brazil* (1983).

Additional Bibliography

Livingston-Isenhour, Tamara Elena, and Thomas George Caracas Garcia. *Choro: a Social History of Brazilian Popular Music.* Bloomington: Indiana University Press, 2005.

Tinhorão, José Ramos. *Pequena história da música popular: Da modinha ao tropicalismo.* São Paulo: Art Editora, 1986.

Valença, José Rolim. *Modinha: Raízes da música do povo.* São Paulo: Dow, 1985.

JOHN COHASSEY

MODOTTI, TINA (1896–1942). Tina Modotti (*b.* 16 August 1896; *d.* 6 January 1942), photographer and political activist. Italian-born Modotti immigrated to California in 1913, and then to Mexico in 1923. She and the American photographer Edward Weston set up a portraiture business, and from him she learned photographic techniques, especially formal composition. Modotti's early still lifes and light studies reveal Weston's example. In Mexico, Modotti was influenced by the Movimiento Estridentista. Her photographs of telephone poles and oil tanks reflect their modernist, machine aesthetic.

Modotti joined the Communist Party of Mexico in 1927. Among her politically charged photographs are images of campesinos demonstrating, workers holding tools or reading the Communist organ *El Machete,* and women with children. Her carefully composed still lifes of a bandolier, guitar, ear of corn, and sickle were seen as "revolutionary icons." Modotti also documented the murals of her friends Diego Rivera, David Alfaro Siqueiros, and José Clemente Orozco, thus giving international exposure to the Mexican mural movement. Modotti's political activities led to her deportation in 1930. She gave up photography and worked for the International Red Aid in Moscow and in Spain during the civil war. In 1939 she returned to Mexico, where she died.

See also **Photography: 1900–1990.**

BIBLIOGRAPHY

Margaret Hooks, *Tina Modotti: Photographer and Revolutionary* (1993).

Sarah M. Lowe, *Tina Modotti: Photographs* (1995).

Additional Bibliography

Albers, Patricia. *Shadows, Fire, Snow: The Life of Tina Modotti.* New York: Clarkson Potter, 1999.

Argenteri, Letizia. *Tina Modotti: Between Art and Revolution.* New Haven, CT: Yale University Press, 2003.

Lowe, Sarah M., Tina Modotti, and Edward Weston. *Tina Modotti and Edward Weston: The Mexico Years.* London, New York: Merrell, in association with Barbican Art Gallery, 2004.

SARAH M. LOWE

MOGROVEJO, TORIBIO ALFONSO DE

MOGROVEJO, TORIBIO ALFONSO DE (1538–1606). Toribio Alfonso de Mogrovejo (*b.* 16 November 1538; *d.* 23 March 1606), also known as Santo Toribio, second archbishop of Lima. Born in Mayorga, in the province of León, Spain, he studied law at the universities of Valladolid and Salamanca. In 1574 he was named president of the Tribunal of the Inquisition in Granada. Even though he was a layman, he was named archbishop of Lima in 1578, where, after his ordination as priest and bishop, he arrived in 1581. He convoked the third of the Lima church councils (1582–1583). The council, which brought together bishops from all over South America, as well as the leading theologians of colonial Peru, aimed to systematize the evangelization process and to lay down norms for Christianizing the Indians more effectively.

Toribio considered himself primarily a missionary bishop called to reach the Indians, and secondarily a pastor for the Spanish population. He spent seventeen of his twenty-five years as archbishop outside of Lima, visiting his vast archdiocese. The longest of his four trips, 1584–1590, took him through the Callejón de Huaylas in the north central Andes. He preached to the Indians, baptized, confirmed, and married them. He wrote to the king criticizing local Spanish officials who abused the Indians. In 1584 he founded the seminary in Lima that bears his name. He died in the *villa* of Saña. In 1726 he was canonized.

See also **Catholic Church: The Colonial Period.**

BIBLIOGRAPHY

Enrique Bartra, *Tercer concilio limense, 1582–1583* (1982).

Enrique Dussel, *El episcopado latinoamericano y la liberación de los pobres, 1504–1620* (1979).

Mary McGlone, "The King's Surprise: The Mission Methodology of Toribio de Mogrovejo," in *The Americas* 50 (July 1993): 65–83.

Vicente Rodríguez Valencia, *Santo Toribio de Mogrovejo: Organizador y apóstol de Sur-América,* 2 vols. (1957).

Additional Bibliography

Benito Rodríguez, José Antonio, editor. *Libro de visitas de Santo Toribio Mogrovejo, 1593–1605.* Lima, Peru: Pontificia Universidad Católica del Perú, Fondo Editorial 2006.

Vargas Alzamora, Augusto. *Santo Toribio y la nueva evangelización.* Lima, Peru: Conferencia Episcopal Peruana: Centro de Investigaciones Teológicas de la Facultad de Teología Pontificia y Civil de Lima, 1991.

JEFFREY KLAIBER

MOHR, NICHOLASA

MOHR, NICHOLASA (1938–). The award-winning author, playwright, and accomplished visual artist Nicholasa Mohr has written thirteen books, primarily for children and young adults. She was born in New York City's El Barrio to parents who had immigrated to the United States from Puerto Rico. Her father died when she was only eight years old, leaving her mother with seven children to care for on her own.

Mohr was the youngest child in the family, and by the time she went to kindergarten her eldest brother had already taught her to read and write. Mohr also loved drawing pictures, and she used her artistic talents and fantastic imagination to escape the poverty of her surrounding community. As a result, Mohr earned a great deal of praise in school, which gave her the confidence that would eventually lead to her success, initially as a visual artist, and later as a writer.

Mohr wrote her first book, *Nilda* (1974), after her art agent urged her to write a book about her experiences growing up in El Barrio. *Nilda* received a great deal of critical acclaim, having been described by scholars as an important new contribution to the long tradition of bildungsroman literature. In 1999 and 2000 stories adapted from Mohr's *El Bronx Remembered* (1975) ran on New York City stages. A musical adaptation of *Nilda* was sponsored in 1999 through a grant from the New York State Council on the Arts.

Mohr resides in El Barrio of New York City, where she continues to write and serve as a witness to the diversity of the American experience.

See also **Feminism and Feminist Organizations; Hispanics in the United States; Literature: Spanish America; Puerto Rico; Women.**

BIBLIOGRAPHY

Primary Works

Nilda. New York: Harper and Row, 1973.

El Bronx Remembered: A Novella and Stories. New York: HarperCollins, 1975.

In Nueva York. New York: Dial, 1977.

Felita. New York: Dial, 1979.

Rituals of Survival: A Woman's Portfolio. Houston, TX: Arte Publico, 1985.

Going Home. New York: Dial, 1986.

All For the Better: A Story of El Barrio. Austin, TX: Steck-Vaughan, 1992.

Growing Up Inside the Sanctuary of My Imagination. New York: J. Messner, 1994.

The Magic Shell. New York: Scholastic, 1995.

The Song of El Coquí and Other Tales of Puerto Rico. With Antonio Martorell. New York: Viking, 1995.

Old Letivia and the Mountain of Sorrows. New York: Viking, 1996.

A Matter of Pride and Other Stories. Houston, TX: Arte Publico, 1997.

Secondary Works

Bellver Sáez, Pilar. "*Nilda* de Nicholasa Mohr: El Bildungsroman y la aparición de un espacio puertorriqueño en la literatura de los EEUU." *Atlantis: Revista de la Asociación Espanola de Estudios Anglo-Norteamericanos* 28, no. 1 (June 2006): 101–113.

Muñiz, Ismael. "Bildungsroman Written by Puerto Rican Women in the United States: Nicholasa Mohr's *Nilda: A Novel* and Esmeralda Santiago's *When I Was a Puerto Rican.*" *Atenea* 19, no. 1–2 (June 1999): 79–101.

Zarnowski, Myra. "An Interview with Author Nicholasa Mohr." *Reading Teacher* (October 1991): 100.

Ethriam Cash Brammer

MOJICA, JOSÉ DE JESÚS (1896–1974). José de Jesús Mojica (*b.* 14 September 1896; *d.* 20 September 1974), Mexican operatic tenor, film actor, and singer. Born in San Gabriel, Jalisco, Mojica attended the Escuela Nacional de Agricultura; when it closed during the Revolution, he entered the Conservatorio Nacional de Música. He then trained with Alejandro Cuevas and made his solo debut in *La Traviata.* After touring the republic, he sang his first lead role in *The Barber of Seville* in 1916 (Teatro Arbeu, Mexico City).

Mojica appeared with Enrico Caruso when the latter visited Mexico City (1919). Caruso's recommendation resulted in an invitation to perform with the Chicago Opera, where Mojica acquired a notable reputation, especially in French operas, with the famed soprano Mary Garden, and in the world premiere of Sergei Prokofiev's *Love for Three Oranges* (1921). During the 1920s Mojica sang in Chicago and Mexico. He was a favorite tenor of Thomas Edison, for whose company he recorded arias and Hispanic folk songs.

In 1930 Mojica went to Hollywood and began a career in musical films with *One Mad Kiss,* followed by some dozen other movies, made in both the United States and Mexico. Following his mother's death, Mojica abandoned his career to become a Franciscan friar (1943). In order to build a training center for priests in Peru, he raised funds through additional films and concerts. He last appeared in Mexico City's Bellas Artes Theater (1969), celebrating his fifty years as a singer. He died in Lima, Peru.

See also **Music: Art Music.**

BIBLIOGRAPHY

José de Jesús Mojica *I, a Sinner,* translated by Fanchon Royer (1963).

Additional Bibliography

Arauco Travezán, Ernesto. *José Mojica: mundo, arte y espíritu.* Lima, Peru: Editorial Bruño, 1999.

Koegel, John. "Del Rancho Grande y a través del Río Grande: músicos mexicanos en Hollywood y en la vida musical norteamericana, 1910–1940." *Heterofonía* 128 (January–June 2003): 51–99.

RONALD H. DOLKART

MOJOS. Mojos, region located in the foothills and plains of the Andes, extending from northern to central southeastern Bolivia, and its Indian inhabitants. The Rio Mamoré runs through the center of the region, connecting its tropical savannas to the Amazon basin. The Mojos region, named after the local tribe, beckoned into its inhospitable realms numerous Spanish explorers in search of El Dorado. But its inaccessibility, harsh climate, local resistance, and disputes among the explorers thwarted most efforts of conquest and settlement. Nevertheless, each expedition, whether sponsored by Peruvian authorities or led by Paraguayan competition, pressed further on, establishing outposts where possible. By 1563, although far from pacified, Mojos was officially incorporated into the Audiencia of Charcas.

The Jesuits, who entered the area in 1595, fared better than their civil and military counterparts. They persevered in their attempts at pacification, and in 1667, Brother Juan de Soto made friendly contact with the Mojos. By 1682, the Jesuits had founded the first of twenty-six missions. The Jesuits' activity in Mojos is often compared to their acclaimed and controversial missionary work in Paraguay. With the expulsion of the Jesuits in 1767, the region remained relatively untouched until the late-nineteenth-century development of its rubber industry.

See also **Amazon Region; Andes.**

BIBLIOGRAPHY

Josep M. Barnadas, *Charcas: Orígenes históricos de una sociedad colonial* (1973), pp. 61–62, 466.

Herbert S. Klein, *Bolivia: The Evolution of a Multi-Ethnic Society* (1982); pp. 7–8, 35.

Francisco J. Eder, *Breve descripción de la reducciones de Mojos,* translated and edited by Josep M. Barnadas (1985), pp. xlii-xliii.

Additional Bibliography

Cortés, Jorge. *Caciques y hechiceros: Huellas en la historia de Mojos.* La Paz, Bolivia: Plural Editores: Universidad de la Cordillera, 2005.

Guzmán Torrico, Ismael. *Provincia Mojos: Tierra, territorio, y desarrollo.* La Paz, Bolivia: Fundación Tierra, 2004.

Roca, José Luis. *Economía y sociedad en el Oriente Boliviano, siglos XVI–XX.* Santa Cruz, Bolivia: COTAS, 2001.

LOLITA GUTIÉRREZ BROCKINGTON

MOLINA, ARTURO ARMANDO (1927–). Arturo Armando Molina (*b.* 6 August 1927), Salvadoran military officer and president (1972–1977). Born into a military family, Molina began his primary education in Sonsonate and graduated from the military school in San Salvador in 1949 as a sublieutenant of infantry. He advanced through the ranks on schedule and served in a variety of positions: comandante of Santa Anna, subdirector of the military school, and professor of tactics, strategy, and military history until Fidel Sánchez Hernández chose him as his successor in 1972. The 1972 "stolen elections" were a milestone in Salvadoran history as the government's Party of National Conciliation denied the victory to the civilian UNO slate led by José Napoleón Duarte. As president, Colonel Molina was distrusted by both the oligarchy and the right-wing military, as well as resented by the opposition from whom he had stolen power. Molina dubbed his presidency a period of "national transformation," a slogan that reflected his commitment to making visible changes not only in roads and ports but also in foreign investment incentives and administrative reforms. Molina's tenure saw the polarization of Salvadoran society as the Left began to form guerrilla groups and the Right countered with paramilitary "death squads." His attempts to silence opposition included the 1972 military occupation and closure of the university, violence directed against those protesting the 1975 Miss Universe pageant in San Salvador, and overt attacks on the church, including the assassination of priests. Molina's presidency set the stage for the civil war of the 1980s in El Salvador. Although after his term was over in 1977, he left the country, and in 1992 he returned to El Salvador.

See also **El Salvador.**

BIBLIOGRAPHY

Stephen Webre, *José Napoleón Duarte and the Christian Democratic Party in San Salvadoran Politics, 1960–1972* (1979).

Enrique A. Baloyra, *El Salvador in Transition* (1982).

James Dunkerley, *The Long War: Dictatorship and Revolution in El Salvador* (1982).

Philip L. Russell, *El Salvador in Crisis* (1984).

Additional Bibliography

Grenier, Yvon. *The Emergence of Insurgency in El Salvador: Ideology and Political Will.* Basingstoke: Macmillan, 1999.

Molina, Arturo Armando. *Política de transformación agraria del presidente Molina.* San Salvador: Ministerio de Agricultura y Ganadería, Departamento de Información Agropecuario, 1976.

KAREN RACINE

MOLINA, JUAN RAMÓN (1875–1908). Juan Ramón Molina (*b.* 17 April 1875; *d.* 2 November 1908), Honduran modernist poet. Born in Comayaguela, twin city of Tegucigalpa, Molina studied in Guatemala, where he met Rubén Darío, the great modernist poet, in 1891. Molina began writing at age seventeen and later edited several journals and newspapers. He served as undersecretary of public works for the government of Dr. Policarpo Bonilla (1895–1899). In 1900 he went to prison for criticizing President Terencio Sierra. In the revolution of 1903, Molina fought and earned the rank of colonel. In 1906 he participated along with Rubén Darío in the Pan-American Conference in Rio de Janeiro and for the first and only time experienced the creative environment of a large urban center. Another revolution in 1907 defeated Bonilla, and Molina was exiled to El Salvador. Throughout his life Molina felt stifled by his surroundings and suffered depression augmented by alcohol abuse. In 1908, at age thirty-three, he died from an overdose of morphine, an apparent suicide. After his death his poems and short prose pieces were collected by his friend and fellow writer, Froylan Turcios, in *Tierras, mares y cielos* (1911). Miguel Ángel Asturias called Molina the greatest Central American modernist poet after Darío.

See also **Honduras.**

BIBLIOGRAPHY

Miguel Ángel Asturias, "Juan Ramón Molina: Poeta gemelo de Rubén," in *Antología de Juan Ramón Molina* (1959).

Julio Escoto in *Tierras, mares y cielos* (1977).

Additional Bibliography

Molina, Juan Ramón, Arturo Oquelí, and Elisea Pérez Cadalso. *Juan Ramón Molina: su obra y su vida.* Tegucigalpa, Honduras: El Comité Pro Monumento a Juan Ramón Molina, 1994.

Reina Argueta, Marta. *Nací en el fondo azul de las montañas hondureñas: Ensayo sobre Juan Ramón Molina.* Tegucigalpa, Honduras: Editorial Guaymuras, 1990.

ANN GONZÁLEZ

MOLINA, MARCELO (1800–1879). Marcelo Molina (*b.* 19 February 1800; *d.* 20 May 1879), Guatemalan lawyer, political leader, and first governor of Los Altos, the sixth state of the Central American Federation. The son of a notable Quetzaltenango family, Molina obtained a degree in 1821 from the Tridentine College and a law degree from the University of San Carlos in 1824. After a year of law practice in his hometown, he began his career in public service as syndic for Quetzaltenango and as a provincial judge, participating in 1831 in the unsuccessful experiment with trials by jury espoused by the Liberal government of Dr. Mariano Gálvez. When Los Altos proclaimed its secession from Guatemala in 1838, Molina resigned his post as attorney general of the State of Guatemala and returned to Quetzaltenango to become governor of the new state in 1839. His political and diplomatic efforts on behalf of Los Altos proved fruitless, however, and the sixth state was forcibly restored to Guatemala by the Conservative dictator Rafael Carrera in January 1840. Following a brief period of detention in Guatemala City, he went into exile in Mexico, where he remained until 1847. Back in Guatemala, he resumed his public service career, serving as member of the Supreme Court of Justice from 1847 to 1849. Molina then worked as a teacher of Latin in Quetzaltenango before being reappointed to the Supreme Court in 1856, where he served until his retirement in 1874.

See also **Central America, United Provinces of.**

BIBLIOGRAPHY

Manuel Aparicio Mérida, "La familia Molina establecida en Quetzaltenango desde el siglo XVIII," in *Revista de la Academia guatemalteca de estudios genealógicos, heráldicos, e históricos,* no. 2 (1968): 239–274.

Marcelo Molina, *Ligeros apuntamientos acerca de los principáles sucesos de la carrera literaria y vida pública* (1971).

JORGE H. GONZÁLEZ

MOLINA, MARIO (1943–).

Mario Molina is a Mexican scientist who won the Nobel Prize in chemistry in 1995. Born March 19, 1943, the son of a prominent lawyer who later became a diplomat, Molina obtained his bachelor's degree from the National University of Mexico in 1965 and his Ph.D. in physical chemistry from the University of California, Berkeley, in 1972. He took a position at the University of California, Irvine, where he and his colleague, F. Sherwood Rowland, published research demonstrating that chlorofluorocarbons, which were widely used in spray cans and air conditioners, were harmful to the ozone layer, eventually leading to efforts to ban their use. From 1982 to 1989 he worked for the Jet Propulsion Laboratory in Pasadena, and then taught at MIT beginning in 1989. In 2005 he took a teaching position at the University of California at San Diego and also established a strategic studies center in energy and the environment in Mexico City. He is the only Mexican to have won a Nobel Prize in the sciences.

See also **Environment and Climate; Science.**

BIBLIOGRAPHY

Molina, Mario. Nobel Lecture, December 8, 1995. Available from http://nobelprize.org/nobel_prizes/chemistry/laureates/1995/molina-lecture.html.

RODERIC AI CAMP

MOLINA, PEDRO (1777–1854).

Pedro Molina (*b.* 29 April 1777; *d.* 21 September 1854), Guatemalan scholar, revolutionary, and statesman. Born in Guatemala City of illegitimate parentage, Molina studied humanities at an early age under the tutelage of one of the great Guatemalan scholars of the late eighteenth century, Fray Antonio de Liendo y Goicoechea (1735–1814). Never abandoning the Enlightenment ideas of his teacher, he later studied medicine and surgery, and received his degree on 11 June 1798. In the first decade of the nineteenth century, Molina served as a surgeon in Nicaragua. He returned to his native Guatemala in 1811 to assume the chair of professor of medicine at the University of San Carlos. In 1819, the colonial government awarded him the degree of doctor and the office of *protomédico,* or chief surgeon general, of the province of Guatemala.

In the years prior to independence from Spain, Molina became increasingly involved in politics. He eventually came to lead an unlikely alliance of conservative oligarchs and middle-class elements. Born out of opposition to the captain-general, José de Bustamante y Guerra, this political faction later became the most radical one of the era, actively urging independence. Molina had no close ties to the oligarchy but was an ardent and capable representative of the creole professional classes. The elite, especially the influential Aycinena family, supported Molina, only because the return to power of the Spanish liberals threatened its position of prestige and monopoly. Both factions of the coalition, the professionals and the aristocrats, viewed the opposition to their political dreams as a conspiracy of *peninsulars.*

The voice of this nascent political party, known derisively by its opponents as the *cacos,* or thieves, was the newspaper *El Editor Constitucional,* edited by Molina, who also wrote the column on physical and moral education. On the eve of independence (14 September 1821), Molina, a talented political activist and rabble-rouser, and the aristocratic Mariano Aycinena (1789–1855) worked through the night to ensure that a mob would gather at the palace the next morning. Molina scattered his supporters throughout Guatemala City to stir up the masses to clamor for independence. After independence, however, the elite broke its alliance with Molina and the radical liberals and formed a truly conservative party.

Molina nonetheless continued to play an active role in politics and government. In 1825, as plenipotentiary to Bogotá, he signed the first treaty concluded by the newly created United Provinces of Central America, ensuring a defensive alliance with Colombia. In 1826 he served in another diplomatic post as one of the representatives of the Central American republic to the Panama Conference called by Simón Bolívar. After the bloody civil war between conservatives and liberals from 1826 to 1829, Molina was elected chief of the state of Guatemala and almost immediately clashed with the federal government, under the leadership of Francisco Morazán, over the question of reconstituting Guatemala City as a federal district and over Molina's project to reform the confederation. Molina favored the model of the Swiss republic, abolishing the expensive machinery of a federal government that was often in conflict with the different states. He called for a federal congress that would wield power in only foreign affairs.

The provinces showed little interest in these proposals, and many powerful men who either held or aspired to hold federal offices, the most prominent being Morazán, actively opposed the latter. In retribution, Molina was suspended as chief of state on false charges and actually brought to trial. Although he was acquitted, he was never allowed to return to his post. The failure of the reform scheme and Molina's inability to counter successfully his political enemies dealt a terrible blow to his political career.

Although less influential during the last two decades of his life than he had been, Molina remained an important political force. He supported the radical liberal administration of Guatemalan chief of state Mariano Gálvez until Gálvez formed a coalition with conservatives in an effort to avert a popular insurgency. Thereafter, until the end of his life, Molina wrote political commentary, often under the pseudonym Liberato Cauto.

See also **Guatemala.**

BIBLIOGRAPHY

Antonio Cacua Prada, *Pedro Molina: Patricio centroamericano* (1978).

José Joaquín Pardo Gallardo, ed., *Bibliografía del doctor Pedro Molina* (1954).

Rubén Leyton Rodríguez, *Doctor Pedro Molina o Centro América y su prócer* (1965).

Pedro Molina, *Escritos del doctor Pedro Molina conteniendo la reproducción integra de los escritos del primer semestre del periódico "El Editor Constitucional" y "El Genio de la Libertad"...Guatemala,* 3 vols. (1969).

Additional Bibliography

Salazar, Ramón A. *Biografía del doctor Pedro Molina.* Guatemala: CENALTEX, Ministerio de Educación, 1985.

MICHAEL F. FRY

MOLINA BEDOYA, FELIPE (1812–1855). Felipe Molina Bedoya (*b.* 30 April 1812; *d.* 17 February 1855). Central American politician and diplomat. He was born in Granada, Nicaragua, into the family of the independence heroine Dolores Bedoya and the prominent Guatemalan patriot and statesman Pedro Molina. As a member of the Liberal government that was deposed in April 1839, Molina was forced to immigrate to Quetzaltenango. In 1843 he joined his father and brother, José, in Costa Rica. A more stable political climate allowed the family to return to Guatemala in 1845. Molina was able to obtain his law degree before a new political crisis compelled him to leave Guatemala once again in 1847. He traveled in Chile and Peru before settling in Costa Rica. In 1849, President José María Castro appointed him to serve as Costa Rican ambassador to Nicaragua and then to England. Through his efforts, Costa

Rica was able to secure an advantageous commercial treaty with England. He then spent some time in France and Spain before moving to the United States in 1851, the year in which his *History of Costa Rica* was published. He died in Washington, D.C.

See also **Bedoya de Molina, Dolores; Molina, Pedro.**

BIBLIOGRAPHY

Carlos C. Haeussler Yela, *Diccionario general de Guatemala,* vol. 2 (1983).

Federico Hernández de León, *El libro de las efemérides,* vol. 5 (1925).

Felipe Molina, *Bosquejo de la República de Costa Rica, seguido de apuntamientos para su historia* (1851) and *Costa Rica and New Granada* (1853).

JORGE H. GONZÁLEZ

MOLINA ENRÍQUEZ, ANDRÉS (1868–1940).

Andrés Molina Enríquez (*b.* 30 November 1868; *d.* 1 August 1940), Mexican land reformer and lawyer. Portrayed in Mexico as the "Father of Agrarian Reform" and the "Rousseau of the Mexican Revolution," Andrés Molina Enríquez made important contributions, both ideologically and politically, to the official land-reform program of the Mexican Revolution. Molina Enríquez studied Mexico's agrarian problems in depth during the fifteen years prior to the Revolution while working as a land notary and judge in various rural locations in the state of Mexico. As early as 1905 he had arrived at the legal basis for land reform in Mexico in a proposed water law that mandated national control of natural resources for the common good and regulated foreign ownership of Mexican resources. He included these principles in his seminal book, *Los grandes problemas nacionales,* written on the eve of the Mexican Revolution in 1909, warning the *hacendados,* or large landowners of Mexico, that they faced land reform or revolution. Molina Enríquez appeared in Querétaro at the 1917 constitutional convention and wrote the first draft of Article 27, which followed his pre-Revolutionary land-reform ideas. The provisions limited foreign ownership of Mexican land and resources, called for the restitution of Ejido lands despoiled during the Porfiriato, and directed state governments to establish laws limiting the size of individual landholdings.

See also **Mexico, Constitutions: Constitution of 1917.**

BIBLIOGRAPHY

D. A. Brading, "Social Darwinism and Romantic Idealism: Andrés Molina Enríquez and José Vasconcelos in the Mexican Revolution," in his *Prophecy and Myth in Mexican History* (1984).

Andrés Molina Enríquez, *Los grandes problemas nacionales [1909] [y otros textos, 1911–1919]* (1978), includes the best general introduction to Molina Enríquez's life and ideas in Spanish in the prologue by Arnaldo Córdova.

Stanley F. Shadle, *Andrés Molina Enríquez: Mexican Land Reformer of the Revolutionary Era* (1994).

Additional Bibliography

Basave Benítez, Agustín Francisco. *México mestizo: Análisis del nacionalismo mexicano en torno a la mestizofilia de Andrés Molina Enríquez.* Mexico City: Fondo de Cultura Económica, 1992.

Kouri, Emilio H. "Interpreting the Expropriation of Indian Pueblo Lands in Porfirian Mexico: The Unexamined Legacies of Andres Molina Enríquez." *The Hispanic American Historical Review* 82:1 (February 2002): 69-117.

Sánchez Arteche, Alfonso. *Molina Enríquez: La herencia de un reformador.* Toluca, Mexico: Instituto Mexiquense de Cultura, 1990.

STANLEY F. SHADLE

MOLINA GARMENDIA, ENRIQUE (1871–1964).

Enrique Molina Garmendia (*b.* 4 August 1871; *d.* 8 March 1964), Chilean philosopher and educator. Enrique Molina graduated in 1892 from the University of Chile's Instituto Pedagógico, a leading teacher-training institution that launched a generation of secularly oriented secondary school teachers. Their aim was to further undermine the influence of the church in education. Molina, however, became critical of both Catholicism and the dominant secular school of positivism. He developed a philosophical approach that emphasized secular spiritual values. His most important work was *De lo espiritual en la vida humana* (1937), which brought to Chile the emphasis on human values that changed the philosophical landscape in several Latin American nations. In this and other writings he introduced a distinction between spiritual and materialistic concerns that had a significant impact on the nature of philosophical studies in Chile: spiritual values came to be seen as the proper emphasis of philosophy. Molina was also a historian of Chilean philosophy. In his *La filosofía en Chile en la primera mitad del siglo XX* (1953), Molina reviewed the development of philosophy and advanced an interpretation of the discipline as removed from social and political concerns. An institution builder, Molina presided over the University of Concepción, the first private secular university, for nearly forty years (1919–1956). He also founded the journal *Atenea* and was instrumental in the creation of the Sociedad Chilena de Filosofía in 1948. Despite his antipolitical stands, he served as minister of education during the increasingly anti-Communist administration of Gabriel González Videla (1946–1952). He gave philosophical expression to the rejection of Marxism but retained a commitment to the reform of society through education.

See also **Universities: The Modern Era.**

BIBLIOGRAPHY

Iván Jaksić, *Academic Rebels in Chile: The Role of Philosophy and Higher Education in Chile* (1989).

Solomon Lipp, *Three Chilean Thinkers* (1975).

Additional Bibliography

Costa Leiva, Miguel da. "Enrique Molina Garmendia: Sus ideas pedagógicas (1871–1964)." *Revista Pensamiento Educativo* 34 (June 2004): 135–161.

IVÁN JAKSÍC

MOLINARI, DIEGO LUÍS (1889–1966). Argentine politician and historian Diego Luís Molinari was a close associate of Argentine presidents Hipólito Irigoyen and Juan Domingo Perón. Molinari began his political career in the Unión Cívica Radical, becoming the undersecretary of foreign relations during the first Irigoyen administration (1916–1922). In this capacity Molinari defended Argentine neutrality during World War I and led several diplomatic and commercial missions to neighboring countries before leaving the post to assume the presidency of the National Labor Department in 1922. He was elected national deputy for the federal capital in 1924 and to the Senate in 1928. Molinari's Senate term was cut short by the September 1930 military coup that ousted Irigoyen.

As part of a dissident Radical faction that supported Juan Domingo Perón, Molinari regained his Senate seat in 1946. He became head of the Peronist majority in the Senate and played a key role in early attempts to fuse the pro-Perón political organizations into what would become the Partido Peronista. In addition, Molinari played an active role in defending Argentina's protectionist commercial policy at the 1947–1948 United Nations Conference on Trade and Employment in Havana. Molinari withdrew from electoral politics with the fall of Perón in 1955.

Molinari's historical scholarship contributed to an important nationalist reevaluation of nineteenth-century caudillo politics, and his work stands with that of Rómulo Carbia, Ricardo Levene and Emilio Ravignani as part of the "New Historical School." In 1938 Molinari became a vice dean of the Universided de Buenos Aires, and from 1947 to 1955 headed the University's Instituto de Investigaciones Históricas.

See also **Irigoyen, Bernardo de; Perón, Juan Domingo.**

BIBLIOGRAPHY

Molinari, Diego Luís. *Antecedentes de la Revolución de Mayo.* Buenos Aires: Peuser, 1922.

Molinari, Diego Luís. *"¡Viva Ramírez!" El Despotismo en las Provincias de la Unión Del Sur (1816–1820).* Buenos Aires: Coni, 1938.

Molinari, Diego Luís. *El nacimiento del Nuevo Mundo, 1492–1534: Historia y cartografía.* Buenos Aires: Editorial Kapelusz, 1941.

Pagano, Nora. "Un intelectual entre la academia y la política: Diego Lúis Molinari." In *Estudios de historiografía argentina.* Vol. II, edited by Julio Stortini, Nora Pagano, and Pablo Buchbinder. Buenos Aires: Editorial Biblos, 1999.

JAMES CANE

MOLINARI, RICARDO E. (1898–1996). Ricardo E. Molinari (*b.* 20 May 1898; *d.* 31 July 1996), Argentine poet. Born in Buenos Aires, Molinari began writing poetry in the 1920s, making him a contemporary of Jorge Luis Borges and the postwar *ultraístas* who sought to initiate a vanguard movement against neoclassicist monumental poetry by implanting in Argentina a movement that would be both culturally nationalistic and internationalistically modernist. While Borges's ironic postmodernism *avant la lettre* quickly led him to abandon such a project, Molinari went on to establish himself as a major voice in Argentine poetry, for poetry as an objective art in which national cultural material is always a constant, as is especially to be noted in the key collection *Mundos de la madrugada* (1943). Molinari's poetry can be studied as virtually an academic showcase of the modernist lyric, with its utilization of complex metaphors, a hermetic style, the romantic nostalgia of the lone poetic voice, and the image of poetry as privileged expression. In 1968 he was nominated to the Argentine Academy of Letters. In 1984, the Konex Academy awarded him a Merit Diploma for his poetry, and also presented him with the Platinum Konex Award.

See also **Literature: Spanish America.**

BIBLIOGRAPHY

Julio Arístides, *Ricardo E. Molinari o la agonía del ser en el tiempo* (1965).

Günter Lorenz, *Diálogo con América Latina* (1972), pp. 91–108.

Angélica Beatriz Lacunza, *La dimensión temporal en algunos poemas de Ricardo E. Molinari* (1973).

Marta Scrimaglio, *Literatura argentina de vanguardia, 1920–1930* (1974), pp. 244–257.

Thorpe Running, *Borges' Ultraist Movement and Its Poets* (1981), pp. 123–127.

Emilio Sosa López, "Tres poetas argentinos modernos: Molinari, Molina y Girri," in *Sur*, no. 348 (1981): 81–88.

Additional Bibliography

Cincotta, Héctor Dante. *El tiempo y la naturaleza en la obra de Ricardo E. Molinari.* Buenos Aires: Corregidor, 1992.

González Gandiaga, Nora. *Poesía y estilo en las odas de Ricardo E. Molinari.* Santa Fe, Argentina: Universidad Nacional del Litoral, 1983.

Herrera, Ricardo H. *La ilusión de las formas: Escritos sobre Banchs, Molinari, Mastronardi, Wilcock, y Madariaga.* Buenos Aires: El Imaginero, 1988.

DAVID WILLIAM FOSTER

MOLINA SOLÍS, OLEGARIO (1843–1925).

Olegario Molina Solís (*b.* 6 March 1843; *d.* 28 April 1925), governor of Yucatán, Mexico (1902–1909), Mexican minister of development (1907–1911). Born and raised in Bolonchenticul, in present-day Campeche, Molina moved with his family to Yucatán's capital, Mérida, in 1857, after the Caste War of Yucatán ravaged his family's properties. After securing degrees in law and topographical engineering, Molina served as secretary to Liberal General Manuel Cepeda Peraza, who defeated Emperor Maximilian's forces in the peninsula in 1867. During the 1870s Molina became an engineer, superintendent, and later a partner in the first railroad built in Yucatán, the Mérida–Progreso railway, which he helped complete. Later he established a profitable import-export company, O. Molina y Compañía, that largely exported Yucatán's principal crop, henequen, a fiber used by North American cordage and binder twine manufacturers. Some scholars contend that in 1902, Molina y Compañía became the International Harvester Company's agent—at the time Harvester was the largest buyer of fiber in the United States. It is believed that Molina and his son-in-law, Avelino Montes, worked to depress fiber prices to benefit their North American partners (and themselves). Molina and Montes used their dominant position in the fiber trade to expand the investment base of their company dramatically. Ventures in real estate, import/exports, and speculation in local industry, commerce, and infrastructure made Molina and Montes, and their extended network of family and friends, an economic octopus in turn-of-the-century Yucatán.

It is noteworthy that Molina's financial success coincided with his political rise to Yucatán's statehouse. Driven by the desire to make his native state a dynamic partner in the modernization of Mexican society, Governor Molina is best remembered in the peninsula as "the builder." An indefatigable public servant, he is lionized for the number of schools he built, the paving and draining of Mérida's streets, and a spate of capital improvement projects in Mérida, including the O'Horan Hospital, the Juárez Penitentiary, the Peón y Contreras Theater, and the Ayala Asylum. (O. Molina y Compañía received lucrative contracts for many of these capital projects.) He also reorganized the property registry, rewrote the state constitution, reformed the penal and civil codes, and reorganized the state National Guard and Mérida police force.

The embodiment of nineteenth-century positivism, Yucatán's own *científico* (technocrat), Molina reasoned that, to the extent that he and his affluent class prospered, so would Yucatán. His regard for Yucatán's Maya Indians might best be described as paternalistic; he did little to provide education or other services to the tens of thousands of peons who lived on haciendas throughout the countryside. In 1906 President Porfirio Díaz visited Mérida, and after marveling at all of the impressive physical changes, rewarded Molina by bringing him to Mexico City to serve as minister of development. After Díaz was ousted in 1911 by revolutionaries, Molina, like many of Díaz's *científicos*, went into exile, living out his life in Cuba.

BIBLIOGRAPHY

Francisco A. Casasús, "Ensayo biográfico del licenciado Olegario Molina Solís," in *Revista de la Universidad de Yucatán* 14 (1972): 68–95.

Diane Roazen-Parrillo, "Las elites de México durante el siglo diecinueve en una economía regional: El ascenso de la familia Olegario Molina Solís de Yucatán hasta 1902," in *Sociedad, estructura agraria y estado en Yucatán*, edited by Othon Baños Ramírez (1990), pp. 257–295.

Allen Wells, "Family Elites in a Boom-And-Bust Economy: The Molinas and Peóns of Porfirian Yucatán," in *Hispanic American Historical Review* 62 (1982): 224–253.

Additional Bibliogrpahy

Pérez de Sarmiento, Marisa. *Historia de una elección: La candidatura de Olegario Molina en 1901.* Mérida, Mexico: Ediciones de la Universidad Autónoma de Yucatán, 2002.

Wells, Alan, and Gilbert M. Joseph. *Summer of Discontent, Seasons of Upheaval: Elite Politics and Rural Insurgency in Yucatán, 1876–1915.* Stanford, CA: Stanford University Press, 1996.

ALLEN WELLS

MOLINA UREÑA, JOSÉ RAFAEL

MOLINA UREÑA, JOSÉ RAFAEL (1921–2000). José Rafael Molina Ureña (*b.* 1921; *d.* May 2000), provisional president of the Dominican Republic (1965). The president of the Chamber of Deputies, José Rafael Molina Ureña was installed as provisional president of the Dominican Republic by the "constitutionalist" group of the Dominican Revolutionary Party (PRD) in 1965. The PRD government of Juan Bosch had been overthrown by the military after just seven months in office in 1963. The civilian triumvirate under Donald Reid Cabral that replaced it then fell victim to a coup in 1965. Meeting in secret, the dissolved Dominican Congress declared Molina Ureña the constitutional president of the republic. As a result, Molina Ureña was arrested and exiled to Puerto Rico by anti-Bosch and anti-PRD "loyalists." After the constitutionalists ousted the military triumvirate, Molina Ureña returned from exile and was sworn in as the interim president until Juan Bosch could return from exile in Puerto Rico.

The fighting between the Bosch and Molina Ureña constitutionalists and the anti-PRD loyalists caused great concern in Washington, which considered the PRD a Communist-influenced party. As the constitutionalists made headway against the loyalists and looked to win the struggle, the U.S. Marines arrived on 28 April 1965 to suppress the constitutionalists and establish order.

See also **Dominican Republic, Dominican Revolutionary Party (PRD).**

BIBLIOGRAPHY

Selden Rodman, *Quisqueya: A History of the Dominican Republic* (1964).

Howard J. Wiarda, *The Dominican Republic: Nation in Transition* (1969).

Ian Bell, *The Dominican Republic* (1981).

Howard J. Wiarda and M. J. Kryzanek, *The Dominican Republic: A Caribbean Crucible* (1982).

Additional Bibliography

Franco, Franklin J. *La revolución constitucionalista de 1965: Vista por actores y testigos.* Dominican Republic: Editora Universitaria, 2005.

Rosa, Jesús de la. *La revolución de abril de 1965: Siete días de guerra civil.* Santo Domingo, Dominican Republic: Editora Nacional, 2005.

HEATHER K. THIESSEN

MOLONY, GUY

MOLONY, GUY (1884–1972). Guy Molony ("Machine Gun" Molony; *b.* 1884; *d.* 13 February 1972), North American soldier of fortune. Molony ran away to South Africa during the Boer War. He fought alongside Lee Christmas in the Honduran invasion of January 1911 and subsequently returned to New Orleans and became police chief in 1921. Four years later, he abruptly resigned and went back to Honduras, where he served as bodyguard to the president. He acquired plantations, an automobile dealership, and a post in the national brewery. In the mid-1930s, he fought rebels trying to overthrow President Tiburcio Carías Andino. He operated a rice plantation in Honduras until the early 1960s, then retired to New Orleans, where he died.

See also **Christmas, Lee; Zemurray, Samuel.**

BIBLIOGRAPHY

Hermann Deutsch, *Incredible Yanqui: The Career of Lee Christmas* (1931).

Additional Bibliography

Langley, Lester D., and Thomas Schoonover. *The Banana Men: American Mercenaries and Entrepreneurs in Central America, 1880-1930.* Lexington: University of Kentucky Press, 1995.

LESTER D. LANGLEY

MOMPOX DE ZAYAS, FERNANDO

(c. 1690–c. 1745). Fernando Mompox de Zayas (*b.* c. 1690; *d.* c. 1745), Spanish-born revolutionary and participant in the Paraguayan Comunero Revolt of 1721–1735. Of shadowy origins, Mompox had been imprisoned in the late 1720s by inquisitorial authorities in Lima. In jail, he made the acquaintance of José de Antequera y Castro, former leader of the anti-Jesuit faction of the Spanish residents of Paraguay. Shortly thereafter, Mompox escaped, and in 1730, armed with letters of introduction from Antequera, made his way to Asunción, where he began to resuscitate the popular opposition to the Jesuits. Passing himself off as a lawyer, he soon gained fame for his loud oratory in the streets of the town.

Though an outsider, Mompox quickly became the most important actor in Paraguayan politics, taking Antequera's movement in a new, radical direction. Mompox denounced the entire artifice of absolute government, claiming that only the *común,* the "free-born" residents of Asunción, could speak for Paraguay. This declaration threatened not only the power of the Jesuits, but also that of the king's representatives. When word came that a new governor, Ignacio Soroeta, was due to arrive, Mompox organized a plot against him. Armed Comuneros took over the Paraguayan capital and made it clear to Soroeta that they intended to retain power no matter what. Shortly thereafter, however, Mompox was betrayed and handed over to loyal officials. Later, while en route back to Lima, the prisoner escaped and managed to get across the Brazilian frontier. Mompox spent the rest of his life as a retailer in Rio de Janeiro. His Comunero associates, however, went down in defeat by early 1735.

See also **Antequera y Castro, José de.**

BIBLIOGRAPHY

James Schofield Saeger, "Origins of the Rebellion of Paraguay," in *Hispanic American Historical Review* 52 (1972): 215–229.

Adalberto López, *The Revolt of the Comuñeros, 1721–1735* (1976).

Carlos Zubizarreta, *Cien vidas paraguayas,* 2d ed. (1985), pp. 67–69.

Additional Bibliography

Montezuma Hurtado, Alberto. *Comuneros del Paraguay.* Bogotá, Colombia: Ediciones Tercer Mundo, 1983.

Romero, Roberto A. *La revolución comunera del Paraguay: Su doctrina política.* Asunción, Paraguay: s.n., 1995.

THOMAS L. WHIGHAM

MONAGAS, JOSÉ GREGORIO

(1791–1858). José Gregorio Monagas (*b.* 1791; *d.* 15 July 1858), president of Venezuela (1851–1855). Monagas owed his presidency to his brother, José Tadeo Monagas. In 1848 the latter, a military chief, or caudillo, from eastern Venezuela, seized power from the Conservative coalition headed by José Antonio Páez and put the Liberal Party in power. In 1851, José Gregorio succeeded his brother and ran a basic caretaker government, which, like his brother's, was characterized by widespread corruption.

On 25 March 1854, José Gregorio Monagas achieved a permanent place in Venezuelan history when he emancipated the nation's slaves by a presidential proclamation. That act, like most of his decisions, owed as much to political expediency as anything.

See also **Slavery: Abolition.**

BIBLIOGRAPHY

Francisco González Guinán, *Historia contemporánea de Venezuela,* vols. 5–6 (1954).

John V. Lombardi, *Venezuela: The Search for Order, the Dream of Progress* (1982).

William D. Marsland and Amy L. Marsland, *Venezuela Through Its History* (1954).

Guillermo Morón, *A History of Venezuela,* edited and translated by John Street (1964).

Additional Bibliography

Banko, Catalina. *Las luchas federalistas en Venezuela.* Caracas, Venezuela: Monte Avila, 1996.

Ferrer, Dilian. *Maracaibo durante el gobierno de los Monagas: Relaciones de poder y autonomía, 1848–1858.* Maracaibo, Venezuela: Gobernación del Estado Zulia, Secretaría de Gobierno, Acervo Histórico del Estado Zulia: Comisión V Centenario del Lago de Maracaibo, 2000.

Moreno Molina, Agustín. *Entre la pobreza y el desorden: El funcionamiento del gobierno en la presidencia de José Gregorio Monagas.* Caracas, Venezuela: Universidad Católica Andrés Bello, 2004.

WINTHROP R. WRIGHT

MONAGAS, JOSÉ TADEO (1785–1868).

José Tadeo Monagas (*b.* 28 October 1785; *d.* 18 November 1868), president of Venezuela (1847–1851, 1855–1858). Monagas, who fought in the wars of independence, became a powerful regional leader in eastern Venezuela. In 1831, he led an abortive rebellion against President José Antonio Páez. Four years later, he took part in the failed Revolution of Reform.

Despite rifts with Páez, the latter allowed Monagas to succeed Carlos Soublette as president in 1847. In 1848, Monagas shifted to the Liberal faction when he dismissed Conservatives from his cabinet. The National Congress attempted to censure Monagas, but on 24 January 1848 violence broke out and several deputies died in the fighting. Monagas immediately assumed dictatorial powers.

In 1851, Monagas chose his brother, José Gregorio, as his successor. The latter met one Liberal objective in 1854 when he emancipated the slaves. In 1855, José Tadeo returned as president. A revolt in 1858 led by moderate Liberals and Conservatives under General Julián Castro ended the Monagas dictatorship. Monagas fled to the French embassy. Threats to remove him from the embassy led to an international crisis. French and British gunships eventually guaranteed international protocol, and enabled Monagas to leave Venezuela under a safe conduct pass issued by the Minister of Foreign Affairs, Wenceslao Urrutia.

In 1864, Monagas returned to Venezuela, and as a leader of the unsuccessful Blue faction, tried to restore his power. In 1868, he entered Caracas and proclaimed a short-lived presidency that lasted one month. He died shortly after his defeat.

See also **Venezuela: Venezuela since 1830.**

BIBLIOGRAPHY

Juan Bautista Querales D., comp., *Repertorio histórico-biográfico del Gral. José Tadeo Monagas (1785–1868),* 3 vols. (1983).

Ricardo Becerra, *José Tadeo Monagas. Breves apuntes biográficos* (1979).

Rafael E. Castillo Blomquist, *José Tadeo Monagas* (1987).

Francisco González Guinán, *Historia contemporánea de Venezuela,* vols. 2, 4–9 (1954).

John V. Lombardi, *Venezuela: The Search for Order, the Dream of Progress* (1982).

William D. Marsland and Amy L. Marsland, *Venezuela Through Its History* (1954).

Robert Paul Matthews, Jr., *Violencia rural en Venezuela, 1840–1858: Antecedentes socio-económicos de la Guerra Federal* (1970).

Guillermo Morón, *A History of Venezuela,* edited and translated by John Street (1964).

Additional Bibliography

Banko, Catalina. *Las luchas federalistas en Venezuela.* Caracas, Venezuala: Monte Avila, 1996.

Ferrer, Dilian. *Maracaibo durante el gobierno de los Monagas Venezuala: Relaciones de poder y autonomía, 1848-1858.* Maracaibo: Gobernación del Estado Zulia, Secretaría de Gobierno, Acervo Histórico del Estado Zulia: Comisión V Centenario del Lago de Maracaibo, 2000.

WINTHROP R. WRIGHT

MONCADA, JOSÉ MARÍA (1871–1945).

José María Moncada (*b.* 1871; *d.* 23 February 1945), president of Nicaragua (1929–1933). Moncada rose to fame as one of the principal Conservative generals responsible for the overthrow of the Liberal dictator José Santos Zelaya in 1909. He was not, however, a professional military man; he had begun his career in Nicaraguan politics as a journalist for a Conservative newspaper published in Granada. During the Zelaya dictatorship, Moncada published a pro-government newspaper, but by 1906 he had fallen out with the dictator and had fled to Honduras. There he served as undersecretary of the interior until the Conservative revolt against Zelaya began. After Zelaya's ouster, Moncada served as secretary of the interior in the Conservative government from 1910 to 1911. Moncada, however, fell out with the Conservatives and switched his allegiance to the Liberal Party. He was elected to the Senate in 1924. In 1926 Moncada supported the return from Mexico of former Liberal vice president Juan Bautista Sacasa, not only by supplying arms and ammunition but also by serving as Sacasa's minister of war in his campaign against the Conservative government headed by Adolfo Díaz. The ensuing civil war led to increased U.S. intervention. As a consequence Moncada and his generals accepted the terms of the Tipitapa Agreements (1927) that Moncada and U.S. representative Henry L. Stimson negotiated to end hostilities.

In 1928, Moncada won the presidential election supervised by the U.S. The reemergence of Augusto César Sandino, the only one of Moncada's generals who had refused to accept the terms of the Tipitapa Agreements and to lay down his arms, however, overshadowed the Moncada presidency. Nonetheless, the U.S. entrusted Moncada to hold elections in 1932. Sacasa was elected president, and the U.S. Marines left Nicaragua on 2 January 1933.

See also **Nicaragua; Tipitapa Agreements.**

BIBLIOGRAPHY

William Kamman, *A Search for Stability: United States Diplomacy Toward Nicaragua, 1925–1933* (1968).

Neill Macaulay, *The Sandino Affair* (1985).

Additional Bibliography

Mercado, Gustavo. *José María Moncada: Vivir haciendo historia.* Managua, Nicaragua: Fondo Editorial CIRA, 2002.

Moncada Fonseca, Manuel. "Pensamiento y acción de José María Moncada." *Cuadernos Americanos* 86 (March–April 2001): 114–127.

SHANNON BELLAMY

MONCAYO GARCÍA, JOSÉ PABLO (1912–1958).

José Pablo Moncayo García (*b.* 29 June 1912; *d.* 16 June 1958), Mexican composer. Born in Guadalajara, Moncayo García studied piano with Eduardo Hernández Moncada and composition with Candelario Huízar and Carlos Chávez at the National Conservatory in Mexico City (1929–1935). He was pianist and percussionist for the Mexico Symphony Orchestra (1932–1944) and from 1949 until his death conductor of the Mexico National Orchestra. He studied composition with Aaron Copland at Tanglewood in Massachusetts (1942). With Blás Galindo, Salvador Contreras, and Daniel Ayala he formed the Grupo de los Cuatro (Group of the Four) to promote new music styles. Moncayo's works are built on diatonic and polytonal harmony with the use of parallel chords of impressionist influence. He also used impressionist orchestral timbres. Moncayo's most important works are *La mulata de Córdoba,* an opera, which premiered at the Mexico City Palacio de Bellas Artes (October 1948); and *Amatzinac* (1935), *Huapango* (1941), based on three folk dances, Symphony (1944), and *Tres piezas* (1947), all for orchestra. He died in Mexico City.

See also **Music: Art Music.**

BIBLIOGRAPHY

Gérard Béhague, "Music in Latin America" (1979); *New Grove Dictionary of Music and Musicians,* vol. 12 (1980).

John Vinton, ed., *Dictionary of Contemporary Music* (1974).

Additional Bibliography

Alcaraz, José Antonio, and Héctor Anaya. *En la más honda música de selva.* México, D.F.: CONACULTA, 1998.

Ruiz Ortiz, Xochiquetzal. *Blas Galindo: Biografía, antología de textos y catálogo.* México, D.F.: CENIDIM, 1994.

SUSANA SALGADO

MONÇÕES. Monções, annual canoe flotillas covering the river routes between São Paulo and the gold mines of Mato Grosso in eighteenth-century Brazil. Setting out from Porto Feliz on the Tietê River near São Paulo, convoys ranging from 50 to 300 canoes transported as many as 3,000 persons and several tons of cargo to the mining districts. The outbound voyage ordinarily lasted between five and seven months, as crews conducted their crowded and heavily packed vessels through scores of rapids and over at least one rough portage. Passengers included colonists, with their Indian and African slaves, hoping to strike fortunes in the mines, as well as royal officials assigned to the remote outposts of the Portuguese Empire.

The return trip was much quicker, taking around two months, due mainly to favorable river currents but also to far fewer passengers and a lighter cargo in gold. In the 1720s and 1730s the return convoys frequently were attacked by Paiaguá Indians, who sought iron for their weapon heads and gold to trade with the Spanish of Paraguay. The *monções* became less frequent with the decline in mining returns during the second half of the eighteenth century.

BIBLIOGRAPHY

Sergio Buarque De Holanda's brilliant *Monções* (1945) was the first and most important work to point out the significance of the movement to Brazilian history. Part of this work appears in English in Richard Morse, ed., *The Bandeirantes* (1965). See also Charles Ralph Boxer, *The Golden Age of Brazil* (1962), chap. 10. On the Paiaguá and other Indian groups affected by the movement, see John Hemming, *Red Gold* (1978), chap. 17.

Additional Bibliography

Guimarães, Acyr Vaz. *Quinhentas léguas em canoa: De Araraitaguaba às minas do Cuiabá: As monções paulistas.* Campo Grande, MS: Editora UCDB, 2000.

JOHN M. MONTEIRO

MONEDA PALACE. The Moneda Palace (La Moneda)—the Mint in English—is located in the central area of Santiago, Chile. It is the symbol of political power par excellence, because that is where the office of the president of the nation is located.

Construction started in 1784, during the Spanish colonial administration, under the supervision of the Italian architect Joaquín Toesca. It was opened in 1805 as the colony's mint. Its style is neoclassical with some Roman doric influences. In 1846 President Manuel Bulnes moved the office of the president to the building. Minting did not stop, however; in fact, it continued until 1922, when new premises for the mint were built.

Between 1930 and 1934 the Moneda Palace underwent a thorough restructuring: A new wing, which doubled its size, was added on its southern side, and a third story was added on its northern side. During the September 11, 1973, military coup that overthrew President Salvador Allende, the palace was bombarded by the air force and entirely destroyed by rockets and fire. Reconstruction took eight and a half years.

The palace was partially remodeled again during the presidency of Ricardo Lagos (2000–2006). Also during his presidency an old tradition, suspended in 1969, was restored: Chileans could once again cross from Moneda Street to the Plaza de la Ciudadanía (from north to south) by walking along the palaces corridors and patios.

See also **Allende Gossens, Salvador; Bulnes Prieto, Manuel; Chile: The Twentieth Century; Lagos, Ricardo; Santiago, Chile.**

BIBLIOGRAPHY

Collier, Simon D., and William F Sater. *A History of Chile 1804–1994.* Cambridge, U.K., and New York: Cambridge University Press, 1996.

Loveman, Brian. *Chile: The Legacy of Hispanic Capitalism*, 3rd edition. New York and Oxford: Oxford University Press, 2001.

LUIS ORTEGA

MONEY. *See* **Coinage (Colonial Spanish America); Currency.**

MONGE ÁLVAREZ, LUIS ALBERTO (1926–). Luis Alberto Monge Álvarez (*b.* 1926), president of Costa Rica (1982–1986). Of humble origin and little formal education beyond the secondary level, Monge Álvarez, at age twenty-three, served in the constitutent assembly that drafted the Constitution of 1949. Two years later he was a founding member of the National Liberation Party (PLN), Costa Rica's dominant political party. He became secretary-general of the Inter-American Regional Organization of Workers (ORIT) in 1952.

During the 1960s, Monge Álvarez almost gave up politics. In 1959 he and PLN leader José Figueres Ferrer established the Inter-American Institute of Political Education, a collaborative effort of Latin American social-democratic parties. Monge Álvarez was dismayed by the disclosure that the institute was secretly funded by the U.S. Central Intelligence Agency. His disillusionment grew during the presidency of Francisco José Orlich Bolmarcich (1962–1966) because he believed that Orlich Bolmarcich was abandoning PLN goals. Figueres Ferrer managed to pull Monge Álvarez out of the doldrums and in 1966 encouraged him to become PLN secretary-general, a post he held for twelve years.

Monge Álvarez used his position to build a solid base within the PLN. During Figueres Ferrer's presidency (1970–1974), he gained additional stature as president of the Legislative Assembly. In 1978, challenging the party's old guard, he ran for president, but lost. Four years later, he won by the highest percentage in Costa Rican presidential elections.

Monge Álvarez's policies as president surprised those who knew his politics and his attitude toward U.S. intervention. He assumed office amid an economic crisis. Working with the International Monetary Fund, Monge Álvarez instituted a stabilization program that brought inflation under control and restored economic growth. But he did it by raising rates charged by government-owned utilities, cutting social programs, trimming the public sector, and reducing the huge bureaucracy. He did it also by cooperating with U.S. efforts against the Sandinista government of Nicaragua.

See also **Costa Rica, National Liberation Party.**

BIBLIOGRAPHY

Charles D. Ameringer, *Democracy in Costa Rica* (1982).

Harold D. Nelson, ed., *Costa Rica; A Country Study,* 2d ed. (1983).

Frank Mc Neil, *War and Peace in Central America* (1988).

Marc Edelman and Joanne Kenen, eds., *The Costa Rica Reader* (1989).

Additional Bibliography

Eguizábal, Cristina. *Entre la alianza y la crísis: Administración Monge Alvarez: Reconstrucción del proceso de toma de decisiones en política exterior: Mayo 1982–noviembre 1983.* San José: Instituto de Investigaciones Sociales, Universidad de Costa Rica, 1990.

Hernández, Gerardo. *Partidos políticos en Costa Rica: Trayectoria, situación y perspectivas para el cambio.* San José: CEDAL, 2005.

Mongüe Aguero, Jorge and Juan Manuel Villasuso E. *Procesos de cambio en Costa Rica: Reflexiones al inicio de siglo XXI.* San José: Friedrich Ebert Stiftung, 2003.

Mora A., Jorge A. *Luis Alberto Monge Alvarez: Su pensamiento político.* Costa Rica: Universidad Interamericana de Costa Rica, 2001.

Charles D. Ameringer

MONKEY. The monkey is a member of the order Primates. Like humans, monkeys can see in depth and in color and can grasp objects with hands and feet. They usually eat leaves, insects, fruits, and bird eggs.

New World monkeys, found from Mexico to South America, are smaller and lighter than Old World monkeys and have flat noses. The family Cebidae generally has a rounded head and thirty-six teeth. The legs are longer than the arms, and the limbs end in five digits. The family Callitrichidae are the New World's smallest monkeys. They have small, round heads and thirty-two teeth. The tail is longer than the head and body together.

Most species of the marmoset and tamarin families are threatened with extinction, due mainly to loss of habitat. Especially threatened are the golden lion tamarins of Brazil (*Leontopithecus rosalia*), fewer than five hundred of which are estimated to live in the wild.

BIBLIOGRAPHY

Baschieri Salvatori, Francesco. *Rare Animals of the World.* New York: Mallard Press, 1990.

Bates, Marston. *The Land and Wildlife of South America.* New York: Time Inc., 1964.

Boitani, Luigi, and Stefania Bartoli. *Simon and Schuster's Guide to Mammals*, trans. Simon Pleasance, pp. 95–105. New York: Simon and Schuster, 1983.

Patzelt, Erwin. *Fauna del Ecuador*. Quito: Banco Central del Ecuador, 1989.

Kay, Richard F., Blythe A. Williams, and Federico Anaya. "The Adaptations of *Branisella boliviana*, the Earliest South American Monkey." In *Reconstructing Behavior in the Primate Fossil Record*, ed. J. Michael Plavcan et al., pp. 339–370. New York: Kluwer Academic/Plenum 2002.

RAÚL CUCALÓN

MONROE DOCTRINE. Monroe Doctrine, a fundamental principle of U.S. foreign policy that rejects European expansion in the Western Hemisphere. The immediate causes for the doctrine's pronouncement were the fear that Spain might find European powers willing to assist with the restoration of her Latin American empire lost to wars for independence and concern over Russian activities on the northwestern coast of North America. At the same time, British foreign secretary George Canning did not want the Spanish colonies restored because of the trading links Britain had established with them. Anxious to placate the United States, Canning proposed a joint Washington-London declaration. To ensure that Spain would not receive help from other European nations, Canning secured a promise from France's ambassador to London, Prince Polignac, not to assist Spain with the recovery of her colonies, an agreement not known to the United States. In Washington, President James Monroe consulted with former presidents Thomas Jefferson and James Madison, who favored a joint declaration with the British, and Secretary of State John Quincy Adams, who favored an independent course. Monroe determined that the United States should act independently of Britain. Therefore, in his message to Congress on 2 December 1823, Monroe asserted that the Western Hemisphere was not open to future European colonization, that Europe could no longer extend political control to any portion of the Western Hemisphere, and that the United States would not interfere in the affairs of Europe. While the principles dealt with contemporary issues—the possibility that the European powers would recover Spain's lost colonies in the New World, Russia's claims on the northwestern coast, and U.S. neutrality in the Greek Revolution—their origins predated the War of Independence in the United States and the belief that Europe's monarchical political system should not be extended to the New World. Since the time of independence, presidents George Washington, Jefferson, and Madison had enunciated similar statements.

Monroe's declaration was not well received in the capitals of Europe, and the Latin Americans were puzzled at the unilateral pronouncement. They all understood that Britain, not the United States, was the major supporter of the Latin American struggle for independence. In the nineteenth century, the doctrine did not deter European expansion in the Americas. The Clayton–Bulwer Treaty (1850) recognized the British presence in Central America. The Monroe Doctrine failed to prevent Spain from reannexing Santo Domingo in 1861 or the French from placing Austrian Archduke Maximilian in the Mexican presidential palace in 1864. In Mexico, Secretary of State William H. Seward recognized the European right to debt collection, but held out the threat of future retribution should Napoleon maintain a European presence. Seward's threat kept Napoleon worried about a possible conflict with the United States once its civil war was over. Still, when the French withdrew from Mexico in 1866–1867, it was because of Mexican opposition to the French imposition, not due to U.S. policy. Corollaries have been attached to the Monroe Doctrine. In 1845, President James K. Polk declared that if any North American people desired to join the United States, the matter would be one for them and the U.S. government to determine without foreign interposition. Polk's declaration referred to British and French efforts to prevent the annexation of Texas, to the dispute with Britain over Oregon, and to suspicions that Britain intended to limit U.S. interests in California. In 1904, President Theodore Roosevelt added a corollary. He asserted that if any Latin American state behaved in a manner that invited European intervention, it was the obligation of the United States to intervene first, in order to prevent the European action. The Roosevelt Corollary justified intervention by the United States in the Caribbean region through 1933. In each instance the United States acted to put regional political and financial houses in order, in an effort to prevent possible European intervention, which might threaten the Panama Canal. In 1928, State Department official J. Reuben Clark repudiated the Roosevelt Corollary as a justifiable extension of the Monroe Doctrine, because the corollary dealt with inter-American affairs, not European relations.

In 1912, when a Japanese company considered the acquisition of a large land tract in Baja California, Mexico, Senator Henry Cabot Lodge introduced a resolution to the Senate disapproving the transfer of American territory to non-American private firms that could be serving as agents of foreign nations. Following World War II, many U.S. policymakers argued that the Monroe Doctrine became hemispheric policy with the Rio de Janeiro Treaty (1947), the Act of Bogotá (1948), and a resolution at the Caracas Conference (1954), all of which established a hemispheric defense system against foreign aggression and subversion. The United States, however, often acted unilaterally to remove what it perceived to be a European threat, specifically communism, to the security of the Western Hemisphere; among such interventions were Guatemala (1954), the Bay of Pigs (1961), the Cuban Missile Crisis (1962), the Dominican Republic (1965), and support of the Nicaraguan Contras (1980–1989). The paternalistic attitude embodied in the Monroe Doctrine, coupled with the unilateral actions of the United States, contributed to Latin America's nationalistic response to Washington's policies.

See also **Clark Memorandum; Dollar Diplomacy; Good Neighbor Policy.**

BIBLIOGRAPHY

Alejandro Alvarez, ed., *The Monroe Doctrine: Its Importance in the International Life of the States of the New World* (1924).

Dexter Perkins, *A History of the Monroe Doctrine,* rev. ed. (1963).

Donald M. Dozer, ed., *The Monroe Doctrine: Its Modern Significance* (1965).

Harold Molineu, *U.S. Policy Toward Latin America: From Regionalism to Globalism* (1986).

Alonso Aguilar Monteverde, *Pan-Americanism from Monroe to the Present: A View from the Other Side* (1988).

Lester D. Langley, *America and the Americas: The United States in the Western Hemisphere* (1989).

Additional Bibliography

Dent, David W. *The Legacy of the Monroe Doctrine: A Reference Guide to U.S. involvement in Latin America and the Caribbean.* Westport, CT: Greenwood Press, 1999.

Hilton, Sylvia-Lyn. "La 'nueva' doctrina Monroe de 1895 y sus implicaciones para el Caribe español: Algunas interpretaciones coetáneas españolas." *Anuario de Estudios Americanos* 55:1 (January–June 1998): 125–151.

LaFeber, Walter. *Inevitable Revolutions: The United States in Central America.* 2nd ed. New York: W.W. Norton, 1993, pp. 19–85.

Smith, Gaddis. *The Last Years of the Monroe Doctrine, 1945–1993.* New York: Hill and Wang, 1994.

THOMAS M. LEONARD

MONSERRAT, COLEGIO DE. Colegio de Monserrat, Argentine secondary school. The Colegio de Monserrat was founded in Córdoba in 1687 as the Real Colegio Convictorio de Nuestra Señora de Monserrat (Royal College and Convent of Our Lady of Monserrat) as an institution of secondary education and a seminary. It replaced the Colegio Máximo of the Society of Jesus (founded in 1610), which became the University of Córdoba in 1622. The Colegio Monserrat is thus the oldest extant secondary school in Argentina. It was first located in an ornate colonial building bequeathed to the Jesuits by a leading citizen of Córdoba, Ignacio Duarte de Quirós. The Colegio de Monserrat worked closely with the university with which it later shared buildings. Run by the Jesuits from 1687 to 1767, its faculty excelled in teaching classical studies, theology, and mathematics.

Higher education in South America suffered a setback with the expulsion of the Jesuits, upon which control of Monserrat was transferred to the Franciscan Order until 1807. From 1807 to 1820 Monserrat was placed in the hands of the secular clergy, where it flourished under Gregorio Funes, a learned friar, statesman, historian, and alumnus of Monserrat. The school was administered by the province until 1854, when it was incorporated into the National University of Córdoba as a college preparatory school in 1907. Argentine presidents who studied at Monserrat include: Nicolás Avellaneda, Santiago Derqui, Roque Sáenz Peña, and José Figueroa Alcorta. Other prominent alumni include the statesmen Juan José Castelli, Juan José Paso, Tomás Godoy Cruz, Viceroy Santiago Liniers, and jurist Dalmacio Vélez Sársfield. Besides being declared an international historic monument in 1938, the United Nations declared the colegio international cultural patrimony in 2000.

See also **Argentina, University Reform; Córdoba, University of; Franciscans; Funes, Gregorio; Jesuits.**

BIBLIOGRAPHY

Fernando Beato et al., *El Monserrat: Trecientos años, 1687–1987* (1987).

Additional Bibliography

Aguiar de Zapiola, Liliana. *Cultura liberal, cultura autoritaria: El Colegio Monserrat (1943/1955).* Córdoba: Editorial Universidad Nacional de Córdoba, 1998.

Vera de Flachs, María Cristina. *Finanzas, saberes y vida cotidiana en el Colegio Monserrat: Del antiguo al nuevo regimen.* Córdoba: Universidad Nacional de Córdoba, 1999.

GEORGETTE MAGASSY DORN

MONSIVÁIS, CARLOS (1938–).

Carlos Monsiváis (*b.* 4 May 1938) is a Mexican writer. One of the leading cultural essayists and editorialists in Latin America, Monsiváis completed studies in economics and literature at the National Autonomous University of Mexico (UNAM). His works include the editorship of *Antología de la poesía mexicana* (1966), and the authorship of *Díaz de guardar* (1971), *Amor perdido* (1977), *Escenas de pudor y liviandad* (1981), and *Entrada libre* (1987). He has published numerous interpretative articles on a multitude of cultural subjects in Latin America, the United States, and Europe. Widely respected and influential, he is regarded as one of the most authoritative, insightful, and independent voices of Mexico and Latin America. Monsiváis is a regular contributor to *La Jornada* and *Proceso.* Subcomandante Marcos, the spokesman/leader of the Zapatista Army of National Liberation in Chiapas, has cited Monsiváis as an influence. In 2006, Monsiváis was involved in a movement of leading Latin American authors and cultural figures that demanded sovereignty for Puerto Rico.

See also **Journalism in Mexico.**

BIBLIOGRAPHY

Egan, Linda. *Carlos Monsiváis: Culture and Chronicle in Contemporary Mexico.* Tucson: University of Arizona Press, 2001.

García, Cristina, ed. *Bordering Fires: The Vintage Book of Contemporary Mexican and Chicano/a Literature.* New York: Vintage Books, 2006.

DAVID MACIEL

MONTALVO, JUAN (1832–1889).

The Ecuadoran writer Juan Montalvo was born on April 13, 1832, in Ambato. His formal schooling ended after two years at the University of Quito. Subsequently he educated himself by extensive reading and travel. He lived in Europe, chiefly France, from 1857 to 1860 and from 1881 until his death on January 27, 1889.

Montalvo dedicated himself primarily to fighting for liberal democratic causes. Though he wrote some minor dramatic works, a few poems, and a novel, he earned his fame as an essayist. In his journalistic work he crusaded against corruption, injustice, and tyranny, employing a writing style that was often combative, polemical, and hyperbolic. After publishing a caustic denunciation of President Gabriel García Moreno entitled *La dictadura perpetua* (1874), Montalvo claimed that his pen had killed the dictator.

Montalvo's most notable works were *Las catilinarias* (1880–1882), *Siete tratados* (1882–1883), *El espectador* (1886–1900), and a novel, *Capítulos que se olvidaron a Cervantes* (1895). In addition he published two periodicals, *El Cosmopolita* (1866–1869) and *El Regenerador* (1876–1878), that made him famous for vehement attacks on García Moreno and other public figures, including prominent liberals. The four-hundredth anniversary in 2005 of Cervantes's *Don Quijote* offered new opportunities for interest in Montalvo's *Capítulos que se le olvidaron a Cervantes,* perhaps his most mature work.

See also **Literature: Spanish America.**

BIBLIOGRAPHY

Anderson Imbert, Enrique. *El arte de la prosa en Juan Montalvo.* Mexico: El Colegio de México, 1948.

Esteban, Ángel. "Introducción." *Capítulos que se le olvidaron a Cervantes,* by Juan Montalvo, 13–85. Madrid: Cátedra, 2004.

Reyes, Oscar Efrén. *Vida de Juan Montalvo.* Quito, Ecuador: Talleres Gráficos de Educación, 1943.

Sacoto, Antonio. *Juan Montalvo: El escritor y el estilista,* 3rd edition. Quito: Sistema Nacional de Bibliotecas, 1996.

Yerovi, Agustín L. *Juan Montalvo, ensayo biográfico.* Paris: Imprenta Sudamericana, 1901; repr. 1932.

MARK J. VAN AKEN

MONTALVO Y AMBULODI ARRIOLA Y CASABENTE VALDESPINO, FRANCISCO

MONTALVO Y AMBULODI ARRIOLA Y CASABENTE VALDESPINO, FRANCISCO (1754–1822). Francisco Montalvo y Ambulodi Arriola y Casabente Valdespino (*b.* 18 May 1754; *d.* 1822), viceroy of New Granada. A Cuban-born noble, Francisco Montalvo had an active military career before being named captain-general of New Granada in 1812. He reached a royalist-held section of the Caribbean coast of New Granada in mid-1813. Following the arrival of the expeditionary force under Pablo Morillo in 1815, Montalvo entered Cartagena, which remained his headquarters even after the position of viceroy was reestablished and he was named to it. Montalvo sought to limit the rigors of repression imposed on the defeated by Morillo and by Juan Sámano, whom Morillo established as military governor in the interior. However, Montalvo had scant success, for his authority in most of the colony was little more than nominal. Succeeded as viceroy by Sámano in March 1818, Montalvo departed for Cuba and then Spain, where he died.

See also **New Granada, Viceroyalty of.**

BIBLIOGRAPHY

José María Restrepo Sáenz, *Biografías de los mandatarios y ministros de la Real Audiencia (1671 a 1815)* (1952), pp. 250–259.

Germán Bleiberg, ed., *Diccionario de historia de España,* 2d ed. (1968–1969), vol. 2, pp. 1105–1106.

Brian R. Hamnett, "Popular Insurrection and Royalist Reaction: Colombian Regions, 1810–1823," chap. 10 in *Reform and Insurrection in Bourbon New Granada and Peru* (1990), edited by John Fisher, Allan J. Kuethe, and Anthony McFarlane.

Additional Bibliography

Lasso, Marixa. *Myths of Harmony: Race and Republicanism during the Age of Revolution: Colombia, 1795–1831.* Pittsburgh, PA: University of Pittsburgh Press, 2007.

Rodríguez Gonzalez, Ana Luz. *Cofradías, capellanías, epidemias y funerales: Una mirada al tejido social de la Independencia.* Bogotá, Colombia: El Ancora Editores, 1999.

Sosa Abella, Guillermmo. *Representación e independencia, 1810-1816.* Bogotá, Colombia: Instituto Colombiano de Antropología y Historia, 2006.

DAVID BUSHNELL

MONTAÑA

MONTAÑA. Montaña, the region east of the Andes in Peru encompassing almost two-thirds of the country's territory and only one-tenth of its population. According to the studies of geographer Javier Pulgar Vidal, it is classified as one of the three official natural regions of Peru, together with the Coast and the Sierra. The easternmost Andean slopes, known as the upper Montaña, steep and thickly forested, pose formidable obstacles to land and river transportation. The lower Montaña, a lowland tropical forest, is traversed by navigable rivers such as the Amazon, Marañón, Ucayali, and Huallaga. Different ethnic groups account for a dwindling population of approximately 150,000 Amazonians still living on the wide variety of animals, vegetation, and fish in the region. The major export products of the Montaña include coca leaves, oil, and rubber.

See also **Andes.**

BIBLIOGRAPHY

Javier Pulgar Vidal, *Geografía del Perú: Las ocho regiones naturales del Perú* (1972).

Additional Bibliography

Arana Freire, Elsa, and Roberto Frantozzi. *Perú secreto.* Lima: BienVenido Editores, 2000.

Raimondi, Antonio, and Luis Felipe Villacorta O. *La sierra y selva central: Morococha, Cerro de Pasco, y Chanchamayo.* Lima: Universidad Mayor de San Marcos, 2006.

Zapata, Florencia. *Memorias de la comunidad de Vicos: Así nos recordamos con alegría.* Huaraz, Peru: Corporación Gráfica Andina, 2005.

ALFONSO W. QUIROZ

MONTE, DOMINGO DEL

MONTE, DOMINGO DEL (1804–1853). Domingo del Monte (*b.* 4 August 1804; *d.* 4 November 1853), Cuban literary critic and poet. Domingo del Monte y Aponte was the most important literary critic in nineteenth-century Cuba. A humanist and respectable poet in his own right, Del Monte was the initiator of Cuba's national literature. Born in Maracaibo, Venezuela, Del Monte and his family immigrated to Santiago de Cuba in 1810 and later lived in Havana, where he studied philosophy at the university from 1816 to 1820 and received an advanced degree in civil law in 1827.

Having developed an interest in literature, Del Monte promoted a Cuban-based form of education on the island. With the Spanish writer J. Villarino, Del Monte founded and published the weekly *La Moda o Recreo Semanal del Bello Sexo* (1829–1831), a magazine about culture and literature. He was a member of the prestigious and powerful Sociedad Económica de Amigos del País and was in charge of the education section from 1830 to 1834. He was also named secretary and, in 1842, president of the Comisión de Literatura of the Sociedad Económica. With other Cuban intellectuals, Del Monte helped to make the Sociedad Económica's *Revista Bimestre Cubana* (1831–1834) one of the most important publications in the Spanish language. He and others supported a national culture and transformed the Comisión de Literatura into the Academia Cubana de Literatura. Literature became a vehicle for expressing a national culture and changing society. Supporters of slavery and others hostile to Cuban-born nationals suppressed the academy, but this did not stop Del Monte from pursuing his literary interests.

Del Monte, who married Doña Rosa de Aldama of the powerful Aldama family, is better known for his famous literary circle, which he began in his hometown of Matanzas in 1834 and continued in Havana after 1835. At his home, young and progressive writers gathered and looked to him for inspiration and guidance. Del Monte encouraged his writer friends to abandon romanticism, accept realism, write about Cuban society and culture, and condemn the evils of slavery. His ideal of Cuban literature was reflected in the antislavery narratives written between 1835 and 1839 by himself, Anselmo Suárez y Romero, and Félix Tanco y Bosmeniel, among others.

Because of his friendship with the British abolitionist David Turnbull, Del Monte traveled to Philadelphia in 1842. In his absence, he was falsely accused by the mulatto poet José de la Concepción Valdés (Plácido) of participating in the Ladder Conspiracy of 1844, a failed slave rebellion. Refusing to go before the military tribunal, Del Monte was never allowed to return to Cuba and died in exile in Madrid, Spain.

See also **Slave Revolts: Spanish America; Slave Trade, Abolition of: Spanish America.**

BIBLIOGRAPHY

Salvador Bueno, *Las ideas literarias de Domingo del Monte* (1954), *Figuras cubanas del siglo XIX* (1980), and *Domingo de Monte* (1986).

William Luis, *Literary Bondage: Slavery in Cuban Narrative* (1990).

Jesús Saíz de la Mora, *Domingo del Monte: Su influencia en la cultura y literatura cubana* (1930).

Carlos Valdés Miranda, *Domingo del Monte y Aponte* (1941).

Additional Bibliography

Martínez Carmenate, Urbano. *Domingo del Monte.* La Habana, Cuba: Ediciones UNIÓN, 1997.

Paz Sánchez, Manuel de. "'El Lugareño' contra la esclavocracia: las cartas de Gaspar Betancourt y Cisneros, 1803–1866." *Revista de Indias* 58:214 (Sept.–Dec. 1998): 617–636.

WILLIAM LUIS

MONTEAGUDO, BERNARDO DE

MONTEAGUDO, BERNARDO DE (1789–1825). Bernardo de Monteagudo (*b.* 1789; *d.* 28 January 1825), prominent Argentine political leader at the time of independence. Monteagudo became involved very early in the movement for independence and was arrested several times. In 1808, he wrote *Diálogo entre Atahualpa y Fernando VII,* in which he criticized the colonial system. Monteagudo talked about the need for independence and favored the use of terror and the death penalty for those who opposed it. He also favored the installation of a dictatorship responsible to a popular assembly to ensure independence and freedom. As a consequence of his radicalism, Monteagudo was opposed by other independence leaders and was sent into exile several times. In 1817, he went to Chile, where José de San Martín gave him an important governmental position. He accompanied San Martín on his expedition to Peru. There, he became minister of war, following a hardline policy against the Spaniards and those suspected of opposing independence. His policies created such resentment that a rebellion broke out on 25 July 1822. He was murdered in Lima, Peru.

See also **San Martín, José Francisco de.**

BIBLIOGRAPHY

Mariano de Vedia y Mitre, *La vida de Monteagudo* (1950).

Juan Pablo Echagüe, *Historia de Monteagudo* (1950).

Eduardo María Suárez Danero, *Monteagudo: La servidumbre del poder* (1968).

Additional Bibliography

Assis de Rojo, M. Estela. *Del Foro Romano al Cabildo de Mayo: Estudios sobre el discurso político de B. de Monteagudo.* Tucumán, Argentina: Instituto Interdisciplinario de Literatura Argentina, 1998.

Herrero, Fabián. *Monteagudo: Revolución, independencia, confederacionismo.* Buenos Aires: Ediciones Cooperativas, 2005.

O'Donnell, Pacho. *Monteagudo: La pasión revolucionaria.* Buenos Aires: Planeta, 1995.

JUAN MANUEL PÉREZ

MONTE ALBÁN. Monte Albán is the ancient Zapotec capital located in the present-day state of Oaxaca, in southwestern Mexico. The archaeological site covers 2.51 square miles of rugged hilltops that rise over 1,300 feet. Shortly after its foundation (500 BCE), Monte Albán reached urban proportions, becoming one of the first cities in the Americas. When the Spaniards reached the central valleys of Oaxaca in the 1520s, the ancient site was abandoned. The site's Zapotec name is unknown, as are the origins of the present-day name Monte Albán.

Monte Albán is among the most intensively studied pre-Hispanic sites, notably in Alfonso Caso's excavations begun in the 1930s and Richard Blanton's surface survey in the 1970s. The ancient city was organized into residential wards, with most people living on terraces cut from the hillside. Water was procured by channeling rainfall into communal cisterns. Monumental stone masonry buildings made with earthen fill and large public spaces covered the hilltop, forming the city's ceremonial, elite residential, and administrative core. Pyramids were decorated with stucco reliefs and carved stones inscribed with hieroglyphs. Houses varied in size and construction materials with the more elaborate surrounding enclosed patios. The city's inhabitants buried their dead underneath their dwellings. Heads of noble families were placed inside subfloor tombs with painted murals and Zapotec funerary urns. Zapotec script—the earliest form of writing in the New World (dating from 600 BCE)—remains largely undeciphered, but notations at Monte Albán give the names of rulers and calendar dates. Other inscriptions refer to conquered territories beyond the confines of the central valleys of Oaxaca. Explanations of the site's origins and early political growth cite expansionist warfare as a leading factor.

Monte Albán's peak population is estimated at 30,000. The hieroglyphic inscriptions and pottery from Monte Albán suggest contact with other leading centers in ancient Mexico, including the city of Teotihuacan. By 800 CE Monte Albán had collapsed, and most of the city's population had relocated to competing centers within the surrounding valley. The causes of its collapse are unknown. The present-day archaeological site is partially reconstructed and a major tourist attraction. The modern inhabitants of Oaxaca City are recolonizing its lower slopes.

See also **Archaeology; Caso y Andrade, Alfonso.**

BIBLIOGRAPHY

Blanton, Richard E., et al. *Ancient Oaxaca: The Monte Albán State.* Cambridge, U.K., and New York: Cambridge University Press, 1999.

Caso, Alfonso, Ignacio Bernal, and Jorge R. Acosta. *La Cerámica de Monte Albán.* Mexico City: Memorias del Instituto Nacional de Antropología e Historia 13, 1967.

Marcus, Joyce, and Kent V. Flannery. *Zapotec Civilization: How Urban Society Evolved in Mexico's Oaxaca Valley.* New York: Thames and Hudson, 1996.

JAVIER URCID
ANDREW BALKANSKY

MONTE ALEGRE, JOSÉ DA COSTA CARVALHO, MARQUÍS DE (1796–1860).

José da Costa Carvalho, Marquis de Monte Alegre (*b.* 7 February 1796; *d.* 18 September 1860), Brazilian statesman. Monte Alegre was one of the Coimbra-trained magistrates central to the early monarchy. In the opposition to Pedro I, he represented Bahia in the Constituent Assembly of 1823 and in the legislatures that obstructed Pedro I to the point where he chose to abdicate in 1831. As president of the Chamber of Deputies, Monte Alegre was a natural choice of the *moderados* for one of the three "permanent" regents during Pedro II's minority (1831–1840). Like many Moderados he shifted to the right under the subsequent regency of Diogo Antônio Feijó and emerged as a São Paulo deputy in the Conservative-majority Chamber of Deputies of 1837, whence he was elevated to the Senate (for Sergipe) in 1839. As provincial president, he was the Conservatives' point man during the 1842 Liberal revolt in São Paulo, the province where he had served as a judge (1821–1822), edited the periodical *Farol Paulistano* (1827–1831), directed the faculty of law (1835–1836), and married (twice) into the planter elite. A councillor of state in 1842, he also served (1849–1852) as the prime minister and minister of the empire in an administration dominated by the Saquarema reactionaries. That cabinet is credited with internal peace, reforms, and stability; the end of the slave trade; and the war against Juan Manuel de Rosas.

See also **Brazil, Political Parties: Moderados.**

BIBLIOGRAPHY

Joaquim Nabuco, *Um estadista do império,* vols. 1 and 2 (1898–1899).

Roderic J. Barman, *Brazil: The Forging of a Nation* (1988).

Additional Bibliography

Barman, Roderic J. *Citizen Emperor: Pedro II and the Making of Brazil, 1825–1891.* Stanford: Stanford University Press, 1999.

Dennison, Stephanie. *Joaquim Nabuco: Monarchism, Panamericanism and Nation-Building in the Brazilian Belle Epoque.* Oxford, New York: Peter Lang, 2006.

Vidigal, Gerardo de Camargo. *O marquez de Monte Alegre: Alvorecer de um estadista.* São Paulo: IBRASA, 1999.

JEFFREY D. NEEDELL

MONTEALEGRE FERNÁNDEZ, JOSÉ MARÍA (1815–1887).

José María Montealegre Fernández (*b.* 19 March 1815; *d.* 26 September 1887), president of Costa Rica (1859–1863). Montealegre was brought to the presidency as a consequence of the overthrow of his former brother-in-law, Juan Rafael Mora Porrás. He served until 1863 as the representative of the wealthiest coffee planters and traders. His father, Mariano Montealegre Bustamante, had been the colonial-era tobacco administrator and one of the first coffee planters. The younger Montealegre continued the large-scale development of coffee plantings begun by his father, in the 1830s, to the west of San José in former municipal lands. One of the largest coffee producers of the day, he was also a leading export merchant and processor, as was common among the wealthiest growers of the time.

As part of a long political career Montealegre was deputy from the province of Guanacaste (although he never lived there) seven times (Chamber of Representatives, 1846–1848; Senate, 1863–1868). His partisan activities eventually led to his exile by strongman Tomás Guardia in 1872. He died in San José, California, 26 September 1887.

Montealegre was the son of Jerónima Fernández Chacón and Mariano Montealegre Bustamante. He was the first Costa Rican to study medicine in the United Kingdom (1827–1838), graduating from the University of Edinburgh in 1838. He returned home in 1839 and married Ana María Mora Porrás in 1840; they had ten children prior to her death in 1854. He then married the tutor of his children, Sofía Matilde Joy Redman, with whom he had two children.

See also **Guardia Gutiérrez, Tomás; Mora Porrás, Juan Rafael.**

BIBLIOGRAPHY

The essential source for Montealegre is the biography by Carlos Meléndez Chaverri, *Dr. José María Montealegre* (1968). Further details are in Lowell Gudmundson, *Costa Rica Before Coffee* (1986); and Samuel Z. Stone, *La dinastía de los conquistadores* (1975).

Additional Bibliography

Díaz Arias, David. *Construcción de un estado moderno: Política, estado, e identidad nacional en Costa Rica, 1821–1914.* San José: Editorial de la Universidad de Costa Rica, 2005.

Fallas Santana, Carmen María. *La política y la elite cafetelera en la década de Mora Porras, 1849–1859.* Ciudad Universitaria, Costa Rica: Facultad de Ciencias Sociales, 1994.

LOWELL GUDMUNDSON

MONTE ALTO.

MONTE ALTO. The archaeological site of Monte Alto, located in the department of Escuintla on the south coast of Guatemala, has long attracted attention because of its eleven sculptures, six in the form of colossal heads and five as "potbellies," rendered in what has come to be known as "Monte Alto" style. The site was occupied from Middle Preclassic times, circa 800 BCE, until the beginning of Early Classic, circa 300 CE, during which period strong relationships were maintained with other coastal sites and Kaminaljuyu in the highlands. During the Early Classic period, Monte Alto succumbed to hostile invasions and was abandoned.

Potbelly sculptures are distributed along the piedmont zone of the Guatemala south coast, into the highlands at Kaminaljuyu, extending as far as western El Salvador. They date to the Late Preclassic period, circa 400 BCE to 100 CE. Within their wider distribution they show sufficient resemblance to one another to indicate a shared cult or belief system. Their concentration at Monte Alto suggests it was a major cult center, probably for pilgrimages and special ceremonies.

The Monte Alto style pertains to boulder sculptures carved on a portion of a rough natural stone to portray colossal heads and potbelly figures. One head at Monte Alto is somewhat different, representing a stylized jaguar distantly related in theme to the Olmec Middle Preclassic style. The others exhibit a consistent non-Olmec design scheme, the style of the large heads being portrayed in a manner similar to those on the potbelly bodies. The face is characteristically sculpted in relatively flat relief and displays closed eyes, usually puffy or with an eye covering. It bears heavy jowls, straight lips, with a deep crease running from the bridge of the nose to the lower edge of the cheek. On the potbellies the chest and abdomen merge to form an enlarged rounded swollen body. The arms and legs are executed in low relief and extend across the large belly, almost as though appliquéd onto the surface. These sculptures lack the navel, collar (with one exception), and crossed legs that are often found on potbellies at other sites. The significance of these figures is not known.

See also **La Democracia; Mesoamerica; Olmecs.**

BIBLIOGRAPHY

Parsons, Lee Allen. *The Origins of Maya Art: Monumental Stone Sculpture of Kaminaljuyu, Guatemala, and the Southern Pacific Coast.* Studies in Pre-Columbian Art and Archaeology, No. 28. Washington, DC: Dumbarton Oaks Research Library and Collection, 1986.

Popenoe de Hatch, Marion. "A Seriation of Monte Alto Sculptures." In *New Frontiers in the Archaeology of the Pacific South Coast of Southern Mesoamerica,* edited by Federick Bove and Lynette Heller. Anthropological Research Papers No. 39. Tempe: Arizona State University, 1989.

MARION POPENOE DE HATCH

MONTEIRO, PEDRO AURÉLIO DE GÓIS

MONTEIRO, PEDRO AURÉLIO DE GÓIS (1889–1956). Pedro Aurélio de Góis Monteiro (*b.* 12 December 1889; *d.* 26 October 1956), Brazilian general. Born into an influential family of planters in the northeastern state of Alagoas, Góis spent about a decade in Rio Grande do Sul (1906–1916) as a young officer. In the 1920s he taught in the army's Command and General Staff College and served in the forces pursuing the Prestes Column throughout the Brazilian interior. Family ties (through marriage) and his long experience in Rio Grande do Sul led to his involvement in the uprising against the administration of Washington Luís in October 1930. Head of the triumphant rebel forces, Góis was promoted to general in 1931. He then led the government siege of rebel forces in São Paulo in 1932 and served as minister of war in 1934–1935.

Góis played a key role in the military coup of November 1937 that imposed the Estado Novo dictatorship, following which he served as the chief of staff of the Brazilian army (1937–1943). While serving a second tour (1945–1946) as minister of war, he personally organized the forced resignation of Getúlio Vargas in October 1945 and oversaw national elections in December. From 1947 to 1951 he served as senator from Alagoas, failing in a reelection bid in 1950. During his second term, President Vargas appointed him chief of staff of the armed forces in 1951, a position he held until 1952.

See also **Estado Novo; Rio Grande do Sul; Vargas, Getúlio Dornelles.**

BIBLIOGRAPHY

Lourival Coutinho, ed., *O general Góes depõe* (1955).

Plínio de Abreu and Marcos Penchel, "Góis Monteiro," in *Dicionário histórico biográfico* (1983).

Peter Seaborn Smith, *The Brazilian Army in 1925: A Contemporary Opinion* (1981).

Additional Bibliography

Freixinho, Nilton. *Instituicões em crise: Dutra e Góes Monteiro, duas vidas paralelas.* Rio de Janeiro: Biblioteca de Exército Editora, 1997.

Suano, Marcelo José Ferraz. *Para inserir o Brasil no reino da história: O pensamento político e militar do General Góes Monteiro.* Manaus, Brazil: EDUA, 1999.

MARSHALL C. EAKIN

MONTEIRO, TOBIAS DO RÊGO

MONTEIRO, TOBIAS DO RÊGO (1866–1952). Tobias do Rêgo Monteiro (*b.* 29 July 1866; *d.* 3 August 1952), Brazilian historian. Born in Natal, Monteiro abandoned studies at Rio's Faculdade de Medicina in 1889 for journalism and key bureaucratic sinecures in the 1890s. He became an editor of the *Jornal do Commércio* (1894–1907), where he championed the emergent Paulista republicans at the century's turn. He also served as President Manuel Ferraz de Campos Sales's secretary and apologist. His public life was crowned by election as a senator for Rio Grande do Norte (1920–1922). He began publishing history in 1913, studying the monarchy's decline; he is celebrated, however, for his work on the early monarchy. He remains noteworthy for his use of primary sources and his research in Brazilian and European archives.

See also **Campos Sales, Manuel Ferraz de; Rio Grande do Norte.**

BIBLIOGRAPHY

Percy Alvin Martin, *Who's Who in Latin America,* 2d ed. (1940).

Tobias do Rêgo Monteiro, *Pesquisas e depoimentos para a história* (1913).

Tobias do Rêgo Monteiro *História do império—a elaboração da independência* (1927).

Tobias do Rêgo Monteiro, *O presidente Campos Salles na Europa* (1928).

Tobias do Rêgo Monteiro, *O primeiro reinado,* 2 vols. (1939–1946).

Additional Bibliography

Marcondes, Ayrton Cesar. *Campos Salles: Uma investigação na República Velha.* Bauru, SP, Brazil: EDUSC, 2000.

JEFFREY D. NEEDELL

MONTEIRO LOBATO, JOSÉ BENTO

MONTEIRO LOBATO, JOSÉ BENTO (1882–1948). The Brazilian writer and publisher Monteiro Lobato was born in Taubaté on April 18, 1882, the son of José Bento Marcondes Lobato and Olympia Monteiro Lobato. As a child he liked to draw and to leaf through books, and he worked on student publications. He studied law in São Paulo, and in the interim published articles and illustrations. He graduated in 1904, returning to Taubaté.

He was a prosecutor, then a rancher, writing all the while. In 1914 he wrote a profile of the rural Brazilian laborer Jeca Tatu (The country bumpkin), which earned him acclaim. He worked with *Revista do Brasil* magazine from its inception, contributing reviews, articles, and stories.

In 1917 he sold the farm and moved to São Paulo, concentrating on his journalistic endeavors. *Sacy-Perêrê: Resultado de um inquérito* (Sacy-Perere: The Outcome of an Inquiry) was his first publishing venture at the end of the year, when he would also publish a critique of the painter Anita Malfatti's exhibit that would lead to a falling out with modernists.

The following year he became immersed in publishing, purchasing *Revista do Brasil* and printing his first collection of short stories, *Urupês,* which caused a sensation on the market and was reprinted in multiple editions. His rise in business was meteoric. He published new writers and set higher standards for the bookselling industry, combining refined graphics with literary quality. He also decided to write for children. In December 1920 he launched *A menina do narizinho arrebitado* (The Girl with the Turned-up Nose) and struck gold. From then on, the people and adventures of Sítio do Picapau Amarelo (Yellow Woodpecker Farm) would win a place in the hearts of generations of young Brazilians.

Business, however, was not always stellar. The Companhia Gráfico-Editora Monteiro Lobato (the Monteiro Lobato Graphics-Publishing Company) went bankrupt in 1925. But Lobato continued pursuing his dream. He moved to Rio de Janeiro and, by artfully maneuvering behind the scenes, established the Companhia Editora Nacional (National Publishing Company) that same year; it would publish the country's most important work in ensuing decades.

In 1927 he was named commerce attaché in New York. Living in this metropolis was the jolt that his restless and curious spirit was missing. In addition to pursuing new experiences, he continued his writing for children, even incorporating such foreign characters as Felix the Cat and Peter Pan. With the 1930 revolution, he lost his post and returned to the country determined to fight for economic modernization. The oil campaign (in which Lobato traveled across Brazil delivering speeches, sending letters, and making the whole country aware of the importance of oil to national development) ended up pitting him against the Vargas dictatorship, and he was imprisoned in 1941. This was quite a difficult period in his life, during which two of his children died as well. Grief-stricken, in 1946 he tried living in Argentina, but the cold proved too much for his health. When he died on July 4, 1948, he left behind more than fifty literary works, the majority for children, in addition to his countless translations, generally from English, of literary classics.

See also **Literature: Brazil; Modernism, Brazil.**

BIBLIOGRAPHY

Azevedo, Carmen Lucia de, Marcia Camargos, and Vladimir Sacchetta. *Monteiro Lobato: Furacão na Botocúndia*. São Paulo: SENAC, 1997.

Penteado, J. Roberto Whitaker. *Os filhos de Lobato*. Rio de Janeiro: Dunya Editora, 1997.

CARMEN LUCIA DE AZEVEDO

MONTEJO, FRANCISCO DE (1479–1553).

Francisco de Montejo (*b.* 1479; *d.* 1553), conquistador, important associate of Hernán Cortés, and conqueror of Yucatán and Honduras. Born in Salamanca, Montejo came to America in about 1514 and served as a conquistador under Pedro Arias de Ávila, Diego de Velásquez, and Juan de Grijalva (in 1518) before joining Cortés as one of the latter's most important lieutenants. On the eve of the conquest of Mexico, Cortés sent Montejo to Spain to represent him before Charles V in order to legalize the expedition. After several years Montejo accomplished his mission, and in return Cortés rewarded him with a large share of the booty of the Conquest, including the *encomienda* (landed estate) of Atzcapotzalco in the valley of Mexico.

In 1526 the crown granted Montejo the title of governor-captain-general adelantado (*gobernador capitán general adelantado*) and the right to conquer Yucatán and Honduras. Montejo undertook the conquest of Yucatán the same year, but failed because of Maya resistance. He then passed the Yucatán expedition on to his son, Franciso Montejo y León (1507–1565), whose 1537 expedition also failed. That same year, Montejo succeeded in conquering Honduras. The family's third attempt in Yucatán succeeded in 1542. In 1548 the crown, as part of an attempt to reduce the power of the original conquistadores throughout America, stripped Montejo of his political offices and encomiendas in Yucatán and Honduras. In 1551 he returned to Salamanca, Spain, where he died two years later.

See also **Conquistadores; Cortés, Hernán.**

BIBLIOGRAPHY

Robert S. Chamberlain, *The Conquest and Colonization of Yucatán, 1517–1550* (1948).

Robert S. Chamberlain, *The Conquest and Colonization of Honduras, 1502–1550* (1953).

Juan Francisco Molina Solís, *Historia del descubrimiento y conquista de Yucatán,* 2 vols. (1896).

Additional Bibliography

Clendinnen, Inga. *Ambivalent Conquests: Maya and Spaniard in Yucatan, 1517-1570.* New York: Cambridge University Press, 2003.

Montell, Jaime. *México: El inicio, 1521–1534.* México, D.F.: Editorial Joaquín Mortiz, 2005.

ROBERT W. PATCH

MONTEMAYOR, CARLOS (1947–).

The Mexican writer Carlos Montemayor is an award-winning novelist, essayist, poet, short-story writer, literary critic, and translator. He is nationally known for his contributions to indigenous literatures, and for addressing a broad range of topics, from his personal experiences in rural Mexico to the Tlatelolco massacre of October 1968 to the current conflict in Chiapas. In 1997 the Writers Association in Indigenous Languages (Asociación de Escritores en Lenguas Indígenas) honored him for his contributions to the dissemination of indigenous literatures in Mexico.

A decisive experience in his literary career was his interaction with a community of writers and scholars in Mexico City that included Rosario Castellanos (1925–1974), Ruben Bonifaz Nuño (b. 1923), Salvador Elizondo (1932–2006), Alí Chumacero (b. 1918), and Juan Rulfo (1917–1986). Although Montemayor's narratives are not historical, they are based on a strong reelaboration of oral traditions, personal interviews, and extensive research in rural areas. In addition, Montemayor has also translated into Spanish a plethora of twentieth-century English, Portuguese, and other European texts, as well as classical Latin and Greek poetry.

A member of the Academia Mexicana de la Lengua, the Real Academia Española, and the Asociación de Escritores en Lenguas Indígenas, Montemayor has received numerous literary awards and fellowships in Europe, the United States, and Mexico. He is the author of the poetry collections *Las Armas del Viento* (1977), *Abril y otros poemas* (1979), *Finisterra* (1982), *Abril y otras estaciones* (1989), *Poesía* (1997), *Antología personal* (2001), and *Los amores pastoriles*; the short story collections *Las llaves de Urgell* (1971), *El alba y otros cuentos* (1986), *Operativo en el trópico* (1994), *Cuentos gnósticos* (1997), and *La tormenta y otras historias* (1999); the novels *Mal de Piedra* (1980), *Minas del Retorno* (1982), *Guerra en el Paraíso* (1991), *Los informes secretos* (1999), and *Las armas del alba* (2003); and the essay collections *La rebelión indígena de Mexico* (1998), *Rehacer la historia* (2000), and *Los pueblos indios de Mexico* (2001).

See also **Bonifaz Nuño, Rubén; Castellanos, Rosario; Chumacero, Alí; Elizondo, Salvador; Literature: Spanish America; Rulfo, Juan.**

BIBLIOGRAPHY

Cortéz, Eladio, ed. *Dictionary of Mexican Literature.* Westport, CT: Greenwood Press, 1992.

JUAN CARLOS GRIJALVA

MONTENEGRO Y NERVO, ROBERTO (1887–1968).

Roberto Montenegro y Nervo (*b.* 19 February 1887; *d.* 1968), Mexican artist. Montenegro, a native of Guadalajara, began his artistic studies at an early age in his hometown. Later, he traveled to Mexico City and enrolled in the Academy of San Carlos. In 1905, he was given a fellowship for European study by the Education Ministry and stayed, initially in Paris, later in Madrid, until 1920, becoming friends with the most important artistic and literary figures of the time, some of whom he met through his cousin, the poet Amado Nervo.

Upon his return to Mexico, Montenegro y Nervo developed a strong interest in folk art, in pursuit of which he published *Pinturas mejicanas 1800–1860;* painted murals in such important locations as the Colegio de San Pedro y San Pablo, the Ministry of Education, and other distinguished venues; and in 1921, along with Dr. Atl and others, he held the first exhibit of folk art in Mexico. Throughout his adult life he gathered a superb collection of masks, which he donated to the Ministry of Education. In 1934 he became director of the Museum of Popular Art and head of the department of plastic art at the National Institute of Fine Arts. At the same time, Montenegro pursued an interest in the ballet, designing scenery for the screen version of *Coppélia* and helping Marc Chagall with the sets for the ballet *Aleko.* In 1958 he completed a mosaic, *Apollo and the Muses,* for the Teatro Degollado in Guadalajara. Throughout his career he was also known as a distinguished portraitist, capturing such celebrities as Diego Rivera, Carlos Chávez, Lázaro Cárdenas, and Alfonso Reyes. In 1967 he won the National Prize for the Fine Arts. He died on a train traveling between Mexico City and Pátzcuaro.

See also **Art: The Twentieth Century.**

BIBLIOGRAPHY

Erika Billeter, ed., *Images of Mexico: The Contribution of Mexico to Twentieth Century Art* (1987).

Justino Fernández, *Roberto Montenegro* (1962).

Additional Bibliography

Balderas, Esperanza. *Roberto Montenegro: La sensualidad renovada*. Coyoacán, México: CENIDIAP, 2001.

Ortiz Gaitán, Julieta. *Entre dos mundos: Los murales de Roberto Montenegro*. México: Instituto de Investigaciones Estéticas, Universidad Nacional Autonóma de México, 1994.

BARBARA A. TENENBAUM

MONTEPÍOS. *Montepíos*, Spanish and Spanish American pension bureaus and pensions for public officials, sometimes referred to as *montes*. In the second half of the eighteenth century in an effort to provide regular pensions for public servants, Charles III created *montepíos*. Prior to the establishment of these institutions, the crown had granted pensions to public officials or to the military and their survivors primarily on an ad hoc basis, but in the early 1760s it initiated a systematic new plan to provide retirement income for those in the military (*montepío militar*) and high bureaucratic positions (*montepío de ministros*). A short time later the plan was extended to lesser state officials (*montepío de oficinas*). A board consisting of a director and four members chosen from the councils of Castile, Indies, Orders, and Hacienda administered the pension fund and certified individuals eligible for stipends.

Montepíos were introduced into the Indies virtually at the same time as in Spain. In Cuba, Santo Domingo, and Puerto Rico, royal treasury officials began pension deductions from military salaries in the mid-1760s at the same time they were put into effect in New Granada. Far to the south in Buenos Aires, engineers—probably from Spain—working on fortifications in the Río de la Plata region paid into a pension fund (*montepío de ingenieros*) in 1764; soon thereafter public officials and the military began doing the same. In Mexico in the mid-1770s the authorities put in place a military *montepío* first, and then almost immediately thereafter established *montepíos* for government bureaucrats. In Lima, however, the state pension program took hold more slowly. The first salary deductions for the *montepío militar* appeared in the Lima account ledgers in 1780 and for officials in 1787. Thus, expansion of the pension system varied from region to region, but between the early 1760s and 1780, *montepíos* had been set up virtually everywhere in the empire for a whole host of public servants: major and minor bureaucrats; those serving in the army and navy; naval, army, and civilian surgeons performing public service; arsenal personnel; and ship pilots in Spanish American ports.

Montepíos were aimed at providing pensions equal to one-quarter of an official's salary. Salary deductions were based on the wages earned by the government official. Unfortunately, in setting deduction rates and the size of a retiree's pension, *montepío* directors had no actuary to predict life expectancy for the pensioner, his widow, or surviving children, nor could they know if a widow would remarry. Thus, the *montepíos* became a financial nightmare. Funds built up initially when the pension plans were put into effect quickly ran out, particularly in those *montepíos* with a small base of contributors, such as the *montepío de ministros*. When funds were exhausted, pension administrators either had to lower or suspend payment of stipends or borrow money to meet their obligations. For these reasons, by the time of the Wars of Independence, the pension program for government servants was floundering virtually everywhere in the Indies. On the positive side, despite these failures, establishment of the *montepíos* demonstrated the new paternalistic commitment of the Spanish state to a seemingly rational system for providing old-age support for those who had performed faithfully in the public service.

BIBLIOGRAPHY

Dewitt S. Chandler, *Social Assistance and Bureaucratic Politics: The Montepíos of Colonial Mexico, 1767–1821* (1991).

Additional Bibliography

Acevedo, Edberto Oscar. *Funcionamiento y quiebra del sistema virreinal: Investigaciones.* Buenos Aires: Ciudad Argentina, 2004.

Marichal, Carlos, Daniela Marino, and Ana Lidia García. *De colonia a nación: Impuestos y política en México, 1750-1860.* México: El Colegio de México, Centro de Estudios Históricos, 2001.

Sánchez Santiró, Ernest, Luis Jáuregui, and Antonio Ibarra. *Finanzas y política en el mundo iberoamericano: Del antiguo régimen a las naciones independientes, 1754-1850.* México, D.F.: Universidad Autónoma de México, Facultad de Economía: Instituto de Investigaciones Mora, 2001.

JOHN JAY TEPASKE

MONTERREY. According to its charter, Monterrey became the capital of the Mexican state of Nuevo León on September 20, 1596. Located 565 miles (930 km) north of Mexico City, this small, relatively insignificant outpost on a frontier only weakly held against hostile Indians and changed little during its first 250 years. In the twenty-first century, Monterrey is the dominant metropolitan center of northeastern Mexico and is characterized by a rapidly growing population and an expanding industrial economy. Its population of 3.5 million makes the city the third-largest in Mexico, and, excepting the industrial complex focused on Central Mexico and Mexico City, it has the highest concentration of manufacturing in the country. Monterrey has earned this distinction by taking advantage of some important factors. These include effective transportation links to other parts of Mexico, the proximity of metallic ores to support a century of industrial development, and an entrepreneurial spirit characteristic of the *regiomontanos,* as citizens of Monterrey are called. The *regiomontanos* are known for their commitment to hard work, self discipline, ambition, and frugality.

Situated in the dry basin of the Río Santa Catarina, the city lies at an altitude of 538 meters (1765 ft). Monterrey has a subtropical climate, with warm, wet summers and cool, dry winters. The city is ringed by mountains that give it a dramatic backdrop but also trap air, exacerbating the atmospheric pollution. In the mid-nineteenth century, and especially during the United States Civil War, Monterrey began a textile industry that traded to some degree with the Confederates. Real change to its economy began, however, when the railroad reached Monterrey in 1888, and the city soon became a hub for rail lines reaching out in all directions.

Monterrey's heavy industrial development began in 1890 when the Cervecería Cuauhtémoc opened and quickly grew into the largest and most important brewery in Mexico. Its success also provided the investment capital for such related industries as Vidriera de Monterrey in 1899. In 1903 Latin America's first iron and steel plant opened in Monterrey, and the industry was well-established by the 1920s. Other new businesses contributed to the city's rapid growth, and Monterrey's 1900 population of 50,000 had increased to nearly 80,000 by 1910. Monterrey now has a diversified economic base, and the city is a major financial, manufacturing, and transportation center for the country.

Another significant contribution to Monterrey's successful economy has been its business community, especially the Garza and Sada families, who have dominated the Monterrey economy since the early 1900s. Through intermarriage and strategic business decisions, these families built a powerful unified coalition—known as the Monterrey Group—that was involved in virtually every aspect of the city's commercial life. The *regiomontanos* have stringently opposed any socialist orientation or communist influence. In 1973 communist guerrillas assassinated the Monterrey Group's chief officer; fearing a communist victory in the resultant political struggle, area businessmen dissolved the Monterrey Group. Today, the Garza and Sada families continue to play significant roles in the commercial scene of Monterrey. Furthermore, along with northeastern and western Mexico, Monterrey is a stronghold of the conservative National Action Party (PAN), adherents of which are often at great odds with policies of the central government in Mexico City.

See also **Nuevo León.**

BIBLIOGRAPHY

Cerutti, Mario. "Division capitalista de le produccion, industrias, y Mercado interior: Un studio regional: Monterrey (1890–1910)." In *El Siglo XIX en México,* edited by Doménico Síndico and Mario Cerutti. Mexico: Claves Latinoamericanas, 1985.

Riding, Alan. *Distant Neighbors: A Portrait of the Mexicans.* New York: Knopf, 1985.

Saragoza, Alex M. *The Monterrey Elite and the Mexican State, 1880–1940.* Austin: University of Texas Press, 1988.

Scott, Ian. *Urban and Spatial Development in Mexico.* Baltimore, MD: Johns Hopkins University Press, 1982.

JOHN J. WINBERRY

MONTERROSO, AUGUSTO (1921–). Augusto Monterroso (*b.* 21 December 1921), Guatemalan short-story writer, considered one of Latin America's contemporary masters of the genre. Completely self-taught, Monterroso had no more than elementary schooling in his native country. He moved to Mexico City in 1944, where he has lived ever since, except for a brief period as Guatemalan consul in La Paz, Bolivia (1951–1954), and a short stay in Santiago, Chile (1954–1956). A very exact, demanding, precise, and well-read writer, Monterroso published his first book, *Obras completas y otros cuentos,* in 1959. A ten-year silence followed, during which he worked as an editor for Editorial Universitaria, then published a contemporary renewal of the fable genre in *Oveja negra y demás fábulas* (1969). This book won the Magda Donato Award in 1970 and was translated into English as *The Black Sheep and Other Fables* (1971). In 1972 Monterroso won the Xavier Villaurrutia Award for *Movimiento perpetuo.* Monterroso organized a creative writing workshop for the Instituto Nacional de Bellas Artes (National Institute of Fine Arts) and has had a hand in training most young Mexican writers. He became a best-selling author in Spain in the 1980s. Additional books by Monterroso are *Lo demás es silencio* (1978); *Viaje al centro de la fábula* (1981); *La palabra mágica* (1984); and *La letra E* (1987). In 1992, along with his wife, Bárbara Jacobs, he published *Antolog'a del cuento triste.* He won numerous awards in the 1990s, including the Guatemalan Journalists Association's Quetzal de Jade Maya, and the Juan Rolfo Prize for Latin American and Caribbean Literature. He was also awarded an honorary doctorate from the University of San Carlos in Guatemala. In 2000, he was recognized for his life's work with the prestigious Premio Principe de Asturias de las Letras. He died in Mexico City on February 8, 2003.

See also **Literature: Spanish America.**

BIBLIOGRAPHY

Wilfrido Corral, *Lector, sociedad y género en Monterroso* (1985) and *La literatura de Augusto Monterroso* (1988).

Additional Bibliography

González Zenteno, Gloria Estela. *El dinosaurio sigue all': Arte y política en Monterroso.* México, DF: Taurus, 2004.

Méndez Vides. *Presencia y obra de Augusto Monterroso.* Guatemala: Editorial Cultura, 2000.

Noguerol Jiménez, Francisca. *La trampa en la sonrisa: Sátira en la narrativa de Augusto Monterroso.* Sevilla: Universidad de Sevilla, 1995.

Sánchez Zepeda, Gustavo and Gloria Hernández. *Los nuevos escritores y Augusto Monterroso.* Guatemala: Editorial Universitaria, Universidad de Guatemala, 2004.

ARTURO ARIAS

MONTES, CÉSAR (1941–). César Montes (*b.* 1941) is a Guatemalan guerrilla leader. Nicknamed "El Chirís," a Mayan term meaning "kid," Montes began to rebel at the age of thirteen, when he was expelled from a Catholic school for his reaction to the overthrow of the Jacobo Arbenz government. Montes later attended law school and was imprisoned for his role in a student demonstration. At the age of twenty he became an active member of the Communist PGT (Guatemalan Labor Party) youth wing. By the time he was twenty-five, he had succeeded Luis Augusto Turcios Lima as the leader of the Rebel Armed Forces (FAR). After breaking with the PGT on 10 January 1968, the FAR declared its total and definitive unification with the 13th of November Revolutionary Movement (MR-13), led by Marco Antonio Yon Sosa (February 1968). The new group based its operations in the Sierra de las Minas. In 1972 he founded the Guerrilla Army of the Poor (EGP). However, due to ideological disagreements he left the Guatemalan groups and went to fight with the Farabundo Martí National Liberation Front (FLMN) army in El Salvador. He lived there on and off until 1996, at which point he returned to Guatemala to assist in peace negotiations. He continues to live and work on behalf of the poor in Guatemala City.

See also **Guatemala, Political Parties: Guatemalan Labor Party (PGT).**

BIBLIOGRAPHY

Eduardo Galeano, *Guatemala: Occupied Country* (1967), esp. pp. 18–19 and 24–25.

Jim Handy, *Gift of the Devil* (1984), esp. p. 232.

Additional Bibliography

Aguilera Peralta, Gabriel. *Realizar un imaginario: La paz en Guatemala.* Guatemala: Cultura de Paz, UNESCO Guatemala, 2003.

Brett, Roderic Leslie. *Movimiento social, etnicidad y democratización en Guatemala, 1985–1996.* Guatemala: F&G Editores, 2006.

Brockett, Charles D. *Political Movements and Violence in Central America.* Cambridge: Cambridge University Press, 2005.

Zepeda López, Raúl. *El espacio político en que se construye la paz.* Guatemala: FLASCO Guatemala, 2004.

DOUGLAS R. KEBERLEIN

MONTES, ISMAEL (1861–1933). Ismael Montes (*b.* 5 October 1861; *d.* 18 December 1933), president of Bolivia (1904–1909 and 1913–1917). Born in La Paz, Montes was the most important leader of the Liberal Party, which he dominated during much of its twenty years in power. As prosperity reigned during his first term because of the boom in tin exports, Montes continued a railroad building program and provided money for other infrastructure projects. During his first term the most liberal land-grant policy in Bolivian history was put into effect; during his second term, however, he oversaw the cessation of land grants on the frontiers. His banking reforms of 1917 and the creation of a state bank based in La Paz undermined Sucre's role as the financial center of the nation. Montes's intransigence led to a split in the Liberal Party in 1914 and the creation of the Republican Party, which in 1921 took over the government in a coup.

See also **Bolivia, Political Parties: Liberal Party.**

BIBLIOGRAPHY

Herbert S. Klein, *Parties and Political Change in Bolivia: 1880–1952* (1969).

Juan Albarracín Millán, *El poder minero en la administración liberal* (1972).

Additional Bibliography

Antezana Salvatierra, Alejandro Vladimir. *Los liberales y el problema agrario de Bolivia, 1899-1920.* La Paz, Bolivia: Plural Editores, 1996.

ERICK D. LANGER

MONTES DE OCA, CONFUCIO (1896–1925). Confucio Montes de Oca (*b.* 1896; *d.* 1925), Honduran painter of the Generation of '20. Montes de Oca painted scenes of his native La Ceiba. Largely self-taught, his paintings of the tropical scenes of the north coast of Honduras were especially noteworthy. In 1919 he went to Paris, where he perfected his style, and in 1921 his best-known painting, *The Blacksmith,* won international acclaim. In the same year he moved to Rome, where his romantic paintings of both urban and rural scenes were recognized for their beauty, harmony of forms, and forceful use of color. In Italy his style became more impressionistic with little trace of his early Honduran style remaining. In 1925 he returned to Honduras, but died two months after his arrival there. His brother, Zoroastro Montes de Oca (*b.* 1893), who survived him, was also a popular painter in Tegucigalpa, but he never received the international recognition of Confucio.

See also **Art: The Twentieth Century.**

BIBLIOGRAPHY

J. Evaristo López and Longino Becerra, *Honduras: 40 pintores* (1989).

Additional Bibliography

Argueta, Mario. *Diccionario de artistas plásticas hondureños.* Choluteca, Honduras: Ediciones Subirana, 1996.

RALPH LEE WOODWARD JR.

MONTESINOS, ANTONIO DE (?–c. 1530). Antonio de Montesinos (Montesino, Montezinos; *d.* c. 1530), a Dominican priest who was the first public exponent of the rights of the Indians in the New World. Montesinos criticized Spanish treatment of the indigenous inhabitants on Hispaniola during the early sixteenth century. In his

Christmas sermon of 1511, he denounced the maltreatment of the Indians, refused communion to the Spaniards he viewed as most responsible for such activities, and threatened them with damnation.

On 20 March 1512, King Ferdinand of Spain ordered Governor Diego Columbus to silence Montesinos and other Dominicans. On 23 March an official communication from the Dominican superior in Spain, Alonso de Loaysa, was received. It reprimanded Montesinos and ordered him to cease his public criticism. Should Montesinos refuse, he would be returned to Spain and no further Dominicans would be sent to the New World.

It is known that Montesinos spoke at the royal court in Spain in defense of the Indians. Most important, he convinced Bartolomé de Las Casas to renounce his *encomienda* and commercial interests on the island. Ordained as a Dominican priest, Las Casas undertook the most famous defense of the New World's indigenous population. Montesinos died in Venezuela while working to protect the Indians of that region from Spanish abuses.

See also **Catholic Church: The Colonial Period.**

BIBLIOGRAPHY

Bartolomé De Las Casas, *Historia de las Indias,* edited by Gonzalo de Reparaz (1927).

Lewis Hanke, *The Spanish Struggle for Justice in the Conquest of America* (1949).

James Lockhart and Stuart B. Schwartz, *Early Latin America: A History of Colonial Spanish America and Brazil* (1983).

Leslie Bethell, ed., *Colonial Spanish America* (1987).

Mark A. Burkholder and Lyman L. Johnson, *Colonial Latin America* (1990).

Additional Bibliography

Montesinos, Antonio de, Domingo de Betanzos, et. al. *Three Dominican Pioneers in the New World: Antonio de Montesinos, Domingo de Betanzos, Gonzalo Lucero.* Lewiston, NY: E. Mellen Press, 2002.

Nesvig, Martin A., ed. *Local Religion in Colonial Mexico.* Albuquerque: University of New Mexico Press, 2006.

Wood, Stephanie Gail. *Transcending Conquest: Nahua Views of Spanish Colonial Mexico.* Norman: University of Oklahoma Press, 2003.

HEATHER K. THIESSEN

MONTESINOS, VLADIMIRO (1945–).

Vladimiro Montesinos was the de facto head of Peru's National Intelligence Service during the government of Alberto Fujimori (1990–2000). Over those ten years, Montesinos amassed millions of dollars and thousands of videotapes compromising a significant swath of Peru's elites, and was often considered more powerful than Fujimori himself.

Born in Arequipa on May 20, 1945, by the early 1970s Montesinos was an army captain and aide to one of the highest-ranking officials in the leftist military government of Juan Velasco. Suspected of spying for the Central Intelligence Agency (CIA), he was cashiered. In 1978 he became a lawyer, primarily for drug traffickers. During the 1990 presidential campaign, Montesinos arranged for the dropping of legal charges against Fujimori and soon became one of the president's chief advisers. Peru was facing a major insurgency and increased coca production; reestablishing his relationship with the CIA, Montesinos became Peru's most powerful policy maker on counterinsurgency and antinarcotics issues.

After Fujimori decided to seek an unconstitutional third term, Montesinos masterminded the avalanche of bribes and abuses for this purpose. Although Fujimori's third inauguration was achieved in July 2000, in August Montesinos was implicated in illegal arms sales to Colombian guerrillas, and in September a video showing Montesinos bribing a congressman was broadcast on Peruvian television. Montesinos fled Peru but was captured in Venezuela in June 2001. Imprisoned as of 2007, he has been found guilty of several charges, including embezzlement, and continues to face additional charges, including his responsibility in human-rights violations committed by a death squad during the early 1990s.

See also **Fujimori, Alberto Keinya; Peru: Peru Since Independence.**

BIBLIOGRAPHY

Bowen, Sally, and Jane Holligan. *The Imperfect Spy: The Many Lives of Vladimiro Montesinos.* Lima, Peru: PEISA, 2003.

Conaghan, Catherine M. *Fujimori's Peru: Deception in the Public Sphere.* Pittsburgh, PA: University of Pittsburgh Press, 2005.

McClintock, Cynthia, and Fabián Vallas. *The United States and Peru: Cooperation at a Cost.* New York: Routledge, 2003.

CYNTHIA MCCLINTOCK

MONTEVIDEO. Montevideo, department and capital city of Uruguay. With 1,345,010 inhabitants (2006), the department has 41 percent of Uruguay's total population, and the expansion of Greater Montevideo has encroached upon the neighboring department of Canelones. With a concentration of 1,485 inhabitants per square mile, Montevideo is one of the most densely populated capitals in South America. The funnel-shaped bay on which the city is located was first sighted in 1514 by the Portuguese navigators Nuño Manuel and Juan de Haro, who named the place Monte de Santo Ovidio. The bay was visited in 1516 by Juan Díaz de Solís and in 1520 by Ferdinand Magellan, who is said to be responsible for the name of the city, having commented: "Mountain I saw" ("Monte vide eu"). In 1580 Juan de Garay established the settlement of Santa María del Buen Ayre (present-day Buenos Aires) on the southern shore of the Río De La Plata estuary, which became the focus of colonization. The northern shore was neglected, no doubt owing to the presence of the belligerent Charrúa Indians.

When the Portuguese established themselves in Colônia do Sacramento in 1680, and when their possession was confirmed by the Treaty of Utrecht in 1713 and new attempts were made at founding a second settlement on the estuary, authorities in Buenos Aires awoke to the threat, and Governor Mauricio de Zabala ordered the establishment of the City of San Felipe del Puerto de Montevideo on 9 November 1724. In 1726 families from Teneriffa and from Santa Fé and Buenos Aires were among the first settlers. Remnants of the old city's fortification still stand. Soon the emplacement became the major center of hide exports from the interior and a military outpost charged with intercepting the smuggling activities of the Portuguese, French, and English in Colônia do Sacramento. During the turbulent years spent in gaining independence—first from Spain, then from the United Provinces of the Río De La Plata, and finally from Brazil—Uruguayans displayed admirable military fortitude.

After 1828, when Uruguay gained relative stability as an independent republic, Montevideo was sought out by European merchants to establish lucrative enterprises: the Falkland Islands, for example, were exploited and administered from Montevideo and not from Buenos Aires. The ensuing immigration of Europeans and the growing importance of agrarian activities in the interior of the country reinforced the city's relevance as a centralized capital. A good share of the national income went into constructing modern port installations and social services for Montevideo, to the detriment of the development of the rest of the country. Promenades, wide avenues, and magnificent buildings in the tradition of southern European architecture were built during the halcyon years of agrarian export. Residential development occurred along avenues General Flores and 8th of October, as well as along the picturesque Rambla Costanera running east along the Río de la Plata in the direction of Carrasco, where the international airport is located (some 13 miles from downtown), and along the famous beaches of Pocitos, Buceo, Los Ingleses, Malvin, and Carrasco. A small Afro-Uruguayan community famous for its candombé, a drum-based musical rhythm, is centered in the capital, as well as a sizeable Jewish population. The low-income sectors extend east of the Cerro, to the north of the city in the direction of Canelones, and into the industrial area to the west.

City services employ more than half of the labor force, compared with 34.5 percent in manufacturing and processing activities. A majority of the country's industrial establishments are located in Montevideo and its suburbs, though in the twenty-first century there has been some diversification. Besides the federal and local government, the city is the headquarters for Mercosur. Primary activities such as agriculture, mining, and fishing are scarcely represented, and nearly 7 percent of the economically active population of Montevideo reports no specific occupation. Well-maintained roads connect Montevideo with Punta Del Este, with Río Branco, Rivera, and Artigas on the Brazilian border, and with cities on the Uruguay River. The railroad system has only two major lines, one traveling to Rivera and Porto Alegre, Brazil, and the other to Río Branco. Communications with Buenos Aires are extremely busy, with hourly services of ferries and hydrofoils from Montevideo and

The Plaza Independencia in downtown Montevideo, 2006. Montevideo is the political, financial, and cultural capital of Uruguay, home to more than 40 percent of the country's total population. © JON HICKS/CORBIS

Colonia and numerous commuter flights from the Carrasco airport. Citizens of Montevideo enjoy a high quality of life, though an economic crisis in 2001 created some decline, which is evident in the increase in informal employment.

See also **Candomblé; Magellan, Ferdinand; Uruguay, Geography.**

BIBLIOGRAPHY

Marta Canessa, *La ciudad vieja de Montevideo* (Montevideo, 1976).

Grupo De Estudios Urbanos, *La ciudad vieja de Montevideo: Posibilidades de rehabilitación* (Montevideo, 1983).

Ricardo Alvarez, *El Montevideo de la expansión, 1868–1915* (Montevideo, 1986).

Intendencia Municipal, *Montevideo: Capital del Uruguay* (Paris, 1990).

Additional Bibliography

Alfaro, Milita. *Carnaval: Una historia social de Montevideo desde la perspectiva de la fiesta.* 2 vols. Montevideo: Ediciones Trilce, 1991.

Barrán, José Pedro. *Amor y transgresión en Montevideo, 1919–1931.* Montevideo: Ediciones de la Banda Oriental, 2001.

Betancur, Arturo Ariel. *El puerto colonial de Montevideo.* Montevideo: Universidad de la República Departamento de Publicaciones, 1997–1999.

Giménez Rodríguez, Alejandro. *Breve historia de Montevideo.* Montevideo, Uruguay: Ediciones El Galeón, 2003.

Goldaracena, Ricardo. *Montevideo es así: Historia de sus calles.* Montevideo: Ediciones El Galeón, 2006.

Pineo, Ronn F., and James A. Baer. *Cities of Hope: People, Protests, and Progress in Urbanizing Latin America, 1870–1930.* Boulder, CO: Westview Press, 1998.

Salgado, Susana. *The Teatro Solís: 150 Years of Opera, Concert, and Ballet in Montevideo.* Middletown, CT: Wesleyan University Press, 2003.

CÉSAR N. CAVIEDES

MONTEVIDEO CONFERENCE (1933).

See **Pan-American Conferences: Montevideo Conference (1933).**

MONTEZUMA.

See **Motecuhzoma II.**

MONTONERA.

MONTONERA. Civil wars marred the first several decades of independence in the Río de la Plata. Regional caudillos often led *montoneras,* uprisings attacking the government or another military chieftain. Irregular gaucho cavalrymen, called *montoneros,* did most of the fighting in these bloody wars. Wielding lance, Boleadoras, and Facón, gauchos fought well and viciously. Such mounted raids often degenerated into the generalized looting of towns and *estancias,* as well as rape and murder of the inhabitants. The *montonera* became a way of life and source of income for some gauchos. The centralizing efforts of Justo José de Urquiza in the 1850s suppressed most regional caudillos and the destructive raids.

See also **Montoneros.**

BIBLIOGRAPHY

Madaline Wallis Nichols, *The Gaucho* (1968), pp. 53–57.

Ricardo Rodríguez Molas, *Historia social del gaucho* (1968).

Additional Bibliography

Deniri, Jorge Enrique. *Orígenes de las ideas federales en la provincia de Corrientes, 1810–1824.* Corrientes, Argentina: Moglia Ediciones, 2002.

Titto, Richard de. *Los hechos que cambiaron la historia argentina en el siglo XIX.* Buenos Aires: Editorial El Ateneo, 2006.

RICHARD W. SLATTA

MONTONEROS.

MONTONEROS. Montoneros, the best-known guerrilla arm of Argentine Peronism. The Montoneros emerged in 1964 in the clandestine Movimiento Revolucionario Peronista (Peronist Revolutionary Movement, MRP), dedicated to struggle against the current regime and to making a revolution following the seizure of power. MRP members styled themselves Montoneros after the gaucho bands of the Wars of Independence. The MRP's initial struggle was against the reformist followers of Juan Perón headed by Augusto Vandor of the Confederación General del Trabajo (General Confederation of Labor, CGT). When the military overthrew President Arturo Illía in June 1966, the CGT supported the coup and sought an immediate understanding with the military. In 1968 the CGT split in two, and in May 1969 the conflict deepened with the outbreak of the Córdoba insurrection (the Cordobazo). Vandor, who failed to support the insurrection, was murdered by revolutionaries. Armed bands emerged in the aftermath: The Fuerzas Armadas Peronistas (Peronist Armed Forces) and the Juventud Peronista (Peronist Youth) Montoneros. The latter, deeply influenced by Juan García Elorrio and soon under the leadership of Mario Firmenich, fused the views of Che Guevara and the revolutionary Catholicism of the Colombian priest Camilo Torres. On the anniversary of the Cordobazo the Montoneros announced they had executed former President Pedro Aramburu for alleged crimes against the Argentine people. The Communist Fuerzas Armadas de la Liberación (Liberation Armed Forces), the Trotskyite Ejército Revolucionario del Pueblo (People's Revolutionary Army), and the Peronist Fuerzas Armadas Revolucionarias (Revolutionary Armed Forces) also took the field; the latter merged with the Montoneros in 1973, creating the largest of the armed groups. Robberies, kidnappings, municipal insurrections, and other actions against the military government increased in 1971 and 1972.

General Alejandro Lanusse entered into negotiations with Juan Perón—still in exile in Madrid—with a view to restoring him to power in return for a commitment to control revolutionary Peronism. Perón's return from Spain was marked by a pitched battle among Peronist factions at Ezeiza Airport. Denying his sympathies to youthful radicals and to a "Socialist fatherland," Perón during his brief incumbency (July 1973 to his death one year later) failed to resolve the struggle between revolutionaries and reformists, much less the nation's socioeconomic crisis. The Montoneros went underground in September 1974; in November the government of Isabel Perón declared a state of siege. Peronist violence and the government's counteroffensive of terror, the dirty war, escalated during 1975. Restored to rule by a coup in March 1976, the armed forces took direct charge of antiguerrilla operations. These were so successful that by 1978 the Left organizations had been dispersed or destroyed; thousands of militants (and thousands of passive leftists or innocent citizens) had been kidnapped, imprisoned without charge, tortured, raped, exiled, or murdered. One who escaped was Mario Firmenich; in 1984, following Argentina's return to parliamentary democracy, he was extradited from Brazil and jailed. He was amnestied (with a group of military criminals) by President Carlos Saúl Menem in 1990.

See also **Guevara, Ernesto "Che"; Lanusse, Alejandro Augusto; Perón, Juan Domingo; Vandor, Augusto.**

BIBLIOGRAPHY

Donald C. Hodges, *Argentina, 1943–1987: The National Revolution and Resistance* (rev. ed. 1988).

Additional Bibliography

Amorín, José. *Montoneros: La buena historia*. Buenos Aires: Catálogos, 2005.

Calveiro, Pilar. *Política y/o violencia: Una aproximación a la guerrilla de los años 70*. Buenos Aires: Norma, 2005.

Chaves, Gonzalo Leonidas, and Jorge Omar Lewinger. *Los del 73: Memoria montonera*. La Plata: Editorial de la Campana, 1998.

Flaskamp, Carlos. *Organizaciones político-militares: Testimonio de la lucha armada en la Argentina, 1968-1976*. Buenos Aires: Ediciones Nuevos Tiempos, 2002.

Lewis, Paul H. *Guerrillas and Generals: The "Dirty War" in Argentina*. Westport: Praeger, 2002.

Moyano. María José. *Argentina's Lost Patrol: Armed Struggle, 1969-1979*. New Haven, CT: Yale University Press, 1995.

Zamorano, Eduardo. *Peronistas revolucionarios: Un análisis político del apogeo y crisis de la organización Montoneros*. Buenos Aires: Distal, 2005.

RONALD C. NEWTON

MONTOYA, JUAN PABLO (1975–). Born in Bogotá, Colombia, on September 20, 1975, Juan Pablo Montoya was strongly encouraged by his architect father to race. He began on the kart level at age ten and first drove a car at fourteen. Inspired by his heroes Roberto Guerrero (Colombia) and Ayrton Senna (Brazil) and supported by his entire family, he attended the Skip Barber Racing School, then moved skillfully through various classifications in Colombia, Mexico, Britain, and the United States. He won seven races and the title as a rookie in the CART open-wheel circuit in 1999, captured the Indianapolis 500 in 2000 in his first attempt, and as a rookie in Formula One in 2001 won the Italian GP. Over six seasons he won seven F1 races but never finished better than third in the championship standings. Frustrated by the F1 style and by the dominance of seven-time champion Michael Schumacher, the outspoken Montoya signed with NASCAR in late 2006. His first season (2007) driving a Dodge for the NEXTEL Cup found him sixteenth overall after six races and first among rookies. In addition, his Chip Ganassi team won the Rolex 24 at Daytona in January, and he drove aggressively to victory in the Busch Series Telcel-Motorola 200 in Mexico City in March. His first Nextel win came at Infenion Raceway in Sonoma, California, in June, and he finished second in the Allstate 400 at Indianapolis in July. Although auto racing is a secondary sport in Colombia, Montoya's success has aroused widespread national pride.

See also **Sports.**

BIBLIOGRAPHY

Hilton, Christopher. *Juan Pablo Montoya*. Newbury Park, CA: Haynes North America, 2003.

Juan Pablo Montoya: Official Web site. Available from http:// www.jpmontoya.com.

JOSEPH L. ARBENA

MONTSERRAT. Montserrat is a 40-square-mile island of the British West Indies in the Leewards, southwest of Antigua. Montserrat's history is one of conflict between the French and the British, and between the planter and slave classes.

Columbus discovered the island in 1493, but it was not until 1625 that Charles I of England issued letters patent for its settlement. Irish colonists arrived in 1632 and immediately suffered raids by the Caribs of Dominica. In 1666 hostilities between the British and the French broke out in the Leeward Islands, and after the French captured Montserrat in 1667, the Irish defenders swore loyalty to the Catholic French sovereign. In 1737 the English governor William Mathew began removing the disabilities of Roman Catholics in the Leewards. Further conflicts led to the Treaty of Versailles (September 1783), which returned Montserrat to the British crown. In 1805 French troops ransomed the island for £7500.

A British decree in 1816 divided the Leeward Islands into two governorships, and in 1834 the colony of Antigua (including Montserrat and Barbados) became the first West Indian colony to declare all slaves free. The Leeward Islands Act of 1956 dissolved the colonies in the Leeward Isles, although Montserrat elected to remain a British crown colony. Although Montserrat's population was once estimated at twelve thousand, as of the early years of the twenty-first century it was roughly one-third of what it had been. This was due to a number of natural disasters in the late twentieth century. In September 1989 Hurricane Hugo damaged over 90 percent of the structures on the island. These were rebuilt, but in July 1995 the island's Soufrière Hills volcano erupted, burying the capital city of Plymouth in over forty feet of mud, destroying the island's airport, and rendering the entire southern half of the island unfit for human habitation. A new airport opened in 2005.

See also **Leeward Islands.**

BIBLIOGRAPHY

J. B. Labat, *The Memoirs of Père Labat,* translated by John Eaden (1931).

Alan Burns, *History of the British West Indies* (1954).

Howard A. Fergus, *History of Alliouagana: A Short History of Montserrat* (1985).

Additional Bibliography

Britnor, L. E., and Charles Freeland. *Montserrat to 1965.* Hail Weston, U.K.: British West Indies Study Circle, 1998.

Farnsworth, Paul, ed. *Island Lives: Historical Archaeologies of the Caribbean.* Tuscaloosa: University of Alabama Press, 2001.

O'Shaughnessy, Andrew Jackson. *An Empire Divided: The American Revolution and the British Caribbean.* Philadelphia: University of Pennsylvania Press, 2000.

CHRISTOPHER T. BOWEN

MONTT ÁLVAREZ, JORGE (1846–1922). Jorge Montt Álvarez (*b.* 22 April 1846; *d.* 8 October 1922), Chilean admiral and president of Chile (1891–1896). A career naval officer, Montt entered the navy at twelve. He served with distinction in the war with Spain of 1865–1866 as well as in the War of the Pacific. During the 1891 revolution he commanded the congressionalist flotilla and served as the head of the insurgent movement's governing board. Montt led the fleet during the key battles of Concón and Placilla.

Following the victory of the congressionalists over José Manuel Balmaceda, the legislature unanimously elected Montt president of Chile. An apolitical supporter of the parliamentary cause, Montt did not want the post but was prevailed upon to take it in the interest of fostering national unity. He may have regretted giving up the simple life of a naval officer for the tumultuous one of ruling a nation beset by domestic problems and besieged by foreign enemies such as the United States and Argentina.

As president, Montt nonetheless managed to quell unrest, integrate the forces of Balmaceda into the country's political life, oversee honest elections, resolve the Baltimore Incident, and avoid war with Buenos Aires. He tried but failed to return the nation to the gold standard. This former admiral, perhaps out of deference to the new political system, did not rule Chile but left its administration in the hands of the eight cabinets that governed the nation.

After the completion of his presidential term, Montt returned to the fleet, where he labored to reform the navy's administrative system. Following his retirement from active duty after more than fifty years of naval service, he directed the Chilean Red Cross and served as an alderman in Valparaíso, where he attempted to reform municipal politics. An honest man who, unlike other parliamentary regime politicians, did not use public service to enrich himself, he died virtually penniless.

See also **Chile, Revolutions: Revolution of 1891.**

BIBLIOGRAPHY

Rodgrigo Fuenzalida Bade, *Marinos ilustres y destacados del pasado* (1985), pp. 143–148.

Manuel Rivas Vícuña, *Historia política y parlamentaria de Chile,* 3 vols. (1964), vol. 1, pp. 13–46.

Additional Bibliography

Castedo, Leopoldo. *Chile: vida y muerte de la república parlamentaria (de Balmaceda a Alessandri).* Santiago de Chile: Editorial Sudamericana, 2001.

Núñez P., Jorge. *1891, crónica de la guerra civil.* Santiago de Chile: LOM Ediciones, 2003.

WILLIAM F. SATER

MONTT TORRES, MANUEL (1809–1880). Manuel Montt Torres (*b.* 5 September 1809; *d.* 21 September 1880), president of Chile (1851–1861) and key political figure of his period. The relative poverty of his upper-class family meant that he had to make his own way in life. He became deputy rector of Santiago's prestigious Instituto

Nacional in 1832 and rector in 1835, also serving as senior official in the Ministry of the Interior. He was minister of the interior in 1840–1841 and again in 1845–1846, winning a deserved reputation for toughness toward opposition. His reputation was undoubtedly enhanced by his own austere and rather inflexible character—although his numerous enemies always acknowledged his intelligence and administrative talent.

Montt's presidential candidacy for the ruling Conservative party provoked political agitation on a scale unseen in Chile since 1830. His election was marked by the outbreak of civil war, the most serious feature of which was a menacing revolt in the southern provinces. The government won, but Montt's repeated use of emergency powers thereafter gradually alienated many of his Conservative supporters. His administration, much of which coincided with a commercial boom, was noted for its industriousness. During Montt's two terms, Chile's first railroads were built, gaslights appeared in the streets of Santiago, banking developed, the mail system was modernized, and the number of schools greatly increased. Material progress, however, did little to reconcile the Liberal opposition. With the Question of the Sacristan in 1856, it became impossible for Montt to contain political tensions. A large section of his Conservative party now defected, joining forces with the Liberals in the Liberal-Conservative Fusion (1858). Montt's own reduced following formed the new National Party.

In 1858 political agitation once again intensified. In the end, as usual, Montt imposed emergency powers. This was followed early in 1859 by rebellion in the northern provinces and rural guerrilla attacks in the Central Valley. The guerrillas were soon crushed, but in the north, where the rich miner Pedro León Gallo (1830–1877) improvised an army of a thousand soldiers, the outcome was only decided four months later at the battle of Cerro Grande (29 April 1859). Military victory was followed by political stalemate. Montt could not secure the presidential succession for his closest associate, Antonio Varas (1817–1886: minister of the interior, 1850–1856 and 1860–1861). The man selected, the easygoing patrician José Joaquín Pérez (1800–1889), soon called the Fusion into government (1862), thus displacing the Nationals (or *Montt-Varistas,* as these were now nicknamed).

Montt's main job after his decade of power was as president of the Supreme Court. His enemies tried, in vain, to impeach him in 1868–1869, proving that the strong passions Montt had aroused in the 1840s and 1850s were still very much alive. Montt also represented Chile at the American Congress held in Lima in 1864–1865, and did so with great dignity.

See also **Chile, Political Parties: Conservative Party.**

BIBLIOGRAPHY

Alberto Edwards, *El gobierno de don Manuel Montt, 1851–1861* (1933).

Januario Espinosa, *Don Manuel Montt* (1944).

Additional Bibliography

Bravo Lira, Bernardino. *El Absolutismo ilustrado en Hispanoamérica: Chile (1760-1860) de Carlos III a Portales y Montt.* Santiago de Chile: Editorial Universitaria, 1994.

Guzmán Traverso, Andrés. "Manuel Montt Torres, un presidente con vocación de educador." *Revista Pensamiento Educativo* 34 (Junio 2004): 50–75.

SIMON COLLIER

MONTÚFAR, LORENZO (1823–1898).

Lorenzo Montúfar (*b.* 11 March 1823; *d.* 21 May 1898), Guatemalan author, diplomat, educator, and government minister. Montúfar was the quintessential nineteenth-century Central American liberal. Deeply committed to isthmian union, anticlericalism, and the modernization of education and the law, and a proponent of constitutional government, he nevertheless supported authoritarian rule when it served his purposes. Son of Sergeant-Major (later General) Rafael Montúfar y Coronado, and nephew of Colonel Manuel Montúfar y Coronado, the author of *Memorias para la historia de la revolución de Centro-América* (*Memorias de Jalapa*), Lorenzo Montúfar received the standard, church-dominated education available to members of the elite at the time and was graduated with a law degree in 1845. Anticlerical writings and active opposition to the dictator Rafael Carrera, however, quickly forced him into exile in Costa Rica.

In what became his second home, Montúfar practiced law and served in various government positions and in the university. Drawn back to Guatemala following the Liberal Revolution of 1871, he held ministerial posts and the rectorate of the University of San Carlos. In 1876, as a member of the Constituent Assembly, he made his famous defense of dictatorship, successfully recommending that rather than create a document the caudillo would violate, and thus weaken respect for the law, the assembly should allow Justo Rufino Barrios four more years of unfettered rule.

In 1878 Montúfar began his most influential scholarly work, the seven-volume *Reseña histórica de Centro-América* (1878–1887), which offered a spirited argument for Central American unification and a defense of Liberal rule. Montúfar held the post of minister of foreign affairs from 1877 to 1881 and served as special envoy to Washington, D.C., but broke with Barrios over the question of Guatemala's boundary claims against Mexico and again went into exile in Costa Rica. A brief return in 1885 provoked a confrontation with the church and expulsion, but Montúfar soon returned and ended his public career in 1891 as the unsuccessful Liberal Party candidate for president.

See also **Guatemala.**

BIBLIOGRAPHY

Robert Claxton, "Lorenzo Montúfar: Central American Liberal" (Ph.D. diss., Tulane University, 1970).

Lorenzo Montúfar, *Reseña histórica de Centro-América,* 7 vols. (1878–1887), and *Memorias autobiográficas* (1888).

Additional Bibliography

Clegern, Wayne M. *Origins of Liberal Dictatorship in Central America: Guatemala, 1865–1873.* Niwot, CO: University Press of Colorado, 1994.

Santacruz Noriega, José. *Barrios, dictador: Gobierno del general J. Ruffino Barrios.* Guatemala: Tipografia Nacional, 1996.

DAVID MCCREERY

MONTÚFAR MONTES DE OCA, LORENZO (1743–1808).

Lorenzo Montúfar Montes de Oca (*b.* 1743; *d.* 7 May 1808), Guatemalan soldier and politician. Montúfar was born in Santiago de Guatemala and earned his bachelor's degree in philosophy from San Carlos University in 1763. He served as provisional magistrate of Quezaltenango, magistrate of Tecpán-Atitlán and of Verapaz, and first mayor of Guatemala City in 1783. As lieutenant field marshal and magistrate of Sacatepéquez, he was a major figure in the Terronistas, who between 1773 and 1776 opposed moving the capital of the realm to Valle de la Ermita after the destruction of Santiago de los Caballeros (Antigua) by earthquakes. In 1793, as mayor of Antigua, he firmly opposed the order of the Royal Tribunal to destroy the ruins of the former capital, in gratitude for which his portrait in oil has hung in the chapter room of city hall in Antigua since 1936. He was the father of historian, soldier, and conservative politician Manuel Montúfar y Coronado.

See also **Antigua (La Antigula Guatemala).**

BIBLIOGRAPHY

Edgar Juan Aparicio y Aparicio, "Los Montúfar," in *Anales de la Academia de Geografía e Historia de Guatemala* 56 (1982): 303–319.

José Arzú, *Pepe Batres íntimo. Su familia, su correspondencia, sus papeles* (1940).

Julio Galicia Díaz, *Destrucción y traslado de la ciudad de Santiago de Guatemala* (1976).

Agustín Estrada Monroy, ed., *Hombres, fechas y documentos de la patria* (1977).

Pedro Pérez Valenzuela, *La nueva Guatemala de la Asunción* (1934).

Additional Bibliography

Alvarez P., Rafael V. *Terremotos en Antigua: Secuencias y secuelas.* Guatemala: s.n., 2001.

ARTURO TARACENA ARRIOLA

MONTÚFAR Y LARREA, JUAN PÍO DE (1759–1816).

Juan Pío de Montúfar y Larrea (*b.* 20 June 1759; *d.* 31 July 1816), leader of an uprising against Spanish authority in Quito. Montúfar, son of the marquis of Selva Alegre, who was president of the Audiencia of Quito (1753–1761), was born in Quito. He served in 1809 as the leader of a small group of antiroyalist conspirators who organized a Sovereign Junta of Quito on 10 August with Montúfar as president. The junta opposed French rule over Spain, declaring its loyalty to jailed Spanish monarch Ferdinand VII. Few in Quito or elsewhere in the *audiencia* supported these actions. The rebellion ended in October 1809 when Spanish troops arrived from Lima. Royal authorities executed all involved except for the noblemen on the Sovereign Junta of Quito.

Montúfar left for exile in Cádiz, Spain, where he died. The tenth of August is celebrated as Ecuadorian independence day, the uprising remembered as the "first cry of independence." However, most historians now depict the movement as one for greater autonomy from Spain, not complete independence.

See also **Quito Revolt of 1809.**

BIBLIOGRAPHY

Roger Paul Davis, "Ecuador Under Gran Colombia, 1820–1830: Regionalism, Localism, and Legitimacy in the Emergence of an Andean Republic" (Ph.D. diss., University of Arizona, 1983).

Martin Minchom, *The People of Quito, 1690–1810* (1994).

Additional Bibliography

Mena V., Claudio. *El Quito rebelde (1809–1812).* Quito, Ecudor: Abya-Ayala, Letranueva, 1997.

RONN F. PINEO

MON Y VELARDE, JUAN ANTONIO

MON Y VELARDE, JUAN ANTONIO (1747–1791). Juan Antonio Mon y Velarde (*b.* August 1747; *d.* 1 September 1791), *oidor* of the Audiencia of Guadalajara (1775–1778) and the Audiencia of Santa Fe (1781–1790), *visitador* of the province of Antioquia (1785–1788), and president of Quito (1790–1791).

Born into Asturian aristocracy in the town of Mon, Mon studied law at the universities of Oviedo and Salamanca. In 1778, after serving three years as *oidor* on the Audiencia of Guadalajara, he was assigned to Santa Fe, although he did not assume his position on the audiencia until three years later. Mon is best remembered for his work as judge-visitor of the province of Antioquia.

Commissioned by Viceroy Antonio Caballero y Góngora to impose order on the royal administration and treasury and to foment mining, agriculture, and commerce, he discharged his obligations with uncommon energy and enlightened vision. He also championed education and public works and founded towns. Mon was promoted to president of the Audiencia of Quito in 1790 but soon thereafter was recalled to Spain to assume a position on the Council of the Indies. His promising career ended prematurely owing to a fatal bout with food poisoning soon after his arrival in Cádiz.

See also **Quito, Audiencia (Presidency) of.**

BIBLIOGRAPHY

José María Restrepo Sáenz, *Biografías de los mandatarios y ministros de la Real Audiencia, 1671–1819* (1952), especially pp. 368–379.

Emilio Robledo, *Bosquejo biográfico del Señor Oidor Juan Antonio Mon y Velarde, visitador de Antioquia (1785–1788)* (1954).

Ann Twinam, *Miners, Merchants, and Farmers in Colonial Colombia* (1982).

Additional Bibliography

Borchart de Moreno, Christiana Renate. *La Audiencia de Quito: aspectos económicos y sociales (siglos XVI–XVIII).* Quito, Ecuador: Ediciones del Banco Centro del Ecuador, 1998.

ALLAN J. KUETHE

MOOG, CLODOMIRO VIANNA

MOOG, CLODOMIRO VIANNA (1906–1988). Clodomiro Vianna Moog (*b.* 28 October 1906; *d.* 16 January 1988), Brazilian intellectual, novelist, and diplomat. His comparative study of national characters in the Americas, *Bandeirantes e pioneiros* (1954; *Bandeirantes and Pioneers,* 1964), contrasted the predatory style of Brazilian colonizers with the settler style of American pioneers.

Moog's experience of contrasts within the nation led him to define Brazil as a "cultural archipelago." After political exile in the Amazon, from 1932 to 1934, he published *O ciclo do ouro negro* (1936; The Cycle of Black Gold), depicting the challenge of nature to colonization of the Amazon. Upon return to his native Rio Grande do Sul, he directed the newspaper *A Folha da Tarde.* His novel *Um rio imita o Reno* (1939; A River Imitates the Rhine), reflecting on Brazil's assimilation of German immigrants, won him election to the Brazilian Academy of Letters in 1945. Thereafter, his career was that of a diplomat and man of letters, representing Brazil on economic and social commissions at the United Nations and the Organization of American States.

See also **Brazilian Academy of Letters.**

BIBLIOGRAPHY

Vianna Moog, *Obras completas* (1966).

Richard M. Morse, ed., *Bandeirantes: The Historical Role of the Brazilian Pathfinders* (1964), includes criticism and a review of Moog's comparative frontiers thesis.

Additional Bibliography

Monteiro, John M. *Negros da terra: Índios e bandeirantes nas origens de São Paulo.* São Paulo, Brazil: Companhia das Letras, 1994.

Weinstein, Barbara. "Racializing Regional Difference: São Paulo versus Brazil, 1932." In *Race and Nation in Modern Latin America.* Nancy P. Appelbaum, et al., eds. Chapel Hill: University of North Carolina Press, 2003.

DAIN BORGES

MOQUEGUA. Moquegua is a city and department centered in the Osmore River valley of southern Peru. In 2005 the population of the valley region was 159,306. Moquegua, home to an estimated 73,000 people (2003), is capital of Mariscal Nieto province. Garcilaso de la Vega writes of the Incas establishing a settlement called *Moquehua* along the river. After the Spanish Conquest, the valley first belonged to Chucuito province and then in the 1570s became the independent *corregimiento* (province) of Ubinas, for the most populous local Indian group. As to the city itself, Spaniards began residing there as early as 1541, although they did not receive official authorization to found the villa of Santa Catalina de Moquegua until 1625.

Moquegua gained greatest renown as a viticultural center. By 1587, Spaniards established vineyards in the valley, where they flourished. After 1600, Moqueguans sold most of their wine in Potosí, La Paz, and other highland districts. In the eighteenth century, they distilled much of the wine into brandy. At its height the Moqueguan industry had storage capacity for more than 3 million gallons of wine and brandy. The region suffered from occasional earthquakes and volcanic eruptions, but in the late 1800s an epidemic of phylloxera and the Chilean invasions during the War of the Pacific (1879–1883) devastated the vineyards.

In June 2001 an earthquake caused extensive damage throughout the city, leaving an estimated 100,000 people homeless. Part of the restoration process involved rebuilding family kilns long used in the region.

See also **Wine Industry.**

BIBLIOGRAPHY

J. A. Montenegro y Ubaldi, "Noticia de la ciudad de Moquegua," in *Revista histórica* 1 (1906): 70–109.

Luis E. Kuon Cabello, *Retazos de la historia de Moquegua* (1981).

Kendall W. Brown, *Bourbons and Brandy: Imperial Reform in Eighteenth-Century Arequipa* (1986).

Don S. Rice, Charles Stanish, and Phillip R. Scarr, eds., *Ecology, Settlement, and History in the Osmore Drainage, Peru,* 2 vols. (1989).

Additional Bibliography

Gutiérrez Flores, Juan, and Teresa Cañedo-Argüelles Fabrega. *La visita de Juan Gutiérrez Flores al Colesuyo y Pleitos por los cacicazgos de Torata y Moquegua.* Lima: Pontificia Universidad Católica del Perú Fondo Editorial, 2005.

Lozada, María Cecilia, and Jane E. Buikstra. *El señorío de Chiribaya en la costa sur del Perú.* Lima: Instituto de Estudios Peruanos, 2002.

Pinto Vargas, Ismael. *Moquegua: Perfil de una ciudad.* San Antonio, Peru: Red Eléctrica del Sur, 2000.

Vining, Benjamin R. *Social Pluralism and Lithic Economy at Cerro Baúl, Peru.* Oxford, U.K.: John and Erica Hedges, 2005.

KENDALL W. BROWN

MORA, FERNANDO DE LA (1785–1835). Fernando de la Mora (*b.* 1785; *d.* 23 August 1835), Paraguayan statesman. One of the most highly educated and influential Paraguayans of his time, de la Mora failed to gain the fame he deserved only because he stood in the shadow of José Gaspar de Francia, the country's first great authoritarian dictator of the nineteenth century. Born in Asunción, de la Mora attended school at the University of Córdoba, Argentina. He later aided in the defense of the viceregal capital during the English invasions of 1806–1807.

Returning to Asunción some time before 1810, de la Mora operated a successful distillery, dabbled in commerce, and held a seat on the *cabildo* of the province. With independence in 1811, he joined the first revolutionary junta alongside Francia. Unlike his isolationist colleagues, de la Mora openly favored some confederal arrangement for Paraguay with the other Platine states, especially Buenos Aires. This attitude drew much criticism at the time, however, and with increasing tensions along the rivers, it grew more unpopular as the months passed.

In 1812, the other junta members sent him as a civilian representative on a punitive expedition against hostile Mbayá Indians. During his absence, de la Mora's administrative powers were stripped from him at Francia's specific request. Then, in August 1813, he was forced to resign from the junta, again at the behest of Francia, who went on one year later to establish a "supreme dictatorship" that lasted until 1840.

De la Mora withdrew from politics to devote himself to his business affairs. He was not, however, permitted to enjoy his retirement. Branded as pro-*porteño* in sympathy, he was the object of constant police scrutiny. In 1820, though they had no clear proof of wrongdoing, the police accused him of complicity in an antigovernment plot. He was arrested and all his property confiscated. De la Mora died wretchedly in prison, forgotten by all save his family.

See also **Paraguay: The Nineteenth Century.**

BIBLIOGRAPHY

Jerry W. Cooney, "The Rival of Dr. Francia: Fernando de la Mora and the Paraguayan Revolution," in *Revista de Historia de America* 100 (1985): 201–229.

Carlos Zubizarreta, *Cien vidas paraguayas,* 2d ed. (1985), pp. 119–123.

Additional Bibliography

Duarte Barrios, Miguel Angel. *Los perfiles de un pueblo: de Zavala-Cué a Fernando de la Mora.* Asunción, Paraguay: M. A. Duarte Barrios, 2003.

Enríquez Gamón, Efraín. *Francia, un hombre interminable.* Asunción, Paraguay: El Lector, 1994.

THOMAS L. WHIGHAM

MORA, JOSÉ MARÍA LUIS (1794–1850).

José María Luis Mora (*b.* 1794; *d.* 14 July 1850), Mexican politician and political theorist. Born in Chamacuero, Guanajuato, Mora studied theology, and was ordained a priest in 1829 when he obtained a doctorate. A moderate constitutionalist, Mora became a journalist and politician after independence. Elected to the legislature of the state of Mexico, he participated in writing that state's constitution. However, he became more significant as a journalist, a publicist for the *escoceses* (Scottish rite Masons), and an apologist for Nicolás Bravo and the rebels against the government in 1828.

A supporter of the repressive administration of Anastasio Bustamante (1830–1832), Mora nevertheless emerged as an advocate of reform in 1834 during the vice presidency of Valentín Gómez Farías, achieving distinction when he synthesized widely published criticisms of the church and when he joined liberals in favoring education reform. When that regime fell Mora traveled to Paris and subsequently represented his country in France and in England. He remained in France until his death. There he published three volumes of his projected four-volume *Méjico y sus revoluciones* (1836) and his *Obras sueltas* (1837), in which he claims to have played a key role in his country's politics. His works which criticize the excesses of the independence era and favor moderate liberalism, exerted great influence in the late 1840s and 1850s among a new generation of liberals who sought an antidote to the powerful conservative arguments of Lucas Alamán. As a result, although a minor political figure, Mora has become known as the "liberal theorist" of early Mexico.

See also **Mexico: 1810–1910.**

BIBLIOGRAPHY

Michael P. Costeloe, *La primera república federal de México, 1824–1835* (1975).

Charles Hale, *Mexican Liberalism in the Age of Mora* (1968).

Charles W. Macune, *El Estado de México y la federación mexicana, 1823–1835* (1978).

Additional Bibliography

González Oropeza, Manuel. *José María Luis Mora y la creación del estado de México.* Toluca, México: Instituto de Estudios Legislativos, 2000.

Lugo Plata, Eliseo. *Fuera de serie: José María Luis Mora de Lamadrid 1794–1850.* México: Universidad Autónoma del Estado de México, 1995.

JAIME E. RODRÍGUEZ O.

MORA FERNÁNDEZ, JUAN (1784–1854).

Juan Mora Fernández (*b.* 12 July 1784; *d.* 16 December 1854), first president of Costa Rica (1824–1833). He was chosen head of state of Costa Rica by the Constituent Assembly of 1824 and reelected in 1829. His major achievement was survival amid the turbulence of the Central American Federation civil wars. His administrations kept as much distance as possible from Guatemalan authorities while seeking British commercial and political support.

Mora was able to convince Central American Federation leaders to provisionally accept the annexation of Guanacaste province (1825) over Nicaraguan opposition. Costa Rica's first formal constitution was enacted under his rule in 1825. Mora's ability to negotiate compromises on the conflict-laden issue of the location of the nation's capital helped prevent the collapse of constitutional authority locally, despite the repeated civil wars in the rest of Central America.

The son of San José residents Mateo Mora Valverde and Lucía Encarnación Fernández Umaña, Mora studied in Léon, Nicaragua, before returning to Costa Rica in 1806. He married Juana Castillo Palacios in 1819. He continued to be active in politics throughout his life, serving as a member of Congress eleven times between 1821 and 1848, representing San José and outlying Pacific coast districts of Boruca/Térraba. He served as vice president in the brief presidency of Manuel Aguilar and was exiled along with Aguilar by the revolt of 27 May 1838 led by Carrillo. He returned to political life after Carrillo's fall, as a congressman (1842–1848).

See also **Costa Rica, Constitutions.**

BIBLIOGRAPHY

Carlos Monge Alfaro, *Historia de Costa Rica,* 16th ed. (1980), pp. 178–191.

Carmen Lila Gómez, *Los gobiernos constitucionales de don Juan Mora Fernández (1825–1833)* (1974).

Niní De Mora, *Obras de Juan Mora Fernández* (1970).

Jorge Sáenz Carbonell, *El despertar constitucional de Costa Rica* (1985).

Carlos Jinesta, *Juan Mora Fernández* (1938).

Additional Bibliography

Gudmundson, Lowell, and Héctor Lindo-Fuentes. *Central America, 1821–1871: Liberalism before Liberal Reform.* Tuscaloosa: University of Alabama Press, 1995.

Villalobos, José Hilario, Luz Alba Chacón de Umaña, and Jorge Francisco Sáenz Carbonell. *Braulio Carrillo.* San José, Costa Rica: s.n., 1998.

LOWELL GUDMUNDSON

MORAIS, VINÍCIUS DE (1913–1980).

Vinícius de Morais (*b.* 19 October 1913; *d.* 9 July 1980), Brazilian writer and songwriter. Born in Rio, Morais studied in Jesuit schools. He graduated from law school with a bachelor's degree in 1933, when he published his first book of poetry. Influenced by Catholic intellectuals, his first efforts were in the Christian mystical vein of the second generation of Brazilian modernism. He wrote film criticism and worked as a government film censor before spending an academic year at Oxford (1938–1939), where he studied English literature. In the 1940s, with increasingly secular and material texts, he established a literary reputation. He entered the diplomatic corps in 1943. Serving in Los Angeles, he was able to cultivate further interests in film and jazz. On assignment in Paris, he wrote his widely read books of sonnets and the verse play *Orfeu da conceição* (1955), whose film adaptation by Marcel Camus, *Black Orpheus* (first place award, 1959 Cannes Film Festival), brought worldwide attention to Brazil, to Brazilian popular music, and to Morais as a lyricist.

In the early 1960s, Morais participated in a movement for sociopolitical awareness in poetry and began to perform as a vocalist. He gained wide public attention as the leading cowriter of bossa nova compositions, including "Garota de Ipanema" (The Girl from Ipanema). While his increasing involvement in popular music and bohemian lifestyle led to his departure from diplomatic service (he served in Montevideo until 1969), his application of his literary skills to songwriting and his support of song as an essential manifestation of national culture helped impart a new status and dignity to popular music. In the 1960s and 1970s, he published new books of poetry and *crônicas* (journalistic prose pieces) and made two dozen recordings. His standing as a cultural hero was enhanced by his criticism of the military regime.

See also **Bossa Nova.**

BIBLIOGRAPHY

Ashley Brown, "Vinícius de Morais, 1913–1980: A Tribute," in *World Literature Today* 56 (Summer 1982): 472–473.

David W. Foster and Virginia Ramos Foster, *Modern Latin American Literature,* vol. 1 (1975), pp. 78–80.

Charles A. Perrone, *Masters of Contemporary Brazilian Song: MPB, 1965–1985* (1989).

Additional Bibliography

Castello, José. *Vinicius de Morais: O poeta da paixão: uma biografia.* São Paulo, Brazil: Companhia das Letras, 1994.

Castro, Ruy. *A onda que se ergeu do mar: Novos mergulhos na bossa nova.* São Paulo, Brazil: Companhia das Letras, 2001.

Garcia, Walter. *Bim bom: A contradictção sem conflitos de João Gilberto.* São Paulo, Brazil: Paz e Terra, 1999.

CHARLES A. PERRONE

MORAIS BARROS, PRUDENTE JOSÉ DE

MORAIS BARROS, PRUDENTE JOSÉ DE (1841–1902). Prudente José de Morais Barros (*b.* 4 October 1841; *d.* 3 December 1902), president of Brazil (1894–1898). Morais rose to political prominence as a distinguished provincial legislator representing São Paulo's Partido Republicano Paulista, the most important Republican party of the Brazilian Empire. As a legislator, Morais was a strong advocate of coffee planters' rights and foreign immigration. Following the proclamation of the Republic on 15 November 1889, Morais served as the first republican governor of São Paulo, subsequently rising to national distinction as the president of the Constituent Assembly of 1891. In March 1894 Morais became the first civilian president of the fledgling republic. While serving as president, Morais promoted the economic and political interests of São Paulo.

The Morais presidency was characterized by the slow and painful consolidation of the decentralized, federalist political system sought by the most powerful state Republican parties. The consolidation of stable civilian rule was hampered by a civil war in Rio Grande do Sul (1893–1895) and several revolts. By far, the most famous armed insurrection centered in Canudos, Bahia, where state and federal troops experienced enormous difficulties in subduing the ragtag *sertanejo* followers of the self-proclaimed prophet, Antônio Conselheiro. Morais himself narrowly escaped death in a failed assassination attempt made by a disgruntled federal soldier returning from Canudos. Morais later used the attempt on his life to justify clamping down on political opponents.

Amid these political upheavals, a serious economic crisis prompted the federal government to secure the 1898 funding loan, which primarily aided the powerful coffee interests of São Paulo and Minas Gerais. Nevertheless, inflation, high prices, and low wages meant that few Brazilians prospered under Morais. But, despite these political and economic difficulties, when Morais stepped down from office in 1898, he was celebrated as the leader who pacified the Republic. In poor health, Morais returned to São Paulo, where he died four years later.

See also **Sertão, Sertanejo.**

BIBLIOGRAPHY

Raúl Alves da Souza, *História política dos governos da república* (1927), pp. 55–74.

E. Bradford Burns, *A History of Brazil* (1980).

José Eugênio de Paula Assis, *Prudente de Morais, sua vida e sua obra* (1976).

Joseph L. Love, *São Paulo in the Brazilian Federation, 1889–1937* (1980), pp. 104–114.

Additional Bibliography

Dobroruka, Vicente. *Antônio Conselheiro, o beato endiabrado de Canudos.* Rio de Janeiro: Diadorim, 1997.

Perissinotto, Renato M. *Classes dominantes e hegemonia na República Velha.* Campinas, SP, Brazil: Editora da UNICAMP, 1994.

São Paulo Assembléia Legislativa. *Prudente de Moraes: Parlamentar da Província de São Paulo (1868-1889).* São Paulo, Brazil: Imprensa Oficial, 2004.

DARYLE WILLIAMS

MORALES, AGUSTÍN (1808–1872).

Agustín Morales (*b.* 11 May 1808; *d.* 27 November 1872), president of Bolivia (1871–1872). Morales's military career exemplified *caudillismo* in Bolivia. Born in La Paz, Morales at age twenty-two joined the army under Andrés de Santa Cruz and participated in the wars of the Peru-Bolivian Confederation. After Santa Cruz was deposed in 1839, Morales fought alongside José Ballivián and occupied the posts of commandant of Potosí and Cochabamba. When Ballivián's rival, Manuel Isidoro Belzu, seized power in 1848, Morales's commercial house in Cochabamba was sacked by the victorious troops. Vowing revenge, Morales attempted to assassinate Belzu in 1850. Failing to kill him, he fled into exile.

Returning a decade later, Morales joined with another *caudillo,* José María Linares, in 1859 and then another, Mariano Melgarejo, in 1865. Driven into exile again in 1865, Morales returned in 1870 and led a popular movement in La Paz that deposed Melgarejo. After Morales became president in early 1871, he supported the newly emerging silver barons of southern Bolivia. He legalized free trade in silver, thereby ending a government monopoly in force since the beginning of the colonial era. His intemperate behavior toward his subordinates, however, led to his assassination by his nephew, Frederico Lafaye, in 1872.

See also **Caudillismo, Caudillo.**

BIBLIOGRAPHY

Moisés Ascarrunz, *De siglo a siglo, hombres celebres de Bolivia* (1920), pp. 113–117.

Julio Díaz Arguedas, *Los generales de Bolivia (rasgos biográficos) 1825–1925,* pp. 214–218.

Herbert S. Klein, *Bolivia: The Evolution of a Multi-Ethnic Society* (1992), pp. 141–142.

Additional Bibliography

Arteaga Cabrera, Walter. "La muerte del Presidente Pedro Agustin Morales." *Archivos Bolivianos de Historia de la Medicina* 6:2 (July–Dec. 2000): 131–142.

Salmón, Josefa, and Guillermo Delgado, eds. *Identidad, ciudadanía y participación popular desde la colonia al siglo XX.* La Paz, Bolivia: Plural Editores, Asociación de Estudios Bolivianos, 2003.

ERWIN P. GRIESHABER

MORALES, ARMANDO (1927–).

Armando Morales (*b.* 1927), Nicaraguan painter. Born in Granada, Morales studied under Rodrigo Peñalba at the School of Fine Arts in Managua (1948–1953). He received the Ernest Wolf Award for best Latin American artist at the Fifth Biennial in São Paolo (1959). With a Guggenheim Fellowship he studied engraving at the Pratt Institute Graphic Center in New York City (1960) and in 1965 he won a gold medal for painting from the Association of American Writers and Artists in Managua. He taught at the Cooper Union in New York City from 1972 to 1973, and in 1982 he moved to Paris. During that time he was a UNESCO representative for the Nicaraguan revolutionary government. When the Sandinista rebel government lost the 1990 elections, he left this position and opened a studio in London. The Museo Rufino Tamayo in Mexico City showcased an exhibition of his lithographs in 1993.

Even in Morales's most abstract paintings there are allusions to the landscape—forest, sea, sky, and beach. Some of his paintings incorporate animate and inanimate forms, frequently architectural. His work became more figurative, focusing on the depiction of the female figure, for example *Woman About to Return* (1972). Since then he has painted jungle scenes of overlapping trees (*Tropical Forest II,* 1984) and female figures, often with segmented limbs. He painted *Farewell to Sandino* (1985), an iconic image of the Nicaraguan revolutionary surrounded by other militants.

Morales's carefully crafted technique, consisting of glazes and polished brushstrokes, endows his images with a patina of archaic fragility, often reinforced by the inclusion of painted architectural fragments, reminiscent of Central American pre-Conquest architecture. Morales's work is particularly distinguished by his refined control of tonal variation.

See also **Art: The Twentieth Century.**

BIBLIOGRAPHY

Gilbert Chase, *Contemporary Art in Latin America* (1970), pp. 56–57.

Félix Angel, "The Latin American Presence," in *The Latin American Spirit: Art and Artists in the United States, 1920–1970,* by Luis R. Cancel et al. (1988), pp. 246–247.

Oriana Baddeley and Valery Fraser, *Drawing the Line: Art and Cultural Identity in Contemporary Latin America* (1989), pp. 25, 95, 111–112.

Additional Bibliography

Ashton, Dore. "Y los sueños sueños son …" *Correo de los Andes* 46 (Aug.–Sept. 1987): 66–72.

Bayón, Damián Carlos. "El espacio próximo y palpable en la pintura de Armando Morales." *Plural (Mexico)* 36 (Sept. 1974): 51–54.

Craven, David. "Armando Morales." *Latin American Art* 1 (Fall 1989): 45–49.

Morales, Armando and Lily S. de Kassner. *Morales.* Italy: Américo Art Editores, 1995.

MARTA GARSD

MORALES, BELTRÁN (1945–1986).

Beltrán Morales (*b.* 1945; *d.* 1986), Nicaraguan poet. Born in Jinotega, Nicaragua, Morales formed part of the so-called Betrayed Generation of the 1960s. His first book of poetry, *Algún sol* (Guatemala, 1969), consists largely of humorous and cynical love poems. His second collection, *Agua regia* (Costa Rica, 1972), is increasingly cynical, political, and experimental. *Juco final/ Andante* (Nicaragua, 1976) collects his later poetry (1966–1975), which is often short, cryptic, and contemplative of the artistic process itself. Morales studied education and Spanish at the Universidad Nacional Autonoma de Nicaragua and was sent to Madrid (1964–1965) by the Instituto de Cultura. His prose and critical articles were collected in 1975 in *Sin páginas amarillas* and republished posthumously (1989) along with previously unpublished essays on poetry and poets. His reputation in Nicaragua is such that shortly after his sudden death in 1986 his complete works were collected and republished as *Poesía completa* (1989).

BIBLIOGRAPHY

"Cinco libros" in *Sin páginas amarillas/Malas notas* (1989).

Jorge Eduardo Arellano, *Panorama de la literatura nicaragüense,* 5th ed. (1986).

Additional Bibliography

Valle-Castillo, Julio. *El siglo de poesís en Nicaragua.* Managua, Nicaragua: Uno, 2005.

Wellinga, Klaas. *Entre la poesía y la pared: Política cultural sandinista, 1979–1990.* Costa Rica: FLACSO, 1994.

ANN GONZÁLEZ

MORALES, EUSEBIO A. (1865–1919).

Eusebio A. Morales (*b.* 1865; *d.* 1919), Panamanian lawyer and politician and one of the leading figures in the Liberal Party. He served in many government posts, including minister to the United States and secretary of the treasury. He wrote many essays on contemporary politics, which were later published in the book *Ensayos, documentos y discursos* (1977). Morales had presidential aspirations, but he had to abandon them after his supporters failed to change an article in the constitution that required presidents to be Panamanians by birth (he was born in Colombia).

See also **Panama, Constitutions.**

BIBLIOGRAPHY

Ernesto De Jesús Castillero Reyes, *Historia de Panamá,* 7th ed. (1962).

Additional Bibliography

Pizzurno Gelós, Patricia, and Celestino Andrés Araúz. *Estudios sobre el Panamá republicano: 1903–1989.* Panamá: Manfer, 1996.

Tack, Juan Antonio. *Ilusiones y realidades en las negociaciones con los Estados Unidos de América.* Panamá: Manfer, 1995.

JUAN MANUEL PÉREZ

MORALES, EVO (1959–).

Evo Morales was elected president of Bolivia in 2006, after an improbable and meteoric rise through the ranks of Bolivian politics. In some quarters his election to the presidency has been cited as an example of a turn to the left in Latin America and of the ascendancy of the indigenous majority in his own country.

Born in an obscure, Aymara-speaking village on the Altiplano, on October 26, 1959, "Evo," as he is known throughout Latin America, and his family lived as subsistence agropastoralists until they joined a drought-induced migration that led many campesinos to the Chapare region in the early 1980s. A gifted athlete, Morales used soccer as his calling card to enter local politics and was elected general secretary of the San Francisco peasant syndicate in 1985. His skill as an organizer and a negotiator propelled him into the national arena, first as head of the six Chapare Coca Federations in 1996 and then to a seat in the house of deputies a year later. As a deputy, Morales achieved notoriety in resisting attempts to eradicate coca production in the Chapare, a stance that would lead to his brief expulsion from the legislature. However, Morales's surprisingly strong showing in the 2002 presidential campaign, in which he deftly deflected criticism by the U.S. ambassador to establish himself as an anti-imperialist, resulted in his reinstatement and in establishing him and his Movimiento al Socialismo (Movement toward Socialism; MAS) party as viable contenders for national leadership.

In 2003 and 2004 Morales vigorously opposed the imposition of neoliberal economic policies in his country. This stance enhanced his credentials as a nationalist and set the stage for a second presidential campaign. In December 2005 Bolivians went to the polls in record numbers and gave Morales 53.7 percent of the vote, an unprecedented majority in a multiparty contest. In May, during the first year of his presidency, Morales gained notoriety by his move to nationalize Bolivia's gas reserves. However, his most enduring legacy may emerge from ongoing negotiations with Chile over extending Bolivian territory to the Pacific coast.

See also **Chapare; Bolivia, Political Parties: Movimiento al Socialismo (MAS); Neoliberalism.**

BIBLIOGRAPHY

Evo Morales. Available from http://www.evomorales.org.

Stefanoni, Pablo, and Hervé Do Alto. *Evo Morales, de la coca al palacio.* La Paz, Bolivia: Malatesta, 2006.

DAVID BLOCK

MORALES, FRANCISCO TOMÁS

(1781–1845). Francisco Tomás Morales (*b.* 20 December 1781; *d.* 5 October 1845), officer in the Spanish army during the War for Independence. The proprietor of a tavern in the town of Piritu, Venezuela, Morales joined the royalist ranks under the command of José Tomás Boves in 1813. On Boves's death he proclaimed himself commander of the royalist forces, joined the troops of Pablo Morillo, and accompanied him in operations into New Granada. Morales later participated as troop commander in various campaigns against the republican forces. He was commander of the Spanish offensive against Venezuela after the republican victory at Carabobo in 1821. Meeting with no success, he returned to Spain after being defeated in the naval battle of Maracaibo in 1823. On his return to Spain, he was appointed commander in chief of the Canary Islands and subsequently president of the royal *audiencia* in 1827.

See also **Boves, José Tomás; Morillo, Pablo.**

BIBLIOGRAPHY

Analola Borges, *Francisco Tomás Morales, general en jefe del ejército realista en Costa Firme, 1820–1823* (Madrid, 1965).

Additional Bibliography

Pérez Tenreiro, Tomás. *Para acercarnos a don Francisco Tomás Morales, mariscal de campo, último capitalán general en Tierra Firma, y a José Tomás Boves, coronel, primera lanza del Rey.* Caracas: Academia Nacional de la Historia, 1994.

INÉS QUINTERO

MORALES, MARIO ROBERTO

(1947–). Mario Roberto Morales (*b.* 5 September 1947), Guatemalan novelist. Morales came of age during the first cycle of the armed revolutionary struggle in Guatemala in the 1960s and 1970s. His participation in the guerrilla movement resulted in his arrest in Mexico in 1982 and subsequent deportation to Costa Rica, where he lived until 1991. Improved political conditions have allowed him to reestablish residency in Guatemala. His prize-winning novels combine autobiographical experiences with the linguistic, temporal, and structural experimentation found in Latin American "Boom" fiction. He is ranked by Seymour Menton as one of the leading representatives of the Guatemalan "new" novel. His experimental first novel, *Obraje* (1971), won the Floral Games Competition for Novel in Quetzaltenango; *Los demonios salvajes* (1978; 2d ed., 1993), which recounts his growing political awareness, won the Premio Unico Centroamericano de Novela: "15 de septiembre"; *El esplendor de la pirámide* (1985), about a love affair between a Mexican girl and a Guatemalan guerrilla, won the Latin American EDUCA Prize for the novel; and *El ángel de la retaguardia* (unpublished), about a Guatemalan expatriate in Italy, was a finalist for the Nueva Nicaragua Prize. His recent works, *Señores bajo los árboles,* a novelized testimony of Guatemalan Indian voices, and *La ideología y la lírica de la lucha armada,* a critical study of Guatemalan literature during the two decades of the armed struggle, were published in 1994. Several of his short stories and his *Epigramas para interrogar a Patricia* (1982) have been translated into English. In 1990 he published another work of poetry, *Epigramas.* In 1999, he published a collection of essays entitled *La articulación de las diferencias o el síndrome de Maximón.* In 2000, his *Face of the Earth, Heart of the Sky* was published in English. As of 2007, he taught in the department of Modern Languages at the University of Northern Iowa. In 2007, he won the National Miguel Angel Asturias Literature Prize.

See also **Literature: Spanish America.**

BIBLIOGRAPHY

For a detailed review of the life and works of Morales, see Ann González, "Mario Roberto Morales," in *Dictionary of Literary Biography: Modern Latin-American Fiction Writers* (1994). For analyses specifically of *Los demonios salvajes,* see Ann González "La formación de la conciencia social en *Los demonios salvajes* de Mario Roberto Morales," in *La literatura centroamericana,* edited by Jorge Román Lagunas (1994), and Seymour Menton, *Historia crítica de la novela guatemalteca,* 2d ed. (1985). Morales discusses his own work, along with that of contemporary Guatemalan writers Marco Antonio Flores and Arturo Arias, in "La nueva novela guatemaleca y sus funciones de clase: La política y la ideología," in Ileana Rodríguez, Ramón Acevedo, and Mario Roberto Morales, *Literatura y crisis en Centroamérica: Ponencias* (1986). The English translation of his epigrams is "Epigrams to Interrogate Patricia," in *Latin American Literary Review* 18 (July–December 1990): 87–103.

Additional Bibliography

Asturias, Miguel Angel, and Mario Roberto Morales. *Cuentos y leyendas.* Madrid: Alica XX, 2000.

Volek, Emil. *Latin America Writes Back: Postmodernity in the Periphery (An Interdisciplinary Perspective.)* New York: Routledge, 2002.

ANN GONZÁLEZ

MORALES, MELESIO (1838–1908). Melesio Morales (*b.* 4 December 1838; *d.* 12 May 1908), Mexican composer. Morales was born in Mexico City and began his studies with Felipe Larios, Agustín Caballero, Antonio Valle, and Cenobio Paniagua. He began composing operas to Italian libretti while in his teens; his first, *Romeo e Giulietta,* was premiered in 1863 by an Italian company. His second opera, *Ildegonda* (1865), was produced under the sponsorship of Emperor Maximilian. Morales spent three very successful years in Italy composing and attending performances of his operas. Upon his return, he established his own opera department "alla Napolitana" at the National Conservatory in Mexico City, training many of the composers of the next generation. Morales was the first to conduct Beethoven's symphonies in Mexico. He himself wrote a symphonic fantasy entitled *La locomotora,* celebrating the inauguration of the Puebla railroad service (November 1869). Most of his works were published in Italy. He died in Mexico City.

See also **Music: Art Music.**

BIBLIOGRAPHY

Enrique De Olavarría y Ferrari, *Reseña histórica del teatro en México,* 2 vols. (1961); *New Grove Dictionary of Music and Musicians,* vol. 12 (1980).

Robert Stevenson, *Music in Mexico* (1952).

Additional Bibliography

Maya, Aurea, and Melesio Morales. *Melesio Morales, 1838-1908: Labor periodística.* México, D.F.: CENIDIM, 1994.

Morena Rivas, Yolanda. *La composición en México en el siglo XX.* México, D.F.: Consejo Nacional para la Cultura e las Artes, 1994.

SUSANA SALGADO

MORALES BERMÚDEZ, REMIGIO (1836–1894).

Remigio Morales Bermúdez (*b.* 1836; *d.* 1894), president of Peru (1890–1894). His death before the end of his term in office led to a civil war between caudillos Andrés A. Cáceres and Nicolás de Piérola. Morales Bermúdez was born in Tarapacá and worked in his father's nitrate business in what was Peruvian territory before the War of the Pacific (1879–1883). Trained for a career in the military beginning in 1854, Morales Bermúdez participated in several struggles for power among military chieftains. During the War of the Pacific he fought at the side of Cáceres in the resistance campaign in the Peruvian highlands. Supporting Cáceres's bid for power against Miguel Iglesias, Morales Bermúdez became vice president and, at the end of Cáceres's term in 1890, president until his sudden death in Lima. His son, Lieutenant Colonel Remigio Morales Bermúdez, army commander in Trujillo, was allegedly killed by Aprista militants in 1939.

BIBLIOGRAPHY

Jorge Basadre, *Historia de la República del Perú* (1963).

David Werlich, *Peru: A Short History* (1978).

Additional Bibliography

Farcau, Bruce W. *The Ten Cents War: Chile, Peru, and Bolivia in the War of the Pacific, 1879–1884.* Westport, CT: Praeger, 2000.

ALFONSO W. QUIROZ

MORALES BERMÚDEZ CERRUTI, FRANCISCO (1921–).

Francisco Morales Bermúdez Cerruti (*b.* 4 October 1921), military president of Peru (1975–1980) who took power from ailing nationalist General Juan Velasco Alvarado and led the military government, in power since 1968, through a gradual transition—the so-called second phase—to a revived democracy, inaugurated in 1980. Son of Remigio Morales Bermúdez, commander of Trujillo who was killed in 1939, Francisco graduated with the highest honors from the Chorrillos Military Academy and specialized as an engineer. Promoted to general in 1968, he was minister of finance during the first term of Fernando Belaúnde (1963–1968). After the 1968 coup against Belaúnde, Morales Bermúdez was again minister of finance in charge of refinancing Peru's foreign debt and, in 1975, prime minister. In 1975, he led the coup that ousted Velasco Alvarado. In 1978, after intense labor and social protests, Morales Bermúdez devised a schedule for the return of democracy through elections to a constituent assembly (1978–1979) and general elections in 1980. He was an unsuccessful candidate for president in 1985. After that, he avoided public appearances.

See also **Morales Bermúdez, Remigio.**

BIBLIOGRAPHY

Daniel Masterson, *Militarism and Politics in Latin America: Peru from Sánchez Cerro to "Sendero Luminoso"* (1991).

Additional Bibliography

Gonzales, Osmar. *Señales sin respuesta: Los Zorros y el pensamiento socialista en el Perú, 1968–1989.* Lima: Ediciones PREAL, 1999.

Gorriti Ellenbogen, Gustavo. *The Shining Path: A History of the Millenarian War in Peru.* Chapel Hill: University of North Carolina Press, 1999.

Martín Sánchez, Juan. *La revolución Peruana: Ideología y práctica política de un gobierno militar, 1968–1975.* Sevilla: CSIC, 2002.

ALFONSO W. QUIROZ

MORALES CARRIÓN, ARTURO (1913–1989).

Arturo Morales Carrión (*b.* 16 November 1913; *d.* 24 June 1989), Puerto Rican historian, teacher, diplomat. Morales Carrión was born in Cuba and came to Puerto Rico as a child. Trained in political science and in the history of Latin America at the universities of Puerto Rico, Texas (Austin), and Columbia, he excelled in various fields. He taught both in Puerto Rico and the United States and also served both governments. In the 1950s, Morales Carrión was Puerto Rico's undersecretary of state, and in 1961 President John F. Kennedy named him deputy assistant secretary for Inter-American Affairs. He wrote various books on Puerto Rico, most of which are considered classics and are still in use in Puerto Rico and the United States. He died in San Juan, Puerto Rico.

BIBLIOGRAPHY

Puerto Rico Office Of Federal Affairs, *Puerto Rico USA: Biographies* (1980).

Tomás Sarramía, *Nuestra gente: Apuntes y datos biográficos de personajes representativos de Puerto Rico* (1993).

Additional Bibliography

Cancel, Mario R. *Puerto Rico y occidente: Obra historiográfica de Arturo Morales Carrión.* San German, P.R.: Universidad Interamericana de Puerto Rico, 1994.

Rivera Quiñones, Eladio. *Doctor Arturo Morales Carrión: Aspectos culturales y bibliografía.* San Juan, P.R.: Fundación Puertorriqueña de las Humanidades, 1999.

OLGA JIMÉNEZ DE WAGENHEIM

MORALES LEMUS, JOSÉ (1808–1870).

José Morales Lemus (*b.* 2 May 1808; *d.* 13 June 1870), Cuban independence figure. A wealthy lawyer and businessman born in Gibara, Morales Lemus professed moderate liberal ideas. He freed his own slaves but was only a qualified abolitionist. He disliked Spanish domination, and for a time favored Cuba's annexation to the United States. However, after the U.S. Civil War made this impossible, he joined the reformists, a group of prominent creoles who advocated constitutional reforms within the framework of Spanish rule. In 1866 he led the group of reformists who went to Madrid to negotiate with the Spanish government. After this effort failed, he cast his lot with the planters who initiated the Ten Years' War (1868–1878). As a result he had to seek refuge in New York, where he became president of the Cuban junta in exile. Later he served as minister of the Cuban Republic in Arms to the U.S. government. Because his properties were confiscated when he fled Cuba, he died penniless in New York City.

See also **Ten Years' War.**

BIBLIOGRAPHY

Enrique Piñeyro y Berry, *José Morales Lemus y la revolución cubana* (1871).

Additional Bibliography

Casanovas, Joan. *Bread or Bullets!: Urban Labor and Spanish Colonialism in Cuba, 1850–1898.* Pittsburgh: University of Pittsburgh Press, 1998.

Pérez, Louis A. *Cuba and the United States: Ties of Singular Intimacy.* Athens, GA: University of Georgia Press, 1997.

JOSÉ M. HERNÁNDEZ

MORA OTERO, JOSÉ ANTONIO (1897–1975).

José Antonio Mora Otero (*b.* 22 November 1897; *d.* 26 January 1975), Uruguayan diplomat. Mora Otero had an extremely active international career, especially in Pan-American organizations. He was born in Montevideo, where he received his law degree in 1925. He joined the foreign service in 1926 and served in the Ministry of Foreign Affairs from 1933 to 1941. He was appointed minister to Bolivia in 1942. Starting in 1945, he played an active role in meetings that gave rise to the United Nations. In 1946 he was appointed minister to Washington and Uruguayan delegate to the United Nations. In 1951 he remained in Washington, now in the post of ambassador. In 1954 he was appointed chair of the Organization of American States (OAS) and from 1956 to 1968 served as secretary general of that organization. Returning to his country, he served as minister of foreign affairs from 1971 to 1972 before retiring. His writings include *Sentido internacional del Uruguay* (1938) and *From Panama to Punta del Este* (1968).

BIBLIOGRAPHY

Enrique Arocena Olivera, *Evolución y apogeo de la diplomacia uruguaya, 1828–1948* (Montevideo, 1984).

Additional Bibliography

Caetano, Gerardo, Gabriel Bucheli, and Jaime Yaffé, eds. *Cancilleres del Uruguay: Reseña biográfica de los ministros de relaciones exteriores de la República Oriental del Uruguay, 1828–2002.* Montevideo: República Oriental del Uruguay, 2002.

JOSÉ DE TORRES WILSON

MORA PORRÁS, JUAN RAFAEL (1814–1860).

Juan Rafael Mora Porrás (*b.* 8 February 1814; *d.* 30 September 1860), president of Costa Rica (1849–1859). Mora is best remembered for his leading role in defeating the filibuster William Walker in the National Campaign of 1856.

Along with his brother, José Joaquín (1818–1860), Mora was the primary military commander of the expeditionary force which engaged Walker in southern Nicaragua and northern Costa Rica. Some 9,000 troops were raised in Costa Rica and, along with local, British, Peruvian, and Guatemalan financial assistance, they were instrumental in the eventual collapse of Walker's puppet state in Nicaragua.

The impact of the military campaign on Costa Rica was enormous, in terms of both political mythology and material life. In purely demographic terms perhaps 10 percent of the nation's nearly 100,000 inhabitants died in the cholera epidemic which broke out with the return of the troops. As a tribute to Mora's leadership the border province of Guanacaste was briefly renamed Moracia (1854–1860). Subsequent generations have referred to him by the diminutive of "Don Juanito" and have considered him perhaps the true founder of Costa Rican sovereignty.

Mora was one of the few early political leaders in Costa Rica without a university education. By the time his father died in 1836, Mora was already embarked on a business rather than an academic career. By the late 1830s Mora had become a significant property owner and one of the leading wholesale traders. He was also one of the first to undertake large-scale coffee plantings, west of San José on former municipal lands.

He was elected deputy from San José province (1846–1847) and assumed the presidency in 1849. He engineered his reelection in 1853 over semipublic military conspiracies against him. A similar reelection was staged in April 1859, but on 14 August 1859 he was deposed by a barracks revolt and exiled to El Salvador. He returned, leading an exile invasion force, on 17 September 1860, but after they landed at Puntarenas and secured a small coastal strip, the campaign fizzled. He was taken prisoner and ordered shot by the government headed by his former brother-in-law, José María Montealegre, in Puntarenas.

Opposition to Mora was led by rival coffee planter-merchants fearful of a state bank intended to provide smaller growers with crop loans, as well as to heighten Mora's control of finance and export activities. Mora and his associate in this endeavor, the Spaniard-Argentine Crisanto de Medina, were the targets of intense criticism by commercial competitors after the decree of 1 July 1858 established the Banco de Medina.

The Mora regime had also angered the church hierarchy by not responding to the creation of an archdiocese for Costa Rica in 1850 with a willingness to negotiate the application of the tithe to coffee production, disregarded locally since the beginnings of the industry in the 1830s. Church-state tensions reached new heights with the December 1858 expulsion of Archbishop Anselmo Llorente y Lafuente for too vigorously defending family members involved in political disputes with the president.

A final element of discontent with the Mora regime was based on his ill-advised campaign to auction certain of the remaining common lands, often close associates. This decree, of 6 August 1859, threatened lands surrounding San José and Alajuela long occupied by farmers paying nominal annual rents. Public protests broke out and were used as justification by the military forces who deposed Mora the following week. In this, as in other areas, Mora followed classically liberal policies in Costa Rica's internal economic affairs, despite his identification in Central America with the conservative forces opposed to Morazán and later to Walker.

Juan Rafael Moras Porrás was the son of San José residents Camilo Mora Alvarado and Ana María Porrás. He married Inés Aguilar de Coeto, who survived him by several decades and successfully administered the couple's many properties. She was subsequently one of the major suppliers of sugarcane to the state liquor monopoly established by her husband while he was president. Their children were Camilo and Juana Mora Aguilar.

See also **Costa Rica.**

BIBLIOGRAPHY

Lowell Gudmundson, *Costa Rica Before Coffee* (1986).

Carlos Meléndez Chaverri, *Dr. José María Montealegre* (1968).

Rafael Obregón Loría, *Conflictos militares y políticos de Costa Rica* (1951).

Rafael Obregón Loría, *Costa Rica y la guerra del 56: La campaña del transito,* 2d ed. (1976).

Armando Rodríguez Porras, *Juan Rafael Mora y la guerra contra los filibusteros* (1955).

Additional Bibliography

Botey, Ana María. *Costa Rica, estado, economía, sociedad y cultura desde las sociedades autoóctonas hasta 1914.* San José, Costa Rica: Editorial de la Universidad de Costa Rica, 2002.

Chacón M., Euclides. *Indice cronológico de la Campaña Nacional, 1856-1857.* Alajuela, Costa Rica: Museo Histórico Cultural Juan Santamaría, 2002.

LOWELL GUDMUNDSON

MORA VALVERDE, MANUEL (1910–1994). Manuel Mora Valverde (*b.* 1910; *d.* 29 December 1994), the leading figure and one of the founding fathers of communism in Costa Rica, elected to five terms in the national congress (1934–1948, 1970–1974), and twice candidate for the presidency (1940, 1974).

Manuel Mora's life and career have been intertwined with the communist movement in his native Costa Rica. His active political career began while he was still a young law student at the School of Law in San José. In 1930 he played a leading role in the organization of the Workers and Peasants Bloc, which rather quickly evolved into the Costa Rican Communist Party (PC).

Along with Carlos Luis Fallas Sibaja, Jaime Cerdas Moran, and others, Mora capitalized on the deteriorating economic conditions during the Great Depression to bring the Communist Party to the forefront of labor union organization. With his segment of the labor movement as a voting base, he made the Communist Party a force to be reckoned with in national politics. Never a true contender for power, it has been a militant and influential minority party.

Mora contributed to his country through his dedication, writings, austerity, and ability to change the agenda of Costa Rican politics. Political leaders from León Cortés Castro (1936–1940) through Rafael Angel Calderón Guardia (1940–1944), Otilio Ulate Blanco (1949–1953), and José Figueres Ferrer (1948–1949, 1953–1958, 1970–1974) felt it necessary to respond ideologically to the communist challenge. Even though they rejected Mora's party and its links to the Soviet Union, most respected him as a national leader. Mora's program did not become the nation's program; however, the challenge that he posed led his political opponents to formulate their own responses to the socioeconomic problems of Costa Rica. He thus contributed to the great progress that has characterized Costa Rica since 1940.

Mora reached the apex of his power and influence during the administrations of Calderón Guardia (1940–1944) and Teodoro Picado Michalski (1944–1948). After changing the name of his party to the Popular Vanguard (PVP) and receiving the approval of Archbishop Víctor M. Sanabria Martínez, he entered into a political alliance with the governing National Republican Party. This alliance, which called itself the Victory Bloc, enacted wide-ranging social legislation, which has been maintained and enhanced by subsequent administrations.

With the overthrow of Picado by the Figueres-led revolution in 1948, Mora was forced into exile and his party was outlawed. He later returned to Costa Rica and renewed his political activities, but neither his own party nor the various leftist coalitions in which it participated ever achieved the strength and influence that the Popular Vanguard enjoyed during its alliance with the government between 1942 and 1948. In 1993, the University of Costa Rica presented him with its Rodrigo Facio prize. The following year he was the recipient of an honorary doctorate from the Universidad Estatal a Distancia.

See also **Communism.**

BIBLIOGRAPHY

John Patrick Bell, *Crisis in Costa Rica* (1971).

Charles D. Ameringer, *Don Pepe* (1978).

William Krehm, *Democracies and Tyrannies of the Caribbean* (1984).

Richard Biesanz, Karen Zubris Biesanz, and Mavis Hiltunen Biesanz, *The Costa Ricans* (1982; rev. ed. 1988).

Marc Edelman and Joanne Kenen, *The Costa Rica Reader* (1989), pp. 74–114 and 309–313.

Additional Bibliography

Merino del Rio, José. *Manuel Mora y la democrácia costarricense: Viaje al interior del Partido Comunista.* Heredia, Costa Rica: Editorial Fundación UNA, 1996.

Salas, Addy. *Con Manuel: "Devolver al pueblo su fuerza."* San José: Editorial de la Universidad de Costa Rica, 1998.

JOHN PATRICK BELL

MORAVIAN CHURCH.

MORAVIAN CHURCH. Moravian Church, or the Church of the United Brethren, a German pietist sect that originated in Saxony and spread to the Americas during the mid-nineteenth century. In Central America, the Moravians are found almost exclusively along Nicaragua's Atlantic Coast, where they work with people of Zambo heritage (collectively known as the Miskito Indians). Although based in Bluefields, Nicaragua, the Moravian Church maintains missions as far north as southern Honduras.

The Moravians first came to Nicaragua in 1849, when they established missions and schools for the Miskitos, Afro-Caribbeans, (Costeños) and British Protestants who lived along the coast when the country was a British protectorate. After Britain abandoned its claim to the coast in the Clayton-Bulwer Treaty of 1850, the Moravians confined their work to the Miskitos. Throughout the nineteenth and twentieth centuries, the Moravians, who advocate "separation from the world" for religious reasons, encouraged the Miskitos to maintain their identity separate from that of the Catholic, Hispanic society of western Nicaragua. This practice has periodically caused friction between the Nicaraguan government and the Moravian Church, as evidenced in 1900, when Nicaragua's president, José Santos Zelaya, temporarily closed Moravian schools for failing to teach the Miskito to be "faithful subjects of the government."

Although the Moravian Church advocates pacifism, Nicaraguan Moravians from the Atlantic coast were instrumental in forming the first popular resistance to the Sandinista government in 1981. This ethnically based movement for Miskito autonomy was known as Misurasata, an acronym for Miskito, Sumo, Rama, and Sandinista. Since 1985, Nicaragua's north and south Atlantic coasts function as self-governing, autonomous regions.

See also **Nicaragua.**

BIBLIOGRAPHY

Humberto Belli, *Nicaragua: Christians Under Fire* (1984).

John Booth, *The End and the Beginning: The Nicaraguan Revolution,* 2d ed. (1985).

George Irwin Ferris, Jr., "Protestantism in Nicaragua: Its Historical Roots and Influences Affecting Its Growth" (Ph.D. diss., Temple University, 1981).

Additional Bibliography

Gordon, Edmund T. *Disparate Diasporas: Identity and Politics in an African Nicaraguan Community.* Austin: University of Texas Press, Austin, Institute of Latin American Studies, 1998.

Hale, Charles. R. *Resistance and Contradiction: Miskitu Indians and the Nicaraguan State, 1894-1987.* Stanford: Stanford University Press, 1994.

Robertson, C. Alton. *The Moravians, the Miskitu, and the Sandinistas on Nicaragua's Atlantic Coast: 1979-1990.* Bethlehem, PA: Moravian Church in America, 1998.

Smith, Calvin L. *Revolution, Revival, and Religious Conflict in Sandinista Nicaragua.* Boston: Brill, 2007.

VIRGINIA GARRARD-BURNETT

MORA Y DEL RÍO, JOSÉ (1854–1928).

José Mora y del Río (*b.* 24 February 1854; *d.* 22 April 1928), archbishop of Mexico, 1908–1928. A native of Pajcuarán, Michoacán, Mora y del Río studied in Rome and rose rapidly to become bishop of Tehuantepec (1893), a poor rural area. As bishop, he supported Catholic Social Action to benefit the peasantry. He was sympathetic to the presidency of Francisco Madero (1911–1913), the collapse of which threw Mexico into a period of civil strife in which the Catholic Church became identified with conservatism.

After five years in exile, Mora y del Río returned to Mexico in 1919 to confront growing anticlericalism. In 1926 he openly rejected the restrictions on the church in the Mexican constitution which President Plutarco Elías Calles energetically enforced through closure of church primary schools and required registration of priests. The archbishop called a church strike which ended public religious services. Calles exiled Mora y del Río, who died in San Antonio, Texas, barely a year before the conflict ended through a negotiated settlement.

See also **Religion in Mexico, Catholic Church and Beyond.**

BIBLIOGRAPHY

David Bailey, *¡Viva Cristo Rey! The Cristero Rebellion and the Church-State Conflict in Mexico* (1973), esp. pp. 44, 47–75, 142–149, 198–199.

Robert Quirk, *The Mexican Revolution and the Catholic Church, 1910–1929* (1973), esp. pp. 18–19, 30–33, 50–74, 125–228.

Additional Bibliography

Butler, Matthew. *Popular Piety and Political Identity in Mexico's Cristero Rebellion: Michoacán, 1927-1929.* Oxford; New York: Published for the British Academy by Oxford University Press, 2004.

Krauze, Enrique. *Mexico: Biography of Power: A History of Modern Mexico, 1810–1996.* New York: Harper Perennial, 1998.

JOHN A. BRITTON

MORAZÁN, FRANCISCO (1792–1842). Francisco Morazán (*b.* 3 October 1792; *d.* 15 September 1842), president of the Federation of Central America (1830–1834, 1835–1839). The armed conflict between Central American Liberals and Conservatives after 1826 brought Morazán, a native of Tegucigalpa, Honduras, from provincial obscurity to leadership of the Liberal cause. In a military campaign (November 1827–April 1829) he drove the Conservative federal armies from Honduras and El Salvador, invaded Guatemala, and overthrew the "intrusive" governments there. Temporarily assuming power as chief executive of both state and federation, he restored to office the "legitimate" Liberal state and federal authorities displaced in 1826, imprisoned the deposed officials, and exiled the principal prosecutors of the war. He was elected president (16 September 1830), and continued for a second term when in 1834 death removed José Cecilio del Valle, chosen to succeed him. Until the federation collapsed, Morazán commanded the federal forces and either occupied the presidency or exercised the power that sustained it.

Morazán's victory temporarily established Liberal ascendancy, but it provided neither a working consensus nor an atmosphere of mutual toleration that enabled him to govern. As Liberal leader he championed reforms intended to restructure traditional Central American institutions to emulate the most advanced contemporary models, and sought to maintain Liberal regimes that would promote such reforms in each state. Mariano Gálvez, for example, inaugurated in Guatemala a notably comprehensive restructuring of society for which Morazán shared responsibility. Tensions generated by a growing body of Liberal innovations that forced accommodation to unfamiliar institutions and draconian measures, such as the exile of leading Conservatives, including the archbishop of Guatemala and friars of three regular orders, drove offended and scandalized citizens into the domestic opposition and created a body of aggrieved and resentful exiles plotting invasion from abroad.

Grave operational defects in the political structure of the Central American Federation restricted Morazán's options. The federal constitution was not universally accepted as appropriate to Central America, and modification or abandonment of the system was widely sought but never accomplished. Chronic financial exigency hampered both federal and state governments, and states not infrequently withheld federal revenues collected within their jurisdictions. Some states dared to nullify federal laws and, in the absence of legal penalties for counterfeiting, to mint spurious coins. Frictions generated by regional jealousies and rivalries between and among states subverted unity and severely strained the federal structure. Particularly destructive was a provincial distrust of Guatemala. The traditional seat of power, its population (which entitled it to overwhelming representation in the federal Congress), wealth, and economic suzerainty enabled it to dominate the federation. Guatemala successfully resisted an attempt to diminish its influence by creating a federal district around Guatemala City, and Morazán's attempt (1834) to achieve a more equitable balance among states by transfer of the capital to San Salvador produced little improvement. States frequently threatened revolt and occasionally seceded.

The outbreak of cholera in 1837 was a fatal blow to the federation, already threatened by dissolution. Terrorized by the advance of the disease and distrustful of the control measures, the peasants of eastern Guatemala erupted in a popular revolt from which José Rafael Carrera emerged the natural leader. Divided counsels among Liberals paralyzed action, and when Morazán assented to a dissident faction's proposal to negotiate with Carrera rather than respond to an urgent appeal from Gálvez for military intervention, a Carrera force entered Guatemala City (30 January 1838). Gálvez resigned (1 February 1838), the federation lost its major source of support, and the unpredictable Carrera kept the state and the union in turmoil until Morazán entered the war (November 1838). To buy time, Carrera accepted peace, only to resume the offensive to displace the Liberal government Morazán had installed.

Recognizing that the federation was approaching the final stages of disintegration, the federal Congress formally released the states (30 May 1838) to adopt regimes of their choosing, and held the final session (30 July 1838) of the last federal Congress. When Morazán's second term expired (1 February 1839), no competent authority existed to call an election to choose a successor, so he transferred power to his brother-in-law, Vice President Diego Vijil (10 February 1839).

Elected head of state of El Salvador (June 1839), Morazán attempted with such troops as he could muster to force together the fragments of the broken union. He first had to defeat the allied armies of Nicaragua and Honduras (September 1839), sent to deprive him of his base of power. Then he invaded Guatemala to confront Carrera, and occupied the plaza of Guatemala City (18 March 1840), only to be routed by Carrera the following day. He fled into exile but, refitted in Peru, he returned to Central America (1842) and usurped the government of Costa Rica. He soon fell victim to a popular uprising, and in San José a firing squad ended his career.

As president, Morazán hoped to achieve the domestic stability and order necessary for sustained progress. Circumstances, however, determined that his energies went principally to sustain Liberal regimes, put down civil wars, remove opposition leaders who seized state governments, and cajole or coerce state authorities to honor their federal obligations. These activities provided the basis for his admirers to construct a portrait of an unswervingly loyal champion of the federation, unselfishly dedicating his life and sterling talents to its development and protection, and devoting his broad-visioned statesmanship and his unmatched prowess as a military leader to its defense.

As Morazán's tenure lengthened, criticism of the federal regime focused increasingly on the person of the leader rather than on institutional deficiencies or Liberal ideology. Critics charged that Morazán maintained a nepotistic monopoly of positions of power, that his zeal in sustaining the federation reflected determination to preserve his monopoly of privilege rather than loyalty or devotion to the union, that he manipulated office to his personal profit in such instances as sale of ecclesiastical properties. They charged that for profit Morazán sold out his country to the British by fueling the increased British presence and renewed assertion of suzerainty on the Mosquito Coast through his sales to Belize cutters of mahogany trees within the extensive tract the government of Honduras (1835) granted him there.

These disparate characterizations of Morazán's career and character rest largely on contemporary intuitive interpretations of his public life. Natural disasters and, if partisan allegations are credited, partisan purges of archives have so truncated the sources that the prospect that objective scholarship will be able significantly to resolve the discrepancy or flesh out the portrait is not promising.

See also **Liberal Party (Central America).**

BIBLIOGRAPHY

Robert. S. Chamberlain, *Francisco Morazán, Champion of Central American Federation* (1950).

Miguel Ángel Gallardo, comp., *Papeles históricos,* 3 vols. (1954–1964).

William J. Griffith, "The Personal Archive of Francisco Morazán," Middle American Research Institute, *Philological and Documentary Studies,* vol. 2, no. 6 (1977), pp. 197–286.

Alberto Herrarte, *La unión de Centroamérica: Trajedia y esperanza* (1955).

Thomas L. Karnes, *Failure of Union: Central America, 1824–1960* (1961).

Clemente Marroquín Rojas, *Francisco Morazán y Rafael Carrera* (1965).

Agustín Mencos Franco, *Rasgos biográficos de Francisco Morazán,* 4th ed. (1906).

Lorenzo Montúfar y Rivera Maestre, *Morazán,* 3d ed. (1982).

Ralph Lee Wooward, in *Rafael Carrera and the Emergence of the Republic of Guatemala, 1821–1871* (1992).

Additional Bibliography

Gudmundson, Lowell, and Héctor Lindo-Fuentes. *Central America, 1821–1871: Liberalism before Liberal Reform.* Tuscaloosa: University of Alabama Press, 1995.

Umaña, Helen. *Francisco Morazán en la literature hondureña.* San Pedro Sula: s.n., 1995.

WILLIAM J. GRIFFITH

MORÉ, BENY (1919–1963). Beny Moré was the greatest male vocalist during the golden age of Cuban music. Born in Santa Isabel de las Lajas to a poor family, he received no formal musical training, but his family connections led him to become part of Afro-Cuban fraternal organizations. In Havana after 1940, Moré sang on the streets and in cafés. He became associated with groups led by Miguel Matamoros. He traveled to Mexico in 1945 as a member of Los Matamoros but chose to stay on for the next five years. While there he performed with a number of Mexican and Cuban bands, most notably that of Dámaso Pérez Prado. He began to record with RCA Victor and also appeared in a number of motion pictures. He returned to Cuba in 1950, and in 1953 formed his Banda Gigante, which had a series of hits and performed internationally in North America and throughout the Caribbean.

Known as "*el bárbaro del ritmo*" (the barbarian of rhythm), Moré was admired for the impressive range and rich sound of his voice and for his precise sense of timing. He was the master of a wide variety of Cuban musical styles, from *son* to mambo to bolero. Among other fine songs, he wrote "Qué Bueno Baila Usted," "Bonito y Sabroso," and "Dolor y Perdón." His extensive discography remains an essential component of any serious Latin American music collection. He is believed to have died from cirrhosis of the liver.

See also **Bolero; Mambo; Music: Popular Music and Dance; Son.**

BIBLIOGRAPHY

Contreras, Félix. *Yo Conocí a Benny Moré.* Havana, Cuba: Ediciones Unión, 2002.

Loza, Steven. *Tito Puente and the Making of Latin Music.* Urbana: University of Illinois Press, 1999.

Orovio, Helio. *Cuban Music from A to Z.* Durham, NC: Duke University Press, 2004.

ANDREW J. KIRKENDALL

MOREAU DE JUSTO, ALICIA (1886–1986). Alicia Moreau de Justo (*b.* 11 October 1886; *d.* 1986), Argentine physician, socialist, and feminist. She was born in London to French parents, who were exiled in England for their activities in the Paris Commune. The family immigrated to Buenos Aires in 1890, where her father worked for progressive causes and the Socialist Party, founded by Juan B. Justo (1896). At fifteen Alicia Moreau helped to establish the Socialist Women's Center with Fenia Cherkov, believing that the fight for women's education should take precedence over civil or political equality. She taught child care and hygiene at the Socialist Women's Center in Buenos Aires and fought against prostitution. She wrote for the journal *Humanidad Nueva* and the socialist daily *La Vanguardia,* which she directed from 1956 to 1962. Moreau studied medicine, taught anatomy, graduated from the University of Buenos Aires in 1914, and practiced in working-class clinics. A lifelong socialist, Moreau put the fight for social-justice issues above individualistic goals. After the death of Juan B. Justo's first wife (Mariana Cherkov), Moreau married him in 1922, despite the objections of Justo's sister Sara, a dentist and prominent feminist. Moreau wrote influential books, including *La emancipación civil de la mujer* (1919), *El feminismo en la evolución social* (1911), *El socialismo según la definición de Juan B. Justo* (1946), and *¿Qué es el socialismo en la Argentina?* (1983). The influence of the Socialist Party declined in the 1930s after the defeat of the de la Torre–Repetto presidential ticket, splits in the party, and political repression. Although they belonged to different political camps, Moreau and the writer Victoria Ocampo led the women's movement in the 1930s and fought proposed changes in the Civil Code. Moreau opposed Peronism and said in a 1977 interview that she never understood completely the importance of nationalism to Argentines. In 1984 she was named Woman of the Year and Physician of the Century, and her one-hundredth birthday was celebrated throughout the nation.

See also **Argentina, Political Parties: Socialist Party.**

BIBLIOGRAPHY

Blas Alberti, *Conversaciones con Alicia Moreau de Justo y Jorge Luis Borges* (1985).

Marifrán Carlson, *Feminismo! The Woman's Movement in Argentina from Its beginning to Eva Perón* (1988).

Mirta Henault, *Alicia Moreau de Justo: Biografía* (1983).

Lily Sosa De Newton, *Diccionario biográfico de mujeres argentinas* (1986).

Additional Bibliography

Cichero, Marta. *Alicia Moreau de Justo.* Buenos Aires: Planetas, 1994.

Henault, Mirta. *Alicia Moreau de Justo: "Dad paso a la honradez, al trabajo, a la justicia."* Argentina: CUATA Ediciones, 2002.

GEORGETTE MAGASSY DORN

MOREIRA DA COSTA RIBEIRO, DELFIM (1868–1920). Delfim Moreira da Costa Ribeiro (*b.* 7 November 1868; *d.* 1 July 1920), president of Brazil (November 1918–July 1919). Moreira was a native of Minas Gerais, one of the most influential states of Brazil's First Republic (1889–1930). In the years following graduation from the São Paulo School of Law, the premier training ground for the Republican elite, Moreira garnered the support of the Partido Republicano Mineiro in several successful campaigns for state office. From 1914 to 1918 Moreira served as *presidente* (governor) of Minas Gerais, where he gained a national reputation as a skillful leader of the state's powerful political and economic interests.

In 1918 Moreira was elected vice president of Brazil on a ticket with *Paulista* presidential candidate Rodrigues Alves. However, Moreira was sworn in as interim president when Alves was too ill to assume the presidency on the day of inauguration. Alves died on 18 January 1919, and Moreira's interim presidency was extended pending the appointment of a new president. During his eight-month presidency, Moreira himself fell ill and the majority of daily presidential duties were carried out by the minister of the interior, Afrânio de Melo Franco. In July 1919 the federal legislature voted Epitácio Pessoa president and Moreira resumed his position as vice president, which he held until his death a year later.

BIBLIOGRAPHY

Raúl Alves Da Souza, *História política dos governos da república* (1927).

John D. Wirth, *Minas Gerais in the Brazilian Federation, 1889–1937* (1977).

E. Bradford Burns, *A History of Brazil* (1980).

Additional Bibliography

Beattie, Peter M. *The Human Tradition in Modern Brazil.* Wilmington, DE: SR Books, 2004.

Schnieder, Ronald M. *Order and Progress: A Political History of Brazil.* Boulder, CO: Westview Press, 1991.

DARYLE WILLIAMS

MOREJÓN, NANCY (1944–). Nancy Morejón (*b.* 7 August 1944), Cuban poet. Born in Havana to Angélica Hernández and Felipe Morejón, she received a degree in French from the University of Havana. A translator, journalist, editor, and director of the Centro de Estudios del Caribe at Casa de las Américas, Morejón has published four critical studies and eleven collections of poetry. Her lyrical verse, shaped by an Afro-Cuban sensibility and a feminist consciousness, evokes the intimacy of family, the ephemerality of love, and the significance of Cuban history. Poems like "Black Woman" and "I Love My Master" have been widely anthologized and translated. In 1986, her work *Piedra pulida* won the *Cuban Premio de la Crítica.* She was the first black woman to win Cuba's National Prize for literature, in 2001.

See also **Literature: Spanish America.**

BIBLIOGRAPHY

Translations include *Grenada Notebook,* translated by Lisa Davis (1984); *Where the Island Sleeps Like a Wing,* translated by Kathleen Weaver (1985); and *Ours the Earth,* translated by J. R. Pereira (1990). On Morejón, see Susan Willis, "Nancy Morejón: Wrestling History from Myth," in *Literature and Contemporary Culture* 1 (1984–1985): 247–256; Claudette Rosegreen-Williams, "Re-writing the History of the Afro-Cuban Woman: Nancy Morejón's 'Mujer negra,'" in *Afro-Hispanic Review* 8, no. 3 (1989): 7–13; Yvonne Captain-Hidalgo, "Nancy Morejón," in *Spanish American Women Writers,* edited by Diane Marting (1990); Keith Ellis, "Nancy Morejón," in *Spanish American Authors: The Twentieth Century,* edited by Angel Flores (1992).

Additional Bibliography

Pérez Sarduy, Pedro, and Jean Stubbs. *Afro-Cuban Voices: On Race and Identity in Contemporary Cuba.* Gainesville: University Press of Florida, 2000.

Rowell, Charles H. *Making Callaloo: 25 Years of Black Literature, 1976–2000.* New York: St. Martin's Press, 2002.

Tapscott, Stephen. *Twentieth-Century Latin American Poetry: A Bilingual Anthology.* Austin: University of Texas, 1996.

MIRIAM DECOSTA-WILLIS

MORELOS. Morelos, Mexican state created in 1869. Covering 1,976 square miles, Morelos borders on the states of Puebla, Guerrero, Mexico, and the Federal District. Altitudes range from 17,700 feet above sea level in the mountainous north to 2,624 feet in the south.

Between 1430 and 1437 the Triple Alliance, dominated by Tenochtitlán, conquered the indigenous Tlahuica and Xochimilca peoples of Morelos. After Spaniards entered the area in 1521, the conqueror Hernán Cortés incorporated its most prosperous communities into his *encomienda.* By 1550, epidemics of European diseases had reduced the local population from a precontact estimate of 725,000 to about 158,000. The cultivation of sugarcane, introduced in the 1520s, expanded rapidly between 1580 and 1630 as aspiring *hacendados* accumulated land through governmental grants and other means. Throughout the colonial period, indigenous villagers produced fruits, vegetables, and maize for Mexico City markets, while prospects for small-scale commercial agriculture attracted many Spaniards, mestizos, and mulattoes to the area. By 1800 non-Indians outnumbered Indians in most major communities.

Late colonial expansion of sugar haciendas accelerated competition for land and water, and spawned local support for the insurgent José María Morelos y Pavón. After 1821 the area formed part of the state of Mexico. Outbursts of discontent continued: in the 1850s local villagers endorsed Juan Álvarez's Revolution of Ayutla, hoping that a liberal victory would help them defend their lands and water from the *hacendados.* However, the liberals who came to power in 1854 forcefully stifled agrarian unrest in the region. In 1869 the government of Benito Juárez created the state of Morelos, appointing the liberal general Francisco Leyva as governor.

The introduction of railroads and steam-powered equipment in the 1880s further stimulated sugar cultivation at the expense of village agriculture. By 1910 national political ferment provided an opening for local leaders, led by Emiliano Zapata, to challenge the power of the *hacendados.* Heavy fighting during the 1910 Revolution destroyed many haciendas, while the state's population declined from 180,000 in 1910 to 103,500 in 1921. Overturning an earlier redistribution sponsored by Zapata, the government of Álvaro Obregón formalized local land reform, creating 120 *ejidos* on three-fourths of the state's arable land.

After 1930 the numbers of landless peasants rapidly increased. By 1960 the state's population had reached 386,000, and by 2005, it had reached 1,612,899. Since the 1930s commercial agriculture has remained the economic mainstay of Morelos. Sugarcane continues to be important, with many *ejidos* producing for the cooperative mill at Zacatepec. Other crops include rice, sorghum, peanuts, maize, fruits, and vegetables. Tourism has grown, as entrepreneurs have converted colonial haciendas into lavish resorts.

See also **Sugar Industry.**

BIBLIOGRAPHY

John Womack, *Zapata and the Mexican Revolution* (1969).

G. Michael Riley, *Fernando Cortés and the Marquesado in Morelos* (1973).

Arturo Warman, *"We Come to Object": The Peasants of Morelos and the National State,* translated by Stephen K. Ault (1980).

Guillermo De La Pena, *A Legacy of Promises: Agriculture, Politics, and Ritual in the Morelos Highlands of Mexico* (1981).

Cheryl E. Martin, *Rural Society in Colonial Morelos* (1985).

Additional Bibliography

Hernández Chávez, Alicia. *Mexico: A Brief History.* Berkeley: University of California Press, 2006.

Scharrer Tam, Beatriz. *Azúcar y trabajo: Tecnología de los siglos XVII y XVIII en el actual estado de Morelos.* Mexico: CIESAS: Instituto de Cultura de Morelos: Miguel Angel Porrua, 1997.

CHERYL ENGLISH MARTIN

MORELOS Y PAVÓN, JOSÉ MARÍA (1765–1815). José María Morelos y Pavón (*b.* 30 September 1765; *d.* 22 December 1815), foremost Mexican insurgent leader in the struggle for independence. Born in Valladolid, he worked as a scribe and accountant from 1779 to 1790, when he began ecclesiastical studies at the College of San Nicolás, where he met Miguel Hidalgo y Costilla (1753–1811). In 1795 he entered the Tridentine Seminary and presented his bachelor of arts exam at the University in Mexico City. In 1796, he went to Uruapan as an auxiliary priest. He was ordained presbyter in December 1799 and served as parish priest of Churumuco and La Huacana and later of Carácuaro and Nocupétaro. Upon learning of the Hidalgo revolt, he joined the insurgent leader in Charo and Indaparapeo in October 1810. When Hidalgo commissioned him to raise troops in the south, Morelos solicited leave from the See of Valladolid, returned to Carácuaro, and began his first campaign. With twenty-five men, he moved through Nocupétaro, Huetamo, Coahuayutla, Zacatula, and Petatlán, where he obtained men and weapons. In Tecpan, he was joined by Galeanas, including Hermenegildo Galeana (1762–1814), who later became his lieutenant. After obtaining his first cannon there, he then marched toward Acapulco. En route, in Coyuca, he was joined by Juan Álvarez (1790–1867).

José Maria Morelos y Pavón (1765–1815), 1812–1813 (oil on canvas), Mexican School painting (19th century). MUSEO NACIONAL DE HISTORIA, MEXICO CITY, MEXICO/ PHOTO: MICHEL ZABE / AZA/ INBA/ THE BRIDGEMAN ART LIBRARY

In addition to organizing troops, Morelos addressed political and social questions. On 17 November 1810, he issued an order abolishing slavery, the caste system, and *cajas de comunidad* (community treasury). He also engaged the royalists in battle in various places, among them El Veladero and La Sabana. Unable to capture Acapulco in February 1811, Morelos laid siege to the port. He returned to Tecpan, where he organized the government of that province. He then headed toward Chilpancingo and while still en route sent two commissioners to the United States to seek aid. Joined by the Bravos (Leonardo, Víctor, Máximo, Miguel, and Nicolás) at the Hacienda of Chichihualco, Morelos entered Chilpancingo on 24 May and two days later took Tixtla, where Vicente Guerrero (1783–1831) joined him. There he ordered the creation of a national copper currency and wrote Ignacio Rayón (1773–1832) about forming a governing junta. In August 1811, Morelos sent José Sixto Verduzco as his representative to a meeting convened by Rayón to establish such a junta. At that time he took Chilapa, leaving the south, with the exception of Acapulco, in insurgent hands.

In mid-November, he marched toward Tlapa, thereby initiating his second campaign. He took Chiautla de la Sal and Izúcar, where he was joined by Mariano Matamoros (1770–1814). He proceeded to Cuautla and then to Taxco and Tenancingo. In February 1812, he returned to Cuautla, where he was besieged by Félix María Calleja (*c.* 1755–1828). He successfully defended the town, despite the royalist assault, lack of supplies, and lack of assistance from other insurgents. Forced to break the siege on 2 May, he left for Chiautla, from where he initiated his third campaign on 1 June.

Later that month, La Suprema Junta appointed Morelos captain-general and the fourth member of the body. After assisting Valerio Trujano (1760–1812) in Huajuapan de León, he moved to Tehuacán, where he reorganized his troops. He named Matamoros second in command and appointed Galeana marshall. He also worked on the political organization of the insurgent movement. In October he marched to Ozumba, but was repulsed by the royalists in Ojo de Agua. On 29 October he took Orizaba. Upon his return to Tehuacán he was once again defeated and lost his artillery. But on 25 November he captured Antequera de Oaxaca, where he organized the government of that province, established a mint, and published the paper *El Correo Americano del Sur.* His fourth campaign began in February 1813 when he marched to Acapulco, which he captured on April 12, and then laid siege to the fortress of San Diego, which capitulated on August 20.

Concerned about the disagreements among the members of the junta, Morelos sought to mediate among them. After realizing that the governing body of the insurgency needed to be completely restructured, he instructed the provinces under insurgent control to designate representatives to the Supremo Congreso Nacional Americano. Meeting in Chilpancingo on 14 September 1813, the body structured itself following the guidelines Morelos set forth in his *Reglamento* and his *Sentimientos de la nación.*

After the Congress elected him *generalísimo* in charge of executive power, he initiated his fifth campaign. On 23 December Ciriaco de Llano and Agustín de Iturbide (1783–1824) defeated him in Valladolid. On 5 January 1814, he suffered defeat once again in Puruarán, where Matamoros was captured. In February, Congress removed him as *generalísimo* in Tlacotepec, where he was defeated once more and where he also lost his equipment and papers. Congress then sent him to Acapulco to save the artillery at San Diego, and the following March, removed him from the executive. After burning Acapulco, Morelos marched to Tecpan, Petatlán, and Zacatula. He then moved on to Atijo and to Ario, joining the Congress at Tiripitío. From there they moved to Apatzingán, where the Congress proclaimed the Constitution on 22 October 1814 and named an executive consisting of Morelos, José María de Liceaga (1785–1870) and José María Cos y Pérez (*d.* 1819). During 1815 Morelos remained with the Congress while it wandered, pursued by the royalists. In September Congress decided to move to Tehuacán and charged Morelos with its defense. On 5 November Manuel Concha captured him in Temalaca. He was then taken to Atenango, Cuernavaca, and Mexico City, where he was imprisoned first in the Inquisition and then in the Ciudadela. He was tried, found guilty, and condemned to death after first being defrocked from the priesthood. He was shot in San Cristóbal Ecatepec. His imprisonment and death were the worst blows the insurgent movement received and marked the end of the organized insurgency. In 1823, Morelos was declared *Benemérito de la Patria.* His native city was named Morelia in 1828; the state that bears his name was formed in 1869.

See also **Chilpancingo, Congress of.**

BIBLIOGRAPHY

Virginia Guedea, *José María Morelos y Pavón, Cronología* (1981).

Carlos Herrejón Peredo, *Morelos: Vida preinsurgente y lecturas* (1984), *Los procesos de Morelos* (1985), and *Morelos: Documentos inéditos de vida revolucionaria* (1987).

Ernesto Lemoine, *Morelos: Su vida revolucionaria a través de sus escritos y de otros testimonios de la época* (1965).

Ernesto Lemoine, *Morelos y la revolución de 1810,* 2d ed., (1984).

Alfonso Teja Zabre, *Vida de Morelos* (1959).

Wilbert H. Timmons, *Morelos: Priest, Soldier, Statesman of Mexico* (1963).

Additional Bibliography

Benítez, Fernando. *Morelos.* México: Fondo de Cultura Económica, 1998.

González-Polo, Ignacio. *La estirpe y el linaje de José María Morelos.* México: Universidad Nacional Autónoma de México, 1997.

Hurtado, Alfonso. *Morelos.* Las Rozas, Madrid: Dastin, 2003.

VIRGINIA GUEDEA

MORENO, FULGENCIO (1872–1935).

Fulgencio Moreno (*b.* 9 November 1872; *d.* 1935), Paraguayan journalist, diplomat, and historian. Moreno was descended on his maternal side from several of the founders of the Paraguayan republic, and much of his most important historical work centered on the early period of Paraguay's independence. Born in Asunción, he early decided on a career in journalism and served on the staffs of four major newspapers between 1893 and 1901. Journalism, however, turned out to be a stepping-stone to important political and diplomatic posts. In 1901 he became finance minister, and in 1903, senator. Four years later, the government appointed him to a technical commission to study the rights of Paraguay in the Chaco boundary dispute with Bolivia. Afterward, Moreno turned his efforts to diplomacy more narrowly defined: he served as minister first to Chile and Peru (1913), then to Bolivia (1918), and then back to Chile (1919).

These experiences gave Moreno ample material for his historical pursuits. He was prolific in his production of articles, pamphlets, and books. Among the latter were several works that are still read and admired in Paraguay today. These include *Diplomacia paraguaya-boliviana* (1904), *Estudio sobre la independencia del Paraguay* (1912), *Paraguay-Bolivia,* 3 vols. (1917–1920), and *La ciudad de la Asunción* (1926). Unlike many Paraguayan historians of his era, Moreno concentrated less on military heroes than on literary figures and movements—and thus his work is noteworthy for its appealing cultural emphases.

See also **Paraguay: The Twentieth Century.**

BIBLIOGRAPHY

William Belmont Parker, *Paraguayans of To-Day* (1921), pp. 163–165.

Jack Ray Thomas, *Biographical Dictionary of Latin American Historians and Historiography* (1984).

Carlos Zubizarreta, *Cien vidas paraguayas,* 2d ed. (1985), pp. 228–231.

Additional Bibliography

Farcau, Bruce W. *The Chaco War: Bolivia and Paraguay, 1932–1935.* Westport, CT: Praeger, 1996.

Scavone, Ricardo. *Las relaciones entre el Paraguay y Bolivia en el siglo XIX.* Asunción: Servi Libro, 2004.

THOMAS L. WHIGHAM

MORENO, MARIANO (1778–1811). Mariano Moreno (*b.* 23 September 1778; *d.* 4 March 1811), one of the leading figures of Argentina's independence movement. He studied theology and law in Chuquisaca (now Sucre), Upper Peru, and wrote his dissertation on Indian service, in which he favored their freedom. He was sickly, but what he lacked in physical strength he made up for in a powerful intellect. He became the Jacobin of the May 1810 revolution in Argentina. In 1809 he wrote the *Representación de los hacendados y labradores,* in which he criticized colonial policy and defended free trade. The book represented creole aspirations, and in a way it was written as a criticism of the new viceroy, Baltasar Hidalgo de Cisneros, who had replaced Santiago de Liniers and had repealed many of the latter's liberal policies.

Moreno was appointed secretary to the First Junta, headed by Cornelio de Saavedra. He favored a tough policy toward Spaniards and toward anyone engaged in counterrevolutionary activities. In July 1810, Liniers and his followers rose in revolt against the revolutionary government. The revolt was crushed by Buenos Aires, and as a result of Moreno's insistence, the leaders, including Liniers, were executed. This action led to much criticism against Moreno because Liniers was still considered a hero by many for his contributions to the defense of Buenos Aires against the invading British armies in 1806–1807. Moreno was a firm believer in democratic government, but his radicalism and uncompromising attitude earned him many enemies, even in the junta itself. The showdown occurred when Saavedra imposed reactionary delegates from the provinces on the junta in face of Moreno's opposition. This may very well have been the first confrontation between *unitarios* and *federales.* Faced with a growing Federalist opposition, Moreno resigned from the junta at the end of 1810. His resignation almost caused a rebellion, and to avoid bloodshed, he accepted a diplomatic mission to England and died at sea en route. While in office he helped found the national library and a census bureau and published the *Gaceta de Buenos Aires.*

See also **Liniers y Bremond, Santiago de; Saavedra, Cornelio de.**

BIBLIOGRAPHY

Julio Delfín Martino, *Vida de Mariano Moreno* (1954).

Ricardo Levene, *Historia de Moreno* (1945).

Manuel Moreno, *Vida y memorias del doctor Mariano Moreno, Secretario de la Junta de Buenos Ayres, capital de las provincias del Río de la Plata* (1812).

Additional Bibliography

Egües, Carlos. *Mariano Moreno y las ideas político-constitucionales de su época.* Córdoba, Argentina: Academia

Nacional de Derecho y Ciencias Sociales de Córdoba, 2000.

Dürnhöfer, Eduardo O. *Mariano Moreno.* Buenos Aires: Editorial Dunken, 2000.

JUAN MANUEL PÉREZ

MORGAN, HENRY (c. 1635–1688). Henry Morgan (*b.* c. 1635; *d.* 25 August 1688), the most famous buccaneer of the West Indies from the mid- to late seventeenth century. A bold and brilliant tactician, Henry Morgan, a Welshman, assumed the leadership of the Port Royal, Jamaica, buccaneers after 1665. He first came to the New World, to Barbados, as an indentured servant (c. 1655–1660). Later, Morgan escaped and joined the buccaneers, becoming a prominent leader by his late twenties. A heavy drinker, Morgan acquired wealth and land, was knighted, and after his buccaneering activities ended became lieutenant governor of Jamaica and helped suppress buccaneering.

Morgan's fame reached its height in the late 1660s and early 1670s. In 1668 the governor of Jamaica, Sir Thomas Modyford, commissioned him to carry out a reconnaissance mission in Cuba and then to attack Porto Bello with four hundred buccaneers. After arriving in Cuba, Morgan moved on toward Porto Bello, on the Isthmus of Panama. Although the port was well fortified, with 300 men defending it, Morgan successfully surprised the Spanish by entering at night from a swampy, forested area behind it. In killing the 300 defenders he solidified his reputation for brutality. His followers pillaged and debauched the town.

Instead of moving on to attack Cartagena, Colombia, the center of Spanish naval power, Morgan chose to assault Maracaibo, Venezuela, instead. The booty there was minimal, as the town had been pillaged only a year earlier. Upon leaving, however, he encountered three Spanish ships carrying silver, which he and his men plundered and destroyed or beached.

Morgan mounted his third, final, and biggest expedition, which was also commissioned by Governor Modyford, in 1670. With 1,500 men, one third of whom were Frenchmen from Tortuga, Morgan sacked Santa Marta and Río Hacha, Colombia, and Porto Bello. In December 1670 he marched across the isthmus to attack Panama, where he tortured and murdered most of the inhabitants and destroyed the city.

Following the Treaty of Madrid (1670) peace agreement between England and Spain, the two Jamaican governors, Lord John Vaughan and the Earl of Carlisle, employed Morgan in 1674 as their lieutenant governor, giving him the responsibility of suppressing buccaneers. The lack of military support meant that it was not until 1685, with the arrival of a new naval squadron, that Morgan was able to achieve much success in his effort to combat buccaneering. Morgan died three years later. Despite his later efforts against the buccaneers, in his earlier career, Morgan had carried out a reign of terror and brutality hitherto unsurpassed in the Caribbean.

See also **Buccaneers and Privateers; Piracy.**

BIBLIOGRAPHY

Père P. F. X. Charlevoix, *Histoire de L'Isle Espagnole ou de S. Domingue,* 2 vols. (1731, repr. 1943).

A. D. Exquemelin, *The Buccaneers of America* (1678, repr. 1972).

C. H. Haring, *The Buccaneers in the West Indies in the XVII Century* (1910).

Nellis Maynard Crouse, *The French Struggle for the West Indies, 1665–1713* (1943).

J. H. Parry et al., *A Short History of the West Indies,* 4th ed. (1987).

Dudley Pope, *The Buccaneer King: The Biography of Sir Henry Morgan, 1635–1688* (1978).

Additional Bibliography

Breverton, Terry. *Admiral Sir Henry Morgan: "King of the Buccaneers."* Gretna, LA: Pelican, 2005.

Lane, Kris E. *Pillaging the Empire: Piracy in the Americas, 1500-1750.* Armonk, NY: M.E. Sharpe, 1998.

Petrovich, Sandra Marie. *Henry Morgan's Raid on Panama: Geopolitics and Colonial Ramifications, 1669–1674.* Lewiston, NY: E. Mellen Press, 2001.

BLAKE D. PATTRIDGE

MORGA SÁNCHEZ GARAY Y LÓPEZ, ANTONIO DE (1559–1636). Antonio de Morga Sánchez Garay y López (*b.* 29 November 1559; *d.* 21 July 1636), *oidor* (civil justice) of the Audiencia of the Philippines

(1593–1603), *alcalde del crimen* (criminal judge) of the Audiencia of Mexico City (1603–1615), and president of the Audiencia of Quito (1615–1636). Born in Seville to a wealthy merchant family, this energetic jurist received his doctorate at the University of Salamanca in 1580. After holding several minor judicial posts in Spain, Morga attained first the governorship of the Philippines and later a judgeship in the Audiencia of Manila. He served with some distinction in the Philippines and in 1603 received a coveted promotion to the position of *alcalde del crimen* in the viceregal capital of Mexico City. He escaped blame in the numerous scandals surrounding that court, and in 1615 the crown named him president of the Audiencia of Quito.

During his presidency, Morga battled with the viceroys in Lima to secure more autonomy for the Audiencia in legal and political affairs. He sponsored an unsuccessful effort to build a road from Quito to the coast, through the frontier province of Atacames, to facilitate the export of highland foodstuffs and textiles. He also supported efforts to reorganize the labor and management systems of the highland *obrajes* (textile mills) and to reform Spanish–Native American relations.

Despite Morga's accomplishments, disturbing rumors of dissension on the court and of the president's illegal activities and personal immorality prompted a *visita general* (general investigation) in 1624. The visitor-general, Juan de Mañozca, and his successor, Juan Galdós de Valencia, charged Morga with seventy-three infractions, including illicitly introducing Chinese silks in 1615, carrying on disreputable gambling operations, engaging in unauthorized business ventures, living a scandalous personal life, and failing to observe the normal procedures and regulations governing the audiencia. In 1636 the Council of the Indies found Morga guilty on fifty-six of the charges, levied fines of 31,300 ducats, and suspended him from office for six years. The disgraced president was spared this final indignity, for he had died earlier in the year.

See also **Audiencia; Quito, Audiencia (Presidency) of.**

BIBLIOGRAPHY

Morga's career in Quito is concisely summarized in Federíco González Suárez, *Historia general de la República del Ecuador* (1970): 527–571. The seminal work on the life and times of this controversial jurist is John Leddy Phelan, *The Kingdom of Quito in the Seventeenth Century* (1967).

Additional Bibliography

Andrien, Kenneth J. *The Kingdom of Quito, 1690–1830: The State and Regional Development.* Cambridge: Cambridge University Press, 1995.

Lodoño, Jenny. *Entre la sumisión y la resistencia: Las mujeres en la audiencia de Quito.* Quito: Abya-Yala, 1997.

Ortiz de Tabla Ducasse, Javier. *Los encomenderos de Quito, 1534–1660: Origen y evolución de una elite colonial.* Sevilla: Escuela de Estudios Hispano-Americanos, 1995.

KENNETH J. ANDRIEN

MORILLO, PABLO (1778–1837). Pablo Morillo (*b.* 5 May 1778; *d.* 27 July 1837), Spanish general. General Pablo Morillo was sent to northern South America by Ferdinand VII in 1815 with the title of Pacificador de Tierra Firme. His orders included the charge that he replace General Juan Manuel de Cajigal as captain-general of Venezuela. Morillo's career and meteoric rise to the rank of general paralleled that of many of the generals serving in Ferdinand's army. From the lower class, young Morillo became an officer in 1808 at the age of thirty due to leadership and loyalty displayed against the French at the Battle of Bailén. He was made a general just three years later.

The 1815 expedition to Venezuela under his command included ten thousand men and a fleet of sixty ships. The end of the Napoleonic Wars allowed the metropolitan authorities to confront the Venezuelan insurrection with considerably more manpower. The first military confrontations between Morillo's forces and those of the Venezuelan patriots in April 1815 changed the nature of the war. No longer a civil war between factions of Venezuelans, the hostilities became more directed toward complete separation from Spain. Morillo allied himself with the wealthy planter class that had called for the break with Spain in 1811. Unfortunately for Morillo, too much had changed between 1811 and 1815. The forces unleashed in 1811, especially the *castas,* were too powerful to be ignored, and Morillo's vision of a royalist Venezuela—perhaps a realistic alternative in 1811—was no longer possible. In effect, the arrival of this expeditionary force ended royalist government in Venezuela. The lack of efficient bureaucracy forced Morillo to confiscate property to supply his army of pacification. Relying on terror and the military prowess of his experienced corps, Morillo conquered Venezuela and most of New Granada. He is perhaps best remembered today in Venezuela as a tyrant who ordered the execution of such men as Dr. Camilo Torres and the scientist Francisco de Caldas.

It soon became clear that the final chapter in the war between Spain and Venezuela would be settled by force of arms. The patriot victory at the battle of Boyacá in August 1819 caused Morillo to see the end was at hand. After the liberal rebellion in Spain in 1820, he was ordered to negotiate with the patriots on the basis of the Constitution of 1812. In November 1820 representatives of Símon Bolívar and Morillo signed a six-month armistice. Morillo then returned to Spain, where he was granted the titles of conde de Cartagena and marqués de la Puerta and during the next decade held a number of government offices.

See also **Venezuela: The Colonial Era.**

BIBLIOGRAPHY

Miguel Izard, *El miedo a la revolución: La lucha por la libertad en Venezuela, 1777–1830* (1979).

Stephen K. Stoan, *Pablo Morillo and Venezuela, 1815–1820* (1974).

Francisco Xavier Arámbarri, *Hecos del general Pablo Morillo en América* (1971).

Additional Bibliography

Archer, Christin I. *The Wars of Independence in Spanish America.* Wilmington, DE: Scholarly Resources, 2000.

Quintero Saravia, Gonzalo M. *Pablo Morillo: General de dos mundos.* Bogotá: Planeta, 2005.

GARY MILLER

MORÍNIGO, HIGÍNIO (1897–1983).

Higínio Morínigo (*b.* 1897; *d.* 1983), Paraguayan president (1940–1948) and military leader. Born into a middle-class family in the interior town of Paraguarí, Morínigo decided early on a military career. In 1906 his family moved to Asunción, where he later entered the national military academy.

As a young junior officer in the early 1920s, Morínigo received orders to intervene in a civil conflict then raging between rival groups within the ruling Liberal Party. Though he obeyed these orders, he did so with much resentment—and this experience embittered him toward civilian politicians and their penchant for embroiling the army in their various power struggles. Perhaps because he failed to cater to such politicians, Morínigo soon found himself posted to a series of obscure frontier forts, most of them in the disputed Gran Chaco region.

The Chaco War fought with Bolivia over this same territory (1932–1935) gave Morínigo the chance for rapid promotion. A brief assignment as a regional field commander earned him the rank of major, and in 1936, the Rafael Franco government promoted him to colonel and gave him command of the important garrison of Concepción. By this time, Morínigo had developed considerable popularity among the growing *revolucionario* faction of the officer corps, a base that he used to advance to the post of army chief of staff in 1938 and then to interior minister in 1939 under Félix Paiva. Finally, in May 1940, radicals in the army pressured José Félix Estigarribia to accept Morínigo as war minister. It was from this position that he was forced upon the Liberals as the new president when Estigarribia died in an airplane crash four months later.

As president, Morínigo erected a repressive police state with clear pro-Axis overtones. Despite Paraguay's official neutrality, the government permitted Nazi agents to work more or less openly in the country. At the same time, the United States attempted to woo Morínigo with the promise of aid for highway construction and other projects. In the end, Paraguay declared war on Germany, but only in February 1945.

By that point, Morínigo had chosen to compromise in domestic politics and had begun to ease out the far-right members of his wartime cabinet. He compromised still further in 1946, when he called for a coalition government that included Colorados and Febreristas. This coalition lasted only a few months before radical elements among the Colorados (especially the Guion Rojo group) were battling the Febreristas, Liberals, and Communists in the streets of Asunción.

Unable to control events any longer, Morínigo watched Paraguay slip into the bloody civil war of 1947. Aided by Colorado militias and arms sent from Perón's Argentina, he managed to defeat the rebels, but in so doing became little more than a figurehead for the Colorados. Their own infighting, in turn, made Morínigo's continued presence in the country inconvenient. In 1948, he agreed to retire from politics and went to live in permanent exile in Buenos Aires.

See also **Paraguay, Political Parties: Colorado Party.**

BIBLIOGRAPHY

Harris Gaylord Warren, *Paraguay: An Informal History* (1949), pp. 331–353.

Michael Grow, *The Good Neighbor Policy and Authoritarianism in Paraguay* (1981).

Oscar Peyrou, *Morínigo: Guerra, dictadura, y terror en Paraguay* (1971).

Additional Bibliography

Amaral, Raúl. *Los presidentes del Paraguay (1844–1954): Crónica política.* Asunción: Centro Paraguayo de Estudios Sociológicos, 1994.

Caeiro, Daniel. *Crónica de un matrimonio politico: La relación histórica entre peronistas y colorados.* Asunción: Intercontinental Editora, 2001.

Farcau, Bruce W. *The Chaco War: Bolivia and Paraguay, 1932–1935.* Westport, CT: Praeger, 1996.

THOMAS L. WHIGHAM

MORLEY, SYLVANUS GRISWOLD

MORLEY, SYLVANUS GRISWOLD (1883–1948). The American archaeologist Sylvanus Griswold Morley was an expert in Maya hieroglyphic writing and the public face of Maya studies from the 1920s to late 1940s. Born in Chester, Pennsylvania, on June 7, 1883, Morley earned a BA (1907) and MA (1908) from Harvard and later an honorary doctorate from the Pennsylvania Military College. While still an undergraduate, he undertook archaeological fieldwork in the U.S. Southwest, under the supervision of Edgar L. Hewett. Shortly after finishing his graduate degree, Morley moved to Santa Fe, New Mexico, and accepted a position at the newly founded School of American Archaeology (later the School of American Research). In 1914 he joined the staff of the Carnegie Institution of Washington as the head of a new research program focusing on the ancient Maya. In 1923 he began the Chichén Itzá Project (1924–1940), which excavated and reconstructed many important structures at that ruined city in Yucatan. Until 1929 Morley directed the entire Carnegie Maya program, with archaeological projects at Uaxactún, Guatemala, and elsewhere in Mexico and Central America. A great majority of Maya archaeologists in the first half of the twentieth century trained under Morley and at Carnegie projects.

Morley was the foremost world expert in Maya hieroglyphic writing in the first half of the twentieth century. Although he wrote a still-useful introduction to ancient Maya writing (1915), his scholarly legacy rests upon his great compendia of the inscriptions at Copan, Honduras (1920), and of the Petén, Guatemala (1937–1938). Morley lived and wrote in a time when even the experts thought that the ancient Maya used their writing to record nothing beyond dates and astronomical events, and more than anything, these works are excellent guides to the archaeological sites described and to the chronology of the thousands of Maya inscriptions then known. In an earlier paper on the Lunar Series in Maya dates (1916), Morley proposed a technique of analyzing texts using substitution patterns that decades later became one of the keys to the phonetic decipherment of Maya hieroglyphic writing.

Every fall for forty years, Morley presented public lectures about the ancient Maya to audiences in the United States, Europe, and Latin America. He also wrote much for general audiences, with articles in the *National Geographic Magazine* and a classic book, *The Ancient Maya* (1946), that is still in print. Morley also collaborated on an English-language version (1950) of Adrian Recinos's Spanish translation of the Quiché Maya epic the *Popol Vuh.* And in 1944 he was the impetus behind the monumental English translation of Bernardino de Sahagún's Florentine Codex, completed by Arthur J. O. Anderson and Charles E. Dibble (1950–1982), Morley died on September 2, 1948.

See also **Archaeology; Maya, The; Mayan Epigraphy; Popol Vuh.**

BIBLIOGRAPHY

Primary Works

An Introduction to the Study of the Maya Hieroglyphs. Washington, DC: Government Printing Office, 1915.

"The Supplementary Series in the Maya Inscriptions." In *Holmes Anniversary Volume*, 366–396. Washington, DC: J. W. Bryan Press, 1916.

The Inscriptions at Copan. Washington, DC: Carnegie Institution of Washington, 1920.

The Inscriptions of Petén. 5 vols. Washington, DC: Carnegie Institution of Washington, 1937–1938.

With Delia Goetz and Adrián Recinos. *Popol Vuh: The Sacred Book of the Quiché Maya.* Norman: University of Oklahoma Press, 1950.

Secondary Works

Brunhouse, Robert L. *Sylvanus G. Morley and the World of the Ancient Maya.* Norman: University of Oklahoma Press, 1971.

Harris, Charles H., III, and Louis R. Sadler. *The Archaeologist Was a Spy: Sylvanus G. Morley and the Office of Naval Intelligence.* Albuquerque: University of New Mexico Press, 2003.

Kidder, Alfred Vincent. "Sylvanus Griswold Morley, 1883–1948." *El Palacio* 55, no. 9 (1948): 267–274.

Thompson, J. Eric S. "Sylvanus Griswold Morley, 1883–1948." *American Anthropologist* 51, no. 2 (1949): 293–297.

KHRISTAAN D. VILLELA
EUGENE V. THAW

MORONES, LUIS (1890–1964). Luis Morones (*b.* 11 October 1890; *d.* 6 April 1964), Mexican labor leader of the 1920s. Morones experienced a meteoric rise from electrical worker to the nation's most powerful labor leader within a period of fifteen years. Born in the Federal District, he joined the anarchist-led House of the World Worker (Casa del Obrero Mundial), but ambition soon drove him in another direction. Morones founded a small group within this splintering organization which then formed a separate union, the Regional Confederation of the Mexican Worker (Confederación Regional Obrera Mexicana) in Saltillo, Coahuila, in May 1918.

Using a pragmatic approach in politics through alliances with key figures, Morones supported Álvaro Obregón in the maneuvering which led to the overthrow of President Venustiano Carranza (1917–1920). Morones organized strikes against the Carranza administration and sent armed workers into combat. During the Obregón presidency (1920–1924) Morones headed Mexico's vital government-operated munitions industry. During the administration of Plutarco Elías Calles (1924–1928), Morones reached the pinnacle of his career. He continued as head of the Confederation, by then the nation's largest labor organization, at the same time that he was minister of industry, commerce, and labor. He made decisions in his government post that favored his union and weakened its rivals.

Morones's accomplishments were marred by his flagrant displays of personal wealth and persistent accusations of corrupt and violent methods. Critics also charged that he undermined the autonomy of the labor movement when he tied it to the national government.

Morones fell from power quickly. His opposition to Obregón's successful campaign for the presidency in 1928 factionalized his organized support. Political enemies wrongly accused him of complicity in Obregón's subsequent assassination. Morones's career as a labor leader was effectively ended. He became conservative in later years but had limited influence in labor and political affairs.

See also **Calles, Plutarco Elías; Carranza, Venustiano; Obregón Salido, Álvaro.**

BIBLIOGRAPHY

Barry Carr, *El movimiento obrero y la política en México, 1910–1929,* translated by Roberto Gómez Ciriza (1976), esp. vol. 1, pp. 121–220, vol. 2, pp. 5–63, 115–181.

Marjorie Ruth Clark, *Organized Labor in Mexico* (1934; repr. 1973).

John W. F. Dulles, *Yesterday in Mexico: A Chronicle of the Revolution, 1919–1936* (1961), esp. pp. 236–389, 659–681.

John M. Hart, *Anarchism & the Mexican Working Class, 1860–1931* (1987), esp. pp. 128–129, 151–160, 170–175.

Harvey Levenstein, *Labor Organizations in the United States and Mexico* (1971).

Additional Bibliography

Caulfield, Norman. *Mexican Workers and the State: From the Porfiriato to NAFTA.* Fort Worth, TX: Texas Christian University Press, 1998.

Hodges, Donald Clark. *Mexican Anarchism after the Revolution.* Austin, TX: University of Texas Press, 1995.

Rivera Castro, José. *En la presidencia de Plutarco Elías Calles (1924–1928).* México: Siglo Veintiuno, UNAM, 1996.

JOHN A. BRITTON

MORROW, DWIGHT WHITNEY (1873–1931). Dwight Whitney Morrow (*b.* 11 January 1873; *d.* 5 October 1931), U.S. ambassador to Mexico (1927–1930). Morrow was born in Huntington, West Virginia, and was educated at Amherst College and Columbia University Law School. A Wall Street banker with international experience, he dealt with the troubled relations between Mexico and the United States. He cultivated a positive image for himself in Mexico and for Mexico in the United States as he hosted humorist Will Rogers and aviator Charles Lindbergh at the U.S. embassy in Mexico City. He also had a close working relationship with Mexican President Plutarco Elías Calles, who continued as a powerful influence after his term ended in 1928.

Morrow quickly arranged a temporary settlement of the dispute concerning privately owned oil properties. U.S. oil companies feared confiscation under the Constitution of 1917, but Morrow and Calles devised a compromise in which private concessions remained secure indefinitely if the holders had taken positive acts to exploit the oil before 1917.

Morrow believed that the conflict between the government and the Catholic Church could cause widening chaos. Its most disruptive aspect was the bloody Cristero Rebellion in rural areas of Jalisco and surrounding states. Morrow struggled with complex negotiations involving the papacy, Catholics in the United States, the Mexican government, and the Catholic hierarchy and lay leaders in Mexico before aiding in a settlement in 1929.

In spite of his calming diplomatic influence, Morrow ended his tenure amid controversy. He had advised a slowing of land reform and an increase in the payment of the nation's foreign debt. When the Mexican government discussed these policies (although not entirely because of Morrow), his critics accused him of unwarranted meddling in Mexico's internal affairs.

See also **Cristero Rebellion.**

BIBLIOGRAPHY

L. Ethan Ellis, "Dwight Morrow and the Church-State Controversy in Mexico," in *Hispanic American Historical Review* 38 (1958): 482–505.

Harold Nicholson, *Dwight Morrow* (1935).

Stanley Robert Ross, "Dwight Morrow and the Mexican Revolution," in *Hispanic American Historical Review* 38 (1958): 506–528.

Ronald Steel, *Walter Lippmann and the American Century* (1980), esp. pp. 235–244.

Additional Bibliography

Cárdenas N., Joaquín. *Morrow, Calles, y el PRI: Chiapas y las elecciones del '94.* México, D.F.: Editorial Pac, 1995.

Collado, María del Carmen. *Dwight W. Morrow: Reencuentro y revolución en las relaciones entre México y Estados Unidos, 1927–1930.* México: Instituto de Investigaciones Dr. José María Luis Mora, 2005.

JOHN A. BRITTON

MORSE, RICHARD (1922–2001). Richard McGee Morse (June 26, 1922–April 17, 2001), pensador and pioneering historian, was a unique figure among the first Latin Americanists in the postwar United States. After studying literature, Spain, and Spanish America at Princeton University, Morse took his doctorate at Columbia University, where he first taught and also led in revising and teaching its contemporary western civilization core curriculum. He left to found the University of Puerto Rico's Caribbean studies institute, and then chaired the new history department at State University of New York Stony Brook, taught at Yale and Stanford Universities, and headed the Wilson Center's Latin American program. A key leader in early Latin Americanist institutions by the 1960s, Morse nonetheless criticized their trends as deracinated, instrumentalist, and narrow. He advocated broad, humanistic training, literature, and history practiced as transdisciplinary study. His noted analyses of Latin American political thought and practice emphasized their sense of being part of a larger, natural, moral order, their post-colonial search for charismatic political legitimacy, and their perception of the state as an integrating, patrimonial, symbolic center. His foundational urban work, begun with his "biography" of São Paulo, turned on cities' critical role as cultural and political foci, expressing and shaping their communities and countries. Both the political and the urban studies were interwoven with his abiding preoccupation with Latin American culture. He argued for the humane character of Latin American civilization, beholden to a vital matrix first conceived in seventeenth-century, Catholic Iberia. He suggested that this civilization served as an illuminating contrast to the oppressive, alienated, mechanistic qualities he found in Anglo-American modernity.

See also **Cities and Urbanization.**

BIBLIOGRAPHY

Primary Works

From Community to Metropolis: A Biography of São Paulo, Brazil. Gainesville: University of Florida Press, 1958.

"The Heritage of Latin America." In *The Founding of New Societies: Studies in the History of the United States, Latin America, South Africa, Canada, and Australia*, edited by Louis Hartz, Kenneth D. McRae, Richard Morse, et al. New York: Harcourt, Brace, 1964.

"The Care and Grooming of Latin American Historians, Or, Stop the Computers I Want to Get Off." In *Latin America in Transition: Problems of Training and Research*, edited by Stanley R. Ross. Albany: State University of New York Press, 1970.

"A Prolegomenon to Latin American Urban History." *Hispanic American Historical Review* 52, no. 3 (August 1972): 359–394.

"The Development of Urban Systems in the Americas in the 19th Century." *Journal of Interamerican Studies and World Affairs* 17, no. 1 (1975): 4–26.

El espejo de Próspero: Un estudio de la dialéctica del Nuevo Mundo, translated by S. Mastrangelo. México: Siglo Veintiuno, 1982.

New World Soundings, Culture, and Ideology in the Americas. Baltimore: Johns Hopkins University Press, 1989.

"The Multiverse of Latin American Identity, c. 1920–c. 1970." In *The Cambridge History of Latin America*, vol. 10, edited by Leslie Bethell. New York: Cambridge University Press, 1995.

Secondary Works

Borges, Dain. "Introduction: A Field Guide to Richard Morse's Brazil." *Luso-Brazilian Review* 32, no. 2 (Winter 1995): 3–14.

Needell, Jeffrey D. "Obituary: Richard M. Morse (1922–2001)." *Hispanic American Historical Review* 81, no. 3–4 (Aug.–Nov. 2001): 759–763.

JEFFREY D. NEEDELL

MOSCOTE, JOSÉ DOLORES (1879–1958).

José Dolores Moscote (*b.* 1879; *d.* 1958), Panamanian legal scholar. Moscote gained notoriety in the 1920s for his influential writings on the nature of the state. He opposed the classical tenets of nineteenth-century liberalism and favored a state more active in the life of the country. He participated in the drafting of the highly regarded 1946 constitution. Moscote was rector of the National Institute and vice rector of the National University. His most important works are *Introducción al estudio de la constitución* (1929), *Orientaciones hacia la reforma constitucional* (1934), and *Estudios constitucionales* (1938).

See also **Panama, Constitutions.**

BIBLIOGRAPHY

Carlos Bolívar Pedreschi, *El pensamiento constitucional del Dr. Moscote* (1959).

Jorge Conte Porras, *Diccionario biográfico ilustrado de Panamá*, 2d ed. (1986).

Additional Bibliography

Szok, Peter A. *La última gaviota: Liberalism and Nostalgia in Early Twentieth-century Panama.* Westport, CT: Greenwood Press, 2001.

JUAN MANUEL PÉREZ

MOSHINSKY BORODIANKSKY, MARCOS (1921–).

Marcos Moshinsky Borodianksky (*b.* 20 April 1921), Mexican nuclear physicist. A native of Kiev, Ukraine, his father immigrated to

Mexico in 1928 and became a naturalized citizen five years later. Moshinsky received most of his education in Mexico City, graduating with a chemistry degree from the National University in 1944 before studying physics as an Allen Nun fellow at Princeton University (1946–1949). He became a professor at the National University and a research scientist at the Institute of Geophysics. Moshinsky directed the theoretical nuclear physics section at the National University and edited the Mexican physics review. He was awarded the National Prize in Sciences in 1968 and named a member of the National College in 1972. He often writes for the popular media, including *Excélsior.* In 1985, the Universidad Nacional Autónoma de México (UNAM) awarded him its Prize for the Exact Sciences. He donated the cash portion of the prize to the victims of the September 1985 Mexico City earthquake. He won the Prince of Asturias Prize for Scientific and Technical Investigation in 1988. He is currently a professor of theoretical physics and a researcher at the Physics Institute of UNAM.

See also **Science.**

BIBLIOGRAPHY

Colegio Nacional, *Memoria,* vol. 7 (1973), pp. 271–274.

RODERIC AI CAMP

MOSQUERA, MANUEL JOSÉ (1800–1853).

Manuel José Mosquera (*b.* 11 April 1800; *d.* 10 December 1853), Colombian prelate and reformer. Born in Popayán into southern Colombia's most distinguished family, he studied at its seminary until 1819. He later received his bachelor's degree and his doctorate at Quito, and was ordained in 1823. He served successively as vicar general of the diocese of Popayán (1828), a canon of the Bogotá cathedral (1829), and rector of the University of Cauca (1829–1835). A domestic prelate from 1832, Mosquera was elected archbishop of Bogotá in 1834 and assumed office in September 1835. His erudition and prideful manner combined to alienate many of his subordinates, since he demanded strict canonical behavior of them.

Mosquera revitalized the seminary (1841–1850) and sponsored the Jesuits' return to Colombia (1844). The presidency of his brother Tomás (1845–1849) further politicized his image, already compromised in Liberal eyes. The regime of the Liberal José Hilario López (1849–1953) expelled the Jesuits (May 1850), secularized tithe collections (January 1851), and ended the seminary's autonomy (January 1852). It then demanded archepiscopal acceptance of secular election of the clergy. Mosquera refused. Thereupon the Senate voted his exile (May 1852). In poor health, he left for Rome (September 1852). After visiting New York and Paris, he died in Marseilles.

See also **Mosquera, Tomás Cipriano de.**

BIBLIOGRAPHY

Terence B. Horgan, *El arzobispo Manuel José Mosquera, reformista y pragmático* (1977).

José María Arboleda Llorente, *Vida del illmo: Señor Manuel José Mosquera, arzobispo de Santa Fe de Bogotá,* 2 vols. (1956).

José Restrepo Posada et al., eds., *Antología del ilustrísimo Señor Manuel José Mosquera, arzobispo de Bogotá y escritos sobre el mismo* (1954).

Additional Bibliography

Castrillón Arboleda, Diego. *Tomás Cipriano de Mosquera.* Bogotá: Planeta, 1994.

Lofstrom, William Lee. *La vida íntima de Tomás Cipriano de Mosquera, 1798–1830.* Bogotá: Banco de la República, 1996.

J. LEÓN HELGUERA

MOSQUERA, TOMÁS CIPRIANO DE

(1798–1878). Tomás Cipriano de Mosquera (*b.* 26 September 1798; *d.* 7 October 1878), Colombian president (1845–1849, 1861–1863, 1863–1864, 1866–1867). Born into the Popayán elite, Mosquera had served only briefly in the military (1815–1816) before becoming a captain in 1820. He was a lieutenant colonel by 1822, and colonel by 1824. Severely wounded at Barbacoas, Cauca, in 1824, Mosquera lost most of his left jaw and as a result suffered from a lifelong speech defect. His ambition, dedication, and family connections brought him the intendency of Guayaquil, where in August 1826 he proclaimed Bolívar's dictatorship. He became intendant of Cauca in 1828. His forces routed by Colonel José María Obando in November 1828 at Popayán, he was publicly humiliated by General José María Córdoba before leaving, now a general, as envoy to Peru (1829–1830). Mosquera was in Europe and the United States from 1831 to 1833. Back in Colombia, he was elected to Congress, where, from 1834 to 1837, he opposed Francisco de Paula Santander's administration while sponsoring initiatives for material improvements.

Mosquera's political importance began in 1839, when he became minister of war and, from 1840 to 1842, played a major part in the War of the Supremes. His military reputation secured, he won the presidency in 1845. His term was marked by fiscal, political, and educational reforms and infrastructural advances. Mosquera lived in New York (1851–1854); when his business failed, he returned to Colombia and helped defeat General José María Melo. After being elected senator (1855–1857), Mosquera espoused federalism and founded Cauca State, of which he became governor in 1858. He also organized Bolívar State. By 1860, now a Liberal, he led a revolution against the regime of Mariano Ospina Rodríguez and captured Bogotá in July 1861. Mosquera decreed a harsh program of anticlerical measures, culminating in the abolition of mortmain. The Rionegro Convention of 1863 elected him president once again. He defeated an Ecuadoran army (6 December 1863) at Cuaspud, Nariño.

After a diplomatic mission to Europe (1864–1865), Mosquera was again elected president. His authoritarianism and grandiose military schemes clashed with the Liberal-dominated Congress. Mosquera dissolved it and, a month later, was overthrown by a coup (23 May 1867). He spent 1868–1870 in Peruvian exile. Cauca again elected him governor in 1871, and he served as senator from Cauca in 1876–1877. He died at Coconuco, his estate, about thirty miles from Popayán.

See also **War of the Supremes.**

BIBLIOGRAPHY

Ignacio Arizmendi Posada, *Presidentes de Colombia, 1810–1990* (1989), pp. 79–83.

J. León Helguera, *Mosquera, 1827 a 1842: Un ensayo sobre sus actuaciones políticas*... (1972).

J. León Helguera, "General Mosquera as President," in *South Eastern Latin Americanist* 25 (June 1981): 1–14.

J. León Helguera, "General Mosquera and Cartagena, 1817–1875," in *South Eastern Latin Americanist* 33 (December 1989): 1–15.

John W. Kitchens, "General Mosquera's Mission to Chile and Peru," in *The Americas* 9 (October 1972): 151–172.

Additional Bibliography

Castrillón Arboleda, Diego. *Tomás Cipriano de Mosquera.* Bogotá: Planeta, 1994.

Lofstrom, William Lee. *La vida íntima de Tomás Cipriano de Mosquera, 1798–1830.* Bogotá: Banco de la República, 1996.

J. LEÓN HELGUERA

MOSQUERA Y ARBOLEDA, JOAQUÍN

MOSQUERA Y ARBOLEDA, JOAQUÍN (1787–1878). Joaquín Mosquera y Arboleda (*b.* 14 December 1787; *d.* 4 April 1878), Colombian president (1830), vice president, diplomat, and educator. The eldest sibling of southern Colombia's leading family, Mosquera studied in his native Popayán and in Bogotá, where he received his law doctorate in 1804. After supporting independence in 1810–1814, he traveled in Europe (1815–1817) and engaged in trade in Jamaica and Cartagena (1817–1818) before returning home. He and his father, forced to immigrate to Quito by royalists (1819–1820), became supporters of Bolívar (1821). Mosquera was named minister plenipotentiary for Colombia by Bolívar and negotiated treaties of alliance and friendship with Peru (6 July 1822), Chile (21 October 1822), and Buenos Aires (10 June 1823). He served in the Senate (1825–1826). In 1828 he was a moderating influence in the Ocaña Congress between the forces of Bolívar and Santander and was chosen president, succeeding Bolívar, by the 1830 ("Admirable") Congress. Mosquera proved to be a vacillating president (12 June–5 September 1830) and he was overthrown by General Rafael Urdaneta. He spent 1831–1832 and part of 1833 in Europe and the United States. His intercession with Bolívar (1828–1830) probably saved the life of General Francisco de Paula Santander, and may explain Mosquera's election as Santander's vice president (1833–1835). In that office, he promoted primary and secondary education. Back in

Popayán, he served as rector of Cauca University (1835–1836). Mosquera died in Popayán.

See also **Bolívar, Simón.**

BIBLIOGRAPHY

José M. De Mier, ed., *Testimonio de una amistad. Francisco de Paula Santander y Joaquín Mosquera* (1984).

Guillermo Valencia, "Joaquín Mosquera," in *Colombianos ilustres,* compiled by Rafael M. Mesa, vol. 1 (1916), pp. 243–268.

Additional Bibliography

Castrillón Arboleda, Diego. *Tomás Cipriano de Mosquera.* Bogotá: Planeta, 1994.

Lofstrom, William Lee. *La vida íntima de Tomás Cipriano de Mosquera, 1798–1830.* Bogotá: Banco de la República, 1996.

Reales Orozco, Antonio. *Santander, fundador del estado colombiano.* Bogotá: Tercer Mundo Editores, 1994.

J. León Helguera

MOSQUITO COAST. Historically, the Mosquito Coast (or Mosquito Shore) was an ill-defined, isolated strip of the Caribbean coast of Central America that occasionally became a focus of international confrontation. Centering on Cape Gracias a Dios, where the Coco River bisects the hump of the Central American isthmus, the Mosquito Coast stretched in endless monotony west to Black River in Honduras and south to Bluefields Lagoon in Nicaragua. The partly alluvial and partly coralline, low shoreline was fringed with coconut palms and mangrove trees, dotted with many small islands and reefs, and protected by treacherous shoals and sandbars. Hot and humid, the desolate region was infested with black sand flies, drenched with heavy rains, interrupted by swamps, heavily overgrown, and rife with yellow fever and malaria, to which Europeans proved highly susceptible. Behind the coastal barrier the land rose slightly and opened into a series of broad savannas and heavily wooded pine barrens that were eventually swallowed up by mountains.

The Mosquito Coast was inhabited by a number of Sumu peoples of obscure origins who were basically hunters. The men pursued game, fished the rivers and coastal waters, and harpooned turtles from dugout canoes. The women gathered wild fruits and coconuts and tended rudimentary garden plots of cassava and plantains. Polygynous, basically egalitarian, and lacking formal government, the Sumu peoples lived in scattered clusters.

The Mosquito people were one of the smaller but more aggressive communities living at Cape Gracias a Dios. Some of them absorbed the African survivors of a slave ship wrecked off the coast. These Sambo-Mosquitos emerged as the dominant element on the shore and responded positively to European interlopers in the seventeenth century.

The Spanish did not establish themselves on the Mosquito Coast. Settled on the Pacific side of the isthmus, separated from the Caribbean coast by rugged terrain and hostile indigenous peoples, they lacked any incentive to penetrate the isolated region. During the heyday of buccaneering, European freebooters coasting the region were seen by the Mosquitos as allies against the Spanish. Eventually a few Englishmen settled at Black River on the Honduran coast and provided a refuge for British trespassers in neighboring Belize whenever they were forced by the Spanish to suspend their illegal woodcutting activities. The security of the Black River settlement relied on the Sambo-Mosquitos, who had expanded into that area from Cape Gracias a Dios. Wars with Spain prompted the British to strengthen their position in the Bay of Honduras by forging an interdependent commercial, military, and political triangle linking Jamaica, Belize, and the Mosquito Coast.

From 1749 to 1786 the governors of Jamaica maintained a formal protectorate over the Mosquito Coast to better defend the Belize dyewood and mahogany cutters from Spanish attack. British superintendents befriended the Sumus and Mosquitos and encouraged their resistance to Spanish incursions. Attempting to systematize relations with the various headmen competing for British favor, the superintendents designated one of the numerous chiefs as "king of Mosquitia" and the others as "admirals, governors, and generals." But the nature of the Indian society made this hierarchical organization artificial and ineffective. After a long struggle, the Spanish and British signed the Convention of London on 14 July 1786, whereby the British evacuated the Mosquito Coast in return for permission to cut wood in Belize. Spanish attempts to occupy the region failed because of poor planning, ignorance, and resistance by the local inhabitants.

For the next fifty years, the British government was indifferent to the Mosquito Coast. Some Belize residents, however, continued to maintain ties with the Sumus or Mosquitos, and in 1816 they arranged for the crowning in Belize of Jamaica-educated George Frederick as the "king" of the Mosquito Nation. But the new "nation" continued to complain of British neglect. The Mosquito Coast was unaffected by Central American independence in 1823. Although the new republic presumed sovereignty over the region, it made no attempt to exercise it despite a brief flurry of canal talk. For the next twenty-five years British interest in the Mosquito Coast was limited to various private schemes, beginning with Gregor McGregor's futile attempt to establish a tropical Eden at Black River.

As the mahogany trade became more competitive following a series of reforms in England that challenged the restrictive policies of mercantilism, enterprising Belize cutters in 1836 resurrected the position of Mosquito "king" in order to receive from him permission to cut wood on the Honduran coast. This maneuver raised questions in international circles regarding the nature and extent of the so-called Mosquito Kingdom. Persuaded by local interests of historic British ties with the region, the British government upheld Mosquito sovereignty, thereby encouraging an assortment of mahogany cutters, marginal traders, land speculators, and naive colonizers to secure concessions from the king, Robert Charles Frederick. The anarchy that followed his death in 1842 prompted the British government to appoint an agent, Patrick Walker, to administer the region behind the facade of an underage Mosquito king.

The Mosquito Coast was a mere geographic convenience serving private British interests. Actually, there were two Mosquito Coasts that overlapped at Cape Gracias a Dios. The north coast, oriented toward Belize, was dominated by Sambo-Mosquitos and served the interests of mahogany cutters and land speculators. The eastern coast, oriented toward Jamaica, was inhabited by pure Mosquitos and black Creoles settled around Bluefields, and served the interests of itinerant traders and canal promoters. British attention focused on the western extremity beyond Black River and the southern extremity below Bluefields, two areas that were never an integral part of the Mosquito Coast either historically or culturally.

War between the United States and Mexico had repercussions for the Mosquito Coast. The California gold rush of 1849 flooded Nicaragua with transients en route to California and revived interest in an oceanic canal. The United States rejected Mosquito claims to the San Juan River outlet as a British ploy to control the Caribbean terminus. The United States and England clashed over the nature and extent of the Mosquito nation, the former denying and the latter reaffirming its existence. Finally persuaded that neither was seeking to monopolize the canal project, the two nations signed the Clayton–Bulwer Treaty in 1850, agreeing that neither party would build, operate, or fortify a canal on its own or for its own purposes. Over the next decade England gradually disengaged from the Mosquito Coast and terminated its protectorate. Treaties were signed with Nicaragua and Honduras recognizing their sovereignty over the Coast. Nicaragua accepted responsibility for the welfare of the region's people and recognized the Mosquito king as a tribal chief over an autonomous reservation.

For the next thirty years the Mosquitos remained isolated and ignored by everyone. Local government was monopolized by the Anglicized blacks at Bluefields. Incoming Americans generated a brief boom with the banana industry in the 1880s, but it was confined to the Bluefields area and bypassed native peoples. Britain accepted the Americanization of its former protectorate and the incorporation of the Mosquito reservation into Nicaragua by President José Zelaya in 1894. After 200 years the Mosquito Coast ceased to exist as a separate political entity. In the twentieth century the Mosquitos remained outside the mainstream and were still resisting assimilation in the 1980s, when they were involuntarily drawn into the Contra/Sandinista war. In that war the English-speaking Mosquitos were aligned with the Contras, or were perceived to be aligned with the Contras. This perception led the Sandinista government to respond with a relocation campaign that was devastating to the Mosquito people. The Sandinistas later apologized for their error.

See also **Clayton-Bulwer Treaty (1850).**

BIBLIOGRAPHY

Charles N. Bell, "Remarks on the Mosquito Territory, Its Climate, People, Productions etc., with a Map," in *Journal of the Royal Geographical Society of London* 32 (1862): 242–268.

Eduard Conzemius, *Ethnographical Survey of the Miskito and Sumu Indians of Honduras and Nicaragua* (1932).

José Dolores Gámez, *Historia de la costa de Mosquitos (hasta 1894)*. (1939).

V. Wolfgang Von Hagen, "The Mosquito Coast of Honduras and Its Inhabitants," in *Geographical Review* 30 (1940): 238–259.

Troy Floyd, *The Anglo-Spanish Struggle for Mosquitia* (1967).

William S. Sorsby, "Spanish Colonization of the Mosquito Coast, 1787–1800," in *Revista de historia de América* no. 73–74 (1972): 145–153.

Bernard Nietschmann, *Between Land and Water: The Subsistence Ecology of the Miskito Indians, Eastern Nicaragua* (1973).

Mary W. Helms, "Negro or Indian?: The Changing Identity of a Frontier Population," in *Old Roots in New Lands,* edited by Ann M. Pescatello (1977), 157–172.

Philip Dennis, "The Costeños and the Revolution in Nicaragua," in *Journal of Inter-American Studies and World Affairs* 23, no. 3 (1981): 271–296.

Craig Dozier, *Nicaragua's Mosquito Shore: The Years of British and American Presence* (1985).

Robert A. Naylor, *Penny Ante Imperialism: The Mosquito Shore and the Bay of Honduras, 1600–1914* (1989).

Carlos Maria Vilas, *State, Class, and Ethnicity in Nicaragua: Capitalist Modernization and Revolutionary Change on the Atlantic Coast,* translated by Susan Norwood (1989).

Additional Bibliography

Frazier, Samuel Vincent. *Commerce, Contraband, and Control: Illicit Trade on Nicaragua's Mosquito Coast, 1860–1910.* Austin: University of Texas Press, 2005.

Pineda, Baron L. *The "Port People" of Bilwi: Ideologies of Race, Lexicons of Identity, and the Politics of Peoplehood in the Mosquito Coast.* Chicago: University of Chicago Press, 1998.

Pineda, Baron L. *Shipwrecked Identities: Navigating Race on Nicaragua's Mosquito Coast.* New Brunswick, NJ: Rutgers University Press, 2006.

Waterfield, Robin, and Paul Theroux. *The Mosquito Coast.* Harlow, U.K.: Pearson Education, 1999.

Robert A. Naylor

MOTECUHZOMA I (c. 1397–1468).

Motecuhzoma I (Motecuhzoma Ilhuicamina; *b.* ca. 1397; *d.* 1468/69), Aztec emperor from 1440 to 1468. The elder Motecuhzoma ("He Becomes Angry Like a Lord") was the fifth Mexica ruler, or *tlatoani,* and the first who can be called an emperor: his conquests extended Aztec rule beyond the Valley of Mexico and ensured a luxurious tribute supply. He was the son of Huitzilihuitl, the second *tlatoani,* and Miahuaxihuitl, a Cuauhnahuac (Cuernavaca) princess; the legend of his birth reflects Huitzilihuitl's temporary control over Cuauhnahuac, later reestablished by Motecuhzoma. Miahuaxochitl's sorcerer father sent scorpions and other vermin to guard her. Huitzilihuitl attached a precious greenstone to an arrow he shot over the wall; when Miahuaxihuitl swallowed the stone Motecuhzoma was conceived. The name Ilhuicamina, "He Shoots Arrows at the Sky," by which he was probably known during his lifetime, may have suggested the tale.

According to native histories, Motecuhzoma sent envoys to the mythical origin-places of the Mexica and their deity Huitzilopochtli. With his half-brother Tlacaelel, he codified Aztec law and instituted the Flowery Wars, periodic skirmishes that provided sacrificial victims. The worst crisis of Motecuhzoma's reign was the famine of 1450–1454, which emptied the imperial granaries and forced people to flee to the humid lowlands; intensification of agriculture helped to prevent further famines.

See also **Aztecs; Flowery Wars.**

BIBLIOGRAPHY

Burr Cartwright Brundage, *A Rain of Darts: The Mexica Aztecs* (1972).

Nigel Davies, *The Aztecs: A History* (1980).

Diego Durán, *The Aztecs: The History of the Indies of New Spain,* translated by Doris Heyden and Fernando Horcasitas (1964).

Susan D. Gillespie, *The Aztec Kings: The Construction of Rulership in Mexica History* (1989).

Additional Bibliography

Kaibara, Yukio. *Motecuhzoma Xocoyotzin.* México, D.F.: Ediciones Taller Abierto, 1997.

Read, Kay Almere, and Jason J. González. *Mesoamerican Mythology.* Oxford: Oxford University Press, 2002.

Tsouras, Peter. *Montezuma: Warlord of the Aztecs.* Washington, DC: Potomac Books, 2005.

LOUISE M. BURKHART

MOTECUHZOMA II (c. 1466–c. 1520).

Motecuhzoma II (Moctezuma, Montezuma; *b.* ca. 1466; *d.* ca. 30 June 1520), ninth Mexica ruler (ca. 1502–1520). Motecuhzoma Xocoyotl (or Motecuhzoma the Younger, often designated Motecuhzoma II) was described by an early chronicler as "a man of medium stature, with a certain gravity and royal majesty, which showed clearly who he was even to those who did not know him" (Cervantes de Salazar). Also described as deeply religious, very aware of his status as head of the Mexica ruling hierarchy, and rigid and elitist in his application of law and custom, Motecuhzoma was leader of the Mexica and their empire when, bent on conquest and colonization, Hernán Cortés led an army of Spaniards into Tenochtitlán in 1519.

Motecuhzoma II has long been depicted as superstitious, weak, and vacillating in contrast to the "determined" and "bold" Cortés. This picture is overdrawn and does not accurately portray the multiple, though ultimately ineffective, ways that Motecuhzoma II sought to protect his people and empire in the face of an enemy far different than any he had faced before.

He was chosen as his uncle Ahuitzotl's successor in about 1502. Almost every Mexica *tlatoani* (or supreme ruler) had enlarged the territorial holdings of the empire. Motecuhzoma II did so, though he did not gain as much territory as his immediate predecessor. His conquests followed the general geographic patterns of Ahuitzotl's conquests and lay largely to the east and south of the Valley of Mexico, concentrating especially on central and southern Oaxaca and northern Puebla and adjoining areas of latter-day Veracruz. He ignored areas lying to the west and north of central Mexico, and left the southern regions of the empire still only loosely tied. Continuing warfare with Tlaxcala—and the inability of the Tenochca Mexica and their allies to subdue it—created a political wedge that the Spanish were later able to use to their advantage during the Conquest.

While Motecuhzoma II is reported to have believed that Cortés was the returning deity Quetzalcoatl, it is unlikely that Motecuhzoma or his advisers still thought this when the Spaniards reached Tenochtitlán. Motecuhzoma tried to discourage the Spaniards from their inland march in search of the center of his empire. Unfortunately, one of Motecuhzoma's means of discouraging them was to send gifts such as gold, which only further excited Spanish interest. As the Spaniards moved closer to Tenochtitlán, the Mexica leader attempted to have them captured but to no avail.

When Motecuhzoma II and Cortés finally met, Motecuhzoma again tried to discourage Spanish interest in his empire. But in his much quoted address to Cortés, he acknowledged Spanish military skill and apparently stated that the Mexica would obey the Spanish. Inexplicably, Motecuhzoma allowed himself to be taken captive by Cortés and some of his soldiers. Although Motecuhzoma II sought to form an alliance with Pánfilo de Narváez while imprisoned, he had lost control of events and died in 1520. The Spanish sources generally state that he was stoned by other Mexica and died from his wounds. There is disagreement among Indian sources, though some, such as Chimalpahin, state that the Spaniards killed him. It was left to his successors, Cuitlahua (Cuitlahuac) and Cuauhtemoc, to mount a military opposition, which ultimately failed.

See also **Aztecs; Mesoamerica.**

BIBLIOGRAPHY

Francisco Cervantes De Salazar, *Crónica de Nueva España* (1914).

Bernal Díaz Del Castillo, *The Conquest of New Spain,* translated by J. M. Cohen (1963).

Francisco De San Antón Muñón Chimalpahin Cuauhtlehuanitzin, *Relaciones originales de Chalco Amaquemecan,* translated and edited by Silvia Rendón (1965).

Hernán Cortés, *Letters from Mexico,* translated and edited by Anthony Pagden (1971).

Ross Hassig, *Aztec Warfare: Imperial Expansion and Political Control* (1988).

Additional Bibliography

Carrasco Pizana, Pedro. *The Tenocha Empire of Ancient Mexico: The Triple Alliance of Tenochtitlan, Tetzcoco, and Tlacopan.* Norman: University of Oklahoma Press, 1999.

Carrillo de Albornoz, José Miguel. *Moctezuma, el semidiós destronado.* Madrid: Espasa, 2004.

Headrick, Annabeth. *The Teotihuacan Trinity: The Sociopolitical Strucutre of an Ancient Mesoamerican City.* Austin: University of Texas Press, 2007.

SUSAN KELLOGG

MOTOLINÍA, TORIBIO DE (c. 1487–1569). Toribio de Motolinía (also Toribio de Paredes and Toribio de Benavente; *b.* ca. 1487; *d.* 1569), one of the first twelve Franciscan friars ("Los Doce") who arrived in New Spain in 1524. Born in Paredes, near Benavente, León, Spain, he proudly took "Motolinía," (Nahuatl for "poor") as his name after hearing the indigenous people use it to describe the barefoot Franciscans in their tattered habits as they walked from Veracruz to Mexico City. Converting the local people to Christianity was his primary aim, but he studied and wrote at length about their culture before and after European contact in order to be more effective in his evangelical task.

During the years 1524–1540, Motolinía wrote either three large religious chronicles or three different versions of the same chronicle. Two survive today in modified form as the *Historia de los indios de la Nueva España* and *Memoriales;* the third has been referred to as the *De moribus indorum.* Read and quoted by other colonial chroniclers, these works are valuable to modern ethnohistorians for their depth of detail on indigenous society, religion, food and artisanal production, modes of transportation, and calendrics. In volume and detail, as early first-hand accounts, Motolinía's writings are possibly second only to those of Bernardino de Sahagún.

See also **Franciscans.**

BIBLIOGRAPHY

Toribio de Motolinía, *History of the Indians of New Spain* translated by Elizabeth Andros Foster (1950) and Francis Borgia Steck (1951).

Edmundo O'Gorman, *La incognita de la llamada "Historia de los indios de la Nueva España" atribuida a Fray Toribio Motolinía* (1982).

Georges Baudot, *Historia de los indios de la Nueva España* (1985).

Additional Bibliography

Mosquera, Daniel O. *Motolinía, Olmos, and the Staging of the Devil in Sixteenth-century New Spain.* Ph.D. diss., 1998.

STEPHANIE WOOD

MOVIMIENTO CHAMULA 1869. Between 1865 and 1867 the indigenous people of the district of Ciudad Real, Chiapas, protested to the authorities about excessive taxes and other various abuses inflicted on them by the community's parish priests and teachers. In 1867 they formed a non-Catholic religious cult in the region's town of Chamula, and with it a barter-based market independent of the church, teachers, merchants, and hacienda owners of Ciudad Real. In December 1868, when the authorities of Ciudad Real captured the group's leaders, their supporters organized an army to rescue them. The indigenous army laid siege to Ciudad Real on June 17, 1869, and then entered into negotiations with the city authorities. The leaders were freed in exchange for the teacher and engineer Ignacio Fernández Galindo, his wife Luisa Quevedo, and his helper Benigno Trejo, all of whom had joined the indigenous movement. The government executed Galindo and Trejo, then moved to eradicate the indigenous movement. The rebellion spread to other regions of Chiapas, and after intense battles between indigenous people and government troops aided by the militias of hacienda owners, it ended in the 1870s.

See also **Chalco Agrarian Rebellion of 1868; Chiapas; Díaz, Porfirio; San Cristóbal de las Casas.**

JOSÉ R. PANTUJA REYES

MOVIMIENTO DE MAESTROS 1958. The Movimiento de Maestros of 1958 was a social movement led by Mexican primary and preschool teachers who were members of the National Educational Workers Union. They had two demands: an increase in salaries and union democracy. They opposed the vertical, authoritarian control exercised by the union leaders, who were part of the Institutional Revolutionary Party. The teachers were led by Professor Otón Salazar, who was influenced by the Mexican Communist Party. The movement had some triumphs, but the repression and jailing of its leaders, as well as errors of leadership, caused internal wrangling that led to the movement's defeat in 1960 (Loyo Brambila 1990). The movement is considered to have been a significant precursor of the struggles of the 1980s and a landmark in the collective memory of leftist teachers (Cook 1996).

See also **Mexico, Political Parties: Institutional Revolutionary Party (PRI); Mexico, Political Parties: Partido Comunista Mexicano; Movimiento Ferrocarrilero.**

BIBLIOGRAPHY

Cook, María Lorena. *Organizing Dissent: Unions, the State and Democratic Teachers' Movement in Mexico.* University Park: Pennsylvania State University Press, 1996.

Loyo Brambila, Aurora. *El movimiento magisterial de 1958 en México.* 2nd ed. México D.F.: Ediciones Era, 1990.

Aurora Loyo

MOVIMIENTO DE UNIDAD PLURINACIONAL PACHACUTIK (MUPP).

In 1995 indigenous leaders in Ecuador founded the Movimiento de Unidad Plurinacional Pachacutik (Pachacutik Movement for Plurinational Unity; MUPP) to campaign for political office. Emerging out of years of debate among indigenous organizations over whether to enter the electoral realm and whether to put forward their own candidates or join existing parties, Pachacutik represented a third option, in which indigenous peoples organized as equals with other popular movements. Pachacutik assumed a center-left ideology that opposed neoliberal economic policies and favored a more inclusive and participatory political system.

In its first ten years, Pachacutik had mixed success. In 1996 its leader, Luis Macas, was elected a national deputy in the national assembly, becoming the first indigenous person elected to national office. In 2002, however, he lost a race for the Andean parliament and in 2006 received barely 2 percent of the vote in a presidential bid. Pachacutik achieved more success on a local level. Activists continued to debate hotly whether social justice was best achieved by organizing as part of civil society or as an electoral movement.

See also **Indigenous Organizations; Macas, Luis.**

BIBLIOGRAPHY

Collins, Jennifer. "Linking Movement and Electoral Politics: Ecuador's Indigenous Movement and the Rise of Pachakutik." In *Politics in the Andes: Identity, Conflict, Reform*, edited by Jo-Marie Burt and Philip Mauceri, pp. 38–57. Pittsburgh, PA: University of Pittsburgh Press, 2004.

Marc Becker

MOVIMIENTO FERROCARRILERO.

In February 1958 Mexico's Railroad Workers' Union (Sindicato de Trabajadores Ferrocarrileros, or STF) demanded a salary hike, which was resisted by trade union leaders, business owners, and the government. On June 26, the workers began a strike that led to an agreement with President Adolfo Ruiz Cortinez. Because the STF executive committee (Comité Ejecutivo General, or CEG) was led by trade unionists who had been coopted by management, another mobilization, on July 2, attempted to democratize the union; one of its achievements was the election of Demetrio Vallejo as president of the CEG. The union's collective contracts were subsequently revised, and when workers' demands remained unresolved, another strike was called in March 1959. This time the movement was harshly repressed, with thousands of workers fired and their leaders thrown into jail.

See also **Campa Salazar, Valentín; Mexico, Organizations: Federation of Mexican Labor (CTM); Mexico, Political Parties: Institutional Revolutionary Party (PRI); Mexico, Political Parties: Partido Comunista Mexicano; Movimiento de Maestros 1958.**

BIBLIOGRAPHY

Barrios, Elías. *El escuadrón de hierro.* México: Cultura Popular, 1978.

Campa, Valentín. *Mi testimonio. Experiencias de un comunista mexicano.* México: Cultura Popular, 1978.

Vallejo, Demetrio. *Las luchas ferrocarrileras que conmovieron a México. Orígenes hechos y verdades históricas.* México: Editorial del Movimiento de Liberación Nacional, 1967.

Enrique Esqueda

MOVIMIENTO INDÍGENA PACHACUTIK. The Indigenous Pachacutik Movement (Movimiento Indígena Pachacutik, MIP), a radical and separatist stream of *katarismo* in Bolivia, was founded in 2000 by the often flamboyant and unpredictable Aymara leader Felipe Quispe, el Mallku ("the condor"). In the 2002 elections, MIP won 6 of 130 congressional seats. Quispe, as its presidential candidate, attained 6.1 percent of the popular vote. By the 2005 elections, its influence having waned, it won only 2.2 percent of the popular vote. With the election of indigenous leader Evo Morales to the presidency in January 2006, Quispe and the MIP, which considered Morales a reformer, dropped from active public participation.

See also **Aymara; Katarismo; Morales, Evo; Quispe, Felipe.**

BIBLIOGRAPHY

Albó, Xavier. "El Alto, La Vorágine de Una Ciudad Única." *Journal of Latin American Anthropology* 11, no. 2 (2006): 329–350.

Albro, Robert. "Bolivia's 'Evo Phenomenon': From Identity to What?" *Journal of Latin American Anthropology* 11, no. 2 (2006): 408–428.

Goodale, Mark. "Reclaiming Modernity: Indigenous Cosmopolitanism and the Coming of the Second Revolution in Bolivia." *American Ethnologist* 33, no. 4 (2006): 634–649.

LINDA FARTHING
BENJAMÍN KOHL

MOVIMIENTO JARAMILLISTA. The movimiento Jaramillista (1943–1962) was a peasant movement led by Rubén Jaramillo Ménez (1898–1962) in the state of Morelos, Mexico. Jaramillo had served in the revolutionary forces of General Emiliano Zapata. At the end of the war, around 1920, Jaramillo began a legal battle to acquire land and loans for rice and sugarcane producers, and organized the building of a sugar refinery in Zacatepec that started operations in 1938. Jaramillo's followers (Jaramillistas) came up against land bosses (*caciques*), monopolies, and regional politicians. In 1943, after escaping an assassination attempt, Jaramillo began the first phase of his armed conflict, adopting a strategy of guerrilla warfare. In 1945 his followers accepted amnesty and founded the Morelense Farm and Labor Party (Partido Obrero Agrario Morelense, or PAOM), nominating Jaramillo to run for state governor. Following allegations of electoral fraud and another attempt on his life, Jaramillo returned to armed conflict. In 1951 to 1952 Jaramillo's followers went back to the polls in alliance with the presidential candidate Miguel Henríquez, but the federal government repressed the Henriquista Movement and so began another phase of guerilla action (1952–1958). After another amnesty, the Jaramillistas returned to mostly peaceful means of struggle from 1959 to 1962 (although they invaded the plains of Michapa and El Guarín in 1961, and were defeated). On May 23, 1962, Jaramillo, his pregnant wife, and three of his children were kidnapped in Tlaquiltenango by officers of the Military Judicial Police and executed in the vicinity of the Xochicalco archaeological site.

See also **Mexico: Since 1910; Zapata, Emiliano.**

BIBLIOGRAPHY

Jaramillo, Rubén. *Autobiografía y asesinato.* México: Editorial Nuestro Tiempo, 1967.

Macín, Raúl. *Rubén Jaramillo, profeta olvidado.* México: Diógenes, 1984.

Ravelo, Renato. *Los jaramillistas.* México: Editorial Nuestro Tiempo, 1978.

ADELA CEDILLO

MOVIMIENTO REVOLUCIONARIO TÚPAC AMARU (MRTA). The Movimiento Revolucionario Túpac Amaru (MRTA) is a Peruvian guerrilla organization formed by the 1982 merging of the Partido Socialista Revolucionario–Marxista Leninista and the Movimiento de Izquierda Revolucionaria–El Militante. Rejecting the civilian regime established in 1980, the MRTA advocated social revolution through armed struggle. Leaders of the organization included Víctor Polay Campos (b. 1951), Néstor Cerpa Cartolini (1953–1997), Peter Cárdenas Schulte, Alberto Gálvez Olaechea, and Miguel Rincón Rincón, among others. Although it was never as strong as the Shining Path, the MRTA achieved notoriety through publicity-seeking acts, relying heavily on kidnappings to fund its activities. It developed a network of "people's prisons" where prominent business people were held captive while their ransoms were being negotiated. In the early 1990s the organization suffered severe military setbacks, including the capture of Polay. In an effort to free its jailed comrades, a group of seventeen militants seized the residence of the Japanese ambassador to Peru on December 17, 1996, holding hostage the ambassador and many other high officials. The siege finally came to an end on April 22, 1997, when the Peruvian military stormed the residence and killed all of the MRTA guerillas, including its leader, Cerpa. After this, the MRTA declined significantly.

See also **Polay Campos, Víctor.**

BIBLIOGRAPHY

"Peru State Attorney Seeks Fujimori Murder Charges." Cable News Network, March 9, 2001. Available from http://www.latinamericanstudies.org/peru/fujimori-mrta.htm.

Tulchin, Joseph, and Gary Bland. *Peru in Crisis: Dictatorship or Democracy?* Boulder, CO: Lynne Rienner, 1994.

JULIO CARRION

MOVIMIENTO REVOLUCIONARIO TUPAJ KATARI DE LIBERACIÓN (MRTKL).

The most electorally successful party of the Bolivian Aymara nationalist movement, known as Katarismo, was the Movimiento Revolucionario Tupaj Katari de Liberación (MRTKL), which first competed in 1985 national elections, winning two deputies' seats. Víctor Hugo Cárdenas, an Aymara intellectual and educator, held one seat, and under his leadership the MRTKL joined a winning electoral alliance in 1993. Cárdenas then became the country's first indigenous vice president, serving until 1997. Seeking a distinct identity for Indians, the MRTKL also sought incorporation into the existing political process. After 1997 Cárdenas failed to institutionalize the MRTKL, and it faded from prominence.

See also **Aymara; Bolivia: Bolivia Since 1825; Cárdenas, Víctor Hugo; Movimiento Indígena Pachacutik.**

BIBLIOGRAPHY

Patzi Paco, Félix. 1999. *Insurgencia y sumisión. Movimientos indígeno-campesinos (1983-1998).* La Paz, Bolivia: Muela del Diablo Editores.

Ticona Alejo, Estaban, Gonzalo Rojas Ortuste, and Xavier Albó. 1995. *Votos y Wiphalas: Campesinos y pueblos originarios en democracia.* La Paz, Bolivia: CIPCA Cuadernos de Investigación.

Van Cott, Donna Lee. 2003. "Institutional Change and Ethnic Parties in South America." *Latin American Politics and Society.* 45, no. 2: 1–40.

BENJAMÍN KOHL

MOVIMIENTO SINARQUISTA.

The Movimiento Sinarquista (synarchist movement) was a popular, nationalist, Catholic movement that began in May 1937 in the city of León, Guanajuato, Mexico. Its leading party, the Unión Nacional Sinarquista (National Synachist Union, or UNS), succeeded the National Catholic Party (1910–1913) and the Catholic organization La Base, and opposed the anticlerical principles and the social program of the government of President Lázaro Cárdenas (1934–1940). The movement's founders and principal leaders were José Antonio Urquiza (?–1938), who had collaborated with the Phalange in the Spanish civil war, José Trueba Olivares, Manuel Zermeño, and Salvador Abascal (1910–2000). Its support came from peasants and the middle class of Mexico's west-central region of Bajío. It received recognition from the Anti-Communist Center, founded in 1936 by the Nazi sympathizer Helmut Oskar Schreiter, and had ties to the Mexican Revolutionary Action Party, the Social Democrat Party, the Mexican Nationalist Vanguard Party and anti-Communist, anti-Semitic, and pro-Franco organizations. The UNS began to decline in 1943 due to internal divisions, agreements between the state and the Catholic Church hierarchy, and the lack of an economic and political program.

See also **Cárdenas del Río, Lázaro; Mexico, Political Parties: National Action Party (PAN).**

LAURA PEREZ ROSALES

MOVIMIENTO VASCONSELISTA 1929–1930.

José Vasconcelos Calderón (1882–1959), Mexico's first secretary of education during the government of Álvaro Obregón (1920–1925), laid the foundations of the national education system, promoted the National Teachers School, embarked on cultural missions in the country's poorest and most marginal regions, and reorganized the National University.

Vasconcelos distanced himself from the group in power and decided to leave the country when Obregón was reelected president. He returned in 1928 to launch a campaign for the presidency. Supported mainly by university students, he led a highly successful electoral campaign and won Mexico's main cities, but amid allegations of fraud the regime handed the presidency to its official candidate, Pascual Ortiz Rubio, and Vasconcelos went into exile once again. Before leaving the country he called on his fellow party members to take up arms to defend his triumph at the polls, through a manifesto issued on December 10, 1929. This was the end of the Vasconcelos movement.

See also **National Autonomous University of Mexico (UNAM).**

José R. Pantoja Reyes

MOYA DE CONTRERAS, PEDRO

(c. 1530–1591). Pedro Moya de Contreras (*b.* 1530?; *d.* December 1591?), first inquisitor (1570–1573) and third archbishop of Mexico (1573–1591?), interim viceroy (1584–1585), and president of the Council of the Indies (1591). Moya was born in the village of Pedroche, in the province of Córdoba, Spain. After studies at Salamanca (1551–1554) he came under the patronage of Juan de Ovando, later the president of the Council of the Indies. In 1570 he was appointed first inquisitor of Mexico and in 1573 he was named archbishop of Mexico. From 1583 until 1586 he conducted a visita of the civil government of New Spain, the most exhaustive of the colonial period. His most important achievement was the Third Mexican Provincial Council of 1585, which established the organization of the church in New Spain. After his return to Spain in 1586, he acted as unofficial adviser to Philip II. He died in Madrid.

See also **Council of the Indies.**

BIBLIOGRAPHY

Cinco cartas del illmo. y excmo. Señor D. Pedro Moya de Contreras, arzobispo-virrey y primer inquisidor de la Nueva Espanna. Precedidas de la historia de su vida segun Cristóbal Gutiérrez de Luna y Francisco Sosa (1962).

Stafford Poole, C.M., *Pedro Moya de Contreras: Catholic Reform and Royal Power in New Spain, 1571–1591* (1987), and "The Last Years of Archbishop Pedro Moya de Contreras, 1586–1591," in *The Americas* (July 1990): 1–38.

Additional Bibliography

Cummins, Victoria Hennessey. "Blessed Connections: Sociological Aspects of Sainthood in Colonial Mexico and Peru." *Colonial Latin American Historical Review* 3:1 (Winter 1994): 1–18.

Traslosheros Hernández, Jorge E. *Iglesia, justicia y sociedad en la Nueva España: La audiencia del arzobispado de México, 1528-1668.* México D.F.: Editorial Porrúa: Universidad Iberoamericana, 1994.

Stafford PooleC.M.

MOYANO, MARÍA ELENA

(1958–1992). María Elena Moyano, a community leader and activist of Afro-Peruvian descent, was murdered by Shining Path guerrillas on February 15, 1992. Moyano's activism was forged in her youth in the shantytown of Villa El Salvador (VES), renowned for its community organization. A founding member of the Popular Federation of Women of Villa El Salvador (FEPOMUVES), Moyano helped organize hundreds of communal soup kitchens and women's groups in VES. An active member of the United Left, Moyano was elected deputy mayor of VES in 1989 and became a vocal opponent of both Shining Path violence and government repression. Moyano's murder epitomizes the terrorist violence of Shining Path; her life exemplifies the struggles of poor Peruvians to improve their circumstances amid a brutal and degrading internal conflict.

See also **Peru, Revolutionary Movements: Shining Path; Villa El Salvador; Women.**

BIBLIOGRAPHY

Moyano, María Elena. *The Autobiography of María Elena Moyano: The Life and Death of a Peruvian Activist*, edited and annotated by Diana Miloslavich Túpac, translated by Patricia S. Taylor Edmisten. Gainesville: University Press of Florida, 2000.

Burt, Jo-Marie. "Shining Path and the 'Decisive Battle.' In Lima's *Barriadas: The Case of Villa El Salvador.*" In

Shining and Other Paths: War and Society in Peru, 1980–1995, edited by Steve J. Stern, pp. 267–306. Durham, NC: Duke University Press, 1998.

JO-MARIE BURT

MOZIÑO, JOSÉ MARIANO

MOZIÑO, JOSÉ MARIANO (1757–1820). José Mariano Moziño (*b.* 24 September 1757; *d.* 19 May 1820), natural scientist, theologian, and author. Moziño, born in Temascaltepec, Mexico, to Spanish parents, received a bachelor of philosophy degree from the Seminario Tridentino in 1776 and was awarded an academic degree in scholastic theology and ethics in 1778. Turning his attention to other fields, Moziño earned his bachelor of medicine from the Royal and Pontifical University in 1787 and completed the course in botany at the Royal Botanical Garden in Mexico City in 1789. In 1792 he joined the expedition of Juan Francisco de la Bodega y Quadra to the Pacific Northwest, where he wrote a description of the Nootka Sound area of Vancouver Island that included a detailed history of the native peoples. Upon returning to Mexico in 1793, Moziño conducted field trips throughout southern Mexico and Guatemala before traveling to Spain in 1803. He served as president of Spain's Royal Academy of Medicine and director of the Royal Museum of Natural History. Caught up in the problems of the French invasion, Moziño was exiled to France in 1812. He received permission to return to Madrid in 1817, but he died en route in Barcelona. Moziño was a dedicated scientist who, under different circumstances, could have brought international recognition to Spain and Mexico in the fields of botany and ethnography.

See also **Bodega y Quadra, Juan Francisco de la.**

BIBLIOGRAPHY

Iris H. W. Engstrand, *Spanish Scientists in the New World: The Eighteenth-Century Expeditions* (1981).

Rogers McVaugh, *Botanical Results of the Sessé and Mociño Expedition, 1787–1803* (1977).

José Mariano Moziño, *Noticias de Nutka: An Account of Nootka Sound in 1792,* translated and edited by Iris H. W. Engstrand (1970, 1991).

Additional Bibliography

Aceves Pastrana, Patricia. *Química, botánica, y farmacia en la Nueva España a finales del siglo XVIII.* México, D.F.: Universidad Autónoma Metropolitana, Unidad Xochilmico, 1993.

Lozoya, Xavier. *Plantas y luces en México: La real expedición científica a Nueva España (1787–1803).* Barcelona: Ediciones del Serbal, 1984.

IRIS H. W. ENGSTRAND

MPB: MÚSICA POPULAR BRASILEIRA

MPB: MÚSICA POPULAR BRASILEIRA. "MPB" designates contemporary middle-class popular music in Brazil beginning with a generation that emerged around 1965. It is a hybrid body of music first produced during the second generation of bossa nova, when many composers and performers turned away from the jazzy sophistication of the original style toward more heritage-derived arrangements. MPB identifies urban popular music—that is, separate from the folkoric, traditional, or rural—yet with a broadly defined national orientation, so as to be distinct from foreign imports and other new national forms considered to be foreign-inspired. The acronym denotes not a discrete style but a general practice of modern popular music, usually acoustic and politically aware, setting it apart from local renditions of Anglo-American rock 'n' roll called *iê-iê-iê* ("yeah-yeah-yeah") that were marketed as part of a scheme called *Jovem Guarda* ("young guard").

As bossa nova diversified in the early to mid-1960s, regional rhythms, traditional instruments, and models of oral poetry were integrated into new schemes. In keeping with the prevailing attitudes of the educated middle-class in the mid-1960s, typical MPB lyrics spoke of social injustice, political repression, and folk culture. The initials "MPB" began to be used in 1965 during festivals of popular music, songwriters' competitions with live performances, and televised final rounds. At these events, electric instruments and music in the rock mode were not initially permitted or accepted by the audience. As early as 1967, however, electric guitars were introduced into the festival format by *tropicalismo*, a musical movement that changed the face of MPB by challenging facile divisions between "nationalistic" and "foreign" music. Even though some tropicalist songs had evident nontraditional elements, the music could still be considered MPB in comparison to overtly imitative *iê-iê-iê*.

With the assimilation of rock into Brazilian popular music in the 1970s, lines dividing "nationalistic" from "foreign-inspired" became increasingly blurred. In the mid-1980s national rock became dominant in the marketplace, and "MPB" began to be employed differently. It largely came to be used to distinguish the music of the rock-dominated 1980s generation from that of the previous generation. "MPB" thus designated less a musical orientation and more the work of musicians born in the 1940s who made their names in the 1960s or early 1970s. Since the 1980s some have employed the term "MPB" in a historically less discriminating sense to refer to Brazilian popular music in general, with no distinction of decade or stylistic orientation. From the 1990s into the 2000s, "MPB" has been used to refer to diverse singer-songwriters, including those associated with neo-Afro-Brazilian material in Bahia (*axé* music) and even local hip-hop and rap artists.

What characterizes MPB in the most general sense, over the years, is an originality of composition that may diversify samba, the traditions of northeastern Brazil, Afro-Bahian folklore, and international trends; if the immediate source was bossa nova, some MPB artists went on to incorporate rock elements. The prime singer-songwriters of MPB are Chico Buarque, Caetano Veloso, Gilberto Gil, Milton Nascimento, Jorge Ben, Edu Lobo, João Bosco, Djavan, and Ivan Lins. Younger artists of note include Chico César, Zeca Baleiro, and Chico Science (d. 1996) and his band Nação Zumbi, all of whom hail from the northeastern region and form part of a "new generation." The vanguard rock-inflected efforts of Arnaldo Antunes are legendary. Leading vocalists whose selection of repertoire best reflects the contemporary music of the country are Elis Regina (d. 1981), Maria Bethânia, Gal Costa, Simone, Elba Ramalho, Marisa Monte, and Daniela Mercury. MPB was an important expression of politics and art in the 1960s and embodied cultural modernization during the military regime (1964–1985); in the age of digital recording and the Internet, it reflects local and global changes in music-making.

See also **Bossa Nova; Buarque, Chico; Gil, Gilberto; Music: Popular Music and Dance; Nascimento, Milton; Regina, Elis; Samba; Tropicalismo; Veloso, Caetano.**

BIBLIOGRAPHY

Dunn, Christopher. *Brutality Garden: Tropicália and the Emergence of a Brazilian Counterculture.* Chapel Hill: University of North Carolina Press, 2001.

McGowan, Chris, and Ricardo Pessanha. *The Brazilian Sound: Samba, Bossa Nova and the Popular Music of Brazil,* new edition. Philadelphia: Temple University Press, 1998.

Perrone, Charles A. *Masters of Contemporary Brazilian Song: MPB, 1965–1985.* Austin: University of Texas Press, 1989.

Perrone, Charles A., and Christopher Dunn, eds. *Brazilian Popular Music and Globalization.* Gainesville: University Press of Florida, 2001.

CHARLES A. PERRONE

MUCKERS' REBELLION. Muckers' Rebellion, millenarian uprising (1872–1874) organized by a second-generation German Protestant immigrant couple, Jacobina and João Jorge Maurer, in the community of Ferrabrás, in Rio Grande do Sul, Brazil. João Maurer gained fame as a healer throughout the municipality, and Jacobina had gathered a following by interpreting biblical passages and entering a trance state at will. The rebellion's roots date to 1872, when the Maurers and their followers began preaching an end of the world and advising a separatist existence. This alienated other residents of Ferrabrás. By 1873, the Maurers and their growing sect were living as a commune at Ferrabrás, with Jacobina claiming to be the reincarnation of Christ. Tensions heightened when local inhabitants labeled them "os Muckers," a term synonymous with "fanatic" or "hypocrite," and many viewed their activities as a threat to the entire province. Jacobina was derided as "the Sainted Christ" and violent behavior (including murder) was attributed to the Muckers.

Believing that they could get no help from local or provincial authorities, the Muckers appealed directly to the emperor but received no reply. Desperate, they purchased arms to protect themselves, declaring that the end of the world was near and that God had chosen them to exterminate their enemies. After the burning of thirteen homes by the Muckers on June 25, 1874, the district chief of police responded on June 26 by attacking the Mucker premises. On August 2, after a major assault by National Guard troops, 120 members of the sect either were killed, surrendered, or escaped. Jacobina was among those killed. Her husband's whereabouts were never discovered.

The Muckers' rebellion was one of a series of movements in late-nineteenth-century Brazil, including Quebra-Quilos (1874–1875), the millenarian movements of Juazeiro (1899–present), Canudos (1893–1897), and the later Contestado Rebellion (1912–1916), which resulted from the shifting political climate of the Brazilian Empire, church-state conflicts, the modernization of transportation systems that brought in new immigrants and so increased the conflict between new and old settlers, and tensions among Catholic and Protestant immigrants.

See also **Messianic Movements: Brazil.**

BIBLIOGRAPHY

Leopoldo Petry, *O episódio do Ferrabráz (Os Mucker)* (1966).

Moacyr Domingues, *A nova face dos Muckers* (1977).

Janaína Amado, *Conflito social no Brasil: A revolta dos "Mucker," Rio Grande do Sul 1868–1898* (1978).

Additional Bibliography

Amado, Jana'na. *A revolta dos Mucker: Rio Grande do Sul, 1868–1898.* Sao Leopoldo, Brasil: Editora Unisinos, 2002.

Sant'Ana, Elma. *Jacobina, a l'der dos Mucker.* Porto Alegre: AGE, 2001.

Sant'Ana, Elma. *Minha amada Maria: Cartas dos Mucker.* Canoas: Editora da Ulbra, 2004.

NANCY E. VAN DEUSEN

MÚGICA, FRANCISCO JOSÉ (1884–1954).

MÚGICA, FRANCISCO JOSÉ (1884–1954). Francisco José Múgica (*b.* 3 September 1884; *d.* 12 April 1954), Mexican revolutionary and presidential candidate. Múgica served as a deputy to the constitutional convention of 1916–1917, where he established his reputation as a radical ideologue. A close friend of Lázaro Cárdenas, he joined his cabinet as secretary of public works (1935–1939) and became a precandidate in 1939 for the presidential nomination of the government party against Manuel Ávila Camacho. Because Múgica was so strongly identified with radical elements in the party, Cárdenas, despite their close friendship, chose the moderate Camacho to succeed himself.

Born in Tinguindín, Michoacán, Múgica studied in the Zamora seminary until 1904, after which he taught school. Politically active in his home state, he joined Francisco Madero's forces as a second lieutenant in 1910. He served as an assistant to Venustiano Carranza and in 1913 joined the Constitutionalists. Becoming a career officer in the new revolutionary army, he commanded numerous military zones in the 1930s. He served as governor of his home state (1920–1922) and of Baja California del Sur (1940–1946). In 1952 he supported the presidential bid of General Miguel Henríquez Guzmán.

See also **Cárdenas del Rio, Lázaro; Carranza, Venustiano.**

BIBLIOGRAPHY

Armando De María y Campos, *Múgica: Crónica biográfica* (1939).

Magdalena Mondragón Aguirre, *Cuando la Revolución se cortó las alas (Intento de una biografía del General Francisco J. Múgica)* (1967).

Francisco J. Múgica, *Hechos, no palabras* (1982); *Francisco J. Múgica: Compromiso histórico con la Revolución mexicana* (1985).

Additional Bibliography

Boyer, Christopher R. *Becoming Campesinos: Politics, Identity, and Agrarian Struggle in Postrevolutionary Michoacán, 1920–1935.* Stanford: Stanford University Press, 2003.

Navarro, Aaron William. *Political Intelligence: Opposition, Parties and the Military in Mexico, 1938–1954.* Ph.D. diss., 2004.

RODERIC AI CAMP

MUISCA. Muisca refers to Chibcha-language-speaking societies that inhabited the eastern highlands of central Colombia at the time of the Spanish Conquest in 1536. Muisca chiefdoms derived subsistence from intensive agriculture of maize, potatoes, and other plants adapted to high altitudes. Most of the population lived in the high plateaus above 8,250 feet. The Muisca, however, also controlled lands at lower altitudes where cotton and coca were grown.

The basic units of production and consumption were the *capitanías.* Frequently, several *capitanías* made up a unit called a *pueblo* by the Spaniards. The heads of some larger *pueblos* began a process of expansion by which lesser *pueblos* were incorporated under their domain. In the early sixteenth century, four chiefs were struggling to achieve regional prominence—those of Bogotá, Duitama, Sogamoso, and Tunja. Instability was a main feature of political centralization. *Pueblos* incorporated into confederations were able to retain much autonomy. Anytime regional chiefs delegated power, internal strife erupted as lesser chiefs attempted to gain regional power.

The Muisca elite had privileged access to resources. Chiefs were given tribute in goods and helped with the construction of their dwellings, storehouses, and a palisade that surrounded their villages. As the degree of social stratification increased beyond the level of local *pueblos,* large proportions of surplus were accumulated by regional chiefs. This surplus was invested in the support of chiefly needs and the maintenance of craft specialists. Nonetheless, some portion of the tribute was redistributed to the people at large, mainly in the form of communal feasts.

How the features of social organization that the Spaniards described came to be knowledge remains scant. Research in a portion of the Valle de Fúquene, north of Santa Fe de Bogotá, establishes a sequence of development from 300 BCE to CE 1600. The earliest occupation of the area dates from 300 BCE to CE 800. Population density was very low and settlement patterns consisted of two small villages twelve acres in size. The Early Muisca period ranges from CE 800 to about CE 1300. Population more than doubled and most of it was concentrated in a large village of about thirty-seven acres that probably dominated the region. The Late Muisca period (CE 1300 to 1600) is characterized by a population increase, evidence of long-distance trade, and the emergence of several large villages (twelve to twenty-five acres in size) in the area. The largest village that predominated during the Early Muisca period increased further in size, reaching some fifty acres.

The importance of the Muisca cannot be ignored. In spite of the fact that the Muisca were conquered by the Spaniards early in the sixteenth century, some of their traditions survive today. Currently, most of the population in the eastern highlands, including that of Santa Fe de Bogotá, Colombia's capital, is of mixed Muisca-Spanish ancestry.

Colombia's 1991 constitutional reforms were favorable to indigenous groups on matters of land rights and autonomy, recognition and protection of cultural and social rights, self-governance, and participation in national politics; Colombia is thought to be the most progressive Latin American nation in its legislative attitude toward indigenous peoples. Regardless of official policy and new legislation, however, the 2,000 Muisca residing near Bogotá continue to struggle to protect their land, revitalize and strengthen language and cultural practices, and to develop small-scale community based businesses.

See also **Indigenous Peoples.**

BIBLIOGRAPHY

Descriptions of Muisca social organization may be found in Sylvia M. Broadbent, *Los chibchas: Organización socio-política.* (1964) and Juan Villamarín, "Encomenderos and Indians in the Formation of Colonial Society in the Sabana de Bogotá, 1537–1740." (Ph.D. diss., Brandeis University, 1972). Information on Muisca economy is provided by Carl Henrik Langebaek, *Mercados, poblamiento e integración étnica entre los muiscas, siglo XVI* (1987) and "Highland Centre and Lowland Periphery in 16th Century Eastern Colombia," in *Research in Economic Anthropology* 13 (1991): 323–337. The basic source for archaeology in the Muisca territory is Marianne Cardale, *Las salinas de Zipaquirá: Su explotación indígena* (1981). A broad picture of historical developments in the eastern highlands and neighboring areas is found in Carl Henrik Langebaek, *Noticias de Caciques muy Mayores: Origen y desarrollo de sociedades complejas en el nororiente de Colombia y norte de Venezuela* (1992).

CARL HENRIK LANGEBAEK R.

MULES AND MULE RAISING. *See* **Livestock.**

MUNGUÍA, CLEMENTE DE JESÚS

(1810–1868). Clemente de Jesús Munguía (*b.* 23 November 1810; *d.* 14 December 1868), bishop and later archbishop of Michoacán, opponent of the Reform Laws. Munguía, reputedly born in Zamora, Michoacán, represented the new breed of mid-nineteenth-century bishops determined to defend the rights and independence of the church from state encroachments. Ordained in 1841, he became rector of the seminary in Morelia in 1843, and was consecrated bishop of Michoacán in 1852. He wrote thirty-six pastoral letters during his time as bishop. He managed only a partial diocesan visit and recommended the establishment of new dioceses and parishes.

During Santa Anna's last régime (1853–1855) Munguía was president of the Council of State, a position that led him in November 1855 to oppose the Ley Juárez and argue for the church's right to the *fuero*. He believed that the government had exceeded its powers and should first have consulted the Holy See. He protested against the Ley Lerdo (1856) and the Ley Iglesias (1857), and denounced the government requirement of an oath to the 1857 Constitution. Munguía protested against General Epitacio Huerta's sack of the cathedral in Morelia on 22 September 1858 and occupation of the seminary building on 10 May 1859. He was the principal author of the 30 August 1859 bishops' manifesto condemning the Veracruz Reform Laws and refuting Liberal claims that the episcopate consisted of subversives. Expelled from Mexico by Juárez in 1861, he returned with the French Intervention in September 1863. When Pope Pius IX raised Michoacán to an archdiocese in January 1863, he appointed Munguía its first archbishop. An opponent of Maximilian's ecclesiastical policy, Munguía was exiled to Rome in June 1865, where he died in poverty.

See also **Ley Iglesias; Ley Lerdo.**

BIBLIOGRAPHY

José Bravo Ugarte, *Munguía* (1967).

Michael P. Costeloe, *Church and State in Independent Mexico* (1978).

Additional Bibliography

Chowning, Margaret. *Wealth and Power in Provincial Mexico: Michoacán from the Late Colony to the Revolution.* Stanford: Stanford University Press, 1999.

Ivereigh, Austen. *The Politics of Religion in an Age of Revival: Studies in Nineteenth-century Europe and Latin America.* London: Institute of Latin American Studies, 2000.

Matute, Alvaro, Evelia Trejo, and Brian Francis Connaughton Hanley. *Estado, Iglesia y sociedad en México, siglo XIX.* México, D.F.: Facultad de Filosofía y Letras, UNAM: Grupo Editorial, Miguel Angel Porrúa, 1995.

BRIAN HAMNETT

MUNICÍPIO, MUNICÍPIO NEUTRO.

Município, Município Neutro, the area of jurisdiction associated with an incorporated town (vila) in Brazil. The municipality was the basic administrative unit of the Portuguese Empire. During the colonial period, municipal councils were limited formally to local administration, but the *municípios* of the interior developed extralegal political and judicial powers to the point of challenging crown governors and viceroys. Under the Empire, the municipal councils were formally reduced to administrative entities by the law of 1 October 1828. The *município neutro* was created in 1834 under the Additional Act to the constitution, which created the provincial legislative assemblies. It designated the municipality of Rio de Janeiro as a separate entity without independent municipal representation, analogous to a federal district.

BIBLIOGRAPHY

Edmundo Zenha, *O município no Brasil, 1532–1700* (1948).

Richard M. Morse, "Brazil's Urban Development: Colony and Empire," in *From Colony to Nation: Essays on the Independence of Brazil,* edited by A. J. R. Russell-Wood (1975).

Additional Bibliography

Bieber, Judy. *Power, Patronage, and Political Violence: State Building on a Brazilian Frontier, 1822-1889.* Lincoln: University of Nebraska Press, 1999.

Ferreira, Marieta de Moraes, ed. *A República na velha província: Oligarquias e crise no estado do Rio de Janeiro (1889 1930).* Rio de Janeiro: Rio Fundo, 1989.

O'Dwyer, Eliane Cantarino. *Quilombos: Identidade étnica e territorialidade.* Rio de Janeiro: Editora FGV, 2002.

Santos Junior, Orlando Alves dos. *Democracia e governo local: Dilemas da reforma municipal no Brasil.* Rio de

Janeiro: Observatório IPPUR/UFRJ-FASE: Editora Revan, 2001.

JUDY BIEBER FREITAS

MUÑOZ, JOSÉ TRINIDAD (?–1855).

José Trinidad Muñoz (*d.* 18 August 1855), Nicaraguan military officer. Muñoz, a veteran of the Central American civil wars of the 1840s, received military training in Mexico under Antonio López de Santa Anna. He established a military academy in León, Nicaragua, and gained a reputation as the best tactician in Central America. On 4 August 1851 Muñoz overthrew the government of José Laureano Pineda in León but was subsequently ousted and left Nicaragua.

This large, handsome, but egotistical officer was generally on the Democratic (Liberal) side, but he was less ideologically committed than many of his contemporaries. After Máximo Jerez retreated from Granada in early 1855, Francisco Castellón, head of the Democratic government at León, brought Muñoz back to relieve Jerez as commander of his army. William Walker arrived to support the Democrats soon afterward. Seeing Walker as a rival for power, Muñoz took an instant dislike to him. They argued over strategy and tactics, and Walker accused Muñoz of sabotaging his campaign.

Some Nicaraguan historians have viewed Muñoz as a defender of Nicaraguan sovereignty in his efforts to undermine Walker while also opposing the Conservative forces that came from the other Central American states to fight against Walker. Muñoz sought a peaceful settlement between the *legitimistas* (Conservatives) and *democráticos* (Liberals). His death in August 1855 at the battle of El Sauce, where he had defeated Santos Guardiola, opened the way for Walker to become the Democrats' leading general.

See also **Nicaragua; Walker, William.**

BIBLIOGRAPHY

Albert Z. Carr, *The World and William Walker* (1963), pp. 122–128.

Francisco Ortega Arancibi, *Cuarenta años (1838–1878) de historia de Nicaragua,* 3d ed. (1975).

Marco A. Soto Valenzuela, *Guerra nacional de Centroamérica* (1957).

William Walker, *The War in Nicaragua* (1860), pp. 35–85.

Andrés Vega Bolaños, *Gobernantes de Nicaragua: Notas y documentos* (1944), pp. 157–209.

Additional Bibliography

Burns, E. Bradford. *Patriarch and Folk: The Emergence of Nicaragua, 1798–1858.* Cambridge, MA: Harvard University Press, 1991.

Montúfar, Lorenzo, and Raúl Aguilar Piedra. *Walker en Centroamérica.* Alajuela: Museo Histórico Cultural Juan Santamaría, 2000.

RALPH LEE WOODWARD JR.

MUÑOZ CAMARGO, DIEGO (1529–1599).

Diego Muñoz Camargo, an early Mexican chronicler and businessman, was one of the first mestizo intellectuals in New Spain. Although there has been some controversy regarding his identity (both his father and son were also Diego Muñoz Camargo), his life and his writing have generally been documented. His parents were a Spanish conquistador and a Tlaxcalan noblewoman; after becoming an adult, he also took a Tlaxcalan bride. These inherited and conjugal links gave Muñoz Camargo two special connections with Tlaxcala, in business and in culture. Regarding the latter he had access to pre-Conquest historical documents and testimonies and some of the writings of Bernadino de Sahagún. He wrote for some forty years, sometimes expanding on previous manuscripts he had submitted to the king, sometimes drafting responses to a questionnaire. The result is several interrelated works: the *Descripción*, *Suma y Epíloga*, *Historia Natural*, *Relació de la Gran Cochinilla* and, the most familiar, the *Historia de Tlaxcala*.

What makes Muñoz Camargo interesting and different from other mestizo chroniclers such as Fernando de Alva Ixtlilxóchitl and Hernando Alvarado Tezozómoc is his writing's pronounced adherence to the Spanish view of things. He is also important as an early chronicler of Tlaxcala, a polity that aided Hernán Cortés in his conquest of Tenochtitlan. His perspective on historical episodes such as the massacre on the religious holiday of Toxcatl offers keen insight into the complex reality of the Conquest, when the Spanish inserted themselves into a web of Nahua internal politics. He is also noteworthy for his tutoring of the indigenous peoples Cabeza de Vaca brought with him to Mexico from the lands that would later become the United States.

See also **Alva Ixtlilxochitl, Fernando; Alvarado Tezozomoc, Hernando; Cabeza de Vaca, Alvar Núñez; Tlaxcala; Torquemada, Juan de.**

BIBLIOGRAPHY

Gibson, Charles. "The Identity of Diego Muñoz Camargo." *Hispanic American Historical Review* 30, no. 2 (1950): 195–208.

Mignolo, Walter D. "El mandato y la ofrenda: La *Descripción de la ciudad y provincia de Tlaxcala*, de Diego Muñoz Camargo, y las relaciones de Indias." *Nueva Revista de Filología Hispánica* 35, no. 2 (1987): 451–484.

Miller, Marilyn. "Covert *Mestizaje* and the Strategy of 'Passing' in Diego Muñoz Camargo's *Historia de Tlaxcala*." *Colonial Latin American Review* 6, no.1 (1997): 41–58.

Mörner, Magnus, and Charles Gibson. "Diego Muñoz Camargo and the Segregation Policy of the Spanish Crown." *Hispanic American Historical Review* 42, no. 4 (1962): 558–568.

Muñoz Camargo, Diego. *Historia de Tlaxcala: Ms. 210 de la Biblioteca Nacional de París*, edited by Luis Reyes García y Javier Lira Toledo. Tlaxcala, Mexico: Gobierno del Estado de Tlaxcala/Universidad Autónoma de Tlaxcala, 1998.

Velazco, Salvador. *Visiones de Anáhuac: Reconstrucciones historiografías y etnicidades emergentes en el México colonial: Fernando de Alva Ixtlilxóchitl, Diego Muñoz Camargo y Hernando Alvarado Tezozómoc.* Guadalajara, Mexico: Universidad de Guadalajara, 2003.

Ward, Thomas. "Expanding Ethnicity in Sixteenth-Century Anahuac: Ideologies of Ethnicity and Gender in the Nation-Building Process." *MLN* 116, no. 2 (2001): 419–452.

Ward, Thomas. "From the 'People' to the 'Nation': An Emerging Notion in Sahagún, Ixtlilxóchitl and Muñoz Camargo." *Estudios de Cultura Náhuatl* 32 (2001): 223–234.

THOMAS WARD

MUÑOZ LEDO LAZO DE LA VEGA, PORFIRIO

MUÑOZ LEDO LAZO DE LA VEGA, PORFIRIO (1933–). Porfirio Muñoz Ledo Lazo de la Vega is a Mexican politician and one of the founders of the Democratic Revolutionary Party (PRD). An important political figure since the 1970s, Muñoz Ledo abandoned the government party after he and Cuauhtémoc Cárdenas failed to reform it from within in 1987. A key organizer of Cárdenas's campaign in the 1988 presidential elections, he was elected as one of the first opposition senators in modern times. In 1993 he became president of PRD.

Born on July 23, 1933, in Mexico City, Muñoz Ledo studied at the Centro Universitario Mexicano with a distinguished generation of future politicians and graduated with a law degree from the National Autonomous University of Mexico (UNAM) in 1955. He obtained a doctor of laws degree at the University of Paris in 1958. After teaching political science at UNAM and the Colegio de México, as well as holding other teaching positions, he entered public life, serving in the secretariat of public education and the social security institute. He rose to the post of undersecretary of the presidency (1970–1972) and then secretary of labor (1972–1975) under Luis Echeverría. He became president of the Institutional Revolutionary Party (PRI) in 1975–1976 and briefly served as secretary of education (1976–1977) before being fired by President José López Portillo. He later served as ambassador to the United Nations (1979–1985) under López Portillo and Miguel de la Madrid.

In 1986 he co-founded the Democratic Current in the PRI, serving as its national coordinator, before supporting Cárdenas's 1988 presidential campaign. He was elected senator and served from 1988 to 1994. In 1988 Muñoz Ledo co-founded the PRD, becoming president of the party in 1993, the only politician in modern times to preside over two of the three major parties. From 1997 to 2000, he served as leader of the PRD congressional delegation. He remains an active figure in the PRD.

See also **Mexico, Political Parties: Democratic Revolutionary Party (PRD).**

BIBLIOGRAPHY

Bruhn, Kathleen. *Taking on Goliath: The Emergence of a New Left Party and the Struggle for Democracy in Mexico.* University Park: Pennsylvania State University Press, 1997.

Langston, Joy. *Three Exits from the Mexican Institutional Revolutionary Party: Internal Ruptures and Political Stability.* Mexico: CIDE, 1994.

Muñoz Ledo, Porfirio. *Sumario de una izquierda republicana.* Mexico: Océano, 2000.

RODERIC AI CAMP

MUÑOZ MARÍN, LUIS (1898–1980).

Luis Muñoz Marín (*b.* 18 February 1898; *d.* 30 April 1980), the first elected governor of Puerto Rico (1948–1964). Muñoz Marín, the son of political leader Luis Muñoz Rivera, spent much of his young life in the United States as a student, a writer, and an advocate of Puerto Rican independence. His political outlook gradually underwent a transformation, however, and he came to believe that economic development was more vital than immediate independence. In 1938, alienated from the political parties dominant in Puerto Rico, Muñoz Marín founded the Popular Democratic Party (PPD), whose motto was "Bread, Land, and Liberty." Following a strong PPD showing in the 1940 elections, Muñoz became president of the Puerto Rican Senate in 1941. He immediately pushed through basic reforms in land tenancy, natural resources, transportation, and education. The PPD, with Muñoz Marín as its president, swept the 1944 elections, but the independence issue ultimately divided the party. Muñoz Marín remained with the less radical PPD, favoring economic and social reform with U.S. assistance.

The first gubernatorial elections took place on 2 November 1948, and Muñoz Marín won with a clear majority, becoming the first Puerto Rican to be elected governor of the island. He vigorously promoted industrial development as part of his program Operation Bootstrap, but eventually he rejected independence as an option for Puerto Rico, favoring instead a permanent union with the United States. After holding the office of governor for four terms, he declined to run again in 1964, though he remained an active figure in Puerto Rican politics for many years.

See also **Operation Bootstrap; Puerto Rico, Political Parties: Overview.**

BIBLIOGRAPHY

Thomas Aitken, Jr., *Poet in the Fortress: The Story of Luis Muñoz Marín* (1964).

Lieban Córdova, *Luis Muñoz Marín y sus campañas políticas* (1984).

Manuel De Heredia, *Luis Muñoz Marín: Biografía abierta* (1973).

Arturo Morales Carrión, ed., *Puerto Rico: A Political and Cultural History* (1983), pp. 221–304.

Additional Bibliography

Maldonado, A. W. *Luis Muñoz Marín: Puerto Rico's Democratic Revolution.* San Juan: Editorial Universidad de Puerto Rico, 2006.

Villaronga, Gabriel. *Toward a Discourse of Consent: Mass Mobilization and Colonial Politics in Puerto Rico, 1932–1948.* Westport: Praeger, 2004.

SARA FLEMING

MUÑOZ RIVERA, LUIS (1859–1916).

Luis Muñoz Rivera (*b.* 17 July 1859; *d.* 15 November 1916), Puerto Rican journalist, poet, and political leader. Born in Barranquitas, Puerto Rico, Muñoz Rivera completed his primary schooling in local schools and began his career in politics in 1887. He rose to prominence as a leader of the Autonomist Party. In 1890 he founded the newspaper *La Democracia,* which became the voice of the autonomist movement. He successfully negotiated a pact with the Spanish Liberal Fusionist Party in 1896 that ultimately resulted in the granting of autonomy to Puerto Rico. Muñoz Rivera and the autonomists won the first elections, but U.S. occupation in 1898 prevented the new government from assuming office. Renewing his struggle to procure political rights for Puerto Rico, Muñoz Rivera founded the Federalist Party in 1898 and became Puerto Rico's resident commissioner in Washington (1910–1916). He was instrumental in formulating the Jones Act (signed 4 March 1917), which increased Puerto Rico's powers of self-government, but he did not live to see its passage.

See also **Puerto Rico, Political Parties: Overview.**

BIBLIOGRAPHY

Harold J. Lidin, *History of the Puerto Rican Independence Movement,* vol. 1 (1981).

Arturo Morales Carrión, *Puerto Rico: A Political and Cultural History* (1983), pp. 118–199.

Additional Bibliography

Maldonado, A. W. *Luis Muñoz Marín: Puerto Rico's Democratic Revolution*. San Juan: Editorial Universidad de Puerto Rico, 2006.

SARA FLEMING

MURILLO TORO, MANUEL (1816–1880).

Manuel Murillo Toro (*b.* 1 January 1816; *d.* 26 December 1880), Liberal president of Colombia (1864–1866 and 1872–1874). Murillo was born in Chaparral, Tolima, and received his law degree in Bogotá in 1836; he became a protégé of Francisco de Paula Santander. Murillo served as secretary of the interior and as finance secretary during the regime of José Hilario López (1849–1853), and was the first president (i.e., governor) of Santander (1857–1858). After the Liberal triumph of 1861 he served as minister to France, the United States, and Venezuela. During his first presidency Murillo achieved tenuous reconciliations with the church and the defeated Conservatives and recognized the Conservatives' dominance in Antioquia. During his second term he pushed for railroad development and other infrastructure projects, giving rise to serious interregional rivalries. Ideologically, Murillo shifted from radical popular sovereignty (ca. 1850) to laissez-faire libertarianism (ca. 1858); by the late 1860s he espoused a government role in economic development and a moderated role for popular participation.

See also **Berrío, Pedro Justo; Colombia, Political Parties: Radical Olympus.**

BIBLIOGRAPHY

Ignacio Arizmendi Posada, *Presidentes de Colombia, 1810–1990* (1990), pp. 121–124.

Gerardo Molina, *Las ideas socialistas en Colombia* (1987), pp. 123–124.

James William Park, *Rafael Núñez and the Politics of Colombian Regionalism, 1863–1886* (1985).

Additional Bibliography

Eastman, Jorge Mario. "Murillo Toro, reformador social." *Boletín de Historia y Antigüedades* 87:808 (January–March 2000): 119–141.

RICHARD J. STOLLER

MURRA, JOHN V. (1916–2006).

Anthropologist John Victor Murra pioneered the study of the historical anthropology of the Inca empire and its subject peoples. His influential early insights into the "redistributive" nature of Inca power were stimulated by wide study of other precapitalist states, especially those of Africa. In 1972 he published an equally influential model of the adaptive bases of Andean society, rooted in discontinuous "vertical archipelagos" of resource bases up and down rugged mountain landscapes.

Born in Odessa on August 24, 1916, Murra took his Ph.D. at Chicago in 1956, after a turbulent period as a Republican soldier in the Spanish Civil War. All modern study of high-Andean adaptation and statecraft draws on his works: his articles in the *Handbook of South American Indians*, his dissertation (*The Economic Organization of the Inka State*, an unpublished classic until 1978), his archival discoveries and ecologically oriented analyses of sixteenth-century Inca sources, and his critical edition of the works of indigenous chronicler Felipe Guamán Poma de Ayala. Murra pioneered the use of early colonial *visitas* (house-by-house inspections) of Andean communities, initially as a complement to his 1963–1965 fieldwork (with Craig Morris and Donald Thompson) at the giant Inca site of Huánuco Pampa.

Committed to building research infrastructure in the Andean countries, Murra published largely with Peruvian institutions. His teaching, however, was mainly done in the United States: at Vassar (1950–1961), Yale (1961–1963, 1970–1971), and Cornell (1968–1982). Murra served as President of the American Ethnological Society (1972–1973) and of the Institute of Andean Research (1977–1978). As emeritus he held honors from the University of Barcelona and from the University of San Marcos in Lima. In 2000 the Instituto de Estudios Peruanos published a conversational autobiography under the Quechua-Spanish title *Nispa ninchis/Decimos diciendo* (Speaking We Say). He died on October 16, 2006.

BIBLIOGRAPHY

Works by Murra

Survey and Excavations in Southern Ecuador (with Donald Collier). Chicago: Field Museum of Natural History Anthropological Series, vol. 35, 1943.

"The Historic Tribes of Ecuador." In *Handbook of South American Indians*, Vol. 2: *The Andean Civilizations*, ed. Julian H. Steward. Washington, DC: U.S. Government Printing Office, 1946–1959.

"The Cayapa and the Colorado." In *Handbook of South American Indians*, Vol. 4: *The Circum-Caribbean Tribes*, ed. Julian H. Steward. Washington, DC: U.S. Government Printing Office, 1946–1959.

Visita hecha a la provincia de Chucuito por Garci Diez de San Miguel en el año 1567. Lima: Casa de la Cultura del Perú, 1964.

Visita de la Provincia de León de Huánuco en 1562. Huánuco, Perú: Universidad Nacional Hermilio Valdizán, 1967, 1972.

Formaciones económicas y políticas del mundo andino. Lima: Instituto de Estudios Peruanos, 1975.

La organización económica y política del estado inca. México, D.F.: Siglo XXI, 1978. Republished in English as *The Economic Organization of the Inka State.* Greenwich, CN: JAI Press, 1980.

Guamán Poma de Ayala, Felipe. [1615] *El primer nueva corónica y buen gobierno.* Edited by John V. Murra and Rolena Adorno, trans. Jorge L. Urioste. 3 vols. México, D.F.: Siglo XXI, 1980.

Works about Murra

Castro, Victoria, Carlos Aldunate, and Jorge Hidalgo, eds. *Nispa ninchis/decimos diciendo: Conversaciones con John Murra.* Lima: Instituto de Estudios Peruanos; New York: Institute of Andean Research, 2000.

FRANK SALOMON

MURTINHO, JOAQUIM DUARTE

(1848–1911). Joaquim Duarte Murtinho (*b.* 7 December 1848; *d.* 19 November 1911), minister of finance of Brazil (1898–1902). As minister of finance under Manuel Ferraz de Campos Sales, Murtinho, a native of Cuiabá, Brazil, based his economic policies upon the reestablishment of the gold standard of 1846. He pursued this policy in reaction to the inflation surrounding the financial crisis of 1891, following the financial market reforms of 1890 (the *encilhamento*). Since the mil-réis had depreciated 257 percent between 1855 and 1896, the necessary deflation (and depression) to achieve this parity was dramatic (around a 72 percent fall in the price level). Some historians feel that Murtinho's motivations were more than economic. According to Carlos Peláez and Wilson Suzigan (1981), Murtinho believed that the racial inferiority of the inhabitants of Brazil (compared with those of the United States and Western Europe) rendered industrialization an untenable policy goal. Murtinho also argued that the overabundant coffee production at the time was due to market inefficiencies and too many producers. The appreciation of the currency would rid Brazil of the small industry developed since 1886 and weed out inefficient coffee producers by making imports cheaper and coffee exports more expensive. Murtinho's restrictive monetary policies contracted economic activity to an extent only seen in the depressions of 1981–1982 and 1990. Murtinho's other credentials include that of medical doctor (to Marshal Deodoro da Fonseca), campaigner for the Republic, senator from Mato Grosso (1890), member of the Constituent Congress (1891), senator (1903–1906), and vice president of the Senate (1905–1906). He died in Rio de Janeiro.

See also **Campos Sales, Manuel Ferraz de; Coffee Industry; Economic Development.**

BIBLIOGRAPHY

Werner Baer, *The Brazilian Economy: Growth and Development,* 3d ed. (1989).

João Manoel Cardoso De Mello and Maria Conceição Tavares, "The Capitalist Export Economy of Brazil 1884–1930," in *The Latin American Economies: Growth and the Export Sector, 1880–1930,* edited by Roberto Cortés Conde and Shane J. Hunt (1985).

Celso Furtado, *The Economic Growth of Brazil,* translated by Ricardo W. de Aguiar and Eric Charles Drysdale (1965).

Paulo Neuhaus, *História monetária do Brasil, 1900–1945* (1975).

Carlos Manuel Peláez and Wilson Suzigan, *História monetária do Brasil* (1981).

Wilson Suzigan and Anníbal Villanova Villela, *Política do governo e crescimento da economia brasileira* (1973).

Steven Topik, *The Political Economy of the Brazilian State* (1987).

Additional Bibliography

Hanley, Anne G. *Native Capital: Financial Institutions and Economic Development in Sao Paulo, Brazil, 1850–1920.* Stanford: Stanford University Press, 2005.

JOHN H. WELCH

MUSA, SAID (1944–). Said Musa (b. March 19, 1944) has been prime minister of Belize since 1998. In the national election of March 5, 2003, Musa became the first of all incumbent prime ministers to lead his party, the People's United Party (PUP), to victory since Belize gained independence in 1981. The fourth of eight children of Hamid Musa and Aurora Gibbs, he grew up in San Ignacio, in the Cayo District of western Belize. He is half Palestinian on his father's side (his father emigrated from El Bireh near Ramallah in 1930) and a combination of Scottish and Maya on his mother's. After attending primary school in San Ignacio, the family moved to Belize City, where Said distinguished himself as a student at the Jesuit-run St. John's College.

Musa studied law at Manchester University in the United Kingdom, graduating with an honors degree in law, and was called to the bar at Gray's Inn, London. While there he met and married Joan Pearson and started a family. Returning to Belize in 1967, he served as circuit magistrate and as a crown counsel in the Office of Public Prosecutions. His concern with the well-being of civil servants led to his election as president of the Public Service Union.

Musa entered private practice, first with Assad Shoman, and subsequently with Lawrence "Ronnie" Balderamos, founding the law firm of Musa and Balderamos in 1970. With Evan X. Hyde, he became an activist in the United Black Association for Development (UBAD), and in the early 1970s he and Assad Shoman founded the People's Action Committee (PAC) and the Society for the Promotion of Education and Research (SPEAR).

Musa's long political career began when he joined the PUP and ran for office of the National Assembly in 1974. Although he lost, Premier George Price appointed him senator for the 1974–1979 term. In 1979 he defeated the chief opposition leader, Dean Lindo, of the United Democratic Party (UDP), winning the Fort George constituency, which he retains. He was appointed attorney general, minister of education and sports, and, later, minister of foreign affairs and minister of economic development during two periods of PUP domination, 1979–1984 and 1989–1993. He was a key figure in drafting the Belize constitution of 1981.

In 1996 Musa succeeded George Price as leader of the PUP and led his party to victories in elections on August 27, 1998, and on March 5, 2003. Once in office he made foreign affairs and political reform his top priorities. In January 2000 his government approved the establishment of the University of Belize. Seeking a second consecutive mandate, he campaigned on a slogan of "no turning back," promising to create 20,000 new jobs and to give locals access to the same investment incentives as foreigners. At his swearing in for a second term, he stated that economic and social development would continue to be the main thrust of his government and promised to improve access to and quality of education.

Since 2004 the Musa government has been mired down in a series of domestic controversies. On March 23, 2004, his government made the fateful decision to sell 15 percent of its 52 percent share in Belize Telecommunications Ltd. to ECOM Ltd., a Carlisle Company, for US$14.5 million. The government was to retain three seats on the board. Innovative Communication, owned by Jeffrey Prosser, agreed to purchase the government's remaining shares in BTL for US$89 million. In November 2004 *Forbes* magazine reported that Prosser was in Washington, D.C., trying to stave off creditors and regulators. After Prosser defaulted on his payment to the government of Belize, the prime minister announced he was taking back BTL on February 10, 2005. Protests about these scandals championed by the opposition party turned violent in April 2005, sabotaging the telecommunications system and causing other damage.

Continuing problems with BTL, investigations off misconduct involving the Social Security Board and the Development Finance Corporation, and poor economic performance prompted Standard and Poor and Moodys to downgrade Belize's credit rating. On October 1, 2005, the IMF expressed concern that the country's fiscal and external deficits remained unsustainably high. This growing economic crisis had a political toll when the opposition UDP party won 64 of 67 seats in two cities and seven towns in the municipal elections of March 2, 2006. Adding to this gloomy news was a report from the International Narcotics Control Strategy, which complained that Belize continued to be a transshipment point in the cocaine trade.

On September 21, 2006, Belize celebrated its twenty-fifth anniversary of political independence.

Prime Minister Musa announced that his government was implementing a complex package of fiscal, monetary, and financial sector reforms. With national elections looming in 2008, the best news of the year came on January 11, 2007, when Belize began its first crude old exports to the United States. However, civil unrest boiled over again on May 18 because of strong objections to the government's move to settle a US$33 million debt for Universal Health Services with public monies. Musa fired two members of his cabinet their for lack of support of the proposed settlement. With further protests in the offing, the payoff plan was abandoned. On July 1 the PUP held its national convention in Corozal. Musa promised to take the fight to each of the thirty-one constituencies in the 2008 election.

See also **Belize.**

BIBLIOGRAPHY

BELIZEmagazine.com. "Twenty Questions—The January Interview with Prime Minister Hon. Said Musa." January 2004. Available from http://www.belizemagazine.com/edition01/english/e01_05guestions.htm.

Conway, Janelle Conway. "Looking for Balance in Belize: Celebrating its First Twenty-Five Years." *Americas* (English ed.) 58, no. 6 (November–December 2006): 10–18.

Smith, Godfrey P., ed. *Belize: A Caribbean Nation in Central America: Selected Speeches of Said Musa.* Kingston, Jamaica: Ian Randle, 2006.

BRIAN E. COUTTS

MUSIC

This entry includes the following articles:

ART MUSIC

INTRODUCTION

Art music—broadly defined as music, whether sacred or secular, of serious artistic intent, written by trained composers—arrived in the Americas with the first missionaries, who brought with them the church music of the European Renaissance. The Spanish and Portuguese crowns gave the Catholic Church a preeminent role in introducing European culture into the New World. As early as the second half of the sixteenth century missionaries were instructing the Indians in the fundamentals of music. Although the first missionaries were Franciscans, Dominicans, and Augustinians, it was the Jesuits who dominated in introducing European art and music into the New World.

About 1750, when Latin America was divided into viceroyalties, the political division of the Spanish colonies was: (1) the Viceroyalty of New Spain, from Florida and the western bank of the Mississippi River to present-day Costa Rica and the isles of the Caribbean; (2) the Viceroyalty of New Granada, embracing the lands of present-day Venezuela, Colombia, Panama, and Ecuador; (3) the Viceroyalty of Peru, which included the *audiencias* of Lima, Cuzco, and Chile; and (4) the Viceroyalty of the Río De La Plata, formed by present-day Argentina, Uruguay, Paraguay, and part of Bolivia. Portugal created the Viceroyalty of Brazil and divided it into *capitanías generales.* With the building of the first cathedrals in the capitals of the viceroyalties, music rose to a new level of importance. From the simple religious chants of the missions to the heights of the polyphonic mass, and with the introduction of the organ and the proliferation of choruses in the churches, sacred art music flourished in the Americas. The chapelmasters and organists of the cathedrals became the leaders of cultural activity.

The theater was the second outlet for musical development in Latin America. The regal palaces of the viceroys were the first stages for musical plays, beginning in the early seventeenth century. The high point was the premiere of the first opera produced in America: *La púrpura de la rosa* by Tomás de Torrejón y Velasco, at the viceroyal palace in Lima in 1701. Interest in music was not limited to the royal and the prominent. The populations of the cities were avid for musical entertainment, and thus started, in the mid-eighteenth century, the building of the first public theaters. These were primitive, rustic constructions, with an unfurnished orchestra—the public brought their own chairs—and a few boxes with armchairs and some embellishment, reserved for the authorities. There were performances of *tonadillas escénicas* and *zarzuelas,* both Spanish genres that alternate singing with musical interludes and spoken parts.

Around this time instrumental and vocal music began to be heard in the salons of the colonial mansions, and musical soirées in the European romantic tradition, with songs accompanied by piano, harp, guitar, or violin, became widely popular. These informal ensembles were the roots of chamber music and of the first primitive orchestras in the New World.

At the beginning of the nineteenth century, and coincidental to the emergence of ideas of freedom and independence, Italian opera came to America. Initially overtures and some arias and choruses were performed; later there were complete performances of opera. By 1830 virtually every country in America had heard at least one complete work by Rossini. With the arrival of opera, the old theaters were replaced by elaborately decorated opera houses to rival those of Europe. And a century and a half later, many still endure, a tribute to the permanence of opera in the cultural life of America.

Most of the musicians who arrived as orchestra members of the Italian opera companies took up residence in America and became the teachers of a new generation of national composers. As a result, the works of the first American composers were entirely European in technique and style. The second generation studied for the most part in conservatories in Europe. Upon their return to their native countries, many found inspiration for their compositions in the tunes, rhythms, and themes of the native American populations and in the popular music of their ancestors, thereby transforming folk materials into the elements of art music. As a result, a new musical trend was born in America by the beginning of the twentieth century: nationalism. Nevertheless, with the frequent interchange of composers and musicians between Europe and America, the new European styles were rapidly assimilated by American composers. After impressionism, the most dramatic change in musical style came during the 1950s with the arrival of new technologies, aesthetics, and musical countercurrents: serialism, aleatorism, computerized music, and a variety of electronic techniques.

The Inter-American Music Festivals, created by the Colombian conductor Guillermo Espinosa, chief of the Music Division of the Organization of American States, and held in Washington, D.C., from 1958 to 1974, discovered and promoted the works of many of today's prominent composers.

MEXICO AND THE CARIBBEAN COUNTRIES

Mexico. During the colonial period and after the early period of the Franciscan missions, the development of music in Mexico took place at three cathedrals: Mexico City, Puebla, and Morelia. Starting with the production of *villancicos,* psalms, *coplas,* and Nativity and Passion plays in the Spanish tradition, religious music reached its most elaborate forms in the polyphonic masses, Te deums, requiems, and Magnificats of the mid-sixteenth century. Organists and chapelmasters were the composers of that period: Francisco López Capillas (ca. 1615–1673), Antonio de Salazar (ca. 1650–1715), Manuel de Zumaya (ca. 1678–1756), and Juan Gutiérrez De Padilla (ca. 1590–1664). Built around 1500, Mexico City's old Casa de Comedias was replaced in 1670 by the Teatro Coliseo, which presented Spanish plays, *tonadillas,* and *zarzuelas* for half a century until it burned down on 16 January 1722. The Teatro Coliseo Nuevo opened in 1735 and continued the tradition of presenting Spanish comedies, dramas, *sainetes,* songs, dances, and *fines de fiesta.* At the beginning of the nineteenth century, this repertoire became mixed with and quickly replaced by operatic arias of Rossini, Bellini, and Donizetti plus some of the most well-known Rossini overtures. But the real operatic vogue began in 1827, when the legendary Manuel García and his family sang *Il barbiere di Siviglia.* In Mexico City, the Teatro Principal became the leading house for opera performances around 1831. In the 1850s the Gran Teatro de Santa Anna shared the yearly opera seasons with the Principal, and, since then, opera and *zarzuela* have been presented on all Mexican stages.

With the founding in 1866 of a private musical conservatory that eventually became, in 1877, the Conservatorio Nacional de Música, instrumental music came to prominence. The better-known composers during the nineteenth century were Cenobio Paniagua, Melesio Morales, Luis Baca, and Aniceto Ortega, whose opera *Guatimotzin* (1871), using Italian technique, incorporated Indian tunes. Piano salon-music was in vogue at the beginning of the twentieth century; Juventino Rosas (1868–1894) became famous for his universally popular waltz

Sobre las olas. Manuel Ponce (1882–1948) was the leader of the nationalist style, which continued with Silvestre Revueltas (1899–1940). A unique case is that of composer and theoretician Julián Carrillo (1875–1965), who developed a microtonal system and the "Sonido 13." Carlos Chávez (1899–1978), a dominant authority until the 1950s, was also a celebrated conductor and the founder of the Orquesta Sinfónica de México (1928). The contemporary and avant-garde generations are represented by Daniel Ayala-Pérez (1908–1975), José Moncayo (1912–1958), Blás Galindo (1910–1993), Luis Sandi (*b.* 1905), Manuel Enríquez (1926–1994), Héctor Quintanar (*b.* 1936), Mario Kuri-Aldana (*b.* 1931), and Eduardo Mata (1942–1995).

Cuba. Sacred music began at the Santiago de Cuba cathedral about 1544 with organist Miguel Velázquez, and later was continued by chapelmaster Domingo de Flores (*b.* 1682). However, the first composer of importance was Esteban Salas y Castro (1725–1803), who left a vast production of masses, motets, psalms, and *villancicos.* The Havana parish church became a cathedral in 1788, and achieved its musical climax around 1850. Opera and symphonic and piano music dominated in the nineteenth century. The first playhouse, Teatro Coliseo, opened in 1776 and was remodeled in 1803 as Teatro Principal. From 1810 on, after brilliant seasons of *tonadillas* and *zarzuelas,* opera became the public favorite, and an active national opera company was established. Moreover, with the opening of Teatro de Tacón on 28 February 1838, opera seasons became the height of fashion.

The first Havana conservatory (1885) was replaced by the Conservatorio Municipal Amadeo Roldán (1935), and the Orquesta Sinfónica Nacional was founded in 1960. Antonio Raffellín (1796–1882) and Nicolás Ruiz Espadero (1832–1890) were the two major composers of the classical and romantic generations. Cuba's leading nationalist composer Ignacio Cervantes (1847–1905) was followed by Eduardo Sánchez de Fuentes (1874–1944), Amadeo Roldán (1900–1939), and Alejandro García Caturla (1906–1940). José Ardévol (1911–1981), the prominent composer of the 1930s, founded the Grupo Renovación. The major twentieth-century composers, Harold Gramatges (*b.* 1918), Julián Orbón (1925–1991), and Aurelio de la Vega (*b.* 1925), were followed by the younger generation, represented by Juan Blanco (*b.* 1920) and Leo Brouwer (*b.* 1939).

Puerto Rico. Sacred music was developed after the Conquest. The first theater on the island, San Juan's Teatro Municipal (renamed Teatro Tapia in 1937), opened in 1832. Soon thereafter the first Sociedad Filarmónica was created. Among the earlier composers, Felipe Gutiérrez y Espinosa (1825–1899) was known for his opera *Guarionex, zarzuelas,* and religious music. Juan Morel Campos (1857–1896) was considered one of the most significant musicians of his time for his prolificness, with about five hundred works, and for including in his compositions the *danza puertorriqueña.* The leader of nationalism, Héctor Campos-Parsi (*b.* 1922), who had studied with Copland, Messiaen, and Nadia Boulanger in Paris, changed to neoclassicism and later to avant-garde techniques. He won France's Maurice Ravel Prize (1953).

Dominican Republic. The composition and performance of Spanish sacred and secular music was encouraged during the colonial period. Later Juan Francisco García (*b.* 1892), professor, composer and musicologist, incorporated the Dominican folk song into his symphonies and piano works. Manuel Simó (*b.* 1916), composer and conductor, wrote numerous symphonic works. Margarita Luna (*b.* 1921), an organist and composer, trained at the Juilliard School of Music in New York City and taught musical analysis and the history of music at the National Conservatory of Santo Domingo.

Venezuela. Sacred music in Venezuela developed from the last part of the eighteenth century to the early twentieth. A prominent group of colonial composers included José Francisco Velázquez, José Antonio Caro de Boesi, Juan José Landaeta, Pedro Nolasco Colón, and José Cayetano Carreño, all of whom were active at the beginning of 1800. José Ángel Lamas (1775–1814), with laudable works, was the most significant of them all. While the first opera season opened in Caracas in 1808, the operatic tradition reached its first period of prominence with the building of the Teatro Caracas (1854) and later with the fifteen-hundred-seat Teatro Municipal (1881). The musicians of that period were pianist Felipe Larrazábal

(1816–1873); José Ángel Montero (1839–1881), the Caracas cathedral chapelmaster and composer of *Virginia,* the first Venezuelan opera; and Federico Villena (1835–ca. 1900), who wrote sacred and orchestral works as well as several *zarzuelas.* Two musicians, the pianist Teresa Carreño (1853–1917) and the composer Reynaldo Hahn (1875–1947), achieved international fame.

In 1868 the first conservatory was founded, followed by the Academy of Music of the Instituto de Bellas Artes in 1877. From the 1920s to the 1960s Vicente Emilio Sojo (1887–1974), composer, teacher, and musicologist, led the musical life of Venezuela. In addition to his important works, he was founder and director of both the Orquesta Sinfónica Venezolana (1930) and the Orfeón Lamas, director of the Escuela Superior de Música José Ángel Lamas (1936), and the teacher of three generations of major Venezuelan composers. One of Sojo's pupils was Juan Bautista Plaza (1898–1965), renowned nationalist composer and musicologist, who published important essays on Venezuelan colonial music. Other nationalist composers were Carlos Figueredo (*b.* 1910), Evencio Castellanos (*b.* 1915), Antonio Estévez (*b.* 1916), Inocente Carreño (*b.* 1919), and Gonzalo Castellanos (*b.* 1926). The creation of the Conservatorio Nacional de Música (1972) by the Instituto Nacional de Cultura y Bellas Artes (INCIBA) and the establishment of the Caracas Music Festival gave great impetus to Venezuelan music. Starting in the 1960s, a group of composers experimented with avant-garde techniques, among them Rhazes Hernández-López (*b.* 1918), José Luis Muñoz (*b.* 1928), Alexis Rago (*b.* 1930), and the Greek Yannis Ioannidis, who settled in Caracas in 1969.

CENTRAL AMERICA

Beginning in 1573, Hernando Franco (1532–1585), a well-trained Spanish musician, directed the musical life of the Guatemala cathedral as chapelmaster, becoming the leading composer of the southern area of the Viceroyalty of New Spain in the sixteenth century. The first Central American composers incorporated indigenous themes, rhythms, and tunes into their works, which also drew on European romantic and impressionist techniques. The first Guatemalan composer to combine these stylistic elements was the pianist Luis Felipe Arias (1870–1908), who wrote principally piano works. Jesús Castillo (1877–1946), a forerunner of his generation, wrote symphonic music and operas, and José Castañeda (1898–1983) was the first to experiment with polytonality, microtonality, and other avant-garde trends. Jorge Sarmientos (*b.* 1933), who studied at the Di Tella Institute in Buenos Aires, used serial techniques and is today a major composer.

The first military band in Honduras, organized in 1876, became the Banda de los Supremos Poderes. Manuel de Adalid y Gamero (1872–?) composed the *Suite tropical* and also wrote several essays around 1940 about the music of his country. In El Salvador, Gilberto Orellana (*b.* 1942) has experimented with and composed in the serial technique.

Presently the major composer of his country, San Salvador's Germán Cáceres (*b.* 1954) is also an orchestra conductor and oboist. He earned undergraduate and graduate degrees at New York's Juilliard School of Music (1973–1978) and a doctorate in composition (1989) at the University of Cincinnati. His works have been performed in the United States, France, Holland, Switzerland, Germany, Austria, and Latin America, where he also performed and conducted. He has been invited to participate in numerous forums and contemporary music festivals and has been awarded several international prizes, among them Germany's International Gertrud Ramdohr Prize (1986). Currently he is the music director of the Sinfónica Nacional in San Salvador. In 1991, he won a fellowship from the Rockefeller Foundation.

Luis A. Delgadillo (1887–1964), who studied at the Milan Conservatory, is the major Nicaraguan composer of the twentieth century. He was director of the Escuela Nacional de Música in Managua, taught in Mexico and Panama, was the conductor of the Orquesta Nacional, and composed more than four hundred works in the nationalist style.

The early Costa Rican composers included Manuel María Gutiérrez (1829–1887), creator of the national anthem, the bandleader Rafael Chávez Tórrez (1839–1907), and Pedro Calderón Navarro (1864–1909), who composed principally religious music. Julio Fonseca (1885–1950), trained in Milan and Brussels, was the major Costa Rican composer of the first half of the twentieth century.

In 1964, Bernal Flores (*b.* 1937), who received his musical education at the Eastman School of Music in Rochester, New York, was appointed professor of music at the University of Costa Rica. Benjamín Gutiérrez (*b.* 1937), who attended the New England Conservatory in Boston and the Di Tella Institute in Buenos Aires, is a pianist and orchestra conductor. Together the two have trained numerous young Costa Rican composers.

Roque Cordero (*b.* 1917), a Panamanian, is the most prominent composer of Central America. He studied composition with Krenek and conducting with Chapple, Barzin, and Mitropoulos. In 1964 he founded and directed the Orquesta Nacional de Panamá. An adherent of nationalism in his early works, he turned, in 1946, to serialism. From 1972 to 1987 he was professor of composition at Illinois State University.

ANDEAN AREA

Colombia. Cartagena de Indias, founded in 1533, and Bogotá, founded five years later, were the two places where sacred music developed during the colonial period in the then Viceroyalty of New Granada. Juan Pérez Materano (*d.* 1561) was the first musician to conduct and perform sacred music in Cartagena. But during the rest of the colonial age the musical center of the region was the Bogotá cathedral, where Gutierre Fernández Hidalgo (1553–1620), the eminent sixteenth-century composer, was appointed chapelmaster in 1584. José de Cascante and Juan de Herrera continued the musical tradition after Fernández left for Quito and Sucre. The composer Roberto Pineda-Duque (1910–1977) devoted much of his life to writing and performing sacred music.

During the nineteenth century, music developed around opera and the European symphonic style. The first Sociedad Filarmónica was founded in 1847. Henry Price (1819–1863), an Englishman, settled in Colombia and began teaching music. His son Jorge Price (1853–1953) founded the Academia Nacional de Música in 1882. José María Ponce de León (1846–1882), composer of the first Colombian operas, *Ester* (1874) and *Florinda* (1880), and also of symphonic works, was a pioneer of nationalism in music. In 1909 the Academia Nacional became the Conservatorio Nacional and ever since brilliant composers have been associated with the institution, especially Guillermo Uribe Holguín (1880–1971), who was its director for twenty-five years, considered the most significant composer of his era. Andrés Martínez Montoya (1869–1933) and Santos Cifuentes (1870–1932) belonged to the same generation. Guillermo Espinosa (1905–1990), a conductor trained in Europe, founded the Orquesta Sinfónica Nacional in 1936 and served as its first director. Later, while chief of the OAS Music Division in Washington, D.C., he created the Inter American Music Festivals (1958–1974). Antonio María Valencia (1902–1952), a pianist trained in Paris, wrote songs and chamber music based on Colombian themes but with an impressionist influence. Two other internationally known Colombian composers are Luis Antonio Escobar (1925–1993) and Blás Emilio Atehortúa (*b.* 1933).

Ecuador. As early as 1550 Flemish monks of the Franciscan order founded the Colegio de San Andrés in Quito to instruct the sons of Indian chiefs in European polyphony and Gregorian chant. As a consequence, Diego Lobato (ca. 1538–ca. 1610), a mestizo and one of the sons of the Inca Atahualpa, became chapelmaster of the Quito cathedral in 1574. In 1588, Fernández Hidalgo arrived in Quito and served briefly as chapelmaster. Presumably, during the remainder of the colonial era, the performance of sacred music was divided between Quito and Guayaquil.

Although the Conservatorio Nacional de Música had been founded in 1870, it wasn't until 1903, when the Italian Domenico Brescia came to Quito to direct the conservatory, that the serious study of music began in Ecuador. A composer himself, he started the nationalist style along with his pupil Segundo Luis Moreno (1882–1972), who was also an ethnomusicologist and a folklorist. Pedro Pablo Traversari (1874–1956) continued in the same trend with a more romantic language. The leading composer of that period, however, was Luis H. Salgado (1903–1977), who composed two operas and several major symphonic works based on Indian legends. The Ecuadorian Mesías Maiguashca (*b.* 1938) studied at the Quito Conservatory and at the Eastman School of Music. He was a pupil of Messiaen and Ginastera at the Di Tella Institute in Buenos Aires and is internationally known for his experiments in avant-garde techniques. Since 1990 he has been the director of the Studio for Electronic Music in Freiburg's Musikhochschule.

Peru. On a par with Mexico, Peru was the other politically important entity in the Spanish colonies of the New World. Consequently, from the 1500s to the end of the colonial period, Lima and Cuzco became important centers of musical development. The chapelmasters and organists of the cathedrals of both cities were responsible for the diffusion of the polyphonic style of the High Renaissance. Gutierre Fernández Hidalgo (1553–1620)—the most influential sixteenth-century composer in Latin America—was the dominant figure in sacred music in Cuzco until a native American, José de Orejón y Aparicio (1706–1765), took control of the direction of Peruvian music. The viceroyal palace became famous for staging the first operas, concerts, and plays, including Tomás de Torrejón y Velasco's (1644–1728) *La púrpura de la rosa,* the first opera produced in America, in 1701. During the late 1700s Roque Ceruti (ca. 1683–1760) was the leading composer of both sacred and secular music. Italian opera owed a great deal to the Italian Carlo Enrico Pasta (1855–1898) and his opera *Atahualpa* (1877), which sparked an interest in that genre among the native Peruvians, particularly following the opening of Lima's Nuevo Teatro Principal (1889) and the Teatro Municipal (1904). The works of Daniel Alomía Robles (1871–1942), based on Indian melodies, spawned a nationalist movement that was continued by other composers, such as Teodoro Valcárcel (1902–1942).

Peruvian art music flourished in the late 1920s when two important European composers and musicologists, Andrés Sas (1900–1967) and Rudolf Holzmann (1910–1992), took up residence in Peru. They developed a solid school of composition based on European pedagogy that produced a generation of highly trained composers. A new breed of musicians, trained in the United States and Europe, is committed to experimenting with advanced techniques in the search for a new musical language. They are Enrique Iturriaga (*b.* 1918), Enrique Pinilla (*b.* 1927, *d.* 1989), César Bolaños (*b.* 1931), Edgar Valcárcel (*b.* 1932), and the Chilean born Celso Garrido-Lecca (*b.* 1926).

Bolivia. Called Audiencia de Charcas, or Alto Perú, during the viceroyalty, Bolivia depended on Lima for its musical life until the founding of the capital city of La Plata (later Chuquisaca, and since 1839, Sucre). As one of the wealthiest cities in the New World, La Plata became an important intellectual and musical center in Spanish America. Juan de Araújo (1646–1712), chapelmaster of the cathedral, was the most notable composer during the seventeenth century; the cathedral music library was improved with valuable manuscripts from European and American composers. A century later sacred music was directed by Manuel Mesa y Carrizo (*d.* 1773). After La Paz became the capital of Bolivia, musical activity became centered there. The first institutions founded were the Military School of Music (1904), the Conservatorio Nacional (1908), and the Círculo de Bellas Artes (1910). The Orquesta Nacional was created in 1940 by the leading nationalist composer José María Velasco-Maidana (*b.* 1900). Better known worldwide from that period were Eduardo Caba (1890–1953) and Simeón Roncal (1870–1953). Atiliano Auza-León (*b.* 1928) and Alberto Villalpando (*b.* 1940), both pupils of Ginastera's at the Di Tella Institute, experimented with serial and other avant-garde techniques.

Chile. During the seventeenth and eighteenth centuries the music of the church in Chile developed from simple plainchant and *villancicos* with guitar and flute accompaniment to complex polyphonic choral works, including pontifical masses. The secular music of the period of independence sounded strong echoes of European romanticism, especially in the piano pieces. And Italian opera found an avid and loyal audience among the general population. Two major institutions were founded in Santiago: the Conservatorio Nacional de Música (1849) and the Teatro Municipal (1857). In Valparaíso, the city that shared cultural life with the capital, the first opera stage was the Teatro de la Victoria (1844). In early 1800 the Sociedades Filarmónicas gave public concerts at Santiago, Valparaíso, Valdivia, Copiapó, Antofagasta, and Concepción. Composers of that era wrote instrumental music in the European romantic style and used the Italian technique when composing opera. Aquinas Ried (1810–1869) was a German native and author of the first Chilean opera, *La* *telesofra* (1846). Other musicians of that time were Manuel Robles (1780–1837), José Zapiola (1802–1885), Isidora Zegers (1803–1869), Federico Guzmán (1837–1885), and another German, Guillermo Frick (1813–1896).

A postromantic period was headed by Enrique Soro (1884–1954) and Alfonso Leng (1894–1974). Pedro H. Allende (1885–1959), a leader of nationalism, composed in an impressionistic style and incorporated Indian tunes into his works. Próspero Bisquertt (1881–1959), Carlos Lavin (1883–1962), and Carlos Isamitt (1887–1974) composed in a similar manner. Chilean art music, however, is the least nationalist of all in Latin America. Domingo Santa Cruz (1899–1987), a very influential composer, teacher, and administrator between 1920 and 1960, became a proponent of Hindemith's method of composition. An active promoter of academic institutions in Chile, he organized the Facultad de Artes Musicales and was its dean until 1965. In his footsteps came Jorge Urrutia-Blondel (*b.* 1905) and Alfonso Letelier (1912–1994). Juan Orrego-Salas (*b.* 1919) is well known outside Chile for his considerable output of interesting works, and for his work as director of the Latin American Music Center at Indiana University (1961–1990). The younger generation of Chilean composers, all of them experimenting with the lastest compositional techniques, includes Gustavo Becerra (*b.* 1925), León Schidlowsky (*b.* 1931), Fernando García (*b.* 1930), Miguel Aguilar-Ahumada (*b.* 1931), Juan Aménabar (*b.* 1922), and José Vicente Asuar (*b.* 1933).

BRAZIL, PARAGUAY, AND THE RÍO DE LA PLATA AREA

Brazil. Sacred music was introduced by the Franciscan monks but from 1550 on, the Jesuits were more influential in musical training in Bahia. The first organs were built in Pernambuco and Minas Gerais, and the first colonial composition (1759) was written in Bahia by Caetano de Mello Jesus, one of the chapelmasters (1740–1760) of the Bahia cathedral, the center of musical development at that time. In the late eighteenth century Minas Gerais was the social, artistic, and commercial center of the country. The music composed there came to a peak with the important religious works written by José Lôbo de Mesquita (ca. 1740–1805), Ignacio Parreiras Neves (ca. 1730–ca. 1793), Marcos Coelho Netto (*d.* 1823), Francisco Gomes da Rocha (*d.* 1808), and the prolific Bahian composer Damião Barbosa de Araújo (1778–1856). The most prominent religious composer of the colonial period was José Mauricio Nunes García (1767–1830), who wrote many masses and a famous requiem, and was chapelmaster of the Rio de Janeiro cathedral (1798).

Opera bloomed early in Bahia with the Casa da Opera da Praia (1760), followed by the Casa da Opera (1798), Teatro do Guadalupe, and Teatro São João (destroyed 1922). In Rio de Janeiro opera houses included the Royal Theater (later Imperial), San Pedro de Alcantara (1824), and Teatro Municipal (1909). Antonio Carlos Gomes (1836–1896) became the most prominent South American opera composer of the nineteenth century; his *Il Guaraní* premiered at the Teatro alla Scala (1870).

Itiberé da Cunha (1846–1913) was considered a nationalist composer, but it was Alberto Nepomuceno (1864–1920) who created the basis of a national movement. This trend was continued by Heitor Villa-Lobos (1887–1959), who composed more than one thousand works, and by Oscar Lorenzo Fernândez (1897–1948) and Luciano Gallet (1893–1931). In the next generation Francisco Mignone (1897–1986) and Camargo Guarnieri (*b.* 1907) both gained international reputations. Claudio Santoro (1919–1989) explored dodecaphonic theory and later the Bahian Group of Composers, founded in 1966, dedicated itself to experimenting with most advanced techniques. Carlos Nobre (*b.* 1939), who studied at the Di Tella Institute with Ginastera, Messiaen, Malipiero, and Dallapiccola, has achieved international recognition.

Paraguay. French operetta was performed at the Asunción Teatro Nacional in 1875, and Italian opera arrived, on the same stage, around 1877. The Orquesta Sinfónica de Asunción was founded (1951) by composer and conductor Carlos Lara-Bareiro (*b.* 1914), a music professor trained in Brazil, who settled in Buenos Aires (1960). His compositions, like those of Herminio Giménez (*b.* 1905), who studied at the Williams Conservatory in Buenos Aires, are nationalist and evoke Guaranian legends and tunes.

Uruguay. Sacred music was first heard in Montevideo at the Church of San Francisco in 1724 and later at the cathedral (1804). Hymns, *villancicos,* and psalms were performed early on, while more ornate polyphonic music developed in the 1800s. The San Francisco archives contain primitive liturgical works and elaborate masses of European and American origin. Fray Manuel Ubeda (ca. 1760–1823) wrote the *Misa para día de difuntos* (1802), the first religious work written in Uruguay. Three major chapelmasters settled in Montevideo, the Spaniards Antonio Sáenz (1829) and Carmelo Calvo (1871), and the Italian José Giuffra (1850). Theater music started with performances of Spanish *tonadillas escénicas* and *zarzuelas* at the Casa de Comedias (1793). In the 1820s Italian opera arrived in Montevideo, resulting in the construction of the *Teatro Solís* (1856), one of the largest opera houses in South America (2,800 seats) and site of the Montevideo debuts of Toscanini and Caruso (1903) and Richard Strauss conducting his *Elektra* (1923). Opera and concerts were also performed at the Teatro San Felipe (1879), Politeama (1890), Cibils (1893), and Urquiza, later the SODRE (3,000 seats), which opened in 1905 (destroyed by fire in 1971). The public's appetite for chamber and symphonic music was satisfied by the Sociedades Filarmónicas (1827–1853); the Orquesta Beethoven (1897); the Orquesta Nacional (1908); the Sociedad Orquestal (1929); OSSODRE (1931), the first official symphony orchestra. The Cuarteto La Lira (1873) initiated chamber music in Montevideo.

The three leading composers of the nineteenth century were Tomás Giribaldi (1847–1930), author of *La parisina* (1878), the first Uruguayan opera; León Ribeiro (1854–1931), who wrote the first string quartet; and Luis Sambucetti (1860–1926), who studied at the Paris Conservatory and composed the *Suite d'orchestre* (1899), the best symphonic work of that period. Nationalism started with three major composers: Alfonso Broqua (1876–1946), Eduardo Fabini (1882–1950), and Luis Cluzeau Mortet (1889–1957). César Cortinas (1890–1918) and Carlos Estrada (1909–1970) wrote in a universal style that, especially in Estrada's works, approached neoclassicism. The next generation was made up of both nationalistic composers and those experimenting with more advanced techniques, and included Vicente Ascone (1897–1979), Carlos Giucci (1904–1958), and Guido Santórsola (*b.* 1904). Héctor Tosar (1923–2002), the principal composer in the 1950s, has become universally well known since then. To the same generation belong Jaurés Lamarque Pons (1917–1982), Pedro Ipuche-Riva (*b.* 1924), Ricardo Storm (*b.* 1930), León Biriotti (*b.* 1929), and Antonio Mastrogiovanni (*b.* 1936). José Serebrier (*b.* 1938) and Sergio Cervetti (*b.* 1941), both living in the United States, are active as conductor and teacher, respectively.

Argentina. Religious music performed by the organ was heard in the church of Santiago del Estero as early as 1585, but the zenith of the colonial music period came with the Italian composer and organist Domenico Zipoli (1688–1726), when he arrived in Córdoba in 1717, then the most cultivated city in Argentina. Sacred music in Buenos Aires was introduced by the Jesuits (1611) and performed in the cathedral beginning in 1622. Stage music began to flourish with performances of *tonadillas escénicas* and *zarzuelas* at the Casa de Operas y Comedias (1757), and later at the Teatro de la Ranchería (1783). But it was at the Coliseo Provisional (1804), the Teatro de la Victoria (1838), the old Teatro Colón (1857–1888), and the Teatro de la Opera (1872) that Italian opera began its reign. *La gatta bianca,* the first Argentine opera, was performed at the Teatro de la Opera in 1877. With the opening of the new Teatro Colón (1908), which seats about four thousand spectators, international opera seasons began.

At the same time, there was enthusiastic popular interest in symphonic and chamber music not only in Buenos Aires, home of the Conservatorio Nacional, founded in 1880, but in Córdoba, Mendoza, Rosario, and other cities. The most celebrated composers of the nineteenth century were Juan Pedro Esnaola (1808–1878), Amancio Alcorta (1805–1862), and Juan Bautista Alberdi (1810–1884). The work of Alberto Williams (1862–1952), the most influential composer and teacher of that era, began a period of great advancement in music education. Arturo Berutti (1862–1938), whose operas, which premiered in Italy, were based on native plots, was a pioneer of nationalism in opera. He was followed by Felipe Boero (1884–1958), composer of *El matrero* (1929). Carlos López Buchardo (1881–1948) and Floro Ugarte (1884–1975) continued to refine the nationalist style, while Juan Carlos Paz (1897–1972), together with the composers Jacobo Ficher (1896–1978), Juan José Castro (1895–1968) and his brothers José María (1892–1964) and Washington Castro (*b.* 1909), Gilardo Gilardi (1889–1963), and Luis Gianneo (1897–1968), created the Grupo Renovación (1929) to search for new techniques and styles.

Roberto García Morillo (*b.* 1911) and Carlos Guastavino (*b.* 1914) belong to the next generation, which culminated with Alberto Ginastera (1916–1983), the most significant Latin American composer of the twentieth century. Rodolfo Arizaga (1926–1985), Roberto Caamaño (1923–1993), Francisco Kröpfl (*b.* 1928), and Alcides Lanza (*b.* 1929) are noteworthy representatives of the 1950s generation. The crop from the 1960s, many of them Ginastera pupils at the Di Tella Institute, includes Antonio Tauriello (*b.* 1931), Mauricio Kagel (*b.* 1931), Gerardo Gandini (*b.* 1936), Juan Carlos Zorzi (1936–1999), Armando Krieger (*b.* 1940), and Alicia Terzián (*b.* 1936).

See also **Campos-Parsi, Héctor; Fernández Hidalgo, Gutierre; García Morillo, Roberto; Gutiérrez y Espinosa, Felipe; Morales, Melesio; Nepomuceno, Alberto; Rosas, Juventino; Theater.**

BIBLIOGRAPHY

Renato Almeida, *Compendio de história da música brasileira,* rev. ed. (1942).

Luiz H. Corrêa De Acevedo, *Música e músicos do Brasil* (1950).

Lauro Ayestaran, *La música en el Uruguay* (1953).

Alejo Carpentier, *La música en Cuba,* 2d ed. (1961).

Robert Stevenson, *The Music of Peru* (1960), *Renaissance and Baroque Musical Sources in the Americas* (1970), and *Music in Mexico,* 2d ed. (1971).

Rodolfo Arizaga, *Enciclopedia de la música argentina* (1971); *Dictionary of Contemporary Music* (1974).

Claro and J. Urrutia Blondel, *Historia de la música en Chile* (1979).

Gérard Béhague, *Music in Latin America* (1979); *New Grove Dictionary of Music and Musicians* (1980).

Susana Salgado, *Breve historia de la música culta en el Uruguay,* 2d ed. (1980); *New Grove Dictionary of Opera* (1992).

Additional Bibliography

Olsen, Dale A., and Daniel E. Sheehy, eds. *The Garland Encyclopedia of World Music.* Vol. 2: *South America, Central America, Mexico and the Caribbean.* New York: Garland, 1988.

Rodicio, Emilio Casares, et al., eds. *Diccionario de la música española y hispanoamericana.* Madrid: Sociedad General de Autores y Editores, 1999.

Sadie, Stanley, ed. *The New Grove Dictionary of Music and Musicians.* London: Macmillan, 2001.

SUSANA SALGADO

POPULAR MUSIC AND DANCE

Popular music is generally distinguished from folk music, although it often has roots in folk traditions. Its commercial dimension and its unavoidable connection with radio, TV, the cinema, and above all sound recording make it essentially a phenomenon born of the twentieth century. This essay focuses primarily on distinctly Latin American popular music (and, where appropriate, associated dance forms), with a final note on the music and dance related to the international, Anglo-American mainstream, that is, the various musical trends deriving from the rock-and-roll revolution of the 1950s and 1960s. This music, of essentially North American provenance (with some notable British inputs), has proved just as popular in Latin America as elsewhere (as a visit to any large Latin American music store will reveal). From the 1960s onward, the international mainstream stimulated a host of local imitations and creative musical fusions of variable quality. Some trends of this sort (Argentina's *rock nacional* of the 1980s, for instance, or Brazil's more recent techno-samba) have won growing international attention. Such trends have made an obvious and important contribution to the overall pattern of Latin American popular music, and apparently satisfied many Latin American tastes since the 1980s, especially among youth; but their regional characteristics are less pronounced than other popular musics, drawing as they do (often eclectically) on foreign influences.

Alongside the international mainstream and its local reformulations, a great variety of regional and national musical and dance forms and styles have displayed great vitality and staying power. Indeed, some Latin American trends have had great influence on popular music and jazz in North America and Europe. The tango, the samba, and the bossa nova, for example, made their marks internationally, whereas the longer and more continuous influence of Cuban dance music has had a pervasive effect on the taste of Latin American communities in the United States. No Latin American country has had quite the same overseas impact in these matters as has Cuba, especially the Cuba of the period from the 1920s to the 1950s.

The two primary influences on Latin American popular music and dance have been European and African. European influence has for obvious reasons been strongly Hispanic, but by no means exclusively so, for nineteenth-century dance forms such as the waltz, the polka, and the mazurka have all played an important part. The impact of indigenous folk traditions has been much less marked, and the extent to which such traditions can be said to be "pure" is still a matter for debate. Plenty of highly attractive Native American folk music can still be heard, especially in the Andean countries, but it is hard to argue that these folkloric traditions have influenced major modern trends, except locally, as in the urban popular music of Peru, where Andean-style *huaynos* and *carnivalitos*, for instance, are present in both the performed and recorded repertoires. Indigenous influence achieved a wider international effect in the use made of traditional Andean instruments, such as the *quena* and the *charango*, in certain "neofolk" traditions, notably in the Southern Cone. The international impact of such music, especially after the 1960s, helped folk ensembles from Peru and in particular Bolivia (Los Jairas, Rumillajta, Inti-Raymi, and others) to win applause far from South America.

MEXICO

Indigenous influence is not in the least discernible in the popular music of Mexico. This largest of the Spanish-speaking nations has a rich profusion of Hispanic-mestizo folk traditions, some of which (such as the *corridor*, the ballad form often associated with the Revolution) overlap the boundary between folk and popular music. Mexico's preponderant modern forms have been international (ballads and love songs, for example). The Cuban bolero, transformed into the lilting and sentimental ballad popular throughout Spanish America from the 1940s, was perhaps more cultivated in Mexico than elsewhere, not least at the hands of the legendary composer-performer Agustín Lara and later the Chilean-born singer Lucho Gatica. Nonetheless, certain distinctively Mexican kinds of music may be found, including some of which have achieved immense local popularity. The so-called *canción ranchera* (country song) enjoyed a great vogue in the middle decades of the century, when the flourishing Mexican movie industry gave a particular boost to this simple type of song, which typically focuses on patriotism (and sentiment for the *patria chica*) and masculinity. The favored vocal style is open and rather exaggerated; the vocalists are accompanied by mariachi ensembles (brass, violin, guitar) or by accordion-based groups. (Mariachi ensembles may take their name from the French *mariage*, assimilated at the time of the French occupation of the 1860s, though this etymology has been disputed.) Jorge Negrete, Pedro Infante, and Pedro Vargas sang in this tradition, and others, to very good effect. Negrete, a noted film star as well as a singer, was one of the great heartthrobs of his generation.

A distinctive Mexican regional form is the so-called *música norteña* (northern music), with its accordion-led groups specializing in polkas, waltzes, and *corridos*. Its close musical relative across the border, Tex-Mex, is best considered a regional U.S. form. The popular music of Mexico's southern neighbor, Guatemala, and of other Central American republics has been strongly marked by Mexican influence; it is also noted for its prominent use of the marimba, probably an African-derived large form of xylophone, which has become the Guatemalan national instrument. It is not surprising that the main manifestations of Euro-African fusion have occurred where contact between Europeans and Africans was historically greatest: the Caribbean and Brazil.

CUBA

In the Caribbean, it is important to highlight the vital role of Cuba—a great musical crossroads and a fertile source of trends, attributable to the assimilation of African elements (syncopation, heavy use of percussion) into a magnificent series of dance forms. The first of these was the early nineteenth-century *habanera*, partly derived from the French *contredanse* imported into Cuba by refugees after the Haitian revolution. In Cuba it soon acquired the repeated short phrases that are a clear sign of African influence. Its successor in popularity, the *danzón*, dominant from the 1880s to the 1920s, was played by ensembles known as *charangas francesas*, or simply *charangas* (piano, violin, flute, bass, percussion). The more purely Afro-Cuban *rumba* dance and song, with its strongly percussive accompaniment, developed at roughly the same time. In due course the *danzón* was displaced by the *son*, the most influential of all Cuban dance forms. It became entrenched in the 1920s and 1930s with some first-rate bands, such as Sexteto Habanero, Septeto Nacional, and Trío Matamoros. The instrumental lineup in such ensembles—the forebears of the great midcentury dance bands—included trumpets, bass, guitar (or the *tres*, the Cuban nine-stringed variant), and a strong percussion section. From this point on, Cuban dance music proved thoroughly exportable; it was popularized in Europe by bands such as the Lecuona Cuban Boys and (more briefly) Don Azpiazú's Havana Casino Orchestra, whose hit recording of "El manicero" ("The Peanut Vendor"), a *son* often misleadingly labeled as a rumba, took the United States by storm in 1931. Mention should be made of two great bandleaders, the Spaniard Xavier Cugat (who grew up in Cuba) and the Scottish-Venezuelan Edmundo Ros (born in Trinidad, brought up in Venezuela), who made Cuban music familiar (albeit in clearly attenuated form) to large audiences in both the United States and Britain, respectively. Since the 1940s, Cuban dance music has been prevalent in many parts of Africa, especially west and central Africa, where Cuban influence was fundamental, though less so after the 1960s.

Alongside the ubiquitous *son*, other noteworthy Cuban dance forms are the cha-cha, adopted by the *charangas* in the 1950s and especially popular (in somewhat modified form) in the United States; the lively *guaracha*, and the mambo, which incorporated U.S.-swing influence and was popularized in the 1950s by prominent bandleaders such as Pérez Prado. In the 1950s numerous distinguished Cuban dance bands flourished, in New York City as well as Cuba, and the *son* and the rumba fused to create the authentic midcentury "Cuban sound."

Salsa music (a generic label) stems in large part from the midcentury Cuban *son*-rumba fusion and became extraordinarily popular in Latin America and among Latin Americans in the United States from the 1960s on. Its best-known stars were the Cuban-born Celia Cruz (who left Cuba in 1960) and the Puerto Rican New Yorker Willie Colón. Musically, salsa has been both diverse and constantly changing. In Cuba itself, where the salsa label was intensely disliked, the years following the 1959 Revolution saw relatively little innovation in the traditional rhythms that had given the island so much international fame. Groups such as Irakere and Los Van Van later developed interestingly eclectic combinations of styles, while the Nueva Trova movement, whose internationally best known figure was the singer Silvio Rodríguez, derived much of its impetus from the Latin American *nueva canción* ("new song") tendency of the later 1960s.

PUERTO RICO

The development of Puerto Rico's popular music is similar to that of Cuba's in important respects—the *danza* to some extent paralleling the *danzón*, the *bomba* and *plena* clearly related to the original Afro-Cuban rumba, and so on—though it has been argued that the African influence was even stronger in Puerto Rico. The island's political link with the United States, coupled with the diplomatic and commercial isolation of revolutionary Cuba, allowed Puerto Rican musicians, such as the instrumentalists Bobby Valentín, Luis "Perico" Ortiz, and Tommy Olivencia, and the singer Hector Lavoe, to play a leading part in the salsa explosion of the 1970s, in the United States as well as Puerto Rico itself and elsewhere in Latin America.

DOMINICAN REPUBLIC

In the Dominican Republic, the national form has been the merengue, with its fast-moving 2/4 rhythm and simple choreography. In its original rural environment, the merengue was played on *tambora* drums, *guiros* (scrapers), and the guitar or *tres*. In the town, accordions and, later, saxophones were included in the instrumental lineups. This dance music was strongly encouraged for nationalistic reasons (though the lyrics added to it were strictly controlled) during the thirty-year dictatorship of General Rafael Trujillo. In the 1970s and 1980s the merengue had a considerable international impact with such talented musician-entrepreneurs as Johnny Ventura (singer) and Wilfrido Vargas (trumpeter).

COLOMBIA

In similar fashion, in Colombia during the 1940s and 1950s, popular taste was captured by the insistent 4/4 rhythm (with accent on the second beat) of the *cumbia*, a dance originally from the Caribbean coast and Panama. Like salsa and the merengue, the *cumbia* soon became well known all over Spanish America. (The Guatemalan marimba repertoire, for instance, quickly incorporated both *cumbias* and merengues.) Another important Colombian tradition, *vallenato* music, is a "country" style from the north of the republic, with Hispanic rather than Afro-Hispanic roots, and with the accordion prominent in its instrumental ensembles.

BRAZIL

The other great area of Euro-African fusion is, of course, Brazil, where, as in Cuba, slavery survived longer than elsewhere in the Americas. Here the earliest domestic forms of popular music were the *choro*, an instrumental form (from *chorar*, "to weep," not *coro* "chorus"), and *maxixe* (a Brazilian polka adaptation) of the nineteenth century. A key figure at the turn of the century was the highly talented pianist-composer Ernesto Nazareth, who labeled some of his *choros* and *maxixes* "Brazilian tangos," which should not be confused with the Argentine tango, though in both cases the influence of the Cuban habanera was strong.

Samba. A new and soon hegemonic national song-dance form emerged in the early twentieth century in the samba. (A masculine noun in Portuguese, its etymology is uncertain.) It probably originated in the heavily Afro-Brazilian Northeast but soon became inseparably associated with Rio de Janeiro. There have been numerous samba variants and derivatives. The "street samba," accompanied by formidable polyrhythmic percussion (Brazil has easily the highest number of percussion instruments of any country in the Americas) was complemented from the 1920s by the somewhat slower *samba-canção* (samba-song). Prominent writers of sambas during the acknowledged golden age (1920s–1950s) include Pixinguinha (Alfredo da Rocha Viana) and Ary Barroso, whose "Aquarela do Brasil" (1939) several times became a hit (under the title "Brazil") in the United States. An early star of the tradition, with numerous hit recordings in the 1930s, was the legendary Carmen Miranda, who later transferred her talents to the screen in Hollywood. The role of the samba in Brazilian carnivals—the samba schools (from the later 1920s), lavish costumes, and ornate floats—has often attracted international notice, achieving worldwide exposure through the 1959 film *Orfeu negro* (*Black Orpheus*). Samba lyrics are often very topical, and even political, and the form has proved open to manipulation by governments, most notably during the Getúlio Vargas regime and the military dictatorship of 1964–1985, through subsidies to the samba clubs and the monitoring and censorship of songs.

Bossa Nova. The bossa nova, a samba derivative that emerged toward the end of the 1950s, incorporated "cool" jazz influence from the United States. Among those who gave it worldwide fame in the early 1960s was João Gilberto, who, along with the singer Antônio Carlos Jobim and the poet Vinícius de Morais, was a principal begetter of the new form; Astrud Gilberto had striking international success with the song "A garota de Ipanema" ("The Girl from Ipanema"), which would have to go on any list of the Latin American Top Twenty of the twentieth century.

Tropicalismo. Another outstanding Brazilian artist, Chico Buarque, usually considered the finest Brazilian songwriter since the 1960s and a central figure of the *musica popular Brasileira* (commonly referred to as MPB) movement of the late 1960s, both wrote and performed songs whose sheer poetic quality has often been remarked on, though they also frequently ran afoul of the military censors of the period. MPB built upon bossa nova and encompassed a diversity of styles, which shared in common their Brazilian musical roots and often politically inflected lyrics. Another important singer-songwriter to emerge from the MPB movement was Milton Nascimento, who by the 1990s had gained international renown by collaborating with musicians such as Paul Simon and Pat Metheny. Also of great importance in Brazil after the later 1960s was the short-lived Tropicália, or *tropicalismo*, movement. Its two leading figures were Caetano Veloso and Gilberto Gil, both of whom were briefly imprisoned by the military regime, and who became superstars by the 1980s; Maria Bethania also built a major career stemming from this trend. Tropicalismo was identified with no single form or style. Indeed, its principal exponents consciously wished to create a "universal sound," drawing on whatever national or international trends took their fancy, and often successfully fusing rock with local rhythms.

Despite the predominance of the samba and its variants and derivatives, Brazilian popular music (easily the most successful of Latin American traditions in terms of sales in Europe and the United States in the 1980s and 1990s) continues to be marked by rich diversity, as befits the enormous size of the country. A prominent local form, actually a series of forms, largely unnoticed outside Brazil is *música sertaneja*, a "country" tradition comparable to its U.S. equivalent, accounting for more than one-third of record sales in the 1980s. In Salvador, Bahia, as part of the Afro-Brazilian cultural upsurge of the 1970s and 1980s, black carnival associations (*blocos afros*) elaborated new carnival-related musical forms, including the samba-reggae hybrid.

At another level, Brazilian music (including tropicalismo) has been more than somewhat influenced by the international mainstream, which has produced several more or less respectable local variants, especially strong in the São Paulo megalopolis. As with elsewhere in Latin America, punk rock of the 1970s exercised a particularly strong influence on Brazilian rock music, or *iêiêiê*, as it is often called locally (from the Beatles' "yeah, yeah, yeah"). This can be explained by the rapid development of Brazilian mass society and the growth of a flourishing mass media, including huge recording and TV industries.

Tango dancers, Buenos Aires, Argentina. Developed in the poor areas of Buenos Aires in the late nineteenth century, the tango became a popular cultural export across the world with its blend of European and Afro-Argentinean dance steps and music. © JON HICKS/CORBIS

ARGENTINA

Argentina was the first Latin American country to undergo the transition to mass society (1920s–1930s). The republic's spectacular economic boom, its urbanization, and the purchasing power of its people meant that a large market for records and radios existed earlier than elsewhere in Latin America. This occurred before the explosion of the electronic media that took place after World War II and before the appearance of the international mainstream. Certainly U.S. popular music was well known in Argentina, especially with the coming of "talkies" (a very solid local jazz tradition also developed early), but it was in no sense hegemonic. It was possible for a locally created form to become predominant among the mass public, as occurred with the tango, the first Latin American musical form to win universal renown. The tango as a dance triumphed spectacularly on European dance floors in 1913–1914. A combination of European and (in its choreography) Afro-Argentine elements, the tango originated in the poor outer districts of Buenos Aires in the 1880s, and a rich musical tradition developed at the turn of the century. Initially played in 2/4 time, the dance slowed down after the 1910s, and the music (usually in 4/8 from then on) became more sentimental and tinged with melancholy. From the 1910s to the 1950s this was the popular music of Argentina and Uruguay.

The tango's golden age (roughly 1920–1950) produced a great profusion of distinguished bands (Julio de Caro, Francisco Canaro, Osvaldo Fresedo, Aníbal Troilo, and many more), with the German-made bandoneon a key instrument in such ensembles. (A cousin of the accordion, the fully developed bandoneon has seventy-one buttons, each of which produces two tones, depending on whether the instrument is being inflated or deflated; it is very difficult to play well.) Like so many Latin American dance forms, the tango soon became a form of popular song. Vocalists who added to the tradition included Ignacio Corsini, Agustín Magaldi, Francisco Fiorentino, Azucena Maizani, Mercedes Simone, and Ada Falcón. This popular musical tradition can hold its own with any in the world this century for sheer quality, and can easily lay claim to being Latin America's greatest. The absolute superstar of the tango tradition, and indeed Latin America's first twentieth-century superstar, was the baritone Carlos Gardel. Rising to local fame in the 1910s as a folksinger, he specialized in tangos from the early 1920s. His richly expressive voice and endearing personality won him huge popularity; sixty years after his death, he remained for millions of Latin Americans quite simply the best popular singer ever.

The tango's hegemony in Argentina and Uruguay eventually waned. Although the avant-garde tango musician Astor Piazzolla was to win great international distinction in the 1970s and 1980s, his standing with the Argentine public up to that point was ambiguous, and his work really transcended the limits of popular music. The tango was challenged in the 1950s not only by international pop music but also by a new and very distinguished Argentine trend often labeled "neofolklore." Musicians in Argentina, as elsewhere, were able to tap into a rich tradition of rural music, and not only recaptured songs and rhythms on the point of disappearing, but made them the basis for songs in folk idiom yet with sophisticated arrangements and instrumental lineups. This process occurred independently in several countries, but was perhaps most prominent in Argentina, with groups such as Los Chalchaleros and Los Fronterizos, singers such as Atahualpa Yupanqui (noted for his left-wing commitment), and writers like Ariel Ramírez. The neofolk approach continues to inspire musicians all over Latin America, and it has been applied to a great variety of purposes. In the 1950s and 1960s, for instance, there was a rash of folk masses, the most celebrated being Ramírez's *Misa criolla*, the album of which sold all over the world. The neofolk idiom has also had a readily discernible influence on the music used in church services, Catholic and Protestant alike.

CHILE

Argentine neofolklore had a special impact on Chile, always a country receptive to trans-Andean influence in music and in slang (though never in politics). By the early 1960s a Chilean version of neofolklore had emerged, rather smooth and prettified though technically admirable. Groups such as Los Huasos Quincheros held their own against the rising tide of imported foreign music, which at that period included a discernible Mexican component (including the wave of *rocancol*, Spanish-language derivative bands, such as Los Teen Tops and Los Locos del Ritmo). Meanwhile, a number of devoted Chilean *folkloristas* had been collecting and transcribing rural folk songs, Margot Loyola and Violeta Parra being the best known. Parra also composed and performed her own songs in folk idiom, usually with guitar or *charango* accompaniment. These songs represent a high point of Chilean (and Latin American) culture in the 1960s—some surely as beautiful as any written anywhere during the twentieth century.

Parra's two children, Angel and Isabel, continued the tradition, and by the time their mother died in 1967, a new trend was crystallizing in Chile. It was not until a year or two later that it acquired the label *nueva canción chilena* ("new Chilean song"). Its emphases and priorities were later extensively imitated all over Latin America. (The Cuban Nueva Trova group, for instance, was much influenced.) The new Chilean song had certain definite aims: to break from commercial popular music; to purify Chilean neofolklore from its prettification and innocuousness; to experiment with instruments, especially by incorporating such Andean instruments as the *quena* and the *charango* into ensembles; and to diversify the subject matter of popular songs, specifically to give them a strong social and political edge. The sympathies of the movement inclined it to support the Socialist and Communist parties in Chile and the ill-fated Allende government, elected in 1970. The trend produced some notable groups (Inti-Illimani, Quilapayún) and some good singers: the Parra children themselves, Rolando Alarcón, Patricio Manns, and above all Víctor Jara, a poet-singer of genius who was brutally murdered by the Chilean military at the time of its seizure of power in September 1973. After Allende's overthrow, the surviving musicians continued their work in exile, while the new dictatorship strove to expunge all memory of them.

Although the "new song" never came near to establishing itself as a dominant musical tendency in Latin America, and had less of an international impact than, say, midcentury Cuban dance music, its fresh and vital contribution is beyond question. Like the Argentine tango, this was popular music of high quality, standing out amid the pandemonium of the international mainstream. Indeed, many Latin American contributions to the world's popular music of the twentieth century were of a consistently high quality and a true measure of the region's astonishing creativity.

SINCE THE 1980S

Rock underwent a renaissance in the 1980s and reflected a firmer grounding in Latin American cultural esthetics, as well as sonic and political sensibilities. Groups such as the Mexican band Café Tacuba creatively fused regional styles (such as *son jarocho*) with international trends (such as ska and metal), to produce a cosmopolitan rock sound with national, regional, and international appeal. Indeed, such fusion has carried itself across the border and is reflected in the convergence of U.S. and Latin American popular musical styles, through groups such as Ozomatli, Lila Downs, and others. Also in the 1980s the Dominican performer Juan Luis Guerra popularized a commercialized form of merengue that ushered in a resurgent interest across the region among all social classes for *música tropical*—salsa, merengue, *cumbia*, *bachata*. Since the late 1990s two new trends in popular music can be discerned. The first is hip-hop, whose emphasis on lyrics and sparse technical requirements allowed it to spread rapidly, especially among the lower classes. Cuba and Brazil, notably, have exceptionally strong *rapero* (rap) scenes and the Cuban government has even sponsored an annual hip-hop festival. The second trend is *reggaetón*, a dance style said to have originated in Puerto Rico (others suggest Panama) and which melds reggae-derived beats with rap lyrics and a cross-section of other Latin American dance rhythms, such as salsa and *bomba*. This inclusiveness has made *reggaetón* immensely popular not only across Latin America, but also in the United States.

See also **Barroso, Ary; Bolero; Bossa Nova; Choro, Chorinho; Corrido; Cruz, Celia; Cugat, Xavier; Cumbia; Gardel, Carlos; Gil, Gilberto; Gilberto, João; Jara, Víctor; Jobim, Antônio Carlos "Tom"; Lara, Agustín; Mambo; Mariachi; Marimba; Maxixe; Merengue; MPB: Música Popular Brasileira; Parra, Violeta; Patria Chica; Pixinguinha; Samba; Samba Schools; Son; Tango; Tropicalismo; Veloso, Caetano.**

BIBLIOGRAPHY

Austerlitz, Paul. *Merengue: Dominican Music and Dominican Identity.* Philadelphia: Temple University Press, 1996.

Azzi, María Susana, et al. *Antropología del tango: Los protagonistas.* Buenos Aires: Ediciones de Olavarría, 1991.

Chasteen, John Charles. *National Rhythms, African Roots: The Deep History of Latin American Popular Dance.* Albuquerque: University of New Mexico Press, 2004.

Clark, Walter A., ed. *From Tango to Tejano: Essays on Latin American Popular Music.* New York: Routledge, 2002

Collier, Simon. *The Life, Music, and Times of Carlos Gardel.* Pittsburgh: University of Pittsburgh Press, 1986.

Glasser, Ruth. *My Music Is My Flag: Puerto Rican Musicians and Their New York Communities, 1917–1940.* Berkeley: University of California Press, 1997.

Guillermoprieto, Alma. *Samba.* New York: Knopf, 1990.

Jara, Joan. *An Unfinished Song: The Life of Victor Jara.* New York: Ticknor and Fields, 1983.

Manuel, Peter. *Popular Musics of the Non-Western World: An Introductory Survey.* New York: Oxford University Press, 1988.

Moore, Robin. *Nationalizing Blackness: Afrocubanismo and Artistic Revolution in Havana, 1920-1940.* Pittsburgh: University of Pittsburgh Press, 1997.

Moore, Robin. *Music and Revolution: Cultural Change in Socialist Cuba.* Berkeley: University of California Press, 2006.

Pacini Hernandez, Deborah; Héctor Fernández L'Hoeste; and Eric Zolov, eds. *Rockin' Las Américas: The Global Politics of Rock in Latin/o America.* Pittsburgh: University of Pittsburgh Press, 2004.

Perrone, Charles A. *Masters of Contemporary Brazilian Song: MPB, 1965–1985.* Austin: University of Texas Press, 1989.

Perrone, Charles A., and Christopher Dunn, eds. *Brazilian Popular Music and Globalization.* Gainesville: University Press of Florida, 2001.

Roberts, John Storm. *The Latin Tinge: The Impact of Latin American Music on the United States,* 2nd edition. New York: Oxford University Press, 1999.

Veloso, Caetano. *Tropical Truth: A Story of Music and Revolution in Brazil.* Translated by Barbara Einzig. New York: Knopf, 2002.

Vianna, Hermano. *The Mystery of Samba: Popular Music and Identity in Brazil.* Translated and edited by John C. Chasteen. Chapel Hill: University of North Carolina Press, 1999.

Waxer, Lise. *Situating Salsa: Global Markets and Local Meanings in Latin Popular Music.* New York: Routledge: 2002.

Zolov, Eric. *Refried Elvis: The Rise of the Mexican Counterculture.* Berkeley: University of California Press, 1999.

Eric Zolov
Simon Collier

PRE-COLUMBIAN MUSIC OF MESOAMERICA

From the beginning of civilization on the American continent, music was linked to almost every human activity. Religion, war, ceremonies, births, feasts, games, love, and death had unique and unmistakable musical contexts. In ancient times, the character of music was more functional than aesthetic. For this reason, instruments were conceived in accordance with the spiritual requirements of each situation, and great attention was paid to the acoustical quality. The forms of animals, metaphysical entities, and people of the time were incorporated into many instruments. The oldest known musical instrument originated in the Olmec civilization (Veracruz and Tabasco, Mexico, 1500–100 BCE).

Musician-artisans devoted their inventive efforts chiefly to wind and percussion instruments. The best-known instruments were flutes, whistles, and ocarinas of clay; the horizontal wooden drum called *tunkul* and the slit wooden drum called *teponaztli;* the three-legged, vertical wooden drum called *huéhuetl;* and the Mayan *timbal,* a small, U-shaped, clay drum. Some of these percussion instruments are still in use today. Musical instruments were decorated with symbolic figures, and for this reason they had specific purposes. During the colonial period any instrument whose use was thought to be linked to the ancient religions was banned as heretical by the Inquisition.

In pre-Columbian times, the voice was also an important musical element. In schools of music, dance, and poetry, vocal arts were also taught. Musicians were often singers, and poets frequently sang about their uncertainties and pleasures. And in the shamanistic singing of the priests and witch doctors, the initiate sought to reveal the words of the divine world through the spiritual trance.

WIND INSTRUMENTS

The shapes of the wind instruments were extraordinarily varied. There are whistles and ocarinas representing crabs, iguanas, frogs, ocelots, chameleons, snakes, coyotes, dogs, crickets, turtles, pelicans, parrots, turkeys, and a great number of other birds. The form of the animal gave the instrument its shape and volume. Whistles and ocarinas were generally small and could be suspended from a cord around the neck.

Flutes had from two to five holes, and their ranges went from sweet and innocent to dark echoes of the pre-Columbian inner world. The majority of those between 4 and 8 inches long were cheerful and songlike, and could also be made to sound like birds. Those from 8 to 12 inches long had a medium sound, neither high-pitched nor deep. Those more than 12 inches long tended toward a mysterious sound. They were made of clay, and almost all were decorated with human or animal images. Flutes also could consist of two, three, or four parallel tubes connected to one mouthpiece. Reed flutes, which are still played today, were quite common.

Conch shells were used in the worship of the sun god, as well as to call the people together. Clay facsimiles of conch shells were made that replicated the sounds of the natural ones.

Small trumpets were made of clay, medium-sized ones were fashioned from large calabashes, and the largest, like those depicted in the Mayan mural at Bonampak, were of wood. These large trumpets had a very deep and muffled sound compared with the shrillness of the small clay trumpets.

PERCUSSION INSTRUMENTS

The horizontal log drum, or *teponaztli,* is sometimes described as a two-keyed xylophone. It resembled a wooden log enclosed at each end and was often covered with carved designs. An I-shaped slit cut in the top allowed the tongues on each side to produce a different warm watery tone when struck by mallets with natural rubber tips called *olmaitl.* An "I" was also cut in the base to increase volume. A drummer usually stood upright to play the *teponaztli,* which was placed on a support.

The skins of deer, jaguars, and monkeys were combined with wood and clay in a great many shapes and sizes to make drums. An example notable for its expressive power and ritual use is the *huéhuetl,* or *zakatán,* a large, three-legged, vertical drum that the musician played with the hands while standing.

The *teponazhuéhuetl* was a combination instrument similar to the *teponaztli* but with a skin at each end of the cylindrical body. Small clay bongos with sharp, cheerful tones also were made.

An unusual percussion instrument was the water drum, so called because it consisted of a vessel containing water on which floated half of a hollowed-out calabash, its convex side facing the musician. This was beaten with a stick covered with corn leaves.

The turtle shell was played with a deer antler, a rubber stick, or a tree branch. Different shells produced different tones.

A stone became a percussion instrument when struck against a smaller one. The sound was crystalline and quite resonant, very similar to bottles containing water.

Probably the clay vessel was played as an instrument before the Conquest, since it is still heard today in the indigenous music of various regions and cultures with roots in the Mesoamerican past. However, no documented proof of this exists.

STRING INSTRUMENTS

Whether or not string instruments existed is unknown, except for (probably) the musical bow. This was a type of hunting bow whose cord was beaten with two arrows, using a large calabash as a resonator. Today this is known as the *tepehuano* bow.

BIBLIOGRAPHY

Robert Stevenson, *Music in Aztec and Inca Territory* (1968).

Norman Hammond, *Classic Maya Music* (1972).

Sibyl Marcuse, *Musical Instruments: A Comprehensive Dictionary* (1975).

Luis Antonio Escobar, *La música precolombina* (1985); *Instrumentos musicales de América Latina y el Caribe* (1988).

Additional Bibliography

Archaeology, Inc. *Secrets of the Maya.* New York: Hatherleigh Press, 2003.

Gómez, Luis Antonio. *El libro de música Mexica a través de los cantares mexicanos.* México: Colegio Nacional de Bibliotecarios: Información Científica Internacional, 2001.

ANTONIO ZEPEDA

PRE-COLUMBIAN MUSIC OF SOUTH AMERICA

Music once illuminated secular and sacred life throughout South America. Today we have nothing but the archaeological remains of musical instruments and iconography, which have been preserved mainly in the Andean region. Those remains give us information of some possible sounds and their relations with specific cultural spheres. Early Spanish accounts and the ethnographic study of living Indian traditions enable us to interpret their musical meaning.

Instrumentation developed mainly in the flute realm, with a rich variety of shapes, timbres, and musical possibilities. Some flutes produced melodies and others produced harsh timbres and dissonant chords between two adjacent tones. The first were represented by the siku, a reed panpipe that existed as early as the Chorrera culture (1000–300 BCE) and reached a great development during the Moche culture (CE 100–800), lasting to the present in the Andean region from Bolivia to Panama. The siku was sometimes played in complimentary pairs, sometimes in big orchestras of many pairs of musicians, as in modern Aymara usage, to produce very elaborated melodies. Another popular flute to play melodies was the *kena* (quena), a reed or bone-notched, end-blown flute. It appeared around 5000 BCE and gained great popularity in Moche and Inca times and is still played. Outstanding chord-flutes include the delicately sound-balanced double ocarina found in the Andes between Ecuador and Peru (300 BCE–CE 500) and the antara, a ceramic panpipe in which each tube produces a shrill, vibrating tone. It appeared in Paracas (700–200 BCE), developed in Nazca (100 BCE–CE 400) and later in Atacama and southward, up to the Inca conquest (1400–1535). Stone flutes of the Mapuche region show a wide variety of forms. Another interesting flute, of unknown use, is the whistling ceramic vessel, a Chorrera invention that uses a hydraulic system to produce sound. It became very popular in the coastal central Andean region between 500 BCE and CE 1470 and reached Mesoamerica to the north. Conch-shell trumpets appeared in Chavín (1000–200 BCE) and existed up to Inca times. They were precious objects obtained by trade in Ecuatorial coasts and reaching the Peruvian highlands. Straight trumpets of metal, wood, cane, and ceramic, of diverse shapes, were also used throughout the Andes.

Cylindrical double-headed drums existed in the Andean region. They were played with a single stick or sometimes with a notched rope. Idiophones of different shapes were also common; the most important type was the rattle of gourd, ceramic, metal, or other materials. It was an important shamanistic instrument. Ecuatorian stone percussive chimes appeared between 500 BCE and CE 500. There is no definite evidence of pre-Columbian clarinets, oboes, or chordophones, although there may have been a pre-Columbian musical bow. It is probably safe to say that, as in present-day Indian music, the most important element in pre-Columbian music was the human voice, especially shamanic trance-songs, including rituals using psychoactive plants. Scales were varied, including three-, five-, and six-tone scales, and melodies had a tendency toward tonal development. Whereas Western music presents a tendency toward the use of different voices in a coordinate tonal and rhythmic manner, avoiding parallel motion and noncoincidence, in pre-Columbian music the probable tendency was the opposite, toward the use of parallel motion or of discoordinated tonality and rhythm, avoiding coincidence. The "vertical" conception of sound was developed to produce sound clusters, probably related to the search for altered states of consciousness. Outside the Andes there is no archaeological evidence of pre-Columbian music in South America, although ethnographic data shows a rich and varied musical life in the great Amazonian region. The Selk'nam had a vocal music tradition with no musical instruments.

BIBLIOGRAPHY

Latin America lacks a general survey on pre-Columbian music. An unsurpassed general survey on archaeological and ethnographic instruments is Karl G. Izikowitz, *Musical and Other Sound Instruments of the South American Indians* (1934). See also Robert Stevenson, *Music in Aztec and Inca Territory* (1968). A summary on recorded sounds is the cassette José Pérez De Arce, *Instrumentos precolombinos* (1982).

Additional Bibliography

Bejar, Ana Maria, and Raúl R. Romero. *Música, danzas, y máscaras en los Andes.* Lima: Pontificia Universidad Católica del Perú: Instituto Riva-Aguero, Proyecto de Preservación de la Música Tradicional Andina, 1993.

Harcourt, Raoul d' and Marguerite d'. *La música de los Incas y sus supervivencias.* Lima: Occidental Petroleum Corp. of Peru, 1990.

José Perez de Arce

MUSICAL INSTRUMENTS. This article will focus on musical instruments used in post-Columbian times, regardless of their period of origin. Because Latin America is a mosaic of various cultures, the musical instruments will be discussed in relation to the music cultures to which they belong: Indian-derived, European-derived, and African-derived. Cross-cultural elements, however, are present in most Latin American music, and therefore it is difficult to classify instruments in one of the three cultures exclusively.

INDIAN-DERIVED CULTURES

In Indian-derived music cultures, rhythms are played on instruments such as gourd rattles used by shamans, bell rattles in northern Chile (*chorromón*), water drums among the Chaco Indians (northern Argentina and Paraguay), wooden drums filled with pebbles (*kultrún*) among the Mapuche shamans of Chile and Argentina, double-headed frame drums used in the Andes, Central American kettle drums, the Maya *teponaztli* (two-tongue slit drum) and turtle shells played with antlers.

Among the wind instruments from Indian-derived music cultures are side-blown bamboo trumpets with gourd or metal bells like the *erke* of Peru and Ecuador; natural horn trumpets like the *putu* of northern Chile; long, end-blown bamboo trumpets like the Argentine and Chilean *trutruka;* conch-shell trumpets of the Central American Indians; flutes, whistles, and pipes of wood, clay, bone, or reed used by the Guatuso, Mayas, and other Central American Indians; clay globular flutes (ocarinas), transverse flutes with both ends stopped or opened, Andean vertical flutes such as the *kena* (end-blown notched flute) and *pinkillo* (end-blown duct flute), the 8-foot-long paired flute *uruá* among the Kamaiura of Brazil; panpipes in the Andes and among the Kuna of Panama; clarinets of probable post-Columbian origin among groups from Guyana, Brazil, Bolivia, and northern Argentina (the *erkencho*).

It is believed that string instruments were brought to the Americas by Europeans and Africans. Some string instruments used by the Indians and mestizos as accompaniment in Andean folk music are the European harp and guitar, and the mestizo *charango,* a small, fretted lute that sometimes is constructed with an armadillo shell as resonator.

EUROPEAN-DERIVED CULTURES

European-derived music cultures have used string instruments such as the harp, violin, and guitar, all over Latin America. The harp has been widely used throughout Latin America since colonial times: from Mexico and Central America through the plains of Colombia and Venezuela to Peru, Paraguay, Argentina, and Chile. The guitar, too, is found in many countries (e.g., Argentine folk dances such as the *chacarera, zamba,* and *gato;* the Ecuadorian *pasillo;* the Peruvian *vals;* the Chilean *cueca;* and the Mexican mariachi ensemble).

Other string instruments used in European-derived music cultures are various types of *tiples* (treble guitars; Colombia, Guatemala, Puerto Rico, and Venezuela), *bandolas* (flat-backed lutes; Guatemala, Colombia, and Venezuela), the *bandurria,* a plucked lute (Peru, Venezuela), the *jarana* (small guitar; Yucatán and Veracruz, Mexico), the *guitarrón* (large, five-string bass instrument with convex body that is accompaniment for the mariachi ensemble), various types of *cuatro* (a small, four-string guitar of Venezuela and a larger, ten-string guitar of Puerto Rico), and the *tres* (a small, three-double-string guitar of Cuba).

European-derived music cultures use wind instruments such as the accordion (played for the Colombian *vallenato* and the Argentine tango [in the latter it is called *bandoneón*]), flutes, brass instruments (Mexican and Colombian *bandas*), and *chirimías* (shawm) played by *conjuntos* of Mexico, Guatemala, and Colombia.

AFRICAN-DERIVED CULTURES

African-derived music cultures are found throughout Latin America but more particularly in Brazil, the Caribbean, and coastal areas of northern South America, Central America, and Mexico. Percussion instruments such as drums, bells, and rattles are important elements in African-derived music. For example, in Venezuela there are drum ensembles called *mina* (6.5-feet-tall Tambor De Mina or *tambor grande* and *curbata* drum), *culo 'e puya* (double-headed *tambor redondo* and *culo 'e puya* drum), *golpe de tambor* (*cumaco* drum and *campana* drum); and *fulia* (drums of three different sizes).

Drums are also the principal musical instruments in African-derived religions. In some religions such as Candomblé and Umbanda in Brazil, Santería in Cuba, vodun in Haiti, and shango in Trinidad, most drums are played in groups of three, together with a bell and/or a rattle. These drums vary in size and shape, but most are of three sizes: the largest drums, played by the master drummer; the medium-sized drums and the smallest ones keep a steady rhythm. The bell (*agogo*) or the rattle generally sets the fundamental beat. This complex combination of different rhythms, played simultaneously, is called polyrhythm.

Wind instruments can be included in African-derived drum ensembles as melodic instruments. For example, on the Atlantic coast of Colombia, we find two drum ensembles comprised of *repicador, llamador, tambora* or *bombo* drums, *guache* (tubular rattles), and maracas. One ensemble uses as melodic instrument the *caña de millo,* probably an African-derived transverse clarinet. The other uses the *gaita,* an Indian-derived end-blown duct flute.

Three other important percussion instruments in African-derived music cultures are the Marimba, the *güiro*, and the *claves*. The marimba, a xylophone of African origin, is the national instrument of Guatemala, and is a popular instrument in other African-derived and Indian-derived traditions of Latin America as well. In nineteenth-century Brazil, *marimba* was the name for a portable lamellophone played with the thumbs. The *guiro* is a scraper (*reco-reco*) used in the Caribbean, Panama, and South America; the *claves,* consisting of two cylindrical hardwood sticks, is used in Cuba. Tambourines and *cuicas* are widely used in Brazilian Carnival music.

A string instrument in the African-derived tradition is the *berimbau,* a gourd-resonated bow used in Brazil as part of the music for the martial art/dance Capoeira. African bow lutes were played in nineteenth-century Brazil.

See also **Music: Pre-Columbian Music of Mesoamerica; Music: Pre-Columbian Music of South America.**

BIBLIOGRAPHY

Karl Gustav Izikowitz, *Musical and Other Sound Instruments of the South American Indians* (1935), Carlos Vega, *Los instrumentos musicales aborígenes y criollos de la Argentina* (1946).

Fernando Ortiz Fernández, *Los instrumentos de la música afrocubana,* 5 vols. (1952–1955).

Alceu Maynard Araújo, *Instrumentos musicais e implementos* (1954).

Gilbert Chase, *A Guide to the Music of Latin America* (1962; 2d ed., 1972).

Isabel Aretz De Ramón y Rivera, *Instrumentos musicales de Venezuela* (1967).

Joan Rimmer, "The Instruments Called Chirimia in Latin America," in *Studia instrumentorum musicae popularis,* 4 (1973); 101–110.

Sibyl Marcuse, *Musical Instruments: A Comprehensive Dictionary* (1975).

Instituto Nacional De Musicología "Carlos Vega," *Instrumentos musicales etnográficos y folklóricos de la Argentina* (1980).

Fradique Lizardo, *Instrumentos musicales folklóricos dominicanos* (1980).

Dale A. Olsen, "Folk Music of South America—A Musical Mosaic," in *Music of Many Cultures,* edited by Elizabeth May (1980).

Carlos Alberto Coba Andrade, *Instrumentos musicales populares registrados en el Ecuador,* 2 vols. (1981).

Egberto Bermúdez, *Los instrumentos musicales en Colombia* (1985).

René De Maeyer, ed., "Musique et influences culturelles réciproques entre l'Europe et l'Amérique Latine du XVIe au XXe sicèle," in *Brussels Museum of Musical Instruments Bulletin* 16 (1986).

Centro Para Las Culturas Populares y Tradicionales, *Instrumentos musicales de América Latina y el Caribe* (1988).

Jesús Muñoz-Tábora, *Organología del folklore hondureño* (1988).

Bruno Nettl, ed., *Folk and Traditional Music of the Western Continents,* 3d ed. (1990), chaps. 9, 10.

Guillermo Abadía, *Instrumentos musicales: Folklore colombiano* (1991).

Revista Musical Chilean, *Bibliografía musicológica latinoamericana,* no. 1 (1992).

Additional Bibliography

Olsen, Dale A. *Music of El Dorado: The Ethnomusicology of Ancient South American Cultures.* Gainesville: University Press of Florida, 2002.

Olsen, Dale A., and Daniel Edward Sheehy. *The Garland Handbook of Latin American Music.* New York: Garland, 2000.

Orovio, Helio. *Cuban Music from A to Z.* Durham, NC: Duke University Press, 2004.

MANUEL FERNÁNDEZ

MÚSICA POPULAR BRASILEIRA.

See **MPB: Música Popular Brasileira.**

MUSLIMS.

See **Islam.**

MUTIRÃO.

Mutirão, one of the most important spontaneous manifestations of solidarity in rural Brazilian society. It consists of mutual, free assistance among unskilled laborers through work meetings for purposes such as clearing land, planting, mixing and applying adobe, building houses, processing foodstuffs, harvesting pisciculture ponds, and fighting fires. Originally, the person being helped expressed surprise when the neighbors came "against his or her wishes." Now the participants are expected. They arrive very early with their tools and work in a festive atmosphere until nightfall. The person being helped provides food and spirits and organizes a party. The women prepare the food and distribute water and spirits to the workers. After work, everyone participates in a religious feast that can include litanies, the rosary, and pagan rituals. They may dance the *pagode* to the sound of the harmonica, the flute, or the violin. In recent years, some grass-roots public administrations rely on popular mobilization and direct participation of their constituents, who hold *mutirãoes* for the construction of community centers, health clinics, community gardens, and sewers.

Synonyms and variations for *mutirão* include: *ademão, adjunto, adjutório, ajuri, arrelia, bandeira, batalhão, estalada, mutirom, mutirum, muxirão, muxirã, muxirom, muquirão, putirão, putirom, putirum, pixurum, ponxirão, punxirão, puxirum,* and *traição.*

BIBLIOGRAPHY

Clovis Caldeira, *Mutirão, formas de ajuda mútua no meio rural* (1956).

Hélio Galvão, *O mutirão no nordeste* (1959).

Antônio Cândido, *Os parceiros do Rio Bonito,* 4th ed. (1977).

Edagard De Vasconcelos, *Sociologia rural* (1977).

Walney Moraes Sarmento, *Sociologia rural: Seleção de textos,* 2d ed. (1978).

Márcio Moreira Alves, *A força do povo: Democracia participativa em Lages* (1980).

Carlos Rodrigues Brandão, *Campesinato goiano: Três estudos* (1986).

Additional Bibliography

Freitas, Marcos Cezar de, and Dermeval Saviani. *A reinvenção do futuro: Trabalho, educação, política na globalização do capitalismo,* São Paulo: Cortez Editora, 1996.

Muçoucah, Paulo Sergio de C., and Marco Antônio de Almeida. *Mutirão e autogestão em São Paulo: Uma experiência de construção de casas populares.* São Paulo: POLIS-Instituto de Estudos, Formação e Assessoria em Políticas Sociais, 1991.

DALISIA MARTINS DOLES

MUTIS, ALVARO

(1923–). Alvaro Mutis (*b.* 29 August 1923), Colombian novelist and poet. Known as a poet most of his life, Mutis, a native of Bogotá, blossomed as one of Colombia's major novelists during the 1980s and 1990s. He has published more than fifteen books of poetry and fiction. Mutis began publishing poetry in the 1940s, and continued in the 1950s and 1960s, describing a decaying world, often in a satirical tone. Many of his prose poems are narrated in the bitter and ironic voice of a character named Maqroll el Gaviero. One of Mutis's major books of poetry is *Los trabajos perdidos* (1965). He has lived most of his adult life in Mexico.

In 1986, at the age of sixty-three, Mutis published his first novel, *La nieve del almirante,* followed by *Ilona llega con la lluvia* (1987). Following the pattern and tone established in his prose poems, Mutis made Maqroll el Gaviero the protagonist of these two novels. Maqroll travels by ship to several countries, and the reader follows his spiritual voyage. Maqroll's mysterious and secretive travels continued in *Un bel morir* (1989), *La última escala del Tramp Steamer* (1989), and several other works of fiction. In all of his writing, Mutis tends to portray failure as a form of triumph. In 1989, he won the Prix Médicis in France, and the following year he won the Premio Príncipe de Asturias de Letras in Spain. In 2001, the Spanish government awarded him the Miguel de Cervantes prize for achievement in literature. In 2002, he won the Neustadt Prize for Literature in the United States. His work has been translated in English, Portuguese, Dutch, French, German, Italian, and Swiss, among other languages.

See also **Literature: Spanish America.**

BIBLIOGRAPHY

Giuseppe Bellini, *Historia de la literatura hispanoamericana* (1985).

George R. McMurray, *Spanish American Writing Since 1941* (1987).

J. G. Cobo Borda, *Alvaro Mutis* (1989).

Additional Bibliography

Cobo Borda, J.G. *Para leer a Alvaro Mutis.* Bogotá, Colombia: Espasa, 1998.

García Aguilar, Eduardo. *Celebraciones y otras fantasmas: Una biografía intelectual de Alvaro Mutis.* Barcelona, Spain: Casiopea, 2000.

Siemens, William L. *Las huellas de lo trascendental: La obra de Alvaro Mutis.* México: Fondo de Cultura Económica, 2002.

RAYMOND LESLIE WILLIAMS

MUTIS, JOSÉ CELESTINO (1732–1808). José Celestino Mutis (*b.* 6 April 1732; *d.* 11 September 1808), distinguished figure of the Spanish American Enlightenment. Born in Cádiz, one of the cities in Spain most receptive to the new ideas of the Enlightenment, Mutis studied first at the Colegio de San Fernando in his hometown and later at the University of Sevilla. Mutis concentrated on botany—he evidently had some correspondence with Linnaeus—although he also studied physics, mathematics, astronomy, and medicine. A licensed physician, he went to the Indies in 1760 as doctor to the new viceroy of New Granada, Pedro de Messía De La Cerda.

Immediately after his arrival in Bogotá, Mutis began collecting and studying New World plants for their medicinal value. As the premier physician in New Granada—there were only two licensed in the realm—he became *protomédico* (medical examiner) in Bogotá, dedicating himself to improving public health and controlling epidemics. In 1773 he entered the clergy. Like the first *protomédico* of New Spain (Francisco Hernández) two hundred years earlier, Mutis combined his medical training with his botanical expertise.

Late in 1783, with the title of First Botanist and Astronomer of the King from Charles III, Mutis headed a team of eighteen distinguished scientists who traversed virtually all of what is now Colombia, collecting samples of the flora, making drawings, and ascertaining the practical uses of the 130 families of plants and twenty thousand herbs they studied. To disseminate the findings of his expedition, Mutis planned a series of thirteen volumes, including color drawings, but he never saw his prodigious labors put into print. Overwhelmed by a multitude of scientific, clerical, and medical responsibilities in New Granada, he had no time to see to publication. Fortunately, however, after his death, almost seven thousand of his drawings and four thousand pages of manuscripts were shipped to the archive of the Real Jardín Botánico (Royal Botanical Garden) in Madrid.

A typical figure of the Spanish American Enlightenment, Mutis was interested in promoting all useful knowledge: the effectiveness of quinine against malaria, Spanish dictionaries of Indian languages, barometric pressure as it affects the growth of plants, and ways to control epidemics. When the renowned German scientist Alexander von Humboldt came to Bogotá during his travels in Spanish America, he was greatly impressed by Mutis's breadth of learning, referring to him at one point as the "patriarch of botanists" and later dedicating one of his scientific treatises to the Spanish American scientist. In 1803, engaging in yet another intellectual enterprise, Mutis established an astronomical observatory in Bogotá, the highest in the world at the time. He died in Bogotá at seventy-six.

See also **Medicinal Plants; Protomedicato.**

BIBLIOGRAPHY

José Celestino Mutis, *Diario de observaciones de José Celestino Mutis, 1760–1790,* 2d ed. (1983).

José Celestino Mutis, *Flora de la Real Expedicíon Botánica del Nuevo Reino de Granada* (1987).

José Celestino Mutis, *Viage a Santa Fe* (1991).

María Pilar De San Pío Aladrén, ed., *Mutis y la Real Expedición del Nuevo Reyno de Granada*, 2 vols. (Madrid, 1992).

Additional Bibliography

España, Gonzalo. *Mutis y la expedición botánica*. Santafé de Bogotá: Panamericana Editorial, 1999.

Hernández de Alba, Gonzalo. *Quinas Amargas: El sabio Mutis y la discusión naturalista del siglo XVIII.* Colombia: Asesoría Editoria, 1996.

JOHN JAY TEPASKE

MUZO EMERALD CONCESSION.

Muzo Emerald Concession, mines located in the Colombian department of Boyacá that produce some of the world's finest and best-known emeralds—famous for their deep green color. The concession itself originated with the Spanish conquest of the Muzo Indians in 1559 and the discovery of nearby emerald deposits that began to be mined eight years later in the name of the Spanish crown. With the defeat of the Spanish (1819) by forces fighting for Colombian independence, it passed into the hands of Colombia's republican government in 1821–1822. Over the next 122 years, the government leased the mines to various private companies, domestic and foreign. In 1945 the government sought to increase its control over emerald production by placing the concession under the sole administrative authority of Colombia's central bank, the Banco de la República.

See also **Gems and Gemstones.**

BIBLIOGRAPHY

Victor Oppenheim, "The Muzo Emerald Zone, Colombia, S.A.," in *Economic Geology* 43, no. 1 (1948):31–38.

Rafael Domínguez, *Historia de las esmeraldas de Colombia* (1961).

Additional Bibliography

Uribe, María Victoria. *Limpiar la tierra: Guerra y poder entre esmeralderos.* Bogotá, D.C., Colombia: CINEP, 1992.

PAMELA MURRAY

NABORÍA.

NABORÍA. Naboría, a word originally denoting an indigenous noble's dependent. A Caribbean term, perhaps *Taíno*, *naboría* was transferred by Spaniards to mainland colonies, where in the sixteenth century it was applied to the evolving and slowly expanding indigenous servant/worker class. *Naborías* became in effect the first wage laborers of the hemisphere, a minority group of individuals who left indigenous communities to perform semi-skilled jobs in colonists' homes, mines, estates, textile workshops, and other enterprises. The term is freely used in the chronicles of the sixteenth century.

As the functions of the *naborías* became increasingly varied and specialized over time, the term was gradually replaced with more specific labor categories, such as *gañán* (estate worker) or *criado* (domestic servant).

See also **Colonialism.**

BIBLIOGRAPHY

Ida Altman and James Lockhart, *Provinces of Early Mexico: Variants of Spanish American Regional Evolution* (1976), pp. 18–19, 24, 26, 44–46, 103, 217.

James Lockhart, *The Nahuas After the Conquest* (1992), pp. 113–114.

Additional Bibliography

Díaz del Castillo, Bernal. *Historia verdadera de la conquista de la Nueva España.* Edited by Carmelo Sáenz de Santa María. Madrid: Instituto "Gonzalo Fernández de Oviedo," C.S.I.C., 1982.

Horn, Rebecca. *Postconquest Coyoacan: Nahua-Spanish Relations in Central Mexico, 1519–1650.* Stanford, CA: Stanford University Press, 1997.

Pastrana Flores, Miguel. *Historias de la Conquista: Aspectos de la historiografía de tradición náhuatl.* Mexico City: Universidad Nacional Autónoma de México, 2004.

Schwartz, Stuart B., ed. *Victors and Vanquished: Spanish and Nahua Views of the Conquest of Mexico.* Boston: Bedford/St. Martin's, 2000.

STEPHANIE WOOD

NABUCO DE ARAÚJO, JOAQUIM

NABUCO DE ARAÚJO, JOAQUIM (1849–1910). Joaquim Nabuco de Araújo (*b.* 19 August 1849; *d.* 17 January 1910), Brazilian abolitionist and diplomat. Nabuco was born in Recife. His mother came from Pernambuco's planter elite, and his father, José Tomás Nabuco de Araújo, was a deputy, senator, Progressive League chieftain, Liberal leader, minister, councillor of state, and jurist. Nabuco was expected to assume his place. As a student at the Colégio D. Pedro II (1857–1866) and at law school in São Paulo and Recife (1866–1870), Nabuco was drawn to both literature and sociopolitical reform. He spent the 1870s indecisively, writing, touring Europe, and serving as a diplomatic attaché in London and New York. Upon his father's death in 1878, his family pressed him to seek election in Pernambuco as a deputy.

Nabuco conceived of himself as an English Liberal reformist. He found his cause in abolition, an issue that had attracted him since his student days.

Slavery's destruction, he argued in *O Abolicionismo* (1883), was the most important of the reforms necessary to the empire's survival and progress. The abolition movement (1879–1888) involved sustained mobilization of the urban middle class and worker elements paralleled by plantation agitation, slave resistance and revolt, and flight.

Nabuco, using and attacking traditional politics, was an indispensable leader. A superb speaker and propagandist, charismatic and well-connected, he led the movement in parliament, public meetings, and international conferences. His commitment and political moralism cost him defeats, European self-exile, and party ostracism, but they also brought him romantic glory and a commanding position among reformists. Abolition was realized in 1888 by a Conservative cabinet, which completed the disarray of the traditional parties, produced reaction, and encouraged republicanism. Nabuco sought the monarchy's survival through further reform, but he was unsuccessful.

Nabuco interpreted the 1889 Republic as the reactionary work of the planters. He refused to participate in the new regime, and turned to journalism, law, and literature (1889–1899). In these years, he completed *Um estadista do império* (1897–1900), a biography of his father and the classic study of the monarchy, and *Minha formação* (1900), an intellectual autobiography. Nabuco helped found the Brazilian Academy of Letters in 1897.

When the Republic had painfully reconstructed political consensus, Nabuco allowed himself to be wooed into diplomacy to defend Brazil in an imperialistic era that he thought threatened his much weakened nation. His first mission, an arbitration with Britain over the Guyana border (1899–1904), ended in failure. Nonetheless, Nabuco, who was appointed minister to Great Britain (1900–1904) during the arbitration, was subsequently appointed Brazil's first ambassador to the United States (1905–1910). Nabuco was very successful; he lectured widely, and he secured a hemispheric partnership with the United States. His crowning achievement was the Pan-American Conference held in Rio (1906). This was his last, triumphant return to Brazil before his death in Washington, D.C., four years later.

See also **Slave Trade, Abolition of: Brazil.**

BIBLIOGRAPHY

The most scholarly and complete biography is Nabuco's daughter's treatment, Carolina Nabuco, *The Life of Joaquim Nabuco* (1950). Emília Viotti Da Costa, *Da senzala à colônia,* 2d ed. (1982), gives us the best analysis of the abolitionist movement; her *The Brazilian Empire* (1988) has chapters that focus on the politics and ideological problems that make the movement's context comprehensible. Robert E. Conrad, *The Destruction of Brazilian Slavery* (1971), is useful for its political analysis. Jeffrey D. Needell studies Nabuco's political thought in "A Liberal Embraces Monarchy," in *The Americas* 48, no. 2 (1991): 159–179. E. Bradford Burns, *The Unwritten Alliance* (1966), explores Nabuco's diplomatic partnership with Rio Branco vis-à-vis the United States.

Additional Bibliography

Costa, Milton Carlos. *Joaquim Nabuco entre a política e a história.* São Paulo: Annablume, 2003.

Dennison, Stephanie. *Joaquim Nabuco: Monarchism, Panamericanism and Nation-building in the Brazilian Belle Epoque.* New York: Peter Lang, 2006.

Silveira, Helder Gordim da. *Joaquim Nabuco e Oliveira Lima: faces de um paradigma ideológico da americanização nas relações internacionais do Brasil.* Porto Alegre: EDIPUCRS, 2003.

JEFFREY D. NEEDELL

NACAOME. Nacaome, the capital of the department of Valle in Honduras, traversed by the river of the same name. Founded in 1535, Nacaome was the site of a battle in which Francisco Ferrera and Francisco Malespín joined to defeat an invading Nicaraguan Liberal force on 24 October 1844. Malespín then led a combined Honduran-Salvadoran army to capture León, Nicaragua, on 24 January 1845, bringing a temporary respite to the fighting. The city was host to a conference beginning 6 July 1847 between Honduras, Guatemala, and El Salvador, during one of many attempts to reunite the United Provinces of Central America. The Pact of Nacaome was signed there on 7 October 1847. The pact provided for the reconstitution of the federal government, but was never implemented because of the absence of representatives from Nicaragua and Costa Rica.

BIBLIOGRAPHY

Lorenzo Montúfar, *Reseña histórica de Centro America,* vol. 4. Guatemala: El Progreso, 1881.

Thomas Karnes, *The Failure of Union.* Chapel Hill: University of North Carolina Press, 1961.

Mario Argueta and Edgardo Quiñónes, *Historia de Honduras,* 2d ed. Tegucigalpa: Escuela Superior del Profesorado Francisco Morazán (1979).

Additional Bibliography

Sierra Fonseca, Rolando. *Colonia, independencia y reforma: Introducción a la historiografía hondureña (1876-2000.)* Tegucigalpa: Universidad Pedagógica Nacional Francisco Morazán, Fondo Editorial, 2001.

Woodward, Ralph Lee. *Central America: A Nation Divided.* Cambridge: Oxford University Press, 1999.

JEFFREY D. SAMUELS

NACIÓN, LA (BUENOS AIRES).

Throughout the twentieth century, the Buenos Aires morning paper *La Nación* (Buenos Aires) has played a major role in the political, social, and cultural world of Argentina. It has had a wide circulation and has presented itself as a serious paper expressing the ideas of the economic and social elite. Although not without major inconsistencies, it has supported politics that can be best labeled conservative. Its cultural and social pages have carried tremendous weight.

The politician, historian, and general Bartolomé Mitre founded *La Nación* in 1870 to support his political ambitions. In 1909, upon the death of Bartolomé's son Luis, the heirs transformed the paper into a representative of elite classes. The Mitre family still controls the paper and continues to play an active role. By 1922 *La Nación* had the second-largest circulation—almost 200,000—of any newspaper in Argentina. It did not shrink from criticizing governments, either that of Hipólito Irigoyen (1916–1922, 1928–1930) or the Neo-Conservatives of the 1930s, but its attacks on the Peronist government (1946–1955) were muted after the seizure by the regime of its great rival, *La Prensa*, in 1951. In the long run, *La Nación* was able to capture many of its rival's readers and become the example of an elite-oriented, serious paper.

During the military regime of the 1970s, *La Nación* became, along with two other papers, partners with the government in a company that produced newsprint. Many felt that the papers' independence had been compromised. In the early twenty-first century *La Nación* remains a strong voice and is one of three national papers.

See also **Journalism; Mitre, Bartolomé.**

BIBLIOGRAPHY

Sidicaro, Ricardo. *La política mirada desde arriba: Las ideas del diario La Nación, 1909–1989.* Buenos Aires: Editorial Sudamericana, 1993.

JOEL HOROWITZ

NACOGDOCHES.

Nacogdoches, a city and county in eastern Texas, named for the Nacodoche Indians, a Caddoan tribe that had occupied the area since CE 1250. In response to French interest in the area, Fray Antonio Margil De Jesús founded Mission Nuestra Señora de Guadalupe de los Nacogdoches in June 1716 to establish Spain's claim. After lapsing, the mission was reestablished in 1721 by the Marques de Aguayo. Following the pronouncement of the New Regulation of the Presidios (1772), Governor Juan María Vincencio de Ripperda ordered the evacuation of the area. In 1779, Antonio Gil Y'Barbo led several hundred settlers back to the mission site and founded the town of Nacogdoches. It became an important gateway to and from the United States for smugglers, filibusters, and, later, legal settlers. Nacogdoches was the site of the Fredonia Rebellion (1826–1827), when Texas was still under Mexican control, and the site of the first newspaper published in Texas (1812).

BIBLIOGRAPHY

Archie P. Mc Donald, *The Bicentennial Commemorative History of Nacogdoches* Nacogdoches: Nacogdoches Jaycees, 1976. and *Nacogdoches: Wilderness Outpost to Modern City (1779–1979)* Burnet, TX: Eakin Press, 1980.

Additional Bibliography

Borders, Gary B. *A Hanging in Nacogdoches: Murder, Race, Politics, and Polemics in Texas's Oldest Town, 1870-1916.* Austin: University of Texas, 2006.

Reynolds, Richard. *Texas, Then & Now.* Englewood, CO: Westcliffe Publishers, 2005.

ARCHIE P. MCDONALD

NAFTA.

See **North American Free Trade Agreement.**

NAHUAS. Nahuas, a people bound together by a shared culture and language (Nahuatl) dominated central Mesoamerica in 1519. The best-known members of this group are the Mexicas of Tenochtitlán (popularly referred to as Aztecs), but there were a large number of individual Nahua states in the Basin of Mexico and adjacent areas, including Texcoco, Cholula, and Tlaxcala.

The Nahuas were originally non- or perhaps semi-sedentary people, collectively known as Chichimecs, who entered central Mexico in waves from a northern region known in legend as Aztlán. Each succeeding ethnic group learned sedentary ways from the center's native inhabitants; the Mexicas claimed descent of this sort from the Toltec. Over time, the Nahuas developed a complex polity, whose basic corporate building blocks were the Altepetl (regional states), the Calpulli or Tlaxilacalli (*altepetl* subdivision), and the family. Society was heavily stratified, from the *altepetl* ruler (Tlatoani) and nobility (Pipiltín) to the commoners (Macehualli), who were internally ranked from the relatively wealthy Pochteca (merchants) to slaves. Most commoners fell in between, and owed tribute in goods and services to the state, formed the rank and file of armies, and received access to land by virtue of *calpulli* membership.

The two centers of *Nahua* life were the market and the temple compound, which was the site of outdoor ceremonials, including various forms of human sacrifice dedicated to the many deities of the intricate Nahua religion. Inter-*altepetl* warfare, sometimes waged to capture sacrificial victims, was endemic, but by the late fifteenth century the Triple Alliance of Tenochtitlán, Texcoco, and Tlacopán (dominated by the Mexicas) had formed an extensive empire.

Yet the Nahuas remained a micropatriotic people, a fact that undermined the cohesion of this empire; lacking any collective identity, individual ethnic groups, such as the Tlaxcalans, made alliances with Cortés against the Mexicas, unwittingly bringing about their own subjugation. The Nahua *altepetl* bore the brunt of reorganization under the *congregación* program, the imposition of Iberian-style municipal government, and the replacement of temple compounds and deities by Catholic churches, the Trinity, the Virgin Mary, and the saints. The Nahuas were among the first to suffer the terrible effects of European epidemic diseases, which drastically reduced population by the early seventeenth century.

Yet the Nahuas and their culture survived. They continued to control their *altepetl,* even when traditional structures were modified by colonial innovations, and elites learned to manipulate the imposed legal system (which granted them certain rights) to their own and the corporate entities' benefit. The fact that Nahuatl came to be written in European script, and that much of the business of the indigenous world was carried out in this language, facilitated survival. Historian James Lockhart has identified three major stages in this process: in the first, during the initial post-Conquest generation, little changed in Nahua organization; in the second, to the mid-seventeenth century, an increasing number of Spanish elements were adapted to preexisting traditions; and in the third, continuing stage, expanding contact with outsiders created a more thorough cultural mixture.

See also **Aztecs.**

BIBLIOGRAPHY

The definitive study of the Nahuas, especially after 1519, is James Lockhart, *The Nahuas After the Conquest: A Social and Cultural History of the Indians of Central Mexico, Sixteenth through Eighteenth Centuries* (1992). Otherwise, there are more important works dealing with specific groups among the Nahuas: Bernardino De Sahagún, *Florentine Codex: General History of the Things of New Spain,* translated by Arthur J. O. Anderson and Charles E. Dibble, 12 vols. (1950–1982); Charles Gibson, *The Aztecs Under Spanish Rule* (1964); George A. Collier, Renato I. Rosaldo, and John D. Wirth, eds., *The Inca and Aztec States: Anthropology and History* (1982); Susan D. Gillespie, *The Aztec Kings: The Construction of Rulership in Mexica History* (1989); Inga Clendinnen, *Aztecs, an Interpretation* (1991); James Lockhart, *Nahuas and Spaniards: Postconquest Central Mexican History and Philology* (1991); and Miguel Léon-Portilla, *The Aztec Image of Self and Society: An Introduction to Nahua Culture,* edited by J. Jorge Klor de Alva (1992).

Additional Bibliography

León-Portilla, Miguel. *La filosofía náhuatl estudiada en sus fuentes, 3ª ed.* México: Universidad Nacional Autónoma de México, Instituto de Investigaciones Históricas, 1966.

López-Austin, Alfredo. *Cuerpo humano e ideología: las concepciones de los antiguos nahuas.* México: Universidad Nacional Autónoma de México, Instituto de Investigaciones Antropológicas, 1980.

Ward, Thomas. "Expanding Ethnicity in Sixteenth-Century Anahuac: Ideologies of Ethnicity and Gender in the Nation-Building Process." *MLN* 116.2 (March 2001): 419-452.

ROBERT HASKETT

NAHUATL. Nahuatl, a Uto-Aztecan language dominant in Mesoamerica at the time of the Spanish Conquest. Spoken by the Nahuas of central Mexico, it became something of a lingua franca as their economic and political influence spread, especially during the time of the empire of the Triple Alliance. The Nahuas developed a tradition of secular and sacred record keeping in a partly pictographic, partly phonetic form in "paper books."

While overly zealous Spanish clergy destroyed most pre-Hispanic records after 1521, to facilitate Christian conversion some of them learned Nahuatl (and about Nahua culture) and taught indigenous people to write their language in European script. The *Florentine Codex,* a massive compilation of Mexica culture and history by indigenous informants under the direction of the Franciscan friar Bernardino de Sahagún, is a landmark of this process. Sahagún and other clergy produced Nahuatl-language confessional guides, sermons, grammars, and dictionaries. Indigenous writers preserved Nahuatl poetry and drama, and composed significant annals and histories in the native tradition.

But as important as such major works are, workaday Nahuatl records provide an even more intimate portrait of colonial indigenous society. By the later sixteenth century, community-based Indian notaries were producing thousands of testaments, petitions, land records, and the like that were recognized by the Spanish as legal documentation. Such documents are not important to modern scholars solely for their contents, though such information is often unobtainable elsewhere. Just as crucial is their linguistic evolution, marked by three major stages linked to the process of Hispanicization. As identified by linguist Frances Karttunen and historian James Lockhart, the first stage, coincident with the initial post-Conquest generation, involved the adoption of a few Spanish nouns and Nahuatl adapted to describe foreign objects. The second stage, lasting to the mid-seventeenth century and reflecting closer contact with Spaniards, was characterized by freer borrowing of Spanish nouns. In the third stage, continuing today and linked to increased culture sharing and growing bilinguality, verbs, participles, and the translation of Spanish idioms, as well as even more nouns, entered Nahuatl.

After independence, Nahuatl persisted as a principal language of the indigenous people, especially those living away from concentrations of Spanish speakers: during the Mexican Revolution, Emiliano Zapata had announcements translated into Nahuatl to accommodate the large number of monolingual Morelos citizens. In the twenty-first century Nahuatl is still spoken, though the continuation of third-stage borrowing would make it unintelligible to a sixteenth-century Nahua.

BIBLIOGRAPHY

Nahuatl is now receiving a good deal of attention from scholars in several disciplines. An important study of the language is Frances Karttunen and James Lockhart, *Nahuatl in the Middle Years: Language Contact Phenomena in Texts of the Colonial Period* (1976). James Lockhart, *The Nahuas After the Conquest: A Social and Cultural History of the Indians of Central Mexico, Sixteenth Through Eighteenth Centuries* (1992), discusses the nature of the language, its evolution during the Spanish era, as well as the sociocultural implications of this evolution. A number of collections of English translations of Nahuatl documents with accompanying commentaries are available, including Arthur J. O. Anderson, Frances Berdan, and James Lockhart, *Beyond the Codices: The Nahua View of Colonial Mexico* (1976); S. L. Cline and Miguel León-Portilla, trans. and eds., *The Testaments of Culhuacán* (1984); James Lockhart, Arthur J. O. Anderson, and Frances Berdan, *The Tlaxcalan Actas: A Compendium of the Records of the Cabildo of Tlaxcala (1545–1627),* (1986); Frances Karttunen and James Lockhart, trans. and eds., *The Art of Nahuatl Speech: The Bancroft Dialogues,* (1987). Significant ethnohistorical studies that have relied heavily on Nahuatl documentation include S. L. Cline, *Colonial Culhuacán, 1580–1600: A Social History of an Aztec Town* (1986); Louise M. Burkhart, *The Slippery Earth: Nahua-Christian Moral Dialogue in Sixteenth-Century Mexico* (1989); Robert Haskett, *Indigenous Rulers: An Ethnohistory of Town Government in Colonial Cuernavaca* (1991). Among the most important colonial-era resources are the great dictionary of Alonso De Molina, *Vocabulario en lengua castellana y mexicana y mexicana y castellana* 2d ed., *estudio preliminar de Miguel León-Portilla* (1977); Andrés De Olmos, *Arte para aprender la lengua mexicana,* (1972); and Horacio Carochi, *Arte de la lengua mexicana* (1645).

Additional Bibliography

Andrews, J. Richard. *Introduction to Classical Nahuatl.* Rev. ed. Norman: University of Oklahoma Press, 2003.

Carochi, Horacio. *Grammar of the Mexican Language: With an Explanation of Its Adverbs (1645).* Ed. James Lockhart. UCLA Latin American Studies, v. 89. Stanford, CA: Stanford University Press, 2001.

Chimalpahin Cuauhtlehuanitzin, Domingo Francisco de San Antón Muñón, Arthur J. O. Anderson, Susan Schroeder, and Wayne Ruwet. *Codex Chimalpahin: Society and Politics in Mexico Tenochtitlan, Tlatelolco, Texcoco, Culhuacan, and Other Nahua Altepetl in Central Mexico: The Nahuatl and Spanish Annals and Accounts Collected and Recorded by don Domingo de San Antón Muñón Chimalpahin Quauhtlehuanitzin.* 2 v. Norman: University of Oklahoma Press, 1997.

Flores Farfán, José Antonio. *Cuatreros somos y toindioma hablamos: Contactos y conflictos entre el náhuatl y el español en el sur de México.* Tlalpán, D.F.: CIESAS, 1999.

García Escamilla, Enrique. *Neologismos nahuas: Incorporación de voces de la vida actual al vocabulario de la lengua azteca.* México, D.F.: Plaza y Valdés Editores, 1999.

Hernández Sacristán, Carlos. *Introducción a la lengua y cultura nahuas.* València: Universitat de València, Departament de Teoria dels Llenguatges: Instituto Valenciano de Lenguas y Culturas Amerindias, 1997.

Lockhart, James. *Nahuatl as Written: Lessons in Older Written Nahuatl, with Copious Examples and Texts.* Stanford: Stanford University Press, 2001.

Ruiz González, Francisco Javier. *Nahuatlismos en el español de México.* Zapopan: SIMA Editores, 2001.

Siméon, Rémi. *Diccionario de la lengua nahuatl o mexicana.* Trad. Josefina Oliva de Coll. México: Siglo Veintiuno, [1885] 1999.

Robert Haskett

NAIPAUL, V. S. (1932–). The celebrated novelist and winner of the Nobel Prize in Literature in 2001, Vidiadhar Surajprasad Naipaul, of Indian Brahman descent, was born a British citizen on August 17, 1932, in Chaguanas, Trinidad. Seepersad Naipaul, a journalist, embraced and encouraged his son's aspiration to become a writer before the former's unexpected death in 1953. After graduating from Queen's Royal College in Port of Spain in 1948, V. S. Naipaul studied literature at Oxford with a scholarship from the Trinidadian government. At Oxford he met Patricia Hale; they married in 1955. After his Oxford years (1950–1953), Naipaul worked as a journalist for the British Broadcasting Corporation's program *Caribbean Voices* and wrote reviews for *The New Statesman*, a progressive literary journal founded in London in 1913.

Naipaul's first novel, *The Mystic Masseur* (1957), follows the winding journey of an East-Indian young man in Trinidad who dreams of becoming a writer. The semiautobiographical novel saw little success initially but later became a renowned work; the novelist Caryl Phillips wrote the screenplay for the 2002 film of the same name. His second novel, *Miguel Street* (1959), the story of a young boy in Trinidad who leaves the island to study abroad, also was met with little fanfare. *A House for Mr. Biswas* (1961), also a story of a Brahman Indian in Trinidad, was Naipaul's breakthrough success and propelled what would become an illustrious career of both fiction and nonfiction. As early as the 1950s Naipaul was writing essays and descriptions of his travels among fellow West Indians. His notable nonfiction books include *The Middle Passage* (1962), *India: A Wounded Civilization* (1977), *Among the Believers: An Islamic Journey* (1981), and *Beyond Belief: Islamic Excursions among the Converted Peoples* (1998). Naipaul reinforced his credentials as a novelist with *A Way in the World* (1994) and *Half a Life* (2001). Naipaul's wife died in 1996; he subsequently married Nadira Alvi, a Pakistani journalist. Apart from the Nobel Prize, Naipaul's other honors include the Booker Prize in 1971, British knighthood in 1989, and the David Cohen British Literature Prize in 1993. As of 2007 Naipaul resides in England.

See also **Literature: Spanish America; Travel Literature.**

BIBLIOGRAPHY

Dooley, Gillian. *V. S. Naipaul, Man and Writer.* Columbia: University of South Carolina Press, 2006.

Feder, Lillian. *Naipaul's Truth: The Making of a Writer.* Lanham, MD: Rowman and Littlefield, 2001.

Kamra, Shashi. *The Novels of V. S. Naipaul: A Study in Theme and Form.* New Delhi: Prestige Books, 1990.

Theroux, Paul. *V. S. Naipaul, an Introduction to His Work.* London: Deutsch, and New York: Africana Pub. Corp., 1972.

PATRICK BARR-MELEJ

NALÉ ROXLO, CONRADO

NALÉ ROXLO, CONRADO (1898–1971). Conrado Nalé Roxlo (*b.* 15 February 1898; *d.* 2 July 1971), Argentine journalist, poet, and dramatist. Born in Buenos Aires, Nalé Roxlo contributed to a wide array of literary genres, but for the most part only his epigrammatic poetry and his works for the theater continue to be read. As a journalist and literary critic, he wrote for *La Nación, El Mundo,* and other such journals. His dramatic efforts corresponded to the enormously significant developments in theatrical activity in Buenos Aires in the 1930s, 1940s, and early 1950s known as the Teatro Independiente, a movement that affirmed a noncommercial (but very public) art theater in the tradition of Pirandello, O'Neill, and Shaw. (Nalé Roxlo's play *Judith y las rosas* [1954] won the Primer Premio Nacional de Comedia for 1954–1956.) Nalé Roxlo brought to his theatrical efforts the dominant emphases of his multifaceted poetry: a concern for the human comedy seen in often markedly farcical terms, the contradictions of fragile and transient individual endeavor, the interplay between illusion and anguished uncertainty, and a jocose manipulation of language that underscores life's existential ambiguities. The result is a highly original form of literary humorism that reveals a profound preoccupation with the human condition during a period of intense international and national moral, social, and political turbulence.

El grillo (1923), Nalé Roxlo's first book of poetry, possesses a significant metapoetic dimension that evokes the literary vanguard of the period and the emphasis on the privileged, primordial voice of the poet even when dealing with mundane reality and unpretentious natural elements. Other works by Nalé Roxlo include *Antologías apócrifas* (1943), *De otro cielo* (1952), and *El pacto de Cristina* (1945).

See also **Literature: Spanish America.**

BIBLIOGRAPHY

María Hortensia Lacau, *El mundo poético de Conrado Nalé Roxlo: Poesía y estilo* (1954) and *Tiempo y vida de Conrado Nalé Roxlo: Entre el ángel y el duende* (1976).

Arturo Berenguer Carisomo, *Conrado Nalé Roxlo* (1986).

David William Foster, *The Argentine Teatro Independiente, 1930–1955* (1986), pp. 70–85.

Additional Bibliography

Dubatti, Jorge, and Laura Cilento. *Poéticas argentinas del siglo XX: Literatura y teatro.* Capital Federal: Editorial de Belgrano, 1998.

Pickenhayn, Jorge Oscar. *El Tema del amor en ocho poetas argentinos.* Buenos Aires: Editorial Plus Ultra, 1997.

DAVID WILLIAM FOSTER

NAMBIKWÁRA

NAMBIKWÁRA. Nambikwára, Nambiquara, or Nambicuara, a term that designates a minor linguistic family with a geographical distribution limited to Brazil. It extends from northeastern Mato Grosso to southeastern Roudônia. The Nambikwára linguistic family contains three distinct languages: Sabanê, Northern Nambikwára, and Southern Nambikwára. The latter two constitute, in reality, dialects. Northern Nambikwára is comprised of four dialects: Tawandê or Tagnaní, Lacondê, Mamaindê, and Nagarotú. Southern Nambikwára, which has the greatest variety of dialects, can be clustered into four groups: Mundúka, Nambikwára do Campo, Nambikwára do Guaporé, and Nambikwára do Sararé (also called Kabixi). Within the languages of the Nambikwára family, Sabanê appears to be the most different from the rest. Nambikwára languages employ an abundance of high and low sounds.

The name "Nambikwára," which means "They who have holes in their ears," is a generic designation bestowed by the neighboring Tupi groups on all of the groups who belong to the Nambikwára linguistic family. Nevertheless, those groups refer to themselves by the name "Anunsu."

During periods of dry weather, the Nambikwára live as hunter-gatherers; in the rainy season, they cultivate fields along riverbanks, where they plant manioc, millet, cotton, and weepers. From the root of the *Strychnos* shrub they extract a poison that they use on their arrows. Among the beliefs of the Nambikwára is one of an abstract force called *nande* that is found in solid objects and magical or real poisons. The thunder is the greatest of the supernatural beings, with whom the *pajé* (shaman) can communicate by means of visions. The inevitable coming of death is linked to the appearance of a mythical being named *atasu*, who can take the form of a jaguar. The Nambikwára have been visited and studied by various anthropologists and ethnologists, among whom were Edgard Roquette Pinto (1912), Claude Lévi-Strauss (1939), K. Oberg (1949), and L. Bolgar (1959).

BIBLIOGRAPHY

Additional Bibliography

Gomes, Mércio Pereira. *The Indians and Brazil.* 3rd ed. Gainesville: University Press of Florida, 2000.

Lévi-Strauss, Claude. *Family and Social Life of the Nambikwara Indians.* New Haven: Human Relations Area Files, 1970s.

Pereira, Adalberto Holanda. *Os espíritos maus dos Nanbikuára.* São Leopoldo: Instituto Anchietano de Pesquisas, 1973.

Pinto, Edgard Roquette. *Rondonia.* 4th ed. São Paulo: Companhia Editora Nacional, 1938.

Price, David. *Before the Bulldozer: The Nambiquara Indians and the World Bank.* Cabin John, MD: Seven Locks Press, 1989.

Roosevelt, Anna Curtenius. *Amazonian Indians from Prehistory to the Present: Anthropological Perspectives.* Tucson: University of Arizona Press, 1994.

CHARLOTTE EMMERICH

NAMUNCURÁ, CEFERINO (1886–1905).

Ceferino Namuncurá (*b.* 1886; *d.* 1905), Argentine Araucanian (mapuche) proposed as a candidate for beatification. Descendant of the great Araucanian military leaders Calfucurá and Manuel Namuncurá, Ceferino was educated in Salesian missions established near *reservas* set aside for subjugated Indians in Argentina in the 1880s. Ceferino Namuncurá's excellence as a student attracted the attention of his teachers, and he was sent to Rome for seminary studies. He died there of tuberculosis short of his twentieth birthday.

See also **Mapuche.**

BIBLIOGRAPHY

Adalberto A. Clifton Goldey, *El cacique Namuncurá: Último soberano de la pampa,* 2d ed. (1964).

Judith Ewell and William Beezeley, eds., *The Human Tradition in Latin America: The Nineteenth Century* (1989), pp. 175–187.

Additional Bibliography

Noceti, Ricardo. *La sangre de la tierra: Para una nueva visión de Ceferino Namuncurá.* Rosario: Ediciones Didascalia, 2000.

KRISTINE L. JONES

NAMUNCURÁ, MANUEL (?–1908).

Manuel Namuncurá (*d.* 1908), leader of Araucanian confederation in the Argentine pampas from 1873 until final defeat in 1883. Namuncurá assumed leadership of the confederation of the Araucanian and Pampas tribes in the Argentine pampas after the death of his father, Calfucurá, in 1873. Originally chosen to serve as one of a triumvirate elected by Araucanian elders, Manuel Namuncurá emerged as the most effective leader in achieving Araucanian hegemony in Argentina. In the five years following his ascendance, Namuncurá's followers maintained a strong line of defense against creole expansion and conducted highly organized and effective malones against their enemies. Following the military operations of Argentine generals Adolfo Alsina (1877) and Julio A. Roca (1878–1879), Araucanian resistance crumbled, and the last straggling forces under the leadership of Namuncurá finally surrendered in 1883.

See also **Araucanians.**

BIBLIOGRAPHY

Adalberto A. Clifton Goldney, *El cacique Namuncurá: Último soberano de la pampa,* 2d ed. (1964).

Judith Ewell and William Beezeley, eds., *The Human Tradition in Latin America: The Nineteenth Century* (1989), pp. 175–187.

Additional Bibliography

Martínez Sarasola, Carlos. *Los hijos de la tierra: Historia de los indígenas argentinos.* Buenos Aires: Emecé, 1998.

KRISTINE L. JONES

NANAWA, BATTLE OF.

In 1933 two major battles of the Chaco War (1932–1935) between Bolivia and Paraguay occurred around a fortified Paraguayan position known as Nanawa. The Bolivian commander Hans Kundt envisioned the first assault on Nanawa as an opportunity to turn the southern flank of the Paraguayans. Nanawa was a position strengthened by barbed wire, mines, shallow trenches, and log redoubts. The Bolivian Seventh Division sought to envelop and destroy the Paraguayan Fifth Division. The assault began on January 20, 1933, and ground to a halt on January 26, 1933, with a Paraguayan counterattack. After the battle a stalemate developed involving prolonged trench warfare. In July 1933 Kundt again decided to concentrate on the seizure of Nanawa. The Bolivians marshaled 7,600 soldiers; the Paraguayans had 6,000 defenders. The Bolivian army unleashed its attack on July 4, 1933. By the end of July 8, Kundt called a halt to the assault. After the second battle, the Paraguayans admitted to 150 men killed; the Bolivians reported 2,000 to 3,000 casualties. The second Bolivian failure at Nanawa allowed the strategic initiative to swing in favor of the Paraguayans; the Paraguayan commander José Félix Estigarribia immediately launched successful offensives to the northwest.

See also **Chaco War.**

BIBLIOGRAPHY

Farcau, Bruce W. *The Chaco War: Bolivia and Paraguay, 1932–1935.* Westport, CT: Praeger, 1996.

Vergara Vicuña, Aquiles. *Historia de la Guerra del Chaco.* 7 vols. La Paz, Bolivia: Litografías e Imprentas Unidas, 1944.

ROBERT SMALE

ÑANDUTÍ.

ÑANDUTÍ. *Ñandutí*, from a Guarani word, *ñánduti*, meaning "spider web," is very fine white lace similar to a woven spider web. A handicraft of Paraguay, it is estimated to date back to the eighteenth century. Its original form was an adaptation by the indigenous people of Paraguay of the fine ornamental garments introduced by the Spanish during the colonization of America. *Ñandutí* differed fundamentally from European laces in that the latter are made by removing threads from the fabric, while *ñandutí* is made by weaving threads on a frame separate from the fabric. In the early twenty-first century it is made with a great variety of stitches and is considered to be a local cultural expression.

See also **Textiles, Indigenous.**

BIBLIOGRAPHY

Sanjurjo, Annick. *Ñandutí: The Flower in the Spider's Web.* Organization of American States, 1978.

ELENA MOREIRA

NAÓN, RÓMULO S.

NAÓN, RÓMULO S. (1876–1941). Rómulo S. Naón (*b.* 17 February 1876; *d.* 29 December 1941), Argentine politician and diplomat. Having served in the cabinet of José Figueroa Alcorta, Naón in 1910 began an eight-year diplomatic posting in Washington, D.C., first as envoy extraordinary and, after 1914, as Argentina's first ambassador to the United States. Naón represented Argentine interests in Washington in a time of rapid changes in U.S.-Argentine relations. Naón was a supporter of increased bilateral trade and financial ties, and his expertise in international law helped facilitate the growing American dominance of many Argentine commercial markets.

During the First World War Naón began to influence Argentine foreign policy, exceeding the normal ambassadorial role. In 1917 and 1918, as relations between the United States and Argentina deteriorated over the issue of Argentine neutrality, Naón worked hard to convince American officials that the nationalist rhetoric of President Hipólito Irigoyen and Foreign Minister Honorio Pueyrredón was of little practical significance. For a time, and on the basis of his success in negotiating an important wheat sale agreement between Argentina and the Allied powers, Naón succeeded in defusing this antagonism. But in 1918, after having played a major role in the strengthening of U.S.-Argentine economic ties, Naón resigned his post in a rejection of what he regarded as Irigoyen's intransigent anti-Americanism.

See also **Irigoyen, Hipólito; Pueyrredón, Honorio; United States-Latin American Relations.**

BIBLIOGRAPHY

Harold F. Peterson, *Argentina and the United States, 1810–1960* (1964).

Joseph S. Tulchin, *Argentina and the United States: A Conflicted Relationship* (1990).

Additional Bibliography

Lanús, Juan Archibaldo. *Aquel apogeo: Política internacional argentina, 1910–1939.* Buenos Aires: Emecé Editores, 2001.

Siepe, Raimundo. *Yrigoyen, la Primera Guerra Mundial y las relaciones económicas.* Buenos Aires: Centro Editor de América Latina, 1992.

DAVID M. K. SHEININ

NAPOLEON I (1769–1821). Napoleon I (*b.* 15 August 1769; *d.* 5 May 1821), first consul of France (1799–1804) and emperor of the French (1804–1814). Napoleon Bonaparte essentially ruled France and much of Europe from 1799 through 1814, when his armies were defeated by an alliance of British and continental forces. Born in Corsica, Napoleon rose through the ranks of army officers and became leader of the French Revolution through a coup in 1799. He reformed and exported the legal system that came to be known as the Napoleonic Code. By 1808 he commanded the European continent directly or through representatives.

Napoleon's first signs of weakness appeared in the Peninsular War (1807–1814), which was fought against Great Britain and Portugal with the help of Spanish guerrillas after Napoleon forced both Charles IV and Ferdinand VII into abdication and exile and placed his brother Joseph Bonaparte on the Spanish throne. In the ensuing struggle, Madrid changed hands several times, but ultimately the combination of the duke of Wellington's forces and relentless guerrilla warfare triumphed. By 1810, Napoleon had also been defeated in Portugal; the Portuguese royal family, however, had already fled to Brazil.

The various governments of resistance to Napoleonic rule in Spain—beginning with the central junta—had a vested interest in retaining the empire and its revenue. Some in the liberal Cortes of Cádiz suggested that the colonies be placed on a more representative and equal footing with the peninsula. But, in the end, the Cortes denied demands for equal representation and free trade, and promises for reform turned out to be empty.

See also **Louverture, Toussaint.**

BIBLIOGRAPHY

Gabriel H. Lovett, *Napoleon and the Birth of Modern Spain,* 2 vols. (1965).

Vincent Cronin, *Napoleon Bonaparte: An Intimate Biography* (1977).

Additional Bibliography

Castells, Irene, and Antoni Moliner i Prada. *Crisis del Antiguo Régimen y Revolución Liberal en España, 1789–1845.* Barcelona: Editorial Ariel, 2000.

Esdaile, Charles J. *Fighting Napoleon: Guerrillas, Bandits and Adventurers in Spain, 1808–1814.* New Haven, CT: Yale University Press, 2004.

SUZANNE HILES BURKHOLDER

NAPOLEON III (1808–1873). Napoleon III (*b.* 20 April 1808; *d.* 9 January 1873), founder of the Second Empire of France. Born the third son of Louis Bonaparte, king of Holland, and Queen Hortense, daughter of Empress Joséphine, he spent the early part of his life in Italy, Switzerland, and Germany. In the early 1830s, he declared his intention to claim the Napoleonic inheritance. He was twice imprisoned, in Strasbourg (1836) and in Ham (1840–1846), from which he escaped. His ideas of a liberal political system, social reform, and revived French power (*Des idées napoléoniennes,* 1839) took shape during his imprisonment and exile. In 1844 he wrote *On the Extinction of Poverty.* He solicited support for a canal scheme across the Nicaraguan lakes in 1847 without success. The scheme to establish a French protectorate over Mexico was conceived also in these years.

On 10 December 1848 Napoleon was elected president of the Second French Republic with over 5 million votes (74.2 percent). In a coup on 2 December 1851 he dispensed with the constitutional system. A new constitution (14 January 1852) prepared the way for the establishment of the Second Empire. On 2 December 1852 Louis Napoleon Bonaparte assumed the title Napoleon III, and on 30 January 1853 he married Eugenia de Montijo, the daughter of Cipriano de Montijo, count of Teba, who had fought for King Joseph Bonaparte in the Peninsular War (1808–1814).

Imperial expansion in Algeria and Indochina accompanied an interventionist foreign policy in the Crimea (1854–1856) and Italy (1859). Work on the Suez Canal (1859–1869) complemented designs for an interoceanic American canal. Only one aspect of the Mexican scheme, the proposed canal, however, came to assume great importance for Napoleon between 1861 and 1867. Weakened by the disastrous outcome of the French Intervention in Mexico, his regime finally was destroyed by internal opposition and the Prussian military victory in 1870–1871. Napoleon III died in exile in England.

Napoleon III was execrated by French and Mexican republicans alike; he was equally unpopular among French and Mexican Catholics. He is usually viewed as a supreme opportunist, with self-promotion as his principal political skill. Nevertheless, Bonapartism in mid-nineteenth-century France did have popular roots (particularly rural) and sought to exclude both the traditionalist Right and the revolutionary Left from power. In spite of the failure of the Mexican policy, French power was extended in Southeast Asia and North Africa during the Second Empire. However, the fundamental weakness of the French army could not sustain the empire at home during the Franco-Prussian War.

See also **Maximilian.**

BIBLIOGRAPHY

F. A. Simpson, *The Rise of Louis Napoleon,* 3rd ed. (1951).

J. M. Thompson, *Louis Napoleon and the Second Empire* (1954).

Frédéric Bluche, *Le Bonapartisme: Aux origines de la droite autoritaire* (*1800–1850*) (1980).

James. F. Mc Millan, *Napoleon III* (1991).

Additional Bibliography

Black, Shirley Jean. *Napoleon III and Mexican Silver.* Silverton: Ferrell Publications, 2000.

Cunningham, Michele. *Mexico and the Foreign Policy of Napoleon III.* New York: Palgrave, 2001.

Price, Roger. *The French Second Empire: An Anatomy of Political Power.* Cambridge: Cambridge University Press, 2001.

BRIAN HAMNETT

NARANJO, CARMEN (1928–). Carmen Naranjo is a Costa Rican writer. Born in Cartago on January 30, 1928, Naranjo introduced existentialist themes and innovative narrative techniques into Costa Rican prose. She obtained a doctorate in Spanish philology and has held several positions in public administration while also writing novels, short stories, poems, and essays. During the second presidency of José Figueres, Naranjo was the assistant administrative manager of the Costa Rican Bureau of Social Security cashier's office and ambassador to India (1972–1974). Naranjo was also the director of the Museo del Arte Costarricense, was the only woman to hold a cabinet position, and served as secretary-general of the Bureau of Social Security. She became known with her first novel, *Los perros no ladraron* (1966), which focuses on the circumstances of the modern world's bureaucratic system, in which monotony, selfishness, and lack of fraternal feeling give rise to pessimism in the human being. Naranjo's other novels include *Memorias de un hombre palabra* (1968), *Responso por el niño Juan Manuel* (1971), *Diario de una multitud* (1974), *Mi guerrilla* (1984), *Sobrepunto* (1985), *El caso 117.720* (1987), *En partes* (1994), *Más allá del Parismina* (2000), and *Marina Jiménez de Bolandi: Recordándola* (2002). Her short story collections include *Ondina* (1985), *Otro rumbo para la rumba* (1989), and *Ventana de indicios sobre una ciudad perdida* (1995). Her poetry anthologies are *Idioma del invierno* (1972) and *Homenaje a don Nadie* (1981). Her essays are collected in *Cinco temas en busca de un pensador* (1977), *Cultura* (1978), and *El Café* (1993).

See also **Literature: Spanish America.**

BIBLIOGRAPHY

Virginia Sandoval De Fonseca, *Resumen de literatura costarricense.* (1978), pp. 39–52.

Lourdes Arizpe, "Interview with Carmen Naranjo: Women and Latin American Literature," in *Signs* 5 (1979): 98–110.

Evelyn Picón Garfield, "La luminosa ceguera de sus días: Los cuentos 'humanos' de Carmen Naranjo," in *Revista iberoamericana* 53 (1987): 287–301.

Additional Bibliography

Ras, Barbara, ed. *Costa Rica: A Traveler's Literary Companion.* San Francisco: Whereabouts Press, 1994.

Santos, Rosario, ed. *And We Sold the Rain: Contemporary Fiction from Central America*, 2nd edition. New York: Seven Stories Press, 1996.

JUAN CARLOS GALEANO

NARCOTRÁFICO. *See* Drugs and Drug Trade.

NARDONE, BENITO (1906–1964).

Benito Nardone (*b.* 1906; *d.* 1964), Uruguayan radio personality and political figure who rose to political prominence in the late 1960s. His political vehicle was the Federal League of Rural Action (LFAR), the official name for the political movement known as *ruralismo.* The LFAR was an interest group ostensibly representing small farming and ranching interests even though its founder, Domingo R. Bordaberry, was a large ranch owner. Bordaberry started the newspaper *Diario Rural* in 1940 and hired Nardone, then a young journalist, as its editor. In 1951 Bordaberry and Nardone founded a radio station, Radio Rural, which quickly thrust Nardone into the public eye. He became the first important media personality in Uruguay.

By the mid-1950s, Nardone held mass public rallies in Montevideo, which he called *cabildos abiertos,* a reference to the rural protests of the past. *Ruralismo* was basically a conservative, nonpartisan movement until the 1958 election, when, disenchanted with the politics of Colorado President Luis Conrado Batlle Berres, Nardone joined the Herrerist faction of the Blancos (National Party). Nardone's support proved crucial to the Blanco victory and thrust him into an even more prominent role in national life. His writings under the name Chico-Tazo (Crack of the Whip) became more strident, reflecting a virulent anticommunism and a championing of the "little guy." In this respect, the movement can be compared to Poujadism in France. He attacked Batllismo and all the liberal, urban values it represented while extolling the virtues of the small farmer and of rural society.

Nardone and a new close collaborator, a rich wood producer named Juan José Gari, continued to support the Blancos in their successful 1962 campaign, publishing the magazine *Mundo Americano,* whose slogan was "with democracy and against communism." The magazine echoed Nardone's attacks on liberalism and the Left. Nardone's movement dissipated quickly following his death. Radio Rural remained on the air, utilizing Nardone's widow as a symbol of continuity, but with rapidly diminished appeal and influence, *ruralismo* was not a factor in the 1966 elections.

See also **Radio and Television; Ruralismo; Uruguay, Political Parties: Blanco Party.**

BIBLIOGRAPHY

Benito Nardone, *Peligro rojo en América Latina* (1961).

Martin Weinstein, *Uruguay: The Politics of Failure* (1975).

Additional Bibliography

Costa Bonino, Luis. *La crisis del sistema político uruguayo: Partidos políticos y democracia hasta 1973.* Montevideo: Fundación de Cultura Universitaria, 1995.

Jacob, Raúl. *Brevísima historia del Partido Ruralista.* Montevideo: Arpoador, 2006.

Traversoni, Alfredo, and Diosma Piotti. *Historia del Uruguay siglo XX.* Montevideo: Ediciones de la Plaza, 1993.

MARTIN WEINSTEIN

NARIÑO, ANTONIO (1765–1823).

Antonio Nariño (*b.* 9 April 1765; *d.* 13 December 1823), Colombian independence leader. A member of the creole upper class of Santa Fe de Bogotá, Nariño was a prosperous merchant who served as *alcalde* and as royal treasurer of tithes. He also headed a group that met to discuss the issues of the day in the light of new intellectual currents emanating from the European Enlightenment, whose principal authors were represented in Nariño's extensive personal library.

When Nariño first toyed with the idea of independence is unclear, but he gained political notoriety when he was arrested in 1794 for having printed and secretly distributed a Spanish translation of the French revolutionary Declaration of the Rights of Man. He was tried and convicted of subversive activity and sentenced to exile in Spanish North Africa. However, Nariño escaped his captors on reaching Spain. From there he traveled to France and ultimately to England, where he attempted to sound out the British concerning possible help in case a revolution broke out in Spanish America. In 1797 he returned to New Granada, where he boldly surrendered to the authorities. He was not sent back to exile, but over the following years he was in and out of jail on suspicion of revolutionary activities; Nariño was in the dungeon of the Inquisition at Cartagena when the independence movement began in 1810.

By the end of 1810, Nariño was again in Santa Fe. He plunged into revolutionary politics, first as journalist—calling in the pages of his newspaper, *La Bagatela,* for outright separation from Spain and for creation of a strong centralist regime in New Granada. From September 1811 he was president-dictator of Cundinamarca, comprising Santa Fe and its surrounding area but not the outlying provinces, which were either committed to federalism or under royalist control. Conflict between Nariño's Cundinamarca and the federalist United Provinces of New Granada soon degenerated into civil war. Fortunes swung back and forth until in May 1814 Nariño, having led an army south to overcome the royalist bastion of Pasto, was taken prisoner by the enemy and shipped to Spain.

The Spanish liberal revolution of 1820 led to Nariño's freedom. He returned home to aid the cause of independence and served briefly in 1821 as provisional vice president of Gran Colombia, by appointment of Simón Bolívar. However, he was defeated for a full term by Francisco de Paula Santander, who became acting chief executive in Bolívar's absence and waged a campaign in Congress and the press to undermine the influence of his older rival. Although Nariño is revered today as "Precursor" of Colombian independence, he died in bitter disappointment at Villa de Leiva.

See also **Alcalde; Bolívar, Simón; Colombia: From the Conquest Through Independence; Gran Colombia.**

BIBLIOGRAPHY

Jesús María Henao and Gerardo Arrubla, *A History of Colombia,* translated by J. Fred Rippy (1938), esp. pp. 180–184, 193–195, 222–226, 242–253.

Raimundo Rivas, *El andante caballero, don Antonio Nariño,* 2d ed. (1938).

Jorge Ricardo Vejarano, *Nariño: Su vida, sus infortunios, su talla histórica* (1945).

Guillermo Hernández De Alba, *El proceso de Nariño a la luz de documentos inéditos* (1958) and *Diez años en la vida de Nariño* (1965).

Thomas Blossom, *Nariño, Hero of Colombian Independence* (1967).

Additional Bibliography

Cacua Prada, Antonio. *Antonio Nariño y Eugenio Espejo: Dos adelantados de la libertad.* Guayaquil: Archivo Histórico del Guayas, 2000.

Santos Molano, Enrique. *Antonio Nariño, filósofo revolucionario.* Santafé de Bogotá: Planeta, 1999.

DAVID BUSHNELL

NARVÁEZ, PÁNFILO DE (c. 1478–1528).

Pánfilo de Narváez (*b.* ca. 1478/80; *d.* 1528), Spanish soldier. Born in Valmanzano, Segovia, Spain, Narváez came to the New World around 1498. A veteran of military engagements in Jamaica, he helped to lead the bloody conquest of Cuba in 1510–1514. In 1520 he vied with Hernán Cortés in Veracruz for the opportunity to raid portions of Mexico. He lost, and was imprisoned for two and a half years.

In 1526 Narváez received a royal contract to explore La Florida. After landing near Tampa Bay in April 1528, he and three hundred men marched north to Apalachee, where they suffered illness and were attacked by natives. Retreating, they moved to the nearby coast to build vessels in which they could sail to Mexico. The Spaniards tried to follow the coastline west but were either swept out into the Gulf or washed ashore, where some lived among native groups. Four survivors, including Alvar Núñez Cabeza De Vaca, who wrote an account of the expedition, eventually walked westward nearly to the Pacific Ocean and were rescued near the Río Yaqui in 1536.

See also **Cabeza de Vaca, Alvar Núñez; Cortés, Hernán; Explorers and Exploration: Spanish America.**

BIBLIOGRAPHY

Alvar Núñez Cabeza De Vaca, *The Journey of Alvar Núñez Cabeza de Vaca and His Companions from Florida to the Pacific, 1528–1536* (1905, repr. 1964).

Morris Bishop, *The Odyssey of Cabeza de Vaca* (1933).

Robert S. Weddle, *Spanish Sea: The Gulf of Mexico in North American Discovery, 1500–1685* (1985), esp. pp. 27–33, 116–119, 185–207.

Additional Bibliography

Adorno, Rolena, and Patrick Charles Pautz. *Alvar Núñez Cabeza de Vaca: His Account, His Life, and the*

Expedition of Pánfilo de Narváez. Lincoln: University of Nebraska Press, 1999.

Thomas, Hugh. *Rivers of Gold: The Rise of the Spanish Empire, from Columbus to Magellan.* New York: Random House, 2003.

Wood, Michael. *Conquistadors.* Berkeley: University of California Press, 2000.

JERALD T. MILANICH

NASCA. Nasca, the name given by archaeologists to the culture that inhabited the valleys of Ica, Chincha, Pisco, Nazca, and Acarí on the south coast of Peru during the Early Intermediate Period (ca. 370 BCE–CE 540). The Nasca people, descended from the Paracas, flourished for nearly a millennium until being absorbed by the Huari (Wari) Empire around 540.

The nature of Nasca society, and in particular its political organization, has been the subject of much debate. Like other Peruvian coastal peoples, the Nasca farmed the river valley bottoms and irrigated their fields, growing a large inventory of crops. Their sophisticated water delivery systems, called *puquios,* allowed them to tap underground rivers and streams and redirect the water through a series of canals to their fields. Throughout the area of the five valleys between Ica and Acarí, the Nasca produced a remarkably uniform culture, which seems to suggest that this area may have been controlled by a small empire or state-level government. The frequent artistic depictions of warriors and trophy heads perhaps suggest a conquest-oriented political organization.

The capital of the Nasca polity is believed to be the site called Cahuachi, in the Nazca valley, where there are a large pyramid and several other ceremonial structures. Work at Cahuachi has indicated that this site was probably an empty ceremonial center, a fact that seems to argue against a state-level society. It has been suggested that the site functioned as a ritual center where people came together periodically to celebrate religious festivals. The social organization may have been along the lines of a complex chiefdom controlled by priests in a pattern similar to that postulated for the organization of society during the Early Horizon (1000–500 BCE). One of the problems in attempting to understand the organization of Nasca society is that it is known primarily from cemeteries. Almost no habitation sites with architecture have been preserved. As a result, it is very difficult to determine the function of many of the Nasca archaeological sites.

Nasca iconography varies from simple naturalistic designs to extremely varied and complex expressions of religious and mythical themes. The simpler designs often represent plants, such as beans, chili peppers, maize, and San Pedro cactus. Also shown are animals, including felines, various species of birds, many types of fish, and occasionally camelids. Humans are often depicted in scenes from daily life, including fishing, farming, and warfare. One of the most common representations is of human trophy heads taken from defeated enemies or sacrificial victims. Not only are the heads depicted on painted and modeled vessels, but a number of actual mummified heads have been recovered from offering caches. After decapitation the brains were removed and the mouth was fastened shut with thorns and yarn. A rope was then passed through a hole in the forehead to form a handle for carrying.

The more complex iconographic representations in Nasca art involve depictions of supernatural beings with the characteristics of humans, felines, serpents, birds, and killer whales. These creatures seem to be associated with trophy heads and perhaps warfare, as well as with plants and fertility. The elaborate representations with multiple discrete elements, including arms, legs, heads, eyes, and feline mouths, recall the complex kennings of Chavín art. Some of these creatures may represent a priest dressed in a costume identified with a deity. Regalia found in tombs suggest that priests costumed themselves as these mythical beings.

In addition to iconographic representations on ceramics and textiles, the Nasca created major works of art in the huge ground drawings found on the plain known as the Pampa de Nazca, which is adjacent to the Nazca valley. Here the mythical themes are reproduced in figures on a gigantic scale on the dry desert plain, together with geometric figures and hundreds of straight lines covering some 200 square miles. These were formed by scraping away the dark surface stones and gravel to reveal the lighter earth beneath. It has been proposed that the lines had astronomical significance referring to stars or planets, perhaps related to a calendrical system, but recent work has shown that very few of the lines are aligned with any celestial objects. Another explanation is that they may be ritual pathways relating to some specific religious celebration. It seems probable that there is some religious significance to the ground drawings since they include sacred iconography that also occurs on the ceramics.

See also **Archaeology; Art: Pre-Columbian Art of South America; Nasca Lines.**

BIBLIOGRAPHY

Sources on the Nasca include Maria Reiche, *Mystery on the Desert* (1968); Tony Morrison, *Pathways to the Gods: The Mystery of the Andes Lines* (1978); Donald Proulx, "The Nasca Style," in *Art of the Andes: Precolumbian Sculptured and Painted Ceramics from the Arthur M. Sackler Collections,* edited by L. Katz (1983); Evan Hadingham, *Lines to the Mountain Gods: Nazca and the Mysteries of Peru* (1987); Helaine Silverman, "Cahuachi: Non-urban Cultural Complexity on the South Coast of Peru," in *Journal of Field Archaeology* 15, no. 4 (1988): 403–430, and "Beyond the Pampa: The Geoglyphs of the Valleys of Nazca," in *National Geographic Research* 6, no. 4 (1990): 435–456; Persis Clarkson, "The Archaeology of the Nazca Pampa, Peru: Environmental and Cultural Parameters," in *The Lines of Nazca,* edited by Anthony Aveni (1990); Helaine Silverman, "The Early Nasca Pilgrimage Center of Cahuachi and the Nazca Lines," in *The Lines of Nazca,* edited by Anthony Aveni (1990); Kroeber, A. L., Donald Collier, and Patrick H. Carmichael, *The Archaeology and Pottery of Nazca, Peru: Alfred L. Kroeber's 1926 Expedition* (1998). A more esoteric interpretation can be found in Däniken, Erich von, *Arrival of the Gods: Revealing the Alien Landing Sites of Nazca* (2002).

GORDON F. MCEWAN

NASCA LINES. Nasca Lines, geoglyphs, or very large, desert ground drawings that are visible from hilltops or in aerial photographs. Among the best preserved in the Andean area, the lines are situated in the Río Grande de Nazca drainage area on the south coast of Peru. They include figures of living plant and animal forms (a bird, fish, monkey, flower, and killer whale, for example); geometric and abstract figures, such as trapezoids, rectangles, spirals, and concentric ray systems; and straight lines, which far outnumber the other two types. Ground markings are also found in different parts of the central Andes, such as the Santa and Casma River valleys in Peru, in Bolivia, and in northern Chile. Many of the Nasca geoglyphs date to the Nasca culture.

There is general consensus regarding how the lines were made. The producers relied upon both subtractive and additive methods. The first involved the removal of the small black and angular desert pebbles and topsoil to reveal a light-colored, coarse, sandy subsurface. In the additive approach, rocks and cobbles were collected from the immediate vicinity to shape circular stone piles that are evenly spaced across uncultivated sand flats, or they appear as lines with evenly spaced single stones or as cairns.

From the time of their discovery by Alfred Kroeber in 1926 and for the following fifty years, the prevailing interpretation was that the lines held astronomical and calendrical significance. Torribio Mejía Xesspe initially suggested (1940) that the lines may have been used as ceremonial paths or roads. But it was Paul Kosok (1965) who actually recorded the desert markings through aerial photography and who believed that the ground drawings were aligned with astronomically important points on the horizon. This theory was supported by the research of a German mathematician, Maria Reiche (1974), who has spent her life studying, measuring, and protecting the ground drawings.

Rituals that involve the use of the geoglyphs as ceremonial pathways remain the common thread that unites most studies concerned with explaining the creation of the Nasca lines. Recent studies have discredited the astronomical alignment theory and have revealed that the lines, particularly those with concentric ray clusters, indicate a strong correlation with points where water is available.

Ceramics that are found with the figural ground drawings can be dated through correspondence with Nasca ceramic styles of the Nasca culture that flourished during the Early Intermediate Period (c. 200 BCE–CE 600). Disagreement concerning the chronology of the lines and other geometric forms persists. Some believe the lines to be of a later date because they often cross over life-form figures. More recent dates are based on the analysis of desert varnish, the natural dark coating that has accumulated on the surface of stones on the Nasca lines over time. Dates

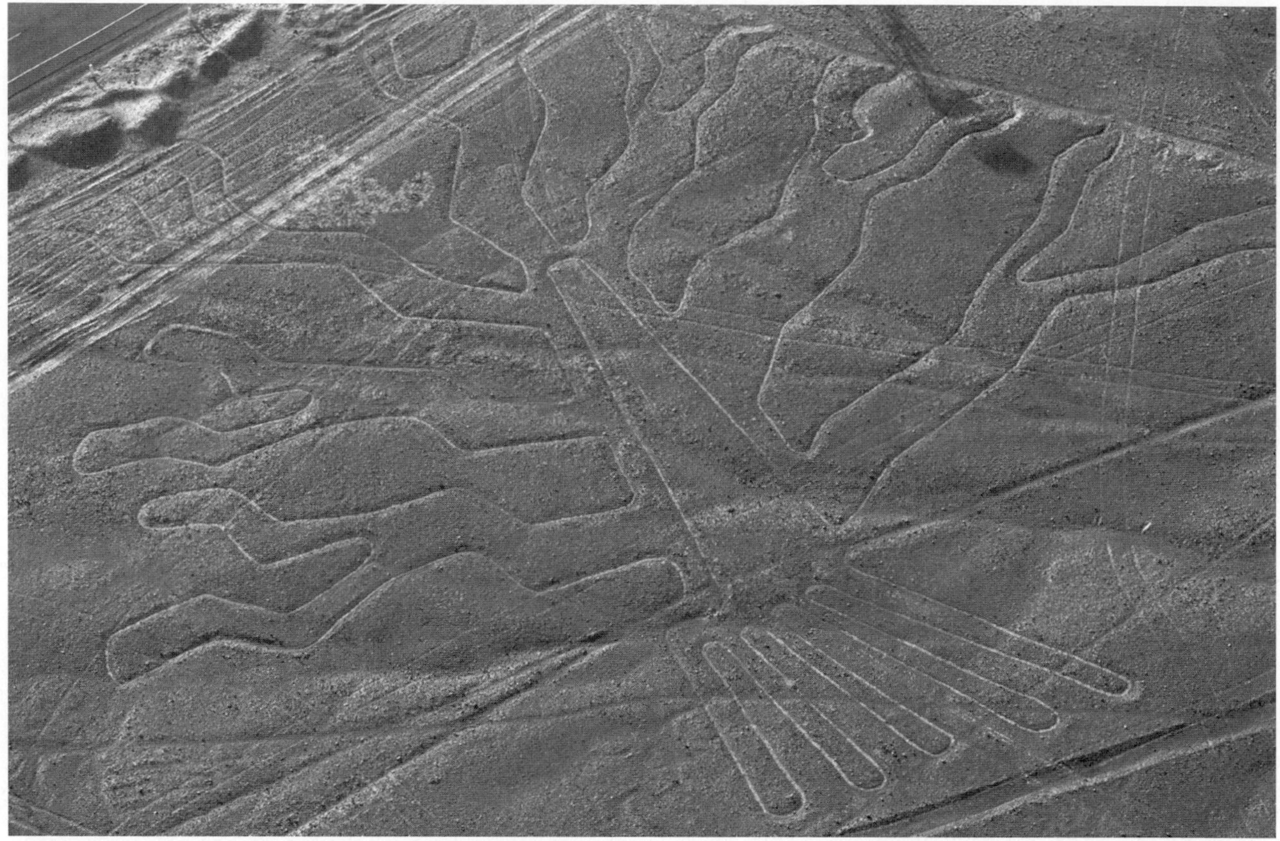

Aerial view of Nasca lines, southern Peru, late 20th century. The meaning of these lines, depicting a variety of animal figures, remains unknown. © YANN ARTHUS-BERTRAND/CORBIS

provided by this method indicate line production occurred between 193 BCE and CE 648.

See also **Archaeology; Nasca.**

BIBLIOGRAPHY

Torribio Mejía Xesspe, "Acueductos y caminos antiguos de la hoya del Río Grande de Nasca," in *Actas y trabajos científicos del XXVII Congreso,* International Congress of Americanists, vol. 1 (1939): 559–569.

John Howland Rowe, "Alfred Louis Kroeber, 1876–1960," in *American Antiquity* 27, no. 3 (1962): 395–415.

Paul Kosok, *Life, Land, and Water in Ancient Peru* (1965).

Maria Reiche, *Peruvian Ground Drawings* (1974).

R. I. Dorn and T. M. Oberlander, "Microbial Origin of Desert Varnish," in *Science* 213 (1981): 1245–1247.

Johan Reinhard, *The Nazca Lines: A New Perspective on Their Origin and Meaning,* 4th ed. (1988).

Anthony F. Aveni, ed., *The Lines of Nazca* (1990).

Helaine Silverman, "Beyond the Pampa: The Geoglyphs in the Valleys of Nazca," in *National Geographic Research* 6, no. 4 (1990): 435–456; "Estudio de los patrones de asentamiento y reconstrucción de la antigua sociedad Nasca," in *Boletín de Lima* 82 (1992): 33–44.

ANITA COOK

NASCIMENTO, ABDIAS DO (1914–). Abdias do Nascimento is a Brazilian playwright, educator, and political activist. Nascimento was born on March 14, 1914, in Franca, São Paulo, and received a degree in economics from the University of Rio de Janeiro in 1938.

Among his first political actions was his participation in the Frente Negra Brasileira, which he joined in the late 1930s. In 1944 Nascimento founded the Teatro Experimental do Negro (TEN), initiating a twenty-four-year career as a theater director and playwright. TEN won critical acclaim with its productions of such works as Eugene O'Neill's *The Emperor Jones* and Nascimento's own play, *O sortilégio.* TEN also served as a vehicle for Nascimento's political activism. As a complement to TEN, Nascimento formed the Comité Democrático Afro-Brasileiro in 1945, to lobby the Brazilian Congress for the enactment of antidiscrimination legislation. Nascimento's efforts in this regard presaged the passage of the Afonso Arinos Law of 1951, Brazil's first law against racial discrimination. Nascimento also displayed leadership in the Brazilian arts by establishing the Museu de Arte Negra in 1968.

In 1969 Nascimento established residence in the United States, where he held several academic posts. He was visiting professor at Yale and Wesleyan universities, and subsequently was named professor in the department of Puerto Rican Studies at the State University of New York, Buffalo. During the 1970s Nascimento traveled widely in the United States and Africa, speaking on behalf of blacks in Brazil and the Pan-African movement. He was instrumental in organizing several conferences of Afro-Latin American intellectuals under the banner of the Congress of Black Cultures in the Americas. Nascimento was elected President of the Third Congress of Black Cultures, which was held in São Paulo in 1982.

After returning to Brazil in 1979, Nascimento was named professor of black studies at the Pontifical Catholic University in São Paulo. While there, he created the research institute known as IPEAFRO (Afro-Brazilian Studies and Research Institute). In 1982 he was elected to Congress as a candidate of the Partido Democrático Trabalhista (PDT), led by Leonel Brizola, with whom Nascimento had been closely associated.

In 1983 Nascimiento was elected to the federal chamber of deputies. In that post he supported legislation to address racial problems. He then served in the senate, from 1994 to 1999. In 2004 he was nominated for the Nobel Prize for Peace and was awarded UNESCO's Toussaint Louverture Prize, for contributions to the struggle against racism.

Nascimento has written or edited some fourteen books, plays, and collections of essays on Afro-Brazilian culture and politics. His wife, Elisa Larkin Nascimento, has collaborated with him in several of these enterprises.

See also **African-Latin American Relations; Theater.**

BIBLIOGRAPHY

Abdias Do Nascimento, *Teatro Experimental do Negro: Testemunhos* (1966); *O negro revoltado* (1968); *Racial Democracy in Brazil: Myth or Reality?* (1977); *Brazil: Mixture or Massacre?: Essays in the Genocide of a Black People,* 2nd rev. ed., translated by Elisa Larkin Nascimento (1989); *Quilombismo* (1980).

Abdias Do Nascimento and Elisa Larkin Nascimento, *Africans in Brazil: A Pan-African Perspective* (1992). See also Elisa Larkin Nascimento, ed., *Dois negros libertários: Luiz Gama e Abdias do Nascimento* (1985).

Additional Bibliography

Nascimento, Abdias Do. *Orixás: Os deuses vivos da Africa (Orishas: The Living Gods of Africa in Brazil).* Rio de Janeiro: IPEAFRO/Afrodiaspora; Philadelphia: Temple University Press, 1997.

MICHAEL MITCHELL

NASCIMENTO, MILTON (1942–). Milton Nascimento is a Brazilian singer and songwriter. Born on October 26, 1942, in Rio de Janeiro, Nascimento moved with his adoptive family at the age of three to Três Pontas, Minas Gerais, where he spent his formative years. He became a leading figure of the post–bossa nova musical generation and one of Brazil's most popular composers and performers in the 1970s and 1980s.

Nascimento's voice is rich in timbre and wide in range, and many critics consider him the greatest Brazilian vocalist of his time. His music merges influences from rural *toadas,* Minas church choral music, bossa nova, *nueva canción,* the Beatles, jazz, and classical music; his songs feature strong melodies, elaborate harmonies, unusual rhythms, and a pronounced lyricism. He collaborated on songwriting with fellow Minas musicians Wagner Tiso, Beto Guedes, Lô Borges, Márcio Borges, Tavinho Moura, and Fernando Brant.

Nascimento gained national fame at the 1967 International Song Festival in Rio, when he was named best performer and his "Travessia" took the second-place song award; his debut album *Milton Nascimento* appeared that year. Important later albums include: *Clube da esquina* (with Lô Borges, 1972), *Minas* (1975), *Native Dancer* (with Wayne Shorter, 1975), *Geraes* (1976), *Clube da esquina 2* (1978), *Sentinela* (1980), *Missa dos quilombos* (1982), and *Miltons* (with Herbie Hancock and Naná Vasconcelos, 1989). In the mid-1990s he signed with Warner Bros. and released *Angelus* (1995); *Amigo* (1996); *Nascimento* (1997), which won a 1998 Grammy for Best World Music Album; and *Crooner* (1999), which won a 2000 Latin Grammy for Best Contemporary Pop Album. In 2006 the label released *The Essential Collection: The Best of the EMI Odeon Years (1969–78)*.

Nascimento's songs have been recorded by Paul Desmond, Wayne Shorter, Paul Simon, Quincy Jones, Sarah Vaughan, Herbie Mann, the Manhattan Transfer, George Duke, and dozens of other musicians outside of Brazil. His concert appearances, from stadiums in Brazil to clubs in New York, continue to draw enthusiastic audiences.

See also **Music: Popular Music and Dance.**

BIBLIOGRAPHY

José Eduardo Homem De Mello, *Música popular brasileira* (1976).

Ana Maria Bahiana, *Nada será como antes* (1980).

Vasco Mariz, *A canção brasileira,* 5th ed. (1985).

Charles Perrone, *Masters of Contemporary Brazilian Song: MPB, 1965–1985* (1989).

Additional Bibliography

McGowan, Chris, and Ricardo Pessanha. *The Brazilian Sound: Samba, Bossa Nova, and the Popular Music of Brazil*, new edition. Philadelphia: Temple University Press, 1998.

Motta, Nelson. *Noites Tropicais: Solos, improvisos e memórias musicais.* Rio de Janeiro: Objetiva, 2000.

CHRIS MCGOWAN

NATAL.

NATAL. Natal, the capital and principal commercial center of the state of Rio Grande do Norte in Brazil, has a population of 712,317 (2000 est.). Founded on Christmas Day (hence its name) 1598, near a Portuguese fort, Natal was occupied by the Dutch from 1633 until their expulsion in 1654. After Brazil's independence, the city's political importance increased, but even regionally under the empire and during the republic, it was not of major importance. In the twentieth century, however, for various reasons, the city took on larger historical significance.

Capitalizing on political and economic turmoil in the early 1930s, militants of the Brazilian Communist Party fostered unrest in army garrisons at Natal and elsewhere, culminating in revolts in the city as well as in Recife in November 1935. The rebels established a "popular" government in Natal but, isolated and facing the arrival of troops from Paraíba and Alagoas, the government collapsed within a few days.

The city's geographic location on the Atlantic coast made it ideal for an air base, which became known as the "trampoline to victory" in World War II. Natal served as a stop on air ferry routes to Africa, in particular Dakar, to help the Allied campaign in North Africa. The South Atlantic Wing of the United States Air Transport Command based its headquarters near the city, maintaining an airport at Parnamirim that was temporarily the busiest in the world. The city was subject to nightly blackouts from March 1942 to May 1943. President Franklin Delano Roosevelt met with Brazil's president Getúlio Vargas in the city in January 1943. The wartime experience temporarily increased commercial activity and U.S. cultural influence there. In the early twenty-first century, Brazil maintains a military base near the city, and the rocket base of Barreira do Inferno is twelve miles to the south. Natal is a center of tourism, with the nearby historic Portuguese fort and the local sand dunes among its popular attractions.

See also **Rio Grande do Norte.**

BIBLIOGRAPHY

Cascudo, Luís da Câmara. *História do Rio Grande do Norte.* Rio de Janeiro: Ministério de Educação e Cultura, 1955.

McCann, Frank D., Jr. *The Brazilian-American Alliance, 1937–1945.* Princeton, NJ: Princeton University Press, 1973.

Medeiros, Tarcísio. *Aspectos geopolíticos e antropológicos da história do Rio Grande do Norte.* Natal, Brazil: Imprensa Universitária, 1973.

ANDREW J. KIRKENDALL

NATIONAL AUTONOMOUS UNIVERSITY OF MEXICO (UNAM). The Royal and Pontifical University of Mexico, the precursor of UNAM, was patterned after Spain's

University of Salamanca. It was founded by royal decree on 21 September 1551 and opened officially in Mexico City on 25 January 1553. It offered courses in theology, scripture, canon law, jurisprudence, arts, rhetoric, and the Justinian Code, all of which were taught in the scholastic tradition that stressed dogma over the discovery of truth. During the colonial period, it added chairs in medicine, Native Indian and Asian languages, and astronomy and astrology, first held by the legendary savant Carlos de Sigüenza y Góngora. By 1636, when the first university in the United States (Harvard College) was founded, it had already awarded more than 8,000 bachelor's degrees.

During the later colonial period, the university continued in its role as firm supporter of tradition and order. When it failed to support the Spaniards against the Creole insurgency in 1810, Viceroy Venegas De Saavedra expelled its faculty and students and converted its buildings into a barracks. As part of his anticlerical program, Vice President Valentín Gómez Farías closed the university in 1833. President Antonio López de Santa Anna reopened it in 1834 and reorganized it in 1854, but it was closed once more by President Ignacio Comonfort in 1857. Félix Zuloaga reopened it in 1858, but Benito Juárez shut it down again in 1861, an action that Emperor Maximilian upheld in 1865.

On 26 May 1910 Minister of Education Justo Sierra Méndez created the modern university, the National University of Mexico, which was allied with the National Preparatory School and the schools of law, medicine, engineering, fine arts, and advanced studies. In 1929 the word "autonomous" was added to its name, but true independence from civil authority was not granted until 19 August 1933. After replacing university leadership on 30 December 1944, President Manuel Ávila Camacho proclaimed new regulations on 9 March 1945 whereby the university was reorganized to include a wide array of educational institutions that incorporated the schools of philosophy and letters, sciences, law, political and social sciences, economics, business, medicine, and the National Library. As a result, UNAM became a de facto agency of the government and received increased financial support.

Ensuing years saw peace with government and steady funds. The opening of a new campus in 1952 reflected the determination to build a true university out of diverse professional faculties. Ten years later, rector Ignacio Chávez instituted educational reforms to strengthen academic requirements but faced a confrontation between academic modernizers and students. UNAM's low point came with the 1968 government slaughter of over 300 protesting students. Seeking to shore up its legitimacy, the government financed systemwide growth of 13 percent per year in the 1970s, which was cut in half in the 1980s before slowing to a trickle the following decade.

This growth stripped UNAM of its overwhelming dominance. It fell from 50 percent of enrollments in 1960 to 30 percent by the early 1970s to 12 percent as of 2007. States founded or greatly expanded their own public universities and technical institutions. In 1973 the government created another public university with several branches right in the federal district. Meanwhile, a surge in private universities wrested away privileged applicants, status, and graduates' job prospects—breaking the near monopoly UNAM graduates had possessed on obtaining top political positions. The power shift called pointed attention to UNAM's laxness: automatic access for its own preparatory school students; free tuition; scandalous attendance and teaching policies; and so forth. Rector Jorge Carpizo's sober assessment of the need for change revived the student movement, albeit temporarily, in the late 1980s. And tangible progress made by UNAM in academic matters was undermined by rapid growth (from 40,000 students in 1960 to 135,000 in 1994, and double that with the preparatory level) that left it with more unprepared students and fewer key resources per student. Still only one-eighth of its professors are full-time, about half the national average.

Despite these problems, UNAM remains Mexico's preeminent educational institution. It is much larger than any other such facility in Mexico; has more top professors, graduate students, and especially researchers; garners one-fourth of the system's total resources; offers the most fields of study (sixty-one); and still boasts all modern Mexican presidents as alumni. If reforms of the 1970s failed to bring envisioned pedagogical innovation, they at least brought decentralization, with new campuses and activities. Even the main campus has diversified, as shown by an array of research units.

Whether UNAM can be "national" in more than mere nomenclature depends not on recapturing its past status, but on whether it leads or lags behind the higher education system's modernization efforts to establish quality, evaluation, merit-rewarded performance; private-public partnerships; and internationalization. However, policy reforms to those ends have met with resistance. In 1999, the rector of UNAM tried to raise fees, but a group of students launched a strike disrupting classes for several months. While many Mexicans found the strikers' demands unreasonable and the federal government arrested the protesters, the activities did limit privatization attempts.

See also **Ávila Camacho, Manuel; Education: Overview; Sierra Méndez, Justo; Sigüenza y Góngora, Carlos de; Universities: The Modern Era.**

BIBLIOGRAPHY

Thomas Noel Osborn, II, *Higher Education in Mexico: History, Growth, and Problems in a Dichotomized Industry* (1975).

Daniel C. Levy, *University and Government in Mexico: Autonomy in an Authoritarian System* (1980); Dirección General de Asuntos Personales, UNAM, ed., *Diagnóstico del personal académico de la UNAM* (1984).

Roderic A. Camp, *Intellectuals and the State in Twentieth-Century Mexico* (1985).

Daniel C. Levy, *Higher Education and the State in Latin America: Private Challenges to Public Dominance* (1986), pp. 114–170; Rollin Kent, *Modernización conservadora y crisis académica en la UNAM* (1990).

David E. Lorey, *The University System and Economic Development in Mexico Since 1929* (1993).

Additional Bibliography

Aranda Sánchez, José María. *Un movimiento estudiantil contra el neoliberalismo: UNAM 1999–2000.* Toluca, Mexico: Universidad Autónoma del Estado de México, 2001.

Babb, Sarah L. *Managing Mexico: Economists from Nationalism to Neoliberalism.* Princeton, NJ: Princeton University Press, 2001.

Mendoza Rojas, Javier. *Los conflictos de la UNAM en el siglo XX.* Mexico City: Centro de Estudios sobre la Universidad, Universidad Nacional Autónoma de México: Plaza y Valdés, 2001.

Ordorika Sacristán, Imanol. *Power and Politics in University Governance: Organization and Change at the Universidad Nacional Autónoma de México.* New York: RoutledgeFalmer, 2003.

DANIEL C. LEVY

NATIONAL COUNCIL OF LA RAZA.

The National Council of La Raza (NCLR) is a nonpartisan civil rights organization founded in Phoenix, Arizona, in 1968 as the Southwest Council of La Raza. Then funded by the Ford Foundation, the National Council of Churches, and the United Auto Workers, in 1972 the organization changed its name to reflect its intentions to serve Mexican Americans in all parts of the country. It moved its headquarters to Washington, D.C., and obtained federal funding for several projects.

With a membership of more than 300 affiliated community-based organizations, the NCLR considers its constituency to be all Hispanics. It has issued position papers and commissioned research reports to inform policy makers about issues affecting the familial, educational, economic, and political health of Latinos in the United States. The NCLR's stated goal is to be an advocate for Latinos on the national level, taking controversial positions such as opposing immigration restrictions and increased funding for the border patrol. It has been effective in lobbying federal and state officials to protect the civil rights of Latinos and to enact laws that will improve their social condition.

See also **Hispanics in the United States.**

BIBLIOGRAPHY

Hernandez, Roger. "Hispanic Organizations: Searching for Unity." *Hispanic* (1991): 18–22.

Martinez, Douglas R. "Hispanic Organizations: Meeting the Challenge of the 1980s." *La Luz* 8, no. 6 (February–March, 1980): 8, 9–43.

RICHARD GRISWOLD DEL CASTILLO

NATIONAL ENDOWMENT FOR DEMOCRACY (NED).

The National Endowment for Democracy is a private, nonprofit organization established by the U.S. government in 1983 to promote democracy around the world. The NED is primarily funded by a congressional appropriation that goes to the NED through the U.S. Department of State. For many years it operated with an annual budget of approximately $30 million, a figure that increased sharply after 2000 and by 2005 stood at approximately $100 million. Most of NED's funds go to four core grantees representing the two main U.S. political parties, U.S. business, and U.S. labor: the International Republican Institute (IRI), the National Democratic Institute for International Affairs (NDI), the Center for International Private Enterprise (CIPE), and the American Center for International Labor Solidarity (ACILS). The rest of NED's funds go to discretionary grants, primarily prodemocratic, nongovernmental organizations based in or working in new or potential democracies.

NED's programs in Latin America focus on promoting free and fair elections, political party development, democratic civic education, political and civil rights, women's political participation, union-building, and market-oriented economic reform policies. Since 2000, NED's Latin America work has been largely concentrated in the Andean region, Central America, Cuba, and Mexico.

NED maintains that its work is nonpartisan and serves a broad prodemocratic agenda, not U.S. foreign policy interests with respect to particular foreign governments. Nevertheless, NED's activities sometimes provoke accusations of political interventionism, such as NED's support for the political opposition in the 1990 Nicaraguan elections, which ended Sandinista rule, and NED's support for civic and political activists challenging the government of Venezuelan President Hugo Chavez.

See also **Democracy; United States-Latin American Relations.**

BIBLIOGRAPHY

Carothers, Thomas. *Aiding Democracy Abroad: The Learning Curve.* Washington, DC: Carnegie Endowment, 1999.

THOMAS CAROTHERS

NATIONAL INSTITUTE OF ANTHROPOLOGY AND HISTORY. The National Institute of Anthropology and History (Instituto Nacional de Antropología e Historia; INAH) is a public institution entrusted with rescuing, exploring, safeguarding, restoring, conserving, researching, and disseminating Mexico's tangible and intangible cultural heritage. Through a presidential decree, Lázaro Cárdenas (1934–1940) founded the Institute on December 31, 1938, under the ministry of public education. It was a product of the Mexican nationalism that had developed through the Mexican Revolution of 1910 and stemmed from the union of two nineteenth-century institutions: the Office of Archeological and Colonial Monuments and the National Museum of Archeology, History, and Ethnology.

The Federal Law on Archeological and Historical Monuments and Zones was decreed in 1972 to provide a framework for similar laws in various nations. The National Institute of Anthropology and History has two important educational institutions: the National School of Anthropology and History (with one campus in the Federal District and another in the city of Chihuahua) and the National School of Conservation, Restoration, and Museography. The Institute is represented in each one of Mexico's states through the INAH Centers. In the early twenty-first century it is responsible for some 150 archeological zones that are open to the public, and over one hundred museums throughout Mexican territory. The research done at its different centers, specializing by area and supported by prestigious libraries, provides resources for its schools, museums, and publications.

See also **Anthropology.**

BIBLIOGRAPHY

Biblioteca Nacional de Antropología e Historia. Available from http://www.bnah.inah.gob.mx.

Dirección de Estudios Históricos. Available from http://www.estudioshistoricos.inah.gob.mx.

Olivé, Julio César, and Augusto Urteaga, coords. INAH: Una Historia. México: MINAH, 1988.

Olivé, Julio César, and Bolfy Cottom, coords. INAH: Una Historia, 3 vols. México: INAH, 2003.

Sistema Nacional de Fototecas. Available from http://www.sinafo.inah.gob.mx.

LILIA VENEGAS AGUILERA

NATIONALISM. By the early twentieth century, nationalism emerged as a major force with the potential of reshaping Latin America. Combining the power of pride with a sense of mission, nationalism exerted a formidable influence on politics, culture, literature, and economics. Despite its significance, nationalism as a concept defies easy definition. Clearly, it embodies an emotional identification of the individual citizen with the nation-state. By varying means, that identification forges a group consciousness that attributes great value to the nation-state and thereby elicits unswerving devotion to it. In short, citizens feel their well-being intertwines with and depends upon that of the nation-state. The Brazilian scholar Júlio Barbuda reduced the complexities of nationalism into a pithy observation, "Nationalism is the emotional synthesis of the fatherland" (*Literatura Brasileira,* 1916).

The roots of nationalism derive from the long colonial past. Already in the sixteenth century, Iberians born in the New World identified with their locality. That identification accompanied by a sense of pride constituted nativism, a kind of precursor to nationalism. Bernardo de Balbuena expressed such nativism in his book *Grandeza mexicana* (Grandeur of Mexico) in 1604. He praised all things Mexican and concluded that Mexico equaled—even surpassed—Spain. In 1618, Ambrósio Fernandes Brandão interpreted Brazil in a similar fashion in *Diálogos das grandezas do Brasil* (Dialogues of the Grandeurs of Brazil). Perhaps he even foretold of future economic nationalism by criticizing those Portuguese who arrived in Brazil to exploit its riches and return wealthy to Europe. In his studies of the colonial past, the Peruvian historian Jorge Basadre spoke of the "self-consciousness" exhibited by the Europeans born in the Americas and by their mestizo and mulatto descendants. That characteristic increasingly separated them from the Iberians.

Over the course of more than three centuries of colonial governance, the psychology of the Latin Americans, particularly the elite, changed from a feeling of inferiority before the Iberian-born to one of equality and then to superiority. They reflected the symbolic observation about the importance of the New World made by the Brazilian intellectual Sebastião de Rocha Pita: "The sun now rises in the West." The Latin Americans thus challenged Europe.

The struggles for independence began in Haiti in 1791 and ended in Peru in 1824. In Haiti, Mexico, and northwestern South America these wars were lengthy, and in general they aroused the basic emotion that gives rise to nationalism—hatred of the outsider. They forced many Latin Americans to explain why they believed they should be free of European governance and what they expected from their own constitutions, governments, and societies. Incipient political nationalism accompanied the emergence of the new nations.

After Independence began the difficult task of creating nation-states, a challenge that lasted through much of the nineteenth century. The elites sought to maintain the unity, independence, and sovereignty of the nation-states they governed. They imposed the symbols of nationality—flags, anthems, and heroes—and developed a rhetoric of nationalism. Wars, boundary disputes, and foreign threats imposed an us-versus-them mentality on much of the citizenry, thereby intensifying political nationalism. From 1829 to 1854, for example, Juan Manuel de Rosas ably manipulated the Argentine distrust of foreigners to weld diverse and querulous regions into a national union. Mexico suffered disastrous invasions of the French in 1838, the United States from 1846 to 1848, and again the French from 1862 to 1866. Memories of these events aroused a combination of resentment of foreign intrusion and pride in local resistance, basic ingredients of political nationalism.

With sufficient political control and growing economic prosperity, the elites, in the names of the nations they governed, pursued certain broad, common goals during the last half of the nineteenth century. They wanted to modernize and chose Western Europe, whose technology, prosperity, and life-styles they admired, as their model. Some aspects of modernization contributed to both nation building and nationalism. Improvements in communication and transportation, notably after 1860, better unified the nations, thereby enhancing a greater sense of nationality. To the degree that the elites achieved some of their goals, they felt a pride and satisfaction akin to nationalism.

The high rate of miscegenation among peoples of indigenous, African, and European heritage also contributed to nationalism, although it took the elite a long time to accept the connection. The accelerating rate of mixture obscured both racial and ethnic origins to create a more homogeneous Mestizo population. Some racial combinations were even unique to specific countries. While becoming more conscious of the traits of their distinctive populations, the citizens of diverse nations developed a stronger sensibility about national identity. Defending racial mixing against the poisonous North Atlantic doctrines of racial hierarchy which glorified the Caucasian, intellectuals at the close of the century further honed nationalism. As a positive contribution, nationalism eventually defended racial equality, at least in theory. Otherwise, the Latin Americans would be accepting an inferior status. In turn, attention to racial contributions to nationality focused attention on cultural diversity.

With its emphasis on the Nahua past, the Mexican Revolution promoted cultural nationalism. Indeed, the revolution marked the rise of the mestizo to political power. In the 1920s, the intellectual José Vasconcelos celebrated the triumph of the new mestizo "race" (*la raza cósmica*), characterized by beauty, spirituality, and harmony. He declared Mexico's cultural independence: "Tired, disgusted of all this copied civilization, we wish to cease being Europe's spiritual colony." As minister of education, he commissioned Diego Rivera, José Clemente Orozco, and other young visionary artists to paint monumental murals glorifying the indigenous past. Musicians and writers further developed those themes. Mexican genius flowered and cultural nationalism soared.

Simultaneously, young Brazilian intellectuals declared their nation's cultural independence. A new generation announced its intentions clearly during Modern Art Week in 1922: "We are the sons of the hills and forests. Stop thinking of Europe. Think of America," exhorted Ronald de Carvalho. Art, music, and literature of a distinctive indigenous flavor flourished, an outpouring exemplified by the paintings and murals of Cândido Portinari, the compositions of Heitor Villa-Lobos, and the prose and poetry of Mário de Andrade. The intellectuals left the coastal cities, at least temporarily, to explore the countryside and interior, enriching the arts with hearty injections of folklore, in an effort to draw inspiration from ordinary people and folk culture rather than exclusively from Europe. Similar movements sprouted elsewhere in Latin America. The original contours of Latin American literature excited international acclaim. In 1945, Gabriela Mistral of Chile was the first Latin American to receive the Nobel Prize for literature. In the following half-century, four more won the accolade: Miguel Ángel Asturias, Pablo Neruda, Gabriel García Márquez, and Octavio Paz.

The financial failure of the Western world in 1929 and the consequent depression shook the always fragile, monocultural, export economies of Latin America. Their collapse ignited the smoldering fires of economic nationalism. They inspired hopes of decreasing dependency by initiating economic development. Nationalists looked to the governments for plans to diversify the economy, making it less dependent on the gyrations of the international market. They urged greater industrialization, a goal appealing to both pride and common sense that promised to broaden the economy as well as keep foreign exchange from being spent to import what could be manufactured at home. The nationalists also called for the recovery of Latin American natural resources held and exploited by foreigners. They regarded those resources as too fundamental to local economic well-being to remain outside of national control. Bolivia's nationalization of the foreign-owned petroleum industry in 1937 and Mexico's similar action in 1938 initiated a process of resource recovery characteristic of economic nationalism for the remainder of the century.

The goals of economic nationalism required governments to play a more active role. They introduced long-range planning. Wider governmental participation shifted the leadership of nationalism from the intellectuals to the governments themselves, which understood the power it conferred. At the same time, the support for nationalism widened to include the middle class and the urban working class. Sensing that trend, astute leaders such as Getúlio Vargas of Brazil, Lázaro Cárdenas of Mexico, and Juan Perón of Argentina combined nationalism with populism to gain wide support for programs to nationalize foreign-owned property, to increase government planning and participation in the economy, to industrialize, and to institute social welfare programs.

During the last half of the twentieth century, the most salient characteristics of nationalism were four. First, populists or the Left dominated the leadership. The military and the elites, groups that once had played vital roles as nationalists, became more closely identified with foreign interests. They seemed more inclined to preserve the institutions of the past and less interested in pursuing economic development that would benefit larger numbers of the population. Second, criticism of foreign economic penetration dominated, intensified by the debt crises of the final

Hugo Chávez beneath a painting of Simón Bolívar, Caracas, Venezuela, December 5, 2001. Chávez gained attention through his Bolivarian Revolution, named after the Venezuelan revolutionary Simón Bolívar. In his reforms, Chávez promotes a socialist agenda, nationalizing industries and providing more government services for the poor. JUAN BARRETO/AFP/GETTY IMAGES

quarter of the century. Despite the poverty of a majority of its inhabitants, Latin America exported capital. For example, the U.N. Economic Commission reported in 1988 that fully $147 billion flowed from Latin America to "developed countries" between 1982 and 1988 as a "net transfer of resources." That flow from poorer to richer nations outraged the nationalists. Third, criticism of the United States mounted because it was the metropolis and the largest single investor and creditor. And fourth, questions of economic development absorbed the lion's share of attention. The nationalists showed a greater impatience with the ideologies of the past and more interest in experimenting with new ones. In the late 1960s, the secretary-general of the Organization of American States (OAS), Galo Plaza, concluded, "One of the most powerful forces in Latin America today, and one of the least understood outside the region, is the upsurge of economic nationalism."

Over the course of a century, the thrust of nationalism altered. While nationalists once contented themselves with tracing the historical roots of their nationality and in glorifying the potential wealth and natural beauty of their land, their focus has shifted to the future. They take seriously the advice José Martí proffered at the end of the nineteenth century: "A people economically enslaved but politically free will end by losing all freedom, but a people economically free can go on to win its political independence."

In the twenty-first century both cultural and economic nationalism continue but have been reshaped by changes brought by globalization. In the case of Mexico, the state embraced free trade with United States and Canada. This policy shift greatly weakened the protectionist policies of economic nationalism. However, opposition to strong trading ties with United States has bolstered the leftist Party of the Democratic Revolution (PRD), which remains wary of these recent economic changes. Venezuela's President Hugo Chávez has promoted a regional identity, with a focus on economic nationalism, in opposition to U.S. hegemony.

While many intellectuals feared that globalization meant that U.S. culture would overwhelm national traditions, the results have been more complex. U.S. companies have succeeded in Latin America by adapting to the national culture rather than simply imposing the same practices and standards from the United States. In Brazil, musicians have mixed U.S. musical traditions and Brazilian styles to create one of the most vibrant music scenes in the world. With some support from international organizations, indigenous groups claiming their own identities (as in Chiapas, Mexico) have rejected national identities. Consequently, new subregional identities have emerged. While globalization might have fractured nationalism, it continues to be a potent force politically, economically, and culturally.

See also **Balbuena, Bernardo de; Basadre, Jorge; Colonialism; Globalization; Mestizo; United States-Latin American Relations.**

BIBLIOGRAPHY

Gerhard Masur, *Nationalism in Latin America* (1966).

Arthur P. Whitaker and David C. Jordan, *Nationalism in Contemporary Latin America* (1966).

Victor Alba, *Nationalists Without Nations* (1968).

E. Bradford Burns, *Nationalism in Brazil: A Historical Survey* (1968).

Frederick C. Turner, *The Dynamic of Mexican Nationalism* (1968).

Samuel L. Baily, ed., *Nationalism in Latin America* (1971).

Additional Bibliography

Appelbaum, Nancy P., Anne S. Macpherson, and Karin Alejandra Rosemblatt, eds. *Race and Nation in Modern Latin America.* Chapel Hill: University of North Carolina Press, 2003.

Chacon, Vamireh. *A construção da brasilidade: Gilberto Freyre e sua geração.* São Paulo, Brazil: Marco Zero, 2001.

Florescano, Enrique. *Etnia, estado y nación: Ensayo sobre las identidades colectivas en México.* México, D.F.: Aguilar, 1997.

Mallon, Florencia E. *Peasant and Nation: The Making of Postcolonial Mexico and Peru.* Berkeley: University of California Press, 1995.

Shumway, Nicolas. *The Invention of Argentina.* Berkeley: University of California Press, 1991.

Tenorio-Trillo, Mauricio. *Mexico at the World's Fairs: Crafting a Modern Nation.* Berkeley: University of California Press, 1996.

Ward, Thomas. "From the 'People' to the 'Nation': An Emerging Notion in Sahagún, Ixtlilxóchitl and Muñoz Camargo." *Estudios de Cultura Náhuatl* 32 (2001): 223–234. Available from http://www.ejournal.unam.mx/cultura_nahuatl/ecnahuatl32/ECN03212.pdf.

E. BRADFORD BURNS

NATIONAL WAR. National War (1856–1857), the Central American response to William Walker's filibustering expedition to Nicaragua (1855–1857). Walker's invasion and subsequent takeover of Nicaragua in alliance with Nicaraguan liberals stimulated a strong reaction from conservatives in all of the Central American states. Some liberals who opposed the foreign intervention in Central America joined them. By February 1856 the governments of the four other states had agreed to send troops. Costa Rica led the way with a declaration of war on 1 March of that year, and Costa Rican President J. Rafael Mora headed the coalition that carried on the "National Campaign" against Walker. He received especially strong support from Rafael Carrera in Guatemala, the state that sent the most troops to the campaign.

Carrera declined command of the Central American army, leaving that to Mora. The Guatemalan expeditionary force was first commanded by Mariano Paredes, who died in the campaign, and then by José Víctor Zavala. Honduran troops, led by Santos Guardiola, were among the first to enter the war against Walker; Salvadoran troops were led by Ramón Belloso and Gerardo Barrios Espinosa. These troops supported the Nicaraguan *legitimistas* (Conservatives) who had been fighting the *democráticos* (Liberals). Great Britain and several South American countries gave material aid to the anti-Walker coalition.

The Costa Ricans turned the tide against Walker, who had initially enjoyed great success. On 20 March 1856 they repelled a Walker force under Louis Schlessinger at the Santa Rosa hacienda, in Guanacaste, and then pushed into Nicaragua in early April, occupying the transit route from San Juan del Sur to Virgin Bay. They won a major victory at Rivas on 11 April but failed to follow it up with a pursuit of Walker that might have brought a quick end to the war.

Troops from the other states were now arriving, however, besieging Walker from the north and west, forcing him to fight on two fronts. Both sides suffered heavy losses, but the Central Americans soon outnumbered Walker's American phalanx by a large margin. By November 1856 this large, united Central American army forced Walker to evacuate Granada. The heavy fighting in and around Granada resulted in the virtual destruction of that old city, and Walker ordered it burned after abandoning it.

New North American recruits for the Walker forces prevented the Central Americans from bringing an earlier end to the conflict, but in December the Costa Ricans gained control of the

Río San Juan when they seized Fort Castillo Viejo. At Rivas, surrounded and battered by the Central American forces and decimated by a serious cholera epidemic, Walker finally surrendered his remaining 463 men on 1 May 1857 to a U.S. naval detachment under Commander Charles Davis.

The unity engendered by the National War spawned efforts to create a conservative-oriented Central American union, but in the face of resistance from special interests in each state, they failed. In Nicaragua, they resulted in conservative domination for more than three decades.

See also **Filibustering.**

BIBLIOGRAPHY

There is a large volume of publication on the Walker episode: among the best accounts is William O. Scroggs, *Filibusters and Financiers: The Story of William Walker and His Associates* (1916). A more useful account is Albert Z. Carr, *The World and William Walker* (1963). Frederic Rosengarten, Jr., *Freebooters Must Die!* (1976), is especially useful for its many photos, maps, and drawings. James T. Wall, *Manifest Destiny Denied: America's First Intervention in Nicaragua* (1981), offers additional information and insight. Central American views are provided by Rafael Obregón, *La campaña del tránsito, 1856–1857* (1956).

Marco Antonio Soto Valenzuela, *Guerra nacional de Centroamérica* (1957).

J. Ricardo Dueñas Van Severen, *La invasión filibustera de Nicaragua y la guerra nacional,* 2d ed. (1962), among many others, including a collection of documents edited by Angelita García Peña, *Documentos para la historia de la Guerra Nacional contra los filibusteros en Nicaragua* (1958). E. Bradford Burns, *Patriarch and Folk: The Emergence of Nicaragua, 1798–1858* (1991), provides a new perspective on the period. Ralph Lee Woodward, Jr., *Rafael Carrera and the Emergence of the Republic of Guatemala, 1821–1871* (1992), provides detail on Guatemalan participation in the war.

Additional Bibliography

Montúfar, Lorenzo, and Raúl Aguilar Piedra. *Walker en Centroamérica.* Alajuela, Costa Rica: Museo Histórico Cultural Juan Santamaría, 2000.

RALPH LEE WOODWARD JR.

NATIONHOOD AND THE IMAGINATION.

Latin American nations belong in their own right to the first wave of independent constitutional states that emerged from the crisis of the ancien régime. By 1825, at the end of the wars of independence, the Spanish colonial empire in America had disaggregated into eight separate polities: Mexico, the United Provinces of Central America, Grand Colombia, Peru, Bolivia, Paraguay, Chile, and the United Provinces of the River Plate. However, the political instability of the new states soon gave way to a larger set of independent countries. Between 1838 and 1840 the United Provinces of Central America broke up into five new republics: Guatemala, El Salvador, Honduras, Nicaragua, and Costa Rica. In 1830 the Grand Colombia split up into Colombia, Venezuela, and Ecuador. Non-Spanish domains fared differently: A slave rebellion won Haiti its independence from France in 1804, whereas the transfer of the imperial government from Lisbon to Rio de Janeiro in 1807 and dynastic continuity in the person of Pedro I allowed Brazil to undergo a rather pacific transition to sovereignty in 1822 and preserved Portuguese America as a unified polity. The creation of new states continued during the nineteenth and twentieth centuries with the separation of Uruguay from Brazil in 1825 and of the Dominican Republic form Haiti in 1844; the Spanish-American War in 1898, which resulted in the independence of Cuba; the secession of Panama from Colombia in 1903; and the progressive decolonization of the British possessions in the Caribbean since the 1960s.

Yet political independence from colonial rule did not always come hand in hand with the corresponding national imagination. This was clearly the case of the countries that achieved sovereignty during the early nineteenth century. Whereas the reasons for colonial revolt and the ideologies that influenced it have been an issue of discussion, historians generally agree that nationalism did not create the first independent states in Latin America. Political independence was ultimately attained as a result of territorial and social cleavages, but it was not fought for in the name of the nation. National identity was rather the result of the efforts by political and cultural elites to represent the nation and make it meaningful to the citizens. However, the relationship between nationhood and nationalism has been a divisive issue among specialists in the field. The so-called modernist theorists of nation, such as Benedict Anderson, Ernest Gellner, and Eric Hobsbawm, conceived of it mainly as a political construct whose cultural meaning was brought about by modern social change—markets, urbanization, social mobility, mass literacy, and public spheres. On the contrary, advocates of a stronger ethnocultural approach, such as Anthony Smith, have insisted on the symbolic patrimony inherited from pre-modern times as a condition for the existence of modern nation-states. In the opinion of such scholars, the mobilization of cultural resources is a process beyond the reach of nationalist elites and their modernizing efforts. The discrepancy between the two approaches is less significant than it might seem at first glance: Both accept that it is impossible to imagine a national community in an entirely arbitrary way, and both concede that an ethnic social structure needs to develop a cultural imagination of its own in order to have a subjective meaning.

Historians' interpretations of nationhood must in any case be assessed when applied to Latin America. The Iberian conquistadors had encountered a heterogeneous range of peoples and polities on the continent: from the great Aztec and Inca empires in septentrional (northern) America and the Andes to the bands of hunters and gatherers of the tropical rainforests and the pampas. Empires proved easier to conquer and colonize than nomadic populations, and the territories gained were worthless without labor to exploit them. The legal status of the Indians was therefore a key issue during the first years of colonization. Bartolomé de las Casas struggled and ultimately succeeded in defending the free status of the Indians as Spanish subjects, although that did not exonerate them from paying tribute to the crown and serving forced labor in the *encomienda*. The decimation of native populations during the sixteenth century encouraged the use of slave labor imported from Africa, which further increased the ethnic complexity of the colonial world. But important as they were for the internal structure of colonial society, ethnic divisions played no significant role in the differentiation of the American territories under the authority of the Spanish Crown. The first batch of independent states basically reproduced the jurisdictional space of the colonial administrative bodies (viceroyalties, captaincies, and *audiencias*) and territorial conflicts were subsequently settled following the principle of *uti possidetis* (as you possess), which meant that national frontiers should follow the boundaries of the old colonial territories from which they emerged.

Colonial society was internally structured along ethnic and corporative lines. Legal privileges, customs, dwelling places, and dressing codes identified the different ethnosocial groups. Relevant organizations such as guilds, militias, and *cofradías* (religious brotherhoods) reflected such cleavages. *Limpieza de sangre* (alleged blood purity) remained a prerequisite for access to the upper positions of certain corporate bodies—universities, the Church, and the army—until the end of the colony. Miscegenation did occur (mainly outside wedlock) and became a key element of social change, but it was not officially encouraged nor socially endorsed. Even if a recognizable gap separated the white settlers from the mestizos, *castas* (multiracial subjects of African descent), and Indians, the distance between Creole elites and lower-class whites was vast.

Geographical provenance was an additional marker within the white elite. The appointment to official positions proved to be a recurrent matter of resentment among the Creoles (born in the New World), especially since the mid-eighteenth century, when the Bourbon reforms tried to limit the selling of key bureaucratic posts and tended to favor peninsular over local candidates. But whatever the tensions between settlers and Crown officials were, Creoles and *peninsulares* (living in the New World but born in Spain) constituted the economic, administrative, and cultural elite of colonial society. The interplay of alliances across social and ethnic boundaries proved also to be a decisive factor during the independence revolts. Whereas Creoles usually nourished the ranks of the insurgents, this was not always the case. There were also *peninsulares* who supported the rebels while, on the other hand, natives and *mulato* groups sometimes fought on the side of the Royalists, as in the case of the Pasto Indians in Nueva Granada and the Venezuelan *llaneros*. This was the reason why Creole patriots had to take local, regional, and status-group identities into consideration before they could convincingly imagine the nation.

THE SOURCES OF CREOLE PATRIOTISM

Creole political imagination had to ripen into a specific cultural and social identity before it could develop a political meaning. The first colonial texts reflected the shock of the European encounter with American native civilizations. These texts were mostly chronicles of the conquest and histories of the ancient American kingdoms gained for the glory of the European kings and emperors. Emerging from a society then ruled by the principles of status, honor, and lineage, such texts should be read as a plea by the conquistadors and their descendants for the recognition of their privileges as lords of a New World. Bernal Díaz del Castillo (1492–1584), a soldier in the troop that conquered Mexico, openly claimed in his *Historia verdadera de la conquista de la Nueva España* (True Story of the Conquest of New Spain, 1575) a part of the honor and glory that the official chronicle of Francisco López de Gómara had mainly attributed to Hernán Cortés. But an increasing tone of resistance against Old World prejudices can soon be recognized in these kinds of texts. Creole literature subtly enhanced the dignity and pride of the Spanish subjects born overseas and embellished the deeds of conquest and the natural wonders of a land no less worthy of praise than the mother country. In the case of *El Inca* Garcilaso de la Vega (1539–1616), a son of a Spanish conquistador and a Peruvian princess, his *Comentarios reales de los Incas* (Royal Commentaries of the Incas, 1609) described the history of Tawantinsuyu (the Inca empire) and its conquest by Pizarro in order to vindicate his noble heritage to the Spanish authorities and public. In the same period can also be found in Portuguese America the first *História do Brasil* (1627), written by Vicente do Salvador, a Creole friar.

Although Garcilaso de la Vega was the only mixed-heritage chronicler to become part of the intellectual canon (except while he was banned during the late colonial era), there were a number of unrecognized indigenous and mestizo authors whose work was recovered in later centuries. In New Spain authors such as Diego Muñoz Camargo, who wrote a history of Tlaxcala (*Historia de la Ciudad y República de Tlaxcala*), and Fernando de Alva Ixtlilxóchitl, the author of a history of the Chichimeca nation, were conversant with Nahua/Aztec culture and past. The narratives they composed offer a window into ancient Nahua concepts of the nation as well as into the mestizo national imagination. In Peru, Felipe Guamán Poma de Ayala, the author of a long manuscript addressed to King Philip III (*Nueva corónica y buen gobierno*), devised a scheme whereby Peru would remain Catholic under the authority of the Spanish monarch, but its administration would revert to Inca rule. The two Nahua/Novo-Hispanic authors were not published until the nineteenth century, and the Peruvian was not even discovered until the twentieth century. Nevertheless, these three authors (and others as well) are important receptacles of early nationalist-leaning thought.

Creole patriotism, a process of sentimental affirmation of local belonging whose roots can be traced back to the seventeenth century, lacked in any case the connotations usually ascribed to the modern national conscience. In an environment where the Church permeated every pore of social life, the Creoles found in religion the basic references of their shared identity. Not only were priests the main managers of cultural resources in colonial society, but they also counted themselves among the administrators of the Empire. For this reason the early imagination of Latin America was predominantly implemented by a group of intellectual clerics. The cult devoted to Our Lady of Guadalupe is the clearest example of a religious icon turned into a prenational mirror of collective identity. Her purported apparition to a Mexican Indian in 1531 gave the natives their own connection to the Catholic Church and a separate dignity in the divine plan of salvation. In a tract published in 1648, *Imagen de la Virgen María* (Image of the Virgin Mary), Miguel Sánchez, a local priest, introduced some apocalyptic elements in the interpretation of the image of Guadalupe and presented Mexico as the predestined land for the Virgin to manifest herself. An analogous religious dignification of local affiliation by the Peruvian Creoles can be perceived in the worship of St. Rose of Lima, the first saint of the Americas. The role of *guadalupanismo*, the cult of the Virgin of Guadalupe, grew so important as an agent of social cohesion that during and after the independence it became the main symbol of Mexican national identity.

Cultural vindications run at the same pace as religious ones. Although the traces of *criollismo* in the writings of Sor Juana Inés de la Cruz (born Juana Inés de Asbaje y Ramírez de Santillana, 1651–1695) are debatable, her defense of intellectual freedom and her mastery of the Spanish language projected an aura of cultural respectability beyond the borders of her Novohispanic homeland. Her contemporary, the polymath Carlos de Sigüenza y Góngora (1645-1700), speculated on the idea of Thomas the Apostle having evangelized the American natives before the arrival of the Spaniards and defended the political virtues of the ancient *tatloanis* (Aztec kings) as a model for modern princes. The allegory of Sigüenza was represented in a triumphal arch commissioned by the municipal council of Mexico in 1680 to welcome the new viceroy, the Marquis de la Laguna. Lorenzo Boturini's inclusion of the Aztec nation in the course of universal history in his *Idea de una nueva historia de la América septentrional* (Idea of a New History of the Septentrional America, 1746) using the new historical method of Gianbattista Vico, the envisagement of a pre-Hispanic classicism by Francisco Javier Clavijero in his *Historia Antigua de México* (A History of Old Mexico, 1780) and the attribution of a biblical genealogy to the Aztec religion by Servando Teresa de Mier in his famous sermon on December 12, 1794, are all milestones of a recognizable ideological process that reached its maturity during the eighteenth century: the elaboration of a specific and dignified historicity for New Spain under the approved canons of universal history.

The expulsion of the Jesuits from the Portuguese and Spanish domains in 1759 and 1767, respectively, was a crucial episode in the pre-romantic imagination of the Americas. Its relevance does not have so much to do with the alleged role of the Jesuits as precursors of Latin American independence as with the consequences of their intellectual belligerence in correcting the prejudices the Europeans maintained about the New World. The European bias against the alleged inferiority of the American continent reached its peak with the eighteenth-century naturalist writings of the Dutch philosopher Cornelius de Pauw and the French naturalist Georges-Louis Leclerc, Comte de Buffon. Such prejudices were not only directed against the plants, the animals, and the natives, whose natural faculties supposedly degenerated on American soil, but against the Creoles as well, who were often branded as indolent and vain. The writings of exiled Jesuits such as the Chilean Juan Ignacio Molina (1740–1829), with his essays on the natural and civil history of Chile, of the Peruvian Juan Pablo Viscardo (1748–1798), who published a widely read *Letter to the Spanish Americans*, or the historical essay on Mexico from Clavijero, helped to create the first Latin American intellectual community with a sense of continental identity.

POLITICAL INDEPENDENCE AND NATION-BUILDING

The issue of representation was central during the last part of the colonial period, when the system of tacit consultation and noninstitutionalized checks and balances started to show its limitations. The traditional Spanish world was traversed by a thick network of corporative links. Between the Crown and its subjects well over a dozen intermediate bodies could be counted, but colonial institutions such as the *audiencias*, *cabildos*, and viceroyalties were hardly of a representative character. During the Habsburg period their positions had often been open to acquisition, which reinforced the oligarchic structure of overseas societies. On the bureaucratic side, the functional principles and boundaries of such institutions did not correspond to the modern patterns of what the German sociologist and political economist Max Weber (1864–1920) called "formal rationality"—that is, goal-attainment, specialization, and accountability—but rather to a "substantive rationality" by which particular needs were identified and met in different ways. Local administration worked through the gracious intercession of a distant king legitimated by faith and tradition. This also explains the underlying meaning of the formula "*se acata pero no se cumple*" (orders are obeyed but not put into practice), of which the colonial authorities so often availed themselves when they received royal instructions: the "real" goals of the Crown had to be interpreted and implemented beyond the literal and often dysfunctional content of its commands. Accordingly, the role of the viceroy was to coordinate, rather than to directly run the different administrative hierarchies. This combination of corporative privileges, juridical conventions, decentralized competencies, and functional overlapping shaped the elastic and often contradictory frame within which the interests of colonial society found their expression. The reforms introduced by the Bourbon dynasty had a limited success for the Crown's interests, but they created further grievances among its American subjects.

In 1808 the old Spanish monarchy collapsed under the joint pressure of its internal contradictions and external aggression. The French invasion of the Iberian Peninsula and the refusal of several overseas territories to recognize the new authorities fighting Napoleon undermined the customary complicities that generated political acquiescence and demolished the juridical and territorial structures of the colonial world. The vacuum of power produced by the forced abdication of Ferdinand VII, who was held prisoner in France, and the promulgation of the Cadiz constitution by Spanish and Creole patriots in 1812, ignited a process in which the dream of a Spanish transcontinental nation-state could not outlive the juridical imagination of its "founding fathers." In Spain the proclamation of national sovereignty could simply proceed by submitting the royal will to the rule of law, but state structure had to be created in the Americas from below, asserting a central authority over a series of competing elites and regional powers. Between 1810 and 1850 more than sixty constitutions were proclaimed in the new republics. Such proliferation reflected the failure to recreate political order after the end of the ancien régime. Political instability was mainly induced by internal rivalries among the new elites and power games between the officers of the victorious armies, but there was a territorial component as well, as was witnessed in the struggle between federalist and centralist projects of nation attested to for more than half a century.

The independence of Spanish America consisted of a series of concurrent and locally generated rebellious movements with countless leaders, fluctuating periods, limited coordination, and a changing ideological justification. The view of pre-existing American nations struggling to free themselves from the imperial yoke cannot therefore be accepted. The notion of Latin American independence as an enlightened southern extension of the "Atlantic revolution" should also be reconsidered. The ideological references of the Creole patriots actually covered a wide range. Miguel Hidalgo, who mobilized the Indian masses of Mexico behind the image of the Virgin of Guadalupe, was a parish priest in whom scholastic and Enlightenment influences combined, whereas José San Martín was a military Creole with monarchical inclinations who developed his early career in the peninsular Royal Army before returning to his native Argentina. The ideology expressed in the colonial institutions evolved with time as well. Given the absence of the king, the *audiencias* and *cabildos* generally resorted to the traditional categories of Catholic natural law to claim the reversion of sovereignty. According to Francisco Suárez, the influential sixteenth-century Spanish scholastic philosopher, the attributes of social life do not originate in single individuals, but in the political community as a whole. The civil power of the monarch was thus vested in him through a *pactum subjectionis*, a conditional alienation of sovereignty by the people. It was precisely the royal abdication therefore that allowed the American *juntas* to invoke a state of "natural necessity" to legitimately reassume sovereignty. This was purportedly done to preserve the rights of the legitimate king while in captivity; but after the restoration of absolutism in 1814 the ideological arguments of Creole patriots turned to open rebellion.

Simón Bolívar, a member of the *mantuano* elite, the planters' aristocracy of Caracas, expressed himself in the political language of civic republicanism. His idea of liberty, shaded with the colors of Greco-Roman classicism, was that of the antique republics. For him the new American *patrias*, in order to fulfill their emancipatory duty, should be created ex nihilo, leaning exclusively on the civic virtue of their citizens. In his *Jamaica Letter* (1815) Bolívar recognized the ambiguities affecting the whole process of independence, for the Spanish American *demos* was yet to be clearly defined. Insurgent political projects very often embodied an oligarchic spirit. In his speech in Angostura in 1819, Bolívar publicized his plans for an independent republic of Venezuela, which included a life-term presidency, an indirect representative system, and a hereditary senate. This was, however, a more participative model than the one the coastal planters who first seized power in Caracas had attempted to develop in 1811. The first Venezuelan constitution, while admitting the indigenous and the *pardos* (free subjects of black/white mixed race) into citizenship, at the same time biased the possibilities of political influence in favor of the landed proprietors by restricting voting rights to property owners. This system of censitary suffrage marked a sharp contrast to the Mexican constitution of Apatzingán (1814), which removed caste distinctions and envisaged the unencumbered incorporation of all adult males in the body politic. In fact, one of the consequences of popular recruitment for the separatist cause during the war was the inclusion of non-white racial groups into the political process.

Compared with the ancien régime, the modern "national imagination" implied a radical change in the symbolic universe within which individuals were politically socialized. For three centuries, religion, church ceremonial, and local semifeudal institutions provided the main sources of socialization in the Latin American colonial world. The inauguration of the new "national period" and of the corresponding sentiment therefore required the creation of a "national culture"—that is, that Creoles, *castas*, and Indians alike ceased to identify themselves through the old corporative and ethnic molds of colonial society and started to understand themselves as Mexicans, Venezuelans, Peruvians, and so on. Such a radical change in the social imagination was mainly a state-induced phenomenon. However, for a long time the control that the new independent governments could exert on the territories and populations under their nominal jurisdiction was quite limited. One thing was the defense of the borders through occasional military campaigns and the promulgation of new legislation from the capital of the country. A different thing altogether was to be able to reach the minds and properties of the new national subjects by means of schools, taxes, and civil servants throughout vast and ill-communicated territories.

The "nationalization" of history and its diffusion through public education was a key element of this cultural process. The *historias patrias* (patriotic national histories) reproduced a teleological scheme in which the colonial emancipation was presented as the inevitable fate of a series of preexisting American nations. Historical texts such as those written by Bartolomé Mitre on Argentina, Diego Barros Arana on Chile, Rafael María Baralt on Venezuela, and José Manuel Restrepo on Colombia coincided in structuring national history around the primordial episode of independence. The political course of the nation was thus presented as an accumulative process toward emancipation and, after it, as the fulfillment of a particular destiny. In this context, the writing of history could not be dissociated from its political function. The Creole scholars who replaced the Catholic Church after independence as the "organic intellectuals" of the new society were recruited from a relatively homogeneous group in terms of their social origin and education. Presidents, diplomats, and parliamentary representatives, often the only ones with access to the necessary documents and archives, abounded in the first generation of Latin American historians. But beyond their social background, what nineteenth-century national histories reflect is a deep change in the meaning of historiography itself. In opposition to the traditional function of sacred history, which was aimed at the salvation of the souls, or to the old chronicles of the conquest, which sought to claim privileges and demonstrate lineages, the new national historiography built upon the romantic canons imported from Europe was driven by an edifying purpose: to present history as a school of civic virtue and a source of political wisdom. Their institutionalization turned these narratives into moral chronicles whose mission was to certify the integral fulfillment of the promises made with the proclamation of independence.

Germán Colmenares has tried to show the distorting effect that such patterns had on the self-perception of Latin American societies. The *historias patrias* were written in a context in which the values of colonial times had lost their prestige. The new topics imposed by the European canon, such as the search for the "noble Indian," social evolution, and scientific progress, were thus actively pursued by the Latin American historians. However, their insistence in comparing their own countries with northern Europe and the United States under circumstances that were completely different led them to envisage a congenital deficit in their inner constitution. On the other hand, their personal insertion in a class structure that was still of a colonial character moved this generation of intellectuals to adopt an elitist approach: The keys to social progress were restricted to a small learned minority. The first independent intelligentsia was thus concealing an ideological solution to a deep-rooted cultural conflict: The attempt to perform a radical break with a colonial past that systematically reemerged in the way of life of the Latin American masses. Whereas Iberoamerican baroque culture had asymmetrically, but functionally, integrated different socioethnic groups in the body of colonial society, the new elites were unable either to substitute this corporative structure for a liberal association of individuals or, by means of a hegemonic ideology, to conciliate the conflicts of the post-colonial world. The result was an exclusionary approach that divided national societies into "civilized people" and the rabble, an unassimilable and increasingly angry throng. Local intellectuals often came to represent their own societies as an alien object whose evolution responded to motives that only a select minority could interpret. This was true of Bolívar, who became frustrated by the ailing civic virtues of the emancipated Americans; of the positivists, worried by the retarded development of the continent; and of twentieth-century Marxists, disappointed by the reticent revolutionary commitment of the rural and native masses.

THE CULTURAL MOLD OF NATIONHOOD

The founders of new postcolonial states have often faced an uneasy choice when adopting an official cultural pattern for the purpose of nation-building. This is what the American anthropologist Clifford Geertz (1926–2006) branded the essentialism-versus-epochalism dilemma: the choice between the mobilization of autochthonous culture and the promotion of a more developed but usually foreign one. The dynastic crisis that ignited Latin American independence soon revealed the deep divisions than ran through the new republics. In fact, the social structure inherited from the colony would last much longer than the ideologies used to scorn it. During the nineteenth-century struggles between liberals and conservatives, the landed and the commercial interests, the city and the countryside, the coast and the inland, it became clear that the social order of the colony still held deep roots in important segments of the independent societies. The obstinate resistance of the newly emancipated citizens to behave in accordance with the civic patterns of Greco-Roman antiquity was a constant motive of frustration for modern republicans. Bolívar saw in it a lack of political character caused by three centuries of colonial despotism, and also a reason to institute dictatorship as a means of implementing the general will against the spirit of factionalism. A later liberalism, such as that held by Juan Bautista Alberdi in Argentina, would resort to the language of commercial humanism to transform the art of government into demographic planning. Under the banner of *gobernar es poblar* (to govern is to populate), he sought to import political virtue through massive immigration and to introduce "civilized" forms of life in the scarcely inhabited, and therefore "barbarian," pampas. Ultimately this would also be the argument used to legitimate the genocide of the Indian population during the Conquest of the Desert in Argentina's southern territories.

The early debates of the Latin American intelligentsia after the dissolution of the political links with the metropolis reflect a division over the value of the Spanish heritage. What is known as the Generation of 1837 in Argentina was particularly explicit in its rejection. Domingo Faustino Sarmiento, a member of this group, not only avowed during his exile in Chile—fleeing from the dictatorship of Juan Manuel Rosas—the orthographic reform of the Spanish language according to the Latin American phonetic, but also scandalized the local public by declaring Spanish itself as a dead language for the cause of civilization. This was a motive of dispute with Andrés Bello, the respected Venezuelan *pensador* living in Chile, who warned against the dangers of losing a common language by the arrival of (mainly French) neologisms that altered its structure and might reproduce with American Spanish the process of corruption the Latin language suffered in medieval Europe.

The animosity against the Spanish cultural heritage was generally shared, although in different tones, by the intellectuals of a liberal inclination, such as the Argentine Alberdi, the Chileans José Victorino Lastarria and Francisco Bilbao Barquín, José María Samper in Colombia, and Carlos María de Bustamante in Mexico. It was not only the social legacy of the colonial period they questioned; they also deemed a spiritual legacy responsible for the historical backwardness of the hemisphere. Nothing reflects this view better than the essay for which Lastarria was given an award by the University of Chile in 1843: *Investigaciones sobre la influencia social de la conquista y del sistema colonial de los Españoles en Chile* (Research on the Social Influence of the Spanish Conquest and Colonial System in Chile). In this republican tract, Lastarria asserted that the Chilean people, before independence, were morally degraded by the submissive character of colonial institutions, which were designed "to breed slaves." In one way or another, all these intellectuals proposed to abandon the Spanish tradition as the fastest way for their countries to access the cultural, political, and economic modernity then envisaged in France, England, and the United States. Spain, as they saw it, had simply isolated itself from the process of modern culture and could no longer offer solutions to the new problems.

There were, however, authors such as Lucas Alamán in México, Sergio Arboleda in Colombia, and Bello in Chile who, while criticizing the Spanish colonial domination, nevertheless defended the right of the Spanish Americans to participate in a common heritage held valuable for the development of the incipient national institutions. In this context, the Spanish legacy functioned as a cultural refuge for the social groups more closely attached to the traditional order. It is not surprising then that, by the end of the nineteenth century, Latin American conservatism took hispanophilia, and particularly the ideas imported from Spanish Catholic traditionalism, and made it an instrument of political resistance. Gabriel García Moreno, president of Ecuador between 1859 and 1875, constitutes the best example of a Catholic ultramontane government in Latin America. But it is the Colombian period known as the Regeneración (1880–1899) that best illustrates the intellectual features of political Catholicism during the nineteenth century. The Regeneration consisted of a series of institutional reforms carried out under the auspices of a group of conservative Catholic intellectuals. Their leader was Miguel Antonio Caro, who settled the doctrinal bases of the Colombian constitution of 1886. The constitution declared God as the source of all forms of authority and established Colombia as a confessional state. In his writings Caro also vindicated the Spanish heritage, which together with the Catholic religion, the Spanish language, and a strong central power, would constitute the pillars of Colombian nationhood.

SUPRANATIONAL IDEOLOGIES

The challenge of integrating the different socio-ethnic groups of colonial society into a unified national culture has been a permanent matter of political concern in Latin America since independence. But nationalism has traditionally had to compete in this realm with other kinds of supranational ideologies. Bolívar himself dreamed of an American federation of sovereign states, for which a congress was summoned in Panama, without much success, in 1826. Since then Latinoamericanism has been a powerful rhetorical resource in the politics of the region. During the twentieth century, however, it had to rival the pan-American initiatives of several U.S. governments and the Catholic ideology of the *hispanidad*, the belief in a common Hispanic character molded by history and religion.

Ariel, the famous essay published in 1900 by the Uruguayan José Enrique Rodó, and the intellectual movement that it initiated, are usually signaled as the starting point of a new Latin American cultural conscience and of the vindication of its Greco-Latin values against Anglo-Saxon purported utilitarianism. The truth is, however, that by the end of the nineteenth century, liberalism, with its view of modern society as a contract of free individuals, had given way to positivism and its idea of the nation as a homogeneous social body endowed with a common destiny. Ethnic cleavages, now under the aegis of a biologistic interpretation of social behavior, reentered the political agenda of the independent nations. In countries with a small proportion of indigenous population, native American culture played no significant role in the national imagination. Argentine positivists such as José Ingenieros and Carlos Octavio Bunge drew on social Darwinism, and on the tradition formerly set by Sarmiento and Alberdi, in considering miscegenation as a process conducive to the physical and moral degeneration of society. On the contrary, a positivist historian such as Manoel Bomfim conceived of Brazil's nation-building "not as a mere social, political, civic and moral development, but as a deep and prolonged physio-psychological process" (1997, p. 327; author's translation) in which the different races combined their energies and traditions.

In other countries the positivist concern with "racial quality" produced different ideological outcomes. The political assumptions of *indigenismo*, understood as a public policy for integrating the Indians into mainstream society, differed with time and place, but in general its aim was the social dilution of the indigenous peoples through miscegenation and acculturation. In his essay *Pueblo enfermo* (A Sick People, 1909) and in the novel *Raza de bronce* (A Race of Bronze, 1919), Alcides Arguedas depicted the exploitation of Bolivian Indians by the local landowners, and also his pessimism about the country's ability to escape its historical prostration. Andrés Molina Enríquez, an early mentor of Mexican indigenism, also saw racial heterogeneity as the main obstacle to national development, but envisioned a long term solution in the turning of the Indians into mestizos. José Vasconcelos Calderón developed such a view into a full-fledged nationalist ideology according to which a new "cosmic race" would ultimately become the subject of the Mexican nationhood fashioned by the 1910 revolution. Around the same time, socialist theorists Raúl Haya de la Torre and José Carlos Mariátegui in Peru made the connection between indigenism and Marxism by recognizing the specificity of surviving pre-Columbian cultures: The Indians could after all not be equated to the Western industrial proletariat and deserved special consideration in the strategy for a Latin American socialist revolution.

By the 1930s new ideologies linked to ethnicity entered the political arena. In the Caribbean, Afrocentric creeds proved particularly prolific. The idea of *négritude* (blackness), developed in the French-speaking realm by Senegalese president Léopold Senghor, the Martinican poet Aimé Césaire, and the Guyanese writer León Damas, expressed the rejection by Third World black intellectuals of Western neocolonial domination. But whereas indigenism emerged and consolidated in some countries as a state policy, *négritude* remained as a mainly cultural and literary movement that soon found in Nicolás Guillén and the Cuban *negrismo* a Spanish-speaking equivalent. In the English Caribbean and the United States, Jamaican-born Marcus Garvey promoted a current of black nationalism that encouraged the return to Africa as a way of redemption from the legacy of slavery. Garvey's vision was contested by other African-American leaders and did not render long-term political results; but it was rapidly incorporated into the symbolic structure of Rastafarianism, and his image has since been preserved as a cultural icon in Anglo-Caribbean popular imagination.

Different as they are, all these pan-ethnicist movements coincided in considering the nation-state as an insufficient frame for political action. This is by no means an exclusive attribute of regional identity politics, but a familiar feature in Latin American ideologies pushed by an emancipatory and anticolonial spirit. In the 1950s the implementation of the United Nations development plans through the Economic Commission for Latin America and the Caribbean (CEPAL) planted the seeds for what later would come to be known as dependency theory. Although developed in Latin America by CEPAL economists such as Fernando Henrique Cardoso and Enzo Faletto, some of its prescriptions, like the import-substitution program, were readily applied in several African and Asian developing countries. Dependency theory can be summarily described as a center-periphery critical approach to the economic relations between advanced capitalist countries and the Third World. The structure of such relations was accused of systematically undermining the economic autonomy of the developing countries, and the implicit political corollary was the encouragement of Latin American nationalism as a way to escape underdevelopment.

Postcoloniality and its related poststructuralist theories, such as subaltern studies, can be considered the latest academic paradigm applied to the understanding of Latin American political imagination. To a large extent they have come to occupy the gap left by the decline of Marxism as a critical knowledge. According to this new perspective, the traditional alienation of Latin American elites from their own societies—the political and intellectual syndrome produced by a never-to-be-achieved modernity—was the product of a neocolonial cultural logic that since the nineteenth century condemned a series of nonhegemonic subjects—women, Indians, blacks, homosexuals, peasants, and so on—to a structurally subaltern condition. The postmodern agenda for emancipatory politics in Latin America should therefore address more restricted social categories, rely on subaltern forms of self-knowledge, and adopt a new postnational general outline.

See also **Alamán, Lucas; Alberdi, Juan Bautista; Alva Ixtlilxóchitl, Fernando; Arguedas, Alcides; Baralt, Rafael María; Bello, Andrés; Bilbao Barquín, Francisco; Bolívar, Simón; Bunge, Carlos Octavio; Bustamante, Carlos María de; Cardoso, Fernando Henrique; Caro, Miguel Antonio; Césaire, Aimé; Clavigero, Francisco Javier; Conquest of the Desert; Dependency Theory; Díaz del Castillo, Bernal; García Moreno, Gabriel; Garcilaso de la Vega, El Inca; Garvey, Marcus; Guadalupe, Virgin of; Guaman Poma de Ayala, Felipe; Guillén, Nicolás; Haya de la Torre, Víctor Raúl; Indianismo; Indigenismo; Ingenieros, José; Jesuits; Juana Inés de la Cruz, Sor; Lastarria, José Victorino; Mariátegui, José Carlos; Mitre, Bartolomé; Muñoz Camargo, Diego; Négritude; Peninsular; Peru: Peru Since Independence; Positivism; Restrepo, José**

Manuel; Rodó, José Enrique; Rosa de Lima; Rosas, Juan Manuel de; Salvador, Vicente do; Samper, José María; Sarmiento, Domingo Faustino; Sigüenza y Góngora, Carlos de; Tlatoani; Vasconcelos Calderón, José; Viscardo y Guzmán, Juan Pablo.

BIBLIOGRAPHY

Primary Sources

Alva Ixtlilxóchitl, Fernando de. *Historia de la nación Chichimeca.* Madrid: Historia 16, 1985.

Bello, Andrés. *Selected Writings of Andrés Bello.* Edited by Iván Jaksić. Translated by Frances M. López-Morillas. New York: Oxford University Press, 1997.

Bolívar, Simón. *El Libertador: Writings of Simón Bolívar.* Edited by David Bushnell. Translated by Frederick H. Fornoff. Oxford and New York: Oxford University Press, 2003.

Bomfim, Manoel. *O Brasil na América: Caracterição da Formação Brasileira.* Rio de Janeiro: Topbooks, 1997.

Boturini Benaducci, Lorenzo. *Historia general de la América Septentrional,* 2nd edition. Edited by Manuel Ballesteros Gaibrois. México: Instituto de Investigaciones Históricas, Universidad Nacional Autónomo de México, 1990.

Clavigero, Francisco Javier. *Historia antigua de México: Facsimilar de la edición de Ackermann, 1826.* Puebla, México: Gobierno del Estado de Puebla, Secretaría de Cultura, 2003.

Cardoso, Fernando Henrique, and Enzo Faletto. *Dependencia y desarrollo en América Latina: Ensayo de interpretatión sociológico.* México: Siglo Veintiuno Editores, 1969.

De la Torre Villar, Ernesto, and Ramiro Navarro de Anda, eds. *Testimonios históricos guadalupanos.* México: Fondo de Cultura Económica, 2004.

Díaz del Castillo, Bernal. *The Bernal Díaz Chronicles.* Garden City, NJ: Doubleday, 1956.

Guamán Poma de Ayala, Felipe. *Nueva corónica y buen gobierno.* México: Fondo de Cultura Económica, 1993.

Juana Inés de la Cruz, Sister. *Poems, Protest, and a Dream: Selected Writings.* Translated by Margaret Sayers Peden. New York: Penguin, 1997.

Lastarria, José Victorino. "Investigaciones sobre la influencia social de la Conquista y del sistema colonial de los españoles en Chile." In *Obras Completas,* vol. 7. Santiago de Chile: Imprenta Barcelona, 1909.

Muñoz Camargo, Diego. *Descripción de la Ciudad y Provincia de Tlaxcala de las Indias y del Mar Océano para el buen gobierno y ennoblecimiento dellas.* México: Instituto de Investigaciones Filológicas/Universidad Nacional Autónoma de México, 1981.

Salvador, Frei Vicente do. *História do Brasil, 1500–1627,* 6th ed. São Paulo: Edições Melhoramentos, 1975.

Sarmiento, Domingo Faustino. *Facundo: Civilization and Barbarism.* Translated by Kathleen Ross. Berkeley: University of California Press, 2003.

Sigüenza y Góngora, Carlos de. *The Misadventures of Alonso Ramírez.* Translated by Edwin H. Pleasants. Mexico: Imprenta Mexicana, 1962.

Silva, José Bonifacio de Adrada e. *Projetos para o Brasil.* Edited by Miriam Dolhnikoff. São Paulo: Companhia das Letras, 1998.

Vega, Garcilaso de la. *The Incas: The Royal Commentaries of the Inca, Garcilaso de la Vega, 1539–1616.* Translated by Maria Jolas from the French edition of Alain Gheerbrant. New York: Orion Press, 1961.

Secondary Sources: Nationalism

Anderson, Benedict. *Imagined Communities: Reflections on the Origin and Spread of Nationalism,* rev. ed. London and New York: Verso, 2006.

Castro-Klarén, Sara, and John Charles Chasteen, eds. *Beyond Imagined Communities: Reading and Writing the Nation in Nineteenth-Century Latin America.* Washington, DC: Woodrow Wilson Center Press; Baltimore: Johns Hopkins University Press, 2003.

Colom, Francisco, and Ángel Rivero, eds. *El altar y el trono: Ensayos sobre el catolicismo político iberoamericano.* Barcelona: Anthropos, 2006.

Gellner, Ernest. *Nations and Nationalism,* 2nd edition. Malden, MA: Blackwell, 2006.

Gutiérrez Chong, Natividad, ed. *Mujeres y nacionalismos en América Latina: De la independencia a la nación del nuevo milenio.* México: Universidad Nacional Autónoma de México, 2004.

Hobsbawm, Eric J. *Nations and Nationalism since 1780: Programme, Myth, Reality,* 2nd edition. Cambridge, U.K., and New York: Cambridge University Press, 1992.

McEvoy, Carmen. *Forjando la nación: Ensayos de historia republicana.* Lima: Pontificia Universidad Católica del Perú; Sewanee, TN: University of the South, 1999.

Smith, Anthony D. *The Ethnic Origins of Nations.* Oxford and New York: Blackwell, 1987.

Ward, Thomas. *La resistencia cultural: La nación en el ensayo de las Américas.* Lima: Universidad Ricardo Palma, 2004.

Secondary Sources: Historiography

Colmenares, Germán. *Las convenciones contra la cultura: Ensayos sobre la historiografía latinoamericana del siglo XIX,* 4th edition. Colciencias: TM Editores, 1997.

Batllori, Miguel. *El abate Viscardo: Historia y mito de la intervención de los Jesuitas en la independencia de Hispanoamérica.* Madrid: Mapfre, 1995.

Rojas-Mix, Miguel. *El fin del Milenio y el sentido de la historia: Lacunza y Molina.* Santiago de Chile: LOM, 2001.

Secondary Sources: Indigenismo

Favre, Henri. *El indigenismo.* México: Fondo de Cultura Económica, 1998.

Villoro, Luis. *Los grandes momentos del indigenismo en México.* México: Fondo de Cultura Económica, 1998.

Secondary Sources: Nacional Imagination

Annino, Antonio, and François-Xavier Guerra, eds. *Inventando la nación: Iberoamérica siglo XIX.* México: Fondo de Cultura Económica, 2003.

Colom-González, Francisco, ed. *Relatos de nación: La construcción de las identidades nacionales en el mundo hispánico.* Madrid: Iberoamericana; and Frankfurt: Vervuert, 2005.

Geertz, Clifford. *The Interpretation of Cultures: Selected Essays.* London: Hutchinson, 1975.

Lafaye, Jacques. *Quetzalcóatl and Guadalupe: The Formation of Mexican National Consciousness, 1531–1813.* Chicago: University of Chicago Press, 1976.

Secondary Sources: Coloniality

Mignolo, Walter. *The Darker Side of the Renaissance: Literacy, Territoriality, and Colonization*, 2nd edition. Ann Arbor: University of Michigan Press, 2003.

FRANCISCO COLOM GONZÁLEZ

NAVA, GREGORY (1949–). Gregory Nava, a Mexican-American film director, writer, and producer, aims to bring Hispanic stories and characters into the mainstream of U.S. popular culture. Nava was born on April 10, 1949, in San Diego, and attended the UCLA film school. His first major success as a director was *El Norte* (1984), which he co-wrote with his wife, Anna Thomas. The film tells the story of a Guatemalan brother and sister who immigrate illegally to the United States. In many of his films Nava places Hispanic characters at the center of the action in stories that contain a universal message. *Selena* (1997) is a biopic of the Texas-born singer who became a Latin music star; *Why Do Fools Fall in Love* (1998), also the story of a popular singer, in this case focuses on an African American, Frankie Lymon. The feature film *My Family/Mi familia* (1995) and the PBS drama *American Family* (2002, 2004) offer multigenerational portraits of Mexican families in the United States. Although his work has been described by some as melodramatic, he has won critical praise as well as Oscar and Emmy nominations. His film *Bordertown* (2006) was nominated for a Golden Bear at the 2007 Berlin Film Festival. Nava has worked with well-known Latino actors from the United States and Latin America, including Sonia Braga, Jennifer Lopez, Esai Morales, Edward James Olmos, and Raquel Welch.

See also **Cinema: Since 1990; Hispanics in the United States.**

BIBLIOGRAPHY

André, María Claudia. "Familia y comunidad como bases del proceso de adaptación social en tres largometrajes chicanos: *. . . y no se lo tragó la tierra, El Norte y My Family.*" In *The Ties That Bind: Questioning Family Dynamics and Family Discourse in Hispanic Literature*, ed. Sara E. Cooper, 127–154. Lanham, MD: University Press of America, 2004.

Fojas, Camilla. "Schizopolis: Border Cinema and the Global City of Angels." *Aztlán: A Journal of Chicano Studies* 31, no.1 (2006): 7–31.

Nava, Gregory. Interview by Bill Moyers for the PBS program *NOW*, February 15, 2002. Transcript available from http://www.pbs.org/now/transcript/transcript_nava.html.

Williams, Bruce. "The Bridges of Los Angeles County: Marketing Language in the Chicano Cinema of Gregory Nava." *Canadian Journal of Film Studies/Revue Canadienne D'Etudes Cinématographiques* 14, no. 2 (2005): 54–70.

CARYN C. CONNELLY

NAVAJOS. Navajos (also Navahos and Diné) are an Athapaskan tribe that settled in the American Southwest between 1000 and 1525 CE. The Navajos likely experienced some demographic decline after Spanish contact, but their isolation contributed to a rapid resurgence in their numbers. Relations between the Spaniards and the Navajos were marked by bitter warfare, fueled by the trade in captives in which both groups participated. Navajos allied with the Puebloans in the Pueblo Rebellion of 1680, after which their lands became a refuge for those who resisted the Spanish reconquest (1692–1693). Many of the fugitives remained among the Navajos, exposing Navajo culture to Hopi and Pueblo influences.

Internal division resulted from conflicts between Puebloan and Athapaskan values within the Navajo Nation. Tensions were exacerbated by drought and the increasing incidence of Ute attacks. Together these pressures led to a revitalization of Navajo culture. By 1774 the Navajos had driven the Spaniards from much of their traditional lands in northwestern New Mexico and settled down to a life of agriculture, animal husbandry, hunting, and gathering.

After Mexican independence (1821), the Navajos became the target of slave traders from New Mexico. Warfare between the Navajos and the New Mexicans escalated rapidly in the 1830s as did the trade in Navajo captives. The burdens of war fell heaviest on the isolated Navajos, who again experienced internal division as a result of outside pressure.

The Navajos' fate did not improve when the United States usurped Mexico's position as the dominant force in the Southwest in 1846. In an ill-conceived plan to relocate the Navajos, the tribe was moved to Bosque Redondo, New Mexico, in the infamous Long Walk of 1864. The resettlement plan was a disaster: the Navajos suffered from drought, disease, blight, and ultimately starvation. In 1868 the Navajos returned to their reservation, which was now only a fraction of their former homelands.

Over the twentieth century the Navajo Nation slowly recovered in both population numbers and land base. In 2002, the Navajo Nation counted 250,000 members, and their territory spanned approximately 25,000 square miles in southern Utah, northern Arizona, and northern New Mexico. All Navajo land is communally owned and administered by the Nation's government. Although poverty and unemployment continue to plague Navajo communities, rich mineral deposits on Navajo land and the construction of the Navajo Nation's first casino may improve the local economy.

See also **Indigenous Peoples; Pueblo Indians; Pueblo Rebellion; Slavery: Indian Slavery and Forced Labor.**

BIBLIOGRAPHY

Frank McNitt, *Navajo Wars: Military Campaigns, Slave Raids, and Reprisals* (1972, 1990).

Myra Ellen Jenkins and Ward Alan Minge, *Navajo Activities Affecting the Acoma-Laguna Area, 1746–1910* (1974).

Peter Iverson, *The Navajo Nation* (1983).

AARON PAINE MAHR

NAVAL CLUB, PACT OF THE. Pact of the Naval Club, an agreement reached on August 3, 1984, between Uruguay's military and a majority of the political opposition. The agreement was the culmination of a series of meetings in the Naval Club that sought to transfer power from the military to democratically elected civilians. This process had included a plebiscite in 1980, internal party elections in 1982, and successive attempts at negotiation. Participating groups among the opposition included the Frente Amplio (some organizations of which were returned to legal status by the agreement) and the Colorado Party, but not the Blanco (National) Party, whose principal leader was in prison at the time. The agreement confirmed November 1984 as a date for general elections that would involve the active participation of all political forces, although not of all of their leaders. It also confirmed concessions by the military to accept an advisory council on matters of national security dominated by the president and his cabinet and a one-year period during which they would be able to name commanders in chief. In political terms, the agreement was a triumph for the Colorado strategy of transition, which was crowned by its success at the polls in the 1984 election. It also provided important guarantees for the military in the future democracy, especially concerning the possibility of trials for human rights violations.

See also **Uruguay, Political Parties: Blanco Party; Uruguay, Political Parties: Colorado Party.**

BIBLIOGRAPHY

Martin Weinstein, *Uruguay: Democracy at the Crossroads* (1988).

Charles Gillespie, *Negotiating Democracy* (1991).

FERNANDO FILGUEIRA

NAVARRA Y ROCAFUL, MELCHOR DE (1626–1691). Melchor de Navarra y Rocaful (duke of Palata), born in Aragon, was one of the most energetic and innovative but ultimately unsuccessful administrators of colonial Peru. As viceroy, from 1681 to 1689, Palata focused on reorganizing indigenous communities in order to increase tribute income and to maximize the *mita*, the state labor levy. Concerned with the continued decline in the mining industry, Palata initiated a series of proposals to stimulate production. He also undertook a major review of labor practices within the viceroyalty aimed at stabilizing the work force and combating the chronic shortfalls in the *mita*. Palata ordered a comprehensive census of indigenous society that would include individuals living within or outside of the communities through which their tribute and labor should be paid. Palata issued a series of orders designed to eliminate the protected status of various groups of Indians (such as forasteros and vanaconas) who were avoiding their obligations to the Crown. Under the Palata reforms, the *reducción* (resettlement) system of the 1570s was effectively abandoned and Indians then required to pay tribute and serve *mita* duty through the communities in which they currently resided.

Palata's efforts were ultimately frustrated by resistance from those who benefited from private arrangements with these Indians—employers (particularly miners in Upper Peru), clergy, and some indigenous community leaders—and from Indian communities as well. When the Palata reform proposals threatened these arrangements and increased indigenous migration from areas subjected to *mita* demands, he was forced to abandon his program. The new tribute and labor assessments were first reduced and then revoked by Palata's successor, the count of Monclova. In 1691, his administration came to an end: He sailed for Spain to become president of the Council of Aragon but died en route on April 13.

See also **Mita; Portocarrero y Lasso de la Vega, Melchor; Viceroyalty, Viceroy.**

BIBLIOGRAPHY

Jeffrey A. Cole, *The Potosí Mita, 1573–1700: Compulsory Indian Labor in the Andes* (1985).

Ann M. Wightman, *Indigenous Migration and Social Change: The Forasteros of Cuzco, 1570–1720* (1990), esp. pp. 9–44.

ANN M. WIGHTMAN

NAVARRO, (FÉLIX) MARTÍN ANTONIO

NAVARRO, (FÉLIX) MARTÍN ANTONIO (1738–1793). Martín Antonio (Félix) Navarro (*b.* 20 November 1738; *d.* 26 May 1793), treasurer, contador and first intendant of Louisiana. Born in La Coruña, Galicia, Spain, Navarro accompanied the first Spanish expedition to Louisiana on 5 September 1765 and remained there for the next twenty-two years. During the war against Great Britain, Navarro oversaw supplies and munitions for Governor Bernardo de Gálvez's victorious expeditions against Baton Rouge (1779), Mobile (1780), and Pensacola (1781).

In 1780 Navarro became the first intendant in Louisiana; on 29 August of that year he wrote "Political Reflections on the Current Condition of the Province," recommending increased population and free trade. Consequently, the crown approved a new commercial code in 1782 permitting Louisiana direct trade with France and the Spanish West Indies as well as with designated ports in Spain. When Navarro granted licenses to Panton, Leslie, and Company to trade, critics protested his giving such rights to foreigners. In 1784 he and Governor Esteban Miró went to Pensacola and Mobile, where they met with the Creek, Choctaw, Alibamone, and Chickasaw Indians and drew up tariff arrangements for the pelt trade. Navarro left Louisiana on 10 May 1788 and returned to Spain. The following year he was appointed special commissioner of the crown and visited factories throughout Europe. His report concluded that Spain could manufacture most of the goods traded in Louisiana. Navarro died intestate in Madrid. The total value of his estate was 3,711,330 reales de vellon. His daughter Adelaide and her husband Louis Demarest used their share to build Frances Plantation near present day Franklin, Louisiana. Two governors of Louisiana are descendants.

See also **Gálvez, Bernardo de; Louisiana.**

BIBLIOGRAPHY

Brian E. Coutts, "Martín Navarro: Treasurer, Contador, Intendant, 1766–1788" (Ph.D. diss., Louisiana State University, 1981); "Flax and Hemp in Spanish Louisiana, 1777–1783," in *Louisiana History* 26 (Spring 1985): 129–139; and "Boom and Bust: The Rise and Fall of the Tobacco Industry in Spanish Louisiana, 1770–1790," in *The Americas* 42 (January 1986): 289–310.

Additional Bibliography

Din, Gilbert C. *The Spanish Presence in Louisiana, 1763-1803.* Lafayette: Center for Louisiana Studies, University of Southwestern Louisiana, 1996.

Montero de Pedro, José. *The Spanish in New Orleans and Louisiana*. Gretna Pelican Pub., 2000.

BRIAN E. COUTTS

NAVARRO WOLFF, ANTONIO

NAVARRO WOLFF, ANTONIO Antonio Navarro Wolff (*b.* ca 1948), Colombian political leader. After training as a sanitary engineer at the Universidad del Valle in Cali, Navarro joined the M-19 guerrilla movement, participating in a number of its operations against government and private targets over the next dozen years. In May 1985, Navarro was badly wounded, losing his left leg and suffering some speech impairment. Following Carlos Pizarro Leongómez's assassination in April 1990, leadership of the M-19 passed to Navarro, who brought it into open political participation. He was the Left's presidential choice in the 1990 elections and won 700,000 votes, better than 10 percent of the total. Navarro served for a few months as President César Gaviría's health minister before resigning to enter the Constituent Assembly elections of December 1990. M-19 garnered 27 percent of the vote, and Navarro became a major force in the Assembly, helping to shape the constitution adopted in July 1991. His party did not fare well in the October 1991 congressional elections, but Navarro returned as a presidential candidate in 1994. After losing this election, Navarro went onto become mayor of Pasto (1995–1997), then a federal representative (1998–2002) and finally a senator (2002–2006). M-19 began loosing power in the 1990s but much of its membership, including Navarro, formed the Alternative Democratic Pole. In the party's internal election, Navarro ran to be the party's presidential candidate in 2006 but lost this campaign. The party's nominee, Carlos Gaviria, came in second in the presidential race.

See also **Betancur Cuartas, Belisario; Colombia, Revolutionary Movements: M-19; Gaviria Trujillo, César Augusto.**

BIBLIOGRAPHY

Patricia Lara, *Siembra vientos y recogerás tempestades* (1982), pp. 215–247.

Phil Gunson, Andrew Thompson, and Greg Chamberlain, *The Dictionary of Contemporary Politics of South America*, (1989), 172–173, 248–249.

Jenny Pearse, *Colombia: Inside the Labyrinth* (1990), pp. 170–182.

Additional Bibliography

Cárdenas Rivera, Miguel E. *La construcción del posconflicto en Colombia enfoques desde la pluralidad*. Bogotá: FESCOL, 2003.

Livingstone, Grace. *Inside Colombia: Drugs, Democracy, and War*. London: Latin America Bureau, 2003.

J. LEÓN HELGUERA

NAZARETH, ERNESTO

NAZARETH, ERNESTO (1863–c. 1934). Ernesto Nazareth (Júlio de Nazareth; *b.* 20 March 1863; *d.* ca. 2 February 1934), Brazilian salon pianist and composer. Nazareth's father, Vasco Lourenzo da Silva Nazareth, was a customs official, and his mother, Carolina Augusta Pereira da Cunha, a pianist who gave her son his first piano lessons. After his mother's death in 1873, Nazareth continued his musical studies with Eduardo Madeira and Lucien Lambert. An early intense interest in the music of Chopin continued to grow and became an important factor in the development of his compositional style. From 1920 to 1924 he played daily in the Cinema Odeon in Rio de Janeiro, where one of the cellists, Heitor Villa-Lobos, admired Nazareth's salon style of playing. When describing the *choro* as a musical genre, Villa-Lobos frequently spoke of his own compositions as music in the style of Nazareth and other salon musicians of the late nineteenth and early twentieth centuries.

Although Nazareth's compositions are exclusively piano pieces in salon style, Nazareth was the most important composer of popular music of his time. His approximately 220 compositions were an important source of ideas for composers in the emergent nationalist school of music. His works often bore a sophisticated or whimsical title of subtle meaning comprehensible only to a "carioca" (urban resident of Rio de Janeiro), such as *Odeon, Espalhafatoso,* and *Esta chumbado.* Subtitles were names of dances, provided in what often appeared to be a haphazard fashion, resulting in a fusion of dance forms such as maxixe, polka, polka-maxixe.

During his lifetime Nazareth's music was performed only for entertainment in salon settings, but his music achieved a much wider audience after his death, often appearing on concert programs.

See also **Music: Art Music.**

BIBLIOGRAPHY

Gérard Béhague, "Popular Musical Currents in the Art of Music of the Early Nationalistic Period in Brazil, c. 1870–1920" (Ph.D. diss., Tulane Univ., 1966).

Additional Bibliography

Nazareth, Ernesto. *Ernesto Nazareth: A Collection of His Finest Piano Works.* San Francisco: Guitar Solo Publications, 2001.

Newman, Paul Jared. *Ernesto Nazareth: Brazilian Tangos.* Pacific, MO: Mel Bay, 2001.

DAVID P. APPLEBY

NAZIS. The first Nazi *Landesgruppe* ("country organization") in Latin America was founded among German settlers in Paraguay in 1929; other such groups were created in Latin America prior to Hitler's accession to power in 1933. Activists in these organizations were recent German and Austrian immigrants who had experienced war, revolution, and inflation in Europe; most did not yet feel themselves established, or did not intend to remain, in the New World. Created at local initiative, country organizations had to be approved by the *Auslands-Organisation* ("foreign organization") of the Nazi Party in Germany; furious personal and factional disputes ensued. In total numbers, the Brazilian and Argentine *Landesgruppen* were two of the four largest Nazi organizations (with Holland and Austria) outside Germany; however, the ratio of party members to German citizens—theoretically, only German citizens were eligible for membership—resident in the country was much greater in Venezuela and Panama. In mid-1937, 143,640 Reichsdeutsche (German nationals) resided in Latin America; of them, 7,602 (5.3%) were party members.

Enthusiasm for Hitler's Third Reich probably reached its peak among overseas Germans around 1936, by which time Hitler had restored order and eliminated the restrictions of the Treaty of Versailles; this would suggest, perhaps, that nationalism counted for more than ideology. Nazis (and other German agencies) proselytized actively among Latin Americans, but since most of the latter were repelled by Nazi attitudes of racial superiority and hostility to religion, they made few converts. They also proselytized among partly assimilated settlers in older German-speaking communities, particularly in the Southern Cone. Their efforts to propagate Nazi and German nationalist dogma in German-language schools proved offensive to the Argentine, Brazilian, and Chilean governments. The resultant conflicts led, in 1938 and 1939, to legislation restricting the political activities and cultural autonomy of all foreign-language groups; between 1938 and 1942 the party itself was banned everywhere.

During World War II, individual Nazis participated in Germany's clandestine-warfare operations in the Americas, but the party as such was a negligible factor. After 1945 German Nazis and ex-collaborators made their way to South and Central America. Most lived in quiet obscurity, but a few joined with local right-wing radicals to perpetuate the Nazi ideology in marginal, though occasionally violent, sects.

See also **Germans in Latin America.**

BIBLIOGRAPHY

Hans-Adolf Jacobsen, *Nationalsozialistische Aussenpolitik, 1933–1938* (1968).

Donald M. Mc Kale, *The Swastika Outside Germany* (1977).

Ronald C. Newton, *The "Nazi Menace" in Argentina, 1931–1947* (1992).

Holger M. Meding, *Flucht vor Nürnberg? Deutsche und österreichische Einwanderung in Argentinien, 1945–1955* (1992).

Additional Bibliography

Ben-Dror, Graciela. *Católicos, nazis y judíos: La Iglesia argentina en los tiempos del Tercer Reich.* Buenos Aires: Lumiere: Universidad de Tel Aviv, Instituto de Historia y Cultura de América Latina, 2003.

Friedman, Max Paul. *Nazis and Good Neighbors: The United States Campaign against the Germans of Latin America in World War II.* Cambridge: Cambridge University Press, 2003.

RONALD C. NEWTON

NEBEL, CARL (1805–1855). Carl Nebel (*b.* 1805; *d.* 1855), German painter of Mexican scenes. After studying architecture and design, Nebel traveled through Mexico from 1829 to 1834, exploring various locations with the object of drawing rural and urban landscapes, archaeological sites, and folkloric scenes. Nebel was the first to draw Tajín, Xochicalco, and other sites. Due to his academic education, his drawings are excellent, and his folkloric scenes particularly outstanding.

Returning to Europe, Nebel worked in Paris on publishing his first book on Mexico. Consisting of fifty color lithographs and text based on observations by Alexander Von Humboldt, who was a possible inspiration for Nebel's work, the book first appeared in grand format in 1836, and a Spanish translation entitled *Viaje pintoresco y arqueológico: Sobre la parte más interesante de la República Mexicana* was published in 1840. Another book illustrated by Nebel, *The War Between the United States and Mexico,* was published in Philadelphia in 1851. The drawings were done from memory, perhaps from notes that Nebel had taken or that were supplied to him. The book contains photographs of the Mexican-American War, some of the first photography to serve as testimony of a military clash.

See also **Art: The Nineteenth Century; Mexico, Wars and Revolutions: Mexican-American War; Xochicalco.**

BIBLIOGRAPHY

Manuel Romero De Terreros, *México visto por los pintores extranjeros de siglo XIX* (1959).

Renate Löschner et al., *Artistas alemanes en latinoamérica: Pintores naturalistas del siglo XIX ilustran el continente* (1978).

Additional Bibliography

García Rubio, Fabiola. *La entrada de las tropas estadunidenses a la ciudad de México: La mirada de Carl Nebel.* México, D.F.: Instituto Mora, 2002.

ESTHER ACEVEDO

NEGRETE, JORGE (1911–1953). Jorge Negrete (*b.* 30 November 1911; *d.* 5 December 1953), Mexican actor and singer. Born in Guanajuato, Negrete began his studies in a military academy, but dropped out to pursue a music career. Throughout the 1930s he had a series of successful singing engagements in Mexico and the United States. In 1937 Negrete debuted in the film *La madrina del diablo.* His good looks, deep masculine voice, and self-assurance quickly propelled him to stardom. Negrete, along with Pedro Infante, dominated the *ranchera* films. Known as the "immortal *charro mexicano,*" he starred in over forty films. Among his classic features are *El peñón de las ánimas; El cementerio de las ánimas; La Valentina; ¡Ay, Jalisco, no te rajes!; Historia de un gran amor; El rapto;* and *Dos tipos de cuidado.* He was also a founder and president of the cinema workers' union.

See also **Cinema: From the Silent Film to 1990; Music: Popular Music and Dance.**

BIBLIOGRAPHY

Luis Reyes De La Maza, *El cine sonoro en México* (1973).

E. Bradford Burns, *Latin American Cinema: Film and History* (1975).

Carl J. Mora, *Mexican Cinema: Reflections of a Society: 1896–1980* (1982).

John King, *Magical Reels: A History of Cinema in Latin America* (1990).

Additional Bibliography

Barajas Sandoval, Carmen. *Jorge Negrete.* México: EDAMEX, 2001.

Serna, Enrique. *Jorge el bueno: La vida de Jorge Negrete.* México: Clío, 1993.

DAVID MACIEL

NÉGRITUDE. Négritude, term invented by Aimé Césaire in Paris in 1934, in order to emphasize the important role of black creativity in human history, a role that had been denied by colonialism and Christianity. In the magazine *L'étudiante Noir,* Césaire claimed that he possessed a miraculous weapon, a poetry that spoke not to the reason but to the heart. Césaire was then one of a group of black students from the Caribbean and Africa who studied in Paris and were interested in the work of black artists from all over the world, especially Africa. The most famous members of the group were Léopold Sédar Senghor (1906–1990?) and Ousmane Socé

(1911–1973) from Senegal and Léon-Gontran Damas (1912–1978) from Guyana.

The group around the magazine was greatly influenced by the controversy over the novel *Batouala* (1921), written by the Guyanese René Maran. This "really black novel," with its anticolonial allusions, caused a scandal while at the same time winning the prestigious Prix Goncourt. Inspired by this controversy, some students founded the anticolonalist magazine *Légitime Défense* (1932–1934), which borrowed its name from surrealism and engaged in the debate about communism and sociopolitical alternatives. Of course, for Senghor, Damas, and Césaire this alternative was closely involved with the process of political decolonization, an orientation that distinguished their concept of "marvelous realism" from that of André Breton and André Masson, two exponents of French-oriented surrealism.

Senghor felt closer to the existentialism of Jean-Paul Sartre, who debated French colonialism in his magazine *Les Temps Modernes* and wrote the famous preface "Black Orpheus" for Senghor's *Anthologie de la nouvelle poésie nègre et malgache de langue française* (1945). Senghor became the first president of the Republic of Senegal in 1960 and served for two decades as head of the government. Nevertheless, he continued working on the elaboration of the poetical concept of *négritude,* in order to confront western ideological models with humanistic African traditions.

Black pride, considered by Senghor and Césaire as the sine qua non for *négritude,* maintained its influence in the younger generation of students coming from Africa and especially, from the Caribbean. Frantz Fanon and Édouard Glissant, both former students of Césaire's in Martinique, developed their own ideas, although they did not adopt the term *négritude.* Fanon was very much involved with the independence movement in Africa, which inspired his *Les Damnées de la terre* (1961), again published with a preface by Sartre. Glissant searched for a broader view of cultural networks under the label "poétique de la rélation," which literally means a poetics of networks.

In the French- and Creole-speaking areas of Africa and the Caribbean, the term continues to offer an important motif for discussion, especially in relationship with nation-building and political independence. The writer René Dépestre from Haiti, a country with a long tradition of *négritude* and marvelous realism since the 1920s, took the concept up in his long essay "Bonjour et adieu à la négritude," published in the anthology *Africa en las Américas* (1977). Three years later, in a revised version of this text edited in Paris as a collection of essays, Dépestre declared that *négritude* was meant to demystify the terms "black" and "white" imposed by the colonial past. He believed that such concepts would one day be replaced by a syncretistic mutation he termed *créolité.* This implies a decentralization of European views and the possibility of a new imaginative faculty. With the decline of national social identities, Dépestre claims that *créolité* would be a worldwide process of escape from slavery and radical denial of oppressive models of colonialism. The critic James Clifford commented on this process and its relation to Césaire's *négritude:* "Césaire makes rebellion and the remaking of culture—the historical maroon experience—into a *verb.* A necessary new verb names the New World poetics of continuous transgression and cooperative cultural activity."

The extensive literature on *négritude* continues to grow. It describes cultures inspired by African values, emphasizing their importance in contemporary situations and their creative capacities, all too often kept from public view in the past.

See also **Césaire, Aimé; Race and Ethnicity.**

BIBLIOGRAPHY

Frantz Fanon, *Black Skin, White Masks,* translated by Charles Markmann, (1989); and *Les Damnés de la terre* (1968).

Léopold Sédar Senghor, *Liberté.* Vol. 1, *Négritude et humanisme* (1964) and Vol. 3, *Négritude et civilisation de l'universel* (1977).

Manuel Moreno Fraginals, *Africa en América Latina* (1977).

A. James Arnold, *Modernism and Négritude: The Poetry and Poetics of Aimé Césaire* (1981).

René Dépestre, *Bonjour et adieu à la négritude* (1990).

James Clifford, "A Politics of Neologism: Aimé Césaire," in *The Predicament of Culture* (1988), pp. 175–182.

Édouard Glissant, *Le discours antillais* (1981).

Additional Bibliography

Jack, Belinda Elizabeth. *Negritude and Literary Criticism: The History and Theory of "Negro-African" Literature in French.* Westport: Greenwood Press, 1996.

INEKE PHAF

NEGRO, RIO. Rio Negro, an Amazonian tributary. Beginning as the Rio Guainía in southeastern Colombia, the Rio Negro meanders in an eastwardly direction for 1,400 miles. It serves as the natural boundary between Colombia and Venezuela before entering the Brazilian state of Amazonas. A mulch of tannin-bearing leaves, which drop and cover the rain-forest floor, discolors the Negro. The blue-black water of the Rio Negro flows into the light brown waters of the Solimões at the Encôntro das Aguas (meeting of the waters) 11 miles below Manaus. The two rivers flow side by side for about 4 miles before their waters finally merge.

Francisco de Orellana named the Negro when he first reached it on 3 June 1451. In 1657 Jesuits inhabited the river banks, where they found Manau, Aruák, and Tarumá Indians. In 1669, the Portuguese established a small outpost, Fort São José do Rio Negro, at the mouth of the Negro. After 1700, slaving along the river was common until many Indians succumbed to European diseases and forced labor. At the end of the eighteenth century, explorers Alexandre Rodrigues Ferreira and Baron Alexander von Humboldt traveled along the river. Richard Spruce spent from 1864 to 1870 wandering up the Negro, and he saw rubber being gathered the entire length of the river. Seringueiros still collect rubber and other rain-forest products, such as Brazilnuts from the banks of the Negro, but poor soils prevent it from supporting a dense population.

See also **Brazil, Geography.**

BIBLIOGRAPHY

Henry Bates, *The Naturalist on the River Amazon* (1863).

Alex Shoumatoff, *The Rivers Amazon* (1986).

Leslie Bethell, ed., *Colonial Brazil* (1987).

Additional Bibliography

Little, Paul E. *Amazonia: Territorial Struggles on Perennial Frontiers.* Baltimore: Johns Hopkins University Press, 2001.

Smith, Anthony. *Explorers of the Amazon.* London: Viking, 1990.

Smith, Nigel J.H. *The Amazon River Forest: A Natural History of Plants, Animals, and People.* New York: Oxford University, 1999.

CAROLYN JOSTOCK

NEGRO, RÍO. Río Negro, stream at the southern edge of the Pampa, created by the confluence of the Limay and Neuquén rivers flowing out of the Argentine Andes. After a 400-mile course, the Río Negro empties into the Atlantic Ocean north of Viedma. Its flow is kept steady and regular by winter rains and by snowmelt in the spring. Several hydroelectric plants have been constructed along the river, and since 1908 numerous regulating channels have increased the area of the Río Negro valley under cultivation to include 232,500 acres of fruit orchards. Export-quality apples, pears, peaches, and almonds are grown in the valley. Río Negro is the northern boundary of Argentine Patagonia and constitutes the main artery of the Río Negro Province. Among its major population centers are the city of Neuquén and the towns of Cipolletti, General Sosa, General Conesa, and Viedma.

See also **Argentina, Geography.**

BIBLIOGRAPHY

César A. Vapnarsky, *La formación de un area metropolitana en la Patagonia: Población y asentamiento en el Alto Valle del Río Negro* (Buenos Aires, 1987).

Additional Bibliography

Koon, Ricardo. *Pioneros judíos en el desierto: Neuquén y Río Negro, 1879-1939: investigación histórica.* Argentina: R. Koon, 2000.

Maida, Esther L. *Inmigrantes en el Alto Valle del Río Negro.* General Roca, Río Negro, Patagonia, Argentina: PubliFadecs, 2001.

Rafart, Gabriel, and Enrique Masés. *El peronismo desde los territorios a la nación: Su historia en Neuquén y Río Negro (1943-1958).* Neuquén, Argentina: Editorial de la Universidad Nacional del Comahue, 2003.

CÉSAR N. CAVIEDES

NEGROES. *See* **African Brazilians, Color Terminology.**

NEOLIBERALISM. In the centuries-old debate on how to organize an economy, neoliberalism is the ideology that advocates giving preference to market forces over state intervention in most areas of economic activity. Neoliberals believe that Adam Smith's classic, liberal economic dictum—that supply and demand forces are better left unencumbered—can be fruitfully adapted to contemporary realities. More than having just a blind faith in markets and private property, neoliberals in the early twenty-first century share a profound distrust of economic intervention by the state, which they regard as neither omniscient nor free of political bias and thus ill-suited to decide on its own the proper allocation of resources in a society. For neoliberals, the most serious economic problems of the present time—inflation and unsustainable macroeconomic environments, lack of competitiveness, clientelistic and inefficient public spending, poverty, and corruption—result from misguided state interventions that distort market incentives.

Neoliberalism in economics should not be confused with "liberalism" in U.S. politics, which is an ideology in favor of using state regulation to advance socially progressive agendas and lessen inequalities. In economics, neoliberalism stands instead for reducing government influence especially in the areas of price controls, trade restrictions, and productive activities. For neoliberals, government cannot be trusted as a truly public-minded regulator because it is too easily captured by self-serving political forces, such as biased ruling parties, trade unions, rent-seeking lobbyists, and unaccountable bureaucrats. Neoliberals do accept some state intervention (e.g., to stabilize the monetary supply, fund social programs and infrastructure, enforce property rights), but they prefer to leave most economic decisions to producers and consumers.

Between the 1930s and 1970s, neoliberals were considered extreme, and their influence in policy circles was secondary to that of rival ideologies such as Keynesianism, protectionism, populism, socialism, and even Marxism. But as countries that embraced these rival ideologies began to experience crippling economic crises in the 1970s and 1980s, neoliberals began to gain ascendancy, first in Chile (under Augusto Pinochet) and then in the United Kingdom (under Margaret Thatcher), and the United States (under Ronald Reagan). In 1974 and 1976, respectively, two leading proponents of neoliberalism, Friedrich von Hayek and Milton Friedman, won Nobel prizes in economics, further boosting the renaissance of these ideas. In the 1980s former socialists leaders in advanced democracies began to embrace neoliberal policies (Felipe González in Spain, Bob Hawke in Australia). By the early 1990s, neoliberals dominated policy circles in most Latin American, former Soviet, and Asian nations, as well as in leading international financial institutions such as the International Monetary Fund and the World Bank.

Neoliberals advocate confronting economic malaises with a package of reforms that includes, among other policies, tight fiscal discipline (through expenditure and debt reduction) and tax simplification, avoidance of currency overvaluation, privatization, trade and capital account liberalization, and deregulation. This set of reforms came to be known in the early 1990s as the Washington Consensus.

In the first decade of the twenty-first century, neoliberal policies again became a matter of acrimonious debate. Critics contend that neoliberalism has deprived vulnerable economic sectors and social groups of protection against the negative impacts of globalization and failed to deliver economic growth robust enough to alleviate poverty and inequality. Neoliberals retort that economic growth under neoliberal guidelines is qualitatively better than other forms of growth because it is more sustainable and has fewer distortions (e.g., inflation, nebulous regulations) that disproportionately harm the poor. Adherents insist that most observed shortcomings are due to spotty policy implementation, rather than to flaws in neoliberal policy prescriptions themselves.

See also **Chicago Boys; Economic Development.**

BIBLIOGRAPHY

Kuczynski, Pedro-Pablo, and John Williamson. *After the Washington Consensus: Restarting Growth and Reform in Latin America.* Washington, DC: Peterson Institute for International Economics, 2003.

Von Hayek, Friedrich. *The Road to Serfdom.* Chicago: Chicago University Press, 1994.

Williamson, Wolf, Martin. *Why Globalization Works.* New Haven, CT: Yale University Press, 2005.

Yergin, Daniel, and Joseph Sanislaw. *The Commanding Heights: The Battle for the World Economy.* New York: Free Press, 2001.

JAVIER CORRALES

NEPOMUCENO, ALBERTO (1865–1920). Alberto Nepomuceno (*b.* 6 July 1865; *d.* 16 October 1920), Brazilian composer and conductor, the "Father of Brazilian music." In an era in which the most important Brazilian music critic, Oscar Guanabarino, championed the Italian language as the language of art songs, Nepomuceno frequently stated that "a people who do not sing in their own language have no native land." In spite of fierce resistance from Guanabarino and other critics, Nepomuceno wrote arts songs in Portuguese now recognized as some of the finest works of the genre. Nepomuceno's wide range of musical activities were not confined to championing works by Brazilian composers. He helped Heitor Villa-Lobos, a young and very controversial composer at the time, get his works published by Sampaio Araújo, a Brazilian publisher, but he also conducted the first Brazilian performance of Debussy's *Prélude à l'après-midi d'un faune;* he not only arranged to have Arnold Schoenberg's *Harmonielehre* translated into Portuguese but also had it adopted at the National Institute of Music, in spite of the fierce resistance of members of the faculty and critics. One of Nepomuceno's most significant contributions in providing Brazilian musicians with a historical sense of their heritage was his revival of the works of Padre José Maurício Nunes Garcia, the most important Brazilian composer of the early nineteenth century. Nepomuceno's contributions as a composer included several operas; string quartets and chamber music; instrumental, vocal, and piano music. His orchestral composition *Série brasileira* greatly offended Brazilian critics by utilizing the reco-reco, a percussion instrument commonly employed only in popular music. The incorporation of rhythmic patterns previously used only by salon composers was, moreover, an important element in the emerging nationalist music.

See also **García, José Maurício Nunes; Music: Art Music; Villa-Lobos, Heitor.**

BIBLIOGRAPHY

Marcos Antônio Marcondes, ed., *Enciclopédia da música brasileira,* vol. 1 (1977).

David P. Appleby, *The Music of Brazil* (1983).

Additional Bibliography

Martins, Floriano. *Alberto Nepomuceno.* Fortaleza: Edições Demócrito Rocha, 2000.

DAVID P. APPLEBY

NERUDA, PABLO (1904–1973). Pablo Neruda (*b.* 12 July 1904; *d.* 23 September 1973), Chilean poet. Born Neftalí Eliecer Ricardo Reyes Basoalto in Parral, southern Chile, Neruda is the most renowned poet of modern Latin American literature and one of the major poets of the twentieth century. Winner of the Nobel Prize for literature in 1971, Neruda's fifty-some books, produced in as many years, established his reputation as a writer of prodigious output and creative power, as well as a poet of remarkably varied styles. His work reflects in many ways the twentieth-century history of poetry in the Spanish language, moving from *modernismo* to more traditional verse forms and meters as well as free verse, only to plunge deeply into vanguard tendencies, especially surrealism. He employed a baroque, hermetic style as well as an epic stance with elements of the chronicle, and wrote in a lyrical mode as well as a conventional style. These movements did not necessarily coincide with nor were they limited to specific periods of his life. Some critics have assigned his work to the categories of nature poetry, public poetry, erotic poetry, and personal poetry; again, these are poetic stances rather than chronological designations. Neruda himself eschewed all such critical classifications, but they are not without validity in establishing his range.

Neruda's life reflects a constant series of voyages from his native Chile, with his country providing a constant geographical and emotional center for his poetic and political concerns. At the age of twenty-three, he was appointed consul in Rangoon, Burma. From 1928 to 1936 he filled consular posts in Sri Lanka (Ceylon), Indonesia (Java), Singapore, Buenos Aires, Barcelona, and Madrid. Because of his sympathy with the Republican cause in the Spanish Civil War and his support of the Communist Party, he lost his position as consul in Madrid and traveled to Paris to edit with Nancy Cunard the magazine *The Poets of the World Defend the Spanish People.* In 1937, after founding the Spanish American Society to Aid Spain with César Vallejo he returned to Chile and Buenos Aires. In 1939 he was named consul for Spanish emigration in Paris, and in 1940 he was appointed consul to Mexico. Following several short trips to Cuba (1942), the United States (1943), and Colombia (1943), Neruda's visit to Inca ruins in Peru in 1943 inspired one of his most celebrated poems, "The Heights of Machu Picchu" (1945). In 1949, as a Communist Party member since 1945 and a senator

Pablo Neruda reads from his work in a radio interview, mid-twentieth century. A prolific writer, Neruda's poems explored many themes, including nature, women, and politics. In 1971, Neruda received the Nobel Prize for literature. © CORBIS

in the Chilean government, he was forced into exile by the González Videla regime. He returned to Chile in 1952, and continued to travel extensively while maintaining his base there. He had three homes, in Valparaíso, Santiago, and Isla Negra.

In 1971, the government of Salvador Allende named Neruda ambassador to France. He returned to Chile in 1973, and died in Santiago, only twelve days after the Chilean army overthrew Allende's Popular Unity Government in a coup d'état supported by elements of the U.S. government and business community. Though Neruda had bitterly criticized U.S. involvement in Latin American affairs, in his poetry and prose he was deeply influenced by Walt Whitman in both the thought and form of his poetry, and he was a great admirer of Abraham Lincoln, who he believed represented the finest aspects of the American democratic tradition.

Neruda's first published work, *Crepusculario* (1920; Twilight Book), was written in the received aesthetics of Hispanic *modernismo* (not yet the vanguard aesthetic implied by the Anglo-American term "modernism"), but he moved immediately, in the most popular book of poems ever published in Spanish, *Veinte poemas de amor y una canción desesperación* (1924; *Twenty Love Poems and a Song of Despair,* 1969, 1976), to a more individual style that moved between elaborate structures and imagery, and free verse. Here his two lifelong obsessions, nature and sex, are clearly revealed. With the first two volumes of *Residencia en la tierra* (1933; *Residence on Earth,* 1935), he achieved international recognition. Written during the Spanish Civil War, Neruda's *España en el corazón* (1937; Spain in My Heart) demonstrated a profound commitment to political concerns.

Tercera residencia (1947; Third Residency), the third volume in the *Residencia en la tierra* series, and *Canto general* (1950; General Song) were his next important books. The latter, his longest and most ambitious work, is an attempt to write the epic, both historical and mythical, of Latin America from a Marxist perspective. In the 1950s his work underwent another notable change as he turned from the epic style to the ode to express joy in the simple things of life. His four volumes in this form include *Odas elementales* (1954; Elementary Odes), *Nuevas odas elementales* (1956; New Elementary Odes), *Tercer libro de odas* (1957; Third Book of Odes), and *Navegaciones y regresos* (1959; Voyages and Homecomings). This series demonstrates Neruda's tendency to write in cycles, as do the *Residencia* volumes and *Canto general.*

Neruda continued to publish new volumes of poetry with extraordinary regularity, producing during his last years a number of notable works, including *Estravagario* (1958; *Extravagaria,* 1974), a word coined by Neruda to suggest extravagant, even eccentric, poetic moves and modes: "Of all my books, *Estravagario* is not one that sings the most, but rather the one that skips about the best.... Because of its irreverence it is my most personal book." The work's impudence, eclecticism, and humor make it his most individualistic work.

Between *Estravagario* and his death in 1973 Neruda produced nineteen books. Eight volumes of posthumous verse and his prose memoirs were released in 1974. Some of these works are varied in subject (*La barcarola,* 1967; *Las piedras del cielo,* 1970), others develop only one theme (*Arte de pájaros,* 1966, translated as *The Art of Birds,* 1985; *Las piedras de Chile,* 1961). Introspection is a dominant note in his later work, and his most ambitious work after *Estravagario* is the autobiographical *Memorial de Isla Negra* (1964; *Isla Negra: A Notebook,* 1981) whose five volumes, another cycle, constitute a long nostalgic look back at his life.

Neruda's final major work was his prose autobiography *Confieso que he vivido: Memorias* (I Confess That I Have Lived: Memoirs, translated as *Memoirs,* 1977) written in the last decade of his life and published posthumously in 1974. The twelve *cuadernos* (notebooks) that comprise the work essentially take the form of confessions united by the perennial passions of the poet's life: his love of women and nature, his interest in politics, his affection for simple things, his devotion to life. As in much of his later poetry, there is humor, nostalgia, and a constant introspection joined to a profound commitment to the world about him. In various ways, Neruda's life exemplifies many aspects of the historical, literary, and cultural process of the political left in Latin America in the twentieth century.

See also **Literature: Spanish America.**

BIBLIOGRAPHY

Collections of Neruda's works available in English include: *The Elementary Odes of Pablo Neruda,* translated by Carlos Lozano, 1961; *The Early Poems,* translated by David Ossman and Carlos B. Hagen, 1969; *A New Decade (Poems: 1958–1967),* translated by Ben Belitt and Alastair Reid, 1969; and *New Poems: 1968–1970,* translated by Ben Belitt, 1972. See also Amado Alonso, *Poesía y estilo de Pablo Neruda: Interpretación de una poesía hermética* (1940); Jaime Alazraki, *Poética y poesía de Pablo Neruda* (1965); Angel Flores, *Aproximaciones a Pablo Neruda* (1974); René De Costa, *The Poetry of Pablo Neruda* (1979); Manuel Durán and Margery Safir, *The Poetry of Pablo Neruda* (1981); Alain Sicard, *El pensamiento poético de Pablo Neruda,* translated from the French by Pilar Ruiz Va (1981); Marjorie Agosin, *Pablo Neruda,* translated by Lorraine Ross (1986); Emir Rodríguez Monegal and Enrico M. Santí, eds., *Pablo Neruda* (1986); Hensley C. Woodbridge and David S. Zubatsky, *Pablo Neruda: An Annotated Bibliography of Biographical and Critical Studies* (1988); Harold Bloom, ed., *Pablo Neruda* (1989).

Additional Bibliography

Feinstein, Adam. *Pablo Neruda: A Passion for Life.* New York: Bloomsbury, 2004.

Longo, Teresa, ed. *Pablo Neruda and the U.S. Culture Industry.* New York: Routledge, 2002.

Neves, Eugenia. *Pablo Neruda: La invención poética de la historia.* Providencia: RiL Editores, 2000.

Olivares Briones, Edmundo. *Pablo Neruda, los caminos de oriente.* Santiago: LOM Ediciones, 2000.

Vidal, Virginia. *Neruda, memoria crepitante.* Valencia: Ediciones Tilde, 2003.

KEITH MCDUFFIE

NERVO, AMADO (1870–1919). Amado Nervo (*b.* 27 August 1870; *d.* 24 May 1919), Mexican writer. Born in Tepic, Nayarit, Nervo excelled as a student at the Colegio de San Luis Gonzaga in Jacona, Michoacán. In 1886 he began seminary in Zamora, Michoacán, but soon abandoned this path in order to help support his family. He moved to Mexico City in 1894 where he launched his literary and journalistic career. Nervo began his literary career writing in a romantic style with naturalist tendencies, but he soon fell under the influence of the *modernista* movement at the turn of the century. In this vein, he coedited the important cultural journal *Revista Moderna* (Modern Review [1898–1911]) with Jesús Valenzuela. He traveled internationally as a journalist. He was an associate of the Nicaraguan *modernista* poet Rubén Darío in Paris. After 1905, Nervo worked as a member of the diplomatic service. Although extremely popular at the turn of the century, Nervo's poetry and narrative have been disparaged by subsequent generations because of its overly sentimental and anti-intellectual characteristics. Nervo's first novel, *El bachiller* (The Student, 1895), attracted much attention because of its sexual theme. In 1898 he published his first important collections of poetry, *Perlas negras* (Black Pearls) and *Místicas* (Mystical Poems). Although the Mexican Revolution interrupted diplomatic services in 1914 and left Nervo in a financially difficult position in Madrid, in 1918 the Mexican government recalled him from Spain and then sent him to Argentina and Uruguay on a diplomatic mission. He died in Montevideo.

See also **Literature: Spanish America.**

BIBLIOGRAPHY

Manuel Durán, *Genio y figura de Amado Nervo* (1968).

Almudena Mejías Alonso, "Amado Nervo," in *Historia de la Literatura Hispanoamericana*. Vol. 2, *Del neoclasicismo al modernismo,* edited by Luis Iñigo Madrigal (1987), pp. 647–654.

Frank Dauster, "Amado Nervo," in *Latin American Writers,* edited by Carlos A. Solé and Maria Isabel Abreu, vol. 1 (1989), pp. 425–429.

Additional Bibliography

Urbina, Luis G., Miguel González Lomelía, and Lourdes C. Pacheco Ladrón de Guevara. *Visiones críticas de Amado Nervo.* Nayarit: Gobierno del Estado, Secretaría de Educación Pública, Consejo Estatal para la Cultura y las Artes de Nayarit, 2004.

DANNY J. ANDERSON

NETZAHUALCÓYOTL. Ciudad Netzahualcóyotl, or "Netza," is a municipality of the state of Mexico. It was created in 1964 to incorporate more than forty separate *colonias populares,* illegal settlements on part of the desiccated bed of Lake Texcoco that formed a large, low-income tract on Mexico City's eastern corridor. Originally state-owned, the land was conditionally privatized for agricultural improvements that were never undertaken. Instead the lands were acquired by unscrupulous real estate companies that sold off some 160,000 lots of between 150 and 300 square meters, without services or titles, to low-income families, who then built their own homes.

The population of the nascent municipality was 70,000 in 1964; by 1970 it had grown to 610,000 and by 1990 to 1.26 million, stabilizing thereafter (actually showing a slight decline to 1,140,528, according to the midterm census in 2005). Population densification, lot subdivision, and the expansion of rental accommodation have converted Netza into a tract of high-density *colonia popular* neighborhoods. The total lack of services in the late 1960s and 1970s caused a major political crisis that eventually led the government to establish a trust fund for the installation of services by the local municipal authorities, and for the transfer of legal titles to the de facto owners. In the early twenty-first century, the area is fully serviced, most roads are paved, and a growing proportion of the population rent one or two rooms in small informal tenements or share a lot with kinsmen. The low-income homeownership frontier has moved farther east and northeast.

Patron-clientelism originally made this a bastion of support for the Institutional Revolutionary Party (PRI). However, the municipality has come to be run by a sequence of mayors from the Democratic Revolutionary Party (PRD), which has also dominated the Federal District of Mexico City since direct elections were implemented in 1997.

See also **Mexico City; Mexico, Political Parties: Democratic Revolutionary Party (PRD); Mexico, Political Parties: Institutional Revolutionary Party (PRI).**

BIBLIOGRAPHY

De la Rosa, Martín. *Netzahualcoyótl, un fenómeno.* Mexico: Fondo de Cultura Económica, 1974.

Gilbert, Alan, and Peter M. Ward. *Housing, the State, and the Poor: Policy and Practice in Three Latin American Cities.* Cambridge, U.K., and New York: Cambridge University Press, 1985.

Garza, Gustavo, ed. *La Ciudad de México en el fin del segundo milenio.* Mexico: El Colegio de México y el Gobierno del Distrito Federal, 2000.

Ward, Peter. *Mexico: Megaciudad—Desarrollo y política, 1970–2002*, 2nd edition. Mexico: Colegio Mexiquense y Miguel Angel Porrúa, 2004.

PETER M. WARD

NEUQUÉN.

Neuquén is a province in Patagonia, in southwest Argentina, the so-called Comahue. It has approximately 470, 000 inhabitants (2001 census) with some 200,000 of them in its capital city, also called Neuquén. A small portion of the Neuquén province belongs to the Mapuche indigenous group. Since the 1970s, local politics have been dominated by the Neuquén Popular Movement (Movimiento Popular Neuquino). This movement, which has its origins in Peronism, took root exclusively in the provinces and is headed by the Sapag family.

The Spaniards first entered in the area in the sixteenth century, but it was not until the dessert campaign (1879) commanded by general Julio Argentino Roca that the indigenous people lost control over the territory. From the 1960s onward, the province experienced great economic and demographic expansion, absorbing population from other regions of Argentina. Social indicators rank it above the national average. Its principle economic resources are petroleum and hydropower. Neuquén is an important provider of electrical power to the country and power royalties are a significant component of its financial resources. Fruit crops are important. Tourist activity located along the Andean range, with its forests and lakes, also brings in considerable revenue. Winter sports in San Martín de los Andes, Villa La Angostura, and the Nahuel Huapi National Park are its main attractions.

See also **Argentina: The Nineteenth Century; Argentina: The Twentieth Century; Mapuche; Patagonia.**

BIBLIOGRAPHY

Favaro, Orienta, ed. *Neuquén: La construcción de un orden estatal.* Neuquén: Centro de Estudios Históricos de Estado, Política y Cultura, Universidad Nacional del Comahue, 1999.

Palermo, Vicente. *Neuquén. La construcción de una sociedad* Buenos Aires: Centro Editor de América Latina, 1988.

VICENTE PALERMO

NEVE, FELIPE DE

(1728–1784). Felipe De Neve (*b.* 1728; *d.* 21 August 1784), Spanish governor of California. Born in Bailén, Spain, Neve entered military service as a cadet in 1744, subsequently serving in Cantabria, Flanders, Milan, and Portugal. He came to New Spain in 1764, and saw duty in Querétaro and Zacatecas as a captain; he was promoted to lieutenant colonel in 1774. Neve assumed the governorship of the Californias 4 March 1775 at Loreto, and on 3 February 1777 he moved to establish a separate government for Alta California at Monterey. He founded the civilian towns of San José (29 November 1777) and Los Angeles (4 September 1781). He launched an attack against the Yuma Indians after they had massacred the party of Fernando de Rivera y Moncada at the Colorado River, 18 July 1781. In 1782 Neve was named inspector general of the Provincias Internas del Occidente, and commandant general in 1783. He died at the Hacienda Nuestra Señora del Carmen de Peña Blanca, Chihuahua.

See also **Rivera y Moncada, Fernando de.**

BIBLIOGRAPHY

Hubert H. Bancroft, *History of California*, vol. 1 (1884).

Edwin A. Beilharz, *Felipe de Neve: First Governor of California* (1971).

Additional Bibliography

Gutiérrez, Ramón A., and Richard J Orsi. *Contested Eden: California before the Gold Rush.* Berkeley: University of California Press, 1998.

W. MICHAEL MATHES

NEVES, TANCREDO DE ALMEIDA

(1910–1985). Tancredo de Almeida Neves was elected president of Brazil in 1985 but died before taking office. Born in São João del Rei, Minas Gerais, Neves moved in 1928 to Belo Horizonte to attend law school. In 1932 he returned to his hometown and opened a law office. He married and had three children. He served as public prosecutor for the local judicial district and in 1934 was elected city council member, acceding to the office of president of the municipal legislature. Following the 1937 coup that mandated the closing of all legislative bodies, Neves lost his position and resumed practicing law.

In 1947 his political career was launched anew when he was elected state deputy on the Social Democratic Party (PSD) ticket. In 1950 he took a seat as a federal deputy and served on the committee for transportation, communication, and public works from 1951 to 1953. Neves gave up his seat to head the ministry of justice under President Getúlio Vargas. He opposed any attempts to remove Vargas from office in 1954 and returned to the chamber of deputies after Vargas's suicide.

Supported by a center-labor coalition, Neves won the governorship of Minas Gerais in 1960. In 1961 he was appointed prime minister of Brazil by President João Goulart but willingly relinquished the post in 1962, and was soon elected majority leader of the Social Democratic Party. In the 1966 elections Neves, now affiliated with the opposition Brazilian Democratic Movement (MDB), was elected to Congress and represented Minas Gerais for many years. In 1982 he was elected vice president of the new centrist Brazilian Democratic Movement Party (PMDB) and once again became governor of Minas Gerais.

A consummate politician with a unique ability to bring together factions from the right and the left, Neves prevailed against the handpicked candidate of the military administration and in January 1985 was declared president by the electoral college. On the eve of taking office in March 1985, Neves became ill and underwent surgery but did not recover. His running mate, José Sarney, assumed the presidency. Neves's death had a powerful emotional effect on much of the Brazilian population.

See also **Brazil, Political Parties: Brazilian Democratic Movement (MDB); Brazil, Political Parties: Brazilian Democratic Movement Party (PMDB).**

BIBLIOGRAPHY

Bandeira, Luiz Alberto Moniz. *O Governo João Goulart: As lutas sociais no Brasil, 1961–1964*, 7th edition. Rio de Janeiro: Revan, 2001.

Dulles, John W. F. *Vargas of Brazil*. Austin: University of Texas Press, 1967.

Silva, Vera Alice Cardoso, and Lucília de Almedia Neves Delgado. *Tancredo Neves: A trajetória de um liberal*. Petrópolis, Brazil: Universidade Federal de Minas Gerais, 1985.

Skidmore, Thomas E. *Politics in Brazil, 1930–1964: An Experiment in Democracy*. New York: Oxford University Press, 1967.

Skidmore, Thomas E. *The Politics of Military Rule in Brazil, 1964–85*. New York: Oxford University Press, 1988.

ÍÊDA SIQUEIRA WIARDA

NEW AUSTRALIA. In September 1893, 254 Australian immigrants arrived in Paraguay to found an agricultural colony based upon communitarian principles. Hard economic times in Australia and a recent failed general strike prompted William Lane, a prominent social reformer and Labour Party publicist, to propose a new society free from social and economic oppression. Isolated from worldly corruption, the society would be based upon shared wealth and work, women's equality, and prohibition of alcohol.

Paraguay was selected for the site of the new colony, and its government awarded the New Australian Cooperative Settlement Association fifty square leagues in the remote Ajos region. Paraguay, desiring agricultural immigrants, demanded only that 600 families be settled in the new colony. Soon a second party of 195 men arrived.

The government had appointed William Lane intendant of New Australia and he had sole and full control over the colony's finances. He insisted upon a rigid interpretation of the association rules, particularly the ban on alcohol. His demand that all wealth be shared equally met opposition. And his racist prohibition against hiring Paraguayan labor for fear of "contamination" of the new society delayed development. Rapidly, some eighty-five of the original party had either been expelled or simply left. The second party allied themselves with remaining discontented original settlers and forced Lane to step aside and depart in April 1894. The New Australians then reorganized the colony on a business basis, abandoning much of the socialism inherent in the original project.

In Australia news of the colony's turmoil, and better economic times, precluded any further significant immigration, and by 1897 only 150 New Australians remained. The association was dissolved with its property distributed among remaining members and the colony became open to all settlers. Some Australians remained there; others returned to their homeland. Those staying in Paraguay and their descendants melded with the general Paraguayan population, leaving only the memory of an idealistic, but failed, social experiment.

See also **Paraguay: The Nineteenth Century; Paraguay: The Twentieth Century.**

BIBLIOGRAPHY

Kleinpenning, Jan M. G. *Rural Paraguay, 1870–1932.* Amsterdam: CEDLA, 1992.

Livermore, Harold. "New Australia." *Hispanic American Historical Review* 30:3 (August 1950): 290–313.

Souter, Gavin. *A Peculiar People: The Australians in Paraguay.* Sydney, Australia: Angus & Robertson, 1968.

JERRY W. COONEY

NEW CHRISTIANS (BRAZIL).

See **Inquisition: Brazil.**

NEW GRANADA, TREATY OF (1846).

See **Bidlack Treaty (Treaty of New Granada, 1846).**

NEW GRANADA, UNITED PROVINCES OF.

United Provinces of New Granada. The first general government created by New Granadan patriots was the United Provinces of New Granada, established in November 1811. The pact of union was signed by representatives of only five provinces, the most important being Cartagena. Bogotá was conspicuously absent, as were several others. The failure to include all of New Granada reflected the intensity of the interprovincial rivalries that had erupted since the independence movement began in 1810. Rejection by Bogotá further reflected the insistence of the former colonial capital on adopting a highly centralized system of government. The United Provinces, by contrast, was a loose confederation whose members retained full control of their internal affairs and alone could implement (or not implement) the policies of the federal authorities, who lacked administrative agencies of their own.

By the middle of 1812 the United Provinces were engaged in civil warfare with the centralists of Bogotá, led by Antonio Nariño. The conflict sputtered on and off until 1814, when Bogotá was subdued by federalist forces led by Simón Bolívar. Still unable to assert effective control over New Granada, the union easily fell victim to the Spanish reconquest of 1815–1816.

See also **Wars of Independence, South America.**

BIBLIOGRAPHY

Manuel José Forero, *La primera república* (1966).

Thomas Blossom, *Nariño: Hero of Colombian Independence* (1967).

Additional Bibliography

Santos Molano, Enrique. *Antonio Nariño, filósofo revolucionario.* Santafé de Bogotá, Colombia: Planeta, 1999.

DAVID BUSHNELL

NEW GRANADA, VICEROYALTY OF.

Viceroyalty of New Granada. Following a failed start (1717–1723), the Viceroyalty of New Granada, with its capital in Santa Fe de Bogotá, was reestablished in 1739 both to convert northern South America into an economic asset for Spain and to strengthen its military posture in the face of imminent war. Viceroy Sebastián de Eslava led Cartagena's defenders in repulsing a massive British invasion in 1741, and the viceroyalty endured thereafter.

As constituted in 1739, New Granada included the presidencies of Quito and Panama, although the latter's audiencia was suppressed in 1751. The eastern provinces of Maracaibo, Cumaná, and Guayana were joined to Caracas to form an autonomous captaincy general in 1777. In 1803, Guayaquil, Mainas, and Quijos were detached to the Viceroyalty of Peru for strategic reasons. Militarily, commandants-general exercised regional authority. These included the governors of Cartagena and Panama and, after 1767, the president of Quito. Cartagena exercised supervisory power over the governorships of Santa Marta and Riohacha; Panama over Portobelo, Veragua, and Darién; and Quito over the jurisdictions subordinate to its *audiencia*, including Guayaquil and Popayán. An archbishop resided in Santa Fe and bishops in Cartagena, Popayán, Santa Marta, Panama, Quito, and, after 1779, Cuenca; the latter three were subordinate to the archbishop of Lima.

Despite a significant population, the viceroyalty (Caracas excluded) failed to become an important asset to the imperial system either commercially or fiscally. The census of 1778 recorded New Granada's population at 1,280,000 inhabitants, 324,000 of them whites, 459,000 Indians, 427,000 free mixed-bloods and blacks, and 70,000 slaves. The viceroyalty lost much of its importance commercially when the southern fleet system was abandoned following the War of Jenkins's Ear, and contraband dominated its external commerce as before.

Between 1782 and 1796, during the era of imperial free trade, New Granada absorbed only about 8 percent of Spain's exports to its American colonies and accounted for just 3 percent of its imports, principally gold and lesser amounts of cotton, tobacco, cacao, cascarilla, and sugar. Totaling just under one million in 1772, royal income rose to 3,350,000 pesos by the late 1780s, largely driven by the tobacco and Aguardiente monopolies, and then leveled off at three million after 1800.

Plagued by chronic deficits during its earlier history, fiscal reform permitted the viceroyalty to generate small surpluses for Spain during the 1790s. New Granada did not accept the yoke of colonialism easily, producing the massive Comunero Revolt against royal revenue reform in 1781 and multiple conspiracies inspired by the French Revolution during the 1790s.

VICEROYS OF NEW GRANADA

Jorge de Villalonga, conde de la Cueva, 1719–1724
Sebastián de Eslava, 1740–1748
José Alonso Pizarro, marqués del Villar, 1749–1753
José Solís Folch de Cardona, 1753–1761
Pedro Mesía de la Cerda, marqués de la Vega de Armijo, 1761–1773
Manuel de Guirior, 1773–1776
Manuel Antonio Flores, 1776–1782
Juan de Torrezal Díaz Pimienta, 1782
Juan Francisco Guttiérrez de Piñeres, 1782
Antonio Caballero y Góngora, 1782–1788
Francisco Gil de Taboada, 1789
José Manuel Ignacio Timoteo de Ezpeleta, 1789–1797
Pedro de Mendinueta y Múzquiz, 1797–1803
Antonio Amar y Borbón, 1803–1810
Manuel Bernardo de Álvarez, 1810–1811
Benito Pérez Brito, 1811–1813
Francisco Montalvo y Ambulodi Arriola, 1813–1818
Juan José de Sámano y Urribarri, 1818–1819
Juan de la Cruz Mourgeón y Achet, 1819–1821

BIBLIOGRAPHY

Historia extensa de Colombia, especially vol. 4, Sergio Elías Ortiz, *Nuevo reino de Granada: El virreynato* (1970).

Allan J. Kuethe, *Military Reform and Society in New Granada, 1773–1808* (1977).

John R. Fisher et al., eds., *Reform and Insurrection in Bourbon New Granada and Peru* (1990).

Additional Bibliography

McFarlane, Anthony. *Colombia before Independence: Economy, Society, and Politics under Bourbon Rule.* Cambridge, U.K.: Cambridge University Press, 2002.

ALLAN J. KUETHE

NEW JEWEL MOVEMENT. New Jewel Movement, Grenadian revolutionary movement (1973–1983). The New Jewel Movement (NJM) was formed in opposition to Eric M. Gairy's bizarre and corrupt rule. It resulted from a merger of two populist organizations: the urban-based Movement for Assemblies of the People (MAP), directed by lawyers Maurice Bishop and Kenrick Radix, and the rural-based Joint Endeavor for Welfare, Education, and Liberation (JEWEL), led by economist Unison Whiteman. Upon the merger of the two organizations on 11 March 1973, the NJM issued a special manifesto that promised to develop a program to help the common people. After the Grenadian Revolution of 13 March 1979, the leadership of the New Jewel Movement (as the People's Revolutionary Government) ruled Grenada until the fatal internal schism between Bishop and his deputy Bernard Coard, during the autumn of 1983. Bishop was executed and, shortly thereafter, Grenada was invaded by U.S. and Caribbean forces.

See also **Bishop, Maurice; Gairy, Eric.**

BIBLIOGRAPHY

Gregory Sandford, *The New Jewel Movement: Grenada's Revolution, 1979–1983* (1985).

Kai P. Schoenhals and Richard A. Melanson, *Revolution and Intervention in Grenada: The New Jewel Movement, the United States, and the Caribbean* (1985).

Additional Bibliography

Heine, Jorge. *Revolución y intervención en el Caribe: Las lecciones de Granada.* Buenos Aires: Emece Editores, 1990.

Sanford, Gregory W. *Granada, la historia secreta.* Madrid: Editorial Playor, 1986.

Steele, Beverly A. *Grenada: A History.* Oxford: Oxford University Press, 2003.

KAI P. SCHOENHALS

NEW LAWS OF 1542. New Laws of 1542, general legislative code designed to protect the Indians and to restrain the *encomenderos.* Clerical denunciation of Spanish mistreatment of the Indians began on Hispaniola and became more strident when the Dominican friar Bartolomé de Las Casas, a former conquistador and *encomendero,* entered the fray. Las Casas's lobbying influenced Charles I's promulgatation of the New Laws in 1542.

The New Laws authorized a viceroy for Peru and audiencias in Lima and Guatemala to create a more effective administrative and judicial system. They are best known for prohibiting Indian slavery, attacking the *encomenderos* in general, and ordering that individuals responsible for the civil war in Peru be stripped of their *encomiendas.* This last provision, coupled with one prohibiting new assignments of *encomiendas* and ordering the reversion of existing ones to the crown upon the death of the holders, angered the *encomenderos* and led to a rebellion in Peru and the death of the region's first viceroy. In New Spain a wiser viceroy, Antonio de Mendoza, refrained from enforcing contested provisions of the laws to avoid a rebellion.

Faced with the unexpectedly violent reaction, the Crown relented and, by allowing succession for a second "life" in 1545, enabled the *encomenderos* to pass on their grants for another generation.

See also **Charles I of Spain; Encomienda; Las Casas, Bartolomé de; New Spain, Viceroyalty of; Slavery: Spanish America.**

BIBLIOGRAPHY

John H. Parry and Robert G. Keith, eds., *New Iberian World: A Documentary History of the Discovery and Settlement of Latin America to the Early 17th Century,* 5 vols. (1984), vol. 1, *The Conquerors and the Conquered,* pp. 348–359.

Additional Bibliography

Casas, Bartolomé de las. *An Account, Much Abbreviated, of the Destruction of the Indies, with Related Texts.* Edited by Franklin W Knight. Trans. Andrew Hurley. Indianapolis, IN: Hackett Pub., 2003.

Charles, Holy Roman Emperor, Fred W. Lucas, and Henry Stevens. *The New Laws of the Indies for the Good Treatment and Preservation of the Indians.* London: Privately printed at the Chiswick Press, 1893.

Cieza de León, Pedro de. *Crónica del Perú.* 4 v. Lima: Pontificia Universidad Católica del Perú, Fondo Editorial: Academia Nacional de la Historia, 1984.

MARK A. BURKHOLDER

NEW MEXICO. New Mexico, a colony of Spain (1598–1821), province of Mexico (1822–1846), territory (1846–1912), and state (1912) in the southwestern United States. The colony, or kingdom and provinces of New Mexico, with its capital at Santa Fe (1610), represented Spain's grandiose but ill-defined claim to the far north of New Spain. Founded in 1598 by Juan de Oñate under contract with the Spanish crown, New Mexico offered no easily exploitable resource, so Oñate resigned as governor in 1607. Its status changed from proprietary to royal colony in 1609 when it became, in effect, a government-subsidized Franciscan ministry to the Pueblo nation. A momentous event, the Pueblo Rebellion (1680–1696), caused a readjustment of human relations, as crusading intolerance gave way to practical military cooperation against common enemies. The purpose of the colony, which was still subsidized, shifted from missionary to military, when it began serving as buffer against Frenchmen and Englishmen, Apaches and Comanches.

About 1750 the Hispanic population surpassed that of the Pueblos for the first time and by 1800 stood at about 20,000. A series of alliances with non-Pueblo groups negotiated by Governor Juan Bautista de Anza, the most important of which was that with the Comanches in 1786, permitted a century of unprecedented expansion. In 1821, Mexican independence and encouragement of foreign commerce gave rise to the Santa Fe trade and to the economic reorientation of New Mexico from Chihuahua to Missouri. As a result, the United States faced only sporadic resistance when its Army of the West occupied New Mexico in 1846 during the Mexican-American War. Although it was the most populous of the Mexican provinces that fell to the United States, New Mexico was long considered by Congress a wasteland between the great states of Texas and California. Given their familiar boundaries in the 1850s and 1860s, New Mexico and Arizona did not achieve statehood until 1912. As of 2006, New Mexico's population was estimated at 1,954,599. As of 2000, it was 42 percent Hispanic, and 9.5 percent Native American.

See also **Anza, Juan Bautista de; Comanches; Missions: Spanish America; Oñate, Juan de; Pueblo Rebellion; Santa Fe, New Mexico.**

BIBLIOGRAPHY

See *Handbook of North American Indians,* vols. 9 and 10, *Southwest,* edited by Alfonso Ortiz (1979; 1983); Marc Simmons, *New Mexico: An Interpretive History* (1988); Jerry L. Williams, ed., *New Mexico in Maps,* 2d ed. (1986); and Charles L. Briggs and John R. Van Ness, eds., *Land, Water, and Culture: New Perspectives on Hispanic Land Grants* (1987).

Additional Bibliography

Chavez, Thomas E. *An Illustrated History of New Mexico.* Albuquerque: University of New Mexico Press, 2002.

Chavez, Thomas E. *New Mexico Past and Future.* Albuquerque: University of New Mexico Press, 2006.

Will de Chaparro, Martina. *Death and Dying in New Mexico.* Albuquerque: University of New Mexico Press, 2007.

JOHN L. KESSELL

NEW ORLEANS. New Orleans, capital of Spanish Louisiana (1763–1803). In 1718 the governor of Louisiana, Jean Baptiste Le Moyne, Sieur de Bienville, selected a site along the banks of the Mississippi River for a new settlement. Four years later the French colony's capital was moved from Biloxi to New Orleans. The limited prosperity the colony enjoyed under the French prompted its cession to Spain on 13 November 1762.

Spain was slow to take possession: The first official Spanish ship to reach New Orleans did not arrive until 5 March 1766, carrying a new governor, Don Antonio de Ulloa, and a small number of Spanish officials. Less than two and a half years later, during the Revolt of 1768, Ulloa was forced out of the colony by dissident French groups. To put down the rebellion, a sizable expedition commanded by Alejandro O'Reilly reached New Orleans on 18 August 1769. After reestablishing Spanish control and executing the ringleaders of the revolt, O'Reilly set to work to establish Spanish institutions in the colony. For the city of New Orleans he abolished the French superior council and replaced it with one of Spain's ancient municipal institutions, the *cabildo* (town council), whose first meeting was held 1 December 1769.

In 1769 the city consisted of sixty-six blocks, eleven fronting the river by six squares in depth, of which thirty had been subdivided into lots and had houses or buildings. Most of the buildings were constructed of wood and were in bad repair. There was no public lighting, no drainage system, no fire department, and no night watch. The stockade that surrounded part of the city, fronted by a small ditch, was dilapidated.

Entirely rebuilt after the great fires of 1788 and 1794, the city boasted many well-built houses and public buildings by 1803 and was much better fortified with an earthwork and five small forts. City regulations issued after 1788 required that all houses more than one story be constructed of brick.

Stimulated by a special "free trade" *cedula* of 1782, exports from New Orleans, principally indigo, tobacco, lumber, and pelts, reached 313,549 pesos in 1784. The *cedula* also encouraged the growth of merchant companies in the city. Prominent among these were Juan Baptista Macarty, Pablo Segond, Jerome Lachapelle, and Reaud and Fortier Company.

By 1803, when Louisiana was ceded first to France and then sold to the United States, the city's population stood at some 11,000, with most of the growth coming from immigration from Spain, Ireland, Acadia, and England.

The presence of more than 380 regular troops in the city made drinking, gambling, and dancing popular affairs, especially on All Saints Day, Christmas Day, New Year's Day, and Holy Week. Public dances originally held in the king's warehouse before 1782 moved to the Tremoulet Hotel around 1784. The famous Conde Street Ballroom opened 4 October 1792 on the site of the former public market. By 1800 there were so many ballrooms that an attempt was made to restrict them. The first public theater opened 4 October 1792 on St. Peter Street. Four years later, on 22 May 1796, the first opera premiered, a performance of *Sylvain* by André Gretry. The earliest parades date from 1787 and occurred with regularity on Mardi Gras and other holidays.

On 30 November 1803, Spanish authority in the city and colony officially ended when the colony was transferred to France at a ceremony held in the Cabildo. Twenty days later, following the sale of Louisiana to the United States, William Clairborne and General James Wilkinson accepted the city and colony for the United States.

See also **Spanish Empire.**

BIBLIOGRAPHY

Research on Spanish New Orleans has been accelerating in recent years although few monographs have as of 2007 been published. John G. Clark, *New Orleans 1718–1812.* Baton Rouge: Louisiana State University Press, 1970, describes its economy principally from printed sources. Edwin A. Davis, *Louisiana: A Narrative History,* 3d ed. Baton Rouge: Claitor's Book Store, 1971, has chapters on social and cultural life in the city and on the economy. The best accounts, however, are in dissertations: John Harkins, "The Neglected Phase of Louisiana's Colonial History: The New Orleans Cabildo" (Ph.D. diss., Memphis State University, 1976), and Thomas Ingersoll, "Old New Orleans: Race, Class, Sex, and Order in the Early Deep South, 1718–1819" (Ph.D. diss., UCLA, 1990). Two travelers, Captain Philip Pittman, *The Present State of the European Settlements on the Mississippi: With a Geographical Description of That River.* Gainesville: University of Florida Press, 1977, and James Pitot, *Observations on the Colony of Louisiana, from 1796 to 1802.* Baton Rouge: Published for the Historic New Orleans collection by the Louisiana State University Press, 1979, describe the city at the beginning and end of the Spanish period.

Additional Bibliography

Baker, Liva. *The Second Battle of New Orleans: The Hundred-year Struggle to Integrate the Schools.* New York: Harper Collins Publishers, 1996.

Hirsch, Arnold R; Logsdon, Joseph. *Creole New Orleans: Race and Americanization.* Baton Rouge: Louisiana State University Press, 1992.

Hollandsworth, James G. *An Absolute Massacre: The New Orleans Race Riot of July 30, 1866.* Baton Rouge: Louisiana State University Press, 2001.

Johnson, Walter. *Soul by Soul: Life inside the Antebellum Slave Market.* Cambridge, MA: Harvard University Press, 1999.

Montero de Pedro, José. *Españoles en Nueva Orleans y Luisiana.* Madrid: Ediciones Cultura Hispánica del Centro Iberoamericano de Cooperación, 1979.

Schafer, Judith Kelleher. *Becoming Free, Remaining Free: Manumission and Enslavement in New Orleans, 1846–1862.* Baton Rouge: Louisiana State University Press, 2003.

BRIAN COUTTS

NEW SAINT ANDREW. *See* **Caledonia.**

NEW SPAIN, COLONIZATION OF THE NORTHERN FRONTIER. In the eighteenth and nineteenth centuries, the Spanish and later the Mexican governments were concerned over the fact that the northern frontier provinces of New Spain or Mexico were underpopulated and thus vulnerable to foreign invasion and occupation. This concern was particularly important in its impact on the colonization of Texas and Alta California, thought to be most vulnerable to foreign invasion.

In the eighteenth century the royal government organized groups of colonists to populate the sparsely settled frontier. The government also established military garrisons along the border, hoping that the soldiers stationed in the forts would establish families and remain in the area once they retired. From about 1710 to 1740 the viceregal government in Mexico City considered Texas, located on the border with French Louisiana, to be the most vulnerable part of the northern frontier. In 1716 a large expedition occupied east Texas, establishing missions and military garrisons. Then in the early 1720s the government established several presidios in the San Antonio area. In 1731 it sent a group of Canary Islanders to establish the Villa de Bexar at San Antonio.

In 1769, Visitor-General José de Gálvez, responding to the potential threat of the English and Russian presence in the Pacific Basin, organized the so-called Sacred Expedition to occupy Alta California. This expedition consisted of five Franciscan missionaries, sixty-six soldiers recruited in northwestern New Spain, twenty-seven Catalán volunteers from Spain, and several individuals of indigenous heritage recruited from the Baja California missions.

Over the next thirty years efforts were made to populate Alta California. In 1775–1776, Captain Juan Bautista de Anza, a military commander in Sonora, led some 240 colonists and soldiers overland from Sonora to Alta California. The settlers established a civilian town at San José in 1777, and the soldiers formed the garrison of the presidio at San Francisco in 1776. In 1781, Fernando de Rivera y Moncada led a second group of about 230 settlers overland from Sonora. These colonists established the pueblo of Los Angeles that year. Finally, in 1797 a group of some thirty colonists recruited in the Guadalajara region of central Mexico founded the Villa de Branciforte. The three pueblos in Alta California were among a larger group of planned communities established in frontier provinces. In the 1780s, for example, the viceregal government had established another such planned community at Horcasitas in central Sonora.

After the Louisiana Purchase in 1803, with the U.S.–Spanish border in east Texas in dispute, U.S. citizens posed the greatest threat to the northern frontier. The Spanish (and later the Mexican government) still felt that Texas and California were underpopulated. Organized in New Orleans, a number of filibustering expeditions to Texas only reinforced the Spanish government's growing sense of paranoia. In 1821, Stephen F. Austin received a grant of land in Texas and brought a group of colonists to settle in the eastern part of the province. In addition, thousands of Anglo-Americans migrated to Texas, New Mexico, and Alta California illegally. Because these Anglo-American settlers were a potentially subversive element, the Mexican government attempted to use incentives to attract Mexican settlers to the frontier. Two colonization laws passed in the 1820s facilitated the granting of land to settlers. In the 1830s and 1840s, following the secularization of the missions, the governors of Alta California made more than 800 grants of land in the province.

In the 1830s the Mexican government sent one last group of colonists to Alta California. A group of 250 colonists recruited in central Mexico arrived in California in 1834 to establish a town at the site of modern Santa Rosa, north of San Francisco. Mariano G. Vallejo, the military commander of the northern section of the province, wanted to fortify the Mexican presence in the region to counter the Russian-American Company's outpost at Fort Ross, but the community shortly collapsed.

Ultimately, the attempt to colonize the northern frontier, especially Texas and Alta California, failed, and the pattern of Anglo-American settlement in both provinces undermined Mexican control. In 1821 the settler populations of Texas and Alta California were 8,000 and 3,500, respectively. In 1836, some 20,000 Anglo-Americans living in Texas organized the revolt that led to the creation of an independent republic in that year. And the hundreds of Anglo-American settlers in Alta California in 1846 contributed materially to the U.S. conquest of that province at the beginning of the Mexican-American War. New Mexico, also conquered by the United States during the war, was the most populous of the far northern frontier provinces, with some 28,000 settlers living there in 1821. With the failure of population politics, the frontier region of northern Mexico remained sparsely settled, and the frontier fell to U.S. expansion in the early and mid-nineteenth century.

See also **Borderlands, The.**

BIBLIOGRAPHY

Peter Gerhard, *The North Frontier of New Spain* (1982, rev. 1993).

David J. Weber, *The Mexican Frontier, 1821–1846: The American Southwest Under Mexico* (1982).

Robert H. Jackson, "Demographic Change in Northwestern New Spain," in *The Americas* 41:4 (Apr. 1985): 462–479.

Additional Bibliography

Weber, David J., and Jorge Ferreiro. *La frontera española en América del Norte.* México: Fondo de Cultura Económica, 2000.

ROBERT H. JACKSON

NEW SPAIN, VICEROYALTY OF. Viceroyalty of New Spain, the first viceroyalty created in the Americas. Antonio de Mendoza was appointed its viceroy in 1530 but did not actually occupy the position until 1535. New Spain was defined to include all of Mexico north of Chiapas, incorporating the *audiencias* of Mexico and Nueva Galicia and the interior provinces of the far north. For governmental purposes, the viceroy's authority theoretically extended over the Caribbean, Central America, and even the Philippines; in actual fact, however, the three jurisdictions outside of New Spain were effectively ruled by their governors and *audiencias,* and the viceroy concentrated on governing Mexico. Viceroys have often been portrayed as ruthless tyrants brutally repressing the indigenous population. However, twenty-first-century scholars have questioned this extreme portrait by looking at the limitations of viceregal power. With minimal resources to govern such a large territory, a viceroy could not arbitrarily impose his will. Academics have therefore studied how the government directed public rituals to symbolically establish the authority of the viceroy and the Spanish colonial state. The truth of the position probably lies between the two extremes. Beyond governance, some viceroys are also of consequence because they left behind important historical accounts. Lorenzo Suárez de Mendoza, for example, ordered the compilation of Nahua knowledge known as the Codex Mendoza, which offers a wealth of data about the pre-contact culture of Anáhuac.

VICEROYS OF NEW SPAIN

Antonio de Mendoza, 1535–1550
Luis de Velasco, 1550–1564
Audiencia, 1564–1566
Gastón de Peralta, marqués de Falces, 1566–1567
Martín Enríquez de Almansa, 1568–1580
Lorenzo Suárez de Mendoza, conde de la Coruña, 1580–1582
Luis de Villanueva y Zapata, 1582–1583
Pedro Moya y Contreras, 1583–1585
Álvaro Manrique de Zúñiga, marqúes de Villamanrique, 1585–1590
Luis de Velasco, marqués de Salinas, 1590–1595 (first term)
Gasper de Zúñiga y Acevedo, conde de Monterrey, 1595–1603
Juan Manuel de Mendoza y Luna, marqués de Montesclaros, 1603–1607
Luis de Velasco, marqués de Salinas, 1607–1611 (second term)
Francisco García Guerra, 1611–1612
Pedro de Otálora, 1612
Diego Fernández de Córdoba, marqués de Guadalcázar, 1612–1621
Diego Carrillo de Mendoza y Pimental, marqués de Gelves y conde de Priego, 1621–1624
Rodrigo Pacheco y Osorio, marqués de Cerralvo, 1624–1635
Lope Diáz de Armendáriz, marqués de Cadereyta, 1635–1640
Diego López Pacheco Cabrera y Bobadilla, duque de Escalona, 1640–1642
Juan de Palafox y Mendoza, 1642
García Sarmiento de Sotomayor, conde de Salvatierra y marqués de Sobroso, 1642–1648
Marcos de Torres y Rueda, 1648–1649
Matías de Peralta, 1649–1650
Luis Enríquez de Guzmán, conde de Alba de Liste y marqués de Villaflor, 1650–1653
Francisco Fernández de la Cueva, duque de Albuquerque, 1653–1660
Juan de Leyva y de la Cerda, marqués de Leyva, conde de Baños, 1660–1664
Diego Osorio de Escobar, 1664
Antonio Sebastián de Toledo, marqués de Mancera, 1664–1673
Pedro Núñez Colón de Portugal, duque de Veragua y marqués de Jamaica, 1673
Payo Enríquez de Rivera, 1673–1680
Tomás Antonio Manrique de la Cerda y Aragón, conde de Paredes y marqués de Laguna, 1680–1686
Melchor Portocarrero y Lasso de la Vega, conde de la Monclova, 1686–1688

Gaspar de Sandoval y de la Cerda Andoval Silva y Mendoza, conde de Galve, 1688–1696
Juan de Ortega y Montañes, 1696–1697 (first term)
José Sarmiento de Valladares, conde de Moctezuma y de Tula, 1697–1701
Juan de Ortega y Montañes, 1701–1702 (second term)
Francisco Fernández de la Cueva Enríquez, duque de Albuquerque, 1702–1711
Fernando de Alencastre Noroña y Silva, duque de Linares, 1711–1716
Baltasar de Zúñiga y Guzmán, marqués de Valero y duque de Arión, 1716–1722
Juan de Acuña y Bejarano, marqués de Casafuerte, 1722–1734
Juan Antonio de Vizarrón y Equiarreta, 1734–1740
Pedro de Castro y Figueroa, duque de la Conquista y marqués de Gracia Real, 1740–1741
Pedro Malo de Villavicencio, 1741–1742
Pedro Cebrián y Agustín, conde de Fuenclara, 1742–1746
Juan Francisco de Güemes y Horcasitas, conde de Revillagigedo, 1746–1755
Agustín de Ahumada y Villalón, marqués de las Amarillas, 1755–1760
Francisco de Echévarri, 1760
Francisco Cajigal de la Vega, 1760–1761
Joaquín de Monserrat, marqués de Cruillas, 1761- 1766
Carlos Francisco de Croix, marqués de Croix, 1766–1771
Antonio María de Bucareli y Ursúa, 1771–1779
Martín de Mayorga, 1779–1783
Matías de Gálvez, 1783–1784
Vicente de Herrera y Rivero, 1784–1785
Bernardo de Gálvez, conde de Gálvez, 1785–1786
Eusebio Sánchez Pareja Beleño, 1786–1787
Alonso Núñez de Haro y Peralta, 1787
Manuel Antonio Flores, 1787–1789
Juan Vicente de Güemes Pacheco y Padilla, conde de Revillagigedo, 1789–1794
Miguel de la Grúa Talamanca y Branciforte, marqués de Branciforte, 1794–1798
Miguel José de Azanza, 1798–1800
Félix Berenguer de Marquina, 1800–1803
José de Iturrigaray, 1803–1808
Pedro Garibay, 1808–1809
Francisco Javier de Lizana y Beaumont, 1809–1810
Francisco Javier Venegas, 1810–1813
Félix María Calleja del Rey, marqués de Calderón, 1813–1816
Juan Ruíz de Apodaca, conde del Venadito, 1816–1821
Francisco Novella, 1821
Juan O'Donojú, 1821

See also **Anáhuac; Audiencia; Viceroyalty, Viceroy.**

BIBLIOGRAPHY

Peter Gerhard, *A Guide to the Historical Geography of New Spain* (1972).

Additional Bibliography

Barrios, Feliciano, ed. *El gobierno de un mundo: Virreinatos y audiencias en la América hispánica.* Cuenca: Ediciones de la Universidad de Castilla–La Mancha, 2004.

Berdan, Frances F., and Patricia Rieff Anawalt. *The Codex Mendoza.* 4 vols. Berkeley: University of California Press, 1992.

Cañeque, Alejandro. *The King's Living Image: The Culture and Politics of Viceregal Power in Colonial Mexico.* New York: Routledge, 2004.

JOHN E. KICZA

NEWSPAPERS AND MAGAZINES.

See **Journalism; Journalism in Mexico.**

NEZAHUALCOYOTL (c. 1402–1472).

Nezahualcoyotl (*b.* ca. 1402; *d.* 1472), ruler of Texcoco, Mexico (1431–1472). Nezahualcoyotl ("Fasting Coyote") ruled the Nahuatl-speaking Acolhua polity centered at Texcoco, on the eastern shore of the Valley of Mexico lake system. Though he is one of the most renowned pre-Conquest Mexican rulers, part of his fame undoubtedly results from post-Conquest revision. According to native histories, Nezahualcoyotl witnessed the assassination of his father, Ixtlilxochitl, in 1418, during a conflict between the Acolhuas and their Tepanec overlords. He fled to his mother's people, the Mexica royal dynasty at Tenochtitlán. In 1428 he became a key player in the alliance of Mexicas, Acolhuas, and rebellious Tepanecs that defeated the Tepanec ruler Maxtla. Installed by the Mexica in his father's place and with a Mexica princess as his principal wife, Nezahualcoyotl remained a junior partner in the Aztec Empire. He became a wise judge and lawgiver, a master builder, a poet, and a philosopher, while fathering over one hundred children by his forty wives. Claims that he was a monotheist and that he composed several Nahuatl songs recorded in the sixteenth century are probably unfounded. He was succeeded by his seven-year-old son, Nezahualpilli; his line continued into the colonial period and included the historian Fernando de Alva Ixtlilxochitl (1578–1650).

See also **Aztecs; Nezahualpilli.**

BIBLIOGRAPHY

Alva Ixtlilxochitl, Fernando De, *Obras históricas,* edited by Edmundo O'Gorman (1975).

Nigel Davies, *The Aztecs: A History* (1980).

Jerome A. Offner, *Law and Politics in Aztec Texcoco* (1983).

Diego Durán, *The Aztecs: The History of the Indies of New Spain,* translated by Doris Heyden and Fernando Horcasitas (1964).

Additional Bibliography

Elizondo, Carlos. *Nezahualcóyotl.* México, D.F.: Planeta, 2005.

LOUISE M. BURKHART

NEZAHUALPILLI (1465–1515).

Nezahualpilli (*b.* 1465; *d.* 1515), ruler of Texcoco, Mexico (1472–1515). Nezahualpilli ("Fasting Child" or "Fasting Noble") succeeded Nezahualcoyotl as ruler of Texcoco, one of three polities heading the Aztec Empire, which was dominated by the Mexica of Tenochtitlán. Son of a Mexica noblewoman, Nezahualpilli was seven years old when his father died, having designated him as heir. His right to the office protected by his Mexica relatives from jealous older brothers, Nezahualpilli matured into a capable statesman and lawmaker, master builder, and renowned diviner. In a famous (though likely legendary) episode, Nezahualpilli predicted to Motecuhzoma II that Mexico would soon be ruled by foreigners. Motecuhzoma's own diviners claimed otherwise. Nezahualpilli challenged Motecuhzoma to a series of ball games in order to settle the argument; Nezahualpilli won the match. He died without naming an heir. The ensuing dispute between his sons Cacama and Ixtlilxochitl left the polity divided. Motecuhzoma installed Cacama; a few years later Ixtlilxochitl became one of Cortés's principal allies.

See also **Mesoamerica.**

BIBLIOGRAPHY

Fernando De Alva Ixtlilxochitl, *Obras históricas,* 3d ed. (1975).

Jerome A. Offner, *Law and Politics in Aztec Texcoco* (1983).

Additional Bibliography

Coe, Michael D., and Rex Koontz. *Mexico: From the Olmecs to the Aztecs.* New York: Thames & Hudson, 2005.

LOUISE M. BURKHART

NIAGARA FALLS CONFERENCE.

Niagara Falls Conference, meeting convened May to July 1914 in Niagara Falls, Canada, after the U.S. seizure of Veracruz, Mexico, in April 1914. The conference was initiated by the government in Washington, D.C., and representatives of Argentina, Brazil, and Chile, who offered to mediate the U.S.–Mexico dispute. While the mediators wished to confine the agenda to this dispute, Woodrow Wilson's administration insisted on including Mexican internal affairs.

The United States sought to use the conference to negotiate the removal of General Victoriano Huerta from power and the transfer of government control to the revolutionary forces under Venustiano Carranza. After initially seeking to confine the issue to the withdrawal of U.S. troops, Huerta offered to resign in favor of a compromise candidate if the United States pledged to support the resulting government against the Carrancistas. Carranza refused to participate, rejecting the call for an armistice, denying the legitimacy of the sessions, and sending envoys to confer only with the U.S. representatives.

The sessions produced a protracted stalemate, yielding little more than a formal armistice between the United States and the Mexican government.

See also **Huerta, Victoriano; Wilson, Woodrow.**

BIBLIOGRAPHY

Kenneth J. Grieb, *The United States and Huerta* (1969); and "The A.B.C. Mediation Conference at Niagara Falls, Ontario, in 1914," in *Niagara Frontier* 16, no. 2 (1969): 42–54.

Additional Bibliography

Eisenhower, John S. D. *Intervention!: The United States and the Mexican Revolution, 1913-1917.* New York: W.W. Norton, 1993.

Suárez Argüello, Ana Rosa. *Pragmatismo y principios: La relación conflictiva entre México y Estados Unidos, 1810-1942.* México, D.F.: Instituto Mora, 1998.

KENNETH J. GRIEB

NICARAGUA. Modern Nicaragua has struggled through natural disasters, dictatorship, civil war, revolutionary promise, and political corruption to establish itself as a constitutional democracy in Central America. Although in area (59,998 square miles), Nicaragua is the largest Central American state, its population (5.7 million in 2005) ranks among the poorest in the Western Hemisphere. Nicaragua is bordered on the north by Honduras, on the south by Costa Rica, on the east by the Caribbean Sea, and on the west by the Pacific Ocean. The country comprises three major geographic zones: the Pacific Slope, the Central Highlands, and the heavily forested Atlantic Coast. Lake Managua, the largest lake in Central America, and Lake Nicaragua are in the southwest. A string of approximately forty volcanoes runs along the Pacific Coast. Another notable feature of Nicaragua's geography is the break in this mountain chain that made Nicaragua one of the most probable sites for an interoceanic canal. Moreover, this geography has meant that unlike most of the major cities of Central America, which are in the highlands, Nicaragua's population centers—Granada, León, Masaya, and Managua—are all located near sea level. The distinctive physical and climatic characteristics of each region have resulted in varied economic and demographic patterns. Western Nicaragua is the demographic and economic heartland of the country. Managua (population 1 million) has served as the country's capital since 1852. The majority of Nicaragua's population is mixed European and Indian ancestry, and the resulting mestizo culture is centered in the Pacific lowlands and the adjacent interior highlands, where the climate is drier and more comfortable than in the tropical lowlands of the Caribbean watershed. The population of the Caribbean shore is predominantly African and West Indian, with significant enclaves of native Miskito, Sumu, and Rama Indians. In the mid-1980s the central government divided the eastern part of the country into two autonomous regions and gave the indigenous populations there limited self-rule.

Nicaragua is one of the least industrialized countries in Latin America, yet more than half of the population is urban-based. Although it is predominantly Roman Catholic, the country has a rapidly growing Evangelical Protestant population. Traditional agricultural exports including indigo, coffee, bananas, cotton, beef, and sugar have dominated economic development, though fishing, timber, and gold mining also have been somewhat important in its history. Most recently, there has been interest in the potential of hydro- and geothermal power and the growth of tourism.

INDEPENDENCE AND THE EARLY YEARS OF THE REPUBLIC

In the nineteenth century Nicaragua's political development followed the rise of León and Granada. By the close of the colonial period, León, the colonial capital, had become the focus of strong liberal sentiment and the site of the only university in Central America outside the capital city of Guatemala. Granada, in contrast, was the conservative bastion of the landed elite and the center of clerical privilege. In 1811 a creole-dominated junta in León led the first attempt at Nicaraguan independence following the French occupation of Spain in 1808. Royalist forces crushed this attempt. Division among the Creole elite again flared after a junta in Guatemala City declared Central America independent on September 15, 1821, in accordance with Agustín de Iturbide's Plan De Iguala. León favored joining Iturbide's Mexican Empire, whereas Granada favored a separate Central American nation. These diverging visions ushered in four

decades of intense conflict between Conservative Granada and Liberal León, in which family feuds became an important component. Before any resolution was reached, however, Iturbide's empire collapsed, and in 1823 Nicaragua joined in the formation of the United Provinces of Central America. Torn by regional factionalism, this federation was doomed to disintegrate. On April 30, 1838, a Nicaraguan constituent assembly declared the state to be "independent and sovereign," and despite Nicaraguan Liberal attempts to resurrect the union in the 1840s, all attempts failed. Although the Conservative politician Fruto Chamorro proclaimed the Republic of Nicaragua on February 28, 1854, frequent civil wars left the country politically exhausted and economically devastated.

It was hoped that plans for an interoceanic canal would fuel Nicaraguan economic development, but the Anglo-American rivalry for control of such a route contributed to further disruption of the country. On the Caribbean coast, the British followed an

Nicaragua

Population:	5,700,000 (2005 est.)
Area:	59, 998 sq mi
Official language(s):	Spanish
Language(s):	Spanish, Miskito, other; English and indigenous languages spoken on the Atlantic coast
National currency:	gold cordoba (NIO)
Principal religions:	Roman Catholic, 72.9%; Evangelical, 15.1%; Moravian, 1.5%; Episcopal, 0.1%; other, 1.9%; none, 8.5%
Ethnicity:	mestizo (mixed Amerindian and European), 69%; European, 17%; African, 9%; Amerindian, 5%
Capital:	Managua (pop. 1,098,000; 2005 est.)
Other urban centers:	Granada, León, Chinandega, Esteli, Masaya, Matagalpa, Chichigalpa, Tipitapa, Juigalpa
Annual rainfall:	The Mosquito Coast often receives 100–250 in; Managua, 45 in, while the Pacific coast averages over 40 in.
Principal geographic features:	*Bodies of water:* Lake Nicaragua, Lake Managua, Coco (or Segovia) River, San Juan River *Mountains:* Cordillera Isabelia, Cordillera Dariense, Cordillera Chontaleña, Serranías Huapí
Economy:	*GDP per capita:* $3,100 (2006 est.)
Principal products and exports:	*Agriculture:* coffee, bananas, sugarcane, cotton, rice, corn, tobacco, sesame, soy, beans; beef, veal, pork, poultry, dairy products; shrimp, lobsters *Industries:* food processing, chemicals, machinery and metal products, textiles, clothing, petroleum refining and distribution, beverages, footwear, wood
Government:	Constitutionally defined as a democracy. As of 2006 the Sandinista constitution of 1987 was in effect; it provides for a democratic system in which elections are held every six years, with executive, legislative (National Assembly), judiciary, and electoral council (Consejo Supremo Electoral—CSE) branches. There are also two other levels of elected government—municipal councils (153 as of 2006) and the two autonomous Atlantic coast regional councils.
Armed forces:	14,000 active personnel in 2005. *Army:* 12,000 *Navy:* 800 *Air force:* 1,200
Transportation:	As of 2002, 11,639 mi of roads, of which 1,322 mi were paved, including the Inter-American Highway and the Pacific Highway. As of 2004, only 3.7 mi of narrow gauge railway in operation, mostly for carrying passengers from Chichigalpa to Ingenio San Antonio. Air transportation is important because of limited road and railway facilities. In 2004, there were an estimated 176 airports, only 11 of which had paved runways as of 2005. A state-owned airline, Aerolíneas de Nicaragua (AERONICA), provides services to El Salvador, Costa Rica, Panama, and Mexico. The principal airport is Augusto Sandino, an international terminal at Las Mercedes, near Managua.
Media:	In 2004, there were 210 chartered radio stations in the country, 52 AM stations and 158 FM. The Voice of Nicaragua is the primary government station. There were 10 television stations based in Managua and 63 cable television franchises. There were two major daily newspapers in 2004 including, *La Prensa,* with a circulation of 37,000, and *El Nuevo Diario,* circulation 30,000. Press censorship ended with the departure of the Sandinista government.
Literacy and education:	*Total population:* 67.5% (2003 est.) Primary and secondary education is free and compulsory for 6 years between the ages of 6 and 12. There were a total of 14 universities in Nicaragua in 1998, including the National Autonomous University of Nicaragua, the Central American University, affiliated with Georgetown University, and the Polytechnic University of Nicaragua.

aggressive policy begun by seventeenth-century buccaneers. A British protectorate over the Miskito Indians left an English-speaking legacy there that remains to this day. In 1816 the British formally founded the autonomous Kingdom of Mosquitia with the crowning of George Frederick II in Belize. They occupied San Juan del Norte from 1848 to 1850 and did not acknowledge Nicaraguan sovereignty over the region until 1860, when the Treaty of Managua ended the British protectorate. By 1894 the British had relinquished all claims to the coast, although they did not finally abandon the region until 1904.

The United States's interest in Nicaragua accelerated following its acquisition of the Pacific coast of North America. In 1850 Cornelius Vanderbilt (1794–1877) established the profitable Accessory Transit Company that ferried California-bound gold prospectors across Nicaragua, while British, French, and U.S. interests competed for control of the canal route.

In response to the Conservatives' victory in 1854, Nicaraguan Liberal leaders invited North American filibusters to aid them in regaining control. In 1855 William Walker brought fifty-eight men from California into the country and quickly took over the leadership of the Liberal armed forces. Within a year he made himself president of Nicaragua, as thousands from the southern United

Manati Hunting, Lake Nicaragua, 1867 (w/c on paper) by F. Deiezmann (fl. 19th century). PRIVATE COLLECTION/ © MICHAEL GRAHAM-STEWART/ THE BRIDGEMAN ART LIBRARY

States joined his army in hopes of Nicaraguan land grants and other concessions. A combined Central American army, led by Costa Rican president Juan Rafael Mora Porrás with heavy backing from Guatemala's José Rafael Carrera and the British, defeated Walker in 1857. Walker attempted to return in two subsequent invasions, but was repelled each time. He ultimately was captured by the British and executed by Honduran authorities in 1860.

With the Liberals discredited by their association with Walker, Nicaragua entered a period of relative political stability under Conservative Party rule, referred to as "Los Treinta Anos" (the Thirty Years, 1863–1893). Managua rose to increased political influence, decreasing the historical competition between León and Granada. Under a new constitution, Conservative Party presidents were elected every four years. Foreign investment supported the establishment of railroads and the development of coffee and banana plantations and the timber industry. Gold production increased, and concessions were made to foreign investors in return for infrastructure development. Throughout the period, coffee planters took land from Indians and mestizo peasants. In the 1881 War of the Comuneros, the government brutally crushed a rebellion resisting these land expropriations.

JOSÉ SANTOS ZELAYA, 1893–1909

In 1893 divisions among the Conservatives enabled the Liberal José Santos Zelaya to seize power and rule until 1909. Characterized as a tyrant and a xenophobic nationalist, Zelaya implemented reforms, persecuted political opposition, and alienated foreign interests. His reforms included a new constitution that separated church and state, established civil marriage and divorce, reformed the judiciary, and set up state-controlled education. His economic policies promoted export production, but he also put the country deeply in debt. Zelaya encountered growing opposition from both Conservatives and foreign economic interests that had prospered under the Conservatives' laissez-faire administration. His meddling in the politics of the other Central American states alarmed U.S. business interests, and his anti-U.S. sentiment and taxation of U.S. investors led to a cooling of relations. His challenge to the landed Nicaraguan elite decreased his support within the country. The execution of two U.S. "adventurers" who attempted to blow up two Nicaraguan ships ultimately resulted in a U.S.-backed Conservative revolt led by Juan Estrada. In 1909 Estrada captured Managua and ousted Zelaya.

INTEROCEANIC CANAL

A recurrent theme of nineteenth-century Nicaragua was the effort to establish an interoceanic canal via the San Juan River and Lake Nicaragua. The Clayton-Bulwer Treaty of 1850 had restrained the rivalry between British and U.S. interests, with both agreeing neither to acquire territory in Central America nor to block the other from building a canal, but the agreement also prevented Nicaragua from pursuing a national project for the development of the canal. After the U.S. Maritime Canal Company collapsed in the early 1890s, having failed to build a canal through Nicaragua, Zelaya began to court German and Japanese financial interests for the project. Such actions contributed further to the alienation of the United States. Ultimately, the United States began constructing a canal in Panama in 1904, but in 1913 the United States renewed its interest in the Nicaraguan site, perhaps merely to prevent construction of a rival canal. The resulting Bryan-Chamorro Treaty granted exclusive rights to the United States for canal construction and military privileges in the country. Nicaragua received $3 million to help pay its foreign debt. The treaty was abrogated in 1970. Most recently, former president Enrique Bolaños (b. 1928) presented a plan to build a new interoceanic canal, but with his 2006 loss in the presidential elections, the future of new canal plans for Nicaragua is unclear.

U.S. INTERVENTION

Following the ousting of Zelaya in 1909, the Conservatives found themselves with a very tenuous grip on political power. The Nicaraguan congress named a Liberal, José Madriz (1867–1911), as president, but the United States forced his resignation and imposed a quadrumvirate dominated by Conservatives. A Conservative-dominated congress elected General Estrada president in 1911, but he resigned in protest against excessive U.S. political involvement. Vice President Adolfo Díaz took over and began to implement traditionally Conservative policies. When the Liberals under Benjamín Francisco Zeledón revolted and engulfed Nicaragua in a serious political and financial crisis, the Conservatives again turned to the United States. In 1912 U.S. Marines crushed Zeledón's rebellion, took over the operation of the railways, and garrisoned the main cities. The United States supervised the election of Díaz as president and signed the Knox-Castrillo Treaty of 1911, which required Nicaragua to surrender control over its customs collection and other important elements of its financial system to U.S. administrators. In return, the Nicaraguan government received $14 million in loans. The United States also gained the right to intervene on behalf of U.S. interests and to arbitrate any dispute in which Nicaragua became involved. Following patterns already established by the United States in Cuba, Panama, and the Dominican Republic, Nicaragua essentially became a U.S. protectorate, with concomitant control of the Nicaraguan economy by U.S. investors.

By 1914 coffee was Nicaragua's major export, and foreign investment in bananas and gold mining had grown. In 1916 General Emiliano Chamorro Vargas was elected president, and Conservative policies continued as foreign investment grew rapidly. By the 1920s the Standard Fruit and Steamship Company had surpassed United Fruit as the largest single private employer and source of foreign exchange in Nicaragua. Initially, Standard had focused on the timber industry, but once it had cleared the land it turned to and dominated banana production.

Despite Zeledón's death and a ban on Liberal Party electoral activity, the Liberals continued to oppose both the Conservative government and the U.S. presence in the country. A series of Conservative presidents ruled Nicaragua during the early 1920s with U.S. support. The U.S. Marines withdrew in 1925 as political stability seemed assured, but immediately new revolts erupted. Fear of leftist Mexican support for the Liberals influenced U.S. president Calvin Coolidge to send the Marines back in 1926 to protect American lives and business interests. General Chamorro ousted President Carlos Solórzano, but the Liberal vice president, Juan Bautista Sacasa, opposed Chamorro's takeover.

The U.S. State Department negotiated a settlement that returned Adolfo Díaz to the presidency, but U.S. military presence increased as Liberal rebels continued fighting government troops. In 1927 the Tipitapa Agreement provided for U.S.-supervised elections in 1928, which were won by Liberal General José María Moncada. Moncada had opposed U.S. military intervention, and in 1931 a gradual withdrawal of U.S. troops began. But the fact that Moncada had taken office during the U.S. occupation alienated many of his supporters, including Lieutenant Augusto César Sandino.

Sandino had fought under General Moncada against the Conservatives and the U.S. Marines. Moncada's collaboration with the Conservatives and U.S. officials and his ultimate election as president convinced Sandino that he had betrayed the Liberal cause and Nicaragua. Sandino withdrew into the hills around Matagalpa in northeastern Nicaragua and launched his nationalist guerrilla struggle against the Marines, which by 1930 included more than 5,000 rebels. Despite aerial bombing, the Marines could not defeat Sandino's peasant army. In the last U.S.-supervised election, in 1932, Sacasa came to the presidency, and in 1933 the Marines left.

U.S. military occupation left three legacies: U.S. economic domination; a guerrilla war; and the development of Nicaragua's National Guard. The United States established and trained the National Guard to assist the Marines in repressing the Sandino Revolt and to maintain order in the country after U.S. military withdrawal. By 1934 it was apparent that Anastasio Somoza García, commander of the National Guard since 1932, had eclipsed the state in terms of power and control. Increasingly, Somoza and Sacasa came into conflict over numerous issues, one of which was Sandino.

In 1934 Sacasa arranged a meeting with Sandino to negotiate a peace that would include the gradual disarming of Sandino's forces. After the meeting, members of the National Guard assassinated Sandino, ostensibly on Somoza's orders. Sandino became a folk hero and a martyr whose cause and symbol was resurrected in the 1960s.

THE SOMOZA DYNASTY

In 1936 Somoza forced Sacasa to resign and arranged for Carlos Brenes Jarquín (1884–1942) to be elected president. The new government implemented traditional Liberal policies, but ties with the United States were strengthened. Although the United States gained economic and financial concessions under Somoza's rule, it was primarily the Somoza family that monopolized the Nicaraguan economy, showing little interest in using their power to promote the general welfare of the population.

Anastasio Somoza García became president in January 1937 and began a regime in which the state, inextricably tied to him, became an increasingly repressive instrument used to prevent opposition participation and economic betterment for any Nicaraguan outside the Somoza circle. Somoza's Nationalist Liberal Party controlled Nicaraguan politics. In 1947 Leonardo Argüello won the presidency with Somoza's backing, but when he attempted to exert his independence, Argüello was ousted after only four weeks in office. His successor, Benjamín Lacayo Sacasa (1884–1959), suffered the same fate. Finally Somoza turned to a member of his own family, Victor M. Román y Reyes, to fill the office, and in 1950 Somoza himself returned to the presidency. The economy expanded, supported by the World War II cotton boom, but the country's stability was increasingly the result of political repression.

Somoza consolidated the state and its administrative, social, and judicial branches in his single person. Through the National Guard, he controlled the military, police, and judges; the awarding of business licenses; the arms, tobacco, prostitution, and liquor trades; the national health services; broadcasting; the collection of taxes; and the leading financial institutions.

Somoza's success continued as long as he maintained the support of the traditional pillars of Nicaraguan society: the ecclesiastical hierarchy; agricultural and commercial elites; the traditional party leadership; and the military. However, his candidacy for a fifth presidential term in 1956 came at a point when the political and economic environment was changing in Nicaragua. Previous support from the emerging middle class began to weaken as Somoza's vast commercial network became a major obstacle to its advancement. In addition, the repressive tactics of the Somoza state had negative repercussions among the general populace. Social discontent ultimately found its voice. On 21 September 21, 1956, a young poet, Rigoberto López Pérez

(c. 1929–1956), assassinated Somoza in León. Under a state of siege, the National Assembly unanimously elected Somoza's eldest son, Colonel Luis Somoza Debayle, to complete his term, and a younger son, Anastasio "Tachito" Somoza Debayle took over the National Guard. A popular election confirmed Luis as president in 1957.

A political modernizer, Luis Somoza Debayle sought to remove his family from public office but not from influence. In 1959 he approved a law barring any individual from serving consecutive terms and from being succeeded by a blood relative. In 1963 a family associate, René Schick Gutiérrez of the Nationalist Liberal Party, won the presidential election. Schick died in office in August 1966, and his term was completed by Vice President Lorenzo Guerrero Gutiérrez (1900–1981), but the Somozas held the real power. Tachito consolidated control of the National Guard and carried out a purge of military and civilian subversives. Opposition leaders were arrested, and despite a 1950 power-sharing arrangement between the Liberals and Conservatives that maintained a sham of democracy, the Chamorro family and its supporters found their influence in the political arena was dwindling despite their control of the leading daily newspaper, *La Prensa.*

The Somozas' economic interests continued to compete unfairly with other economically powerful sectors of Nicaraguan society. Capitalist investment in agriculture and industry and the worsening conditions of the majority of Nicaraguans presented a persistent contradiction that the Somoza-dominated state dealt with through increasing brutality and repression. As Gutiérrez neared the end of his term, Tachito Somoza announced his candidacy. Popular reaction was negative, and even his brother, Luis, urged him not to run. January 1967 saw mass demonstrations outside the presidential palace. The National Guard fired on the demonstrators, killing hundreds. Tachito became president of Nicaragua in February 1967, defeating, according to the official tally, the National Opposition Union coordinated by Pedro Joaquín Chamorro Cardenal, editor of *La Prensa.* A heart attack killed Luis in April, removing the only restraining influence over Tachito.

THE RISE OF THE FSLN

The Sandinista National Liberation Front (FSLN) began its opposition to the Somozas in 1961 when Carlos Fonseca Amador, Tomás Borge Martínez, and Silvio Mayorga, influenced by Fidel Castro's Cuban Revolution, founded a small organization that would grow into a major guerrilla force. By 1963 the FSLN was active, but it suffered under the repressive rule of Luis Somoza. By the end of 1967 most of its leaders had been killed or imprisoned, but the remnants regrouped in the northern hills and by 1970 were again actively opposing the government. Initial support for the movement came from leftist students, but the guerrillas also drew on backing from peasants, for whom the image of Sandino was still a strong symbol. The FSLN also attracted the youth of the middle and upper-middle classes, and by 1978 it had about 3,000 members.

Other opposition to Somoza increased. In 1971 the Social Democrats and other leftist parties formed the National Civic Alliance, but the Congress, dissolving itself, transferred all executive and legislative power to the office of the president. U.S. ambassador Turner Shelton helped negotiate an agreement that a triumvirate of two Liberals (General Robert Martínez Lacayo and Alfonso López Cordero) and one Conservative (Fernando Agüero) would succeed Somoza as president in 1972. Somoza, however, remained supreme commander of the National Guard, and announced his intention to stand for reelection to the presidency in 1974.

Then, on December 23, 1972 a massive earthquake destroyed Managua. Between 12,000 and 20,000 died and 300,000 were left homeless. Somoza used the emergency to extend his political and economic power, naming himself the chairman of the National Emergency Committee. His blatant misuse of relief funds further alienated Nicaraguans. His wealth increased while the Nicaraguan population became one of the poorest in Central America. Unemployment reached 36 percent, illiteracy was 74 percent, and 60 percent of the population suffered from malnutrition. Because the Constitution banned active military officers from the presidency, Somoza resigned as directive head of the National Guard in 1973 but remained its administrative head. Amid widespread repression and the imprisonment of many opposition leaders, Somoza won the 1974 election, but the breakdown of the social and economic order and an increase in crime brought rising opposition from within the middle and upper classes.

Outdoor market, Managua, Nicaragua. UNITED NATIONS. REPRODUCED BY PERMISSION

On January 10, 1978, the vocal and popular Pedro Joaquín Chamorro Cardenal, editor of *La Prensa* and founder of the opposition Democratic Liberation Union (UDEL), was assassinated. There followed three days of demonstrations, which the National Guard put down violently. UDEL demanded Somoza's resignation and supported a general strike. Somoza answered with a news blackout and press closures. The Catholic Church stepped up its opposition to Somoza as priests began preaching against the government from the pulpit. Student protests increased throughout the late 1970s, and clashes with the National Guard occurred. In July 1978 UDEL joined with Alfonso Callejo's Nicaraguan Democratic Movement (MDM) and Los Doce (Group of Twelve) to form the Broad Opposition Front (FAO) under the leadership of Rafael Cordova Rivas. Los Doce emerged in November 1977, when twelve prominent Nicaraguans declared in *La Prensa* that there could be no solution to the crisis without the full participation of the FSLN. The church, led by Archbishop Miguel Obando y Bravo, openly supported the FAO, which now demanded Somoza's resignation.

The FSLN, meanwhile, organized the United People's Movement (MPU), which incorporated trade unions, student groups, and progressive Christian activists into the revolutionary struggle. By December 1974 the FSLN had emerged as a major guerrilla force in Nicaragua. A daring raid on a Somoza associate's Christmas party in that year and the 1978 occupation of the National Palace under the leadership of Comandante Cero (Edén Pastora Gómez) brought the release of FSLN prisoners (including Daniel Ortega Saavedra), huge ransom payments, public broadcast of Sandinista objectives, and wage increases. Although Somoza retaliated with new rounds of repression, the FSLN's actions widely publicized its cause and enhanced its popularity, enabling the Sandinistas to become the largest and best-organized opposition group in the country.

By spring 1979 it was apparent that Somoza had lost control, but he was unwilling to admit defeat. His orders to bomb civilian areas left hundreds dead or homeless and merely strengthened his opponents' resolve. In May leading Somocistas fled Nicaragua, and the United States attempted unsuccessfully to impose a plan called by opponents "Somocismo sin Somoza." After terrible violence in which an estimated 50,000 Nicaraguans died, Somoza finally fled to the United States and then to Paraguay. On July 19, 1979, the FSLN took control of Nicaragua, ending the forty-six-year Somoza dynasty.

After the overthrow of Somoza, the FSLN set up a three-person junta that shared power with the Council of State, chosen in 1980 by the various interest sectors. The FSLN also dominated the legislature, although other political and economic groups were represented. Effective power was held, however, by the nine-person FSLN National Directorate. There was popular participation through organizations of workers, peasants, farm laborers, women, youth, professionals, and neighborhood Committees for the Defense of Sandinismo. Although Marxist influence was obvious and Nicaragua established close diplomatic and trade links with Cuba and the Soviet Union (USSR), the FSLN followed a nationalist party line, formally affiliating with the Socialist International in London rather than the Comintern in Moscow. But the subsequent U.S. embargo and efforts to overthrow the Sandinista government resulted in greater dependency on Cuba and the USSR.

The early years of FSLN rule were marked by successful literacy and primary health campaigns that established schools and clinics throughout the nation. An agrarian reform redistributed land, and other restructuring measures promoted a mixed capitalist-socialist economy. National elections in 1984 gave the FSLN an overwhelming victory. At the United States's urging, opposition parties boycotted the election, but international observers deemed the elections fair. Daniel Ortega was elected president of the republic with 68 percent of the votes cast.

THE CONTRA WAR

Relations with the United States deteriorated throughout the Sandinista decade. U.S. president Jimmy Carter provided some aid, but Ronald Reagan's hard-line anticommunism led him in to suspend assistance and to block International Monetary Fund (IMF) and World Bank assistance in 1981. The Reagan administration depicted Nicaragua as a destabilizing influence in the region and linked the FSLN to the guerrilla movement in El Salvador. In December 1981 the White House secretly authorized the Central Intelligence Agency (CIA) to spend $19.8 million to aid FSLN opponents and to create counterrevolutionary forces—the Contras. The Contras operated from camps in Honduras and Costa Rica. Their military operations seriously hampered the Sandinistas' ability to focus on the revolution's social and economic reforms. The CIA mined Nicaraguan harbors, and despite a May 1984 International Court of Justice ruling against the actions of the United States, it continued to support hostilities, even after the U.S. Congress, through the Boland amendments (1982–1984), had prohibited such support. In what became a major scandal for the Reagan administration, the United States began channeling funds received from illicit sale of arms to Iran to CIA-trained Contras. In May 1985 President Reagan inaugurated a total embargo on trade with Nicaragua that continued until March 1990.

The Sandinistas were receptive to international efforts to end the growing civil war, especially to the Mexican-sponsored Contadora Plan, but the United States resisted. Finally, in 1989 all sides agreed to a Central American peace plan proposed by Costa Rican president Oscar Arias Sánchez with strong support from the other Central American states. The Arias Plan brought an end to the Contra war with the promise of another free election in Nicaragua.

The last years of the FSLN's revolutionary period in power were marked by spiraling inflation and a weak economy, stemming from the financial and human costs of the Contra war, U.S. financial and trade embargoes, and government mismanagement. A rollback of many of the revolution's gains occurred as the FSLN leadership implemented an austerity program. By 1989 the currency had been devalued and prices had skyrocketed. Shortages and rationing were common. The FSLN was able to undermine support for the Contras through modifying land-reform policies, improving relations with Atlantic Coast indigenous groups, and implementing grassroots discussions of constitutional reform. The Contras suffered major military reverses as the Nicaraguan government led a sustained but costly offense, but the conflict demoralized the population. From 1983 to 1987, 40,000 lives were lost in the fighting. The damage caused by the Contra war by 1987 was estimated at between $1.5 and $4 billion. Sixty-two percent of government expenditures went to defense, which necessitated reductions in previous priority areas such as education and health care.

VIOLETA BARRIOS DE CHAMORRO AND THE UNO

As proposed by the Arias Peace Plan, Nicaragua prepared for elections in 1990, a time of extreme economic hardship. The GDP had fallen 11.7 percent from 1988 to 1990, and the country faced a $1.2 billion trade deficit. Per capita income plummeted and unemployment reached 35 percent, and the traditional support base of the FSLN was eroding as a result of the austerity measures imposed by the government to regain control over the economy. Despite pre-election polls favoring the Sandinistas, Violeta Barrios de Chamorro, the widow of the slain newspaper publisher Pedro Chamorro, won the national elections. She received the overt backing of the (George H. W.) Bush administration in Washington and was the candidate of the United Nicaraguan Opposition (UNO), a coalition of fourteen political parties from the Left to far Right. On April 25, 1990, Chamorro took office and U.S. aid to Nicaragua was restored.

Despite winning 51 of 92 National Assembly seats, internal divisions within UNO prevented a unified mandate. The FSLN remained the most unified and popular single party (with 39 seats) and was in control of the army under the command of Humberto Ortega Saavedra. Chamorro's political approach was national reconciliation, but her first year in office was characterized by private-sector and public-employee strikes and challenges from both the Right and the Left. UNO's tenuous coalition splintered; the Contras refused to disarm; and the FSLN and labor unions continued to defend the gains of the revolution. In March 1991 the Chamorro government implemented a recommended IMF policy similar to the 1988 FSLN plan, but hoped some of the negative economic repercussions would be softened with substantial U.S. aid. But the United States was slow to respond to aid requests, claiming Chamorro was not taking adequate steps to suppress the FSLN or privatize the economy. In November 1991 there was a resurgence of violence when former Contras, dissatisfied with the terms of the peace accord and opposed to the ongoing presence of the FSLN in Chamorro's government, organized themselves as the "Re-Contras." Supporting Chamorro was the Committee on Nicaraguan Recuperation and Development (CORDENIC), founded by Foreign Minister Enrique Dreyfuss and Minister to the President Antonio Lacayo. This think tank of businessmen and intellectuals advocated a moderate political approach and prepared economic policies and programs aimed at rebuilding the country.

As for the FSLN, it was headed in the early 1990s by a triumvirate of Luis Carrión, Bayardo Arce Castaño, and Henry Ruíz. Humberto Ortega resigned from the Sandinista Directorate and Sandinista Assembly to remain as head of the Nicaraguan army. Although the 1990 election forced the FSLN to reexamine its organization and policies, it emerged from the electoral loss as the best-organized political party in Nicaragua and the key to ensuring political stability.

THE RISE OF NEOLIBERALISM AND THE RETURN OF THE LEFT

As the postrevolutionary era began, the greatest threat that President Chamorro and the process of democracy faced in Nicaragua was not from the Left but from the Right. In 1994 the "Group of Three" (Vice President Virgilio Godoy, Managua mayor Jose Arnoldo Alemán Lacayo, and legislative president Alfredo César) embarked upon an international campaign to oust Chamorro, and attempted to use illegal congressional sessions to undercut her position. Chamorro's government suffered from persistent trade and budget deficits, which were exacerbated by the impact of a 1992 earthquake. Nicaragua's political system stabilized in 1995 with the reform of the 1987 Sandinista constitution, resulting in new powers for the National Assembly, including a presidential veto override for the Assembly and a more even distribution of power among the four branches of government. In 1996 Arnoldo Alemán (b. 1946) was elected president as the leader of a conservative coalition called the Liberal Alliance. Alemán accelerated the neoliberal policies of the postrevolutionary era, focusing on privatization and free trade. But the impact of 1998's Hurricane Mitch, which killed thousands, left two million homeless, and caused $10 billion of damage, undercut the modest economic gains of the 1990s. By 2000 Nicaragua was identified as a "Heavily Indebted Poor Country" (HIPC) by the IMF and qualified for a debt-relief initiative. The opposition parties benefited, and in local elections the FSLN swept the Managua municipal elections. In the 2001 presidential elections Alemán was ousted by the Liberal Constitutional Party leader, Enrique Bolaños, who narrowly defeated the FSLN candidate Daniel Ortega Saavedra. Despite three consecutive presidential defeats since 1990 and the taint of corruption charges, the FSLN retained Ortega as party leader.

While Bolaños continued on the neoliberal economic path, the main focus of his administration was a vigorous anticorruption campaign. In 2002 former president Alemán was convicted of corruption and embezzlement and sentenced to twenty years imprisonment, which was later changed to house arrest. Nicaragua's dire economic situation was relieved somewhat in 2004 when the World Bank erased 80 percent of Nicaragua's debt and Russia wrote off its Soviet-era debt. Negotiations with the United States and other regional powers resulted in the 2005 approval of the Central American Free Trade Agreement (CAFTA), but this was not enough to promote real economic recovery. Economic growth remained centered on agricultural export production, some increase in foreign investment, remittances from Nicaraguans living abroad, and an emerging tourism economy. None of this was able to offset increasing the popular discontent that boiled over in 2005, ignited by fuel-price and cost-of-living increases. Bolaños's government faced a political crisis over a plan initiated by Congress to decrease the power of the executive through a constitutional reform. A full-blown crisis was avoided when Congress agreed to back off on the reforms until after Bolaños left office in 2007.

The political fallout of Bolaños's anticorruption campaign and continuing economic crisis provided the backdrop for the November 2006 presidential elections. A center-Right vote split resulted in Daniel Ortega Saavedra's return to the presidency. Although the Marxism of his revolutionary years has been moderated, Ortega stated that he will challenge the "savage capitalism" of the previous administrations, and he has established relations with Venezuela's Hugo Chávez and Cuba's Fidel Castro. Nicaragua's recent election results seem to reflect a swing to the Left occurring throughout Latin America. Although constitutional democracy has been clearly established in Nicaragua, and the FSLN was able to recast itself as an effective political opposition party, it will be interesting to see if the FSLN can resurrect the pragmatic socialism of the past to effectively address the economic and social problems facing Nicaragua in the twenty-first century.

See also **Barrios de Chamorro, Violeta; Bryan-Chamorro Treaty (1914); Central America; Central Intelligence Agency (CIA); Chamorro Cardenal, Pedro Joaquín; Chamorro Vargas, Emiliano; Clayton-Bulwer Treaty (1850); Contras; Estrada, Juan José; Filibustering; Iturbide, Agustín de; Knox-Castrillo Treaty (1911); Managua; Miskitos; Moncada, José María; Mora Porrás, Juan Rafael; Nicaragua, Sandinista National Liberation Front (FSLN); Ortega Saavedra, Daniel; Ortega Saavedra, Humberto; Plan of Iguala; Prensa, La (de Nicaragua); Sandino, Augusto César; Solórzano, Carlos; Somoza Debayle, Luis; Somoza García, Anastasio; Tipitapa Agreements; United States-Latin American Relations; Walker, William; Zelaya, José Santos; Zeledón, Benjamín Francisco.**

BIBLIOGRAPHY

Anderson, Leslie, and Lawrence Dodd. *Learning Democracy: Citizen Engagement and Electoral Choice in Nicaragua, 1990–2001.* Chicago: University of Chicago Press, 2005.

Babb, Florence. *After Revolution: Mapping Gender and Cultural Politics in Neoliberal Nicaragua.* Austin: University of Texas Press, 1994.

Black, George. *The Triumph of the People: The Sandinista Revolution in Nicaragua.* London: Zed Press, 1981.

Booth, John A. *The End and the Beginning: The Nicaraguan Revolution*, 2nd edition. Boulder, CO: Westview Press, 1985.

Burns, E. Bradford. *Patriarch and Folk: The Emergence of Nicaragua, 1798–1858.* Cambridge, MA: Harvard University Press, 1991.

Cabezas, Omar. *Fire from the Mountain: The Making of a Sandinista.* New York: Plume, 1986.

Crawley, Eduardo D. *Dictators Never Die: A Portrait of Nicaragua and the Somoza Dynasty.* New York: Palgrave Macmillan, 1979.

Dickey, Christopher. *With the Contras.* New York: Simon and Schuster, 1987.

Dore, Elizabeth. *Myths of Modernity: Peonage and Patriarchy in Nicaragua.* Durham, NC: Duke University Press, 2006.

Dozier, Craig L. *Nicaragua's Mosquito Shore: The Years of British and American Presence.* Birmingham: University of Alabama Press, 2002.

Gilbert, Dennis. *Sandinistas: The Party and the Revolution.* London: Basil Blackwell, 1990.

Gobat, Michel. *Confronting the American Dream: Nicaragua under U.S. Imperial Rule.* Durham, NC: Duke University Press, 2005.

Gould, Jeffrey. *To Lead as Equals: Rural Protest and Political Consciousness in Chinandega, Nicaragua, 1912–1979.* Chapel Hill: University of North Carolina Press, 1991.

Harrison, Brady. *Agent of Empire: William Walker and the Imperial Self in American Literature.* Athens: University of Georgia Press, 2004.

Kinzer, Stephen. *Blood of Brothers: Life and War in Nicaragua.* Cambridge, MA: Harvard University Press, 2007.

Millett, Richard. *Guardians of the Dynasty.* New York: Orbis Books, 1977.

Navarro-Genie, Marco A. *Augusto "César" Sandino: Messiah of Light and Truth.* Syracuse, NY: Syracuse University Press, 2002.

Ortega Saavedra, Humberto. *Cincuenta Años de lucha Sandinista.* Havana, Cuba: Editorial de Ciencias Sociales, 1980.

Ramirez, Sergio, and Robert Edgar Conrad, eds. *Sandino: The Testimony of a Nicaraguan Patriot, 1921–1934.* Princeton, NJ: Princeton University Press, 1990.

Randall, Margaret. *Sandino's Daughters Revisited.* New Brunswick, NJ: Rutgers University Press, 1994.

Walker, Thomas W., ed. *Revolution and Counterrevolution in Nicaragua, 1979–1990.* Boulder, CO: Westview Press, 1991.

Walker, Thomas W. *Nicaragua: The Land of Sandino.* 4th edition. Boulder, CO: Westview Press, 2003.

HEATHER THIESSEN-REILY

NICARAGUA, CONSTITUTIONS.

Nicaragua was an original signatory of the Federal Constitution of the Central American Federation in 1824. In April 1838, it left the union and promulgated its first constitution in November of that year. Ideas of liberty, sovereignty, and individual rights were borrowed from the French Revolution and the U.S. Constitution. A new constitution was written in November 1857, after the Conservative General Tomás Martínez came to power in a coup. Separation of church and state was incorporated into the constitution drafted by the Liberal government of General José Santos Zelaya in 1893.

The first three decades of the twentieth century were marked by U.S. intervention in Nicaragua. The next constitution was not written until March 1939, two years after National Liberal Party leader Anastasio Somoza García became president. In 1950 Somoza and Conservative leader Emiliano Chamorro reached a peace settlement and modified the 1939 document. From that point, the Somoza family ruled arbitrarily until the Sandinistas ousted Anastasio Somoza Debayle in 1979.

In July 1979 the Governing Junta of National Reconstruction abolished the constitution and governed by decree until 1986. On 9 January 1987 the National Assembly promulgated the current constitution. The Sandinista principles of self-determination, political pluralism, a mixed economy, and a nonaligned foreign policy imbue the legal framework.

See also **Central America; Chamorro Vargas, Emiliano; Martínez, Tomás; Somoza García, Anastasio; Zelaya, José Santos.**

BIBLIOGRAPHY

Thomas Karnes, *The Failure of Union: Central America, 1824–1960* (1961).

Ralph Lee Woodward, Jr., *Central America: A Nation Divided,* 2d ed. (1985).

Kenneth J. Mijeski, *The Nicaraguan Constitution of 1987* (1991).

Additional Bibliography

Esgueva Gómez, Antonio. *Las constituciones políticas y sus reformas en la historia de Nicaragua.* Managua: IHNCA, 2000.

MARK EVERINGHAM

NICARAGUA, ORGANIZATIONS

This entry includes the following articles:

MARITIME CANAL COMPANY OF NICARAGUA
SANDINISTA DEFENSE COMMITTEES

MARITIME CANAL COMPANY OF NICARAGUA

The Maritime Canal Company was incorporated by an act of U.S. Congress in 1889 for the purpose of constructing a transisthmian canal through Nicaragua. After the Civil War, U.S. interest in an interoceanic canal intensified, but the government re-mained unwilling to participate in the project. When Congress incorporated the Maritime Canal Company, it excluded the government from any fiscal responsibilities. The project began on 23 March 1887, when Aniceto G. Menocal, a civil engineer with the U.S. Navy, negotiated an agreement with the Nicaraguan government that allowed his company to construct a canal within a ten-year period and to own it for ninety-nine years, after which it would revert to Nicaragua. Construction began at Greytown in 1889, and by 1893 the company had spent approximately $4 million on dredging the Greytown harbor, clearing the jungle, and other preliminary work. The project then collapsed owing to a lack of continued funding, corruption, and Nicaragua's political turmoil. Menocal's project officially came to an end in 1899, when the Maritime Canal Company defaulted on its contract. By that time other forces emerged that contributed to the U.S. government's undertaking of a transisthmian canal project.

See also **Panama Canal.**

BIBLIOGRAPHY

United States Isthmian Canal Commission, *Report of the Isthmian Canal Commission*, 1899–1901 (1904).

Gerstle Mack, *The Land Divided: A History of the Panama Canal and Other Isthmian Canal Projects* (1944).

Roscoe R. Hill, "The Nicaraguan Canal Idea Until 1898," *Hispanic American Historical Review* 28 (1948): 197–211.

Additional Bibliography

Gobat, Michel. *Confronting the American Dream: Nicaragua under U.S. Imperial Rule*. Durham: Duke University Press, 2005.

Herrera, René. *Relaciones internacionales y poder político en Nicaragua*. México, D.F.: Colegio de México, 1992.

THOMAS M. LEONARD

SANDINISTA DEFENSE COMMITTEES

The Sandinista Defense Committees constituted the largest popular mass organization in Nicaragua during the Sandinista administration (1979–1990). A grassroots organization, Sandinista Defense Committees (CDSs) arose from a nucleus of prerevolutionary clandestine neighborhood groups known as Civil Defense Committees that promoted support for the Sandinista National Liberation Front (Frente Sandinista de Liberación Nacional—FSLN). Serving as independent yet integral components of the Sandinista Party, CDSs were conduits between the government and the people, and in the immediate postwar period they assumed traditional responsibilities of the state, including social and administrative services.

Early objectives of the CDS included unification of the populace and advancement of the revolution. Through the achievement of these goals, the CDS hoped to alleviate many societal problems. Immediate concerns included the implementation of basic social, educational, and health services. Under the guidance of the Sandinista Party, the CDS helped to direct literacy campaigns, vaccination programs, food distribution, construction, and civil defense projects. Open to any individual over the age of fourteen, regardless of party affiliation or social status, membership in the CDS soared to more than one-half million in the early 1980s. Organized by neighborhood blocks and by rural areas, the CDS included zonal, regional, and national committees through which information, ideas, and complaints flowed between the people and the state.

As its strength in numbers increased, so did charges of corruption, favoritism, and abuses of power. To its supporters, the CDS was a true form of participatory democracy. To its critics, it functioned as a dictatorial association. Four years after the revolution, approximately half of the CDSs were defunct. It took the threat of external counterrevolutionary attacks on the FSLN to revive the CDS. After reorganization in the mid-1980s, democratically elected CDS leaders worked more closely with local and state governments. Following the 1990 election of the opposition president Violeta Barrios De Chamorro, the CDS officially disbanded.

See also **Barrios de Chamorro, Violeta; Nicaragua, Sandinista National Liberation Front (FSLN).**

BIBLIOGRAPHY

Luis Hector Serra, "The Sandinista Mass Organizations" *Nicaragua in Revolution,* edited by Thomas W. Walker (1979), pp. 105–106.

Carlos María Vilas, *The Sandinista Revolution: National Liberation and Social Transformation in Central America* (1986), pp. 239–244.

Gary Ruchwarger, *People in Power: Forging a Grassroots Democracy in Nicaragua* (1987), pp. 90–94, 148–186.

Luis Hector Serra, "Grassroots Organizations," *Revolution and Counterrevolution in Nicaragua,* edited by Thomas W. Walker (1991), pp. 64–75.

Additional Bibliography

Hoyt, Katherine. *The Many Faces of Sandinista Democracy*. Athens: Ohio University Center for International Studies, 1997.

Vargas, Oscar-René. *El sandinismo: veinte años después*. Managua: ANE: NORAD: CNE, 1999.

Wellinga, Klaas. *Entre la poesía y la pared: Política cultural sandinista, 1979–1990.* Costa Rica: FLACSO; Amsterdam: Thela, 1994.

D. M. SPEARS

NICARAGUA, SANDINISTA NATIONAL LIBERATION FRONT (FSLN).

The Sandinistas are the revolutionaries who toppled the Somoza dictatorship in Nicaragua in July 1979. In July 1961 Carlos Fonseca Amador, Tomás Borge, and Silvio Mayorga formed the Sandinista National Liberation Front (Frente Sandinista de Liberación Nacional, FSLN). Their military actions in the 1960s were failures. In 1975 the Sandinistas divided into three ideological factions. The dominant Prolonged Popular War (GPP) faction was led by Fonseca, Borge, and Henry Ruíz. The Proletarian Tendency of Jaime Wheelock Román, Luis Carrión (b. 1952), and Carlos Nuñez (1951–1990) rejected the GPP's Maoist notion of voluntarism and focused on factory workers and barrio dwellers. The third (Tercerista) faction of Humberto Ortega Saavedra, Daniel Ortega Saavedra, and Víctor Tirado (b. 1940) sought tactical alliances with businessmen, religious leaders, and professionals in 1977 and 1978. The three factions publicly united in March 1979. On July 19, they marched into Managua to assume political power.

The Sandinistas pursued the goals of national sovereignty, social security, agrarian reform, literacy, and a nonaligned international status. By 1982 they were confronted by a counterrevolutionary force supported by the Reagan administration. The Sandinistas dominated the first free election in Nicaragua's history, held in November 1984. They became the minority party in the National Assembly after losing the February 1990 election to the Nicaraguan Opposition Union. The Sandinistas held their first party congress in July 1991.

Serious political differences emerged within the party in the mid-1990s. The debate between orthodox leftists and moderate elements culminated in a confrontation at a special party congress in May 1994. Daniel Ortega was reelected party general secretary, and his orthodox faction won control of the Sandinista Assembly and two-thirds of the National Directorate, the party executive committee. The moderate elements described the results as a setback for democracy within the party and for the country at large. Prominent intellectuals and moderate professional and working-class members of the FSLN resigned in the latter 1990s, and many of them joined the Sandinista Renewal Movement (MRS). The split also led to the closing of the party newspaper, *Barricada*.

In September 1997 the FSLN and the Nicaraguan government under the Constitutionalist Liberal Arnoldo Alemán (b. 1946) announced an accord on the controversial issue of property. The accord created a tribunal system to rule on the properties in dispute on a case-by-case basis, consistent with provisions of Law 209 passed by the National Assembly in November 1995. On May 18, 1998, the 103rd anniversary of the birth of the Nicaraguan revolutionary Augusto Sandino, the FSLN held its second party congress that shifted power decidedly in favor of the orthodox position. During the administrations of Alemán (1996–2001) and Enrique Bolaños (2002–2007), the FSLN held about 40 percent of the National Assembly, and important municipal and departmental offices throughout the country. In 2005 an alliance between the FSLN and the Constitutionalist Liberal Party restricted the power of President Bolaños. Representatives loyal to Alemán and Ortega cooperated to block constitutional reforms and policy initiatives in the National Assembly in a veto-proof majority.

During the electoral campaign in May 2006 the FSLN presented a plan of government that promised to address problems with employment, health, poverty, and education, to reject the Central American Free Trade Agreement (CAFTA), and to reconsider economic reforms requested by the International Monetary Fund. FSLN candidate Daniel Ortega won the presidency on November 5, 2006, with just under 38 percent of the national vote, and was inaugurated on January 10, 2007. The FSLN won departmental control of Estelí, Leon, Matagalpa, Chinandega, Managua, and Jinotega, among others, and thirty-seven of ninety-one legislative seats in the National Assembly. FSLN loyalists were named to the Supreme Court of Justice and the Supreme Electoral Council.

In March 2007 the FSLN complied with an agreement with the Constitutionalist Liberal Party to lift completely the conditions of house arrest and movement imposed on former president Arnoldo

Alemán in 2003 for corruption and misappropriation of funds. During the first months of the Ortega government, the FSLN clashed with the United States on an array of issues related to trade and economic policy, immigration, and extradition of criminals. The Ortega administration named Sandinista Samuel Santos (b. 1938) foreign minister. Santos began an immediate review of loan conditions from international financial institutions, and sought to improve diplomatic relations with leftist governments in Latin America such as Venezuela and Bolivia.

See also **Communism; Nicaragua; Nicaragua, Organizations: Sandinista Defense Committees; Ortega Saavedra, Daniel.**

BIBLIOGRAPHY

Cardenal, Ernesto. *La Revolución Perdida*. Managua, Nicaragua: Anama, 2003.

Gilbert, Dennis. *Sandinistas: The Party and the Revolution*. New York: Basil Blackwell, 1988.

Laramée, Pierre. "Differences of Opinion: Interviews with Sandinistas." *NACLA Report on the Americas* 28, no. 5 (March–April 1995).

United States Department of State, Bureau of Western Hemisphere Affairs. "Background Note: Nicaragua." January 2007. Available from http://www.state.gov/r/pa/ei/bgn/1850.htm

Vilas, Carlos M. *The Sandinista Revolution*. New York: Monthly Review Press, 1986.

Walker, Thomas W., ed. *Reagan versus the Sandinistas: The Undeclared War on Nicaragua*. Boulder, CO: Westview Press, 1987.

MARK EVERINGHAM

NICARAO. The Nicarao are an ethnic group of Mexican Nahuatl origin. The Nicarao settled in Classic and Postclassic times around Lake Managua and Lake Nicaragua, where they established a number of towns, some of which later became the foundations for the Spanish cities of León, Managua, Granada, and Chinandega. They developed commerce and other relations with native peoples already in the region. These activities led to a war with the Chorotegans that ended about CE 1200 with the establishment of the Nicarao around Lake Nicaragua and especially on Ometepe Island. Gil González Dávila, who encountered these people on his 1523 expedition to Nicaragua, referred to their chief as Nicarao. On his peaceful visit he claimed to have baptized more than thirty-two thousand. There is controversy over the population of the Nicarao at the time of the Conquest, but it appears to have been in the range of one hundred thousand to two hundred thousand among a total Indian population of Pacific Nicaragua of about a half million. Slave exports to other colonies and disease quickly decimated their numbers, although enough survived to become a part of the ethnic foundation of modern Nicaragua.

See also **González Dávila, Gil; Indigenous Peoples; Slave Trade.**

BIBLIOGRAPHY

Doris Stone, *Pre-Columbian Man Finds Central America: The Archaeological Bridge* (1972).

William L. Sherman, *Forced Native Labor in Sixteenth-Century Central America* (1979).

Linda Newson, *Indian Survival in Colonial Nicaragua* (1987).

William R. Fowler, Jr., *The Cultural Evolution of Ancient Nahua Civilizations: The Pipil-Nicarao of Central America* (1989).

Additional Bibliography

Chapman, Anne MacKaye. *Los Nicarao y los Chorotega según las fuentes históricas*. San Juan, Costa Rica: Ciudad Universitaria, 1974.

Pérez Estrada, Francisco. *Los nahuas de Nicaragua*. Managua: Talleres Nacionales, 1962.

RALPH LEE WOODWARD JR.

NICUESA, DIEGO (1464–c. 1511). Diego de Nicuesa (*b.* 1464; *d.* ca. 1 March 1511), Spanish explorer. Born in Baeza, Spain, and raised in the house of Don Enrique Enríquez, uncle of Ferdinand V, Nicuesa was appointed on June 9, 1509, as governor of the reportedly rich Veragua, or Castilla del Oro (between Cape Gracias a Dios, at the border of Nicaragua and Honduras, and the middle of the Gulf of Darién). He left Hispaniola in November 1509 with 700 men, but shipwreck and hunger quickly reduced their numbers. Nicuesa continued on foot from a river near Carreto, eventually establishing a small fort at Nombre de Dios. He departed upon learning that Martín Fernández de Enciso had encroached on his territory to establish the colony of Santa María la Antigua de Darién. Initially welcomed by the colonists to settle a dispute between Enciso and Vasco Núñez de Balboa, Nicuesa lost his popularity by ordering the surrender of all gold. He was forced to leave for Santo Domingo on an unseaworthy vessel on 1 March 1511, the last time he was seen.

See also **Explorers and Exploration: Spanish America.**

BIBLIOGRAPHY

D. León Fernández, *Historia de Costa Rica durante la dominación española, 1502–1821* (1889).

Ricardo Fernández Guardia, *History of the Discovery and Conquest of Costa Rica,* translated by Harry Weston Van Dyke (1913).

Ricardo Blanco Segura, *Historia eclesiástica de Costa Rica, 1502–1850* (1983).

Ralph Lee Woodward, Jr., *Central America: A Nation Divided,* 2d ed. (1985), pp. 26–27.

Additional Bibliography

Ruiz, Bruce. *Diego de Nicuesa: 1464–1511.* 2002. http://www.bruceruiz.net/PanamaHistory/diego_de_nicuesa.htm.

PHILIPPE L. SEILER

NIEMEYER SOARES FILHO, OSCAR

(1907–). Oscar Niemeyer Soares Filho is a Brazilian architect. Niemeyer was born on December 15, 1907, in Rio de Janeiro and attended the National School of Fine Arts there from 1930 to 1934. He began to work with Lucio Costa and Carlos Leão, leaders of the modern movement in Brazilian architecture, in 1934. From 1937 to 1943, he collaborated with and ultimately succeeded Costa as head of the design team for the Ministry of Education and Health building in Rio, which brought Niemeyer into contact with Le Corbusier, the Swiss-born French architect who consulted on the design. The raised peristyle design of the building infuses many of the characteristic Corbusian elements (rooftop garden, sun roof, and inverted roof) with Brazilian baroque expression.

In the late 1930s, Niemeyer once again worked with Costa. The Brazilian Pavilion for the 1939 New York World's Fair catapulted Costa, Niemeyer, and the whole Brazilian movement into the world spotlight. A fluid plan centers on an exotic garden layout, the work of the painter Roberto Burle Marx. In 1947, Niemeyer was asked to represent Brazil on a commission in the planning of the United Nations buildings in New York City. In the 1940s, the architect Walter Gropius named Niemeyer the "bird of paradise" of the architectural world.

Niemeyer's first major solo project was the plan for a group of buildings in Pampulha, a new suburb in Belo Horizonte, the capital of the state of Minas Gerais. The project was commissioned in 1941 by Juscelino Kubitschek de Oliveira (1902–1976), then mayor of Belo Horizonte and later president of Brazil (1956–1961). It incorporates the use of free forms, the interplay of light and shade, painting, and sculpture into the architectural formula. The complex includes the casino, which some have called Niemeyer's masterwork. It is a "narrative" building with ramps, elliptical corridors, promenades, and labyrinthine accessways to direct the flow, while colorful stones, glass, and textures paint the mood. The building has served as an art museum since the interdiction on gambling. The other buildings in the Niemeyer group are a circular restaurant with a sun roof, the yacht club with an inverted slope roof, and the São Francisco de Assis Chapel adorned with parabolic shells.

Niemeyer's 1955 design for the Museum of Modern Art in Caracas serves as an aesthetic watershed in his career. Borrowing design elements and forms, such as pyramidal shapes, reminiscent of neoclassicism, he distances himself somewhat from the informal functional focus of his earlier free-form designs. To the detriment of function and social need, this tendency is reiterated and extended further in the free-form modernism of the new capital city, Brasília, the plans for which were initiated following the election of Kubitschek to the presidency in 1956. Niemeyer served as chief architect for Novacap, the government building authority, between 1956 and 1961. Responsible for designing the public buildings, Niemeyer helped fulfill Lucio Costa's master plans for the new city. Between 1958 and 1961, he designed the president's residence of Alvorada Palace, the Supreme Court building, the Presidential

Chapel, the Three Towers Square, the National Theater, a group of buildings for the University of Brasília, the Arches Palace, and the Ministry of Justice.

Niemeyer returned to private practice in 1961 and worked on civic, commercial, and governmental projects, on large and small scales. In the mid-1960s, he designed urban redevelopment plans for Grasse, France, the Algarve in Portugal, and Algiers. In 1966 he designed the French Communist Party headquarters in Paris. He returned to Brazil in 1968 to lecture at the University of Rio de Janeiro. While there, he designed Satetyles, a telecommunications complex in Rio, Cuiabá University in Mato Grosso, and the Ministry of Defense in Brasília. In the 1970s and 1980s, he designed the Hotel Nacional in Rio, the cathedral in Brasília, numerous office buildings in Brazil and in France, the Anthropological Museum in Belo Horizonte, a zoo in Algiers, a samba stadium, sixty schools in the state of Rio de Janeiro, and a project for a convention center in Abu Dhabi in the United Arab Emirates.

Niemeyer has always lived in Rio de Janeiro, except for international commissions that take him abroad. Niemeyer resides in an apartment overlooking Copacabana. The house he designed in São Conrado, a suburb of Rio, has been named a city landmark. There are plans to redesign it as a museum for his work. He also designed a theater in São Paulo, an annex to the Supreme Court in Brasília, and a theater complex for the state of São Paulo.

Beyond his architectural planning and teaching, Niemeyer was the founder of the magazine *Modulo* in the 1950s. He has also received many international awards. They include the Lenin Peace Prize in 1963, the Benito Juárez Award for the Mexican Revolution Centennial in 1964, the Medal of the Polish Architectural Association in 1967, a gold medal from the American Institute of Architects in 1970, and a gold medal from the Parisian Académie d'Architecture in 1982. In 1988 he split the Pritzker Architecture Prize with Gordon Bunshaft of Skidmore, Owings, and Merrill.

His membership affiliations include honorary member of the American Academy of Arts and Sciences, Legion of Honor officer, commander of the Ordre des Arts et Lettres, honorary member of the Academy of Arts of the USSR, member of the European Academy of Arts, Sciences, and Humanities, and member of the Comitate Internazionale dei Garanti.

As of 2007, at the age of ninety-nine Niemeyer was still actively designing sculptures and making adjustments on his existing older works, many of them protected by historic heritage regulations from modifications by anyone other than himself.

See also **Architecture: Modern Architecture; Burle Marx, Roberto; Costa, Lúcio.**

BIBLIOGRAPHY

Oscar Niemeyer, *Minha experiencia em Brasília* (1961).

Rupert Spade, *Oscar Niemeyer* (1971).

Oscar Niemeyer, *A forma na arquitetura* (1977).

Alan Hess, "Perspectives: Back to Brasília," in *Progressive Architecture* 72 (October 1991): 97–98; "Interview with Oscar Niemeyer," in *Progressive Architecture* 72 (October 1991): 98–99.

David Underwood, *Oscar Niemeyer and Brazilian Free-form Modernism* (1994).

Additional Bibliography

Graça, Eduardo. "The Last of the Modernists." *Metropolis Magazine* (May 2006).

Hess, Alan. *Oscar Niemeyer Houses.* Photographs by Alan Weintraub. New York: Rizzoli, 2006.

Niemeyer, Oscar. *The Curves of Time: The Memoirs of Oscar Niemeyer.* London: Phaidon, 2000.

CAREN A. MEGHREBLIAN

NIEVES Y BUSTAMANTE, MARÍA

(1865/1871–1947/1948). The Peruvian writer María Nieves y Bustamante is best known for her two-volume masterpiece, *Jorge; o, El hijo del pueblo* (1892). Besides being a historical novel—that is to say, a narrative whose action takes place before the author's birth—*Jorge* also breaks ground as both a *costumbrista* and *regional* novel. Its history centers on the 1856–1858 civil war between the caudillos Ramón Castilla and Manuel Ignacio Vivanco, the author taking sides with the latter. Its *costumbrismo* resides in the portrayal of the people and their customs and specifically in practices associated with class and race, for the novel's protagonist, Jorge, is a mestizo. It is regionalist because the action does not concentrate on Lima (as was common for that time), nor on the Andes as a rural society (an up-and-coming trend during the period), but on Arequipa, Peru's second-largest city. Arequipa is portrayed as having a sophisticated, albeit culturally insensitive elite. The idea of a regional novel was both new and controversial. Clorinda Matto de Turner also dealt with this war in her second novel *Indole*, which she subtitled "Peruvian Novel," thereby taking sides with General Castilla's nation-building stance.

See also **Castilla, Ramón; Literature: Spanish America; Matto de Turner, Clorinda; Vivanco, Manuel Ignacio.**

BIBLIOGRAPHY

Primary Works

Matto de Turner, Clorinda. *Índole*. Lima: Tipo Litograrafía, 1891.

Nieves y Bustamante, María. *Jorge; o, El hijo del pueblo.* Arequipa: Imprenta de la Bolsa, 1892.

Secondary Works

Ferreira, Rocío. "Nación y narración/Historia y ficción en *Jorge o El hijo del pueblo.*" *Lucero: A Journal of Iberian and Latin American Studies* 8 (Spring 1997): 23–37.

Ward, Thomas. "Perú y Ecuador." *La narrativa histórica de escritoras latinoamericanas*, edited by Gloria da Cunha, 271–305. Buenos Aires: Ediciones Corregidor, 2004: 271–305.

THOMAS WARD

NIMUENDAJÚ, CURT (1883–1945).

Curt Nimuendajú (*b.* 17 April 1883); *d.* 10 December 1945), German-born immigrant who devoted his life to the study and defense of Brazil's indigenous peoples. Though not formally trained as an anthropologist, Nimuendajú is recognized for his prolific contributions to Brazilian ethnology and for his ability to immerse himself in indigenous cultures. Born Curt Unkel, he came to Brazil in 1903 at the age of twenty. Two years later he took up residence with the Apopocuva Guaraní, among whom he lived as an adopted member until 1908 and from whom he acquired the name Nimuendajú. His first significant ethnological publication (1914), dealing with Guaraní religion, resulted from these years.

Throughout his life, Nimuendajú lived among and visited numerous Brazilian indigenous groups. He received financing from foreign institutions such as the University of California at Berkeley and the Carnegie Institute through his collaboration with the American anthropologist Robert Lowie and from European museums for artifact collection. His collaboration with Lowie, initiated in the early 1930s, stimulated a period of intensive study of social organization among Gê groups and produced several scholarly publications, among them three monographs (*The Eastern Timbira; The Apinayé; The Serente*). He was also occasionally employed by the Indian Protection Service (SPI) where he left copious ethnographic documentation in field reports, and for whom, from 1921 to 1923, he led the team that established peaceful contact with the Parintintin of the Madeira River. In his later years, he received support from the Museu Goeldia (Belém) and the Museu Nacional (Rio de Janeiro). In Belém, a year before his death, Nimuendajú completed his monumental *Ethnohistorical Map of Brazil and Adjacent Regions* and the accompanying *Guide*. He died among the Tukuna Indians of the Solimões River.

See also **Indigenous Peoples; Pacification.**

BIBLIOGRAPHY

Herbert Baldus, "Curt Nimuendajú," in *Sociologia* 8, no. 1 (1946): 46–52.

D. Maybury-Lewis, ed., *Dialectical Societies: The Gê and Bororo of Central Brazil* (1979), pp. ix–xiv; *Mapa etno-histórico de Curt Nimuendajú* (1981), pp. 13–21.

Darcy Ribeiro, *Os índios e a civilização: A integração das populações indígenas no Brasil moderno* (1982), pp. 164–175.

Additional Bibliography

Correa, Filho Virgílio, "Curt Nimuendaju, 1883–1945: Un homem que fez o seu própio lar." In *Jangada Brasil* no. 32 (2001): 1–3.

Nimuendajú, Curt. "The Eastern Timbira." Translated and edited by Robert Lowie. In *American Archaeology and Ethnology,* Volume 41. Berkeley and Los Angeles: University of California Press, 1946.

Nimuendajú, Curt. *The Tukuna*. Los Angeles: University of California Press, 1952.

LAURA GRAHAM

NIÑO, PEDRO ALONSO

NIÑO, PEDRO ALONSO (c. 1468–c. 1505). Pedro Alonso Niño was a Spanish explorer known as el Negro. A native of Moguer, Spain, Niño acted as pilot of the Santa María during the first voyage of Christopher Columbus. In 1499 Niño and Christopher Guerra received permission from Bishop Juan Rodríguez De Fonseca to explore the Gulf of Paria. On the island of Margarita they bartered for a considerable quantity of pearls and then made their way to the Cubagua Islands, which they believed to be part of Tierra Firme. There they traded for a substantial amount of pearls and returned to Spain in April 1500, only to be imprisoned for allegedly concealing part of the wealth they had acquired in the New World. Niño was exonerated of all charges, was set free, and gained fame for participating in one of the most lucrative voyages to the New World.

See also **Conquistadores; Explorers and Exploration: Spanish America.**

BIBLIOGRAPHY

Samuel Eliot Morison, *The Great Explorers: The European Discovery of America* (1978), pp. 385 and 388.

Washington Irving, *Voyages and Discoveries of the Companions of Columbus,* edited by James W. Tuttleton (1986), pp. 19–22.

MICHAEL POLUSHIN

NIÑOS HÉROES

NIÑOS HÉROES. Niños Héroes, the young men killed at Cerro de Chapultepec on 13 September 1847, during the Mexican-American War. The public sculpture of these young heroes is Mexico's premier emblem of nationalism; the monument, at the west end of Mexico City's Paseo de la Reforma, symbolizes the greatness of a people. The staff and cadet volunteers of the Military Academy contributed seventy of the 1,000 or so defenders of Chapultepec Castle. Of these seventy, six were killed, three wounded, and one taken prisoner. Five of the Niños Héroes were cadets.

The seventy Military Academy defenders of Chapultepec were initially honored on 11 November 1847 by a medal; on 23 December another decoration was authorized for the group. The six who died in this action were not recognized until 3 March 1884, an action that was not ratified until 31 July 1926. Remains claimed to be those of the Niños Héroes were discovered on 25 March 1947 in Chapultepec Park; six months later (9 September 1947) the find was officially recognized (not without controversy) by congressional decree.

The six Niños Héroes are Lieutenant Juan de la Barrera, nineteen years old; Cadet Juan Escutia, less than nineteen, a cadet for five days; Cadet Francisco Márquez, at thirteen the youngest casualty; Cadet Agustín Melgar, younger than nineteen, who had been a cadet, expelled, then readmitted five days before he was killed; and Cadet Fernando Montes de Oca, younger than nineteen, found wrapped in a flag three days after the engagement, who had apparently jumped to his death to avoid capture; and fourteen-year-old Cadet Vicente Súarez Ferrer.

See also **Mexico, Wars and Revolutions: Mexican-American War.**

BIBLIOGRAPHY

Alberto María Carreno, *El Colegio militar de Chapultepec: 1847–1848,* 2d ed. (1972).

José Rogelio Álvarez, *Enciclopedia de México,* vol. 10 (1988), pp. 3,809–5,811.

Additional Bibliography

Heidler, David Stephen, and Jeanne T. Heidler. *The Mexican War.* Westport, CT: Greenwood Press, 2006.

Henderson, Timothy J. *A Glorious Defeat: Mexico and Its War with the United States.* New York: Hill and Wang, 2007.

Vázquez, Josefina Zoraida. *México al tiempo de su guerra con Estados Unidos, 1846-1848.* México: Secretaría de Exteriores: El Colegio de México: Fondo de Cultura Económica, 1997.

ROBERT HIMMERICH Y VALENCIA

NITRATE INDUSTRY

NITRATE INDUSTRY. Historically a crucial industry for Chile, nitrates were an important product for European and American farmers. Nitrates, the principal component of fertilizer and explosives, became an important commodity in the late nineteenth century. Discovered in large quantities in the Bolivian portion of the Atacama Desert and the Peruvian province of Tarapacá in the mid-nineteenth century, these deposits became important sources of income. It is not surprising, then, that Chile would annex these territories after defeating Peru and Bolivia during the War of the Pacific (1879–1883).

Through its military triumph, Chile acquired a monopoly on the world's supply of natural nitrates. Rather than retain ownership, however, which would have required assumption of a large debt, the Chilean government sold off the nitrate mines to private interests. Thus freed of the problems of running the industry, the government levied an export duty on its sales. For the next forty years this tax provided the Chilean government with approximately half its ordinary revenues.

The processing of nitrates was a labor-intensive procedure employing at its height approximately sixty thousand men. With a combination of dynamite and brute force, these laborers dug the nitrate from the hard desert floor, then transported it to refineries. Using the British-derived Shanks process of producing carbonate of soda, the ore was crushed and mixed with water, permitting the extraction of the pure nitrates. The mining and refining of nitrates was a dangerous enterprise which cost the lives of many miners. The high wages and relatively low cost of living at the mines, however, attracted large numbers of laborers, many of whom regarded working in the nitrate pampa as an opportunity to amass enough capital to start their own businesses in the south.

Although the producers of nitrates, the *salitreros,* had no competition, they did have to deal with the laws of supply and demand. The price of nitrates fluctuated, depending on the needs of agriculture and the presence of war. When demand declined, the producers reduced output to stabilize prices. This somewhat cumbersome tactic generally worked. After World War I, however, the Haber–Bosch process, an inexpensive method of producing synthetic nitrates, severely damaged the nitrate producers. First Germany, then Great Britain and Norway increased the output of nitrate substitutes, driving down the world price.

The Guggenheims, an American mining family, breathed new life into the *salitreros* after World War I by employing new techniques to refine low-grade ore. These processes, whose improvements relied heavily upon technology, merely slowed but did not arrest the collapse of the Chilean nitrate industry. What the Haber process began the Great Depression completed: after 1930, world demand for nitrates collapsed, devastating the Chilean economy. Still, nitrate production continues and Chile produces 69 percent of world production, as of the mid-1990s. The industry, at the end of the twentieth century, employed directly and indirectly about 100,000 people. Nitrate is used in production of gunpowder, construction materials, and in small quantities as a nutritional supplement.

See also **Mining: Modern; Privatization.**

BIBLIOGRAPHY

Markos Mamalakis, "The Role of Government in the Resource Transfer and Resource Allocation Processes: The Chilean Nitrate Sector, 1880–1930," in *Government and Economic Development,* edited by Gustav Ranis (1971), pp. 181–215.

A. Lawrence Stickel, "Migration and Mining: Labor in Northern Chile in the Nitrate Era, 1880–1930" (Ph.D. diss., Indiana University, 1979).

Michael Monteón, *Chile in the Nitrate Era* (1982).

Thomas F. O'Brien, *The Nitrate Industry and Chile's Crucial Transition: 1870–1891* (1982) and "'Rich Beyond the Dreams of Avarice': The Guggenheims in Chile," in *Business History Review,* 63 (1989): 122–159.

Additional Bibliography

Pinto Vallejos, Julio. *Trabajos y rebeldías en la pampa salitrera: El ciclo del salitre y la reconfiguración de las identidades populares (1850-1900).* Santiago de Chile: Editorial Universidad de Santiago, 1998.

Robles-Ortiz, Claudio. "Agrarian Capitalism in an Export Economy: Chilean Agriculture in the Nitrate Era, 1880–1930." PhD diss., University of California, Davis, 2002.

WILLIAM F. SATER

NIZA, MARCOS DE (?–1558). Marcos de Niza (*d.* 25 March 1558), Franciscan explorer and chronicler who searched for the Seven Cities of Cíbola. From the French Franciscan province of Aquitaine, Niza arrived in the Americas by 1531, serving in Peru and Guatemala before going to New Spain. In 1539, following his guide, Esteban, Niza traveled north from San Miguel de Culiacán in Sinaloa as far as Arizona and New Mexico, perhaps to within sight of the Zuni pueblo of Hawikuh. His

Relación del descubrimiento de las siete ciudades (Report of the Discovery of the Seven Cities) told of seven magnificent cities on the order of Mexico City and Cuzco and of vast quantities of gold and turquoise. The account was influential in kindling interest in the exploratory expedition undertaken by Francisco Vázquez de Coronado in 1540. Though serving as minister provincial in Mexico City, Niza accompanied Coronado, but when his claims about Cíbola proved false, he returned to New Spain. Ill and depressed, Niza completed his term as minister provincial, which concluded in 1543, at San Francisco de México. For the next few years he spent time in Jalapa, Xochimilco, and Mexico City, where he died and was buried.

See also **Seven Cities of Cíbola.**

BIBLIOGRAPHY

Fray Angelico Chávez, *Coronado's Friars* (1968).

Cleve Hallenbeck, *The Journey of Fray Marcos de Niza* (1987).

Additional Bibliography

Montané Martí, Julio C. *Por los senderos de la quimera: El viaje de fray Marcos de Niza.* Hermosillo: Instituto Sonorense de Cultura, 1995.

RICK HENDRICKS

NOBOA BEJARANO, GUSTAVO (1937–).

Gustavo Noboa served as vice-president of Ecuador under Jamil Mahuad (1998–2000) and was named interim president by Congress following a coup that overthrew Mahuad in January 2000. Born in Guayquil and trained as a lawyer, Noboa has served as provincial governor (1983–1984) and academic with ties to the business sector. Noboa resisted presidential politics until 1998, when he joined the Popular Democracy-Christian Democratic Union party (DP-UDC) and was nominated as Jamil Mahuad's vice-president.

Twenty-four hours after the three-man junta had removed Mahuad in January 2000, constitutional rule was restored with the nomination of Noboa, the sixth president in four years. A self-proclaimed political independent and devout Catholic, Noboa promised to restore credibility to Ecuador. He tried to revive the struggling economy by continuing to promote the dollarization of the economy, freeing US$400 million in frozen assets and privatizing state-owned industries. While Noboa briefly stabilized the economy, the country continued to be marred by political instability. After the election of junta leader Lucio Gutierrez in 2002, Noboa left office in January 2003.

In 2003, a judicial investigation declared irregularities in Noboa's handling of the external debt negotiations (July 2000) that cost the country US$9 billion. Protesting innocence and claiming to be the victim of an "unfair persecution" (BBC News 2003), Noboa received political asylum in the Dominican Republic, where he lived from 2003 to 2005. He returned to his hometown of Guayaquil when the Supreme Court cleared his charges but was soon was placed under house arrest. Ten months later he was released but in April 2007 the Supreme Court decided to uphold charges for his mishandling of the foreign debt negotiations (Associated Press 2007). As of 2007 he resides in Guayaquil with his wife, Isabel Baquerizo.

See also **Mahuad, Jamil.**

BIBLIOGRAPHY

Gerlach, Allen. *Indians, Oil, and Politics: A Recent History of Ecuador.* Wilmington, DE: Scholarly Press, 2003.

Political Database of the Americas. Georgetown University. 2007. http://pdba.georgetown.edu/Executive/Ecuador/pres.html.

SUZANNE CASOLARO

NOBOA Y ARTETA, DIEGO (1789–1870).

Diego Noboa y Arteta (also Novoa; *b.* 15 October 1789; *d.* 3 November 1870), president of Ecuador (1850–1851). A wealthy Guayaquil-born merchant and landowner, Noboa joined the governing Liberal triumvirate after the 6 March 1845 overthrow of President Juan José Flores. He was a candidate in the 1850 presidential election, which ended in a deadlock, with support in Congress evenly divided between Noboa and General Antonio de Elizade. When Vice President Manuel de Ascásubi assumed authority, Noboa's ally General José María Urbina led a revolt that placed Noboa in power. In 1851 Congress ratified the coup. Largely ineffectual during his brief tenure in office, Noboa is chiefly remembered for allowing the Jesuits to return to

Ecuador. In July 1851 his erstwhile friend Urbina (president, 1851–1856) staged a coup, sending Noboa into exile in Costa Rica. He died in Guayaquil.

See also **Ecuador: Since 1830; Flores, Juan José; Urbina, José María.**

BIBLIOGRAPHY

Frank MacDonald Spindler, *Nineteenth Century Ecuador: An Historical Introduction* (1987).

Mark J. Van Aken, *King of the Night: Juan José Flores and Ecuador, 1824–1864* (1989).

Additional Bibliography

Ayala Mora, Enrique. *Historia de la revolución liberal ecuatoriana.* Quito: Corporación Editora Nacional, 1994.

Maiguashca, Juan. *Historia y región en el Ecuador, 1830–1930.* Quito: Corporación Editora Nacional, 1984.

RONN F. PINEO

NOBRE, MARLOS (1939–).

NOBRE, MARLOS (1939–). Marlos Nobre is a Brazilian composer, conductor, and pianist. Born on February 18, 1939, Nobre began his musical studies at the age of five in the Pernambuco Conservatory in Recife and graduated in piano and theory in 1955. For his piano work *Nazarethiana,* he won an award and a scholarship for study in Teresópolis in the state of Rio de Janeiro, where he studied composition with Hans Joachim Koellreutter. Subsequent studies with Camargo Guarnieri, Alberto Ginastera, and Aaron Copland proved decisive in the development of his compositional style.

In 1962 Marlos Nobre established residence in Rio de Janeiro, where for several years he was director of the Radio Ministério Educação e Cultura, whose broadcasts showcased the works of Brazilian composers, including his own. Nobre's work with various major musical organizations within Brazil and in Europe has made him one of the best-known contemporary Brazilian musicians. His most significant major commissioned work is *Cantata del Chimborazo,* written for the celebration of the bicentennial of the birth of Simón Bolívar. Works such as *Rhythmetron* and *Ukrinmakrinkrin* have demonstrated enormous rhythmic vitality and a powerful creative imagination. In 1992 he led the Royal Philharmonic in the premiere of his *Columbus* oratorio, commemorating the quincentennial of the discovery voyage.

In the 1980s and 1990s Nobre served as visiting professor at Yale, the Juilliard School, and Indiana University, and as guest composer at the University of Georgia and Texas Christian University. In addition to composing commissioned works, he has appeared both as conductor and pianist with major orchestras in South America and Europe. Among his many awards for composition are the Gold Medal of Merit of the Joaquim Nabuco Foundation of Pernambuco (1999) and the Tomás Luis de Victoria Prize of Spain (2006). As of 2007 he was president of the National Music Committee of IMC/UNESCO, director of contemporary music programs at Radio MEC-FM of Brazil, and president of the Musica Nova Editions of Brazil.

See also **Music: Art Music; Radio and Television.**

BIBLIOGRAPHY

Gérard Béhague, *Music in Latin America* (1979).

David P. Appleby, *The Music of Brazil* (1983).

Additional Bibliography

Barce, Ramón. "Marlos Nobre." *Ritmo* 634 (1992): 48–49.

Bethell, Leslie, ed. *A Cultural History of Latin America: Literature, Music and the Visual Arts in the 19th and 20th Centuries.* Cambridge, U.K., and New York: Cambridge University Press, 1998.

Brown, Royal S. "An Interview with Marlos Nobre." *Fanfare* 18, no.1 (1994): 60–65.

Cáurio, Rita. *Brasil musical (básico).* Rio de Janeiro: Art Bureau, 1989.

Moore, Tom. "An Interview with Marlos Nobre." December 2002. Available from Música Brasileira (June 2007), http://www.músicabrasileira.org/marlosnobre/.

DAVID P. APPLEBY

NÓBREGA, MANUEL DA (1517–1570).

NÓBREGA, MANUEL DA (1517–1570). Manuel da Nóbrega (*b.* 18 October 1517; *d.* 18 October 1570), Jesuit missionary. Manuel da Nóbrega was the leader of the first Jesuit mission to Brazil in 1549. Born in Minho in 1517 to a noble Portuguese family, he joined the Society of Jesus in 1544, after being educated at the universities of Salamanca and Coimbra. He spent more than twenty years in Brazil, dedicating his life to founding missions among the Indians and schools for the children of the white population.

Arriving in Brazil on the fleet carrying the first governor, Nóbrega headed a group of six Jesuit missionaries. He concentrated on learning the Indian languages and gathering small tribes into segregated missions, or *aldeias*, where they were converted and protected from enslavement. In 1553 Nóbrega was selected as the first provincial general of the Jesuits in Brazil. In 1554, in the captaincy of São Vicente, Nóbrega helped to found a mission and *colégio* near the village of Piratininga, modern São Paulo.

Nóbrega's greatest accomplishment was the founding of local schools, missions, and the College of São Paulo. In 1560, after Nóbrega was relieved of his duties as provincial general, he helped the Portuguese regain control of Rio de Janeiro by securing valuable Indian allies to expel the French pirates from Guanabara Bay. In 1567, in the newly established city of Rio de Janeiro, he founded another Jesuit *colégio* to educate the sons of Indian chiefs and white settlers. Nóbrega served as rector of the *colégio* until his death.

Nóbrega's letters and his two works, *Informação das Terras do Brasil* (Information about Brazil [1550]) and *Diálogo sobre a Converso do Gentio* (Dialogue about the Conversion of the Heathen [1556])—the first true literary works on Brazil—give glowing descriptions of the natural beauty of the New World, the "simplicity" of the Indians, and their "receptivity" to Christianity. As the first superior of the Jesuits in Brazil, he supervised the missionary activities in the south of Brazil and throughout the colony. A good diplomat and politician as well as an organizer of missions and schools, he left colonial Brazil a rich legacy.

See also **Missions: Brazil.**

BIBLIOGRAPHY

Serafim Leite, *História da Companhia de Jesus no Brasil,* 10 vols. (1938–1950), and *Novas páginas da história do Brasil* (1965).

Helio Vianna, *História do Brasil colonial* (1975).

John Hemming, *Red Gold: The Conquest of the Brazilian Indians, 1500–1760* (1978).

Additional Bibliography

Mariz de Moraes, José. *Nóbrega: O primeiro jesuita do Brasil.* Rio de Janeiro: Relume Dumará, 2000.

Souza, Miguel Augusto Gonçalves de. *O descobrimento e a colonização portuguesa no Brasil.* Belo Horizonte: Editora Itatiaia, 2000.

PATRICIA MULVEY

NOCHE TRISTE. Noche Triste, the "sad night" of 30 June 1520, an episode marking the end of the first phase of the Spanish Conquest, when the Aztec confederation slaughtered a large Spanish force and its native allies, the Tlaxcalteca, as they fled from the imperial city of Tenochitlán-Tlatelolco. Less than a year earlier, the Spanish expedition led by Hernán Cortés made landfall in Veracruz and with the help of coastal and Tlaxclan allies marched inland and seized control of the Aztec capital. For months, the Spaniards reigned through Moctezuma, the Aztec ruler. Not long after, Cortés left the city to defeat and incorporate a larger Spanish force charged with arresting him. In his absence, the Spaniards under Pedro de Alvarado massacred unarmed warriors dancing in the temple festival of Toxcatl, triggering a massive revolt.

Cortés returned to find Spanish control of the city lost. Besieged in the heart of Tenochtitlán by tens of thousands of Aztec warriors, Cortés and his approximately 1,100 men had to flee to avoid complete destruction. To prevent their escape, the Aztecs had destroyed many of the bridges throughout the canal-crossed island city. The Spanish decided to try to sneak out during the night but Aztec sentinels soon spread the alarm. Attacked as they proceeded along the Tacuba causeway, the Spanish and Tlaxcalans found it hard to resist the onslaught by their opponents in canoes. Perhaps half of the Spanish force was killed, or captured and later sacrificed, along with more than 1,000 Tlaxcalans. The Spanish rout could be attributed to cunning Mexican military, but it also resulted from their greed—overloaded with booty, their progress was slow and cumbersome and their escape all the more difficult. The survivors successfully retreated to Tlaxcala to regroup. In May 1521, Cortes returned to lay siege on Tenochtitlán.

See also **Aztecs; Cortés, Hernán; Tenochtitlán; Tlaxcala.**

BIBLIOGRAPHY

Hugh Thomas, *Conquest of Mexico* (1993).

Additional Bibliography

Cortés, Hernán. *Letters from Mexico.* Translated by Anthony Pagden. New Haven, CT: Yale University Press, 1986.

Díaz del Castillo, Bernal. *The Discovery and Conquest of Mexico, 1517–1521.* Translated by A. P. Maudslay. New York: Farrar, Straus, and Cudahy, 1956.

León Portilla, Miguel, ed. *The Broken Spears: The Aztec Account of the Conquest of Mexico.* Translated by Lysander Kemp. Boston: Beacon Press, 1992.

Lockhart, James, ed. *We People Here: Nahuatl Accounts of the Conquest of Mexico.* Berkeley: University of California Press, 1993.

Schwartz, Stuart B., ed. *Victors and Vanquished: Spanish and Nahua Views of the Conquest of Mexico.* Boston: Bedford/St. Martin's, 2000.

JOHN E. KICZA

NOÉ, LUIS FELIPE (1933–). Luis Felipe Noé is an Argentine artist. Born on May 26, 1933, in Buenos Aires, Noé studied with Horacio Butler. Preoccupied with the chaotic modern world, Noé expressed his concerns by making figure and background hardly distinguishable from each other by using gestural brushstrokes, accidental painting, collage, and fragmented canvases. He was a cofounder of the New Figuration group in 1961, the same year that he painted his *Federal Series,* which includes *Agonic Image of Dorrego* and *General Quiroga Travels to His Death,* a depiction of the anarchy that characterized the Federal period in Argentine history. In these paintings he used primarily black and red to convey a climate of passion and death.

In 1964 Noé moved to New York City, where he had a Guggenheim Fellowship (1965–1966). During this period he wrote *Antiestética* (Antiesthetic), in which he argued that artists must focus on the act of creation rather than on traditional composition and techniques. At this time he began to experiment with concave mirrors to create chaotic environments but abandoned art in 1968 and devoted his time to teaching and organizing public painting experiences. In 1971 he published *Una sociedad colonial avanzada* (An Advanced Colonial Society), a satirical view of Argentina and Latin America. He resumed painting in 1975 with *Nature and Myths* and *Conquest and Destruction of Nature,* two series of colorful natural landscapes populated by mythical creatures in a state of metamorphosis. In 1976 he moved to Paris, where he lived until 1986, exhibiting frequently in Buenos Aires. After he made a trip to the Amazon in 1980, nature prevailed over mythical references in his work.

In 1987 Noé returned to Buenos Aires, where he further explored the genre of landscape on oversized canvases. He was invited to present his work at La Bienal de Cuenca, in Ecuador, in 1994 and at the Salón Nacional de la Provincial de Santa Fé, in Buenos Aires, in 1995. The Museo Nacional de Bellas Artes, in Buenos Aires, organized a retrospective of his work in 1995. In 2007 Noé was at work on a book, *La pintura desnuda* (Naked painting), and compiling essays for a book to be titled *No escritos.*

See also **Art: The Twentieth Century.**

BIBLIOGRAPHY

Gilbert Chase, *Contemporary Art in Latin America* (1970), pp. 153–154.

Mercedes Casanegra, *Luis Felipe Noé* (1988).

Additional Bibliography

Glusberg, Jorge. "Luis Felipe Noé: La Asunción del Caos." *ArteUna* (1995). Available from http://www.arteuna.com/Info.htm.

Glusberg, Jorge, and Luis Felipe Noé. *Lectura Conceptual de una Trayectoria.* Buenos Aires: Centro de Artes y Comunicación, 1993.

Melazzini, Santiago. *El pintor Luis Felipe Noé.* Buenos Aires: La Marca Editora, 2005.

Noé, Luis Felipe. *A Oriente por Occidente.* Bogotá: Dos Gráficos, 1992.

Noé, Luis Felipe. "El otro, la otra y la otredad." Buenos Aires: IMPSAT, 1994.

Noé, Luis Felipe. *Una Sociedad Colonial Avanzada: 1971–2003.* Buenos Aires: Asunto Impreso, 2003.

MARTA GARSD

NORD, PIERRE ALEXIS (1820–1910). Pierre Alexis Nord (*b.* 1820; *d.* 1 May 1910), president of Haiti (1902–1908). Nord came to power after the abdication of Simon Sam and the subsequent civil war between forces led by Nord and those led by Antenor Firmin. After the victory of Nord's forces, he became president in December

1902. Nord's introduction of reforms such as punishment of looters of the national treasury made him unpopular.

In March 1908 an uprising resulted in almost fifty deaths. The government responded with a reign of terror. Four nations sent warships to Port-au-Prince to protect their citizens. In November 1908, Nord ordered General Antoine Simon, commander of the army in the south, to come to the capital to confer on the political situation. Instead Simon led a revolt, taking possession of Port-au-Prince on 2 December. Nord fled to Jamaica, where he died. Simon succeeded him as president (1908–1911).

See also **Haiti; Sam, Tirésias Augustin Simon; Simon, Antoine.**

BIBLIOGRAPHY

Robert D. Heinl, Jr., and Nancy G. Heinl, *Written in Blood: The Story of the Haitian People* (1978).

Additional Bibliography

Berloquin-Chassany, Pascale. *Haïti, une démocratie compromise, 1890–1911.* Paris: Harmattan, 2004.

DARIÉN DAVIS

NORIEGA MORENO, MANUEL ANTONIO

NORIEGA MORENO, MANUEL ANTONIO (1934–). Manuel Antonio Noriega Moreno was commander in chief of the Panamanian National Guard (1983–1989) and a highly controversial figure of the late twentieth century. Born on February 11, 1934, in a poor Panama City neighborhood, he attended public school, graduating in 1955 near the top of his class. He then attended the Peruvian Military Academy, graduating in 1962, the same year he became a National Guard Officer. He completed his education in 1967 at the U.S. School of the Americas in Panama, where he received counterintelligence training. An associate of fellow officer Omar Torrijos Herrera, Noriega was instrumental in suppressing a December 1969 coup attempt, thereby enabling Torrijos to return from Mexico to put down the revolt. As a reward, Torrijos promoted Noriega several ranks to lieutenant colonel and placed him in command of the guard's Intelligence Division G2.

Torrijos's death in an airplane crash on July 31, 1981 provided Noriega his opportunity. A participant in the 1983 coup that removed Colonel Rubén Darío Paredes, Noriega signed an agreement with several colonels, each of whom would resign at specified times, thus rotating the guard command among them. Professing loyalty to the revolution of General Torrijos, he continued projects benefiting urban labor and rural peasants and promoted their integration into the political system.

After becoming guard commander on August 12, 1983, Noriega established complete control of the nation. Concentrating power in his own hands and using tactics of intimidation perfected during his days as intelligence chief, he ruthlessly eliminated rivals, installed presidents at will, and rigged the 1983 election. He used the National Assembly to impeach a president who dared suggest his removal in 1988, appointed and dismissed several provisional presidents, and finally annulled the elections of 1989.

It is evident that during his career Noriega served as an intelligence operative for a number of causes, though specifics are hard to obtain. He was a paid informant of the U.S. Central Intelligence Agency for many years, apparently beginning as early as his days as a cadet in Peru. After involvement in the transit of arms from Cuba to the Sandinista rebels in Nicaragua, at one point Noriega aided U.S. arms shipments to their enemies, the Contras, although he later reversed himself and prevented further arms shipments through Panama. He provided intelligence to both Israel and Cuba in return for training his personal bodyguards. He was accused of working with the Medellín drug cartel, allegedly facilitating international drug smuggling and money transfer and laundering through Panama. A U.S. grand jury in Miami indicted him on narcotics charges, and he was convicted in 1992.

The combination of Noriega's annulment of the 1989 elections (an act condemned by the Organization of American States [OAS]), the drug indictment, and his support of the Sandinistas in Nicaragua led to a break with Washington. In support of deposed president Eric Arturo Delvalle, the United States initiated a financial and economic boycott, while Noriega engaged in intimidating U.S. military personnel in Panama. After the failure of several attempted coups in Panama, the United States intervened militarily on December 20, 1989. Noriega took refuge in the Papal Nunciate, later surrendering to U.S. troops on January 3, 1990, to be taken to Miami for trial on the narcotics indictment. He was convicted in 1992 and sentenced to 40 years in prison. The United States then installed a new government, headed by Guillermo Endara.

Noriega was to have been released from prison on September 9, 2007, after serving fifteen years of a thirty-year sentence for drug trafficking. However, his release was delayed because of an extradition request from France on charges of money laundering. As of 2007 he was also still wanted in Panama, where he is charged in connection with the 1985 murder of Hugo Spadafora, a political activist who had criticized him for his protection of drug trafficking.

See also **Central Intelligence Agency (CIA); Contras; Drugs and Drug Trade; Nicaragua; Panama; Torrijos Herrera, Omar; United States-Latin American Relations.**

BIBLIOGRAPHY

Reliable sources on Noriega are Steve C. Ropp, "Panama's Struggle for Democracy," in *Current History* (December 1987); "Panama's Defiant Noriega" in *Current History* (December 1988); and "Military Retrenchment and Decay in Panama," in *Current History* (1990). See also Frederick Lempe, *Divorcing the Dictator* (1990).

Additional Bibliography

Dinges, John. *Our Man in Panama: How General Noriega Used the United States and Made Millions in Drugs and Arms.* New York: Random House, 1990.

Koster, R. M., and Guillermo Sánchez. *In the Time of the Tyrants: Panama, 1968–1990.* New York: Norton, 1990.

Noriega, Manuel, and Eisner, Peter. *America's Prisoner: The Memoirs of Manuel Noriega.* New York: Random House, 1997.

KENNETH J. GRIEB

NORONHA, FERNÃO DE (c. 1460–1505). Fernão de Noronha (*b.* ca. 1460; *d.* after 1505), a Portuguese nobleman of Jewish descent who held the first royal concession to develop trade with Brazilian Indians. A wealthy merchant, he was an important investor in Portugal's far-flung empire, operating outlets in Africa, India, and Belgium. In 1502, he headed a group of financiers who leased a three-year monopoly contract to exploit Brazil. The consortium sponsored at least two voyages to Brazil, the second of which built the first European settlement there. The fortified trading post (*feitoria*) was located on an island near Cabo Frio; stories of the island's inhabitants are said to have inspired Thomas More's *Utopia.* The venture also inspired Portuguese Jews, then suffering from persecution, to envision the establishment of a safe haven in the Brazilian northeast. In 1504, Noronha was made captain of the coastal islands near Natal, which were later named for him. Although his contract expired in 1505, the trade in brazilwood, Indian slaves, and exotic animals was profitable enough to entice his continued investment.

See also **Brazilwood; Explorers and Exploration: Brazil; Slave Trade.**

BIBLIOGRAPHY

Bailey W. Diffie, *A History of Colonial Brazil, 1500–1792* (1987).

H. B. Johnson, "Portuguese Settlement, 1500–1580," in *Colonial Brazil,* edited by Leslie Bethell (1987), pp. 1–38.

Additional Bibliography

Lourenço, Elias José. *Judeus: Os povoadores do Brasil colônia.* Brasília: ASEFE, 1995.

CLIFF WELCH

NORTE CHICO. Norte Chico, the region of transverse valleys created by numerous streams—Copiapó, Huasco, Elqui, Limarí, Choapa, Petorca, and Aconcagua—north of Chile's Central Valley, between 27 and 33 degrees south latitude. It is a transitional region in terms of climate and economic activities: the aridity of the Norte Grande gives way to increased winter rains toward the south, and mining is gradually replaced by agriculture as the focus of activity. The silver of Chañarcillo, copper of Potrerillos and Río Blanco, iron of El Tofo and Romeral, cement of Juan Soldado and La Calera are the region's main mineral resources. In the Elqui and Huasco valleys grow the choicest grapes, which together with *pisco,* the Chileans' favorite brandy, count among the region's most valuable exports. The major centers are Copiapó, the mining capital of Chile during the nineteenth century; Vallenar, an active agricultural town on the Huasco River; La Serena and

Coquimbo, two cities at the mouth of the Elqui River that were of great significance in colonial times; and Ovalle. In the twenty-first century, cities such as La Serena have doubled in size owing to the growth from tourism that has attracted visitors to the beach and the clear night skies.

See also **Chile, Geography; Pisco.**

BIBLIOGRAPHY

Leland Pederson, *The Mining Industry of the Norte Chico, Chile* (1966).

Roland Paskoff, *Le Chili semi-aride* (Bordeaux, 1970).

Additional Bibliography

Gallardo Fernández, Gloria L. *Communal Land Ownership in Chile: The Agricultural Communities in the Commune of Canela, Norte Chico (1600–1998).* Burlington, VT: Ashgate, 2002.

Mayo, John, and Simon Collier, eds. *Mining in Chile's Norte Chico: Journal of Charles Lambert, 1825–1830.* Boulder, CO: Westview Press, 1998.

Tuozzo, Celina. *Efectos sociales de las migraciones internas en Chile: Una experiencia histórica: el Norte Chico a principios del siglo XX.* Buenos Aires: La Crujía Ediciones: Instituto Torcuato di Tella, Programa de Naciones Unidas para el Desarrollo, 2003.

CÉSAR N. CAVIEDES

NORTE CHICO (PERU).

NORTE CHICO (PERU). Consisting of the adjacent valleys of the Huaura, Supe, Pativilca, and Fortaleza rivers, the Norte Chico (Little North) is so named for its position between the North Coast and the Central Coast regions of Peru. The Norte Chico has gained prominence, since important discoveries there in the mid-1990s, for the dense concentration of archaeological sites with monumental architecture; these date to the third millennium BCE, the earliest known in the Western hemisphere. Within the bounds of this region, measuring 1,800 square kilometers, archaeologists have identified thirty sites dating to the Late Archaic period (3000–1800 BCE) that are distinguished by the presence of truncated pyramids associated with sunken circular plazas and upright stone monoliths. These features are notable not only for their early date but also for their tight clustering. Sites range from a single mound or mound-plaza complex to those covering more than 100 hectares with two or three mound-plaza groups arranged in a U and surrounded by extensive residential remains.

For more than a thousand years, what appears to have been a stable society maintained a way of life dependent on farming irrigated fields and trading agricultural products for marine resources. Evidence of hierarchy is present, though there is no evidence of regional centralization or a "capital" city. The eventual expansion of large-scale irrigation techniques to other regions, coupled with the development of increasing centralization and economic specialization, resulted in diminished pyramid-building after 1800 BCE and the end of the cultural distinctiveness and prominence of the Norte Chico.

See also **Archaeology.**

BIBLIOGRAPHY

Creamer, Winifred, Alvaro Ruiz, and Jonathan."Archaeological Investigation of Late Archaic (3000–1800 B.C.) in the Pativilca Valley, Peru." *Fieldiana Anthropology* 40 (monograph). Chicago: Field Museum, 2007.

Engel, Frederic André. *De las begonias al maíz: Vida y producción en le Perú antiguo.* Lima: Ediagraria, Universidad Agraria La Molina, 1987.

Haas, Jonathan, and Winifred Creamer. "Crucible of Andean Civilization, the Peruvian Coast from 3000 to 1800 BC." *Current Anthropology* 47, no. 5 (2006): 745–775.

Haas, Jonathan, Shelia Pozorski, and Thomas Pozorski, eds. *The Origins and Development of the Andean State.* Cambridge, U.K., and New York: Cambridge University Press, 1987.

Kosok, Paul. *Life, Land, and Water in Ancient Peru.* New York: Long Island University Press, 1965.

Shady, Ruth, and Carlos Levya, eds. *La ciudad sagrada de Caral-Supe: Los orígenes de la civilización andina y la formación del estado prístino en el antiguo Perú.* Lima: Instituto Nacional de Cultura, 2003.

Williams, C. "A Scheme for the Early Monumental Architecture of the Central Coast of Peru." In *Early Ceremonial Architecture in the Andes: A Conference at Dumbarton Oaks, 8th to 10th October 1982,* ed. Christopher B. Donnan, pp. 227–240. Washington, DC: Dumbarton Oaks Research Library and Collection, 1985.

WINIFRED CREAMER

NORTE GRANDE.

NORTE GRANDE. Norte Grande, the northernmost desert region of Chile, whose two major administrative regions, Tarapacá and Antofagasta, have a combined population of 747,635 (1990). The Norte Grande region was not a part of Chilean territory until after the War of the Pacific (1879–1884), when the victorious Chileans claimed the land and its rich copper and nitrate deposits from the beaten Bolivians. By the early twentieth century the region was in the midst of an unprecedented nitrate boom, which just as quickly deflated when European companies developed new petroleum-based fertilizers. Thereafter, the copper industry experienced an upswing, and in the early twenty-first century many copper mines dotted the landscape, including the world's largest open pit copper mine, Chuquicamata.

The physical features of the Norte Grande are the coastal strip, where most of the important centers are located (Arica, Iquique, Mejillones, and Antofagasta); the central basin, or Pampa del Tamarugal, and the extended interior high basin of the Loa River; the Chilean Altiplano in the upper Andes; and the Chilean segment of the Puna de Atacama. The coastal cities are mainly dedicated to trade and to the export of minerals from the interior and from Bolivian mines. Fisheries in Arica and Iquique also contribute to the economy. In the interior basins, nitrate (María Elena, Pedro de Valdivia, and Mantos Blancos), iodine, and copper mining (Chuquicamata and El Salvador) are dominant. The Chilean Altiplano is populated by Aymara people engaged mostly in pastoral activities. In the Puna de Atacama, natural salt and borax are the principal extractive resources. Agriculture thrives in some river oases fed with the snowmelt from Andean volcanoes. Valued crops are the vegetables and olives from the Azapa Valley, north of Arica, and the citrus fruits and tomatoes from Pica and Matilla, in the Pampa del Tamarugal.

See also **Agriculture; Chile, Geography; Mining: Modern; Nitrate Industry; War of the Pacific.**

BIBLIOGRAPHY

Instituto Geográfico Militar, "Región de Tarapacá," in *Geografía de Chile,* vol. 22 (Santiago, 1986).

Sara Larraín, *Norte Grande: 500 años después* (Santiago, 1989).

Instituto De Investigaciones Del Patrimonio Nacional, Universidad De Chile, *El Norte Grande.* Vol. 3, *Jornadas territoriales* (Santiago, 1989).

Additional Bibliography

Jordá, Eduardo. *Norte Grande: viaje por el desierto de Atacama.* Barcelona: Ediciones Península, 2002.

Melcher, Gerardo. *El norte de Chile: su gente, desiertos, y volcanes.* Santiago de Chile: Universitaria, 2004.

Rector, John Lawrence. *The History of Chile.* Westport, CT: Greenwood Press, 2003.

César N. Caviedes

NORTH AMERICAN FREE TRADE AGREEMENT. Ratified in 1993, the Tratado de Libre Comercio, or Free Trade Agreement, bound Canada, Mexico, and the United States into a vast and unprecedented trade accord. When the treaty went into effect on 1 January 1994, it provided the framework to liberalize the flow of commerce and investment within the member nations. At that time it represented the largest free-trade zone on earth, with more than 360 million people and a Gross National Product in excess of 6.5 trillion dollars. The North American Free Trade Agreement (NAFTA) is an improved and expanded version of the Canada-U.S. Free Trade Agreement, signed in 1988, and incorporates the experience of that treaty by addressing its major problems.

NAFTA comprises a basic trade alliance signed in 1992 by the heads of government of the three countries and three side agreements approved in September 1993 that the Clinton administration thought were necessary to ensure the Free Trade Agreement's passage by Congress. The essence of NAFTA is the elimination of barriers to trade in goods and services, the promotion of fair competition, and the creation of increased investment opportunities—aspects that are monitored by a commission based in Mexico. The provisions on environmental issues address the prevention of pollution and the enforcement of environmental laws and is overseen by a review board established in Canada. A commission located in the United States has the responsibility for enforcing the laws and regulations dealing with labor conditions. The treaty includes a parallel agreement to assess import surges that could harm specific sectors of the three countries' economies and to take measures to ameliorate their negative impact.

The free trade process began when Mexican president Carlos Salinas De Gortari proposed the idea to U.S. president George Bush in March 1990. The Canadians later expressed their desire to participate in the negotiations in order to protect their interests and improve their own free trade agreement with the United States. Despite official support, the prospect of such an agreement elicited unexpected and strong opposition in the United States and Canada from an array of partisans on both the left and the right of the political spectrum. In the United States these groups consisted mainly of labor unions (with AFL-CIO president Lane Kirkland expressing strong opposition); protectionist special interest groups in industry and agriculture; environmental and nongovernmental organizations of a diverse nature, including the Sierra Club, consumer advocate Ralph Nader, African-American political leader Jesse Jackson, third-party presidential candidate Ross Perot, and such dissident Republicans as Pat Buchanan. Those who supported the agreement were the usual free-trade advocates in the business community, academia, and the government, who saw not only its economic implications but also its strategic and political ramifications, and the high end of the workforce, confident of widening the opportunities for jobs and improving intellectual property protection. In Mexico there was widespread support for the agreement except among the backers of Cuauhtémoc Cárdenas and other left-wing politicians who believed that nothing sponsored by a government led by the Institutional Revolutionary Party (PRI) could be beneficial for the country.

The economic consequences of the Free Trade Agreement have been mixed. For Mexico, foreign investment and its exports have increased dramatically. However, Mexico's overall economic growth has been lackluster. In 1993, Mexico devalued its peso causing a severe economic downturn. The economy recovered and has been stable but not robust. Due to the lack of job opportunities, Mexican immigration to the United States increased dramatically in the 1990s and early twenty-first century. Also, politicians in Mexico have complained that U.S. agricultural subsidies give U.S. farmers an unfair advantage over Mexico's rural sector. Finally, NAFTA primarily benefited Mexico's northern states, while Mexico's south has received little new investment.

Some analysts predicted that NAFTA would create hundreds of thousands of jobs in the U.S. and Canada, whereas detractors argued that employers in large numbers would leave the United States for Mexico. In reality, NAFTA, although slightly positive, has had a less dramatic impact on the economies of the United States and Canada because of their much larger sizes. Thus, NAFTA has generally been seen as a letdown. Part of the disappointment with NAFTA stems from the very optimistic predictions leaders in all three countries made before the agreement passed. Nevertheless, majorities in Canada, the United States, and Mexico still support the treaty. Also, these nations continue to pursue free trade agreements with other countries. The United States signed free trade pacts with Central America and Colombia. Mexico has likewise signed trade agreements with many Spanish American countries, Japan, and the South American trading block (Mercosur). All three countries are involved in a potential pact called the Free Trade Area of the Americas (FTAA). However, disagreements between Brazil and the United States means that the completion of FTAA will be several years away, if at all.

See also **Cárdenas Solorzano, Cuauhtémoc; Economic Development; Free Trade Area of the Americas (FTAA); Mercosur; Mexico, Political Parties: Institutional Revolutionary Party (PRI); United States-Latin American Relations.**

BIBLIOGRAPHY

Sydney Weintraub, *A Marriage of Convenience: Relations Between Mexico and the United States* (1990).

Luis Rubio, *¿Cómo va a afectar a México el Tratado de Libre Comercio?* (1992).

Gary C. Hufbauer and Jeffery J. Schott, *North American Free Trade: Issues and Recommendations* (1992), and *NAFTA: An Assessment,* rev. ed. (1993).

Manuel Suárez-Mier, "The NAFTA and Its Impact on the U.S. and the Mexican Economies," in *Global Competitor* 1, no. 1 (1993): 33–38.

Additional Bibliography

Borja Tamayo, J. Arturo, Judith Mariscal, and Miguel Angel Valverde. *Para evaluar al TLCAN.* México: Tec de Monterrey, Campus Ciudad de México, 2001.

Hufbauer, Gary Clyde, and Jeffrey J. Schott. *NAFTA Revisited: Achievements and Challenges.* Washington, DC: Institute for International Economics, 2005.

Kirton, John J., and Virginia White Maclaren, eds. *Linking Trade, Environment, and Social Cohesion: NAFTA Experiences, Global Challenges.* Aldershot, Hampshire, England: Ashgate, 2002.

Manuel Suárez- Mier
Byron Crites

NOSSA SENHORA DA APARECIDA. Nossa Senhora Da Aparecida (Our Lady of Aparecida), the Virgin of Conception, is the patron saint of Brazil. She first appeared in 1717 as a terra-cotta image in the net of three poor fishermen in the Paraíba River between Rio de Janeiro and São Paulo. The 15-inch image is said to have miraculously provided large catches to supply the table for visiting Dom Pedro Miguel, then governor of São Paulo and Minas Gerais. A chapel built in 1745 was replaced by a church in 1852 and by a larger edifice in 1888. Pope Pius XI proclaimed Aparecida the patron saint of Brazil in 1930. Today, hundreds of thousands of pilgrims annually visit the Basilica of Aparecida in São Paulo, especially in May, October, and December.

Rubem César Fernandes views Aparecida as a weak national symbol for two major reasons. The first is Brazil's strong regionalism, based on geographic and historical differences. Other religious figures, such as Padre Cícero in the northeast and Nosso Senhor do Bonfim in Salvador, are evidence of this regionalism. Aparecida is recognized as the principal religious shrine in the south-central region, comprised by the states São Paulo, Rio de Janeiro, and Minas Gerais, whose importance in national politics may help explain why Aparecida was chosen as the national patron saint. The second reason Aparecida is considered a weak national figure is because the clergy and the majority of the faithful worship her in different ways. The pilgrims see themselves as depending on her protection in exchange for a promise, while the clergy views her more as a mediator and in terms of sacred mysteries.

See also **Catholic Church: The Colonial Period.**

BIBLIOGRAPHY

Luís Da Câmara Cascudo, *Dicionário do folclore brasileiro,* 2d ed. (1962), pp. 56–57.

Rubem César Fernandes, "Aparecida: Nossa rainha, senhora e mãe, saravá!" in Viola Sachs et al., *Brasil & EUA: Religião e identidade nacional* (1988), pp. 85–111.

Additional Bibliography

Brustolini, Júlio. *A Senhora da Conceição Aparecida: História da imagem, da Capela, das romarias.* Aparecida: Editora Santuário, 1981.

Macca, Marcelo, and Andréa Vilela de Almeida. *Nossa Senhora Aparecida: Padroeira do Brasil.* São Paulo: Editora Planeta do Brasil, 2003.

ESTHER J. PRESSEL

NO-TRANSFER RESOLUTION. No-Transfer Resolution, the first U.S. government statement, for the purpose of its own security, expressing opposition to the transfer of territories in the Western Hemisphere from one European power to another. With the Spanish colonial empire crumbling, the United States faced the possibility that the Floridas, particularly West Florida, where Americans had settled under Spanish land grants, might fall under British or French control. With Spanish authority weakened, President James Madison in 1810 placed the territory between the Mississippi and Perdido rivers under U.S. control. In response to British and Spanish protests, Congress, on 15 January 1811, quickly passed a resolution and legislation that empowered the president to take the land in question until future negotiations settled the issue. In so doing, Congress set a fundamental principle of U.S. policy toward the Spanish Borderlands, which Secretary of State John Quincy Adams extended in 1823 to include Cuba, and Monroe, in his doctrine, extended to all Latin America. In 1940, following the outbreak of the European war, Congress passed a resolution calling for joint hemispheric action in case of transfer or attempted transfer of colonies. The no-transfer principle was adopted by the Latin American governments at the Havana Meeting of Consultation of Ministers of Foreign Affairs in July 1940.

See also **Monroe Doctrine.**

BIBLIOGRAPHY

John A. Logan, *No Transfer: An American Security Principle* (1961).

Dexter Perkins, *A History of the Monroe Doctrine,* rev. ed. (1963).

Additional Bibliography

Dent, David W. *The Legacy of the Monroe Doctrine: A Reference Guide to U.S. Involvement in Latin America and the Caribbean.* Westport, CT: Greenwood Press, 1999.

Hilton, Sylvia-Lyn. "La 'nueva' doctrina Monroe de 1895 y sus implicaciones para el Caribe español: Algunas interpretaciones coetáneas españolas." *Anuario de Estudios Americanos.* 55:1 (January-June 1998): 125-151.

Smith, Gaddis. *The Last Years of the Monroe Doctrine, 1945-1993.* New York: Hill and Wang, 1994.

THOMAS M. LEONARD

NOVA FRIBURGO. Nova Friburgo, city in a high mountain valley of the state of Rio de Janeiro. Founded in 1819 by immigrants from the Swiss canton of Fribourg, this settlement was part of an active government program, initiated by the government of Dom João VI, to promote and support agricultural colonies in Brazil. Based on the belief that settling small communities of European farmers would encourage the spread of agriculture, the government offered generous inducements to potential immigrants, and succeeded in attracting some two thousand Swiss Catholic colonists to the region. The colony at Nova Friburgo was successful, but costly to maintain, which discouraged similar ventures by the throne. In the second half of the nineteenth century, Nova Friburgo was a popular refuge from the yellow fever epidemics that ravaged Rio de Janeiro. The city is now an attractive summer resort northeast of Rio de Janeiro. As of 2006, it had an estimated population of 178,102.

See also **Brazil: The Colonial Era, 1500-1808.**

BIBLIOGRAPHY

Additional Bibliography

Burns, E. Bradford. *A History of Brazil.* 3d edition. New York: Columbia University, 1993.

Fausto, Boris. *A Concise History of Brazil.* Cambridge, U.K.: Cambridge University Press, 1999.

Levine, Robert M. *The History of Brazil.* Westport, CT: Greenwood Press, 1999.

Page, Joseph A. *The Brazilians.* Boston: Addison-Wesley, 1996.

Skidmore, Thomas E. *Brazil: Five Centuries of Change.* New York: Oxford University Press, 1999.

SHEILA L. HOOKER

NOVARRO, RAMON (1899–1968). Silent film actor Ramon Novarro (February 6, 1899–October 30, 1968), best-known for his portrayal of the title role in *Ben Hur* (1925), was born José Ramón Gil Samaniego in Durango, Mexico. Although he seriously considered becoming a priest, it was a desire to become a musician, along with the violence of the Mexican Revolution, that brought him to the United States in 1915. Needing to find employment immediately, he began working as an extra in the burgeoning Hollywood film industry. After a number of uncredited roles, his breakthrough came with *The Prisoner of Zenda* (1922) and was followed by the critically acclaimed *Trifling Women* (1922), both directed by studio director Rex Ingram, under whose direction Novarro "prove[d] his worth as a performer" (Soáres 2002, p. xi).

Novarro' next picture with Ingram, *Where the Pavement Ends* (1923), led to his signing a lucrative five-year contract with Metro Studios, where the goal was to make him a star. *Scaramouche* (1923), also directed by Ingram, was his most popular film to date. However, in 1924 he began filming the epic blockbuster *Ben Hur*, playing the title role of Judah Ben-Hur, which would cement his stardom. He spent the next decade enjoying success in the film industry, often being typecast in a "Latin lover" role. However, his contract with MGM Studios expired in 1935, and the studio chose not to renew it. He lived in California until his murder in 1968 by two young men attempting to rob him at his house.

See also **Cinema: From the Silent Film to 1990.**

BIBLIOGRAPHY

Ellenberger, Allan R. *Ramon Novarro: A Biography of the Silent Film Idol, 1899–1968, with a Filmography.* London: McFarland, 1999.

Soares, André. *Beyond Paradise: The Life of Ramon Novarro.* New York: St. Martin's Press, 2002.

STACY LUTSCH

NOVÁS CALVO, LINO (1905–1983). Lino Novás Calvo (*b.* 22 September 1905; *d.* 24 March 1983), Cuban short story writer, novelist, translator, and essayist. Born in Spain, Novás Calvo immigrated to Cuba as a young boy and lived there until 1980, when he moved to the United States. His works often reflect the plight of people trapped by events beyond their control. In spite of their usual regional setting, his works ascend always to a universal level because of his themes of the basic loneliness of the individual and the uncertainties of human life. His narratives, while usually written in the first person and characterized by colloquial language, nonetheless avoid narrow regionalism. His best known novel is *El negrero* (1933; The Slave Trader). However, it is his short stories, collected mainly in *La luna nona y otros cuentos* (1942; The Ninth Moon and Other Stories), *Cayo Canas* (1946; Palm Key), and *Maneras de contar* (1970; Narrative Manners), that place him among the great writers of Latin America. They are characterized by magical realism, a deceptively simple narrative style, varied perspective, and unexpected developments and imagery.

See also **Literature: Spanish America.**

BIBLIOGRAPHY

Seymour Menton, *Prose Fiction of the Cuban Revolution* (1975), pp. 235–239.

Raymond D. Souza, *Lino Novás Calvo* (1981).

Lorraine E. Roses, *Voices of the Storyteller: Cuba's Lino Novás Calvo* (1986).

Raymond D. Souza, "Lino Novás Calvo," in *Dictionary of Twentieth Century Cuban Literature,* edited by Julio A. Martínez (1990), pp. 318–323.

Additional Bibliography

Febles, Jorge M. "La ineludible voz tácita del otro en 'El negrero': Vida novelada de Pedro Blanco Fernández de Trava." *Hispania* 84:4 (December 2001): 758–766.

Habra, Hedy. "El negrero como personaje romántico en 'Pedro Blanco, el negrero' de Lino Novás Calvo." *Afro-Hispanic Review* 18:1 (Spring 1999): 46–52.

OTTO OLIVERA

NOVO, SALVADOR (1904–1974). Salvador Novo (*b.* 30 July 1904; *d.* 13 January 1974), Mexican writer. Born in México City, Salvador Novo was one of the first Mexican authors to demonstrate that a Mexican writer could earn a living by the pen. Novo entered the world of letters as a poet at a time when artists supported themselves by means of government appointments as teachers or bureaucrats. He led the way in breaking this dependence on the government when he became a professional essayist and editoral writer, as well as a playwright/director. Throughout most of his writing career his journalistic fee was "cinco centavos la palabra." He estimated that by the time he was fifty he had earned 425,250 pesos at this rate. He is known today primarily for his theater direction and for the incisive wit of his several plays, as well as for his autobiographical travel books and his essays.

With characteristic self-mockery, Novo described his youthful artistic posture as that of "an old, world-weary author whose writings deliberately betrayed the youth of the penman." He contrasted this with the creative stance he assumed during his middle years which he described as "a youthfulness only half-trying to disguise the venerable mind of the penman."

Along with Xavier Villaurrutía and Rodolfo Usigli, Salvador Novo is one of the pillars of contemporary Mexican theater. His first work for the stage was *El Tercer Fausto* (1934, French; 1956, Spanish), and his best-known plays include *La culta dama* (1951), *Yocasta, o casi* (1961), and *La guerra de las gordas* (1963). He also wrote a collection of dialogues and short plays. Novo directed well over fifty stage productions and even wrote a text on acting, *Diez lecciones de técnica de actuación* (1951). Novo's best-known works of poetry are *XX poemas* (1925) and *Nuevo amor* (1933); his travel book is *Return Ticket* (1928). His critical writings have been collected in several anthologies.

See also **Journalism; Journalism in Mexico; Theater.**

BIBLIOGRAPHY

See Salvador Novo, *Nuevo amor,* translated into English by Edna Worthley Underwood (1935). For a thorough bibliography see the appendix of Novo's *Yocasta, o casi* (1985).

Additional Bibliography

Acero, Rosa María. *Novo ante Novo: Un novísimo personaje homosexual.* Madrid: Editorial Pliegos, 2003.

Monsiváis, Carlos. *Salvador Novo: Lo marginal en el centro.* México, D.F.: Ediciones Era, 2004.

WILLIAM I. OLIVER

NUCLEAR AMERICA. Nuclear America, the term applied to the early high-culture areas of the Western Hemisphere that arose before the Spanish Conquest. It incorporates Mesoamerica, a culture area that includes most of Mexico, all of Belize and Guatemala, and portions of Central America, as well as the areas of South America in which high cultures first appeared.

The early cultures to which it refers include those of the Olmec, Maya, Teotihuacán, Toltec, and Aztec in Mesoamerica, and the Inca, Chimu, and Chavín of the Andean region of South America. In both areas the cultures flourished within the span 1250 BCE–CE 1500.

See also **Aztecs; Incas, The; Indigenous Peoples; Maya, The.**

WALTER R. T. WITSCHEY

NUCLEAR INDUSTRY. Early attempts to develop a national capability in nuclear science and technology in Brazil, Argentina, and Mexico date back as far as the 1950s. Research on alternative fuel cycles and reactor prototypes preceded negotiations with foreign suppliers for the acquisition of "turn-key" plants. Argentina negotiated the acquisition of its first nuclear power plant in 1968 from the West German firm Siemens, its second in 1973 from Atomic Energy of Canada, and its third in 1979 from Kraftwerk Union (KWU), a subsidiary of Siemens. The first two (Atucha I, near Buenos Aires, and Embalse, in Córdoba) began operation in 1974 and 1983 respectively. The share of national Argentine components for these plants increased from over 30 percent for Atucha to over 50 percent for Embalse. The third nuclear power plant, Atucha II, was expected to be completed by 2010. All three are fueled with natural uranium and moderated with heavy water. In addition, Argentina has five small research reactors, a pilot heavy-water-producing plant, a uranium-enrichment facility, and a commercial heavy-water plant and small (plutonium-separating) reprocessing facility under construction.

Brazil acquired its first and only operating reactor (Angra I) from Westinghouse in 1971, a pressurized water reactor (fueled by enriched uranium) that came on line in 1985. In 1975 Brazil signed a large-scale agreement with KWU for the purchase of up to eight plants as well as complete fuel-cycle technology, from uranium mining and enrichment to fuel reprocessing. The share of domestic inputs for the power plants was to grow considerably beyond the initial (30 percent) contribution. Angra I and Angra II are operating and Angra III is still under construction as of 2008.

Brazil became the site of the largest factory of heavy components for nuclear reactors in the third world (Nuclep). In addition to the pilot enrichment plant contracted for in 1975, the navy operates an indigenous enrichment plant at Aramar, linked to a nuclear submarine program (the program succeeded in enriching uranium in 1986 and led to a pilot centrifuge facility at the Aramar Research Center). In 2006, Brazil opened a new centrifuge called Resende. Both Argentina and Brazil are capable of exporting certain components and services for nuclear industries, including uranium exploration, mining, and processing; training in nuclear safety; power and research plant equipment; and engineering. Argentina has sold nuclear reactors to Egypt, Australia, Algeria, and Peru.

Ambiguous nuclear policies persisted in Argentina and Brazil for many decades, when both countries upheld a long-standing rejection of the NPT as a discriminatory tool. The 1968 Non-Proliferation Treaty (NPT) provides for the transfer of peaceful nuclear technology to the developing world but compels the recipients not to obtain or produce nuclear weapons nor export sensitive materials without international safeguards implemented by the International Atomic Energy Agency. Nor did Brazil nor Argentina become an effective party to the 1967 Treaty of Tlatelolco for many years either. Chile and Cuba remained outside Tlatelolco for decades as well. Brazil and Chile signed and ratified the treaty but did not waive the conditions required for the treaty to enter into force on their territories.

The democratic administrations of Raul Alfonsin and Jose Sarney in Argentina and Brazil made joint declarations of peaceful intentions and exchanged visits to sensitive facilities but did not abandon opposition to the NPT, refusals to ratify Tlatelolco, or rights to peaceful nuclear explosions. On 28 November 1990, Carlos S. Menem of Argentina and Fernando Collor De Mello of Brazil, took the unprecedented step of signing an agreement renouncing the manufacture of nuclear weapons and pledging to open all their nuclear power facilities to reciprocal inspections. The declaration implied a common intention to conclude a "full-scope" safeguards agreement with the International Atomic Energy Agency, whereby all their present and future nuclear facilities would be open for international inspection.

Argentina and Brazil also committed themselves to take initiatives leading to the full entry into force of the Tlatelolco Treaty provisions. A Common Accounting and Control System signed in July 1991 was followed by an agreement on the Exclusively Peaceful Use of Nuclear Energy (Guadalajara, 1991), which created an Agency for Accounting and Control of Nuclear Materials (ABACC, *Agência Brasileiro-Argentina de Contabilidade e Controle de Materiais Nucleares*). Joint declarations committed both countries to put into effect an updated version of the regional NWPZ Tlatelolco Treaty. In 1992 Argentina, Brazil and Chile agreed on amendments designed to facilitate their adherence to the Tlatelolco Treaty (Cuba signed the treaty in 1995). Argentina ratified the NPT in 1994 and Brazil in 1998.

The Treaty of Tlatelolco is the product of Mexican regional diplomacy. An NPT-signatory, Mexico contracted in 1972 for its first power plant, a boiling-water reactor, from General Electric. Laguna Verde was connected to the electric power distribution network in 1990, after intense antinuclear activities by ecological groups. Such activities became more common in Brazil and Argentina only after democratic regimes assumed power in the mid-1980s. Finally, Cuba had ambitious plans to generate more than a quarter of its energy from nuclear power but has only two partially constructed nuclear reactors, Juragua 1 and 2.

See also **Collor de Mello, Fernando Affonso; Menem, Carlos Saúl; Nuclebrás; Science; Technology; Weapons Industry.**

BIBLIOGRAPHY

John R. Redick, "The Tlatelolco Regime and Nonproliferation in Latin America," in *International Organization* 35, no. 1 (Winter 1981).

Etel Solingen, *Industrial Policy, Technology, and International Bargaining: Designing Nuclear Industries in Argentina and Brazil.* Stanford, CA: Stanford University Press, 1996.

Additional Bibliography

Rojas Nieto, José Antonio. *Desarrollo nuclear de Mexico.* Mexico, D.F.: Universidad Nacional Autónoma de México, 1989.

Solingen, Etel. "Macropolitical Consensus and Lateral Autonomy in Industrial Policy: Nuclear Industries in Brazil and Argentina." *International Organization* 47:2 (Spring, 1993).

Valle Fonrouge, Marcelo F. *Desarme nuclear regímenes internacional, latinoamèricano y argentino de no proliferación.* Ginebra: UNIDIR, 2003.

ETEL SOLINGEN

NUCLEBRÁS. Nuclebrás, state holding company created in Brazil in 1975 during negotiations with the West German firm Kraftwerk Union (KWU), a subsidiary of Siemens, to manage nuclear industrial activities. The comprehensive agreement signed with KWU and associated firms established five joint ventures under the Nuclebrás umbrella: Nuclen (75 percent Nuclebrás, 25 percent KWU) was responsible for nuclear engineering; Nuclep (75 percent Nuclebrás, with the remaining 25 percent in the hands of KWU, GHH, and Voest Alpine) became the largest producer of heavy components for nuclear plants in the third world; Nuclam (51 percent Nuclebrás, 49 percent Urangessellschaft) specialized in uranium mining; Nuclei (75 percent Nuclebrás, 25 percent Steag and Interatom) was responsible for an isotopic enrichment demonstration plant; and Nustep (50 percent Nuclebrás, 50 percent Steag) engaged in isotopic enrichment research and development. In addition to these joint ventures, Nuclebrás managed two other subsidiaries: Nucon, in power-plant construction, and Nuclemon in extraction and processing of heavy minerals, as well as a nuclear technology research and development center, a fuel element fabrication plant, and yellowcake production facilities. Eight 1,100-megawatt pressurized water reactors were to be built in Brazil under this structure.

The nature of the joint ventures, in which the foreign partners preserved substantial control over operations, provoked considerable opposition within the Brazilian scientific community and segments of engineering and capital-goods producers, who felt excluded from the large-scale program, estimated at between $12 billion and $18 billion in 1975. Critics of Nuclebrás denounced the overall cost of the ambitious program, as well as its tendency to rely on newly created state rather than private-sector firms. Nuclebrás became a symbol of the military-technocratic regime's modus operandi, a pattern that developed after the 1964 takeover from civilian President João Goulart.

Following intense political pressures, budgetary contractions, and the turn toward privatization, Nuclebrás was dissolved in 1988. The two power plants under construction, Angra II and Angra III, and the engineering subsidiary Nuclen were transferred to the jurisdiction of the state utility Eletrobrás. Nuclep and Nuclemon were privatized, Nustep and Nuclam dissolved, and the yellowcake and fuel-element facilities were placed under a new enterprise, Industrias Nucleares do Brasil S.A. In 2000 Angra II was completed. Because of environmental concerns and the inefficiency of nuclear plants, the Brazilian government is still debating the funding of Angra III.

See also **Energy; Nuclear Industry; Privatization.**

BIBLIOGRAPHY

Etel Solingen, "Macropolitical Consensus and Lateral Autonomy in Industrial Policy: The Nuclear Sector in Brazil and Argentina," in *International Organization* 47, no. 2 (Spring 1993): 263–298.

Additional Bibliography

Malheiros, Tania. *Histórias secretas do Brasil nuclear.* Rio de Janeiro: WVA, 1996.

Solingen, Etel. *Industrial Policy, Technology, and International Bargaining: Designing Nuclear Industries in Argentina and Brazil.* Stanford, CA: Stanford University Press, 1996.

ETEL SOLINGEN

NUEVA BURDEOS, COLONY OF.

Colony of Nueva Burdeos, an abortive colonization experiment in the Paraguayan Chaco during the 1850s aimed to improve relations with Europe and increase agricultural production, but failed on both counts. The opening of Platine waterways after the fall of the Argentine dictator José Manuel de Rosas in 1852 enabled Paraguay to reach out to foreign nations for diplomatic and commercial contacts. The 1853–1854 European tour of Francisco Solano López sealed several such agreements and also opened the door to immigration into Paraguay. French representatives, responding to López's overtures, agreed to permit the transport from Bordeaux of some four hundred settlers who, with the material aid of the Asunción government, would build an agricultural colony in the Gran Chaco region (at the site of the present–day town of Villa Hayes).

The French settlers began to arrive in May 1855, but from the first everything went wrong. Few of the immigrants had had farming experience and none were prepared for the climate, the insects, and the rigors of life in the Chaco. With little help from the Paraguayans, many settlers simply abandoned the rudimentary colony and drifted into Asunción, where they were arrested for having failed to live up to a contract that few had even seen.

The poor treatment meted out to these individuals created a diplomatic impasse with France, though, at the last moment, Paraguayan officials relented and allowed the hapless colonists to leave the country. With the dissolution of the Nueva Colonia Burdeos settlement at the end of 1855, the Paraguayan presence in the Chaco was reduced to two or three minor military posts. New immigration into the same area had to wait until the arrival of the Mennonites early in the next century.

See also **Chaco Region.**

BIBLIOGRAPHY

John Hoyt Williams, *The Rise and Fall of the Paraguayan Republic, 1800–1870* (1979), pp. 192–193.

Efraím Cardozo, *Paraguay independiente* (1987), pp. 136, 152.

Additional Bibliography

Guerra, Sergio. *Paraguay: De la independencia a la dominación imperialista, 1811–1870.* Paraguay: C. Schauman, 1991.

THOMAS L. WHIGHAM

NUEVA GALICIA. Nueva Galicia, province of New Spain, including all of the present-day Mexican states of Aguascalientes, Zacatecas, Nayarit; a large part of Jalisco; and the northwest corner of San Luis Potosí, with an area of some 72,000 square miles and a population in 1520 estimated at 855,000. Its conquest began in 1524; by the following year, indigenous communities were being given out to conquistadores in *encomiendas* and the Franciscan order was converting the local people. From February to June 1530, Nuño de Guzmán, the first president of the *audiencia* of Mexico, and an army of Spaniards, indigenous allies from central Mexico, and Tarascan slaves waged a ferocious campaign of killing, torture, and enslavement against the largely unresisting local population. This strategy continued into the 1540s until the local population fought back in a full-scale rebellion, known as the Mixtón War (1541), and drove the Spaniards out. The viceroy eventually restored order, but the indigenous population had declined significantly to perhaps as few as 220,000. By 1560 both *audiencia* and bishopric were firmly established in Guadalajara, although the entire area was not subdued until 1722 with the surrender of the Cora nation of Nayarit.

In 1574 the first *gobernador* arrived in Guadalajara and took control over the area, although he soon lost the power of making official appointments in his jurisdiction to the viceroy. By the mid-seventeenth century, the population stood at a mere 130,000. Half of it consisted of indigenous people, while the rest were two-thirds Spaniards and mestizos and one-third slaves of African descent brought in as the original population declined. The new population settled either near the mines in the northeast or on cattle, wheat, and sugar estates in the south.

By the early eighteenth century, the area boasted large multiracial cities such as Zacatecas, Guadalajara, Aguas-Calientes, Sombrerete, and Fresnillo along with smaller towns and even smaller autochthonous villages. In 1789, with the implementation of the intendancy reform, Nueva Galicia, with a population of approximately 450,000, was divided between the intendancies of Guadalajara, Zacatecas, and San Luis Potosí.

See also **Audiencia; Encomienda; Guadalajara; Indigenous Peoples; New Spain, Viceroyalty of; Slavery: Indian Slavery and Forced Labor.**

BIBLIOGRAPHY

María Del Carmen Velázquez, "La jurisdicción militar en la Nueva Galicia," in *Historia Mexicana* 9, no. 33 (1959): 15–34.

Peter Gerhard, *The North Frontier of New Spain,* rev. ed. (1993).

Additional Bibliography

Aceves Ortega, Raul. *Hospitales de indios y otras fundaciones civiles y religiosas en Nueva Galicia*. Guadalajara, Jalisco: Universidad de Guadalajara, Editorial Universitaria, 2004.

Berthe, Jean-Pierre, Thomas Calvo, Agueda Jimenez Pelayo. *Sociedades en construcción: la Nueva Galicia según las visitas de oidores, 1606–1616.* Guadalajara, Jalisco, México: Universidad de Guadalajara, Coordinación Editorial; México, D.F.: Centre Français d'Études Mexicaines et Centraméricaines, 2000.

Burciaga, José Arturo. *Las flores y las espinas: perfiles del clero secular en el noroeste de Nueva Galicia (1750–1810.)* México,D.F.: Universidad Autónoma de Zacatecas; Instituto Zacatecano de Cultura, 2006.

Carmen Ramos-Escandón

NUEVA VIZCAYA. Named after conqueror Francisco de Ibarra's native Vizcaya, this province (*reino*) of colonial Mexico at first encompassed all of the territory claimed by Spain north of Zacatecas. Even after Nuevo México and Sonora y Sinaloa were detached from it in 1598 and 1733, respectively, Nueva Vizcaya still comprised an enormous territory extending from the central plateau in southern Durango to northern Chihuahua, and from the high peaks and deep canyons of the Sierra Madre Occidental in the west to the deserts of Coahuila in the east. Except in judicial matters, which came under the Audiencia of Guadalajara, the governor of Nueva Vizcaya reported to the viceroy until 1777, and from then on to the *comandante general* of the Provincias Internas. In 1787, Nueva Vizcaya (with Parras and Saltillo severed) became the intendancy of Durango. The capital was located in Durango for the period 1632–1739, when the governors resided in Parral. Nueva Vizcaya was the most populous and economically productive northern province, encompassing silver mining centers like Parral and Chihuahua as well as livestock- and grain-producing areas surrounding the Valley of San Bartolomé, Parras, and Saltillo.

See also **Audiencia; Intendancy System; Mexico: The Colonial Period; Viceroyalty, Viceroy.**

BIBLIOGRAPHY

Guillermo Porras Muñoz, *Iglesia y estado en Nueva Vizcaya* (1966).

Peter Gerhard, *The North Frontier of New Spain* (1982).

Oakah L. Jones, Jr., *Nueva Vizcaya: Heartland of the Spanish Frontier* (1988).

Additional Bibliography

Deeds, Susan M. *Defiance and Deference in Mexico's Colonial North: Indians under Spanish Rule in Nueva Vizcaya.* Austin: University of Texas Press, 2003.

Olveda, Jaime. *Los vascos en el noroccidente de México, siglos XVII–XVIII.* Jalisco: Colegio de Jalisco, 1998.

Teja, Jesus F. de la, and Frank Ross. *Choice, Persuasion, and Coercion: Social Control on Spain's North American Frontiers.* Albuquerque: University of New Mexico Press, 2005.

Susan M. Deeds

NUEVO LEÓN. Nuevo León, a province in northeastern Mexico. The Hispanic settlement of Nuevo León followed patterns developed elsewhere in northern New Spain: the search for silver, the enslavement of nonsedentary indigenous peoples, the attempts to pacify the frontier through colonization by sedentary Tlaxcalans (more a northeastern phenomenon), and the development of livestock raising as the major economic activity of the colony. The Hispanic presence dates from the 1580s and 1590s, when Luis de Carvajal and later Diego Montemayor established settlements in the vicinity of present-day Monterrey. By the mid-seventeenth century, Indian slaving in the region gave way to the raising of sheep and cattle and the exploitation of relatively limited silver deposits at Boca de Leones, Cerralvo, and Vallecillo. Livestock and mining remained mainstays of the economy at least through Independence.

While little affected by the independence struggle, subsequent wars—Texas independence, the U.S. invasion in 1846, the U.S. Civil War, and the French Intervention—transformed Nuevo León, particularly in commerce. Monterrey merchants acted as middlemen in the trade with the United States, especially inensuring an outlet for Southern cotton during the blockade of Confederate ports in the 1860s. Although many of the mercantile fortunes were dissipated in the depressed Mexican economy of the 1870s and 1880s, some survived to provide the basis for Nuevo León's economic revival, spurred by the expansion of railroads in the northeast in the late 1880s. This extensive railroad network, with Monterrey as its northeastern hub, prompted the revival of mining and stimulated the growth of an industrial sector funded almost exclusively by local capital. Monterrey's present role as a major industrial center had its roots in the latter years of the nineteenth century.

Close cooperation between the region's business elite and politicians facilitated Nuevo León's development, with governors Santiago Vidaurri and General Bernardo Reyes Ogazón particularly supportive of business interests. But such support was difficult to secure after 1910. By late 1913, Nuevo León felt the violence of the civil war, as armies of the various revolutionary chieftains contended for power; industrial production and trade declined precipitously. Even the relative stability of the postwar period brought scant comfort to business interests: the pro-labor provisions of the 1917 Constitution and the perceived anticapitalist stance of Mexican presidents between 1920 and 1940 deepened the conservatism of the business sector and the nascent middle class alike. The region's staunch opposition to Lázaro Cárdenas in 1934 and the elite's support of Partido Acción Nacional (PAN) candidate Juan Andreu Almazán in the 1940 election contributed to the rightward tilt of the government Partido de la Revolución Mexicana (PRM) after 1940 (the PRM was later renamed Partido Revolucionario Institucional, PRI). Nuevo León remains among the more politically conservative states, and Monterrey's industrial elite are among the most prominent supporters of the PAN. When the PRI began a slow process of democratization in the 1990s, the PAN won the election for governor in 1997. Reflecting the competitive electoral landscape, the PRI in 1993 surprisingly took back the governor position. Also, in the 1990s, Mexico opened up its economy, which increased foreign investment and trade. Generally, Nuevo León has benefited from this transition. Despite global competition, in the early twentieth century large Mexican corporations, such as cement producer CEMEX and the food company Bimbo, have thrived. With this economic success, Nuevo León has the highest standard of living in Latin America.

See also **Cárdenas del Río, Lázaro; Carvajal, Luis de; Cementos de Mexico; Mexico, Political Parties: National Action Party (PAN).**

BIBLIOGRAPHY

Vito Alessio Robles, *Monterrey en la historia y en la leyenda* (1936).

Eugenio Del Hoyo, *Historia del nuevo reino de León (1527–1723)* (1972).

Peter Gerhard, *The North Frontier of New Spain* (1982), esp. pp. 344–357.

Alex M. Saragoza, *The Monterrey Elite and the Mexican State* (1988).

Stephen Haber, "Assessing the Obstacles to Industrialization: The Mexican Economy, 1830–1940," in *Journal of Latin American Studies* 24, no. 1 (1992): 1–32.

Additional Bibliography

Cavazos Garza, Israel. *Breve historia de Nuevo León.* México: Colegio de México, 1995.

Hernández, Marie Theresa. *Delirio: The Fantastic, the Demonic, and the Reél: The Buried History of Nuevo León.* Austin: University of Texas Press Austin, 2002.

Mora-Torres, Jua. *The Making of the Mexican Border: The State, Capitalism, and Society in Nuevo León, 1848–1910.* Austin: University of Texas Press, 2001.

LESLIE S. OFFUTT

NUEVO SANTANDER. Nuevo Santander, a northeastern province of New Spain stretching northward beyond the Nueces River in present-day Texas and southward to the Río Pánuco in the Mexican state of Tamaulipas. Francisco de Garay began the colonization of the area in 1519. After Hernán Cortés conquered the Huasteca Indian inhabitants in 1523, the Spaniards started selling them into slavery in the Central Valley of Mexico and in the Caribbean. Following the height of the slave trade under Governor Luis de Carvajal in 1581–1586, the region slowly became depopulated and both colonies and missionaries lost interest. Beginning in the mid-1740s, José de Escandón reestablished control over the area, founding over twenty towns and colonies. From its establishment as a separate political jurisdiction in 1748, Nuevo Santander was under the direct control of the viceroy except in 1788–1792 and 1813–1821, when it formed part of the Provincias Internas and fell under a separate authority. With the promulgation of the Mexican Constitution of 1824, Nuevo Santander disappeared into the new state of Tamaulipas.

See also **Carvajal, Luis de; Escandón, José de; Garay, Francisco de; New Spain, Colonization of the Northern Frontier; Tamaulipas.**

BIBLIOGRAPHY

Vicente De Santa María, *Relación histórica de la colonia del Nuevo Santander* (1973).

Lionel Garza, *The Kingdom of Nuevo Leon, the Cradle of Coahuila, Tejas, and Nuevo Santander* (1989).

Juan Fidel Zorrilla, *El poder colonial en Nuevo Santander* (1989).

Peter Gerhard, *The North Frontier of New Spain,* rev. ed. (1993).

Additional Bibliography

Cavazos Garza, Israel. *Nuevo León y la colonización del Nuevo Santander.* Monterrey, N.L., México: Sección 21 del SNTE, 2004, 1994.

López de la Cámara Alta, Agustín. *Descripción general de la colonial de nuevo Santander.* México, DF: Universidad Autónoma Nacional de México, 2006.

Osante, Patricia. *Orígenes del Nuevo Santander.* México: Universidad Nacional Autónoma de México, Instituto de Investigaciones Históricas, 1997.

CARMEN RAMOS-ESCANDÓ N

NUFIO, JOSÉ DOLORES (?–?). José Dolores Nufio, one of the principal leaders of the 1848 *montaña* revolt of the Lucíos in Guatemala. As military commander of Chiquimula, Nufio's defection to the liberals at the end of July 1848 was important in bringing about Carrera's resignation on 15 August. Nufio promised to place his forces under the orders of the new assembly but separated himself from Guatemalan authority until that body covened, allying himself with rebels in Los Altos. Nufio then seized Izabal, where his control of the port and customs house made Carrera's position untenable.

Following Carrera's departure, however, the liberal assembly failed to meet the demands of Nufio and other rebel commanders, who in turn refused to submit to the new government and continued the revolt. This division among the liberals helped Carrera eventually to return in 1849. In collaboration with José Francisco Barrundia, Gerardo Barrios, and Trinidad Cabañas, Nufio joined forces with liberals in Los Altos, El Salvador, and Honduras. His "National Army" raided and attacked Guatemala from sanctuaries in El Salvador and Honduras through 1850. These activities eventually led to a showdown at San José la Arada, Guatemala, on 2 February 1851, where Carrera dealt the liberal allies a stunning defeat, thus assuring the security of conservative rule in Guatemala.

See also **Guatemala.**

BIBLIOGRAPHY

Pedro Tobar Cruz, *Los montañeses: La facción de los Lucíos* (1971), esp. pp. 145–285.

María Eugenia Morales, *Movimiento de los Lucíos: Un acercamiento histórico sociológico* (1983).

RALPH LEE WOODWARD JR.

NUNES, CLARA (1943–1983). The Brazilian singer Clara Nunes was one of the foremost samba interpreters of her time. She was born in Paraopea in the state of Minas Gerais on August 12, 1943. Orphaned at a young age, she moved to Belo Horizonte at age 16, where she found employment in a factory and sang in local church choirs. Her first professional break came in 1960 when she won the Minas Gerais section of the Voz de Ouro ABC (ABC Golden Voice) talent competition and went on to place third in the national finals in São Paulo. She moved to Rio de Janeiro in 1965 and signed with Odeon Records, which released her debut album *A Voz Adorável de Clara Nunes*, a mix of boleros and romantic sambas. Her first commercial hit came in 1968 with Ataulfo Alves' song "Você passa e Eu Acho Graça," and in 1974 her album *Alvorecer* sold 500,000 copies, a previously unheard of number for a female vocalist in Brazil. Nunes followed this achievement with a number of commercially and critically successful albums including *Claridade* (1975), *Canto de Três Raças* (1976), *Guerreira* (1978), and *Brasil Mestiço* (1980), and toured throughout Europe and Japan.

Nunes's commercial success is often credited with paving the way for other female samba singers such as Beth Carvalho and Alcione. Her repertoire mixed compositions from the older generation of composers such as Ataulfo Alves, Dorival Caymmi, and Nelson Cavaquinho with songs by younger artists such as Paulinho Viola, Paulo César Pinheiro (whom she married in 1975), and Chico Buarque. She also had a long association with the Portela samba school and recorded several of its carnival theme songs, including "Ilu Ayê" and "Portela na Avenida." A follower of the Afro-Brazilian religion Candomblé, Nunes displayed her religious devotion through the white costumes and extensive jewelry she often wore onstage and in songs such as "A Deusa dos Orixás," and "Ijexá (Filhos de Gandhi)." She died in 1983 in Rio de Janeiro from complications following surgery for varicose veins. In addition to those listed above, her numerous hits include "Juizo Final," "Menino de Deus," "Coração Leviano," and "Morena de Angola."

See also **Buarque, Chico; Candomblé; Caymmi, Dorival; Music: Popular Music and Dance; Samba; Samba Schools; Viola, Paulinho.**

BIBLIOGRAPHY

Autran, Margarida. "Samba, artigo de consumo nacional." In *Anos 70: Ainda sob a tempestade*, ed. Adauto Novaes. Rio de Janeiro: Aeroplano, Editora Senac Rio, 2005.

Marcondes, Marcos Antônio, ed. *Enciclopédia da Música Brasileira: Popular, Erudita e Folclórica*, 2nd edition. São Paulo: Art Editora, Publifolha, 1998.

McGowan, Chris, and Ricardo Pessanha. *The Brazilian Sound: Samba, Bossa Nova, and the Popular Music of Brazil.* New York: Billboard Books, 1991.

ANDREW CONNELL

NÚÑEZ MOLEDO, RAFAEL (1825–1894). Rafael Núñez Moledo (*b.* 28 September 1825; *d.* 18 September 1894), president of Colombia (1880–1882, 1884–1886, 1887, 1888). As the dominant political leader of Colombia from 1880 until his death in 1894, Rafael Núñez left a major imprint on his nation's history by bringing to a close a period of Liberal hegemony, inaugurating an era of Conservative rule lasting until 1930, and imposing the Constitution of 1886 (which remained in force until 1991). A native of Cartagena, Núñez received a law degree in the mid-1840s from the University of Cartagena. He remains an intriguing figure in Colombian history because of his apparent betrayal of a lifelong devotion to liberalism, his impressive intellect, his voluminous writings, including *Ensayos de crítica social* (Rouen, 1874) and *La reforma política en Colombia* (Bogotá, 1945–1950), and a private life that left him vulnerable to political attack.

The Liberal and Conservative parties had achieved clear definition by mid-century, and after a turbulent decade marked by liberal reform, dictatorship, and intermittent civil war, Liberals gained control of the government and held it from 1863 to 1885, a period characterized by extreme federalism, severe limitations on the church, free trade, and provisions for wide-ranging individual freedom. During this period there was also a division in Liberal ranks that deepened in 1875, when Núñez returned to his homeland after twelve years in the United States and Europe, where he served as Colombian consul and as a writer for Latin American newspapers. He launched an unsuccessful bid for the presidency as a Liberal representing the interests of the coastal region against the incumbent Liberals of the interior.

Upon his election as president in 1880, Núñez, concerned over a weakening federal system, civil turmoil, and a worsening economy, began moving against key elements of the Liberal program and calling for constitutional reform. Following his election again in 1884, Núñez, faced with rebellion by the bulk of the Liberal Party, summoned Conservatives to the aid of his administration, the Regeneration. Following the success of Núñez and his adherents in the war of 1884–1885, Núñez presided over implementation of the unitary Constitution of 1886, restoration of government protection of the church, and the undoing of the Liberal program.

See also **Colombia, Constitutions: Overview; Colombia, Political Parties: Liberal Party.**

BIBLIOGRAPHY

Charles W. Bergquist, *Coffee and Conflict in Colombia, 1886–1910* (1978).

Helen Delpar, *Red Against Blue: The Liberal Party in Colombian Politics, 1863–1899* (1981).

James William Park, *Rafael Núñez and the Politics of Colombian Regionalism, 1863–1886* (1985).

Additional Bibliography

Lemaitre, Eduardo. *Contra viento y marea: La lucha de Rafael Núñez por el poder*. Bogotá: Instituto Caro y Cuervo, 1990.

Uribe Uribe, Rafael, and Otto Morales Benítez. *La Regeneración Conservadora de Nuñez y Caro*. Santafé de Bogotá: Instituto para el Desarrollo de la Democracia Luis Carlos Galán, 1995.

JAMES WILLIAM PARK

NÚÑEZ VARGAS, BENJAMIN (1915–1994).

NÚÑEZ VARGAS, BENJAMIN (1915–1994). Benjamin Núñez Vargas (*b.* 1915; *d.* 19 September 1994), Catholic priest, sociologist, labor organizer, cabinet minister, diplomat, educator.

Father Benjamin Núñez Vargas entered public life as a protégé of Archbishop Víctor M. Sanabria Martínez, who had both encouraged and facilitated his sociological studies in the United States, first at Niagara University and then at the Catholic University in Washington, D.C. At Sanabria's request Núñez returned to Costa Rica to form the labor union federation Rerum Novarum, named for Pope Leo XIII's encyclical that dealt with social problems, an activity that placed him in direct competition with the existing communist-oriented unions.

Núñez's social concern and activism propelled him into political action. His early commitment to the National Liberation Movement and the 1948 revolution catapulted him into political leadership, where he remained for over thirty years. He served as labor minister in the revolutionary junta (1948–1949). He took part in the formation of the National Liberation Party (PLN), which quickly became the dominant force in Costa Rican politics. He served in many party and national capacities, including ambassador to Israel and to the United Nations, as well as representative to UNESCO.

His special concern for the development of new leaders inspired a career in education that included a distinguished position as a professor at the University of Costa Rica, appointment as the first rector of the National University, and his establishment of a political training institute in San Isidro de Coronado for rising Latin American democratic leaders. Throughout his career he has been a confidant of all PLN presidents from José Figueres Ferrer through Oscar Arias Sánchez.

See also **Costa Rica, National Liberation Party.**

BIBLIOGRAPHY

John Patrick Bell, *Crisis in Costa Rica* (1971).

James Backer, *La iglesia y el síndicalismo en Costa Rica* (1975).

Charles D. Ameringer, *Don Pepe* (1978).

Additional Bibliography

Berle, Adolph. "Navigating the Rapids, 1918–1971." *American Historical Review* (April 1974), Vol. 79, No. 2 pp. 603–604.

Bulmer-Thomas, Victor. *The Political Economy of Latin America since 1920.* New York: Cambridge University Press, 1988.

Núñez Vargas, Benjamin. "Del Volcán Irazú al Monte Sión." *Heredia, EUNA* (1992).

Núñez Vargas, Benjamin. "Epicentro del Alma Humana y Corazón del Pueblo judío." *KADIMA Instituto Cultural Costarricense-Israelé* (1980).

Núñez Vargas, Benjamin. "Vida de Sacerdote." *Heredia, EUNA,* (1992).

Núñez Vargas, Benjamin and Villegas Hoffmaister, Guillermo. *El Espíritu del 48.* Costa Rica: Editorial Costa Rica, 1987.

JOHN PATRICK BELL

NÚÑEZ VELA, BLASCO (?–1546). Blasco Núñez Vela (*d.* 18 January 1546), ill-fated first viceroy of Peru. From Ávila de los Caballeros, Núñez Vela had served as *veedor general de las guardias de Castilla* before his appointment as first viceroy of Peru. A large fifty-ship fleet carrying the viceroy and justices (*oidores*) of the first Royal Audiencia of Lima sailed from Sanlúcar on 3 November 1543 and reached Nombre de Dios, on Panama's coast, on 10 January 1544. Entrusted with the application of the famous New Laws of 1542 for the protection of the Indians, the newly appointed viceroy quickly set out to enforce the legislation to the letter, in spite of vocal opposition from settlers. He freed Indian slaves in Panama, and on 24 January headed for Peru, arriving relatively quickly at Tumbes on 4 March 1544. From there he marched overland toward Lima.

Encomenderos and previous royal officials began to grow wary of Núñez Vela's seemingly intransigent character. He announced a full *residencia* (official inquiry) to examine the tenure of Governor Cristóbal Vaca De Castro. In Piura he ordered the *tambos,* the old way stations manned by natives, closed. In Trujillo he removed Indians from some *encomenderos* and mandated that natives could not be used to transport Europeans. As he entered Lima, the royal factor, Illan Suárez de Carbajal, asked the viceroy to respect city rights. Tension rose between the viceroy and other officials. The viceroy ignored and insulted his chief advisers, the *oidores.* Meanwhile Gonzalo Pizarro, the Peruvian rebel leader who had been proclaimed governor by the Audiencia in Lima, slowly moved toward the city, his ranks swelling with disaffected settlers. The turning point came when the viceroy, in a fit of anger, assassinated Suárez de Carbajal. The *oidores* decided that by this act the viceroy had threatened the stability of royal government in Peru, and they imprisoned him on 18 September 1544. They asked the crown for review of the New Laws and a trial for Núñez Vela, whom they planned to return to Spain to face charges before the Council of the Indies.

He was imprisoned for a time on an island off Lima, before his opponents shipped him to Panama. During the voyage north, however, the crafty viceroy convinced the ship's captain to land him at Tumbes, where he began to collect men and weapons to retake the viceroyalty. Hoping to engage quickly and defeat the still weak and disorganized Núñez Vela, Gonzalo Pizarro set out from Lima in March 1545. The viceroy retreated northward as far as Pasto, in modern Colombia, trying to unite with Sebastián de Belalcázar, an old Pizarro enemy. A final engagement of rebel and royalist forces took place not far from Quito, in Ecuador. The viceroy was finally defeated and killed by the rebels at the battle of Añaquito on 18 January 1546.

See also **Peru: From the Conquest Through Independence.**

BIBLIOGRAPHY

José Antonio De Busto Duthurburu, *Historia general del Perú,* vol. 2, *Descubrimiento y conquista* (1978).

Alexandra Parma Cook and Noble David Cook, *Good Faith and Truthful Ignorance: A Case of Transatlantic Bigamy* (1991).

Additional Bibliography

Ramírez, Susan E. *The World Upside Down: Cross-Cultural Contact and Conflict in Sixteenth-Century Peru.* Stanford, CA: Stanford University Press, 1996.

NOBLE DAVID COOK

NUSDORFFER, BERNARDO (1686–1762). Bernardo Nusdorffer (*b.* 17 August 1686; *d.* 18 March 1762), German missionary and writer. Nusdorffer, one of several non-Spanish Jesuits who worked as a missionary (in the Paraguay reductions), was born in Plattling, Bavaria, and entered the Jesuit order in 1704. He arrived with eight other German missionaries in the Río de la Plata in 1717 and spent most of his life in Paraguay as a missionary among the Indians. From 1732 to 1739 he was in charge of all of the Jesuit Guaraní reductions. In 1745, when he was the superior of the reduction of San Nicolás de Loreto, he wrote about the effects of alcohol among the Pampas Indians. He thought that its easy availability was leading to their destruction as a people. In 1747, again the provincial superior of the reductions, he wrote a lengthy account of the effects of the Treaty of Limits (1750), which transferred seven Guaraní missions to the Portuguese. In his *Relación de todo lo sucedido en estas Doctrinas en orden a las mudanzas de los Siete Pueblos* (1750–1756), Nusdorffer wrote that after receiving the order of transfer, he immediately took steps to find other land for the thousands of Indians who were being moved from their towns. Among Nusdorffer's writings are accounts of theatrical productions in Jesuit colleges of Paraguay, descriptions of the Indians within and outside the reductions of Paraguay, and several reports of the proceedings surrounding the opposition of the Indian towns to their forced evacuation. He died in San Carlos reduction in 1762.

See also **Missions: Jesuit Missions (Reducciones).**

BIBLIOGRAPHY

Guillermo Furlong Cardiff, *Bernardo Nusdorffer y su "Novena parte" (1760)* (1971).

Additional Bibliography

Ganson, Barbara Anne. *The Guaraní under Spanish Rule in the Río de la Plata.* Stanford, CA: Stanford University Press, 2003.

Several, Rejane da Silveira. *A Guerra Guaranítica.* Porto Alegre: Martins Livreiro-Editor, 1995.

NICHOLAS P. CUSHNER

NUTRITION. Human adaptation to the diverse geography of Latin America has produced many types of nutritional regimes. In Mesoamerica and the Andes, complex agricultural systems supported the growth of densely settled, culturally elaborate civilizations. In the less densely populated Caribbean islands, tropical lowlands, and plains, hunting and gathering in addition to agriculture provided the basis for the diet. European expansion in the sixteenth century altered these civilizations and their nutritional regimes. Interpretations of the nutritional impact of the Conquest and of colonization differ, partly because of varying interpretations of pre-Columbian diets. Some scholars emphasize extreme protein deficiencies, or at least serious undernutrition; others argue the prevalence of nutritionally complete diets, and suggest that pre-Columbian diets were both more balanced and of more nutritional value than those of today. Recent research offers significant evidence supporting the thesis of good diets in pre-Columbian Mesoamerica, the Andes, and in some areas of the tropical lowlands, but more research is needed before definitive claims can be made.

There is little doubt that diets changed beginning in 1492. The introduction of new plants and animals and the displacement of traditional ones initiated nutritional changes in Latin America, and subsequently in the rest of the world. For the first time in history, nutritional regimes incorporated foods from around the world. Latin America enjoyed these advantages first, followed by Europe, Africa, and Asia. Most significant from a nutritional standpoint were the new sources of protein, specifically the cattle, sheep, goats, pigs, and fowl introduced by the Europeans. Then came the new sources of carbohydrates, the grains, fruits, and vegetables of the conquerors. Bananas and plantains emerged as especially important sources of carbohydrates, vitamins, and minerals. Through much of tropical Latin America, land planted in plantains and bananas produced twenty times as much food as the same land planted in grain.

The variety of foods available in Latin America created the potential for the best nutritional regimes in the world in the sixteenth century, though social and political forces that influenced the production, distribution, and consumption of nutrients could undermine the realization of that potential. The rapid decline of the Amerindian population, for example, lessened the pressure on food resources but restricted the number of workers available for food production. As the Indian population declined, new labor and tribute demands emerged. The Spanish and Portuguese regimes relied on the control of labor, Indian and black, for the building and maintenance of cities, mines, factories, and plantations.

Many accounts emphasize the exploitative aspects of colonialism as evidence of widespread malnutrition during the period. They also emphasize monopolistic practices, high prices, short weighing, and adulteration of foodstuffs as contributing to poor nutrition. To combat these practices, Spain and Portugal transferred many of their regulatory institutions and policies to Spanish America and Brazil. When enforced, laws requiring adequate supplies at fair prices did help to ensure a suitable diet. Access of the worker, free or slave, to small garden plots and to hunting and gathering was also an important factor in determining diet.

Population decline and disease are often linked to nutrition. For Latin America, poor nutrition is frequently offered as an explanation for disease and death. While the lack of research on the quantity and quality of early Latin American diets makes this relationship difficult to prove for most social and ethnic groups, the evidence for black slaves in the Caribbean and Brazil is convincing. Slaves suffered severe vitamin A and B complex deficiencies when their diets were limited to root crops and dried fish and meat. Despite adequate caloric intake, there were deficiencies of vitamins and minerals that led to the widespread incidence of beriberi, pellagra, yaws, and other diseases. Other evidence suggests that the poor—when they had control over their own diets—ate as well as or better than the rich. They relied more heavily on unrefined foods, fish, and fresh fruits and vegetables. And as anthropological research has shown, the diets of twentieth-century tropical peoples still adhering to traditional ways are nutritionally adequate. Complex biospheres provide rich and varied diets, including adequate sources of protein, often with less labor cost than in modern industrial societies. The emphasis on protein deficiency as an explanation for cultural practices such as cannibalism and warfare has been balanced by an emphasis on sufficient protein in indigenous diets.

Hunting and gathering declined as the cattle, pigs, and sheep introduced by Europeans became more important in the diet. Where abundant cattle continued to roam—the great range lands of the pampas, the São Francisco River basin, the llanos of Venezuela—there was surplus protein. Those areas with dense populations, especially the expanding urban centers in the Caribbean, Mexico, Brazil, and the Andes, experienced more difficulty in securing adequate supplies of protein and other nutrients by the end of the colonial period. Population growth, increasing production for export, deforestation and soil erosion, and the problems of supplying ever larger urban centers made securing an adequate diet more difficult. Adding to the difficulties were climatic problems (the recurring droughts of northeastern Brazil, for example) that limited food production.

By the late nineteenth century, Latin America was experiencing a nutritional transition, the time and intensity of which varied from region to region. While Europe entered a period of increased consumption of calories and protein, Latin America faced increased shortages. In the Andes and Middle America, in particular, hunger became more persistent. Reports of increased food prices, declines in production of subsistence foods, and monotonous, simple diets suggest a decline in nutrition over earlier years. Control over land and labor were the critical issues. As haciendas, plantations, and cities expanded and rural people became a part of increasingly complex production and labor arrangements, diets suffered. Increased commercial agriculture and rapid urbanization were the main trends undermining diets. This interpretation has merit, but the diversity of regions, resources, and labor arrangements makes generalizations about nineteenth-century diets difficult.

By the 1920s, nutritional deficiencies, along with alcohol abuse, illiteracy, and lack of adequate sanitary conditions, emerged as widely discussed social problems. Gradually, national and international organizations began to focus on the inadequacy of the Latin American diet. Studies began to reveal the extent of nutritional-deficiency diseases. The Tercera Conferencia Internacional de la Alimentación, held in Buenos Aires in 1939, concluded that "Latin America lived a true tragedy due to the malnutrition that affects all the countries." Fully 25 percent of the population could not afford recommended diets. The International Labor Office provided comparative information, demonstrating the weakness of the Latin American diet when compared with that of other regions in the hemisphere. In the 1930s, Chilean wage earners spent 71.1 percent of all expenditures on food, residents of Bogotá, 63.7 percent, of Mexico City, 56.4 percent, compared with 33.5 percent in the United States. The surveys, which seem to suggest poor nutrition, at times conflict with detailed analyses of the balanced diets of poor villages, where the staples of maize, tubers, beans, and chilies were only infrequently supplemented by eggs, milk, and meat. The advantage that these poor rural people had was that they followed the traditional custom of consuming wild foods—weeds, insects, grubs, and worms—that helped to balance the diet.

It is as difficult to generalize about diets in the twentieth century as it is regarding earlier periods. At the national level in the early 1960s, Argentines consumed 3,600 calories and 100 grams of protein per day, higher than residents of the United States, who consumed 3,220 calories and 97 grams of protein. No other Latin American country achieved the consumption levels of Argentina; most fell far below. Central American and Andean countries had particularly severe problems of malnutrition. Marasmus was not widespread, but there were increasing examples of protein-calorie malnutrition, and the deficiency diseases of beriberi, endemic goiter, xerophthalmia, and ariboflavinosis. Low birth weight and small stature were also signs of the extent of malnutrition in many regions. So were the incidence and severity of infectious and parasitic diseases.

Reports from the 1960s predicted a "Malthusian crisis" in Latin America if food production was not increased. Most regions have achieved the increase in production. In addition, national and international organizations have sponsored nutritional research, food distribution systems, and educational efforts. New foods (such as Incaparina, a nutritious soybean substitute for milk introduced by the Institute of Nutrition of Central America and Panama (INCAP) in the 1950s in Guatemala) have been developed to reduce malnutrition. This does not mean an improvement in nutrition. Indeed, in some regions, Central America and the Andes, for example, nutritional levels have declined, despite increased food production. Even traditionally food-wealthy countries such as Argentina have experienced severe food shortages in recent years.

Two problems undermining nutrition are the increasing production of foods for export and the increasing inequality in the distribution of income. Since the 1970s, soybean production has grown significantly, reaching nearly 100,000 metric tons (a jump from 12,927 metric tons in 1978), putting it ahead of cassava, wheat, rice, and banana production—traditional food crops in Latin America. The decreasing income of the poor aggravated by the global recession of the early 1970s, limited purchasing power for food. To these difficulties can be added a host of problems: displacement of traditional foods; increased reliance on processed, imported foods; control by transnational food corporations; marketing directed to middle- and upper-class incomes; food policies that subsidize urban and neglect rural populations; and counterproductive food-aid policies. Seldom are the traditional explanations of peasant ignorance and conservatism, lack of capital and technology, and climate and soil deficiencies used to explain nutrition today.

Demography also influences nutrition, though the extent of its influence is debated. Once rural societies have become overwhelmingly urban. The rapid population increase that began during the interwar years nearly tripling the region's inhabitants, increased pressure on food resources. Without political and social mechanisms to ensure the equitable distribution of food, hunger and nutritional deficiencies followed. In the twenty-first century, people in the Latin American region have seen improvements in overall health care and quality of life. Yet new problems related to an aging and urban society have also arisen. The effects of this can be seen with increases in conditions like obesity, diabetes, hypertension, and cardiovascular disease. Still, malnutrition continues to be a challenge, particularly for poor urban and rural residents. Stunted growth, a consequence of inadequate nutrients, continues to be evident in children throughout the Andean region. Many impoverished children rely upon federal- and state-sponsored public school lunch programs for their basic nutritional needs. Indeed, most of the recent research on hunger in Latin America confirms the conclusions of the Conference on Food and Agriculture, a forerunner of the Food and Agriculture Organization of the United Nations, held in the United States in 1943, which declared that "the primordial cause of hunger and poor nutrition is poverty."

See also **Banana Industry; Cuisines; Diseases; Fruit Industry; Income Distribution; Maize; Medicine: The Modern Era; Population: Brazil; Population: Spanish America; Soybeans.**

BIBLIOGRAPHY

Bernard R. Ortiz De Montellano, *Aztec Medicine, Health and Nutrition* (1990), presents an excellent analysis of diets in central Mexico before the Conquest. For comparison with the Maya, see Luis Alberto Vargas, "La alimentación de los mayas antiguos," in *Historia general de la medicina en México* vol. 1, edited by Fernando Martínez Cortés (1984), pp. 273–282. Alfredo Castillero Calvo surveys early diets in "Niveles de vida y cambios de dieta a fines del período colonial en América," in *Anuario de Estudios Americanos* 44 (1987): 427–475. Mary C. Karasch, *Slave Life in Rio de Janeiro, 1808–1850* (1987) and Kenneth F. Kiple and Virginia H. Kiple, "Deficiency Diseases in the Caribbean," in *Journal of Interdisciplinary History* 11, no. 2 (1980): 197–215, assess slave diets. John C. Super and Thomas C. Wright, eds., *Food Politics, and Society in Latin America* (1985) analyzes historical and current issues of food supply. The works by Jacques M. May and Donna L. McLellan, *The Ecology of Malnutrition in Mexico and Central America* (1972) and *The Ecology of Malnutrition in Eastern South America* (1974) are convenient summaries of information on nutrition. Still very much worthwhile reading is the early classic statement on nutrition in Latin America by Josué De Castro, *The Geography of Hunger* (1952). Charles D. Brockett incorporates recent theoretical and interdisciplinary work on food, nutrition, and social and economic change in *Land, Power, and Poverty: Agrarian Transformation and Political Conflict in Central America* (1988). For recent nutritional data consult the yearly Food and Agriculture Organization of the United Nations reports, *The State of Food and Agriculture*.

Additional Bibliography

Arcondo, Aníbal B. *Historia de la alimentación en Argentina: Desde los orígenes hasta 1920.* Buenos Aires: Ferreyra Editor, 2002.

Bartell, Ernest J., and Alejandro O'Donnell. *The Child in Latin America: Health, Development, and Rights.* Notre Dame, IN: University of Notre Dame Press, 2001.

Food and Agriculture Organization of the United Nations. *Globalization of Food Systems in Developing Countries: Impact on Food Security and Nutrition.* Rome: Food and Agriculture Organization of the United Nations, 2004.

Sawaya, Ana Lydia, and Alexandre Archanjo Ferrari. *Desnutrição urbana no Brasil em um período de transição.* São Paulo: Cortez Editora: Centro de Recuperação e Educação Nutricional: Núcleo Salus Paulista, 1997.

Lima, Eronides da Silva. *Mal de fome e não de raça: Gênese, constituição e ação política da educação alimentar, Brasil 1934–1946.* Rio de Janeiro: Editora Fiocruz, 2000.

Lima Junior, Jayme Benvenuto, Lena Zetterströ, and Flávio Luiz Schieck Valente. *Extrema pobreza no Brasil: A situação do direito à alimentação e moradia adequada.* São Paulo: Edições Loyola, 2002.

Long, Janet, and Luis Alberto Vargas. *Food Culture in Mexico.* Westport: Greenwood Press, 2005.

Ochoa, Enrique. *Feeding Mexico: The Political Uses of Food since 1910.* Wilmington, DE: Scholarly Resources, 2000.

Pollitt, Ernesto. *Consecuencias de la desnutrición en el escolar peruano.* Lima: Pontificia Universidad Católica del Perú: Fondo Editorial, 2002.

Prudencio B., Julio. *Soberanía o inseguridad?: El problema alimentario en Bolivia.* La Paz: Gisvol, 2005.

Remedi, Fernando Javier. *Consumo de alimentos, condiciones sanitarias y políticas públicas en la Ciudad de Córdoba en las primeras décadas del siglo XX.* Córdoba: EMCOR. Editorial de la Municipalidad de Córdoba, 2003.

World Bank. *Nutritional Failure in Ecuador: Causes, Consequences, and Solutions.* Washington, DC: World Bank, 2007.

Wright, Lori E. *Diet, Health, and Status among the Pasión Maya: A Reappraisal of the Collapse.* Nashville, TN: Vanderbilt University Press, 2006.

JOHN C. SUPER

O, GENOVEVO DE LA (1876–1952).

Genovevo de la O (*b.* 3 January 1876; *d.* 12 June 1952), Mexican revolutionary. The leader, in 1910, of an autonomous rebellion in the northwestern corner of the state of Morelos, de la O joined the movement of Emiliano Zapata shortly after the promulgation of the Plan of Ayala in 1911. He soon became one of Zapata's fiercest fighters and most important generals. Because he frequently struck north to the mountainous fringes of Mexico City, de la O was one of the Zapatistas most feared in the capital. In particular, he developed a reputation as a destroyer of trains. After the revolution he pursued a more conventional military career before retiring to his farm in 1941.

See also **Plan of Ayala; Zapata, Emiliano.**

BIBLIOGRAPHY

John Womack, *Zapata and the Mexican Revolution* (1968).

Salvador Rueda, "La zona armada de Genovevo de la O," in *Cuicuilco* 2, no. 3 (1981): 38–43.

Samuel Brunk, *Revolution and Betrayal in Mexico: A Life of Emiliano Zapata* (1995).

Additional Bibliography

Avila Espinosa, Felipe Arturo. *Los orígenes del zapatismo.* México: El Colegio de México, Centro de Estudios Históricos, 2001.

Hart, Paul. *Bitter Harvest: The Social Transformation of Morelos, Mexico, and the Origins of the Zapatista Revolution, 1840–1910.* Albuquerque: University of New Mexico Press, 2005.

SAMUEL BRUNK

OAXACA (CITY).

Oaxaca is the capital of the state of Oaxaca, located in the heart of the Central Valleys district, 328 miles southeast of Mexico City. In 2007 its population was estimated at 437,634.

Founded as a fort in 1486 by the Aztecs, Huaxyacac was resettled by a group of Spanish conquistadores who received title to it as the Villa of Antequera in 1528. However, Hernán Cortés continually disputed Antequera's legality, insisting that it fell within the domain of his marquesado del Valle. In 1532 Charles V decreed Antequera to be an independent city, but by 1560, it had only 500 Spanish and other inhabitants. Ten years later, construction began on the exquisite Santo Domingo church.

Antequera survived as an administrative center on the royal highway to Central America and as the center of a regional marketing system dating from the pre-Columbian period. As capital of the Intendancy of Oaxaca in the late eighteenth century, the city of Oaxaca ("Antequera" fell into disuse) grew dramatically as a result of textile manufacturing and the cochineal dye trade. José María Morelos established his government there for a few months during the struggle for independence, and in 1824 Oaxaca became the state capital. Its Instituto de Ciencias y Artes, inaugurated in 1827, educated many of Mexico's leading liberals, among them Benito Juárez and Porfirio Díaz. In 1955 the institute became the Universidad Autónoma "Benito Juárez" de Oaxaca.

A cradle of Mexican liberalism, on 10 October 1872 Oaxaca affixed "de Juárez" to its name to honor the state's preeminent liberal. During the Porfiriato, the capital prospered from mining and coffee exports. The local merchant and landowning oligarchy intermarried with arriving foreign investors and their families to broaden its base.

In 1931 a brutal earthquake destroyed half the city, but most buildings (many of green limestone) were later repaired to restore Oaxaca's colonial splendor. A 1976 presidential decree declared the center of the city a national monument, and in 1987 the United Nations included Oaxaca in Humanity's Cultural Patrimony. Today it is a major center of tourism and distribution of indigenous artisanry.

In 2006, a series of strikes turned violent when peacefully protesting local teachers were forcibly removed from the city's main square by Oaxaca police. Some media reports claim that at least four people died in these clashes, although the Oaxacan government denies this. As of 2007 the teachers were still lobbying for better pay and a series of measures to help the city's poor students, and they are supported by a group known as the Popular Assembly of the Peoples of Oaxaca (APPO), a coalition of union, women's, peasant and indigenous movements.

See also **Earthquakes; Intendancy System; Mexico: The Colonial Period.**

BIBLIOGRAPHY

Jorge Fernando Iturribarría, *Oaxaca en la historia*. Mexico: Editorial Stylo,1955.

John Chance, *Race and Class in Colonial Oaxaca*. Stanford, CA: Stanford University Press, 1978.

José Iñigo Aguilar Medina, *El hombre y la urbe: La ciudad de Oaxaca*. Mexico: Secretaría de Educación Pública, Instituto Nacional de la Antropología e Historia, 1980.

Additional Bibliography

Basques, Jeremy. *Indians, Merchants, and Markets: A Reinterpration of the Repartimiento and Spanish-Indian Economic Relations in Colonial Oaxaca, 1750–1821*. Stanford, CA: Stanford University Press, 2000.

Marcus, Joyce, and Kent V. Flannery. *Zapotec Civilization: How Urban Society Evolved in Mexico's Oaxaca Valley*. New York: Thames and Hudson, 1996.

Murphy, Arthur D., and Alex Stepick. *Social Inequality in Oaxaca*. Philadelphia: Temple University, 1993.

Terraciano, Kevin. *The Mixtecs of Colonial Oaxaca: Nudzahui History, Sixteenth through Eighteenth Centuries*. Stanford, CA: Stanford University Press, 2001.

FRANCIE CHASSEN-LÓPEZ

OAXACA (STATE). The state of Oaxaca covers 36,820 square miles and contained 3,506,821 inhabitants in 2005. Crossed by the Sierra Madre Oriental and Sierra Madre del Sur, Oaxaca's rugged terrain accounts for its isolation and division into seven distinct geographical regions (Central Valleys, Sierra Juárez, Cañada, Mixteca, Costa, Isthmus of Tehuantepec, and Papaloapan River basin) and partially for the survival of sixteen indigenous groups.

Zapotecs and Mixtecs, the two most numerous groups today, are descendants of major Mesoamerican civilizations. Zapotec culture reached its height in the classic period at Monte Albán (200–900), and the Mixtecs flourished during the postclassic period (1000–1521). The advancing Aztec Empire established a garrison in 1486 at Huaxyacac (today the city of Oaxaca). Francisco de Orozco and Pedro de Alvarado conquered the Central Valleys in 1521–1522. A large part of Oaxaca fell within Hernán Cortés's marquesado del Valle, ceded to him by Charles V in 1529. Oaxaca was evangelized by the Dominican order and continues to be a stronghold of Catholicism.

The economy languished until cochineal dye, textile manufacture, and silver production generated prosperity in the latter eighteenth century. Owing to its geographical isolation, lack of transportation, and the tenacity of its indigenous population to retain communal lands, haciendas existed precariously. A commercial elite, based in the capital city, has dominated economics and politics since this period. The Bourbon Reforms established Oaxaca as one of Mexico's twelve intendancies.

During the struggle for independence, José María Morelos ruled briefly from the city of Oaxaca, where a native son, Carlos María de Bustamante, published the insurgent *El Correo del Sur*. In 1824 Oaxaca became a state. In 1853, after a local rebellion, a Conservative government created a separate federal territory straddling the states of Oaxaca and Veracruz. Although the state was abolished by Benito Juárez in 1857, isthmian separatism remains a latent problem.

Two Oaxacan Liberals (who also served as state governors) dominated Mexican politics during the latter half of the nineteenth century. President Benito Juárez guided the nation's Liberal reform movement through civil wars and the French Intervention. President Porfirio Díaz fostered economic liberalism:

infrastructure, commercial agriculture, and foreign investment. During his rule, a railway connected Oaxaca to Mexico City, thus facilitating a mining boom and the exportation of cash crops. Commercial agriculture expanded at the expense of the communal landholdings of the indigenous villages.

Although urban and rural middle sectors seconded the 1910 Revolution in Oaxaca, support for Díaz was strong in his native state. In 1915 the conservative Oaxacan oligarchy, opposed to the increasing domination of Mexico by the Constitutionalists led by Venustino Carranza, attempted to distance itself from the civil war by temporarily withdrawing recognition from his government and resuming state sovereignty. However, by mid-1916, Constitutionalist forces controlled most of the state's territory.

After the revolution, Oaxaca continued to export coffee, especially the highly prized Pluma Altura bean. Nevertheless, neglected by revolutionary regimes and failing to industrialize (producing only 1 percent of the nation's industrial goods in 1990), Oaxaca became Mexico's poorest state, suffering from high infant mortality, malnutrition, and illiteracy, especially among its indigenous population. With the restoration of archaeological sites and colonial architecture, the recent development of coastal attractions (Huatulco), and distribution of indigenous artisanry, tourism has developed into a major source of income. The prominent Mexican artists Miguel Cabrera, Rufino Tamayo, and Francisco Toledo were born in Oaxaca. Controversy and political strife erupted in Oaxaca city in May 2006, when teachers striking for higher wages occupied and held buildings. By October, the movement had garnered the support of tens of thousands of people and supporters called for the resignation of Oaxaca's governor. On October 27, government paramilitary troops fired into a crowd of protesters and killed three of them. Two days later, President Vicente Fox authorized police and military officers to use bulldozers and water cannons to push back the protestors and to regain control of the city. Disputes between protestors and troops continued, but as of 2007 all actions had been peaceful.

See also **Cortés, Hernán; Díaz, Porfirio; Juárez, Benito; Mexico: The Colonial Period; Mexico: Since 1910; Mixtecs; Monte Albán; Zapotecs.**

BIBLIOGRAPHY

Jorge Fernando Iturribarría, *Oaxaca en la historia* (1955).

William B. Taylor, *Landlord and Peasant in Colonial Oaxaca* (1972).

José María Bradomín, *Monografía del estado de Oaxaca* (1980).

Leticia Reina, ed., *Historia de la cuestíon agraria: Estado de Oaxaca,* 2 vols. (1988).

Margarita Dalton, comp., *Oaxaca: Textos de su historia,* 5 vols. (1990).

María De Los Angeles Frizzi, comp., *Lecturas históricas del estado de Oaxaca,* vols. 2–4 (1990).

Víctor Raúl Martínez Vázquez, ed., *La revolución en Oaxaca, 1900–1930* (1993).

Additional Bibliography

Baskes, Jeremy. *Indians, Merchants, and Markets: A Reinterpretation of the Repartimiento and Spanish-Indian Relations in Colonial Oaxaca, 1750–1821.* Stanford, CA: Stanford University Press, 2000.

Chassen de López, Francie R. *From Liberal to Revolutionary Oaxaca: The View from the South: Mexico, 1867–1911.* University Park: Pennsylvania State University Press, 2004.

Guardino, Peter F. *The Time of Liberty: Popular Political Culture in Oaxaca, 1750–1850.* Durham, NC: Duke University Press, 2005.

Overmyer Velázquez, Mark. *Visions of the Emerald City: Modernity, Tradition, and the Formation of Porfirian Oaxaca, Mexico.* Durham, NC: Duke University Press, 2006.

Terraciano, Kevin. *The Mixtecs of Colonial Oaxaca: Nudzahui History, Sixteenth through Eighteenth Centuries.* Stanford, CA: Stanford University Press, 2001.

FRANCIE CHASSEN-LÓPEZ

OBALDÍA, MARÍA OLIMPIA DE (1891–1985). María Olimpia de Obaldía (*b.* 9 September 1891; *d.* 15 August 1985), Panamanian poet. Obaldía was born in Dolega, Panama. She completed her high school studies in a small school in the city of David. In 1913 she was awarded a teaching certificate by the Normal de Institutoras, and shortly after, was appointed to teach in Dolega by the mayor of the city. She returned in 1915 to her alma mater to occupy the position of superintendent, remaining in this post until 1917.

With the appearance of her first book of poems, *Orquídeas* (Orchids, 1926), and with the publication three years later of *Brevario Lírico* (Lyrical Breviary), she attained recognition and a distinguished place in Panamanian letters as a representative poet of the postmodernist movement. Her greatest contribution to Panamanian letters is not only the development of the theme of conjugal, maternal, fraternal, and filial love in Panamanian literature, but also the creation of a new space for the feminine voice in Panamanian poetry. The universality of her poetic message is another one of her major contributions to Latin American literature.

Obaldía was a distinguished member of the Panamanian Academy of the Spanish Language and a delegate at international conferences. Her works have appeared in anthologies published in Latin America and abroad.

See also **Literature: Spanish America.**

BIBLIOGRAPHY

Gloria Guardia, *Obras completas de doña María Olimpia de Obaldía* (1975).

Diane E. Marting, ed., *Women Writers of Spanish America* (1987).

ELBA D. BIRMINGHAM-POKORNY

OBANDO, JOSÉ MARÍA (1795–1861).

José María Obando (*b.* 8 August 1795; *d.* 29 April 1861), acting president (23 November 1831–10 March 1832) and president of Colombia (1853–1854). The illegitimate son of a member of an elite Popayán family, Obando was adopted by members of the Pasto gentry but educated in Popayán. He was a royalist guerrilla officer (1819–1822) in the Pasto-Popayán region, forming networks of personal friendship through his charismatic personality. In 1822, he joined the patriots as a lieutenant colonel and eventually emerged as the caudillo of southern Colombia. Obando led populist rebellions in 1828, 1831, and 1840–1842 (the latter the War of the Supremes), then fled into exile in Peru and Chile (1842–1849). General Tomás Cipriano de Mosquera attempted, unsuccessfully, to extradite him. Obando, a hero to Colombia's Liberals, was elected president in 1853. Caught between their doctrinaire agenda and his own populist sympathies, and hamstrung by the Constitution of 1853, his presidency foundered. When, in April 1854, General José María Melo rebelled, Obando remained passive. He was removed from office by the Senate on 4 April 1855 and returned to Popayán. He joined his former enemy, Mosquera, in the revolution of 1859–1861. He died in an ambush near Bogotá.

See also **Colombia: From the Conquest Through Independence; Colombia: Since Independence; Melo, José María.**

BIBLIOGRAPHY

Horacio Rodríguez Plata, *José María Obando íntimo* (1958).

Antonio José Lemos Guzmán, *Obando: De cruz verde a cruz verde, 1795–1861* (1959).

J. León Helguera, "José María Obando," in *Encyclopedia of Latin America,* edited by Helen Delpar (1974).

Francisco U. Zuluaga R., *José María Obando* (1985).

Additional Bibliography

Sant Roz, José. *El Jackson granadino, José María Obando: Recuento político-religioso del asesinato de Sucre.* Mérida: Kariña Editores, 2000.

J. LEÓN HELGUERA

OBANDO Y BRAVO, MIGUEL (1926–).

Miguel Obando y Bravo was the archbishop of Managua, Nicaragua, from 1970 to 2005. A member of the Salesian religious congregation, Obando, born on February 2, 1926, was consecrated auxiliary bishop of Matagalpa in 1968 and then became archbishop of Managua. In 1985 Pope John Paul II named him the first and only cardinal in Central America; many regarded the pope's decision as an effort to strengthen Obando's hand against the Sandinista revolutionary government.

During the 1970s Obando and other bishops criticized the Somoza dictatorship, but the National Guard's dubbing him "comandante Miguel" was not accurate; he was more aligned with the oligarchy's opposition to Somoza than with the Sandinistas' revolutionary struggle. During hostage-taking actions by the Sandinistas in 1974 and 1978, Obando served as mediator between the Sandinistas and the government. After the 1979 takeover by the Sandinistas, Obando turned against them, objecting to their Marxism and secularism. In the late 1980s he continued his role as a mediator, this time between the Sandinista government and the U.S.-supported contras. In the 1990 elections he supported the winning United Nicaraguan Opposition (UNO), led by Violeta Barrios de Chamorro, and in the early 1990s he served as a verifier of the peace accords between her government and groups that were continuing paramilitary activity.

During Obando's tenure as archbishop there were bitter conflicts within the church. Many Christian-based communities, which supported the Sandinista revolutionary government as a means toward greater justice for the poor, criticized Obando as a supporter of the violent counterrevolution; his defenders considered him a champion of freedom. His resignation from the post of archbishop did not remove him from the realm of controversy. In 2004, the year before his resignation, he held a mass to honor the memory of those killed during the wars of the 1970s and 1980s, publicly forgiving the Sandinistas. In 2006 Sandinista leader Daniel Ortega won the presidential election, returning him to power for the first time since 1990, and reconciled with the Catholic Church. He then named Obando y Bravo head of a Peace and Reconciliation Committee, a move regarded by some as politically expedient for both leaders.

See also **Nicaragua; United States-Latin American Relations.**

BIBLIOGRAPHY

Roger N. Lancaster, *Thanks to God and the Revolution* (1988).

Irene Selser, *Cardenal Obando* (1989).

Miguel Obando y Bravo, *Agonía en el bunker,* 2d ed. (1990).

Michael Dodson and Laura Nuzzi O'Shaughnessy, *Nicaragua's Other Revolution* (1990).

Joseph E. Mulligan, *The Nicaraguan Church and the Revolution* (1991).

Additional Bibliography

Urtasun, Domingo. *Miguel Obando Bravo, Cardenal por la paz.* Managua: Editorial Hispamer, 1994.

JOSEPH E. MULLIGAN

OBIN, PHILOMÉ (1892–1985). Philomé Obin (*b.* 1892; *d.* 1985), Haitian painter. Obin was the head of an extensive family of artists in Haiti whose brothers Othan and Senêque and their children continue the tradition. Obin founded the school of northern realists in Haiti and is linked stylistically and thematically with the naïfs movement. His bright colors, voodoo-inspired scenes, and tropical lighting share much with the later works of Wilson Bigaud. Obin became a Mason in 1918 and subsequently abandoned Catholicism for the Baptist church. He considered himself to be both a historian and an artist, because many of his best works deal with historical events and people: the revolutionary epoch, King Christophe, and the building of the Citadelle. Obin's masterpiece is *The Funeral of Charlemagne Péralte* (1947).

See also **Art: The Twentieth Century; Vodun, Voodoo, Vaudun.**

BIBLIOGRAPHY

Selden Rodman, *The Miracle of Haitian Art* (1974).

Eleanor Ingalls Christensen, *The Art of Haiti* (1975).

Madame Shishi, *"Les Naïfs Haitiens": An Introduction to Haitian Art and History* (1982).

Additional Bibliography

Grandjean, Michèle. *Artistes en Haïti: Cent parmi d'autres.* Marseille: Art et coeur, 1997.

KAREN RACINE

OBRAJE. Obraje, a single enterprise that incorporated most, if not all, of the processes of wool cloth manufacture: dyeing, carding, spinning, weaving, fulling, and finishing. First established in Puebla, Mexico, during the 1530s, by the 1560s *obrajes* had developed in Peru. *Obraje* buildings were large: the examples Richard Salvucci gives for Mexico range from 5,600 to almost 40,000 square feet. Andean *obrajes* could be even bigger: Manuel Miño Grijalva cites the *obraje* of Pichuichuro (1777), which had five patios and weaving and spinning galleries, each 250 yards long. An *obraje* could house between 4 and 40 looms, and employ from 40 to 250 men, women, and children. Early in the colonial period *obrajes* were often owned and managed by clothiers from the wool-producing towns of Castile. By the eighteenth century, *obrajes* were more likely to be immigrant merchants from northern Spain. By then it had become common in Mexico and the Andes for *obrajes* to form part of broader, vertically integrated rural enterprises. Technology resembled that current in Spain: backward but an advance upon native techniques. Thus expenditures for wages and short-term credit greatly exceeded investment in fixed capital.

The real strength of the *obraje* lay in its control over labor in an imperfect labor market. *Obrajes* produced all kinds of woolen cloth, from coarse serges and blankets to fine *paño de primera.* The fine cloth originally produced in Puebla and Quito for distant markets gave way in time to cheaper, ordinary cloth produced closer to the source of the wool supply and meant for local markets. By the end of the colonial period, most *obrajes* in Mexico were on the point of collapse in the face of foreign competition and labor indiscipline; few survived independence. Ecuador's *obrajes* proved more resilient but underwent a continuing decline during the nineteenth century.

See also **Textile Industry: The Colonial Era.**

BIBLIOGRAPHY

Richard E. Greenleaf, "The Obraje in the Late Mexican Colony," in *The Americas,* 23 (1967): 227–250.

John C. Super, "Querétaro Obrajes: Industry and Society in Provincial Mexico," in *Hispanic American Historical Review,* 56 (1976): 197–216.

Javier Ortiz De La Tabla Ducasse, "El obraje colonial ecuatoriano: Aproximación a su estudio," in *Revista de Indias,* 37 (1977): 471–541.

W. P. Glade, "Obrajes and the Industrialisation of Colonial Latin America," in *Economics in the Long View: Essays in Honour of W. W. Rostow,* edited by Charles P. Kindleberger and Guido di Tella, vol. 2 (1982).

Richard Salvucci, *Textiles and Capitalism in Mexico: An Economic History of the Obrajes, 1539–1840* (1987).

Manuel Miño Grijalva, "El obraje colonial," in *European Review of Latin American and Caribbean Studies,* 47 (December 1989): 3–19.

Additional Bibliography

Silva Santiesteban, Fernando. *Los objajes en el virreinato del Perú.* Lima: Publicaciones del Museo nacional de Historia, 1964.

Gómez Galvarriato, Aurora. *La industria textil en México.* México, D.F.: Instituto Mora: Colegio de Michoacán: Colegio de México, 1999.

Ramos-Escandón, Carmen. *Industrialización, género y trabajo femenino en el sector textil mexicano: el obraje, la fábrica y la compañía industrial.* México, D.F.: CIESAS, 2004.

Guy P. C. Thomson

OBRAS PÍAS.

OBRAS PÍAS. Obras Pías, charitable foundations for the support of hospitals, convents, missions, and schools, as well as chaplaincies, which were established during the colonial period and continued through the first part of the nineteenth century. Other usages of the term include provisions in wills for perpetual masses established for the repose of the souls of the dead and members of his or her family. These became *obras pías* when the church established the mechanism whereby the funds could be invested in agriculture, urban real estate, or trade. Dowries for all brides, religious or secular, might also be characterized as *obras pías.* The idea derives ultimately from the conception of charity embodied in the Judeo-Christian tradition. The Council of Trent (1545–1563) established procedures for these charitable foundations. The wording of the documents of donation indicates that donors believed such deeds could release one's own soul and that of members of one's family from purgatory. Wills reflected additional aspects of *obras pías,* sometimes making it difficult to differentiate between voluntary donations and those that were so widespread as to be characterized as taxation, such as the almost universal provision in testaments in New Spain for the beatification of Gregorio López.

BIBLIOGRAPHY

John Leddy Phelan, *The Hispanization of the Philippines* (1959).

Michael P. Costeloe, *Church Wealth in Mexico: A Study of the "Juzgado de Capellanías" in the Archbishopric of Mexico: 1800–1856* (1967).

John Frederick Schwaller, *The Origins of Church Wealth in Mexico* (1985).

Additional Bibliography

Ludlow, Leonor, and Jorge Silva Riquer. *Los negocios y las ganancias de la colonia al México moderno.* México: Instituto de Investigaciones Dr. José María Luis Mora: Instituto de Investigaciones Históricas-UNAM, 1993.

Martínez de Sánchez, Ana María. *Cofradías y obras pías en Córdoba del Tucumán.* Córdoba: Editorial de la Universidad Católica de Córdoba, EDUCC, 2006.

Martínez López-Cano, María del Pilar, Gisela von Wobeser, and Juan Guillermo Muñoz Correa. *Cofradías, capellanías y obras pías en la América colonial.* México, D.F.: Universidad Nacional Autónoma de México, 1998.

Edith Couturier

OBREGÓN, ALEJANDRO (1920–1992). Alejandro Obregón (*b.* 4 June 1920; *d.* 11 April 1992), Colombian artist. Born in Barcelona, Spain, Obregón always considered himself self-taught although he studied art in England, the United States, and France. His career was difficult at its inception because of his inability to master pictorial techniques. In 1943 he had his first solo show and launched his career. He developed special symbols—like the falcon and colorful flowers—to depict the Colombian landscape and its inhabitants. His figures are painted in large and strong brush strokes.

In 1948–1949 Obregón served as director of the School of Fine Arts at the National University of Bogotá. In the following decades he participated in group shows: the Bienal Hispanoamericana (Madrid, 1958), receiving first prize; the Gulf Caribbean International Exhibition (Houston, 1959); the Salon of National Artists (Bogotá, 1962 and 1966); and the São Paulo Bienal (1967), where he received the grand prize. In 1981 a retrospective of his work was held at the Avianca Cultural Center in Barranquilla, Colombia, and in 1985 another large retrospective traveled from Bogotá to Paris and Madrid.

See also **Art: The Twentieth Century.**

BIBLIOGRAPHY

Museum of Modern Art of Latin America (Art Museum of the Americas, Oas), *Alejandro Obregón; Recent Paintings* (1983).

Juan Gustavo Cobo Borda, *Obregón* (1985).

Additional Bibliography

Jaramillo, Carmen María. *Alejandro Obregón: El mago del Carib.* Bogotá: Asociación de Amigos del Museo Nacional de Colombia, 2001.

BÉLGICA RODRÍGUEZ

OBREGÓN, JOSÉ (1832–1902). José Obregón (*b.* 1832; *d.* 1902), Mexican painter. Obregón received his education at the Academia de San Carlos, where he was a student of Pelegrín Clavé for more than fifteen years. In his youth, his pictorial themes corresponded with his desire to appreciate universal culture through biblical themes. In the 1860s, Obregón was the first painter to use themes involving early national episodes. His *The Discovery of Pulque*, a painting of undoubted historical significance, took its place in the moralist line of historical paintings. Its novelty lay in that, rather than being derived from a biblical or Greco-Roman episode, its theme sprang from a national event. This work interested other figure painters at the academy in the idea of using Mexican historical themes.

By order of Maximilian, Obregón painted the portrait of General Mariano Matamoros, as well as that of José María Morelos, for the Gallery of Heroes in the National Palace. He was likewise commissioned for the portraits of Maximilian and Carlota, which served as models in Europe for the coining of currency that bore their effigies. He enjoyed much success as a portraitist of Mexican society. He remained as a master at the academy until 1891, when the loss of his eyesight forced him to leave his post.

See also **Art: The Nineteenth Century; Matamoros y Guridi, Mariano; Maximilian; Morelos y Pavón, José María.**

BIBLIOGRAPHY

Justino Fernández, *El arte del siglo XIX en México,* 3d ed. (1983).

Fausto Ramirez, *La plástica del siglo de la independencia* (1985).

Additional Bibliography

Soler, Jaime, and Esther Acevedo. *La fabricación del Estado, 1864-1910.* México, D.F.: Museo Nacional de Arte, 2003.

ESTHER ACEVEDO

OBREGÓN SALIDO, ÁLVARO (1880–1928). Álvaro Obregón Salido (*b.* 19 February 1880; *d.* 17 July 1928), president of Mexico (1920–1924). The poor relation of one of southern Sonora's most prominent families, Obregón struggled to achieve a modest prosperity by 1910. Though he initially withheld active support of the Revolution, Obregón soon rose to national prominence through his military exploits outside the state. He built a wide base of popular support through much of the country and joined it to the alliance of revolutionary chiefs in northwestern Mexico in order to challenge successfully the attempt by Venustiano Carranza to establish hegemony over the national government. He was elected president in 1920, and again in 1928, but was assassinated before taking office.

Obregón's birth (he was the last of eighteen children) coincided with the culmination of the gradual loss of his father's small fortune. Francisco Obregón's business partner's affiliation with the empire of Maximilian had resulted in the confiscation of all his holdings in the interior of the country. The great flood of 1868 and Yaqui Indian raids thereafter had ruined his hacienda in the Mayo Valley. His death three months after Álvaro's birth left the family with only one important resource: his wife's family, the Salidos.

The Salidos owned the most important haciendas in the Mayo Valley. Through their close ties to the political circle that controlled the state government as subordinate allies of the Porfirio Díaz regime, the Salidos occupied the posts of district political prefect, state legislator, and state school inspector. Three of Obregón's sisters and a brother secured teaching positions in the emerging town of Huatabampo, to which the family moved. Obregón received his schooling from his siblings and from a Salido relative in the district seat of Álamos. As a boy, he worked at odd jobs to help support the family, developing mechanical interests and abilities. He began work as a mechanic at the flour mill of his uncles. In 1898, he moved to central Sinaloa to work in a similar capacity at the largest sugar refinery in that state, owned by an in-law of the Salido family. Two years later he returned to the Mayo Valley, briefly teaching school, then became mill manager on his uncles' hacienda. In 1904, recently married, he struck out on his own. After renting land for a year, he purchased a farm of nearly 450 acres, in part with a loan from the Salidos. He concentrated on chick-peas, a rapidly emerging export crop; and in 1909 he invented a chick-pea planter that eventually was manufactured and marketed by a Mazatlán foundry. He also worked on the extension of railroad lines and irrigation works.

Obregón did not participate in the Maderista movement in Sonora, though his cousin Benjamín Hill urged him to do so. His years of working closely with small farmers, rural workers, and industrial laborers had cultivated in him a concern for their plight. But, finally, after years of struggle, he and his family had achieved a measure of prosperity and stature in Huatabampo. They were considerably beholden to the Salidos for their success. Moreover, he was then a widower with two small children. Though he did not sign an act of adherence to the Porfirista regime, as two of his brothers had done under pressure, he chose not to risk the personal interests of his family. Nevertheless, with the Revolution's triumph and his brother's appointment as interim municipal president, Obregón challenged the candidate of the ruling clique for the town's top office. He won the disputed post (the election was decided by the legislature), largely through the support of small farmers and agricultural workers. They included many Mayo Indians, whose language he spoke and with many of whom he had been friends since boyhood. These groups also formed the majority of armed recruits who enabled Obregón to establish himself in the revolutionary movement. In response to the Orozco Revolt (1912), he raised a local force of 300, the largest in the state and one of the few willing to serve wherever needed. Having distinguished himself militarily, Obregón was named chief of the state's forces to oppose the Huerta coup against Francisco Madero in early 1913. Some of the more veteran Maderista commanders disputed this appointment, but Benjamín Hill proved a valuable intermediary.

Bypassing the Revolution's political struggles in Sonora, Obregón used his military success beyond the state as a springboard to national power, as one of Venustiano Carranza's three leading constitutionalist commanders. He sought to mediate the growing divisions between Carranza, Pancho Villa, and Emiliano Zapata, most notably at the Aguascalientes Convention (1914). But when forced to choose, he allied with Carranza and was named commander in chief. He led a decisive series of battles in the Bajío region (1915), during which the Villistas' military power was broken. The following year he was named secretary of war in response to Villa's raid into New Mexico and the subsequent U.S. military expedition led by General John Pershing. At the same time, Obregón had been working to secure a power base of his own. Unable to establish singular control over Sonora, he was forced to ally with Plutarco Elías Calles and Adolfo De La Huerta. But he was successful in mobilizing support among labor and agrarian movements, young professionals, and revolutionary chiefs across the country, who were joined in the Revolutionary Confederation and the Liberal Constitutional Party in support of major reform. In the Constitutional Convention of 1917, Obregón lent his military protection and accumulated prestige—as the Revolution's most noted military hero, as international negotiator (with the U.S. officials), and as a charismatic supporter of popular grievances—to the more radical group of delegates who prevailed on the major points of the Constitution of 1917.

With Carranza's election as constitutional president, Obregón retired to private life to mend his health (still suffering from the severe wound in 1915 that had led to mental fatigue and the amputation of an arm); to expand his agricultural interests in southern Sonora; and to consolidate political support within the state and the nation for his candidacy in the 1920 presidential elections. As Carranza increasingly concentrated political control and ignored the reforms promised in the new constitution, Obregón's candidacy (announced in June 1919) rose in popularity. Carranza's attempt to impose a successor provoked the Agua Prieta Revolt, which brought the revolutionary faction headed by the Sonoran revolutionary chiefs to power, and Obregón to the presidency (1920–1924).

Throughout his revolutionary career, Obregón had almost always opted for moderation over radical change. Moreover, as president, he, more than the other Sonoran chiefs, recognized that the national regime they now headed possessed neither the internal cohesion, the fiscal capacity, nor the political control to pursue aggressively the reform options which the 1917 Constitution empowered a strong interventionist state to undertake. Obregón pursued with firm resolve only education (and, to a lesser extent, the agrarian option). Instead, he focused his efforts on political consolidation. He made significant strides in depoliticizing the regional armed forces and professionalizing the army. Through the Bucareli Treaty with the United States (1923), he secured diplomatic recognition. The financial and economic instabilities of a decade of civil war and the post–World War I depression were mitigated. However, Obregón's support of Calles as successor galvanized a rebellion led by de la Huerta in 1923.

That revolt was a serious but unsuccessful challenge to Obregón's forging of a personalist governing coalition that to a large degree reestablished the centralized state apparatus of the Díaz regime. And like Díaz, Obregón could not abide the no-reelection principle. By 1928, with Calles's official leadership, Congress reintroduced the six-year term and unlimited (but not immediate) reelection. Though successful, Obregón's candidacy provoked another rebellion and led to his assassination before taking office. Obregón's death initiated the demise of the Sonorans' personalist coalition. To retain control, Calles moved expediently toward the institutionalization of the governing coalition through the National Revolutionary Party.

See also **Carranza, Venustiano; Díaz, Porfirio; Mexico: 1810-1910; Pershing Expedition; Villa, Francisco "Pancho"; Zapata, Emiliano.**

BIBLIOGRAPHY

E. J. Dillon, *President Obregón: A World Reformer* (1923).

Roberto Quiros Martínez, *Álvaro Obregón: Su vida y su obra* (1928).

Juan De Dios Bojórquez, *Obregón: Apuntes biográficos* (1929).

Rubén Romero, ed., *Obregón: Aspectos de su vida* (1935).

Álvaro Obregón, *Ocho mil kilómetros en campaña* (repr. 1970).

Randall George Hansis, "Álvaro Obregón, the Mexican Revolution, and the Politics of Consolidation, 1920–1924" (Ph.D. diss., University of New Mexico, 1971).

Francisco R. Almada, *La Revolución en el Estado de Sonora* (1971).

Hector Aguilar Camín, *La frontera nómada: Sonora y la Revolución Mexicana* (1977).

Linda B. Hall, *Álvaro Obregón: Power and Revolution in Mexico, 1911–1920* (1981).

Additional Bibliography

Collado, María del Carmen. *Empresarios y políticos, entre la restauración y la revolución, 1920–1924.* México: Instituto Nacional de Estudios Históricos de la Revolución Mexicana, 1996.

Gonzales, Michael J. *The Mexican Revolution, 1910–1940.* Albuquerque: University of New Mexico Press, 2002.

Sánchez González, Agustín. *El general en La Bombilla: Alvaro Obregón, 1928, reelección y muerte.* México, D.F.: Editorial Planeta Mexicana, 1993.

STUART F. VOSS

OCAMPO, MELCHOR (1813–1861). Melchor Ocampo (*b.* 1813; *d.* 3 June 1861), Mexican liberal politician and cabinet minister. Ocampo was born to unknown parents on the hacienda of Pateo in the state of Michoacán. He was raised by the owner of the hacienda, Doña Francisca Xaviera Tapia, from whom he later inherited the property. After his return from a trip to Europe in 1840, Ocampo turned to politics and was elected to represent Michoacán in the national legislature in 1842. As governor of Michoacán during the war with the United States, Ocampo supported the Mexican forces and offered more troops to continue resisting the invaders, arguing that the Treaty of Guadalupe Hidalgo should be rejected. In 1851, Ocampo was involved in a bitter dispute with the church over the refusal of a parish priest to bury a man whose widow could not pay the clerical fees for burial. He then began a campaign to reform parochial fees but was deposed as governor of Michoacán and exiled by Santa Anna in 1853. In New Orleans, Ocampo met Benito Juárez and other exiled liberals.

With the triumph of the Revolution of Ayutla, he returned to Mexico. He served as President Juan Álvarez's first minister of foreign relations (October 1855) but resigned over differences with Ignacio Comonfort. Ocampo was elected to the Constitutional Convention of 1856–1857 and served on the committee that drafted the constitution. When Juárez assumed the presidency in 1858, Ocampo served as minister of foreign relations (1858–1859, 1859–1860, 1860–1861) as well as minister of other departments. In 1859 Ocampo bitterly denounced the Ley Lerdo for inhibiting the transfer of property to those of modest means and for actually strengthening the church and increasing its wealth. He also feared that the wars between liberals and conservatives would make it impossible to pay Mexico's foreign creditors, thereby encouraging foreign intervention. To raise capital, Ocampo negotiated the controversial McLane-Ocampo Treaty, signed on 14 December 1859. The treaty has been criticized for giving the United States the right to transport troops and merchandise across the isthmus of Tehuantepec and from Matamoros to Mazatlán, and to use its own troops to protect U.S. citizens and their property in those areas in return for a payment of $4 million to Mexico. Others argue that the McLane-Ocampo Treaty only reaffirmed U.S. transit rights already conceded under the Treaty of Guadalupe Hidalgo and the Gadsden Purchase agreement. Although the McLane-Ocampo Treaty was eventually rejected by the U.S. Senate, it increased dissension in Juárez's cabinet, principally between Ocampo and Miguel Lerdo De Tejada. On 22 January 1860, Ocampo resigned his post as minister of foreign relations and traveled to the United States to determine what help that nation might provide should the Mexican liberals be unable to defeat the conservatives on their own. He returned to the cabinet as minister of foreign affairs on 27 September 1860. Although the liberals had defeated the conservatives by December 1860, Ocampo's increasingly bitter disputes with Lerdo led to him to resign from the cabinet again on 17 January 1861. Ocampo retired to his hacienda, from which he was kidnapped by conservative guerrillas in May. A few days later he was shot on the orders of Leonardo Márquez, who had his corpse hung from a tree. His murder led the liberals to take more extreme measures to repress the conservatives and carry out their reforms.

See also **Juárez, Benito; McLane-Ocampo Treaty (1859); Mexico: 1810-1910.**

BIBLIOGRAPHY

Jesús Romero Flores, *Don Melchor Ocampo, el filósofo de la Reforma,* 2d ed. (1953).

José C. Valadés, *Don Melchor Ocampo, reformador de México* (1954).

Walter V. Scholes, *Mexican Politics During the Juárez Regime, 1855–1872* (1957).

Richard N. Sinkin, *The Mexican Reform, 1855–1876: A Study in Liberal Nation-Building* (1979), pp. 45–57, 52–59, 77–78, 83–84, 127, 151–155, 177; *Diccionario Porrúa de historia, biografía y geografía de México,* 5th ed. (1986).

Additional Bibliography

Matute, Alvaro, Evelia Trejo, and Brian Francis Connaughton Hanley. *Estado, Iglesia y sociedad en México, siglo XIX.* México, D.F.: Facultad de Filosofía y Letras, UNAM: Grupo Editorial, Miguel Angel Porrúa, 1995.

Medina Peña, Luis. *Invención del sistema político mexicano: Forma de gobierno y gobernabilidad en México en el siglo XIX.* México, D.F.: Fondo de Cultura Económica, 2004.

D. F. STEVENS

OCAMPO, VICTORIA (1890–1979). Victoria Ocampo (*b.* 7 April 1890; *d.* 27 January 1979), Argentine essayist, critic, publisher, and promoter of cultural activities. Born in Buenos Aires into a well-established, aristocratic family, Ocampo inherited a considerable fortune, which she used mainly to promote literature and art. In 1931, at the insistence of her friend, the Spanish philosopher José Ortega y Gasset, and with the help of two other friends, Waldo Frank and Eduardo Mallea, Ocampo founded the cultural journal *Sur*. To help defray the expenses of the review, she also started a publishing house, also called Sur. A believer in universalist culture, she befriended the most distinguished literary figures of her time, invited them to her home, and had their work translated and published in her journal or by her publishing house. Rabindranath Tagore, Graham Greene, Albert Camus, and Aldous Huxley are the most important writers whose work she published. In 1953 Ocampo was imprisoned for her steadfast opposition to the authoritarian regime of President Juan Perón; protests were published in newspapers all over the world. She was the first woman to become a member of the Argentine Academy of Literature. In 1967, Harvard conferred upon her an honorary doctor of letters degree.

Although Ocampo was treated with respect and admired for her opposition to the Nazi and Fascist governments during World War II and for her support of feminism and women's suffrage, she was also bitterly criticized for her literary taste, considered elitist by leftists, as well as for her strong dislike of Castro's Cuba and Communism in general. Many thought her eccentric and *extranjerizante* (a lover of the foreign). A great believer in translation and a supporter of translators, Ocampo published numerous translations herself, as well as twenty-six volumes of essays, nine of which are called *Testimonios.*

See also **Feminism and Feminist Organizations; Literature: Spanish America; Women.**

BIBLIOGRAPHY

Fryda Schultz De Mantovani, *Victoria Ocampo* (1963).

Marcos Victoria, *Un coloquio sobre Victoria Ocampo,* 2d ed. (1963).

Doris Meyer, *Victoria Ocampo: Against the Wind and the Tide* (1979).

David William Foster, "Bibliography of Writings By and About Victoria Ocampo, 1890–1979," *Revista Interamericana de Bibliografía* 30, no. 1 (1980): 51–58.

Alba Omil, *Frente y perfil de Victoria Ocampo* (1980).

Blas Matamoro, *Genio y figura de Victoria Ocampo* (1986).

Laura Ayerza De Castilho and Odile Felgine, *Victoria Ocampo* (1991).

Additional Bibliography

López Viñuela, Ana Cristina. *Victoria Ocampo: De la búsqueda al conflicto.* Mendoza: EDIUNC, 2004.

Ruggiero, Kristin. *The Jewish Diaspora in Latin America and the Caribbean: Fragments of Memory.* Portland: Sussex Academic Press, 2005.

Steiner, Patricia Owen. *Victoria Ocampo: Writer, Feminist, Woman of the World.* Albuquerque: University of New Mexico Press, 1999.

ROLANDO COSTA PICAZO

OCHOA REYES, LORENA (1981–). Born on November 15, 1981, in Guadalajara, Mexico, Lorena Ochoa Reyes began her golfing life as a child at her hometown country club in the state of Jalisco. Winning numerous national and international events, she enrolled at the University of Arizona to study sports psychology and play golf. There she won twelve events and never finished more than three strokes from the top; she was NCAA Freshman of the Year in 2001, First-Team All-American in 2002, and twice NCAA Player of the Year. She turned professional in 2002, finishing first on the Futures Tour money list and qualifying for the LPGA Tour. The following year she received the Louise Suggs Rolex Rookie of the Year Award. Reflective of her celebrity, she was twice honored with Mexico's National Sports Award: in 2001 as an amateur, the first golfer and youngest recipient ever, and again in 2006. That year she made the cut in all twenty-five tournaments played, leading the tour in eagles, birdies, times in top ten, rounds in the 60s, average low score, and money winnings (almost \$2.6 million). She won six tournaments, including the Tournament of Champions by a record ten strokes, bringing her professional total to nine and replacing Annika Sorenstam as LPGA Player of the Year. The Associated Press also designated her Female

Athlete of 2006. She opened the 2007 LPGA tour tying for fourth at the SBS Open in Kahuku, Hawaii, and later that year moved to number one in the LPGA rankings. Off the course, Ochoa has represented Banamex, Rolex, Office Depot, Coca-Cola, and Audi, and is officially Jalisco's sports ambassador and promoter of the 2011 Pan American Games. A source of both national pride and rising public interest in golf, Ochoa, with her coach, Rafael Alarcón, inaugurated the Ochoa Golf Academy in Guadalajara.

See also **Sports.**

BIBLIOGRAPHY

Berra, Lindsay. "To Know Her Is to Love Her." *ESPN: The Magazine* (March 12, 2007): 116–121. Available from the Official Web site of Lorena Ochoa, http://www.lorenaochoa.com/article_espnmagazine0307.asp.

Juárez Cedillo, Héctor. "Lorena Ochoa: La nueva reina del golf." *Caras Golf* 2, no. 1 (2006): 24–27.

JOSEPH L. ARBENA

ODIO, EUNICE (1919–1974).

Eunice Odio (*b.* 18 October 1919; *d.* 15? March 1974), Costa Rican poet. Overlooked by her compatriots during her lifetime, Odio, a native of San José, was later recognized as one of Costa Rica's greatest poets. Because she lived in several countries, including Guatemala and Mexico, she became a citizen of each. Her work as a journalist appeared in magazines throughout Latin America and France. Odio's books of poetry are *Los elementos terrestres* (1948), for which she won the Central American "15 de septiembre" prize; *Zona en territorio del alba* (1953); and *El tránsito de fuego* (1957); her poetry has been compared to the biblical Song of Songs in its tone and images. Odio also published the essays *En defensa del castellano* (1972) and *Los trabajos de la catedral* (1971) and a short story, "El rastro de la mariposa" (1970). She died in Mexico.

See also **Literature: Spanish America.**

BIBLIOGRAPHY

Collections that contain an English translation of "El rastro de la mariposa" are Victoria Urbano, ed., *Five Women Writers of Costa Rica* (1978).

Enrique Jaramillo Levi, ed., *When Flowers Bloomed* (1991). Collections of her work include Italo López Vallecillos, ed., *Territorio del alba y otras poemas* (1974).

Juan Liscano, ed., *Antología: Rescate de una gran poeta* (1975). Critical studies are Rima De Vallbona, *La obra en prosa de Eunice Odio* (1980), "Eunice Odio," in *Women Writers of Spanish America,* edited by Diane Marting (1987), and "Eunice Odio," in *Spanish American Women Writers,* edited by Diane Marting (1990).

Mario Esquivel Tobar, *Eunice Odio en Guatemala* (1983).

Additional Bibliography

Chen Sham, Jorge, and Rima de Vallbona, editors. *La palabra innumerable: Eunice Odio ante la crítica.* San José: Editorial de la Universidad de Costa Rica, 2001.

SUSAN E. CLARK

O'DONNELL, GUILLERMO (1936–).

Guillermo O'Donnell is a leading theorist of authoritarianism and democratization and one of the most distinguished Latin American social scientists. Born in Buenos Aires, he received a law degree from the National University of Buenos Aires and a Ph.D. in political science from Yale University. After teaching at various universities in Argentina between 1958 and 1975, he became a founding member of the Centro de Estudios de Estado y Sociedad (CEDES) in Buenos Aires, where he was a researcher from 1975 to 1979; from 1980 to 1991 he worked as a researcher in Brazil; and since 1983 he has taught at the University of Notre Dame, where he was also academic director of the Kellogg Institute for International Studies (1983–1998). He served as president of the International Political Science Association (1988–1991) and vice president of the American Political Science Association (1999–2000), and was elected to the American Academy of Arts and Sciences in 1995.

O'Donnell's *Modernization and Bureaucratic-Authoritarianism* (1973) offered a pioneering analysis of the breakdown of democracies in South America in the 1960s that challenged the prevailing modernization theory and emphasized the political conflicts generated by an import-substitution model of industrialization. To capture the distinctiveness of the form of authoritarianism that ensued, O'Donnell coined the term "bureaucratic authoritarianism." O'Donnell also made seminal contributions to the study of democratization. *Transitions from Authoritarian Rule: Tentative Conclusions about Uncertain Democracies* (1986), co-authored with Philippe Schmitter, was one of the most widely read works in political science during the 1980s and 1990s. Moreover, the book's analysis of the strategic choices faced by anti-authoritarian groups influenced many opposition leaders around the world. O'Donnell's research since the early 1990s has explored the question of the quality of democracy. His concept of "delegative democracy" highlights the concentration of power in the hands of elected presidents in contemporary Latin American democracies; he has also drawn attention to deficiencies in horizontal accountability and in the rule of law, and the failure of the state to guarantee the rights of citizenship.

See also **Democracy.**

BIBLIOGRAPHY

O'Donnell, Guillermo. *Modernization and Bureaucratic-Authoritarianism: Studies in South American Politics.* Berkeley: Institute of International Studies, University of California, 1973.

O'Donnell, Guillermo. *Counterpoints: Selected Essays on Authoritarianism and Democratization.* Notre Dame, IN: University of Notre Dame Press, 1999.

O'Donnell, Guillermo, and Philippe C. Schmitter. *Transitions from Authoritarian Rule: Tentative Conclusions about Uncertain Democracies.* Baltimore: Johns Hopkins University Press, 1986.

O'Donnell, Guillermo, Philippe C. Schmitter, and Laurence Whitehead, eds. *Transitions from Authoritarian Rule: Prospects for Democracy*, 4 vols. Baltimore: Johns Hopkins University Press, 1986.

O'Donnell, Guillermo, Jorge Vargas Cullell, and Osvaldo Iazzetta, eds. *The Quality of Democracy: Theory and Applications.* Notre Dame, IN: University of Notre Dame Press, 2004.

GERARDO L. MUNCK

O'DONOJÚ, JUAN

O'DONOJÚ, JUAN (1762–1821). Juan O'Donojú (*b.* 1762; *d.* 8 October 1821), Spanish army officer and politician. Born in Seville, O'Donojú became a liberal Mason, serving as minister of war during the first constitutional period (1801–1814). Unique among Spanish liberals, O'Donojú supported Spanish Americans in their quest for home rule. When the constitution was restored in 1820, leading Mexican liberals such as Miguel Ramos Arizpe arranged to have him appointed *Jefe Político Superior,* the office that replaced the viceroy in the new system.

When he arrived in Veracruz in July 1821, O'Donojú discovered that most of the country was in the hands of the insurgents. As a liberal, he attempted to ensure that constitutional rule was firmly implanted in Mexico; as a Spaniard, he sought to retain whatever ties were possible with the mother country. Therefore, on 24 August 1821 he signed the Treaty of Córdoba, which recognized Mexican independence. He became a member of the new regency and entered Mexico City peacefully in September. Unfortunately for his new land, he died of pleurisy shortly thereafter.

Besides assuring Mexican independence, O'Donojú was also responsible for consolidating and expanding Masonry in Mexico.

See also **Masonic Orders.**

BIBLIOGRAPHY

Jaime Delgado, *España y México en el siglo xix,* vol. 1 (1950), pp. 25–79.

William Spence Robertson, *Iturbide of Mexico* (1952), esp. pp. 105–129.

Jaime E. Rodríguez O., *The Emergence of Spanish America: Vicente Rocafuerte and Spanish Americanism, 1808–1832* (1975), esp. pp. 38–42.

Additional Bibliography

Rodríguez O., Jaime, editor. *Mexico in the Age of Democratic Revolutions, 1750–1850.* Boulder, CO: Lynne Rienner, 1994.

JAIME E. RODRÍGUEZ O.

ODRÍA, MANUEL APOLINARIO

ODRÍA, MANUEL APOLINARIO (1897–1974). Manuel Apolinario Odría (*b.* 26 November 1897; *d.* 18 February 1974), military dictator and president of Peru (1948–1956) who represented the rise to power of technocratic forces among the Peruvian army. Born in Tarma, he was educated in the military academy of Chorrillos (1915–1919) and trained in the Peruvian Advanced War School and in the United States. He rose to notoriety through his leadership as lieutenant colonel in the victorious battle of Zarumilla during the war between Peru and Ecuador in 1941, which was settled by international agreement in 1942.

Because of his military training, Odría was vehemently opposed to the populist Aprista Party. In 1946, Odría became the chief commander of the army. General Odría performed briefly as minister of government under President José Luis Bustamante y Rivero (1945–1948) before his resignation in opposition to the Apristas' growing influence. Odría led the coup d'état that overthrew Bustamante's beleaguered regime in 1948. By 1950, Odría maneuvered his "election" as constitutional president. He adopted the economically liberal recommendations of U.S. adviser Julius Klein, resumed servicing Peru's foreign debt, which had been in default since 1931, and enticed foreign (mainly U.S.) investment by liberalizing the mining and petroleum codes. This coincided with the favorable position of Peruvian export prices in the early 1950s to produce an economic boom.

In the domestic terrain Odría combined severe repressive measures, especially against the Aprista Party and its leader, Víctor Raúl Haya De La Torre, who sought a long asylum in the Colombian embassy, with demagogic acts and public works. His wife, María Delgado de Odría, became the leading figure of the regime's social charity. Housing, school, and health insurance projects were carried out, and concessions granted to slum dwellers. However, the growing opposition, even among the social elite led by Pedro Beltrán, resulted in the need to call elections in 1956. Odría handed power to Manuel Prado (1956–1962). Odría participated in the elections of 1962 with his own party, the Odriista National Union, which paradoxically established an alliance with Odría's former foe, the Aprista Party, in opposition to the election and regime of Fernando Belaúnde (1963–1968). He died in Lima.

See also **Peru: Peru Since Independence.**

BIBLIOGRAPHY

David Collier, *Squatters and Oligarchs: Authoritarian Rule and Policy Change in Peru* (1976).

Rosemary Thorp and Geoffrey Bertram, *Peru, 1890–1977: Growth and Policy in an Open Economy* (1978).

David Werlich, *Peru: A Short History* (1978).

Gonzalo Portocarrero Maisch, *De Bustamante a Odría* (1983).

Additional Bibliography

Guerra, Margarita. *Manuel A. Odría.* Lima: Editorial Brasa, 1994.

Tamariz Lúcar, Domingo. *La ronda del general: Testimonios inéditos del Cuartelazo de 1948.* Lima: J. Campodonico Editor, 1998.

Alfonso W. Quiroz

ODUBER QUIRÓS, DANIEL (1921–1992).

Daniel Oduber Quirós (*b.* 25 August 1921; *d.* 1992), president of Costa Rica (1974–1978), founding member of the Center for the Study of National Problems and the National Liberation Party (PLN).

San José–born Oduber began his political career as a young law student and participated actively in the epoch-making events of the revolutionary decade (1940–1950). He helped organize and sustain the Center for the Study of National Problems (1940), the Social Democratic Party (1945), the United Opposition in the 1948 election, the inner circle of the Figueres Ferrer–led revolution, and the PLN. He became nationally prominent when he was named general secretary of the revolutionary junta (1948–1949) and after that played a prominent role in party and national affairs.

Oduber held many positions in government and the PLN, including president of the legislative assembly (1970–1973), president of the PLN (1970–1977), foreign minister (1962–1964), vice president of the Socialist International, and president of Costa Rica (1974–1978).

In addition to his law degree, he earned a master's degree from McGill University and a doctorate from the Sorbonne.

See also **Costa Rica, National Liberation Party.**

BIBLIOGRAPHY

Alberto Baeza Flores, *Daniel Oduber: Una vida y cien imágenes* (1976).

Charles D. Ameringer, *Don Pepe* (1978).

Richard Biesanz, Karen Zubris Biesanz, and Mavis Hiltunen Biesanz, *The Costa Ricans* (1982; rev. ed. 1988).

Additional Bibliography

Fernández Alfaro, Joaquín Alberto. *Oduber: El hombre, el político, el estadista, su pensamiento.* San José: Editorial Universidad Estatal a Distancia, 1997.

Obregón Valverde, Enrique. *Semblanzas: Dirigentes históricos del Partido Liberación Nacional.* San José: [s.n.], 1998.

JOHN PATRICK BELL

OGÉ, JACQUES VICENTE (1755–1791).

Jacques Vicente Ogé (*b.* 1755; *d.* 25 February 1791), Haitian revolutionary. Ogé, a coffee merchant and owner of half a plantation in the northern parish of Dondon, was in Paris when the French Revolution broke out. The leader of the free mulattoes who fought for the civil rights of the *gens de couleur* (people of color), he was a vociferous member of Les Amis des Noirs.

When Ogé's requests for funds for the Haitian revolutionaries were rejected by the French, he turned to the British abolitionist Thomas Clarkson, who arranged for cash and letters of credit to be used to buy arms and ammunition in the United States. His forces landed on Haiti on 21 October 1790. After their defeat, Ogé fled to the Spanish part of the island. He was captured by the Spanish authorities and extradited by the French, who subsequently executed him.

See also **Haiti.**

BIBLIOGRAPHY

Cyril L. R. James, *The Black Jacobins* (1963), is a classic study. More recent works are Robert D. Heinl, Jr., and Nancy G. Heinl, *Written in Blood: The Story of the Haitian People* (1978).

Michel-Rolph Trouillot, *Haiti: State Against Nation* (1990).

Additional Bibliography

King, Stewart R. *Blue Coat or Powdered Wig: Free People of Color in Pre-Revolutionary Saint Domingue.* Athens: University of Georgia Press, 2001.

Nicholls, David. *From Dessalines to Duvalier: Race, Colour, and National Independence in Haiti.* New Brunswick: Rutgers University Press, 1996.

DARIÉN DAVIS

O'GORMAN, CAMILA (1828–1848).

Camila O'Gorman (*b.* 1828; *d.* 18 August 1848), a national heroine. Born to an aristocratic *Rosista* family of Buenos Aires, Camila lived in a society dominated by the rules of the dictatorial regime of General Juan Manuel de Rosas, who later ordered her execution in the name of "law and order." At nineteen, she fell in love with Uladislao Gutiérrez, a young and attractive priest from Tucumán, then serving her Parish of the Virgen del Socorro. After some hesitation and knowing that they were defying the moral and civil codes of their time, they decided to elope on 12 December 1847, thus confronting family, political authorities, and the Catholic Church. Their action threatened to provoke a major scandal that had the potential of tearing apart the Rosas regime. Using assumed names, the couple ran away to San Fernando in order to reach Goya, Corrientes province, where they settled and opened an elementary school, thus becoming part of that community. They were discovered by chance and were taken to Buenos Aires in August 1848.

While they were in jail in Santos Lugares, the Rosas government, in compliance with the request of Camila's father, ordered their immediate execution. The tragic end of these young lovers was made even more dramatic by the fact that, according to most accounts, Camila was pregnant. This government action transformed a much-debated social transgression into one of the major crimes of Argentine history. Much has been written about the fatal journey of these lovers. Among the most interesting accounts in recent times are *Una sombra donde sueña Camila O'Gorman* (A Shadow Where Camila O'Gorman Dreams, 1973), a novel by the Argentine poet Enrique Molina, and the film *Camila* (1984), directed by Argentine filmmaker María Luisa Bemberg.

See also **Bemberg, María Luisa; Rosas, Juan Manuel de.**

BIBLIOGRAPHY

Leonor Calvera, *Camila O'Gorman, o, El amor y el poder* (1986).

Additional Bibliography

Batticuore, Graciela. *Mujeres argentinas: El lado femenino de nuestra historia.* Buenos Aires: Alfaguara, 1998.

Luna, Félix. *Camila O'Gorman.* Buenos Aires: Planeta, 2001.

MAGDALENA GARCÍA PINTO

O'GORMAN, EDMUNDO (1906–1995). Edmundo O'Gorman (*b.* 24 November 1906; *d.* 28 September 1995), Mexican historian of ideas and institutions. Born in Mexico City, O'Gorman was the grandson of the third commissioner of the first British mission to Mexico, Charles O'Gorman. Edmundo O'Gorman spent the first ten years of his professional life as a lawyer following completion of his degree at the National University (UNAM) in 1928. After working at the Archivo General de la Nación, he received his Ph.D. in history from UNAM in 1951. He published extensive original research on colonial Mexico, historiography, and intellectual history as well as editions of the writings of sixteenth-century historians such as Bartolomé de Las Casas, José de Acosta, and Fr. Toribio de Motolinía. O'Gorman's major subjects include the Conquest of the New World and America as a European cultural creation. He debated these topics extensively with the highly regarded social theorists Silvio Zavala, Marcel Batallion, Georges Baudot, Miguel León-portilla, and Octavio Paz. He served as a member of the governing board of the National University and as director of a seminar at the Archivo General de la Nación. In 1967 he was named professor emeritus at UNAM. He died in 1995.

O'Gorman's most important works include *La idea del descubrimiento de América* (1951), which argues that America was not discovered but rather constructed by its early chroniclers, a proposition continued in *La invención de América* (1958). Some of his other important contributions include *La supervivencia política novo-hispana* (1969), a look at monarchism as a political concept in nineteenth-century Mexico, and *Destierro de sombras* (1986), an analysis of the devotion to the Virgin of Guadalupe.

See also **Guadalupe, Virgin of; Mexico: The Colonial Period.**

BIBLIOGRAPHY

Patrick Romanell, *The Making of the Mexican Mind: A Study in Recent Mexican Thought* (1952), pp. 176–185.

Francisco Larroyo, "El ser histórico de América de Edmundo O'Gorman," in *Conciencia y autenticidad históricas: Escritos en homenaje a Edmundo O'Gorman,* edited by Juan Antonio Ortegy y Medina (1968), pp. 41–47.

Carmen Ramos, "Edmundo O'Gorman como polemista," in *Conciencia y autenticidad históricas: Escritos en homenaje a Edmundo O'Gorman,* edited by Juan Antonio Ortega y Medina (1968), pp. 49–67.

Additional Bibliography

Celorio, Gonzalo. *Ensayo de contraconquista.* Mexico City: Tusquets, 2001.

Elizundia Ponce, María del Carmen. *Cultura mexicana: Antología de textos.* México: Universidad Anáhuac del Sur, 1999.

Jaimes, Héctor. "La visión del la historia en el ensayo hispanoamericano contemporáneo: Germán Arciniegas, Ezequiel Martínez Estrada, Octavio Paz, Edmundo O'Gorman, Leopoldo Zea, Mariano Picón-Salas." Ph.D. diss., University of Pennsylvania, 1998.

Lozoya, Jorge Alberto. *La miel de la piedra: Reflexiones sobre la invención de Iberoamérica.* Barcelona: Lunwerg Editores; SECIB, 2003.

CARMEN RAMOS-ESCANDÓN

O'GORMAN, JUAN (1905–1982). Juan O'Gorman (*b.* 6 July 1905; *d.* 8 January 1982), Mexican painter and architect. A great admirer of Frida Kahlo and the nineteenth-century landscape artist José María Velasco, Juan O'Gorman came from a wealthy and aristocratic Irish family with relatives in Mexico. His father, who arrived in Mexico at age twenty-four, was an amateur portrait painter and taught his son drawing and painting; his mother was Mexican born. Trained as an architect, O'Gorman introduced the functional international style to Mexico and built a number of schools and residences in this mode until he turned to the mosaic ornamentation of surfaces. His best-known buildings are the house-studio for Diego Rivera in San Angel, Mexico City (1931), his own organic mosaic-covered home in San Angel (1949, destroyed 1969), and the narrative mosaic-covered library at the University of Mexico (1950–1951), which has been compared to a codex.

In 1931, O'Gorman began a series of murals in tempera and fresco, the most important of which are *The History of Aviation* (1937–1938; partially destroyed), the *History of Michoacán* (1941–1942), and *Altar of Independence* (1959–1961). Several of his murals were destroyed for political or anticlerical imagery. O'Gorman also produced a large body of easel paintings, many in tempera, which include portraits and imaginary landscapes with surreal qualities.

O'Gorman's mural style was strongly influenced by Diego Rivera but was even more complex and layered, though carefully organized for legibility. He frequently used textual references, reproducing lines from manuscripts, or injecting his own commentaries. His imaginary landscapes, however, are freer and more flowing in design, though painted with the same minute attention to detail as the murals.

See also **Architecture: Modern Architecture; Art: The Twentieth Century; Kahlo, Frida; Rivera, Diego; Velasco, José María.**

BIBLIOGRAPHY

Antonio Luna Arroyo, *Juan O'Gorman: Autobiografía, antología, juicios críticos, y documentación exhaustiva sobre su obra* (1973) and *Homenaje a Juan O'Gorman, 1905–1982* (1983).

Additional Bibliography

Burian, Edward R. "Modernity and Nationalism: Juan O'Gorman and Post-Revolutionary Architecture in Mexico, 1920-1960." In *Cruelty & Utopia: Cities and Landscapes of Latin America*, Jean-François Lejeune, editor. New York: Princeton Architectural Press, 2005.

Eggener, Keith L. "Settings for History and Oblivion in Modern Mexico, 1942–1958: The City as Imagined by Juan O'Gorman, Luis Barragán, Mathias Goeritz, and Mario Pani." In *Cruelty & Utopia: Cities and Landscapes of Latin America*, Jean-François Lejeune, editor. New York: Princeton Architectural Press, 2005.

Jiménez, Víctor. *Juan O'Gorman: Vida y obra*. Mexico City: Universidad Nacional Autónoma de México, Facultad de Arquitectura, 2004.

Masters, Hilary. *Shadows on a Wall: Juan O'Gorman and the Mural in Pátzcuaro*. Pittsburgh: University of Pittsburgh Press, 2005.

SHIFRA M. GOLDMAN

O'HIGGINS, AMBROSIO (1720–1801). Ambrosio O'Higgins (*b.* 1720; *d.* 18 March 1801), viceroy of Peru (1796–1801). Although best known as the father of Bernardo O'Higgins, Chile's first president, Ambrosio was an important figure in his own right, particularly as captain-general of Chile from 1789 until his promotion to Peru.

The details of O'Higgins's early career are obscure. Born in Ireland, he was taken to Spain as a child and initially pursued a commercial career—in Cádiz, Lima, Buenos Aires, and Santiago—before making a name for himself in the 1760s as an officer leading campaigns against the Araucanians on Chile's southern frontier. He secured rapid promotion, becoming intendant of Concepción in 1786 and field marshal in 1789. His term as viceroy of Peru was complicated by the financial and commercial difficulties arising from Spain's declaration of war against Britain in 1796, but he was able to undertake a number of major public works, including the improvement of the Callao–Lima road, before dying in office.

See also **Chile: Foundations Through Independence; O'Higgins, Bernardo; Peru: From the Conquest Through Independence.**

BIBLIOGRAPHY

Ricardo Donoso, *El marqués de Osorno, don Ambrosio O'Higgins* (1941).

Rubén Vargas Ugarte, *Historia del Perú: Virreinato (Siglo XVIII)* (1957), esp. pp. 49–74.

Additional Bibliography

Edwards, David Hugh. "Economic Effects of the Intendancy System in Chile: Captain-General Ambrosio O'Higgins as Reformer." Ph.D. diss., University of Virginia, 1973.

González Santis, Aurelio. *El gobernador Ambrosio O'Higgins*. Santiago de Chile: Editorial Salesiana, 1980.

JOHN R. FISHER

O'HIGGINS, BERNARDO (1778–1842). Bernardo O'Higgins (*b.* 20 August 1778; *d.* 24 October 1842), liberator and national hero of Chile. Born at Chillán, he was the natural son of a Chilean mother, Isabel Riquelme, and an Irish father, Ambrosio Higgins (later O'Higgins, 1720–1801), a colonial official who later rose to be governor of Chile and viceroy of Peru. It is doubtful if Bernardo saw his father more than once, and he was separated from his mother at ten, when he was taken to Lima to start his education. In 1795 he was sent to England, where he continued his studies under tutors at Richmond-on-Thames. A decisive influence on the young creole's life was his meeting, in London, with Francisco de Miranda (1750–1816), from whom he eagerly imbibed subversive ideas of independence. In 1802 he returned to Chile and inherited Las Canteras, his father's large estate near the Araucanian frontier. He also petitioned to be allowed to assume his father's surname and titles of nobility; the surname was allowed, the titles were not.

An active and enterprising *hacendado* (landowner), O'Higgins became friendly with the tiny handful of separatists in the south of Chile. The crisis of the Spanish Empire and the installation of a patriot government in Santiago (September 1810) gave him a chance to further his ideas. As a representative of the radical minority, he was elected to the first national congress (1811), but José Miguel Carrera's (1785–1821) seizure of power (November 1811) soon compelled him to return to Las Canteras.

The outbreak of the Wars of Independence in 1813 drew O'Higgins into action at the head of militia forces he himself organized. He distinguished himself in a number of battles, including that at El Roble on 17 October 1813, in which he was wounded. When Carrera was dismissed as commander in chief early in 1814, O'Higgins assumed his role. Faced with another royalist offensive, he signed a peace treaty with the royalist commander, General Gabino Gaínza, at Lircay (May 1814), but this treaty was repudiated by the viceroy of Peru. Meanwhile, Carrera had seized power in Chile once again (23 July 1814), but O'Higgins refused to recognize the new regime. Civil war would have broken out had not a new royalist expedition launched a strong offensive. O'Higgins chose to make his stand at the town of Rancagua (1–2 October 1814), where his forces were totally overwhelmed. Patriot Chile collapsed.

O'Higgins himself escaped from the carnage and took refuge across the Andes in Argentina. There he became a close associate of José de San Martín (1771–1850), who selected him for a key role in the liberation of Chile. When San Martín's Army of the Andes undertook its epic crossing of the Cordillera, O'Higgins was a divisional commander. His audacious cavalry charge secured victory at Chacabuco on 12 February 1817. In Santiago, four days later, he was appointed supreme director of Chile.

Portrait of Bernardo O'Higgins. The sword in O'Higgins's hand hints at the daring military role he played in achieving Chile's independence from Spain. © CORBIS

O'Higgins's first three years in power were dominated by the need to prosecute the war of independence. Only after the decisive battle of Maipú (5 April 1818) was Chile finally secure from the royalists. However, the struggle for independence was not over yet. Great efforts had to be made to create a navy and to mount the expedition San Martín was to lead to the Viceroyalty of Peru. With Argentina descending into chaos, most of the burden of organizing and financing the expedition fell on O'Higgins's government. The expedition's departure in August 1820 was probably his supreme personal moment. From then on, he was obliged to give full attention to domestic issues.

O'Higgins's government was commendably vigorous. It restored those patriot institutions abolished during the Spanish reconquest, such as the Instituto Nacional and the National Library. It abolished titles of nobility and the public display of coats of arms. It completed the San Carlos Canal, a public works project dating from colonial times and designed to irrigate the land to the south of Santiago. It made plans to convert a sheep track running down one side of the city into a tree-lined avenue—today the Avenida Bernardo O'Higgins. O'Higgins also launched a number of diplomatic missions, though his envoy in London failed to secure British recognition of Chile's independence. (The United States extended recognition in 1822.)

While O'Higgins retained much of his personal prestige, his government provoked increasing antipathy. In some quarters, the supreme director was suspected of being under excessive Argentine influence. His support for the execution of the three Carrera brothers alienated a powerful faction. Some of his ecclesiastical measures (prohibition of burial in church, temporary banishment of the bishop of Santiago, approval of a Protestant cemetery) aroused clerical hostility. His appointment of José Antonio Rodríguez Aldea (1779–1841) as finance minister in 1820 also incurred disapproval from those who distrusted this slippery ex-royalist.

More serious, perhaps, was the personal and somewhat cliquish nature of the regime, which seemed to discourage the bulk of the creole elite from taking an active part in public life. O'Higgins's first constitution (1818) was minimal, and allowed no element of popular election, although its nominated senate was by no means a subservient body. Pressure for political reform eventually compelled O'Higgins to summon a constituent convention. This body produced his second constitution (October 1822), which provided for elections, a congress, and similar liberal desiderata. It also included a clause that would have enabled O'Higgins to remain in office for another ten years, a prospect most creoles found unacceptable. The final blow to the regime came from the war-ravaged south, where a desperate economic situation breeding frustration and resentment toward the capital prompted General Ramón Freire (1787–1851), intendant of Concepción, to launch a rebellion against O'Higgins. The northern province of Coquimbo followed suit. In Santiago, leading creoles conspired against the dictator. On 28 January 1823, in a scene of compelling drama, he was persuaded to abdicate. Six months later he was finally permitted to leave the country, never to return.

Abandoning a plan to visit Ireland, the land of his forebears, O'Higgins settled in Peru. In 1824 he accompanied Simón Bolívar (1783–1830) during part of the final patriot campaign in the highlands, but soon afterward doffed his uniform forever. The Peruvian government had awarded O'Higgins a couple of haciendas in the fertile Cañete Valley, to the south of Lima. Here and in Lima the exiled liberator lived out his final years in tranquillity, enjoying the company of his mother (until she died in April 1840), his half-sister Rosa, and his own natural son Pedro Demetrio, the fruit of a brief love affair that took place during the patriot campaigns of 1817.

O'Higgins was an amiable man with a simple, straightforward, unsubtle character. His many friends were devoted to him, and his followers very loyal. O'Higgins himself probably entertained few hopes of restoration to power. In 1826 he gave halfhearted support to a military insurrection in Chiloé, an ill-advised gesture that led the Chilean congress to strip him of his rank. In 1830 the successful Conservative rebellion led by his old protégé Joaquín Prieto (1786–1854) may have briefly revived his aspirations. He was touched by the attentions of Chilean soldiers occupying Lima during the war between Chile and the Peru-Bolivia Confederation. In 1842 the Manuel Bulnes government (1841–1851) restored his rank and emoluments, news of which reached O'Higgins shortly before his death. He was buried in Lima, and in January 1869 his remains were repatriated to Chile. Just over three years later, in May 1872, an equestrian statue of the hero was inaugurated in Santiago. Appropriately, it shows him in desperate action at the battle of Rancagua.

See also **Carrera, José Miguel; Chile: Foundations Through Independence; Chile: The Nineteenth Century; Miranda, Francisco de; O'Higgins, Ambrosio; Peru: From the Conquest Through Independence; San Martín, José Francisco de; Wars of Independence, South America.**

BIBLIOGRAPHY

Simon Collier, *Ideas and Politics of Chilean Independence, 1808–1833* (1967), chap. 6.

Jay Kinsbruner, *Bernardo O'Higgins* (1968).

Stephen Clissold, *Bernardo O'Higgins and the Independence of Chile* (1969).

Luis Valencia Avaria, *Bernardo O'Higgins, el "buen genio" de América* (1980).

Additional Bibliography

Cacua Prada, Antonio. *Vivir con honor o morir con gloria!: Bernardo O'Higgins Riquelme.* Bogotá: Publicaciones Universidad Central, 1994.

Díaz-Trechuelo Spínola María Lourdes. *Bernardo O'Higgins: El padre de la patria chilena.* Madrid: Anaya, 1988.

Díaz-Trechuelo Spínola, María Lourdes. *Bolívar, Miranda, O'Higgins, San Martín: Cuatro vidas cruzadas.* Madrid: Encuentro Ediciones, 1999.

Ibáñez Vergara, Jorge. *O'Higgins, el Libertador.* Santiago de Chile: Instituto O'Higginiano de Chile, 2001.

Valenzuela Ugarte, Renato. *Bernardo O'Higgins: el estado de Chile y el poder naval: En la independencia de los países del sur de América.* Santiago de Chile: Editorial Andrés Bello, 1999.

SIMON COLLIER

O'HIGGINS, PABLO

O'HIGGINS, PABLO (1904–1983). Pablo O'Higgins (*b.* 1904; *d.* 1983), American artist who worked primarily in Mexico. Born Paul O'Higgins in Salt Lake City, Utah, he was raised and educated in the United States. In 1924 O'Higgins traveled to Mexico, where he was attracted to the muralist movement, then in its early years. He became a studio assistant of Diego Rivera, and from 1925 to 1927 participated in the creation of Rivera's murals at Chapingo and Mexico City. In 1927 he joined the Communist Party, and from 1931 to 1932 he studied at the Moscow Academy of Arts. Upon returning to Mexico, he began to create his own murals, the first in 1933. His major public work, *La explotación del campesino y del obrero,* was executed at the Mercado Abelardo Rodríguez, Mexico City, in 1934–1936. He also produced murals in the United States, including one for the Ship Scalers' Union Hall, Seattle, in 1945. O'Higgins was a founding member in 1933 of the leftist artists' group Liga de Escritores y Artistas Revolucionarios, and in 1937 of the graphics collaborative Taller de Gráfica Popular. He died in Mexico City.

See also **Art: The Twentieth Century; Rivera, Diego.**

BIBLIOGRAPHY

Elena Poniatowska and Gilbert Bosques, *Pablo O'Higgins* (1984).

Museo Del Palacio De Bellas Artes, *Exposición homenaje Pablo O'Higgins, artista nacional (1904–1983)* (1985).

Dawn Ades, *Art in Latin America: The Modern Era, 1820–1980* (1989).

James Oles, *South of the Border: Mexico in the American Imagination, 1914–1947* (1993).

Additional Bibliography

Celorio, Gonzalo, Teresa del Conde, and Pablo O'Higgins. *Pablo O'Higgins: Hombre de siglo XX.* Mexico City: Difusión Cultural, UNAM, 1992.

Reyes Palma, Francisco. *Pablo O'Higgins: De estética y soberanía.* Mexico City: Fundación Cultural María y Pablo O'Higgins, 1999.

Uranga López, Lourdes. *El tema campesino en la pintura de Pablo O'Higgins.* Chapingo: Universidad Autónoma Chapingo, Dirección de Difusión Cultural, Coordinación de Extensión Universitaria, 1987.

ELIZABETH FERRER

OIDOR

OIDOR. Oidor, a judge of an audiencia. *Oidores* were the judges of the *audiencias* in the New World. After the appointment of *alcaldes del crimen* (judges whose responsibilities were limited to criminal cases), to the courts in Lima and Mexico City in 1568, the *oidores* on those tribunals were limited to civil cases. Prior to this date and in the other *audiencias,* they heard both civil and criminal cases.

While their judicial duties are best known, *oidores* also had legislative and executive responsibilities. They formed the core of the Acuerdo and thus participated in making political decisions. Regularly they were appointed by the region's chief executive to serve on commissions making inspection tours of the region or to serve as the judge of a corporate body.

By virtue of their high office, *oidores* were part of the elite in the capital where they served and, consequently, became attractive marital partners. Many obtained dispensations from restrictive legislation in order to marry local women of prestigious and well-to-do families and became directly involved in the local economy. When the crown sold *audiencia* appointments from 1687 to 1750, numerous Americans purchased appointments as *oidores* along with dispensations allowing them to marry and invest locally.

Unlike viceroys and other chief executives who were named for a specified term in office, *oidores* served at the pleasure of the king, occasionally for more than forty years. Since typically a viceregal *audiencia* had *oidores* who had served for years before the arrival of a new viceroy, the new executive could ignore their advice only at his peril.

See also **Judicial Systems: Spanish America.**

BIBLIOGRAPHY

Recopilación de leyes de los reynos de las Indias, 4 vols. (1681; repr. 1973), *libro* II, *título XVI;* Mark A. Burkholder and D. S. Chandler, *Biographical Dictionary of Audiencia Ministers in the Americas, 1687–1821* (1982).

Additional Bibliography

Barrios, Feliciano. *El gobierno de un mundo: Virreinatos y audiencias en la América hispánica.* Cuenca: Ediciones de la Universidad de Castilla-La Mancha: Fundación Rafael del Pino, 2004.

Hawkins, Timothy. *José De Bustamante and Central American Independence: Colonial Administration in an Age of Imperial Crisis.* Tuscaloosa: University of Alabama Press, 2004.

Sanciñena Asurmendi, Teresa. *La audiencia en México en el reinado de Carlos III.* México: Universidad Nacional Autónoma de México, 1999.

MARK A. BURKHOLDER

OIL INDUSTRY. *See* **Petroleum Industry.**

OITICICA, HÉLIO (1937–1980).

Hélio Oiticica (*b.* 26 July 1937; *d.* 22 March 1980), Brazilian painter and sculptor. Born in Rio de Janeiro, Oiticica began his artistic training as a student of Ivan Serpa, a pioneer in the Brazilian concrete art movement. In 1954 he joined Grupo Frente, whose members included Serpa, Lygia Pape, Lygia Clark, and other neoconcrete artists. Like his friend and colleague Clark, Oiticica was preoccupied with color and real space. In both *The Penetrables,* a series of tunnels, and a sculptural garden made of sand and color, he used diverse materials and objects to create an environment allowing spectator participation. Intrigued by the visceral effect achieved by color, he experimented with three-dimensional, solid, penetrable objects of color. In his *Fireball Box,* the red color mass has an energy field drawing the spectator into it.

In 1967 Oiticica participated in a neoconcrete exhibition entitled "New Brazilian Objectivity." His other exhibitions included the 1967 Paris Biennial, a 1969 retrospective of his work at London's Whitechapel Gallery, a 1970 exhibition at the Museum of Modern Art in New York, and a traveling retrospective in 1992.

See also **Art: The Twentieth Century; Clark, Lygia.**

BIBLIOGRAPHY

Hélio Oiticica, *Hélio Oiticica* (1992).

Additional Bibliography

Basualdo, Carlos, editor. *Hélio Oiticica: Quasi-cinemas.* Ostfildern-Ruit: Kölnischer Kunstverein, New Museum of Contemporary Art, Wexner Center for the Arts in association with Hatje Cantz Publishers; New York: Distributed Art Publishers, 2001.

Jacques, Paola Berenstein. *Estética da ginga: A arquitetura das favelas através da obra de Hélio Oiticica.* Rio de Janeiro: Editora Casa da Palavra: RIOARTE, 2001.

Justino, Maria José. *Seja marginal, seja herói: Modernidade e pós-modernidade em Hélio Oiticica.* Curitiba: Editora UFPR, 1998.

Zelevansky, Lynn, and Valerie L. Hillings. *Beyond Geometry: Experiments in Form, 1940s–70s.* Cambridge: MIT Press, 2004.

CAREN A. MEGHREBLIAN

OJEDA, ALONSO DE (c. 1466–1516).

Alonso de Ojeda (*b.* ca. 1466; *d.* 1516), Spanish navigator and conquistador. Ojeda traveled with Christopher Columbus on his second voyage in 1493 and partook in explorations of Guadalupe and Hispaniola. Years later he obtained permission to travel to the mainland following the route of Columbus's third voyage. Ojeda set sail in 1499, accompanied by Amerigo Vespucci. They arrived near the equator, explored the coast of Trinidad and the entire Venezuelan coast, the mouth of the Orinoco, and the island of Margarita. After Ojeda returned to Spain, information from his expedition was incorporated into Juan de la Cosa's map of 1500, on which the name *Venezuela* appeared for the first time.

Ojeda made other expeditions in 1501 and 1509. In 1501 he was appointed governor of

Coquivacoa, and in 1502 he explored the area of La Guajira. Francisco Pizarro accompanied him on his 1509 voyage, in which Juan de la Cosa and one hundred other Spaniards perished in a skirmish with natives near Cartagena Bay. Ojeda finally occupied the Gulf of Urabá and founded the city of San Sebastián, but the expedition was chaotic overall and had little commercial success. Nevertheless, Ojeda was among the most important navigators and discoverers of the New World.

See also **Columbus, Christopher; Explorers and Exploration: Spanish America; Pizarro, Francisco.**

BIBLIOGRAPHY

On Ojeda see Ricardo Majo Framis, *Alonso de Ojeda* (1972), and Hermano Nectario María, *Descubrimiento del Lago de Maracaibo por Alonso de Ojeda y Juan de la Cosa, 24 de agosto de 1499: Rasgos biográficos de ambos descubridores* (1978). On the general theme of the discovery and conquest of the territory of Venezuela, see the classic work of José Oviedo y Baños, *The Conquest and Settlement of Venezuela* (1987), translated by Jeanette Johnson Varner.

Additional Bibliography

Alvarez Perelló, Eduardo. *El conquistador Don Alonso de Ojeda.* Santo Domingo [?]: Taller, 1990.

Florencia, María Christen. *El caballero de la virgen: La narración de Alonso de Ojeda en la Historia de las Indias de fray Bartolomé de las Casas.* Iztapalapa [Mexico City]: Universidad Autónoma Metropolitana, 1988.

Szászdi León-Borja, István. *Los viajes de rescate de Ojeda y las rutas comerciales indias: El valor económico del Señorío del Mar de los Reyes Católicos.* Santo Domingo: Ediciones Fundación García Arévalo, 2001.

INÉS QUINTERO

OLANCHO. Olancho, an eastern border province of Honduras that once covered the northeastern third of the country and is still the largest department in Honduras. Although in many respects the least developed region of the country, Olancho is relatively rich in natural resources. Grassy valleys nestle between the jumbled mountain ranges. The gold-bearing Guayape, Guayambre, and Jalán tributaries of the Patuca River system bisect the larger of these valleys.

Before the Spanish Conquest, nomadic hunter-gatherers ranged the mountains and valleys of "Greater" Olancho. In the mid-1520s, rival bands of conquistadores from Panama, Cuba, and Mexico entered the region to battle for glory, gold, and dominion, during which most Olancho natives were killed or enslaved.

Pedro de Alvarado of Guatemala eventually extended his hegemony over Olancho and promptly discovered abundant gold in the sand beaches of various rivers that cut through the area. Soon Indian and black slave gangs were put to work panning for gold in Olancho. The initial bonanza soon gave way to a more prosaic but stable economy of cattle ranching, sporadic gold panning by washerwomen wielding *bateas* (wooden wash tubs), and missionary campaigns to evangelize the remaining pockets of natives.

After the late-sixteenth-century silver strikes at nearby Tegucigalpa, mule trails running through Olancho to Trujillo provided the principal outlet for silver exports. Most of the mules and horses that plied these trails came from Olancho. Herds of Olancho cattle were driven to mining camps and to markets as far away as El Salvador and Guatemala. The rawhide ambience of the isolated cow towns along these trails disguised the fact that Olancho remained one of the richest provinces in Honduras well past the mid-1800s. The redirection of export trade through the ports of Puerto Cortés (on the North Coast) and Amapala (on the Fonseca shore) in the late nineteenth century, confirmed Olancho's isolation from the rest of the country and fostered a sense of regional autonomy. That desperadoes sought haven among the hill folk, and gold-crazed adventurers sought the fortune in the Olancho gold-panning sites, which are more famous than they are productive, only added to the region's badlands aura.

Since 1950, various quixotic international development schemes, voracious North American and Japanese logging operations, sprawling purebred cattle spreads, and land-hungry peasant cooperatives have collided in a race to stake out prime resources along and beyond the modern limited-access highway that cuts diagonally across the department.

See also **Honduras; Mining: Colonial Spanish America.**

BIBLIOGRAPHY

William V. Wells, *Explorations and Adventures in Honduras* (1857).

Lester D. Langley, "Welcome to the Free Republic of Olancho," in his *Central America: The Real Stakes—Understanding Central America Before It's Too Late* (1985).

Additional Bibliography

Foster, Lynn V. *A Brief History of Central America.* New York: Facts on File, 2000.

Holden, Robert H. *Armies without Nations: Public Violence and State Formation in Central America, 1821–1960.* Oxford: Oxford University Press, 2004.

Sheilds, Charles J. *Honduras.* Philadelphia: Mason Crest Publishers, 2003.

KENNETH V. FINNEY

OLAÑETA Y GÜEMES, JOSÉ JOAQUÍN CASIMIRO (1795–1860).

José Joaquín Casimiro Olañeta y Güemes (*b.* 3 March 1795; *d.* August 1860), Bolivian politician, who is often considered the real father of the country. Olañeta was the key figure in the creation of independent Bolivia and the most influential politician in the new nation's first decades. Born in Chuquisaca (now Sucre) into the small colonial elite of Upper Peru, he studied in Córdoba, Argentina, and at the University of San Francisco Xavier, where he received a degree in law. He became the secretary of the fierce royalist general Pedro Antonio de Olañeta, his uncle, whom he adroitly manipulated. In 1824, when it became apparent that the Spanish cause was doomed, he deserted and encouraged Antonio José de Sucre and Simón Bolívar to establish an independent Bolivia. Later he conspired against Sucre's Bolivarian government.

Never wanting to be president, Olañeta preferred to exercise power by Machiavellian means. During seven presidencies he held a variety of government posts in the executive, legislative, and judicial branches as well as that of diplomat. His shifty behavior earned him the sobriquet of Dos Caras (Two-Faced).

See also **Bolivia: Bolivia Since 1825.**

BIBLIOGRAPHY

Charles W. Arnade, *The Emergence of the Republic of Bolivia* (1957).

Additional Bibliography

Ortiz de Zevallos, Paz-Soldán. *Negociación Ferreyros-Olañeta; Arequipa, 28 de septiembre de 1830–13 de febrero de 1831.* Lima, Perú: Ministerio de relaciones exteriores del Perú, 1958.

CHARLES W. ARNADE

OLAYA HERRERA, ENRIQUE (1880–1937).

Enrique Olaya Herrera (*b.* 12 November 1880; *d.* 18 February 1937), president of Colombia (1930–1934). Born in Guateque, Boyacá, Olaya received his law degree in 1903. During the administration of Carlos E. Restrepo (1910–1914), he was foreign minister and later minister to Argentina. From 1922 to 1929 he was Colombian minister to the United States, a delicate position for a Liberal in a Conservative regime. In 1930, with the Conservatives divided, Olaya won the presidency under a "National Concentration" banner, promising a coalitionist government. His regime was faced with serious partisan violence, particularly in the northeast. He faced the Great Depression with orthodoxy; only in April 1933 did he suspend interest payments on Colombia's foreign debt. In social matters Olaya was weakly reformist, as seen in the 1931 Labor Code. He responded to the Peruvian seizure of the Amazon port of Leticia with a large-scale mobilization, but the matter was settled by negotiation. After his term, Olaya was minister to the Vatican; before his death he was a likely Liberal candidate for the presidency in 1938.

See also **Colombia: Since Independence.**

BIBLIOGRAPHY

Gustavo Humberto Rodríguez, *Olaya Herrera: Político, estadista, caudillo* (1980).

Terrence B. Horgan, "The Liberals Come to Power *por debajolde la ruana:* A study of the Enrique Olaya Herrera Administration, 1930–1934" (Ph.D. diss., Vanderbilt University, 1983).

Ignacio Arizmendi Posada, *Presidentes de Colombia, 1810–1990* (1990), pp. 229–232.

RICHARD J. STOLLER

O'LEARY, DANIEL FLORENCIO (1801–1854).

Daniel Florencio O'Leary (*b.* 1801; *d.* 24 February 1854), Irish officer in the Venezuelan Liberating Army and close aide of Simón Bolívar. In 1817, at the age of sixteen, O'Leary traveled to Venezuela as a member of the British volunteers who united to fight for the cause of independence in America. He came to Venezuela by way of the town of Angostura and rapidly gained the confidence of Simón Bolívar, who included him in his honor guard in 1818. O'Leary participated in the New Granada campaign in 1819, and in 1820 Bolívar appointed him as his aide-de-camp. He took care of Bolívar's correspondence and records, and remained very close to him throughout the Southern campaign. In the November 1820 negotiations that concluded with the Trujillo armistice, O'Leary acted as Antonio José de Sucre's secretary. When Bolívar and Pablo Morillo, leader of the royalist armies, met on 27 November 1820 in the town of Santa Ana to ratify the treaty, O'Leary acted as Bolívar's emissary in arranging the details of the meeting. O'Leary participated in the liberating campaigns of Venezuela (1821) and Ecuador (1822) and closely collaborated with Bolívar in his political projects concerning the integration of the Americas. He accompanied the leader until the latter's last days in Cartagena.

After Bolívar's death, O'Leary organized and compiled his voluminous archive, augmenting it with a great number of documents solicited from men who had been involved in the War of Independence. In Spain he visited Morillo, who handed over the documentation in his possession for inclusion in the collection. After O'Leary's death, his family gave the archive to the Venezuelan government. It was published in thirty-two volumes under the auspices of the Antonio Guzmán Blanco administration and was known as the *Memorias del General Daniel Florencio O'Leary* (1879–1888).

After 1833 O'Leary undertook various diplomatic missions as Venezuelan minister to England, Spain, France, and the Vatican. As a diplomat in the service of the British government, he was named chargé d'affaires in Caracas in 1841 and in Bogotá in 1843.

See also **Bolívar, Simón; Morillo, Pablo.**

BIBLIOGRAPHY

Alfonso Rumazo González, *O'Leary edecán del Libertador* (1956).

Manuel Pérez Vila, *Vida de Daniel Florencio O'Leary, primer edecán del Libertador* (1957).

R. A. Humphreys, ed., *The "Detached Recollections" of General D. F. O'Leary* (1969).

Additional Bibliography

Rayfield, Jo Ann. "Después del Santuario: La pacificación de Antioquia por O'Leary, 1829." *Boletín de Historia y Antigüedades* 70 (January-March, 1983): 291–320.

Rumazo González, Alfonso. *Ocho grandes biografías,* 3 vols. Caracas: Ediciones de la Presidencia de la República, 1993.

Inés Quintero

O'LEARY, JUAN EMILIANO (1880–1968).

Juan Emiliano O'Leary (*b.* 13 June 1880; *d.* 1968), Paraguayan historian, poet, and polemicist. Born in Asunción of mixed parentage, O'Leary received his education at the Colegio Nacional and the university, where he specialized in history. He later went on to teach history and geography at the *colegio* and the normal school. He was also for many years director of Paraguay's Archivo Nacional and Biblioteca Nacional.

As a historian, O'Leary saw as his particular goal the rehabilitation, even glorification, of Francisco Solano López, nineteenth-century field marshal and president of Paraguay during the War of the Triple Alliance and the object of heated criticism in its aftermath. Despite the fact that some members of his family had suffered under Marshal López, O'Leary spent years developing a portrait of the dictator as the supreme hero of the Paraguayan nation. Under the pseudonym Pompeyo González, O'Leary frequently wrote articles for the Partido Colorado's daily newspaper, *Patria.* His nationalist polemics were especially significant in channeling patriotic feelings in Paraguay during the Chaco War (1932–1935).

O'Leary lived to see his right-wing version of Paraguayan history adopted as official dogma during the Alfredo Stroessner regime (1954–1989). On several occasions O'Leary participated more directly in government as a Colorado deputy. Still, it is for his historical works that O'Leary is chiefly remembered. They include *Páginas de historia* (1916), *Nuestra epopeya* (1919), *El libro de los héroes* (1922),

El mariscal López (1925), and *El héroe del Paraguay* (1930). He died in Asunción.

See also **López, Francisco Solano; Paraguay: The Twentieth Century.**

BIBLIOGRAPHY

William B. Parker, *Paraguayans of To-Day* (1921).

Harris G. Warren, *Rebirth of the Paraguayan Republic: The First Colorado Era, 1878–1904* (1985), esp. p. 293.

Additional Bibliography

Amaral, Raúl. *Antecedentes del nacionalismo paraguayo: El grito de Piribebuy (12 de agosto de 1919).* Asunción: Fundación Asunción, 1995.

Centurión Morínigo, Ubaldo. *Raúl Amaral, el discípulo intelectual de Juan E. O'Leary.* Asunción: Impr. Alber, 2000.

THOMAS L. WHIGHAM

OLID, CRISTÓBAL DE (1488–1524).

Cristóbal De Olid (*b.* 1488; *d.* 12 May 1524), conquistador of Mexico and Central America. A trusted captain of Hernán Cortés, Olid later betrayed him in order to claim for himself regions he had explored in Honduras.

Born in Baeza, in the Andalusian region of Spain, Olid left for America in 1518 to search for gold and other wealth. Arriving in Cuba, he joined Cortés's expedition to Mexico. Olid was made quartermaster of Cortés's army, and in 1519 participated in the founding of Veracruz and in campaigns to Tlaxcala and Tenochtitlán (the capital city). Cortés appointed Olid captain of the guard in Tenochtitlán, and when the Spaniards captured Motecuhzoma II, Olid became the ruler's personal guard.

During the siege of Tenochtitlán, Olid became one of Cortés's most trusted captains. He distinguished himself as a loyal and capable soldier, rising quickly to the rank of camp commander, a position of both administrative and judicial power. In addition, he was given the command of a large company of his own, heading campaigns in Texcoco, Chapultepec, and Coyoacán. Following the conquest of Tenochtitlán in 1521, Olid led an expedition to Michoacán, extending Spanish control outward from the Mexican capital.

In 1524 Cortés sent Olid south to take possession of Honduras, which was believed to contain great wealth. He was also instructed to capture Gil González Dávila, a conquistador who had claimed for himself the area surrounding Lake Nicaragua. After gathering provisions in Cuba, Olid sailed down the coast, arriving in the Gulf of Honduras in May 1524. He claimed the land in Cortés's name and established the town of Triunfo de la Cruz. Soon after, he renounced Cortés's authority and claimed the region for himself. When Cortés learned of his captain's betrayal, he sent out an expedition under the leadership of Francisco de las Casas with instructions to capture Olid. Cortés began his own journey south in November 1524 to handle the matter.

Olid moved west into the Valley of Naco, where he encountered González Dávila. The arrival of Francisco de las Casas in the Gulf of Honduras, however, prevented an immediate pursuit. Olid tried to stall de las Casas's landing by proposing a truce. The ploy proved successful. A storm decimated de las Casas's forces, giving Olid the chance to capture both de las Casas and González Dávila. The two men later managed to escape, attempting unsuccessfully to assassinate Olid, who fled, seriously wounded, to the mountains. He soon was found, however. After a perfunctory trial, Olid was sentenced to death and beheaded.

See also **Cortés, Hernán; Explorers and Exploration: Spanish America; Michoacán; Tenochtitlán.**

BIBLIOGRAPHY

Rafael Heliodoro Valle, *Cristóbal de Olid, conquistador de México y Honduras* (1950).

Bernal Díaz Del Castillo, *The Discovery and Conquest of Mexico, 1517–1521,* edited by Genaro García, translated by A. P. Maudslay (1956).

Robert S. Chamberlain, *The Conquest and Colonization of Honduras, 1502–1550* (1966).

William H. Prescott, *The History of the Conquest of Mexico* (1966), edited by C. Harvey Gardiner.

Additional Bibliography

Montell, Jaime. *México: El inicio, 1521–1534.* Mexico City: Editorial Joaquín Mortiz, 2005.

SARA FLEMING

OLINDA. Olinda, the old capital of Pernambuco, founded in 1537 and center of colonial Brazilian economic activity. Between 1630 and 1654 it was occupied by the Dutch. In the early 1700s, Olinda was the site of the War of the Mascates (1709–1711), a bitter struggle between its resident sugar planters and Recife-based *mascates,* or merchants, who were their creditors. The planters of Olinda attempted to trade directly with Dutch and English ships, thus bypassing the *mascates* and crown duties. The Portuguese-born merchants who resided in Recife objected to their lack of representation in the Senado da Câmara of Olinda, which levied the taxes of Recife. Revolt erupted when the crown gave Recife its own *câmara* in 1710 and hence independence from the political control of Olinda. Its planters retaliated by attacking and capturing the port, but Recife ultimately prevailed as Pernambuco's principal city. Olinda is now a national monument notable for its finely restored churches, monasteries, and convents. As of 2006, Olinda's population was estimated at 387,494.

See also **Pernambuco.**

BIBLIOGRAPHY

Bailey W. Diffie, *A History of Colonial Brazil.* Malabar, FL: R.E. Krieger Pub. Co.,1987.

Bethell, Leslie, ed. *Colonial Brazil (Cambridge History of Latin America).* Cambridge: Cambridge University, 2004.

Burns, E. Bradford. *A History of Brazil,* 3d ed. New York: Columbia University, 1995.

Page, Joseph A., *The Brazilians.* Reading, MA: Addison-Wesley, 1995.

ORLANDO R. ARAGONA

OLINDA, MARQUESS OF. *See* **Araújo Lima, Pedro de, Marquis of Olinda.**

OLIVARES, CONDE-DUQUE DE (1587–1645). Conde-Duque de Olivares (Gaspar de Guzmán y Pimental; *b.* 6 January 1587; *d.* 22 July 1645), Spanish statesman and chief minister of Philip IV (1621–1643). Unlike the monarch he served, Olivares intimidated contemporaries with his tireless energy spent in pursuit of victory in European conflicts and centralization of the Spanish state. Of primary concern in European affairs was the defense of the Low Countries, which drew Spain into costly participation in the Thirty Years War (1618–1648). Although Spain lacked the revenue to support such military involvement, Olivares never allowed fiscal limitations to deter him from an aggressive foreign policy aimed at fulfilling Spain's destiny as a world power. He undertook the Mantuan war in Italy (1628–1631) to prevent the French successor from claiming the throne and to maintain Spain's control over northern Italy, but was unable to accomplish either. In 1626 he inaugurated the Unión de Armas in an effort to get the non-Castilian provinces in Europe and the New World to contribute to imperial defense.

Olivares's attempt to force Catalonian participation in the war between Spain and France resulted in the revolt of the Catalans in 1640. A revolt against Spanish rule in Portugal later in the year coincided with a collapse in transatlantic trade and sealed Olivares's fate. He willingly resigned for health reasons on 24 January 1643 and died two years later.

See also **Philip IV of Spain.**

BIBLIOGRAPHY

John H. Elliott and José F. De La Peña, *Memoriales y cartas del Conde duque de Olivares* (1978–1980).

John H. Elliott, *The Count-Duke of Olivares: The Statesman in an Era of Decline* (1986).

Additional Bibliography

Alcalá-Zamora, José N. *Felipe IV: El hombre y el reinado.* Madrid: Real Academia de la Historia: Centro de Estudios Europa Hispánica, 2005.

Domínguez Ortiz, Antonio. *Historia de la caída del conde-duque de Olivares: Manuscrito del siglo XVII.* Málaga: Editorial Algazara, 1992.

González Duro, Enrique. *Demonios en el convento: El conde-duque de Olivares frente a la Inquisición.* Madrid: Oberón, 2004.

SUZANNE HILES BURKHOLDER

OLIVEIRA, GERALDO TELES DE (1913–1990). Geraldo Teles de Oliveira (*b.* 1 January 1913), Brazilian sculptor. Rarely leaving the state of Minas Gerais where he was born,

Oliveira began to experiment with wood sculptures in 1965. Although he worked in relative isolation, in 1975 a commission from the French government threatened to end his obscurity. With only one exception, a gilded head of Tiradentes, which was a commission for the town of São João del Rey, his sculptures integrate African art and the Brazilian popular ex-voto tradition. All signed with the acronym of Oliveira's full name, "GTO," they almost exclusively depict human figures carved and interwoven within an architectural form, such as a wheel or column. In his *Living Wheel,* done in 1968, human figures serve as spokes and fill in the empty spaces of a circular form. He participated in the 1969, 1971, and 1975 São Paulo Bienals. Belo Horizonte's Salão Global presented him with a travel grant to France in 1975, to be on hand for the exhibition of his sculpture for the French government. While in Europe, Oliveira exhibited works in the 1978 Venice Biennale and in group shows in Paris and Brussels. He died in 1990.

See also **Art: The Twentieth Century.**

BIBLIOGRAPHY

Selden Rodman, *Genius in the Backlands* (1977), esp. pp. 96–108.

Dawn Ades, *Art in Latin America* (1989), esp. pp. 287, 358.

Additional Bibliography

Rasmussen, Waldo and Fatima Bercht. *Latin American Artists of the Twentieth Century.* New York: Museum of Modern Art, 1993.

Zaya, Octavio. *The Garden of Forking Paths: Contemporary Artists from Latin America.* København: Kunstforeningen, 2002.

CAREN A. MEGHREBLIAN

OLIVEIRA, MANUEL BOTHELHO DE

OLIVEIRA, MANUEL BOTHELHO DE (1636–1711). Manuel Bothelho De Oliveira (*b.* 1636; *d.* 5 January 1711), Brazilian writer and politician. Born to a wealthy plantation family that belonged to the petty aristocracy, Oliveira studied law at the University of Coimbra in Portugal, where he knew Gregório de Matos. He practiced law on his return to Bahia, and eventually entered politics and held several important offices. Oliveira's importance comes largely from his being the first Brazilian to publish his poetry in book form. His *Música do Parnasso* (1705) contains a variety of poems written in Spanish, Italian, and Latin, as well as Portuguese. Its emphasis on linguistic and formal virtuosity, including both cultism and conceptism, identifies it aesthetically as a late baroque work in the European tradition. Only the 325-line *silva* "Ilha da mare" is notably Brazilian in content. (A collection of poems on religious themes, *Lira sacre,* was posthumously published in 1971.)

Admitting that Oliveira is a minor though skillful poet, Wilson Martins has nevertheless identified him as the writer who, given his dates, consciousness of his profession, and responsiveness to a specific literary theory, became the founder of the Brazilian literary tradition. He also wrote two plays in Spanish, both imitative of contemporary Spanish *comedias.* Although lightly regarded today, they secure him a place in the history of Brazil's secular theater.

See also **Literature: Brazil.**

BIBLIOGRAPHY

Claude L. Hulet, *Brazilian Literature,* vol. 1 (1974), pp. 51–57.

Wilson Martins, *História da inteligência brasileira,* vol. 1 (1977), pp. 259–269.

Additional Bibliography

Muhana, Adma, editor, and Manuel Botelho de Oliveira. *Poesia completa: Música do parnasso, Lira sacra.* São Paulo: Martins Fontes, 2005.

Teixeira, Ivan, editor. *Musica do Parnaso.* Cotia: Ateliê Editorial, 2005.

NORWOOD ANDREWS JR.

OLIVEIRA, WILLY CORREIA DE

OLIVEIRA, WILLY CORREIA DE (1938–). Willy Correia de Oliveira (*b.* 11 February 1938), Brazilian composer and teacher. Oliveira has been associated with the Santos-based group of composers Música Nova (notably Gilberto Mendes, Rogério Duprat, Damiano Cozzella, and Julio Medaglia). The works of Pierre Boulez and Karlheinz Stockhausen were the focus of intense discussion within the group, which rejected the prevailing nationalist trends. Oliveira became interested not only in providing a unique formal structure for each work but also in forming a unique conceptual framework in which the actual sounds are of secondary importance. In the *Five Kitschs* (1967), for example, a series of pitches and a harmonic progression form the basis for all five pieces ("Background," "Nocturne," "Make It Yourself," "Jazztime," and "Narcissus"). The manner of repetition of the series is serialist in nature. The striving for maximum unity of structure and harmonic tension is minimalist in conception. Oliveira's approach to composition belongs to the postnationalist generation of composers who reject the idea of writing works with a clearly identifiable national element.

See also **Music: Art Music.**

BIBLIOGRAPHY

Gérard Béhague, *Music in Latin America* (1979).

Additional Bibliography

Correia de Oliveira, Willy, and Héctor Olea. *Para sorprano e percussaio.* São Paulo: Editora da Universidad de São Paulo, 1980. Also available online http://www.edusp.com.br.

Correia de Oliveira, Willy, and Franta Richter. *Com ilustracoes de Franta Richter: sete pequeninas pecas para piano.* São Paulo: Editora da Universidad de São Paulo, 1996.

Nepomuceno, Alberto y Pignatari. *Canções para Voz e Piano.* Brazil, EDUSP, 2006.

DAVID P. APPLEBY

OLIVEIRA LIMA, MANUEL DE (1867–1928).

Manuel de Oliveira Lima (*b.* 25 December 1867; *d.* 24 March 1928), Brazilian historian and diplomat. Although he was born in Recife, Oliveira Lima received most of his education in Portugal, where he began his diplomatic career in 1890 as an appointee of the new republican government. He later occupied many posts in Europe, the Americas, and Asia. A notable speaker and an engaging but outspoken conversationalist, he acted on several other occasions as an ambassador of Brazilian culture abroad. In 1920, he retired from public service and established himself in Washington, D.C., where he taught at the Catholic University of America. He donated over forty thousand books and manuscripts, which he had collected from his many travels, as a token of international peace and friendship to found the Oliveira Lima Ibero-American Library at the Catholic University. Most of the works focus on the history and culture of Portugal, Spain, and their American domains.

Oliveira Lima published a historical drama and several works on his diplomatic experience and many conferences on Brazilian history and literature, some of which he wrote in French. His first historical study, *Pernambuco, seu desenvolvimento histórico* (The Historical Development of Pernambuco [1895]) is a remarkable history of the province from its beginnings to 1848. Still useful are the notes he appended in 1917 to Francisco Muniz Tavares's *Historia da Revolução de Pernambuco em 1817* (History of the 1817 Revolution in Pernambuco, [1840]). It is in his masterpiece, *Dom João VI no Brasil* (*King John VI in Brazil,* 1908), that scholarship, literary skill, and sociological insight are matched to a degree rarely attained in Brazilian historical writing.

See also **Brazil: Since 1889; Pernambuco.**

BIBLIOGRAPHY

Manuel De Oliveira Lima, *Memórias* (*Estas minhas reminiscências*...), edited by Gilberto Freyre (1937), includes James A. Robertson's memorial address on Oliveira Lima, which was delivered at the International Association of Arts and Letters.

Additional Bibliography

Freyre, Gilberto. *Oliveira Lima, Don Quixote gordo*, 2nd edition. Recife: Universidade Federal de Pernambuco, 1970.

Lyra, Heitor. *A diplomacia brasileira na Primeira República, 1889-1930; e outros ensaios.* Rio de Janeiro: Instituto Histórico e Geográfico Brasileiro, 1992.

GUILHERME PEREIRA DAS NEVES

OLIVEIRA VIANA, FRANCISCO JOSÉ DE (1883–1951).

Known for his cultural and sociological studies of his native Brazil, Oliveira Viana was born in Saquarema on June 20, 1883. He graduated in 1906 from the Rio de Janeiro School of Law and went on to become a professor there in 1916. He was a member of the Brazilian Academy of Letters and the Brazilian Historical and Geographic Institute.

Oliveira Viana took up journalism in the first decades of the twentieth century, writing for the newspapers *Diário Fluminense* and *A Capital* as well as for *A Imprensa, O Paiz*, and *Revista do Brasil.* He seldom practiced law, instead devoting himself to studying domestic issues, especially questions of Brazilian development. In 1920 he published *Populaçoes meridionais do Brasil* (Meridional Populations of Brazil), a seminal work on Brazilian culture that became a benchmark for his generation.

Throughout his life Oliveira Viana was intensely engaged in both professional and intellectual activities. Among other positions, he served as director of the Rio de Janeiro State Development Institute (1926); legal adviser to the Ministry of Labor; member of the State Advisory Board, Special Constitutional Review Commission, and Law Review Commission of the Ministry of Justice and Domestic Commerce; and minister of the Federal Audit Court. He died in Niterói, on March 28, 1951.

Oliveira Viana's writings are considered a milestone of a new phase in Brazilian conservative thought, based on an interpretation of Brazilian society from an analysis that valued national authors and references, searching to understand Brazil through its internal dynamics. They include *Pequenos estudos de psicologia social* (1921), *O idealismo na evolução política do Império e da República* (1922), *Evolução do povo brasileiro* (1923), *O idealismo na Constituição* (1927), *Problemas de política objetiva* (1930), *Raça e assimilação* (1932), *As novas diretrizes da política social* (1939), *Os grandes problemas sociais* (1942), and *Instituições políticas brasileiras* (1949).

See also **Journalism.**

BIBLIOGRAPHY

Bastos, Elide Rugai, and João Quartim Moraes, eds. *O pensamento de Oliveira Viana.* Campinas, Brazil: Editora da Unicamp, 1993.

Torres, Vasconcellos. *Oliveira Viana: Sua vida e sua posição nos Estudos Brasileiros de sociologia.* Rio de Janeiro and São Paulo: Freitas Bastos, 1956.

Vélez Rodríguez, Ricardo. *Oliveira Viana e o papel modernizador do Estado Brasileiro.* Londrina, Brazil: Editora da Universidade Estadual de Londrina, 1997.

FERNANDO VALE CASTRO

OLLANTÁY.

OLLANTÁY. *Ollantáy* is the title of the most important play in the Quechua language. Its author and the exact date it was written are unknown, but it can satisfactorily be situated in the first half of the eighteenth century (around 1735). This would make it a colonial period work, impregnated with the Baroque aesthetic.

Ollantáy must have been written by a mestizo priest and substantially modified by Antonio Valdez, a parish priest of Yanaoca. It is unique in that it lacks romance, despite being a work about a passionate love affair, while the political powers, in which the church is the mediator, are deployed during its development and culminate in the denouement. Addressing political themes, this drama differs from other similar works of its time, among them the *auto sacramental* or allegorical religious play *Uska pawkar* (*The Poorest Rich Man*), also anonymous, and other dramas of a mythical or religious nature such as *El rapto de Proserpina y sueño de Endimión* or *El Hijo Pródigo* by Juan Espinosa Medrano (El Lunarejo), to whom *Ollantáy* has been unjustifiably attributed, and *El pobre más rico* by Gabriel Centeno de Osma.

There are several known versions of the work, arising from changes in its performances during the colonial era, when it was banned as a result of the revolt led by Tupac Amaru II in 1781. The main versions are known as the First Dominican (around 1755) and the Second Dominican (1940), clearly referring to an earlier manuscript, now lost. The work also has been translated into German, Spanish, English, French, Italian, Czech, Latin, Russian, and Catalan (in that order).

Ollantáy consists of 1,868 verses (in Calvo's critical edition of 1998). The verse is generally octosyllabic, with consonant rhyme, and has some lovely *décimas* and three magnificent *yaravíes* (sweet and sad songs of Indians). In the story, Ullanta, a general of the cruel Inca Pachacutec, secretly marries the Inca's daughter. This results in his exile from the fortified city of the same name, Ollantaytambo, while Kusi Quyllur, his pregnant wife, is confined for life in the Acllawasi (House of the Chosen) as punishment for her disobedience. When the Inca Pachacutec dies, he is succeeded by his son, Tupac. Yupanqui, who, in contrast to the former Inca, takes pity on his enemies. After defeating the already rebel Ullanta through cunning actions of his general Rumi Ñahui Tupac Yupanqui pardons him at the same time that Ullanta's now ten-year-old daughter, Ima Sumac (How Beautiful!), is horrified to discover that her mother, she did not know, is living awfully chained in prison, also in the Acllahuasi. The Inca orders her freed and bestows on the family his best wishes for the rest of their lives.

See also **Quechua.**

BIBLIOGRAPHY

Calvo Pérez, Julio. *Ollantay. Edición crítica de la obra anónima quechua.* Monumenta Linguistica Andina, 6. Cuzco, CERA "Bartolomé de las Casas". 1998.

Markham, Clements R. *Ollan:. An Ancient Ynca Drama.* Translated from the original *Quechua.* Londres, Tübner and Co., 1871.

Meneses, Teodoro L. *Teatro quechua colonial: Rapto de Proserpina y Sueño de Eudimión, Usca Paucar, Apu Ollantay, El pobre más rico, Tragedia del fin de Atahuallpa.* Lima, Edubanco, 1983.

JULIO CALVO PÉREZ

OLLANTAYTAMBO.

OLLANTAYTAMBO. Located in the Urubamba valley, sometimes called the "Sacred Valley of the Incas," Ollantaytambo lies about midway between Cuzco and Machu Picchu. The site is one of the best surviving examples of a planned Inca town and is the only major Inca town in which the structures have been continuously inhabited since before the Conquest. Ollantaytambo was built as an estate for the Inca Pachacuti on the site of an earlier non-Inca settlement that strategically controlled two of the three routes into the *montaña* region. During the Spanish conquest the forces of Manco Inca defeated the Spanish at Ollantaytambo.

See also **Machu Picchu; Manco Inca; Pachacuti.**

BIBLIOGRAPHY

John Hemming, *The Conquest of the Incas* (1970).

Graziano Gasparini and Luise Margolies, *Inca Architecture,* translated by Patricia J. Lyon (1980).

Jean-Pierre Protzen, *Inca Architecture and Construction at Ollantaytambo* (1993).

Additional Bibliography

Bengtsson, Lisbet. *Prehistoric Stonework in the Peruvian Andes: A Case Study at Ollantaytambo.* Göteborg: Göteborg University, Dept. of Archaeology: Etnografiska museet, 1998.

Cárdenas Arroyo, Felipe, and Tamara L. Bray, eds. *Intercambio y comercio entre costa, andes y selva: Arqueología y etnohistoria de suramérica.* Santafé de Bogotá: Universidad de Los Andes, Departamento de Antropología, 1998.

Glave Testino, Luis Miguel, and María Isabel Remy. *Estructura agraria y vida rural en una región andina: Ollantaytambo entre los siglos XVI-XIX.* Cusco: Centro de Estudios Rurales Andinos "Bartolomé de las Casas," 1983.

Thomson, Hugh. *The White Rock: An Exploration of the Inca Heartland.* Woodstock: Overlook Press, 2003.

GORDON F. MCEWAN

OLMECS. Olmecs, a Mesoamerican people who created an early pre-Columbian archaeological culture and art style. The Olmec archaeological culture was centered in a heartland stretching for some 90 miles along the southern shore of the Mexican Gulf Coast in the vicinity of the modern border between the Mexican states of Veracruz and Tabasco. Geographically, this heartland is a well-watered coastal plain whose swampy and riverine character is interrupted only by the centrally located volcanoes and low-lying hills that comprise the Tuxtla Mountains. Between roughly 1200 and 400 BCE, along the many rivers and streams that cut through this Gulf Coast heartland, the inhabitants of a number of centers (Laguna de Los Cerros, La Venta, San Lorenzo and Tres Zapotes) had constructed the enormous earthen platforms equipped with complex drainage systems and had carved the huge basalt heads, thrones, stelae, and other monuments that have become the hallmarks of Olmec culture.

The immense scope of public works at these heartland centers indicates that Olmec social structure was stratified in such a way as to allow for a complex system of labor control. The nonegalitarian nature of the heartland Olmec political structure is indicated not only by the magnitude of the public works found in the centers but also by the large number of monumental stone sculptures that have human rulers as their central theme. The exact

Jade figurine of an Olmec jaguar spirit. This figurine displays the almond-shaped eyes, notched forehead, and downturned mouth typical of Olmec art. WERNER FORMAN/ ART RESOURCE, NY

level of the political complexity is still a matter of debate, with scholarly opinion ranging from chiefdom to fully developed state. The ethnic identification of the people who inhabited the Gulf Coast Olmec heartland is also far from certain, but recent linguistic prehistorical reconstruction has compiled evidence that strongly suggests that the archaeological Olmec culture was developed by speakers of an ancestral form of the Mixe-Zoquean linguistic family.

In contrast to the geographical limits of the Gulf Coastal archaeological culture, objects created in the Olmec art style are found throughout Mesoamerica. To a considerable degree, the origins of the Olmec art style can be traced to the Gulf Coast heartland, but there is also evidence to support a Mexican highland origin for many of the symbols and motifs that constitute an essential part of the Olmec style. This same evidence also supports the hypothesis that the Olmec art style spread throughout Mesoamerica through long-distance trade and ideological interaction.

The Olmec art style is famous for its many exquisitely carved jades. The symbols and motifs incised on many of these jades are also found on monumental stone sculptures and on portable objects of clay, wood, and stone. Olmec-style objects often depict distinctive supernatural creatures who are strikingly portrayed with almond-shaped eyes, cleft foreheads, and strangely drooping mouths. The symbol system that was an integral part of the Olmec art style functioned ultimately as a politically and ideologically motivated communication system. Essentially, the mission of this communication system was to convey, define, and sanctify the charter of rulership in what was then a nonliterate Mesoamerican political landscape.

The Olmec art style and the Gulf Coastal centers of the archaeological Olmec culture ceased to function sometime after 500 BCE. Most scholars agree that the Olmec art style with its accompanying symbol system is the very first preserved material expression of the ideological concepts that are the underpinnings of much of later Mesoamerican civilization. More specifically, the political legacy of the archaeological Olmec played an important part in the development of supernaturally chartered hereditary rulership that was developed by the Classic Period Maya. The influence of the Olmec style can be seen in the later art styles of Itzapa and the Zapotecs, as well as in the Classic Maya. The Olmec symbol system was most certainly the point of origin for the recently recognized Isthmian system of hieroglyphic writing and provided a number of glyphs for the highly sophisticated Maya hieroglyphic system.

See also **La Venta; Precontact History: Emergence of Complex Society; San Lorenzo.**

BIBLIOGRAPHY

Michael D. Coe, "The Olmec Style and Its Distribution," in *Handbook of Middle American Indians,* vol. 3, edited by Gordon R. Willey (1965), pp. 739–775, and *America's First Civilization* (1968).

Robert J. Sharer and David C. Grove, eds., *Regional Perspectives on the Olmec* (1989).

Additional Bibliography

Bernal, Ignacio. *El mundo olmeca.* México: Editorial Porrúa, 1968.

F. KENT REILLY III

OLMEDO, JOSÉ JOAQUÍN DE

OLMEDO, JOSÉ JOAQUÍN DE (1780–1847). An Ecuadorian statesman, neoclassical poet, and lawyer, Olmedo was born on March 20, 1780, in Guayaquil and completed a law degree at the University of San Marcos in Lima in 1805. One of the American deputies elected to the first Spanish Cortes in 1810, he served as secretary the deputies' assembly and participated in the writing of the Liberal Constitution of 1812. He returned to Ecuador in 1816 and was a deputy of the Peruvian Congress. Simon Bolívar appointed him diplomatic agent to the European courts (Great Britain and France), and Olmedo stayed in London until 1828.

He returned to Ecuador and headed the provisional government formed at Guayaquil in October 1820 that liberated the Audiencia of Quito in 1822. When the Republic of Colombia was disbanded he was elected vice president of the Republic of Ecuador. But he resigned to become prefect of Guayas province in 1830, president of the 1835 Constituent Congress, and member of the triumvirate of Liberals that ousted Juan José Flores in March 1845.

Olmedo was one of the great lyric poets of the nineteenth century. From 1802 to 1847 he wrote close to one hundred poetic compositions, the most famous of which are "La victoria de Junín: Canto a Bolívar" (1825) and "Al General Flores, vencedor en Miñarica" (1835). His complete works were published in Valparaíso (1848), Paris (1853), and Mexico (1862). He is considered, along with Andrés Bello, an outstanding member of the Spanish American Enlightenment. He died on February 19, 1847.

See also **Ecuador: Conquest Through Independence; Ecuador, Constitutions; Literature: Spanish America.**

BIBLIOGRAPHY

Andrade Reimers, Luis. *Olmedo el estadista.* Quito: Editorial Ediguías, 1993.

Conway, Christopher. "Gender, Empire, and Revolution in 'La victoria de Junín.'" *Hispanic Review* 69, no. 3 (Summer 2001): 299–317.

Espinosa Pólit, Aurelio. *Olmedo en la historia y en las letras.* Quito: Editorial Casa de la Cultura Ecuatoriana, 1980.

Rosero, Rocío. *José Joaquín Olmedo: ¿Patriota, político o desertor? 1800–1847.* Quito: Eskeletra, 1994.

Smith, Carolyn F. "The Sacred-Historical Role of the Inca in Olmedo's 'Canto a Bolívar.' " *Hispania* 56 (April 1973): 212–216.

LINDA ALEXANDER RODRÍGUEZ
WILL H. CORRAL

OLMOS, ANDRÉS DE

OLMOS, ANDRÉS DE. *See* **Sahagún, Bernardino de.**

OMAGUACA

OMAGUACA. Omaguaca, an indigenous people whose existence was first evident around 1000 CE. In the second half of the fifteenth century, they were incorporated into the Incan state, and a hundred years later they were conquered by the Spanish armies. The center of what was once their territory is today called Quebrada de Humahuaca in the province of Jujuy in the northwest extremity of Argentina. Their territory also extended eastward along the woody slopes of the sub-Andean sierras. The population was concentrated in hamlets and fortified settlements (*pucarás*) inhabited by distinct kinship groups. The economic base of this society was provided by intensive agriculture, mainly corn cultivation, and the tending of *auchenidos* (llama, alpaca, vicuña, and guamoco). Like other Andean societies, the Omaguaca were organized into two great halves. The northern half had as its capital the town of Humahuaca and at the time of the Spanish conquest was governed by the chief Tuluy. The southern half was under the control of the chief Viltipoco, who resided in the town of Tilcara. During the Incan domination, Tilcara functioned as a provincial administrative center. Power remained within certain determined lineages, and authority was transmitted by inheritance. With respect to language, we know only that at the outset of Spanish domination they were catechized in the Aymara tongue. Their religion, springing from deep Andean roots, was based on the worship of the sun and atmospheric phenomena.

See also **Incas, The; Indigenous Peoples.**

BIBLIOGRAPHY

José Antonio Pérez, *Concerning the Archaeology of the Humahuaca Quebrada* (1978).

Alberto Rex Gonzales and Jose Antonio Perez, *Argentina indígena en vísperas de la conquista* (1990).

Additional Bibliography

Reboratti, Carlos E. *La Quebrada: Geografía, historia y ecología de la Quebrada de Humahuaca.* Buenos Aires: Editorial La Colmena, 2003.

Zanolli, Carlos Eduardo. *Tierra, encomienda e identidad: Omaguaca (1540–1638).* Buenos Aires: Sociedad Argentina de Antropología, 2005.

José Antonio Pérez Gollá

OMBÚ.

OMBÚ. Ombú, *Phytolacca dioica*, is a giant shrub probably transplanted by the Spanish to the pampa from the Andean foothills. Highly adaptable, it grows in virtually any terrain and became common on the pampa, in the Chaco, and beyond. The odd plant has soft, spongy wood unusable for building or fuel. Its leaves, fruit, and flowers have little use except as purgatives. The overhanging branches offer shade to humans and livestock on the largely treeless plains. Visible from miles away, the shrubs served as landmarks to help travelers navigate across the plains. Like the ceibo, the *ombú* became fabled in regional folklore. Superstitious gauchos attributed supernatural powers to the shrub, some believing that it could cause a person harm or make someone fall in love.

See also **Andes.**

BIBLIOGRAPHY

Coluccio, Félix. *Diccionario folklórico argentino*, vol. 2. Buenos Aires: L. Lasserre, 1964.

Slatta, Richard W. *Gauchos and the Vanishing Frontier.* Lincoln: University of Nebraska Press, 1983.

Richard W. Slatta

ONA. *See* **Selk'nams.**

OÑA, PEDRO DE (1570–c. 1643). Pedro de Oña was Chile's first known poet. The son of a Spanish captain killed in the Araucanian wars in Chile, Oña was born at Los Confines. At around the age of twenty he went to Lima to study at the University of San Marcos. Viceroy García Hurtado De Mendoza (1535–1609), who had been offended by his portrayal in *La Araucana*, by the Spanish poet Ercilla y Zúñiga (1533–1594), encouraged Oña to write an epic poem to recount the Viceroy's earlier exploits as governor of Chile (1557–1561). The resulting work, *Arauco domado,* in nineteen cantos, was published in Lima in 1594. The first poem published by a Chilean creole author, it covers some of the events already narrated in Part 2 of *La Araucana,* but fails to carry the story through, and the bulk of the poem is based on episodes (such as a revolt in Quito and the viceroy's actions against English sea dogs) that are irrelevant to the Araucanian wars. Oña promised a second part, which never appeared. He died in Lima.

Oña, whose other works include *El vasauro* (1635), a religious poem, and *El Ignacio de Cantabria* (1639), a pious work celebrating St. Ignatius of Loyola, was not a truly talented poet. *Arauco domado* does not bear comparison with *La Araucana,* which it sought to emulate and perhaps imitate (its meter is similar but not identical). However, Oña cannot be denied his rightful place as the first Chilean poet.

See also **Hurtado de Mendoza, García; Literature: Spanish America.**

BIBLIOGRAPHY

Castillo Sandoval, Roberto. "'Una misma cosa con la vuestra'?: El legado de Ercilla y la apropriación postcolonial de la patria araucana en el Arauco domado." *Revista Iberoamericana* 61, no. 170–171 (1995): 232–247.

Díaz, Miguel Angel. *Ayer y Hoy: Ercilla y Oña en la épica chilena.* Chile: Rengo, 1998. Available from http://www.memoriachilena.cl.

Gutiérrez, Juan María. *El Arauco Domado, poema por Pedro de Oña:, 1809–1878.* [1848.] Madrid: Ediciones Cultura Hispánica, 1944.

Simon Collier

OÑATE, JUAN DE (c. 1550–c. 1630). Juan de Oñate was the founder and first governor of New Mexico (1598–1609). Born in New Spain, he was the son of the Basque Cristóbal de Oñate, the developer of the Zacatecas silver mines. Oñate negotiated a contract with Viceroy Luis de Velasco in 1595 for the pacification of New Mexico, receiving the privileges of *adelantado* in return for the heavy investment of his family consortium. He led his colonizing caravan of several hundred people, among them ten Franciscan missionaries, north across the Chihuahua desert, striking the Rio Grande downriver from present-day El Paso, where he took formal possession of the colony on 30 April 1598. Some 350 miles up river, he established a settlement near San Juan Pueblo. When the Indians of Acoma killed his nephew in an open challenge to the Spaniards, Oñate dispatched seventy armed men to punish them, which, even though outnumbered, they succeeded in doing. Hoping to discover an exploitable resource to help support his colony, he ventured far out into the Great Plains and to the Gulf of California; he failed in his mission.

In 1607, with the colony in poor condition and financial distress, Oñate resigned his office but remained to complete the establishment of the town of Santa Fe. The year before, accusations against Oñate of cruelty to both Indians and colonists had reached King Philip III; the king appointed a new governor and, in 1608, ordered Oñate to Mexico City. In 1613 Oñate was fined and banished from New Mexico for life, and from Mexico City for four years. Over subsequent years he attempted to clear his name and was at least partly successful. He eventually traveled to Spain, where, on a tour as royal inspector of mines, he died.

See also **Adelantado; Franciscans; New Mexico; Philip III of Spain.**

BIBLIOGRAPHY

Gaspar Pérez De Villagrá, *History of New Mexico by Gaspar Pérez de Villagrá, Alcalá, 1610,* translated by Gilberto Espinosa (1933).

George P. Hammond and Agapito Rey, eds., *Don Juan de Oñate, Colonizer of New Mexico, 1595–1628,* 2 vols. (1953).

Marc Simmons, *The Last Conquistador: Juan de Oñate and the Settling of the Far Southwest* (1991).

Additional Bibliography

Crespo-Francés y Valero, José Antonio. *El legado de Juan de Oñate: Los últimos días de adelantado.* Seville, Spain: Arboleda Ediciones, 2003.

Millares Carlo, Agustín. "Repertorio bibliográfico de los archivos mexicano y de los europeos y norteamericanos de interés para la historia de México." *Instituto Bibliográfico Mexicano* 24 (1959): 367.

JOHN L. KESSELL

ONCENIO. Oncenio, the common term for Augusto B. Leguía's dictatorial second administration as president of Peru (1919–1930). During this period, considered by some "the birth of modern Peru," there was a decline in the power of the traditional elite, rapid social change, a major increase in the size and scope of government, and subtle but effective political repression. Leguía initially enjoyed broad support from artisans, the middle class, and reformist intellectuals. In return, his handpicked Congress wrote a comparatively progressive constitution (1920), legally recognized Peru's indigenous communities, and legislated benefits for white-collar employees. Public works were Leguía's obsession: new streets, sewers, public buildings, and residential suburbs were built in Lima, and rural infrastructure was expanded through the controversial use of forced Indian labor. These programs were financed by heavy borrowing and direct foreign investment, though some of the money, critics argued, lined the pockets of Leguía's friends. Over time, moderate reformers became disillusioned with the regime and radical opponents were emboldened—both the populist APRA movement of Víctor Haya De La Torre and the Socialist Party of José Carlos Mariátegui were founded during the *oncenio.* Ultimately, the Great Depression put an end to Leguía's free-spending policies, and sparked his overthrow by Luis Sánchez Cerro.

See also **Peru, Political Parties: Peruvian Aprista Party (PAP/APRA).**

BIBLIOGRAPHY

Howard Laurence Karno, "Augusto B. Leguía: The Oligarchy and the Modernization of Peru, 1870–1930" (Ph.D. diss., University of California, Los Angeles, 1970).

Julio Cotler, *Clases, estado, y nación en el Perú* (1978).

Steve Stein, *Populism in Peru: The Emergence of the Masses and the Politics of Social Control* (1980), pp. 18–82.

Peter Klarén, "The Origins of Modern Peru, 1880–1930," in *The Cambridge History of Latin America,* vol. 5 (1986).

Additional Bibliography

Johnson, Carlos A. *Leguía, Fujimori, el miedo y la trafa en el Perú: El trágico derrotero de los gobiernos peruanos.* Nueva York: Ediciones Español, Ya!, 2000.

DAVID S. PARKER

ONETTI, JUAN CARLOS Juan Carlos Onetti (*b.* 1 July 1909; *d.* 30 May 1994), Uruguayan novelist and short-story writer. Onetti's semantic and technical experimentation place him among the inaugurators of the "new novel" in Latin America. His anguished, alienated characters are archetypes of the existential novel. Born in Montevideo, Uruguay, Onetti settled in Buenos Aires when he was twenty-one. His first novel, *El pozo* (The Pit, 1991), appeared in 1939. The protagonist, Eladio Linacero, expressed his estrangement from a bizarre, hostile world through a long, interior monologue. *El pozo* marks a significant transition from the telluric to the urban novel, in which the city is viewed as hostile and dehumanizing. *Tierra de nadie* (1941; *No Man's Land,* 1994), which won second place in the Losada competition, expressed resentment toward both reality and existential absurdity. In *La vida breve* (1950; *A Brief Life,* 1976), which catapulted him into the international limelight, Onetti uses a fragmentary structure to express the existential anguish of his character, Brausen, who, through his imagination, flees from Buenos Aires to the fictitious world of Santa María. Onetti's attitude is extremely pessimistic, for he rejects traditional values, while offering only an unsatisfying, absurd alternative. The short novel *Los adioses* (1954; *Farewells,* 1992) also expresses existential alienation, this time through a love story.

In *Para una tumba sin nombre* (1959; *A Grave with no Name,* 1992), set once again in Santa María, Onetti suggests that objective reality is impossible to know. In 1962, he won Uruguay's National Prize for Literature. In *El astillero* (1961; *The Shipyard,* 1968) and *Juntacadáveres* (1964; *Body Snatcher,* 1964) the author returns to Santa María. Onetti's later works include *La novia robada y otros cuentos* (1963), *Las máscaras del amor* (1968), *La muerte y la niña* (1973), *Tiempo de abrazar y los cuentos de 1933 a 1950* (1974), *Tan triste como ella y otros cuentos* (1976), and *Dejemos hablar al viento* (1979). In 1974, he and several other writers were imprisoned by Uruguay's military dictatorship, charged with selecting a short story with an anti-military message as the winner of a literary contest they were judging. He served six months in a mental institution and left Uruguay upon his release. He fled to Spain, and while there was awarded the Premio Cervantes, the most prestigious literary prize in the Hispanic world. He died in 1994 in Madrid.

See also **Literature: Spanish America; Uruguay: The Twentieth Century.**

BIBLIOGRAPHY

Helmy Giacoman, ed., *Homenaje a Juan Carlos Onetti* (1974).

Michael Ivan Adams, *Three Authors of Alienation: Bombal, Onetti, Carpentier* (1975).

Djelal Kadir, *Juan Carlos Onetti* (1977).

Josefina Ludmer, *Onetti: Los procesos de construción del relato* (1977).

Omar Prego, *Juan Carlos Onetti, o, la salvación por la escritura* (1981).

Mark Millington, *Reading Onetti: Language, Narrative, and the Subject* (1985).

José Pedro Díaz, *El espectáculo imaginario: Juan Carlos Onetti y Felisberto Hernández* (1986).

Beatriz Bayce, *Mito y sueño en la narrativa de Onetti* (1987).

Sonia Mattalia, *La figura en el tapiz: Teoría y práctica narrativa en Juan Carlos Onetti* (1990).

Jack Murray, *The Landscapes of Alienation: Ideological Subversion in Kafka, Celine, and Onetti* (1991).

Additional Bibliography

Blixen, Carina. *Bienvenido, Juan: Textos críticos y testimonios sobre Juan Carlos Onetti.* Montevideo, Uruguay: Librería, Linardi y Risso: Biblioteca Nacional del Uruguay, 2007.

Craig, Linda. *Juan Carlos Onetti, Manuel Puig, and Luisa Valenzuela: Marginality and Gender.* Woodbridge, Suffolk: Rochester, NY: Tamesis, 2005.

Flores, Reyes E. *Onetti: Tres personajes y un autor.* Madrid: Editorial Verbum, 2003.

BARBARA MUJICA

ONGANÍA, JUAN CARLOS (1914–1995). Juan Carlos Onganía Carballo (March 17, 1914–June 8, 1995) was a member of the

Argentine military who served as military president of the nation from 1966 to 1970. He was a general in the cavalry and emerged as a military leader in the serious armed conflicts of 1962 between two Army factions known as the Blues—the "legalistic" faction, which thought to reintegrate the banned peronist sectors to a military supervised constitutional regime, and the Reds—the antiperonist faction. Onganía, a blue supporter, was promoted to commander in chief of the army following their victory in 1963, but was retired in 1965 by President Arturo Illia.

In June 1966, invoking the doctrine of national security, Onganía led the coup d'état that installed an authoritarian regime that was ideologically conservative and pro-development, with extensive ambitions to lead a so-called Argentine revolution. The press was censored, national universities were taken over, professors and students were severely repressed (notably during the 1966 incident known as the Night of the Long Batons, when students at the University of Buenos Aires were beaten and arrested by police), and academicians and intellectuals were forced into exile.

The government's relations with the powerful unions and with Peronism began to deteriorate in 1968 when the General Confederation of Labor (Confederación General de Trabajadores; CGT) split in two: the Argentinean CGT and the Azopardo CGT. The Argentinean CGT took a combative position. In 1969 discontent with the government among important social sectors came to a head with worker and student protests in Corrientes and Santa Fe and later with the uprising in the city of Córdoba known as *El Cordobazo.* Although they were violently repressed, the disturbances weakened Onganía's ability to remain in power. The execution of former dictator Pedro Eugenio Aramburu by the Montoneros (Peronist guerrillas) convinced military leaders to remove Onganía. In June 1970, General Roberto Marcelo Levingston assumed the presidency and Onganía retired from military activity.

See also **Aramburu, Pedro Eugenio; Argentina: The Twentieth Century; Argentina, Organizations: General Labor Confederation (CGT); Cordobazo, El; Levingston, Roberto Marcelo; Montoneros; Perón, Juan Domingo.**

BIBLIOGRAPHY

O'Donnell, Guillermo. *El estado burocrático autoritario.* Buenos Aires: Editorial de Belgrano, 1982.

Riz, Liliana de. *La Política en suspenso, 1966–1976.* Buenos Aires: Paidós, 2000.

VICENTE PALERMO

OPERATION BOOTSTRAP. Operation Bootstrap (known in Spanish as "Operación Manos a la Obra"), an economic incentives program created by the government of Puerto Rico during the 1940s to attract outside investment to the island to industrialize the economy. Faced with a growing population, high unemployment, and widespread poverty, the island's leaders sought to resolve these problems by changing the basis of the economy from agriculture to manufacturing. The plan to industrialize the economy was implemented in stages, with both public and private capital participation. The government first used public funds to establish various state-owned manufacturing firms, in an effort to demonstrate their viability. These firms were under the direction and supervision of Pridco (Puerto Rico Development Company), a state agency founded in 1942 to promote the industrialization project commonly referred to as "Fomento." Lack of sufficient public funds to create the industries necessary to employ the growing population led Pridco in 1945 to devise the strategy of "industrialization by invitation." Incentives such as low wages and rent-subsidized factory space were offered to potential investors.

To accelerate the investment flow, Pridco, which set up an office in New York in 1945, added a tax exemptions package that included exemptions from both local and federal corporate taxes for U.S. subsidiaries willing to invest in Puerto Rico. The local tax holiday was made possible by the Industrial Incentives Act passed by the Puerto Rican legislature in 1947. Exemptions from federal income taxes for U.S. industries in Puerto Rico were permitted by laws that govern the island's relations with the U.S. Under article 14 of the Foraker Act (1900) and article 9 of the Jones Act (1917), individuals and corporations earning income in Puerto Rico were exempted from federal income taxes. In addition, Section 931 of the Internal Revenue Code of 1921 allowed subsidiaries of U.S. corporations in Puerto Rico to exclude the income they earned there from their corporate tax bill, under the heading of "possessions corporations." Adjustments to the Internal Revenue Code in 1976 led to the creation of Section 936, which permits both the federal tax exemption for subsidiaries and the repatriation of profits to the parent company in the United States.

For Puerto Rico, the combined effects of the tax laws, the absence of tariff or quota barriers on trade between the island and the United States, and the various programs designed by the local government have achieved the desired goal—industrialization of the economy. Manufacturing in 2007 represented 42 percent of the island's gross domestic product and employed 139,000 workers (11% of the workforce), compared with 24,000 in 1953. Similarly, the number of factories multiplied from eighty-three in 1953 to more than 2,000 in 1992. Meanwhile, agricultural jobs have declined sharply. One result of this dramatic economic transformation is an income per capita of $6,400 in 1992 compared with $125 in 1940. But despite obvious economic growth, the island's unemployment rate has remained relatively high, fluctuating between 22 percent in 1982 and 12 percent in 2007.

Since the 1990s, federal legislation and global competition have brought new challenges to Operation Bootstrap. U.S. tax reforms in 1982 and 1993, spurred by the massive federal budget deficit, threatened the future of the program, as they reduced incentives offered to investors under Section 936. In the late 1990s, Section 936 was phased out, and the federal government applied higher minimum wage laws. To counter these changes, Puerto Rico's government implemented local tax incentives. Federally, the government proposed to ease the loss of tax incentives through Section 30A of the tax code, which enabled firms to claim 60 percent of wages and capital investment as nontaxable. In 1994 the North American Free Trade Agreement (NAFTA) raised job competition between Puerto Rico and Mexico. Thus, despite the safeguards, many low-skill, labor-intensive factories closed. However, the allowances in Section 30A gave high-tech industries an advantage. Consequently, capital-intensive manufacturing in pharmaceuticals and machinery increased, offsetting the decrease in labor-intensive branches like clothing and food. Section 30A expired in December 2005, although the pharmaceutical industry continues to expand. The erosion of incentives had the effect of reformulating manufacturing, the widely acknowledged "engine" of the Puerto Rican economy.

See also **Economic Development; Globalization; Industrialization; Puerto Rico.**

BIBLIOGRAPHY

A critical interpretation of Operation Bootstrap appears in James Dietz, *Economic History of Puerto Rico* (1986), pp. 206–212, 240–255. See also a different perspective in Gary Martin, "Industrial Policy by Accident: The United States in Puerto Rico," in *Journal of Hispanic Policy* 4 (1989–1990): 93–115. For an official version of the facts, see the Puerto Rico Industrial Development Company (Pridco), *Annual Report* (1992).

Additional Bibliography

Collins, Susan Margaret, Barry Bosworth, and Miguel A. Soto-Class, eds. *The Economy of Puerto Rico: Restoring Growth.* San Juan: Center for the New Economy; Washington, DC: Brookings Institution Press, 2006.

Curet Cuevas, Eliézer. *Economía política de Puerto Rico: 1950–2000.* San Juan: Ediciones M.A.C., 2003.

Maldonado, A. W. *Teodoro Moscoso and Puerto Rico's Operation Bootstrap.* Gainesville: University Press of Florida, 1997.

OLGA JIMÉNEZ DE WAGENHEIM

ORBEGOSO, LUIS JOSÉ DE (1795–1847). Luis José de Orbegoso (*b.* 1795; *d.* 1847), military leader and president of Peru (1833–1835). Orbegoso was born to a notable family of northern Peru. At the time of independence he was an officer of the royalist army, but he offered early support to José de San Martín. Promoted to colonel and then general by Simón Bolívar, Orbegoso was appointed prefect of Trujillo in 1824 and 1827. As an active and popular participant in one of the most complex struggles for power among nineteenth-century Peruvian military leaders, Orbegoso fought under the banner of the constitutional resistance to military caudillismo. Having been elected president of the republic by the National Convention in 1833, Orbegoso withstood attempts by Generals Agustín Gamarra and Pedro Bermúdez to oust him in 1834. A civil war ensued that was initially favorable to Orbegoso. However, General Felipe Santiago Salaverry rebelled against Orbegoso in 1835. Orbegoso responded by allying himself with Bolivian General

Andrés de Santa Cruz. The alliance defeated Salaverry and established the Peru-Bolivia Confederation (1836–1839), in which Orbegoso performed as president of the newly created state of Northern Peru. However, Orbegoso rebelled against the confederation in 1838, an action that led to his exile.

See also **Peru: From the Conquest Through Independence; Salaverry, Felipe Santiago; Santa Cruz, Andrés de; Trujillo.**

BIBLIOGRAPHY

Evaristo San Cristóbal, *El gran mariscal, Luis José de Orbegoso: Su vida y su obra* (1941).

Jorge Basadre, *Historia de la República del Perú,* vol. 1 (1963).

Additional Bibliography

Méndez G., Cecilia. "Tradiciones liberales en los Andes: Militares y campesinos en la formación del estado peruano." *Estudios Interdisciplinarios de América Latina y el Caribe* 15:1 (January–June, 2004): 35–63.

ALFONSO W. QUIROZ

ORBIGNY, ALCIDE DESSALINES D'

(1802–1857). Alcide Dessalines d'Orbigny, (*b.* 6 September 1802; *d.* 30 June 1857), French naturalist and explorer. Orbigny, a native of Couëron, France, was commissioned by the Paris Museum of Natural History to explore much of South America between 1826 and 1834. He spent the first year collecting plants and animals in Brazil and Uruguay. From 1827 to 1828, Orbigny traversed the Paraná River through Brazil, Paraguay, and Argentina. In 1828 the government of Argentina commissioned him to study the pampas in order to determine the region's agricultural value. After completing this assignment, Orbigny went to Patagonia to continue his studies in natural history. During his stay, he spent time with a native tribe and took part in an intertribal war. Afterward, he investigated the land, plants, and animals of Bolivia and Peru.

In 1834 Orbigny returned to France, where he won the grand prize of the Paris Geographical Society for his work. The French government published his research in nine volumes titled *Voyage dans l'Amérique méridionale* (1834–1847). In addition to its description of flora, fauna, and geography, it provides important ethnographical data on various Indian populations. Orbigny's travels through South America enabled him to produce a comprehensive map of the area in 1842. He died at Pierrefitte-sur-Seine, France.

See also **Pampa; Patagonia; Science.**

BIBLIOGRAPHY

Heinz Tobein, "Orbigny," in *Dictionary of Scientific Biography,* edited by C. G. Gillispie, vol. 10 (1974).

Additional Bibliography

Albarracín Millán, Juan. *Una visión esplendorosa de Bolivia: Las exploraciones de Alcides d'Orbigny en Bolivia.* La Paz: Plural Editores, 2002.

Arze Aguirre, René Danilo. *El naturalista francés, Alcide Dessaline d'Orbigny en la visión de los bolivianos.* Lima: Institut Français d'Etudes Andines, IFEA; La Paz: Plural Editores, 2002.

Baptista Gumucio, Mariano. *Alcides d'Orbigny en la tierra prometida: Sus viajes por Bolivia, 1830–1833.* La Paz: Anthropos, 1997.

Potelet, Jeanine. "En la huella de Humboldt: Naturalistas, comerciantes y artistas franceses en Brasil." *Cuadernos Americanos* 13:73 (January–February, 1999): 113–131.

JOSEPHINE DELORENZO

ORBÓN, JULIÁN

(1925–1991). Julián Orbón (*b.* 7 August 1925; *d.* 20 May 1991), Cuban composer, essayist, and educator. Orbón received his musical education in Spain, Cuba, and the United States, where he studied with Aaron Copland. In Havana he was a member of the Grupo Renovación Musical (1942–1949) and director of the Orbón Conservatory from 1946 until 1960, when he left Cuba. After teaching in Mexico from 1960 to 1963, he moved to New York City, where he taught composition at Columbia University. A composer of orchestral, piano, and choral works, he received commissions from various foundations. His compositions earned numerous prizes and were selected for inclusion in international festivals. Although he occasionally employed Cuban elements, his wide musical interests, originally rooted in the Spanish tradition, ranged from neoclassic to a restrained romantic expression.

See also **Music: Popular Music and Dance.**

BIBLIOGRAPHY

Guillermo Espinosa, ed., "Julián Orbón: Classified Chronological Catalog of Works by the Cuban

Composer," in *Composers of the Americas,* vol. 6 (1960), pp. 83–87.

Gérard Béhague, *Music in Latin America: An Introduction* (1979), pp. 260–261.

Aurelio De La Vega, "Julián Orbón," in *New Grove Dictionary of Music and Musicians* (1980).

Velia Yedra, *Julián Orbón: A Biographical and Critical Essay* (1990).

Additional Bibliography

Estrada, Julio. "Tres perspectivas de Julián Orbón." *Pauta: Cuadernos de Teoría y Crítica Musical* 6:21 (January–March, 1987): 74–104.

Mata, Eduardo. "Julián Orbón: Hacia una música latinoamericana." *Pauta: Cuadernos de Teoría y Crítica Musical* 5:19 (July-September, 1986): 15–24.

Orbón, Julián. *En la esencia de los estilos y otros ensayos.* Spain: Editorial Colibrí, 2000.

Orovio, Helio. *Diccionario de la música cubana.* Havana, Editorial Letras Cubanas, 1992.

OTTO OLIVERA

ORDENAÇÕES DO REINO.

Ordenações do Reino (Afonsinas, Filipinas, Manuelinas), the laws of the realm of Portugal and its territories, first compiled in the fifteenth and sixteenth centuries to systematize the complex legal inheritance of the early modern state. The first collection, *Ordenações afonsinas* (1446–1448), was instigated by petitions of the Cortes to King Duarte, and issued in the reign of Afonso V. Although it was soon outdated and remained in manuscript form until the eighteenth century, it was a notable work for its time, manifesting the centralizing tendencies of the Aviz dynasty. Disparate elements of law, which included proclamations of previous rulers, Roman and canon law, and local custom, were brought together in five "books," subdivided by titles and paragraphs according to the following scheme: (1) royal, municipal, and other administrative bodies' decrees, including regulations emanating from the treasury, justice, and military; (2) rights and duties of the monarchy, nobility, clergy, Jews, and Moors; (3) civil procedure; (4) civil law; and (5) criminal law and procedure.

The need for revision was recognized in the reign of Manuel I, which resulted in the first printing of the *Ordenações manuelinas* (1514–1521). A further revision, the *Ordenações filipinas* (1603), was published during the Hapsburg era. It rescinded all legislation that was not incorporated into the revised compilation with the exception of treasury laws (*Ordenações da fazenda*), tax regulations (*Artigos das sisas*), and those registered by the superior appeals tribunal at court, the Casa Da Suplicação. Despite being marred by numerous errors, characterized as *filipismos,* which stem from incorrect transcription and failure to eliminate obsolete regulations, the code was confirmed by the Bragança dynasty in 1643 and remained in effect in Portugal and its colonies, and even in the ex-colony of Brazil (after 1822) until the issuance of the first modern codifications of the law, in 1867 in Portugal and 1917 in Brazil.

See also **Judicial Systems: Brazil; Judicial Systems: Spanish America.**

BIBLIOGRAPHY

See Mário Júlio De Almeida Costa, *História do direito português* (1989). Facsimile editions have been published by the Fundação Calouste Gulbenkian: *Ordenações afonsinas,* 5 vols. (1984), reprint of *Ordenações do Senhor Rey D. Afonso* (1792); *Ordenações Manuelinas,* 5 vols. (1984), reprint of *Ordenações do Senhor Rey d. Manuel* (1797); *Ordenações filipinas,* 5 vols. (1985), and reprint of *Ordenações filipinas* (1870).

Additional Bibliography

Nazzari, Muriel. *Disappearance of the Dowry: Women, Families, and Social Change in São Paulo, Brazil (1600–1900).* Stanford, CA: Stanford University Press, 1991.

CATHERINE LUGAR

ORDENANZA DE INTENDENTES.

In 1782 Charles III declared the establishment of Intendancies in the newly created viceroyalty of the Río de la Plata (1776). This administrative innovation, originally adopted from French Bourbon experience, had earlier been tested in Cuba. Intendants were projected as a new layer of bureaucrats between viceroys and such local administrators as *corregidores.* In their respective jurisdictions, these eight new officials, aided by a small number of bureaucrats, were responsible for royal justice, military preparedness, certain rights of church patronage, public works, the encouragement of commerce, and especially the collection of revenue.

Intendants paid close attention to local institutions, particularly the *cabildos* of important urban areas. Spanish-born immigrants, often merchants in vocation, were favored by intendants for posts in these *cabildos* and, with urging, did much to revitalize urban life in the Río de la Plata. At much the same time, intendants carried out various important militia reforms throughout the viceroyalty. Economic reforms attendant upon the creation of the viceroyalty gave these new administrators the opportunity to promote commerce, and thus royal revenues. This viceroyalty demonstrated solid economic progress by the 1790s, and while general imperial reforms had been quite important, intendants nonetheless contributed greatly to the vigorous commercial life.

The greatest failure of the intendants was their inability to effect real reforms in the countryside. *Subdelegados* (replacing in many instances the old *corregidores*) retained much of the earlier oppressive power over Indians in regions such as Alto Perú, Salta, Tucumán, and Paraguay; and little could even be attempted in the vast emptiness of the pampas. Still, the *Ordenanza de Intendentes* did represent a moderately successful attempt to provide more efficient local administration in this vast region.

BIBLIOGRAPHY

John Lynch, *Spanish Colonial Administration, 1782–1810: The Intendant System in the Viceroyalty of the Río de la Plata* (1958).

Additional Bibliography

Acevedo, Edberto Oscar. *Funcionamiento y quiebra del sistema virreinal: Investigaciones.* Buenos Aires: Ciudad Argentina, 2004.

JERRY W. COONEY

ORDÓÑEZ, JOSÉ (?–1819). José Ordóñez (*d.* 8 February 1819), Spanish army officer. Ordóñez fought in the Peninsular War and was briefly a prisoner of war in France. During the Spanish reconquest of Chile, he served as intendant of Concepción, arriving there in August 1815. When Chile was liberated, he successfully defended Talcahuano against stubborn assaults from the patriots. In 1818, with the arrival of General Mariano Osorio's expedition from Peru, Ordóñez took part in the final Spanish offensive in the Chilean Central Valley. He masterminded the surprise attack at Cancha Rayada (19 March 1818) that nearly destroyed the patriot army, and fought tenaciously at the battle of Maipú (5 April 1818). He was the last senior Spanish officer to surrender. With other royalist prisoners Ordóñez was sent across the Andes to San Luis in Argentina. He and a number of accomplices were executed after a daring but frustrated attempt to assassinate the provincial governor, Vicente Dupuy.

See also **Cancha Rayada, Battle of.**

BIBLIOGRAPHY

Arroyo Alvarado, Guillermo. *Historia de Chile: Campana de 1817–1818: Gavilan, Talcahuano, Cancha Rayada, Maipo (contribución a la historia militar de Chile).* Santiago-Valparaiso: Sociedad imprenta-litografia "Barcelona," 1918.

SIMON COLLIER

ORÉ, LUIS GERÓNIMO DE (c. 1554–1630). Luis Gerónimo de Oré (*b.* ca. 1554; *d.* 30 January 1630), Peruvian Franciscan, linguist, and first American-born bishop of Concepción, Chile. Luis Gerónimo was born in Guamanga. His father, Antonio de Oré, was one of Peru's early settlers; his mother, Luisa Dias de Roxas y Rivera, inherited the *encomienda* of Hanan Chilques. The family's fortune was based on Indian tributes and labor and on silver mines in the Guamanga district. Luis Gerónimo had several brothers and sisters; four brothers became Franciscans; three sisters were founders of the Poor Clares Convent in Guamanga. At fourteen Oré journeyed to Cuzco to become a Franciscan novice. He continued his studies in Lima at the University of San Marcos and was ordained by Archbishop Toribio de Mogrovejo on 23 September 1581.

Oré was fluent in Latin, Quechua, and Aymara and probably participated in the preparation of a Peruvian catechism ordered by the Third Church Council of Lima and published in 1584. In the mid-1580s Oré was assigned to the Collaguas Doctrina near Arequipa, where he perfected his translation skills and finished important dictionaries and grammars in Quechua and Aymara (now lost), as well as the *Sýmbolo Cathólico Indiano* (1598) and the *Rituale seu Manuale Peruanum*

(1607). By 1600 he was preaching in the mining center of Potosí, Bolivia, and later received an Indian parish in Cuzco. Cuzco's Bishop Antonio de la Raya appointed Oré to represent the diocese in Europe in a jurisdictional dispute with Charcas. Oré spoke before the Council of the Indies in Valladolid, Spain, in the spring of 1605. By winter Oré was in Rome, where the massive *Rituale,* a manual for the administration of the sacraments in Andean America, was published.

In 1611 Oré was back in Spain, and was appointed to lead a group of missionaries to Florida. While collecting a contingent of friars, he met Peruvian historian El Inca Garcilaso De La Vega in Córdoba in early 1612. The two discussed Peru's past and Florida's prospects. Unable to set out on his mission in 1612, Oré helped collect another group of Franciscan friars for the Venezuelan missions later that year. He also was ordered to conduct an inquiry into the Andalusian years of Francisco Solano, a Franciscan whose beatification was advocated by many. Oré quickly finished the *Relación de la vida y milagros del Venerable Padre Fr. Francisco Solano de la Órden de San Francisco* (1614).

Oré reached Saint Augustine, Florida, in the latter part of 1614, and again for a second inspection in November 1616. He conducted a thorough inspection of the province and held the first general chapter of the order in Florida. Before completing his work as general commissioner, he collected material for his *Relación de los mártires de la Florida* (1619). Perhaps during his return voyage to Spain he composed a long poem dedicated to the Virgin: *Corona de la sacratíssima Virgen María…* (1619).

On 17 August 1620 he was appointed bishop of La Imperial (Concepción, Chile). He traveled to Chile via Panama and Peru. When he arrived there in 1623, Concepción was a modest garrison on the Araucanian frontier. Oré's last years were troubled by conflict with both secular and religious authorities. He conducted an inspection of the distant Chiloé missions and established a seminary at Concepción. He consistently required solid training for mission clergy, stressing knowledge of native languages. He advocated peaceful Indian-European relations. His death in Concepción in early 1630 ended a period of peaceful coexistence on the Bío-Bío frontier.

See also **Franciscans; Missions: Spanish America; Saint Augustine.**

BIBLIOGRAPHY

Antonine Tibesar, *Franciscan Beginnings in Colonial Peru* (1953).

Noble David Cook, "Beyond the Martyrs of Florida: The Versatile Career of Luis Gerónimo de Oré," in *Florida Historical Quarterly* 71 (October 1992).

Additional Bibliography

Cook, Noble David. "Tomando posesión: Luis Gerónimo de Oré y el retorno de los Franciscanos a las doctrinas del Valle del Colca." In *El hombre y los Andes. Homenaje a Franklin Pease*, vol. 2., Rafael Varón Gabai and Javier Flores Espinoza, editors. Lima: Pontificia Universidad Católica del Perú, 2002.

Oré, Luis Jerónimo de. *Symbolo Catholico Indiano.* Lima: Australis, 1992.

Richter, Federico. *Fr. Luis Jerónimo de Oré, O.F.M., Obispo de Concepción.* Santiago de Chile: Archivo Franciscano, 1990.

NOBLE DAVID COOK

OREAMUNO, YOLANDA (1916–1956).

Yolanda Oreamuno (*b.* 8 April 1916; *d.* 8 July 1956), Costa Rican writer. Born in San José, Yolanda Oreamuno was one of the initiators of the contemporary Costa Rican narrative. Her psychological novel *La ruta de su evasión* (1950) won the Guatemalan 15 de Septiembre Prize. Finding it difficult to establish herself as a writer and intellectual in her own country, which she outspokenly criticized for its provincial attitudes and overly folkloric literature, from 1943 on she resided alternately in Guatemala, where she became a citizen in 1948, and in Mexico, where she died. In 1933, she composed a fiery essay on the role of women, which was later published in the literary journal *Repertorio Americano,* as were most of her essays and stories. The existence and location of her other novels, possibly as many as four, remain uncertain. Some of her stories have been translated into English and are included, with critical comments, in Victoria Urbano, editor, *Five Women Writers of Costa Rica* (1978), and Enrique Jaramillo Levi, editor, *When New Flowers Bloomed* (1991). Other writings are in her collection *A lo largo del corto camino* (1961) and in Alfonso Chase, editor, *Relatos escogidos* (1977).

See also **Literature: Spanish America.**

BIBLIOGRAPHY

Victoria Urbano, *Una escritora costarricense* (1968).

Rima De Vallbona, *Yolanda Oreamuno* (1972).

Additional Bibliography

Macaya, Emilia. *Espíritu en carne altiva.* San José: Editorial de la Universidad de Costa Rica, 1997.

Vallbona, Rima de. *La narrativa de Yolanda Oreamuno.* San José: Editorial Costa Rica, 1995.

SUSAN E. CLARK

O'REILLY Y MCDOWELL, ALEJANDRO (1723–1794). Alejandro O'Reilly y McDowell (Alexander; *b.* 24 October 1723; *d.* 23 March 1794), governor of Louisiana (1769–1770) and inspector general of the Spanish Army. A native of Beltrasna, county Meath, near Dublin, Ireland, O'Reilly was schooled in Spain at the Colegio de las Escuelas Pías de Zaragoza. His military career began at the age of ten, when he became a cadet in the Hibernian Infantry Regiment. He took part in the Italian campaigns of Isabella, queen consort of Philip V, from 1734 to 1736 and again from 1740 to 1748, and was seriously wounded in the latter affair.

Following service in two European wars, O'Reilly studied Austrian, Prussian, and French military organization. As a military consultant, he introduced Prussian tactics to the Spanish army. He was promoted to brigadier and then to inspector general and field marshal of the army. In his role as inspector general he accompanied Spain's captain general of Cuba, the Conde de Ricla, to Cuba and Puerto Rico in 1763 and 1765. Reaching Havana on 30 June 1763, O'Reilly participated in the restoration of Havana to Spanish control following the Treaty of Paris (10 February 1763) in which Havana, under British occupation, was exchanged for Florida. He reformed the Cuban militia, setting up a system that endured for nearly a century. Returning to Spain, O'Reilly won favor with King Charles III when he commanded troops accompanying the king in his flight to Aranjuez during the riots of March 1766 against Esquilace.

Three years later, on 16 April 1769, while in La Coruña, he was appointed to head an expedition to put down a revolt in Louisiana, where dissident elements had expelled the Spanish governor, Antonio de Ulloa, in 1768. Arriving in Havana on 24 June 1769, O'Reilly commanded a force of 2,056 men and twenty-one ships. The fleet sailed on 6 July, reaching New Orleans on 18 August to take control of the colony. An immediate investigation and trial of the conspirators took place and on 24 October the ringleaders of the revolt were condemned to death.

The rapid conclusion of the trial enabled O'Reilly to devote his remaining months in the colony to a thorough reorganization of Louisiana's administration, including political, military, and fiscal reforms, the promulgation of a new legal code, the Code O'Reilly, as well as religious and commercial reforms. The most important of O'Reilly's reforms was his integration of Louisiana into the Spanish commercial system.

O'Reilly departed New Orleans in March of 1770, and in April returned to Spain, where he established a military academy at Ávila for infantry, cavalry, and engineers. On 28 January 1772 Charles III bestowed on him the title of Conde de O'Reilly y Vizconde de Cavan.

O'Reilly's later career was marked by failure. He commanded the ill-fated expedition to Algiers in 1775, which historian John Lynch has called "a model of military incompetence." Uninformed about the strength of the enemy, and following an ill-advised battle plan, some 5,000 Spanish troops were killed or wounded. When O'Reilly later blamed this defeat on the cowardice of his troops, protests took place in several cities. O'Reilly was subsequently referred to as "General Disaster."

In 1780 he was appointed captain-general of Andalusia and governor of Cádiz. With the death of Charles III in 1788, he lost much of his support, resigning his post in 1789 and retiring to Valencia. When the French National Convention declared war against Spain in 1793, he was called back to service to command the Spanish Army in the Eastern Pyrenees. He died en route at Murcia and was buried in Cádiz.

See also **Louisiana Revolt of 1768; Militias: Colonial Spanish America.**

BIBLIOGRAPHY

O'Reilly's role in Cuban military reform is detailed in Allan J. Kuethe, *Cuba, 1753–1815: Crown, Military, and Society* (1986), esp. pp. 31–51. His Louisiana career is described in John Preston Moore, *Revolt in Louisiana: The Spanish Occupation, 1766–1770* (1976), and Bibiano Torres Ramírez, *Alejandro O'Reilly en las Indias* (1969). The disastrous Algiers campaign is described in John Lynch, *Bourbon Spain, 1700–1808* (1989). Also useful is Jack D. L. Holmes, "Alexander O'Reilly," in *The Louisiana Governors: From Iberville to Edwards,* edited by Joseph G. Dawson III (1990), pp. 49–52.

Additional Bibliography

Ingersoll, Thomas N. *Mammon and Manon in Early New Orleans: The First Slave Society in the Deep South, 1718–1819.* Knoxville: University of Tennessee Press, 1999.

BRIAN E. COUTTS

OREJONES. Orejones, a term used by the Spanish conquistadores to refer to the Inca and other native nobility of ancient Peru. The term, which literally means "big ears," derives from the custom of noble males wearing very large, cylindrical spools or plugs in their pierced earlobes as a badge of rank. These plugs were often made of wood, gold, or silver, depending on rank, and measured as much as two inches in diameter. The Inca equivalent of *orejones* was the Quechua term *pakoyoq,* which means literally "earplug man." The custom of wearing earplugs as a badge of nobility or rank is an ancient one in Peru, going back to at least a millennium before the time of the Incas.

See also **Incas, The.**

BIBLIOGRAPHY

See John H. Rowe, "Inca Culture at the Time of the Spanish Conquest," in *Handbook of South American Indians,* vol. 2 (1946), pp. 236, 261.

GORDON F. MCEWAN

OREJÓN Y APARICIO, JOSÉ DE (1706–c. 1765). José de Orejón y Aparicio (*b.* 1706; *d.* ca. 7–21 May 1765), Peruvian composer and organist. Born in Huacho, Orejón was considered to be a child prodigy; at the age of nine he replaced an adult singer at the Lima Cathedral Choir. He was probably a pupil of Tomás de Torrejón y Velasco, the Lima cathedral's *maestro de capilla,* and studied organ with Juan de Peralta. After Orejón was ordained a priest, he became chief organist at the cathedral in 1742. Gifted with extraordinary technical proficiency and musicality, Orejón was named alternate *maestro de capilla* at Lima upon the death of Roque Ceruti in December 1760, becoming full *maestro de capilla* in 1764.

As a composer Orejón wrote in the Neapolitan style, with an affinity for Giovanni Battista Pergolesi's sacred works. His natural talent and excellent technical skills surpassed those of any other colonial composer born in the Americas during his lifetime. His most significant piece is the *Passion* [sic] *del Viernes Santo* (Good Friday Passion) for triple chorus and orchestra (1750). Written in a homophonic style, it has thirteen segments, with the voices moving in thirds and doubling. The *Cantata al Santísimo Sacramento "Mariposa de sus rayos"* for soprano, continuo, and two violins is in the baroque style. Among his duets are *A del día, Enigma divino,* and *Jilguerillo sonoro.* Although Orejón's compositions never reached Spain in his lifetime, they were widely heard in South America, reaching as far as the La Plata cathedral in Sucre (Bolivia). Orejón's works are kept in two archives: the Archivo Arzobispal de Lima and the Catedral de La Plata (Sucre). He was without question the finest composer in the Americas during the eighteenth century. He died in Lima.

See also **Music: Art Music.**

BIBLIOGRAPHY

Gérard Béhague, *Music in Latin America* (1979).

Robert Stevenson, *The Music of Peru* (1960); *New Grove Dictionary of Music and Musicians,* vol. 13 (1980).

Additional Bibliography

Casares Rodicio, Emilio, ed. *Diccionario de la música española e hispanoamericana.* Madrid: Grupo Anaya Comercial, 2004.

Sas, Antonio. "Las investigaciones de Andrés Sas sobre la música de la colonia." *El Comercio,* Lima, (1954).

SUSANA SALGADO

ORELLANA, FRANCISCO DE (c. 1511–1546). Francisco De Orellana (*b.* ca. 1511; *d.* November 1546), leader of the first European

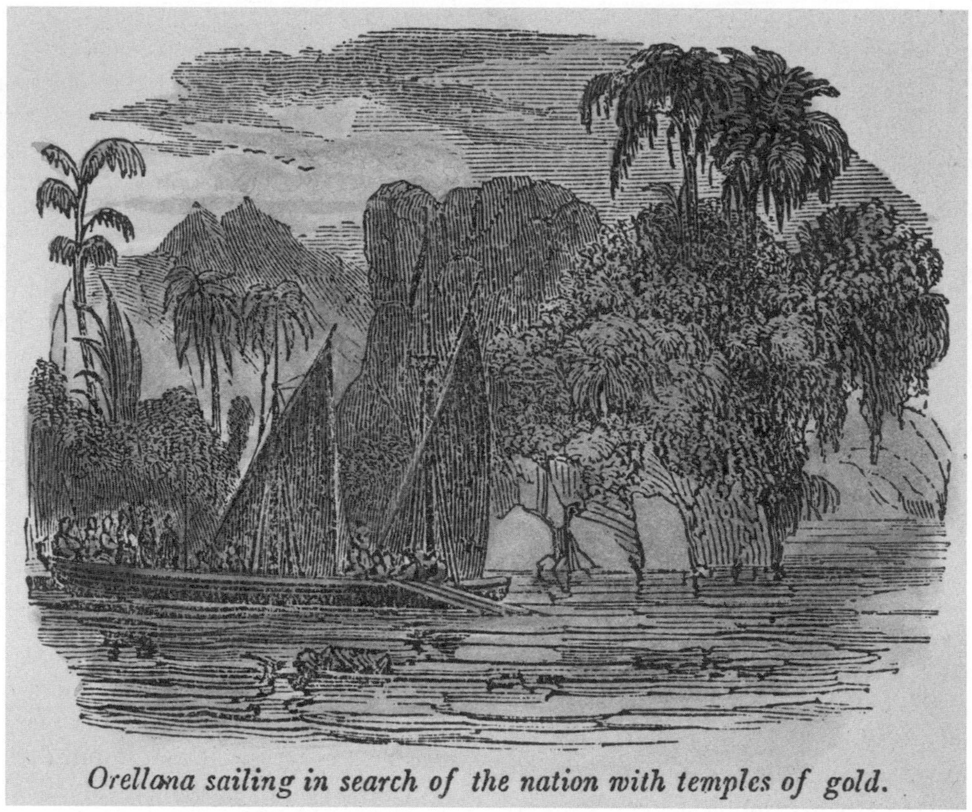

Orellana's voyage down the Amazon River, from an American engraving, 1848.
THE GRANGER COLLECTION, NEW YORK

descent of the Amazon River. Born in Trujillo, Spain, Orellana was in Panama in 1528 and probably joined Alonso de Alvarado's expedition to Peru in 1535. He fought against the native inhabitants in the siege against Lima in 1537 and two years later was one of the founders of Guayaquil, in present-day southwest Ecuador.

During this period, following the battle of Salinas (west Ecuador) on 6 April 1538, Gonzalo Pizarro made his way to Ecuador and organized an expeditionary force to find the wealthy kingdom of El Dorado, the "Land of Cinnamon." Orellana joined as second in command. The 1541 expedition (about 180 Spaniards and 4,300 Indian auxiliaries) entered the upper Amazon basin through the province of Quixos, descending tributaries of the great river. The men failed to encounter Indian groups worthy of note and suffered great hardships, exhausting both food and other supplies. Realizing that a vast jungle stretched before them and that return upriver was daily becoming more difficult, Pizarro sent Orellana downstream in a brigantine that had been constructed earlier to search for supplies, expecting him to return within twelve days. Orellana's group consisted of fifty-seven men, including the Dominican friar Gaspar de Carbajal, who would become the chronicler of the expedition. They left the main camp on 26 December 1541, but did not find an Indian village with food for eight days. Swift currents had carried them so far downstream that they believed it impossible to return to the Pizarro camp within the allotted time. After waiting briefly for Gonzalo Pizarro's forces to descend, they decided to continue on. They reached the mouth of the Napo near present-day Iquitos in Peru on 14 February 1542 and stopped in a village they called Aparia la Mayor, where they constructed a second brigantine.

On 1 March, Orellana and his men signed a document declaring their independence from Pizarro. Setting sail in mid-April, they passed through the Omaguas territory, where from 12 May on they faced almost continuous attacks by Indians until they reached the mouth of the Purus River on 23 May.

For three months they sailed downriver, passing many large villages with hostile warriors. On 24 June they engaged in combat with a powerful force that included women fighters whom they compared to the Amazons of classical mythology. Carvajal's account of these warriors and of a nearby kingdom where women ruled prompted European cartographers to name the river the Amazon. The group reached the broad mouth of the river on 8 August but no salt water until the 26th. From here they sailed northwesterly along the coast, reaching the island of Cubagua in September and continuing on to Santo Domingo.

Orellana returned to Spain and in May 1543 reported directly to Prince Philip and the Council of the Indies. Meanwhile, Gonzalo Pizarro had managed to struggle back to Quito, losing most of his men to hunger and disease. Complaints of treason were lodged against Orellana, but he secured an appointment (13 February 1544) to return and conquer the vast new land.

With his new wife, Ana de Ayala, Orellana left Spain in May 1545, leading a small fleet. Two of the four ships were lost in the crossing, and illnesses took a severe toll. About half the group sailed up the Amazon, with fifty-seven companions dying of hunger and another ship lost. Orellana himself came down with "fevers" and died in the arms of his wife. The remnants of the expedition sailed to the island of Margarita, off the coast of present-day Venezuela.

See also **El Dorado; Explorers and Exploration: Spanish America; Pizarro, Gonzalo.**

BIBLIOGRAPHY

José Antonio Del Busto Duthurburu, *Historia general del Perú: Descubrimiento y conquista* (1978), pp. 245–258.

John Hemming, *Red Gold: The Conquest of the Brazilian Indians* (1978), pp. 185–194.

Additional Bibliography

Latorre, Octavio. *La expedición a la Canela y el descubrimiento del Amazonas.* Quito: O. Latorre, 1995.

Muñiz, Mauro. *Orellana: El tuerto del Amazonas.* Madrid: Alderabán, 1998.

Pérez, María Teresa. *El descubrimiento del Amazonas: Historia y mito.* Seville: Ediciones Alfar, 1989.

NOBLE DAVID COOK

ORELLANA, JOSÉ MARÍA (1872–1926).

José María Orellana (*b.* 11 July 1872; *d.* 26 September 1926), president of Guatemala (1921–1926). Born to humble rural parentage in El Jícaro, in the eastern department of Zacapa, Orellana was a military man for most of his life. As a youth, according to legend, Orellana attracted the attention of Guatemalan president Manuel Estrada Cabrera, who became the boy's mentor and sent him to Guatemala's military academy, the Escuela Politécnica. After Orellana graduated as an officer and an engineer, he served his mentor in several military and political capacities. Although Orellana remained close to the dictator during his rule, he was still highly respected for his honesty and fairness as an officer and a politician. He was described as broad minded, tolerant, hard working, and sincere.

At the time of the overthrow of Estrada Cabrera in 1920, Orellana was a member of the Guatemalan National Assembly and the dictator's minister of public instruction. In his capacity as minister, Orellana opposed many of Estrada Cabrera's actions, contributed to the momentum of the uprising, and, thereby, was recognized as a friend and supporter of the Unionists—the coalition opposing Estrada Cabrera.

Nonetheless, Orellana, like many senior military officers, became disillusioned with the Unionists' experiment with democracy and the unrest that was associated with their government (1920–1921). Consequently, with the support of several senior members of Guatemala's Liberal Party, he agreed to participate in the coup that ousted the government of Carlos Herrera on 5 December 1921. Early in 1922, General Orellana achieved an overwhelming victory as the Liberal candidate in the presidential election and served as president until a heart attack resulted in his death.

See also **Estrada Cabrera, Manuel; Guatemala; Guatemala, Political Parties: Unionist Party.**

BIBLIOGRAPHY

Joseph A. Pitti, "Jorge Ubico and Guatemalan Politics in the 1920's" (Ph.D. diss., Univ. of New Mexico, 1975).

Wade Kit, "Precursor of Change: Failed Reform and the Guatemalan Coffee Elite, 1918–1926" (Master's thesis, Univ. of Saskatchewan, 1989).

Additional Bibliography

Aguilar de León, Juan de Dios. *Semblanza de José María Orellana Pinto.* Guatemala: Llerena F&G Editores, 1998.

WADE A. KIT

ORFILA, ALEJANDRO (1894–1958). Argentine politician Alejandro Orfila, born February 27, 1894, was elected governor of the province of Mendoza in 1926. A member of the Unión Cívica Radical, Orfila held to the party's dissident reformist current, led by José Néstor Lencinas and his son Carlos Washington Lencinas. During Orfila's brief term in office, the province enacted one of the country's first minimum-wage laws and began the construction of public housing for workers. The last of the "lencinista" governors, Orfila was removed from office in 1928 by the federal government. Following the military coup of September 1930, he largely withdrew from politics to practice law. He died on December 11, 1958. Orfila's only son, (Washington) Alejandro Orfila, served as secretary general of the Organization of American States from 1975 to 1984.

See also **Argentina, Political Parties: Radical Party (UCR); Lencinas, Carlos Washington; Orfila, Washington Alejandro José Luis; Organization of American States (OAS); Panama Canal; United States-Latin American Relations.**

BIBLIOGRAPHY

Rodríguez, Celso. *Lencinas y Cantoni: El populismo cuyano en tiempos de Yrigoyen.* Buenos Aires: Editorial de Belgrano, 1979.

JAMES CANE

ORFILA, WASHINGTON ALEJANDRO JOSÉ LUIS (1925–). Alejandro Orfila, an Argentine diplomat, served as secretary general of the Organization of American States. Born on March 9, 1925, in the city of Mendoza, Orfila's father was then governor of Mendoza Province. In 1946, when Federico Cantoni became the first Argentine ambassador appointed to the USSR, Orfila was assigned to Cantoni's staff. This early experience was followed by consular posts in Varsovia (1947), San Francisco (1948) and New Orleans (1949). Orfila's diplomatic career began in the Argentine embassy in Washington. In 1960 he was appointed ambassador to Japan; as such he returned to Washington in 1973. On May 17, 1975, Orfila was elected secretary general of the Organization of American States, and reelected for the period 1980–1985, but resigned in 1984. During his tenure as secretary general of the OAS, the treaties between Panama and the United States were signed (1977), by which full sovereignty over the Panama Canal reverts to Panama in 1999. He authored *The Americas in the 1980s* (1980). In 1994 Orfila purchased a winery in southern California, where he continues to live.

See also **Organization of American States (OAS).**

BIBLIOGRAPHY

Atkins, G. Pope. *Encyclopedia of the Inter-American System.* Westport, CT: Greenwood Press, 1997.

CELSO RODRÍGUEZ

ORGANIZATION OF AMERICAN STATES (OAS). The Organization of American States (OAS) is the world's oldest regional organization, whose antecedents can be traced to the First International Conference of American States, held in Washington, D.C., from October 1889 to April 1890. The participants at that gathering set up the Bureau of American Republics, which by 1910 had evolved into the Pan-American Union (PAU). For half a century the PAU provided an arena in which to establish the legal conventions and agreements underlining inter-American economic, social, and cultural collaboration. The experiences of the Great Depression and World War II led to a strengthening of inter-American cooperation and a general agreement for stronger multilateral response to the threats to peace and security in the Americas. To address these mutual concerns, the Ninth International Conference of American States, held in Bogotá, Colombia, in 1948, adopted the Charter of the OAS. The charter was subsequently amended by the Protocol of Buenos Aires, signed in 1967, which established the subsequent structure of the OAS General Secretariat, and by the Protocol of Cartagena de Indias, signed in 1985, which strengthened its political role in the hemisphere. The Protocol of Washington, which renewed the commitment of the member states to the strengthening, defense, and promotion of representative democracy and human rights in the hemisphere, was signed in 1992, to take effect upon ratification by two-thirds of the member states.

The technical-cooperation activities of the OAS received a powerful impulse with the declaration of the Alliance for Progress in 1961. The OAS effectively executed the multilateral development projects of the alliance and, more importantly, of programs developed as a result of the alliance that continued for decades after its demise. Since its creation, the OAS has been the regional international organization most active in conflict resolution and in dealing with low-violence disputes and internal conflicts. It has monitored human rights and, since 1988, elections.

Since the revision of its charter in 1985, the OAS has been increasingly involved in the peaceful resolution of conflicts, the process of social reconciliation, and the promotion of democracy. The OAS has based its efforts on respect for the sovereignty of, recognition of the equality of, and the principle of nonintervention in the internal affairs of member states. Given these precepts, the OAS did not sanction the U.S. interventions in Grenada (1983) and Panama (1989).

In 1994, the OAS had thirty-five member states: Antigua and Barbuda, Argentina, the Bahamas, Barbados, Belize, Bolivia, Brazil, Canada, Chile, Colombia, Costa Rica, Cuba, Dominica, the Dominican Republic, Ecuador, El Salvador, Grenada, Guatemala, Guyana, Haiti, Honduras, Jamaica, Mexico, Nicaragua, Panama, Paraguay, Peru, Saint Christopher-Nevis, Saint Lucia, Saint Vincent and the Grenadines, Suriname, Trinidad and Tobago, the United States, Uruguay, and Venezuela. In addition, the organization has granted permanent observer status to twenty-nine states as well as the European Economic Community.

The basic purposes of the OAS are: (1) to strengthen the peace and security of the continent; (2) to promote and consolidate representative democracy, with due respect for the principle of nonintervention; (3) to prevent possible causes of difficulties and to ensure the peaceful settlement of disputes among the member states; (4) to provide for common action in the event of aggression; (5) to seek the solution of political, juridical, and economic problems among member states; (6) to promote, by cooperative action, economic, social, and cultural development; and (7) to achieve an effective limitation of conventional weapons that will make it possible to devote the largest amount of resources to the economic and social development of the member states.

The OAS accomplishes its goals through the following organs: the General Assembly; the Meeting of Consultation of Ministers of Foreign Affairs; the Permanent Council; the Inter-American Economic and Social Council; the Inter-American Council for Education, Science, and Culture; the Inter-American Juridical Committee; the Inter-American Commission on Human Rights; the General Secretariat; and specialized conferences and organizations and other entities established by the General Assembly.

The General Assembly holds regular sessions once a year. Under special circumstances it meets in special session. The Meeting of Consultation is convened to consider urgent matters of common interest and to serve as Organ of Consultation under the Inter-American Treaty of Reciprocal Assistance (Rio Treaty), the main instrument for joint action in the event of aggression. The Permanent Council deals with matters that are entrusted by the General Assembly or the Meeting of Consultation and implements the decisions of both organs when their implementation has not been assigned to any other body. It also monitors the maintenance of friendly relations among the member states and the observance of the standards governing operations of the General Secretariat, and it acts provisionally as Organ of Consultation under the Rio Treaty. The purpose of the other two councils is to promote cooperation among the member states in their respective areas of competence. These councils hold one annual meeting and meet in special sessions when convoked in accordance with the procedures provided for in the charter. The General Secretariat is the central and permanent organ of the OAS. The headquarters of both the Permanent Council and the General Secretariat are in Washington, D.C. The secretary general of the OAS is elected to a five-year term by the General Assembly.

See also **Inter-American Organizations; Pan-Americanism; United States-Latin American Relations.**

BIBLIOGRAPHY

Carnegie Endowment For International Peace, Division of International Law, *International Conferences of American States,* 3 vols. (1934, 1940, 1954).

Inter-American Institute of International Legal Studies, *The Inter-American System* (1966).

John E. Fagg, *Pan Americanism* (1982).

Organization of American States, *Charter of the Organization of American States* (1992).

Additional Bibliography

Bouvier, Virginia Marie. *The Globalization of U.S.-Latin American Relations: Democracy, Intervention, and Human Rights.* Westport, CT: Praeger, 2002.

Cooper, Andrew Fenton, and Thomas Legler. *Intervention without Intervening? The OAS Defense and Promotion of Democracy in the Americas.* New York: Palgrave Macmillan, 2006.

Marichal, Carlos. *México y las conferencias panamericanas, 1889–1938: Antecedentes de la globalización.* Mexico: Secretaría de Relaciones Exteriores, 2002.

Shaw, Carolyn M. *Cooperation, Conflict, and Consensus in the Organization of American States.* New York: Palgrave Macmillan, 2004.

Sheinin, David. *Beyond the Ideal: Pan Americanism in Inter-American Affairs.* Westport, CT: Greenwood Press, 2000.

JAMES PATRICK KIERNAN

ORGANIZATION OF CENTRAL AMERICAN STATES (ODECA). Organization of Central American States (ODECA), a loose affiliation of Costa Rica, El Salvador, Guatemala, Honduras, and Nicaragua established in 1951. The body's long-term objective was to bring about the long-cherished, but elusive, goal of Central American unification, a condition that prevailed for a time after the region attained independence from Spain. Short-term objectives, intended to promote unification, were peaceful settlement of intra–Central American disputes; joint solution of common problems; and promotion of the region's economic, social, and cultural development.

The agreement establishing the organization, headquartered in San Salvador, set an elaborate institutional structure: Meeting of Heads of State, Conference of Foreign Ministers, Executive Council, Legislative Council, Court of Justice, Economic Council, Cultural and Educational Council, Defense Council, and Secretariat.

Despite the ideal of Central American union, the organization never proved effective in meeting its objectives. Most notably, it had little or no success in dealing with the many disputes between member countries. Additionally, from the outset, it was marked by political bickering. Operation of ODECA halted with the turmoil and violence of the late 1970s and 1980s. In 1993, with more stability in the region, Central American nations formed the Central American Integration System (SICA) to promote peace and democracy in the region. In 2005 the Central American countries signed a free trade agreement with the United States.

See also **Central America.**

BIBLIOGRAPHY

Ralph Lee Woodward, Jr., *Central America: A Nation Divided,* 2d ed. (1985).

G. Pope Atkins, *Latin America in the International Political System,* 2d ed. (1989).

Additional Bibliography

Antillón Salazar, Alvar. *La ODECA y el Parlamento Centroamericano.* San José, Costa Rica: Editorial Juricentro, 1996.

JAMES D. COCHRANE

ORIBE, EMILIO (?–1975). Emilio Oribe (*b. ca.* 1890s; *d.* 1975), Uruguayan poet, writer, literary critic, and educator. After completing his medical studies in Montevideo, Oribe was posted to Brussels as scientific attaché at the Uruguayan embassy. While there, he published his first book of poetry, *Alucinaciones de belleza* (1912). He never practiced medicine, but taught philosophy and worked for the National Council of Education of Uruguay. Oribe's poetry and essays were informed by the work of classical Greek and medieval philosophers, as is shown in *Transcendencia y platonismo en poesía* (1948) and *Tres ideales estéticos* (1958).

Essayistic works such as *Teoría del nous* (1934) and *El mito y el logos* (1945) focus primarily on topics relevant to the process of writing poetry and on "eternal" concerns such as time, death, and immortality. Characteristic of most of

Oribe's thirty-seven published collections is an intellectual or metaphysical focus. Other poems, however, treat more earthy topics, such as the emotion experienced in the countryside, personal confidences, nature, history, customs, and the mystery of life.

Other important works by Oribe include *Fugacidad y grandeza* (1941), *La medusa de Oxford* (1950), *Ars magna: Poemas* (1950), and *Antología poética* (1965). He is considered one of the outstanding intellectuals of his generation.

See also **Buenos Aires; Montevideo; Uruguay, Political Parties: Blanco Party.**

BIBLIOGRAPHY

Homenaje a Emilio Oribe en la Academia Nacional de Letras (1958).

Sarah Bollo, *Literatura uruguaya, 1807–1965,* vol. 2 (1965).

Norma Suiffet, *Tres poetas de Cerro Largo: Emilio Oribe, Juana de Ibarbourou, José Lucas* (1978).

Additional Bibliography

Sesto Gilardoni, Isabel. *Emilio Oribe: El poeta.* Montevideo: Barreiro y Ramos, 1981.

WILLIAM H. KATRA

ORIBE, MANUEL (1792–1857). Manuel Oribe (*b.* 26 August 1792; *d.* 12 November 1857), second president of Uruguay (1835–1838) around whom the Blanco Party was formed, one of the two traditional political parties in Uruguay. The name Blanco derived from the white ribbons worn by Oribe's men. Oribe became involved very early in the military. In 1812, when he was just twenty years old, he participated in the second siege of Montevideo by patriot troops. The following year he went to Buenos Aires to study as a cadet at the Escuela de Matemáticas. He went back to Montevideo in 1814 during the last stage of the siege. In September, several months after the fall of the city, he was promoted to lieutenant in the First Grenadier Regiment, and a few days later he became an aide to the governor. Oribe was growing increasingly uncomfortable with the way Buenos Aires was treating Montevideo. In February 1815, the city passed into the hands of José Gervasio Artigas, and Oribe remained there and accepted his authority. In 1817, when Montevideo was in the hands of the Portuguese, who had invaded the country in 1816, Artigas named Fructuoso Rivera commander of the irregular forces to the south of the Río Negro to fight the Portuguese in guerrilla warfare. Oribe did not like this appointment and left for Buenos Aires, where he remained until 1821.

In Buenos Aires, Oribe became associated with a society called the Caballeros Orientales, founded in 1819 to promote Uruguayan independence. This group came to be dominated by the *cabildo* of Montevideo. It took advantage of the divisions in the enemy ranks caused by the Brazilian declaration of independence in September 1822. In 1823, Oribe led an unsuccessful revolt and returned to Buenos Aires in 1824.

In 1825, he organized an invasion force that has come to be known in Uruguayan history as La Cruzada de los Treinta y Tres. By the end of the same year the Brazilians were being engaged in battle by the Uruguayans. The conflict evolved into a regional one when Buenos Aires entered the war on the side of the Uruguayans. Oribe fought the Brazilians successfully in various campaigns during 1825 and 1826. In 1828, he was sent to arrest Rivera, who had invaded the Misiones Orientales at the time when a peace treaty was being negotiated, and the rivalry between the two men began. In 1832, Oribe was appointed chief of staff and the following year minister of war.

In March 1835, Oribe was elected president and tried to initiate a period of national reconstruction. His administration was in sharp contrast with that of Rivera (1830–1835), who paid very little attention to the affairs of government. Oribe's problems began when he attempted to bring the interior under Montevideo's control, an area that Rivera considered his own. On 16 July 1836, Rivera rose in rebellion against him. Oribe had some initial success, but in 1838 he was totally defeated and was forced to resign in October. He went to his ally, Juan Manuel de Rosas of Argentina, for help, and in 1839 Rivera declared war on Rosas, initiating the Guerra Grande (1839–1852), which started out as a political dispute and turned into a regional war with the involvement of Brazil and Argentina and later into an international conflict joined by France and England. Oribe defeated Rivera in December 1842, and in February 1843 he laid siege to Montevideo, which lasted until October 1851. When an agreement was reached with Justo José de Urquiza, Oribe retired to private life, but in 1853 he was forced into exile, not returning until 1855.

See also **Uruguay, Political Parties: Blanco Party; Uruguay: Before 1900.**

BIBLIOGRAPHY

Aquiles B. Oribe, *Brigadier General D. Manuel Oribe,* 2 vols. (1912).

Mario Andrés Raineri, *Oribe y el estado nacional* (1960).

José A. Torres Wilson, *Oribe: El drama del Estado Oriental* (1976).

Additional Bibliography

Aguirre Ramírez, Gonzalo. *Tres aportes históricos.* Montevideo: Ediciones de la Plaza, 1996.

Medere Larrosa, Aristides I. *Oribe y su tiempo.* Montevideo: Taller Gráfico Barreiros y Ramos, 1994.

Torres Wilson, José de. *Oribe, el Uruguay en la lucha de los imperios.* Montevideo: Ediciones de la Planta, 1986.

JUAN MANUEL PÉREZ

ORIENTALES. Orientales, a term used for Uruguayans. It comes from the term Banda Oriental, which was used during the period of Spanish colonization to refer to the area along the eastern bank of the Uruguay River. In the Revolution of 1811, this area began to be called the Provincia Oriental, a name arising from the federalist ideas of José Artigas. After a war (1825–1828) between the United Provinces of the Río De La Plata (among which was the Provincia Oriental) and the Brazilian Empire, the Preliminary Peace Pact was signed, with the mediation of Great Britain, on 27 August 1828. This pact formed the basis out of which was to come Uruguay, officially called the República Oriental del Uruguay.

See also **Banda Oriental.**

BIBLIOGRAPHY

Ariosto González, *¿Orientales o Uruguayos?* (1943).

Brother Damasceno, *Ensayo de historia patria,* vol. 1 (1955).

Washington Reyes Abadie and Andrés Vázquez Romero, *Crónica general del Uruguay,* vols. 1–2 (1984).

Additional Bibliography

Maiztegui Casas, Lincoln R. *Orientales: Una historia política del Uruguay.* Montevideo: Planeta, 2005.

JOSÉ DE TORRES WILSON

ORIENTE (BOLIVIA). Oriente (Bolivia), a vast tropical plain located east of the Bolivian Andes (formerly Charcas), stretching from north to east, with its farthest reaches bordering Brazil. It includes the Mojos-Chiquitos tropical savannas, the Grigotá plains, and the tropical slopes to the southeast once held by the aggressive Chiriguano people. Mojos villages were scattered throughout the northern part of the Oriente along rivers and tributaries connecting the area to the Amazon basin. The Chiquitos dwelled in the southeastern tropical forests, while the Yuracarés lived in what is now the coca-producing Chaparé region northeast of Cochabamba.

Legends of vast treasures in this almost mythical region kindled Spanish interest, and by the 1540s expeditions into the jungles were under way. Treasure seeking aside, royal authorities encouraged explorers to push into the untamed frontier for pacification and possible settlement. Most of the expeditions failed. Conflicts between Charcas and Paraguayan interests, harsh physical conditions, and the ever present Chiriguanos, who fiercely withstood Spanish incursion into their territory, prevented permanent settlement. Soon, the primary government objective became containment of the Chiriguanos. Thus, authorities urged settlement of the intermediate, fertile subpuna valleys where Mizque, Tarija, Tomina, and El Villar were established as defense zones.

Meanwhile, in the Oriente proper, outposts and fortresses became towns and points of departure for expeditions into the Mojos and Chiquitos territories. In 1561 the first Santa Cruz de la Sierra was established, followed by La Barranca del Guapay, San Lorenzo de la Frontera, Santiago del Puerto, the second Santa Cruz, and, in 1603, Santísima Trinidad. Some of these towns were soon abandoned, destroyed, or moved to other locations. Overall, the missionaries (Dominicans, Franciscans,

Augustinians, and particularly the Jesuits) were more successful with regional settlement and pacification than their nonecclesiastical counterparts. The region has yet to develop its full potential.

See also **Chiriguanos.**

BIBLIOGRAPHY

Josep M. Barnadas, *Charcas: Orígenes históricos de una sociedad colonial* (1973), pp. 24, 26, 47, 49, 62, 469.

Enrique Finot, *Historia de la conquista del Oriente boliviano,* 2d ed. (1978), pp. 13, 17.

Ray Henkle, "The Move to the *Oriente:* Colonization and Environmental Impact," in *Modern-Day Bolivia: Legacy of the Revolution and Prospects for the Future,* edited by Jerry R. Ladman (1982), pp. 277, 295.

Humberto Vázquez Machicado, José De Mesa, and Teresa Gisbert, *Manual de historia de Bolivia,* 2d ed. (1983), pp. 166–167.

Brooke Larson, *Colonialism and Agrarian Transformation in Bolivia: Cochabamba, 1550–1900* (1988), pp. 246–249.

Additional Bibliography

Baptista Gumucio, Mariano. *Las misiones Jesuíticas de Moxos y Chiquitos: Una utopía cristiana en el oriente Boliviano.* La Paz: Newylibros: CENDES, 2003.

Roca, José Luis. *Economía y sociedad en el Oriente boliviano, siglos XVI-XX.* Santa Cruz: COTAS, 2001.

Steinbach de Loza, Ingrid, and Franca Calmotti Crevanti. *Investigaciónes históricas sobre el Oriente Boliviano.* Santa Cruz de la Sierra, Bolivia: Facultad de Comunicación Social y Humanidades–UPSA, Centro de Investigaciónes Humanísticas y Sociales, 2003.

Urioste Fernández de Cordova, Miguel, and Cristóbal Kay. *Latifundios, avasallamientos y autonomías: La reforma agraria inconclusiva en el Oriente.* La Paz: Fundación Tierra, 2005.

Lolita Gutiérrez Brockington

ORIENTE (ECUADOR). Oriente (Ecuador), the eastern slopes of the Andes and the tropical rainforest lowlands of Amazonia, covering some 56,000 square miles, and including the provinces of Napo, Pastaza, Morona-Santiago, and Zamora-Chinchipe. The most thinly populated zone in Ecuador (about 3 percent of the total), the region is home to several independent Indian groups (the Shuar, Cofan, Waorani, and lowland Quechua), hunter-gatherers who have never been effectively subjugated by Europeans. Despite the region's remoteness and lack of European settlement, Ecuador and Peru have repeatedly fought over ownership of it. In 1967 a significant oil strike in northern Oriente brought dramatic changes. Settlers from the crowded sierra followed the highways cut into the oil-producing zones. Oriente oil is now Ecuador's leading export.

See also **Ecuador-Peru Boundary Disputes.**

BIBLIOGRAPHY

On the history of Oriente oil, see John D. Martz, *Politics and Petroleum in Ecuador* (1987). On boundary disputes in the Oriente, see David Hartzler Zook, Jr., *Zarumilla–Marañón: The Ecuador–Peru Dispute* (1964).

Additional Bibliography

Tapia, Luis. *Territorio, territorialidad, y construcción regional amazónica.* Quito: Abya-Yala, 2004.

Trujillo Moncalvo, Patricio. *Salvajes, civilizados y civilizadores: La Amazonia ecuatoriana: El espacio de las ilusiones.* Quito, Ecuador: Fundación de Investigaciones Andino-Amazónicas: Ediciones Abya-Yala, 2001.

Ronn F. Pineo

ORINOCO RIVER. The Orinoco River runs some 1,600 miles from the Guiana highlands at the Brazilian border to the Gulf of Paria. Historically it constituted part of Venezuela's waterway transportation between Ciudad Bolívar and Maracaibo. The Orinoco drains most of the country.

In the late sixteenth century, Walter Raleigh raided the Orinoco region. During the wars of independence, Simón Bolívar used the river as a means of attacking and defeating the Spanish forces in Venezuela. The river basin now comprises an important part of Venezuela's modern economy. It produces some 21 percent of Venezuelan oil. In 1970, the Guri dam on the Caroní River, one of the Orinoco's major tributaries, began to generate tremendous hydroelectric power. The river also facilitates Venezuelan exploitation of rich iron ore deposits and expansion of steel production in eastern Venezuela.

See also **Guiana Highlands.**

BIBLIOGRAPHY

Demetrio Ramos Pérez, *El tratado de límites de 1750 y la expedición de Iturriaga al Orinoco* (1946).

Rafael Gómez Picón, *Orinoco, río de libertad: Biografía, aspectos geográficos, históricos, socioeconómicos,* 2d ed. (1978).

Additional Bibliography

Belton, Benjamin Keith. *Orinoco Flow: Culture, Narrative, and the Political Economy of Information.* Lanham, MD: Scarecrow Press, 2003.

Penn, James R. *Rivers of the World: a Social, Geographical, and Environmental Sourcebook.* Santa Barbara: ABC-CLIO, 2001.

Roosevelt, Ana Curtenius. *Amazonian Indians from Prehistory to the Present: Anthropological Perspectives.* Tucson: University of Arizona Press, 1994.

WINTHROP R. WRIGHT

ORIXÁS. Orixás, deities of several major religions in the the African diaspora, of Yoruban influence. Besides Candomblé in Brazil and Santería in Cuba, Orixás figure in the pantheon of religions found in Trinidad and Tobago, Haiti, and several Caribbean island states, as well as the African countries where they originated. Orixás act as intermediaries between humans and the supreme being, Olodumare (or Olorun), who rules over all. Every living being and natural phenomenon was created by Olodumare, and is therefore infused with his sacred energy, known as *axe* (ah-SHAY), or life-force. Because his powers and responsibilities are so vast, Olodumare does not involve himself directly in human affairs. Legend maintains that for this purpose he created the orixás. Each orixá embodies an aspect of Olodumare's creative power in personalized form, representing both natural phenomena and human qualities. Parables about the personified orixá help teach basic cultural values.

Orixá worship is an integral part of Candomblé, for it is through the assistance of the orixás that problems are analyzed and resolved. An individual may consult the orixás through the ancient system of divination known as *Ifa,* in which the answer to a problem is contained in a series of verses and parables, or may turn to other methods of divination. The individual orixás are also regularly invoked through possession ritual. The *axe* of each orixá may be tapped through songs, dances, and drum rhythms particular to them. In ceremonies called *batuques, toques,* or *festas,* orixás are summoned to temporarily possess initiated devotees, although they sometimes select an uninitiated individual of their own choosing. Once an orixá has arrived, it may communicate directly with worshippers or indirectly through the assistance of a senior initiate.

Every individual is said to have a special affinity with at least one orixá, who is considered the "ruler of the head" and a personal guardian. The relationship between a person and his or her orixá is symbolized by strings of beads (*contas*) worn around the necks of initiates and bearing each orixá's personal colors. Devotees bring gifts and offerings to orixás on the days sacred to them. Many rites of orixá worship have become part of Brazilian popular culture, such as Rio de Janeiro's annual tribute to Iemanjá, goddess of the sea waters, in which gifts and flowers are sent to the ocean on miniature boats with prayers for the new year.

Of the more than 600 orixás worshipped in Nigeria and Benin, little over a dozen major orixás are recognized throughout Brazil. Others have been developed in Brazil, sometimes through incorporation of indigenous deities. These other deities, such as the Negro Velho and various Exús of Umbanda, or the Caboclo (indigenous) deities of Candomblé Caboclo, function similarly to orixás, but are not considered part of traditional Candomblé.

Principal orixás of Afro-Brazilian Candomblé include:

Exú: guardian of crossroads and divine messenger. All ceremonies begin with an offering to Exú so that he will open the path of communication and carry the prayers of the devotees to the orixás. He is represented with red and black.

Oxalá: eldest orixá, symbol of creativity and purity, represented by the color white. Oxalá is regarded as the father of all orixás.

Xangô: represented by thunder, lightning, and fire, symbolizing his passion and temper, although Xangô whose colors are brown, red, and white, is also known for his profound sense of justice.

Oxossi: orixá of hunters and the hunt, protector of ecological balance, symbolized by the color green. Oxossi is celebrated on Thursday.

Ogum: deity of iron, metallurgy, tecnhologyand warfare, whose color is green.
Omolu: orixá of smallpox and disease, his colors are red and black.
Iemanjá: Mother of the orixás, associated with maternity and the sea (hence, her association with the Middle Passage among slaves). She isrepresented with clear blues and greens.
Oxunmare: keeper of the rainbow.
Iansã: warrior goddess, keeper of the winds, wife of Xangô, symbolized with the color red.
Oxum: young goddess of sweetness, sensuality, beauty, and wealth, associated with fresh rivers and streams, also wife of Xangô. Associated with fertility, her colors are gold and yellow.

See also **Yoruba.**

BIBLIOGRAPHY

Raymundo Nina Rodrigues, *O animismo fetichista dos negros bahianos* (1935).

Donald Pierson, *Negroes in Brazil: A Study of Race Contact at Bahia* (1942).

Edison Carneiro, *Candomblés da Bahia,* 3d ed. (1961).

Roger Bastide, *The African Religions of Brazil: Toward a Sociology of the Interpenetration of Civilizations,* translated by Helen Sebba (1978), and *O Candomblé da Bahia,* 2d ed. (1978).

Gary Edwards and John Mason, *Black Gods: Orisa Studies in the New World* (1985).

Manuel Querino, *Costumes africanos no Brasil,* 2d ed. (1988).

Additional Bibliography

Daniel, Yvonne. *Dancing Wisdom: Embodied Knowledge in Haitian Vodou, Cuban Yoruba, and Bahian Candomblé.* Urbana: University of Illinois Press, 2005.

Falola, Toyin, and Ann Genova. *Orisa: Yoruba Gods and Spiritual Identity in Africa and the Diaspora.* Trenton: Africa World Press, 2005.

Henry, Frances. *Reclaiming African Religions in Trinidad: The Socio-Political Legitimatization of the Orisha and Spiritual Baptist Faiths.* Barbados: University of the West Indies Press: London, 2003.

Lachatañeré, R. and Christine Ayorinde. *Afro-Cuban Myths: Yemayá and other Orishas.* Princeton: M. Wiener Publishers, 2003.

Nascimento, Abdias do. *Orixás: os deuses vivos da Africa.* Rio de Janeiro: IPEAFRO/Afrodiaspora, 1995.

Prandi, J. Reginaldo. *Mitologia dos orixás.* São Paulo: Companhia das Letras, 2001.

Voeks, Robert A. *Sacred Leaves of Candomblé: African Magic, Medicine, and Religion in Brazil.* Austin: University of Texas Press, 1997.

KIM D. BUTLER

ORLICH BOLMARCICH, FRANCISCO JOSÉ (1907–1969). Francisco José Orlich Bolmarcich (*b.* 1907; *d.* October 1969), president of Costa Rica (1962–1966). Born in San Ramón, a member of one of Costa Rica's wealthiest families, "Chico" Orlich Bolmarcich studied accounting and business administration in New York in the 1920s. Orlich, along with José Figueres Ferrer, his close friend and collaborator since childhood, dominated Costa Rican politics for two decades following the 1948 civil war. He and Figueres founded Costa Rica's principal political party, the National Liberation Party (PLN), in 1951. During Figueres's presidency (1953–1958), Orlich served as party leader in the Legislative Assembly. He lost the election for president in 1958, but ran successfully four years later.

Regarded as the more conservative of the two, particularly in the area of government intervention in the economy, Orlich nonetheless tackled the difficult issues of agrarian reform and housing for the poor that Figueres had avoided. He sponsored Costa Rica's membership in the Central American Common Market. Orlich's presidency was hampered by the eruption of the volcano Irazú (1963–1965), which caused grave economic hardship for over two years and led to charges of mismanagement of disaster relief, which contributed to the PLN's defeat in the presidential election of 1966.

See also **Costa Rica; Figueres Ferrer, José.**

BIBLIOGRAPHY

Carlos Araya Pochet, *Historia de los partidos políticos: Liberación Nacional* (1968).

Charles D. Ameringer, *Don Pepe: A Political Biography of José Figueres of Costa Rica* (1978).

Harold D. Nelson, ed., *Costa Rica: A Country Study,* 2d ed. (1983).

Additional Bibliography

Obregón, Clotilde María. *Semblanza de Don Francisco J. Orlich B.* San José: Partido Liberación Nacional, Editorial Raíces, 2003.

CHARLES D. AMERINGER

ORO, JUSTO SANTA MARÍA DE

ORO, JUSTO SANTA MARÍA DE (1772–1836). Justo Santa María de Oro (*b.* 3 September 1772; *d.* 19 October 1836), Dominican priest, patriot, first bishop of Cuyo. In 1789 Oro, a native of San Juan, Argentina, entered the Dominican order. He was ordained to the priesthood in 1794 and went to Spain in 1809 for further studies and to get permission to establish schools in Argentina. The next year, after the May Revolution broke out, he returned and worked with José de San Martín in the formation of the Army of the Andes. Oro was a member of the Congress of Tucumán and adamantly opposed any form of monarchy that did not have the approval of the people. He supported the Chilean independence movement under Bernardo O'Higgins. In 1818 he was made superior of the Dominicans in Chile. Oro was sent to Juan Fernández Island in 1825 because of his suspected involvement in a movement against the government of General Freire. Permitted to leave Chile in 1828, he returned to San Juan, Argentina, where he was named apostolic vicar by Pope Leo XII. In 1834, he was named bishop of the newly formed diocese of Cuyo.

See also **Cuyo; Dominicans; San Martín, José Francisco de.**

BIBLIOGRAPHY

Antonio B. Toledo, *Las ideas republicanas de fray Justo Sant Maria de Oro* (1926); *Emilio Maurin Navarro, Fray Justo de Santa María de Oro* (1960); and *Forjadores de la República* (1967).

Additional Bibliography

Carril Quiroga, Pablo Alberto del. *El corazón de fray Justo de Santa María de Oro y otros temas conexos.* San Juan: Academia Provincial de la Historia, 1971.

NICHOLAS P. CUSHNER

OROZCO, JOSÉ CLEMENTE

OROZCO, JOSÉ CLEMENTE (1883–1949). José Clemente Orozco (*b.* 23 November 1883; *d.* 7 September 1949), Mexican muralist. Orozco grew up in Mexico City, where he attended the Escuela Nacional de Agricultura, the Escuela Nacional Preparatoria, and the Escuela Nacional de Bellas Artes (San Carlos). His first exhibit in Mexico City in 1916 showed the influence of the popular engraver and illustrator of Porfirian broadsides, José Guadalupe Posada. Because of its popular inspiration and controversial subject matter (he depicted several prostitutes), it was not well-received by the public.

In 1917, Orozco worked in a doll factory in New York City, where he tried to establish himself as an artist. A declared enemy of the decorative folk nationalism then in vogue among young Mexican artists, Orozco sought an art that would address the emotional intensity of Mexico's cataclysmic revolutionary reality. Called upon in 1922 by Education Minister José Vasconcelos to paint the walls of the Escuela Nacional Preparatoria as part of the artistic Renaissance, Orozco emerged as a major artist of the twentieth century, depicting the agony of war from a peasant perspective and initiating the pictoral history of Mexico as an interracial drama of struggle and sorrow. In 1923, with Diego Rivera, David Alfaro Siqueiros, and others, Orozco formed the Syndicate of Revolutionary Painters, which declared war on "bourgeois individualism" and committed itself to the creation of a monumental art for and about the Mexican people to capture "the moment of transition from a decrepit order to a new one."

Painting in the early 1930s at Pomona College in California, the New School for Social Research in New York City, Dartmouth College, and Mexico's Palacio de Bellas Artes, Orozco developed New World historical themes with an outraged sense of tragedy over the destructiveness of the contemporary world, an interpretation at odds with his fellow muralists' Marxist optimism about progress. Between 1936 and 1939, he painted in Guadalajara. His work in the university auditorium displays a stinging critique of political leaders. In the Palacio de Gobierno, he painted his famous image of Miguel Hidalgo. His most outstanding work, and one of the greatest works of twentieth-century art, is in the Hospicio Cabañas in Guadalajara, where he synthesizes his understanding of human history and nature in the Promethean figure of a man consuming himself by fire.

Additional murals by Orozco are in the Palacio de Justicia, the Hospital de Jesús Nazareno, the Jiquilpán revolutionary museum, the Escuela Nacional de Maestros, and the Museo Nacional de Historia in Chapultepec. When he died in Mexico City, he was buried in the Rotonda de los Hombres Ilustres in the Panteón de Dolores, the first artist to have had this honor.

See also **Art: The Twentieth Century.**

BIBLIOGRAPHY

Justino Fernández, *Orozco: Forma e idea* (1942).

MacKinley Helm, *Man of Fire: J. C. Orozco* (1953).

Alma Reed, *Orozco* (1955).

Luis Cardoza y Aragon, *Orozco* (1959).

José Clemente Orozco, *An Autobiography,* translated by Robert C. Stephenson (1962).

Dawn Ades, *Art in Latin America* (1989).

Additional Bibliography

Anaya Wittman, Marcela Sofia. *José Clemente Orozco, el Orfeo mexicano.* Guadalajara: Universidad de Guadalajara, Centro Universitario de Arte Arquitectura y Diseño, División de Artes y Humanidades, Departamento Teorías e Historias, 2004.

Folgarait, Leonard. *Mural Painting and Social Revolution in Mexico, 1920-1940: Art of the New Order.* Cambridge and New York: Cambridge University Press, 1998.

Rochfort, Desmond. *Mexican Muralists: Orozco, Rivera, Siqueiros.* San Francisco: Chronicle Books, 1998.

Tibol, Raquel. *José Clemente Orozco: Una vida para el arte: breve historia documental.* Mexico City: Fondo de Cultura Económica, 1996.

MARY KAY VAUGHAN

OROZCO, OLGA (1920–1999).

OROZCO, OLGA (1920–1999). Olga Orozco (*b.* 17 March 1920–15 August 1999), Argentine poet. Born in La Pampa, she began her career as a student of literature in the Faculty of Philosophy and Letters at the University of Buenos Aires. She joined a group of writers that published their work in the literary magazine *Canto,* which later would be identified with the Generation of 1940. Her first publication was *Desde lejos* (1946; From Far Away), followed by *Las muertes* (1951; The Deaths), and *Los juegos peligrosos* (1962; Dangerous Games). In 1964 she won the first Municipal Prize for Poetry. *La oscuridad es otro sol* (1967; Darkness Is Another Light) won the second Municipal Prose Award, and in 1971 she received the Grand Prize of Honor from the Argentine Foundation for Poetry. Her next works were *Museo salvaje* (1974; Wild Museum), *Cantos a Berenice* (1977), and *Mutaciones de la realidad* (1979; Mutations of the Reality).

In 1979, in recognition of her poetic development, the first collection of her complete poetry was published, establishing her as one of the main voices in Argentine poetry. *Obra poética* was awarded the Grand Prize of the National Fund of the Arts in 1980 and the Esteban Echeverría Award in 1981. Two later books are *La noche a la deriva* (1983; Night Adrift) and *En el revés del cielo* (1987; In the Underside of Heaven). Among the themes that characterize Orozco's poetry are the religious concerns of a poet searching for primordial unity and the incorporation of elements from astrology, witchcraft, alchemy, and the tarot, which in combination create metamorphic imagery that displays uncanny perceptions of reality.

See also **Literature: Spanish America.**

BIBLIOGRAPHY

Stella Maris Colombo, *Metáfora y cosmovisión en la poesía de Olga Orozco* (1983).

Additional Bibliography

Orozco, Olga *Eclipses y fulgores: Antología,* (Eclipses and Splendors: Anthology). Colección Tierra Firme, Buenos Aires, 1998.

Orozco, Olga. *También luz es un abismo,* (Also Light Is an Abyss). Buenos Aires: Emece Editores, 1994.

Orozco, Olga, and Zabaljauregui. *Relámpagos de lo invisible: Antología,* (Flash of Lighten of the Invisible: Anthology). Buenos Aires: Colección Tierra Firme, 1997.

MAGDALENA GARCÍA PINTO

OROZCO, PASCUAL JR. (1882–1915).

OROZCO, PASCUAL JR. (1882–1915). Pascual Orozco, Jr. (*b.* 28 January 1882; *d.* 30 August 1915), guerrilla army leader in the state of Chihuahua during the early years of the Mexican Revolution. Born near San Isidro, Chihuahua, Orozco learned to read and write at a local public school. Working as a muleteer for various mining companies, he gained a reputation as a good worker and honest man.

His popularity as a leader in his home state, his ability to recruit and secure the allegiance of his followers, his knowledge of the local terrain, and his tactical ability in guerrilla combat made Orozco a key figure in the Revolution. He was one of the early leaders of the anti-reelectionist movement against General Porfirio Díaz and part of the initial group that rallied around Revolutionary leader Francisco I. Madero. When Madero launched his rebellion after escaping from prison following the fraudulent elections of 1910, Orozco immediately rose to support Madero's Plan of San Luis Potosí (5 October 1910).

Orozco was responsible for some of the initial successes of the movement, including the first Revolutionary victory over federal troops at Pedernales (27 November). He later led the attack against Ciudad Juárez, which resulted on 10 May 1911 in the capture of that city, the key victory of the uprising. As a result, Orozco enjoyed prominence as a hero of the Revolution. He was also responsible for putting down several revolts against the Madero regime.

Impatient with Madero, Orozco disavowed the administration and launched his own rebellion on 3 March 1912. Gaining control of much of the north, his movement constituted the strongest threat to the Madero administration, and his troops repelled an attack by a federal army led by the minister of war, General José González Salas. A few months later, however, Orozco was defeated by a federal army commanded by General Victoriano Huerta in a series of battles at Rellano (23 May) and Bachimba (3 July).

When Huerta deposed Madero (February 1913), Orozco supported the Huerta regime and commanded troops opposing Madero's successors. His controversial campaigns on behalf of the Huerta regime gained him several promotions, carrying him ultimately to the highest rank in the Mexican Army, general of division, and also earning him the enmity of his former Revolutionary colleagues, who felt he had betrayed their movement.

After the fall of Huerta (15 July 1914), Orozco opposed both the interim regime and the Revolutionary government of General Venustiano Carranza. Forced to flee to the United States, Orozco joined with Huerta and other exiles in seeking to launch a new rebellion. The rebellion was forestalled when Orozco and Huerta were arrested by U.S. marshals on 27 June 1915. Escaping from custody, Orozco was shot by a U.S. posse in Culberson County, Texas.

See also **Huerta, Victoriano; Madero, Francisco Indalecio; Mexico, Wars and Revolutions: Mexican Revolution.**

BIBLIOGRAPHY

Michael C. Meyer, *Mexican Rebel: Pascual Orozco and the Mexican Revolution, 1910–1915* (1967), provides the most detailed study. See also Charles C. Cumberland, *Mexican Revolution: Genesis Under Madero* (1952); and Kenneth J. Grieb, *The United States and Huerta* (1969).

Additional Bibliography

Katz, Friedrich. *The Life and Times of Pancho Villa.* Stanford: Stanford University Press, 1998.

Knight, Alan. *The Mexican Revolution*, 2 volumes. Lincoln: University of Nebraska Press, 1990.

KENNETH J. GRIEB

OROZCO Y BERRA, MANUEL (1818–1881). Manuel Orozco y Berra (*b.* 1818; *d.* 27 January 1881), Mexican historian, engineer, and statistician. Born in Mexico City, the son of an insurgent captain who served under Mariano Matamoros during the Mexican War of Independence, Orozco attended the Colegio de Minería as an engineer topographer. While in Puebla as *maestro mayor* of public works, he received his licenciate in law (1847). His friend José Fernando Ramírez secured a post for him at the Archivo General de la Nación, of which he later became director. In 1856, he became senior official in the Secretaría de Fomento.

A contributor to literary and political journals since his youth, he wrote on geographical and historical subjects for the seven-volume *Diccionario universal de historia y geografía* (1853–1856). Between 1853 and 1857, he edited the *Documentos para la historia de México* in twenty volumes. A minister of the Supreme Court of Justice (1863), he declined appointment to the Assembly of Notables but in 1864 he accepted membership in the Scientific Commission of Mexico.

Under the empire, he again worked at the Secretaría de Fomento and became director of the National Museum created by Emperor Maximilian, who appointed him to the Council of State in September 1865. Rehabilitated by 1870 (he had never been a Conservative), he rejoined the Society of Geography and Statistics and the Academy and Literature and Sciences. His last years were dedicated to his magnum opus, the four-volume *Historia antigua de la conquista de México* (1880). His interest in the pre-Columbian era distinguished him as part of the Mexican historiographical revival of the latter part of the nineteenth century.

See also **Mexico: 1810-1910.**

BIBLIOGRAPHY

Manuel Orozco y Berra, *Historia de la dominación española en México* (1938).

Additional Bibliography

García, Rubén. *Biografía, bibliografía e iconografía de don Manuel Orozco y Berra.* Mexico City: [?], 1934.

Uribe Ortiz, Susana. *Manuel Orozco y Berra en la historiografía mexicana.* Mexico City: Universidad Nacional Autónoma de México, Facultad de Filosofía y Letras, 1963.

BRIAN HAMNETT

ORPHÉE, ELVIRA (1930–). Elvira Orphée is an Argentine writer. Born in San Miguel de Tucumán, she grew up in Tucumán and Buenos Aires. She suffered from health problems as a child, an experience from which she drew frequently to build her fictional world.

Orphée published her first collection of short stories, *Dos veranos* (Two Summers), in 1956. In 1961 she published *Uno,* a novel, followed by *Aire tan dulce* (1966; When the Air is Soft), which is considered her best work for its innovative language and her treatment of love and hate. *En el fondo* (1969; At the Bottom) received the first Municipal Prize for the Novel. In 1973 she published a collection of short stories, *Su demonio preferido* (His Preferred Devil), followed in 1977 by *La última conquista de El Angel* (*El Angel's Last Conquest*), a novel in episodes whose main character is a member of the Buenos Aires secret police in charge of torture and abuse of political prisoners. Later works include *Las viejas fantasiosas* (1981; The Old Ladies' Tales); *La muerte y los desencuentros* (1990; The Death and the Separation); *Ciego de cielo* (1990; Blind of Heaven), a collection of short stories that deal with justice; and *Basura y luna* (1996; Garbage and Moon).

See also **Literature: Spanish America.**

BIBLIOGRAPHY

Orphée, Elvira. *El Angel's Last Conquest.* Translated by Magda Bogin. New York: Ballantine Books, 1985.

Additional Bibliography

Pellerin, Gilles, and Oscar Hermes Villordo. *Encuentros: Escritores y artistas de la Argentina y Quebec.* Quebec: Editions Sans Nom, 1989.

MAGDALENA GARCÍA PINTO

ORREGO-SALAS, JUAN ANTONIO (1919–). Juan Antonio Orrego-Salas, a Chilean composer, was born on January 18, 1919, in Santiago. His composition teachers at the National Conservatory of Music in Chile were Humberto Allende and Domingo Santa Cruz. He received degrees in arts and letters and in architecture. With fellowships from both the Rockefeller and Guggenheim Foundations he studied in the United States from 1944 to 1946 with Paul Henry Lang, Randall Thompson, and Aaron Copland. From 1949 to 1961 he edited the well known *Revista musical chilena.* He wrote articles on music folklore and theoretical topics and essays on Copland, Villa-lobos, and the Chilean composers Leng and Santa Cruz. He was the director of the Latin American Music Center and professor of composition at Indiana University from 1961 to 1987.

Orrego-Salas's early musical language had influences of Spanish popular dances with their characteristic rhythms and harmonies. He utilized more experimental techniques and atonality in his larger works. Beyond some stylistic similarities with works of de Falla and Hindemith, the composer has done significant work with rhythmical relationships characterized by polyrhythms and multimetric layers. Nevertheless, Orrego-Salas's use of dodecaphonic techniques has never attained the level of strict twelve-tone writing. From his first period: *Cantata de Navidad* (1945) and *Canciones castellanas* (1948), both for soprano and chamber orchestra; Symphony no. 1 (1949); *El retablo del rey pobre* (1949–1952), an opera-oratoria. He began experimenting with more contemporary languages in *Serenata concertante* for orchestra (1954); *Dúos concertantes* for cello and piano (1955); and particularly with his Symphony no. 2 (1954). Among his piano works are Suite no. 1 (1946); *Variaciones sobre un pregón* (1954); *Rústica* (1952); *Sonata* (1967); and *Rondo-Fantasia* (1984).

In his *Missa "In Tempore Discordiae"* (1968–1969), a large work for chorus, tenor, and orchestra, he uses spoken effects, whispering, quasi-parlando and aleatoric procedures. A prolific composer, Orrego-Salas created *Biografía mínima de Salvador Allende* for voice, guitar, trumpet, and percussion (1983); Concerto for violin and orchestra (1984); Fantasia for piano and wind orchestra (1986); and *Partita* for alto saxophone and piano trio (1988). He wrote the opera *Widows* (1987–1990), based on the novel by Ariel Dorfman. In 1992 Orrego-Salas was awarded the Premio Nacional del Arte, the Chilean government's highest honor in the arts and humanities.

Orrego-Salas has continued to receive commissions from foundations, universities, ensembles, and soloists around the world. Among his numerous later works are his fifth and sixth symphonies (1995 and 1997); oratorios and cantatas, including *La ciudad Celeste* (2004), for baritone soloist, chorus, and orchestra; and compositions for chamber orchestra with soloists, small chamber ensembles, singers, and solo instruments. In 2004 the Latin American Music Center and the Center for Latin American and Caribbean Studies at Indiana University held a colloquium, combining discussions and the premiere of *La ciudad Celeste*, in honor of Orrego-Salas's eighty-fifth birthday. In 2005 he published *Encuentros, visiones y repasos*, a memoir of his life as well as reflections on music in general and on his own work.

See also **Music: Art Music.**

BIBLIOGRAPHY

John Vinton, ed., *Dictionary of Contemporary Music* (1974), pp. 548–549.

Gérard Béhague, *Music in Latin America: An Introduction* (1979), pp. 269–270, 315–319; *New Grove Dictionary of Music and Musicians* (1980); *Octavo festival internacional de música contemporánea* (1992), pp. 69–70, 123.

Additional Bibliography

Orrego-Salas, Juan Antonio. *Encuentros, visiones y repasos: Capítulos en el camino de mi música y de mi vida.* Santiago: Ediciones Universidad Católica de Chile, 2005.

Orrego-Salas, Juan Antonio. "Mi camino de la vocación al hallazgo." *Revista Musical Chilena* 58, no. 202 (2004): 63–74.

ALCIDES LANZA

ORTEGA DEL VILLAR, ANICETO

(1825–1875). Aniceto Ortega del Villar (*b.* 1825; *d.* 17 November 1875), Mexican composer and physician. Born in Tulancingo, Hidalgo, the son of a statesman, Ortega was educated in Mexico City at the Seminario Conciliar de México (1837), the Seminario de San Ildefonso (1840), and the School of Medicine (1841–1845). He founded the Sociedad Filarmónica Mexicana in 1866. In 1867 his march *Zaragoza* was published; later it became, unofficially, Mexico's second national anthem. Two other marches, *Republicana* and *Potosina,* premiered at the Gran Teatro Nacional. His nationalistic opera *Guatimotzin,* based on a libretto by José Cuellar, told the story of the defense of Mexico by the Aztecs. It was first performed on 13 September 1871, at the Gran Teatro Nacional, with the Mexican soprano Angela Peralta and the tenor Enrico Tamberlik in the leading roles. This opera is generally considered the first in Mexico to incorporate indigenous elements into the Italian format then prevalent. Ortega also wrote several piano pieces, among them *Invocación a la Beethoven, op. 2* (1867). This work, performed in 1867 and published by Wagner and Levien, created an interest in that composer that resulted in a Beethoven Festival, held in Mexico City in 1871. Ortega died in Mexico City.

See also **Music: Art Music.**

BIBLIOGRAPHY

Robert Stevenson, *Music in Mexico* (1952; 2d ed., 1971); *New Grove Dictionary of Music and Musicians,* vol. 13 (1980).

Additional Bibliography

Kuss, Malena. "The 'Invention' of America: Encounter Settings on the Latin American Lyric Stage." *Revista de Musicología* 16:1 (1993): 185–204.

SUSANA SALGADO

ORTEGA SAAVEDRA, DANIEL (1945–). Daniel Ortega Saavedra is the principal leader of the Sandinista Front of National Liberation (FSLN), was president of Nicaragua from 1985 to 1990 and was reelected as president in 2006. Ortega was born in La Libertad in the department of Chontales. His father was an accountant for a mining firm and fought with Augusto César Sandino's army in the 1920s. His parents were arrested by Anastasio Somoza García in the 1940s. Ortega attended private church schools in Managua and met Jaime Wheelock at the Christian Brothers Pedagogic Institute. He studied briefly for the priesthood in El Salvador, under the direction of the Nicaraguan bishop Miguel Obando y Bravo. However, Ortega soon returned to Nicaragua and increased his activities in the Nicaraguan Patriotic Youth organization in the early 1960s. For a short time he attended law school at the University of Central America, where he focused on organizing student protests.

Ortega made contact with the Sandinista leadership and joined the guerrilla ranks in 1963. He was arrested for trying to seize a National Guard post and for bombing vehicles at the U.S. embassy. In 1964 Ortega was detained in Guatemala for illegal political activity and turned over to the Nicaraguan government. He was severely tortured; this led to his involvement in the assassination of a National Guard officer in October 1967. The following month he was charged with bank robbery and sentenced to eight years in prison. While in jail he studied law, history, and geography. He also wrote poems, one of which was titled "I Never Saw Managua When the Miniskirt Was in Style." A Sandinista raid on the Christmas party of a wealthy landowner freed Ortega in a prisoner-hostage exchange in December 1974. He joined the Sandinista National Directorate in 1975, and helped his brother Humberto develop the Tercerista insurrectionist strategy that was successful against the National Guard in the late 1970s. He rarely made statements for attribution before the victory, and allowed Humberto to speak for the Terceristas. He was part of the reunified guerrilla leadership that directed the final offensive from March to July 1979.

After the fall of the Somoza regime, Ortega became a member of the Governing Junta of National Reconstruction. He emerged as the principal representative of the junta and the Sandinistas, and traveled frequently in Latin America, Europe, and Asia as Nicaragua's chief diplomat. Following the resignation of two non-Sandinista members of the junta in April 1980, Ortega became a dominant political figure of the revolution. He was selected as the Sandinista presidential candidate for the November 1984 election, which he won by a landslide with 67 percent of the popular vote after the main opposition candidate pulled out of the race in protest of alleged press restrictions and intimidation.

Ortega assumed the presidency in January 1985 for a six-year term. One of his first acts was to centralize economic planning in the Executive Committee of the President. The foremost tasks of his government were creating a new constitution and defending the country from counterrevolutionary threats. Ortega divided his time between the constitutional debate, national economic planning, and international diplomacy. He gained the reputation of a pragmatist with a knack for political gamesmanship. His good relationship with the Soviet president Mikhail Gorbachev (b. 1931) brought economic and military aid to Nicaragua from the Soviet Union at the height of the war with the Contras, the armed opponents of the Sandinista government.

The Contras formed in 1980 and 1981 around two dozen national guard officers of the ousted Somoza regime. As the civil war intensified, the United States Central Intelligence Agency assisted in the expansion of the Contra leadership to disaffected moderate supporters of the revolution and the broadening of its popular base among peasants and indigenous peoples of the Caribbean coast of Nicaragua. Ortega frequently traveled to Eastern Europe to consult with heads of state and secure support for Nicaragua against the United States. Moreover, he played a key role in the negotiation of the Central American peace plan that was initiated by Costa Rican president Oscar Arias in February 1987.

Toward the end of his term, Ortega implemented an economic austerity plan intended to control hyperinflation, encourage greater productivity, and reduce public spending. At the same time, Ortega opened lines of communication with the internal opposition and business community. Much of his political behavior in the late 1980s was in anticipation of the presidential election of February 1990. Ortega had to confront the military threat of the Contra force and the electoral challenge of a fourteen-party opposition coalition, the Nicaraguan Opposition Union (UNO). Once again, Ortega headed the Sandinista ticket. A large part of the female population and many peasants and young males rejected Ortega in favor of UNO candidate Violeta Barrios de Chamorro. In the wake of defeat, Ortega promised supporters that his party would "govern from below," and that the Sandinista revolution would continue.

Ortega retained his place on the Sandinista National Directorate and his title "Commander of the Revolution." At the first party congress in July 1991 he was elected general secretary by a unanimous vote. This was the first time the Sandinistas had chosen a party secretary to oversee day-to-day activities. At the meeting Ortega delivered a three-hour speech that recognized the mistakes of the Sandinista revolutionary government but called on the members to defend their right to rebellion. In September 1991 he replaced Sergio Ramírez Mercado as leader of the Sandinista deputies in the National Assembly. This was attributed to Ortega's role as head of the party and his more aggressive political style. He has traveled widely as a self-proclaimed emissary of peace, most notably during the Iraqi occupation of Kuwait in late 1990.

Ortega maintained his authority in the FSLN, but alienated several elements of the party base in rural areas and among intellectuals and professionals. He ran unsuccessfully for the presidency as the Sandinista candidate in 1996 and 2001. In 1999 the FSLN reached an agreement with the government of Arnoldo Alemán and the Constitutionalist Liberal Party to reduce the minimum percentage of the national vote required by the constitution to win the presidency from 45 percent to 35 percent.

As the November 2006 presidential election approached, Ortega declared publicly that he was no longer a revolutionary and changed the banner colors displayed in his campaign from the distinctive Sandinista red and black. He courted conservative Catholic voters with his support of a national law banning abortion under any circumstances. He also selected Jaime Morales Carazo as his vice presidential running mate in a move to gain the confidence of the business sector. Morales Carazo is a prominent business figure whose property was confiscated by the FSLN in the 1980s, including his house in Managua in which Ortega continues to live. On November 5, 2006, Ortega won just under 38 percent of the national vote, carrying him to the presidency for a five-year term. The FSLN won 37 of 91 legislative seats, and pluralities or majorities in 12 of 19 departments.

See also **Barrios de Chamorro, Violeta; Nicaragua; Nicaragua, Sandinista National Liberation Front (FSLN).**

BIBLIOGRAPHY

"Carter destaca integridad de elecciones." *La Prensa* (Managua), November 7, 2006. Available from http://www.laprensa.com.ni/archivo/2006/noviembre/17/elecciones/noticias/154838.shtml.

Frente Sandinista de Liberación Nacional. *Informe central de la dirección nacional del FSLN.* Author, 1991.

García Márquez, Gabriel, ed. *Los Sandinistas.* Bogotá, Colombia: Editorial veja Negra, 1979.

Gilbert, Dennis. *Sandinistas: The Party and the Revolution.* New York: Basil Blackwell, 1988.

Selser, Gabriela. "Defender nuestro derecho a la rebelión." *Barricada*, July 1, 1991.

United States Department of State, Bureau of Public Affairs. *Nicaraguan Biographies: A Resource Book.* Washington, DC: Author, 1988.

Vargas, Vargas, Oscár René. *Adónde va Nicaragua?* Managua, Nicaragua: Ediciones Nicarao, 1991.

MARK EVERINGHAM

ORTEGA SAAVEDRA, HUMBERTO

(1942–). Humberto Ortega Saavedra (*b.* September 1942), Nicaraguan leader and chief of the Sandinista Popular Army. Ortega, brother of Daniel Ortega, was born in the department of Chontales in central Nicaragua. He attended private Catholic schools and later taught catechism classes in Managua. He joined the radical student movement in the late 1950s and became the leader of the Nicaraguan Patriotic Youth organization in 1962. He joined the Sandinista National Liberation Front in 1965. After participating in the Sandinista defeat at Pancasán in 1967, Ortega fled to Cuba, where he remained for two years. He contributed to the refinement of the Sandinista strategy and objectives during this time. In December

1969, he was captured after trying to free Carlos Fonseca from a Costa Rican jail. He was handed over to the Nicaraguan National Guard and severely tortured. As a result, he partially lost the use of his right arm and some motor skills. He was freed in October 1970 after Sandinistas hijacked an airplane in Nicaragua.

Ortega became a prominent intellectual force in the revolutionary movement in the 1970s. He argued for a strategy of popular armed revolt throughout the country and worked closely with Carlos Fonseca. After Fonseca's death in 1976, Ortega emerged as the primary advocate of an urban-based insurrection. This plan was the basis for the "General Political-Military Platform of the Struggle of the Sandinista National Liberation Front," published in May 1977. The document coincided with the ascendancy of Ortega's Tercerista faction and efforts to recruit business, religious, and professional figures into the revolution. Tactical alliances with the middle and upper classes were critical factors in the Sandinistas' success during the civil war of 1978 and 1979. Ortega directly coordinated guerrilla attacks on the National Guard with business strikes and urban demonstrations until the July 1979 victory.

Ortega was named commander in chief of the Sandinista Popular Army in October 1979. He became minister of defense in January 1980, a post giving him control over the air force, air defense, navy, and Sandinista militia. He held the title Commander of the Revolution and was the only four-star general in the Nicaraguan military. He managed the military buildup and recruitment process during the war against the counterrevolutionary force. He established excellent relations with the officer corps and was popular among the soldiers.

After the Sandinistas' electoral defeat in February 1990, President Violeta Barrios De Chamorro named herself minister of defense but retained Ortega as head of the military; in return he promised not to participate in partisan politics while head of the armed forces. This decision was harshly criticized by the far right of the fourteen-party coalition that backed Chamorro's candidacy. Ortega supported Chamorro's desire to eliminate obligatory military service and to reduce the armed forces to one-third of their size at the height of the conflict with the Contras. In September 1991 Ortega officiated at the celebration of the twelfth anniversary of the Sandinista Popular Army, accompanied by President Chamorro and Cardinal Miguel Obando y Bravo.

At the Sandinista Party congress in July 1991, Ortega gave a strong speech in support of the neoliberal economic stabilization plan for Nicaragua. He also reiterated his assurances that the army would remain behind the administration under any circumstances. The Sandinista Assembly unanimously reelected him to the National Directorate during the congress, but he refused to reassume the post he had held since 1975. On account of political pressure from opponents in the National Assembly and legal difficulties linking him to the murder of the son of a wealthy family, Ortega agreed to step down as army chief in late 1994.

See also **Nicaragua, Sandinista National Liberation Front (FSLN).**

BIBLIOGRAPHY

Humberto Ortega, *Cincuenta años de lucha sandinista* (1979).

Shirley Christian, *Nicaragua: Revolution in the Family* (1985).

Gabriele Invernizzi, Francis Pisarri, and Jesús Ceberio, *Sandinistas: Entrevistas a Humberto Ortega Saavedra, Jaime Wheelock Román y Bayardo Arce Castaño* (1986).

Dennis Gilbert, *Sandinistas: The Party and the Revolution* (1988).

Humberto Ortega, "El ejército jamás volverá a ser el brazo armado del partido sandinista," in *Semanario* 1, no. 32 (1991): 8–12.

Additional Bibliography

Ortega, Humberto. *La epopeya de la insurreción. Nicaragua Siglo XX, pesamiento y acción, análisis histórico, narración inédita.* Managua: Lea Grupo Editorial, 2004.

MARK EVERINGHAM

ORTIZ, FERNANDO (1881–1969). Fernando Ortiz (*b.* 16 July 1881; *d.* 10 April 1969), Cuban scholar, public servant, and political activist. No three words can describe the life and activities of this multifaceted Cuban intellectual. He studied law in Havana, completed his studies in Barcelona, and began his career as a criminal law specialist. His interests soon broadened to include sociology, archaeology, history, philology, anthropology, musicology, and ethnology. He served as a consular official in Italy, as public prosecutor for Havana, as a professor of law and, later, anthropology at the University of Havana, and as a representative for several terms in Congress. A tireless political agitator, he directed the Junta Cubana de Renovación Nacional against governmental corruption in 1923 and organized the Cuban Alliance for a Free World Against Fascism in 1945. In answer to the fascist claim of Aryan superiority, he wrote *El engaño de las razas* (*Deception of the Races*) in 1945.

Ortiz is best known for his studies on African-Cuban culture and as a prosecutor of sugar monoculture. His studies of the African contribution to Cuban life have marked him as the "greatest definer of the Cuban identity." In his first study of colonial blacks, *Hampa afro-cubano: Los negros brujos* published in 1906, he introduced the term "afro" as a prefix in sociological and anthropological studies. He further initiated use of the term "transculturation" to replace the many other terms used to describe the symbiosis of cultures. He founded the Society of Afro-Cuban Studies as a forum to promote awareness of the importance of Africans to the Cubans. His works span the colonial period to the modern, slavery to music and dance, and he laid the foundation for the unique national identity of the Cuban people.

His book best known to North Americans is *Cuban Counterpoint: Tobacco and Sugar* in which he condemns the sugar industry and describes its evils and calls for promotion of the Cuban tobacco industry. He strongly opposed the United States' growing influence on Cuba and accused it of using sugar to increase its dominance over Cuban people. His criticisms brought to light the political and economic dependence of Cuba on the United States.

See also **Cuba: The Republic (1898-1959); Economic Integration.**

BIBLIOGRAPHY

The majority of Ortiz's many works have not been translated to English but are available in Spanish. Two in English are his *Cuban Counterpoint: Tobacco and Sugar,* translated by Harriet de Onis (1947), and his *On the Relations Between Blacks and Whites* (1943). An examination of his writings and philosophy is available in Diana Iznaga, *Transculturación en Fernando Ortiz* (1989). A study of his life and works is Araceli García Carranza, ed., *Bio-bibliografía de don Fernando Ortiz* (1970).

Additional Bibliography

Castellanos, Jorge. *Pioneros de la etnografía afrocubana: Fernando Ortiz, Rómulo Lachatañeré, Lydia Cabrera.* Miami: Ediciones Universal, 2003.

Font, Mauricio A., and Alfonso W. Quiroz. *Cuban Counterpoints: The Legacy of Fernando Ortiz.* Lanham: Lexington Books, 2005.

Iznaga, Diana. *Transculturación en Fernando Ortiz.* Havana: Editorial de Ciencias Sociales, 1989.

Salermo Izquierdo, Judith. *Fernando Ortiz: Notas acerca de su imaginación sociológica.* Havana: Centro de Investigación y Desarrollo de la Cultura Cubana Juan Marinello, 2004.

Santí, Enrico Mario. *Fernando Ortiz: Contrapunteo y transculturación.* Madrid: Colibrí Editorial, 2002.

Toro, Carlos del. *Fernando Ortiz y la Hispanocubana de Cultura.* Havana: Fundación Fernando Ortiz, 1996.

JACQUELYN BRIGGS KENT

ORTIZ, ROBERTO MARCELINO

(1886–1942). Roberto Marcelino Ortiz (*b.* 24 September 1886; *d.* 25 July 1942), cabinet minister and president of Argentina (1938–1942). Born in Buenos Aires, Ortiz received a law degree from the University of Buenos Aires in 1909. After establishing a successful law practice in the Argentine capital, he sought public office. He first served as a city councilman in Buenos Aires between 1918 and 1920. He then advanced to the Argentine Chamber of Deputies, where he represented Buenos Aires until 1924. In 1925, President Marcelo T. de Alvear (1922–1928) appointed him minister of public works.

Active in national politics through the 1920s, Ortiz became one of the leading Anti-Personalist Radicals. He returned to public service during the Concordancia, when President Agustín P. Justo (1932–1938) named him minister of finance (1935). Justo selected him as his successor, and in 1938 he was elected president. In office, Ortiz tried to curtail the fraudulent electoral practices that had undermined Argentine democracy after 1930. Before substantive changes were introduced, diabetes forced him to delegate power in 1940 to Ramón Castillo and then to resign in June 1942.

See also **Argentina: The Twentieth Century; Argentina, Political Parties: Antipersonalist Radical Civil Union.**

BIBLIOGRAPHY

Mark Falcoff and Ronald H. Dolkart, eds., *Prologue to Perón: Argentina in Depression and War, 1930–1943* (1975).

Félix Luna, *Ortiz: Reportaje a la Argentina opulenta,* 6th ed. (1982).

DANIEL LEWIS

ORTIZ DE AYALA, SIMÓN TADEO

ORTIZ DE AYALA, SIMÓN TADEO (1788–1833). Simón Tadeo Ortiz de Ayala (*b.* 18 October 1788; *d.* 18 October 1833), Mexican entrepreneur and diplomat. Born in Mascota, Jalisco, Ortiz de Ayala visited Spain, where in 1810 he became a champion of independence and initiated a decade of travels in search of aid for his country that took him to the United States, much of South America, and England. In 1822 he published *Resumen de la estadística del Imperio Mexicano.*

After a mission to Guatemala in 1822, Ortiz de Ayala became a land speculator in Texas as well as in Coatzacoalcos in the south. Although he developed a number of schemes to colonize both areas, none was successful. While the Mexican consul in Bordeaux he published another important analysis, *México considerado como nación independiente y libre* (1832).

See also **Mexico: 1810-1910.**

BIBLIOGRAPHY

Wilbert H. Timmons, "Tadeo Ortiz, Mexican Emissary Extraordinary," in *Hispanic American Historical Review* 51 (August 1971): 463–477 and his *Tadeo Ortiz: Mexican Colonizer and Reformer* (1974).

Additional Bibliography

Chanes Nieto, José. *Uno de los primeros teóricos del México independiente: Simon Tadeo Ortiz de Ayala.* Mexico City: Universidad Nacional Autónoma de México, Centro de Investigaciones en Administración Pública, 1983.

Ortiz, Tadeo, and Fernando Escalante Gonzalbo. *México considerado como nación independiente y libre: O sea algunas indicaciones sobre los deberes más esenciales de los mexicanos.* Mexico City: Consejo Nacional para la Cultura y las Artes, 1996.

Torre Villar, Ernesto de la. "La política americanista de Fray Servando y Tadeo Ortiz." In *Estudios de historia moderna y contemporánea de México.* Mexico City: Universidad Nacional Autónoma de México, 1980.

JAIME E. RODRÍGUEZ O.

ORTIZ DE DOMÍNGUEZ, JOSEFA

ORTIZ DE DOMÍNGUEZ, JOSEFA (1768–1829). Josefa Ortiz de Domínguez (*b.* 5 September 1768; *d.* 1829), Mexican insurgent heroine, known as "la Corregidora." Born in Morelia, she was the wife of Miguel Domínguez (1756–1830), who became corregidor (provincial magistrate) of Querétaro. She was in contact with various autonomists and participated in the conspiracy of 1810. When the conspiracy was denounced, Domínguez apprehended several of the participants and locked up his wife to prevent her from informing the others. But Josefa was able to send word of the danger to Ignacio Allende (1769–1811). Upon receiving the news, Miguel Hidalgo y Costilla (1753–1811) initiated the rebellion of 16 September. Confined to the convent of Santa Clara, Josefa was freed shortly thereafter. She continued aiding the insurgency. In 1813 the authorities initiated proceedings against her, believing her to be the "Anne Boleyn" of the movement, and she was imprisoned in Mexico City in the convent of Santa Teresa until 1817. When Agustín de Iturbide (1783–1824) proclaimed himself emperor in 1822, she refused to be a maid of honor of the empress. She died in Mexico City in 1829. In 1878, the Congress of Querétaro declared her *Benemérita de la Patria.*

See also **Mexico, Wars and Revolutions: Mexican Revolution.**

BIBLIOGRAPHY

Francisco Sosa, *Biografías de mexicanos distinguidos* (1985), pp. 773–783.

Hugh M. Hamill, Jr., *The Hidalgo Revolt: Prelude to Mexican Independence,* 2d ed. (1970); *Diccionario Porrúa de historia, geografía y biografía de México,* vol. 2 (1986), p. 2152.

Additional Bibliography

Agraz García de Alba, Gabriel. *Los corregidores Don Miguel Domínguez y Doña María Josefa Ortiz y el inicio de la independencia.* Mexico City: G. Agraz García de Alba, 1992.

Zárate Toscano, Verónica. *Josefa Ortiz de Domínguez, La Corregidora.* Mexico City: Comisión Nacional para las Celebraciones del 175 Aniversario de la Independencia Nacional y 75 Aniversario de la Revolución Mexicana, 1985.

VIRGINIA GUEDEA

ORTIZ DE ZÁRATE, JUAN AND JUANA

ORTIZ DE ZÁRATE, JUAN AND JUANA (1521–1576). Juan Ortiz de Zárate (*b.* 1521; *d.* 26 January 1576) and Juana (*d.* 1584), Adelantado of Río de la Plata and heir thereof. Ortiz de Zárate was born in Vizcaya, Spain, to a prominent family. He went to America with the first viceroy of Perú, Blasco Núñez De Vela, and became a wealthy man in Chuquisaca.

In 1567, Diego López de Zúñiga y Velasco, count of Nieva, viceroy of Peru, gave Ortiz de Zárate a temporary *adelantazgo* (governorship) of the Río de la Plata. He returned to Spain to be confirmed by the crown, and disembarked again on 17 October 1572, arriving in the Río de la Plata in November of the following year. After suffering many hardships, he finally reached Asunción in February 1575 to take charge of the government. He died the following year.

Ortiz de Zárate named Juana, his daughter with the Inca Princess Leonor Yupanqui, his universal heir. The government of the *adelantazgo* would be in the hands of the person whom his daughter married, granted he follow all the capitulations made between Ortiz de Zárate and Philip II.

Juana had many suitors, and finally married *licenciado* Juan de Torres de Vera y Aragón in December 1577. She died seven years later.

See also **Peru: From the Conquest Through Indepnendence.**

BIBLIOGRAPHY

Pedro Tadeo Acevedo and Ernesto J. Colombres, *Los amores de la princesa Ynca Leonor Yupanqui y el romance de la indohispana Juana Ortiz de Zárate* (1935), and *Los adelantados del Río de la Plata* (1936).

JUAN MANUEL PÉREZ

ORTIZ MENA, ANTONIO

ORTIZ MENA, ANTONIO (1907–2007). Antonio Ortiz Mena, was a Mexican and international financial figure. As secretary of the treasury under two consecutive administrations (1958–1970), Ortiz Mena presided over the longest period of consistently high rates of economic growth in Mexico. He is regarded as the architect of the economic model, known as "stabilizing growth," that Mexico adopted during this period; leftist intellectuals see him as the true organizer of the new bourgeoisie. In 1963 and again in 1969 he was considered a possible candidate for the official Institutional Revolutionary Party (PRI) nomination for president.

Born on April 16, 1907, in Parral, Chihuahua, Ortiz Mena was a member of a third generation of important political figures, his grandfathers having been active in politics and his father treasurer of the Federal District. Ortiz Mena was the political disciple of President Adolfo Ruiz Cortines (1952–1958) and the uncle of President Carlos Salinas (1988–1994). He attended the National Preparatory School and the National School of Law, where, along with future president Miguel Alemán (1946–1952), he was a member of the distinguished Generation of 1925–1928. Early in his career he was associated with the Guanajuato political group, led by José Aguilar y Maya. Aided by his mentor in the 1930s, he held a number of minor positions in the federal bureaucracy before joining Ruiz Cortines's cabinet as director general of the Mexican Institute of Social Security (1952–1958). After leaving the treasury secretariat in 1970, he headed the Inter-American Development Bank from 1971 through 1988. In 1988 Salinas appointed him director general of Banamex, one of Mexico's largest banks, where he served until 1990. Ortiz Mena died in Mexico City on March 12, 2007.

See also **Economic Development; Inter-American Development Bank (IDB); Mexico: Since 1910; Ruiz Cortines, Adolfo; Salinas de Gortari, Carlos.**

BIBLIOGRAPHY

Raymond Vernon, *The Dilemma of Mexico's Development* (1963).

Roger D. Hansen, *The Politics of Mexican Development* (1971); *Excélsior,* 3 June 1984, 16.

Additional Bibliography

Ortiz Mena, Antonio. *Development in Latin America, a View from the IDB: Addresses and Documents, 1971–75.* Washington, DC: Inter-American Development Bank, 1975.

Ortiz Mena, Antonio. *Development in Latin America, a View from the IDB: Addresses and Documents, 1976–80.*

Washington, DC: Inter-American Development Bank, 1985.

Ortiz Mena, Antonio. *El desarrollo estabilizador: Reflexiones sobre una época.* Mexico: Colegio de México, Fideicomiso Historia de las Américas, Fondo de Cultura Económica, 1998.

RODERIC AI CAMP

ORTIZ RUBIO, PASCUAL (1877–1963). Pascual Ortiz Rubio (*b.* 10 March 1877; *d.* 4 November 1963), Mexican president. He was elected in a hotly contested presidential race with José Vasconcelos in 1929, after president-elect Álvaro Obregón was assassinated before taking office. Some analysts believe he actually lost to Vasconcelos. During his administration (5 February 1930 to 4 September 1932), former president Plutarco Elías Calles (1924–1928) remained so powerful behind the scenes and his influence so openly pervasive that Ortiz Rubio resigned in protest against his lack of presidential sovereignty and authority. Ortiz Rubio was the second of three presidents to fill out the first six-year presidential term, 1928–1934.

Ortiz Rubio was born in Morelia, Michoacán, the son of lawyer Pascual Ortiz, from a landowning family, and Leonor Rubio. He was related by marriage to President José López Portillo. He attended preparatory school at the famous Colegio de San Nicolás in Michoacán, and as a student leader opposed the reelection of Porfirio Díaz in 1896. He completed his topographical engineering degree at the National College of Mines (later the National School of Engineering) in 1902 and returned to Morelia, where he soon involved himself in local politics. Elected to the 1912–1913 federal legislature after Madero's victory, he became a member of the "Renovation Group." After Madero's murder, Victoriano Huerta imprisoned him in 1913.

After his release, Ortiz Rubio joined the Constitutionalists as a colonel of engineers. In 1914, he was in charge of enemy properties for the Mexican government and directed the federal stamp bureau. By 1915, he had risen to the rank of brigadier general, responsible for engineering supplies. He later directed the department of military engineers for the secretariat of war before becoming governor of his home state (1917–1920). He served presidents Adolfo de la Huerta and Obregón as secretary of communications and public works (1920–1921) and president Calles appointed him ambassador to Germany and then Brazil. He became the National Revolutionary Party's presidential candidate in 1929. After resigning the presidency in 1932, the only Mexican to do so since 1913, he went to the United States. He returned to Mexico in 1935.

See also **Mexico: Since 1910; Mexico, Political Parties: National Revolutionary Party (PNR).**

BIBLIOGRAPHY

John W. F. Dulles, *Yesterday in Mexico: A Chronicle of the Revolution, 1919–1936* (1961).

Pascual Ortiz Rubio, *Memorias, 1895–1928* (1963).

Lorenzo Meyer, *Historia de la Revolución mexicana,* vols. 12 and 13 (1978).

Tzvi Medin, *El minimato presidencial: Historia política del maximato* (1982).

Additional Bibliography

Mijangos Díaz, Eduardo Nomelí. *La Revolución y el poder político en Michoacán, 1910–1920.* Morelia: Univerisdad Michoacana de San Nicolás de Hidalgo, Instituto de Investigaciones Históricas, 1997.

Mijangos Díaz, Eduardo Nomelí. *Pascual Ortiz Rubio: Compendio de vida y obra.* Morelia: Archivo Histórico, Universidad Michoacana de San Nicolás de Hidalgo, 1997.

Oikión Solano, Verónica. *El constitucionalismo en Michoacán: El periodo de los gobiernos militares, 1914–1917.* Mexico City: Consejo Nacional para la Cultura y las Artes, 1992.

RODERIC AI CAMP

ORURO. Oruro, city and department of Bolivia. Officially founded in 1606, the city lies north of Lake Poopó at an altitude of 12,150 feet. The region ranked second to Potosí during the remainder of the colonial period as a silver producer in the Audiencia of Charcas.

The Aymara reportedly worked mines in the region during Inca times. Around 1557 Indians from Paria revealed their location to Lorenzo de Aldana, the Spanish *encomendero,* but Potosí's competition for workers and resources handicapped their development. When the major lodes of San Miguel and San Cristóbal were discovered in 1595, thousands flocked to the vicinity, including the priest of Colquemarca, Francisco de Medrano, who played an important role in exploiting the mineral wealth and populating the region. Manuel Castro Padilla, *oidor* (judge) of the Audiencia (high court) of Charcas, founded the Royal Villa of St. Philip of Austria of Oruro on 1 November 1606. The following year a royal treasury office opened in Oruro to collect taxes on the silver output.

In contrast to Potosí, Oruro received little attention from Spain. Mine operators at Oruro petitioned the government to assign them a Mita (cheap forced labor). But Viceroy Francisco de Toledo had already assigned the region to send *mita* workers to Potosí. Thus Oruro's demands could only be satisfied at the expense of its more famous competitor. The upshot was that on the one hand Oruro's operators had to hire costly free workers. On the other hand, Oruro, closer to the mercury mines at Huancavelica, paid less than Potosí for mercury to amalgamate its silver ores. But in times of shortage, Potosí's influence probably enabled its refiners to obtain extra mercury to the detriment of smaller camps such as Oruro.

Oruro's initial boom quickly ran its course. Miners had worked the rich, oxidated silver chloride ores on the surface but had not discovered how to refine efficiently the *negrillos* (deeper silver sulphide ores). In January 1627 Antonio de Salinas adapted the techniques used to amalgamate ores at Potosí to Oruro conditions and touched off another boom. Based on tax records, silver production more than doubled after 1610, reaching more than 3.5 million pesos de ocho (pieces of eight) in 1632. Output then declined rapidly to about half a million pesos per year and then remained stagnant. A modest rise began around 1690, but the great pan-Andean epidemic ended it in 1719. After the crown halved the tax on silver to 10 percent in 1736, Oruro's output doubled to nearly 1.2 million pesos in 1762.

Following the Túpac Amaru uprising near Cuzco and the murder of Tomás Catari in Chayanta, rebellion convulsed Oruro on 10 February 1781. Led by Juan de Dios Rodríguez, Jacinto Rodríguez, and Sebastián Pagador, creoles attacked Oruro's Spaniards. With Indians recruited from outside, the rebels looted, destroyed, and killed for several days before order was partially restored.

Oruro's decayed condition at independence reflected a general exhaustion of its ores and the destruction suffered in rebellions and wars. In 1810 the city revolted against the crown. Royalist forces later destroyed most of the mining infrastructure. Oruro's population declined from 75,920 in 1678, of whom half were Indians, to only 8,000 or less at independence.

In 1826 the city became the administrative center of the department of Oruro. Besides silver, demand for tin and tungsten helped reinvigorate the mining industry. In the late nineteenth century Oruro became a railroad center, linking much of Bolivia with Peru and Chile. The city's population rose from 13,575 in 1900 to more than 175,000 in 1988. As of 2005, its population was projected to be 433,481.

Of all Bolivian cities, Oruro enjoys fame for its folkloric celebrations, especially its carnival. Masked dancers portray the Spanish conquest of the Andes, including Pizarro's execution of Atahualpa. In honor of the Virgin of the *Socavón* (Mine), figures represent a myriad of saints and demons, Spaniards and Indians, in a colorful union of native and Christian lore.

See also **Aymara; Carnival.**

BIBLIOGRAPHY

Marcos Beltrán Avila, *Capítulos de la historia colonial de Oruro.* La Paz, 1925.

Lillian Estelle Fisher, *The Last Inca Revolt, 1780–1783.* Norman: University of Oklahoma Press, 1966, esp. pp. 140–157.

Mario Montaño Aragón, *Síntesis histórica de Oruro* (1972).

Luis Guerra Gutiérrez, *Elarte en la prehistoria orureña: Síntesis* (1977).

Additional Bibliography

Condarco Santillán, Carlos; Llanque, Ricardo Jorge. *El Carnaval de Oruro.* Oruro: Casa Municipal de Cultura: Latinas Editores, 2002.

Cornblit, Oscar. *Power and Violence in the Colonial City: Oruro from the Mining Renaissance to the Rebellion of Tupac Amaru, 1740-1782.* New York: Cambridge University Press, 1995.

Robins, Nicholas A. *El mesianísmo y la rebelión indígena de Oruro en 1781.* La Paz, Bolivia: Hisbol, 1997.

KENDALL W. BROWN

OSÓRIO, MANUEL LUÍS (1808–1879). Manuel Luís Osório (*b.* 10 May 1808; *d.* 4 October 1879), Brazilian military hero and politician. The son of a modest rancher, Osório overcame his relatively humble origin and almost complete lack of formal education to become one of his country's greatest military figures and leading Liberal politicians. His military career began with his participation as a low-ranking officer in the Cisplatine War (1825–1828). In the Farroupilha Revolt (1835–1845), his distinguished service on the Loyalist side caught the attention of the military commander and sped his rise through the ranks. By 1852 he was entrusted with the command of the Brazilian division sent to Argentina to combat Juan Manuel de Rosas. He also led the Brazilian force that occupied Montevideo in 1864. When the War of the Triple Alliance broke out the following year, Osório was in charge of the Brazilian military contingent, coordinating the first wave of attacks on Paraguayan forces with the Argentine Bartolomé Mitre. After leading his troops to a series of victories, Osório was wounded twice and left the front. On both occasions he returned to battle after short periods of recovery. In the midst of that war, he uttered his famous phrase: "It is easy to command free men; it is enough to show them the path of duty."

As reward for his service, he received titles of nobility, being named first baron, then viscount, and finally marquês de Erval. At the close of the Farroupilha Revolt he served in the provincial legislature of his native Rio Grande do Sul. In 1862 he helped found a reformulated Liberal Party in that province and later won a seat in the national Senate. A year after achieving his country's highest military rank in 1877, Osório assumed the post of minister of war in the Sinimbú cabinet, a position he held until his death.

See also **Brazil: 1808-1889; Farroupilha Revolt; Rosas, Juan Manuel de; War of the Triple Alliance.**

BIBLIOGRAPHY

Joseph L. Love, *Rio Grande do Sul and Brazilian Regionalism, 1882–1930* (1972).

Helga I. L. Piccolo, *A política rio-grandense no II Império (1868–1882)* (1974).

João Baptista Magalhães, *Osório: Síntese de seu perfil histórico* (1978).

ROGER A. KITTLESON

OSORIO, OSCAR (1910–1969). Oscar Osorio (*b.* 1910; *d.* 6 March 1969), president of El Salvador (1950–1956). A graduate of the Escuela Politécnica Militar, he rose through the ranks until exiled to Mexico for conspiracy in 1945. Returning in 1948, he joined the young officers who overthrew President Salvador Casteñeda Castro in 1948. An admirer of the Mexican PRI (Partido Revolucionario Institucional), he organized the military-civilian coalition that, through the PRUD–PCN (Revolutionary Party of Democratic Unification–National Coalition Party), dominated Salvadoran politics for thirty-one years.

Osorio led the military junta of 1948–1949 and was elected to the presidency in 1950. As president he launched what Charles Anderson termed the "controlled revolution," namely, a strategy in which the government would seek to satisfy growing middle-class demands for change by enacting a moderate program of socioeconomic reforms without seriously disrupting the existing social and economic structure. Limited political opposition would be allowed by permitting a few accepted political parties to participate in elections.

See also **El Salvador; El Salvador, Political Parties: National Conciliation Party (PCN).**

BIBLIOGRAPHY

Raymond Ashton, "El Salvador and The 'Controlled Revolution': An Analysis of Salvadorean Development, 1948–1965" (M.A. thesis, Tulane University, 1968).

Charles Anderson, "El Salvador: The Army as Reformer," in *Political Systems of Latin America,* 2d ed., edited by Martin C. Needler (1970).

Enrique Baloyra, *El Salvador in Transition* (1982).

José Z. García, "El Salvador: Recent Elections in Historical Perspective," in *Elections and Democracy in Central America,* edited by John A. Booth and Mitchell A. Seligson (1989).

Additional Bibliography

Leistenschneider, María. *Teniente coronel Oscar Osorio y su administración.* San Salvador: Ministerio del Interior, 1981.

ROLAND H. EBEL

OSORNO. Osorno, province of the Los Lagos region in southern Chile. Its 221,509 inhabitants (2002) are mostly concentrated in the city of Osorno, advantageously located in the Central Valley. The settlement of Osorno was begun in 1558 by Governor García Hurtado De Mendoza, the successor of Pedro de Valdivia, who was killed by the Araucanians in 1553. In 1692 the settlement was destroyed by the Indians, but recognizing its strategic value, Governor Ambrosio O'Higgins ordered its reconstruction in 1796. After 1860 several German and Swiss families settled in the province and started successful wheat and dairy farms. At the turn of the century Osorno was famed for its flour, breweries, and leather industries. After decades of recession Osorno has recovered economically and has become an active dairy and sugar beet production center.

See also **Chile, Geography; Hurtado de Mendoza, García; O'Higgins, Ambrosio.**

BIBLIOGRAPHY

Additional Bibliography

Armstrong, Alberto. *Evolución del conflicto laboral en Chile: 1961–2002.* Santiago: Ediciones Universidad Católica de Chile, 2006.

Lazzara, Michael J. *Chile in Transition: The Poetics and Politics of Memory.* Gainesville: University Press of Florida, 2006.

Villalobos R., Sergio. *Historia de los chilenos.* Santiago de Chile: Taurus, 2006.

César N. Caviedes

OSPINA, PEDRO NEL (1858–1927). Pedro Nel Ospina (*b.* 18 September 1858; *d.* 1 July 1927), Conservative Party leader and president of Colombia (1922–1926). Ospina was born in Bogotá's presidential palace, the son of President Mariano Ospina Rodríguez. He spent much of his childhood in Guatemala and received a degree in mining engineering from the University of California. Settling in Antioquia, Ospina joined his brothers in managing the family businesses, which were concentrated in coffee but also included mining. Elected to Congress in 1892, he allied himself with the Historical wing of the Conservative Party. He distinguished himself as a Conservative commander during the War of the Thousand Days and was named minister of war in 1901 by Vice President José Manuel Marroquín, who had seized power from President Manuel A. Sanclemente. Ospina's participation in an abortive plot to restore Sanclemente led to his banishment. While in exile, he studied cotton cultivation and textile manufacturing in Mexico, the United States, and Europe. He was later a founder of the country's first modern textile factory, established near Medellín in 1906.

In the presidential race of 1922 Ospina defeated Liberal Benjamín Herrera. The most important achievement of his administration was the adoption of banking and fiscal reforms recommended by Edwin W. Kemmerer, who spent six months in Colombia in 1923. The reforms included establishment of a central bank, the Banco de la República; modernization of the budgeting process; and the creation of the office of national comptroller. Ospina was the father of the economic historian Luis Ospina Vásquez (1905–1977).

See also **Banco de la República (Colombia); Colombia, Political Parties: Conservative Party; Textile Industry: Modern Textiles; War of the Thousand Days.**

BIBLIOGRAPHY

Emilio Robledo, *La vida del General Pedro Nel Ospina* (1959).

Jorge Sánchez Camacho, *El General Ospina* (1960).

Paul W. Drake, *The Money Doctor in the Andes: The Kemmerer Missions, 1923–1933* (1989), esp. pp. 30–60.

Additional Bibliography

Mejía de López, Angela. *Algunos aspectos de la administración: Pedro Nel Ospina, 1922–1926.* Bogotá: Universidad Nacional de Colombia, 1978.

Murray, Pamela. "Engineering Development: Colombia's National School of Mines, 1887–1930." *Hispanic American Historical Review* 74:1 (February, 1994): 63-82.

Tirado Mejía, Alvarado. *Nueva Historia de Colombia.* Bogotá: Planeta, 1989.

Helen Delpar

OSPINA PÉREZ, MARIANO (1891–1976). Mariano Ospina Pérez (*b.* 24 November 1891; *d.* 14 April 1976), president of Colombia

often cited as one of the most beautiful towns in South America. Otavalo is famous for the production of beautiful handwoven woolen tapestries, ponchos, and blankets by the Otavalo peoples. When the Crown created the Audiencia of Quito in 1563, it named Otavalo as one of the *corregimientos.* During the colonial period, the Otavalons were not reduced to haciendas under conditions of debt peonage, as were most other highland natives. Instead, they used their skills as artisans to secure a measure of freedom and dignity otherwise unknown to sierra natives.

Outgoing and friendly, the Otavalans are today less deferential to Europeans than are most other sierra Indians. The men are known for their distinctive dress: shin-length white pants, and hair worn in a long braid. Perhaps the best artisans in Ecuador, Otavalans travel to Quito and Guayaquil in Ecuador, and to Colombia, to sell their wares. In turn, the Otavalan weavers from the villages of Peguche, Iluman, and Quinchuqui journey to Otavalo for the weekly Saturday market.

Today, the Otavalans are noted for their ability to participate in a global marketing of their ethnic identity as musicians and craftsmen. While many young people from the community have moved to Quito and abroad to engage in fully "modern" lifestyles, at the same time of the Otavalans continue to practice the agricultural and weaving techniques of their ancestors. Scholars have noted the community's ability to sustain its traditions while participating in modern society and economies.

See also **Sierra (Ecuador); Textiles, Indigenous.**

BIBLIOGRAPHY

Colloredo-Mansfeld, Rudolf Josef. *The Native Leisure Class: Consumption and Cultural Creativity in the Andes.* Chicago: University of Chicago Press, 1999.

Korovkin, Tanya. "Commodity Production and Ethnic Culture: Otavalo, Northern Ecuador." *Economic Development and Cultural Change* 47, no. 1 (October 1998): 125–154.

Meisch, Lynn. *Andean Entrepreneurs: Otavalo Merchants and Musicians in the Global Arena.* Austin: University of Texas Press, 2002.

Wibbelsman, Michelle Cecilia. "Otavaleños at the Crossroads: Physical and Metaphysical Coordinates of an Indigenous World." *Journal of Latin American Anthropology* 10, no. 1 (April 2005): 151–185.

Ronn F. Pineo

OTERO, ALEJANDRO (1921–1990). Alejandro Otero (*b.* 7 March 1921; *d.* 13 August 1990), Venezuelan artist. Born in El Manteco, Otero was the son of a rubber worker who died soon after the artist's birth. He grew up in the small provincial town of Upata and then in Ciudad Bolívar. Although he began to study agriculture, he also took courses in art at the Cristóbal Rojas School of Fine and Applied Arts, in Caracas, where he taught painting and stained glass from 1943–1945. In 1945, on a government fellowship, he traveled to Paris, where he studied cubism and the Dutch neoplasticist artists. He completed a series of forty still lifes entitled *Las Cafeteras,* and exhibited them at the Organization of American States in Washington, D.C. (1948) and the Museo de Bellas Artes in Caracas (1949), where they produced a critical uproar among the conservative Venezuelan art world. In 1950 Otero along with other Venezuelan artists in Paris formed the group *Los Disidentes,* which published five issues of an art review promoting geometrical abstraction as the way to reach a universal art.

In 1952 he returned to Caracas, where he taught at the School of Fine and Applied Arts (1954–1959), and joined with the artists Calder, Vasarely, Arp, Léger, and Soto in designing the University City. In 1959 and 1975 he participated in the Venezuelan group show at the São Paulo Bienal. In 1960 he returned to Paris, where he produced a series of assemblages and collages. Back in Caracas he became vice president of the Instituto Nacional de Cultura de Bellas Artes (1964). In 1966 he began his famous series *Coloritmo,* an experiment with a striped pattern of industrial color on rectangular pieces of wood to produce a moving visual interaction of vertical lines of color. That year, and again in 1982, he represented Venezuela at the Venice Biennale.

In the mid-1960s, Otero began work on large-scale outdoor kinetic sculptures like *Delta solar* (Washington, D.C.), *Ala Solar* (Bogotá), and *Terra solar* (Guri Dam, Venezuela). In 1971 he received a Guggenheim Memorial Fellowship to research sculptural ideas at the Center for Advanced Visual Studies at the Massachusetts Institute of Technology. He participated in international group shows such as the Hayward Gallery's Art in Latin America

(London, 1989) as well as many solo shows at the Museum of Contemporary Art (1985) and the National Gallery of Art (1990) in Caracas.

See also **Art: The Twentieth Century.**

BIBLIOGRAPHY

Bélgica Rodríguez, *La pintura abstracta en Venezuela, 1945–1965* (1980).

Consejo Nacional De La Cultura (conac), *Alejandro Otero, representación venezolana* (1991), introduction by Elena Ramos.

Additional Bibliography

Calzadilla, Juan. "Alejandro Otero y la enseñanza del arte." *Revista Nacional de Cultura (Venezuela)* 59: 306–307 (July–Dec 1997): 209–217.

Otero, Alejandro. *He vivido por los ojos: Correspondencia Alejandro Otero Alfredo Boulton 1946–1974.* Caracas: Museo Alejandro Otero, 2001.

BÉLGICA RODRÍGUEZ

OTERO, MARIANO (1817–1850). Mariano Otero (*b.* 1817; *d.* 1850), Mexican politician and cabinet minister. A native of Guadalajara, Jalisco, Otero studied law there and received his degree in 1835. His intelligence, eloquence, and energy soon attracted the attention of local liberals, and in 1841 Otero was elected to the Junta de Representantes de los Departamentos. As a deputy for Jalisco to the special national congress in 1842, he opposed the projected centralist constitution. That year he also published one of the most important analyses of Mexico's postindependence trauma, *Ensayo sobre el verdadero estado de la cuestión social y política que se agita en la República mexicana.*

Otero believed that Mexico was essentially different from European countries. The Mexican aristocracy had not exercised civil jurisdiction and had no political influence. Mexico's colonial experience was a "true despotism, without intermediate classes, and this power [colonial despotism] was essentially foreign." This despotism created a society in which each corporation, group, and class sought only its own prerogatives, thereby making coherent political action impossible. Otero proposed that Mexico's condition was the result of its historical development, and he stressed the underlying property relationships as the root of the problem. Otero's thought shows the influence of utopian socialism.

Otero wrote frequently for the newspaper *El siglo XIX* and other periodicals. After the liberal revolt of 1846, he returned to Congress, where he led the effort to pass the Reform Acts, which restored the federal Constitution of 1824 with some alterations. After the United States invasion, Otero was one of four deputies in Querétaro who opposed the Treaty of Guadalupe Hidalgo. He resigned from the senate in 1848 to become minister of foreign relations in the government of President José Joaquín de Herrera. He died in the cholera epidemic of 1850.

See also **Guadalupe Hidalgo, Treaty of (1848); Mexico: 1810-1910.**

BIBLIOGRAPHY

Mariano Otero, *Ensayo sobre el verdadero estado de la cuestión social y política que se agita en la República mexicana* (1842; repr. 1979).

Jesús Reyes Heroles, *El liberalismo mexicano,* 3 vols. (1957–1961), vol. 2, pp. 89–136.

Charles A. Hale, *Mexican Liberalism in the Age of Mora, 1821–1853* (1968), pp. 12–15, 34–35, 46, 75, 183–187, 206, 212; *Diccionario Porrúa de historia, biografía y geografía de México,* 5th ed. (1986), vol. 2, p. 2160.

Additional Bibliography

Villeneuve, Anne. *Mariano Otero.* Dinard: Editions Vue ser mer, 1996.

Zavala Castillo, José Francisco, and José Rodolfo Arturo Vega Hernández. *Fórmula Otero?: Exegesis del Artículo 25 de la Acta de Reformas de 1847.* Santiago de Querétaro, México: Fundación Universitaria de Derecho, Administración y Política, 2005.

D. F. STEVENS

OTERO VÉRTIZ, GUSTAVO ADOLFO (1896–1958). Born in La Paz, Bolivia, on September 8, 1896, Otero Vértiz was a politician (minister of education), diplomat (representing his country in Barcelona, Colombia, and Ecuador), and bureaucrat (director, National Library). But he is most important for his historical, sociological, and literary writing. As a historian he wrote *La vida social en el* *coloniaje* (*Esquema de la historia del Alto Perú, hoy Bolivia, de los siglos XVI, XVII, y XVIII*; 2nd ed., 1958), a work frequently cited and republished. In this vein he edited an anthology of colonial chronicles under the title *Tihuanacu* (1943). As a sociologist/anthropologist he effected studies such as *La piedra mágica: Vida y costumbres de los indios callahuayas de Bolivia* (1951), creating a rubric for *ethnocostumbrismo.* In addition, as a novelist, he cultivated the historical novel with *Horizontes incendiados* (1933), a work that deals with the Chaco war. His writing was well known in Bolivia and was also disseminated to the far reaches of Latin America (Mexico and Argentina) as well as Spain. Unfortunately, he has been largely passed over by scholarship in the United States. Otero Vértiz died in La Paz on July 1, 1958.

See also **Literature: Spanish America.**

BIBLIOGRAPHY

Arnade, Charles W. "Gustavo Adolfo Otero (1896–1958)." *Hispanic American Historical Review* 40, no. 1 (February 1960): 85–89.

Valdez, Abraham. "Gustavo Adolfo Otero y su Contribución a la Sociología Boliviana." *Revista Mexicana de Sociología* 21, no. 1 (January 1959): 31–47.

THOMAS WARD

OTOMÍ. Otomí, a broad designation referring to various distinct indigenous groups and languages that have existed from pre-Hispanic times through the present, principally in the areas west and north of the Valley of Mexico. It is a designation that includes the more sedentary peoples whom the Nahuas called the Otomí, Mazahua, Matlatzinca, and Ocuilteca, particularly numerous in the Valley of Toluca, plus other sedentary and less sedentary groups in what are now the states of México, Hidalgo, Querétaro, and San Luis Potosí, including the southern Chichimec zone. There are also pockets known to exist in Puebla, Tlaxcala, Michoacán, Jalisco, and elsewhere. Macro-Otomanguean languages include Mixtec and Zapotec of Oaxaca.

Many Otomí groups resembled Nahuas except in language, since they lived in close proximity and all claimed descent from the Toltecs. But the proud Nahuas refused to recognize any similarities, taking every opportunity, as in the Florentine Codex, to deprecate their rivals. The Otomí had strong ties to the Tepanecas, imperial rulers based in the city of Azcapotzalco, who were defeated by the Mexica and Acolhuas in 1430. The Nahuas also disdained what they saw as a barbarian strain in the Otomí, who had experienced a late Chichimeca penetration. Still, they respected the Chichimec and Otomí prowess in war, creating high military titles bearing the names of those cultures.

Given the Nahua rivalry, it is not surprising that the Otomí aided the Spanish in the conquest of Mexico, but they also served on the Chichimec frontier as a buffer, settling model communities and taking the brunt of the fighting there.

See also **Aztecs; Chichimecs; Indigenous Peoples.**

BIBLIOGRAPHY

Pedro Carrasco Pizana, *Los Otomíes: Cultura e historia prehispánicas de los pueblos mesoamericanos de habla otomiana* (1950).

H. R. Harvey, "The Relaciones Geográficas, 1579–1586: Native Languages," in *The Handbook of Middle American Indians,* vol. 12, pt. 1, edited by Howard F. Cline (1972), pp. 301–302.

James Lockhart and Stuart B. Schwartz, *Early Latin America: A History of Colonial Spanish America and Brazil* (1983), p. 292.

STEPHANIE WOOD

OTTAWA AGREEMENT (1932). Ottawa Agreement (1932), a series of trade policy initiatives enacted by Britain and its dominions. Out of the 1932 Ottawa Conference came not one, but seven separate agreements, which Argentines called the "black pacts." Although the rabidly anti-Argentine press baron Lord Beaverbrook saw no distinction between these pacts and an eighth one between London and Buenos Aires, there was, nevertheless, a crucial difference. While the dominions were pressing to maximize an advance in the U.K. market, the Argentines were struggling to minimize a retreat. The former mustered telling arguments: First, Britain had long enjoyed preferences in imperial markets and conceded little in return. With free trade suspended and tariffs imposed, the dominions could press for much more. With the Great Depression demanding compassion and the

Statute of Westminster (1931) weakening political control from London, subsequent imperial consolidation had to be economic.

The main implications of the Ottawa agreements for Argentina were that 33.2 percent of British imports were now subject to duties in comparison to 17.3 percent just before the conference. (Prior to 1930 none were subject.) There were also severe cuts in Argentina's exports, allowing the dominions more exports to Britain. It was in a bid to counter these slashes that the controversial Roca-Runciman Pact was negotiated between London and Buenos Aires in 1933.

See also **British-Latin American Relations; Roca-Runciman Pact (1933).**

BIBLIOGRAPHY

Ian M. Drummond, *Imperial Economic Policy, 1917–1939* (1974).

Additional Bibliography

Lobell, Steven E. "Second Image Reversed Politics: Britain's Choice of Freer Trade or Imperial Preferences, 1903–1906, 1917–1923, 1930–1932." *International Studies Quarterly* 43 (1999): 671-694.

ROGER GRAVIL

OTTONI, TEOFILO BENEDITO (1807–1869). Teofilo Benedito Ottoni (*b.* 27 November 1807; *d.* 17 October 1869), Brazilian statesman and entrepreneur, perhaps the foremost radical Liberal ideologue of his time. As a student at the Naval Academy, Ottoni associated with many of the leaders of the opposition to Pedro I. He began his apprenticeship as a liberal polemicist and a journalist in the 1820s. In the early regency, he separated from his *moderado* mentors as a radical, calling for constitutional reform; as a Minas Gerais provincial deputy in 1835, and a national deputy for Minas Gerais after 1838, his star in the emergent Liberal Party rose high. Ottoni was a stalwart of the Majority movement (1840) and the Liberal Revolt of 1842, and was seen as the party chieftain in the Chamber of Deputies during the failed Liberal interregnum of the 1840s.

As a merchant and entrepreneur, Ottoni had called for infrastructural development since 1832; by the mid-1840s, he had begun to shift his interest from the disappointments of Liberal politics to steamship and road linkage between northern Minas Gerais and the coast. From 1846 to 1858, he devoted himself to this Mucuri project, which brought him both failure and success. His subsequent return to politics quickly restored him to prominence, again on the party's left. By 1860 he was widely considered the most popular chief of the Liberals, and his campaign writing enjoyed general renown. A senator for Minas Gerais by 1864, he led the party's radical wing in the era of renewed ideological definition, figuring in the rebirth of the Liberal Party in 1868 and influencing the Liberal Manifesto of 1869, which defined the party's program in opposition.

See also **Brazil, Political Parties: Liberal Party.**

BIBLIOGRAPHY

Joaquim Nabuco, *Um estadista do império,* vols. 1 and 2 (1898–1899).

Paulo Pinheiro Chagas, *Teofilo Ottoni, ministro do povo,* 2d rev. ed. (1956).

Leslie Bethell, ed., *Brazil: Empire and Republic* (1989), chaps. 2 and 3.

Additional Bibliography

Prado, Maria Emília. *O estado como vocação: Idéias e práticas políticas no Brasil oitocentista.* Rio de Janeiro: Access Editora, 1999.

Vespucci, Ricardo. *Rebeldes brasileiros: Homens e mulheres que desafiaram o poder.* São Paulo: Editora Casa Amarela, 2001.

JEFFREY D. NEEDELL

OURO PRÊTO. Ouro Prêto, a city in the mountains of southeastern Brazil in the state of Minas Gerais, particularly famous for its eighteenth-century baroque architecture. Established by gold prospectors in 1698, the town became the capital of the newly created captaincy of Minas Gerais in 1720.

The enormous wealth generated in the surrounding region by the Western world's first great gold rush financed the construction of many churches, public buildings, and private homes in a distinctive baroque style. Some of the churches were designed and built by Brazil's most famous artist of the colonial period,

Antônio Francisco Lisboa, better known as Aleijadinho (The Little Cripple), in the late eighteenth century.

With the drastic decline in gold production after 1770, the city experienced decades of economic stagnation and slow growth. In 1897 the state capital was moved to Belo Horizonte, thus depriving the city of its political importance. The Brazilian government declared the city a national historic monument in the 1930s, and it is also recognized by UNESCO as a world historic monument. The architectural beauty of the central city has been very well conserved, and today the city is an important tourist attraction. In 2005, the population was estimated at 58,300.

BIBLIOGRAPHY

Charles R. Boxer, *The Golden Age of Brazil, 1695–1750.* Berkeley: University of California Press, 1969.

A. J. R. Russell-Wood, "The Gold Cycle, ca. 1690–1750," in *Colonial Brazil,* edited by Leslie Bethell. New York: Cambridge University Press, 1987, pp. 190–243.

Additional Bibliography

Castro, Yeda Pessoa de. *A língua mina-jeje no Brasil: Um falar africano em Ouro Preto do século XVIII.* Belo Horizonte: Sistema Estadual de Planejamento, 2002.

Pereira, Edimilson de Almeida; Núbia Pereira Magalhães Gomes. *Ouro Preto da Palavra: Narrativos de preceito do congado em Minas Gerais.* Belo Horizonte: Editora PUC Minas, 2003.

MARSHALL C. EAKIN

OUVIDORES. Ouvidores, judges in the captaincies of colonial Brazil. In the sixteenth century they were appointed by one of the Portuguese proprietors of colonial Brazil or by one of the military orders in areas under their control. *Ouvidores* had both judicial and administrative functions. Besides having the power to arrest, sentence, and punish lawbreakers within their jurisdiction, *ouvidores* could review the roll of citizens eligible to serve on municipal councils. As a result, they exercised considerable influence in the selection of municipal officers. An *ouvidor* did not need legal training, and they often were military officers.

In 1549 the king of Portugal centralized government in Brazil and gave the governor-general authority to appoint an *ouvidor geral,* a superior crown magistrate who could exercise authority over *ouvidores.* The *ouvidor geral* generally was a member of the royal magistracy, appointed by the king of Portugal, and had wide jurisdiction and powers. He had both judicial and administrative functions, including the power to spend funds from the colonial treasury.

In the twenty-first century, ouvidores can be found throughout ministerial branches at the federal, state, and municipal levels. They hear, transmit, and follow-up on complaints received within their offices.

See also **Judicial Systems: Brazil; Portuguese Empire.**

BIBLIOGRAPHY

Stuart B. Schwartz, *Sovereignty and Society of Colonial Brazil* (1973).

Additional Bibliography

Sá, Adísia, Fátima Vilanova, and Roberto Maciel. *Ombudsmen, ouvidores: Transparência, mediação e cidadania.*Fortaleza: Edições Demócrito Rocha, 2004.

Russell-Wood, A.J.R. "Ambivalent Authorities: The African and Afro-Brazilian Contribution to Local Governance in Colonial Brazil" *The Americas* Vol. 57, No. 1 (July, 2000): 13-36.

ROSS WILKINSON

OVANDO, NICOLÁS DE (1451–1518). Nicolás de Ovando (*b.* 1451; *d.* 1518), governor of Hispaniola. Born in Cáceres, in Extremadura, Spain, Ovando was a member of the military Order of Calatrava. On 3 September 1501 the crown ordered him to Hispaniola to investigate the administration of Francisco de Bobadilla and to reestablish order. Ovando arrived in April 1502; his large fleet had departed Sanlúcar de Barrameda, Spain, with some twenty-five hundred colonists, including Bartolomé de Las Casas, a man who would later achieve fame as the Protector of the Indians. Using ample force and authority, Ovando completed the "pacification" of the island, subduing both native Americans and Spanish malcontents, and returning unruly colonists to Spain in chains.

Ovando also exercised some more positive imperatives. He sought to establish new towns and cities, following a general gridiron pattern that later came to characterize town planning in Spanish America. Santo Domingo was refounded on the opposite bank of the Ozama River. Ovando also ordered continued exploration of Hispaniola and nearby islands: Andrés Morales prepared a detailed map; Sebastián de Ocampo completed the circumnavigation of Cuba; Juan Ponce De León was authorized to explore Puerto Rico. Ovando was generally interested in protecting Amerindians and experimented to see if they could live freely as Europeans. By a royal cedula of 20 December 1503, he instituted a division (*repartimiento*) of Indians, which was the foundation for the *encomienda* system.

On the outgoing fourth expedition of Columbus, Ovando refused the explorer safe admission to the port of Santo Domingo. Had it been possible for Columbus to refit and repair ships and perhaps purchase better ones, the Jamaica disaster might have been averted. In 1508 Ovando was replaced by Diego Colón.

See also **Columbus, Christopher; Encomienda; Las Casas, Bartolomé de; Militias: Colonial Spanish America; Ponce de León, Juan; Repartimiento; Santo Domingo.**

BIBLIOGRAPHY

Ursula Lamb, *Frey Nicolás de Ovando* (1956).

Carl Ortwin Sauer, *The Early Spanish Main* (1967).

Additional Bibliography

Mira Caballos, Esteban. *Nicolás de Ovando y los orígenes del sistema colonial español, 1502–1509.* Santo Domingo, República Dominicana: Patronato de la Ciudad Colonial de Santo Domingo, 2000.

NOBLE DAVID COOK

OVANDO CANDÍA, ALFREDO (1917–1982).

Alfredo Ovando Candía (*b.* 1917; *d.* 1982), army officer and president of Bolivia (1964–1966, 1969–1970). Ovando graduated from the Bolivian Military Academy in 1936, after having been in active service during the Chaco War. He pursued further military studies in Bolivia and Argentina. He rose regularly in rank, before and after the Bolivian National Revolution of 1952. He became a division general in 1952 and was named army chief of staff in 1957 and commander in chief of the armed forces in 1962.

When President Víctor Paz Estenssoro was overthrown in November 1964, the deposed president was confident of Ovando's loyalty, but Ovando was, in fact, the major co-conspirator with General René Barrientos in Paz Estenssoro's ouster. Ovando and Barrientos became copresidents from 1964 to 1966, when Barrientos resigned to become a candidate for election as president. During Barrientos's administration, Ovando continued as commander in chief of the armed forces. When Barrientos died in April 1969, Vice President Luis Adolfo Siles Salinas took over, but late in September, Ovando ousted Siles and assumed the presidency.

In his second presidential term, Ovando launched a "nationalist" program, the centerpiece of which was the nationalization of the Gulf Oil Corporation's holdings in Bolivia, for which he promised to compensate the company. He also encouraged the reorganization of the labor movement and patronized several new leftist parties. He extended diplomatic relations to, and received a loan from, the Soviet Union.

In October 1970 a right-wing military coup resulted in Ovando's resignation. He had second thoughts and attempted to resume his office, but it was too late. After several days of confusion, a more leftist-oriented general, Juan José Torres, became president. Ovando was named ambassador to Spain. After Torres's own overthrow in August 1971, Ovando resigned.

See also **Barrientos Ortuño, René; Bolivia, Political Parties: Nationalist Revolutionary Movement (MNR); Paz Estenssoro, Víctor.**

BIBLIOGRAPHY

Christopher Mitchell, *The Legacy of Populism in Bolivia* (1977).

Additional Bibliography

Grindle, Merilee Serrill, and Pilar Domingo. *Proclaiming Revolution: Bolivia in Comparative Perspective.* Cambridge, MA: David Rockefeller Center for Latin American Studies, Harvard University, 2003.

Soto S., César. *Historia del Pacto Militar Campesino.* Cochabamba, Bolivia: Ediciones CERES, 1994.

ROBERT J. ALEXANDER

OVERSEAS COUNCIL (PORTUGAL).

The standing orders (*regimento*) of the Portuguese Overseas Council (Conselho Ultramarino) were drawn up and dated 14 July 1642, but a year elapsed before the council was officially created. The formal inauguration did not take place until 2 December 1643. By an *alvará* (royal decree) of 22 December, the king ordered that henceforth all official overseas correspondence be directed to the council. However, it was not fully functioning until the following year, when it took over most of the overseas responsibilities of the Council of the Treasury (Conselho da Fazenda), founded in 1591 during the reign of Philip II, first of the Hapsburg monarchs to rule Portugal.

In particular, the Overseas Council based its organization and regulations on the short-lived Conselho Da India (1604–1614). The Overseas Council had authority over all overseas possessions except North Africa and the Atlantic Islands of Madeira and the Azores. Initially, it was composed of a president who was always a member of the titled nobility, two councillors with military experience, a councillor with a law degree, and a secretary. All exercised voting power except the secretary. Later the number of councillors was increased. At times, the councillors themselves were serving overseas. In fact, all those serving on the council were expected to have had overseas experience. Therefore the number of members fluctuated, at times reaching six; initially, a quorum of three was required. The council met at the Royal Palace every morning (except for Sundays and holidays) from seven to ten o'clock in the summer and eight to eleven o'clock in the winter. Thursdays and Fridays were reserved for matters dealing with Brazil. One morning a week was also set aside to review petitions for rewards of overseas services and to make recommendations to the crown.

The council made personnel recommendations for most of the overseas positions in the administrative, fiscal, and military spheres as well as for the overseas bishoprics. The council both initiated recommendations to the king and consulted on problems handed them by the monarch. The members had authority over Portuguese America until November of 1807, when the royal court was transferred to Brazil. It is estimated that during that time the Overseas Council had approximately 13 presidents and 126 councillors, although several members never officially took office.

See also **Portuguese Overseas Administration.**

BIBLIOGRAPHY

The only available study of the Portuguese Overseas Council is the brief one by Marcello Caetano, *O Conselho Ultramarino: Esboço da sua história* (1967). Because Salvador de Sá was named to the Overseas Council in 1644 and served on it until his death, Charles R. Boxer, *Salvador de Sá and the Struggle for Brazil and Angola, 1602–1686* (1952) is also useful. For the Overseas Council's role in recommending Brazilian bishops, see Francis A. Dutra, "The Brazilian Hierarchy in the Seventeenth Century," in *Records of the American Catholic Historical Society,* 83, nos. 3–4 (1972): 171–186. A good example of the various kinds of issues handled by the Overseas Council is found in Luiza Da Fonseca, "Indice abreviado dos documentos do século XVII do Arquivo Histórico Colonial de Lisboa," in *Anais do I° Congresso de História da Bahia 2* (1950): 7–353.

Additional Bibliography

Bethencourt, Francisco, and Diogo Ramada Curto. *Portuguese Oceanic Expansion, 1400-1800.* Cambridge [England]: Cambridge University Press, 2007.

Silva, Maria Beatriz Nizza da. *De Cabral a Pedro I: Aspectos da colonização portuguesa no Brasil.* [Oporto, Portugal?]: Universidade Portucalense Infante D. Henrique, 2001.

FRANCIS A. DUTRA

OVIEDO Y VALDÉS, GONZALO FERNÁNDEZ

OVIEDO Y VALDÉS, GONZALO FERNÁNDEZ (1478–1557). Gonzalo Fernández Oviedo y Valdés (*b.* August 1478; *d.* 26 June 1557), chronicler of the Indies. Born in Madrid, Oviedo was one of the earliest and most astute chroniclers of the Indies, combining a critical understanding of the historical method with first-hand experience. In 1490 he entered the service of Alfonso de Aragon, duke of Villahermosa, who presented him to the court. He witnessed the surrender of Granada. In 1493 he entered the service of Prince Don Juan, who was his own age. After the prince's untimely death six years later, Oviedo participated in the Italian campaigns. In 1500 he was admitted to the court of Don Fadrique, king of Naples. Oviedo returned to Madrid in 1502 and married Margarita de Vergara, who died within ten months of the union. In 1503 Oviedo entered the service of the duke of Calabria and fought in Rousellon. He remarried in 1509 and had a son.

King Ferdinand named Oviedo secretary to Gonzalo Fernández de Córdoba, the Great Captain, in Italy. Oviedo and others, frustrated by lack of action and tardy pay, returned to Spain and joined an expedition to Castilla del Oro. With two thousand men on twenty-two vessels, the group departed Spain on 11 April, reaching Santa Marta on 12 July 1514, and continued on to Santa María de la Antigua. There, within a few weeks, with insufficient food and supplies and suffering illness, many settlers died. Oviedo returned to Spain to give full account of the disastrous expedition. In the meantime, King Ferdinand had died, so Oviedo traveled to Flanders to report to the young Charles. The question of inheritance in Spain led to long delays at Darién in the review of what happened, but Oviedo was vindicated and given fresh assignments in the Indies (1519). He also received royal support to complete a general history that he had already begun.

Oviedo returned to the Indies with his wife, two children, and eight servants, to assume administrative duties at Santa María de la Antigua. Conflict led to a *residencia* (investigation) of his activities. Although he was not found guilty of improprieties, he decided to return to Spain to give account of his services. Gravely ill, he left Panama for Cuba on 3 July 1523. While recuperating in Santo Domingo, he met Diego Colón. After reaching Sanlúcar, Spain, on 5 November, he journeyed north to Vitoria, where he held an audience with Charles, now emperor. At this time he secured fresh information from Juan Sebastián de El Cano on the circumnavigation begun by Magellan. Although granted a position in Darién, Oviedo remained at court, pressing claims against Dávila.

In 1525 he returned to the Indies a third time, stopping first in Castilla del Oro and then Nicaragua before finally settling in Santo Domingo. At the end of 1530 he returned to Spain again. It was then that Charles V named him "cronista general de Indias." In 1532 he returned to Santo Domingo, where he was *alcaide* of the city's fort. On his fourth return to Spain in mid-1534, he carried the completed first part of the *Historia general y natural de las Indias,* which was published in September 1535. Oviedo returned to Santo Domingo, where he remained from 1536 to 1546 while he finished the second and third parts of the history. He also collected a series of important new documents, including Diego de Almagro's report on the Chilean expedition. He returned again to Spain (late 1546 to early 1549), carrying to court important reports on the Peruvian civil wars. Oviedo then returned to Santo Domingo, where he remained until his death. In addition to his *Historia general y natural de las Indias* and the *Sumario de la historia natural de las Indias,* he prepared several other histories.

See also **Explorers and Exploration: Spanish America; Santo Domingo; Spanish Empire.**

BIBLIOGRAPHY

Francisco Esteve Barba, *Historiografía indiana* (1964).

Additional Bibliography

Ares Queija, Berta, and Serge Gruzinski, eds. *Entre dos mundos: Fronteras culturales y agentes mediadores.* Seville: Escuela de Estudios Hispano-Americanos, 1997.

Pardo Tomás, José. *Oviedo, Monardes, Hernández: El tesoro natural de América: Colonialismo y ciencia en el siglo XVI.* Madrid: Nivola, 2002.

NOBLE DAVID COOK